India

THE ROUGH GUIDE

There are more than eighty Rough Guide titles
covering destinations from Amsterdam to Zimbabwe

Forthcoming titles include
China • Jamaica • New Zealand • South Africa
Southwest USA • Vienna • Washington DC

Rough Guide Reference Series
Classical Music • The Internet • Jazz • World Music • Rock Music

Rough Guide Phrasebooks
Czech • French • German • Greek • Italian • Mexican Spanish • Polish
Portuguese • Spanish • Thai • Turkish • Vietnamese

Rough Guides on the Internet
http://www.roughguides.com/
http://www.hotwired.com/rough

Rough Guide to India Credits

Text editor:	Lemisse Al-Hafidh and Samantha Cook
Series editor:	Mark Ellingham
Production:	Link Hall and Nicola Williamson
Cartography:	Melissa Flack, Sam Kirby, David Callier

Acknowledgments:

Thanks to Daniel Jacobs and Nick Edwards for their invaluable work on this edition; Lemisse, who ploughed so stoically through the bulk of the book, and Sam C, for stepping into the breach and pulling it all together; Link and Nicola for patient, creative and good-humoured production; Melissa and Sam K for deciphering some very messy map specs, Jean McNeil and Helen Ostick for keying, Rosemary Morlin and Elaine Pollard for proofreading, and Narrell Leffman and Ann Muchnick for work on *Basics*. For their continuing contributions thanks to Gareth Williams, Dave Crawford, Ravi S Vasudevan, Tony Stones, Jameela Siddiqi, David Muddyman and such a fine job of editing the first edition. Thanks, too, to *Somak Holidays*; Dr Dandapani of *SD Enterprises*, and especially the India Government Tourist Office, particularly Mr Lakhanpal (Director, London), for help and hospitality at key moments. We're also grateful to the many readers who took the trouble to write to us about the last edition; a full list appears on p.iv. Individually the authors would like to thank:

David: thank you, once again, Menaxshi Mehta and her helpful colleagues at the India Government Tourist Office in Bombay; Agnelo Godinho in Panjim and staff at the British High Commission of Bombay for getting me out of a scrape in Kerala; Naom, Lis, Cathy and the Walcot posse for road-testing the South India additions; and to Tracy Walker, for checking out pools a-plenty along the way.

Devdan: I dedicate my part of this book to the memory of my mother, my cousin Arjun Soni and to the memory of my friend and mentor, Malcolm Smith. Writing my part of this book would not have been possible without vital support from Pauleen. Special thanks to Jai Chand Mahtab and family in Calcutta, Nisha and Rajiv Kehr in UP, June Lal, Kanika Dumraon and Samjit Dasgupta, the Government of India Tourist Board, especially Mr Raj Mittal of the Department of Tourism and the Indian tourist offices at Agra, Varanasi and Patna.

Harriet: thanks to family and friends for standing by throughout, particularly Dee, the Podgers, the Cheema family and Gabi. Also Atul and Seema Seth in Delhi, Mr Raj Mittal for support and advice, and staff at Janpath Tourist Office. In Ladakh thanks to Nawang and family for hospitality and to Uwe, Nina and Kyle for their adventurous spirit. Also Nigel Eggo, Michael Willis, Shyam Prasad, Franz Rollinger and Stanto Bombek. I'm indebted to Yunis Khan for company and guidance in Pachmarhi. I'd like to thank all the staff at the MPTDC hotels and tourist offices, in particular Mr Chahal and Mr Choudhary (Bhopal), Mr Vivek Mathur and Rajendra Singh (Mandu), Mr Dixit and Mr Shad (Orchha), Mukesh Kapoor in Ujjain, and in HP Mr Thakur and Pramode Paul, and Alex, Friddly and Isabelle.

Nick: thanks to Mrs Murlidhavan and staff, GITO, Madras; all the TTDC tourist offices and hotels; Mr Shyam Sundar, *Indian Airlines*, Madras; Mr Sherad, APTDC, Hyderabad; Mr Jogendra Patra and Mr DN Panigrahi, OTDC, Bhubaneshwar; staff of OTDC *Panthaniwas*, Bhubaneshwar, Konarak, Puri and Chandipur; Mr Kumar, *Broadlands*, Madras; Francis, *Metro Tours*, Mamallapuram; Alexander Oilman of *MV Pilobhati*, Andaman Islands; Yugabrata (Bubu), *Heritage Tours*, Puri; Ashok and Anita Gupta and sons; and Steve Thompson.

Daniel: thanks to Lakshmikant Jangir (Jhunjhunu), *Thar Safari* (Jaisalmer), Robin Laloo (Shillong).

> The publishers and authors have done their best to ensure the accuracy and currency of all the information in *The Rough Guide to India*, however, they can accept no responsibility for any loss, injury or inconvenience sustained by any traveller as a result of information or advice contained in the guide.

This second edition published November 1996 by Rough Guides Ltd, 1 Mercer Street, London WC2H 9QJ.

Distributed by the Penguin Group:

Penguin Books Ltd, 27 Wrights Lane, London W8 5TZ

Penguin Books USA Inc., 375 Hudson Street, New York 10014, USA

Penguin Books Australia Ltd, 487 Maroondah Highway, PO Box 257, Ringwood, Victoria 3134, Australia

Penguin Books Canada Ltd, 10 Alcorn Avenue, Toronto, Ontario, Canada M4V 1E4

Penguin Books (NZ) Ltd, 182–190 Wairau Road, Auckland 10, New Zealand

Typeset in Linotron Univers and Century Old Style to an original design by Andrew Oliver.

Printed by Bath Press, Bath. Illustrations in Part One & Part Three by Edward Briant.

1312pp, includes index

A catalogue record for this book is available from the British Library.

ISBN 1-85828-200-4

India

THE ROUGH GUIDE

Written and researched by
**David Abram, Devdan Sen, Harriet Sharkey
and Gareth John Williams**

With additional accounts by
Nick Edwards and Daniel Jacobs

THE ROUGH GUIDES

HELP US UPDATE

We've gone to a lot of effort to ensure that the second edition of *The Rough Guide to India* is up-to-date and accurate. However things do change, and any corrections, comments or suggestions will be greatly appreciated. We'll credit all contributions, and send a copy of the next edition (or any other *Rough Guide* if you prefer) for the best. Please mark all letters "Rough Guide to India update" and send to:

Rough Guides, 1 Mercer St, London WC2H 9QJ or
Rough Guides, 375 Hudson St, 9th floor, New York, NY 10014 or
india@roughtravl.co.uk.
Online updates about this book can be found on Rough Guides' website at
http://www.roughguides.com/

Among those whose letters were invaluable on this edition were: Alan Ambrose, Bente Amundsen, Kathryn Anderlie, Victoria Armstrong, Hans Arya, Meiko Asahi, Nick Atkinson, Phil Baarda, Adam Bailey, Ben & Rupinder, Bhagvati of Tika Gumru, Chris Bannister, Richard Boily, Susan & John Bowman, Jane Brace, Simon Broughton, Martin Bryant, John Bushaway, Mr Baldev S Chauhan, Lisa Clift, Pat Colbert, Michelle Coles, Jim Cook & Ulli, Michelle Cursley, Aparna Datta, Anant Dhotrekar, Marc Dyer & Karen Cooper, Clive Errington-Watson, Galadriel Frond, G Gardner, John R Gee, Dr Gautam Ghosh, Philip Giles, Nigel & Savi Goodall, Steve Gordon, Dara Gorelick, Jane Graham, Judith Gregory, Lydia Hassall & Dodie Khurshid, Andrea Hechle, Nicholas Holloway, Peter Holmes, Rachel Hurford & Michael Ormiston, Carolina Jareno, CM Jones, Conor Kilgallan, Hans Kollmann, Dr Thoms Leitha, Petra Lindheim, Liz & Anne (Australia), Donal McMonagle, Kevin McSweeny, Neil Manley, Clare Mason, DM Mazumdar, Annette Miller, Suzanne Mrozik, Ole Jacob Nilsen, Rebecca Norman, Annika Orjmark, Gillian Ottet, D Patel, Alexandra Pateman, Jill Prescott, Sub Lietenant MH Rajesh, Peter Ras, JP Robertson, Ad van Schaik, Ansgar Schoberl, Steven Schwartz, Tracey Schwartz, Dr Keith & Mrs Jenny Selkirk, Phil Shirely, Brijraj Singh, Graham Smitheram, Rob Sperring, Tod Stansburg, Kay Starr, Andrew Starkie, Stephanie (Australia), Cyril Stephen, Andrew Stephens, Andrew Stoneman, Godfrey Talbot, Michel Tanis & Manja Thiry, Geoffrey Taunton, N Theobold, DV Tindale, Thomas Toll, Paola Topliss & Ben Rose, Edwin Towill, Ross Tucker, AJ Tyrrell, Francis Uhlman, Ariadne van de Ven & John Prescott, Richard Waghorn, Mark Wallace, Johnny Whitright, SJ Wise, Lindsay Wright, R Wyburn, Justin Zaman and Ulrika Ziesmer.

ROUGH GUIDES

Travel Guides • Phrasebooks • Music and Reference Guides

We set out to do something different when the first **Rough Guide** was published in 1982. Mark Ellingham, just out of university, was travelling in Greece. He brought along the popular guides of the day, but found they were all lacking in some way. They were either strong on ruins and museums but went on for pages without mentioning a beach or taverna. Or they were so conscious of the need to save money that they lost sight of Greece's cultural and historical significance. Also, none of the books told him anything about Greece's contemporary life – its politics, its culture, its people, and how they lived.

So with no job in prospect, Mark decided to write his own guidebook, one which aimed to provide practical information that was second to none, detailing the best beaches and the hottest clubs and restaurants, while also giving hard-hitting accounts of every sight, both famous and obscure, and providing up-to-the-minute information on contemporary culture. It was a guide that encouraged independent travellers to find the best of Greece, and was a great success, getting shortlisted for the Thomas Cook travel guide award, and encouraging Mark, along with three friends, to expand the series.

The Rough Guide list grew rapidly and the letters flooded in, indicating a much broader readership than had been anticipated, but one which uniformly appreciated the Rough Guide mix of practical detail and humour, irreverence and enthusiasm. Things haven't changed. The same four friends who began the series are still the caretakers of the Rough Guide mission today: to provide the most reliable, up-to-date and entertaining information to independent-minded travellers of all ages, on all budgets.

We now publish 100 titles and have offices in London and New York. The **travel guides** are written and researched by a dedicated team of more than 100 authors, based in Britain, Europe, the USA and Australia. We have also created a unique series of **phrasebooks** to accompany the travel series, along with an acclaimed series of **music guides**, and a best-selling **pocket guide to the Internet and World Wide Web**. We also publish comprehensive travel information on our two **web sites**: http://www.hotwired.com/rough and http://www.roughguides.com/

THE AUTHORS

Born in Cardiff, Wales, **David Abram** first travelled to India aged 18, returning with the first of several notoriously soporific slide shows and a desire to return, which he did a couple of years later while a student of French at Warwick University. Subsequent attempts to make a living out of travel have taken him as an English teacher to various southern European countries, as a post-graduate anthropologist to a Native American reservation in the US, and as a *Rough Guide* author to Goa, the Scottish Highlands and Corsica. When not trapped in front of a word processor, he spends as much time as possible playing music in his home town Bath, UK.

Devdan Sen, born in West Bengal, travelled extensively in his own country before leaving to study at the School of Oriental and African Studies in London. He is now based in Surrey, England, though writing, climbing and photography give him plenty of excuses to get back to India as much as possible.

In 1989 **Harriet Sharkey** taught English in Pakistan and travelled through India and Nepal for seven months. Back home, she took a degree in Comparative Religion at Manchester University, specializing in Buddhism, Sanskrit and Pali, and has returned to India almost every year since then, fitting trekking and wildlife-viewing around research trips for the *Rough Guide*. She lives with her husband, Dee, in the English Lake District where she makes a living from writing, for *Rough Guides* among others.

Following his work in the early 1980s with experimental band *this heat*, **Gareth John Williams** moved to south India to study classical theatre and music. Later he studied Indian religion, art, archeology and music at London University. His writing about, and fascination with, Indian arts, culture and mythology continues unabated.

KASHMIR

Due to the current political unrest in the region, this edition of *The Rough Guide to India* does not include an account of **Kashmir** and its capital, Srinagar, nor the area around the troubled city of **Jammu**. We felt it would be irresponsible to encourage readers to travel through the east of Jammu & Kashmir, particularly with so many tempting, and politically stable, destinations accessible in other areas of the north-west Himalaya.

The current spate of disturbances first came to a head in the late 1980s, after nearly forty years of separatist agitations for an independent Muslim state. Orchestrated by Pakistani-backed paramilitary groups, the violence targeted Indian government buildings and personnel, as well as army and police posts, and provoked a robust response from New Delhi. Huge numbers of troops were drafted into the region, curfews implemented, and thousands of suspected "militants" detained without trial. Widespread riots, sieges and killings ensued, both in the Kashmir valley, and the area around Jammu, further south, which has been plagued by bombings and shootings since the early 1990s.

The impact of the troubles on **tourism** has been catastrophic. Before 1987, 150,000 visitors poured through the valley each summer, relaxing on Dal Lake's famous houseboats and hiking in the surrounding mountains. Now, virtually the only foreigners to be seen in Kashmir are journalists, or the odd tourist forced into the valley when the fragile Manali–Leh road is closed by snowfalls and landslides. The Kashmiris claim that the tourist boycott has been actively encouraged by the Indian government in an attempt to strangle the valley's economy. However, the militants have played their part, too, by abducting foreigners to gain publicity for their cause. The latest kidnapping involved five Westerners, one of whom was killed by his captors; when this book went to press, the remaining four hostages had been missing for more than eighteen months, and are believed to be dead.

The chances of getting caught up in any violence should you visit Kashmir are, of course, considerably less than the risk of a traffic accident on almost any Indian highway. Nevertheless, we strongly recommend that you avoid travelling to the region until peace returns. Quite apart from the danger, Kashmir these days is far from the appealing prospect it used to be, marred by roadblocks, sandbagged machine-gun emplacements and police posts.

CONTENTS

MAP SYMBOLS

REGIONAL MAPS

- Railway
- Main Road
- Minor Road
- Track or Trail
- River
- Ferry
- International boundary
- State boundary
- Chapter division boundary
- Mountains
- Peak
- Pass
- Waterfall
- Viewpoint
- Mudflats
- Marshland
- Beach
- Town
- Place of interest
- Airport
- Lighthouse
- Hut
- Glacier

STREET MAPS

- Railway
- Main Road
- Secondary Road
- Lane
- Track
- Path
- River
- Fortified wall
- Park
- Building
- Church
- Tourist Office
- Post Office
- Telephone
- Hotel or Restaurant
- Bus Stand

COMMON SYMBOLS

- Mosque or Muslim Monument
- Buddhist Temple
- Hindu or Jain Temple
- Ghat

LIST OF MAPS

INTRODUCTION

The home of one of the world's oldest civilizations, and several of the world's great religions, India has been changing and re-shaping itself for as long as anywhere on earth, forever producing new forms of culture and absorbing new influences. Visiting the subcontinent, you'll see Kipling-esque visions of spectacular carved temples and gleaming marble palaces, lonely Himalayan lamaseries and far-flung dusty villages where council meetings are held under the shade of a *banyan* tree, plodding camels and man-eating tigers, holy cows, snake charmers and wild-haired *sadhus*: you'll also find a dynamic state racing towards the twenty-first century. The boundaries of modern India, fixed less than fifty years ago, are merely the latest in a four-thousand-year sequence of redefinitions that have produced one of the most heterogenous societies in the world. The land where the Buddha lived and preached, and where the Moghul Muslims erected the Taj Mahal, has recreated itself as both a majority Hindu nation and the world's largest secular democracy, home to almost one thousand million people.

Many first-time visitors cannot see past the grinding poverty of the country's most disadvantaged citizens. Others expect a timeless ascetic wonderland and are indignant to find that materialism has its place here too. Still more find themselves intimidated by what may seem, initially, an incomprehensible and bewildering continent.

This book sets out, chapter by chapter, to guide you through the states, cities and towns of India, offering historical, architectural and cultural information to enrich your trip, whether you intend to travel for a few weeks or several months. The guide's intention is to spare you the mistakes and anti-climaxes that can spoil the best-laid plans, and to direct you towards off-beat delights as well as world-famous landmarks. Each chapter covers a specific state or region, starting off by introducing its major sights, surveying its history, and summarizing its major travel routes. In each town we've detailed the best places to stay and eat, reviewing palace hotels of faded grandeur alongside inexpensive lodges and simple pilgrim guesthouses, and Mughlai

ROUGH GUIDES FAVOURITES

Wildlife Parks and Nature Reserves

Bandhavgahr (MP) Hilly grassland; probably your best chance of seeing a tiger. p.408.

Corbett (UP) Tiger sanctuary in the high Himalayan wilderness. p.287.

Gir Forest (Guj) The last refuge of the rare Asiatic lion, symbol of Buddhist emperor Ashoka. p.596.

Ranthambore (Raj) Jungle cats, paradise fly-catchers, a medieval fort, *chhatris* and palaces. p.160.

The Sunderbans (WB) Where crocodiles and amphibious man-eating tigers lurk in the marshes of West Bengal. p.805.

Beaches

Kovalam (Ker) Friendly hang-out a rickshaw-ride away from the relaxed south Indian town of Thiruvananthapuram. Increasingly commercialized, with scores of restaurants and places to stay. p.1064.

Mamallapuram (TN) Long, empty beaches overlooked by ancient shore temple, and a stone's throw from superb rock carvings. p.981.

Palolem (Goa) Exquisite crescent-shaped palm-backed bay in Goa's relaxed south. p.766.

Varkala (Ker) Kerala's low-key alternative to Kovalam; sheer red cliffs and amazing sea views. p.1071.

restaurants next to village food stalls that dish up spicy *dals* in spotless tin trays. We haven't set out to list the cheapest options everywhere, because here, as anywhere else, the cheapest can easily be the worst. As well as providing detailed accounts of all the major sights, we provide the information you need to search out performing arts, enjoy Indian cinema, explore ashrams and religious centres, and get swept away by the fervour of the great festivals.

The best Indian **itineraries** are the simplest. To imagine that there is some set list of places you must go, or things you must see, is a sure way to make your trip self-defeating. You couldn't see everything in one expedition, even if you spent a year trying. Far better then, to concentrate on one or two specific regions, and above all, to be flexible. Although it requires a deliberate change of pace to venture away from the cities, rural India has its own very distinct pleasures. In fact, while Indian cities are undoubtedly adrenalin-fuelled, upbeat places, it is possible – and certainly less stressful – to travel for months around the subcontinent and rarely have to set foot in one.

The **Basics** section, which takes up the first 75 pages of this book, provides an overview of the practical aspects of travelling in India. To put it simply, it's not as difficult as you may imagine, or may be told. Some travellers impose an exhausting sequence of long-distance journeys and other privations upon themselves that no Indian would dream of attempting, and then wonder why they're not enjoying their trip. Although becoming overtired is an almost inevitable part of travelling around India, getting ill – despite the interminable tales of Delhi-belly and associated hardships so proudly told by a certain type of India bore – certainly isn't. If you give yourself time to rest there's no reason why you should pick up anything worse than a headache. **Food** is generally extremely good, especially in south India, famed for its creative vegetarian cuisine; **water** can be bought in bottles, just like anywhere else in the world, and there are plenty of comfortable, inexpensive places to **stay**. Though the sheer size of the country means that **travel** is seldom straightforward, the extensive road, rail and air links ensure that few destinations are inaccessible, and fares are invariably cheap. Furthermore, the widespread use of English makes communication easy for the majority of Western visitors. Journeys may be long – a four-hour bus ride is normal, and travelling constantly for thirty hours not uncommon – but they can provide some of the very best moments of a trip: punctuated with frequent food stops and memorable encounters, and passing through sleepy villages and an everchanging landscape. For

---

Monuments

Ajanta caves (M) Vibrant murals in caves chiselled into basalt cliffs. p.683.

Alchi gompa (L) Ancient Buddhist murals and wood sculpture, hidden away in a hamlet beside the River Indus. p.517.

Darasuram (TN) Exquisite Chola temple near the holy city of Kumbakonam. p.1008.

Ellora caves (M) Buddhist, Hindu and Jain caves, and the Hindu Kailash temple, carved from a single rock. p.676.

Hampi /Vijayanagar (Kar) Deserted city of one of the greatest Hindu empires, scattered over a bizarre landscape of giant golden-brown boulders. p.1163.

Khajuraho (MP) Superbly restored temples, famed for erotic carvings. p.387.

Konarak (Ori) Ruined temple – an enormous chariot dedicated to the sun god Surya. p.933.

Mamallapuram (TN) Dazzling bas-reliefs and caves with south India's earliest stone-built temple on the seashore. p.981.

Orchha (MP) Deserted medieval city of palaces, carved *havelis*, temples and cenotaphs in peaceful riverbank setting. p.384.

Palitana (Guj) Almost nine hundred Jain temples crowning a hill. p.604.

Sanchi (MP) Immaculate Buddhist *stupa*, one of India's earliest religious structures, surrounded by intricate sculpture. p.360.

Taj Mahal (UP) Simply the world's greatest monument: this anthem to romantic love fully matches all expectations. p.226.

long hauls, much the best way to go is by **train**; with computerized booking now established almost everywhere, the Indian rail network is as efficient as almost any in the world. Rail journeys also offer the chance to meet other travellers and Indians from all walks of life, and a constant stream of activity as *chai*-wallahs, peanut-sellers, musicians, astrologers and mendicants wander through the carriages. The travel details in each chapter will help you decide on the most convenient transport, show you the best way to book tickets, and save a great deal of time and frustration.

Finally, the **Contexts** at the end of the book draw together the many facets of Indian life and culture discussed throughout the *Guide*, including summaries of the subcontinent's **history** and manifold **religions**, and overviews of Indian **music** and **cinema** – among the least understood art forms in the world. We also recommend further reading to enjoy before you go and as you travel.

When and where to go

Before you decide exactly **where** you go in India, you need to take into account **when** you're going. Broadly speaking, the **best time to visit** most of the country is after the monsoon, and before the summer heat returns – effectively, between October and March. At that time, conditions in the hottest regions, such as Rajasthan and Madhya Pradesh, are at their mildest, and major festivals are held all over the country, while the scenery of southern India is a delight. Between April and September, you should either expect to have to pace yourself even more slowly than at other times, or head for the

---

Pilgrimage Sites

Amritsar (H&P) Site of the fabled Golden Temple, the Sikhs' holiest shrine. p.540.

Bodh Gaya (B) Where the Buddha gained enlightenment; visited by pilgrims from all over the world. p.841.

Gangotri (UP) Where the sacred Ganga springs from a Himalayan ice-cave; desolate, craggy scenery, a short walk to one of the most beautiful glaciers in the inner Himalayas. p.271.

Gokarn (Kar) Traditional temple town within walking distance of superb beaches. p.1158.

Madurai (TN) Definitive south Indian city, centred on its vibrant, compelling medieval temple. p.1023.

Puri (Ori) Gigantic pyramidal Jagannath Temple, one of the four Hindu "Abodes of the Divine". p.923.

Pushkar (Raj) Atmospheric desert town; *ghats* lead down to a shimmering lake, and boasts one of two temples in the world dedicated solely to Lord Brahma. p.165.

Sravanabelgola (Kar) Extraordinary hilltop naked Jain colossus. p.1147.

Varanasi (UP) City of Light, founded by Shiva, where the bathing *ghats* beside the Ganga teem with pilgrims. p.322.

Great Journeys

Camel treks (Raj) Wonderfully romantic, if utterly touristy, way to experience the deserts of Rajasthan; sleep under the stars and visit desert villages. p.179.

Kalka–Shimla: The Viceroy's Toy Train (HP) Tiny blue-and-white diesel locomotive rattling up to the popular summer hill station, deep in the Himalayan foothills. p.437.

Kettuvallam backwaters (Ker) Long lazy boat trips through lush tropical waterways. p.1078.

The Manali–Leh Highway (HP/L) India's greatest high-Himalayan road trip, along the second highest road in the world. p.490.

Neral–Matheran (M) Train up to Maharashtra hill station along 20km of track with 281 sharp bends; hard wooden benches are the price you pay for extraordinary views. p.699.

The Palace on Wheels (Raj) India's answer to the *Orient Express*; one of the most magnificent, opulent train journeys in the world, taking travellers in one pampered week to Rajasthan's major cities and to Agra. p.133.

high mountains, as this is the trekking season in the Himalayas. For more on the general topography of India, and the temperatures and rainfall to expect at different times of the year, see p.52.

The most-travelled circuit, combining spectacular monuments with the flat arid landscape that for many people is archetypally Indian, is the so-called "Golden Triangle" in the north – **Delhi** itself, the capital, and within easy reach of it **Agra**, the home of the Taj Mahal, and the Pink City of Rajasthan, **Jaipur**. **Rajasthan** is probably the single most popular state with travellers, who are drawn by its desert scenery, and the romantic Rajput past epitomized by the fort of Jaisalmer, the palaces of Udaipur, and the hilltop temples of Mount Abu.

North of Delhi stretch the mighty **Himalayas**. Kashmir was until the recent escalation of tensions the most touristed region of the mountains; on p.vi we explain why we do not include a chapter on the state in this book. We do, however, include very detailed accounts of the other Indian Himalayan regions, which partly as a result of government policy are rapidly developing their facilities for visitors. Both **Himachal Pradesh** – where Dharamsala is the home of a Tibetan community that includes the Dalai Lama himself – and **Uttar Pradesh** – where the glacial source of the sacred River Ganges has attracted pilgrims for over a thousand years – offer magnificent trekking, while deeper in the mountains, **Ladakh** and **Sikkim** are scattered with remote Buddhist monasteries.

East of Delhi, the Ganges meanders through some of India's most densely populated regions to reach the extraordinary holy Hindu city of **Varanasi** (also known as

Music and Festivals

Dussehra: Kullu (HP) Village deities brought to Kullu and led in procession by the master god of them all, Raghunathji. Folk music and funfairs. p.471.

Hemis Setchu (L) Two days in summer when this peaceful *gompa* comes alive, crowded with Ladakhi villagers: monks mime out ancient Buddhist texts, while children scamper to join them. p.511.

Khajuraho (MP) Springtime classical dance festival in the ancient city of the Chandellas. p.395.

Konarak (Ori) Odissi dance performances beside the Sun Temple. p.936.

Nizamuddin (D) Medieval district of Delhi, where you can catch hypnotic *qawwali* performances in the exquisite marble courtyard of a Sufi shrine. p.97.

Pushkar camel mela (Raj) The sacred desert city becomes a flurry of life, when camel traders flock from all over the state to race and sell their animals. p.168.

Shantiniketan (WB) Rabindranath Tagore's traditions continue, in the home of the itinerant Baul musicians. p.808.

Thrissur Puram (Ker) Spangled elephants and fireworks accompanied by ear-shattering south Indian drums. p.1104.

Palaces and Forts

Amber Palace (Raj) Breathtaking palace complex: ivory and sandalwood carvings, glittering mirror mosaics and best of all, elephant rides. p.145.

City palace, Jaipur (Raj) Resplendent Rajasthani palace in the wonderful Pink City. p.138.

Daulatabad (M) Imposing Muslim fort that briefly replaced Delhi as capital in the 1300s. p.672.

Golconda (AP). Resolutely elephant-proof stronghold of the Qutb Shahs. p.1190.

Jaisalmer (Raj) Honey-coloured fairy-tale fort, emerging from the desert sands. p.178.

Jai Vilas, Gwalior (MP) Shamelessly eccentric nineteenth-century palace crammed with fusty antiques. p.377.

Junagarh Fort, Bikaner (Raj) Behind a modest exterior, this sixteenth-century fort shelters magnificent murals and sculpture. p.185.

Padmanabhapuram (Ker) Archetypal south Indian tiled-roofed palace, notable for its religious murals. p.1069.

Stok palace (L) Dignified residence of the Ladakhi royals. p.508.

Benares), where to witness the daily rituals of life and death focused around the water-front *ghats* (bathing places) is to glimpse the continuing practice of India's most ancient religious traditions. Further east still is the great city of **Calcutta**, the capital until early this century of the British Raj, and now a vibrant centre of Bengali culture that also epitomizes contemporary India's most pressing problems, poverty and over-population.

Heading south from Calcutta along the coast, you come first to **Orissa**, where Puri's Jugganath temple is the scene of one of India's greatest festivals, and the temple at Konarak has re-emerged from beneath the sands to re-state its claims as one of the most fabulous achievements of the medieval stonemasons. **Tamil Nadu**, further south, has its own tradition of magnificent architecture, with towering *gopura* gateways dominating towns whose thriving temple complexes are still the focus of everyday life, scuttling with devotees, tourists, gaily painted elephants, and clattering musicians. **Kerala**, near the southernmost tip of the subcontinent on the western coast, is India at its most tropical, and relaxed, with lush backwaters teeming with simple wooden craft of all shapes and sizes, and red-roofed towns and villages all but invisible between the verdant canopy of palm trees. Here, in south India, you will dine on what is simply one of the finest cuisines on earth. Further up the coast is **Goa**, the former Portuguese colony whose 100km-coastline is fringed with beaches to suit all tastes and budgets, from upmarket package tourists to zonked-out ravers, and whose towns hold whitewashed Christian churches that might have been transplanted from Europe.

Some of India's most memorable monuments lie far inland, on long-forgotten trading routes across the heart of the peninsula – the abandoned city of **Vijayanagar** (or **Hampi**) in **Karnataka**, whose ruins are scattered across a primeval boulder-strewn landscape; the painted and sculpted Buddhist caves of **Ajanta** and **Ellora** in Maharashtra; the deserted temples of **Khajuraho** and palaces of **Orchha** in Madhya Pradesh. Finally, there's much-maligned **Bombay**, an ungainly beast that has been the major focus of the nationwide drift to the big cities. Centre of the country's formidable popular movie industry, it reels along on an undeniable energy that, after a few days of acclimatization, can prove compelling.

As we've said, however, to appreciate your travels to the full you'll need to conserve your energies. On a long trip, it makes sense to pause and rest a while every few weeks. Certain places have fulfilled that function for generations. Dotted across the continent are the Victorian **hill stations**, resorts designed to escape the summer heat, created by the British towards the end of the last century wherever a suitable stretch of hills stood conveniently close to the workaday cities of the plains. Within the last thirty years, a network of "alternative" hang-outs for young budget travellers has also developed. These are often places where a tourist infrastructure had already been created, such as the beach resort of **Mamallapuram** in Tamil Nadu, which is also the site of some of India's earliest surviving experiments in temple architecture, or Hampi, mentioned above, or **Manali**, a former hill station in Himachal Pradesh. Elsewhere, the presence of sand and sea is enough, as with many of the beaches of Goa, or **Kovalam** or **Varkala** in Kerala.

PART ONE

THE

BASICS

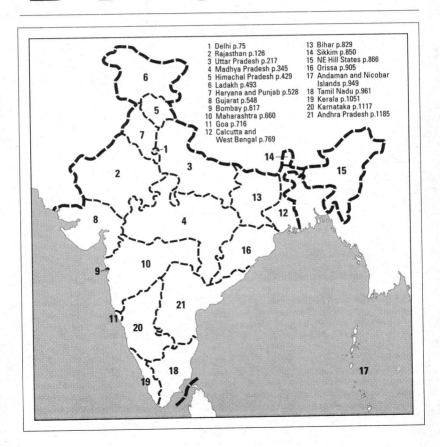

GETTING THERE FROM BRITAIN AND IRELAND

Direct flights to India from Britain – the quickest, if not necessarily the least expensive, way to reach the subcontinent – serve Delhi, Bombay, Madras and Calcutta. Although Delhi and Bombay are that bit nearer and that bit cheaper, which city you choose to fly to will obviously depend on the area(s) of the country you're intending to explore. If cutting costs is a major priority, investigate the possibilities opened up by taking an indirect flight. As this involves a change of plane, it inevitably takes a few hours longer at the very least, though it may also allow you the option of a stopover on the way out or back. For short stays only, there are also ever-increasing numbers of charter flights to Goa and Kovalam in Kerala. However you go, though, be sure to shop around, as prices can vary wildly between agents.

Most days, around three direct flights leave **London** for **Delhi**, with *Air India*, *British Airways*, *Air Canada* and *Thai Airways* among airlines flying the route. Discounted return fares on these vary from just under £450 in low season (roughly Jan, Feb, March, May, June & Nov) to upwards of £550 in high season (July, Aug & Dec). *Air Canada* tend to be the cheapest, but *Air India* and *BA* sometimes have off-season special offers, which can drop as low as £400 or less.

Cheaper fares – down to as little as £330 return out of season – can usually be found if you're prepared to take an indirect flight with an airline such as *Aeroflot*, *Tarom*, *Air Uzbekistan*, or *Syrian Arab Airlines*. However, there has been a lot of concern expressed recently about the safety records of some of these (notably *Aeroflot*). Also they can involve long late-night or multi-day stopovers in unlikely and inhospitable places, and have been known to leave passengers stranded for weeks waiting for a seat on the return flight (this is liable to happen at peak periods, so book your return flight as soon as possible). Consequently, many agents refuse to deal with them. *Royal Jordanian* is another important discount airline flying via Amman.

BA and *Air India* also fly direct daily from **London to Bombay**. Prices are much the same as those to Delhi. *Egyptair*, with a change in Cairo, charge one fare year round, which usually makes them the cheapest option in high season. You can extend the stopover in Cairo for around £100. *Singapore Airlines* fly direct twice weekly from Manchester to Bombay.

BA's three weekly direct flights from **London to Madras** cost upwards of £550 return in low season, £650 high season, sometimes reduced as low as £420. Going *Air India* and changing at Bombay may save a little, or you can fly *Air Lanka* and change at Colombo (£550–600; they also fly to Tiruchirapalli and Thiruvananthapuram).

Only *BA* fly direct from **London to Calcutta**, twice weekly; fares with them and with *Air India* cost slightly less than to Madras. *Tarom* and *Aeroflot* are bargain-basement alternatives, at around £350–400 return.

There are no direct flights to India from any **other British cities**. You could fly *BA*, changing at London, but add-on fares are high. From Manchester, your best bet is with *Emirates* to Delhi or Bombay via Dubai for £420–520, depending on season, or with *Singapore* for £450. You can also pick up *KLM* flights to India by flying first to Amsterdam; either fly *KLM* from Belfast, Birmingham, Bristol, Cardiff or Manchester, or *Air UK* from Aberdeen, Edinburgh, Glasgow, Humberside, Leeds/Bradford, Norwich, or Newcastle. Similarly, *Air France* fly to Paris from Birmingham, Bristol, Edinburgh and Glasgow; in general, both *KLM* and *Air France* beat *BA* by about £50–100, with return tickets often discounted to as low as £420.

British companies operating winter (Oct–May) **charters to Goa** include *Hayes and Jarvis*,

AIRLINES AND AGENTS IN BRITAIN

Airlines

Aeroflot ☎0171/355 2233
70 Piccadilly, London W1.

Air Canada ☎0990/247226
7–8 Conduit St, London W1R.

Air France ☎0181/742 6600
177 Piccadilly, London W1Z.

Air India ☎01753/368 4828
Mathison Building, Colnbook, Slough SL3 OHF.

Air Lanka ☎0171/930 4688
22 Regent St, London SW1.

Air UK ☎01345/666777
Stansted Airport, Essex CM24

Biman Bangladesh Airlines ☎0171/629 0252
17 Conduit St, London W1.

British Airways ☎01345/222111
156 Regent St, London W1.

Egypt Air ☎0171/734 2395
296 Regent St, London W1R.

Emirates ☎0171/930 5356
125 Pall Mall, London SW1Y.

Gulf Air ☎0171/408 1717
14 Albermarle St, London W1X.

KLM ☎0181/750 9000
Plesman House, 190 Great South West Rd, Bedfont,
Middlesex TW14 9RL.

Pakistan International Airways ☎0171/734 5544
45-46 Piccadilly, London W1

Royal Jordanian ☎0171/734 2557
177 Regent St, London W1.

Singapore Airlines ☎0181/747 0007
143–147 Regent St, London W1.

Swissair ☎0171/434 7300
Swiss Centre, 1 Swiss Court, London W1V.

TAROM Romanian Airlines ☎0171/224 3693
27 New Cavendish St, London W1M.

Thai Airways ☎0171/491 7953
41 Albermarle St, London W1X.

Uzbekistan Air ☎0171/935 1899
72 Wigmore St, London W1.

Discount Flight Agents

Campus Travel
52 Grosvenor Gardens, London SW1.
☎0171/730 8111

541 Bristol Rd, Birmingham ☎0121/414 1848
39 Queen's Rd, Clifton, Bristol ☎0117/929 2494
5 Emmanuel St, Cambridge ☎01223/324283
53 Forest Rd, Edinburgh ☎0131/668 3303
166 Deansgate, Manchester ☎0161/833 2046
105-106 St Aldates, Oxford ☎01865/242067
61 Ditchling Rd, Brighton ☎01273/570226
*Student/youth travel specialists, with branches also
in YHA shops and on campuses all over Britain.*

Flightfile ☎0171/700 2722
49 Tottenham Court Rd, London W1.
Recommended for budget flights.

Global Travel ☎0171/629 5123
10 Maddox St, London W1.
*Competitive rates for India and neighbouring coun-
tires with most carriers.*

Globe Air ☎0171/493 4343
93 Piccadilly, Mayfair, London W1.
Competitive fares, particularly for cheaper airlines.

STA Travel
74 Old Brompton Rd, London SW7.
☎0171/361 6262

25 Queen's Rd, Bristol ☎0117/929 4399
38 Sidney St, Cambridge ☎01223/366966
75 Deansgate, Manchester ☎0161/834 0668
*Discount fares, with particularly good deals for stu-
dents and young people.*

Trailfinders
42–50 Earls Court Rd, London W8. ☎0171/938 3366
194 Kensington High St, London W8.
☎0171/938 3939
58 Deansgate, Manchester ☎0161/839 6969
48 Corn St, Bristol ☎0117/929 9000
*One of the best-informed and most efficient agents
dealing with Asia; good for RTW tickets, too.*

Travel Bug ☎0161/721 4000
597 Cheetham Hill Rd, Manchester.

USIT ☎01/679 8833
Aston Quay, O'Connell Bridge, Dublin 2, Ireland.

Somak, Manos, Thompson and *Kuoni*. Leaving from Gatwick (5 weekly), Manchester (Thurs), and Glasgow and Newcastle (Tues), these are usually for stays of two weeks (though 1–6 weeks are also possible) and often work out cheaper than a stan-dard scheduled deal to Bombay. Your fare must include some form of accommodation (even if it isn't advertised as such), which you can occupy on arrival and then ditch when you're ready to move on. Charter tickets are generally sold through high-

SPECIALIST TOUR OPERATORS IN BRITAIN

Abercrombie and Kent ☎0171/730 9600
Sloane Square House, Holbein Place, London SW1W
8NS. *Upmarket sightseeing and tailor-made holidays, plus ExplorAsia's trekking and wildlife trips.*

Alfred Gregory Holidays ☎0114/272 9428
c/o Woodcock Travel, 25–31 Wicker, Sheffield S3
8HW. *Annual photographic trip from a firm founded by Tensing and Hillary's official snapshot man.*

Asia Experience ☎0171/636 4343
83 Mortimer St, London W1N 7TB. *Tailor-made and regular tours for individuals or groups.*

Bales ☎01306/740048
Bales House, Junction Rd, Dorking, Surrey RH4 3EJ.
Well-established India tour operator with a range of sightseeing and wildlife trips.

Butterfield's Indian Railway Tours
☎01262/470230
Burton Fleming, Driffield, Yorks YO25 0PQ. *Train tours of north or south India in the company's own special "bogie" (carriage).*

Coromandel ☎01572/821330
Andrew Brock Travel Ltd, 54 High St, Uppingham,
Rutland LE15 9PZ. *Car tours, textile tours to village craft workshops, plus David Sayer's botanical and horticultural tours, and Himalaya treks.*

Cox & Kings ☎0171/873 5000
4th Floor, Gorden House, 10 Greencoat Pl, London
SW1P. *Tailor-made itineraries with operators established in the days of the Raj.*

Cygnus Wildlife Worldwide ☎01548/856178
96 Fore St, Kingsbridge, Devon TQ7 1PY.
Birdwatching and tiger-watching tours.

Discover India ☎0181/429 3300
29 Fairview Cres, Rayners Lane, Harrow, Middx HA2
9UB. *Tailor-made trips including tours arranged for pilgrims and cricket teams.*

Encounter Overland ☎0171/370 6845
67 Old Brompton Rd, London SW5. *Whistlestop tours of Indian regions in Bedford trucks.*

Exodus Expeditions ☎0181/675 5550
9 Weir Rd, London SW12 0LT. *Mountain-biking in Ladakh, hiking in the Himalayas and truck tours by established experts.*

Explore Worldwide ☎01252/319448
1 Frederick St, Aldershot, Hants GU11 1LQ. *Trekking, walking and sightseeing.*

Global Link ☎0171/409 7766
Colette House, 52–55 Piccadilly, London W1V 9AA.
Run a gourmet food tour as well as standard and tailor-made sightseeing.

Highlife Holidays ☎0181/452 3388
79 Cricklewood Bdy, London NW2 3JR. *Sightseeing tours with optional Goa beach extensions.*

High Places ☎0114/275 7500
The Globeworks, Penstone Rd, Sheffield S6 3AE.
Specialists in trekking and mountaineering.

Holt's Battlefield Tours ☎01304/612248
15 Market St, Sandwich, Kent. *Annual Raj and military history tours – on the Mutiny, for example – usually in Jan.*

Indian Encounters ☎01929/480548
Creech Barrow, East Creech, Wareham, Dorset BH20
5AP. *Set tours including golf, painting, textiles, and camel safaris, and tailor-made itineraries.*

Interchurch Travel Ltd ☎0800/300444
Saga Building, Middleburg Sq, Folkestone, Kent
CT20 1AZ. *Interdenominational religious-interest visits.*

Karakoram Experience ☎017687/73966
32 Lake Rd, Keswick, Cumbria CA12 5DQ. *High-altitude trekking and mountaineering.*

Maxwell Scott Agency ☎01347/878566
Foss House, Strensall, York YO3 4TU. *Fishing, trekking and other tailor-made tours.*

Munjeeta Travel ☎01483/773331
12 Cavendish Rd, Woking, Surrey GU22 0EP.
"Homestay" holidays, lodging with Indian families.

Mysteries of India ☎0181/574 2727
92 The Green, Southall, Middlesex UB2 4B6. *A choice of a dozen or so imaginatively put-together 5-star tours, some to off-track destinations.*

Pettits India ☎01892/515966
14 Lonsdale Gardens, Tunbridge Wells, Kent TN1
1NU. *Tailor-made holidays off the beaten track.*

The Romance of India by Rail ☎01232/329477
c/o *Williams Travel,* Whitehead, Co. Antrim BT38
9PZ. *Set itineraries and tailor-made tours by train.*

Somak Holidays ☎0181/423 3000
Somak House, Harrovian Village, Bessborough Rd,
Harrow-on-the-Hill, Middx HA1 3EX. *Goa beach holidays; optional sightseeing and wildlife extensions.*

Swan Hellenic ☎0171/800 2200
77 New Oxford St, London WC1A 1PP. *Art tours with specialist guides.*

Top Deck Travel ☎0171/370 4555
131–135 Earls Court Rd, London SW5 9RH. *Extensive 5-week tours – kicking off in Kathmandu – in a double-decker bus.*

Trans Indus Travel ☎0181/566 2729
Northumberland House, 11 The Pavement, Popes
Lane, London W5 4NG. *Fixed and tailor-made tours from various Indian cities; specialists in wildlife, cricket, fishing and trekking.*

Travel Alternative ☎01865/791636
27 Park End St, Oxford OX1 1HU. *Textile and handicraft tour of Rajasthan and Gujarat every February.*

street travel agents, and are also advertised in the travel pages of newspapers. **Note** that Indian passport holders cannot fly charter.

FLIGHTS FROM IRELAND

There are no direct flights to India **from Ireland**. Apart from *BA* via London, **Dublin** is also served by *Royal Jordanian* to Delhi, *Swissair* to Bombay or a combination of *Air Inter* and *Air France* to both. Of these, *Royal Jordanian* will be the cheapest in low season at IR£530 return (rising to IR£700 in high season), *Swissair* cheapest in high (around IR£600 all year). *Aeroflot's* daily flight from Shannon is the rock-bottom alternative, at around IR£500 all year round. Finally, flying *KLM* from **Belfast** to Delhi or Bombay costs the same as from London.

DISCOUNT AGENTS

The best deals on tickets to India are normally to be found through **discount agents**, who sell off excess seats for airlines at rock-bottom prices. Some of these (such as *STA*, *Campus Travel*, and *Trailfinders*) specialize in youth and student travel, and often have cheap insurance packages on offer too. When dealing with smaller agents, or **bucket shops**, make sure to get details in writing of the flight you've enquired about. Try the agents listed on the following pages, or check the ads in the Sunday newspapers.

At certain times (Christmas for one), the best-value flights can get booked up weeks, even months, in advance, so plan ahead. If you're flying on to Southeast Asia or the Middle East, it may even be possible – but unlikely to be any cheaper – to get your onward ticket in India rather than at home.

PACKAGES

A large number of operators run **package holidays** to India, covering such activities as trekking and safaris as well as sightseeing and sunbathing. Specialist minority-interest tours range from steam locomotives and war history to religion and food. Even among straight sightseeing tours, most firms have a good range of options usually including the "Golden Triangle" of Delhi, Agra and Jaipur, or a tour of Rajasthan, or a southern tour taking in Bangalore, Hyderabad, Madras and Kochi. Some also offer wildlife tours, the *Palace on Wheels* train journey (see p.31),

take in Nepal or Bhutan, or have various combinations of all these. In addition, many companies will arrange **tailor-made tours**, and can help you plan your own itinerary.

Of course, any package holiday is a lot easier than going under your own steam, particularly if you only have a short time and don't want to use it up on making your own travel bookings. On the other hand, a typical sightseeing tour can rather isolate you from the country, shutting you off in air-conditioned hotels and buses. Specialist trips such as trekking and tailor-made tours will work out rather expensive, compared to what you'd pay if you organized everything independently, but they do cut out a lot of hassle. However, Goa beach holidays, and packages to Kovalam in Kerala, particularly with charter operators, can work out cheaper than a normal flight, and usually offer tour options as extras.

FLIGHTS FROM EUROPE

Direct flights connect Delhi and Bombay with Amsterdam, Paris, Rome, Frankfurt, Geneva, Zurich and Moscow. In addition, there are flights from Bucharest to Delhi with *TAROM*, and Athens to Bombay with *Biman*. The only direct flights to Madras are from Paris (with *Air India*) and Frankfurt (with *Lufthansa*); there's also one weekly to Calcutta from Moscow (with *Aeroflot*). Amsterdam and Athens have their own array of discount agents, but Europeans may find it worthwhile to get to London and buy tickets there: try calling the UK agents listed on p.4 and comparing their prices to those available where you live.

ROUND THE WORLD

Other possibilities include taking in India as a stopover while flying, for example, between Britain and Australasia, or on a **round-the-world ticket**, which makes a lot of sense if you are planning a long trip with several stops in Asia. A typical one (£800–1400), open for a year, would depart and return to London, taking in Delhi, Bangkok, Sydney, Honolulu and LA; variations could include doing a leg from Delhi to Kathmandu overland. Among the airlines who allow you to slot such "surface sectors" in to your itinerary are *Thai* (who fly through Delhi) and *Singapore* (via Bombay), both good choices if you plan to explore Southeast Asia, as they fly in and out of five different cities in the region.

FLIGHTS PER WEEK BETWEEN INDIA AND SOUTHEAST ASIA

	Delhi	Bombay	Madras	Calcutta
Dhaka	British Airways (1) Biman (4)	Biman (2)	via Calcutta	Indian Airlines (5) Biman (24)
Karachi	PIA (3) MAS (2)	PIA (5) Indian Airlines (2) Air Lanka (1)	via Bombay	via Delhi
Kathmandu	Royal Nepal (15) Indian Airlines (7) Druk Air (1)	Royal Nepal (2)	via Calcutta	Indian Airlines (4) Royal Nepal (3)
Colombo	Air Lanka (2)	Air Lanka (2)	Air Lanka (11) Indian Airlines (7)	via Madras
Bangkok	Thai (5) Indian Airlines (2) Aeroflot (1) Air India (1) Singapore Airways (2)	Cathay (4) Air India (2)	via Kuala Lumpur or Colombo	Indian Airlines (5) Thai (3) Air India (1) Druk Air (2)
Kuala Lumpur	MAS (2) Air India (1)	Air India (2)	MAS (6) Indian Airlines (2) Air India (2)	via Bangkok or Madras
Singapore	Air India (5) Singapore (3) Aeroflot (1)	Singapore (5) Air India (22)	Air India (10) Singapore (10) Indian Airlines (3)	Royal Brunei (1) Singapore (2)
Hong Kong	Air India (5) United Airlines (6)	Cathay (4) Air India (5) Swissair (3) Air France (1)	via Singapore or Kuala Lumpur or Bombay	via Bangkok

Chittagong (Bangladesh)–Calcutta	Biman (3); Indian Airlines (1)	US$95/£65
Lahore (Pakistan)–Delhi	PIA (4)	US$65/£45
Kathmandu–Varanasi	Indian Airlines (7)	US$80/£55
Colombo–Tiruchirappalli	Air Lanka (2)	US$45/£30
Colombo–Thiruvananthapuram	Air Lanka (6); Indian Airlines (3)	US$45/£30
Penang (Malaysia)–Madras	MAS (1)	US$255/£175
Malé (Maldives)–Thiruvananthapuram	Indian Airlines (7); Air Maldives (1)	US$45/£30

There are no direct flights from **Rangoon** to India.

OVERLAND ROUTES TO INDIA

The classic Asia **overland trip** is still alive and kicking, despite periodic re-routings in the face of political circumstances. Leaving Europe at Istanbul, the usual route traverses Turkey, angles down through Iran (check beforehand that this route is open), entering Pakistan via Quetta (Afghanistan is still off-limits), thence to Lahore and across into India at Amritsar, where in the

OVERLAND EXPEDITION OPERATORS

Encounter Overland ☎0171/370 6845
267 Old Brompton Rd, London SW5 9JA .
*11-week trips to Kathmandu including 1–3 weeks in
India. No discount for getting off at Delhi (except on
a last-minute deal). Also trips within India.*

Exodus Expeditions ☎0181/675 5550
9 Weir Rd, London SW12 0LT.
*15 weeks to Kathmandu. Discount given if you get
off at Islamabad (9 weeks), but not in India.*

Hinterland Travel ☎01883/743584
2 Ivy Mill Lane, Godstone, Surrey RH9 8NH.
*London to Delhi almost entirely by train, and London
to Kathmandu by bus (3 weeks in India, discount for
getting off there).*

Top Deck Travel ☎0171/370 4555
131–135 Earls Court Rd, London SW5 9RH.
*11 weeks to Kathmandu by double-decker including
1–3 weeks in India.*

days of Partition, half the population of the Punjab used the same route: Muslims one way, Hindus and Sikhs the other. Thanks to this, crossing the border is rather an abrupt exit from the more austere world of Islam into the multi-coloured cacophony of India.

Iran is still off-limits, however, to US passport holders, who must therefore find **another route**. One way might be on the trans-Siberian express to China, thence down the Karakoram Highway – if it's open – into Pakistan; another might be to negotiate a ride on a *dhow* from the Gulf to Karachi. It may just be possible to find a cargo ship or a private yacht to take you from the Red Sea or East Africa, but don't count on it.

If you are considering coming by car, motorbike or bicycle, you'll find further information under "Driving" and "Cycling" in the "Getting Around" section on p.28.

Overland expedition operators in the UK (see box below) run 6- to 18-week trips in special vehicles along the overland trail, most finishing in Kathmandu, Nepal. Expect to pay £2000–3000 for the one-way trip from London, depending on the length of the journey (some detour around the Middle East) and the level of luxury.

GETTING THERE FROM NORTH AMERICA

India is on the other side of the planet from North America. If you live on the East Coast it's somewhat shorter to go via Europe, and from the West Coast it's shorter via the Pacific; but either way it's a long haul, involving one or more intermediate stops, and you'll arrive fresher and less jet-lagged if you can manage to fit in a few days' layover somewhere en route.

Delhi and **Bombay** are the busiest – and, in general, the cheapest – air gateways to India, and either one makes a good starting/ending point for a tour of the whole country or of the popular north and west. Some airlines fly into **Madras**, the main port of entry for the south, and **Calcutta**, in the east; *Air India* also offers direct flights to Goa, on the west coast, and *Gulf Air* flies to Thiruvananthapuram in the south. You should be able to ticket a connecting internal flight on *Indian Airlines*, the domestic carrier, at the same time as your international flight. Some typical one-way add-on fares: Delhi to Agra $35; Delhi to Bangalore $246; Delhi to Bombay $130; Bombay to Bangalore £103. (*Indian Airlines'* unlimited-travel air passes can also be purchased in advance for around $500 for 21 days, good for one-way only – see "Getting Around".)

Air fares from North America to India are highest from the beginning of June to late August, which is fortunate since not too many travellers want to go then anyway. They drop during the "shoulder" seasons (Sept to early December and during the last half of May), but you'll get the best deals during low season (mid-Dec to mid-May, excluding Christmas). Note that flying on weekends ordinarily adds about $100 to the round-trip fare; price ranges quoted in the sections below assume midweek travel.

If India is only one stop on a longer journey, you might want to consider buying a **round-the-world ticket**. Some travel agents can sell you an "off-the-shelf" RTW ticket, touching down in about half a dozen cities (Delhi is on most itineraries); others will have to assemble one for you, usually more expensive. Figure on $1500 for a minimum RTW ticket including India and Europe. A more extensive RTW ticket will cost around $3000.

SHOPPING FOR TICKETS

Airline tickets are sold through many channels, and there's no magic rule for predicting which will be cheapest. Whatever the airlines are offering, however, any number of specialist travel agents set out to beat it. These are the outfits you'll see advertising in the Sunday newspaper travel sections, and they come in several forms. **Consolidators** buy up large blocks of tickets to sell at a discount. Besides being cheap, they don't normally impose advance purchase requirements (although in busy times you'll want to book ahead to be sure of getting a seat), but they do often charge very stiff fees for date changes; note also that airlines generally won't alter tickets after they've gone to a consolidator, so you can only make changes through the consolidator. Also, as these companies' margins are pretty tiny, they make their money by dealing in volume – don't expect them to entertain lots of questions. **Discount agents** also wheel and deal in blocks of tickets offloaded by the airlines, but typically offer a range of other travel-related services such as insurance, youth and student ID cards, car rentals, tours and the like. They tend to be most

---

MAJOR AIRLINES IN NORTH AMERICA

Aeroflot ☎1-800/995 5555
Flights from several US cities and Montreal to Moscow; connections to Delhi only.

Air Canada ☎1-800/776-3000
All major Canadian cities to London, and on to Delhi. Only direct flight is Vancouver to Delhi.

Air France ☎1-800/237 2747
To Paris from several US cities, Montreal and Toronto; connections to Delhi and Bombay.

Air India ☎1-800/223 7776 or 212/751 6200
New York and Toronto to Delhi, Bombay, Madras and Calcutta; also New York to Goa.

British Airways ☎1-800/247 9297
From major US cities and Montreal and Toronto to London, and on to Delhi, Bombay, Madras and Calcutta.

Cathay Pacific ☎1-800/233 2742
From New York, LA, Toronto and Vancouver to Hong Kong; connections to Bombay.

Egypt Air ☎1-800/334 6787
New York (and LA once a week) to Cairo and on to Bombay.

Gulf Air ☎1-800/553 2824
New York and Houston to various Gulf capitals; connections to Delhi, Bombay and Thiruvananthapuram.

KLM ☎1-800/374 7747 (US)
☎1-800/361 5073 (Canada)
Major US and Canadian cities to Amsterdam; connections to Delhi, Bombay and Calcutta.

Kuwait Airways ☎1-800/458 9248
New York to London, London to Kuwait, and on to Delhi and Bombay.

Lufthansa ☎1-800/645 3880
From 12 US cities and Toronto, Vancouver and Calgary to Frankfurt; connections to Bombay, Delhi and Madras.

Malaysia Airlines ☎1-800/421-8641
Flies from LA and Vancouver to Kuala Lumpur (stopover); connections to Delhi and Madras.

Northwest Airlines ☎1-800/225 2525
From several US and Canadian cities to India in cooperation with Air India and KLM.

PIA ☎1-800/221 2552
New York to Karachi/Lahore, on to Delhi and Bombay.

Singapore Airlines ☎1-800/742 3333
LA, San Francisco, New York or Vancouver to Singapore; connections to Delhi, Bombay, Calcutta and Madras.

Thai International ☎1-800/426 5204
LA to Bangkok; connections to Delhi and Calcutta.

worthwhile to students and under-26s. **Discount travel clubs**, offering money off air tickets, car rental and the like, are an option if you travel a lot. Most charge annual membership fees.

Don't automatically assume that tickets bought through a travel specialist will be cheapest – once you get a quote, check with the airlines and you may turn up an even cheaper promotion. Be advised also that the pool of travel companies is swimming with sharks – exercise caution with any outfit that sounds shifty or impermanent, and *never* deal with a company that demands cash up front or refuses to accept credit cards.

NORTH AMERICAN TOUR OPERATORS

Above the Clouds ☎1-800/233 4499
PO Box 398, Wooster, MA 01602. *Treks to remote areas.*

Adventure Center ☎1-800/227 8747
1311 63rd St, Emeryville, CA 94608. *Trekking and cultural tours.*

Cox & Kings ☎1-800/999 1758
511 Lexington Ave, Suite 388, New York, NY 10017. *Deluxe and special interest sightseeing.*

Himalayan Travel ☎1-800/225 2380
110 Prospect St, Stamford, CT 06901. *Custom regional tours.*

Geographic Expeditions ☎1-800/777 8183
2627 Lombard St, San Francisco, CA 94123. *Unusual tours including sea kayaking in the Andamans.*

Journeyworld International ☎1-800/635 3900
119 West 57th St, Penthouse N, New York, NY 10019. *Regional tours.*

Mercury Travels Limited ☎1-800/223 1474
820 2nd Ave, Suite 1302, New York, NY 10017. *Custom regional tours.*

Mountain Travel/Sobek ☎1-800/227 2384
6420 Fairmount Ave, El Cerrito, CA 94530. *Trekking and camel safaris. Cultural trip to Ladakh.*

Nature Expeditions International
☎1-800/869 0639 or 503/484 6529
474 Wilamette St, Suite 203, Eugene, OR 97401. *Wildlife and cultural tours.*

Tours of Distinction ☎1-800/888 8634
141 East 44th St, New York, NY 10017. *Regional and all-India tours.*

Wilderness Travel ☎1-800/368 2794
801 Allston Way, Berkeley, CA 94710. *Rajasthan camel safari and elephant research expedition.*

Worldwide Adventures ☎1-800/387 1483
36 Finch Ave West, North York, ON M2N 2G9. *Sightseeing plus trekking, cycling and camel safari.*

DISCOUNT AGENTS, CONSOLIDATORS AND TRAVEL CLUBS

Air Brokers International ☎1-800/883 3273
323 Geary St, Suite 411, San Francisco, CA 94102. *Consolidator.*

Council Travel ☎212/254 2525
Head Office: 205 E 42nd St, New York, NY 10017. *Nationwide US student travel organization. Branches (among others) in San Francisco, Washington DC, Boston, Austin, Seattle, Chicago, Minneapolis.*

CUC Travel Services ☎1-800/548 1116
PO Box 1015, Turnbull, CT 06611-9938. *Discount travel club.*

Fly Time ☎212/760 3737
25 West 45th St, Suite 1003, New York, NY 10036. *Consolidator specializing in tickets to India.*

Hariworld Travel ☎212/997 3300
30 Rockefeller Plaza, Shop 21, Mezzanine Floor, New York, NY 10012. *Biggest Indian consolidator; agent for Indrail passes.*

HighTime Travel ☎212/684 7700
303 5th Ave, Suite 204, New York, NY 10016. *Consolidator specializing in tickets to India.*

Moment's Notice ☎718/234 6295
7301 New Utrecht Ave, Brooklyn, New York, NY 11204. *Discount travel club.*

New Frontiers (US)
☎1-800/366 6387 or 212/779 0600
Nouvelles Frontières (Canada) ☎514/526 8444
12 E 33rd St, New York, NY 10016.
1001 Sherbrook East, Suite 720, Montreal , H2L 1L3. *French discount travel firm. Other branches in LA, San Francisco and Quebec City.*

STA Travel ☎212/627 3111
Head office: 10 Downing St, New York, NY 10014. *Worldwide specialist in independent youth and student travel. Other offices in Los Angeles, Boston.*

Travel Cuts ☎416/979 2406
Head office: 187 College St, Toronto, ON M5T 1P7. *Nationwide Canadian student travel organization .*

Worldwide Travel
☎1-800/343 0038 or 202/659 6430
1026 16th St, NW, Washington, DC 20036. *Ticket consolidator.*

FROM EASTERN AND CENTRAL USA

Flying eastwards, you'll stop over somewhere in Europe (usually London), and probably again somewhere in the Gulf. Figure on at least 18 hours' total travel time from the East Coast. *Air India* has the only **direct flights** to India (from New York); on all other airlines, you'll change planes in their hub city.

Air India and *PIA* discount their tickets heavily through a few specialist, understaffed New York consolidators (see box). Marked-down tickets on European carriers – notably *British Airways*, *Air France* and *Lufthansa* – are frequently sold by other discount agents. Other airlines flying between the eastern US and India include *KLM*, *Aeroflot*, *Gulf Air*, *Kuwait*, *Egypt Air* and *Tower Air*. Or you can simply hop on any of the dozens of airlines that fly to London and pick up a flight to India from there.

Prices are most competitive out of **New York**, where the cheapest low-season fares to **Delhi** or Bombay hover around $1300 ($1400 high season). From **Washington** or **Miami**, figure on $1380/$1500; from **Chicago**, $1400/$1500; and from **Dallas/Ft Worth**, $1620/$2300. Fares to Madras, Calcutta or Goa run about $100 to $150 higher.

FROM THE WEST COAST

From the West Coast, it takes about as long to fly eastwards or westwards – a minimum of 22 hours' total travel time – and if you're booking through a consolidator there may not be much difference in price, either. *Thai*, *Cathay*, *Malaysia* and *Singapore* are the main carriers flying over the Pacific to India, via their respective hubs. *Air India* doesn't do the trans-Pacific route, but can book passengers on *Northwest* to any of several Asian capitals and then fly them the rest of the way. For eastbound routings, see above.

From **Los Angeles** or **San Francisco**, you're looking at a minimum of $1500 to fly to Delhi or Bombay in low season ($1600 in high season). Flights to Madras, Calcutta or Goa cost about $50 more (Goa is only served by *Air India*, via London).

FROM CANADA

At the time of writing, the only **direct flights** from Canada to India were Toronto–Delhi on *Air India* and Vancouver–Delhi on *Air Canada* (both via London, and both taking under 20hr). All other routings involve a plane change and more layover time. *Air Canada* flies from all major Canadian cities to London, where passengers can join the Vancouver–Delhi flight. Other airlines offering services to India, via their capitals, include *British Airways*, *Air France*, *Lufthansa*, *KLM* and *Aeroflot*. This list doesn't convey the full range of possibilities, however. A discount agent will probably break the journey into two, using one of dozens of carriers for the transatlantic (or trans-Pacific) leg.

Typical discounted low and high season fares to Delhi or Bombay: from **Montreal** or **Toronto**, CDN$1350/$1550; from **Vancouver**, CDN$1400/$1600. Add $100 for Madras, Calcutta or Goa.

PACKAGES AND ORGANIZED TOURS

Wrapping India up into a tidy **package** makes it less daunting and more comprehensible to many first-time tourists. A tour company can also shield you from the subcontinent's many little frustrations, enabling you to cover more ground than if you were going it alone. Of course, you'll have to be prepared to forgo independence and spontaneity, and accept that there will be only fleeting and predominantly mercenary encounters with local people.

Tours of India work best when they focus on one region of the country, or when based on an activity or a special interest. A fairly standard best-seller list is offered by many companies: Rajasthan palaces, Rajasthan camel safaris (often timed to coincide with the Pushkar Camel Fair), Agra–Varanasi–Khajuraho (often packaged with a few days in Nepal), wildlife parks, Goa, temples and/or beaches of the south, and the *Palace on Wheels* railway. Quite a few companies specialize in trekking in the Himalaya, although they invariably offer many more itineraries in Nepal than in India.

Tour prices are always wildly out of line with the cost of living in India, and whether you take one will depend on which is tighter, your budget or your schedule. Excluding airfare, a two-week tour is likely to cost at least $2000, and a three-week trip with all the bells and whistles can cost $3500 or more. The *Palace on Wheels* is the ultimate in expense – $1850 for eight days. Your local travel agent should be able to book any tour for you at no additional cost.

GETTING THERE FROM AUSTRALASIA

One of the best-value air fares **from Australia** to India is on *Qantas* and *Air India* from the east coast, Perth and Darwin: flying via Singapore to Bombay or Delhi costs around Aus$1400 in low season (Feb 1–Nov 21), and $1750 high season (Nov 22–Jan 31), while via Kuala Lumpur to Madras or Calcutta is more like $1350. An *Indian Airlines* airpass for 21 days' unlimited travel (see p.32) can be added on for another US$500. For most of the year there are two flights weekly; in the peak season, that rises to around five.

Of possible alternatives, *Thai International* fly via Bangkok to Delhi from eastern Australia ($1480/$1850) and to Calcutta ($1400/$1800). Also via Bangkok, *British Airways* and *Air France* combine for Bombay ($1400 in low season). *Malaysian Airlines* fly from eastern Australia via Kuala Lumpur to Madras or Delhi ($1400/$1750).

Singapore fly to Bombay or Delhi for $1550/$1950 from eastern Australia, $1350 (low season) from Perth or Darwin. *Cathay Pacific* charge $1560 (low season) to Bombay via Hong Kong from the east coast or Perth. There's also a weekly *Qantas* and *Royal Nepal* deal to various destinations in India via Kathmandu ($1900).

Flying **from New Zealand**, the cheapest fares to India are: *Singapore* daily from Auckland via Singapore to Bombay or Delhi (NZ$2000/$2300); *Air New Zealand–Air India* from Auckland to Bombay or Delhi via Singapore, Hong Kong or Bangkok (NZ$2000/$2300); *Thai* to Delhi via Bangkok (NZ$2100/$2400). **Add on** a fare of NZ$150 for flights from Wellington.

Round-the-world fares from Australia and New Zealand using the above airlines can take in India; for example, *Thai, Air New Zealand, Quantas* or *Malaysian* can route you through Delhi or Bombay as part of a RTW deal from around A$2400/NZ$2700.

BY LAND AND SEA THROUGH SOUTHEAST ASIA

It's barely possible to get from Australasia to India without flying at least part of the way. Flights from Darwin to Timor or Bali can in any case be rather more convenient than the boat trip, but your real barrier is Burma (Myanmar), still impassable by land. With the return of the boat service between Penang (Malaysia) and Madras as yet still no more than a rumour, the only solution is to fly from Singapore, KL or Bangkok to Calcutta, Dhaka or Kathmandu.

AIRLINES AND AGENTS IN AUSTRALASIA

Airlines

Aeroflot
388 George St, Sydney ☎02/9233 7911

Air France
12 Castlereagh St, Sydney ☎02/9321 1000
57 Fort St, Auckland ☎09/303 1229

Air India
Level 18, 44 Market St, Sydney ☎02/9299 1983
57–59 Customs St East, Auckland ☎09/303 1301

Air New Zealand
5 Elizabeth St, Sydney ☎02/9223 4666
Quay St, Auckland ☎09/357 3000

British Airways
Level 26, 201 Kent St, Sydney ☎02/9258 3300
154 Queen St, Auckland ☎09/356 8690

Cathay Pacific
Level 12, 8 Spring St, Sydney ☎02/9931 5500

11f Arthur Andersen Tower,
205–209 Queen St, Auckland ☎09/379 0861

Malaysian Airlines
16 Spring St, Sydney ☎13 2627
12–26 Swanson St, Auckland ☎09/373 2741

Qantas
Hunter and Phillip St, Sydney ☎02/9957 0111
154 Queen St, Auckland ☎09/357 8900

Singapore Airlines
17–19 Bridge St, Sydney ☎13 1011
Lower Ground Floor, West Plaza Building, cnr
Customs and Albert streets, Auckland ☎09/379 3209

Thai Airways
75–77 Pitt St, Sydney ☎02/9844 0999
22 Fanshawe St, Auckland ☎09/377 3886

Specialist Agents

Flight Centres
Circular Quay, Sydney ☎02/241 2422
Bourke St, Melbourne ☎03/650 2899
205–225 Queen St, Auckland ☎09/309 6171
50–52 Willis St, Wellington ☎04/472 8101
Branches throughout Australia and NZ.

STA Travel
732 Harris St, Ultimo, Sydney ☎02/212 1255
256 Flinders St, Melbourne ☎03/347 4711
10 High St, Auckland ☎09/309 9995
233 Cuba St, Wellington ☎04/385 0561
223 High St, Christchurch ☎03/379 9098
Branches throughout Australia and NZ.

Abercombie and Kent
90 Bridport St, Albert Park, Victoria ☎03/9699 9766
*Specialist in individual mid–upmarket holidays,
away from the main tourist trails.*

Adventure World
73 Walker St, Sydney ☎02/956 7766
101 Great South Rd,
Remuera, Auckland ☎09/524 5118
*Tailor-made air-accommodation packages, rail pass-
es and regional tours. NZ agents for Exodus and
Peregrine.*

Exodus
Suite 5, level 5, 1 York St, Sydney ☎02/9251 5430
*Overland expeditions and Himalayan trekking from
gentle walks around Darjeeling to climbs among the
Ladakh peaks.*

India/Nepal Adventure Travel
1st Floor, 132 Wickham St, Brisbane ☎07/3854 1022
All travel arrangements. Agent for Peregrine.

Integrity Tours
Level 4, 491 Kent St, Sydney ☎02/9621 3320
*Grass-roots level budget tours using local transport.
Also Himalayan cross-country trekking and skiing.*

Peregrine
258 Lonsdale St, Melbourne ☎03/663 8611
407 Great South Rd,
Penrose, Auckland ☎09/525 3074
Extensive tailored group and individual tours.

San Michelle Travel
81 York St, Sydney ☎02/9299 1111
Adelaide Embankment Arcade,
Melbourne ☎03/9629 4961
Cinema Arcade, Perth ☎08/9325 1288
*Budget to upmarket air-accommodation packages,
rail tours and land based designer tours for groups
or individual travellers.*

St Kilda Road Travel
346 St Kilda Rd, Melbourne ☎03/9690 1877
*All aspects of travel, from air-accommodation deals
to 5-star packages.*

Top Deck Travel
8th Floor, 350 Kent St, Sydney ☎02/9299 8844
4 Durham St East, Auckland ☎09/377 4586
*Overland double-decker bus adventures in India. NZ
agent: Destinations Adventure.*

VISAS AND RED TAPE

Gone are the days when Commonwealth nationals could stroll visa-less into India and stay for as long as they pleased: nowadays everybody needs a visa, except Nepalis and Bhutanis.

There are two kinds of Indian visa, and different restrictions apply to each. **Three-month** (aka "tourist") **visas** cost £13/$40 and are valid from the date of entry, while **six-month visas**, valid from the date of issue, cost £26/$60. As you're asked to specify whether you need a single-entry or a multiple-entry visa, and the same rates apply to both, it makes sense to ask for the latter, just in case you make a side trip to Nepal or another neighbouring country.

Much the best place to get a visa is in your country of residence, from the embassies and high commissions listed on p.15. Embassies in India's neighbouring countries often drag their feet, demand letters of recommendation from your embassy (expensive if you are, for example, British), or make you wait and pay for them to send your application to Delhi. Tourist visas are available by post in most countries, though in the US, for example, this takes a month as opposed to two days if you do it in person – check your nearest embassy, high commission or consulate to be sure. Make sure that your visa is signed by someone at the embassy, as you may be refused entry into the country.

It's also possible in many countries, and usually faster, to pay a **visa agency** to obtain them on your behalf; this can cost anywhere between £15–20/$35 (plus the price of the visa). In Britain, try *The Visa Service*, 2 Northdown St, Kings Cross, London N1 (☎0171/833 2709), or *Visa Express*, 31 Corsham St, London N1 (☎0171/251 4822). In the US, try *Express Visa Service*, 2150 Wisconsin Ave, Suite 20, Washington (☎202/337 2442).

It is no longer possible to extend a visa in India, though exceptions may be made in special circumstances. Note too that Indian embassies in neighbouring countries are unlikely to grant a new visa if you have just finished a six-month one. However, this is likely to change in the future, so check before leaving your home country.

If you do stay more than 180 days, before you leave the country you are supposed to get a **tax clearance certificate**, available at the foreigners' section of the income tax department in every major city. They are free, but you should take bank receipts to show you have changed your money legally. In practice, tax clearance certificates are rarely demanded, but you never know.

The only way to spend more than six months in India (unless you are eligible for a five-year visa – see below), is to head for a neighbouring country, such as Nepal or Sri Lanka, and apply for a brand new visitors' visa from there; the fact that you already have a recently used visa in your passport doesn't prevent you from obtaining a new one.

For details of other kinds of visas – foreigners of Indian origin, business travellers, and even students of yoga, can get five-year visas – contact your nearest Indian embassy.

Duty-free allowances for travellers arriving in India are covered on p.69.

SPECIAL PERMITS

In addition to a visa, **special permits** may be required for travel to certain specific areas of the country (notably parts of Sikkim, Ladakh, the Andaman Islands, Lakshadweep and some northeastern hill states) while others (some northeastern hill states, areas of Sikkim, and the Indo-Chinese-Pak border region in Jammu-Kashmir) remain out of bounds altogether to foreign nationals. If you have some special reason for going to any of these latter areas, apply for a permit to the Ministry for Home Affairs Foreigners' Section, Lok Nayak Bhavan, Khan Market, New Delhi 110 003, at least four weeks in advance.

> For more details of **permit** requirements, see the relevant chapters of this book.

Permits for those areas of **Sikkim** that are open to tourists are easily available at all foreigners' registration offices, immigration offices at the main international airports, all Indian embassies, consulates and high commissions abroad, and at offices in nearby Darjeeling and Siliguri. Sikkim is the only place where you need a special **trekking permit**.

In the northeast, Assam, Meghalaya and Tripura are now routinely open to tourists, and Nagaland is still effectively closed. Permits to visit Mizoram and parts of Maripur and Arunchal Pradesh are issued to tourists travelling in groups of four or more by representatives of the relevant state goverments. Permits for individual travel to these places are much harder to get, and are issued by the Ministry for Home Affairs (see above). For full details of the northeast permit situation, see p.868.

Should you get your hands on a visa for **Bhutan**, you'll also need a transit permit for the border area from the Ministry of External Affairs.

INDIAN DIPLOMATIC REPRESENTATIVES ABROAD

UK
High Commission: India House, Aldwych, London WC2B 4NA, ☎0171/836 8484; fax 836 4331.
Consulate: 20 Augusta St, Birmingham B18 6GL, ☎0121/212 2782; fax 212 2782.
Consulate: St Andrew House 141 West Nite St, Glasgow G1 2RN, ☎0141/333119; fax 333 1116.

USA
Embassy of India (Consular Services): 2536 Massachusetts Ave NW, Washington DC 20008, ☎202/939 9839; fax 939 7027.
Consulates: 3 East 64th St, New York, NY 10021, ☎212/879 7800; fax 988 6423; 540 Arguello Blvd, San Francisco, CA 94118, ☎415/668 0657; fax 668 2073; 150 N Michigan Ave, Suite 1100, Chicago, IL 60601, ☎312/718 6280; 201 St Charles Ave, New Orleans, LA 70170, ☎504/582 8106; 2051 Young St, Honolulu, HI 96826, ☎808/947 2618.

Canada
High Commission: 10 Springfield Rd, Ottawa, ON K1M 1C9, ☎613/744 3751; fax 744 0913.
Consulates: 2 Bloor St W, #500, Toronto, ON M4W 3E2, ☎416/960 0751; 325 Howe St, 2nd floor, Vancouver, BC V6C 1Z7, ☎604/662 8811.

Australia
High Commission: 3–5 Moonah Place, Yarralumla, Canberra, ACT 2600, ☎06/273 3999; fax 273 3328.
Consulates: 25 Bligh St, Sydney, NSW 2060, ☎02/9223 9500; fax 9929 6058; 13 Munro St, Coburg, Melbourne, Vic 3058, ☎03/384 0141; fax 9384 1609; c/o *Magic Carpet Tours & Travels Ltd*, 4th floor, 195 Adelaide Terrace, East Perth, WA 6004, ☎09/221 1207; fax 221 1206.

New Zealand
Indian High Commission: 180 Molesworth St (PO Box 4005), Wellington, ☎04/473 6390; fax 499 0665.

Netherlands
Buitenrustweg 2, 251 KD, Den Haag, ☎070/346 9771; fax 361 7072.

ASIA
Bangladesh House 120, Rd 2, Dhanmondi Residential Area, Dhaka, ☎02/503606; fax 863662; 1253–1256 OR Nizam Rd, Mehdi Bagh, Chittagong, ☎031/211007; fax 225178.

Burma (Myanmar) Oriental Assurance Building, 545-547 Merchant St (PO Box 751), Rangoon, ☎01/82550.

Japan 2-11, Kudan Minami 2-Chome, Chiyoda-ku, Tokyo 102, ☎03/3262 239; fax 89562.

Malaysia 2 Jalan Taman Dlita (off Jalan Duta), PO Box 10059, 50704 Kuala Lumpur, ☎03/253 3504; fax 253 3507.

Nepal Lainchaur (off Lazimpath), PO Box 292, Kathmandu, ☎01/410940; fax 413132. Mon–Fri 9.30–11am, allow a week – plus extra fee – to fax Delhi; Brits and some Europeans need letters of recommendation.

Pakistan G-5, Diplomatic enclave, Islamabad, ☎051/814371; fax 820742; India House, 3 Fatima Jinnah Rd (PO Box 8542), Karachi, ☎021/522275; fax 568 0929.

Singapore India House, 31 Grange Rd (PO Box 9123), Singapore 0923, ☎737 6777; fax 732 6909.

Sri Lanka 36-38 Galle Rd, Colombo 3, ☎01/421605; fax 446403; 31 Rajapihilla Mawatha, PO Box 47, Kandy, ☎08/24563.

Thailand 46 Soi 23 (Prasarn Mitr), Sukhumvit Rd, Bangkok 10110, ☎02/258 0300; fax 258 4627; 113 Bumruangrat Rd, Chiang Mai 50000, ☎053/243066; fax 247879. Visas take five working days to issue.

TRAVEL INSURANCE

In the light of the potential health risks involved in a trip to India – see p.18 – travel insurance is too important to ignore. In addition to covering medical expenses and emergency flights, it also insures your money and belongings against loss or theft.

Flights paid for with a major credit or charge card offer some automatic cover, but usually only while travelling to and from your destination. Some package tours too may include insurance, but package operators more commonly offer an insurance deal as an extra: it might be worth checking against alternative policies, though differences in price and cover are likely to be slight.

Always **check the fine print** of a policy. A 24-hour medical emergency contact number is a must, and one of the rare policies that pays your medical bills directly is better than one that reimburses you on your return home. The per-article limit for loss or theft should cover your most valuable possession (a camera for example) but, conversely, don't pay for cover you don't need – such as too much baggage or a huge sum for personal liability. Make sure, too, that you are covered for all the things you intend to do. Activities such as trekking or rafting are usually specifically excluded, but can be added on for a supplement.

Frequent travellers may benefit from **annual** insurance policies, but these almost invariably put an upper limit on the duration of any single trip, likely to be 90 days at most.

Among **UK insurers**, *Worldwide Travel Insurance Services Ltd* are about the cheapest,

offering a month's complete cover for around £35. Their policies – which cover a minimum of two months, or a maximum of eighteen – are sold direct from their head branch at Elm Lane Offices, Elm Lane, Tonbridge, Kent TN10 3XS (☎01732/ 773366). *Endsleigh*, whose policies are sold by most major youth/student travel agents or through their office at 97–107 Southampton Row, London WC1B 4AG (☎0171/436 4451), are recommended for shorter trips. *Columbus Travel Insurance* (☎0171/375 0011) also offer competetive rates.

Travellers from the **US** should carefully check their current insurance policies before taking out a new one. You may discover that you are already covered for medical and other losses while abroad. Holders of ISIC cards are entitled to be reimbursed for $3000-worth of accident coverage and 60 days of in-patient benefits of up to $100 a day for the period the card is valid. If you do want a specific travel insurance policy, there are numerous kinds to choose from: short-term combination policies covering everything from baggage loss to broken legs are the best bet and cost around $25 for ten days, plus $1 per day for trips of 75 days or more. Companies you might try include *Travel Guard*, 1145 Clark St, Stevens Point, WI 54481 (☎715/345 0505 or 1-800/826 1300), *Access America International*, 600 Third Ave, New York, NY 10163 (☎212/949 5960 or 1-800/284 8300), and *Travel Assistance International* (☎1-800/821 2828).

In **Australia** and **New Zealand**, travel insurance is put together by the airlines and travel agent groups such as *UTAG, AFTA, Cover-More*, at 32 Walker St, Sydney (☎02/9202 8000), *and Ready Plan*, 141–147 Walker St, Victoria (☎1-800/337 462), or 63 Albert St, Auckland, who give the best coverage. Most adventure sports are covered, but check your policy first. A typical policy will cost AUS$150/NZ$170 for one month.

If you need **to claim**, you *must* have a police report in the case of theft or loss, and supporting evidence of medical treatment in the form of bills, though with some policies, doctors and hospitals will be able to bill your insurers direct. Keep photocopies of everything you send to the insurer and don't allow months to elapse before informing them. Write immediately and tell them what's happened; you can usually claim later.

HEALTH

A lot of visitors get ill in India, and some of them get very ill. However, if you are careful, you should be able to get through the country with nothing worse than a mild dose of "Delhi belly". The important thing is to keep your resistance high and to be very aware of health risks such as poor hygiene, untreated water, mosquito bites and undressed open cuts.

What you **eat** and **drink** is crucial: a poor diet lowers your resistance. Ensure you eat a balance of protein, energy, vitamins and minerals. Meat and fish are obvious sources of protein for non-vegetarians in the West, but not necessarily in India; eggs, pulses (lentils, peas and beans), rice and curd are all protein sources, as are nuts. Overcooked vegetables lose a lot of their vitamin content; eating plenty of peeled fresh fruit helps keep up your vitamin and mineral intake. With all that sweating, too, make sure you get enough salt (put a bit extra on your food) and drink enough water. It's also worth taking daily multi-vitamin and mineral tablets with you. Above all, make sure you eat *enough* – an unfamiliar diet may reduce the amount you eat – and **get enough sleep** and rest: it's easy to get run down if you're on the move a lot, especially in a hot climate.

> In Britain, travellers who call the "**Health Line**" run by **Masta** – the Medical Advisory Service for Travellers Abroad – on ☎0171/631 4408 receive the latest detailed health advice by return of post; if you specifically want information about malaria prevention, call ☎0891/224100. *Masta* is based at the London School of Hygiene and Tropical Medicine, Keppel St, London WC1E 7HT.

PRECAUTIONS

The lack of sanitation in India can be exaggerated. It's not worth getting too worked up about or you'll never enjoy anything, but a few **common-sense precautions** are in order, bearing in mind that things such as bacteria multiply far more quickly in a tropical climate, and your foreign body will have little immunity to Indian germs.

For details on the **water**, see the box on p.18. When it comes to **food**, it's quite likely that tourist restaurants and "Western" dishes will bring you grief. Be particularly wary of prepared dishes that have to be reheated – ask yourself how long they've been on display in the heat and the flies. Anything that is boiled or fried (and thus sterilized) in your presence is usually all right, though meat can sometimes be dodgy, especially in towns or cities where the electricity supply (and thus refrigerators) frequently fails; anything that has been left out for any length of time is definitely suspect. Raw unpeeled fruit and vegetables should always be viewed with suspicion, and you should avoid salads unless you know they have been soaked in an iodine or potassium permanganate solution. As a rule of thumb, stick to cafes and restaurants that are doing a brisk trade, and where the food is thus freshly cooked, and you should be be fine.

Be vigilant about **personal hygiene**. Wash your hands often, especially before eating, keep all cuts clean, treat them with iodine or antiseptic, and cover them to prevent infection. Be fussier about sharing things like drinks and cigarettes, and never share a razor or toothbrush. It is also inadvisable to go around barefoot – and best to wear flip-flop sandals even in the shower.

Among items you might wish to take with you – though all are available in India itself, at a fraction of what you might pay at home – are hypodermic needles and sterilized skin wipes (more for the security of knowing you have them with you, than any fear that an Indian hospital would fail to observe basic sanitary precautions), antiseptic cream, plasters, lints and sealed bandages, a course of *Flagyl* antibiotics, a box of *Immodium* (*Lomotil*) for emergency diarrhoea treatment, rehydration sachets, insect repellent and cream such as *Anthisan* for soothing bites, paracetamol or aspirin (useful for combating the effects of altitude), and a mild oral anaesthetic such as *Bonjela* for soothing ulcers or mild toothache.

Advice on avoiding **mosquitoes** is offered under "Malaria" below. If you do get bites or itches try not to scratch them: it's hard, but infection and tropical ulcers can result if you do. Tiger balm and even dried soap may relieve the itching.

Finally, especially if you are going on a long trip, have a **dental check-up** before you leave home – you don't want to go down with unexpected tooth trouble in India. If you do, and it feels serious, head for Delhi, Bombay or Calcutta, and ask a foreign consulate to recommend a dentist.

WHAT ABOUT THE WATER?

One of the chief concerns of many prospective visitors to India is whether the **water** is safe to drink. To put it simply, no, though your unfamiliarity with Indian micro-organisms is generally more of a problem rather than any great virulence in the water itself. The fact is, if you are in the country for a while, your stomach will have to get used to local bugs, and you will probably get diarrhoea a few times. By exercising reasonable caution, however, you can minimize the risk of going down with anything more serious.

It is generally not a good idea to drink **tap water**, although in big cities it is usually chlorinated. However, it is almost impossible to avoid untreated tap water completely: it is used to make ice, which may appear in drinks without being asked for, *lassis* are made with it, utensils are washed with it, and so on. **Bottled water** is widely available. Always check that the seal is intact, as refilling bottles is not uncommon.

If you plan to go somewhere with no access to bottled drinks – which really only applies to travellers venturing well off the beaten track – find an appropriate method of **treating water**, whether your source is tap water or natural groundwater such as a river or stream. **Boiling** it for a minimum of five minutes (longer at higher altitudes) is sufficient to kill micro-organisms, but is not always practical and does not remove unpleasant tastes. **Chemical sterilization** is cheap and convenient, but dirty water remains dirty, and still contains organic matter or other contamination. You can sterilize water by using chlorine or iodine tablets, but these leave a nasty after-taste (which can be masked with lemon or lime juice) and are not effective in preventing such diseases as amoebic dysentery and giardia. Tincture of iodine is better; add a couple of drops to one litre of water and leave to stand for twenty minutes. Pregnant women, babies, and people with thyroid problems should avoid using iodine sterilizing tablets or iodine-based purifiers, or use an additional iodine-removal filter. The various kinds of **filter** only remove visible impurities and the larger pathogenic organisms (most bacteria and cysts). However fine the filter, it will not remove viruses, dissolved chemicals, pesticides, herbicides etc.

Purification, a two-stage process involving both filtration and sterilization, gives the most complete treatment. Portable water purifiers range from pocket-size units weighing 60g, up to 800g. Some of the best water purifiers on the market are made in Britain by **Pre-Mac**; for suppliers, contact:

Pre-Mac (Kent) Ltd ☎01892/534361
40 Holden Park Rd, Southborough, Tunbridge Wells,
Kent TN4 0ER, England.

All Water Systems Ltd ☎01/456 4933
Unit 12, Western Parkway Business Centre, Lr.
Ballymount Rd, Dublin 12, Ireland.

Outbound Products ☎800/663 9262
1580 Zephyr Ave, Box 56148, Hayward CA 94545,
USA.

Outbound Products ☎604/321 5464
8585 Fraser St, Vancouver, BC V5X 3Y1, Canada.

VACCINATIONS

No **inoculations** are legally required for entry into India, but meningitis, typhoid, and hepatitis A jabs are recommended, and it's worth ensuring that you are up to date with tetanus, polio and other boosters. All vaccinations can be obtained in Delhi, Bombay and other major cities if necessary; just make sure the needle is new.

Hepatitis A is not the worst disease you can catch in India, but the frequency with which it strikes travellers makes a strong case for immunization. Transmitted through contaminated food and water, or through saliva, it can lay a victim low for several months with exhaustion, fever and diarrhoea – and may cause liver damage if mixed with alcohol. The *Havrix* vaccine has been shown to be extremely effective; though expensive, it lasts for up to ten years. The protection given by gamma-globulin, the traditional serum of hepatitis antibodies, wears off quickly and the injection should therefore be as late as possible before departure: the longer your planned stay, the larger the dose.

Symptoms by which you can recognize hepatitis include a yellowing of the whites of the eyes, general malaise, orange urine (though dehydration could also cause that) and light-coloured stools. If you think you have it, avoid alcohol, try to avoid passing it on, and get lots of rest. More serious is **hepatitis B**, passed on like AIDS through blood or sexual contact (though it is more infectious than AIDS). There is a vaccine, but it is only recommended for those planning to work in a medical environment. Otherwise, your chances of getting hepatitis B are low – assuming you take the precautions you should be taking to avoid AIDS.

Typhoid, also spread through contaminated food or water, is endemic in India, but rare outside the monsoon. It produces a persistent high fever with malaise, headaches and abdominal pains, followed by diarrhoea. Vaccination can be by injection (two shots are required, or one for a booster), giving three years' cover, or orally – tablets are more expensive but easier on the arm.

Cholera, spread the same way as hepatitis A and typhoid, causes sudden attacks of watery diarrhoea with cramps and debilitation. It is endemic in the Ganges basin, but only during periodic epidemics. If you get it, take copious amounts of water with rehydration salts and seek medical treatment. There is a vaccination but it offers very little protection (the vaccine used in India is usually stronger than at home, with longer-lasting after-effects).

Most medical authorities now recommend vaccination against **meningitis** too. Spread by airborne bacteria (through coughs and sneezes for example), it attacks the lining of the brain and can be fatal.

You should have a **tetanus** booster every ten years whether you travel or not. Tetanus (or lockjaw) is picked up through contaminated open wounds; if you cut yourself on something dirty and are not covered, get a booster as soon as you can.

Assuming that you were vaccinated against **polio** in childhood, only one (oral) booster is needed during your adult life. Immunizations against mumps, measles, TB, and rubella are a good idea for anyone who wasn't vaccinated as a child and hasn't had the diseases.

Although **rabies** is a problem in India, the best advice is to give dogs and monkeys a wide berth, and not to play with animals at all, no matter how cute they might look. A bite, a scratch or even a lick from an infected animal could spread the disease; wash any such wound immediately but gently with soap or detergent, and apply alcohol or iodine if possible. Find out what you can about the animal and swap addresses with the owner (if there is one) just in case. If the animal might be infected, act immediately to get treatment – rabies is invariably fatal once symptoms appear. There is a vaccine, but it is expensive, which serves only to shorten the course of treatment you need anyway, and is only effective for a maximum of three months.

Diseases you won't need vaccinations for include: smallpox (now virtually eradicated in India), cholera (because the vaccine offers very little protection) and yellow fever (only necessary if you're visiting Africa).

MALARIA

Protection against **malaria** is absolutely essential. The disease, caused by a parasite carried in the saliva of female *Anopheles* mosquitoes, is endemic everywhere in India except high-altitude regions of Himachal Pradesh, Kashmir and Sikkim, and is nowadays regarded as *the* big killer in the subcontinent. It has a variable incubation period of a few days to several weeks, so you can become ill long after being bitten. Programmes to eradicate the disease by spraying mosquito infested areas and distributing free preventative tablets have proved disastrous; within a short space of time, the *Anopheles* develop immunities to the insecticides, while the malaria parasite itself constantly mutates into drug-resistant strains, rendering the old cures ineffective.

Nevertheless, it is vital for travellers to take **preventative tablets** according to a strict routine, and to cover the period before and after your trip. The drug used is chloroquine (trade names include *Nivaquin*, *Avloclor* and *Resochin*), usually two tablets weekly, but India has chloroquine-resistant strains, and you'll need to supplement it with daily proguanil (*Paludrine*) or weekly *Maloprim*. A new weekly drug, mefloquine (*Lariam*), is supposed to replace all these, but is not currently recommended for journeys of more than two months because of its side-effects (see below). Australian authorities are now prescribing the antibiotic Doxycycline instead.

As the malaria parasite can incubate in your system without showing symptoms for more than a month, it is essential that you continue to take preventative tablets for at least four weeks after you return home: the most common way of catching malaria is when travellers forget to do this.

If you do go down with malaria, you'll know soon enough. The shivering, burning fever and headaches are like severe flu and come in waves, usually beginning in the early evening. Anyone who develops such symptoms should get to a doctor for a blood test as soon as possible. Malaria is not infectious, but some strains are dangerous and occasionally even fatal when not treated promptly, in particular, the choloquine-resistant **cerebral malaria**. This virulent and lethal strain of the disease, which affects the brain and often proves fatal if left untreated, is treatable, but has to be diagnosed early. If you are unable to see a doctor, you may have to treat yourself with two 600mg quinine tablets three times daily for seven days, then three *Fansidar* tablets, also sold in India as *Metakelfin*. Where quinine isn't available, take ordinary chloroquine (10mg per kilo body weight up to 600mg maximum, usually four tablets), then half as much eight hours later. If you improve, repeat the second dose for the next two days; if not, your malaria is chloroquine-resistant, so see a doctor or obtain and take three *Fansidar tablets*.

Side-effects of anti-malaria drugs may include itching, rashes, hair loss, sight problems, and even (in the case of *Larium*) depression, and it is probably not advisable to use them for prolonged periods. However, on a three-month trip, it is just common sense. Chloroquine and quinine are safe during pregnancy, but *Maloprim, Fansidar*, mefloquine and Doxycycline should be avoided then. Note that the doses we quote apply to adults: children will want lower ones.

The most important thing, however, is to **avoid mosquito bites**. Sleep under a net if possible – one which can hang from a single point is best (you can usually find a way to tie a string across your room to hang it from), burn mosquito coils (easily available, but easy to break in transit), and use repellent (an Indian brand called *Odomos* is widely available and very effective, though most travellers bring their own from home, usually one containing the noxious but effective compound DEET. Mosquito "buzzers" are pretty useless. Though active from dusk till dawn, female *Anopheles* mosquitoes prefer to bite in the evening, so be especially careful at that time. Wear long sleeves, skirts and trousers, avoid dark colours, which attract mosquitoes, and put repellent on all exposed skin.

Another illness spread by mosquito bites is **dengue fever**, whose symptoms are similar to those of malaria, plus a headache and aching bones. The only treatment is complete rest, with drugs to assuage the fever. **Japanese encephalitis**, yet another mosquito-borne viral infection causing fever, muscle pains and headaches, has been on the increase in recent years in wet rural rice-growing areas. However, there have been no reports of travellers catching the disease, and you shouldn't need the vaccine (which has several potentially nasty side-effects) unless you plan to spend much time around paddy fields during and immediately after the monsoons.

INTESTINAL TROUBLES

Diarrhoea is the most common bane of travellers. When mild and not accompanied by other major symptoms, it may just be your stomach reacting to

unfamiliar food. Accompanied by cramps and vomiting, it could well be food poisoning. In either case, it will probably pass of its own accord in 24–48 hours without treatment. In the meantime, it is essential to replace the fluids and salts you're losing down the drain, so take lots of water with oral rehydration salts (commonly referred to as ORS, or called *Electrolyte* in India). If you can't get them, use half a teaspoon of salt and three of sugar in a litre of water. It's a good idea to avoid greasy food, heavy spices, caffeine and most fruit and dairy products; but some say bananas and pawpaws are good, as is coconut water, while curd or a soup made from *Marmite* or *Vegemite* (if you happen to have some with you) are forms of protein that can be easily absorbed by your body when you have the runs. We advise against drugs like *Lomotil* or *Immodium*, which simply plug you up – they undermine the body's efforts to rid itself of infection – but they can be a temporary stop-gap if you have to travel. If symptoms persist for more than a few days, a course of antibiotics may be necessary; this should be seen as a last resort, following medical advice.

Sordid though it may seem, it's a good idea to look at what comes out when you go to the toilet (and it makes an endless topic of polite meal-time conversations with your fellow travellers). If your diarrhoea contains blood or mucus, the cause may be dysentery or giardia. With a fever, it could well be caused by **bacillic dysentery**, and may clear up without treatment. If you're sure you need it, a course of antibiotics such as tetracycline should sort you out, but they also destroy "gut flora" in your intestines (which help protect you – curd can replenish them to some extent), and if you start a course, be sure to finish it, even after the symptoms have gone. Similar symptoms without fever indicate **amoebic dysentery**, which is much more serious, and can damage your gut if untreated. The usual cure is a course of metronidazole (*Flagyl*), an antibiotic which may itself make you feel ill, and should not be taken with alcohol. Similar symptoms, plus rotten-egg belches and farts, indicate **giardia**, for which the treatment is again metronidazole. If you suspect that you have any of these, seek medical help, and only start on the metronidazole (750mg three times daily for a week for adults) if there is definitely blood in your diarrhoea and it is impossible to see a doctor.

Finally, bear in mind that oral drugs, such as malaria pills, and *the* pill, are likely to be largely ineffective if taken while suffering from diarrhoea.

BITES AND CREEPY CRAWLIES

Worms may enter your body through skin (especially the soles of your feet), or food. An itchy anus is a common symptom, and you may even see them in your stools. They are easy to treat: if you suspect you have them, get some worming tablets from any pharmacy.

Biting insects and similar animals other than mosquitoes may also aggravate you. The obvious ones are **bed bugs** – look for signs of squashed ones around cheap hotel beds. An infested mattress can be left in the hot sun all day to get rid of them, but they often live in the frame or even in walls or floors. Head and body **lice** can also be a nuisance but medicated soap and shampoo (preferably brought with you from home) usually sees them off. Avoid scratching bites, which can lead to infection. Bites from ticks and lice can spread **typhus**, characterized by fever, muscle aches, headaches and, later, red eyes and a measles-like rash. If you think you have it, seek treatment (tetracycline is usually prescribed – for adults, a single 1g dose followed by 300mg four times daily for five days).

Snakes are unlikely to bite unless accidentally disturbed, and most are harmless in any case. To see one at all, you need to search stealthily – walk heavily and they usually oblige by disappearing. If you do get bitten, remember what the snake looked like (kill it if you can), try not to move the affected part, and seek medical help: antivenoms are available in most hospitals. A few **spiders** have poisonous bites too. Remove **leeches**, which may attach themselves to you in jungle areas, with salt or a lit cigarette rather than just pulling them off.

HEAT TROUBLE

The sun and the heat can cause a few unexpected problems. Many people get a bout of **prickly heat** rash before they've acclimatized. It's an infection of the sweat ducts caused by excessive perspiration that doesn't dry off. A cool shower, zinc oxide powder (sold in India) and loose cotton clothes should help. **Dehydration** is another possible problem, so make sure you're drinking enough liquid, and drink rehydration salts frequently, especially when hot and/or tired. The main danger sign is irregular urination (only once a day for instance), but dark urine also probably means you should drink more, although it could indicate hepatitis.

The **sun** can burn, or even cause sunstroke, and a high-factor sun-block is vital on exposed skin, especially when you first arrive, and on areas newly exposed by haircuts or changes of clothes. A light hat is also a very good idea, especially if you're doing a lot of walking around in the sun.

Finally, be aware that overheating can cause **heat-stroke**, which is potentially fatal. Signs are a very high body temperature without a feeling of fever, but accompanied by headaches and disorientation. Irrational behaviour by your travelling companions may be down to this. Lowering body temperature (a tepid shower for example) is the first step in treatment.

ALTITUDE SICKNESS

At high altitudes, you may develop symptoms of **acute mountain sickness (AMS)**. Just about everyone who ascends to around 4000m or more experiences mild symptoms, but serious cases are rare. The simple cure – descent – almost always brings immediate recovery, but never descend too quickly.

AMS is caused by the fact that at high elevations there is not only less oxygen, but also lower atmospheric pressure. This can have all sorts of weird effects on the body: it can cause the brain to swell and the lungs to fill with fluid, and even bring on uncontrollable farting. The syndrome varies from one person to the next, but symptoms include breathlessness, headaches and dizziness, and nausea and appetite loss. More extreme cases may cause disorientation and loss of balance, and the coughing up of pink frothy phlegm.

AMS strikes without regard for fitness – in fact, young people seem to be more susceptible, possibly because they're more reluctant to admit they feel sick. Most people are capable of acclimatizing to very high altitudes but the process takes time and must be done in stages. The golden rule is not to go too high, too fast; or if you do, spend the night at a lower height ("Climb High, Sleep Low"). Above 3000m, you should not ascend more than 500m per day; take mandatory acclimatization days at 3500m and 4000m – more if you feel unwell – and try to spend these days day-hiking higher. If you fly direct to a high-altitude destination such as Leh, be especially careful to acclimatize; you'll certainly want to avoid doing anything strenuous at first.

Other precautions to take at high altitudes include drinking more liquid, and protecting your skin against UV solar glare.

Some of the illnesses and parasites you can pick up in India may not show themselves immediately. If you become ill within a year of returning home, tell whoever treats you where you have been.

HIV AND AIDS

Aids is still an unknown quantity in India, and often regarded as a foreign problem, but indications are that HIV levels are already high among prostitutes, and the same presumably applies to intravenous drug users. You are also of course at risk from your fellow travellers. It is extremely unwise to contemplate casual sex without a condom – carry some with you (preferably brought from home as Indian ones may be less reliable; also, be aware that heat affects the durability of condoms), and insist on using them. They also protect you from other sexually transmitted diseases, and even work as a contraceptive.

Should you need an injection or a transfusion in India, make sure that new, sterile equipment is used; any blood you receive should be from voluntary rather than commercial donor banks. If you have a shave from a barber, make sure he uses a

clean blade, and don't submit to processes such as ear-piercing, acupuncture or tattooing unless you can be sure that the equipment is sterile.

GETTING MEDICAL HELP

Pharmacies can usually advise on minor medical problems, and most doctors in India speak English. Also, many hotels keep a doctor on call. Basic medicaments are made to Indian Pharmacacopoea (IP) standards, and most medicines are available without prescription (always check the sell-by date). Hospitals vary in standard. Private clinics and mission hospitals are often better than state-run ones, but may not have the same facilities; hospitals in the big cities are generally pretty good, university or medical school hospitals best of all. Indian hospitals require patients (even emergency cases) to buy necessities such as plaster casts and vaccines, and to pay for X-rays, before procedures are carried out. However, charges are usually so low that for minor treatment the expense may well be lower than the initial "excess" on your insurance. Addresses of clinics and hospitals can be found in our "*Listings*" sections for major towns in this book.

AYURVEDIC MEDICINE

Ayurved, a five-thousand-year-old holistic medical system, is widely practised in India. Ayurvedic doctors and clinics in large towns deal with foreigners as well as their usual patients, and some pharmacies specialize in Ayurvedic preparations, including toiletries such as soaps, shampoos and toothpastes.

The "knowledge of life" assumes the fundamental sameness of self and nature. Unlike the allopathic medicines of the West, which depend on finding out what's ailing you and then killing it, *ayurved* looks at the whole patient: disease is regarded as a symptom of imbalance, so it's the imbalance that's treated, not the disease. Ayurvedic theory holds that the body is controlled by three forces, which reflect the forces within the self: *pitta*, the force of the sun, is hot, and rules the digestive processes and metabolism; *kapha*, likened to the moon, the creator of tides and

rhythms, has a cooling effect, and governs the body's organs; and *vata*, wind, relates to movement and the nervous system. The healthy body is one that has the three forces in balance. To diagnose an imbalance, the Ayurvedic doctor goes not only to the physical complaint but also to family background, daily habits and emotional traits.

Imbalances are typically treated with herbal remedies designed to alter whichever of the three forces is out of whack. Made according to traditional formulae, using indigenous plants, Ayurvedic medicines are cheaper than branded or imported drugs. In addition, the doctor may prescribe various forms of yogic cleansing to rid the body of waste substances. To the uninitiated, these techniques will sound rather offputting – for instance, swallowing a long strip of cloth, a short section at a time, and then pulling it back up again to remove mucus from the stomach.

INFORMATION AND MAPS

The Indian government maintains a number of tourist offices abroad, where you can pick up a range of pamphlets. Their main purpose is to advertise rather than inform, but they can be extremely helpful and knowledgeable.

Other sources of information include travel agents (who are in business for themselves, so their advice may not always be totally unbiased), and the *Indian Railways* representatives listed on p.31.

Inside India, both national and local governments run **tourist information offices**, providing general travel advice and handing out an array of printed material, from city maps to glossy leaflets on specific destinations. The Indian government's tourist department, whose main offices are on Janpath in New Delhi and opposite Churchgate railway station in Bombay, has

branches in most regional capitals. These, however, operate independently of the information counters and bureaux run by the **state tourism development corporations**, usually referred to by their initials (eg MPTDC in Madhya Pradesh, RTDC in Rajasthan, etc), who offer a wide range of travel facilities, including **guided tours**, **car rental**, and their own **hotels** (which we identify with the relevant acronyms throughout this book).

Just to confuse things more, the Indian government tourist office has a go-ahead corporate wing too. **ITDC** (Indian Tourism Development Corporation), is responsible for the *Ashok* chain of hotels, and operates tour and travel services, frequently competing with its state counterparts.

MAPS

Getting good **maps** of India, in India, can be difficult; the government forbids the sale of detailed maps of border areas, which include the entire coastline. It makes sense to bring a basic one with you, such as ***Bartholomew's*** 1:4,000,000 map of South Asia, which has coloured contours and serves as a reliable **route map** of the whole country. *Lascelles* also produce one on the same scale, as do *Nelles Verlag*, who show good road detail but can be less accurate; *Nelles* also cover parts of the country with 1:1,500,000 regional maps. These are generally excellent, with colour contours, road distances, inset city plans and even the tiniest places marked, but cost a fortune if you buy the complete set. ITDC does a very basic country map for free.

INDIAN GOVERNMENT TOURIST OFFICES ABROAD

Australia ☎02/9232 1600; fax 9223 3003
Level 1, 17 Castlereagh St, Sydney NSW.

Canada ☎416/ 962 3787
60 Bloor St West, #1003, Toronto, Ontario M4W 3B8.

Malaysia ☎03/242 5285; fax 242530
2nd floor, Wisma HLA, Lot 203, Jalan Raja Chulan 500200, Kuala Lumpur.

Netherlands ☎020/620 8991; fax 383059
Rokin 9–15, 1012 KK, Amsterdam.

Singapore ☎235 3800; fax 235 8677
20 Karamat Lane, 01–01A United House, Singapore 0922.

Thailand ☎02/235 2585
Singapore Airlines Bldg, 3rd floor, 62/5 Thaniya Rd, Bangkok.

UK ☎0171/437 3677; fax 494 1048
7 Cork St, London W1X 1PB.

USA
3550 Wiltshire Bd, Suite #204, Los Angeles, CA 90010, ☎213/380 8855; fax 380 6111.

30 Rockefeller Plaza, Room 15, North Mezzanine, New York, NY 10020, ☎212/ 586 4901 or 4902; fax 582 3274.

If you need larger-scale **city maps** than the ones we provide in this book — which are keyed to show recommended hotels and restaurants — you can sometimes get them from tourist offices. The *TT* company, 328 GST Rd, Chromepet, Madras 600044, also publish state and city maps, while the *Survey of India*, Janpath Barracks A, New Delhi 110 001 (☎332 2288), have authoritative town plans at scales of 1:10,000 and 1:50,000 (whose export is illegal, so they may be unwilling to sell you them).

As for **trekking maps**, the US Army Map Service produced maps in the 1960s which remain superbly accurate on topography, but are of course out-dated on the latest road developments. Most other maps that you can buy are based on their work, and no single series is especially worth recommending above the others. The official Indian mapping organization, the *Survey of India* (based in Dehra Dun in Uttar Pradesh) has issued a rather poor new 1:250,000 series for trekkers in the Uttar Pradesh Himalayas; they are simplified versions of their own infinitely more reliable maps, produced for the military, which it is absolutely impossible for an outsider to get hold of.

BOOK AND MAP OUTLETS

IN THE UK
Books from India   ☎0171/405 3784
45 Museum St, London WC1A 1LY.

John Smith and Sons   ☎0141/221 7472
57–61 St Vincent St, Glasgow

National Map Centre   ☎0171/222 4945
22–24 Caxton St, London SW1.

Stanfords   ☎0171/836 1321
12–14 Long Acre, London WC2.
Mail order service

Thomas Nelson and Sons Ltd   ☎0131/557 3011
51 York Place, Edinburgh EH1 3JD.

IN AUSTRALASIA
Bowyangs   ☎03/670 4383
372 Little Bourke St, Melbourne, VIC 3000.

Hema   ☎07/221 4330
239 George St, Brisbane, QLD 4000.

The Map Shop   ☎08/231 2033
16a Peel St, Adelaide, SA 5000.

Perth Map Centre   ☎09/322 5733
891 Hay St, Perth, WA 6000.

Travel Bookshop   ☎02/241 3554
20 Bridge St, Sydney, NSW 2000.

IN NORTH AMERICA:
British Travel Bookshop   ☎212/490 6688
551 5th Ave, New York NY 10176.

The Complete Traveler Bookstore
199 Madison Ave,   ☎212/685-9007
New York NY 10016.

3207 Fillmore St,   ☎415/923 1511
San Francisco CA 92123.

Elliot Bay Book Company   ☎206/624 6600
101 South Main St, Seattle WA 98104.

Open Air Books and Maps   ☎416/363 0719
25 Toronto St, Toronto M5C 2R1.

Rand McNally
444 N Michigan Ave,   ☎312/321 1751
Chicago IL 60611.

150 East 52nd St,   ☎212/758 7488
New York NY 10022.

595 Market St,   ☎415/777 3131
San Francisco CA 94105.

7988 Tysons Corner Center,   ☎703/556 8688
McLean, VA 22102.

Ulysses Travel Bookshop   ☎514/843 9447
4176 St-Denis, Montreal.

World Wide Books and Maps   ☎604/687 3320
736 Granville St, Vancouver.

COSTS, MONEY AND BANKS

India is, unquestionably, one of the least expensive countries for travellers in the world; a little foreign currency goes a long way. That means you can be confident of getting consistently good value for your money, whether you're setting out to keep your budget to a minimum or to enjoy the opportunities that spending a bit more will make possible.

While we attempt below to suggest the kind of sums you can expect to pay for varying degrees of comfort, it is vital not to make a rigid assumption at the outset of a long trip that whatever money you bring to India will last for a certain number of weeks or months. On any one day it may be possible to spend very little, but cumulatively you won't be doing yourself any favours if you don't make sure to keep yourself well rested and properly fed.

What you spend depends on you: where you go, where you stay, how you get around, what you eat and what you buy. On a budget of as little as US$8/£5 per day, you'll manage if you stick to the cheapest of everything and don't move about too much; double that, and you can permit yourself the odd splurge meal, the occasional mid-range hotel, and a few souvenirs. If you're happy spending US$20–30 (£15–20) per day, however, you can really pamper yourself; to spend much more than that, you'd have to be doing a lot of travelling, and consistently staying in the best hotel in town and eating in the top restaurant.

Accommodation ranges from US$2/£1.50 per night upwards (see p.36), while a mid-range vegetarian **meal** in an ordinary restaurant is unlikely to cost even that much. Rice and *dal* can be had for well under 50cents, but you wouldn't want to live on that alone. Transport in town costs pennies (even by taxi or the most over-charging rickshaw), while a 12-hour train journey might cost $3–4 (£2) in second class, $15 (£10) in first.

Where you are makes a difference: Bombay is notoriously pricey, especially for accommodation, while tourist enclaves like the Goa beaches will not be cheap for things like food, and there will be more souvenirs to tempt you. Delhi too is substantially more costly than most parts of the country. Out in the sticks, on the other hand, and particularly away from your fellow tourists, you will find things incredibly cheap, though your choice will obviously be more limited.

Some independent travellers tend to indulge in wild and highly competitive penny-pinching, which Indian people find rather pathetic – they know how much an air ticket to Delhi or Bombay costs, and they have a fair idea of what you can earn at home (not much more than most Indians!). Bargain where appropriate, but don't begrudge a few rupees to someone who's worked hard for them: consider what their services would cost at home, and how much more valuable the money is to them than it is to you. Even if you get a bad deal on every rickshaw journey you make, it will only add at most one percent to a $1500/£1000 trip. Remember too, that every pound or dollar you spend in India goes that much further, and luxuries you can't afford at home become possible here: sometimes it's worth spending more simply because you get more for it. At the same time, don't pay well over the odds for something if you know what the going rate is. Thoughtless extravagance can, particularly in remote areas that see a disproportionate number of tourists (such as Ladakh), contribute to inflation, putting even basic goods and services beyond the reach of local people.

INDIAN MONEY

India's unit of currency is the **rupee**, usually abbreviated "Rs" and divided into a hundred paise. You may also hear the odd reference to an old unit, the anna (16 to a rupee, so four annas is 25 paise). Almost all money is paper, with notes of 1, 2, 5, 10, 20, 50, 100 and 500 rupees. Coins start at 1 paisa (for temple offerings), then range up to 5, 10, 20, 25 and 50 paise, and 1, 2 and 5 rupees.

Banknotes, especially lower denominations, can get into a terrible state, but don't accept **torn banknotes**; no-one else will be prepared to take them, so you will be left saddled with the things. You can change them at the *Reserve Bank of India* and large branches of other big banks, or slip them into the middle of a wad when paying for something (which is probably how they'll have been passed to you). Don't pass them on to beggars; they can't use them either, so it amounts to an insult.

Large denominations can also be a problem, as **change** is often in short supply, particularly in small towns. Many Indian people cannot afford to keep much lying around, and you shouldn't necessarily expect shopkeepers or rickshaw *wallahs* to have it (and they may – as may you – try to hold onto it if they do). Paying for your groceries with a Rs100 note will probably entail waiting for the grocer's errand boy to go off on a quest around town trying to change it. Keeping a wad of Rs1 notes handy isn't a bad idea (you can get bundles of a hundred stapled together in banks; holes from the staples don't count as rips, so long as they don't reach the edge of the note).

TRAVELLERS' CHEQUES AND CREDIT CARDS

Carry a mixture of cash and travellers' cheques to cover all eventualities, with a few small denominations for the end of your trip, and for the odd foreign-currency purchase. US dollars are the easiest **currency** to convert, with pounds sterling a close second. Major hard currencies can be changed easily in tourist areas and big cities, less so elsewhere. If you enter the country with US$10,000 or the equivalent, you are supposed to fill in a currency declaration form.

Travellers' cheques aren't as liquid as cash, but obviously more secure (and you get a slightly better exchange rate for them at banks). Not all banks, however, accept them, and those that do can be quirky about exactly which ones they *will* change (well-known brands such as *Thomas Cook* or *American Express* are your best bet).

A **credit card** is a handy back-up, as an increasing number of hotels, restaurants, large shops and tourist emporia as well as airlines now take plastic, *Amex, Access/Mastercard, Visa* and *Diners Club* being the most commonly accepted brands. If you have a selection of cards, take them all; you'll get much the same exchange rate as you would in a bank, and bills can take a surprisingly long time to be charged to your account at home. The *Bank of Baroda* issues rupees against a *Visa* card at all its branches, while *Amex* will issue rupees or travellers' cheques to cardholders against a cheque at their offices. Train tickets can now be paid for by credit card.

It is illegal to carry rupees into or out of India, and you won't get them at a particularly good rate in the West anyhow (though you might in Thailand, Malaysia or Singapore).

TRAVELLERS' CHEQUES AND CREDIT CARDS

American Express		Thomas Cook	
Lost and stolen cards ☎011/687 5050 (open 24hr)		**New Delhi**	☎374 7414
New Delhi	☎332 4149	Rishsya Mook Building, 85-A Panchkuin Rd	
Wenger House, "A" Block, Connaught Place		**Bangalore**	☎558 8038
Bombay	☎204 8291	70 Mahatma Gandhi Rd	
Regal Cinema Building, Shivaji Marg, Colaba		**Bombay**	☎204 8556
Calcutta	☎248 9555	Dr DN Marg, Colaba	
21 Old Court House St		**Calcutta**	☎247 5378
Madras	☎852 3596	Chitrakoot Building, 2nd Floor, 230/A AJ Chandra Bose Rd	
G-17, Spencer Plaza, 769 Anna Salai		**Madras**	☎825 8417
		Ceebros Centre, 45 Montieth Rd, Egmore	

Both *American Express* and *Thomas Cook* have offices in other major cities throughout India (see the relevant accounts in the guide).

BANKS

Changing money in regular banks can be a time-consuming business, involving lots of form-filling and queuing at different counters, so change substantial amounts at any one time. Banks in main cities are likely to be most efficient, though not all change foreign currency, and some won't take travellers' cheques or currencies other than dollars or sterling. You'll have no such problems with private companies such as *Thomas Cook*, *American Express* or *Wall Street Finances*, who have offices in most state capitals. In small towns, the *State Bank of India* is your best bet. Note that if you arrive at a minor airport you may not be able to change anything except cash US dollars or sterling.

Outside **banking hours** (Mon–Fri 10am–2pm, Sat 10am–noon), large hotels may change money, probably at a lower rate. Banks at Delhi, Bombay, Calcutta and Madras airports, and at the *Ashok Hotel* in Delhi, stay open **24 hours** but none of these is very conveniently located. Otherwise, there's always the black market.

Hold on to **exchange receipts** ("encashment certificates"); they will be required if you want to change back any excess rupees when you leave the country, or buy things like air tickets with rupees, and if you need a tax clearance form (see p.14). The *State Bank of India* now charges for these.

Wiring money to India is a lot easier than it used to be. Indian banks with branches abroad, such as the *State Bank of India* and the *Bank of Baroda*, can wire money by telex from those branches to large ones in India in two working days. *Western Union* (information on ☎1-800/325 6000 in the US or ☎0800/833833 in the UK) can transfer cash or banker's drafts paid into their overseas branches to any one of 43 offices in India within fifteen minutes, for a typical fee of around 7.5 percent of the total amount, and similar services are offered by *American Express*, *Thomas Cook*, and foreign banks with branches in India such as *ANZ Grindlays* (who have the most).

THE BLACK MARKET

A **black market** still exists today, but only in the major tourist areas of the biggest cities, with little if any premium over the bank rate, though it is a lot faster. Small denominations are not popular, with the best rates given for notes of US$100, £50 or DM1000; you will, of course, have to haggle.

Always do this kind of business with shopkeepers rather than shady "hello my friend"-types on the street, and proceed with caution. Never hand over your pile until you *yourself* have counted and checked the rupees and have them in your hand; make sure they really are the denominations you think. Unusually high rates suggest a con, as does any attempt to rush you, or sudden claims that the police are coming. Remember what you are doing is illegal; you can be arrested and you may be set up.

At one or two of India's land borders (notably Bangladesh), unofficial money-changers may be your only option; as their rates will not be good, however, only change as much as you need to get you to a bank.

BAKSHEESH

As a presumed-rich *sahib* or *memsahib*, you will, like wealthy Indians, be expected to be liberal with the ***baksheesh***, which takes three main forms.

The most common is **tipping**: a small reward for a small service, which can encompass anyone from a waiter or porter to someone who lifts your bags onto the roof of a bus or keeps an eye on your vehicle for you. Large amounts are not expected – five rupees should satisfy all the aforementioned. Taxi drivers and staff at cheaper hotels and restaurants do not necessarily expect tips, but always appreciate them, of course, and they can keep people sweet for the next time you call. Some may take liberties in demanding *baksheesh*, but it's often better just to acquiesce rather than spoil your mood and cause offence over trifling sums.

More expensive than plain tipping is paying people to **bend the rules**, many of which seem to have been invented for precisely that purpose. Examples might include letting you into a historical site after hours, finding you a seat or a sleeper on a train that is "full", or speeding up some bureaucratic process. This should not be confused with bribery, a more serious business with its own risks and etiquette, which is best not entered into.

The last kind of *baksheesh* is **alms giving**. In a country without a welfare system, this is an important social custom. People with disabilities and mutilations are the traditional recipients, and it seems right to join local people in giving out small change to them. Kids demanding money, pens or the like are a different case, pressing their demands only on tourists. In return for a service it is fair enough, but to yield to any request encourages them to go and pester others.

GETTING AROUND

Inter-city transport in India may not be the fastest or the most comfortable in the world, but it's cheap, goes more or less everywhere, and generally gives you the option of train or bus, sometimes plane, and occasionally even boat. Transport around town comes in even more permutations, ranging in Calcutta for example from rickshaws still pulled by men on foot to a spanking new metro system.

Whether you're on road or rail, public transport or your own vehicle, India offers the chance to try out some classics: narrow-gauge railways, steam locomotives, the *Ambassador* car and the *Enfield Bullet* motorbike, they're all here. Some people come to India for these alone.

BY TRAIN

Travelling by train is one of the great experiences of India. There may be railway systems that are faster, more punctual and more comfortable (though perhaps none cheaper), but nowhere will you find one that is more, well, Indian!

Indian railways are a frenetic, crowded, yet in some ways rather quaint world of "up" trains and "down" trains, carrying untold masses of people in barrack-like carriages, echoing to the ubiquitous cries of the *chai-wallahs* as they dispense tea in

At the start of each chapter in this book, you'll find a chart of **"Travel Details"** summarizing major transport connections in the relevant state. In addition, boxes at the end of each major city detail **"Moving On"** from that city.

disposable clay cups, and food hawkers whose stalls spring into action on every railway platform as each train arrives and they jostle for position with sellers of coconuts, *bidis*, newspapers and magazines. From tiny country stations where the daily train is the big event, to massive labyrinthine city terminals where families make their homes on the platforms as the new broom of computer technology sweeps through the dusty offices of railway functionaries and station officials, it's a system which looks like chaos, but it works, and well. Trains are often late of course, by hours rather than minutes, but they do run, and with amazing efficiency too: when the train you've been waiting for rolls into the station, the reservation you made halfway across the country several weeks ago will be on a list pasted to the side of your carriage, and when it's time to eat, the packed meal you ordered down the line will be ready at the next station, put on the train and delivered to your seat.

Once rolling, you can settle down to enjoy an excellent view of the countryside as it slips past, fall into conversation with your fellow passengers, enjoy a nice cup of *chai*, or relax with a book or newspaper. It's worth bearing in mind too, with journeys frequently lasting 12 hours or more, that an overnight train can save you a day's travelling and a night's hotel bill, assuming you sleep well on trains. While carriages can be jam-packed during the day, between 9pm and 6am anyone with a bunk reservation is entitled to exclusive use of their bunk. When travelling overnight, always padlock your bag to your bunk.

ROUTES AND CLASSES

The railway network covers almost the entire country; only a few places (such as Sikkim, Ladakh, and most of Himachal Pradesh and Goa) are inaccessible by train. **Inter-city trains**, called "express" or "mail", vary a lot in the time taken to cover the same route. Slow by Western standards, they're still much faster than local **"passenger" trains**, which you need only use to get right off the beaten track. There are also one or two special "super-fast" a/c trains, such as the Delhi–Bombay and Delhi–Calcutta *Rajdhani* expresses; these can cut journey times by as much as 50 percent.

Most lines are either metre-gauge or broadgauge (1.676m, or 4'6"), the latter being faster;

many metre-gauge lines are now being converted to broad-gauge. There are also a few narrow-gauge lines (often referred to as "toy trains"), notably to the hill stations of Darjeeling, Shimla, Matheran and Ootacamund. **Steam locomotives** are still used on the first and last (the latter on Sundays only) of these, as well as on some local lines and goods services, and you may well see some in use in shunting yards, but they are fast disappearing; almost all trains nowadays are diesel-hauled.

Indian Railways distinguishes between no less than seven **classes** of travel, though you'll seldom have more than three to choose from on mainline services: first, second and air-conditioned first (or air-conditioned two- or three-tier). **First class**, in comfortable compartments of two or four berths, is used mainly by English-speaking business travellers and insulates you to a certain extent from the chaotic hustle and bustle – which you may or may not consider to be an advantage. It costs about 3.5 times as much as **second class**, which can be unbearably crowded during the day, even if you reserve a seat, and never lacks activity, be it peanut, *chai* or coffee sellers, travelling musicians, beggars or sweepers passing through each carriage. Overnight trips in second-class **sleeper** compartments are reasonably comfy (provided the berths are foam and not wooden), and there's the option of a little privacy for women in ladies' compartments on most long-haul journeys. **Air-conditioned first class**, at about 2.5 times the price of ordinary first, has little extra to offer apart from the eponymous air-conditioning. Finally, there's **second class unreserved**, painfully crowded and noisy with no chance of a berth overnight, and incredibly cheap: just Rs205 (that's $7 or £4) for a 5000km journey.

One or two services also have second-class air-conditioned "chair cars" with reclining seats, which cost about double the usual second-class fare, and second-class air-conditioned sleepers (a/c three-tier) at about five times more than normal second (and 25 percent more than non-a/c first). On the superfast *Rajdhani* and *Shatabdi* expresses, which provide meals and free mineral water, only a/c accommodation is available. Less celebrated services, and all local services, have second-class only, and no air-conditioning.

In general, most travellers (not just those on low budgets) choose to travel second class, and prefer not to be in a/c compartments; an open window keeps you cool enough, and brings you into contact with the world outside, while air-conditioning by definition involves being sealed away behind glass, often virtually opaque. Doing without a sleeper on an overnight journey is however a false economy. Bed rolls (sheet, blanket and pillow) are available in first class and a/c second for that extra bit of comfort – book these with your ticket, or before you board the train.

TIMETABLES AND TICKETS

Indian Railways publish an annual **timetable** of all mail and express trains – in effect, all the trains you are likely to use. Called *Trains at a Glance*, it is available from information counters and newsstands at all main stations, and from *IR* agents abroad. *Thomas Cook's International Timetable Vol II* (the blue one) has a limited selection of timetables, while the elusive monthly *Indian Bradshaw* covers every scheduled train in the country. In theory, this is available at major termini, but it is often difficult to get hold of (Calcutta seems to be the best place); complete regional timetables are widely available however.

All rail **fares** are calculated according to the exact distance travelled; *Trains at a Glance* prints a chart of fares by kilometres, and also gives the distance in kilometres of stations along each route in the timetables, making it possible to calculate what the basic fare will be for any given journey. Endless poring over the columns reveals little more than that fares are very cheap indeed.

Each individual train has its own name and number, prominently displayed in station booking halls. When buying a ticket, it makes sense to pay the tiny extra fee to reserve a seat or sleeper (the fee is already included in the price of a first-class sleeper). To do so, you fill in a form specifying the train you intend to catch, its number, your date of travel, and the stations you are travelling to and from. Most stations (listed in *Trains at a Glance*) have computerized booking counters, and you will be told immediately whether or not seats are available. In larger cities, the major stations have special tourist sections to cut the queues for foreigners and Indian citizens resident abroad buying tickets, with helpful English-speaking staff; however, if you don't pay in pounds sterling or dollars (travellers' cheques or cash), you must produce an encashment certificate to back up your rupees. Elsewhere, buying a ticket can often involve a long wait, though women can cut this down immeasurably at ticket counters which have "ladies' queues". Some stations also operate a number system of queuing, allowing you to repair to the chai stall or check the timetable until your number is called. Failure to buy a ticket at the point of departure will result in paying a far higher fare when the ticket inspector finds you.

It's important to plan your train journeys in advance, as the demand often makes it impossible to buy a long-distance ticket on the same day that you want to travel. Travellers following tight itineraries tend to buy their departure tickets from particular towns the moment they arrive, to avoid having to trek out to the station again. At most large stations it's possible to reserve tickets for journeys starting elsewhere in the country; whenever you've worked out your schedule a few days ahead, try to buy all the tickets you'll need in one. In fact, you can even book tickets for specific journeys (if you buy an *Indrail* pass) before you leave home, with *Indian Railways* representatives abroad (see box). They accept bookings up to six months in advance, with a minimum of one month for first class, and three months for second.

If you have to **cancel your ticket**, the fare is refunded up to a day before departure, minus a fee for the reservation (Rs10 in second class, Rs20 in first, Rs30 a/c first). Between a day and four hours before scheduled departure, you get 75 percent back; you can still claim a 50 percent refund if you present your ticket up to twelve hours after the train actually leaves on a journey of over 500km, or three hours after a short journey.

If there are **no places available** on the train you want, you have a number of choices. First, some seats and berths are set aside as a "tourist quota" – ask at the tourist counter if you can get in on this, or else try the stationmaster. Failing that, other special quotas, such as one for VIPs, may remain unused – however, if you get a booking on the VIP quota and a pukka VIP turns up, you lose the reservation. Drawing a blank there, a "reservation against cancellation" (RAC) ticket will give you priority if sleepers do become available – the ticket clerk should be able to tell you your chances – or you could get a plain unreserved ticket, get on the train and go and see the ticket inspector as soon as possible. You may be able to persuade them to find you a place if one is free: something usually is, but you'll be stuck in unreserved if it isn't. Alternatively, and especially if you get on where the train starts its journey, *baksheesh* may persuade a porter to "reserve" you an unreserved seat or, better still, a luggage rack where you can stretch out for the night. You

---

INDRAIL PASSES

Indrail passes, sold to foreigners and Indians resident abroad, cover all fares and reservation fees for periods ranging from half a day to 90 days. Even if you travel a lot, this works out considerably more expensive than buying your tickets individually (especially in second class), but it will save you queuing for tickets, allow you to make and cancel reservations with impunity (and without charge), and generally smooth your way in, for example, finding a seat or berth on a "full" train: passholders, for example, get priority for tourist quota places. *Indrail* passes are available, for sterling or US dollars, at main station tourist counters, in India, and outside the country at *IR* agents (see box on p.31). If you're travelling from Britain, Mr Dandapani of *SD Enterprises Ltd* (see box on p.31) is an excellent contact, providing information on all aspects of travel on Indian railways, and also sells *Indrail* passes.

RATES IN US$

	a/c First Class		First Class or a/c Sleeper, or a/c Chair car		Second Class	
	Adult	Child	Adult	Child	Adult	Child
1 day*	86	43	39	20	17	9
4 days*	220	110	110	55	50	25
7 days	300	150	150	75	80	40
15 days	370	185	185	95	90	45
21 days	440	220	220	110	100	50
30 days	550	275	275	140	125	65
60 days	800	400	400	200	185	95
90 days	1060	530	530	265	235	120

*For sale outside India only; half-day & 2-day pass also available. Note that these prices are liable to rise a further 10 percent.

INDIAN RAILWAYS SALES AGENTS ABROAD

Australia: Adventure World ☎02/956 7766
73 Walker St (PO Box 480), North Sydney, NSW 2059.

Bangladesh: Omaitrans Internat'l ☎02/834401
70/1 Inner Circular Rd, Kakrail, Dhaka.

Malaysia: City East West Travels ☎03/293 0569
Sdn Bhd No 135-A, Jalan Bunus, 50100 Kuala Lumpur.

Thailand: SS Travels Service ☎02/236 7188
10/12–13, SS Building, Convent Rd, Bangkok 10500.

Canada: Hari World Travel Inc ☎366 2000
1 Financial Place, Adelaide St East, Toronto M5C 2V8.

UK: SD Enterprises Ltd ☎0181/903 3411
103 Wembley Park Drive, Wembley, Middx HA9
8HG. (Mon–Fri 9am–5.30pm, Sat 9am–2pm).

USA: Hariworld Travels Inc ☎212/957 3300
30 Rockefeller Plaza, #21, New York, NY10112.

could even fight your way on and grab one your-self, although we don't rate your chances. As for attempting to **travel unreserved**, for journeys of any length it's too uncomfortable to be worth seri-ously considering on any major route.

Ladies' compartments exist on all overnight trains for women travelling unaccompanied; they are usually small and can be full of noisy kids, but can give untold relief to women travellers who otherwise have to endure incessant staring in the open section of the carriage. On the other hand, particularly if you like (or are with) children, they can be a good place to meet Indian women. Some stations also have ladies-only waiting rooms.

THE PALACE ON WHEELS

Should you fancy something a bit posher than a normal scheduled train, the Rajasthan Tourist Development Corporation (RTDC) run the *Palace on Wheels*, a luxury, refurbished, air-conditioned train that goes on weekly tours of Rajasthan, departing from Delhi Cantonment station every Wednesday evening between September and April, and returning the following Wednesday morning, with accommodation on board. For more details see p.133. Bookings can be made through *Indian Railways* representatives abroad or RTDC, Bikaner House, Pandara Rd, New Delhi (☎011/381884 or 383837); rates start at £1400 per person for two weeks. Some package opera-tors include it in tours.

Such has been the success of the *Palace on Wheels* that seven similar (less expensive) train services are currently planned to start touring dif-ferent regions of India. A *Temple on Wheels* tour of Tamil Nadu has been announced: others being set up will cover the Buddha trail in Uttar Pradesh (aimed primarily at East Asian tourists), and Gujarat, which is already up and running.

As an alternative to these, British travel opera-tors *Butterfields* (see p.5) run tours in their own

specially converted carriages, which are attached to a series of scheduled trains and hauled around the country. These must be booked in the UK.

CLOAKROOMS

Most stations in India have "cloakrooms" (some-times called "parcel offices") for passengers to leave their baggage. These can be extremely handy if you want to go sightseeing in a town and move on the same day. In theory, you need a train ticket or *Indrail* pass to deposit luggage, but they don't always ask; they may however refuse to take your bag if you can't lock it. Losing your reclaim ticket causes problems; the clerk will be assumed to have stolen the bag if he can't pro-duce it, so there'll be untold running around to obtain clearance before you can get your bag without it. Make sure, when checking baggage in, that the cloakroom will be open when you need to pick it up.

BY AIR

Though obviously more expensive than going by train or bus, **flying** can save a lot of time: Delhi–Madras, for example, takes 36 hours' hard travelling by train, a mere 1hr 40min by plane. Delays and cancellations can whittle away the time advantage, especially over small distances, but if you're short of time and plan to cover a lot of ground, you should definitely consider flying for longer journeys.

India has just one national internal air carrier, **Indian Airlines**, (*IA*) which serves 147 routes, and also flies to the southeast Asian destinations listed on p.7. In addition, *Air India* runs shuttles between the four main cities (from the interna-tional, not the domestic, terminals), and private operators such as *Jagson*, *Archana*, *Modiluft* and *East-West* offer links with smaller towns such as Porbander, Kullu, Dharamsala and Jaisalmer: all

MULTI FLIGHT DEALS – INDIAN AIRLINES

Discover India Fare
Unlimited travel on all internal flights for 21 days;
$500 (no single route twice).

India Wonderfare
Seven days' travel in one given region; $200 ($300
including Port Blair).

21 Days South India Excursion
30% discount on dollar tariff for 21 days.
30% discount on south Indian journeys if you fly in
from Colombo or Maldives.

NB: *Disabled passengers with stretchers must pay
three times the normal fare.*

very convenient, but more expensive than *IA*. (You
may see references to *Vayudoot*, who disappeared
in 1993; confusingly many of its offices remain
open, selling tickets for former *Vayudoot* routes
now taken over by *IA*.) Short flights can be cheap,
often less than $50, but longer ones are hardly
less than equivalent distances anywhere else:
Delhi–Madras is currently $168 with *IA*. *IA* has a
number of special deals that are worth knowing
about; in addition to 25 percent discount for under-
30s and students, and 50 percent for over-65s,
they offer three multi-flight discounts (see box).

One problem with flying is that you may have to
spend a massive amount of time queuing at the airline office to get a reservation; it's often quicker to
book through a hotel or travel agent, which is the
norm for booking on private carriers. If you haven't
got a confirmed seat, be sure to get to the airport
early and keep checking your position in the queue;
even if you *have* got a confirmed seat, be sure to
always reconfirm 72 hours before your flight.

Airlines have offices or representatives in all
the places they fly to; all are listed in this book in
the relevant city sections. *IA* tickets must be paid
for in hard currency or with a credit card. Children
under 12 pay half fare, and under-twos (one per
adult) pay 10 percent. There are no cancellation
charges if you pay in foreign currency, but tickets
are not replaceable if lost. **Timetables** for all
internal flights (with fares) are published in *Divan*
and *Excel* magazines, and shown on teletext if
you can get access to that, while each operator
stocks their own timetables.

BY BUS

Although the railway is the definitive way to travel in India, and generally more comfortable than a

bus, there are places (such as most Himalayan
valleys) where trains don't go, where they are
awkward and inconvenient, or where buses are
simply faster (as in most of Rajasthan and other
places without broad-gauge track). Alternatively,
you might just fancy a change or the train you
want might be booked up. In that case, the bus is
for you; and you'll be pleased to know that they
go almost everywhere, more frequently than
trains (though mostly in daylight hours), with
state-government-operated services everywhere,
and plenty of private firms besides.

Buses vary somewhat in price and standards.
Government-run ramshackle affairs, packed to
the gunwales with people, livestock and luggage,
cover short and very long distances – in remote
mountain regions, for example, they rattle along
un-tarmacked roads for up to 24 hours. In more
widely travelled areas there's usually a (welcome) alternative, a private or government-run
bus that should be less crowded, and more comfortable, and doesn't make quite so many stops.
It's worth asking when booking if your bus will
have a video or music system, as their deafening
noise ruins any chances of sleep. Popular tourist
routes (eg. Delhi–Manali, Delhi–Pushkar), are
now covered by rather smart **private buses**
which cost a little more than government "tourist
coaches" (booked through tourist offices), and
often carrying more Western than Indian tourists.
However, even luxury coaches can have broken
seats, recliners that don't recline, and windows
that don't close, so be prepared, and always try
to avoid the back seats – they accentuate bumpy
roads and launch you into the air several times a
minute. Smaller private bus companies may be
only semi-legal and have little backup in case of
breakdown.

Luggage travels in the hatch of private buses,
but more usually on the roof (you may be able to
travel up there yourself if the bus is too crowded,
though it's dangerous and illegal); check that it's
well secured (ideally, lock it there) and not liable
to get squashed. *Baksheesh* is in order for whoever puts it up there for you.

Buying a bus ticket is usually less of an
ordeal than buying a train ticket, although at large
city bus stations there may be 20 or so counters,
each assigned to a different route. When you buy
your ticket you'll be given the registration number
of the bus and, sometimes, a seat number. As at
railway stations, there is usually a separate,
quicker, ladies' queue, although the sign to indi-

cate it may not be in English. Prior booking is usually necessary for express and private services, but often tickets can be bought on the bus itself.

BY BOAT

Apart from river ferries, few **boat services** run in India. The Bombay–Panjim boat has been out of action for years, though there are always rumours of its imminent reappearance.

The Andaman Islands are connected to Calcutta and Madras by boat – as well as to each other – and there are luxury services between Kochi and Lakshadweep, but the only part of mainland India with a regular passenger boat system is **Kerala**, where a number of services operate out of Alappuzha and Kollam, including the popular "backwater trip" between the two.

BY CAR OR MOTORBIKE

It is much more usual for tourists in India to be driven than it is for them to drive; car rental firms operate on the basis of supplying **chauffeur-driven vehicles**, and taxis are available at cheap daily rates. Arranged through tourist offices, local car rental firms, or branches of *Hertz, Budget* or *Europcar*, a chauffeur-driven car will run to about US$30 per day. On longer trips, the driver sleeps in the car. The big international chains are the best bet for self-drive car rental; in India they charge around 30 percent less than chauffeur-driven, with a Rs1000 deposit against damage, though if you pay in your home country it can cost a whole lot more. In one or two places, motorbikes or mopeds may be rented out for local use, but for biking around the country, it is a much better idea to buy (see below).

Driving in India is not for beginners. If you do drive yourself, expect the unexpected, and expect other drivers to take whatever liberties they can get away with. Traffic circulates on the left, and don't expect road regulations to be obeyed. Traffic in the cities is heavy and undisciplined; vehicles cut in and out without warning, and pedestrians, cyclists and cows wander nonchalantly down the middle of the road as if you didn't exist. In the country the roads are narrow, in terrible repair, and hogged by overloaded *Tata* trucks that move aside for nobody, while something slow-moving like a bullock cart or a herd of goats can easily take up the whole road. To overtake, sound your horn – the driver in front will signal if it is safe to do so; if not, he will wave his hand, palm down-

wards, up and down. A huge number of potholes don't make for a smooth ride either. Furthermore, during the monsoon roads can become flooded and dangerous; rivers burst their banks and bridges get washed away. Ask local people before you set off, and proceed with caution, sticking to main highways if possible.

You should have an **international driving licence** to drive in India, but this is often overlooked if you have your licence from home (but beware of police in Goa, who are quick to hand out fines). Insurance is compulsory, but not expensive. Car seat belts and motorcycle crash-helmets are not compulsory but very strongly recommended; helmets are best brought from home. Accident rates are high, and you should be on your guard at all times. It is very dangerous to drive at night – not everyone uses lights, and bullock carts don't have any. If you have an **accident**, it might be an idea to leave the scene quickly and go straight to the police to report it; mobs can assemble fast, especially if pedestrians or cows are involved.

Fuel is reasonably cheap compared to home, but the state of the roads will take its toll, and mechanics are not always very reliable, so a knowledge of **vehicle maintenance** is a help, as is a check-over every so often to see what all those bone-shaking journeys are doing to your conveyance. Luckily, if you get a flat tyre, puncture-*wallahs* can be easily found almost everywhere.

To import a car or motorbike into India, you'll have to show a *carnet de passage*, a document intended to ensure that you don't sell the vehicle illegally. These are available from foreign motoring organizations such as the *AA*. It's also worth bringing a few basic spares, as spare parts for foreign makes can be hard to find in India, although low-quality imitations are more widely available. All in all, the route is arduous (see p.7), and bringing a vehicle to India something of a commitment.

The classic **Indian automobile** is the Hindustan *Ambassador* (basically a *Morris Oxford*), nowadays largely superseded by more modern vehicles such as the Japanese-style *Maruti*. Renting a car, you'll probably have a choice of these two or others. If you're interested in buying one, the *Ambassador* is not famed for its mod cons or low mpg, but has a certain style and historical interest, and later models make little sense as prices are higher and quality lower than in the West.

Buying a motorbike is a much more reasonable proposition, and again, if it's an old British classic you're after, the *Enfield Bullet* (350 model), sold cheapest in Pondicherry, leads the field. If low price and practicality are your priorities, however, a smaller model, perhaps even a moped or a scooter, might better fit the bill. Many Japanese bikes are now made in India, as are *Vespas* and *Lambrettas*, and motorcycles of various sorts can easily be bought new or secondhand. Garages and repair shops are a good place to start; see Delhi "Listings" for details of the city's Karol Bagh area, renowned for its motorcycle shops, as well as Bales Rd in Madras. Obviously, you will have to haggle for the price, but you can expect to pay half to two-thirds the original price for a bike in reasonable condition. Given the right bargaining skills, you can sell it again later for a similar price – perhaps to another foreign traveller, by advertising it in hotels and restaurants. A certain amount of bureaucracy is involved in transferring vehicle ownership, but a garage should be able to put you on to a broker ("auto consultant") who, for a modest commission (around Rs250), will help you find a seller or a buyer, and do the necessary paperwork. A motorbike can be taken in the luggage car of a train for the same price as a second-class passenger fare.

BY BICYCLE

Ever since Dervla Murphy's *Full Tilt*, a steady but increasing trickle of travellers have either themselves done the overland trip **by bicycle**, or else bought a bike in India and ridden it around the country. In many ways it is the ideal form of transport, offering total independence without loss of contact with local people. You can camp out, though there are cheap lodgings in almost every village – take the bike into your room with you – and, if you get tired of pedalling, you can put it on top of a bus as luggage, or transport it by train (it goes in the luggage van: get a form and pay a small fee at the station luggage office).

Bringing a bike from abroad requires no *carnet* or special paperwork, but spare parts and accessories may be of different sizes and standards in India, and you may have to improvise. Bring basic spares and tools, and a pump. Panniers are the obvious thing for carrying your gear, but fiendishly inconvenient when not attached to your bike, and you might consider sacrificing ideal load-bearing and streamlining technology for a backpack you can lash down on the rear carrier.

Buying a bike in India presents no great difficulty; most towns have cycle shops and even cycle markets. The advantages of a local bike are that spare parts are easy to get, locally produced tools and parts will fit, and your vehicle will not draw a crowd every time you park it. Disadvantages are that Indian bikes tend to be heavier and less state-of-the-art than ones from abroad (bikes with gears, let alone mountain bikes, are unheard of). Selling should be quite easy: you won't get a tremendously good deal at a cycle market, but you may well be able to sell privately, or even to a rental shop.

Bicycles can be **rented** in most towns: this is a good way to find out if your legs and bum can survive the Indian bike before buying one. Rs10–20 per day is the going rate, usually more in tourist centres, and you may have to leave a deposit, or even your passport as security. Most bicycle-rental firms rent bikes for in-town use only; they won't take too kindly to you disappearing round the country on them. If you want to do that, buying would be a much better option.

IBT, 4887 Columbia Drive S, Seattle WA 98108-1919 (☎206/628 9314), publish information and offer advice on bicycle travel around the world. In India, the *Cycle Federation of India*, C-5A/262, DDA Flats, Janak Puri, New Delhi 110058 (☎553006), is the main cycle-sports organization.

CITY TRANSPORT

Transport around town takes various forms, with **buses** the most obvious. These are usually single-decker, though double-deckers (some articulated) exist in Bombay and elsewhere. City buses can get unbelievably crowded, so beware of pickpockets, razor-armed pocket-slitters, and "Eve-teasers" (see p.64); the same applies to **suburban trains** in Bombay (Madras is about the only other place where you might want to use trains for local city transport).

You can also take **taxis**, usually rather battered *Ambassadors* (painted black and yellow in Delhi and Bombay). With luck, the driver will agree to use the meter; in theory you're within your rights to call the police if he doesn't, but the usual compromise is to agree a fare for the journey before you get in. Naturally, it helps to have an idea in advance what the fare should be, though any figures quoted in this or any other book should be treated as being the broadest of guidelines only. From places such as main stations, you may be able to find other passengers to share a taxi to the town centre; many stations, and certainly most airports operate pre-paid taxi schemes with set fares that you pay before departure; more expensive pre-paid limousines are also available.

The **auto-rickshaw**, that most Indian of vehicles, is the front half of a motor-scooter with a couple of seats mounted on the back. Cheaper than taxis, better at nipping in and out of traffic, and usually metered (again, they probably won't use them and you should agree a fare before setting off), auto-rickshaws are a little unstable and their drivers often rather reckless, but that's all part of the fun. In major tourist centres rickshaws can however hassle you endlessly on the street, often shoving themselves right in your path to prevent you ignoring them, and once you're inside they may take you to several shops before reaching your destination. Moreover, agreeing a price before the journey will not necessarily stop your rickshaw *wallah* reopening discussion when the trip is under way, or at its end. In general it is better to hail a rickshaw than to take one that's been following you.

One or two cities also have larger versions of auto-rickshaws known as **tempos**, with six or eight seats behind, which usually ply fixed routes at flat fares. In Delhi they are built onto old *Harley Davidson* motorbikes. Here and there you'll also come across horse-drawn carriages, or **tongas**. Tugged by underfed and often lame horses, these are the least popular with tourists.

Slower and cheaper still is the **cycle rickshaw** – basically a glorified tricycle. Foreign visitors often feel squeamish about travelling this way, and with good reason; except in the major tourist cities, cycle rickshaw *wallahs* are invariably emaciated pavement dwellers who earn only a pittance for their pains. In the end, though, to deny them your custom on those grounds is spurious logic; they're the least expensive form of transport and will earn even less if you don't use them. Only in Calcutta do the rickshaw *wallahs* continue to haul the city's pukka rickshaws on foot.

If you want to see a variety of places around town, consider hiring a taxi, rickshaw or auto-rickshaw for the day. Find a driver who speaks English reasonably well, and agree a price beforehand. You will probably find it a lot cheaper than you imagine: the driver will invariably act as a guide and source of local knowledge, and tipping is usually in order.

ACCOMMODATION

There are far more Indians travelling around their own country at any one time – whether for holidays, on pilgrimages, or for business – than there are foreign tourists, and a vast infrastructure of hotels and guest houses caters for their needs. On the whole, accommodation, like so many other things in India,

provides **extremely good value for money, though in the major cities, especially, prices are soaring for luxury establishments that provide Western-style comforts and service.**

Throughout this book we recommend places to stay in cities, towns and villages that range from lavish lakeside palaces to the most basic dormitory accommodation. Travellers on all budgets are looking to get the best return for what they're prepared to spend, and we set out to spotlight bargains in every category. However, we have not slavishly listed the very cheapest rooms, regardless of quality; there's usually a reason why specific hotels have much lower rates than the others, and part of the function of this book is to spare you from finding out what that reason is.

INEXPENSIVE HOTELS

While accommodation prices in India are generally on the up, there's still an abundance of **cheap hotels**, catering for backpacking tourists and less well-off Indians. Most charge Rs100–150 for a double room, and some outside the big cities have rates below Rs100 ($3/£2). The cheapest option is usually in a dormitory of a hostel or hotel, where you'll be charged anything from Rs20 to Rs100.

Budget accommodation varies from filthy fleapits to homely guest houses and, naturally, tends to be cheaper the further you get off the beaten track; it's most expensive in Delhi and Bombay, where prices are at least double those for equivalent accommodation in most other cities.

Cold showers or "bucket baths" are the order of the day – not really a problem in most of India for most of the year – and it's always wise to check out the state of the bathrooms and toilets before taking a room. Bed bugs and mosquitoes are other things to check for – splotches of blood around the bed and on the walls where people have squashed them are tell-tale signs.

If a taxi driver or rickshaw *wallah* tells you that the place you ask for is full, closed or has moved, it's more than likely that it's because he wants to take you to a hotel that pays him commission – added, in some cases, to your bill. Hotel touts operate in some major tourist spots, working for commission from the hotels they take you to; this can become annoying, but sometimes paying the little extra can be well worth it, especially if you arrive alone in a new place at night.

Finally, if you find yourself disagreeing with our review of a particular hotel, it was probably true when it was written; one unavoidable effect of books such as this is that the hotels we recommend may well change in character as a result. Many of the long-standing "backpackers' haunts" around the country are these days so inundated

with foreign budget travellers as to have lost any sense of being in India – or even on this planet. To a lesser extent, they may also decide to raise their prices or lower their standards. And make sure you've got the right place; another spin-off is that imitators spring up to cash in on the popularity of well-known budget hotels.

MID-RANGE HOTELS

Even if you value your **creature comforts**, you don't need to pay through the nose for them. A large clean room, freshly made bed, your own spotless (often sit-down) toilet, and hot and cold running water can still cost under Rs200 ($6/£4). Extras that bump up the price include TV, mosquito nets, a balcony, and, above all, **air-conditioning**. Abbreviated in this book and in India itself as **a/c**, air-conditioning is not necessarily the advantage you might expect – in some hotels you can find yourself paying double for a system that is so dust-choked, wheezy and noisy as to preclude any possibility of sleep – but providing it entitles a hotel to consider itself mid-range. Some also offer a halfway-house option known as "**air-cooled**". Many medium-priced hotels also have attached restaurants, and even room service.

New hotels tend to be lined inside, on floors and walls, with marble (or an approximation thereof), which can make them feel totally characterless. They are, however, much cleaner than older hotels, where dirt and grime clings to cracks and crevices, and damp quickly devours paint.

Most state governments run their own "**tourist bungalows**", similar to mid-range hotels, but often also offering pricier a/c rooms and cheaper dorms. They are usually good value, though they vary a lot from state to state (Rajasthan's, for example, tend to be rather run-down, whereas Tamil Nadu's, all called *Hotel Tamil Nadu*, are as a rule very well kept), and even within states. If you're on a medium budget, it's not a bad idea to think first of staying in the state-run hotel in any town; to make that easier, we've consistently indicated such places through this guide by including the state acronym in the name – eg MPTDC *Palace*. Bookings for state-run hotels can be made in advance by telephone, or through the state tourist offices throughout the country.

UPMARKET HOTELS

Most luxury hotels in India fall into one of two categories: old-fashioned institutions brimming with class, and modern jet-set chain hotels, largely confined to large cities and tourist resorts.

The faded grandeur of the **Raj** lingers on in the venerable edifices of British imperial hangouts such as Calcutta and the hill stations. These can be well worth seeking out for their olde-worlde charm, and their knack of being somehow more quintessentially British than the British ever managed. In addition, in states such as Rajasthan, UP and Madhya Pradesh, magnificent old forts and palaces (*thikanas*) from feudal estates, and *havelis*, the former homes of aristocratic families, have been designated "**heritage hotels**."

Modern deluxe establishments – slicker, brighter, faster and far more businesslike – tend to belong to chains, as often Indian as international. The *Taj* in Bombay for example, the country's grandest hostelry, has a number of offshoots, including former palaces in Rajasthan. Other chains include *Oberoi, Holiday Inn, Meridien, Hyatt* and *Sheraton*, as well as ITDC's *Ashok* chain. You'll find such hotels in most state capitals and some resorts favoured by rich Indian and foreign tourists. It's becoming more common for these to quote tariffs in US dollars, starting at $90, but sometimes bringing the price for a double room up to an astonishing $300. In palaces and heritage hotels however, you'll still get excellent value for money, with rates only just beginning to approach those of their counterparts back home.

Bookings for many of the larger hotel chains can be made in offices around the world. The *Taj, Oberoi* and *Sheraton* chains are among those with outlets in the UK and the US. Otherwise, bookings can be made by mail or fax to:

Ashok Group, Ashok Reservation Service, *Hotel Samrat*, Chanakyapuri, Delhi 110021; ☎011/603030, fax 011/687 3216.

Oberoi Group, *Oberoi Maidens*, 7 Sham Nath Marg, Delhi 110054; ☎011/252 5464, fax 011/292 9800.

Taj Group, *Taj Mahal Intercontinental*, Apollo Bunder, Bombay 400039; ☎022/202 3366, fax 022/287 2711.

Welcomgroup (Sheraton), *Maurya Sheraton*, Diplomatic Enclave, New Delhi; ☎011/303 0101, fax 011/301 2892.

YS AND YHS

Official and non-official **youth hostels**, some run by state governments, are spread haphazardly across the country. Often run-down and often full (though on occasion completely empty), they'll

YOUTH HOSTEL ASSOCIATIONS

Australia
Australian YHA ☎02/9565 1325
Level 3, 10 Mallett St, Camperdown, Sydney.

Canada
HI Canadian Hostelling Association ☎613/237-7884
#400, 205 Catherine St, Ottawa, Ontario K2P 1C3.

England and Wales
Youth Hostel Association (*YHA*) ☎017278/45047
8 St Stephen's Hill, St Alban's, Herts AL1.
London shop and information office ☎0171/836 1036
14 Southampton St, London WC2.

Ireland
An Oige ☎01/363111
39 Mountjoy Square, Dublin 1.

New Zealand
YHA of New Zealand ☎03/3799970
PO Box 436, Christchurch 1.

Northern Ireland
YHA of Northern Ireland ☎0232/324733
56 Bradbury Place, Belfast, BT7.

Scotland
Scottish YHA ☎01786/511817
Glebe Crescent, Stirling, FK8 2JA.

USA
American Youth Hostels (*HI-AYH*) ☎202/783-6161
733 15th St NW, PO Box 37613, Washington DC 20005.

give *HI* cardholders a discount, but rarely exclude non-holders, nor do they usually impose daytime closing or other silly rules. Prices match the cheapest hotels; where there is a youth hostel, it usually has a dormitory and may well be the best budget accommodation available – which goes especially for the *Salvation Army* ones.

YMCAs and YWCAs, confined to big cities, are plusher and pricier, comparable to a mid-range hotel. They are usually good value, but often full, and sometimes only take members of one sex.

OTHER PLACES

Many railway stations have **"retiring rooms"** for passengers to sleep. These can be particularly handy if you're catching an early morning train, but tend to get booked up well in advance. They vary in price, but generally charge roughly the same as a budget hotel, and have large, clean, if somewhat institutional rooms; dormitories, where you can bank on being woken at the crack of dawn by a morning chorus of throat-clearing, are often available.

In one or two places, you can rent **rooms in people's homes**. In Rajasthan, the state tourist development corporation runs a "Paying Guest Scheme" to place tourists with families offering lodging, while *Munjeeta Travel* in London (see p.5) organize "Homestay Tours" across India – an excellent way to get to know an Indian family and see how they live. **Houseboats** were the thing in Srinagar, Kashmir, but going there is not a particularly good idea at present.

Camping is possible too, although in most of the country it's hard to see why you'd want to be cooped up in a tent overnight when you could be sleeping on a cool *charpoi* (a sort of basic bed) on a roof terrace for a handful of rupees – let alone why you'd choose to carry a tent around India in the first place. Except possibly on treks, it's not usual simply to pitch a tent in the countryside, but

many hotels allow camping in their grounds. The *YMCA* run a few sites, as do state governments (Maharashtra in particular), and the Scouts and Guides.

Finally, some temples, particularly Sikh *gurudwaras*, offer accommodation for pilgrims and visitors, and may put up tourists. A donation is often expected, and certainly appreciated. Pilgrimage sites, especially those far from other accommodation, also have **dharamshalas** where visitors can stay – very cheap and very simple, almost always with basic, communal washing facilities.

PRACTICALITIES

Check-out time at most hotels is noon. Always confirm this when you arrive: some expect you out by 9am, while others operate a 24-hour system, under which you are simply obliged to leave by the same time as you arrived. Some places let you use their facilities after the official check-out time, sometimes for a small charge, others won't even let you leave your baggage after then unless you pay for another night.

Unfortunately, not all hotels offer **single rooms**, so it can often work out more expensive to be travelling alone; in hotels that don't, you may be able to negotiate a slight discount. It's not unusual to find rooms with three or four beds however – great value for families and small groups.

In cheap hotels and hostels, you needn't expect any **additions to your basic bill**, but as you go up the scale, you'll find taxes and service charges creeping in, sometimes adding as much as a third on top of the original tariff. Service is generally 10 percent, but taxes are a matter for state governments and vary from state to state.

Like most other things in India, the price of a room may well be open to **negotiation**. If you think the price is too high, or if all the hotels in town are empty, try haggling. You may get nowhere – but nothing ventured, nothing gained.

EATING AND DRINKING

Indian food has a richly deserved reputation throughout the world for being aromatic and delicious. Visiting India, you should exercise a little caution as to where and what you eat, but most travellers develop a level of tolerance after a period of controlled exposure.

If you're a **vegetarian**, you've come to the right place. Indians are used to people having special dietary requirements: yours will be respected, and no-one will think you strange for having them. Indeed, some of the very best food India has to offer is vegetarian, and even the most confirmed meat-eaters will find themselves tucking into delicious *thalis*, *dals* and veg curries with relish. Most religious Hindus, and the majority of people in the south, do not consume the flesh of animals, while some orthodox Brahmins will not eat food cooked by anyone outside their household (or onions or garlic, as they inflame the baser instincts), and Jains are even stricter. Veganism as such is not common, however; if you're vegan, you'll have to keep your eyes open for eggs and dairy products.

Many eating places state whether they are vegetarian or non-vegetarian ("veg" or "non-veg"); sometimes, as with station canteens, there are both, and on public transport, you always get the option of veg or non-veg food; "pure veg" means that no eggs or alcohol are served. As a rule,

For advice on **water** in India, see p.18.

meat-eaters should exercise caution in India: even when meat is available, especially in the larger towns, its quality is not assured and you won't get much in a dish anyway – especially in railway canteens where it's mainly there for flavouring. Hindus, of course, do not eat beef and Muslims shun pork, so you'll only find those in a few Christian enclaves such as the beach areas of Goa. Note that what is called "mutton" on menus is in fact goat.

Broadly speaking, there are three types of eating establishments. *Dhabas* or *bhojanalayas* are **cheap Indian diners**, where food is basic but often good, consisting of vegetable curry, sometimes meat, *dal* (a lentil soup pronounced "da'al"), and rice or Indian bread (the latter more standard in the north). These places can be grubby – look them over before you commit yourself – and they have a bit of a tendency to pile on the *garam masala* as a substitute for fresh and appropriate spices. They do, on the other hand, have the advantage of being dirt cheap.

Restaurants as such vary in price and quality, and can be veg or non-veg, offering a wide choice of dishes, much like Indian restaurants anywhere else in the world. If you're in a group, you can order a variety of dishes and sample each one. Deluxe restaurants such as those in 5-star hotels can be very expensive by Indian standards, but they offer a chance to try classic Indian cooking of a very high standard: rich, subtle, mouthwatering, and still a fraction of the price you'd pay for such delights at home – assuming you could find Indian food that good. Try a meal in one at least once.

The third type of eating place caters specifically for foreign travellers with unadventurous taste-buds: the **tourist restaurant**, found in beach resorts, hill stations and travellers' meccas across India. Here you can get pancakes and fritters, omelettes and toast, chips, fried prawns, cereal, and fruit salad. The downside is that they can be a little bit pricey, some miss the mark by a long way, and they are not, of course, authentically Indian.

Finally, should you be lucky enough to be invited into someone's home, you will get to taste the most authentically Indian food of all. Most Indian women are professional cooks and housewives, trained from childhood by mothers, grandmothers and aunties, and aided by daughters and nieces.

They can quite easily spend a whole day cooking, grinding and mixing the spices themselves, and using only the freshest ingredients.

INDIAN FOOD

What Westerners call a **curry** covers a variety of dishes, each made with a different *masala*, or mix of spices. Curry powder does not exist in India, the nearest equivalent being *garam masala* ("hot mix"), a combination of dried ground black pepper and other spices in theory added to a dish at the last stage of cooking to spice it up, but often used as a substitute for other aromatics. Commonly used **spices** include chilli, turmeric, garlic, ginger, cinnamon, cardamom, cloves, coriander – both leaf and seed – cumin and saffron. These are not all added at the same time, and some are used whole, so beware of chewing on them. The spice that gives British and Caribbean curry powder its distinctive taste, fenugreek, is used much more sparingly in India.

It's the Indian penchant for **chilli** that alarms many Western visitors. The majority of foreigners develop a tolerance for it; if you don't, you'll just have to stick to mild dishes such as *kurma* and *biryani* where meat or vegetables are cooked with rice, and eat plenty of *chapati*. Indians tend to assuage the effects of chilli with chutney, *dahi* (curd) or *raita* (curd with mint and cucumber, or other herbs and vegetables). Otherwise, **beer** is one of the best things for washing chilli out of your mouth; the essential oils that cause the burning sensation dissolve in alcohol, but not in water.

Vegetarian curries are usually identified (even on menus in English) by the Hindi names of their main ingredients. Terms like "curry" and "*masala*" don't really tell you what to expect; meat curries are more often given specific names such as *kurma* or *dopiaza*, to indicate the kind of *masala* used or the method of cooking.

Regional variety is vast: the Bengalis love fish and cook a mean *mangsho* (meat) curry as well as exotic vegetable dishes such as *mo-cha* – cooked banana flower. They also like to include fish bones for added flavour in their vegetable curries – a nasty surprise for vegetarians. Biharis are known for their *satu* – a staple flour used instead of rice. Tibetans and Bhotias from the Himalaya have a simple diet of *thukpa* (meat soup), and *momo* (meat dumplings), as well as a rancid salty tea. In Punjab and much of northern India, home cooking consists of *dal* and vegetables along with

roti (bread) and less rice than the Bengalis. Food in Gujarat, predominantly veg, is often cooked with a bit of sugar.

In the north of India especially, but as far south as Hyderabad, the influence of the Moghuls lives on in the form of Mughlai cooking. Mostly non-veg, the food is extremely rich, using ingredients such as cream, almonds, sultanas and saffron. Mughlai as the name of a *masala* normally indicates a mild, creamy one. *Mughlai paratha* is spicy fried bread with egg.

The other big northern style is *tandoori*. The name refers to the deep clay oven (*tandoor*) in which the food is cooked. *Tandoori* chicken is marinated in yoghurt, herbs and spices before cooking. Boneless pieces of meat, marinated and cooked in the same way are known as *tikka*; they may be served in a medium-strength *masala* (*tikka masala*), one thickened with almonds (*pasanda*), or in a rich butter sauce (*murg makhani* or butter chicken). Breads such as *nan* and *roti* are also baked in the *tandoor*.

Certain combinations are traditional and seasonally repeated, such as *makki ki roti* (fried corn bread) with *sarson ka sag* (mustard-leaf greens) around Punjab and other parts of north India. *Baingan bharta* (puréed roast aubergine) is commonly eaten with plain yogurt and *roti* (plain bread). In good Muslim cooking from the north, delicately thin *rumali roti* (handkerchief bread) often accompanies rich meat and chicken dishes. *Dal* is a safe bet with almost any meat or vegetable dish, and easy to eat with rice or bread.

In the south, where fish is more abundant, meat much less so, and all food generally spicier, the most common meal is *thali*, a mound of rice surrounded by various delicious vegetable curries, *sambar dal*, chutney and curd, and usually accompanied by *poppadums* and *vadas*. Traditionally served on a round metal tray (also found in north India), with each side dish in a separate metal bowl, it is sometimes dished out on a rectangle of banana leaf instead. In most traditional restaurants, you can eat as much as you want, and staff circulate with refills of everything. In the south even more than elsewhere, eating with your fingers is *de rigueur* (you want to feel the food as well as taste it) and cutlery may be unavailable.

Wherever you eat, remember to use only your right hand, and wash your hands before you start. Try and avoid getting food on the palm of your hand by eating with the tips of your fingers.

SNACKS AND STREET FOOD

Feeling peckish should never be a problem, with all sorts of snack meals and finger food to choose from. Of the sit-down variety, *chana puri*, a thin chick-pea curry with a *puri* (or sometimes other breads) to dunk, is a great favourite in the north of the country; *idli sambar* — lentil and vegetable sauce with rice cakes to dunk — is the southern equivalent. But the great snack meal of the south is *masala dosa*, a potato and vegetable curry wrapped in a crispy rice pancake.

Street finger food includes *bhel puris* (a Bombay speciality of small vegetable-stuffed *puris* with tamarind sauce), *pani puris* (the same *puris* dunked in peppery and spicy water — only for the seasoned), *bhajis* (deep-fried cakes of vegetables in chick-pea flour), *samosas* (meat or vegetables in a pastry triangle, fried), and *pakoras* (vegetables in potato dipped in chick-pea flour batter and deep-fried). Kebabs are common in the north, most frequently *seekh kebab*, minced lamb grilled on a skewer, but also *shami kebab*, small minced lamb cutlets. Kebabs rolled into griddle-fried bread are popular in Calcutta, where they are known as *kathi* rolls. With all street snacks, though, remember that food left lying around attracts germs — make sure it's freshly cooked.

You won't find anything called "Bombay mix" in India, but there's no shortage of dry spicy snack mixes, often refered to as *channa chur*. You'll also find the constituents on sale separately at shops and stalls. Jackfruit chips are sometimes sold as a savoury snack, though they are rather bland, and cashew nuts are a real bargain. Peanuts also known as "monkey nuts" or *mumfuli* usually come roasted and un-shelled and can cause a lot of litter in railway carriages.

NON-INDIAN FOOD

Chinese food has become widespread in large towns, where it is cooked by local chefs and is not what you'd call authentic. Still, it can make a pleasant change, and simple, unspiced dishes are safe options if you have an upset stomach. A few cities, like Calcutta, have large Chinese communities, and you can get very good Chinese cuisine indeed.

Western food is either dire or expensive, or often both. *McDonald's* has yet to reach India, but *Wimpy* in Delhi will do you a "lamburger" (what did you expect, beef?), or a plate of unlimited salad for a price high by local standards but cheap compared to elsewhere in the world. *Kentucky Fried Chicken's* outlets in Delhi and Bangalore were closed by suspicious and politically motivated authorities who claimed that their methods and ingredients were suspect! Delhi and Bombay also offer international cuisine such as Thai, Japanese, Italian and French, but it doesn't come cheap.

BREAKFAST

Unreconstructed Westerners seem to get especially homesick around breakfast time; but getting your fry-ups and hash browns is likely to be a problem. *Chana puri* is an option in the north, if a little spicy for some, and *alu paratha* with *dahi* is another traditional start to the day. *Iddli sambar* and *masala dosa* is the most common equivalent in the south, where members of the *India Coffee House* chain can be depended upon for some decent coffee and toast.

In those towns which have established a reputation as hang-outs for "travellers", budget hotels

PAAN

You may be relieved to know that the red stuff people spit all over the streets isn't blood, but juice produced by chewing **paan** — a digestive, commonly taken after meals, and also a mild stimulant, found especially in the northeast where it is fresh and much stronger.

A *paan* consists of chopped or shredded nut (always referred to as *betel* nut, though in fact it comes from the areca palm), wrapped in a leaf (which *does* come from the betel tree) that is first prepared with ingredients such as *katha* (a red paste), *chuna* (slaked white lime), *mitha masala* (a mix of sweet spices, which can be ingested), and *zarda* (chewing tobacco, not to be swallowed on

any account, especially if made with *chuna*). The triangular package thus formed is wodged inside your cheek and chewed slowly, spitting out the juice as you go.

Paan, and *paan masala*, a mix of betel nut, fennel seeds, sweets and flavourings, are sold by *paan-wallahs*, often from tiny stalls squeezed between shops. *Paan-wallahs* develop big reputations; those in the tiny roads of Varanasi are the most renowned of all, asking astronomical prices for *paan* made to elaborate specifications including silver and even gold foil. *Paan* is an acquired taste; novices should start off, and preferably stick with, the sweet and perfectly harmless *mitha* variety.

A GLOSSARY OF FOOD TERMS

General Terms and Requests

bhat	cooked rice	hath dhoney ka pani	water for washing hands	mehti	spicy
chamach	spoon	jaggery	unrefined sugar	mirch	pepper
chawal	uncooked rice	jhal	chilli hot	murgi	chicken
cheeni	sugar	kala mirch	black pepper	namak	salt
cheeni mat dhalna	do not put sugar (eg in tea)	kam or kamti	less – eg jhal kam (less hot)	pani	water
cheeni nehin	no sugar!	kanta	fork	peeney ka pani	drinking water (not mineral water)
chhoori	knife	khaana	food	plate	plate
dudh	milk	lal mirch	red pepper	sabji	any vegetable curry
garam	hot	macchi	fish	thanda	cold
gosht	meat, usually mutton			ziadah or awr	more

Vegetables

adrak	ginger	dal	lentils	paneer	Indian cheese
alu	potatoes	gaajar	carrot	piaz	onions
baingan or brinjal	eggplant (aubergine)	gobi	cauliflower	sabzi	literally greens; used for all vegetables
		kadoo	pumpkin		
bhindi	okra (ladies finger, gumbo)	karela	bitter gourd	sag	general term for green vegetables
		lasoon	garlic		
chana	chick peas (garbanzo beans)	mattar	peas	tamatar	tomato
		palak (or sag)	spinach		

Dishes and cooking terms

alu baingan	potato and aubergine; mild to medium	keema	scrambled eggs
alu methi	potato with fenugreek leaves; usually medium-hot	kofta	balls of minced vegetables or meat in a curried sauce
bhindi bhaji	fried okra; gently spiced	kurma	meat braised in yoghurt sauce, mild
bhuna	roasted first and thickened-down medium-strength curry	maacher jhol	mild fish stew, often with the entire fish – a Bengali delicacy
biryani	rice with saffron or turmeric, whole spices, and meat (sometimes vegetables), and often hard-boiled egg; mild	malai kofta	vegetable kebabs in a rich cream sauce; medium-mild
Bombay duck	dried bummelo fish	molee	curry with coconut, usually fish, originally Malay (hence the name), now a speciality of Kerala; hot
chingri	prawns		
chop	minced meat or vegetable surrounded by breaded mashed potato	mulligatawny	curried vegetable soup, a classic Anglo-Indian dish rumoured to have come from "Mulligan Aunty" but probably south Indian; medium-strength
cutlet	cutlet – often minced meat or vegetable fried in the form of a flat cake		
dahi maach	fish curry with yoghurt, ginger and turmeric; a mild Bengali dish	pathia	thickened curry with lemon juice; hot
		pomfret	a flatfish popular in Bombay and Calcutta
dal gosht	meat cooked in lentils; hot	pulau	rice, gently spiced and prefried
dhansak	meat and lentil curry, a Parsi speciality; medium-hot	rogan josh	deep red lamb curry, a classic Mughlai dish; medium-hot
dopiaza	with onions added at two different stages of cooking; medium-mild	sambar	soupy lentil and vegetable curry with asafoetida and tamarind
dum	steamed in a casserole	subje	white coconut chutney often served with vada
jalfrezi	with tomatoes and green chilli; medium-hot		
jeera	cumin; a masala so described will usually be medium-hot	tarka dal	lentils with a masala of fried garlic, onions and spices
karahi	cast-iron wok which has given its name to a method of cooking meat with dry masala and dishes of medium-strength	vindaloo	Goan vinegared meat (sometimes fish) curry, originally pork; very hot (but not as hot as the kamikaze UK version)

Breads and Pancakes

appam*	rice pancake speckled with holes, soft in the middle	papad or poppadum	crisp, thin chick-pea flour cracker
batura	soft bread made of white flour and traditionally accompanying *chana* (chickpeas); common in Delhi	paratha	wholewheat bread made with butter, rolled thin and griddle-fried; a little bit like a chewy pancake, sometimes stuffed with meat or vegetables
chapati	unleavened bread made of wholewheat flour and baked on a round griddle-dish	puri	crispy, puffed-up, deep fried wholewheat bread
dosa*	rice pancake; should be crispy		
iddli*	steamed rice cake, usually served with *sambar*	roti	loosely used term; often just another name for chapati, though it should be thicker, chewier, and baked in a *tandoor*
kachori	small thick cakes of salty deep fried bread especially good in Varanasi		
loochi	delicate *puri* often mixed with white flour; cooked in Bengal	uttapam*	thick rice pancake often cooked with onions
nan	white leavened bread baked in a *tandoor*	vada*	doughnut-shaped deep-fried lentil cake

*South Indian terminology; all other terms are either in Hindi or refer to North Indian cuisine.

and restaurants serve up the usual hippy fare – banana pancakes, muesli, etc – as well as omelettes, toast, porridge (not always oatmeal), cornflakes, and even bacon and eggs.

SWEETS

Most Indians have rather a sweet tooth; Indian **sweets** can be very sweet. Of the more solid type, *barfi*, a kind of fudge made from milk which has been boiled down and condensed, varies from moist and delicious to dry and powdery. It's often sold covered with silver leaf (which you eat). Smoother-textured, round *penda* and thin diamonds of *kaju katri*, plus moist *sandesh* and the harder *paira*, both popular in Bengal, are among many other sweets made from *chhana* or boiled-down milk. Crunchier *mesur* is made with chickpeas; numerous types of gelatinous *halwa*, not the Middle Eastern variety, include the rich *gajar ka halwa* made from carrots and cream.

Getting softer and stickier, those circular orange tubes dripping syrup in sweet-shop windows, called *jalebis* and made of deep-fried treacle, are as sickly as they look. *Gulab jamuns*, deep-fried sponge balls soaked in syrup, are as unhealthy. Common in both the north and the south, *ladu* consists of balls made from semolina flour with raisins and sugar and sometimes made of other grains and flour, while among Bengali sweets, widely considered to be the best are *ras-gullas*, rosewater-flavoured cream cheese balls floating in syrup. *Ras malai*, found throughout north India, is similar but soaked in cream instead of syrup.

Chocolate is improving rapidly in India and you'll find various *Cadbury's* and *Amul* bars. None of the various indigenous brands of imitation Swiss and Belgian chocolates appearing on the cosmopolitan markets are worth eating.

Among the large **ice-cream** vendors, *Kwality*, *Vadilal's*, *Gaylord* and *Dollops Bounty* bar (coconut choc-ice) stand out. Uniformed men push carts of ice-cream around and the bigger companies have many imitators, usually quite obvious. Some have no scruples – stay away from water ices unless you have a seasoned constitution. Ice-cream parlours selling elaborate concoctions including sundaes have really taken off; Connaught Circus in Delhi has several. Be sure to try *kulfi*, a pistachio- and cardamom-flavoured frozen sweet which is India's answer to ice-cream; *bhang kulfi*, not available everywhere, has an interesting kick to it, but should be approached with caution.

FRUIT

What fruit is available varies with region and season, but there's always a fine choice. Ideally, you should **peel all fruit**, or soak it in strong iodine or potassium permanganate solution for half an hour. Roadside vendors sell fruit which they often cut up and serve sprinkled with salt and even *masala* – don't buy anything that looks like it's been hanging around for a while.

Mangoes of various kinds are usually on offer, but not all are sweet for eating – some are used for pickles or curries. Indians are picky about their mangoes, which they feel and smell before buying; if you don't know the art of choosing the fruit, you could be sold the leftovers. Among the species appearing at different times in the season, which lasts from spring to summer, look out for *Alphonso* and *Langra*. Bananas of one sort or another are also on sale all year round, and oranges and tangerines are generally easy to come by, as are sweet melons and thirst-quenching watermelons.

Tropical fruits such as coconuts, pawpaws and pineapples are more common in the south, while things such as lychees and pomegranates are very seasonal. In the north, temperate fruit from the mountains can be much like that in Europe and North America, with strawberries, apricots and even rather soft apples available in season.

Among less familiar fruit, the *chiku*, which looks like a kiwi and tastes a bit like a pear, is worth a mention, as is the watermelon-sized jackfruit, whose spiny green exterior encloses sweet, slightly rubbery yellow segments, each containing a seed. Individual segments are sold at roadside stalls.

DRINKS

India sometimes seems to run on **tea (chai)**, grown in Darjeeling, Assam and the Nilgiri Hills, and sold by *chai-wallahs* on just about every street corner. However, although it was introduced from China by the East India Company in 1838, its use was only popularized by a government campaign in the 1950s.

Tea is usually made by putting tea dust, milk and water in a pan, boiling it all up, straining it into a cup or glass with lots of sugar and pouring back and forth from one cup to another to stir. Ginger and/or cardamoms are often added. If you're quick off the mark, you can get them to hold the sugar. English tea it isn't, but most travellers get used to it: "Just don't think of *chai* as tea," advise some. Sometimes, especially in tourist spots, you might get a pot of European-style "tray" tea, generally consisting of a tea bag in lukewarm water – you'd do better to stick to the pukka Indian variety.

Instant coffee is becoming increasingly common, and in some cases is more popular than tea. At street stalls and on trains the familiar cry of "*garam chai*" (hot tea) is giving way to "*kofi*", while the *bhand*, a disposable mud tea cup, is gradually disappearing in preference to inferior plastic cups. In the north, most coffee is instant, even that advertised as "espresso".

In the south, **coffee (kofi)** is certainly more common than tea, and far better than it is in the north. One of the best places to get it is in outlets of the *India Coffee House* chain, found in every southern town, and apparently creeping ever northwards. A whole ritual is attached to the drinking of milky Keralan coffee in particular, poured in flamboyant sweeping motions between tall glasses to cool it down.

With **bottled water** so widely available, you may have no need of **soft drinks**. These have long been surprisingly controversial in India. *Coca Cola* and *Pepsi* have recently made comebacks, after being banned from the country for 17 years. That policy was originally instigated by socialists in the Janata government, in part to prevent the expatriation of profits by foreign companies; since their return, militant Hindu groups such as the BJP and the RSS have threatened to make them the focus of a new boycott campaign against multinational consumer goods. The absence of *Coke* and *Pepsi* spawned a host of Indian colas such as *Campa Cola* (innocuous), *Thums Up* (not unpalatable), *Gold Spot* (fizzy orange), and *Limca* (rumoured to have dubious connections to Italian companies, and to contain additives banned there). All contain a lot of sugar but little else: adverts for Indian soft drinks have been known to boast "Absolutely no natural ingredients!" None will quench your thirst for long.

More recommendable are straight water (treated, boiled or bottled; see also p.18), and cartons of *Frooti Jumpin* and similar brands of fruit juice drinks, which come in mango, guava, apple and lemon varieties. If the carton looks at all mangled it is best not to touch it as it may have been recycled. At larger stations, there will be a stall on the platform selling Himachali apple juice. Better still, **green coconuts** are cheaper than any of these, and sold on the street by vendors who will hack off the top for you with a machete and give you a straw to suck up the coconut water (you then scoop out the flesh and eat it). You will also find street stalls selling freshly made sugar-cane juice: delicious, and not in fact too sweet, but not always as safe healthwise as you might like.

India's greatest cold drink, **lassi**, is made with curd and drunk either sweetened with sugar, salted, or mixed with fruit. It varies widely from smooth and delicious to insipid and watery, and is sold at virtually every cafe, restaurant and canteen in the country. Freshly made milk shakes are also commonly available at establishments with blenders. They'll also sell you what they call a fruit juice, but which is usually fruit, water and sugar (or salt) liquidized and strained; also, street vendors selling fresh fruit juice in less than hygenic conditions are apt to add salt and *garam masala*! With all such drinks, however appetizing they may seem, you should exercise great **caution** in deciding where to drink them; find out where the water is likely to come from.

ALCOHOL

Prohibition, once widespread in India, is now only fully enforced in Gujarat, Andhra Pradesh and some of the northeastern hill states, although Tamil Nadu and some other states, retain partial prohibition in the form of "dry" days, high taxes, restrictive licences, and health warnings on labels ("Liquor – ruins country, family and life," runs Tamil Nadu's). There is a trend to reintroduce prohibition, with rules extended recently in Delhi, where the right-wing Hindu BJP local government has introduced 48 dry days and extraordinary taxes.

Alcoholic enclaves in prohibition states can become major drinking centres: Daman and Diu in Gujarat, and Pondicherry and Karaikal in Tamil Nadu are the main ones. Goa, Sikkim and Mahé (Kerala) join them as places where the booze flows especially freely and cheaply. Interestingly, all were outside the British Raj. **Liquor permits** – free, and available from Indian embassies, high commissions and tourist offices abroad, and from tourist offices in Delhi, Bombay, Calcutta and Madras, and even at airports on arrival – allow those travellers who bother to apply for one to evade certain restrictions in prohibition states.

Beer is widely available, if rather expensive by local standards. Price varies from state to state, but you can usually expect to pay around Rs50 for a 650ml bottle. *Kingfisher* is the leading brand, but there are plenty of others. All lagers, which tend to contain chemical additives, are usually pretty palatable if you can get them cold. In certain places, notably unlicensed restaurants in Tamil Nadu, beer comes in the form of "special tea" – a teapot of beer, which you pour into and drink from a teacup to disguise what it really is. A cheaper, and often delicious, alternative to beer in Kerala and one or two other places is *toddy* (palm wine). In Bengal, it is made from the date palm, and is known as *tadd*. Sweet and non-alcoholic when first tapped, it ferments within twelve hours.

Spirits usually take the form of "Indian Made Foreign Liquor" (IMFL), although the recently legitamized foreign liquor industry is expanding rapidly. Some Scotch, such as *Seagram's Hundred Pipers*, is now being bottled in India and sold at a premium; *Smirnoff* vodka is also available and other known brands are soon to follow. Some of the brands of Indian whisky are not too bad and are affordable in comparison; gin and brandy can be pretty rough, while Indian rum is sweet and distinctive. In Goa, *fene* is a spirit distilled from coconut or cashew fruit. You are warned, however, to steer well clear of illegally distilled *arak*, which often contains methanol (wood alcohol) and other poisons. A look through the press, especially at festival times, will soon reveal numerous cases of blindness and death as a result of drinking bad hooch (or "spurious liquor" as it's called). Licensed country liquor, sold in several states under such names as *bangla*, is an acquired taste. In the Himalaya, the Bhotia people, of Tibetan stock, drink *chang*, a beer made from millet, and one of the nicest drinks of all – *tumba* where fermented millet is placed in a bamboo flask and topped with hot water, then sipped through a bamboo pipe.

MAIL, TELECOMMUNICATIONS AND MEDIA

There is no need to be out of touch with the rest of the world while you're in India. The mail service is pretty reliable if a little slow; international phone calls are surprisingly easy. There are a number of decent English-language newspapers, and more people and places than you might imagine have access to satellite TV in English too.

MAIL SERVICES

Mail can take anything from three days to four weeks to get to or from India, depending largely on where exactly you are; ten days is about the norm. Stamps are not expensive, and aerogrammes and postcards cost the same to anywhere in the world. Ideally, you should have mail franked in front of you. Most post offices are open Mon–Fri 10am–5pm and Sat 10am–noon, but big city GPOs keep longer hours (Mon–Fri 9.30am–6pm, Sat 9.30am–1pm). You can also buy stamps at big hotels.

Poste Restante (General Delivery) services throughout the country are pretty reliable, though exactly how long individual offices hang on to letters is more or less at their own discretion; for periods of longer than a month, it makes sense to mark mail with your expected date of arrival. Letters are filed alphabetically; in larger offices, you sort through them yourself. To avoid misfiling, your name should be printed clearly, with the surname in large capitals and underlined, but it is still a good idea to check under your first name too, just in case. Have letters addressed to you c/o Poste Restante, GPO (if it's the main post

office you want), and the name of the town and state. In Delhi, you will probably want to specify "GPO, New Delhi", since "GPO, Delhi" means Old Delhi GPO, a lot less convenient for most tourists. Sometimes too, as in Calcutta and Madras, local tourist offices might be more convenient than the GPO. Don't forget to take ID with you to claim your mail. *American Express* offices also keep mail for holders of their charge card or travellers' cheques.

Having parcels sent out to you in India is not such a good idea – chances are they'll go astray. If you do have a parcel sent, have it registered.

Sending a parcel out of India can be quite a performance. First you have it cleared by customs at the post office (they often don't bother, but check), then you take it to a tailor and agree a price to have it wrapped in cheap cotton cloth (which you may have to go and buy yourself), stitched up and sealed with wax. In big city GPOs, people offering this service will be at hand. Next, take it to the post office, fill in and attach the relevant customs forms (it's best to tick the box marked "gift" and give its value as less than Rs1000 or "no commercial value", to avoid bureaucratic entanglements), buy your stamps, see them franked, and dispatch it. Parcels should not be more than a metre long, nor weigh more than 20kg. Surface mail is incredibly cheap, and takes an average of six months to arrive – it may take half, or four times that, however. It's a good way to dump excess baggage and souvenirs, but don't send anything fragile this way.

As in Britain, North America and Australasia, books and magazines can be sent more cheaply, unsealed or wrapped around the middle, as **printed papers** ("book post"). Alternatively, there are numerous courier services but it is safest to stick to known international companies such as *DHL*. Packages sent by air are expensive. Couriers are not as reliable as they should be and there have been complaints of packages going astray. Remember that all packages from India are likely to be suspect at home, and searched or X-rayed: don't send anything dodgy.

PHONES

Privately run **phone services** with international direct dialling facilities are very widespread. Advertising themselves with the acronyms

International Codes

	From India:	To India:
UK	☎00 44	☎00 91
Irish Republic	☎00 353	☎00 91
US and Canada	☎001	☎011 91
Australia	☎00 61	☎0011 91
New Zealand	☎00 64	☎00 91

STD/ISD (standard trunk dialling/international subscriber dialling), they are extremely quick and easy to use; some stay open 24 hours per day. Both national and international calls are dialled direct. To call abroad, dial the international access code (00), the code for the country you want – 44 for the UK, for example – the appropriate area code (leaving out any initial zeros), and the number you want; then you speak, pay your bill, which is calculated in seconds, and leave. Prices vary between private places and are slightly cheaper at official telecommunications offices; many have fax machines too. Calling from hotels is usually more expensive.

Home country direct services are now available from any phone to the UK, the USA, Canada, Ireland, Australia, New Zealand, and a growing number of other countries. These allow you to make a collect or telephone credit card call to that country via an operator there. If you can't find a phone with home country direct buttons, you can use any phone toll-free, by dialling 000, your country code, and 17 (except Canada which is 000-127).

To **call India** from abroad, dial the international access code, followed by 91 for India, the local code minus the initial zero, then the number you want.

THE MEDIA

India has a large number of **English-language daily newspapers**, usually either regional or in regional editions. The most prominent of the nationals are *The Hindu, The Statesman*, the *Times of India, The Independent*, the *Economic Times*, and the *Indian Express* (usually the most critical of the government). All are pretty dry and sober, and concentrate on Indian news; the *Independent* and the *Calcutta Telegraph* tend to have better coverage of world news than the rest. *Asian Age*, published simultaneously in India, London and New York, is emerging as one of the best of a new breed of papers.

India's press is the freest in Asia and attacks on the government are often quite outspoken. However, as in the West, most papers can be seen as part of the political establishment, and are unlikely to print anything that might upset the "national consensus".

In recent years, a number of *Time/Newsweek*-style **news magazines** have hit the market with a strong emphasis on politics. The best of these are *India Today* and *Frontline*, published by *The Hindu*. Others include *Sunday* and *The Week*. As they give more of an overview of stories and issues than the daily papers, you will probably get a better idea from them of what is going on in Indian politics, and most tend to have a higher proportion of international news too. *Business India* is more financially orientated and *The India Magazine* more cultural. Film fanzines and gossip mags are very popular (*Screen* is one of the best, though you'd have to be reasonably *au fait* with Indian movies to follow a lot of it), but magazines and periodicals in English cover all sorts of popular and minority interests, so it's worth having a look through what's available. One publication of special interest is *Amar Chitra Katha*'s series of Hindu legends, Indian history and folk tales in comic form for children.

Foreign publications such as the *International Herald Tribune, Time, Newsweek, The Economist* and the international edition of the British *Guardian* are all available in the main cities, and in the most upmarket hotels, but they are rather costly. For a read through the British press, try the British Council in Delhi, Bombay, Calcutta and Madras; the USIS has a similar national bias with an American perspective.

BBC World Service radio can be picked up on short wave on 15.31MHz (19.6m) between about 8.30am and 10.30pm (Indian time). Alternative frequencies if reception is poor include 17.79MHz (16.9m), 15.56MHz (19.3m) and 11.96MHz (25.1m).

The government-run **TV** company, *Doordarshan*, which broadcasts a sober diet of edifying programmes, has tried to compete with the onslaught of mass access to **satellite TV** and cheap DIY cable networks by revamping its second channel, but with little success. The main broadcaster in English is Rupert Murdoch's *Star TV* network, which incorporates the BBC World Service, *Zee TV*, which presents a progressive blend of Hindi oriented chat, film, news and music programmes; others include *CNN*, some sports channels, and a couple of American soap and chat stations.

TREKKING

For many visitors, the opportunity to trek in the magnificent mountains is one of the main reasons to come to India. Though trekking is less commercialized, but less well organized than in neighbouring Nepal, well-tried routes can be found throughout the Himalayas, from Kashmir to Sikkim, as well as in other parts of the country, and are detailed at the appropriate points throughout this book. Routes vary in length and difficulty from short but rewarding treks around Darjeeling to long and challenging high-altitude trails through Ladhak and Zanskar. Guides are recommended whenever possible, especially on more difficult and less frequented routes; you must carry all necessary equipment and supplies and research the route in advance.

One or two operators run **package trekking holidays**, and trekking agencies exist at such places as Manali, Darjeeling and Gangtok, but most people go under their own steam and organize guides, plus porters or ponies, privately. A trek normally lasts a week or two; the longer it is, in general, the more you'll get out of it.

Himachal Pradesh, which issues trekking maps, brochures and trekking guides, is the most efficient state in which to trek; the Mountaineering Institute is on hand in Dharamsala to offer advice. Himalayan **Uttar Pradesh** sees fewer trekkers, but there are plenty of opportunities to wander off the beaten track and escape the hordes of pilgrims who come to the mountains of Garhwal and Kumaun every summer. Kashmir itself is not the best place to venture at present, but there are exciting and exotic treks through the ancient Buddhist kingdoms of **Ladakh** and **Zanskar**. At the eastern end of the Himalaya, Darjeeling offers a good base from which to explore the surrounding mountains, while nine- and twelve-day treks in **Sikkim** require a permit issued by the Foreigners' Registration Office in Gangtok, and a guide from a recognized agency to be taken with you (the dollar fees are high). Shorter and less strenuous treks are available in the Ghats and the Nilgiri hills of **southern India**.

CHECKLIST OF TREKKING EQUIPMENT

The checklist below is based on staying in rest houses or *chai* shops. This may not be possible, especially on treks lasting over 3–4 days. If you plan to **camp** (tents are easy to rent) or climb you'll need more.

Essentials
Backpack
Compass and map (most maps are woefully inadequate)
Pocket knife
Sleeping bag
Sunblock and lip balm
Sunglasses (UV protective)
Toiletries and toilet paper
Torch/Flashlight
Water bottle

Other useful items
Candles
Emergency snack food
Insect repellent
Insulation mat
Large mug and spoon
Plastic bag or heavy-duty bin-liner (to rainproof your pack)
Sewing kit
Small towel

Spare bootlaces
Stuff-sacks or plastic bags (for keeping dirty clothes and separating belongings)
Umbrella to keep off the sun

Health care equipment
Aspirin/Paracetamol
Crepe bandage
Knee supports
Muscle balm
Plasters
Rehydration sachets
Water purification (see p.18)

High-altitude gear
Crampons (rarely needed on usual treks)
Gaiters
Ice axe (rarely needed on usual treks)
Salopettes

Telescopic ski poles (to help carry large loads over snow)

Clothes
Cotton hat with brim
Leggings (for women)
Mittens or ski gloves
Parka (down or lightweight fibre)
Shirts/T-shirts
Skirt/Dress (mid-calf length is best)
Thermal underwear
Trousers
Weather-proof shell jacket (Gortex or other breathable fabric preferable)
Woolly hat/Balaclava (should cover ears)
Woolly sweater

Footwear
Cotton and woollen socks
Trekking boots

For advice on the potential **health hazards** of mountain trekking, see p.21.

Having the right **equipment** for a trek is important, but high-tech gear isn't essential – bring what you need to be comfortable but keep weight to a minimum. In some places, such as Darjeeling, you can rent equipment, but otherwise, you'll have to buy what you need or bring it with you. Make sure everything (zips for example) is in working order before you set off. Clothes should be lightweight and versatile, especially considering the range of temperatures you might encounter: dress in layers for maximum flexibility.

Mountaineering is a more serious venture, requiring planning and organization; if you've never climbed, don't start in the Himalayas. Mountaineering institutes at Darjeeling, Uttarkashi (UP) and Dharamsala (HP), run training courses, though only the one at Dharamsala usually accepts foreigners; it also organizes high-altitude treks. Permission for mountaineering expeditions should be sought at least six months in advance from the *Indian Mountaineering Federation*, Anand Niketan, Benito Juarez Rd, New Delhi 110021 (☎011/671211). Peak fees range from $600 to $3000, according to height, and expeditions must be accompanied by an *IMF* liaison officer equipped to the same standard as the rest of the party. The *IMF* can also supply lists of local mountaineeering clubs; climbing with such clubs enables you to get to know local climbers, and obtain permits for otherwise restricted peaks.

WILDLIFE VIEWING

With habitats running the gamut from high mountain to tropical jungle, there are all sorts of plants and animals to see in India. Tigers and elephants are just the two most obvious species. The Indian elephant, distinguished from its African cousin by its smaller ears, is still used as a beast of burden, and in temple processions and ceremonies. In the wild, it is not currently under threat.

The elephant's co-pachyderm, the one-horned **rhinoceros**, retains a foothold in the east of the country, but the tiger's fellow **big cats** have not fared so well. The cheetah is now extinct in India, while the Asiatic lion clings on in one tiny patch of Gujarat. The snow leopard is increasingly rare too, although the **leopard** (aka panther) of the plains can still be found in several places. Other indigenous felines include the jungle cat, the fishing cat of Bengal, and a kind of lynx called the caracal.

The larger cats' prey, deer and antelope, are much more abundant. The largest of the **deer** is the *sambar*, usually a solitary animal. Smaller and more gregarious are the spotted deer or *cheetal*, and others include the *muntjac* (barking deer) and *para* (hog deer). The smallest deer in India is the *chevrotain*, known from its size as the mouse deer. The swamp deer is rarer, while the *hangul* (Kashmiri red deer) is now an endangered species and so is the much sought after musk deer. **Antelopes** include the *nilgai* or bluebull, the black buck, the four-horned *chowsingha*, and the Indian gazelle known as the *chinkara*.

Among other animals you might hope or expect to see in India, the triple-striped palm squirrel is very common, as are **monkeys** (particularly macaques and langurs) which are also found thriving in built-up urban areas such as Varanasi. There are wild **buffalo**, and also *gaur*, the massive Indian bison. Indian wild dogs are called *dhole*, and there are also wolves and foxes. **Wild boar** are reasonably common too. Harder to spot are the shaggy sloth bear, and Asia's answer to the armadillo, a scaly anteater called a *pangolin*. **Reptiles** run from common-or-garden lizards to cobras, massive pythons, monitor lizards and

SELECTED INDIAN WILDLIFE PARKS

Park or Reserve	State	Terrain	Wildlife	Best Season
Bandhavgarh NP	Madhya Pradesh	hilly grassland	tiger, leopard, sloth bear, *sambar, chital, gaur, muntjac, nilgai, chinkara, drongos*	Feb–June (cl July–Oct)
Corbett NP	Uttar Pradesh	lake and forested foothills	tiger, leopard, elephant, sloth bear, *sambar, chital, muntjac*	Dec–May
Dudhwa NP	Uttar Pradesh	*sal* forest & marshland	tiger, leopard, sloth bear, *nilgai, barasingha*	Dec–May (cl June–Nov)
Flower Valley NP	Uttar Pradesh	alpine valley	mountain flowers	July & Aug
Hazaribagh NP	Bihar	*sal*-forested hills	tiger, leopard, *sambar, chital*	Feb–April
Jaldapara Wildlife Sanctuary	West Bengal	tropical forest & grassland	rhino, leopard, elephant, boar, *gaur*	Dec–May
Jawahar NP (Bandipur, Nagarhole, Mudumalai, Wayanda)	Karnataka, Kerala & Tamil Nadu	mixed forest	tiger, leopard, elephant, *sambar, chital, gaur, muntjac, chowsingha*, pangolin	Dec–June & Sept–Oct (open all year)
Kanha NP	Madhya Pradesh	*sal* forest & grassland	tiger, leopard, boar, *chital, gaur*, black buck, *barasingha, chowsingha, dhole*, birdlife	Feb–June (cl July–Oct)
Kaziranga NP	Assam	grassland, swamp and forest	rhino, tiger, leopard, elephant, bear, buffalo	Nov–March (cl April–Oct)
Keoladeo Bird Sanctuary	Rajasthan	marshland	resident & migratory water-fowl, pythons, deer	Oct–March
Krishnagiri Upavam NP	Maharashtra	marshland	water birds	Oct–June
Little Rann of Kutch Wildlife Sanctuary	Gujarat	desert	wild ass, wolf, caracal, desert wildlife	Oct–June
Manas Wildlife Sanctuary	Assam	rainforest & grassland	rhino, tiger, elephant, buffalo, golden langur, pygmy hog	Jan–March
Nal Sarovar Bird Sanctuary	Gujarat	lake	flamingoes, migratory water birds	Nov–Feb
Palama Tiger Reserve	Bihar	deciduous hilly forest	tiger, leopard, elephant, jungle cat, *sambar, chital*, wolf	Oct–April (open all year)
Periyar Wildlife Sanctuary	Kerala	forest with large (dam-created) lake	elephant, boar, *sambar, chital, gaur*, black langur	Dec–May
Point Kalimere Bird Sanctuary	Tamil Nadu	tidal mud flats	flamingoes, herons, teals, curlews, plovers	Nov–Feb (open all year)
Ranthambore NP	Rajasthan	deciduous forest	tiger, leopard, crocodile, sloth bear, *sambar, nilgai*	Nov–May (cl June–Sept)
Sariska NP	Rajasthan	deciduous forest	tiger, leopard, *sambar, chital, nilgai*, black buck	Nov–June (cl July & Aug)
Sasan Gir NP	Gujarat	forest & lake	Asiatic lion, leopard, *sambar, nilgai, chinkara, chowsingha*	Jan–May (cl May–Oct)
Shivpuri NP	Madhya Pradesh	deciduous forest with lake	tiger, leopard, *nilgai, chinkara, chowsingha*	Jan–May
Similipal Tiger Reserve	Orissa	*sal* forest	tiger, leopard, elephant, *sambar, chital, muntjac*, wolf	Nov–May (cl June–Oct)
Sunderbans Tiger Reserve	West Bengal	mangrove swamp & delta forest	crocodiles & other reptiles, Bengal tiger, fishing cat, boar, spotted deer, dolphin	Dec–March (cl July to mid-Sept)
Tadoba NP	Maharashtra	teak forest & lake	tiger, leopard, *sambar, chital, nilgai*, nocturnal life	March–May
Vedanthangal Water Bird Sanctuary	Tamil Nadu	forest & marsh-land	cormorants, herons, storks, pelicans, glebes, spoonbills	Oct–March
Velvadar	Gujarat	grassland	black buck	Oct–June

crocodiles. In the Ganges, notably at Varanasi, river dolphins can be seen.

Among India's spectacular **birdlife**, both resident and migratory, waterfowl such as flamingoes, spoonbills and pelicans are the biggest draw, but eagles and peacocks are at least as spectacular,

and herons, storks, ibises, hornbills and vultures are all there if you know where to look.

National Parks and **Wildlife Reserves** cover all of India's natural environments, and offer a chance to see a huge variety of birds, mammals and plants. Entrance fees and facilities vary, as do the seasons at which they are best visited, though October to June is usually the best time and parks are generally closed during the monsoon. The more popular places can get quite packed at weekends, so it is usually better to visit them during the week.

Park accommodation, if it exists, is rather spartan and often full (book ahead, especially for weekends), so you may well be staying at a town or village on the edge of the reserve rather than in the park itself. Park tours by jeep can generally be arranged with the park authorities, and boat trips, even elephant rides, are available at some parks too.

Corbett National Park (UP), is the country's first (it opened in 1935) and most popular. It was here that "Project Tiger" was launched in 1973 to protect the stripy felines, whose numbers had fallen to a low of 1830 across the country (see box p.50). Of the 19 reserves in the project, others where you might catch a glimpse of the elusive tigers include Dudhwa (UP), Kanha and Bandhavgarh (Madhya Pradesh), Betla (Bihar), Bandipur (Karnataka), and Manas and Kaziranga (Assam). The most famous and the most ferocious of all are the Royal Bengal tigers of the **Sunderbans** (West Bengal) which are difficult to spot due to the difficult terrain consisting of estuaries and mangrove swamps. According to the last census figures (1994) the tiger population now stands at anywhere between 2750 and 3750 but unofficial reports suggest an even lower figure. Ranthambhore (Rajasthan), once one of India's most evocative tiger sanctuaries, today has no tigers left.

Elephants can be most easily seen at Periyar (Kerala), where you'd be lucky to spot a tiger, Similipal (Orissa), also a tiger reserve, and Manas (Assam). India's main **bird sanctuary** is at Keoladeo Ghana (Rajasthan), a monsoon wetland favoured by both resident and migratory waterfowl, but there are others at Govind Sagar (Himachal Pradesh), and Vedanthangal and Point Kalimere (Tamil Nadu). Two rather different parks are both to be found in Gujarat: Gir, the last remaining home of the **Asiatic lion**, and the desert sanctuary of the Rann of Kutch, where flamingoes and wild asses may be seen.

As for **mountain flora**, the Valley of Flowers (UP) comes into stunning multicoloured bloom from June to September every year and, though only accessible on day trips as camping isn't allowed, makes an excellent short trek.

For more on India's **wildlife**, see *Contexts*.

SPORTS

India is not perhaps a place that most people associate with sports, but cricket, hockey and football (soccer, that is) all have their place.

Cricket is the most popular of these, and a fine example of how something quintessentially British (well, English) has become something quintessentially Indian. International test matches in particular are followed avidly and you'll see games being played on open spaces around the country. Unless it's a special match, you'll probably be welcome to join in, provided you know how to play.

India was the first country outside the British Isles to have a **golf** course, at the Royal Calcutta Golf Club, opened in 1829. Other record-breaking courses include the world's highest at Gulmarg (Kashmir), and there are now so many courses that you can even go on golfing tours of the country.

Horseracing can be a good day out, especially if you enjoy a flutter. Most race courses are quite large, though Darjeeling's is an exception, being the smallest in the world. Calcutta's racecourse is the most popular, often attracting crowds of over 50,000, but there are several others around the country, mostly in larger cities such as Bombay, Pune, Hyderabad, Mysore and Bangalore. Other (mainly) spectator sports include **polo**, originally from upper Kashmir, but taken up by the British to become one of the symbols of the Raj, and **hockey**, which regularly furnishes India with Olympic medals.

A great variety of other sports are available in India, from **tennis** and **squash,** in private clubs and big hotels, to sea and river **fishing**, white-water **rafting** in the mountains, and even **hang-gliding**, for which several clubs exist around the country (the climate and landscape give excellent thermals).

One indigenous sport you're likely to see being played in north India is **kabaadi**, played formally at national level on a small (badminton-sized) court, and informally on any suitable open area.

The game consists of a player from each team alternately attempting to "tag" as many members of the opposing team as possible in the space of a single breath (cheating is impossible; the player has to maintain a continuous chant of *kabaadikabaadikabaadikabaadi* etc), and getting back to his/her own side of the court without being caught. The game can get quite rough as slaps and kicks in tagging are allowed and the defending team must try to tackle and pin the attacker so as not to allow him or her to even touch the dividing line. Tagged victims are required to leave the court.

Finally, though India may be a far cry from Colorado or the Alps, you can **ski** here too. With the Kashmiri resort of Gulmarg currently out of action due to the political situation, skiing is still on at Narkanda and Manali in Himachal Pradesh, and Auli in Uttar Pradesh, at prices that are also a far cry from those of Europe or North America. The season is January to March.

CLIMATE AND GEOGRAPHY

India's range of climate and season is enormous. In the far north, the mountain valleys of the Himalaya experience the four seasons of northern temperate zones, while down at the other end of the country, the Deccan peninsula is tropical. With the northern Gangetic plain, it shares a long dry season building up in heat and intensity until the monsoon douses it in massive quantities of rain.

THE LIE OF THE LAND

Sweeping across the top of India, the massive barrage of the **Himalaya**, backed by the plateau of Tibet, marks the country's northern boundary. The water that flows off these mountains feeds the basin of the **River Ganges**, which flows westwards across the plain of Uttar Pradesh into the Bay of Bengal. The mountains support a range of climates from barren and inhospitable at the highest altitudes to pleasantly alpine in the foothills, while the Ganges sustains a largely dry sub-tropical **plain** right across the north of the country. To its west is the valley of the Indus, which, though now in Pakistan, gives India its name. The watershed between the two river systems is the Thar Desert (**desert** characterizes much of the northwestern states of Rajasthan and Gujarat), which also separates India from Pakistan; to its north, the Punjab (literally "five rivers"), split between the two countries, is irrigated by tributaries of the Indus. East of the Ganges basin, the River Brahmaputra waters the **jungles of Assam**. Beyond, the north–south line of the Naga Hills constitutes India's eastern boundary with Myanmar (Burma). The Brahmaputra and the Ganges join forces at their lower reaches to form the massive **delta** that is Bengal, the eastern half of which is Bangladesh.

South of the northern plain rise the Vindhya and Satpura hills of Madhya Pradesh, drained by the River Narmada, and behind them, the great southern plateau called the **Deccan** (also sometimes known as the Indian Peninsula). This is bounded on both sides by ranges of hills called the **Eastern** and **Western Ghats**. The Western Ghats being the higher of the two ranges, most Deccan rivers flow east. Parts of the coastal stretch along the edge of the Western Ghats harbour Mediterranean climates while in the far south lies the lush state of Kerala.

CLIMATE

The **mountain valleys** of the Himalayan foothills are usually snowed in in winter and pleasantly warm in summer. Some passes are closed in winter and places such as Ladakh and Zanskar (really part of the Tibetan plateau) are extremely cold and hard to reach. Spring is very pleasant, with trees in blossom (avalanches are a danger at higher altitudes during the thaw), while in the summer the snows have melted and all the passes are open. The mountains of northeast India, Sikkim and Uttar Pradesh bear the brunt of the monsoon rains, heaviest in July and August, when landslides frequently cut vulnerable mountain roads. Despite the hazards, the best time to see the high Himalayan flora in bloom is towards the end of the rainy season around early September. Autumn brings the harvest, with fresh produce available in every mountain valley.

In the rest of India, the most important feature of the climate is the wet season, or **monsoon**.

AVERAGE TEMPERATURES AND RAINFALL

		Jan	Feb	Mar	Apr	May	June	July	Aug	Sept	Oct	Nov	Dec
Agra	Av daily max (°C)	22	26	32	38	42	41	35	33	33	33	29	24
	Rainfall (mm)	16	9	11	5	10	60	210	263	151	23	2	4
Ahmedabad	Av daily max (°C)	29	31	36	40	41	38	33	32	33	36	33	30
	Rainfall (mm)	4	0	1	2	5	100	316	213	163	13	5	1
Bangalore	Av daily max (°C)	28	31	33	34	34	30	28	29	28	28	27	27
	Rainfall (mm)	4	14	6	37	119	65	93	95	129	195	46	16
Bombay	Av daily max (°C)	31	32	33	33	33	32	30	29	30	32	33	32
	Rainfall (mm)	0	1	0	0	20	647	945	660	309	17	7	1
Calcutta	Av daily max (°C)	26	29	34	36	36	34	32	32	32	31	29	27
	Rainfall (mm)	13	22	30	50	135	263	320	318	253	134	29	4
Darjeeling	Av daily max (°C)	9	11	15	18	19	19	20	20	20	19	15	12
	Rainfall (mm)	22	27	52	109	187	522	713	573	419	116	14	5
Delhi	Av daily max (°C)	21	24	30	36	41	40	35	34	34	34	29	23
	Rainfall (mm)	25	22	17	7	8	65	211	173	150	31	1	5
Gangtok	Av daily max (°C)	14	15	19	22	22	23	23	23	23	22	19	15
	Rainfall (mm)	44	56	142	222	493	644	663	588	476	152	35	15
Hyderabad	Av daily max (°C)	29	31	35	37	39	34	30	29	30	30	29	28
	Rainfall (mm)	2	11	13	24	30	107	165	147	163	71	25	5
Jaipur	Av daily max (°C)	22	25	31	37	41	39	34	32	33	33	29	24
	Rainfall (mm)	14	8	9	4	10	54	193	239	90	19	3	4
Jaisalmer	Av daily max (°C)	24	28	33	38	42	41	38	36	36	36	31	26
	Rainfall (mm)	2	1	3	1	5	7	89	86	14	1	5	2
Kochi	Av daily max (°C)	31	31	31	31	31	29	28	28	28	29	30	30
	Rainfall (mm)	9	34	50	139	364	756	572	386	235	333	184	37
Madras	Av daily max (°C)	29	31	33	35	38	37	35	35	34	32	29	28
	Rainfall (mm)	24	7	15	25	52	53	83	124	118	267	309	139
Madurai	Av daily max (°C)	30	32	35	36	37	37	36	35	35	35	31	30
	Rainfall (mm)	26	16	21	81	59	31	48	117	123	179	161	143
Nagpur	Av daily max (°C)	29	33	36	40	43	38	31	30	31	32	30	29
	Rainfall (mm)	15	2	25	20	10	174	351	277	181	62	9	2
Nainital	Av daily max (°C)	10	13	17	19	24	24	21	21	21	19	16	13
	Rainfall (mm)	117	44	54	25	75	273	769	561	331	305	7	35
Panjim (Goa)	Av daily max (°C)	31	32	32	33	33	31	29	29	29	31	33	33
	Rainfall (mm)	2	0	4	17	18	580	892	341	277	122	20	37
Pune	Av daily max (°C)	31	33	36	38	37	32	28	28	28	32	32	30
	Rainfall (mm)	2	0	3	18	35	103	187	106	127	92	37	5
Puri	Av daily max (°C)	27	28	30	31	32	31	31	31	31	31	29	27
	Rainfall (mm)	9	20	14	12	63	187	296	256	258	242	75	8
Shimla	Av daily max (°C)	9	10	14	19	23	24	21	20	20	18	15	11
	Rainfall (mm)	65	48	58	38	54	147	415	385	195	45	7	24
Varanasi	Av daily max (°C)	23	27	33	39	41	39	33	32	32	32	29	25
	Rainfall (mm)	23	8	14	1	8	102	346	240	261	38	15	2

The main ("southwest") monsoon strikes the coast of Kerala at the very end of May, working its way northwest across the country over the next month and a half. While it lasts, expect rain every day – heavy tropical rain (as in rainforest). Most days, the rain will last a couple of hours, then the sun will come out and eveything will be steamy and flooded. At the height of the season, especially in jungle regions like Assam and Bengal, the rain may seem endless, and it certainly has a major impact on communications, disrupting road and rail services, causing floods, homelessness, death and destruction, but also bringing life to the parched land and putting a carpet of green on even desert areas like Rajasthan.

By September, the monsoon has started to recede, but it takes a good three months before it finally withdraws from the Deccan. The east of Tamil Nadu and southern Andhra Pradesh – the coastal plain of the Eastern Ghats – and the Andaman and Nicobar islands, are subject to a different monsoon (the "northeast") which begins in mid-October, ending around the new year.

Down on the plain, the heat begins to build up as the **dry season** gets under way. In the north, it is still tempered by the winter, and doesn't really get going until February, leaving a cool period in between. Delhi in particular can get quite surprisingly nippy at this time, especially at night. It is at this time of year that many travellers head south, before the heat there gets serious.

From February onwards, the temperature begins to rise, reaching its peak just before the monsoon. April and May can be unbearably hot and dusty, with a debilitating dry heat (temperatures over 40°C/100°F are quite normal) that saps you of energy and dehydrates you fast. Many head up to the mountains to escape it. The Raj used to move its capital yearly for this reason: originally from Calcutta to Darjeeling, later from Delhi to Shimla. In the south, travellers make for hill stations up in the Ghats. As the hot season draws on, everyone anxiously awaits the return of the monsoon. Finally, heralded by high clouds and electric storms, it is back and the cycle starts again.

The **best time** to see most of the country is between the monsoon and the height of the hot season, that is between about October and March, spending the mid-part of that time in the south. Come April or May, it makes sense to head up into the mountains.

Unfortunately, it is not always possible to fit the seasons in with your travel plans and sometimes you will have to visit places where the weather is not at its optimum. That is not the end of the world; so long as you are prepared for India's extremes of climate and the limits they may place on your movements and activities, anywhere can be rewarding all year round. What's more, visiting at the "wrong" time of year avoids the other tourists, while getting the best air fares (though it probably won't affect the price of accommodation). Nonetheless, it is a good idea to take weather conditions into account if possible when planning your trip.

CRIME AND PERSONAL SAFETY

In spite of the crushing poverty and the yawning gulf between rich and poor, India is on the whole a pretty safe country in which to travel. As a tourist, however, you are an obvious target for thieves (who may include some of your fellow travellers), and stand to face serious problems if you do lose your passport, money and ticket home.

Common sense therefore suggests a few precautions.

Carry valuables in a money belt or a pouch around your neck at all times. If the latter, the cord should be hidden under your clothing and not be easy to cut through (a metal guitar string is good). Beware of crowded locations, such as packed buses or trains, in which it is easy for pickpockets to operate – slashing pockets with razor blades is quite common – and don't leave valuables unattended on the beach when you go for a swim. Backpacks in dormitory accommodation are also obvious targets.

Budget travellers would do well to carry a padlock, as these are usually used to secure the doors of cheap hotel rooms and it's reassuring to know you have the only key; strong combination locks are ideal. You can also lock your bag to seats or racks in trains. Don't put valuables in your luggage for bus or plane journeys: keep them with you at all times. If your baggage is on the roof of a bus, make sure it is well secured. On trains and buses, the prime time for theft is just before you leave, so keep a particular eye on your gear then,

DRUGS

Future is black if sugar is brown – Bombay anti-drugs poster.

India is a centre for the production of **cannabis** and to a lesser extent **opium**, and derivatives of these drugs are widely available. *Charas* (hashish) is produced all along the Himalayas, where the harvest is around September. East of Kashmir, it is rubbed from the plant; westwards it is threshed. Kashmir itself produces both varieties: rubbed *attar*, and threshed *garda* (known as "twist"). The best-known growing area is Manali and the surrounding region, but Almora (UP) also produces a crop. *Ganja* (marijuana) is available in all these areas too, as well as Kerala (especially), West Bengal, Rajasthan and Orissa.

Charas and *ganja* are normally smoked in a *chillum*, originally the bowl of a hookah pipe, used by the poor, who would cup their hands around it to make a smoke-cooling chamber. Nowadays, *chillum*-making has become something of an art form, with centres at Pondicherry, Hampi and Pushkar.

The use of cannabis is frowned upon by respectable Indians – if you see anyone in a movie smoking a *chillum*, you can be sure it's the baddie. *Sadhus*, on the other hand, are allowed to smoke *ganja* legally as part of their religious devotion to Shiva, who is said to have originally discovered its narcotic properties.

Bhang (a preparation made from marijuana leaves) is legal and widely available in *bhang* shops: it is used to make sweets and drinks such as the notoriously potent *bhang lassis* which have waylaid many an unwary traveller. *Bhang* shops also frequently sell *ganja*, low-quality *charas*, and opium (*chandu*), mainly from Rajasthan and Madhya Pradesh. Its derivatives, morphine and heroin, are widespread too, with addiction an increasing problem among the urban poor. "Brown sugar" that you may be offered on the street is number three heroin; Varanasi is becoming notorious for its heroin problem. Use of other illegal drugs such as LSD, ecstasy and cocaine is largely confined to tourists.

All of these drugs except *bhang* are strictly controlled under Indian **law**, with a minimum sentence of ten years for possession. Anyone arrested with less than five grams of cannabis which they are able to *prove* is for their own use is liable to a six-month maximum, but cases can take years to come to trial (two is normal, and eight not unheard of). Police raids and searches are particularly common at the following places: Manali, the Kulu valley and Almora, and buses from those places to Delhi, especially at harvest time; buses and trains crossing certain state lines, notably between Gujarat and Maharastra; budget hotels in Delhi's Paharganj; the beach areas of Goa; and around Idukki and Kumily in Kerala. "Paying a fine now" *may* be possible with one or two officers on arrest (though it will probably mean *all the money* you have), but once you are booked in at the station, your chances are slim.

beware of deliberate diversions, and don't put your belongings next to open windows. Remember that routes popular with tourists tend to be popular with thieves too; knifepoint muggings are on the increase in Goa.

However, don't get paranoid. Crime levels in India are a long way below those of Western countries, and violent crime against tourists is extremely rare. Virtually none of the people who approach you on the street intend any harm: most want to sell you something (though this is not usually made apparent immediately), some want to practise their English, others (if you're a woman) to chat you up, while more than a few just want your address in their book. Anyone offering wonderful-sounding money-making schemes, however, is almost certain to be a con artist. Be wary of **credit card fraud**; a credit card can be used to make duplicate forms to which your account is then billed for fictitious transactions, so don't let shops or restaurants take your card away to process – insist they do it in

front of you. Even **monkeys** rate a mention here – it is not unknown for them to steal things from hotel rooms with open windows, or even to snatch bags from unsuspecting shoulders.

It's not a bad idea to keep US$100 or so separately from the rest of your cash, along with your travellers' cheque receipts, insurance policy number and phone number for claims, and a photocopy of the pages in your passport containing personal data and your Indian visa. This will cover you in case you do lose all your valuables.

If the worst happens and you get robbed, the first thing to do is report the theft as soon as possible to the local **police**. They are very unlikely to recover your belongings, but you need a report from them in order to claim on your travel insurance. Dress smartly and expect an uphill battle – city cops in particular tend to be jaded from too many insurance and travellers' cheque scams.

Losing your passport is a real hassle, but does not necessarily mean the end of your trip. First, report the loss immediately to the police, who will issue you with the all-important "complaint form" you need to travel around and check into hotels, as well as claim back any expenses incurred in replacing your passport from your insurer. A complaint form, however, will not allow you to change money or travellers' cheques. If you've run out of cash, your best bet is to ask your hotel manager to help you out (staff will have seen your passport when you checked in, and the number will be in the register). The next thing to do is telephone your nearest embassy or consulate in India (see p.15).

Normally, passports have to be applied for and collected in person, but if you are stranded, it is usually possible to arrange to receive the necessary forms in the post. However, you still have to go to the embassy or consulate to pick it up. "Emergency passports" are the cheapest form of replacement, but are normally only valid for the few days of your return flight. If you're not sure when you're leaving India, you'll have to obtain a more costly "full passport"; these can only be issued by embassies and larger consulates in Delhi or Bombay, not those in Madras, Calcutta or Panjim.

CULTURAL HINTS AND ETIQUETTE

Cultural differences extend to all sorts of little things. While allowances will usually be made for foreigners, visitors unacquainted with Indian customs may need a little preparation to avoid causing offence or making fools of themselves. The list of do's and don'ts here is hardly exhaustive: when in doubt, watch what the Indian people around you are doing.

EATING AND THE RIGHT HAND RULE

The biggest minefield of potential *faux-pas* has to do with **eating**. This is usually done with the fingers, and requires practice to get absolutely right. Rule one is: **eat with your right hand only**. In India, as right across Asia, the left hand is for wiping your bottom, cleaning your feet and other unsavoury functions (you also put on and take off your shoes with your left hand), while the right hand is for eating, shaking hands, and so on.

Quite how rigid individuals are about this tends to vary, with Brahmins (who at the top of the hierarchical ladder are one of the two "right-handed castes") and southerners likely to be the strictest. While you can hold a cup or utensil in your left hand, and you can usually get away with using it to help tear your *chapati*, you should not eat, pass food or wipe your mouth with your left hand. Best is to keep it out of sight below the table.

This rule extends beyond food. In general, do not pass anything to anyone with your left hand, or point at anyone with it either; and Indians won't be impressed if you put it in your mouth. In general, you should accept things given to you

with your right hand – though using both hands is a sign of respect.

The other rule to beware of when eating or drinking is that your lips should not touch other people's food – *jhuta* or sullied food is strictly taboo. Don't, for example, take a bite out of a *chapati* and pass it on. When drinking out of a cup or bottle to be shared with others, don't let it touch your lips, but rather pour it directly into your mouth. This custom also protects you from things like hepatitis. It is customary to wash your hands before and after eating.

TEMPLES AND RELIGION

Religion is taken very seriously in India; it's important always to show due respect to religious buildings, shrines, images, and people at prayer. When entering a temple or mosque, remove your shoes and leave them at the door (socks are OK and protect your feet from burning-hot stone ground). Some temples – Jain ones in particular – do not allow you to enter wearing or carrying leather articles, and forbid entry to menstruating women. Dress conservatively (see below), and try not to be obtrusive; cover your head with a cap or cloth when entering a *dargar* (Sufi shrine) or Sikh *gurudwara*. In a mosque, you'll not normally be allowed in at prayer time; in a Hindu temple, you are not usually allowed into the inner sanctum; and at a Buddhist *stupa* or monument, you should always walk round clockwise (ie, with the *stupa* on your right). Hindus are very superstitious about taking **photographs** of images of deities and inside temples; if in doubt, desist. Do not take photos of funerals or cremations.

DRESS

Indian people are very conservative about **dress**. Women are expected to dress modestly, with legs and shoulders covered. Trousers are acceptable, but shorts and short skirts are offensive to many. Men should always wear a shirt in public, and avoid shorts (a sign of low caste). These rules go double in temples and mosques.

Never mind sky-clad Jains or *naga sadhus*, **nudity** is not acceptable in India. The mild-mannered people of Goa may not say anything about nude bathing (though it is in theory prohibited), but you can be sure they don't like it. If you respect them, you will not bathe in the nude, and certainly not where there are Indian families.

In general, Indians find it hard to understand why rich Western sahibs should wander round in ragged clothes, dress shamelessly like prostitutes, or imitate the lowest ranks of Indian society, who would love to have something more decent to wear. Staying well-groomed and dressing "respectably" (and you don't have to go over the top) vastly improves the impression you make on local people, and reduces sexual harassment too.

OTHER POSSIBLE GAFFES

Kissing and **embracing** are regarded in India as part of sex: do not do them in public. It is not even a good idea for couples to hold hands, though Indian men can sometimes be seen holding hands as a sign of "brotherliness". Be aware of your feet. When entering a private home, you should normally remove your shoes (follow your host's example); when sitting, avoid pointing the soles of your feet at anyone. Accidental contact with one's foot is always followed by an apology.

Indian English can be very formal and even ceremonious. Indian people may well call you "sir" or "madam", even "good lady" or "kind sir". At the same time, you should be aware that your English may seem rude to them. In particular, **swearing** is taken rather seriously in India, and casual use of the F-word is likely to shock.

MEETING PEOPLE

Westerners have an ambiguous status in Indian eyes. In one way, you represent the rich *sahib*, whose culture dominates the world, and the old colonial mentality has not completely disappeared: in that sense, some Indians may see you as "better" than them. On the other hand, as a non-Hindu, you are an outcaste, your presence in theory polluting to an orthodox or high-caste Hindu, while to members of all religions, your morals and your standards of spiritual and physical cleanliness are suspect: in that sense Indians may see themselves as "better" than you. Even if you are of Indian origin, you may be considered to suffer from Western corruption, and people may test you out on that score.

Indians are irrepressibly inquisitive and as a traveller, you will constantly come across people who want to strike up a conversation. English not being their first language, they may not be familiar with the conventional ways of doing this, and thus their opening line may seem abrupt if at the same time very formal. "Excuse me good gentleman, what is your mother country?" is a typical one. It is also the first in a series of questions that Indian men seem sometimes to have learnt from a single book in order to ask Western tourists. Some of the questions may baffle at first ("What is your qualification?" "Are you in service?"), some may be queries about the ways of the West or the purpose of your trip, but mostly they will be about your family and your job.

You may find it baffling or even intrusive that complete strangers should want to know that sort of thing, but bear in mind that their culture is different from yours and they do not see it the same way. For one thing, these are subjects which interest them (showing photos of your family always goes down well, especially between women). Secondly, they are considered polite conversation beween strangers in India, and help people place each other in terms of social position. Thirdly, your family, job, even income, are not considered "personal" subjects in India, and it is completely normal to ask people about them. Asking the same questions back will not be taken amiss – far from it. Being curious does not have the "nosey" stigma in India that it has in the West: taking an interest in other people's lives is totally up front and considered quite normal. And don't forget that for the majority of Indians travelling abroad is inconceivable, as, indeed, is holiday and leisure time.

Things that Indian people are likely to find strange about you are lack of religion (you could adopt one), travelling alone, leaving your family to come to India, being an unmarried couple (letting people think you are married can make life easier), and travelling second class or staying in cheap hotels when, as a tourist, you are relatively rich. You will probably end up having to explain the same things many times to many different people; on the other hand, you can ask questions too, so you could take it as an opportunity to ask things you want to know about India. English-speaking Indians and members of the large and growing middle class in particular are usually extremely well informed and well educated, and often far more *au fait* with world affairs than

Westerners, so you may even be drawn into conversations that are way out of your depth.

India can mean many things to many people, and visitors who come here searching can easily fall into the trap of imagining they have found the "real" India, one that the materialistic city-dwelling Indian has lost. This mixture of religion and fantasy is best kept under control by getting to know the people who actually live here.

SHOPPING

So many beautiful and exotic souvenirs are on sale in India, at such low prices, that it's sometimes hard to know what to buy first. On top of that, all sorts of things (such as made-to-measure clothes) that would be vastly expensive at home are much more reasonably priced in India. Even if you lose weight during your trip, your baggage might well put on quite a bit – unless of course you post some of it home.

WHERE TO SHOP

Quite a few items sold in tourist areas are made elsewhere and, needless to say, it's more fun (and cheaper) to pick them up at source. Best buys are noted in the relevant sections of the guide, along with a few specialities that can't be found outside their regions.

Virtually all the state governments in India run handicraft "**emporiums**", most with branches in Delhi. There are also *Central Cottage Industries Emporiums* in Delhi, Calcutta and Bombay. Goods in these places are generally of a high quality, even if their (fixed) prices are a little expensive, and they are worth a visit to get an idea of what crafts are available and how much they should cost.

BARGAINING

Whatever you buy (except food and cigarettes), you will almost always be expected to **haggle over the price**. Bargaining is very much a matter of personal style, but should always be lighthearted, never acrimonious. There are no hard and fast rules – it's really a question of how much something is worth to you. It's a good plan, however, to have an idea of how much you want, or ought, to pay.

Don't worry too much about initial prices. Some guidebooks suggest paying a third of the opening

price, but it's a flexible guideline depending on the shop, the goods and the shopkeeper's impression of you. You may not be able to get the seller much below the first quote; on the other hand, you may end up paying as little as a tenth of it. If you bid too low, you may be hustled out of the shop for offering an "insulting" price, but this is all part of the game, and you'll no doubt be welcomed as an old friend if you return next day.

Don't start haggling for something if you know you don't want it, and never let any figure pass your lips that you are not prepared to pay. It's like bidding at an auction. Having mentioned a price, you are obliged to pay it. If the seller asks you how much you would pay for something, and you don't want it, say so.

Sometimes rickshaw *wallahs* stop unasked in shops; they get a small commission simply for bringing customers. In places like Jaipur and Agra where this is common practice, tourists often strike a deal with their drivers – five shops, say no buying, and a split in the commission! Obviously if you're taken to a shop by a tout or driver and buy something, you pay around 50 percent extra.

METALWARE AND JEWELLERY

Artisans have been casting **bronze statues** of Hindu gods for over a thousand years. The images are produced by the lost-wax process, in which a model is first carved out of wax, then surrounded in clay, and finally fired. That melts the wax to leave a terracotta mould; small pieces can be cast from a single mould, but larger ones have to be assembled from up to a dozen pieces, the joins concealed by ornate ornamentation. The best-quality images will have carefully detailed fingers and eyes, and the metal should not have pits or spots. The south is one major area for them (dancing Shivas a favourite here – check out the quality in the palace art gallery at Thanjavur), the Himalayas another.

Brass and copperware can be very finely worked, with trays, plates, ashtrays, cups and bowls among products available. The best trays – which should be forty years old or more – are from Varanasi. In the north, particularly in Rajasthan, enamel inlays (*meenakari*) are common. **Bidri work**, named after Bidar (Karnataka), where it originated, is a method of inlaying a gunmetal alloy with fine designs in brass or silver, then blackening the gunmetal with sal-ammoniac, to leave the inlay work shining. *Bidri* jewellery boxes, dishes and *hookah* pipes, among other things, are widely sold, especially in Karnataka and Andhra Pradesh; while the Orissan filigree *tarakashi* is worth looking out for. **Stainless steel** is less decorative and more workaday: *thali* sets and spice tins are among the possible buys, available throughout the country.

Among precious metals, silver is generally a better buy than **gold**. The latter is usually 22 carat and very yellow, but relatively expensive due to taxes (smuggling from the Gulf to evade them is rife) and to its popularity as a form of investment – women traditionally keep their wealth in this form, and a bride's jewellery is an important part of her dowry. Indian gold jewellery too is a little garish for Western tastes. **Silver** varies in quality, but is usually reasonably priced, with silver jewellery generally heavier and rather more folksy than gold. Rajasthan and Bengal are its main centres, and Tibetan silver jewellery is also popular. Gold and silver are usually sold by weight, the workmanship costing very little.

Gemstones can be something of a minefield; scams abound, and you would be most unwise to even consider buying gems for resale or as an investment without a basic knowledge of the trade. That said, some precious and semi-precious stones can be a good buy in India, particularly those which are indigenous, such as garnets, black stars and moonstones. Jaipur is a major centre for gems (and con tricks), while Hyderabad specializes in sorting **pearls**, which can therefore be picked up at low prices.

WOODWORK, CERAMICS AND STONE

Wooden furniture, if a little heavy to carry with you, can be a real bargain, and is especially good in the mountainous areas of the north. Carvings of gods (often in sandalwood) are particularly common in the south, and those of elephants are always a favourite. Old wooden carvings from houses or temples that are being refurbished are usually available at reasonable prices, if sometimes a little weathered.

Terracotta figures are a speciality of Bengal and Bihar, but the finest **ceramic** work is the glazed pottery of Jaipur, Kurja, and Delhi. Brightly painted clay and plaster gods are another souvenir possibility, while marble and soapstone are both used for sculpture (though big pieces weigh a ton), and marble items inlaid in the style of the Taj Mahal are popular souvenirs in Agra. Somewhat less weighty than these are papier-mâché items sold in Kashmiri shops that have sprung up around the country (most of which seem to get their supplies in Delhi).

CARPETS AND RUGS

If you get dragged into a Kashmiri arts shop, chances are it's a **carpet** they really want to sell you. Kashmiri rugs are among the best in the world (up there with Iran) and, given a little bit of caution and scepticism, you can get yourself a bargain in India (though you can also get shafted if you're not careful). A pukka Kashmiri carpet should have a label on the back stating that it is made in Kashmir, what it is made of (wool, silk, or "silk touch" – wool combined with a little cotton and silk to give it a sheen), its size, density of knots per square inch (the more the better), and the name of the design. To tell if it really is silk, scrape the carpet with a knife and burn the fluff – real silk shrivels to nothing and has a distinctive smell. Even producing the knife should cause the seller of a bogus silk carpet to demur. Carpets in styles such as Bokhara (Afghan) are now produced in Rajasthan, but tend not to be as fine as the original.

The surest way to make sure a carpet reaches home is to take it away and post it yourself; a seller may offer to post it to you and bill you later, which is fair enough, but be aware that your carpet will be sent immediately, whatever you say (will someone be there to receive it?), and if you use a credit card, your account will also be billed immediately, whatever is said. Be aware of import tax being levied on arrival.

Dhurries (woven carpets or kilims), traditionally made of wool, are an older art form, and a less expensive one. UP is the main centre for these, particularly Agra and Mirzapur, but they are also made in Rajasthan, Gujarat, the Punjab, and Andhra Pradesh. Tibetan rugs are available in areas with a large Tibetan community, such as Himachal Pradesh. Many foreigners prefer carpets in "tasteful" earthy colours, assuming them to be traditional and therefore "ethnic". In fact, Indian carpets traditionally come in bright colours, though the synthetic dyes used nowadays are of course new-fangled.

TEXTILES AND CLOTHING

Textiles are so much a part of Indian culture that Gandhi wanted a spinning wheel put on the flag. The kind of cloth he had in mind was the plain white homespun material worn by Nehru, whose hat, jacket and *dhoti* remain a mark of support for the Congress Party to this day. Homespun, hand-loom-woven hand-printed cloth is called **khadi**, and is sold in government shops called *Khadi Gramodyog* all over India. Methods of dying and printing this and other cloth vary from the tie-dying (*bhandani*) of Rajasthan to block printing and screen printing of calico (from Calicut – now Kozhikode, Kerala) cotton, and of silk.

Saris are normally made of cotton for everyday use, although **silk** is used for special occasions, and quite common in the south. Western women are notoriously inept at wearing this most elegant of garments – it takes years of practice to carry one properly – but silk is usually a good buy in India, provided you make sure it is the real thing (the old test was to see whether it was possible to pull the whole garment straight through a wedding ring; however, some synthetics apparently go through too, so burn a thread and sniff it to be sure). Varanasi silk is world famous, but the best nowadays comes from Kanchipuram and Madurai in Tamil Nadu.

Other popular fabrics include the heavy mirror-embroidered cloth of Rajasthan, Bengali *baluchari* brocade, and Indonesian-style ikat and batik from Orissa, Madhya Pradesh and Gujarat, while clothing to take home includes *lunghis* in the south (as much a sheet as a garment), thick Tibetan sweaters from Darjeeling, and *salwar kamise*, the elegant pyjama suits worn by Muslim women, with trousers (*pajamas*) of various styles. Long loose shirts – preferably made of *khadi*, and known as *kurta* or *panjabi* – are practical in the heat of India, and traditionally worn, by men, with

white pyjamas. Tourist shops sell versions in various fabrics and colours. Block-printed bedsheets, as well as being useful, make good wall-hangings, as do Punjabi *phulkari* (originally wedding sheets), but every region has its own fabrics and its own methods of colouring them and making them up – the choice is endless.

On top of this, with **tailoring** so cheap in India, you can choose the fabric you want, take it to a tailor, and have it made into whatever you fancy. For formal Western-style clothes, you'll probably want to see quite a posh tailor in a big city (Calcutta is probably the best), but tailors in almost every village in the country can run you up a shirt or a pair of pyjama-type trousers in next to no time. Many tailors will also copy a garment you already have.

PAINTINGS AND ANTIQUES

Art and antiques are another field where only experts should look for an investment, but where a souvenir hunter is very likely to find a bargain. Silk and cotton paintings are popular in Rajasthan and the north, but vary vastly in quality, so check out a few before you buy. The village of Kishangarh (Rajasthan) is known for them; otherwise, they are sold in Udaipur.

Most Tibetan **thangkas** (Buddhist religious paintings mounted on brocaded silk) are mass produced (usually in Nepal) and modern, whatever the seller says, but even the cheapest can't hide the dense Buddhist symbolism inherent in the form. You'll find them in the north, where there are Tibetan communities, and a little investigation of the range of styles is well worthwhile.

Leaf skeleton paintings, originally from southern Kerala, are much cheaper and widely available, though they too vary somewhat in quality. **Miniatures** in the traditional style, often masquerading as antiques, are common in tourist shops too, but subject to the same provisos as *thangkas*.

When it comes to **antiques**, if they really are genuine – and, frankly, that is unlikely – you'll need a licence to export them, which is virtually impossible to get. The same applies to "art treasures". Age and status can be verified by the **Archaeological Survey of India**, Janpath, New Delhi 110011 (☎011/301 9451); Sion Fort, Sion, Bombay 400022(☎022/407 1102); 27 Biplabi Trailokya Maharaj Sarani, Narayani Building, Calcutta 700001 (☎033/261933); Fort St

George, Madras 600009 (☎044/560396); Old Town, Bhubaneshwar 751002, Orissa (☎0674/56575); #364, 16th Main, 4th T Block, Jayanagar, Bangalore 560041, Karnataka (☎080/645901), who also issue export clearance certificates.

ODDS AND SODS

Of course, not everything typically Indian is old or traditional. **Tapes or records** of classical, *bhangra*, *filmi*, and Western music are very popular; the actual cassettes fall apart all too readily, so it's well worth copying any you buy once you get home. **Videos** too are widely available, though often bad quality, unsubtitled, and so ridden with adverts as to be almost unwatchable. Insist on watching before you buy; southern films are more likely to be subtitled than Hindi ones.

Books are excellent buys in India, whether by Indian writers (see *Contexts*) or writers from the rest of the English-speaking world. They are likely to be much cheaper than at home, if not so well printed or bound.

Leatherware can be very cheap and well-made, though the leather doesn't normally come from cows, of course: Rajasthani camel-hide *moja-di* slippers go down well, as do distinctive *kholapuri* slippers, which need to be broken in, and *chappal* (sandals). Otherwise, buffalo-hide belts and bags can be very reasonable compared to similar items made of cowhide in the West; Madras and Pondicherry are good places to go looking.

Bamboo flutes are incredibly cheap, while other **musical instruments** such as *tabla*, *sitar* and *sarod* are heavy to carry and available in the West anyway. The quality is crucial; there's no point going home with a *sitar* that is virtually untunable, even if it does look nice. Students of music purchase their instruments from master craftsmen or established shops; get advice before you buy, and never buy one from a tourist shop.

Other possibilities include kitchen implements, wind-up clockwork tin toys, film posters, tea (especially from Darjeeling, Assam and Nilgiri), coffee, spices, peacock feather fans (though these are considered unlucky), and anything which reminds you of India – which needn't be expensive or arty.

Things not to bring home include ivory and anything made from a rare or protected species, including snakeskin and turtle products. As for drugs – don't even think about it.

FESTIVALS AND HOLIDAYS

Virtually every temple in every town or village across the country has its own festival. The biggest and most spectacular include Puri's Rath Yatra festival in June or July, Pushkar's camel fair in November, Kullu's Dussehra, and Madurai's three annual festivals. **While mostly religious in nature, merrymaking rather than solemnity are generally the order of the day, and onlookers are usually welcome. Indeed, if you are lucky enough to coincide with a local festival, it may well prove to be the highlight of your trip.**

Alas, we cannot list here every festival in every village across India, but local festivals are listed throughout the body of the guide. Below is a list of the main national and regional celebrations. It requires a little explanation. Hindu, Sikh, Buddhist and Jain festivals follow the Indian **lunar calendar** and their dates therefore vary from year to year against the plain old Gregorian calendar. Determining them more than a year in advance is a highly complicated business best left to astrologers. Each lunar cycle is divided into two *paksa* (halves): "bright" (waxing) and "dark"

PRINCIPAL INDIAN FESTIVALS

India has only four national public holidays as such: Jan 26 (Republic Day); Aug 15 (Independence Day); Oct 2 (Gandhi's birthday); and Dec 25 (Christmas Day). Each state, however, has its own calendar of public holidays, and you can expect most businesses to close on the major holidays of their own religion, marked with an asterisk below.

Although not all the festivals below are Hindu, we have divided them according to the Hindu calendar; most dates vary against the Gregorian calendar, as is explained on p.61.

Key: B=Buddhist; C=Christian; H=Hindu; J=Jain; M=Muslim; N=non-religious; P=Parsi; S=Sikh.

Magha (Jan–Feb)

H Pongal (1 Magha): Tamil harvest festival celebrated with decorated cows, processions and *rangolis* (chalk designs on the doorsteps of houses). *Pongal* is a sweet porridge made from newly harvested rice and eaten by all, including the cows. The festival is also known as Makar Sankranti, and celebrated in Karnataka, Andhra Pradesh and the east of India.

H Ganga Sagar: Pilgrims come from all over the country to Sagar Dwip, on the mouth of the Hooghly 150km south of Calcutta, to bathe during Makar Sankranti.

H Vasant Panchami (5 Magha): One-day spring festival in honour of Saraswati, the goddess of learning, celebrated with kite flying, yellow *saris*, and the blessing of schoolchildren's books and pens by the goddess.

N Republic Day (Jan 26)*: A military parade in Delhi typifies this state celebration of India's republic-hood, followed on Jan 29 by the "Beating the Retreat" ceremony outside the Presidential Palace in Delhi.

N International Kite Festival at Aurangabad (Maharashtra).

H Floating Festival (16 Magha) at Madurai (Tamil Nadu).

M 1st Ramadan (Jan 10, 1997; Dec 31, 1997; Dec 20, 1998 ; Dec 11, 1999): The start of a month during which Muslims may not eat, drink or smoke from sunrise to sunset, and should abstain from sex. Towards the end of the month it takes its toll, so be gentle with Muslims you meet at this time.

Phalguna (Feb–March)

B Tibetan New Year (1 Phalguna): Celebrations among Tibetan communities, especially at Dharamsala.

H Shivratri (10 Phalguna): Anniversary of Shiva's *tandav* (creation) dance, and his wedding anniversary. A *sadhu* festival of pilgrimage and fasting, especially at important Shiva temples.

H Holi (15 Phalguna)*: Water festival held during Dol Purnima (full moon) to celebrate the beginning of spring, most popular in the north. Expect to be bombarded with water, paint, coloured powder and other mixtures; they can permanently stain clothing, so don't go out in your Sunday best.

M Id ul-Fitr (Feb 9, 1997; Jan 30, 1998; Jan 20, 1999: 1 Shawwal)*: Feast to celebrate the end of Ramadan, after 28 days.

N Khajuraho (Madhya Pradesh) Dance Festival.

C Carnival (Mardi Gras): The last day before Lent, 40 days before Easter, is celebrated in Goa, as in the rest of the Catholic world.

Chaitra (March–April)

H Gangaur (3 Chaitra): Rajasthani festival (also celebrated in Bengal and Orissa) in honour of Parvati, marked with singing and dancing.

H Ramanavami (9 Chaitra)*: Birthday of Rama, the hero of the *Ramayana*, celebrated with readings of the epic and discourses on Rama's life and teachings.

C Easter (movable feast)*: Celebration of the resurrection of Christ. Good Friday in particular is a day of festivity.

P Pateti: Parsi new year, also known as No Ruz, celebrating the creation of fire. Feasting, services and present giving.

P Khorvad Sal (a week after Pateti): Birthday of Zarathustra (aka Zoroaster).

H Chittirai, Madurai (Tamil Nadu): elephant-led procession.

Vaisakha (April–May)

HS Baisakhi (1 Vaisakha): To the Hindus, it's the solar new year, celebrated with music and dancing; to the Sikhs, it's the anniversary of the foundation of the *Khalsa* (Sikh brotherhood) by Guru Gobind Singh. Processions and feasting follow readings of the *Granth Sahib* scriptures.

J Mahavir Jayanti (13 Vaisakha)*: Birthday of Mahavira, the founder of Jainism. The main Jain festival of the year.

M Id uz-Zuha (April 17, 1997; April 5, 1998; March 25, 1999: 10 Zoul Hagga)*: Pilgrimage festival to commemorate Abraham's preparedness to sacrifice his son Ismail. Celebrated with slaughtering and consumption of sheep.

H Puram Festival, Thrissur (Kerala): frenzied drumming and elephant parades.

B Buddha Jayanti (16 Vaisakha)*: Buddha's birthday. He achieved enlightenment and *nirvana* on the same date. Sarnath (UP) and Bodh Gaya (Bihar) are the main centres of celebration.

Jyaishtha (May–June)

H Ganga Dussehra (10 Jyaishtha): Bathing festival to celebrate the descent to earth of the goddess of the Ganges.

M Muharram: Festival to commemorate the martyrdom of the (Shi'ite) Imam, the Prophet's grandson and popular saint, Hussain.

Ashadha (June–July)

H Rath Yatra (2 Ashadha): Festival held in Puri (and other places, especially in the south) to commemorate Krishna's (Lord Jaggernath's) journey to Mathura.

H Teej (3 Ashadha): Festival in honour of Parvati, to welcome the monsoon. Celebrated particularly in Rajasthan.

B Hemis Festival, Leh (Ladakh): July 15 & 16, 1997; July 4 & 5, 1998; June 23 & 24, 1999.

Shravana (July–Aug)

H Naag Panchami (3 Shravana): Snake festival in honour of the *naga* snake deities. Mainly celebrated in Rajasthan and Maharashtra.

H Raksha Bandhan/Narial Purnima (16 Shravana): Festival to honour the sea god Varuna. Brothers and sisters exchange gifts, the sister tying a thread known as a *rakhi* to her brother's wrist. Brahmins, after a day's fasting, change the sacred thread they wear.

N Independence Day (15 Aug)*: India's biggest secular celebration, on the anniversary of her Independence from Britain.

Bhadraparda (Aug–Sept)

H Ganesh Chaturthi (4 Bhadraparda): Festival dedicated to Ganesh, especially celebrated in Maharashtra. In Bombay, huge processions carry images of the god to immerse in the sea. 1995's festival was on Aug 29–Sept 8; in 1996, Sept 16–Sept 26; in 1997, Sept 6–Sept 15.

H Onam: Keralan harvest festival, celebrated with snake-boat races, especially at Alappuzha.

H Janmashtami (23 Bhadraparda)*: Krishna's birthday, an occasion for fasting and celebration, especially in Agra, Bombay, Mathura (UP) and Vrindaban (UP).

H Avani Mula festival, Madurai (Tamil Nadu): Celebration of the coronation of Shiva.

Ashvina (Sept–Oct)

H Dussehra (1–10 Ashvina)*: Ten-day festival (usually two days' public holiday) associated with vanquishing demons, in particular Rama's victory over Ravana in the *Ramayana*, and Durga's over the buffalo-headed Mahishasura (particularly in West Bengal, where it is called Durga Puja). Celebrations include performances of the *Ram Lila* (life of Rama). Best in Mysore (Karnataka), Ahmedabad (Gujarat) and Kullu (Himachal Pradesh).

N Mahatma Gandhi's Birthday (2 Oct)*: Rather solemn commemoration of Independent India's founding father.

Kartika (Oct–Nov)

H Diwali (Deepavali) (15 Kartika)*: Five-day festival of lights to celebrate Rama and Sita's homecoming in the *Ramayana*. Festivities include the lighting of oil lamps and firecrackers, and the giving and receiving of sweets.

J Jain New Year (15 Kartika): Coincides with Diwali, so Jains celebrate alongside Hindus.

S Nanak Jayanti (16 Kartika)*: Guru Nanak's birthday marked by prayer readings and processions, especially in Amritsar and the Punjab, and at Patna. Nov 7 1995.

Margashirsha, or Agrahayana (Nov–Dec)

H Sonepur Mela: World's largest cattle fair at Sonepur (Bihar).

N Pushkar (Rajasthan) Camel Fair.

Pausa (Dec–Jan)

CN Christmas (Dec 25)*: The Christian festival the whole world celebrates, popular in Christian areas of Goa and Kerala, and in big cities.

N Posh Mela (Dec 27): held in Shantiniketan near Calcutta, a festival renowned for *baul* music.

Movable

H Kumbh Mela: Major three-yearly festival held at one of four holy cities: Nasik (Maharashtra) in Shravana, Ujjain (Madhya Pradesh) in Kartika, Allahabad (UP) in Magha, or Haridwar (UP) in Chaitra. In 1998, it's at Hardwar.

(waning), each consisting of fifteen *tithis* ("days" – but a *tithi* might begin at any time of the solar day). The *paksa* start respectively with the new moon (*ama* or *bahula* – the first day of the month) and the full moon (*purnima*). Lunar festivals, then, are observed on a given day in the "light" or "dark" side of the month. The lunar calendar adds a leap month every two or three years to keep it in line with the seasons. Muslim festivals follow the **Islamic calendar**, whose year is shorter and which thus loses about eleven days per annum against the Gregorian.

You may, while in India, have the privilege of being invited to a **wedding**. These are jubilant affairs with great feasting, always scheduled on auspicious days. A Hindu bride wears red for the ceremony, and puts a *bindi* on her forehead for the rest of her married life. Although the practice is officially illegal, large dowries change hands. These are usually paid by the bride's family to the groom, and can be contentious; poor families feel obliged to save for years to get their daughters married.

Funeral processions are much more sombre affairs, and should be left in peace. In Hindu funerals, the body is normally carried to the cremation site within hours of death by white-shrouded relatives (white is the colour of mourning). The eldest son is expected to shave his head and wear white following the death of a parent. At Varanasi and other places, you may see cremations; such occasions should be treated with respect, and photographs not taken.

WOMEN TRAVELLERS

India is not a country that provides huge obstacles to women travellers, petty annoyances being more the order of the day. In the days of the Raj, upper-class eccentrics started a tradition of lone women travellers, taken up enthusiastically by the flower children of the hippy era. Nineties women still do it, and come through the challenge perfectly unscathed. However, few women get through their trip without any hassle, and it's good to prepare yourself to be a little thick-skinned.

Indian streets are almost without exception male dominated – something that may take a bit of getting used to, particularly when you find yourself subjected to incessant staring and name calling. Most of your fellow travellers on trains and buses will be men who may start up most unwelcome **conversations** about sex, divorce and the "freedom" of relationships in the West. At its worst in larger cities, all this can become very tiring. You can get round it to a certain extent by joining women in public places, and you'll notice an immense difference if you join up with a male travelling companion. In this case, expect Indian men to approach him (assumed, of course, to be your husband – an assumption it is sometimes advantageous to go along with) and talk to him about you quite happily as if you were not there. Beware, however, if you are (or look) Indian with a non-Indian male companion: this may well cause you grief and harassment, as you will be seen to have brought shame on your family by adopting the loose morals of the West.

In addition to staring and suggestive comments and looks, **sexual harassment**, or "Eve teasing" as it is bizarrely known, is likely to be a nuisance, but not generally a threat. It is nowadays widely recognized as a social problem, which is a start, but it remains a daily fact of life for Indian women. Expect to get groped in crowds, and to have men "accidentally" squeeze past you at any opportunity. It tends to be worse in cities than in small towns and villages, but anywhere being followed can be a real problem. In time you'll learn to gauge a situation – sometimes wandering around on your own may attract so much unwanted attention that you may prefer to stay in one place until you've recharged your batteries or your male fan club has moved on. When you're alone it's best to dress modestly – a *salwar kamise* is perfect – and refrain from smoking in public, which only reinforces suspicions that Western women are "loose" and "easy".

Returning an unwanted touch with a punch or slap is perfectly in order (Indian women often become aggressive when offended), and does serve to vent a little frustration. It should also attract attention and urge someone to help you, or at least deal with the offending man – a man transgressing social norms is always out of line, and any passer-by will want to let him know it. If you feel someone getting too close in a crowd or on a bus, brandishing your left shoe in his face can be very effective.

Violent sexual assaults on tourists are extremely rare, but unfortunately the number of reported cases of **rape** is rising. Though no assault can be predicted, you can take precautions: at night avoid quiet, dimly lit streets and alleys, and try to get someone to accompany you to your hotel whenever possible. While Indian women are still quite timid about reporting rape – it is considered as much a disgrace to the victim as to the perpetrator – Western victims should always report it to the police, and before leaving the area try to let other tourists, or locals, know, in the hope that pressure from the community may uncover the offender and see him brought to justice. At present there's nowhere for tourists who've suffered sexual violence to go for sanctuary (though you could try the *Women's Resource Centre* or *FRC* in Bombay); most victims seek support from other travellers, or go home.

The **practicalities of travel** take on a new dimension for lone women travellers. Often you can turn your gender to your advantage. For example, on buses the driver and conductor will often take you under their wing, watch out for you and buy you *chai* at each stop, and there will be countless other instances of kindness wherever you travel. You'll also be more welcome in some private houses than a group of Western males, and may find yourself learning the finer points of Indian cooking round the family's clay stove. Women frequently get preference at bus and railway stations where they can join a separate "ladies' queue", use ladies' waiting rooms, and on overnight trains the enclosed ladies' compartments are peaceful havens (unless filled with noisy children). Finally however, in **hotels** watch out for "peep-holes" in your door (and in the common bathrooms), and be sure to cover your window when changing *and* when sleeping. And do bring your own supply of tampons, not widely available outside Indian cities.

INDIAN WOMEN

The role of a woman in Indian society is in theory very well-defined by a tradition that does not encourage independence. It is to marry a man approved (if not chosen) by her parents, join his

---

WOMEN'S ORGANIZATIONS IN INDIA

Centre for Women's Development Studies, B-43, Panchseel Enclave, New Delhi 110017 (☎643 8428).

Feminist Resource Centre (FRC), 13 Carol Mansion, 35 Sitladevi Temple Rd, Mahim, Bombay 400016. Feminist-perspective research on wide-ranging issues (eg, health, sexuality, violence against women, discrimination at work).

Forum against the Oppression of Women, c/o Vibhuti Patel, K8 Nensey Colony, Express Highway, Borivili East, Bombay 400066.

Indian Council of Social Science Research (ICSSR), 3F Shah Rd, New Delhi 110001 (☎383186). Organize workshops and symposia on feminist themes and run a women's studies programme.

Indian Social Institute (ISI) Programme for Women's Development, Lodi Rd, New Delhi 110003 (☎622379).

Kali for Women, N84 Panchshila Park, New Delhi 110017. Feminist publisher.

Self-Employed Women's Association (SEWA), Textile Workers' Union Building, Ahmedabad, Gujarat. Self-help union mentioned in text below.

Streelekha (International Feminist Bookshop and Information Centre), #67, 2nd floor, Blumoan Complex, MG Rd, Bangalore 560001, Karnataka. Stocks books, journals, posters; provides space for women to meet.

Women's Centre, 307 Yasmeen Apartments, Yashwant Nagar, Valoka, Santa Cruz East, Bombay.

family, bear and bring up his children and look after their home. Before marriage, contact between the sexes is rigorously controlled, something that is becoming less easy among the middle classes with mixed gender universities. Even then, inter-religion or inter-caste marriages are rare and difficult – a daughter marrying out of her social class is likely to face ostracism.

Women are, however highly visible in everyday life and you will see women in India doing all sorts of jobs that you may not have expected, though they are unlikely to earn as much as men of the same social class. Fieldworkers and roadside labourers are often women, but most of them belong to the "scheduled castes" and are paid next to nothing. Women do have a lot of power and influence in Indian society, but in general it is through the family unit, not independently.

A small number of women are exceptions to this rule and have made great headway in the professions (Indira Gandhi, one of the modern world's first women political leaders, among them), but most women with such ambitions are held back by tradition, poverty or both. At the other end of the economic scale women have organized themselves with sometimes astounding success. One example is Ahmedabad's Self-Employed Women's Association (SEWA), a cooperative that has managed to rescue its low-caste low-income members from economic dependence on money-lenders, and act as a pressure group for their rights (see p.561).

Aside from these, however, tradition still rules. Dowries are illegal, but still demanded by prospective in-laws, thus putting a price on daughters that many families simply can't afford. Despite protests, sex determination is extremely popular and female foeticide very common, as is female infanticide; both, it is hoped, can be curbed by effective education before it is too late. Even *sati* (immolation of a widow on her husband's funeral pyre, banned by the British in 1829) is still not unheard of – indeed, it has gone through something of a revival in states controlled by the BJP –, and accusations of "bride-burning" all too frequent. Girls may be allowed an education, but this is more often to attract a husband than to enter a career. Women's groups exist – mainly composed of educated middle-class women, but the network is widening and awareness of the power of female unity is growing in thousands of villages. City based groups concentrate on issues such as dowries, discrimination, pay differentials, education and sexual harassment. They may not always see themselves as akin to Western feminists.

As for **publications** of interest to women, India has plenty of "women's magazines" along pre-Cosmo Western lines. *Femina* is the best known, but has scores of imitators. They won't tell you how to pick up Indian men, but they might give you an idea of what interests Indian women are supposed to have. In addition, look out for the following:

Manushi, c/o 202 Lajpat Nagar, New Delhi 110024. Excellent Hindi and English journal of information and analysis on women's issues in India.

Newsletter of the Institute of Social Studies (ISS), 5 Deen Dayal Upadhyaya Marg, New Delhi 110002. Research on women's organizations, access to employment, role in development.

Quarterly Newsletter of the Research Unit on Women's Studies, SNDT, Women's University, 1 Nathibai Thackersey Rd, Bombay 400020.

GAY TRAVELLERS

Homosexuality is not generally open or accepted in India, and "carnal intercourse against the order of nature" (anal intercourse) is an offence under article 377 of the penal code, while laws against "obscene behaviour" are used to arrest gay men for cruising or liaising anywhere that could be considered a public place. The same law could in theory be used against lesbians, but that is unlikely as lesbian liaisons are much more clandestine.

Physical contact between members of the same sex, such as holding hands, is commonplace in India and should not necessarily be taken as sexual. On the other hand, as in many countries where heterosexual contact outside of marriage is difficult, homosexual behaviour is frequent among people who do not consider themselves gay, and a surprising number of Indian men are bisexual. For this reason, however, one-offs are much more likely than long-term relationships.

For lesbians, **making contacts** will be rather difficult: the *Sakhi* resource centre in Delhi (details below) is the only public face of a very hidden scene. For gay men, a network exists in most big cities, especially Bombay, where gay parties are a regular event. Contact the *Khush Club*, PO Box 573551, Bombay 400058 – which does not have fixed premises – for details of forthcoming social activities in the city.

Cruising areas are strictly defined by time and place, with police harassment frequent and sometimes brutal. Male prostitution also exists, but robberies are common.

Some Indian gay male couples make their relationship acceptable by one of them becoming a **eunuch** (eunuchs are semi-accepted as a kind of "third sex"), but such a step would probably be a little drastic for most Western visitors. Gay Westerners contemplating a relationship should be aware that they will not be able to bring their lovers home with them.

Contacts (write in advance for information – most addresses are PO boxes):

Bombay Dost, 105A Veena-Beena Shopping Centre, Bandra Station Rd, Bandra (West), Bombay 400050. Publish a newsletter and have contacts nationwide.

Shakhi, PO Box 3526, Lajpat Nagar, New Delhi 110065. Lesbian guest house and resource centre.

Arambh, c/o Aalok, PO Box 9522, New Delhi 110095.

The Counsel Club, PO Bag 10237, Calcutta 700016.

Pravartak, PO Box 10237, Calcutta 700 019. Publish a newsletter.

Friends of India, PO Box 59, Mahanagar, Lucknow 226006, ☎0522/247009.

Sneha Sangama, PO Box 3250, Bangalore 560032. Gay men's group.

Gay Info Centre, c/o Owais, PO Box 1662, Secunderabad HPO 500003, Andhra Pradesh.

Good As You, 201 Samaraksha, 2nd Floor Royal Corner, 1+2 Lalbang Rd, Bangalore. Gay support group.

Saathi, PO Box 571, Putlibowli PO, Hyderabad, Andhra Pradesh.

Udaan, 'Box Holder' (do not address to Udaan), PO Box 6793 Sion, Bombay. Working class gay support group.

Men India Movement, PO Box 885, Kochi 682005, Kerala.

DISABLED TRAVELLERS

Disability is common in India; many conditions that would be treatable in the West, such as cataracts, are permanent disabilities here because people can't afford the treatment. Disabled people are unlikely to get jobs (though there is a famous blind barber in Delhi), and the choice is usually between staying at home being looked after by your family, and going out on the street to beg for alms.

For the disabled traveller, this has its advantages: disability and disfigurement, for example, do not get the same embarrassed reaction from Indian people that they do from able-bodied Westerners. On the other hand, you'll be lucky to see a state-of-the-art wheelchair or a disabled loo (major airports usually have both, though the loo may not be in a usable state), and the streets are full of all sorts of obstacles that would be hard for a blind or wheelchair-bound tourist to negotiate independently. Kerbs are often high, pavements uneven and littered, and ramps non-existent. There are potholes all over the place, open sewers and all sorts of unexpected obstacles from cows to heaps of rubbish to negotiate your way around. Some of the more expensive hotels have ramps for the movement of luggage and equipment, but if that makes them accessible to wheelchairs, it is by accident rather than design.

If you walk with difficulty, you will find street obstacles and steep stairs hard going. Another factor that can be a problem is the constant barrage of people proffering things at you (hard to wave aside if you are for instance on sticks or crutches), and all that queuing, not to mention heat, will take it out of you if you have a condition that makes you tire quickly. A light, folding camp-stool is one thing that could be invaluable if you have limited walking or standing power.

Then again, Indian people are likely to be very helpful if, for example, you need their help getting on and off buses or up stairs. Taxis and rickshaws are easily affordable and very adaptable; if you rent one for a day, the driver is certain to help you on and off, and perhaps even around the sites you visit. If you employ a guide, they may also be prepared to help you with steps and obstacles.

If complete independence is out of the question, going with an able-bodied companion might be on the cards. In the UK, the charity *Holiday Care Service*, 2nd Floor, Imperial Buildings, Victoria Rd, Horley, Surrey RH6 7PZ (☎01293/774535), provides information and lists of tour operators and should be able to help you get in touch with someone; *Tripscope* (☎0181/994 9294) is a free telephone information service giving advice and assisting with journeys. Specialist tour operators for the disabled include *Can Be Done*, 7-11 Kensington High St, London W8 5NP (☎0181/907 2400) and *Carefree Holidays*, 64 Florence Rd, Northampton NN1 4NA (☎01604/34301). Otherwise, some package tour operators try to cater for travellers with disabilities – *Bales, Butterfield's* and *Somak* among them – but you should always contact any operator and discuss your exact needs with them before making a booking. You should also make sure you are covered by any insurance policy you take out.

DISABLED ORGANIZATIONS

India *India Rehabilitation Co-ordination – India*, A–2 Rasadhara Co-operation Housing Society, 385 SVP Rd, Bombay 400004.
USA *SATH*, 347 Fifth Ave, Suite 610, New York NY10016, ☎212/447 7284.
Travel Information Service, Moss Rehab Hospital, 1200 West Tabor Rd, Philadelphia PA 19141, ☎215/456 9600).
Canada *Easter Seals/March of Dimes National Council*, 90 Eglinton Ave E, Suite 511, Toronto, Ontario M4P 2Y3, ☎416/932 8382.

UK *RADAR*, 12 City Forum, 250 City Rd, London EC1V 8AS, ☎0171/250 3222.
Ireland *National Rehabilitation Board*, 25 Clyde Road, Ballsbridge, Dublin 4, ☎01/668 4181.
Australia *ACROD*, PO Box 60, Curtain, ACT 2605, ☎06/682 4333.
Barrier Free Travel, 36 Wheatley St, North Bellingen, NSW 2454, ☎066/551733.
New Zealand *Disabled Persons Assembly*, PO Box 10–138, The Terrace, Wellington, ☎04/472 2626.

TRAVELLING WITH KIDS

Travelling with kids can be both challenging and rewarding. Indians are very tolerant of children so you can take them almost anywhere without restriction, and they always help break the ice with strangers.

The main problem with children, especially small children, is their extra vulnerability. Even more than their parents, they need protecting from the sun, unsafe drinking water, heat and unfamiliar food. All that chilli in particular may be a problem, even with older kids, if they're not used to it. Remember too, that diarrhoea, perhaps just a nuisance to you, could be dangerous for a child: rehydration salts (see under "Health", p.17) are vital if your child goes down with it. Make sure too, if possible, that your child is aware of the dangers of rabies; keep children away from animals, and consider a rabies jab.

For babies, nappies (diapers) and places to change them can be a problem. For a short visit, you could bring disposable ones with you; for longer journeys, consider going over to washables. A changing mat is another necessity. And if your baby is on powdered milk, it might be an idea to bring some of that: you can certainly get it in India, but it may not taste the same. Dried baby food too could be worth taking – mix it with hot (boiled) water that any cafe or *chai wallah* should be able to supply you with.

For touring, hiking or walking, child-carrier backpacks such as the *Tommy Lightrider* are ideal, start at around $45/£30, and can weigh less than 2kg. If the child is small enough, a fold-up buggy is also well worth packing – especially if they will sleep in it (while you have a meal or a drink . . .). If you want to cut down on long journeys by flying, remember that children under 2 travel for 10 percent of the adult fare, and under-12s for half price.

DIRECTORY

low-denomination ones) and credit cards are also acceptable. This tax also applies to international sea departures.

Cigarettes Indian cigarettes, such as *Wills, Gold Flake, Four Square* and *Charms*, are OK once you get used to them, and hardly break the bank (Rs4–Rs15 per pack), but if you find them too rough, stock up on imported brands such as *Marlboro* and *Benson and Hedges*, or some rolling tobacco, available in the bigger towns and cities. One of the great smells of India is the *bidi*, the cheapest smoke, made of a single low-grade tobacco leaf. If you smoke roll-ups, stock up on good papers as Indian *Capstan* cigarette papers are thick and don't stick very well and Rizlas, where available, are pretty costly.

Airport Departure Tax As you depart from any Indian airport, you are expected to pay a tax of either Rs300 – for most international flights – or Rs150, for domestic flights and flights to Pakistan, Bangladesh, Nepal, Sri Lanka, Myanmar (Burma), the Maldives and Afghanistan. Ideally you'd pay with left-over rupees kept for that purpose, but travellers' cheques (so hang on to some

Duty Free Allowance Anyone over 17 can bring in 1 US quart (0.95 litre – but nobody's going to quibble about the other 5ml) of spirits, or a bottle of wine and 250ml spirits; plus 200 cigarettes, or 50 cigars, or 250g tobacco. You may be required to register anything valuable on a Tourist Baggage Re-export Form to make sure you can take it home with you, and to fill in a currency declaration form if carrying more than US$10,000 or the equivalent. There is a market for duty free spirits in big cities: small retailers are the best people to approach.

Electricity Generally 220V 50Hz AC, though direct current supplies also exist, so check before plugging in. Most sockets are triple round-pin (accepting European-size double round-pin plugs). British, Irish and Australasian plugs will need an adaptor, preferably universal; American and Canadian appliances will need a transformer too, unless multi-voltage. Power cuts and voltage variations are very common; voltage stabilizers should be used to run sensitive appliances such as portable computers.

Initials and acronyms Widely used in Indian English. Thus, the Janata Party Prime Minister, Vishwana Pratap Singh, was always "VP", and many middle-class Indian men bear similar monikers. The United Provinces, renamed Uttar Pradesh after independence, have always been UP. More recently, and less universally, Himachal Pradesh is HP, Madhya Pradesh MP, and Andhra Pradesh (not Arunchal Pradesh) AP. State and national organizations such as ITDC, RTDC and so on are always known by their acronyms. MG Road means Mahatma Gandhi Road, Victoria Terminus in Bombay is VT, and the only reason Calcutta has come to accept the new name for Dalhousie Square is because they can call it BBD Bagh (that's Benoy Badal Dinesh).

Laundry In India, no-one goes to the laundry: if they don't do their own, they send it out to a *dhobi-wallah*. Wherever you are staying, there will either be an in-house *dhobi-wallah*, or one very close by to call on. The *dhobi-wallah* will take your dirty washing to a *dhobi ghat*, a public clothes-washing area (the bank of a river for example), where it is shown some old-fashioned discipline: separated, soaped and given a damn good thrashing to beat the dirt out of it. Then it is hung out to dry in the sun and, once dried, taken to the ironing sheds where every garment is endowed with razor-sharp creases and then matched to its rightful owner by hidden cryptic markings. Your clothes will come back from the *dhobi-wallah* absolutely spotless, though this kind of violent treatment does take it out of them: buttons get lost and eventually the cloth starts to fray. For more on *dhobi-wallahs*, see our box on p.630 in the Bombay chapter; if you'd rather not

entrust your Savile Row made-to-measure to their tender mercies, dry-cleaners do exist in large towns

Meditation Meditation courses and retreats are on offer all over India, held by numerous schools and sects, involving various Hindu disciplines such as Vedanta as well as Buddhist practices.

For Buddhist meditation, the *Root Institute* (☎0631/400714), in the important centre Bodh Gaya (Bihar), organizes short courses throughout the winter and spring, while in Dharamsala (HP), there's a choice between Tibetan and Hinayana (Indian and Southeast Asian) traditional teachings. Tibetan or Mahayana Buddhist meditation is usually taught through monasteries in Dharamsala and Darjeeling (WB). Institutions such as *Sivananda Ashram* in Rishikesh (UP) organize courses throughout the country.

Vipassana centres, which offer Hinayana meditation courses of varying lengths, are dotted around the country; enquire through the *Vipassana Centre*, Dharmaghetta, in Kusumnagar, Hyderabad (☎0842/530290), or by calling the *Vipassana International Academy* in Igatpuri, Maharashtra (☎0253/72592). In England, contact the *Vipassana Trust*, Dharmadipa, Harewood End, Hereford (☎01989/730234); in the US, *Dharmamahavana*, PO Box 1167, North Fork, CA 93643 (☎2209/877 4386).

Numbers A hundred thousand is a *lakh* (written 1,00,000); ten million is a *crore* (1,00,00,000). Millions, billions and the like are not in common usage.

Opening Hours In theory, standard shop opening hours in India are Mon–Sat 9.30am–6pm. Most big stores, at any rate, keep those hours, while smaller shops vary from town to town, religion to religion, and one to another, but usually keep longer hours. Government tourist offices are open in principle Mon–Fri 9.30am–5pm, Sat 9.30am–1pm, though these may vary slightly; state-run tourist offices are likely to be open Mon–Fri 10am–5pm.

Photography Beware of pointing your camera at anything that might be considered "strategic", including airports and anything military, but even at bridges, railway stations and main roads. Remember too that some people prefer not to be photographed, so it is wise to ask before you take a snapshot of them – and only common courtesy after all. Camera film, sold at average Western prices, is widely available in India (but check the date on the box, and note that false boxes containing outdated film are often sold – *Konica* have started painting holograms on their boxes to prevent this), and it's fairly easy to get films developed, though they don't always come out as well as they might at home. If you're after slide film, slow film or fast film, buy it in the big cities, and don't expect to find specialist brands such as *Velvia*. Also, remember to guard your equipment from dust – it can get everywhere.

Time India is all in one time zone: GMT+5hr 30min all year round. In principle this makes it 5hr 30min ahead of London, 10hr 30min ahead of New York, 13hr 30min ahead of LA, and 4hr 30min behind Sydney; however, summer time in those places will vary the difference by an hour.

Toilets A visit to the loo is not one of India's more pleasant experiences: toilets are often filthy and stink. They are also, of course, major potential breeding grounds for disease. And then there is the squatting position to get used to; this is the natural position for defecation and once you get the hang of it, you may even prefer it, especially since it involves no physical contact with the toilet (you don't need loo-seat paranoia to prefer

avoiding that). Paper, if used, often goes in a bucket next to the loo rather than down it. Indians use instead a jug of water and their left hand, a method you may also come to prefer, but if you do use paper, keep some handy – it isn't usually supplied, and it might be an idea to stock up before going too far off the beaten track as it is not available everywhere.

Yoga While hatha yoga – the physical form – is the most renowned, there are several other major forms of yoga involving meditation, mental and philosophical traditions; these include vedanta, rajya yoga, kriya yoga and bhakti. Varanasi (UP) and Rishikesh (UP) are the centres for yoga but there are numerous institutions throughout the country. One- or two-week yoga courses for visitors, involving physical and mental practices based on Hindu philosophy (usually the *Bhagavad Gita*), are run in major centres. Ashrams often tend to be self-interested and demand a level of personal commitment that may not always be healthy or something you may want to give; studying yoga and adopting a guru can often be two distinctly different experiences.

THINGS TO TAKE

Many things are of course easy to find in India and cheaper than at home, but here is a miscellaneous and rather random list of items you should consider taking to India with you:

A padlock (to lock rooms in budget hotels, and attach your bag to train fittings)

A universal electric plug adaptor and a universal sink plug (few sinks or bathtubs have them)

A mosquito net

A sheet sleeping bag (made by sewing up a sheet – so you don't have to worry about the state of the ones in your hotel room)

A small flashlight

Earplugs (for street noise in hotel rooms and music on buses)

High-factor sunblock

A pocket alarm clock (for those early morning departures)

An inflatable neck-rest, to help you sleep on long journeys

A multi-purpose penknife

A needle and some thread (but dental floss is better than cotton for holding baggage together)

Plastic bags (to sort your baggage, make it easier to pack and unpack, and keep out damp and dust)

Tampons (those available in India aren't too great)

Condoms

Multi-vitamin and mineral tablets

Suggestions for a general **medical kit** are listed on p.17; details of **trekking** prerequisites are on p.48.

PART TWO

THE
GUIDE

CHAPTER ONE

DELHI

Delhi is the symbol of old India and new . . . even the stones here whisper to our ears of the ages of long ago and the air we breathe is full of the dust and fragrances of the past, as also of the fresh and piercing winds of the present.

Jawaharlal Nehru

On first impressions, **DELHI**, with its tower blocks and temples, forts, mosques and colonial mansions, and jam-packed streets, can be as disorienting as it is fascinating. It certainly takes a while to find your feet – literally – as you attempt to weave a path through buses, trucks, nippy modern cars, mopeds, rickshaws, nonchalant cows, bullock carts and hand-pulled trolleys. Unlikely juxtapositions are everywhere you look; suit-and-tie businessmen rub shoulders with traditionally dressed orthodox Hindus and Muslims, groups of young Delhi-ites wearing *Levi's* pile into burger-joints, bars and discos, turbaned snake charmers tease hypnotizing moans out of curved pipes, pundits pontificate while *sadhus* smoke their *chillums*, and ragged beggars clutching dusty children plead for a little help towards a meal.

The daunting scale of Delhi becomes more manageable as you start to appreciate that geographically as well as historically it consists of several distinct cities – if anything, more than the **Seven Cities** of tradition. The hub of the metropolis is **Central New Delhi**, an orderly plan of wide roads lined with sturdy colonial buildings which was established as the capital of British India in 1911. Many of the city's hotels are here, concentrated amid the columned facades of **Connaught Place**, and just north of the **parliamentary buildings**, the architectural jewels in the Imperial crown. **Old Delhi**, Shah Jahan's seventeenth-century capital (Shahjahanabad), lies 2km or so further north. This is Delhi at its most quintessentially Indian, where the traditional lifestyle of its predominantly Muslim population has changed little over two hundred years. A visit to Old Delhi's mighty **Red Fort** and **Jami Masjid**, India's largest mosque, is a must, and should be combined with a stroll through the old city's bazaars, a warren of clustered houses, buzzing with commotion, and infused with aromatic smells drifting from open-fronted restaurants, spice shops and temples.

The other five of Delhi's ex-capitals, further south, are today all but deserted, standing as impressive reminders of long-vanished dynasties. Among them you'll find the towering free-standing column erected by Qutb-ud-din Aibak, the **Qutb Minar** (twelfth century), that marks the first capital, Dhillika, and that signalled the development of the city that visitors see today. Walls and dilapidated pillars survive from the fourteenth-century city of **Tughluqabad**, and **Purana Qila**, the sixth capital. Interspersed between these historic ruins are the grand **tombs** of Delhi's former rulers, plus a plethora of Hindu **temples**, and domed **mosques**, introduced by the Muslims, which dramatically changed the conventional mould of Indian cities. Perhaps the finest expressions of the Moghuls' architectural genius were the grand *charbagh* (quartered garden) mausoleums of **Humayun's Tomb**, and, most famously, the Taj Mahal in Agra. The major monument of the great Moghul period is **Lal Qila**, the "Red Fort", in Old Delhi.

As befits a national capital, Delhi provides plenty of opportunities to learn about the rest of the country, not least in its admirable range of political, historical and art **museums**. **Shops** trade in goods from every corner of India, and with a little legwork you can find anything from Tibetan carpets, antiques, and jewellery to modern art and designer clothes. Unlike Bombay, Delhi has little nightlife to speak of – only a handful of discos and an assortment of congenial bars – but its auditoria host a wide range of **national music** and **dance** events, featuring India's most accomplished performers.

Delhi's crowds and stifling, heavily polluted atmosphere soon become tiring, if not unbearable, and few tourists stay longer than a week. However, its long history and firmly rooted traditions ensure that the city never seems quite so much on the brink as Bombay, and many people grow to enjoy its diversity and vivacity.

History: The Seven Cities of Delhi

Growing popular belief has it that Delhi was the city of the Pandavas, the heroes of the *Mahabharata* – though as the Hindu epic is essentially mythology, any attempt to place it within a specific landscape has to be questionable. Nonetheless, the earliest known settlement in the Delhi area, thought to have stood close to the River Yamuna (near the Purana Qila) between 1000 BC and the fourth century AD, has been identified with the city of **Indraprastha**, mentioned in the *Mahabharata*. There's also evidence that Delhi lay on an important trunk route of the Mauryan period, and Ptolemy, who came here in the second century AD, mentions "Dilli".

However, modern Delhi is usually said to have come into being when the Tomara Rajputs founded **Lal Kot** in 736 AD. That was extended, and renamed **Qila Rai Pithora**, the first city of Delhi, in 1180, after a rival Rajput clan, the Chauhans, had ousted the Tomaras; only a few walls of Lal Kot now remain, at the Qutb Minar complex in southwest Delhi. Soon afterwards, in the two successive battles of Tarain in 1191, the Rajputs first managed to hold off an invading force from Afghanistan led by Muhammad Ghuri, and then succumbed to it a few months later.

Unlike other invaders from Central Asia who swept into the north Indian plains, Muhammad Ghuri had come to stay and not merely to plunder. He was assassinated in 1206, and his kingdom did not survive long in Afghanistan, but his Indian provinces remained more or less intact in the hands of his Turkish general, Qutb-ud-din Aibak. This ex-slave, who founded the **Delhi Sultanate** (or Slave Dynasty – the first major Muslim rulers of the subcontinent), established himself at the site of Lal Kot, and commenced the construction of the **Qutb Minar**. His successor, **Iltutmish** (1211–27), was arguably the greatest of the early Delhi Sultans.

In 1290, another group of Turks came to power – the Khaljis. Inspired by **Ala-ud-din-Khalji** (1296–1316), they extended their dominion to the Deccan in central India. His reign, the pinnacle of the Delhi Sultanate, was marked by agrarian reforms, and the establishment of **Siri**, the second city of Delhi in 1303. Near present-day Hauz Khas, it grew into a flourishing commercial centre. Ala-ud-din died a disappointed man, as cracks appeared in his dream of empire; the ensuing period of confusion only ended when **Ghiyas-ud-din Tughluq** proclaimed himself Sultan in 1320.

Ghiyas-ud-din in turn built a city fortress, at **Tughluqabad**, 8km east of Qutb, but Delhi's third city was occupied for just five years from 1321; apart from the ramparts encompassing the crumbling ruins, and the odd building and tomb, little of it now remains. It was replaced by the fourth, **Jahanpanah**, built between Lal Kot and Siri by the eccentric Muhammad bin Tughluq to protect the vulnerable open plain; that scheme also failed, and the capital was briefly and unsuccessfully transferred south 1100km to Daulatabad in the Deccan in 1328. The energies of the next Sultan, **Firuz Shah**, were taken up with suppressing rebellion, as the Sultanate began to disintegrate, but his reputation as an iconoclast is belied by his keen interest in Indian culture and history. Fascinated by the Ashokan pillars of Meerut and Topra, he had them moved to the new capital, the fifth city of **Firozabad**, built beside the river in 1354.

The Tughluq line came to an end in 1398, when **Timur** (Tamerlane), a Central Asian Turk, sacked Delhi. His successors, the Sayyids (1414–50), were ousted by Buhlul **Lodi**, who established a dynasty that left behind the fine pieces of architecture still to be seen in the **Lodi Gardens**. Ibrahim Lodi made many enemies, and the governors of Punjab and Sind invited **Babur**, a descendant of Genghis Khan and Timur, who was seeking his fortune in Afghanistan, to come to their aid. Lodi died in battle, fighting the brilliant and enigmatic Babur on the plain of Panipat just north of Delhi in 1526. That heralded the start of Babur's new dynasty, the **Moghuls** (a derivative of Mongol), who eventually achieved the dream of an Indian empire that had eluded the Delhi Sultans. Babur's reign was brief, and he moved his capital to Agra not long after taking Delhi; his *Babarnama*, a chronicle of the times, makes fascinating reading.

Babur was succeeded in 1530 by his son, Humayun, a scholar and astronomer who moved to Delhi in 1534. Here he built the fort, **Din-Panah**, or Asylum of Faith, which still stands on the banks of the Yamuna in the southwest of modern Delhi and is known as **Purana Qila**. All the signs indicated that Humayun's reign would be prosperous, but in 1540 the Afghan Sher Shah laid siege to Delhi and he fled to Persia. Sher Shah began the construction of a new citadel around Humayun's fort – the sixth city of **Shergarh** – but the string of bickering power-thirsty relatives who followed him were overcome when Humayun returned from Kabul to retake Delhi in 1555. When Humayun died in a fall in 1556, his son **Akbar** (who could not read or write) took over as emperor, and the capital was moved once more to Agra.

Delhi once again became capital under Prince Khurrum, Akbar's grandson, in 1628, who assumed the title **Shah Jahan**, "Ruler of the Universe", and began a fruitful reign that oversaw the construction of some of the finest Moghul monuments, including the Taj Mahal in Agra. The new walled capital of **Shahjahanabad**, the seventh city, which is now Old Delhi, incorporated the mighty Red Fort with its opulent courts and the huge Jami Masjid mosque, fringed by bazaars. Shah Jahan was deposed (and imprisoned in Agra) by his ruthless son, **Aurangzeb**, who ruled from Delhi until 1681, when he transferred the capital to the Deccan.

For the next sixty years Delhi's government was controlled by courtiers, and the city fell victim to repeated invasions. In 1739 Nadir Shah, the emperor of Persia, swept across north India and overcame Muhammad Shah in the Red Fort, taking away precious booty and wiping out much of the local population. Soon after, in 1760, the Hindu Marathas and Jats, unhappy with Moghul supremacy, combined forces against the rulers and besieged and looted the Red Fort, but did not take power.

The Moghul rulers were reduced to puppet kings, and the **British**, who had already gained footholds in Madras and Bengal under the guise of the East India Company, moved to Delhi in 1803 during the reign of the blind Moghul emperor,

Bahadur Shah. They swiftly took control, leaving Bahadur with his palace and his pension, but no power. British forces fended off a number of Maratha attacks in the next decade, and faced determined opposition during 1857 when the Indian Mutiny (or "First War of Independence") broke out. Bahadur Shah was proclaimed Hindustani Emperor in the Red Fort, and it took much bloodshed before the British regained the city.

The British retained a hold on Delhi while administering affairs of state from their capital in Calcutta. When King George V came to India from England to be crowned as Emperor in 1911, it was decided to make Delhi India's new **capital**. Fervent construction of grand houses, parliamentary buildings and public offices followed, and in 1931 Delhi was officially inaugurated as the capital of Britain's largest colonial possession.

With India's declaration of **Independence** in 1947, the British, represented in Delhi by the Viceroy Lord Mountbatten, lost all authority, and the democratically elected Congress Government came to power with Nehru at its head. The recent history of Delhi is entwined with that of the country as a whole, and the capital continues to grow as a commercial and governmental centre.

Arrival

Delhi is India's main point of arrival for overseas visitors, and has two **airports**. **State buses** from all over the country pull into the Inter-state Bus Terminal in Old Delhi, while private buses stop in the more central location close to New Delhi Railway Station. **Trains** arrive at the railheads in Old or New Delhi, both well-connected to Connaught Place, the commercial centre of the city, by rickshaws and taxis.

For a summary of the kinds of accommodation available in different areas of the city, which may well determine where you head first, see p.101. In short, **Connaught Place**, the heart of New Delhi and packed with banks, restaurants and shops, caters for all budgets, while there are cheaper options in **Paharganj**, close to New Delhi railway station, and **Old Delhi**. See also the colour **map** of Delhi in the centre of the book.

By air

International flights land at **Indira Gandhi International Airport** (☎329 4410 or 565 2011), 23km southwest of the centre (formerly Palam airport). The *State Bank of India* in the airport is open 24 hours for changing money; be sure to get some small change for taxis and rickshaws. If you want to book accommodation, head for the 24-hour **ITDC** desk in the departure hall which has a list of approved hotels and will secure reservations by phone on the spot. **Beware** of bogus booking counters: there have been many cases of trickery and overcharging. Not all budget hotels accept telephone bookings; for these you'll have to make your own way into town (see below). There's another small tourist office at the **domestic airport**, 15km southwest of town (☎329 5126). **Retiring rooms** at both airports are convenient if you wish to stay overnight to make an early connection (④–⑤), but are issued on a first-come-first-served basis.

From the international airport, the least expensive and least convenient way to **get into Delhi** is by **bus**. Tickets for the *Ex-servicemen's* shuttle (*EATS*) are issued in the departure hall, while State Transport buses wait outside; both take roughly thirty minutes to reach the city centre. Expect to pay Rs20, plus an additional Rs5 for luggage. All buses go via the domestic terminal, from where it is a twenty-minute ride into the city (18 daily; Rs12), and stop at Janpath, in New Delhi. The driver may be able to drop you close to your chosen hotel.

Taxis are faster (20min) and more comfortable, and should certainly be taken if you arrive late at night. Book at the pre-paid kiosk just outside the departure hall. Fixed

ONWARD TRANSPORT CONNECTIONS

For details of **onward transport connections** from Delhi, both international and domestic, and including specific train recommendations, see p.119 onwards.

rates (Rs200–250) apply, with a 25 percent surcharge between 11pm and 5am. Picking up a non-registered taxi near the bus rank is not recommended; this frequently results in extortionate prices and even claims that your hotel is full, closed, or even burned down. Ignore such assertions – and remember it's best to phone ahead. The **rickshaws** that wait in line at the departure gate are less expensive than taxis (Rs100–150), but constitute the most precarious and least reliable form of transport from the airport. Many tourists have complained of being taken to a hotel other than the one requested, and being hassled for more money on arrival. It makes sense to settle in for a while before you try using one.

By train
Delhi has two major **railway stations**. **New Delhi Station** is east of Paharganj (Main Bazaar), and within walking distance of many of the area's hotels, though tourists burdened with luggage often prefer to hail a cycle rickshaw to reach their hotel, which shouldn't cost more than Rs15 – negotiate the fare in advance. If you're heading for hotels south of the station, however, bear in mind that cycle rickshaws cannot enter Connaught Place. You can take an auto-rickshaw (insist the meter is turned on or negotiate a price) or book a reliable pre-paid taxi at the booth, close to the main road at the front of the railway station. **Delhi Station** in Old Delhi, west of the Red Fort, is connected to the city hotels by taxis (not pre-paid) and auto-rickshaws. Both stations have **retiring rooms** (②–③), and are notorious for theft: don't take your eyes off your luggage for a moment. Lesser stations in the Delhi area include **Hizrat Nizamuddin**, south of the centre on the main line into New Delhi.

By bus
State buses pull in at the Inter-state Bus Terminal, north of the train station in Old Delhi. Auto-rickshaws to New Delhi or Paharganj take about fifteen minutes (around Rs50), cycle rickshaws twice that (around Rs30). **Private buses** from all over India terminate outside New Delhi train station; some will drop passengers in Connaught Place if they pass that way.

Information and communications

There are reasonably helpful tourist offices at the international and domestic airports, railway stations and bus terminals. However, the best place to pick up information on Delhi's sites, city tours, shopping, cultural events and accommodation, and free maps – which are also sold at negotiable prices on the street – is the **Government of India tourist office** at 88 Janpath, just south of Connaught Place (Mon–Fri 10am–5pm, Sat 10am–2pm; ☎332 0005). Steer clear of tourist offices along the same road that claim to be "government authorized" – there is no such authorization and you're likely to end up paying well over the odds for any services.

The telephone **area code** for Delhi is ☎011.

Banks and currency exchange

You can exchange money at the international airport's 24-hour branch of the **State Bank of India**, but there are no facilities for withdrawing money on a credit card. Banks in the city (Mon–Fri 10am–2pm & Sat 10am–noon or 1pm) include *American Express*, A-Block, Connaught Place (Mon–Sat 9.30am–7pm); *ANZ Grindlays*, 10 E-Block, Connaught Place; *Andhra Bank*, 35 M-Block, Connaught Place; *B Bank of Baroda* (for *Visa* encashments); *State Bank of India*, Sansad Marg; and *Thomas Cook* at the *Hotel Imperial* on Janpath. In addition, all major **hotels** offer exchange; the *Ashoka* in Chanakyapuri changes currency for non-residents even on Sundays.

Mail services

Delhi's main **poste restante** is at the back of the **Foreign Post Office** (Mon–Sat 10am–4.30pm) on Bhai Vir Singh Marg (formerly Market Rd), easier to reach by rickshaw than by foot. You must show your passport to claim mail, and check the register for parcels. Letters sent to "Poste Restante, Delhi", rather than to New Delhi, may end up in **Old Delhi GPO**, north of the railway line on Mahatma Gandhi Rd. You can also have mail sent to the Government of India tourist office, 88 Janpath, who pass any parcels to the Foreign Post Office.

Other **post offices** are on Janpath and on A-Block, Connaught Place; all have a **speed post** service, and you can guarantee next-day delivery of parcels and papers to all international destinations with *Overnite Express Pvt Ltd*, whose office is in Kanishka Shopping Plaza, Janpath.

Telephone and fax

Making international **telephone** calls from Delhi has become increasingly easy in recent years. STD booths, marked with yellow signs, have direct-dialling facilities and display the length and cost of each call. Several will allow you to receive incoming calls.

More and more STD booths are installing **fax** machines which are clearly advertised. Most of the booths in Paharganj operate round the clock and store incoming faxes until collection. You can also send faxes from post offices and outlets in Connaught Place. Rates are usually by the page, with around Rs10 charged for incoming faxes. Expensive hotels let residents use their fax machines at inflated prices.

Publications

For details of exhibitions or cultural events in Delhi, pick up a local **magazine** from any bookstore or street stall (and see p.116). The excellent weekly *Delhi Diary* lists useful information on current events, lectures, exhibitions, films and what's on TV, and has a comprehensive directory and map; *First City* is packed with listings, articles and a city directory.

The pocket-sized *Genesis – The City Guide* also has articles and listings, plus a clear guide to what's on and a basic **map**. Travel tips, and train and airline timetables within Delhi and further afield, can be found in the monthly *Travel Links*. *City Scan* (monthly) has features on topical issues from sports and arts to politics and industry.

City transport

In the absence of the much-promised underground metro system, Delhi's **public transport** remains ill-equipped to cope with the city's size and ever-increasing complexity. Buses and a few suburban trains carry most of the burden, though many visitors prefer to pay more for auto-rickshaws and taxis.

Buses

Despite running more than 300 different routes, the *Delhi Transport Corporation*'s vast centralized **bus network** can seem totally inadequate. Guides (in Hindi) to their own routes, and those run by other state transport corporations, are available from their office, near the tourist office at Scindia House, Janpath (☎251 9083 or 331 9847). The first digit of each three-digit route number shows the direction of each bus – thus routes starting with "5" head south from the centre towards Mehrauli, and those starting with "4" travel southeast towards Kalkaji. Specific services useful for tourists include #454 between Connaught Place and Nizamuddin, #505 to Mehrauli and the Qutb Minar, #620 to Chanakyapuri, and #101 and #139 between the *Regal Cinema* bus stand (beside *Park Hotel*) and the Red Fort. **Night buses** start with the digit "0", such as #055 which passes Nizamuddin on its way to Connaught Circus. All buses are liable to get hideously overcrowded – **women** travellers will appreciate the row of seats on the left of each which is reserved exclusively for their use.

Minibuses and private buses, such as the **"Green"** and the slightly more expensive **"White"** lines ply many of the same routes, and are often less congested. A Ring Service runs around the Ring Road, both clockwise (marked with a "+") and anti-clockwise ("-"). **Railway Specials** connect outlying stations with the centre; #42 to Tughluqabad is handy for visitors to the ancient fort.

Auto-rickshaws and cycle rickshaws

Auto-rickshaws (or "autos") – scooters converted into three-wheeler taxis – can be extremely useful in Delhi's chaotic traffic, though they catch the worst of the polluting exhaust fumes since their open sides are level with larger vehicles' exhaust pipes. In theory they should charge what's shown on the meter, but even on the rare occasions when their meters are working, the rates tend to be out of date, and liable to supplements according to a table which drivers are required to carry but sometimes don't (saying "chart dekhao" – show me the chart – can help). For most journeys, it's simplest just to agree on a price before you set out; by way of example, at the time this book went to press Paharganj to Connaught Place cost Rs15 maximum, Red Fort to Connaught Place is more like Rs30. Try to avoid catching the rickshaws that hang around major tourist centres: even crossing the road from a hotel entrance can make for a better price.

Four- or six-seater autos, some built on ancient but immaculately kept **Harley Davidsons**, also ply certain fixed routes for flat fees. The most useful link is between the Red Fort (Old Delhi) and Palika Bazaar (Connaught Place) which will set you back a mere Rs5. **Cycle rickshaws** are not allowed in Connaught Place and parts of New Delhi, but are handy for short routes in outlying areas and in Paharganj, and nippier than motorized traffic in Old Delhi.

Taxis

Taxis, which charge around 70 percent more than auto-rickshaws – thus Red Fort to Connaught Circus costs in the region of Rs55 – are considered to be the most reliable mode of transport. Drivers belong to local taxi stands, where you can make bookings and fix prices; if you flag a taxi down on the street you're letting yourself in for some hectic haggling. Between 11pm and 5am, there is a surcharge of around 25 percent.

Car and cycle rental

The cheapest and most reliable outlets for chauffeur-driven *Ambassador* cars, for local sightseeing and journeys beyond the city confines, are the tourist office, 88 Janpath, and the booths at the southern end of the Tibetan Market on Janpath; most are willing to negotiate a price. Private travel agencies throughout Delhi usually charge more, but can be excellent value. If you want the option of self-drive, and don't mind paying extra to brave Delhi's notoriously dangerous roads, try *Budget*, G3 Arunchal Building, Barakhamba Rd (☎331 8600), which charges around $50 per day for self drive and $20 for chauffeur driven, or *Wheels*, 4–5 Kanchenjunga Building, Barakhamba Rd (☎331 8695), whose prices are slightly lower at $35 per day, self drive.

Cycling in the large avenues of New Delhi takes some getting used to, but a bike can be handy for reaching the various sites. **Bicycle rental** is surprisingly difficult to come by; there's a small hire shop a few doors down from *Hotel Vivek* in Paharganj.

City and regional tours

The tourist office, 88 Janpath, organizes morning tours of New Delhi (daily 8am–1pm; Rs80) and afternoon tours of Old Delhi (daily 2.15pm–5.00pm; Rs70), and a combined tour of Old and New Delhi (8am–5pm; Rs140), all starting at *Ashok Yatri Niwas Hotel*, Janpath, and can supply guides if you prefer to travel under your own steam. Alternatives include those run by *American Express Travel Service*, A-Block, Connaught Place (☎332 4119), whose *Delhi Durbar* tour, led by an English speaking guide and supplemented by leaflets in 5 languages, includes a discounted lunch at *The Holiday Inn* (full day Rs250; half-day Rs150). All the 5-star hotels offer their own, more expensive, tours. Longer trips to destinations such as Agra and Jaipur can be arranged through the tourist office, or any reputable travel agent, such as *Royal Express*, Moghul Tours and Travels, 16 KG Marg, Connaught Place (☎371 6611).

The City

Delhi is both daunting and alluring, a sprawling metropolis with a stunning backdrop of ancient architecture. One you've found your feet and got over the initial impact of the commotion, noise, pollution and sheer scale of the place, the city's geography slowly slips into focus. Monuments in sandstone and marble, which stand in assorted states of repair, make Delhi a veritable museum of Indo-Islamic architecture, seen at its best in the frenetic streets of **Old Delhi** and the venerable sites of **South Delhi**. Delhi today, however, as experienced by its many thousands of visitors, centres very much around the imperial city built by the British from 1911 onwards. Most foreign travellers to India find it necessary to call in at some of the myriad of administrative offices that fill the formal buildings of **Connaught Place**, the heart of **New Delhi**. From here it's easy to visit one of many outstanding **museums**, stocked with artistic treasures from all over the country and recording the lives of India's political figureheads. For a map of Delhi, see colour insert no.3 in the centre of the book.

Old Delhi (Shahjahanabad)

Alhough it's not in fact the oldest part of Delhi, the seventeenth-century city of **Shahjahanabad**, built by the Moghul emperor, Shah Jahan, is known as **OLD DELHI**. The original city walls spread for seven miles, enclosing the sprawling fort, **Lal Qila**, and the formidable **Jami Masjid**, or "Friday Mosque". Old Delhi's main thoroughfare, **Chandni Chowk**, a seething mass of hooting, pushing cars, tempos, cycle rickshaws and ox carts, was once a sublime canal lined with trees and some of the most opulent bazaars of the East. Today the city walls have crumbled, and houses and shops have long since spilled beyond the remaining five of the fourteen old gates.

On the west bank of the River Yamuna northeast of the modern centre, Old Delhi resembles an overgrown village of tight-knit communities, alive with intriguing contradictions and contrasts. Photographers huddled at the east end of Chandni Chowk using rickety equipment left over from the days of the Raj are overlooked by garish film

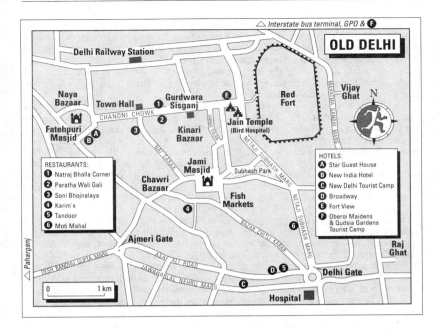

boards and advertisements for sex clinics, while the bazaars in the back alleys have changed little since the eighteenth and nineteenth centuries. It's a fascinating area, but you'll need stamina, patience and time to endure the crowds and traffic, and pursue a rewarding exploration of the city's streets, mosques, temples and *guradwaras*.

Lal Qila (Red Fort)

The largest of Old Delhi's monuments is **Lal Qila**, or Red Fort (daily dawn–dusk; Rs0.50), whose thick red sandstone walls, bulging with turrets and bastions, rise above a wide dry moat in the northeast corner of the original city of Shahjahanabad. The fort covers a semi-octagonal area of almost 2km, its longest walls facing the town in the west and the River Yamuna in the east. Work was started on the fort – modelled on the royal citadel in Agra – in 1639, and it was completed by 1648. It contains all the expected trappings of the centre of Moghul government: halls of public and private audience, domed and arched marble palaces, plush private apartments, a mosque, and elaborately designed gardens. Today the Yamuna no longer flows close to the east wall, the "Stream of Paradise" no longer trickles through each palace, copper-plated domes have been replaced with plainer marble domes, and there are few signs of the precious stones and gems once set into the marble walls. Nevertheless, the fort remains an impressive testimony to Moghul grandeur, despite being attacked and plundered by the Persian emperor Nadir Shah in 1739, and by British soldiers during the battles of 1857 – as well as being rubbed, touched and worn down by marvelling tourists.

Entrance to the fort is through the mighty three-storey **Lahori Gate** in the centre of the west wall. A booking office sells tickets just outside, and eager guides will offer their services at negotiable prices (Rs20–50) – generally more than twice the price that you'd pay within. The main entrance opens onto **Chatta Chowk**, a covered street flanked with arched cells that used to house Delhi's most talented jewellers, carpet makers, goldsmiths and silk weavers, but now stock the usual souvenirs: miniatures, *hookahs*, brass ornaments, stone and wood carvings and low-quality jewellery. Just beyond a small restaurant at the end of Chatta Chowk, the road stretches past the military colony into the heart of the fort, coming to an end at **Naubhat Khana**, the erstwhile "drum house", where music was once played five times a day and which now bears scant remains of its original painting.

From Naubhat Khana, a path runs east through wide lawns to the hall of public audience, the **Diwan-i-Am**. This lofty hall, with sturdy pillars supporting its roof and its floor raised on a high platform, was the scene of daily public appearances by the emperor until the custom was stopped by Aurangzeb. When in use it was laid with silk carpets and partitioned with hanging tapestries and curtains. Set against the west wall is "the seat of the shadow of God", a marble throne surrounded by twelve panels inlaid with precious stones. It was designed by an artist from Bordeaux, whose frieze of the Greek god Orpheus with his lute makes a surprising departure from the more usual floral designs of the Moghuls. Lord Curzon, Viceroy of India from 1898 to 1905, restored the hall and returned the emperor's seat from the British Museum in 1909.

The **palaces** in the fort along the east wall face spacious gardens in the west and overlook the banks of the Yamuna, once the scene of animal fights laid on to entertain the royal occupants. Immediately east of the Diwan-i-Am, **Rang Mahal**, the "Palace of Colour", housed the emperor's wives and mistresses. "The crowning jewel of Shah Jahan's seraglio" was crowned with gilded turrets, delicately painted and decorated with intricate mosaics of mirrors, and with a ceiling overlaid with gold and silver that was reflected in a central pool in the marble floor. Unfortunately, it was greatly defaced when the British used it as an Officers' Mess after the Mutiny, and today is a shadow of its former glory. The similar **Mumtaz Mahal**, south of the main *zenana*, or women's quarters, and probably used by princesses is now a **museum** (daily except Fri 10am–5pm) housing weaponry, textiles, carpets, ornate chess sets and *hookahs*.

On the northern side of Rang Mahal, the marble **Khas Mahal** was the personal palace of the emperor, divided into separate apartments for worship, sleeping and sitting. The southern chamber, **Tosh Khana** (robe room), has a stunning marble filigree screen on its north wall, carved with the scales of justice. Viewing the screen from the north you'll see suns surrounding the scales, but from the south these look more like moons. The octagonal tower projecting over the east wall of the Khas Mahal was used by the emperor, who would appear here daily before throngs gathered on the river banks below. In 1911, when Delhi was declared capital, King George V (Emperor of India) and Queen Mary sat here before the citizens of Delhi.

North of Khas Mahal, in the large **Diwan-i-Khas** (hall of private audience), the emperor would address the highest nobles of his court. Today it's the finest building in the fort, a marble pavilion shaded by a roof raised on stolid pillars embellished with amber, jade and gold, meeting in ornate scalloped arches. On the north and south walls you can still make out the Persian inscription attributed to Shah Jahan's prime minister:

Agar Firdaus bar ru-e-zamin ast
Hamin ast o hamin ast o hamin ast.

(If there be paradise on the face of earth,
It is this, Oh, it is this, Oh, it is this.)

A marble and gold peacock throne inlaid with rubies, sapphires and diamonds once stood on the central pedestal, bypassed by a stream that gurgled through the cool chamber. It took seven years to construct, and was the pride of the fort, but the Persian Nadir Shah took it back to his kingdom as booty after a raid in 1739.

A little further north are the **hammams**, or royal baths, sunken into the marble floor inlaid with delicate patterns of precious stones, and dappled in jewel-coloured light that

SOUND AND LIGHT SHOWS

Each night a **Sound and Light Show** takes place in the **Red Fort**: the palaces are dramatically lit, and a historical commentary blares from crackly loudspeakers. The show starts after sunset and lasts an hour (Rs10 and Rs20; in **Hindi** 7pm Feb–April & Sept–Oct, 7.30pm May–Aug, 6pm Nov–Jan; in **English** 8.30pm Feb–April & Sept–Oct, 9pm May–Aug, 7.30pm Nov–Jan; ☎327 4580). Heavy monsoon rains may affect summer shows.

filters through stained-glass windows. The western chamber contained hot baths while the eastern apartment, with fountains of rose water, was used as a dressing room.

West of the baths the tiny **Moti Masjid**, built by Aurangzeb, is beautifully proportioned, but desperately in need of maintenance. In the gardens beyond, pavilions stand among symmetrical flower beds and neat lawns intersected by stream-beds that once bubbled with water drawn from the Yamuna.

Jami Masjid

Old Delhi's red and white **Jami Masjid** (Rs10; Rs5 camera), dominating the surrounding markets around 500m to the west of the Red Fort, may look huge from a distance, but feels nothing short of immense once you've climbed the wide staircases to the arched gateways and entered the open courtyard, large enough to accommodate the bending bodies of up to 25,000 worshippers. This is India's largest mosque, designed by the eminent architect Shah Jahan, and built by a workforce of 5000 between 1644 and 1656. Originally called *Masjid-i-Jahanuma* ("mosque commanding a view of the world"), this grand structure stands on Bho Jhala, one of Shahjahanabad's two hills, and looks east to the sprawling Red Fort, and down on the seething streets of Old Delhi all around. Broad red sandstone staircases lead to gateways on the east, north and southern sides, where all visitors must remove their shoes and pay the entrance fee. If you're wearing shorts, you'll have to rent a *lunghi* to wrap around your legs and hide your knees.

Once inside the stadium-like courtyard, your eyes will be drawn to the three bulbous marble domes crowning the **main prayer hall** on the west side (facing Mecca), fronted by a series of high cusped arches, and sheltering the *mihrab*, the central niche in the west wall reserved for the prayer leader. Worshippers use the prayer hall on most days, extending into the courtyard and even filling it on Fridays and other holy days: it's particularly busy during Ramadan. The pool in the centre is used for washing feet, hands and faces before prayer. At each corner of the square yard a slender minaret crowned with a marble dome rises to the sky, and it's well worth climbing the tower south of the main sanctuary (Rs5; Rs5 camera) for an unrivalled view over Delhi, ancient and modern. In the northeast corner a white shrine protects a collection of Muhammad's relics, shrouded in pungent rose petals and watched over by keepers who are keen to reveal the contents, for a small *baksheesh*: two sections of the Koran written on deerskin by relatives of the prophet, a red beard-hair of Muhammad's, his sandals, and his "footprint" miraculously embedded in a marble slab.

Digambara Jain temple and Jain Bird Hospital

Delhi's oldest **Digambara Jain temple**, directly opposite the entrance to the Red Fort, at the east end of Chandni Chowk, was built in 1526, but modified and added to ever since, and remains a haven of tranquillity amid the noise and chaos of the main street. Though not as ornate as the fine temples in Gujarat and Rajasthan, it does boast detailed carvings, and gilded paintwork in the antechambers surrounding the main shrine to Parshvanath, the twenty-third *tirthankara*. You'll have to remove your shoes, and hand them over with your bags and all leather articles to a kiosk before entering.

THE BAZAARS OF OLD DELHI

Old Delhi's trading is carried out in bustling **bazaars**, where shops huddle together in open houses or beneath makeshift awnings, and between them stock an incredible array of goods ranging from fish and spices to currency garlands and giant candles. If you take time to amble down streets branching off **Chandni Chowk** and running south of the mosque, you'll come across lively markets of all kinds, each concentrating on one particular trade.

Chor Bazaar A curious bazaar behind the old ramparts of the Red Fort, which comes to life on Sundays to trade a mix of "second-hand" and allegedly stolen goods.

Kinari Bazaar A colourful street set behind the *guradwara* on Chandni Chowk, and connected to the main road by Dariba Kalan, "the street of incomparable pearl", which is the centre for jewellers. The shops in Kinari Bazaar overflow with bright wedding finery, including garlands made of rupee notes, grooms' turbans, rosettes and glistening tinsel used by Hindus, Christians and Muslims in vivid and noisy marriage ceremonies. In October (the month of Ram Lila) the shops stock props for the annual theatre productions – bows and arrows, cardboard swords and fake heads for the evil nine-headed King Ravana.

Naya Bazaar Spice market on Khari Baoli, near Fatehpuri Masjid, clouded with the fine dust of flour and spices, and heavy with rich aromas. The nuts, spices and dried fruits sold here are said to be the best in Delhi, and many are sold to wholesalers by the sack; weighed-down porters load their burdens onto ox carts which trundle off to other parts of the city through the mass of motorized traffic. The covered **Gadodia Market**, just off Khari Baoli, is a gathering place for wholesalers who weigh their goods on huge old-fashioned scales. Among the spices and condiments you can find aniseed, turmeric, pomegranate, dried mangoes, ginger, saffron, *reetha* nuts (used for washing hair and cleaning silver), lotus seeds, pickles, sugars, chutneys and edible leaves of silver paper used to coat sweets and cakes.

Meena Bazaar A distinctively Islamic bazaar of cramped shops clustered around the base of the Jami Masjid, full of clothes, domestic implements and smells not found in Hindu regions of the city. Here you can buy *burquas, dupattas, topis*, caged chickens, bangles, kebabs, sticky sweetmeats and devotional pictures of shrines.

Car Parts Bazaar South of the Jami Masjid, the stalls that make up this bazaar stock, or rather pile high, new and secondhand automobile parts from all models, ranging from speedometers and the all-important horn to complete engines.

Chawri Bazaar Named after the Marathi word *chawri* (meeting place), a street running west from the Jami Masjid that was once flanked by huge mansions, destroyed by the British after the Mutiny. In the nineteenth century it was famous for its "dancing girls", who looked into the streets below from arched windows and balconies and beckoned men with enticing glances; they were moved out by the Delhi Municipal Corporation in the twentieth century. Today the shops specialize in copper and brass Buddhas, Vishnus, Krishnas, bells, lamps, ashtrays, masks and boxes. The long road, **Nai Sarak**, which connects Chawri Bazaar with Chandni Chowk, is lined with nineteenth- and twentieth-century buildings whose lower storeys are used for making and selling paper, and houses shops stocking educational books and stationery.

Kalan Mahal A small market street further south of the Jami Masjid near the Kalan Masjid, Kalan Mahal is the gathering place for brass polishers, and also has stalls displaying intricately carved bone necklaces.

Poultry and Fish Markets East of Kalan Mahal the air is filled with the unmistakable smell of fish. Piled high on lorries and stored in barrels of ice, transported between cramped stalls on the heads of porters, every imaginable kind of fish is traded here before finding its way onto plates all over the city. In between fish stalls, chickens lie cramped in stacked cages before being slaughtered and plucked. Head towards **Netaji Subash Marg** to get into the thick of the poultry scene, and watch out for the "cul-de-sacs" in the fish market. While most traders sleep at the back of their pungent patches, few visitors can stand more than half an hour in Old Delhi's smelliest corner.

The **Jain Bird Hospital**, in the temple courtyard, puts into practice the Jain principle that all life is sacred, admitting up to sixty sick birds per day. It serves as a rescue sanctuary for partridges, caught and wounded by fowlers and bought in bulk by Jain merchants who bring them here to recover, and there are separate wards for pigeons, parrots, sparrows (notoriously vulnerable to deadly whirring ceiling fans) and domestic fowl. Squirrels, who will not hurt the birds, are also treated here, but birds of prey are seen on a strictly out-patient basis, as they are not vegetarian. Most of the cages are home to pigeons with a disease that brings on paralysis. As their condition improves they are moved to larger cages closer to the roof, and eventually released. There's no entrance fee, but donations are appreciated.

Gauri Shankar temple

Tucked behind fragrant mounds of marigolds, roses and jasmine blossoms sold on Chandni Chowk just west of the Jain temple, the large marble **Gauri Shankar temple**, dominated by its eight-hundred-year-old *lingam*, is Delhi's holiest Shiva temple. Devotees enter up a narrow flight of marble steps, flanked by pillars carved with chains and bells, that opens onto a spacious courtyard, always a scene of animated devotional activity. Inside, offerings for sale include *bilva* (wood apple) leaves, *chandan* (sandalwood paste), marigolds, red powder, rice, and cotton threads. The main sanctuary holds bejewelled statues of Gauri (Parvati) and Shankar (Shiva) standing beneath a silver canopy, and the ancient brown stone *lingam* resting on a marble *yoni* encased in silver and draped with silver serpents. Shrines to other deities line the south wall.

Raj Ghat

When Shah Jahan established his city in 1638, its eastern edges bordered the River Yamuna, a line of *ghats*, or steps leading to the water, was installed along the river banks. *Ghats* have been used in India for centuries, primarily for worship, but also for washing clothes and bathing, and for the final ritual, cremation. **Raj Ghat**, the site of the cremations of three of modern India's most revered figures, Mahatma Gandhi (1948), Indira Gandhi (1984) and her son Rajiv (1991), is more of a park than a *ghat*, lying well away from the river bank. The Mahatma's *samadhi*, a low black plinth, receives the attentions and prayers of an almost constant stream of visitors, many of them pilgrims. Walk northwards from here to the quieter memorials of the two former prime ministers, Rajiv remembered in a striking frieze and his mother marked by a red-grey stone monolith. You can continue through the park all the way to the southern end of the Red Fort, roughly 1km to the north.

Mahatma Gandhi is further remembered at his *samadhi* by prayers held every Friday evening, and on the anniversaries of his birth and death (Oct 2 & Jan 30), and by the small **Gandhi Memorial Museum** (daily except Thurs 9.30am–5.30pm) opposite Raj Ghat. On Sundays you can watch a film on Gandhi's political and personal life (Hindi 6pm, English 7pm; 4 & 5pm in winter) after taking in the displays of photographs and writings in the museum.

Firoz Shah Kotla

The prosperous fifth city of Delhi, **Firozabad**, was founded in 1354, and stretched from the north ridge to Hauz Khas in the south, but few traces survive save the remains of the palace of Firoz Shah Kotla, set amid ornamental gardens 500m east of Delhi Gate. Its most incongruous and yet distinctive element is the single polished sandstone **Ashokan Column** (third century BC), carried down the Yamuna by raft from Ambala to grace a palace that is now a crumbling ruin. The 14m-high column, the second brought to Delhi, continues to protrude above the surroundings, withstanding the ravages of time and dominating the ill-kept gardens. Next to a *baoli* (step-well) lie the massive ruins of a mosque which once accommodated over 10,000 worshippers; Timur (Tamerlane) is said to have been so impressed by it that it served as the model for his great mosque in Samarkand. Today, surrounded by large and busy roads, the gardens and their monuments lie almost forgotten and few tourists stop by.

North of the Old City

Just north of Old Delhi, not far from the Inter-state bus terminal, the peaceful **Qudsia Gardens** are a fading reminder of the magnificent pleasure gardens commissioned in the mid-eighteenth century by Queen Qudsia, favourite mistress of Muhammad Shah, and mother of Ahmed Shah. The original mosque still stands, but part of the park was taken over by the British Freemasons, who built a hall and banned Indians from entering the park in the afternoons. There's also a Hindu monument here; a mounted figure represents the valiant Pratap Singh who is famed for his unfaltering defiance of Akbar. Near the gardens, on Commissioner's Lane, is **Mother Teresa's Orphanage**, "Missionaries of Charity" where voluntary help is welcomed (see p.118).

Just west of Qudsia Gardens, on Qudsia Rd, Delhi's oldest burial ground, **Nicholson Cemetery**, is named after Brigadier General John Nicholson who led the attacks on Delhi in 1857 when the British were striving to regain the city from the Nationalists. The graveyard is still used, but most of the headstones show the names of British residents killed defending this outpost of the British Empire, or stricken as young children by fatal diseases at the start of the twentieth century.

Central New Delhi

The modern area of **CENTRAL NEW DELHI**, with its wide tree-lined avenues and solid colonial buildings, has been the seat of central government since 1931. At its hub, the royal mall, **Rajpath**, runs from the palatial **Rashtrapati Bhavan**, in the east, to **India Gate** war memorial, in the west. At the north edge of the new capital is the thriving business centre, **Connaught Place**, where neon advertisements for *Wimpy*, *American Express*, hotels and countless airline offices adorn the flat roofs and colonnaded verandahs of high white buildings that curve around a central park to form an almost perfect circle. Central New Delhi also has its fair share of more recent high-rise offices and hotels, standing close to pre-British constructions such as the open-air observatory, **Jantar Mantar**, and a generous smattering of excellent museums covering arts and crafts and the lives of India's post-Independence politicians.

Rashtrapati Bhavan and Rajpath

After George V, king of England and emperor of British India, decreed in 1911 that Delhi should replace Calcutta as the capital of India, the talented and ambitious English architect, **Edwin Lutyens**, was commissioned to plan the new governmental centre. **Rashtrapati Bhavan**, the official residence of the president of India, is one of the largest and most grandiose of the Raj constructions, built by Lutyens and Sir Herbert Baker between 1921 and 1929. Originally the Viceroy's House, this salmon-pink H-shaped structure on the gentle slope of Raisina Hill was built to dominate: a symbol asserting imperial power in the face of its doomed struggle against Indian Nationalism, it was home to Lord Mountbatten, appointed Viceroy in 1947 to supervise the transition to Independence. Its grandeur was considered nothing more than "vulgar ostentation and wasteful extravagance" by Motilal Nehru, while Mahatma Gandhi claimed that the construction of such "architectural piles" was "in conflict with the best interests of the nation".

Despite its classical columns, Moghul-style domes and *chhatris*, and Indian filigree work, the whole building is unmistakably British in character. The majestic proportions are best appreciated from India Gate to the east, from where you can see the perfectly balanced residence slightly raised on the hill, flanked in pleasing symmetry by the two Secretariat buildings below – though with increasing pollution, the view is often clouded by a smoggy haze. At closer quarters the height and multitude of pillars supporting the front verandahs are clearly seen, while the immensity of the central crowning copper dome, the dominating feature of the whole complex, is quite overwhelming. Between the entrance gates and the east side of the residence, the slender **Jaipur**

Column, donated by the Maharaja of Jaipur, rises to a height of 145m, piercing the sky with a glass star balanced on a bronze lotus blossom. Close to its base an early plan of New Delhi is etched onto a square panel. Troops and guards parade before the iron-grille gates each Saturday (9.35–10.15am) in a ceremony that is Delhi's answer to London's Changing of the Guard.

The apartments inside are strictly private, but the **gardens** at the west side are open to the public each February. Modelled on Moghul pleasure parks, with a typically ordered square pattern of quadrants dissected by waterways and refreshed by fountains, Lutyens' gardens extend beyond the normal confines to include eight tennis courts, butterfly enclosures, vegetable and fruit patches and a swimming pool. The immaculate flowerbeds contain many English varieties, and trees lining walkways are trimmed into perfect oblongs. In 1947, 418 staff worked in the gardens, fifty of whom were specifically employed to frighten away birds.

The **Secretariats** on the north and south side of Raisina Hill are an interesting synthesis of Moghul and colonial styles, topped with baroque domes overlaid with low-relief lotus motifs and elephants. Built by Baker, today they house the Home and Finance Ministries and the Ministry of Foreign Affairs.

Vijay Chowk, immediately in front of Rashtrapati Bhavan, leads into **Rajpath**, the wide straight road once known as King's Way, flanked with gardens and fountains that are floodlit at night, and the scene of annual **Republic Day** celebrations (Jan 26).

THE PARLIAMENT OF INDIA

The **Indian Parliament** in Delhi was formed under the British in 1931, and later tailored to the needs of the newly independent nation under the leadership of Jawaharlal Nehru. Today, Delhi's parliament closely follows the English model. It is made up of a politically neutral president, an upper house, the **Rajya Sabha** ("Council of States"), and a lower house, the **Lok Sabha** (literally "People's House"). Members represent all India's seventeen states and ten Union Territories, in numbers proportionate to each district's population. Thanks in part to the influence of Mahatma Gandhi, a quota of seats is reserved for "untouchables", or *Harijans*. Members of the Lok Sabha are elected every five years, and every two years elections replace one-third of the Rajya Sabha. The 1996 electoral results saw Congress lose their majority – which has been fairly constant since 1947 – and a fundamentalist BJP Prime Minister stepped in, only to resign after twelve days. The confusion created will ensure more unsettled debates in the future, as stability seems an unlikely prospect for the new government, whichever party takes over.

The Lok Sabha, the larger of the two houses, comprises up to 525 members, at least fifty of whom must be present to propose and pass bills. Only two or three times a year does the whole house attend. While bills may be put forward in either house, most originate in the Lok Sabha, and are passed to the Rajya Sabha for approval. Taxation, spending, budgets and government economy are discussed only in the lower house. Each day in the Lok Sabha begins with an hour of questions to the Speaker, when government policies are clarified, and opposition parties criticize and push for change.

The smaller Rajya Sabha, with 250 members, serves as more of an advisory body. It does, however, have the power to create or abolish states and alter boundaries – issues that were of particular importance between 1953 and 1956, when 562 principalities acceded and Congress demanded that territories should be determined by common language. The more recent formation of Punjab and Nagaland states and the Union Territory of Himachal Pradesh was also determined by the Rajya Sabha.

Despite their separate roles, the two houses meet for collective votes on bills that have not been passed by a majority, and to elect the parliamentary president. While the large membership and exhaustive screening of bills ensures the fullest consideration of political issues, government critics argue that the two-house system wastes energy, and thickens India's already stifling web of bureaucratic confusion.

Rajpath runs directly east to **India Gate**, the "All India War Memorial" designed by Lutyens in 1921. The high arch, reminiscent of the Arc de Triomphe in Paris, commemorates the 90,000 Indian soldiers killed fighting for the British in World War I, and bears the names of over three thousand British and Indian soldiers who died on the Northwest frontier and in the Afghan War of 1919. The extra memorial beneath the arch honours the lives lost in the Indo-Pakistan War of 1971.

Parliament House (Sansad Bhavan)

Northeast of Rashtrapati Bhavan at the end of Sansad Marg is **Parliament House**, now known as **Sansad Bhavan**. Planned by Lutyens and built under the supervision of Baker, the low circular structure covers more than five acres. Obliged to respond to complaints about its extravagant design and large costs, Baker himself referred to the unusual building as a "merrie-go-round", but successfully completed a momentous project. From outside, Parliament House presents an unbroken circle of high buff pillars, and a higher storey (not originally planned) that screens a central dome.

Inside, three semicircular chambers were built to house the Council of State, the Assembly Chamber and the Council of Princes. Today the latter, where leaders from India's princely states gathered until Independence, contains a **library** with a comprehensive collection of books and records detailing political history from the 1920s onwards. Vistors can look round when parliament is not in session; ask one of the desk-clerks in reception for permission. It's suitably formal, stuffy even, its walls overlaid with convex teak panels positioned at a downward angle to improve acoustics, and the coats of arms of India's royal families. The **Lok Sabha** now meets in the Assembly Chamber, and with permission from the reception office on Raisina Rd (and a letter of introduction for foreigners from a relevant embassy), visitors can watch debates from seats in the public gallery.

Connaught Place

The hub of New Delhi, **Connaught Place** could not be more different from the crowded centre of Old Delhi that it replaced. Conceived by Robert Tor Russell, Chief Architect of the Government of India, it is one of the few areas of the new city that was not designed by Lutyens, though its lofty facades and classical columns are derivative of the style he established with Rashtrapati Bhavan. Originally designed in the shape of a horseshoe, Connaught Place now forms a full circle, divided into blocks A–N by seven radial roads and rimmed by a busy outer Ring Road known as **Connaught Circus**. Note also that the whole area, from *Plaza Cinema* in the north to Jantar Mantar and Tolstoy Marg in the south, is commonly referred to as Connaught Place. Recent suggestions that the commercial districts should be renamed Indira Gandhi Chowk and Rajiv Gandhi Chowk gained popularity in 1995, but were later opposed on the grounds that *chowk* means square.

Connaught Place is rather grand for a commercial centre, with shops and offices housed in colonnaded buildings almost as splendid as the parliamentary headquarters further south. Unsurprisingly, considering its wealth of tourist facilities, including a glut of hotels and most of Delhi's restaurants, the area buzzes with touts and salesmen selling anything from airline tickets to five-metre-long leather whips.

From Connaught Place, **Sansad Marg** runs southwest to the parliamentary buildings, while southbound **Janpath**, with the busy Tibetan Market at its northern end, is lined with several modern hotels, Russell's majestic Eastern and Western Courts, and the Central Post and Telegraph Office. The park at the core of Connaught Place, and the grassy area over the underground Palika Bazaar, close to Janpath, offer respite from the busy streets, and provide the perfect arena for Delhi's ice-cream sellers, shoe-shiners, masseurs and flower-vendors, who peddle their wares from dawn to dusk.

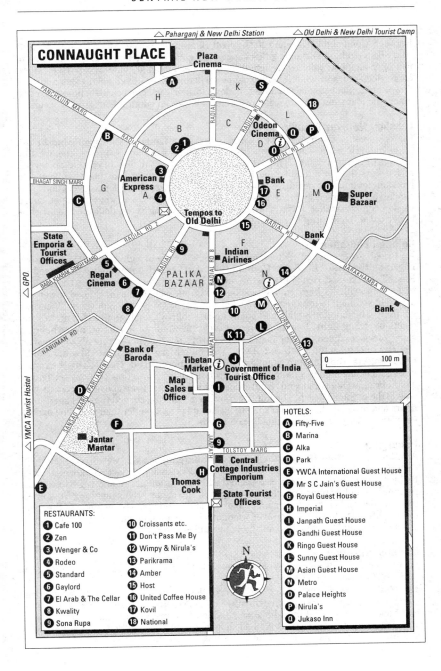

CONNAUGHT PLACE

△ Paharganj & New Delhi Station   △ Old Delhi & New Delhi Tourist Camp

Plaza Cinema

PANCHKUIN MARG

BHAGAT SINGH MARG

Odeon Cinema

American Express

Tempos to Old Delhi

Bank

Super Bazaar

State Emporia & Tourist Offices

GPO

Regal Cinema

PALIKA BAZAAR

Indian Airlines

Bank

BARA KHARAK SINGH MARG

BARAKHAMBA RD

Bank

HANUMAN RD

Bank of Baroda

Tibetan Market

Government of India Tourist Office

Map Sales Office

YMCA Tourist Hostel

SANSAD MARG (PARLIAMENT ST)

Jantar Mantar

JANPATH

KASTURBA GANDHI MARG

TOLSTOY MARG

Central Cottage Industries Emporium

Thomas Cook

State Tourist Offices

0   100 m

N

HOTELS:
- **A** Fifty-Five
- **B** Marina
- **C** Alka
- **D** Park
- **E** YWCA International Guest House
- **F** Mr S C Jain's Guest House
- **G** Royal Guest House
- **H** Imperial
- **I** Janpath Guest House
- **J** Gandhi Guest House
- **K** Ringo Guest House
- **L** Sunny Guest House
- **M** Asian Guest House
- **N** Metro
- **O** Palace Heights
- **P** Nirula's
- **Q** Jukaso Inn

RESTAURANTS:
- **1** Cafe 100
- **2** Zen
- **3** Wenger & Co
- **4** Rodeo
- **5** Standard
- **6** Gaylord
- **7** El Arab & The Cellar
- **8** Kwality
- **9** Sona Rupa
- **10** Croissants etc.
- **11** Don't Pass Me By
- **12** Wimpy & Nirula's
- **13** Parikrama
- **14** Amber
- **15** Host
- **16** United Coffee House
- **17** Kovil
- **18** National

Jantar Mantar

Between Connaught Place and Rashtrapati Bhavan on Sansad Marg, **Jantar Mantar** (daily 9am–7pm; Rs1) stands little changed since its construction in 1725 as the first of five open-air observatories designed by the ruler of Jaipur, Jai Singh II (see p.134). Huge deep-red and white slanting stone structures loom over palm trees and neat flower beds, giant sundials that cast shadows formerly used to calculate time, solar and lunar calendars and astrological movements, all with an admirable degree of accuracy.

Lakshmi Narayan Mandir

Directly west of Connaught Place on Mandir Marg, **Lakshmi Narayan Mandir** is a large modern temple also known as Birla Mandir after its sponsors, the wealthy Marwari Birla merchants. The extravagant temple, built mainly of marble on several raised tiers, lies in attractive gardens. In front of the main sanctuary, dedicated to Lakshmi (goddess of wealth), a large prayer hall is the scene of silent prayers and jovial singing accompanied by *tabla* and *bhaja*. Marble passages, stairways and open courtyards connect smaller shrines, which include a dazzling room dedicated to Krishna bedecked with coloured stones and mirrors.

Colonial churches

No British governmental centre could be complete without a church, and in 1927 work began on the **Church of the Redemption**, east of Parliament House. Designed by Russell's successor, Henry Medd, the robust structure owes more than a passing nod to Lutyens with its high curved vaults, and subtle yet dominant domed tower – it appealed so much to the then-Viceroy, Lord Irwin, that it became known as "Viceroy's Church". The exterior is plain and boldly linear, while within, high rounded arches and shafts of strong light streaming through crescent windows impart an overwhelming sense of space. A company of angels looks down from the curved roof above the altar.

Further north, at the south end of Bhai Vir Singh Marg, is one of Medd's more ambitious projects, the Roman Catholic **Church of the Sacred Heart**. This betrays a strong Italianate influence, with a facade of white pillars supporting a canopy set against a dark brick background, and circular colonnaded turrets rising above the roof to each side of the entrance porch. The lofty interior has a towering curved roof, polished stone floors and broad arches set into smooth walls, and is far grander than would be expected from the largely stark and unadorned facade.

Paharganj

Also known as **Main Bazaar**, the bazaar of **Paharganj**, leading west from New Delhi railway station, lies a few minutes' walk north of Connaught Place. Renowned for its budget hotels (see p.103), it's also packed with restaurants, fruit and vegetable stalls, pharmacies, public phone booths, travel agents, and shops selling anything from brass bells, kettles and clothes to perfumed bath oil and wooden massage kits. Off the main thoroughfare tall houses teeter over winding alleys, where children play among chickens and pigs, and the commercial city seems miles away.

National Museum

Janpath. Tues–Sun 10am–5pm. Admission free. Guided tours daily 10.30am, 11.30am, noon &2pm. ☎301 9538.

The **National Museum**, Delhi's largest, provides the best general overview of Indian culture and history. Packed with exhibits ranging over five thousand years, it takes several hours to get around the whole place, which follows a circular plan, with galleries arranged around a central yard. A small shop in the entrance hall sells postcards, books and souvenirs, and has details of daily film shows (2.30pm).

The **ground floor** is dominated by architectural displays, setting off with simple stone **Neolithic** tools (3000–1500 BC), and shell and bone jewellery excavated from **Indus Valley civilization** sites such as Mohenjo Daro and Harappa in Pakistan, Lothal (Gujarat) and Kalibangan (Rajasthan). Carved pillars and statues from the **Mauryan** empire (250 BC) feature typical designs such as the Emperor Ashoka's lion motif and common Buddha symbols: lotus blossoms, *bodhi* trees, *stupas*, footprints and wheels. An assortment of **Gupta** (400AD) terracottas includes imposing statues of the river goddesses, Ganga and Yamuna, who stand with water vessels in their hands, and can often be seen guarding temple sanctuaries. **South Indian** temple architecture is represented by a series of bold rounded sandstone figures from Pallava temples, dominated by Shiva and his consort, and some more intricate dark grey stone friezes from later Chola constructions. Stone and bronze **Buddhist** statues from India are set beside exquisitely designed Thai figurines, such as the elegant Tara (Goddess of Wisdom), fashioned in jade and crowned with a jewelled tiara. Take a little time to absorb the complexity of the Tibetan manuscripts, painted in sweeping black-ink characters and illustrated in extraordinarily minute detail.

Another gallery on the ground floor holds a superb collection of bejewelled clothes, dark-wood boxes inlaid with mother-of-pearl, fierce swords, daggers and spears, silk tapestries and ivory ornaments, all of which belonged to the powerful **Moghul** rulers who combined art forms from Persia, Afghanistan and India to create a unique and elaborate style. The Moghul theme is continued on the **first floor**, where Persian and Arabic manuscripts include the handwritten memoirs of Emperor Jahangir (1605–27). Other paintings on this floor show the work of several Indian schools, the most distinctive of which are the **Pahari** miniatures of the Himalayan regions of Gharwal and Kangra – simple yet striking scenes of courtly life and loving couples, whose fine lines were often drawn using a single hair. Continuing through the first-floor galleries you'll come across a section devoted entirely to models and masks made in **Nagaland**, whose long straight noses, square set faces and slanted eye-slits evoke Peruvian art: the assorted masks and religious statues from Morocco, Peru and Costa Rica on the second floor make for interesting comparison. Also tucked away on the upper floor are several thick-set and intricately carved wooden doors, lintels and window shutters, examples of the elaborate carpentry that remains a strong tradition in **Gujarat**. The three hundred musical instruments on display in the adjoining gallery represent only part of India's vast musical tradition – it's a good collection, but if you want an even better insight into Indian music, head for *Sangeet Natak Akademi* (see below).

Nehru Memorial Museum and Library

Teen Murti House, Teen Murti Marg. Tues–Sun 9.30am–4.45pm. Admission free. ☎301 6734.

Built in 1930 as the residence for the British Commander in Chief, the grand and sombre Teen Murti House later became home to India's first Prime Minister, Jawaharlal Nehru, and is now the **Nehru Memorial Museum and Library**. A tour of the house leads through rooms laden with photographs recording Nehru's life, from his childhood and student years at Harrow and Cambridge to his formal appointment as leader of India's government in the presence of the king and queen of England in 1948. The years between were dominated by the growth of the Congress party and calls for Independence, decisive periods in India's history that are documented here with excellent displays and reference to all the political activists involved. While Nehru's political life is brought to the fore, his personal effects in a simple bedroom, office and sitting room give some idea of the character of the father of a dynasty that hasn't left the political arena since Independence. Even Sonia Gandhi, reluctant to enter politics, is now something of a figurehead among many Indians.

Another of Nehru's passions was astronomy, an interest reflected in the planetarium (daily astronomy shows 11am & 3pm; Rs3) in the formal grounds of the house. Inside, the exhibition has little of striking interest, save the descent module used by the first Indian cosmonaut in 1984, its heat-shield charred by re-entry into the atmosphere.

National Gallery of Modern Art

Jaipur House, near India Gate. Daily 10am–5pm. Admission free. ☎338 2835.

Once the residence of the Maharaja of Jaipur, the extensive **National Gallery** is a rich showcase of Indian contemporary art. Its ground floor, focusing on post-1930s work, has many of the best exhibits, including pieces by the "Bengali Renaissance" artists Abanendranath Tagore and Nandalal Bose, the great poet and artist, Rabindranath Tagore, and Jamini Roy, whose work, reminiscent of Modigliani, reflects the influence of Indian folk art. Also on show are the romantic paintings and etchings of Thomas Daniell and his nephew William, British artists of the Bombay, or Company, School. An **Art Reference Library** has quite a large collection of art books, journals and periodicals.

Indira Gandhi Memorial Museum

1 Safdarjung Rd. Tues–Sun 9.30am–5pm. Admission free. ☎301 0094.

Although at times uncompromisingly harsh in her politics, Indira Gandhi was a much loved mother-figure of her country during the long years of her leadership, and it is with deep respect that she is remembered at the **Indira Gandhi Memorial Museum**. It was in this house that she was assassinated by her own Sikh body guards in 1984; her bloodstained *sari*, which has been chemically preserved, is on display. The collection of letters, press cuttings, photos (many taken by Rajiv) and possessions is both informative and moving. It's supplemented by a section devoted to Rajiv, including the clothes he was wearing when he was killed, that winds up the exhibition on a rather tragic note. So popular is the former Gandhi home that you may well find yourself caught up in a fast moving line of Indian tourists; arrive early and you can view the exhibition at a leisurely pace.

National Museum of Natural History

FICCI Building, Barakhamba Rd. Mon–Sun 10am–5pm. Admission free. ☎331 4849.

Galleries at the **National Museum of Natural History** illustrate natural resources and ecology from all over the world, and especially India. Along with models of dinosaurs, stuffed animals and birds and fossils, there are supervised activity rooms in which children learn to model animals and handle specimens. Such appreciation of ecological issues is all too rare in India, where forests and natural habitats are fast disappearing, and the list of endangered species is growing rapidly.

National Philatelic Museum

Dak Bhavan, Post Office, Sansad Marg. Mon–Fri 9.30am–12.30pm & 2.30–4.30pm. Admission free.

To get to the **National Philatelic Museum**, go to the post office on Sansad Marg and approach the head postmaster who can lead you to an extensive collection of rare stamps, first day covers and special cancellations behind the main counters. It's worth a visit just to pick up some commemorative stamps, featuring events such as space visits and UN achievements and figures like Nehru and Gandhi, to liven up your letters.

Sangeet Natak Akademi

Rabindra Bhavan, Firoz Shah Rd. Mon–Fri 9.30am–6pm. Admission free. ☎338 7246.

India's premier institution for music (*sangeet*), dance (*natak*), and the performing arts, **Sangeet Natak Akademi** is more of a resource centre than a museum, with a large audio-visual archive, photographs and films. A gallery also displays an extensive collection of folk and classical musical instruments, masks and costumes, while its library holds all sorts of rare and otherwise unobtainable volumes.

Tibet House

1 Institutional Area, Lodi Rd. Mon–Fri 9.30am–1pm & 2–5.30pm. Rs1. ☎461 1515.

Tibet House, a cultural centre that organizes seminars and monthly lectures (mostly in Hindi), also has a small and somewhat limited museum of Tibetan art. Displays include *thangkas* (painted scrolls), old currency notes, costumes, objects of prayer and musical instruments, and a shop sells clothes, jewellery, medicines, incense and curios.

Crafts Museum

Pragati Maidan, Bhairon Rd. Daily 10am–5pm. Admission free. ☎331 8287 or 7641.

Immediately north of Purana Qila, the **Crafts Museum** is a uniquely dynamic exhibition of the rural arts and crafts of India. Its village complex displays an assortment of building traditions, bringing together cultures from throughout the subcontinent to provide a unique if artificial insight into rural life. Authentically constructed mud huts are beautifully decorated with folk art, and exhibits include wood carvings, paintings, papier mâché, embroidery and a full-sized wooden *haveli* from Gujarat. Live demonstrations by the artisans offer close-up glimpses of the folk arts that can be all too difficult to obtain elsewhere in the country. You can buy ritual objects, ornaments, rugs, shawls and books from the craftsmen and women or from the excellent museum shop.

South Delhi

Most of the early settlements of Delhi, including its first cities, are to be found not in "Old Delhi" but in **SOUTH DELHI**, the area south of Connaught Place. Although the rapid expansion of suburban Delhi is swallowing up the countryside, it remains littered with monuments from the past, and pockets of almost untouched rural peace make it a fascinating blend of the contemporary, the pastoral and the historic. This mix of urban and rural is at its most startling in the housing enclaves and shopping precincts springing up throughout the vast area, such as the fashionable **Hauz Khas**.

Early Muslim kingdoms built their cities on the foundation of earlier settlements, creating the **Qutb Minar Complex**; the later developments of **Siri**, **Tughluqabad**, **Jahanpanah**; **Firozabad**, north along the river; and **Shergarh**, around the **Purana Qila**. **Humayun's Tomb**, which heralded the great Moghul period in architecture, is not far from the elegant **Lodi Gardens** and one of the holiest shrines of Sufism, **Hazrat Nizamuddin**. Development has been haphazard, so communications have not always kept pace, and access to sites is not always easy.

Purana Qila

Daily, dawn–dusk. Admission free. Served by buses between Delhi Gate and Sundernagar such as #423 and #438. The #411 continues to Nizamuddin, and #482 goes on to Kalkaji.

The majestic fortress of **Purana Qila**, whose crumbling ramparts dominate the busy **Mathura Rd**, 4km southeast of Connaught Circus, is often said to stand on the site of **Indraprastha**, the city of the Pandavas, of *Mahabharata* fame. More certainly, it was the centre of the sixth city of Delhi, created by Humayun, the second Moghul emperor, as **Din-Panah**, and renamed **Shergarh** by Sher Shah, who briefly displaced him.

Two principal buildings survive to hint at the former glories of the fortress. The **Qila-i-Kuhna Masjid** is one of Sher Shah's finest monuments. Constructed in 1541 in the Afghan style, influenced by Indo-Islamic architecture, it consists of five elegant arches, embellished with white and black marble to complement the red sandstone. The **Sher Mandal**, a red sandstone octagonal observatory and library, was the scene of the death of Humayun, just a year after he defeated Sher Shah and returned to power. He stumbled down its treacherously steep steps in 1556 as he answered the *muezzin*'s call to prayer; visitors today can climb to the top for panoramic views of Delhi and the River Yamuna to the east. The fortress is entered through the lofty south gate, **Lal Darwaza**, just inside which a small museum houses sculpture from the Mauryan era (daily 8am–6.30pm; free).

The few other remains of the once-extensive sixth city include the grey and red arch known as **Sher Shah's Gate**, and **Khair-ul-Manzil Masjid**, built in 1561 during the reign of Akbar for use as a *madrasa* or seminary, whose cloistered courtyard is reached via an elegant large sandstone gateway opposite Lal Darwaza and the zoo.

The Yamuna formerly flowed along the eastern base of Purana Qila; the moats it fed are now dry, save a lake to the west used for boating. During the painful Partition of India in 1947, hordes of Muslim refugees gathered within the confines of the fort, in extremely unhygienic conditions and amid great trepidation, to await transportation to the newly created nation of Pakistan.

Zoo

Daily except Fri; summer 8am–6pm, winter 9am–5pm. Admission Rs0.50.

Below the southern ramparts of the Purana Qila, the open-air enclosures and cages of **Delhi Zoo** cover an extensive area. Although it may look attractive, a visit may well severely disappoint anyone who loves animals. It does house some magnificent white tigers, but nothing is done to educate visitors, and as a result the disdainful creatures have to submit to prods and taunts all day long. Recent allegations of corruption against zoo officials regarding the sale of animals further taint the picture.

Lodi Gardens

The leafy, pleasant **Lodi Gardens** (previously Lady Willingdon Park; daily 5am–8pm; free), 4km south of Connaught Circus, form part of a belt of fifteenth- and sixteenth-century monuments that now stand incongruously amid golf greens, large bungalows and privileged estates. The park is especially full in the early mornings and early evenings, when middle-class fitness enthusiasts come for brisk walks or to jog through the manicured gardens against a backdrop of much-graffitied medieval monuments.

Near the centre of the gardens is the imposing **Bara Gumbad** (large dome), a square late-fifteenth-century tomb capped by the eponymous dome. While its monotonous exterior is relieved by grey and black stones, the inside is adorned with painted stucco work. The mosque alongside was built in 1494, with a rectangular prayer hall faced by five arched openings. Heavily ornamented with coloured tiles, foliage and Koranic inscriptions, the tapering Tughluq-style minarets next to the *mihrab* seem to herald the octagonal towers of the coming Sur and Moghul periods. **Shish Gumbad** (Glazed Dome), a similar tomb 50m north, still bears a few traces of the blue tiles liberally used to form friezes below the cornice and above the entrance. Inside, plasterwork is inscribed with ornate Koranic inscriptions.

The octagonal **tomb of Muhammad Shah** (1434–44) of the Sayyid dynasty, stands 300m southwest of Bara Gumbad, surrounded by verandahs and pierced by arches and sloping buttresses. Accented by turrets at each corner, a sixteen-sided drum supports a majestic dome. Enclosed within high walls and a square garden, 300m north of Bara Gumbad, the **tomb of Sikandar Lodi** (1517–18) repeats the octagonal theme, with a central chamber encircled by a verandah. **Athpula** (eight piers), a sixteenth-century ornamental bridge, lies east, in the northwest corner of the park.

Nizamuddin

Now engulfed by a busy road network and plush suburbs, the *mahalla* (neighbourhood) of **Nizamuddin** is almost isolated from the rest of the city; to enter it is like passing through a time warp into the Middle Ages. The heart of the village is just off the busy Mathura Rd, 6km south of Connaught Circus, and easily accessible by public transport such as the #454 bus, which passes Paharganj and Palika Bazaar.

QAWWALI

Of all Indian art forms, **qawwali**, whose prime purpose is to gain *hal* (spiritual ecstasy), is among the most adaptable and versatile, appearing as popular entertainment at modern weddings and on concert platforms. Musically, *qawwali* is linked to the north Indian classical form of vocal music, *khyal*, deriving its melody from such sources as classic *ragas* (modal compositions) and its own forms based on central Asian roots. Comprising a chorus led by solo singing accompanied by clapping and usually a harmonium combined with *dholak* (double-membraned barrel drum) and *tabla* (paired hand-drums), the resulting hypnotic rhythm can inspire its audience into a state of *mast* (spiritual intoxication), manifested by wild swaying and swinging of the head. The simple but effective drum patterns used include *qawwali tal*, *dadra*, and *keherwa* – respectively four-, six- and eight-beat rhythmic cycles.

Most performers, or *qawwals*, are hereditary musicians who trace their lineage back to **Amir Khusrau**, to whom several songs are attributed. Some compositions have become universal hymns, such as the haunting *Dam-a-dam mast Qalandar* (constantly intoxicated Qalandar) and the robust *hamd* (a eulogy in praise of God, the Prophet, or a saint), *Allah Hu*. Musical gatherings, or *Mehfil-e Sama*, are held regularly in *dargahs* such as Nizamuddin and in Ajmer, with especial poignancy during the *urs* (anniversary) of the saint in question.

Alleys lead past shops selling flowers and accoutrements of worship to the marble courtyard of one of Sufism's greatest shrines, **Hazrat Nizamuddin Dargah**. The tomb of the fourth saint of the Chishtia order, Sheikh Nizamuddin Aulia (1236–1325), was built the year he died, but has been through several renovations, and the present mausoleum dates from 1562. A distinctive white marble dome ornamented with vertical black lines, crowns its small square chamber surrounded by marble-faced verandahs. Lattice screens and arches in the inner sanctum surround the actual tomb, enclosed by a marble rail and a canopy of mother-of-pearl. Religious song and music play an important role among the Chishtias, and *qawwals* (bards) gather to sing in the evenings (especially on Thursdays and feast days). Sheikh Nizamuddin's disciple, the poet and chronicler **Amir Khusrau** – considered to be the first Urdu poet and the founder of *khyal*, the most common form of north Indian classical music – lies in a contrasting red sandstone tomb in front of his master's mausoleum.

Anyone entering either building should cover their heads with a handkerchief or cap bought or borrowed from one of the stalls selling offerings. *Sheikhs* hover about ready to assist and take donations from visitors. Twice a year, on the anniversaries of the deaths of Sheikh Nizamuddin and Amir Khusrau, an *urs* (religious fair) draws thousands of pilgrims, and Nizamuddin resounds to the sound of *qawwali*.

The oldest building in the area, the red sandstone mosque of **Jam-at Khana Masjid**, looms over the main *dargah* on its western side. It was built in 1325 by Khizr Khan, the son of Ala-ud-din-Khalji. Enclosed by marble lattice screens next to Amir Khusrau's mausoleum, the tomb of **Princess Jahanara**, the favourite daughter of Shah Jahan, is topped by a hollow filled with grass in compliance with her wish to have nothing but grass covering her grave. At the north gate of the *dargah's* compound is a holy *baoli* (step-well), next to the mosque **Chini-ka-Burj** (tower of tiles) named for its upper chamber profusely decorated with coloured tiles.

Prominent Muslims buried in Nizamuddin include **Mirza Ghalib**, the nineteenth-century poet whose work lives on in *ghazals* (devotional and love poetry, often set to music) popular throughout the Urdu-speaking world. Alongside is the elegant marble pavilion of **Chausath Khamba** (sixty-four pillars), built in 1625.

Humayun's Tomb

Close to the medieval Muslim centre of **Nizamuddin**, 2km from Purana Qila and 500m from Nizamuddin railway station, **Humayun's Tomb** stands at the crossroads of the

Lodi and Mathura roads. Delhi's first Moghul tomb was constructed from 1564 onwards, after the death of the second Moghul emperor, under the watchful eye of Haji Begum, Humayun's senior widow and mother of Akbar, who camped here for the duration. The grounds were later used to inter several prominent Moghuls, and served as a refuge for the last emperor, Bahadur Shah II, captured here by the British in 1857.

Though later eclipsed by the Jama Masjid and the Taj Mahal, its sombre, Persian-style elegance marks this as one of Delhi's finest historic sites. Constructed of red sandstone, inlaid with black and white marble, on a commanding podium looking towards the Yamuna, it stands in the centre of the formal *charbagh*, or quartered garden. The enclosure is dissected into quarters by causeways and channels, and each square is further quartered. Rising on an arcaded platform, the octagonal structure is crowned with a double dome that soars to a height of 38m – the inner shell forms the vaulted ceiling. Porches on each side rise to 12.2-metre-high pointed arches, flanked by outer bays and recessed windows with lattice screens of stone and marble. Below the cenotaph, inside the building, are the graves of Humayun and Haji Begum.

Among tombs of uncertain origin nearby is **Nila Gumbad** (Blue Dome), an octagonal tomb with a dome of blue tiles, to the southeast outside the enclosure. Nila Gumbad was supposedly built by one of Akbar's nobles to honour a faithful servant but may possibly predate Humayun's Tomb. Within the grounds southeast of the main mausoleum, another impressive square tomb has a double dome and two graves inscribed with verses from the Koran. It is tentatively considered to be that of **Babur**, the first Moghul Emperor and father of Humayun. Immediately south of Bu Halima's Garden (who exactly Bu Halima was remains a mystery), which marks the entrance to Humayun's Tomb, the central dome of the tomb of **Isa Khan**, a nobleman of Sher Shah, rises from a 32-sided drum.

Safdarjang's Tomb

The tomb of **Safdarjang**, the Moghul viceroy of Avadh under Muhammad Shah (1719–48), and the father of the Nawab of Avadh, Shuja-ud-Daula, stands at the end of the Lodi Rd, 5km southwest of Connaught Place. Built between 1753 and 1774, it is one of the last in the tradition of Moghul garden tombs. At the centre of another *charbagh*, reached through a grand double-storeyed gateway off a busy main road to the east, the double-storeyed mausoleum, made of red and buff sandstone and relieved by marble, rises on a dramatic platform overlooking the adjacent airport of the *Delhi Flying Club*. However, its inordinate height and bulbous dome somehow lack the grandeur of Humayun's Tomb. A single cenotaph in the square central hall marks the underground tombs of Safdarjang and his wife. Immediately to the south is the site of the battlefield upon which Timur (Tamerlane) routed Muhammad Shah Tughluq in 1398.

Hauz Khas

Hauz Khas, the Soho of Delhi, is a wealthy suburban development, packed with boutiques and restaurants, 12km southwest of Connaught Circus. The "village" is just off Aurobindo Marg (or the Delhi–Mehrauli Rd), which leads from the centre to the Qutb Minar Complex, and adjacent to a pleasant deer park. From the shopping enclave, a small road leads to the ruins of Ala-ud-din-Khalji's large tank (enclosed reservoir), built early in the fourteenth century to supply the inhabitants of Siri, Delhi's second city. It was expanded almost fifty years later by Firoz Shah, who added a two-storey *madrasa* (seminary), and a mosque at its northern end. The entire complex was constructed in an L-shape, with latticed windows, and deep stone niches for books.

In among the anonymous tombs scattered throughout the area is that of Firoz Shah himself, next to the southeast corner of the *madrasa*. Its high walls, lofty dome, and doorway spanned by a lintel with a stone railing outside, are fine examples of Indian traditions effectively blended with Islamic architecture. Once the site of Timur's camp, the bed of the tank is used today to hold concerts and dance recitals for wealthy tourists who dine against this impressive backdrop (see p.110).

Moth-ki-Masjid

The **Moth-ki-Masjid**, built during the reign of Sikandar Lodi (1488–1517), is now all but abandoned, isolated in a rural setting within the rapidly spreading suburbs of south Delhi, 2km from Hauz Khas off the Delhi–Mehrauli Rd. A milestone in the evolution of the Moghul mosque, its three domes, ornate *mihrab* and arches stand on a raised plinth, enclosed by walls pierced by an elegant red sandstone gate to the east. Legend has it that Sikandar Lodi picked a grain of *moth* (a type of lentil), sown by his minister Miyan Bhuwa; doubled and sold again and again, it financed the construction of the mosque. Some houses in the village of the same name still have mangers.

Khirki-ki-Masjid

Firoz Shah's **Khirki-ki-Masjid**, "The Mosque of Windows", famous for its heavy stone lattice windows, lies close to the site of Jahanpanah, Delhi's fourth city, 4km east of Qutb Minar and 13km south of Connaught Circus. The battered bastions of the squat double-storeyed mosque, flanked by short minarets, give it a fortress-like aspect. Its unusual roof, consisting of 25 squares capped by domes and flat sections, is open at the centre to allow light into a dark pillared courtyard, plagued by bats.

Baha'i Temple and Kalkaji

Often compared to the Sydney Opera House, on open ground atop Kalkaji Hill 12km southeast of Connaught Place, Delhi's modern **Baha'i temple** has become yet another symbol of the city. Dominating the haphazard suburban sprawl, giant white petals of Rajasthani Macrana marble in the shape of an unfolding lotus spring from nine pools and walkways, to symbolize the nine spiritual paths of the Baha'i faith. Inside, uniformed tour guides lead you to the central hall, which rises to a height of 30.5m without the distraction of supporting columns. Set amid well-maintained gardens, the temple is at its most impressive when the rays of the setting sun catch the lotus petals. Remove your shoes on entering, and keep silence. Otherwise open from dawn to dusk, the temple is closed to tourists during morning and evening prayers, which last an hour (Tues–Sun 10am & 4pm).

The domed twelve-sided *shakti* **Kalkaji** temple (also known as Kalika or Kalka Devi) lies on the same hill as the Baha'i temple. Though of no architectural significance, this popular Kali shrine is at the heart of a village that has somehow ignored the march of time, and the Hindu worship of its *mahants* (important *sadhus*) makes a fascinating contrast with the brash new faith of the Baha'is. Kalkaji is a major bus depot – among buses from the centre are #433 and #440 from Connaught Circus.

Ashoka's Rock Edict

The emperor **Ashoka's Rock Edict** was discovered in 1966, engraved on a rock overlooking the Yamuna near Srinivaspuri, 11km southeast of Connaught Circus, not far from Kalkaji. A ten-line epigraph in the ancient Brahmi script, one of many such placed at important sites and crossroads throughout Ashoka's vast empire, the inscription proves that Delhi was occupied during the Mauryan period, prior to both Muslim and Rajput settlement. It states that the emperor's exertions in the cause of *dharma* had brought the people of India (*Jambudvipa*) closer to the gods; and that through their efforts, irrespective of their station, this attainment could be increased even further.

Tughluqabad

On a rocky escarpment, 8km east of Qutb Minar and 15km southeast of Connaught Place on the Mehrauli–Badarpur Rd, stand the crumbling 6.5-kilometre-long battlements of the third city of Delhi, **Tughluqabad**, built during the short reign of Ghiyas-ud-din Tughluq (1321–25). The huge ruins are almost entirely abandoned, overgrown with scrubland and home to nomadic Gujars and rhesus monkeys – which is seen by some as a fulfilment of a curse by the Sufi saint, Sheikh Nizamuddin Aulia (see p.97).

Divided into three main portions, Tughluqabad had its high-walled citadel to the south near the present entrance off the main road; only a long underground passage, the ruins of several halls and a tower, now remain. The grid pattern of some of the city streets to the north is still traceable, while the palace area is to the southwest. The southernmost of its thirteen gates still looks down on a causeway, breached by the modern road, that rises above the flood-plain, to link the fortress with **Ghiyas-ud-din Tughluq's Tomb**. Itself resembling a small fortress, it has withstood the ravages of time, rising beyond a massive red sandstone gateway on a high plinth, surrounded by pentagonal stone walls. The distinctive mausoleum consists of sloping walls topped with a marble dome and contains the graves of Ghiyas-ud-din, his wife, their son Muhammad Shah II, and even what is purported to be Ghiyas-ud-din's favourite dog – although dogs are traditionally held to be unclean. The later fortress of **Adilabad**, built by Muhammad Shah II and now in ruins, can be seen on a hillock to the southeast.

Tughluqabad is awkward to get to by **bus**; either take #451 bus from Jantar Mantar to Badarpur, and change onto a Mehrauli-bound service, or take #505 to Mehrauli/Qutb Minar Complex, and catch a bus going east.

Qutb Minar Complex

Daily, dawn–dusk. Admission Rs3. On bus route #505 from Ajmeri Gate.

Above the foundations of **Lal Kot**, settled in the eighth century by the Tomara Rajputs and developed in the twelfth century by the Chauhans, the first monuments of Muslim India, now known as the **Qutb Minar Complex**, stand in well-tended grounds 13km south of Connaught Circus. One of Delhi's most famous landmarks, the fluted red sandstone tower of the Qutb Minar tapers upwards from the ruins, covered with intricate carvings and deeply inscribed verses from the Koran, to a height of 72.5m.

Work on the Qutb Minar started in 1199 as Qutb-ud-din Aibak's victory tower, celebrating the advent of the Muslim dominance of Delhi (and much of the subcontinent) that was to endure until 1857. For Qutb-ud-din, who died four years after gaining power, it marked the eastern extremity of the Islamic faith, casting the shadow of God over east and west. It was also a minaret, from which the *muezzin* called the faithful to prayer. Only the first storey of the Qutb Minar has been ascribed to Qutb-ud-din's short reign; the rest were built by his successor Iltutmish, and the top was restored in 1369 by Firoz Shah, who used marble to face the red sandstone. Access to the balconies via the staircase inside has been closed after a spate of accidents and suicides.

Adjacent to the tower lie the ruins of India's first mosque, **Quwwat-ul-Islam** ("the might of Islam"), built by Qutb-ud-din using the remains of 27 Hindu and Jain temples and the help of Hindu artisans – their influence can be seen in the detail of the masonry and the indigenous corbelled arches. Steps lead to an impressive courtyard flanked by cloisters and supported by pillars unmistakeably taken from a Hindu temple, while especially fine ornamental arches, rising as high as 16m, remain of what was once the prayer hall. Beautifully carved sandstone screens, combining Koranic calligraphy with the Indian lotus, form a facade immediately to the west of the mosque, facing Mecca. Iltutmish and his successors extended the mosque, enlarging the prayer hall and the cloisters and introducing such Islamic architectural traditions as geometric designs, calligraphy, glazed tiles set in brick, and squinches (arches set diagonally to a square to support a dome).

In complete contrast to the mainly Islamic surroundings, an **Iron Pillar** (7.2m) bearing fourth-century inscriptions of the Gupta period, stands in the courtyard of the mosque. Once topped with an image of the Hindu bird god, Garuda, the extraordinary and virtually rust-free pillar, made of 98 percent pure iron, is a puzzle to metallurgists. It must have been transplanted here, but its origins remain hazy. Tradition has it that anyone who can encircle the column with their hands behind their back will have their wishes granted.

Ala-i-Darwaza, a mausoleum-like gateway with stone lattice screens, was added by Ala-ud-din Khalji (1296–1316). Its inlaid marble embellishments are owed to an influx of artisans from Byzantine Turkey, and the import of Seljuk influences – the true arches were the first in India. The south entrance to the complex is marked by yet another tower, **Alai Minar.** Planned as grander and larger than the Qutb Minar, it was left abandoned after the construction of its 24.5-metre-high first storey.

On a plinth west of Quwwat-ul-Islam, the **Tomb of Iltutmish,** built in 1235 by the ruler himself, was the first Muslim mausoleum in India – something new to the subcontinent, as Hindus cremate their dead rather than bury them. A relatively plain exterior blending Indian and Muslim styles, with three ornate arches, hides an interior nine metres square with geometric arabesque patterns combined with calligraphy and lotus and wheel motifs. The square red-sandstone chamber was once covered by the dome that now lies in pieces around the site; only its corbelled squinches bear witness to a flawed method of early Indo-Islamic building.

Ala-ud-din-Khalji's Tomb and **Madrasa** (theological college), lies on the southwest perimeter of Quwwat-ul-Islam, its L-shaped structure reflecting the Seljuk influence. To the southeast of the Ala-i-Darwaza is the small and attractive tomb of the Sufi saint Imam Muhammad Ali, better known as **Imam Zamin,** a native of Turkestan who came to India during the reign of Sikandar Lodi (1488–1517).

The octagonal Moghul tomb of Muhammad Quli Khan, one of Akbar's courtiers, 150m southeast of the Qutb Minar, was occupied and converted by **Charles Metcalfe,** resident at the Moghul Court, into a country house but is now in ruins. Outside the complex, north of the Qutb Minar, **Adham Khan's Tomb** stands on the remains of the walls of Lal Kot. A general in Akbar's army, he was hurled from the ramparts of Agra Fort on the orders of the emperor after some murderous court feuding.

Cafes and a good restaurant at the complex offer refreshments, while Mehrauli, adjacent to it, is developing as a chic shopping centre.

Rail Transport Museum

Chanakyapuri. Tues–Sun 9.30am–5.30pm. Adults Rs3; cameras Rs10.

Venerable trains remain in use throughout the country, but to see the cream of India's royal coaches and her oldest engines, you should head for the **Rail Transport Museum** in Chanakyapuri. Outside, 27 locomotives and 17 carriages stand on short tracks in the open air. Look out for the ornate gold-painted saloon car of the Maharaja of Baroda (1886), the teak carriage of the Maharaja of Mysore, trimmed in gold and ivory, and the cabin used by the Prince of Wales in 1876. Steps beside each carriage enable visitors to peer in without damaging the well-preserved interiors.

The covered section of the museum is a delight for train buffs, with models of famous engines and coaches, explanations of the workings of narrow- and broad-gauge lines, displays of old tickets, and even the skull of an elephant hit by a train near Calcutta in 1894. The pride of the museum is a model of India's very first train, a steam engine which made its inaugural journey of 21 miles from Bombay to Thana in 1853. Train spotters who wish to delve deeper can ask the curators to open the library.

Accommodation

As befits a capital city, Delhi has a healthy mix of **places to stay,** and you'll have no difficulty finding anything from a dirt-cheap lodge to an extravagant international hotel. Bookings for upmarket hotels can be made at the tourist desks at the airports and railway stations, but budget travellers have to do their searching on their own.

The hotels of **Connaught Circus** cover all price ranges, are handy for banks, restaurants and shops, and have good transport connections to all the main sights. North of Connaught Circus, the busy market area of **Paharganj**, close to New Delhi railway station, has the best of the budget accommodation, and **Old Delhi** has some even cheaper hotels. The main youth hostel is in the **south**, where you'll find Delhi's top **luxury hotels**, most complete with bars, discos, swimming pools and health clubs, and many charging upwards of $100 a night. The accommodation listed below is marked on the **maps** on p.91 and p.104 and on the colour map of Delhi in the centre of the book.

Central Delhi

Staying in **central Delhi** makes sense if you want to take ITDC tours which start from Janpath, catch the airport bus, or get to Old Delhi on the cheap and bumpy *tempos* that gather near Palika Bazaar. The area is also somewhat quieter than Paharganj.

The circular **Connaught Place**, Delhi's commercial hub, and the southbound radial road, **Janpath**, both have a full cross-section of accommodation. The least expensive lodges, huddled around the north end of Janpath, near the Government of India tourist office, offer dorms as well as rooms, are cramped but friendly, and often full. Within the curved colonial lanes of Connaught Place you'll find moderately priced hotels of varying standards. Further south the upmarket towers on and around Janpath and along **Sansad Marg** cater mainly for business travellers and tourist groups. Most of these have plush restaurants, bars, and **American-plan** rooms (which include meals), and some have pools – all add heavy taxes to their bills, which we have included in our price guide, and many require foreigners and non-Indian residents to pay in foreign currency, although *Visa* cards and travellers' cheques will also be accepted.

ACCOMMODATION PRICE CODES

All **accommodation prices** in this book have been coded using the symbols below. In principle the prices given are for the least expensive double rooms in each establishment; however, some hotels, usually in category ①, offer rates per bed rather than per room. Local taxes are not included unless specifically stated. For more details, see p.35.

① up to Rs100	④ Rs225–350	⑦ Rs750–1200
② Rs100–150	⑤ Rs350–500	⑧ Rs1200–2200
③ Rs150–225	⑥ Rs500–750	⑨ Rs2200 and above

Inexpensive

Gandhi Guest House, 80 Tolstoy Lane, behind Scindia House (☎332 1113). Less cramped than the neighbouring lodges, with larger rooms and a tiny roof area. Rooms have shared bath and hot water in winter. Rumoured renovations should improve standards, but probably raise prices. ③.

Mr SC Jain's Guest House, 7 Pratap Singh Building, Janpath Lane (no phone). Large, plain rooms with shared bathrooms in a laid-back family bungalow, away from the noise and bustle of Janpath and overlooking Jantar Mantar. ③.

Ringo Guest House, 17 Scindia House (☎331 0605). Cramped but friendly lodge, popular for its rooftop dorms. Individual rooms are poky and airless, but offer privacy and undisturbed sleep. Open 24hr – knock on the door if you arrive after midnight. ①–④.

Royal Guest House, 44 Janpath (☎332 9485). Above *Royal Nepal Airlines* office. Quiet and clean, with spacious singles. Some a/c rooms. ④.

Sunny Guest House, 152 Scindia House (☎331 2909). Similar layout to *Ringo Guest House*, with very friendly staff, sociable rooftop seating and a range of dorm beds and rooms, some a/c. Clean bathrooms, hot showers, good food and booking facilities for private buses. Open 24hr. ①–④.

Moderate

Alka, 16/90 G-Block, Connaught Circus (☎34 4328). Stuffy but comfortable carpeted rooms, all with TV and a/c, few with windows. Excellent in-house veg restaurant. ⑦.

Asian Guest House, 14 Scindia House (☎331 0229). The least appealing of the lodges off Janpath, with stuffy, overpriced rooms. The a/c rooms are OK. ④–⑥.

Hotel Fifty-Five, 55 H-Block, Connaught Place (☎332 1244). A moderate hotel that has seen better and cleaner days. Reasonably sized a/c rooms, bar and balcony terrace. ⑦.

ITDC Ashoka Yatri Niwas, 19 Ashoka Rd (☎332 4511). The airport bus stops here, but it really should be a last resort. Rooms are spacious and quiet, with good views, but service is poor and the lifts, to all 15 storeys, slow. Check-in and -out can take an hour. ⑥.

Janpath Guest House, 82–84 Janpath (☎332 1935). Spacious but stuffy carpeted rooms, all with private bath and some with a/c. ⑤–⑥.

Jukaso Inn, L-Block, Connaught Place (☎332 4977). Pristine but unimaginative marble-walled a/c rooms with attached bath. No lift to higher floors, and small rooms that hardly justify the price. ⑧.

Metro, 49 N-Block, Connaught Place (☎331 3856). Despite visible ageing and lack of maintenance, the large shabby rooms of this once-grand hotel retain a little of their former charm. ⑦.

Nirula's, L-Block, Connaught Place (☎332 2419). Fairly smart hotel, with a handful of small, cosy a/c rooms and a variety of restaurants. Often full. ⑧.

Palace Heights, D-Block, Connaught Place (☎332 1419). Very central. Small rooms, some with windows, some a/c, and a cosy atmosphere. Pleasant balcony terrace. ⑥.

YMCA Tourist Hostel, Jai Singh Rd (☎31 1915). Staid and sterile place with sermons played on loudspeakers. Good restaurants, swimming pool and attractive gardens. Ordinary and a/c rooms, and a reliable hot water suppply in both the common and private bathrooms. ④–⑦.

YWCA International Guest House, 10 Sansad Marg (☎31 1561). Clean and airy a/c rooms with private bathrooms, most, but not all, occupied by women. Set meals in the hostel's restaurant. Foreign currency preferred. ⑦.

Expensive

Holiday Inn, Barakhamba Rd (☎332 0101). American-style towers, extremely spacious, with efficient service, fussy decor and several good restaurants; a bit impersonal. Prices start at $300 for a double room. ⑨.

Imperial, Janpath (☎332 5332). Plush, well-maintained rooms with an unmistakably European flavour. Swimming pool, shops, beauty parlour and several restaurants. Non-resident Indians must pay in foreign currency for rooms starting at $150. ⑨.

ITDC Kanishka, 19 Ashoka Rd (☎332 4422). The best government-run hotel in the area. Comfortable but unimaginative rooms, on 18 storeys, all with TV and clean bathrooms. Swimming pool, bars and food halls, including a rooftop restaurant. Foreigners pay in foreign currency: $90. ⑨.

Janpath, Janpath (☎332 0070). Moderate hotel with large carpeted rooms and some exceptionally good restaurants. ⑨.

Marina, 59 G-Block, Connaught Circus (☎332 4658). Old but refurbished hotel with sizeable rooms and good service, at inflated rates. Rooms facing the road are constantly invaded by traffic noise. The travel counter organizes tours, and books onward journeys. ⑨.

Le Meridien, Windsor Place (☎371 0101). Posh hotel, with tax on everything. Glitzy futuristic design, swimming pool, health club, restaurants, bars and disco. Prices start at $200 per double. ⑨.

Park, 15 Sansad Marg (☎35 2477). Comfortable but soulless carpeted rooms, with bathtubs, fridges, TV and room service, and views over Jantar Mantar from the front. Not the best of its category. Over $100 for a double. ⑨.

Paharganj

The **Paharganj** area running west from New Delhi railway station, a popular hunting ground for inexpensive and mid-range accommodation, is a lively scene of typical Indian city life – see p.92 – that you'll miss if you stay in Connaught Circus, just ten minutes' walk south. It's also a place where you can buy from other travellers things they

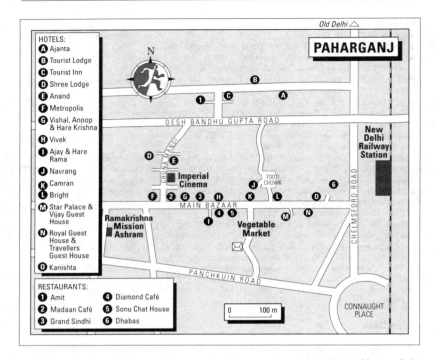

HOTELS:
- Ⓐ Ajanta
- Ⓑ Tourist Lodge
- Ⓒ Tourist Inn
- Ⓓ Shree Lodge
- Ⓔ Anand
- Ⓕ Metropolis
- Ⓖ Vishal, Anoop & Hare Krishna
- Ⓗ Vivek
- Ⓘ Ajay & Hare Rama
- Ⓙ Navrang
- Ⓚ Camran
- Ⓛ Bright
- Ⓜ Star Palace & Vijay Guest House
- Ⓝ Royal Guest House & Travellers Guest House
- Ⓞ Kanishta

RESTAURANTS:
- ❶ Amit
- ❷ Madaan Café
- ❸ Grand Sindhi
- ❹ Diamond Café
- ❺ Sonu Chat House
- ❻ Dhabas

PAHARGANJ

Old Delhi

New Delhi Railway Station

DESH BANDHU GUPTA ROAD

Imperial Cinema

TOOTI CHOWK

MAIN BAZAAR

Ramakrishna Mission Ashram

Vegetable Market

PANCHKUIN ROAD

CHELMSFORD ROAD

CONNAUGHT PLACE

0   100 m

no longer need: *Enfield* motor bikes, rucksacks, camping gear, malaria tablets and so forth. However, some hotels, particularly those with all-night restaurants, are becoming more like 24-hour parties, so if you want to sleep, choose carefully.

Lodges at knock-down prices are invariably poky, stuffy and grubby, with rickety beds, moth-eaten mattresses and thin partition walls, but if you're intent on finding a budget room, there are exceptions in the alleys off the **Main Bazaar**, which runs west from New Delhi railway station for roughly 1km. The area lacks the space enjoyed by hotels further south, and the noisy narrow main street is constantly blocked with cars, rickshaws, and mopeds billowing exhaust fumes into the air and fighting for space with cycles, carts and wandering bovines. Each day sees several crashes and mini pile-ups.

Note, too, that Paharganj is notorious for its hotel **touts**, and it's not uncommon for rickshaw drivers to announce that the hotel you're heading for has burnt down, gone bankrupt, changed its name, or simply never existed. Be firm and stand your ground.

Ajay Guest House, 5084-A Main Bazaar (☎777 7617). Marble decor and clean, small rooms, most with baths but no windows. Good-value dorms and airy roof terrace (24-hr service). ③–④.

Anand, 2537/48 Chuna Mandi (☎52 6911). A passable but declining lodge north of *Imperial Cinema*, with long balconies on each floor. Some rooms with fridge, all with bath. ③.

Anoop, 1566 Main Bazaar (☎73 5219). Clean, modern lodge with a rooftop restaurant. ③.

Bright, 1089–1090 Main Bazaar (☎752 5852). Very basic, but clean and very cheap, and often full. Small rooms around a courtyard – extra charges for blankets and hot water. ①.

Camran Lodge, 1116 Main Bazaar (☎52 6053). Small lodge with an interesting carved facade and more character than the newer hotels, despite being dim and a little poky. Good-value singles. ②.

Hare Krishna, 1572–1573 Main Bazaar (☎753 3017). Friendly, clean and cosy, and fairly quiet. ③.

Hare Rama Guest House, 298 Main Bazaar (☎752 9293). Modern, marble-slab lodge, popular with the party crowd. Clean rooms and dorms. Helpful service, left-luggage and airport taxis. ③.

Kanishta, 22 Main Bazaar (☎52 5365). Uninspiring place close to the railway station, with cosy double rooms. Though some are airless, those with balconies are good value. ④.

Metropolis, 1634 Main Bazaar (☎52 5492). Main bazaar's most upmarket and comfortable hotel. Dorms are a bit pricier and quieter than elsewhere, with lockers provided. Some double rooms have a/c, large windows, and a shower with constant hot water. No singles. A good restaurant on site (not 24-hr). ⑤–⑦.

Navrang, 644-C Mahalla Bowali, 6 Tooti Chowk (☎52 1965). Basic, inexpensive and friendly lodge tucked off the main street. ①.

Royal Guest House, 4464 Main Bazaar (☎753 5880). Clean and very friendly, with a selection of a/c and non a/c rooms, all with private bathroom. ④–⑤.

Shree Lodge, 2012–2015 Chuna Mandi (☎52 6864). In a quiet alley off Chuna Mandi, with all the character of a family house. Simple cosy rooms, some with attached bath, and precarious stairs. ②.

Star Palace, 4590 Main Bazaar (☎752 4849). One of Paharganj's more salubrious hotels, with small, clean rooms around a central courtyard, TVs, and constant hot water in private bathrooms. The rooftop restaurant is overpriced, but the rooms are good value. ④–⑤.

Travellers Guest House, 4362 Main Bazaar (☎354 4849). A smart, well-kept hotel above *Madan's Store* not far from the railway station, with unremarkable decor but friendly service. ④.

Vijay Guest House, 4459 Katra Raiji, Main Bazaar (☎751 9611). Fresh, well-kept 4-storey hotel with constant hot water, blankets, a pleasant roof terrace and friendly management. ③–④.

Vishal, 1600 Main Bazaar (☎753 2079). Unoriginal marble decor, but clean and comfortable, with a good restaurant and larger rooms than similar lodges. ③–④.

Vivek, 1534–1550 Main Bazaar (☎777 7062). Popular place, with a 24-hr rooftop restaurant, and unremarkable rooms. Most have attached bath and hot water, and room service. The best rooms have windows facing the street, and some are a/c. ③.

Ram Nagar

Directly north of Paharganj, five minutes' walk from New Delhi railway station, under the flyover section of D B Gupta Rd, is **Ram Nagar**, lined with hotels and a few restaurants. Within easy reach of the bazaar, but spared the incessant noise and commercial atmosphere, hotels in Ram Nagar are beginning to make a name for themselves among Western tourists, and are worth considering if you want to stay near the station, but don't fancy Paharganj. However, crossing D B Gupta Rd to get to the Main Bazaar can be more than nerve wracking; it's wise to go the long way round, under the flyover.

Ajanta, 36 Arakashan Rd (☎752 0925). Clean and efficiently run place with spacious rooms, some a/c, but not much atmosphere. Good attached restaurant/ice-cream bar. ④–⑤.

Tourist Inn, 8502 Arakashan Rd (☎777 7112). Very smart and clean, for the price, with carpets, room service and good food. Some a/c. ⑤–⑥.

Tourist Lodge, 26 Arakashan Rd (☎753 2990). Sizeable rooms with attached bathrooms. Reasonably clean, and better value than some on the Main Bazaar. ③–④.

Old Delhi and north of Connaught Circus

If you find Paharganj too much of a travellers' hangout, or Connaught Circus too impersonal, head for **Old Delhi**, where foreign tourists seldom stay. Here you'll find yourself swamped by the noise and smells of the least modernized area of the capital. Prices are low and standards not very high, but the hotels are well-sited for visits to the Red Fort and Jami Masjid, and you can guarantee constant activity on the crowded streets, excellent food from long-established restaurants, and superb sweets from Muslim roadside stalls. If the noise of Chandni Chowk proves too much, you could choose one of the smarter hotels nearby that give easy access to the bazaars and New Delhi.

Broadway, Asaf Ali Rd (☎327 3821; fax 326 9966). Midway between Old and New Delhi, close to Delhi Gate, this is a great top-range hotel with high standards, an excellent restaurant specializing in Kahmiri feasts and two bars. Some rooms look out over the Jami Masjid. Tours through Old Delhi can be organized for guests. ⑤.

Fort View Hotel, Chandni Chowk (no phone). Small, basic rooms opposite the fort at the eastern end of the main street. Great views from the balconies, but tacky decor and low standards of cleanliness – only for the thick skinned. ②.

New Delhi Tourist Camp, Jawaharlal Nehru Marg (☎327 2898; fax 326 2326). Small bungalows, with cramped but clean, windowless rooms – fearful heat traps in summer. Camping, and ample parking space; you can sleep in your vehicle on site for a minimal fee. A restaurant serves Western, Indian and Chinese food, and there's laundry service, left-luggage, trekking equipment for rent, travel agency, mail and fax pick-up and a daily airport bus. Communal washing blocks have hot showers. Good value, and connected to Connaught Place (10min) by *tempos* and rickshaws. ②–④.

New India Hotel, 172 Katra Bariyan, Fatehpuri (☎23 5117). Old house, opposite Fatehpuri mosque, where large simple rooms, steeped in the character of the old city, open onto a central courtyard: some double rooms have their own balcony. Basic communal washing facilities. ③.

Oberoi Maidens, 7 Sham Nath Marg (☎252 4422). Top-notch hotel in a colonial mansion north of Old Delhi, not far from the Inter-state Bus Terminal. Pleasant rooms, but not terribly smart. Leafy gardens, swimming pool, a fine restaurant and bar till midnight. ⑨.

Qudsia Gardens Tourist Camp, opposite the Inter-state Bus Terminal (☎252 3121). Camping facilities and dank huts. A feasible option only if you arrive late or need to leave early by bus. ①–③.

Star Guest House, 186 Katra Bariyan, Fatehpuri (☎292 1127). Poky, characterless rooms in a fairly new hotel overlooking the narrow street that winds past Fatehpuri mosque. Worth considering if you can't get into *New India Hotel*. ③.

South Delhi

Most of the accommodation **south of Connaught Circus** lies firmly in the luxury category, although there are a few guest houses in Sundernagar, the odd mid-range hotel tucked away in a residential area, and the modern **youth hostel** near the exclusive diplomatic enclave. The 5-star hotels provide Delhi's best restaurants, bars, health centres, nightclubs and most exclusive discos – facilities otherwise lacking in a town that dies early each evening. As a result, the city's high society uses them to entertain, be seen in and hold lavish weddings, cocooned from the outside world. Prices here are some of the highest in India; those in this section encompass a range of Rs2200 to Rs22,000.

Ambassador, Sujan Singh Park (☎463 2600). Next to Khan Market, recently acquired by the *Taj Group*. Comfortable and friendly; no frills and large old-fashioned rooms. Showing its age. ⑨.

Centaur, Delhi Airport (☎565 2223). Serves transit passengers and airline crews. Large and comfortable, with airy rooms and all services, but otherwise characterless. Rs4000. ⑨.

Claridges, 12 Aurangzeb Rd (☎301 0211). An elegant Thirties-style facade leads into the marble foyer of one of Delhi's oldest and finest establishments. Tennis courts and swimming pool. Around Rs4000. ⑨.

Hyatt Regency, Bhikaiji Cama Place, Ring Rd (☎688 1234). Smart, elegant and not too brash, with all the comforts of this renowned chain. Excellent eating, plus a fitness and health centre. Prices start at $250. ⑨.

ITDC Ashok, Chanakyapuri (☎60 0121). A landmark in the grand pseudo-Moghul style, finished in red sandstone. One of Delhi's finest, but not as efficient as some of the new pretenders. Prices over $250. ⑨.

ITDC Lodhi, Lala Lajpat Rai Marg (☎436 2422). Built in mock-Tughluq style but otherwise characterless and showing its age, though it does have an open-air swimming pool. ⑧.

Maharani Guest House, 3 Sundernagar (☎469 3128). Experience residential Delhi in a pleasantly sited, exclusive colony with a good shopping arcade. A good alternative to the usual hotels. ⑦.

Maurya Sheraton and Towers, Diplomatic Enclave (☎301 0101). Extremely plush, exclusive and very grand, imposing and very expensive. ⑨.

Oberoi, Dr Zakir Hussain Marg (☎436 3030). One of Delhi's first in the super league; manages to retain its elegance without being loud and brash. Highly recommended if you can afford it. Prices of $350 and over. ⑨.

Qutab, off Sri Aurobindo Marg (☎66 0060). Concrete and characterless, but otherwise comfortable. All mod cons including tennis courts, swimming pool and the only bowling alley in Delhi. ⑨.

Samrat, Chanakyapuri (☎60 3030). Comfortable place, behind the *Ashok*, with pretentious 5-star treatment aimed at business users. ⑨.

Sartaj, A-3, Green Park (☎66 7759). An unusual location in a southern suburb, this garish hotel is essentially nouveau-riche Indian in taste. ⑧.

Shyama, C 5/32, Safdarjang Development Area (☎66 5222). Small and friendly, away from the traditional tourist areas in a residential area near the *Indian Institute of Technology* in south Delhi. ⑦.

Surya Sofitel, Friends Colony (☎683 5070). The only 5-star accommodation in this part of southeast Delhi; comfortable, but rather isolated. ⑨.

Taj Mahal, 1 Mansingh Rd (☎301 6162). Ornate and luxurious in the typical grand style of the *Taj Group*, with marble foyer and chandeliers, and an excellent choice of restaurants. Expect to pay at least $300 a night. ⑨.

Taj Palace, 1 Sardar Patel Marg (☎301 0404). Grand, imposing, very comfortable and exclusive, but otherwise lacking the character of the flagship *Taj Mahal*, though similarly priced. ⑨.

Youth Hostel, 5 Naya Marg, Chanakyapuri (☎301 6285). Away from the bustling city centre, this ultra-modern building in grey concrete, with dorms (Rs25) and doubles, is the showpiece-cum-administration centre of the Indian YHA. Non-members pay an extra Rs250 to enrol. ①.

Eating

Delhi's **restaurants** cater for floods of tourists and business travellers, and menus cover an exhaustive array of dishes from all over the world. There's something for every budget, from delicious Indian snacks from roadside stalls in Paharganj, Palika Bazaar and Janpath, to Western food in the 5-star hotels where expert cooking and presentation is reflected by high prices. Note that most restaurants close early by Western standards, but those with bars usually stay open until midnight. If you're looking for a **late-night** meal, you can either eat in a top hotel, try a snack in Paharganj's round-the-clock roof-top cafes, or head to the markets of south Delhi. Wherever you eat, be careful of the **water**. The restaurants listed below are marked on the **maps** on p.91, p.104 and on the colour map of Delhi in the centre of the book.

Connaught Place

Connaught Place has snack bars for quick stops, and plenty of upmarket restaurants, as well as budget sit-down joints that attract a largely Western clientele. Even if you can't afford a meal in an expensive restaurant, it's worth going into air-conditioned comfort and treating yourself to silver-service tea, filter coffee, or a cool milkshake. For patties, sandwiches and take-out meat and veg dishes, head behind the market at the top of Janpath, where you'll find great snacks at incredibly good value. Larger restaurants remain closed on Sunday mornings.

Amber, 19 N-Block, Connaught Circus. Typical dimly lit, a/c restaurant catering for wealthy Indians and tourists. Refreshing chilled beer and great food: veg and non-veg lightly spiced Indian and Western choices. Pricey, but good value.

Cafe 100, B-Block, Connaught Place. Ice-creams galore, plus pizzas, burgers, and fries to take away or eat in (standing). Long lunchtime queues; buy a meal ticket before you reach the counter.

The Cellar, beneath *El Arab*. Gastronomic delights for meat eaters: unbeatable steaks, German salads, roasts and desserts – and outrageously filling bacon-sausage-egg breakfasts (from 10am).

Croissants etc, 9 Scindia House. Delicious hot-filled croissants, ice-creams, cakes and pizzas just round the corner from *Ringo* and *Sunny* guest houses.

Don't Pass Me By, Scindia House. Friendly, inexpensive veg and non-veg Chinese restaurant just off Janpath, popular with travellers staying nearby. Opens early for breakfast – fresh juices, huge bowls of porridge, curd and muesli, eggs, toast, and great Tibetan bread. Also good for lunch and dinner, with prompt service and tasty food. Reliable travel service run from the restaurant.

El Arab, Sansad Marg. Great place for Middle-Eastern dishes on the corner of Sansad Marg and the outer ring of Connaught Circus, with prices ranging from medium to high. Tasty *hummus, baba ghanoush* and Lebanese salads.

Gaylord, Connaught Circus, off Sansad Marg. High-quality Indian cuisine in plush surroundings lit by glittering chandeliers. Fairly expensive, but good value.

Host, F-Block. A/c relief from the Indian heat, and a good place to sit with a beer, silver-service tea, or strong filter coffee. Meals, however, are overpriced, and the portions stingy.

Kovil, 2 E-Block, Connaught Place. Fresh, no-smoking restaurant serving exclusively south Indian veg dishes, with great *dosas*, and full *thalis* (for around Rs150) at lunch time.

Kwality, Regal Building, Sansad Marg. High standards of service and hygiene, with good but unspectacular international cuisine.

National, opposite L-Block, Connaught Circus. The best of a bunch of inexpensive sit-down restaurants, with great fiery curries, and an endless supply of *chapati*.

Nirula's, 135 L-Block, Connaught Circus. Quality food, including salads and pastries, in downstairs snack bar (serving packed lunches) and first-floor restaurant. The open ground-floor parlour serves over 50 flavours of Delhi's best ice-cream. A second branch on N-Block, near the *Wimpy*, is a quick-snack bar, with wonderfully smooth ice-cream shakes.

Parikrama, Kasturba Gandhi Marg. Novel revolving restaurant higher than most of New Delhi's modern buildings. Delicious Indian and Western meals and snacks, and superb views over Delhi; a single rotation takes 100 minutes. Great place for a splurge, particularly at sunset. Full meals served from noon–3pm & 7–10.30pm.

Rodeo, 12 A-Block, Connaught Circus. New-Mexican restaurant with Wild West waiters, swinging saddle bar stools, pitchers of beer and excellent *fajitas*. Moderately priced.

Sona Rupa, 46 Janpath. Undoubtedly the best in the area for good north and south Indian and Chinese food, extremely popular with families. Unfussy surroundings, no-nonsense prices, great food and dramatic *dosa*-flinging in the open-fronted kitchen downstairs. Beer and north Indian food upstairs; buy a food ticket at the till and present it to the cooks.

Standard, 44 Regal Buildings, Connaught Circus. Five minutes' walk from Janpath and close to *Regal* Cinema, with two main foodhalls, one for the best-value south Indian *thalis* in town (Rs40), and the other for north Indian and *tandoori* specials and chilled beer on tap.

Surang, *Alka Hotel*, P-Block, Connaught Circus. A minor treat – *tandoori* and Mughlai specialities.

United Coffee House, 15 E-Block, Connaught Circus. Together with the *Host*, this is a longstanding favourite, and does great coffee. The food is mediocre.

Vega, *Alka Hotel*, P-Block, Connaught Circus. Delicious, varied pure veg dishes, and a terrace.

Wenger & Co, 16 A-Block, Connaught Circus. Mouthwatering patties, pasties, rolls, cutlets, sandwiches, sweet cream cakes and a variety of bread to take away. Great value.

Wimpy, 5 N-Block, Connaught Circus. American-style joint with burgers, fries, shakes and chicken nuggets. Popular with students and tourists, but not that great, and pricey for what you get.

Zen, 25 B-Block, Connaught Circus. Excellent Chinese and Japanese meals served in traditional style, with chopsticks, and Western snacks (3–7pm). Distinctly upper-class, with prices to match, and a selection of wines, spirits and beers. Noon–3pm & 7–11.30pm.

Paharganj

Food comes inexpensive and unelaborate in the lively market area of **Paharganj**. You can guarantee finding some excellent wholly Indian joints, particularly in the alleys opposite the railway station which waft with the aroma of pungent spices, and where hot *dhals,* meat and veg dishes are freshly cooked nearly all day. Restaurants geared to tourists offer typically poor Western imitations and under-spiced "curries", but are popular hangouts, and good for a tame breakfast of toast, porridge, muesli or cereal if you can't stomach chillies too early. Many of the hotels in the centre of the main street have cafes serving light meals through the night. Look out too, for meat cuts hanging in shop fronts where you can choose a piece to be grilled or *tandooried,* and mobile stalls dishing out French fries seasoned with *masala*, salt, pepper and lemon juice, and served in a bowl made of dried leaves (Rs5). Roadside juice stalls stock *Mars Bars, Snickers, Yoplait* yoghurt, European cheeses, and all brands of international cigarettes.

Amit, 8674 Arakashan Rd, Ram Nagar. Pure veg Gujarati *thalis* served in this unassuming traditional restaurant close to *Ajanta Hotel*. Great value meals noon–3pm & 7–10pm.

Appetite, *Hotel Vishal*, 1600 Main Bazaar. Popular travellers' restaurant serving pizzas in addition to the usual Indo-Western food. The cable TV is switched on during international sports matches.

Diamond Cafe, opposite *Hotel Vivek*. Small and simple cafe-cum-restaurant.

Grand Sindhi Restaurant, opposite hotels *Ajay* and *Hare Rama*. Great place for a lazy coffee, with filling desserts and a whole range of meals.

Lord's Cafe, *Hotel Vishal*, 1600 Main Bazaar, next to *Appetite*. International cuisine, some Israeli dishes, and inexpensive steaks.

Madaan Cafe, Main Bazaar. Inexpensive and unelaborate open-fronted food house where the seating overflows onto the pavement. A good place to sit and watch the chaos of the main street. Filling breakfasts and large cups of *chai*.

Metropolis, 1634 Main Bazaar. Cosy a/c ground-floor restaurant. Paharganj's priciest venue serves full breakfasts, great curries and *tandoori* specials on rooftop terrace.

Sonu Chat House, Main Bazaar. Noodles, soup, *samosas* and red-hot curries in cramped but clean surroundings.

EATING IN THE TOP HOTELS OF DELHI

For superlative food, comfortable a/c surroundings, unbeatable service, and hefty bills, head for any of Delhi's luxury hotels. In some, you'll be expected to dress the part.

Ambassador, Sujan Singh Park. *Dasaprakash* is considered one of the best south Indian restaurants in Delhi, while mouth-watering Manchurian and Cantonese snacks are the order of the day in the *Chinese Room*.

Claridges Hotel, 12 Aurangzeb Rd. The Chinese *Jade Garden* complements the *Dhaba*, designed to look like a trucker's cafe, with a reconstructed truck to add atmosphere – for those who want to eat really good *dhaba* cooking without having to go on to the streets.

Holiday Inn, Barakhamba Rd. *Grill Room* is strong on steak and seafood; *Baluchi* serves *tandoori* and food from the Northwest Frontier; the *Rendezvous* is a coffee shop and piano bar with an expensive, limited menu; *Silk Orchid* is a popular Thai restaurant, and *Top Deck* is a salad bar.

Imperial, Janpath. The open-air *Garden Party Restaurant & Bar* has a pleasant atmosphere and good food.

Janpath, Janpath. The *Mandarin Room* for excellent Chinese dishes, *The Gulnar* for Indian and Mughlai food with accompanying live music, *The Orbit* for buffet spreads at lunch and dinner, and a 24-hr coffee shop.

Kanishka, 19 Ashoka Rd. The *Dilkusha Restaurant*, serves international food. It also has a tea lounge, a cocktail bar, and a 24-hr coffee shop.

Le Meridien, Windsor Place. The *Pierre* and the nouvelle cuisine *Le Belvedere* are two very good French restaurants; also *Pakwan Restaurant* for *tandoori* and Mughlai, *Aloha Bar*, *La Brasserie* coffee shop and Cantonese and Szechwan dishes in the *Golden Phoenix*. All exceptionally high standard, and very expensive.

Oberoi, Dr Zakir Hussain Marg. Besides *La Rochelle*, specializing in French cuisine and the *Taipan* serving Chinese food, *Baan Thai* is Delhi's second and newest Thai restaurant with traditional floor seating known as *khuntoke* as well as contemporary tables and chairs in a teak-lined dining room.

Taj Mahal, 1 Mansingh Rd. A good choice includes the *Casa Medici*, primarily an Italian restaurant but also offering other cuisines at its lunch buffets; the exclusive Chinese *House of Ming*; and *Haveli*, serving Mughlai to the accompaniment of live Indian music and folk dances (try *karhai paneer* – cheese cubes cooked in a wok).

Taj Palace, 1 Sardar Patel Marg. *Tea House of the August Moon*, as featured in the *Goon Show*, serves excellent Chinese regional cooking; and *Handi* has Indian and Mughlai food.

Old Delhi

Among the shops, offices and houses in **Old Delhi**'s crowded streets, simple, grubby, unadvertised hole-in-the-wall food halls serve surprisingly good, and invariably fiery Indian dishes for less than Rs15. There are few upmarket places in the heart of Old Delhi, but a number of larger, cleaner restaurants on the outskirts offer surroundings more conducive to leisurely and relaxed eating.

Chor Bizarre, *Hotel Broadway*, Asaf Ali Rd. The best place in Delhi to sample pure, but pricey, Kashmiri *tarami* and *wazwan*, made all the more enjoyable by comfortable decor and a servery made from a 1927 Vintage *Fiat*. Easily accessible from the *Tourist Camp*.

Karim's, Matya Mahal. In a side street opposite the south gate of the Jami Masjid, with the best and widest range of meat dishes in the city. Four eating halls round a courtyard all serve delicious fresh kebabs, hot breads and curries. Has been a favourite of Delhi-ites for years; there's another branch in Nizamuddin.

Moti Mahal, Netaji Shubash Marg, Darya Ganj. On the noisy main road south of Jami Masjid, this smart restaurant, established in 1947, is a little scruffy now, though it still serves delicious food, with a strong emphasis on meat. An average full meal will cost you around Rs200.

Natraj Bhalla Corner, Chandni Chowk. Right next to Central Bank, midway along Chandni Chowk. Cosy first-floor snack bar with a few window seats and a limited menu comprising Indian, Western and Chinese options.

Paratha Wali Gali, Chandni Chowk. Opposite Central Bank, tucked down an alley that leads behind *Kanwarji Raj Kumar Sweet Shop*. Follow the smell of rich *ghee* (the restaurant's hallmark) to a tiny room squeezed behind a counter displaying pure veg food. Here you choose a *paratha* to go with standard veg dishes, filled with anything from *paneer* and *gobi* to *mutter* and *masala*, all cooked to order. A culinary treat that will set you back less than Rs30.

Soni Bhojnalaya, Nai Sarak. First-floor restaurant at the top of a yellow staircase opposite *Bina Musical Stores*, 30m off Chandni Chowk. Great *thalis* in typically Indian unfussy surroundings.

Tandoor, *Hotel President*, Asif Ali Rd. Traditional Indian food, plush decor, live Indian classical music and snappy service. Pricey, with meals starting at Rs300.

Vig Coffee House, Chandni Chowk. A small snack stall just over from the Red Fort serving excellent coffee, cold drinks, *samosas*, toasties and veg burgers.

South Delhi

The enclaves and villages spread across the vast area of **South Delhi** offer countless eating alternatives. Trendy **Hauz Khas**, with its Village Bistro restaurant complex, is renowned as one of Delhi's best areas for dining out, where visitors can combine eating with shopping and sightseeing. The small, chic **Santoshi Shopping Complex** near the diplomatic enclave has one of Delhi's most raved-about restaurants – *Basil & Thyme* – while Chankyapuri, better known for its embassies and top hotels, holds a cluster of **Tibetan** *dhabas* selling *momos* (dumpling) and *thukpa* (soup). The alleys and lanes of the medieval village of **Nizamuddin** conceal cafes and restaurants of varying standards, with the extraordinarily rich Muslim cooking of *Karim's* as the real highlight. Part of the **Asiad Games Village**, built 5km south of Connaught Circus to house the mid-1980s Asian Games, has been converted into a small restaurant complex.

Finally, some **late-night** alternatives, if you don't want to pay 5-star prices. The popular cafes of **Bengali Market** on Tansen Rd, near Connaught Circus and New Delhi railway station, keep going until about 11pm, when much of Delhi has closed up. The restaurants of **Pandara Road Market**, close to India Gate, are not especially good but they do stay open until 2am.

Aangan, Asiad Games Village. Smart and upmarket, Indian food.

Al Capone, the Village Bistro, Hauz Khas Village. Western cuisine.

American Pie, Asiad Games Village. Fast-food outlet selling burgers and the like.

Angeethi, Asiad Games Village. Specializes in dishes from the Northwest Frontier.

Basil & Thyme, Santushti Shopping Complex. Popular with Delhi's jet set, serving Western and Parsi food at very reasonable prices.

Bengali Sweet House, Bengali Market. More than a sweet shop; busy cafe whose menu ranges from *dosas* to onion *kulcha* and *channa* (bread and chickpeas), plus ice-creams and milk shakes. Also take-away *makki-ki-roti* (cornbread) with *sarson ka sag* (mustard-leaf spinach) and yogurt.

Chicken Inn, Pandara Rd Market. Dimly lit but comfortable – the only restaurant in the market selling Chinese food.

Chopsticks, Asiad Games Village. Airy and smart with excellent Chinese food.

Dakshin, the Village Bistro, Hauz Khas Village. A good south Indian restaurant.

Darbar, the Village Bistro, Hauz Khas Village. Mughlai cuisine, good views from atop Hauz Khas.

Ghalib's Kabab Corner, Nizamuddin. As its name suggests a budget cafe strong on kebabs in a strongly Muslim corner of New Delhi.

Great Wall of the Village, the Village Bistro, Hauz Khas Village. Great, but pricey Chinese food.

Karim's, Nizamuddin. Legendary, unmissable Mughlai cooking, though the sumptuous food is very rich. Much-renowned specialities, plus kebabs, *korma* and *rumali roti* (super-thin bread).

Khas Bagh, the Village Bistro, Hauz Khas Village. *Tandoori* food and kebabs.

Nathu's Sweets, Bengali Market. A busy, similar, rival to the *Bengali Sweet House* across the road.

Osaka, Main Square, Hauz Khas Village. Chinese and Japanese food with a pleasant ambience; gentle on the pocket.

Top of the Village, the Village Bistro, Hauz Khas Village. Popular *tawa* (griddle) and barbecues.

Triveni Kala Sangam, 205 Tansen Marg, near Bengali Market. Excellent little art-centre cafe serving Indian food. Go for lunch, but be prepared to share a table and put up with frantic service.

Shopping

Although the traditional places to shop in Delhi are around **Connaught Place** and **Chandni Chowk**, a number of the suburbs created by the rapid growth of the city are emerging as fashionable shopping districts. The best known of these is the "ethnic chic" shopping area of **Hauz Khas Village**, 12km southwest of Connaught Place, with its boutiques, excellent restaurants, jewellery shops and galleries, some pretentious and others well worth a browse. Well-heeled visitors to this leafy, exclusive residential area can also take in evening dance and music performances, set against the picturesque backdrop of the ruins of Ala-ud-din Khilji's fourteenth-century tank.

The garden complex of **Santoshi Shopping Arcade**, just inside Wellington Barracks next to the *Samrat Hotel* in Chanakyapuri, and run by Air Force officers' wives, is another trendy place, patronized by embassy officials. **Mehrauli**, a new precinct near the Qutb Minar, also holds boutiques and curio shops, as does **Greater Kailash**, a hot spot for "ethnic chic" designer clothes. Elsewhere, self-contained local precincts ranging from bookshops to European vegetables include **Khan Market**, 500m south of India Gate, and **Bengali Market**, off Barakhamba Rd, which is especially renowned for its sweet shops and large bustling cafes.

Unlike the **markets of Old Delhi** (see p.86), shops in New Delhi take credit cards.

Art, antiques, crafts and jewellery

Much the best area to go shopping for **art and antiques** – even if sceptics do consider it vastly overpriced and rarely authentic – is the small **Sunder Nagar Market**, in a wealthy residential area near Purana Qila and the zoo. However, you shouldn't expect a bargain – the antique and art trade in India is a cut-throat business – and bear in mind that it is illegal to take art objects over 100 years old out of India.

Elsewhere, **curio shops** aimed at tourists sell everything from carpets and fabrics to handicrafts and collectors' items. Few locals bother to venture to the stretch of Janpath known as **Tibetan Market**, packed with vendors feeding off the tourist trade; in fact its shops have a fine assortment of **jewellery**, using semi-precious stones and even silver. Be sure you can tell the difference between silver and white metal.

Central Cottage Industries Emporium, Janpath. Popular and convenient government-run complex, with handicrafts, carpets, leather and reproduction miniatures at fixed (if fractionally high) rates. Jewellery ranges from tribal silver anklets to costume jewellery and precious stones.

Cottage of Arts and Jewels, 50 Hauz Khas Village. Interesting, eccentric jewellery and papier-mâché. A sift through Mrs Jain's semi-precious stones and trinkets is highly recommended.

Ellora, Shop 9, Sundernagar. Silver specialists; jewellery and Indian handicrafts.

Friends Electric Company, Shop 25, Sunder Nagar Market. Makers and exporters of brassware and handicrafts. An interesting array of white metal furniture, plus brass, metal, trinkets, chandeliers and a few antique watches. You never know what you may find.

Jain Super Store, 172 Palika Bazaar, Gate #6. Perfumes, bottles, tea, incense, spices and the like at very reasonable prices.

Kumar Gallery, Sunder Nagar Market. Specializes in antique bronzes and paintings.

Lotus Eaters, Santoshi Shopping Complex. Fashion boutique stocking excellent silver jewellery.

M Zee Handicrafts, 48 Palika Bazaar, Gate 3, Connaught Place. Good for silver jewellery.

Nav-Rattan Arts, Shop 26, Sunder Nagar Market. As the name ("nine gems") suggests, an emphasis on gems, jewellery, silver, bronze, tapestries, and antique perfume bottles.

Poonam Backliwal, Shop 5, Sunder Nagar Market. Established in 1880, boasting exceptional original miniatures, bronze and stone sculptures, Tanjore glass paintings and medieval jewellery. You may find rare and exquisite Bundi drawings or a miniature of a Moghul emperor.

R-Expo, 1115 Main Bazaar, Paharganj. Aromatic oils, bath stuff, scented candles, sandalwood, massage implements, *chillums*, solid and liquid perfumes; dubious quality, but great presentation.

Works of Art, 1 Hauz Khas Village. Upmarket gallery with an interesting collection of brass, papier-mâché and frames.

Books

Delhi has a wide selection of places to buy books and magazines. **Pavement vendors** around Connaught Circus will sell you anything from Sidney Sheldon to Vivekananda, as well as guidebooks. **Bookstores** generally lack the Western trivia, but sell all kinds of publications in English, Hindi, and other European languages. You'll find books on all aspects of Indian history and culture, and an evergrowing supply of short works by Indian authors published by *Penguin India*. Upmarket **hotels** often have their own bookshops, which usually tend towards the coffee-table market; *Khazana*, at the *Taj Mahal*, and *Jainson's* at *Janpath Hotel*, are worth perusing. Several budget hotels have multi-lingual collections of **secondhand** books for sale, swap or part exchange.

Amrit Book Co, 21 N-Block, Connaught Circus. Vast stock of novels and books on history, philosophy and religion.

Book World, Shop #7, Palika Bazaar. A wealth of glossy hardbacks, architectural books, travelogues and novels. Credit cards accepted.

Moti Lal Benarsi Das, Nai Sarak, Chandni Chowk. One of India's premier publishing institutions, retailing as well as publishing academic books on India.

Oxford Book & Stationery Co, Scindia House. Old and new philosophy and history books, plus a few coffee-table copies, a bulging stock of British classics, and a hoard of language dictionaries.

People Tree, 8 Regal Buildings, Parliament St. Pamphlets and books covering poverty, environmental issues, women's issues and controversial politics, as well as students' art work, T-shirts and jewellery. Also details forthcoming films and lectures at centres such as the Max Mueller Bhavan.

Rajiv Book House, Shop #30, Palika Bazaar. Expensive photo-packed hardbacks, great for gifts and collections, and often reduced in price, as well as cheaper novels and paperbacks.

The Bookshop, Khan Market. One of the best of a few good bookshops in this popular market.

The New Book Depot, 18 B-Block, Connaught Place. Well-stocked shop with international *Penguin* titles, bargain hardbacks and a good selection of books covering religion, environment and society in India.

Fabrics and clothes

In Delhi you can buy anything from high-quality silks, homespun cottons and Kashmiri jackets and shawls to traditional everyday wear and multi-coloured tie-dyed Western-style outfits. Buyers are expected to **bargain** in most street-side stalls, which can make shopping all the more fun. Be wary of high prices – the same item is often available in different shops at varying rates. Shops with fixed prices should have a sign to prove it. For Western-style trousers, skirts and shirts, try **Paharganj**, the **Tibetan Market** at the north end of Janpath, and **Palika Bazaar**. Beautiful silks and fine cotton are at their best in **government emporia**, most of which are on Baba Kharak Singh Marg.

Delhi also holds a few upmarket **boutiques**, trading in *haute couture* and furnishings; some, such as *Anokhi*, now have shops all around the world.

Anokhi, Santoshi Shopping Arcade. Clothes and soft furnishings; particularly renowned for hand-block printed cottons combining traditional and contemporary designs.

Bata, 16 B-Block, Connaught Place. Reliable and hardy sandals, trainers and smarter leather shoes, that will survive in India much longer than flimsy leather flip-flops sold in most bazaars.

The Bina Ramani Collection: Twice Upon a Time, 12 Hauz Khas and H5/6 Mehrauli Rd. One of India's leading designers, Ramani's clothes are very chic, very exclusive and very expensive (notice the pun on *Armani*).

Cashmeir Galleri, 50 Hauz Khas Village. Handmade oriental carpets in silk and wool, chain stitch rugs, shawls and papier-mâché.

Central Cottage Industries Emporium, Janpath. Tucked behind the Tibetan Market, this has one of the best ranges of raw silks and cottons in town, and stocks traditional Indian dress, silk ties and finely-tailored jackets and suits.

Dastkar, 1A/1 Hauz Khas Village. Reasonably priced terracotta, block prints, *saris*, patchwork, toys, leather, basketry, weaves, and beautiful folk-art Madhubani prints on cloth.

Handloom House, 9 A-Block, Connaught Circus. Exquisite silks; top quality, sky-high prices.

Khadi Gramodyog Bhavan, 24 Regal Building, corner of Sansad Marg and Connaught Circus. Great place to pick up hardy, lightweight travelling clothes. Reasonably priced, ready-made, traditional Indian garments include *salwar kamise* (trousers and shirt), woollen waistcoats, *kurta pygama*, shawls and caps, plus rugs, material by the metre, incense, cards and tablecloths.

New Kashmir Stores, 225B Village Lado Sarai, Mehrauli. One of those places rental car drivers take you to against your will. The reward is a fine collection of carpets, some of which are antique – the problem is to guess which ones.

Shyam Ahuja, Santoshi Shopping Arcade. Exclusive rugs and *dhuris* by a world-famous rug designer, patronized by shops such as *Liberty* of London.

Tibetan Carpets and Handicrafts, HH the *Dalai Lama's Charitable Trust Handicraft Exports*, 16 Jor Bagh, Lodi Rd. Carpets of all sizes, seamless and runners, woollen pullovers, jackets, bags, *chuba* (Tibetan women's dress), incense and other gifts.

Vastra, 12 Hauz Khas Village. Essentially a clothes store, selling *salwar kamise*, some in antique silk – also sells frames and old photographs.

Musical instruments and cassettes

Delhi has a lively classical **Indian music** scene; the *Triveni* arts centre (see p.115) is a good place to catch live performances as well as to get information on instrument makers. Among classical recordings, the *Music Today* series has an excellent collection of both north and south Indian classical music. For popular Western music on tape and CD at bargain prices, head for any one of the music stalls in Palika Bazaar.

Blue Bird & Co, 9 Regal Buildings, Sansad Marg. Cassettes, CDs, videos and hi-fis.

Lahore Music House, Netaji Subhash Marg, Darya Ganj. North Indian musical instrument-makers who have a long reputation and have been exporting instruments for years.

Rangarsons, Outer Circle, Connaught Circus. Extraordinary shop that once boasted regiments of the British Indian army among its patrons. A collection of brass and other marching band instruments as well as contemporary *tablas* and *sitars*.

Rhythm Corner, 16 N-Block, Connaught Place. Much like *Blue Bird*; copious quantities of CDs, cassettes, and videos of contemporary and classical music, including international chart hits.

Ricki Ram, Outer Circle, Connaught Circus. Once *sitar*-makers to the likes of Ravi Shankar, they maintain their exclusive airs and produce quality instruments, but have lost the leading edge.

Nightlife and entertainment

There's surprisingly little to do after dark in Delhi; outside the city's restaurants, your best bet for a drink is in the **bars** of the upmarket hotels, where you can get shorts and often cocktails as well as the more easily available *Kingfisher* and *Eagle* beers. A sprinkling of **discos** in the 5-star hotels cater for the city's yuppies, who can meet here outside family confines and dance the night away to Western and Indian popular music.

The city fares much better on the cultural front. A few venues host performances of classical dance such as **Bharatnatyam** and **Kathakali**, and there are nightly shows at Hauz Khas in the south of the city. Check any of the listings magazines detailed on p.80 to see what's on at **India International Centre**, a good place to catch lectures and films on all aspects of Indian culture and environment, and the city's principal venue for musical performances.

Bars

Broadway, *Hotel Broadway*, Asif Ali Rd, New Delhi. Decked out in an attempt to recreate the New York scene in the 1960s. Beers and a variety of "American" cocktails. *Thugs Bar* upstairs is more English in style. Both are convenient if you're staying in the *Tourist Camp* just over the road.

THE FESTIVALS OF DELHI

India's annual **religious celebrations** are a large part of Delhi social life, and it's well worth trying to time your visit to enjoy their whirl of rowdy activity, traditional dances and vibrant costumes. In addition, several **secular festivals** are particular to the capital, and India's top performers gather for **music, dance and drama** festivals.

January

Lohri (Jan 13). The climax of winter is celebrated with bonfires and song.

Republic Day Parade (Jan 26). The first event in a week of celebrations. Soldiers, musicians and dancers from every state parade down Rajpath, salute the president, then pass India Gate, and head north to the Red Fort. Tickets (Rs100) for seats on Rajpath can be bought from travel agents and hotels – arrive early to get a good view. The "dress rehearsal" 2–3 days before the event is free and less crowded. Fanfares of "Beating the Retreat" in Vijay Chowk, close to Rashtrapati Bhavan, round things off on Jan 29.

Martyr's Day (Jan 30). Songs and prayers throughout the morning at Raj Ghat, which is surrounded by a guard of honour, to remember Mahatma Gandhi (who died on this day in 1948) and others who lost their lives in the Independence struggle.

Delhi Rose Festival (end of Jan). Roses from all the world displayed at Safdarjang's tomb.

Shankarlal Sangeet Sammelan (end of Jan). A festival of Indian music with performances in several venues: check local magazines for details.

February

Basant Panchami (Feb 2). The official date of the first day of Spring, when the Moghul gardens behind Rashtrapati Bhavan are opened for the month, after a great deal of watering and pruning.

Delhi Flower Show. Held in the sublime Purana Qila grounds; horticulturalists exhibit flowers and hybrids from all over the world.

Id-ul-Fitr (Feb 9, 1997; Jan 30, 1998; Jan 20, 1999). A day of Muslim feasting and celebrations at the end of the Ramadan fast. Thousands gather for prayers at Jami Masjid.

Thyagaraja Festival. An enthusiastic display of south Indian music and dance, opposite Nehru University in Vaikunthnath temple.

Jazz Bar, *Maurya Sheraton Hotel*, Diplomatic Enclave. Live jazz of varying standards from Indian musicians. Serves beer in pitchers, and cocktails such as New Orleans Surprise and Cool Jazz.

Maikada, *Hotel Marina*, 59 G-Block, Connaught Circus. Comfortable bar with a small outside terrace and well-presented but pricey drinks.

Le Meridien, Windsor Place. Two exclusive bars, *Aloha* and *Henri's*, with extortionate prices but nothing less than five-star treatment.

Rodeo, 12 A-Block, Connaught Circus. Cosy atmosphere in restaurant bar serving a full range of drinks, including tequila slammers. Mock saddle seats at the bar bring out the rodeo theme.

Saqi, *Hotel Alka*, G-Block, Connaught Circus. Very dimly-lit bar that's a little sleazy, but you can take your drink out onto a small verandah.

Tavern, *Hotel Imperial*, Janpath. A restaurant-cum-bar, with tolerable live music and a moderate range of drinks.

Dance performances

Dances of India, Parsi Anjuman Hall, Bahadur Shah Zafar Marg (☎331 7831). Excellent classical, folk and tribal dance. Daily 7–8pm.

Hauz Khas. Lavish meals accompanied by open-air dance shows. US$10 a head.

India International Centre, 40 Lodi Estate (☎461 9431). Regular dance shows. Performances often repeated several nights in a row; enquire by phone.

Triveni Theatre, 205 Tansen Marg (☎371 8833). A popular venue for dance shows by professionals and highly talented student groups.

March

Holi. March, when spring reaches its height, is celebrated with the random flinging of coloured powder and squirting of coloured liquids. Great fun, but can be a little over the top, especially when drunken men are involved.

April

Amir Khusrau. Prayers and *qawwali* singing in Nizamuddin, on the anniversary of the birth of the famous musician.

Id-ul-Zuhr (April 17, 1997; April 5, 1998; March 25, 1999). Muslims recall the sacrifice of Ibrahim's son with animal sacrifice, feasting on mutton and sweet vermicelli, and prayers.

National Drama Festival. Classical and modern dance, music and drama, at Rabindra Bhavan.

May

Buddha Jayanti. The birth of the Buddha is celebrated on the first night of the full moon with prayers at Ladakh Buddha Vihara, Ring Rd, and the Buddha Vihara next to Lakshmi Narayan Mandir on Mandir Marg.

July

International Mango Festival. A peculiar event, with over 500 types of mango on show, usually in Talkatora Stadium. Free tastings.

August

Crafts Mela. Shops and stalls are set up at Suraj Kund just after the monsoon, to display handicrafts and fabrics from all over India.

Janmasthami. Krishna's birthday, celebrated throughout the city; festivities are grandest at Lakshmi Narayan Mandir.

Independence Day (15 Aug). Huge crowds gather to watch the Indian flag hoisted at the Red Fort amid cheering and singing.

October

Gandhi Jayanti (2 Oct). Mahatma Gandhi's birth; singing and prayers at Raj Ghat.

Dussehra. Celebrated in Delhi, and all India, with ten nights of festivities and stage plays of the *Ramayana*. Spectacular performances of the *Ramlila Ballet* at Delhi Gate (all month). The effigy of the demon king Ravana is burnt on the ninth night of the festival.

Diwali. "Festival of lights", with funfairs in parks and in front of the Red Fort. Night skies are lit by dazzling firework displays.

December

Christmas and **New Year**. Although neither Hindu nor Muslim, Christmas is a public holiday, and a good excuse for parties, when many hotels lay on special buffet spreads.

Cinemas

After gloriously hyped releases, Bollywood movies make their way to the capital where there is passionate enthusiasm for burly heroes and red-lipped maidens. If you're interested in enjoying a classic Indian experience, the best **cinemas** to head for are the *Odeon* and *Plaza* in Connaught Place. Both show popular films with the compulsory goodies and baddies, a generous dose of manly courage and shy love, much singing and dancing, and happy endings. In addition you may be able to see dubbed classics exported from America and Britain. Films in non-Indian languages are shown at many of the cultural centres listed below.

Auditoria and cultural centres

There is nearly always some cultural activity going on in Delhi – check at the tourist office, or get hold of local newspapers and publications like *City Scan* and *City Guide*.

Alliance Francaise, D13 NDSE Part II (☎644 0128). Hosts film shows and has an art gallery.

American Centre, 24 Kasturba Gandhi Marg (☎331 6841). Concerts, talks and films.

British Council, 17 Kasturba Gandhi Marg (☎371 1401). Talks, film shows and concerts, plus a good library and reading room.

India International Centre, 40 Lodi Estate, Max Mueller Marg (☎461 9431). Originally designed for academics but now an exclusive club. Regular concerts, lectures, seminars and film shows and a very good reading room.

Italian Culture Centre, 2 Golf Links (☎462 7807). Seminars and film shows, plus a library.

Japan Cultural Centre, 32 Firoz Shah Rd (☎332 9838). Lectures, seminars, exhibitions, and a library.

Kamani Auditorium, Copernicus Marg (☎338 8084). Concerts and theatre.

Lalit Kala Akademi, Rabindra Bhavan, 35 Firoz Shah Rd (☎38 7241). Delhi's premier art academy, with an extensive collection of paintings, sculpture, frescoes and drawings. Also hosts films and seminars, and has a photographic section and a sales counter.

Max Mueller Bhavan, 3 Kasturba Gandhi Marg (☎332 9506). Along with hosting concerts and exhibitions which include Indian artists, this German government cultural centre also has a library.

Russian Cultural Centre, 24 Firoz Shah Rd (☎332 9102). Holds exhibitions, talks and films and houses the *Eisenstein Film Club* and the *Botwinnik Chess Club*, which organizes chess competitions.

Sahitya Akademi, Rabindra Bhavan, Firoz Shah Rd (☎338 6626). An excellent library devoted to Indian literature through the ages, with some books and periodicals in English.

Sangeet Natak Akademi, Rabindra Bhavan, Firoz Shah Rd (☎338 7246). The premier performing arts institution with a large archive and collections (see p.94).

Siri Fort, Asian Village Complex (☎649 3370). Cultural programmes and film shows.

Triveni Kala Sangam, 205 Tansen Marg (☎371 8833). Two galleries devoted to dance and fine art, two theatres (one open-air), a bookshop, a good cafe, music archives, a sculpture park, and a collection of terracotta; and they also organize classes in art, classical music and dance.

Discos

Most, if not all, of the **discos** popular with elite Delhi-ites are in the luxury hotels; expect to pay around Rs250 for entrance and to follow some sort of dress code.

CJ's, *Le Meridien* (☎371 0101). Selective entry.

Ghungroo, *Maurya Sheraton* (☎301 0101). For residents only.

My Kind of Place, *Taj Palace* (☎301 0404). Nostalgia for the over 30s.

Number One, *Taj Mansingh* (☎301 6162). Young and flash local crowd.

Oasis, *Hyatt Regency* (☎688 1234). Flashy basement atmosphere; women-only night Wed.

Swimming, sports and outdoor activities

The recreational activity most likely to appeal to visitors in the pre-monsoon months has to be a dip in one of Delhi's **swimming pools**, but local diversions for the athletically minded include **bowling**, **golf**, and even **rock climbing** on crags on the outskirts of the city, during the cooler months.

Bowling Alley, *Qutb Hotel*, off Sri Aurobindo Marg (☎66 0060). Four-lane bowling alley.

Delhi Flying Club, Safdarjang Airport (☎461 8271). Temporary membership available.

Delhi Gliding Club, Safdarjang Airport (☎461 1298). Call for details of a day's flying.

Delhi Golf Club, Dr Zakir Hussein Marg (☎436 2768). Busy and beautiful 220-acre golf course on the fifteenth-century estate of the Lodhi dynasty, planted with over 200 varieties of trees, which also acts as a bird sanctuary. Monuments and mausoleums, such as the ruined *barakhamba* on a hillock next to the seventh green, dot the grounds. Temporary membership is available.

Delhi Lawn Tennis Association, Africa Ave, Asian Games Village (☎65 3955).

Delhi Riding Club, Safdarjang Rd (☎301 1891). Morning rides start at 6.30am and afternoon rides at 2pm; open to the public but with prior arrangement through the Club Secretary.

Delhi Tourism, N-36 Bombay Life Building, Middle Circle, Connaught Place (☎331 5322). Local activities such as rock climbing, paragliding and water sports, plus treks as far afield as Sikkim.

Indian Mountaineering Foundation, Benito Juarez Marg (☎67 1211). Official organ governing mountaineering and permits throughout India, with a library and an outdoor climbing wall. Some equipment can be rented here, and you can get information on local crags and climbing groups.

Swimming Pools, *Hotel Imperial*, Janpath, Rs300 for non-residents; *Hotel Samrat*, Chanakyapuri, Rs200 per day. Other hotels, such as *Ashok*, and *Claridges*, usually allow non-residents to swim in their pools, for Rs200–300 per day, but they tend to alter their rules so check first. The city's main public swimming baths are the *NMDC Pools*, in Nehru Park, Chanakyapuri.

Listings

Ambulance ☎1099.

Airport enquiries International ☎565 2011; domestic ☎329 5126.

Banks Most open Mon–Fri 10am–2pm (see p.80).

Bus enquiries *Delhi Transport Corporation* (☎251 5543), will also provide enquiry numbers for buses run by other state transport corporations.

Churches *Church of the Redemption*, Church Rd; *Sacred Heart Free Church*, Parliament St.

Embassies & consulates *Australia* 1/50-G Shantipath, Chanakyapuri (☎688 8232); *Bangladesh*, 56 Ring Rd, Lajpat Nagar III (☎683 4668); *Bhutan*, Chandragupta Marg, Chanakyapuri (☎60 9217); *Canada*, 7/8 Shantipath, Chanakyapuri (☎687 6500); *China*, 50-D Shantipath, Chanakyapuri (☎60 0328); *Indonesia*, 50A Chanakyapuri (☎611 8642); *Malaysia*, 50M Satya Marg, Chanakyapuri (☎60 1291); *Nepal*, Barakhamba Rd (☎332 8191); *Netherlands*, 6/50-F Shantipath, Chanakyapuri (☎688 4951); *New Zealand*, 50-N Nyaya Marg (☎688 3170); *Pakistan*, 2/50G Shantipath, Chanakyapuri (☎60 0603); *Singapore*, E6 Chandragupta Marg, Chanakyapuri (☎688 5659); *Sri Lanka*, 27 Kautilya Marg, Chanakyapuri (☎301 0201); *Thailand*, 56-N Nyaya Marg, Chanakyapuri (☎605679); *UK*, Shantipath, Chanakyapuri (☎687 2161); *USA*, Shantipath, Chanakyapuri (☎60 0651).

Hospitals *All India Institute of Medical Sciences*, Ansari Nagar, Sri Aurobindo Marg (☎66 1123), 24-hr emergency service and good treatment; *East West Medical Centre*, 38 Golf Links Rd (☎69 6229), good private clinic; *Dr Ram Manohar Lohia Hospital*, Baba Kharak Singh Marg (☎86 5525), also private; *Lok Nayak Jaya Prakash Hospital*, Jawaharlal Nehru Marg, Old Delhi (☎331 4352), a government hospital opposite the *Tourist Camp*.

Immigration and foreigners' registration For visa renewal and permits for restricted states, go to the Foreigners' Registration office, Hans Bhavan, Mathura Rd, near Tilak Bridge railway station (9.30am–1.30pm & 2–4pm; ☎331 9489 or 8179), with four passport photographs. Be sure to wait in the right line – to pay either in rupees (backed up by exchange certificates), or foreign currency – and take plenty of change. If you've been in India more than 120 days, you'll need to get a tax clearance certificate before you can leave, from the foreign section of the Income Tax Office, Indraprastha Estate (10am–1pm & 2–5pm; ☎331 7826) in the Central Revenue Building next to the FRO; bring bank certificates.

Left luggage Left luggage counters at the railway stations are expensive. To deposit your bags long-term ask at your hotel; most charge Rs2–4 per day. Hotels *Hare Rama*, *Anoop*, and *Ajay* in Paharganj offer access to a 24-hr lock up, for a maximum period of six months.

Libraries For a bit of hearty reading or access to foreign newspapers, try the *British Council*, 17 Kasturba Gandhi Marg, *India International Centre*, 40 Lodi Estate, or *Max Mueller Bhavan*, 3

TRAVEL AGENTS IN DELHI

NB: *Booking flights and excursions through street-side touts, particularly along Janpath, is not recommended. Student travel Information centre for students at* Thomas Cook, Hotel Imperial, *Janpath; issue and renewal of student cards and details of travel reductions.*

American Express, A Block, Connaught Place (☎332 4119). Expensive, tailor-made tours of the capital, and sites further afield.

Amber Tours, 606 Akash Deep, Barakhamba Rd (☎331 3229). Expensive adventure tours with rafting, trekking, wildlife safaris and fishing.

Ashoka Tours and Travels, Kanishka Shopping Plaza, 19 Ashoka Rd (☎332 4422). Package tours, car rental.

Cox and Kings, Indra Palace, Connaught Place (☎332 0067). International operators.

Don't Pass Me By Tours and Travels, 79 Scindia House, Nr Janpath (☎335 2942). Reliable and inexpensive tour operator specializing in road trips to Agra and through Rajasthan.

Hans Travel Service, *Vishal Hotel*, Main Bazaar, Paharganj (☎52 7629). Friendly and reasonably priced taxi rental; private long distance buses; and tours by private car.

Mercury, Jeevan Tara Building, Parliament St (☎373 2866). Expensive, well organized tours by private car.

Nepal Travel Information Centre, 203–204 Adhanik Chambers, 13/29 East Patel Nagar (☎576 4223). Specialize in trips to and within Nepal.

Peak Adventure Tours, B 29A, Kailash Colony (☎643 2894). Established tour and trekking agency.

Rajasthan Tourism Development Corporation, Bikaner House, Pandara Rd (☎38 3837). Package tours of Rajasthan by bus or car, including a wildlife tour of Sariska, Ranthambore and Bharatpur.

Shantum Seth, 309-B, Sector 15-A, Noida, UP 201301 (☎892 1520). Shantum operates a unique circuit of the Buddhist sites of UP, Bihar and Nepal.

Sita World Travel, F12 Connaught Place (☎331 1122). International and domestic flights and package tours.

Student Travel Information Centre, *Hotel Imperial*, Janpath (☎332 4789 or 7582). Agents for a number of international airlines. Student discounts given to those with cards, though you can get better bargains.

Thomas Cook, *Hotel Imperial*, Janpath (☎332 8468).

Travel Corporation of India, N49 Connaught Circus (☎332 7468). Established and efficient tour operators.

Tripsout Travels, Tolstoy Lane, 72/7 Janpath, behind tourist office (☎332 2654). Popular and trustworthy travel service dealing with international airlines and sometimes offering discounts.

Y's Tours & Travels, YMCA, Jai Singh Rd (☎31 1662 ext 4426). Why bother to queue up when you can get your train tickets from here.

Youth Hostelling International, 5 Nyaya Marg, Chanakyapuri (☎301 6250). Extremely good-value treks in the mountains of Himachal Pradesh.

Kasturba Gandhi Marg. *Sahitya Akademi*, Rabindra Bhavan, Firoz Shah Rd, stocks all genres of Indian literature, and a number of periodicals, many in English.

Maps The *Survey of India Map Sales Office*, in Janpath, sells guide maps of a number of cities and states, some of which are grossly out of date and lack detail (see *Basics*. pp.23–24).

Mother Teresa hostels The orphanage inspired by Mother Teresa close to Qudsia Gardens north of Old Delhi accepts voluntary help with teaching, which should be pre-arranged. Contact *Missionaries of Charity*, 12 Commissioner's Lane, Shishu Bhavan, Delhi 110054, or call ☎251 8457.

Motorcycles The Karol Bagh area is known for its many good motorcycle shops; new or second-hand *Enfields* can be bought at the reliable *Inder Motors*, 1744/1755 Hari Singh Nalwa St, Abdul Aziz Rd (☎572 8579), while *Lucky Auto Accessories*, 53/1767 Shri Kishan Dass Rd (☎73 8815), offers excellent renovations of secondhand (ex-army) *Enfield Bullets*.

Opticians *Bon-Ton Opticians*, 13 Janpath Market and *Lawrence & Mayo*, 76 Janpath both offer good, expensive glasses and sunglasses; *Medikos Opticians*, 1588 Main Bazaar, Paharganj, has cheap computerized eye-tests, prescription lenses and sunglasses made up in half a day.

Pharmacies Nearly every market has at least one pharmacy. Those in *Super Bazaar*, Connaught Place, and the *All India Medical Institute*, Ansari Nagar, Sri Aurobindo Marg, are open 24hr.

Photographic studios *Delhi Photo Company*, 78 Janpath, for high-quality developing, printing, and slide processing, is second only to *Kinsey Brothers* beneath *India Today* offices at 2-A Block, Connaught Circus.

Police ☎100.

State Tourist Offices *Andaman and Nicobar Islands*, F105 Curzon Rd Hostel, Kasturba Gandhi Marg (☎38 7015); *Andhra Pradesh*, Andhra Bhavan, 1 Ashoka Rd (☎338 1293); *Arunachal Pradesh*, Arunchal Bhawan, Kautilya Marg (☎301 3915); *Assam*, State Emporia Complex, Kharak Singh Marg (☎34 5897); *Bihar*, 216 Kanishka Shopping Plaza, 19 Ashoka Rd (☎372 3371); *Goa*, Goa Sadan, 8 Amrita Shergill Marg (☎462 9967); *Gujarat*, A6 State Emporia Building, Baba Kharak Singh Marg (☎373 2017); *Haryana*, Chandralok Building, 36 Janpath (☎332 4911); *Jammu & Kashmir*, 202 Kanishka Shopping Plaza, 19 Ashoka Rd (☎332 5373); *Karnataka*, C4 State Emporia Building, Baba Kharak Singh Marg (☎34 3862); *Kerala*, Information Centre, 219 Kanishka Shopping Plaza (☎331 6541); *Madhya Pradesh*, 204–205 Kanishka Shopping Plaza (☎332 1187); *Maharashtra*, A8 State Emporia Building, Baba Kharak Singh Marg (☎34 3773); *Manipur*, C7 State Emporia Building, Baba Kharak Singh Marg (☎334 4026); *Meghalaya*, Meghalaya House, 9 Aurangzeb Rd (☎301 4417); *Mizoram*, Mizoram Bhawan, Circular Rd, Chanakyapuri (☎301 5951); *Nagaland*, Government of Nagaland, 29 Aurangzeb Rd (☎301 5638); *Orissa*, B4 State Emporia Building, Baba Kharak Singh Marg (☎34 4580); *Punjab*, 214–215 Kanishka Shopping Plaza (☎332 3055); *Rajasthan*, Bikaner House, near India Gate (☎338 3837); *Sikkim*, New Sikkim House, 14 Panch Sheel Marg, Chanakyapuri (☎301 5346); *Tamil Nadu*, C1 State Emporia Building, Baba Kharak Singh Marg (☎373 5427); *Tripura*, Tripura Bhavan, Kautilya Marg, Chanakyapuri (☎301 4607); *Uttar Pradesh*, Chanderlok Building, 36 Janpath (☎332 2251); *West Bengal*, A/2 State Emporia Building, Baba Kharak Singh Marg (☎373 2840).

Yoga centres *Yoga Shakti Mission*, 14–20 Ajit Arcade, Kailash Colony (☎641 2379); *Yoga Vishwatayan*, Ashoka Rd (☎371 8866).

Onwards from Delhi

Delhi has good domestic and international travel connections. Anyone heading from the south to the western Himalaya (Himachal Pradesh, Kullu, Manali, Ladakh) will pass through Delhi; it seldom takes more than a day to arrange the onward journey. Scores of **travel agents** (see box) sell bus and air tickets, and many hotels (budget or otherwise) will book private buses for you; **touts**, concentrated at the top of Janpath, waylay tourists with promises of cheap fares, but can't always be trusted.

Travel within India

Whichever direction you're heading in, there'll be a plane, train or bus to get you there. Buses leave Delhi extremely frequently, and tourists are usually ensured places on trains in a reserved **tourist quota**. Flights should be booked as far in advance as possible, but since most routes are covered daily, nobody should have to wait too long.

By plane
Indian Airlines, whose main office is in the Malhotra Building on F-Block, Connaught Circus, near *Wimpy*, operate the most frequent, and the least expensive **internal flights**, though private carriers (see box below) serve more destinations: tickets can be bought through travel agents or the main offices. All flights leave from the domestic terminal, 15km southwest of town, easily reached by the convenient *EATS* bus service (Rs15 plus charge for luggage; 20min) that departs from Palika Bazaar, just outside *Wimpy*. Rickshaws and taxis are more expensive, but slightly quicker. Passengers on domestic flights must check in two hours prior to departure. A simple food counter sells tea, coffee and snacks.

FLIGHTS FROM DELHI

	Indian Airlines	Private Airlines	Journey time
Agra	1 daily		40min
Ahmedabad	2–3 daily	1–2 daily	1hr 25min–2hr
Amritsar	3 weekly		50 min
Aurangabad	4 weekly		3hr 35min
Bagdogra (Siliguri)	4 weekly	3 weekly∞	1hr 55min
Bangalore	2 daily	2–3 daily	2hr 30min
Bhopal	1 daily	4 weekly●	1hr 10min–2hr
Bhubaneshwar	1 daily		3hr 20min
Bombay	8–10 daily*	6–10 daily	2–4hr
Calcutta	2–3 daily*	2–4 daily	2–3hr 40min
Chandigarh		1 daily††	1hr
Dehra Dun	1 daily‡		50min
Dhaka	2 weekly§		2hr 30min
Gagal (Dharamsala)		3 weekly§	2hr 40min
Goa	1 daily	1–2 daily, exc Sat	2hr 25min
Guwahati	4 weekly**	1–3 daily	2hr 25min–5hr 25min
Gwalior	4 weekly†		50min
Hyderabad	2 daily	1 daily exc Sat	2hr
Indore	6 weekly††	1–2 daily††	1hr 45min–3hr 10min
Jaipur	1–2 daily‡	1–4 daily	30–45min
Jaisalmer		3 weekly§	2hr 50min
Jammu	1 daily	1–2 daily	1hr 10min–2hr 40min
Jodhpur	4 weekly●●	3 weekly§	1hr 30min–1hr 50min
Kathmandu	1 daily	1–2 daily	1hr 45min
Khajuraho	1 daily	4 weekly▢	1–1hr 55min
Kochi (Cochin)	1 daily		4hr
Kullu		1–3 daily	1hr 10min–1hr 40min
Leh	1 daily (in seaon)		1hr 10min
Lucknow	1–2 daily***	2 daily	55min
Ludhiana		3 weekly°°	1hr 10min
Madras	2 daily*	2 daily	2hr 40min
Nagpur	5 weekly°		1hr 25min
Pune	1 daily	4 weekly●	2hr–3hr 55min
Ranchi	1 daily exc Mon		2hr 55min
Shimla		1 daily	1hr
Srinagar	1–2 daily	1 daily	1hr 15min–2hr 30min
Thiruvananthapuram	1 daily		5hr 10min
Udaipur	1–2 daily‡	1 daily	1hr 55min–4hr 45min
Vadodara	1 daily exc Tues & Thurs		1hr 25min
Varanasi	1–2 daily	1–2 daily exc Wed	1hr 15min–3hr

Key:

*some flights also with *Air India*   **not Wed, Fri or Sat   ***not Thurs   †not Wed, Sat or Sun
††not Sun   ‡not Tues   §Tues, Thurs & Sat   ∞Wed, Sat, Sun   ●not Tues, Thurs or Sat
●●not Tues, Thurs or Sun   °not Wed & Thurs   °°Mon, Wed & Fri   ▢Tues, Thurs, Sat & Sun

For details of flight connections between Delhi and **Southeast Asia**, see p.7.

RAIL ROUTES FROM DELHI

To Rajasthan			To the Punjab and Himachal Pradesh		
Abu Road	4 daily	13hr 20min–19hr	Ambala Cantt	13 daily	2hr 20min–4hr
Ajmer	5 daily	10hr 20min–15hr	Amritsar	9 daily	7hr 20 min–12hr
Bharatpur	4 daily	4hr–5hr 10min	Chandigarh	3 daily	3hr–6hr 10min
Bikaner	3 daily	11hr–12hr 25min	Firozpur	2 daily	8hr 30min
Chittaurgarh	2 daily	12hr/16hr	Jalandhar	8 daily	6hr 20min–9hr
Jaipur	8 daily	5hr–13hr 25min	Jammu Tawai	3–4 daily	13hr 15min–15hr
Jhunjhunu	1 daily‡	5hr 50min	Kalka, for Shimla	2 daily	4hr–5hr 20min
Jodhpur	2 daily	12hr–14hr 35min	Ludhiana	6 daily	5hr 20min–8hr
Kota	6 daily	8hr–11hr 40min	Pathankot	3–4 daily	10hr 15min–12hr
Sawai Madhopur	4 daily	7–8hr			
Sikar	1 daily‡	8hr 25min	**To central India**		
Udaipur	2 daily	15hr 30min/20hr	Bhopal	14 daily	7hr 45min–15hr
			Gwalior	15 daily	3hr 15min–7hr
To Uttar Pradesh			Hyderabad	2–3 daily	24hr 25min–28hr
Agra	15 daily	2hr–4hr 15min	Indore	1 daily	27hr 40min
Allahabad	9 daily	7–14hr	Jhansi	15 daily	4hr 25min–9hr
Dehra Dun	1–2 daily	7hr 30min–10hr			
Gorakhpur	1 daily	13hr 20min	**To Gujarat and Bombay**		
Kanpur	15 daily	5–10hr	Ahmedabad	4 daily	17hr–24hr 30min
Lucknow	5–6 daily	6hr–9hr 45min	Bombay	8 daily	16hr 30min–29hr
Mathura	11 daily	2hr 50min	**To the south**		
Varanasi	6 daily	13–18hr	**From New Delhi Station**		
			Bangalore	1 daily	40hr 35min
To the east			Ernakulam	1 daily†	48–50hr
Bhubaneshwar	1 daily	29hr 35min–34hr	Kanyakumari	1 on Mon	57hr 20min
Cuttack	1 daily	28hr 30min–33hr	Madras	2–3 daily	33hr 20min–43hr
Gaya	3 daily	15hr–17hr 20min	Thiruvananthapuram	1 daily†	53–55hr
Guwahati	1 daily	36hr	**From Hizrat Nizamuddin Station**		
Howrah, Calcutta	1–2 daily§	18hr–34hr 15min	Pune	1 daily	26hr 35min
Puri	1 daily	36hr 50min–38hr	Vasco Da Gama*	1 daily	41hr 35min
Vijayawada	6 daily	27hr 30min–37hr	*change at Miraj		

Key: ‡ not Sun   § not Mon   † 2 on Mon

By train

Delhi's main railhead, **New Delhi Station** at the eastern end of Paharganj, less than 1km north of Connaught Circus, has regular departures to all corners of India, and a very efficient **booking office** (Mon–Sat 7.30am–5pm) for tourists on the first floor of the main departure building. They'll give you advice on the fastest trains, and you should have little difficulty finding a seat or berth: **women** travelling alone in second class may prefer to ask for a berth in the ladies' carriage. Foreigners must show passports, and pay in foreign currency or in rupees backed up by exchange certificates. **Ignore** roadside advice to book train tickets elsewhere, and don't try buying one at the Reservations building down the road, a confusion of queues and crowds.

   Southbound trains leave from New Delhi, many stopping also at **Old Delhi** station, where you can board the train if it's more convenient. All trains to **Rajasthan**, except those to Bharatpur, Kota and Sawai Madhopur, begin their journey at Old Delhi. Bookings can be made at the tourist office in New Delhi station and at the bus terminal. If you're going to Pune or Vasco da Gama, you'll have to start the journey at **Hizrat Nizamuddin station**, a rickshaw ride away, southeast of Purana Qila.

RECOMMENDED TRAINS FROM DELHI

Frequent trains connect Delhi with all parts of India; see the summary opposite. Those below are recommended as the fastest and/or most convenient for specific cities. All are daily if not otherwise marked.

	Name	No.	From	Departs	Total Time
Agra	Shatabdi Express*	2002	ND	6.15am	1hr 55min
	Taj Express	2180	HN	7.15am	2hr 30min
	Punjab Mail	1038	ND	6am	3hr 15min
	A.P. Express	2724	ND	5.50pm	2hr 30min
Ahmedabad	Ashram Express	2905	OD	6pm	18hr 40min
Ajmer	Shatabdi Express ‡	2015	ND	6.15am	7hr 15min
	Ahmedabad Mail	9901	OD	9.10pm	12hr
Bombay	Rajdhani Express§	2952	ND	4.05pm	16hr 30min
Calcutta	Rajdhani Express	2302/ 2306	ND	5.15pm	17hr 30min–20hr
	Kalka–Howrah Mail	2312	OD	6.30am	24hr 15min
Jaipur	Shatabdi Express	2015	ND	6.15am	4hr 45min
	Garib-Nawaz Express	2915	OD	6am	6hr
	Ahmedabad Mail	9901	OD	9.10pm	8hr 20min
Jhansi	Shatabdi Express	2002	ND	6.15am	4hr 25min
	Punjab Mail	1038	ND	7.15am	6hr 30min
Madras	Tamil Nadu Express	2622	ND	10.30pm	33hr 20min
Udaipur	Garib-Nawaz Express	2915	OD	6am	17hr 30min
	Chetak Express	9615	OD	1.20pm	20hr 15min
Varanasi	New Delhi–Howrah Express∞	2382	ND	4.30pm	13hr 15min
	Delhi–Muzaffarpur Exp•	4008	OD	4.45pm	16hr 15min
	Delhi–Muzaffarpur Shaheed Expⁿ	4650	OD	9pm	15hr 15min
Vasco da Gama	Goa Express†	2480	HN	3pm	36hr 45min

OD Old Delhi   **ND** New Delhi   **HN** Hizrat Nizamuddin
* a/c only   † Change to connecting train at Miraj
‡ Does not run Sun   § Does not run Tues   ∞ runs Mon, Tues & Fri only
• exc. Mon, Wed & Sat   ⁿ runs Mon, Wed & Sat

By bus

Delhi is at the centre of an extensive **bus** network covering much of the neighbouring states in north India. Buses can often be quicker than trains, but the long-distance ones especially tend to be uncomfortable. On long-distance routes there's usually a choice between ramshackle state-run buses and smart soft-seated coaches run by tourist offices, hotels and private agents. Use these as much as you can – outside the main cities, all buses are state run.

The vast majority of **state-run buses** depart from the **Inter-state Bus Terminal** near Kashmiri Gate in Old Delhi (☎251 9083), which has a cafe and left luggage counter. To be on the safe side, arrive at the terminal an hour or so before your bus leaves. You have to book seats before getting on the bus, which involves a frustrating search for the relevant counter (there are over thirty), where you may well be turned away, having arrived just when the attendant decides to take a break. Make sure you book yourself on the correct bus: most leave frequently and it's usual practice to take the next service. Ask for the registration number and departure platform. Besides

Delhi Transport Corporation, the terminal holds offices of *Rajasthan Roadways* (☎251 4417), *Haryana Roadways* (☎252 1262), *Punjab Roadways* (☎251 7842), and *Himachal Pradesh Roadways* (☎251 6725), and is also used by *Jammu & Kashmir Roadways*, based at *Hotel Kanishka* (☎332 4422 ext 2243), and *UP Roadways*, at Ajmeri Gate (☎251 8709).

Both *UP* and *Haryana Roadways* run deluxe buses to **Agra** (5hr) every half-hour, but the train is much more convenient. Basic *Rajasthan Roadways* buses leave half hourly for **Jaipur** (6hr; Rs45) and **Ajmer** (9hr; Rs70); deluxe services for Jaipur are quicker (5hr; Rs80). *Haryana Roadways* also serves Jaipur, and lays on an a/c bus. Some *Rajasthan Roadways* deluxe buses run to Jaipur from the more pleasant environs of Bikaner House, Pandara Rd near India Gate (☎38 3469). Other *Rajasthan Roadways* destinations include **Alwar** (half hourly; 4hr), **Bikaner** (1 daily at 6am; 11hr), **Chittaurgarh** (3 daily; 12hr), **Jodhpur** (3 daily; 12hr), **Kota** (4 daily; 10hr), and **Pushkar** (1 daily at 11pm; 10hr).

Ordinary *HP* and *Haryana Roadways* buses leave for **Manali** (9 daily; 16hr), calling at **Kulu** en route; a deluxe *HP Roadways* service departs at 8.30pm, and a less smart "semi-deluxe" leaves at 6.30pm. Regular basic *DTC*, *HP* and *Haryana Roadways* buses to **Shimla** (10 daily; 9–10hr) are supplemented by *HP*'s a/c service (9.30am; Rs190), which leaves from their offices at Chanderlok Building, 36 Janpath. Both *DTC* and *HP Roadways* also run to **Dharamshala** (6 daily; 12hr; Rs75), with a deluxe service at 5.30pm, and a semi-deluxe at 6.40pm. Note that the above Himachal Pradesh destinations can all be reached on private buses.

UP Roadways buses into the mountains include frequent departures to **Haridwar** (half hourly; 5hr), and **Rishikesh** (every 45min; 6hr). Services to **Nainital** (8–9hr) range from the excruciating ordinary bus (leaves 7.30am; Rs60) to the *Super Deluxe* (nightly; Rs110); avoid the *Video Coach*. There are also plenty of buses to **Dehra Dun**, **Mussoorie** (2 daily), and to **Almora** (4 daily) – an overnight deluxe bus leaves at 9.15pm (10hr; Rs120). To get to **Corbett National Park**, head for **Ramnagar** (7–8hr; Rs60); the buses are pretty basic but there's little alternative. *DTC*, *Punjab*, *Haryana* and *HP Roadways* buses to **Chandigarh** take 5 or 6 hours; an excellent a/c service costs around Rs140. *J&K Roadways* has a single deluxe bus leaving for **Srinagar** at 5pm (14hr; Rs80).

Private **deluxe buses**, in theory faster and more comfortable than state buses, usually depart from Chelmsford Rd, opposite New Delhi railway station, but some pick up passengers at hotels. They often delay departure to ensure a full quota, and many boast extremely loud video systems that blare throughout the night. Even so, the seats are soft, and usually recline, and some are air-conditioned. Popular destinations include Kulu, Manali, and Dharamsala, which are not accessible by train, as well as Srinagar, towns in the UP hills, and Pushkar. Prices are at least double those charged on state buses. Buy tickets a day or two ahead at the agencies on Chelmsford Rd or Paharganj.

Leaving India

Delhi is well connected to neighbouring Asian countries, and to distant continents, and has no shortage of agents selling tickets. Most travellers leave India by **plane**, while the most likely overland destination from Delhi is Pakistan, and it's not uncommon to head straight for Nepal.

Anyone travelling to a country that requires a **visa** should get the necessary documentation from the embassy concerned (see *Listings*, p.117). Before going to the embassy, call to check opening hours, how many photos you'll need, and the likely waiting period.

By air

If you don't already have a ticket for a **flight** out of India, you'll have little trouble finding one, except between December and March when it may be difficult to get one at

AIRLINE OFFICES IN DELHI

International Airlines

Aeroflot, 1st Floor, BMC House, N-1 Connaught Place, Middle Circle (☎331 0426).

Air Canada, Site No.1421, Holiday Inn Crown Plaza (☎372 0014).

Air France, 7 Atma Ram Mansion, Scindia House, Connaught Circus (☎331 7054).

Air India, Jeevan Bharati Building, opposite Palika Bazaar, Connaught Circus (☎331 1225).

Air Lanka, Room 1, *Hotel Janpath*, Janpath (☎332 6843).

Air Ukraine, C-37, Hauz Khas (☎686 7545).

Alitalia, Surya Kiran Building, 19 Kasturba Gandhi Marg (☎331 1019).

American Airlines, 105 Indra Prakash Building, Barakhamba Rd (☎332 5876).

Bangladesh Biman, c/o *Jet Air*, N-40 Connaught Place (☎331 2119).

British Airways, 1A DLF Centre, Parliament St (☎332 7428).

Canadian Airlines, 66 Janpath (☎371 2266).

Cathay Pacific, Tolstoy House, Tolstoy Marg (☎332 5789).

Continental Airlines, Room No. 5, *Hotel Janpath*, Janpath (☎372 2162).

Emirates, Kanchenjunga Building, 18 Barakhamba Rd (☎331 6644).

Ethiopian Airlines, Room No.2, *Hotel Janpath*, Janpath (☎372 2162).

Gulf Air, G-12 Marina Arcade, Connaught Place (☎332 7814).

Japan Airlines, 36 Chandralok Building, Janpath (☎332 4922).

KLM, 7 Prakash Deep, Tolstoy Marg (☎332 4489).

Kuwait Airways, 2C, DCM Building, 16 Barakhamba Rd (☎331 4221).

Lufthansa, 56 Janpath (☎332 3310).

Malaysian Airlines, G-55 Connaught Place (☎332 4308).

North West Airlines, Indra Prakash Building, Barakhamba Rd (☎371 6006).

Qantas Airways, Mohandev Building, 13 Tolstoy Marg (☎332 9732).

Royal Jordanian, G-56 Connaught Place (☎332 7418).

Royal Nepal Airlines, 44 Janpath (☎332 0817).

SAS, Amadeep Building, Kasturba Gandhi Marg (☎335 2299).

Saudi Arabian Airlines, 15 Hansalaya Building, Barakhamba Rd (☎331 0466).

Singapore Airlines, G-11 Connaught Circus (☎332 0145).

Swissair, DLF Centre, Sansad Marg (☎332 5511).

TAROM, 16 GF Antrikash Building, 22 Kasturba Gandhi Marg (☎335 442).

Thai Airways, Ambadeep Building, 14 Kasturba Gandhi Marg (☎332 3638).

United Airlines, 66 Janpath (☎371 2266).

US Air, 622 Indra Prakash Building, 21 Barakhamba Rd (☎371 4621).

Domestic Airlines

Indian Airlines main office, Safdarjang Airport (☎462 2220). Open around the clock. General enquiries ☎141; pre-recorded information ☎142; departures ☎143.

Indian Airlines Booking Offices: PTI Building, Sansand Marg (Mon–Sat 10am–5pm; ☎371 9168); Malhotra Building, Janpath (daily except Sat 10am–5pm; ☎331 0517); Kanchenjunga Building, Barakhamba Rd (Mon–Sat 10am–5pm; ☎331 3732).

Archana Airways, 41A Friends Colony East, Mathura Rd (☎684 2001).

Damania, UG 26A Somdutt Chambers, 5 Bhikaji Cama Place (☎688 1122).

East West DCM Building, 16 Barakhamba Rd (☎375 5167).

Jagson Airlines, 12E Vandhana, 11 Tolstoy Marg (☎372 1593).

Jet Airways, 3E Hansalaya Building, Barakhamba Rd (☎372 4727).

Modiluft, Vandana Building, Tolstoy Marg (☎371 9347).

Sahara Indian Airlines, Amadeep Building, Kasturba Gandhi Marg (☎332 6851).

Vayudoot, Malhotra Building, Janpath (☎331 2729). No longer flying, but sells tickets.

short notice. While you can buy tickets directly from the airlines, who all have offices around Connaught Place, it saves time and leg work to book through an **agency** (see p.118); reputable agents abound in Paharganj, and there are several on Janpath. The cheapest deals are to be had from touts on the street; make sure they're genuine by ringing the airline to check you have a seat. In any case, confirm your flight 72 hours before leaving.

Airport buses to the international airport, running from outside *Indian Airlines* office at the top of Janpath, cost Rs20 plus Rs5 per item of baggage. You can book tickets in advance at the small office next to *Indian Airlines*. The journey takes around 40 minutes. Departures are as follows: 4am, 5.30am, 7.30am, 2pm, 3.30pm, 6pm, 7.30pm, 9pm, 10.10pm & 11.30pm.

Make sure you arrive two hours prior to departure for all international flights, and put aside Rs300 for the obligatory **airport tax**. Most tourists taking night-time flights book a **taxi** in advance (Rs200–250) to avoid sleeping at the airport, where there's only a minimal food stall. It's a good idea to take a little food and drink in any case – delays are very common. If you're travelling on your own, you should have no difficulty finding someone who will share a taxi.

Overland travel

For journeys to neighbouring countries, there's always the alternative of **overland** travel, a long haul by train and/or bus. Crossings to **Pakistan** should be made from Amritsar, 10 hours by train from Delhi, where buses cross the border and head to Lahore (lifts with trucks are no longer easy to find). Those travelling overland to **Nepal** should make for **Gorakhpur**, to pick up a bus that crosses the border, and drives on to Kathmandu. In addition, several agencies now offer direct bus services to Kathmandu from Delhi – a gruelling two- or three-day journey that is convenient, but rarely comfortable. Connections east to **Bangladesh** can be made via Calcutta or Chittagong.

CHAPTER TWO

RAJASTHAN

Southwest of Delhi, fertile plains roll into the sharp tree-covered crags of the Aravalli mountains, which stretch from the northeastern corner of **RAJASTHAN** down to the south. They peter out in the west of the state, to give way to the parched, forbidding **Thar** or **Great Indian Desert**, whose sands extend west to Pakistan and north to Punjab and Haryana. By contrast, near its southern border with Gujarat, Rajasthan is characterized by verdant hills and fertile fields.

This diverse landscape, until recently a realm of kings, princes, heroic battles, and extravagant merchants, is littered with illustrious palaces, crumbling forts, and sprawling mansions, and emboldened with the vivid, almost luminous, hues of bulging turbans, flowing skirts and pleated scarves and veils. Outside the princely capitals, Rajasthan's vast rural population continues to live in close-knit communities, raising livestock and tending fields of wheat, sugar cane, castor, millet, pulses and rice.

Rajasthan is among India's most popular tourist destinations, with an abundance of palace-hotels that reaches the height of luxury in **Jaipur**, the capital, and **Udaipur**, where one of several palaces glistens white in the centre of a lake. Forts adorn almost every town and city, and range from modest bastions to immense citadels, such as that at **Chittaurgarh**. Thanks to the erstwhile rulers of the palaces and forts, who earmarked land for private hunting expeditions – and tribes such as the Bhils and Bishnois – the outlying countryside offers a rich assortment of wildlife. Tigers, leopards, and a host of other animals and birds can be sought out in the grassy **Sariska National Park** not far from Delhi, and in **Ranthambore National Park** further south, which affords vistas over the lakes and forested hills beyond. The wetlands of **Keoladeo National Park** near Bharatpur boast India's densest concentration of migratory birds, and attract almost three hundred species in the cool winter months. Outside the major cities, where pushy touts and tradesmen can quickly become tiresome, visitors can enjoy quiet, leisurely towns and villages, where camels pad lazily through the streets, and few locals speak English. Many harbour spectacular temples, forgotten forts and exquisite, if faded, mansions, such as the Marwari heartland of

Shekhawati, north of Jaipur, where painted houses, temples and palaces bring life to the endless deserts.

Rajasthan's **climate** reaches the extremes common to desert regions. Temperatures can rise unbearably to over 45°C between May and June, before the heavy skies over central and east Rajasthan break with a fierce monsoon that revitalizes the arid land and fills empty river beds. The summer heat remains until mid-September or October, when night temperatures drop considerably and you'll need a shawl or thick jumper if you're outdoors, and a sleeping bag for night journeys and hotels that don't provide blankets. The best time to visit is between November and February, when daytime temperatures rarely exceed 30°C, and celebrations at fairs and festivals such as Gangaur and Holi fill the streets with swirls of colour.

Getting around the state is rarely problematic, though there's no avoiding some tedious long hauls. The efficient state-run road transport system has regular **bus** services between cities; routes via small towns and villages take longer, and breakdowns and delays are often due to the poor state of the roads rather than a failing in the vehicle. If you don't want to subject yourself to sleepless nights on buses and the din of video coaches, **trains** connect all major cities and many smaller towns – always book ahead for night journeys. Only Jaipur, Jodhpur and Udaipur have **airports**.

Rajasthan, the first state to instigate the **"Paying Guest Scheme"**, is one of the best places to enjoy this unique opportunity to get to know an Indian family and see how they live – most rewarding if you are going to be here for a while rather than just a day or two. Tourist offices across the state keep names and addresses of local families who take part in the scheme, along with details of family members, languages spoken and diet (veg or non-veg). Prices are similar to those of a mid-range hotel.

Some history

People of the Indus Valley Civilization are known to have spread into western India as far as the Gujarati coast, from their base of Mohenjo Daro in Pakistan, but few Rajasthani sites – such as Kali Bangan in the north, thought to have been settled by the **Harappans** before 2500 BC – have been discovered. Similarly, the Buddhist influence of the powerful Mauryan empire, who rose to prominence in Gujarat between 360 BC and 210 BC, touched only the southernmost districts of Rajasthan.

The turbulent history of Rajasthan, characterized by courtly intrigue and inter-state warfare, only really begins in the sixth and seventh centuries AD, with the emergence of warrior clans such as the Sisodias, Chauhans, Kuchwahas and Rathores – the **Rajputs** ("sons of princes"). These heroic fighters seem originally to have been denied positions of power by a rigid caste system, due to low social status or foreign birth, but claimed to be able to cleanse themselves of impurities by complex fire rituals. Never exceeding 8 percent of the population, they were to rule the separate states of **Rajputana** for centuries. Their code of honour set them apart from the rest of society – as did the popular belief that they were descended from the sun and moon – but did not invite excessive hostility. The Rajputs provided land, employment and trading opportunities for their subjects, and are still praised as gods in some communities.

The Rajput codes of chivalry that lay behind endless clashes between clans and family feuds found their most savage expression in battles with Muslims. **Muhammad of Ghori**, the first to march his troops through Rajasthan, met with the fierce defiance of the Chauhan Rajputs at Ajmer; however, the success of his second onslaught gained him the foothold that enabled him to establish the **Sultanate** in Delhi. During the 350 years that followed, much of central, eastern and western India came under the control of the Sultans, but, despite all the Muslims' efforts and victories, Rajput resistance precluded them from ever undermining family solidarity and taking over Rajputana.

Ghori's successors were pushed out of Delhi in 1483 by the Moghul Babur, whose grandson **Akbar** came to power in 1556. Aware of the futility of using force against the

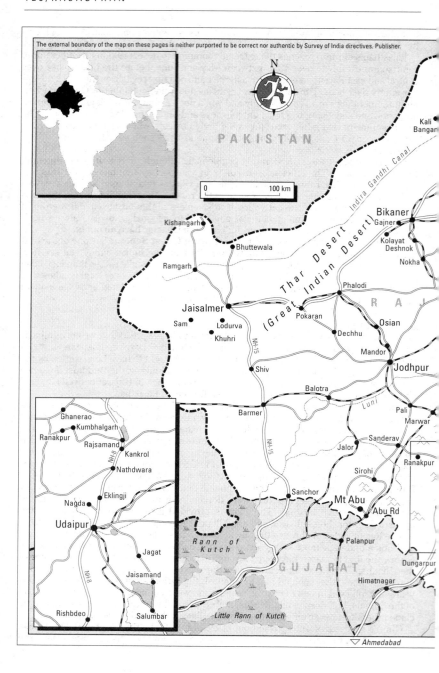

The external boundary of the map on these pages is neither purported to be correct nor authentic by Survey of India directives. Publisher.

N

PAKISTAN

0   100 km

Kali Bangan

Indira Gandhi Canal

Kishangarh

Bhuttewala

Ramgarh

Bikaner
Gajner
Kolayat
Deshnok
Nokha

Thar Desert

(Great Indian Desert)

Phalodi

Jaisalmer
Sam   Lodurva
Khuhri

Pokaran

Dechhu

Osian

Mandor

Shiv

Jodhpur

Balotra

Luni

Pali

Barmer

Marwar

Ghanerao
Kumbhalgarh
Ranakpur
Rajsamand
Kankrol
Nathdwara
Eklingji
Nagda
Udaipur
Jagat
Jaisamand
Rishbdeo
Salumbar

Sanderav
Jalor
Sirohi
Ranakpur

Sanchor

Mt Abu
Abu Rd

Palanpur

GUJARAT

Rann of
Kutch

Dungarpur

Himatnagar

Little Rann of Kutch

▽ Ahmedabad

NH-15
NH-15
NH-8
NH-8
R A J

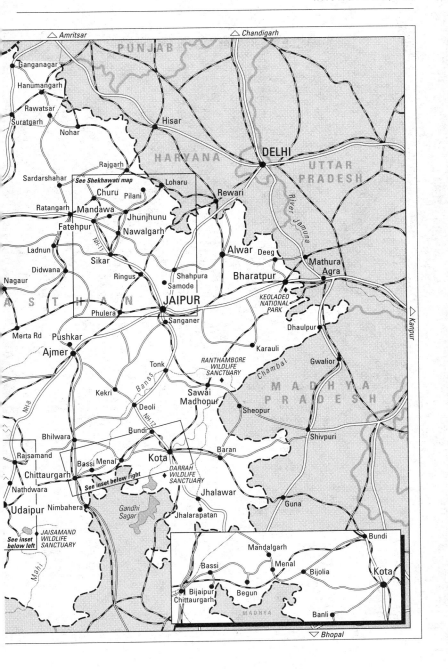

RAJASTHAN TRAVEL DETAILS

	Trains		Buses		Flights	
	Frequency	Time	Frequency	Time	Frequency	Time
To and from JAIPUR						
Agra	1–2 daily	7hr	8 daily	5hr		
Ahmedabad	2 daily	16hr	1 daily	16hr	5 weekly	50min
Ajmer	5 daily	3hr 10min–4hr	every 30min	2hr 30min		
Alwar	7 daily	2hr 35min–4hr	hourly	4hr		
Aurangabad					4 weekly	2hr 20min
Bharatpur			every 30min	4hr		
Bikaner	3 daily	6hr 30min–10hr	11 daily	7hr		
Bombay	1 daily	18hr 20min			22 weekly	1hr 30min
Calcutta	1 daily	29hr			5 weekly	4hr 15min
Chittaurgarh	2 daily	8hr 30min	7 daily	8–9hr		
Churu	3 daily	5hr 20min	every 30min	4hr 30min		
Delhi	8 daily	5hr–8hr	every 15 min	5hr 30min	21 weekly	40min
Indore	1 daily	16hr 10min				
Jaisalmer			1 daily	13hr		
Jhunjhunu	3 daily	4hr 40min–6hr	every 30min	5hr		
Jodhpur	4–5 daily	4hr–5hr	every 30min	7–8hr	4 weekly	45min
Kota	3 daily	4hr	38 daily	6hr	1 daily	30min
Mount Abu*	2 daily	11hr	2 daily	10hr		
Pushkar**			9 daily	3hr 30min		
Sawai Madhopu***	5 daily	2hr 30min	2 daily	5hr		
Sikar	5 daily	3hr	every 15min	3hr		
Udaipur	2 daily	10–12hr	hourly	10hr	8 weekly	45min–1hr15min
To and from JODHPUR						
Ahmedabad	3 daily	9hr 30min	4 daily	12hr		
Ajmer	1 daily	5hr 25min	hourly	5hr		
Alwar	2 daily	8hr 20min				
Bharatpur			2 daily	12hr		
Bikaner	2 daily	4hr 30min	13 daily	6hr		
Bombay					4 weekly	2hr 20min
Delhi	2 daily	11hr 10min	3 daily	14hr	7 weekly	1hr 30min–2hr 20min
Jaisalmer	1 daily	8hr 50min	7 daily	6hr	3 weekly	50min
Kota	1 daily	15hr 40min	5 daily	10hr		
Mount Abu*	2 daily	6hr 35min	1 daily	7hr		
Osian	1 daily	2hr 30min	every 30min	2hr		
Ranakpur			6 daily	6hr		
Udaipur	2 daily	12hr 30min	10 daily	7–9hr	4 weekly	40min
To and from UDAIPUR						
Ahmedabad	2 daily	9hr 40min–13hr 25min	hourly	7hr		
Ajmer	3 daily	7hr 45min–12hr 35min	hourly	8hr		
Aurangabad					4 weekly	1hr 5min
Bikaner			1 daily	12hr		
Bombay					22 weekly	1hr 10min
Chittaurgarh	4 daily	3hr 20min–4hr	6 daily	3hr		
Delhi	2 daily	16hr 40min–20hr 30min	2 daily	17hr	22 weekly	1hr 55min
Kota			6 daily	6hr		
Mount Abu*			6 daily	6hr		
Ranakpur			6 daily	3hr		

Note that no individual route appears more than once in this chart; for any specific journey, check against where you want to get to as well as where you're coming from.

	Trains		Buses		Flights	
	Frequency	Time	Frequency	Time	Frequency	Time
To and from Ajmer						
Ahmedabad	5 daily	10hr–22hr 30min	6 daily	12hr		
Bikaner			12 daily	7hr		
Bharatpur			8 daily	6–8hr		
Chittaurgarh	5 daily	4hr–6hr 15min	every 30min	5–6hr		
Delhi	6 daily	9hr 30min–12hr 20min	18 daily	9–12hr		
Jaisalmer			2 daily	12hr 30min		
Kota			23 daily	5hr		
Pushkar**			every 15min	40min		
To and from Alwar						
Agra	3 weekly	4hr	hourly	2hr		
Ajmer	1 daily	4hr 45min	4 daily	6–7hr		
Bharatpur			every 15min	2hr 30min		
Deeg	1 daily	2hr	every 15min	1hr 30min		
Delhi	4 daily	3hr	15 daily	4–5hr		
To and from Bharatpur						
Agra	2 daily	2hr	hourly	2hr		
Ahmedabad			1 daily	14hr		
Bombay	4 daily	19h–27hr				
Delhi	4 daily	5–6hr	15 daily	4–5hr		
Mathura	8 daily	25min–1hr				
Sawai Madhopur***	6 daily	2hr 15min–5hr				
To and from Bikaner						
Barmer			3 daily	11hr		
Churu	5 daily	4hr	3 daily			
Delhi	3 daily	10hr 30min	4 daily	11hr		
Fatehpur (Shekhawati)	1 daily	6hr	14 daily	5hr 30min		
Gajner			9 daily	1hr		
Jaisalmer			6 daily	7hr 30min		
Jhunjhunu			5 daily	6hr 30min		
Kota			3 daily	9hr		
Mandawa			3 daily	6hr		
Mount Abu*			1 daily	10hr		
To and from Kota						
Ahmedabad	1 daily	10hr 15min				
Bombay	8 daily	11hr 40min–21hr				
Bundi	1 daily	1hr	every 30min	1hr		
Chittaurgarh	1 daily	4hr 30min	7 daily	4hr		
Delhi	7 daily	5hr 30min–11hr	3 daily	9hr	1 daily	1hr 50min
Jhalawar			hourly	2hr 30min		
Mathura	7 daily	4hr 10min–10hr 5min				
Sawai Madhopur***	13 daily	1hr 30min	4 daily	4hr		
Ujjain	1 daily	4hr 40min	2 daily	4hr		
To and from Mount Abu*						
Ahmedabad	7 daily	4hr 30min–6hr	10 daily	7hr		
Ajmer	5 daily	5hr 15min–12hr 35min	2 daily	7hr 30min		
Bhuj	1 daily	15hr				
Delhi	3 daily	13hr 45min–21hr 45min	1 daily	18hr		
Jaisalmer			1 daily	10hr		
Ranakpur			6 daily	3hr		

* Trains for Mount Abu use the **Abu Road** station, 1hr away on regular buses; see p.204.
** Long-distance travel connections for **Pushkar** are best made via Ajmer; see p.165.
*** For Ranthambore National Park

FESTIVALS IN RAJASTHAN

Rajasthan's striking juxtaposition of vibrant local costumes against the arid sandscape is most dazzling during the state's **festivals**, which accompany cattle markets and celebrate nationwide religious events, local folk heroes and village deities. In addition to intoxicating blazes of colour, the festivals invariably feature traditional dancing, singing and the music of pipes, drums and rickety stringed instruments. Some are geared particularly towards foreign visitors, and many of the most important celebrations fall in the tourist season (the cool months between November and March). For dates of specific events, ask at tourist offices; most festivals fall on days determined by the lunar calendar.

Most **weddings** are held between April and June; noisy, communal affairs when out-of-tune bands and dancing relatives jostle through the streets waving rupee notes, and mobile strip lights illuminate dapper bridegrooms decked in turbans and tinsel.

Tilwara Cattle Fair (Jan). The small town of Barmer comes alive during Rajasthan's largest cattle market that draws traders from all over the state.

Nagaur Cattle Fair (Feb). Dancing, singing and sales of local handicrafts accompany the trading of cows, buffalo, donkeys and horses at Nagaur, 100km south of Bikaner.

Desert Festival (Feb). Jaisalmer's own two-day event when camel races, handicraft stalls, folk dances and competitions are laid on primarily to attract tourists, but also help sustain traditional arts and crafts.

Holi (Feb/March). A festival celebrating the end of winter and the destruction of evil demons, held throughout northern India. Dancing and drumming (especially good in Churu) continue for several days before the final day of manic coloured-powder throwing.

Elephant Festival (March). Parades of mounted elephants bedecked in jewels march through the streets of Jaipur and into the City Palace to the accompaniment of drums and trumpets.

Eid-ul-fitr (March). Muslims celebrate the end of Ramadan, a month of fasting, with special milk sweets, *sheer kurma*, and gather for prayers in the mosques.

Mewar Festival (March/April). The Ranas of Udaipur commemorate their long line of rulers with dance and music and a bellowing refrain from a bagpipe orchestra in the *Shiv Niwas Palace* hotel.

Gangaur (April). A festival unique to Rajasthan, when women pray for their husbands, and unmarried girls wish for good ones. Effigies of Gauri (Parvati) and Isa (Shiva) – the ideal couple – are carried through the streets along with potted rice and flowers which hark back to the days when this was primarily a harvest festival. Excellent in Jaisalmer, when the local Raja heads the procession amid an entourage of camels.

Urs Mela (April/May). Thousands of Muslims and Hindus converge on the Dargah in Ajmer to commemorate the life of the Sufi saint and teacher Muin-ud-din Chisti, who died here in 1236. Much drumming, praying and feasting.

Muharram (April/June). Shi'a Muslim festival remembering the death of Hussain. Concentrated in Muslim quarters of cities and in Fatehpur, Jhunjhunu and Churu. Models of saints' tombs are led through the streets in grand procession after a night of vigorous drumming, especially in Churu.

Rani Sati Mela (Aug). A day of prayers and dances in Jhunjhunu, in memory of a merchant's widow who committed *sati*, sacrificing her life on her husband's pyre, in 1595.

Gugaji Mela (Aug). A festival held in honour of the local goddess in Churu.

Dussehra (Oct). Nine days of dancing and singing dedicated to the goddess Durga. Scenes from the *Ramayana* are acted out on makeshift stages, but in Bissau (Shekhawati) these are replaced by silent dances at dusk.

Diwali (Nov). A five-day festival of lights celebrated across India but of particular importance to the merchant community, especially in Shekhawati, since it marks the start of the financial year and includes a day of praises to Lakshmi, goddess of wealth. Hundreds of delicious sweets are cooked and exchanged by families and friends.

Pushkar Camel Fair (Nov). Rajasthan's largest event, when traders of camels, oxen, buffaloes, cows and donkeys are joined by handicraft sellers and thousands of tourists who are accommodated in specially erected tent cities. Camel races, dances and fireworks continue for four days.

Chandrabhaga Fair (Nov). The full moon of Kartika is celebrated in Jhalawar at the temples on the banks of the Chandrabhaga, and devotees bathe in the river.

Rajputs, Akbar chose instead to negotiate in friendship, and married Rani Jodha Bai, a princess from the Kuchwaha family of Amber. As a result, Rajputs entered the Moghul courts, and the influence of Moghul ideas on art and architecture remains evident in palaces, mosques, pleasure gardens and temples throughout the state.

When the Moghul empire began to decline after the accession of Aurangzeb in 1658, so too did the power of the Rajputs. Aurangzeb sided with a new force, the **Marathas**, who plundered Rajput lands and extorted huge sums of protection money from territories as strong as Mewar, whose capital was Udaipur, and Marwar, whose ruling family in Jodhpur had never submitted to any other power. The Rajputs eventually turned for help to the Marathas' chief rivals, the **British**, and signed formal treaties as to mutual allies and enemies. Although in theory the Residents who represented British authority in each state were supposed to be neutral communicators, they were soon wielding more power than the Rajput princes. However, the Rajputs were never denied their royal status, and relations were so amicable that few joined the Mutiny of 1857. Wealth from overland trade enabled them to festoon their palaces with silks, carpets, jewels and furnishings far beyond the imagination of most ordinary citizens, while the prosperous **Marwari** merchants of the northwest built and decorated stylish mansions, temples and meeting halls. Murals depicting British ministers with Indians, British hunting parties, ladies, motor cars and black-capped bobbies are firm reminders of the strong alliance between the two ruling powers.

The nationwide clamour for Independence in the years up to 1947 eventually proved stronger in Rajasthan than Rajput loyalty; when British rule ended the Rajputs were left out on a limb. With persuasion from the new Indian government including the offer of "privy purses", they agreed one by one to join the Indian Union, and in March 1949 the 22 states of Rajputana finally merged to form the state of **Rajasthan**.

But for three brief years of Janata domination from 1977 onwards, Congress held sway over Rajasthan from its first democratic elections in 1952 until 1994, when the **BJP** won a decisive victory. Central control soon exposed the Rajputs' neglect of their

THE PALACE ON WHEELS

To enjoy the life of Rajasthan's former maharajas and maharanis, you have two options: either splash out and stay a night in one of the illustrious palace hotels, or go the whole hog and spend a week travelling like royalty between the state's finest cities on the **Palace on Wheels**. India's answer to the *Orient Express*, the *Palace on Wheels* is among the most luxurious trains in the world, and offers an unrivalled tour of beautiful countryside and stupendous monuments. In 1993 the maharajas' carriages were updated into modern coaches, still decorated with original designs. Within the air-conditioned train, twin bedrooms, spacious lounges, dining rooms and bars are all decked out in classic Rajput style, using local cloths and soft bolsters to complement the traditional carved wood and stone inlay designs that cover the walls. Each group of tourists is attended by hosts in full royal livery, often greeted with garlands and trumpets in the larger cities, and courteously guided around forts and palaces.

The whistle-stop tour (Sept–April only) starts each week in Delhi, with stops at Jaipur, Chittaurgarh, Udaipur, Jaisalmer, Jodhpur, Bharatpur and Agra. The price ($300 per person per day double occupancy, $450 per person per day single occupancy, $240 triple occupancy) includes all meals, buffet lunches at the palace hotels of Udaipur and Jaipur, and a camel ride and dance show in Jaisalmer. The trip is brief, and extortionately expensive, but it's a must for train buffs, upmarket travellers with limited time, and anyone who simply likes to be pampered.

Bookings can be made through RTDC offices, or in railway offices in the US, Australasia, Thailand, the UK and other European countries. Addresses are given in *Basics* on p.31 and details of similar services elsewhere in India.

subjects, whom they had entrusted to power-thirsty landowners (*jaghidars*), and village councils (*panchayats*) were set up to organize local affairs. Nonetheless, several princes still maintain splendid households amid great honour. Since 1947 the literacy rate has risen from 8.95 percent to 25 percent, and several universities have been established – though female illiteracy is still higher than elsewhere in India. New industries benefit from an increased electricity supply that once only met the needs of palaces, and now reaches most villages, while irrigation schemes such as the Indira Gandhi Canal, which brings water from Punjab across the northern deserts to Bikaner and Jaisalmer, have improved crop production, and provided relief in times of inadequate monsoon.

Jaipur

A flamboyant showcase of Rajasthani architecture and flair at its most irresistible, the **Pink City** of **JAIPUR** has long been established on tourist itineraries as the third corner of India's "Golden Triangle", just 300km southwest of Delhi and 200km west of Agra. Though the "Pink City" label applies specifically to the old walled quarter of the Rajasthani capital, in the northeast of town, glorious palaces and temples, in an assortment of styles that span the centuries, are scattered throughout the whole urban area. The walled city is suffused with a gentle pink light, flashed through by bright turbans and *saris*, while in the pink shops and houses that line its orderly streets, craftsmen create objects of delicate beauty with time-honoured traditional skills, in full view of the hectic swirl of shoppers and tourists outside.

Lying on the bed of a long-dry lake, Jaipur laps against hills in the north, east and west, and rolls across the open plains to the south towards Bundi. Getting and keeping your bearings is simple; even if you can't see the high walls of the Pink City, the hills behind it in the northeast, topped by **Nahagarh Fort**, are always conspicuous.

The **Pink City** houses the principal tourist attractions – the Palace of Winds or **Hawa Mahal**, and Jai Singh's **City Palace** and **Observatory** – while the **Ram Niwas Garden, zoo, Albert Hall (Central Museum)** and **Modern Art Gallery** are a short way south of the walls, within easy walking distance of its gates. Broad and widely spaced roads in the newer areas outside the walls accommodate the industries and businesses that underlie the economy of the modern city, as well as most of Jaipur's hotels. **Mirza Imail Road** is the main route from west to east (south of the old city), on which you'll find the GPO, hotels and restaurants and some of the larger boutiques and jewellery shops. **Station Road** runs from the railway station in the west, past the bus stand and on to Chand Pole, the westernmost gate of the old city.

For all its appeal, Jaipur's heavy traffic, combined with the aggression of over-eager traders, tends to reduce the appeal of a long stay. Few travellers find it easy to relax here, though most spend a good few days visiting the sublime palaces, exploring the ruins and wandering through the bazaars, renowned for carpets, clothes, and the best selection of precious stones and metals in India.

If you're anywhere near Jaipur in March, don't miss the **Elephant Festival**, one of India's most flamboyant parades, celebrated with full Rajput pomp. Makar Sankranti (14 Jan), predominantly celebrated in the east of India, here takes the form of a **kite festival**, filling the air with gaudy paper kites for days leading up to it.

A brief history

Jaipur is one of Rajasthan's younger cities, founded in 1727. In 1700, **Jai Singh II** succeeded at the tender age of thirteen to the throne of the **Kuchwaha Rajputs** in Ajmer, inheriting a realm that encompassed Shekhawati to the north, and spread east to the borders of the kingdom of the Jats at Bayana, south to Aligarh, and west to Kishangarh where its boundaries met the mighty kingdoms of the Mewars (Udaipur) and Marwars

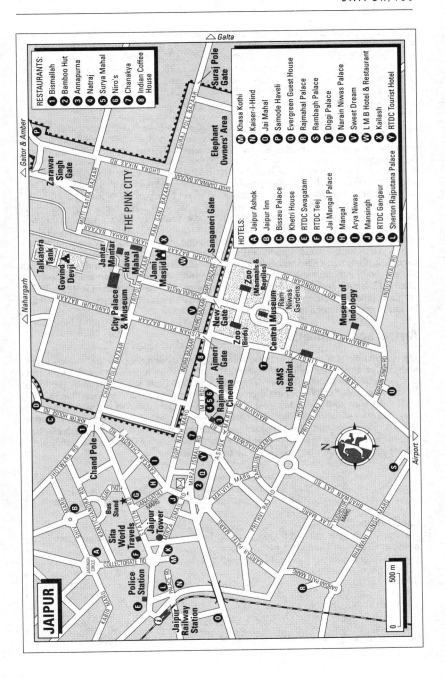

△ *Galta*

JAIPUR

THE PINK CITY

RESTAURANTS:
1 Bismallah
2 Bamboo Hut
3 Annapurna
4 Natraj
5 Surya Mahal
6 Niro's
7 Chanakya
8 Indian Coffee House

HOTELS:
A Jaipur Ashok
B Jaipur Inn
C Bissau Palace
D Khetri House
E RTDC Swagatam
F RTDC Teej
G Jai Mangal Palace
H Mangal
I Arya Niwas
J Mansingh
K RTDC Gangaur
L Sherton Rajputana Palace
M Khasa Kothi
N Kaiser-I-Hind
O Jai Mahal
P Samode Haveli
Q Evergreen Guest House
R Rajmahal Palace
S Rambagh Palace
T Diggi Palace
U Narain Niwas Palace
V Sweet Dream
W L M B Hotel & Restaurant
X Kailash
Y RTDC Tourist Hotel

△ *Gaitor & Amber*
△ *Nahargarh*

Suraj Pole Gate
Zarawar Singh Gate
Elephant Owners' Area
Sanganeri Gate
Talkatora Tank
Govind Devji
Jantar Mantar
Hawa Mahal
Jami Masjid
City Palace & Museum
New Gate
Ajmeri Gate
Zoo (Birds)
Zoo (Mammals & Reptiles)
Ram Niwas Gardens
Central Museum
Museum of Indology
SMS Hospital
Rajmandir Cinema
Chand Pole
Bus Stand
Jaipur Tower
Sita World Travels
Police Station
Jaipur Railway Station

Airport ▷

N

0   500 m

(Jodhpur). Although the Kuchwaha Rajputs had been the first to ally themselves with the Moghuls, in 1561, thereby inviting contempt from other Rajput clans, the free flow of trade, art and ideas with their obliging overlords had by this time won them great prosperity. Jai Singh's sharp wit greatly impressed the Moghul emperor Aurangzeb, who bestowed upon him the title of "Sawai" (one and a quarter), to imply his superlative potential. Jai Singh proved his distinction, excelling in battle, politics and learning, and quickly showing an aptitude for astronomy and an extraordinary passion for symmetry.

When Jai Singh decided to move his capital south from the cramped hilly area of Amber, he drew up plans for the new city of Jaipur, named after himself, in accordance with the ancient Hindu treatise *Shilpa Sashtra*, a formal exposition on architecture written soon after the compilation of the *Vedas*. With the aid of the superb Bengali architect Vidyadhar Bhattacharaya, he had the city built in under eight years, following the sacred guidelines with unrivalled precision. The **City Palace** was also designed by him, as was **Jantar Mantar**, the largest stone-built observatory in the world.

After Jai Singh's fruitful 43-year reign came an inevitable battle for succession between the offspring he had fathered with 28 wives and four concubines, and the state was thrown into turmoil. Much of its territory was lost to Marathas and Jats, and the British quickly moved in to take advantage of Rajput infighting, gaining power for themselves while forming alliances with the Rajputs to avoid inconvenient conflict. Unlike their neighbours in Delhi and Agra, the rulers of Jaipur remained loyal to the British during the bloody uprisings of 1857. Following Independence, Jaipur merged with the states of Bikaner, Jodhpur and Jaisalmer; it became capital of Rajasthan in 1956. Today, with a population bordering on two million, the state's most advanced commercial and business centre remains as prosperous as ever.

Arrival and information

Jaipur's **airport**, 15km south of the centre, is served by domestic *Indian Airlines* flights and one or two independent operators. An airport bus into town costs Rs20; taxis charge more like Rs100. The very cheapest way to get into town is to walk 1km or so to the roundabout called Airport Circle, and take city bus #113 from there for Rs3.

The **railway station** is 1km west of the Pink City, very close to the main concentration of hotels, while ordinary and "deluxe" **buses** from all over Rajasthan and further afield arrive at the central **Inter-state bus terminal** on Station Rd. Rickshaws at both stations will take you to your lodgings, invariably asking over the odds; for hotels along MI Rd and Station Rd the fare *should* be between Rs7 and Rs12.

The telephone **area code** for Jaipur is ☎0141.

Information

For information and guided tours of Jaipur, head for the main **RTDC tourist information office** on Platform 1 of the railway station (daily 6am–8pm; ☎315714). They can also help find accommodation, and have good local maps. There's a second branch at the *Tourist Hotel* (☎375466), and a Government of India Tourist Office at the *Khasa Kothi* hotel (Mon–Fri 9am–6pm, Sat 9am–1.30pm; ☎372200). The monthly **Jaipur Vision**, listing hotels, restaurants, sights, events, shopping hints and fair rickshaw prices, should be in stock in *Books Corner* on MI Rd (Rs20).

Changing **travellers' cheques** can be time-consuming. **Banks** (Mon–Fri 11am–2pm) include *Bank of Baroda*, Johari Bazaar; *State Bank of India*, Sanganeri Gate, MI Rd; *Punjab National Bank*, near Hawa Mahal, and *State Bank of Bikaner and Jaipur*

(Mon–Fri noon–6pm). *Thomas Cook* in Jaipur Towers, on MI Rd (Mon–Sat 9.30am–6pm; ☎360940), are much faster and more courteous than any bank, and give better rates; or you could try *Transcorp International*, in Shanti Sedan on Church Rd, off MI Rd just west of Sardar Patel Marg (Mon–Sat 9.30am–6.30pm, Sun 9.30am–1.30pm). Upmarket hotels offer exchange, usually at poor rates, and often only to their guests.

For **poste restante** go to the GPO on MI Rd (Mon–Sat 9am–6pm). Parcels or registered mail is kept at the sorting office behind the main desks. Most hotels offer direct dial **phone calls** to other states and abroad, but calls are cheaper in shops offering STD/ISD/PCO. Look for the yellow signs. Some such shops also offer **fax** facilities.

City transport

Jaipur's frenzied flow of vehicles is at its heaviest during the morning and evening peak periods; it's best to avoid rush hours if you want to enjoy the sights and street activity without gripping your seat in fear. Jaipur is fairly spread out, and although it's pleasant to walk around the Pink City, you may need some form of transport to get you there.

Unmetered yellow-top **taxis** have stands on MI Rd. Precarious **tempos** can be hailed along all the main thoroughfares in and out of the Pink City; the flat rate is Rs2 or 3. Cheaper (and fuller) **minibuses**, some of them light pink, ply the same routes, zig-zagging and jerking through the chaotic jumble of traffic. For a less hair-raising experience, try an **auto-rickshaw**, which should be metered, or a **cycle rickshaw**.

Many budget hotels rent out **bicycles** to their guests; failing that, you can rent them for Rs20 a day from a place in the passage by 286 Kishan Pole Bazaar, about 100m north of the Ajmeri Gate. The use of an RTDC **car** (with driver) costs from Rs100 for one hour to Rs500 for twelve; they can be picked up at the *Tourist Hotel*, MI Rd.

City tours

One efficient way to see Jaipur's main attractions is on a **guided tour**. The inexpensive RTDC tours can be a trifle rushed, but they are good value and the guides are very informative. **Half-day** tours, starting from the railway station and the RTDC *Tourist Hotel* on MI Rd, take in Hawa Mahal, Observatory, City Palace and Museum, Amber Fort, Jaigarh Fort and Central Museum (daily 8am, 11.30am & 1.30pm; 5hr, book the day before; Rs60). The **full-day** tour (daily 9am–6pm; Rs90) also includes the Dolls' Museum, Birla Mandir and Nahagarh Fort – getting to the fort alone costs more than the tour itself, unless you walk. RTDC plans to make the morning and afternoon half-day tours different, so that you can see everything in two separate half days without exhausting yourself. ITDC *Ashok Travels and Tours* at the gates of the *Khasa Kothi* hotel offers full-day tours (daily 9.30am–5.30pm; Rs70) which also take in Amber.

The Pink City

For anyone familiar with other Indian cities, the rigorous geometry of Jaipur's **Pink City** may come as a surprise. High walls with ten gates enclose the old city, which is divided into seven sectors, with the City Palace at its heart. Maharaja Jai Singh clearly aimed for architectural perfection when he planned the city in 1727; instead of a maze of narrow winding alleys, the spacious streets are completely straight and laid out at right angles, in accordance with calculations laid down in the *Shilpa Shastra*. All roads are of prescribed widths and the shops are equally proportioned; even the mosques and temples slot neatly into place between shops and houses. The only buildings to stray from the structural uniformity are the City Palace and the Hawa Mahal.

The single most striking feature of the old city, its **pink** colour, did not in fact form part of Jai Singh's plans. Although many people think the rosy hue is as old as the buildings themselves, they were in fact originally a sallow yellow. Pink is traditionally the colour of hospitality in Rajasthan, but the wash, now regularly reapplied, has only been compulsory since the city was spruced up in preparation for the visit of Prince Albert from England in 1856.

Each quarter in the Pink City is home to a particular centre of activity or commerce. **Surajpole Bazaar** in the southeast corner houses elephants and their owners; **Nehru Bazaar** (closed Tues) and **Bapu Bazaar** (closed Sun) are special centres for textiles, perfumes and locally styled camel skin shoes; shops in **Tripolia Bazaar** and **Chaura Rasta** sell textiles and household utensils. For Jaipur's much celebrated silver, sparkling gems and tie-dyed *saris*, go to **Johari Bazaar** (partly closed on Sun & Tues). Behind the City Palace, to the north, spacious gardens surround Govind Devji Temple and the vast Talkatora water tank.

Hawa Mahal

Jaipur's most acclaimed landmark, the tapering **Hawa Mahal**, or "Palace of Winds", stands to the west of the City Palace, where it exudes an orangey pink glow in the rays of the rising sun. Built in 1799 to enable the women of the court to watch street processions while remaining in a strict state of *purdah*, its five-storey facade, decked with no less than 593 finely screened windows and balconies, makes the building seem far larger than it really is; in fact it is little more than one room thick in most parts.

Though the primary source of its appeal is undoubtedly the fantastic honeycomb pink and white face, visitors can go inside (enter from the back) to see exactly where the women sat, and take a close look at the detailed stone work (daily except Fri 10am–4.30pm; Rs2, camera Rs30, video Rs70).

City Palace

Daily 9.30am–4.45pm. Rs30 (students, athletes and jounalists with ID, and everyone on holy days, Rs15), camera Rs50, video Rs100.

The magnificent **City Palace**, open to the public as the **Sawai Man Singh Museum**, stands enclosed by a high wall in the centre of the city amid fine gardens and court-yards. The royal family still occupies part of the palace, advancing in procession on for-mal occasions through the grand **Tripolia Gate** in the centre of the southern wall. Less regal visitors must enter through **Atish Gate** left of the main gate or **Nakkar Gate** in the west, passing the food stalls and souvenir shops in **Jalebi Chowk**.

The palace was conceived and built by Jai Singh, but many of the apartments and halls were added by his successors. The exhibits and interior design have lost none of the pomp and splendour of their glory days. Each door and gateway is heavily deco-rated, each chandelier intact and each hall guarded by sentinels decked in full royal liv-ery, so that Jaipur's palace, unlike any other in Rajasthan, impresses upon the visitor the continuity of a living royal presence.

An ornate gateway in the southwest corner of the complex leads into the first court-yard, with the solid marble **Mubarak Mahal** in its centre. This elegant palace, built in 1890, holds the textile section of the museum, where stylish clothes include those worn by Madho Singh I (one of Jai Singh's sons) who stood a full 2m tall. Musical instru-ments used to entertain the rulers are also on display. The first floor of the building next to the Mubarak Mahal houses the royal **arsenal**. Inside what was once the harem, with its delicate paintings on the walls and mirrors glittering on the ceilings, is laid out a menacing array of spears, swords, shields and daggers. The terrifying blades conjure up images of raging battles, but inscriptions and bejewelled decorations on handles and shields make them surprisingly attractive on purely aesthetic grounds.

As you enter the second courtyard you're confronted by the raised **Diwan-i-Khas**, the Hall of Private Audience, built in sandstone and marble. Open sided, with its roof raised on marble pillars, the hall contains two silver urns, reputedly the largest crafted silver objects in the world, each more than 1.5m high. When Madho Singh II went to England to attend the coronation of King Edward VII in 1901, he was so reluctant to trust the water in the West that he had these urns filled with Ganges water and took them along with him.

In the centre of the compound, with balconies and windows studding its seven-storey facade, **Chandra Mahal** is the residence of the royal family. You can see it best from **Pritam Niwas Chowk**, known as Peacock Courtyard, to the west of the Diwan-i-Khas. Against the ochre walls of this court, four gateways provide a shock of dazzling colour, decorated with peacocks and regular patterns in red, green, blue and gold.

The last, and largest, section of the museum is housed in the **Diwan-i-Am**, once the Hall of Public Audience, where ornate pillars support the high ceilings. The walls, intricately painted with touches of deep red and gold, provide perfect mounts for immense medieval Afghan and Pakistani carpets. Miniatures from the Moghul and Jaipur schools, and Jai Singh's translations in Arabic and Sanskrit of the astronomical treatises of ancient scientists such as Euclid and Ptolemy, are displayed in glass cases, all under the breeze of huge fans and the shimmer of chandeliers.

Jantar Mantar

Daily 9am–4.30pm. Rs4 (free on Mon), camera Rs50, video Rs100.

The incredible brick curves, slants, circles and pillars of Jai Singh's astronomical **observatory**, overlaid with sherbet-yellow gypsum, are solidly planted in the southern courtyard of the palace complex. A total of eighteen instruments were erected between 1728–34 by Jai Singh; some are triangular, some are circular or semicircular, and all are very large. Although Jai Singh was influenced by the works of foreign astrologers and the advice of his teachers – one of whom was his mother – many of the devices were of his own invention.

It's a good idea to pay (Rs25–50) for the services of a guide to explain how the observatory works. The instruments are built so that shadows fall onto marked surfaces, identifying the position and movement of stars and planets, telling the time, and even predicting the intensity of the monsoon. The time calculated is unique to Jaipur, between ten and forty-one minutes (depending on the time of year) behind Indian standard time, but is used to calculate the Hindu (lunar) calendar. Probably the most impressive of Jai Singh's constructions is the sundial, **Samrat Yantra**. Its slanting centrepiece, or *gnomon*, reaches a height of 27m, casting shadows onto curved stone faces that are graduated in hours. Each hour is divided into thirty parts, so the time calculated is accurate to within two minutes.

A more original device, the **Jaiprakash Yantra**, consists of two hemispheres laid in the ground, each composed of six curving marble slabs with a suspended ring in the centre whose shadow marks the day, time and zodiac symbol. This is vital in calculations of auspicious days for marriage; when unfavourable planets are in influential positions, for example between August and October, marriages have always been avoided.

Outside the Pink City

Jaipur's attractions outside the Pink City include museums, temples and cenotaphs, which can be reached from the centre of town on foot or by rickshaw.

Ram Niwas Public Gardens

South of the Pink City, on the road leading out of New Gate, lie 36 acres of lush gardens, named **Ram Niwas Public Gardens** after the planner, Ram Singh, who ruled Jaipur from 1835–80. The gardens represent but a small fraction of Ram Singh's successful efforts to improve public services, and originally covered 76 acres.

As well as providing parks for the citizens, the gardens now house a number of institutions, the most notable being the **Albert Hall**, in which you'll find the **Central Museum** (daily except Fri 10am–4.30pm; Rs3, free on Mon), designed by the British architect Sir Samuel Jacob. This remarkable stately construction, built over several years from 1867 onwards, drew heavily on contemporary British models, but its arched verandahs and rooftop domed pavilions hint at the Moghul background of its artisans. The exhibits within, including miniature paintings, rocks, clothes and ornamental wooden boxes, are not quite as inspiring as the building itself, but it's worth seeking out the highly original display of *yoga* postures demonstrated by tiny clay *sadhus*. Also within the gardens is a **zoo** (daily except Tues; summer 8am–6pm, winter 8am–5.30pm), with an aviary on one side, an animal section on the other, and a small crocodile-breeding farm. The beasts are kept in the usual poor conditions.

To the south of these, off Jawaharlal Nehru Rd, the **Museum of Indology** (daily 10am–5pm; Rs30 including guided tour) holds an outrageous collection of assorted curiosities maintained by writer and painter Acharya Vyakul, including a map of India painted on a grain of rice, letters written on a hair, a glass bed, textiles, manuscripts, stamps, coins and the largest collection of tantric art in the world, as well as a gallery of modern art. A larger premises is planned 7km out on the road to Amber.

Birla Mandir

One of Jaipur's newer temples, **Birla Mandir**, was built in the southeast of town in 1985, funded by the affluent Birla family. The large marble structure houses ornate statues of Lakshmi and Narayan dressed in gaudy robes, representing the Hindu vision of heavenly luxury. Carvings in the temple and on pillars supporting covered walkways include images of the Hindu pantheon and Jesus, Mary and St Francis of Assisi. The design leans towards the idea of universal religion, but architecturally its standard is nowhere near as high as India's ancient temples.

Gaitor

A short distance north of the City Palace, and just over 6km from central Jaipur on the Amber road, the walled complex of **Gaitor** contains the stately marble *chhatris* of Jaipur's ruling family. Built by Jai Singh II, the complex contains memorials to himself and his successors, including his son and grandson, with room set aside for a future memorial to the present head of the family.

Unless a ruler should happen to die an untimely death, the construction of his cenotaph is normally well under way during his lifetime, and traditionally each ruler takes exceptional pains to ensure that the marble carving on his own tomb is of an appropriately high standard. That of Jai Singh is inlaid with scenes from Hindu mythology, and processions from his reign, depicting among other things the Hawa Mahal.

Nahagarh

Teetering on the edge of the hills northeast of Jaipur, **Nahagarh**, or "Tiger Fort" (10am–4.30pm; Rs2) was built by Jai Singh II in 1734 as a retreat for his wives, the maharanis. Its unique design, regular and repetitive, stands in contrast to the other royal dwellings in Jaipur, and the views are breathtaking.

All the queens' apartments are identical, arranged around the central courtyard in perfect symmetry, each with a room for a personal maidservant. Ram Singh, who in 1868 built more apartments on the upper floor, continued Jai Singh's tradition of orderly design by constructing another set of identical rooms. These bear traces of paintings, and their slightly damaged stained-glass windows are still quaint.

Vehicles of any kind can only get to the fort along a road that branches off Amber Rd, a nine-kilometre journey from Jaipur. However, if you're feeling energetic, it's possible to **walk** there along a two-kilometre footpath that starts northwest of the City Palace. A very reasonably priced cafe by the fort serves meals and snacks.

If you want to **stay** somewhere a little out of the ordinary, the old buildings next to the fort hold one double room for rent (④; best booked in advance ☎320538): the room is simple but the views spectacular, with six windows facing west and south.

Galta

Nestling in a steep-sided valley 2km west of Jaipur, **GALTA** is a picturesque collection of temples, two hundred and fifty years old. You can either get there by road, following a route that winds around the hills for 16km, or take a fairly gruelling walk from town, leaving by **Suraj Pole** and climbing up to the Surya temple on the crest of the hill before dropping down into the valley below.

Galta owes its sacred status in large part to a freshwater spring that seeps constantly through the rocks in the otherwise dry valley, keeping two tanks fresh and full, and hordes of monkeys (associated with the monkey god Hanuman) happy. Humans bathe in the upper water tank, while monkeys jump and splash in the lower pool.

The temples themselves are intricately and vividly painted. Friezes around the top of pavilions that face the monkeys' tank show scenes from religious festivals and stately occasions; behind one procession the City Palace is sketched in dubious proportions. Inside the roofs, swirling red, yellow and blue clouds ring more of Michelangelo than of traditional Hindu style.

The long road to Galta passes **Sisodia Rani ka Bagh** (daily 8am–6pm; Rs1), 8km east of Jaipur. Landscaped with fountains and painted pavilions, these gardens are part of a palace complex built in the eighteenth century by Jai Singh II for the Udaipur princess he married to secure relations with his neighbouring Sisodia Rajputs. When the political alliance weakened, the queen lost favour with the Jaipur household and moved to a private palace with her son, Madho, who later succeeded his father.

Temples at the back of the gardens, coated with the sherbet-yellow wash that covers the whole compound – the original colour of the Pink City – and enhanced with naturalistic designs, are open midday and early evening for worship.

Accommodation

As a major centre for business and tourism, Jaipur has a wide selection of **hotels**, most of them scattered south and west of the Pink City. Dull but adequate options and elaborate old palaces share roads with hotels that wouldn't seem out of place in any Western capital. Some have swimming pools, most have restaurants, and the more expensive hotels offer taxi services to and from the airport. At busy times of year, such as Christmas and the Elephant Festival (first half of March), it's prudent to book ahead.

ACCOMMODATION PRICE CODES

All **accommodation prices** in this book have been coded using the symbols below. In principle the prices given are for the least expensive double rooms in each establishment; however, some hotels, usually in category ①, offer rates per bed rather than per room. Local taxes are not included unless specifically stated. For more details, see p.35.

① up to Rs100	④ Rs225–350	⑦ Rs750–1200
② Rs100–150	⑤ Rs350–500	⑧ Rs1200–2200
③ Rs150–225	⑥ Rs500–750	⑨ Rs2200 and upwards

Inexpensive

Diggi Palace, Diggi House, Shivaji Marg, Hospital Rd (☎374265; fax 370359). A welcome respite from the dust and noise. Clean, well-managed 200-year-old palace with budget rooms, a/c options and cottages facing beautiful lawns. Excellent meals in terrace restaurant, and a party in the grand hall at Christmas. ②–⑥.

Evergreen Guest House, Chameliwala Mkt, MI Rd (☎363446; fax 371934). Crowded and shabby, but popular with young travellers. Exceptionally poor dorms and variable rooms, most with private bath. Pleasant garden area, mediocre restaurant and tiny swimming pool. Often full. ①–③.

Jaipur Inn, Shiv Marg, Bani Park (☎316821). An informal budget travellers' favourite, with a selection of rooms and an excellent dorm, all spotlessly clean. Camping on the lawn (Rs25 per person). Tasty and filling evening meals, also served on rooftop; great views. ①–④.

Kaiser-I-Hind, Palace Rd, opposite the *Sheraton Rajputana* (☎310195). Characterful old house whose huge suites and musty dining hall still ring of the days of the Raj, and which boasts airy verandahs and a garden with peacocks. The manager claims that guests have included Mark Twain (who wrote about room #6 in his autobiography), Henry Ford, Gandhi and Benito Mussolini. ③.

RTDC Tourist Hotel, MI Rd (☎360238). Large place with tatty rooms, dorm, and vast lawns. ①–④.

Moderate

Arya Niwas, behind Amber Complex, Sansar Chandra Rd (☎372456; fax 364376). Extremely clean, family-run place; very large and slightly impersonal. All rooms have private bath and running hot water. The guests-only restaurant serves lightly spiced home cooking, and there's a bar overlooking the lawn, on which you can take tiffin or dinner. Tours, bicycle and car rental. ④–⑤.

Jai Mangal Palace, Station Rd, opposite the bus stand (☎378901). Simple, clean rooms, private baths with hot water, TV and uninspired decor. Bar, restaurant, pool and beauty parlour. ④–⑥.

Kailash, Johari Bazaar (☎565372). One of the few hotels in the heart of the Pink City, opposite the Jama Masjid. Though a little cramped, the rooms are OK; the most expensive have private bathrooms with showers, and windows overlooking the constantly active street. ③–④.

Khetri House, Khetri House Rd, outside Chand Pole; up to the end of the road, then though a gate marked "Dharohar Paying Guest House", and on to the end of the drive (no phone). Very eccentric tatty pile with huge suites, complete with antique furniture, in an old house where you can feel the centuries. Not to all tastes, but some will love it. ⑤–⑥.

Mangal, Sansar Chandra Rd (☎375126 or 7). Great location near the bus stand, off the main road. The rooms, all with TV, are carpeted and stuffy. Restaurant on site, but overpriced ④–⑥.

RTDC Gangaur, MI Rd (☎371641 or 2). Smart hotel with comfortable, carpeted, tasteful rooms; some deluxe, some a/c. Good restaurant and snack bar. ④.

RTDC Swagatam, Station Rd (☎310595). Moderately comfortable place, near the railway station. Uninspiring but clean rooms, and a dorm. ①–⑥.

RTDC Teej, Collectorate Rd, Bani Park (☎374373). Extremely well-kept, clean and comfortable, with cheaper beds in spacious, fresh dorms. It also has a good restaurant. ①–⑤.

Sweet Dream, Nehru Bazaar, just inside the New Gate in the Pink City (☎314409). Friendly lodge, with clean rooms on several floors, some with balcony, some a/c, and a rooftop restaurant. ④–⑥.

Expensive

Bissau Palace, Khetri House Rd, outside Chand Pole (☎304371; fax 304628). The summer home of the Thakurs of Bissau, built in 1919 and decorated with artefacts of the heroic fighting days before Independence. Rajasthan's first heritage hotel, with tasteful rooms, some a/c, plus gardens, swimming pool, tennis and badminton courts. Adequate parking space, and dining facilities. ⑦.

Jai Mahal, Jacob Rd, Civil Lines (☎371616; fax 365237). Plush hotel southwest of the railway station. Regal atmosphere, swimming pool, gardens and restaurant. ⑨.

Jaipur Ashok, Jai Singh Circle, Bani Park (☎390091 or 2; fax 322999). Immaculate a/c rooms, en-suite bathrooms, luxurious pool (Rs100 for non-residents), bar, coffee shop and restaurant – plus resident astro-palmist. ⑧–⑨.

Khasa Kothi, just south of the junction of Station Rd and MI Rd (☎375151; fax 374040). Faded but comfortable, if a little expensive. Mediocre open-air restaurant amid spacious lawns. ⑦–⑧.

L M B, Johari Bazaar (☎565844; fax 562176). Plush a/c rooms in the Pink City, some facing the road; duller ones at the back. Excellent veg restaurant. Foreigners pay in foreign currency. ⑦.

Mansingh, Sansar Chandra Rd (☎378771; fax 377582). Luxurious a/c rooms with large windows. Swimming pool, health club, restaurant and bar. Foreigners pay in foreign currency; 50 percent discount for single occupancy March–Aug. ⑨.

Narain Niwas Palace, Kanota Bagh, Narayan Singh Rd (☎561291; fax 563448). Delightful old palace, almost 2km from the Pink City. Individually styled rooms feature original paintings on walls and ceilings, and classic furniture including four-poster beds in some. Well-maintained, with patios and shady gardens. Food available. ⑦.

Rajmahal Palace, Sardar Patel Marg (☎381757; fax 381887.). Stylish grand hotel, sensitively converted from the former British Residency. Pool and bar, and suites from $300 per night. ⑨.

Rambagh Palace, Bhawani Singh Marg (☎381919; fax 381098). Spectacular palace hotel, popular with Indian movie stars, in fountained gardens. Bar, restaurant, indoor swimming pool, tennis and squash courts, and nightly open-air folk music and dance performances. Foreigners pay in foreign currency; rates start at well over $100 per night. ⑨.

Samode Haveli, Gangapole (☎540370; fax 42407). Beautiful old mansion in the northeastern corner of the city, formerly a residence of the Rawals of Samode. ⑧.

Sheraton Rajputana Palace, Palace Rd (☎360011; fax 367848). High-standard, business-oriented hotel with high security, a fountained lobby, bar and restaurant. Rooms cost $140 per night. ⑨.

Eating and drinking

Jaipur's **restaurants** serve an assortment of Indian, Chinese and Western cuisine. Plenty of sumptuous dishes are on offer in the top hotels, where you can relax in a bar before and after a meal. There are few street snack sellers, but inexpensive roadside eating-houses around the bus stand and on MI Rd, opposite Chameliwala Market, sell highly spiced and tasty *dhals* and sloppy curries.

For a cool refreshing drink, the *Milk Stop*, on Station Rd by the main crossroads, has velvety thick **milkshakes**, soft ice-cream and a genuine certificate to prove its ice and water are free from bacteria.

Annapurna, behind *Raj Mandir* cinema on Bhagwan Das Rd (no sign in English). Tasty Gujarati veg *thalis* at low prices. Open 11am–3pm & 6–11pm.

Ashiana, Nehru Bazaar. Veg restaurant with small roof terrace, above *Hotel Sweet Dream*, with views to the Albert Hall. Good Indian and Chinese food, and south Indian snacks. Open 7am–11pm.

Bamboo Hut (aka *Handi*), MI Rd. Open-air restaurant for very good north Indian non-veg at reasonable prices. Basic standards of hygiene. Open 10am–11pm.

Bismallah, Chand Pole. One of a group of restaurants bordering the busy meat and vegetable market, serving distinctly Islamic cuisine. Cheap meat and some veg options. Open 7am–11pm.

Chanakya, MI Rd. Delicious high-class veg food – superb stuffed *parathas*. Open noon–11pm.

Indian Coffee House, MI Rd, 100m west of Ajmeri Gate. The usual fine coffee, reasonable snacks, and decent breakfast options from the south Indian co-operative. Open 7.30am–9pm.

L M B, Johari Bazaar. Very popular veg restaurant of the purest and highest standards using special *deshi ghee*, but no garlic or onion. Outstandingly tasty food in comfortable a/c surroundings; live classical music after 7pm. Open 11.30am–3.30pm & 7–11pm, snacks only 4–7pm.

Natraj, MI Rd. A/c place for good veg food and Chinese dishes in the upper price bracket. Open 11am–2pm & 7–10pm.

Niro's, MI Rd. Superior non-veg food – Chinese, Western and speciality Mughlai dishes – with prices to match. Open 10am–11.30pm.

Rambagh Palace Hotel, Bhawani Singh Marg (☎381919). Top-notch food from all over the world, at very steep prices. Beautiful gardens and an outdoor bar make a meal here a real treat.

Surya Mahal, MI Rd. Veg restaurant next to *Natraj*, and very similar; its menu also offers pizza. Open 8am–11pm.

Listings

Airlines See "Moving on from Jaipur".

Bicycle repairs In an enclosure just west of Ajmeri Gate.

Bookstores *Books Corner* on MI Rd just past *Niro's* has up-to-date magazines, newspapers and books in all major European languages. *Evergreen Guest House* has a secondhand stall.

Cinemas Jaipur is packed with picture palaces including the huge, famous and very plush *Raj Mandir* on Bhagwan Das Rd just off MI Rd. Four daily showings, and there's always a queue.

Dance *Panghat Theatre* at *Rambagh Palace Hotel* has nightly performances of Rajasthani dance and music, from 7pm.

MOVING ON FROM JAIPUR

From Jaipur there are several daily flights to **Delhi** (*Indian Airlines, Modiluft, NEPC, UP Airways & Sahara*), **Bombay** (*Indian Airlines, Modiluft* and *NEPC*) and **Udaipur** (*Indian Airlines* and *Modiluft*), five weekly to **Ahmedabad** (*Sahara*) and several to **Jodhpur** (*Indian Airlines*), **Aurangabad** (*Indian Airlines*) and **Calcutta** (*Sahara*). **Bookings** can be made at *Indian Airlines* in Nehru Place, Tonk Rd, the southward continuation of Sawai Ram Singh Rd (☎514500), *NEPC* (☎362278), *Modiluft* (☎363373) and *Sahara* (☎620781). *UP Airways* are c/o *Anukampa* on MI Rd near Ajmeri Gate. Other **airline offices** include *Air India* (☎368569), *British Airways* (☎370374) and *Alitalia* (☎369120), all on MI Rd near Jaipur Towers; *Thai Airways* and *KLM* (both ☎370062), and *Air France, Singapore Airlines* and *Gulf Air* (all ☎377051) are in Jaipur Towers.

Train bookings should be made at least a day in advance (call ☎131 for enquiries). The fastest service to **Delhi**, and the only one serving New Delhi station, is the a/c *Shatabdi Express* #2015, which leaves daily except Thursday. Three trains serve Old Delhi station (around 5hr). Others, which operate on metre gauge, are rather slower, and terminate at Delhi's Sarai Rohilla station; of these, you might just want to opt for the overnight *Delhi Mail* #9902. To **Bombay**, there is only one direct train, the *Gangaur Express* #2956. Otherwise, connections can be made at Sawai Madhopur or Ahmedabad, but they take around 22hr. To **Calcutta**, the *Howrah Mail* also serves **Agra**, arriving early in the morning. The three-times weekly *Marudhar Express* #2464 is the only other direct service to Agra. Two daily trains serve **Abu Road** (11hr), and **Ahmedabad** (16hr) from where there are good services south to Madras, Secunderabad, Kochi and Thiruvananthapuram (but this entails staying a day or a night in Ahmedabad). To **Udaipur**, the *Garib Nawaz Express* #2915 and the overnight *Chetak Express* also serve **Chitttaurgarh** (8hr 30min). **Ahmedabad** and Udaipur trains also serve **Ajmer**, the fastest being the *Garib Nawaz Express*, which only takes 3hr10min; the others take around 4hr.

For **Jodhpur**, the *Intercity Express* #2465 and the *Superfast* #2307 are supplemented by a thrice-weekly express and two local trains, all of which are much slower. Two expresses also serve **Bikaner**: the *Intercity Express* #2468, and the *Bikaner Express* #4737. The local train is far slower. The fastest train to **Sawai Madhopur** (for Ranthambore National Park) is the *Gangaur Express* #2956. For **Shekhawati**, your best bet is the *Shekhawati Express* #9704 which calls at Sikar and Jhunjhunu en route to Delhi Sarai Rohilla.

Shorter journeys to Agra, Ajmer, Pushkar and Bharatpur are best made on the frequent *RSRTC* **buses** from the Inter-state bus stand. For longer routes, faster "deluxe" services guarantee seats and may be a/c. Enquiries can be made by phone (☎375834), but it's less hassle to turn up at the bus stand in person, and head for the relevant booking office (destinations are listed outside each cabin). Some **travel agents** have their own services, or will book a seat for you, on desperately uncomfortable **video buses** to Bombay, Lucknow, and even further afield. Cowboy companies tout for business along Station Rd near the station.

Emergency services Police ☎100; Ambulance ☎102; Fire ☎101.
Hospitals The most reliable is *SMS Hospital*, Sawai Ram Singh Rd (☎560291 or 564222).
Immigration The foreigners' registration office is at the Rajasthan Police Head Office behind the Hawa Mahal. **Visa extensions** should be applied for at least a week before expiry.
Photography *Fuji* outlet on Kishan Pole Bazaar, near Ajmeri Gate; *Konica* on MI Rd almost opposite *Niro's*, *Kodak* by *Sweet Dream* hotel, and various others.
Police stations The main station is on Station Rd opposite the railway station (☎311677).
Swimming pools *Hotel Jai Mangal Palace* and *Evergreen Guest House* charge non-residents Rs40 for use of their pools, but you may prefer to pay more (Rs100–150) at posher establishments such as the *Jaipur Ashok* or *Raj Mahal*, where lawns, deck chairs and refreshments are available.
Travel agents *GSA Janta Travels*, MI Rd (☎368569). *Sita World Travels*, Station Rd (☎368226 or 361404; fax 321522), an agent for *Indian Airlines* and also *Western Union*, deals with international and domestic flights very efficiently. The *Thomas Cook* office is in Jaipur Towers, MI Rd (☎ 360940). *Rajasthan Tours*, at the *Rambagh Palace* (☎381041), is a reputable agent for trips out of Jaipur.

Around Jaipur

Forts, palaces, temples and ruins from a thousand years of Kuchwaha history adorn the hills and valleys near Jaipur. The superb palaces of **Amber** provide the most obvious destination for a day trip, but you can also visit **Amber Fort** – or Jaigarh – that crowns the hills to the north, the temples strewn in the valley east of Jaipur at **Galta**, or travel south to search out the traditional potters and dyers of **Sanganer**.

Organized tours go north and visit Amber and Jaigarh in a day; Amber is accessible by public transport, and minibuses run to Sanganer. Rickshaw *wallahs* who offer tours are likely to stop at shops and factories to get the commission vital to their livelihood. Although this can prove irritating, it enables you to watch Jaipur's artisans at work, probably see carpets in the making and stop wherever you want en route.

Amber

On the crest of a rocky hill behind Maota Lake, 11km north of Jaipur, the Rajput stronghold of **AMBER** was the capital of the Kuchwaha Rajputs from 1037 until 1728. Fortified by natural hills, high ramparts and a succession of gates along a cobbled road, Amber's magnificent palaces are distinctly Rajput, but it's clear that Moghul ideas crept in to influence the design. The practice of covering walls with mosaics of mirrors is purely Moghul, first introduced to India at Agra and Fatehpur Sikri.

It's worth visiting Amber independently, as there's so much to see; tour groups rarely get enough time to view the entire compound, let alone to scramble into the village behind it, dotted with fascinating temples and ruins. Regular **public buses** to Amber (#113) leave from outside Jaipur's Hawa Mahal, stopping on the main road below the palaces, where there's a **tourist office** (☎530264). From there you can either enjoy a pleasant twenty-minute uphill walk, take a jeep for Rs65 (up to four people), or waddle like the royals of yesteryear on an elephant for Rs250 (again, four people). You can also take your own vehicle up for Rs25.

THE PALACE COMPLEX
Entering the **palace complex** (daily 9am–4.30pm; Rs4, camera Rs 50, video Rs100) from the east through Suraj Pole (Sun Gate), you step into the main courtyard, **Jaleb Chowk**, where there's another opportunity to ride an elephant (Rs50 round the courtyard). In its southwest corner, the Shri Sila Devi temple was the Kuchwaha shrine to the goddess of war, Sila, an aspect of Kali; the image inside was brought to Amber from Bengal in 1604. Next to this, at the head of a flight of steps, Singh Pole (Lion Gate) provides access to the palaces.

The lofty Hall of Public Audience, **Diwan-i-Am**, used by Raja Jai Singh I and his successors from 1639 onwards, stands in the entrance courtyard, while opposite in the south wall of the yard, the exquisitely painted **Ganesh Pole** leads through narrow passages into the charming royal apartments. Here, protruding from the east wall, the dazzling **Sheesh Mahal** houses what were the private chambers of the Maharaja and his queen. Shards of mirror and coloured glass form an intricate mosaic that entirely covers the inner and outer walls and ceilings of the rooms. From a distance they seem to be covered in jewels, tinted with pastel shafts of sunlight that seep through the Arabic-style stained-glass windows. Above the Sheesh Mahal, the small chamber of the brilliant **Jas Mandir** radiates with the light and colour of similar mosaics. Guarded from the glare of the sun in the east by delicate marble screens, it served as a cool refuge in summer.

A fountained garden separates the mirrored palace from the "pleasure palace" opposite, **Sukh Mahal**, where marble rooms are cooled by water cascading through fine perforations in the centre of the wall – an early and very efficient system of air conditioning. The doors are inlaid with ivory and sandalwood.

The oldest part of the complex, the **Palace of Man Singh I**, lies south of the main quadrangle. The pillared *biradiri* in the centre of the courtyard was once a meeting area for the maharanis, shrouded from men's eyes by flowing curtains. Narrow passages and stairwells connect small rooms and open balconies on all sides.

Walking down the hill behind the palace complex – via the elephant stable in the western corner of Jaleb Chowk – brings you to the temples and ruined mansions of **Amber village**.

AMBER FORT

The mighty **Amber Fort** (Jaigarh), built in 1600, stands high on the hill behind Amber (daily 9am–4.30pm; Rs10, camera Rs10, video Rs50). As the Kuchwahas were on friendly terms with the Moghuls, the fort saw few battles, and its immense cannon – the largest in Asia, which needed 100 kilos of gunpowder for one shot and could send a ball 35km – was never fired in anger. The small museum ("collection") displaying artillery, old maps, medals, stamps and photographs, plus the odd fifteenth-century spitoon, is unspectacular, but has an interesting hand-drawn floor plan of the palaces at Amber. The fort's robust bastions command a view unrivalled in the whole of Rajasthan.

Most people walk to Amber Fort from the village, but it's quite a long climb; the alternative is to descend to the valley and follow by vehicle the much longer road that leads to both Jaigarh and Nahagarh.

Sanganer

At **SANGANER**, 16km south of Jaipur and the busiest crafts centre in the region, you can visit artisans in their workshops and pick up bargains from the makers themselves. Block and screen printing are among the techniques used to adorn locally made cloth, while offcuts are recycled into paper.

Artists also decorate pottery in Jaipur's distinctive style; graceful floral designs in white or deep-sea green are painted over a traditional inky-blue glaze. Within the town there are ruined palaces and a handful of elegant Jain **temples**, most notably the Shri Digamber temple near the Tirpolia Gate. Minibuses (Rs4) leave for Sanganer from Chand Pole, or you can take city bus #113 from Ajmeri gate.

Samode

SAMODE, 42km northwest of Jaipur on the outskirts of Shekhawati but normally visited as a day trip from the city, is notable for a superb restored eighteenth-century **palace** with exquisite murals and delicate stonework. The centre of attention here is the main hall, **Sheesh Mahal**, or mirror palace, where the glasswork is even more stunning than at Amber. The Samode palace is now a **heritage hotel**, a luxurious stop en route to Shekhawati (℡01423/4113; fax 4113; ⑨) – bookings can also be made at *Samode Haveli*, in Jaipur.

North of Jaipur: Shekhawati

Beyond the last ripples of the Aravalli range, north of Jaipur, lies the easternmost extent of the Thar Desert, where small dusty towns sit between sand dunes and infertile expanses of parched land. This is **SHEKHAWATI**, a region of strange, profound beauty. While the terrain is barren, dry and hostile, the architecture and painting of the local buildings possess a richness unparalleled in all India, with an incredible number of mansions, palaces and cenotaphs decorated inside and out with detailed and vivid colourful **murals**. The murals, executed between the 1770s and the 1930s, are unusual in that they were commissioned not for Maharajahs or religious institutions, but largely for the region's merchants, the Marwaris. Their subject matter covers not only traditional themes, scenes from folk tales and religious stories, animals and local customs, but also local cities, merchants and their families, British *sahibs* of the Raj, and Victorian technology (trains are a great favourite), each mural bordered with delightful floral designs. Sadly, nowadays, many are going to pot, faded, defaced, covered with posters or even just whitewashed over, but there are so many – and the towns are so small – that you cannot fail to see a work of art virtually wherever you look.

As Shekhawati has not yet become part of the Rajasthan's well-trodden tourist trail – few local people speak English, accommodation is thin on the ground, and there's little prospect of Western food – the region presents great scope for exploration. Only the main towns have been covered here, but – perhaps with the help of Ilay Cooper's *The Painted Towns of Shekhawati*, produced by *Mapin* in Ahmedabad, and available in Delhi, Jaipur and Mandawa – you should be able to find exciting sites in any town or village you pass through. Most of the buildings are still privately owned, and many are homes; ask permission to enter any house, and respect the custom of removing your shoes before you do so.

THE HAVELIS OF SHEKHAWATI

The magnificent houses built by the rich merchants of Shekhawati were called **havelis** after the Persian word for "enclosed space". Each house, anything from one to four storeys high, is entered from the street through huge arched porches with carved brass or wooden doors. Inside, you come into the forecourt, where visitors were received. Beyond, through the most ornate doorway of the house, is the main courtyard, where the women of the family could live in *purdah*, shielded from the eyes of the street. The forecourt is flanked by large pillared reception areas called *baithak*, where guests could recline in the shade, each surmounted by a gallery where the women could if they wanted be privy to the business conducted below, and there is often a window by the door to the inner courtyard so that they could see whoever came in. More extravagant Marwari mansions might have up to four large courtyards, as well as grand domed facades and overhanging upper storeys supported on sturdy stone brackets. The tradition of wood carving that produced the imposing doors and window shutters is still strong, particularly in Churu.

The meticulous painting of the interiors was executed by craftsmen from outside the region, using a vast array of intense hues, often highlighted with gold or silver leaf and mirrored designs. Religious themes, especially episodes from the life of Krishna, were common, and often feature along the lintels above the main doors. The outer walls were usually decorated by the masons who built the *haveli*, employing bolder designs and weather-hardy green, maroon and yellow ochres, with the occasional flash of blue.

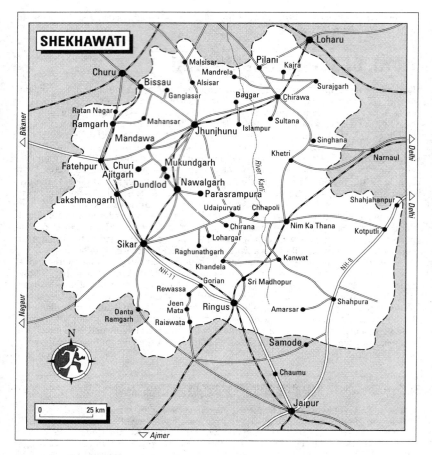

A brief history of Shekhawati

The first people to settle the lands north of Jaipur, Muslims of the Khaimkani clan, established two small states based at **Jhunjhunu** and **Fatehpur** in 1450. Their hold on the region was broken in 1730, when the Rajput **Sardul Singh** of the Shekawat clan took over Jhunjhunu. Two years later he consolidated Shekhawati rule by helping his brother (already ruler of Sikar) to seize Fatehpur from its Muslim Nawab.

Although the area is known as Shekhawati, the Shekawat Rajputs were only responsible for the construction of the forts in each town. The caravan route known as the "spice road" passed through the region on its way between China and the coast of Gujarat, and it was the local **merchants** – the Marwaris, Hindus of the *vaisya* caste, and Jains – who funded the building and painting of family houses (*havelis*), temples, wells and rest houses (*dharamshalas*). The Marwaris were often rivals in influence to the local Rajputs, and it was this that led the Shekawats to turn a blind eye to, and even sponsor, brigandry against them. In response, the merchants formed an alliance with the British, ever eager for means to get a foothold in this fiercely independent region. In 1835, and with funding from the Maharajas of Jaipur and Bikaner (to whom the Marwaris had also applied for help), a small force of cavalry called the Shekhawati Brigade was set up under the command of Henry Forster and based in Jhunjhunu to control the brigands. This gave the Marwaris the security they needed to build their magnificent *havelis*, and though many of them moved, encouraged by the British, to Bombay, Madras and especially Calcutta, they continued to send their profits back to Shekhawati, erecting elaborate buildings either to prove their worth as prospective bridegrooms, or simply as aid projects during times of famine.

When the British left India a number of Marwaris bought British industries, and such names as *Birla* and *Poddar* remain prominent in business today. However, many merchant families have now left Shekhawati and settled more permanently in the major urban centres, which is why so many of their buildings have been allowed to deteriorate. The region's current inhabitants continue to rear goats and sheep for their wool, and reap what they can from the dry earth, while maintaining traditional crafts: tie-and-dye, screen printing, lacquer work, wood carving and silverwork.

Arrival and local transport

Travelling to Shekhawati **from Jaipur**, your most likely point of arrival is **Sikar**, two hours' journey by road (110km) or almost twice that by train. With only basic lodging available, it's best to limit your stay here to a couple of hours and head northwest to **Nawalgarh**, where you'll find better hotels and a more relaxed, rural atmosphere. Buses also run from Jaipur to **Fatehpur** (48km north of Sikar) – approaching **from Bikaner** (see p.184), this will almost certainly be your point of arrival.

Unless you happen to coincide with the right train, **travelling around Shekhawati** by rail is far less convenient than by bus; slow and infrequent trains arrive at stations on the outskirts of towns. Fairly regular local **buses**, always overcrowded, also usually stop on the outskirts of town; few operate after dark. **Jeeps** run according to demand, picking up as many passengers as physically possible. For less congested and precarious transport, you can rent a jeep in Jhunjhunu, but by far the most comfortable (and most costly) way to get round the area is by **taxi** from Jaipur.

Within the small towns the semi-rural life runs at a leisurely pace, and there is little traffic apart from the odd moped dodging between meandering donkey and camel carts. In larger centres such as **Churu**, tempos and tongas cover the distance between the bus station and the centre of town.

Sikar

As an introduction to Shekhawati, **SIKAR** is disappointing, sprawling beyond the old city walls and having lost much of its original charm. Though the *havelis* are by far from being the best in the region, the **New Palace** in the centre of the old city is worth a look. Its murals include a picture-map of the town in the Sheesh Mahal (mirror room) and a series of fine portraits in the Chini Mahal, or "China Palace", decorated with blue-and-white porcelain tiles.

There's nowhere worth staying in Sikar, but luckily it's easy to move on: the **bus stand** is southeast of town, about 2km from the fort at the centre of the old city, with departures to Jaipur (every 15min), Nawalgarh and Fatehpur (both every 30min), and less frequent services to Bikaner, Delhi, and Ajmer. Sikar's **railway station**, in the northeast of town, has services to Jaipur (5 daily; 3hr), Churu (4 daily; 3hr), Fatehpur (1hr 10min), Ramgarh (1hr 50min), Jhunjhunu (2hr) and Nawalgarh (45min).

Fatehpur

The charming, compact and bustling market town of **FATEHPUR** has the feel of a crumbling open-air museum. In 1450 Fateh Khan, a Muslim Khaimkani Nawab, claimed leadership of the small settlement and held it until it passed into the hands of the Shekawats in the eighteenth century.

Fatehpur's merchant community left a rich legacy of remarkable buildings; almost every street is flanked with the painted outer walls of *havelis*, and their interiors are among the finest in Shekhawati. A common theme for paintings is Lakshmi, the goddess of wealth, attended by mighty, regal elephants, and set against a rich azure background. Friezes in several temples depict scenes from the great Hindu epics.

The most celebrated of Fatehpur's *havelis* is the small but exquisite **Goenka Haveli**, built in the mid-nineteenth century by a Jain merchant, Mahavir Prasad, and reached by following the main road north from the bus stand and turning left at the first main crossroads. While the inner courtyard is beautifully painted, the first-floor room is dazzling, its walls and ceiling decorated in the finest detail with a myriad of colours, gold leaf and mirrors. Panels to either side of the door show Krishna riding an elephant (on the right) and a horse (on the left), each animal made up of contorted female figures. A room next door shows further scenes from Krishna's life, and women spinning, churning butter and decorating each other's feet with spidery henna patterns. A later building to the left of Goenka Haveli has superb mirrorwork in the front porch.

If you rejoin the main northbound road at the crossroads, and turn right after 20m, you'll come to **Nand Lal Devra Haveli**, whose splendid ceiling panels in the reception area were copied by many other merchant families. The murals on the courtyard walls, and the complex carving of the wooden doors and shutters, are equally impressive.

To the north of town, distinctive Shekhawati **wells** stand raised on square platforms, with domed shelters on each corner, so they could be seen from afar. Once the lifeline of the community, and still common meeting places, these wells have not suffered the decay seen elsewhere since the advent of more sophisticated plumbing systems.

Practicalities

Fatehpur's **bus stand** is in the centre of town on the main Sikar–Churu (north–south) road. Buses serve Bikaner (14 daily; 5hr 30min), Jaipur (25 daily; 3hr 30min), and Churu via Ramgarh (hourly). Private buses from Mandawa and Jhunjhunu (both every 30min) stop further north. The **railway station**, east of town, has four daily **trains** to Churu, one continuing to Bikaner, and four to Sikar, of which two go on to Jaipur.

A kilometre south of town on NH-11, the modern RTDC *Hotel Haveli* (☎01571/20293; ①–③) has ordinary or air-cooled rooms and a dorm. It's clean, comfortable and offers meals and beer. Between the two bus stands, on the other side of the street, the *Kedia Guest House* (☎01571/21088; ①) is the basic but clean alternative. There's no sign in English but it stands opposite a *haveli* of the same name. If you don't eat at the *Ratangarh*, try any of the *dhabas* near the bus stands; the food is good, but meals are only cooked around noon and after 6 or 7pm.

Ramgarh and Lakshmangarh

The two small towns of Ramgarh and Lakshmangarh, near Fatehpur, boast rich selections of *havelis*. Neither has any accommodation, but each can be easily visited in a day, using local buses or jeeps.

RAMGARH, 20km north of Fatehpur, was founded in 1791 and developed almost as a status symbol by the Poddar merchant family, who made every effort to make their new town outshine Churu. They were successful; there's hardly a bare wall in town, even among the shops in the bazaar. Most of the grand Poddar *chhatris* beside the main Churu–Sikar road preserve attractive murals within their domes, while the family *havelis* in the north of town, west of Churu Gate, are decorated with scenes from local folk stories, and a three-fish motif that is unique to Ramgarh. Temples such as Natwar Niketan, Ram Lakshman temple and Ganga temple cherish excellent depictions of scenes from the *Ramayana, Bhagavad Gita* and local legends; the **Shani temple** in the northwest of town also holds some elaborate mirrorwork.

The most imposing feature of the quaint little desert community of **LAKSHMAN-GARH**, 20km south of Fatehpur, is the nineteenth-century **fort**, hewn from steep, smooth grey rocks, that dominates the west side of town. It is now empty and dim inside, though you can climb the ramp to the summit to enjoy a spectacular view. Lakshmangarh is easy to explore, thanks to a symmetrical street grid inspired by that of Jaipur. It holds three principal squares, several wells and temples, and plenty of richly painted *havelis*. Just below the fort, near the bus stand with its snack stalls and fruit sellers, stands the huge **Char Chowk Haveli**. Built around four large courtyards (*chowks*), it remains in private ownership, and access is therefore restricted. In any case, it's best seen from the fort, from where its peculiar design can be appreciated.

Other excellent – and amusing – frescos in town include the heavily painted **Kyal** and **Naria** *havelis* in the southeast of town, the scenes of European women on walls near the clock tower, and **Sanganeeria Haveli**, east of the Radha Murlimanohar temple. In the far east of town, near a *chhatri* and a well, the bright but dilapidated **Pansari Haveli** shelters a semi-permanent settlement of *lohars*, nomadic iron workers.

Mandawa

Small, attractive **MANDAWA**, 20km east of Fatehpur, was founded by the Shekhawats in 1755, though most of its paintwork dates from the early nineteenth century. The town's original **fort**, right in the centre, now houses the finest **hotel** in the region (see below), as well as a small museum of royal artefacts.

The outer walls, jutting balconies, alcoves and overhanging upper storeys of the **Goenka Double Haveli** in the west of town are replete with patterns and paintings, ranging from traditional Rajasthani women and religious motifs to Europeans in stylish hats and Victorian finery. In the **Nand Lal Murmuria Haveli** next door, paintings of trains, cars, George V, and Venice were executed during the 1930s by Balu Ram, one of

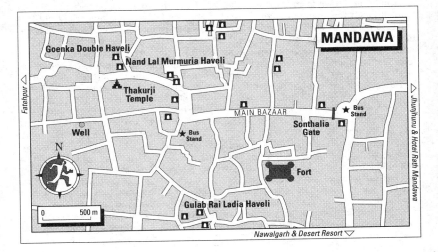

the last working artists of the region. Murals in the **Thakurji temple** opposite these two mansions include soldiers being shot off the mouths of cannons, a reflection of the horrors of the Mutiny. Further west are a couple of *chhatris*, and a step-well, still used today and bearing paintings inside its decorative corner domes.

Another *haveli* worth asking for by name is **Gulab Rai Wadia Haveli**, in the south of town, where the decoration of the outer and inner walls is perhaps the finest in Shekhawati. Blue washes here and there betray twentieth-century censorship of the erotic scenes that had been commonly acceptable one hundred years earlier.

Mandawa is rather more geared up for **tourism** than the other towns of the region, with a fair share of well-heeled European visitors. There is also a smattering of souvenir shops, urgent salesmen, self-styled guides, and commission agents. The only really good buy, however, is the local **tie-dyed fabric**.

Practicalities

Buses from Jhunjhunu and Nawalgarh (at least hourly), as well as Jaipur and Bikaner (3 daily) stop at Sonthalia Gate in the east of town. From Fatehpur, most buses pull in at a stand in the centre of town, just off the main bazaar. Jeeps ply the same routes.

Accommodation in Mandawa is the best in Shekhawati, and the priciest. In the fort, *Hotel Castle Mandawa* (☎01592/23124; fax 23171; ⑧), with its authentically furnished rooms complete with original murals, is one of the most appealing luxury hotels in Rajasthan. If you can't afford to stay, pop in for a buffet **dinner** (around Rs250). The less luxurious *Hotel Rath Mandawa* on the Rath road, 1km east of Sonthalia Gate (☎01592/23140; ④), lacks the palatial atmosphere, but offers comfortable rooms with attached bathrooms, balconies and desert views. Bookings for the *Desert Resort* (☎01592/23151; ⑧), a complex of huts south of town on the Mandawa–Nawalgarh road, can be made at *Castle Mandawa*.

Nawalgarh

NAWALGARH, 30km southeast of Fatehpur, came into its own in 1737, when the Shekawat Nawal Singh claimed what was then a small village as the site for a fort. Thick stone walls, pierced by four gateways, were erected to encircle the town.

Coming into town from the bus stand, you enter the southern gateway, or **Nansa Gate** (though the sign on it actually reads, "Ramilas Podar [sic] Memorial Gate"). If you turn left just inside the gate and follow the street round for about 250m, you come to an enclosure on your left, surrounded by painted walls, many of which form part of **Aath Haveli**, a complex of seven *havelis* (eight – *aath* – were planned). The murals here feature trains, carts, false windows (very common in Nawalgarh) and barbers at work. Taking a right turn just inside Nansa Gate and then the second right, you come to **Surajmal Chhauchharia Haveli**, where murals include a picture of Europeans floating past in a hot-air balloon. The painter was obviously unclear about the mechanics involved; the two passengers are blowing into the balloon to power their journey.

The third right turn after entering Nansa Gate brings you to the **fort**, housing banks and offices around a central yard crowded with vegetable vendors. The *Hotel Raj Hans*, next to the *State Bank of Bikaner and Jaipur*, boasts the magnificent mirrored **Sheesh Mahal**, with a ceiling mural that includes maps of Nawalgarh and Jaipur. Despite its name, the *Raj Hans* is a restaurant; they will let you see the *Sheesh Mahal* for Rs10, or have a meal for not much more. Straight on from the Nansa Gate takes you, after 300m, to a little square, beyond which stands the colourful **Lakshminarayan temple**. A right turn at the square brings you to the **eastern gateway**, called Poddar Gate.

Other *havelis* in Nawalgarh include **Goenka Haveli**, in the north of town near Bowri Gate, and the magnificent **Anandi Lal Poddar Haveli**, east beyond Poddar Gate (follow the main road, bearing left and then round to the right after 50m, past a trio of rather delapidated *havelis*, and it's down a turning on your right). Built in 1920 and now a school, it treasures some excellent paintwork, especially in the forecourt, and has recently been restored to its original glory.

Practicalities

Nawalgarh's **bus** and **jeep** stand is about 2km west of town, served by buses from Jhunjhunu (every 15min; 1hr 15min) via Dundlod (15min) and Mukundgarh (20min); Sikar (every 30min; 1hr); Jaipur (every 30min; 4hr), and Ajmer (1 daily; 5hr). The **railway station** is about 500m beyond the bus stand with four daily services in each direction from Sikar (three of them from Jaipur) and Jhunjhunu (one of which comes from Delhi). There are jeeps from Nawalgarh to smaller towns; for Mandawa, change to a jeep or another bus at Mukundgarh.

Much the most comfortable **accommodation** in Nawalgarh is in the spacious, smart *Roop Niwas Palace* (☎01594/22008; fax 22491; ⑥–⑧), set in attractive gardens 1km or so east of town along the main road leading out of Poddar Gate, which provides a taste of how Shekhawati's ruling class lived in days gone by. Pricey meals are served in the plush dining room. The basic *Natraj Hotel* stands in Sabzi Mandi, in the heart of town near the entrance to the fort (☎01594/23154; ①), while the pleasant *Nawal Hotel*, out by the bus stand on Mandawa Rd (☎01594/22155; ①–②), is a good option if you arrive late. As well as a cheap dorm, it has two rooms to each common bath, plus a couple of rooms with private bath – rooms at the back are quieter – and prepares decent food.

You can also stay at the much smaller town of **Dundlod**, 7km north of Nawalgarh, which has its own interesting murals. Although not as palatial as *Roop Niwas Palace* or *Castle Mandawa*, Dundlod's fort, *Dera Dundlod Kila* (☎01594/52519; ⑦–⑧), captures the Shekawat style with its own painted rooms and a grand diwan-i-khas. Frequent buses and jeeps run to Dunlod from Nawalgarh (15min) and Jhunjhunu (1hr).

Parasrampura

The life of the Shekhawati Rajput **Sardul Singh** is commemorated by more painted buildings in the quiet and unassuming village of **PARASRAMPURA**, just over 10km southeast of Nawalgarh, where he lived and died. Murals in the **Gopinath temple**, built in 1742, include depictions of the torments of hell (a common theme in the eighteenth century), and Sardul Singh with his five sons; flocks of Persian-style angels look down from the ceilings. The frescos are unfinished, as the artists were diverted to decorate the **Chhatri of Sardul Singh** when he died that same year. The large dome of his cenotaph, supported by twelve pillars, contains a flourish of lively and well-preserved murals. Once again there are images of hell, and of Sardul Singh with his sons; this time he's also seen smoking a hookah and enjoying a tiger hunt. Parasrampura's modest **fort**, in reasonable repair, is on the west bank of the dry river bed.

Jhunjhunu

The large settlement of **JHUNJHUNU**, taken over by the Shekawats in 1730 as the capital of their newly formed territory, not only features some of the finest murals in the region, but also has managed to retain much of the tranquillity and appeal of the smaller towns. The quiet, narrow and dusty streets within its old boundaries hold a profusion of fabulously designed and painted buildings, spanning five centuries, and remain relatively unaffected by the twentieth-century accretions that have helped to make Jhunjhunu one of the major business centres of modern Shekhawati.

The main bazaar, not far north of the bus station, is sandwiched between the outer walls of two large private mansions, decorated with striding camel trains, elephants, women and religious scenes. The ornate gateway of **Modi Haveli**, the larger of the two, can be reached by a grand flight of steps from the shops built into the base of its walls; its murals are considered to be the very best in Shekhawati. Inside, through an entrance porch embellished with scenes from the life of Krishna, the forecourt features more paintings of Krishna and several portraits of Maharajahs and British *sahibs*, while the pillared reception area or *baithak* has superb murals on the ceiling and soft mattresses and bolsters on the floor. The door to the inner courtyard is lavishly carved, bordered with exquisite designs including a scene of Jaipur. Nearby, the similar **Kaniram Narsinghdas Tibrewala Haveli** boasts coloured glass windows around the top of its *baithak*, while the **Bihari temple** features some of the oldest Shekhawati murals, painted in 1776 in vegetable pigments. Dating to a time before the Marwaris took over from the Rajputs as the dominant social class, they feature Sardul Singh's five sons, each of whom built a fort in the town.

Further west, the unique **Khetri Mahal** palace, built in 1760, is ageing and empty, but there's no mistaking the originality of its design: marble pillars stand in place of walls wherever possible, and a covered ramp, wide enough for horses, winds up to the roof. Views over Jhunjhunu from here stretch to the old **Muslim sector**, Pirzada Mahalla, where a grand mosque is surrounded by tombs dating back to 1500. Many of Jhunjhunu's Muslims – still an important sector of the population – were wealthy merchants who built painted *havelis* of their own. A wander through Pirzada Mahalla leads past mosques, *dargahs* and meat markets, as well as neat rows of shops painted in pastel greens, blues and pinks unlike anywhere else in Shekhawati.

West of the Khetri Mahal, at the foot of the conical Kana Pahar hill, are **Badalgarh** – the only remaining fort from the Nawab period – and the **Dargah of Kamaruddin Shah**, where a mosque, *madrasa* and collection of tombs stand in a small complex. Behind the *madrasa* stands a monument to the infant son of Henry Forster, commander of the British-run Shekhawati Brigade, who died in 1841. Only one of the five gates of "Forster Gunge", the Shekhawati Brigade's cantonment, survives. In the north of Jhunjhunu, the **Mertani Bawri** is the region's most impressive step-well.

Practicalities

Buses from the sprawling stand in the south of town run throughout Shekhawati, and to Bikaner (5 daily; 5hr 30min), Jaipur (every 30min; 5hr) and Delhi. The stand for private buses is east of the main bazaar. Four **train** services arrive at the station on the southern edge of town from Sikar via Nawalgarh, three of them from Jaipur. There are also four services the other way from Loharu, one of which starts in Delhi.

The local **tourist office**, which produces maps of most of Shekewati's main towns, is attached to the *Shiv Shekhawati Hotel* (Mon–Sat 10am–5pm, closed 2nd Sat in the month; ☎01592/32909). Jhunjhunu is quite spread out, and walking around can be tiring, but many of the streets of the old town are too narrow for cars; **rickshaws** operate as taxis, picking up as many passengers as they can. **Bicycles** can be rented from a small shop near the park in the south. **Taxis** to explore further afield gather at a rank outside the bus stand, costing around Rs3 or 4 per kilometre.

The best inexpensive **accommodation** is the *Hotel Sangam* (☎01592/32544; ①–④), which has clean, spacious rooms. It's set back from the bus stand, so doesn't get the noise that infiltrates the nearby *Naheen* (☎01592/32544; ①) and *Kulhari* (☎01592/34525; ②), both of which are pretty basic. Further east, the *Shiv Shekhawati Hotel* (☎01592/32651; fax 32603; ③), is a smart, well-kept lodge with a touch of Shekhawati character; nearby, on the eastern edge of town, the owner has opened the *Jamuna Resort* (☎01592/32871; ⑥), where you can stay in beautifully decorated "cottages", or eat the best **food** in Jhunjhunu on the lawn or in a marquee-style dining hall. There are also numerous food stalls concentrated around the bus stand, and basic sit-down joints such as *Nehru's Hotel* and *Amber Restaurant* in Gandhi Chowk.

North from Jhunjhunu

The first significant stop on the road northwest of Jhunjhunu, after 40km, is the small and atmospheric town of **BISSAU**, 10km northeast of Ramgarh. Opposite the bus stand here, the **Chhatri of Hammir Singh** commemorates the son of Shyam Singh, a brigand leader. It's fenced in, but you can get the key from a barber shop just outside the gate. Several domes stand above a high basement structure, where decaying murals adorn the walls. Of the heavily painted *havelis* in town, **Kedia Haveli** in the west has some distinctive depictions of Europeans on elephants, a Gangaur procession and relaxed hookah-smoking. Nearby, the **Jhunjhunuwala Haveli**, currently used as a student hostel, holds wonderful detailed paintings, especially in its porticoed forecourt. During **Dussehra** (Oct), all-but-silent dances in Bissau's bazaar, to honour Durga, take the place of the more usual stage play.

The much larger town of **CHURU** is 10km further on. Though Churu has never been part of Shekhawati, being officially in Bikaner territory, it too was home to many merchant families – including the Poddars, before they left for Ramgarh. It also has a strong Muslim presence, with several prominent turquoise mosques. Noteworthy (if rather scattered) buildings and murals here include some attractively decorated temples (open before 10am and after 5pm) around the clock tower in the central square. *Havelis* around the bazaar, just west, include **Kanhaiyal Bagla Haveli**, whose south wall is decorated with a grand frieze showing Dhola and Maru, lovers from local folklore, fleeing on camels, preceded by a couple from a Punjabi tale on horseback. The frieze is behind the compound wall; if you can get permission, you'll get an excellent view from the walls of the Jami Masjid nearby. The red-ochre-painted fort at the eastern end of town houses the police station and various other official buildings. Probably the best time to visit Churu is during the Shi'a festival of **Muharram** (April/June), when the local Muslim drummers come into their own.

Churu practicalities

Churu is on the Delhi–Bikaner and Jaipur–Bikaner lines, so **train services** are good, with departures to Bikaner (5 daily; 4hr), Sikar (4 daily; 3hr), Delhi (3 daily; 6hr), Jaipur (3 daily; 5hr 20), and Sawai Madhopur (1 daily; 9hr). The station is 3km south of the centre. Opposite, the old bus stand serves private buses; many state buses still call here before terminating at the new bus stand 1km northeast. Shared auto-rickshaws run between the two. **Buses** arrive at least hourly from Fatehpur, half-hourly from Jaipur, three times daily from Delhi and Bikaner, and twice from Jodhpur and Alwar.

The best **place to stay** in Churu is the basic but spotless *dharamshala* attached to the Ram Mandir temple in the west of town, about 1km south of the fort and a similar distance northwest of the railway station (☎01562/5024; ①). There are a trio of dirty and overpriced places just east of the railway station, but the **railway retiring room** is a much better bet (there is only one, with two beds; ①). The *Rajend Restaurant* almost opposite the station (slightly to the left, with a sign in Hindi only) is open round the clock for tasty, endlessly refilled and unbelievably cheap **thalis**.

East of Jaipur

The fertile area **east of Jaipur**, interspersed with the forested slopes of the Aravalli hills, holds an inviting mixture of historic towns and wildlife sanctuaries. The fortified town of **Alwar** to the northeast, fought over for centuries before its incorporation into Rajasthan in 1949, served as refuge for the exiled Pandava brothers of the *Mahabharata* during their thirteenth year of hiding, before Krishna helped them in the fierce battle against their cousins, the Kauravas, chronicled in the *Bhagavad Gita*.

Not far from Alwar, **Sariska Wildlife Sanctuary** is renowned for its tigers, while further east are the former princely capitals of **Deeg** and **Bharatpur**, and India's finest bird sanctuary, **Keoladeo National Park**. The wildlife sanctuary at **Ranthambore**, southeast of Jaipur, has lost most of its tigers to poachers, but the old palaces in its grounds, plus the rich vegetation and fauna, still attract many visitors.

Alwar

Roughly 140km northeast from Jaipur towards Delhi, **ALWAR** rests peacefully in a valley, overlooked by a fortress that stretches along a high craggy ridge to the northwest. Alwar was not always so calm; its strategic position on the Rajput border resulted in incessant warfare between the Jats of Bharatpur and the Kuchwahas of Amber, from the tenth to seventeenth centuries. It later fell to the Marathas and then the British, before Pratap Singh, the shrewd Rana of Mewar, brought it under Hindu control. The fort, now a radio station, can only be visited with police permission; the buildings within are in any case unspectacular, though the views make the climb worthwhile.

Construction of Alwar's Indo-Islamic **Vinay Vilas Palace** began under Bhaktawar Singh, Pratap Singh's successor. Although time has worn away much of its glory, it remains flamboyant, with domed roofs, lavish verandahs decorated in gold leaf, and delicate balconies facing a huge tank flanked by symmetrical *ghats* and pavilions. The stately sandstone and marble **Moosi Maharani Chhatri** here was built in memory of Bhaktawar Singh's mistress, who sacrificed her life on his funeral pyre. A **museum** on the top floor of the palace (daily except Fri 10am–5pm; Rs1) houses a collection of courtly memorabilia, including remarkable Arabic and Sanskrit manuscripts, tenth-century statues, ivory ornaments, fine embroidery and the inevitable weapons and stuffed animals.

Much of the palace is now taken up with government offices; in the main courtyard, used as the venue for the local courts, typists, lawyers and advisors huddle round rickety tables under banyan trees, drinking tea and filing through endless piles of paper.

Practicalities

The **bus stand** in the west of Alwar sees services to and from Deeg and Bharatpur (every 15min), and Sariska (every 30min or so). Frequent buses also run north to Delhi and south to Jaipur (both 2–3hr). Several food stalls at the bus stand sell drinks and fiery curries, and there's a **bike rental** shop near the exit. The **railway station**, receiving trains from Delhi, Jaipur, Jodhpur, Ahmedabad, Deeg and Ajmer, is a few kilometres away on the east side of town, and has retiring rooms.

The **tourist office** on Raghu Marg opposite Company Bagh (Mon–Sat 10am–5pm; ☎0144/21868) has dusty piles of aged leaflets about Rajasthan, and information on Alwar's **hotels**. Near the bus stand on Manu Marg, the best for your money is *Ashoka Hotel* (☎0144/21780; ①–⑤), which has basic rooms with or without bath, and better rooms upstairs. Within spitting distance are the noisy, dull but large *Imperial* (☎0144/21430; ②), and the *Alankar* (☎0144/20027; ③), with acceptable spacious rooms. Two hundred metres from the station, the much smarter *Aravali Hotel* (☎0144/332883; ③–⑦) offers dorm beds, basic rooms and more expensive doubles. Its bar and good **restaurant** are useful, as Alwar has little else to offer a hungry traveller.

Around 20km west – either by rickshaw, or on a Sariska-bound bus which can drop you off at a turning 3km short – the RTDC *Lake Palace Hotel* in **Siliserh** (☎0144/22991; ⑤–⑥, dorm ①), is housed in a former palace beside a lake. It's very relaxing, with a restaurant, bar and boating facilities.

Sariska

Alwar is the jumping-off point for the beautiful wooded **Sariska Tiger Reserve and National Park**, surrounded by barren hills tipped with ancient temples, and under the charge of Project Tiger (see p.161). Though the sanctuary has an abundance of **wildlife** – including *nilgai* (blue bulls), *sambar* (antelope), *chital* (spotted deer), wild boar, mongooses, monkeys, peacocks, parrots and other birds – poaching has regrettably decimated its population of **tigers**. The best prospect of seeing one is around the water holes that attract animals in the dry season when other sources of moisture dry up. Access to the park (closed July & Aug) is limited to daylight hours (dawn–dusk), to protect tigers from surreptitious night poaching.

Practicalities

The 37-kilometre journey by **bus** to Sariska from Alwar (1hr) can be very crowded. Tours run by the *Aravali Hotel* in Alwar cost well over the odds for a trip in a packed minibus that rushes through the park, with a minimal chance of any sightings.

If you choose to **stay** in Sariska there are two options. RTDC *Hotel Tiger Den* (☎0144/41342; ①–⑤), set in peaceful gardens right next to the park entrance, offers well-kept spacious rooms and a dorm, while the more extravagant *Sariska Palace* (bookings in Jaipur ☎0141/66804; ⑦), one of the largest hunting lodges in India, has a total of 27 rooms, some a/c.

An **entrance fee** (Rs25, camera Rs10, video Rs50, plus Rs100 per jeep) is payable at the park gate. **Tours** around the 480-square-kilometre central area can be arranged at either of the two hotels. *Hotel Tiger Den* charges Rs425 per jeep (excluding entrance fee) for a three-hour tour, *Sariska Palace* is slightly more expensive. Jeeps hold five people and drivers are usually prepared to slow down or stop on request.

Deeg

Few foreigners visit **DEEG** (also spelt Dig), around 50km east of Alwar, 30km north-west of Bharatpur, and only 95km from Agra. However, its sublime complex of summer palaces, intended to represent a "paradise on earth", really is worth seeing, perhaps as a pause for a few hours on a longer journey.

Construction of the royal retreat began in 1730, when the Jat ruler Badan Singh established Deeg as the second capital of Bharatpur state. There's a commanding view from the high fortified walls of his citadel, and you can still see some of the original cannons. The delicate design of the **palaces** or *bhawans* (daily 8am–noon & 1–7pm), with arches, pillars and domes reflected in surrounding water tanks, and the leafy gardens interspersed with two thousand fountains, is typical of the Jats. Most were built by the king Surajmal in 1756, and even the oldest, **Purana Mahal**, still bears traces of wall paintings. The largest, **Gopal Bhawan**, near the entrance to the complex, was Surajmal's summer residence. Its spacious, plushly furnished hall is built in graceful proportion, with majestic archways, sculpted pillars and intricate balconies overlooking the tank **Gopal Sagar**. A pavilion stands on either side of the *bhawan*; the deliberate resemblance of the whole ensemble to a pleasure barge is best appreciated from the west.

In the east of the complex, overlooking Rup Sagar, **Kesav Bhawan** is an open-sided square pavilion, designed to recreate the freshness of the monsoon. In Surajmal's time, fountains played within it, producing a shimmering rainbow in the sunshine, while cooling water showered from the roof to the accompaniment of artificial rolls of thunder. The reservoir for the fountains took a week to fill and only a matter of hours to empty, and nowadays they are only switched on during local festivals.

Practicalities

Deeg fell into decline along with the Jat rulership at the beginning of the nineteenth century, and remains very small, though it is served by bus (every 15min; 1hr 30min) and train (daily; 2hr) from Alwar. Permission to **stay** at the *Dak Bungalow* (①) must be obtained in advance from the Overseer in the Public Works Department office, Kama Darwaja. The only place to **eat** is the *Tamolia Restaurant*, just past Lakshman Mandir.

Bharatpur and Keoladeo

The compact town of **BHARATPUR** is just a stone's throw from the border with Uttar Pradesh, 150km east of Jaipur, and a mere 18km from Fatehpur Sikri, Akbar's deserted citadel (see p.238). Though it may not hold any especially distinguished attractions, it's fun to explore by bike or foot, with traditional markets dotted with mosques and temples and a massive fort encircled by a wide and murky moat.

However, the real reason anyone comes here is to visit **Keoladeo National Park**, a large expanse of wetland 7km south of town, which welcomes thousands of indigenous and migratory birds every year. Other common wildlife such as antelope and deer roam freely within the marshy sanctuary, and, even for the non-ornithologist, it's not to be missed.

Arrival and information

Bharatpur's **bus stand** is in the west of town near Anah Gate, just off NH11. Buses run to all major centres in Rajasthan and to Delhi, Agra and Fatehpur Sikri. Two kilometres northwest, the **railway station** lies on the main Delhi–Bombay line. There are also two fast trains to Agra (2hr) and one to Amritsar (14hr). The town's **tourist office** (Mon–Sat 10am–5pm; ☎23700), where you can pick up good state maps and

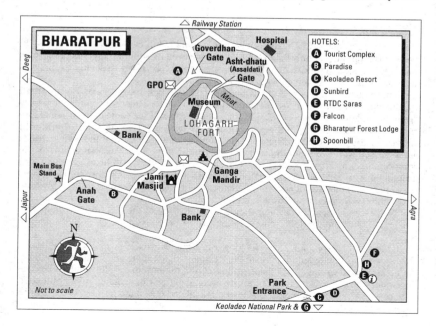

information on Bharatpur and the sanctuary, is nearer the park in the *Saras Tourist Bungalow*.

Cycle rickshaws are the main form of transport within the city, but fares for the long haul in and out of town soon mount up, and it makes sense to rent a **bicycle**, either from your hotel (around Rs30 per day) or the shop on NH11 outside the *Spoonbill Restaurant*. If you need to **change money**, head for the *State Bank of Bikaner and Jaipur*, Binarayan Gate (Mon–Fri 10am–2pm, Sat 10am–noon).

The telephone **area code** for Bharatpur is ☎05644.

The City

Bharatpur itself was founded by the Jat leader Surajmal, who built the virtually impregnable **Lohagarh Fort** at its heart in 1732; known as the eastern gateway to Rajasthan, it soon developed into a busy market centre. Although the original moat, 45m wide and up to 15m deep, still encircles the town, little remains of the thick eleven-kilometre walls that protected it – the British spent four months in 1805 trying in vain to penetrate them, before suffering their heaviest defeat in Rajasthan.

As you enter the fort from the north, through Assaldati Gate, you'll see a jumble of old and new buildings, among them the three palaces built by the Jats between 1730 and 1850. Of these, the **Maharaja's Palace** with its stone lattice windows, painted walls and a curious collection of *hammams* (sunken baths) on the ground floor, is the most aesthetically appealing. The **Kamra Palace** in the west of the fort now houses the government museum (daily except Fri 10.30am–5pm), with a well-stocked gallery of Jain sculptures, a copious assortment of weaponry and graphic manuscripts in Arabic and Sanskrit. Among its collection of statues from the region is a figurine of a *yaksha* from the first century BC. From the shade of a lofty pavilion on the roof of the palace you can enjoy great views of the surrounding countryside.

South of the fort, in the main market area, lie the **Jama Masjid**, fronted by a magnificent arched portal, and **Ganga Mandir**, a large, elaborate temple of pure sandstone.

Keoladeo National Park

KEOLADEO NATIONAL PARK, formerly known as Bharatpur Bird Sanctuary, was originally reserved by the royal family for hunting – despite sixty years of which, the avian population flourished. It became a sanctuary in 1956 and received total protection in 1981 on recognition as a national park. Keoladeo's 29 square kilometres of swamp and lakes constitute one of the most important **heronries** in the world, with such species as the dazzling purple heron, the common grey and the tiny brown pond heron. Other residents include orange-headed painted storks, snake-like darters, spoonbills, white ibis and grey pelicans. Some are vegetarian, but many feed on frogs, beetles and fish, and soon after the breeding season (July–Oct), birds of prey home in on the vulnerable fledglings to supplement their usual diet.

Between October and March, the 120 species of Indian birds who live in the park year-round are joined by a further 130 species from as far afield as the Russian steppes and Central Asia. The finest and rarest of these migratory birds, all of whom spend the winter in Bharatpur building up reserves of fat before the long flights back to their breeding grounds, are the five pairs of Siberian cranes who nest in the south of the park each winter. Only 125 such cranes, pure white with crimson bills and facial patches, are estimated to survive in the entire world.

You may also glimpse wild boar, mongoose, *chital* (spotted deer), *nilgai* (blue bulls) and *sambar* (antelope) along the paths, and may spot jungle cats, hyenas, jackals, otters and Indian black buck. Langorous rock pythons sun themselves at Python Point, just past Keoladeo temple, and in the dry bush land off the main road close to the entrance barrier.

The park (daily 6am–6.30pm; Rs25, camera Rs10, video Rs250) is at its most picturesque at dawn and dusk, and fullest between October and March. In summer you miss the migratory flocks, but should catch some busy nesting activity. A single metalled road passes through the sanctuary; numerous small paths lined with *babul* trees cut across lakes and marshes and provide excellent cover for bird-watching. If you need help identifying the birds, or finding vantage points, you can hire a **guide** at the gate (Rs50 per hour for up to 10 people), who will probably have binoculars. The best way to get around is by bike – also available at the sanctuary gate – or by cycle rickshaw – drivers are very clued up and know the main nesting areas. Tongas (Rs40 per hour) carry up to six people. During the winter, gondola-style **boats** provide a superb opportunity to get really close to the birds in the heart of the wetland.

Accommodation and eating

Few people stay in Bharatpur proper – the entrance to the park is 7km south of the railway station on the far side of town, and it makes more sense to spend the night in one of several assorted hotels along NH11, which passes by the northern edge of the park. The two hotels actually inside the park are quite upmarket, but most of the rest are inexpensive, and all offer snacks or full meals.

Bharatpur Forest Lodge, in the park (☎22760). Immaculate a/c rooms with balcony. Staying here, surrounded by bird song and avian activity, is a treat. Bar, bank, post office, and a fine restaurant with sumptuous buffets, open to non-residents when the hotel isn't full. Book in advance. ⑨.

Eagle's Nest, NH11 (☎25144). Situated at a noisy junction, not far from the park. Comfortable, carpeted rooms with bath (hot water). ⑤.

Falcon, set back from the main road near the park (☎23815). Small, quiet and clean place, with home cooking by friendly family. Bikes from shop opposite. ②.

Keoladeo Resort, NH11 (☎22251). The nearest to the park entrance. Rooms are supplemented in season by a tented compound with hot showers, garden and camp fire. ③–⑧.

Paradise, NH11, near the bus station in town (☎23791). Smart rooms, convenient if you're catching an early-morning bus. ⑤.

Pelican, NH11, near park entrance (☎24221). Small, homely rooms with or without bath. ①–⑤.

RTDC Saras Tourist Bungalow, NH11, at junction of main road near the park (☎23700). Poorly maintained, with large, cleanish rooms and a dorm. Restaurant and bar for residents only. Off-season discounts. ①–⑥.

Spoonbill, near the *Saras*. Basic rooms and fine restaurant. Friendly owners and bikes for rent. ①.

Tourist Complex, in town, near the railway station and Goverdhan Gate (☎32546). Basic rooms with a reasonable restaurant. ③–⑤.

Ranthambore National Park

One of Rajasthan's last sizeable stretches of verdant bush land, **Ranthambore National Park** lies 10km east of **SAWAI MADHOPUR**, a small junction town between Kota and Bharatpur, 180km north. Unlike Sariska to the north (see p.157), Ranthambore is fed by several perennial rivers, so the park never becomes a yellow expanse of dry grasses, and a number of lakes, haunted by crocodiles and attracting hundreds of water-birds, remain full year round. The tenth-century Chauhan fort and quaint pavilions, palaces and *chhatris* give the hill-fringed sanctuary a unique charm.

Although the fort was conquered by Ala-ud-din-Khalji's army in 1031 AD, and Akbar in 1569, for most of its existence Ranthambore has been controlled by the Rajputs, and was set aside by the rulers of Jaipur for royal hunting jaunts. Soon after Independence the area was declared a sanctuary, becoming a national park under **Project Tiger** (see *Contexts*) in 1972. Ranthambore used to be famous for its "friendly" tigers, who often hunted in full daylight, and rarely shied from cameras and jeep-loads of tourists. However, relentless poaching to satisfy Chinese demand for tiger bones and tiger-penis soup has decimated the tiger population, and made those who remain more elu-

The telephone **area code** for Sawai Madhopur and Ranthambore is ☎07462.

sive, and wary of human presence. Realistic estimates of their current number vary between sixteen and twenty. However, Ranthambore is still home to *chital*, *nilgai*, jackals, panthers, jungle cats and a wide selection of birds, among which you may see crested serpent eagles, paradise fly-catchers and more common painted storks.

Next to the impressive **fort**, which is built on a crag of solid rock, is a temple to Ganesh, where people from all over the country write to the elephant-headed god to invite him to their weddings. All the letters are read aloud to Ganesh (or at least to his image) by the temple priest.

Arrival and information: Sawai Madhopur

Most tourists arrive at Sawai Madhopur by **train**; the station, and the **bus stand**, are in the market area, near the cheapest hotels. About 100m southwest along the train track (towards Bombay and Jaipur) is a bridge carrying the road to Ranthambore (left) and the area called **Sawai Madhopur City**. The "city", where buses from Shivpuri stop, boasts the only **banks** that change money. Just beyond the bridge, to the left of the track, is the **tourist office** (Mon–Sat 10am–5pm; ☎20808) and the **Project Tiger** office (daily 10.30am–2pm & 6–7.30pm); on the other side of the line, *Prakash Talkies*, one of Sawai Madhopur's three cinemas, is housed in what was once the Maharajah of Jaipur's private station.

Getting to Ranthambore National Park

Ranthambore National Park is open between October and June. To visit, you will either have to rent a five-passenger **jeep** (referred to as a "Gypsy"), for Rs630 (including compulsory guide and jeep entrance fee), or else pay Rs60 for a place on a twenty-seater open **truck** (called a "canter"). Jeeps and canters must be booked at the *Project Tiger* office, preferably a day in advance. Jeeps can be booked for any time, but only ten can enter the park at once. Canters enter the park at 6.30am and 3.30pm in summer, 7am and 2.30pm in winter for the three-hour jaunt; they will pick up from any hotel on the Ranthambore Rd, but not from those in Sawai Madhopur, so if you're staying there, you'll have to get up to the Project Tiger office before departure time. Jeep and canter fees do not include **entrance fees** (Rs25 for foreigners, camera Rs10, video Rs50).

To **visit the fort**, you do not need to be in a vehicle, nor do you have to pay the park entrance fee. You could either arrange for your jeep to wait for you at the entrance on your way in or out, or else take a bus from the railway station.

Accommodation and eating

The range of **hotels** in Sawai Madhopur has something to appeal to all budgets, generally increasing in price and luxury the closer you get to the park. RTDC hotels are often cheaper between April and June. Though the **food** isn't special in the cheaper lodges, you'll be glad it's there at all; there's precious little alternative other than the *Hotel Garden View*, on the Ranthambore Rd, 1km out of town, which serves inexpensive Chinese, veg and non-veg food.

Ankur Resort, Ranthambore Rd, 1.5km from town (☎20792; fax 5553). Modern complex of clean, comfortable rooms with bath. Filling meals served in its dining room. Discounts out of season. ⑥.

Anurag Resort, Ranthambore Rd, 1.5km from town (☎20451; fax c/o PO, 20697). Decent rooms with bath, as well as camping (Rs25) and a small dorm – very good value for budget travellers. The hotel grows most of its own food, and has a fascinating kitchen garden. ①–⑤.

Hamir Wildlife Resort, Ranthambore Rd, 7km from town (☎20562). Reasonable fall back if the *Ankur* and the *Anurag* are full; the rooms are far better value than the outside "cottages". ⑤.

Pink Palace, Bal Mandir Colony, just northeast of the bridge (☎20722). Candy pink inside and out. The rooms are otherwise fairly ordinary – the pricier ones not even pink – with attached bath. ③.

RTDC Castle Jhoomar Baori, on a hillside 7km out of town (☎20495). In a great location, with 11 comfortable rooms in a former royal hunting lodge, with suites, a plush lounge and airy roof terrace (from which you *may* even spot the odd tiger). Book ahead; discounts April–June. ⑤–⑥.

RTDC Vinayak, Ranthambore Rd, 8km from town (☎21333). New, very comfortable hotel. ⑤.

Swagat, main road, market area, about 500m northeast of the railway station (☎-20601). Cheap and a bit grubby, but with friendly, efficient staff. The upstairs rooms are best. Each room has private bath, but don't expect any hidden comforts. The *Vishal* (☎20504), two doors away, is pretty similar. ①.

MOVING ON FROM SAWAI MADHOPUR

Leaving Sawai Madhopur, there are **trains** to Kota (13 daily; 1hr 30min) and the other way to Bharatpur (6 daily; 4–6hr), and eight each to Bombay (16hr) and New Delhi (5hr 30min). There are also five daily trains to Jaipur (2–3hr), one to Jodhpur (8hr 30min), and three to Agra (5hr), one of which continues to Calcutta Howrah (34hr). **Buses**, slower and less comfortable, run to Jaipur (2 daily; 5hr), Kota (4 daily; 4hr), and Ajmer (3 daily; 8hr) from a stand on the market area's main street, just before the bridge. For Shivpuri, however, you'll have to trek out to the city bus stand in Sawai Madhopur City.

West of Jaipur

Heading west out of Jaipur, NH8 passes through an arid landscape that is largely barren for all but that fraction of the year when the rains tease growth out of the desert soils. As it approaches **Ajmer**, craggy ridges of the northern Aravalli range break out of the sandy plains to shelter larger settlements such as **KISHANGARH**. This small and busy market town, 30km east of Ajmer, won fame for the miniature paintings produced in its fort during the seventeenth century. Decorated within by murals of the life of Krishna, the fort today stands almost empty just outside the town, beside a lake that brims with lotus flowers during the monsoon.

Thousands of pilgrims converge on the area each year for its **festivals**. Muslims flock to Ajmer during Urs Mela (April/May), while Hindus and local traders commune in **Pushkar**, a little northwest, for Karttika Purnima, the **camel fair** (Oct/Nov). In April, acres and acres of **roses** make startling flashes of colour in the desert sands before being collected to be sprinkled by devotees over the tomb of the Sufi saint Khwaja Muin-ud-din Chisti in Ajmer. Carpets of dazzling pink cover the flat rooftops of Ajmer and Pushkar, where the roses are laid to dry before being packaged and sent to Mecca for use in worship, and made into incense.

Ajmer

The unspectacular town of **AJMER** is famous throughout India as the former home of the Sufi **Khwaja Muin-ud-din Chisti**, founder of the Chistiya Order – still India's foremost Sufi order. He died here in 1236, at a time when Ajmer was under Muslim rule, the forces of the fearsome Muhammad of Ghori having successfully besieged what was previously a stronghold of the Rajput Chauhans in 1191. To this day, Chisti's tomb, the **Dargah**, remains one of the most fascinating and holy Muslim shrines in the country.

Ajmer belonged to the Sultanate until 1326, but from then until the advent of the British, it was constantly fought over by neighbouring states, with just a century of peace under Akbar and Jahangir. Though its dusty main streets now burst with traffic,

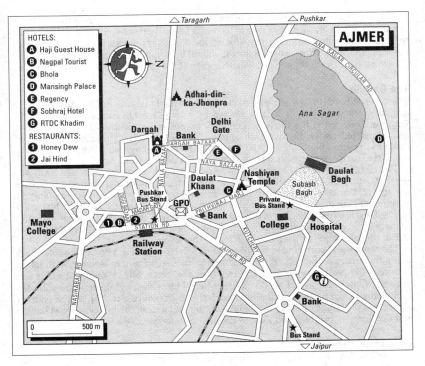

HOTELS:
- **A** Haji Guest House
- **B** Nagpal Tourist
- **C** Bhola
- **D** Mansingh Palace
- **E** Regency
- **F** Sobhraj Hotel
- **G** RTDC Khadim

RESTAURANTS:
- **1** Honey Dew
- **2** Jai Hind

the narrow lanes of the bazaars and residential quarters are almost medieval, throng-ing with pedestrians. Near the Dargah, bazaar stalls overflow with offerings and sou-venirs, while the streets of Nalla Bazaar are lined with shoe shops, clothes and sewing machines. **Ana Sagar**, a sprawling artificial lake west of town, freshens the desert, and the gardens on its southern edge are popular for picnics and evening strolls.

Arrival and information

Ajmer's **railway station** is in the centre of town, with regular services from the rest of Rajasthan, and points south; the main **bus stand**, with an exhaustive array of routes, is about 2km south. Tempos connect the two. Buses to **Pushkar** also leave every fifteen minutes from outside Gandhi Bhawan, a few hundred metres east of the railway station. Seats on private buses – many of which have connecting services from Pushkar – can be reserved at Ajmer bus station, Pushkar hotels, or at any of the travel agents along Kutchery Rd between the bus stand and railway station.

The efficient **tourist office** (Mon–Sat 8am–noon & 3–6pm; ☎52426) adjoins RTDC *Hotel Khadim*, not far from the bus stand. *State Bank of India*, near the bus stand, will change *Thomas Cook* and *Amex* (but not *Visa*) travellers' cheques and most currencies; *Bank of Baroda*, on Station Rd near the GPO, will only change travellers' cheques if you have the receipt.

The telephone **area code** for Ajmer and Pushkar is ☎0145.

Ajmer's chief attractions lie within walking distance of each other, in the centre of town, and are easily visited in a day. To rent a **bike**, there are a couple of places just west of Delhi Gate (expect to pay around Rs10 per day). Fares for cycle rickshaws, more popular here than auto-rickshaws, should be negotiated in advance. If you don't plan to stop for the night you can leave luggage at the railway station or the bus stand.

The Dargah

The revered Sufi, Khwaja Muin-ud-din Chisti, who died in Ajmer in 1236, was buried in a small brick tomb that is today engulfed by a large marble complex known as the **Dargah**. Founded in the thirteenth century by Sultan Iltutmish of the slave dynasty, and completed under the sixteenth-century Moghul emperor Humayun, the Dargah contains mosques built by rulers such as Shah Jahan, Jahangir and Akbar (who visited the shrine on numerous occasions and even walked twice from Agra).

The complex is entered from Dargah Bazaar, through a high gateway that leads into the first courtyard. Once inside, you'll see two immense cauldrons, known as *degs*, each 3m across. Donations are thrown in and later shared among the poor, continuing the tradition of giving succour to the needy that was so important to the saint. During the saint's **Urs festival**, the *degs* are filled with sweetened rice and sold to devotees by "looters" who receive the profits. To the right is the marble mosque donated by Akbar, and to the left stands an assembly hall for the homeless.

The tomb itself, surrounded by silver railings, is enshrined in a domed marble chamber in the centre of the second courtyard, near the magnificent mosque of Shah Jahan. Devotees file past, some sprinkling roses over the grave, others simply standing and praying. Visitors are asked for donations, offered blessings, lightly brushed with peacock feathers and given the chance to touch the cloth covering the tomb. The continual murmur of singing, praying, sobbing, laughter and music, the heady scent of flowers and the flurry of bright-robed women creates an unforgettable spectacle.

Islamic monuments

The **Adhai-din-ka-Jhonpra**, or "two-and-a-half-day mosque", slightly north of the Dargah, is the oldest survivor of Ajmer's days under Muslim rule; built in 1200 and now no longer in use, it remains one of the finest examples of medieval architecture in Rajasthan. Although probably named after a festival, tradition holds that the mosque was constructed as quickly as its name suggests. Its arched facade is covered with Islamic calligraphy, while many of its bricks and pillars were taken from nearby Hindu and Jain temples, considered of little worth by the new Muslim governors.

The most recent of Ajmer's Islamic relics is the squat sandstone **Daulat Khana** palace in the heart of the city, used by Akbar and his son Jahangir. Here, in 1616, Sir Thomas Roe became the first British ambassador to be given an official audience. It now houses the government **museum** (daily except Fri 10am–4.30pm; Rs2), which displays Rajasthani statues dating back to the eighth century, and pieces excavated from Mohenjo Daro (second millennium BC). Exhibits in the Jain gallery include a beautiful statue of Saraswati from Banswara.

Other attractions

When Ajmer came under British control in 1818, it was one of the few cities in Rajputana outside the hegemony of the princely states. Monuments still standing as echoes of its colonial past include the **Jubilee clock tower** opposite the railway station, **Edward Memorial Hall** a little to the west and the famous **Mayo College**, originally built as a school for princes, and now a leading educational institution.

About 3km west of the Dargah, high above the city, the **Taragarh** or "Star Fort" was built in 1100 AD as one of India's first hill forts. It's now badly ruined, and the only reward for the steep climb to the crest of the hill is the panoramic view.

Perhaps the most bizarre sight in Ajmer is the mirrored **Soniji-ki-Nashiya** hall adjoining the Nashiyan Jain temple, or "red temple" (daily 8am–5pm; Rs2). The hall commemorates the life of Rishabha (or Adinath), the first Jain *tirthankara*, believed to have lived countless aeons in the past. From the uppermost of the three storeys that surround it you can look down on musicians flying above the sacred Mount Sumeru on swans, peacocks and elephants. The whole display is in gold, extravagantly detailed in fantastic proportions appropriate to the realm of legend. Admission to the main temple alongside is restricted to Jains, of whom there is a large number in Ajmer.

Accommodation

Ajmer has many **hotels** to house the flow of pilgrims visiting the Dargah. Most are full during Urs Mela, but at other times rooms are in plentiful supply. A collection of modest rest houses stand opposite the railway station, and there are also a few hotels in the bazaar area. If you want to stay in style, try the grand *Mansingh Palace*.

Bhola, Agra Gate, Subzi Mandi (☎23844). The best-value cheap hotel, very clean, with a good restaurant. ②.

Haji Guest House, Nalla Bazaar (☎23835). Right next to the Dargah in lively bazaar area. Spotless rooms, some with balconies; most doubles have attached bathroom. ②.

Mansingh Palace, Ana Sagar Circular Rd (☎425702). Lavish hotel in ideal surroundings, a few kilometres northwest of town. ⑧.

Nagpal Tourist, Station Rd (☎21603). Bright and breezy modern hotel, where the cheaper rooms have TV but no hot water. ③.

Regency, Delhi Gate (☎30296). Smart air-cooled and a/c rooms with TVs. ⑤.

RTDC Khadim, near the bus stand (☎52490). Good value place, with cheap dorm. ①–④.

Sobhraj Hotel, Delhi Gate (☎23488). A once-plush hotel on the decline, with some a/c rooms; not to be confused with the grotty *Sobhraj Guest House* opposite. ④.

Eating

In addition to the snack and fruit-juice places around Dargah Bazaar and Delhi Gate, Ajmer has a handful of larger restaurants.

Bhola, see above. Excellent pure veg food, including good-value *thalis*. Open 8am–11pm.

Honey Dew, Station Rd. Veg, non-veg and pizza at middling prices, next to the King Edward Memorial. There's a garden, and a good selection of *Kwality* ice-cream. Open 7am–11pm.

Jai Hind, Station Rd, tucked in an alley beside the clock tower opposite the station. Opened in 1949 by Hindu refugees from Sind. Very good veg food, in smart surroundings; special dishes every month. Open 8.30am–10.30pm.

Mansingh Palace Hotel, see above. Pricey, delicious international cuisine in a clean and fresh dining hall in lush surroundings. Open 12.30–3pm & 7.30–11pm.

Pushkar

With its smooth spread of white-domed houses and temples reflected in a tranquil lake, **PUSHKAR**, just 13km northwest of Ajmer, resembles nothing so much as a pearl dropped in the desert. Although during the annual **camel fair**, held during the full moon in October or November, Pushkar is transformed into a crowded hive of activity, for the rest of the year this profoundly peaceful town makes a welcome respite from the din and hassle of the cities. One of those destinations where travellers tend to stay considerably longer than they originally envisage, it is also a popular place to relax before flying out of Delhi, a night's train or bus journey away.

No one knows quite how old Pushkar is: **legend** relates that at the beginning of time, Brahma dropped a lotus flower (*pushkara*) from the sky, declared the lake that sprang from the arid desert sands to be holy, and promised that anyone who bathed in it would be freed from their sins. As the site of one of only two temples in the world dedicated

Tourist Village at time of Camel Festival

PUSHKAR

Camel Market during Festival

Gayitri Mandir & Ajmer

Savitri Temple

Hospital
Marwar Bus Stand
GPO
N

0   200 m

BADI BASTI (MAIN BAZAAR)

Gau Ghat
Varah Ghat

Brahma Mandir
Brahma Ghat

Bank

Pushkar Lake

Vishnu Temple
Ajmer Bus Stand
Hanuman Tower

AJMER RD

HOTELS:
Ⓐ Everest Guest House
Ⓑ Amar
Ⓒ Bharatpur Palace
Ⓓ Navratan Palace
Ⓔ Lake View
Ⓕ Payal Guest House
Ⓖ Lotus
Ⓗ RTDC Sarovar Tourist Bungalow
Ⓘ Pushkar Palace
Ⓙ Om
Ⓚ Oasis
Ⓛ Peacock
Ⓜ Siva
Ⓝ Prince

RESTAURANTS:
❶ R S
❷ Rainbow & Krishna
❸ Sanjay
❹ Sarovar
❺ Venus
❻ Raju Garden
❼ Raju
❽ Moondance

solely to the Lord Brahma, Pushkar attracts a constant flow of pilgrims to worship and bathe from its 52 lakeside *ghats*. Records of visits go back as far as the second century, when the Kshatrapa ruler of western India came to immerse himself and present gifts to the *brahmins*.

The streets of Pushkar are too narrow for traffic, and there are no rickshaws; a lazy stroll around the shores of the lake and through the main bazaar takes little more than an hour. **Shopping** is the prime pastime for visitors; you're encouraged to take all the time you want browsing at the countless small roadside stalls, choosing from a vast assortment of clothes, jewellery, second-hand books, *chillums,* Indian classical music CDs and cassettes, and Rajasthani paintings. You'd do better, however, to buy the latter in Udaipur; clothes here (especially of the hippy variety), are usually much better buys.

Arrival and information

Most long-distance journeys to and from Pushkar have to be made via Ajmer; Pushkar does not have a railway station. The **Ajmer bus stand** in the east of town is served by buses from Ajmer and Jaipur, while travellers from destinations further afield, such as Delhi, Jodhpur and Bikaner, arrive in the north of town at **Marwar bus stand**, to be besieged by eager accommodation touts. The lack of rickshaws means that you'll have to walk to your hotel (though there are **bicycles** for rent right by the Ajmer bus stand).

There is no **tourist office** in Pushkar. The **GPO** for parcels and poste restante is in the north of town, and there's a smaller one on the market square. The *State Bank of Bikaner and Jaipur* (Mon–Fri 11am–3pm) in the square near Varah Ghat is the best bet for **currency exchange**.

In addition to the state buses, a number of **private bus firms** run daily buses to Delhi, Agra, Jaipur, Abu, Jaisalmer, Udaipur, Jodhpur and Ahmedabad, and some have connecting services from Pushkar. All can usually be booked from hotels. The management at the *Peacock Hotel* will book onward **rail** journeys from Ajmer for a small charge (and book, cancel or change air tickets). Otherwise go to Ajmer to book for yourself well in advance; trains to Delhi in particular are often reserved days ahead.

Temples

There are more than four hundred temples in and around Pushkar; many had to be rebuilt after pillaging during the merciless rule of Moghul Emperor Aurangzeb (1656–1708), while others are recent additions. Some, like the splendid **Vishnu temple**, are out of bounds to non-Hindus.

Pushkar's most important temple, **Brahma Mandir**, may not be architecturally astounding, but its layout is superb. The main sanctuary, raised on a stepped platform in the centre of a courtyard, is surrounded on three sides by chambers and smaller shrines topped with flat roofs providing views across the desert west to **Saivitri Mandir** on the summit of a nearby hill. The two-hour climb to the top of that hill is rewarded by superb vistas over the town, surrounded on all sides by desert, and is best done in the evening, to reach the summit for sunset. **Gayitri Mandir**, on the other hand, set on a hill east of the town, faces east and should ideally be visited at sunrise.

The ghats

The sacred **ghats** of Pushkar – broad flights of steps leading down into the water – constitute a vital link between temple and lake. Each is named after an event or person, and three in particular bear special significance. Primary among them is **Gau Ghat** (sometimes called Main Ghat), where visiting ministers and politicians come to worship, and from which ashes of Mahatma Gandhi, Jawaharlal Nehru and Shri Lal Bahadur Shastri were sprinkled into the lake. **Brahma Ghat** marks the spot where Brahma himself is said to have worshipped, while at the large **Varah Ghat**, just off the market square, Vishnu is

---

BRAHMA

Brahma, revered as the Creator from later Vedic times onwards, was seen as one of the most important gods, together with Shiva (Destroyer) and Vishnu (Preserver). The three served in anthropomorphic terms to represent the powerful, non-conceptual Brahman – an unchanging and eternal force associated with cosmic unity. As the concept of *samsara* came to be at the heart of Hindu philosophy, however – and life was envisaged as endless transmigration with no beginning – Brahma's role as Creator was questioned by later philosophers. His importance as a cult god dwindled until it had almost ceased to exist by the nineteenth century, but he is still regarded as a major divinity.

Stories of Brahma's exploits are still told and retold in **Pushkar**, site of a temple dedicated exclusively to the deity. One such tale reveals the significance of the temples named after Brahma's wives, **Saivitri** and **Gayitri**. According to this, Brahma was waiting on the *ghats* for his wife Saivitri, in order that he could perform *puja* at the appointed time. She did not arrive soon enough, and Brahma insisted that he perform the ritual accompanied by a wife. So an unmarried woman was found and bathed in cow's milk as a means of purification, and the ritual commenced. The woman was named after the sacred cow, *Gau*. Saivitri in her anger withdrew to the mountain in the west of town where a temple now stands in her honour, and Gayitri is remembered by the hill-top temple to the east.

believed to have appeared in the form of Varaha (a boar), one of his nine incarnations. At all the *ghats*, it is a respected and unspoken request that visitors should remove their shoes at a reverential distance from the lake, and refrain from smoking and taking photos.

Indian and Western tourists alike are urged by local Brahmin priests to worship at the lake, that is, to make **Pushkar Puja**. This involves the repetition of prayers while scattering rose petals into the lake, and then being asked for a donation (these days often an astronomically high one) which *usually* goes to temple funds, or to the priest who depends on such benefaction. On completion of the *puja*, a red thread taken from a temple is tied around your wrist. Labelled the "Pushkar Passport" by locals, this simple token means that you'll no longer attract pushy Pushkar priests, and can wander unhindered onto the *ghats*.

Accommodation

Pushkar has numerous *dharamshalas* for pilgrims. For the ever-growing influx of Western tourists, there's a wide choice of **hotels**, many of them in family homes. Most are pretty basic, but they're comfortable, and some provide well-furnished rooms with private bath. Views over the lake are rare, but many have rooftops looking across

KARTTIKA PURNIMA AND PUSHKAR CAMEL FAIR

Hindus visit Pushkar year round to take a dip in the redemptory waters of the lake, but there is one particular day when bathing here is believed to relieve devotees of all their sins, and ultimately free them from the bonds of *samsara*: the full moon (*purnima*) of the **Karttika** month (usually Nov). For five days leading up to and including the full moon, Pushkar hosts thousands of celebrating devotees, following prescribed rituals on the lakeside and in the Brahma Mandir. To add to the flurry of colour and activity, a few days before the main religious festival a large **camel fair** is held in the sandy flats west of the town, when hordes of traders from all over Rajasthan gather to parade, race and trade their camels, horses and cattle. The transformation of Pushkar from a peaceful desert town is complete and overwhelming – the streets are packed with swarms of devotees, eager traders and hundreds of tourists; hotels and restaurants are choc-a-bloc, and prices soar. Families from all over Rajasthan struggle through the crowded lanes laden with children, blankets, food and makeshift tents, setting up camp west of town where night fires, delicious open-air cooking smells and harmonious tunes drifting through the starlit night create an unforgettable experience.

Once trading is under way camels and cattle are meticulously groomed, lined up and auctioned, while women dressed in mirrored skirts and vivid shawls lay out embroidered cloth, jewellery, pots and ornaments beside the herds, stopping trade occasionally to gather dung to fuel the evening fires. Cattle, poultry, sheep and goats are entered for competitions, and prizes given for the best displays of fruit and vegetables. Away from the main activity, the dusty ground is stirred up by vigorous **camel races**, noisily urged on by gamblers. Things become even more animated as acrobats balance precariously on tight ropes and cartwheel between the crowds, and insouciant jugglers toss fire batons before enthralled onlookers. Photo-opportunities are limitless, and anyone with a camera should definitely over-budget on films, which may not be on sale in Pushkar.

The fair attracts up to 200,000 people, many of whom are tourists. Hotels hike their rates and are usually full well before the start, but extra **accommodation** is provided by RTDC in tented compounds outside town where there's a choice between dormitory beds (③), deluxe tents (⑨), or huts (⑨) complete with private bathrooms. Be sure to book ahead by contacting the RTDC office in Jaipur (☎ & fax 0141/316045) or by writing well in advance to the Manager, CRO, RTDC, Usha Niwas, Kalyan Path, Jaipur. The tent village has an information counter (☎72074), exchange facilities, safes, shops and a medical centre. Not surprisingly, **food** stalls spring up everywhere during the fair, serving freshly cooked regional specialities.

Pushkar to the distant hills. Some hotels operate 11pm curfews, and most are visited regularly by cheeky, inquisitive monkeys. Note that **prices** soar during the camel fair.

Amar, set back from the main road in the centre of town (no phone). A delightful little place, with ground-floor rooms facing a lush jasmine-filled garden. ①.

Bharatpur Palace, Brahma Temple Rd (☎72320). Large house bordering the lake with spacious roof area and simple, charming rooms; more expensive ones face the lake, including a special detached "Maharaja's Room". ②–④.

Everest Guest House, near the Marwar bus stand (☎72080). Cheap and popular, though not as homely as some. ①.

Lake View, Main Bazaar (☎72106). Simple rooms on a large rooftop, right by the lake. ①.

Lotus, south shore of the lake (no phone). In gardens on the lake's edge. Welcoming, cramped and grubby; popular for long stays, and often full. There's an annexe on the main bazaar. ①.

Navratan Palace, Brahma Temple Rd, near Brahma Mandir (☎72145; fax 72225). New, characterless place with large comfy rooms with bath; great views towards the hills. Cleanish, with a pool. ④.

Oasis, Ajmer Rd (☎72100). Right next to the Ajmer bus stand, but comfortable and clean, with an interior courtyard and 360° view from the roof. All rooms have attached bathroom with hot water on tap, some have mosquito nets. There's also a swimming pool (Rs25 for non-residents). ③.

Om, Ajmer Rd (☎72143). Ramshackle place with central courtyard. Basic rooms, with or without bathroom. Non-residents can use the small pool for Rs50 (or free if dining). ①–③.

Payal Guest House, Main Bazaar (☎72163) Small central hotel with rooms around a fresh, leafy courtyard. Good value and no night curfew. ②.

Peacock, Ajmer Rd (☎72093; fax 32974). A little out of town past Ajmer bus stand, and popular mainly for its pool, which non-residents can pay Rs40 to use. Decent rooms but nothing special, plus cheap dorms and more expensive suites, and a restaurant. They also run the *Royal Camp* resort 2km out of town, with deluxe tents & "cottages". ②–⑥.

Prince, on the road leading off the market square by the post office (no phone). Quiet place with unelaborate rooms around a verdant courtyard; roof area and restaurant. ①.

Pushkar Palace (☎72401 or 2; fax 72226). On the east side of the lake, with panoramic views from a peaceful garden. Rooms range from tiny and basic to large and lavish – the general atmosphere is somewhat upper class. There's also a good restaurant. ⑦.

RTDC Sarovar, Ajmer Rd (☎72040). Entered at the end of Ajmer Rd, but set back from the street in peaceful gardens, just east of the lake. Pleasant and well maintained; rates include evening meal, but the food is notoriously poor. Dorms available. ①–④.

Siva, on the road leading off the market square by the post office (☎72120). Popular and very friendly little place with a leafy courtyard and roof top, but small rooms. If it's full, try the similarly priced *Sai Baba* and *Shanti Palace* across the street. ①.

Eating

As Pushkar is sacred to Lord Brahma, all food is strictly veg: meat, eggs and alcohol are banned (and taking drugs is considered highly offensive). However, its **restaurants** cater for both Indian and foreign palates, offering national dishes as well as pizza, spaghetti and apple pie. Be wary of the many buffets offering tempting all-you-can-eat menus; most are likely to consist of terribly unhealthy reheated food, and it's safer to stick to the more expensive places. This does not apply to **buffet breakfasts**, however, with unlimited supplies of cereal, toast and curd – try the *Omshiva Buffet*, on the fourth floor, above *Hotel VK*, near the *Pushkar Palace*. If you fancy a change, stalls opposite *Gau Ghat* sell sumptuous freshly made sweets.

Krishna, Brahma Temple Rd. Tasty Indian dishes, including south Indian *dosas* at breakfast, and Israeli-style *falafel* and *hummus*. Open 8am–10.30pm.

Moondance, opposite Vishnu temple. Nepali-run, with nothing Indian on the menu. Attempts at Thai and "Maxican" food are tasty but nothing like the real thing; the pizza and pasta is the best in town. Taking over from *R S* as the "in" place for travellers. Open 8.30am–11pm.

R S, opposite the Brahma Mandir. Long-standing favourite, with a small garden area and patio seating. Try its inexpensive but high-quality *thalis* (after 6pm) or veg curries. Open 7am–10pm.

Rainbow, Brahma Temple Rd. Rooftop restaurant above the *Krishna*, serving veg curries, pasta, pizza, *falafel*, Chinese dishes and even attempts at *enchiladas* and *moussaka*. Open 8am–midnight.

Raju, Ajmer Rd. Not to be confused with *Raju Garden Restaurant*, this small basic place serves very cheap curries and good *thalis*. Open 7am–10pm.

Raju Garden Restaurant, off Main Bazaar near Ram Ghat. Delicious Indian, Chinese and Western food of a standard rarely matched by other restaurants. Set breakfasts for Rs25. Open 8am–11pm.

Sanjay, Main Bazaar. Rooftop seating overlooking the lake; the food – veg curries, *thalis*, pizza – is nothing special, but the buffet breakfasts (Rs25) are good. Open 7am–11pm.

Sarovar, Ajmer Rd. Good Western, Indian, Chinese and Tibetan food in pleasant garden surroundings, next to the Ajmer bus stand. Open 7am–10pm.

Venus, Ajmer Rd. Set back from the lake, with a garden and a roof terrace. The Indian dishes are good, and the "sizzler hotplate" is their speciality, but they haven't quite got the hang of Western cooking. Open 7am–10.30pm.

Jodhpur

On the eastern fringe of the Thar Desert, the city of **JODHPUR** sprawls across the sandy terrain, watched over by a mighty walled fort that emerges from a high rocky outcrop. Jodhpur was once the centre of Marwar, the largest princely state in Rajputana, and today has a population close to half a million.

Most of the tourists that stop in Jodhpur only stay for a day, squeezing in a visit to the fort and palaces before heading west to Jaisalmer (300km) or east to Jaipur (320km). It's a shame to rush the place though, and if you spend more time you'll be able to explore the bazaars of the old city, search out puppeteers and dyers, and get a taste of rural Rajasthan by taking a trip to the surrounding villages.

A brief history

In 1459, Rao Jodha of the Rathore clan moved the capital of Marwar state several kilometres from the exposed site of **Mandore** to a massive steep-sided escarpment, where he named his new capital after himself. The high barricaded fort proved virtually impregnable, and the city soon amassed great wealth from trade en route to the ports of Gujarat. Not surprisingly, the Moghuls were eager to take over Jodhpur, but realizing there was little prospect of that they presented treaties and riches to the Rathores in exchange for military aid in their onslaught on Gujarat. A marriage alliance between Udai Singh's sister and Akbar in 1561 ensured the most friendly of terms.

However, the tide turned in the mid-seventeenth century, after Jaswant Singh joined Shah Jahan's forces in an unsuccessful bid for power against his fellow Moghul Aurangzeb. Aurangzeb set out to purge his enemies, and demanded the death of Jaswant's young son, **Ajit Singh**. That demand was not satisfied, but Jodhpur was sacked in 1678 and its inhabitants forcibly converted to Islam. In the finest romantic tradition, Ajit Singh eventually recaptured his rightful kingdom after thirty years in hiding. The performance of *sati* on his funeral pyre by six wives and fifty-eight concubines in 1731 may seem shocking now, but at the time was testimony to his heroism. The eighteenth century saw many bloody battles between Jodhpur, Jaipur and Udaipur, despite their policy of unification against the Moghuls. At its close, Jodhpur passed first into the hands of the Marathas and then the British; the signing of a friendship treaty with the East India Company in 1818 guaranteed its safety, albeit at great cost to Rathore honour.

The last Maharaja before Independence, **Umaid Singh**, is commemorated by his immense Umaid Bhawan Palace; he set 3000 citizens to work for sixteen years on its construction, in part to alleviate problems during a severe famine by creating employment. Jodhpur is now a democratic union within the independent India, but its social fabric remains tinged with feudalism and a medieval atmosphere prevails.

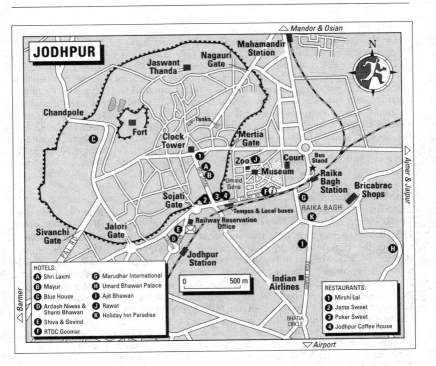

Arrival and information

Jodhpur's main **railway station** is in the south of town, close to several basic hotels, and a couple of kilometres from the fort. Just two trains (including the Jodhpur–Jaisalmer service) stop at Raika Bagh station on the eastern edge of town, near the state **bus stand**. Private buses drop you near the main railway station. From the **airport**, 4km south, the only form of public transport into town is **auto-rickshaw**; in town these are supplemented by tempos and small minibuses that follow fixed routes along the main roads. **Bicycles** can be rented from shops near the railway station (Rs7 per day), and **cars** from *Hotel Ardash Niwas*, Station Rd (☎26936). *Rajasthan Tours*, Hospital Rd (☎32694 or 36942) is a reliable agent for **tours** around the state.

The **tourist office** (Mon–Sat 10am–5pm; ☎45083), in the RTDC *Goomar Tourist Bungalow* on High Court Rd, has city maps and information on private bus services. The *State Bank of India* is behind the Collectorate, off High Court Rd (Mon–Fri 10am–2pm, Sat 10–noon).

The telephone **area code** for Jodhpur is ☎0291.

The City

Life in Jodhpur focuses very much around the fort, still almost completely encircled by the strong walls erected by Rao Maldeo in the 1500s. The blue wash on houses in the old city originally signified that they belonged to *brahmins*, who made up most of the city's inhabitants. Nowadays, however, the colour has caught on, and there is even a blue-wash mosque on the road from the Jalori Gate to the west side of the fort.

The bazaars of the old city are gathered around the tall **clock tower**, with different areas assigned to different trades. Locally made goods include tie-dye, puppets and lacquered jewellery. **Jalori Gate** and **Sojati Gate** lead out of the old city to the south, close to the railway station, GPO and hospital. Beyond the walls, more modern buildings spread east and west of the old boundaries, the domes of the splendid **Umaid Bhawan** dominating the scene to the southeast. Immediately to the east of the old city, by the Mertia Gate, the **Umaid Gardens** (daily 5am–10pm) house the rather uninteresting **Government Museum** (daily except Fri 10am–4.30pm; Rs2), and a **zoo** with larger than usual enclosures (daily except Tues 9am–noon & 3–6pm; free).

Meherangarh Fort

Daily summer 8.30am–5.30pm, winter 9am–5pm; Rs50, camera Rs50, video Rs100, elevator to the top Rs10 (free if you have a walking disablity); guides Rs100 for 1–5 people, Rs150 for 6 or more.

Jodhpur's **Meherangarh Fort** provides what must be the most authentic surviving taste of the ceaseless round of war, honour and extravagance that characterized Rajputana. Unlike the fort in Jaisalmer, it is uninhabited, its paths trodden only by visitors to the temples and palaces within its high crenellated walls. On the wall next to **Loha Pole**, the sixth of seven gates designed to hinder the ascent of enemies up a steep winding cobbled road, are the handprints of Maharaja Man Singh's widows. Following the Rajput code of honour, they voluntarily ended their lives in 1843 on their husband's pyre, in defiance of the law against *sati* passed in 1829 by the British.

Beyond the massive **Suraj Pole**, the final gate, lie the palaces that now serve as the **Meherangarh Museum** (closed 1–2.30pm). From the courtyards, you can see the fantastic *jali* (lattice) work that almost entirely covers their sandstone walls and balconies. The exotic names of the palaces evoke a courtly society that between violent battles loved to indulge in beauty and elegance. In the **Jhanki Mahal**, or "Queen's Palace", there's a colourful array of cradles of former rulers, while **Moti Mahal** (Pearl Palace) houses the majestic marble coronation seat upon which all the rulers apart from Jodha have been, and still are, crowned. One prize exhibit in the museum is a 250-year-old pure silk tent seized during a raid on the Moghul court in Delhi. The most elaborate of the apartments is **Phool Mahal** (Flower Palace), a dancing hall for the entertainment of the Maharaja and his guests. Pictures of dancers, deities and rulers look out from its walls and wooden ceilings, brightly painted with touches of gold. Other palaces have sandalwood ceilings, mirrored walls and decorated archways, and the last section displays solid silver *howdahs* (elephant seats) and palanquins, perfectly carved and very, very heavy.

The fascinating walk up to the fort from the old city passes through busy bazaars and communal living areas, where some of the streets are so narrow that pedestrians have to advance in single file, vying for right of way with goats and chickens. You can also reach the fort by taxi or rickshaw along the much longer road (5km) that enters the old city at Nagauri Gate.

Jaswant Thanda

North of the fort, and connected to it by road, **Jaswant Thanda** is a pillared marble memorial to the popular ruler Jaswant Singh II (1878–95), who purged Jodhpur of dacoits, initiated irrigation systems and boosted the economy. The cenotaphs of members of the royal family who have died since Jaswant are close by his memorial; those who preceded him are remembered by *chhatris* at **Mandor** (see p.175).

Accommodation

Hotels in Jodhpur are grouped in three main areas. With the exception of the *Ardash Niwas* and the *Govind*, those along the noisy **Station Rd** are acceptable only to thick-skinned budget travellers; the hotels on **Nai Sarak** (also called New Rd) in the old city are better bets. More refined lodgings – including two palaces – are in the **southeast** of town in and around the area known as Raikabagh.

Station Road area

Ardash Niwas, Station Rd (☎26936). Modern, clean, comfortable, and convenient for the station, but uninspiring. Marble decor and few windows. Hot water and TV in all rooms, some a/c. ⑥–⑦.
Govind, Station Rd (☎22758). Excellent budget hotel – not to be confused with the *Rada Govind* – opposite the GPO (look for the tree in front), near the station. Clean, friendly and has a dorm. ①–④.
Shanti Bhawan, Station Rd (☎21689). Right opposite the railway station; rooms range from bare and cramped to spacious and comfortable. Friendly management. ①–④.
Shiva, Station Rd (☎24774). Clean, characterless rooms with bath around small courtyard. ④.

Old City

The Blue House, Novechokiya (☎22758). Friendly little budget hotel in the shadow of the fort, in a blue-washed house from 1458, with a handful of basic rooms, a dorm and tasty home cooking. ①.
Mayur, 140 Nai Sarak (☎47511). Simple, quite clean rooms; some with balconies. ②.
Shri Laxmi, 132–133 Nai Sarak, near the clock tower (☎47047). Rooms (with bath) are small but clean and adequate. ③.

Raikabagh and around

Ajit Bhawan, Airport Rd (☎37410; fax 37774). Grand a/c palace suites, set in leafy gardens and still used by the royal family, plus spotless and characterful round huts for two designed to a village theme. Regal treatment and a true taste of Rajasthani tradition; evening buffets (see below) feature performances by villagers. Also daily village excursions. ⑦.
Holiday Inn Paradise Guest House, Raikabagh (☎24097). Clean, plain rooms, and a dorm, with running hot water. ①–⑤.
Marudhar International, opposite KN Hall, Raikabagh (☎32061). Plain, comfortable rooms (some a/c), a little out of the centre, set around a lawn. Clean and quiet, with a reasonable restaurant. ⑤.
Rawat, north gate of Umaid Gardens (☎42622). Bright new mid-range place in a lovely setting. ⑤.
RTDC Goomar, High Court Rd (☎40810 or 20). Fairly typical RTDC hotel with large, bare rooms in need of a spring clean. Cheap dorm, alcohol shop, restaurant and travel counter. ①–⑤.
Umaid Bhawan Palace, southeast of town (☎33316; fax 35373). For those with extravagant tastes and bulging purses. The building is awesome and rooms are expansive, but some lack the style you'd expect for the price. Numerous bars, huge gardens and an underground swimming pool. The buffet spreads are overpriced and disappointing. Rooms start at $180. ⑨.

Elsewhere

Raj Basera, Residency Rd, 2km southwest of town (☎ & fax 31973). Popular with tour groups. New village-style cottages with interesting decor; swimming pool and open-air restaurant. ⑦.

Eating

Jodhpur's **restaurants** cater for all tastes and all budgets. The cheapest places, for surprisingly tasty food are the small dimly lit stalls opposite the railway station, beneath *Shanti Bhawan*, and at the other side of the GPO, by the main private bus stand. **Local specialities** include *mawa* sweets and *dhood fini*, a sweet mixture of wheat strands and milk. The best place to sample these is at *Janta Sweet* and *Poker Sweet*, both on Nai Sarak near the corner of High Court Rd (look for the crowds). These places also sell *mirchi bada*, a chilli in wheatgerm and potato, deep-fried like a *pakora*, available at *samosa* stalls elsewhere in Rajasthan, but originally from here. *Mirshi Lal*, in the gateway just south of the clock tower, is the most famous purveyor of **Makhania Lassi**, made with cream, saffron and cardomom, but in fact theirs is rather sickly – the lighter version available at the *Fort View* restaurant is better.

Ajit Bhawan, Airport Rd. Delicious evening buffets (7–10.30pm; Rs200) accompanied by folk music and dance. Best book ahead. Buffet lunches also available, but must be pre-booked.

Fort View, on the roof of the *Govind* hotel, Station Rd. A cut above the usual tourist places, with good veg curries, *thalis*, Chinese food and great views of the fort. It's open round the clock, and you can hang out here while waiting for the bus or train (baggage storage facilities available).

Jodhpur Coffee House, High Court Rd, near the corner of Nai Sarak. South Indian snacks and coffee similar in style to the *Indian Coffee House* chain, but with less choice. Closed for lunch.

Kalinga, Station Rd. Smart restaurant next to *Ardash Niwas*, with tasty veg and non-veg food plus set breakfasts (7–11am) including egg, bacon and sausage. Open 7am–10pm.

Midtown, Station Rd. New veg place attached to the *Mayur* hotel, for curries, south Indian snacks, pizza and *thalis*. Special Rajasthani dishes at the weekend. Open 8.30am–10.30pm.

Punkhaj, Station Rd, two doors from the corner opposite the station. Grubby hole-in-the-wall place, known for its superb *tandoori* nans. Sign in Hindi only. Open 7am–midnight.

MOVING ON FROM JODHPUR

The best **train** from Jodhpur to **Jaipur** is the *Intercity Express #2466*. There are two more daily trains to Jaipur and two to **Delhi** Sarai Rohilla, of which the overnight *Mandor Express #2462* is the faster (11hr 10min). The slower *Delhi Mail #4894* runs via **Ajmer** (5hr 25min), while **Agra** (12hr 10min) and **Lucknow** (14hr 25min) are served by the *Howrah Express #2308*, which continues to Calcutta's Howrah station (35hr 30min), and also by the thrice weekly *Marudhar Express #2464*. To **Ahmedabad** the most convenient train is the overnight *Surya Nagri Express #2907*. Two daily expresses run to **Barmer** (5hr), and one to **Bikaner** (4hr), while **Udaipur** is served by two daily passenger steam trains, one of them overnight (12hr 30min). The passenger train to **Jaisalmer** goes via Osian. The **reservation** office is next to the GPO in Station Rd (8am–1.45pm & 2–8pm).

The *RSRTC* **bus stand** is at the eastern end of High Court Rd, with services to Jaipur, Delhi, Ahmedabad, Jaisalmer, Bikaner via Nagaur (2hr 30min), Udaipur, Ranakpur, Abu Road, Kota and Osian. You can also get to Pushkar (3 daily; 5hr), Chittaurgarh (3 daily, 9hr), and Agra (1 daily; 14hr). Daily deluxe *Silver Line* buses leave for Jaipur and Jaisalmer – tickets are sold at the tourist office. **Private buses** depart by Station Rd, where numerous agents sell tickets for destinations including Jaipur, Delhi, Ahmedabad, Jaisalmer, Udaipur, Pushkar, Bikaner and Mount Abu.

Jodhpur's **airport** (☎30617) is 4km south of town. *Indian Airlines* fly to Jaipur and Delhi, Udaipur and Bombay. Their office is on Airport Rd near Bhatia Circle (☎36757). *Jagson Airlines* (☎44010 ext 360) have three weekly non-stop flights to Delhi and Jaisalmer.

Around Jodhpur

Should you stay in Jodhpur for longer than a day, and be tempted to see more than the fort and the medieval bazaars, you can visit the gardens in the old capital of **Mandor** on the outskirts of town, where former rulers are remembered by elaborate temple-like constructions, or a remarkable collection of early Jain and Hindu temples further afield at **Osian**, an hour's drive away.

Jodhpur's arid surroundings can also be explored on organized **village safaris**, which take small groups of tourists out into rural Rajasthan for a taste of traditional life. With several very dubious agencies around, much the most enlightening option is the

THE BISHNOIS

The **Bishnoi** people follow 29 principles laid down by Guru Jambhoji, who made environmental and wildlife protection a "religion" in the fifteenth century. Common throughout Rajasthan and Gujarat, they are renowned for a concern for nature, particularly for their refusal to harm the black buck, which now survives only in Bishnoi areas.

Bishnoi beliefs came to the political forefront in 1730, when the king of Jodhpur ordered his men to collect wood for a new palace. Despite the pleas of the Bishnois, felling commenced in the small village of Khejadali near Jodhpur. In desperation Amritdevi, a Bishnoi woman, hugged a tree. The fellers, assuming that the king's request was to be respected, ignored her plea. She and 362 of her fellow people lost their lives trying to protect the forests. On hearing the news the king recalled his men and accorded state sanction to the Bishnoi religion, a turning point in history remembered each September when thousands attend a festival at Khejadali.

daily half-day trip from the *Ajit Bhawan* hotel (book at least a day in advance; 8.30am–1 or 2pm; Rs400, including lunch). Each tour visits nearby villages, set in scrubland where the rare black buck, a beautiful indigenous antelope that is a menace to crops, is protected by the local Bishnoi tribe. In desert dwellings, mostly circular thatched huts, you can taste traditional food, learn about herbal remedies, and watch crafts such as spinning and carpet-making. The Maharaja encourages the fair sale of Bishnoi handicrafts in the hope that they can thereby avoid the emigration to the city that has destroyed the traditional way of life of so much of India's rural population.

Mandor

Most of Jodhpur's minibuses head for the royal cenotaphs, or *dewals*, of the maharajas in the fertile gardens 9km north of the city at **MANDOR**, the capital of the Parihar Rajputs between the sixth and fourteenth centuries. The Parihars were ousted when the Rathore Rao Chauhan in 1381 established the seat of government for his new kingdom at Mandor, and little remains of their fortified city. The dark red sandstone *chhatris*, memorials to Jodhpur's rulers, grew in size and grandeur as the Rathore kingdom prospered, culminating with the last and largest, that of **Maharaja Dhiraj Ajit Singh** (died 1763). It's Shaivite in style, fronted by a balustraded porch and topped with a towering roof crowned with four faces of Shiva. By the *chhatris*, opposite a rather dull museum, you'll find the **Hall of Heroes**, a strange display of life-sized gods and Rajput fighters that were hewn out of the rock face early in the eighteenth century.

A path leads over the hill behind the gardens to another set of cenotaphs, seemingly neglected on a sandy slope among twisted cacti. These commemorate the ranis of Jodhpur and though smaller, are more stately than those of the men, with exquisitely detailed carving on the pillars and domed roofs.

Osian

Rajasthan's largest group of early Jain and Hindu temples lies on the outskirts of the small town of **OSIAN**, 64km north of Jodhpur. Half-hourly buses (2hr) drop you on the main road south of town; the railway station (served by the Jodhpur–Jaisalmer train, 2hr30min out of Jodhpur) is 1km west.

The oldest group, the **Vishnu and Harihara temples**, built in the Pratihara period of the eighth and ninth centuries, are right by the bus stop. All three retain a considerable amount of decorative carving: twisted serpents coil around the doorways to the sanctuaries, and friezes on the outer walls include pictures of Krishna and various deities. Where the main road from Jodhpur to Phalodi bends round to the right, the smaller road straight ahead leads to the town centre, where you'll find the **Sachiya Mata temple**, at the top of a large staircase, overlooking the whole of Osian, and still used for worship. This temple dates back to the twelfth century, and features a hall for large gatherings. The main shrine, to Sachiya, an incarnation of Durga, is surrounded by smaller, earlier ones to Ganesh and Shankar (an aspect of Shiva), and, on the right, to Surya and Vishnu. The latter in particular is decorated with fine sculptures, including fierce mythical beasts. The main hall is full of mirror-tiled pillars, the ceiling borne by sixteen finely carved figures, and the whole ensemble is surrounded by battlements giving views over the whole town.

Coming out of the Sachiya Mata temple, the third group of temples, rather more spread out, is roughly straight ahead. The first is the **Mahavira Jain temple**, built in the eighth century, and renovated in the tenth. The gateway embellished with figurines was added in 1015. Twenty elegantly carved pillars hold up the main portico. The usual rules (no leather, don't enter during menstruation) apply. Fifty metres beyond is the **Surya temple**, surrounded by gargoyle-like projecting elephants. Its inner sanctum contains an image of Surya, flanked by Ganesh and Durga. Another 50m brings you to the **Sun temple**, where the carvings around the doorway have suffered the ravages of time (and graffiti), but those in the surrounding niches are very fine. A little way behind it is a massive Pratihara period step-well, currently under restoration.

If you want to **stay** in Osian, the ashram at the Sachiya Maya temple will put you up for a donation, while one of the temple's *brahmins*, Vimal Sarma, runs a one-room guest house (①) opposite the Mahavira temple, where home-cooked food is also available if you ask him in advance.

Jaisalmer

The westernmost town of Rajasthan, a good 100km beyond its closest neighbour Pokaran, **JAISALMER** is a desert city *par excellence*, its honey-coloured fort emerging from the flat dry sands like a fairy-tale kingdom, abounding in ancient palaces, temples and delicately sculpted houses. This is one of Rajasthan's most enchanting destinations, tranquil and beautiful, its soft desert-yellow streets spiced with bright oranges, reds, yellows and blues of turbans, scarfs and skirts. As the sun sets, the sandstone buildings emit the lustrous glow that makes Jaisalmer the "Golden City".

After its foundation as a Rajput stronghold by Rawal Jaisal of the Bhatti clan in 1156, a turbulent and heroic history unfolded. Initially there were constant wars with the neighbouring Rajput states of Jodhpur and Bikaner; later, in 1294, Muslim invaders attacked and conquered Jaisalmer, inducing large-scale *johar* (voluntary death by sword and fire) by the warriors and their womenfolk. In the fourteenth century the Bhatti Rajputs retook the city, but provoked a second sacking when they challenged the Muslims at Ajmer. Relations with the Muslims improved, and in 1570 the ruler of Jaisalmer married one of his daughters to Akbar. From the seventeenth century the city prospered as a market centre for traders on the overland routes between India and Central Asia; the magnificent *havelis* of the merchants bear witness to those times. However, with the emergence of Bombay as a major port, overland trade diminished, and so did Jaisalmer's wealth. After Independence, the city was left almost stranded, but its location so close to the newly sensitive border gave it significance during the Indo-Pakistan wars of 1965 and 1971, and it is now a major military outpost.

The telephone **area code** for Jaisalmer is ☎02992.

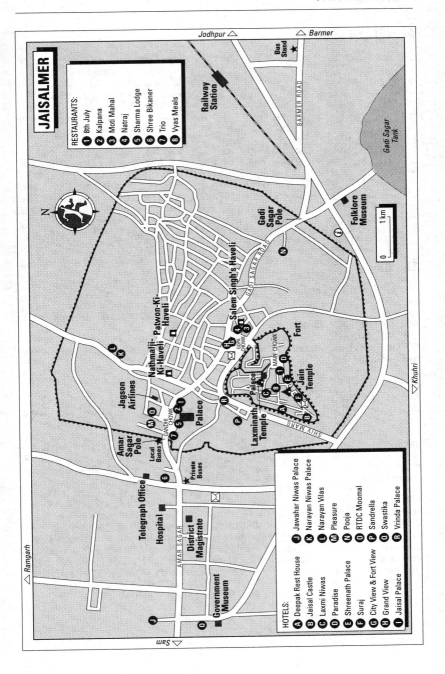

Arrival and information

Jaisalmer's **railway station** is 2km east of the city. Over-eager touts, hoping to entice you onto a shoddy and overpriced camel safari, accost arriving passengers with offers of free taxi services and low rents at their hotels. If you don't feel like facing all this, walk or pay Rs3 to get into town by jeep and choose a hotel yourself. Arriving at the **RSRTC bus stand** nearby, you will not be met with quite such a gauntlet of touts, rickshaw-*wallahs* and commission agents; the **private bus stand** by Amar Sagar Pole in the west of town is easy walking distance from most accommodation. There are **bike rental** shops in the main street, and opposite *Fort View Hotel*.

There's a **tourist office** (Mon–Sat 8am–6pm; ☎52406), southeast of town not far from Gadi Sagar Pole, but *Thar Safari* (☎52722) in Gandhi Chowk is equally good at providing information, with bus timetables, details of hotels and camel safaris, and tips on local sights and history. The **GPO**, with poste restante, is west of town, 100m south of the private bus stand; a more convenient office stands shaded by a huge banyan tree in Gopa Chowk in the centre. **Banks** are concentrated on Gandhi Chowk; *Bank of Baroda* (Mon–Fri 11am–3pm, Sat 11am–1pm) changes money and torn notes.

Jaisalmer's flourishing tourist trade has helped keep alive many **local crafts**; good buys include woven jackets, dyed cloth, wooden boxes and ornaments, and Western-style clothes.

The City

Getting lost in the narrow winding streets of Jaisalmer is both easy and enjoyable, though the city is so small that it never takes long to find a familiar landmark. Main roads lead around the base of the fort from the central market square, **Gopa Chowk**, east to **Gadi Sagar Tank**, and west to **Gandhi Chowk**.

Within the fort the streets are yet narrower, but orientation is simple: head west from the main *chowk* and **Maharawal's Palace** to reach the **Jain temples** and hotels nestled within the walls.

Jaisalmer fort

Every part of Jaisalmer **fort**, from its outer walls to the palace, temples and houses within, is made of soft yellow sandstone. The narrow winding streets are flanked with carved sandy facades, and from the bastions, some of which still bear cannons, you can see the thick walls that drop almost 100m to the town below. Today the fort stands strong, housing nearly a quarter of the town's population, and strict rules limit additional building.

A paved road punctuated by four huge gateways winds up to the fort, built when the city was founded in 1156. By the second gate stands a "death well", down which traitors and criminals were thrown to their doom back in days of yore. The fourth gateway leads into Main Chowk, which these days becomes a crowded mass of colour and life during festive celebrations, but was once the scene of the gathering of troops, marriage parties and the terrible act of *johar* when women chose death rather than dishonour for themselves and their children after their husbands left for the battlefield. The *chowk* is dominated by the old **palace of the Maharawal** (daily 10am–3pm), whose five-storey facade of balconies and windows displays some of the finest masonry work in Jaisalmer, while the interior is painted and tiled in typical Rajput style. The monarch would address his troops and issue orders from the large ornate marble throne to the left of the palace entrance.

Although the fort holds temples dedicated to Surya, Lakshmi, Ganesh, Vishnu and Shiva, none is as impressive as the **Jain temples** (daily 7am–noon; free, camera Rs25, video Rs50; usual restrictions on leather and menstruation apply), built between the twelfth and fifteenth centuries in the familiar Jurassic sandstone, with their yellow and white marble shrines. Walls, ceilings and pillars bear exquisite sculpted motifs, and small corridors and stairways connect one temple to another. In a vault beneath the

CAMEL SAFARIS

Few visitors who make it as far as Jaisalmer pass up the opportunity to go on a **camel trek**, which provides the wonderfully romantic chance to cross the barren sands on a sturdy ship of the desert, sleep under the stars, and sing traditional desert songs. Sandstorms and sore backsides aside, the safaris are usually great fun.

Treks last for one, two, three or four days, at **prices** varying from Rs80 to Rs900 per night. In general the less you spend the less you get, in terms of food, blankets, fitness of camel, and so forth. A lot depends on whether the guides are friendly, how big the group is, and what expectations you have. Freelance camel owners, working for extremely low prices, may stop you in the street and offer their services, and most hotels offer their own versions, though increased demand has resulted in high prices and very poor service from some. All in all, you'll do better to go through an agency. A couple of reputable operators are mentioned below, and you should check with your fellow travellers: ask around to see who has just had a successful trek of the standard you're after. Things to make sure of are an adequate supply of blankets, to sleep on and under (it can get very cold at night), a quota of fruit if you're paying anything over the average, and whether there will be a camp fire. If you're only going for a day, none of this applies, but be sure to wear a hat and take high-factor sun-protection lotion.

Following government restrictions on **routes**, most safaris head west of Jaisalmer through places such as Sam sand dunes, Lodurva, Amar Sagar, Bada Bagh and assorted small villages. Some visitors feel this puts too much emphasis on sightseeing; it's possible to arrange a few days' amble through the desert without stopping at any monuments if you'd prefer to leave them out. Taking a **jeep** at the start or end of the trek enables you to go further in a short time, and some travellers prefer to begin their trek at Khuhri (see p.183). Longer safaris to Pokaran, Jodhpur or Bikaner can also be arranged. Firms running treks into into restricted areas (see "Around Jaisalmer" p.182) should fix the necessary permits for you, but check this in advance.

Thar Safari (☎52722; fax 53214) in Gandhi Chowk is the oldest established and most reputable **agency**, offering a range of safaris, many with tents provided, and reliable guides. They will also organize treks to Jaisalmer from Pokaran if given at least ten days' notice, and are among the few agents who genuinely take care to protect the desert environment. Less expensive operators include *Sahara Travels* in Gopa Chowk near the first fort gate (☎52609). Of the **hotels**, *Paradise* has a good reputation, and for alternative routes, try *Deepak* and *Grand View*.

Sambhavnath temple, the **Gyan Bhandar** (daily 10–11am) contains Jain manuscripts, paintings and astrological charts dating back to the eleventh century.

The havelis

The streets of Jaisalmer are flanked with numerous honey-pale facades, covered with lattice work and floral designs, but the city's real showpieces are its **havelis**. Each of these extravagant mansions, comprising three or more storeys around a central courtyard, was commissioned by a wealthy merchant during the eighteenth or nineteenth centuries. Their stonework was the art of *silavats*, a community of masons responsible for much of Jaisalmer's unique sculpture.

The large **Patwon-ki-Haveli** (daily 10am–5pm; free), not far from *Narayan Niwas* in the north of town, was constructed over fifty years by the Patwa merchants, traders in brocades. Five separate suites with individual entrances facing a narrow street are connected from within, and all have flat roof areas – the views are excellent. Traces of stylish wall paintings survive in some rooms.

Salim Singh's small *haveli* provides Jaisalmer's only favourable memory of the tyrannical Salim Singh Mohta, prime minister in 1800, who impoverished the citizens through vigorous taxation and extortion rackets. His curious family home is topped with small bluish domes; its upper floor, enclosed by a protruding balcony, is best seen from the roof of *Natraj Restaurant*. The house is still lived in, but you can go inside. On the road to Malka Pole, you pass the decorative facade of the late nineteenth-century **Nathmalji-ki-Haveli**, also built for a prime minister of Jaisalmer. No visitors are allowed, so you won't be able to view the skilful paintings on the interior walls.

Gadi Sagar Tank and the Folklore Museum

South of the city through an imposing triple gateway, **Gadi Sagar Tank**, built in 1367, was once Jaisalmer's sole water supply. Its north and east banks are flanked with *ghats* and temples whose sandstone bricks glow with a warm deep ochre in the evening light. This peaceful place is the focus of the festival of Gangaur in March, when women fling flowers into the lake and pray for a good husband, and the Maharawal heads a procession amid a pomp and splendour unchanged for generations.

The delightful little **Folklore Museum** near the tank's main gate (daily 8am–7pm; Rs5) has some interesting displays of folk art, much of it religious. The locally styled wooden statues of Krishna and Radha, musical instruments, paintings and travelling temple (*kavad*) are all from the personal collection of its proprietor, who will probably be on hand, and happy to talk about them. The cursory collection of fossils and cultural artefacts in the small **Government Museum** west of town by the RTDC *Moomal Hotel* (daily except Fri 10am–4.30pm; free) however, hardly merits the effort.

The desert festival

In January or February, depending on the lunar calendar, RTDC organizes a huge **desert festival**, more for the sake of tourists than out of tradition, which features camel racing, dances, music, puppet shows and moustache competitions. Prices for rooms and food soar – rates at the *Moomal*, for example, are four times higher than usual – and extra accommodation is provided in a special "tourist village" (⑧). Further details are available from Rajasthan Tourism, Government Hostel Building, Jaipur (☎0141/376362), the Deputy General Manager, Rajasthan Tourism, Bikaner House, Pandara Rd, New Delhi (☎011/383837), or the tourist office in Jaisalmer.

Accommodation

Jaisalmer has plenty of places to stay, most of them in the **budget** category. Almost all offer **camel treks**, which vary in standard and price, and some managers can be uncomfortably pushy if you don't want to arrange a safari through them, suddenly hiking room rates or turfing you out. The most notorious hotels for this are those currently calling themselves the *Ringo* (opposite the *Pleasure*) and the *Peacock* (opposite the *Swastika*), whose reputations got so bad that they had to change their names, and will probably do so again. The *New Tourist Hotel* and the *Henna* are others, and in general you should avoid anyone touting for business at the station or bus stand. Many visitors prefer the peaceful, atmospheric hotels among the jumble of sandstone houses and *havelis* within the **fort**, whose roofs offer splendid desert vistas. However, there are moves afoot to ban these places, so their days may be numbered. Below the fort in the **town**, hotels generally have less character, but many are small and intimate with lovely roof terraces. Except where stated, most places operate a 9am **checkout**.

In the fort

Deepak Rest House, in the west of the fort (☎52665; fax 52070). Small and friendly, with basic rooms (one with balcony), dorm, and roof terrace. "Off the beaten track" camel treks. ①–④.

Jaisal Castle, in the southern corner of the fort (☎52362; fax 52101). Old *haveli* with great views, but overpriced and not that clean. Noon checkout; full board available. ⑤–⑧.

Laxmi Niwas, north of the Jain temples (☎52758). Small, basic and clean, with beds and mattresses on the floor, shared bathrooms and tiny roof terrace. The annexe has more facilities, but dull rooms.①–⑤.

Paradise, off the Main Chowk (☎52674). Well-run, comfortable hotel with grassy courtyard and some excellent rooms with balcony and private bath. The best has a double view. Large roof terrace for budget travellers. 10.30am checkout. ①–⑥.

Shreenath Palace, near the Jain temples (☎52907). Small stylish family home in an old *haveli* with large rooms and a small roof terrace with nice view. Very basic shared toilet facilities. ④.

Suraj, near *Shreenath* (☎53023). Superbly carved sandstone *haveli* with real style. Five spacious, comfortable rooms all with hot shower and some with original wall-paintings, in family atmosphere. Excellent rooftop view. ④.

In the town

City View, off Gopa Chowk (☎52804). Next door to the *Fort View*, with small but clean rooms; the larger ones take 3 or 4 people. ①.

Fort View, off Gopa Chowk (☎52214). Large and reasonably clean, with a view of the fort, oddly enough, from the roof terrace. Some triple rooms; discounts to readers carrying this book. ①.

Grand View, off Central Mkt (☎52533). One of the most basic, but with great hot showers. ①.

Jaisal Palace, behind Royal Palace (☎52717). Clean modern hotel, a bit sterile. Large roof area. ④.

Jawahar Niwas Palace, Amar Sagar Rd (☎52208; fax 52259). Old palace less than 1km west of town with grand but musty rooms; they charge you Rs100 extra for "welcome drinks and garland". Veg and non-veg restaurant; full board available. ⑧.

Narayan Niwas Palace, Malkaprol Rd (☎52408; fax 52101). On the northern edge of town with a large grass courtyard and pleasant bar. Overpriced a/c rooms are clean but unimaginative and often without outside windows; again, it's Rs100 extra for your "welcome drinks and garland". ⑧.

Narayan Vilas, Malkaprol Rd (☎52283). Old, characterful *havel* next to the *Narayan Niwas*. Comfortable and clean. ⑤.

Pleasure, off Gandhi Chowk (☎52323). OK rooms in house with tiny courtyard and roof terrace. ①.

Pooja, off Gadi Sagar Rd (☎ 52068 – a neighbour's number). Beautiful old *haveli* in typically carved sandstone, with a small roof terrace. A few more pricey and atmospheric rooms. ①.

RTDC Moomal, Amar Sagar Rd (☎52392). Clean, spacious rooms in well-run hotel. Round huts in the grounds, each with double room and bathroom, are less pricey and great value, and there's a dorm. Good restaurant, free outdoor dance show on Sun evenings. Noon checkout. ①–⑤.

Sandrella, off Shiv Marg (no phone). Homely budget place in the shadow of the fort. Rooms are basic but clean with attached bathroom. ①.

Swastika, Chainpura (☎52152). An old favourite still going strong; cheap, clean and cosy with free morning tea and hot showers. Great view from roof; dorm available. Discount of 40 percent March–June, 20 percent July–Sept. ①–②.

Vrinda Palace, Shiv Marg (☎53025). One of the cleaner and more modern cheapies. Rooms with bath (not all with outside window), and rooftop restaurant. Pay more for a Western-style loo. ②–⑤.

Eating

Being so popular with foreign tourists, Jaisalmer offers peanut butter, vegemite, pizza, pancakes and apple pie and cakes on its menus alongside typical Indian dishes. The choice of **places to eat** is thin, however, and it only takes a day or two to find one you'll want to stick with. Many are rooftop restaurants with a view, often attached to hotels, but officially these have been banned, and it remains to be seen how far that ban will be enforced.

8th July, in the fort. Veg restaurant overlooking Main Chowk, where the extensive and imaginative menu includes thalis, pizza, vegeburgers, thick, milky smoothies and massive fruit salads – but no curries. Open 9.30am–3pm & 6–10pm.

Cinera, off Gopa Chowk on the roof of the *Grand View Hotel*. Veg food, plus eggs – nothing special, with the usual curries, *thalis* and Chinese, but the view of the fort really is grand.

Kalpana, Gandhi Chowk. Tasty, good-value veg and non-veg Punjabi and north Indian dishes with open-air seating. Some Chinese options. Open 7am–10.30pm.

Moti Mahal, opposite Salim Singh's *haveli*. Small ground-floor veg restaurant for the best-value tourist breakfasts in town. Some tables face the street from the front verandah. Open 8am–10pm.

Natraj, facing the top floor of Salim Singh's *haveli*. Pleasant rooftop and indoor non-veg restaurant; the only a/c place in town. The food is of a high standard and moderately priced. Open 8am–11pm.

Sharma Lodge, Gandhi Chowk. Very cheap hole in the wall by *Thar Safari* for excellent *chai* and basic *thalis*. Open 7am–10.30pm.

Shree Bikaner, just north of the private bus stand. Popular place for veg specialities from all over India. Open 8.30am–10.30pm.

Trio, Gandhi Chowk. Sumptuous Mughlai food, tasteful decor, snappy service and live folk music make this a wonderful place to dine; excellent value for its price range. The safari soup is, as the menu claims, memorable. Open 7.30am–10pm, meals noon–3pm & 6.30–10pm.

Vyas Meals, in the fort by the handicraft shops on the way to the Jain temples. Small, unpretentious place doing home-style veg *thalis* and snacks. Open 10am–10pm.

MOVING ON FROM JAISALMER

Jaisalmer's only **rail** connection is to Jodhpur, more than 250km east. All other long-distance trips involve tedious **bus** journeys. The *RSRTC* bus stand, round the corner from the station, has departures for Jaipur, Jodhpur, Bikaner, Barmer, Mount Abu and Ahmedabad. "Deluxe" private buses are the best options, and leave from the crossroads just outside Amar Sagar Gate, where you'll find the booking offices. There are buses from here to Jodhpur (18 daily; 6hr), Bikaner (4 daily; 7hr 30min) and one or two daily to Jaipur (14hr), Delhi (20hr), Bombay (30hr), Ajmer (12hr 30min), Pushkar (13hr) and Udaipur (14hr). Frequent but much slower **local buses**, which can't be booked, use the stand a little northeast of the crossroads. They include three daily to Khuhri (1hr 30min).

The **airport** is 8km west of town on the Sam road. *Jagson Airlines*, based just off Ghandi Chowk opposite the *State Bank of India*, flies to Jodhpur and Delhi.

Around Jaisalmer

The sandy, barren terrain around Jaisalmer harbours some unexpected architectural sights, looming out of the sweeping sands. Infrequent buses negotiate the dusty roads, and you can rent a jeep, but the best way to visit these places, and see villages and abandoned towns inaccessible by road, is on a camel trek (see p.179). Being close to the Pakistani border, the area west of Highway NH15 is a **restricted area**. Tourists are allowed to visit Amar Sagar, Sam, Bada Bagh, Lodurva, Akal fossil park, Khuri, Rampunda and Kuldera without a permit, but if you want to go anywhere beyond those places, you should apply to the District Magistrate's Office just west of the private bus stand in Jaisalmer (Mon–Fri & sometimes Sat 10am–5pm). On the few camel treks where this is necessary, however, the organizers will usually get permits for you.

Amar Sagar

A short distance northwest of Jaisalmer, **AMAR SAGAR** is a small peaceful town set around a large lake (empty during the dry season). A former palace and large complex of Jain temples, currently being restored to their former magnificence, stand on the lake edges. Both are built of sandstone.

Sam

The huge, rolling sand dunes 40km west of Jaisalmer are known as **SAM**, though strictly this is the name of a small village further west. The dunes are so famous in Rajasthan that most tourists don't realize that there are others throughout the desert; consequently they have become a prime attraction. There's even a *Tourist Bungalow* (no phone; ③), bookable through the RTDC *Moomal Hotel* in Jaisalmer, but given the inexorable advance rate of the dunes, it will more than likely be buried by sand within the next decade. Sunset at Sam can be breathtaking, though drink sellers, musicians and numerous camel trains somewhat dilute the romance. The undulating sandscape also looks spectacular at sunrise, so it's worth sleeping the night here if you're on a camel safari. A **bus** does run to Sam, but it doesn't return until the next day. Those visitors who aren't travelling on camels usually make the journey by jeep.

Bada Bagh and royal cenotaphs

Six kilometres north of Jaisalmer, in the fertile area of **Bada Bagh**, a collection of cenotaphs built in memory of Jaisalmer's rulers stand clustered on a hill. Domed roofs shade small marble or sandstone slabs bearing inscriptions and equestrian statues. The green gardens below are where most of the fruit and vegetables of the region are grown – a surreal sight amid the hostile waste of sand and scrub.

Lodurva

Another 10km north of Bada Bagh, **LODURVA** was the capital of the Bhatti rulers until the foundation of Jaisalmer in the twelfth century. Of the city's fine buildings, only a few **Jain temples**, rebuilt in the 1970s, remain (8am–6pm; camera Rs25, video Rs50). The *toran* (archway) at the entrance to the temple compound is the most exquisite in the Jaisalmer district. The main structure has detailed tracery work in the stone walls and a finely carved exterior. A smaller temple, built on a series of diminishing square platforms, stands to its right.

THE LOVERS OF LODURVA

Lodurva is the scene of Rajasthan's answer to *Romeo and Juliet*, the story of **Moomal** and **Mahendra**. Moomal was a princess whose legendary beauty brought her many suitors, none of whom succeeded in gaining her affections, until the handsome prince Mahendra, with the aid of Moomal's maid, gained access to her bedroom and won her heart. Every night he visited her, and in the morning he left. One day Moomal's sister, who was dying to meet him, persuaded Moomal to let her attend her bedchamber disguised as a minstrel. That night however, Mahendra's wives, suspicious of his absence, kept him from leaving, and he didn't arrive at Moomal's until dawn. On finding her asleep in bed with a minstrel boy, he stormed out in disgust, and in the months that followed, though ill from grief, refused to so much as open her letters. Finally, Moomal disguised herself as a man and set out to find him. She eventually tracked him down and, joining him in a game of *chokar* (a board game), noticed that he was crying and asked him why. "It's the birthmark on your hand", he explained, "it reminds me of my lost true love." Revealing her identity, Moomal explained to Mahendra what had happened, and they fell into each others' arms. But alas, it was too much for them, and they both died there and then from the emotion of it all. Scant remains of Moomal's palace can still be seen by the bank of the River Kak, which they say has never flowed since that day.

Akal Fossil park

The scattered remains of Jurassic tree fossils up to 180 million years old in the **fossil park**, 17km south of Jaisalmer (daily Nov–Feb 8am–5pm, March–Oct 8am–6pm) are of interest only to the most avid paleobotanists. Eighteen trees, none of them standing, and most of them pretty shattered, lie around the site. Buses to Barmer pass through, but for a quicker visit it's best to take a jeep, which costs about Rs200 round trip.

Khuhri

Though most camel treks start in Jaisalmer, a handful of travellers prefer to begin their safari out in the desert at the rustic, laid-back village of **KHUHRI**, just 1km from the dunes. It can be reached on three daily buses (1hr 30min) from the local bus stand in Jaisalmer. Safaris are organized by the two basic **guest houses** (though you may need permits from Jaisalmer; see p.182). *Mama's Guest House* (no phone; ② full board) is the older of the two, offering tasty home cooking, and is now marginally undercut by a newcomer, the *Khuhri Guest House* (no phone; ①).

Barmer

BARMER, 158km south of Jaisalmer, is another important desert outpost, but has little to offer tourists. It's usually a dusty backwater, where the manufacture of handicrafts, forming its main export, occupies much of the population. In January however, the place is transformed during the hectic **Tilwara Cattle Fair**, held on the banks of a saltwater river nearby. This is the largest cattle market in Rajasthan, attended by villagers and traders from all over the state.

Accommodation and **food** stalls in Barmer are scarce; if you need to **stay the night**, try the basic *Krishna Hotel* (☎02982/20785; ③) near the railway station, or the rather better *Hotel Kelas Sarowar* (☎02982/20730; ③).

Buses run to Barmer from Jaisalmer (12 daily; 3hr), and there are two expresses (5hr) and a passenger train (7hr) from Jodhpur.

Pokaran

POKARAN, with its red sandstone fort and superb *havelis*, is a quiet, seldom-visited desert town 110km east of Jaisalmer, situated at the road and rail junctions between Jodhpur, Bikaner and the west. Once included in the territory of Jodhpur, it passed into the huge state of Jaisalmer after Independence. The fort has a maze of passages behind its ornate facades, and you can stay within its walls in the charming *Hotel Pokaran Fort*. For a less expensive room try the *Monika* (☎0294/22269; ③). Not far from Pokaran, in **Ramdevra**, a tiny town consisting mostly of *dharamshalas*, an old temple dedicated to Ram is the scene of celebrations on Ram's birthday (end March or the beginning of April) and during a fifteen-day festival in October.

Bikaner

The commercial city of **BIKANER** may not quite possess the aesthetic attraction of its more venerable neighbour, Jaisalmer, over 200km southwest, but it does boast a spectacular fort and an old city dotted with *havelis* and surrounded by 7km of high walls. In addition, simply because Rajasthan's fourth largest city receives fewer visitors than other major settlements, it has a certain "unspoilt" feel.

The city was founded in 1486 as a link in the overland trading route, by **Bika**, one of fourteen sons of Rao Jodha, the Rathore king who established Jodhpur as the centre of the state of Marwar. Under Rai Singh, who came to the throne in 1573, **Junagarh Fort** was built and closer ties were forged with the Moghuls; Rai Singh gave his daughter in marriage to one of Akbar's sons. Later, during the reign of Ganga Singh in the early 1900s, new agricultural schemes, irrigation work, town planning and the construction of a rail link with Delhi helped Bikaner's economic advance; it has long since outgrown the confines of the city wall, and has tripled in size since 1947.

Arrival and information

Rickshaws ply the route between the **bus stand**, opposite Lalgarh Palace a few kilometres north of the centre, and the south of town, where you'll find the railway station and most hotels. The **tourist office** (daily 10am–5pm; ☎27445) is in the RTDC *Dhola Maru Hotel* at Pooran Singh Circle. For trips around town, use any of the cycle or auto-

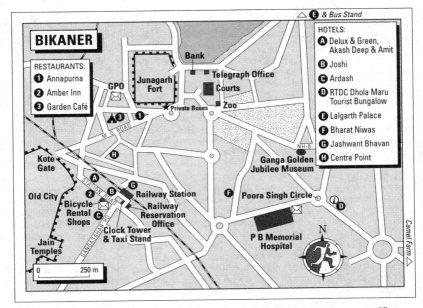

rickshaws, or rent a bike; you'll find two **bike rental shops** outside the **post office** on Station Rd. **Travellers' cheques** can be changed at the *State Bank of Bikaner and Jaipur* (Mon–Fri 10am–2.30pm) opposite the entrance to the fort.

    Camel treks are not as established in Bikaner as they are in Jaisalmer (see p.179), but the idea is catching on. Local firms include (in roughly ascending order of price and comfort) *Victor Travels and Tours* in GS Rd, Transport Line, not far from the railway station (☎524117), *Camelman* opposite Sophia School on the Jaipur road about 1km east of the Ganga Golden Jubilee Museum (☎26494), and *Rajasthan Safaris and Treks* in Purani Ginani (☎28557). Treks go from about Rs250 to about Rs1000, or you can take a leisurely tour of the city itself on a camel for around Rs150.

The City

It's worth spending a day or two just wandering around Bikaner, watching dyers at work, visiting the ancient **Jain temples**, and **Junagarh Fort**. Bikaner is also famous for its skilled lacquer work and handicrafts, and the **markets** are brimming with bargains.

Junagarh Fort

Built on ground level, defended only by high walls and a wide moat, **Junagarh Fort** (daily except Fri 10am–4.30pm; R30, camera Rs20, video Rs50) is not as immediately imposing as the mighty hill forts elsewhere in Rajasthan. But the decorative interiors and sculpted stone of the palaces, temples and 37 pavilions within its walls are almost unrivalled in their magnificence.

    The fort was built between 1587 and 1593, during the rule of Rai Singh, and later rulers added their own palatial suites, temples and plush courtyards. The **Karan Mahal**, with gold-leaf paintings adorning its pillars and walls, was built in the seventeenth century to commemorate a victory over the Moghul emperor Aurangzeb, while the **Chandra Mahal** and the dazzling **Phool Mahal** were erected by Gaj Singh, a hundred years later. Stained-glass windows, finely carved stone and wood balconies, and brightly painted walls and ceilings around the fort demonstrate the extravagant tastes of these rulers. The **Anup Mahal** is the most opulent construction, with wooden ceilings inlaid with mirrors, Italian tiles and delicate lattice work on the windows and balconies. The huge carpet is one of many made by inmates of Bikaner jail, a manufacturing tradition that has only recently ceased.

Although it was never conquered, the fort was attacked – handprints set in stone near the second gate, **Daulat Pole**, bear witness to the voluntary deaths of royal women, remembered as *satis*, whose menfolk had lost their lives in battle.

Visitors are escorted through the fort by English- and Hindi-speaking guides, with the tour finishing in the huge **Ganga Singh Hall**. The most recent part of the fort, dating from 1937, it houses part of the **museum**, whose exhibits include the inevitable weaponry and an unexpected World War II aeroplane, still in tip-top condition.

The old city

Kote Gate at the west end of MG Rd is the main entrance through the high city walls into the atmospheric **old city**, where the clashing and banging of metalworkers resonate through winding streets tinted with the hues of local dyers. The main attractions here are the two **Jain temples** in the southeast corner (daily 7am–1pm & 5–8pm). Built by two merchant brothers, both are remarkable for the sheer mass of colour and intricate wall paintings, a rare feature in Rajasthan's Jain temples. The ground floor of **Bhandreshwar temple** (1571) has a cluster of pillars; some are decorated with gilded floral designs known as *usta* typical of Muslim artisans, others with embossed male and female sculptures common in medieval India. A statue of Lord Suminath, the fifth *tirthankara*, stands on the second floor. **Sandeshwar temple**, dedicated to Neminath (the 22nd *tirthankara*) and dated to 1536, houses rows of saints shaped from solid marble, and has enamel and gold-leaf paintings on the walls.

The sixteenth-century **Laxminath temple** nearby was built by Lunkaran Singh, the third ruler of Bikaner, on the edge of the high city wall. It overlooks a Muslim community of dyers and screen printers, with the barren desert in the distance.

Lalgarh Palace

The sturdy red-sandstone **Lalgarh Palace** in the north of the town is home to the royal family of Bikaner, although parts now serve as a hotel. It was built during the reign of Ganga Singh, who lived there from 1902, using the fort only for private business, and despite some detailed carving, its modern aspect makes it fairly dull in comparison to other Rajasthani palaces. The enormous collection of photographs of the golden days of the Raj in its **Shri Sadul Museum** (daily except Weds 10am–5pm) is dull in the extreme, and the stuffed animals offer little relief. If time is short, head instead for the **Anup Sanskrit Library** (same hours) which has a small selection of unique and well-preserved manuscripts, parchments and engraved copper, plus gold and silver plaques.

Ganga Golden Jubilee Museum

The small **Ganga Golden Jubilee Museum** (daily except Fri 10am–4.30pm; Rs2) on NH8 not far from the *Dhola Maru Hotel* contains a moderately interesting display of costumes, weapons, ornaments, ancient statues and paintings, one of which depicts the signing of the Versailles Treaty by Ganga Singh. Older exhibits include terracottas from the Gupta period (fourth and fifth centuries).

Accommodation

Bikaner has a narrow range of **hotels**. A group of cheap and dingy places stands opposite the station, but in this area the **railway retiring rooms** (①) are a better bet. More acceptable hotels line Station Rd, but for upmarket accommodation you'll have to go further afield. The extremely posh *Lalgarh Palace* is the only option near the bus stand.

Akash Deep, Station Rd (☎26024). Cleaner and quieter than its neighbours. ①.

Amit, Station Rd (☎28064). Small but clean, set back a little from the noisy road. ②.

Bharat Niwas, Sadul Colony (☎23025; fax 523674). New hotel near PB Memorial Hospital. Bright and spotless with all the necessary comforts; the only minus is that the windows face inward. ④.

Jashwant Bhavan, Alakhsagar Rd, behind the station (☎521834). Peaceful family-run place, lined with old photos of the owner's father, who was a founding member of the Lok Sabha. ⑥.

Joshi, Station Rd (☎527700; fax 521213). Smartest in the area. Clean carpeted rooms, some a/c. ④.

Lalgarh Palace (☎523963; fax 522253). Expansive, richly furnished rooms. Swimming pool, tennis courts and restaurant for guests only. ⑧.

RTDC Dhola Maru Tourist Bungalow, Pooran Singh Circle (☎28621). Well-kept rooms ranging from ordinary to super deluxe with balconies, and a cheap dorm. ①–③.

Eating

Bikaner has only a few **restaurants** outside the hotels, serving mostly veg dishes. For quick, low-priced food try any of the open-air shacks on Station Rd, which always have several cauldrons of constantly warmed curries to choose from.

Annapurna, MG Rd. Inexpensive and unpretentious veg place serving south Indian and continental dishes. No smoking. Open 10am–9pm.

Chhotu Motu Joshi, Station Rd, next to the *Joshi Hotel*. Not a restaurant, but a popular place for *lassi*, sweets and snacks. Open 8am–10pm.

Delux and **Evergreen**, Station Rd. Two hotels next door to each other, both serving veg snacks, breakfast, and light south Indian meals. Open 8am–10pm.

Dhola Maru, Pooran Singh Circle. The only place apart from roadside stalls that sells good, inexpensive meat. Beakfast 8–10am, lunch noon–2.30pm, tea 4–6pm, supper 7–10pm.

Garden Cafe, off MG Rd by Ratan Bihariji Temple. Pleasant open-air park cafe serving ice-cream, milk shakes and south Indian snacks. Open 10am–10pm.

Joshi, Station Rd. Upstairs hotel restaurant serving good-value *thalis* (12.30–3pm & 7.30–10pm) and all-day breakfasts (6am–10pm).

MOVING ON FROM BIKANER

RSTRC buses run to to Jodhpur via Nagaur (2hr 30min), Jaisalmer, Jaipur via Sikar, Fatehpur, Jhunjhunu, Ajmer, Kota, Barmer, Delhi, Udaipur, and Ahmedabad via Abu Road (10hr). **Private buses** leave from MG Rd, just below the fort. **Trains** include three to Delhi Sarai Rohilla (two by night, one by day) via Churu (4hr). Services to Jaipur include the fast early-morning *Intercity Express* #2467 (6hr) and the slow overnight *Bikaner Jaipur Express* #4738 (10hr 30min). The latter also serves Churu, Fatehpur and Sikar. The best train to Jodhpur is the *Kalka Express* #4587, leaving late morning.

Around Bikaner

Several places of interest close to Bikaner can be visited in a day. The most unusual are the **camel breeding farm** and **Karni Mata temple**, a scurrying mass of sacred rats. Memorials of the rulers of Bikaner stand at **Devi Kund Sagar**; further out of town in **Gajner** their former royal hunting ground is now a wildlife reserve.

Devi Kund Sagar

The majestic cenotaphs or *chhatris* of sandstone and marble that commemorate the rulers of Bikaner stand around an artificial lake at **Devi Kund Sagar**, about 8km west of the city. The most recent cenotaph in the enclosure, which dates back to the eighteenth century, is that of Sadul Singh, the last Maharaja, who died in 1950.

Camel breeding farm

What is probably Asia's largest **camel breeding farm** (daily 3–5pm) lies out in the desert 10km south of Bikaner, an easy round trip by rickshaw that should cost around Rs50. Although Bikaner has long been renowned for its famously sturdy beasts, and the camel corps was a much-feared component of the imperial battle formation, the farm itself was only founded in 1975. Its propagation programme has been so successful that it now provides 50 percent of India's camels, hundreds of whom, young and old, can be seen strutting their knock-kneed way across the sands.

Karni Mata temple

Devotees at the unique **Karni Mata temple** (daily 7am–9pm daily; free; camera Rs10, video Rs25) in **Deshnok** – 30km south of Bikaner and served by hourly buses – believe that departing souls are saved from the wrath of Yama, the god of death, by being reincarnated as **rats**. Teeming hordes of free-roaming holy rodents, known as *kabas*, are accordingly worshipped and fed by visitors; the experience of having one run over your feet is considered a great privilege. It is also deemed auspicious to eat *prasad* (blessed food from the main shrine) after it has been nibbled by the *kabas*.

The large black-and-white-marble temple is named after the patron goddess of the Bikaner dynasty Karni Mata, an incarnation of the fearsome Durga, and features a stunning set of solid silver doors donated by Maharaja Ganga Singh. On the last night of the festival of Navratri (March), crowds from nearby villages and towns flock here to pay homage to the goddess.

Gajner sanctuary and Kolayat

Once the imperial hunting ground of Ganga Singh, the lake and wooded area in **Gajner**, 32km west of Bikaner, is now a protected sanctuary that shelters *nilgai*, black buck, *chinkara* and gazelles all year round. In winter it's a popular spot for migratory birds, particularly the Siberian grouse. Buses leave Bikaner every half hour for Gajner, where double **rooms** are available in the *Gajner Palace Hotel* on the shore of the lake (☎01521/23263; fax 25963; ⑦).

Nearby, at the temple-studded pilgrimage centre of **Kolayat**, devotees and wandering *sadhus* worship and bathe in an artificial lake that never dries up.

Nagaur

The grand mosques and painted palaces of the heavily fortified little town of **NAGAUR**, 100km south of Bikaner, are testimony to years of both Hindu and Muslim sovereignty. Nagaur is famous for its stout breed of bullock, and holds a week-long **cattle fair** (late Jan–early Feb) that attracts camel, horse and bullock traders from all over Rajasthan, with festivities, races and dances in the lead up to the sales. Connections with Bikaner are straightforward by both road and rail, and if you want to stay more than a day, there's an RTDC **hotel**, *Khurja* (☎01582/2681; ④), southwest of the centre.

Udaipur

> *The valley of Oodipur, the most diversified and most romantic spot on the continent of India . . .*
>
> James Tod, *Annals and Antiquities of Rajasthan* (1829)

Set around the vast Pichola Lake and dominated by dramatic palaces, **UDAIPUR** is Rajasthan's most atmospheric and picturesque city. High whitewashed houses and narrow winding alleys lend it an almost medieval charm, even if the newer quarters with their wide roads and squat buildings are less aesthetically pleasing. Prevailing over all else is the peaceful influence of the shimmering lake, and the joy of relaxing on a roof terrace in the cool of the evening tempts many travellers to forget their tight schedules. In any case, it takes a good week to explore the city's monuments, and the temples, forts, palaces and scenery of the hills and valleys nearby.

The smooth rolling hills that surround Udaipur like sleeping armadillos were once covered with forests. Widespread felling, instigated by the Indian government in the 1970s after it took possession of the Mewar lands, left them irreversibly barren and have added to the dry and dusty desert conditions of the Udaipur valley.

A brief history

Udaipur takes pride in having been the capital of the state of **Mewar**, the only one of the seven major Rajput states to uphold its Hindu allegiance in the face of Muslim invasions and political compromises. Its present ruler is the seventy-sixth in the unbroken line of Mewar suzerains, which makes the Mewar household the longest lasting of all ruling powers in Rajasthan, and perhaps the oldest surviving dynasty in the world.

The history of Udaipur itself stretches back far beyond its foundation in the sixteenth century, for the actions and policies of its Sisodia maharanas follow a code of honour laid down by the very first in line, **Guhil**, who established Mewar in 568 AD. Legend claims that Guhil was of local stock, but he seems at the time to have been fleeing south Gujarat during Muslim invasions. Either way, Guhil dwelt in the forest where he was trained in leadership and devotion by a hermit. His successors set up their capital at **Nagda**, which now stands in ruins just over 30km north of Udaipur. Chittaurgarh (also known as Chittor; see p.208) replaced Nagda as capital in the eighth century, and its hill-top fort protected the Sisodia Rajputs for almost 800 years.

By the time **Udai Singh II** inherited the throne of Mewar and the leadership of the Sisodia Rajputs in 1537, it was clear that the magnificent fortress of Chittor was doomed; his mother had sacrificed her life two years previously during its second major sacking. Udai scanned the surrounding countryside for a suitable site for a new capital, and settled for the area beside Lake Pichola, protected on all sides by outcrops of the Aravalli range. Having laid the foundation stones in 1559, he fled the battlefield when Chittor finally fell to the Moghuls eight years later to his new city of **Udaipur**. On his death in 1572 Udai was succeeded by his son **Pratap**, a legendary hero whose refusal to recognize the Moghul **Akbar** as emperor led to the battle of Haldighati, in which Akbar's forces were outwitted and peace in Udaipur was guaranteed.

As the city prospered, the arts flourished; Mewar's superior school of miniature painting became firmly rooted and the awesome palaces on the lake and its shore were constructed. However, in 1736 Mewar was attacked by the destructive Marathas whose pillage had by the turn of the century reduced the city to poverty and ruin. The British, whose role in the East India Company had until then been purely commercial, stepped

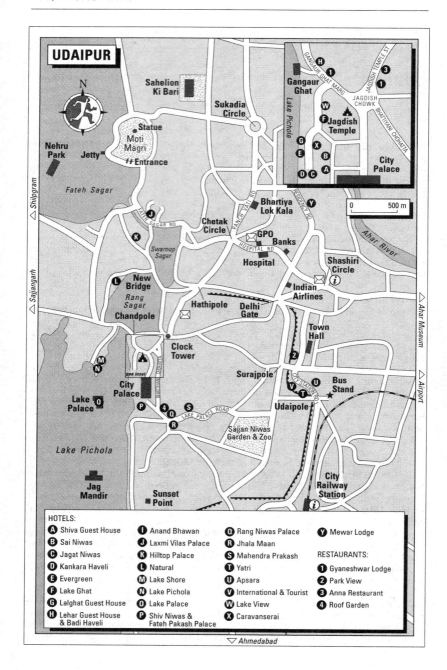

UDAIPUR

Sahelion
Ki Bari

Sukadia
Circle

Nehru
Park

Statue

Moti
Magri

Jetty

Entrance

Fateh Sagar

Shilpgram

Sajjangarh

Ahar River

Gangaur
Ghat

Lake Pichola

GANGAUR GHAT MARG

JAGDISH TEMPLE ST

H

W

F Jagdish
Temple

G

E X

D C

A

B

JAGDISH
CHOWK

BHATTIYAN CHOHATTA

City
Palace

0   500 m

Bhartiya
Lok Kala

Chetak
Circle

GPO

Banks

Hospital

Y

RESIDENCY RD

ANAT YATRI RD

HOSPITAL RD

Shashiri
Circle

Swaroop
Sagar

New
Bridge

Rang
Sagar

Chandpole

Hathipole

Delhi
Gate

Indian
Airlines

Town
Hall

2

Clock
Tower

see inset

City
Palace

Lake
Palace

Surajpole

CITY STATION RD

V T

U

Bus
Stand

Udaipole

P

4

S

R

LAKE PALACE ROAD

Sajjan Niwas
Garden & Zoo

City
Railway
Station

Lake Pichola

Jag
Mandir

Sunset
Point

Ahar Museum

Airport

HOTELS:

A Shiva Guest House
B Sai Niwas
C Jagat Niwas
D Kankara Haveli
E Evergreen
F Lake Ghat
G Lalghat Guest House
H Lehar Guest House
  & Badi Haveli

I Anand Bhawan
J Laxmi Vilas Palace
K Hilltop Palace
L Natural
M Lake Shore
N Lake Pichola
O Lake Palace
P Shiv Niwas &
  Fateh Pakash Palace

Q Rang Niwas Palace
R Jhala Maan
S Mahendra Prakash
T Yatri
U Apsara
V International & Tourist
W Lake View
X Caravanserai

Y Mewar Lodge

RESTAURANTS:

1 Gyaneshwar Lodge
2 Park View
3 Anna Restaurant
4 Roof Garden

Ahmedabad

in to pick up the pieces, presenting the Maharana with a treaty of "perpetual alliance and friendship" in 1818. Guaranteeing protection from invaders and restoration of all its hereditary territories, this treaty and the support of the British helped to put Udaipur on the road to recovery. Yet the principle of refusing to bow down to a foreign power persisted and the maharanas never allowed the British to displace them.

The promises of "perpetual" protection had of course to be dissolved when Britain withdrew from India in 1947. The Maharana of Udaipur spearheaded the movement by the princely states to join the new democratic and independent India, and was later at the forefront of a campaign to persuade Indira Gandhi's Congress government to retain the privy purses that funded the upkeep of Rajputana's historic monuments. Congress was however determined to reduce the Rajput princes to the status of normal citizens, and political recognition of royalty came to an end.

Centuries of loyalty between rulers and subjects have been kept alive by songs, stories and paintings; the Maharana may now lack political power, but he remains as respected by the people of Udaipur as were his forefathers. His personal funding and income from tourism are invested in the *Maharana of Mewar Trust*, which subsidizes local hospitals and educational institutions, and supports environmental projects.

Arrival, information and city transport

Daily flights connect **Dabok Airport** (☎23011), 25km east of Udaipur, with Bombay, Delhi, Aurangabad, Jaipur and Jodhpur. Taxis and infrequent buses run to the city itself. **Trains** from Delhi and Ahmedabad pull in at **Udaipur City Station** a little to the south of the town centre (don't get off at Udaipur Station, much further north). The **bus stand** is a few hundred metres north of here, directly opposite **Udaipole**, the westernmost gate of the old city. The best way to get to a hotel from either point is to take a rickshaw: if you want to avoid paying extra for the driver's commission, head for a particular area and check out the hotels yourself. The moderately helpful **tourist office** (Mon–Sat 10am–5pm; ☎411535) at Surajpole, has some useful literature, and there are branch offices at the airport (☎655433) and City railway station (Mon–Sat 7.30–11.30am & 4–7pm; ☎412974). Most hotels offer maps and tips on local sightseeing.

Money can be changed at *State Bank of Bikaner and Jaipur*, Chetak Circle, or *Canara Bank*, Hospital Rd (both Mon–Fri 10am–2pm). The *State Bank of India*, also in Hospital Rd, only deals with dollars or sterling cash, or *Amex* dollar cheques, but does change torn notes. For **poste restante**, go to the **GPO** on Chetak Circle (Mon–Sat 10am–3pm); the City Post Office is on Shastri Circle (Mon–Sat 10am–4pm).

> The telephone **area code** for Udaipur is ☎0294.

City transport

Rickshaws and **taxis** (available from any tour operator) are the usual means of transport. Rickshaw prices are relatively high and it's worth renting a **bicycle**: try *Shri Averi Cycle Works*, Lake Palace Rd, or a few stores near the clock tower.

RTDC, based at the tourist office, offers car rental and tours around the city (daily 8am–1pm, Rs30), and to Haldighati, Nathdwara and Eklingji (daily 2–7pm; Rs70). In addition, Udaipur's **travel agencies** – mostly located around Lalghat, Lake Palace Rd and Chetak Circle (a selection are listed on p.198) offer city tours (Rs30–40), airport transfer (Rs125), private car rental, and booking services for trains and buses. All charge similar rates. **Taxi tours** include visits to Sajjangarh (2hr; Rs375), Nagda, Eklingji and Nathdwara (4hr for Rs450; 9hr for Rs900 including Ranakpur). For longer hauls, charges per car are approximately Rs3 per kilometre.

The City

The original settlement of Udaipur focussed around the grand **City Palace**, bordering the west shore of **Lake Pichola**. Immediately to the north is the maze of tightly winding streets that constitute the **old city**. It takes a few days of wandering before this labyrinth becomes intelligible; start by getting acquainted with the gates and circles that form traffic islands at the major crossroads. From the clock tower that marks the northern edge of the old city, roads lead east to the tourist information bureau and Ahar, west to the lake, and north to the GPO at Chetak Circle. Continuing north, the road passes the excellent folk art museum, Bharatiya Lok Kala, and heads to Sahelion-ki-Bari, the gardens of the royal ladies.

The road that encircles **Lake Fateh Sagar** north of Lake Pichola carries on west to the superb crafts village of **Shilpgram**, a showcase for all types of traditional Indian art. It's a good cycling route; you can stop off at **Pratap Memorial Gardens** on the eastern shore of the lake, visit **Nehru Park** in its centre and cool off with an ice-cream or drink from mobile stands near the jetty. In the far west of the city, **Sajjangarh** – the "Monsoon Palace" – commands superb views across the plains, while to the east both the royal cenotaphs and **Ahar museum** with its fifth-century BC relics can be visited in a morning.

Lake Pichola

The serene lakeside location chosen by Udai for his new capital made a welcome change from the craggy heights of Chittaurgarh. He enlarged the lake, which drew water from mountains up to 160km away, and now covers eight square kilometres. Later rulers added dams and canals to prevent flooding during the monsoon.

The two islands in the lake, topped with the ivory-white domes and arches of private palaces, are the most familiar and photogenic features of Udaipur. **Jag Niwas**, now the **Lake Palace Hotel**, is the larger of the two, built as a summer palace during the reign of Jagat Singh (1628–52). Even if you aren't staying here, you can visit the palace for lunch, dinner or afternoon tea; the price includes the boat ride from the mainland (booking advisable; see p.196).

The larger **Jag Mandir**, on the island to the south, has changed little since its construction by Karan Singh in 1615. It takes its name from Jagat Singh who added to the initial structure. Intended as a small Rajput palace, it was never used as such; Karan Singh offered refuge here to the Moghul prince Khurum (later Emperor Shah Jahan), exiled by his father, Emperor Jahangir, in the 1620s. Khurum succeeded his father while still in Udaipur, and the Moghul gathering for the occasion defied the established code of Rajput–Moghul enmity. During the Mutiny (1857) the island once again served as a safe haven, this time for European women and children.

The main building facing the City Palace has detailed stone inlay work within its domed roof. In front of it a green marble *chhatri* carved with vines and flowers is the centrepiece of a garden guarded by stone elephants. The island's only inhabitants other than flocks of birds are three royal servants who tend the gardens and grow flowers for the Maharana's celebrations.

Half-hour **boat rides** around the lake depart from the jetty behind the City Palace (hourly, April–Sept 8–11am & 3–6pm, Oct–March 10am–noon & 2–5pm; Rs45), while an hour's trip (hourly, 2–6pm; Rs110) includes a stop at Jag Mandir. The view of the palaces and shoreline from the lake at sunset is one of the most memorable images of Rajput splendour.

The City Palace

Udaipur's fascinating **City Palace** stands moulded in soft yellow stone on a rocky promontory on the northwest shore of Lake Pichola, its thick windowless base crowned with ornate turrets and canopies. Eleven constituent *mahals* (palaces), constructed by successive maharanas during the three hundred years that followed the foundation of Udaipur in 1559, and characterized throughout by their exemplary workmanship, together form the largest royal complex in Rajasthan.

Part of the palace is now a museum (daily 9.30am–4.30pm; Rs15, camera Rs30, video Rs200), entered through **Toran Pole** from the massive courtyard where elephants once lined up for inspection before battle. Although **guided tours** (Rs60 for a non-Indian language) are not compulsory, they do serve to illuminate the chronology of the palaces, the significance of the paintings, and details of the lives of the maharanas.

Everywhere you look the marble and granite walls are laden with brilliant miniature paintings, decorated with tiles or overlaid with spangling mosaics of coloured glass and mirrors, and each room glows with sunlight filtering through stained-glass windows. Narrow low-roofed passages connect the different *mahals* and courtyards, creating a haphazard effect, designed to prevent surprise intrusion by armed enemies.

Each of the three large peacocks (*mor*) set into the walls of the seventeenth-century **Mor Chowk**, placed there by Sajjan Singh 200 years after the palace was built, is composed of 5000 pieces of glass, glittering in green, gold and blue. The pillared apartments that face Mor Chowk are adorned with scenes from Krishna legends, a favourite theme of the paintings in the **Zenana Mahal**, the women's quarters. With alcoves, balconies, coloured windows, tiled walls and floors, these are the most splendid rooms in the palace. Other chambers include **Kanchi-ki-Burj**, decorated throughout with a mosaic of mirrors, and **Chandra Chowk** (Moon Square) which although right at the top of the palace manages to enclose its own garden – it rests on the crest of a hill that rises in the heart of the palace. **Krishna Vilas**, an apartment full of miniatures, honours a nineteenth-century Udaipur princess who poisoned herself to avoid the dilemma of choosing a husband from the two rival households of Jodhpur and Jaipur.

Adjoining the palace, the dusty **Government Museum** (daily except Fri 10am–5pm; Rs2) displays clothes, unlabelled relics and a stuffed and decaying two-headed deer. It's worth passing through to the last room to see a good selection of temple statues, dating back to the eighth century, but otherwise the museum does not merit a detour.

Jagdish temple

Raised above the main crossroads a little north of the City Palace, **Jagdish temple** is a centre of constant activity. Built in 1652 and dedicated to Lord Jagannath, an aspect of Vishnu, its outer walls and towering *shikhara* are heavily carved with figures of Vishnu, scenes from the life of Krishna, and dancing *apsaras* (nymphs). The spacious *mandapa* leads to the sanctuary where a black stone image of Jagannath sits shrouded in flowers, while a small raised shrine in front of the temple protects a bronze Garuda, the half-man, half-bird vehicle of Vishnu. Smaller shrines to Ganesh and Hanuman stand to either side of the main temple.

Bharatiya Lok Kala

Udaipur's folk museum, **Bharatiya Lok Kala** on Panch Vati Rd just north of Chetak Circle (daily 9am–6pm; Rs7, camera Rs10, video Rs50), provides an inspiring introduction to Rajasthani arts and folklore. Exhibits include village paintings, puppets of all descriptions, printing blocks, terracottas, costumes, musical instruments, toys, jewellery and photographs of local Bhil and Garasia tribal people. Short amusing **puppet shows** (free) continue throughout the day, and are easy to follow even if you don't understand Hindi; longer performances take place between 6pm and 7pm (Rs20). The museum also runs short courses in puppet-making and theatre; call ☎24296 for details.

Sahelion-ki-Bari

The "garden of the maids of honour", **Sahelion-ki-Bari**, roughly 2km north of Hathi Pole (daily 9am–7.30pm; Rs2), was laid out by Sangram Singh early in the eighteenth century for the diversion and entertainment of the ladies of the royal household. Surrounding a shady courtyard, the fountained garden must once have made a delightful retreat, but today the fountains only play at the request of visitors, and the focus of attention is the wide range of indigenous trees and flowers. During the monsoon the lotus pond behind the courtyard is ablaze with colour.

Fateh Sagar

Not far west of Sahelion-ki-Bari is **Fateh Sagar**, a lake fringed by sharp hills and connected to Lake Pichola by a canal built shortly after the turn of the century. At the jetty on the western shore, you can hop on the boat that ferries tourists across the water to **Nehru Park** in the centre of the lake (daily summer 8am–6.30pm, winter 8am–6pm; Rs3). The park, constructed in 1937 as a famine relief project, is nothing special, but pleasant enough if you want to get away from the bustle of the town.

A two-minute walk from the boat moorings towards Udaipur brings you to **Moti Magri** (daily summer 7.30am–8pm, winter 7.30am–7pm; Rs5). In theory, the gardens here preserve the memory of Maharana Pratap Singh, who denied Akbar control of Udaipur and is remembered for his courage in the battle of Haldighati (see p.200). However, they are now in such a sorry state as to be barely worth a visit. A statue of Chetak, Pratap's faithful steed, stands at the top of the hill.

Shilpgram

The road running around the north of Fateh Sagar leads to the rural arts and crafts centre of **Shilpgram** (daily 9.30am–6pm; Rs2), near the village of Havala, 5km out from town and best reached by bike. This exemplary crafts village – one of the best in the country – was set up to promote and preserve the traditional architecture, music and crafts of the tribal people of western India, and holds rare displays of the diverse traditional lifestyles and customs of India's rural population.

Dwellings arranged in the compound include a solid two-storey wooden house from northern Gujarat, exquisitely carved throughout, circular painted huts from Kutch (Gujarat), thick-walled low-roofed houses from the Rajasthani deserts, and Goan potters' huts. Musicians and dancers – *hijras* (eunuchs) among them – perform around the houses, while weaving, potting, puppetry and embroidery continue as they would in their original localities. Allow at least an hour to walk round the compound; the best time to go is at weekends, when the centre is filled with artisans.

Sajjangarh

High on a hill 5km west of the city, the "Monsoon Palace", **Sajjangarh**, was abandoned by the royal family soon after its construction in 1880. It had been found to be impossible to pump water to the palace, which is now used as Udaipur's radio station and closed to visitors. The views over Udaipur from the courtyards of the palace are unrivalled, however, especially if you can make it up there for sunrise, when the surrounding countryside looks its most magical. That said, getting up the hill requires a bit of effort, as the climb is too steep to tackle by bicycle. The journey takes a good fifteen minutes by rickshaw or taxi, and costs more than Rs50 for the round trip.

Royal cenotaphs and Ahar museum

Across the narrow Ahar River, 2km east of Udaipur, domed cenotaphs huddle together on the site of the royal cremation ground. Raised on platforms, some of which are decorated with *shivalingams*, many of the *chhatris* are falling into disrepair, and the site is pretty dirty. Even so, it's a good place to pick up on local history, featuring an ornate memorial to the prodigious builder Jagat Singh (1628–52) and the cenotaph of Amar

THE EUNUCHS OF INDIA

Every country in the world has its share of transvestites, hermaphrodites and sexual ambivalents, but rarely do they play such a prominent a social role as India's eunuchs – the **hijras**. Numbering well over 400,000, with 150,000 in Delhi alone, the *hijras* have been around for centuries; they are mentioned in the *Mahabharata*, and the *Kama Sutra* outlines the best ways to have sex with a eunuch.

The *hijras* gather in clans that supplant the ties of family and caste renounced at initiation, and usually live in well-defined territories within major cities. Most *hijras* are effeminate, since castration results in hormonal changes, but they are not by definition homosexual. They are easy to recognize, gaudily made-up, unusually tall and often making crude gestures, and their dances to harsh rhythmic music are unmistakeably sexual. Popularly despised for their abnormality and vulgar behaviour, they are also feared for the strange power implied by their ambiguity: their curses are dreaded. Some earn their living as temple beggars or prostitutes, but most dance and sing at weddings and births, being paid *badhai* (tips) either to pronounce blessings or simply to go away. Their presence at the birth of a child, especially a boy, is particularly auspicious – the *hijra* is believed to absorb any homosexual tendencies from the infant, and in certain towns any family that refuses to invite a eunuch to a birth risks gossip among the local community that they may be hiding a hermaphrodite child.

Each *hijra* clan has a guru, an older eunuch who presides over initiation ceremonies, protects the socially vulnerable group, and corners a high proportion of any money earned. Members of the **All India Hijra Kalyan Sabha**, a social-work group formed in 1984 to protect the rights of *hijras*, have recently revealed that at least 1000 young men each year – some homeless, some married with children – are kidnapped, pushed into prostitution and eventually forcibly gelded. The Hijra Kalyan Sabha believes that the gurus make much of their money by auctioning off fresh eunuchs, so it pays them to pick healthy and attractive men. Horrendous castrations, performed by ill-equipped backstreet doctors, are carried out on heavily drugged patients whose wounds are later tended with substances such as herbs, mustard oil and cow dung. No anaesthetic is used, more than a hundred stitches are often needed, and the death rate may be as high as 75 percent (though a "doctor" accused of performing castrations recently claimed that only one of the 1000 operations he had performed was fatal).

In 1993 the Hijra Kalyan Sabha backed up the claims of a number of eunuchs who courageously spoke out against those who forcibly castrated them. As *hijra* mafias compel silence with death threats, filing charges is no mean feat. Indian law does not recognize emasculation as an offence (the nearest equivalent listed under the penal code is "abduction and grievous injury with a sharp weapon"); police are reluctant to interfere, and providing conclusive evidence of abduction and castration is extremely difficult. Local courts have been more cooperative, and have begun to force police to complete efficient investigations, but few cases have resulted in conviction, and the victims continue to face a struggle in a society where they will never be fully accepted.

Singh (died 1620) who contributed so much to the City Palace, embellished with friezes depicting the immolation of his wives.

Less than 1km south of here, archeological exhibits at the **Ahar museum** (daily except Fri 10am–5pm; Rs2) include locally unearthed pottery from the first millennium BC. Among more recent statues is a handsome tenth-century Surya image.

Accommodation

Udaipur has literally hundreds of places to stay, ranging from simple lodges near the bus stand, unexciting but handy for early-morning departures, to extravagant palaces. Most hotels are sandwiched between the **City Palace** and **Jagdish temple** on the east side of Lake Pichola; all offer excellent views over the lake to the west. Hotels around the smaller lakes **Rang and Swaroop** are peaceful and homely, most of them only ten minutes' walk from Jagdish temple. Behind the City Palace along Lake Palace Rd, the hotels have larger rooms and gardens but lack views across the lake. Note that budget hotels in Udaipur tend to have 10am **checkout**.

If you don't mind staying some way from the lakeside and the sights, the **best budget option** is the *Mewar Inn*, 42 Residency Rd (☎522090; ①), where even the deluxe rooms cost next to nothng; YHA cardholders get a further discount.

Near the bus stand

Apsara, City Station Rd (☎523400). Relatively quiet, set back a little from the road. Decent enough rooms, with attached bathrooms done out in marble. Car parking.①.

Tourist, 21 City Station Rd (☎28055). Noisy and basic roadside hotel; 9am checkout. ①.

Yatri, City Station Rd, opposite bus stand (☎27251). Moderate standard, but a little musty. ③.

Jagdish temple area/East side of Lake Pichola

Badi Haveli, 86 Gangaur Ghat Marg (☎412588; fax 520008). Delightful hotel in 350-year-old *haveli* with individual rooms, garden restaurant, and excellent views of the lake and palace. ③.

Caravanserai, 14 Lalghat (☎ & fax 521252). Bright, modern hotel done out in marble, very clean and pleasant with all mod cons and services. ⑥.

Evergreen, 32 Lalghat (☎27823). Popular lakeside place with basic rooms set around a grassy courtyard; very reasonable rates and a rooftop restaurant. ①.

Jagat Niwas, 25 Lalghat (☎29728). Right on the lakeside, entered down a narrow alley. Quiet, comfortable and relaxing, with shady courtyards, rooftop and restaurant. ③–⑥.

Kankarawa Haveli, 26 Lalghat (☎ & fax 411457). Nicely restored old *haveli* with comfortable rooms and modern attached bathrooms. ⑥.

Lake View, Lalghat (☎23527). Cheap and popular with a good roof restaurant. ①.

Lalghat Guest House, 34 Lalghat (☎525301; fax 523493). Popular, long-established place, with immaculate bathrooms, roof terrace overlooking the lake and cooking facilities. ②–⑤.

Lehar Guest House, 86 Gangaur Ghat Marg (no phone). Basic, spacious rooms in an old house with plenty of character. Roof terrace and restaurant. ①.

Sai Niwas, 75 Navghat (☎524909). Beautiful rooms with hand-painted decorations and classic furniture; some have lake-facing balconies. Romantic atmosphere and excellent management. ⑥.

Shiva Guest House, 74 Navghat (no phone). Small three-storey hotel with comfy rooms, some with balcony; shared bathrooms (constant hot shower) and roof terrace; Hindi lessons available. ①.

Along Lake Palace Road

Jhala Maan, Lake Palace Rd (☎27235). Pleasant, good-value hotel surrounded by trees. Large fresh rooms with bathroom (hot water); the best has huge windows, bath tub and balcony. ②.

Mahendra Prakash, Lake Palace Rd (☎29370). All rooms are spacious, with bathroom (hot water guaranteed). A large garden, central courtyard, roof terrace and parking facilities. ②.

Rang Niwas Palace, Lake Palace Rd, opposite the gate leading to *Shiv Niwas* (☎523890 or 1). Palatial old building with dorms, basic rooms, and suites. The large garden, friendly atmosphere and pool (Rs50 residents, Rs100 non-residents) make up for the lack of views. ①–⑥.

West side of Lake Pichola, Rang Sagar and Swaroop Sagar

Lake Pichola, outside Chand Pole (☎29197; fax 410575). Lovely, stately place with superb lake-facing rooms and posh dining hall. ⑥.

Lake Shore, outside Chand Pole (no phone). Next to *Lake Pichola Hotel*. Small peaceful hotel; doubles have trellissed windows overlooking the lake. Roof terrace with beautiful view. ②.

Natural, near New Bridge, Rang Sagar (☎527879). Basic but large and clean rooms at knock-down prices, many with balconies over the lake. A beautiful and peaceful budget location. ②.

Around Fateh Sagar

Anand Bhawan, off Fateh Sagar Rd (☎523256; fax 523247). Excellent hotel with carpeted rooms and commanding view. Good value. ⑥.

Hilltop Palace, Ambavgarh (☎561664; fax 525106). Smart, luxurious hotel, above Fateh Sagar. ⑧.

Luxury accommodation

Fateh Pakash Palace, City Palace (☎528016 or 7; fax 528006). True regal style in wonderfully decorated rooms and suites; splendid yet homely. Guests enjoy breathtaking views from turrets, and use of the facilities at the *Shiv Niwas*. Rooms cost around $100–200. ⑨.

Lake Palace, Lake Pichola (☎527961 or 73). With its central swimming pool, royal suites and lakeside dining area this has to be the most romantic of the smart hotels, glittering in the heart of the lake. Not to be missed if you have the money ($160, say). Book at least a month ahead. ⑨.

Laxmi Vilas Palace, off Fateh Sagar Rd (☎529711 or 2; fax 525536). Expensive (starting at $120) and comfortable. Snappy service, excellent view, luxurious swimming pool (Rs165 for non-residents) and good (pricey) restaurant and bar. ⑨.

Shiv Niwas, City Palace (☎528016 or 7; fax 528006). Live like a monarch in this architecturally perfect palace, still occupied in part by the royal family, and host to the regal Mewar festival every spring. An assortment of rooms and suites, all with their original interior design, starting at $65. All mod cons in traditional setting; pool, bar and restaurant. ⑨.

Eating

Eating prospects in Udaipur are gradually improving and some excellent **restaurants** have sprung up, most open all day and catering for all budgets. Restaurants abound between the **City Palace** and **Jagdish temple** on the east side of Lake Pichola, though you get better value for money in less patronized areas. Several of the cheaper ones show the James Bond movie *Octopussy*, with its manic boat chase on Pichola Lake, every evening, usually at 7pm. Many hotels have rooftop restaurants, and the *Lake Palace* tempts many travellers to drift over for a rather extravagant meal on the terrace.

Anna Restaurant, 151 Jagdish Temple Rd. Excellent Indian veg and Western food (delicious *malai kofta*), and *Octopussy* every night in the back. Open 7.30am–10pm.

Fateh Pakash Palace, City Palace. English tea is served in the gallery 3–5pm daily with a choice of fine teas available. The full Monty, with cream and scones costs around Rs100.

Gyaneshwar Lodge, Lalghat. Small, cheap place with the best *thalis* in town. Open 9am–midnight.

Jagat Niwas, 25 Lalghat. Charming hotel restaurant jutting over the lake. Tasty Indian meals and great continental breakfasts at fairly high prices. Open 7am–2pm & 6.30–10pm.

Lake Palace, Lake Pichola. Pricey wining and dining in plush palace surroundings, but you may be disappointed by the buffet food. Booking is essential; guests have priority. Dinner 7.30–10pm.

Natural, near New Bridge, Rang Sagar. Hotel restaurant in picturesque location, with reasonable attempts at a range of cuisines including Mexican (with *chapatis* for *tortillas*). Also breakfasts of *huevos rancheros* and hashbrowns, Tibetan and Italian dishes, and beer. Open 8am–11pm.

Park View, Town Hall Rd, opposite the Town Hall. Mid-priced softly lit restaurant, popular with locals and offering a very high standard of Indian veg and meat dishes. Open 8.30am–11pm.

Roof Garden Restaurant, Lake Palace Rd. Bustling non-veg rooftop restaurant with a view of the palace and a largely Western clientele, bedecked with fairy lights at night. Live classical music from 7.30pm. Open 8.30am–9.30pm.

Sai Niwas, 75 Navghat. Carefully prepared non-veg food on a lake-facing terrace. Relatively pricey but very tasty. Dinner served 6–10pm, breakfast and snacks at other times.

Listings

Bookshops *Mayur Book Paradise*, Bhattiyati Chohatta; coming from Jagdish temple, 400m on the left. There's a second-hand bookshop on Lalghat opposite the *Lake View* hotel.

Cultural entertainment Folk dance performances (daily except Sun 7pm; Rs30) at *Meera Kala Mandir*, Meera Bhawan, Sector 11, on the Ahmedabad road (☎583176); puppet shows and folk dances (daily 6–7pm; Rs20) at *Bharatiya Lok Kala Mandal*, Panch Vati Rd (☎24296).

Opticians *Best Optical*, Surajpole, on the north side of the square.

Pharmacies *Bansal Department Stores*, inside Surajpole (20m west of the gate); *Vijay Medical Store*, opposite the hospital entrance on Hospital Rd. *Laxmi General Store*, Bhattiyani Chohatta, 300m coming from Jagdish temple, on the right, is a useful general pharmacy selling almost anything you could need, including *Marmite*, tiger balm and rizlas.

Photographic stores *Unique Camera Image*, 103 Bhattiyani Chohatta, is among many that sell good-quality films, take pictures and offer a developing service.

Travel agents Tour operators to choose from include the very efficient *Haveli Tours & Travels*, 82 Gangaur Ghat Marg, opposite the corner of Lalghat (☎523525), who will also book and confirm flights, *Gangaur Tours & Travels*, 28 Gangaur Ghat Marg (☎411476) and *Taldar Travels*, Town Hall Rd, 50m north of the *Park View* restaurant and next to the pick-up point for private buses (☎28160). *Rajasthan Tours* (☎25777), is a reputable agency offering longer tours around Rajasthan.

MOVING ON FROM UDAIPUR

Indian Airlines, on Dhan Mandi, off Delhi Gate (Mon–Fri 10am–1.15pm & 2-5pm; ☎410999) **flies** to Jaipur, Delhi and Bombay, Jodhpur and Aurangabad. *UP Airways* and *Moduluft* each have daily morning flights to Bombay and evening flights to Jaipur and Delhi. *Moduluft* are represented by *Techno Tours* on Hospital Rd by Chetak Circle (daily 10am–1pm & 2–6pm; ☎526564), *UP* by *Anukampa Tours*, Circle View Apartments, just north of Sukadia Circle (Mon–Sat 9am–1pm & 2–5pm; ☎370266).

Eight **trains** leave Udaipur daily, six of them steam-hauled – romantic perhaps, but slow. The exceptions are the the *Garib Nawaz Express* #2916 (5.40am) and *Chetak Express* #9616 (6.10pm) to Delhi Sarai Rohilla (17hr) via Chittaurgarh (3hr 20min), Ajmer (8hr), Jaipur (11hr) and Alwar (14hr 30min). For Ahmedabad, take the *Udaipur-Ahmedabad Express* #9643 at 7pm (14hr 50min). Jodhpur is served by two daily passenger trains.

Buses connect Udaipur with Ahmedabad, Delhi, Jaipur via Ajmer (8hr), Jodhpur, Kota via Chittaurgarh, and Mount Abu. Comfortable **private buses** operate daily services to these destinations (also Pushkar) in less time, departing from Town Hall Rd by *Taldar Travels* (see *Listings*), who can supply tickets and times.

Around Udaipur

You'd need to have a lot of time on your hands before you could hope to see more than a fraction of the ruins, palaces, temples, forts, lakes and wildlife sanctuaries that abound in the countryside around Udaipur.

Day trips northeast of the city can take in such destinations as **Nagda**, **Eklingji**, **Nathdwara**, and **Kankroli** along NH8 towards Bhilwara, or the peaceful wooded surroundings of **Ranakpur** and **Kumbalgarh**, which also make appealing stopovers before you join NH15 en route to Jodhpur. Renting a car saves time, but regular and efficient local buses, as well as private tour companies, serve both routes.

Southeast from Udaipur, an easy drive leads to **Jaisamand** lake and wildlife sanctuary and the ruined temples at **Jagat**. A poor road continues south to the palaces at **Dungarpur**, set on a high and rocky plateau and festooned with wall paintings.

Nagda

The ragged remnants of the ancient capital of Mewar, **NAGDA**, which date back to 626 AD, stand next to a lake 20km northeast of Udaipur, a couple of kilometres short of

Eklingji. Buses from Udaipur set down passengers for Nagda shortly before the road drops into the valley that shelters the Eklingji temple, beside a *chai* stall and bicycle shop. Nagda itself is a short ride away, west of the lake.

Most of the buildings were either destroyed by Moghul zealots or submerged by the lake, which has naturally accumulated over the centuries. All that survives is a majestic pair of tenth-century Vaishnavite temples, known as **Saas-Bahu** – literally "Mother-in-law" and "Daughter-in-law". Each has a main sanctuary fronted by a *mandapa* (pillared entrance hall) and topped by a pyramidal roof. The larger (Mother-in-law) has an astounding wealth of carving in its interior. Within the *mandapa*, a marriage area is marked by four pillars bearing images of the gods to which a couple must pay homage: Brahma, Vishnu, Shiva and Surya. On the northeast pillar you can make out representations of Sita's trial by fire, a favourite episode from the *Ramayana*, while scenes from the *Mahabharata* cover the ceilings. The outer walls of both temples display images of the entire Hindu pantheon, nubile *apsaras* (heavenly maidens), and even a few couples engaged in erotic acts.

The quickest route to Eklingji from the cycle shop is along a path that leads behind the old protective walls and downhill, passing shaded tanks and half-preserved muddy-brown temples.

Eklingji

The god **Eklingji**, a manifestation of Shiva, has been the protective deity of the rulers of Mewar ever since the eighth century, when Bappa Rawal was bestowed with the title *darwan* (servant) of Eklingji by his guru. To this day, the Maharana of Udaipur still visits his temples at the eponymous **EKLINGJI** every Monday evening – the day traditionally celebrated all over India as being sacred to Shiva. Lesser mortals can make the straightforward half-hour trip northeast of Udaipur by taxi, or on very frequent buses from the main bus stand.

The milky-white marble main temple (daily 4.30–6.30am, 10.30am–1.30pm & 5.30-6.45pm), dominating the compound with an elaborate two-storey *mandapa* guarded by stone elephants, surrounds a four-faced black marble *lingam* that marks the precise spot where Bappa Rawal received his accolade. Images of Shiva and his fellow deities, *apsaras* and musicians are etched into the walls both outside and within, where silver doors, chests and lamps glint in the shady halls, and a solid silver (Nandi) bull faces the main sanctuary. The temple had to be rebuilt under Maharana Raimal at the end of the fifteenth century, and again two hundred years later after the ravages of Aurangzeb's iconoclastic forces. Numerous smaller shrines, some also composed of white marble, house images of deities such as Ganesh and Vishnu.

Behind the temple complex to the north, the temples of **Indra Lake**, bordered by *ghats* on its southern shore, resonate with drum beats and singing each Monday. *Kailash Guest House* near the bus stand has a few simple rooms (①).

Nathdwara

The temple dedicated to Krishna – known also as **Nath**, the favourite *avatar* (incarnation) of Vishnu – at **NATHDWARA**, "Gateway to God", is a major goal for Vaishnavite pilgrims. Nathdwara was called Sihar until the moment in the seventeenth century when a chariot laden with an image of Krishna became stuck in the mud 26km north of Eklingji. The idol was being carried from Krishna's birthplace Mathura to Udaipur to spare it almost certain destruction by Aurangzeb; its bearers interpreted the event as a divine sign and established a new temple where it had stopped.

Nathdwara is on NH8, and welcomes a constant flow of buses en route north and south, as well as two daily trains to Udaipur. Although the area around the bus stand

---

HALDIGHATI

At **Haldighati**, west of Nathdwara, Hindu pilgrims pause to pay homage to **Maharana Pratap Singh** at the site of the famous battle he fought with the forces of the Moghul emperor Akbar in 1576. Pratap epitomizes the role of the maharanas of Mewar as defenders of the Mewari people, sworn never to submit to foreign power.

Although wounded and obliged to withdraw, Pratap remained in hiding protected by Bhil tribesmen, and succeeded in preventing supplies from reaching the nominally victorious Moghul warriors. They were left with no choice but to surrender, an act which put an end to their arrogant certainty of sweeping all the Rajput states under Moghul suzerainty.

For the casual visitor, there's little to see except the dark yellow sands of the battlefield in a narrow pass between the hills, a cenotaph to Pratap's valiant horse, **Chetak**, and the tomb of **Hakim Khan Suri**, the leader of Pratap's forces.

---

is grim, a short ride on a rickshaw west brings you to narrow streets where stalls display incense, beads, perfumes and small Krishna statues, and blossom with the pinks, yellows and reds of temple decorations. In the centre of town the **Shri Nathji temple** opens for worship eight times daily, when the image is woken, dressed, washed, fed and put to bed. The most elaborate session, *aarti*, takes place between 5pm and 6pm. Don't miss the radiant *pichwai* paintings in the main sanctuary, made of handspun cloth and coloured with strong vegetable pigments: these original hangings possess a brilliance unmatched by the numerous copies available all over Rajasthan.

Rooms are at a premium during the festivals of **Janmasthami** (Aug/Sept) and **Diwali** (Oct/Nov).

Accommodation

Hotels in Nathdwara and the surrounding valley, whose primary function is to serve the needs of pilgrims, include the RTDC *Hotel Gokul* (☎02953/2685; ①–④) in the north of town overlooking Lal Bagh, which offers reasonable deluxe and ordinary rooms and a dorm. In the central Naya Bazaar, *Hotel Vindra* (☎02953/2218; ④) has pleasant rooms and serves tasty meals in its own restaurant.

Kankroli and Rajsamand

Northeast of Nathdwara, NH8 winds through another 17km of undulating scrub before reaching **KANKROLI**, 65km from Udaipur. This small dusty market town stands on the shores of the vast deep blue **Rajsamand Lake**, whose construction was commissioned by Maharana Raj Singh in the seventeenth century after a terrible drought swept Rajasthan, leaving a trail of death and pestilence. He hoped the lake would prevent the recurrence of such a large-scale disaster.

On the lake's western shore, a few kilometres out of town, is **Nauchowki**, a collection of nine *chowks* (pavilions), on platforms above the steps leading to the water. With carved pillars and ceilings showing scenes from the life of Krishna, these *chowks* were erected by Raj Singh to commemorate his marriage to Princess Charumati of Kishangarh, an act that saved her from the matrimonial clasp of Aurangzeb.

The **Dwarkadish temple** overlooking the southern shore houses an image of Krishna installed by Raj Singh in 1676, and has a sanctuary similar to that at Nathdwara. It forms part of an old palace whose passages wind through low-ceilinged rooms to covered walkways beside the lake. On steps descending to the water you can buy grain to feed the flocks of pigeons who survive on the charity of pilgrims.

The best views of the lake are to be had from the **Digambara Jain temple**, dedicated to Adinath, which crowns a steep hill between Nauchowki and the bus stand. From here you can see the Dwarkadish temple, Nauchowki, scattered old palaces on the nearby hills, and the Aravalli landscape rolling south as far as the eye can see.

J & K Guest House (①), east of the bus stand, has very basic **rooms**.

Ranakpur

Surprisingly few foreign visitors to Rajasthan take the time to venture out to the absolutely stupendous complex of **Jain temples** couched in the small wooded valley of **RANAKPUR**, 60km north of Udaipur. There is nothing else in this secluded spot except a small *chai* stall, and an RTDC tourist bungalow on a hill to the west.

The main temple (open for worship 10am–5pm) is dedicated to the first *tirthankara* **Adinath**, whose four-faced image is enshrined in its central sanctuary. Built in 1439 on land donated to the Jains by Rana Kumbha, the temple is two or three storeys high in parts, and its roof, topped with five large *shikharas*, undulates with tiny spires that crown the small shrines to Jain saints lining the temple walls. Within, 29 halls, some octagonal and many more than one storey high, are dissected by 1444 pillars, each sculpted with unique designs. The carving on the walls, columns and the domed ceilings is absolutely superb. Friezes depicting the life of the *tirthankara* are etched into the walls, while musicians and dancers have been modelled out of brackets between the pillars and the ceiling.

Two smaller temples dedicated to **Parshvanath** and **Neminath** nestle among the trees close by; the sculptures within are of a similarly high standard. Also in the compound is a contemporary Hindu temple dedicated to **Surya**, inside which carvings depict racing chariots commanded by the solar deities.

Practicalities

Ranakpur is a long day's journey out from Udaipur on the road towards Jodhpur, and can also be reached from Mount Abu. Its *dharamshala* asks overnight guests for donations, and provides lunch (noon–1pm) and dinner (5–6pm) for a small fee. The RTDC *Hotel Shilpi* (☎02934/3674; ①–④) has clean rooms, a dorm and a restaurant serving acceptable, if pricey, food. Private **buses** from Ranakpur run to Jodhpur and Jaipur, and there's a state bus to Jodhpur.

Kumbalgarh

The remote and mighty hill-top fort of **KUMBALGARH**, 84km north of Udaipur, is perhaps the most formidable of the thirty-two constructed by Maharana Kumbha in the fifteenth century. Protected by a series of seven thick ramparts, it was only successfully besieged once, when Akbar poisoned the Sisodias' water supply – he later returned it to them anyway.

Sandy brown crenellated walls encircle the crest of the hill to protect the palace on its summit. The crumbling **Jain temples** among the reservoirs and gardens within are said to have been erected in the second century; the **tombs** of Kumbha (murdered by his eldest son) and his grandson Prithviraj (poisoned by his brother-in-law) stand just to the east. A guide can show you the room where Udai Singh was raised by his nurse after fleeing Chittaurgarh in 1535, and the topmost Cloud Palace, restored and furnished by Udaipur's Fateh Singh early this century.

Practicalities

Kumbalgarh's **heritage hotel**, the *Aodhi* (☎02954/4222; ⑨; 20–30 percent discount April–July) provides some relief after the long journey from Jodhpur or Udaipur. From the hotel you can take a 6-hour horse trek (Rs1200) or 5-hour jeep safari (Rs1500) to a crocodile park, passing through a wildlife sanctuary that protects one of India's few families of wolves, as well as leopards and flying squirrels. Cheaper three-hour treks to Kumbalgarh fort are also available. Bookings can be made through the *Aodhi* hotel, or the *Shiv Niwas Palace* in Udaipur. There is also a delightful palace hotel, the *Royal Castle*, in the nearby town of **Ghanerao** (☎02934/7335; ⑨),

South of Udaipur

Asia's largest artificial lake, **Jaisamand**, created by Jai Singh as a summer retreat in the seventeenth century and measuring 10km by 15km, is 48km southeast of Udaipur. Apart from a few ruined palaces, there's not much to see, though a boat trip on the lake (Rs20), skirts a few islands inhabited by **Bhil tribespeople**. The surrounding area was declared a sanctuary in 1957, for *chital, chinkara* and the odd leopard. Tucked away in the woods at **Jagat**, between Udaipur and Jaisamand, an elaborate tenth-century temple dedicated to Ambika Mata is crammed with images of Hindu goddesses.

NH8 leads directly south to the village of **RISHABDEO**, 40km from Udaipur, where a temple to the Jain *tirthankara* Rishabha (Adinath) attracts Jains, Vaishnavites (who worship him as an incarnation of Vishnu) and Bhils. There is an RTDC **hotel**, the *Gavri* (☎029072/245; ④).

THE BHILS

Numbering some 2.5 million people, the **Bhils** – who also live in parts of Madhya Pradesh, Gujarat and northern Maharashtra – are concentrated in the south of Rajasthan, especially around Dungarpur, Udaipur and Chittaurgarh. Formerly hunter-gatherers, the Bhils are now mostly farmers, but still renowned for their **archery skills** (Bhil originally means "bow"), mentioned in the great Hindu epics. They several times proved invaluable in the defence of the Rajputs against the Marathas and Moghuls, and even the East India Company sought their services. The Bhils' **language** is related to Gujarati and Hindi rather than to the Dravidian tongues spoken by most "tribal peoples", but their **religion**, with its own gods, bears only the faintest resemblance to Hinduism.

DUNGARPUR, which traces its roots back to a Sisodia Rajput who left Udaipur in the thirteenth century after a family dispute, is a further 30km south and connected to Udaipur and Ahmedabad by road and rail. However, you'll need your own transport to get to the old city, built on a rocky hill 2km above the forested plains. Its thirteenth-century palaces, built of grey-green granite and marble, are bedecked with arched windows, ornate balconies, and pillars twisted like barley sugar. Inside, the walls are bright with remarkably well-preserved paintings, tiles and mirror mosaics.

Mount Abu

Set amid craggy outcrops on a high southwestern plateau, Rajasthan's only hill station, **MOUNT ABU**, is named for a mountain whose mythological past (if not its recorded history) is central to the development of the state. Mount Abu was long a favourite summer home for the rulers of Rajasthan and Gujarat, who built affluent summer palaces here, and for the British, who used it as a recuperation centre. These days, like many hill stations, it remains a popular resort for Indian honeymooners, although foreign tourists may feel it has little to offer beyond a welcome respite from the heat of the plains and the proximity of the extraordinary Jain temples at **Dilwara**.

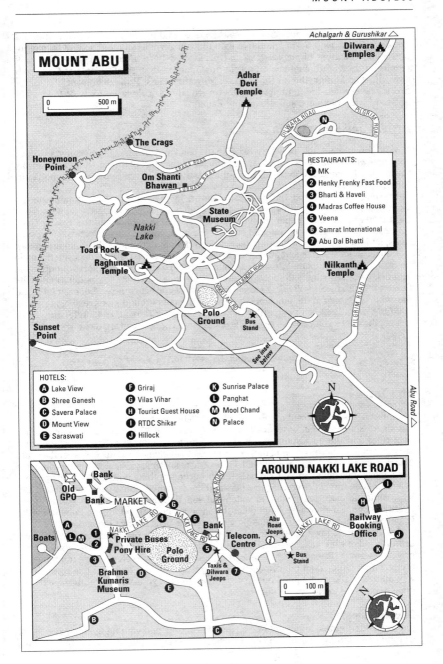

MOUNT ABU

0   500 m

Achalgarh & Gurushikar △

Dilwara Temples

Adhar Devi Temple

The Crags

Honeymoon Point

Om Shanti Bhawan

State Museum

Nakki Lake

Toad Rock

Raghunath Temple

Sunset Point

Polo Ground

Bus Stand

Nilkanth Temple

Abu Road △

See inset below

RESTAURANTS:
1 MK
2 Henky Frenky Fast Food
3 Bharti & Haveli
4 Madras Coffee House
5 Veena
6 Samrat International
7 Abu Dal Bhatti

HOTELS:
A Lake View
B Shree Ganesh
C Savera Palace
D Mount View
E Saraswati
F Griraj
G Vilas Vihar
H Tourist Guest House
I RTDC Shikar
J Hillock
K Sunrise Palace
L Panghat
M Mool Chand
N Palace

AROUND NAKKI LAKE ROAD

Old GPO

Bank

Bank

MARKET

Boats

Private Buses
Pony Hire

Brahma Kumaris Museum

Polo Ground

Bank

Telecom. Centre

Taxis & Dilwara Jeeps

Abu Road Jeeps

Bus Stand

Railway Booking Office

0   100 m

The focal point of Mount Abu is **Nakki Lake**, said to have been formed when the gods scratched away at the mountain with their fingernails (*nakh*). Legend tells of the powerful ceremony of *yagna agnikund* performed here after the fall of the Gupta empire in the eighth century, on a spot now marked by a small temple at Gaumukh, 3km short of Mount Abu on the road up from the plains. Prayers in front of a sacred fire (*agni*) created the fighting clans that were later to rule large parts of India – the Solankis, the Chauhans, and the mighty Rajputs.

Arrival and information

Mount Abu is accessible only by road. Aim to spend as little time as you can in the uninspiring town of **Abu Road**, the nearest railhead, at the start of the one-hour ascent from the plains. It has a few typically Rajasthani bazaars, but very poor accommodation. Entering Mount Abu itself, you have to pay a Rs5 fee.

Passengers arriving at the main **bus stand** in the southeast of Mount Abu are swamped by hotel touts and would-be luggage porters pushing pram-like trolleys. Turn right to get to the more expensive hotels, the RTDC *Shikar Hotel* and the *Tourist Guest House*; left for the large central polo ground, the main bazaar, budget hotels and restaurants, and the lake (the road up the east side of the polo ground is the quickest route).

Details on local sights and guides are available at the **tourist office**, opposite the main bus stand (Mon–Sat 10am–1.30pm & 2–5pm; ☎3151). To **change travellers' cheques** the best bet, if you're lucky, is the *State Bank of Bikaner and Jaipur* at the northern end of the bazaar; the nearby *State Bank of India* changes most hard currencies, but cash only, and the *Bank of Baroda* at the junction southeast of the polo ground gives cash against *Visa* or *Mastercard*. There's a **post office** next to the *Bank of Baroda*, and a **telecom** centre just south, where you can also receive faxes, though connections are dicey.

> The telephone **area code** for Mount Abu is ☎02974.

The Town

Mount Abu has a significant number of religious sites, whether Jain, Hindu or otherwise; but all are some way out of town. Nearer the centre, **Nakki Lake** is a pleasant spot for boat rides and the eucalyptus woods nearby are great for walks. Keep an eye out for strange granite outcrops around the lake such as the looming Toad Rock; Camel Rock and Nandi Rock are not so easily identified. Of several panoramic viewpoints on the fringes of town above the plains, **Sunset Point** is the favourite – with its hordes of holidaymakers, peanut sellers, camel drivers, cart pushers and horse owners, it has to be the noisiest and least romantic place imaginable to watch the sun sink over the horizon. **Honeymoon Point**, also known as Ganesh Point (after the adjacent temple) and Anadra Point (after the village it overlooks), has a breathtaking view over the plain at any time of day.

Further out of town are several Hindu temples and the spectacular Jain **Dilwara temples**, all of which can be seen by taking a half-day tour from the tourist office or any private operator (8.30am–1.30pm or 2–7pm; Rs30–40). However, if you're interested in architecture rather than pilgrimage sites, forget the rushed tour and make your own way up there, allowing a good one or two hours to pick your way through the extraordinary wealth of intricate carving.

Dilwara temples

Jains consider temple building to be an act of devotion, and without fail their houses of worship are lovingly adorned and embellished, but even by Jain standards, the **Dilwara**

temples 3km northeast of Mount Abu (daily noon–6pm; free; no leather, cameras, transistors, tape recorders, or menstruating women), are some of the most beautiful in India. All five are made purely from marble, and the incredibly fine carving, especially in the two main structures, is breathtakingly intricate, unparalleled in its lightness and delicacy. Each little section stands on its own as a work of art, inspiring a stunned response from even the most temple-jaded tourists. For sheer aesthetic splendour, only the temples at Ranakpur 200km northwest (see p.201) come close.

The oldest temple, **Vimala Vasahi**, named after the Gujarati minister who funded its construction in 1031AD, is dedicated to Adinath, the first *tirthankara*, whose image sits cross-legged in the central sanctuary guarded by tall statues of Parshvanath (the twenty-third *tirthankara*). Although the exterior is simple, inside not one wall, column or ceiling is unadorned; the work, carried out by almost 2000 labourers and sculptors, took fourteen years to complete. Eight of the forty-eight pillars in the front hall form an octagon that supports a domed ceiling arranged in eleven concentric circles, alive with dancers, musicians, elephants and horses. Within the sanctuary and the cloisters that surround it, small shrines, countless pillars, brackets and wall niches are imaginatively decorated, and each section of the roof is adorned; deities among the lotus designs and dancing maidens include Saraswati, Ganesh and Krishna. In front of the entrance, a portico shelters marble statues of ten elephants, a horse and their riders.

The later **Neminath temple** (1231 AD) imitates that dedicated to Adinath, but its carvings are yet more precise and detailed. The large dome over the entrance hall is unprecedented. Friezes etched into the walls depict cosmological themes, stories of the *jinas* (saints) and grand processions. Sculptures near the entrance porch commemorate the temple's patrons, the two brothers Vastupala and Tejapala. Said in legend to have discovered a huge treasure, they were advised by their wives – also portrayed here – to build temples, and funded many on the holy hill of Shatrunjaya in Gujarat.

The remaining three fifteenth-century temples are less spectacular. Although the **Adinath temple** – not to be confused with Vimala Vasahi – which houses a four-and-a-half-ton brass image of the *tirthankara*, has some fine carving, much of it is unfinished; the one consecrated to Parshvanath has ornate ceilings and *jinas* etched into the outer walls, and is topped by a high grey stone tower. Five hundred metres beyond the temples is a small **wildlife sanctuary** (Rs10), with a pair of crocodiles and allegedly sixteen leopards and eighty sloth bears, though you'll be lucky to see any of them with the noisy crowd who usually gather round the waterhole for a look.

To **get to Dilwara**, you can charter a jeep (Rs20), or take a place in a shared one (Rs2), from main junction at the southeastern end of Mount Abu's polo ground. The walk up there is also pleasant, though many prefer to save their energies for the downhill walk back into town.

Hindu temples

Beyond the Brahma Kumaris University, about 3km northeast of town, a flight of more than 400 steps climbs up to **Adhar Devi temple** (dedicated to Durga), cut into the rocky hill-top. The milk-coloured water of the **Doodh Baori** well at the foot of the steps is the traditional source of pure milk (*doodh*) for gods and sages.

A further 8km northeast, the temple complex at **ACHALGARH** is dominated by the **Achaleshwar Mahadeo** (Shiva) temple. Its sanctuary holds neither an image of Shiva nor a *lingam*, only a *yoni* with a hole in it said to reach into the netherworld, watched over by figures of Parvati and Ganesh on the walls. Statues of Parvati flank the entrance, faced by an unusually large metal Nandi bull. Subsidiary shrines include one dedicated to Vishnu, in which detailed plaques depict the familiar reclining Vishnu and his nine incarnations. The large tank lined with stone buffaloes outside the temple, intended to contain purifying water, is the legendary scene of the slaying of demons disguised as buffaloes who stole purifying *ghee* from the tank.

BRAHMA KUMARIS

The religious sect **Brahma Kumaris** (children of Brahma) preach that all religions reach for the same goal, but label it differently. At about 2000 centres around the world they teach Raja Yoga – meditation that directs people to knowledge of an inner light, the "divine spark" or soul, that is part of, and one with, the all-encompassing soul, Shiva. Belief in the five evils – anger, ego, attachment, greed and lust – is shared with Buddhism and Hinduism, with the ultimate goal being their elimination, and the advent of a **Golden Age** of peace, prosperity and purity.

The **Brahma Kumaris Spiritual University** at **Om Shanti Bhawan** to the north of Nakki Lake (☎3348) aims to foster awareness, tolerance, love and "God-consciousness" in a meditative atmosphere where smoking, alcohol, meat and sex are avoided. Classes range from three-day Raja Yoga camps, to advanced six-month courses; lectures are translated into ten languages. The **Brahma Kumaris Museum** by the private bus stand between the polo ground and the lake (daily 8am–8pm; free) holds daily meditation classes.

Another important Hindu pilgrimage site is the Atri Rishi temple at **Guru Shikar**, 15km northeast of town, which at 1772m above sea level marks the highest point in Rajasthan. Depending on how energetic you're feeling, you can enjoy superb panoramic vistas either from the temple itself, or the drinks stall at the bottom of the steps that lead up to it.

Accommodation

The steady stream of pilgrims and honeymoon couples ensures that Mount Abu has plenty of **hotels**. A fair sprinkling offer luxuries for newly-weds in special "couple rooms"; the *Samrat International*, for example, takes pride in its curtained four- or six-poster beds and deep marble bathtubs, and even boasts swings for two in some rooms. Though in **low season** you can live in stylish comfort for little more than you might otherwise pay for rock-bottom accommodation, prices rocket in **high season** (April–June & Sept–Dec), reaching their peak during Diwali (Oct/Nov). We have indicated below where the difference in seasonal rates is drastic.

Note that **checkout** time is usually 9am, and the flow of hot water can be sporadic.

Inexpensive

Giriraj, near main bazaar (☎3501). Quiet, cramped rooms with bath. Good value low-season. ①/⑤.

Lake View, Nakki Lake (☎3659). Fresh, clean rooms; the more expensive ones facing the lake have the best view in town. Roof terrace. ③/⑤.

Mool Chand, Nakki Lake Rd (☎3591). Basic, grubby and dirt-cheap rooms with tiny bathrooms. Two have lake-view balconies. ①/③.

Mount View, opposite the polo ground (☎38279). Very pleasant rooms in a two-storey building, with courtyard and front lawn. Hot water available in the morning. No high season increase. ②.

Panghat, Nakki Lake Rd (☎3386). Reasonable rooms with bathrooms and TV, at the end of the road leading to Nakki Lake, Roof terrace overlooking the lake. ①/③.

RTDC Shikar, opposite the *Tourist Guest House*. (☎3219; fax 3526). Large impersonal rooms or cottages, a year-round cheap dorm, and restaurant, all set in agreeable gardens. ③/④–⑥.

Saraswati (☎3237). Large fresh rooms with bathroom and sitting area. Fine views from upper floors. Restaurant serving good veg Gujarati food. ④/⑦.

Shree Ganesh, near Sophia High School (☎3591). The cleanest and best value of the budget hotels, in a quiet location. ①/④.

Tourist Guest House, near *HP* petrol pump (☎3200). Newly rebuilt with full facilities and a flowery courtyard. ④/⑤.

Vilas Vihar, Shivaji Marg (☎3585). Quiet rooms with attached bathrooms and optional piped music. Running hot water and room service. ①/④.

Moderate to expensive

Hillock, Abu Rd (☎3277; fax 3467). Smart new high-rise hotel. Carpeted rooms are immaculately clean, and provide great views over the Abu hills. Restaurant, bar, and parking facilities. ⑧.

Palace Hotel, Bikaner House (☎3121; fax 3674). Half a kilometre before the Dilwara temples, a former summer palace equipped with private lawns and tennis courts, plus its own lake. A luxurious and peaceful treat. Some discounts off-season. ⑦.

Savera Palace (☎ and fax 3354). Modern bungalow with carpeted, dusty rooms offering steam baths and swimming – you may have to share the pool with several hundred midges. ⑤/⑥.

Sunrise Palace, Bharatpur Kothi (☎3573; fax 3775). Huge, opulent rooms in a former palace, on the crest of a hill behind the *Hillock*. A glass-walled restaurant surveys the valley below. ⑤/⑥.

Eating and drinking

Nakki Lake Road, between the bus stand and the market, is lined with inexpensive **restaurants** with open-air seating, serving veg food from Gujarat, Punjab and south India. Nearer the lake, ice-cream stalls and "fast food" stops neighbour restaurants with indoor seating. The classier hotels serve **alcohol**; it is also available at the wine and beer shops near the crossroads at the bottom of town. There are a trio of cheap *dhabas* doing good low-priced veg curries on the main road 200m southeast of the polo ground, opposite the telecom centre: the one in the middle (*Abu Dal Bhatti*; Hindi sign only; 7am–10pm) is the best. A number of omelette-*wallahs* have stalls opposite the *Madras Cafe* on the street leading into the market.

Aangan, Nakki Lake Rd. Attached to the *Samrat International Hotel*. Well-known for its very reasonably priced Gujarati veg*thalis* and comfortable atmosphere. Open 8am–3pm & 6–10pm.

Ambika, Nakki Lake Rd. Inexpensive Punjabi and south Indian snacks. Open 9am–10pm.

MOVING ON FROM MOUNT ABU

Buses leave Mount Abu for **Abu Road** every hour; jeeps leave when full (from opposite the bus stand), and taxis are available on request (from the junction at the southeastern corner of the polo ground; Rs200 for a full car).

If you plan to travel onwards by **train**, there's an information and **booking office** (Mon–Sat 9am–1pm & 2–4pm; ☎3353) on the main road by the *HP* petrol pump, about 200m southeast of the tourist office. The fastest and most convenient service to Ahmedabad is the *Ashram Express* #2905, currently passing through at 8.30am. This train does not call at Mehsana, but most of the others do (around 4hr). In the other direction, of the three trains to Delhi Sarai Rohilla via Ajmer (5hr 35min), your best bet is the overnight *Ashram Express* #2906. A slower overnight service for Ajmer, the *Sarai Rohilla Express* #9904, gets you there at a more civilized hour, when Pushkar buses are running. There's also a night train to Jodhpur.

RSRTC and *GSTC* run services from the state **bus** stand, about 200m southeast of the polo ground on the main road. Most buses to Ahmedabad go via Palanpur (3hr, change for Bhuj) and Mehsana (4hr), with a couple continuing to Vadodara (9hr), and one to Surat (12hr). Other destinations include Udaipur, Jaipur via Ajmer (7hr 30min) and Chittaurgarh (2 daily; 9hr), with morning departures to Delhi, Jodhpur, and Jaisalmer via Barmer (8hr).

Many small companies offer daily tours and **private buses** to Abu Road and further afield, though not all are reliable. *Shobha Travels*, near *Samrat Hotel* (☎3302), run daily services, mostly overnight, to Udaipur, Ahmedabad, Jaipur, Ajmer, Vadodara, Surat and Bombay. Private buses operate from a stand north of the polo ground.

Haveli, Nakki Lake Rd. Really two separate restaurants tucked away on the main street between the private bus stand and Nakki Lake. The one on the left does low-priced Gujarati *thalis*, while the one on the right serves mainly Punjabi food. Very good quality. Open 8am–10pm.

Henky Frenky Fast Food, Nakki Lake Rd, on the right of the main road leading to the lake. Incongruous place serving good south Indian veg dishes, cutlets and burgers.

Veena, Nakki Lake Rd. Open-air seating next to the main road. High quality, inexpensive south Indian and Gujarati meals, plus pizza and vegeburgers. Open 7am–3pm & 6pm–midnight.

Madras Cafe, Nakki Lake Rd. Good filter coffee, if slightly over the odds pricewise, with reasonable south Indian snacks taken indoors or out, and Gujarati and Punjabi dishes upstairs. Try the special pau bhaji for Rs20. Open 8am–10pm.

MK Restaurant, Nakki Lake Rd. Good Indian and Chinese food at reasonable prices, with some great fish dishes; indoor seating.

Mayur, at the *Hillock Hotel*. Fine non-veg food, including "Rajasthani speciality" *thalis* in a pleasant atmosphere. Open noon–3pm & 7–11pm. The hotel also has a coffee shop, the *Chit Chat*, serving breakfast and snacks 7–11am & 3–7pm.

East of Udaipur

The belt of hilly land east of Udaipur is the most fertile in Rajasthan, watered by several perennial rivers; at the tail end of the monsoon cliffs and ravines resound with the rush of waterfalls. Although you need your own vehicle to penetrate the countryside, the historic town of **Chittaurgarh**, which preceded Udaipur as the seat of Mewar's rulers, is easily accessible. Further east, clusters of time-worn temples mark the sites of ancient cities. In the far southeast, the heartland of the princely state of Kota, palaces and forts in **Kota** and **Bundi** stand sentinel over fields of wheat, groundnut, castor-oil plants and poppies.

Chittaurgarh

The colossal fort at **CHITTAURGARH**, also known as **Chittor**, sits on a rocky plateau high above the smooth plains of southern Rajasthan, 115km northeast of Udaipur. Steeped in the terrors and triumphs of Rajput battles, its crenellated walls and buildings are hewn from the same yellow-brown stone that comprises its rocky foundation. Seen from afar, only a few towers and turrets, protruding above the protective walls, betray its existence.

Below the fort, the town is severed by the River Ghambiri, alive with leaping fish, and fringed with the bright *saris* laid out to dry on its banks. Apart from the usual turmoil of its crowded back streets, the **old city** east of the river has little to grab your attention, and some tourists choose to squeeze a tour of Chittaurgarh into a day trip from Udaipur. A one-night stop, however, leaves time for a more leisurely visit to the fort and a stroll through the town or along the river.

Some history

Of all the Rajput capitals, Chittaurgarh stands out as the strongest centre of Hindu resistance. The uncompromising policy of death before submission followed by its **Sisodia** overlords ensured that its history brims with tales of loyalty and terrible sacrifice. Its origins are however shrouded in legend; some claim that **Guhil**, the first of the Mewar leaders, founded the city in the sixth century, others favour the popular eighth-century **Bappa Rawal**, true forefather of the Sisodia Rajputs.

From a battle-scarred past, three devastating attacks are most remembered. The first, in 1303 during the reign of **Ratan Singh**, was launched by **Ala-ud-din-Khalji**, the

---

The **telephone area code** for Chittaurgarh is ☎01472.

fiercest of the Delhi Sultans. Having besieged the city, and all but starved the Rajputs out, he offered to withdraw – if he could take Ratan's queen, **Padmini**, with him. After being permitted to glimpse the queen's reflection in a mirror, the Sultan took Ratan prisoner. Padmini left the fort accompanied by an army of men disguised as maids of honour, but the Rajputs lost the ensuing battle. Thirteen thousand women, led by Padmini, committed *johar* by throwing themselves and their children onto a huge funeral pyre. The angry Sultan destroyed most of the fort's temples and palaces.

After returning to Rajput hands in 1326, Chittaurgarh saw two hundred years of prosperity. However, in 1535, an unexpected onslaught led by **Sultan Bahadur Shah** from Gujarat once again decimated the Rajput warriors, and the women surrendered their lives in another ghastly act of *johar*. The young heir, **Udai Singh**, who had been whisked away to safety by his nursemaid Panna Dai, returned to Chittaurgarh at the age of thirteen. Aware of its vulnerability, he searched for a new site for his capital, and in 1559 founded **Udaipur** on the shore of Lake Pichola. This proved to be a prescient decision. **Akbar** laid siege to Chittaurgarh in 1567. His forces killed 30,000 of the fort's inhabitants, the women once again sacrificed themselves on a raging pyre, and many of the buildings within the fort were devastated. Although Chittaurgarh was ceded back to the Rajputs in 1616, the royal family never resettled there.

Arrival and information

Chittaurgarh's **railway station** is in the western corner of the city. From here it's about 2km to **Roadways bus stand** on the west bank of the Ghambiri, and a further 2km to the base of the fort.

For maps and information on accommodation and tours of the fort, head for the RTDC **tourist office** near the railway station on Station Rd (Mon–Sat 10am–6pm; ☎41089). The **GPO** (Mon–Sat 10am–6pm) is on Shri Gurukul Rd near *Pratap Palace Hotel*.

Tours of the fort can be made by rickshaw (Rs50), complete with jangly pop music and silky curtains, or tonga (Rs25); both can be rented through the tourist office, with a driver who will act as guide. However, tours tend to take in only the most famous monuments rather than the entire fort, which extends 5km long by 1km wide. To see the whole thing – which takes a good three hours – you'd do best to rent a **bike** from the shop beneath the *Hotel Sanvaria*, almost opposite the station. The initial climb is steep, but most of the roads on the plateau itself are flat.

Moving on, there are two express trains a day to Udaipur; the *Chetak Express* #9615 at 6.35am, and the *Garib Nawaz Express* #2915 at 8.05pm (3hr 30min); the passenger train takes rather longer and is still steam-hauled part of the way. In the opposite direction, the same two expresses go to Delhi (13hr) via Jaipur (7hr). There are also five daily trains to Indore (8–12hr) including an express and an overnight service.

The fort

The ascent to the fort, protected by massive bastions, begins at **Padan Pole** in the east of town and winds upwards through a further six gateways (*pols*). Close to the second *pol* stand the *chhatris* of **Kalla** and **Jaimal**, heroic fighters who lost their lives in the final sacking of 1567. The houses of the small community that still inhabits the fort are huddled together near the final gate, **Rama Pole**.

As you enter the fort, you pass the fifteenth-century **Shingara Chauri Mandir**, a highly adorned Jain temple dedicated to Shantinath, the sixteenth *tirthankara*. Ahead of this, the slowly deteriorating fifteenth-century **Palace of Rana Kumbha** – built by the ruler who presided over the period of Mewar's greatest prosperity – remains a classic example of Rajput architecture, and is immortalized as one of the scenes of *johar*. Nearby the modern **Fateh Prakash Palace**, built for the Maharana in the 1920s, is the site of a small, dimly lit **archeological museum**, filled with weapons (daily

10am–4.30pm; Rs2). Also in the palace compound is the **Kumbha Shyama temple**, crowned by a pyramidal roof and lofty tower, whose eighth-century sanctuary enshrines an image of Varaha, the boar incarnation of Vishnu. A smaller temple slightly to the south with a delicate curved tower, also constructed by Rana Kumbha, is dedicated to **Meerabai**, a Jodhpur princess-poet famed for her unrelenting devotion to Krishna.

The main road within the fort continues south to its focal point, **Jaya Stambh**, the soaring "tower of victory", erected by Kumbha to commemorate his 1437 victory over the Muslim Sultan Mehmud Khilji of Malwa. This magnificent sand-coloured tower, whose nine storeys rise 36m, took a decade to build; its walls are lavishly carved with mythological scenes and images from all Indian religions, including Arabic inscriptions in praise of Allah. You can climb the dark narrow stairs to the very summit for Rs0.50 (daily dawn–dusk; free on Fri): watch for low ceilings. Kumbha himself wrote a detailed study of the style and purpose of the Jaya Stambh.

A path leads from the tower through more fine but ruined temples to **Gaumukh Kund**, a large reservoir fed by an underground stream that trickles through carved mouths (*mukh*) of cows (*gau*). This quiet spot, away from the main road, commands superb views across the plains. Buildings further south include the **Kalika Mata Temple**, originally dedicated to **Surya** in the eighth century, but rededicated to the Mother Goddess afer renovations in 1568. Carvings on the outer wall include images of Surya, the guardians of the eight directions (such as Indra, Yama, Agni and Vayu), and friezes depicting the churning of the ocean by the gods and demons, a popular creation myth. An image of Surya guards the main entrance to the temple. **Padmini's Palace**, now rather dilapidated, stands opposite in the centre of a pool. From a building on the shore, you can look into the mirror that revealed the queen to Ala-ud-din-Khalji.

The road continues south past the deer park to the point used for hurling traitors to their deaths, and returns north along the eastern ridge. Several temples line the route, but the most impressive monument is **Kirti Stambh**. The inspiration for the tower of victory, this smaller "tower of fame" was built by Digambaras as a monument to the first *tirthankara* Adinath, whose unclad image is repeated throughout its six storeys.

Accommodation and eating

While Chittaurgarh's mid- and upper-range **hotels** cost more than elsewhere, places at the lower end of the price scale are pretty dingy; if you want to stay near the railway station, your best bet is the **retiring rooms**. As for **food**, the only alternative to the hotel-restaurants is the group of stalls around the bus station, where the usual spicy vegetable dishes vary in standard from day to day.

Laxmi Lodge, Fort Rd (☎2987). Grey rooms with bath, and hot water by the bucket. Unexciting food in restaurant. The *Meera Guest House* next door (☎2059) is similar, also with a restaurant. ①.

Natraj, City Rd, next to *Roadways* bus stand (☎41855). Dull but passable, and very cheap. ①–③.

Padmini Palace, Chanderiya Rd (☎41718). On the Ajmer road, just across the Bairach River. Peaceful place with views towards the fort, and a nice restaurant. ⑥.

Pratap Palace, Shri Gurukul Rd, opposite GPO (☎40099; fax 41042). Fresh, expansive and attractive. Running hot water; some bath tubs. Decent restaurant on site. ⑤.

RTDC Panna, Station Rd (☎41238). A short way from the station, with spacious, comfortable rooms, a cheap dorm, and a restaurant. ①–⑤.

Birla Dharamshala, in the fort, near the archeological museum (no phone). The only place to stay in the fort, basic but clean and incredibly cheap with home-cooked food (guests only). The only sign in English says "Drinking is strictly prohibited". ①.

From Chittaurgarh to Kota

The stretch of countryside east of Chittaurgarh towards Kota harbours some interesting small places that can be reached by public transport, but are more easily visited if you rent your own vehicle. A turning at the small lakeside town of **Bassi**, 25km out of Chittaurgarh, leads to **BIJAIPUR**, a quaint village whose elegant 200-year-old **palace** is now the idyllic *Hotel Castle Bijaypur* (☎01472/81222; ⑥) book through *Pratap Palace Hotel*, Chittaurgarh. The walled palace, all domed ceilings, alcoves, and antique furniture, is wonderful; little but birdsong and distant voices disturb the peace, and the food is excellent. Other brief detours from the main road lead to the walled town of **Begun** (served by local buses from Chittaurgarh and Bijolia), whose palace is now a hotel, and the fifteenth-century fort at **Mandalgarh**.

On the edge of a deep gorge that rumbles with the sound of vigorous waterfalls after the monsoon, the tiny village of **MENAL**, 90km east of Chittaurgarh harbours a group of well-preserved twelfth-century temples. The main compound is dominated by a temple to Shiva, surrounded by sculptures and friezes, some of them erotic, and fronted by a hornless but otherwise very impressive Nandi. Around the lip of the gorge is a second, but less well-preserved temple, also dedicated to Shiva in the form of the *lingam*. There's nowhere to stay in Menal, and not all buses stop there.

BIJOLIA, 20km east of Menal, was the centre of the Chauhan kingdom in the tenth century. It once had a hundred temples; the three that survive are beautifully fashioned in a style common in central India at the time. To get to them from the bus stand, head west towards Chittaurgarh for about 200m, take a left through the market and go straight on past the gate of the walled city and around the outside of the walls. The **Hajashwar temple**, nearest the wall, is the simplest, comprising just a single *shikhara*. The **Mahakaleshwar temple**, next to it, is larger and more elaborate, with a *yoni* rather than a *lingam* in the inner sanctum, but it is the **Undeshvara temple**, furthest from the wall, which really excels in its carving. From the main chamber, seven steps lead down to the small *lingam* in the inner sanctum. There are three basic **guest houses** in Bijolia, all with signs in Hindi only. The best is the *Mewara*, a pink building 50m west of the bus stand (☎01489/6743; ①); the ridiculously cheap *Kushal Raj* directly opposite the bus stand (no phone; ①) is also clean and comfortable.

The main road from Bijolia continues northeast to **Bundi**, while a smaller route heads directly to **Kota**, 70km east. Both cities originated as part of the thirteenth-century **Hadaoti** state, ruled by the Hadachauhan Rajputs from a hill-top stronghold at Bundi; Kota became capital of its own princely state in 1625. Bundi is much the more attractive as a destination, but Kota is the usual base for visits not only to Bundi but also the imposing tenth-century temples in **Baroli** and **Jhalrapatan** to the south.

Kota

KOTA, 230km south of Jaipur on a fertile plain fed by Rajasthan's largest river, the Chambal, is one of the state's dirtier and less stimulating cities, and foreign visitors are sufficiently unusual to attract stares in the streets. But it does have some beautiful gardens, and its old **palaces** house the best museum in all Rajasthan.

In the seventeenth century, when Kota was declared capital of a newly independent princely state by the Moghul Emperor Jahangir, it was ruled by Rao Madho Singh of the Hadachauhan Rajputs. Today it is one of Rajasthan's major commercial and industrial cities, with hydro, atomic and thermal power stations along the banks of the Chambal, and Asia's largest fertilizer plant. The nuclear plant of Rawat Bhata, protected by stringent security 60km southwest, is notorious for its impact on local villagers.

Greatly prized *saris* from the village of **Kaithoon**, 20km southeast of Kota, are sold in all the bazaars. Made of tightly woven cotton or silk, and often highlighted with golden thread, they are known here as *masooria* and elsewhere as *Kota doria sari*.

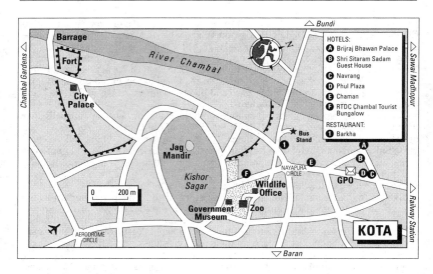

HOTELS:
A Brijraj Bhawan Palace
B Shri Sitaram Sadam Guest House
C Navrang
D Phul Plaza
E Chaman
F RTDC Chambal Tourist Bungalow

RESTAURANT:
1 Barkha

Arrival and information

Kota's **railway station** is in the north of town, a few kilometres from the central **bus stand**. As well as the usual auto-rickshaws, tempos run throughout town collecting as many passengers as possible for Rs2 per head. They get unbearably crowded towards noon. Private **cars** (with drivers) can be rented from *Hotel Navrang* (☎23294).

For information on local sites, accommodation and transport head for the **tourist office** (Mon–Sat 8am–6pm; ☎27695) in *Chambal Tourist Bungalow*, Kshar Bagh, not far from the bus stand. There, you can join a four-hour sightseeing tour (Sun–Thurs; 9am). Changing **money** is a tedious, time-consuming process. The *State Bank of India* on Aerodrome Circle will change travellers' cheques: other banks do not. The **post office** is on Station Rd (Mon–Sat 6am–6pm).

The City

The residential areas, bazaars, fort, City Palace and museum east of the Chambal face harsh buildings and factory smokestacks across the river. **Kishor Sagar**, an artificial lake built in 1346, gives picturesque relief. The red and white palace in its centre, **Jag Mandir**, was commissioned by Prince Dher Deh of Bundi in 1346 and can be visited only with permission from the Superintendent Engineer of Kota; ask at the tourist office. Gardens to the north of the tank are lush with viridescent mango trees, dahlias and palms, and crocodiles and gharial sun themselves in a shallow pond in the **Chambal Gardens** on the edge of the river a few kilometres south of the fort. Efforts are being made to increase their numbers after excessive hunting.

In the Brijvilas Palace on the northern edge of the lake, the **Government Museum** (daily except Fri 10am–5pm; Rs2) has a small collection of clothes, weapons and miniature paintings and a fascinating hand-drawn plan of Kota's manoeuvres during the Mutiny of 1857 that shows positions of defence and attack in minute detail. Behind the

The **telephone area code** for Kota is ☎0744.

museum is a pleasant park, containing a small **zoo** (daily except Tues, summer 8am–6.30pm, winter 8.30am–6pm; Rs2).

Kota's **fort**, raised above the flat bank of the Chambal 2km south of the bus stand, was built in 1264 by Rajkumar Jait Singh of Bundi. Construction of the **City Palace** and offices of state within the fortifications began in 1625, and continued sporadically until the early years of this century. Although the older fort ramparts are falling into disrepair, the palaces are still in excellent condition. Apartments in the heart of the palaces house the excellent **Maharao Madho Singh Museum** (daily except Fri 11am–5pm; Rs25; camera Rs10, video Rs25), approached through a brightly painted gateway flanked by elephants. Among a vast collection of carefully decorated weapons, the size and severity of which is out of this world, are spears, daggers, firearms, arrows in fine quivers and shields adorned with the solar symbol of the Hadachauhan Rajputs, large enough to protect an elephant. Solid silver artefacts and fading sepia photographs of viceroys, maharajas, polo teams and Queen Victoria record the extravagance of royalty, and there are some outstanding examples of *Kota Kamba*, miniatures from Kota's school of painting. A sorry array of stuffed animals in the basement is accompanied by photographs of proud hunters. The most spectacular apartment is **Raj Mahal**, which contains the royal throne. Its walls, decked with eighteenth-century paintings of the exploits of Krishna, hunting parties and maharajas, glow with mosaics of gold and glass, while the ceiling glitters with silver and mirrors.

Accommodation and eating

Kota's **hotels** cater mainly for passing business travellers, and the cheaper rest houses reflect the dustiness and neglect that prevails in the town. Inexpensive dives are grouped around the railway station and the areas known as Civil Lines and Nayapura close to the bus stand and main market. In addition to the hotel **restaurants** – the *Navrang* and *Chaman* both have reasonable dining rooms open to non-residents – try the cheap but good veg *Barkha Restaurant* on Nayapura Circle. Failing that, you'll have to settle for a roadside stall – there are a couple of decent ones outside *Hotel Navrang*.

Brijraj Bhawan Palace (☎450529; fax 450057). Home to the Maharaja of Kota; an oasis in beautiful gardens on the banks of the Chambal. Lovely rooms and suites, plus a restaurant for residents; full board available. ⑦–⑧.

Chaman, Nayapura (☎23377). Reasonable accommodation; the surface dirt makes it look worse than it is. Quieter rooms at the back, away from the road. ①.

RTDC Chambal Tourist Bungalow, Kshar Bagh (☎26527). Large place, with attractive gardens and uninspiring but spacious clean rooms. ④.

Meghraj, Ram Mandir Rd, first left off the main street coming from the railway station (☎441444; fax 441177). Average, cramped three-storey hotel, quite clean. Rooms with bathroom and TV. ②.

Navrang, Civil Lines (☎23294; fax 450044). Above average, big rooms with bath and hot water. ⑥.

Shri Sitaram Sadam Guest House, by the gate to the *Brijraj Bhawan Palace* (☎23715). Quiet, peaceful and old-fashioned, with large spotless a/c rooms and proper bathtubs. ⑦.

Phul Plaza, Civil Lines (☎22356). New hotel next door to the *Navrang*; not as stylish, but with a wider range of rooms. ④–⑦.

MOVING ON FROM KOTA

Kota is well-connected by **bus** to destinations in Rajasthan and inter-state. There are also six daily **trains** to Delhi and to Bombay, the best of which is the *Rajdhani Express* #2951/2952 for New Delhi and Bombay Central. Of services to Jaipur, the best is the *Bombay-Jaipur Superfast* #2995. There are even direct trains to Amritsar and Jammu Tawi. From Kota's **airport**, in the south of town, just about walking distance from the centre, and a lot closer than the station, there is just one flight a day to Jaipur and Delhi.

Bundi

The walled town of **BUNDI**, 37km north of Kota, lies in the north of the former Hadaoti state, shielded on the north, east and west by jagged outcrops of the Vindhya range. Visible only from the south and guarded by the tremendous **Taragarh** or "star fort" high in the north of town, Bundi made a perfect capital for the Hadachauhans, perched in their immense turreted **palace**, beneath the lofty walls of the fort. However, although settled in 1241, 25 years before Kota, Bundi never amounted to more than a modest market centre, and remains relatively untouched by modern developments.

From the **bus stand** in the south of town a short walk north through the central bazaar leads to the hillside **palace** at the base of the fort, built during the sixteenth and seventeenth centuries in authentic Rajput style, untainted by Moghul influence. A short steep path winds to the entrance, **Hathi Pole**, flanked by the elephants that are so common in the Hadaoti region. From the small courtyard within, steps lead to **Ratan Daulat**, the Diwan-i-Am or Hall of Public Audience, with its simple marble throne. These are closed to the public, but can be seen from the forecourt of the **Chittra Shala**, a courtyard enclosed by cloisters vivid with blue, green, turquoise and white. Guides are available to show you around. Many of the palace apartments are walled up, which helps to stoke rumours of a vast undiscovered treasure, said to be hidden far below in subterranean labyrinths. Views over Bundi from the palace take in the **Nawal Sagar** tank with its half-submerged temple. The best views of all are from the Taragarh, though it's a steep climb to see them.

A walk from the palace westwards through the walled bazaar and old gateways takes you to Rajasthan's most spectacular step-well, **Raniji-ki-Baori**, built in 1699 by Nathwati, wife of Rao Raja Singh. It lies deep beneath the surface of a small park, reached by a flight of steps punctuated by platforms and embellished pillars. Watch out for stones thrown from above by mischievous children.

East of town, a few kilometres by rickshaw, the beautiful **Sukh Niwas** – summer palace – on the northern shore of **Jait Sagar** tank cannot be visited. You can however take a pleasant stroll in the adjoining gardens, and continue to a collection of cenotaphs at the far end of the lake.

Practicalities

Buses run between Kota and Bundi (1hr) every halfhour, and cover the journey to Chittaurgarh (6hr) via Menal and Bijolia three times a day, two of them continuing to Udaipur. There are also hourly buses to Ajmer (165km; 6hr) and Jaipur (210km; 8hr). **Trains** call at the station south of town off the Kota road; currently there's only one a day in each direction, to Chittaurgarh in the morning and Agra in the evening.

The **tourist office** by the Circuit House just south of the bus stand (☎0747/22697), should be able to give you a glossy pamphlet with a map of Bundi. You can also pick up a **guide** here: one local who comes highly recommended for trips around the region is Billu, who lives almost opposite the water tower in Azad Park, and can be contacted through the *Hotel Bundi Tourist Palace*.

Although usually seen as a day-trip from Kota, Bundi is a delightful place to **stay**. Below the palace, the 150-year-old rooms at *Haveli Braj Bhushanjee* (☎0747/32322; fax 32142; ④–⑦) – the former home of the prime-ministers of Bundi – are comfortable and full of character; the hotel serves good meals and has a shop selling local crafts. You can also stay in the former stables of the palace, the *Royal Retreat* (☎0747/441193; ⑤), whose terrace is not a bad place to stop for a cup of tea or a snack on the way up (or down). The best budget option is the *Bundi Tourist Palace* (☎0747/32650; ①) facing Azad Park. Cheap **veg meals** are available at the *Diamond Hotel*, also near Azad Park.

South of Kota

The inviting smaller towns of the former Kota state merit a longer stay in the district. **Baroli**'s temples are still in use after more than a thousand years, while **Jhalrapatan**, near **Jhalawar**, abounds with the bustle of lively bazaars, and boasts some superbly ornate tenth-century temples.

Baroli

Local buses make the one-hour journey southwest from Kota to **BAROLI** (hourly; 40km), dropping passengers off a little short of the village beside a group of elaborate tenth-century temples on a small grassy patch surrounded by fields of wheat and castor-oil plants.

Though ruined, these temples are the finest to remain from the Pratihara period (*c.* 900 AD), and still shelter a resident priest – plus several hoopoes and jewel-coloured peacocks. The central, and best-preserved, **Ghateshvara temple** has a high pyramidal roof and a columned porch leading to the main sanctuary. Within the doorway, decorated with dancing Shivas, Vishnus and river goddesses, five natural stones serve as *lingams*. A particularly exquisite statue of Chamunda is set in the north wall. Geometric and foliate designs cover the ceiling of the porch whose shafts are bursting with busty maidens. The other temples are in a state of disrepair, many of their better statues having been removed to the Kota museum, but doorways and walled shrines still display some magnificent carving. It's best to visit the temples early, when the reddish stone glows in the morning light. Buses for the return journey can be hailed as they pass along the road.

Alternatively, the **Darrah Wildlife Sanctuary** 10km beyond Baroli covers more than 250 square kilometres of woodlands, peppered with ruins. Between February and May, visitors have a good chance of seeing the rare Indian wolf, leopard, sloth bear and chinkara. To visit, you'll need permission from the Wildlife Office by the zoo in Kota, who should also be able to tell you about availability of rooms at the *Forest Rest House* in the park (①).

Jhalawar and Jhalrapatan

Beyond the sanctuary, the southbound road arrives at **JHALAWAR**, 85km from Kota and accessible by local bus (hourly; 2hr 30min). The medium-sized **fort** in the centre of town now houses government offices, which grant permission to visit the **Janana Khas** (daily except Fri 10am–4.30pm), a room in the fort decorated with coloured glass, mirrors and bright paintings of Jhalawar's turbaned rulers. In the winter the fields are carpeted with opium poppies.

From Jhalawar, local buses or tempos continue 7km south to the colourful walled town of **JHALRAPATAN**. Once evocatively and appropriately known as the "city of temple bells", Jhalrapatan may no longer have 108 temples, but many do survive. The most elaborate is the large sandy eleventh-century **Surya temple** in the main street, with a wide entrance hall dissected by sculpted pillars and crowned with domed pavilions in a style common in central India. Open for worship in the morning and evening, at other times it's a hectic meeting place. Other notable central temples include **Shantinath Jain Mandir**, displaying typically expert Jain carving and, less typical, some unusual Jain painting, and **Dwarkadish temple** on the western edge of town, where images of Krishna attract devotees from all over India.

On the banks of the **River Chandrabagha**, 1km south, is a collection of **temples** dating from the seventh and eighth centuries. Time and battle have eroded many of the superb images lining their lintels and roofs, but resident priests still tend some of the temples by the small *ghats* on the river's edge. The simple beauty of the compound makes this among the most serene spots in Rajasthan – except during the festival of the **Karttika Purnima** (full moon Oct/Nov), when bathing in the Chandrabagha is considered especially auspicious.

CHAPTER THREE

UTTAR PRADESH

Although **UTTAR PRADESH** – "the Northern State", known as **UP** since the days of the United Provinces, under the Raj – is only the fourth largest state in India, it is the most varied and heavily populated, dominating the nation in culture, religion, language, and politics. Geographically, it has almost everything except the sea, stretching from the Himalayan snows in the northwest to the vast steamy Gangetic plains in the east. The **history** of UP is very much the history of India, and its temples and monuments – Buddhist, Hindu and Muslim – are among the most impressive in the country. It holds some of Hinduism's most venerated sites, including the source of the holy Ganga – the **River Ganges**, deep in the Himalayas. UP is also the heartland of **Hindi**, the principal indigenous language of India, and the official language of government.

Not far from Delhi, in the west of the state, **Agra**, home of the Taj Mahal, and deserted **Fatehpur Sikri**, stand as poignant reminders of the great Moghuls. Nearby, on the other hand, somehow sheltered from successive waves of Muslim conquest, the much-mythologized Hindu land of **Braj**, centered on **Mathura** and **Vrindavan**, was the childhood playground of the god Krishna.

Northeast of Delhi, on the borders with Nepal and Tibet, the mountains of **Garhwal** and **Kumaun** rise from the fertile sub-Himalayan plains. Every summer, pilgrims flock to the high temples known as the **Char Dham – Badrinath**, **Kedarnath**, **Yumnotri** and **Gangotri** – while trekkers and mountaineers explore newly de-restricted trails that lead to the glaciers of the inner Himalayas. Hill stations such as **Nainital** in Kumaun and **Mussoorie** in Garhwal retain their Victorian charm, their promenades thronging with

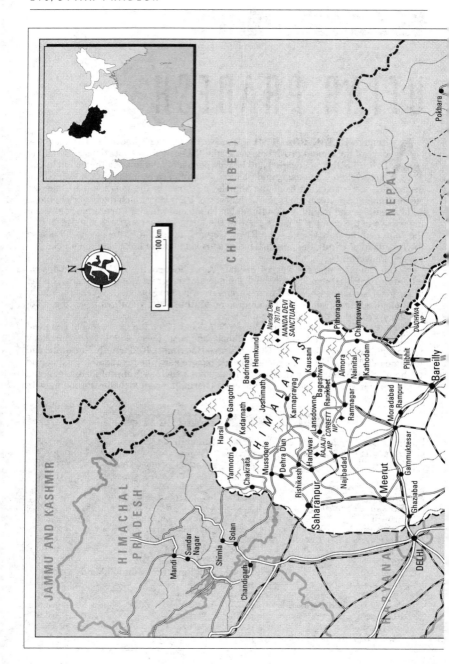

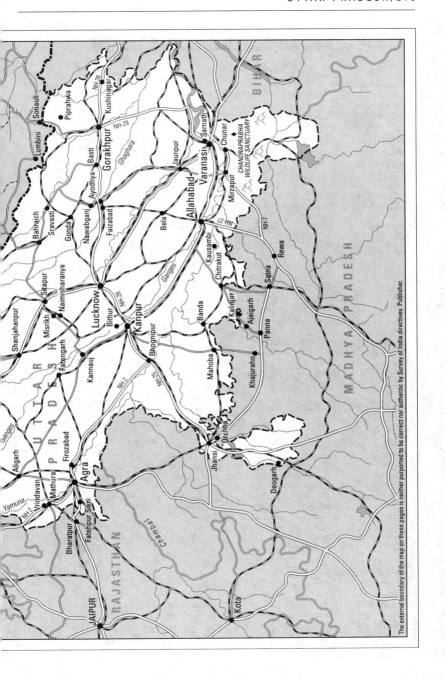

The external boundary of the map on these pages is neither purported to be correct nor authentic by Survey of India directives. Publisher.

UTTAR PRADESH TRAVEL DETAILS

	Trains		Buses		Flights	
	Frequency	Time	Frequency	Time	Frequency	Time
To and from AGRA						
Ahmedabad	1 weekly	27hr 30min				
Alwar	1 daily	4hr	hourly	3hr		
Bhopal	16–19 daily	5hr 30min–9hr				
Bhubaneshwar	1 daily	39hr				
Bombay	2 daily	23hr 30min–27hr			1 daily	6hr
Calcutta	1 daily	30hr			1 daily	6hr
Delhi	15 daily	2hr–4hr 15min	hourly	4–6hr	2 daily	40min
Gwalior	15–19 daily	1hr 20min–2hr	hourly	2hr 30min		
Haridwar			2 daily	10hr		
Indore	1 daily	14hr 25min				
Jaipur	3 daily	6hr	20 daily	5hr		
Jalgaon	3–4 daily	14hr 20min–19hr				
Jhansi	15–19 daily	2hr 15min–5hr				
Kanpur	4 daily	7hr	1 daily	10hr		
Khajuraho					2 daily	45min
Lucknow	3 daily	7hr–8hr 30min	4 daily	8hr 30min		
Madras	1–2 daily	34hr–42hr				
Mathura	12 daily	1hr 30min–2hr	hourly	1hr 30min		
Nainital	1 daily	11hr	1 daily	10hr		
Puri	1 daily	40hr				
Ujjain	2 daily	14hr 30min–17hr 30min				
Varanasi	2 daily	16hr			2 daily	2hr
To and from VARANASI						
Allahabad	5–8 daily	2hr 30min–4hr	hourly	2hr 30min		
Ahmedabad	1 daily	43hr				
Bhubaneshwar	Tues, Fri & Sun	22hr 30min			6 weekly	1hr 15min
Bombay	4 daily	30hr–33hr			1–3 daily	3hr 20min–9hr
Calcutta	5–8 daily	11hr–18hr			1–2 daily	2hr
Dehra Dun	2 daily	20hr				
Delhi	18 daily	14–16hr 30min			2 daily	1hr 15min–3hr
Gaya & Bodhgaya	5–8 daily	3hr 40min–5hr	6 daily	6hr		
Gorakhpur	4 daily	5–10hr	8–12 daily	6hr		
Gwalior	1 daily	19hr 20min				
Haridwar	2 daily	19hr				
Jabalpur	7 daily	8hr 30min–11hr				
Jalgaon	4 daily	18hr–22hr 25min				
Jhansi	2 daily	17–19hr				
Kanpur	5–6 daily	8–9hr	2 daily	10hr		
Kathmandu					1 daily	1hr 10min
Khajuraho					1 daily	45min
Lucknow	8 daily	5–7hr	4 daily	8hr	3 weekly	45min
Madras	Mon, Wed & Sat	36hr–42hr				
New Jalpaiguri	4 daily	11hr 30min–17hr				
Patna	1 daily	5hr	4 daily	6hr	3 weekly	45min
Puri	Tues, Fri & Sun	24hr 30min				
Ujjain	1 daily	33hr 25min				
To and from Haridwar						
Bombay	1 daily	40hr				
Calcutta	1 daily	33hr				
Dehra Dun	8 daily	2hr	hourly	1hr 15min		
Delhi	4 daily	4hr 15min–8hr	4–6 daily	5–6hr		
Nainital			2 daily	9hr		
Rishikesh	2 daily	30min	20 daily	30min		

	Trains		Buses		Flights	
	Frequency	Time	Frequency	Time	Frequency	Time
To and from Jhansi						
Bombay	4 daily	19–23hr				
Calcutta	4 weekly	23hr 25min				
Delhi	16–20 daily	4hr 25min–9hr				
Goa	1 daily	35hr				
Indore	1 daily	10hr 45min				
Khajuraho			4 daily	7hr–8hr		
Madras	5 daily	28–38hr				
Orchha	3 daily	15min	hourly	30min		
Ujjain	2–3 daily	8–14hr				
To and from Lucknow						
Bombay	2 daily	26hr 30min–30hr			1–2 daily	2hr–3hr 30min
Calcutta	5–6 daily	21hr 45min–28hr			9 weekly	2hr 20min–3hr 40min
Dehra Dun	2 daily	14–18hr				
Delhi	17 daily	6hr 30min–9hr 45min	2 daily	9hr	2–4 daily	1hr
Gorakhpur	13 daily	5hr	5 daily	6hr		
Haridwar	2 daily	10hr–12hr	4 daily	10hr		
Kanpur	15 daily	1hr	hourly	1hr 15min		
Kulu					1 daily	3hr 15min
Nainital	1 daily	9hr 15min	4 daily	10hr		
Patna	3 daily	9hr				3 weekly
1hr						
Sonauli (for Nepal)			8 daily	10–12hr		
To and from Nainital						
Almora			4 daily	2hr 30min		
Dehra Dun			1 daily	10hr 30min		
Delhi	1 daily	10hr	4 daily	8hr		
Kausani			4 daily	5hr		
Ramnagar			4 daily	3hr 30min		
Ranikhet			4 daily	3hr		

Note that no individual route appears more than once in this chart. For any specific journey, check against where you want to get to as well as where you're coming from.

For details of connections to **Delhi** – especially services between Delhi and the UP Hills – see p.248 onwards. Most important trains to Varanasi stop at Moghul Sarai requiring a change of trains or a connecting bus or taxi (see p.337). Trains to Nainital terminate at Kathgodam or Lalkuan (see p.286).

refugees from the heat of the plains. At **Haridwar**, not far from the tiger-inhabited forests of **Corbett National Park**, the Ganges thunders out from the foothills on its long journey to the sea. Nearby **Rishikesh** is familiar from one of the classic East-meets-West images of the 1960s; it was where the Beatles came to stay with the Maharishi.

Central UP, and especially **Lucknow**, the state capital, is redolent with memories of the lavish and ultimately decadent last days of the Muslim rule, when the Kingdom of Avadh faded away before the advance of the British imperialists in the nineteenth century. The scars of the First War of Independence – the "Mutiny", a despairing reaction to the British usurpation of power – have in places yet to heal. To the east, **Allahabad** is the site of one of the world's largest religious fairs, when millions congregate at the confluence of the Ganges and the Yamuna to mark the auspicious occasion of **Kumbh Mela**. Along the southern borders of the state, the rugged Vindhya Mountains mark the end of the Deccan plateau. Once the domain of the Chandela Rajputs, the belt known as **Bundelkhand** harbours forgotten fortresses such as gigantic **Kalinjar**; the fort at **Jhansi** remains a symbol of the struggle for Independence.

The Ganges meanders across the vast plains of **Eastern UP** to the holiest Hindu city of all – the sacred *tirtha* (crossing-place) of **Varanasi**, where death transports the soul to final liberation. Even before Hinduism, this land was sacred; the Buddha himself, and Mahavira, the founder of Jainism, frequented Varanasi, and the whole state, from Mathura to **Sarnath**, on the outskirts of Varanasi, and beyond to the great schools of learning in Bihar, was long under the influence of Buddhism.

Although UP was once a thriving centre of Islamic jurisprudence and culture, many Muslims departed during the painful years after Independence, and the Muslim population is now just 16 percent. In recent years, Gangetic UP, known derisively elsewhere as the "cow belt", has been plagued by caste-politics and is dominated by the right-wing Hindu BJP, who for a brief period controlled its government. The state acquired an unfortunate reputation as the focus of bitter communal tensions, most notoriously in the destruction of the Babri Masjid mosque in **Ayodhya** in 1992. Since then, however, a series of coalition governments have come to power supported by the lower caste and Muslim votes, and so BJP extremism has been checked.

With an efficient if basic state bus system and an excellent railway network, **travelling around** the state is generally straightforward (exception for Bundelkhand in the south). The main road from Delhi to Kathmandu passes through Gorakhpur, while Garhwal and Kumaun, in the Himalayas, are also well-connected to the capital, and have local buses to penetrate the interior. The major tourist cities, **Agra** and **Varanasi**, have been coping with visitors and pilgrims for centuries; and today have good transport connections and facilities the traveller could require.

WESTERN UP

Western Uttar Pradesh, on the fringes of Delhi, and serving as the gateway to the heartland of the sub-continent, has always been close to the centre of power in India. Once the Moghul capital, **Agra** is renowned for the most stunning mausoleum in the world – the **Taj Mahal** – as well as the stupendous battlements of the **Agra Fort**. Not far away, the beautiful sandstone pavilions of **Fatehpur Sikri**, built by the Moghul emperor Akbar and abandoned after only fifteen years, remain perfectly preserved in the dry desert-like air.

The earliest records of the area date back 2500 years, when Gautama Buddha visited the ancient city of **Mathura**, whose strategic position at the junction of several major trade routes had already earned it the prosperity that was to attract numerous adventurers and conquerors. Later, Mathura was incorporated at the centre of the Hindu mythological landscape of **Braj**, associated with the childhood of Krishna.

Immediately north and east of Delhi, an industrial belt of commercial and administrative towns on busy road and railway networks includes **Meerut**, which is only noteworthy as the place where the "Mutiny" of 1857 began.

Agra

The river Yamuna flows through it for five Kos, and on either bank are delightful villas and pleasant stretches of meadows. Filled with people from every country, Agra is the crossroads of the world. His majesty [Akbar] has built a fort of red sandstone, the like of which travellers have never recorded.

Court historian and chronicler, early eighteenth century

The splendour of **AGRA** – capital of all India under the Moghuls – remains undiminished, from the massive fort to the magnificent **Taj Mahal**. Along with Delhi, 204km

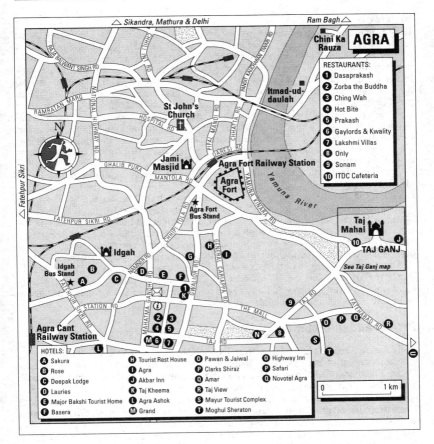

Sikandra, Mathura & Delhi · Ram Bagh

AGRA

Chini Ka Rauza

RESTAURANTS:
1. Dasaprakash
2. Zorba the Buddha
3. Ching Wah
4. Hot Bite
5. Prakash
6. Gaylords & Kwality
7. Lakshmi Villas
8. Only
9. Sonam
10. ITDC Cafeteria

Itmad-ud-daulah

St John's Church

Jami Masjid

Agra Fort Railway Station

Agra Fort

Yamuna River

Agra Fort Bus Stand

Idgah

Idgah Bus Stand

Taj Mahal

TAJ GANJ

See Taj Ganj map

Agra Cant Railway Station

THE MALL

TAJ RD

0 · 1 km

HOTELS:
- A Sakura
- B Rose
- C Deepak Lodge
- D Lauries
- E Major Bakshi Tourist Home
- F Basera
- H Tourist Rest House
- I Agra
- J Akbar Inn
- K Taj Kheema
- L Agra Ashok
- M Grand
- O Pawan & Jaiwal
- P Clarks Shiraz
- Q Amar
- R Taj View
- S Mayur Tourist Complex
- T Moghul Sheraton
- U Highway Inn
- P Safari
- Q Novotel Agra

northwest, and Jaipur in Rajasthan, Agra is the third apex of the "golden triangle", India's most popular tourist itinerary. It fully merits that status; the Taj effortlessly transcends all the frippery and commercialism that surrounds it, and continues to have a fresh and immediate impact on all who see it.

Most of Agra is on the west bank of the **River Yamuna**, with the fort and the Taj at its nucleus. The city radiates outwards from here, to the **Taj Ganj** area, directly south of the Taj, which has the most hotels and amenities, and southwest to the commercial centre around the **Sadar Bazaar** and **Cantonment** areas. Of its monuments, **Agra Fort** provides an insight into the private lives of the Moghuls, its high ramparts crowded with exquisite pavilions, while the beautifully inlaid marble tomb of **Itmad-ud-daulah**, across the river, offers a refreshing tranquillity. **Akbar's Mausoleum** at Sikandra, 10km northwest, and the eerie abandoned city of **Fatehpur Sikri**, 32km west, are further unforgettable echoes of a grand and eloquent past. Although it's possible to see Agra in a day trip from Delhi, the Taj alone deserves so much more; a fleeting visit would miss the subtleties of its many moods, as the light changes from sunrise to sunset.

History

Little is known of the pre-Muslim history of Agra; one of the earliest chronicles, dated to the Afghan invasion under Ibrahim Ghaznavi in 1080 AD, describes a robust fort occupying a chain of hills, with a flourishing city strategically placed at the crossroads between the north and the centre of India. However, Agra remained a minor administrative centre until 1504, when the Sultan of Delhi, **Sikander Lodi**, moved his capital here, to keep a check on the warring factions of his empire. The ruins of the Lodis' great city can still be seen on the eastern bank of the Yamuna. After defeating the last Lodi Sultan, Ibrahim Lodi, at Panipat in 1526, **Babur**, the founder of the Moghul empire, sent ahead his son **Humayun** to capture Agra. In gratitude at their benevolent treatment at his hands, the family of the Raja of Gwalior rewarded the Moghul with jewellery and precious stones – among them the legendary **Kohinoor Diamond**, now among the crown jewels of England.

Agra's greatest days arrived during the reign of Humayun's son, **Akbar the Great** (1556–1605), with the construction of Agra Fort. The city maintained its position as the capital of the empire for over a century; even when **Shah Jahan**, Jahangir's son and successor, built a new city in Delhi, his heart remained in Agra. He pulled down many of the earlier red sandstone structures in the fort, replacing them with his hallmark – exquisite marble buildings. Although the empire flourished under his heir Aurangzeb (1658–1707), his intolerance towards non-Muslims stirred a hornets' nest. Agra was occupied successively by the Jats, the Marathas, and eventually the British.

After the uprising in 1857, the city lost the headquarters of the government of North-Western Provinces and the High Court to Allahabad. Agra began to decline, but its medieval treasures ensured its survival and today, the city is once again prospering, as an industrial and commercial centre, as well as a tourist destination.

Arrival and information

Daily *Indian Airlines* flights arrive from Delhi, Khajuraho and Varanasi at the **airport**, 16km northwest of the city; daily *Moriluft* flights link Agra with Bombay as well as Delhi, Khajuraho and Varanasi. Accommodation can be booked on arrival, and taxis wait in line to carry passengers into town (Rs80–100).

Agra has six **railway stations**. The most important station and most convenient place to alight is **Agra Cantt Station**, in the southwest, serving Delhi, Gwalior, Jhansi and points south, which has a tourist information counter and is near most hotels. Trains from Rajasthan pull in close to the fort at **Agra Fort Station**, further from the main hub of hotels. Don't be persuaded to get off at Agra City Station, an expensive rickshaw ride away from town.

To get to a hotel, use the prepaid auto-rickshaw booth at Agra Cantt Station (Rs25–40) or flag down one of the rickshaws (Rs15–20), auto-rickshaws or taxis (up to Rs60) that wait outside the station; avoid the drivers who dash onto the platform to find passengers. They invariably demand an inflated price and can get quite aggressive. Most rickshaw and auto drivers will try and gain commission by taking you to a hotel and may even tell you that the hotel of your choice is closed.

Buses usually stop at **Idgah bus stand** close to Agra Cantt Station, though services from Mathura arrive at **Agra Fort bus stand**, just west of the fort. Some buses from Delhi stop outside the fort gate, where you'll have no trouble finding a rickshaw.

Information

Agra has two **tourist offices**, one run by the Government of India, at 191 The Mall (Mon–Fri 9am–5.30pm, Sat 9am–1pm; ☎363377), and one run by UPTDC, close to the *Clarks Shiraz*, at 64 Taj Rd (same hours; ☎360517); there is also an information booth

The telephone **area code** for Agra is ☎0562.

at the Cantt station. The Government of India office is better organized and provides information about other destinations, though both supply information on hotels and local sights, and details of **tours** that start and end at Agra Cantt railway station.

For information on **festivals** in Agra, contact either one of the tourist offices or phone UPT ☎360517. UP Tourism organizes an annual arts and crafts fair each February, the **Taj Mahotsava** held at Shilpgram near the East Gate, with cultural performances including dance and music. Another similar festival, the **Shardotsav**, held in early October and staged at various historic locations such as the Diwan-i-am in Agra Fort and at Fatehpur Sikri. The festival features some of the country's best dancers and musicians and incorporates a programme of yoga classes.

Banks, including the *State Bank of India, Andhra*, the *Central Bank of India* (*Taj Ganj*) and the *Allahabad* (in the *Hotel Clarks Shiraz*), congregate on Taj Rd; money transfers can also be arranged through *Sita World Travel*, also on Taj Rd (☎363013). The main **post office** is on the Mall, near the Government of India Tourist Office; there is another in the Taj Mahal complex and another in Taj Ganj. Poste restante at the main post office is inefficient and you may be better off using the Government of India tourist office's address, on the Mall.

City transport

Plans are being considered to create a two-kilometre pollution-free exclusion zone around the Taj banning the petrol and diesel-powered vehicles which choke the city and spoil its architecture. The only pollution-controlling measure currently in operation is an **electric bus** for tourists, connecting the fort to the Taj (Rs1). Although becoming fairly scarce, **tongas**, horse-drawn carriages, may also be re-introduced as part of the pollution control scheme, though the sight of skinny near-lame horses, often covered in open sores, will put most people off. Another alternative is the dwindling **cycle rickshaw** which provides a means of transport pedalling slowly and noiselessly from place to place. Cycle rickshaw drivers often offer their services for day tours, and they'll more often than not have a book full of encouraging comments from delighted tourists. If you want to **walk**, expect an unending stream of offers from cycle and auto-rickshaw *wallahs*. Early-morning rides to the Taj should be booked the night before.

Auto-rickshaws provide a faster, and more expensive, alternative for short trips, and can be good value if rented for the day. Although you may have to bargain, prices, including waiting time, are still reasonable (upwards of Rs60), but rise sharply if you want to visit Akbar's tomb and other monuments on the outskirts of the city. **Taxis** are less popular, though handy for longer trips to the airport or Fatehpur Sikri. Expensive hotels have their own fleet of taxis, and there are taxi ranks at the stations and airport.

Whichever form of transport you choose, you'll be expected to **bargain**. Agra sees so many "fresh" tourists that the drivers will always quote high prices – if you object, the price falls. Also, take note that many rickshaw and taxi drivers will stop at jewellers, craft shops and the like to earn extra commission. After dark, rickshaw *wallahs* converge in the centre of town, so if you want to get out of Taj Ganj after an evening meal, you may be faced with a long walk before you find a rickshaw.

To save the hassle of taking public transport, you could rent a **bicycle**, and do everything at your own pace. Try the rental shop near *Taj View Hotel* or others scattered around Taj Ganj, where charges are Rs3 per hour, and no more than Rs16 per day. **Car rental** is also an option, though cars are more useful for driving out of Agra than for getting around town. Chauffeur-driven cars can be rented from the reliable *Travel*

Corporation of India, whose office is in *Hotel Clarks Shiraz* (☎361122) and from *Pleasure Tours*, 507 The Mall (☎364103). Self-drive cars are available from *Budget Rent a Car*, at *Mansingh Hotel* on Fatehbad Rd (☎361771), but they're expensive.

Tours

Agra's surprising lack of organized **tours** of the city is more than made up for by the cycle and auto-rickshaws who offer their services for a full day. For a more comfortable sightseeing jaunt, rent a taxi from a high-class hotel: around Rs350–550 for a full day.

There is currently just one official tour run by *UPT* (half day Rs80; full day Rs100), which is designed to coincide with the main train connections to and from Delhi. Pickup starts at 9.15am at the Government of India tourist office on The Mall, with the second stop at Agra Cantt Railway Station at 10.15am. The tour then proceeds to Fatehpur Sikri before returning to *Taj Kheema* for lunch (not included in the price) at 2pm; the afternoon tour takes in the Taj Mahal and Agra Fort and finishes around 6pm back at the station to connect with the *Taj Express* to Delhi. Though useful for those with limited time, the tour is rather rushed and doesn't cover Akbar's mausoleum and the tomb of Itmad-ud-Daulah. Similar itineraries are offered on demand at higher prices by other agents, such as *Ashok Tours and Travels* at *Agra Ashok*, The Mall (☎361223), and *Mercury Travels* (☎360282) and *Travel Corporation of India* (☎361122), both at *Clarks Shiraz*.

The Town

Agra city centres on the **old town**, a sprawling web of alleys, bazaars, mosques and cramped houses, but its focal point is the mighty **fort** immediately to the south, rising above the River Yamuna at the sharp bend where it changes its course to flow past the **Taj Mahal**, 2km east. Although Agra stretches for ten kilometres north to south, most tourists concentrate their attention on the district south of the fort, where hotels, restaurants and tourist amenities are conveniently located for the main sights.

If you want to walk between the fort and the Taj, take the path that runs through **Shahjahan park**, with its lofty trees and well-tended flower beds.

The Taj Mahal

Daily, dawn–dusk. Admission Rs10.50 8am–5pm, Rs100 before 8am and after 5pm. Free on Friday. No tripods.

Described by the Indian classical poet Tagore as a "tear on the face of eternity", the **Taj Mahal** is undoubtedly the zenith of Moghul architecture and quite simply one of the world's most marvellous buildings. Volumes have been written on its perfection, and its image adorns countless glossy brochures and guide books; nonetheless, the reality never fails to overwhelm all who see it, and few words can do it justice.

The glory of the monument is strangely undiminished by the crowds of tourists who visit each day, as small and insignificant as ants in the face of this immense and captivating monument. That said, the Taj is at its most alluring in the relative quiet of early morning, shrouded in mists and bathed with a soft red glow. As its vast marble surfaces fall into shadow or reflect the sun, its colour changes, from soft grey and yellow to pearly cream and dazzling white; it's well worth visiting at different times. This play of light is an important decorative device, symbolically implying the presence of Allah, who is never represented in anthropomorphic form.

There's no time limit on visits to the Taj, and some people spend most of the day here, sitting, reading, dozing or picnicking in the beautifully kept gardens. Hawkers and salesmen are not allowed in, and official guides are not available on site, but can usually be provided by hotels, and always accompany organized tours. The ticket office, just outside the western gate, is rarely blocked by long queues, except between 4 and

5pm before the admission fee increases; bring the right amount of money as the ticket booth attendants rarely have change and tend to pocket the difference.

Overlooking the River Yamuna, and visible from the fort in the west, the Taj Mahal stands at the northern end of vast gardens enclosed by walls. Though its layout follows a distinctly Islamic theme, representing Paradise, it is above all a monument to romantic love. **Shah Jahan** built the Taj to enshrine the body of his favourite wife, Arjumand Bann Begum, better known as Mumtaz Mahal ("Elect of the Palace"), who died shortly after giving birth to her fourteenth child, in 1631. The Shah was devastated by her death, and set out to create an unsurpassed, eternal monument to her memory. Of all the Moghuls, only Shah Jahan, who had been designing palaces and forts since the age of sixteen, could have come up with such a magnificent design. The name of the chief architect is unknown, but Amanat Khan, who had previously worked on Akbar's tomb, was responsible for the calligraphic inscriptions that adorn the gateways, mosque and tomb. Construction by a workforce of some 20,000 men from all over Asia commenced in 1632, and the tomb was completed in 1653. Marble was brought from Makrana, near Jodhpur, in Rajasthan, and precious stones for decoration – onyx, amethyst, malachite, lapis lazuli, turquoise, jade, crystal, coral and mother-of-pearl – were carried to Agra from Persia, Russia, Afghanistan, Tibet, China and the Indian Ocean.

The story is given an exquisite poignancy by the fate of Shah Jahan himself, who became a tragic and inconsolable figure. Eventually, his devout and austere son Aurangzeb seized power, and Shah Jahan was interned in Agra Fort, where he lived out his final years gazing wistfully at the Taj Mahal in the distance. He died there in January 1666, with his daughter, Jahanara Begum, at his side; his body was carried across the river to lie alongside his beloved wife in his peerless mausoleum.

The walled complex is approached from the south through a red sandstone forecourt, Chowk-i Jilo Khana, whose wide paths, flanked by arched kiosks, run to high gates in the east and west. The original entrance, a massive arched gateway topped with delicate domes and adorned with Koranic verses, stands at the northern edge of Chowk-i Jilo Khana, directly aligned with the Taj, but shielding it from the view of those who wait outside. Today's entrance, complete with security checks, is through a narrow archway in the southern wall to the right of the gate.

Once beyond the southern wall, you'll see the mighty marble tomb at the end of superb gardens designed in the *charbagh* style so fashionable among Moghul, Arabic and Persian architects. Dissected into four quadrants by waterways, they evoke the Islamic image of the Gardens of Paradise, where rivers flow with water, milk, wine and honey. The "rivers" converge at a marble tank in the centre that corresponds to *al-Kawthar*, the celestial pool of abundance mentioned in the Koran. Today only the watercourse running from north to south is full, and its precise, glassy reflection of the Taj is a favourite photographic image. Views from the paths lining the east-west canal, lined with lofty trees, ferns and deep red and pink flowers, are equally sublime. To the west of the tomb is a domed red-sandstone mosque, and to the east a replica (*jawab*), probably built to house visitors, and necessary to achieve perfect symmetry.

Essentially square in shape, with peaked arches cut into its sides, the Taj Mahal surmounts a square marble platform marked at each corner by a high minaret. Topped with a huge central dome, it rises for over 55m, its height accentuated by a crowning brass spire, itself almost 17m high. Steps lead to the platform, and visitors must remove their shoes before climbing to the tomb. The marble floor can be icy cool in the morning, but at midday it gets extremely hot – you may want to wear socks, or rent a cloth foot-cover from the shoe attendants. On approach, the tomb looms ever larger and grander, but not until you are close do you appreciate both its awesome magnitude and the extraordinarily fine detail of relief carving, highlighted by floral patterns of precious stones. Carved vases of flowers including roses, tulips and narcissi, rise subtly out of the marble base, a pattern repeated more colourfully and inlaid with precious stones around the four great arched recesses (*pishtaqs*) on each side. Arabic verses praising the glory of Paradise fringe the archways, proportioned exactly so that each letter appears to be the same size when viewed from the ground.

The south face of the tomb is the main entrance to the interior: a high, echoing octagonal chamber flushed with pallid light reflected by yellowing marble surfaces. A marble screen, cut so finely that it seems almost translucent, and decorated with precious stones, scatters dappled light over the cenotaph of Mumtaz Mahal in the centre of the tomb, and that of Shah Jahan next to it. Inlaid stones on the marble tombs are the finest in Agra; attendants gladly illuminate the decorations with torches. No pains were spared in perfecting the inlay work – each petal or leaf may comprise up to sixty separate stone fragments. Ninety-nine names of Allah adorn the top of Mumtaz's tomb, and set into Shah Jahan's is a pen box, the hallmark of a male ruler. These cenotaphs, in accordance with Moghul tradition, are only representations of the real coffins, which lie in the same positions in an unadorned and humid crypt below that's heavy with the scent of heady incense and rose petals. Have a few coins ready for a respectful donation to an attendant priest who will lay the offering on the graves.

If you're spending a full day at the Taj and want a break from the sun, make a small detour to the **museum** (daily 10am–5pm) in the western wall of the enclosure. The interior contains exquisite miniatures, two marble pillars believed to have come from the fort, and portraits of Moghul rulers including Shah Jahan and Mumtaz Mahal. Further into the building a gallery shelters architectural drawings of the Taj Mahal, a display of elaborate porcelains, seventeenth-century coins and examples of stone inlay work, though you'll more than likely have seen enough in the Taj.

POLLUTION THREATENING THE TAJ MAHAL

Although the Taj Mahal may appear to the untrained eye almost as perfect as the day it was completed, the marble is undeniably sullen and yellow in parts, and empty casings here and there betray lost precious stones. These are the early effects of the threat posed by environmental **pollution** from traffic and industry, and the thousands of tourists who visit each day of the year. While marble is all but impervious to the onslaught of wind and rain that erodes softer sandstone, it has no natural defence against the sulphur dioxide that lingers in a dusty haze and shrouds the monument; sometimes the smog is so dense that the tomb cannot be seen from the fort. Sulphur dioxide mixes with atmospheric moisture and settles as sulphuric acid on the surface of the tomb, making the smooth white marble yellow and flaky, and forming a subtle fungus that experts have named **"marble cancer"**.

The main sources of pollution are the 1700 **factories** in and around Agra, and the continuous flow of vehicles along the national highways that skirt the city. Chemical effluents belched out of factory chimneys are well beyond safety limits laid down by environmental committees. Despite laws demanding the installation of pollution-control devices, and an exclusion zone marking 10,400 square kilometres around the Taj Mahal that should be free of any new industrial plants, pollutants in the atmosphere have continued to rise, and new factories have been set up illegally. In September 1993, the Supreme Court finally took action and ordered 212 plants to shut down until emissions fell to legal limits.

Cleaning work on the Taj Mahal rectifies the problem to some extent, but the chemicals used will themselves eventually affect the marble. Already attendants shine their torches on repaired sections of marble to demonstrate that they have lost their translucency. The doubtful methods of the Archaeological Survey of India, such as scrubbing with toothbrushes, may prove disastrous in the long term. Hopes for proper care of the Taj Mahal have been raised since the government turned its attention to the plight of India's greatest monument, and entry fees have been increased in an attempt to regulate the flow of tourists, but the fate of the Taj Mahal hangs in the balance.

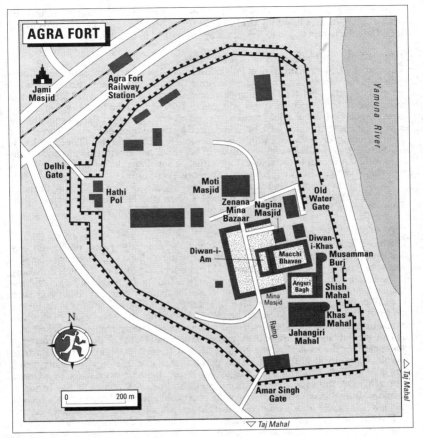

AGRA FORT

Jami Masjid

Agra Fort Railway Station

Yamuna River

Delhi Gate

Hathi Pol

Moti Masjid

Zenana Mina Bazaar

Nagina Masjid

Old Water Gate

Diwan-i-Am

Macchi Bhavan

Diwan-i-Khas

Musamman Burj

Anguri Bagh

Shish Mahal

Mina Masjid

Ramp

Khas Mahal

Jahangiri Mahal

N

0   200 m

Amar Singh Gate

▷ Taj Mahal

▽ Taj Mahal

Agra Fort

Daily 7am–6pm. Admission Rs10.50. Free on Friday.

The high red-sandstone ramparts of **Agra Fort**, stretching for almost 2.5km, dominate a bend in the River Yamuna, 1.6km northwest of the Taj Mahal. Akbar laid the foundations of this majestic citadel, built between 1565 and 1573 in the form of a half moon, on the remains of earlier Rajput and Suri fortifications. Agra Fort developed as the seat and stronghold of the Moghul empire for successive generations: Akbar constructed the walls and gates, his grandson, Shah Jahan, had most of the principal buildings erected, and Aurangzeb, the last great emperor, was responsible for the ramparts.

The curved bastions of the sandstone ramparts are interrupted by massive gates, of which only the **Amar Singh Gate** is open to the public. Ornamented with glazed tiles, and with impressive double walls and a forecourt, this gate was used by the victorious General Lake when he entered the fort in 1803. The original and grandest entrance was through the western **Delhi Gate**, leading to the inner portal, **Hathi Pol** or "Elephant Gate", now flanked by two red sandstone towers faced in marble, but once guarded by colossal stone elephants with riders – destroyed by Aurangzeb in 1668.

Access to much of the fort is restricted, so masterpieces of Moghul architecture such as Shah Jahan's beautiful **Moti Masjid** (Pearl Mosque) are out of bounds to visitors. Only those parts open to the public are described in detail below.

DIWAN-I-AM AND THE GREAT COURTYARD

The graceful **Diwan-i-Am** (Hall of Public Audience), open on three sides, stands immediately to the east as you approach from Amar Singh Gate. Replacing an earlier wooden structure, the sandstone building was constructed by Shah Jahan in 1628. After use as an arsenal by the British, it was restored in 1876 by Sir John Strachey. Three rows of white polished stucco pillars topped by peacock arches support the flat roof; the elegance of the setting would have been enhanced by the addition of brocade, carpets and satin canopies for audiences with the emperor. The ornate throne alcove is inlaid in marble decorated with flowers and foliage in bas-relief, and connects to the royal chambers within. Adjacent to the alcove, the Baithak, a small marble block, is where ministers would sit to deliver their petitions and receive commands.

An incongruous intrusion in the centre of the great courtyard is a gothic Christian tomb marking the **grave of John Russel Colvin**, the Lieutenant-Governor of the North-Western Provinces who died here during the rebellion of 1857.

THE ROYAL PAVILIONS

Clustered around a high terrace overlooking the river, the **royal pavilions** were designed to catch the cool breeze wafting across the Yamuna – and for ease of access to a water supply. The **Macchi Bhavan** (Fish Palace), approached through the alcove in the Diwan-i-Am, has suffered through the ages. During the period of Jat control, the Maharaja of Bharatpur removed some of its marble fixtures to his palace in Deeg; later, Lord William Bentinck auctioned off much of the original mosaic and fretwork, including parts of the **Hammam-i-Shahi**, the Royal Bath. The palace was once strewn with fountains and flower beds, interspersed with tanks and water channels stocked with fish for the angling pleasure of the emperor and courtiers. In the northwest corner of the enclosure, the exquisite little **Nagina Masjid** (Gem Mosque) is entirely made of marble. Capped with three domes and approached from a marble-paved courtyard, it was built by Shah Jahan for the ladies of the *zenana*. Below it, overlooked by a beautiful marble balcony with carved lattice screens and peacock arches, is the **Inner** or **Zenana Mina Bazaar,** where ladies of the court could browse through goods such as silk, jewellery and brocade offered by merchants, without being seen themselves.

The **Chitor Gate**, salvaged by Akbar as a trophy from the horrific sacking of the Rajput stronghold of Chitor and installed in 1568, leads to the **Mandir Raja Ratan**, erected in 1768 during the Jat occupation of the fort. Past this is the Hall of Private Audience, the **Diwan-i-Khas**, where the emperor would receive kings, dignitaries and ambassadors. Built in 1635, the building was badly damaged when it came under bombardment by General Lake in 1803, but the hall – with its ornate pillars and arches inlaid with lapis lazuli and jasper – survives. Two thrones adorn the large terrace in front of the Diwan-i-Khas, one of black slate and the other of white marble. Shah Jahan apparently took his evening repose in the white throne; from the black one, the emperor would amuse himself by watching elephant fights in the eastern enclosure. Tucked away by the west wall of the hall, approached by a staircase, is the tiny **Mina Masjid** (Heavenly Mosque), the emperor's personal mosque, where Shah Jahan prayed during his imprisonment.

A doorway from the rear of the Diwan-i-Khas leads to a two-storeyed pavilion or tower known as **Musamman Burj**, famous in Moghul legend as the spot where, in the open octagonal chamber atop the highest of the riverside bastions, Shah Jahan caught his last glimpse of the Taj Mahal before he died. Surrounded by a verandah, the elegant chamber has a lattice-screen balustrade with ornamental niches; exquisite inlay covers almost every surface, and a marble *chhatri* adds the finishing touch. In front of the tower a courtyard, paved with marble octagons, has a *pachisi* board at its centre, where the emperor played a rather bizarre version of the game (a form of backgammon) using dancing girls as pieces.

To the south of Musamman Burj lies the marble building known as **Khas Mahal** (Private Palace), possibly used as a drawing room or the emperor's sleeping chamber. Khas Mahal is designed for comfort, with cavities in its flat roofs to insulate against the searing heat of an Agra summer, and with soothing riverside and garden views. The palace is flanked by two **Golden Pavilions**, their curved roofs covered with gilded copper tiles, in a style similar to the thatched roofs of Bengali village huts. Stretching in front of the Khas Mahal to the west is **Anguri Bagh** (Grape Garden), a miniature *charbagh*, with its quarters delineated by wide marble pavements. In the northeast corner, the **Shish Mahal** (Palace of Mirrors) was where royal women bathed, steeped in the soft lamplight reflected from the mirrorwork mosaics that covered the walls and ceiling. Connected to the Khas Mahal by an extensive corridor, the **Shah Jahani Mahal** (Shah Jahan's Palace) is supported by wooden beams; its four chambers were originally painted in bright colours and embossed in gold.

THE PALACES OF JAHANGIR AND AKBAR

Immediately southwest of the Shah Jahani Mahal is the robust, square **Jahangiri Mahal**. This red sandstone palace, built either by Jahangir or by Akbar on his son's behalf, is almost entirely Hindu in its interior design. In the Assembly Hall, carved ornamental brackets support beams, wide eaves and ceilings with struts; the serpentine form being emitted from a dragon's mouth is reminiscent of a Gujarati temple.

Rooms to the west are thought to have been the temple and drawing room of Jahangir's Rajput wife Jodhbai. Below the palace, three storeys of basement chambers were used to escape the heat; this dark unpleasant labyrinth hides secrets of a long-forgotten harem and includes a guillotine. **Jahangir's Hauz** or cistern, a giant bowl made in 1611 from a single block of porphyry and inscribed in Persian, was unearthed in the nineteenth century and stands in the courtyard in front of the Jahangiri Mahal.

Returning towards Amar Singh Gate to the left, an assembly hall, a verandah overlooking the river and excavations are all that remain of the southernmost palace, the once extensive **Akbari Mahal**, built in 1571.

Jami Masjid

Opposite the fort and overlooking the railway station, the **Jami Masjid** – "Friday" mosque as found in almost every city, especially the Muslim ones – was built by Shah Jahan in 1648 and dedicated to his favourite daughter, Jahanara Begum. Standing on a high plinth approached by stairs, and with five arched entrances to the courtyard, the mosque is crowned by three large sandstone domes distinguished by their zigzag bands of marble. Still in use today, the mosque is impressive in size but otherwise not as spectacular as those in Delhi or Fatehpur Sikri.

Itmad-ud-daulah

Dawn-dusk. Admission Rs10.50, free on Friday.

Itmad-ud-daulah, the beautiful tomb of Mirza Ghiyath Beg, an important member of Akbar's court and later *wazir* to Emperor Jahangir, stands amid gardens with scampering monkeys on the east bank of the Yamuna, less than 3km from the city. The first building to be constructed of pure marble in Moghul India, this charming two-storey mausoleum is small but perfectly executed, with translucent stones etched into its walls and tracery work. It's unmistakably feminine, having been designed by Ghiyath Beg's daughter, the favourite queen of Jahangir, and the most powerful woman in Moghul history, named Nur Jahan, "Light of the world", by Jahangir. He respected her intellect and talent so much that he ordered coins to be minted in her name, and by the time of her father's death in 1622 she had substantial control over the empire.

The square mausoleum, with an octagonal turret at each corner, foreshadows the Taj Mahal in its exclusive use of marble, but is more daintily proportioned, and has a pavilion on its roof rather than a dome. However, recent "restoration" work has resulted in poor-quality plaster obscuring some of the exquisite detail, and in other places semi-precious stones that were once embedded into the marble have been winkled out and stolen. Ghiyath Beg's grave is underground, next to his wife's sarcophagus, shrouded in flowers and sallow light. A pierced and intricately carved wall in front of the entrance to the grave casts a soft hazy light over paintings of flowers, cypresses, vases and wine vessels, all symbols of paradise, in the inner chamber. From the garden you can look over the Yamuna. Wide and vigorous during the monsoon, for most of the year it trickles in a shallow stream. *Saris* are laid to dry on its sandy bed and melancholy buffalo wallow in its waters.

Chini-ka-rauza

Less than 1km north of Itmad-ud-daulah is **Chini-ka-rauza**, built in 1635 and reputed to be the mausoleum of Afzal Khan, a Persian poet and Shah Jahan's prime minister. Neglected and decaying, its soft brown stone is victim to the elements and its eaves shelter pigeons. Topped with a bulbous dome the dull earth-coloured tomb is a far cry from Nur Jahan's delicate work, but is distinctive as Agra's sole Persian construction. Parts of the walls are still covered with the coloured enamel tiles (*chini*) that once enhanced the whole of the exterior and gave the tomb its name, while traces of paintings and Islamic calligraphy can still be made out on the high domed ceiling.

Ram Bagh

Ram Bagh, laid out by Babur in 1528 and probably the first pleasure garden of its kind, is only a few kilometres north of Chini-ka-rauza. Reputedly the resting place of Babur's body before it was taken to Kabul, the garden is now dilapidated and overgrown, and only a few tattered columns and walls remain of the stone pavilions that once sheltered the royal family. Its original name, Aram Bagh (garden of rest), was corrupted to Ram, after the Hindu god.

Akbar's mausoleum

Sikandra. Dawn–dusk. Admission Rs10.50, free on Friday.

Given the Moghul tradition of building magnificent tombs for men and women of high status, it comes as no surprise that the mausoleum of the most distinguished Moghul ruler was one of the finest and most ambitious structures of its time. **Akbar's mausoleum**, a majestic composition of deep-red sandstone and cool marble designed by Akbar and modified in 1605 by his son, Jahangir, borders the roadside at Sikandra, 10km northwest of Agra. Rickshaws charge at least Rs50 to make the round trip, or you could hop on any bus bound for Mathura from the Agra Fort bus stand.

The most overwhelming feature of the complex is its huge south gate, **Buland Darwaza**, "Gateway of Magnificence" – so high that it obstructs any view to the tomb beyond. Surmounted by four tapering marble minarets, and overlaid with marble and coloured tiles set in repetitive geometrical patterns, it bears the Koranic inscription "These are the gardens of Eden, enter them and live forever." Buy a ticket at the office set into the left face of the gate, then walk through to the gardens, divided by wide paved walkways into four equal quadrants in typical Moghul fashion, and enclosed by high walls. Along the paths friendly long-tailed langur monkeys laze in the sunshine and groom one another, and black buck roam through the tall grasses.

ACCOMMODATION PRICE CODES

All **accommodation prices** in this book have been coded using the symbols below. In principle the prices given are for the least expensive double rooms in each establishment; however, some hotels, usually in category ③, offer rates per bed rather than per room. Local taxes are not included unless specifically stated. For more details, see p.35.

① up to Rs100	④ Rs225–350	⑦ Rs750–1200
② Rs100–150	⑤ Rs350–500	⑧ Rs1200–2200
③ Rs150–225	⑥ Rs500–750	⑨ Rs2200 and upwards

In the centre of the gardens, directly in front of Buland Darwaza, the broad-based square mausoleum has arcaded cloisters along each side and pavilions enhanced by delicate marble domes rising above its centre. A high marble gateway in the southern face draws attention to meticulous lattice screens shielding a small vestibule, once painted with rich sea-blue frescoes and Koranic verses. From here a ramp leads to a subterranean crypt, where Akbar's grave lies sprinkled with roses and bathed in a cool yellow light. Akbar's mausoleum may not be as grand nor as awesome as the indomitable Taj, but it possesses a serenity sometimes lost among the throngs of tourists at Agra's most visited monument. It also marks the important transition in Moghul design after Akbar's death, replacing his bold, masculine red stone monuments with more ethereal and sensuous marble buildings, epitomized and perfected in the Taj Mahal.

Accommodation

The cluster of narrow streets just south of the Taj Mahal is known as **Taj Ganj**. Away from the worst of the city's traffic, and with plenty of restaurants, shops and auto-rickshaws to hand, it's a great place to stay. However, its hotels only cater for **budget** travellers; if you're looking for greater comfort, most of the tourist-class hotels are dotted around in the more spacious locales further south. Luxury hotels, as well as a few cheaper bargains, remain aloof in the **Cantonment**, near Agra Cantt railway station. **Sadar Bazaar**, around the commercial hub, has hotels in all price ranges.

Taj Ganj

Gulshan Lodge, South Gate (☎369918). Dingy but passable low-priced rooms with attached bath. The restaurant here is popular. ①.

Host, West Gate (☎361010). Simple, small rooms including one cheap a/c room, and a view of the Taj from the roof. Good as an overspill from the *Siddhartha* next door. ①–③.

Jahangir Lodge, Taj Rd, Purani Mandi. Further from the Taj than most, but homely and clean. ②.

Kamal, Chowk Kagzi, South Gate (☎360926). Fresh, clean rooms and a great view from the rooftop restaurant. ②–③.

Noorjahan, South Gate. Closest to the south gate of the Taj, the rooms here are plain and simple. To sample the acclaimed view, you'll have to climb a rickety ladder to the roof. The restaurant on the ground floor has good-value breakfasts. ①–③.

Pink, East Gate (☎360677). Painted entirely in pink, this friendly hotel has adequate rooms, some with attached baths, some with hot water geysers, and a restaurant. ①.

Raj, South Gate (☎260979). Extensive new hotel under the same management as the *Sikander*, opposite. A variety of rooms; those on the roof (shared baths) are good value. *Shivam* restaurant on the ground floor is good. ①–③.

Shah Jahan, South Gate (☎366869). A selection of clean rooms; the best are on the roof. ①–③.

Shanti Lodge, Chowk Kagzi, South Gate (☎361644). Rooms of varying standards, most with smelly bathrooms hidden by thin partitions, some with balconies; one of the best views of the Taj. ③.

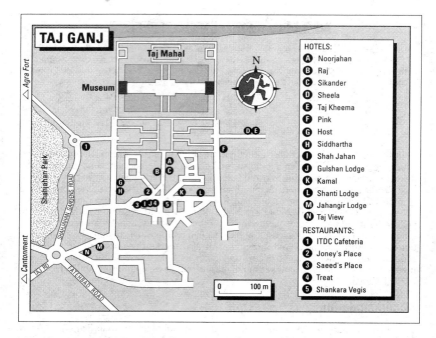

TAJ GANJ

Taj Mahal

Museum

N

HOTELS:
- **A** Noorjahan
- **B** Raj
- **C** Sikander
- **D** Sheela
- **E** Taj Kheema
- **F** Pink
- **G** Host
- **H** Siddhartha
- **I** Shah Jahan
- **J** Gulshan Lodge
- **K** Kamal
- **L** Shanti Lodge
- **M** Jahangir Lodge
- **N** Taj View

RESTAURANTS:
- **1** ITDC Cafeteria
- **2** Joney's Place
- **3** Saeed's Place
- **4** Treat
- **5** Shankara Vegis

0   100 m

Sheela, East Gate (☎361794). The best bet for budget travellers; no views, but only 200m from the east gate of the Taj. Ground-floor rooms with attached bath, amid colourful gardens; air-cooled rooms are only slightly more expensive. ①–③.

Siddhartha, West Gate (☎360238). A homely and clean hotel with spacious rooms set around a leafy courtyard cafe, all with attached baths and some with hot water. ①–②.

Sikander, 2/10 South Gate (☎260979). Clean budget rooms, some carpeted with attached bath, and a spacious roof for excellent views. Great value. ②.

Taj Kheema, East Gate (☎360140). Misconceived government-run hotel with a small handful of uninspiring airless rooms, some a/c. Superb views of the Taj from a grassy mound in the parched gardens, but non-residents have to pay just to sit there. ③–⑤.

Taj View, Taj Rd, Purani Mandi. Not to be confused with the luxury hotel of the same name. Fairly cheap, though extremely spartan, and has no view of the Taj. ①.

Sadar Bazaar and Cantonment

Agra, F M Cariappa Rd (☎363331). Chaotic, old-world hotel in a garden setting, with views of the Taj Mahal from the patio. Now showing their age, the rooms (some a/c) are dim and musty but spacious, with large bathrooms and hot showers. ③–④.

Agra Ashok, 6B The Mall (☎361223). Carpeted comfort with large luxurious rooms arranged around gardens and a swimming pool; choice of high-standard expensive restaurants. ⑨.

Akbar Inn, 21 The Mall (☎363212). Reasonably priced with a garden and a small campsite; the annexe has cheap, basic rooms; pleasant open-air cafe. ①–③.

Basera, 19 Ajmer Rd, Baluganj (☎363641). In the busy bazaar area, small and well equipped, with a range of rooms, but a bit expensive for what it is. ④–⑥.

Clarks Shiraz, 54 Taj Rd (☎361421). Pleasant setting with extensive grounds, including swimming pools and golf; restaurants, bar, shopping arcade, banks and travel services on the premises. ⑨.

Deepak Lodge, 178 Ajmer Rd, Pratap Pura. Small but pleasant enough, with a garden; close to all amenities but far from the Taj. ①–②.

Grand, 147 Station Rd (☎364014). Large hotel with a pleasant garden, restaurant and bar, but a bit tacky and expensive for what it is. ⑤–⑦.

Lauries, Mahatma Gandhi Rd (☎364536). One of Agra's legendary hotels which has seen better days. Open-air swimming pool and pleasant grounds and gardens; camping facilities. ⑥.

Major Bakshi Tourist Home, 33–38 Ajmer Rd (☎363829). Sikh-run and friendly, clean and pleasant, with a dormitory and good home cooking; recommended. ③–⑤.

Pawan & Jaiwal, 3 Taj Rd, Sadar Bazaar (☎363716). Two recently amalgamated hotels, with clean air-cooled and a/c rooms in the heart of the busy restaurant belt of Sadar Bazaar. ④–⑥.

Rose, 21 Old Idgah Colony, located down a quiet lane behind the *Sakura* (☎367562). Mr Gulati goes out of his way to welcome foreigners – this is by far the best accommodation available in the Idgah bus stand area. The cheaper rooms are good value and there is also a dorm. You can see the Taj Mahal from the rooftop cafe. ①–⑤.

Sakura, 49 Old Idgah Colony (☎369793). Close to Idgah bus stand – Rajasthan buses leave from the forecourt. Some rooms are poky, but it's handy and has a pool. Pasta and Mexican food. ②–③.

Tourist Rest House, Baluganj (☎363961). Popular budget place to meet other travellers. Ageing rooms (some with private bathrooms) set around a cramped but green courtyard; hot showers in common bathroom, and dreary vegetarian food. ①–②.

South of Taj Ganj

Amar, Fatehbad Rd (☎360695). All mod cons including a health club and swimming pool, but unattractive and garish. ⑦–⑧.

Highway Inn, opposite radio station behind *Hotel Amar*, Vibhav Nagar (☎360458). Campsite-cum-motel being converted into a hotel. Basic but friendly, and popular with overlanders. ①–③.

Mayur Tourist Complex, Fatehbad Rd (☎360302). Extraordinary pseudo-Moghul cottages set in extensive grounds. Restaurant, bar, swimming pool and camping facilities. ⑥–⑦.

SHOPPING

Agra is renowned for its marble table tops, vases and trays, inlaid with semi-precious stones in lavish floral designs, in imitation of that found in the Taj Mahal. It is also an excellent place to buy **leather**: Agra's shoe industry supplies all India, and its tanneries export bags, briefcases and jackets. **Carpets** and **durries** are manufactured too, and traditional embroidery continues to thrive. *Zari* and *zardozi* are brightly coloured, the latter building up three-dimensional patterns with fantastic motifs; *chikan* uses more delicate overlay techniques.

There are several large emporiums such as the official-sounding *Cottage Industries Exposition* on the Fatehabad Rd, which is lavish and well-presented but outrageously expensive and is one of the places you may be taken to by a commission-seeking driver. Shops in the big hotels may be expensive, but their quality and service are usually more reliable. *UP Handicrafts Palace*, 49 Bansal Nagar, have a wide selection of marble; other state emporia round the Taj include UP's *Gangotri*, which has fixed prices. Close to the East Gate, *Shilpgram* is an extensive crafts village with arts and handicrafts from all over India, and occasional live music and dance performances.

Shopping or browsing around The Mall, MG Rd, Munro Rd, Kinari Bazaar, Sadar Bazaar and the Taj Complex is fun, but you need to know what you're buying and be prepared to haggle; you should also be wary of ordering anything to be sent overseas. Commission payable by shops to rickshaw- and taxi-drivers and tour guides inflate prices. You are advised never to let your credit card out of your sight, even for the card to be confirmed, and you should make sure that all documentation regarding the card is filled in correctly and fully so as not to allow unauthorized later additions. Several serious cases of credit card fraud have been reported in Agra.

Moghul Sheraton, Fatehbad Rd (☎361701). Opulent, lavish and extremely expensive, the fake Moghul splendour feels overdone. Excellent restaurants, bar and a pleasant pool. ⑨.

Novotel Agra, Tajnagri Scheme, Fatehbad Rd (☎368282). Tasteful, efficient and comfortable, with good restaurant and swimming pool. Less ostentatious and cheaper than the other luxury hotels. Recommended, but far from centre, and 3km from the Taj. ⑨.

Safari, Shaheed Nagar, Shamsabad Rd (☎360013). Friendly and relaxed; under the same management as the *Tourist Rest House*. The more expensive rooms are good value, and you get great views of the Taj Mahal from the rooftop cafe. ②–③.

Taj View, Fatehbad Rd, Taj Ganj (☎361171). All the hallmarks of the Taj Group of luxury hotels – marble lobby, comfortable rooms – lavish, yet understated, with all facilities. ⑨.

Eating

Some of the best eating is to be had in the luxury hotels, but at a price. Agra's speciality, Mughlai cuisine, imitated in Indian restaurants throughout the world, is known for its rich cream and curd-based sauces, kebabs, *naan* and *tandoori* breads roasted in earthen ovens, rice dishes and milky sweets such as *kheer*. A constant flow of tourists ensures that Agra has a wide choice to suit most budgets. Taj Ganj has the main concentration of cheap restaurants aimed at travellers. For mid-priced restaurants, head for Sadar Bazaar, where an average meal will cost around Rs150; for more expensive food in opulent surroundings, the larger hotels are your best option.

Taj Ganj

Gulshan Lodge, South Gate. Roadside seating, bargain breakfasts and reasonable snack food, including crêpes.

ITDC Cafeteria and Restaurant, Western Gate. Large government-sponsored restaurant and cafe serving Indian and international food, though can be a bit expensive.

Joney's Place, South Gate. Tiny and very popular restaurant with a minute kitchen dishing up some unusually good vegetarian food, including spaghetti, aubergine bake and delicious *hummus*.

Pink, East Gate. Hearty Indian dishes and a few alternatives such as chips; good value.

Saeed's Place, South Gate. A simple but cosy restaurant specializing in Israeli food – and Israeli music. The menu includes *falafel*, *hummus*, pitta (and great chips).

Shankara Vegis, Chowk Kaghzi, South Gate. Friendly, relaxed and a good place to meet other travellers and catch up on reading. Extensive vegetarian menu.

Treat, South Gate. Opposite *Joney's Place* and one of several new travellers' cafes, all in competition. Its best feature is the pleasant rooftop overlooking the busy square. Serves good *lassi*.

Sadar Bazaar & Cantonment

Ching Wah, Gopi Chand Shivare Rd (opposite *Zorba*), Sadar Bazaar. Popular Chinese garden restaurant with thatched huts and a varied menu of reasonable Chinese food.

Dasaprakash, Meher Theatre Complex, 1 Gwalior Rd. Close to the *Hotel Agra Ashok*, comfortable, well-decorated specializing in mid-priced south Indian food with an extensive ice-cream menu.

Gaylords, Sadar Bazaar. Mid-price Chinese and Indian food similar and close to *Kwality*, though not as comfortable.

Hot Bite, 7 Shopping Arcade, Sadar Bazaar. A/c restaurant opposite *Kwality*, with Indian, Chinese and international dishes, including a selection of pizzas and burgers.

Kwality, Sadar Bazaar. Renovated a/c branch of the large chain, with predictable, mid-priced food. Specializes in Indian and Chinese food, and ice-creams.

Lakshmi Villas, Sadar Bazaar. Traditional south Indian cafe with an established reputation.

Only, 45 Taj Rd, Phool Syed Crossing. Well-presented, smart and by far the best of the independent restaurants, with good food and reasonable service. Popular with day tour groups from Delhi.

Prakash, 49 Taj Rd, Sadar Bazaar. South Indian dishes and Punjabi cuisine with excellent value *thalis* and non-veg alternatives.

MOVING ON FROM AGRA

The two main daily **flights** from Agra are north to **Delhi** (4.30pm; 40min), and east to **Khajuraho** and on to **Varanasi** and **Kathmandu** (9.25am); bookings can be made at the *Indian Airlines* office (☎360948, 360153) in the *Clarks Shiraz*, which also holds *Jet Air* and *Lufthansa* offices.

If you're leaving Agra by train, book well in advance at Agra Cantt Station. The fastest, and most expensive, train to **Delhi** is the fully a/c *Shatbadi Express* #2001 (8.18pm; 2hr); in the other direction as #2002 (8.15am), it travels to **Gwalior** and on to **Jhansi** from where you can catch a bus to **Khajuraho**. A convenient early-morning service to Delhi is the *A.P. Express* #2723 (5.30am; 3hr); the fastest midday train is the *Kerala Express* #2625 (noon; 3hr). Although the *Udyan Abha Toofan Express* #3008 travels all the way to **Calcutta** (12.40pm; 30hr) via Moghul Sarai and **Patna**, it is nearly always late. The best train for Varanasi is *Bhiwani–Malda Town Farakha Express* (11.15pm; 15hr 30min). You can also pick up trains to **Madras** (1–2 daily; 34–42hr) and **Thiruvananthapuram** (1–2 daily; 50hr 30min– 52hr 40min) from Agra Cantt.

Trains to **Rajasthan** include the *Marudhar Express* #2463, which leaves Agra Cantt 3 times a week for Jaipur and Jodhpur. Others depart from Agra Fort station but the line is being currently upgraded; check to see if regular services have been reinstated. Also from Agra Fort, the daily *Kumaon Express* #5311 (10pm; 12hr 10min) travels to Lalkua and **Kathgodam**, the nearest railhead to the hill station of **Nainital** in northern Uttar Pradesh. Several trains connect Agra Fort with Kanpur and Lucknow.

Onward journeys by **bus** are best made on deluxe vehicles and *Rajasthan Roadways* buses that leave from **Idgah bus stand** in the southwest of town. Seats on *Rajasthan Roadways* buses should be booked at the bus stand: for any destinations further afield than Jaipur, take a bus to **Jaipur** (every 15min 6am–2pm, then every 2hr; via Bharatpur) and pick up a connecting service. Deluxe and a/c buses for Jaipur leave from the forecourt of *Shital Lodge*, next to the bus stand (around Rs80 and Rs110 respectively, 5hr). There's a booking office in the lodge for fast and direct buses to **Delhi** (hourly; 5–6hr; via Mathura) and **Gwalior** (5 daily; 3hr 30min), and early morning departures for **Khajuraho** (12hr), **Lucknow** (9hr 30min) and **Nainital** (10hr). Additional buses to the same destinations leave from the tourist office on Taj Rd: book a day in advance at the office.

Agra Fort bus stand, chaotic, dusty and potholed, has extremely frequent services (several each hour) on rickety, often windowless, buses heading for Delhi, Mathura, Gwalior, Jhansi, Kanpur and as far afield as Indore. Here it's a case of locating the bus you want, jumping on, finding a seat, and then buying a ticket.

Unless you fly, getting to **Khajuraho** involves a 12hr bus journey (daily; 5am), or a train to Jhansi (2hr 45min–3hr 50min), and then a 6hr bus ride.

Priya, 4/17A Baluganj. Near the *Tourist Rest House*; multi-cuisine (Indian and Chinese), strongest on south Indian food.

Savitri, Gopi Chand Shivare Rd, Sadar Bazaar. Indian cuisine; speciality kebabs and chicken *tikka*.

Sonam, 51 Taj Rd. Mid-price garden restaurant and bar. Chinese and international menu, buffets in winter, and a budget section featuring *thalis*, but the Indian cooking is the best, attempting to recreate medieval Mughlai cuisine. Credit cards accepted.

Zorba the Buddha, E-13 Shopping Arcade, Gopi Chand Shivare Rd, Sadar Bazaar. A popular, no-smoking veg restaurant, whose staff are clearly enthused; delicious Indian and Western food and perfect *roux* sauces – not the cheapest, but worth at least one visit. Open noon–3pm & 6–9pm.

Listings

Emergency Ambulance ☎102; police ☎100.
Foreigners' Registration Office 16 Idgah Colony (☎367563).

Hospitals *Lady Lyall Hospital*, Noori Gate Rd (☎72658); *Modern Hospital*, The Mall (☎360196); *S N Hospital*, Hospital Rd (☎361318).

Photographic supplies *Agra Color Lab*, E6–7 Shopping Arcade, Sadar Bazaar (☎363221), and 34/2 Sanjay Place, opposite Soor Sadan, offers one-hour processing.

Trains Enquiries ☎131; Reservations ☎364244.

Swimming Agra's exclusive hotels sometimes let non-residents swim in their pools, for daily fees of up to Rs200. Try *Clarks Shiraz*, *Agra Ashok* or the *Taj View* on Fatehbad Rd; *Lauries* and *Mayur* are cheaper at around Rs100.

Fatehpur Sikri

The ghost city of **FATEHPUR SIKRI** straddles the crest of a rocky ridge, 37km southwest of Agra. Built between 1569 and 1585 by the great Moghul emperor Akbar, it has lain silent for almost four centuries; by 1600, its meagre water supply had proved incapable of sustaining the population. Now deserted, it is almost perfectly preserved – a masterpiece in sandstone, glowing in subtly changing shades of pink and red as the day progresses and the light fades. The very embodiment of Akbar's unorthodox court, the city fuses Hindu and Muslim artistic traditions; Hindu buildings such as **Birbal's Palace** and **Jodhbai's Palace** mingle with the pavilions and halls of the grand court, while the **Jami Masjid**, the only building of exclusively Muslim derivation, houses one of the most exquisite mausoleums of the Moghul period, the marble **Tomb of Sheikh Salim Chishti**.

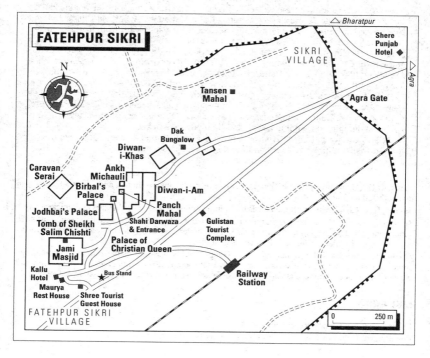

Fatehpur Sikri was originally intended to be joint capital with Agra; although it receives only a fraction of the visitors of its rival, the stunning elegance of its palace and courts ensure that it remains as powerful a testimony to Moghul grandeur.

The Royal Palace

Sprawling along the crest of the hill for around 1km, the main **Royal Palace** and court complex (daily dawn–dusk; Rs10.50, free on Fri), unused and uninhabited since its abandonment but still more or less intact, is best entered via the **Shahi Darwaza**. As there are no signs within the compound, you may prefer to hire an official guide at the booking office, for around Rs15.

Inside the magnificent complex, whose layout was inspired by that of a Moghul camp, you wander into a world resonant with echoes of the forgotten palace. The spacious courtyard of the **Diwan-i-Am** (Hall of Public Audience) lies at its heart, surrounded by colonnades, with the emperor's platform at the western end. Adjacent to the Diwan-i-Am, west of the main imperial residence, the **Daulat Khana** (Abode of Fortune), comprises a series of buildings distinguished by exquisite stone screens, elaborate brackets, broad eaves, and columns mounted on carved bell-shaped pedestals. Behind the library, Akbar's beautiful sleeping chamber, the **Khwabgah** (House of Dreams), is decorated with faded inscriptions of Persian verse. Separating the Daulat Khana from buildings to the north is the **Pachisi Court**, a giant stone board for the game known as *pachisi* or *chawpai,* similar to ludo; Akbar is said to have indulged in the odd game, using slave girls dressed in colourful costumes as live pieces.

At the centre of the otherwise unremarkable **Diwan-i-Khas** (Hall of Private Audience), an extraordinary carved column, the **Throne Pillar**, supports a large circular platform from which four balustraded bridges radiate outwards. From the central throne platform, the emperor would debate with representatives of diverse religions seated at the four corners, before an audience congregated on the floor below. Access to the pillar and balconies is via steps on the exterior of the building. Close by lies the three-roomed **Treasury**, its brackets embellished by mythical sea creatures, guardians of the treasures of the deep; it was apparently used to play the game of **Ankh Michauli** (Hide and Seek), the origin of the building's other name. Next to it is the Astrologer's Seat, a small pavilion with elaborate Jain carvings.

To the northeast of the Diwan-i-Khas, the **Anup Talao Pavilion**, also known as the **Turkish Sultana's House**, is thought to have been the palace of one of Akbar's favourite wives, the Sultana Ruqayya Begum. With balconies and Kashmiri-style woodcarvings, this exquisite building betrays Persian, Turkish and even Chinese influences, and may have been a *hammam* (bath) or pleasure pavilion. Legend has it that the great musician **Mian Tansen** once sang *Deepak*, the *rag* of fire, on its central dais. So effective was his performance that he grew hotter and hotter, until his daughter had to come to the rescue by performing the rain *rag*, *Malhar*. Understandably nervous at this onerous responsibility, she faltered on the seventh note of the scale, thereby creating one of the most famous and stirring *ragas* of north India – *Mian ki Malhar*. Happily, the *rag* had the desired effect; rain fell, and Tansen was saved. The southern aspect overlooks the Anup Talao or "Peerless Pool" where, on a central dais surrounded by perfumed water, Akbar is believed to have taken repose.

One of Fatehpur Sikri's most famous structures, the **Panch Mahal** or Five-Storeyed Palace, looms northwest of Anup Talao. The palace tapers to a final single kiosk and is supported by 176 columns of varying designs; the ground floor contains 84 pillars – an auspicious number in Hindu astrology. At one time, the Panch Mahal also had stone lattice screens, which would have been augmented by layers of dampened *khas*, a scented grass still harvested and used to cool verandahs throughout northern India.

The Women's Quarters

Next to the Daulat Khana, a courtyard garden reserved for the *zenana*, the ladies of the harem, signals the start of the women's area of the palace complex. The adjoining **Sunahra Makan** (Golden House) is variously thought to have been the home of the emperor's mother or the palace of one of Akbar's wives – hence its alternative names of the **Palace of the Christian Queen** and **Mariam's House** – although no record exists of Akbar's marriage to a Christian called Mariam. Once adorned with gilded murals, the only ornamentation that survives are some inscriptions of verse penned by Fazl, Akbar's court poet.

Solemnly presiding over the whole complex, the main harem, known as **Jodhbai's Palace**, blends elements of traditional Islamic architecture with influences from Gujarat and Gwalior, incorporating an elegant tulip motif characteristic of Fatehpur Sikri. The **Hawa Mahal** (Palace of the Winds), a small screened tower with a delicately carved chamber, was designed to catch the evening breeze, while a covered walkway gave the imperial ladies of the court access to the lake, now dry, to the north.

The third women's palace, part of the **Haram Sara** (Imperial Harem) is called **Birbal's Palace** – a misnomer, as Birbal, Akbar's favourite courtier, was a man and would have been most unwelcome in this area. It may in fact have been the residence of two of Akbar's senior wives. The palace's profuse carvings include a ceiling crafted to resemble a canopy of blossoms.

Jami Masjid

At the southwestern corner of the palace complex, with the village of Fatehpur Sikri nestling at its base, stands **Jami Masjid**, also known as Dargah Mosque. The alignment of the entire palace complex was determined by the orientation of the mosque's *mihrab* (prayer niche) towards Mecca. Housing the tomb of Sheikh Salim Chishti, the mosque is unusual in that it is also a living Sufi shrine.

The main approach is through the imposing **Buland Darwaza** (Great Gate), though you may choose to use the Shahi Darwaza once again to escape the attentions of touts, unofficial guides and hawkers. Built around 1576, possibly to commemorate Akbar's brilliant campaign in Gujarat, the spectacular gate reaches a height of 54m and is scaled by an impressive flight of steps. Flanked by domed kiosks, the archway of the simple sandstone memorial is inscribed with a message from the Koran:

> *Said Jesus Son of Mary (peace be on him): The world is but a bridge – pass over without building houses on it. He who hopes for an hour hopes for eternity; the world is an hour – spend it in prayer for the rest is unseen.*

Before entering the mosque itself, visitors are required to remove their shoes, but cloth sandals can be borrowed for a small fee. The gate leads into a vast cloistered courtyard containing the **Zenana Rauza** (Tomb of the Royal Ladies), and the lattice-screen **Tomb of Islam Khan**, one of many nobles buried here. The focus of the Sufi shrine or *dargah* is the relatively small but exquisite **Tomb of Sheikh Salim Chishti**, much of which was originally crafted in red sandstone and only later faced in marble: the lattice screens are among the most intricate and beautiful in the world, with striking serpentine brackets supporting the eaves.

Sheikh Salim played a crucial role in the founding of Fatehpur Sikri: the site of the city was primarily determined by its connections with the saint, who had prophesied the birth of a son to the emperor. When one of Akbar's wives, Rani Jodh Bai, a Hindu Rajput princess from Amber, became pregnant she was sent here until the birth of her son Salim, who later became the emperor Jahangir. Fatehpur Sikri was constructed in the saint's honour and, some historians believe, abandoned when Akbar's faith changed. The *dargah* still attracts women who come here to pray for offspring, tying string onto the marble screen; when entering the main chamber, visitors cover their heads with cloth as a mark of respect. During Ramadan, an *urs* is held here, attracting *qawwals* (singers of Sufi songs; see p.97) from all over the country.

Practicalities

Buses to and from Agra run every half-hour from about 5.45am until 6.30pm, and take between forty minutes and one hour. Regular buses also leave for Bharatpur (30min).

Though well worth a day or two, Fatehpur Sikri has a limited choice of places to **stay**. The *Gulistan Tourist Complex*, about 1.5km from the Buland Darwaza, on Agra Rd (☎05619/2490; ⑤–⑥), is a comfortable if slightly impersonal state-run complex, with food at reasonable prices, and beer available. Among the handful of poky rooms at the small *Maurya Rest House*, Buland Darwaza (☎05619/2348; ②–③), just one has an attached bath; the leafy courtyard serves reasonable snacks including good vegetable pakoras. A few metres down the lane near the bus stand, the *Shree Tourist Guest House & Restaurant*, Main Market, Dargah Gali (☎05619/2276; ①–②), is a no-frills lodge and cafe. Although a bit far from the main site and suffering from an unflattering location on the main road, the *Shere Punjab*, Bypass Rd (☎05619/2238; ③), is clean, friendly and welcoming and has an excellent up-market *dhaba* serving good Punjabi food and ice-cream. *Dak Bungalow* (①), bookable through the Archaeological Survey at 22 Mall Rd in Agra, is extremely good value and quite comfortable. Abdul Ghani Arif at the *Kallu Hotel*, next to the car park below the Buland Darwaza, produces standard *dhaba* cooking as well as good Mughlai *parathas*.

Braj: Mathura and Vrindavan

Although the holy land of **BRAJ** can be precisely located on the map – centred around the city of **Mathura**, it lies in the southwestern corner of the Gangetic valley, extending 75km north to south and 50km east to west, with its northern boundary roughly 80km south of Delhi – its prime significance is on a metaphysical plane, as the mythological backdrop to the idyllic childhood of **Krishna**.

Early texts only mention Mathura itself – Krishna's birthplace – the forest tract of **Vrindavan**, the hill of **Govardhan**, and the **River Yamuna**. However, in the sixteenth century, Bhakti saints such as Chaitanya and Vallabha "rediscovered" the area and identified it with "Braj", Krishna's legendary pastoral playground. By then Vrindavan had already been decimated by deforestation, but they gave the myths a new spatial reality by mapping out the sites of Krishna's youthful adventures, pinpointing twelve smaller "forests", various woods, and assorted lakes and ponds. The fact that Braj lay between Delhi and Agra, and thus had borne the brunt of the Muslim conquests, provided a historical explanation for the previous "loss" of these sacred sites.

Braj became, and remains, one of the most important pilgrimage centres for devotees of Krishna, who tour the twelve forests – now reduced to groves on the outskirts of towns and villages – on foot. This great circular pilgrimage, known as the **Ban Yatra** ("Forest Pilgrimage"), or the **Chaurosi Kos Parikrama** (which refers to the circumambulatory distance of 84 *kos*, equivalent to 224km), can take several weeks. Less energetic or devout visitors may prefer to explore the major sites by bus.

Mathura

The sprawling city of **MATHURA**, 141km south of Delhi and 58km northwest of Agra, is celebrated above all as the place where Krishna was born, on the banks of the River Yamuna that features so prominently in tales of his boyhood. Hindu mythology claims that it was founded by Satrugna, the youngest brother of another incarnation of Vishnu,

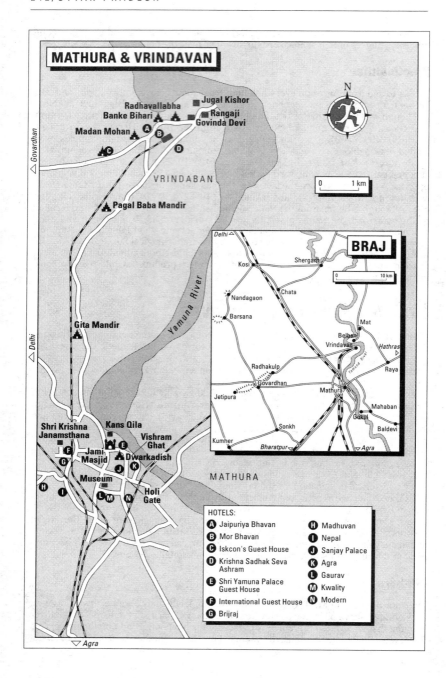

MATHURA & VRINDAVAN

Radhavallabha
Banke Bihari
Madan Mohan
Jugal Kishor
Rangaji
Govinda Devi

Ⓐ Ⓑ

Ⓒ Ⓓ

VRINDABAN

0   1 km

Pagal Baba Mandir

Gita Mandir

Yamuna River

Shri Krishna
Janamsthana

Kans Qila

Vishram
Ghat

Jami
Masjid

Dwarkadish

Museum

Holi
Gate

MATHURA

△ Govardhan

△ Delhi

▽ Agra

BRAJ

Delhi △

Kosi

Shergarh

0   10 km

Nandagaon

Chata

Barsana

Mat

Belban
Vrindavan

Hathras
▷

Radhakulp

Raya

Govardhan

Mathura

Jetipura

Mahaban

Sonkh

Gokul

Baldevi

Kumher

Bharatpur ▽

▽ *Agra*

Yamuna River

HOTELS:

Ⓐ Jaipuriya Bhavan
Ⓑ Mor Bhavan
Ⓒ Iskcon's Guest House
Ⓓ Krishna Sadhak Seva
    Ashram
Ⓔ Shri Yamuna Palace
    Guest House
Ⓕ International Guest House
Ⓖ Brijraj

Ⓗ Madhuvan
Ⓘ Nepal
Ⓙ Sanjay Palace
Ⓚ Agra
Ⓛ Gaurav
Ⓜ Kwality
Ⓝ Modern

Rama – the king of Ayodhya, and hero of the *Ramayana*. However, Mathura's earliest historical records date back around 2500 years, before the conquests of Alexander. Buddha himself founded monasteries here, in what was known to later Greeks as *Madoura ton Theon* ("Mathura of the Gods"). The city reached an early peak under the Indo-Bactrian Kushan people, whose greatest ruler Kanishka came to power in 78 AD. Fa Hian, the Chinese pilgrim, reported that in 400 AD it held twenty Buddhist monasteries, with about three thousand resident monks.

The enduring prosperity and sophistication of Mathura, which lay on a busy trade route, attracted such adventurers as the Afghan Mahmud of Ghazni in 1017, whose plundering and destruction signalled the death knell of Buddhism. Sikander Lodi from Delhi wrought further havoc in 1500, as did Aurangzeb. Mathura has grown in recent years into a multi-faceted urban sprawl, incorporating the teeming **old city** with its many Krishna-associated sites, a vast British military cantonment, known as the **Civil Lines**, to the south, and haphazard industrial development on the outskirts.

Arrival and information

The city's principal railway station, **Mathura Junction**, lies southwest of the centre, around 4km from Holi Gate and the old city. It's on the main Delhi–Agra line, 2hr 30min from Delhi on the fast *Taj Express* #2179, and only 30 minutes short of Agra; Mathura is also served by several Delhi–Bombay trains such as the *Punjab Mail* #1038 via Agra and the super-fast *August Kranti Rajdhani Express* #2953, which travels every day except Wednesdays; both *Rajdhani* and *Pashchim Express* #2925 stop at Sawai Madhopur (if you're heading for the wildlife park of Ranthambore; see p.160) and Kota.

Mathura has two bus stands; the **Old Bus Stand**, near Holi Gate, has hourly connections to Agra and serves **Govardhan**, 25km west, while the **New Bus Stand**, a little way west is used by Delhi and Jaipur buses as well as more Agra services.

Cycle and auto-rickshaws are always on hand for local journeys, and shared tempos and horse-drawn tongas are also available. The **tourist information** office (Mon–Sat 9.30am–5pm) at the Old Bus Stand hands out dusty leaflets and not much else; **foreign exchange** is handled by the *State Bank of India*, Railway Station Rd (☎405814).

> The telephone **area code** for Mathura is ☎0565.

The Town

Despite its history and the its religious heritage, Mathura today must be one of the most crowded and dusty cities in India.

The ornate sandstone **Holi Gate** at the entrance to the old city is Mathura's major landmark, now plastered with political and other posters as well as years of dust and grime. To the east, the riverfront is minute compared to Varanasi, the bathing *ghats* are much smaller, and the streets are not as interesting. Along the river towards the north lie the remains of **Kans Qila**, a fort built by Raja Man Singh of Amber and rebuilt by Akbar – little is left apart from the foundations, and no traces survive of the astronomical observatory constructed by Jai Singh (as seen in Jaipur, Delhi, and Varanasi).

To the south, the brightly coloured **Vishram Ghat** is the "*ghat* of rest" where Krishna is said to have recuperated after killing the evil Kamsa. Several shrines around its marble-paved courtyard include one in the corner to Krishna Balava, and another to the river goddess Yamuna in a small annexe. **Boats** for river excursions can be rented at the *ghat*. Just south, on the riverbank, the square red-sandstone tower of **Sati Burj** is alleged to have been built in 1574 to commemorate the *sati* (self-immolation) of the wife of the Raja of Amber on her husband's funeral pyre. This unremarkable seventeen-metre-high edifice has been the subject of some abysmal repair work.

Heading through the network of narrow streets that radiates from Vishram Ghat brings you (by way of several bangle shops) to Radha Dhiraj Bazaar, and the large and ostentatious turn-of-the-century **Dwarkadhish** temple, approached by steep steps off the busy main road. The **Jami Masjid**, on a plinth raised above street level a little way north, was completed in 1661 by Aurangzeb's governor Abd-un-Nabi. It has long since lost its original vivid glazed tiles, but remains surrounded by four minarets and assorted outer pavilions. Around 500m west, stands another of Aurangzeb's mosques, the impressive red sandstone **Katra Masjid**. This was erected on the foundations of the once-famous Kesava Deo temple, destroyed by the Moghul emperor, which had itself been built on the ruins of a Buddhist monastery. Some traces of the Hindu temple can be seen around the back, where the **Shri Krishna Janamsthan** or Janambhoomi complex now stands. Directly behind the mosque, approached through a corridor, a shrine marks Krishna's exact birthplace (*janamsthan*); its cage-like surround signifies that he was born in captivity, when his parents were prisoners of the tyrant king Kamsa. Inside the adjacent **Bhagwat Bhavan** – a modern, towering, flamboyant great hulk also known as **Gita Mandir** – a garishly painted ceiling depicts scenes from Krishna's life. No cameras are allowed into the complex, where although the shops and shrines combine to produce a park-like atmosphere, nothing obscures the heavy paramilitary presence – a reminder of underlying Hindu-Muslim tensions. Nearby, the impressive stepped sandstone tank of **Potara Kund** is believed to have been used to wash Krishna's baby clothes.

KRISHNA – THE MYTH

One of the most popular gods of the Hindu pantheon, appearing in numerous forms in a vast body of mythological literature, **Krishna** was probably originally a tribal chieftain who was later deified and came to be recognized as an *avatar* or incarnation of Vishnu. Although he is represented as a warrior hero in the *Mahabharata*, even that incorporates the Song of the Lord – the **Bhagavad Gita** – of which the Lord is Krishna. In the *Bhagavad Gita* he is represented initially as a profound seer, living in Dwarka, who teaches Arjuna about Ultimate Reality; however, Krishna later reveals himself to be not simply an incarnation of Vishnu, but the Supreme Lord of the Universe, and first propounds the **Bhakti** religion of selfless loving devotion to the Supreme Lord.

Legend tells how, over three thousand years ago, the throne of Mathura was usurped by Krishna's uncle, the tyrannical **Kamsa**. When Kamsa came upon a prophecy that he would meet his end at the hands of the son of his sister Devaki, he incarcerated Devaki and her husband Vasudev and set out to slaughter every newborn baby. However, under the cover of a stormy night, Vasudev managed to smuggle the infant Krishna across the River Yamuna.

Krishna grew up as an enchanting but mischievous boy in the nomadic encampment of the cowherders (*gopa*) of **Braj**, which as **Gokul** provided the setting of the childhood pranks during which he first revealed his divinity. Later, the nomads moved on to the mythical forest of **Vrindavan**, where he further demonstrated his omnipotence by defeating demons sent by the wicked Kamsa. Eventually, Kamsa found out about the remarkable boy, and realizing his identity invited him to match his skills at a tournament. Krishna won easily, killed Kamsa, and took his body to the banks of the Yamuna for cremation.

The image of the irresistibly charming adolescent Krishna, cavorting with the milk-maids (*gopi*) amid a verdant pastoral landscape, recurs throughout Hindu iconography and popular performing arts. It traditionally culminates in an autumnal moonlit tryst in the sacred basil groves, with Krishna captivating the *gopi* with his magical flute. Allegories of the human soul yearning for a selfless union with the Divine Lord, the *gopis* perform the **Maharasalila**, the Great Circular Dance. The divine Krishna multiplies himself so that each milkmaid, who has abandoned her husband to be with the Lord, imagines him to be dancing with herself alone.

Close to the centre of Mathura in Dampier Park, the **Archeological Museum** (Tues–Sat 10.30am–4.30pm; free), places a particular emphasis on Buddhist and Jain sculpture, dating from the Kushan (first–third centuries AD) and Gupta periods (fourth–sixth centuries). Known collectively as the **Mathura school**, the sculpture, characterized by its spotted red sandstone, reflects in its fusion of styles the fluctuating history of the region. Building on the skill of earlier craftsmen, sculptors assimilated primitive cults within the Jain, Buddhist and Hindu pantheons. The museum's highlight, one of the finest examples of Gupta art, is a miraculously intact standing Buddha. Shown with a beautiful benign expression, an ornate halo, and delicate fluted robes, he is making the Abhaya *mudra* ("fearless") hand gesture. Both this and a seated Buddha, also in red sandstone and this time depicted as the Enlightened One, are thought to have been created by the monk Dinna around 434 AD. Kushana art on display includes a headless image of King Kanishka in a foreign-styled tunic and boots, and some exquisite railings carved with floral motifs and human figures, while contemporaneous pieces of Gandhara sculpture, originally from northwest Pakistan but discovered locally, prove early contact between the two centres of civilization. A well-presented **terracotta** gallery is built around the work of the German Archaeological Mission, which has been digging at **Sonkh**, 35km west of Mathura, since 1966.

Accommodation

Despite being an important pilgrimage centre and a large industrial and military city, Mathura offers a very limited choice of **accommodation**, and none of its mid-range or luxury hotels is especially worthy of recommendation. Neighbouring Vrindavan (see p.247) has a small but more pleasant range.

Agra, Bengali Ghat (☎403318). Small place, overlooking the river in the old city and redolent of the atmosphere of the *ghats*. Bengali food, and a choice of rooms but expensive for what it is. ③–④.

Brijraj, opposite Shri Krishna Janamsthan (☎406232). Reasonable accommodation although the prices are creeping up, with some affordable a/c rooms, and a good cafe downstairs. ③–④.

Gaurav, Dampier Nagar (☎406192). Small but clean rooms and with the advantage of being near the station in a comparatively quiet and pleasant neighbourhood. ③.

International Guest House, Shri Krishna Janamsthan (☎405888). Large institution-like building beside the temple. Very affordable and clean, with a good *bhojanalaya*, or vegetarian cafe. ①.

Kwality, near Old Bus Stand (☎406195). Claims to be the oldest hotel in the city – and may well be, considering its dire need of refurbishment. The restaurant has seen better days. ③.

Madhuvan (☎404064). Probably the best hotel Mathura has to offer, thanks only to the lack of competition. Facilities include a good restaurant and a swimming pool open to non-residents. ⑥–⑦.

Modern, Agra Rd (☎404747). Close to the town centre, opposite the New Bus Stand. Has a popular dimly-lit bar but is otherwise quite ordinary. ②.

Nepal, Delhi Rd (☎404308). Once a dependable and pleasant budget hotel but now temporarily closed due to family wrangles; it may open again. ①–③.

Sanjay Palace, Sanjay Market, Arya Samaj Rd (☎407867). Near Holi Gate and not far from the river. Run-of-the-mill accommodation above shops within a commercial precinct that can be a bit noisy. Some a/c rooms. ③.

Shri Yamuna Palace Guest House, Radha Dhiraj Bazaar (no phone). Dilapidated former property of the Maharajah of Bharatpur, near Vishram Ghat, set around a courtyard. A couple of atmospheric but basic rooftop rooms overlook the river. ①.

Eating

Due to the city's spiritual significance for Vaishnavas, restaurants and cafes in Mathura tend to serve **vegetarian** food only. As a result, many tourists restrict themselves to eating in their hotels, with perhaps the occasional foray into the numerous sweetshops.

Brijraj, Shri Krishna Janamsthan. Hotel and cafe which serves *dosas* and snacks.

Brijwasi Mithai Wala, Shri Krishna Janamsthan. Appealing sweetshop opposite *International Guest House*.

Kwality, near Old Bus Stand. Formerly part of the famous chain, and retaining much of its typical look and feel, but now poorly maintained and run by indifferent management. Serves veg food.

Madhuvan. The hotel's restaurant, serving mid-priced Indian and Chinese cuisine, is perhaps the best that Mathura has to offer.

Around Mathura

At the very heart of Braj, Mathura is the obvious base for peregrinations in the pastoral landscape associated with the adolescent Krishna, where the sacred temple-crowned hills of **Govardhan**, **Barsana** and **Nandagaon** stand in striking contrast to the prevailing flatness. Very little survives of its idyllic legendary forests, and only serious pilgrims would choose to walk rather than catch local buses.

Mahaban and Gokul

Across the Yamuna from Mathura, 10km southeast of the city and reachable by boat or bus, **Mahaban** and **Gokul** are associated with Krishna's foster parents, Nanda and Yashoda. **MAHABAN**, "the Great Forest", was sacked by Mahmud of Ghazni at the beginning of the eleventh century, and a fort built in the fourteenth century was also soon occupied by the Muslims. Of temples here, the most interesting is **Nanda's Palace**, also known as **Assi Khamba** or "Eighty Pillars", an amalgam of several influences including Buddhist. Rebuilt as a mosque under Aurangzeb, the temple's pillars resemble the Qutb Minar in Delhi, and probably date back to the tenth century.

On a high bank overlooking the river 2km from Mahaban, **GOKUL**, the cowherd encampment to which the newborn Krishna was smuggled, is the headquarters of the followers of the sixteenth-century saint Vallabha. This is where Krishna first revealed his divinity to his foster mother Yashoda – she made him open his mouth after catching him eating earth, only to peer in and see the entire universe. All of Gokul's sixteenth- and seventeenth-century temples are in a very bad state of repair.

Govardhan

GOVARDHAN, 25km west of Mathura, is significant as Krishna is said to have lifted the hill of the same name on the tip of one finger, to shelter the inhabitants of Braj from a deluge caused by the wrath of the god Indra. A popular Vaishnavite icon, the entire hill is circumambulated by thousands of pilgrims each year.

The eponymous town is clustered close to a masonry tank known as Mansi Ganga, in a gap towards the hill's northern end. Two impressive cenotaphs immediately opposite the tank commemorate Randhir Singh and Baladeva Singh, two of the Bharatpur rajas, while the temple of Hari Deva, founded during the reign of Akbar, lies nearby. At the northern extremity of the hill, the twin tanks of **Radhakund**, "rediscovered" by Chaitanya, are said to have been manifested for Krishna's expiatory ablutions after he had killed the demon bull, Arishta; on the hill's southern crest, above the village of Jatipura, the ruined temple of **Sri Nath** was founded by Vallabha in 1520.

Barsana and Nandagaon

The hill sites of **Barsana** and **Nandagaon**, 25km and 32km north of Govardhan respectively, were originally dedicated to Brahma and Shiva before being appropriated into the Krishna myth.

An impressive stone staircase leads from the town at the base of the hill at **BARSANA** to an extensive ridge, where temples include that of **Lali Ji**, a local name for Krishna's mistress, Radha. Priya Kund, on the outskirts of the town, is a sacred bathing tank. Similarly, the eighteenth-century temple of **Nand Rae** dominates the smaller hill and town of **NANDAGAON**, identified as the village of Krishna's foster father Nanda; it too can be reached by stairs, which also provide access to the sacred lake of Pan Sarovar nearby. A curious local ritual takes place each year during the spring festival of Holi. First the menfolk of Nandagaon invade Barsana, to taunt the women with lewd songs and be beaten with long wooden staffs for their pains; then on the next day the procedure is reversed, and the men of Barsana pay courting calls to the women of Nandagaon.

Vrindavan

The dusty little town of **VRINDAVAN**, on the banks of the Yamuna, 11km north of Mathura, is among the most important pilgrimage sites in Braj, attracting an estimated 500,000 pilgrims each year. In practice, most of these come during the spring Holi festival, which in Braj is extended for up to a month, and during the two months of celebrations for the birthdays of Krishna and Radha, his mythical mistress, in the autumn.

Although Vrindavan is in theory a *tirtha* or holy crossing place on the Yamuna, in fact it has been progressively abandoned by the river, as it meanders away from the original two-kilometre-long waterfront, and all but five of its 38 *ghats* are now without water. Neither is there much trace of the forests of the Krishna legend, and only a few sacred basil groves remain at the spot where he cavorted with the *gopis*. Nevertheless, as a *tirtha*, the town attracts elderly Vaishnavas who believe that to die here earns instant *moksha* or liberation. Along with its many *dharamshalas*, Vrindavan holds several "widow houses", maintained by wealthy devotees, which provide food and shelter for the poor women who find solace in devotion to Krishna. Two thousand of them congregate in the **Mirabai Ashram** twice a day to sing *bhajans* (devotional songs).

If not exactly boasting the thousand temples of popular exaggeration, the town does hold numerous shrines, many of them now neglected and crumbling. Close to the centre, on the main Mathura–Vrindavan road, **Govinda Deva**, known locally as "Govindji", is one of northern India's most impressive medieval Hindu edifices, though worship here is low-key in comparison to some of the other shrines of Vrindavan. Erected by Raja Man Singh in 1590, its main tower is said to have been seven storeys high; the three storeys that survived the depredations of Aurangzeb leave it with a squat and truncated look. An impressive *mandapa* (front hall), with open balconies on two floors, sports elaborate columns, brackets and overhanging eaves. Adopting traditions from mosque architecture, Govinda Deva's sharply cut mouldings and sculptured detail avoid depicting any human form, utilizing true arches and a domed interior (now housing a flock of bats).

At the western end of town, the direly neglected temple of **Madan Mohan** overlooks the river from the small hill of Dwadashaditya Tila. Next to its octagonal *shikhara* (spire), adorned with square motifs and threatened with vegetation, stands a smaller and much more recent, egg-shaped *shikhara*. Close to **Keshi Ghat** at the northern end of Vrindavan, another neglected temple, **Jugal Kishor**, is distinguished by a large *shikhara* capped with an *amalaka* – a flat cylindrical crown – and an entrance arch which has an image of Krishna holding up the hill of Govardhan.

Although of much later design, and rebuilt in the nineteenth century, **Banke Bihari** (9am–noon & 6pm–9pm), off Purana Bazaar, is Vrindavan's most popular temple, renowned for impressive floral decorations of the deity. Banke Bihari's image was supposed to have been worshipped by the musician saint, Swami Hari Das, who as a musician was Tansen's guru, and who was visited by the emperor Akbar. The temple here is a great place to experience a theatrical display of *darshan* (sight or blessing) where the curtains are momentarily drawn aside revealing the *murthi* (idol) and relieving the pent-up expectations of the worshippers. Women should watch out, however, for surreptitious groping in the crowds. Stalls on the corner of the lane leading to the temple serve excellent *malai* (cream) and *kesar* (saffron) lassis in *bhands* (un-fired clay cups).

Close by, the temple of **Radhavallabha**, founded by the followers of the medieval poet-saint Hit Hari Vans, is hidden behind a nondescript exterior and entered via an impressive archway. Worship here follows the same pattern as that of Banke Bihari, but is a bit more low-key and friendly to women.

Opposite Govinda Deva, across the main road, lies the lavish new south-Indian-style temple of **Shri Ranganatha**, also known as **Rangaji Temple**, where ostentatious displays include the numerous gold-plated embellishments that crown its lofty *shikhara*, and the gold-plated **Dhwaja Stambha** column in the inner courtyard (no admittance to non-Hindus). An electronic puppet show enlivens the entrance gate, and a small museum inside houses processional images and chariots (Rs0.50). Also within the large courtyard, a subsidiary image of **Tirupathi Balaji** is bathed in milk every Friday. The ceremonial **Gajendra Muksh Kund** tank, adjacent to the temple, holds an image of an elephant and crocodile fighting; bathing is forbidden.

ISKCON, the International Society of Krishna Consciousness, has recently completed a lavish new temple complex, the **Krishna Balaram Mandir**, around 3km west of Vrindavan at Raman Reti. Built in Bengal Renaissance style with bright frescoes depicting episodes from Krishna's life, the temple is approached through an ornate marble gateway and incorporates a marble mausoleum in honour of the society's founder, Swami Prabhupada, who died in 1977. His private chambers have been made into a museum. ISKCON, which provides a squeaky-clean, Westernized alternative Krishna worship, runs courses here all year round, ranging from meditation to Ayurvedic medicine (☎82478).

Among the new temples springing up along the Mathura–Vrindavan road is the **Gita Mandir** which houses the Gita Stambh, a pillar with the entire *Bhagavad Gita* carved on its surface. The imposing temple, built by one of the country's leading industrial families, the Birlas, is overshadowed by the outrageous multistoreyed, spaceship-like edifice known as the **Pagal Baba Mandir** just down the road.

Practicalities

Getting to Vrindavan from Mathura is straightforward; frequent **buses**, shared **tempos**, and **taxis** ply the route and three local **trains** leave Mathura Junction each day (6.30am, 3.40pm & 7.40pm) for the station in the south of Vrindavan (they return at 7.30am, 4.35pm & 8.05pm).

Besides the numerous *dharamshalas*, several ashrams offer good value **accommodation** at fixed rates, as well as **food**. Away from the centre, the *Krishna Sadhak Seva Ashram* on Gurukul Rd (①–③), set in extensive grounds, is quiet and has comfortable suites; more central is the *Mor Bhavan*, in Ahir Para near Banke Bihari (①–②), while the nearby *Jaipuriya Bhavan* (①–③), built around a pleasant garden courtyard, is larger though slightly more expensive. ISKCON's *Guest House* (☎0565/442478; ①–②), immediately behind their temple, offers rooms on a suggested donation system which works out a real bargain, but you may need to book ahead as it can get busy. Their vegetarian restaurant serves some of the best food in the region.

THE UP HILLS

Within easy access of Delhi, the **UP Hills** – also known as **Uttaranchal** or increasingly as **Uttarkhand** – consist of the two regions of **Garhwal** in the west and **Kumaun** in the east. Both are progressively opening up to visitors, with the slow demilitarization of the Tibetan border regions to the north. Although not as high as the giants of Nepal, further east, or the Karakoram, the snow peaks here rank among the most beautiful mountains of the inner Himalayas, forming an almost continuous chain that culminates in Nanda Devi, at 7816m the highest complete mountain in India. Perhaps the single most enticing spot is **Gangotri Glacier** in north-central Garhwal – just a day's walk from the road, and revered as the source of the Ganges.

Rising from the steamy sub-Himalayan plains (*terai*) towards the permanent snows of Tibet, both Garhwal and Kumaun have preserved their own distinct languages and cultures. Successive deep river valleys shelter fascinating micro-civilizations, where Hinduism meets animism and the Buddhist influence is never too far away. The high alpine meadows known as **bugyals** – the summer pastures, where rivers are born and paths meet – play an important role in the life of the mountain communities. Local pilgrimages and shrines honour their spirits, and classic treks such as the Kuari Pass trail cross them through the heart of the mountains.

Every year the monsoons play havoc with the roads, causing giant landslides and avalanches. In 1992 the huge **Uttarkashi earthquake** devastated central Garhwal, and scientists predict another by the end of the century. Nonetheless, the government is going ahead with a plan to dam the River Bhagirathi at Tehri, with potentially disastrous consequences way beyond the evacuation of the fertile and well-populated valley.

A brief history of the mountains

The first known inhabitants of the Uttaranchal were the **Kuninda** in the second century BC, who seem to have had a close affinity with contemporary Indo-Greek civilization. Essentially a central Himalayan tribal people, practising an early form of Shaivism, they traded in salt with Tibet. A second-century Ashokan edict at Kalsi in western Garhwal shows that Buddhism made some inroads in the region, but Garhwal and Kumaun remained Brahmanical. The Kuninda eventually succumbed to the **Guptas** around the fourth century AD, who despite controlling much of the north Indian plains failed to make a lasting impact in the hills. Between the seventh and the fourteenth centuries, the Shaivite **Katyuri** dominated lands of varying extent from the Katyur-Baijnath valley in Kumaun, where their stone temples still stand. Under them **Jageshwar** was a major pilgrimage centre, and Brahmanical culture flourished. Eastern Kumaun prospered under the **Chandras**, from the thirteenth to the fifteenth centuries, when learning and art took on new forms and the Garhwal school of painting was developed. Later on, the westward expansion of the **Gurkha** empire was brought to an end by British annexation in the nineteenth century.

The call for an autonomous **Uttarkhand**, separate from UP, has grown steadily in recent years into an explosive issue. Things came to a head in October 1994 when a peaceful protest march to Delhi was violently disrupted by the UP police. It has taken two years to bring some of those police responsible to justice. Strikes or *bandhs* (closures) for the cause of Uttarkhand can bring the region to a standstill and have become increasingly common.

Garhwal

GARHWAL, which holds the sources of the mighty Ganges and Yamuna rivers, is the holy land of **Uttarkhand**. In the wake of the decline of Buddhism in northern India, the ninth-century reformer Shankara incorporated many of the mountains' ancient shrines into the fold of Hinduism. He founded the four main **yatra** (pilgrimage) **temples**, deep within the Himalayas, known as the **Char Dham – Badrinath**, **Kedarnath**, and the less-visited pair of **Gangotri** and **Yumnotri**. Each year, between May and November, once the snows have melted, streams of pilgrims penetrate high into the mountains, passing by way of **Rishikesh**, the land of *yogis* and ashrams.

For over a millennium, the *yatris* (pilgrims) came on foot. However, the annual event has been transformed in the last few years; roads blasted by the military through the mountains during the war against China in the early 1960s are now the lifelines for a

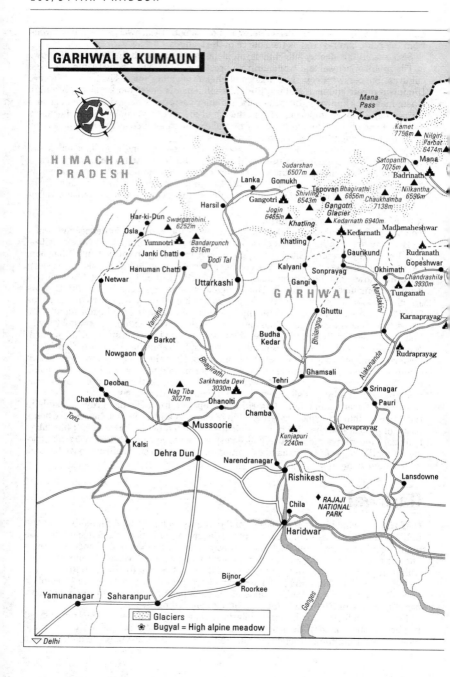

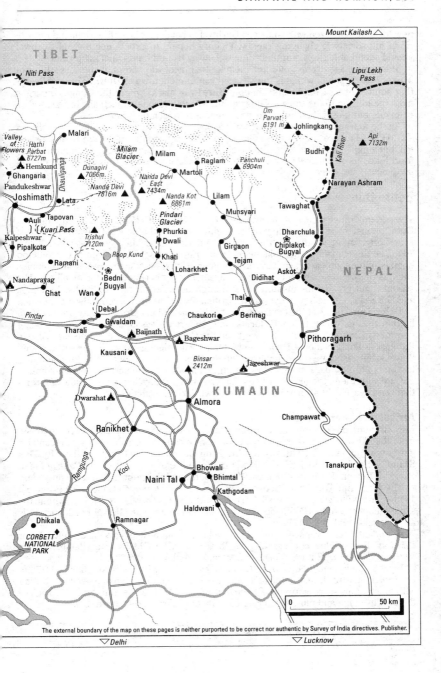

Mount Kailash △

TIBET

Niti Pass

Lipu Lekh Pass

Om Parvat 6191 m ▲ Johlingkang

Api ▲ 7132m

Valley of Flowers

Hathi Parbat ▲ 6727m

Malari

Milam Glacier

Milam

Raglam

Panchuli ▲ 6904m

Budhi

Kali River

▲ Hemkund

● Ghangaria

Pandukeshwar

Dunagiri ▲ 7066m

Nanda Devi East ▲ 7434m

Martoli

Narayan Ashram

Joshimath

Lata

Dhauliganga

Nanda Devi ▲ 7816m

Lilam

Tawaghat

Auli ● Tapovan

(Kuari Pass)

Nanda Kot ▲ 6861m

Munsyari

Kalpeshwar

Pipalkota

Trishul ▲ 7120m

Pindari Glacier

Phurkia

Dwali

Dharchula

Chiplakot Bugyal

Askot

NEPAL

Girgaon

● Ramani

Roop Kund

Khati

Loharkhet

Tejam

Nandaprayag

Bedni Bugyal

Didihat

Ghat

Wan

Thal

Pindar

Debal

Chaukori ●

Beringa

Tharali

Gwaldam

Baijnath

Bageshwar

Pithoragarh

Kausani ●

Binsar ▲ 2412m

Jageshwar ▲

KUMAUN

Dwarahat ▲

Almora

Champawat ●

Ranikhet

Tanakpur ●

Ramgunga

Kosi

Bhowali

Naini Tal

Bhimtal

Kathgodam

Haldwani

● Dhikala

CORBETT NATIONAL PARK

Ramnagar

0 _____ 50 km

▽ Delhi

▽ Lucknow

new form of motorized *yatra*. Eastern Garhwal in particular is getting rich, and the fabric of hill society is changing rapidly. Visitors hoping to experience the old Garhwal should spend at least part of their time well away from the principal *yatra* routes.

Many travellers from Delhi get their first sight of the snows at the hill station of **Mussoorie**. Just below that is the pleasant cantonment town of **Dehra Dun**, while further south, not far from Rishikesh, holy **Haridwar** marks where the Ganges emerges from the hills on to the Indian plains; technically the town is not actually in Garhwal or Kumaun, but its spiritual links are strong enough to include it here.

All the tourist bungalows in Garhwal are operated by Garhwal Mandal Vikas Nigam – **GMVN**. Most are concentrated along the pilgrimage routes, although their network has been expanding, and takes in the ski area at Auli. Standards vary widely, but the **food** tends to be particularly poor. GMVN also organize **tours** (often over-priced and inefficient), and offer expensive **car rental**.

Dehra Dun

The administrative centre of Garhwal and the UP Hills, **DEHRA DUN**, 255km north of Delhi, tends to be seen simply as a staging post on the way to the hill station of Mussoorie, 34km north, and the Garhwal interior. Pleasantly located at just below 700m, as the Himalayan foothills begin their dramatic rise, Dehra Dun never gets too hot in summer, and snows only rarely in winter. With its vast open spaces and colonies such as the Cantonment, this popular retirement spot is renowned for its elite public schools, and prestigious institutions. Although occupied in turn by Sikhs, Moghuls, and Gurkhas, it is clearly an overgrown British town, with its Raj roots always showing.

Dehra Dun stands at the centre of the 120-kilometre-long **Doon Valley** (*dun* or *doon* literally means "valley"), famous for its long grain rice – *basmati* – and unique in being hemmed in by the Yamuna to the west and the Ganges at Rishikesh to the east. Also in the east is Rajaji National Park, known for its wild elephants, while the low-forested Shivalik hills separate the valley from the dusty plains to the south. The local administration is fighting back against devastating deforestation; the springs are returning to life and with them, the dry river beds that criss-cross the valley. Those tracts of forests that remain are best seen at its eastern and western extremities.

Arrival and information

Jolly Grant **airport**, 24km east of Dehra Dun, is a stop on the regular bus route to and from Rishikesh; if you do arrive on one of its rare and over-priced flights, you can also get to town by taxi. The **railway station** is on Gandhi Rd, just south of the **City Bus Stand**, which is next to the Clock Tower in the centre of town. The *State Bank of India*, Rajpur Rd (Mon–Fri 10am–2pm, Sat 10am–noon), and the **post office** are alongside.

The **Regional Tourist Office**, at the GMVN *Hotel Drona*, 45 Gandhi Rd (Mon–Sat 10am–5pm; ☎653217), covers all Garhwal and *Drona Travels* (☎654371), within the same complex, books GMVN accommodation and tours. The GMVN headquarters is at 74/1 Rajpur Rd (☎26817).

Abundant local transport includes cycle and auto-rickshaws and multi-seater *Vikrams*. Better-value **car rental** than that offered by GMVN is available through *Ventures Rent-a-car*, 8 BMS Business Centre, 7B Astley Hall (☎22724).

If you're looking to fix up a **trek**, *Garhwal Tours & Trekking*, 151 Araghar (☎627769), run by KP Sharma, is an established and experienced organization and used to working with tour groups such as *Exodus*. *Paramount*, 16 Moti Market, behind Paltan Bazaar, are the best trekking and mountaineering equipment dealers in the entire region.

The telephone **area code** for Dehra Dun is ☎0135.

The Town and around

Most of Dehra Dun's busy markets lie near the tall Victorian **Clock Tower**, from where Rajpur Road, the lifeline to Mussoorie, stretches northwards. Four kilometres along is the vast leafy colony occupied by the **Survey of India**, founded in 1767. Its greatest achievement was to determine the height of Mount Everest – and name it after the Surveyor General, Sir George Everest. Most of the stock in its **map shop** is old and out of date, and anything interesting you might pick up will almost certainly be stamped "Not For Export" if it includes such sensitive areas as any portion of India's coastline. Their new trekking series of the UP Himalayas is very poor (see p.24).

Crossing the rainy-season river bed of Bindal Rao, Kaulagarh Rd progresses northwest past Dehra Dun's top private school, the Doon School, to the expansive grounds of the chateau-like **Forest Research Institute**, devoted to the preservation of India's much-threatened woodlands (Mon–Fri 10am–5pm; free). Along with a library and bookshop, there's a large and interesting museum, holding wood samples, insects, furniture, and wildlife – even a few stuffed animals. **Tapkeshwar Mahadev**, Dehra Dun's only significant temple, lies 2km further north, 6km from the centre. Steps lead down to a rocky and wooded river, beside which a cave with water dripping from its ceiling contains a Shiva shrine. According to the *Mahabharata,* Shiva made milk flow from this cave for Ashwathama, the son of the guru Dronacharya.

Somewhat further afield, **Rajpur**, 12km to the north, past the Survey of India and well connected by Vikrams, has a sizeable Tibetan community with a striking *gompa* (temple) – the **Shakya Centre** – decorated with ornate frescoes and a centre of Tibetan medicine next door. Another *gompa* is located on the main road around 5km towards Mussoorie.

Accommodation

Dehra Dun has a good selection of mid-range **hotels**, many of them strung along Rajpur Rd as it heads north to Mussoorie. What little budget accommodation there is can be found near the town centre – or in the old-fashioned railway retiring rooms.

Ajanta, Rajpur Rd, opposite *Great Value* (☎659595). Comfortable, clean and well-managed with an excellent restaurant and pleasant bar and the only hotel, at present, with a swimming pool. ⑦.

Chandra, Old Mussoorie Rd (☎684360). Excellent, atmospheric place (if a bit damp), set in the hills 14km north of Dehra Dun and 2km from Rajpur; now a bit neglected as a result of the new bypass to Mussoorie. Nice garden and grand views. ②–③.

Embassy, 18 Dhamawala (☎654453). Down a series of lanes, not far from the centre and well worth seeking out. A good range of rooms. ③.

GMVN Drona, 45 Gandhi Rd (☎654371). Drab, large government-run hotel which is central and close to all amenities, and has tourist information and tour and travel operators on the premises; the range includes a dorm and a/c rooms. ④–⑥.

Great Value, 74C Rajpur Rd (☎654086). Now belonging to the *Clarks Group*, a much improved amalgamation of two earlier but newish hotels, with good facilities. ⑥–⑧.

Kwality, 19 Rajpur Rd (☎657001). A landmark near the centre of Dehra Dun, established in the motel-influenced 1960s, with large comfortable, if old fashioned, rooms, good restaurant and bar. ⑤.

Madhuban, 47 Rajpur Rd (☎656041). A large, imposing yet characterless hotel with two popular restaurants, a bar, and a travel desk; some considered this as Dehra Dun's best but it is certainly the most expensive. A favourite with the few tour groups that come through. ⑧.

Meedo, 71 Gandhi Rd (☎627088). Close to the station gates. Reasonably priced and moderately comfortable with the best rooms at the back away from the sleazy bar in front. Their upmarket branch, the *Meedo Grand*, is on Rajpur Rd. ③.

Nishima, 59 Gandhi Rd (☎626640). Reasonable if ordinary budget accommodation close to the station and bus stand, but slightly better than the poky *Dinex* (☎625192) next door.

Osho Resorts, 111 Rajpur Rd (☎659544). Extraordinary place on the road to Mussoorie – part hotel, part restaurant and part ashram, with wooden cottages and a good multi-cuisine restaurant. The piped audio-visual channels include lectures by Osho, once known as Bhagwan Rajneesh. ⑥.

Victoria, 70 Gandhi Rd, near railway station (☎623486). Simple, central, lodge, with a courtyard. ②.

Eating

Dehra Dun has several commendable mid-priced eating places, such as the *Kwality*, and also a bunch of adequate cheaper cafes around the bus and train stations.

Daddy's, 3 Astley Hall, Rajpur Rd. Above *The Vegetarian* but not vegetarian itself. Multi-cuisine from pizzas to *thalis* in a friendly atmosphere.

Heaven's Garden, Osho Resorts, 111 Rajpur Rd. Part of the Bhagwan Rajneesh complex with Indian, Chinese and Western. Barbeque, fast food counter and a rooftop restaurant.

Kumar Vegetarian, 15B Rajpur Rd, near *Kwality*. Excellent vegetarian cooking at reasonable prices in comfortable surroundings. Popular and recommended.

Kundan Palace, opposite *Madhuban*, Rajpur Rd. Open-air multi-cuisine place, popular with locals.

Kwality, 19 Rajpur Rd. Good and reliable multi-cuisine chain restaurant with bar, next to the motel.

Pushp, 65 Gandhi Rd. A well-priced cafe offering a wide range from *dosas* to omelettes.

Tripti, 72 Gandhi Rd. Clean *dhaba* opposite the station gates with ordinary cooking and strong competition from similar places serving *thalis* such as *Samman Veg Restaurant*, close by.

The Vegetarian, Astley Hall, Rajpur Rd. South Indian and Punjabi cooking in a canteen-like atmosphere.

MOVING ON FROM DEHRA DUN

Jolly Grant airport, 24km east of Dehra Dun, is currently not served by any airline and is unlikely to resume operations for commercial flights in the near future.

Major **trains** back down to the plains include the *Dehra Dun–Varanasi Express* #4266, through **Lucknow** to **Varanasi**, the *Doon Express* #3010 through Varanasi to **Calcutta**, the *Mussoorie Express* #4042 to **Delhi**, the *Dehra Dun–Bombay Express* #9020, and the *Ujjain–Dehra Dun Ujjaini Express* #4310, which stops at **Agra**. **Train reservations** are available at the computerized booking office, opposite the railway station.

Hourly **buses** from the Mussoorie (City) Bus Stand near the station gates head to **Mussoorie**, while buses to Delhi leave from the Gandhi Road Bus Stand; a deluxe bus costs around Rs100. You can also get buses to **Shimla**, **Dharamsala**, **Chandigarh**, **Kulu**, **Manali**, as well as numerous services to **Rishikesh** and **Haridwar**, and one early morning bus to **Nainital**.

Mussoorie

Spreading for 15km along a high serrated ridge, **MUSSOORIE** is the closest hill station to Delhi, just 278km north of the capital, and 34km north of Dehra Dun (from where it is clearly visible). At an altitude of 2000m, it provides travellers from the plains with a long-awaited first glimpse of the snow-covered Himalayan peaks of western Garhwal, as well as dramatic views of the Dehra Dun Valley below. Established in 1823 by a certain Captain Young, Mussoorie soon became a typical Victorian resort, centering on its long promenade – **the Mall** – and boasting an Anglican church, library and club.

These days, Mussoorie is very popular with Indian tourists; although some of the old settlement can still be seen, much of the centre is now congested and unattractive. Dominated by the long Banderpunch Massif (6316m), with Swargarohini (6252m) in the west and the Gangotri Group in the east, Mussoorie's mountain panorama may not be as dramatic as some other hill stations, but it forms a pleasant backdrop to rambling walks when you feel like escaping the busy holiday town.

Arrival, transport and information

As Mussoorie's two-kilometre-long **Mall** is closed to motor vehicles during the tourist season, its two ends – the **Library** area at the west end, and the **Kulri** area in the east – serve as distinct transport hubs. Buses and shared taxis from Dehra Dun, the plains and the rest of Garhwal arrive either at the **Library Bus Stand** at Gandhi Chowkh, or

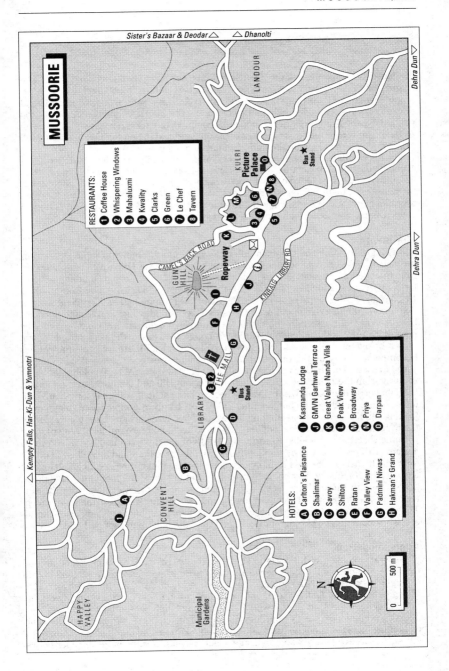

MUSSOORIE

Sister's Bazaar & Deodar △   △ Dhanolti

LANDOUR

Dehra Dun ▷

Dehra Dun ▷

△ Kempty Falls, Har-Ki-Dun & Yumnotri

RESTAURANTS:
1 Coffee House
2 Whispering Windows
3 Mahaluxmi
4 Kwality
5 Clarks
6 Green
7 Le Chef
8 Tavern

KULRI
Picture Palace
Bus Stand ★

CAMEL'S BACK ROAD
GUN HILL
Ropeway

KINCRAIG LIBRARY RD

THE MALL

LIBRARY

Bus Stand ★

HOTELS:
A Carlton's Plaisance
B Shalimar
C Savoy
D Shilton
E Ratan
F Valley View
G Padmini Niwas
H Hakman's Grand
I Kasmanda Lodge
J GMVN Garhwal Terrace
K Great Value Nanda Villa
L Peak View
M Broadway
N Priya
O Darpan

CONVENT HILL

HAPPY VALLEY

Municipal Gardens

N

0   500 m

> The telephone **area code** for Mussoorie is ☎0135.

the **Kulri** or **Masonic Lodge Bus Stand**, but not both. At the smaller **Tehri Bus Stand**, east of Landour 5km from the Mall, buses pull in from Tehri, Chamba and points east. Shared taxis and cars are available at the bus stands, while ponies and hand-drawn carriages – glorified rickshaws – run along the Mall itself. Ponies can also carry you around the Camel's Back Rd, but cross-country pony trekking has yet to catch on. *Bertz* (no, not *Hertz;* no phone), near Darpan in Kulri and in London House on the Mall, rent 100cc **motorcycles** by the hour, half-day and full day.

Facilities along the Mall include the information-only **Tourist Bureau** (daily 10am–5pm; ☎632863) next to the cable-car, **post offices** at the Kulri end and another at Library, and a GMVN transport office at Library which runs **tours** of the town and further afield. *Ambica Travels* (☎632238) and *Kulwant Travels* (☎632717) are approved tour and car rental operators and the *Kamal Taxi Service, Hotel Ratan* (☎632719) provides a similar service which includes one-way trips to Delhi.

The Town

Surprisingly, the Mall and the main hub face away from the snows towards Dehra Dun; the distant peaks can best be seen from the flat summit of **Gun Hill**, which rises like a volcano from central Mussoorie. This can be ascended on foot or pony on a bridle path that forks up from the Kutcheri, or on the 400-metre "Ropeway" cable-car ride from the Mall (Rs25 return). Alternative prospects of the mountains can be had on a peaceful stroll or ride around the three-kilometre-long **Camel's Back Road**, which girdles the northern base of Gun Hill, passing by the distinctive **Camel's Rock**. Another vantage point, the highest in the immediate vicinity, is **Childer's Lodge**, 5km east of the Mall above Landour.

Just below the Mall, beside the *Padmini Niwas* hotel, a **Tibetan street market** has become something of a fixture, with traders selling sweaters and woollens to unprepared tourists. The markets of Kulri and Landour provide more local colour.

Away from the noise and bustle, close to Convent Hill and 3km west of the Library, the Tibetan settlement of **Happy Valley** holds a large school, a shop selling hand-knitted sweaters and the small but beautiful **Tchechen Choling** *gompa* (monastery), overlooking the Doon Valley and surrounded by gardens. It makes an enjoyable walk from the Mall along wooded roads, but you can also catch a taxi (around Rs60 return).

Somewhat further afield, **Kempty Falls**, 18km northwest on the road down to Yamuna Bridge, is served by regular buses from the Library stand as well as a GMVN tour which costs Rs25. This local beauty spot has been all but ruined by its deluge of day-trippers. In theory they come to take a dip in the pool at the foot of the falls themselves, though there always seem to be a lot more people watching from the surrounding tea shops (which rent out towels and swimming costumes) than swimming. The steps down to the pool from the road lead past shops, beggars and snake charmers, while commercial photographers lie in wait at the bottom to capture holiday snaps.

Accommodation

Mussoorie is packed with **hotels** to suit all budgets – most of them clustered around the Mall. Room rates fluctuate between three rather vague **seasons**; lean (Jan–March & July-Sept, when the rains come), shoulder or mid-season (Christmas, April and the "Bengali season" of Oct & Nov), and peak (May–July), when prices can quadruple. Prices below reflect lean season with an indication of high season fluctuations.

If you are unable to carry your luggage to your hotel, porters from either the Kulri or Library bus stands charge under Rs20 to most locations along the Mall. Mussoorie still suffers from a severe water shortage which may affect some of the cheaper hotels.

HARKI DUN VALLEY TREKS

A relatively undemanding but superb trek **from Mussoorie** takes four days (including one on the bus) to reach the sparsely populated "Valley of the Gods", **HAR-KI-DUN**, in the **Fateh Parvat** region of northwestern Garhwal. In the valley itself if not higher in the mountains, accommodation is widely available, and food can usually be bought.

The rivers and streams of Har-ki-Dun drain the glaciers and snowfields that cloak the peaks of Swargarohini (the "ascent to heaven"; 6252m) and Bandarpunch (the "monkey's tail"; 6316m). Local people trace their lineage to the *Mahabharata*, claiming descent from Duryodhana and his followers. Like the Pandavas of the epic, they practise a form of polyandry, and follow intriguing religious customs. Worship at Taluka's Duryodhana temple, for example, consists of throwing shoes at the idol, while at Pakola, the image has its back to the congregation. Their distinctive alpine buildings have beautifully carved wooden doors and windows, with the mortar construction punctuated by wooden slats.

The trek to Har-ki-Dun

Starting out from Mussoorie on **DAY 1**, catch a Yumnotri bus and change at Nowgaon to continue via **Netwar** (9km short of Barkot, from where a road climbs to Hanuman Chatti) to **Purola** – a total of 154km. You can stay in Purola at a PWD bungalow, set amid a patchwork of wheat and rice terraces, which is where to get permission to stay at the forest rest houses further on. Simple cafes can be found around the bus stand.

Early the next morning – **DAY 2** – take the bus to the roadhead at **Sankri**, which also has a bungalow. A gentle trail from here leads the 12km to **Taluka** (1900m), where there is another bungalow and simple food.

On **DAY 3**, the trail follows the River Tons through beautiful forests. Although you can get tea at the hamlet of Gangari, no food is available until you've walked the full 11km to **Osla** (2259m). Osla too has a *Forest Rest House*, where security is unfortunately doubtful; from here on you have to carry your food, so stock up.

A steep 14km climb from Osla on **DAY 4** brings you finally to the campground at **Har-ki-Dun** (3560m) – an excellent base from which to explore the *bugyals* below the Swargarohini to the east, and the Jaundhar Glacier (3910m) at the head of the valley.

Returning along the same route takes two days, or one if you're really fit.

Across Yumnotri Pass

From the head of Har-ki-Dun valley, a challenging trail – only to be tackled by fully equipped and acclimatized trekkers, with local guides – winds for 30km over the **Yumnotri Pass** (4890m). Take the trail that forks off above **Osla**, and head 10km east along the Ruinsar Nala gorge to the mountain lake of **Ruinsara Tal** (3350m). From here, it takes a full day to climb to a campsite just below the pass at 4135m; on the second day you cross the pass and camp on the far side at 4000m; the third ends at **Yumnotri** itself (see p.269).

From here, the gentle 14km trek outlined on p.268 leads down to **Hanuman Chatti** (2134m), from where you can either embark on the Dodi Tal trek to create a two-week expedition through stunning mountain scenery, or catch a bus out.

Broadway, Kulri. Small, old guest house which retains much of its charm. A good bet for budget travellers. ①–②.

Carlton's Plaisance, Happy Valley Rd (☎632800). Great old building, full of character, but in need of attention. Has a pleasant garden. Threatened by the expansion of the civil service college. ⑥–⑦.

Darpan, near *Picture Palace*, Kulri (☎632483). Reasonable and clean, with good mountain views from the rooms and a good vegetarian restaurant. ③–⑤.

Deodar Inn, Sister's Bazaar (☎632644). Recently refurbished, beautiful hotel in secluded site on outskirts of town. Popular with visiting teachers to the nearby language school and so can get full – book in advance and you may even get collected from the bus stop. ⑨.

Great Value Nanda Villa, Camel's Back Rd, Kulri (☎631442). Comfortable and central chain hotel, reasonably priced for its range. Good views, close to all amenities and quiet. ⑥–⑦.

Kasmanda Lodge, Vayu Theatre, The Mall (☎632424). A short but stiff climb leads to an ex-Maharajah's summer palace now opened as a period hotel. Comfortable and quiet with a beautiful garden; recommended if you don't mind being surrounded by hunting trophies. ⑥–⑦.

Padmini Niwas, Library, The Mall (☎632793). Just below the Mall with beautiful grounds and garden, one of Mussoorie's better and more established addresses; the cottage is attractive. ⑤–⑦.

Peak View, opposite *State Bank of India*, Camel's Back Rd (☎632052). Quiet budget hotel close amenities, comfortable with an open terrace and views of the snows. ②–③.

Priya, The Mall, Kulri (☎632477). Spacious and good-value rooms with hot water; good views over the market to the hills beyond, but otherwise neglected and without food. ①–②.

Ratan, Gandhi Chowkh (☎632719). In the busy Library area, friendly, clean and excellent value with a terrace looking onto the snows. ③–⑤.

Residency Manor, Baluganj (☎631800). Large, brash and unmistakable new complex below town off the Dehra Dun Road; the most luxurious of all with all mod-cons and a swimming pool. ⑨.

Savoy, The Mall (☎632010). Above the Library, a driveway leads to pleasant grounds with large period buildings steeped in history; captures all the ambience of Victorian Mussoorie. ⑧.

Shalimar, Charliville Rd (☎632410). Good-value, old world, place, below the road to Kempty. ③–④.

Valley View, The Mall (☎632324). Sunny disposition with terrace overlooking the Doon Valley and a good restaurant; clean and close to all amenities – recommended. ③–④.

Eating

Cafes and **restaurants** all along the Mall and around Kulri serve everything from hot dogs to Chinese specialities; we recommend several below, but there are more good restaurants in hotels such as the *Valley View* and the atmospheric *Savoy* (see above).

Clarks, The Mall, Kulri. Period atmosphere with a multi-cuisine restaurant and bar.

Coffee House, near *Carlton's*, Happy Valley Rd. Pleasant cafe away from the noise and bustle on the way to Happy Valley, with Chinese and Tibetan food.

Green, The Mall, Kulri. Justifiably popular vegetarian restaurant.

Kwality, The Mall, Kulri. Part of the large chain; the usual good Indian, Western and Chinese food and *Star TV* while you eat.

Le Chef, The Mall, Kulri. Fast food, hot dogs, burgers and pizzas.

Mahaluxmi, The Mall, Kulri. On the corner near the GPO – nice place, with tasty vegetarian *thalis*.

Momos, Landour Bazaar. A small Tibetan-run cafe that remains closed in the low-season.

Tavern, The Mall, Kulri. Near the Kulri bus stand, a mediocre multi-cuisine restaurant but good for a beer; occasional live bands and dancing during the high season.

Whispering Windows, Gandhi Chowkh (☎632611). Also a hotel, one of Mussoorie's better restaurants – lively with piped music and a bar.

Haridwar

At **HARIDWAR** – the Gates (*dwar*) of God (*Hari*) – 214km northeast of Delhi, the **River Ganges** emerges from its final rapids past the Siwalik Hills, to start the long slow journey across northern India to the Bay of Bengal. Stretching for roughly 3km along a narrow strip of land between the craggy wooded hills to the west and the river to the east, Haridwar is especially revered by Hindus, for whom the **Har-ki-Pairi** *ghat*, literally the "Footstep of God", marks the exact spot where the river leaves the mountains. Looking north along the vast Doon Valley, the faint lines of the Himalayan foothills can be discerned rising above Rishikesh in the distance, while Haridwar itself faces east across the river to the hills of the Rajaji National Park. A major road and rail junction, linking Delhi and the Gangetic plains with the mountains of Uttarkhand and their holy *yatra* network, Haridwar may not be administratively part of the mountain districts, but it possesses a crucial spiritual and geographical significance.

Along with Nasik, Ujjain, and the holiest of them all, Prayag in Allahabad, Haridwar is one of the four holy *tirthas* or "crossings" that serve as the focus of the massive **Kumbh Mela** festival. Every twelve years, thousands of pilgrims come to bathe at a pre-ordained moment in the turbulent waters of the channelled river around Har-ki-Pairi. The Kumbh Mela is next due to take place here in 1998. Busy at the best of times, Haridwar can become unbearably congested during the Mela, when surging crowds around the bathing areas can create stampedes.

Arrival and information

Haridwar's **railway station** and **Station Bus Stand**, southwest of the centre, face each other across the main thoroughfare that channels all traffic through to meet the river at Har-ki-Pairi. **Trains** and **buses** connect Haridwar with Rishikesh, Dehra Dun and the mountains, and run back down to Delhi. You can also get to Rishikesh in shared taxis, while *Vikrams* and tempos ply the few roads in town. To arrange a **tour** of Garhwal by bus or car, call in at *Konark Tourist Service*, Jasaram Rd (☎427210).

An information booth at the station operates at arrival times. Information is also available at the **Regional Tourist Office**, near Lalta Rao Bridge on Upper Rd (Mon–Sat 10am–5pm; ☎427370), which has a GMVN booking office, and at the **UP Tourist Information Bureau**, near the bus stand at *Rahi Motel*, Station Rd (Mon–Sat 10am–5pm, closed 2nd Sat each month; ☎427370). There's a **post office** on Upper Rd, opposite *Ram Panjawani* (☎427266), the local agents for *Indian Airlines*. You can change **money** at the *State Bank of India*, near *Chitra Talkies* on Sadhu Bela Marg (☎426103).

> The telephone **area code** for Haridwar is ☎0133.

The Town

Split by a barrage north of Haridwar, the Ganges flows in two principal channels, divided by a long sliver of land. The main natural stream lies to the east, while the embankment of the fast-flowing canal to the west holds *ghats*, ashrams and buildings that seem to emerge out of the water. Promenades, river channels and bridges create a pleasant riverfront ambience, with the major *ghats* and religious activity clustered around **Har-ki-Pairi**, which bears a distinct resemblance to a railway station. Bridges and walkways connect the various islands, and metal chains are placed in the river to protect bathers from being swept away by ferocious currents. Non-Hindus are not allowed onto the actual Har-ki-Pairi *ghat*, where Vishnu left his footprints in stone, but the platform-like island opposite it, topped by a clocktower, provides an excellent vantage point, especially for evening worship. At dusk, the spectacular daily ceremony of **Ganga Arati** draws a crowd of thousands onto the islands and bridges. Lights float down the river, and priests perform elaborate choreographed movements, swinging torches in an ancient ritual to the accompaniment of gongs and music.

Near Vishnu Ghat in the centre of town, the uninspiring **Shri Mayadevi** temple, built on a site that dates back to the eleventh century, is dedicated to a form of Shakti. Further north along the Rishikesh road, the pool of **Bhimgoda** was gorged out by Bhima, one of the Pandava heroes of the *Mahabharata*. Haridwar's teeming network of **markets** are the main other focus of interest. **Bara Bazaar**, at the top of town, is strong on brass, cane and bamboo-ware – a good place to buy a *danda* (bamboo staff) for lengthy treks in the mountains. Stalls in the colourful **Moti Bazaar** on the Jawalapur road sell everything from clothes to spices.

High above Haridwar, on the crest of a ridge, the gleaming white *shikhara* of the **Mansa Devi** temple dominates both town and valley. The temple is easily and enjoy-

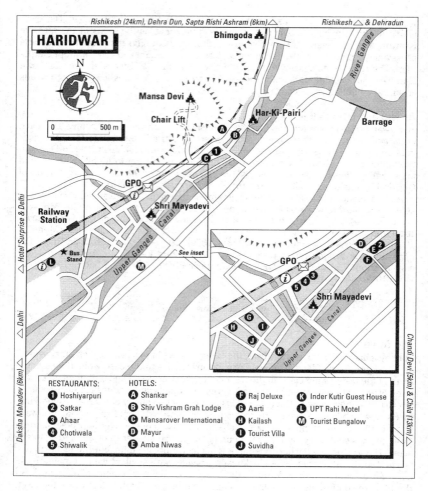

RESTAURANTS:
1 Hoshiyarpuri
2 Satkar
3 Ahaar
4 Chotiwala
5 Shiwalik

HOTELS:
A Shankar
B Shiv Vishram Grah Lodge
C Mansarover International
D Mayur
E Amba Niwas

F Raj Deluxe
G Aarti
H Kailash
I Tourist Villa
J Suvidha

K Inder Kutir Guest House
L UPT Rahi Motel
M Tourist Bungalow

ably reached by **cable car** (daily 8am–noon & 2–5pm; Rs13 return), from a base station off Upper Rd in the heart of town, though the steep 1.5-kilometre walk is pleasant enough early in the morning. None of the shrines and temples up top holds any great architectural interest, but you do get excellent views along the river. An elaborate queuing system leads pilgrims to *darshan* of the main image, showing Mansa Devi – a tripleheaded image of Shakti as the goddess Durga. Photography is taboo.

The extraordinary modern seven-storeyed **Bharat Mata** temple, 5km north of Haridwar and reachable in shared *Vikrams* for around Rs3, is dedicated to "Mother India". A temple with a similar name and intent can be found in Varanasi, but this one is much newer, and much more garish – and is obviously doing very nicely. Each of its various floors – connected by elevators – is dedicated to a celestial or political theme, and populated by life-like images of heroes, heroines and Hindu deities.

The **Shri Dakheshwar** temple, also known as **Daksha Mahadev**, 6km south of Haridwar in Khankhal, is beautifully situated with large trees above a *ghat*. The new main temple contains a gilded image of a snake symbolizing Shiva; legend relates Shiva's wife Sati was so enraged when her father snubbed Shiva by failing to invite him to a sacrifice performed on this spot that she sacrificed herself by self-immolation. A few hundred metres away, within the impeccable retreat of **Anandamoyee Ma Ashram**, a marble mausoleum is dedicated to the recently deceased Bengali woman guru. An adjacent bookshop sells literature connected with her life and work.

Across the river 5km east of Haridwar and on the edge of Rajaji National Park, **Chandi Devi**, another Shakti *pith* (temple) on a high ridge, looks down on the valley; its final rise can only be negotiated on foot.

Accommodation

Although it has no luxury hotels, Haridwar has **accommodation** to suit most budgets and temperaments. It's a small place, so wherever you stay the river and the bazaars are never too far away. Most hotels are within a Rs5 rickshaw ride northeast of the station; some, like the *Rahi*, are within walking distance.

Aarti, Railway Rd (☎427456). Quite a reasonable hotel on a busy main road, convenient for the railway station and bus stand. ④–⑤.

Amba Niwas, Choti Sabzi Mandi, Vishnu Ghat (☎423639). Small hotel in a crowded bazaar, with hot and cold running water in attached bathrooms. ③.

Inder Kutir Guest House, Sharwan Nath Nagar (☎426336). A family home, near the river being extended upwards with small rooms off the terrace. A change from the usual hotels. ③–④.

Kailash, Shiv Murti (☎427789). Central hotel near the railway station, with a handy counter for rail and bus tickets. Around 70 rooms, some air-cooled, and a vegetarian restaurant. ③–⑤.

Mansarover International, Upper Rd (☎426501). Comfortable, well-equipped hotel in the heart of the old town. ④–⑥.

Mayur, near Ropeway (☎427586). Ordinary place; good value during the lean season but overpriced during May and June. ②–④.

Raj Deluxe, Vishnu Ghat (☎427755). Large, busy and moderately comfortable hotel at the heart of a busy market, close to the river and bridge. ④–⑦.

Shankar, Upper Rd, near Post Office (☎427849). Poky rooms but the a/c makes it slightly more attractive, especially at this price. ②–④.

Shiv Vishram Grah Lodge, Upper Rd, near Har-ki-Pairi (☎427618). Large, quiet courtyard off the busiest part of town, with reasonable if somewhat shabby, air-cooled, budget rooms. ②.

MOVING ON FROM HARIDWAR

Major **trains** passing through include the excellent *Mussoorie Express* #4042 between Dehra Dun and **Delhi**, which leaves Haridwar at 10.50pm and takes 7hr to reach Delhi. Other trains to Delhi include the *Dehra Dun–Bombay Express* #9020; the *Ujjain–Dehradun Express* #4310 stops at **Agra**. The *Dehra Dun–Varanasi Express* #4266, covers the 850km to **Varanasi** in 20hr. The *Doon Express* #3009, which travels through **Lucknow** to **Calcutta**, is notoriously late. Local trains on the branch line to Rishikesh aren't that useful in view of the excellent and more frequent road connections.

Buses to **Delhi** leave from the **Station Bus Stand** almost every half-hour (5–6hr; fares from Rs53.50). Five or six buses a day leave for **Agra**, 368km south (10hr; around Rs90). Similarly, numerous buses go to **Rishikesh**, 24km north, and **Dehra Dun**, 57km northwest, as well as **Shimla**, **Nainital** and **Almora**. The **taxi** association near the railway station sets prices slightly higher than quoted elsewhere; a taxi to Delhi costs Rs1200, and Rs300 to Rishikesh. Shared Vikrams or tempos ply the route to Rishikesh and provide a cheap and interesting alternative for Rs10. Travellers heading into the mountains should go to Rishikesh to pick up onward transport.

Suvidha, Sharwan Nath Nagar, behind *Chitra Talkies Cinema* (☎427423). Pleasant location, near the river, away from the bustle of the bazaars and main roads. Comfortable and plush. ⑤–⑥.

Tourist Bungalow, Belwala, on the main island (☎426379). One of the few places on the east bank, in a pleasant garden overlooking the river away from the noise. Rooms range from a cheap dorm to a/c. ①–⑥.

Tourist Villa, Himalaya Depot Gali, Sharwan Nath Nagar (☎426391). Popular and quite new with a range of rooms. The ones at the top are less noisy. Food available as room service only. ③–④.

UP Tourism Rahi Motel, Station Rd (☎426430). Large modern bungalow next to the bus stand, with a dorm plus a restaurant set in pleasant gardens. ④–⑤.

Eating

Haridwar is a strictly **vegetarian** town; if you're happy with that, the food is very good, whether in the cafes around Har-ki-Pairi or the restaurants of Upper Rd and Station Rd.

Ahaar, Upper Rd. Mid-range Sikh-run restaurant, with a wood-panelled ambience, and serving good *thalis*, Chinese food and superb Punjabi cuisine such as the traditional and seasonal *makki-ki-roti* (corn *paratha*) with *sarson ka saag* (mustard-leaf spinach).

Chotiwala, Lalta Rao Bridge, near *Big Town Hotel*, Upper Rd. Next to *Ahaar* and another good restaurant, offering Indian food and good *thalis*. Established in 1937, and with a branch in Swarg Ashram, Rishikesh, it's still one of the best around. Is many imitators include one near Har-ki-Pairi.

Hoshiyarpuri, Upper Rd. Legendary and popular *dhaba*-like restaurant close to Har-ki-Pairi.

Satkar, Vishnu Ghat. Half-restaurant, half-*dhaba*, but quite pleasant, with Indian and Chinese food.

Shiwalik, Station Rd. One of a row of three good restaurants. Don't take its breakfast sign too seriously as it tends to open late; tasty south Indian snacks like *dosas*.

Rajaji National Park

Around 830 square kilometres of the Himalayan foothills immediately east of Haridwar are taken up by **RAJAJI NATIONAL PARK** (mid-Nov to mid-June; Rs100, plus Rs20 per vehicle, and camera fees), which belongs to the same forest belt as Corbett National Park, 180km east. Although not geared for tourism to the same extent as Corbett, the park is absolutely beautiful, with a similar range of wildlife – most notably elephants, but also tigers and even a rare species of ant-eater.

There are eight entry gates into the national park including **Kunnao** close to Rishikesh and the main gates at **Chila**, 9km east of Haridwar by road, across the Ganges. **Accommodation** is available at ten Forest Rest Houses (②–④), within the park and bookable through the Rajaji National Park Office, 5/1 Ansari Marg, Dehra Dun (☎23794). However, visitors don't have to go into the core area to experience the jungles, as it's possible to venture in from Chila or Rishikesh, or from the road between the two, paralleling the canal that marks the boundary of the huge fringe forest.

Chila

To get to **CHILA** from Haridwar, catch a Kandi- or Kandra-bound **bus** from the stand opposite the railway station, or a shared **jeep** from Chandi Ghat opposite Har-ki-Pairi. You could even **walk**; Chila is visible from Haridwar, and taking a short cut from Har-ki-Pairi via the riverbeds and a bridge makes it just four kilometres east. **Elephant rides** from here cost around Rs200 for two hours.

The town itself is neither attractive nor interesting, located right beside the Ganges barrage and its massive electricity pylons. However, it makes a good base for explorations of the park, and **Chila Beach** – occasionally used by large river turtles – lies within walking distance through the woods, 1km north along the Ganges.

Accommodation is available at the large GMVN *Chila Tourist Centre* (①–④), which has a dorm, standard and a/c rooms, huts and camping facilities.

Bindevasani and forest trails

Along the Kimsar road, which penetrates the deep *sal* forests northeast of Chila, visitors have a reasonable chance of glimpsing **wild elephant**. Elephant herds migrate here seasonally from as far away as Corbett, and can sometimes be seen in the forests behind Swarg Ashram in Rishikesh. The tiny hamlet of **BINDEVASANI**, 14km northeast of Chila and linked to both Chila and Haridwar by regular buses, stands at the foot of steep hills. Besides a small *dharamshala* and a tea shop, there's little here to detain travellers, but it's possible to camp in the covered forecourt of the small clifftop Durga temple, which affords dramatic views over the confluence of the Bindedhara and Nildhara rivers. For around 4km before Bindevasani, the road follows a vast riverbed, dry and extremely hot in summer, and still fordable during the rainy season.

A copious network of **trails** laces through the hills around Bindevasani. Possible routes include one to the village and temple of **Nilkantha** (14km north; see p.267); one to **Lakshmanjhula** (20km northwest; see p.265), the bridge and roadhead near Rishikesh; and one to the remote hamlet of **Yamkeshwar** (22km northeast), where a small Shiva temple on the banks of the Ravasan is surrounded by deep forest.

Rishikesh

RISHIKESH – forever famous as the spot where the Beatles met the Maharishi – is 238km northeast of Delhi and 24km north of Haridwar, at the point where the wooded mountains of Garhwal rise abruptly from the low valley floor, and the Ganges crashes onto the plains. Its many ashrams – some very clearly ascetic, some verging on the opulent – continue to draw devotees and followers of all sorts of weird and wonderful gurus, with the large **Shivananda Ashram** in particular renowned as a yoga centre.

Rishikesh has one or two ancient shrines, but its main role has always been as a way station for *sannyasin*, *yogis* and *sadhus* heading for the high Himalayas. The arrival of the Beatles was one of the first manifestations of the lucrative expansion of the *yatra* pilgrimage circuit; these days it's all too easy to see why Ringo thought it was "just like Butlin's". By far the best times to visit are in winter and spring, when the mountain temples are shut by the snows. In the absence of the *yatra* razzmatazz, you can get a sense of the tranquillity that was the original appeal of the place. At other times, a walk upriver leads easily away from the bustle to secluded spots among giant rocks ideally suited for yoga, meditation or an invigorating dip in the cold water.

Confusingly, the name Rishikesh is applied to a loose association of five distinct sections, encompassing not only the town but also hamlets and settlements on both sides of the river – **Rishikesh** itself, the commercial and communications hub; sprawling suburban **Muni-ki-Reti**; **Shivananda Nagar**, just north; the multi-storeyed and multi-coloured temples of **Lakshmanjhula**, straddling the river a little further north; and the assorted ashrams around **Swarg Ashram** on the east bank.

Arrival, transport and information

Far more visitors arrive in Rishikesh by road or rail than at the airport, 18km west (see p.252). The **Main Bus Stand**, used by Haridwar and Dehra Dun government buses, as well as direct services to and from Delhi (6hr), is on Bengali Mandir Rd, close to the centre; buses for the Garhwal hills use the **Yatra Bus Stand**, also known as the **Tehri Bus Stand**, off the Dehra Dun Rd. Rishikesh is at the end of a small branch **railway** line, served by trains to and from Haridwar. Advance reservations can be made from the station, which only has a small quota.

Local transport connecting the main areas includes cycle and auto-rickshaws and shared *Vikrams*. Some head south towards Haridwar, but few go all the way. **Cars** and **taxis** can be rented through *Ajay Travels*, at the *Hotel Nilkanth*, Haridwar Rd (☎30644),

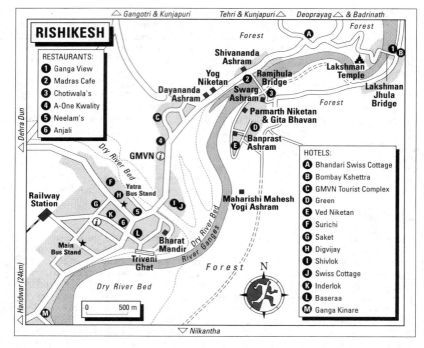

RISHIKESH

△ *Gangotri & Kunjapuri*   *Tehri & Kunjapuri*△   *Deoprayag* △ *& Badrinath*

Forest   *Forest*

RESTAURANTS:
❶ Ganga View
❷ Madras Cafe
❸ Chotiwala's
❹ A-One Kwality
❺ Neelam's
❻ Anjali

Forest

Shivananda Ashram

Yog Niketan   ❷ Ramjhula Bridge   Lakshman Temple

Dayananda Ashram   Swarg Ashram ❸   Lakshman Jhula Bridge

△ *Dehra Dun*

❸ Parmarth Niketan & Gita Bhavan   *Forest*

Dry River Bed

❻ GMVN ⓘ   ❹   Ⓓ

❹   Ⓔ Banprast Ashram

❺   **HOTELS:**
Ⓐ Bhandari Swiss Cottage
Ⓑ Bombay Kshettra
Ⓒ GMVN Tourist Complex
Ⓓ Green
Ⓔ Ved Niketan
Ⓕ Surichi
Ⓖ Saket
Ⓗ Digvijay
Ⓘ Shivlok
Ⓙ Swiss Cottage
Ⓚ Inderlok
Ⓛ Baseraa
Ⓜ Ganga Kinare

Ⓕ
Ⓗ Yatra Bus Stand

Railway Station   Ⓖ   Ⓘ Ⓙ

Maharishi Mahesh Yogi Ashram

Ⓚ   ❺   ❻
ⓘ
Ⓛ

Bharat Mandir

Main Bus Stand ★

Triveni Ghat   *River Ganges*   *Dry River Bed*

Forest   N

Dry River Bed

0 ━━━━━━━ 500 m

Ⓜ

△ *Haridwar (24km)*

▽ *Nilkantha*

or *Neelam's* restaurant, just off Haridwar Rd. Long-distance journeys can be booked at *Triveni Travels*, Shop No 1, opposite *PNB*, Haridwar Rd (☎30989).

The friendly and helpful **UPT Tourist Office**, Nehru Park, Railway Rd (Mon–Sat 10am–5pm, closed 2nd Saturdays of each month; ☎30209), provides information only. **GMVN** in theory exist to promote tourism in the region from their headquarters in Muni-ki-Reti (☎30372), but in practice restrict themselves to selling their own tours or booking accommodation in one of their tourist lodges. Their Mountaineering and Trekking division (☎30799), however, rents basic equipment, arranges guides, and provides information which may not always be conclusive; they also organize skiing breaks at Auli (see p.280). You may find one of the private operators situated around here such as Vicky Tiwari at the *Tourist Information & Facilitation Desk*, opposite *PNB*, Muni-ki-Reti (☎31654), more use; they also organize **rafting** on the Ganges.

Banks in town include the *State Bank of India*, Railway Lok, near *Inderlok Hotel* (☎30114), and *Bank of Baroda*, Dehra Dun Rd (both Mon–Sat 10am–2pm).

The Town

Most of the pilgrims who pass through Rishikesh on their way to the Himalayan shrines of the Char Dham pause for a dip and *puja* at what is left of the large sandy expanse of **Triveni Ghat**, close to the centre of town. Large, outlandish statues of the heroes of Hinduism have recently sprouted up along the *ghat* giving it an air of a theme

The telephone **area code** for Rishikesh is ☎01364.

ASHRAMS, YOGA AND MEDITATION

Due to an ongoing dispute with the government, Maharishi Mahesh Yogi's beautifully situated **Shankaracharya Nagar Transcendental Meditation Centre**, home to the Beatles in February 1968, is not presently open to foreigners; it stands empty on a high forested bluff above the river. However, plenty of other ashrams in Rishikesh welcome students of yoga, and don't charge the US$350 per day John Lennon et al. had to pay.

Shivananda Ashram Large institution, with branches all over the world, run by the *Divine Life Society* and founded by the remarkable Swami Shivananda (who passed into what his followers refer to as *maha samadhi*, final liberation, in 1963). It places an emphasis on the philosophy of Advaitya Vedanta, based on the belief of the non-dual Brahman, or godhead as the undivided self, and has a well-stocked library, a forest retreat, and a charitable hospital with allopathic, homeopathic and Ayurvedic treatment. Courses in meditation and other forms of yoga, plus other activities, are always going on. To arrange a long-term stay, write one month in advance to the Secretary.

A Yoga Week is held at the *Hotel Ganga Kinare* (☎30566) every year around the first week in February. The intensive course, based on Iyengar Yoga, costs US$500 per head, which includes all accommodation and food.

Brahma Niwas Towards the river near Kailash Gate in Muni-ki-Reti, Swami Kaivalyananda delivers a no-nonsense, shoot-from-the-hip interpretation of Vedanta that may not agree with some.

Dayananda Vedanta Ashram Near Shivananda Ashram; lectures on Vedanta and yoga classes.

Omkarananda Ashram Above Yoga Niketan, and also known as Durga Mandir; kindergarten school, plus classes which include classical Indian music and dance.

Vanamli Gita Yogashram On an idyllic site overlooking the river at Tapovan near Lakshmanjhula and offering short courses on different aspects of yoga.

Ved Niketan Huge ashram, across the river south of Swarg Ashram. Yoga classes early in the morning and evening lectures.

Yoga Niketan Meditation centre, reached by a path adjacent to Shivananda Ashram. Founded by the late Swami Yogeshwarananda, it offers a range of courses, with accommodation if necessary.

Yoga Study Centre Reputable school for the Iyengar form of Hatha Yoga, 1km south of central Rishikesh at Koyelgati.

---

park. The river here looks especially spectacular during *arati* (evening worship), when *diya* lights float on the water. Nearby, at **Bharat Mandir**, Rishikesh's oldest temple, a black stone image of Vishnu is supposed to have been consecrated by Shankara in the ninth century; the event is commemorated during Basant Panchami, to mark the first day of spring.

The dense-knit complex of cafes, shops and ashrams collectively known as **Swarg Ashram**, opposite Shivananda Nagar, is the most attractive part of Rishikesh, backing on to forest-covered hills where caves are still inhabited by *sadhus*. The river can be crossed at this point either on the new Ram Jhula footbridge, or more romantically on **ferries**, which operate between 8am and 7pm according to demand (Rs2.50 one-way, Rs4 return). The eponymous **Swarg Ashram** itself, popularly referred to as Kale Kumbli Wale, was founded in honour of Swami Vishudhanand, who came here in 1884 and habitually wore a black (*kala*) blanket (*kumble*). The most conspicuous of the other ashram-temples is **Parmarth Niketan**, whose large courtyard is crammed with bright-ly-clad gods and goddesses. Gita Bhavan runs a free Ayurvedic dispensary here, as well as selling books and *khadi*, handloom cloth.

Around 2km north of Swarg Ashram, a path skirts the east bank of the river, and beautiful sandy beaches sheltered by large boulders, en route to **Lakshmanjhula**. A footbridge named after the brother of Ram spans the river here as it negotiates its final rocky course out of the mountains. Many of the temples and ashrams around both ends

---

CHAR DHAM BUSES

During the April to November pilgrimage season, when the **Char Dham** temples are open in the Garhwal Hills, direct buses connect Rishikesh's Yatra Bus Stand with Badrinath (297km), Kedarnath (210km, via Gaurikund), Gangotri (250km), and Yumnotri (280km, via Hanuman Chatti). Buses leave around 4am and few complete the journey in a day; the roads are treacherous and tedious, so you might prefer to break the journey along the way.

GMVN in Muni-ki-Reti organize **package tours** (a four-day trip to Badrinath, including bus, food and lodging, costs around Rs1320), as well as very expensive car rental. *Sharma Travels*, Haridwar Rd (☎30364), has a fleet of press cars leaving around 5am to carry newspapers to various points in the mountains including Joshimath and Uttarkashi. Slightly more expensive and often cramped and uncomfortable, this is nevertheless, a much faster way of getting to the interior than by bus.

---

of the bridge – such as the extraordinary futuristic **Kailashananda Ashram**, with each of its thirteen storeys dedicated to a different deity – are complete eyesores.

Accommodation

Choosing a place to **stay** depends where you want to be – the hotels of Rishikesh are the nearest to the buses and general amenities, and Muni-ki-Reti is not too far either. Swarg Ashram and the east bank of the river, away from the noise and near the ashrams, are more pleasant, but quite a way from town; Lakshmanjhula is further still. There are also a couple of international ashrams, including the *Italian Ashram* (ask Mr Singh at *Neelam's* restaurant).

Arvind Lodge, Yatra Bus Stand. Simple budget accommodation, with unflattering rooms but very handy for early-morning buses to the hills. ①.

Banprast Ashram, next to Ved Niketan, Swarg Ashram. Well maintained bungalows at very good rates, in attractive grounds within a walled enclosure. Entry is discretionary. ①.

Baseraa, 1 Ghat Rd (☎30767). Comfortable modern hotel in the heart of the market area. ④–⑦.

Bhandari Swiss Cottage, Lakshmanjhula. Pleasantly located above the main road; the small block facing the orchard is preferable to the main building. Not to be confused with *Swiss Cottage*. ②.

Bombay Kshettra, Lakshmanjhula. Basic accommodation with shared baths. Handy for exploring the unspoilt upper reaches of this stretch of the river. ①.

Digvijay, Yatra Bus Stand (☎31528). Good value, pleasant and roomy – possibly the best of the budget hotels around the bus stand. ②–③.

Ganga Kinare, 2km south of Rishikesh, Barrage Rd (☎30566). Large, comfortable but overpriced. Hosts the International Yoga Week (see above), and runs yoga classes. ⑦.

GMVN Tourist Complex, Rishilok, Rishikesh (☎30373). Pleasant setting with garden and cottages away from the main centres. Busy during the *yatra* season. ④–⑤.

Green, Swarg Ashram (☎31242). Popular little hotel tucked behind *Gita Bhavan*. All rooms have attached baths, and a restaurant serves under-spiced Indian and Chinese food. ①–④.

Inderlok, Railway Rd (☎30555). Long-established and recommended central hotel. Comfortable rooms open onto an inner well, plus restaurant, roof garden, and foreign exchange. ⑤–⑥.

Saket, 154 Ashutosh Nagar (☎31776). Off the Dehra Dun Rd, down a quiet lane opposite the Yatra Bus Stand, with a small restaurant. The ordinary rooms share bathrooms without hot water. ②–④.

Shivlok, Lakshmanjhula Rd, Muni-ki-Reti (☎31055). Moderately comfortable, mid-priced hotel lying close to the bridge and handy for town. ④–⑤.

Surichi, Yatra Bus Stand (☎30356). Modern and well-maintained hotel, with good restaurant and an eager manager. Convenient for buses for the Char Dham, if a bit far from the river. ④.

Swiss Cottage, Chandra Bhaga. Run by the affable Swami Brahmananda, once one of Swami Shivananda's inner group of disciples. Near the bridge and down unnamed lanes towards the river, a small but peaceful haven with nine rooms in a motley selection of buildings. Not an ashram, but popular with long-term visitors, and extremely good value, so often booked up. ①.

PANCH PRAYAG – THE FIVE HOLY CONFLUENCES

As **Ganga** descended to earth at the behest of the gods, she fell onto Shiva's head and flowed down his matted locks; these strands are the mountains, where the separate ribbons of rivers meet to form the holy river before she emerges onto the plains of northern India. Five sacred **confluences** mark successive stages on the journey.

The Alaknanda, which rises near Badrinath, meets the Dhauli Ganga 10km north of Joshimath at **Vishnuprayag**, in a deep valley hidden from the sun for most of the day. A few shrines are all that mark the dramatic, rocky confluence.

The next confluence, where the river is joined by the Nandakini, is at the small town of **Nandprayag**, on the road from Uttarkashi that descends alongside the Alaknanda.

A further 21km downstream, the Alaknanda meets the Pindar, dropping from Nanda Devi, at the market town of **Karnaprayag**, named after a character in the *Mahabharata*.

The Alaknanda continues on its turbulent way to join the Mandakini at **Rudraprayag**, 34km from Karnaprayag. Rudraprayag has expanded haphazardly over recent years; the plaque that marks the famous spot where Jim Corbett shot a man-eating leopard is today at the heart of the noisy and bustling commercial centre. Crossing the river, a road forks up the valley, towards the source of the beautiful deep-blue Mandakini at Kedarnath.

After Rudraprayag, the Alaknanda descends through the open valley of Srinagar before its final and most dramatic mountain confluence, **Deoprayag**. Here it meets the Bhagirathi, a river of equal importance, descending from Gomukh on the glacier above Gangotri, and the two become the Ganges as it heads first to Rishikesh, 68km away, and then Haridwar, where it emerges on to the northern plains. The two mighty rivers meet with great force at a promontory of rock, where temples and a *ghat* in the shape of India extend into the confluence.

Ved Niketan, Swarg Ashram. Enormous and brightly painted ashram, well south on the east bank of the river, and very popular with low-budget Westerners. ①.

Eating

In addition to the restaurants in the larger hotels, Rishikesh has plenty of cafes and *dhabas. Neelam's* is an all-time favourite with an almost exclusively Western clientele.

A One Kwality, Kailash Gate, Muni-ki-Reti. Close to the Tourist Complex with a varied and extensive menu aimed at travellers. Especially good for breakfast.

Anjali, Railway Rd. Popular cross between a *dhaba* and a restaurant.

Chotiwala's, Swarg Ashram. *The* place to eat on this side of the river – large, busy and famous cafe that has spawned imitators throughout the region. An extensive menu includes ice-cream, sweets and cold drinks, while a special *thali* costs around Rs22.

Ganga View, Phoolchatti Rd, Lakshmanjhula. Popular traveller's cafe with a very pleasant little terrace overlooking the river.

Madras Cafe, Shivananda Nagar. Near the ferry, and strong on south Indian food but not particularly hygenic.

Neelam's, off Haridwar Rd. Towards the bridge and Muni-ki-Reti, this legendary Sikh-run *dhaba* is always filled with foreign travellers. The food and prices are worth braving the crowds, and Mr Singh is extremely helpful.

Around Rishikesh: local treks

Although a road has now been blasted through the forest to the small Shiva shrine in the hamlet of **Nilkanth Mahadev** or simply Nilkantha, east of Rishikesh, it's still possible to walk there along the old pilgrim path. This beautiful forest track rises through the forests behind Swarg Ashram, passes Mahesh Yogi's ashram, and eventually crosses a spur before descending to Nilkantha. There's a chance you may encounter wildlife along the way; keep a safe distance from wild elephants. Nilkantha itself is changing, as an ever-growing number of pilgrims travel along the new road that has cut a swathe through the forests from Lakshmanjhula. Its small bazaar and *dharamshala* become especially animated for around a month from mid-July, when pilgrims flock to the temple, which commemorates the time when the god drank the poison of creation and ended up with a blue (*nil*) throat (*kantha*). The motorable track north of Lakshmanjhula follows the river, passing several good beaches before arriving at the beautiful ashram of **Phulcchatti** (10km) on a bend in the river with giant boulders and excellent swimming.

Another hike leads high above Lakshmanjhula for ten kilometres to the small white Shakti temple of **Kunjapuri**, at the sharp point of an almost perfectly conical hill with stupendous views of the Himalayas to the north and towards Haridwar in the south. Try to catch the sunrise from the top, before the haze seeps into the atmosphere. A less strenuous alternative is to take the bus to Hindola Khal on the road to Tehri and walk the remaining 3km to the temple.

The Trek to Yumnotri

Cradled in a deep cleft in the lap of Bandarpunch, and thus denied mountain vistas, the temple of **Yumnotri** (3291m), 223km northeast of Rishikesh, marks the source of the Yamuna, India's second holiest river after the Ganges. As the least dramatic of the four *dhams* of Garhwal, it's also the most unspoiled and the least commercial, and the undemanding 14-km (5hr) trek up to it from **Hanuman Chatti** is one of the region's most popular short hikes. The trail leads through attractive countryside, following the turbulent river as it runs below terraced fields, with snowy peaks in the distance.

Hanuman Chatti

The roadhead for the Yumnotri trek, **HANUMAN CHATTI**, is connected by bus with Dehra Dun, Mussoorie, and Rishikesh. Some routes necessitate a change at **Barkot**, 29km short, which has a scattering of accommodation. Buses and shared taxis run the last leg up from there along a poor-condition road that is prone to landslides. Hanuman Chatti itself holds an over-priced GMVN *Tourist Bungalow* (②–③), between the bus stand and the river, and a couple of better-value basic hotels nearby. Food is available either at the bungalow or at cafes around the bus stand.

The path leads up across a bridge from Hanuman Chatti to meet the trail to Dodi Tal (see p.269), then veers left along the Yamuna for 6km, passing one or two small hamlets with tea shops, to **Phul Chatti**, where a couple more tea shops serve food. If you're planning any more ambitious trekking than the hike up to Yumnotri you're strongly advised to secure the aid of a local **guide**; Tota Ram and the older Shankar Singh are based in Phul Chatti, and others can be found in Hanuman Chatti.

Janki Chatti

The main trail from Phul Chatti continues along the river and over a bridge. A short and narrow section then traverses a landslide high above the river, before widening to reach **JANKI CHATTI**, 3km out of Phul Chatti. As the village gets a lot more sun than Yumnotri, just 5km further up, and is significantly larger and more hospitable, a lot of trekkers choose to stay here. Its GMVN *Tourist Bungalow* (②–④) is friendly, if a bit overpriced, and has its own cafe. GMVN also run a simpler hostel with dormitories (①), down by the river, and farther along the main trail, the *Ganga Jamuna* (①–②) provides a new alternative, with a cafe.

While you're in Janki Chatti, it's worth making the one-kilometre detour across the river to the traditional Garhwali village of **Kharsali**, home to the *pandas* (pilgrim priests) of Yumnotri. Its dry-stone buildings, with their beautifully carved wooden beams, contrast sharply with the characterless concrete structures cropping up all over the *yatra* trails of Garhwal. However, the unique three-storey Shiva temple – dedicated to Someshwar, lord of the mythical intoxicant Soma – has developed a slight tilt since the terrible earthquake of 1990. You can also hike to Kharsali direct from Phul Chatti.

Yumnotri

A short way beyond Janki Chatti, the trail begins to get really interesting. One especially hair-raising stretch involves negotiating a vertical cliff-face on a path 50 metres above the river, which when not hacked into the rock is built out over the abyss on concrete slabs. It's straightforward enough if you keep your head, but some of the path is in poor condition and the railings are often inadequate. You can only sympathize with the pilgrims who come this way mounted on ponies; as well having to duck to avoid the overhanging roof, they are under strict instructions never to look down.

After a final climb through some beautiful rocky forested crags, the path rounds a bend to offer the first glimpse of the small and dingy hamlet of **YUMNOTRI**, just a few hundred metres away. Sited near the river, around three piping-hot sulphur springs, Yumnotri's **temple** is new and architecturally uninteresting; it has to be completely rebuilt every few years due to the impact of heavy winter snows and monsoon rains. Its

---

THE DODI TAL TREK

The relatively short **Dodi Tal trek**, which links the Gangotri and Yumnotri regions without straying into high glacial terrain, is one of Garhwal's all-time classics. It's not a difficult hike, but local villagers are keen to offer their services as porters or guides, and you should definitely avail yourself of their help if you want to wander off the beaten track. Carry as much of your own food as possible, and also your own tent.

The trek is described below from east to west, starting from **Uttarkashi** on the way to Gangotri, and ending at **Hanuman Chatti**, the roadhead for Yumnotri.

On **DAY 1**, catch one of the three daily buses from Uttarkashi to **Kalyani** via Gangotri (the first is at 7am, and takes 1hr). From Kalyani, a good but steep trail rises through open fields to **Agoda**, 7km on. Stop for the night at the basic *Tourist Bungalow* (①), at the far end of the village, however tempted you may be to press on. You'll need a carry-mat to sleep on.

On **DAY 2**, the trail from Agoda climbs beside a river and then zig-zags steadily upwards through lush pine and spruce forests, with a couple of *chai* shops en route. After 14km and a final undulation, it arrives at **Dodi Tal** (3024m), a lake set against a backdrop of thickly forested hills. The basic forest bungalow in the clearing here, severely damaged by the earthquake, has yet to be repaired, so there's just a *chai* shop and some simple accommodation, which can get cramped – so you may prefer to use your own tent.

Some trekkers consider the full 18km from Dodi Tal to Shima on **DAY 3** to be too long and arduous, and prefer to split it into two days. Follow the well-marked path along (and often across) the stream that feeds Dodi Tal, which can get steep and entail scrambling; continue straight ahead, ignoring tracks that cross the trail, until you emerge above the treeline. After a further 1.5km the trail heads left to a small pass then zig-zags up scree to **Darwa Top** (4130m). This is the highest point of the trek, providing superb panoramas of the Srikanta range. If you're ready to rest here, a leftward path beyond the top leads to camping and water. The main route goes down to a valley and then climbs sharply again. **Shima**, where you re-join the treeline, has basic hut accommodation; bring your own food.

The beautiful 12km trail down from Shima on **DAY 4** kicks off with a steep 1.5km scramble alongside a stream, then eases past forest and *bugyal*, where shepherds have their huts. A well-defined rocky path drops steadily through two villages and zigzags down to the Hanuman Ganga river. It emerges at **Hanuman Chatti** (see p.268), from where buses run via Barkot to Uttarkashi, Mussoorie and other points in Garhwal.

The Dodi Tal trek can be easily be tied in with hikes in the **Har-ki-Dun** and **Yumnotri** areas; see also pages pp.257 and 269.

main shrine – actually part of the top spring, worshipped as the source of the river – holds a small silver image of the goddess Yamuna, bedecked with garlands. The daughter of Surya, the sun, and Sangya, consciousness, Yamuna is the twin sister of Yama, the lord of death; all who bathe in her waters are spared a painful end, while food cooked in the water is considered to be *prasad* (divine offering).

Technically, the source of the Yamuna is the glacial lake of **Saptarishi Kund**. This is reached via a hard twelve-kilometre trek, which heads straight up the mountain alongside the river until finally easing towards the base of Kalinda Parbat. Both this trek, and the route over the challenging Yumnotri Pass to Har-ki-Dun (see p.257) necessitate at least one day's acclimatization, adequate clothing, supplies and a guide.

If you choose to **stay** in Yumnotri, there's a simple dormitory at the GMVN *Tourist Bungalow*, near the temple (①). Probably the best of the few *dharamshalas* is the *Ramananda Ashram* (①), commanding good views from the hill above the temple, and owned by the head priest. Simple food arrangements can be made through the ashrams and the bungalow. Below the temple, a bridge leads across the river to a small complex of tea stalls and shops selling paraphernalia for worship.

Uttarkashi

The largest town in the interior of Garhwal, **UTTARKASHI**, occupies the flat and fertile valley floor of the Bhagirathi. Most pilgrims pass through without bothering to stop, but it can make a warm and sunny break in the long journey between Rishikesh, 148km south, and Gangotri, 100km northeast. *Uttar* Kashi ("northern Kashi"), like Varanasi (also known as "Kashi"), centres around the Shiva temple of **Vishwanatha**, although the unassuming temple complex here, surrounded by large trees, has much less spiritual significance. In fact, Uttarkashi was little known to the outside world until it lent its name to the massive nearby earthquake in 1991.

Uttarkashi's busy and well-stocked market is ideal for stocking up on supplies before high-altitude treks, and the town is also a good place to contact experienced mountain **guides** – mostly graduates of its Nehru Institute of Mountaineering. The going rates stand at around Rs150 per porter and Rs150–350 for a guide. Specialist operators include *Mount Support*, PO Box 2, B D Nautial Bhawan, Bhatwari Rd (☎01374/2419), on the main road near the bus stand, who also have equipment for rent.

Practicalities

All **buses** to and from Uttarkashi – which has hourly services to both Gangotri and Rishikesh between May and November – stop on the main highway, near the bazaar between the road and the river. **Taxis** can be picked up in the market area; the round trip to Gangotri costs around Rs1200. On the main drag, the information-only **Tourist Bureau** (☎01374/2290) is almost hidden behind the queues of noisy buses.

Good and reasonably priced **lodges** in the main bazaar include the *Hanslok* (②–④), and the *Meghdoot*, next door (②–④). Both have some a/c rooms. GMVN's poorly run *Tourist Bungalow* (③–⑤), around 1km away near the bridge, is a large faceless complex with a garden, where the spacious rooms have attached baths. Away from the bustle, in a pleasant location overlooking the valley 3km north of Uttarkashi just off the Gangotri road, the *Monal* (①–②) has cheap and comfortable rooms, but no restaurant.

Among the many *bhojanalaya* (vegetarian cafes) in central Uttarkashi, *Roopam* on the main road serves healthy local cuisine with *dal* and fresh *roti*.

Gangotri and around

Set amid tall *deodar* pine forests at the head of the Bhagirathi gorge, 248km north of Rishikesh at 3140m, **Gangotri** is the most picturesque of the four *dhams* (pilgrimage sites) of Garhwal. Although the Alaknanda, which flows past Badrinath, has in some ways a better claim to be considered the main channel of the Ganges, Gangotri is for Hindus the spiritual source of the great river, while its physical source is the ice cave of **Gomukh** on the Gangotri Glacier, 14km further up the valley. From here, the **River Bhagirathi** begins its tempestuous descent through a series of mighty gorges, carving great channels and cauldrons in the rock and foaming in white-water pools.

The road up

Several daily buses run from **Uttarkashi** to Gangotri. The first significant town en route, **Gangnani**, has a welcome hot spring above the road and a temple, plus a couple of *dharamshalas*, *chai* shops and a simple GMVN *Tourist Bungalow* (②). An Italian "baba", or *sadhu*, and his family have taken up residence here, and have become a well-known curiosity throughout Garhwal.

Parts of the road beyond, where the vast and fertile Bhagirathi flood plain is famous for its apple orchards, were damaged by the earthquake; gigantic blocks of rock almost dammed the river and created a lake. Off the main road down a rough track 31km along, **Harsil** marks the bottom limit of the Gangotri gorge. The village itself is grubby and depressing, with a large army base, but there's a newish *Tourist Bungalow* (②–④) pleasantly situated beside the river. A stone path leads along the valley floor and over a couple of bridges to an appealing Bhotia village. Prayer flags flutter over the small Buddhist temple of Vagori, standing amid the apple trees in a small garden.

Ten kilometres beyond Harsil, the road crosses the deep Bhagirathi gorge at **Lanka**, on a dramatic bridge said to be among the highest in the world. This is an army area, so don't take any photographs. At the hamlet of **Bhaironghati**, 3km further on and 11km short of Gangotri, the Rudragaira emerges from its own gorge to meet the Bhagirathi. A small temple stands in towering *deodar* forests, and there are a few tea shops as well as a barely used GMVN *Tourist Bungalow* (②–③).

Gangotri

Although most of the nearby snow peaks are obscured by the desolate craggy mountains looming immediately above **GANGOTRI**, the town itself is redolent of the atmosphere of the high Himalayas, populated by a mixed and ever-changing cast of Hindu pilgrims and foreign trekkers. Its unassuming **temple**, overlooking the river just beyond a small market on the left bank, was built early in the eighteenth century by the Gurkha general Amar Singh Thapa. Capped with a gilded roof, consisting of a squat *shikhara* surrounded by four smaller replicas, it commemorates the legend that the Ganga was enticed to earth by acts of penance performed by King Bhagirath, who wanted her to revitalize the ashes of his people. As she fell from heaven, Shiva braced the impact by entangling her in his locks; she was released by Brahma in answer to further prayers from the pious king. Inside the temple is a silver image to the goddess, while a slab of stone adjacent to the temple is venerated as **Bhagirath Shila**, the spot where the king meditated. Steps lead down to the main riverside *ghat*, where the devout bathe in the freezing waters of the river to cleanse their bodies and souls of sin.

Across the river, a loose development of ashrams and guest houses leads down to **Dev Ghat**, overlooking the confluence with the Kedar Ganga. Not far beyond, at the impressive waterfall-fed pool of **Gaurikund**, the 20-kilometre-long gorge starts to get into its stride. Beautiful forest paths lead through the dark *deodar* woods and past a bridge along the edge of the gorge to a flimsy rope-bridge, commanding great views of the ferocious river below.

Several **teashops** and **lodges**, whose rates rise wildly in high season, lie below the final car park and bus stand at the Gangotri roadhead. Most of the nicer guest houses lie across the river from here, reachable either via a beautiful footbridge or the main cantilever bridge near the temple; this bank is leafier and more pleasant, even if it doesn't catch so much sun.

GANGOTRI ASHRAMS

Although most of the so-called "ashrams" in Gangotri are in reality boarding houses, a few *sadhus* offer rooms on a donation basis for visitors looking for a quiet retreat.

The simple, atmospheric **Kailash Ashram**, overlooking the confluence of the Kedar Ganga and the Bhagirathi, is run (along with a small Ayurvedic clinic) by the affable Bhim Yogi, who welcomes guests for medium- and long-term stays. Nearby, **Nani Mata's Ashram** belongs to an English *mataji* (woman *sadhu*), who has lived in Gangotri for many years and is held in high esteem. Above Kailash Ashram, the larger **Yoga Niketan Ashram**, set in an attractive garden, operates along much more regimented lines, with fixed meal times and meditation periods, and a fixed though nominal fee.

GMVN's *Tourist Bungalow* (①–④), over the footbridge, has a reasonably cheap dorm. Nearer the main bridge, the large and popular *Ganga Niketan* (①–③) has a cafe overlooking the river, and *Birla Mangal Niketan* (①) is a large faceless block opposite the temple, where rates for the spacious rooms with attached baths remain fixed all season. The most attractive of the bungalows, the *Forest Guest House* (①) is a beautiful new log cabin in immaculate gardens; it can only be booked through the Forestry Department in Uttarkashi.

Meat is not available in Gangotri; the best places to eat are the large terrace at the *Ganga Niketan*, where the open-air seating comes with colourful umbrellas, and the *Manisha*, near the bus stand, which serves simple south and north Indian food.

Gomukh and Gangotri Glacier

A flight of steps alongside the temple at Gangotri leads up to join a large pony path that rises gently, providing stunning mountain vistas, towards the **Gangotri Glacier** – one of the most beautiful and accessible glaciers in the inner Himalayas, within 17km of the road. As the path emerges from the trees just beyond Gangotri, and the day progresses, you know you're in for a long hot climb in the high-altitude sun.

Approaching the oasis of **Chirbasa**, 7km out of Gangotri, the skyline is dominated by magnificent buttresses and glass-like walls, culminating in the sharp pinnacles of Bhagirathi 3 (6454m) and Bhagirathi 1 (6856m). Chirbasa amounts to no more than a few tea shops strung along the path for around 500m, as it winds through a rocky sheltered section. These provide basic meals and mattresses, or tents – the best are on the Gomukh path out of town – and there's also a basic forest lodge (①), below the road.

The path then climbs above the treeline, continuing along the widening valley to enter a high mountain desert. A number of accidents have been reported at the point just beyond Chirbasa where the trail across a cliff face has badly deteriorated, so great care is called for. Soon after crossing a stream, the path rounds a shoulder to offer a glimpse of the glacier's snout near Gomukh, the ever-present Bhagirathi peaks, and the huge expanse of the Gangotri Glacier – 24km long, and up to 4km wide – sweeping like a gigantic highway through the heart of the mountains.

Down below on the flat valley bottom, 5km from Chirbasa, is the cold grey hamlet of **Bhojbasa**, where most visitors spend the night before heading on to Gomukh. For once, the GMVN *Tourist Bungalow* here (①–③) comes out on top – even though mice run riot, and there's no electricity. As well as a dormitory and basic double rooms, some with attached bathrooms, there are some chilly but rodent-free tents. Guests huddle in the evening in the small but friendly cafe, which is where to arrange a mountain **guide** if you plan to cross the glaciers. Accommodation in the only competitor, *Lal Baba's Ashram* (①), is even more basic – just mattresses on the floor.

A good track continues from Bhojbasa for 5km to **Gomukh** ("the Cow's Mouth"), where the river emerges with great force from a cavern in the glacier. As the ice is constantly in flux, the huge greyish-blue snout of the glacier continually changes in appear-

TREKKING IN TEHRI GARHWAL: KHATLING GLACIER

The **Khatling Glacier**, source of the Bhilangana, lies at the head of a remote valley between the Gangotri and Kedarnath regions. It forms a huge watershed, with Jaonli (6632m) to the west, the Jogin group (6465m) to the north, and the striking peaks of Kirti Stambh (6270m) and Bharte Kunta (6578m) to the east. The upper Bhilangana valley is virtually unspoiled, with vast tracts of forest, beautiful waterfalls, and mountain streams descending from high *bugyals*.

Trails radiate from the nearest roadhead, **Ghuttu**, 147km north of Rishikesh, to the Bhagirathi to the west, and Sonprayag and the Mandakini valley to the east, while high mountain routes lead to Kedarnath via Khatling, and Uttarkashi via Gomukhi Tal.

Most long-distance bus journeys to Ghuttu involve a change at **Ghansyali** on the Uttarkashi-Rudraprayag road, three hours' drive west of Tehri (served by regular buses to and from Rishikesh). Simple hotels and cafes can be found at Ghansyali and Ghuttu.

The Khatling Glacier trail

DAY 1 of the moderately strenuous trail up to **Khatling Glacier** is a gentle introduction, with an ascent of just 650m in the 10km hike from Ghuttu to **Reeh**. You can stay above Reeh in the *Forest Rest House* (①) at Buranshchauri. An arduous trek of 10km on **DAY 2** brings you to the last inhabited village of the valley, **Gangi**. Continue 6km to camp at **Kalyani**, a village used by shepherds during the grazing season. **DAY 3** leads 14km from Kalyani, beyond Kharsoli, to **Bhelbagi** – at 3110m, the base camp for the glacier. On **DAY 4**, follow a rough trail up to Khatling Glacier (3658m), for a grand view (weather permitting) of the amphitheatre of snow peaks, and back to **Bhelbagi** – a 14km round trip.

On to Kedarnath

Using local guides, acclimatized and well-equipped trekkers can continue beyond Khatling Glacier to **Kedarnath** (see p.276), past a succession of mountain lakes. From **Bhelbagi**, a difficult track leads 7km to **Maser Tal** (4572m), where pilgrims bathe in the freezing waters. Camping here is recommended, as the icy conditions get extreme at the high **Pain Tal** (5629m), 7km further on. From there, a track descends through rough terrain for 6km to **Vasuki Tal** (4328m); you could camp here, but if you're going well and are dying for a *chai* shop and a bed, Kedarnath is just 9km further along a well-marked pony track. However, the descent to 3584m can be hard on the legs. From **Kedarnath** a 14km pony track, often full of pilgrims, leads to the Sonprayag roadhead and a hot spring.

Sahastra Tal

The seven small lakes known as **Sahastra Tal** lie close to each other, high on the divide between the Bhilangana valley in Tehri Garhwal and the Philangana valley in Uttarkashi, and cradled within rough rocky ground, covered with snow for much of the year. The lakes are venerated by local people in the belief that the Pandavas of the *Mahabharata* inhabited their shores, and built the natural stone terraces to sow their grain. During the rainy season, villagers from both sides of the divide carry deities to the lakes in an annual pilgrimage and perform ceremonies for their dead ancestors.

Although the lakes can be reached along a 35km trek from Malla on the Uttarkashi-Gangotri road, via Shilla and the simple refuge of Dharmshala, the path from **Gangi** to the highest lake – **Gomukhi Tal**, on the Bhilangana side – is shorter, and can be combined with the trip to Khatling Glacier. From **Kalyani** (see above), a rough track that becomes progressively harder to discern rises for 8km to the campsite at Tari Udiyar.

The Sonprayag trail

The major pilgrim path that linked the Gangotri and Uttarkashi region with Kedarnath until the motor road opened leads east from Ghuttu to **Sonprayag** (see p.275), with simple shelter and food available along the way. The first stop is the village of Panwali Kanta, 10km out of Ghuttu. Maggu is 6km further on, and the popular temple village of **Triyugi Narayan**, with its eternal flame (see p.275), is 5km beyond that. A rough motor road connects Triyugi Narayan to the main road, and a trail of around 3km cuts through the forest to Sonprayag.

ance, and chunks of ice tumble into the gushing water – be careful of standing above the cave. Two or three *chai* shops near here provide food and basic shelter.

Tapovan and Nandanvan

The campsites of **Tapovan** and **Nandanvan**, 6km beyond Gomukh on slightly divergent glacier-side routes, are popular objectives for lightweight trekking and mountaineering, as a rule best attempted using guides engaged from Gangotri or Bhojbasa.

A difficult track leads past the last tea shop at Gomukh to ascend the moraine on the left edge of the glacier, following it for 1km before crossing the glacier diagonally towards a high point in the middle, in line with Shivling. Depending on the season, this stage can be confusing and dangerous; heavy snow can conceal deep crevasses and the cairns that mark the way. From the high point, you should be able to see a stream coming down the high bank opposite. Use this as a marker; an extremely steep and strenuous climb up unstable ground runs to its left, to top out eventually on the grassy meadow of **TAPOVAN**, where you're greeted by the fantastic sight of Shivling (6543m) towering above. With its herds of grazing, almost tame *bharal* (mountain goats), and a tranquil stream, the meadow makes a bizarre contrast to the sea of ice below.

Many trekkers arrive in Tapovan without camping equipment, expecting to shelter in either of its two ashrams. However, although Mataji, a female *sadhu* who lives here throughout the year, and Shimla Baba do indeed have small hermitages with blankets, and are prepared to feed visitors, their resources are greatly stretched. Whether or not you stay with them, please carry supplies, which will always be welcome, and bring camping and cooking equipment if you plan to be here more than a day or two.

NANDANVAN lies on a similar but less frequented meadow below the Bhagirathi Peaks, at the junction of the glacier known as the Chaturang Bamak and the Gangotri Glacier. From here you get magnificent views of Bhagirathi, Shivling, and the huge snowy mass of **Kedar Dome** (6831m), hiding a steep sheer rocky face. The trail up follows the same path from Gomukh, but instead of the diagonal slant towards Tapovan, continues across the Raktaban Glacier and follows the left bank of the Gangotri Glacier. If you do get confused and find yourself in Nandanvan by mistake, an indistinct 3km trail across Gangotri Glacier leads back to Tapovan.

Kedar Tal

Kedar Tal, the source of the Kedar Ganga – an emerald lake 5000m above sea level, surrounded by a grand amphitheatre of mountains – makes a challenging objective. Although it's only 17km from Gangotri, the 2000m climb to such an altitude means that trekkers should be well equipped and fully acclimatized to the height.

A steep rough trail through the forest from Dandi Chetra, near Gangotri's Dev Ghat, follows the right bank of the Kedar Ganga for 7.5km to the meadow of **Bhoj Kharak**. At this point – a good campground – the pine woods give way to *bhoj* (birch), whose bark was used to write on before the introduction of paper. Continuing along a stretch made treacherous by rockfall and avalanche, the path rises for 4km above the treeline to reach another *bugyal* (meadow) suitable for camping – **Kedar Kharak**.

From Kedar Kharak, the gruelling 5km ascent to Kedar Tal scrambles over difficult loose terrain directly towards the rocky pinnacle of Thalesagar. Surrounding the beautiful glacial lake at the head of the valley, the cirque of mountains include, from left to right, Bhrigupanth (6772m), Thalesagar (6904m) and the Jogin group.

The route to Kedarnath

It's hard to imagine a more dramatic setting for a temple than **Kedarnath**, 223km north of Rishikesh, close to the source of the Mandakini at 3583m above sea level, and overlooked by tumbling glaciers and huge buttresses of ice, snow and rock.

Kedarnath – the "field" (*kedara*) where the crop of *moksha* (liberation) is sown – is the most important shrine in the Himalayas, and among the major Shiva temples of all India. According to the *Puranas*, when the Pandavas were searching for Shiva to grant them absolution, they succeeded in tracking him down to Kedarnath, where he disguised himself as a bull in a herd of cattle. One of the brothers, Bhim, then straddled the valley and allowed the herd to pass beneath him, reasoning that the only bull to refuse must be Shiva himself. When Shiva was unmasked, he dived into the ground; Bhim grabbed him from behind, and held on tight. However, all that remained of the god was his rear; his *lingam* appeared in Varanasi (Kashi), while assorted other pieces of his anatomy are commemorated by the Panch Kedar temples (see p.277).

As one of India's twelve *Jyotrilinga* – *lingams* of light – Kedarnath attracts hordes of pilgrims in summer, undeterred by the gruelling fourteen-kilometre trek up from the roadhead at **Gaurikund** that forms the final leg of the journey. So popular is it on the *yatra* trail that the path up has been all but stripped of vegetation, used for fuel and to feed the ponies that carry wealthier pilgrims. *Chai* shops that provide food and shelter along the route, especially in the upper sections, add to the environmental damage.

The road up

The main road to Kedarnath heads north from Rudraprayag towards Sonprayag. Deep in the Mandakini valley, the temple of **Kalimath** is one of the few temples devoted to Kali in the region. Beyond it, on the road to Gopeshwar, is the pleasant town of **Okhimath**, to which the population of Kedarnath decamps in winter, to continue worship when the high temple is snowed in.

Larger **Sonprayag** was, until the road was pushed another 5km up to Gaurikund in the late 1970s, the transport junction for Kedarnath, which explains its sizeable bus stand and plentiful amenities, including a pretentious hotel-like *Tourist Lodge* (②–④). From Sonprayag, a rough but drivable road rises 3km to the temple of **Triyugi Narayan**, outside which an eternal flame burns on the spot where Shiva and Sati are said to have been married in the presence of Vishnu (also known as Narayan).

Gaurikund

GAURIKUND, formerly a charming village, but since the advent of the motor road and the expansion of its *yatra* trade rapidly growing into a small ugly town, is for the moment the starting point of the trek up to Kedarnath (although there are plans to extend the road to Rambara). En route to or from chilly Kedarnath, a dip in the **Tapt Kund** hot springs can be very welcome, although sadly they are not well maintained. The small temple of Gauri Devi, adjacent to the pool, is dedicated to Parvati.

Direct buses run to Gaurikund all the way from Rishikesh, but most visitors arrive on local buses and taxis from the larger bus terminal at **Guptkashi**, 29km lower down. This receives services from Rudraprayag, 109km south on the busy main Rishikesh–Joshimath–Badrinath route, and Gopeshwar, 138km southeast.

Inexpensive *dharamshalas* and rest houses in Gaurikund itself include the large grey *Bharat Seva Ashram* (①), *Punjab Sindh* (①–②), where some rooms have attached baths, and the smaller *Sanjay Lodge* and *Sunil Lodge* (both ①–②). Rates for the very cosy rooms in the GMVN *Tourist Centre* (①–④) are pricier, but remain constant even in high season (when it's advisable to book in advance), and it also has a cheap dorm. The *Gauri's Grand* **restaurant** is a complete culture shock, with MTV piped through the sound system – however, it is comfortable and clean and its wide-ranging menu even extends as far as veggie burgers.

The trail from Gaurikund

A large pony track, dotted with *chai* shops, climbs from Gaurikund, traversing the hillside through the disappearing forests, to the village of **Rambara**, 7km up and halfway to Kedarnath. With its many cafes and rest houses (and open sewers), Rambara signals the end of the treeline and the start of the alpine zone. Several conspicuous short cuts scar the hillside as the track rises steeply to Garur Chatti, then levels off roughly 1km short of Kedarnath. Suddenly, rounding a corner, you come face to face with the incredible south face of the peak of Kedarnath (6940m) at the end of the valley, with the temple town dwarfed beneath it and almost insignificant in the distance.

Kedarnath: town and treks

KEDARNATH is not in itself a very attractive town – in fact it's almost unbearable at the height of the pilgrimage season (May, June & Sept). It's a grey place, consisting of a central thoroughfare stretching for 500 metres between the temple and the bridge, lined with rest houses and *dharamshalas*, pilgrim shops, and administrative offices. However, the sheer power of its location tends to sweep away any negative impressions, and it's always possible to escape to explore the incredible high-altitude scenery.

At the head of the town, the imposing **temple** is constructed along simple lines in stone, with a large *mandapa* (fore-chamber) housing an impressive stone image of Shiva's bull, Nandi. Within the inner sanctum, open to all, *pandas* sit around a rock considered to be the hindquarters of Shiva, left as he plunged head-first into the ground. Mendicant *sadhus* congregate in the elevated courtyard in front of the temple.

A solid path from near the main bridge, before the town, crosses the Mandakini to the left of the valley, and ends 4km away at the **glacier**. At its edge, the **Chorabari Tal** lake is now known as **Gandhi Sarovar**, as some of Mahatma Gandhi's ashes were scattered here. Close by, around 800m before the lake, is the source of the Mandakini; it emerges from a hole in the moraine on extremely suspect ground, which should not be approached. You could also cross the river by the small bridge behind the temple, and scramble up the rough boulder-strewn moraine to meet the main track.

East of town, a well-marked path rises diagonally along the hillside to the prayer flags that mark a small shrine of the wrathful emanation of Shiva – **Bhairava**. The cliff known as **Bhairava Jhamp** is said to be somewhere nearby; until the British banned the practice in the nineteenth century, fanatical pilgrims used to leap to their deaths from it in the hope of gaining instant liberation.

The most challenging of all the Kedarnath excursions is the 9km-trek to the lake of **Vasuki Tal** (4328m). From the *Tourist Bungalow*, a well-marked pony track zigzags in clear view of Kedarnath, heading up the hill for around 1km before negotiating scree

---

SHANKARA IN GARHWAL

Immediately behind the temple at Kedarnath, towards the glacier, a gigantic hand holding an ascetic's staff protrudes from a marble wall. This modern monument – which, it has to be said, is a complete eyesore – commemorates the ninth-century Hindu philosopher and reformer, **Shankara**, who is said to have died here.

Shankara travelled through the region as the Buddhist era came to a close, introducing sweeping reforms that helped to create the order of *sanyas* (monkhood). Much of his philosophy adheres to the principles of Advaitya Vedanta and its belief in non-dual Brahman or unified consciousness which some modern philosophers see as borrowing heavily from Buddhism. In Garhwal, he converted fertility and animist cults into Shaivite and Vaishnavite shrines, and helped to establish the great pilgrimage centres such as Kedarnath. Today, the **Rawal**, who heads both Badrinath and Kedarnath, continues to be chosen from the same Nambudiri sect of Keralan *brahmins* that he belonged to. Among the four major seats of learning set up by Shankara in the four corners of India, each headed by a *Shankaracharya*, was the one in Joshimath.

and rough ground near the crest, and descending slightly to Vasuki Tal. Don't be surprised to find wealthier pilgrims being led most of the way on horseback. Beyond Vasuki Tal, a challenging trail – only to be attempted with full supplies, appropriate clothing and an experienced guide – continues to the **Khatling Glacier**, via the high lakes of Pain Tal and Maser Tal (see p.273).

Practicalities

Kedarnath's GMVN *Tourist Bungalow* (①–④), standing like a disused railway station before the bridge that leads into town, has a cheap dorm and standard doubles. Alternatives include the clean and comfortable *Bharat Seva Ashram* (①), a large red building beyond the temple on the left; the pleasantly located bungalow of *Modi Bhavan* (②), behind and above the temple near the monument, which has large rooms and kitchenettes; and *Punjab Sindh* (①–②), next to the post office.

Food in the cafes along Kedarnath's main street is simple but expensive, as all supplies have to be brought up from the valley on horseback. The canteen run by the temple committee, *Shri Badrinath Kedarnath Mandi Samiti,* behind the temple, serves meals and *alu paratha*. It is also a good place to contact a mountain **guide**, if you plan to attempt the Vasuki Tal and Khatling crossing.

Panch Kedar

Pilgrim trails cross the heart of Garhwal from Guptkashi in the west to Gopeshwar and the Alaknanda valley in the east, winding their way far above the steamy valleys and terraced fields, up through beautiful forests to the sharp grassy ridges that hold the widely scattered Shiva temples collectively known as **Panch Kedar**.

The Panch Kedar temples almost certainly started life as shrines to fertility gods, and had little to do with each other until Shankara passed this way in the ninth century and incorporated them into the framework of Hindu mythology, saying that they represent the five (*panch*) parts of Shiva's body left protruding from the earth when he escaped the Pandavas by fleeing into the underworld (see p.275). Strictly speaking, the five include Kedarnath, but the term usually refers only to the other four, which have escaped the commercialism of the main *yatra* trails.

These four – **Madhmaheshwar** in the northwest; **Tunganath** (3680m), the highest temple in India, in the centre; and **Rudranath**, with **Kalpeshwar** below it, overlooking the Alaknanda valley in the east – can be taken in on a long circular trek. However, most visitors use vehicles along the Okhimath–Gopeshwar road to avoid the hike between the separate areas. Even so, getting to the temples themselves involves a bit of trekking, although **Tunganath** is only 3km above Chopta on the main road. One daily **bus** leaves Gaurikund, near Kedarnath, at 5am, for Badrinath, and stops at access points for Panch Kedar en route; a local bus connects Gopeshwar and Guptkashi.

Madhmaheshwar

The most remote of the Panch Kedar temples, at **MADHMAHESHWAR**, north of **Okhimath**, is also the least visited. One of Garhwal's most beautiful roads climbs up from the Mandakini valley beyond Okhimath for 10km through dense forest to the tiny hamlet of **Sari**, the start of the 5km trail to the wooded lake of **Deoria Tal**.

Beyond Deoria Tal, the trail continues for 15km, through the village of Mansuna and across the Madhmaheshwar Ganga river, to Lank and Ransi. At this point, a poor trail, only to be attempted with a guide, branches left across the high ridges to Kedarnath. The main path from Ransi, however, continues 3km to Gondhar, crosses a river, then climbs 10km to the hamlet of Madhmaheshwar, set in pleasant meadows at 3497m. The small temple here, a simple stone structure with colourfully painted woodwork on the door and on the top of the *shikhara*, is dedicated to the middle (*madhya*) of the bull-Shiva. The village offers simple pilgrim shelter and food.

Chopta and Tunganath

The beautiful little village of **CHOPTA** is situated amid dark *deodar* forests and sweeping alpine meadows on the road between Okhimath (21km) and Gopeshwar (40km). This quiet and peaceful spot holds a few simple *chai* shops and the region's one – overpriced – GMVN *Tourist Bungalow* (①–④), where the rooms have attached baths, with hot water available by the bucket. They also run camping facilities and a rather poor roadside cafe. Alternative accommodation available at the adjacent village is basic but much more atmospheric.

A steep three-kilometre trail climbs up from Chopta, winding through a dense forest of pine and rhododendron before emerging onto open meadows along a well-marked pony track as the view towards the Yumnotri, Gangotri and Kedarnath peaks gradually unfolds. The virgin forests around teem with wildlife such as leopard and bear. As you approach, a tiny dot near the top of the ridge, reveals itself to be the stone temple of **Tunganath**, associated with Shiva's hand (*bahu*). Simple accommodation and food is available here; due to its exposed position, it can get very cold, even in summer.

Beyond Tunganath, a well-marked path skirts the edge of the precipitous ridge, and zigzags for 1km up the steep *bugyal* to culminate at the grassy knoll of **Chandrashila Peak** (3930m), with an incredible 180° panorama of Himalayan snow peaks.

Kalpeshwar and Rudranath

The unspoiled temples of **Kalpeshwar** and **Rudranath** are most easily accessible from the Badrinath–Rishikesh highway as it runs through the Alaknanda valley, although tackling the route from the other end, starting at Mandal on the Chopta–Gopeshwar road, makes it easier to combine with Tunganath. Either way, the criss-crossing mountain paths can get very confusing, and enlisting the aid of a guide is advisable.

Buses along the Badrinath–Rishikesh highway serve the village of **Helang**, 14km south of Joshimath, from where a path sets off across a footbridge over the Alaknanda and winds for 9km to **Urgam**. As well as its own temple, Urgam has simple accommodation and food. A 1.5km side trail leads to the temple of **KALPESHWAR**, dedicated to the *jata* (hair) of the bull-Shiva, beside a cave with a beautiful waterfall.

A little further beyond, in **Dumak**, the last village before Rudranath, it's possible to stay in the postmaster's house. Several trails split off; but the main trail first rises, then descends to cross a river, and rises once more to the lake of **Toli**, after 9km. Used for pasture, this has no accommodation; continue to **Panar**, where a *sadhu* provides accommodation in a cave beyond two small Shiva temples, and there's also excellent camping, with a good supply of water. From here on you'll have to be self-sufficient.

Beyond Panar, the path follows the high ridge visible from Tunganath, sometimes left and sometimes right of the crest, to the junction of several trails. After 3km, you come to a col; the hamlet of **RUDRANATH** lies a short distance right of the crest, with some small stone shrines dedicated to the mouth of the bull-Shiva. There are a few houses up here, but the whole place closes during the long winters – check whether anyone will be around before you set off.

Back at the col on the ridge, you should be able to pick out the 16km track that descends to the Shakti temple of **Anasuya Devi**, set on a shelf in a spellbinding spot in the woods. Below Anasuya Devi and its few basic *dharamshalas*, the path drops to a crystal-clear river, where you can bathe in the pools of a waterfall amid bamboo and dense forest. **Mandal** village, 6km below Anasuya Devi on the Chopta-Gopeshwar road, has a few *chai* shops and very basic rooms, and there's a *Forest Rest House* (①) at Pangar Basa 1km away. **Buses**, and the odd shared taxi, run to Gopeshwar, 11km east.

Joshimath and Auli

The scattered administrative town of **JOSHIMATH** clings to the side of a deep valley 250km northeast of Rishikesh, with tantalizing glimpses of the snow peaks high above, and the prospect far below of the road disappearing into a sunless canyon at Vishnu Prayag, the confluence with the Dhauli Ganga. Few of the thousands of pilgrims who pass through en route to Badrinath linger here, but Joshimath has close links with **Shankara**, the ninth-century reformer, who attained enlightenment here beneath a mulberry tree, before going on to establish **Jyotiramath**, one of the four centres of Hinduism (*dhams*) at the four cardinal points. In winter, when Badrinath is closed, the Rawal, the head priest of both Badrinath and Kedarnath, resides at Joshimath.

Joshimath consists of a long drawn-out upper bazaar, and, around 1km from the main square on the Badrinath road, a lower bazaar holds the colourful **Narsingh**, **Navadurga**, **Vasudev** and **Gauri Shankar** temples. Narsingh, dedicated to Vishnu as a lion, is the largest, with brightly painted woodwork reminiscent of Badrinath. In addition, **Tapovan**, 11km north of Joshimath along the Dhaul Ganga Valley and named after its hot springs, is the end of the **Curzon Trail** over Kuari Pass.

Practicalities

Most **buses** up to Joshimath stop in the upper bazaar. All motorized transport onwards to Badrinath – and there are plenty of buses during the *yatra* season – is obliged to move in **convoys**. A gate system controls traffic in each direction, in two equal 24-kilometre stages – the first between Joshimath and Pandukeshwar, the second between Pandukeshwar and Badrinath. Several convoys leave Joshimath each day, forming around the Narsingh temple complex. At night the road remains closed.

Rooms at the GMVN *Tourist Rest House* (☎01389/2118; ①–④), at the north end of the upper bazaar, include a dorm, and a cafe serves simple meals; the unattractive annexe up the lane at Gandhi Maidan is a converted school. Also at Gandhi Maidan, the local **tourist office** (Mon–Sat 10am–5pm) is friendly enough, but no longer rents out trekking gear and guides – this service has been shifted to Auli. *Nanda Devi Mountain Travel*, *Hotel Nanda Devi*, Main Bazaar (☎01389/2170), organizes **treks** and **river rafting** and provide guides and equipment; they also have offices in New Delhi and Manali.

Bang next door to the *Tourist Rest House*, *Shailja* (☎01389/2208; ①–②) is popular with travellers as the prices are negotiable. Small hotels around the main square include the basic *Kamet* (☎01389/2155; ①–③): rooms facing the square are the cheapest. A short way south, *Jyoti Lodge* (☎01389/2133; ②–④) is excellent value, while the older *Neelkanth* (☎01389/2131; ②–④), opposite, has quiet pleasant rooms overlooking the valley. Further south of the centre, *Dronagiri* (☎01389/2254; ④–⑥;) may be characterless but it's the most comfortable in town, with a clean restaurant. At the bus stand near the Narsingh temple in the lower bazaar, *Kedar Holy Home* (☎01389/2246; ①–③) is simple but clean and handy for early morning buses to Badrinath. The traveller-friendly *Paradise* cafe, next to the *Tourist Rest House*, has a good range plus porridge for breakfast, while down at the main square the *Marwari* is a busy and reasonable vegetarian *dhaba* with a small hotel upstairs.

Auli

A rough road winds fifteen kilometres up through the *deodar* forest from Joshimath to **AULI**, which has been recently developed as a **ski** resort, partly in the hope of replacing the ski areas rendered inaccessible by the war in Kashmir. With the introduction of a cable-car in 1994, the extensive meadows of **Auli Bugyal** will never be the same again. One of the longest cable-cars in Asia, the trolley, as it is known locally, connects Joshimath with **Gorson**, above Auli (Rs150 return, no singles) from where Auli's only chair-lift travels to the base lodge below (Rs50). A short distance beyond Gorson lies the hill of Gorson Top, which provides excellent mountain vistas and is on the 24-kilometre trail to **Kuari Pass** (see below). At present, all the pistes empty into one central run, arriving at the badly sited GMVN *Tourist Centre*, which faces the wrong way and has no views. Skiing here is cheap and packages are available at competitive rates; you can ski on a day trip for around Rs200, including lift charges and the rental of (rather poor) equipment. Note that Auli's season is short and starts around New Year. For up-to-date information on skiing contact GMVN at Rishikesh (☎01364/30799).

The *Tourist Centre* (☎01389/2226; ②–⑥) has two large dorms with lockable cubicles, and comfortable, if pricey, rooms and suites in its outbuildings. The friendly staff in the dining hall try their best, but don't expect any *après-ski* activity.

Badrinath

The most popular of the four main temples of Garhwal, 298km northeast of Rishikesh and just 40km south of Tibet, is that of **BADRINATH** – "Lord of the Berries". One of Hinduism's holiest sites, it was founded by Shankara in the ninth century, not far from the source of the Alaknanda, the main tributary of the holy Ganga. Although the temple has a stunning setting, beneath the sharp snowy pyramid of Nilkantha (6558m), the town that has grown up around it is grey, grubby and unattractive. Set in a deep valley, it remains in shade for most of the day.

Until a few years ago, Badrinath was a remote and evocative place, where legends spoke of mysterious *sadhus* such as the Englishman who lived high in the mountains amid the snow and ice. Now, however, it has grown out of all proportion to its infrastructure. The army-built road up from Joshimath, 48km south, brings endless convoys of buses and taxis, and the temple turns over astronomical amounts of money. Pilgrims crowd in, the streets are lined with mendicant *sadhus* and beggars, and roadside stalls sell all sorts of religious paraphernalia.

Badrinath is still presided over by a Nambudiri *brahmin* from Kerala – the Rawal, who also acts as the head priest for Kedarnath. According to myth, the two temples were once close enough together for the priest to worship at both on the same day. The **temple** itself, also known as Badri Narayan, is dedicated to Vishnu, who is said to have done penance in the mythical Badrivan ("Forest of Berries"), that once covered the mountains of Uttarkhand. Unusually, it is made of wood; the entire facade is repainted each May, once the snows have receded and the temple opens for the season. From a distance, its bright colours resemble a Tibetan *gompa*; there's some debate as to whether the temple was formerly a Buddhist shrine. Inside, where photography is strictly taboo, the black stone image of **Badri Vishal** is seated like a *bodhisattva* in the lotus position (some Hindus regard the Buddha as an incarnation of Vishnu). *Pandas* (pilgrim priests) sit around the cloisters carrying on the business of worship and a booth enables visitors to pay in advance for rituals chosen from a long menu. This site, on the west bank of the turbulent Alaknanda, may well have been selected because of the sulphurous **Tapt Kund** hot springs on the embankment right beneath the temple, which is used for ritual bathing. Immediately south of the temple, the **old village** of Badrinath is still there, its traditional stone buildings and a small market seeming like relics from a bygone age. A sign on the main road north of Badrinath prohibits foreigners from proceeding further towards Tibet. However, visitors can normally – check the current situation – take local buses to the end of the road at the Bhotia village of **Mana**, 4km on, where a small army camp on the far side of the river effectively bars your way. It's also possible to walk this far along a footpath. The village itself consists of a warren of small lanes and buildings piled virtually on top of each other; the local Bhotia people, Buddhists of Tibetan origin who formerly traded across the high Mana Pass, now tend livestock and ponies. A path drops from the village to cross a bridge, then continues west along the side valley towards the mountain of Satopanth on the divide between the Mana and Gangotri regions, to the base of the impressive high waterfall of **Vasudhara**. Dropping from a hanging valley, this is considered to be the source of the Alaknanda, where it falls from heaven.

Practicalities

At the **Information Centre**, run by Badrinath's **Temple Committee**, on the east bank opposite the temple, you can book rooms in the various pilgrim rest houses they manage, such as the nearby *Modi Bhavan* (②), and *Gujarat Bhavan* (③), next to the temple on the west bank. *Kale Kambli Wale's Ashram* (①), behind the temple, is also excellent value. The most comfortable option in town is the large GMVN *Devlok* (④), at the top car park; **GMVN** have another, simpler, lodge near the post office between the two car parks; with dorms as well as rooms (①–②), and a large brash development near the bus stand, currently under construction. The most atmospheric area for cafes and *chai* shops is the old section close to the temple, but the more commercial east bank holds a few more upmarket neon-lit restaurants, such as *Kwality* and *Saket*, along with numerous *dhabas*, none of them very special.

Traffic back down to Joshimath, including the regular local buses, moves in the same convoy system as on the way up (see p.279). Long-distance buses run direct to Rishikesh – the nearest railway station – with an overnight halt en route, and to Gaurikund near Kedarnath (14hr), bookable at the bus stand office above the town.

Hemkund and the Valley of the Flowers

Starting from the hamlet of **Govind Ghat**, 28km south of Badrinath on the road to Joshimath (local buses will stop on request), an important pilgrim trail winds for 21 steep kilometres up to the snow-melt lake of **HEMKUND** (4329m). In the Sikh holy book, the *Guru Granth Sahib*, Govind Singh recalled meditating at a lake surrounded by seven high mountains; only this century was Hemkund discovered to be that lake. A large *gurudwara* (Sikh temple), and a small shrine to Lakshmana, the brother of Rama of *Ramayana* fame, now stand alongside. However, to protect the *deodar* forests along the trail, visitors can no longer spend the night.

Instead, the overgrown village of **Ghangaria**, 6km below Hemkund, serves as a base for day-hikes. It has several *chai* shops, basic lodges, *gurudwaras* and even a GMVN *Tourist Bungalow*, complete with dormitory (check it's open before hiking here out of season; ①–④). Govind Ghat too has a large *gurudwara*, run on a donations system.

An alternative trail forks left from Ghangaria, climbing 5km to the mountain *bugyals* of the Bhyundar valley – the **VALLEY OF THE FLOWERS**. Starting at an altitude of 3352m, the valley was discovered in 1931 by the visionary mountaineer, Frank Smythe, who named it, not surprisingly, on account of its multitude of rare plants and beautiful flowers. The meadows are at their best towards the end of the monsoons, in early September; they too have suffered at the hands (or rather feet) of large numbers of visitors, so camping is not allowed here either. As a result, it is not possible to explore the ten-kilometre valley in its entirety, in the space of a day's hike from Ghangaria.

Nanda Devi Sanctuary

The majestic twin peaks of **Nanda Devi** – at 7816m, the highest complete mountain in India – dominate a large swathe of northeastern Garhwal and Kumaun. The eponymous goddess is the most important deity for all who live in her shadow, a fertility symbol also said to represent Durga, the virulent form of Shakti. Surrounded by an apparently impenetrable ring of mountains, the fastness of Nanda Devi was long considered inviolable; when mountaineers Eric Shipton and Bill Tilman finally traced a way through, along the difficult **Rishi Gorge**, in 1934, it was seen as a defilement of sacred ground. A string of catastrophes followed; as recently as 1976, an attempt on the mountain by the father and daughter team of Willi and Nanda Devi Unsoeld ended in tragedy, when Nanda Devi Unsoeld died below the summit for which she was named.

The beautiful wilderness around the mountain now forms the **NANDA DEVI SANCTUARY**. In theory, it's a magnificent place to camp, but it has been closed since 1983 for environmental reasons. Although the Indian Mountaineering Foundation in Delhi has declared the sanctuary open, local wardens do not allow access into the inner sanctuary past Lata Kharak and the Dharansi Pass. As the entire area lies comfortably in India, away from the Tibetan frontier, there is hope that the current easing of border tensions may soon lead to the reopening of the sanctuary; check with KMVN or GMVN, and don't try to go it alone. If the trail does reopen, be prepared for a gruelling sixty-kilometre haul from the village of **Lata**, on the Joshimath–Malari road.

Gwaldam

Straddling a pass between Garhwal and Kumaun, surrounded by pine forests 61km east of Karnprayag, the peaceful hamlet of **GWALDAM** looks down upon the beautiful valley of the Pindar, a world away from the hectic *yatra* trails. This picturesque spot, with stunning views of the triple pointed peak, Trisul (7120m), used to be a tea plantation; now, thanks to its position on the main road to Almora, 90km southeast, it makes an ideal base for treks, especially following the ten-day **Curzon Trail** across the high mountain *bugyals* of northeastern Garhwal, over **Kuari Pass** to Tapovan and Joshimath.

The unassuming little Buddhist **Khamba Temple**, or **Drikung Kagyu Lhundrup Ling**, stands alongside orchards in the middle of a Tibetan settlement about 1.5km from Gwaldam's main crossroads. On the ridge above the village, the small shrine of **Badhangari**, dedicated to the goddess Durga and not far from the remnants of a Chand stone fort, commands superb views of the mountains of Kumaun and Garhwal. To reach it, take a bus for 4km to the village of **Tal**, then trek another 4km – some of which is quite steep – through rhododendron forests.

Practicalities

The GMVN *Tourist Rest House* (①–④), above the crossroads in Gwaldam, has an old cottage equipped with two exceptionally comfortable suites, and a new block with ordinary rooms and dorms; only limited food is available. This is the place to arrange guides for local treks. Alternatively try the good-value *Trishul* (①–③), where a pleasant little garden offers views of the snows. The new extension upstairs is more luxurious but less characterful.

Roop Kund: the mysterious lake

The high mountain lake of **Roop Kund** (4778m), a few days out of Gwaldam, lies in the lap of Trisul. Though it is the goal of the Raj Jat Yatra, a pilgrimage from the village of Nauti, led by a four-horned ram and held every twelve years, Roop Kund is not one of the most attractive spots in the mountains; during the short summer thaw, when the snow and ice on its surface melts, it reveals a grisly secret. Three hundred **skeletons**, thought to be six hundred years old, can be seen in the water. Some say that they are what remains of the army of a Dogra general, Zorawar Singh, who tried to invade Tibet, but they probably belonged to a party of royal pilgrims caught by bad weather while making the Nanda Jat pilgrimage to the lake of **Hom Kund**, 13km away, to propitiate the goddess Nanda Devi. The route from Gwaldam to Roop Kund passes through **Wan** and the beautiful alps of **Badni Bugyal**, taking in some of the finest scenery of the region and should not be attempted without a local guide and adequate supplies.

KUARI PASS AND THE CURZON TRAIL

Named after a British Viceroy who trekked parts of the **Curzon Trail** and renamed after Independence as the **Nehru Trail**, the long route over **KUARI PASS** (4268m), in northeastern Garhwal provides some stunning mountain views. Traversing the high ranges without entering the permanent snowline, the ten-day trail starts on the border with Kumaun at Gwaldam above the River Pindar and ends around 150km north, at the hot springs of Tapovan in the Dhauli Ganga valley near Joshimath. Numerous variations and shorter trails approaching the pass include one of around 24km from Auli.

An ideal expedition for those not equipped to tackle glacial terrain, the trail over Kuari Pass follows alpine meadows and crosses several major streams, skirting the outer western edge of the Nanda Devi Sanctuary. Along the way you'll get excellent views of Trisul (7120m), the trident, Nanda Ghunti (6309m), and from the pass itself, Nanda Devi (7816m) and the elusive tooth-like Changabang (6864m), while to the far north on the border with Tibet rises the unmistakable pyramid of Kamet (7756m).

On a major bus route between Karnaprayag and Almora and with comfortable accommodation, **Gwaldam** makes a good base for the start of the trek. Camping equipment is needed, especially on the pass. Guides can be negotiated here (see p.282), available at several points along the route. You can either take local transport from Gwaldam, including shared jeeps via Tharali or trek down through beautiful pine forests and cross the River Pindar to **Debal** 8km away, where there is a forest rest house and a tourist lodge. Motorized transport is available from Debal to **Bagrigadh**, just below the beautiful hamlet of **Lohajung**, which has a pleasant tourist lodge. Also here is the shrine of *lohajung* – a rusted iron bell suspended from a cypress tree and rung to announce your arrival to the *devta* or local spirit.

Following the river **Wan** for 10km the trail arrives at the large village of Wan, where there's a choice of accommodation, including a tourist bungalow and a forest rest house. The small village of **Sutol** is 14km from Wan, along a trail following pleasant cypress and deodar forests. From Sutol to **Ramni**, a gentle 10km trail passes through several villages. A steep trail rises for 4km through dense forest from Ramni to the pass of **Sem Kharak** before descending for a further 9km to the small village of **Jhenjhenipati**, from where a rough track continues to the village of **Panna** 12km away, passing the beautiful **Gauna Lake**. From Panna a relentlessly steep trail rises for 12km to **Kuari Pass** (4298m) on the high divide between the lesser and the greater Himalayas, with rewarding views of Nanda Devi and Trisul. Using Kuari Pass as a base, a climb to the peak of **Pangerchuli** (5183m), 12km up and down, is thoroughly recommended – the views from the summit reveal almost the entire route, including breathtaking mountain vistas. Although snow may be encountered on the climb, it is not a technical peak and no special equipment is necessary, save a good stick. From Kuari, a gruelling, knee-grinding 22km descent brings you straight down to the small village of **Tapovan**, overlooking the Dhauli Ganga, which has a hot spring-fed tank. From here, local buses run to Joshimath, 11km away with several bus connections back towards Karnaprayag and Rishikesh. An alternative descent from Kuari Pass is the long but picturesque route through forest to the ski centre of **Auli** via **Chitrakantha** – a trek of 24km – that avoids the dramatic decrease in altitude to Tapovan.

Kumaun

The Shaivite temples of **KUMAUN**, such as **Jageshwar**, **Bhageshwar** and **Baijnath**, do not attract the same fervour as their equivalents in Garhwal. Instead they remain frozen in time, undisturbed by the throngs from the plains. Hill towns like **Almora**, **Ranikhet** and **Kausani** have a charm of their own, with views towards the snows, while in **Corbett National Park**, southeast of the resort of Nainital, vast jungles continue to protect tiger and huge herds of wild elephant. To the east, Kumaun's border with Nepal follows the Kali valley to its watershed with Tibet; threading through it is the holy trail (closed to foreigners) to the ultimate pilgrimage, Mount Kailash in Tibet, the abode of Shiva and his consort Parvati.

Kumaun Mandal Vikas Nigam, or **KMVN**, are in charge of tourism in Kumaun, providing a similar (and equally patchy) range of services to GMVN in Garhwal.

Nainital

The dramatic lake of **NAINITAL** (*tal* means lake), set in a mountain hollow at an altitude of 1938 metres, 277km north of Delhi, gives its name to the largest and most important town in Kumaun. Discovered for Europeans in 1841 by Mr Barron, a wealthy sugar merchant, Nainital swiftly became a popular escape from the summer heat of the lowlands, and continues to be one of India's main hill stations. Throughout the year, and especially between March and July, hordes of tourists and honeymooners pack the **Mall**, the promenade that links **Mallital** (head of the lake), the older colonial part of Nainital at the north end, with **Tallital** (foot of the lake).

Nainital's position within striking range of the inner Himalayas – visible from vantage points above town – makes it a good base for exploring Kumaun; Corbett National Park, Almora and Ranikhet are all within easy access. When the town's commercialism gets a bit much, it's always possible to escape into the beautiful surrounding country, to lakes such as **Sat Tal** where the foothills begin their sudden drop towards the plains to the south, or to the forested ridges around **Kilbury**.

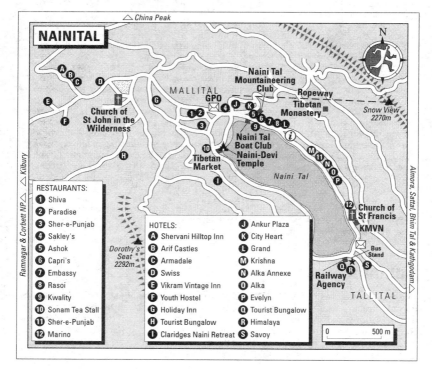

Arrival and information

Two main highways approach Nainital from opposite ends – one arrives at Mallital from Ramnagar and Corbett National Park, the other, which brings in most of the traffic, comes in at Tallital in the south. **Buses** and **taxis** from Tallital travel with great frequency to the closest railhead at Kathgodam near Haldwani, 40km south. The nearest airport, at **Pantnagar**, 72km south, is rarely used and best reached by taxi.

Parvat Tours and Tourist Information Centre, Tallital (☎05942/2656), run by KMVN, organizes tours, car rental and books accommodation at all KMVN lodges. Cars can also be rented from agencies along the Mall, such as *Hina Tours & Travels* (☎05942/2860), though cycle rickshaws are the most convenient means of local transport. The **UP tourist office**, on the Mall near the Mallital end (Mon–Sat 10am–5pm; ☎05942/2337), hands out leaflets and has a KMVN representative who books tours. For specialist advice on **trekking** and **mountaineering**, call in at *Naini Tal Mountaineering Club*, CRST Inter College Building (☎05942/2051), or their representative Anit Sah at the *Allied Stores*, The Mall, Mallital, or at *Altitudes*, in the *Hotel Konark*, Bara Bazaar, Mallital (☎05942/2112). **Banks** in town include the *State Bank of India* and *Allahabad Bank*, on the Mall in Mallital.

The Town

Most of the activity around the crater lake of Nainital takes place along the 1.5-kilometre-long **Mall**. Basic **boat rental** starts at around Rs30 per hour out of season; dinghies, arranged at the boat club on the northwest corner of the lake in Mallital, cost more like Rs50. The large area known as the **Flats** here, now used as a play and meeting ground, was hit by a huge landslide in 1880, which buried the *Victoria Hotel* along with 150 people. Beside the boat club stand a large onion-domed *gurudwara* (Sikh temple), and an unremarkable new temple dedicated to one of Kumaun's most important deities, **Naina Devi**. This marks the spot where Sati's eyes (*naina*) fell as Shiva carried her disintegrating body; steps lead down from it to the water's edge. Also in Mallital, the **Tibetan Market** sells clothing to shivering tourists up from the plains,

A **ropeway** climbs from near the *Mayur* restaurant on the Mall to **Snow View** (2270m); the return ticket covers a one-hour stay (7am–1pm & 2–6pm; Rs30 return, Rs15 one way). Otherwise it's a two-kilometre hike along a choice of steep trails, which can also be undertaken on ponies for a similar fee. At the top, which gets overcrowded in season, you'll find a promenade and cafes; views of the snow peaks are most assured early in the morning. Trails lead on for six kilometres to **Naina Peak** (2611m) one of the best vantage points around, and to the isolated **China Peak** (pronounced "Cheena"), the craggy rise to the west. About halfway up to Snow View, conspicuous thanks to its abundant prayer flags, lies the small Tibetan *gompa* (monastery) of **Gadhan Kunkyop Ling**, which has recently been rebuilt in traditional *gompa* style.

Accommodation

As a holiday town, Nainital is full of **hotels**; however, budget accommodation is hard to come by, and a hefty 15 percent tax on top is levied almost everywhere. Prices are high between March and July, peaking in June, but you can normally find discounts at other times. On the whole, room rates are cheaper in Tallital than in Mallital.

Alka, The Mall (☎05942/2220). Ornate, large and comfortable, with a restaurant strong on Gujarati and Punjabi food. Rates are lower in the *Annexe* (☎05942/2225; ③), 300m towards Mallital. ⑥–⑦.

Ankur Plaza, above Mallital rickshaw stand (☎05942/2448). Good value especially low-season, with friendly management. The best rooms are off a great roof-terrace overlooking the lake. ③–⑥.

Arif Castles, above Mallital (☎05942/2801). An extraordinary affair, part Gothic, part space age. Well-furnished rooms with luxurious bathrooms. Garden restaurant and coffee shop, plus a disco for couples only – no single men allowed. ⑧.

Armadale, Waverley Rd, Mallital (☎05942/2855). Quiet location. Reasonably comfortable mid-range rooms, with free transport on arrival. ③–⑥.

City Heart, above Mallital rickshaw stand (☎05942/2228). Upper rooms are over-priced during the high season, but have superb lake views. No food, but near amenities. ③–⑤.

Claridges Naini Retreat, Ayarpatta Slopes (☎05942/2108). Beautifully situated high above the lake, with extensive and immaculate grounds. The best Nainital can offer. ⑨.

Evelyn, The Mall (☎05942/2457). Overlooking the lake, with excellent views from the large roof patio. Spacious and well kept. Recommended. ④–⑥.

Grand, The Mall (☎05942/2406). One of Nainital's oldest establishments, where time seems to stand still – period atmosphere but a bit musty. ⑥.

Himalaya, Tallital (☎05942/2258). Above the bus stand with good views of the lake from an assortment of cottages and a large characterless block with a vast range of rooms. ①–⑦.

KMVN Tourist Bungalows, booked through *Parvat Tours*, The Mall (☎05942/2656). Two lodges with rooms and dorms at either end of town, and a cottage at Snow View. The lodge at Tallital is the most conveniently situated, near the bus stand. ①–⑥.

Krishna, The Mall (☎05942/2662). The more expensive lake-view rooms upstairs are comfortable and clean but overpriced. ④–⑤.

Holiday Inn, Grasmere Estate (☎05942/2531). One of Nainital's finest, with all mod cons including the only bar in town, a discotheque, and good Szechuan food in the *Lotus Garden* restaurant. ⑨.

Savoy, Tallital (☎05942/2721). Amalgamated with *Ashok* next door. No views, and unflattering rooms but has hot water and is handy for buses. ③–④.

Shervani Hilltop Inn, Mallital (☎05942/3304). Once a Maharajah's palace, below China Peak and next door to *Arif Castles*. Extensive gardens, and cottage accommodation as well. ⑧.

Swiss, Mallital (☎05942/3013). Popular family-run place. Spacious old-fashioned rooms and plenty of atmosphere if a bit chaotic, with food included. ⑧.

Vikram Vintage Inn, Mallital (☎05942/3177). Full-featured hotel; billiards and snooker and smart and comfortable rooms. No views, but surrounded by pines and away from the bustle. ⑧.

Youth Hostel, Mallital (☎05942/3353). Two doubles and 44 dorm beds, in charming secluded spot above Mallital. Slightly more expensive for non-*YHA* members. Excellent value. ①.

Eating

Nainital has plenty of places to **eat**, with restaurants and fast-food options along the Mall geared to tourists, and everyday *dhabas* (local cafes) in the bazaars at either end.

Ashok, near the Boat House, The Mall, Mallital. Good veg *dhaba*; cheap considering its location.

MOVING ON FROM NAINITAL

Shared taxis regularly ply the route between Tallital, Haldwani and Kathgodam, the main railway station for Nainital. **Buses** leave every 30 minutes and take around 1hr 30min to Haldwani. The **Road cum Railway Out Agency** (☎0594/2518), at the Tallital bus stand, handles railway reservations. Among the trains that depart from Kathgodam are the *Delhi–Kathgodam Express* #5014 to **New Delhi**, the *Kathgodam–Howrah Express* #3020 passing through **Lucknow** to **Calcutta**, and the *Kumaun Express* #5312 to **Agra**; *the Nainital Express* #5307 is a convenient overnight train to Lucknow leaving from Lalkuan, 14km south.

Delhi is an eight-hour ride away with either *UPSRTC* **buses** (8am & 7pm) or the *Delhi Transport Corporation* (9am & 7pm), while private operators run more comfortable coaches at around twice the price (you'll have to put up with non-stop videos). **Almora**, 67km north, is served by a few direct buses (4 daily; 2hr 30min) and shared taxis from Bhowali, 11km from Nainital. There is one direct bus to **Dehra Dun** (11hr) and **Mussoorie** (13hr), with a stop at **Haridwar** (9hr). Buses from Nainital connect with **Pithoragarh** (9hr) and **Kausani** (5hr), as well as an early morning start for **Song** on the route to Pindari Glacier.

To get to **Corbett National Park**, 113km southwest, take a bus for 66km to **Ramnagar** (3hr), from where local transport is available (see p.288). KMVN's *Parvat Tours* (☎05942/2656) organizes cheap package tours of Corbett from Rs140 per head per day.

Embassy, The Mall, Mallital. One of Nainital's better restaurants with wood-panelled interior; serves pizzas and baked dishes, but strongest on Mughlai cooking.

Kwality, The Mall, Mallital. Lakeside restaurant; tables overlook the water. The usual multi-cuisine.

Marino, The Mall, Tallital. A very good selection of vegetarian *thalis*.

Paradise, Bara Bazaar, Mallital. Next to *Shiva*, has good *dhaba* and excellent vegetarian cooking.

Rasoi, The Mall, towards Mallital. Mid-priced vegetarian cooking but otherwise unexceptional.

Sakley's, The Mall, Mallital. Versatile restaurant, with Western food on the menu, plus a bakery and confectioners.

Sher-e-Punjab, The Mall. Good Indian food, halfway along between Mallital and Tallital. Another branch near the main bazaar of Mallital is just as good and a bit cheaper.

Shiva, Bara Bazaar, Mallital. Cheap but good and popular *dhaba* in the bazaar.

Sonam Tea Stall, Tibetan Market, Mallital. Roadside cafe in the covered section of the market selling *momos* (steamed meat dumplings) and *thukpa* (soup).

Corbett National Park

CORBETT NATIONAL PARK, based at **Ramnagar**, 250km northeast of Delhi and 63km southwest of Nainital, is one of India's premier wildlife reserves. Established in 1936 by Jim Corbett among others as the Hailey National Park, India's first, and later renamed in his honour, it is one of Himalayan India's last expanses of wilderness. Almost the entire 521-square-kilometre park, spread over the foothills of Kumaun, is sheltered by a buffer zone of mixed deciduous and giant *sal* forests, which provide impenetrable cover for wildlife. Most of the Core Area of 330 square kilometres at its heart remains out of bounds, and many visitors are disappointed to find that safaris on foot are strictly forbidden; they are only permissible in the fringe forests.

Corbett is most famous for its large cats, and in particular the **tiger** – this was the first designated Project Tiger Reserve, in 1973 – but its tigers are extremely elusive.

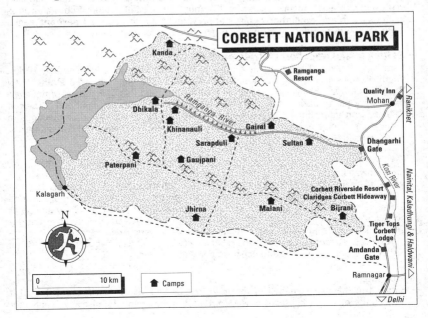

ENTRY INTO CORBETT NATIONAL PARK

All visitors to Corbett National Park have to obtain **permits** from the park administration centre at Ramnagar. Indians pay less than overseas visitors. Rates tend to go up every couple of years, but as a rough idea the **entrance fee** for foreigners as this book goes to press is Rs100 for the first three days at Dhikala, excluding board and lodging. Each additional day is Rs50, use of a still camera costs Rs50 and a video camera is Rs500. Elephant rides are Rs50 per head or Rs200 per elephant.

Note that Corbett is **closed** between 16 June and 14 November, when the monsoons flood the river beds and cut the fragile road links.

Sightings are very far from guaranteed, and should be regarded as an unlikely bonus. Nonetheless, although there have been problems elsewhere with the project, and the very survival of the tiger in India is in serious jeopardy (see *Contexts*), Corbett does at least seem to be prioritizing the needs of tigers over those of other wildlife – and of tourists – and claims to have poaching under control.

The park holds a great assortment of other animals. Large **elephant** herds have been confined within its boundaries since the construction of the Ramganga Reservoir blocked migratory routes that formerly ranged as far as Rajaji National Park, 200 kilometres west. The best place to see them is around the picturesque Dhikala camp near the reservoir, especially in spring, when the water level drops and the animals have more space to roam. The reservoir shelters populations of **gharial**, a long-snouted, fish-eating crocodile, and **maggar**, a large marsh crocodile, and other reptiles. **Jackal** is common, and **wild boar** run through the camps in the evenings. The grasslands around Dhikala are home to deer species such as the spotted deer known as **chital**, **hog deer** and the larger **sambar**. **Rhesus** and **common langur** are both abundant, representing the two main classes of Indian monkeys. Bird life ranges from water birds such as the **pied kingfisher** to birds of prey, including the **crested serpent eagle**, **Pallas's fishing eagle** and **Himalayan greyheaded fishing eagle**.

Getting to and from Corbett National Park

Ramnagar is served by frequent **buses** to and from Nainital and Ranikhet, 100km north. Buses arrive every half-hour or so after the eight-hour trip from **Delhi**; *Delhi Transport Corporation* run a semi-deluxe service (around Rs90), and most of the alternatives are pretty basic. The only direct **train** to Delhi leaves at 8pm and arrives at 6.30am, with interminable stops along the way. For faster trains and connections to other parts change at Moradabad. The nearest airport, at Pantnagar, 80km southeast, is rarely used.

The closest of the various **gates** into the park, 1km from central Ramnagar, is on the road to **Bijrani** camp, 11km away, a base for day trips. **Dhangarhi Gate**, 18km along the highway north to Ranikhet, provides access to the northern and northwestern portion of the park along the Ramganga river valley, and the main camp of **Dhikala**.

Jeeps, the most convenient way to travel within the park, can be rented for around Rs800 per day in Ramnagar from the KMVN *Tourist Lodge* (☎05945/85225) and other agencies such as *Bharat Hotel* (☎05945/85775) near the bus stand. One bus each day goes to Dhikala from Ramnagar, stopping at the *Forest Rest Houses* en route.

KMVN's *Parvat Tours* (☎05942/2656) organizes cheap package tours (from Nainital) of Corbett from Rs140 per head per day.

Ramnagar

Situated in the rich farm-belt of the *terai*, on the southeastern fringes of the great forests, the busy market town of **RAMNAGAR** is the main administrative centre for

JIM CORBETT (1875–1955)

Jim Corbett – hunter of man-eating tigers, photographer, conservationist and author – was born in Nainital of English and Irish parentage. A childhood spent around the Corbett winter home of Kaladhungi (halfway between Nainital and Ramnagar, and now a rather disappointing memorial to him) brought young Jim into close communion with nature, and an instinctive understanding of jungle ways. After working on the railways, he joined the Indian Army in 1917 at the age of forty; he rose to the rank of Lieutenant Colonel, and saw action in Flanders at the head of the 70th Kumaun Company.

Known locally as "Carpet Sahib", a mispronunciation of his name, Jim Corbett was called upon time and time again to rid the hills of Kumaun of man-eating tigers and leopards. Normally shy of human contact, such animals turn man-eaters when infirmity brought upon by old age or wounds renders them unable to hunt their usual prey. Many of those killed by Corbett were found to have suppurating wounds caused by porcupine quills embedded deep in their paws; tigers always seem to fall for the porcupine's simple defensive trick of walking backwards in line with its lethal quills.

One of Corbett's most memorable exploits was the killing of the Rudraprayag leopard, which accounted for 125 human lives between 1918 and 1926, and was bold enough to steal its victims from the midst of human habitation; he also terminated the careers of the Chowgarh tigress, the Talla Des and the Mohan man-eaters. Corbett described his adventures in books such as *My India, Jungle Lore* and *Man-Eaters of Kumaun*; Martin Booth's *Carpet Sahib* is an excellent biography of a remarkable man. Awarded the Order of the British Empire in recognition of his lifelong work with nature, Jim Corbett was unhappy in post-Independence India, and left to settle in East Africa.

Corbett National Park and Project Tiger. There's little to do around Ramnagar itself except go **fishing**. At Lohachaur, 15km north along the River Kosi, good anglers are in with a chance of landing the legendary mahseer, a redoubtable battling river carp. Permits to have a go must be sought from the Project Tiger office in Ramnagar; most resorts also arrange all-inclusive fishing trips.

Although most tourists head straight to Dhikala in the park as soon as they arrive, Ramnagar does have some **accommodation**. The KMVN *Tourist Lodge* (☎05945/85225; ①–④), next to the Project Tiger offices, is not bad as such places go, with a dorm as well as basic doubles, while the *Everest* (①–③), at the bus stand, has a variety of decent good-value rooms. On the main road opposite the bus stand, *Govindas* is a surprisingly good multi-cuisine **restaurant**, strongest on Indian food. Across from the *Tourist Lodge*, *Corbett Jungle Outpost*, more of a bar than a restaurant, is good for a cold beer and serves food.

Dhikala

Corbett's main camp, **DHIKALA**, beautifully situated, overlooking the Ramganga reservoir and the forested hills beyond, is 40km northwest of Ramnagar. As you can only stray beyond the confines of the camp under armed guard, on elephant back or in a car or jeep, the whole place has something of the air of a military encampment. **Accommodation** ranges from the 24 bunk beds in the *Log Huts* (①) and other assorted spartan huts (④), to more comfortable bungalows and cabins (④–⑤). **Food** is available in a canteen either per day, with higher prices for Western food, or on a *Janta* ("peoples") meal basis. There's also a library and reading room, where film shows on wildlife are run.

It's normally possible to see plenty of animals and birds from the **lookout tower** beside a waterhole 1km from the camp; bring binoculars, remain quiet, and don't wear loud colours or perfume. *Chital, sambar,* and various other deer species find refuge in the savannah grasslands known as the "maidan", behind the camp to the south, and tigers are occasionally drawn in looking for prey. Two-hour **elephant rides** (Rs50 per head, less for Indian citizens; in theory, rides are first-come-first-served) explore this sea of grass, rarely penetrating far into the deep jungles beyond; try to convince your *mahout* (elephant driver) to venture in, as they can be quite magical. Come at dusk or dawn; in the heat of the day you probably won't come across much more than deer among the tall grass. Tiger sightings are few and far between, but you may be rewarded with fresh pug marks.

On the way to Dhikala from the Dhangarhi gate, the road passes through magnificent forest – if you have your own transport, stop at the **High Bank** vantage point, and try to spot crocodile or even elephant on the river below. The *Sultan* (③), *Gairal* (⑤) and *Sarapduli* (⑤) forest rest houses on the road are bookable through Project Tiger, but you have to make your own food arrangements and there is no electricity. The bungalows are surrounded by deep forest; as movement on foot is restricted, you'll only see wild animals that stray close to or into the compound. The beautifully sited *Kanda* (②) rest house stands on a hill above the Ramganga reservoir and Dhikala.

Resort accommodation around Corbett

A number of self-contained resorts are springing up on the fringes of Corbett, providing a higher standard of accommodation – at a price – as well as guides for expeditions in the forests, which can be as rich in wildlife as the park, without the restrictions. Impossible to get to without pre-arranged transport, the most secluded is the *Ramganga Resort*, 13km off the main road from Mohan.

Camp Corbett, Corbett Nagar, Kaladhungi (☎05942/4227). Far from the park gates but close to Jim Corbett's house and large tracts of fringe forest. Less ostentatious than most of the others with a central building and comfortable semi-permenant tents. Food is included in the price which is a bit more reasonable for the tents. Safaris and park tours arranged. ⑦–⑧.

Claridges Corbett Hideaway, Garija, Ramnagar (☎05945/85959; reservations 011/3010211). Luxurious with all mod cons; pretending to be rustic without success. Terracotta huts dotted around a pleasant orchard on a bluff overlooking the river. Safaris and the usual tours arranged. ⑨.

Corbett Riverside Resort, Garija, Ramnagar (☎05945/85960). A picturesque setting, 10km north of Ramnagar, looking across the River Kosi to forest-covered cliffs. Much of the complex was washed away not long ago, when the river dramatically changed course. Now rebuilt, with some buildings sited on a ledge above the extensive beach area, the rustic-looking huts are luxurious inside and expensive. Safaris arranged; full board. Off-season discounts. ⑧–⑨.

Quality Inn Corbett Jungle Resort, Kumeria Reserve Forest, Mohan (☎05945/85219). Wood-panelled stone cottages in a leafy mango orchard above the Kosi, 29km from Ramnagar on the road north to Ranikhet, 9km beyond the Dhangarhi gate. Elephant rides into the forest and safaris into the park itself. Full board; good off-season discounts from June to November. ⑨.

Tiger Tops Corbett Lodge, Dhikala, Ramnagar (☎05945/85279). Corbett's most ostentatious resort, overlooking the Kosi and the forested hills beyond. Large comfortable rooms, a library, a well-stocked bar and a swimming pool. Activities include nature trails with the resort's own naturalists, jungle rides, fishing, trekking and films. Not related to the famous *Tiger Tops* in Nepal. ⑨.

Ranikhet

The scattered and deliberately undeveloped town of **RANIKHET**, 50km west of Almora, is one of UP's pleasantest hill stations. Essentially, it's an army cantonment, the home of the Kumaun Rifles. New construction is confined to the hectic **Sadar Bazaar** area, while the rest of the town above it, climbing up towards the crest of the hill, retains pine woods that lend it a dark but leafy atmosphere. Beautiful forest trails abound, including short cuts from the bazaar to the Mall; leopards still roam some of the more remote areas within the town boundaries, despite efforts by army officers to prove their skill at hunting. Ranikhet is for some reason only marginally popular with Indian tourists, so its parade grounds, churches and beautifully maintained golf course, within sight of the snows, remain unspoiled, making it an ideal place for a quiet break.

Arrival and information

Buses from all over Kumaun including the railhead at Kathgodam, 84km away, arrive at the **bazaar**, at either of two bus stops. The **KMOU stand**, on the Haldwani road, is the base for buses to Haldwani (10–12 daily; 4hr), the nearest town to Kathgodam; to get to Nainital, change at Bhowali, or take one of the three daily direct services (10am, 11am & 4pm; 3hr). The **Roadways (Almora) Bus Stand**, 500m on, is used by regular services to Almora (2hr) with shared jeeps providing a crowded but slightly faster alternative. Buses between the bazaar and the Mall, 3km away, run every ninety minutes, stopping outside the *Hotel Meghdoot*; shared taxis travel the same route.

KMVN provide the usual Kumaun-wide services from their *Tourist Bungalow* on the Mall (☎05966/2297), while the UP Tourist Bureau, above the Almora Bus Stand, offers a haphazard assortment of leaflets. There's a *State Bank of India* on Gandhi Chowkh, but they are unlikely to change money so you may have to go to Nainital.

The Town

Although in India the word "Mall" normally conjures up images of a busy promenade with shops and joy-rides, visitors to Ranikhet will be pleasantly surprised; its Mall, running along on the wooded crest of the ridge, has few buildings apart from leafy officers' messes and a sprinkling of hotels. Parade grounds and the occasional sound of gunfire from the adjacent firing ranges are evidence of the strong military presence, which otherwise does not seem overbearing. Traces of the colonial past remain evident everywhere, in the form of large bungalows and church steeples.

At the **Shawl & Tweed Factory and Outlet**, above the Narsingh Stadium Parade Ground – an old church equipped with looms and wheels – you can buy herringbone and houndstooth tweed. Kumaun has a tradition of weaving, and the Gandhi Ashram in the bazaar, has a selection of local fabric including *pankhis*, plain shawls for men.

Local tourist authorities heavily promote the idea of a visit to the orchards of **Chaubatia**, 10km east beyond the Mall. It's a scenic enough spot, with good views of the snows, and a pleasant short walk leads along a lofty pine-covered ridge to the small lake of **Bhaludam**. On the way up to Chaubatia, the temple of Jhula Devi, dedicated to Shakti (here a sister of **Nanda Devi**), would be unremarkable but for the huge collection of **bells** fixed to the shrine as offerings – a custom found throughout Kumaun. At Chilianaula, 7km west, commanding an incredible panorama of the snows, the brash new temple and ashram of **Haidarkhan** is a modern hybrid amalgamating various religious traditions into a new-age interpretation.

Accommodation and eating

Hotels in Ranikhet readily divide into two sections, clustered either around the busy bazaar, or in quieter locations along the Mall. Seasonal fluctuations can double prices especially around June and July. The prices listed here apply to low season. The choice of **eating** is pretty limited; the best food is found in the better hotels, but there are a few simple cafes and *dhabas* in the market area, such as the *Mayur* by Almora Bus Stand, a good-value vegetarian place.

Himadri Tourist Rest House, Chilianaula (☎05966/2588). A spanking new and modern KMVN-run bungalow next to the Haidarkhan complex, 7km from town; huge prices, hikes in season. ③.

Meghdoot, The Mall (☎05966/2475). Comfortable suites with running hot water, parking and room service, plus a good mid-price restaurant. Recommended. ③–④.

Moon, Bazaar (☎05966/2258). Extensive place in the heart of the bazaar, with suites, two cottages and a multi-cuisine restaurant. ⑤–⑦.

Norton's, The Mall (☎05966/2377). Large characterful family-run hotel that has seen better days; just down from the *Meghdoot*. ②–④.

Parwati Inn, Ratan Palace Compound (☎05966/2325). Brash modern edifice above the Almora Bus Stand. Best of all are the balconied rooms looking onto the snows. ④–⑥.

Rajdeep, Bazaar (☎05966/2447). Opposite the *Moon*; one of the best budget hotels around here and nearly always busy. A bit noisy, but clean. ①–③.

Tourist Bungalow, the Mall (☎05966/2297). Comfortable cottages and dorms, tucked away 4km from the bazaar in a beautiful wooded spot that enjoys the best of Ranikhet. ④–⑤.

Tribhuwan, KMOU Bus Stand (☎05966/2524). Plain but pleasant rooms with a verandah and great views of the snows. ③.

West View, Mahatma Gandhi Rd (☎05966/2261). Grand old-world establishment in an idyllic spot among the pines on the outskirts of town. Spacious if a bit musty, with fireplaces. ⑦–⑧.

Almora

ALMORA, 67km north of Nainital, is one of the rare Kumauni towns that conspicuously pre-dates the Raj, with its cobbled alleyways and wood and stone buildings. Founded by the Chand dynasty in 1560, and occupied successively by the Gurkhas and the British, it remains a major market town, and is considered the cultural capital of the region. Set at a pleasant altitude of 1646m on rambling ridges that look towards the inner Himalayan snows, Almora's peaceful environs have attracted an eclectic assortment of visitors over the years, such as Swami Vivekananda, Timothy Leary and the Tibetologist and author of *The Way of the White Clouds*, Lama Angarika Govinda.

Arrival and information

Almora has regular **bus** connections with Nainital (6 daily; 3hr), Ranikhet (hourly; 2hr 30min), Kathgodam (2 daily; 4hr), the nearest railhead, and Kausani (4 daily; 2hr 30min). Most buses use either of two adjacent stands on the Mall, which has a **taxi stand** close by if you're heading for distant accommodation, such as the *Holiday Home*. However, most hotels are within walking distance. Access to much of the centre, including the market area above the Mall, is restricted to pedestrians. Another bus stand at Dharanaula, on the other side of the market, is for buses to the interior of Kumaun, with most leaving in the afternoon.

UP Tourism maintain an information-only **tourist office**, next to the *Savoy Hotel*, above the GPO (Mon–Sat 10am–5pm; ☎05962/22180). The KMVN HQ is at the *Holiday Home*; another office near the Gandhi statue at Chaudhan Pata, the Mall (☎05962/22706), assists in booking their packages and accommodation throughout Kumaun. The best places to find out about local **treks** are *Discover Himalaya* (☎05962/23507), opposite the GPO on the Mall, who supply equipment and guides, and *High Adventure* (☎05962/23445), next door. The *State Bank of India*, on the Mall, provides an erratic service, and hasn't been changing money for some time; the only official money-changing facility in Kumaun at present is in Nainital.

The Town

Although most of Almora's official business is conducted along the **Mall**, the **market area** immediately above and parallel to it along the crest of the saddle, holds much more of interest. Exploring its well-stocked bazaars, knitted together with lanes flanked by beautifully carved wooden facades, you feel as though you're drifting into the distant past. Among items you might want to buy are *khadi* (home-spun) cotton textiles and ready-mades from the Gandhi Ashram near the bus stands, and local woollens from *Garur Woollens* or *Kumaun Woollens* on the Mall. However, the great local tradition is the manufacture of **tamta**, beaten copper pots plated with silver, which are sold in the busy Lala Bazaar and the Chowk area at the northeast end of the market.

Towards the top of town, beyond Chowk, a compound holds a group of Chand-period stone **temples**. The main one, a squat single-storey structure, is dedicated to **Nanda Devi**, the goddess embodied in the region's highest mountain. More typical of

Kumauni temple architecture are two larger Shaivite painted stone temples, capped with umbrella-like wooden roofs covering their stone *amalaka* (circular crowns). During Sravana (Jul/Aug), a large fair is held here in honour of Nanda Devi.

Enclosures amid the tall pine woods of **Deer Park**, a pleasant three-kilometre walk northeast of the Mall, house assorted deer, as well as Himalayan black bear and sorry-looking leopards. Following the Mall southwest for three kilometres, on the other hand, brings you to the hill called **Bright End Corner**, where you may, weather permitting, catch views of the hills and vales of Kumaun, and the distant snow peaks.

Moving on 8km east of Almora, a pleasant walk or bus ride away, the small Durga temple of **Kasara Devi**, surrounded by pines, on a commanding hill above the Binsar Rd is an idyllic spot. Swami Vivekananda meditated and gained enlightenment here but the tranquillity has been shattered by the intrusion of a new telephone exchange.

Accommodation

Accommodation in Almora itself is largely centered along the Mall. However, it is also possible to "go native" in village houses in the region around Kasara Devi; enquire about places to rent at the *chai* shops in Kalimath nearby.

Deodar Holiday-Inn, Sister Nivedita Cottage, The Mall (☎05962/23295). Home to Swami Vivekananda and his disciple Nivedita between 1890 and 1898, which time seems to have forgotten and where little has changed; the garden is pleasant, especially with a log fire. ③.

Kailas, The Mall, above the GPO (☎05962/22624). Quaint, brightly coloured and funky place, with an incredibly cheap dormitory, redolent of the eccentricities of its owner Mr Shah, a legend among travellers. Nothing has changed in years – some may like it, others may not. ①.

KMVN Holiday Home, The Mall (☎05962/22250). Set in a nice garden 2km from the centre, this characterless tourist bungalow, has a main building and cottages, and a good-value dorm. ③–④.

Renuka, The Mall, next to the GPO (☎05962/22860). Slightly garish but otherwise pleasant and comfortable hotel which, although relatively new, is already looking frayed at the edges. ③–④.

Savoy, Police Line, above the GPO (☎05962/22329). A quiet place, away from the noise of the Mall and the markets, but handy for all amenities. Spacious rooms, garden and verandah; good off-season discounts. ③–④.

Shikhar, The Mall (☎05962/22253). Almora's central landmark. Don't be put off by the exterior or expensive reputation; a wide range of rooms, some at very reasonable prices, with common baths. Reasonable restaurant serves good breakfasts. ②–⑦.

Eating

Cafes and **restaurants** are strung along the Mall, especially around the bazaar area at its northern end. There should be something for everybody.

Glory, near *Shikhar*, The Mall. Multi-cuisine cafe-cum-restaurant, strong on north Indian cooking.

Madras Cafe, opposite the *Glory*, The Mall. The name is misleading, as the emphasis is on good-value north Indian food. Tasty coffee, too.

Soni Dhaba, The Mall bus stand. Excellent, Sikh-run *dhaba* which can get crowded.

Swagat, next to the *Shikhar*, The Mall. Large cafe, with *dosas* and other snacks as well as meals.

Kausani

Spreading from east to west along a narrow pine-covered ridge, 52km northwest of Almora, the quiet hill resort of **KAUSANI** is more of a loose settlement than a town. It is at its most concentrated in the area around the Mall, where the Almora road crosses the lowest point in the ridge en route north to the Katyur valley and Baijnath.

A popular day trip from Almora, Kausani is renowned as an ideal place for a retreat, and holds several ashrams. Mahatma Gandhi walked here in 1929, thirty years before the road came through; Gandhi-ism continues to be a major influence in these hills and his symbol of self-reliance, the spinning wheel, is still used in homes around Kausani.

Practicalities

Kausani is well connected by bus to Almora and Ranikhet, and to Bageshwar and Gwaldam further north. Guests prepared to observe ashram rules, such as not smoking, are welcome to stay at Gandhi's pleasant but spartan former ashram, known as *Anashakti Ashram* (①), above the Mall. Further up, *Amar Holiday Home* (☎05969/84115; ③–④) is a small and pleasant family-run establishment, a good starting point for forest walks with a beautiful garden and a panorama of the snows. Several new hotels are beginning to crop up around here, and the similarly priced but soulless *Jeetu* (☎05969/84123; ③–④), next door, is handy when the *Amar* is closed in mid-winter. Cheaper options are available below in the bazaar. The KMVN *Tourist Bungalow* (☎05969/84106; ②–⑤), 2km west of the Mall, has the usual tourist lodge atmosphere but is at least secluded, and surrounded by pine forests. The fanciest place to eat is the *Hill Queen*, a mid-priced multi-cuisine restaurant below the *Anashakti Ashram*.

Around Kausani: Baijnath

Halfway between Kausani, 20km southeast, and Gwaldam to the west, the road (served by occasional buses) drops down to a broad valley and the eleventh-century stone temples of **BAIJNATH**, standing at a bend in a beautiful river. This was once an important town of the Katyurs, who ruled much of Garhwal and Kumaun; now it's more like a park, with intrusive lights placed between the temples. Unusually, the main temple is devoted to Parvati, the consort of Shiva, rather than Shiva himself; its 1.5-metre image of the goddess is one of the few in the complex to have withstood the ravages of time. Beside the river, a pristine pool teems with large carp; as they are considered holy, fishing is prohibited. In stark contrast with its surroundings, KMVN's modern *Tourist Rest House* will be the first hotel in Baijnath; at present there are a couple of simple cafes including the *Calcutta*.

Binsar

Known locally as **Jhandi Dhar**, the forest-clad hill of **BINSAR**, 34km north of Almora, rises in isolation to a commanding 2412 metres. A steep road leads 11km up from the main Almora–Bageshwar highway, to a tourist complex near the top of the hill. This was the summer capital of the Chands, but today little remains in the area, except the imposing stone Shiva temple of **Bineshwar** 3km below the summit. Most visitors come for the 300-kilometre panorama of Himalayan peaks along the northern horizon, including from west to east Kedarnath, Chaukhamba, Trishul, Nandaghunti, Nanda Devi, Nandakot, and Panchuli. Closer at hand, you can enjoy quiet forest walks through oak and rhododendron woods. Recently designated a nature reserve, Binsar is rich in alpine flora, ferns, hanging moss and innumerable species of wild flowers.

Practicalities

Binsar is only accessible by public transport if you are willing to walk from the main road; **taxis** from Almora charge from Rs200 for a one-way drop. Besides the poorly maintained KMVN *Tourist Bungalow* (②–④), Binsar's only accommodation is a beautifully situated but lonely *Forest Rest House* (①) above the tourist bungalow, booked through the department in Almora. There are no shops or cafes.

Jageshwar

Surrounded by giant ancient *deodars*, 1870m up, **JAGESHWAR**, 34km northeast of Almora, is the very heart of Kumaun, a place where language and customs seem to have resisted change. An idyllic small river meanders through dark pines into this ancient world, 3km off the main road from Artola, stumbling onto a complex of 124 shrines and ornate stone temples whose construction continued for a thousand years, from the eighth century.

Jageshwar is one of India's twelve *Jyotrilinga*, where the luminous energy of Shiva is epitomized by a *lingam* of light, and was a medieval centre of Lakulisha Shaivism (Shiva with the Club). Its main temple, **Shri Jyotrilinga** or **Mahamrityunjaya**, has a short forechamber and a ten-metre-tall main temple with sculpted motifs on the sides and heavy lattice stone windows. The *dvarpalas* – sculpted stone doorkeepers – that protect the entrance are Nandi and Bhrangi, the wrathful bodyguards of Shiva. Unfortunately, recent pilfering of statues has been rife; local gossip implicates one of the priests. Today, a wall topped with barbed-wire and floodlights serve to protect the monuments but destroy the ambience of this magical place.

Although ugly modern buildings are beginning to intrude, Jageshwar retains much of its traditional charm, with stone paved lanes and beautifully carved wooden doors and windows painted in green, turquoise and other striking colours. Good local **walks** include the steep three-kilometre ascent through beautiful pine forests to the small hamlet and stone temples of **Vriddha** or **Briddh Jageshwar** (Old Jageshwar), with an extensive panorama from the mountains of Garhwal to the massifs of western Nepal. A trail from here leads 12km along an undulating ridge to **Binsar** (see above); the trail finally emerges from the woods near the stone temple of **Bineshwar**.

Practicalities

Two **buses** each day connect Jageshwar with the railhead at Haldwani, via Almora, and buses to destinations all over Kumaun leave from Artola, 3km away on the main highway. The large, brash KMVN *Tourist Bungalow* (②–③) makes no attempt to blend in with its surroundings and is poorly maintained, but inside, it's comfortable enough and has dorms; the food is not too bad. Next to the gate, there's a very basic but atmospheric *dharamshala* (①) in a traditional building. **Accommodation** in village houses can also be negotiated. Jageshwar has a sprinkling of simple *dhabas* and the *Rajmahal* opposite the temple gates is a refreshing little **restaurant**, with a good if limited selection, specializing in *khue-suji* (semolina) and banana fritters.

Bageshwar

In a steamy valley, 90km north of Almora, **BAGESHWAR** is one of Kumaun's most important pilgrimage towns. It's not a particularly attractive spot, despite its setting just before the final rise to the high Himalayas, but its market is a good opportunity to stock up on provisions for long treks.

Overlooking the confluence of the Gomti and Sarayu rivers, a large group of ancient temples and ashrams is dominated by the Shiva temple of **Baghnath** with its *amalaka* (ribbed circular crown) capped with an umbrella-like roof made of wood and slate. As in many Kumauni temples, the fabulous bronze bells at shrines throughout the complex are offerings from devotees. According to legend, Bageshwar was built here in the shadows of Mount Nila, the home of gods, *sadhus, gandharvas* and *apsaras* (celestial musicians), by a certain Chandisa for his master Shiva. When Shiva and Parvati arrived at the confluence they were welcomed by an *akashvani* (celestial song); hence the place was named Vagiswar (the lord of eloquent speech).

Practicalities

Bageshwar has good **bus** connections with Almora, Nainital (156km south), and Gwaldam (43km west); the longer of the two roads to Almora passes through

---

THE TREK TO PINDARI GLACIER

One of the most accessible and varied treks into the heart of the Kumauni Himalayas leads from Bageshwar through forests, valleys and high *bugyals* right up to the Pindari Glacier, 3820 metres above sea level in the shadow of Nanda Devi. Unless you want to spend a night at the glacier itself, there's no need to carry a tent or stove, as the route is amply supplied with KMVN bungalows. These should be booked in advance through the *Tourist Bungalow* in Bageshwar, which can also provide trekking equipment and information.

On **DAY 1**, take a local bus from Bageshwar either to **Bharari**, where there is a basic hotel and a PWD bungalow, and walk for 16km from there along the Sarayu valley to **Song**, or catch the bus all the way. From Song, continue for 3km on foot to **Loharkhet**, which has a basic KMVN *Tourist Bungalow* overlooking the village, and a PWD bungalow.

DAY 2 is considerably more gruelling, involving around 1000m of ascent along a good forest track for 11km over **Dhakuri Pass** (2835m), which has superb mountain views, before dropping 2km down to the KMVN *Tourist Bungalow* at **Dhakuri**.

DAY 3 consists of an 8km walk along the Pindar valley to **Khati**, where the Pindar and Sunderdhanga rivers meet. The last major village along the trail, Khati too has a bungalow.

Continuing beside the Pindar on **DAY 4**, you follow a forested trail past bamboo, fern and spectacular waterfalls, for 11km to **Dwali**, where there is more KMVN accommodation (a trail right from here, with no further facilities of any kind, leads 13km to Kafni Glacier, near the base of the elegant 6860m peak of Nanda Kot). For an early start for Pindari Glacier, head another 5km from Dwali to **Phurkia**, where the treeline gives way to *bugyal*, used for summer pastures, and there's a KMVN *Tourist Bungalow*.

Although it's just 8km from Phurkia up to the glacier, **DAY 5** can prove long and exhausting, because if you don't have a tent you'll have to get back down to Phurkia by nightfall. **Zero Point** (3820m), marks the foot of the **Pindari Glacier**, which consists of two sections; the bottom is dry and crevassed, with a large rubble-strewn lateral moraine, while the top is a severely broken ice-fall, topped by a snowfield known as **Traill's Pass**. Some maps show a route up to the pass, but only expert mountaineers should attempt it.

Kausani. The large, ugly, KMVN *Tourist Bungalow* (③), 2km from the temples across a bridge, is the only hotel, **though** there are basic *dharamsalas* and *dhabas* around the temple.

Chaukori

KMVN are doing their utmost to promote **CHAUKORI**, 132km north of Almora and 48km east of Bageshwar, as a tourist destination in its own right, largely because it can boast UP's only, very dilapidated, tea estate. However, there's so little here that Chaukori is only of interest if you want to spend a day or two doing absolutely nothing – in which case rambling around the gentle local ridges will enable you to enjoy an impressive Himalayan panorama, centered on the twin peaks of Nanda Devi.

Practicalities

The road from Bageshwar to Chaukori, taken by regular **buses**, must be one of the most beautiful roads in Kumaun, following a pine-covered ridge for most of the way. Daily buses leave Chaukori for Almora at 7am and 2pm, and there are several services each morning to Pithoragarh (5hr). The sixteen-bed KMVN *Tourist Bungalow* (③), which has a dormitory and private rooms, is hopelessly inadequate to cope with the increasing number of visitors. Book in advance through KMVN if you plan to come.

TREKKING RESTRICTIONS IN EASTERN KUMAUN

With the gradual shrinking of the Inner Line and the removal of restrictions, the mountains of Pithoragarh District are being opened up to trekkers. Ironically, while on certain routes, foreigners do not require **permits**, Indians, including trekking agents, still do. Starting at Tawaghat, the trail via Nue to Johlingkang near the base of Om Parvat (6191m) aka Chotta ("small") Kailash, is currently open. Although the main Kailash trail to Tibet also starts at Tawaghat, access is allowed, via the idyllic Narayan Ashram, only as far as Budhi. Milam Glacier (see below) north of Munsiyari has also been derestricted. If the local tourist office and local trekking agencies can provide the necessary information regarding current regulations, contact the Sub-Divisional Magistrates (SDM) at Pithoragarh, Dharchula and Munsiyari, who are responsible for issuing permits.

Pithoragarh

PITHORAGARH, the headquarters of the easternmost district of Kumaun, in the beautiful sprawling Sore Valley, 188km northeast of Nainital, is a busy administrative and market town which acts as a gateway to the mountains. With the ongoing removal of restrictions on access to the interior (although foreigners will find it impossible to get permits to trek into Tibet), the town seems certain to grow; for now, however, the planned airport – the only one in the UP hills – is yet to open for regular flights. While the town itself is not particularly attractive, the fringes remain charming with terraced cultivation at an altitude of around 1650m and offering glimpses of Panchuli and the remote mountains of western Nepal.

Above Pithoragarh, in the pine-wooded slopes of the Leprosy Mission at **Chandag** 7km north, a large cross overlooks the valley in benediction, commanding views of the valley and of Saipal and Api massifs in western Nepal. It makes a pleasant walk up from the *Tourist Bungalow*, or you can take local buses en route for Bans.

Practicalities

UPT's low-key **Tourist Office** at the top of the town, at Siltham (☎05964/22527), is useful for information on current trekking restrictions. Hill buses and shared taxis stop here while the main **Roadways Bus Stand**, is close to the centre below the bazaar and a smaller, **KMOU Bus Stand** lies 1km to the north, also servicing hill destinations. Private **bus** companies and *UPSRTC* buses connect the town with Nainital (8hr; 1 daily) and Almora (6hr; 2 daily), as well as the railheads of Tanakpur, 151km south, and Kathgodam, 212km southeast. Pithoragarh's airport at Naini Saini 5km to the west, may now be operating regular flights to Lucknow and Delhi; check the latest schedules. Although amenities in town remain limited, Pithoragarh's busy markets are worth a browse in and are good to stock-up for treks.

Hotel accommodation is basic and for once, the KMVN *Tourist Lodge* (☎05964/22434; ①–③), tucked away in the woods 1.5km above the bazaar on the Chandag Rd, comes out tops. The more central *Ulka Priyadarshani* (☎05964/22596; ①), in the top bazaar close to the Siltham bus stand, is a very decent budget hotel while the *Trishul* (①), nearby, is poky. The nondescript *Utranchal Deep*, above Roadways (☎05964/22654; ①–④), has a wider choice than the *Samrat*, opposite Roadways (☎05964/22450; ①–③), while *Raja*, Takana Rd, near the KMOU Bus Stand (☎05964/22224; ①–③) is possibly the best of the three. Along with simple cafes and *dhabas* in the bazaars, *Cooks*, Link Rd, above Roadways, is about the best that Pithoragarh can offer. *Meghnath*, in Simalgair Bazaar, is a large, decent and very popular snack bar specializing in sweets and *masala dosa*.

The **Milam** trail from **Munsiyari** sets out to explore the beautiful and remote Johar Valley, in the vicinity of the magnificent peak of Nanda Kot (6860m). Lying near the border with Tibet, and policed by the Indo-Tibetan Border Police, Milam has been closed to visitors until quite recently. Foreigners are allowed to follow the main trails but not to stray off them; check current regulations before setting out.

DAY 1 consists of a total walk of 12km. Follow the pony trail from Munsiyari down to Jemighat, and then along the River Gori until a final forested rise for 3km to **Lilam**, a village which has a PWD bungalow, plus a couple of tea shops and cafes.

Another 12km walk on **DAY 2** continues from Lilam beside the Gori along a forested trail for 8km to Railgari (whose unusual name means "railway train"), where simple cafes offer very basic accommodation in season. **Bugdiar**, 4km further on, has a PWD guest house with a kitchen, a few very limited cafes – and an ITBP checkpost.

A steady but gentle rise from Bugdiar on **DAY 3** leads for 7km to mountain *bugyals* and the hamlet of Manpanga, which also has a seasonal tea shop. Press on for 5km to **Railkot**, where there is limited seasonal accommodation and food.

Set off from Railkot on **DAY 4** up a gentle path that reaches the treeline after 6km at the large village of Burfu, where basic accommodation includes a hotel. From Burfu a gentle track leads for 4km to Bilju, with a tea shop and views of Nanda Kot. A further 3km brings you to the large village of **Milam**, home to the Rawats and other groups of Hindu Bhotias; Milam also has a large ITBP presence and a checkpost. Milam Glacier is 2km further on.

Munsiyari

The sprawling and unattractive village of **MUNSIYARI** stands at the threshold of the inner Himalayas, 154km north of Pithoragarh, looking down on the Gori river gorge and deep valleys branching up into the high mountains. Vantage spots throughout the area offer breathtaking views of the five almost-symmetrical Panchuli peaks, which owe their name – the "five cooking pots" – to their plumes of wind-blown snow. These are notorious for their bad weather, but on clear days at Munsiyari, you feel you could almost reach out and touch them.

Among spectacular local high-mountain walks, which are being increasingly de-restricted, is the gentle 11km trail up to the **Kalika Pass** (2700m), where a small Shakti temple stands amid dark pines. More difficult trails lead via the small village of **Matkot**, 12km away, to the glaciers in the Panchuli group, and 30km to the large alpine meadows of **Chiplakot Bugyal**, dotted with tiny lakes, as well as up to the Milam Glacier and the Johar Valley (see box). Many of the local people are Bhotias, of Tibetan stock, who have over the ages absorbed Indian religious and cultural practices, though their origins can still be seen in the Tibetan-style weaving of carpets, adorned with the ubiquitous dragon motif. These are sold in Munsiyari by *Pratpsing Pangtey*, an elderly gentleman who runs a small carpet factory just below the bus stand.

Practicalities

Munsiyari is at the end of the road, so few **buses** come this way and those that do are very basic; there are daily departures to Pithoragarh (5.30am; 8hr) and Almora (5am; 11hr). Along with KMVN's brand new tourist **lodge** (①–③), there are a couple of simple lodges near the bus stand and the PWD *Bungalow* (①) has four very comfortable suites with hot water geysers. Food is usually available, at a price. Cheaper **eating** is available at the simple cafes around the bus stand. A handful of **trekking agencies** are cropping up around the bazaar including *Panchuli Trekking*, while Prem Ram, of Gram

Bunga, Tala, Nayabasti, is a recommended guide who can organize treks including cooks and porters, from around Rs150 per head per day.

CENTRAL UP

Large tracts of **CENTRAL UP**, along the fertile flood-plains of the Doab, constituted the nineteenth-century **Kingdom of Avadh**. Eventually little more than puppets of the British, its wealthy Nawabs focussed their attentions on the arts, and created a unique civilization centred around **Lucknow**. Monuments from those days, and traces of the bitter fighting of the "Mutiny" or "First War of Independence" that coincided with the final eclipse of Avadh, are scattered throughout both city and region. However, Lucknow is now the capital of a Hindu-dominated state far removed from the communal harmony of Avadh – named after the now-notorious holy town of **Ayodhya**, the recent flashpoint of right-wing Hindu militancy. Industrialized **Kanpur**, southwest of Lucknow, was as "Cawnpore" the scene of some of the bloodiest moments of the rebellion of 1857. It's now most worth visiting to explore its near-neighbour **Bithur**, a miniature and forgotten Varanasi beside the Ganges. Further east, the holy river flows towards **Allahabad**, and the sacred confluence at **Prayag**, where it meets the Yamuna and the mythical Saraswati that flows from heaven.

Kanpur

Although the teeming metropolis of **KANPUR**, 438km east of Delhi and 190km west of Allahabad, is among the most polluted cities in the world, it's not a particularly unpleasant place to visit. Its setting is certainly attractive, on a fertile escarpment on the south bank of the Ganges, 1.5km wide at this point, and in the leafy Civil Lines area you can remain happily oblivious to the tanneries, chemical works, engineering and industrial developments that belch on the outskirts. Kanpur has been a textile-manufacturing centre since its cotton mills were established in 1869, and together with its twin city, Lucknow, 76km northeast, it dominates the industrial heartland of Uttar Pradesh.

The problem with Kanpur as a tourist destination is simply that it's not all that interesting. Unlike other points along the Ganges, the riverside is of little significance; its *ghats* are run down, and only those at **Bithur**, 20km upstream, are worth exploring.

Arrival, transport and information

Trains on the main Delhi–Calcutta line pull in regularly at **Kanpur Central**, in the most congested part of the city. **Buses** from Lucknow and points east terminate at the **Collectorganj Bus Stand** (☎0512/63259) in Sadar Bazaar, a short way east, while services from Delhi, Agra, Haridwar and the west arrive at **Chunniganj** (☎0512/63603), 3km west of the Mall. Few people fly to Kanpur, as rail connections, especially with Delhi, are good, but there's an **airport** 12km to the east, a taxi-ride (Rs100) or an auto-rickshaw-ride (Rs30) from the centre. *Indian Airlines* have offices opposite M G College, Civil Lines (☎0512/211430) and at the airport (☎0512/43042).

Local buses use stands such as Ghanta Ghar, near the Mall; **taxis** are plentiful near the station; **cars** can be rented through the larger hotels or from the main taxi stand at Canal Road Crossing on the Mall; and **cycle** and **auto**-rickshaws abound. Noisy diesel-powered *Vikrams* and tempos operate along fixed routes, and horse-drawn tongas can be rented on a shared or exclusive basis.

As the government does not consider Kanpur to be a tourist destination, the city has no official information centre. The **GPO** is at Bara Chaurha on The Mall, and money can be changed nearby at *ANZ Grindlays* **bank**.

The Town

The focus of modern Kanpur is north of the station, where the large avenue known as **The Mall** threads east to west to form a hub for the more cosmopolitan sectors of the city. Further north and west, beyond the exclusive **Civil Lines** area, is the river.

"Cawnpore", among the most vital of the British East India Company's garrisons along the Ganges, was a major focus of the wild revolt of 1857 – what the British call the "**Indian Mutiny**" and Indians the "**First War of Independence**". One thousand or so British residents were besieged throughout June by the forces of Nana Sahib of Bithur, their numbers whittled away by disease, starvation and enemy sharp-shooting. Only a few hundred were still alive when Brigadier-General Wheeler finally managed to negotiate a truce. However, as they boarded boats at Satichaura Ghat, to carry them to Allahabad, they were mown down by gunfire, and any survivors put to the sword. When relief under Brigadier-General Havelock finally reached Kanpur a few days later, on 17 July, they found that two hundred imprisoned women and children had been butchered in revenge for previous British atrocities. Terrifying and equally brutal reprisals by the British included executions of innocent civilians, the razing of villages, and the shooting of captives spreadeagled across the mouths of cannons.

Around 1.5km east of the station, close to the run-down Kanpur Club, broad tree-lined streets lead to the red-brick **All Saints' Memorial Church** (if locked, ask for the keys at the Gate Lodge). Erected in 1875, near the site of General Wheeler's original entrenchment, it serves as a tribute to the British dead. A fine stained-glass window above the west door filters light into the spacious and cool interior, where marble tablets line the walls; the vestry holds a plan of the entrenchment. Outside, enclosed by iron railings, a tiled memorial marks the graves of officers and men, not far from a capped well where many died trying to draw water. Within an enclosure east of the church, the **Memorial Garden** has a Gothic screen designed by Sir Henry Yule, and a touching epitaph in stone by Baron Carlo Marochetti. The memorials originally stood over the site of the terrible Bibighat well in the centre of the city, where Havelock discovered the still-warm remains of the massacred women and children; they were relocated here after Independence.

Although **Kanpur Zoo**, an oasis amid the noisy urban sprawl at Allen Park 5km west of the Mall, might on first sight appear to be just another zoological park, it is far from ordinary (daily except Mon, dawn–dusk; Rs5). This vast area of woodland provides a surreal setting in which wild animals co-exist alongside others in open enclosures and cages. Along the southeast, extensive low-lying marshlands provide grazing for herds of wild deer, and sustain a mixed assortment of birds. During feeding time, in the early evenings, *nilgai* antelope ("blue bull") emerge from the dense surrounding woods to gorge on grain laid out close to their captive cousins.

The new, brash **JK Mandir**, in attractive gardens 4km west of the Mall, not far from the zoo, has become one of Kanpur's principal temples – an object lesson as to where mass religion in India is heading. This extraordinary white marble and alabaster edifice was constructed by a local business family in a hybrid modern style that incorporates north and south Indian elements, capped by five *shikharas* (spires). In separate chapels inside the huge central hall, hung with chandeliers, numerous deities are represented in hyper-realistic detail. The large **Moti Jheel** tank nearby is popular with picnickers.

Accommodation

Several of Kanpur's better **hotels** can be found in and around the Mall, while cheaper accommodation is concentrated near the Central Railway Station – which itself has reasonable retiring rooms.

Attic, 15/198 Vikramjit Singh Rd, Civil Lines (☎0512/311691). Mysteriously misnamed Kanpur landmark, with a distinct whiff of the Raj. Comfortable bungalow and a garden, full of character. ⑤.

Bliss, near Gumti 5, Gurudwara, 11A/5 G T Rd (☎0512/291738). Sikh-run, clean and comfortable with both air-cooled and a/c rooms; 4km from the centre but worth the trek. ③–④.

Ganges, 51/50 Nayaganj (☎0512/352853). Cheap and not far from the station, with a restaurant. ②.
Gaurav, 18/54 The Mall (☎0512/368616). Central hotel, four doors down from the better-known *Geet*, but not as loud and a lot more pleasant. ⑤–⑥.
The Landmark, 10 The Mall (☎0512/317601). Behind Som Dutt Plaza; the closest Kanpur comes to luxury. Features include currency exchange. ⑧.
Meera Inn, The Mall (☎0512/319972). Friendly and comfortable place opposite *Reserve Bank* but showing its age. Despite lacking its own restaurant, it does offer room service. ⑤.
Meghdoot, The Mall (☎0512/311999). Popular business-class hotel opposite Company Bagh, with a small rooftop swimming pool, health club, several restaurants and a bar. ⑦–⑧.
Natraj, 71/150 Suterkhana (☎0512/366907). Reasonable budget accommodation close to the railway station. Some rooms with shared baths and some small but expensive a/c. ①–⑥.
Station View, opposite Railway Station, city side (☎0512/366138). Reasonably-priced basic, budget hotel with air-cooled rooms. ②–③.
Swagat, 80 Feet Rd, Brahm Nagar (☎0512/541923). Far from the centre but newish, with comfortable rooms and several facilities including car rental. ④–⑤.

Eating

While few of the high street **eating places** can be recommended, several of Kanpur's better hotels such as the *Landmark* and the *Meghdoot* have good restaurants.
Budhsen, Virhana Rd, Nayaganj. A popular restaurant with an adjacent sweetshop which, along with the posh *Haveli*, is one of several options on this busy and central shopping street.
Kailash Misthan Bhandar, G T Rd, Gumti 5. The best of a couple of roadside cafes near Moti Jheel, serving snacks such as *dosas* to locals who come here to take the evening air.
Kwalitys, The Mall. Part of the national chain; predictable multi-cuisine food and a separate bar.
Little Chef, Vikramjit Singh Rd, Civil Lines. Modern fast-food place, next to the *Attic*. Burgers, ice-cream, and Indian food, plus piped music. Attracts a well-heeled young crowd, but pleasant enough.
Shanghai, The Mall. Popular Chinese restaurant in the centre of town.
Treat, behind *The Landmark*, Navin Market, The Mall. Popular cafe in a shopping precinct, with a flexible menu including Chinese and South Indian food and ice-creams.

Around Kanpur: Bithur

Some Hindus consider the charming little town of **BITHUR**, set in rich farming country beside the Ganges, 20km west of Kanpur, to be the centre of the world. However, few pilgrims, let alone tourists, come to this miniature Varanasi, where many of the *ghats* have been reclaimed by the river, since being devastated by the British bombardment that followed the uprising of 1857. Bithur's principal shrine, at the main *ghat*, is one of the few in the Hindu world to be dedicated to **Brahma**. The town is also connected to the *Ramayana*, and specifically with Rama's wife Sita – this is where her sons were born, and where she died when the earth opened and swallowed her.

Much the best way to enjoy the ambience of the place is to rent a **boat** at the main *ghat*. Most are owned by the *pandas* (pilgrim priests), whose houses are huddled together with the *dharamshalas* near the *ghat*'s dilapidated gate. Less than a kilometre upriver stands another of the many mosques built on the foundations of devastated Hindu temples during the reign of Aurangzeb. As in Ayodhya (see p.309), this mosque has attracted the attention of Hindu fundamentalists, but the local *pandas* proudly inform visitors that here Hindus and Muslims continue to co-exist in harmony.

Practicalities

Three local **trains** a day connect Brahmavart, 2km from Bithur, with Kanpur Central, while buses and shared auto-rickshaws travel between Kanpur and Mandhana, where local transport to Bithur can be picked up. For the moment, the only way to arrange food and lodging is through the pleasant and helpful *pandas*. During the full moon of Kartika Purnima (Oct/Nov), Bithur plays host to a large and colourful rustic fair.

Lucknow

In the approximate centre of Uttar Pradesh, 516km east of Delhi, the state capital **LUCKNOW** is best remembered for the ordeal of its British residents during the five-month **siege** of 1857. However, the city had earlier witnessed the last heady days of Muslim rule in India, before the final capitulation to the British. In fact the summary British deposition of the incompetent last Nawab of **Avadh** – or Oudh as the British called it – Wajid Ali Shah, is usually numbered among the root causes of the "Mutiny". Today, Lucknow's fading nineteenth-century monuments bear the scars of the fighting, and of the destruction wrought by the British army when they regained control.

The centre of Muslim power shifted gradually from Delhi to Avadh from the middle of the eighteenth century onwards, as the Moghul empire declined. The later Nawabs of Avadh are a byword in India for indolence and decadence, but it has to be acknowledged that under their rule the arts flourished, cocooned from the responsibilities of government. Avadh became a magnet for poets and artists, where Hindus and Muslims worked in harmony, fuelled by wealth and plentiful leisure time. Lucknow was also an important repository of Shi'a culture and Islamic jurisprudence, with its Farangi Mahal school of law attracting students from as far afield as China and Central Asia.

The patronage of the Shi'a Nawabs also produced new expressions of the faith – the annual **Muharram** processions, in memory of the martyrdom of Hussain and his two sons, developed into elaborate affairs with **tazia**, ornate reproductions in paper of the Shi'a Imam's shrine at Karbala in southern Iraq, being carried to the local Karbala for burial. In Lucknow, Muharram is often a time of great tension between the Shi'a and

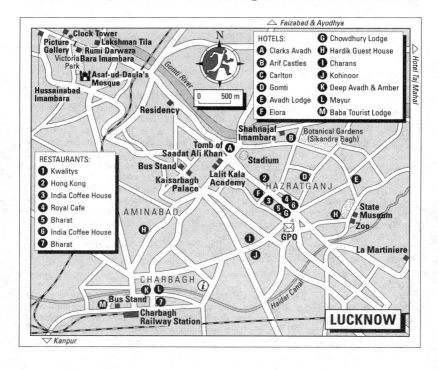

The telephone **area code** for Lucknow is ☎0522.

their rival Sunni Muslims. During the rest of the year the *tazia* images are kept in Imambara ("houses of the Imam"); these range from humble rooms in poor Shi'a households to the **Great Imambara** built by Asaf-ud-Daula in 1784.

Extraordinary sandstone monuments, now engulfed by modern Lucknow, still testify to the euphoric atmosphere of this unique culture. European-inspired edifices too are prominent on the skyline, often embellished with flying buttresses, turrets, cupolas and floral patterns, but the brick and mortar with which they were constructed means that they are not ageing as well as the earlier stone buildings and old Lucknow is, literally, crumbling away.

Arrival, information and transport

From **Amausi Airport** (☎256130), 16km south on the Kanpur Road, a taxi to the centre of Lucknow costs around Rs150. Airport buses connect with flights.

Lucknow's main **Charbagh Railway Station**, 4km southwest of the central hub of Hazratganj, is itself a remarkable building, with prominent *chhatris* above the entrance arcade and a roof inspired by a chess-board. Most **buses** including those from Varanasi, Allahabad, Agra, Jhansi and Kanpur arrive at the main **Charbagh Bus Stand** alongside, while some buses from the Nepal border at Sonauli and from Gorakhpur, Faizabad and Ayodhya pull in at the **Kaisarbagh** stand, near Hazratganj.

City transport and guided tours

The fierce competition for space makes rush hours in Lucknow particularly interesting. Tempos and *Vikrams*, their diesel engines sounding like hundreds of loud rattles, have more or less taken over from city buses, plying regular routes such as from Charbagh

---

THE PERFORMING ARTS OF LUCKNOW

In the eighteenth and nineteenth centuries, Muslim Lucknow saw the emergence of an astounding range of music and dance forms that remain prominent in the performing arts of north India. The period is still considered as a Golden Age of artistic achievement.

Apart from the musicians of the court, and courtiers – among them some of the Nawabs themselves – **tawwaif** (courtesans) took on a vital role in the cultural life of the city, becoming proficient as poets and in dance and song. While *khyal* and *dhrupad* remained the mainstay of classical music, **thumri** – love songs amalgamating classical *ragas* and folk melodies – developed a high degree of sophistication, and forms such as *dadra*, *tappa* and *hori*, influenced by folk traditions, also became widely popular. Often referred to as "semi" or "light" classical music, these latter forms are fading from the repertoire of modern musicians.

Kathak, the main genre of north Indian classical dance, developed under Nawabs such as Shuja-ud-Daula (1756–75) and Asaf-ud-Daula (1775–97). The theme of Krishna cavorting with the milkmaids (*gopis*) became especially important within performances that otherwise rely on strong and energetic footwork around *laikari*, intricate rhythmic compositions accompanied by *tabla* or hand-drums. Some of Avadh's great **Gharana** (schools) of dance and music – including those at Lucknow, Farrakhabad and Rampur – are gradually being assimilated into a new system of patronage, now dependent on the middle classes.

The **Lucknow Festival**, held in February, gives visitors an excellent opportunity to sample the city's vibrant traditions of music and dance. For information, contact UP Tourism.

to the GPO, with depots at Janpath Market, Clarks Avadh Crossing and the Chowk. Adding to the chaos are legions of reasonably priced cycle rickshaws, more common than auto-rickshaws and charging around Rs5 from the station to Hazratganj.

Cars can be rented from various operators, including *Hotel Clarks Avadh*, *UP Tours* at the *Hotel Gomti*, 6 Sapru Marg (☎232659), and *Transworld Travel & Tours*, 98 *Carlton Hotel*, Shah Najaf Rd (☎232145). Comprehensive daily **city tours**, which must be booked in advance through *UP Tours*, leave the *Hotel Gomti* at 9am and return at 2pm. They will also pick up from the station (at 7.45am) and various hotels. Guide and entrance fees are included in the price (Rs50).

Information

The national government's **Regional Tourist Bureau**, close to the railway station at 10 Station Rd (Mon–Sat 10am–5pm, closed 2nd Sat of each month; ☎246205), provides information only; they also operate a stand at the railway station. The **UP Tourism** office, at 3 Newal Kishore Rd (☎228349), has an information counter.

Lucknow's **GPO** is on Vidhan Sabha Marg. Among **banks** for foreign exchange are *Punjab National Bank*, Ashok Marg, Hazratganj (☎21290), and *State Bank of India*, also on Ashok Marg (☎21341) and at Moti Mahal Marg (☎220186).

The Town

Most of Lucknow's monuments are spread along or near the southern bank of the Gomti, a sluggish weed-covered stream when the rains aren't falling. Close to the main central bridge lies the modern economic centre of **Hazratganj**, with the **Shah Najaf Imambara** to its north near the riverbank. Further west, beyond the ruins of the **Residency**, the road passes the majestic **Bara Imambara**, leading through the large gate of **Rumi Darwaza** to the **Hussainabad Imambara**. South of Hussainabad, between Hazratganj and Charbagh, the old city sector of Aminabad holds a maze of busy streets and fascinating markets.

Hussainabad

In the west of the city, in the vicinity of Hardinge Bridge around "old" Lucknow, lie several crumbling relics of the Nawabs of Avadh. Chief among them is the Great or **Bara Imambara** (daily except during Muharram 8am–6.30pm; combined ticket including Hussainabad Imambara and Picture Gallery, Rs10), which boasts one of the largest vaulted halls in the world – 50m long and 15m high. Flat on top, slightly arched inside, and built by Asaf-ud-Daula in 1784 without the aid of a single iron or wooden beam, the roof was constructed using a technique known as *kara dena*, in which bricks are broken and angled to form an interlocking section and then covered with concrete – here several feet thick. The arcaded structure is approached through what must have been an extravagant gate, now pockmarked and on the verge of collapse. Two successive courtyards lead from the gates to the Imambara itself, which, unlike the sombre architecture of mosques, is festive and loud. Steps lead up to a labyrinth of chambers known as *bhulbhulaiya* – the "maze". Adjacent to the Bara Imambara and overlooking it is **Asaf-ud-Daula's Mosque**, set upon a two-tiered arcaded plinth with two lofty minarets. Closed to non-Muslims, it can be readily viewed from the Victoria Gardens that adjoin it to the west (daily except Fri dawn–dusk; Rs6).

Straddling the main road west of the main gates, the colossal **Rumi Darwaza** is an ornamental victory arch modelled on one of the gates to Asia Minor at Istanbul (known to the Islamic world in Byzantine times as "Rumi"). Now decaying, it sports elaborate floral patterns and a few extraordinary trumpets. Steps lead up to open chambers that command a general prospect of the monuments of Hussainabad.

A short distance further west, the lavish **Hussainabad Imambara** is also known as the Chota ("small") Imambara, or the Palace of Lights, thanks to its fairy-tale appearance when decorated and illuminated for special occasions. The raised tank in front of it, which is approached via a spacious courtyard, adds to the overall festive atmosphere. A central gilded dome dominates the whole ensemble, busy with minarets, small domes and arches and even a crude miniature Taj Mahal. Built in 1837 by Muhammad Ali Shah (1837–42), partly to provide famine relief through employment, the Imambara houses a silver-faced throne, plus the tombs of important Avadhi personalities. The dummy gate opposite the main entrance was used by ceremonial musicians, while the unfinished watch-tower is known as the Satkhanda or "Seven Storeys", even though only four were ever constructed. West of the Imambara, and surrounded by ruins, are the two soaring minarets and three domes of the **Jami Masjid**, completed after the death of Muhammad Ali Shah, which does not admit non-Muslims.

Beyond the Hussainabad Tank, east of the Hussainabad Imambara, the isolated 67-metre-high **Hussainabad Clocktower**, an ambitious Gothic tower completed in 1887, carries the largest clock in India. Close to this bizarre monolith lies **Taluqdar's Hall**, built by Muhammad Ali Shah to house the offices of the Hussainabad Trust, and the **Picture Gallery**, also known as the **Muhammad Ali Shah Art Gallery**. Exhibits in its one large hall include old photographs and paintings including a famous portrait of the ineffectual and feeble last Nawab of Avadh, Wajid Ali Shah (1847–56), with his left nipple showing. Dusty and dank, the gallery nevertheless captures the decadent spirit of Avadh – as indeed do the adjacent trust offices. **Aurangzeb's Mosque**, on the high ground towards Hardinge Bridge known as **Lakshman Tila**, was the site of Lucknow's original fifteenth-century settlement.

The Residency

The blasted **Residency** (daily dawn–dusk; Rs0.50, free on Fri) rests in peace amid landscaped gardens southeast of Hardinge Bridge – a battle-scarred ruin left exactly as it stood when the siege was finally relieved by Sir Colin Campbell on November 17, 1857. Its shattered tower became a shrine to the tenacity of the British in India, and continued to be maintained as such even after Independence.

During the siege, every building in the complex was utilized for the hard-fought defence of the compound. The **Treasury**, on the right through the **Baillie Guard Gate**, served as an arsenal, while the sumptuous **Banqueting Hall**, immediately west, was a makeshift hospital, and the extensive single-storey **Dr Fayrer's House**, just south, housed women and children. Most of the original structures, such as **Begum Kothi**, were left standing to impede direct fire from the enemy. On the lawn outside Begum Kothi, a large cross honours the astute but helpless Sir Henry Lawrence, responsible for building its defences, who died shortly after hostilities began.

The pockmarked Residency itself holds a small **museum**. Circular steps descend into its bowels, to the huge cellar known as the *tikhana* where many of the women and children took shelter. On the ground floor, the **Model Room** (daily 9am–4.30pm), the only one with its roof intact, houses a large model of the defences and of the Residency, and a small but excellent collection of etchings and old photographs.

Several victims of the siege are buried in the **Cemetery** next to the ruined church west of the Residency. Not far away east, along the river, the rather dull **Shaheed Smarak** is a corresponding post-Independence memorial to the Indian martyrs who died here fighting the British in the "First War of Independence".

Kaisarbagh

Isolated by the noise and bustle of modern Lucknow, the nineteenth-century monuments around **Kaisarbagh**, south of the Residency, stand forlorn and unattended. Large chunks of the **Kaisarbagh Palace**, built in 1850 by Wajid Ali Shah and intended

THE SIEGE OF THE RESIDENCY OF LUCKNOW

The mutinous *sepoys* who poured across the River Gomti into Lucknow on June 30, 1857 found the city rife with resentment against the recent British takeover of the kingdom of Avadh. The tiny, isolated, **British garrison**, under the command of Sir Henry Lawrence, took refuge in the **Residency**, which became the focus of a fierce struggle for survival.

Less than a thousand of the three thousand British residents and loyal Indians who crammed into the Residency survived the relentless war of attrition. So unhygienic were their living conditions that those who failed to succumb to gangrenous and tetanus-infected wounds were liable to fall victim to cholera and scurvy. While a barrage of heavy artillery was maintained by both sides, a simultaneous **subterranean** battle was being fought. The *sepoys* pinned their hopes of breaching the defences on tunnelling and laying mines, but the British were far more adept at such methods. The skills of the ex-miners of the 32nd (Cornish) Regiment enabled them to follow the sounds of enemy chipping and defuse mines, and even blow up several *sepoy*-controlled buildings on the peripheries of the complex.

Morale remained high among the 1400 **non-combatants**, who included fifty schoolboys from La Martiniere, and class distinctions were upheld throughout. While the wives of European soldiers and non-commissioned officers, children and servants took refuge in the *tikhana* (cellar), the "Ladies" of the Residency occupied the higher and airier chambers, until the unfortunate loss of Miss Palmer's leg, carried off on July 1, persuaded them of the gravity of their predicament. Sir Henry Lawrence was fatally wounded the next day.

The wealthier officers managed to maintain their own private hoard of supplies, living in much their usual style. Matters improved when after three months General Sir Henry Havelock arrived with reinforcements, and the normal round of visits and invitations to supper was resumed despite the inconvenient shortage of good food and wine.

Not until November 17 was the siege finally lifted, by the forces of Sir Colin Campbell. When the Highlanders liberated the Residency, their offers of tea were turned down by the women; they were used to taking milk in their tea, which the soldiers could not supply.

to be the eighth wonder of the world, have vanished, while the nearby **Chattar Manzil**, once the United Services Club, has lost most of its roof. Within the grounds of the Kaisarbagh, beside the grave of his wife **Khurshid Zadi**, is the tomb of **Saadat Ali Khan** (1798–1814). Now overgrown and often locked, it is distinguished by black-and-white marble paving, beneath which a dark narrow stairway drops down to the vault.

Kaisarbagh's **Folk Art Museum**, a large hall devoted to the contemporary arts of UP, is a disappointment. Nearby, the former coronation hall on Lal Baradari is now the **Lalit Kala Academy** (Mon–Fri 9am–5pm; free), the gallery for the government school of art. It too is dilapidated and poorly maintained.

Hazratganj

Along the river, opposite the fading *Carlton Hotel*, on Rana Pratap Marg, squats the huge dome of the **Shah Najaf Imambara** (daily except Fri dawn–dusk; donations), named after the tomb of Ali in Iraq and at its best when adorned with lights during Muharram. Its musty interior holds some incredibly garish chandeliers used in processions, several *tazia*, and the silver-faced tomb of the decadent and profligate Ghazi-ud-din-Haidar (1814–27), buried with three of his queens.

The Imambara was commandeered as a *sepoy* stronghold in 1857, and the crucial battle that enabled the British to relieve the Residency was fought in the adjacent pleasure gardens of **Sikandrabagh** on November 16. It took one and a half hours of bombardment for the soldiers of Sir Colin Campbell to breach the defences of the two thousand *sepoys*; then the Sikhs and 93rd Highlanders poured through, to embark on a rampage of slaughter. There was no escape for the terrified *sepoys*, some of whom are said to have believed the bloodstained, red-faced, kilted Scots to be the ghosts of the murdered European women of Kanpur. Driven against the north wall, they were either bayoneted or shot, and the dead and dying piled shoulder-high. Tranquil once again, Sikandrabagh is now home to the National Botanical Research Institute and the beautiful **Botanical Gardens** (daily 6am–5pm; free), with their conservatories, nurseries, herb, rose and bougainvillea gardens, and manicured lawns.

Towards the east of Lucknow, an extraordinary chateau-like building has become almost a symbol of the city – **La Martiniere**, an exclusive public school in the finest colonial tradition. It was built as a country retreat by Major-General Claude Martin, a French soldier-adventurer taken prisoner by the British in Pondicherry in 1761. The enigmatic Martin later joined the East India Company, made his fortune in indigo, and served both the British and the Nawabs of Avadh. The building is an outrageous but intriguing amalgam, crowned by flying walkways; Greco-Roman figures on the parapets give it a busy silhouette, gigantic heraldic lions gaze across the grounds, and a large bronze cannon graces the front. Martin himself is buried in the basement. During the siege, La Martiniere was occupied by rebels, while its boys were evacuated to the Residency. Entry to the building is by prior arrangement with the Principal.

Close to the centre of Hazratganj, its grounds dotted with derelict Avadhi monuments, Lucknow's small **zoo** also serves as an amusement park with a miniature train to view the animals (daily except Mon dawn–dusk; Rs5). Head through the zoo to reach the **State Museum** (daily except Mon 10.30am–4.30pm; Rs1, cameras Rs5), with its delicate, speckled-red-sandstone sculpture from the Mathura school of the Kushana and Gupta periods (first–sixth centuries AD). Besides sculpture from Gandhara, Mahoba, Nalanda and Sravasti, it boasts a gallery of terracotta and even an Egyptian mummy. Musical instruments, paintings and costumes provide atmosphere in the Avadh Gallery; while the natural history section is a taxidermist's dream.

Shopping

Chikan is a long-standing Lucknavi tradition of embroidery, in which designs are built up to form delicate floral patterns along edges on *saris* and on necklines and collars of *kurtas*. Workshops can be found around the Chowk, the market area of old Lucknow and shops and showrooms in Hazratganj, Janpath Market, Nazirabad and Aminabad. **Bhagwat Das & Sons** are reputable dealers with two shops – one at Chowk and the other at Husseinganj Chaurhai; **Tandon's**, 17/1 Ashok Marg, Hazratganj, is another good outlet. The fixed prices at **Gangotri**, the UP government emporium in Hazratganj, are more expensive than those in the markets, but despite the poor selection, the quality is assured and you don't have to haggle.

Lucknow is also renowned for its **ittar** (or *attar*), concentrated perfume sold in small vials – an acquired (and expensive) taste. Small balls of cotton wool are daubed with the scent and placed neatly within the top folds of the ear; musicians believe that the aroma heightens their senses. Popular *ittar* are *ambar* from amber, *khus* from a flowering plant and *ghulab* from rose. The best place for *ittar* is *Asghar Ali Mohammad Ali*, Aminabad, who have their own factories in Kannauj 150km away.

Accommodation

Budget and mid-range **hotels** are concentrated in the **Charbagh** area, around the bus and railway stations, and along Vidhan Sabha Marg, the main artery feeding into the city centre around the GPO. The more cosmopolitan **Hazratganj** district holds a few bargains. Top-range hotels under construction as this book went to press include the *Taj Palace* in Gomti Nagar and *Arif Castles*, 4 Rana Pratap Marg.

Amber, Naka Hindola (☎215658). Spacious air-cooled rooms, with clean Indian-style toilets. ③–⑤.

Arif Castles, 4 Rana Pratap Marg, near Shah Najaf (☎231313). Comfortable but ostentatious; dripping with chandeliers and reminiscent of a Hindi film set. ⑦–⑧.

Avadh Lodge, 1 Ram Mohan Rai Marg (☎282861). A hall hung with dusty hunting trophies captures the atmosphere of old Lucknow, but the place is musty and showing its age. ③–⑤.

Baba Tourist Lodge, Charbagh Railway Station (☎54357). A stone's throw from the station – turn left and walk 300m; pleasant and reasonably clean Sikh-run option with a range of rooms from shared baths to a/c. ③–⑤.

Carlton, Shah Najaf Rd (☎244021). Fabled Lucknow address, a *fin-de-siècle* Euro-Avadhi edifice with big rooms, ancient plumbing and a pleasant garden restaurant. Expensive for what it is. ⑤–⑦.

Charans, 16 Vidhan Sabha Marg (☎247219). Mid-range and quiet, even though it lies just off the main road, with a choice of air-cooled or a/c rooms. ④–⑥.

Chowdhury Lodge, 3 Vidhan Sabha Marg (☎241911). Close to the GPO, well-priced, pleasant, friendly and justifiably popular. Tea served in bed in the mornings. ②–③.

Clarks Avadh, 8 Mahatma Gandhi Marg (☎220131). An imposing if characterless landmark in the centre of Lucknow, which has lost its crown as the best in town to the *Taj* (see below). ⑨.

Deep Avadh, Naka Hindola, Aminabad Rd (☎216521). New place, with a good multi-cuisine restaurant and a travel desk, in an interesting part of town, close to the station. ③–⑤.

Elora, 3 Lalbagh (☎231307). Popular with travellers, in the busy heart of Lucknow with air-cooled and a/c rooms; the prices, however, are a bit high. ③–⑥.

Hardik Guest House, 16 Rana Pratap Marg, near Jopling Road Crossing (☎272817). Clean, comfortable and recommended little guest house, with a/c rooms and food. ⑤–⑥.

Kohinoor, 6 Station Rd (☎217693). Close to the station and one of the best along this stretch. Although devoid of character, it does have a 24hr-coffee shop. ⑥.

Mayur, Charbagh (☎451824). Opposite the station, next to the Charbagh Bus Stand and above the *Bharat Restaurant*. Unattractive cheaper rooms, while those at the other end of the range are much too expensive for what they are. ③–⑤.

Taj Mahal, Vipin Khand, Gomti Nagar (☎393939). Recently built in Avadhi style; easily Lucknow's most elegant and comfortable, but expensive. ⑨.

UP Tourism Gomti, 6 Tej Bahadur Sapru Marg (☎232291). Showpiece establishment but devoid of character, off the busy centre of Hazratganj; *UP Tours* is also housed here. ⑦.

Eating

The rich traditional Lucknavi **cuisine** – featuring such Mughlai dishes as *shami kebabs, mughlai parathas, sheekh kebabs*, chicken *musallam* and *boti kebab* – is available from food stalls throughout the city, in places such as Shami Avadh Bazaar, near the K D Singh Babu Stadium, and behind the *Tulsi Theatre* in Hazratganj. Standard a/c restaurants are found mostly in Hazratganj, while, of course, hotel restaurants such as the expensive *Clarks Avadh* and the new *Taj Mahal*, serve excellent but pricey food.

Bharat Restaurant, Charbagh. Cheap open-air cafe opposite the station. Good *dosas*.

Chef Restaurant, Vidhan Sabha Marg, near GPO (☎223313). Multi-cuisine restaurant with snacks and an ice-cream parlour.

Hong Kong, Mahatma Gandhi Marg, Hazratganj. Popular Chinese restaurant with good food.

India Coffee House, Ashok Marg. Once a hotbed of Lucknow's intelligentsia; still popular with the faithful, but now dingy and a bit run down. South and north Indian snacks and coffee.

John Hing, opposite *Sahu Cinema*, Mahatma Gandhi Marg, Hazratganj. One of the few reasonable Chinese restaurants in Lucknow.

Kwality, Mayfair Building, Hazratganj. Dimly lit, a/c, the standard menu of this nationwide chain.

Mehman Fast Foods, Charbagh. Open station cafe; Chinese and north and south Indian food.

Royal Cafe, Hazratganj. Popular multi-cuisine a/c restaurant close to *Kwalitys*.

Vyangyan, Ashok Marg, near Ritz. A good a/c vegetarian restaurant, with competition from *Ruchika* next door.

Indian Airlines flights from Lucknow include those to **Varanasi** and **Bombay** (Mon, Thurs & Sat); to **Calcutta** via **Patna** (Mon, Wed & Fri), and several to **Delhi** (daily). *Indian Airlines* have offices at *Hotel Clarks Avadh*, 8 Mahatma Gandhi Marg (☎220927), and at the airport at Amausi (☎256132; information ☎142). The brand new airline, *UPAir* also have their offices at *Clarks Avadh* and another at the airport (☎257826); their schedule, presently erratic, includes flights to **Kullu** via **Delhi**, with a new service planned linking all the major Buddhist sites including **Sravasti**, **Kushinagar**, **Varanasi** and **Bodh Gaya**.

By **rail**, the excellent all a/c *Shatabdi Express* #2003 goes to **Delhi** (Mon–Fri 3.20pm; 7hr); cheaper alternatives include the *Gomti Express* #2419 (daily except Tues; 5.25am, 8hr), and the slower overnight *Lucknow Mail* #4229 (10pm; 9hr 45min). The best choice to **Agra** is the *Avadh Express* #5063 (8.40pm; 7hr). The *Kushinagar Express* #1016 travels to **Bombay** (daily; 0.30am; 30hr). **Calcutta** is served by several trains, such as the *Amritsar–Howrah Mail* #3006 (10.50am; 22hr 15min) and the slower *Amritsar–Howrah Express* #3050 (11.40am; 28hr). Trains to **Varanasi** include the fast evening *Lucknow–Varanasi Varuna Express* #2428 (6pm; 7hr), the overnight *Kashi–Vishwanath Express* #4058 (11.20pm; 8hr), the *Dehra Dun–Varanasi-Express* #4266 (8am; 8hr 30min) and the *Doon Express* #3010, both of which in the opposite direction head for **Dehra Dun** (14hr) via **Haridwar**. Satna, the jumping off point for **Khajuraho**, is serviced by trains such as the *Chitrakoot Express* #5010 (5.25pm; 11hr), which stops at **Chitrakut Dham** in the middle of the night.

Trains such as the *Vaishali*, #2554, *Kushinagar* #1015 and *Sabarmati* #9165 *Expresses* travel to **Gorakhpur** (5hr), where you can catch a bus to the **Nepal** border at **Sonauli** – the choice of buses to **Kathmandu** and **Pokhara** is better on the Nepalese side. This may seem a convoluted way to get to Nepal, but is more comfortable than a single long gruelling direct bus. If you're content to make the 11- to 12-hour journey by road, several buses leave from **Kaisarbagh** and **Charbagh**, from where buses also go to Gorakhpur and to Faizabad. Kaisarbagh also offers **Delhi** buses, and an efficient night service to **Nainital**.

Agents for air, rail and bus tickets include *Hollywood Travels*, Mayfair Building, 29 Hazratganj (☎226559); *Travel Corporation of India*, 3 Shah Najaf Marg (☎233212); and the efficient, friendly *UP Tours*, *Hotel Gomti*, 6 Sapru Marg (☎232659).

Finally, if you're heading for the UP hills, Lucknow holds offices of both **GMVN**, 432/4 New Civil Lines, Old Hyderabad (☎387349), and **KMVN**, near *Kirpa Automobiles*, 2 Gopal Khera House, Sarojini Naidu Marg (☎235903), who organize tours of, and accommodation in, **Garhwal** and **Kumaun** respectively. For more on both, see p.249 and p.283.

Ayodhya

As one of the seven holy cities of the Vaishnavites, the small town of **AYODHYA**, on the south bank of the River Ghaghara, 130km east of Lucknow and 6km east of Faizabad, attracts pilgrims from all over India. Even before the destruction in 1992 of the Babri Masjid mosque catapulted Ayodhya into world prominence, as the putative birthplace of Rama, it was renowned as a potential flashpoint for sectarian violence, and only the foolhardiest of foreign tourists venture out here. The town, housing over 7000 shrines, is permeated by tension and any disturbance should be avoided; so should *Kar Sevaks*, or "volunteers", who mingle with pilgrims and visitors pretending to be temple guides while continuing to dish out their propaganda.

The embattled and heavily-guarded site of what was once Babri Masjid – the **Ram Janmabhumi** – stands just south of the shrine known as **Janam Sthana**, the "birthplace", where Rama is said to have spent much of his early childhood. The contentious site is opened to the public twice a day (7–10am & 3–5pm) attracting huge crowds who throw flowers at the barbed-wire adorned ruins. Other sites associated with the Rama legend include **Lakshmana Ghat**, a river landing near the bridge north of town, where Rama's brother Lakshmana is said to have committed suicide after breaking a vow. Not far away, on the banks of a rivulet, is the prominent and much-venerated temple of **Kala Rama**, while the nineteenth-century **Kanak Bhavan** temple in the centre of town is devoted to Rama and his wife Sita. Further south, towards the railway station 1km east of the Ram Janmabhumi, the **Hanuman Gadhi** temple ("Hanuman's Fortress"), approached by an impressive flight of stairs, is enclosed within a quadrangle protected by massive white bastion-like walls. Embossed silver doorways lead to several shrines of Rama's monkey companion, Hanuman, and one of Sita. Shops on the street below sell religious paraphernalia, gifts and postcards, some of which, clearly aimed by the VHP to shock, are gruesome and graphic photographs of *Kar Sevaks* killed during police firings when, according to them, the river ran red with blood.

Practicalities

Though Ayodhya has a small **railway station** of its own, south of town, most visitors come for the day from busy Faizabad (see below), on buses and auto-rickshaws from the station there. If you want to **stay** in Ayodhya, the *Tourist Bungalow* (②–③), next to the station, has a dorm and a wide range of rooms, as well as a poorly managed restaurant. Alternatively, the *Birla Dharamsala* (①), on the main road, has very cheap and decent accommodation in its "VIP" rooms. Ayodhya is a **vegetarian** town.

BABRI MASJID AND RAM JANMABHUMI

Although legend tells of Ayodhya as the birthplace of **Rama** – an incarnation of Vishnu and hero of the epic *Ramayana* – archeologists have found no proof of the existence of the king or his capital. They have however shown that Ayodhya was inhabited in the seventh century BC, and a Jain settlement dating from the fourth century BC is among the oldest known, said to be the home of the first and fourth Jain *tirthankaras*. The Buddha is also said to have visited the town, but there is little evidence that Ayodhya had any significance prior to the Muslim invasion in the fifteenth century. It can be argued that any earlier Hindu structures would have suffered from the usual practice of razing temples and replacing them with mosques, but the fact that the many shrines today crowded into the small town are relatively new is more likely to be simply because the re-emergence of Rama is a modern development.

Rama has been hijacked as the champion of fundamentalist Hindus, orchestrated by political parties such as the Vishwa Hindu Parishad (**VHP**) and the Bharatiya Janata Party (**BJP**) to advance their campaign for a Hindu homeland or "Hindutva" as opposed by the "secularism" of the Congress Party. They focussed attention on the then quiet and barely used **Babri Masjid** mosque, constructed by the first Moghul emperor Babar in the fifteenth century, which had co-existed for many years alongside the shrine known as **Ram Janmabhumi**, which is considered to be the spot where Rama was born.

After two years of ugly confrontation, Babri Masjid was attacked in 1992 by thousands of Hindu fanatics, who tore it down with their bare hands. Television footage of the onslaught inspired "communalist" riots throughout India, especially in Bombay and Gujarat, leaving hundreds dead. Repercussions were felt wherever in the world Hindu and Muslim communities live side by side, including Britain, and there were violent demonstrations in Muslim countries. The central government of India, still at odds over the issue, has yet to carry out its declared intention of reconstructing the mosque alongside a Hindu shrine; meanwhile, in 1994, the egalitarian *purohit* (priest) of Ram Janmabhumi – according to whom, Hindus and Muslims had shared the premises peacefully for years until the right-wing parties manipulated the issue – was murdered by unknown persons. While the Indian government, committed to secularism, intends to rebuild the mosque, the VHP are chiselling away at stone blocks on the other side of town with dreams of reconstructing the temple and re-igniting the issue.

Around Ayodhya: Faizabad

During the reign of Shuja-ud-Daula (1756–75), as the Moghul empire disintegrated, **FAIZABAD**, 6km southwest of Ayodhya, attracted craftsmen, artists and musicians from Delhi. However, the first capital of Avadh declined in tandem with the rise of Lucknow (see p.304). Among the few monuments to survive is the lofty white marble **Tomb of Bahu Begum**, the widow of Shuja-ud-Daula, close to the Nawab's own mausoleum. Faizabad's cantonment area is a legacy of British rule – caught up in the rebellion of 1857, it was thankfully spared the bloodshed seen in Kanpur and Lucknow.

Cheap central **accommodation** can be found near the *chowk* in the *Hotel Abha*, Moti Bagh (☎0527/812550; ②), the best of a handful along this quiet lane; the *Shan-e-Awadh* (☎0527/813586; ③–⑤), Civil Lines, near the bus stand, has more comfortable a/c rooms while the adjacent *Tirupati* (☎0527/813231; ③–⑤) is newer, with a good restaurant. Faizabad is practically equidistant from Lucknow, Varanasi, Allahabad and Gorakhpur. Buses to all those cities take three to five hours, and there are regular trains to Lucknow and Varanasi.

Allahabad

The administrative and industrial city of **ALLAHABAD**, 135km west of Varanasi and 227km southeast of Lucknow, is also known as **Prayag** ("Confluence"), as the point where the rivers Yamuna and Ganges meet the mythical Saraswati. Sacred to all Hindus, the **Sangam** (which also means "confluence"), east of the city, is one of the great pilgrimage destinations of India. Allahabad comes alive during its *melas*; the annual **Magh Mela** (Jan/Feb), and the colossal **Maha Kumbh Mela**, held every twelve years.

Allahabad is a pleasant city to visit, with vast open riverside scenery and good amenities, but is without major temples or monuments – and there's little evidence that it had any before the Muslims arrived in 1194 either. At the junction of the fertile Doab, the "two-river" valley between the Yamuna and the Ganges, it did however possess a crucial strategic significance; its massive **fort**, built by the emperor Akbar in 1583, is still used by the military. Another Moghul, Jahangir's son Khusrau, was murdered here by his brother Shah Jahan, who went on to become emperor and build the Taj Mahal.

Allahabad played a vital role in the emergence of modern India. After the "Mutiny" of 1857, the British moved the headquarters of their North Western Provinces here from Agra, and the formal transfer of power from the East India Company to the crown took place here the following year. Well-preserved relics of the British impact include **Muir College** and **All Saints' Cathedral**. The city also witnessed the first Indian National Congress in 1885, and the inauguration of Mahatma Gandhi's non-violent movement in 1920. **Anand Bhavan**, the home of Pandit Jawaharlal Nehru, is now a shrine to the Independence movement.

Arrival, information and transport

Allahabad has four **railway stations** (including Prayag, City and Daraganj), but major trains on the broad-gauge Delhi–Kanpur–Calcutta line arrive at the main **Allahabad Junction**. Most of the city's hotels are nearby; be sure to use the exit appropriate to the area where you plan to stay.

Leader Road bus stand, used by **buses** from western destinations such as Agra, Lucknow, Kanpur and Delhi, is just outside the station's south gates on the city side, while the smaller **Zero Road** bus stand, serving Mahoba and Satna to the south – the railheads for Khajuraho – is 1km southeast. Buses from all over and especially points east, including Varanasi, arrive at the **MG Marg** bus stand, next to the *Tourist*

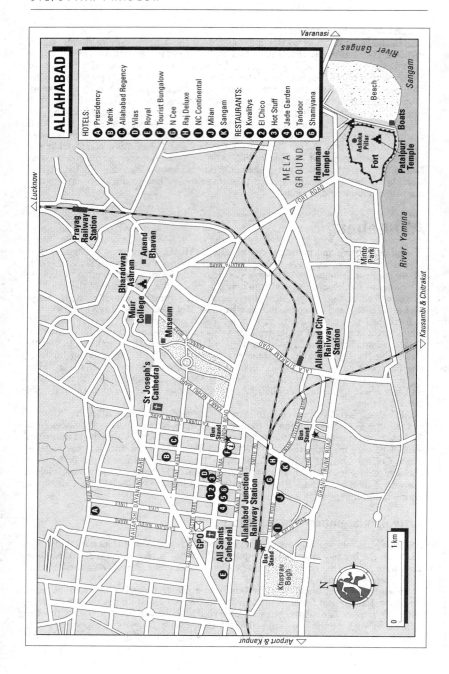

ALLAHABAD

HOTELS:
- Ⓐ Presidency
- Ⓑ Yatrik
- Ⓒ Allahabad Regency
- Ⓓ Vilas
- Ⓔ Royal
- Ⓕ Tourist Bungalow
- Ⓖ N Cee
- Ⓗ Raj Deluxe
- Ⓘ NC Continental
- Ⓙ Milan
- Ⓚ Sangam

RESTAURANTS:
- ① Kwalitys
- ② El Chico
- ③ Hot Stuff
- ④ Jade Garden
- ⑤ Tandoor
- ⑥ Shamiyana

The telephone **area code** for Allahabad is ☎0532.

Bungalow, about 1km east of the Civil Lines. There are no flights currently operating in and out of Bamrauli Airport, 18km west on the road to Kanpur.

Taxis are widely available around the station, but cycle and auto-rickshaws are the most common mode of transport; a trip to the Sangam from the Civil Lines crossing costs around Rs15 (hang on to your vehicle for the return journey). **Car rental** through general travel agencies such as *Kant Travel* (☎605699) and *Krishna Travel* (☎605536), both at 936 Daraganj, costs in the region of Rs400 per day plus mileage. Other reputable travel agents are *Varuna Travels*, Maya Bazaart, MG Marg (☎624323) and *Shree Travels*, 21 Church Lane (☎606021).

The **Tourist Information Office**, at the *Tourist Bungalow*, 35 MG Marg, Civil Lines (Mon–Sat 10am–5pm; ☎601440), can provide useful information during the *melas* but otherwise has little to offer. Allahabad's **post office** (known as the GPO or HPO), is at Sarojini Naidu Marg, near All Saints' Cathedral in the Civil Lines.

The Town

As the railway line crosses the centre, it splits Allahabad in two, with the chaotic and congested **old city** or **Chowk** south of the main station, and the well-defined grid of the **Civil Lines** to the north.

Around one kilometre north of the station, the yellow and red sandstone bulk of the Gothic **All Saints' Cathedral** dominates the surrounding avenues. Designed by Sir William Emerson, architect of the Victoria Memorial in Calcutta, the cathedral retains much of its stained glass and an impressive altar of inlaid marble. Plaques provide interesting glimpses of Allahabad in the days of the Raj, while flying buttresses and snarling gargoyles on the exterior add to the effect of an English county town. Sunday services

---

THE KUMBH MELA

Hindus traditionally regard river confluences as auspicious places, and none more so than the **Sangam** at Allahabad, where the Yamuna and the Ganges meet the River of Enlightenment, the mythical Saraswati. According to legend, Vishnu was carrying a *kumbha* (pot) of *amrita* (nectar), when a scuffle broke out between the gods, and four drops were spilled. They fell to earth at the four *tirthas* of Prayag, Haridwar, Nasik, and Ujjain (*tirtha* means "ford of a river", a place where the devout can cross from this finite world into divine celestial realms; see Varanasi p.322). The event is commemorated every three years by the **Kumbh Mela**, held at each *tirtha* in turn; the Sangam is known as Tirtharaja, the "King of *Tirthas*", and its *mela*, once every twelve years, is the greatest and holiest of all.

The **Maha Kumbh Mela** – the "Great" Kumbh Mela – is the largest religious fair in India, attended by literally millions of rejoicing pilgrims. The vast floodplains and river banks adjacent to the confluence are overrun by tents, organized in almost military fashion by the government, the local authorities and the police. The *mela* is especially renowned for the presence of an extraordinary array of religious ascetics – *sadhus* and *mahants* – enticed from remote hideaways in forests, mountains and caves. Once astrologers have determined the propitious bathing time or *Kumbhayog*, the first to hit the water are legions of **Naga Sadhus** or **Naga Babas**, the ferocious-looking members of the "snake sect" who cover their naked bodies with ash, and wear their hair in long dreadlocks. The *sadhus*, who see themselves as guardians of the faith, approach the confluence at the appointed time with all the pomp and bravado of a charging army. The next Maha Kumbh Mela is due to take place in 2001.

continue to attract large congregations; so too do masses at the flamboyant **St Joseph's Roman Catholic Cathedral**, a short distance west.

On the edge of the pleasant **Chander Shekhar Azad Park**, also in the Civil Lines, the grounds of the **Allahabad Museum** (daily except Mon 10am–5pm, closed 2nd Sat each month; Rs2) are dotted with pieces of ancient sculpture. Inside, you'll find early terracotta artefacts, eighth-century sculptures from the Buddhist site of Kaushambi, and a striking twelfth-century image from Khajuraho of Shiva and Parvati. A copious collection of modern Indian art includes work by Haldar, Sajit Khastgir and Rathin Mitra, as well as Jamini Roy, who was inspired by folk art. European paintings concentrate on spiritual themes, with sombre but naive canvasses by the Russian artist Nicholas Roerich, and further pieces by the Tibetologist Lama Angarika Govinda. A natural history section features stuffed animals and birds, and photographs and documents cover the Independence struggle.

North of the museum rise the nineteenth-century sandstone buildings of Allahabad University, and the Gothic **Muir College**, built in 1870. A 61-metre-high tower accompanies domes clad with blue and white glazed tiles (some of which are missing), and a quadrangle with tall and elegant arches. Just beyond the college, in beautiful grounds roughly 1km northeast of the museum, is **Anand Bhavan** (daily except Mon 9.30am–5pm; Rs2 allows entry to the first floor; planetarium Rs5). This ornate Victorian building, with Indo-Saracenic effects finished in grey and white trim and crowned by a *chattri*, was the boyhood home of the first prime minister of an independent India, Jawaharlal **Nehru**. It is now maintained as a museum, allowing queues of visitors to peer through plate glass into the opulent interior to see how the first family lived. Nehru was the father of one assassinated prime minister, Indira Gandhi, who was born here, and the grandfather of another, Rajiv Gandhi; Mahatma Gandhi (no relation of the family) stayed here when he visited the city. Also within the grounds, as at the Nehru Museum in Delhi (see p.93), is a **planetarium**, which puts on hourly shows.

Not far from Anand Bhavan, down a small road next to a children's park, the **Bharadwaj Ashram** is not an ashram as such but a collection of small temples. None is particularly old, but the ashram is named after the philosopher, scientist and ascetic Bharadwaj, said in the *Ramayana* to have had his hermitage here, and to have been visited by Rama. Legend relates that the ashram once had ten thousand students. Unusually, women are numbered among its *purohits* (priests), and act as caretakers.

A short way south of the main railway station, a lofty gateway leads to the attractive walled gardens of **Khusrau Bagh**, where the remains of Jahangir's tragic son Khusrau rest in a simple sandstone mausoleum, completed in 1622. Khusrau made an unsuccessful bid for power that ended in death at the hands of his brother Shah Jahan, and is buried far from the centre of Moghul power. His mother's two-storeyed mausoleum is a short way west, beyond a tomb reputed to be that of his sister. Once Jahangir's pleasure garden, today much of Khusrau Bagh has been made into an orchard, famous for its guavas, and a rose nursery, but parts are unkempt and overgrown.

Most of Allahabad's river frontage is along the Yamuna, to the south, where women perform *arati* or evening worship at **Saraswati Ghat** by floating *diya*, small oil-filled lamps, downstream. Immediately to the west, in **Minto Park**, a memorial marks the exact spot where the British Raj came into being, when India was taken away from the East India Company in 1858 and placed under the auspices of the crown.

East of Saraswati Ghat, close to the Sangam, loom the huge battlements of Akbar's **Fort** – best appreciated from boats on the river. Much of the fort remains in military occupation, and public access is restricted to the leafy corner around the **Patalpuri temple**, approached through one of the three massive gates that puncture the fort's defences. The catacombs occupied by the temple have been converted into a sort of religious supermarket; its religious figures and deities are reminiscent of an extended

---

THE SANGAM

Around 7km from the centre of the Civil Lines, overlooked by the eastern ramparts of the fort, wide floodplains and muddy banks protrude towards the sacred **Sangam**. At the point at which the brown Ganges meets the greenish Yamuna, *pandas* (priests) perch on small platforms to perform *puja* and assist the devout in their ritual ablutions in the shallow waters. Beaches and *ghats* are littered with the shorn hair of pilgrims who come to offer *pind* for their deceased parents.

Boats to the Sangam, used by pilgrims and tourists alike, can be rented at the *ghat* immediately east of the fort, for the recommended government rate of Rs12 per head. However, most pilgrims pay around Rs36 and can be charged as much as Rs150. Official prices for a whole boat are between Rs100 and Rs120 but can soar to more than Rs250 during peak seasons. On the way to the Sangam, high-pressure aquatic salesmen loom up on the placid waters selling offerings such as coconuts for pilgrims to discard at the confluence. Once abandoned, the offerings are fished up and sold on to other pilgrims – a blatant if efficient form of recycling.

Punch and Judy show. A sapling is said to be descended from the infamous **Akshaya Vata** or "Undying Tree", visited by the Chinese pilgrim Hiuen T'siang in the seventh century, from which desperate pilgrims threw themselves to their deaths in order to gain instant *moksha* (salvation). According to some reports the tree itself is bricked away beyond public access. Much of the superstructure of the fort is neglected; the **Zenana** with its columned hall does survive, but can only be viewed with prior permission. At the main gates to the fort stands a poorly restored polished stone **Ashoka Pillar**, inscribed with the emperor's edicts and dated to 242 BC.

Where the eastern battlements of the fort meet the river, a muddy *ghat* is busy with boatmen jostling for custom from the steady stream of pilgrims to the Sangam. Inland along the base of the fort, with the vast flood-plain of the Sangam to the right, a road leads past rows of stalls catering to pilgrims to the **Hanuman temple**. What's unusual about this otherwise nondescript temple is that its large sunken image of the monkey god is reclining rather than standing erect; the story goes that during the annual floods the waters rise to touch his feet before once again receding.

Accommodation

Allahabad has **hotels** to suit most budgets and temperaments, with cheaper options generally in the old Chowk area to the south, and the mid-range and more expensive ones in the Civil Lines.

Allahabad Regency, 16 Tashkent Marg, Civil Lines (☎601519). Snooty management, but comfortable with a decent restaurant, plus a sauna, jacuzzi, swimming pool and well-kitted gym. Book in advance if possible. ⑥–⑦.

Milan, 46 Leader Rd (☎400021). Close to the station and south of the railway line in the busy bazaar area. Assorted reasonable rooms, with hot and cold running water and telephones. ④–⑤.

N C Continental, Katju Rd (☎652058). Good, clean accommodation south of the railway lines and very handy for the station. A bit more spacious than the *N Cee*. ②–⑤.

N Cee, Leader Rd (☎401166). Sister to *N C Continental*, south of the railway line in the busy bazaar area. The rooms are small, but it's a pleasant and friendly place. ②–③.

Sangam, Johnstonganj Crossing (☎402667). Basic budget accommodation in the old city. ①–②.

Presidency, 19D SN Marg, Civil Lines (☎623308). Plush, comfortable guest house in quiet residential area, run by an ex-MP, with swimming pool and foreign exchange. Book in advance. ⑥–⑦.

Raj Deluxe, 6 Johnstonganj (☎400684). Cheap and basic budget accommodation. ①–③.

Royal, Civil Lines (☎623285). In the centre of the Civil Lines, close to the railway station. Period building with high ceilings but musty and very badly maintained. ③–④.

Tourist Bungalow, 35 MG Marg, Civil Lines (☎601440). The comfortable, cylindrical new block, built around a central well, overlooks the bus stand; choose your room carefully to avoid round-the-clock noise. The older block, now showing its age, is less noisy. Basic but friendly restaurant. ③–⑤.

Vilas, 22C Sardar Patel Marg, Civil Lines (☎622878). Moderately-priced and central, but otherwise quite ordinary. ③.

Yatrik, 33 Sardar Patel Marg, Civil Lines (☎601713). Popular, if a little expensive. Well-run and with a beautiful garden graced with elegant palms. ⑦.

Eating

Most of the better **cafes** and **restaurants** are in the Civil Lines area, within walking distance from each other close to the main crossing.

El Chico, MG Marg, Civil Lines. Smart high-street restaurant, close to *Kwality*. One of the city's best, with good Indian, Chinese and Western cuisine.

Hot Stuff, 15 Elgin Rd, Civil Lines. Popular hang-out for Allahabad's young and trendy, as well as the not-so-young. Burgers, shakes, Chinese food and ice-creams.

Jade Garden, MG Marg, Civil Lines. Small thatched garden restaurant, strong on Chinese food.

Kwality, The Mall, MG Marg. In a corner of a small shopping centre, part of a once-formidable chain, predictable but good multi-cuisine restaurant now succumbing to the competition.

Shamiyana, Civil Lines. Cafe in the centre of town, serving both north and south Indian food.

Tandoor, MG Marg. Tucked into a shopping precinct opposite *Kwality* and *El Chico*. Comfortable and upmarket, it preserves a reputation as one of the best places in the city for Indian food.

Around Allahabad

Just 63km south of Allahabad, on the banks of the Yamuna, are the extensive ruins of **Kausambi**, a major Buddhist centre where the Buddha himself came to preach. The city flourished between the eighth-century BC and the sixth-century AD; archeological evidence suggests even earlier habitation. According to legend, it was founded by descendants of the Pandavas, after floods destroyed their city of Hastinapur. Mud ramparts, originally faced with brick, tower over the fields, running along an irregular 6km perimeter, and sections remain of a defensive moat. Within the complex, excavations have revealed a paved road, brick houses, wells, tanks and drains, a monastery with cloisters and a large *stupa*, and the remains of a palace in the southeast corner. The only standing feature is a damaged sandstone column ascribed to **Ashoka** – a second column, moved by the Moghuls, now graces the gates of the fort at Allahabad.

If you have your own vehicle, Kausambi is a straightforward day trip from Allahabad. Otherwise, bus connections are tedious; head first to Serai Akil, from where several forms of local transport run the remaining 15km. The Buddhist pilgrimage circuit is developing rapidly, so it's worth consulting local tourist authorities to see if any direct services have been introduced since this book went to press.

Allahabad also makes a good base from which to venture into the remoter parts of **Bundelkhand** to the south. The pilgrimage town of **Chitrakut** (see p.321) is 132km south, and easily accessible by both train and bus; **Kalinjar** (see p.319) is 150km away.

SOUTHERN UP: BUNDELKHAND

BUNDELKHAND – the area defined by the craggy Vindhya Mountains, which stretch across southern UP – was carved by the ninth-century Chandella Rajputs into a mighty kingdom that included **Khajuraho** in Madhya Pradesh (see p.387). Today, it abounds in relics of the past – the colossal astrologically aligned fortress at **Kalinjar**, the

Chandella capital of **Mahoba**, the Vaishnavite pilgrimage centre of **Chitrakut**, and the fortified town of **Jhansi**, scene of epic nineteenth-century resistance to the British. However, the sheer difficulty of the terrain, and the all but unbearable heat in the summer, make this the most difficult region of the state to explore.

In fact, the labyrinthine hills and valleys along the border with Madhya Pradesh are also the most difficult region to govern, and even today are home to infamous bands of outlaw **dacoits**. Many of these brigands have become folk-heroes among local villagers, who shelter them from the almost equally brutal police force. The most celebrated in recent years was **Phoolan Devi**, the "Bandit Queen", who, as revenge for being raped, massacred the men of an entire village in 1981, eventually surrendered to the police, and was released in 1994. She is now active in politics. The past couple of years has seen the rise of a fledgling and uncertain movement for a semi-autonomous region of Bundelkhand, separate from both UP and Madhya Pradesh.

Jhansi

Unless you harbour a passion for seventeenth-century forts, you'll find the rail- and road-junction town of **JHANSI**, located in an anomalous promontory of UP that thrusts south into Madhya Pradesh, unremittingly dull. Most visitors only stop long enough to catch a connecting bus to **Khajuraho**, 175km further southeast in Madhya Pradesh.

Until 1742, Jhansi was a sleepy satellite village of the Bundela capital at nearby Orchha, 18km southeast. When the local Raja died without a male heir in 1853, the British enacted the controversial Principle of Lapse to wrest control of the town from his widow. Four years later, resentment at this colonial opportunism bubbled over into a full-blown **rebellion**, sparked off by the Mutiny at Kanpur (see p.299). Once the uprising had been put down by the British, they handed Jhansi over to Maharaja Scindia in exchange for Gwalior, in 1861, then reclaimed it 25 years later.

Arrival and information

Trains on both of the *Central Railway* branches that converge on Jhansi pull in at the station on the west side of town, near the Civil Lines area. Of the two state **tourist information** kiosks on platform one, MP Tourism's (☎0517/442622) is more useful, advising on transport on to **Khajuraho**. In town, the **Regional Tourist Office**, *Hotel Veerangana* (☎0517/44126), provides literature and information on Bundelkhand and the route to Khajuraho (Mon–Sat 10am–5pm, closed every 2nd Sat).

Although Jhansi is the most convenient main railway station, the tourist authorities have discontinued the express bus to **Khajuraho**, leaving travellers at the mercy of the inadequate bus system (7–8hr). Buses for Khajuraho depart from them railway station at 6am and 7am and, later from the **Kanpur Road** bus stand, 4km away, northeast of the main Sadar Bazaar, at 11.45am and 1pm. This is also the place to pick up buses for Datia and Gwalior; **tempos** for **Orchha** (faster than local buses, at 45min, and more frequent) wait alongside. **Car rental** is available through the larger hotels, as well as *Baghel Travels*, Nehru Market (☎441255), *Tourist Travel*, Jai Complex (☎443490) and *Ruby Travels*, near Elite Crossing (☎441136).

If you need to **change money**, the *State Bank of India* (Mon–Fri 10am–2pm, Sat 10am–noon; ☎440534), stands on Jhokan Bagh Rd beside the busy intersection in the centre of town, exactly halfway between the railway station and the bus stand.

The telephone **area code** for Jhansi is ☎0517.

The Town

In common with many former British cities, Jhansi is divided into two distinct areas: the wide tree-lined avenues, leafy gardens and bungalows of the **Cantonment** and **Civil Lines** to the west, and the clutter of brick and concrete cubes, narrow lanes, minarets and *shikharas* of the **old town** to the east.

Dominating it all from a bare brown craggy hill, **Jhansi fort** (daily dawn–dusk; Rs0.25; Fri free) is the obvious place to head if you've time to kill. Built in 1613 by one of the Orchha Rajas, Bir Singh Joo Deo, it's worth visiting primarily for the **views** from the lofty ramparts – down to the densely packed old town on one side, and out across a dusty *maidan* and the Cantonment to the other. The legendary Rani of Jhansi was supposed to have leapt over the west wall on horseback when she escaped from the British – if so, she must have had a pretty unusual horse. Inside the fort are a couple of unremarkable temples, plus an old cistern and the ruins of a palace. The only other attraction is the bizarre model of the 1857 siege of Jhansi fort recently installed beside the main road on the south slope of the hill. An accompanying interpretative panel recounts the story of the battle in very colourful English.

The new **archeological museum** (daily except Mon 10.30am–4.30pm) stands to the left of the road as you head back into town, with an unremarkable collection of Hindu **sculpture** saved from the area's ruined medieval temples. There are a lot more in storage, but the planned expansion of the museum is developing at a comatose pace.

Once the palace of the Rani of Jhansi, the **Rani Lakshmi Mahal** (daily except Mon 10am–5pm) is a small stately home in "Bundela style" (lots of ornate balconies and domed roofs), two minutes' walk from the roundabout directly below the fort. This was the scene of a brutal **massacre** in 1858, when British troops bayoneted all its occupants. These days, the building is a memorial-cum-museum-cum-archeological-warehouse, with unlabelled fragments of antique stone sculpture littered around its attractive interior courtyard. A couple of rooms upstairs, once the Rani's private quarters, harbour traces of seventeeth-century wall and ceiling paintings – now faded and flaking off in the heat.

The grounds of a pleasant seminary in the Cantonment area hold one of the most important Catholic pilgrimage sites in India, **St Jude's Shrine**. A bone belonging to Jude the Apostle, the patron saint of hopeless causes, is said to be buried in the foundations of the sombre grey and white cathedral. On his feast day, 28 October, thousands come to plead their own special causes.

Accommodation

With Orchha just down the road, it's hard to see why you might **stay** in Jhansi unless you arrive too late to move on. Most of its hotels are too far from the railway and bus stations to be easily reached on foot. The cheaper ones operate 24-hour checkout times, as opposed to noon in the mid-price and more expensive hotels.

Jhansi, Shastri Marg (☎441360). Former haunt of British *burra-sahibs*. Comfortable rooms, some a/c, plus *Star TV*, verandahs, and a big garden. The atmospheric colonial bar is currently being renovated, and there is a new restaurant. ⑤.

Prakash, Station Rd, Civil Lines (☎448811). Pleasant if basic bungalow accommodation including some a/c rooms, set around a small garden and very handy for the station. ②–④.

Prakash Guest House, Shri Sardari Lal Market (☎443133). Close to the fort and centre of town. Nothing special despite a revamp, but clean enough with some a/c. A pool is being built. ③–⑤.

Raj Palace, near GPO, Shastri Marg (☎442554). Clean, comfortable and handy for the bus stand. Rooms have attached bathrooms and hot water. Some a/c. 24hr check-out. ③–④.

Rishab, opposite Dhyan Chand Stadium, Civil Lines (☎445106). Simple but airy rooms, and has a lawn and a good cheap restaurant. ②–③.

Sita, Shivpuri Rd (☎442956). Comfortable Western-style hotel close to the station, with well-appointed rooms and a good restaurant. Credit cards accepted. Some a/c. ⑤.

THE RANI OF JHANSI

Rani Lakshmi Bhai, better known as the **Rani**, or Queen, **of Jhansi**, was one of the great nationalist heroines of pre-Independence India. Born the daughter of a Benares *brahmin*, she was married off to Raja Gangadhar of Jhansi, but never bore him children – a fact exploited by the British to force her and her adopted baby son into retirement in 1853. The Rani retaliated in 1857, the year of the "Mutiny", by leading her personal bodyguard of five hundred Afghan-Pathan warriors to seize Jhansi fort. The British dispatched troops to see off the insurgents, but took seventeen days to blow a breach in the walls of the citadel. Three days of fierce hand-to-hand fighting ensued, in which five thousand soldiers were killed. With her son strapped tightly to her back, the Rani somehow managed to slip through the British net and rejoin the main rebel army at Gwalior, where she rode to her death, "dressed as a man . . . using her sword with both hands and holding the reins of her horse in her mouth".

Statues of Rani Jhansi in this heroic pose stand all over northern India. For many in the Independence movement, she was India's Joan of Arc; a martyr and icon whose example set in motion the freedom struggle that eventually rid the subcontinent of its colonial rulers.

UPTDC Veeranganga, near Exhibition Ground, Shivpuri Rd (☎442402). Shabby government-run hotel, five minutes by scooter from the station. Plain rooms, some a/c, plus rock-bottom dorms, a nice lawn and a bar serving ice-cold beer. ③–⑤.

Eating

With the exception of the cheaper lodges, nearly all of Jhansi's hotels have their own **restaurants**. For a cheap alternative, try the *Railway Refreshment Rooms* in the station, which serve freshly cooked ten-rupee *thalis* and budget breakfasts.

Holiday, Shastri Marg. Posh but not all that expensive a/c restaurant, east of the *Jhansi Hotel*. Low light, table cloths, attentive service and classy Indian and Western food.

Nav Bharat, Shastri Marg. Western-style fast food and Indian snacks, behind the post office.

Sharma Sweets, Shastri Marg. Hygienic sweet shop selling delicious take-out *rasgulla, gulabjamun, jalebi* and *barfi*.

Sita, Shivpuri Rd. Spotlessly clean, upmarket hotel restaurant with a wide selection of Indian (and some continental) dishes. The place for a splurge.

Veeranganga, Shivpuri Road. Standard inexpensive veg/non-veg menu served inside in hotel-restaurant or al fresco on the lawn (bring mosquito repellent).

Kalinjar

Deep in the heart of Bundelkhand, in a remote region 150km west of Allahabad and 53km south of Banda, the abandoned star-shaped fortress of **KALINJAR** looks down on the Gangetic Valley from the final escarpments of the craggy Vindhya Hills. Little remains of its huge fortifications, save sections of battlements around the rim of the high forested plateau. Overlooking the dusty town of the same name, much of the fort has been reclaimed by dry shrubby forest, populated by monkeys. Once grand avenues are now rocky footpaths that wind through the few remaining dilapidated buildings.

Possibly one of the oldest forts in India, referred to by Ptolemy as Kanagora, Kalinjar may have started life as a hill shrine before it was converted into a fortress; now devoid of military significance, it is once again becoming a place of worship. Kalinjar is known to have been a stronghold of the Chandellas (ninth to twelfth centuries AD), the creators of Khajuraho, who left their mark in stone sculptures around the temple of Nilkantha, below the western battlements. This strategic location attracted repeated Muslim onslaughts; Mahmud of Ghazni laid unsuccessful siege in 1023, Qutb-ud-din-Aibak destroyed several temples in his conquest of 1202, and Humayun spent fifteen years trying to capture the fort. After Sher Shah Suri, who temporarily wrested power from the Moghuls, died when an exploding shell ignited gunpowder as he attacked Kalinjar in 1545, his son went on to take the fortress. Even the British occupied it for a while, before its strategic importance was finally exhausted, and it was left to decay.

The fortress

Each of the seven gates, sheltered by barbicans, that pierces the walls of Kalinjar symbolizes one of the seven planets. Steep steps lead straight up from **Kalinjar village**, in the valley at the northern base of the fort, to the main gate, known as the **Alam Darwaza**. To the southeast, an unkempt boulder-strewn road gradually climbs across the hillside to approach the southernmost **Panna Gate**, where rock carvings depict seven deer. Beyond Lal Darwaza to the east, the **Bara Darwaza** or "Large Gate" is flanked by two iron cannons. Beneath it, in the artificial cave of **Sita Sej**, a stone couch dating from the fourth century holds some of Kalinjar's earliest inscriptions.

Colossal rambling battlements provide sweeping views of the Gangetic plain to the north and the Vindhya hills to the south, hiding the crumbling remains of a fortress that is almost 1.5km long. Tracing the faint marks of the old avenues, you arrive at its heart, littered with roofless and devastated buildings. **Kot Tirth**, a ceremonial tank with stone steps, is the largest of several bodies of water on the plateau, and still in frequent use by villagers and pilgrims. Above it, beyond a small Hanuman shrine, stands the well-preserved palace-like **Raja Mansingh Mahal**. Further west, beside the bougainvillea-fringed road that passes the PWD bungalow, the small British graveyard holds a monument to Andrew Wauchope, the first Commissioner of Bundelkhand. Paths through desultory woodland head to a gate overlooking the western flank, where steep steps flanked by rock carvings wind down from the massive stone battlements to the temple of **Nilkantha** – the "Blue Throated One", an epithet of Shiva. Although the temple has lost its roof, its *mandapa* (forechamber) sports some beautifully carved stone pillars. Its main shrine is housed within a cave – a *lingam*, worn smooth over centuries. Trickles from the rocky hill drain out near the neck of the image, keeping it perpetually wet.

To the left of the main shrine, within the temple compound, a five-metre-high low-relief rock carving, of primeval intensity, portrays **Bhairava**, the wrathful emanation of Shiva as Destroyer, sporting four arms and brandishing weapons. A gap in the retaining wall provides access to the steps back down to the village. Above the pool of **Bhairan Kund**, adjoining the temple, a walkway leads along the face of the large stone buttresses that fall in tiers from the edge of a plateau to a point where rainwater seeps into a cave. Steps hewn into the rock allow bathers into the flooded interior, supported by carved pillars dating from the Chandella period. Although the cave is no longer than 10m, swimming in the deep water beneath its low roof is an eerie experience.

Practicalities

Kalinjar has no tourist facilities to speak of – accommodation or food is only available in absolutely basic fly-infested tea shops – and precious few tourists. Most of those who do come are either on day trips from Chitrakut or Allahabad, or stay in **Banda**, which is on major train and bus routes and is connected to Kalinjar by local buses.

However, the ruined **PWD bungalow**, looking across from the top of the fortress towards the interior of the Vindhyas, is gradually being rebuilt – check with UP tourist authorities before you set off to see if it's ready for guests.

Chitrakut

The large sprawling town of **CHITRAKUT** stands on the banks of the Mandakini, 128km southwest of Allahabad and 116km east of Mahoba. Together with its twin town of **Karbi**, 8km east, Chitrakut, known also as Sitapur or Chitrakut Dham, is a major Vaishnavite pilgrimage centre. In the *Ramayana*, Rama, his wife Sita, and his brother Lakshmana, sought refuge in a forest that covered this entire area, after being banished from Ayodhya.

Most of Chitrakut's religious and leisure activity revolves around the small, charming, and very central **Ramghat**, where boats with electric-blue mattresses and pillows create a pretty picture against a backdrop of ashrams and *ghats* to either side of the narrow, slow-moving river. Half-hour boat trips cost around Rs2 per person or Rs12 per boat. Among the pilgrim shops and cafes nearby are several **temples**, such as the new **Tulsibedi**, dedicated to the poet saint (see p.333) who apparently spent time here. This was built on the site of an earlier shrine, located in an extended cave up an alley off the *ghat*. Steps above the *ghat* lead to the **Math Gajendranath** Shiva temple, and its picturesque river views. Taking a rickshaw beside the Mandakini to **Sitapur** enables you to see several more riverside temples, as well as waterfront *ghats* much like Ramghat.

Pilgrims to Chitrakut traditionally perform the Parikrama, or ritual circumambulation of the wooded hill of **Kamedgiri**, 3km southwest of town. On its course around the base of the hill, the five-kilometre path passes numerous temples and shrines, including the big **Kantanath Swami** temple, which holds a modern image of Rama and Sita and a more venerated monolithic stone image, black and embellished with large eyes. A long flight of stairs at the **Hanumandhara** hill shrine, 6km east, leads up to a large image of the monkey god Hanuman, a companion of the trio from the *Ramayana*.

Practicalities

Long-distance transport connections are best made via **Karbi**. From the main **Karbi Bus Stand**, several daily buses run to Allahabad, passing through Serai Akil, 15km from the Buddhist ruins of Kausambi, and also to historic Mahoba, a possible stop-off en route to Khajuraho. The **railway station** at Karbi has services to Allahabad and Mahoba, as well as Varanasi, 374km northeast (9hr). From the **Satna Bus Stand** in Chitrakut, buses head south into Madhya Pradesh; connecting buses from Satna itself can also carry you to Khajuraho.

Unless you read Hindi, you may not find the **information** provided by the **UP Tourist Office**, at Karbi Rd, Sitapur (Mon–Sat 10am–5pm, closed 2nd Sat; ☎0519768/218), all that helpful. UPTDC's drab and poorly maintained *Tourist Bungalow* alongside (☎0519768/219; ②—④), has some a/c **rooms**, and only provides food **to** order in its restaurant. MP Tourism's old-fashioned *Tourist Bungalow*, at Satna bus stand in Chitrakut (☎07276/65326; ②), is more welcoming, and serves basic Indian food.

Several simple **hotels**, *dharamshalas* and guest houses can be found around Ramghat; though the accommodation is basic at the *Vishram Grah*, Kamedgiri Bhavan (①) on the *ghat* itself, it's full of atmosphere, with a lovely terrace overlooking the river, and the adjacent *bhojanalaya* – vegetarian cafes – serve simple but wholesome food.

South of Chitrakut

Several further shrines linked with the *Ramayana* are tucked away in the region **south of Chitrakut**. The major **Janki Kund** temple ("pool of Janki", Janki being another name for Sita) is just 2km south of Chitrakut on the Satna road, on the border with Madhya Pradesh. This rocky pool was where Rama's wife bathed in the Mandakini; a path above it leads through a complex of ashrams and shrines to a small footbridge that crosses the picturesque river to the wooded far bank.

Further down the main road, 2km south, a path through a similar complex of ashrams leads to the large flat rock of **Sphatekshila**, protruding onto the river, where Sita used to sit. It supposedly bears the impressions of the feet of Rama which you are advised not to step on. This idyllic spot, with its *ghats* surrounded by large trees, and woods on the other side of the river, powerfully evokes the legend of the *vanvasi* – the forest dwellers that the exiled Rama, Lakshmana and Sita became. Overlooked by dramatic rocky cliffs where the river Mandakini emerges from thick forest cover, **Sati Anasuya**, 14km south of Chitrakut, is by far the most beautiful of all the holy sites.

EASTERN UP

Flowing beyond Allahabad across the plains of **EASTERN UP**, the Ganges turns sharply north at **Chunar** and traces a great arc through ancient **Varanasi**. Even before the Hindus declared this to be the most sacred spot on Earth, it stood at the centre of the Buddhist universe, linked by trading routes from Rajgir in Bihar to Mathura near Delhi. It was on the outskirts of Varanasi, at the deer park at **Sarnath**, that the Buddha delivered his first sermon. North of Varanasi, the much-travelled road to **Nepal** passes through the large administrative town of **Gorakhpur**, not far from **Kushinagar**, where the Buddha achieved final enlightenment.

Varanasi

Older than history, older than tradition, older even than legend, and looks twice as old as all of them put together.

Mark Twain

The great Hindu city of **VARANASI**, also known as **Banaras** or **Benares**, glows golden in the early morning sun. Stretched along the crescent of the holy river Ganga – born in heaven and descended to earth – Varanasi's waterfront is dominated by long flights of stone steps known as *ghats*, literally "landings", where thousands of pilgrims and residents come for their daily ritual ablutions. The *ghats* remain the single major attraction of Varanasi; it does not possess temples or monuments of any antiquity, thanks largely to the destruction wrought by the emperor Aurangzeb.

Known to the devout as **Kashi**, the Luminous – the City of Light, founded by Shiva – Varanasi is one of the oldest living cities in the world. It has maintained its religious life since the sixth century BC in one continuous tradition, in part by remaining outside the mainstream of political activity and historical development of the subcontinent, and stands at the centre of the Hindu universe, the focus of a religious geography that reaches from the Himalayan cave of Amarnath in Kashmir, to Kanyakumari, the southern tip of India, Puri to the east, and Dwarka to the west. Located next to a ford on an ancient trade route, Varanasi is among the holiest of all *tirthas* – "crossing places", that allow the devotee access to the divine and enable gods and goddesses to come down to earth. It has attracted pilgrims, seekers, *sanyasins*, and students of the *Vedas* throughout its history, including sages such as the Buddha, Mahavira, the founder of the Jain faith, and the great Hindu reformer Shankara.

Life and death go hand in hand in Varanasi; in among the bathing *ghats*, smoke rising from the cremation grounds signals the final release of tormented souls from the earthly round of *samsara*, the unceasing cycles of death and rebirth. Anyone who dies in Varanasi, on the banks of the river of life, attains instant *moksha* or enlightenment. Widows and the elderly come here to seek refuge or to live out their final days, finding shelter in the temples assisted by alms given by the faithful.

NAMES OF THE CITY

Numerous names have been given to **Varanasi**, though its recently revived official appellation is mentioned in the *Mahabharata* and in the *Jataka* tales of Buddhism. It probably derives from the two rivers that flank the city, the Varana to the north and the Asi to the south. Many still use the anglicized forms of **Banaras** or **Benares**, while pilgrims refer to **Kashi**, first used three thousand years ago to describe the kingdom and the city outside which the Buddha preached his first sermon; the "City of Light" is also called Kashika, "the shining one", referring to the light of Shiva. Another epithet, **Avimukta**, meaning "Never Forsaken", refers to the city that Shiva never deserted, or that one should never leave. Further alternatives include **Anandavana**, the "forest of bliss", and **Rudravasa**, the place where Shiva (Rudra) resides.

Varanasi's associations with Shiva stretch back to the dawn of time: legends relate how, after his marriage to Parvati, Shiva left his inhospitable Himalayan abode and came to reside in Kashi with all the gods in attendance. Temporarily banished during the rule of the great king Divodasa, Shiva sent Brahma and Vishnu as his emissaries, but eventually returned to his rightful abode guarded by his faithful attendants Kalabhairav and Dandapani. Over 350 gods and goddesses, including a protective ring of Ganeshas form a *mandala* or sacred pattern with Shiva Vishwanatha at its centre.

Each name carries an additional meaning in terms of the sacred symbolism of the city, with each defining a progressively decreasing arc starting and ending on the west bank of the Ganges. While the boundary of **Kashi** is delimited by the circular Panchakroshi Road, **Varanasi** is the main city, extending from Asi Ghat and circling around to the confluence of the Ganges and the Varana. Yet a smaller area, defined as **Avimukta**, starts at Kedara Ghat in the south and ends at Trilochana Ghat. Most important of all is **Antargriha**, the "Inner Sanctum" around the Vishwanatha Temple, which encompasses Dashashwamedha Ghat, Surya Kund, the *lingam* of Bharabhuta, and Manikarnika Ghat. Another, later, interpretation suggests three sectors or *khandas* in the form of Shiva's trident, each centered around a temple – Omkara to the north, Vishwanatha in the centre and Kedara to the south.

Western visitors since the Middle Ages have marvelled at the strangeness of what is perhaps the most alien of Indian cities – at the tight mesh of alleys barely wide enough to accommodate a rickshaw, at the accoutrements of religion, the host of deities great and small, and at the proximity of death. At sunrise, flotillas of camera-clicking tourists peruse the *ghats* in amazement, while the pilgrims and people of Kashi continue their morning rituals without so much as a second glance.

Arrival, information and city transport

An airport bus (Rs25) connects with flights landing at **Babatpur Airport**, 22km northwest of the city and goes to the *Indian Airlines* office, via the Government of India tourist office, both in the Cantonment area. Taxis should charge around Rs200 for the same journey; look for official number plates sporting names such as ITDC and TCI, as you're liable to be overcharged.

The main Delhi–Calcutta **railway** line bypasses Varanasi, but local buses and taxis regularly make the 17km trip from the station at Moghul Sarai. Some major trains do serve the **Varanasi Cantonment station**, which is convenient for the more luxurious hotels and the garden hotels to the north. Beware of ticket touts at the station, and a hotel information counter that overcharges for arranging reservations and buying train tickets. The old city and the *ghats* are 2km south – a Rs15 cycle rickshaw ride. Rickshaw-*wallahs* who offer to take you there for less are getting commission from particular hotels. If you are heading for the old city, one way to avoid the hassle of being

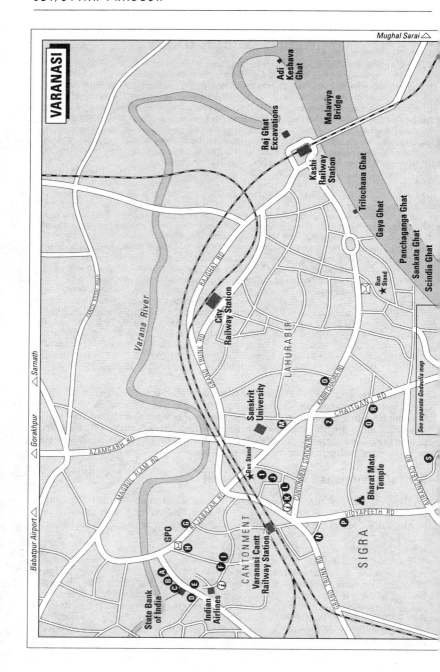

VARANASI

Mughal Sarai △

Adi
Keshava
Ghat

Raj Ghat
Excavations

Malaviya
Bridge

Kashi
Railway
Station

Trilochana Ghat

Gaya Ghat

Panchaganga Ghat

Sankata Ghat

Scindia Ghat

Varana River

PANCH KOSHI ROAD

RAJGHAT RD

City
Railway Station

GRAND TRUNK RD

Bus
Stand
★

LAHURABIR

KABIR CHAURA RD

Sanskrit
University

M

CHAITGANJ RD

2

AZAMGARH RD

CANTONMENT STATION RD

★ Bus Stand

Bharat Mata
Temple

AURANGABAD RD

S

See separate Godaulia map

△ Gorakhpur   △ Sarnath

Babatpur Airport △

MACBUL ALAM RD

HAJARAZAR RD

GPO

G

H

F I

CANTONMENT

Varanasi Cantt
Railway Station

VIDYAPEETH RD

N

SIGRA

GRAND TRUNK RD

State Bank
of India

A
B
C
D E

Indian
Airlines

i

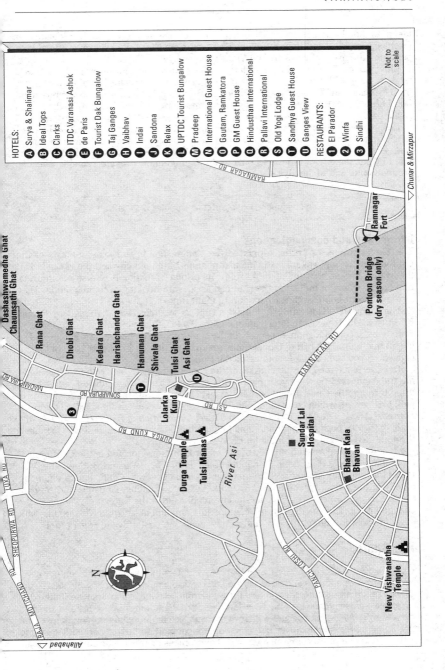

HOTELS:
Ⓐ Surya & Shalimar
Ⓑ Ideal Tops
Ⓒ Clarks
Ⓓ ITDC Varanasi Ashok
Ⓔ de Paris
Ⓕ Tourist Dak Bungalow
Ⓖ Taj Ganges
Ⓗ Vaibhav
Ⓘ Indai
Ⓙ Sandona
Ⓚ Relax
Ⓛ UPTDC Tourist Bungalow
Ⓜ Pradeep
Ⓝ International Guest House
Ⓞ Gautam, Ramkatora
Ⓟ GM Guest House
Ⓠ Hindusthan International
Ⓡ Pallavi International
Ⓢ Old Yogi Lodge
Ⓣ Sandhya Guest House
Ⓤ Ganges View

RESTAURANTS:
❶ El Parador
❷ Winfa
❸ Sindhi

Not to scale

▽ Chunar & Mirzapur

▽ Allahabad

Dashashwamedha Ghat
Chaumsathi Ghat
Rana Ghat
Dhobi Ghat
Kedara Ghat
Harishchandra Ghat
Hanuman Ghat
Shivala Ghat
Tulsi Ghat
Asi Ghat

Ramnagar Fort

Pontoon Bridge
(dry season only)

Lolarka Kund

Durga Temple
Tulsi Manas

River Asi

Sundar Lal Hospital

Bharat Kala Bhavan

New Vishwanatha Temple

RAMNAGAR RD
SONARPURA RD
ASI RD
DURGA KUND RD
MADANPURA RD
LUXA HV
SHEOPURWA RD
RAJA MOTICHAND RD
PANCH KOSHI RD
RAMNAGAR RD

N

taken to hotels against your wishes is to get them to take you to Godaulia or Dashashwamedha and then find your own way from there. Rickshaws are unable to penetrate the maze of lanes around Vishwanatha anyway.

Most **buses** terminate in the vicinity of the station: the **Cantonment Bus Stand** tends to be used by services from Nepal and Gaya, while private operators and buses from Mirzapur and Chunar use the **Pilikothi Bus Stand** and another private bus stand is at **Lahar Tara**, 1km west of the railway station where buses arrive from Lucknow and Allahabad.

Besides cycle and auto-rickshaws and an inadequate and over-crowded city bus system, with terminals at Lanka near BHU and Godaulia, shared auto-rickshaws or tempos are a cheap and efficient way of travelling certain routes such as from the railway station to Godaulia and to the Civil Court in the Cantonment. **Bicycle** rental is available around Lanka and Maldahiya.

> The telephone **area code** for Varanasi is ☎0542.

Information and communications

The **Government of India tourist office** languishes in the leafy suburbs of the Cantonment, a long way from the main attractions of the old city and the *ghats*, at 15B the Mall (Mon–Sat 9.30am–5pm; ☎43744). Its primary function is to dish out information on the whole of India, but the staff can assist with booking accommodation. They also maintain a booth at the airport during flight times.

The main **UP Government tourist office** is at their *Tourist Bungalow*, Parade Kothi (☎43413); there's an information counter (☎46370) at the railway station nearby. Both book accommodation, especially in the state-run tourist bungalows, and provide a useful free map. The **Bihar Government tourist office** on Englishia Line (☎43821), is useful if you're heading east towards the Buddhist centres.

To experience the *ghats* at sunrise, or the peace of Sarnath, you're best off eschewing the conducted bus and your own arrangements. Official tour **guides** can be organized through the Government of India tourist office (Rs200 for a 4hr tour for four people). **Car rental**, which costs around Rs550 per day, is available from *ITDC*, in the *Hotel Varanasi Ashok*, The Mall (☎46032), and *Travel Corporation of India, Hotel Clarks*, the Mall (☎46209), both of which serve as fully fledged tour agencies, and also arranged through the Government of India tourist office (☎43744).

Most foreign-currency branches of the major **banks** are located in the Cantonment area: the *State Bank of India* is behind *Hotel Ideal Tops*, Varuna Bridge, The Mall (☎43445), and the *Allahabad Bank* is near *Takshal Cinema*, Cantt; banks changing money in the old city include *Andhra Bank*, Yelchico Building, Godaulia and *Bank of Baroda, Hotel Ganges Building*, Dashashwamedha Rd – the latter follows an erratic change policy. The main **post offices** are in Cantonment and Bisweswarganj, with other offices throughout the city, and a convenient sub post office in *Hotel Clarks*.

The Ghats

The great river banks at Varanasi, built high with eighteenth- and nineteenth-century pavilions and palaces, temples and terraces, are lined with an endless chain of stone steps – the **ghats** – progressing along the whole of the waterfront, altering in appearance with the dramatic seasonal fluctuations of the river level. Each of the hundred *ghats,* big and small, is marked by a *lingam*, and occupies its own special place in the religious geography of the city. Some have crumbled over the years, others continue to thrive, with early-morning bathers, *brahmin* priests offering *puja*, and people practising meditation and yoga. Hindus regard the Ganges as *amrita*, the elixir of life, which brings purity to the living and salvation to the dead; sceptical outsiders tend to focus on the all-pervasive and extreme lack of hygiene. Ashes of the dead, emissions from open drains and the left-overs from religious rites float by the devout as they go about their bathing and ceremonial cleansing.

For centuries, pilgrims have traced the perimeter of the city by a ritual circumambulation, paying homage to shrines on the way. Among the most popular routes is the **Panchatirthi Yatra**, which takes in the Pancha (five) Tirthi (crossings) of Asi, Dashashwamedha, Adi Keshava, Panchganga and finally Manikarnika. To gain merit or appease the gods, the devotee, accompanied by a *panda* (priest), recites a *sankalpa* (statement of intent) and performs a ritual at each stage of the journey. For the casual visitor, however, the easiest way to see the *ghats* is to follow a south–north sequence either by boat or on foot.

Asi Ghat to Kedara Ghat

At the clay-banked **Asi Ghat**, the southernmost in the sacred city, at the confluence of the Asi and the Ganges, pilgrims bathe prior to worshipping at a huge *lingam* under a *peepal* tree. Another *lingam* visited is that of **Asisangameshvara**, the "Lord of the Confluence of the Asi", in a small marble temple just off the *ghat*. Traditionally, pilgrims continued to **Lolarka Kund**, the "Trembling Sun", a rectangular tank fifteen metres below ground level, approached by steep steps. Now almost abandoned, except during the Lolarka Mela fair (Aug/Sept), when thousands come to propitiate the gods and pray for the birth of a son, Lolarka Kund is among Varanasi's earliest sites, one of only two remaining Sun sites linked with the origins of Hinduism. Equated with the twelve *adityas* or divisions of the sun, which predate the great deities of modern Hinduism, it was attracting bathers in the days of the Buddha.

Much of the adjacent **Tulsi Ghat** – originally Lolarka Ghat, but renamed in honour of the poet Tulsi Das, who lived nearby in the sixteenth century – has crumbled. Continuing north, above **Shivala Ghat**, **Hanuman Ghat** is the site of a new temple built by the *ghat*'s large south Indian community. Considered by many to be the birthplace of the fifteenth-century Vaishnavite saint Vallabha, who was instrumental in the resurgence of the worship of Krishna, the *ghat* also features a striking image of **Ruru**, the dog **Bhairava**, a ferocious and early form of Shiva.

Named for a legendary king said to have almost lost everything in a fit of self-abnegation, **Harishchandra Ghat**, one of Varanasi's two cremation or burning *ghats*, is easily recognizable from the smoke of its funeral pyres.

Further north, the busy **Kedara Ghat** is ignored by pilgrims on the Panchatirthi Yatra. Above its steps, a red-and-white-striped temple houses the **Kedareshvara lingam**, an outcrop of black rock shot through with a vein of white. Mythologically related to Kedarnath in the Himalayas (see p.276), Kedara and its *ghat* become a hive of activity during the sacred month of Sravana (July/Aug), the month of the rains.

Chauki Ghat to Chaumsathi Ghat

Northwards along the river, **Chauki Ghat** is distinguished by an enormous tree that shelters small stone shrines to the *nagas*, water-snake deities, while at the unmistakable **Dhobi** (Laundrymen's) **Ghat** clothes are still rhythmically pulverized in the pursuit of purity. Past smaller *ghats* such as **Manasarovara Ghat**, named after the holy lake in Tibet, and **Narada Ghat**, honouring the divine musician and sage, lies **Chaumsathi Ghat**, where impressive stone steps lead up to the small temple of the **Chaumsathi** (64) **Yoginis**. Images of Kali and Durga in its inner sanctum represent a stage in the emergence of the great goddess as a single representation of a number of female divinities. Overlooking the *ghats* here is Peshwa Amrit Rao's majestic sandstone *haveli* (mansion), built in 1807 and currently used for religious ceremonies and occasionally, as an auditorium for concerts.

Dashashwamedha Ghat

Dashashwamedha Ghat, the second and busiest of the five *tirthas* on the Panchatirthi Yatra, lies past the plain, flat-roofed building that houses the shrine of **Shitala**. Extremely popular, even in the rainy season when devotees have to wade to the temple or take a boat, Shitala represents both benign and malevolent aspects – ease and succour as well as disease, particularly smallpox.

Dashashwamedha is Varanasi's most popular and accessible bathing *ghat*, with rows of *pandas* sitting on wooden platforms under bamboo umbrellas, masseurs plying their trade and boatmen jostling for custom. Its name, "ten horse sacrifices", derives from a complex series of sacrifices performed by Brahma to test King Divodasa: Shiva and Parvati were sure the king's resolve would fail, and he would be compelled to leave Kashi, thereby allowing them to return to their city. However, the sacrifices were so perfect that Brahma established the **Brahmeshvara** *lingam* here. Since that time, Dashashwamedha has become one of the most celebrated *tirthas* on earth, where pilgrims can reap the benefits of the huge sacrifice merely by bathing.

Man Mandir Ghat to Lalita Ghat

Man Mandir Ghat is known primarily for its magnificent eighteenth-century observatory, equipped with ornate window casings, and built for the Maharajah of Jaipur. Pilgrims pay homage to the important *lingam* of Someshvara, the lord of the moon, alongside, before crossing **Tripurabhairavi Ghat** to **Mir Ghat** and the **New Vishwanatha Temple**, built by conservative *brahmins* who claimed that the main Vishwanatha *lingam* was rendered impure when Harijans (untouchables) entered the sanctum in 1956. Mir Ghat also has a shrine to **Vishalakshi**, the Wide-Eyed Goddess, on an important *pitha* – a site marking the place where various parts of the disintegrating body of Shakti fell as it was carried by the grief-stricken Shiva. Also here is the **Dharma Kupa**, the Well of Dharma, surrounded by subsidiary shrines and the *lingam* of **Dharmesha**, where it is said that Yama, the Lord of Death, obtained his jurisdiction over all the dead of the world – except here in Varanasi.

Immediately to the north is **Lalita Ghat**, renowned for its **Ganga Keshava** shrine to Vishnu and the Nepali Temple, a typical Kathmandu-style wooden temple which houses an image of **Pashupateshvara** – Shiva's manifestation at Pashupatinath, in the Kathmandu Valley – and sports a small selection of erotic carvings.

Manikarnika Ghat

North of Lalita lies Varanasi's pre-eminent cremation ground, **Manikarnika Ghat**. Such grounds are usually held to be inauspicious, and located on the fringes of cities, but the entire city of Shiva is regarded as **Mahashmashana**, the Great Cremation Ground for the corpse of the entire universe. The *ghat* is perpetually crowded with funeral parties, as well as the **Doms**, its Untouchable guardians, busy and pre-occupied with facilitating final release for those lucky enough to pass away here. Seeing bodies being cremated so publicly has always exerted a great fascination for visitors to the city, but photography is strictly taboo; even having a camera visible may be construed as intent, and provoke hostility.

Lying at the centre of the five *tirthas*, Manikarnika Ghat symbolizes both creation and destruction, epitomized by the juxtaposition of the sacred well of **Manikarnika Kund**, said to have been dug by Vishnu at the time of creation, and the hot, sandy ash-infused soil of cremation grounds where time comes to an end. In Hindu mythology, Manikarnika Kund predates the arrival of the Ganga and has its source deep in the Himalayas. Vishnu carved the *kund* with his discus, and filled it with perspiration from his exertions in creating the world, at the behest of Shiva. When Shiva quivered with delight, his earring fell into this pool, which as Manikarnika – "Jewelled Earring" –

became the first *tirtha* in the world. Every year, after the floodwaters of the river have receded to leave the pool caked in alluvial deposits, the *kund* is re-dug. Its surroundings are cleaned and painted with brightly coloured folk art, which depicts the presiding goddess, **Manikarni Devi**, inviting pilgrims to bathe and worship at its small Vishnu shrine, and at the *paduka* (footprint) of Vishnu set in marble on the embankment of the *ghat*. The most important of the *lingams* is the remains of **Tarakeshvara**, Shiva as Lord of the Taraka Mantra, a "prayer of the crossing" recited at death.

Strictly speaking, Manikarnika is the name given to the *kund* and to the *ghat,* while the constantly busy cremation ground is Jalasi Ghat, dominated by a dark smoke-stained temple built by Queen Ahalya Bai Holkar of Indore in the eighteenth century.

Scindia Ghat

Bordering Manikarnika to the north is the picturesque **Scindia Ghat**, with its tilted Shiva temple lying partially submerged in the river, having fallen in as a result of the sheer weight of the *ghat*'s construction around 150 years ago. Above the *ghat*, several of Kashi's most influential shrines are hidden within the tight maze of alleyways of the area known as **Siddha Kshetra** (the Field of Fulfilment). Vireshvara, the Lord of all Heroes, is especially propitiated in prayer for a son; the Lord of Fire, Agni, was supposed to have been born here.

Panchganga Ghat to Adi Keshava Ghat

Beyond Lakshmanbala Ghat, with its commanding views of the river, lies one of the most dramatic and controversial *ghats*, **Panchganga Ghat**, dominated by Varanasi's largest riverside building, the great **Mosque of Alamgir**, known locally as Beni Madhav-ka-Darera. With its minarets now much shortened, the mosque stands on the ruins of what must have been one of the city's greatest temples, **Bindu Madhava**, a huge Vishnu temple that extended from Panchganga to Rama Ghat before it was destroyed by Aurangzeb and replaced by an impressive mosque. Panchganga also bears testimony to more favourable Hindu-Muslim relations, being the site of the initiation of the medieval saint of the Sufi-Sant tradition, Kabir, the son of a humble Muslim weaver who is venerated by Hindus and Muslims alike. Along the riverfront lies a curious array of three-sided cells, submerged during the rainy season, some with *lingams*, others with images of Vishnu, and some empty and used for meditation or yoga. One of these is a shrine to the Five (*panch*) Rivers (*ganga*) which, according to legend, have their confluence here: the two symbolic rivulets of Dhutapapa (Cleansed of Sin) and the Kirana (Sun's Ray), which join the mythical confluence of the Yamuna and the Sarasvati with the Ganga.

Above **Trilochana Ghat**, further north, is the holy ancient *lingam* of the Three (*tri*) Eye (*lochana*) Shiva. Beyond it, the river bypasses some of Varanasi's oldest precincts, now predominantly Muslim in character; the *ghats* themselves gradually become less impressive and are usually of the *kaccha* (clay-banked) variety.

At **Adi Keshava Ghat** (the "Original Vishnu"), on the outskirts of the city, the Varana flows into the Ganga. Unapproachable during the rainy season, when it is com-

---

BOAT TRIPS ON THE GANGES

All along the *ghats,* and especially at the main ones such as Dashashwamedha, the prices of **boat** (*bajra*) **rental** are highly inflated, with local boatmen under pressure from touts to fleece tourists and pilgrims. There's a police counter at the top of Dashashwamedha, but the lack of government tourist assistance means that renting a boat to catch the dawn can be a bit of a free-for-all, and haggling is essential. A few boatmen operate on a fixed rate, determined in conjunction with UP Tourism, of about Rs45 per hour.

pletely submerged, it marks the place where Vishnu first landed as an emissary of Shiva, and stands on the original site of the city before it spread southwards; around Adi Keshava are a number of Ganesha shrines.

Vishwanatha Khanda – the Old City

At the heart of Varanasi, between Dashashwamedha Ghat and Godaulia to the south and west and Manikarnika Ghat on the river to the north, lies **Vishwanatha Khanda**, sometimes referred to as the Old City. The whole area rewards exploration, with numerous shrines and *lingams* tucked into every corner, and buzzing with the activity of pilgrims, *pandas* and stalls selling offerings to the faithful.

Approached through a maze of narrow alleys and the **Vishwanatha Gali** (or Lane), the temple complex of **Vishwanatha** or **Visheshwara**, the "Lord of All", is popularly known as the **Golden Temple**, due to the massive gold plating on its *shikhara* (spire). Inside the compound – which is hidden behind a wall, and entered through an unassuming doorway – is one of India's most important *shivalingams*, made of smooth black stone and seated in a solid silver plinth, as well as shrines to the wrathful protectors **Mahakala** and **Dandapani**, and the *lingam* of **Avimukteshvara**, the Lord of the Unforsaken, which predates Vishwanatha and once held much greater significance. The current temple was built in 1777 by Queen Ahalya Bai Holkar of Indore, and is closed to non-Hindus, who have to make do with glimpses from adjacent buildings.

Vishwanatha's history has been fraught. Sacked by successive Muslim rulers, the temple was repeatedly rebuilt, until the grand edifice begun in 1585 by Todar Mal, a courtier of the tolerant Moghul Akbar, was finally destroyed by Aurangzeb. On its foundations, guarded by armed police to protect it from Hindu fanatics, stands the **Jnana Vapi Mosque**, also known as the Great Mosque of Aurangzeb. Its simple white domes tower over the **Jnana Vapi** (Wisdom Well), immediately north, housed in an open arcaded hall built in 1828, where Shiva cooled his *lingam* after the construction of Vishwanatha. Covered by a grate to prevent people jumping in, in search of instant *moksha*, and covered with a cloth to stop coins being thrown in, only the presiding brahmins have access to its waters, considered to be liquid knowledge. Pilgrims offer their *sankalpa* or statement of intent here, before commencing the Panchatirthi Yatra. Slightly north, across the main road, the thirteenth-century **Razia's Mosque** stands atop the ruins of a still earlier Vishwanatha temple, destroyed under the Sultanate.

Close by, the temple of **Annapurna Bhavani** is dedicated to the supreme Shakti ("She, the Being of Plenteous Food"), the queen and divine mother also known in this benevolent form as Mother of the Three Worlds. As the provider of sustenance, she carries a cooking pot rather than the fearsome weapons borne by her horrific forms Durga and Kali; a subsidiary shrine opened only three days a year houses a solid gold image of Annapurna. Nearby is a stunning image, faced in silver against a black surround, of **Shani** or Saturn. Anyone whose fortunes fall under his shadow is stricken with bad luck – a fate devotees try to escape by worshipping here on Saturdays.

The rest of the city

Although it can take years to fully explore the *ghats* and the old city, Varanasi does hold a few other sites of interest, especially in the area south of Godaulia just beyond Asi Ghat. The **Durga Temple** here, and the Bharat Kala Bhavan museum of **Benares Hindu University** (BHU) are easily accessible, while just across the river, **Ramnagar** and its impressive fort continue to play an important role in the life of the city.

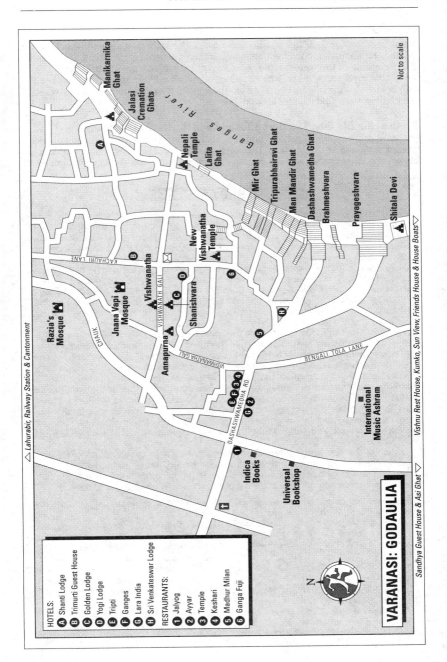

Not to scale

△ Lahurabir, Railway Station & Cantonment

Vishnu Rest House, Kumko, Sun View, Friends House & House Boats ▷

Sandhya Guest House & Asi Ghat ▷

VARANASI: GODAULIA

Manikarnika Ghat

Jalasi Cremation Ghats

Ganges River

Nepali Temple

Lalita Ghat

Mir Ghat

Tripurabhairavi Ghat

Man Mandir Ghat

Dashashwamedha Ghat

Brahmeshvara

Prayageshvara

Shitala Devi

New Vishwanatha Temple

Razia's Mosque

Jnana Vapi Mosque

Vishwanatha

Shanishvara

Annapurna

KACHAURI LANE

VISHWANATH GALI

VISHWANATHA GALI

CHAUK

BENGALI TOLA LANE

DASHASHWAMEDHA RD

International Music Ashram

Indica Books

Universal Bookshop

N

HOTELS:
- Ⓐ Shanti Lodge
- Ⓑ Trimurti Guest House
- Ⓒ Golden Lodge
- Ⓓ Yogi Lodge
- Ⓔ Tripti
- Ⓕ Ganges
- Ⓖ Lara India
- Ⓗ Sri Venkateswar Lodge

RESTAURANTS:
- ❶ Jalyog
- ❷ Ayyar
- ❸ Temple
- ❹ Keshari
- ❺ Madhur Milan
- ❻ Ganga Fuji

Bharat Mata

About 3km west of Godaulia, outside the old city, the modern temple of **Bharat Mata** (Mother India), inaugurated by Mahatma Gandhi, is unusual in that it has a huge relief map in marble of the whole of the Indian subcontinent and the Tibetan plateau, with mountains, rivers and the holy *tirthas* all clearly visible. Pilgrims circumambulate the map before viewing it in its entirety from the second floor. The temple can be reached by rickshaw from Godaulia for around Rs7.

South of the Old City: The Durga Temple and the Hindu University

The nineteenth-century **Durga Temple** – stained red with ochre, and known among foreign travellers as the Monkey Temple, thanks to the aggressive and irritable monkeys that occupy every nook and cranny – stands within a walled enclosure 8km south

---

MUSIC IN VARANASI

Renowned as a centre for north Indian **classical music**, Varanasi attracts students from all over the world, and is famous for its exhilarating school (*gharana*) of *tabla* (paired hand-drum) playing. The city is home to such legendary figures as **Ustad Bismillah Khan** (*sehnai* – oboe) and **Pandit Shanto Prasad** (*tabla*), and **Pandit Ravi Shankar** (*sitar*) has also been based here. Small schools and instrument shops in the alleys off Dashashwamedha try to catch the transient tourist trade, but if you want to probe deeper, the traditional scene, based around student-teacher relationships, continues to thrive. Between Jangambali post office and Bengali Lane, the *International Music Ashram*, D33/81 Khalishpura, holds concerts and organizes classes aimed at foreigners. **Asi Ghat** has always been known for its rapidly changing music scene, and there's a lively performing arts department at BNU.

Varanasi is renowned for big music **festivals**, particularly during winter and spring. Held during Shivratri (Feb/March), the **Dhrupad Mela** is devoted to *Dhrupad*, an archaic form in which the voice, treated as a musical instrument, is accompanied by the double-membrane barrel drum, *pakhawaj*. Pakhawaj solos are particularly vibrant; the drum has a deep and sonorous tone, and performances rise to energetic crescendos. A four-day music and dance festival, the **Ganga Mahotsav** takes place at Rajendra Prasad Ghat near Dashashwamedha and is held around Kartik Purnima – the full moon after Diwali (Oct/Nov); entrance is usually free. Varanasi's large Muslim community also makes its mark: there is an active Sufi tradition, and at *dargahs* (shrines) you may chance upon a **qawwali** performance; these are often given on Thursdays at the Dargah of Chandan Sahid, Raj Ghat.

Most of the best instrument makers are tucked away in the alleys of the old city, known only to practitioners; some also supply the Dashashwamedha tourist shops, who then add on a hefty mark-up. For those in the know, much the best idea is to have an instrument made to order. The following places are worth a look if you're hooked:

Bassaruddin, near Arya Samaj Temple, Lalapura. Run by one of Varanasi's best craftsmen, *tabla* maker to the professionals; expect to pay from Rs1300 for a pair of made-to-order *tablas* and Rs2000 with a case.

Imtiaz Ali, D57/49 Sidh Giri Bagh. Another master craftsman, offering made-to-order *tabla* prices.

Indian Music House, D47/195 Ramapura, opposite *Mazda Movie Hall*. General music shop with a motley collection of instruments. Although prices are reasonable, quality is mediocre, they will arrange better quality instruments on demand – but of course, at a price.

Kesho Prasad, C K 38/5 Gyanwapi, near Dashashwamedha. Specializes in string instruments such as the *sitar* and *tanbura* (drone).

Nitai Chandra Nath, 35/181 Jangambali, near *International Music Ashram*. A good *sitar* maker and once the instrument technician to BHU; good *sitars* for around Rs3500 and cases for Rs1500.

Sur Sangam, D16 Man Mandir Ghat. Aimed at tourists, this shop charges outrageous prices and is best avoided.

of Godaulia, not far from Asi Ghat. It was built in a common north Indian style, with an ornate *shikhara*, consisting of five segments symbolizing the elements, and supported by finely carved columns. The whole ensemble is best seen from across Durga Kund, the adjoining tank. Permeated by a stark primeval atmosphere, it is devoted to Durga, the terrifying aspect of Shiva's consort, Parvati, and the embodiment of *shakti* or female power. In contrast to the benevolent Annapurna, Durga, the unassailable destroyer of demons, clad in red and riding a tiger, is fully armed with Shiva's trident, Vishnu's discus and a sword. A forked stake in the courtyard is used during festivals to behead sacrificial goats, in an early or pre-Hindu form of worship which has now generally been replaced by a symbolic mark in vermilion.

Non-Hindus are admitted to the courtyard, but not the inner sanctum, of the Durga temple, but access to the **Tulsi Manas Temple** alongside is unrestricted (daily 5am–noon & 3pm–midnight). Built in 1964 of white-streaked marble, its walls are inscribed with verses by the poet and author of the *Ramcharitmanas*, the Hindi equivalent of the great Sanskrit epic *Ramayana*. On the second floor, moving images bring to life episodes from the classics.

A little further south, the **Bharat Kala Bhavan** museum (daily except Sun; 11am–4.30pm, May & June 7.30am–12.30pm; Rs5, Rs10 camera) has a fabulous collection of miniature paintings, sculpture, contemporary art and bronzes. Dedicated to the city of Varanasi, a gallery with a stunning nineteenth-century map has a display of the recent Raj Ghat excavations and old etchings of the city. Along with Buddhist and Hindu sculpture and Moghul glass, galleries are devoted to foreign artists who found inspiration in India, such as Nicholas Roerich and Alice Boner. Jamini Roy, the Bengali renaissance painter so influenced by folk art, is also well represented.

Bharat Kala Bhavan forms part of BNU, the campus of which also holds the **New Vishwanatha Temple** (daily 4am–noon & 1–9pm), distinguished by its lofty white marble *shikhara*. The brainchild of Pandit Malaviya, founder of the university and a great believer in an egalitarian and casteless Hindu revival, it was built by the Birlas, a wealthy Marwari industrial family. Although supposedly modelled on the original temple destroyed by Aurangzeb, the building displays characteristics of the new wave of temple architecture, amalgamating influences from various parts of India with a garish interior. Tea shops, flower sellers and other vendors in the small market outside the gates cater for a continuous flow of visitors.

Ramnagar

The residence of the Maharajah of Varanasi, **Ramnagar Fort**, looks down upon the Ganges not far south of the Asi Ghat. The best views of the fortifications – especially impressive in late afternoon – are to be had from the other side of the river, which is reached by a road heading south from the BHU area and over a rickety pontoon bridge. During the monsoon the bridge is dismantled and replaced by a ferry, still preferable to the long main road that crosses the main Malaviya bridge in the north before heading down the eastern bank of the river.

Inside, the fort bears testimony to the wealth of the Maharajah and his continuing influence. A dusty and poorly kept **museum** (daily 9am–noon & 2–5pm; Rs3) provides glimpses of a decadent past: horse-drawn carriages, old motor cars, palanquins, gilded and ornate silver *howdahs* (elephant seats), *hookahs*, costumes and old silk in a sorry state are all part of the collection, along with an armoury, a collection of minute ivory carvings, an astronomical clock and hunting trophies. Some visitors have reported having tea with the affable Maharajah after chance encounters.

Across the courtyard, a section is devoted to the **Ram Lila** procession and festivities, held during Dussehra (Oct). Varanasi is renowned for its Ram Lila, during which episodes from the *Ramayana* are re-enacted throughout the city and the Maharajah sponsors three weeks of elaborate celebrations.

Accommodation

Most of Varanasi's better and more expensive hotels lie on its peripheries, either in the **Cantonment** in the north or in the commercial belt in places like Sadar Bazaar. However, to experience the full ambience and mystery of the city, you have to stay close to the *ghats* and the lanes of **Vishwanatha**. Lodges are ideally suited to the budget-conscious traveller, any lodges have cropped-up over the last few years, all trying to cash in on the success of good ones such as *Golden Lodge*, *Yogi Lodge* and *Vishnu Guest House*. Getting to your hotel can be a headache as rickshaw men get commission from particular hotels and invariably try and dissuade you from your own choice (see "Arrival", on p.323).

Old City

Friends House, Aliyabhai Ghat. Simple and basic with good views of the river. Best approached via Dashashwamedha Ghat past Shitala Devi to the right and up the next *ghat* to a lane. ①.

Ganges, Bank of Baroda Building, Dashashwamedha Rd (☎321097). Off the congested main thoroughfare, in its own yard, this guest house has an excellent reputation. It's as close as you can get to Dashashwamedha Ghat, and is roomier than most around this area. ③–⑤.

Ganges View, Asi Ghat. A great verandah looking out onto the river, a lobby full of interesting books, a pleasant ambience and an interesting landlord mean this popular place is often booked up with visiting musicians and scholars. ③–⑤.

Golden Lodge, D8/35 Kalika Lane (☎323832). Close to the *Yogi Lodge*, a small but pleasant guesthouse, popular with budget travellers, which boasts a rooftop patio. ①.

House boats, Mansarovar Ghat. Very basic and not particularly hygienic, but ideal for soaking up the ambience of life along the river. ①.

Kumiko House (Pension), D24/26 Pandey Ghat, close to *Vishnu Guest House*. Run by an elderly, affable Japanese-speaking Bengali who operates a curfew. Small choice of rooms full of atmosphere, pleasantly situated looking steeply down to the water. ②.

International Music Ashram, D33/81 Kalishpura, near Jangambali Post Office. A few rooms with the added advantage of being part of a music scene (see "Music" box, on p.332). ②–③.

Lara India, Dashashwamedha Rd (☎320323). In the heart of Godaulia, this small place has smart a/c rooms, and a good mid-range restaurant, strong on local Varanasi food ③–⑤.

Old Yogi Lodge, D53/62 Luxa (☎350141). Good budget option with a loyal following. Small but very cheap rooms, but quite a way from the river. ①.

Sandhya Guest House, Shivala Ghat (☎313292). The unfortunate location on a main road does not detract from this friendly and welcoming guest house with a relaxed rooftop cafe. ①–③.

Shanti Lodge, Manikarnika Ghat (☎322568). An old favourite along with *Sindhia Guest House* around the corner at Sindhia Ghat. Large and generally clean, with attached baths and an excellent view from the rooftop cafe. ①–②.

Sri Venkateswar Lodge, D5/64 Dashashwamedha Rd (☎322357). Simple but clean and close to the *ghats* and to Vishwanatha, capturing the ambience of the old city. ①.

Sun View Guest House, B6/105 Kedar Ghat (first floor). Small budget lodge – a bit poky, but with terrace and garden overlooking the river; the riverside rooms are airy and pleasant. *Jogesh Lodge* downstairs has a similar ambience. ①–②.

Trimurti Guest House, near Vishwanatha Temple (☎322616). Good range of rooms (some air-cooled), which can be on the small side. Extensive views from the terrace. ①–③.

Tripti, Dashashwamedha Rd (☎322346). Basic, budget rooms on the roof look down on the crowded and interesting thoroughfare. ①.

Vishnu Rest House, Pandey Ghat (no phone). One of the nicest of the riverside lodges with a lovely patio and cafe overlooking the Ganges, best approached via the *ghats* – turn right at Dashashwamedha. Popular and often booked-up. ①–③.

Yogi Lodge, D8/29 Kalika Gali (☎322588). An old favourite with budget travellers which still retains much of its charm and reputation. ①.

Cantonment and the peripheries

Clarks, The Mall, Cantt (☎46771). Plush and well presented, with all mod cons including swimming pool. The best that Varanasi has to offer. ⑨.

de Paris, 15 The Mall, Cantt (☎46601). Founded by a Frenchman at the turn of the century, and set in extensive gardens, it captures an old-world atmosphere. Large comfortable rooms, but poorly run. ⑦.

Gautam, Ramkatora (☎46239). Clean and moderately comfortable but otherwise characterless and a bit expensive; not far from *Pradeep*. ④–⑤.

GM Guest House, 1 Chandrika Colony, Sigra (☎361292). Away from the old town, but easy to reach. Good-value rooms, large and air-cooled with clean bathrooms, plus good food. ③–⑥.

Hindustan International, C21/3 Maldahiya (☎57075). Plush, characterless business-class hotel, with an atrium at its centre, and good facilities including a swimming pool. ⑧.

Ideal Tops, The Mall (☎348091). Next to *Clarks*, new and comfortable chain hotel. ⑦–⑧.

India, 59 Patel Nagar (☎342912). The old block is very good value while the new extension is smart and comfortable with a bar and a good restaurant and a roof garden; the best in its class. ④–⑦.

International Guest House, C32/4 Vidyapith Rd, opposite Vidyapith University (☎360912). Family home, close to the station, with 4 rooms, a small dorm and camping facilities and a very pleasant garden; overlanders may not be able to get their vehicle down the narrow lane. ①–④.

ITDC Varanasi Ashok, The Mall (☎46020). Next to *Clarks* in the quiet leafy Cantonment; with all mod cons including a swimming pool, but poorly maintained. ⑨.

Pallavi International, Hathwa Place, Chetganj (☎356939). Extensive ex-maharajah's palace behind a busy shopping mall – ornate but a bit tacky; used for weddings. ⑤–⑥.

Pradeep, Jagatganj (☎344963). Comfortable, quite smart and popular with tour groups; away from the *ghats* but within striking distance. Attractive multi-cuisine *Poonam* restaurant. ④–⑤.

Railway Retiring Rooms. Convenient with cheap a/c rooms and dorms; can get booked up. ①–③.

Relax, Parade Kothi, Cantt (☎43503). Good-value budget option near the railway station, just outside the gates of the *Tourist Bungalow* and next to the *Mandarin* Chinese restaurant. ②.

Sandona, S17/331-3 City Bus Depot, Maldahiya (☎46555). Next to *El Parador* restaurant. Airy budget rooms, handy for buses and the station. One of the best around here in its range. ②.

Shalimar, Varuna Bridge, The Mall (☎46227). Overspill for the *Surya*, next door. Simple but a bit expensive. ③–⑤.

Surya, S20/51, A5 Nepali Kothi, Varuna Bridge, Cantt (☎343014). Pleasant garden, a good restaurant and reasonable prices make this place popular with overland groups. ②–⑤.

Taj Ganges, Nadesar Palace Grounds (☎345110). Top hotel, in the grand *Taj* style. Excellent facilities – two restaurants, a bar and a swimming pool – but lacking the character of *Clarks*. ⑨.

UPTDC Tourist Bungalow, Parade Kothi, Cantt (☎43413). Handy for the bus and railway station. Large institutional complex alleviated by the friendly, helpful management and the garden; with a bar and restaurant, and a range of rooms including a dorm. ③–⑤.

Vaibhav, 56 Patel Nagar (☎46466). Quite a smart little establishment with mid-sized rooms. The good *Palki* restaurant serves Indian, Chinese and Western food. ④–⑤.

> For details of the **accommodation price codes** used in this book, see p.35.

Eating

Most of the old city cafes are vegetarian, and alcohol is not tolerated, but the newer Cantonment area is less constrained by religious mores and some of the more expensive hotels have bars. After a trip on the boats in the early morning, try *kachori*, savoury deep-fried pastry bread, in the old city next to the *ghats* – a city tradition. The city is also renowned for its sweets and *paan* (betel leaf), while *bhang*, a potent form of cannabis sometimes mixed in *lassis* and *sharbats* (cold sweet drinks), is available from government-licensed shops. But beware of the food and water in Varanasi, as stomach disorders are a common phenomenon.

Ayyar's Cafe, next to *Banaras Lodge*, Dashashwamedha Rd. At the back of a shopping arcade, a small, cheap cafe serving south Indian food, including *masala dosas*, and filter coffee.

El Parador, Maldahiya Roadways, near Pani Tanki. Run by a Gurkha family from Darjeeling. Remarkable menu ranging from Mexican to Italian, with good pasta, chocolate cake and pancakes and although popular with travellers and recommended, it is not cheap.

Fagin's, D8/35 Kalika Lane, near Vishwanatha, Dashashwamedha. An ideal travellers' haunt, with an extensive menu, reasonable prices, and (recorded) music. Part of *Golden Lodge*.

Ganga Fuji, D5/8 Kalika Gali, near Vishwanatha, Dashashwamedha. Odd name for a pleasant little cafe, serving assorted cuisine and with live music in the evenings.

Garden, opposite *Sushil Cinema*, Godaulia. Cheap, leafy and relaxed rooftop cafe aimed at travellers; good breakfasts.

Jalyog, Dashashwamedha Rd. Long-standing local cafe, serving vegetarian food strong on *puris* (deep fried puffed bread) and the legendary Varanasi *kachoris*.

Keshari, lane opposite *Banaras Lodge*, Godaulia. *Paneer* (cheese) dishes and good-value *thalis*.

Madhur Milan Cafe, Dashashwamedha Ghat. Good for *lassis*, sweets and *kachoris*.

Poonam, *Hotel Pradeep*, Jagatganj. Good *Mughlai* food in a reasonably comfortable environment; but it's not cheap.

Sindhi, Bhelupur Thana. One of Varanasi's most popular restaurants, 1.5km from Godaulia. The rickshaw ride will be rewarded with excellent vegetarian food.

Temple, *Hotel Ganges*, *Bank of Baroda* Building, Dashashwamedha Rd. Piped music, an upbeat ambience and a familiar menu have made it an instant success.

Winfa, near *Prakash Cinema*, Lahurabir. Not much to look at, but the best Chinese food in town.

Shopping

With hustlers and rickshaw drivers keen to drag tourists into shops offering commission, **shopping in Varanasi** can be a nightmare – but it's worth seeking out the city's rich silk-weaving and brasswork. The best areas to browse are the Thatheri Bazaar (for brass), or Jnana Vapi and the Vishwanatha Gali with its *Temple Bazaar* (for silk brocade and jewellery). State-run emporia in Godaulia, Lahurabir and the Chowk – the three *UP Handlooms* outlets at Lahurabir, Nadesar and Neechi Bag, and *Mahatex* in Godaulia – offer fixed prices and assured quality. Housed in a former palace opposite the *Taj Hotel*, Cantt, the *CIE* has a large and impressive selection but, despite its official-sounding name, is an outrageously expensive Kashmiri-run chain aimed exclusively at the five-star market.

Sales pitches tend to become more aggressive when it comes to **silk**, and you need to be wary of the hard-sell. *Qazi Sadullahpura*, near *Chhavi Mahal Cinema*, lies at the heart of a fascinating Muslim neighbourhood devoted to the production of silk. *Upica*, the government-run emporium has the advantage of fixed prices, with outlets at Godaulia and opposite the *Taj Hotel*, Cantt. *Handloom House*, D64/132K Sigra, another government-sponsored chain, is the best and safest place to buy silk with a modern showroom although the sales staff appear disorganized. For tailoring, try *Paraslakshmi Exports*, 71 Chandrika Colony, Sigra (☎361496), a silk business providing a good and prompt service; they'll deliver to your hotel, and also offer ready-made waistcoats and boxer shorts.

Listings

Astrologers *Nila Baba*, Dashashwamedha Ghat; *Dr Sidh Nath Srivastava*, Planet Guide Centre, *Tourist Dak Bungalow*, The Mall (☎42182); *Yogostrology*, D61/26 B-2 Sidhgiribagh (☎358157).

Automobile Association *UP Automobile Association*, Bulanala (☎63500).

Bookshops *Amit (University) Book House*, University Rd, Lanka, with another branch at Assi Ghat; *Indica Books*, D40/18 Godaulia, have a good selection including guides and also provide a useful parcel mailing service; *Universal Book Company*, Godaulia, is a few doors down; *Nandi*, Varanasi Ashok, has a surprisingly good selection including second-hand books bought and sold.

Foreigners Registration Office Srinagar Colony, Sigra (☎351968).
Hospitals *Sir Sunderlal Hospital*, BHU – Benares Hindu University (☎312542), *Birla Hospital*, Machhodari (☎330357); *SSPG Hospital* (government-run), Kabirchaura (☎333723); *Heritage Hospital*, Lanka Market, near BHU Gate (☎313978).
Motorcycles *Jagatganj*, near the Sanskrit University. Mechanics and workshops specializing in *Enfields* are clustered in this area; ask around for a secondhand bike.
Opticians *Gupta Optical*, Godaulia (10am–7pm).
Pharmacies 24hr-*Singh Medical*, near *Prakash Cinema*, Lahurabir, and near the main hospitals.
Photography *Bright Studio*, Godaulia; *Passi Studio*, Lahurabir; *Veer Studio*, Jagatganj, in front of Queen's College.

MOVING ON FROM VARANASI

A full summary of transport connections from Varanasi can be found on p.220.

Indian Airlines' daily **flight** to **Kathmandu** gets very heavily booked in winter; there's also a daily flight to **Delhi**, via Khajuraho and Agra. In addition four flights a week link Varanasi to **Delhi** and **Bhubaneshwar** and three to **Bombay** and **Lucknow**. *Indian Airlines* are behind *Hotel de Paris*, Cantt (Mon–Fri 10am–1pm & 2–5pm; ☎45959), and they also have an airport office (☎43742). Among the private airlines, *Sahara Airlines* flies three times a week to Delhi, Patna and Bombay. *Modi Luft* also flies to Delhi three times a week. The brand new *UPAir* plans to link Varanasi to the Buddhist sites of Bodh Gaya, Kushinagar and Sravasti – check to see if they have taken off. *UPAir* have their office at the airport (☎43742), *Modi Luft* at *Hotel Vaibhav*, Cantt (☎46466) and *Sahara Airlines* at Mint House, opposite the *Taj Hotel* (☎342355). *Air India* are in *Hotel Clarks* (☎46326).

Most of the super-fast **trains** on the main east–west line between Delhi and Calcutta such as the *Rajdhani*, bypass Varanasi but stop at **Moghul Sarai**, a nightmarish 45 minutes away by road or a short train ride. All major trains from Varanasi depart from the Cantt station (reservations daily 8am–2pm & 2.30–7pm; ☎131 or 43404). The daily *Mahanagri Express* #1094 is the fastest service to **Bombay** (11.35am; 28hr). For **Calcutta** via **Gaya**, the daily choice is the *Amritsar–Howrah Express* #3050 (7.50pm; 20hr) or the *Amritsar–Howrah Mail* #3006 (5.25pm; 15hr). Two good trains run to **Delhi**: the *AC Express* #2381 (Tues, Thurs & Sat, 9.15pm; 14hr), and the *Neelachal Express* #8475 (Mon, Wed & Sun, 7.35am; 14hr). For the **mountains** of UP, the daily *Dehra Dun–Varanasi Express* #4265 (9.15am; 20hr) is a better bet than the *Doon Express* #3010 (7.45pm; 20hr), which is nearly always late. Three trains daily leave for Nepal via **Gorakhpur** (8–10hr; see p.342); they're not mainline services, so are subject to infuriating delays. For **Khajuraho**, take a train to Satna such as the *Kurla Express* #4248 (7hr) and change onto a bus (4hr). The same train travels through **Karbi**, the station for **Chitrakut**. Keep an eye out for ticket touts at Varanasi station; also, avoid the hotel information counter here that will try to overcharge you for train tickets.

Avoid direct **buses** to Nepal: buses on the far side of the frontier are generally better. UPSRTC run morning and evening buses, including overnight services, to the border at **Sonauli** (10hr) via **Gorakhpur** from the Cantt Bus Stand. Slightly more luxurious private buses travel through Sonauli to Kathmandu with an all-inclusive price including basic overnight accommodation, but you can take the bus to the Sonauli and get a better choice from across the border to Pokhara or Kathmandu. Several buses depart for Gaya, near **Bodh Gaya** (6hr) from around 6am. Regular services ply the Grand Trunk Road east to **Patna**, and there are good deluxe buses for **Allahabad**, which is an excellent rail link. Regular bus services travel to **Lucknow** (9hr), Faizabad, Ayodhya (7hr) and **Jaunpur** (2hr).

General **travel agencies**, selling tickets and offering car rental, include ITDC, at the *Ashok*, The Mall (☎46032); *Khan Travels*, S20/52, 3A Nepali Kothi (☎46623) and *Hotel de Paris*, The Mall; *Sita Tours and Travels* (☎43421) and *Travel Corporation India* (☎46209), both at *Hotel Clarks*; and *Varuna Travels*, Panday Haveli, near Durga Charan Girls School.

Sarnath

SARNATH, 10km north of Varanasi, is a place of pilgrimage for Buddhists, and has also become popular with day-trippers, who picnic among its ruins and parklands. It was in a quiet grove here, in the sixth century BC, that Siddhartha Gautama – who came to be known as the **Buddha**, the "Awakened One" – gave his first sermon, and set in motion the Wheel of Law, the *Dharmachakra*. During the rainy season, when the Buddha and his followers sought respite from their round of itinerant teaching, they would retire to Sarnath. Also known as **Rishipatana**, the place of the *rishis* or sages, or **Mrigadaya**, the deer park, its name derives from *Saranganatha*, the Lord of the Deer.

Over the centuries, Sarnath flourished as a centre of Buddhist art and teaching, particularly for **Hinayana** Buddhism (the "Lesser Way"). In the seventh century, the Chinese pilgrim Hiuen T'siang recounted seeing 30 monasteries, supporting some 3000 monks, and a life-sized brass statue of the Buddha turning the Wheel of Law.

Buddhism in India floundered under the impact of Muslim invasions and the rise of Hinduism, and except for the vast bulk of the Dhamekh Stupa much of the site lay in ruins for almost a millennium. Prey to vandalism and pilfering, Sarnath remained abandoned until 1834, when Major General Sir Alexander Cunningham, the head of the Archaeological Survey, visited the site. Today it is once more an important Buddhist centre, and its avenues house missions from all over the Buddhist world.

The Main Site and the Dhamekh Stupa

Dominated by the huge bulk of the Dhamekh Stupa, the extensive archeological excavations of the main site of Sarnath are maintained within an immaculate park. Entering from the southwest, the pillaged remains of the **Dharmarajika Stupa** lie immediately to the north: within its core the *stupa* concealed a green marble casket full of human bones and precious objects, including decayed pearls and gold leaf. Commemorating the spot where the Buddha delivered his first sermon, the *stupa* is attributed to the reign of Ashoka in the third century BC, but was extended a further six times.

Adjacent to Dharmarajika Stupa are the ruins of the **Main Shrine**, where Ashoka is said to have meditated. To the west stands the lower portion of an **Ashokan Pillar** – minus its famous capital, now housed in the museum. The ruins of four monasteries, dating from the third to the twelfth centuries, are also contained within the compound; all bear the same hallmark of a central courtyard surrounded by monastic cells.

Most impressive of all is the **Dhamekh Stupa**, also known as the **Dharma Chakra Stupa**, which stakes a competing claim as the exact spot of the Buddha's first sermon. The *stupa* is composed of a cylindrical tower rising 33.5 metres from a stone drum, ornamented with bas-relief foliage and geometric patterns; the eight arched niches halfway up may once have held statues of the Buddha. It dates from the Gupta period, but with evidence of earlier Mauryan construction; some archeologists have conjectured that the *stupa*'s upper brickwork may originally have been plastered over.

The **Sri Digambar Jain Temple**, or **Shreyanshnath Temple**, is believed to mark the birthplace of Shreyanshnath, the eleventh *tirthankara*. Built in 1824, the interior houses a large image of the Jain saint, as well as attractive frescoes depicting the life of Lord Mahavira, the founder of the religion and contemporary of the Buddha.

Museum

Daily 10am–4.45pm. Rs0.50; closed Fridays.

Opposite the gates to the main site, the **museum**, designed to look like a *vihara* (monastery), has a small but renowned collection of Buddhist and Brahmanist antiquities, consisting mostly of sculpture in the excellent medium of Chunar sandstone.

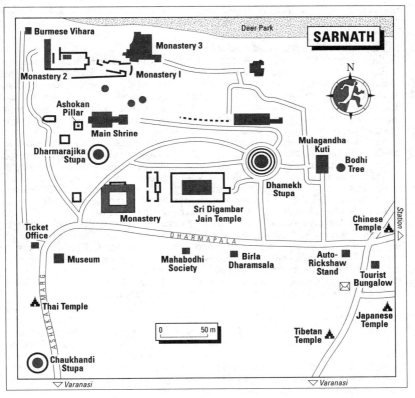

The most famous exhibit is the **lion capital**, removed here from the Ashokan column on the main site. Constructed by Ashoka (273–232 BC), the great Mauryan king and convert to the *dharma*, it has become the emblem of modern India: four alert and beautifully sculpted lions guard the four cardinal directions, atop a circular platform. Belonging to the first and second century AD are two impressive life-size standing *bodhisattvas* – one has a stone parasol with fine ornamentation and emblems of the faith. Among the large number of fifth-century figures is one of the **Buddha**, cross-legged and with his hands in the *mudra* gesture. Perfectly poised, with his eyes downcast in deep meditation, and a halo forming an exquisite nimbus behind his head, the Buddha is seated above six figures, possibly representing his companions, with the Wheel of Law in the middle, to signify his first sermon. Later sculptures, dating from the tenth to twelfth century, include an exceptionally delicate image of the deity **Avalokiteshvara** with a lotus, and another of **Lokeshvara** holding a bowl.

Chaukhandi Stupa

The dilapidated brick remains of the **Chaukhandi Stupa**, 1km south of the main site, date from the Gupta period (300–700 AD), and are said to mark the spot where the Buddha was reunited with the Panchavargiya Bikshus, his five ascetic companions who had previously deserted him. Standing on a terraced rectangular plinth, the *stupa* is capped by an incongruous octagonal Moghul tower, built by Akbar in 1589 AD to commemorate his father's visit to the site.

Mulagandha Kuti Vihara and modern sites

To the east of the Dhamekh Stupa, the lofty church-like **Mulagandha Kuti Vihara** was built in 1931 with donations from the international Buddhist community. Run by the Mahabodhi Society, it drew devotees from all over the world to witness its consecration, and has become one of Sarnath's greatest attractions for pilgrims and tourists alike. The entrance foyer is dominated by a huge bell – a gift from Japan – and the interior houses a gilded reproduction of the museum's famous image of the Buddha, surrounded by fresco-covered walls depicting scenes from his life.

A little way east, shielded by a small enclosure, Sarnath's **Bodhi Tree** is an offshoot of the tree at Bodh Gaya, in Bihar, under which the Buddha attained enlightenment. Sangamitta, Emperor Ashoka's daughter, took a branch from the original tree in 288 BC and planted it in Anuradhapura, in Sri Lanka, where its offshoots have been nurtured through the ages.

Buddhist communities from other parts of the world are well represented in Sarnath. In addition to the long-established **Mahabodhi Society**, the **Central Institute of Tibetan Studies**, founded in 1967, offers degree courses in Tibetan philosophy and the ancient language of Pali. Close to the *Tourist Bungalow* is the traditional-style **Tibetan Temple** with frescoes and a good collection of *thangkas* (Tibetan scroll paintings): its central image is a colossal Shakyamuni, or Buddha Calling the Earth to Witness (his enlightenment). The **Chinese Temple** lies 200 metres east of the main gates; to the west, the **Burmese Temple** houses a white marble image of the Buddha flanked by two disciples. Behind the *Tourist Bungalow* are the **Japanese Temple** and the **Thai Temple**, the latter run by the Mrigdayavana Mahavihara Society.

Practicalities

Sarnath is easily reached by road from Varanasi but, given the sporadic **bus** service, auto-rickshaws might be a better option at Rs40 one-way; shared autos are also available for around Rs10 per person from Godaulia in Varanasi. Sarnath **railway** station, served only by local trains, is around 1km to the east of the sites. The main sites can be quite easily – and pleasantly – explored on foot; the so-called guides who linger outside the main gates and near the museum aren't really necessary.

Close to the main gate, the UPTDC *Tourist Bungalow* (①–③) is a typical government-run affair, with poorly maintained rooms and a dorm. Some of the monasteries, such as the pleasant *Burmese Vihara*, north of the main site, have basic rooms where visitors can stay, for a donation (①). Right in front of the Mahabodhi Temple gates, the *Birla Dharamsala* (①), is a very central option. There are a few simple **cafes and restaurants** outside the main gates near the Mulagandha Kuti Vihara, and a rather institutional restaurant serving *thalis* at the *Tourist Bungalow*. Also at the *Tourist Bungalow* is the UP **Tourist Bureau** (Mon–Sat 10am–5pm). The main **Post Office** is opposite.

Around Varanasi and Sarnath

Besides the trip across the river to Ramnagar (see p.288), other possible attractions around Varanasi include Sher Shah's grand fortress at **Chunar**, and the great Muslim city of **Jaunpur**, with its beautiful mosques, a long day trip to the northwest.

Chunar

From their vantage point at the northern extremity of the Kaimur Hills, the impressive sandstone battlements of **CHUNAR** overlook a bend in the Ganges before the river curves north to Varanasi, 22km away. Evidence of the earliest occupation of the site dates it from Vikramaditya of Ujjain in 56 BC. Chunar sandstone has been used for centuries, most famously in Ashokan pillars – highly polished for sheen and longevity – and is still quarried, leaving the surrounding hills looking ravaged in places.

The almost impregnable citadel, protected by massive Moghul ramparts, looks down onto the river, graced by a beautiful beach of silver sand during the dry season; the views of the sunset are stunning. Akbar stormed the fortress in 1575, and it was presided over by the Nawabs of Avadh until the British took it in 1764. Chunar is also associated with Warren Hastings, who took refuge here from an uprising in 1781; a large British graveyard lies near the western gate by the river. The ramparts and huge gates aside, the buildings themselves are unremarkable, except for a picturesque pavilion, built as a gatehouse during the reign of Sher Shah Suri (*c*.1538). Now a PWD bungalow, it makes an atmospheric and inexpensive stopover (①), bookable through the PWD at Mirzapur or by a private arrangement with the *chowkidar* (caretaker) who may also be able to arrange food.

On the banks of the river, the small, pleasant, traffic-free town of **Balu Ghat** has a small market and a few basic cafes; Chunar village, off the Ramnagar-Mirzapur highway and thronged with sandstone merchants, is a bit more animated.

The best way to get to Chunar is by local bus from Godaulia to Chunar Ghat, 22km south, from where a pontoon bridge crosses to Balu Ghat, at the base of the fortress. During the rainy season, the bridge is dismantled and a ferry takes its place.

Jaunpur

Few tourists visit the large dusty town of **JAUNPUR**, 65km northwest of Varanasi, and founded by Feroz Shah in 1360 to guard the eastern flank of the Delhi Sultanate. The city flourished until a ruthless onslaught by Sikander Lodi spared only its remarkable **mosques** – built in a unique hybrid style, using the plundered remains of previous Hindu and Buddhist structures – and later returned to prominence under the Moghuls.

The River Gomti, which bisects Jaunpur, is spanned by the massive sixteenth-century **Akbari Bridge** congested with hawkers and choked with traffic. Designed by an Afghan architect, the stone structure's fifteen arches have withstood floods and earthquakes; at its southern end, a large sculpture of a lion tussling with an elephant doubles as a provincial milestone.

The older sector, north of the river, is the site of Feroz Shah's original **Fort**, whose stone walls still show traces of coloured and glazed-brick cladding, and the remnants of masonry from an earlier Hindu temple. Little remains of its towers, blown up by the British in 1857. Around 350 metres north of the bridge, **Atala Masjid** is the earliest and finest example of the architecture of the independent Sharqi dynasty. Built by Sultan Ibrahim Sharqi in 1408, and incorporating the remains of the temple of Atala Devi, it holds two-storeyed cloisters, large arches and an open-pillared verandah. Along with three handsome gateways, the most impressive feature of the mosque is the prayer hall to the west: its huge central arch, composed of three pylons and flanked by two tapering towers, reaches a height of 23m.

Less than a kilometre north, the ambitious **Jami Masjid** mosque, built by Sultan Hussain Shah Sharqi (1458–79), sits on a high plinth. Approached by steep steps, its prayer hall has an imposing square chamber capped with a lofty dome; remnants of Hindu structures can be seen embedded in the cloisters and walls. Around six kilometres northwest of Akbari Bridge, the small **Lal Darwaza Mosque**, built around 1450 by Bibi Raji, the queen of Sultan Muhammad Shah (1436–58), is a cut-down version of Atala Masjid, with just one dome over its prayer hall and an almost square arch giving it a squat appearance.

What basic accommodation and food is available is concentrated around the Fort. Most visitors come from Varanasi for the day: both trains and buses take two hours.

Gorakhpur

GORAKHPUR, 230km north of Varanasi, which rose to prominence as a way station on a pilgrim route linking Kushinagar (the place of the Buddha's enlightenment) and Lumbini (his birthplace, across the border in Nepal), is now known primarily as a gateway to Nepal. It was named after the Shaivite yogi Gorakhnath, and holds a large ashram and temple dedicated to him. Tourists and pilgrims tend to hurry through, their departure hastened by the town's infamous flies and mosquitoes; if you do get stranded, there's a bustling bazaar, adequate amenities and a few passable hotels.

Around 5km northwest of the station, along the road to Nepal, the Gorakhnath ashram is an extensive complex of shrines, residences, and meeting halls, all rebuilt this century. On the site of an earlier temple, considered to be the traditional seat of the **Dharmanath** and **Ram Panths** (*panth* means branch or path) of the **Nath Yogi Sampradaya**, the ornate marble **Gorakhnath Temple** is decorated with images in the realistic style now popular throughout India. Surrounded by other shrines to Durga and Bhaironath, and a building that houses an eternal flame, the temple overlooks well-maintained grounds.

Arrival and information

There are three **bus** stands – the main Railway Station bus stand, 1km north of the centre, for buses from the Nepalese border at **Sonauli** and **Kushinagar**; the Kacheri bus stand, 1km southwest of the station, has buses from **Allahabad**, **Lucknow** and from Varanasi, but the main bus stand for **Varanasi** (6hr) is at Pedleyganj, 2km southeast of the station. Buses on their way between Varanasi and Nepal often stop here.

Major daily **trains** servicing Gorakhpur include the fast *Vaishali Express* #2553 to **Lucknow** (5.35pm) and the *Kushinagar Express* #1016 for **Bombay** via Lucknow (6am); among trains to **Varanasi** are a *Fast Passenger* (3am; 9hr), and the *Chauri Chaura Express* #5004 (10pm; 7hr). Station facilities include pleasant retiring rooms, a basic restaurant and a **tourist information** booth (daily except Sun 9am–5pm).

Rickshaws are the main means of **transport**, with few hotels more than one kilometre from the station. **Car rental** can be arranged through *India Tours & Travels*

GETTING TO NEPAL

Gorakhpur is a convenient jumping-off point for western Nepal, offering access to Pokhara and even Kathmandu. Direct **buses** to **Kathmandu** and **Pokhara** are not a very good deal – your best bet is to enter Nepal at the 24-hour crossing at **Sonauli**, where there is a better choice of transport.

Buses for Sonauli (3hr) depart from the bus stand near Gorakhpur railway station between 4.30am and 9pm; deluxe buses leave from in front of the railway station. Take one of the earliest if you want to get a connecting bus to Pokhara (10hr) or Kathmandu (14hr) in daylight, to enjoy the views; night buses also ply the routes. Private buses leave Sonauli almost hourly in the mornings, between 5am and 11am. The most popular service for Kathmandu, the government-run *Saja*, actually operates from **Bhairawa**, 5km away in Nepal; the booking office is near Bhairawa's *Yeti Hotel*. Local buses cover the 24km from Bhairawa to Lumbini (Nepal), the birthplace of the Buddha.

If you want to **break your journey**, UPT's *Hotel Niranjana* (①–④) in Sonauli, a kilometre short of the border, has a dorm and air-cooled rooms; there's more choice over the border in Nepal and in Bhairawa, the *Yeti* and the *Himalayan Inn* are popular.

Nepalese visas, which you should be able to get at the border, cost US$25. There is a *State Bank of India* on the Indian side of the border. Money-changers across the border will cash travellers' cheques.

(☎330915) in the Elora Building, opposite the railway station; beware ticket touts and poor service from most of the agents around here. The main **GPO** is in Golghar, to the southwest. The *State Bank of India* is on Bank Rd (☎334765); foreign-exchange facilities can also be found at some of the more expensive hotels.

Accommodation and eating

Gorakhpur has a wide range of **hotels** from the budget-type near the station to mid-range in the dull commercial hub around Golghar, 1km southwest. During the hot months, air-cooled or the more expensive a/c rooms are welcome, especially if you have just come down from the mountains. Cheap *dhabas* can be found in the vicinity of the station; a row of them stand outside the station gates. Elsewhere, the best eating is in the more expensive hotels.

Avantika, Kushinagar Rd, Mohaddipur (☎0551/338765). On the outskirts, 4km from the (currently dormant) airport and 2.5km from the station; newish and quite comfortable with a good mid-priced international restaurant. ③–⑤.

Bobina, Nepal Rd (☎0551/336663). About 2km from the station; an extraordinary and now rather tacky building where facilities include foreign exchange, a garden, restaurant and bar. ④–⑤.

Elora, opposite Railway Station (☎0551/330647). One of the best of the station hotels, with a range of rooms including a/c and air-cooled. The best rooms are at the back, away from the station. ②–④.

Ganges, *Tarang Cinema* crossing, towards Gorakhnath Temple (☎0551/333530). Pronounced *gang-ez*, one of Gorakhpur's better hotels. All mod cons, including two good restaurants. ③–⑥.

Ganges Deluxe, Cinema Rd, Golghar (☎0551/336330). Newish with all a/c rooms at the same price; the current pride of Gorakhpur. ⑥.

Marina, Golghar (☎0551/337630). Tucked away behind the *President* in the same compound, this place is older, less ostentatious and more pleasant; room service but no restaurant. ③–⑤.

President, Golghar (☎0551/337654). Off the main road, once one of Gorakhpur's ritziest but now showing its age. A range of mid-priced rooms, plus the recommended *Queen's* restaurant. ④–⑥.

Retiring Rooms, Railway Station. Good value with a cheap dorm, ordinary and a/c rooms; recommended if you need to catch an early train. ①–③.

Shalimar, Ghosh Company Chowkha (☎0551/337502). Friendly, good-value budget accommodation in the centre of town, close to all amenities. ①–②.

Standard, Station Rd (☎0551/336439). Reminiscent of station retiring rooms but good value. Opposite the station gates. ②.

Yark Inn, MP Building, Golghar (☎33233). One of several similarly and reasonably priced establishments along this main stretch. ③–⑤.

Kushinagar

Set against a pastoral landscape, the small hamlet of **KUSHINAGAR**, 53km west of Gorakhpur, is revered as the site of the Buddha's **Mahaparinirvana**, his death and cremation that marked his final liberation from the cycles of death and rebirth. During the Buddha's lifetime, **Kushinara**, as it was then called, was a small town in the kingdom of the Mallas, surrounded by forest. It remained forgotten until the late nineteenth century when archeologists rediscovered the site, and began excavations – based on the writings of seventh-century Chinese pilgrims, including Hiuen T'siang.

Set in a leafy park at the heart of Kushinagar, the **Nirvana Stupa**, dated to the reign of Kumaragupta I (413–55 AD), was extensively rebuilt by Burmese Buddhists in 1927. Within the accompanying shrine lies a large gilded **reclining Buddha**, reconstructed from the remains of an earlier Malla image, and the surrounding area is strewn with *stupas* erected by pious pilgrims, and the ruins of four monasteries. At a crossing immediately southwest, excavations continued at the **Mathakunwar** shrine, where a stunning tenth-century blue schist Buddha has been unearthed. About 1.5km southeast of the main site – surrounded by fields of rice, wheat and cane – the crumbling bricks of the **Ramabhar Stupa** are thought to be the original **Mukutabandhana Stupa** erected to mark the spot of the Buddha's cremation.

Today, Kushinagar is rediscovering its roots as a centre for international Buddhism, and is home to many *viharas* (monasteries), including a Tibetan *gompa* devoted to Shakyamuni (the historical Buddha), a Burmese *vihara*, and temples from China and Japan. The strikingly simple **Japanese Temple**, built by the Atago Isshin World Buddhist Cultural Association, consists of a single circular chamber housing a golden image of the Buddha, softly lit through small, stained-glass windows.

Practicalities

Regular **buses** link Kushinagar with **Gorakhpur** (2hr) and **Varanasi** (8hr). Shared **taxis** and jeeps also travel to and from Gorakhpur, but are a lot less comfortable. A recently built airport, 5km east, has been designed to link Kushinagar into a high-flying Buddhist network including Sarnath and Bodh Gaya. Check with *UPAir* or tourist authorities to see whether flights are in operation. **UP Tourism** maintains a low-key office and information desk at the tourist bungalow, *Pathik Niwas*.

Accommodation options are set to change especially with the ambitious *Lotus Hotel*, currently under construction next to the Japanese Temple. For a donation, you can stay in rooms for visiting pilgrims at one of the temples such as the *Myanmar Buddhist Temple* (①); the *Birla Dharamsala* (①), opposite, is similarly basic while the *International Buddhist Guest House* (①), opposite the Tibetan *gompa*, is poorly-maintained but otherwise quiet and pleasant. The relatively expensive state-run tourist bungalow, *Pathik Niwas* (☎05563/2038; ⑤–⑥), has a/c rooms, luxury cottages called "American Huts" and a canteen-like **restaurant**. Food stalls at the Kasia crossing provide inexpensive snacks.

CHAPTER FOUR

MADHYA PRADESH

Hot, dusty **MADHYA PRADESH**, India's largest state, is a vast landlocked expanse of scrub-covered hills, sun-parched plains, and dense tree cover that accounts for one third of India's forests. Stretching between the headwaters of the mighty **River Narmada** at the borders of Orissa and Bihar and the fringes of the Western Ghats, it is a transitional zone between the Gangetic lowlands in the north and the high dry **Deccan plateau** to the south.

Despite its diverse array of exceptional attractions, ranging from ancient temples and hill-top forts to superb isolated wildlife reserves, Madhya Pradesh receives only a fraction of the tourist traffic that pours between Delhi, Agra and Varanasi, being bypassed by many on the grounds of the relative inaccessibility of major sites. The extra effort, though, is well worth it, and while interest from tour groups is rising, the only place you're likely to meet more than a handful of tourists is Khajuraho, one of India's most celebrated temple sites.

Any exploration of central India will be illuminated if you have a grasp of its long and turbulent **history**. Most of the marauding armies that have swept across the peninsula over the last two millennia passed along this crucial corridor, leaving in their wake a bumper crop of monuments. The very first traces of settlement in Madhya Pradesh are the ten-thousand-year-old paintings on the lonely hill-top of **Bhimbetka**, a day trip south of the capital **Bhopal**. Aboriginal rock art was still being created here during the Mauryan emperor Ashoka's evangelical dissemination of Buddhism, in the second century BC. The immaculately restored *stupa* complex at **Sanchi**, not far away, is the most impressive relic of this era, among the finest early Buddhist remains in Asia. Nearby, the rock-cut Jain and Hindu caves at **Udaigiri** recall the dynasties that succeeded the Mauryans, from the Andhras to the Guptas in the fourth century.

By the end of the first millennium AD, central India was divided into several kingdoms: the Paramaras, whose ruler Raja Bhoj founded Bhopal, controlled the southern and central area, known as **Malwa**, while the **Chandellas**, responsible for some of the subcontinent's most exquisite temples, held sway in the north. Lost deep in the coun-

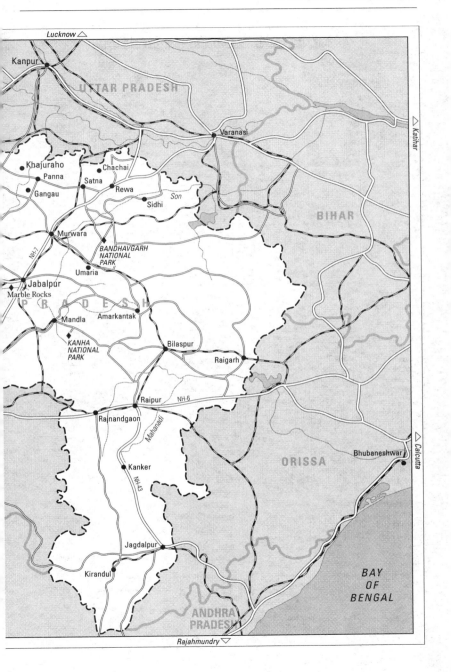

MADHYA PRADESH TRAVEL DETAILS

	Trains		Buses		Flights	
	Frequency	Time	Frequency	Time	Frequency	Time
To and from BHOPAL						
Agra	16–19 daily	5hr 20min–10hr				
Bombay	4 daily	15–18hr			daily exc Sat	2hr 15min
Calcutta	3 weekly	29hr				
Delhi	16–19 daily	7hr 40min–15hr			1–2 daily	1hr 20min–2hr 25min
Dewas			ev 15 min	4–5hr		
Goa	1 daily	26hr 30min				
Gwalior	16–19 daily	4hr 15min–7hr	3 daily	10–11hr	4 weekly	45min
Indore	3–4 daily	5hr 20min–7hr 40min	ev 15min	3hr 30min –4hr	6 weekly	45min
Jabalpur	1–2 daily	6–7hr	7 daily	8–10hr		
Jalgaon	5 daily	7–9hr				
Jhansi	16–19 daily	3hr–5hr 40min				
Madras	2–3 daily	22–32hr				
Manmad+	7–8 daily	9hr–11hr 30min				
Nagpur	8–10 daily	5hr 40min–10hr	5 daily	10–11hr		
Pachmarhi			3 daily	6hr		
Pune	2 daily	15–17hr				
Raisen			5 daily	1hr		
Sanchi			hourly	1–2hr		
Ujjain	4–5 daily	3hr 15min–5hr	hourly	5–6hr		
Vidisha	7 daily	45min	hourly	2–3hr		
To and from Gwalior						
Agra	15–19 daily	1hr 10min–2hr	hourly	3hr		
Bombay	1 daily	20hr 15min			4 weekly	2hr 30min
Calcutta	3 weekly	25hr 30min				
Delhi	16–19 daily	3hr 25min–9hr	1 daily	5–6hr	4 weekly	1hr
Goa	1 daily	32hr 30min				
Indore	1 daily	12hr 30min			2 weekly	1hr 50min
Jabalpur	1 daily	14hr				
Jalgaon	4 daily	13–17hr				
Jhansi	16–20 daily	1hr–2hr 45min	hourly	3hr		
Khajuraho			1 daily	10hr		
Madras	2–3 daily	26hr 15min–39hr				
Pune	2 daily	21hr 40min–24hr				
Puri	1 daily	39hr				
Shivpuri			2 daily	3hr		
Ujjain	1–2 daily	11–14hr	1 daily	14hr		
Varanasi	1 daily	17hr				
Vidisha	7 daily	5hr–8hr 30min				
To and from Indore						
Agra	1 daily	14hr	2 daily	12–15hr		
Ahmedabad					3 weekly	1hr
Ajmer	2 daily	14–15hr				
Aurangabad			1 nightly	10–12hr		
Bombay	1 daily	14hr 45min	1 nightly	12hr	1–3 daily	1hr 10min
Calcutta	3 weekly	36hr				
Chittaurgarh	2 daily	9hr–9hr 45min	1 daily	10hr		
Delhi	2 daily	13hr 45min–19hr			1–3 daily exc Sun	1hr 20min–3hr
Dhar			hourly	30min–1hr		
Jaipur	1 daily	18hr 10min	1 nightly	16hr		
Jhansi	1 daily	10hr 50min				
Kota	1 daily	6hr 25min				

	Trains		Buses		Flights	
	Frequency	Time	Frequency	Time	Frequency	Time
To and from Indore *continued*						
Madras	1 weekly	34hr				
Mandu			2 daily	4hr		
Nagpur	1 weekly	13hr	1 nightly	15hr		
Omkareshwar			4 daily	2hr 30min		
Pune					3 weekly	1hr 45min
Udaipur			3 daily	10hr		
Ujjain	4–6 daily	1hr 30min–2hr	ev 5 min	1hr 30min		
To and from Jabalpur						
Bombay	2–3 daily	18–20hr				
Calcutta	1 daily	23hr				
Delhi	1 daily	20hr				
Indore	1 daily	15hr 45min				
Jhansi	1 daily	12hr				
Kanha			2 daily	5–6hr		
Madras	3 weekly	31hr 25min				
Mandla			hourly	3hr		
Nagpur	6 weekly	10hr	12 daily	7hr		
Patna	1–2 daily	12hr 30min–15hr				
Satna	8–10 daily	3hr	1 daily	8hr		
Ujjain	1 daily	13hr 15min				
Varanasi	4–6 daily	9hr 35min–11hr 30min	1 daily	10hr		
To and from Khajuraho*						
Agra			1 daily	11hr	daily	45min
Bhopal			3 daily	12hr		
Delhi					1–2 daily	1hr 55min–2hr 40min
Gwalior			1 daily	8hr		
Indore			1 nightly	14hr		
Jabalpur			1 daily	11hr		
Jhansi			3–5 daily	6–7hr		
Mahoba			8 daily	3hr 30min–4hr		
Panna			4 daily	1hr		
Satna			5 daily	4hr		
Varanasi					1–2 daily	45min
To and from Ujjain						
Ahmedabad	2–3 daily	9–10hr 30min				
Agra	1–2 daily	12hr 10min–16hr	1 daily	16hr		
Calcutta	3 weekly	34hr				
Delhi	2–3 daily	12hr–21hr 30min	1 daily	20 hr		
Dhar			4 daily	4hr		
Jhansi	2–3 daily	9–14hr				
Kota	1 daily	4hr 40min	1 daily	7hr		
Madras	1 weekly	32hr 45min				
Maheshwar			daily	7hr		
Nagpur	1 weekly	12hr				
Omkareshwar			daily	6hr		
Varanasi	1 daily	34hr 40min				
Vidisha	1 daily	5hr				

* For connections to **Jhansi** in Uttar Pradesh, the major railhead for Khajuraho, see p.221.
+ Go to Manmad for bus links to Ajanta and Ellora

Note that no individual route appears more than once in this chart; for any specific journey, check against where you want to get to as well as where you're coming from.

tryside, equidistant from Agra and Varanasi, their magnificent erotica-encrusted sandstone shrines at **Khajuraho** were erected sufficiently far from the main north–south route to have been overlooked by the iconoclastic warriors who marched past in the eleventh and twelfth centuries. Today, the site is as far off the beaten track as ever; its many visitors either fly in, or make the five- to six-hour bus journey from the nearest railheads at **Satna** (in the east) and **Jhansi** (to the west in Uttar Pradesh, see p.317).

Monuments associated with the long Muslim domination of the region, by contrast, are much easier to get to. The romantic ghost-town of **Mandu**, capital of the Malwa Sultans, can be reached in a day from the industrial city of **Indore**, in western Madhya Pradesh, while **Gwalior**, whose hill-top fort-palace was the lynchpin of both the Delhi Sultanate's and the Moghuls' southward expansion, straddles the main Delhi–Bombay railway in the far north. Finally, between Jhansi and Khajuraho, the atmospheric ruined capital of the Bundella rajas at **Orchha** merits a short detour from the highway.

Under the **British**, the middle of India was known as the "Central Provinces", and administered jointly from Nagpur (now in Maharashtra), and the summer capital, the state's highest hill-station of **Pachmarhi** near Bhopal. Madhya Pradesh, or "MP", only came into being after Independence, when the Central Provinces were amalgamated with a number of smaller princedoms. Since then, the 93 percent Hindu state, with a substantial rural and tribal population, has remained more stable than neighbouring Uttar Pradesh and Bihar. Major civil unrest was virtually unheard of until the Bhopal riots of 1992–93, sparked off by events in Ayodhya. As elsewhere in India, the upsurge in communal tension has been accompanied by a swing towards the Hindu fundamentalist BJP, who ousted Congress in the 1989 state legislature elections. Central rule was imposed by the Indian Prime Minister Narashima Rao in the heat of the crisis, but the BJP were re-elected once the dust settled. In the 1996 elections, Congress lost more seats to the BJP.

In addition to its historic sites, Madhya Pradesh boasts the finest **wildlife reserves** on the subcontinent. In the sparsely populated east, remote savannah grasslands are an ideal habitat for deer and bison, while the shady *sal* forests and *tarai* swamplands that surround the *maidans* provide perfect cover for larger predators such as the **tiger**. Of the **national parks** hidden away in this area, **Kanha** is deservedly popular, though tiger sightings here are on the decline. For the big cats, trek out to **Bandhavgarh** national park to the northwest.

Getting around Madhya Pradesh without your own vehicle invariably involves a lot of bone-shaking bus journeys, usually under the auspices of MPSRTC, the state road transport authority. For longer distances, trains are the way to go. The *Central Railway*, the main broad-gauge line between Bombay and Calutta, scythes straight through the middle of the state between northern Maharashtra and southeast Uttar Pradesh, forking at **Itarsi** junction. One branch veers north towards Bhopal, Jhansi, Gwalior and Agra, while the other continues northeast to Varanasi and eastern India via Jabalpur. In the far west, at Indore and the holy city of **Ujjain**, you can also pick up the *Western Railway*, which heads through eastern Rajasthan to Bharatpur and Delhi.

The **best time to visit** Madhya Pradesh is during the relatively cool winter months between November and February. In the hot season (April, May and June), the region heats up like a furnace, and daytime temperatures frequently exceed 40°C. If you can stand the heat, this is the best time to catch glimpses of tigers in the parks. The rains finally sweep in from the southeast in late June or early July.

CENTRAL MADHYA PRADESH

All roads through the central regions of Madhya Pradesh lead to the state's capital, and its largest and fastest growing city – **Bhopal**. Although not the most attractive of cities – a perception not exactly improved by the appalling industrial disaster of 1984 – it does make a reasonably interesting stopover, within easy access of the unmissable Buddhist *stupa* complex at **Sanchi**, and a number of even older sites. The prehistoric site of **Bhimbetka** is just 45km south of Bhopal while at the attractive, but rarely visited hill station of **Pachmarhi**, further southeast, enjoyable hikes lead through craggy mountains and thick forests littered with more ancient rock-art sites.

Bhopal

With well over a million inhabitants, **BHOPAL**, the capital of Madhya Pradesh, consists of an amorphous mass of minarets, tightly packed streets and ferro-concrete suburbs, sprawling from the eastern shores of a huge artificial lake. Once, the gently sloping barren hills that rise from the southern and western sides of the old town centre lay well beyond its outer limits. Now these, together with acres of flat arid scrubland to the north, have been overtaken by creeping conurbation, industrial zones and miles of makeshift houses thrown up by Bhopal's beleaguered slum-dwellers. Aesthetically, it's not the most inspiring spectacle in central India, but, if you're passing through on the main Delhi–Bombay railway, you could do a lot worse than break your journey here for a day.

In addition to the nineteenth-century mosques that bear witness to Bhopal's enduring Muslim legacy, the packed **bazaars** of the walled old city are well worth a visit. Elsewhere, excellent archeological **museums** house large hoards of ancient sculpture. **Bharat Bhavan**, on the lakeside, is one of India's premier centres for performing and visual arts, with an unrivalled collection of contemporary painting, sculpture and *adivasi* ("tribal") art, while the **Rashtriya Manav Sangrahalaya**, or "museum of man", is an open-air exhibition of *adivasi* houses and technology which aims to challenge prevailing stereotypes of the country's many indigenous groups.

History
Bhopal's name is said to derive from the eleventh-century **Raja Bhoj**, who was instructed by his court gurus to atone for the murder of his mother by linking up the nine rivers flowing through his kingdom. A dam, or *pal*, was built across one of them, and the ruler established a new capital around the two resultant lakes – **Bhojapal**. By the end of the seventeenth century, **Dost Muhammed Khan**, an opportunistic ex-soldier of fortune and erstwhile general of Aurangzeb, had occupied the now-deserted site to carve out his own kingdom from the chaos left in the wake of the Moghul empire. The Muslim dynasty he established eventually became one of central India's leading royal families. Under the Raj, its members were among the select few to merit the accolade of a nineteen-gun salute from the British – a consequence of the help given to General Goddard in his march against the Maharathas in 1778. In the nineteenth century, Bhopal was presided over largely by women rulers. Holding court from behind the wicker screen of *purdah*, successive begums revamped the city with noble civic works, including the three sandstone **mosques** which still dominate the skyline.

Large areas of Bhopal have retained a distinctively Muslim feel. Communal unrest, however, was virtually unheard of here until December 1992, when rioting sparked off by the destruction of the Babri Masjid in Ayodhya led to the imposition of India's longest-ever curfew, lasting eleven days. Things have calmed down considerably since then, although the extreme-right Hindu fundamentalism of the BJP continues to cast its shadow over the mainly Muslim walled city, and after the 1996 elections, remains the strongest party.

Arrival and information

Bhopal's **airport**, served by daily *Indian Airlines* and *Archana* flights from Delhi, Gwalior and Bombay, is around 12km by taxi or auto-rickshaw from the city. The main

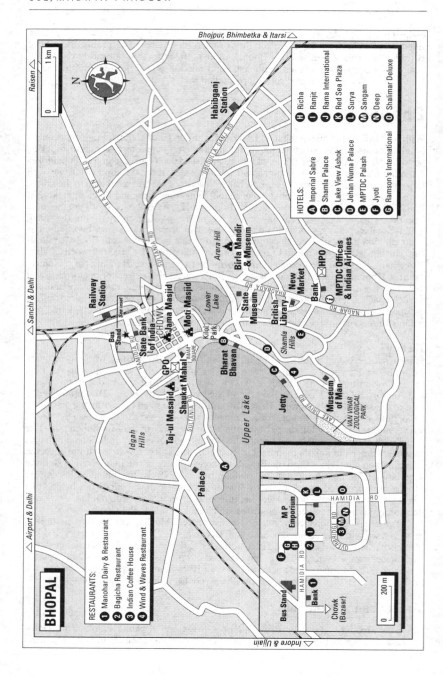

BHOPAL

RESTAURANTS:
1. Manohar Dairy & Restaurant
2. Bagicha Restaurant
3. Indian Coffee House
4. Wind & Waves Restaurant

HOTELS:
A. Imperial Sabre
B. Shamla Palace
C. Lake View Ashok
D. Jehan Numa Palace
E. MPTDC Palash
F. Jyoti
G. Ramson's International
H. Richa
I. Ranjit
J. Rama International
K. Red Sea Plaza
L. Surya
M. Sangam
N. Deep
O. Shalimar Deluxe

railway station, by contrast, is within easy walking distance of the centre; to reach the main hotel district, leave by the exit on platforms four or five, and head past the tonga rank until you reach the busy corner of **Hamidia Rd**. Approaching Bhopal from the south, most trains also stop briefly at **Habibganj station**, a long way out – only get down here if you intend to stay in one of the expensive hotels in Shamla Hills or the New Market area. The **bus stand**, used by long-distance buses from Gwalior, Indore, Jabalpur, Pachmarhi, Sanchi and Ujjain is ten minutes' walk west of the railway station.

 MPTDC have helpful **information** counters in the arrivals hall at the station (platform one exit), and on the fourth floor of the Gangotri Building on TT Nagar, New Market (☎554340), ten minutes by scooter south of the railway station. They don't hand out street maps but are a useful source of travel information, and can pre-book accommodation if you plan to visit Pachmarhi or either of the national parks in eastern Madhya Pradesh.

 There's a Head Post Office on TT Nagar in New Market, and a GPO on Sultania Rd near the Taj-ul Masajid (both Mon–Fri 10am–5pm, Sat 10am–noon). If you want to pick up mail, have it sent to the Head Post Office well in advance – the **poste restante** at the GPO is unreliable. Two *State Banks of India*, one opposite the bus stand and the other on TT Nagar next to the post office, are currently the only places other than the top hotels to **change money** (Mon–Fri 10am–2pm, Sat 10am–12.30pm).

> The telephone **area code** for Bhopal is ☎0755.

City transport

Most of Bhopal's principal places of interest are so far apart (and frequently difficult to find) that the best way of **getting around** has to be by metered **auto-rickshaw**. The **tongas** parked up outside the train station might seem a less expensive option, but few of the emaciated horses look as though they'd make it out of the paddock. **Taxis** can be found outside all of the top hotels, or else arranged through MPTDC. There's also a pre-paid taxi and auto-rickshaw booth outside the station on Hamidia Rd.

 Tickets for MPTDC's **city tours** (Tues, Thurs & Sun 9am–4pm; Rs90) are available at the counter at the train station or the main office on TT Nagar. MPTDC also rent out *Ambassador* or *Maruti* **cars** and minibuses for around Rs1000 per day.

The City

Bhopal has two separate centres. Spread over the hill to the south of the lakes, the **New Market** area, as its name implies, is a recent extension of the city – a modest and largely uninteresting agglomeration of shopping arcades, ice-cream parlours, cinemas and modern office blocks. Once you've squeezed over the strip of land that divides the Upper and (smaller) Lower lakes, sweeping avenues, civic buildings and pleasure gardens quickly give way to the more heavily congested **old city**. Focused around the **Jama Masjid** mosque, or **Chowk** area, the **bazaar** occupies the dense grid of streets between **Moti Masjid Square** to the south and the most chaotic stretches of Hamidia Road to the north. The art **galleries** and **museums** are all well off the beaten track, tucked away down side-roads or on top of the hills that overlook the city.

Chowk

Bhopal's vibrant bazaar, situated in the old **Chowk** district, comes as a very welcome splash of colour after the dismal, traffic-filled streets around the train station. Famous for "*zarda, purdah, garda* and *namarda*" (tobacco, veils, dust, and eunuchs), its bustling back lanes have retained a Muslim ambience absent from most Indian cities. Many of the women only venture out in long black *burkhas*, while the older men, sporting *kurta pajama*, crocheted skull-caps and henna-ed beards, spend much of the day sitting cross-legged on their raised wooden shop-fronts or *haveli* balconies murmuring verses from the Koran. The bazaar is also a great place to shop for *tussar* silk, silver jewellery and the gaudily beaded women's purses for which Bhopal is renowned.

The most straightforward way to approach the northern – Hamidia Road – end of the bazaar is via the lane leading south off the busy crossroads by the main bus stand. Bear right at the bottom and you'll eventually come out near a large **fortified gateway** – one of the last remaining fragments of the walls that once encircled the old city. At the very centre of the bazaar, the rich red sandstone walls and stumpy minarets of the **Jama Masjid** appear at the end of the street. Built in 1837 by Kudsia Begum, the mosque boasts neither age nor great architectural merit, but its whitewashed domes and gleaming gilded pinnacles lend an exotic air to proceedings in the square below. Most of the money that changes hands here does so in the dozens of open-fronted **silver shops** crouched around the base of the mosque itself. Pass through on any day except Friday or Monday (when most of Chowk Bazaar is closed) and you're sure to see large family groups huddled around sets of scales, scrutinizing the elaborate necklaces, belts, anklets and earrings worn by Muslim women on their wedding day.

Each of the narrow streets radiating from the central market square specializes in a different type of merchandise. One has a monopoly on brocaded "Chanderi" silk *saris*, another, west of the square, is given over to the bass-drums and wailing clarinets of Bhopali wedding bands, and others deal in brassware, film cassettes, spices or shoes.

Imam Square to the Taj-ul Masajid

A short way southwest of the Chowk area, **Imam Square** was once the epicentre of royal Bhopal. Nowadays, it's little more than a glorified traffic island, only worth stopping at to admire the **Moti Masjid** on its eastern edge. The "Pearl Mosque", erected in

THE BHOPAL GAS TRAGEDY

Bhopal is notorious as the site of the world's worst **industrial disaster**. In the early hours of December 3, 1984, a lethal cloud of methyl ico-cynate, a toxic chemical used in the manufacture of pesticides, escaped from a tank at the huge Union Carbide plant on the northern edge of the city. The rapidly cooling air and a lack of wind that night kept the gas at ground level as it dispersed through the densely populated nearby residential districts and shanty settlements. By the end of the following day, the leak had left two thousand people dead and many times that number with chronic and incurable health problems.

Lax safety procedures were immediately blamed. Later, the decision by the then Chief Minister, Arjun Singh, not to evict the plant's low-paid workers from illegally built shacks along the perimeter of the factory compound was also singled out as having contributed to the high death toll. Twelve years on, however, with cases of TB, respiratory problems and cancer on the rise – and Bhopal's 13 "gas relief" hospitals swamped with new patients daily – the long term effect of the disaster is becoming alarmingly clear, and its economic impact has proved severe. Though Union Carbide Corporation has finally admitted liability and is shouldering the bill for compensation claims, bureaucratic snarl-ups have meant that these claims are simply not being dealt with adequately. At the time of writing, some 344,000 (more than half those filed) are still awaiting settlement.

Every December there are demonstrations seeking recognition of local problems, partly run by the hundreds of widows who remain uncompensated in purpose-built widows' colonies. The Union Carbide plant, now renamed *Everyready Industries India Ltd*, is unlikely to reopen, but victims may have to wait for as long as twenty years before they see a rupee of what they are owed.

1860 by Sikander Begum, Kudsia's daughter, is a diminutive and much less imposing version of Shah Jahan's Jama Masjid in Old Delhi, notable more for its slender, gold-topped minarets and sandstone cupolas than its size.

Lining the opposite, northern side of the square near the ceremonial archway is a markedly more eccentric nineteenth-century building. The **Shaukat Mahal** palace was originally designed by a French architect (allegedly descended from the Bourbon kings) and is an unlikely fusion of Italian, Gothic and Islamic influences. Unfortunately, neither the palace nor the elegant **Sadar Manzil** ("Hall of Public Audience"), nearby, are officially open to visitors; both have been converted into government offices. No-one, however, is likely to stop you from having a quick look around.

Five minutes' walk west out of Imam Square (under the archway) brings you out at the foot of Bhopal's most impressive monument. With its matching pair of colossal pink minarets soaring high above the city skyline, the **Taj-ul Masajid** certainly lives up to its epithet (denoted by the extra "a" in its name) of "The Mother of All Mosques". Whether it also deserves to be dubbed the biggest in India, as locals claim, is rather less certain. The main **entrance**, on the south side at the end of a stretch of wasteland, opens onto a large walled courtyard and square *dukka* – the fountain and water tank used for ritual ablutions. From here, the bulbous white domes and multi-tiered towers flanking the facade are at their most imposing. Work on the building commenced under the auspices of Sultan Jehan Begum (1868–1901), the eighth ruler of Bhopal. After the death of her domineering husband, the Begum embarked on a spending spree that left the city with a postal system, new schools and a railway, but all but impoverished the royal family – the reason the Taj-ul Masajid was never completed.

The mosque is open to visitors daily except Friday, and during the Muslim festival of Id ul-Fitr (see p.62). If you plan to go inside, make sure you come suitably attired.

The state archeological museum

Hidden away near Raj Bhavan just south of Lower Lake, the modest, poorly labelled collection of ancient sculpture, bronzes and Moghul miniatures at the **Madhya Pradesh state archeological musem**, or *Rajkiya Sangrahalaya* (Tues–Sat 10am–5pm), is only likely to inspire real enthusiasts. If you do end up here, among the more noteworthy exhibits in the main gallery are the second-century BC *yakshis* (female fertility figures), the standing Buddha in black granite and the fifth-century statue of Karttikeya, the Hindu god of war. The far wall in the last gallery holds a reproduction of the famous, now badly damaged, Bagh frescoes – contemporary with those at Ajanta in Maharashtra. On your way out through the main foyer, have a look at the plaster-cast souvenir copies of the exquisite *salabhanjika* figurine from Gyaraspur (see p.368). The original, one of India's most valuable pieces of stone sculpture, is locked away in the vaults of the Gwalior museum (see p.374).

The Birla Mandir museum

Much to the chagrin of the state museum, the **Birla Mandir** collection (Tues–Sun 9am–noon & 2–6pm; Rs2) comprises some of the finest stone sculpture in Madhya Pradesh. It's also more informatively displayed, with explanatory panels in English in the main galleries. The museum is in a detached house beside Birla Mandir, the garish modern Hindu Lakshmi Narayan temple that stands high on the hill overlooking Lower Lake.

As usual, the exhibition is divided between Vishnu, the Mother Goddesses and Shiva. The **Vishnu** section contains some interesting representations of the god's diverse and frequently bizarre reincarnations (*avatars*), though the portly Rajnavahara – the wild boar whose form he adopted in order to rescue the Earth from the depths of the primordial ocean – hardly oozes with the panache one might expect of a cosmic super-hero. In the **Devi** gallery next door, a cadaverous Chamunda (the goddess Durga in her most terrifying aspect) stands incongruously amid a row of voluptuous maidens and fertility figures. Note the dying man writhing at her feet. The **Shiva** room, by contrast, is altogether more subdued. Many of the beautifully carved bas-reliefs show the god of preservation and destruction enjoying moments of marital bliss on Mount Kailash with his consort Parvati – an icon known as *Uma-Maheshwar*.

Finally, have a look at the replicas of the 3500-year-old **Harappan** artefacts encased under the stairs. One of the seals bears an image of the pre-Aryan god Rudra, seated in the lotus position, who archeologists believe was the ancient forerunner of Shiva.

Bharat Bhavan

Inaugurated in 1982 as part of a national bid to promote visual and performing arts, **Bharat Bhavan** (Tues–Sun; Feb–Oct 2–8pm, Nov–Jan 1–7pm; Rs3) was originally intended as one of several such institutions set up in state capitals throughout the country. After Indira Gandhi's death, however, the initiative fizzled out, and Bhopal's contribution emerged as provincial India's most outstanding arts centre.

Once you're within range, the building isn't hard to find. Charles Correa's campus of concrete domes and dour brickwork was designed, apparently, to "merge in exquisite harmony with the landscape, creating a visual impact of spacious and natural elegance"; it might look less out of place on the Maginot Line. Fortunately, the prospect improves when you step inside. In addition to its large and sympathetically displayed collection of modern Indian painting, Bharat Bhavan has one gallery full of sculpture and another devoted exclusively to **adivasis art**. Talent scouts spent months roaming remote regions searching for artists. Among their more famous discoveries was the Gond painter **Jangarh Singh Shyam**, featured by veteran BBC correspondent Mark Tully in his book *No Full Stops In India*. A number of Jangarh's works are on display here, along with a colourful assemblage of masks, terracottas, wood-carvings and ritual paraphernalia. The absence of background information is intentional – the exhibition is intended to represent the objects as works of art in their own right, rather than merely anthropological curios.

If you're wondering how to spend an evening in Bhopal, scan the posters in the foyer for forthcoming **events** at Bharat Bhavan such as theatre productions and music and dance recitals. The pleasant cafe, to the right of the main building, is just the place to pen a couple of the tribal art **postcards** on sale in the office next to the gate.

Rashtriya Manav Sangrahalaya – the "Museum of Man"

The story of India's indigenous minorities – the *adivasis*, literally "original inhabitants" – is all too familiar. Dispossessed of their land by large-scale "development" projects or exploitative money-lenders, the "tribals" have seen a gradual erosion of their traditional culture – a process hastened by proselytizing missionaries and governments that tend at best to regard tribal people as anachronistic and, at worst, as an embarrassment. The **Rashtriya Manav Sangrahalaya** (Tues–Sun 10am–6pm) is an enlightened attempt to redress the balance, setting out to provide genuine insights into ways of life few see at first hand. The aim is twofold: firstly to expose city people to the overall richess and ingenuity of India's tribal culture, and secondly to foster among the participants themselves a greater respect for their own heritage.

Overlooking the city on one side and the majestic sweep of Upper Lake on the other, the two-hundred-acre hill-top site includes a partially reconstructed "coastal village", a rock-art gallery, a research centre and, as its centrepiece, a permanent open-air exhibition of traditional *adivasi* houses, compounds and religious shrines collectively known as the "**tribal habitat**". Specialist *adivasi* craftsmen and women from all corners of India were brought in to construct and maintain authentic replicas of these buildings, using only tools and materials available in their home environments.

Before tackling the exhibition, have a quick look at the **introductory gallery** in the small building opposite the main entrance. From here, a flight of steps leads underneath a thatched gateway (a structure adapted from the "youth dormitory" of the Ao-Naga from Nagaland) up to the top of the hill, where the seventeen or so dwelling complexes are scattered. On a quiet day, the empty mud huts, corral and beaten-earth courtyards form a striking contrast with the teeming city below. Nearly all the **interiors** contain original tools, cooking utensils, baskets and musical instruments, while some are beautifully decorated with intricate **murals**, mouldings and carved beams. Of particular note are the multi-coloured paintings of horses adorning the walls of the Rathwa huts (look out for the picture of the train that carried the artists from their village in Gujarat); the ochre, red, black and yellow rectangular designs inside the Gadaba buildings (from Orissa); and the famous Warli wedding paintings of northern Maharashtra, which show the tribal fertility goddess Palghat framed by complex geometrical patterns. Other highlights include the giant votive terracotta statues of the tribal deities of Tamil Nadu's Ayyanar, and, both from Bastar in southeastern Madhya Pradesh, the wooden sculptures under the eaves of the Mara's shrine and the splendid twelve-metre-high chariot (*rath*) hauled by the Dashahana during their annual religious festival.

The only way of **getting to the museum** without your own vehicle is by auto-rickshaw; drivers are likely to insist on double the meter rate for the twenty-minute ride from the railway station, as they're unlikely to pick up a return fare, so negotiate a flat rate for the round trip, taking at least an hour's waiting time into consideration. A cheaper option is to take a bus from the railway station to New Market, and pick up a rickshaw there.

Van Vihar Zoological Park

If you haven't made it to Madhya Pradesh's bona fide national parks, or if you have and caught the atmosphere but missed the big cats, it's well worth visiting **Van Vihar Zoological Park** (daily 7–11am & 2–5.30pm; Rs10). A trip round the five-square-kilometre sanctuary ties in nicely with a visit to the Museum of Man, just 1km up the hill – keep the same rickshaw for the whole trip. The star of the park is a regal white tiger, but you can also see tortoises, long nosed *gharial*, leopards, Himalayan bears and Indian tigers. The best chance of sightings is from 4pm onwards, when the mighty felines pad and drool close to the boundaries of their enclosures, waiting for their daily feed. *Sambhar* (deer) munch the grass nearby, while egrets, herons, cormorants and ducks take in the evening light on the lake shore. You can get a longer and more peaceful look at the birds by taking a boat from the jetty, half a kilometre from the park gate (7am–sunset; pedal boat Rs25 per 30 min). Set back from the jetty, MPTDC's *Wind and Waves Restaurant* is close at hand for resfreshment.

Accommodation

Visitors not too bothered by the roar of traffic and its accompanying pollution needn't look much further than **Hamidia Road** for a **place to stay**. Bhopal's busy main thoroughfare, within easy walking distance of the bus and railway stations (leave the rail-

---

ACCOMMODATION PRICE CODES

All **accommodation prices** in this book have been coded using the symbols below. In principle the prices given are for the least expensive double rooms in each establishment; however, some hotels, usually in category ①, offer rates per bed rather than per room. Local taxes are not included unless specifically stated. For more details, see p.35.

① up to Rs100	④ Rs225–350	⑦ Rs750–1200
② Rs100–150	⑤ Rs350–500	⑧ Rs1200–2200
③ Rs150–225	⑥ Rs500–750	⑨ Rs2200 and upwards

way station via platforms 4 & 5), is crammed with hotels, ranging from grim "men-only" flea-pits to modern Western-style establishments sporting porters and glitzy reception desks. Bargains are thin on the ground; all, even the dingiest dives, slap a 10 percent "luxury" tax and an equally stiff "service charge" on to your bill. Most of Bhopal's **top hotels** favour congenial locations close to **Upper Lake**, a fifteen-minute ride from the train station. Checkout in all of the following is 24 hours unless otherwise stated.

Deep, behind *Sangam Cinema*, Hamidia Rd (☎535600). Basic but pleasant enough. Economy rooms are much the best value, but there are some with a/c. ③–⑤.

Imperial Sabre, Palace Grounds (☎740542). Former Maharaja's lakeside guest house now gone to seed, with a/c rooms. Might appeal to die-hard Raj-ophiles. ⑥.

Jehan Numa Palace, 57 Shamla Hills (☎540107; fax 551992). Bhopal's most stylish and expensive hotel. Palazzo-style building around central courtyard, set in spacious grounds with top-notch restaurant, coffee shop, bar and foreign exchange, but no lake view. Noon checkout. ⑧–⑨.

Jyoti, 53 Hamidia Rd (☎534898). Small, respectable hotel with "non-alcoholic atmosphere", run by Gujarati family. Recommended for women travellers. Some a/c. Often full. ④–⑤.

Lake View Ashok, Shamla Hills (☎541600). Ugly building, but in a prime site overlooking the lake. All the usual facilities including money changing, swish restaurant and shops. ⑦.

MPTDC Palash, TT Nagar, near New Market (☎553006). Pleasant and popular, with 33 large rooms around a relaxing lawn. Good restaurant, cafe and bar. Book ahead. Noon checkout. ⑥–⑦.

Rama International, Hamidia Rd (☎535542). A shade cleaner and more expensive than the *Gulshan*, but very much in the same mould. Some (cheap) a/c. ③–⑤.

Ramson's International, off Hamidia Rd (☎535298). Well-appointed with satellite TV, restaurant, bar and verandah, though now over-priced and decidedly grubby. Noon checkout. ④–⑥.

Ranjit, Hamidia Rd (☎533511). Plain rooms (all with attached bathrooms), terrace bar and popular cheap restaurant downstairs. Good value. ②–③.

Red Sea Plaza, Hamidia Rd (☎535518). Large, functional hotel conveniently close to the railway station, but poorly maintained, and the tariffs are a little over the odds. ④–⑥.

Richa, 1 Hamidia Rd (☎532564). Clean and efficient, with satellite TV and hot water in all rooms. Very good value. ④–⑥.

Sangam, Overbridge Rd (☎542382). Big building with variously priced, clean rooms on different floors. Good standards, but the deluxe rooms aren't worth the extra. ③–④.

Shalimar Deluxe, Hamidia Rd (☎537063). Nothing deluxe about it. Mentioned only because rock-bottom bathless singles are the cheapest in town. ②–③.

Shimla Palace, 31 Shimla Rd (☎540313). Very pleasant, family-run place in quiet suburban backstreet overlooking the lake. Rooms, some with views, are neat and spacious. ④–⑥.

Surya, Hamidia Rd (☎536925). Better than most: clean standard rooms are the best value. ④–⑥.

Eating

Restaurants in Bhopal's larger hotels serve uniformly spicy north Indian food with a few Chinese dishes thrown in for good measure; the strip-light-and-formica cafes opposite the bus stand do *thalis* and hot platefuls of *subzi*, rice and *dal* for next to nothing.

Bagicha Bar and Restaurant, Hamidia Rd. Mostly Mughlai and Punjabi dishes served al fresco in courtyard. Pleasant but quite pricey.

Bharat Bhavan Cafe. Refreshingly mixed crowd of artists, workers and visitors lounge around on uncomfortable designer furniture. Tea, coffee and light snacks.

Indian Coffee Houses, New Market or next to *Sangam Cinema*. Bhopal's big breakfast venues offer tasty south Indian snacks, eggs and filter coffee served with great style. The New Market branch is brighter and its popular "ladies room" is a haven for women travellers. Cheap.

Jehan Numa Palace, Shamla Hills. The best place to splash out on fine Mughlai-style cuisine. Also has a good Western menu.

Jyoti, 53 Hamidia Rd. Popular hotel-restaurant specializing in inexpensive, traditional (mild, pure veg) Gujarati food. Lunchtime *thalis* are particularly good value.

Manohar Dairy & Restaurant, Hamidia Rd. South Indian snacks, speciality sweets and *namkeen*, plus a full range of ice-cream – the perfect antidote to chilli.

Mehfil, below *Ranjit Hotel*, Hamidia Rd. Dingy-looking restaurant and bar serving up generous piles of no-nonsense northern food to discerning office workers.

Palash, TT Nagar, New Market. Moderately-priced, popular venue for business lunches and formal family dinners. Excellent food – Indian, Western and Chinese – with some great local fish dishes, and a longer-than-usual MPTDC menu.

Listings

Airlines *Indian Airlines* have an office in the Gangotri complex on TT Nagar, New Market (Mon–Sat 9am–5pm, Sun 9am–noon; ☎550480), and a booking counter at the airport.

Bookstores The two English-language bookstores at the top of Bhadbada Rd in New Market stock a reasonable range of paperbacks (mostly popular fiction and Indian authors in translation). A more limited selection is available from the newsstand on platform 1 at the train station.

Hospital Bhopal's main Hamidia hospital (☎72222) is on Sultania Rd, between Imam Square and the Taj-ul Masajid. Doctors are best arranged through the top hotels.

Left luggage Most hotels will look after your bags free of charge. If not, try the parcel office at the train station.

Library The *British Council* have a library in the GTB Complex on Roshanpura Naka, New Market (Tues–Sat 11am–7pm; ☎553767). Non-members are welcome to peruse their collection of British newspapers, magazines and periodicals.

Shopping Chowk (closed Mon & Fri) is the best place for silk and silver; New Market (Tues–Sat) has some bigger stores – *Mrignayani* for handicrafts, men's calico shirts and trendy ethnic *salwar kamises*. The *MP State Emporium* on Hamidia Rd, is the place to buy batiks, *dokra* metalwork, *khadi* clothes, bedspreads and silk *saris*. Check the street stalls on Overbridge Rd for bargains.

MOVING ON FROM BHOPAL

Bhopal is on one of the two broad-gauge **railway** lines between Delhi and Bombay. If you're heading **north** via Jhansi (for Orchha/Khajuraho), Gwalior or Agra, you have a choice between ten or so regular services; and the superfast, completely a/c *Shatabdi Express* #2001 that leaves Bhopal daily at 2.40pm prompt and arrives in **Delhi** a mere 7hr 45min later. The one train (apart from the passenger services) to avoid on this route is the super-slow *Amritsar–Dadar Express* #1457. In the other direction, the 5.25pm *Punjab Mail* #1038 is the best for **Bombay** (14hr 35min). The nightly service to **Jabalpur**, *Narmada Express* #8233 leaves at 11pm and gets in at 6.05am, leaving time to pick up a connecting bus to Kanha. The *Shipra Express* #1172 departs for **Calcutta** on Wed, Thurs and Fri at 2.25am, arriving 34hr 30min later. On other days you'll have to change at **Itarsi Junction**, 92km south, for Calcutta, and for Varanasi.

Most journeys from Bhopal are easier and quicker by train, but the city's good **bus** connections are especially useful for **Indore**, which can be reached either on frequent state buses or the daily MPSRTC superfast luxury coach service, which connects with the arrival of the *Shatabdi Express* (for **Ujjain**, get off at Dewas and pick up a local bus for the remaining 37km). Tickets are sold at the *MPTDC* counter in the train station.

Daily trains to **Sanchi** leave Bhopal at 6am (2hr 45min) and 9.15am (35min); there are also buses (see p.348).

Around Bhopal

A wealth of monuments scattered within a day's reach of Bhopal more than makes up for the state capital's own lack of sights. To the northeast, beyond **Raisen**'s dishevelled hill-top fort, the third-century BC *stupas* at **Sanchi** can be seen in a round trip from Bhopal, or as a stopover as you head north on the *Central Railway*. Sanchi's peaceful setting and good facilities make it an ideal base for visits to **Udaigiri**'s rock-cut caves, combined with a detour to the **Heliodorus pillar** – the last free-standing remains of the Mauryan city that paid for Sanchi. Avid templo-philes with the luxury of their own vehicle may also be enticed by the remote Gupta ruins at **Gyaraspur** and **Udayapur**.

Close to the main road south towards Hoshangabad and the Narmada Valley, the pre-historic cave paintings at **Bhimbetka** can be visited in a day by bus. If you rent a car, the eleventh-century Shiva temple at **Bhojpur**, with its monolithic *shivalingam*, is also worth checking out along the way.

Raisen

Resting on a sheer plateau, high above a sea of parched flat farmland 14km northeast of Bhopal, the ruined fort at **RAISEN** makes a nice break on a bus trip along the scenic back route to Sanchi, 23km further north. The citadel, erected by an independent local ruler around 1200 AD, became a stronghold of the Malwa Sultans two centuries later. The Rajput king Silhadi took over in 1520, but his rule was cut short after only twelve years by the Sultan of Gujarat, Bahadur Shah, who invaded on the pretext that the heathen Hindus had Muslim women locked up in their harem. It seems the rumour was ill-founded, for after the fort's male defenders had all been put to the sword, the seven hundred women inside threw themselves off the cliff rather than fall into the hands of the invaders. Raisen was repeatedly besieged in the years that followed, before being left to rot in the nineteenth century. Today, the once-grand complex of palaces, mosques, temples and tanks lies in ruins, inhabited only by troupes of mangy pink-bottomed monkeys and a lonely ASI caretaker who must be wondering what he did in a past life to deserve a posting in such a forlorn place.

The stony **path** up to the fort from the main road begins behind the improbably named "S & M Convent School", near a small Muslim *dargah*, or shrine-tomb – ask the **bus** between Bhopal and Vidisha to drop you off here and not in the town proper, another kilometre down the road. There is no clean drinking **water** on top of the hill, so take plenty with you – the stiff twenty-minute climb up the rocky hillside can be thirsty work. Beyond a series of fortified **gateways**, surmounted by crumbling pavilions, you come to the imposing battlements that encircle the fort. The main **ruins** are on the far northern end of the plateau, reached along the track to the right. En route to this clutter of tumbledown colonnaded courtyards, corridors and half-col-lapsed buildings, crowned with gently curving Afghan domes, you pass a couple of impressive **tanks**, lined with pond-weed and pools of stagnant green water. In the one wing of the old palace still in good shape, to the right of the main walkway, a court-yard strewn with rusting cannons is surrounded by arched cloisters, and the elegant projecting **balcony** from which Raisen's womenfolk committed suicide during the siege of 1532.

Sanchi

From a distance, the smooth-sided hemispherical object that appears on a hillock overlooking the main railway line at **SANCHI**, 46km northeast of Bhopal, has the surreal air of a space station or an upturned satellite dish. In fact, the giant stone mound stands as testimony to a much older means of communing with the cosmos. Quite apart from being India's finest surviving Buddhist monument, the **Great Stupa** is one of the earliest religious structures in the subcontinent. It presides over a complex of ruined temples and monasteries that collectively provide a rich and unbroken record of the development of Buddhist art and architecture from the faith's first emergence in central India during the third century BC, until it was eventually squeezed out by the resurgence of Brahmanism during the medieval era.

A visit to Sanchi, however, is no dry lesson in South Asian art history. The main *stupa* is surrounded by some of the richest and best-preserved ancient **sculpture** you're ever likely to see *in situ*, while the site itself, floating serenely above a vast expanse of open plains, has preserved the tranquillity that must have attracted its original occupants. Most visitors find a couple of hours more than sufficient to explore the ruins, although you could spend days poring over the four exquisite gateways, or **toranas**, that surround the Great Stupa. Paved walkways and steps lead around the hill-top enclosure (daily 8am–6pm), dotted with interpretative panels and shady trees to relax under if the heat gets the better of you.

The site is connected to the small village at the foot of the hill by a metalled road. Once you've bought a fifty-paise entrance ticket from the booth outside the **museum**, head up the stone steps on the right, past the welcoming posse of postcard-*wallahs*, to the main entrance. From here, the central walkway runs alongside the new Buddhist temple and a cold-drinks stall, before making straight for the Great Stupa.

History
Unlike the other famous Buddhist centres in eastern India and Nepal, Sanchi has no known connection with the life of Buddha himself. It first became a place of pilgrimage when the Mauryan emperor **Ashoka**, who married a woman from nearby **Besnagar**

SANCHI

Vidisha & Udaigiri Caves △

Railway Station
Mahabodhi Society Guest House
Dhabas
Bus Stand
Cycle Rental
Silkworm Farm
Rest House
MPTDC Cafeteria
Ticket Kiosk
Museum
MPTDC Travellers Lodge
Bhopal
Tank
Stupa 2
New Temple
Stupa 3
Vihara 45
Vihara 51
The Great Stupa
Ashok's Pillar
Temple 18
Temple 17
0   300 m
N

(see p.367), erected a polished stone pillar and brick-and-mortar *stupa* here midway through the third century BC. The complex was enlarged by successive dynasties, but after the eclipse of Buddhism Sanchi lay deserted and overgrown until its rediscovery in 1818 by General Taylor of the Bengal Cavalry. In the years that followed, a swarm of heavy-handed treasure hunters invaded the site, eager to crack open the giant stone eggs and make off with what they pictured as their valuable contents. In fact, only *stupas* three and four yielded anything more than rubble; the soap-stone relic caskets containing bone fragments are displayed for one day each December in the new temple. These amateur archeologists, however, left the ruins in a sorry state. Deep gouges gaped from the sides of *stupas* one and two, a couple of ceremonial gateways completely collapsed, and much of the masonry was plundered by the villagers for building materials (one local landlord is alleged to have carted off Ashoka's pillar to use as a roller in his sugar cane press).

Restoration work made little impact until the archeologist John Marshall and the Buddhist scholar Albert Foucher took on the job in 1912. The jungle was hacked away, the main *stupas* and temples were rebuilt, lawns and trees planted and a museum erected to house what sculpture had not been shipped off to Delhi or London.

Getting to and from Sanchi

Although Sanchi is on the main Delhi–Bombay railway line, **getting there** by **train** involves a choice of only two morning services, the painfully slow 6am departure (2hr 45min) and the more convenient 9.15am service (35min). Return services to Bhopal leave at 4.25pm (50min) and 5.20pm (1hr 10min). First-class passengers who have come at least 161km can also arrange to make a "special halt" at Sanchi – except for the "superfast" a/c chair services, like the *Shatabdi Express*, which stop only at Bhopal. The nearest mainline station is **Vidisha**, 10km northeast; there are two daily trains to Bombay and six to Delhi from here.

Buses from Bhopal to Sanchi depart from the main city bus stand more or less hourly, and ply two different routes. The longer and more scenic southern one takes two and a half hours, passing through Raisen (68km), while the more direct northern road follows the *Central Railway* line, taking around ninety minutes. All buses pull into the centre of the tiny bazaar, a handful of wooden stalls surrounding the bus stop square. The low, whitewashed houses of the village proper are on the other side of the main road, huddled below the stupa-covered hill.

Finally, **bicycles** – good for trips to the nearby Udaigiri and Kandagiri caves (see p.367) – can be rented for around Rs3 per hour from a small shop in the bazaar.

Stupa one

Stupa 1, the "Great Stupa", stands on a stretch of level ground at the western edge of the plateau. Fragments of the original construction, a much smaller version built in the third century BC by Ashoka, still lie entombed beneath the thick outer shell of concrete and lime plaster added a century later. The **Shungas** were also responsible for the raised processional balcony, and the two graceful staircases that curve gently around the sides of the drum from the paved walkway at ground level, as well as the aerial-like *chhattra* and its square enclosure which crown the top of the mound. Four elaborate gateways were added next by the **Satavahanas** in the first century BC, followed by the four serene **meditating Buddhas** that greet you as you pass through the main entrances. Carved out of local sandstone, these were installed during the Gupta era, around 450 AD, by which time figurative depictions of Buddha had become acceptable (elsewhere in Sanchi, the Master is euphemistically represented by an empty throne, a wheel, a pair of footprints or even a parasol).

As you move gradually closer to the *stupa*, the extraordinary wealth of sculpture plastered over the **toranas** slips slowly into focus. Staring up at these masterpieces from below, you can see why archeologists believe them to have been the work of ivory craftsmen. Every conceivable nook and cranny of the eight-metre upright posts and three curving cross-bars teems with delicate figures of humans, demi-gods and goddesses, birds, beasts and propitious symbols. Some of the larger reliefs depict narratives drawn from the lives of Gautama Buddha and his six predecessors, the Manushis, while others recount Ashoka's dissemination of the faith. In between, there are plenty of purely decorative panels too, as well as illustrations of heaven intended to inspire worshippers to lead meritorious lives on earth. Start with the *torana* on the south side, which is the oldest, and proceed in a clockwise direction around the *stupa* – as is the custom at Buddhist monuments.

SOUTHERN TORANA

Opening directly onto the ceremonial staircase, the **southern torana** was the Great Stupa's principal entrance, as is borne out by the proximity of the stump of Ashoka's original stone pillar. Over the years, some of the best sculpted panels have dropped off the gateway (and are now housed in the site museum), but those that remain on the three cross-beams are still in reasonable condition. A carved frieze on the middle architrave shows Ashoka, complete with royal retinue, visiting a *stupa* in a traditional show

STUPAS

The hemispherical mounds known as **stupas** have been central to Buddhist worship since the sixth century BC, when Buddha himself modelled the first prototype. Asked by one of his disciples for a symbol to help disseminate his teachings after his death, the Master took his begging bowl, teaching staff and a length of cloth – his only worldly possessions – and arranged them into the form of a *stupa*, using the cloth as a base, the upturned bowl as the dome and the stick as the projecting finial, or spire.

Originally, *stupas* were simple burial mounds of compacted earth and stone containing relics of the Buddha and his followers. As the religion spread, however, the basic components multiplied and became imbued with **symbolic significance**. The main dome, or **anda** – representing the sacred mountain, or "divine axis" linking heaven and earth – grew larger, while the wooden railings, or **vedikas**, surrounding it were replaced by massive stone ones. A raised ambulatory terrace, or **medhi**, was added to the vertical sides of the drum, along with two flights of stairs and four ceremonial entrances, carefully aligned with the cardinal points. Finally, crowning the tip of the *stupa*, the single spike evolved into a three-tiered umbrella, or **chhattra**, standing for the Three Jewels of Buddhism: the Buddha, the Law and the community of monks, or *Sangha*.

The *chhattra*, usually enclosed within a low square stone railing, or **harmika** (a throwback to the days when sacred *bodhi* trees were surrounded by fences) formed the topmost point of the axis, directly above the reliquary in the heart of the *stupa*. Ranging from bits of bone wrapped in cloth, to fine caskets of precious metals, crystal and carved stone, the reliquaries were the "seeds" and their protective mounds the "egg". Excavations on the 84,000 *stupas* scattered around the subcontinent have shown that the solid interiors were also sometimes built as elaborate **mandalas** – symbolic patterns that exerted a beneficial influence over the *stupa* and those who walked around it. The ritual of circumambulation, or **pradhakshina**, which enabled the worshipper to tap into a magical force-field and be transported from the mundane to the divine realms, was always carried out in a clockwise direction from the east, in imitation of the sun's passage across the heavens.

Of the half-dozen or so giant *stupa* sites dotted around ancient India, only **Sanchi** has survived to the present day. To see one in action, however, you have to follow in the footsteps of Ashoka's missionaries southwards to Sri Lanka, northwards to the Himalayas and the Tibetan plateau, or across the Bay of Bengal to Southeast Asia, where, as "**dagobas**", "**chortens**" and "**chedis**", *stupas* are still revered as repositories of sacred energy.

of veneration. On the reverse side, the scene switches to one of the Buddha's previous incarnations. For the **Chhaddanta Jataka**, the *bodhisattva* adopts the guise of an elephant who, in extreme selflessness, helps an ivory hunter saw off his own (six) tusks.

WESTERN TORANA

The **western torana** collapsed during the depredations of the nineteenth century, but has been skilfully restored. Some of Sanchi's liveliest sculpture appears around its two square posts. In the top right panel, a troop of monkeys scurries across a bridge over the Ganges, made from his own body by the *bodhisattva*, their leader, to help them escape a gang of soldiers (below). According to the **Mahakapi Jataka**, the troops were dispatched by the local king to capture a coveted mango tree from which the monkeys had been feeding. You can also just about make out the final scene, where the repentant monarch gets a stern ticking-off from the *bodhisattva* under a *peepal* tree. Meanwhile, high on the top cross-beam, the eight Buddhas, including Maitreya, the Buddha-to-come, appear as a line of *bodhi* trees and *stupas*.

One of the most frequently represented episodes from the life of the Buddha features on the first two panels of the left-hand post facing the *stupa*. In the **Temptation of Mara**, the Buddha, who has vowed to remain under the *bodhi* tree until he attains enlightenment, heroically ignores the attempts of the evil demon Mara to distract him with threats of violence and seductive women (Mara's beautiful daughters). Notice the contrast at the end between Mara's agitated troops and the solemn-faced procession of angels who accompany Buddha after he has achieved his goal.

NORTHERN TORANA

Crowned with a fragmented Wheel of the Law and two tridents symbolizing the Buddhist trinity, the **northern torana** is the most elaborate and best preserved of the four gateways. Scenes crammed onto its two vertical posts include Buddha performing an aerial promenade – one of many stunts he pulled to impress a group of heretics – and a monkey presenting the Master with a bowl of honey. Straddling the two pillars, a bas-relief on both faces of the lowest cross-beam depicts the **Vessantara Jataka**, telling of a *bodhisattva*-prince banished by his father for giving away a magical rain-making elephant. During his exile, the over-generous Vessantara was persuaded to part with everything else that was dear to him, including his wife and kids, before finally being forgiven by the king. A better view of the inner, south-facing side of the plaque can be had from the balcony of the *stupa*'s raised terrace. Note the little tableau on the far right showing the royal family trudging through the jungle: the prince's son is holding his father's hand, while his daughter clings to her mother's hip. The four **elephants** sculpted from the capital supporting the architraves are also very realistic, as are other, smaller elephants, horses and female wood-nymphs separating the three beams.

EASTERN TORANA

Leaning languorously into space from the right capital of the **eastern torana** is Sanchi's most celebrated piece of sculpture, the sensuous **salabhanjika**, or wood-nymph. The full-breasted fertility goddess is one of several such figures that once blessed worshippers as they entered the Great Stupa. Only a few, however, still remain in place, others having been removed to Los Angeles and London. Her *tribhanga*, or hip-shot stance is a classical dance pose which, from this moment onwards, was to become a distinctive feature of all Indian religious sculpture.

Panels on the inner face of the pillar below the *salabhanjika* depict scenes from the life of the Buddha, including his conception when the *bodhisattva* entered the body of his mother, Maya, in the form of a white elephant, shown astride a crescent moon. The front face of the middle architrave picks up the tale some years later, when the young Buddha, represented by a riderless horse, makes his **Great Departure** from the palace where he grew up to begin the life of a wandering ascetic. The reverse side shows the fully enlightened Master, now symbolized by an empty throne, with a crowd of celestial beings and jungle animals paying their respects.

Elsewhere around the enclosure

Of the dozens of other numbered ruins around the 400-metre enclosure, only a handful are of more than passing interest. Smaller, plainer and graced with only one ceremonial gateway, the immaculately restored **stupa 3**, immediately northeast of *stupa 1*, is upstaged by its slightly older cousin in every way but one. In 1851, a pair of priceless reliquaries were discovered deep in the middle of the mound. Turned on a lathe from a fine marble-like soapstone called steatite, the caskets were found to contain relics belonging to two of Buddha's closest disciples. In one, fragments of bone were encased with beads made from pearls, crystal, amethyst, lapis lazuli and gypsum, while on the lid, the initial of the saint they are thought to have belonged to, Sariputra, was painted in ink. Once in the British Museum, along with other treasures pilfered from Sanchi, both are now safely locked in the new Buddhist temple outside the *stupa* enclosure, and are brought out for public view for one day each December. On this day, Sanchi is transformed from a lonely open air museum into a bustling pilgrimage site, with devotees from as far afield as Sri Lanka and Japan.

From *stupa* 3, pick your way through the clutter of pillars, small *stupas* and exposed temple floors nearby to the large complex of interconnecting raised terraces at the far **eastern edge** of the site. The most intact monastery of the bunch, **vihara 45**, dates from the ninth and tenth centuries, and has the usual layout of cells ranged around a central courtyard. Originally, a colossal, richly decorated sanctuary tower also soared high above the complex, but this collapsed to leave the inner sanctum exposed. The river goddesses Ganga and Yamuna number among the skilfully sculpted figures flanking the entrance to the shrine itself – testimony to the mounting popularity of Brahminism at the start of the medieval era. Inside, however, Buddha still reigns supreme. Regally enthroned upon a lotus bloom, his right hand touches the ground to call upon the earth goddess to witness the moment of his enlightenment.

The enclosure's tenth-century eastern **boundary wall** is the best place from which to enjoy Sanchi's serene **views**. To the northeast, a huge, sheer-sided rock rises from the midst of Vidisha, near the site of the ancient city that sponsored the monasteries here (traces of the **pilgrimage trail** between Besnagar and Sanchi can still be seen crossing the hillside below). South from the hill, a wide expanse of well-watered wheatfields, dotted with clumps of mango and palm trees, stretches off towards the angular sandstone ridges of the Raisen escarpment on the distant horizon.

THE SOUTHERN AREA

The **southern area** of the enclosure harbours some of Sanchi's most interesting **temples**. Pieces of burnt wood dug from the foundations of **temple 40** prove that the present apsidal-ended *chaitya* was built on top of an earlier structure contemporary with the Mauryan *stupa* one. **Temple 17** is a fine example of early Gupta architecture and the precursor of the classical Hindu design developed later in Orissa and Khajuraho. Its small, flat-roofed sanctum is entered via an open-sided porch held up by four finely carved pillars with lion capitals. Nearby, directly opposite the Great Stupa's southern entrance, the tall slender pillars of **temple 18** lend it a distinctly Greek air, but in fact, the temple layout follows the usual design for rock-cut Buddhist *chaitya* halls, and resembles the apsidal plan of the caves at Karle and Bhaja (see pp.703–4). Rebuilt several times since its original construction, the present structure dates from the seventh century.

Before leaving the enclosure, hunt out the stump of Ashoka's pillar (#10) to the right of *stupa* one's southern *torana*. Columns such as this were erected by the Mauryan emperor all over the empire to mark sacred sites and pilgrims' trails (see *Contexts*). Its finely polished shaft (made, like all Ashokan pillars, with a sandstone known as Chunar after a quarry on the Ganges near Varanasi) was originally crowned with the magnificent lion capital now housed in the site museum. The inscription etched around its base is in the Brahmi script, recording Ashoka's edicts in Pali, the early Buddhist language and forerunner of Sanskrit.

The western slope

A flight of steps beside *stupa* 1 leads down the **western slope** of Sanchi hill to the village, passing two notable monuments. The bottom portions of thick stone walls of **vihara 51** have been carefully restored to show its floor-plan of 22 cells around a paved central courtyard. Further down, the second-century BC **stupa 2** stands on an artificial ledge, well below the main enclosure – probably because its relics were less important than those of *stupas* 1 and 3. The ornamental railings and gateways around it are certainly no match for those up the hill, although the carvings of lotus medallions and mythical beasts (including some bizarre horse-headed women) that decorate them are worth checking out. The straps that dangle from some of the horse-rider's saddles are believed to mark the first appearance in India of stirrups.

The archeological museum

Sanchi's small **archeological museum** (daily except Fri 10am–5pm; Rs0.50), just behind the admission kiosk to the left of the road up to the hill-top, houses a modest collection of artefacts, mostly fragments of sculpture recovered during successive excavations. Its **main hall** contains the most impressive pieces, including the famous Ashokan lion-capital (see above) and two damaged *salabhanjikas* from the gateways of *stupa* one. Also of note are the distinctive Mathuran red sandstone Buddhas, believed to have been sent to Sanchi from Gandhara in the far northwest of India – source of the first figurative representations of the Master. The best preserved of them dates from the Gupta period around the fourth century AD. Gallery one contains more large pieces of sculpture, while the remaining sections are devoted to smaller antiquities – votive terracotta figurines, stone plaques, jewellery, pottery, weapons and tools.

Accommodation and eating in Sanchi

Cheap **accommodation** can be found in the unusually good *Retiring Room* at the train station (①), or else at the nearby *Sri Lanka Mahabodhi Society Guest House* (☎07592/81239; ①), where a Rs50 donation is requested for a *charpoi* in a bare cell. Moving up the scale, the MPTDC *Tourist Cafeteria* (☎07592/81243; ④), next door to the museum, has two plain, clean rooms with attached shower-toilets. By far the most comfortable option in Sanchi, however, has to be the MPTDC *Tourist Lodge* (☎07592/81223; ④–⑤), five minutes' walk south of the crossroads. Their eight spacious and spotless rooms (two a/c) are excellent value, but often booked; try to reserve at least five days in advance through any MPTDC office, or in Delhi (see p.119). As a last resort, try the *Government Rest House* (①), behind the *Tourist Cafeteria*.

MPTDC also has the monopoly on good **places to eat** in Sanchi. Unless you're staying in the *Tourist Lodge* and can take your dinner at leisure in the courtyard, the best bet is the *Tourist Cafeteria*, with a fresh atmosphere and quick service. This is also a good base for toast-and-egg breakfast. Steaming *chai*, *puri* and *jalebi* are dished up in the stalls by the bus stand from 7am.

Vidisha

The main reason to call in at the bustling railroad and market town of **VIDISHA**, a straightforward 56-kilometre train or bus ride form Bhopal, and also served by buses from nearby Sanchi, is to hop on a tonga to the archeological sites at Udaigiri and Besnagar. However, if you're not pushed for time, the place merits a closer look.

In front of the station a Hindu temple, painted in loud pinks, yellows and blues and decorated with twinkling mirrors, is a fitting introduction to the cheerful bazaar. Overflowing with displays of *saris*, sweetmeats and stainless steel pots, the bazaar spreads into the **old town**, where families chat by piles of vegetables, eggs and jewellery between whitewashed houses. Beyond this, the River Betwa, dappled with *ghats*, white domed temples and commemorative *sati* stones, signals the edge of town and the route to Udaigiri.

The small **museum** (Tues–Sun 10am–5pm; Rs2), hidden away behind the train station in the east of town, is also worth a quick visit. The majority of its prize pieces, such as Kubera Yaksha, the three-metre, pot-bellied male fertility figure in the hallway, are second-century Hindu artefacts unearthed at Besnagar. Attractive Jain *tirthankaras* and lumps of masonry salvaged from the district's plethora of ruined Gupta temples litter the garden.

Vidisha is also known for having financed a prolific third century BC spate of *stupa* construction, including much of the work at Sanchi. By the sixth century AD however, it lay deserted and in ruins, remaining so until the arrival of the Muslims 300 years later when a settlement, called **Bhilsa**, was founded around the flat-topped hill in the centre of the modern town. Vidisha's other rather tenuous claim to fame is that the bricks of a nearby second-century BC Vishnu temple were stuck together with lime mortar, believed to be the world's oldest **cement**.

Udaigiri and Besnagar

The modest collection of rock-cut caves and ruined temples at **Udaigiri** lie 6km west of Vidisha, scattered around a long thin outcrop of sandstone that rises from the surrounding patchwork of yellow and green wheatfields. The most congenial way to explore the area is on one of the tongas that hang around outside Vidisha's bus stand (Rs40–50 round trip), though the site is also an easy cycle ride from Vidisha (bikes are available from shops on the outskirts of the bazaar) or, if your legs are up to it, from Sanchi (1–2hr).

Once across the River Betwa, either turn left to Udaigiri, or head straight on to the ruins of ancient **BESNAGAR** couched in a tiny village half a kilometre along the main road. During the time of the Mauryan and Shunga empires, between the third and first centuries BC, a thriving provincial capital overlooked the confluence of the Bes and Betwa rivers. The emperor Ashoka himself was governor here at one time, and even married a local banker's daughter. Nowadays, a few mounds and some scattered pieces of masonry are all that remain of the houses, stupas, temples and streets. One small monument, however, makes the short detour worthwhile. According to the inscription etched around its base and sixteen sided column, the stone pillar in an enclosed courtyard, known as the **Column of Heliodorus**, was erected in 113 BC by a Bactrian-Greek envoy from Taxila, the capital city of Gandhara (now the northwest frontier region of Pakistan). The shaft, dedicated to Krishna's father Vasudeva, was originally crowned with a statue of Vishnu's vehicle Garuda. Heliodorus converted to the local Vaishnavite cult during his long diplomatic posting here. Most of the other archeological finds dug up on the site – including a colossal fertility god, Kubera Yaksha (see above) – are now at the museum in Vidisha.

Short of Besnagar, a left turn leads along a gently undulating tree-lined avenue for two or three kilometres to the hillside at **UDAIGIRI**, etched with twenty or so fifth-century caves, many decorated by Hindu and Jain mendicants. As it aproaches Udaigiri, the road takes a sharp left turn towards the village. Get off at this corner, at the base of the near-vertical rock face, to climb a steep flight of steps to **cave 19** which has worn but attractive reliefs of gods and demons around the doorways, and a **Jain cave temple** on the northern edge of the ridge. Inside the temple, at the base of an uneven flight of steps, Gupta inscriptions and damaged *tirthankaras* on the back wall look through a natural balcony to the countryside below. From here, a path follows the backbone of the ridge, past a hilltop ruin (possibly a Hindu temple), to the most interesting caves, opposite the small terracotta-roofed village. An ASI *chowkidar* should be around to unlock the doors for you. The site's *pièce de résistance*, a four-metre image of the boar-headed hero Varaha, stands carved into **cave 5**. Vishnu adopted the guise of this long-snouted monster to rescue the earth-goddess, Prithvi (perched on a lotus next to his right shoulder) from the churning primordial ocean – depicted by delicate wavy lines. Varaha's left foot rests on a Naga king wearing a hood of thirteen cobra heads, while the river goddesses Ganga and Yamuna hold water vessels on either side. In the background you can see Brahma and Agni, the Vedic fire-god, plus sundry sages and musicians. The scene, prominent in many contemporary Hindu monuments, is seen as an allegory of the emperor Chandragupta II's conquest of northern India.

Walking around the back of cave five you'll see the waves and curves of Brahmi script etched into the rock, dating from 401AD, and an elegant lute player above the doorway of **cave 4**. A short hike uphill leads to the south, porticoed **cave 1**, constructed in the fourth century, is probably the earliest hermit hide-out here.

Gyaraspur

The middle-of-nowhere market town of **GYARASPUR** may have been an important provincial capital during the Pratihara era, a thousand or more years ago, but it now languishes in obscurity at the end of a sixty-minute ride down a pot-holed back-road from Vidisha, 35km southwest. Daily **buses** connect the two, although as there's nowhere to stay in Gyaraspur, trips from either Sanchi or Bhopal are not really feasible without your own vehicle. Friday, when all the local villagers pour in on their bullock carts for the weekly **market**, is the best day to visit.

The most interesting of the handful of dilapidated monuments that survive is the ninth-century **Maladevi Mandir**, clinging to the scarpside of the steep narrow rocky spur behind the town. Reached via a motorable dirt track, the temple terrace looks over a sweeping vista of geometric farmland and a low, thinly wooded ridge of hills that tapers away southwest. Originally, the building's ornate sandstone surfaces would have included fine individual pieces of sculpture. Over the years, however, many of these have either crumbled away down the hill or been carried off somewhere else. Maladevi's cavernous interior, partially cut from the surrounding hillside, houses a small collection of Buddha-like Jain *tirthankaras* together with a few Hindu fertility goddesses encrusted with bat droppings. There's no need to slip your shoes off before stepping inside; the sanctum is no longer kept as a living shrine.

At the foot of the hill on the opposite side of town, 1500m west, a couple of stone posts and four small seated Buddha figures are all that's left of Gyaraspur's oldest monument, a sixth-century **stupa**. On the way over, look out for eight richly carved columns mounted on a raised plinth in a patch of open ground near the market place – the remains of another ninth-century Hindu temple, the **Atha Khamba**.

Udayapur

Remote, rural **UDAYAPUR**, 73km northeast of Bhopal, is the site of one of Madhya Pradesh's least-visited architectural gems. Unfortunately, to get there from Bhopal or Vidisha, you have to catch a train to **Basoda**, and then a local bus for the final 10km. Check the return times carefully before leaving, as there's nowhere to stay in the town, with the possible exception of the first-class waiting room at the train station.

The magnificent **Neelkantheswara temple**, built in 1080 AD by the Paramara king Udayadita, took 22 years to complete and is considered to be on a par with its illustrious cousins at Khajuraho (see p.387), even if its sculpture is rather more restrained. Its sandstone *shikhara* soars high above the surrounding clutter of dusty streets. Some of the best stonework is to be found in the niches around the huge curvilinear sanctuary tower. A large panel on the front face frames a dancing Shiva, **Nataraj**, surmounted by a sea monster with bulging eyes and the seven mother goddesses, the Sapta Matrikas. The doorways of the three entrance porches of the pyramidal-roofed *mandapa* assembly hall are also richly carved with demigods and goddesses, including several amorous couples. Inside, the pillars are encrusted with garlands of flowers and bells, in marked contrast to the bare shrine room, which still houses a living *shivalingam*.

Bhojpur

Raja Bhoj's legendary mania for hydraulic experiments was by no means confined to Bhopal. At **BHOJPUR**, 28km southeast of the capital (and devoid both of direct bus services and of any accommodation), the eleventh-century Paramara ruler created another enormous tank, this time from the waters of the River Betwa. Enclosed by a ridge of hills on one side and two enormous earth embankments on the other, the 400-square-kilometre artificial lake was eventually destroyed by the second Sultan of

Mandu, Hoshang Shah, when his invading army cut a breach through the smaller of the two dams. Legend has it that the water took three years to seep through the rupture, and that its eventual disappearance transformed the local climate.

With the lake long gone and its stone-lined dams supporting no more than a road to a nearby village, Bhojpur's only real attraction these days is its colossal **Shiva temple** – another of the Raja's large-scale projects. The **Bhojeshwar Mandir** rests unfinished and dishevelled, but not entirely forlorn, on a rocky bluff, amid a patchwork of fertile farmland and tiny hamlets stretching south towards the Vindhya hills. It's a pleasant spot, and one which sees little more than a trickle of visitors. The few who do venture out here come primarily to pay their respects to the temple's imposing centrepiece – a two-and-half-metre-tall polished limestone *shivalingam*, maintained as a living shrine. It rests on an even more enormous pedestal (*yonipatha*), from which the resident *pujari* dispenses smudges of vermillion powder to worshippers. High above his head, the domed ceiling of the sanctuary, though incomplete, is encrusted with some well- preserved sculpture and a couple of appropriately large beehives. A stone's throw away north, beyond a jumble of boulders and collapsed masonry, the ASI have fenced off a flat rock onto which the Raja's architects chiselled their original plans for the temple. This is also a good place to view the remnants of the earthen **ramp** they used to raise chunks of unworked stone up to the roof.

Look out for the yellow pennants of the **Jain shrine** directly behind the sanctuary, at the end of the dirt track up from the village. Its central icon is a giant stone image of **Mahavira**, the sixth-century founder of the faith, represented in the attitude of "immobile bodily discipline" (standing erect, with arms and hands held at the side) similar to the famous seventeen-metre statue of Gommateshvara in Karnataka. This one's a lot smaller than its southern cousin, but is still among the largest of its kind.

Bhimbetka

Shortly after NH12 peels away from the main Bhopal–Hoshangabad road, 45km southeast of the state capital, a long line of boulders appears high on a scrub-covered ridge to the west. The hollows, overhangs and crevices eroded over the millennia from the crags of this malleable sandstone outcrop, harbour one of the world's largest collections of **prehistoric rock art**. Discovered in 1957 by the archeologist Dr V S Wankaner, **BHIMBETKA** is South Asia's equivalent to the cave complexes at Lascaux in southwest France and Altamira in Spain, or the rock paintings of aboriginal Australia. If you have your own transport, or are prepared to do a bit of walking to get there, this rarely visited site makes a fascinating day trip from Bhopal.

Of the thousand **shelters** so far catalogued along the ten-kilometre hilltop, around half contain rock paintings. These date from three different periods, each with its own distinctive style. The oldest fall into two categories: green outline drawings of human figures, and large red images of animals. Lumps of haematite (from which the red pigment was manufactured) unearthed amid the deepest excavations on the site have been carbon-dated to reveal origins in the upper-**paleolithic** era, around ten thousand years ago. The second, and more prolific phase accounts for the bulk of Bhimbetka's rock art, and took place in the late-**mesolithic** – the "stone age" – between 8000 and 5000 BC. These friezes depict dynamic hunting scenes full of rampaging animals, initiation ceremonies, burials, masked dances, sports, wars, pregnant women, an arsenal of different weapons, and even what seems to be a drinking party. No-one is sure why these sophisticated communities of hunter-gatherers decorated their temporary abodes in this way. One theory is that the cave art served the ritual or **magical** function of ensuring a plentiful supply of game; but while abundant depictions of bison, wild boar, antelope and deer lend credence to that notion, animals such as tigers and elephants also appear, that were not on the mesolithic menu.

Shards of pottery found amid the accumulated detritus on the rock-shelter floors show that Bhimbetka's third and final spate of cave painting took place during the early historic period, after its inhabitants had begun to trade with settled agriculturalists. Their stylized, geometric figures bear a strong resemblance to the art still produced by the region's *adivasi*, or tribal groups.

From the car park at the top of the hill, a paved pathway winds through the jumble of rocks containing the most striking and accessible of Bhimbetka's paintings. A *chowkidar* wielding a long stick will, for a bit of *baksheesh*, point out the highlights. As you wander around, look out for the paleolithic images in green, the wonderful "X-ray" animals filled in with cross-hatching and complex geometric designs, and the recurrent image of a bull chasing a human figure and a crab – a motif believed to represent a struggle between the totemic heroes of three different tribes. At the bottom of the track, on the base of a tall column of sandstone not included in the guide's whistlestop tour, there's also a very fine wild boar in black and red.

Practicalities

Without your own vehicle, **getting to Bhimbetka** from Bhopal involves an 80-minute bus journey, with a change 10km short at the market town of **Obaidullaganj**. From there, hop on one of the frequent buses bound for **Hoshangabad** and get off after 7km when you see a sign to the right in Hindi (with "3.2" written on it). The side road runs over a level crossing before starting the gradual three-kilometre climb up to the rocks.

There's nowhere to **eat** or **drink** for miles around Bhimbetka, so bring a day's supply of food and water with you.

Pachmarhi

Halfway between Bhopal and Jabalpur, a forbidding wall of weird blackened sandstone peaks, precipitous ravines and impenetrable forest rears along the south side of the Narmada Valley. The **Mahadeo mountains** were among the last tracts of central India charted by the British. Not until 1857 did the first column of red-coated Bengal Lancers hack their way up from the sweltering plains. Led by the infamous explorer and big-game hunter Captain J Forsyth, the troops were astonished to discover, deep in this wilderness of *sal* trees and sheer red cliffs, an idyllic saucer-shaped plateau strewn with huge boulders and criss-crossed by perennial clear-water streams.

At over 1000m above sea level, **PACHMARHI** had one other quality that appealed to the sun-weary soldiers – deliciously cool air. Within five years Forsyth was back, this time with a gang of surveyors to push a road through the hills from the railhead at **Piparia**. A military sanitorium was established, quickly followed by bungalows, churches, club houses, a race-course, a polo pitch and a network of cart tracks through the woods. By the end of the century, India's newest hill station had become the summer capital of the entire Central Provinces.

The Pachmarhi plateau was, however, inhabited long before it became a fashionable retreat for Nagpur's homesick British contingent. Abundant **prehistoric rock art** scattered across a wide area of remote hills and valleys suggests that this northern spur of the Mahadeos, known as the **Satpuras**, harboured a population of hunter-gatherers as long ago as the late stone age. Finding "the paintings" can be difficult, but enjoyable, involving lots of scrambling through dense forests.

The majority of visitors who venture up to Pachmarhi are either honeymooners from the nearby cities, or elderly English-speaking Bengalis muffled in thick woollen hats and gloves to keep out the chilly morning air. Rarely do they manage much more than a sedate stroll or jeep excursion, and the only time the sleepy hill station sees any real action is during the annual **Shivratri mela** (Jan/Feb), which draws *lakhs* of pilgrims to ancient shrines hidden in the gorges and on the peaks surrounding the plateau. The trail trodden by the exuberant crowds of ragged *yatris* winds through spectacular scenery to the top of **Chauragarh mountain**; out of season, it makes an excellent **day-hike** from the town. Less strenuous saunters along woodland tracks offer an equally rewarding way to sample the area's abundant flora and fauna. The **Satpura National Park** west of town, embracing **Dupgarh**, MP's highest point, encompasses a 247-square-kilometre swathe of old-growth *sal* and teak forest, and supports a wide array of wildlife, including Indian bison (*gaur*), barking deer, sambar, *barasingha*, jackals, wild dogs and a handful of elusive tigers and leopards.

The best **time to visit** Pachmarhi is between September and May, when the cool, clear mountain air makes a refreshing change from the heat and dust at lower elevations. It's especially worth trying to be here for the *mela*, although the bus journeys up from the plains can be nightmarish when the festival is in full swing.

Arrival and information

The nearest railhead to Pachmarhi is the one-horse town of **Piparia**, 47km north. If you're unlucky enough to arrive there after the last bus up the mountain has left, the only decent place to stay is the MPTDC *Tourist Motel* (☎07576/22299; ③), behind the station. Buses also connect Pachmarhi with Bhopal (5 daily; 6hr), Chindwara to the south (2 daily; 4–5hr), en route to Nagpur, and Indore (1 daily; 12hr).

Pachmarhi's small bus stand has an MPTDC **information** counter (Mon–Sat 10.30am–2.30pm) which can book accommodation; their **maps** are wildly inaccurate. Most of the private budget accommodation lies a short walk up the hill in the bazaar and in a cluster close to the bus stand, but a few of the more comfortable MPTDC hotels are a five-minute jeep or rickshaw ride south on the far side of a lotus-filled lake, near the military training area, **Tehsil**. For longer excursions, negotiate with a jeep driver, or rent a **car** (with driver) through the main MPTDC office (☎2100), next to the *Amaltas Hotel*, 1500m south of the bus stand.

Neither the *State Bank of India* nor any of the hotels have foreign exchange facilities. The nearest places to **change money** are in Bhopal, Jabalpur or Nagpur.

The telephone **area code** for Pachmarhi is ☎07578.

Pachmarhi: Town and Hikes

The **town** of Pachmarhi itself is clean, green and pleasant, with a very laid-back feel. Although nothing like India's larger and better-known hill stations, it retains a colonial ambience, enhanced by the elegant British bungalows and Victorian church spires that nose incongruously above the tropical tree-line. The sprawling army training camp, though built after Independence, adds a further touch of the Raj. Military bands march across the spacious *maidans* to the strains of Colonel Bogey, while retired army officers with handlebar moustaches and tweed jackets still enjoy a game of snooker in the old-style gentlemen's clubs.

The web of forest tracks and pilgrim trails that thread their way around Pachmarhi's widely dispersed archeological and religious sites make for excellent **walking**, but few, if any, routes are marked in English. The tourist office, and some hotels and restaurants, can put you in touch with a **guide**, though some sites are known only to academics and the local tribal people. **Bikes**, rented from the repair shop just below the Government Gardens (around Rs20 per day), are a handy way of getting to the trailheads.

Popular short hikes include the 45-minute trip up from the whitewashed Muslim shrine in the Babu Lines area of town (1km southwest of the bus stand) to the top of **Pachmarhi Hill**, from where you have a fine panoramic view over Pachmarhi town on one side, and the thickly forested ravine of Jambu Dwip on the other. The craggy cliffs lining the north side of the uninhabited gorge below are riddled with hidden rock-shelters and caves.

Another 45-minute walk follows a well-beaten track from the bus stand, twisting north from the main bazaar into the hillside through a narrow steep-sided canyon to the sacred **Jatashankar cave**, a prominent point in the Shivratri *yatra*. En route, in a small cluster of prehistoric rock-shelters just off the path, **Harper's cave** is named for a seated figure of a man playing a harp, and also holds an unusual portrait, painted in white and outlined in red, of a man riding an X-shaped horse. From the clearing below Harper's cave, the path picks its way past small temples and a lurid blue effigy of Shiva emerging from a large wayside boulder, to the head of a dark chasm. The Jatashankar cave itself lies deep in the bowels of the mountain at the foot of a long flight of stone steps. Lord Shiva is said to have fled here through a secret passageway under the Mahadeo range to escape the evil demon Bhasmasur. The grotto's name, which literally means "Shiva's hair-style", derives from the rock formation around a natural *lingam* on the cave floor, supposed to resemble the god's matted dreadlocks. Above the *lingam* the rocks resemble a cluster of snakes, *naga*, forming a reverential parasol over the deity. During the week of the *mela*, the claustrophobic cleft in the rock resounds with the ringing of *puja* bells and the raised voices of *yatris* and *sadhus*, whose fires and incense offerings have blackened the sides of the cliff. Off season, a lone *pujari* tends the *shivalingam* inside the tiny cave.

Pandav caves to Dhuandhar

A two- to three-hour walk around the eastern fringes of the plateau strings together a small cluster of ancient rock-cut caves and a prehistoric rock-shelter. First head up to the *Panch Pandav*, or **Pandav caves** (40min), which occupy a nobbly sandstone hillock just east of the road between the ATC cantonment and the petrol pump. Hindu mythology tells that these five (*panch*) simple cells (*marhi*), from which the name Pachmarhi derives, sheltered the infamous Pandava brothers during their thirteen-year exile. Archeologists however maintain that the bare stone chambers and pillared verandahs were excavated by a group of Buddhist monks around the first century BC.

Rejoin the metalled road in front of the caves and head around the back of the hill to the melancholy **British cemetery**. Beyond that, the road peters out into a dusty but jeepable dirt track leading to a small car park. Drop down the hill through the woods from here until you reach a T junction of trails, then turn right. At the fork a little further on, bear left and keep to the path as it winds steeply down the rocky sides of an overgrown gulley.

The **Dhuandhar rock-shelter** is formed by a fifteen-metre slab of sandstone overhanging a dusty, rubble-strewn ledge in the forest. Over the years, the site has suffered abuse at the hands of latter-day graffiti "artists", but plenty of lively prehistoric murals survive. Most of the white-painted forms plastered across the ochre, grey and sand-red surfaces are human figures engaged in warfare or hunting; their dangling loin-cloths, hooped earrings and top-knots suggest the work of the aboriginal **Gonds**, some time between 500 and 800 AD. Dhuandhar's real highlight, however, is considerably older. The red and white bull, or bison, towards the middle of the rock face is thought to date from the late stone age. Note the characteristic "X-ray" style, and the way the artist has rendered the animal's magnificent horns.

If you return from here to the T junction (above), and instead of heading back the way you came, carry straight on through the woods to the stream, you'll eventually arrive at the **Apsara Vihar**, or "Fairy's Pool" – an idyllic bathing place and picnic spot tucked at the foot of a small waterfall nearby. Troupes of black-faced langur monkeys crash through the canopy overhead as you approach the 150-metre **Rajat Prapat**, or "Big Falls", about a five-minute scramble over the boulders further downstream.

Chauragarh

The 23-kilometre climb to the sacred summit of **Chauragarh mountain**, on the south rim of the Pachmarhi plateau, follows the main *yatra* trail used by pilgrims during the Shivratri *mela*. A **bicycle** is definitely recommended, as the trailhead is approached along 8km of surfaced road.

From the main bazaar and bus stand area at the top of town, head south across the lake towards the crossroads in front of the MPTDC *Amaltas Hotel*. Heaped around the trunk of a mango tree nearby are a collection of spatula-shaped wooden memorial plaques placed here by members of the local Gond tribe. Beautifully carved with traditional designs, they're part of the Gond's ancestor-worship cult and should not be disturbed.

The road to Chauragarh runs due south into the woods beyond the MPTDC *New Block Hotel*. Bear left at the fork a few kilometres further on, and keep going until you see a sign on the left to **"Priyadarshini"**, or "Forsyth's Point". The spot from which the explorer first spied the Pachmarhi plateau also looks over the spectacular **Handi Khoh** ravine to the south, supposedly created by Lord Shiva as a prison for a giant serpent that once inhabited the nearby lake. The evil reptile had been hassling pilgrims; to punish it, Shiva drank the lake and forced it into a ravine gouged out with a mighty wallop of his trident. It is often suggested that this legend may be rooted in the events of the sixth and seventh centuries AD, when the plateau's Buddhist occupants, referred to by the *Vedas* as "Snakes", were ousted by Hindus.

After Priyadarshini, the going gets tougher as the road switchbacks up some steep thickly wooded hills. Eventually, it emerges at the head of a sweeping valley, with the striking profile of the Chauragarh peak rising high above the sea of treetops. At the height of the Shivratri *mela*, the bare conical summit that crowns the near-vertical flanks of the mountain shimmers and glints with immense crowds.

The **footpath** proper begins at the very bottom of the valley, after the road has plunged down another sequence of hairpin bends. Before setting off, make a brief diversion up the *khud* behind the modern **temple** to the **Mahadeo cave**, where pilgrims take a purifying dip in the cool perennial spring water that gushes through its pitch-black interior before the strenuous two-hour climb to the top of the holy mountain. The ancient trail passes several other sacred caves sheltering Shaivite *sadhus*, before reaching a knife-edge ridge, where it joins another pilgrim path that scales the mountain from the south. At the very summit, after a flight of concrete steps, a bright blue statue of Shiva is surrounded by a thicket of orange tridents, and a temple houses the all-powerful Chauragarh *lingam*. The view over the verdant Satpuras, to the dusty scrubland and distant flat-topped mountains, is suitably sublime.

Accommodation

Finding **accommodation** in Pachmarhi is only a problem during May and June, when visitors flock to escape the heat of the plains. The tourist information counter at the bus stand can tell you which of the five MPTDC hotels have vacancies, and a handful of private places on or around the main street in the bazaar make good fallbacks.

MPTDC Amaltas, near Tehsil (☎2098). Small hotel with plain but clean rooms, fans, and a so-so bar-restaurant. ③.

MPTDC Holiday Homes, near SADA Barrier (☎2099). No-frills rooms near the bus stand. ③.

MPTDC Panchvati Cottages, near Tehsil (☎2079). Five pricey self-contained chalets in their own gardens, aimed mainly at honeymooners. ⑤.

MPTDC Panchvati Huts, near Tehsil (☎2079). Well-run mid-range hotel set in pleasant grounds with spacious rooms, attached shower-toilets, and on-site restaurant. Good value. ④.

MPTDC Satpura Retreat (☎2097). Pukka British bungalow with six comfortable, old-fashioned rooms, huge white-tiled bathrooms and views over an immaculate flower garden from easy chairs on the verandah. Well worth shelling out for. Some a/c. ⑤–⑦.

New Block, on the Chauragarh road, near the petrol pump. Large but spartan rooms in charmless institutional hotel. A rickshaw ride south of the bazaar. ②–④.
Pachmarhi, Patel Marg (☎2170). One of a batch of budget hotels in the same road. Unexciting clean rooms at assorted prices, and a good restaurant Opposite *Saket*. ③–④.
Saket, Patel Marg (☎2165). Close to *State Bank* in the heart of the bazaar, five minutes from bus stand. Very cheap and clean, with fans and attached bathrooms. Good value. ①.

Eating

All the most congenial **places to eat** in Pachmarhi are run by MPTDC. The best of the bunch, by a long chalk, is at the *Satpura Retreat*, although even there the food is of less note than the bungalow's faded charm. If you're on a tight budget, a couple of cheap little vegetarian cafes can be found in the small square above the bus stand.

Amaltas, near Tehsil. Quiet restaurant with predictable menu and the town's only bar.
China Bowl, near *Panchavati Huts*. Standard MPTDC restaurant, with a few extra soups, *chop sueys* and *chow meins* thrown in for form. Open for breakfast – mainly cutlets, eggs and *iddlis*.
Kalsa, bottom end of bazaar off the main road. Inexpensive, delicious Punjabi and Chinese dishes served inside under strip lights or in the garden. Beer available in side room. Recommended.
Mrignayani, Gandhi Chowk. The most hygenic of the cheap *thali* joints in the bazaar, serving no-nonsense, fiery, pure-veg curries and piping hot *rotis* from large vats.
Satpura Retreat. Regular MPTDC range of veg and non-veg food dished up in TV lounge or al fresco on the atmospheric verandah. A bit of a trek from town if you're not staying here. Moderate.

NORTHERN MADHYA PRADESH

The remoteness of the famous temples at **Khajuraho** means that you could well find yourself travelling through a large tract of **northern Madhya Pradesh**. Given the non-stop coach services and tight train connections from the main Delhi–Agra artery, not many visitors choose to linger in the region. Yet this much-trodden trail passes within striking distance of several sights that are well worth taking time out to see. Foremost among them is the hill-fort at **Gwalior**. In addition to the immaculately restored palaces and ancient Hindu temples within the fort itself, the city also boasts an extravagant European-style palace crammed with quirky art treasures and curios. Just under 100km further south, **Jhansi**, in UP (see p.317), is the main jumping-off point both for Khajuraho and the deserted medieval ghost-town of **Orchha**. Architecture enthusiasts may also want to visit one of the few Indian monuments admired by Lutyens, the brain behind imperial New Delhi. The multi-storey fort-palace at **Datia**, 27km northwest of Jhansi, stands within sight of an even more rarely visited monument, the Jain hill-top temple complex and pilgrimage site of **Sonagiri**.

The region's major rail and road routes arc north from Bhopal, passing through the jigsaw joint with neighbouring Uttar Pradesh at Jhansi, before heading north to Agra and Delhi. In the east, the *Central Railway* connects the state capital with **Satna**, the nearest railhead to Khajuraho, then veers northeast towards Varanasi and the Ganges basin. Cutting between the two on the busy back-country road to Khajuraho enables you to take in Orchha on the way.

Gwalior

Straddling the main Delhi–Bombay railway line, **GWALIOR** is the largest city in northern Madhya Pradesh and the site of India's spectacular hill-top **fort**. The old sandstone citadel, with its temples and palaces, peers down from the edge of a sheer-sided plateau above a haze of petrol fumes, busy streets and cubic concrete houses. Once you've

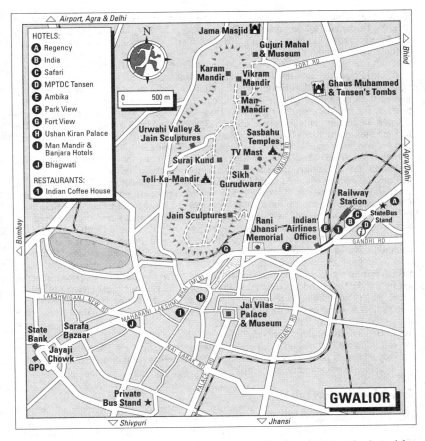

checked out the archeological **museum**, and the rock-cut Jain colossi at the foot of the cliff, the city's other unmissable attraction is the supremely kitsch **Jai Vilas palace** belonging to the local ruling family, the **Scindias**.

Despite its proximity to Agra, 119km north, Gwalior sees few foreigners; in truth, with its drab modern centre and gritty bazaar, it does lack the charm of its counterparts in nearby Rajasthan. Nevertheless, it can be a worthwhile place to pause for a day, particularly around late November and early December, when the old **Moghul tombs** in Gwalior's Muslim quarter host one of India's premier classical **music festivals**.

History

A donative inscription unearthed in a now-defunct sun temple proves that Gwalior was first occupied in the sixth century BC by Hun invaders from the north. Local legend, however, attributes the founding of the fort to the Kuchwaha prince **Suraj Sen**, said to have been cured of leprosy during the tenth century by the hermit **Gwalipa** after whom the city is named. The water tank where the miracle took place, the Suraj Kund, remains intact, as do a pair of ornate temples, the Sasbahu Mandirs, erected by the

Rajput clan. The Kuchwahas' successors, the Parihars, were brutally overthrown in 1232 by **Iltutmish**, following an eleven-month siege. Before the fort eventually fell to the Muslim army, the Rajput women trapped inside committed mass suicide by self-immolation. Afterwards, the Delhi Sultan added to the carnage by ordering the execution, outside his tent, of all seven hundred prisoners taken in the battle.

A third Rajput dynasty, the **Tomars**, retook Gwalior in 1398, and ushered in the city's "golden age". Under **Man Singh**, who ascended to the Tomar *gadi* in 1486, the hilltop gained the magnificent palaces and fortifications that were to earn it the epithet "the pearl in the necklace of the castles of Hind". Skirmishes with neighbouring powers dogged the Rajputs' rule, however, until 1517 when the **Lodis** from Delhi besieged the fort for the second time. On this occasion they were successful. Man Singh was slain, and his son, who managed to fend off the attackers for another twelve months, finally surrendered. Thereafter, Gwalior was ruled by a succession of Muslim overlords, including Babur, Humayun and Sher Shah, before falling to Akbar.

With the decline of the Moghuls, the **Marathas** – a confederacy of Hindu dynasties from the Deccan region – worked their way northwards into the power vacuum. Gwalior became the base of the most powerful of the four Maratha clans, the **Scindias**, in 1754. Twenty-six years later, wily British East India Company troops conquered the fort in an audacious night raid, using rope ladders and socks stuffed with cotton to muffle the sound of their approach. Within hours, the citadel was overrun, and Gwalior became a British feudatory state ruled by a succession of puppet rajas. The most famous of these, the immensely rich Jayaji Rao Scindia (1843–86), remained loyal to the British during the 1858 Mutiny, although 6500 of his troops joined the opposing forces led by Tantia Topia and the infamous **Rani Lakshmi Bai** of Jhansi (see p.319). Both rebel leaders were killed in the ensuing battle, and the Maharaja quickly resumed his role as host to some of the grandest viceregal dinners, royal visits and tiger hunts ever witnessed by the Raj. The Scindias remained influential after Independence, and still live in Gwalior; the Maharaja was until recently a high-ranking minister in the Congress government, while his aged mother is prominent in the far-right Hindu-revivalist BJP. The royal family's political fortunes, quarrels and marriages continue to provide fodder for voracious gossip columnists.

Arrival and information

Gwalior's mainline **railway station**, linked to Delhi, Agra, Jhansi and Bhopal by the fast *Shatabdi Express*, lies in the east of the city, just around the corner from the **government bus stand**. Apart from the handful of cheap lodges nearby, most of the accommodation is an auto-rickshaw ride away to the west, down the busy MLB (Maharani Lakshmi Bai) Rd. If you're travelling light, you could save on the fare by squeezing into one of the inexpensive tempos that run along the main street outside the station. Gwalior **airport**, 9km to the northeast of the centre, is served by both taxis and auto-rickshaws. The **private bus stand** is inconveniently situated on the southwestern edge of town.

MPTDC have a helpful **information** counter at their *Hotel Tansen* (☎34370 or 342606), ten minutes' walk southeast of the train station on Gandhi Rd. If you need to **change money**, and are not staying in a hotel with a foreign exchange facility, the *State Bank of India* (Mon–Fri 10am–2pm, Sat 10am–noon) is at the heart of the bazaar district, on **Jayaji Chowk**, near the **GPO**.

> The telephone **area code** for Gwalior is ☎0751.

The fort

Gwalior's imposing **fort** (daily 8am–6pm; Rs0.50) sprawls over a three-kilometre-long, narrow outcrop of sandstone to the north of the modern city. Its mighty turreted battlements encompass no less than six palaces, three temples, and several water tanks and cisterns, as well as a prestigious public school and a shiny new Sikh Gurudwara.

Two routes wind up the hill. In the west, a motorable track climbs the steep gorge of the **Urwahi valley**, passing a line of rock-cut Jain statues along the way. The other, more accessible entrance is on the northwest corner of the cliff, at the head of a long stepped ramp. The two can be combined by taking a rickshaw to the Urwahi side, then walking across the plateau and dropping down via the northeastern entrance to the museum and Jama Masjid, from where it's easier to pick up a rickshaw back into town.

The northeastern approach and museum

The **northeastern approach** to the fort leads under five successive fortified **gateways**. The first, the **Alamgiri gate**, was built by Matamad Khan in 1660 in honour of the Moghul emperor Aurangzeb. Beyond its small courtyard, the **Badalgarh gate**, named after Man Singh's uncle Badal (also known as the "**Hindola**" after the *hindol*, or "swing", that used to hang from it) is in the same Hindu style as the hill-top palace, with two round turrets raised above its doorway.

The small two-storeyed **Gujuri Mahal**, to the right of the Badalgarh gate, was built by Man Singh to woo his favourite Rani, Mrignayani, when she was still a peasant girl. According to legend, the Raja first became smitten with the "fawn-eyed" Gujur tribeswoman when he saw her wrestle apart a pair of water buffalo during an expedition in the forest; but she would not agree to marry him until he supplied the new palace with water from her village well – the source of her superhuman strength. The elegant sandstone palace now houses Gwalior's **archeological museum** (Tues–Sun 10am–5pm; Rs2), where the large exhibition of sculpture, inscriptions and painting is well worth a look, even if the labels are woefully uninformative. Highlights include the twin lion capitals from Vidisha in gallery two; the massive lintel carved with a depiction of "the humbling of Bali" in gallery seven; and gallery nine's erotic bas-relief, in which a prince is shown gently removing the top of his beloved's *sari*. Unfortunately, the real *pièce de résistance* is locked away in its vaults. The priceless **Salabhanjika** is a small, exquisitely carved female figurine found in the ruins of the temple at Gyaraspur (see p.368). Noted for her sensuous curves and sublime facial expression, the statue is often dubbed "India's Mona Lisa". Plaster casts and photographs are usually on display somewhere in the building.

The next gateway up the hill, the **Ganesh gate**, dates from the mid-fifth century. Close by stand an old pigeon coop, or *kabutar khana*, and (on the far side of the arch) a modern Hindu shrine assembled from the ruins of an earlier one dedicated to the sage **Gwalipa**, which Muhamad Khan replaced with a mosque in 1664. Before arriving at the **Lakshman gate**, you pass a restructured ninth-century Vishnu temple, the **Chatarbhunj** ("four-armed") **mandir**; a Muslim memorial to one of Ibrahin Lodi's nobles who died during the siege of Gwalior in 1518; and a flight of steps up to some unremarkable Jain rock-cut statues. The fifth and final gateway, the **Hathiya** ("Elephant") **Paur**, the most spectacular in the series, forms the entrance to the Man Mandir. Its twin turrets and ornate blue tilework are contiguous with the rest of the massive stone facade.

The Man Mandir

Towering above the northeastern approach to the fort, the **Man Mandir** has to be one of the finest early Hindu palaces in India. Built between 1486 and 1517 by the Tomar ruler Man Singh, it's known as the "Chit Mandir", or "painted palace", for the rich ceramic **mosaics** that encrust its facade. The best preserved fragments of tilework, on its south side, can be seen from the bank left of the main Hathiya Paur gateway. Spread in luxurious bands of turquoise, emerald-green and yellow across the ornate stonework are tigers, elephants, peacocks, banana trees and crocodiles brandishing flowers.

By contrast, the **interior** of the four-storeyed palace is very plain. Some of the larger halls, however, do contain fine pierced-stone *jali* screens, behind which the women of the palace would assemble to receive instruction from Gwalior's great music gurus. The circular chambers in the lower storeys were formerly the palace dungeons. Prisoners incarcerated here in Moghul times were fed on a preparation made with boiled poppy heads called *poust* – a cruelly ingenious form of torture that ensured a protracted and painful death from malnourishment and drug addiction.

Around the Man Mandir

The **Vikram Mandir** (1516), next door to the Man Mandir, is joined to Man Singh's palace by a network of passages hidden in the thick outer walls. The **Karam Mandir**, a two-storeyed Hindu building with a long colonnaded hall at its centre, stands further to the north, a short walk from the remnants of the now-derelict Jehangiri and Shah Jehan palaces. In the far northwestern corner of the enclosure is the large **Jauhar Kund**, the water tank where, in 1232, the women of the Parihar court performed mass suicide by self-immolation, to avoid capture by Iltutmish's advancing army.

The Teli-ka-Mandir and Suraj Kund

The thirty-metre-tall **Teli-ka-Mandir**, on the south side of the plateau, is the oldest surviving monument in the fort. Dating from the mid-eighth century, it consists of a huge rectangular sanctuary tower capped with an unusual vaulted-arch roof, whose *peepal*-leaf shape derives from the *chaitya* windows of much earlier rock-cut Buddhist caves. In the aftermath of the Gwalior Mutiny in 1858, the temple, dedicated to Vishnu, was used by the British as a soda factory. The ASI are now carrying out extensive restoration work.

Set back from the road at the head of the Urwahi ravine, just north of the Teli-ka-Mandir, the **Suraj Kund** is the hundred-metre-long tank whose magical waters are supposed to have cured the tenth-century ruler Suraj Sen, later Suraj Pal, of leprosy.

The Sasbahu Mandirs and Sikh Gurudwara

The **Sasbahu**, or "mother- and daughter-in-law", temples overlook the city from the eastern edge of the fort, near the unsightly TV mast. The larger of the pair has a three-storey *mandapa* (assembly hall), supported by four intricate pillars, while the smaller one consists of an open-sided porch with a pyramidal roof. Both were erected late in the eleventh century and are dedicated, like the Teli-ka-Mandir, to Vishnu.

The huge gold-domed marble building to the south is a modern **Sikh Gurudwara**. Built to commemorate a Sikh hero who was imprisoned in the fort, the temple attracts a constant stream of pilgrims, most of whom drive here in specially converted "Public Carrier" trucks from the Punjab. Along the road leading to it, you'll pass groups of men clad in the traditional garb of Sikh warriors – long blue *kurtas*, bulky turbans, daggers and spears held over their shoulders – filing along like foot-soldiers from a bygone era. The Gurudwara's cool marble courtyard, filled with the strains of devotional music, makes an atmospheric place to escape the heat. Before entering, make sure you cover your arms, legs and head, remove your socks and shoes, and wash your feet in the tank at the bottom of the steps. Tobacco is strictly prohibited inside the complex.

The rock-cut Jain sculptures

The sheer sandstone cliffs around the fort harbour some imposing **rock-cut Jain sculpture**. Carved between the seventh and fifteenth centuries, most of the figures are large honey-coloured icons of the twenty-four Jain Teacher-Saviours – the *tirthankaras*, or "Crossing Makers", depicted in the characteristic standing pose, their arms held stiffly at their sides, or sitting cross-legged, the palms of their hands upturned, staring serenely into the distance. Many lost their faces and genitalia when Babur's iconoclastic army descended on the city in 1527.

The larger of the two main groups lines the southwestern approach to the fort, along the sides of the **Urwahi** ravine. The largest image, to the side of the road near Urwahi Gate, portrays Adinath, 19m tall, with decorative nipples, a head of tightly curled hair, and drooping ears, standing on a lotus bloom beside several smaller statues. Worshippers leave flowers and incense at his colossal feet. The group is well preserved and the statues, including elephants and heavenly *apsaras*, are more or less intact; unfortunately it also doubles as a toilet which can be off-putting. A little further from the fort, on the other side of the road, another company of *tirthankaras* enjoys a more dramatic situation, looking over a natural gorge. All have lost their faces, save a proud trio sheltered by a delicate canopy.

The third collection stands on the southeast corner of the plateau, overlooking the city from a narrow ledge. To get there, follow the main road north along the foot of the cliff from Phool Bagh, near the **Rani Jhansi memorial**, until you see a paved path winding up the hill from behind a row of houses on the left. Once again, the *tirthankaras*, which are numbered, occupy deep recesses hewn from the rock wall. One of the few not defaced by the Muslim invaders, no. #10, is still visited by Gwalior's small Jain community as a shrine. After bathing in the spring in cave no. 1, devotees leave offerings of flowers and rice at the *tirthankara*'s gigantic feet.

The old town

A number of interesting Islamic monuments are tucked away down the narrow, dusty back streets of Gwalior's predominantly Muslim **old town**, clustered around the north and northeast corners of the hill. The **Jama Masjid** stands close to the Gujuri Mahal, near the main entrance to the fort. Erected in 1661 by Muhamad Khan, using sandstone quarried from the plateau above, the beautifully preserved mosque has two slender minarets, and three bulbous onion domes crowned with golden spires.

The city's most famous Muslim building, however, is set amid balding lawns and unruly bougainvillea bushes 1km further east. The sixteenth-century **Tomb of Ghaus Muhammed**, an Afghan prince who helped Babur take Gwalior fort, is a fine specimen of early Moghul architecture and a popular local shrine. Elegant hexagonal pavilions stand at each of its four corners, surrounding a large central dome formerly plastered with blue-glazed tiles; its walls are inlaid with exquisite pierced-stone *jali* screens, whose complex geometric patterns are best admired from the incense-filled interior.

The second and smaller of the tombs in the gardens is that of the famous Moghul singer-musician **Tansen**, one of the "Nine Jewels" of emperor Akbar's court. Every year, performers and aficionados from all over India flock here for Gwalior's annual **music festival** (Nov–Dec). At other times, impromptu recitals of *Qawwaali*, Islamic devotional singing accompanied on the harmonium (see p.97), take place on the terrace outside. Local superstition holds that the leaves of the **tamarind tree** growing on the plinth nearby have a salutary effect on the singing voice, which explains why its bottom branches have been stripped bare. **To get there** from the station, take a rickshaw (Rs15) or a tempo bound for Hazira (Rs2).

The Jai Vilas palace

Due south of the fort, in the heart of Gwalior's upper-class neighbourhood, the **Jai Vilas palace** (Tues–Sun 9.30am–5pm; Rs30; no photos) is one of India's most grandiose and eccentric nineteenth-century relics. It was built in 1875 by Jayaji Rao Scindia. Wanting his residence to rival those of his colonial overlords in Britain, he dispatched his friend Colonel Michael Filose – "Mikul Sahib", the descendant of an Italian mercenary – on a grand tour of Europe to seek inspiration. A year or so later, Filose returned with a vast shipment of furniture, fabric, paintings, tapestries and cut-glass, together with the blueprints for a building that borrowed heavily from Buckingham Palace, Versailles, and a host of Greek ruins and Italian-Baroque stately homes. The result is an improbable blend of Doric, Tuscan and Corinthian architecture, with one of the most shamelessly over-the-top interiors you're likely to see outside Hollywood.

The Scindias, who still occupy parts of the palace, have opened two wings to the public. The one nearest the main entrance has been converted into a **museum** of the more valuable and extraordinary artefacts accumulated by the rulers of Gwalior. Collecting dust in the dozens of rooms and creaky wood-panelled corridors are countless Moghul paintings, Persian rugs, gold and silver ornaments, and pieces of antique furniture acquired by Filose when Louis XVI's estate was sold off piecemeal after the French Revolution. Elsewhere, you'll come across a swing made from Venetian cut-glass which the royal family used to celebrate Krishna's birthday, and a room full of stuffed tigers and sepia photographs that show the Maharaja posing stiffly with rows of pipe-smoking pith-helmeted British guests. Finally, a room upstairs is given over to **erotica**. The *chowkidar* will gleefully point out its centrepiece: a life-size marble statue of a woman succumbing with some elan to the amorous advances of a swan.

The palace's most extravagant wing lies across the courtyard from the museum. The **durbar hall** was where the Maharaja entertained important visitors, among them the Prince of Wales (later Edward VII), who descended on Gwalior in 1875 with an entourage of one thousand people. Displayed in the banquet hall on the ground floor is a silver toy train used by Jayaji Rao Scindia to dispense brandy and cigars after dinner; the Maharaja would tease anyone he didn't like by not stopping the electric locomotive when it reached them. A sweeping Belgian glass staircase leads from the lobby to the gargantuan assembly hall upstairs. Suspended from its ceiling are the world's biggest **chandeliers**. At over three and a half tonnes apiece, they could not be installed until the strength of the roof had been tested with eight elephants – a feat that necessitated the construction of a 500-metre-long earth ramp. The rug lining the floor of the hall is equally enormous. Woven by inmates of Gwalior jail, it took twelve years to complete and, at over forty metres in length, is the largest handmade carpet in Asia.

Accommodation

Most of Gwalior's **hotels** are strung between the railway station and Lashkar, the main bazaar area, along the hectic MLB Rd. Two notable exceptions are the MPTDC *Hotel Tansen*, around the corner from the train station, and the luxurious *Usha Kiran Palace*, tucked away in its own grounds south of the main thoroughfare, near the Jai Vilas palace. Standards at the cheaper end of the market are particularly low, with cramped windowless cells the norm; those we have listed have attached baths (but not all have hot water) and 24-hour checkout, and offer cheaper rates for single travellers.

Ambika, Tansen Rd, Padav (☎326172). Reasonably clean budget hotel fifteen minutes' walk from the train station. The rooms at the back escape the noise from the flyover. ③.

Banjara, High Court Lane (☎321637). Smart hotel next to *Man Mandir*; good restaurant. ④–⑥.

Bhagwati, Anturam Shivari Chowk, Nai Sarak (☎327428). Basic, but best of the budget bunch if you want to be near the bazaar. Rock-bottom rates, and fort views from some rooms. ①.

Fort View, MLB Rd (☎331586). Plain but comfortable and well managed, with light rooms, *Star TV* and some a/c. "Regular" rooms are particularly good value. ③–⑥.

India, Station Rd (☎24983). No-frills lodge run by *Indian Coffee Workers' Co-op*; clean, but noisy rooms overlooking main street. Deluxe rate gets you a Western toilet. Handy for the station. ③.

Man Mandir, High Court Lane (☎321442). Small, friendly, well maintained, and good value, but hard to find. A rickshaw ride from the station. ②.
MPTDC Tansen, 6-A Gandhi Rd (☎340370). Large, efficient hotel in its own gardens near the station, with spacious rooms (some a/c) and a good restaurant. Popular with business travellers, so advance booking is recommended. ⑤–⑥.
Park View, near Rani Jhansi memorial, Phool Bagh Gate, MLB Rd (☎21323). In a dingy basement but clean enough. Some a/c rooms. ④–⑤.
Regency, near bus stand (☎340671). Modern and ritzy, with *Star TV*, foreign exchange, health club (with jacuzzi) and a pool. ⑥–⑧.
Safari, Railway Station Market (☎340638). Identical to *India*, only marginally cheaper and with a more recent lick of paint. ③.
Ushan Kiran Palace, Jayendraganj, Lakshar (☎323213). Former Maharaja's guest house now run by *Welcomgroup* as an opulent 5-star. Period furnishings, large verandahs, and a lawn with wicker chairs preserve some of its original *fin de siècle* feel. ⑧–⑨.

Eating

With a couple of exceptions, all the best **places to eat** in Gwalior are in the mid- and top-of-the-range hotels, where main dishes set you back anywhere between thirty and a hundred rupees. More basic, and much **cheaper** *dal*, *subzi* and *roti* meals are doled up on stainless steel plates at the row of dodgy *dhabas* outside the railway station. Look out too for the **juice bars** dotted around Jayaji Chowk, over in the west end of town, which serve glasses of refreshing, freshly squeezed fruit juice.

Banjara, High Court Lane. A good range of mainly Indian dishes, imaginative daily specials, and efficient service. Western and south Indian breakfasts.
Indian Coffee House, Station Rd. Delicious *dosas* and other south Indian snacks, plain or with "special" nut and veg fillings. Opens 7.30am for breakfast – *iddlis* and eggs.
Tansen, Gandhi Rd. Run-of-the-mill menu includes several *tandoori* and vegetarian options at moderate prices, with some milder *chow meins* and *chop sueys*.
Ushan Kiran, Jayendraganj. Modest selection of (expensive) gourmet Indian and Western food, with lots of mouthwatering Mughlai-style dishes. The buffet lunches are good for a splurge.

Note that the city of **JHANSI**, the major *Central Railway* junction used by travellers heading to the temples at **Khajuraho**, is in Uttar Pradesh, and is thus covered on p.317.

Shivpuri

SHIVPURI, the former summer capital of the Scindias, lies 114km southwest of Gwalior, at a crossroads on the main Jhansi–Jaipur highway. Local rulers from the Moghuls onwards were drawn here by the abundance of game in the area's lush deciduous forests. These days, however, all but a few fragments of woodland remain, and the small market town is now marooned in a landscape of shaly scrub, dried-up riverbeds and escarpments peppered with dusty brown trees. Apart from a couple of nineteenth-century cenotaphs and a minor-league national park, very little remains of Shivpuri's princely past, and the only plausible reason to call in here is to break a journey to Rajasthan's famous Ranthambore wildlife reserve, 180km northwest.

The town's main monuments, the **chhatris**, or tombs, of the Scindia family, stand a two-kilometre tonga ride from the bus stand, by the side of the road leading to the MPTDC *Tourist Village*. Facing each other across an ornamental garden, the brilliant white marble cenotaphs fuse Hindu and Islamic styles, juxtaposing slender temple *shikharas* with Moghul domes and pavilions. The larger of the pair, dedicated to the dowager queen Maharani Raje Scindia, boasts a grand double-storeyed facade that opens onto a water tank intersected by walkways. Her son Madho Rao Scindia's *chhatri* is even more ornate. Standing on a raised platform and flanked by ersatz Victorian street lamps, its intricately carved walls are inlaid with lapis lazuli and onyx. Both enshrine life-size effigies of the Scindias, which local musicians regale with devotional music in the evenings.

Shivpuri's other attraction, the **Madhav national park**, is not worth bothering with unless you have your own vehicle. The most exciting animals you're likely to spot are run-of-the-mill Indian deer: *cheetal, chinkara, nilgai, sambar* and *chausingha*. Jeeps can be rented through MPTDC, at the reception desk of the *Tourist Village*, for full- or half-day tours, and the unexciting **tiger safari** (the animals are captive). Birdwatchers may find Madhav marginally more inspiring, however, as its large artificial (and crocodile-infested) lakes attract several species of migratory wildfowl during the winter. The rare Indian bustard also nests 40km away to the east, in the **Karera bird sanctuary**, which is only accessible by car.

Practicalities

Shivpuri can be reached by **bus** from both Gwalior and Jhansi, 84km east, as well as from Datia (with a change at Karera). Tongas and more expensive unmetered auto-rick-shaws are on hand at the bus stand, in the middle of town, to ferry visitors out to Shivpuri's two best **hotels**, both run by MPTDC. *Chinkara Motel* (☎07492/2297; ④), on the main Bombay–Agra NH3, has four basic but clean non-a/c rooms; the lakeside *Tourist Village* (☎07492/2600; ⑤–⑥), 3km from the bus stand, is more peaceful and comfortable, with spacious and modern chalets, attached bathrooms, a/c on request, and a good licensed restaurant. Ideally, you should reserve at least five days in advance (through any MPTDC office).

The MPTDC hotels are also the best places to **eat**. If you're on a tight budget, there are a handful of grotty *dhabas* on the main street near the bus stand.

Datia

Constructed by Bir Singh Deo at the height of the Bundela's "golden age", the majestic multi-storeyed palace at **DATIA**, 30km northwest of Jhansi, is regarded as one of the finest Rajput buildings in India. Although few of the visitors who spy the exotic hulk of yellow-brown ramparts, cupolas and domed pavilions from the nearby railway line actually stop here, those that do are rarely disappointed. The palace presides from the top of a rocky outcrop at the edge of a busy market town over a mass of white- and blue-washed brick houses, packed tightly onto a saucer-shaped depression in the plains.

The **Nrsing Dev Palace** stands in the north of town, separated from the train and bus stations by a tangle of narrow streets and lanes that are difficult to negotiate without the aid of a rickshaw-*wallah*. Decorated with paintings and stone carving, the main entrance leads into the gloomy bowels of the building under a massive five-storey facade. Half the fun of the labyrinthine palace is trying to find a path from its pitch-black subterranean chambers, hewn out of the solid base of the hill for use during the hot season, to the Rani's airy apartment on the top floor. In between, a maze of cross-cutting corridors, flying walkways, walls encrusted with fragments of green, yellow and turquoise ceramic tiles, hidden passages, latticed screens and archways, pavilions, and suites of apartments lead you in ever-decreasing circles, until you eventually run out of staircases. The views from the upper storeys are breathtaking. Scattered around the town below are several other Rajput monuments, including a sprawling fort, the **Bharat**

Garh, and the stately home of Datia's present ruling family. Although not officially open, you can stroll into the compound where the obliging *chowkidar* may show you round the dusty and disorganized durbar hall, which stands next to a multi-domed whitewashed Govind Mandir (Krishna temple). Immediately to the north, a large tank, the **Karna Sagar**, stands amid *dhobi ghats* and the ruins of temples and *chhatris*. The white pinnacles of Sonagiri are also visible on the horizon.

Nearer the bus stand, the less impressive of Datia's two hill-top palaces, the **Raj Garh**, houses a small **museum** (Tues–Sat 10am–5pm; free), whose dull collection of sculpture and painting is far less inspiring than the views from its balcony.

Practicalities

Datia is on the main Delhi–Bombay railway line, and served by bus or train from both Jhansi and Gwalior. Tongas and cycle-rickshaws ferry passengers into town from the small **railway station**, 2km southwest, while **buses** pull in at a lot on the south side of the centre. If you're coming from Shivpuri, 97km west, you'll have to change buses at Karera. There's no **accommodation** in town; the palace has to be visited as a day trip from Jhansi, or by breaking a journey to or from Gwalior, 71km northwest. The only food available is standard *dhaba* fare.

Sonagiri

SONAGIRI, 61km southeast of Gwalior, is among the more ethereal landmarks punctuating the Delhi–Bombay rail journey. Flowing down the east-facing slope of a solitary hillock, deep in the central Indian countryside, 84 gleaming white shrines mark the spot where the legendary King Nanganang Kumar, together with five-and-a-half *crore* of his followers, achieved liberation from the cycle of rebirth. Today the site, sacred to **Digambar** ("Sky-clad") **Jains**, makes an atmospheric pause for a couple of hours en route to one of the nearby cities.

Minibuses to Sonagiri from the mainline station pull in at the "manager's office" in a small **village square**, where you can check that it's OK to visit. From here, most pilgrims make for the **"mirror temple"**, down the lane to the left, in which artists can be seen fashioning mosaics of *tirthankaras* from coloured glass and mirrors. More somber spiritual pursuits take place in the seminary at the back of the square, next to the main entrance. Old Digambar monks conduct religious discussions with pilgrims in the courtyard, their distinctive yellow wooden water pots (*dariyes*) and peacock-feather whisks beside them. For most of the year, these ascetics wander naked around the country, returning to monasteries for a few months to give and receive teachings. More secular Jains notch up credits on the cosmic balance sheet by making gifts to religious establishments instead – as evidenced by the dozens of donatory plaques set in the **marble walkway** leading up the hill. Crowning the summit of Sonagiri, the main **temple** houses a colossal *tirthankara* icon, while below it, a ceramic scale model of **Mount Meru**, the axial mountain said by Jains to support the cosmos, looks out over the cascade of whitewashed spires and fluttering yellow pennants to the distant plains.

Practicalities

Without your own vehicle, the only way to get to Sonagiri is by **train**. Check the timings of onward services carefully before leaving the station, as there's very little **accommodation**. If you get stuck, the office in the main square will fix you a dorm bed for a night in the Jain *dharamshala*. Pure vegetarian **food**, snacks, *chai* and cold drinks are available at the insanitary-looking stall opposite the bus stand.

Orchha

ORCHHA, literally "hidden place", certainly lives up to its name. Languishing amid a tangle of scrubby *dhak* forest, 18km southeast of Jhansi, the former capital of the **Bundela** dynasty siphons off only a fraction of the tourist traffic bound for Khajuraho on the nearby highway. The deserted medieval town is, nevertheless, an architectural gem, and the ideal place to break the long journey to the temples. Guano-splashed temple *shikharas*, derelict palaces, *havelis* and weed-choked sandstone cenotaphs lie neglected by the banks of the tranquil River Betwa – home to troupes of black-faced langurs, vultures, and wheeling flocks of bright green parakeets.

Clustered around the foot of the exotic ruins, a sleepy village of neatly painted houses, market stalls, and a couple of attractive government hotels provide most of the basic amenities. Orchha doesn't yet have a telephone link with the rest of India, and the electricity supply is intermittent, adding to the sense of isolation that makes this such a fine place to unwind. That said, it's fast catching on as a popular destination for a night-halt; small parties of tourists arrive at lunch time and move on the next morning, but before noon you may find you have the place virtually to yourself.

History

According to one legend, the name of Orchha's founding dynasty, the **Bundelas**, derives from an eleventh-century ancestor who sacrificed five severed heads (or five drops of his own blood) to the mountain goddess Vindhyabatha – a deed that earned him the epithet of "Vindhyela", or "he who offered blood". Expelled by his brothers from their homeland near Varanasi, Vindhyela and his descendants roamed central India until finally settling at **Garkhundar**, the first capital of Bundelkhand. Pushed on by the Delhi Sultan Tuqluq late in the fifteenth century, the Bundelas decamped 45km to a more remote and defensible jungle site. The old Malwan outpost at **Orchha**, astride an island formed by a sharp bend in the River Betwa, proved an ideal platform from which to dominate the region when the Tuqluqs' power eventually declined.

Work on Orchha's magnificent fortifications, palaces and temples was started by Raja **Rudra Pratap** soon after the move, and continued after he was killed in 1531 trying to wrestle a cow from the clutches of a tiger. Thereafter, the dynasty's fortunes depended on the goodwill of their mighty neighbours, the **Moghuls**. After being defeated in battle by Akbar, the proud and pious **Madhukar Shah** nearly signed his clan's death warrant by showing up at the imperial court with a red *tilak* smeared on his forehead – a mark banned by the staunchly Muslim emperor. Luckily for the Bundelas, however, Madhukar's bold gesture earned Akbar's respect, and the two became friends – an alliance fostered in the years that followed by Orchha's most illustrious Raja, **Bir Singh Deo**. Long before he acceded to the throne, the ambitious young Bundela saw the value of keeping on the right side of his counterpart in Delhi, Prince Salim. In 1601, he assassinated the latter's much-loathed adversary, **Abdul Fazal**, and sent Salim the decapitated head on a platter. The murder infuriated Akbar but was never forgotten by his son, who, when he became Emperor Jehangir in 1605, rewarded Bir Singh Deo's brutal act by helping him to seize the Bundela throne from his elder brother Ram Shah.

During his 22-year rule, Bir Singh Deo erected a total of 52 forts and palaces across the region, including the citadel at **Jhansi**, the rambling Nrsing Dev at **Datia** (see p.382), and many of Orchha's finest buildings. After he was killed by bandits while returning from the Deccan with a camel-train full of booty in 1627, however, Bundelkhand's relations with the Moghuls rapidly deteriorated. Attacks by the armies of Shah Jehan, Aurangzeb, and the Marathas ensued, and a spate of eighteenth-century Jat peasant uprisings finally forced the Bundelas to flee Orchha for the comparative safety of **Tikamgarh**. Apart from the Sheesh Mahal, now converted into a small hotel, the magnificent monuments have lain virtually deserted ever since.

Arrival and information

Tightly packed **tempos** and **buses** from Jhansi bus station run regularly to Orchha's main crossroads, 18km away: both take 20 to 40 minutes (depending on the number of stops), and cost Rs5. An auto-rickshaw from Jhansi railway or bus station will set you back around Rs100. Coming from **Khajuraho**, you can ask to be dropped at the Orchha turning on the main road, from where you'll have to hail another bus or rickshaw for the last 7km. If you're heading in the other direction, don't risk flagging the express MPSRTC coaches down on the highway, as they're often full. Instead, get to Jhansi early and arrange a ticket before the Delhi/Agra trains get in. More comfortable private **jeeps** (with drivers) cut the journey time to Khajuraho – they cost upwards of Rs1200 (one way), and can be rented at the bus station, or through the manager of the MPTDC *Sheesh Mahal* hotel, who can also arrange day trips.

Jhansi is the nearest place to **change money** and make STD **telephone calls**.

The monuments

Though the best preserved of Orchha's scattered palaces, temples, tombs and gardens lie within comfortable walking distance of the village and can be seen – at breakneck speed – in a day, to get the most of a trip you should plan on staying the night. If you want to catch up on the history of the palaces and the significance of their wall paintings, it's worth using MPTDC's excellent **walkman tour** of the highlights (2hr; Rs25, plus Rs500 deposit), that sets a lively scene, with medieval Indian music and easy-to-follow commentary. Ask at the reception desk in the *Sheesh Mahal*.

The Raj Mahal and the Rai Praveen Mahal

The first building you come to across Orchha's medieval granite **bridge**, the **Raj Mahal** (daily 10am–5pm), was started by Rudra Pratap, and completed by one of his successors, the indomitable Madhukar Shah. From the end of the bridge, bear left at the main entrance, and then right before reaching the *Sheesh Mahal Hotel*. Of the two rectangular courtyards inside, the second, formerly used by the Bundela ranis, is the most dramatic. Opulent royal quarters, raised balconies and interlocking walkways rise in symmetrical tiers on all four sides, crowned by domed pavilions and turrets. Those apartments projecting into the quadrangle on the ground floor belonged to the most favoured queens. As you wander around, look out for the fragments of mirror-inlay and vibrant **painting** plastered over their walls and ceilings. Some of the friezes are still in remarkable condition, depicting Vishnu's various outlandish incarnations, court and hunting scenes, and lively festivals involving dancers, musicians and jugglers. The resident *chowkidar* is also an excellent guide.

Reached via a path that leads from the Raj Mahal around the northern side of the hill, the **Rai Praveen Mahal** is a small, double-storeyed brick apartment built by Raja Indramani for his concubine in the mid-1670s. The gifted poetess, musician and dancer, Rai Praveen, beguiled the Moghul emperor Akbar when she was sent to him as a gift, but was eventually returned to Orchha to live out her remaining days. Set amid the well-watered lawns of the **Anand Mahal gardens**, it has a main assembly hall on the ground floor (used to host music and dance performances), a boudoir upstairs, and cool underground apartments.

The Jahangir Mahal

Orchha's single most admired palace, the **Jahangir Mahal**, was built by Bir Singh Deo as a monumental welcome present for the Moghul emperor when he paid a state visit here in the seventeenth century. Jahangir had come to invest his old ally with the sword of Abdul Fazal – the emperor's erstwhile enemy whom Bir Singh had murdered some years earlier. Entered through an ornate ceremonial gateway, the main, east-facing facade is still encrusted with turquoise tiles. Two stone elephants flank the stairway, holding bells in their trunks to announce the arrival of the Raja. Once again, three storeys of elegant hanging balconies, terraces, apartments and onion domes are piled around a central courtyard. This palace, however, has a much lighter feel, with countless windows and pierced stone screens looking out over the exotic Orchha skyline to the west, and a sea of treetops and ruined temples in the other direction.

The Sheesh Mahal

Built during the early eighteenth century, long after Orchha's demise, the **Sheesh Mahal** ("Palace of Mirrors") was originally intended as an exclusive country retreat for the local Raja, Udait Singh. Following Independence, however, the property was inherited by the state government, who now run it as a small hotel. The low, rather squat palace stands between the Raj Mahal and the Jehangir Mahal, at the far end of an open-sided courtyard. Covered in a coat of whitewash and stripped of most of its Persian rugs and antiques, the building retains little of its former splendour, though it does offer stunning views from its upper terraces and turrets. The only rooms worth a peep – assuming they're not occupied (check with reception) – are the palatial numbers one and two, which contain original bathroom fittings.

Around the village

Dotted **around the village** below the hill are several other interesting monuments. The **Ram Raja Mandir** stands at the end of the small bazaar, in a cool marble-tiled courtyard. Local legend has it that Madhukar Shah constructed the building as a palace for his wife, Rani Ganesha, and it only became a temple after a Rama icon, which had the queen had dutifully carried all the way from her home town of Ayodhya, could not be lifted from the spot where she first set it down. The god, it seems, had only consented to the move on condition that he be immediately enshrined in his own purpose-built temple. When she got back to Orchha, however, the Rani was dismayed to find the Chatturbuj temple still unfinished. True to its word, when the time came to transport the deity over to the new shrine, it remained stuck to the floor, where it has stood ever since. Nowadays, the pink and yellow Ram Raja Mandir is a popular pilgrimage site. During major Rama festivals, thousands of worshippers gather in front of its ornate silver doors to await *darshan* of the garlanded deity inside.

With its huge pointed *shikharas* soaring high above the village, the temple originally supposed to house Rani Ganesha's icon, **Chatturbuj Mandir**, seems on the face of it well worthy of that honour. In cruciform shape, representing the four-armed Vishnu, with seven stories and spacious courtyards ringed by arched balconies, it epitomizes the regal Bundelkhand style, inspired by the Moghuls, but is also influenced by Rajput, Persian and European tastes. It's unusual for a Hindu temple, with very few carvings and a wealth of space – perhaps to accommodate followers of the **bhakti** cult (a form of worship involving large congregations of people rather than a small elite of priests). You can climb up the narrow staircases between storeys to the temple's roof, pierced by an ornate *shikhara* whose niches shelter nesting vultures.

On the other side of Ram Mandir, a path leads through the Moghul-style **Phool Bagh** ornamental garden to **Hardaul ka Baithaka**, a grand pavilion where Bir Singh Deo's second son, Hardaul, ally of Jahangir and romantic paragon, once held court. Newlyweds come here to seek blessing from Hardaul; he was poisoned by his jealous brother who accused him of intimacy with his sister-in-law. The tall towers rising above the gardens like disregarded bridge supports are *dastgirs* (literally "wind-catchers"), Persian-style cooling towers that provided air-conditioning for the neighbouring palace, Palkhi Mahal; they're probably the only ones of their kind surviving in India.

The Lakshminarayan Mandir

The lone **Lakshminarayan Mandir** (daily 10am–5pm; camera Rs2) crowns a rocky hillock just under 1km west of Orchha village, at the end of a long paved pathway. From the square directly behind the Ram Raja temple, the leisurely fifteen-minute stroll is rewarded with more fine views, and excellent seventeenth- and nineteenth-century **paintings**. For a small tip, the resident *chowkidar* will lead you through the galleries inside the temple. Look out for the frieze depicting the battle of Jhansi, in which the Rani appears in an upper room of the fort next to her horse, while musket-bearing British troops scuttle about below. Another great battle scene is the epic encounter between the ten-headed, twenty-armed demon Ravana and Rama's army of monkey soldiers. Elsewhere, episodes from the much-loved Krishna story crop up, as do portraits of the Bundela rajas and their military and architectural achievements. Finally, a side pillar bears a sketch of two very inebriated English soldiers – as much a parody of the colonials' curious customs as an invective against the evils of drink.

The Chhatris

A solemn row of pale brown weed-choked domes and spires, the riverside **Chhatris** are Orchha's most melancholy ruins and a fitting place to wind up a tour of the town. The fourteen cenotaphs, memorials to Bundelkhand's former rulers, are best viewed from the narrow road bridge or, better still, from the boulders on the opposite bank, where you get the full effect of their reflection in the still waters of the Betwa.

Accommodation and eating

Although Orchha only has a few **places to stay**, new hotels are being planned to cope with the recent rise in tourist traffic. For now, the most atmospheric and stylish is the MPTDC *Sheesh Mahal* (④–⑦), a converted eighteenth-century palace. Formerly the local Raja's country bolt-hole, this small, very friendly hotel has one single and seven non-a/c doubles – all excellent value, with attached bathrooms and superb views. If you can afford it, treat yourself to a romantic night in the royal apartment (⑦). Perks include candlelit dinner on your own private verandah, a bath-tub, and the ultimate loo with a view. Advance booking is recommended. MPTDC also has accommodation at its peaceful a/c and non a/c *Betwa Cottages* (⑤–⑥), each with a double room and modern bathroom, in gardens outside the village on the banks of the river.

Best of the **cheap accommodation** in the heart of the bazaar is *Palkhi Mahal* (②), a beautiful old *haveli* overlooking the Phool Bagh, which has two simple but clean and characterful rooms opening on to a terrace, and a six-bedded dorm (Rs25). Rooms in the *Mansarovar* (①), just off the crossroads above a *chai* shop, are a bit poky, but fine for a night or two. As a fall-back, try the *Prayatak Dharamshala* (①), a spartan lodge intended for Hindu pilgrims, down by the moat.

The smartest **place to eat**, and an attractive place to hang out in the evenings, is the colonnaded dining hall in the *Sheesh Mahal*, which serves a good mix of veg and non-veg food, and *tandoori* specials at lunch time. Alternatives include the *Betwa Cottages* (which has the same MPTDC menu), the rooftop *Betwa Tarang*, by the bazaar cross-roads, and a simple *thali* joint beneath it. You can get hot and spicy dishes and the delicious local speciality, Orchha milkcake, from the small stalls around the gate to the Ram Raja temple forecourt.

Khajuraho

The resplendent Hindu temples of **KHAJURAHO**, immaculately restored after almost a millennium of abandonment and neglect, are despite their inaccessibility, among the most essential stops on any itinerary of India's historic monuments. Famed above all

THE EROTIC ART OF KHAJURAHO

Prurient eyes have been hypnotized by the unabashed **erotica** of Khajuraho ever since the "re-discovery" of the site in February 1838. A young British officer of the Bengal Engineers, **TS Burt**, alerted by the talk of his *palki* (palanquin) bearers, had deviated from his official itinerary when he came upon the ancient temples all but engulfed by jungle – "They reared their sun-burnt tops above the huge trees by which they were surrounded, with all the pride of superior height and age. But the chances are, the trees (or jungle rather) will eventually have the best of it".

Frank representations of oral sex, masturbation, copulation with animals, and such acts may have fitted into the mores of the tenth-century Chandellas, but were hardly calculated to meet with the approval of the upstanding officers of Queen Victoria:

> *I found . . . seven Hindoo temples, most beautifully and exquisitely carved as to workmanship, but the sculptor had at times allowed his subject to grow a little warmer than there was any absolute necessity for his doing; indeed some of the sculptures here were extremely indecent and offensive, which I was at first much surprised to find in temples that are professed to be erected for good purposes, and on account of religion. But the religion of the ancient Hindoos can not have been very chaste, if it induced people under the cloak of religion, to design the most disgraceful representations to desecrate their ecclesiastical erections. The palki [palanquin] bearers, however, appeared to take great delight at those, to them, very agreeable novelties, which they took care to point out to all present.*

Burt found the inscription on the steps of the Vishvanatha temple that enabled historians to attribute the site to the Chandellas, and to piece together their genealogy, but it was several more years before Major General Sir Alexander Cunningham produced detailed plans of Khajuraho, drawing the distinction between "Western" and "Eastern" groups that is still applied today. For Cunningham, "all [the sculptures] are highly indecent, and most of them disgustingly obscene".

The erotic images remain the subject of a disproportionate amount of controversy and debate among academics and curious tourists alike. The task of explanation is made more difficult by the fact that even the Chandellas themselves barely mentioned the temples in their literature, and the very name "Khajuraho" may be misleading, simply taken from that of the nearby village.

Among attempts to account for the sexual content of the carvings have been suggestions of links with **tantric** cults, which use sex as a pivotal part of worship. Some claim that they were inspired by the **Kama Sutra**, and similarly intended to serve as a manual on love, while others argue that the sculptures were designed to entertain the gods, divert their wrath, and thus protect the temples against natural calamities. Alternatively, the geometric qualities of certain images have been put forward as evidence that each represents a *yantra*, a pictorial form of a *mantra*, for use in meditation.

The sixteen large panels depicting sexual union that appear along the northern and southern aspects of the three principal temples – Kandariya Mahadeva, Lakshmana and Vishvanatha – concentrate on the junction of the male and the female elements of the temples, the *mandapa* and the *garbha griha* (the "womb" – see p.390). They might therefore have been intended as a visual pun, elaborated by artistic licence.

A radical new approach that ties history and architecture with living traditions has been proposed by Shobita Punja, in her book *Divine Ecstasy* (Penguin, 1992). Citing historic references to Khajuraho under the name of *Shivpuri* – the "City of Shiva" – she uses ancient Sanskrit texts to suggest that the dramatic temples and their celestial hordes represent the **marriage party of Shiva and Parvati**, taking place in a mythical landscape that stretches along the Vindhya Hills to Kalinjar in the east. Thus Punja argues that the lower panel on Vishvanatha's southern walls shows Shiva as a bridegroom accompanied by his faithful bull, Nandi, while the intertwined limbs of the panel above – the couple locked in *mithuna*, assisted by a maiden to either side – show the consummation, with the lustful Brahma a pot-bellied voyeur at their feet.

for the delicate sensuality – and forthright **eroticism** – of their sculpture, they were built between the tenth and twelfth centuries AD as the greatest architectural achievement of the **Chandella** dynasty. Mysteriously, the Chandellas appear to have forgotten about the temples soon afterwards, and it took "re-discovery" by the British before these masterpieces were fully appreciated in India, let alone internationally.

Although Khajuraho might look central on maps of the subcontinent, 400km southeast of Agra and the same distance west of Varanasi, it remains as remote from the Indian mainstream as it was when the temples were built – which is presumably what spared them the depredations of marauders, invaders and zealots that devastated so many early Hindu sites. No train routes cross this extended flood plain, set against the backdrop of the jagged Dantla Hills, and visitors who don't fly straight here are faced with a long bus journey from either of the nearest railheads.

The exquisite intricacy of the **temples** themselves – of which the most spectacular are **Kandariya Mahadeva**, **Vishvanatha** and **Lakshmana**, all in the conglomeration known as the **Western Group** – was made possible by the soft buff-coloured sandstone used in their construction. Considering the propensity of such stone to crumble, they have withstood the ravages of time remarkably well (suggestions that the 25 temples seen today are all that remain of an original 85 can be discounted, in the face of the lack of debris in the vicinity). Much of the ornate **sculpture** that adorns their walls is in such high relief as to be virtually three-dimensional, with strains of pink in the stone helping to imbue the figures with gentle flesh-like tones. The incredible skill of the artisans is evident throughout, with friezes as little as 10cm wide crammed with naturalistic details of ornaments, jewellery, hairstyles and even manicured nails. A huge congregation of gods and goddesses are everywhere in attendance.

To add to the beauty of the whole ensemble, the temples subtly change hue as the day progresses, passing from a warm pink at sunrise, to white under the midday sun, and back to warm pink at sunset. Dramatic floodlights pick them out in the evening, and they glow white beneath a luminous moon.

Arrival, information and local transport

The easiest way to get to Khajuraho is on one of the daily **flights** with *Indian Airlines* or *Modiluft* from Delhi (via Agra), or Varanasi (connecting with Kathmandu). The local **airport** is 5km south of the main square of Khajuraho town; the taxi ride in costs Rs60. The two nearest railheads are at **Jhansi** to the northwest, covered on p.317 (6hr by bus; 3–5 daily), and **Satna** to the southeast (4hr by bus; 5 daily). Most luxury buses, including the one that meets the *Shatabdi Express* at Jhansi on its way from Delhi via Agra to Gwalior, arrive next to *Raja Cafe* on the main square, while local buses terminate less than 1km southeast at the bus stand, within walking distance of most central hotels.

Information

The Government of India **tourist office**, round the corner from the *Raja Cafe*, provides information only (Mon–Fri 9am–5.30pm, Sat 8am–noon; ☎2047); a counter at the airport operates at flight times. Staff at the *MPTDC* counter at the bus stand can book rooms (Mon–Fri 9am–5.30pm, Sat 8am–noon); their main office is at the *Tourist Village* in the *Chandella Cultural Centre* (☎2051 or 2221).

Money can be changed at the *Canara Bank* near the bus stand (Mon–Fri 10am–2pm), or at the *State Bank of India*, Maqbara Building (Mon–Fri 10.45am–2.45pm & 4–5pm; Sat 10.45am–12.45pm & 2.30–3.30pm). The **post office** is near the bus stand.

The telephone **area code** for Khajuraho is ☎07886.

Local transport

Khajuraho is no more than an overgrown cluster of villages, without public transport, and visitors are dependent on the various rented vehicles in competition with each other. **Taxis** and **rental cars** are available at the main square; through *Raja Cafe*, or from operators such as the reliable Sanjay Jain of the *Hotel Jain* (☎2052), *Khajuraho Tours* (☎2033), in the Maqbara building, or *Travel Bureau* (☎2037), on Jain Temples Rd, near the square. Typical costs are Rs200 for half a day, and Rs250 plus Rs4.50 per km for longer journeys. Cycle **rickshaw** drivers ask around Rs25 per hour; trips to the Eastern or Southern groups from town work out around Rs30.

By far the most enjoyable way of getting around, with virtually empty roads, is by **bicycle**; most budget hotels stock them, as do some restaurants (try *Assi Restaurant* on Jain Temples Rd), charging around Rs20 per day.

Guides and organized tours

Among recommended and highly experienced **guides** who can help you make sense of Khajuraho is Ganga, the owner of *Hotel Harmony* (☎2135). Reliable guides can also be contacted through the *Raja Cafe* – charges average around Rs100 for half a day for a group of up to four. **Organized tours** are laid on by the more expensive hotels, while operators such as *Khajuraho Tours* and *Travel Bureau* (see above) can arrange explorations further afield.

Khajuraho: Town and Village

Facilities for visitors are concentrated in the uncluttered avenues of the small modern town of **Khajuraho**; the gates of the Western Group of temples open immediately onto its main square, which is surrounded by hotels and cafes. Curio shops sell everything from clothes, film and jewellery to Tibetan *thangkas*, but the sales pitch of their owners can be aggressive, and it makes sense to be wary of buying anything. Most local people live a pleasant 1.5-kilometre walk or cycle ride away to the east, in the more rustic setting of **Khajuraho Village**, near the **Eastern Group**. Two further temples, loosely termed the **Southern Group**, lie some distance out. Water is a prominent feature of the landscape, with the lake or tank of **Shivsagar** just south of the Western Group,

THE BODY AND THE WOMB

The **Jangha**, or body, of each temple at Khajuraho – the walls between the base (*adisthana*) and the crowning spire (*shikhara*) – is the realm of the celestial. Their support and protection of the whole structure is symbolized by the strange composite animals, embodying strength and intelligence, depicted on two or three ornate encircling belts known as *bhandas*. Despite the popular belief that the copulating couples of Khajuraho represent the lives of ordinary people, according to Shobita Punja (see p.388) the *jangha* here in fact shows the marriage of Shiva and Parvati. She argues that the beautiful nymphs caught in naturalistic everyday poses are expressing surprise and wonder at seeing the god and the wedding party.

The construction of every temple echoes the creation of life itself, developing from a single seed (*bindu*) placed within its foundations. The central image of the temple, be it a *lingam* or a manifestation in human form, is positioned directly over this seed, and immediately under the highest point, the *shikhara*, in the sacred room known as the **Garbha Griha** – the womb. Though surrounded by the diverse manifestations and shapes of the world of matter – most obviously, on the external walls of the temple – the womb remains simple and without ornamentation, a representation of the dark generative nucleus of life.

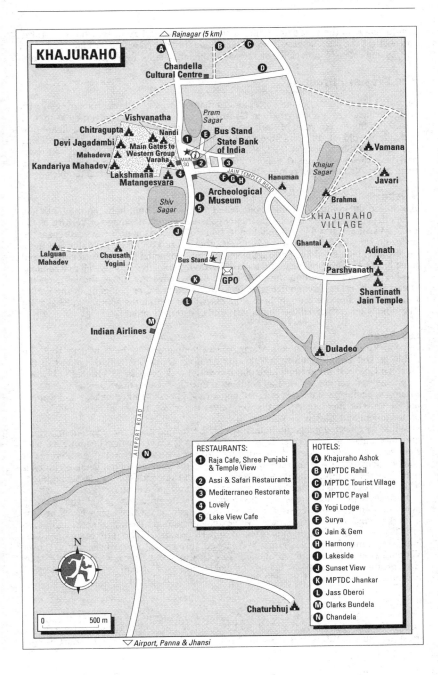

KHAJURAHO

△ Rajnagar (5 km)

Ⓐ Ⓑ Ⓒ
Ⓓ

Chandella
Cultural Centre ▪

Prem
Sagar

Vishvanatha
Chitragupta ▲   Nandi
Devi Jagadambi ▲   ▲
Mahadeva ▲   Main Gates to
Kandariya Mahadev ▲ Western Group
                 Varaha
Lakshmana
Matangesvara

Ⓕ Ⓔ Bus Stand
State Bank
of India
❶
MAIN ❸
SQ. ❷
❹ Ⓕ Ⓖ Ⓗ
JAIN TEMPLES ROAD
Hanuman ▲

▲ Vamana

Khajur
Sagar

Javari ▲

Ⓘ
❺
Archeological
Museum

Brahma ▲

KHAJURAHO
VILLAGE

Shiv
Sagar

Ⓙ

Lalguan
Mahadev ▲

Chausath
Yogini ▲

Bus Stand ★

Ⓚ ✉ GPO

Ⓛ

Ghantai ▲

Adinath
▲
Parshvanath ▲

Shantinath
Jain Temple

Ⓜ
Indian Airlines

▲ Duladeo

N

0   500 m

Ⓝ

RESTAURANTS:
❶ Raja Cafe, Shree Punjabi
   & Temple View
❷ Assi & Safari Restaurants
❸ Mediterraneo Restorante
❹ Lovely
❺ Lake View Cafe

HOTELS:
Ⓐ Khajuraho Ashok
Ⓑ MPTDC Rahil
Ⓒ MPTDC Tourist Village
Ⓓ MPTDC Payal
Ⓔ Yogi Lodge
Ⓕ Surya
Ⓖ Jain & Gem
Ⓗ Harmony
Ⓘ Lakeside
Ⓙ Sunset View
Ⓚ MPTDC Jhankar
Ⓛ Jass Oberoi
Ⓜ Clarks Bundela
Ⓝ Chandela

▽ Airport, Panna & Jhansi

Chaturbhuj ▲

Khajursagar to the east before the village, and the large **Premsagar** on the right to the north of the main square. A few other villages are dotted within striking distance in the flat and rolling countryside; on the whole the inhabitants are pleased to see visitors.

The Western Group

Stranded like a fleet of stone ships, amid pristine lawns and flowerbeds fringed with bougainvillea, Khajuraho's **Western Group** of temples seem oddly divorced from their past. With the exception of **Matangesvara**, just outside the main complex, all are now virtually devoid of religious significance, and they only spring back to life during Shivratri, the Shiva festival (Feb/March). The temples are open daily between dawn and dusk; the entrance fee (Rs0.50; Fri free) also grants access to the museum near the main gates. Visitors must remove their shoes before entering individual temples.

Varaha

Just inside the complex, a small open *mandapa* pavilion, built between the tenth and eleventh centuries, houses a huge, highly polished sandstone image of **Vishnu** as the Boar – **Varaha**. Carved in low relief on its body, 674 figures in neat rows represent the major gods and goddesses of the Hindu pantheon. Lord of the earth, water and heaven, the alert boar straddles Shesha the serpent, accompanied by what Burt conjectured must have been the most beautiful form of **Prithvi**, the earth goddess – all that remains are her feet and a hand on the neck of the boar. Above the image the lotus ceiling stands out in relief. Archeologists suggest that Varaha either belonged to the earlier Gupta period, and was brought here from elsewhere, or that the artisans of Khajuraho may simply have admired the Gupta style and chosen to emulate it.

Lakshmana

Beyond Varaha, adjacent to the Matangesvara temple across the boundary wall, the richly carved **Lakshmana** temple, dating from around 950 AD, is the oldest of the Western Group. It stands on a high plinth covered with processional friezes of horses, elephants and camels, as well as soldiers, domestic scenes, musicians and dancers. Among explicit sexual images is a man buggering a horse, flanked by shocked women onlookers. The sheer energy of the work gives the whole temple an astounding sense of movement and vitality.

While the plinth depicts the human world, the temple itself, the *adhisthana*, brings one into contact with the celestial realm. Two tiers of carved panels decorate its exterior, with gods and goddesses attended by *apsaras*, "celestial nymphs", and figures in complicated sexual acts on the lower tier and in the recesses. Fine detail includes a magnificent dancing Ganesh, the elephant god, on the south face, a master architect with his students on the east, and heavenly musicians and dancers.

Successive pyramidal roofs over the *mandapa* and the porch rise to a clustered tower made of identical superimposed elements. Small porches with sloping eaves project from the *mandapa* and passageway, with exquisite columns, each with eight figures, at each corner of the platform supported by superb brackets in the form of *apsaras*. The inner sanctum, the *garbha griha*, is reached through a door whose lintel shows Vishnu's consort **Lakshmi**, accompanied by **Brahma** and **Shiva**; a frieze depicts the **Navagraha**, the nine planets. Inside, the main image is of Vishnu as the triple-headed, four-armed Vaikuntha, attended by his incarnations as boar and lion.

Kandariya Mahadeva

Sharing a common platform with other temples to the rear of the enclosure, the majestic **Kandariya Mahadeva** temple, built between 1025 and 1050 AD, is the largest and most imposing of the Western Group. A perfect consummation of the five-part design instigated in Lakshmana and Vishvanatha, this Shiva temple represents the pinnacle of Chandellan art, its ornate roofs soaring dramatically to culminate 31m above the base in a *shikhara* that consists of 84 smaller replicas.

Kandariya Mahadeva is especially popular with visitors for the extraordinarily energetic and provocative **erotica** that ornaments its three tiers, covering almost every facet of the exterior. Admiring crowds can always be found in front of a particularly fine image of a couple locked in **mithuna**, sexual intercourse, assisted by a maiden at either side. One of Khajuraho's most familiar motifs, it seems to defy nature, with the male figure suspended upside down on his head; only when considered as if from above do the sinuous intertwined limbs begin to make sense.

An elaborate garland at the entrance to the temple, carved from a single stone, acts as a *torana*, the ritual gateway of a marriage procession. Both inside and out, lavish and intricate images of gods, goddesses, musicians and nymphs celebrate the occasion; within the sanctuary a dark passage leads to the *garbha griha*, and its central *shivalingam*. Niches along the exterior contain images of **Ganesh**, **Virabhadra** and the **Sapta Matrikas**, the Seven Mothers responsible for dressing the bridegroom, Shiva. Wrathful deities and fearsome protectors, the seven consist of Brahmi seated on the swan of Brahma, a female counterpart of Shiva; a three-eyed Maheshvari on Shiva's bull Nandi; Kumari; Vaishnavi, seated on the bird Garuda; Varahi, the female form of Vishnu as the boar; Narasimhi, the female form of Vishnu as lion; and the terrifying Chamunda, the slayer of the *asuras* or "demons" Chanda and Munda, who is the only one of the Sapta Matrikas not a female representation of a major male god.

Devi Jagadambi

North of Kandariya Mahadeva along the platform, the earlier **Devi Jagadambi** temple is a simpler structure, whose outer walls lack projecting balconies. Originally dedicated to Vishnu, its prominent *mandapa* is capped by a massive pyramidal roof. Three *bhandas* (belts) bind the *jangha* (body), adorned with exquisite and sensuous carvings; the erotica on the third is arguably the finest in Khajuraho. Vishnu appears throughout the panels, all decorated with sinuous figures of nymphs, gods and goddesses, some in amorous embrace. Some consider the image in the temple sanctum to be a standing Parvati, others argue that it is the black goddess Kali, known here as Jagadambi.

Between Kandariya Mahadeva and Jagadambi, the remains of **Mahadeva** temple shelter a metre-high lion accompanied by a figure of indeterminate sex. Recurring throughout Khajuraho, the highly stylized lion motif, seen here rearing itself over a kneeling warrior with drawn sword, may have been an emblem of the Chandellas.

Chitragupta

Beyond the platform, and similar to its southern neighbour, Jagadambi, the heavily (and in places clumsily) restored **Chitragupta** temple is unusual in being dedicated to **Surya**, the sun god. Once again its design emphasizes the *mandapa*, which here has large projecting balconies, rather than the main temple. Ornate depictions of hunting scenes, nymphs and dancing girls accompany processional friezes, while on the southern aspect a particularly vigorous ten-headed Vishnu embodies all his ten incarnations. Within the inner chamber, the fiery Surya rides a chariot driven by seven horses.

The small and relatively insignificant temple in front of Chitragupta, also heavily restored and now known as **Parvati**, may originally have been a Vishnu temple, but holds an interesting image of the goddess Ganga riding on a crocodile.

Vishvanatha

Laid out along the same lines as Lakshmana, **Vishvanatha**, in the northeast corner of the enclosure – the third of the three main Western Group shrines – can be precisely dated to 1002 AD, as the work of the ruler Dhangadeva. Unlike some other temples at

Khajuraho, which may have changed their presiding deities, Vishvanatha is most definitely a Shiva temple, as confirmed by the open *mandapa* pavilion in front of the main
temple, where a monolithic seated **Nandi** waits obediently. Hundreds of small *shikharas* resembling miniature temples decorate the *mandapa* roof, sweeping up towards the
climax of the main tower. Large panels between the balconies once more show *mithuna*, with amorous couples embracing among the sensuous nymphs. Idealized representations of the female form include women in such poses as writing letters, playing
music and fondling babies. Decorative elephant motifs appear to the south of
Vishvanatha, and lions guard its northern aspect.

Matangesvara

The simplicity of the **Matangesvara** temple, outside the complex gates, shows it to be
one of Khajuraho's oldest structures; but although built early in the tenth century it
remains in everyday use. Deep balconies project from the walls of its circular sanctuary, inside which a pillar-like *shivalingam* emerges from the pedestal *yoni*, the vulva –
the recurring symbol of the union of Shiva. During the annual festival of Shivratri, the
great wedding of Shiva and Parvati, the shrine becomes a hive of activity, drawing pilgrims for ceremonies that hark back to Khajuraho's distant past.

Shivsagar

A short way south of the complex, a few hundred metres from Matangesvara, the
Shivsagar tank is surrounded by a motley assortment of buildings and open space.
The steps down to it are animated with pilgrims bathing and collecting water from the
"Ocean of Shiva". Cunningham's original map of the temples showed a body of water
that ran north to divide the Western Group into two sections; crossing it to the temples
may have represented a symbolic transition from the finite to the celestial.

Chausath Yogini

Beyond Shivsagar, to the southwest, lie the remains of the curious temple of **Chausath
Yogini** – the "Sixty-Four Yoginis". Dated from the ninth century, Chausath Yogini consists of 35 small granite shrines clustered around a quadrangle; there were originally
64 shrines with the presiding goddess's temple at the centre. Only fourteen other temples, all in northern India, are known to have been dedicated to these wrathful and
bloodthirsty female attendants of the goddess Kali; art historians surmise that the site
was used by an esoteric tantric group. Around 1km further west are the ruins of
Lalguan Mahadev, a small temple dedicated to Shiva.

The Eastern Group

The two separate networks of temples that make up Cunningham's "Eastern Group"
are reached along the two forks of the road east of town. One is the tightly clustered
Jain Group, while slightly north, scattered in the vicinity of Khajuraho Village, are a
number of shrines and the two larger temples of Vamana and Javari.

Left of the road just beyond town, a comparatively new temple holds a 2.1-metre-high
image of the monkey god **Hanuman** that may predate all of Khajuraho's temples and
shrines. As the road forks left along the eastern shore of the murky Khajursagar lake,
at the edge of Khajuraho Village, it passes the remains of a single-room temple erro-
neously referred to as the **Brahma** temple. Often considered to be a Vishnu temple, it
is in fact a shrine to Shiva, as demonstrated by its *chaturmukha* – "four-faced" – *lingam*.
While the eastern and western faces carry benign expressions, and the north face
bears the gentler aspect of Uma, the female manifestation of Shiva, the ferocious southern face is surrounded by images of death and destruction. Crowning the *lingam* is the
rounded form of **Sadashiva**, Shiva the Infinite at the centre of the cosmos.

The dirt road continues to the small **Javari** temple, set on a plain terrace and featuring a double porch and a slender *shikhara*, similar to Chaturbhuj of the Southern Group. Built late in the eleventh century, it may not have the exuberance seen elsewhere but nevertheless contains some fine sculpture, including alluring nymphets in classic Khajuraho style.

The largest of the Khajuraho Village temples, **Vamana**, stands alone in a field 200m further north. Built slightly earlier than Javari, in a fully evolved Chandella style, Vamana has a simple uncluttered *shikhara* that rises in bands covered with arch-like motifs. Figures including seductive celestial nymphs form two bands around the *jangha*, the body of the temple, while a superb doorway leads to the inner sanctum, which is dedicated to Vamana, an incarnation of Vishnu. On the way to the Jain Group, the road runs near what survives of a late tenth-century temple, known as **Ghantai** for its fine columns sporting bells (*ghantai*), garlands and other motifs.

The temple of **Parsvanatha**, dominating the walled enclosure of the **Jain Group**, is probably older than the main temples of Khajuraho, judging by its relatively simple ground plan. Its origins are a mystery; although officially classified as a Jain monument, and jointly administered by the Archaeological Survey and the Jain community, it may have been a Hindu temple that was donated to the Jain community who settled here at a later date. Certainly, the animated sculpture of Khajuraho's other Hindu temples is well represented on the two horizontal bands around the walls, and the upper one is crowded with Hindu gods in intimate entanglements. Among Khajuraho's finest work, they include Brahma and his consort; a beautiful Vishnu; a rare image of the god of love, **Kama**, shown with his quiver of flower arrows embracing his consort **Rati**; and two graceful female figures, one applying *kohl* to her eyes and another removing a thorn from her foot. A narrow strip above the two main bands depicts celestial musicians (*gandharvas*) playing cymbals, drums, stringed instruments and flutes, some carrying garlands, cleverly caught in mid-flight with billowing robes. Inside, beyond an ornate hall, a black monolithic stone is dedicated to the Jain lord Parsvanath, inaugurated as recently as 1860 to replace an image of another *tirthankara*, Adinath.

Immediately south of Parsvanath, **Adinath**'s own temple, similar but smaller, has undergone drastic renovation. Three tiers of sculpture surround its original structure, of which only the sanctum, *shikhara* and vestibule survive; the incongruous *mandapa* is a much later addition. Inside the *garbha griha* stands the black image of the *tirthankara* Adinath himself. The huge 4.5-metre-high statue of the sixteenth *tirthankara*, **Shantinath**, in his newer temple, is the most important image in this working Jain complex. With its slender beehive *shikharas*, the temple attracts pilgrims from all over India, including naked *sadhus*.

THE KHAJURAHO FESTIVAL OF DANCE

The sleepy town of Khajuraho is transformed during the pleasant spring month of Phalguna (Feb/March), when the festival of **Maha Shivratri** draws pilgrims from all over the region to commemorate the marriage of Shiva.

Maha Shivratri also sees one of India's premier dance events – the **Khajuraho Festival of Dance**, a showcase for all forms of classical dance. The festival is typical of a new breed of event, sited at ornate ancient temples to attract visitors by combining tourism with culture (see also Konarak, in Orissa). However, although some performances are presented against the stunning backdrop of the Western Group, most take place in an outdoor arena, away from the temples at the Chandella Cultural Centre.

Precise dates for the festival, which is jointly organized by the Delhi-based Bharatiya Kala Kendra and MPTDC, tend to be confirmed late. Check with Government of India tourist authorities, and book early, as this is the one time of year when Khajuraho is busy. Tickets for specific events cost between Rs50 and Rs250; foreigners should pay in US dollars.

The Southern Group

What is generally referred to as Khajuraho's **Southern Group** consists of two widely separated temples. The nearer to town, **Duladeo**, is down a dirt track south of the Jain Group, 1.5km from the main square – an isolation that stops it achieving the same impact as the great Western Group temples. Built early in the twelfth century, Duladeo in any case bears witness to the decline of temple architecture in the late Chandellan period, noticeable above all in sculpture that lacks the hallmark fluidity of Khajuraho. Nevertheless, its main hall does contain some exquisite carving, and the angular rippled exterior of the main temple is unique to Khajuraho. Rising on a star-shaped ground plan, on which the square inner sanctum dedicated to Shiva is extended by a multifaceted geometrical design, its complex architectural themes are developed only at the expense of becoming rather tediously repetitive. The entire structure, especially the *shikhara* and the pyramidal roof of the *mandapa*, has been extensively renovated.

Across the Khodar stream on the way south towards the airport, a road leads left along a dirt track to the disproportionately tall, tapering **Chaturbhuj**, around 5km south of Khajuraho – the *shikhara* is visible for miles above the trees. A forerunner to Duladeo, built around 1100 AD and bearing some resemblance to the Javari temple of the Eastern Group, Chaturbhuj is plainer than Duladeo and devoid of erotica. A remarkable 2.7-metre-high image of Vishnu graces its inner sanctum.

Museums

Opposite the Western Group, the small **Archeological Museum** is principally noteworthy for a remarkable sculpture of a pot-bellied dancing Ganesh, his trunk swinging with a vibrant sense of motion. Other assorted friezes, brackets and pieces of carving include a panel depicting the transportation and cutting of stone used to build the temples; Vishnu reclining on the endless serpent, Anantha, with a lotus rising from his navel supporting Brahma the originator; a seated Buddha, the only one found in Khajuraho; and of course some erotica. Tickets for the Western Group entitle you to countless visits to the museum (daily 10am–5pm) within a day, and for no extra charge.

Sculpture in the small circular **Jain Museum**, at the entrance to the Jain temples, includes representations of all twenty-four *tirthankaras* (daily 7am–6pm; Rs1).

Accommodation

Khajuraho's more exclusive **hotels** are a bit secluded, but nearly all the mid-range and budget accommodation is close to the town centre, near the Western Group. Khajuraho can get very hot indeed, especially during the run-up to the monsoons, from February towards the end of June, and after the rains between August and November; air-cooled or a/c rooms are a real boon at those times.

A good alternative to Khajuraho itself is *Gile's Tree House* in Madla, 24km southeast (see p.398), which can be booked through the two sisters who run the *Raja Cafe*.

Chandela (☎2054). Khajuraho's grandest address, with every amenity and all the hallmarks of the Taj Group, including a marble foyer and chandeliers. Non-residents can use the pool for Rs150. Puppet shows are held in the evenings. ⑧.

Clarks Bundela, Airport Rd (☎2365). Posh new hotel with all mod cons, and a large pool. Pay in dollars. ⑧.

Gem, Jain Temples Rd (☎2100). Clean and homely, like its neighbours, but without a garden. ④.

Harmony, Jain Temples Rd (☎2135). Neat and clean, with a restaurant. Ask for a room facing the small garden. Run by Ganga, an expert local guide. ⑤.

Jain, Jain Temples Rd (☎2052). Close to the heart of Khajuraho, near the *Harmony*. Reasonable air-cooled rooms, good value singles, and good veg food. ②–③.

Jass Oberoi, By-Pass Rd (☎2085). Elegant but pleasantly understated top-of-the-range place, with tennis courts, swimming pool and a good restaurant. ⑧–⑨.

Khajuraho Ashok, Airport Rd (☎2024). Long-established comfortable hotel, due to be totally refurbished. Carpeted en-suite rooms look over a swimming pool (non-residents Rs100) to the spires of the Western Group. The helpful staff can arrange itineraries and car rental. ⑧.

Lakeside, opposite Shivasagar Lake (☎2120). Assorted rooms not far from the main square, including a dorm. Popular with Japanese tourists. ③–⑤.

MPTDC Jhankar, near the *Oberoi* (☎2063). The best of the MPTDC options; clean with a good restaurant but otherwise plain. ⑤–⑥.

MPTDC Payal (☎2076). Typical, rather charmless mid-range government place; but the rooms are spacious and quiet. The *Camp Ground* alongside can be booked through reception. ⑤–⑥.

MPTDC Rahil (☎2062). More government-run accommodation, once again soulless but in a leafy spot. Offers a dorm (Rs40) and a canteen-like restaurant. ③.

MPTDC Tourist Village (☎2128). Modern mud huts spread across a few acres in imitation of a small village; the mock-rustic restaurant is also in a hut. ③.

Sunset View, opposite Pahil Batika (☎2077). Quite ordinary, with a dorm and budget accommodation as well as more expensive a/c rooms. ②–④.

Surya, Jain Temple Rd (☎2145). Clean, good-value place around a verdant courtyard; does not give commissions to rickshaws. ③–④.

Yogi Lodge (☎2158). Behind the *Raja Cafe*, near the Western Group. Excellent-value budget accommodation with a small courtyard. Similar lodges on either side include *Vikram*, *Marco Polo* and *Natraj*. ①–③.

Eating

Khajuraho is surprisingly good for **food**; it even has an exciting Italian place among its well-priced restaurants and cafes. The budget choices are not bad, and a cold beer never too far away, while the top hotels all provide reasonable to excellent eating.

Assi, Jain Temples Rd. Small, simple and cosy, with no-nonsense Indian food.

MOVING ON FROM KHAJURAHO

To avoid tediously long overland journeys from Khajuraho, you can **fly** with *Modiluft* or *Indian Airlines* to Agra, Delhi and Varanasi: both have offices next to *Hotel Clarks Bundela*. *Indian Airlines* (☎2035; airport ☎2036) has a daily flight at 12.35pm to Varanasi (45min), which returns to pick up passengers at 3.15pm for Agra (1hr) and Delhi (1hr 55min). *Modiluft* has two flights daily (except Mon & Fri; 1 daily) to Delhi and Varanasi. Flights can be heavily booked. Note that with a late reservation you may be promised a confirmation, but can only be sure of a place on the flight at the airport, shortly before departure; allow a little leeway in case your flight is delayed, and be patient.

By far the easiest **road and rail** route out of Khajuraho is by the express a/c tourist bus to **Jhansi**, 175km east (noon; 5hr – cheaper, slower alternatives leave between 5.30am and 4.45pm), then catch the a/c *Shatabdi Express* #2001 train via **Gwalior** and **Agra**, to **Delhi** (departs 5.55pm).

Between 6am and 3.30pm daily, buses set out for **Satna** (4hr), 125km east, which is served by trains on the **Bombay–Varanasi–Calcutta** network, as well as to **Gorakhpur**, from where buses head for the Nepal border. If you're heading to **Varanasi**, 415km east, expect a long wait in Satna: night trains (8hr) leave daily at 8pm, and on Monday, Wednesday and Friday at 10pm as well, while the daily morning departure (7–8hr) leaves at 8.35am. If you need to spend the night in Satna, head for *Hotel USA* (③) or the less expensive hotels *Natraj* and *Park* close to the bus stand (both ①). The best train for **Jabalpur** is the *Mahakosal Express* #1450, which leaves Satna daily at 12.10pm (3hr 15min).

An alternative route to **Varanasi** is to take one of the many daily buses north to **Mahoba** (7.30am–4pm; 3hr; Rs30), from where the #1107 train to Varanasi departs at 10.38pm (12hr).

Finally, a single government bus leaves Khajuraho at 9am for the gruelling 395-kilometre journey to **Agra**, arriving at 8.30pm, with a fare of under Rs100.

Jass Oberoi, By-Pass Rd (☎2085). Comfortably stylish multi-cuisine restaurant in luxury hotel; works out as good value when paid for in foreign currency. Highly recommended.

Lake View Cafe, Airport Rd, Shivsagar. Disappointing food, but good views of the lake.

Lovely Restaurant, near the Western Group gates, Main Square. Reasonable Sikh-run *dhaba*.

Mediterraneo Ristorante Italiano, Jain Temple Rd. Excellent cafe with a pleasant roof terrace, run by an Indian-Italian couple. Fresh pasta makes a welcome change – but you'll miss the wine.

Raja Cafe, Main Square. Where it all happens in Khajuraho. The food might not be all that special, but you can pick up guides, information, and cold beers, and there's a bookstore and curio shop.

Shree Punjabi, Main square. Sociable rooftop seating; filling Punjabi meals, and beer.

Safari, Jain Temple Rd. Popular among travellers, serving chicken and chips and salads.

Temple View, next to the tourist office, off the main square. Large stone chequerboard tables, a good atmosphere and great food at very affordable prices.

Tourist Village (☎2128). Quite a nice place, despite the ersatz setting, with good *thalis*. Not all that cheap, but recommended.

Panna National Park

The vast **Panna National Park**, known for its large cats (including tiger), deer and antelope (*nilgai*), lies a short way east of Khajuraho, spreading across a landscape of rocky hills and ravines covered mostly by scrubby deciduous forest. Access is easier than in some of India's better-known sanctuaries – you can even go in on foot if you take along an armed guide. It's best visited in winter, as the entire area gets extremely hot during summer – though there is a better chance then of seeing tigers as they emerge in search of water. Flowing north through the park towards the Ganges, the **River Ken**, whose rocky islands are bare during the lean seasons, harbours both the two major species of Indian crocodile, *magar* and the long-snouted *gharial*.

The exquisite lake of **Pandava Falls**, couched in a hollow and fed by a waterfall, is 11km east of Madla (see below). Legend has it that the Pandavas of *Mahabharata* fame spent time here. A short road leads left off the main road to a car park and tea shop that overlook a rocky escarpment and the lake. It's an idyllic spot, set within the deep emerald cover of the Panna forest, which offers a good chance of spotting wildlife – tigers are said to frequent the lake to drink. If you descend to the lake and follow a rough track, you'll emerge after a short distance beneath dripping cliffs, where caves have been hewn out of the rock to form shrines.

Park practicalities: Madla

The village of **MADLA**, 24km southeast of Khajuraho near a bridge across the picturesque River Ken, is the most convenient point of access to the park, and has the nearest **accommodation**. Two basic *Forest Rest Houses* can be booked through the Director, Panna National Park, Panna (☎52135); food arrangements must be made separately, which poses a problem in an area that offers only the occasional tea shop.

At *Gile's Tree House* (①), a beautiful open platform in the branches of a large tree on the riverbank, camping and sleeping out beneath the stars are free. Book through *Raja Cafe* in Khajuraho. Be prepared to be woken by the blaring of recorded opera to keep away tigers and other animals; the local crocodile was last seen slinking away to the south. Visitors should either bring food or make a donation towards their meals; a bar serving chilled beer is open long hours. The welcoming, if eccentric, Gile's previous *Tree House* was washed away a few years ago, when the Ken river dam was mistakenly opened and caused a devastating flood. Madla's more upmarket *Ken River Lodge* (②) consists of comfortable modern mud cottages overlooking the river near the bridge, with package deals including meals and a visit to the national park, or longer safaris.

Car rental for a comprehensive tour of the national park costs around Rs1000, and is best booked at Khajuraho – facilities at Madla are extremely limited. To get to Madla by **bus**, take any Panna- or Chhatarpur-bound bus, then change at the T-junction 12km south of Khajuraho and pick up a jeep or a bus east. Allow plenty of time if you want to get from Khajuraho to Pandava Falls and back within a day; there's no accommodation near the falls apart from a friendly caretaker's lodge at the crossing on the main road.

En route to Madla, the Chhatarpur–Panna road passes 1km north of the rambling white **Rajgarh Palace**, perched high on the commanding spur of a hill overlooking the valley. Visitors are allowed to wander the battlements, though plans are afoot to transform it into a private hotel.

EASTERN MADHYA PRADESH

The closest most visitors come to exploring **eastern Madhya Pradesh** is an occasional sleepy glance out of a train window during the interminable trip across the middle of India. Given the drabness of much of the landscape and the virtual absence of places worth breaking a long journey to see, this is hardly surprising. Nevertheless, the comparatively remote and sparsely populated east end of the state can still boast one attraction lost long ago by more heavily industrialized areas: an amazing abundance of **wildlife**. Far off the beaten track, though still accessible by public transport, two of the country's finest **national parks**, **Kanha** and **Bandhavgarh**, enable visitors to dip into some of the few remaining fragments of a forest that until 150 years ago extended right across central India. Both these reserves are among the last strongholds for many endangered species of birds and mammals, including the **tiger**.

Two major **rail networks** cut through the region. The *Central Railway* heads straight up the Narmada Valley to **Jabalpur**, the springboard for Kanha National Park, before veering north to Satna (4hr from Khajuraho) and the Gangetic Plains. The other main route, traced by the *Southeastern Railway*, skirts the top of Bastar (the remote and poor southern extension of the state, dovetailing with Maharashtra, Andhra Pradesh and Orissa) and to the grim industrial cities of Raipur and Bilaspur at the head of the Chhattisgarh Valley. From here, the three big rivers that rise in the coal-rich hills to the north flow eastwards, while the railway makes for the Orissan border.

Jabalpur and around

After running in tandem across an endless expanse of wheat fields and impoverished villages, the main Calcutta to Bombay road and railway lines converge on eastern Madhya Pradesh's largest city. Though an important provincial capital, **JABALPUR**, 330km east of Bhopal, harbours little of interest beyond a half-decent museum, some stalwart Raj-era buildings, and the **marble cliffs** gouged by the River Narmada out of some otherwise featureless countryside nearby. It's only really worth visiting en route to the national parks and tiger reserves, Kanha and Bandhavgarh, a day's journey east.

The city as it stands today is of comparatively recent origin. Formerly, access to the fertile Narmada Valley (and its lucrative trade routes) was controlled from the ancient capital at **Tripuri**, 9km west. The site, occupied from around 2000 BC onwards, rose to prominence under the Kushanas at the start of the Christian era. The Satavahanas (or "Andhras") followed, picking up what pieces their predecessors hadn't frittered away on court intrigues and unbridled debauchery. It was under the powerful and militaristic **Kalchuri** (or "Chedi") dynasty, however, that the city emerged as the region's dominant force. Pre-eminence on the battlefield enabled successive rulers to extend their borders westwards almost to within sight of the Arabian Sea before they were finally

> The telephone **area code** for Jabalpur is ☎0761.

swept aside in the eleventh century by the **Gonds**, descendants of Tripuri's aboriginal inhabitants. Based at **Garha**, on the outskirts of modern Jabalpur, Gond rule gradually spread down the Narmada to Bhopal before it was challenged in 1564 by Asaf Khan, one of Akbar's more ambitious governors. Despite some brave resistance from **Rani Durgavati**, a sixteenth-century Rajput Boadicea, Gondwana was overwhelmed by the imperial army and Asaf Khan installed as its overlord. The **Garha-Mandla Gonds**, as the new ruling dynasty became known, were in turn ousted from their new capital at Mandla by the Marathas late in the eighteenth century, and they by the British, who established a military cantonment and administrative centre in Jabalpur in 1819.

Since then, the city has continued to prosper. Due largely to its location at the centre of India, Jabalpur these days is experiencing a period of intense and chaotic growth, driven by an influx of migrant workers from the poorer rural districts to the east.

Arrival, information and city transport

Central Railway **trains** arrive at the city's only **railway station**, 2km east of the centre. From here, it's a five-minute auto-rickshaw ride into town; less if you plan to stay in either of the slightly more expensive hotels at the top end of the cantonment district. The shambolic city **bus stand** is more in the thick of things, a short way south of the bazaar and west of Naudra Bridge, site of several cheaper hotels.

MPTDC's friendly and efficient **tourist office** (Mon–Fri 10am–5pm; ☎322111) inside the main arrivals hall at the railway station, can provide the usual range of handouts, give advice on travel arrangements, and inform you of vacancies in their hotels in Kanha or Bandhavgarh.

THUGS

With their pot-holes, unlit bullock carts, and suicidal drivers, trunk roads in Madhya Pradesh can be trying at the best of times. For travellers in past centuries, however, a much more sinister threat lurked along the highways of central India. A secret sect of bandits and **Kali**-worshippers known as **Thugs** used to express their devotion to the jet-black four-armed goddess of death (usually shown splattered with blood, wearing a necklace of skulls and a belt of dead men's hands) by committing ritual murders on her behalf. The *thugs* would fall in with hapless travellers, gain their confidence, then summarily throttle them with silk scarves. Any pieces of the corpse not required for offerings were dumped in wells or buried in large pits.

Fear of retribution, and the belief among local rulers and village headmen that *thugee* was in some way the sacred will of the goddess herself, allowed the killing to continue unchecked for generations. Then, in 1830, the British dispatched the zealous sleuth Colonel – later Sir – **William Sleeman** to eradicate the sect. His tactics were ruthless and effective. Using promises of lenient prison sentences, Sleeman recruited a network of "super-grass" informers to expose the identities of the clandestine stranglers. In all, some four thousand *thugs* were captured during the twenty-year campaign, many of whom had notched up three hundred or more murders – one even confessed to killing 931 people in the course of his career. Special courts sent a total of four hundred convicted *thugs* to the gallows, and many more to jail or penal colonies in places such as the Andaman Islands. As for the informers, most ended up with their families in the purpose-built "School of Industry" (now a reform school) at **Jabalpur** where they were taught to turn their hand from silk scarves to carpet weaving. The word "thug" passed into common usage thanks to the characteristically macabre interest in the phenomenon shown by the British press.

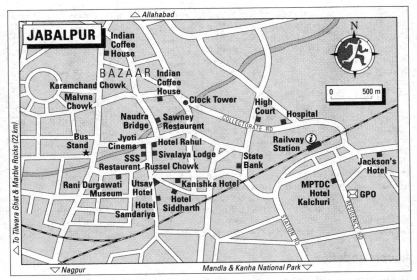

English-language newspapers and magazines are only available on the *Jackson's* hotel campus or from platform 1 in the railway station. The **post office** is a five-minute walk south of the railway station near the *Hotel Kalchuri*. If you need to **change money** (there are no exchange facilities in either national park), the *State Bank of India* (Mon–Fri 10am–2pm, Sat 10am–noon) is a just under a kilometre west of the railway station. The *Samdariya* or *Jackson's* hotels may also agree to help out in emergencies, though officially they're only supposed to change money for residents.

City transport

Jabalpur teems with **auto-** and **cycle rickshaws**, while the rarer *Ambassador* **taxis** can usually be found in front of the *Samdariya*. Vehicles for day trips can be rented through the top hotels. Otherwise, **bicycles** make a good way to get about the city; ask in the repair shops opposite *Hotel Kalchuri*, or on Malvna Chowk in the main bazaar. The dilapidated **tempos** and **minibuses** that chug through the centre of town service outlying suburbs and are only useful for travelling out to the Marble Rocks.

The City

With few real sights to speak of, the best way to kill time in Jabalpur **city** itself is a leisurely tour by bicycle or rickshaw. To the south of the railway line you'll find the remains of the former colonial enclave – now a peaceful suburb of leafy streets, bungalows, churches, British-style boarding schools and barracks. The underpass east of the station opens onto the far end of Collectorate Road. Head west from here, past Madhya Pradesh's Victorian **High Court** building, and you'll eventually arrive at the **clock tower** at the start of Jabalpur's large **bazaar** district. An intricate grid of long dusty streets lined with small shops, factories and disintegrating wooden buildings, the commercial hub is drab by Indian standards, and flooded with raucous traffic.

Due south of the bazaar, a short way down a side-road off Russel Chowk, the **Rani Durgavati Museum** (Tues–Sat 10am–5pm) preserves sculpture and inscriptions in the nineteenth-century home of the local Maharaja. The scruffy garden outside contains Hindu and Jain pieces, the finest being a partially damaged depiction of Shiva and Parvati (as Uma-Maheshwar), to the right of two large Jain statues. Inside, the ground-floor galleries are divided between Shiva and Parvati, Vishnu, and Jain *tirthankaras*, while the upstairs rooms are mostly devoted to bronze plates and seals recording regional dynastic histories. In the last room on the first floor, a small collection of female fertility figures includes a particularly striking *iskalitwashna*, or "naked courtesan bathing", which is a big hit with the bored museum attendants.

Three kilometres west of the centre, the main highway runs alongside a large tank lined with bathing *ghats*, banyan trees and a picturesque row of Hindu shrines crumbling into the water. Opposite, on top of a moraine of enormous granite boulders, stand the ruins of the **Madam Mahal** (pronounced *M'den Mel*) – a fortress-cum-pleasure-palace built by the Gond ruler Madan Shah in 1116. Nowadays, the stony slopes around the bottom of the hill also shelter a sprawl of ramshackle dwellings belonging to a community of potters (whose wares you can see piled up on the roadside), and a couple of immaculately whitewashed **Jain temples**.

The left fork in the main road 1km or so further on drops down to an impressive bridge spanning the River Narmada. Known locally as **Tilwara Ghat**, the handful of shrines near the water's edge below marks one of the sacred places where Mahatma Gandhi's ashes were scattered. The right fork takes you out towards the Marble Rocks.

Accommodation

The majority of Jabalpur's **hotels** are within easy reach of the bus stand – handy for early departures to Kanha. Watch out for "luxury taxes" and "service charges" levied by the pricier places. If you're on a tight budget and don't fancy a seedy windowless cell (par for the course in the cheaper lodges) try the "economy" rooms in the mid-range hotels. The railway station has **retiring rooms** (①–③) and cheap dorms.

Jackson's, Civil Lines (☎323412). This must have cut a fine dash in the Fifties, but is now settling into an advanced, if idiosyncratic, state of decay. A relaxing garden is some compensation for the rather inflated prices. Some a/c. ⑤–⑦.

Kanishka, Russel Chowk (☎29266). Nothing special, but the cheaper "standard" rooms are a good deal, and some rooms are air-cooled. ③–④.

MPTDC Kalchuri, Civil Lines (☎321491). Immaculate and welcoming hotel around the corner from the railway station. Rooms are spacious. Some a/c. ⑤–⑥.

Rahul, opposite *Jyoti Cinema*, Naudra Bridge (☎325525). A slight improvement on rock-bottom, but not much. Most of the cheaper rooms are windowless. Some a/c. ②–④.

Samdariya, off Russel Chowk (☎316800). Plush hotel close to the roundabout, with marble lobby and TVs in all rooms. ⑤–⑧.

Siddharth, off Russel Chowk (☎29247). Well-run and central with simple, light, good-value "standard" rooms. Some a/c. ③–⑤.

Sivalaya Lodge, opposite *Jyoti Cinema*, Naudra Bridge (☎325188). Currently the best-value budget place. Simple, clean rooms with hot water and attached bath, and good value singles. Easy access to bus stand. ①–②.

Utsav, Russel Chowk (☎26038). Efficient, modern hotel in the centre of town. Rooms (all with satellite TV, attached bath and hot water) range from excellent-value "economy" to "super-deluxe" with bath-tubs. Mostly a/c. ③–⑦.

Eating

With a few exceptions, the best **places to eat** in Jabalpur are the hotels. Prices are reasonable and most menus varied, though not all of the restaurants serve alcohol.

The Grub Room, *Jackson's Hotel*, Civil Lines. Jaded and spartan decor, but the moderately priced veg and non-veg grub is good. Some Chinese and adventurous Western options.

Indian Coffee Houses, both in the bazaar district. Great for cheap *dosas, iddlis, uttapams* and other light snacks. Opens at 8.30am for breakfast.

Kalchuri, Civil Lines. Low light, starched table cloths and the usual MPTDC menu: a modest selection of tasty but rather over-priced meat, veg and Chinese dishes. *Tandoori* after 7.30pm only.

Samdariya, off Russel Chowk. The place to splash out on top-notch Indian and Chinese food. Western-style coffee shop does delicious south Indian snacks.

Satyam Shivam Sundaram, near *Jyoti Cinema*, Naudra Bridge. Don't be put off by the bizarre rococo interior. The strictly veg food, including *thalis* and some set menus, is excellent value and some tables overlook the street. Inexpensive.

Sawney, Naudra Bridge. Bustling, unpretentious and cheap. Generous heaps of spicy Punjabi food served mainly to an office crowd. The a/c family room (*Eskimo*) next door is alcohol-free.

Utsav, Russel Chowk. Studiously respectable veg restaurant with an enormous, surprisingly inexpensive menu. The dingy dining room is better for evening meals.

MOVING ON FROM JABALPUR

Kanha National Park is most travellers' next move after Jabalpur. Direct *MPSRTC* services leave the central bus stand twice daily for the main gate at Kisli: the first, at 7am, is faster (5hr); the second (6hr) leaves at 11am. Buses to Mandla, half way to the park, leave every half hour. **Bandhavgarh** is harder to reach; you need to catch a train (4–6 daily; 1hr 20min) or bus (1–2 hourly; 2hr) up to Umaria (via Katni) and take a local bus from there.

To get to **Khajuraho**, catch one of the frequent early-morning trains as far as Satna (3hr), where you can pick up direct state buses. **Varanasi** is on the main Bombay–Calcutta line. Aim for the *Bombay–Varanasi Ratnagiri Express* #1065 (Mon, Wed & Thurs 10.45pm; arrives 8am), or the daily *Mahanagiri Express* #1093 (departs 4.35pm, arrives 4am). Daily trains from Jabalpur to **Patna** help travellers en route to **Nepal**.

Of the five or six daily express trains to **Bombay**, the *Howrah–Bombay Mail* #3003 is the most convenient (depart 5.30pm; 15hr). For **Delhi** (20hr), take the daily *Mahakosal Express* #1449 at 6.35pm, or travel down to Itarsi junction to pick up the more frequent northward services via Bhopal, Gwalior and Agra. There are also three weekly trains to **Madras** (Mon, Wed & Sat, 3.25am; 31hr 30min).

The marble rocks

In a bustling, dusty, Oriental land, the charm of coolness and quiet belonging to these pure cold rocks, and deep and blue yet pellucid waters, is almost entrancing.
Captain J Forsyth, *The Highlands of Central India* (1889).

West of Jabalpur, the Narmada suddenly narrows, plunges over a series of dramatic waterfalls, then squeezes through a seam of milky-white marble before continuing on its westward course across the Deccan. The thirty-metre cliffs and globulous shapes worn by the water out of the rock may not exactly rank as one of the seven wonders of the natural world, but the **MARBLE ROCKS**, known locally as **Bheraghat**, are as good a place as any to while away an idle afternoon.

Bheraghat **village** itself, overlooking the gorge, is a sleepy little place, with few signs of activity beyond the ringing of chisels in the workshops of its many **marble-carvers**. Most pieces on display in the shop-fronts are heavy-duty Hanumans, *shivalingams* and other deities, destined for other parts of India – the local translucent white marble is much in demand for new temples and shrines.

From the main street, a flight of steps leads down to the river and the **ghats**, where **rowing boats** are on hand to ferry visitors up the gorge. Trips take thirty to forty minutes, depending on the water level (if the dams upstream are open, the current can be too strong for boats to pass), though you're more likely to spend at least that long waiting for the requisite fifteen passengers to show up. Once under way, the boatman begins his spiel, pointing out the more interesting **rock formations**. The most appreciative noises from the other passengers are not reserved for the "footprint of the celestial elephant", however, or even the "monkey's leap" (jumped over by Hanuman on his way to Lanka), but for the places where Hindi movie-stars posed in well-known films shot on location here. Look out for the enormous **bees' nests** dangling from the crevices in the rock. One nineteenth-century guidebook urged its readers to refrain from "smoking or firing guns" in the gorge, as an angry swarm once attacked a party of English army engineers who were carrying out survey work for a new railway here. A memorial plaque, still visible on top of the cliffs, was erected to one of their number who drowned trying to shake the bees off. During the evenings the formations are floodlit.

Not surprisingly, Bheraghat is also something of a religious site. From the fork in the river, 107 stone steps lead up to the tenth-century **Mandapur temple**, a circular building known for the 64 beautifully carved tantric goddesses, or **Chausath Yogini**, which stand in its enclosure.

Beyond the temple, at the far end of the gorge, the **Dhaundhar** or "Smoke Cascade" waterfall is particularly dramatic when shrouded in spray after the monsoons. It's reached either by following the main street out through the village, or else via the goat-track that twists along the top of the cliffs below the MPTDC *Motel*. Just above the waterfall, you pass a string of stalls loaded with locally carved marble goods – among them some fine pocket-sized pieces of religious kitsch. Tempos back to Jabalpur start from the open space between the stalls and the village.

Practicalities

Getting to Bheraghat under your own steam from Jabalpur involves picking up a **tempo** from the bus stand next to the museum. Although the 45-minute stop-and-start trip can be excruciating, it's an improvement on the only alternative: a tedious bicycle ride along a busy main road. Clamber off the tempo when you see a row of cold drink and souvenir stalls lining a sharp left-hand bend in the main street.

Accommodation is available if you want to stay the night. Just off the road out to the falls, MPTDC have converted a colonial bungalow, complete with verandah, well-kept lawn and easy chairs, into the very pleasant four-roomed *Motel Marble Rocks* (☎0761/83424; ④). The garden looks out over the gorge and a small **restaurant** serves a standard veg and non-veg menu. The only other option is the much cheaper, if less salubrious *Hotel Rahul Tourist Home* (☎0761/83450; ①–②), opposite the brightly painted Jain temple on the main street (sign in Hindi). Prices start at rock-bottom and increase with the size of the rooms, which are basic but reasonably clean. There's also common roof-space, and a small restaurant that can knock up simple veg food.

From Jabalpur towards Kanha

From Jabalpur, the four-hour bone-shaking bus ride to Kanha takes you into some of eastern Madhya Pradesh's most isolated rural districts. When Captain J Forsyth and his Bengal Lancers pushed through en route to the uncharted interior at the end of the nineteenth century, this landscape was a virtually unbroken tract of *sal* forest teeming with Indian bison, deer and tigers. Since then, the local aboriginal hunter-gatherers have taken up the plough, and all but a few patches of forest clinging to the ridges of nearby hillsides have been logged, cleared for farmland or simply burned as firewood by the burgeoning populations of share-croppers. A further scar on the land was inflicted more recently when several valleys were flooded as part of a large-scale **dam project**. During the short winter dry spell, you occasionally come across desolate stretches of mud and tree stumps where only a decade ago woodland and villages stood.

Shortly after **Narayanganj**, a junction where the bus halts for a ten-minute *chai* stop, the road rejoins the Narmada again, twisting through the patchwork of ripening wheat and sugar-cane planted in the well-watered alluvial soil that lines the river banks. Along the way, look out for the two-tiered terracotta roofs on the village huts – a local design inheriteded from earlier thatching techniques.

It was around these parts, in 1564, that **Rani Durgavati**, the warrior queen of Gondwana, was defeated in battle by Asaf Khan, one of Akbar's right-hand men. When she heard that the viceregal army was advancing on her kingdom, Durgavati rounded up her troops from the harvest, and marched north on elephant-back to waylay the attackers. Unable to hold off the better-armed Moghuls, the Gonds were soon forced to retreat to a place near Mandla where, with the swollen river blocking their only escape, they were finally routed. Asaf Khan allegedly captured 101 cooking pots full of gold and jewels, though not Durgavati, who stabbed herself through the heart to avoid the ignominy of being incarcerated in his harem.

Mandla

Three hours out of Jabalpur, the bus pulls into **MANDLA**, the district headquarters and last sizeable town before Kanha. Travellers rarely, if ever, venture further than the bus stand here, though it's perfectly possible to do so if you catch one of the half-hourly services from Jabalpur early enough to allow time for exploring the town before picking up the 2pm departure for Kanha.

Mandla's easily defensible position, on a narrow tongue of land in the River Narmada, made it an obvious site for the new regional capital when the old one, Garh, was threatened from the north during the seventeenth century. In spite of its **fort** and walls, the Maharathas managed to overthrow the last Garha-Mandla king a hundred years later, torturing him to death in his own castle. A couple of crumbling old gateways are virtually all that's left of the original buildings, overlooking the picturesque **confluence** of the Banjar, Sarasvati and Narmada rivers.

From the bus stand, head straight down the main street, past the market (on the right), as far as the staggered crossroads. The narrow lane opposite takes you past rows of **silver** and "bell-metal" (brass) shops full of jewellery, cooking utensils and smiths bent over blow-torches in the half-light, to a stone bridge spanning an overgrown moat. Once across, you come out alongside the ruined fort – much less noteworthy nowadays than the shiny white temples in its midst. The fortified **gateway** at the far end, which you can climb inside, opens on to a strip of yellow sand from where the ferry-boats push off for the far bank (pay the *chowkidar* sitting under the arch).

Known since the ancient Hindu scriptures as **Trivendi Sangam**, the confluence, said to form the shape of the auspicious "Om" symbol, is a place of pilgrimage and the area's prime site for performing mortuary rituals. It's one of those magical little spots you sometimes come across in central India where the pace and tone of life seems to have changed very little for centuries: *pujaris* (priests) sit cross-legged under rickety bamboo sun-shades, pilgrims bathe in the river, and flat-bottomed canoes paddle past on their way to the market. Just up from the river are a couple of temples, one dedicated to Durga and the other, distinguished by its three oddly tapering towers, to Rama. Assorted ashrams and *mathas* (religious institutions), further around the river bend, can be reached by ferry from the eastern side of the town, where there are also more *ghats* and dilapidated seventeenth-century temples.

Practicalities

Bicycles can be rented for next to nothing from either of two shops opposite the bus stand. Finding somewhere sanitary to **eat** however is more of a problem, the only places being the grim sweet and snack stalls dotted around town.

If, for any reason, you want to **stay** the night, avoid the two filthy dives at the top of the main street and seek out the *PWD Inspection Bungalow* (①), close to the Kanha road up in the north side of the town. Permission normally has to be obtained in advance, though tourists are usually granted special dispensation. Mandla's *State Bank of India* (Mon–Fri 10am–2pm, Sat 10am–noon) only exchanges cash.

Kanha National Park

Often dubbed the greatest of India's wildlife reserves, **KANHA NATIONAL PARK** encompasses nearly two thousand square kilometres of deciduous forest, savannah grassland, hills and gently meandering rivers – home to literally hundreds of species of animals and birds, including the heavily declining population of **tigers**. Despite the arduous overland haul to the park, few travellers are disappointed by its beauty, particularly poignant at dawn, though many feel hard done by when it comes to tiger spotting, as sightings are becoming rarer.

Central portions of the Kanha Valley were designated as a wildlife sanctuary as long ago as 1933. Prior to this, the whole area was one enormous viceregal hunting ground, its game the exclusive preserve of high-ranking British army officers and civil servants seeking trophies for their colonial bungalows. Not until the 1950s though, after a particularly voracious hunter bagged thirty tigers in a single shoot, did the government declare Kanha a bona fide national park. Since then, animal numbers have recovered dramatically, and the park, one of the original participants in Indira Gandhi's **Project Tiger** (see *Contexts*), has expanded to encompass a large protective buffer zone – a move not without its opponents among the local tribal community, who depend on the forest for food and firewood. Over the years, the authorities have had a hard time reconciling the needs of the villagers with the demands of conservation and tourism; but for the time being at least, an equitable balance seems to have been struck. While in no way free of the **poaching** affecting tigers throughout India, Kanha upholds its reputation as a model in wildlife management, and, even if you don't spot a cat, it's a congenial environment in which to enjoy some of central India's most unspoiled and quintessentially Kiplingesque countryside.

The Park

From the main gates, at **Kisli** in the west and **Mukki**, 35km away in the south, a complex network of motorable dirt-tracks fans out across the park, taking in a good cross-section of its diverse terrains. Which animals you see from your open-top jeep largely depends on where your guide decides to take you. Kanha is perhaps best known for the broad sweeps of grassy rolling meadows, or **maidans**, along its river valleys, which support large concentrations of **deer**. The park has several different species, including the rare "twelve-horned" **barasingha** (swamp deer), plucked from the verge of extinction in the 1960s; a handful of *hiran* (blackbuck), now perforce enclosed by tall jackal-proof fences; and the ubiquitous *chital* (spotted deer – the staple diet of Kanha's tigers), which congregate in especially large numbers during the rutting season in early July, when it's not uncommon to see four thousand at one time.

The **woodland** carpeting the spurs of the Maikal Ridge that taper into the core zone from the south, consists of *sal*, teak and moist deciduous forest oddly reminiscent of northern Europe. Troupes of black-faced langur monkeys crash through its canopy, while *gaur*, India's tallest wild buffalo, forage through the fallen leaves. Years of exposure to snap-happy humans seem to have left the awesome, hump-backed bulls impervious to camera flashes, but it's still wise to keep a safe distance. Higher up, you may catch sight of a spiky-horned *nilgai* (blue cow), a porcupine, python, sloth bear, wild boar, mouse deer or a secretive *sambar* – a favourite snack for the nocturnal predators that prowl through the trees. Sightings of **leopards** too are not an impossibility, although these shy animals tend to steer well clear of motor vehicles.

Kanha also boasts an exotic and colourful array of **birds**, including Indian rollers, bee-eaters, golden orioles, paradise fly-catchers, egrets, some outlandish **hornbills** and numerous kingfishers and birds of prey. Enthusiasts should try to stay at Mukki as it's closer to the **River Banjar** area with its many different water-birds.

Kanha's **tigers**, though, are its biggest draw, and the jeep drivers, who are well aware of that, tear around the park in hot pursuit, scanning the sandy tracks for pug marks and responding to other animals' alarm calls. This kind of "chase" gives an idea of the thrill of the hunt that led so many to track the cats, but rarely ends in a sighting. If you're intent on seeing one in the flesh, reckon on making at least two or three excursions, and try to persuade your driver to travel at a slower pace: staying still for a while may give you the time to spot a tiger relaxing in camouflaging brakes of bamboo or the tall elephant grass lining streams and waterholes, and it will definitely improve bird-spotting prospects. One place you're guaranteed to see tigers is on film at the nightly audio-visual show at the **visitors' centre**, by the park gate in Kisli (6.30pm; free).

Park practicalities

Kanha is **open** from dawn to dusk (but closes for 3 or 4 hours around noon) from September 1 until the monsoon arrives at the end of June. During peak season (Nov–Feb), the nights and early mornings can get very **cold**, and there are frequent frosts, so bring a jumper – without one, an open-top jeep safari quickly gets to be a real endurance test. The **heat** between March and June keeps visitor numbers down, but tiger sightings are more common then, when the cats are forced to come out to the waterholes and streams.

Getting there and away

The most straightforward way to **get to Kanha** is via Jabalpur, which is well connected by rail to most other parts of the country. If you're coming from **Orissa**, take a direct train to Katni on the main Bombay–Calcutta line and change there. The nearest airport with scheduled domestic flights is at Nagpur (226km).

Daily **buses** leave Jabalpur for **Kisli** (via Mandla) at 7am (5hr) and 11am (6hr). Both stop briefly at the barrier in **Khatia**, 4km down the road from Kisli; you must register with the park office here. Buses back to Jabalpur leave Khatia at 8am and 12.30pm. If you want to visit the park by car (around Rs2000 for the round trip, with a night halt), you'll have to make arrangements through the tourist office in Jabalpur (see p.400). **Mukki** can only be reached by the daily 12.30pm private bus from Mandla to Malakhand/Khatia.

Getting around

As **walking** inside the park is strictly forbidden, **jeeps**, which leave from Kisli every day at dawn (usually 6am) and in the afternoon, are the only way to **get around**. The fare, worked out according to distance and the fee for the obligatory **guide**, usually comes to around Rs600–800; there are additional charges for cameras and videos. Avoid the diesel jeeps if possible; these are noisier and tend to scare off the animals long before you get anywhere near them. If you can't get a group (up to a maximum of six, though four is more comfortable) together from your hotel and book a jeep direct at the park gate a day in advance, ask your hotel manager about spare seats – he should be able to find you a place.

If you arrive on the early bus and feel up to an evening safari, try asking groups on their way through the main Kisli barrier if they have a spare place. Only parties on package deals from the upmarket hotels are likely to decline, as they usually have their own *Land Rovers* and can afford to shun hitchhikers.

Accommodation and eating

Although MPTDC have a *Forest Lodge* at **Mukki** in the south, their two lodges in **Kisli**, near the western entrance, are easier to reach by public transport, and are situated in a more atmospheric location inside the park proper. Private hotels outside the west gate, in and around **Khatia**, are either first-come-first-served budget lodges, or high style resorts that should be booked at least five working days before arrival. MPTDC accommodation can be booked in advance either by calling into a regional MPTDC tourist office (in Delhi, Bombay, Calcutta, Jhansi, or Jabalpur, or most other major towns and cities in Madhya Pradesh) or by sending a 50 percent advance to: Central Reservations–Tours Division, *MPSTDC Ltd*, Fourth Floor Gangotri, TT Nagar, Bhopal 462 003 (☎0755/554340). However, it's always worth checking availability in Jabalpur before arriving.

Wherever you stay, make sure you tell the bus driver to drop you off at the right place, as the hotels at Khatia and the park gates are scattered along a six-kilometre stretch of road that sees very little traffic during the day.

BUDGET ACCOMMODATION

Machan Complex, Khatia (☎07642/2584). Around half a kilometre from the park gate, this is the cheapest option, and the closest to a family atmosphere, where you'll have to rely on home cooking. Very basic, with dorms, but can arrange jeeps. ①.

Motel Chandan, Khatia (☎07642/4252). Just before the barrier on the roadside. Very basic rooms with fans, old beds and bathrooms. Meals in rough and ready restaurant are part of the deal. More expensive "VIP Deluxe" chalets have bath-tubs and air-coolers. ③–④.

MPTDC Youth Hostel, opposite Kisli's "bus stand". Large rudimentary dorms and communal washrooms; rates include a monotonous diet of *thalis* served in military-style canteen, but you have to pay for second helpings. Pleasant setting, but poor value at over Rs160 per bed. ③.

MODERATE & EXPENSIVE

Indian Adventures, Khatia (book through *IAWR*, 257 SV Rd, Bandra, Bombay 400 050; ☎022/640 8742; fax 640 6399). A similar "all-in" package to *Kipling Camp,* and even further from the park gate. Chalets overlooking river, library, resident experts and al fresco restaurant with occasional dance performances. Pay in US dollars. ⑤–⑨.

Kipling Camp, 4km from Khatia (book through *Tollygunge Club Ltd*, 120 DP Sasmal Rd, Calcutta 700 033; ☎033/473 3306; fax 473 1903). British-owned and run cottage complex offering rustic comfort at absurd prices. "Ethnic" rooms, meals around the fire and pleasant forest location. Full board, safari and guides included. ⑧.

MPTDC Baghira Log Huts, Kisli. Spacious but dark rooms in self-contained chalets in the heart of the forest. Good restaurant, with a varied menu, that also serves beer. ⑥.

MPTDC Kanha Safari Lodge, Mukki. Open all year round. 35km from Kisli at the southern entrance to park, with good access to more remote areas. The best place to get away from it all. Meals, jeeps, guides etc available on site. Some a/c. ⑤–⑥.

Bandhavgarh National Park

With tiger sightings in Kanha on the decline, Madhya Pradesh's second national park at **BANDHAVGARH**, tucked away in the hilly northeast of the state, is receiving more and more attention from tourists, and for good reasons – the park has the highest density of **tigers** of any of India's reserves, shelters a collection of fascinating ruins, and offers the chance of trekking through the jungle on elephant back. It's a long haul to Bandhavgarh from either Jabalpur (195km) or Khajuraho (237km), but worth it – not only to track tigers and deer but also, as all the accommodation is close to the park gates, to watch birds, monkeys and even elephants cooling themselves in the river, without even entering the park.

Bandhavgarh may be one of India's newer national parks, but it claims a long history. Legend dates the construction of its hilltop **fort** to the time of the epic *Ramayana*, when monkey architects built Rama a place to rest on his return from his battle with the demon king of Lanka. Excavations of caves tunnelled into the rock below the fort revealed inscriptions scratched into the sandstone in the first century BC, from which time Bandhavgarh was the base for a string of dynasties. Among them were the **Chandellas**, responsible for the temples at Khajuraho, who ruled from here until the **Bhagels** took over in the twelfth century, staking a claim to the region that is still held by their direct descendant, the Maharaja of Rewa. The dynasty shifted to Rewa in 1617, allowing Bandhavgarh to be slowly consumed by healthy forest and the bamboo and grasslands that provided prime hunting ground for the Rewa Kings. The present maharaja ended his own hunting days in 1968 when he donated the area to the state as parkland. In 1986, two more chunks of forest were added to the original core zone, giving the park a total area of 437 square kilometres.

The Park

Though there are flat grassy *maidans* in the south of the park, Bandhavgarh is predominantly rugged and hilly, clad in *sal* trees in the valleys and mixed forest in the upper reaches, which shelter a diverse avian population. The park headquarters are in the tiny village of **Tala**, a stone's throw from the main gate in the north, connected to Umaria, 32km southwest, by a road slicing through the park's narrow midriff. Jeep tracks wind through the park from the north gate in Tala, circling below the central **fort** through forest and grassland, and passing watering holes and streams, good spots for viewing wildlife.

On the whole, jeep safaris tend to stick to the core area where the chances of spotting one of the thirty or so **tigers** are high, and glimpses of deer and monkeys guaranteed. Species include shy but animated gazelle and small barking deer, as well as the more common *nilgai* (blue cow) and *chital* (spotted deer). Sloth bears, porcupines, *sambhar* and muntjac also hide away in the forest, while hyenas, foxes and jackals appear occasionally in the open country. If you're very fortunate, you may catch sight of an elusive leopard.

Look out too for some very exotic **birds** – one hundred and fifty species at the last count, though no doubt you could add to the list if you stayed long enough. Regular stars include various drongos, fly-catchers, bee-eaters, rollers, parakeets, eagles, vultures and two kinds of rare **hornbills**. A more novel way of game viewing is to ride **elephant-back** in the misty dawn hours, tramping through the undergrowth as the *mahawat* hacks through spider webs and overhanging branches. Elephants have been part of Bandhavgarh society for generations, reared, trained and cared for by *mahawats* and their families in a small compound close to *White Tiger Lodge*. You can watch them tucking into a breakfast of giant 3kg *chapatis* before the morning outing, and enjoying their daily wash in the river each afternoon. The cheeky youngsters receive training beside their forty- to fifty- year old mothers and fathers on the safaris.

One of the best places to do some serious bird spotting is from the crumbling ramparts of the **fort** crowning a hill in the centre of the park, 300m above the surrounding terrain. **Permission** to climb up should be sought at park headquarters, near the main gate – if it's granted you'll need to rent a jeep to take you to the small frog-filled tank guarded by a massive reclining Vishnu at a point called **Shesh Saya**. From here the climb, fairly steep in parts, takes between one and two hours, passing some modest temples and a company of Vishnu's *avatars* carved in stone in the tenth century and still defying the undergrowth. The exotic plantlife en route attracts numerous species of insects which may make your skin crawl, but not as much as the thought that tigers may be watching you as you climb. They're more likely, however, to stick to the lower levels nearer their favourite prey, but the risks are real: permits are usually granted only to serious game viewers.

Park practicalities

Bandhavgarh is **open** from November to June (6.15–10am and 2.15–5.45pm): the **best time to visit**, if you want to spot wildlife, is during the hotter months between March and June, when thirsty tigers and their prey are forced out to the waterholes and the park's three perennial streams. But the heat can be trying, especially when the town's sporadic electricity supply precludes the use of fans or air conditioning before 6pm. Visiting in the cooler months, when wildlife viewing is still excellent, is more comfortable.

Without your own vehicle, **getting there** can be tricky. From Jabalpur, catch a **train** up to Katni, then head a short way down the *Southeast Railway* to Umaria, the nearest railhead to the park. Six daily **buses** (from 8am; 45min–1hr) leave here for **Tala**, 33km northeast. Approaching from Varanasi or Khajuraho, the nearest **airport**, make your way to Satna on the main railway line and pick up a train to Katni where you can change for Umaria. Travelling by bus involves a night in Satna (for hotels see p.397), and a laborious stop-and-start trip on local buses via Amarpatan or Beohari. From Delhi (or Agra), the best train is the *Utkal Express* #8478, which leaves Nizamuddin at 12.50pm and arrives in Katni at 5am the next day: change there for Umaria. Travelling by **rented car** from Khajuraho takes roughly 5 hours, and will cost upwards of Rs2000 for the round trip, plus an extra Rs250–300 for each night you stay.

To cover a reasonable distance within the park, book a **jeep** at the headquarters at the park gate or through your hotel. Up to six people can share a jeep, splitting the cost of Rs550 for a morning or afternoon session; **guides** are part of the deal. **Elephant rides** can also be arranged at the park office or your hotel (Rs200 per hour, shared by a maximum of four people). At present elephant safaris stick to the northern perimeter of the park, but proposals to allow them to cover the whole park are being considered.

Accommodation

Most of Bandhavgarh's new and established hotels, all of which are in Tala, cater for travellers on a higher budget, and offer "jungle-plan" prices – all-in deals including meals and jeep safaris. There's a handful of mid-range hotels, and one budget lodge. The only option for **eating** outside your hotel is the friendly *dhaba* on the main road.

Baghela, Umaria Rd. Small, simple budget option run by a very erratic manager. ③.

Bandhavgarh Jungle Camp, Umaria Rd. One of the oldest resorts, with double-roomed tents, with hot showers and dressing rooms, in the gardens of the old Maharaja's lodge. Al fresco lunch between safaris, and dinner (preceded by a slide show) in the lodge. Book through *Bandhavgarh Wildlife Camp & Safari*, B/21 Greater Kailash Enclave II, New Delhi 110048 (☎011/685 4626; fax 686 4614). Prices ($135 per person at present) payable in dollars. ⑨.

Bandhavgarh Jungle Lodge, close to the river; turn left off Umaria Rd. Characterful huts finished in mud coating and tribal style painting. Residents eat set (Indian) meals al fresco in the pleasant garden. Book through *Tiger Resorts Ltd*, Suite 206 Rakesh Deep, 11 Commercial Complex, New Delhi 110049 (☎011/685 3760; fax 686 5212). Accommodation only ⑤, jungle plan ⑧.

MPTDC White Tiger Forest Lodge, Umaria Rd, next to the barrier over the main road (☎07653/65308). Large complex with clean, cosy rooms, all with attached bath and hot water, and a good restaurant. Rooms 17–21 are in bungalows overlooking the river, where elephants wash and tigers come to drink in the height of summer. ⑤–⑥.

Nature Heritage, down a track forging right from the barrier over the main road. New resort with a sickly colour scheme, but very comfortable rooms, with carpets and baths: bookable through *khajuraho Tours* (see p.390). ⑧.

Tiger Lodge, Umaria Rd. Small and basic lodge opposite Tala's only *dhaba*. The bare rooms have fans, but bathrooms are shared. ②.

V Patel Jungle Resorts, close to *Nature Heritage* (☎07653/65323). Welcoming resort whose four clean rooms have attached bath, hot water and a communal verandah. Flower-filled garden and al-fresco restaurant. Book by phone, or in Jabalpur at 212 Abhaykunj, Narmada Rd (☎0761/26162). Excellent value. ⑤.

WESTERN MADHYA PRADESH

The geography of **western Madhya Pradesh** is dominated by the River Narmada, which drains westwards through a wide alluvial valley, bounded in the south by the Satpura hills and the Maharashtran border, and in the north by the rugged Vindhya range. Forming the major trade corridor between the Ganges plains and the west coast, the region was for nearly a thousand years known as **Malwa** – an independent prince-ly state ruled from the sprawling hill-top fort complex at **Mandu**. The former capital, now deserted, is, with its ruined mosques, tanks and palaces, and its spectacular panoramic views, the area's outstanding tourist attraction.

Most visitors travel to Mandu via the industrial city of **Indore**, then continue north-east to Bhopal, or south on the main Delhi–Bombay railway line towards the jumping-off point for the Ellora and Ajanta caves, Jalgaon. Alternatively, you could head off to the fascinating riverside Hindu pilgrimage centres of **Omkareshwar** and **Maheshwar** – looping east to Mandu, before rejoining the railway at Indore. The sacred city of **Ujjain**, 55km further north, boasts a bumper crop of modern Hindu temples, but little else. You could, nevertheless, choose to pause here on your way to or from southern Rajasthan on the *Western Railway*, the most direct land link with Delhi.

Indore and around

INDORE, the second largest city in Madhya Pradesh, is huge, modern, heavily indus-trialized, and generally dull. If you find yourself with time to kill en route to or from **Mandu**, 105km southwest, however, a couple of worthwhile sights lie hidden among its tangle of ferro-concrete flyovers, expressways and crowded bazaars.

Situated at the confluence of the Kham and Saraswati rivers, the city was for centuries an insignificant stopover on the pilgrimage trails to Omkareshwar and Ujjain, 55km north. In the eighteenth century, it became the capital of the **Holkar** dynasty, whose chief, Malhar Rao, had previously managed to scrounge several choice scraps from the Marathas during their northward advance against the Moghuls. Later, Rao's daughter-in-law, **Ahilya Bai**, took over control of the state, which at its height stretched as far as the Ganges and the Punjab. Described by a contemporary British diplomat as "the most exemplary ruler that ever lived", the Rani was a kind of central Indian Queen Victoria, who, in addition to founding the modern city of Indore, built palaces, temples, *dharamshalas* and charitable institutions all over the country. When she died in 1795, her four grandsons dragged the state into a bloody civil war. A series of skirmishes with the Marathas and East India Company followed, ending in the Treaty of 1818, which secured for the dynasty a small but rich dominion with Indore as the capital. The city's expansion gained momentum in the nineteenth century, fuelled by a lucrative trade in cotton and opium. Despite remaining loyal to the British in the Mutiny, however, the maverick Holkar Maharajas remained firmly under the thumb of their colonial overlords until Independence, when they were finally relieved of their powers by the Congress.

Indore, these days, is the region's biggest business and commercial centre. The nearby industrial estate of **Pithampur**, hyped as "the Detroit of India", hosts numerous

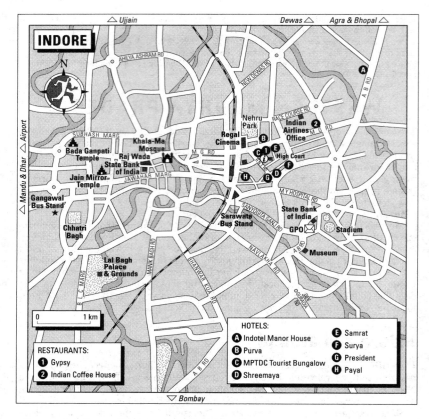

giant steel and auto manufacturers, including *Honda, Bajaj, Hindustan Motors* and *Pratap Steel*. The resulting **affluence** has made a big impact; satellite dishes, luxury hotels and American-style shopping malls are popping up all over the place, while the *nouveaux riches* swan ostentatiously around town on brand-new Japanese scooters. Even the auto-rickshaws seem shinier.

Arrival and information

Trains arriving in Indore on the *Central Railway* pull in at the mainline station in the middle of the city. The principal **bus stand**, "Sarawate" (☎465688), is a short walk south from platform 1, beyond the overpass. Most Mandu buses, however, use the less convenient "Gangawal" bus stand (☎480688), a three-kilometre auto-rickshaw ride west towards the domestic **airport**, 10km out.

The most convenient means of **getting around** is by metered auto-rickshaw; note that the tariffs increase by 50 percent after 10pm. Alternatively, you could brave the traffic yourself by renting a **bicycle** from one of the stalls opposite the train station.

MPTDC's helpful **information** office (Mon–Sat 10am–5pm; closed 2nd and 3rd Sat of the month; ☎430653), behind the Ravindra Natya Griha Exhibition Hall on

The telephone **area code** for Indore is ☎0731.

Rabidranath Tagore Rd (generally referred to as RNT Rd), hands out the usual glossy leaflets and a better-than-average city map. They also have a car for rent (with driver), available for two-day **tours** to Mandu and a one-day tour to Omkareshwar and Maheshwar, all charged at Rs4 per km, plus Rs220 per night halt.

The *State Bank of Indore* (Mon–Fri 10am–2pm, Sat 10am–noon) has a **foreign exchange** office opposite their main branch on Raj Wada. The *Bank of Baroda* (same hours), across town on Agra Bombay (AB) Rd, near the **GPO**, deals with *Visa*. Finally, there's a 24-hour **pharmacy** (☎430301) in the MY Hospital compound, off AB Rd.

The City

With the exception of Indore's museum, over on AB Rd near the GPO, most of the city's sights lie west of the railway line, in and around the bazaar. Two broad thoroughfares, MG Marg and Jawahar Marg, form the north and south boundaries of this cluttered and chaotic district, which is interrupted in the east by the confluence of the Saraswati and Kham rivers – little more than trickles of black slime bordered by *bastees* and heaps of decomposing rubbish. The surrounding suburbs, by contrast, are a much more congenial prospect of detached houses, new apartment blocks and leafy gardens – home to Indore's managerial classes and a couple of old Holkar palaces.

The Lal Bagh palace

Set in its own grounds on the banks of the Kham, the **Lal Bagh palace** (Tues–Sun 10am–5pm; Rs2) is another of those extravagant Neoclassical creations so beloved of the ludicrously rich maharajas of the nineteenth and early twentieth centuries. The building took two generations of the Holkar family around thirty years to complete, and was, in its day, rivalled only by the Scindias' Jai Vilas palace in Gwalior. Granted carte blanche and a limitless budget, its British architects and interior decorators came up with a cross between Brideshead and Versailles – a vast stately home dripping with Doric columns, gilt stucco, crystal chandeliers, and piles of replica rococo furniture. In 1987, the property was inherited by the state government, who installed a small museum in the reception hall and renamed it the Nehru Centre.

Lal Bagh's main entrance is via a pair of grandiose wrought-iron **gates**, modelled on those at Buckingham Palace, which bear the Holkar family arms, with its motto "Success attends he who strives" inscribed in Hindi below. Note the wheat and poppies in the background, symbolizing the two main sources of the dynasty's prosperity. The ground floor of the palace consists of several large chambers: the **durbar hall**, used for royal assemblies, the state banquet hall, and the ballroom, with its specially sprung herring-bone dance floor. Hanging on the wall of the billiards room nearby, a fine picture of Tukoji Rao (1902–25) – the ruler responsible for completing the palace – is encrusted with precious stones. The Maharaja sent his own court artist to France to study European painting so that his portrait could be rendered in the "correct" style. The cherubs, flying nymphs, and Greek and Roman gods that adorn the ceilings of the adjacent rooms are equally convincing. Also worth checking out is the underground passage leading down to the kitchens. One of the rooms hidden away in this vault contains a modest but very colourful collection of **tribal artefacts**, including terracotta votive statues, clothes, jewellery, murals and brass sculpture.

The Raj Wada

The Holkars' Old Palace, the **Raj Wada**, is Indore's principal landmark, presiding over a palm-fringed square in the heart of the city. Built in the style of a western Indian townhouse, the eighteenth-century mansion's most prominent feature is a lofty, seven-storey gateway. Its upper four floors were originally made of wood, which made it particularly prone to fire; most of the palace collapsed after the last one, in 1984. Only the facade and the family temple, immediately inside the main courtyard, survive.

The Kanch Mandir and bazaars

Tucked away deep in the bazaar district, ten minutes' walk west of Raj Wada, the Jain **Kanch Mandir**, or "Mirror Temple" (daily 10am–5pm), is one of the city's more eccentric religious monuments. Surprisingly for a faith renowned for its austerity, the interior of the temple is decked with multi-coloured glass **mosaics**. Vivid tableaux lining the sides of the entrance hall depict the horrors in store for sinners in the afterlife.

The **bazaars** in the vicinity of the Kanch Mandir and Raj Wada are great for a stroll. Rows of stalls and open-fronted shops are jammed beneath picturesque four-storeyed houses with overhanging wooden balconies. The gold and silver jewellery market, Sarafa Bazaar, is Indore's most famous. You'll find it around the corner from the Mirror Temple, near the massive wholesale textile market, where cloth is still sold by weight. Also worth seeking out are shops on Bajaj Khana Chowk that specialize in traditional embroidered and beadwork costumes, and the atmospheric fruit and vegetable market on the river bank beneath the lime-green **Khala-Ma mosque**.

The Central Museum

Indore's **Central Museum** (Mon–Sat 10am–5pm) is over in the southeast of the city, near the GPO. Its large collection includes finds from nearby prehistoric sites, as well as fine Jain and Hindu sculpture from the ruined eleventh- and twelfth-century temples at Hinlajgarh. The downstairs gallery boasts a handful of priceless **Harappan terracottas** unearthed at Mohenjo Daro, in southern Pakistan. None of the exhibits is adequately labelled, but the museum attendants are happy to show you around.

Elsewhere around the city

Several exotic onion-domed cenotaphs dotted around the city are dedicated to former Holkar rulers and their families. The two main concentrations of **chhatris** are near the riverside fruit and vegetable market, below the MG Road bridge, and southwest of the city centre near the Lal Bagh palace. The latter, **Chhatri Bagh**, consists of two weed-infested walled enclosures and can only be visited between 8am and 11am, when offerings are left at the tombs by *pujaris*.

A more state-of-the-art Hindu shrine stands 1km west of Raj Wada, off the busy MG Road. The **Bada Ganpati** temple houses a massive 11-metre seated icon of the elephant-headed god of prosperity, Ganesh. Painted bright orange and decked with sequins, tinsel and garlands of imitation flowers, the idol is made of such unlikely ingredients as cow dung, sugar cane extract, Ganges water, soil from India's seven holiest cities, and ground diamonds, emeralds, rubies, pearls and topaz.

Accommodation

The majority of Indore's **hotels** cater for business visitors, and are scattered around the prosperous suburb of **Tukoganj**, 1km east of the railway station. Competition here is stiff, so standards tend to be high, and prices reasonable. The same cannot be said of the cheaper accommodation, most of which is in the noisy and polluted area between Sarawate and the railway station. Ignore the touts who try to drag you off to the dire lodges opposite the bus stand, and head instead for the better-value budget hotels along **Chhoti Gwaltoli**, a lane beneath the big Patel flyover. All but the absolute rock-bottom lodges levy the mandatory state **luxury tax**.

Indotel Manor House, Agra Bombay Rd (☎537301; fax 392250). The city's top hotel, 4km outside the centre. All mod cons; gourmet restaurant, 24hr coffee shop and exchange counter. ⑥–⑧.

MPTDC Tourist Bungalow, RNT Rd (☎541818). Small, claustrophobic place tucked away behind the *Tagore Natya Griha* exhibition hall; not up to usual standards. No restaurant. Some a/c. ④–⑤.

Payal, 38 Chhoti Gwaltoli (☎463202). By far the best deal among the inexpensive hotels. Airy, clean rooms, with attached shower-toilets and *Star TV*. ③–④.

President, 163 RNT Rd (☎433156; fax 532230). Very glam, and comfortable. All a/c rooms. Health club, excellent veg restaurant and roof-top cafe. Reputable in-house travel agent. ⑦–⑨.

Purva, 1–4 Dhenu Market (☎541149). Small, friendly and spotless hotel, five minutes from the station. Very good value. ④–⑥.

Railway Retiring Rooms, railway station. The recently renovated dorms are cleaner and slightly more expensive than usual. Handy for an early morning departure. ①.

Samrat, 18/5 MG Rd (☎435277). Large, modern hotel geared towards business travellers, and a little frayed at the edges. Restaurant and room service. ⑤–⑥.

Shreemaya, 12 RNT Rd (☎431941). Indore's largest hotel has all the usual facilities, including foreign exchange and a car park. ⑥–⑦.

Surya, 5/5 North Mandi Road (☎431155). A slick businessman's hotel with fresh rooms and balconies, and an above-average restaurant. The best value in its price category. ⑥–⑦.

Eating

Eating out is popular among Indore's middle classes, so there are plenty of quality restaurants around the city centre to choose from. Most are located in the larger hotels, such as the *Shreemaya*, *Surya*, and *President*, and serve the usual Indian and Chinese

---

MOVING ON FROM INDORE

A full summary of Indore's transport connections appears on p.348.

Tickets for *Indian Airlines* **flights** from Indore airport (☎411528 or 411782) can be booked at the office (☎431595), Race Course Rd, 2km northeast of the station. There is no airport bus.

As for **trains**, two broad-gauge branches of the *Western Railway* connect Indore to cities in northern India. The fastest service to **Delhi**, the daily *Indore–Nizamuddin Express* #4005, leaves at 4.15pm and heads north via Ujjain, Kota and Bharatpur, arriving in Delhi at 6am the next day. The other branch, serviced by the daily *Malwa Express* #4667 (departs 5.30pm, arrives 12.30pm the next day), runs east to Bhopal, then north to New Delhi on the *Central Railway* via Jhansi, Gwalior, and Agra.

Trains to **Rajasthan** leave twice daily on the metre-gauge line for Chittaurgarh and Ajmer, and once to Jaipur (*Express* #9770, departs 10.10pm, arrives 4.20pm next day). Getting to **Ellora** and **Ajanta** means catching the 4.40am *Express* #9769 to Kandhwa, arriving at 10.15am, in time to pick up the 11.25am *Lashkar Express* #1162 for Jalgaon (arrive 2pm). There's only one train to **Jabalpur**, for connections to Kanha and Bandhavgarh: the *Narmada Express* #8233 departs daily at 3pm, arriving at 6.05am the next morning.

To get to **Mandu** by **bus** from Indore, take a direct service (1hr 30min–2hr) at 8am from Gangawal bus stand, or from Sarawate at 2.30pm. Failing that, take any of the frequent services from Sarawate bus stand to **Dhar** (45min), which is connected to Mandu by half-hourly buses (30min–1hr).

MPSRTC, whose office is in Sarawate, operate "luxury" buses to **Bhopal** four times daily (6am, noon, 2.45pm & 9pm; 5–6hr), while MPTDC run a single super-fast service leaving the tourist office each morning at 8am (4hr), arriving at Bhopal in time to meet the Delhi-bound *Shatabdi Express*.

Reliable **travel agents** in town include the excellent *President Travels*, at *Hotel President*, 163 RNT Rd (☎533472), *Royal Tourist Service*, 164 RNT Rd (☎434730) and *Taj Tours & Travels*, at *Hotel Taj Regency*, near Scheme 54 (☎438606).

dishes. Thanks to the current "health food" craze, there are a couple of excellent pure-veg places as well, the classiest being *Woodlands* in the *President*. Cheaper food is available at the dingy *dhabas* and canteens around Sarawate bus stand. Stick to the ones doing a brisk trade, and you shouldn't go far wrong.

Apsara, RNT Rd. Popular family place just in front of the *Tourist Bungalow*, serving veg food inside and in the open air. Inexpensive.

Gypsy, MG Rd. American-style fast-food joint near Nath Mandir Crossing, serving mutton-burgers, pizzas and fries, and a range of ice-creams, cakes and pastries at moderate prices.

Indian Coffee House, next to Rampura Building, off MG Rd. The usual south Indian snacks served by waiters in turbans and cummerbunds. Opens at 7.30am for big breakfasts and the papers. There's another branch set in peaceful grounds behind the high court.

Status, below *Hotel Purva*, 565 MG Rd. Superb eat-till-you-burst Rajasthani lunch-time *thalis*, with varied veg dishes, *dals*, breads and chutneys – all for Rs30. Veg *à la carte* later on.

Woodlands, 163 RNT Marg. *Hotel President*'s swanky pure-veg a/c restaurant serves stylish, but pricey south Indian specialities.

Dewas

The dusty, fly-blown town of **DEWAS**, 35km northeast of Indore on NH3, is dominated by a large volcanic hillside that rises from its northern fringes. The site of several ancient rock-cut hermits' caves and a small temple dedicated to the fierce, skeletal goddess Chamunda, the hill inspired the title of E M Forster's autobiographical novel, *The Hill of Devi*. Forster lived in the nearby palace as personal secretary to the local Raja in the 1920s – a post he described as his "great opportunity". Many of the young author's experiences of life in this small central Indian town found their way into *A Passage to India*. The palace is still occupied and not open to visitors, but you can climb (or drive) to the top of the hill to visit its tiny temple, and to appreciate the views.

Although Dewas has no hotels, its frequent bus connections with Bhopal, Ujjain and Indore, aloow you to pause here briefly without running the risk of being stranded.

Dhar

The bustling market town, **DHAR**, 65km west of Indore, was the capital of Malwa before Hoshang Shah moved the royal court to Mandu in 1405. It is here that the first phase of Malwa architecture – often attributed to Mandu – probably originated and it's worth a look, either on a day trip from Mandu, or on the way back to Indore, when you'll be able to compare the two sites. You can safely leave your bags in the conductors' room in the chaotic bus station while you explore on foot or by cycle rickshaw.

Just ten minutes' walk west of the bus stand is **Bhojshala**, a mosque built over a Hindu temple, and completed in 1400. Like Mandu's much grander Jama Masjid, it features shallow domes and low colonnades around a large open courtyard. Note the slate floor slabs engraved with Hindu plays; the Muslim builders probably thought the plays were sacred texts, and wanted to defile them. Officially recognized as an archeological site, the mosque is still used as a place of communal worship – by Muslims on Friday afternoons, and by Hindus on Tuesday mornings – an unusual practice that has continued peacefully for centuries. Remove your shoes before entering the sanctuary.

The town's other notable mosque, **Lat Masjid**, lies 1km away on the southern edge of town, bordering flat agricultural land. Built in 1405 by Dilawar Khan, it lies neglected but not ruined, its nooks and crannies filled with grass and the nests of elegant green parrots. Like Bhojshala it contains segments of earlier Hindu masonry, and bears significance for Hindus: some locals believe the mosque was built on the site of Raja Bhoj's Vijay Mandir, and celebrate the opening ceremonies of Dussehra here each autumn.

Dhar's only other noteworthy monument is the sandstone **fort** that crowns the hill to the east of the bazaar. Built by the Sultans on the site of an eleventh-century Paramara Hindu temple, it is now almost entirely ruined, with a few sorry looking statues propped up in sun-parched grass. It's said that secret passages run from here to Mandu, and provided the escape route for freedom fighters faced with one of the first battles of retaliation launched by British troops after the Mutiny of 1857.

Mandu

Set against the rugged backdrop of the Vindhya hills, the medieval ghost-town of **MANDU**, 98km from Indore, is one of central India's most atmospheric historical monuments. Come here at the height of the monsoons, when the rocky plateau and its steeply shelving sides are carpeted with green vegetation, and you'll see why the Malwa Sultans christened their capital **Shadiabad**, or "City of Joy". Even during the relentless heat of the dry season, the ruins make an exotic spectacle. Elegant Islamic palaces, mosques and onion-domed mausolea crumble beside large medieval reservoirs and precipitous ravines, while below, an endless vista of scorched plains and tiny villages stretches off to the horizon. Mandu can be visited as a day trip from Indore, but you'll enjoy it more if you spend a couple of nights. That not only gives you time to explore the ruins, but enables you to witness the memorable sunset over the Narmada Valley.

History

Archeological evidence suggests that the remote hill-top was first fortified around the sixth century AD, when it was known as Mandapa-Durga, or "Durga's hall of worship" – in time corrupted to "Mandu". Four hundred years later, the site gained in strategic importance when the powerful **Paramaras** moved their capital from Ujjain to Dhar,

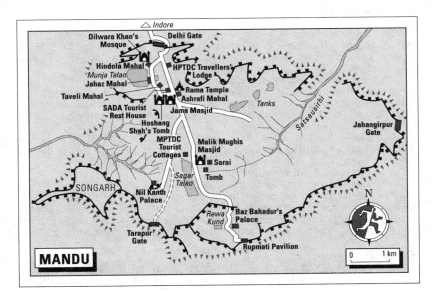

35km north. The plateau's natural defences, strengthened by Raja Bhoj (see p.351), proved, however, unable to withstand persistent attacks by the Muslim invaders during the twelfth century. The fort eventually fell to the Sultans of Delhi in 1305.

When the Sultanate had their hands full fending off the Mongols on their northern borders a century or so later, Malwa's Afghan governor, Dilawar Khan **Ghuri**, seized the chance to establish his own independent kingdom. He died after only four years on the throne, however, leaving his ambitious young son at the helm. During **Hoshang Shah**'s illustrious 27-year reign, Mandu was promoted from pleasure resort to royal capital, and acquired some of the finest Islamic monuments in Asia, including the Jama Masjid, Delhi Gate, and the Sultan's own tomb.

Mandu's golden age continued under the **Khaljis**, who took over from the Ghuri dynasty in 1436, when Mahmud Shah Khalji poisoned Hoshang Shah's grandson. Another building boom and several protracted wars later, Mandu settled down to a lengthy period of peace and prosperity under **Ghiyath Shah** (1469–1500). Famous for his love of cooking and beautiful women, Ghiyath amassed a harem of 15,000 courtesans, and a bodyguard of a thousand Turkish and Abyssinian amazons, whom he accommodated in the appropriately lavish Jahaz Mahal. The sybaritic Sultan lived to a ripe old age, but was poisoned by his son shortly after his eightieth birthday. His successor, Nasir Shah, died of guilt ten years later and Mandu, dogged by feuds and the threat of rebellion, became an easy target for the militaristic Sultan of Gujarat, who invaded in 1526. In the centuries that followed, control over the fort and its rapidly decaying monuments passed between a succession of independent rulers and the Moghuls. It never regained its former prominence, however, and was deserted by the time the Marathas annexed the region in 1732. These days, Mandu is a tranquil backwater that sees far fewer visitors than it deserves. Apart from at weekends, when busloads of exuberant day-trippers breeze in from Indore, the only people you're likely to see picking through the ruins are the Bhil villagers who farm the surrounding fields.

The monuments

Mandu's **monuments** derive from a unique school of Islamic architecture that flourished here, and at the region's former capital, Dhar, between 1400 and 1516. Much admired for their elegant simplicity, the buildings are believed to have exerted a considerable influence on the Moghul architects responsible for the Taj Mahal.

Mandu's platform, a 23km-square plateau, is separated from the body of hills to the north by the **Kakra Khoh**, literally "deep ravine". A narrow causeway forms a natural bridge across the gorge, carrying the present road across and up via a series of subsidiary gates to the fort's modern entrance, beside the original and very grand Delhi Gate. From here, the road runs south past the first and main concentration of monuments, the **Royal Enclave**, to the village square, which stands in the middle of the second, or **village group**. The remaining sites lie further to the south, east of the picturesque **Sagar Talao** tank, and in a fortified enclosure overlooking the Narmada Valley known as the **Rewa Kund group**.

If you don't have your own vehicle, the most pleasant way of **getting around** the fort and its widely dispersed monuments is to rent a bicycle from the *VIP Wine Shop*, just off the main square, or from your hotel (Rs20 per day). Alternatively, you can squeeze into the village's decrepit old tempo that runs between the village square and Rewa Kund group at regular intervals, or rent one of the town's two auto-rickshaws for a complete tour.

The Royal Enclave
Reached via the lane that leads west off the village square, the **Royal Enclave** is dominated by Mandu's most photographed monument, Ghiyath Shah's majestic **Jahaz**

Mahal, or "Ship Palace". The name derives from its unusual shape, and elevated situation on a narrow strip of land between two large water tanks. It originally housed the Sultan's huge harem, and the thousand-strong all-women guard that protected them. A breezy rooftop terrace, crowned with four domed pavilions, looks over **Munja Talao** lake to the west, and the square, stone-lined **Kapur Sagar** in the other direction. From the northern balcony, you also get a good view of the geometric sandstone bathing pools where the palace's inhabitants would have whiled away their long incarceration.

The next building along the lane is the **Hindola Mahal**, or "Swing Palace" – so-called because its distinctive sloping walls supposedly look as though they are swaying from side to side. The design was, in fact, purely functional, intended to buttress the graceful but heavy stone arches that support the ceiling inside. At the far end of the T-shaped assembly hall, a long stepped ramp allowed the Sultan and his retinue to reach the upper storey on elephant-back.

Sprawling over the northern shores of Munja Talao lake are the dilapidated remains of a second royal pleasure palace. The **Champa Baodi** boasts an ingeniously complex ventilation and water-supply system which kept its dozens of subterranean chambers, or *tykhanas*, cool during the long Malwan summers. Immediately to the north stands the venerable **Mosque of Dilawara Khan**, dating from 1405. The chunks of Hindu temple used to build its main doorway and colonnaded hall are still very evident.

The **Hathi Pol**, or "Elephant Gate", was the main entrance to the Royal Enclave. Once past its pair of colossal, half-decapitated elephant guardians, a dusty track heads north to the edge of the plateau and the grand **Delhi Gate**. Built around the same time as Dilawara Khan's mosque, this great bastion, towering over the cobbled road in five sculpted arches, is the most imposing of the twelve that stud the battlements along the fort's 45-kilometre perimeter. The views from its ramparts over Kakra Khoh, the chasm through which invading armies invariably chose to attack Mandu, are spectacular.

The village group

Some of the fort's best-preserved buildings are clustered **around the village**. Work on the magnificent pink sandstone mosque on the west side of the main square, the **Jama Masjid**, commenced during the reign of Hoshang Shah and took three generations to complete. Said to be modelled on the Great Mosque at Damascus, it rests on a huge raised plinth pierced by rows of tiny arched chambers – once used as cells for visiting priests. A flight of steps leads up from the square to the large domed entrance porch. Beyond the ornate *jali* screens and bands of blue-glaze tiles that decorate the main doorway, you arrive in the Great Courtyard, enclosed by rows of pillars and small domes. The prayer hall, or Qibla, at the far end, is surmounted by three larger domes, and houses a small pulpit and some finely carved Koranic inscriptions.

Hoshang Shah's tomb (*c*. 1440), directly behind the Jama Masjid, is this group's real highlight. It stands on a low plinth at the centre of a square-walled enclosure, and is crowned by a squat central dome and four small corner cupolas. Now streaked with mildew and mud washed down from the bats' nests inside its eaves, the tomb is made entirely from milky white marble – the first of its kind in the subcontinent. An inscription on the right door jamb records the visit, in 1659, of the Moghul emperor Shah Jahan, who brought four of his architects to admire the building before they began work on the Taj Mahal. The interior of the tomb is very plain, except for the elaborate pierced-stone windows that illuminate Hoshang's sarcophagus.

On the opposite side of the square to the Great Mosque, the **Ashrafi Mahal**, or "Palace of Coins", was a theological college (*madarasa*) that the ruler Muhammad Shah later converted into a tomb. The complex included a giant marble mausoleum and seven-storey *minar*, or victory tower, of which only the base survives.

Around the Sagar Talao

En route to the Rewa Kund, a further handful of monuments are scattered around the fields east of Sagar Talao. Dating from the early fifteenth century, the **Mosque of Malik Mughis** is the oldest of the bunch, once again visibly constructed using ancient Hindu masonry. Note the turquoise tiles and fine Islamic calligraphy over the main doorway. The high-walled building opposite was a **caravansarai**, where merchants and their camel trains would rest during long treks across the subcontinent.

A short way south of the *sarai*, the octagonal tomb known as the **Dai-ki-Chhoti Bahan-ka-Mahal** looms above the surrounding fields from a raised plinth, still retaining large strips of the blue ceramic tiles that plastered most of Mandu's beautiful Afghan domes. Young couples from the nearby village creep off here during the evenings for a bit of privacy, so make plenty of noise as you approach.

The Rewa Kund group

The road to the **Rewa Kund group** heads past herds of water buffalo grazing on the muddy foreshores of the lake, then winds its way gently through a couple of Bhil villages towards the far southern edge of the plateau. Stately old baobabs line the roadside, like giant upturned root vegetables. The bulbous-bottomed trees, natives of the African Sahel, were introduced to India by Arab traders, and are now used by the local tribespeople for their many medicinal properties.

The **Rewa Kund** itself nestles behind a rise further up the hill. Noted for its curative powers, the old stone-lined reservoir is popular with bus parties of Indian visitors, who picnic under the trees by its banks. Water from the tank used to be pumped into the cistern in the nearby **Baz Bahadur Palace**. Bahadur, the last independent ruler of Malwa, retreated to Mandu to study music after being trounced in battle by Rani Durgavati (see p.400). Legend has it that he fell in love with a Hindu singer named Rupmati, whom he enticed to his hilltop home with an exquisite palace that she could admire from the window of her father's house on the Nirmar Plains below. The couple eventually married, but did not live happily ever after. When Akbar heard of Rupmati's beauty, he dispatched an army to Mandu to capture her and the long-coveted fort. Bahadur managed to slip away from the ensuing battle, but his bride, left behind in the palace, poisoned herself rather than fall into the clutches of the attackers.

The romantic **Rupmati Pavilion**, built by Bahadur for his bride-to-be, still rests on a ridge high above the Rewa Kund. Beneath its lofty terrace, the plateau plunges a sheer 300m to the gently undulating Narmada Valley. The view is breathtaking, especially on a clear day, when you can just about make out the sun-bleached banks of the sacred river as it winds west towards the Arabian Sea.

The Nil Kanth Palace

Another idyllic spot for watching the sun set over the plains is the **Nil Kanth Palace**, an old Shiva temple converted by the Moghuls into a water pavilion. It clings to the top of a steep cliff at the head of a rugged ravine on the western edge of the plateau, and was used by Akbar as royal retreat. Persian verses on the walls of one room record the emperor's military exploits in the Deccan, and, in a more philosophical vein, remind readers of the transience and futility of worldly achievement. It can be reached along a track that forks right off the main road, 500m south of Mandu village square.

Practicalities

Although *MPSRTC* operate direct **buses** to Mandu from Indore, it's quicker to travel to Dhar and pick up a local service to the fort from there – a 35-kilometre journey that takes over one hour. Direct services back to Indore run twice a day. **Taxis** charge around Rs800 for the round trip from Indore, plus a hefty Rs250 waiting charge if you stay overnight – which still works out cheaper than an MPTDC rental car. MPTDC and a couple of private companies also run day-long guided **tours** of Mandu from Indore on weekends (and some weekdays in high season). Ask at the tourist office on RNT Rd in Indore, or in a travel agency (for details see p.413). You can also get to Mandu by state bus from Bhopal, Ujjain and Maheshwar, though the trip to or from Maheshwar is quicker via Indore.

Most **places to stay** inside the fort are managed by MPTDC, who advise visitors to book a couple of days in advance. Their cheapest hotel, the *Travellers' Lodge* (☎07292/63221; ⑨), at the north end of the plateau near the SADA barrier, has scenic views, clean rooms with attached bath and hot water, and very welcoming staff. It's a one-kilometre hike from the main square where the buses pull in, however, so ask to be dropped off en route. In the centre of the village, SADA's ultra-basic *Tourist Rest House* (①), opposite the Jama Masjid, has a few spartan rooms, without running water, for Rs40. The MPTDC *Tourist Cottages* (☎07292/63235; ⑨–⑥), 2km south of the square, is Mandu's most comfortable and expensive hotel. The campus of chalets, over-looking the Sagar Talao tank, boasts twenty large rooms with attached shower-toilets, hot water and some a/c.

The *Tourist Cottages*' pleasant semi-open-air restaurant is the best **place to eat** in the fort. Unlike the cafeteria in the *Tourist Lodge*, you don't have to order your evening meal in advance, and they serve beer in addition to the standard MPTDC menu of moderately priced Indian, Chinese and Western food. Otherwise, the best cheap meals are the vegetarian *thalis*, *subzi* and *chappatis* in the *Shivani Hotel*, halfway between the square and the SADA barrier. The *Relax Point*, on the square, also offers *chai*, cold drinks and greasy fried snacks. Avoid **meat**, though, as frequent power-cuts mean that even places with refrigerators can have problems keeping it fresh.

There is nowhere to **change money**; the nearest bank is in Indore. With persis-tence, you can make **STD calls** from the telegraph office just off the village square.

Ujjain

Situated on the banks of the sacred River Shipra, **UJJAIN**, 80km north of Indore, is one of India's seven holiest cities. Like Haridwar, Nasik and Prayag (near Allahabad), it plays host every twelve years to the country's largest religious gath-ering, the **Kumbh Mela** (see p.313), which in 1992 drew an estimated fifteen million pilgrims here to bathe. Outside festival times, however, Ujjain can be a dull destina-tion for non-Hindus. Despite their manifold mythological associations, its temples are mostly ugly ferro-concrete affairs, while the fabled *ghats* resemble a run-of-the-mill municipal swimming pool. If you come expecting a mini-Varanasi, you'll be dis-appointed. On the plus side, the city is a good place to experience the more lurid side of modern Hinduism: brightly painted temples, colourful *puja* stalls, and the electric devotional music that is nowadays broadcast from virtually every roadside shrine and temple courtyard.

History

Excavations north of Ujjain have yielded traces of settlement as far back as the eighth century BC. The ancient city was a major regional capital under the Mauryans (Ashok was governor here for a time during the reign of his father), when it was known as **Avantika** and lay on the main trade route that linked northern India with Mesopotamia and Egypt. According to Hindu mythology, Shiva later changed its name to **Ujjaiyini**, "He Who Conquers With Pride", to mark his victory over the demon king of Tripuri. Chandragupta II, renowned for his patronage of the arts, also ruled from here in the fourth and fifth centuries. Among the Nava Ratna, or "Nine Gems", of his court was the

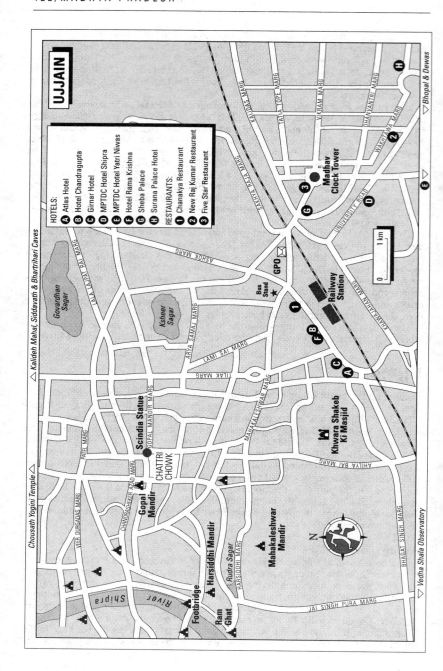

UJAIN

HOTELS:
- Ⓐ Atlas Hotel
- Ⓑ Hotel Chandragupta
- Ⓒ Girnar Hotel
- Ⓓ MPTDC Hotel Shipra
- Ⓔ MPTDC Hotel Yatri Niwas
- Ⓕ Hotel Rama Krishna
- Ⓖ Sheba Palace
- Ⓗ Surana Palace Hotel

RESTAURANTS:
- ❶ Chanakya Restaurant
- ❷ New Raj Kumar Restaurant
- ❸ Five Star Restaurant

illustrious Sanskrit poet **Kalidasa**, whose much-loved narrative poem *Meghduta* ("Cloud Messenger") includes a lyrical evocation of the city and its inhabitants.

Ujjain was sacked in 1234 by Iltutmish, of the Delhi Slave Dynasty, who razed most of its temples. Thereafter, the Malwan capital was governed by Sultans of Mandu, the Moghuls, and by **Raja Jai Singh** from Jaipur, who designed, along with many renovation projects elsewhere in India, the Vedha Shala observatory (Ujjain straddles the Hindu first meridian of longitude). Ujjain's fortunes declined from the early eighteenth century onwards, except for a sixty-year renaissance between the arrival of the Scindia dynasty in 1750 and their departure to Gwalior. These days, nearby Indore sees the lion's share of the region's industrial activity, leaving Ujjain's 367,000-strong population to make its living by more traditional means.

Arrival and information

Trains arriving in Ujjain on both broad-gauge branches of the *Western Railway* pull in at the station in the centre of town, two minutes' walk west of the state **bus** stand. The city is fairly spread out, so you'll need to **get around** by auto-rickshaw, or by renting a **bicycle** from the shop opposite the bus stand. **Taxis** can be arranged through the MPTDC *Hotel Shipra* (☎51495), in the cantonment area, which is also the best source of **information**. The *State Bank of India* (Mon–Fri 10.30am–2pm, Sat 10.30am–noon) is on Udwaria Rd, east of the main bazaar.

> The telephone **area code** for Ujjain is ☎0734.

The City

The *Western Railway* cuts straight through the centre of **the city**, forming a neat divide between the spacious and affluent residential suburbs to the south, and the more interesting, densely packed streets northwest of the station. Unless you spend all day wandering through the bazaar, sightseeing in Ujjain usually means treading the temple trail, with a brief foray south of the *ghats* to visit the Vedha Shala observatory.

The Mahakaleshwar Mandir and the Harsiddhi Mandir

Ujjain's chief landmark, the **Mahakaleshwar Mandir**, crowns a rise above the river, and is the logical place to start a tour of the town. Its gigantic saffron-painted sanctuary tower, a modern replacement for the one destroyed by Iltutmish in 1234, soars high above a complex of marble courtyards, water tanks and fountains, advertising the presence below of one of India's most powerful *shivalingams*.

Housed in a claustrophobic subterranean chamber, the *lingam* is mounted on a solid silver base and piled high with floral offerings left by a constant stream of worshippers. One of India's twelve **jyotrilinga** – "*linga* of Light" – whose essential energy, or *shakti*, derives from the earth, rather than from the rituals performed around it, it is considered particularly potent, especially by Tantric followers, due to its unusual southfacing position. A narrow passage leads out of the sanctum to an adjacent courtyard, where several more modern accessory shrines are dedicated to Shiva's consort, Parvati, and their two sons, Ganesh, the elephant-headed god of prosperity, and Kartikeya, the god of war.

From the Mahakaleshwar Mandir, head west down the hill past the Rudra Sagar tank to another auspicious temple. Hindu mythology identifies the **Harsiddhi Mandir** as the spot where Parvati's elbow fell to earth while Shiva was carrying her burning body from the *sati* pyre. The temple has been a centre of Devi worship ever since. Its main shrine, erected by the Marathas in the eighteenth century, houses (from left to right) images of Mahalakshmi (the goddess of wealth), Annapurna (an incarnation of Durga), and Saraswati (the goddess of wisdom). The two odd-shaped pillars flanking the entrance to the courtyard also date from the Maratha era, and feature in the annual Dussehra festival, when the dozens of tiny butter lamps that encrust their soot-blackened surfaces are lit to celebrate Rama's victory over the demon Ravana.

Ram Ghat

A dip in the Shipra at **Ram Ghat** is the reason most devout pilgrims still travel to the city. During the 1992 Kumbh Mela, the waterfront was jammed solid with naked *sadhus* waiting to wash away several lifetimes of accumulated bad *karma*. Most days, however, very little of note happens here. Soapy kids splash in and out of the shallows, while sleepy *pujaris* ply their trade beneath the rows of orange and whitewashed riverside shrines. The large ceremonial archway on the opposite (west) bank – writhing with multi-coloured gods and goddesses – was erected as part of the *mela* celebrations.

The Gopal Mandir and the Vedha Shala

Standing at the end of a chaotic market square, in the heart of the bazaar, the picturesque **Gopal Mandir** was erected by one of the Scindia Ranis in the early nineteenth century. With its distinctive blend of Moghul domes, Moorish arches and lofty Hindu sanctuary tower, the temple makes a fine example of late Maratha architecture. Inside, the sanctum's silver-plated doors were put here by Mahaji Scindia, who rescued them from Lahore after they had been carried off by Muslim looters. The shrine room itself, lined with marble, silver and mother-of-pearl, contains icons of the presiding deity, Gopal (Ganesh), together with his parents, Shiva and Parvati.

In addition to being a major religious centre, Ujjain was the birthplace of mathematical astronomy in India. Research into the motion of the stars and planets has been carried out here since the time of Ashok. Later, Hindu astronomers fixed both the **first meridian** of longitude and the Tropic of Cancer in the city – the reason why Raja Jai Singh of Jaipur, governor of Malwa under the Moghul emperor Muhammed Shah, chose it as the site for another of his surreal open-air observatories. Built in 1725, the **Vedha Shala** lies 1km southwest of the train station, overlooking a bend in the River Shipra. The complex is nowhere near as large as its more famous cousins in Delhi and Jaipur, the Janta Mantars, but remains in excellent condition. Local astronomers continue to use its five instruments, or *yantras*, to formulate ephemerides (charts predicting the positions of the planets), which you can buy at the site.

The northern outskirts

The **Kalideh Mahal**, a summer retreat built in 1458 by the Sultans of Mandu, rests on an island in the Shipra, 9km north of the city centre. Though renovated by the Scindias early this century, the once grand water palace and its adjacent tank are now boarded up. You might, however, choose to come out here simply to enjoy a ride through pleasant countryside, past some minor religious sites. Near a colony of dyers and batik experts, **Siddavath**, a sacred banyan tree, stands beside the Shipra just north of the city limits next to a red and white shrine, draped in fresh flowers. Shiva's consort, Parvati, is believed to have performed penances here, and during big *melas*, thousands of pilgrims hack through a thick layer of pondweed to bathe in holy water below.

Finally, the **Bhartrihari caves**, burrowed into the rock on the east bank of the river near the Gadkalika temple, are recommended for serious *sadhu* spotters. Local legend has it that King Vikramaditya's stepbrother, the great poet and scholar Bhartrihari, lived here as a hermit in the fifth century. Today, the caves, some with "natural" *linga* emerging from the stone floor, are home to a rare sect of *yogis*. The Kanphatas, or "Split-ears", are named after their arcane initiation rite, which involves cutting holes into the middle of novices' ears with a double-edged knife. You can tell a Kanphata-*yogi* by his large hooped earrings.

Accommodation

Most of Ujjain's limited **accommodation** is within easy walking distance of the railway station, so ignore the auto-rickshaw *wallahs* when you arrive unless you plan to stay in one of the two upmarket hotels, both 2km southeast in the cantonment area. Luxury tax of between 10 and 15 percent is charged on all rooms costing over Rs100. If you plan to stay a while, you could try an **ashram**; *Shri Ram Mandir* (①) close to Rudra Sagar, is one of the best.

Atlas, Station Rd, Indore Gate (☎25873). Respectable, well-managed hotel with restaurant close to the station. All rooms have windows, attached bathrooms and comfortable beds. ③–⑤.

Chandragupta, Subhash Marg (☎25500). Cell-block-style lodge opposite the station, with passably clean, but small rooms. ①–②.

Girnar, Station Rd, Indore Gate (☎25873). Next door to the *Atlas*. Clean and quiet, with comfortable, good-sized rooms. Some attached shower-toilets. Recommended. ②–③.

MPTDC Shipra, University Rd (☎51496). Immaculately tidy and peaceful, with relaxing inner courtyard-cum-garden, and a good licensed restaurant. Some a/c. ⑤–⑥.

MPTDC Yatri Niwas, off Lal Bahadur Shastri Marg (☎51498). Large, peaceful institutional block, almost 2km out of town, with partitioned dorms (Rs40) and four simple doubles (no hot water). Restaurant on site. ③.

Rama Krishna, Subhash Marg (☎25912). In the same mould as the *Chandragupta* next door, with a/c rooms too. ①–⑤.

Sheba Palace, Free Ganj, near Madhav Clock Tower (☎25742). Ex-Maharaja's guest house; pretty shabby despite renovation. Large rooms with huge tiled bathrooms, but not that comfortable. ④–⑤.

Surana Palace, 23 GDC Rd, Dushera Maidan (☎57411). Not a palace, but a large block of a hotel, with comfortable rooms, luxurious suites, attentive service and a good restaurant. ⑤–⑧.

Eating

Ujjain suffers from a dearth of decent **places to eat**. Most visitors either stick to their hotel restaurant, or else chance a plate of veg curry, rice and *chappatis* in one of the cheap places opposite the train station.

Chanakya, Subhash Marg. The best of several no-frills restaurants opposite the station. Spicy, inexpensive, veg food, and chilled beer. The popular *Ankur* next door offers more of the same.

Five Star, Madhav Clock Tower Square. Inexpensive south Indian snack bar serving filling *dosas*, *iddlis* and *waddas* in cramped first-floor cafeteria, or on a roof-top overlooking the square. The sign's in Hindi; look for the glossy ice-cream and *Cadbury* signs.

Nauratan, *Shipra Hotel*, University Rd. Stylish MPTDC restaurant with the usual menu of tasty veg, Mughlai, *tandoori* and Chinese dishes, plus some Western options and a wide choice of beers and spirits.

New Raj Kumar, 20 Bhaktawar Ganj, Dushera Maidan. Low-priced and unpretentious pure veg joint, tucked away down a suburban backstreet near *Surana Palace*.

White House, *Surana Palace*, 23 GDC Rd. Wide range of carefully prepared Indian and Chinese dishes at moderate prices, served indoors or on the lawn. Well worth the rickshaw ride if you're not staying here.

Maheshwar

Overlooking the north bank of the mighty River Narmada, 91km southwest of Indore, **MAHESHWAR** has been identified as the site of King Kartvirajun's ancient capital, **Mahishmati**, a city mentioned in both the *Mahabharata* and *Ramayana*. In the eighteenth century, Maharani **Ahilya Bhai** (see p.411) built a palace and several temples here, giving the town a new lease of life. Today, it's a prominent port of call on the Narmada Hindu pilgrimage circuit, but well off the region's tourist trail.

The waterfront **ghats** that line the river below an old sandstone palace, however, make a quintessentially Indian spectacle. Parties of *yatris* take holy dips, drying their clothes in the breeze blowing off the river, while *pujaris* and groups of *sadhus* sit around murmuring prayers under raffia sunshades. If you're not pushed for time, you could enjoy a fifteen-minute ferry trip across the river to the hamlet of **Navdatoli** on the far bank, where archeologists have uncovered evidence of settlement dating from the Lower Paleolithic era – not that there's much to see when you get there.

Once you've had a look at the whitewashed shrines and the **sati stones** dotted around the *ghats*, head for the flight of steps leading under the ornate sandstone facade of the palace to a raised courtyard, where you'll find a pair of eighteenth-century temples. The larger of the two, the Ahilya Bhai Mandir, has an overhanging balcony wrapped around its tower with a great bird's eye view over the waterfront.

The **palace** and **fort** complex itself, further up the steps, houses the workshops of the Rewa Society, established by the Maharani 250 years ago to promote the local handloom industry. Maheshwari **saris** are famous all over India for their distinctive patterns and superior quality; check out the designs for yourself by visiting the weavers' workshops (Mon–Fri 10am–5pm), which are sponsored by a German aid project. Though descendants of the old ruling family still occupy parts of the building, a couple of rooms around the entrance courtyard have been given over to a small **museum**. Exhibits include a life-size effigy of the devout Ahilya Bhai (shown seated on her throne, or *rajgadi*), a couple of moth-eaten palladins, old photographs of the Holkar dynasty, and the shrine from which Maheshwar's annual Dussehra festival begins.

Practicalities

Accommodation in Maheshwar is limited to the *Ahilya Trust Guest House* (①), a charitable institution near the palace, and the handful of rudimentary *dharamshalas* around the small square behind the *ghats*. This, in part, explains why many visitors prefer to visit on MPTDC guided tours, or as a day trip from Indore. **Buses** from Indore are fairly frequent, taking three and a half hours with a change at the market town of Dhamnod, 76km southwest of Indore on the NH3. The nearest railhead is at **Barwaha**, 39km west. You can also call in at Maheshwar en route between the area's other religious centre, Omkareshwar, and Mandu, from where there are direct, but painfully slow, buses.

Places to eat are thin on the ground, as the majority of visitors to the town are pilgrims who cook their own food. Try a vegetarian meal in one of the *dhabas* on the square if your digestive system is up to it.

Omkareshwar

East of the main river crossing at Barhawa, the Narmada dips southwards, sweeps north again to form a wide bend, and then forks around a two-kilometre-long wedge-shaped outcrop of sandstone. Seen from above, the island, cut by several deep ravines, bears an uncanny resemblance to the "Om" symbol. This, coupled with the presence on its sheer south-facing side of a revered *shivalingam*, has made **OMKARESHWAR**, 77km south of Indore, one of the most sacred Hindu sites in central India.

Since ancient times, pilgrims have flocked here for *darshan* and a holy dip in the river. Until recently, however, few foreign visitors knew of the village's existence; but it is among the region's most atmospheric spots, and anyone who can survive for a couple of days without a comfortable hotel room is likely to enjoy it. Ruined temples, wayside shrines, bathing places, and caves inhabited by chillum-smoking Shaivite *sadhus* are dotted around the island, strung together by an old paved pilgrims' trail.

From the bus stand at the bottom of the village, Omkareshwar's only street runs 400m uphill to a ramshackle square, where you'll find most of the *dharamshalas*, *chai* shops, and a handful of stalls hawking lurid *puja* paraphernalia (including the excellent stylized **maps** taken home by pilgrims as souvenirs of their visits). The island itself is connected to the mainland by a high concrete footbridge, and by flat-bottomed ferries that shuttle between the *ghats* crouched at the foot of the river gorge. Once across, you're soon swallowed up by the crowded narrow lane leading to the main temple.

The prominent white *shikhara* that now soars above the **Shri Omkar Mandhata Mandir** is a relatively new addition to the dense cluster of buildings on the south side of the island. Below it, the ornate pillars in the assembly hall, or *mandapa*, are more representative of the shrine's great antiquity. Myths relating to the origins of the deity in the low-ceilinged sanctum date back to the second century BC. Another of India's twelve **jyotrilinga** ("*linga* of light"; see p.423), it is said by Hindus to have emerged spontaneously from the earth after a struggle between Brahma, Vishnu and Shiva.

Around the island

Traditionally, the *parikrama* (circular tour) of Omkareshwar begins at the *ghats* below Shri Mandhata and proceeds clockwise **around the island**. The walk takes at least a couple of hours, so carry plenty of water if you plan to do the whole thing at one go.

The first section of the trail is a leisurely half-hour stroll from the footbridge to the pebble-strewn western tip of the island, where you'll find a small *chai* stall and a couple of insignificant shrines. The **Trivendi Sangam**, or "Three-rivers confluence", is an especially propitious bathing place, where the Narmada forks as it merges with the Kaveri. From the confluence, the path climbs above the fringe of fine white sand lining the northern shore until it reaches level ground. The ruins of the **Gaudi Somnath temple** stand in the middle of the plateau, surrounded by a sizeable collection of sculpture mounted on concrete plinths. The sanctuary houses a colossal *shivalingam*, attended by an equally huge Nandi bull. At this point, drop down a steep flight of steps to the village, or continue east, towards the old fortified town that crowned the top of the island before it was ransacked by Muslims in the medieval era. Numerous chunks of temple sculpture, lying discarded among the rubble, include a couple of finely carved gods and goddesses, used for shade by families of black-faced langur monkeys.

After scaling the sides of a gully, the trail leads under the large ornamental archway of the **Surajkund Gate**, flanked by three-metre figures of Arjun and Bheema, two of the illustrious Pandava brothers. The tenth-century **Siddhesvara temple** stands five minutes' walk away to the south, on a patch of flat ground overlooking the river. Raised on a large plinth decorated with rampaging elephants, it has some fine *apsaras*, or female fertility figures, carved over its southern doorway, and a donatory Sanskrit inscription that the resident *chowkidar* will, for some *baksheesh*, point out to you.

Of the two possible routes back to the village, one takes you along the top of the plateau, before dropping sharply down, via another ruined temple and the **Maharaja's palace**, to the Shri Mandhata temple. The other follows a flight of steps to the river bank, and then heads past a group of *sadhus*' caves to the main *ghats*.

Practicalities

Omkareshwar is connected by state **bus** to Khandwa (4 daily; 2hr), Maheshwar (1 daily; 2hr 30min), and Indore (7 daily; 2hr 30min). You can also get there by catching the Indore to Khandwa bus as far as **Omkareshwar Road**, a junction and *chai* stop on the NH3, from where a beaten-up local bus runs the remaining 15km. Omkareshwar Road is also the nearest railhead, but only slow passenger services stop here. Barhawa, on the north bank of the Narmada, is the closest mainline railway station.

Finding **somewhere to stay** can be a problem if you're fussy about space and hygiene. The only hotel-style place, the peaceful *Yatrika Niwas* (③), behind the bus stand, has spartan but clean rooms, some with bathrooms; the distance from the *ghats* reduces the impact of devotional music played there early each morning. Most visitors end up in the central *dharamshalas*, which are cheap (Rs20–50), sociable and offer close-hand experience of pilgrim culture. On the down side, *dharamshala* rooms tend to be windowless cells, with washing facilities limited to a standpipe in the yard (to encourage people to use the river), and communal toilets. One of the best is *Jat Samaj* (①), facing the river, to the right of the bridge on the main square – look for the roof-top figure on horseback. Another favourite is *Ahilya Bhai* (①), tucked away behind the Vishnu temple off the road to Mamaleshwar temple and the *ghats*. This and its close neighbour, *Tirole Kunbi Patel* (①), have great views over the river to the *Om* island from their balconies and roof terraces. If these are full, try the massive *Raja Pratap* (①) that towers over the main square. It's the only one with a sign in English, and is fine for a night's stay.

If you can't face a spell in a *dharamshala*, there are a couple of alternatives. Just off the square before it joins the bridge a flight of stone steps leads to *Shiv Niwas*, a delightful house shaded by bougainvillea whose four simple rooms look over the river. Quiet and cosy, it's very popular, and has a welcome supply of running water (①–③). Visitors with their own vehicle may also manage to talk their way into the large, pink, and very pukka *Irrigation Project Guest House* (④) at the top of the hill, whose clean, comfortable rooms are normally reserved for visiting engineers. At the attractive *PWD Rest House* (③) nearby, special permission to stay is required from the nearby village of Sanawad.

Long-stay visitors and pilgrims tend to opt for cooking their own meals, using stoves provided by the *dharamshalas*, or bought at minimal cost in the bazaar, where you can buy basic provisions. The alternatives are fiery, greasy veg dishes (no meat or eggs at this sacred spot) from the grungy *chai* stalls around the square; the best, which cooks dishes to order, is just by the bridge, or you could try the friendly *Jay Ambe Bhojnalaya* cafe by the bus stand. Don't risk eating at the food stalls on the island.

Omkareshwar's token STD telephone booth in the main square close to the bridge works erratically. The nearest **bank** with a foreign exchange counter is at Indore. A small **post office** on the main street, however, offers reliable poste restante.

CHAPTER FIVE

HIMACHAL PRADESH

Ruffled by the lower ridges of the Shivalik Range in the far south, cut through by the Pir Panjal and Dhauladhar ranges in the northwest, and dominated by the great Himalaya in the north and east, **HIMACHAL PRADESH** (HP) is India's most popular and easily accessible hill state, sandwiched between the Punjab and Tibet. Lowland orchards, sub-tropical forests and maize fields peter out in the higher reaches where pines cling to the steep slopes of mountains whose inhospitable peaks soar in rocky crags and forbidding ice fields to heights of over 6000 metres.

Together with deep gorges cut by rivers crashing down from the Himalaya, these mountains form natural boundaries between the state's separate districts. Each has its own architecture, from rock-cut shrines and *shikhara* temples to colonial mansions and Buddhist monasteries. Roads struggle against the vagaries of the climate to connect the larger settlements, which are way outnumbered by remote villages, many of which are home to semi-nomadic **Gaddi** and **Gujjar** shepherds.

An obvious way to approach the state is to head north from Delhi to the state capital, **Shimla**, beyond the lush and temperate valleys of **Sirmaur**. The former summer location of the British government, Shimla is a curious, appealing mix of grand homes, churches and chaotic bazaars, with a favourable climate and breathtaking views. The main road **northeast** from Shimla tackles a pass just north of **Narkanda**, then follows the River Sutlej east to **Sarahan**, with its spectacular wooden temple, and enters the eastern district of **Kinnaur**, most of which is accessible only to those holding **Inner Line permits** (see p.446). Alpine and green in the west, Kinnaur becomes more austere and barren as it stretches east to the Tibetan plateau, its staggering beauty enhanced by delicate timber houses, temples, and fluttering prayer flags.

Another road from Shimla climbs slowly northwest to **Mandi**, a former market town that is still a major crossroads. To the north is Himachal's most popular tourist spot, the **Kullu Valley**, an undulating mass of terraced fields, orchards and forests overlooked by snowy peaks. Its epicentre is the rapidly expanding tourist town of **Manali**, just sixteen hours by bus from Delhi. Long a favourite hang-out of Western "hippies", Manali is set in idyllic mountain scenery, cloaked in apple orchards and murmuring with bubbling rivers. As well as being a perfect starting point for treks, Manali offers **white-water rafting** between May and June, and relaxing sulphurous springs in nearby **Vashisht**.

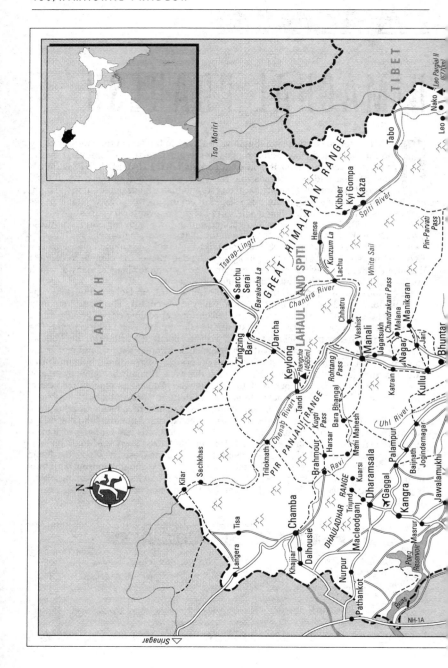

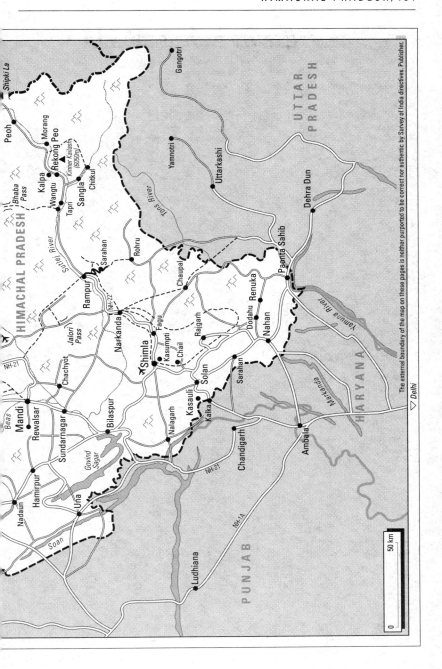

The external boundary of the map on these pages is neither purported to be correct nor authentic by Survey of India directives. Publisher.

HIMACHAL PRADESH TRAVEL DETAILS

	Trains		Buses		Flights	
	Frequency	Time	Frequency	Time	Frequency	Time
To and from SHIMLA						
Ambala			hourly	6hr		
Ani			1 daily	8hr		
Chail			4 daily	3hr		
Chamba			4 daily	15hr		
Chandigarh			every 30min	3hr 30min–4hr		
Dalhousie			1 daily	16hr		
Dehra Dun			4 daily	9hr		
Delhi			hourly	10–12hr	1 daily	1hr 10min
Dharamsala			5 daily	9–10hr	3 weekly	1hr 20min
Haridwar			4 daily	10hr		
Jammu			2 daily	16hr		
Kalka	4–7 daily	5hr 30min–7hr	every 30min	3hr		
Kangra			10 daily	8hr		
Kasauli			hourly	2hr 30min		
Kullu			7 daily	7–8hr	3 daily	25min
Manali			7 daily	9–10hr		
Mandi			7 daily	4hr 30min–5hr		
Nahan			4 daily	6hr		
Narkanda			5 daily	3hr		
Pathankot			5 daily	12hr		
Rampur			5 daily	6hr		
Rekong Peo			3 daily	8–11hr		
Sangla			1 daily	11hr		
Sarahan			2 daily	7hr		
Solan	3–6 daily	2hr 30min–3hr	every 30min	1hr 30min		
To and from DHARAMSALA						
Baijnath			hourly	3hr 30min		
Chamba			1 daily	9hr		
Chandigarh			6–15 daily	7–8hr		
Dalhousie			1 daily	6hr–7hr 30min		
Delhi			7 daily	12hr	3 weekly	2hr 30min
Dehra Dun			1 daily	9hr		
Haridwar			1 daily	14hr		
Jawalamukhi			8 daily	2hr 30min		
Kangra			every 15min	45min–1hr		
Kullu			1 daily	8hr	3 weekly	25min
Manali			1 daily	11hr		
Mandi			4 daily	6–7hr		
Mcleodganj			every 20min	40min		
Nahan			1 daily	12hr		
Pathankot			12 daily	3hr 30min		

	Buses				Buses	
	Frequency	Time			Frequency	Time
To and from Chamba				**To and from Dalhousie**		
Brahmour	5 daily	3hr		Amritsar	2 daily	5hr 30min
Dalhousie	5 daily	2hr 30min		Jammu	1 daily	6hr
Delhi	1 nightly	18hr		Jullundhar	1 daily	6hr
Kangra	2 daily	6hr		Khajjiar	2 daily	1hr
Khajjiar	3 daily	1hr 30min		Pathankot	hourly	3hr 30min
Mandi	1 daily	15hr				
Pathankot	hourly	5hr				

	Buses			**Buses**	
	Frequency	Time		Frequency	Time
To and from Kangra			**To and from Manali**		
Delhi	every 30min	12hr	Amritsar	1 daily	16hr
Jawalamukhi	every 15min	1–2hr	Chandigarh	8 daily	8–11hr
Manali	4 daily	12hr	Darcha	1 daily	12hr
Mandi	4 daily	6hr	Dehra Dun	1 daily	16hr
Masrur	3 daily	2hr	Delhi	6 daily	14–17hr
Pathankot	10 daily	3–4hr	Haridwar	1 daily	16hr
			Jammu	1 daily	16hr
To and from Kasauli			Kangra	4 daily	12hr
Chandigarh	5 daily	2hr 30min	Kaza	1 daily	12hr
Delhi	3 daily	7hr 30min	Keylong	8 daily	6hr
Kalka	3 daily	1hr 30min	Mandi	1 hourly	4hr
Solan	5 daily	40min	Manikaran	9 daily	3hr 30min
			Nagar	hourly	2hr
To and from Kullu			Nahan	1 daily	12hr
Amritsar	1 daily	16hr	Pathankot	5 daily	12hr
Bhuntur	every 10min	30min	Udaipur, Lahaul	1 daily	7hr
Chandigarh	8 daily	6hr 30min			
Dehra Dun	1 daily	14hr	**To and from Nahan**		
Delhi	6 daily	12–14hr	Ambala	1 daily	2hr 30min
Haridwar	1 daily	14hr	Chandigarh	6 daily	2hr
Manali	every 10min	1hr 15min–2hr	Dehra Dun	6 daily	3hr
Mandi	hourly	3hr	Delhi	3 daily	6hr
Manikaran	9 daily	2–3 hr	Mandi	1 daily	8hr
Nagar	hourly	1hr 30min–2hr	Mussoorie	6 daily	5hr
			Renuka	6 daily	2hr

For more details of transport connections from **Delhi**, see p.119 onwards; for **Pathankot** connections, see p.532.

Note that most individual routes appear only once in this chart; check against where you want to get to as well as where you're coming from.

Beyond the Rohtang Pass in the far north of Kullu district, the valleys of **Lahaul and Spiti** stretch beneath mighty peaks in vast brown, bare expanses, where remote settlements are surveyed by stark *gompas*, or monasteries. Although **permits** are needed for trips into the far-flung regions of Lahaul and Spiti, without one you can follow unmatched trekking routes from **Kaza** or **Kibber**, or continue north on the road to Leh.

Visitors to the densely populated **Kangra Valley** invariably make a bee-line for **Dharamsala**, whose large community of Tibetan exiles includes the Dalai Lama himself. Trekking paths lead east from here to the tea-growing district of **Palampur**, and north across the treacherous passes of the Dhauladhar mountains into the **Chamba Valley**.

Finding guides and porters for **treks** is rarely difficult. The season begins as the monsoon washes away the snow in early June, and lasts until late November in the west, and late October in the north and east. In **winter**, all but the far south of the state lies beneath a thick blanket of snow, enticing groups of adventurous skiers to try out remote pistes. The region north of Manali is accessible only from late June to early October when the roads are clear. Even in **summer**, when the days are hot and the sun strong, northern Himachal is beset with cold nights; always carry warm clothes, or pick up a locally made shawl.

Some history

The earliest known inhabitants of the area now known as Himachal Pradesh were the **Dasas**, who entered the hills from the Gangetic plain between the third and second millennium BC, having been pushed out of their homeland by the Indus Valley civilization that swept into India from the West. By 2000 BC the Dasas had been joined by the **Aryans**, and a number of tribal republics, known as *janapadas*, began to emerge in geographically separate regions, where they fostered separate cultural traditions.

The terrain made it impossible for one ruler to hold sway over the whole region. The **Guptas** forged inroads into the mountains between the second and fifth centuries AD, only to be ousted in turn by Vardhana rulers, then petty Rana and Thakhur chieftains, and ultimately the Hindu **Rajputs**. As early as 550 AD Rajput families had gained supremacy over the northwestern districts of Brahmour and Chamba, just two of the many princely states created between the sixth and sixteenth centuries. Of these, the most powerful was **Kangra**, where the Katoch Rajputs held off attacks on their treasure-stocked fort from the Sultans, Mahmud of Ghazni (1009 AD), and the Tughluqs (fourteenth century) before finally falling to the Moghuls in the sixteenth century.

During the medieval era, **Lahaul and Spiti** remained aloof, governed not by Rajputs, but by Jos of Tibetan origin, who introduced Tibetan customs and architecture, and profited from trade between India, Lhasa and Samarkand. After a period of submission to Ladakh, Lahaul and Spiti came under the Rajas of **Kullu**, a central princely state that reached its apogee in the seventeenth century. Further south, the region around **Shimla** and **Sirmaur** was divided into over thirty independently governed *thakurais*. In the late seventeenth century, the newly empowered **Sikh** community, based at **Paonta Sahib** (Sirmaur), added to the threat already posed by the Moghuls. By the eighteenth century, under **Maharaja Ranjit Singh**, the Sikhs had gained strongholds in much of western Himachal, and considerable power in both Kullu and Spiti.

Battling against Sikh expansion, Amar Singh Tapur, the leader of the **Gurkha** army set on extending his own Nepalese dominion, failed to take Kangra, but consolidated power in the southern Shimla hill states. The *thakurai* chiefs turned to the **British** for help, and forced the last of the Gurkhas back into Nepal in 1815. Predictably, the British assumed power over the south, thus tempting the Sikhs to battle in the **Anglo-Sikh War**. With the signing of a treaty in 1846 the British annexed most of the south and west of the state, and in 1864 pronounced Shimla, a cool retreat for British officers and their families, the summer government headquarters.

After Independence, the regions bordering present-day Punjab were integrated, named Himachal Pradesh ("Himalayan Provinces"), and administered by a Chief Commissioner. By 1956 HP was recognized as a Union Territory, and in 1966 the state as it exists today was formed, with Shimla as its capital.

Despite being a political unity, Himachal Pradesh is hardly culturally homogenous. With over 90 percent of the population living outside the main towns, and many areas remaining totally isolated during the long winter months, Himachal's separate districts maintain distinct customs, architecture, dress and agricultural methods. Though Hinduism dominates, there are substantial numbers of Sikhs, Muslims and Christians, and Lahaul, Spiti and Kinnaur have been home to Tibetan Buddhists since the tenth century. After the nationwide reactions to the demolition of Ayodhya's mosque in 1993 (see p.310), Himachali support for the BJP rose, particularly among the high-caste landowning Thakhurs, the informal alliance of apple growers whose wealth gives them considerable influence over Himachali politics. However, after a neck-and-neck race, the **Congress** came out on top in the 1993 autumn elections, placing Himachal Pradesh within the fold of the national Congress majority. The Congress was re-elected in the March 1996 elections.

SHIMLA AND AROUND

Shimla, Himachal's capital, is India's largest and most famous hill station, in a region which holds several considerably lesser and duller rivals but a wealth of spectacular scenery. While the city is a favourite spot for Indian families and honeymooners, its size does little to win it popularity among Western tourists who tend to pass through to sample the fading shadow of the Raj before heading east or west into the denser mountains. To the east, the village of **Sarahan**, site of the famous Bhima Kali temple, set against a spectacular backdrop of soaring peaks, can be visited in a two- or three-day round trip, or en-route to the high remote lands of Kinnaur.

Although most travellers from the south come straight from Delhi to Shimla, a possible detour from Ambala in Haryana, or the approach from Uttar Pradesh, involves crossing the low-lying district of **Sirmaur**, the southernmost area of the state, at the edge of the Haryana plains. Cut by the River Giri, on its way to join the Yamuna in the south, this is among the most fertile areas of the state, blessed with an unusually equitable climate. Near the border, the pretty little town of **Paonta Sahib**, where pastel-yellow houses are packed tightly into the cobbled streets, holds an important shrine dedicated to Guru Gobind Singh, the tenth Sikh guru, who lived here. From Punjab or Harayana, the first town on the road is **Nahan**, Sirmaur's capital, connected by bus to Ambala, 105km southwest, and the hill stations further north. Neither Nahan nor the surrounding forests merit more than a short amble, unless you arrive at the end of the rains and happen upon the **Bhawan Dwadashi** festival, when 52 deities are carried to the Jagannath temple, and floated in a pool until dark.

Six daily buses (2hr) make the journey 45km east of Nahan to **Dodahu**, 2km from the secluded lake at **Renuka**, where a **wildlife sanctuary** protects rare deer plus a magnificent pride of Asiatic lions, introduced here in the hope of creating a stable breeding population. Tropical forests flow down to the lake, along which trees and reeds shelter colonies of herons, kingfishers and bee-eaters. Bright carp and snub-nosed turtles flash by, free in this sacred enclave from the threat of poachers. Lilting devotional music and the toll of brass bells echo over the lake at sunrise and sunset from the Hindu temples. HPTDC *Hotel Renuka* (☎8339; ④–⑤), in sloping gardens on the western shore, has rooms opening onto a shady verandah, and serves good food; order in advance, and watch out for cheeky monkeys.

Shimla

Whether you travel by road or rail, the last stretch of the climb up to **SHIMLA** seems interminable. Deep in the foothills of the Himalayas, the hill station is approached via an unfeasibly sinuous route that winds from the plains at Kalka across nearly 100km of precipitous river valleys, pine forests, and mountain sides swathed in maize terraces and apple orchards. It's not hard to see why the British chose this inaccessible site as their summer capital. At an altitude of 2159m, the crescent-shaped ridge over which it spills is blessed with perennially cool air, crisp light, and superb **panoramas** across verdant, undulating country to the snowy peaks of the Great Himalayan range.

Named after its patron goddess, Shamla Devi (a manifestation of Kali), the tiny village that stood on this spot was "discovered" by a team of British surveyors in 1817. Shortly afterwards, groups of battle-weary army officers began to trickle up here between skirmishes with the Gurkhas in the Sutlej valley. Glowing reports of its beauty and climate gradually filtered to the imperial capital, Calcutta, and within a decade, the ridges around Shimla were peppered with bungalows and holiday cottages. The British finally persuaded the local Raja to part with the land in 1830, and the settlement became the subconti-

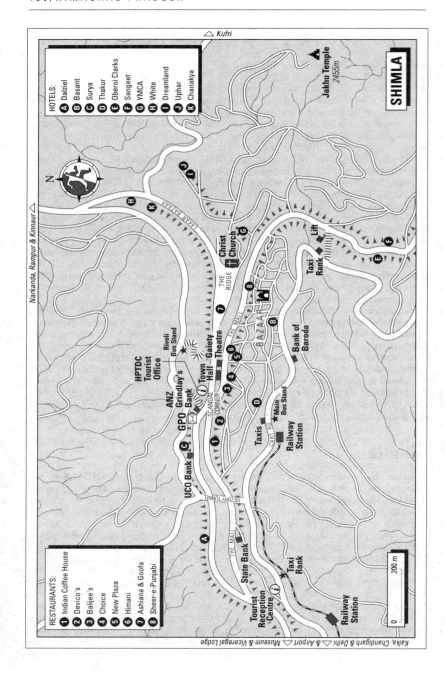

△ *Kufri*

SHIMLA

▲ Jakhu Temple
2455m

HOTELS:
Ⓐ Dalziel
Ⓑ Basant
Ⓒ Surya
Ⓓ Thakur
Ⓔ Oberoi Clarks
Ⓕ Sangeet
Ⓖ YMCA
Ⓗ White
Ⓘ Dreamland
Ⓙ Uphar
Ⓚ Chanakya

Narkanda, Rampur & Kinnaur △

LAKKAR BAZAAR

Christ
Church ✝

THE
RIDGE

Taxi
Rank

Lift

Rivoli
Bus Stand

Gaiety
Theatre

HPTDC
Tourist
Office

Town
Hall

BAZAAR

Bank of
Baroda

ANZ
Grindlay's
Bank

SCANDAL
CORNER

GPO

UCO Bank

Taxis

Main
Bus Stand

Railway
Station

VICTORY TUNNEL

CART RD

THE MALL

State Bank

Taxi
Rank

Tourist
Reception
Centre

Railway
Station

RESTAURANTS:
❶ Indian Coffee House
❷ Devico's
❸ Baljee's
❹ Choice
❺ New Plaza
❻ Himani
❼ Ashiana & Goofa
❽ Sheer-e-Punjabi

Kalka, Chandigarh & Delhi ▽ *Airport* ▽ *Museum & Viceregal Lodge* ▽

0   200 m

THE VICEROY'S TOY TRAIN

Until the construction of the **Kalka–Shimla railway**, the only way to get to the hill station was on the so-called **Cart Road** – a slow, winding trail trodden by lines of long-suffering porters and horse-drawn tongas. Plans for a narrow-gauge railway had been started as early as 1847, but it took the intervention of the Viceroy himself, **Lord Curzon**, to provide the impetus needed to get the massive undertaking off the ground.

By the time the 96-km line was completed in 1897 103 tunnels, 24 bridges, and 18 stations had been built between Shimla and the railhead at Kalka, 26km northeast of Chandigarh. These days, buses may be quicker, but a ride on the "toy train" is far more memorable – especially if you travel first-class, in one of the glass-sided "rail cars". Hauled along by a tiny blue-and-white diesel locomotive, they rattle at a leisurely pace through stunning scenery, taking from five and a half to seven hours to reach Shimla.

Along the route, you'll notice the guards exchanging little leather pouches with staff strategically positioned on the station platforms. The bags they receive in return contain small brass discs, which the drivers slot into special machines to alert the signals ahead of their approach. "**Neal's Token System**", in place since the line was first inaugurated, is a fail-safe means of ensuring that trains travelling in opposite directions never meet face-to-face on the single-track sections of the railway.

For information about train times and ticket booking, see p.442.

nent's most fashionable summer resort. Each year, long trains of packhorses and coolies picked their way up from the plains, bringing with them the Raj's top brass, and legions of grass-widows whose husbands were obliged to sweat it out at lower elevations. The annual migration was finally rubber-stamped in 1864, when Shimla – now an elegant town of mansions, churches and cricket pitches – was declared the Government of India's official hot-season HQ. The civil servants had to carry on business as usual, but for most of its temporary residents, the summer capital was an endless round of garden parties, formal dinners, high teas, balls, bridge games and evening promenades along the main street, the Mall. With the completion of the **Kalka–Shimla Railway** in 1903, Shimla lay only two days by train from Delhi. Its meteoric rise continued after Independence, when, following the reorganization of the Punjab in 1966, it became state capital.

Today, Shimla is still a major holiday resort, popular mainly with *nouveau riche* Punjabis and Delhi-ites who flock here during the May–June run-up to the monsoons. Its jaded colonial charm also appeals to foreigners looking for a taste of the Raj. The *burra-* and *memsahibs* may have moved on, but Shimla retains a decidedly **British feel**: pukka Indian gentlemen in tweeds stroll along the Mall smoking pipes, while neatly turned-out school children scuttle past mock-Tudor shop-fronts and houses with names like *Braeside*. At the same time, the dense, chaotic mass of corrugated iron roof-tops immediately below the ridge, Shimla's **bazaar**, lends an unmistakably Oriental aspect to the town, an active market and gateway for the northwestern Himalayan region.

The **best time to visit** is during October and November, before the Himachali winter sets in, when the days are still warm and dry, and the morning skies are clear. From December to late February, heavy snow is common, and temperatures hover around, or below zero. The spring brings with it unpredictability: warm blasts of air from the plains, and flurries of freezing rain from the mountains. Avoid **high season**, in May, June and July, when accommodation is scarce and expensive. Whenever you come, though, bring plenty of warm clothes as the nights can get surprisingly chilly.

Arrival and information

Buses arriving on the main Chandigarh and Manali highways approach Shimla from the west, via Cart Rd. Before pulling in to the chaotic main **bus stand**, halfway around the hill, they stop briefly outside HPTDC's helpful **tourist reception centre** (daily 10am–5pm), just above the **railway station** – the place to head for general advice on transport and trekking around the state. Unless you plan to stay in the bazaar, which sprawls above the bus stand, get off here; it's a far less strenuous walk away from the top of the town and most of the accommodation. Buses from Narkanda, Rampur and Kinnaur arrive at the **Rivoli**, or "Lakkar Bazaar" **bus stand** on the north side of the Ridge. Shimla's **airport** lies 21km southeast of town on the Mandi road. If your budget won't stretch to a Rs300 taxi ride, take the city bus (Rs35), which meets every flight.

HPTDC's main **tourist office** (daily 10am–5pm; ☎78311), on the Mall near Scandal Corner, hands out the usual glossy leaflets, and sells tickets for their sightseeing tours (see below) and daily luxury and deluxe coaches to Manali and Dharamsala. The green-painted, Swiss-chalet-style **GPO** (Mon–Sat 10am–7pm, Sun 11am–4pm), with its efficient poste restante counter, stands just off Scandal Corner on the Mall. Nearby, the *UCO* is the cheapest and most efficient bank in Shimla with a **foreign exchange facility**. Otherwise, try the *State Bank of India*, halfway between Scandal Corner and the train station; expect a long wait, and to be charged Rs20 for an encashment certificate. *Visa* encashments can be made at the *Bank of Baroda* on Cart Rd, 5 minutes' walk east of the bus stand.

> The telephone **area code** for Shimla is ☎0177.

Local transport

Wherever you arrive in Shimla, you'll be mobbed by Kashmiri **porters**. Most of the town is pedestrianized, so you may be glad of one to lug your gear up the hill. Fix the fee in advance, and ignore claims that your chosen hotel is full. The tourist office keeps a list of "coolie rates for important places" such as Scandal Corner (20min; Rs15–20).

Taxis, which line up outside the tourist reception centre on Cart Rd, are the best way to get to the pricier hotels on the outskirts. The main *Taxi Drivers' Union* rank (☎77136) is 1km east of the bus stand, below the foot of the **elevator** that connects the east end of Cart Rd with the Mall (Rs3 each way). Their published list of set fares applies to high season; at other times, you should be able to negotiate discounts.

HPTDC organizes whistlestop **sightseeing tours** to destinations around Shimla, including Kufri, Chail, Narkanda and Sarahan. For **trekking, mountaineering, and jeep safaris** to Kinnaur and Spiti, contact Mr Pramode Paul at *Ibex Adventures & Travels* next to *Hotel Dreamland* (☎77377) – Shimla's most experienced and reliable adventure tourism outfit.

The Town

Although Shimla and its satellite districts sprawl over the flanks of five or more hills, the centre is fairly compact, on and immediately beneath a shoulder of high ground known as the **"Ridge"**. From here, a tangle of roads and lanes tumbles down in stages, each layer connected to the next by precipitous stone steps. **The Mall**, the main pedestrian thoroughfare, curves around the south slope of the hill, above the fascinating warren of a bazaar, the railway line and **Cart Road**, the upper limit for motor traffic, which encircles the base of the town.

The Ridge

Shimla's busy social scene revolves around the broad and breezy piazza that straddles **the Ridge**, overlooking impressive rippling foothills with the jagged white peaks of the Pir Panjal and Great Himalayan ranges on the horizon. In the afternoon, when the mountains are enveloped in cloud, honeymooners have their photos taken in brilliantly patterned *puttoos* (homespun blankets), while vacationers stroll by, watched by rows of shoeshine boys and Kashmiri porters, their arms tucked inside long woollen *pherans*.

The Victorian-Gothic spire of **Christ Church** in the square, for some reason recently painted a bright yellow, is Shimla's most prominent landmark. Built to accommodate the peak-season Europeans, it was never quite able to cope with the crush: on one occasion, the vicar complained to the assembled *memsahibs* that their copious crinolines took up too much space. The five **stained-glass windows**, the finest in British India, depict (from left to right) Faith, Hope, Charity, Fortitude, Patience and Humility.

At the other end of the square, **Scandal Corner** is the focus of Shimla's famous midafternoon *volta*, when crowds of locals gather in front of *ANZ Grindlay's* to gossip. Watched over by a statue of the Punjabi nationalist hero Lala Lajpat Rai, the intersection takes its name not from all this tongue-wagging, but from the elopement of a highranking British official's daughter with a handsome Indian prince that began here.

The Mall

At Scandal Corner, the road from the railway station finally arrives at **the Mall**, having run past ice-cream parlours, shawl shops, and department stores stuffed with electronic gadgets. The *HP State Emporium* is worth a browse for its discounted woollen goods, which include Kullu shawls and green-felt-fronted Kinnauri caps. Flanked by a long row of unmistakably British half-timbered buildings, Shimla's main shopping street was, until World War I, strictly out-of-bounds to all "natives" except royalty and rickshaw pullers. These days, rickshaws, man-powered or otherwise, are banned, and white faces are few. The quintessentially colonial **Gaiety Theatre**, however, looks exactly as it did in the heyday of the Raj. The *Shimla Amateur Dramatic Company* still performs here, while in the gentlemen's club next door, the talk still revolves around cricket and share prices.

The bazaar

Walk down any of the narrow lanes leading off the Mall, and you're plunged into a warren of twisting backstreets. Shimla's **bazaar** is the hill station at its most vibrant – a maze of dishevelled shacks, brightly lit stalls, and minarets, cascading in a clutter of corrugated iron and rotting timber to the edge of Cart Rd. Little has changed since the nineteenth century, when Rudyard Kipling, in his novel *Kim*, said: "A man who knows his way there can defy all the police of India's summer capital, so cunningly does verandah communicate with verandah, alley-way with alley-way, and bolt-hole with bolt-hole." Apart from being a good place to shop for authentic souvenirs, this is also one of the few areas of town that feels Himalayan: multi-coloured Kullu caps (*topis*) bob about in the crowd, alongside the odd Lahauli, Kinnauri or Tibetan face.

The museum

Tucked away on the western edge of town, the HP state **museum** (Tues–Sun 10am–1.30pm & 2–5pm, closed second Sat of each month) is a bit of a hike out of the centre, but well worth the effort; it's diverse collection includes contemporary, as well as antique works of art, well displayed in an elegant colonial mansion.

The ground floor is given over largely to temple sculpture, and a gallery of magnificent **Pahari miniatures** – examples of the last great Hindu art form to flourish in northern India before the deadening impact of Western culture in the early nineteenth century. An offspring of the Moghul painting tradition, the Pahari or "Hill" school is renowned for subtle depictions of romantic love, inspired by scenes from Hindu epics.

Among the museum's **paintings** are dozens of Moghul and Rajasthani miniatures and a couple of fine "Company" watercolours. Produced for souvenir-hunting colonials by the descendants of the Moghul and Pahari masters, the *fakirs*, itinerant *sadhus* and

THE HIKE TO THE JAKHU TEMPLE

The early-morning hike up to the **Jakhu**, or "monkey" **temple** is something of a tradition in Shimla. The top of the hill (2455m) on which it stands offers a superb panorama of the Himalaya – particularly breathtaking before the bubbles of cloud blister up later in the day. The relentlessly steep climb takes from twenty to forty minutes. Visitors with mobility problems may want to arrange a horse; a couple usually hang around in the main square opposite the Gandhi statue. The path starts just left of Christ Church. When you arrive at the *Dreamland Hotel*, turn right, follow the handrail up the hill, then bear left five minutes later at a fork in the lane. The summit is another ten to fifteen minutes' walk through the woods, beyond a colourful shrine that blasts out electric devotional music.

After the hard hack up, the temple itself, a red-and-yellow brick affair crammed with fairy lights and tinsel, comes as something of an anticlimax – the resident *pujari* doubles as a telephone attendant. The shrine inside houses an image, and what are believed to be the footprints of **Hanuman**, commander-in-chief of the monkey army that helped Rama in his struggle against the arch-demon Ravana – the subject of the *Ramayana*. Legend has it that the monkey god, adored by Hindus for his strength and fidelity, rested on Jakhu after collecting healing Himalayan herbs for Rama's injured brother, Lakshmana. These mythological connections explain the troupes of mangy monkeys around the temple. Pampered by generations of pilgrims and tourists, they have become a real pest; hang on to your bags, and don't carry food or wear bright clothes.

mendicants they depict could have leapt straight from the pages of Kipling. Also worth checking out are the striking contemporary oils of the Himalayas, a small collection of nineteenth- and twentieth-century deity masks from Kullu (see p.470) and Sarahan (see p.445), and a remarkable collection of temple bronzes. One room is devoted to Mahatma Gandhi, packed with fascinating photos of his time in Shimla, and amusing cartoons of his political relationship with the British.

To get there, follow the Mall past the post office and down hill, passing *Dalziel* and *Classic* hotels, then bear right at the first intersection and left at the second, where a signpost guides you up the last, short ascent.

The Viceregal Lodge and Prospect Hill

Shimla's single most impressive colonial monument, the old **Viceregal Lodge** (daily April–July 9.30am–8.30pm; Aug–March 9.30am–5pm; Rs5), summer seat of British government until the 1940s and today home to the Institute of Advanced Studies, is a fifteen-minute walk west of the museum. Perfectly placed on the flattened wooded top of Observatory Hill, its elevated location could not have been more apt for the high seat of imperial power in British India. From here, streams trickle into the Sutlej and Arabian Sea in one direction, and down to the Jamuna, the Ganges, and the Bay of Bengal in the other.

Here is Shimla at its most British. The solid grey mansion, built in Elizabethan style with a lion and unicorn set above the entrance porch, surveys trimmed lawns fringed by healthy pines and kaleidoscopic flower beds. Inside, the lodge is just as ostentatious, though only sections of the ground floor are open to the public: a vast teak-panelled entrance hall, an impressive library (formerly the ballroom), and the guest room, notable for its intricately carved walnut ceiling and period furniture. The **conference room**, hung with photos of Nehru, Jinnah and Gandhi, was the scene of crucial talks in the run-up to Independence. On the stone terrace to the rear of the building, a bronze plaque profiles and names the peaks visible in the distance.

The short hike up to **Prospect Hill** (2176m), a popular picnic spot, ties in nicely with a visit to the Lodge. By cutting through the woods to the west of the mansion, you can drop down to a busy intersection known as **Boileauganj**, from where a tarmac path climbs steeply up to the small shrine of Kamana Devi. The summit gives fine views across the entire south side of Shimla ridge, and over the hills and valleys of southern HP towards the plains of the Punjab – a murky brown haze on the horizon.

Accommodation

Most travellers only spend a couple of nights in Shimla – long enough to see the sights, and to book a ticket somewhere else. There's little to detain you any longer, and **accommodation** is, in the main, phenomenally expensive. Between mid-April and mid-September, tariffs double; during May, June and July, finding anywhere at all to stay is impossible if you haven't booked in advance. At other times it's worth trying to negotiate a **discount**: a 50 percent reduction is usual from November to early April.

ACCOMMODATION PRICE CODES

All **accommodation prices** in this book have been coded using the symbols below. In principle the prices given are for the least expensive double rooms in each establishment; however, some hotels, usually in category ①, offer rates per bed rather than per room. Local taxes are not included unless specifically stated. For more details, see p.35.

① up to Rs100	④ Rs225–350	⑦ Rs750–1200
② Rs100–150	⑤ Rs350–500	⑧ Rs1200–2200
③ Rs150–225	⑥ Rs500–750	⑨ Rs2200 and upwards

The least expensive lodges tend to be very scruffy, with a few exceptions – we've listed the best below. Mid-range accommodation is scattered around the Mall, or on the edge of the bazaar near the bus stand, and there are also a couple of old-style **luxury hotels**. If you're heading for a hotel up the hill it's a good idea to accept the offers of porters – if you've booked ahead make sure you negotiate the porter's fee before setting off.

Basant, Cart Rd, east of the bus stand (☎78341). Best of the rock-bottom bunch in the bazaar area, with cleanish rooms (attached or common shower-toilets). The road can be noisy. Some singles. ④.

Chanakya, Lakkar Bazaar (☎203338). Cosy, clean and central. Cheapest rooms are a good deal. ⑤.

Chapslee, Lakkar Bazaar (☎77319). Old manor house in its own grounds on the edge of town, stuffed with antiques. Six luxurious suites, library, card room, tennis court, and croquet lawn. ⑧–⑨.

Dalziel, The Mall (☎72691). Old and slightly shabby wooden building five minutes' walk uphill from the train station. Spotless, tiled bathrooms, and fine views from the back balconies. ⑤–⑥.

Dreamland, The Ridge, above the church (☎5057). One of the best-value, friendliest budget hotels, with clean rooms, most with geysers, *Star TV*, and superb morning views of the Himalayas. ④–⑤.

Oberoi Clarks, The Mall (☎212991). Period building converted into a very comfortable, formula 5-star. Pay in US dollars: prices start at $130. ⑨.

Sangeet, The Mall (☎202506). Swanky modern hotel, a cut above its peers, and good value. ⑤.

Surya, Circular Rd (☎78191). Popular and comfortable mid-range hotel on the north side of the Victory tunnel. Room service, restaurant, and *Star TV*. ⑥–⑦.

Thakur, just above the bus stand (☎77545). Large, blue wooden building with some original fittings. Good if you can't face the climb up the hill from the bus stand, but often full. ③.

Uphar, The Ridge, near the *Dreamland* (☎77670). Basic, but sizeable, rooms. The pricier ones come with *Star TV* and balcony: all have geysers. ⑤

White, Lakkar Bazaar (☎5276). Centrally located and well-managed hotel, with immaculate, light rooms, most with views. No off-season discount. Recommended. ⑤–⑦.

Woodville Palace, Raj Bhavan Rd (☎72763). Elegantly old-fashioned, 1930s mansion on the peaceful western side of town, with huge rooms, period furniture, lawns and a badminton court. Members of the former royal family still live upstairs. ⑧–⑨.

YMCA, The Ridge (☎72375). Large rooms (with shared bathrooms), and in-house dining hall, *Star TV*, snooker tables and sun-terrace. A little shabby, except for the more modern west wing. No dorms or singles. A good option during high season. ③.

Eating

Few **restaurants** in Shimla retain the colonial ambience you might expect. Catering mainly for Indian visitors, they are heavily Punjabi-oriented, with rich, spicy, meat-based menus. If you're looking for a really cheap and filling meal, try a tin plate piled high with fried potato patties (*tikki*) or chickpea curry and *puris* (*channa batura*) at one of the snack bars that line the steps opposite the *Gaiety Theatre*. An ice-cream or cake from one of the many **bakeries** along the Mall rounds off the evening nicely.

Ashiana, The Ridge. HPTDC restaurant in a converted bandstand offering mainly non-veg Indian food, including tasty chicken *makhanwalla*, pizzas, and a few Chinese dishes.

Balijee's, 26 The Mall. A landmark on Shimla's culinary and social map, this hectic smart-set coffee house does a roaring trade in snacks, sweets, especially in the evenings, but serves no alcohol. Try the piping hot *gulab jamuns*, served to after-dinner strollers at their take-away counter.

MOVING ON FROM SHIMLA

Most travellers bypass Shimla on their way between Delhi and Manali, but HP's capital is a perfect halfway house if you're heading up country to the Kullu Valley, or back in the other direction towards the plains of Haryana-Punjab. It's also the starting post for forays into the remoter regions of Kinnaur, Lahaul and Spiti (see p.466).

The **toy train** leaves Shimla for **Kalka** (4–7 daily; 5hr 30min–7hr), where you can change onto the main broad-gauge line for **Chandigarh** and **New Delhi**. The 11.55am departure from Shimla will get you into Kalka just in time to catch the 4.45pm *Himalayan Queen* #4096, arriving in New Delhi at about 10pm. The 11.30pm departure gets into Delhi at 6.30am (but doesn't stop at New Delhi station). **Reservations** for onward journeys from Kalka can be made at Shimla.

The Cart Rd **bus stand**, below the bazaar, handles services to Chandigarh, Delhi, Mandi, Kullu, Dharamsala, Manali, and elsewhere, while "Lakkar Bazaar" bus stand (reached via the path that drops behind *ANZ Grindlay's Bank* on Scandal Corner) is the place to pick up departures to Narkanda, Ani, Rampur, Sarahan, and Kalpa (for Kinnaur).

Passengers for **Manali**, **Chandigarh**, or **Delhi** can choose between "luxury" (a/c) and "deluxe" (non-a/c) services run by HPTDC and others, or *HPSTC*'s standard boneshaking "express" buses. Tickets for the former should be booked a day in advance at travel agents on the Mall, or through the tourist office on Scandal Corner, which also has a hatch (daily 10am–1pm & 2–4pm) to reserve seats on all state buses from Shimla (including regular expresses to Dharamsala, Chandigarh and Delhi). Alternatively, join the rucks at the reservation counters at the main bus stand on Cart Road.

Note, that the first leg of the journey to **Mandi** (for Kangra, Dharamsala and Manali) can be an ordeal if you suffer from **travel sickness**, as the bus drivers pelt down the switchbacks at incredible speeds. Keep nausea at bay by sitting at the front of the bus (another reason to book early), and by eating a large breakfast before you set off.

Flights between Delhi and Shimla (1hr 10min) are operated by *Jagson Airlines* (Tues, Thurs & Sat) and *Archana Airways* (Mon, Wed, Fri & Sun) on 8-seater planes for around $100. Seats are nearly always available: bookings for *Archana* flights are handled by the tourist office, while *Jagson's* main agent in Shimla is a good all-round **travel agent**, *Stan Travel*, 4 The Mall (☎5222).

Permits for travel into the restricted **"Inner Line" zone**, the recently opened road loop through Kinnaur and Spiti, are issued at the District Commissioner's office below the Mall. Unless you're travelling in a group of four or more, under the auspices of a reputable travel agent (who should arrange your permit), your chances of getting one are virtually nil.

Choice, Middle Bazaar (follow the steps down the side of *Balijee's* and look for the sign on the left). Tiny, no-nonsense Chinese restaurant with an exhaustive menu of cheap and delicious dishes.

Devico's, The Mall. Impeccably clean, Western-style fast food joint serving south Indian snacks, including delicious *rawa masala dosas*, as well as veggie-burgers, and shakes. Good views, too.

Fascination, 26 The Mall. *Balijee's* swish à la carte wing (upstairs) offers a good selection of Indian and Chinese dishes, including non-veg options such as brains curry, and sausage, egg and chips.

Goofa, The Ridge. The *Ashiana*'s dreary veg sibling – directly below in a cavernous basement – filling, moderately priced *thalis*.

Himani, 48 The Mall. *Balijee's* main rival has a lively (mostly male) bar downstairs, and a swanky restaurant on the top floor. Menu includes tasty *tandoori* dishes and south Indian options.

Indian Coffee House, The Mall. Pleasant, slightly shabby cafe with colonial ambience, offering the usual *Coffee House* package of veg snacks, coffee, and attentive service from turbaned waiters.

New Plaza, 60/1 Middle Bazaar, down the steps opposite the *Gaiety*. Deservedly popular, unpretentious family restaurant. Drab decor, but the mostly Indian dishes are fresh, tasty and good value.

Sher-e-Punjabi, Lower Bazaar. One of a string of cheap and basic *dhabas* just below the Mall. The veg branch dishes up hearty ladles of spicy bean, chickpea, and *dal* dishes, for next to nothing.

Kasauli

Though it sees few tourists, the small, slow-paced town of **KASAULI**, cradled by pine forests 77km southwest of Shimla (3hr by bus), and with a touch of Raj architecture, makes a good stop-off point on the way north. Raised high enough above the plains to afford good views south over the glinting lights of Chandigarh at night, as well as north to the Himalayas, it is still low enough to maintain a pleasant climate. Criss-crossed by spindly cobbled streets, spreading along low ridges carpeted with forests and flower-filled meadows, Kasauli abounds in gentle short strolls; the hike to the summit of nearby Monkey Point (4km) is as energetic as most tourists get.

The best way to wind up a visit to Kasauli is to trek along 12km of easy narrow paths through the woods to **Kalka**, railhead for the **toy train** to Shimla. Details of the paths, plus train and bus times, are available at the small **tourist office** by the bus stand. You can **change money** at the *Bank of Baroda* (Mon–Fri 11am–3pm) on Lower Mall.

Accommodation and eating

Kasauli's small cache of **hotels** is enough to cater for the thin trickle of tourists passing through. Aside from the cheapest lodges, most hotels offer high-ceilinged rooms with fire places, carpets and balconies, in true Raj style. Few have built-in water heaters, and supply hot water in buckets. Apart from in the larger hotels, **food** here is monotonous. *Dhabas* in Sadar Bazaar dish up standard *aloo mutter, aloo gobi* and *dal*, plus fresh *puris* in the morning, and there are a couple of good snack stops by the bus stand.

Alasia, Lower Mall (☎01793/2008). Musty Raj-era house, facing north to the distant mountains. Large rooms with balconies, plus a couple of special suites. ⑤.

Anchal, Post Office Rd (☎01793/2052). Good-value option. Some rooms are poky and dim, but others have balconies and views south over the lowlands. One room holds six people. ③.

Gian, Post Office Rd (☎01793/2244). Unremarkable, but homely. Some private bathrooms, and balconies. ①–②.

HPTDC Ros Common, Lower Mall (☎01793/2055). Very smart hotel almost 1km east of town, with beautiful gardens and silver-service tea and coffee all day. Six well-maintained and spotless rooms. Often full – call ahead or book through Shimla's *Hotel Holiday Home* (☎0177/212890). The restaurant, open to non-residents, has Kasauli's most expensive and extensive menu. ⑤–⑦.

Maurice, Lower Mall (☎01793/2974). Well-kept Raj house; towering ceilings and airy balconies. ④.

R Maidans, Lower Mall (☎01793/2128). Stylish but ageing Raj mansion with spacious rooms. Some have balconies, and some fireplaces. ④–⑥.

Narkanda

Another hill town seeing few foreign visitors is **NARKANDA**, a scruffy collection of corrugated-iron and timber houses, *chai* stalls, and wayside *dhabas*, 65km northeast of Shimla. This former staging post on the old Hindustan–Tibet caravan route became, during the Raj, a popular weekend retreat for sporting Shimla-*wallahs* who came to bag bears; you won't see many bears today (the surrounding forests have been mercilessly logged) but the **views** of the Himalayas, rising in snowy ranks from the far side of the valley to the north, are superlative.

Straddling the main Rampur road, NH22, just below the pass that leads from the foothills into the Sutlej Valley, the town (2725m) is the roadhead and market for the area's widely dispersed apple and potato growers, and also functions as one of the state's few **skiing** resorts (Dec–Feb). HPTDC run inexpensive ten-day packages in the *High Altitude Trekking & Skiing Centre*, near the bus stand – but they won't take groups of less than ten. The deal (book by writing in advance) includes rental, tuition, and a room in HPTDC's dour *Hotel Himview* (③–④). Smaller groups, or solo travellers, should contact local mountaineer and ski instructor, Jampa Tsondu (c/o the *High Altitude Trekking and Skiing Centre*, or through the town's biggest and best *dhaba* opposite the centre; ☎01782/8426). The *dhaba's* owner rents out large en-suite north-facing rooms (③) which are better value than those up the hill at *Hotel Snow View* (③).

Narkanda, three hours' bus ride from Shimla, makes a good resting point on the long, bumpy journey to Sarahan (6hr by bus from Narkanda) and Kinnaur further northeast. If you arrive at noon there's time to make an easy and rewarding 7km hike from town to **Hatu Peak** (3143m), crowned by a lonely hilltop **Durga temple**. Marking the highest point for many miles, it looks out over the winding Sutlej to a string of white tipped mountains to the north and east, and to the just-visible Shimla radio pylon in the west.

THE BASHLEO PASS TREK

The four- to five-day trek from Rampur over the **Bashleo Pass** to Banjar – one of the trails followed by Penelope Chetwode in her famous travelogue *Kullu: The End of the Habitable World* (*Time Books International*, Delhi 1989) – is a good alternative to the busier Ani–Jalori Pass route to the Kullu Valley, now somewhat spoiled for walkers by the introduction of a motorable road. The trail up to the pass is comparatively easy, and several forest resthouses allow the luxury of hiking without a tent. A number of picturesque villages, clustered around old wooden tower temples, also lie at regular intervals along the route. The largest, **Sarahan** (not to be confused with the village of the same name on the opposite side of the Sutlej Valley; see p.445), is usually reached at the end of the second day. Stage three takes you over the pass and down the other side to **Bathad**. After passing through **Bandal** and **Gushaini** villages on the fourth or fifth days, you finally arrive at the main road, from where daily buses head south, via **Banjar** and the Jalori Pass, to **Luri**, on NH22, and northwards to **Larji** in the Kullu Valley.

Rampur

Once over the pass at Narkanda, the highway winds steadily down the south side of the Sutlej Valley, passing through several fragrant stands of *deodar* and pine forest. As you approach the river, the trees thin out and the mountainside grows increasingly sun-parched and bare, except for the rice terraces that swirl, in stripes of green and pale yellow, around the banks of the roaring milky-turquoise torrent below.

The river – the border between Shimla and Kullu districts – can be crossed at this point. A fair-weather jeep track climbs up the *nala* to the north towards the village of

Ani and the **Jalori Pass** – for centuries the principal route north to the Kullu Valley. The main road, meanwhile, veers east along the even floor of a grandiose, V-shaped defile towards **RAMPUR**, 132km northeast of Shimla. Formerly the capital of the princely state of Bhushur, the town was once a prosperous and picturesque settlement, thronging with merchants from China, Yarkhand, and Tibet. Today, however, it's a gritty and cheerless cluster of unfinished concrete houses hemmed in by a forbidding wall of rock. The only time you may want to stop is during the **Lavi mela** (late Oct or early Nov), when hill-folk from the remote interior gather in their finest garb to trade bundles of wool, homespun shawls, and sacks of dried fruit and nuts.

If you find yourself stuck in Rampur for an hour or two, check out the gabled **Padam Palace**, home of the local ruling family, the Bahadurs, who trace their lineage back 123 generations to Lord Krishna. Built in 1919, the palace encloses an older Moghul-style building and a grand *durbar* hall – complete with silver throne and slits in its wood-panelled walls to allow the women of the court to spy on proceedings within. Across the main road from the bus stand, a small Buddhist **gompa** crowned with gold is cramped between newer concrete buildings and opens for prayers once or twice a day. Within, the tiny space is almost completely taken up by a huge metal prayer wheel, but also shelters a rock reputedly bearing ten million minute inscriptions of the *mantra* "Om Mane Padmi Hum". If you're unlucky enough to have to **spend the night** in Rampur, try the best of the budget lodges near the bus stand, the poky *Rama Guest House* (②), or the marginally more comfortable *Hotel Bhagavati* (③), at the bottom of the bazaar. Don't expect a feast at the local *dhabas*, whose generous greasy meals are filling but uninspired.

Sarahan

Secluded **SARAHAN**, erstwhile summer capital of the Bhushar rajas, sits astride a 2000-metre ledge above the River Sutlej, near the Shimla–Kinnaur border. Set against a spectacular backdrop, the village harbours one of the northwestern Himalaya's most exotic spectacles – the twin wooden pagodas of the gilt-pinnacled **Bhima Kali temple**. Until the opening of the "Inner Line" to tourists in 1992, only die-hard architecture buffs and the odd Spiti-bound trekking party ever passed through here. Now, with the nearby road no longer a "dead end", and despite a trickle of jeep safaris, it remains an off-track destination, an excellent two-day foray from Shimla, 174km southwest.

With its two multi-tiered sanctuary towers, elegantly sloping slate-tiled roofs, and gleaming golden spires, **Bhima Kali** is the most majestic of the few early timber tem-

---

BLOOD SACRIFICE IN SARAHAN

The **Bhima Kali** deity, a local manifestation of the black-faced, bloodthirsty Hindu goddess Kali (Durga), has for centuries been associated with **human sacrifice**. Once every decade, until the disapproving British appeared on the scene in the 1800s, a man was killed here as an offering to the *devi*. Following a complex ceremony, his newly spilled blood was poured over the goddess's tongue for her to drink, after which his body was dumped in a deep well inside the temple compound. If no victim could be found, it is said that a voice used to bellow from the depths of the pit, which is now sealed up.

The tradition of blood sacrifice continues in Sarahan to this day, albeit in less extreme form. During the annual **Astomi** festival, two days before the culmination of **Dussehra** (see p.471), a veritable menagerie of birds and beasts are put to the knife, including a water-buffalo calf, a sheep, a goat, a fish, a chicken, a crab, and even a spider. The gory spectacle draws large crowds, and is a memorable alternative to the Dussehra procession in Kullu, which takes place at around the same time in mid-October.

ples left in the Sutlej Valley – an area renowned for its unusual tradition of housing holy shrines on raised wooden platforms. Although most of the structure dates from early this century, parts are thought to be more than eight hundred years old. The same **construction technique**, of stacking dry stone blocks between logs, has been used throughout, giving the walls their distinctive brown-and-grey stripes.

The main entrance, through a pair of elaborately decorated metal doors in the west of the compound, opens onto a large courtyard flanked by rest rooms and a small carved-stone **Shiva shrine**. Leave shoes and any leather articles at the racks, and head up the steps to a second, smaller yard. Beyond another golden door, also richly embossed with mythical scenes, the innermost enclosure holds the two **sanctuary towers**. The one on the right houses musical instruments, flags, palladins and ceremonial weapons used in religious festivals, a selection of which is on show in the small "museum" in the corner of the courtyard. Non-Hindus who want to climb to the top of the other, more modern tower for *darshan*, a ritual viewing of the highly polished gold-faced deity, have to leave cameras with the *chowkidar*, and don a saffron cotton cap. On your way across the yard, note the delicate carving that surrounds the main tower's projecting wooden balconies, and the gargoyles that gape from the eaves of its gabled roof – crowned with crimson pennants to advertise the presence of the goddess within. **Bhima Kali** herself is enshrined on the top floor. Decked with garlands of flowers, she peers out from behind clouds of *dhoop* smoke, tended not by ordinary villagers, as is normally the case in Himachal, but by bona fide *brahmin* priests.

Practicalities

If you're travelling to Sarahan from Narkanda, you can take any Rampur-bound bus and change, or pick up one of the two direct buses from Shimla (daily 4.30pm & 10.40am). From Shimla the best option is to catch the 7.30am Sangla bus and change at Rampur (6hr) for the final leg to Sarahan, or failing that get as far as Jeori (pronounced *Jewri*), a dismal town linked to Sarahan by five or six daily buses. If you miss the last bus from Jeori to Sarahan (6pm), you could **hike** for 90 minutes up along a well-worn mule track, a far less daunting prospect than a night in Jeori, whose only accommodation is a flea-infested room above a sweet shop.

Sarahan itself only has two **places to stay**. The first, and more expensive is HPTDC's *Hotel Shirkhand* (④), a concrete monster in quasi-traditional Sutlej style. Rooms here are clean, comfortable, and come with hot-water geysers, and valley views. The small, moderately priced restaurant has a good veg menu, and a relaxing terrace commands fine views over the mountains to the north. If you're on a tighter budget, try one of *Temple Rest House*'s clean pleasant rooms (②–③), inside the Bhima Kali's main courtyard. If the temple kitchens aren't dishing up their usual cheap, filling pilgrims' food, the only places to **eat** are the grubby *dhabas* around the square outside.

KINNAUR

Before 1992, the remote backwater of **KINNAUR** was strictly off-limits to tourists. A rugged buffer zone between the Shimla foothills and the wild western extremity of Chinese-occupied Tibet, it was considered too sensitive for foreigners to wander around unsupervised. To some extent this still holds true. Although visitors are now allowed to travel through the "Restricted Area", and onwards to complete the loop through Spiti and Lahaul to the Kullu Valley, special permission must first be obtained. At present, **"Inner Line permits"**, issued at Shimla, Kullu, Rampur, and the district headquarters, **Rekong Peo**, are only granted to groups of four or more who have organized their trip through government-approved tour operators – which effectively renders most of the region out of bounds to independent travellers. Even if you can't afford a "jeep safari", however, those areas of Kinnaur that lie outside the no-go zone still offer incentives to brave the region's minimal infrastructure – notably the **Baspar Valley**, and sacred **Kinner-Kailash** massif, visible from the mountain village of **Kalpa**.

Straddling the mighty River Sutlej, which rises on the southern slopes of Shiva's winter abode on the Tibetan plateau, Mount Kailash, Kinnaur has for centuries been a major trans-Himalayan corridor. Merchants travelling between China and the Punjabi plains passed through on the **Hindustan–Tibet caravan route**, stretches of which are still used by villagers and trekkers. The bulk of the traffic that lumbers east towards the frontier, however, uses the newer fair-weather road, veering north into Spiti just short of the ascent to Shipki La Pass, on the Chinese border, which remains closed.

In the well-watered, mainly Hindu west of the region, the scenery ranges from subtropical to almost alpine: wood-and-slate villages, surrounded by maize terraces and orchards, nestle beneath pine forests and vast blue-grey mountain peaks. Further east, beyond the reach of the monsoons, it grows more austere, and glaciers loom on all sides. The hospitable Buddhist inhabitants of middle and upper Kinnaur are descendants of aboriginal peoples pushed into the mountains by the Aryan invasions of the second millennium BC. **Buddhism** arrived thanks to the tenth-century kings of Guge, who ruled what is now southwestern Tibet. **Rinchen Zangpo** (958–1055), the "Great Translator" credited with the "Second Spreading" of the faith in Guge, passed through here on his way home from the plains, where he had been sent by the ruler Yeshod to absorb the traditions of Indian Buddhism. In his wake, he left behind several monasteries, and a devotion to a pure form of the Buddhist faith that has endured here for nearly one thousand years. In the sixteenth century, after Guge had fragmented into dozens of petty fiefdoms, the **Bhushar kings** took control of Kinnaur. They remained in power throughout the British Raj, when this was one of the battlegrounds of the espionage war played out between agents of the Chinese, Russian and British empires – the "Great Game" evocatively depicted in the novels of Rudyard Kipling.

Rekong Peo

East of Jeori, the road climbs high above the Sutlej, traversing the sheer ravines that run into the valley from the south by means of flimsy-looking *jhulas*, or cable bridges. Tiny wooden villages, each with a pagoda-roofed temple, cling to the mountain sides – many at gradients beyond which human habitation would seem impossible. At **Wangtu** bridge, the old Inner Line, and trailhead for the Kinnaur–Pin Valley–Kaza trek (see p.449), the highway switches to the north bank of the river before running due east to the dishevelled, claustrophobic village of **Tapri**. Travelling by bus, you'll probably have to stop here to catch onward transport to Rekong Peo, or to Sangla, in the Baspar Valley. It's no place to get stuck, however, as there's no accommodation.

The district headquarters of Kinnaur, **REKONG PEO**, lies ninety minutes further up the valley, 4km above the main road. A batch of hastily constructed concrete houses and government buildings around a small *maidan*, it has the air of a dismal frontier settlement – a nightmare posting for the junior officials that stroll dejectedly along the main street. The only reason to stop is to buy trekking supplies, or to pick up the trail to Kalpa. Peo's **bazaar** is, however, a good place for crowd-watching, particularly in late afternoon when it fills up with dusty villagers waiting for the bus home. Many of the women don traditional Kinnauri garb for their trip to town – green velvet jackets, heavy homespun blankets with intricate borders, raw-silk cummerbunds, stacks of elaborate silver jewellery, and caps set at at jaunty angles above their long black plaits.

Practicalities

Rekong Peo's **buses** are fairly frequent considering its relative isolation. Five daily services ply between here and Shimla; there's a 4.30am departure for Mandi, and a direct bus at 2pm to Sangla. With an Inner Line permit, you can flag down the Tapri–Kaza bus as it passes Poberi, the Rekong Peo turn-off on the main road, at around 7am.

Accommodation is limited to the PWD *Rest House* (④) near the *maidan*, and, next best, the *Hotel Fairyland* (③), above the main street where the buses pull in. Rooms here are clean and aired, some with private baths, and views across to Kinner-Kailash. Avoid the grungy *Mayur Guest House* (①–②), just down the road. Between the two, the small *Chinese Restaurant* is the village's only decent **place to eat**, serving filling meat-based noodle dishes, spicy veg stews, and Tibetan salt-butter tea. You can't get mineral water or soft drinks this far up the valley.

Kalpa (Chini)

Almost 250km northeast of Shimla, **KALPA** – known, when it was the British district heaquarters, as **Chini** – can be reached by road, or on foot along the steep mule track up the mountain from behind Rekong Peo's small *gompa* (look for the large yellow standing Buddha). After a stiff hour's hike through *deodar* trees, orchards and farm terraces, you rejoin the road just before it reaches a bazaar. A scruffy collection of market stalls and slate-roofed farmhouses, Kalpa would not be worth the climb were it not for for its dramatic location, astride a rocky bluff high above the right bank of the Sutlej. Opposite, the magnificent **Kinner-Kailash** massif sweeps 4500m up from the valley floor – a rugged ridge of sharp grey peaks flecked with folds of ice and snow. The mountain in the middle, Jorkaden (6473m) is the highest, followed by the sacred summit of Kinner-Kailash (6050m) to the north, and the needle point of Raldang (5499m) in the south. Up the valley you'll see remains of the Hindustan–Tibet road.

Practicalities

Kalpa is a far more attractive place to stay than Rekong Peo, although finding **accommodation** can involve a lot of walking. The best place is the *Forest Rest House* (④), a splendid ex-British bungalow at the top of the village, with large rooms, superb views from its garden and a resident *chowkidar*-cum-cook. Head up the dirt track that turns right off the metalled road 400m below the bazaar, and follow the path past the school and Forest Department Office. On the way, you pass Kalpa's only budget option, the *Vicky Guest House* (②), whose sole (four-bedded) room is tacked onto the side of a family house. In the unlikely event of both these places being full, you can find a cheap bed for the night by asking around the bazaar on the other side of the village.

Apart from the *Rest House*, the only **places to eat** in Kalpa are its grubby *chai* shops, or the stores on and around the square, where you can buy fresh fruit, biscuits, lentils and rice, but little else; a camping stove is useful.

The Baspar Valley

Hemmed in by the pinnacles of Kinner-Kailash to the north, and the high peaks of the Garhwal range to the south, the seventy-kilometre River Baspar rises in the mountain wilderness along the Indo-Tibetan border, to flow through one of Kinnaur's most beautiful, secluded areas. Despite its comparative accessibility, the **Baspar Valley** sees few visitors, as its remotest reaches lie beyond the Inner Line. Nevertheless, the picturesque villages lower down the valley merit a detour from the main Rampur–Spiti road.

The valley's largest settlement, **SANGLA**, overlooks the right bank of the Baspar from the lower slopes of Kinner-Kailash. Served by daily **buses** from Shimla and Tapri, its chief attractions are a small saffron farm, and the wood-and-stone, gable-roofed **Kamru fort**, a thirty- to forty-minute walk above the village. You can **stay the night** at the rather overpriced and spartan *Baspar Guest House* (③), or, during high season, at the *Trekkers Lodge* (①), just down the road. Sangla also boasts one of India's swankiest government bungalows, the *Electricity Rest House* (④), set apart from the village centre.

TREKKING IN KINNAUR

Unfrequented mountain trails criss-cross Kinnaur, offering **treks** ranging from gentle hikes to challenging climbs over high-altitude passes. The routes along the **Sutlej Valley**, punctuated with government rest houses and villages, are feasible without the aid of ponies, but away from the main road you need to be completely self-sufficient. **Porters** can usually be hired in Rampur and Rekong Peo for around Rs100–150 a day, except in early autumn (Sept/Oct), when they and their horses are in great demand for the apple harvest.

Sarahan to Wangtu

This sedate four- to five-day hike along the path of the old Hindustan–Tibet road is an ideal introduction to the scenery and culture of the Sutlej Valley. The trail begins just below **SARAHAN** (see p.445), peeling away to the right after a sharp switchback in the metalled road that leads down to Jeori. Beyond several kilometres of pine and oak forest, it crosses a couple of mountain streams lower down the valley, before continuing northeast towards the first night-halt, the rest house at **Chaura** village, site of the picturesque Hirmal Devi temple. The second day takes you as far as **Tranda** (8km), or onwards another 10km, via the steep-sided Solding *nala*, or stream-gorge, to the rest house at **Paunda**. The third/fourth stage is an easy 12km amble through the village of Sungra, with its ancient *devi* temple, to **Nechar** *Rest House*. From here, the track drops 5km to meet the main highway. At **Wangtu**, where it crosses the river, you can pick up transport back to Shimla, or further up the Sutlej to Rekong Peo and Kalpa.

The Kinner-Kailash circuit

The five- to seven-day circumambulation of the majestic **Kinner-Kailash** massif, a sacred pilgrimage trail, makes a spectacular trek, for which you need an **Inner Line permit** (see p.446). The circuit starts at the village of **MORANG**, on the left bank of the Sutlej, served by buses from Tapri or Rekong Peo. A jeepable track runs southeast from here alongside the Turung Gad torrent to **Thangi**, the trailhead. The first night halt, a level patch of ground beside the confluence of two streams at **Rahtak**, lies 12km up the valley. The gruelling second stage takes in the stiff climb up to the **Charang La Pass** (5266m), after which the path plunges steeply through a glacial moraine to the village of **Chitkul** in the **Baspar Valley** (see opposite), where there's a small forest rest house. At this point, the Inner Line ends and the trail follows the river down to the beautiful village of **Sangla**. If you're not pushed for time, a number of worthwhile day hikes can be slotted in here: up to **Kamru fort** behind the village, or the steep ascent to the **Shivaling La Pass**, on the opposite (west) side of the valley to Sangla, from where there are superb views of Raldang (5499m), the southernmost peak on the Kinner-Kailash massif. The final stage of the circuit passes through the lower, greener end of the Baspar Valley, via Shang and Brua on the left bank of the river, to **Karcham**, which overlooks the main highway.

Wangtu to Kaza, via the Pin Valley

This challenging route across the Great Himalayan range, via the Kalang Setal glacier and the Shakarof La Pass, is a dramatic approach to Spiti and the **Pin Valley**. The trail, which is very steep, snow-covered, and hard to follow in places, should definitely not be attempted without ponies, porters, adequate gear, and a **guide** – preferably one arranged through a reputable trekking agency (for an address in Shimla, see p.438).

The first day, starting at **WANGTU** on the main highway, is an easy 8km hike up the valley to **Kafnoo** village. Stage two (12km) leads beyond the tree-line to a Gaddi grazing ground called **Mulling**, from where it's another 12km uphill through high pastures to **Phustirang** (3750m), the camp ground below the **Bhaba Pass** (4865m). Day four (or three if you're acclimatized) is a gruelling slog over the pass through eternal snowfields and down the other side into the beautiful and isolated **Pin Valley**. **Kaza** (see p.488), the district headquarters of Spiti, lies a further three or four days' hike to the north. On its way to the main road, the trail winds through remote settlements such as the village of **Kharo**, within striking distance of the ancient Buddhist *gompa* at **Khungri**.

Trekkers and campers should, however, bring their own food and fuel, so as not to over-burden the village's subsistence-oriented economy.

Further up the Baspar Valley the settlements become smaller, and the scenery more dramatic, but the chances of getting a **room** are thinner. In **Rakchham**, forty minutes by bus (2daily) from Sangla, a small rest house has a couple of rooms and the town's only indoor washing facilities. A day's hike away, **Chitkul** is as far up the valley as you can go without an Inner Line permit. The tiny village, which has a basic rest house, sits at the bottom of a sprawling glacial moraine, crossed by the trail that winds up to **Charang La Pass** – the route of the Kinner-Kailash *parikarma*, or pilgrimage circuit, described on p.449.

Upper Kinnaur

Access to **upper Kinnaur**, the remote region east of Kalpa, is restricted. Only visitors with Inner Line permits can travel beyond the checkpoint at Khangi, and on towards the confluence of the Sutlej and Spiti rivers. Five to six hours by jeep from Rekong Peo, within a day's hike of the frontier, the tiny hamlet of **PEOH** (or **Puh**) is the area's main settlement, chosen by the Dalai Lama in summer 1992 as the venue for the rarely performed **Kalachakra ceremony**. Buddhists from all over the world – including Richard Gere and Cindy Crawford, whose arrival almost upstaged the great man himself – flocked here to listen to Tibet's leader-in-exile read from a secret and highly auspicious text, which is believed to divulge a super-fast short-cut to Enlightenment.

Beyond Peoh, the road bends north, crossing the Sutlej for the last time at **Khabo**, near the Spiti confluence. To the northeast, **Leo Pargial II** (6770m), Kinnaur's highest peak, rises in a near-vertical 4000-metre wall of cream-coloured buttresses and pinnacles to mark the international frontier. The mountain also overlooks the old Indo–Tibet road as it enters China via the **Shipki La pass** (5569m). The present road, meanwhile, winds north above the Spiti through the barren wastes of the Hanglang Valley. Within the rain shadow of the Himalayas, this far-eastern edge of Himachal Pradesh, with its deep blue skies, crisp clear light and arid mountain scenery, closely resembles Ladakh. Its only settlements are small scatterings of cubic dry-stone houses piled high with fuel and fodder, and surrounded by thickets of shimmering poplars, apricot groves, and terraces of barley. **NAKO**, the largest village, nestles high above the east side of the river around the banks of a small circular **lake**. Its eleventh-century *gompa*, founded by Rinchen Zangpo, houses ancient Buddhist statues and paintings.

NORTHWEST HIMACHAL

From Shimla the main road winds west and north to the riverside market town of **Mandi**, a crossroads more or less in the centre of the state linking the northeastern Kullu Valley and the hills to the **northwest**. Less dramatic and considerably lower than Himachal's eastern reaches, the rolling foothills in the northwest are generally warmer, and more easily accessible, though the area sees little tourism outside **Dharamsala**, the British hill station turned Tibetan settlement, and home to His Holiness the Dalai Lama. Dharamsala is also an excellent base for treks over the soaring Dhauladhar range to the **Chamba Valley**, harbouring uniquely styled Hindu temples in **Brahmour** and **Chamba**, and beyond to Lahaul and Ladakh. Close to Chamba, **Dalhousie** may have lost its former glory, but still has a certain ex-Raj charm, enticing visitors with its cool tree-clad heights and sublime views, and is well placed for short ambles through the surrounding hills.

The section which follows traces the River Beas and NH21 as they weave from Mandi to Dharamsala, linking a string of quiet mountain towns and villages. Just outside Mandi, sacred **Rewalsar** is great for a few days' rest, while further along the route you could stop at **Jogindernagar** to pick up the narrow-gauge train that weaves through patchwork fields and light forest to the **Kangra Valley**. The main town here, **Kangra**, huddles round its ancient fort, dwarfed by the distant backdrop of sheer mountains rising behind Dharamsala, just one hour away.

Mandi to Dharamsala

The road northwest from Mandi skirts the edges of the hills, passing through thick pine forests and lush tea gardens. While most visitors make the six-hour journey to Dharamsala in one go, on one of the nine daily **buses**, those with more time can pause at the small towns of **Baijnath** and **Palampur**, or pick up the narrow-gauge train as it trundles slowly through the fertile valleys between **Jodindernagar** and **Kangra**.

Mandi

At the point where the southern plains meet the Kullu and Kangra valleys, 158km north of Shimla, **MANDI** straddles the River Beas, its houses clinging to the rising slopes of the gorge. Once a major trading post for Ladakhis heading south – *mandi* means market – the town boasts few sights, though the riverside *ghats* dotted with stone temples where *sadhus* and pilgrims pray present a colourful scene. Mandi also holds a collection of sixteenth-century Nagari-style temples, raised above the town on **Tarna Hill**. To **get there**, climb the 160 steps next to the rifle shop facing the market square, or take the road which winds up from the bridge close to the *Bank of Baroda*. On the summit is the main Kali temple, decorated with garish paintings of the fierce mother goddess draped in skulls and blood; in the sanctuary, gold-clad walls surround a black stone Kali.

Mandi's chief function is as a crossroad. Buses from north and south arrive at a **bus stand** on the east bank, where an excellent cafe cooks delicious veg food all day. Services to Rewalsar leave from here, and also from a smaller depot, near Guntur Ghar on the west bank. The town has plenty of **hotels**, most a rickshaw- or taxi-ride away from the main bus stand, across the river. *The* place to stay is the ramshackle *Raj Mahal* (☎01905/2041; ④), overlooking the town square, a period-furnished palace set in shady gardens, with a few singles, a good restaurant and the only bar in town. Less expensive options nearby include the simple and rather grotty *Standard* (☎01905/22948; ①), opposite the small Rewalsar bus depot, and *Siva* (☎01905/24211; ②–④), on the main road by the town square. Nearer the river on the east bank, the simple *Vyas Guest House* (☎01905/23409; ③) has a few cosy doubles.

Rewalsar

If you've any interest in Buddhism it's worth taking a detour 24km southeast of Mandi to the **monasteries** of **REWALSAR**, which belong to the Nyingma sect, the original school of Tibetan Buddhism. The peaceful village comprises less than a hundred low slate-roofed houses, ranged around a lake. Red, yellow and white **Buddhist temples** crowned with gold-fringed pagodas, are reflected in pleasing symmetry in the waters. Monks and nuns circumambulate the sacred lake beneath fluttering prayer flags, and amble through lanes that echo with the clinks of stone cutters, the hum of hand-powered sewing machines and the toll of bells from Hindu and Buddhist temples.

According to Buddhist legend, the eighth-century monk Padmasambhava wanted to train the daughter of the local Hindu raja in meditation. Her incensed father struck Padmasambhava down in flames, but the powerful monk manifested himself as a lotus flower surrounded by water. Suitably impressed, the king allowed his daughter to train under

Padmasambhava, who set up a Buddhist centre here before embarking on the pilgrimage during which he introduced the faith to Tibet. It's believed that he left his footprint in one of the many caves cut into the hills around the lake, used today as isolated meditation retreats.

For Hindus, on the other hand, Rewalsar lake dates back to the post-Vedic era, and specifically the writing of the *Puranas* (possibly sixth-century), one of which refers to Rewalsar as the abode of the sage Lomas, for whose sake the lake was created with waters from the Ganga and Yamuna. Emerging from a canopy of trees on the west shore, the newer Sikh **gurudwara** attracts pilgrims who retrace the steps of Guru Gobind Singh; this is one of the few sites associated with his life in Himachal. To the south a small **sanctuary** protects deer and Himalayan black bears.

The HPTDC *Rewalsar Inn* (①–③), a short way back from the north shore, has comfortable **rooms**, each with bath and hot showers, and a small dorm; visitors who plan to **stay** for a while can also sleep in the Nyingma monastery (①, and **eat** at a small Tibetan restaurant which serves *thukpa*, *momo* and noodles, just opposite. Standard greasy north Indian food is prepared at *dhabas* along the main road.

Jogindernagar and Bir

JOGINDERNAGAR, 63km northwest of Mandi, is an uninviting little town holding little more than two streets flanked by wooden-fronted houses, and a crowded, disorganized bus stand. The main reason to get off a bus here is to pick up one of the three daytime **trains** that make the slow journey through the Kangra valley to Baijnath and Kangra. Rickshaws near the bus stand cover the three-kilometre journey west to the station; train timetables and comfortable **accommodation** can be found at the smart HPTDC *Hotel Uhl* (☎2002; ④–⑥), at the eastern end of the main road.

Jogindernagar is the place to stay if you want to visit **BIR**, 15km west, where the community weave carpets, and grow potatoes, rice and apples in patchy fields dissected by trickling brooks. Below the village a Tibetan settlement supports a handicraft centre, a school and a community of monks who live in a grand temple. A couple of simple stalls brew acrid Tibetan butter tea and sweet *chai*, but little else. **Treks** from Bir over the Dhauladhars lead west to Chamba or east to Manali (see p.453).

Baijnath

BAIJNATH, 30km west of Jogindernagar, is an unattractive, cramped and dirty place, where the streets seem always to be blocked with traffic, and clusters of hanging electricity wires imperil passengers travelling on the roofs of buses. The town is only noteworthy for its grey stone **Vaidyanath temple**, dedicated to Shiva as Lord of Physicians, whose round-edged *shikhara* is easily visible from the main road, a few hundred metres from the bus stand. It stands in a walled compound set off by the distant backdrop of severe Dhauladhar slopes; niches at regular intervals in the outer walls shelter images of Hindu deities, and there's a stone *lingam* within. Carvings on the sides depict Surya (the sun-god), Karttikeya (the god of war, Shiva's second son), and an emaciated Chamunda (a terrible form of Durga), garlanded with skulls. It's a short, steep walk to the temple from Baijnath station, just over 1km west of town.

Palampur

Further into the Kangra valley, tree-clad slopes give way to rolling deep green fields, as the westbound road enters Himachal's prime tea-growing area, around the small town of **PALAMPUR**, less than 30km northwest of Baijnath. This is the trailhead for walks to nearby hills, tea fields and gorges, and **treks** into the Kullu and Chamba valleys, but sees few Western tourists.

The best of Palampur's **hotels** is HPTDC *Hotel T-Bud* (☎2081; ⑤–⑥), surrounded by lawns and pine trees 1km north of town, where the rooms are spacious and immaculate,

TREKKING FROM PALAMPUR DISTRICT

Palampur is an ideal starting point for a **trek**; scenery nearby includes lush tea gardens, alpine meadows and the harsh and rocky crags of the Dhauladhar range. Passes north of the town offer unrivalled views of the Kangra valley to the south. There are, however, **no trekking companies** in Palampur: if you choose to start a trek here, it's best to organize supplies, guides and porters in Dharamsala. One easy four-day hike leads **from PALAMPUR** over **Waru Pass** (3850m), the "gateway of wind", via Satchali, Thanetar and Dhog to **Holi**; continuing for two more testing days brings you to the sacred **Manimahesh Lake** near Brahmour. From Dhog it's possible to continue east to Barabhangal and as far as Manali.

A pleasant but difficult seven- or eight-day trek **from PALAMPUR** starts by crossing **Sunghar Pass** (4473m), then leads back across the Dhauladhars at **Jalsu Pass** (3600m) and south to Baijnath. In fact **Baijnath**, only 40km from Palampur by road, is itself a good trailhead for treks to Chamba or Bharabhangal, following paths that traverse glaciers, waterfalls, the high Thamsar Pass (4665m) and the River Ravi.

Other long-distance treks start north of the main road **at BIR**, half an hour on frequent buses from Baijnath or Jogindernagar. Once there, a 14km-journey by jeep or foot brings you to **Billing**, 2600m up, from where a 12km-track winds north to the potato farms at Rajgunda, and on to Palachak, where a flat shady campground and a huddle of *dhabas* stay open all summer. A gentle track then ascends wooded paths for 9km to **Panihardu**, where you can rest before tackling the steeper route to Thansar Pass, which takes at least five hours. There's a campground at the snout of the glacier at **Marhu**, below the pass across tricky boulder fields. At this point green meadows and thin tree-cover replace rocky expanses on the route to **Bharanbhangal**, a knot of flat-roofed barns and wooden houses hemmed in by mountains and completely cut off in winter.

Routes head west **from MARHU** to **Chamba** (3 days) and **Manimahesh** (3 days), and southeast to **Manali** over Kalihan ("black ice") Pass. This latter, strenuous, route takes a further six days, and is suitable only for experienced trekkers. A gradual ascent through forests and over streams and frequent ridges leads to the lofty meadows of **Sukha Parao**, with views of snowy peaks on all sides. A 9km-climb up the thin path to **Lama Parao** (3150m) brings you to the upper limit of the forests, before the track weaves across treeless hillsides to **Gwari** (3750m). This is the final stop before the pass, reached after a demanding ascent of 7km over boulders and the bed of a glacier. Once across, the descent traverses a snow field and drops to **Sanghor**, where small but flat fields are perfect for camping. The next leg crosses ridges and streams to **Railli** (9km), and continues through thick clusters of *deodar* and pine to **Sangchur** (22km). After three days' hard trekking, you'll be glad of the easy walk down through villages, bright valleys and pine woods along the River Beas for 12km to **Manali**.

and the restaurant serves excellent food. Options along the main road closer to the new bus stop include the reasonable *Hotel Sawhney* (☎2555; ③–④) and *Palampur Guest House* (①), one of a bunch of very basic lodges. A good short hike heads 2km north of the *T-Bud* to the spectacular 300-metre-wide **Neugal Gorge**, which rises up from the rushing River Bundla, overlooked by HPTDC's *Neugal Cafe*.

Kangra

Though **KANGRA**, above the valley of the Banganga and below the Dhauladhar hills, is usually just passed through by travellers on their way to Dharamsala, 18km north, it certainly merits a day's visit. **Buses** from all over Kangra valley, and further east and west, pull into the bus stand 1km north of the town centre. Frequent services make the journey to Dharamsala (1hr). If you arrive by train, get off at **Kangra Mandir station**; as rickshaws don't usually wait here, you'll probably have to walk 3km over the river, and up the hill.

Before the creation of Himachal Pradesh state, Kangra was capital of a district of the same name; it fell prey for centuries to invasions of Sikhs and Muslims, before the British took control in 1847 and reinstated the Katoch rajas in the town that they had founded in the tenth century. Amid the crowded streets, the **central bazaar** brims with *puja* paraphernalia – red powder, coconuts, tinsel and sugar. Behind it, against the precipitous Dhauladhars, the **Bajreshwari Devi temple** dominates a courtyard chequered in marble and black stone. The temple's legendary wealth invited much Muslim interest between the twelfth and fifteenth centuries; Mahmud of Ghazni, Feroz Shah Tughluq and Sikander Lodi all took their turn sacking and looting. It was finally laid low by an earthquake in 1905; what you see today is the result of extensive rebuilding, and holds little architectural appeal. The only remaining valuable possessions are the silver parasols that shade the idol, though the site is still important to devotees of Shakti, the female embodiment of Shiva's energy.

Kangra's crumbling yet still sturdy **fort**, accessible by rickshaw, imperiously surveys the river valley from 4km south. It too was damaged by the earthquake, and is a shadow of its former self, overgrown and inhabited by screeching green parrots that flit through a few simple temples still tended by priests. High gates, some British-built, span a cobbled path to the deserted ramparts. It was the fort (*garh*), incidentally, supposedly built over the ear (*kan*) of Shiva, that gave the name to town and district.

If you want to stay the night in Kangra, it has a few unelaborate lodges. **Hotels** along Dharamsala Rd, which runs from the bus stand into town, include the simple *Ashoka* (☎25147; ①), the less-clean *Gaurav* (☎25176; ①) and *Preet* (☎5260; ①), and the nicer *Maurya* (☎5244; ③), with airy rooms and private baths. In Nehru Bazaar near the temple, *Hotel Anand* (☎25243; ②–④), up a deceptively dirty flight of stairs at the top of a noisy shopping complex, has reasonably clean rooms, and serves good **meals**. Several *dhabas* in the bazaar have an almost constant supply of spicy local dishes. The *State Bank of Patiala* (Mon–Fri 11am–2pm), next to the post office on Dharamsala Rd, handles **foreign exchange**.

Masrur

Southwest of Kangra a narrow road skirts low rippling hills for 30km to the tiny hamlet of **MASRUR**, the only place in the Himalayas to feature **rock-cut Hindu temples** like those found at Ellora in Maharashtra. While nowhere near as impressive as their distant cousins, these weather-worn monolithic bulks have survived the centuries remarkably well. Hewn out of natural rock formations during the ninth and tenth centuries, the fifteen temples devoted to Shiva, Sita, Ram and Laxman bear eroded carvings of meditating mendicants and busty maidens guarding dim cavernous sanctuaries. Passages cut into the rocky mounds wind up to a flat roof above the main temple, pierced by a vast *shikhara* adorned with solemn faces of Hindu deities. Statues and column bases litter the site and line the low walls of a large tank, but most of the better statues have been removed to state museums.

If you don't have your own vehicle, you can get to Masrur by catching a bus to Pir Bindu and then hiking the last 3km up to the temples on foot, a journey that is too arduous for all but the most inquisitive architectural buffs. Taxis from Dharamsala cost Rs450 return, a little less from Kangra.

Jawalamukhi

One of north India's most important Hindu shrines is protected by a simple whitewashed temple in the otherwise nondescript town of **JAWALAMUKHI**, 35km south of Kangra. The sanctuary, crowned with a squat golden spire, contains a blue gas flame, considered a manifestation of the goddess of fire, Jawalamukhi. Priests are eager to light emissions of gas in smaller chambers for expectant devotees, but only the main flame is kept alight continuously. The HPTDC *Jawalaji Hotel* (☎2080; ③–⑤) offers smart a/c **rooms**, and a restaurant serving local and north Indian food.

Dharamsala

As the home of the Dalai Lama and the Tibetan government in exile, and the starting point for some exhilarating treks into the high Himalayas, **DHARAMSALA** is one of Himachal's most irresistible destinations, and is refreshingly free of the noise and turmoil of most Indian towns. As well as playing host to casual tourists, it is a place of pilgrimage that attracts Buddhists and interested parties from all over the world, many of whom visit India specifically to come here.

Spread across wooded ridges, beneath the stark rock faces of the Dhauladhar range, 150km east of Pathankot and 160km northwest of Mandi, Dharamsala is divided into two distinct and widely separated sections, which differ in height by almost a 1000m. Originally a British hill station, the town has been transformed by the influx of refugees fleeing Chinese oppression in Tibet. They have been arriving since 1960, when their welcome, here and elsewhere, by the Indian government owed much to their propaganda value at a time of great tension between India and China.

Most Tibetans now live in **McLeodganj**, the upper town and the real heart of Dharamsala, where monks and nuns stroll through lanes lined with trading stalls and restaurants. You won't find a "Little Lhasa" here, but the Tibetan influence is undeniably strong: their achievements include the creation of temples, schools, monasteries, nunneries, and meditation centres, and an excellent library of Tibetan history and religion. Staying in McLeodganj for a while is easy; it's relaxed and very friendly.

Despite heavy snows and low **temperatures** between December and March, McLeodganj receives visitors all year round. The summer brings torrential rains that linger in dribs and drabs for much of the year; even then, the days may be hot, but you'll need warm clothes for the chilly nights.

Arrival and information

State run **buses** from Manali, Mandi, Pathankot, Kangra and Delhi pull into the bus stand in the very south of the lower town, though some run all the way up to McLeodganj the usual termination point for private buses from Delhi and Manali. The nearest point of arrival for **trains** from Delhi, Punjab and Jamu Tawai is Pathankot; the narrow-gauge train up from Jogindernagar terminates at Kangra. It's also possible to get here by **air**: three weekly *Jagson* flights leave the airport, 11km south of town at Gaggal, for Delhi (2hr 30min) via Kullu (25min) and Shimla (1hr 10min).

The **tourist office** (Mon–Sat 10am–5pm; ☎22363), stocked with information on accommodation and transport, is at the foot of the main bazaar in the lower town, just a few minutes' walk from the bus stand. For enquiries about the Tibetan settlement, call in at the **Welfare Office** on Bhagsu Rd in McLeodganj, where donations of clothes, books, blankets and pens for new Tibetan arrivals are always gratefully accepted.

McLeodganj's **post office**, on Jogibara Rd (Mon–Fri 9am–5pm, Sat 9am–3.30pm), has a poste restante counter that holds letters for up to a month. Letters not addressed to McLeodganj, Upper Dharamsala, end up in the **GPO** (same hours), a steep 1km out of the lower town. STD telephones are widely available. The *State Bank of India* in McLeodganj (Mon–Fri 10.30am–1pm), will change *Thomas Cook* and *American Express* travellers' cheques; there's another branch in lower Dharamsala (also open Sat 10am–noon). The *Bank of Baroda*, in the lower town, issues money to *Visa* card holders, with one or two days' delay.

The telephone **area code** for Dharamsala is ☎01892.

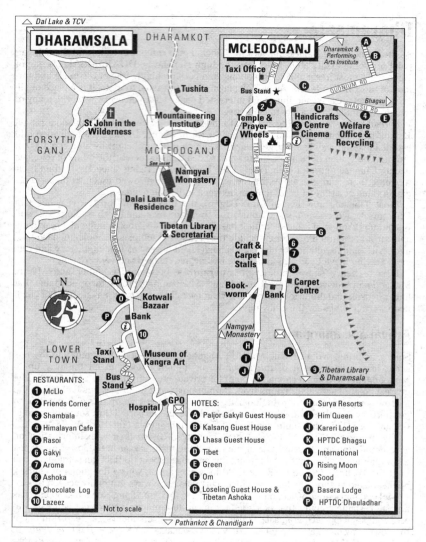

Dal Lake & TCV

DHARAMSALA

DHARAMKOT

MCLEODGANJ

Dharamkot & Performing Arts Institute

A

B

Taxi Office

TIPA RD

QUONIUM RD

Bus Stand ★

C

Bhagsu

Tushita

BHAGSU RD

Mountaineering Institute

St John in the Wilderness

Temple & Prayer Wheels

Handicrafts Centre

D

Welfare Office & Recycling

E

FORSYTH GANJ

Cinema

i

MCLEODGANJ

See inset

F

TEMPLE RD

JOGIBARA RD

Namgyal Monastery

Dalai Lama's Residence

5

Tibetan Library & Secretariat

G

Bus Route to Mcleodganj

Craft & Carpet Stalls

6

7

N

M

N

8

Book-worm

Bank

Carpet Centre

O

Kotwali Bazaar

P

Bank

Namgyal Monastery

H

LOWER TOWN

i

10

Taxi Stand ★

Museum of Kangra Art

I

L

Bus Stand ★

J

K

9 Tibetan Library & Dharamsala

RESTAURANTS:
1 McLlo
2 Friends Corner
3 Shambala
4 Himalayan Cafe
5 Rasoi
6 Gakyi
7 Aroma
8 Ashoka
9 Chocolate Log
10 Lazeez

Hospital

GPO

HOTELS:
A Paljor Gakyil Guest House
B Kalsang Guest House
C Lhasa Guest House
D Tibet
E Green
F Om
G Loseling Guest House & Tibetan Ashoka

H Surya Resorts
I Him Queen
J Kareri Lodge
K HPTDC Bhagsu
L International
M Rising Moon
N Sood
O Basera Lodge
P HPTDC Dhauladhar

Not to scale

Pathankot & Chandigarh

The lower town

It's easy to see why most visitors bypass Dharamsala's **lower town**, a haphazard jumble of shops, offices and houses. Although it holds the tourist office and banks, the only place of interest is the small **Museum of Kangra Art** (Tues–Sun 10am–5pm), and even that, with its scanty collection of Kangra miniatures, supplemented by some modern art, merits the briefest of visits.

From the bus stand at the southern limit of the lower town, a road takes buses and cars north through the crowded bazaars and continues for ten kilometres of hairpin bends to the northern edge of McLeodganj. On foot, the quickest route is a shorter (3km) but much steeper track winding up to McLeodganj's southern end from behind the vegetable market, passing the Tibetan Library and the Dalai Lama's residence.

McLeodganj

The tiny settlement of **Mcleodganj** extends along a slender high ridge that juts out over the valley below. Despite being named after David McLeod, the Lieutenant Governor of Punjab when the hill station was founded in 1848, it now shows little evidence of former British occupation. Intersected by two narrow potholed roads, the focal point of McLeodganj is its Buddhist **temple**, ringed with spinning red and gold prayer wheels. The ramshackle buildings of the town are decked with white, red, green, blue and yellow flags, printed with prayers, that flutter constantly in the wind, and the streets are coloured with the ruby robes of monks and nuns. Today Indian residents are outnumbered by Tibetans, who still stream in after long journeys across Nepal from the Tibetan plateau. For them McLeodganj is not simply a haven, but also the home of their spiritual leader, the Dalai Lama, and a place where children are free to learn Tibetan language, history and religion without breaking the laws imposed by the Chinese in Tibet.

It's easy to find your way around McLeodganj. At its northern end, the road up from the lower town arrives at a small square that serves as the bus stand. Roads radiating from here head south to the Dalai Lama's residence and the Library of Tibetan Works and Archives, north to the village of Dharamkot and Tushita Retreat Meditation Centre, and to the Tibetan Children's Village next to Dal Lake, and east to the small hamlet of Bhagsu.

MEETING HIS HOLINESS THE DALAI LAMA

The **Dalai Lama** is in great demand. Tibetans fleeing their homeland come to him for blessing and reassurance; monks and nuns from all over India and Nepal look to him for spiritual guidance; and an ever-increasing number of Westerners arrive in Dharamsala hoping for a moment of his attention. Ten or twenty years ago it might have been possible for people to meet His Holiness on an individual basis; now casual visitors should count on attending a **public audience**, when he greets and shakes the hands of up to three hundred people. These are scheduled according to demand, taking place when His Holiness has the time, and sufficient personal requests to make it worthwhile have been handed in at the Branch Office in McLeodganj (above the Welfare Office on Bhagsu Rd).

Private audiences are granted to a select few, and can only be arranged by writing at least four months in advance. The Dalai Lama's secretary receives hundreds of such letters each day, and each case is reviewed on its merits. Spiritual enquiries are referred to a resident *lama* who can give advice on specific points, and secretaries and community leaders are usually able to answer queries about Tibetan issues.

The Residence of the Dalai Lama

The Dalai Lama settled temporarily in McLeodganj in 1960; a third of a century later he's still there, and his **residence** on the south edge of town has become his permanent home in exile. His own quarters are modest, and most of the walled compound overhanging the valley is taken up by government offices. In front of the private enclosure Dharamsala's main Buddhist temple, **Tsuglagkhang**, shelters images of Shakyamuni (the historical Buddha), Padmasambhava (who took Buddhism to Tibet) and Avalokitesvara (the *bodhisattva* of compassion): all sit in meditation postures, surrounded by offerings from devotees – packets of biscuits, fruit, incense and prayer flags. After paying homage to the Buddha inside, devotees tap the wheels behind the temple, setting them turning to scatter their prayers with the wind. Each afternoon monks from the nearby Namgyal monastery hold fierce but disciplined debates in the courtyard opposite the temple, amid shouts, claps and gestures that make up the traditional art of discussion.

Library of Tibetan Works and Archives

Dharamsala's **Library of Tibetan Works and Archives** (April–Sept Mon–Fri 9am–5.30pm; Oct–March Mon–Fri 9am–5pm) has one of the world's most extensive collections of original Tibetan manuscripts of sacred texts and prayers, books on all aspects of Tibet, copious information on Indian culture and architecture, and a rich cache of old photos. Decorated on the exterior with bright Tibetan motifs, it is housed in the Tibetan Central Administration compound, below the southern end of McLeodganj. Its literature is not the only attraction – Tibetan language and philosophy **courses** are held each weekday, and usually run for a month. Classes on *dharma*, or Buddhist thought and precepts, are given by Tibetan monks and translated; they run for an hour before noon most weekdays, and are open to anyone interested.

On the first floor of the library, a small **museum** displays Buddhist statues, finely moulded bronzes, and *mandalas* (symmetrical images, used in meditation to symbolize inner spiritual journeys and the pattern of the universe), among which is the only wooden *mandala* outside Tibet. In front of the library, a small cafe serves hot drinks and cakes. An information centre in the **Tibetan Secretariat** beside the entrance to the compound has recent news about the Tibetan community in Tibet and around the world. Just outside, the small **Astro Medical Institute** is staffed by monks who diagnose symptoms by examining the eyes, pulse and urine, and prescribe pills made of herbs, precious stones and sometimes animal products, some of which are mixed on particularly auspicious lunar dates.

North and east of McLeodganj

A minor road winds northwards from the McLeodganj bus stand to **Dharamkot**, a huddle of squat houses tucked between trees and rocks, passing the mountaineering institute and the **Tushita retreat centre**, which holds meditation courses throughout the year. Dharamkot is the starting point for short walks to the high plateau at **Triund** (2975m), or further over the high passes to the Chamba valley.

The small, murky **Dal Lake**, connected to Dharamkot by a path down through the wooded slopes, is the scene of an animal fair and Shaivite festival in September. It stands behind the **Tibetan Children's Village** (TCV), a huge complex providing education and training in traditional handicrafts for around 2000 students, many of whom are orphans or have been brought to safety by parents who have returned to Tibet.

Bhagsu road heads east from McLeodganj's main square, skirting the hillside for two kilometres before reaching **Bhagsu**, a village on the banks of a mountain stream. A path meanders up boulder-strewn slopes from here, through a slate quarry, to the **waterfall** that feeds the stream, where there's a small *chai* stall. Pilgrims come to bathe in the waters of the tank of Bhagsu's Shiva temple each September. Sadly a couple of incidents on the Bhagsu road recently make it unadvisable for women to walk alone between Bhagsu and McLeodganj at night.

Accommodation

Most visitors stay in **McLeodganj**; it's only worth staying in the **lower town**, where the choice is smaller and the standards lower, if you have an early bus to catch, or arrive

LHAMO – THE FOLK OPERA OF TIBET

Exiled Tibetan communities everywhere, and Dharamsala above all others, remain determined to keep alive their traditional arts and crafts, suppressed at home by the Chinese. The **Tibetan Institute of Performing Arts**, fifteen minutes' walk north of McLeodganj bus stop, especially nurtures **lhamo**, a form of folk opera so popular in nineteenth-century Tibet that each district had its own troupe.

In Dharamsala, open-air performances take place on national holidays throughout the year, and for a full week at the start of each April. Singers dress in exotic costumes, loosely modelled on the clothing of the Lhasa aristocracy, and wear elaborate hats and masks, either flat and made of cloth, or moulded as faces with caricatured expressions. Some are made by children at the Centre for Tibetan Arts and Crafts at the Tibetan Children's Village, who are also trained in *thangka* painting and wood carving. If you come across a performance, don't pass it by – the experience is too good to miss.

Before each performance the stage – a flat piece of ground sheltered by a canopy – is purified. This complex procedure involves seven Ngonpa characters, dressed in black baggy trousers, white shirts with red sashes, and flat black masks, and six dancing fairies, or Ringas. They sing praises to Thangtong Gyalpo, the patron saint of *lhamo*, a statue of whom is always placed in the centre of the stage, often accompanied by a juniper branch and a bowl of *tsampa* (a staple food made from barley flour). The narrator, Shung Shangen, then enters the stage, which holds no other props, and offers a résumé of the opera in classical Tibetan (now understood by very few), culminating with a high shout.

The performers themselves enter to the sound of drums and cymbals. The main characters appear first: the **hero** (a prince or king), dressed in dragon-patterned brocade and a wide-brimmed hat; the **heroine**, draped in golden silk and wearing a hat of flowers; the **villain**, often a witch, dressed in black and hiding behind a black-and-white mask, followed by a retinue of ghoulish **demons** whose masks show wide staring eyes, blood-red lips and sharp fangs. Each character has a special dance, and sings in a drawn-out, droning manner known as *namthar* – throaty, high and resonant and so strong that the voice carries beautifully, riding clearly over the accompanying drums and cymbals. The plots revolve around tales from early Buddhist texts, re-enactments of the Buddha's life and the deeds of great Tibetan saints, or stories from the courts of the emperor Songsten Gampo, under whom Buddhism was established in Tibet. Even if you don't know what's going on, you'll catch the drift of it from the bursts of laughter and expectant faces in the audience.

Lhamo instructors from the institute carry the art to other Tibetan settlements in India and Nepal, and also teach non-Tibetan students. Other classes in traditional art forms, plus lectures and study courses, are held in the **Norbulingka Institute** in the valley below Dharamsala; enquire at the Department of Culture and Religion (☎22685).

late. Hotels fill up between October and March, and especially at Tibetan New Year (Feb/March). Tourists planning long stays often head to **Bhagsu** or **Dharamkot**, where farmers let simple huts for a minimal sum; if you do stay out here, expect to cook your own meals, and to queue with the locals for a supply of kerosene at the beginning of each month (wood collecting is restricted). A handful of rooms in the Tibetan Library are available to students on courses, and for fervent Buddhists, there's always the possibility of staying at a monastery or nunnery.

McLeodganj

Green, Bhagsu Rd. Well-kept and comfortable, with good views over the valley, and a good choice of single rooms (Rs80). ④.

Him Queen, south end (☎24961). A selection of ordinary, deluxe and VIP rooms, all with balcony and TV, carpets and an air of freshness. ⑦–⑧.

HPTDC Bhagsu, at southern extremity (☎23191). Smart, well-run hotel, with comfortable carpeted rooms. Small gardens. ⑥–⑧.

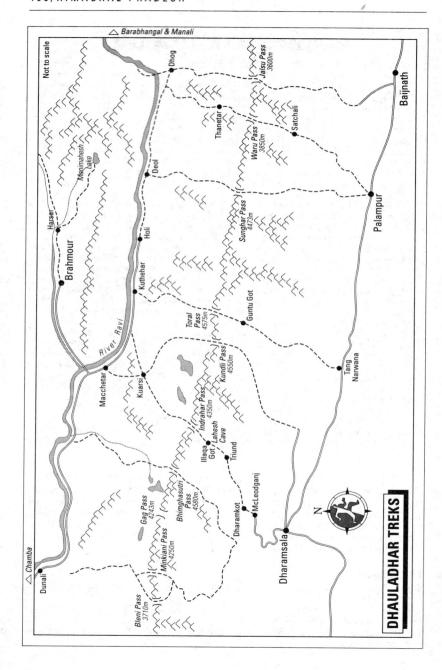

DHAULADHAR TREKS

TREKKING FROM DHARAMSALA

Dharamsala is one of the most popular starting points for **treks** over the rocky ridges of the Dhauladhar range, which rise steeply from the Kangra valley, surmounted by passes as high as 4600m. Most of the routes are used by **Gaddi shepherds**, who cross from north to south in the winter, cradling bundles of lambs and kids in their jackets, and return to the northern pastures in summer. Trails pass through forests of *deodar*, pine, oak and rhododendron, cross streams and rivers, and wind along vertiginous cliff tracks, passing the occasional lake, waterfall and glacier.

Villages en route, most of them temporary Gaddi settlements, are largely agricultural, growing rice, maize, potatoes and even apples; the gently slanting rooftops of the houses are often ablaze with the bright reds and yellows of chillies and maize laid out to dry in the midday sun.

Only attempt treks with the help of guides, cooks and porters. The **Mountaineering Institute**, on Dharamkot Rd, supplies guides, and rents equipment at very reasonable prices; you can pay per day, and buy food yourself in the bazaar before you set off. **Yeti Trekking** (☎2887), also on Dharamkot Rd, offers fixed-price treks (roughly US$20 per day) and has plenty of equipment. Meet your guide before you settle anything. Despite the availability of rough huts and caves, it's best to take a tent. For general advice on trekking, see p.48.

The best **season** to trek is from mid-August to late October. Trekking during the monsoon itself (June–Aug) is more difficult, as paths are frequently washed away and wet equipment gets very heavy, but at this time the fields and forests are at their freshest, and alpine meadows burst with colour. Winter climbing should only be attempted by experienced trekkers, comfortable using crampons and ice picks.

Dharamsala to Chamba over Indrahar Pass (4350m)

The most frequented route from Dharamsala to the Chamba valley, over the **Indrahar Pass** (4350m), is arduous in places, but most novice trekkers manage it in around five days. The first section, from Dharamkot, winds through thick forest and steep rocky terrain for 9km to a grassy plateau at **Triund**. To stay in the forest rest house, book at Dharamsala's forest office.

From Triund, the path climbs less steeply to **Illaqa Got**, a grassy rise at the treeline, fed by glacial waters flowing from the ridge above. Staying a little higher, in the low-roofed but well-sheltered **Lahesh Cave**, saves time and effort before the ascent to the pass early the next day. This is a trying scramble over scattered boulders on ill-defined paths, but the view, south over the Kangra valley and north to the snowy Pir Panjal peaks, is breathtaking. From the pass the descent along the Ravi valley, through alpine meadows and pine woods, is difficult only where paths across sheer rock faces are all but worn away. After re-entering the forests and passing waterfalls, you reach the Gaddi village of **Kuarsi**, from where a 6hr walk along the steep river gorge drops to dusty **Macchetar**, connected to Brahmour and Chamba by road.

Other routes from Dharamsala to Chamba

Several **other routes** cross the Dhauladhar range. To head over **Toral Pass** (4575m), start from **Tang Narwana** (1150m), 10km from Dharamsala. A long ascent leads through scrub, pine and oak woods to **Guntu Got** (3385m), from where the demanding climb to the pass is more difficult during May and June when snow still covers the slopes, and during the monsoon when there's a risk of flash floods. The two-day descent from the pass traverses treacherous boulder fields before meeting a forest and reaching the verdant Gaddi pastures at Kuthehar, 6km from the nearest road, to Chamba and Brahmour.

The most difficult route north is the five- or six-day trek across **Bhimghasutri Pass** (4580m), covering near-vertical rocky ascents, sharp cliffs and dangerous gorges. A much easier four- or five-day trek from Dharamsala crosses **Bleni Pass** (3710m) in the milder ranges to the northwest, weaving through alpine pastures and woods and crossing a few streams, before terminating at **Dunali**, on the Chamba road.

Kalsang Guest House, Quonium Rd (☎22609). Simple rooms and common bathrooms. Large roof with good views. ③–④.

Kareri Lodge, south end (☎24330). New hotel with four spotless rooms, two with superb balcony views. ⑦.

International, Jogibara Rd. Officially the *Kalsang Tsomo International Guest House*. Welcoming and cosy, with carpeted rooms and constant hot water. Good value. ②–③.

Lhasa Guest House, Bhagsu Rd. A large collection of simple rooms set off a warren of corridors, but invaded by noise from the bus stop. Very grotty singles. ③–④.

Loseling Guest House, Jogibara Rd. Standard lodge, well-maintained and unelaborate. Good views from an open roof terrace. Sightly overpriced. ③–④.

Om, near bus stand (☎24313). Simple, quiet and very friendly lodge on the western edge of town, with a few homely rooms on the upper terrace and a cosy restaurant. ①.

Paljor Gakyil Guest House, Quonium Rd (☎22571). Immaculate lodge with plain or carpeted rooms, dorm beds and great views. ①–④.

Surya Resorts, south end (☎22768). Big modern hotel, with some large glass-fronted rooms facing west. Carpets, low-level double beds and plush bathrooms. ⑧–⑨.

Tibet, Bhagsu Rd (☎22587). Excellent hotel overlooking the valley, with a superb restaurant. ⑤–⑥.

Tibetan Ashoka, Jogibara Rd. Friendly and congenial. Rooms vary from simple without bath to deluxe with bathroom and hot shower. Superb views from roof patio. ①–④.

The lower town

Basera Lodge, Kotwali Bazaar (☎22234). The best of the cheap lodges in the bazaar, with clean rooms, each with bathroom and TV. ②.

HPTDC Dhauladhar, near bus stand (☎22889). Spacious rooms with private baths (constant hot water) and balconies giving superb views over the plains to the south. Cheap beds in a small dorm. Delicious mid-priced food in the restaurant and a bar with garden terrace. ④–⑤.

Rising Moon, Kotwali Bazaar (☎22635). The cheapest in the lower town, with spartan rooms and shared bathrooms. Its small restaurant serves good low-priced Indian and Chinese food. ①.

Sood, Kotwali Bazaar (☎22456). Four adequate rooms overlooking bazaar area, each with a bathroom and hot water. ②.

Dharamkot

Hotel Blue Heaven, off the main path below the tea shop. Cosy family house, with excellent views, but a bit tricky to get to after dark. ①.

Nirma Guest House, in the heart of the village, just off the road. Spacious house has rooms with attached bathrooms. Relaxing lawns. Great value. ①.

Eating

McLeodganj is one of those places where sitting and chatting in **restaurants** is a favourite activity; many have sound systems, and the food is varied. Not surprisingly, Tibetan dishes are prominent, along with Chinese options such as egg noodles, drop soup, *chow chow*, *momo* and stir fry. Look out for the bakery opposite *Namtso Guest House* on Temple Rd, which sells fresh-baked Tibetan bread and cakes every morning, and the new *Take Out* bakery on Bhagsu Rd that specializes in croissants and "French" bread. If you're yearning for Western food you'll find fries, toast, veggie-burgers or even vegetable *au gratin* and roast chicken, while several restaurants specialize in Israeli dishes. In **lower Dharamsala** there's no shortage of snack stalls, but less choice of cuisine; your best bet for Indian and Western dishes is *Hotel Dhauladhar*, or *Lazeez Restaurant*, in Kotwali Bazaar, for spicy kebabs and curried vegetables. All the restaurants listed below are in **McLeodganj**.

Aroma, Jogibara Rd. Spicy Indian dishes, plus Israeli specialities at unbeatable prices. Great *hummus*, fresh salads, thick pitta breads and tasty schnitzel (breaded chicken pieces).

Ashoka, Jogibara Rd. Friendly place; the town's best Indian food and beers, pricier than average.

Chocolate Log, Jogibara Rd. Delicious cakes, pies and truffles plus savouries such as spinach pizza. Eat inside or laze on deckchairs on an open roof terrace. Reasonably priced. Closes 6pm.

Friends' Corner, Temple Rd. Popular, comfortable place by the bus stop, with a tasty range of food and beers, but small portions. Excellent *chow chow*. Dimly lit and with a good sound system.

Gakyi, Jogibara Rd. Humble and homely, with great Tibetan and Western veg dishes, and the town's best fruit muesli and Tibetan bread.

Himalayan Cafe, Bhagsu Rd. Standard menu, but excellent south-facing terrace.

Hotel Tibet, Bhagsu Rd. Without doubt Dharamsala's best venue for Tibetan and Chinese food, veg and non-veg. High prices, but worth every *paise*.

McLlo, Central Square. Comfortable first-floor seating overlooking the bus stop. Unmatched selection of Western dishes; hearty portions, fairly high prices, good service, and lots of beer.

Om, *Om Hotel*. Friendly, comfortable restaurant jutting out over the hillside with the town's only west-facing roof terrace. Generous portions of good Tibetan and Chinese veg food and a few Western-style snacks. Great value.

Rasoi, Temple Rd. A small unpretentious place with a wide balcony facing the plains. Specialities include filling *thalis* (standard or special) and pizzas.

Shambala, Jogibara Rd. Cramped seating but good veg food, with fresh cakes and filled pancakes.

Listings

Medical help Lower Dharamsala has the Zonal Hospital (☎22333), but most sick travellers head for the *Tibetan Medical and Astrological Institute*, 10min from the library. A former physician of the Dalai Lama, Dr Yeshi Dhondhen, has a clinic off Jogibara Rd in the main bazaar.

Meditation Besides staying in a monastery, it's possible to take week- or month-long meditation courses following the tenets of Tibetan Buddhism, at the *Tushita Retreat Centre*, a collection of simple wooden huts in a leafy enclosure near Dharamkot, north of McLeodganj (Rs2500 for 2 weeks). The *Vipassana Centre*, also in Dharamkot, follows teachings more akin to Theravada Buddhism, and insists on silence during one- and two-week courses (voluntary donations). Check noticeboards in restaurants for dates, and details of yoga courses.

Publications Tibet-focused magazines published in Dharamsala include *The Tibet Journal*, the glossy *Cho-Yang*, and the *Tibetan Bulletin*, published in Hindi, French and English.

Shopping Stalls and little shops along the main streets offer Tibetan trinkets, inexpensive warm clothing, incense, prayer bells, rugs and books. The large handicrafts shop on Jogibara Rd sells *thangkas* of all sizes, and prayer flags. *Nowrojee* store by the bus stand, unchanged since the nineteenth century, doles out sweets from ancient thick glass jars, along with its own bottled pop. The *Green Shop*, Bhagsu Rd, sells recycled painted cards, hand-painted T-shirts, books on environment and filtered boiled water for Rs5.

Taxis. McLeodganj and Dharamsala have unions with fixed prices clearly displayed. A taxi from McLeodganj to Dharamsala is Rs70, and from Dharamsala to Gagal airport Rs100.

Train bookings Train journeys from Pathankot can be booked through travel agents, or by turning up at the office in the bus stand (10–11am), which has a meagre quota of two tickets per train.

Travel agents The helpful *Himachal Travels*, a tiny office on TCV Rd (☎22723), books local and private buses, trains from Pathankot, and domestic flights, and confirms or alters international flights. You can also rent taxis for journeys within HP or beyond, and enquire about treks.

Dalhousie and around

The quiet, relaxed hill station of **Dalhousie** spreads over five low-level hills at the western edge of the Dhauladhar range. While the town itself, interspersed with Raj-era buildings, low-roofed stalls and hotels, is unremarkable, the pine-covered slopes around it are intersected with paths and tracks ideal for short undemanding walks.

From Dalhousie the road east zigzags in and out of deep copses, skimming the hillsides. After 30km it arrives at sleepy **Chamba**, perched above the rushing River Ravi.

Though seldom visited, it's a good place to recuperate after a trek, with some fascinating temples, and a small art museum. **Brahmour**, three hours further east by bus and the final settlement on the road into the mountains, holds more Hindu temples. Both towns make good bases for **treks** into the remote **Pangi Valley**.

Dalhousie

DALHOUSIE owes its name to Lord Dalhousie, Governor General of Punjab (1849–56), attracted by the cool climate to establish a sanitorium here for the many British, who, like himself, suffered ill health. Early in the twentieth century, it made a popular alternative to crowded, expensive Shimla, but thereafter it declined. A small population of Tibetans has grown up since the Chinese invaded Tibet in 1959; some have moved to Dharamsala, but many have stayed, selling sweaters, watches, bags and ornaments. Today Dalhousie is a favourite summer retreat for holidaying Punjabis, but receives only a handful of Western tourists, few staying longer than a day or two.

The town is spread over a ripple of hills interlaced with winding roads connecting the focal points, the *chowks*. The most central, Gandhi Chowk, with a cluster of restaurants, and the post office, sees the most activity. From here The Mall and Garam Sarak dip and curve to Subhash Chowk, a popular place to eat at the top end of the largely Muslim Sadar Bazaar. North of here, the bus stand and information office mark the main road out of town. You don't have to follow the main roads though, as forest tracks snake around the hillsides; the track connecting Gandhi and Subhash *chowks* dips beneath overhanging pines, and passes rocks painted in bold bright colours with images of the Tibetan Buddhist goddess Tara, and short Tibetan prayers.

Walks in and around Dalhousie include a short stroll south of Gandhi Chowk to **Panch Pulla,** where five bridges span a rushing stream and a drab memorial commemorates the freedom fighter Ajit Singh, a firm supporter of the left-wing Congressman Subash Chandra Bose who raised the Indian National Army to fight alongside the Japanese during World War II. The road north out of Gandhi Chowk meanders up the hill to **Bakrota**, where a small community of weavers make traditional Tibetan carpets.

Practicalities

Dalhousie is usually approached by **bus** from Pathankot in the Punjab, 80km southwest (see p.539), or Chamba, 30km north; the tortuous journeys through the Himalayan foothills from Dharamsala (7hr 30min) and Shimla (18hr) are not recommended. The steep path that climbs the hill from the bus stand towards the Mall is the shortest route to the centre; if you're not up to the hike you should have little trouble getting a lift in one of the local *Maruti* taxis.

Numerous **hotels** cater for Dalhousie's summer visitors; in winter, when most lie empty, many offer substantial **discounts**, so beautiful suites cost little more than simple lodges in larger cities. *Aroma & Claire's*, on Court Rd, a 1930s house sprawling over the hillside south of Subhash Chowk, is the most atmospheric hotel in town, with a library and leafy patios (☎018982/2199; ⑦–⑧). Others include the Raj-esque 1920s *Grand View,* up the hill from the bus stand, whose huge rooms have north-facing balconies (☎018982/2123; ⑦), and the plush modern *Chaanakya* on the Mall (☎018982/2670; ⑧). Of the budget hotels *Moonlight*, on Panch Pulla Rd off Gandhi Chowk, is the most homely (☎018982/2439; ②–⑤), while the *Youth Hostel* five minutes' walk west of the bus stand has extremely cheap, very basic dorms.

Outside hotel restaurants the best **places to eat** are *Milan* on The Mall near Gandhi Chowk, which serves imaginative dishes, and has great views from the upstairs tables; *Preet Palace* on Subhash Chowk, which has a range of south Indian dishes, and any of the *dhabas* between Subhash Chowk and Sadar Bazaar. On the whole, meat in

Dalhousie is of poor quality, though the *Punjabi* just off Gandhi Chowk manages to produce some hearty meaty dishes.

Khajjiar and Kalatope wildlife sanctuary

It's possible to trek 30km from Dalhousie to Chamba along the eastbound road from Gandhi Chowk. En route, in the flat Khajjiar valley, **Khajjiar** itself consists of a few single-storey houses overlooking a vast green, with a modest and grimy lake at its centre. HPTDC *Hotel Devdar* (☎018992/233; ⑤), sheltered by pines and spruce on the edge of the green, has a six-bed dorm (Rs50), comfortable doubles with big windows, and good food. The ridge above the valley holds the **Kalatope wildlife sanctuary**, whose ibex, deer, bears and leopards rarely come out of hiding. The last 20km from Khajjiar to Chamba, across thickly wooded hillsides, can be walked in a day.

Chamba

Shielded on all sides by high mountains, and protected by forces in Kangra to the south, **Chamba** was ruled for over a millennium by kings descended from Raja Singh Varma, who founded it in 920 AD. Unlike Himachal states further south it was never formally under Moghul rule, and its distinct Hindu culture remained intact until the first roads were built to Dalhousie in 1870. When the state of Himachal Pradesh was formed in 1948, **CHAMBA** became the capital, and only large town, of Chamba district. Today, only a handful of visitors make it out here, passing through before or after trekking, or stopping off to see the unique temples.

In summer, **Gujjars**, nomadic Muslim dairymen, wheel great urns of milk through the streets, and migratory Gaddi shepherds gather in Chamba before moving south to Kangra. The *chowgan*, a large green used for sports, evening strolls and festive celebrations, marks the centre of town, overlooked by the **Rang Mahal** palace, now a college.

CHAMBA FESTIVALS

Chamba's annual **Suhi Mata Festival**, which lasts for four days in early April, commemorates Rani Champavati, the wife of the tenth-century Raja Sahil Verman, who gave her name to the town. A curious legend relates that when water from a nearby stream failed to flow through a channel supposed to divert it to the town, local *brahmins* advised Raja Verman that either his son or his wife would have to sacrifice themselves. The queen obliged; she was buried alive at the head of the channel, and the water flowed freely. Only women and children participate in the festival, dancing on the *chowgan* before processing with an image of Champavati and banners of the Rajput solar emblem to the Suhi Mata temple in the hills behind town.

Minjar, a week of singing and dancing at the start of August to celebrate the growth of maize, is also peculiar to Chamba. Its climax comes on the last day, when a rowdy procession of locals, Gaddis and Gujjars, dressed in traditional costumes, leaves the palace and snakes down to the riverbank, where bunches of maize are thrown into the water.

Lakshmi Narayan temples

The intimate complex of **Lakshmi Narayan temples**, behind Dogra Bazaar west of the *chowgan*, is of a style found only in Chamba and Brahmour. Three of its six earth-brown temples are dedicated to Vishnu and three to Shiva, all with profusely carved outer walls and curious curved *shikharas* (spires), topped with overhanging wooden canopies and gold pinnacles added in 1678 in defiance of Aurangzeb's order to destroy all Hindu temples in the hill states. Niches in the walls contain images of deities, but many stand empty, some statues lost in the earthquake of 1905 and others looted more

TREKS IN THE PANGI VALLEY TO LAHAUL

Few trekkers make it to the spectacular, all-but-inaccessible **Pangi valley**, sandwiched between the soaring Greater Himalayan Range in the north and the Outer Himalayan Range in the south. With its deep river gorges and barren mountain peaks, it offers a wide range of scenery and vegetation: cultivated fields give way to forests of pine, *deodar*, spruce and silver oak, and beyond that hardy shrubs. Inhabited by nomadic Gaddi shepherds, the valley maintains a unique village culture. Several peaks within it have never been climbed, and onward paths lead to Kashmir, Lahaul and Zanskar.

The valley itself starts 140km northeast of **Chamba**. The last villages accessible by road are **Trella**, 90km north of Chamba below **Sach Pass** (4390m; May–Nov), and **Brahmour**, 80km east of Chamba, en route to the high passes of the **Pir Panjal**. Equipment, porters and guides can be obtained at Chamba and Brahmour.

From Chamba to Udaipur (Lahaul) over Sach Pass (4390m)

Trekkers already acclimatized can complete this moderately difficult trek in nine or ten days. After the 5hr-bus ride to Trella, on a poor road that twists tightly up precipitous escarpments, the walk begins with a steep climb to the treeline at **Satrundhi** (3500m). This is the last stop before a tricky 3–4hr ascent to the high pass, across boulder fields that are covered with snow in May and June, and have no well-defined tracks. Flower meadows at **Dunai** below the pass make a perfect camping spot before you cross the fresh fast waters of the River Chenab, and gradually descend from the grasslands into forests for 14km east to **Killar**. The next section of the trek is a tiring walk of 12km up and down the steep sides of the Chandra Bhaga gorge, to **Sach Khas**, a campground with a small forest rest house where you can relax before heading east to Purthi (15km) through deep and humid jungle. The last stage follows an unnerving path that clings to almost vertical rock faces; a precarious ropeway spans the Chandra Bhaga before **Raoli**. You can take a bus from here to Tindi, but the final hike is an undemanding and enjoyable amble along the river valley. Motorable roads link Tindi with Udaipur (25km), from where buses head over Rohtang Pass to Keylong and Manali.

Treks from Brahmour

Trekking routes lead north from Brahmour (2130m) across passes covered with snow for most of the year. The challenging trek over **Kalichho Pass** (4990m), aptly named "the abode of Kali" (the goddess of death), starts with a gradual ascent of 24km to **Badagram** (2325m). On the next stage you climb 900m through a lush stream-filled *deodar* forest to **Dhikla** (3300m). The next day's walk of 11km crosses steep ridges interspersed with rich forest along the Bana Diva gorge to a campground at **Bhansar Got**. From here a steep hike climbs to an inhospitable campground at **Alyas**, separated from Kalichho Pass by ice fields. The ascent to the pass is tiring and time-consuming – you have to cut steps as you go – but once over the summit it's not far to a suitable spot to pitch a tent. The last leg of the trek crosses stony ground and descends along the Kalichho valley to verdant pastures, with views over the Pattan valley, cut by the River Chandra Bhaga, and ahead to a panorama of high snow-capped mountains. The village at the end of the trail is **Triloknath**, whose ancient temple to three-faced Shiva is sacred to both Hindus and Buddhists. Buses run from here to Udaipur, and on to Keylong and Manali.

Another demanding route crosses the **Kugti Pass**, "that which makes one miserable to reach", at an awesome 5040m. From **Harsar**, an hour by bus from Brahmour, the path follows the River Budhil for 12km to **Kugti**, known for fine yak milk and curds. Rolling alpine meadows and terraced fields overshadowed by Kailash peak line the second day's route, culminating at **Kuddi Got**, a vast flower-filled meadow (4000m). The next stage, over the pass, requires crampons and ice axe for an incredibly taxing 6hr-climb. Having enjoyed the views of the towering peaks of Lahaul and Zanskar from the summit, you plummet once again to the head of a glacier at **Khardu**. For the next 12km the track traverses loose scree, fording a couple of streams, before reaching the orchards and terraces of **Raape**, 7km from Shansha, which is linked to Udaipur and Keylong by road.

recently. The ensemble is roamed by friendly cats, and murmurs with the prayers of devotees and the laughter of children playing in the cool waters of the tank.

Entering the compound, you're confronted by the largest and oldest temple, built in the tenth century. It enshrines an idol of Lakshmi Narayan (Vishnu), sculpted in Rajasthani marble. The buxom maidens flanking the entrance to the sanctuary, each holding a water vessel, represent the goddesses Ganga and Yamuna, while inside a frieze depicts scenes from the *Mahabharata* and *Ramayana*. One shows Vishnu with a lotus stem emerging from his navel that blooms with six flowers, each supporting a separate god. Temples dedicated to Shiva, watched over by a ferocious statue of half-man half-bird Garuda, the destroyer of obstacles who also serves as Vishnu's mount, fill the third courtyard. Among the images on the outer walls, Shiva's consort is depicted in her various forms as Parvati, Durga, Gauri and Uma. In the inner sanctuary, once your eyes are accustomed to the dim light, you'll see sturdy brass images of Shiva, Parvati and Nandi, inlaid with silver and copper brought from mines nearby.

Other temples

Of Chamba's other temples, the most intriguing is the tenth-century **Chamunda Devi temple** high above the town in the north, a steep half-hour climb up steps that begin near the bus stand. Decorated with hundreds of heavy brass bells and protecting a fearsome image of the blood-thirsty goddess Chamunda, the temple is built entirely of wood, and commands an excellent view up the Ravi gorge and to the hills in the north. Panels cut into the wooden ceiling depict such scenes as Krishna stealing butter, four-armed Shiva wearing a tiger's skin, and comely maidens surrounded by birds.

Back in town, south of the *chowgan* near the post office, the small, lavishly carved **Hariraya temple** contains a smooth brass image of Vaikuntha, the triple-headed aspect of Vishnu. Though often obscured by cloth and vermilion, it is a fine example of the excellent bronze work that has become Chamba's hallmark.

Bhuri Singh Museum

Although small and poorly maintained, the **Bhuri Singh museum** (daily except Mon 10am–5pm; free), opposite Sham Singh hospital at the south end of the *chowgan*, holds a reasonable display of local arts and crafts. Its eighteenth- and nineteenth-century **Kangra miniature paintings**, depicting court life and amorous meetings, and men and women smoking elaborate *hookahs*, are much bolder than their Moghul-influenced Rajasthani equivalents. Temple statues and sculptures, pillars and lintels are displayed alongside silver jewellery, heavy bronzes from Chamba, early coins, and murals taken from the palace. Inscribed copper plates record land and property grants and temple donations from the tenth to the eighteenth centuries.

The museum's best feature is its small cache of **rumals**. Made by women since the tenth century, used in ceremonial exchanges to cover gifts, *rumals* are like embroidered paintings, depicting scenes from popular myth rather than the geometric and floral patterns more common elsewhere in India. Today only a few women continue this tradition, but a weaving centre in the old palace is attempting to revitalize the art.

Practicalities

Buses arrive at the cramped bus stand in the north of town, overlooked by *Thakur* and *Natraj* lodges (avoid at all costs, unless you enjoy sleeping with bugs), and the much better, though slightly shabby *Hotel Chamunda* (π6267; ③–⑤). Chamba's best **hotel** is the HPTDC *Hotel Iravati* (π2671; ⑤–⑥) on the northwest edge of the *chowgan*, where the spotless, carpeted rooms have private bathrooms with hot water. Budget options include the less salubrious but passable *Rishi* (π4343; ②–③) opposite the Lakshmi Narayan temples. The best and most filling **meals** can be found at the *Iravati* or *Rishi*; both serve local specialities such as *madhra*, a rich, oily, and slightly bitter mix of beans, curd and *ghee*, or *gucchi*, mushrooms served with fried rice. The string of *dhabas* south of the *chowgan* dish up cheaper north Indian and local food in less hygienic surroundings, as well as juicy kebabs and freshly puffed *puris*.

Brahmour

BRAHMOUR is a one-horse town of shiny slate-roofed houses, apple trees and small maize fields, shadowed on all sides by high snowy peaks. The **temples**, whose curved *shikharas* dominate the large neatly paved central square, are more dramatic and better preserved than their rivals at Chamba. The sanctuaries are unlocked only for *puja* in the mornings and evenings, permitting a glimpse of bold bronze images of Ganesh, Shiva and Parvati, unchanged since their installation in the seventh and eighth centuries when Brahmour was capital of the surrounding mountainous region.

The efficient **Mountaineering Institute** has details of local **treks**, reliable guides and porters, and equipment for rent. The most popular route begins at **Harsar**, a bumpy one-hour bus journey from Brahmour, and leads to **Manimahesh Lake**, high in the mountains one or two days' walk away. This tarn is held sacred by Shaivites who worship at its waters and follow the ritual circumambulatory path. Hundreds of pilgrims flock to its shores for the *mela* each August. Dharamsala lies five or six days' walk south, a fairly easy route that crosses the Dhauladhars at Indrahar pass (see p.461).

Rooms can be found at the *Mountaineering Institute* (①), north of town, and the congenial *Hotel Amit* (③) at the bottom of the only road, which runs from the square to the bus stand, where food stalls dish up hearty meals all day, but close soon after dark.

THE KULLU VALLEY

The majestic **KULLU VALLEY** is cradled by the Pir Panjal to the north, the Parvati Range to the east, and the Barabhangal Range to the west. This is Himachal at its most idyllic; roaring rivers, pretty mountain villages, orchards and terraced fields rising in fastidious steps to deep green pine forests and high snow-flecked ridges.

Known in the ancient Hindu scriptures as **Kulanthapitha**, or "End of the Habitable World", the Kullu Valley extends 80km north from the mouth of the perilously steep and narrow **Largi Gorge**, near Mandi, to the foot of the **Rohtang Pass** – gateway to the arid mountain wastes of Lahaul and Ladakh. For centuries, it formed one of the major **trade** corridors between Central Asia and the Gangetic plains. Local rulers, based first at **Jagatsukh** and later at **Nagar** and Sultanpur (now **Kullu**), were able to rake off handsome profits from the through-traffic, extending their kingdom as far south as Mandi, east to the Sutlej, and north into Lahaul and Spiti. This trade monopoly, however, also made it a prime target for invasion, and in the eighteenth and early nineteenth centuries, the Kullu rajas were forced to repulse attacks by both the Raja of Kangra, and by the Sikhs, and finally saw their lands annexed by the British in 1847.

Over the following years, colonial families crossed the Jalori Pass from Shimla, making the most of the valley's alpine climate to grow the **apples** that, along with **cannabis** cultivation, today form the mainstay of the rural economy. The first road, built to export the fruit, wriggled up to Kullu in 1927. Improved communications brought greater prosperity, but spelled the end of the peace and isolation, prompting many settlers to pack up and leave long before Independence. The population expanded again in the 1950s and 1960s, however, swollen by **Tibetan refugees**.

In spite of the changes wrought by roads, immigration and, more recently, mass tourism, the Kullu Valley's way of life is maintained in countless timber and stone villages. Known as **paharis** ("hill people"), the locals – high-caste landowning Thakhurs,

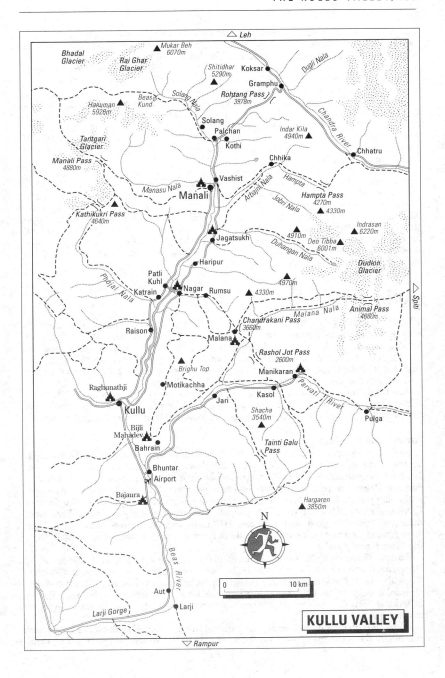

KULLU VALLEY

and their (low-caste) share-cropping tenant farmers – still sport the distinctive Kullu cap, or *topi*. The women, meanwhile, wear colourful headscarves, and *puttoos* fastened with silver pins and chains. Venture into the lush meadows above the treeline, and you'll cross paths with nomadic **Gaddi** shepherds who follow their flocks between pastures, invariably with an orphaned lamb muffled inside their long woollen coats.

Few of the tourists that pour in during the summer, however, bump into a bona-fide nomad. After a gruelling bus journey from Delhi or Leh, most make a beeline for a bed in **Manali**, where the closest you'll get to a Gaddi is a picture on a post-card. With its burgeoning hotels, restaurants, and travel agents, the area's chief resort, entrepot and trekking hub is a convenient base from which to explore India's most accessible and – since the outbreak of unrest in Kashmir – most frequented high-Himalayan valley.

Although **Kullu** itself is largely uninteresting, the recent introduction of **flights** from Delhi, Shimla and Gaggal to Bhuntur, south of Kullu, offers a welcome alternative to long overnight bus journeys. North of town, **Nagar**'s castle and ancient temples make a pleasant change from the claustrophobic concrete of modern Manali, as do **Manikaran**'s sacred hot springs, up the spectacular **Parvati Valley**. **Trekking** opportunities range from day hikes up the Beas River's side valleys, or **nalas**, to challenging long hauls over high-altitude passes and glaciers. Away from the roads, you step into a medieval time warp little altered since the days when the Kullu Valley was one of the most remote places on earth.

Kullu

KULLU, the valley's capital since the mid-seventeenth century, became district head-quarters after Independence. Despite being the region's main market and transport hub, however, it is deservedly eclipsed as a tourist centre by Manali, 40km north. A dishevelled, lacklustre collection of shops and concrete houses stacked around the right bank of the Beas, Kullu is noisy, polluted, and grim: a world away from the tranquil villages that peer down from the surrounding hillsides.

Most travellers stay just long enough to pick up transport for somewhere else. If you find yourself with time to kill, the old pilgrims' paths that lead to any of the unspectacular **temples** around the town provide an escape, and take in some fine valley views.

Arrival and information

Long-distance **buses** heading up and down the valley pull in at the **main bus stand**, on the north side of the Sarvari Nala, which flows through the town from the west. Local services heading north also drop and pick up passengers opposite the congested **Akhara Bazaar depot**, in the north end of town, and at the top of **Dhalpur maidan**, at the south end. This is closer to most of the hotels and restaurants, and the District Commissioner's office (Mon–Fri 10am–5pm) – the place to apply for **Inner Line permits** for travel to Spiti and Kinnaur. HPTDC's **tourist office** (daily 9am–6pm; Nov–June closed Sun) is on the west side of Dhalpur *maidan*, two minutes' walk from the *State Bank of India*.

Anyone **flying** to Kullu from Delhi, Shimla or Gaggal (Dharamsala) will arrive at **Bhuntur**, thirty minutes' south of Kullu by bus (every 10min) or taxi (around Rs100). Taxis should be booked in the union office on the main road close to the tourist office. Onward reservations with *Jagson Airlines* can be made through their office in the *Bijleshwar View Hotel* (Mon–Sat 9.30am–5pm; ☎01902/4830), while *Archana's* office is in the airport.

If you're travelling on to **Nagar**, catch one of the frequent Manali-bound buses that run north along the main road, on the west side of the valley, and jump off at **Patli**

DUSSEHRA IN THE VALLEY OF THE GODS

In the Kullu region, often dubbed "**the Valley of the Gods**", the village deity reigns supreme. No one knows how many *devtas* and *devis* inhabit the hills south of the Rohtang Pass, but nearly every hamlet has one, each with its own history, foibles and temple. Legend has it that they originally descended from the Chandrakani Pass. Jamlu, the maverick god of Malana (see p.485), lifted the lid of the chest in which they were all trapped, and a gust of wind scattered the small circular icons around the villages.

The part each one plays in village life depends on his or her particular **powers**; some heal, others protect the "parish" borders from evil spirits, summon the rains, or ensure the success of the harvest. Nearly all, however, communicate with their devotees by means of **oracles**. Drawn from the lower castes, the village shaman, or **gaur**, is subject to prohibitions that forbid him, among other things, to cut his hair, wear leather, or spread manure on his fields. When called upon to perform, he strips to the waist and, accompanied by the trumpets and drums of the temple band, enters a trance in which the *devta* uses his voice to speak to the congregation. The deity, carried out of the temple on a ceremonial palanquin, or *rath*, rocks back and forth on the shoulders of its bearers as the *gaur* speaks. His words are always heeded, and his decisions final; the *devta*-oracle decides the propitious dates for marriages, and for sowing crops, and arbitrates disputes.

The single most important outing for any village deity is **Dussehra**, which takes place in the town of **Kullu**, every October after the monsoons. Although the week-long festival ostensibly celebrates Rama's victory over the demon-king of Lanka, Ravana (in the local dialect, *dushet hera* means "the demon killed"), it is also an opportunity for the *devtas* to reaffirm their position in the grand pecking order that prevails among them – a rigid hierarchy in which the Kullu Raja's own tutelary deity Rama, alias **Raghunathji**, is king.

The Kullu Dussehra is thought to date from the seventeenth century, when the valley's Hindu rulers set out to weaken the hold of indigenous "nature cults": the worship of animist spirits residing in mountain peaks, rocks, trees, streams, and caves. Judging by the turn-out for the festival, the Raja's ruse worked a treat. On the tenth day of the new, or "white" moon in October, between 150 and 200 *devtas* make their way to Kullu to pay homage to the Raghunathji. As befits a region that holds its elderly women in high esteem, the procession proper cannot begin until **Hadimba**, the grandmother of the royal family's chief god, arrives from the Dunghri temple in Manali. Like her underlings, she is borne on an elaborately carved wooden *rath* swathed in glittering silk and garlands, and surmounted by a richly embroidered parasol, or *chhatri*. Facing each of the four directions, eight or twelve gold and silver **masks** are strapped to the side of the deities, preceded by raucous trumpets, standard bearers, priests, and bare-chested *gaurs*.

Raghunathji leads the great **procession** in his six-wheeled *rath*. Hauled from the Rupi palace on long ropes by a team of 200 honoured devotees, the palanquin lurches to a halt in the middle of Kullu's dusty *maidan*, to be circumambulated by the Raja, his family, and retinue of priests. Thereafter, the festival's more secular aspect comes to the fore. **Folk dancers**, decked out in traditional Himachali dress, perform for the vast crowds; the *maidan* by this time has acquired all the trappings of an Indian fun fair, with market stalls, sweet-sellers, itinerant snake charmers, astrologers, *sadhus* and tawdry circus acts, all serenaded by a deafening barrage of drumming and Hindi film music. The revelries finally draw to a close six days later on the full moon, when the customary **blood sacrifices** of a young buffalo, a goat, a cock, a fish and a crab are made to the god.

Kullu's Dussehra, now a major tourist attraction, has become increasingly staged and commercialized. Book accommodation in advance, and be prepared for a crush if you want to get anywhere near the *devtas*.

Khul, 5km north of Katrain, where you can pick up a shared taxi or local bus for the remaining 6km. Buses also run direct to Manali via Nagar, from the end of the Tapu suspension bridge, across the river from the Akhara Bazaar bus depot. This service, which leaves more or less hourly, is slower, but far more scenic.

The temples

Kullu's most famous temple, the **Raghunathji Mandir**, overlooks the Sarvari *nala* from the steep hillside to the north, in the **Sultanpur** district. To get there, cross the main road outside the bus stand and follow the lane up the hill opposite the *Kailash* cinema. The temple, a long low building tucked away behind the Kullu Raja's **Rupi Palace**, is surprisingly plain considering the pre-eminence of the deity behind its sanctum's iron grille. Lord Raghunathji, a manifestation of Rama, was brought to Kullu from Ayodhya in Oudh by Raja Jagat Singh in the mid-seventeenth century. The Raja had been advised by his priests to install the sacred icon here and crown it king in his place, as a penance for causing the death of a local *brahmin* (thereby ridding himself of a punitive curse that had been turning all his food into worms). To this day, the Kullu rajas consider themselves mere viceroys of Raghunathji, the most powerful *devta* in the valley and the focus of the Dussehra procession. Half an hour's walk further up the paved trail leads beyond Sultanpur to a high ridge, with excellent views over the Beas to the snow peaks in the east. **Vaishno Devi Mandir**, a small cave-temple that houses an image of the goddess Kali (Durga), is a stiff 3km on.

Another important temple stands 8km southeast of town, atop the bluff that overlooks the sacred confluence, or *sangam*, of the Beas and Parvati. Although it's far closer to Bhuntur than Kullu, you have to approach the **Bijli Mahadev Mandir** via the Akhara Baza–Tapu suspension bridge and a well-worn track south along the left bank of the Beas. Bijli Mahadev is renowned for its extraordinary *lingam*. Bolts of lightning, conducted into the inner sanctum by means of the twenty-metre, trident-tipped pole, are said periodically to shatter the icon, which later, with the help of invocations from the resident *pujari*, magically reconstitutes itself. The temple is most memorable though, for its situation, with superb panoramic views of the Parvati and Kullu valleys and Himachal's highest peaks. You can **stay** in the temple rest house (donations welcome), a simple affair with a single cold tap, and no toilets, and walk down into the Parvati Valley the next day.

Accommodation and eating

It's hard to think why, with Nagar and Manali just up the valley, anyone would choose to spend the night in Kullu, but – except during Dussehra – the town has a reasonable choice of **accommodation**. The rates quoted are for high season; at other times discounts of up to 50 percent may be given. Most of the hotels have small, moderately priced **restaurants**. Otherwise, there are rock-bottom *dhabas* in the bazaar: the *Radha*, on the town side of the footbridge, is the cleanest. For a pit stop between buses, try the *Kapoor Chinese Hut*'s tasty Tibetan food, in a shack on the bus stand square.

Ankara, above the telegraph office, Ankara Bazaar. A homely place set off the main road in the heart of the bazaar, five minutes' walk from the bus stand, in the Manali direction. ③.

Bijleshwar View, behind the tourist office, Dhalpur. Quiet, clean, central and friendly, with baths and fireplaces in large rooms, and some dorm beds. Recommended. ④–⑤.

Daulat, Circuit House Rd, Dhalpur (☎01902/2358). Run-of-the-mill, recently renovated hotel, with en-suite rooms and good off-season discounts. ④.

HPTDC Hotel Sarvari, Dhalpur, off the *maidan*. Large, efficient hotel with some dorms. ①–⑤.

Shobla, Dhalpur (☎01902/2800). Kullu's top hotel, overlooking the river. Large rooms, a good mixed-cuisine restaurant – expensive by Kullu standards – and a relaxing lawn. ⑥–⑧.

The Parvati Valley

Hemmed in by giant-pinnacled mountain peaks, the **Parvati Valley**, which twists west from the glaciers and snowfields on the Spiti border to meet the Beas at Bhuntur, 8km south of Kullu, is the Kullu Valley's longest tributary. Picturesque hamlets perch precariously on its sides, amid lush terraces and old-growth pine forests. Only those along the road, however, see many visitors – an incongruous combination of Western hippies and van-loads of Sikh pilgrims bound for the *gurudwara* at **Manikaran**, 32km northeast of the Beas-Parvati confluence. Crouched at the foot of a gloomy ravine, this ancient religious site, sacred to Hindus as well as Sikhs, is famous for the sulphurous **hot springs** that bubble out of its stony river banks.

To make the most of Parvati's stunning scenery you'll have to **hike**. Two popular trails thread their way up the valley: one heads north from **Jari**, over the Chandrakani Pass to Nagar, passing through the remote, fascinating hill village of **Malana** (see p.485); the other follows the River Parvati east to another sacred hot spring and *sadhu* hang-out, **Khiraganga**, and on to the pass that leads into Spiti's remote **Pin Valley**.

Jari

Spilling over the main road and down the south side of the Parvati Valley, **JARI**, 15km from Bhuntur, looks across to the precipitous Malana *nala* in the north, and to the snow-flecked needles of the Baranagh range on the eastern horizon. Like many of its lookalike cousins, the tatty settlement supports a transient population of stoned Westerners, attracted by the village's *charas*, who spend much of the day in the dreary *Deepak Cafe* on the square where the buses pull in. If you're tempted to **stay**, the *Village Guest House*, a traditional wooden-balconied house ten minutes' walk from the square, is the best bet (①–②). *Ratna Guest House* (①), above the square is also good, but doesn't have the views afforded by the newer *Krishna Guest House* (②), five minutes' walk back towards Bhuntur, which overlooks the valley.

Manikaran

Beyond Jari, the road winds down towards the rushing grey-green Parvati, which it meets at **Kasol**. HPTDC's small *Tourist Hut* (③) stands in the centre of the village, and several small cafes and guest houses tucked away in the woods cater for the trickle of trekkers that plod through on their way to or from Rashol Jot (2440m). The pass, a hard day's climb up the north side of the valley, provides an alternative approach to Malana and the Chandrakani route to the Kullu Valley, described on p.485.

Clouds of pungent steam billowing from the rocky riverbank 10km upstream herald the Parvati Valley's chief attraction. Hindu mythology identifies **MANIKARAN** as the place where the serpent king Shesha stole Parvati's earrings, or *manikara*, while she and her husband Shiva were bathing in the river. When interrogated by the god of destruction, the snake, who had slithered away to hide in his subterranean kingdom, Patala, flew into a rage and snorted the earrings out of his nose. Ever since, boiling water has poured out of the ground. The site is also venerated by Sikhs, who have erected a massive green and white onion-domed concrete *gurudwara* over the springs.

Boxed in at the bottom of a vast, sheer-sided chasm, Manikaran is a damp, dark and claustrophobic place where you're unlikely to want to spend more than a night – long enough for a soak in a hot tub, and a chat to the *babas* who congregate on the riverbank. Most of the action revolves around the springs themselves, reached via the lane that leads through the village from the footbridge: just follow the stench of sulphur. On the way, check out the finely carved pale-grey stone **Rama temple** just past the main square, and the pans of rice and *dal* cooking in the steaming pools on the pavements. Down at the riverside **Shiva shrine**, a brightly painted concrete box whose accessory deities have also been left to stew in the hot springs, semi-naked *sadhus* sit in the sulphurous vapours smoking *chillums* and bumming cigarettes from the curious Westerners who wander past. Sikh pilgrims, meanwhile, make their way to the nearby **gurudwara**, where they take a purifying dip in the underground pool, then congregate upstairs to listen to musical recitations from the Sikhs' holy book, the *Guru Granth Sahib*. If you visit, keep your arms, legs and head covered; tobacco is prohibited inside the complex.

Practicalities

Buses leave Bhuntur every couple of hours for Manikaran (1hr 30min), which is as far east as the road goes. The last bus for Kullu, via Bhuntur, leaves at 6pm. *Maruti*-van **taxis** are also available for the trip, costing Rs450, or less out of season.

Except during May and June, when Manikaran fills up with Punjabi visitors, **accom-modation** is plentiful and inexpensive; all hotels listed here have a steaming indoor hot tub. Manikaran's abundance of moisture and sulphurous fumes has affected most hotels, however, leaving them feeling damp and dirty. Two notable exceptions are the HPTDC *Hotel Parvati* (⑤–⑥), near the Raghunath temple on the main street, with large, well-furnished rooms, a restaurant, and a riverside lawn, and the *Sharma Sadan Guest House* (①), opposite, which has four spotless rooms and overlooking the square. The comfortable *Sharma Guest House* (③), at the other end of the bazaar, near the *gurud-wara*, has attached doubles; the *Padha Family Guest House* (②), opposite, is similar, with rooms around a courtyard, but the noise of the river can keep you awake.

Places to eat range from the *Parvati*'s pricey Punjabi restaurant, to the no-frills makeshift *dhabas* along the main street. The best of the tourist cafes catering for trekkers and budget travellers is the Tibetan-run *Shiva Cafe*, near the springs, which serves Indian and Chinese food, plus brown bread, pizza, porridge, pancakes and apple pie. The dimly lit *Holy Palace*, back towards the square, is similar, with a juice bar next door selling *lassis* and glasses of freshly squeezed mangoes, oranges and apples. The small *O-Rest* overlooking the river is more airy, but the food is mediocre.

Nagar

Stacked up the lush terraced lower slopes of the valley as they sweep towards the tree-line from the left bank of the Beas, **NAGAR**, 6km from the main road, is the most scenic and accessible of the hill villages between Kullu and Manali. Clustered around an old **castle**, this was the regional capital before the local rajas decamped to Kullu in the mid-1800s. A century or so later, European settlers began to move in.

Seduced by the village's ancient **temples**, tranquil setting and unhurried pace, many visitors find themselves lingering in Nagar – a far less hippyfied village than those fur-ther north – longer than they intended. Numerous tracks wind up the mountain to more remote settlements, providing a choice of strenuous, enjoyable **hikes**.

Arrival and information

Nagar is connected by regular **buses** to Kullu and Manali. The direct services that ply the left-bank road, on the eastern side of the valley, are slower (2hr from Manali, or 1hr 30min from Kullu), but more scenic and straightforward than the more frequent ser-vices along the main highway on the opposite, west side. These drop at **Patlikuhl** (5km north of Katrain), from where taxis and hourly buses cross the Beas to climb up to Nagar (6km). If you arrive in daylight and are not weighed down with bags, you can also walk from Patlikuhl on the old mule track – a hike of up to an hour.

The castle, Roerich Gallery, temples, and most of Nagar's accommodation lie above the small bazaar where the buses pull in: hop into a waiting rickshaw, or head on foot uphill along the metalled road for about 100m, then turn right onto the steep concrete path. If you have your own vehicle, you can drive all the way up to the Roerich Gallery at the top of the village – the trailhead for the Nagar–Chandrakani Pass–Malana–Parvati Valley **trek** (see p.485). Finally, Nagar has a good supply of guides and porters for treks, amd an STD booth for long-distance phone calls.

The castle

Since it was erected by Raja Sidh Singh (*c.*1700), Nagar's central **castle**, astride a sheer-sided bluff, has served as palace, colonial mansion, court house and school. These days it houses a small state-run hotel; non-residents can wander in to admire the views from its balconies. Built in the traditional "earthquake-proof" *pahari* style (layers of stone bonded together with cedar logs), the castle surrounds a central courtyard, next to which stands a small museum, and an even smaller shrine. The **Jagti Patt temple**'s amorphous deity, a triangular slab of rock strewn with rose petals and rupee notes, is said to have been borne here from its home on the summit of Deo Tibba by a swarm of wild honey bees – the valley's *devtas* in disguise.

The Nicholas Roerich Gallery

Perched on the upper outskirts of the village and shaded by lofty palms, the **Nicholas Roerich Gallery** (daily 9am–1pm & 2–5pm; Rs10) houses an exhibition of paintings and photographs dedicated to the memory of its former occupier, the Russian artist, writer, philosopher, archeologist, explorer and mystic. Around the turn of the century, Roerich's atmospheric landscape paintings and esoteric philosophies – an arcane blend of eastern mysticism and *fin de siècle* humanist-idealism – inspired a cult-like following in France and the US. Financed by donations from devotees, Roerich, variously compared by his admirers to Leonardo and Buddha, was able to indulge his obsession with Himalayan travel in a series of lengthy expeditions to far-flung corners of Tibet and Central Asia. He retired to Nagar in 1929, dying here eighteen years later.

The exhibition, in a small room on the ground floor, comprises a dozen or so evocative oil paintings of the Himalayas, and a few old photos of the self-styled guru, pictured in Chinese silk robes, cossack boots and burly beard, posing on the front lawn with visiting dignitaries such as Jawaharlal Nehru.

The temples

The largest and most distinctive of Nagar's ancient Hindu **temples** and shrines, the wooden pagoda-style **Tripuri Sundri**, stands in a small enclosure at the top of the village, just below the road to the Roerich Gallery. Like the Dunghri temple in Manali, it is crowned with a three-tiered roof, whose top storey is circular. Animal carvings project from the eaves of the shrine, which houses an image of the Mother Goddess – "Beauty of the Triple World". Its *devta* is the focus of an annual *mela* (May 18–24) in which deities from local villages are brought in procession to pay their respects.

Ten minutes' walk further up the hill – follow the stone steps that lead right from the road – brings you to a clearing where the old stone **Murlidhar** (Krishna) **Mandir** looks down on Nagar, with superb views up the valley to the snow peaks around Solan and the Rohtang Pass. Built on the ruins of the ancient town of Thawa, the shrine is strictly off-limits to non-Hindus.

Finally, on your way to or from the bus stand at the bottom of the village, look out for the finely carved stone *shikharas* of the **Gaurishankar Mandir**. Set in its own paved courtyard below the castle, this Shiva temple, among the oldest of its kind in the valley, houses a living *lingam*, so slip off your shoes before approaching it.

Accommodation and eating

Nagar's most popular place to **stay**, the HPTDC *Hotel Castle* (①–⑤), offers well-furnished en-suite doubles (some with superb views from spacious wooden balconies), and cheap dorm beds. Book in advance at any HPTDC tourist office to secure one of the more expensive rooms in the west wing – which is allegedly haunted by the **ghost** of a young rani, who threw herself off the balcony after her jealous husband beheaded an itinerant musician whom she had complimented. Non-residents can eat in its small **restaurant**. A good fall-back is the *Sheetal Guest House* (☎01902/83319; ⑤; reductions off-season), across the road, where rooms come with balconies, bathrooms and hot water; there's the reasonable Indian-Western-Chinese *Cinderella Restaurant* next door. The equally comfortable *Hotel Poonam* (④), around the corner, offers bargain dorms as well as cosy doubles, a good non-veg restaurant, and a shady garden cafe serving pure veg food al fresco.

The rest of Nagar's accommodation is ten minutes away at the top of the village. The friendly *Snow View Guest House* (①–③), adjacent to the Tripuri Sundri temple at the end of a lane branching off the road, has doubles that open on to a pleasant garden, along with cheaper non-attached rooms, and a handful of clean dorm beds. You can eat here in their inexpensive rooftop cafe. The best budget option is the *Alliance Guest House* (①–②), halfway between the Tripuri Sundri and the Roerich Gallery. Run by a Frenchman who settled here in the 1970s, the *Alliance* has simple, clean rooms (shared bathrooms), and a warm family atmosphere, with kids and dogs scampering around its airy terrace. Tasty, inexpensive food – generous breakfasts, *thalis* and Western dishes – is also available.

Manali

Himachal's main tourist resort, **MANALI**, stands at the head of the Kullu Valley, 108km north of Mandi. Despite lying at the heart of the region's highest mountain ranges, it remains easily accessible by road from the plains; after one hour on a plane and a short hop by road, or sixteen hours on a bus from Delhi, you could be staring from your hotel verandah across apple orchards and thick pine forests to the eternal snowfields of Solang Nala, which shine a tantalizing stone's throw away to the north. Alternatively, your room may overlook several other hotels: with the troubles continuing in Kashmir, Manali has taken over as a chief resort for domestic tourists, and new buildings have been hastily erected with apparent disregard for the traditional character of mountain homes, submerging in the process the riverine meadows that once fortified mule trains heading north.

All this has dampened the appeal that lured travellers in the 1970s, though the majestic mountain scenery and the area's seemingly limitless supply of inexpensive *charas* haven't changed, and some of the old charm does remain in **Old Manali** and in the nearby village of **Vashisht**, visited by an annual exodus of "freaks" each June. Set at the foot of the **Rohtang Pass**, gateway to the rugged regions of Lahaul and Spiti, Manali is also the roadhead for the trans-Himalayan highway, and thus the best place to pick up transport for the near-legendary two-day journey to Ladakh's capital, **Leh**.

TAXIS AND TOURS

Manali's *Taxi Operators' Union* kiosk (☎2450) stands on the east side of the square at the top of town, just up from the tourist office. Out of season you should be able to negotiate reductions on the normal "fixed" rates (around Rs1000 for a full day) to local landmarks.

Weather and road conditions permitting, HPTDC run daily bus **tours** to the **Rohtang Pass** (leaves 9am, returns 4pm; Rs80). The trip, popular with domestic tourists eager to experience snow for the first time, provides a good opportunity to take in the views north over the Chenab Valley to the stark mountain scenery of Lahaul. Other daily tours include day trips to **Nagar**, via Jagatsukh (9am–4pm; Rs100), and **Manikaran** in the Parvati Valley (9am–6pm; Rs125). Tickets can be booked ahead at the tourist office.

If you're planning a **trekking or rafting** trip (see p.481), shop around to compare prices and packages; many agencies are fly-by-night operators who make their money from mark-ups on long-distance bus tickets to Delhi, Chandigarh and Leh. Long-established **reliable agents** include *Himalayan Adventurers* (☎2182), opposite the tourist office and *Himalayan Journeys* (☎2365), next to the *State Bank of India* , who also have their own rafting gear and mountain bikes, and organize heli-skiing holidays in the thick of winter.

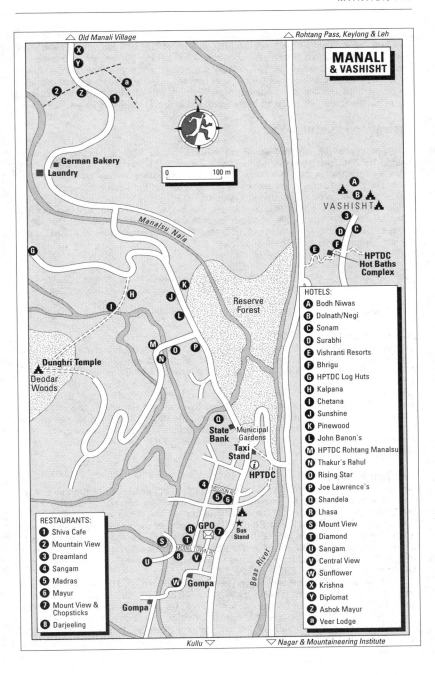

△ Old Manali Village   △ Rohtang Pass, Keylong & Leh

MANALI & VASHISHT

German Bakery
Laundry

Manalsu Nala

VASHISHT

HPTDC Hot Baths Complex

Reserve Forest

Dunghri Temple
Deodar Woods

HOTELS:
- Ⓐ Bodh Niwas
- Ⓑ Dolnath/Negi
- Ⓒ Sonam
- Ⓓ Surabhi
- Ⓔ Vishranti Resorts
- Ⓕ Bhrigu
- Ⓖ HPTDC Log Huts
- Ⓗ Kalpana
- Ⓘ Chetana
- Ⓙ Sunshine
- Ⓚ Pinewood
- Ⓛ John Banon's
- Ⓜ HPTDC Rohtang Manalsu
- Ⓝ Thakur's Rahul
- Ⓞ Rising Star
- Ⓟ Joe Lawrence's
- Ⓠ Shandela
- Ⓡ Lhasa
- Ⓢ Mount View
- Ⓣ Diamond
- Ⓤ Sangam
- Ⓥ Central View
- Ⓦ Sunflower
- Ⓧ Krishna
- Ⓨ Diplomat
- Ⓩ Ashok Mayur
- ⓐ Veer Lodge

State Bank
Municipal Gardens
Taxi Stand
HPTDC

MISSION RD

GPO
Bus Stand

MODEL TOWN RD

Gompa
Gompa

Beas River

RESTAURANTS:
- ① Shiva Cafe
- ② Mountain View
- ③ Dreamland
- ④ Sangam
- ⑤ Madras
- ⑥ Mayur
- ⑦ Mount View & Chopsticks
- ⑧ Darjeeling

0   100 m

Kullu ▽   ▽ Nagar & Mountaineering Institute

Manali may not be a textbook example of town planning, but it makes an ideal **trekking** base. Whether you're embarking on a short hike or a long expedition, you'll find the streets packed with potential companions, guides, porters and provisions, as well as countless agencies keen to put a package together for you. The relaxing hotels in Manali's cleaner greener outskirts, and dozens of sociable cafes and restaurants, ranged around a well-stocked **bazaar**, provide a welcome antidote to the austerities of the mountain trails. For more on treks around Manali and the Kullu Valley, see p.484.

Arrival and information

Buses pull in to Manali's **bus stand** in the middle of the Mall, a short walk from the helpful HPTDC **tourist office** (daily 10am–5pm; ☎2325), where you can make reservations for the town's state-run hotels. If you need to **change money**, the *State Bank of India* (Mon–Fri 10am–1.30pm, Sat 10–11.30am) is just off the square at the top of town. The main **post office**, off Model Town Rd, has a reliable poste restante counter (Mon–Sat 9am–5pm, Sun 9–10am & 2–3pm). The best places to make long-distance and international **calls** are the phone booths next to the tourist office and the bank, which charge standard "government-approved" rates. The *Monalisa Restaurant* has STD facilities at a higher rate, and allows call-back.

The telephone **area code** for Manali is ☎01901.

The Town

Manali's main street, **the Mall**, quite unlike its namesake in Shimla, is a noisy scene of constant activity, fronted by the bus station, several shopping markets, a line of hotels and restaurants, and travel agents. Settle in to a window seat at one of the Mall's many glass-fronted cafes and take in the strange mixture of people – Kulluis in brightly patterned *puttoos*, Tibetan women wearing ankle-length rainbow-striped pinafores, Nepali porters, Buddhist monks, and even the odd party of Zanskaris swathed in fusty woollen *gonchas*, muddled together with souvenir-hunting Indian tourists and an odd mix of Westerners. Most people staying a while in Manali stick to the quieter areas, lodging in the old town, and take daily strolls through the surrounding woods and hills, where villagers at work in the fields seem untroubled by the racy pace of the Mall.

The Dunghri temple

Resting on a wide stone platform in a dense stand of old *deodar*, fifteen minutes' walk northwest of the bazaar, the **Dunghri temple** is Manali's oldest shrine and the seat of **Hadimba** (or "Hirma Devi"), the "grandmother" of the Kullu raja's tutelary deity, Raghunathji. Legend has it that Bhima (the strongest of the five Pandava brothers of *Mahabharata* fame) fell in love with this "mountain belle", the only sister of the fierce demon Tandi, killed by Bhima in hand-to-hand combat. Considered to be an incarnation of Kali, Hadimba is worshipped in times of adversity, and also plays a key role in the Dussehra festival (see p.471).

The **temple** itself, a giant triple-tiered wooden pagoda crowned by crimson pennants and a brass ball and trident (Shiva's *trichul*), dates from 1553, and is a replica of earlier ones that burned down in successive forest fires. Its facade writhes with wonderful wood carvings of elephants, crocodiles and folk deities, as well as scenes from a legend in which a raja chops the hands off the royal sculptor to prevent him from repeating his masterpiece elsewhere. Entered by a door surmounted by wild ibex horns, the gloomy

SHOPPING IN MANALI

Manali's days as an "authentic" *pahari* bazaar ended when the mule trains were superseded by *Tata* trucks, but it is still an excellent place for souvenir **shopping**.

Woollen goods are the town's real forte, particularly the brilliantly patterned **shawls** for which Kullu Valley is famous. The NSC (New Shopping Centre) market near the bus stand sells a good selection. What you pay for a shawl depends on its size, age, the quality of the wool, the number of hours' work that have gone into its manufacture, and, most important of all, your ability to haggle. The cheapest, which can be bought from Tibetan street stalls for between Rs150–200, are machine-woven, thin, and neither warm nor durable. Genuine pure-wool handloom shawls with intricately embroidered borders start at around Rs500, but can cost up to Rs4000 if they are made from finest *pashima* – an exquisitely soft wool shorn from the underbelly of Himalayan goats. A good place to familiarize yourself with fair prices at the top of the range is the *Bodh Shawl Factory Shop*, just off the Mall south of the bus stand, which sells high-quality shawls at fixed rates. While there, try out the acid-test for *pashima*: if it creases when crumpled, it isn't pure.

Elsewhere around the bazaar innumerable stalls are stacked with hand-woven goods and pillbox Kullu *topis*. Those with gaudy multi-coloured up-turned flaps and gold piping are indigenous to the valley, but you can also pick up the plain-green velvet-fronted variety favoured by Kinnauris (and by the state's "men-of-the-people" politicians).

Manali's other speciality is Himalayan **handicrafts**: mainly assorted **Tibetan curios** such as prayer wheels, amulets, *dorjes* (thunderbolts), masks, musical instruments and *thangkas*. Few of the items hawked as antiques in the NSC market and the souvenir shops on or behind the Mall are genuine, but it takes an expert eye to spot a fake. The same applies to silver **jewellery** inlaid with turquoise and coral, which can nonetheless be attractive and relatively inexpensive.

shrine is dominated by several large boulders, one of which shelters the stone on which goats and buffalo are sacrificed during important rituals. The hollow in its middle, believed to be Vishnu's footprint, channels the blood to Hadimba's mouth.

The gompas

Manali harbours the highest concentration of **Tibetan refugees** in the Kullu valley, which accounts both for the abundance of *mani* poles and strings of bedraggled prayer flags fluttering over the approach roads to the town, and the presence, on its southern edge, of two shiny new **gompas**, or Buddhist monasteries.

Capped with polished golden finials, the distinctive yellow corrugated-iron pagoda roof of the **Gadhan Thekchhokling gompa** is an exotic splash of colour amid the ramshackle huts of the Tibetan quarter. Built in 1969, the monastery is maintained by donations from the local community and through the sale of **carpets** hand-woven in the temple workshop. When they are not looking after the **shop**, the young *lamas* huddle in the courtyard to play *cholo* – a Tibetan dice game involving much shouting and slamming of wooden *tsampa* bowls on leather pads. The brightly painted *lakhang*, or prayer hall, dominated by a large seated Shakyamuni, stands on the west side of the quadrangle and is open to visitors. Photography is permitted; leave a donation in the box as you leave. Beside the main entrance a roll of honour recounts the names of Tibetans killed during the violent political demonstrations that wracked China in the late 1980s.

The smaller and more modern of the two *gompas* stands nearer the bazaar, in a garden that in late summer blazes with sunflowers. Its main shrine, lit by dozens of bare electric bulbs and filled with fragrant Tibetan incense, houses a colossal gold-faced Buddha, best viewed from the small room on the first floor. Downstairs, monks sit on the verandah block-printing brightly coloured prayer flags.

Old Manali

Old Manali, the village from which the modern town takes its name, lies 3km (half an hour's walk) north of the Mall, on the far side of the Manalsu *nala*. Unlike its crowded, unsightly offspring, the settlement retains an unhurried and traditional feel. To get there, head past the *State Bank*, bear right at the fork in the road, and keep going through the pine woods until you reach the iron bridge across the river.

You'll pass a string of small guest houses and cafes before reaching the village proper, clustered on top of a steeply shelving ledge of level ground above the *nala*. It is also known as **"Manaligarh"** after its ancient citadel – a now-ruined fort surrounded by a patchwork of maize terraces and deep-green orchards that fan down to the Beas. Built in the old *pahari* style, most of the houses have heavy stone roofs and wooden balconies hung with bushels of drying herbs and tobacco. Handlooms holding half-woven woollen shawls stand outside doorways whose lintels are painted with folk murals, while cows chew their way through bales of sweet-smelling hay scattered across smoky courtyards. The only indication that tourism has not entirely passed Old Manali by are the bands of scruffy kids that accost you in the damp cobbled lanes, thrusting lumps of *charas* and demanding "one pen, one pen".

Accommodation

Manali's older, characterful hotels are dotted around the northern and western outskirts of town. The only **budget** places of note are in **Old Manali**, where rough-and-ready family-run guest houses nestle amid the orchards. Although the *charas*-induced torpor that hangs over some of them (especially the dismal small hotels ranged along the stream near the bridge), and the trek to and from town, can pall, the peace and quiet, and views from their flower gardens, more than compensate. **Women** should be wary of walking along the lane from town to Old Manali after dark, which has been the scene of several attempted **rapes** in recent years.

Tariffs rocket in Manali during **high season** (April–July & Sept–Nov). At other times, a 50 percent reduction on the advertised rates (listed below) for more expensive hotels is standard. The few hotels that stay open in **winter** cater mainly for skiing parties, and charge around Rs50 per day extra for heating.

Ashok Mayur, Old Manali. A small, simple guest house opposite *Shiva* cafe, with balconies warmed by the morning sun. ②.

Chetana, below the Dunghri temple, near *Log Huts* (☎2245). Spruce red and white building with large, neat rooms, lawns, verandahs, a boiler system and peaceful situation. ⑥.

Diplomat, Old Manali. Large modern building with spacious rooms and verandahs. ③.

HPTDC Log Huts, overlooking Manalsu Nala (☎2339). "Honeymoon Huts" and two-bedroomed wooden holiday cottages tucked away in the woods. *Star TV*, and most comforts, but overpriced. ⑧.

MODEL TOWN HOTELS

As soon as you step off the bus in Manali, you'll be assailed by "card-*wallahs*" clamouring to drag you off to one of the **hotels** crammed into the grid of narrow streets immediately behind the Mall, the quarter known as **Model Town**. Though bland and boxed-in, these carbon-copy mid-range places make good bases from which to hunt around for more congenial better-value accommodation once you've found your feet. The majority offer generous off-season discounts, too; a little haggling should get you a clean room with extra blankets and a geyser for around Rs150. Recommended Model Town clones include: the *Central View* (☎2319; ④), the *Diamond* (☎3058; ④), the *Lhasa* (☎2134; ④), the *Sangam* (☎3019; ⑥), the *Mount View* (☎2465; ④), and the *Ambika* (☎2203; ④).

RAFTING IN MANALI

Considering the abundant white water that thrashes down the Kullu Valley during the spring snow melt, Manali's **rafting** scene is surprisingly low-key. Nevertheless, more companies are following the example of their Nepalese counterparts and investing in quality equipment. Raft trips down the River Beas occur between the end of May and early July, when water levels are highest, beginning at Bhuntur (just south of Kullu) and ending 14km downstream at the mouth of the Larji gorge. The price for the day, around Rs700, should include meals, lifejackets, helmets, and return travel; check exactly what you're paying for, as some unscrupulous operators expect you to make your own way back to town after the trip. Reputable agents-cum-rafting outfits are listed on p.476.

Joe Lawrence's, Old Manali Rd. Five-star comfort with a difference: an old colonial campus converted into separate cottages. Stylish, but pricey. ⑦–⑧.

John Banon's, Old Manali Rd. Old guest house, something of an institution. Impeccable rooms, easy chairs, valley views, and a convivial host who keeps a fine table. "Strictly no riff-raff". ⑤.

Kalpana, near the *Chetana Hotel* (☎2413). Large, well-furnished, variously priced rooms ranged around a central lawn at the tranquil top end of town. ⑤–⑥.

Krishna, Old Manali (☎3071). Small, friendly place with wide balconies and hot water in common bathrooms. Connecting doors between rooms make it handy for small groups. ②.

Laxmi, Old Manali. Large, clean, and simple budget rooms ensconced amid shady flower gardens and orchards. Shared bathrooms only. Recommended. ②.

Pinewood, off Old Manali Rd (☎2118). Colonial building with furniture and garden to match. Popular with tour parties and trekking groups. Excellent value, particularly out of season. ⑥.

Rising Star, near *Rohtang Manalsu* (☎2381). Budget back rooms boast big verandahs that overlook a leafy garden. Among the best deals in town. ③.

Shandela, near PSEB office (☎2426). Big, light rooms with views, baths and 24hr-hot water. ④.

Sunflower, Tibetan quarter (☎2419). Friendly family-run hotel with en-suite rooms. ③–④.

Sunshine, off Old Manali Rd (no phone). The last word in understated colonial elegance: old double-storey wooden building with period furniture, fireplaces, and magnificent views from spacious balconies. Meals served on request in common dining room. ⑥.

Thakur's Rahul, opposite *Rohtang Manalsu* (☎2180). Modern building, with an old wing on the opposite side of a relaxing garden. The cheaper rooms are good value. ④–⑥.

Veer, Old Manali. The cheapest of the budget bunch and excellent value, with fine views down the valley from a lovely leafy garden. Some attached bathrooms, too. ①–②.

Eating

Manali's wide range of **restaurants** reflect the town's melting-pot credentials: Tibetan *thukpa* joints stand cheek-by-jowl with south Indian coffee houses, Gujarati *thali* bars, and Nepalese-run German pastry shops. Whatever their ostensible speciality, though, most offer mixed menus that include Chinese and Western dishes alongside standard north Indian favourites. For rock-bottom budget food, head for one of the *dhabas* opposite the bus stand: the best for a sit-down meal is *Himalaya Dhaba*, while the *Krishna* and *Lakshmi* both do a roaring trade in piping hot *parathas*, *channa batura*, *puris*, and other snacks spooned out of giant woks of bubbling oil.

Virtually every cafe in Manali also serves serious "**tourist breakfasts**" of porridge, pancakes, toast and jam; *chai* and omelette-*wallahs* appear on the Mall before dawn if you need to steel yourself for a long and bumpy bus journey.

Finally, stock up on energy-rich **trekking food** at the local produce stores and bakeries in the bazaar. The state-sponsored co-op, near the temple on the Mall, sells sacks of nuts, dried fruit and pots of pure honey at fixed prices, while *Superbake*, just up the road from the *State Bank*, is the place to binge on home-baked cookies, apple crumble and slabs of sticky chocolate cake.

Chopsticks, The Mall. Manali's top Japanese restaurant, fairly expensive but well worth a splurge.

Darjeeling, Model Town Rd. Popular backstreet cafe serving Tibetan and tourist-oriented food plus Gujarati *thalis* indoors or outside in small terrace garden.

German Bakery, Mission Rd and Old Manali. Both good places to buy trekking supplies, or simply to indulge a sweet tooth: apple pie, strudel, lemon cake, and Western wholefood snacks.

Green Forest Restaurant, next to *Hotel Chetana*. Cheap garden cafe with resident masseur, dishing up indifferent food, mostly *momos* and noodles, to young *charas*-toking tourists.

Madras, Mission Rd. Cheap and fiery south Indian food, and filling Rs25 *thalis*.

Mayur, Model Town. Popular tourist haunt with meat and veg Indian and Chinese food, and a decent sound system.

Monalisa, bazaar area. Cosy, sociable tourist cafe with a fairly priced menu of mainly Indian and Chinese dishes, desserts, soups and light snacks.

Mount View, The Mall. Copious mouthwatering Chinese, Japanese, and authentic Tibetan food served under paper lanterns. Very popular, so arrive early or reserve a table.

Mountain View Cafe, Old Manali. Set away from most of the guest houses with extensive views. Simple yet varied menu; open 24hr in season or when there's demand.

Sangam, Mission Rd. Good-value veg restaurant tucked away at the end of a narrow lane. Try their delicious mixed fruit and veg curries.

Shiva Cafe, Old Manali. Sociable, lazy balcony, an open fire most evenings, and Chinese, Indian and pasta dishes make this Old Manali's most popular budget travellers' joint.

MOVING ON FROM MANALI

Manali is well connected by **bus** to other Himachali towns, and major cities on the plains. Three types of services ply the more popular routes: "luxury" (a/c, reclining seats, videos and limited stops), "deluxe" (non-a/c, less leg-room, no video), and "ordinary" (cramped, rock-hard seats and frequent stops). All of these can be booked at the bus stand. During the summer demand invariably outstrips supply, particularly for the faster services, so book as far in advance as possible, and be prepared for regular and fruitless visits to ticket offices.

The luxury and deluxe buses to **Delhi** (2 daily, 1 nightly; 16hr), **Shimla** (1 daily, 1 nightly; 9hr), and **Chandigarh** (1 daily; 10hr), are all operated by *HPTDC* (who sell tickets), and depart from the tourist office in the centre of town. In addition, travel agents sell tickets for regular services to Dharamsala (10hr), Shimla and Delhi (12–14hr) on "luxury" coaches that sometimes turn out to be fairly shabby; try *Harrisons Travels* (☎2473) and *Monal Himalayan Travels* (☎2315), both on The Mall. Cheaper tickets for "express" services to **Shimla** (1 daily; 9hr) and **Dharamsala** (2 daily; 11hr) are sold by *HPSRTC* at Manali's main bus stand.

Transport to Leh

If you can afford the Rs8–10,000 fare, mini-van **taxis** are the most comfortable way to get to Ladakh from Manali. The vast majority of visitors, however, have to travel the 485km to Leh by **bus** – an arduous, but unforgettable two-day (28hr) trip that involves a night-halt under canvas along the route.

With its cushioned, well-spaced seats, HPTDC's daily "luxury" bus, bookable through the tourist office, is the least gruelling option. If your budget won't stretch to the Rs500 fare, their "deluxe" service is also worth considering. Otherwise, choice is limited to the beaten-up buses operated by *HPSRTC* and their Jammu & Kashmiri equivalents, or even dodgier private mini-buses that sell seats through the travel agents on the Mall.

Officially, the **Manali–Leh Highway** is open when the high passes open in mid-June until September 15, after which the state services are suspended. Many of the private companies, however, continue to operate well into October, when the inflated end-of-season prices they charge encourage them to risk getting stuck in an early snowfall.

Whenever and however you travel, avoid the bumpy back seat of the bus, and take plenty of food, especially in autumn when *chai* stalls and *dhabas* are few and far between.

Vashisht

Famous for its sweeping valley views and sulphurous hot-water springs, the large settlement of **VASHISHT** (formerly Bashist), only 3km from Manali, is an amorphous jumble of traditional timber houses and modern concrete cubes, divided by paved courtyards and narrow muddy lanes. It is the epicentre of the local budget travellers' scene; tranquil and traditional, with a good choice of guest houses and cafes.

You can get to Vashisht either by road, or along the footpath that winds up from the main highway to its principal attraction. Supplied by water piped from underground springs, HPTDC's **Hot Bath Complex** (7am–1pm & 2–8pm; Rs30–80) is *the* perfect place to soak away the aches and pains of a long trek or bus journey, if you don't mind a slight grubbiness. The tiled tubs come in two sizes: regular and deluxe (family). Towels are available for a small extra charge, and you can sip delicious fresh apple juice or *Coca-Cola* on the sun terrace. Vashisht also boasts a pair of old stone **temples**, opposite each other above the main square. Dedicated to the local patron saint Vashista (a deified sage and guru of Raghunathji), the smaller of the two opens on to a partially covered courtyard, and is adorned with elaborate wood carvings. Those lining the interior of the shrine, blackened by years of oil-lamp and *dhoop* smoke, are particularly fine. As you leave, check out the **temple tanks**, the free and communal equivalent of HPTDC's hot tubs. Divided into separate sections for men and women, they attract a decidedly mixed crowd of Hindu pilgrims, Western hippies, semi-naked *sadhus*, and gangs of local kids that splash happily about in the pungent soapy water.

Accommodation

Vashisht is packed with budget **guest houses**, many of them old wooden buildings with broad verandahs and uninterrupted vistas up the valley. If you don't mind primitive plumbing, grungy beds and dope smoke, the only time you'll not be spoilt for choice is during high season, when even floor-space can be at a premium. On the outskirts, a couple of larger hotels offer good value, comfortable rooms. The places below are marked on the map on p.477

Amrit, tucked away behind the temple. Turquoise-painted wooden house with basic amenities and lots of charm. ②.

Bodh Niwas, behind *Dolnath Guest House*. A new and very clean lodge opposite a large wooden temple. Superb views from roof terrace. Common bathrooms. ③.

Bhrigu Hotel, below the village centre, on the roadside (☎8240). Large, slightly shabby hotel whose west-facing rooms all have attached bathrooms and superb views from balconies. ④.

Dharma, 15mins' walk up the lane behind the temples. Secluded guest house with rudimentary rooms, common toilets, and a south Indian snack annexe tacked on its first-storey verandah. ①–②.

Rose Garden Inn, next to HPTDC baths (☎8250). Two cosy chalet-style rooms with carpets and bath tubs, looking over a grassy lawn. ④.

Sonam, just down the road from the square. Cramped and dilapidated, but an old favourite. ①–②.

Surabhi Guest House, just below the main square. Very modern, smart and upmarket. Clean, large rooms with bath tubs and great views, and a roof terrace restaurant. ⑤.

Vishranti Resorts, just above the main highway. A bright white building overlooking the footpath, with large, light, clean rooms, a sunny roof terrace, and restaurant. The best value in its class. ⑤–⑥.

Eating

But for the *Superbake* store, behind the square, which has cornered the lucrative cake and bun market (try the wholewheat bread and apple crumble), most of the places to eat in Vashisht fall into the catch-all category: jacks of all trades, but masters of none.

Damrho, next to the *Sonam*. Poky "travellers" cafe with Western breakfasts and basic veg dishes.

Dreamland, the square. Sociable restaurant serving the usual Indian, Western, and Chinese.

Freedom, on the southern edge of the village. Worth the walk (10min) for its good attempts at Italian food, copious plates of *pulao*, breakfast menu, and *tandoor* oven, which fires up at 2pm.

TREKS AROUND MANALI AND THE KULLU VALLEY

The Kullu Valley's spectacular alpine scenery and proximity to some of HP's most dramatic and accessible peaks make it perfect **trekking** terrain. Ascending from a base altitude of 2000m to passes of 3500m and above, the trails are long and steep, but more than repay the effort with superb views, varied flora, and the chance to visit remote hill villages – an excellent introduction to Himalayan trekking, and the ideal way to acclimatize if you plan to attempt longer hikes at higher altitudes in Lahaul or Zanskar.

Within striking distance of several major trailheads, **Manali** is the most popular place to begin and end treks. While the **package deals** offered by the town's many agencies can save time and energy, however, you can easily and safely keep costs to a minimum by organizing the trip yourself. The tourist office on the Mall, and the Mountaineering Institute at the bottom of town, are both good sources of advice, while porters and packhorse-*wallahs* ply their trade in the square behind the main street. Guides are only hard to come by during September and October, when ponies are needed for the harvests.

However you decide to trek, always take a reliable **guide**, especially on less frequented routes. You cannot rely solely on **maps**, none of which, not even the *US Army Map Service U502* series map #NI 43–16, or *Leomann*'s (less dependable) *Indian Himalayas Map Sheet #5*, is one hundred percent accurate. The *Survey of India*'s *Kullu Valley Trekking Map*, available locally, helps you select a route, but little else.

The optimum **season** to trek is right after the monsoons, from mid-September to late October, when skies are clear and pass-crossings unproblematic. From June to August, you run the risk of sudden, potentially fatal snow, or view-obscuring cloud and rain.

Manali to Beas Kund

The relatively easy trek to **Beas Kund**, a glacial lake at the head of Solang *nala*, is the region's most popular short hike. Encircled by five- to six-thousand-metre peaks, the well-used campground beside the lake, accessible in two days from Manali, makes a good base for side-trips up to the surrounding ridges and passes.

Day 1 begins at the village of **Palchan**, a 30min bus ride north of Manali on the main highway. From the road, a jeep track heads up the valley to **Solang**, site of a small ski station, rest house, and the *Mountaineering Institute*'s log huts. The next two hours take you through pine forests, grassy meadows, and boulder chokes to the streamside campground at **Dhundi** (2743m), Gaddi grazing land dwarfed by the Hanuman Tibba massif (5928m) to the west. **Day 2**, when the trail becomes steeper and harder to follow, is more strenuous, winding across a huge moraine to reach **Beas Kund** after 5–6hr. The hike up to the Tentu La Pass (4996m) and back from here can be done in a day, as can the descent to Manali via Solang. Alternatively, head over Tentu La and down to Tantgari *nala*, to pick up a trail that climbs back into the Kullu Valley further south via the Manali Pass (4880m) – a tough ten-day round trip.

Jagatsukh to Deo Tibba

The base of **Deo Tibba** (6001m), is reached via the forests, alpine meadows, and high grazing pastures of the Jagatsukh *nala* – a return trip of between four and five days that is hard going in places. On **Day 1**, the path climbs from the trailhead at **Jagatsukh**, 11km south of Manali, through small villages and across a broad sweep of scree to a wooded ravine, beyond which lie a high glaciated valley and the campground of **Chikha**. **Day 2** is considerably shorter, taking you up to **Serai**, a lush grassy meadow where sheep graze in summer, from where you can trek further up the *nala* to the ridges that overlook the southwest face of Deo Tibba, and on to Chandra Tal lake (not the same as the one in Lahaul). Allow at least a day for the descent from Serai to Jagatsukh.

Manali to Lahaul, via the Hampta Pass

The trek from the Kullu Valley over the Hampta Pass to Lahaul, the old caravan route to Spiti, is a classic. Rising to 4330m, it is high by Kullu standards; do not undertake it without allowing good time for acclimatization along the way. **Day 1**, from the trailhead at **Prini** (near Manali) to the campground above **Sethen**, via Hampta village, is an easy 4–5hr hike up the verdant, forested sides of the valley. **Day 2**, another 5hr, brings you to **Chikha**, a high Gaddi pasture below the pass; stay put for a day or so if you're feeling the effects of the altitude. **Day 3**'s ascent (700m) to the **Hampta Pass** (4330m) is gruelling, but the views from the top – of Indrasan and Deo Tibba to the south, and the endless moonscape of Lahaul to the north – are sublime recompense. It takes 6–7hr of relentless rock-hopping and stream crossings to reach **Chatru**, on the floor of the Chandra Valley. From here, you can turn east towards Koksar and the Rohtang Pass, or west past the world's largest glacier, Bara Shigri, to **Batal**, the trailhead for the Chandratal–Baralacha trek (see p.487).

Nagar to Jari, via the Chandrakani Pass and Malana

Combining grandiose scenery with varied landscapes and flora, the hike to Jari in the Parvati Valley from Nagar, 21km south of Manali, is quintessential Kullu Valley trekking. At a pinch, the round trip can be completed in three days, but you may be tempted to linger in Malana, to explore the roadless and rugged country to the northeast. A **guide** is essential for this trek, both because the first stage involves crossing a maze of grazing trails, and because Malana is a culturally sensitive spot requiring some familiarity with local customs. Note too that the descent to the Parvati Valley is too steep for pack ponies; porters are available in Nagar (through the *Alliance* and *Sheetal* guest houses), or in Manali.

Beginning at **Nagar**, **Day 1** follows a well-marked track up to the village of Rumsu where cheeky children dash between wooden houses, and then winds through wonderful old-growth forests of mixed chestnut, walnuts, pines and huge *deodar* cedars. The open pasture just above the treeline makes ideal camping ground. **Day 2** starts with a 4km climb up to the **Chandrakani Pass** (3660m), which has fine views west over the top of the Kullu Valley to the peaks surrounding Solang Nala, and north to the Ghalpo mountains of Lahaul. Some people walk to the base of the pass on the first day, camping below the final ascent.

Reached after a steep 7km descent from the pass, **MALANA** comprises seventy or so double-storey timber and stone houses, in three separate areas according to caste. Its inhabitants, distinguished by their plain-black-fronted homespun caps and unique Tibetan-based dialect, are famed for their frostiness, and a staunchly traditional way of life, which remains as far from the mainstream as the village does from the nearest road. Although traditional notions of **caste pollution** (the root of the locals' legendary reluctance to interact with outsiders) are not as strictly adhered to as they once were, you should observe a few basic "**rules**" while in Malana: wait to be invited into the village before you enter; stick to the paths at all times; keep away from the temple; and don't, above all, touch anybody or anything, especially not children or houses. If you do commit a cultural blunder, you'll be expected to make amends: usually in the form of a cash payment for a compensatory sacrificial offering of a young sheep or goat to the village deity, **Jamlu**. One of the most powerful of all the Kullu Valley's gods, Malana's imageless deity is as xenophobic as his devotees. During Dussehra (see p.471), he alone is exempt from paying tribute to the omnipotent Raghunathji, remaining on the far bank of the Beas throughout the week's festivities. His **temple**, only open to high-caste Hindus, is decorated with lively folk carvings, among them images of soldiers – the villagers claim to be the area's sole remaining descendants of Alexander the Great's army. Jamlu also presides over Malana's council of elders, which convenes on the large flat slab of grey rock in the centre of the village; the smaller rock nearby is used exclusively for Jamlu's *gaur*.

In spite of Malana's inhospitable air, a couple of trekkers' **guest houses** have sprung up. *Santu Ram's* (①), in the middle of the Harijan quarter, is the most popular, as its owner is an authority on local trails. Or ask someone to show you to the Pradhan, or village headman's house, part of which has been converted into a small hostel (①). Both offer simple meals. The official campground, the usual stopping place for trekking parties, lies 100m beyond the village spring.

The third and **final stage** of the trek takes you down the sheer limestone and scrub-strewn sides of Malana *nala* to the floor of the Parvati Valley – a precipitous 12km drop. From the hamlet of **Rashol**, you have a choice of three onward routes: either head east up the right bank of the river to **Manikaran** (see p.473); follow the trail southwest to the sacred **Bijli Mahadev Mandir** (see p.472); or climb the remaining 3km up to the road at **Jari**, from where regular buses leave for Bhuntur, Kullu and Manali.

Rose Garden Cafe, next to HPTDC baths. Attached to the small hotel. A good range of moderately-priced food, served in a pleasant garden or in the homely dining hall.

LAHAUL AND SPITI

Few places on earth can mark so dramatic a change in landscape as the **Rohtang Pass**. To one side, the lush green head of the Kullu Valley; to the other, an awesome vista of bare, chocolate-coloured mountains, hanging glaciers and snowfields that shine in the dazzlingly crisp light. The district of **LAHAUL and SPITI**, Himachal's largest, is named after its two sub-divisions, which are, in spite of their numerous geographical and cultural similarities, distinct and separate regions.

Lahaul, sometimes referred to as the Chandra–Bhaga Valley, is the massive trough that divides the Great Himalaya and Pir Panjal ranges. Its principal river, the Chandra, rises deep in the barren wastes below the **Baralacha Pass**, a major landmark on the Manali–Leh road, from where it flows south, veering northwest around the base of the immense **Bara Shigri glacier** towards its confluence with the River Bhaga near Tandi. Here, the two rivers become the Chenab, and crash north out of Himachal to Kishtwar in Kashmir. Lahaul's **climate** is very similar to that of Ladakh and Zanskar, which border it to the north. Beyond the reach of the monsoon, the valley sees little rain in summer, when the sun is strong, and the nights cool. Between late October and late March, heavy snow closes the passes, and seals off the region. Even so, its inhabitants, a mixture of Buddhists and Hindus, enjoy one of the highest per capita incomes in the subcontinent. Using glacial water channelled down the mountains through ancient irrigation ducts, Lahauli farmers manage to coax a bumper crop of **seed potatoes** from their painstakingly fashioned terraces. The region is also the sole supplier of **hops** to India's breweries, and harvests prodigious quantities of wild herbs, used to make perfume and medicine. Much of the profit generated by these cash crops is spent on lavish jewellery, especially seed-pearl necklaces and coral and turquoise-inlaid silver plaques, worn by the women over ankle-length burgundy or fawn woollen dresses.

Lahaul's traditional costume and Buddhism are a legacy of the Tibetan influence that has permeated the region from the east, along the course of the River **Spiti**. From its headwaters below the **Kunzum Pass**, the Spiti drains 130km southeast to within a yak's cough of the border of Chinese-occupied Tibet, where it meets the Sutlej. The valley itself, surrounded by huge peaks and with an average altitude of 4500m, is one of the highest and remotest inhabited places on earth – a desolate, barren tract scattered with tiny whitewashed mud-and-timber hamlets and lonely lamaseries.

Until 1992, Spiti in its entirety lay off-limits to foreign tourists. Now, only its far southeastern corner falls within the "**Inner Line**" – which leaves upper Spiti, including the district headquarters **Kaza**, freely accessible from the northwest via Lahaul. If you are really keen to complete the loop through the restricted area to or from Kinnaur (see p.446), you can do so with a **special permit**, issued only to groups of four or more organized through HPTDC, or a government-approved travel agent (see p.438).

One of the main incentives to splash out on a "jeep safari" through the restricted zone is the chance to visit **Tabo** *gompa*, which harbours some of the oldest and most exquisite Buddhist art in the world. It is one of several *gompas* in Spiti believed to have been founded by **Rinchen Zangpo**, the "Great Translator" who imported Buddhism to western Tibet (Guge) in the tenth and eleventh centuries. The others are even further off the beaten track, tucked away in side valleys. Getting to them is half the fun: footpaths and mule tracks to the more remote areas offer some of India's best **trekking**.

Getting around

State buses run from Manali up the Chandra and Bhaga Valleys to Keylong and Darcha from whenever the Rohtang Pass is cleared, usually in late June, until it snows up again

TREKKING IN LAHAUL AND SPITI

If you have come to the Himalayas to hike across high passes and vast scree-covered mountainsides, you'll be spoiled for choice in **Lahaul** and **Spiti**. The old trade routes to Ladakh and Tibet may have been tarmacked, but most of this remote and spectacular region is still only accessible on foot. Its trails, though well-frequented in high season, are long, hard and high, punctuated by few settlements, so you must be self-sufficient in food, fuel, ponies, and take along a guide. Packhorses and provisions are most readily available in **Manali**; or **Keylong** and **Darcha** (Lahaul) and **Kaza** (Spiti) if you can afford to wait around for a few days. A good rope for stream crossings is also essential on many of the routes, particularly in mid- and late summer after the snow bridges have melted.

The **best time** to trek is from July to early September, when brilliant blue skies make this an ideal alternative to the monsoon-prone Kullu Valley. By late September, the risk of snowfall deters many visitors from embarking on longer expeditions. Whenever you leave, allow enough time to acclimatize to the **altitude** before attempting any big passes: AMS (Acute Mountain Sickness) claims victims here every season (see *Basics*, p.48).

Altitude problems are common on the most popular route: from **DARCHA** in the Bhaga Valley over the **Shingo La** pass (5090m) to Zanskar. The trailhead, on the main highway, can be reached by bus from Manali, 145km south. The trail itself winds up the east bank of the Barai or Khade *nala* over the pass to **Kurgiakh**, the highest village in Zanskar. It can be completed in three stages, with a recommended extra day's acclimatization at Shingo La base camp if this is your first trek at altitude. From Kurgiakh, it takes seven more days to hike down the Tsarap Lingti Valley to **Padum**. Among the more amazing sights en route is the famous **Phuktal gompa**, a 4hr side trip from the main path. In recent years, a string of "hotels" (temporary *chai* stalls-cum-tent camps) have sprung up at one-day intervals along the well-marked path, making it possible to dispense with ponies and guides. This may be a safe way to trek in July and August, but you should definitely not bank on finding food and shelter here at the start or end of the season. In September 1988, a party of ten inexperienced trekkers travelled too light and were killed when a freak blizzard caught them on the notoriously snow-prone Shingo La.

Lahaul's other old-favourite trekking route, which follows the River Chandra north to its source at the **Baralacha Pass** (5100m), makes a good extension to the Hampta Pass hike described on p.484. Alternatively, catch the daily Kaza bus from Manali to the trailhead at **Batal**, a checkpoint and *chai* stop below Kunzum La. About 3km beyond the bridge, a track peels left off the main road to climb towards the beautiful milky-blue **Chandratal** ("Moon") **Lake**, a relentless 7hr slog from Batal. The ascent is enlivened by stunning views south across the world's longest glacier, **Bara Shigri**, and the forbidding north face of the **White Sail** massif (6446m). If you struggled for breath during the first stage, spend the second day acclimatizing with gentle side hikes around the lake before continuing up the valley to the next campground at **Tokping Yongma** torrent. Stage four of the trek takes 6–8hr, depending on how swollen the streams are: ask the Gaddis to show you the best crossing points, and always use a rope. **Tokpo Yongma**, the second of the two big side torrents, is particularly tricky. Most trekkers camp on its south bank and then ford it early in the morning of the final day, a steady climb up to the Baralacha Pass.

From **BARALACHA LA**, crossed by the Manali–Leh highway, catch a bus south to Keylong and the Kullu Valley, or continue north on foot to pick up the trail to Zanskar via the 5435m **Phirtse La** – a challenging alternative to the Darcha–Shingo La–Kurgiak route above. This 10-day trek involves lots of difficult stream crossings and strenuous climbing, and should only be attempted by experienced trekkers. If you travel direct to the trailhead from Manali, take acclimatization breaks after each ascent.

SPITI, a day's bus ride east of the Rohtang Pass, offers fewer appealing long-distance routes. One exception is the **Pin Valley** trek. Starting 24km southeast of Kaza, a trail heads south along the right bank of the River Pin past a string of traditional settlements and monasteries to **Ghurguru**, where it forks in two: the northern path over the Pin-Parvati Pass (4802m) to **Manikaran** in the Parvati Valley (see p.473), and the southern one to Wangtu in **Kinnaur** via the Bhaba Pass (4865m). For more details, see p.449.

in late October. You can also travel through Lahaul on private Leh-bound buses if there are free seats. Traffic to Kaza in Spiti is much lighter, although one bus leaves Manali each morning in summer while Kunzum La is open. The only other way to get around is on foot, or by renting a **jeep** from HPTDC or a reliable travel agency.

Keylong

Lahaul's largest settlement, **KEYLONG**, 114km north of Manali, is a good place to pause on the long road journey to Ladakh. Although of little interest itself, the village lies amid superb scenery, within a day's climb of three large Buddhist **gompas**, visible on the opposite (south) side of the grandiose Bhaga Valley. A couple of basic **stores** sell trekking supplies if you are heading off towards Zanskar.

Lahauli Buddhists consider it auspicious to make a clockwise circumambulation – known as the **Rangcha Parikarma** – of the sacred **Rangcha mountain** (4565m), which soars above the confluence of the Bhaga and Chandra rivers. A well-worn trail that makes a long day hike from Keylong, the route is highly scenic, and takes in the **Khardung gompa** along the way. Rising over 1000m from its base elevation (3348m), the trail is a hard slog if you haven't acclimatized, and should not be undertaken lightly. Carry plenty of food, water, and warm clothing, and be prepared to turn back if you start to feel dizzy and/or acutely short of breath.

Practicalities

Keylong is connected by regular state **buses** to Manali, and (in summer) by private buses to all points north and south along the main highway. Note that onward **transport to Leh** can be difficult to arrange in high season (July & Aug), as most buses are full by the time they get there. Travellers frequently find themselves having to ride on the roof, or hitch a lift on one of the trucks that stop at the *dhabas* on the roadside above the village: neither legal, nor particularly safe.

HPTDC's *Tourist Bungalow* (①–③) has three en-suite doubles, dorms, and tents. Among the numerous places around the bottom of the village, the *Gyespa Hotel*'s basic doubles (②) come with attached shower-toilets. Ten minutes further down the lane is the newer, posher *Dikyid Hotel* (④). All serve simple meals if given advance warning.

Kaza

KAZA, the sub-divisional headquarters of **Spiti**, lies 76km southeast of the Kunzum Pass, overlooking the left bank of the river. Accessible in summer by direct daily buses from Manali (leaving at 5am), 201km southwest, this is the region's main market and roadhead, and a good base from which to explore the remote settlements and monasteries nearby. If you plan to do any **trekking** in the region, Kaza is the place to pick up porters and ponymen: rates are comparable with Kullu. Of the **places to stay** in the old Spitian quarter, the best are *Milarepa's* (②), and *Sakya's Abode* (②) next door, both friendly family-run guest houses that offer modest, clean rooms, and meals. Also worth trying are the Electricity Board *Rest Houses* (④) in the newer part of town.

Kyi gompa

Set against a backdrop of snow-flecked mountains and ochre and brown cliffs, **KYI GOMPA**, whose white buildings stick limpet-like to the steep sides of a windswept conical hillock, is a picture-book example of Tibetan architecture, and one of Himachal's most exotic spectacles. Founded in the sixteenth century, Kyi (pronounced "Kee") is the largest **monastery** in the Spiti Valley, supporting a thriving community of *lamas* whose Rinpoche, Lo Chien Tulk from Nako village in Kinnaur (see p.450), is said to be the current incarnation of the "Great Translator" Rinchen Zangpo. His glass-fronted quarters crown the top of the complex, reached via crumbling stone steps that wind between the *lamas'* houses below. A monk carrying a bunch of old Tibetan-style keys will lead you around a labyrinth of dark passages and wooden staircases to the prayer and assembly halls, where you'll be shown collections of old *thangkas*, weapons, musical instruments, manuscripts, and devotional images.

Kyi lies 12km northwest of Kaza by road, and can be reached in summer by bus (every other day). To get the full force of its dramatic southern aspect, walk at least the last part of the trip, or better still **walk** all the way, along the nine-kilometre footpath.

Kibber

KIBBER (4205m) is reputedly the highest settlement in the world with a motorable road and electricity. Jeep tracks, satellite dishes and the odd tin-roofed government building aside, its smattering of a hundred or so old Spitian houses is very picturesque. Surrounded in summer by lush green barley fields, Kibber also stands at the head of a trail that picks its way north across the mountains, via the high **Parang La** pass (5578m) to Ladakh. Before the construction of roads into the Spiti Valley, locals used to lead ponies and yaks this way to trade in Leh bazaar. These days only the old folks in the village know the path, which is used by shepherds as a route to the pastures above.

Without your own vehicle, the only way to get to Kibber from Kaza, 16km southeast, is to catch the bus that lumbers up the mountain every two days during the summer, or to hike. There are no *pukka* guest houses in the village.

Tabo

If you are lucky enough to get your hands on an **Inner Line permit** for the journey through eastern Spiti and Kinnaur, don't miss **TABO gompa**, 46km east of Kaza. The mud and timber boxes that nestle on the steep north bank of the Spiti may look drab, but the multi-hued murals and stucco sculpture they contain are some of the world's richest and most important ancient Buddhist art treasures: the link between the cave paintings of Ajanta, and the more exuberant tantric art that flourished in Tibet five centuries or so later. According to an inscription in its main assembly hall, the monastery was established in 996 AD, when **Rinchen Zangpo**, an emissary of King Yeshe Od of Guge, was disseminating *dharma* across the northwestern Himalaya. In addition to the 158 Sanskrit Buddhist texts he personally transcribed, the "Great Translator" brought with him a retinue of Kashmiri artisans to decorate the temples. The only surviving examples of their exceptional work are here at Tabo, at Alchi in Ladakh, and Toling and Tsaparam *gompas* in Chinese-occupied western Tibet.

Enclosed within a mud-brick wall, Tabo's **Chogskhar**, or "sacred enclave", contains eight temples and a scattering of twenty-four *chortens* (*stupas*). The largest and oldest structure in the group, the **Sug Lhakhang**, stands opposite the main entrance. Erected at the end of the tenth century, the "Hall of the Enlightened Gods" was conceived in the form of a three-dimensional *mandala*, whose structure and elaborately decorated interior functions as a kind of magical diagram of the universe and its constituent deities. Scan the side walls with your flashlight (don't use a camera flash: they damage the murals), and you can make out three distinct bands of detail. The paintings on the lower level depict episodes in the life of the Buddha and his previous incarnations; above are stucco gods and goddesses, while strung around the top of the hall are lines of meditating Buddhas and *bodhisattvas*. The giant four-armed figure in front of the altar, lit by butter lamps, is **Vairacana**, a manifestation of the primordial Buddha.

The other temples, which the *lama* will unlock for you, date from the fifteenth and eighteenth centuries. Their contents illustrate the development of Buddhist iconography from its early Indian origins to the Chinese-influenced opulence of medieval Tibetan tantricism that still, in a more lurid form, predominates in modern *gompas*.

You can **stay** at Tabo in the *PWD Rest House* (③), or at the monastery, where the monks keep a couple of simple rooms for visitors (leave a donation). The new *gompa*, inaugurated by the Dalai Lama in 1983, houses thirty or so *lamas* and a handful of *chomos* (nuns), some of whom receive training in traditional painting techniques under a *geshe*, or teacher from eastern Tibet.

The Manali–Leh Highway

Since it opened to foreign tourists in 1989, the famous **MANALI–LEH HIGHWAY** has deservedly replaced the old Srinagar–Kargil route as the most popular approach to Ladakh. In summer, a stream of clapped-out government buses, private mini-buses and *Enfield* motorcycles set off from the Kullu Valley to travel along the second highest road in the world, which reaches a dizzying altitude of 5328m. Its surfaces vary wildly, from bumpy asphalt to dirt tracks sliced by glacial streams, running through a starkly beautiful lunar wilderness peopled only by nomadic shepherds, tar-covered road coolies, and the gloomy soldiers that man the isolated military checkpoints.

Depending on road conditions, the 485-kilometre journey can take anything from twenty-six to thirty hours. Bus drivers cover more distance on the first day than the second, stopping for a short and chilly night in one of the "**tent camps**" along the route. These, however, are few and far between after September 15, when the highway officially closes. In practice, all this means is that the Indian government won't airlift you out if you get trapped in snow; plenty of companies run regardless. For more details on **transport** between Manali and Leh, see p.482.

Manali to Keylong

Having made its way past the bleak military installations and wayside settlements above **Manali**, the road crosses the Beas to begin its long ascent of the **ROHTANG PASS** (3978m). The views over the eternal snows of Solang *nala* improve as you progress up the switchbacks, which emerge from the conifers to enter grassy mountain pastures strewn with glacial debris and grazed by herds of *dzos* and wild horses. Just below the pass proper, the buses pull in for breakfast at a row of makeshift *dhabas*. Nearby, a modern Hindu temple, reached via a flight of steps, crowns the top of a bluff from where you get a great panorama of the upper Beas Valley. Though not all that high by Himalayan standards, Rohtang itself, a U-shaped defile between two 5000-metre peaks, is one of the most treacherous passes in the region. Each year, Gaddis and mountaineers are caught unawares by sudden weather changes; hence the vultures wheeling overhead, and Rohtang's name, which literally means "piles of dead bodies". A road-builders' beacon tells you when you've reached the top, upstaged by the breathtaking vista of the dusty dark-brown mountains of **Lahaul** to the north.

The descent from Rohtang to the floor of the **Chandra Valley** affords tantalizing glimpses of the shining White Sail massif (6446m) in the east. **KOKSAR**, where the road finally reaches the river, is little more than a scruffy collection of *chai* stalls with a **checkpoint** where you have to enter your passport details in a ledger – one of many such stops on the road to Leh. At the height of the season in 1993, hundreds of tourists and truckers were trapped here when a freak snow storm blocked the highway: a sobering thought given the normally benign blue skies of the Lahauli summer.

The next few hours are some of the most memorable on the entire trip. Bus seats on the left are best, as the road runs across the northern slopes of the valley through the first Buddhist settlements, hemmed in by towering peaks and hanging glaciers. A sharp descent around the base of the sacred **Rangcha** mountain (see p.488) brings you to the Chandra–Bhaga confluence at **Tandi**, after which the road crosses the river on a Bailey bridge and veers north along the Bhaga Valley to **Keylong** (see p.488).

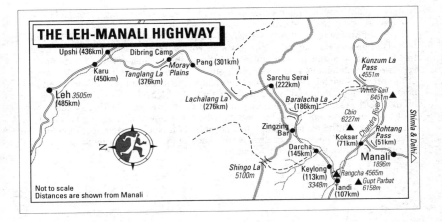

Keylong to Sarchu Serai

Beyond Keylong, the Bhaga valley broadens, but its bare sides support very few villages. By the time you reach **Darcha**, a lonely cluster of dry stone huts and tent camps on the edge of a vast pebbly river confluence, the landscape is utterly denuded. All buses stop here for passengers to grab a hot bowl of Tibetan *thukpa* from a wayside *dhaba*. There's little else to do in Darcha, which would be the definitive one-horse frontier post were it not for all the ponies hanging around on its outskirts near the Shingo La trailhead – the main trekking route north to Zanskar (see p.487 and p.523).

From Darcha, the road climbs steadily northeast across mountain sides of wine-red and pale-green scree. **Zingzing Bar** must be the ultimate punishment posting for Indian soldiers, so be patient if they take their time perusing your passport. However, if you thought Zingzing Bar was desolate, **Baralacha La** will blow your mind. A windswept vale of red-brown rock and grit splashed with streaks of snow, the "four-roads" or "twelve-horned" pass forms the head of three valleys, the Bhaga, the Chandra, and the Yunan, which fall away from its sides in different directions. The only shelter for miles is a couple of corrugated iron government huts.

By the time you get to **Sarchu Serai** you'll be more than ready for your bed, which is likely to be a piece of lumpy ground in a tent made from army-surplus parachutes. HPTDC's *Tent Camp* (①) serves steaming plates of *dal*, rice and *subzi*, in competition with a handful of similarly priced *dhabas* nearby.

Sarchu Serai to Tanglang La

After September 15, Sarchu Serai packs up for the season. Northbound buses have therefore to press on over **Langlacha La** (5059m), the second highest pass on the highway, to the tent camp at **Pang**, which stays open longer. Unfortunately, this means a drive through one of the most dramatic stretches of the route in darkness, arriving at the *serai*, a row of parachute *dhabas* beside a stream at the foot of parched yellow hills, late at night. Nor is the site, at just under 4500m, a sensible place to spend the night if you have come direct from Manali – a net elevation gain of around 2500m.

The army camp at Pang, 3km north of the *serai*, stands at the far southern end of the extraordinary **Moray Plains**: a 45-kilometre-long plateau encircled by rolling hills and, nosing up above them, brilliant white Himalayan peaks. This serene Tibetan landscape is the domain of nomadic *pashima*-rearing herdsmen who migrate here from Rupsu in eastern Ladakh each summer. Look out too for wild ass, po-faced marmots, and the elusive blue sheep (*nabu*) that graze the open grassland.

North of Moray is the dismal **Dibring Camp** where, when they are not bent over barrels of boiling tar, ragged gangs of Bihari roadworkers sit around sipping whisky tea. In a land of a million miserable occupations, theirs must surely rank among the very worst: maintaining a high-altitude highway that never recovers from the ravages of the previous winter. After Dibring, the road starts its ascent of the fourth and final pass. At a head-spinning 5328m, **Tanglang La** is the highest point on the Manali–Leh highway. Drivers pull in at the top for you to visit the "Government Urinals", and to have your photograph taken beside the beacon, whose run-down of Tanglang La's vital statistics ends with the exclamation: "Unbelievable! Is It Not". Staring north beyond the thicket of multicoloured prayer flags across Ladakh to the Karakoram range, just visible on the horizon, you may well agree.

CHAPTER SIX

LADAKH

L ADAKH, the far-flung eastern corner of troubled **Jammu & Kashmir** state, is India's most remote and sparsely populated region: a high-altitude desert cradled by the Karakoram and Great Himalaya ranges, and criss-crossed by line upon line of razor-sharp peaks and ridges. To government servants and soldiers from the plains, charged with the unenviable task of guarding its fragile frontiers with China and Pakistan, this barren, breathless land is a punishment posting. For tourists, however, it offers the chance to experience at first hand a landscape and culture that, until 1974, had only been glimpsed by a few intrepid Western travellers.

Far beyond the reach of the monsoons, Ladakh receives little snow, and less rain (the same amount as the Sahara). Only the most frugal methods enable its inhabitants to farm the thin sandy soil, frozen solid for eight months of the year and scorched by searing sun for the other four. Nourished by meltwater channelled through elaborate irrigation ditches, a single crop of barley (roasted to make the staple **ngamphe**) is sown and harvested between late June and the first October frosts. At lower altitudes, where neat terraced fields are vivid green splashes against the bare rock and mica-flecked scree slopes, this is supplemented by fast-growing strains of wheat, garden vegetables, apricots and walnuts. Higher up, the relentless chill and steep gradients render agriculture impossible, and villagers depend on animals – yaks, goats, sheep and *dzos* (a hybrid of the yak and the domestic cow) – for wool, milk and butter to barter or sell for grain and fuel. Despite the harsh conditions, Ladakhis are unfailingly cheerful and courteous. Rarely do you pass villagers on a trail or working the fields without a chorus of "julay! julay!", the Ladakhi word for "hello" (or "goodbye").

Variously described as "Little Tibet" or "the last Shangri-La", **La-Dags** – "land of high mountain passes" – is one of the last enclaves of Mahayana **Buddhism**, Ladakh's principal religion for nearly a thousand years, now brutally suppressed by the Chinese in its native Tibet. Except near the Kashmiri border, the outward symbols of Buddhism are everywhere: strings of multicoloured prayer flags flutter from the roof tops of houses, while bright prayer wheels and whitewashed *chortens* (the regional equivalent of *stupas*) guard the entrances to even the tiniest settlements. More impressive and mysterious still are Ladakh's medieval **monasteries**. Perched on rocky hilltops and clinging to sheer cliffs, **gompas** are both repositories of ancient wisdom and living centres of worship, whose gloomy prayer halls and ornate shrines harbour remarkable art treasures: giant brass Buddhas, *thangkas*, libraries of antique Tibetan manuscripts, weird musical instruments, and painted walls that writhe with fierce tantric divinities.

The highest concentration of monasteries is in the Indus Valley near **Leh**, the region's capital. Surrounded by sublime landscapes and crammed with hotels, guest houses, and restaurants, this atmospheric little town, a staging post on the old Silk Route, is most visitors' point of arrival and an ideal base for side trips. West of Leh, beyond the windswept **Fatu La** and **Namika La** passes, Buddhism peters out as you approach the predominantly Muslim district of **Kargil**. Ladakh's second largest town, at the mouth of the breathtakingly beautiful **Suru Valley**, marks the halfway stage of the journey to or from Srinagar, and is the jumping-off point for **Zanskar**, the vast and virtually road-free wilderness in the far south of the state that forms the border with Lahaul in Himachal Pradesh.

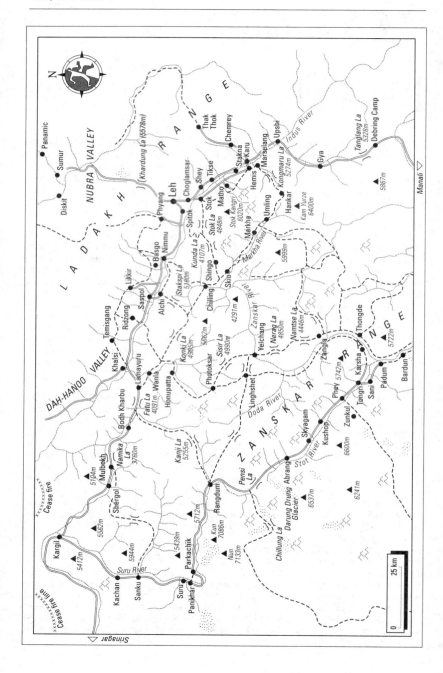

LADAKH TRAVEL DETAILS

To and from LEH	Flights	
Delhi	4 weekly	1hr 15min–3hr
Jammu	3 weekly	1hr
Srinagar	1 weekly	45min

To and from LEH	Buses	
Alchi	1 daily	3hr
Chemrey	2 daily	2hr
Dah	1 daily	9hr
Diskit	1 weekly	6hr
Hemis	1–2 daily	1hr 45min
Lamayuru	1–2 daily	6hr 30min
Likkir	1 daily	3hr
Manali	6–8 daily	28hr
Matho	1 daily	1hr
Panamik	2 weekly	10hr
Phyang	3 daily	1hr 15min

To and from LEH	Buses (continued)	
Shey	hourly	30min
Spitok	4 hourly	20min
Srinagar	1–2 daily except Sun	24hr
Stok	3 daily	45min
Temisgang	1 daily	5hr
Thak Thok	3 daily	2hr 30min
Tikse	hourly	45min

To and from Kargil	Buses	
Drass	2–3 daily	2hr
Mulbekh	2–3 daily	1hr 30min
Padum	2 weekly	18hr
Panikhar	2 daily	3hr
Sankhu	3 daily	1hr 30min
Srinagar	1–2 daily	12hr

The bus details here apply between July 1 and September 15 only.

Two main "highways" connect Ladakh with the rest of India. Due to the unrest in Kashmir, the legendary Srinagar–Leh road now sees far less traffic than the route up from **Manali**, almost 500km south. These two, plus the track from Kargil to Padum in Zanskar, also link the majority of Ladakh's larger settlements with the capital.

Bus services along the main Indus Valley highway are frequent and reliable, but grow less so the further you get from Leh. To get to and from off-track side valleys and villages within a single day, it is much easier to splash out on an *Ambassador* or a jeep **taxi**, available in Kargil and Leh. The alternative, and more traditional, way to get around the region, of course, is on foot. Popular **treks**, which you can organize yourself or through an agency, range from sedate two-day hikes through roadless villages, to gruelling long-distance routes across the mountains to Zanskar, and beyond.

Unless you fly direct to Leh (the world's highest airport), the decision of **when to visit** Ladakh is largely made for you: the passes into the region are only open between late June and late October, when the sun is at its strongest and the weather pleasantly warm. Even then, the nights can be chilly, so bring a sleeping bag. From November onwards, temperatures drop fast, often plummeting to -40°C between December and February, when the only way in and out of Zanskar is along the frozen surface of the river. Another reason to come in summer is to make arguably the most spectacular road journey in the world. The hour-long flight over the Himalayas may be memorable, but is no substitute for the two-day trip from Manali (see p.476) – a crash-course in just how remote and extraordinary this lonely mountain kingdom really is.

History

The first inhabitants of Ladakh are thought to have been a mixture of nomadic herdsmen from the Tibetan plateau and a small contingent of early Buddhist refugees from northern India called the Mons. Sometime in the fourth or fifth centuries, these two groups were joined by the **Dards**, a tribe of Indo-Aryan origin who migrated southeast along the Indus Valley, bringing with them irrigation and settled agriculture.

Details of **treks** in Ladakh and Zanskar appear on p.524.

The first independent kingdom in the region was established in the ninth century by the maverick nobleman Nyima Gon, taking advantage of the chaos after the collapse of the Guge empire of western Tibet. **Buddhism**, meanwhile, had also found its way across the Himalayas from India. Disseminated by the wandering sage-apostles such as Padmasambhava (alias "Guru Rinpoche"), dharma gradually displaced the pantheistic shamanism of the Bön cult (which still holds sway in remote villages north of Khalsi, near Lamayuru). The eastward expansion of the faith towards the Tibetan plateau continued in the tenth and eleventh centuries – the period later dubbed the "**Second Spreading**". Among its key proselytizers was the "Great Translator" **Rinchen Zangpo**, a scholar and missionary associated with the foundation of numerous monasteries in Ladakh, including Alchi (see p.517).

Around the fourteenth century, Ladakh passed through a dark age during which, for reasons that remain unclear, its rulers switched allegiances from Indian to Tibetan Buddhism, a form of the faith deeply invested with esoteric practices drawn from the **Tantra** texts, and possibly influenced by the animated celebrations common to Bön (see *Contexts*). This coincided with the rise to prominence in Tibet of **Tsongkhapa** (1357–1419), who is accepted as founder of the **Gelug-pa** or "Yellow Hat" school. With the Dalai Lama at its head, Gelug-pa is today the most popular school in Ladakh with many more monasteries than sects such as **Kagyu**, which is closely linked with Milarepa, a tantric practitioner (eleventh-century) whose ideas and sonnets have stuck with many Ladakhi Buddhists. Under **Tashi Namgyal** (1555–70), who re-unified the kingdom, Ladakh became a major Himalayan power, and the ascent to the throne of the "Lion", **Sengge Namgyal**, in the seventeenth century, signalled further territorial gains. After being routed by the Moghul-Balti army at Bodh Kharbu in 1639, he turned his energies to civil and religious matters, founding a new capital and palace at Leh, as well as a string of monasteries that included Hemis, seat of the newly arrived **Brugpa** sect, a branch of Kagyu school.

Sengge's building spree created some fine monuments, but it also drained the kingdom's coffers, as did the hefty annual tribute paid to the Moghuls after the Bodh Kharbu debacle. Finances were further strained when Deldan, Sengge's successor, picked a quarrel with his ally, Tibet. The fifth Dalai Lama dispatched an army of Mongolian horsemen to teach him a lesson, and three years of conflict were only ended after the Moghul governor of Kashmir intervened on Ladakh's behalf. This help, however, came at a price: Aurangzeb demanded more tribute, ordered the construction of a mosque in Leh, and forced the Ladakhi king to convert to Islam.

Trade links with Tibet resumed in the eighteenth century, but Ladakh never regained its former status. Plagued by feuds and assassinations, the kingdom teetered into terminal decline, and was an easy target for the **Dogra** (Sikh) general Zorawar Singh, who annexed it for the Maharaja of Kashmir in 1834. The Ladakhi royal family were banished to Stok palace, where they reside to this day.

Ladakh became a part of independent India in 1948, following the first of the three Indo-Pak wars fought in the region. However, both the international frontier, and the so-called "**Cease Fire Line**" that scythes through the top of Jammu & Kashmir remain "unauthenticated": even today, the two armies take periodic pot-shots at each other across the disputed Siachen Glacier in the Karakorams, 100km north. When you consider the proximity of China, another old foe who annexed a large chunk of Ladakh in 1962, it is easy to see why this is India's most sensitive border zone – and why it remained off-limits to tourists until 1974.

Today, Ladakh comprises over 60 percent of the state of Jammu & Kashmir as it stands, and like the other two state districts, the Kashmir Valley and Zanskar, has its own distinct culture, and boundaries formed by mountain ranges that have ensured independent development over several centuries. Long dissatisfied with centralized government from Srinagar, in September 1995 the Ladakhis finally saw the establishment in their region of an **Autonomous Hill Development Council**, localizing government

SUMMER FESTIVALS IN LADAKH

Most of Ladakh's Buddhist **festivals**, in which masked dance dramas are performed by *lamas* in monastery courtyards, take place in January and February, when roads into the region are snowbound. This works out well for the locals, for whom they relieve the tedium of the relentless winter, but it means that few outsiders get to experience some of the northern Himalayas' most vibrant and fascinating spectacles. Recently, however, a few of the larger *gompas* around Leh have followed the example of **Hemis** and switched their annual festivals to the summer, to attract tourists. Proceeds from ticket sales go towards maintenance and restoration work, and the construction of new shrines.

The following festivals are held in summer. Their precise dates, which vary according to the Tibetan lunar calendar, are available through the tourist office in Leh.

Hemis. The largest event of its kind draws huge crowds, and is unmissable if you are within striking distance. July 15/16, 1997; July 4/5 1998; June 23/24 1999. See p.511.

The Festival of Ladakh (early Aug). A popular J&KTDC-sponsored event; archery contests, polo matches, and traditional Ladakhi dance.

Phyang. Featuring the usual *cham* dances, and the ritual exposition of a giant *thangka*. Aug 5/6, 1997; July 25/26, 1998; July 14/15, 1999.

Tikse (late Aug). Put on primarily for tourists, but no less a spectacle than its long-established winter counterpart, one of the most dramatic events of the Ladakhi year.

control. It's hoped that Ladakh's particular needs, dictated largely by climate and tradition, will be better met under the new system. In 1995 and 1996, agitating **Zanskaris**, hoping for a similar sub-hill council, were making travel in the region awkward – it remains to be seen if demands are met and protests dropped (for more see p.523).

Leh

As you approach **LEH** for the first time, via the sloping sweep of dust and pebbles that divide it from the floor of the Indus Valley, you'll have little difficulty imagining how the old trans-Himalayan traders must have felt as they plodded in on the caravan routes from Yarkhand and Tibet: a mixture of relief at having crossed the mountains in one piece, and anticipation of a relaxing spell in one of central Asia's most scenic and atmospheric towns. Spilling out of a side valley that tapers north towards eroded snow-capped peaks, the Ladakhi capital sprawls from the foot of a ruined Tibetan-style palace – a maze of mud-brick and concrete flanked on one side by cream-coloured desert, and on the other by a swathe of lush irrigated farmland.

Leh only became regional capital in the seventeenth century, when Sengge Namgyal shifted his court here from Shey, 15km southeast, to be closer to the head of the Khardung La–Karakoram corridor into China. The move paid off: within a generation, the town had blossomed into one of the busiest markets on the Silk Road. During the 1920s and 1930s, the broad bazaar that still forms its heart received more than a dozen pony- and camel-trains each day. Leh's prosperity, managed mainly by the Sunni **Muslim** merchants whose descendants live in its labyrinthine **old quarter**, came to an abrupt end with the closure of the Chinese border in the 1950s. Only after the Indo-Pak wars of 1965 and 1971, when India rediscovered the hitherto forgotten capital's strategic value, did its fortunes begin to look up. Today, khaki-clad *jawans* (soldiers) and their families from the nearby military and air force bases are the mainstay of the local economy in winter, when foreign visitors are few and far between.

Undoubtedly the most radical shake-up, however, ensued from the Indian government's decision in 1974 to open Ladakh to foreign **tourists**. From the start, Leh bore the brunt of the annual invasion, as busloads of backpackers poured up the road from

HEALTH IN LEH: ALTITUDE SICKNESS AND DIRTY WATER

As Leh is 3505m above sea level, some travellers, and especially those who arrive by plane from Delhi, experience mild **altitude sickness**. If you develop any of the symptoms – persistent headaches, dizziness, insomnia, nausea, loss of appetite or shortness of breath – your body has not yet acclimatized to the comparative lack of oxygen in the thin Ladakhi air; don't worry, it will, probably in as little as twenty-four hours, though it can take longer. In the meantime, take it easy: drink plenty of fluids, lay off alcohol, and don't try to climb any hills for at least a couple of days. For more information, see p.48, or call the hospital's **AMS** (Acute Mountain Sickness) **hotline**: ☎560 (24hr), or ☎212/214 (daily 9am–5pm).

A health problem that affects far more travellers, however, is diarrhoea. **Dirty water** is invariably the culprit – a consequence of the grossly inadequate sewage system, which can't cope with the massive summer influx of visitors. Redouble your normal health precautions while you are here: take extra care over what you drink, and avoid salads and raw vegetables unless you know they have been cleaned in sterilized water. Many hotels now filter their own water making it perfectly safe to drink. Meat of any kind is also a no-no; most of it travels up from Srinagar in unrefrigerated trucks.

Srinagar. Twenty or so years on, though the main approach is now via Himachal Pradesh rather than Kashmir, the summer influx shows no sign of abating. Leh has doubled in size and is a far cry from the sleepy Himalayan town of the early 1970s. During July and August, tourists stroll shoulder to shoulder down its main street, most of whose old-style outfitters and provision stores have been squeezed out by Kashmiri handicraft shops, art emporiums, and Tibetan restaurants. A rapid increase in the number of Kashmiri traders, who have little choice but to seek business outside Kashmir, has led to recent unrest in Leh's bazaar, the first communal violence ever seen in normally peaceful Ladakh.

Leh has nonetheless retained a more tranquil side, and is a pleasant place to unwind after a long bus journey. Attractions in and around the town itself include the former **palace** and **Namgyal Tsemo gompa**, perched amid strings of prayer flags above the narrow dusty streets of the **old quarter**. A short walk north across the fields, the small monastery at **Sankar** harbours accomplished modern tantric murals and a thousand-headed Avalokitesvara deity. Leh is also a good base for longer **day trips** out into the Indus Valley. Among the string of picturesque villages and *gompas* within reach by bus are **Shey**, site of a derelict seventeenth-century palace, and the spectacular **Tikse gompa**. Until you have adjusted to the altitude, however, the only sightseeing you'll probably feel up to will be from a guest-house roof terrace or garden, from where the snowy summits of the majestic **Stok-Kangri massif** (5508m), magnified in the crystal-clear Ladakhi sunshine, look close enough to touch.

Arrival and information

A taxi to the bazaar from Leh **airport**, 5km southwest of town on the main Srinagar highway, will set you back a fixed fare of around Rs80, or Rs100 to Changspa. In theory, an airport bus should also meet incoming flights, but don't bank on it.

State and private **buses** pull into the dusty town bus stand, fifteen minutes' walk, or a short taxi ride (Rs30) south of the bazaar and most of the hotels.

J&KTDC's **tourist reception centre** (Mon–Sat 10am–4pm; ☎2497), 3km from the bazaar on the airport road, is too far out of town and hardly worth visiting. The **Tourist Information Centre** on Fort Rd in the bazaar (Mon–Fri 10.30am–4pm, Sat 10.30am–noon), is far more helpful, with a notice board (useful for finding trekking partners), equipment to rent, and a **money changing** facility at the in-house *State Bank of India*.

The telephone **area code** for Leh is ☎01982.

The **Taxi Operators' Union** rank (daily 7am–6pm; ☎3823) is almost directly opposite. Each driver carries a list of fixed fares to just about everywhere you might want to visit in Ladakh, taking into account waiting time, *gompa* entrance fees, and night halt charges. However, these rates only apply to peak season; reductions of up to 40 percent can be had at other times. Deal directly with the drivers, or their boss in the Union office will take a cut (payable by you). Expect to pay around Rs30–40 to Changspa, Rs800 to Hemis, and Rs5000 to Nubra.

The **post office** is at the Main Bazaar (Mon–Sat 10am–1pm & 2–4pm). For parcels, go to the **GPO** (Mon–Sat 10am–4.30pm), out of town on Airport Rd, whose unreliable **poste restante** counter is tucked around the back. Trunk and international **telephone**

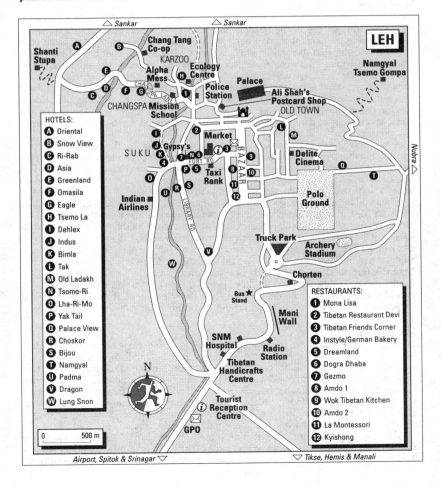

HOTELS:
- Ⓐ Oriental
- Ⓑ Snow View
- Ⓒ Ri-Rab
- Ⓓ Asia
- Ⓔ Greenland
- Ⓕ Omasila
- Ⓖ Eagle
- Ⓗ Tsemo La
- Ⓘ Dehlex
- Ⓙ Indus
- Ⓚ Bimla
- Ⓛ Tak
- Ⓜ Old Ladakh
- Ⓝ Tsomo-Ri
- Ⓞ Lha-Ri-Mo
- Ⓟ Yak Tail
- Ⓠ Palace View
- Ⓡ Choskor
- Ⓢ Bijou
- Ⓣ Namgyal
- Ⓤ Padma
- Ⓥ Dragon
- Ⓦ Lung Snon

RESTAURANTS:
- ❶ Mona Lisa
- ❷ Tibetan Restaurant Devi
- ❸ Tibetan Friends Corner
- ❹ Instyle/German Bakery
- ❺ Dreamland
- ❻ Dogra Dhaba
- ❼ Gezmo
- ❽ Amdo 1
- ❾ Wok Tibetan Kitchen
- ❿ Amdo 2
- ⓫ La Montessori
- ⓬ Kyishong

connections are poor: expect to be cut off at any moment. However, many shops have STD/ISD facilities, most charging higher prices than elsewhere in India.

The Town

With the mighty hulk of the palace looming to the north, it is virtually impossible to lose your bearings in Leh. The broad main bazaar runs north to south through the heart of town, dividing the labyrinthine old quarter and nearby polo ground from the greener and more spacious residential districts of **Karzoo** and **Suku** to the west. **Fort Road**, the other principal thoroughfare, turns west off the main street and then winds downhill past the taxi rank, the *Dreamland Restaurant*, and the arrival and departure point for Himachal Tourism's buses, towards the *Indian Airlines* office on the southern outskirts.

The bazaar and old town

After settling into a hotel or guest house, most visitors spend their first day in Leh soaking up the atmosphere of the **bazaar**. Sixty or so years ago, this bustling tree-lined boulevard was the busiest market between Yarkhand and Kashmir. Merchants from Srinagar and the Punjab would gather to barter for *pashima* wool brought down by nomadic herdsmen from western Tibet, or for raw silk hauled across the Karakorams on Bactrian camels. These days, though the street is awash with kitsch curio shops and handicraft emporiums, it retains a distinctly central Asian feel. Clean-shaven Ladakhi *lamas* in sneakers and shades rub shoulders with half-bearded Baltis and elderly Tibetan refugees whirring prayer wheels, while now and again, snatches of Chinese music crackle out of the shopkeepers' transistor radios. At the bottom of the bazaar, women from nearby villages, stovepipe hats perched jauntily on their heads, sit behind piles of vegetables, spinning wool and chatting as they appraise the passers-by. Even if you are not shopping for trekking supplies, check out the **provision stores** along the street, where bright pink, turquoise, and wine-red silk cummerbunds hang in the windows. Inside, sacks of aromatic spices, dried pulses, herbs and tea are stacked beside boxes of incense, soap, and spare parts for kerosene stoves.

When you have had enough of the bazaar, head past the new green-and-white-painted **Jama Masjid** at the top of the street, and follow one of the lanes that lead into the **old town**. Apart from the odd electric cable, nothing much has changed here since the warren of flat-roofed houses, crumbling *chortens*, *mani* walls, and narrow sandy streets was laid down late in the sixteenth century – least of all the plumbing. One place definitely worth picking through the putrid-smelling puddles to visit, however, is the **Chamba temple**. It's not easy to find on your own; ask at the second row of shops on the left after the big arch for the key-keeper (*gonyer*), who will show you the way. Hemmed in by dilapidated medieval mansions, the one-roomed shrine houses a colossal image of Maitreya, the Buddha to come, and some wonderful old wall paintings.

The palace

Lording it over the old town from the top of a craggy granite ridge is the derelict **palace** of the sixteenth-century ruler Sengge Namgyal (daily 7–9am; Rs5). A scaled-down version of the Potala in Lhasa, it is a textbook example of medieval Tibetan architecture, with gigantic sloping buttressed walls and projecting wooden balconies that tower nine storeys above the surrounding houses. Since the Ladakhi royal family left the palace in the 1940s, damage inflicted by nineteenth-century Kashmiri cannons has caused large chunks of it to collapse. Bring a flashlight, and watch where you walk: in spite of restoration work, holes gape in the floors and dark staircases.

Apart from the flaking murals that decorate the ruined royal apartments and state rooms on the upper levels, very few remnants of the palace's former splendour survive. The main reason to pick your way through its gutted interior is to reach the **roof ter-**

race, which offers spectacular **views** over the mud-brown rooftops of the old town to the wrinkled flanks and snow-covered ridges of the Stok-Kangri mountains.

Also worth a look as you pass is the **Dukhar temple** on the fourth storey (ask the monk to unlock it for you). The gloomy shrine, whose centrepiece is a thousand-armed image of the goddess Tara, houses eerie masks, musical instruments and weapons – props for the recitals and religious ceremonies once held in the courtyard outside.

Namgyal Tsemo gompa

Once you are acclimatized to the altitude, the stiff early-morning hike up to **Namgyal Tsemo gompa** (daily 7–9am), the monastery perched precariously on the shaly crag behind Leh palace, is a great way to start the day. Two trails lead up to "the Peak of Victory", whose twin peaks are connected by giant strings of multicoloured prayer flags; the first and most popular path zig-zags across its south side from the palace road, while a second scales the more gentle northern slope via the village of Chubi (the route followed by the *lama* from Sankar *gompa* who tends to the shrine each morning and evening). Alternatively, you could drive there along the dirt track that turns left off the main Khardung La highway, 2km north of the bus stand.

Approaching the *gompa* from the south, the first building you come to is the red-painted **Maitreya temple**. Thought to date from the fourteenth century, the shrine houses a giant Buddha statue flanked by *bodhisattvas*. However, its wall paintings are modern and of less interest than those in the **Gon-khang** (temple of protector deities) up the hill. Most famous of these, on the left of the door as you enter, is the honorary portrait of Tashi Namgyal, the temple's founder and prolific builder. In the gloomy interior, you can just make out murals of Shakyamuni (the historical Buddha) and Tsong-kha-pa, founder of the Gelug-pa sect. The veiled central deity itself sports a shiny phallus, believed to cure infertility in women.

The Shanti Stupa

A relatively new addition to the rocky skyline around Leh is the toothpaste-white **Shanti Stupa** above Changspa village, 3km west of the bazaar. Inaugurated in 1983 by the Dalai Lama, the "Peace Pagoda", whose sides are decorated with gilt panels depicting episodes from the life of the Buddha, is one of several such monuments erected around India by a "Peace Sect" of Japanese Buddhists. It can be reached by car, or on foot via a steep flight of five hundred steps, which winds up the ridge from the end of Changspa Lane. The site is particularly atmospheric at dusk, when the drums played at evening *puja* seem to set the pace of growing shadows as the sun sinks behind the mountains in the west.

The Ecology Centre

Five minutes' walk north of the main bazaar (next to the *Tsemo-La Hotel*), the **Ecology Centre** (Mon–Sat 10am–5pm) is the headquarters of LEDeG (the Ladakh Ecological Development Group) – a local non-governmental organization that aims to counter the negative impact of Western-style "development" by fostering economic independence and respect for traditional culture. This involves promoting "appropriate" technologies such as solar energy, encouraging organic farming and cottage industries, and providing education on environmental and social issues through village drama, workshops and seminars. A garden hosts an open-air exhibition of solar gadgets, hydraulic pumps, water mills and other ingenious energy-saving devices that have proved successful throughout Ladakh. There's also a small **library**, and a **handicraft shop**, selling locally made clothes, *thangkas*, T-shirts, books and postcards.

Try to catch a screening of LEDeG's short **video** *Ancient Futures: Learning From Ladakh* (check notice boards in hotels for times; usually three weekly, followed by a discussion group), which gives an insightful account of Ladakhi culture and the sweeping changes of the past thirty years, many of them direct results of tourism. Helena

Norberg Hodge, the Swedish-born founder of LEDeG who appears in the film, has written an excellent book on Ladakh's *Ancient Futures*, available at the handicraft shop.

SECMOL

SECMOL (the Students' Educational and Cultural Movement of Ladakh) was founded in 1988 by Ladakhi university students to increase awareness of developmental issues and guide younger students through a problematic educational system. At present the curriculum, devised in Srinagar and taught in Urdu and English, does not cover subjects of local relevance. In the hope of maintaining pride in Ladakh's traditions, SECMOL teaches local history and runs workshops on handicrafts, agriculture and technology. **Volunteer** help from TEFL-qualified visitors is appreciated at the summer schools run just outside Leh. If you'd like to help, or want to meet members of SECMOL, write in advance (to SECMOL, Chubi Katpa, Leh), or drop into their office on the northern outskirts of town (Mon–Sat 2–6pm; ☎3585), ten minutes' walk up the hill from *Ali Shah's Postcard Shop*.

CHORTENS AND MANI WALLS

Among the more visible expressions of Buddhism in Ladakh are the chess-pawn-shaped **chortens** at the entrance to villages and monasteries. These are the Tibetan equivalent of the Indian *stupa* (see p.363) – large hemispherical burial mounds-cum-devotional objects, prominent in Buddhist ritual since the third century BC. Made of mud and stone (now also concrete), many *chortens* were erected as acts of piety by Ladakhi nobles, and like their southern cousins, they are imbued with mystical powers and **symbolic significance**: the tall tapering spire, normally divided into thirteen sections, represents the soul's progression towards *nirvana*, while the sun cradled by the crescent moon at the top stands for the unity of opposites, and the oneness of existence and the universe. Some contain sacred manuscripts that, like the *chortens*, wither and decay in time, illustrating the central Buddhist doctrine of impermanence. Those enshrined in monasteries, however, generally made of solid silver and encrusted with semi-precious stones, contain the ashes or relics of revered *rinpoches* (incarnate *lamas*). Always pass a *chorten* in a clockwise direction: the ritual of circumambulation mimics the passage of the planets through the heavens, and is believed to ward off evil spirits. The largest array is to be found in the desert east of **Shey** (see p.509), the former capital, but look out for the giant, brightly painted specimen between the bus station and Leh bazaar, whose red spire stands out against the snowy Stok-Kangri mountains to the south.

A short way downhill from the big *chorten*, near the radio station, stands an even more monumental symbol of devotion. The 500-metre **Mani wall**, erected by King Deldan Namgyal in 1635, is one of several at important religious sites around Ladakh. Ranging from a couple of metres to over a kilometre in length, the walls are made of hundreds of thousands of stones, each inscribed with prayers or sacred *mantras* – usually the invocation *Om Mani Padme Hum*: "Hail to the Jewel in the Lotus". It goes without saying that such stones should never be removed.

Sankar gompa

Nestled amid the shimmering poplar coppices and terraced fields of barley that extend up the valley behind Leh, **Sankar gompa**, 3km north of the town centre, is among the most accessible monasteries in central Ladakh – hence its restricted visiting hours for tourists (daily 7–10am & 5–7pm; Rs10). You can get there either by car, or on foot: turn left at the junction above *Ali Shah's Postcard Shop*, and then right onto the concrete path that runs alongside the stream. Sankar appears after about twenty minutes' walk, surrounded by sun-bleached *chortens* and a high mud wall.

The monastery, a small under-*gompa* of Spitok, is staffed by twenty monks, and is the official residence of the **Kushok Bakul**, Ladkah's head of the Gelug-pa ("yellow hat") sect. Appropriately for such a high-ranking *rinpoche*, his glass-fronted penthouse enjoys pride of place on top of the main building, crowned with a golden spire and a *dharma chakra* flanked by two deer (symbolizing the Buddha's first sermon in Sarnath). A flight of steps leads from the courtyard to the **Du-khang** (main prayer hall). Beyond the Lords of the Four Quarters and Wheel of Life *mandala* that adorn the verandah, you enter a high-ceilinged hall whose walls writhe with lustrous multicoloured murals. Those on either side of the doorway are the most amazing: many-armed pot-bellied bovine monsters drink blood from skull cups, while the copulating *yab-yum* couples to the right are garlanded with severed heads and engulfed in swirling red and yellow flames.

Above the *Du-khang* stands the *gompa*'s principal deity, Tara, in her triumphant, 1000-armed form as Dukkar, or "Lady of the White Parasol", presiding over a light, airy shrine room whose walls are adorned with a Tibetan calendar and tableaux depicting "dos and don'ts" for monks – some very arcane indeed. Another flight of steps leads to the *gompa* **library** and, eventually, a roof terrace with fine views towards the north side of Namgyal Tsemo hill and the valley to the south.

Accommodation

Leh is absolutely glutted with **accommodation**, most of it refreshingly neat, clean and excellent value. Budget travellers in particular are in for a treat. Gone are the days of bedding down on dusty, tick-infested rooftops. Now most of the town's **cheap guest houses** are immaculately whitewashed traditional houses, set on the leafy outskirts, with sociable garden terraces that look onto green fields. Simple double rooms go for under Rs150, even in high season. For a little more, you can often find a sunny en-suite "glass room" with a view all to yourself. Breakfasts are usually included in the price, served at low Tibetan tables (*chogtse*) in the family kitchen, surrounded by chests full of shiny copper pots, plates and brass and wooden tea urns (*gur-gurs*).

Rooms in Leh's **mid-range hotels** come with en-suite shower-toilets and piped hot water, while **upmarket** accommodation is very poor value for money by Indian standards – unless you see wall-to-wall carpets, room service and (ecologically unsound) bath-tubs as a must. The rates below are for the high season, when they tend to be block-booked by package tour groups, and include both the 10 percent state **luxury tax**, and the extra ten percent "**service charge**" levied by the pricier places, where appropriate. Off season, prices can be slashed by as much as 60 percent.

Inexpensive

Rooms in family houses, grouped in three main areas, account for the bulk of Leh's plentiful **budget accommodation**. **Karzoo** and **Suku**, northwest of the main street, are very central but become tourist ghettos during high season; if you're after peace,

---

ACCOMMODATION PRICE CODES

All **accommodation prices** in this book have been coded using the symbols below. In principle the prices given are for the least expensive double rooms in each establishment; however, some hotels, usually in category ①, offer rates per bed rather than per room. Local taxes are not included unless specifically stated. For more details, see p.35.

① up to Rs100	④ Rs225–350	⑦ Rs750–1200
② Rs100–150	⑤ Rs350–500	⑧ Rs1200–2200
③ Rs150–225	⑥ Rs500–750	⑨ Rs2200 and upwards

quiet, idyllic countryside and mountain views, head for **Changspa** village, fifteen minutes' walk west of the bazaar. More in the thick of things are the mainly Muslim houses of the **old town**. Crouched in the shadow of Leh palace, these are cheap and full of
atmosphere, but the district's dodgy plumbing means that finding your way home after
dark through the maze of narrow unlit lanes can be a trial (especially in flip-flops).

Asia, Changspa. Large, secluded riverside guest house. Sociable terrace-cum-cafe, but no views. ④.

Bimla, Suku (☎3854). Central, though secluded, with nice rooms and plenty of space outside to
lounge around. ③.

Dehlex, Karzoo. An old favourite, now popular with long-stay foreign anthropologists. Run-of-the-
mill rooms, bucket hot water on request, and a large awning in the garden. ③.

Eagle, opposite the army mess, Changspa Lane, Changspa. Plain, but clean and long-established,
with a good-sized terrace around the back, and valley views. ③.

SHOPPING IN LEH

Between June and September, Leh is swamped by almost as many transient Tibetan and
Kashmiri traders as souvenir-hungry tourists. Most of the merchandise hawked in their
temporary boutiques and stalls comes from outside the region too: papier-mâché bowls,
shawls and carpets from Srinagar, jewellery and miniature paintings from Jaipur, and
"Himalayan" handicrafts churned out by Tibetan refugees in Old Delhi. Prices tend to be
high, so haggle hard, and don't be conned into shelling out for cleverly faked "antiques".

Tibetan and Ladakhi **curios** account for the bulk of the goods on sale in Leh's emporiums. Of these, the *Ladakh Art Palace* off the main bazaar, one of only two locally owned
and run souvenir stores, is the least pushy, and a good place to browse. Among its vast
array of articles are Tibetan trumpets (*thumpchen*), cymbals, brass and copper *chang* kettles, prayer wheels, thunderbolts (*dorjes*), *gur-gur* tea churners, *cham* dance masks,
thangkas, and coral and seed-pearl necklaces, to name but a few. If money is no object,
you could even splash out on a **perak**; the long Ladakhi headdresses, encrusted with
turquoises, cost upwards of Rs4000. Stocking fillers such as amulets, butter lamps, beads,
and cheaper silver jewellery inlaid with semi-precious stones are sold from stalls outside
the fresh produce market south of **Fort Road**. However, the best place to head for
thangkas and hand-woven **Tibetan carpets** is the *Tibetan Children's Village Handicraft
Centre*, up the hill from the GPO, which also has racks of cheap woollen Nepali-style jackets, waistcoats, and the whole gamut of "Free Tibet" stickers and posters.

For **authentic Ladakhi souvenirs**, try the outfitters and provision stores dotted
along the main bazaar. The Lahauli-run *Sonambongo Barongpa & Sons*, at the top-right
end of the street, sells traditional costume and religious paraphernalia at fixed prices. If
you've been wondering where to find those dapper stovepipe hats (*tibi*), hand-dyed *gonchas*, raw silk cummerbunds, tie-dyed rope-soled shoes (*pabbu*), Bhutanese cross-button
shirts, prayer flags, real Ladakhi incense, or even monks' robes, look no further.

The **Ecology Centre**'s handicraft shop (with a second branch at the bottom of the
bazaar) is another source of good-quality traditional clothing, including hand-knitted
woollen jumpers, hats and socks. Genuine **pashima shawls**, however, are hard to come
by; start looking in *Chang Tang Co-operative* in Karzoo, five minutes' walk up the lane
past the Ecology Centre. Run by five local women who buy wool direct from nomadic
herdsmen in eastern Ladakh, the co-op was set up to break the Kashmiri's traditional
monopoly of the *pashima* business. Even if you are not in the market for a shawl – they
start at around Rs3500 – the workshop is well worth a visit.

Easily the best **bookshop** in Leh is *Artou's*, who have two branches: one on the main
bazaar, and another between *Tibetan Restaurant Devi* and the Ecology Centre. Both stock
a fair selection of Indian *Penguin* classics, plus dozens of more expensive titles on Ladakh
and the Himalayas. Secondhand paperbacks are sold or part-exchanged at *Parkash* sta-
tioner's opposite the vegetable market. Finally, for **postcards**, black-and-white photographs of Ladakh, and stationery, visit *Ali Shah's Postcard Shop* above the main bazaar.

Greenland, Changspa. Spacious glass rooms or smaller singles downstairs, and a cosy garden. ②.

Indus, Karzoo. Cheap singles and a few doubles, with some attached bathrooms, solar-heated water on tap, and great views from the first floor. ②.

Lung Snon, 1km south of the centre past the *Indian Airlines* office. Old-style, friendly family guest house. Well-placed, but the concret garden is an eyesore. Recommended, but a bit of a walk. ③.

Namgyal, old town. Mud-and-timber town house hemmed in by crumbling *chortens* on the edge of the old town, with basic homely rooms and a newer concrete annexe. ①–②.

Old Ladakh, old town. Ladakh's first-ever guest house is homely and central, and offers a choice of rooms: the kitsch "deluxe" one (pink pillows and Tibetan rugs) is a real winner. ①–③.

Oriental, below the Shanti Stupa, Changspa Lane, Changspa. Congenial guest house with the best of everything: spotless rooms, solar-heated water, superb views, nourishing home-cooked meals, and a warm welcome. Recommended. ②–③.

Padma, off Fort Rd (☎3730). Very traditional by Leh standards: immaculate rooms, a beautiful kitchen, a garden, and mountain views. ②–③.

Palace View, old town. The cleanest of the local rock-bottom bunch. Some en-suite rooms. ①–②.

Tak, old town. Another old favourite, but boxed in beneath the palace and very grubby. Again, its (cheap) glass rooms are by far the best deal. ①–②.

Moderate and expensive

Bijou, Library Rd (☎2331). Spacious, comfortable rooms in large Ladakhi house, five minutes' walk from the centre. Breakfasts served on secluded back terrace. ⑦.

Choskor, Library Rd (☎3626). Traditional timber-frame building whose bright and airy glass rooms are an excellent deal. ⑤.

Dragon, south of the bazaar (☎2339). An ersatz traditional building close to the centre, with plush Western-style rooms ranged around a central courtyard, and a good restaurant. Recommended. ⑦.

Lha-Ri-Mo, Old Leh Rd (☎2377). Tasteful, palatial, repro mansion on the outskirts. Very swish. ⑦.

Ri-Rab, Changspa Lane. Stolid modern hotel with crisp cotton sheets and rooftop views. ⑥–⑦.

Snow View, Karzoo Lane. New, purpose-built hotel on the western outskirts, with superlative views from its large first-floor rooms. Easy road access and parking. Often booked up a year in advance for the summer festival. ⑧.

Tsemo La, near the Ecology Centre (☎2281). A rambling "A"-class hotel: comfortable rooms, lots of garden space, and directors' chairs on a scruffy lawn. ⑦.

Tsomo-Ri, Fort Rd (☎2471). Big and bland, but very central, and with its own generator and reliable water supply. Recommended. ⑧.

Yak Tail (☎2318). Slap in the centre of town, and with most amenities, including money changing and a pricey restaurant that hosts weekly culture shows. ⑦.

Eating

As Leh's thriving restaurant and cafe scene has been cornered by the refugee community, **Tibetan food** has a high profile, alongside tourist-oriented Chinese and European dishes. The most popular Tibetan dish is *momos* – crescent-shaped pasta shells, stuffed with meat, cheese, or vegetables, and (if you're lucky) ginger, then steamed and served with hot soup and spicy sauce. Fried *momos* are called *kothays*. *Thukpa*, another wholesome favourite, is broth made from fresh pasta strips, meat and vegetables. These, and dozens of variations, are dished up in swanky tourist restaurants such as the legendary *Dreamland*, but you can tuck into bigger portions of the same stuff (for a fraction of the price) at modest backstreet "*momo* kitchens".

Most visitors have **breakfast** in their hotel or guest house, where the host family cook small round loaves of Ladakhi wheat-flour bread (*tagi shamos*), eaten piping hot with honey, or jam, and butter. For a truly authentic Leh breakfast, grab a couple of flatbreads from the clay-oven bakeries on the narrow lane at the top of the bazaar; the Tibetan restaurateurs don't mind you turning up with your own. If you fancy a change, apple-pie-and-chocolate-brownie **pastry shops** are dotted all over town.

Finally, the the *Hotel Ibex* and the **liquor store** opposite the taxi stand sell beer. **Chang**, a local barley brew, is harder to come by: ask at your guest house if they can get some in for you. If you're desperate, you might manage to find your way to one of the illegal hole-in-the-wall chang bars tucked away in the backstreets behind the bazaar – not recommended for sensitive stomachs.

Amdo, Main Bazaar. Two Tibetan restaurants overlooking the main street. The one on the east side catches the morning sun, and serves hearty *tsampa* porridge for breakfast.

Dogra Dhaba, Fort Rd (opposite *Dreamland*). Spicy vegetarian Punjabi food at low prices, including beans, *dal*-fry, hot *rotis*, and tasty *tikkis* (potato patties), served up on tin plates.

Dreamland, Fort Rd. A perennial favourite and easily Leh's most popular all-rounder, even though the food is so-so, and pricey.

German Bakery, Fort Rd, Suku. Sister business to its Manali namesake, equally well-stocked with home-baked chocolate cakes, apple strudel, and wholewheat bread.

Gezmo, Fort Rd. Inexpensive street-side cafe popular with postcard and diary scribblers, mainly for its coffee and European breakfasts.

Ibex, Fort Rd (opposite taxi stand). Superb Indian food and a bar for beer and generous measures of spirits.

Instyle, adjoining the *German Bakery* on Fort Rd. Laid-back terrace restaurant. Wholefood breakfasts (muesli, curd, honey), and the standard greasy fried egg option, plus passable espressos, and Chinese meals (tasty garlic-fried noodles) served to tourists under an old parachute.

Kyishong, south of the main bazaar. Arguably the best cheap Tibetan joint in town run by a smiling old chap and his teenage side kick. Groaning portions of freshly cooked food, and as much jasmine tea as you can drink for free. Recommended.

La Montessori, Main Bazaar. Coir mats and minimal decor, but mouth-watering cheese *kothays* figure among the many inexpensive Tibetan dishes.

Mona Lisa, off Changspa Lane, near the Ecology Centre. A Ladakhi-run restaurant serving all the usual stuff, and some ambitious international alternatives (such as Swiss cream cheese, and felafels) indoors or *al fresco* on a sociable terrace. A popular bar, too. Moderate prices.

Tibetan Friends Corner, opposite the Taxi Stand. A bit dingy, but the food is filling and cheap, and a big hit with local *thukpa*-slurping Tibetans.

Wok Tibetan Kitchen, Main Bazaar. Wide choice of Tibetan and Chinese food in clean and airy first-floor restaurant. Reasonable prices (but don't bother with the sandwiches).

Listings

Emergencies For police, ☎2218. There are no ambulances in Leh (see Hospital, below).

Hospital Leh's overstretched, poorly equipped *SNM Hospital* (☎2360), is 1km south of the centre on the main road. For urgent medical treatment, contact a doctor through any upmarket hotel.

Laundry If your hotel or guest house doesn't take laundry, try the *Snow White Dry Cleaners*, opposite the *Dreamland Restaurant*. Avoid the *Ladakh Dry Cleaners* off Changspa Lane, which leaves your clothes stinking of kerosene.

Libraries The Ecology Centre's excellent library (Mon–Sat 10am–4pm) keeps books on everything from agriculture to Zen Buddhism, as well as periodicals, magazines, and files of articles on Ladakh and development issues. Serious students of Buddhism should check out the CIBS library in Choglamsar (Mon–Sat 10am–1pm & 2–4pm), where the helpful librarians speak English.

Meditation Small classes are run by the Mahabodhi society in Changspa.

Mountain bikes Mountain bikes may be rented through *Highland Adventures* in the *Hotel Ibex* complex. Rates are high (around Rs200 per day), but they offer good discounts for longer periods.

Pharmacy *Met Ram Vinay Kumar* at the top of the main bazaar sells a range of allopathic pills and potions, as well as underwear and German-made tampons. For Tibetan medicine, try Dr Tsewang Rigzin Larje, whose clinic is by the old bus stand, south of the main bazaar.

Photography *Ali Shah's Postcard Shop*, two minutes' walk north of the main bazaar, stocks fresh film of all kinds, including slide film. If it's closed, try *ND Dijoo & Sons* on the main street. Check the cases for expiry dates.

Travel agents Reliable travel agents, recommended as trekking operators, include *Adventure North*, *Hotel Dragon* (☎2339); *Gypsy's World Treks and Tours*, Fort Rd (☎3935); *Ladakh Adventure Travels*, *Hotel Ibex* (☎2458); *Highland Adventures*, *Hotel Ibex* (Delhi ☎11/578 2582).

Yoga Small classes for all levels are run by a Western teacher in Changspa (Mon–Fri 10.30am–noon). Ask around Changspa Lane for Thaganj House, or look for posters pinned up in local cafes.

MOVING ON FROM LEH

As befits India's remotest Himalayan town, Leh is singularly hard to get to, and even harder to leave. Fragile road and air links mean visitors all too often find themselves stranded waiting for passes to open, or planes to appear. Wherever and however you travel, book your onward ticket as far in advance as possible, be prepared for delays if the weather changes, and allow plenty of time to connect with onward flights.

The quickest way out of Leh is **by plane**. *Indian Airlines* fly to **Delhi**, **Jammu** and **Srinagar**. Tickets can be booked and confirmed at the *Indian Airlines/Tushita Travels* office beyond *Hotel Lha-Ri-Mo* on Fort Rd (Mon–Fri 10am–5pm, Sat 10am–noon; ☎2276), but you may have to wait: the new computer is "down" a lot more than it's "up". Excessive demand for seats also contributes to the queues, which are worst at the start and end of the tourist season before the passes open, and after the summer festival. It's often a good idea to arrive 30 minutes before the office opens – you can start queuing inside. In addition, due to the altitude of Leh airport (the highest served by jet aircraft in the world), planes arriving here full have to leave with a lighter load (ie empty seats), so some people inevitably get stuck. Even confirmed tickets on outward-bound flights offer no guarantee of a prompt departure as take-offs require near-perfect visibility. The slightest scrap of cloud in the wrong place can result in the last-minute cancellation of the flight, whose passengers are then dumped on to "will-I-won't-I" waiting lists.

Since the Kashmir crisis took a turn for the worse, most **overland** travellers have been reaching Leh via **Manali** in Himachal Pradesh (see p.429). The 485-kilometre journey across the Himalaya takes two days, with a night halt in a tent camp en route. Tickets for *HPTDC*'s comfortable daily "luxury" (a/c) and "deluxe" (non-a/c) buses can be booked in advance (until Sept 15, when they are suspended) at *Yasmin Treks & Tours* opposite the *Dreamland* in Fort Rd, which also provides tickets on private mini-buses at the tail end of the season. Cheaper options include the ramshackle buses run by the *HPSRTC* and *J&KSRTC* state transport corporations, bookable the day before departure at the town bus stand. Don't underestimate the Manali–Leh highway. Even when the road is in good shape, it can be a long hard haul; after it has been recently cleared of snow or landslides the journey can take three or four days. A full account of the route, starting at Manali, is given on p.482.

J&KSRTC buses to **Srinagar** still run in summer (mid-June to late Oct), albeit carrying far fewer tourists than in past years, along a road that is generally kept open longer than the Manali route. The two-day, 434-kilometre trip is broken by an overnight stop in Kargil (see p.520), and long waits at roadblocks while interminable military and civil truck convoys lumber up the one-way sections of the road. Tickets for buses (6am daily except Sun) go on sale between 4pm and 5pm of the day before departure at *J&KSRTC*'s office in the town bus stand. If you're heading for Srinagar, pick up a copy of *Kashmir Times* in the bazaar to catch up on the latest events in the troublesome valley.

If you want to **hitch** (unadvisable for lone women travellers) to either Manali or Srinagar, the truck park in Leh is between the old bus stand and the polo ground. Bear in mind you'll be expected to pay your way (around two thirds of the current bus fare), and chip into toll charges at police checkpoints. Trucks are also liable to break down more frequently than buses, and have more accidents.

For information regarding **local bus services** to destinations in Ladakh, see the relevant account, or consult the "Travel Details" on p.495.

Southeast of Leh

Southeast of Leh, the Indus Valley broadens to form a fertile river basin whose lush geometrical barley fields, interspersed with a tangle of turquoise streams, contrast sharply with the bare brown snow-capped mountains that sweep up from its sides. Among the spectacular Buddhist monuments that crown the rocky knolls and razor-back ridges at the edge of the flat valley floor, and make good **day trips from Leh**, are **Shey**, site of a ruined palace and giant brass Buddha, and the stunning monastery of **Tikse**. Both overlook the main highway and are thus served by regular buses.

With the exception of **Stok Palace**, home of the Ladakhi queen, sights on the opposite (south) side of the Indus, linked to the main road by a relatively unfrequented dirt track, are generally harder to reach by public transport. South of Stok, **Matho** *gompa* is more famous for its winter oracle festivals (Feb/March) than its art treasures, but is well worth a visit, if only for the superb views from its roof terrace. Further south still, either cross the Indus and rejoin the highway, calling in at **Stakna** *gompa* en route, or continue down the left bank to **Hemis**, Ladakh's wealthiest monastery and the venue for one of the few religious festivals held in summer. Finally, if you want to side-step your fellow tourists without spending a night away from Leh, head up the austerely beautiful tributary valley opposite Hemis to **Chemrey** and **Thak Thok** *gompas*. The latter, built around a fabled meditation cave, presides over a tiny village that sees only a trickle of the traffic that rumbles past on the main highway below.

Stok

Just beyond the Tibetan refugee camp at **Choglamsar**, a side road turns left off the highway to cross the Indus on an iron bridge plastered with prayer flags. Visible in the distance, at the top of a huge moraine of pebbles swept down from the mountains, the elegant four-storey **STOK Palace** stands above barley terraces studded with threshing circles and whitewashed farmhouses. Built early in the nineteenth century by the last ruler of independent Ladakh, it has been the official residence of the Ladakhi royal family since they were ousted from Leh and Shey two hundred years ago.

The present *Gyalmo* or "Queen", Deskit Angmo, a former member of parliament and friend of Indira Gandhi, still lives here during the summer, but has converted one wing of her 77-roomed palace into a small **museum** (daily 7am–7pm; Rs20). The fascinating collection comprises some of the family's most precious heirlooms, including antique ritual objects, ceremonial tea paraphernalia, and exquisite sixteenth-century **thangkas** illuminated with paint made from crushed rubies, emeralds and sapphires. The *pièces de résistance*, however, are the *Gyalmo*'s **peraks**. Still worn on important occasions, the ancient headdresses, thought to have originated in Tibet, are encrusted with slabs of flawless turquoise, polished coral, lapis lazuli and nuggets of pure gold. Also of interest are a couple of swords whose blades were allegedly tied in knots as a demonstration of strength by King Tashi Namgyal, and several sacred **dzi stones** – "pearls of pure happiness", said to have fallen from heaven, and worn to ward off evil spirits.

Stok gompa, five minutes' walk up the valley, boasts a collection of dance-drama masks, and some lurid modern murals painted by *lamas* from Lingshet *gompa* in Zanskar – the artists responsible for the Maitreya statue in Tikse (see below).

Buses leave Leh for Stok (40min) at 7.30am, 2pm and 4.30pm. A day in Stok is more than enough to do the museum and the *gompa* justice, and to explore the beautiful side valley behind the village – trailhead for the Markha Valley trek (see p.524). If you are tempted to **stay**, try the *Hotel Highland* (⑤), a palatial two-storey house with fine views from its well-furnished en-suite rooms, or the grubby nameless guest house (①) just above it. Nearby, a collection of *yurts* (tents) make up *Ladakh Sarai* (☎2200; ⑧), luxurious unconventional

RAFTING ON THE RIVER INDUS

While water levels are high, between the end of June and late August, Leh's more entrepreneurial travel agents operate **rafting** trips on the River Indus. The scene is still in its infancy, and the routes tame by comparison with Nepal's, but floating downstream in a twelve-seater rubber inflatable is a hugely enjoyable way to experience the valley's most rugged and beautiful landscape. Two different stretches of the river are used: from **Spitok** to the Indus-Zanskar confluence at **Nimmu** (3hr; Rs850), and from Nimmu to the ancient temple complex at **Alchi** (2hr 30min; Rs1200). Experienced rafters may also want to try the more challenging route between Alchi and Khalsi, which takes in the kilometre-long series of rapids at **Nurla**. The cost of this option is negotiable, as it is rarely undertaken and involves considerably more travelling than either of the other two.

Tickets should be booked at least a day in advance, preferably through the operators themselves to avoid paying an agent's commission. The three best-established and most reliable companies in Leh are: *Ri-Mo Rafting*, who work from the *Hotel Kang-La-Chen* near the Ecology Centre, *Highland Adventures*, on the first floor of the *Hotel Ibex* complex, and *Indus Himalaya*, opposite the *Hotel Yak Tail* on Fort Rd. Make sure when you book that the price includes transport to and from the river, rental of life vests and helmets, and meals, and that the raft has a waterproof strong box for valuables.

accommodation run by an enterprising English couple. The food, served in traditional Ladkahi style, is excellent, but you may miss the family atmosphere of the Leh hotels.

Shey

SHEY, 15km southeast of Leh and once the capital of Ladakh, is now all but deserted, the royal family having been forced to abandon it by the Dogras midway through the last century. Only a semi-derelict palace, a small *gompa*, and a profusion of *chortens* remain, clustered around a bleached spur of rock that juts into the fertile floor of the Indus Valley. The ruins overlook the main highway, and can be reached on the frequent minibuses between Leh bus stand and Tikse.

The **palace**, a smaller and more dilapidated version of the one in Leh, sits astride the ridge below an ancient fort. Crowned by a golden *chorten* spire, its pride and joy is the colossal metal Shakyamuni Buddha housed in its ruined split-level temple (daily 6–9am). Installed in the seventeenth century at the behest of Sengge Namgyal's (*c.*1570–1642) son Deldan, the twelve-metre icon allegedly contains a horde of precious stones, *mandalas*, and powerful charms. Entering from a painted ante chamber lined with shelves of ancient manuscripts, you pass through heavy wooden doors to come face to face with the Buddha's huge feet, soles pointing upwards. The customary circumambulation leads around the base of the statue through a haze of incense smoke, to total darkness behind. Upstairs, from a balcony surrounding the statue's torso, you can see the massive Buddha, painted gold with tightly curled blue hair, in better light, and inspect the magnificent paintings of Buddhas, *bodhisattvas*, *mahasiddhas* and fierce protector deities coating the temple walls. Preserved for centuries by thick soot from votary butter lamps, these are among the finest in the valley, painted in stunning detail and tinted with gold applied with smooth hair-fine brush strokes.

Five minutes' walk across the fields from the palace, in the centre of a surreal *chorten*-strewn plane, stands a **temple**, enshrining another massive Shakyamuni statue (daily 7–9am & 5–6pm). Best viewed from the mezzanine verandah on the first floor, it is slightly older than its cousin up the hill. The descendants of the Nepali metalworkers who made it, brought here by Sengge Namgyal, still live and work in the isolated village of **Chilling**, famous for its traditional silverware. Downstairs, the *gompa*'s *Dukhang* contains dusty old *thangkas* and manuscripts.

Easily missed as you whizz past on the road is Shey's most ancient monument. The **rock carving** of the five Tathagata or "Thus gone" Buddhas, distinguished by their respective vehicles (*vahanas*) and hand positions (*mudras*), appears on a smooth slab of stone on the edge of the highway; it was probably carved soon after the eighth century, before the "Second Spreading". The large central figure with hands held in the gesture of preaching (turning the wheel of *dharma*), is the Buddha Resplendant, Vairocana, whose image is central in many of the Alchi murals (see p.517).

If you want to stay in Shey, there are a few **rooms** by the bottom of the steps leading to the palace. The rooms (②), unlike the fly-ridden **restaurant** below, which has a most unappetizing menu, are clean and fresh, and have great views across the river and flat plains to distant Tikse.

Tikse

Ladakh's most photographed and architecturally impressive *gompa* is at **TIKSE**, 19km southeast of Leh. Founded in the fifteenth century, its whitewashed *chortens* and cubic monks' quarters rise in ranks up the sides of a craggy sun-bleached bluff, crowned by an imposing ochre- and red-painted temple complex whose gleaming golden finials are visible for miles in every direction.

A metalled road cuts up the empty west side of the hill from the main highway to the monastery's small car park. If you arrive by mini-bus from Leh (hourly, from the town bus stand), pick your way across the wasteground below the *gompa* and follow the foot-path up through its lower buildings to the main entrance, where monks issue tickets (Rs15). Tikse's reincarnation as a major tourist attraction has brought it mixed blessings: its constant stream of summer visitors spoils the peace and quiet necessary for meditation, but the income generated has enabled the monks to invest in major refurbishments, among them the spanking new **Maitreya temple** immediately above the main courtyard. Inaugurated in 1980 by the Dalai Lama, the spacious shrine is built around a gigantic gold-faced Buddha-to-come, seated not on a throne as is normally the case, but in the lotus position. The bright murals on the wall behind, painted by monks from Lingshet *gompa* in Zanskar, depict scenes from Maitreya's life.

Tikse's garish modern temple may have had hours of work lavished upon it, but its dingy **Du-khang**, at the far end of the courtyard up a steep flight of steps, hasn't seen a lick of paint in centuries. Faded murals of ghoulish tantric deities peer out of the gloom of the old prayer hall, which contrary to appearances is still in everyday use. The key-keeper will show you around the tiny chapels behind the head *lama*'s throne, pointing out the ancient cloth-bound manuscripts stacked in wooden racks against the side walls. Before you leave the *Du-khang*, check out the enormous *thangkas* stored on the shelf opposite the main doorway. These are unrolled once each year during the annual *chaam* dance festival, Tikse Gustor (November or late October). For most foreign visitors, however, the highlight of a trip to Tikse is the view from its lofty **roof terrace**. A patchwork of barley fields stretches across the floor of the valley, fringed by rippling snow-flecked desert mountains and a string of Tolkien-esque monasteries, palaces, and Ladakhi villages: Shey and Stok to the northwest, Matho on the far side of the Indus, and Stakna crowning a knoll to the south. Come here early enough in the morning, and you'll be able to enjoy this impressive panorama accompanied by primeval groans from the *gompa*'s gargantuan Tibetan trumpets – played on the rooftop at *puja* time.

The last **bus** back to Leh leaves at 6pm. The village's *Skalzang Chamba Hotel* (③) offers **accommodation** and good **food**.

Matho

MATHO, 27km south of Leh, straddles a spur at the mouth of an idyllic side valley that runs deep into the heart of the Stok-Kangri massif. Though no less interesting or scenically situated than its neighbours, the *gompa*, the only representative in Ladakh of the **Saskyapa** sect (that held political power in thirteenth-century Tibet), sees comparatively few visitors. Unlike Tikse, across the Indus, it doesn't lie on the main highway, so is less accessible by bus: services leave Leh daily at 8am and 4pm, returning at 9.30am and 5.30pm. By car, Matho also makes an ideal half-way halt on the bumpy journey along the unsurfaced left-bank road between Stok and Hemis.

Despite its collection of four-hundred-year-old *thangkas*, the monastery is best known for its **oracle festival**, *Matho Nagran*, held on the twenty-fifth and twenty-sixth day of the second Tibetan month (around Feb/March). Two oracles, known as *rongzam*, are elected by lot every three years from among the sixty or so resident *lamas*. During the run-up to the big days, the pair fast and meditate in readiness for the moment when they are possessed by the spirit of the deity. Watched by crowds of rapt onlookers, they then perform all manner of death-defying stunts that include leaping blindfold around the *gompa*'s precipitous parapets while slurping kettle-fulls of *chang*, and slashing themselves with razor-sharp sabres without drawing blood. The events are rounded off with colourful *chaam* dances in the monastery courtyard, and a question-and-answer session in which the *rongzam*, still under the influence of the deity, make prophecies about the coming year.

You can check out the costumes and masks worn by the monks during the festivals in Matho's small **museum**, tucked away behind the *Du-khang*. Men are also permitted to visit the eerie **Gon-khang** on the roof (strictly no photography), where the oracles' weapons and ritual garb are stored. The floor of the tiny temple lies under a deep layer of barley brought as harvest offerings by local villagers.

Hemis

Thanks to the **Hemis Setchu** festival – one of the few held in summer, when the passes are open – **HEMIS**, 45km southeast of Leh, must be the most famous *gompa* in Ladakh. Every year in late June/early July, hundreds of foreign visitors join the huge crowds of locals, dressed up in their finest traditional garb, that flock to watch the colourful two-day pageant. However, at other times, the rambling seventeenth-century *Brugpa* monastery, which oversees Stakna and Chemrey (also of the *Drugpa* sect, part of the Kagyu order), can be disappointingly dull and scant reward for the hassle of getting here by public transport. Only a skeleton staff of monks and novices are resident off-season, giving the impression that the *gompa* is now run largely for the benefit of tourists.

Crouched at the foot of a narrow sinuous ravine, amid a leafy oasis of poplar and willow trees, Hemis stays hidden from view until you are virtually beside it. The only signs of the *gompa*'s existence from the valley are the immense *mani* walls stretching over the rock outflow above you, pointing like giant arrows to the mouth of the gorge.

The main entrance, reached via a long flight of steps, opens onto the large rectangular courtyard where the festival **chaam dances** are performed. Accompanied by cymbal crashes, drum rolls and periodic groans from the temple trumpets, *lamas* dressed in opulently brocaded silk costumes and ghoulish masks mime episodes from Buddhist mythology. Now and again, young novices scamper on to the stage to caricature the stylized gestures of the baddies, egged on by a delighted crowd. The show culminates on the second day with a frenzied dismemberment of a dummy, symbolizing the destruction of the human ego, and thus the triumph of Buddhism over ignorance and evil. Illustrating the basic teachings of Mahayana Buddhism, the dramas are also a form of popular entertainment, eagerly anticipated by Ladakhi villagers.

Once every twelve years, the Hemis festival also hosts the ritual unrolling of a giant *thangka*. The *gompa*'s prize possession, which covers the entire facade of the building, was embroidered by women whose hands are now revered as holy relics. Decorated with pearls and precious stones, it will not now be on show again until 2004. Among the treasures on permanent display is an exquisite Buddha Shakyamuni, also inlaid with jewels. The serene-faced colossus sits in the *Cho-khang* at the far end of the courtyard, along with a couple of richly inlaid silver *chortens.*

Practicalities

By car, Hemis is a possible day trip from Leh. **Bus** services are only frequent during the festival. At other times a single daily service leaves at 9am and returns at 12.30pm, leaving no time to have a good look round. You can **stay** here, either in a small tent camp in the woods below the *gompa*, where you can rent mattresses and blankets, or, if you have your own tent, in one of the many secluded **camping** sites beside the stream. Simple **food** is available at the parachute *dhaba* near the car park.

Chemrey

Clinging like a swallow's nest to the sides of a shaly conical hill, the magnificent *gompa* of **CHEMREY** sees very few visitors because of its location – tucked up the side valley that runs from Karu, below Hemis, to the Chang La pass into Pangong. If you don't have your own vehicle, you'll have to be prepared to do some walking to get here. It takes around fifty minutes to follow the dirt track down to the river and up to the monastery after the Leh–Thak Thok bus drops you off beside the main road.

Founded in 1664 as a memorial to King Sengge Namgyal, the monastery is staffed by a dwindling community of around twenty *Drugpa* monks and their young novices. Its main **Du-khang**, off the courtyard on the lower level, boasts a fine silver *chorten* and a set of ancient Tibetan texts whose title pages are illuminated with opulent gold and silver calligraphy. Upstairs in the revamped **Guru-La-khang**, reached via several flights of rickety wooden steps, sits a giant brass statue of Padmasambhava (founder of the Nyingmapa school), swathed in silk brocade and encrusted with semi-precious stones. Its murals, painted in the early 1980s, are the work of an artist from Nimmu village.

Thak Thok

Clustered around a lumpy outcrop of eroded rocks, 4km up the valley from Chemrey, the small *gompa* of **THAK THOK** (pronounced *Tak-Tak* and meaning "top of the rocks") is the sole representative in Ladakh of the ancient Nyingmapa order. The main shrine here is a cave in which the apostle Padmasambhava is said to have meditated during his epic eighth-century journey to Tibet. Blackened over the years by sticky butter-lamp and incense smoke, the dark and mysterious grotto is now somewhat upstaged by the monastery's more modern wings nearby. As well as some spectacular thirty-year-old wall paintings, the **Urgyan Photan Du-khang** harbours a collection of multi-coloured yak-butter candle-sculptures made by the head *lama.*

For a glimpse of "state-of-the-art" Buddhist iconography, head to the top of Thak Thok village, where a shiny new temple houses a row of huge gleaming Buddhas, decked out in silk robes and surrounded by garish modern murals.

Apart from during the annual **festivals** of Thak Thok Tse Chu (9–11 of the sixth Tibetan month: July/Aug until the year 2000) and Viz Thak Thok Manchog (20–29 of the ninth Tibetan month), the village itself is a tranquil place, blessed with serene views south over the snowy mountains behind Hemis. If you want to stay, **accommodation** is available in the J&KTDC *Tourist Bungalow* (①–②). There are also plenty of ideal camping spots beside the river, although as ever you should seek permission before putting up a tent on someone's field. Three **buses** a day leave Leh for Thak Thok: the first and most convenient at 10.30am, and the last at 4pm, returning at 7pm.

North of Leh: Nubra Valley

Until 1994, the lands north of Leh were off-limits to tourists, and had been unexplored by outsiders since the nineteenth century. Now, **NUBRA VALLEY**, unfolding beyond the world's highest stretch of motorable road (5578m), can be visited for seven days only, enough time to explore the stark terrain and trek out to one or two *gompas*.

The valley's mountain backbone looks east to the Nubra River and west to the Shyok River, which weave southwards to meet amid silver-grey sand dunes and boulder fields. To the north and east, the mighty Karakoram range marks the Indian border with China, a fierce terrain of jagged peaks and snowy passes once crossed by caravans carrying silks, spices, gems and cloth. Now a sensitive area, these heights are a lonely outpost for soldiers who brave the cold and bouts of mountain sickness in the name of duty. In the valley it's relatively mild, though **dust storms** are common, whipping up sand and light debris in choking clouds above the broad river beds.

It's thought that Nubra Valley may once have been filled by a glacier more than 1000m deep. This, and the high altitude climate, have left rocky land that is fertile only at the mouths of ravines, where villages of cosy two-storey houses and whitewashed *chortens* are each overlooked by a monastery. Before the region passed into the administrative hands of Leh, Nubra's ancient kings ruled from a palace in **Charasa**, topping an isolated hillock opposite **Sumur**, home to the valley's principal monastery. Further up the Nubra River, the hot springs of **Panamic**, once welcomed by footsore traders, are blissfully refreshing after ten hours on a bus. By the neighbouring Shyok River, **Diskit**, surveyed by a hillside *gompa*, lies just 7km from **Hundur**, known for its peculiar high-altitude desert camels.

The route to Nubra, a steep unmetalled road that forces painful groans from buses and trucks, keeps Leh in sight for four hours until turning to the north, crossing Khardung-La, and ploughing towards the distant Karakoram range. There's free *chai* at the pass for jeep passengers: buses don't stop until the descent into the northern valley is well under way, and you can measure your relief at a checkpoint and *chai* stall by the young Shyok river. Past the small town of Khardung, the road sweeps above honey-coloured canyons before dropping down towards the river valley at Khalsar, the usual lunch stop.

Practicalities: transport and permits

Buses to Nubra Valley (Rs65) leave Leh for Panamic at 5.30am (Mon & Wed; 10hr), and to Diskit at 6am (Fri; 6hr). Alternatively, **jeeps** can be rented (upwards of Rs5000, maximum five people) from Leh taxi rank or any travel agency. Once in the valley, **hitching** on military or road-builders' trucks is an option, though it's unadvisable for lone travellers. **Permits** – officially for a group of four or more people – are issued free at the Collectors' Office on the far side of the polo ground in Leh. However, it's better to avoid bureaucratic delay by paying a travel agent Rs100 to get your permit, which usually takes a day.

Sumur

Soon after passing Khalsar, the road crosses the confluence of the Shyok and Nubra rivers and follows the Nubra to a patch of green sloping from the river to the base of precipitous mountains. **SUMUR** is home to the valley's most important monastery, **Samstem Ling gompa**, forty minutes' walk behind the village. Built in 1841, the *gompa* is home to over a hundred Gelug-pa (Yellow Hat) monks, aged between 7 and 70. Action centres on the large *Du-khang* which is hung with *thangkas* and dominated by a huge gilded statue of Shakyamuni, accompanied by Maitreya and the protector deity Mahakala. Across the courtyard, the long, low *Gon-khang* is guarded by statues of fierce protector deities strung with wide-eyed skulls and figurines of the 84 *mahasiddhas*, venerated tantric saints.

To catch the morning or evening *pujas* at the *gompa*, you'll have to **stay** in Sumur. Tsering Yangchun, a local schoolteacher, has a couple of simple rooms (①) in the family house, with an earth toilet and sparse washing facilities, and serves home-cooked food. The **camping ground** around the corner is owned by the same family (Rs70 per tent).

Buses leave from the prayer wheel on the main road for Leh (Tues & Thurs; 8hr), Panamic (Mon & Wed; 1–2hr), and for Diskit (Thurs & Sun; 3–4hr).

Panamic

Almost two hours' bus journey (30km) up the valley from Sumur, **PANAMIC** (aka Pinchimik), a dusty hamlet overlooked by the pin point summit of Charouk Dongchen, marks the most northerly point accessible to tourists. Buses stop between the **hot springs** and the only **guest house** (②), just over 1km short of the village proper, where cobbled alleys weave between houses, prayer wheels and thorny scrubs to riverside barley fields. Splitting into wide rivulets at this point, the sapphire Nubra seems shallow and tame, but it's not – heed local advice not to ford it.

After a cleansing trip to the hot springs, where two rooms each have a deep tub filled with piping hot sulphurous water, there's little to do in Panamic save walk. A dot on the mountainside across the river, **Ensa gompa** makes for an obvious excursion. The route, three hours each way, passes through the village and crosses a bridge beyond the vast boulder field 3km upstream, then joins a wide jeep track above the river for 3 to 4km. The final haul up a precipitous gorge hides the *gompa* from view until you stumble upon it, couched in an unexpected valley of willow and poplar trees fed by a perennial sweet water stream. Though the *gompa* is usually locked, the views from rows of crumbling *chortens* nearby make the climb worthwhile. If one of the few semi-resident monks is there, however, you'll be shown inside to see the old wall paintings in the temples, and the footprint of Tsong-kha-pa, allegedly imprinted at this spot when he journeyed from Tibet to India in the fourteenth century.

All **buses** passing through Sumur originate or terminate in Panamic.

Diskit and Hundur

After passing Khalsar, buses and trucks bound for the western villages by the Shyok turn onto a flat, grey expanse of boulders and sand dunes, bumping frantically until the metalled road is joined a few kilometres short of **DISKIT**. A dusty collection of low-roofed houses, Diskit, on first impressions, feels rather dull; the more appealing **old town**, of balconied houses and wind-blown poplars, is fifteen minutes' walk from the centre.

The caramel-brown hillside above the old town supports Diskit's **gompa**, built in 1420 by a disciple of Tsong-kha-pa. If you don't have a jeep to follow the wide track, walk beside the long *mani* wall, which continues on the other side of the road, and trace the path that winds upwards from its end past gullys and waterfalls to the monastery; the walk takes around 30 minutes.

The *gompa*'s steps climb past the monks' quarters to the first of a group of temples (Rs15 ticket gives entry to all, and a monk may offer his services as a guide). Local legend has it that a Mongol demon, a sworn enemy of Buddhism, was slain nearby, but his lifeless body kept returning to the *gompa*. What are reputed to be his wrinkled head and hand, grey and ageless, are now clasped by a pot-bellied protector deity in the spooky **Gon-khang**, a dark and claustrophobic temple, packed with fierce gods and goddesses.

The tiny **Lachung temple**, higher up, is the oldest here. Soot-soiled murals face a huge Tsong-kha-pa statue, topped with a Gelug-pa yellow hat. In the heart of the *gompa*, the *Du-khang*'s remarkable mural, filling a raised cupola above the hall depicts Tibet's Tashilhunpo Gompa, where the Panchen Lama is receiving a long stream of visitors approaching on camels, horses and carts. Finally, the *Kangyu Lang* (bookroom) and *Tsangyu Lang* temples act as storerooms for hundreds of Mongolian and Tibetan texts, pressed between wooden slats and wrapped in red and yellow silk.

The flat rooftop outside the *Gon-khang* affords views across to Sumur to the east, the dunes and boulders of the flat southern valley, and to Kobet peak in the north. **HUN-DUR**, a tiny village in a wooded valley, 7km north, is usually the rest point at the end of a pleasant walk from Diskit; and is most notable for its indigenous lanky camels. Hundur is not yet accessible by bus.

Practicalities

Accommodation in Diskit is all simple. By the south end of the *mani* wall, *Olthang Guest House* (③), with a **camping** ground over the road, has very comfortable rooms, decent washing facilities (hot water on request), and home-grown vegetables for dinner. At the other end of the *mani* wall, opposite the large prayer wheel, the friendly *Happy Valley Guest House* (①), has a few rooms, a wide lawn for camping, and serves meals to guests. Otherwise, you could try the more functional *Sand Dune Guest House* (③) in the village centre, behind *Shahen Hotel*, one of a few unexciting restaurants. In Hundur comfortable rooms are available in the home of Tsering Yangdol Nerchungpa.

Buses return to Leh from Diskit (6hr) on Saturday morning. Make sure to buy a ticket from the bus driver when he arrives from Leh, otherwise you're unlikely to be let on. There's a bus to Sumur and Panamic on Thursday and Sunday. If you're not alone, **hitching** is a good alternative. You can usually get a lift with one of the slow military vehicles running up and down the valley.

West of Leh

Of the many *gompas* accessible by road **west of Leh**, only **Spitok**, piled on a hilltop at the end of the airport runway, and **Phyang**, which presides over one of Ladakh's most picturesque villages, can be comfortably visited as day trips from the capital. The rest, including the unmissable temple complex at **Alchi**, with its wonderfully preserved eleventh-century murals, are usually seen en route to or from **Kargil**. The 231-kilometre journey, taking in a couple of high passes and some mind-blowing scenery, can be completed in a single twelve-hour haul. To do this remarkable stretch of road justice, however, spend at least a week making short forays up side valleys, where idyllic settlements and *gompas* nestle amid swathes of barley fields and stark, shattered mountains.

Among landmarks punctuating the former caravan route is the photogenic monastery of **Lamayuru**. Reached via a nail-biting sequence of hairpin bends as the highway climbs out of the Indus Valley to begin its windy ascent of **Fatu La**, it lies within walking distance of some extraordinary lunar-like rock formations, at the start of the main trekking route south to Padum in Zanskar. Further west still, beyond the dramatic **Namika La** pass, **Mulbekh** is the last Buddhist village on the highway. From here on, *gompas* and *gonchas* give way to onion-domed mosques and flowing *salwar kamises*.

Transport along the main highway is straightforward in summer, when ramshackle state and private buses ply between Leh and Kargil. Getting to more remote spots, however, can be hard. Many travellers resort to paying for a ride on one of the countless *Tata* trucks that lumber past in long convoys; which may save time, but is a far more dangerous way to travel this hair-raising road. Getting a group together to rent a **jeep** from Leh is expensive, but saves time.

Spitok

SPITOK gompa, rising incongruously from the end of the airport runway, makes a good half-day foray from Leh, 10km up the north side of the Indus Valley. If you can't afford the taxi fare, the easiest way to **get there** is to stroll down to the crossroads above the GPO and J&KTDC's tourist reception centre, and then flag down any of the buses heading west along the main Srinagar highway. Travellers who walk the whole way invariably regret it, as the route is relentlessly dull, passing through a string of unsightly military installations hemmed in by barbed-wire fences.

By contrast, the fifteenth-century **monastery**, which tumbles down the sides of a steep knoll to a tight cluster of farmhouses and well-watered fields, is altogether more picturesque. Approached by road from the north, or from the south along a footpath that winds through Spitok village, its spacious roof-tops command superb views.

The main complex, a typical mixture of dusty, dimly lit old prayer halls and vivid modern shrinerooms, is of less interest than **Paldan Lumo** chapel, perched on a ridge above. Probably aimed at the mostly Hindu members of the Indian army posted at Leh, a sign outside warns visitors not to "deliberately mistake" the *Gon-khang* for a Kali temple. Offerings made to the black-faced and bloodthirsty Hindu goddess of death and destruction are, it insists, "not acceptable". The shrine to Vajra Bhairava, a tantric guardian deity of the Gelug-pa order, is distinctly spooky. Lit by flickering butter lamps, the cluttered and cobwebbed chamber houses a row of veiled guardian deities whose ferocious faces are only unveiled once a year. After waving incense smoke before them and muttering a few *mantras*, the key-keeper *lama* will pass around handfuls of sweets newly infused with protective power. If you have a flashlight, check out the 600-year-old paintings on the rear wall of the chapel, which is Spitok's oldest building.

Phyang

A mere 24km west of Leh, **PHYANG gompa** looms large at the head of a secluded side valley that tapers north into the rugged Ladakh range from the Srinagar highway. Of the three daily buses that run here from the capital, the 8am departure (1hr 15min) is the most convenient as it allows you plenty of time to explore the monastery and the pretty nearby village. Buses return to Leh at 9.30am and 5.30pm; between these times, you can walk across the fields to the Kargil-bound road (30min), and hitch a lift on a truck.

The *gompa* itself, a tall buttress-walled building, houses a fifty-strong community of Brigungpa *lamas*, members of the larger Kagyu sect, but few antique murals of note, most having recently been painted over with brighter colours. Its only treasures are a small collection of fourteenth-century Kashmiri bronzes (locked behind glass in the modern **Guru-Padmasambhava temple**), and the light and airy **Du-khang's** three silver *chortens*, one of which is decorated with a seven-eyed coffee-coloured **dzi stone**. The gem, considered to be highly auspicious, was brought to Phyang from Tibet by the monastery's former head-*lama*, whose ashes the *chorten* encases.

Tucked away around the side, the shrine in the *gompa*'s gloomily atmospheric **Gon-khang**, lit by a single beam of dusty sunlight, houses a ferocious veiled protector deity and an amazing collection of weapons and armour plundered during the Mongol invasions of the fourteenth century. Also dangling from the cobweb-covered rafters are various bits of dead animals, including most of a vulture, an ibex skull, and several sets of yak horns, believed to be nine-hundred-year-old relics of the Bön cult (see *Contexts*).

Phyang's annual **festival**, *Phyang Tsedup*, formerly held during the winter but recently switched to summer (Aug 5/6, 1997; July 25/26, 1998; July 14/15, 1999) in order to coincide with the tourist season, is the second largest in Ladakh (after Hemis). Celebrated with the usual masked *chaam* dances, the event is marked with a ritual exposition of a giant ten-metre brocaded silk *thangka*.

Alchi

Driving past on the nearby Srinagar–Leh highway, you'd never guess that the cluster of low pagoda-roofed cubes 3km across the Indus from **Saspol**, dwarfed by a spectacular sweep of pale-brown and wine-coloured scree, is one of the most significant historical sites in Asia. Yet the *Chos-khor*, or "religious enclave", at **ALCHI**, 70km west of Leh, harbours an extraordinary wealth of ancient wall paintings and wood sculpture, miraculously preserved for over nine centuries inside five tiny mud-walled temples. Art historians rave about the site because its earliest murals are the finest surviving examples of a style that flourished in Kashmir during the "Second Spreading". Barely a handful of the monasteries founded during this era escaped the Muslim depredations of the fourteenth century. Of them all, Alchi is the most impressive, the least remote and the only one you don't need a special permit to visit. Nestled beside a bend in the milky blue River Indus, amid some dramatic scenery, it's also a serene spot and the perfect place to break a long journey to or from the Ladakhi capital.

The *Chos-khor* consists of five separate temples, various residential buildings and a scattering of large *chortens*, surrounded by a mud-and-stone wall and a curtain of tall poplar trees. If you are pushed for time, concentrate on the two oldest buildings, the **Du-khang** and the **Sumtsek**, both in the middle of the enclosure. Entrance **tickets** (Rs15) are issued by a pair of elderly *lamas* from nearby Likkir *gompa*, who shuffle around to unlock the doors. To make the most of the paintings' vibrant colours, you'll need a strong flashlight; but don't under any circumstances use a camera flash as it will irreparably damage the murals, last restored in the sixteenth century.

The Du-khang

An inscription records that Alchi's oldest structure, the **Du-khang** or main prayer hall, was erected late in the eleventh century by Kaldan Shesrab, a graduate of the now-ruined Nyarma *gompa* near Tikse, itself founded by the Great Translator Rinchen Zangpo (see p.496). Approached via a walled courtyard and a path that runs under a hollow *chorten*, the square temple's wooden doorway is richly carved with meditating *bodhisattvas*. Once your eyes adjust to the gloom inside, check out the niche in the rear wall where Vairocana, the "Buddha Resplendent", is flanked by the four main Buddha manifestations that appear all over Alchi's temple walls, always presented in their associated colours: Akshobya ("Unshakable"; blue), Ratnasambhava ("Jewel Born"; yellow), Amitabha ("Boundless Radiance"; red) and Amoghasiddhi ("Unfailing Success"; green). The other walls are decorated with six elaborate *mandalas*, interspersed with intricate friezes.

The Sumtsek

Standing to the left of the *Du-khang*, the **Sumtsek** is Alchi's most celebrated temple, and the highest achievement of early-medieval Indian-Buddhist art. Its wood carvings and paintings, dominated by rich reds and blues, are almost as fresh and vibrant today as they were 900 years ago, when the squat triple-storeyed structure was built.

The resident *lama* leads visitors under a delicate wooden facade to the interior of the shrine, shrouded in a womb-like darkness broken only by flickering butter lamps. Scan the walls with a flashlight and you'll see why scholars have filled volumes on this chamber alone. Surrounded by a swirling mass of *mandalas*, Buddhas, demi-gods and sundry other celestials, a colossal statue of **Maitreya**, the Buddha-to-come, fills a niche on the ground floor, his head shielded from sight high in the second storey. Accompanying him are two equally grand **bodhisattvas**, their heads peering serenely down through gaps in the ceiling. Each of these stucco statues wears a figure-clinging *dhoti*, adorned with different, meticulously detailed motifs. Avalokitesvara, the *bodhisattva* of compassion (to the left), has pilgrimage sites, court vignettes, palaces and pre-Muslim style *stupas* on his robe, while that of Maitreya is decorated with episodes from the life of Gautama Buddha. The robe of Manjushri, destroyer of falsehood, to the right, shows the 84 Masters of Tantra, the Mahasiddhas, adopting complex yogic poses in a maze of bold square patterns.

Among exquisite **murals,** some repaired in the sixteenth century, is the famous six-armed green goddess Prajnaparamita, the "Perfection of Wisdom" central to Mahayana thought, and closely associated with Tara. Heavily bejewelled, she sits on a lotus by Avalokitesvara's gigantic left leg. Amazingly, this, and the multitude of other images that plaster the interior of the Sumtsek, resolve, when viewed from the centre of the shrine, into a harmonious whole.

Other temples

The *Chos-khor*'s three **other temples** all date from the twelfth and thirteenth centuries, but are nowhere near as impressive as their predecessors. Tucked away at the far river end of the enclosure, the **Manjushri La-khang** is noteworthy only for its relatively recent "Thousand Buddha" paintings and gilded four-faced icon of Manjushri that fills almost the whole temple. Next door the **Lotsawa La-khang**, with its central image and mural of Shakyamuni, is one of a handful of temples dedicated to Rinchen Zangpo, the "Great Translator", whose missionary work inspired the foundation of Alchi; his small droopy-eared image sits on the right of Shakyamuni. The *lama* may need to be cajoled into unlocking the **La-khang Soma**, the small square shrine south of the Sumtsek, which is decorated with three large *mandalas* and various figures including an accomplished *yab-yum*: the tantric image of the copulating deities symbolizes the union of opposites on a material and spiritual level.

Practicalities

One **bus** per day leaves Leh for Alchi in summer (around 3pm), taking three hours to cover the 70km and returning early the next day. Other buses heading in that direction leave Leh at 6.30am (for Kargil) and 9am (for Dah-Hanoo) – you can catch one of these, get off at **Saspol**, and walk the remaining 2.5km via the motorable suspension bridge west of the village.

Of the two very rudimentary **guest houses** in Alchi, the *Lotsav* (①), left of the main road as you approach the *Chos-khor*, is the most pleasant. Simple rooms with beaten earth floors and *charpois* cost Rs50, and the landlady serves cheap and filling breakfasts and evening meals in the small garden if you give her enough warning. The only other place to stay is the *Zimsgang Hotel* (③), just above the temples, which is an OK place to eat but whose rooms are grungy and overpriced. In the unlikely event of these two being full, return to Saspol and try the four-roomed J&KTDC *Tourist Bungalow* (③), at the top of the lane that leads from the main road past the army depot.

Lamayuru

If one sight could be said to sum up Ladakh, it would have to be **LAMAYURU gompa**, 130km west of Leh. Hemmed in by soaring scree-covered mountains, the whitewashed medieval monastery towers above a scruffy cluster of tumbledown mud-brick houses from the top of a near-vertical, weirdly eroded cliff. A major landmark on the old silk route, the *gompa* numbers among the 108 (a spiritually significant number, probably legendary) founded by the Rinchen Zangpo in the tenth and eleventh centuries. However, its craggy seat, believed to have sheltered Milarepa during his religious odyssey across the Himalayas, was probably sacred long before the advent of Buddhism, when local people followed the shamanical Bön cult (see *Contexts*). Just twenty *lamas* of the Brigungpa branch of the Kagyu school are left now, as opposed to the four hundred that lived here a century or so ago. Nor does Lamayuru harbour much in the way of art treasures. The main reason visitors make the short detour from the nearby Srinagar–Leh road is to photograph the *gompa* from the valley floor, or to pick up the trail to the Prikiti La pass – gateway to Zanskar – which begins here.

The footpath from the highway brings you out near the main entrance to the monastery, where you should be able to find the *lama* responsible for issuing entrance tickets (Rs5), and unlocking the door to the **Du-khang**. Lamayuru's newly renovated prayer hall houses little of note other than a **cave** where Naropa, Milarepa's teacher, is said to have meditated, and a rancid collection of yak-butter sculptures. If you're lucky, you'll be shown through the tangle of narrow lanes below the *gompa* to a tiny **chapel**, whose badly damaged murals of *mandalas* and the Tathagata Buddhas are contemporary with those at Alchi (see above).

Practicalities

Lamayuru lies too far from either Leh or Kargil, 107km west, to be visited in a day trip, so you either have to call in en route between the two, or else spend the night at the monastery itself – not advisable for anyone fussy about hygiene. **Buses** stop opposite the *Dehung Labrang Restaurant*, which serves simple meals and offers a very grubby room for around Rs100. Unfortunately, the *gompa*'s squalid rest house (①), next to the main entrance, is no better, with filthy cells, broken *charpois*, and no running water. A couple of young *lamas* also dish up *dal* and rice downstairs from an insanitary kitchen, eaten crouched over kerosene lamps in a tiny dining room-cum-trekkers' tea shop. Unless you're really on a tight budget, head instead for the more salubrious family-run *Dragon Guest House* (①–②) below the monastery. The newly opened *Meditation Centre*, above the monastery, also has a couple of pleasant rooms (②).

Mulbekh

West of Lamayuru, the main road crawls to the top of **Fatu La** (4091m), the highest pass between Srinagar and Leh, then ascends **Namika** ("Sky-Pillar") **La**, so called because of the jagged pinnacle of rock that looms above it to the south. Once across the windswept ridge, it drops through an Arizona-esque landscape of disintegrating desert cliffs and pebbly ravines to the wayside village of **MULBEKH**. The last sizeable Buddhist settlement along the road is scattered around the banks of the River Wakha, whose glacial waters flow through a lush carpet of barley fields peppered with poplars and orchards of walnut and apricot trees.

Formerly an outpost of the Zangla kingdom of western Ladakh (the deposed monarchs, King Nyima Norbu Namgyal Dey and his Queen, Tashi Deskit Angmo, still live in a dilapidated four-storeyed mansion on the western outskirts of the village), Mulbekh would be a sleepy hamlet were it not for the endless convoys of trucks and tourist buses that thunder through while the passes are open. Those visitors who stop at all tend only to stay long enough to grab a *chai* at a roadside *dhaba*, and to have a quick look at the seven-metre-high **Maitreya** ("Chamba" in Tibetan) **statue** carved from the face of a gigantic boulder nearby. The precise origins of the shapely four-armed Buddha-to-be are not known, but an ancient inscription on its side records that it was carved between the seventh and eighth centuries, well before Buddhism was fully established in Tibet. The best place from which to view the bas-relief is the flat roof of the small *gompa* that partially obscures it. No entrance fee is charged, but the *lamas* appreciate a small donation for showing you their twenty-year-old shrine.

Another incentive to prolong your stay in Mulbekh is the two village **gompas**, perched atop a smooth two-hundred-metre rock 1km west of the Chamba statue. A steep flight of steps winds up to the whitewashed temples, one of which is occupied by a small community of young *chomos* (nuns). Neither houses any great treasures, but the views down the Warkha Valley from their terraces make the climb (a very stiff one if you're not yet acclimatized to the altitude) well worthwhile.

Accommodation in Mulbekh is limited to shabby rooms above the tea shops on the main road opposite the Chamba statue. The one at the end of the row, nearest the temple, is the cleanest and also serves the best *dal*, rice and omelettes.

Kargil

Even though it is surrounded by utterly awe-inspiring scenery, few travellers find anything positive to say about **KARGIL**, capital of the area dubbed "**Little Baltistan**", which rises in a clutter of corrugated iron roof-tops from the confluence of the Suru and Dras rivers. Ladakh's second largest town is largely seen as a charmless rite of passage en route to somewhere more appealing. That reputation, a legacy of the days when tourists poured through in their thousands en route to or from Kashmir, derives from the generally low standard of its budget accommodation, and the fact that the main street doubles as a highway, jammed all summer with cacophonic convoys of *Tata* trucks and buses. If you're overnighting on the way between Leh and Srinagar, this hardly matters. Virtually all you'll see of the town between the time the bus pulls in (around 7pm) and leaves (5am the next morning) is the grim bus stand and, as likely as not, the inside of an equally grotty hotel. If, on the other hand, you're bound for Padum in Zanskar, an eighteen-hour journey south down the Suru Valley, two or three days waiting for a bus is par for the course, allowing plenty of time to sample Kargil's dubious charms.

Unusually for Ladakh, the majority of Kargil's 5500 inhabitants are strict **Muslims**. Unlike their Sunni cousins in Kashmir, however, the locals here are ultra-orthodox **Shias**, which not only explains the ubiquitous Iranian Ayatollah photographs, but also the conspicuous absence of women from the bazaar. Descendants of settlers and Muslim merchants from Kashmir and Yarkhand, Kargilis speak a dialect called **Purig** – a mixture of Ladakhi and Balti. Indeed, had it not been for the daring reconquest of the region by India during the 1948 Indo–Pak war (the Indian army forced their Pakistani adversaries out of town after transporting an entire tank division over the Zoji La pass), Kargil would today be part of Baltistan, the region across the nearby Ceasefire Line which it closely resembles. Prevailing Islamic laws make it strongly advisable to **dress conservatively**. Women especially should not wander around in shorts, sleeveless tops, or even knee-length skirts (without trousers on underneath): wear a *salwar kamise* and a headscarf if you have one.

Once you've found somewhere to stay, there's little to do in Kargil beyond a stroll along the main street. Formerly a major market on the old Samarkhand–Srinagar caravan route, the busy **bazaar** is nowadays a run-of-the-mill string of provision stores, iron-mongers, hole-in-the-wall cafes, and fly-blown butchers whose windows are hung with gruesome sheep carcasses. Here and there, stall-holders sit cross-legged on their raised shop fronts smoking *hookahs*, or murmuring verses from the Koran. Among the bearded and woolly-hatted passers-by you'll also come across the odd white turban of an **Agha**. Kargil's puritanical spiritual leaders, who have banned polo and dancing in the town, still travel to Iran to receive religious training, which they follow up with bouts of study at the famously austere **Imambaras** – Shi'ite theological colleges – at the east end of the main thoroughfare.

Also worth considering if you have time is the short hike up to the picturesque village of **Goma** (Upper) **Kargil**, site of a Shi'ite shrine and a hot spring. From the top of Hospital Rd (turn left up the hill at the end of the bazaar), the trail takes you through a tract of woodland to an open stretch of terraced mountainside, with fine views of the snow peaks to the north. Alternatively, cross the river via the footbridge below the bazaar and follow the track to **Poyen**. The town's oldest satellite settlement, a tumble-down cluster of flat-roofed houses grouped around a small silver-domed mosque, is renowned for its apricots, sold by the sack-load in the bazaar.

Arrival and information

Buses arriving in Kargil from Leh, Srinagar, and Padum either pull in to the main bus stand, immediately below the top (west) end of the bazaar, or at the truck park above the river, two minutes' walk downhill from the main street. If you plan to head off early in the morning, check when you buy your ticket where the bus leaves from.

J&KTDC's **tourist reception centre** (July–Aug Mon–Sat 10am–7pm, Sept–June Mon–Sat 10am–4pm; ☎2266) is on the east side of town, around the corner from the **taxi stand** and most of the hotels. As well as the usual leaflets on Ladakh and Kashmir, they have a well-used travellers' notice board, and rent quality Norwegian **trekking equipment**, including four-season sleeping bags, tents, coats, and boots.

If you need to **change money** (or travellers' cheques), the *State Bank of India* (Mon–Fri 10am–2pm, Sat 10am–noon) is in the middle of the main street. Its rates are poor, but better than at the *Siachen Hotel*, which is the only place to cash currency outside bank hours.

Accommodation

If you've heard anything about Kargil, it is probably that its **hotels** are dreadful – which may be unfair on the few upmarket places, and the J&KTDC *Tourist Bungalows*, but is certainly true of the rock-bottom "guest houses" around the bazaar. The Kashmir crisis, which reduced tourist traffic to a trickle, has aggravated the problem by squeezing half the hotels out of business. Those that remain are either geared towards tour groups, or else are total dives. What's more, room tariffs soar in July and August, when a flea-infested windowless hovel without running water can cost as much as Rs200. The rates quoted below apply to peak season; discounts are usually available at other times.

D'Zoji La, Lankore (☎01985/336). Kargil's top hotel, 2km east of town, offers upmarket accommodation for wealthy trekkers. Phone on arrival for a courtesy coach. ⑦.

Evergreen, below the taxi stand. A good fall-back, but common shower-toilets only. ②.

Greenland, at the end of the lane leading off the east side of the taxi stand. A notch above rock-bottom, with reasonable rooms (some attached bathrooms), and a reliable water supply. ③.

J&KTDC Tourist Bungalow no.1, next to the tourist office, 5 minutes' walk uphill from the crossroads above the bus stand. Clean rooms, clean sheets, and peaceful, with a small dining room. By far the best budget deal in town. If the *chowkidar* says it's full, get a "chit" from the tourist office. ③.

J&KTDC Tourist Bungalow no.2, behind the truck park above the river. Not a patch on its namesake across town, but still good value and convenient for early departures. ①.

Siachen, below (the west side of) the taxi stand (☎01985/221). Large and comfortable, with immaculate en-suite rooms, STD phones, and foreign exchange. Book ahead in July and Aug. ⑥.

Eating

Unless you stay in one of the upmarket hotels, finding somewhere to **eat** in Kargil is a toss-up between the small tourist-oriented cafes on the lane from the truck park to the bazaar, or a *dhaba* on the main street. Choice is even more limited for **breakfast**; all the restaurants are closed, but hot *chapatis* and omelettes are served from 7am onwards at the *chai* stall just up from the *Nuktal* (take your own plate). If you are leaving at the crack of dawn, a couple of *chai-wallahs* also hang around the bus stand.

Nuktal, between the truck park and the bazaar. Pink net curtains and fierce "Ayatollah" decor, but the food – basic Chinese ("spring rods") and some bland Western alternatives (best avoided) – is OK. Generous portions and cheap, too. Try the delicious (bottled) apple juice. Recommended.

Popular Chacha, main bazaar. One of several poky cafes on the high street serving piles of unremarkable-but-safe Chindian food, mostly to men.

Punjabi Jananta & Ruby, east end of main street. Two of a kind: spicy Indian sauces spooned on to groaning platefuls of rice. The cleanest *dhabas* in town.

Shashila Chinese, main bazaar. *Nuktal*'s main rival, with a flashy exterior, but run-of-the-mill food.

The Suru Valley

A spellbinding divide between two of the world's most formidable mountain ranges, the **SURU VALLEY** winds south from Kargil to the desolate Pensi La pass – principal entrepot for Zanskar. Since a fair-weather road was bulldozed all the way to Padum, you can travel to the heart of this remote region by bus (albeit a clapped-out J&K state one), in a single haul of around fourteen hours. The first leg, usually undertaken in the pre-dawn darkness, leads through the broad lower reaches of the Suru Valley, whose fertile floor is strewn with Muslim villages, clustered around gleaming metal mosque domes. By the time the first rays of daylight appear, the surrounding mountains have grown vast, bare and brown, only cultivated along the narrow strip lining the river. Gradually, the pristine white ice-fields and rocky pinnacles of **Nun-Kun** (7077m) nose over the horizon. Apart from a brief disappearance behind the steep sides of the valley at **Panikhar**, this awesome massif dominates the landscape all the way to Zanskar.

Shortly after Panikhar, the Suru veers east around the base of Nun-Kun, passing within a stone's throw of the magnificent **Gangri Glacier**. Having wound across a seemingly endless boulder choke, closed in on both sides by sheer mountain walls, the road emerges at a marshy open plain surrounded by snow peaks and swathes of near-vertical strata. **Juldo**, a tiny settlement whose fodder-stacked rooftops are strung with fluttering prayer flags, marks the beginning of Buddhist **Suru**.

The climb to the pass from **Rangdum gompa**, across the flat river basin from Juldo, is absolutely breathtaking. One glistening 6000-metre peak after another appears atop a series of side valleys, many lined with gigantic folds of rock and ice. The real high point occurs shortly beyond **Pensi La** (4401m), as the road, swinging around dizzying switchbacks, overlooks the colossal S-shaped **Darung Drung Glacier**, whose milky green melt-waters drain southeast into the Stod Valley, visible below.

Panikhar

Although by no means the largest settlement in the Suru Valley, **PANIKHAR**, three hours' bus ride south of Kargil, is a good place to break the long journey to Padum. Before the Kashmir troubles, it was a minor trekking centre, at the start of the Lonvilad Gali–Pahalgum trail. These days, the scruffy collection of roadside stalls and poor mud-brick farm houses sees very few tourists, even in high season.

The main reason to stop is to hike to nearby **Parkachik La**, for panoramic views of the glacier-gouged north face of the mighty **Nun-Kun massif**. The **trail** up to the pass, known locally as Largo ("Nothing") La, begins on the far side of the Suru, crossed via a suspension bridge thirty minutes south of the village. It may look straightforward from Panikhar, but the four-hour round-trip climb to the ridge gets very tough indeed towards the top, especially for those not used to the altitude. However, even seasoned trekkers gasp in awe at the sight that greets them when they finally arrive at the cairns. Capped with a plume of cloud and snow streaming from its huge pyramidal peak, Nun sails 3500m above the valley floor, draped with heavily crevassed hanging glaciers and flanked by its sisters, multi-pinnacled Kun and saddle-topped Barmal.

There are only two **places to stay** in Panikhar. The *Kayoul Hotel & Restaurant* (①), directly opposite the bus stop, has a couple of very basic rooms with fold-away *charpois* and shared "earth" latrines, plus the only place to **eat**, a ramshackle roadside cafe where the affable owner serves freshly cooked veg-noodles and omelettes. For a bit more comfort, try the modest J&KTDC *Tourist Bungalow* (①), 100m further down the road on the left, where a large en-suite room with running water and a Western toilet sets you back a mere Rs40. **Buses** to Kargil leave from the *Kayoul* at 7am and 11am. If you're looking for a lift to Padum, collar the truckers as they leave the *dhaba* after their lunch; the one-way fare costs around the same as the bus (Rs100).

Zanskar

Despite the Indian government dropping restrictions on travel to Dah-Hanoo, Tsomoriri and the Nubra Valley, mountain-locked **ZANSKAR**, literally "Land of White Copper", remains the most stunning and remote corner of Ladakh accessible by road. Hemmed in by the Zanskar range and the Great Himalayan divide, the nucleus of the region is a Y-shaped glacial valley system drained by three main rivers. The **Stod** (or Doda) emerges by the Pensi La pass to flow southeast into a wide triangular plain at **Padum**, the district headquarters, where it merges with the waters of the **Tsarap** (or Lingit) to form the River **Zanskar**. This fast-flowing milky turquoise torrent surges northeast to meet the Indus at Nimmu, gouging a chasm through the jagged mountains en route.

Lying to the leeward side of the Himalayan watershed, Zanskar sees a lot more snow than central Ladakh. Even its lowest passes remain blocked for six or seven months of the year, while mid-winter temperatures can drop to a bone-numbing -40°C. Ten thousand or so tenacious souls subsist in this bleak and treeless terrain – among the coldest inhabited places on the planet – muffled up for half the year inside their smoke-filled whitewashed crofts, a winter's-worth of fodder piled on the roof.

A little over a decade ago, anything the resourceful Zanskaris could not produce for themselves (including timber for building) had to be packed into the region over four- to five-thousand-metre passes, or, in mid-winter, carried along the frozen surface of the Zanskar from its confluence with the Indus at Nimmu – a twelve-day round-trip that is still the quickest route to the Srinagar–Leh road from Padum. Finally, in 1980, a motorable dirt track was blasted down the Suru and over Pensi La into the Stod Valley. Landslides and freak blizzards permitting (Pensi La can be snowbound even in August), the bumpy journey from Kargil to Padum can now be completed in as little as fourteen hours.

Most visitors come to Zanskar to **trek**. Numerous trails wind their way northwards from Padum to central Ladakh, west to Kishtwar, and south to neighbouring Lahaul – all long hard hikes that involve strenuous ups and downs (see p.524). If, on the other hand, you travel down here hoping to use the district headquarters as a comfortable base from which to make short day trips, you'll be disappointed. Only a handful of Zanskar's widely scattered *gompas* and settlements lie within striking distance of the road. The rest are hidden away in remote valleys, reached after days or weeks of walking and surrounded by a shattered wilderness of mountains, where life has altered little since Buddhism first crossed the Himalayas from Kashmir over a thousand years ago.

Improved communications may yet turn out to be a mixed blessing for Zanskar. For while it has undoubtedly brought a degree of prosperity to Padum, the new road has already forced significant changes upon the rest of the valley – most noticeably a sharp increase in tourist traffic – whose long-term impact on the region's fragile ecology and traditional culture has yet to be fully realized. Increased tourism has, in fact, done little to benefit the locals financially, as agencies in Leh, Manali, Srinagar and even Delhi pocket the money paid by trekking groups. **Activists**, weary of seeing their region come second to Kargil (which lies in the same administrative sector), are campaigning for sub-hill council status, a parliamentary representative in Srinagar, and a road following the Zanskar river gorge to Nimmu. Zanskar's isolation makes the demand for semi-independence a difficult one to grant. In 1995 Padum was closed to tourists. Check the situation before arriving, as finding accommodation may be a problem.

TREKKING IN LADAKH AND ZANSKAR

The ancient footpaths that criss-cross **Ladakh** and **Zanskar** provide some of the most inspiring **trekking** in the Himalayas. Threading together remote Buddhist villages and monasteries, cut off in winter behind high passes whose rocky tops bristle with windswept thickets of prayer flags, nearly all are long, hard, and high – but rarely dull. The **best time** to trek is from June to September.

Whether you make all the necessary preparations yourself, or pay an agency to do it for you, **Leh** is the best place to plan a trek. **Equipment**, including high-quality tents, sleeping bags, karrimats, boots and duck-down jackets, can be rented through J&KTDC's tourist information centre on Fort Rd, or at the neighbouring *Himalayan Adventures* in the *Hotel Ibex*. Alternatively, buy your own Indian-made kit in the bazaar and re-sell it again afterwards. To find **ponies** and **guides**, essential for all the routes outlined below, head for the Tibetan refugee camp at **Choglamsar**, 3km south of Leh.

Trekking is undoubtedly the most rewarding way to explore the region, but it can also be highly disruptive. Minimize your impact in culturally and ecologically sensitive areas by respecting the following "golden rules", set out in LEDeG's *Guidelines For Visitors To Ladakh* (see p.501). Be as **self-reliant** as possible, especially with food and fuel. Buying provisions along the way puts an unnecessary burden on the villages' subsistence-oriented economies, and encourages strings of unsightly "tea shops" (invariably run by outsiders) to sprout along the trails. Always burn kerosene, never wood – a scarce and valuable resource. Refuse should be packed up, not disposed of along the route, no matter how far from the nearest town you are, and plastics retained for recycling at the Ecology Centre in Leh. Always bury your faeces and, if you can't convert to water, burn your toilet paper afterwards. Finally, do not defecate in the dry stone huts along the trails; local shepherds use them for shelter during snow storms.

Spitok to Hemis via the Markha Valley

The beautiful **Markha Valley** runs parallel with the Indus on the far southern side of the snowy Stok-Kangri massif, visible from Leh. Passing through cultivated valley floors, undulating high-altitude grassland, and snow-prone passes, the winding trail along it enables trekkers to experience life in a roadless region without having to hike for weeks into the wilderness – as a result, it has become the most frequented route in Ladakh. Do not attempt this trek without adequate wet- and cold-weather gear: snow flurries sweep across the higher reaches of the Markha Valley even in August.

The circuit takes six to eight days to complete, and is usually followed anti-clockwise, starting from the village of **Spitok** (see p.516), 10km south of Leh. A more dramatic approach, via **Stok** (see p.508), affords matchless views over the Indus Valley to the Ladakh and Karakoram ranges, but involves a sharp ascent of **Stok La** (4848m) on only the second day; don't try it unless you are already well acclimatized to the altitude.

From Spitok, the trail crosses the Indus via an iron footbridge, then follows the south bank of the river 7km west to the narrow mouth of the tree-lined Jingchen Valley. Camp beside the stream at **Jingchen** village, 4km further on, or higher up the valley near the **Rumbak**. Day 2 takes you 5hr south down a side valley, via the picturesque village of **Yurutse**, to a camp at the foot of **Kunda La** (4907m), crossed after a long climb on Day 3. **Shingo**, the first settlement below the pass, is a pleasant spot to set up camp if you are doing the trek in short stages. Otherwise, press on 6km down a wild-rose- and willow-lined stream gorge to the **River Markha**. A boggy campsite below the village of **Skiu**, hidden in a side valley 2km further upstream from the confluence, marks the end of this stage.

The next two days' walking are relatively easy, winding west along the river via a series of footbridges and small villages such as **Markha**, where you can visit a ruined fort and small *gompa*. Beyond **Umling**, 3km east, the valley widens, and the peak of **Kang Yurze** (6400m) rears up to the south. **Hankar** stands at the mouth of a side valley which you follow up to the **Nimaling plain**, a rolling pasture criss-crossed by gurgling streams and grazed by the yaks, *dzos*, sheep and horses of nearby villages. The ascent of **Kongmaru La** (5274m), the highest pass on the route, begins shortly after Nimaling on the penultimate leg. It takes 2hr if you are properly acclimatized, and is rewarded with fine views north across the Indus Valley. By the time you reach **Chogdo** after the steep and zig-zagging descent from the ridge, you may well be more than ready to call it a day; if not, carry on through **Sumda** to **Martselang** on the main Indus Valley highway, from where a dusty trail winds up to **Hemis** *gompa* (see p.511). The campsite in the woods below the monastery, serviced by a couple of *chai* stalls, marks the end of the trek.

Likkir to Temisgang

A motorable road along the old caravan route through the hills between **Likkir** and **Temisgang**, north of the main Indus Valley, may be up and running by 1998. For the moment, this leisurely 2-day hike, which takes in three major monasteries (Likkir, Ridzong and Temisgang) and a string of idyllic villages, is a great introduction to trekking in Ladakh, the perfect acclimatizer if you plan to attempt any longer and more demanding routes. Ponies and guides for the trip may be arranged on spec at either Likkir or Temisgang villages, both of which have small guest houses and are connected by daily buses to Leh.

Lamayuru to Alchi

Albeit short by Ladakhi standards, the five-day trek from **Lamayuru** to **Alchi** is one of the toughest in the region, winding across high passes and a tangle of isolated valleys, past a couple of ancient *gompas*, and offering superb panoramic views of the wilderness south of the Indus Valley. It's very hard to follow in places, so don't attempt it without an experienced guide, ponies, and enough provisions to tide you over if you lose your way.

Day 1 follows the main Zanskar traverse (outlined below) southeast from **Lamayuru** (see p.518), to **Wanla** via the Prikit La pass (3810m). Shortly after the campground at **Phanjila**, 3hr beyond Wanla at the confluence of the Spong and Ripchar *nalas*, the trail peels away from the Padum route and heads east up Ripchar Nala to **Hinju**, at the foot of **Konki La** (4905m). Take time out here before the strenuous climb up to the pass. Once across, a zig-zagging descent winds down to the head of Sumdah Chu stream gorge, and thence through the tiny hamlets collectively known as **Sumdah Chunoon**, where there is a small *gompa* and plenty of space to camp. Stage four, to the bottom of the high **Stakspi La** pass (5180m), takes you north up a side valley and can be completed in 8hr. If you are fully acclimatized, the ensuing 3hr ascent should present no problems, although the steep 1000-metre drop down the other side to **Alchi** (see p.517) is tricky in places.

Padum to Lamayuru

The trek across the rugged Zanskar range from **Padum** to **Lamayuru** on the Srinagar–Leh highway, usually completed in ten to twelve days, is a hugely popular but very demanding long-distance route, not to be attempted as a first-time trek, nor without adequate preparation, ponies and a guide. We describe the route from south to north here, but there is no reason not to follow it in the opposite direction, from Lamayuru.

Two trails from **Padum** (see p.527) cover the first half of the trek. The slightly easier one winds along the east bank of the Zanskar via **Thonde** and **Zangla** (where you can detour up to an old palace and monastery), to **Honia**. Then the route ascends **Namtse La** pass (4446m), crossed halfway through the third stage. Day 4 involves a long hard slog over **Nerag La** (4850m) and a steep drop to cross the Zanskar at **Nerag** village. An hour or so north of the river, you meet up near **Yelchang** village with the other path which, after following the Zanskar's west bank to **Karsha** (see p.527), has wriggled over four passes, including the 5000-metre **Hanuma La**. This second and longer route allows you to visit the spectacular **Lingshet gompa**, famous for its *thangka* artists.

From Yelchang, a single track picks its way across a sheer wall of scree to **Sengge La** (the "Lion Pass"; 5000m). **Photokasar** above the River Photang, normally reached on Day 6 or 7, marks the start of the climb up a side valley to **Sisir La** (4990m), after which you drop sharply down to Spong Nala, thence to the campground at **Honupatta** village. Two relatively easy stages round off the trek. The trail follows the river 4km downstream to **Wanla**, and then up the Shilakung Valley and through a rocky gorge to **Prikit La**. **Lamayuru** (see p.518) nestles on the narrow floor of the Sangeluma gorge, 1hr 30min below the pass.

For an outline of the two main approach routes to Zanskar from the south, see **"Trekking in Lahaul and Spiti" (p.466).**

Padum

After a memorable trek or bus ride, **PADUM** comes as an anticlimax. Instead of the picturesque Zanskari village you might expect, the region's administrative headquarters and principal roadhead turns out to be a desultory collection of crumbling mud and concrete cubes, oily truck parks, and incongruous tin-roofed government buildings, scattered around the sides of a stony hillock. The settlement's only real appeal lies in its superb location. Nestled at the southernmost tip of a broad, fertile river basin, Padum presides over a flat patchwork of farm land fringed with grey-pebble river beds and enclosed on three sides by colossal walls of scree and snow-capped mountains.

Straddling a nexus of several long-distance trails, Padum is also an important **trekking hub** and the only place in Zanskar where tourism has thus far made much of an impression. During the short summer season, you'll see almost as many weather-beaten westerners wandering around its sandy lanes as locals – a mixture of indigenous Buddhists and *salwar-kamise*-clad Sunni Muslims descended from the Dogra troops posted here by the Zorawar Singh in the 1840s. Even so, facilities remain very basic, limited to a small tourist office, a handful of temporary tea shops and guest houses, as well as the inevitable rash of Kashmiri handicraft stalls. Nor is there much to see while you are waiting for your blisters to heal or your bum to recover from the bus journey down here. Apart from a small **mosque**, the Jama Masjid, whose plate-metal roof and multicoloured minarets are Padum's most prominent feature, the only noteworthy sight within easy walking distance is a small **Tagrimo gompa**, ensconced amid the poplar trees fifteen minutes' walk to the west.

Arrival and information

Arriving in Padum by bus (twice weekly; 18hr), you'll be dropped in the dusty square at the far south end of the village, close to the old quarter and a couple of the cheaper guest houses. Tickets for the trip (Rs100) go on sale around 2pm the day before departure at Kargil bus stand, or on the bus itself if you are already in Padum. J&KTDC's **tourist reception centre** (July–Sept Mon–Sat 10am–7pm) lies 1km north of the square on the side of the main road, two minutes' walk from the other main concentration of guest houses. Unlike their branches in Leh and Kargil, this one doesn't rent out trekking gear, but is good for general advice.

As yet, there is nowhere in Padum to change money, although you can post letters at the **GPO** next door to the tourist complex.

Basic **trekking supplies** are sold at the two hole-in-the-wall stores above the bus stand. Prices are much higher than elsewhere, so it pays to bring your own provisions with you from Kargil. By mid-October, imported food of any kind is hard to come by.

Most trekkers arrange **horses** through the tourist office or guest house owners. Either way, expect to pay from Rs150 to Rs300 per horse per day, depending on the time of year (ponies transport grain during the harvest, so they're more expensive in October). If you have trouble finding a horse-*wallah*, ask around Pipiting village, thirty minutes' walk north across the fields from Padum, where most of them hang out.

Accommodation

Accommodation in Padum is limited to a handful of grotty guest houses and rooms in private family homes. In both cases, bathrooms are usually shared, and toilets of the "long-drop" variety. One exception is the simple but comfortable J&KTDC *Tourist Bungalow* (②), whose well-maintained en-suite double rooms have running water. A more authentic option is the double-storey farm house nearby, the *Ibex Guest House* (①); its rooms are nothing special, but its very welcoming owners serve breakfast, evening meals, and endless rounds of butter-and-salt tea to guests in their traditional kitchen. The least shambolic of the budget guest houses in the village proper is the *Greenland* (①), which boasts a couple of light and airy rooms.

If you have your own tent and would prefer to **camp**, pitches at the J&KTDC site, up near the tourist reception centre, cost Rs50 per night. Trekkers arriving from Shingo La sometimes camp beside the stream in the Tsarap Valley; ask before you do.

Eating

Finding **food** in Padum only tends to be a problem towards the end of the trekking season; by mid-October, stocks of imported goods (virtually everything except barley flour and yak butter) are low, and even a fresh egg can be a cause for celebration. Earlier in the year, temporary tea-shops and cafes ensure a supply of filling and fairly inexpensive meals. Among the few of these rough-and-ready joints to reappear every year is the popular *Ibex Restaurant*, just south of the tourist office, which dishes up the usual (packet) soups, *dal* and rice, stringy chicken or mutton stew, and "potato *halwa*" (spuds mashed with onions and tomatoes). For cheap Chinese and Tibetan food, try the *Changtang* near the *Tourist Bungalow*, or *Babu Chinese*, back towards the village. Most guest houses also provide half-board if given enough warning.

Around Padum

Public transport around the Zanskar Valley is virtually non-existent, so unless you can afford the vastly inflated fares demanded by Padum's two or three taxi-*wallahs*, you can only get as far into the sweeping plains **around Padum** as you can hike in a day. For all but the most athletic and determined, this leaves just two possible excursions, of which the hike across the fields to **KARSHA gompa**, Zanskar's largest Gelug-pa monastery, is easily the most rewarding. From a distance, this cluster of whitewashed mud cubes clinging to the rocky lower slopes of the mountain north of Padum looks like some strange geological formation. Only close up is it possible to pick out the individual monks' quarters and temples, which date from the tenth to the fourteenth centuries. Of the prayer halls, the recently renovated *Du-khang* and *Gon-khang* at the top of the complex are the most impressive, while the small *Chukshok-jal*, set apart from the *gompa* below a ruined fort on the far side of a gully, contains Karsha's oldest wall paintings, contemporary with those at Alchi (see p.517).

The quickest way to **get to Karsha** on foot is to head north from Padum to the cable bridge across the Stod, immediately below the monastery. Set off early in the morning; the violent icy storms that blow in from the south across the Great Himalayan range around mid-afternoon make the ninety-minute hike across the exposed river basin something of an endurance test.

Karsha can also be reached by road, via the bridge at **Tungri**, 8km northwest of Padum. En route, you pass another large *gompa*, **SANI**, lauded as the oldest in Zanskar, and the only one built on the valley floor. Local legend attributes its foundation to the itinerant Padmasambhava ("Guru Rinpoche") in the eighth century – though the name of the **Kanishka Chorten**, behind the main temple, suggests it may have been established by the Kushan King Kanishka in the first or second century, it is more likely that it was named after the emperor centuries later. There are two small temples in the *Du-khang* grounds: one, in which Naropa is said to have meditated around nine hundred years ago, is permanently locked, while the other, the *La-khang*, has unique painted stucco bas-reliefs whose deep niches enshrine dusty gold-faced icons, most of them manifestations of Padmasambhava. Set apart from the temples a little to the north is a two-metre high Maitreya figure, carved out of local stone some time between the eighth and tenth centuries.

CHAPTER SEVEN

HARYANA AND PUNJAB

Prosperous, but politically unstable, the now separate states of **HARYANA** and **PUNJAB** occupy the flat and fertile tract of river plain that extends from Delhi northwest towards the mountains of Jammu & Kashmir and the border with Pakistan. Divided by the Partition of August 1947, Punjab has been systematically shorn of its once vast territory; losing the Punjab Hills to the newly formed state of Himachal Pradesh (see p.429) and later sacrificing a further chunk to create Haryana. Crossed by the five major tributaries of the **Indus**, the former British-administered region of Punjab ("Land of Five Rivers") was split down the middle at Independence. Indian Muslims fled west into Pakistan, and Hindus east, in an exodus accompanied by horrific massacres. The Sikhs, meanwhile, threw in their lot with India, which they considered a safer option than the homeland of their Muslim arch-enemies. In 1966, prime minister Indira Gandhi, in response to Sikh pressure, further divided the state into two semi-autonomous districts: predominantly Sikh Punjab, and 96 percent Hindu Haryana, both governed from the newly built capital of **Chandigarh**.

The protracted and violent campaign for Sikh self-rule, together with the fact that there's not much to see at the best of times, mean that Haryana and Punjab attract comparatively few foreign visitors. Nevertheless, the "bread basket of the nation" plays a hugely important part in the Indian **economy**. Modern crop technology and irrigation canals, introduced during the **"Green Revolution"** of the 1960s, enable Punjabi farmers to produce nearly a quarter of India's wheat, and one third of its milk and dairy foods, while the cities are major industrial centres. **Ludhiana** churns out 90 percent of the country's woollen goods, and the *Hero* factory in **Jalandhar** manufactures the world's best-selling bicycle. Helped by remittance cheques from millions of expatriates in the UK, US and Canada (and the cheap migrant labour of Bihari *bhaiyas* who took their place), the state's per capita income is now almost double the national average.

Much of the credit for this has to go to the **Sikhs**. Recognizable by their beards and bulky turbans (or, in the case of women, flowing *salwar kamise*), India's most distinctive minority are fiercely independent and proud: their faith explicitly encourages economic self-reliance, family ties, and a readiness to fight for the mother country. Their military tradition, which dates from the days of resistance against the Moghuls, served the Sikhs well during the Raj, when they formed the backbone of the British-Indian army. The eldest sons, however, invariably stayed home to work the land, and Punjabi **Jat** farmers are now the most affluent peasant class in India: nearly every field has a small diesel pump house, while tractors, a rarity elsewhere, are a common sight. In the cities, Sikhs are better known as mechanics, or truck, taxi and auto-rickshaw *wallahs*, particularly in Delhi, where many Punjabi refugees settled after Partition.

Despite the full-bearded fundamentalists you'll see strolling around the **Golden Temple** in the holy city of **Amritsar**, most Sikhs today are non-orthodox. Known as **sahajdharis**, less devout members of the faith are frequently stereotyped as *bon viveurs*, and with some justification: Punjab boasts both India's richest regional cuisine, and its highest per capita consumption of **alcohol**.

Most travellers simply pass through – perhaps with a detour to the beautiful **Golden Temple** – en route to Himachal Pradesh, or to the Indo-Pak border at **Wagha**, near Amritsar. However, if you linger long enough to check out Le Corbusier's experimen-

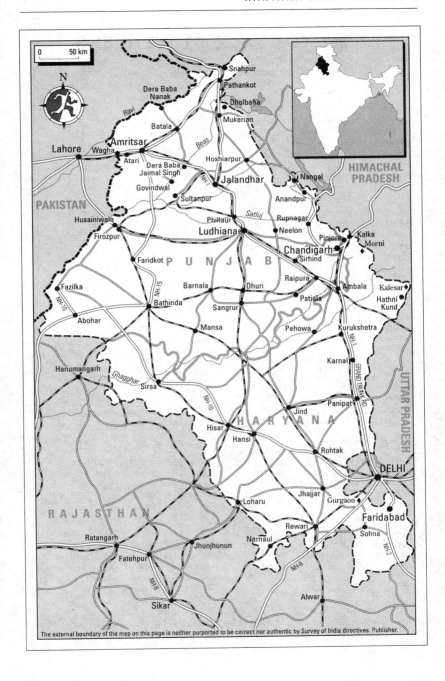

The external boundary of the map on this page is neither purported to be correct nor authentic by Survey of India directives. Publisher.

HARYANA AND PUNJAB TRAVEL DETAILS

	Trains		Buses		Flights	
	Frequency	Time	Frequency	Time	Frequency	Time
To and from AMRITSAR						
Agra	1 daily	15hr 30min				
Allahabad	1 daily	21hr 30min				
Bombay	3 daily	31hr 25min–44hr				
Calcutta	2 daily	38hr 10min–47hr				
Dehra Dun	1 daily	10hr				
Delhi	9 daily	7hr 20min–12hr	8 daily	10hr	4 weekly	55min
Dharamsala			1 daily	7hr		
Ganganagar			2 daily	8hr		
Gwalior	1 daily	18hr 20min				
Jammu	every 30min	5hr				
Jhansi	1 daily	20hr 35min				
Kullu	1 daily	16hr				
Lahore	1 daily	4hr				
Srinagar	4 weekly	50min				
Varanasi	2 daily	23hr 15min–26hr				
Wagha	2 daily	45min				
To and from CHANDIGARH						
Agra			1 daily	10hr		
Amritsar			every 30min	5hr 30min–6hr		
Dehra Dun			2 daily	5hr		
Delhi	3 daily	3hr 10min–6hr	every 20min	5hr 30min–6hr		
Dharamsala			6–15 daily	7–8hr		
Haridwar			2 daily	6hr		
Jaipur			7 daily	11hr		
Jammu			8 daily	10hr		
Kalka	5 daily	50min	every 30min	30min		
Kasauli			5 daily	2hr 30min		
Kullu			8 daily	6hr 30min		
Manali			8 daily	8hr		
Shimla			every 30min	3hr 30min–4hr		
Sirhind			every 20min	1hr 30min		
To and from Pathankot						
Agra	1–2 daily	15hr 38min–19hr				
Ambala	1 daily	7hr 10min	every 20min	7hr		
Amritsar	1 daily	2hr	every 15min	3hr		
Chamba			hourly	5hr		
Dalhousie			hourly	3hr 30min		
Delhi	2–3 daily	11hr 35min–15hr	every 20min	11hr		
Dharamsala			12 daily	3hr 30min		
Gwalior	1–2 daily	17hr 30min–22hr				
Jammu	4 daily	2hr 40min–4hr	every 5min	3hr		
Jogindernagar	3 daily	8hr				
Jullundhar	2 daily	3hr	hourly	3hr		
Kangra	1 daily	3hr 25min	10 daily	3–4hr		
Manali			5 daily	12hr		
Mandi			5 daily	8hr		
Shimla			5 daily	12hr		
Varanasi	2 daily	28–31hr				

Note that no individual route appears more than once in this chart; for any specific journey, check against where you want to get to as well as where you're coming from.

THE GRAND TRUNK ROAD

Crossing Haryana and Punjab en route to, or from, Delhi, you're bound to travel, at some stage, along part of the longest, oldest and most famous highway in India. Stretching 2000km from Peshawar near the rugged Afghan–Pakistan frontier to Calcutta on the River Hooghly, NH1, alias the **Grand Trunk Road**, was described by Kipling in his novel *Kim*, whose hero and his Tibetan *lama* companion set off along it in search of "The River of Arrows", as "the Big Road", and "the Backbone of all Hind".

The first recorded mention of this trade corridor dates from the fourth century BC, when it was known as the **Uttar Path** ("High Way"). A century later, the emperor Ashoka upgraded it with paving stones and watchtowers, placing edict pillars at intervals along the route. Midway through the sixteenth century, the Afghan warlord Sher Shah Suri who briefly usurped power from the Moghuls, added several staging posts (*sarais*) for caravan trains, including **Sirhind** near modern Chandigarh. He also stamped out highway robbery by holding village headmen accountable for crimes committed on their stretch of the road.

In the years to come, the Moghuls sank wells along the Grand Trunk Road, and the British covered it with asphalt. More recently, several sections were converted into 4-lane highways, complete with crash-barriers and neat white lines that everyone ignores. However, the streams of *Tata* trucks and overloaded buses that now tear along NH1 have done little to deter more traditional traffic: donkey carts (*ekkas*), rickshaws, cyclists, and barefoot pilgrims still plod along the hard shoulder, watched by imperious holy cows. The *sarais*, meanwhile, have been overtaken by their twentieth-century counterpart, the roadside *dhaba*, where Sikh truckers in singlets and shorts can wash their long black locks under standpipes, tuck into a plateful of chicken and *chana dal*, and crash out on a *charpoi*. As Kipling put it, "such a river of life . . . exists nowhere in the world."

tal city of Chandigarh, the Moghul monuments at **Sirhind** and **Pinjore**, or the countless brick villages that stud the monotonous plains, you'll find its inhabitants, all of whom seem to have a cousin in Toronto or Southall, extremely hospitable.

Some history

Punjab's arid Chaggar Valley, stretching south from the Shivalik Hills on the HP border to the deserts of Rajasthan, witnessed the rise of urban settlement as early as 3000 BC. Later labelled the **Harappan** civilization, this string of fortified towns was invaded by the Aryans around 1700 BC. Among the Sanskrit scriptures set down in the ensuing "**Vedic**" age was the **Mahabharata**, whose epic battles drew on real-life encounters between the ancient kings of Punjab at **Karnal**, 118km north of Delhi. Conquered by the Mauryans in the third century BC, this became the classic route for Muslim invaders marching on Delhi through the Khyber Pass. These included the mighty Moghul army of Babur, who routed Ibrahim Lodi at **Panipat**, beside the Jamuna, in 1526.

Further north, meanwhile, **Sikhism** was beginning to establish itself under the tutelage of Guru Nanak (1469–1539). Based on the notion of a single Formless God, the Guru's vision of a casteless egalitarian society found favour both with Hindus and Muslims, in spite of Moghul emperor Aurangzeb's concerted attempts to stamp it out. Suppression actually strengthened the Sikh faith in the long run, inspiring the militaristic and confrontational tenth **Guru Gobind Singh** to introduce the Five Ks: part of a rigorous new orthodoxy called the **Khalsa**, or "Community of the Pure" (see *Contexts*).

Having survived repeated seventeenth-century Aghan invasions, the Sikh nation emerged to fill the power vacuum left by the collapse of the Moghuls. Only in the 1840s, after two bloody wars with the British, was the Khalsa army finally defeated. Thereafter, the Sikhs played a vital role in the Raj, helping to quash the Mutiny of 1857. The relationship only soured after the **Jallianwalla Bagh massacre** of 1919 (see p.545), which also ensured that the Punjab's puppet leaders (who hailed the general responsible as a hero) were discredited, leaving the way open for the rise of radicalism.

After the Partition era, things calmed down enough after Independence for the new state to grow wealthy on its prodigious agricultural output. As it did, militant Sikhs began to press for the creation of the separate Punjabi-speaking state they called Khalistan. A compromise of sorts was reached in 1966, when the Hindu district of Haryana and the Sikh-majority Punjab were nominally divided. However, the move did not silence the separatists, and in 1977 Indira Gandhi's Congress was trounced in state elections by a coalition that included the Sikh religious party, the **Akali Dal**.

A more sinister element entered the volatile equation with the emergence of an ultra-radical separatist movement led by **Sant Jaranil Singh Bhindranwale**. Covertly supported by the national government (who saw the group as a way to defeat the Akali Dal), Bhindranwale and his band waged a ruthless campaign of sectarian terror in the Punjab which came to a head in 1984, when they occupied the Golden Temple; Indira's brutal response, **Operation Blue Star** (see p.540), plunged the Punjab into another ugly bout of communal violence. Four years later, history repeated itself when a less threatening occupation of the Temple was crushed by **Operation Black Thunder**. Since then, the Punjabi police have gone on to make considerable advances against the terrorists – helped, for the first time, by the Punjabi peasant farmers, the **Jats**, who had grown tired of the inexorable slaughter. Despite the occasional eruption and the murder of the Governor of Punjab in 1995, these days the situation is calmer, and Haryana and Punjab, previously a no-go zone for tourists, is safe to travel in once again.

Chandigarh

After Partition in 1947, when undivided Punjab's principal city Lahore was claimed by Pakistan, the new state of Punjab found itself without a capital. Premier Jawaharlal Nehru saw this as a golden opportunity to realize his vision of a city "symbolic of the future of India, unfettered by the traditions of the past, [and] an expression of the nation's faith in the future", and dispatched scouts to Europe to search for designers. When their original choice, Polish-born Mathew Nowicki, was killed in a plane crash in 1950, the controversial Swiss-French architect Charles–Edouard Jeanneret, alias **Le Corbusier** (1887–1965), was offered the job.

Begun in 1952, **CHANDIGARH** was to be a ground-breaking experiment in town planning. Instead of the usual amorphous tangle, Le Corbusier's blueprints were for an orderly grid of sweeping boulevards, divided into 29 neat blocks, or **Sectors**, and interspersed with extensive stretches of green: a fusion of "sun, space and verdure". However, far from promoting harmony and accord, the resulting city – situated within sight of the Himalayan foothills between two seasonal rivers – has been a source of controversy since it was completed in the 1960s. Specialists applaud Le Corbusier's brainchild as "the greatest architectural achievement of the twentieth century", while detractors complain that the design was flawed, self-indulgent, and "un-Indian": in a country where only a tiny number of people own cars, Le Corbusier created a city for fast-flowing traffic, complete with dozens of enormous roundabouts and car parks. Nor did he and his team pay much heed to the climate. During the summer, Chandigarh's unfinished concrete office and apartment blocks are like ovens, uninhabitable without expensive air-conditioning. After three decades, many are showing signs of terminal decay, as weeds grow through the cracks in their mildewing walls.

In spite of Chandigarh's infrastructural and aesthetic shortcomings, its 650,000 inhabitants are very proud of their capital, which is cleaner, greener, and more affluent than other Indian cities of comparable size: a sort of south Delhi without the slums. Nor has the orderly American-style street plan entirely eradicated all signs of "Indian-ness", as its critics claim; cycle rickshaw *wallahs* and turbanned *sahajdharis* on scooters add to the traffic chaos, while palmist astrologers ply their trade under the trees on broken pavements.

As a tourist destination, though, Chandigarh is a dud, despite its recent application for UNESCO "World Heritage City" status. Unless you have a penchant for twentieth-century architecture, you'll probably only stay long enough to change buses between Delhi and Himachal Pradesh, or to pick up transport to Amritsar, 240km northwest.

Arrival and information

At the time of going to press, all flights in and out of Chandigarh **airport**, 11km south of the city centre, were indefinitely suspended. When operating, facilities in the terminal building include a small *Indian Airlines* office (☎704539), and a sub-branch of the *State Bank of Patiala*.

Arriving by train, you'll find yourself an inconvenient 8km southeast of the centre. Half-hourly *CTU (Chandigarh Transport Undertaking)* buses stop outside the station, while prepaid auto-rickshaw and taxi booths help to make the journey into town a bit easier. A Chandigarh Industry and Tourism Development Corporation (CITCO) **information counter** hands out maps and leaflets and can make phone bookings for government-approved hotels. The *Northern Railway*'s reservation counter is found at the bus terminal.

Buses from Delhi, HP and Amritsar pull in to the frenetic **Inter-State Bus Terminus** (aka the **ISBT**), on the south edge of the main commercial and shopping district, Sector 17. Only a short walk from most of the hotels, the bus stand also houses *Northern Railway*'s computerized **reservation counter** (Mon–Sat 9am–1pm & 1.30–4pm; ☎704382), on the second floor. The very helpful **tourist office** (Mon–Sat 9am–1pm & 1.30–6pm; ☎704614), with a CITCO Tour & Travel wing (☎703839), is on the first floor – a good place to check bus and train times. Other regional tourist corporations with offices in Chandigarh (all open Mon–Fri 10am–5pm) include Haryana, Sector 17 (☎702955); HP, Sector 22 (☎708569); UP (☎707649); and Punjab, Sector 22 (☎704570).

Several of the banks ranged around the square on the northwest side of Sector 17 **change money**, including the *Andhra Bank*, which also handles *Visa*.

Finally, the 24-hour cloakroom in the bus stand charges Rs1 per article per day for **left luggage**, but will only accept rucksacks if they are securely locked.

> The telephone **area code** for Chandigarh is ☎0172.

City transport
As Chandigarh is too spread out to explore on foot, the most convenient way of **getting around** is to flag down one of its many un-metered blue **auto-rickshaws**: the main rank is beside the bus terminus. **Cycle rickshaws** are almost as ubiquitous, and much cheaper, but find the long haul up to the north end of town very tough going. *Ambassador* **cars** (with drivers) can be rented for half- or full-day sightseeing excursions through the tourist office, or from in front of upmarket hotels such as the *Piccadilly*, *Shivalik View*, and *Mount View*. Expect to pay around Rs500–600 per day.

The City

Chandigarh is made up of 47 numbered **sectors**, subdivided into lettered blocks. Le Corbusier saw the city plan as a living organism, with the imposing **Capital Complex** to the north as a "head", the shopping precinct, **Sector 17**, a "heart", the green open spaces as "lungs", and the cross-cutting network of roads, separated into eight different grades for use by various types of vehicles (in theory only), a "circulatory system". A rickshaw can get around the few noteworthy sights in one or two hours.

The museum and art gallery

Chandigarh's large **museum and art gallery** (Tues–Sun 10am–4.30pm; Rs0.50; camera Rs5), five minutes by rickshaw north of the city centre in Sector 10, houses a sizeable and informatively displayed collection of ancient sculpture, miniature paintings and contemporary Indian art. Among prize pieces on the first floor are a dozen or so standing Buddhas from Gandhara, noted for their delicately carved "wet-look" *lunghis* and distinctly Hellenic features – a legacy of Alexander the Great's conquests. Also Greek-influenced are the beautiful terracotta heads mounted in glass cases at the top of the main staircase; like the Buddhas, they date from the first and second centuries BC.

Art enthusiasts will find plenty to pore over in the adjacent gallery, where abundant exquisite Moghul, Kangra, and Rajasthani miniatures are accompanied by interpretive panels outlining the main features of the respective schools. Modern works featured in the end room include a couple of A N Tagore's atmospheric watercolours, five original Roerichs, and several over-the-top patriotic and devotional Sikh canvasses.

The Capital Complex

Three blocks north of the centre, in the shadow of the Shivalik Hills, the **Capital Complex**, Sector 1, is the site of some of Le Corbusier's most ambitious experiments. The concrete campus, set amid balding sun-parched lawns, was designed to express the strength and unity of independent India. Ironically, the area is now surrounded by barbed wire and patrolled by armed guards, and has been indefinitely closed to tourists since the assassination of the Governor of Punjab, Beant Singh, in front of the Assembly in October 1995. It's a pity as the complex is worth a look, if only to see what inspired all those ferro-concrete university campuses that mushroomed across Europe and the US during the 1960s. Guided **tours** were run by CITCO from the reception desk of the Legislature Assembly (daily 10.30am–12.30pm & 2.30–4.30pm) – check with the tourist office at the bus stand to see if they have been re-instated.

The complex's three most impressive edifices stand to the sides of its giant main piazza. One eminent architect, a fan of Le Corbusier but not of Chandigarh, said that he could see "no possible physical relation between [them]". They were meant to blend together to form a harmonious whole, based on the proportions of the human body (Le Corbusier's **"Le Modulor"** theory); that they don't is largely because the Municipality ran out of money before realizing the plans – hence all the yawning open spaces.

The most imposing edifice in the group is the eight-storey **Secretariat**, Chandigarh's highest building, which houses Haryana and Punjab's ministerial offices, and has a roof garden with good views over the city. The resemblance of the **Legislature Assembly**, or Vidhan Sabha, just north, to a power station is no coincidence: Le Corbusier was allegedly inspired by a stack of cooling towers he saw in Ahmedabad. The most colourful of the three buildings stands opposite the Secretariat. Said to incorporate elements of the Buland Darwaza in Fatehpur Sikri, the **High Court**, whose double roof symbolizes the protective power of the law, is decorated inside with huge woollen tapestries.

Before leaving the Capital Complex, head north from the High Court for a look at the black **Open Hand** monument. Chandigarh's adopted emblem, which revolves on ball-bearings like a weather vane, stands for "post-colonial harmony and peace" – the reason why the army consider it a potential target for Sikh militants.

The rock garden

Close to the Capital Complex, and a refreshing counterpoint to Le Corbusier's drab concrete cityscape, is the bizarre **rock garden** (daily April–Sept 9am–1pm & 3–7pm, Oct–March 9am–1pm & 2–6pm; Rs1), a surreal fantasyland fashioned from fragments

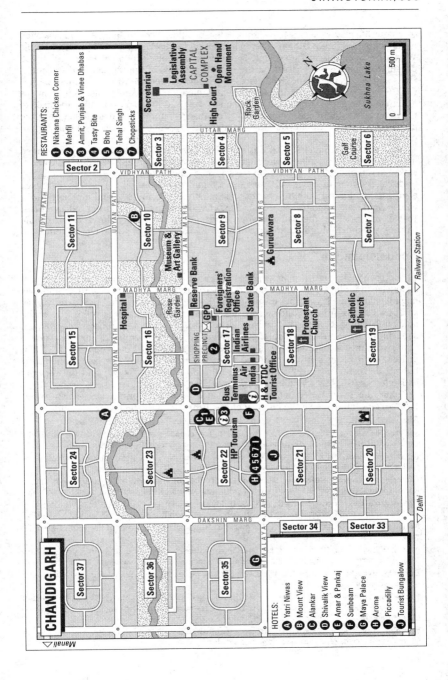

CHANDIGARH

RESTAURANTS:
1. Nikhana Chicken Corner
2. Mehfil
3. Amrit, Punjab & Vinee Dhabas
4. Tasty Bite
5. Bhoj
6. Tehal Singh
7. Chopsticks

HOTELS:
A. Yatri Niwas
B. Mount View
C. Alankar
D. Shivalik View
E. Amar & Pankaj
F. Sunbeam
G. Maya Palace
H. Aroma
I. Piccadilly
J. Tourist Bungalow

of shattered plates, neon strip lights, pots, pebbles, broken bangles and assorted urban-industrial junk. The open-air exhibition is the lifelong labour of retired Public Works Department road inspector, **Nek Chand**. Inspired by a recurrent childhood dream, he spent seven years scouring the stream beds of the Shivalik Hills for materials, and another nine on site before his vision was revealed to the public in 1976. CITCO's leaflet gives a wonderfully romantic rendition of Chand's toils: "Sitting by his hut, under the star-spangled Chandigarh sky, he used to burn cycle and auto-tires to provide him spotlight and, while his eyes profusely watered in the acrid smoke of the improvised fire . . . would patiently shape, stone by stone, an enchanted kingdom of his dreams."

Nearly 40 years on, Nek Chand is still hard at work. His rock garden has expanded into a labyrinthine four-acre site that comprises more than a dozen different enclosures, interconnected by narrow passages, arched walkways, streams, and tiny bridges. Teeming on weekends with excited children and their parents, the complex also features several sculptural set-pieces: mostly birds, animals, and human figures, whose rigid stance and transfixed facial expressions take their cue from Indian *adivasi* (tribal) art. Stick to the path, or you could end up wandering the maze of pebble palaces and mock-Moghul ramparts until the *chowkidar* finds you at closing time.

Accommodation

Chandigarh's sky-high property prices make its **accommodation** among the most expensive in India. Tariffs at the bottom end are particularly inflated, with no improvement in standards. If you want to spend less than Rs150, choice is limited to the railway and bus stations' grim and noisy **retiring rooms** (①), or an airless cell in one of the many unlicensed budget guest houses (alias "tourist bungalows"), tucked away in quiet suburbs or backstreets, which the Municipality are forever trying to close down. Otherwise, try for an economy room in one of the mid-range hotels opposite the ISBT, or look for a vacancy in the cramped modern "**motels**" along the lane immediately behind these (in Sector 22): the best are the *Surya* (☎706037; ④) and the recently expanded and slightly friendlier *Peeush* (☎701090; ③–④).

Luxury tax is not levied in Chandigarh, but several of the pricier places slap 10 percent **service charges** on the bill. **Checkout time** for all the following is noon.

Alankar, Sector 22-A (☎708801). Modern, clean and close to the bus stand. Some a/c. ⑤.

Amar, 806-6 Udyog Path, Sector 22-A (☎602723). The cheapest of 3 identikit hotels in this block (opposite the ISBT). Simple, tidy en-suite rooms with air-coolers, but no single occupancy. ④–⑤.

Aroma, Himalaya Marg, Sector 22-C (☎700045). Reasonably priced 2-star with restaurant, lawn, pastry/coffee shop, and some good value non-a/c rooms. ⑥–⑦.

Chandigarh Tourist Bungalow, 97 Sector 21-A (☎704329). The best of the unlicensed "bungalows". Cleaner than average en-suite rooms (with windows), near the bus stand. Some a/c. ②–⑤.

Chandigarh Yatri Niwas, Sector 24 (☎545904). Municipal hostel, well out of centre. Clean and popular, but spartan, with shared shower-toilets only; call to see if it has vacancies. Some a/c. ③–④.

Maya Palace, SCO 325-28 Sector 35-B (☎600547). Comfortable, and one of the best of the mid-range hotels sprouting up along this strip. ⑦.

Mount View, Sector 10 (☎547882; fax 547120). Chandigarh's top hotel, in its own grounds 2km from the centre. Most amenities, and multi-cuisine restaurant, foreign exchange, and a pool. ⑧–⑨.

Pankaj, Udyog Path, Sector 22-A (☎709891). Slightly more expensive than *Amar* next door, but a bit more comfortable. ⑤.

Piccadilly, Himalaya Marg, Sector 22-B (☎707571). Recently rebuilt, upmarket business-oriented hotel close to the city centre with central a/c, classy restaurant, bar, coffee shop, and in-house travel agent. ⑦–⑧.

Shivalik View, Sector 17 (☎61731). The largest and swankiest hotel in the centre boasts a rooftop Chinese restaurant, 24hr cafe, and shopping arcade. ⑦–⑧.

ACCOMMODATION PRICE CODES

All **accommodation prices** in this book have been coded using the symbols below. In principle the prices given are for the least expensive double rooms in each establishment; however, some hotels, usually in category ①, offer rates per bed rather than per room. Local taxes are not included unless specifically stated. For more details, see p.35.

① up to Rs100	④ Rs225–350	⑦ Rs750–1200
② Rs100–150	⑤ Rs350–500	⑧ Rs1200–2200
③ Rs150–225	⑥ Rs500–750	⑨ Rs2200 and upwards

Sunbeam, Udyog Path, Sector 22-B (☎708100). Top-notch hotel with swish marble lobby and most comforts: central a/c, coffee shop, foreign exchange. Good value for its class. ⑦.

Eating

Chandigarh has no shortage of **places to eat**, whether you just want to grab a quick snack between buses from a rough-and-ready roadside *dhaba*, try some of the new fast food joints serving veggie burgers and ice-cream or splash out on a classy Punjabi meal. Alcohol is widely available and there is a sprinkling of **pubs** around Sector 17 serving mediocre beer on tap in somewhat soulless surroundings.

Amrit, Punjabi & Vinee, opposite the bus stand. Identical rock-bottom but hygienic *dhabas*; spicy piles of no-nonsense south Indian food, Punjabi *tandoori* and filling *chana batura* from formica tables.

Bhoj, #1090-1, Sector 22-B. Classy pure-veg *thali* joint run by Sai Baba devotees. Recommended.

Chopsticks, near *Hotel Piccadilly*, Himalaya Marg. A/c Chinese restaurant with tinted windows and an impressive menu that includes some Indian options. Moderate.

Mehfil, Sector 17 (☎544224). The exclusive preserve of Chandigarh's smart set, *the* place to splurge on rich Mughlai and Punjabi cuisine in a/c comfort. Reservations for dinner.

Nikaha Chicken Corner, Udyog Path, Sector 22-B. No-frills *dhaba* serving large portions of cheap, spicy and delicious chicken (*tandoori*, barbeque or freshly fried) to a beer-swilling male clientele.

Tasty Bite, Himalaya Marg. Snazzy south Indian fast food that specializes in veggie burgers, *dosas*, shakes and other light snacks. Moderate.

Tehal Singh, #1116-17 Sector 22-B. Cheap and very popular *tandoori* restaurant which has a reputation as a hard drinking joint at night. *Singh's Chicken* right next door provides stiff competition.

Listings

Emergency Police ☎100 and 544437; ambulance ☎102.

Foreigners' regional registration office Visas may be extended at the FRRO in the Town Hall Building, Sector 17 (Mon–Fri 10am–5pm).

Hospitals Chandigarh's General Hospital is in Sector 16 (☎43175), but is not as good as the *PGI*, Sector 12 (☎541018).

Optician *Weldon*, SCO 83, Sector 17D (☎703024), provides an efficient same-day service.

Shopping Several states run handicraft emporiums in the Sector 17 shopping complex, among them Haryana, whose *Phulkari* store stocks a good range of embroidered silk, woodwork, and traditional pointed Punjabi shoes (*phulkari*). For quality handloom products, try the nearby UP emporium, or the *Khadi Gramodyog* in the *Shivalik View*'s small arcade: both are strong on block-printed calico garments, especially women's *salwar kamise*. Sector 17 also has a couple of good bookshops including *Capital Book Depot* with a large travel section including maps and *Rough Guides*.

Sport Rowing boats and pedalos can be rented on Sukhna Lake, in the north of the city. There are swimming pools in Sectors 14 (the University campus) & 23, just 5 min by rickshaw from the centre.

MOVING ON FROM CHANDIGARH

Chandigarh's long-distance transport connections are summarized on p.530. As the railway station is 8km from the centre, most travellers **move on** from the city by **bus**. Ordinary state buses operate out of the Inter-State Bus Terminus (ISBT) in Sector 17, as do additional tourist development corporation a/c, deluxe, and semi-deluxe services to destinations such as Delhi, Manali, and Amritsar. Buses run every 20min to **Delhi** (248km; 5hr 30min–6hr), a journey which can be made in as little as 3hr by train on the superfast a/c *Shatabdi Express* #2006 (depart 6.50am).

The quickest way to get to **Shimla** is by bus – direct *Himachal-* or *Haryana-SRTC* "express" services leave every 20–30min from the ISBT (3hr 30min–4hr). You can also get there on the slower but more congenial Viceroys' "Toy Train" (see p.437), but you have to catch a bus 26km northeast to **Kalka** first. For details of connecting services, see p.530.

Tickets for a/c, deluxe, and semi-deluxe bus services have to be pre-booked at the reservation hatches on the ground floor of the ISBT. For ordinary express buses, you can either buy your ticket at the booths on the platform, or pay the conductor. There are no printed timetables but CITCO's tourist office in the ISBT can provide booking information.

Indian Airlines' useful weekly flight to **Leh** has been indefinitely suspended and at the time of going to press there were no civilian flights in or out of the airport. **Airline offices** in Chandigarh include *Air India*, #124, Sector 17 (Mon–Fri 9.30am–1pm & 2–5.30pm, Sat 9.30am–1pm; ☎703510); *Archana Airlines*, Sector 8 (☎44395); *Indian Airlines*, #171-2, Sector 17-C (Mon–Fri 10am–1pm & 2–5pm; ☎704539); *Japan Airlines*, *Onkar Travels*, Sector 17-B (☎704910); *Kuwait Airlines*, *Trans Air Travels*, Sector 17 (☎702833); *Lufthansa*, Sector 17-C (☎702435). *Bajaj Travels*, SCO 96-97 Sector 17-C (☎704500) are agents for international airlines.

Sirhind

Close to the Grand Trunk Road (NH1) and *Northern Railway*, **SIRHIND**, 48km southwest of Chandigarh, was the capital of the Pathan Suri Sultans, and the site of an important *caravansarai* (the name derives from *Sir-i-Hind*, "Frontier of Hind"). Today, only a couple of minor-league Moghul palaces, hot baths, and pleasure pavilions remain from the illustrious past, but it is still a pleasant overnight stop between Delhi and Amritsar, just as it was when the emperors and their entourages passed through.

The Moghul ruins and PTDC's *Maulsarai Tourist Complex*, known collectively as **Aam-Khas-Bagh**, lie 2.5km north of the town proper. Here, Sirhind's best-preserved **monuments** lie, encircled by the high walls of Sher Shah Suri's sixteenth-century **fort**, later developed by Jehangir. Approached via a tree- and fountain-lined walkway, the ruins of the old baths, or **hammam**, enclose a giant circular well whose water used to be hauled up by hand using pulleys, and channelled into geometric bathing pools outside. Nearby, the shell of emperor Shah Jahan's double-storey residence, the **Daulat Khana**, overlooks the leafy gardens and farmland. Originally decorated with ceramic tiles and elaborate stucco, only a few traces of painted plaster still cling to the exposed brickwork on the roof. Just behind the tourist complex, and in much better shape than the ruins at the opposite end of the garden, is the seventeenth-century **Sheesh Mahal**. The elegant "Palace of Mirrors", sometimes used as an Archaeological Survey office, presides over Jehangir's large tank, surrounded by ramparts. For some unfathomable reason, the tank has resisted all recent attempts at being filled and sports a healthy lawn instead.

Across the fields behind the tourist complex garden, 1.5km to the north, is the *gurudwara* (shrine), in the basement of the pristine white **Fatehgarh Sahib**. This important Sikh shrine is in memory of Guru Gobind Singh's two youngest sons who were walled in here alive by the Moghul emperor Aurangzeb for not embracing Islam.

Next door to Fatehgarh Sahib, the fourteenth-century *dargah*, dedicated to a Sufi saint, attracts bus loads of Muslim pilgrims and provides a sharp reminder of the intense friction caused by the proximity of religions so fundamentally opposed.

Practicalities

Regular **buses** run between Chandigarh and Sirhind (every 20min; 1hr 30min); the **railway station**, 5km from the tourist complex (see below), is served by trains from Delhi and Amritsar. Cycle rickshaws will ferry you out to the complex for Rs20, but it's easier to jump off the bus as it passes the turning on the main road. Buses from Amritsar usually drop passengers at the Grand Trunk Road intersection, 7km south of Aam-Khas-Bagh; catch a local bus into town to pick up a cycle rickshaw for the last leg.

Housed in a small eighteenth-century summer palace, the **PTDC tourist complex** overlooks the well-watered garden on one side, and the old tank and Sheesh Mahal on the other. As the Archaeological Survey has repossessed much of the building, there is just one large but shabby room left which at Rs200 per night, is overpriced, but full of character, with high ceilings and lots of peeling plaster. A new purpose-built hotel currently under construction next door threatens to be an intrusion on the medieval surroundings. Inexpensive **food**, chilled beers, and cold **drinks** are served in the dining room, or *al fresco* on the tank-side terrace. **Mosquitoes** can be a problem, so if you do eat outside, slap on plenty of insect repellent.

Pinjore

PINJORE, 22km north of Chandigarh on the Shimla road, is best known for its walled **Yadavindra Gardens**, one of many sites associated with the exile of the Pandavas, chronicled in the *Mahabharata*. The gardens, a well-watered beauty spot at the foot of the Shivalik Hills 4km south of Kalka, originally belonged to the rajas of Sirmaur. Under the Moghuls, it was taken over by Aurangzeb's foster brother, Fidai Khan, who erected three pleasure palaces for his wife amid the cypress trees and lush *maidans*. Legend has it that the Raja reclaimed his summer retreat by sending a female fruit-seller with goitre as a present to the imposters. On being told that the woman's unsightly swelling was caused by the local water, the Begum and her entourage fled.

These days, the walled gardens harbour a small **otter sanctuary**, **aviary**, and **zoo**, and are popular places for a picnic. One of three attractive Moghul summer palaces has been converted by Haryana Tourism into an extensive and comfortable hotel, the *Budgerigar Motel* (☎01733/67759; ④–⑦), which boasts half a dozen a/c rooms and is a convenient place to break a car journey between Delhi and Shimla. Local **buses** connect Pinjore with Kalka and Chandigarh.

Pathankot

The dusty town of **PATHANKOT**, at the end of the northbound railway line from Delhi near the border with Himachal Pradesh, and 270km north of Chandigarh, is only worth passing through to pick up bus connections to Dharamsala, Dalhousie, Chamba and Kashmir, or to take the slow train east across the Kangra Valley. If you're stuck in town waiting for a connection, you can make a short excursion to the pale sandstone fort of **Shahpur Kandi**, 13km north; buses and shared *tempos* are available from the Civil Hospital. Now empty, this was a stronghold of the rajas of Pathan in the sixteenth century.

Practicalities

Pathankot can rustle up a few **hotels**, should you need to spend the night. Rooms at *Hotel Airlines* on Post Office Chowk (☎0186/20505; ②–③) are unspectacular but reasonable, and there's a restaurant-cum-bar; the *Tourist Hotel and Restaurant* (☎0186/20660; ②–③), on Railway Rd, has unelaborate, fairly clean rooms with attached bath but little ventilation. The best bet, if you're lucky enough to find space, are the well-kept *Railway Retiring Rooms* (①–②); in addition to the usual basic ones, a couple of comfortable a/c rooms provide sofa and chairs, carpets, and a private bathroom with hot water. PTDC's *Gulmohar Tourist Complex*, Shimla Pahari, Mission Rd (☎0186/20292; ③–④), exudes an institutional atmosphere but has a wide choice of rooms including a/c, a cheap dorm, a reasonable restaurant and bar and a pleasant garden ideal for breakfast or a beer in the evenings. *Venice*, Dhangu Rd (☎0186/25061; ⑥–⑦), typical of a new breed of plush business hotels, is possibly the most comfortable in Pathankot.

Amritsar

The Sikh's holy city of **AMRITSAR**, site of the fabled **Golden Temple**, is the largest city in Punjab, an inevitable port of call for travellers heading to or from the Pakistani frontier crossing at Wagha, 29km west. If you are arriving from Lahore, you may find it a vibrant yet relaxed place, full of well-stocked bazaars and courteous people. Visitors bound for the border, however, tend to remember Amritsar as a run-of-the-mill Indian city: noisy, dirty, dusty, and hopelessly congested. Its one saving grace, and incentive enough to make a special trip out west, is the Golden Temple, which rises above the melee like an eye in a storm of teeming streets and tenement blocks.

Some history

Amritsar was founded in 1577 by **Ram Das**, the fourth Sikh Guru, beside a bathing pool famed for its healing powers. The land around the tank was granted in perpetuity by the Moghul Akbar to the Sikhs (who paid off the local Jat farmers to avoid any future dispute over ownership). When merchants moved in to take advantage of the strategic location on the Silk Route, Amritsar expanded rapidly, gaining a grand new temple under Ram Das' son and heir, **Guru Arjan Singh**. Sacked by Afghans in 1761, the shrine was rebuilt by the Sikhs' greatest secular leader, **Maharajah Ranjit Singh**, who donated the gold top for which the temple would henceforth be renowned.

Amritsar's history in the **twentieth century** has been blighted by a series of appalling **massacres**. The first occurred in 1919, when thousands of unarmed civilian demonstrators were gunned down without warning by British troops in **Jallianwalla Bagh** – an atrocity that inspired Gandhi's Non-Cooperation Movement. Following the collapse of the Raj, Amritsar experienced some of the worst communal blood-letting ever seen in the subcontinent. The Golden Temple, however, remained unaffected by the volatile politics of post-Independence Punjab until the 1980s. As part of a protracted and bloody campaign for the setting up of a Sikh homeland, heavily armed fundamentalists under the preacher-warrior, Sant Jaranil Singh **Bhindranwale**, occupied the Akal Takht, symbol of Sikh militancy. The siege was brought to an end in early June 1984, when prime minister Indira Gandhi ordered an inept paramilitary attack on the temple, code-named **Operation Blue Star**. An estimated 200 soldiers, and 2000 others, including pilgrims trapped in the *gurudwaras* and Bhindranwale himself, died.

Widely regarded as an unmitigated disaster, Blue Star led directly to the assassination of Indira Gandhi by her Sikh bodyguards just four months later, and provoked the worst riots in the city since Partition. Nevertheless, the Congress government seemed to learn little from its mistakes. In 1987, Indira's son, Rajiv Gandhi, reneged on an

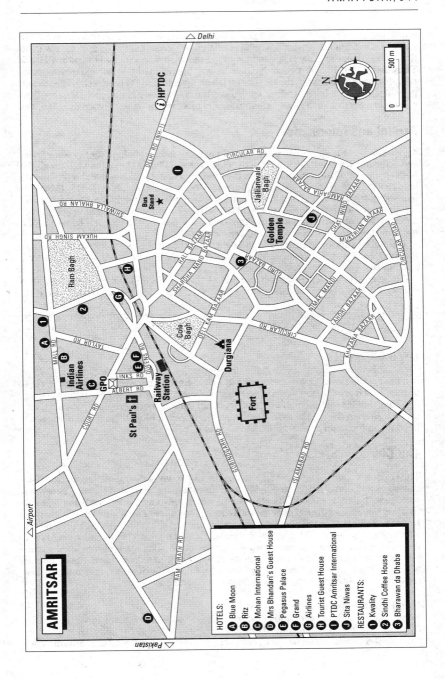

△ Delhi

i HPTDC

CIRCULAR RD

Jallianwala Bagh

HAMGAHA BAZAAR

CHITTI WIND BAZAAR

Golden Temple

MUKERIAN BAZAAR

SHIWALLA BHALAN RD

Bus Stand ★

HUKAM SINGH RD

HALL BAZAAR

SHARDHA MAND BAZAAR

GURU BAZAAR

3

CIRCULAR ROAD

Ram Bagh

NIMAK MANDI

LAHORI BAZAAR

TAYLOR RD

2

G

H

Cole Bagh

DEL TIAN BAZAAR

KHATANA BAZAAR

CIRCULAR RD

MALL RD

A **I**

B Indian Airlines

C GPO

LINKS RD

E **F**

QUEENS RD

ALBERT RD

Durgiana

GOBINDGARH RD

ISTAMABAD RD

COURT RD

St Paul's

Railway Station

Fort

RAM TIRATH RD

D

△ Airport

▽ Pakistan

AMRITSAR

HOTELS:
A Blue Moon
B Ritz
C Mohan International
D Mrs Bhandari's Guest House
E Pegasus Palace
F Grand
G Airlines
H Tourist Guest House
I PTDC Amritsar International
J Sita Niwas

RESTAURANTS:
1 Kwality
2 Sindhi Coffee House
3 Bharawan da Dhaba

0   500 m

N

important accord with the Sikhs' main religious party, the Akali Dal, thereby strengthening the hand of the separatists, who retaliated by occupying the temple for a second time. This time, the army responded with greater restraint, leaving **Operation Black Thunder** to the Punjab police. Neither as well-provisioned nor as well-motivated as Bhindranwale's martyrs, the fundamentalists eventually surrendered. The defeat proved a major set-back for their cause, and today, Amritsar is no more unstable than most other north Indian cities with a culturally mixed population of more than 700,000.

Arrival and information

Amritsar's quiet domestic **airport**, arrival point for *Indian Airlines* flights from Delhi and Srinagar, lies 12km northwest of the city. **Trains** pull in at the railway station on the northern edge of the centre, 2km west of the inter-state bus stand, and a ten-minute auto-rickshaw ride from PTDC's **tourist office**, Mall Mandi, GT Rd (Mon–Fri 9am–5pm; ☎231452). It's hard to think of any reason why you might want to call in here, but the staff are helpful. Another similarly low-key but friendly tourist office can be found at the *Amritsar International Hotel*, near the bus stand. To obtain reliable bus and train information, join the rucks at the respective stations.

Changing money in Amritsar can be a bit of a headache as leading banks such as the *State Bank of India*, halfway between the bus stand and the Golden Temple have a habit of suspending their foreign exchange transactions. Best to try the hotels first.

Luggage can be left for short periods at the Golden Temple's *gurudwaras* (see below), or, provided it is securely locked, at the railway station cloakroom.

The telephone **area code** for Amritsar is ☎0183.

City transport

Amritsar is too large and labyrinthine to negotiate on foot. If you are crossing town or in a hurry, flag down an (un-metered) **auto-rickshaw**. Otherwise, stick to **cycle rickshaws**, which are the best way to get around the narrow, packed streets of the old quarter. Taxi *wallahs* tout for trade outside the train station (northern exit, turn left), and the *Ritz Hotel* in the north of the city. Alternatively, rent a **bicycle** from one of the stalls lined up on the main road outside the bus stand.

The City

The Golden Temple stands in the heart of the **old town**: a disorientating maze of narrow lanes and bazaars encircled by a broad thoroughfare. Eighteen fortified **gateways** punctuate the aptly named **Circular Rd**, of which only one (to the north) is original. Skirting the edge of the old quarter, the railway line, crossed by a series of chaotic road bridges, forms a sharp divide between the bazaar and the more spacious British-built side of the city. Most of the hotels and restaurants are located in this district, around the Maginot-Line-style **railway station**. Further north, long straight tree-lined streets full of fast-moving traffic eventually peter out into leafy residential suburbs, peppered with run-down churches and colonial bungalows. The fastidiously neat military barracks of the **cantonment** form the northwestern limits of the city.

The Golden Temple

Even visitors without a religious bone in their bodies cannot fail to be moved by Amritsar's resplendent **Golden Temple**, spiritual centre of the Sikh faith. Built by Guru **Arjan Singh** in the late sixteenth century, the richly gilded **Hari Mandir** rises from the middle of a rectangular artificial lake, connected to the toothpaste-white marble complex that surrounds it by a narrow causeway. For Sikhs, this serene spectacle is as sacred as the Ka'aba and Mecca are for Muslims. Every devout member of the faith tries to make at least one pilgrimage here in their lifetime for *darshan* of the original Sikh holy book, the *Adi Granth*, and to bathe in the purifying waters of the temple tank, known since the time of the fourth Guru, **Ram Das** (1574–81), as the **Amrit Sarovar** ("Pool of Immortality-Giving Nectar").

The Golden Temple is also renowned for the two bloody battles waged in the 1980s between Sikh militants and the Indian army and police. However, since Operations **Blue Star** and **Black Thunder**, things have calmed down considerably, and life inside the complex has returned to normal. Ugly scars remain, but most of the bullet-holes and shell craters have been patched up, and the once-conspicuous military presence in the surrounding alleys and squares is now very low-key.

The best time to visit the temple is on a weekday morning before it is swamped by crowds. Get here early enough, and you'll catch the first rays of sunlight gleaming on the shrine's bulbous golden domes, whose shimmering reflection in the water of the Amrit Sarovar, enlivened by **kirtans** (devotional songs) emanating from the inner sanctum, is something to savour.

THE PARIKRAMA

The principal north entrance to the temple, the **Darshini Darwaza**, leads under a Victorian **clock tower**, which caught fire during Operation Black Thunder, to the head of a flight of steps, from where you catch your first glimpse of the Hari Mandir, floating serenely above the glassy surface of the Amrit Sarovar. Dropping down as a reminder of the humility necessary to approach God, the steps end at the polished marble **Parikrama** that surrounds the tank, its smooth white stones set with the names of Sikh worthies who contributed to the temple's construction. A long colonnaded verandah opens onto the sacred pavement, always circled in a clockwise direction.

The shrines on the north edge of the enclosure are known as the **68 Holy Places**. Arun Singh, the fifth Guru, told his followers that a visit to these was equivalent to a pilgrimage around all 68 of India's most sacred Hindu sites. Several have been converted into a **Gallery of Martyrs** in which paintings of glorious but very gory episodes from Sikh history are displayed.

Four glass-fronted booths punctuate the Parikrama. Seated in each is a priest, or **granthi**, intoning verses from the *Adi Granth*. The continuous readings are performed in shifts; passing pilgrims touch the steps in front of the booths with their heads and leave offerings of money.

At the east end of the Parikrama, the two truncated **Ramgarhia Minars** – brick watchtowers whose tops were blasted off during Operation Blue Star – overlook the Guru-ka-Langar and the main bathing **ghats**. Hang around here long enough, and you'll see a fair cross-section of modern Sikh society parade past: families of Jat farmers, NRIs (Non-Resident Indians) on holiday from Britain and North America flaunting flash

GOLDEN RULES

Visitors of all nationalities and religions are allowed into the Golden Temple provided they respect a few basic **rules**, enforced by patrolling guards. Firstly, tobacco, alcohol and drugs of any kind are forbidden. Before entering, you should also leave your shoes at the free cloakrooms, cover your head with some kind of cloth (cotton scarves are available free at the entrance gate or at the information office, or sold for Rs5 at the shops outside the main entrance), and wash your feet in the pool below the steps. **Photography** is permitted on the *parikrama*, but not inside any of the shrines.

video cameras, and the odd group of fierce-looking warriors carrying lances, sabres and long curved daggers. Distinguished by their deep-blue knee-length robes and saffron turbans, the ultra-orthodox **nihangs** (literally "crocodiles") are devotees of the militaristic tenth Guru Gobind Singh.

THE GURU-KA-LANGAR

For Sikhs, no pilgrimage to the Golden Temple is considered complete without a visit to the **Guru-ka-Langar**. The giant communal canteen, which overlooks the eastern entrance to the temple complex, provides **free food** to all-comers, regardless of creed, colour, caste or gender. Sharing meals with strangers in this way is intended to reinforce one of the central tenets of the Sikh faith, the **principle of equality**, instigated by the third Guru, **Amar Das**, in the sixteenth century to break down caste barriers.

The tradition of commensality is still practised in *gurudwaras* all over India, but nowhere more forcefully reaffirmed than here at the Langar. Some 10,000 *chapati* and black *dal* dinners are dished up each day in an operation of typical Sikh efficiency, which you can witness for yourself by joining the queues that form outside the hall at meal times (daily 11am–3pm & 7–9pm). When the doors open, up to 3000 pilgrims at a time pile in to take their places on the long coir floor mats. The meal begins only after grace has been sung with great solemnity by a Langar volunteer, or *sevak*, and continues until everyone has eaten their fill. By the time the tin trays have been collected up and the floors swept for the next sitting, another crowd of hungry pilgrims has gathered at the gates, and the cycle starts again. Although the meals are paid for out of the temple's coffers, most visitors leave a small donation in the boxes in the yard outside.

THE AKAL TAKHT

Directly opposite the ceremonial entrance to the Hari Mandir, the **Akal Takht** is the second most sacred shrine in the Golden Temple complex. A symbol of God's authority on earth, it was built by Gobind Singh in the seventeenth century to house the *Shiroman Gurudwara Parbandhak* committee, the religious and political governing body of the Sikh faith, which he founded.

During the 1984 siege, **Bhindranwale** and his army used the golden-domed building as a headquarters, fortifying it with sandbags and machine-gun posts. When Indian paratroopers tried to storm the shrine, they were mown down in their hundreds while crossing the courtyard in front of it: the reason why the army ultimately resorted to much heavier-handed tactics to end the siege. Positioned at the opposite end of the Amrit Sarovar, tanks pumped a salvo of high-explosive squash-head shells into the delicate facade, reducing it to rubble within seconds. The destruction of the Akal Takht offended Sikh sensibilities more than any other aspect of the operation.

The shrine has been largely rebuilt and now looks almost the same as it did before June 6, 1984. Decorated with elaborate inlay, its ground floor is where the *Adi Granth* is brought each evening from the Hari Mandir, borne in a gold and silver *palladin*.

THE JUBI TREE

The gnarled old **Jubi Tree** in the northwest corner of the compound was planted 450 years ago by the Golden Temple's first High Priest, or *Babba Buddhaya*, and is believed to have special powers. Barren women wanting a son hang strips of cloth from its branches, while marriage deals are traditionally struck in its shade for good luck – a practice frowned upon by the modern temple administration.

THE HARI MANDIR

Likened by one Guru to "a ship crossing the ocean of ignorance", the triple-storeyed **Hari Mandir**, the "Golden Temple of God" from which the complex takes its name, was built by Arjan Singh to house the *Adi Granth*, or "Original Book", which he com-

THE JALLIANWALLA BAGH MASSACRE

Only 100m northeast of the Golden Temple, a narrow lane leads between two tall build-ings to **Jallianwalla Bagh** memorial park (summer 9am–5pm, winter 10am–4pm), site of one of the bloodiest atrocities committed in the history of the British Raj.

In 1919, a series of one-day strikes, or *hartals*, was staged in Amritsar in protest against the recent **Rowlatt Act**, which enabled the British to imprison without trial any Indian suspected of sedition. When the peaceful demonstrations escalated into sporadic looting, the Lieutenant Governor of Punjab declared martial law and called for reinforcements from Jalandhar. A platoon of infantry arrived soon after, led by **General REH Dyer**.

Despite a ban on public meetings, a mass demonstration was called by Mahatma Gandhi for April 13, the Sikh holiday of Bhaisakhi. The venue was to be a round-bot-tomed stretch of waste ground in the heart of the city, hemmed in by high brick walls and with only a couple of alleys for access. An estimated 20,000 people gathered in Jallianwalla Bagh for the meeting. However, before any speakers could address the crowd, Dyer and his 150 troops, stationed on a patch of high ground in front of the main exit, opened fire without warning. By the time they had finished firing, ten to fifteen minutes later, thousands of unarmed demonstrators lay dead and dying, many of them shot in the back while clambering over the walls. Others perished after diving for cover into the well that still stands in the middle of the *bagh*.

No one knows exactly how many people were killed. Official estimates put the death toll at 372, with 1200 injured, although the final figure may well have been three to four times higher. Hushed up for over six months in Britain, the Jallianwalla Bagh massacre caused an international outcry when the story finally broke. It also proved seminal in the independence struggle, prompting Gandhi to initiate the widespread civil disobedience campaign that played such a significant part in ridding India of its colonial overlords.

Moving first-hand accounts of the horrific events of April 13, 1919, and contemporary pictures and newspaper reports, are displayed in Jallianwalla Bagh's small **martyrs gallery**. The **well**, complete with chilling bullet holes, has been turned into a memorial to the victims.

piled from the teachings of all the Sikh gurus, and which still forms the lynchpin of the Sikh faith. Instead of the usual single door, the temple has four to indicate that it is open to all four caste divisions of Hindu society. The large dome on its gilded roof, decked with 100kg of gold leaf, is in the form of an inverted lotus, symbolizing the Sikhs' concern for temporal as well as spiritual matters.

The long causeway, or **"Guru's Bridge"**, which joins the Mandir to the west side of the Sarovar, is approached via an ornate archway, the **Darshani Deorhi**, where wor-shippers collect dollops of sticky sweet wheaten porridge on a leaf: **prasad** that will later be placed as an offering in the shrine itself. As you approach the sanctum, check out the amazing Moghul-style marble inlay on its sides, and the beautiful floral gilt above the doors and windows.

The **interior** of the temple, dripping in yet more gold and silver, and adorned with ivory mosaics and intricately carved wood panels, is dominated by the enormous **Adi Granth**, which rests on a sumptuous throne beneath a jewel-encrusted silk canopy. Before his death in 1708, Guru Gobind Singh, who revised the *Adi Granth*, declared that he was to be the last living Guru, and that the tome would take over after him: hence its full title, the *Guru Granth Sahib*. *Granthis* intone continuous readings from the text as the worshippers file past, accompanied by singers and musicians, whose ethereal performance is relayed by loudspeakers around the complex. Known *as Shri Akhand Path*, a single continuous reading of the *Guru Granth Sahib* is carried out in three-hour shifts and takes around forty-eight hours to complete.

Accommodation

Amritsar's numerous **hotels** are spread out all over the city. While mid-range and upmarket accommodation is plentiful, budget options are few and far between, limited to the Golden Temple's rudimentary *gurudwaras* (see below), or the *Tourist Guest House*, on the main road between the bus stand and the railway station, which commission-hungry rickshaw *wallahs* will try to tell you is full.

Airlines, Cooper Rd (☎64848). Solid mid-price hotel with a good Chinese restaurant, en-suite carpeted rooms with TV, some a/c, and swings. Close to the railway station. ④–⑤.

Blue Moon, The Mall (☎220416). Well situated near the main crossroads. Often compared to the more expensive *Ritz* but much cheaper and plainer. ⑤–⑥.

Grand, opposite the railway station (☎62421). Neat, clean, convenient and central: the best deal in its category in the city centre. ⑤–⑤.

Mohan International, Albert Rd (☎227801). Amritsar's top hotel has all the trimmings, including central a/c, swish restaurant, coffee shop, bathtubs, and a pool, but is looking a touch run-down. ⑧.

Mrs Bhandari's Guest House, 10 Cantonment (☎222390). Separate chalets in pukka colonial home, complete with original 1950s fittings, furniture, and feel. Camping/parking space in the garden popular with overlanders. Not cheap, but worth the extra for the novelty. Recommended. ⑥.

Pegasus Palace, opposite the railway station (☎65111). Unappealing, but the cleanest of the dives around the station, and a good fall-back if the *Tourist Guest House* is full. ②.

PTDC Amritsar International, near the bus stand (☎555991). Large, poorly maintained government-run establishment with pretensions of grandeur. Very handy for the bus stand. ④–⑦.

Ritz, 45 The Mall (☎226606). Slightly old-fashioned hotel in quiet suburb just north of city centre, with lawns, gym and a pool. A bit expensive for what it is but otherwise quite pleasant. ⑧.

Sita Niwas, near *Guru Ram Das Niwas* and Golden Temple (☎543092). Budget option in case the *gurudwara* doesn't appeal. Variously priced rooms; some are poky. 24hr hot water and some attached bathrooms also available. ②–④.

Tourist Guest House, Hide Market, near Bhandari Bridge, GT Rd (☎553830). Pitched at budget travellers; a shabby vestige of the "hippy trail" days, run by a retired army officer. Avoid the rooms at the back next to the railway, and the absurdly overpriced food, served on a verandah. ②–③.

THE GURUDWARAS

Undoubtedly the most authentic places to stay in Amritsar are the Golden Temple's two **gurudwaras**. Intended for use by Sikh pilgrims, these charitable institutions also open their doors to foreign tourists, who can stay for a maximum of three nights. Lodging is free, as is the Sikh custom, but donations are gratefully accepted. Of the pair, the *Sri Guru Ram Das Niwas* is the larger, while the neighbouring *Sri Guru Nanak Niwas* (where Bhindranwale and his men holed up prior to the Golden Temple siege in 1984) also offers a limited number of double rooms with attached shower-toilets. A charge is made for these, but they're still a bargain at only Rs15 per night.

Apart from the inevitable dawn chorus of throat-clearing, the downside of staying in a *gurudwara* is that facilities are very basic (*charpoi* beds and communal wash basins in the central courtyard), and **security** a real problem: mug shots of thieves caught stealing pilgrims' possessions are displayed at the main entrance. If space is limited, as it nearly always is during temple festivals, tourists tend to be rounded up and crammed into a bedless, airless dorm, prompting most to decamp for more congenial quarters elsewhere.

Eating

Amritsar boasts a clutch of swish a/c **restaurants**, mostly located in the modern end of town north of the railway. For cheaper food, try the simple vegetarian **dhabas** opposite the Golden Temple, or the bus stand, where a pile of hot *puris* and spicy *chana dal* will set you back less than Rs20. Some local specialities are **Amritsari fish** and *pinnies* and *matthies*, sweets made from lentils available at *Durga's* on Lawrence Rd.

Bharawan da Dhaba, near Town Hall. One of the best *dhabas* in Amritsar, not far from the Golden Temple. Cheap, wholesome and recommended.

Kwality, Mall Rd. Inexpensive, hygienic south Indian snack bar-cum-ice-cream parlour, in addition to the usual dimly lit a/c restaurant.

Mrs Bhandari's, 10 Cantonment (☎222390). Homely "British-style" 3-course meals (pudding and custard for desert) cooked in Mrs B's "Commando Bridge" kitchen. Reservations essential for non-residents. Moderate to expensive.

Palace, ground floor, *Hotel Pegasus Palace*, opposite railway station. A jumped-up *dhaba* serving generous piles of non-veg Indian food, *biryanis* and chicken dishes. Cheap, but low on atmosphere.

Sindhi Coffee House, opposite Ram Bagh. Tinted windows and table cloths, and an exhaustive mixed-cuisine menu that includes several Sindhi specialities. Moderate to expensive.

Listings

Church St Paul's Catholic Church on Albert Rd opposite the train station holds mass daily at 8am during the summer, or 8.30am in winter.

Emergency Ambulance ☎220900.

Hospitals *Kakkar House Hospital*, Green Ave (☎210964), *Sri Guru Nanak Dev*, Majhita Rd (☎220805) and *Madanlal Chpra Hospital*, Mall Rd (☎223046) are the best in the city.

Shopping *Tablas* (hand-drums), harmonia and other musical instruments are available at the shops outside the Golden Temple, where you can also buy cheap cassettes of the beautiful *kirtans* played in the shrine itself. Other possible souvenirs include a pair of traditional *Arabian Nights*-style Punjabi leather slippers – sold at stalls east of the temple's main entrance. While you are there, keep an eye out for the man who distributes religious pamphlets that include: *Cleaning Up The Ganges, The Cow and Peace*, and, most intriguingly, *Human Hair; A Factory Of Vital Energy*.

Swimming pools Both the *Mohan International* and *Ritz* hotels allow discretionary use of their outdoor pools (non-residents Rs100, towels not included).

MOVING ON FROM AMRITSAR

Amritsar is a major hub for traffic heading northeast to Jammu & Kashmir, southeast towards Delhi via Chandigarh (the main jumping-off place for Shimla and central HP), and westwards to India's only land-border crossing point with Pakistan at Wagha.

Buses to Delhi (9 daily; 10hr) are considerably less comfortable and slower than travelling by rail except for the *Maharani Superfast* which takes a comparable 8hr 30min. The best **trains** (8hr 30min) to aim for are the *Amritsar-New Delhi #2014, Shatabdi* (departs 5.10am), the *Amritsar-New Delhi Express #2460* (departs 6.20am) or the *Shane-Punjab Express #2498* (2.25pm). *Indian Airlines* fly on Monday, Wednesday and Sunday between Amritsar and Delhi (55min); *Air India* flies on Tuesday and Thursday mornings, costs less and connects with international flights. The main *Indian Airlines* office is at 367 Green Ave (☎225321) and *Air India* (☎546122) is located at the *Amritsar International Hotel* complex near the bus stand.

Heading for **Pakistan**, you're better off taking the **bus**. Two services each day, at 10.30am and 11.30am, leave Amritsar for **Wagha**, 35km west (45min). Before you get on, make sure the bus goes all the way to Wagha and not just to **Atari**, several kilometres east of the border (daily 9am–4pm). Basic accommodation in the *Neem Chameli Tourist Complex* (③) is available at Wagha if you get stuck; onward connections to Lahore from the Pakistani side of the frontier are generally good. The same trip by **train**, however, invariably takes longer than the scheduled four hours, as the *Indo-Pak Express #4607* (departs Tues and Wed at 9.30am) suffers from cancellations and tends to get fouled up at customs; delays occasionally ruin into the night. Foreign travellers coming from Lahore should also avoid this train, which, if it happens to be carrying a large contingent of Pakistanis (who are not officially allowed to alight in the Punjab), won't stop in Amritsar.

For a full rundown of destinations reachable by train and bus from Amritsar, see p.350.

CHAPTER EIGHT

GUJARAT

The western state of **GUJARAT** – the wealthiest in India – sees relatively few tourists, but it rewards those who do come not only with important temple cities, forts and palaces, but also the chance to search out unique crafts made in tribal communities whose vivid costumes, dances and music remain little affected by modern innovations. Gujarat's foreign trade, started by the **Harappans** in the third millennium BC, was based on the export of goods such as shell jewellery and textiles, many of which still provide major sources of income.

As so often in India, Gujarat's **architectural diversity** reflects the influences of its many different rulers – the Buddhist Mauryans, who also supported the Jain faith, Hindu rajas, and Muslim emperors who combined their skills and tastes with Hindu craftsmanship to produce remarkable mosques, tombs and palaces. **Ahmedabad**, state capital until 1970 and the obvious place to begin a tour, harbours the first mosques to be built in the curious **Indo-Islamic** style, plus richly carved temples and step-wells dating to the eleventh century. Fascinating residential areas are lined with tall wooden residential *havelis*, carved in finest detail by prosperous merchants from the eighteenth century onwards. From Ahmedabad it's an easy trip north to the ancient capital of **Patan** and the Solanki sun temple at **Modhera**, or south to the excavated Harappan site at **Lothal**. In the northwest, the largely barren region of **Kutch** – often cut off from the rest of the state by vast tracts of flooded marshland – was bypassed by Gujarat's successive waves of foreign invaders. Consequently, this intriguing area preserves a village culture where crafts long forgotten elsewhere are practised with age-old skill.

The Kathiawar peninsula, also known as **Saurashtra**, is the true heartland of Gujarat, scattered with temples, mosques, forts and palaces that bear testimony to centuries of rule by Buddhists, Hindus and Muslims. Architectural highlights include superb Jain temples on the hills of **Shatrunjaya**, near Bhavnagar, and **Girnar** close to Junagadh. The coastal temple at **Somnath** is said to have witnessed the dawn of time, and that at **Dwarka** to be built on the site of Krishna's ancient capital. At **Junagadh**, rocks bearing two-thousand-year-old inscriptions from the reign of Ashoka stand a stone's throw from curious mausolea and Gothic mansions built by the Muslims in the 1800s. There's plenty of scope for spotting **wildlife**, too, in particular the lions in **Gir Forest** and herds of strutting black buck at **Velavadar**. Separated from the south coast by a thin sliver of the Arabian Sea, the island of **Diu**, fringed with beaches, leafy palm groves and the whitewashed spires of Portuguese churches, provides an idyllic setting for lazy sun-kissed days. Across the Gulf of Cambay, the thin coastal strip, followed by the main railway line from Ahmedabad to Bombay, features a few towns of lesser interest, among them the old Portuguese port of **Daman** in the far south.

Geographically Gujarat takes a little from each of its neighbours: with forested hilly tracts and fertile plains in the south and east, dry desert sands in the northwest, and a wide stretch of coast, in parts sandy, and in parts rocky and barren, that includes the coral enriched shoreline close to **Jamnagar**. It can become unbearably hot in summer, though a cool sea breeze does relieve the tension of heavy pre-monsoon days along the coast. The **best time to visit** is in the warm pleasant months between October and February, when you may also encounter traditional music and dances at numerous festivals. Thanks to extensive road and train links, **travel** within the state presents few problems, but communication barriers do require a little effort to overcome (few timetables are written in English). You'll also need stamina to negotiate the booking requirements for slow train journeys and to endure long rides on rickety local buses that are supplemented by newer private vehicles in only a few larger towns. Travellers with little time and a lot of cash can protect themselves from the usual rigours of train travel on Gujarat's version of the famed *Palace on Wheels*: the **Royal Orient**, which sets off from Delhi on a high luxury eight-day tour, stopping on the way in Rajasthan.

You'll be hard pushed to find a luxury **hotel** outside Ahmedabad, and many places hold little choice of accommodation beyond spartan lodges. As for **food**, which is predominantly vegetarian, Gujarat's good-value *thalis* are renowned for their size and sweetness. Note that the state operates severe **alcohol restrictions**: to enjoy a cold beer, you'll have to head to the Union Territory enclaves of Daman and Diu.

Some history

The first known settlers in what is now Gujarat were the **Harappans**, who appeared from Punjab in around 2500 BC and established over a hundred towns and cities. Their skilful craftsmanship, combined with important trade links with Africans, Arabs, Persians and Europeans, won them prosperity; despite this, the civilization fell into decline in 1900 BC, largely because of severe flooding around the Indus delta. From 1500 to 500 BC the **Yadavas**, Krishna's clan, held sway over much of Gujarat, with their capital at Dwarka on the western tip of Saurashtra.

Gujarat's political history begins in earnest with the powerful **Mauryan empire**, established by Chandragupta with its capital at Junagadh, then known as Girinagar, and reaching its peak under Ashoka. After his death in 226 BC, Mauryan power dwindled; the last significant Mauryan ruler was Samprati, Ashoka's grandson, a Jain who built fabulous temples at *tirthas* – pilgrimage sites – such as Girnar and Palitana.

In the first century AD the Western **Satraps**, members of the Saka, or Scythian, tribes, gained control over Saurashtra. They ruled it until soon after 388 AD, before being supplanted first by the **Guptas** and then by the **Maitrakas**, who established their capital at Valabhi. The ensuing centuries saw the arrival of the northern Gurjar tribes, who were to give the state its name, and the Kathi tribespeople from the northwest, who established several independent petty states in Saurashtra. The rulers of Sind (now in Pakistan) meanwhile dominated western Gujarat, including Kutch.

In the eleventh and twelfth centuries Saurashtra came under the sway of the **Solanki** (or Chauhan) dynasty; their splendid Jain temples suffered during the raids of Mahmud of Ghazni in 1027, but Muslim rule was not established until the Khalji conquest in 1299.

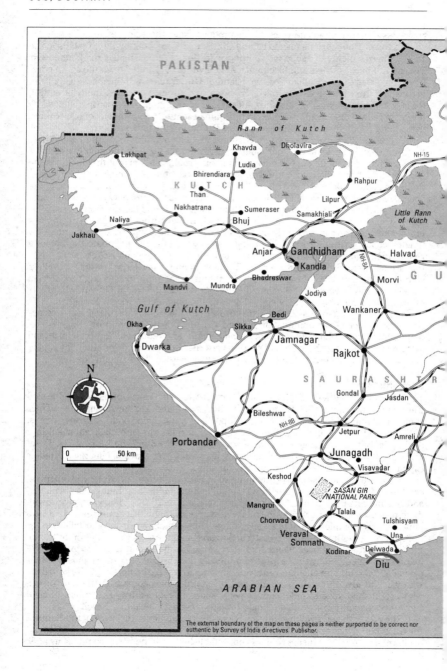

The external boundary of the map on these pages is neither purported to be correct nor authentic by Survey of India directives. Publisher.

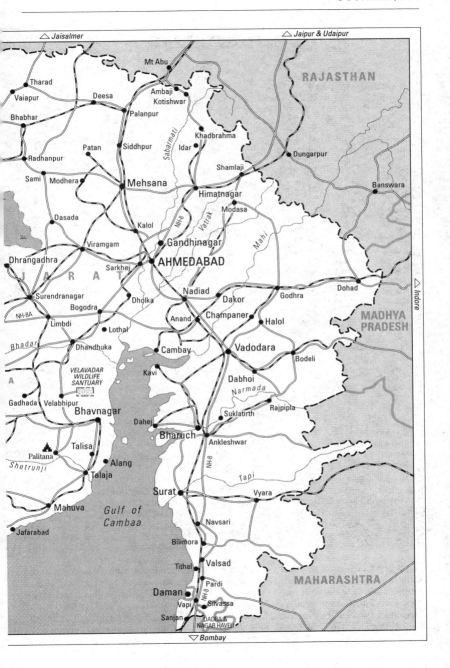

△ Jaisalmer △ Jaipur & Udaipur

Mt Abu

RAJASTHAN

Tharad
Vaiapur
Deesa
Ambaji
Kotishwar
Bhabhar
Palanpur
Khadbrahma
Patan
Siddhpur
Idar
Radhanpur
Dungarpur
Sami
Modhera
Shamlaji
Banswara
Mehsana
Dasada
Himatnagar
Kalol
Modasa
Viramgam
Gandhinagar
Dhrangadhra
Sarkhej
AHMEDABAD
G U J A R A T
Surendranagar
Dholka
Nadiad
Dakor
Godhra
Dohad
Bogodra
NH-8A
Anand
Champaner
Halol
MADHYA
PRADESH
Limbdi
Lothal
△ Indore
Bhadar
Dhandhuka
Cambay
Vadodara
Bodeli
A
Kavi
Dabhoi
Gadhada
Velabhipur
VELAVADAR
WILDLIFE
SANTUARY
Narmada
Bhavnagar
Suklatirth
Rajpipla
Dahej
Talisa
Bharuch
Ankleshwar
Palitana
Shetrunji
Alang
NH-8
Talaja
Tapi
Surat
Vyara
Mahuva
Gulf of
Cambaa
Navsari
Jafarabad
Bilimora
Tithal
Valsad
Daman
Pardi
NH-8
MAHARASHTRA
Vapi
Silvassa
Sanjan
DADRA &
NAGAR HAVELI
▽ Bombay

Sabarmati
NH-8
Vatrak
Mahi

TRAVEL DETAILS

	Trains		Buses		Flights	
	Frequency	Time	Frequency	Time	Frequency	Time
To and from AHMEDABAD						
Abu Road	7 daily	3hr 45min–5hr30min	10 daily	7hr		
Ajmer	5 daily	9hr 15min–13hr	4 daily	14hr		
Bangalore	2 weekly	32hr 20min			6 weekly	2hr
Bhavnagar	3 daily	5hr30min–11hr10min	hourly	4hr		
Bhuj	1 daily	16hr 20min	12 daily	7–10hr	2 weekly	45min–1hr5min
Bombay	8 daily	9hr	1 nightly	12hr	5–6 daily	1hr
Calcutta	1 daily	44hr			4 weekly	5hr 30min
Delhi	3 daily	17hr 45min			3–5 daily	1hr 25min
Diu			1 daily	10hr 30min		
Dwarka	1 daily	10hr	2 daily	11hr		
Indore			1 nightly	10hr		
Jaipur	2 daily	17hr 15min–21hr 45min	1 nightly	16hr	5 weekly	50min
Jamnagar	4 daily	7hr–14hr 15min	2 daily	7hr		
Jodhpur	3 daily	9hr 5min–12hr 30min	4 daily	12hr		
Junagadh	2 daily	9–10hr	7 daily	8hr		
Madras	6 weekly	34hr 40min			6 weekly	3hr 30min
Porbandar	1 daily	10hr	4 daily	10hr		
Rajkot	6 daily	4hr–5hr 30min	6 daily	6hr		
Surat	15 daily	4hr	half-hourly	6hr		
Udaipur	2 daily	9hr–10hr 30min	hourly	7hr		
Una			4 daily	10hr		
Vadodara	24 daily	2hr	every 10min	3hr	3 weekly	25min
Varanasi	3 weekly	30hr				
Veraval	2 daily	11–12hr	4 daily	10hr		
To and from Bhavnagar						
Bhuj			4 daily	8hr		
Bombay			1 daily	17hr	1 daily	50min–1hr 5min
Junagadh			5 daily	7hr		
Palitana	3 daily	2hr	hourly	1hr 15min		
Rajkot	1 daily	8hr 30min	14 daily	4hr		
Una			7 daily	6hr		
To and from Bhuj						
Bombay					4 weekly	1hr
Gandhidham	5 daily	1hr 50min	hourly	1hr		
Palanpur	2 daily	12hr	3 daily	8hr		
Rajkot			3 daily	7hr		
To and from Diu*						
Bombay					2 weekly	1hr
Junagadh	1 daily	6hr 55min	1 daily	5hr 30min		
Rajkot			2 daily	7hr 30min		
Una			half-hourly	40min		
Veraval	1 daily	4hr 15min	2 daily	2hr 30min		

Eight years later, Muzaffar Shah's declaration of independence from Delhi marked the foundation of the **Sultanate of Gujarat,** which lasted until its conquest by the Moghul emperor Akbar in the sixteenth century. In this period Muslim taste and Jain and Hindu styles were melded to produce remarkable Indo-Islamic mosques and tombs, characterized by the elaborate carvings found in Jain temples, and intersected in Hindu fashion by slender pillars meeting in delicate arches. Contrary to impressions encouraged

	Bus		Train		Flight	
To and from Dwarka						
Bombay	1 daily	20hr 10min				
Jamnagar	4 daily	2hr 30min–4hr 40min	8 daily	3hr		
Junagadh			3 daily	5hr		
Porbandar			6 daily	3hr		
Rajkot	4 daily	4hr 40min–7hr 30min				
Veraval			hourly	5–6hr		
To and from Junagadh						
Jamnagar			hourly	5hr		
Palitana			2 daily	6hr		
Porbandar			10 daily	3hr		
Rajkot	4 daily	3hr 30min	half-hourly	2hr		
Sasan Gir	1 daily	2hr 30min	10 daily	1hr 30min		
Una	1 daily	5hr 30min	10 daily	4hr		
Veraval	6 daily	2–3hr	half-hourly	2hr		
To and from Porbandar						
Bombay	1 daily	23hr 30min			daily	1hr 15min
Jamnagar	2 daily	2hr 40min	3 daily	2hr 30min		
Rajkot	2 daily	4hr 30min	10 daily	5hr		
Una			4 daily	6hr 30min		
Veraval			6 daily	3hr		
To and from Rajkot						
Bombay	3 daily	15–19hr			21 weekly	1hr 15min
Jamnagar			half-hourly	2hr		
Una			6 daily	7hr		
Vadodara			12 daily	8hr		
Veraval	2 daily	5hr 15min–6hr	hourly	5hr		
To and from Una						
Palitana			1 daily	5hr		
Sasan Gir	1 daily	3hr	7 daily	3hr		
Veraval	1 daily	4hr	half-hourly	2hr		
To and from Vadodara						
Baruch	28 daily	55min–2hr	half-hourly	2hr		
Bombay	10 daily	7hr	8 daily	14hr	daily	1hr
Calcutta	1 daily	38hr				
Delhi	5 daily	16hr			4 weekly	1hr 30min
Gandhidham	1 daily	8hr 5min				
Indore	1 daily	8hr 15min	2 daily	12hr		
Pune	4 weekly	10hr 25min	3 daily	14hr		
Surat	29 daily	1hr 30min–2hr 30min	half-hourly	3hr		

Note that no individual route appears more than once in this chart; check against where you want to get to as well as where you're coming from.
*To leave Diu by train, use the station at Delvada.

by recent sectarian violence, particularly in Ahmedabad, Islam never eclipsed Hinduism or Jainism, and the three have lived side by side for centuries.

In the 1500s, the **Portuguese**, already settled in Goa, turned their attention to the Gujarati coast, aware of the excellent potential of its ports and its long history of trade. Having captured Daman (1531), they took Diu (1535), building forts and typically European towns and coming to dominate the oceans with the imposition of high taxes and import duties. Fending off Arab and Muslim attacks, the Portuguese governed the ports until they were subsumed by the Indian Union in the 1960s.

The **British East India Company** set up its original Indian headquarters in Surat in 1613, and soon established their first "factory", a self-contained village for labourers' and merchants' houses and warehouses, sowing the seeds of a prospering textile industry. When British sovereignty was established in 1818, governor-generals moved into some of Gujarat's main cities, though the peninsula of Saurashtra never passed into British control and remained an amalgamation of over two hundred petty states until Independence. British rule brought mixed results; while machinery upgraded textile manufacture and brought substantial wealth to the region, many manual labourers were put out of business. Their cause was valiantly fought by Gujarat-born **Mahatma Gandhi**, whose campaigns for Independence and social equality brought international attention to his ashram in Ahmedabad. After Partition, due to its position bordering the new Muslim state of Pakistan, Gujarat received an influx of Hindus from Sind and witnessed terrible sectarian fighting as Muslims fled to their new homeland.

In 1960, after the Marathi and Guajarati **language riots** (demonstrators sought the redrawing of state boundaries according to language, as had happened in the south), Bombay state was split and Gujarat state created. The Portuguese enclaves, along with Goa, were forcibly annexed by the Indian government in 1961. Until recently, Gujarat has been a Congress stronghold, briefly lost to the Janata party in 1977, but the fundamentalists of the BJP have made a lot of headway, taking control of the state in 1991. Today Gujarat's textile industry is still the largest in India, with the trading of the business-minded Jain community helping to maintain its wealth.

Ahmedabad

AHMEDABAD, a mass of factories, mosques, temples and high-rise offices, sprawls along the banks of the River Sabarmati some 90km from its mouth in the Bay of Cambay. First impressions can be poor: Gujarat's largest city is a dirty, polluted place, noisy with a grumbling flow of traffic. Give it a little time, however, and the mix of ancient and modern – along with the combination of thriving Hindu, Muslim and Jain communities – lends the city an undeniable character that can be hard to resist.

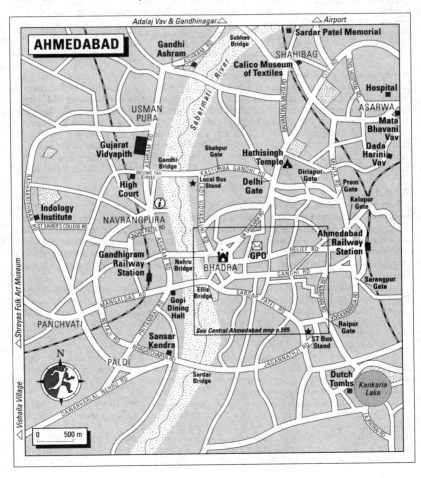

TATTOOS

If you spend any time in the rural areas of Gujarat, or come across tribal people in the cities, you'll notice the heavy blues and blacks of **tattoos** that cover the arms, hands, faces and torsos of most tribal women and many tribal men. This art, **chhundana padavava**, has been practised for centuries, and like *mehandi* – rich red henna patterns stencilled onto hands and feet – is a traditional form of beautification and identification.

For women, the typical rows and symmetrical designs of dots and simple shapes around necks, wrists and earlobes are endowed with the power to attract men and increase chances of love at first sight, as well as ensuring fidelity in a spouse. In some regions, a woman without *chhundana* is thought to have less chance of bearing children, and runs the risk of reincarnation as a camel. Tattoos of scorpions and serpents are believed to protect from bites and stings, while images of churning masts, *ravaiyo*, guarantee a continuous flow of milk from the family cattle. Men who are initiated into the occult and practise "black magic" bear a *narmund*, a human skull, on their chest, while a weighing scale on the palm of a woman's hand indicates that she has been offered in marriage without a dowry demanded from her parents. The actual process of tattooing is often carried out amid dancing, singing and the pulsating beat of *dhola* drums.

Ahmedabad is packed with a pungent diversity of architectural styles: over fifty mosques and tombs, as well as Hindu and Jain temples and grand step-wells (*vavs*). A wander through the bazaars and *pols* (residential areas) of the bustling **old city** is rewarding enough, but the outstanding monuments must be **Sidi Sayyid's Mosque**, **Bhadra citadel** – the site of the original city – the step-well **Dada Harini Vav**, and the hybrid **Jami Masjid** mosque. In addition, assorted **museums** provide a good introduction to Gujarati culture; the extensive **Calico Museum of Textiles** in the northern district of Shahi Bagh rates as one of the world's finest, and Mahatma Gandhi's **Sabarmati Ashram** has an exhibition on his life and the Indian Freedom Movement.

A brief history

When **Ahmed Shah** inherited the Sultanate of Gujarat in 1411, he chose to move his capital from Patan to the site of Asawal village, a small settlement on the east bank of the Sabarmati, renaming it after himself. The city quickly grew, welcoming skilled artisans and traders who were invited to settle. Its splendid mosques were clearly intended to assert Muslim supremacy, and heralded the new **Indo-Islamic** style of architecture, which though best displayed here, is a marked feature of many Gujarati cities.

In 1572, Ahmedabad became part of the growing Moghul empire, regarded as India's most handsome city and profiting from a flourishing trade in textiles that exported velvets, silks and shimmering brocades as far afield as Europe. But after a devastating famine in 1630 and a period of political instability when government passed to and fro between the Muslims and the Hindu Marathas, the city declined. Another famine in 1812 left it almost crippled, but five years later the British arrived, lowering taxes to encourage the return of merchants and traders who had left under Maratha rule. Trade in opium grew – the British needed something to offer the Chinese in return for silk and tea – and the introduction of modern machinery re-established Ahmedabad as a textile exporter that came to be known as "Manchester of the East".

When **Mahatma Gandhi** entered Indian politics in the early 1900s, as a Gujarati and an advocate of self-sufficiency, he was welcomed by Ahmedabad's manual labourers, who under his guidance revitalized their textile production and eventually formed protective trade unions. With the formation of national political parties and the imminence of India's release from British governance, the city became an important seat of political power, and a hotbed for communal tension as parties vied for popularity. Riots instigated by political and religious differences in recent years have sullied Ahmedabad's reputation, but have done little lasting damage to the city's communities.

Arrival, information and city transport

Ahmedabad's **airport** (☎642 5633) is linked to the city, 10km south, by taxi (Rs200–300), auto-rickshaw (Rs60), and city bus #101, which terminates at **Lal Darwaja**, the station for local buses, in the west of the old city near most of the hotels. Long-distance buses arrive at the **ST Bus Stand** in the southeast of the old city, 1km from hotels, while the **railway station** is to the east, at the far end of Relief Rd and MG Rd. Both have taxi stands, and rickshaws are available, as are city buses to Lal Darwaja (#48, #122 and #133 from the railway station; #13/1, #32 and #52/2 from the bus stand).

> The telephone **area code** for Ahmedabad is ☎079.

Information
Most of the action in Ahmedabad is on the east bank of the Sabarmati; however, the main **tourist office** is across the river in HK House, just off Ashram Rd 1km north of Nehru Bridge (daily except Sun and the 2nd & 4th Sat of the month, 10.30am–1.30pm & 2–6pm; ☎449683). **Exchange facilities** for US or sterling cash and travellers' cheques are available at the *Bank of India* in Khas Bazaar, the *Central Bank of India* opposite Sidi Sayyid's Mosque, and the *State Bank of India* opposite Lal Darwaja bus station (all Mon–Fri 11am–3pm, Sat 11am–1pm). *Forexchange* next to the *Hotel Goodnight* is much more convenient, giving bank rates for all major currencies, cash or travellers' cheques (Mon–Fri 10am–6.30pm, Sat 10am–4.30pm). For *Visa* encashments, go to the *Bank of Baroda*'s Ashram Rd branch on the west side of the river, 300m north of Nehru Bridge. The main **post office** is on Salapose Rd (Mon–Sat 8am–8pm, Sun 10.30am–4.30pm).

City transport
It can be fun to amble the narrow backstreets of the old city on foot, but to cover wider distances and avoid the noise and chaos of walking along the main roads you'll need to use public transport. This can be stressful, as the overloaded **buses** which race round town have their destination written in Gujarati, and are numbered in Hindi.

For information call ☎352911. Provided they have more than ten takers (which isn't that often), the municipal corporation run a four-hour **city bus tour** from an office on platform #0 at Lal Darwaja (daily 9.30am & 2pm; Rs30; book a day in advance).

Metered **taxis** can be hailed or picked up at the airport, the railway station and both bus stands, while **auto-rickshaws**, also generally metered, are abundant.

The City

The historic heart of Ahmedabad is the **old city**, an area of about three square kilometres on the east bank of the river, dissected by the main thoroughfares Relief Road and Gandhi Road and reaching its northern limits at **Delhi Gate**. It's the best place to start any exploration, taking in the squat buildings of the original citadel, **Bhadra**, the **mosques** and tombs of Ahmedabad's Muslim rulers, vibrant bazaars and *pols*, labyrinths of high wooden *havelis* and narrow cul-de-sacs that still house families of common caste or trade.

Bhadra and Sidi Sayyid's mosque
The solid fortified citadel, **Bhadra**, built of deep red stone in 1411 as Ahmedabad's first Muslim structure, is relatively plain in comparison to later mosques. The palace inside, now occupied by offices, is off-limits to tourists, but you can climb to its roof via a wind-

ing staircase just inside the main gateway and survey the streets below from behind its weathered bastions. In front of the citadel is a small public garden and **Alif Shah's mosque**, gaily painted in green and white. Further east, beyond the odoriferous meat market in **Khas Bazaar**, is **Teen Darwaja**, a thick-set triple gateway built during Ahmed Shah's reign, that once led to the outer court of the royal citadel. A trio of pointed arches, engraved with Islamic inscriptions and detailed carving, span the busy road below and shelter shoemenders and peddlers.

A prominent feature on the front of glossy city brochures, **Sidi Sayyid's mosque** (1573), famed for the ten magnificent *jali* (lattice work) screens lining its upper walls, sits in the centre of a busy traffic circle in the northwest corner of Bhadra. The two semicircular screens high on the western wall are the most spectacular, with floral designs exquisitely carved out of the yellow stone so common in Ahmedabad's mosques. The eastern face is open, revealing a host of pillars that divide the hall into fifteen areas, each with skilfully carved domed ceilings. Carvings within depict heroes and animals from popular Hindu myths – one effect of Hindu and Jain craftsmanship on an Islamic tradition that rarely allowed the depiction of living beings in its mosques. Women cannot enter, but the gardens around it afford good views of the screens.

Ahmed Shah's mosque

South of Bhadra citadel, not far from Victoria Gardens, **Ahmed Shah's** small and attractively simple **mosque** was the private place of worship for the royal household. Sections of an old Hindu temple, perhaps dating back to 1250 AD, were used in its construction – hence the incongruous Sanskrit inscriptions on some of the pillars in the sanctuary. The *mihrabs*, recesses in the west wall indicating the direction of prayer, are particularly ornate, the central one carved in white and black marble. Hidden behind pierced stone screens above the sanctuary in the northeast corner, the *zenana*, or women's chamber, is entered by steps from outside the main wall.

Jami Masjid

A short walk from Teen Darwaja along Gandhi Road leads to the spectacular **Jami Masjid**, or Friday Mosque. Completed in 1424, it stands today in its entirety, except for two minarets destroyed by an earthquake in 1957. Always buzzing with people, the mosque is fullest on Friday when thousands converge to worship.

A wide flight of steps leads to a vast marble courtyard surrounded on three sides by shady arched cloisters, known as *dalans*. A meeting place as well as an area for prayer, the courtyard has a water tank used for ablutions in its centre, and at the west end, facing Mecca, is the sandstone *qibla*, the main prayer hall, crowned with three rows of five domes. The 260 elegant pillars supporting its roof are covered with profuse, unmistakably Hindu carvings, while close to the sanctuary's principal arch a large black slab is said to be the base of a Jain idol inverted and buried as a sign of Muslim supremacy. The *zenana* is behind finely perforated stone screens above the main sanctuary.

Manek Chowk and the Tomb of Ahmed Shah

East of the Jami Masjid, the jewellers' market, **Manek Chowk**, is a bustling hive of colour where jewellers work in narrow alleys amid newly dyed and tailored cloths. Immediately outside the east entrance of the mosque the square **Tomb of Ahmed Shah I**, who died in 1442, stands surrounded by pillared verandahs. Women are not permitted to enter the central chamber, where his grave, plus those of his son and grandson, lies shrouded in cloth.

Further into the market area, you'll find the mausoleum of Ahmed Shah's queens, **Rani-ka-Hazira**, surrounded by the dyers' colourful stalls. Its plan is identical to Shah's own tomb, with pillared verandahs clearly inspired by Hindu architectural tastes. Inside, the graves are elaborately decorated with metal inlay and mother-of-pearl, now a little faded and worn.

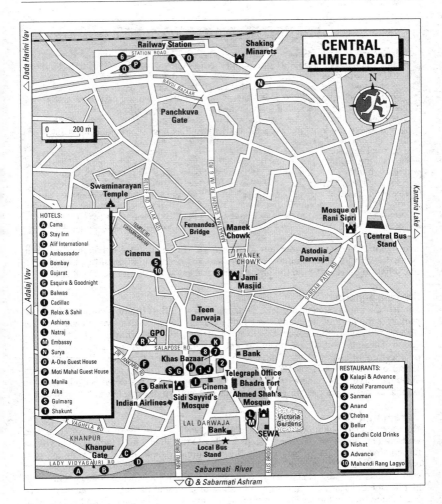

CENTRAL AHMEDABAD

HOTELS:
A Cama
B Stay Inn
C Alif International
D Ambassador
E Bombay
F Gujarat
G Esquire & Goodnight
H Balwas
I Cadillac
J Relax & Sahil
K Ashiana
L Natraj
M Embassy
N Surya
O A-One Guest House
P Moti Mahal Guest House
Q Manila
R Alka
S Gulmarg
T Shakunt

RESTAURANTS:
1 Kalapi & Advance
2 Hotel Paramount
3 Sanman
4 Anand
5 Chetna
6 Bellur
7 Gandhi Cold Drinks
8 Nishat
9 Advance
10 Mahendi Rang Lagyo

Swaminarayan temple

North from Rani-ka-Hazira through a narrow street of material shops, and across Relief Rd, the **Swaminarayan temple** stands behind huge gates and brightly painted walls. Forming a delicate contrast to the many hard stone mosques in the city, both the temple and the houses in the courtyard surrounding it are of finely carved wood, with elaborate and intricate patterns typical of the style of the *havelis* of north and west Gujarat. The temple's main sanctuary is given over to Vishnu and his consort Lakshmi.

Mosque and Tomb of Rani Sipri

Near Astodia Darwaja in the south of the city, the small, elegant **mosque of Rani Sipri** was built in 1514 at the queen's orders. Her grave lies in front, sheltered by a pillared

---

THE KITES OF AHMEDABAD

On January 14, when Gujarat celebrates **Makar Sankrati** to mark the last harvest of winter, Ahmedabad hosts the **International Kite Festival**, the largest of its kind in the world. For weeks in advance shops brim with a splendid assortment of kites of strange and original designs, many painted with animals or the faces of gods and heroes.

India has a long tradition of kite-flying, and during the festival the city comes alive with diving and darting kites flitting through the clear blue skies as families join with enthusiasts from all over Asia and as far afield as America and Japan. On the first day of the festival, crowds of kite-flyers gather in Patang Nagar, a "kite town" – usually in the police stadium – to display models of all sizes, made of paper, cloth, bamboo and fibre glass. There's a carnival atmosphere, with food and crafts stalls and performances of dance and music late into the night. On the second day you can follow the experts to the city's roof terraces and learn to fly kites, and after dark the night sky is ablaze with *tukal* kites strung with coloured lights. The climax of the festival comes on the third day, when kite strings are coated with a lethal mixture of ground glass, egg yolk and boiled rice, and kites are played off against one another in fierce combat. Cries of "kata!" (I've cut!) fill the air as slashed kites fall stricken from the skies and come to rest limply on telegraph wires and trees.

---

mausoleum. The stylish mosque shows more Hindu influence than any other in Ahmedabad, with several Hindu carvings and an absence of arches. Its pillared sanctuary has an open facade to the east and fine tracery work on the west wall.

Shaking minarets

South of the railway station, opposite Sarangpur Darwaja, **Sidi Bashir's minars** are all that remain of the mosque popularly named after one of Ahmed Shah's favourite slaves. Over 21m high, these are the best existing example of the **"shaking minarets"** – built on a foundation of flexible sandstone, probably to protect them from earthquake damage – that were once common to Ahmedabad's skyline. At least two European visitors, Robert Grindlay (1826) and Henry Cousens (1905), reported climbing to the top storey of one minaret, shaking it hard, and causing its twin to shake, but as entry is restricted you'll be lucky to be able to try this yourself, or even to get into the modern mosque beneath the minars.

Dada Harini Vav

Northern Gujarat abounds in remarkable step-wells – deep, with elaborately carved walls and broad flights of covered steps leading to the shaft – but **Dada Harini Vav**, in the northwest of the city, just outside the old boundaries, is among the very finest. It can be reached by taking the bus #111 to Asarwa; ask to be dropped nearby, and either walk or take an auto-rickshaw ride to the well. While it's a Muslim construction, built in 1500 for Bai Harir Sultani, superintendent of the royal harem, the craftsmen were Hindu, and their influence is clear in the lavish and sensuous carvings on the walls and pillars. The best time to visit is an hour or so before noon when the sculpted floral patterns and shapely figurines are bathed in the light of the sun. Bai Harir's lofty mosque and lattice-walled tomb stand west of the well.

A couple of hundred metres north, the neglected **Mata Bhavani Vav** was probably constructed in the eleventh century, before Ahmedabad was founded. It's profoundly Hindu in character, and dedicated to Bhavani, an aspect of Shiva's consort Parvati, whose modest shrine is set in the back wall of the well shaft.

Hathi Singh temple

The Svetambara **Hathi Singh temple** (daily 10am–noon & 4–7.30pm), less than 1km north of Delhi Gate, is easily distinguished by its high carved column, visible from the road. Built entirely of white marble embossed with smooth carvings of dancers, musicians, animals and flowers, this serene temple is dedicated to Dharamnath, whose statue stands in the main sanctuary. He is the fifteenth *tirthankara*, or "ford-maker", one of twenty-four great teachers sanctified by the Jains. Other *tirthankaras* peer out with jewelled eyes from smaller shrines in the pillared cloisters around the courtyard.

Calico Museum of Textiles

Nobody should leave Ahmedabad without visiting the **Calico Museum of Textiles** (daily except Wed, 10.30–11.30am & 2.45–3.45pm; free), in the Sarabhai Foundation, Shahibagh, 3km north of Delhi Gate (bus #101, 101/1 & 103); it's simply the finest collection of textiles, clothes, furniture, temple artefacts and crafts in the country. It's best to arrive early so you can take your time; once inside, you'll be shown round by a guide. Colourful embroidered wall-hangings depicting Krishna legends hang from the second floor right down to ground level. Cloth decorated with tie-dye (*bandhani*), glinting mirror work, screen prints, block prints and intricate embroidery include exquisite pieces made for the British and Portuguese and exported to Bali, while from India's royal households there's an embroidered tent and the robes of Shah Jahan, along with elaborate carpets and plump cushions that furnished Muslim palaces.

SEWA

Of the female workers in India, 89 percent are self-employed. They are particularly subject to exploitation, existing outside the protection of labour laws and national standards of minimum wage. The slide into debt is always a real threat, with all that entails for their children and families. Ahmedabad, however, has since the days of Gandhi maintained a tradition of self-help, and has achieved world recognition as the home base of the ground-breaking **Self-Employed Womens' Association**, or SEWA, founded in the early 1970s by Ela Bhatt. Its original remit, to offer legal advice, training and child care for women, negotiating with police and local government for vendors' licences, and education for the members' children, soon mushroomed. To enable the women of Ahmedabad to buy basic materials and tools, and use their income to live on rather than to pay off loan sharks, SEWA opened its own cooperative *Mahila Bank*, the first to give low interest loans to women, offer savings and deposit accounts and insurance.

In 1984 a major textile industry slump affected 35,000 families, most of them Harijans and Muslims. Many had to resort to rag and paper picking, collecting grimy scraps of paper, polythene and broken glass for recycling, a task which threatened their health and brought in pathetic wages. Setting up training centres in weaving, sewing, dyeing and printing, and providing efficient machinery, SEWA helped to re-establish many women in the textile labour force, and provided an outlet for their products. Contracts with government institutions guarantee a place of work for cleaners and vendors; members now provide vegetables, fruit and eggs to all government hospitals, jails and municipal schools.

SEWA also trained its members in accountancy, management and office skills, and its management committee includes farmers, rag pickers and *bidi*-makers. By the 1980s, members felt confident enough to bring their personal grievances to this approachable team, voicing complaints of verbal and sexual assault in the workplace and at home. Two thousand women registered a protest against *sati* (widow burning) in 1987. A committee was formed to investigate crimes against Muslim women, particularly *talak*, a practice sanctioned by the Koran that allows a man to divorce his wife by uttering the words "I divorce you" three times, often leaving them destitute. Verbal divorce and polygamy, still common elsewhere in India, was banned in Gujarat in 1988. SEWA also strongly opposes sex determination tests that lead to female foeticide, a widespread practice in Gujarat, and its work has now spread to nine other Indian cities.

The SEWA crafts **shop** (mainly clothes) on the east side of Ellis bridge, a few doors from the organization's reception centre (Mon–Sat 10am–7pm), is well worth a browse.

GANDHI'S SALT MARCH

Probably the most famous single act of civil disobedience in India's history, the great **salt march** was organized in Ahmedabad by Mahatma Gandhi as part of his campaign of non-violent resistance (*satyagraha*). Protesting against the British government monopoly on the production and sale of **salt**, Gandhi and almost eighty followers from around the country – among them Hindus, Muslims and Harijans – set off on foot from the Sabarmati Ashram on March 12, 1930.

Gandhi's rousing speeches advocating *swaraj*, or Independence, and the distribution of clothing to the poor, brought the protesters enormous support and international attention. When, after a full month, they finally reached the coastal town of **Dandi**, some 386km south in the Gulf of Cambay, the *satyagrahis*, surrounded by followers who formed a wall against the police, courted arrest by collecting sea water and boiling it to produce salt. They had planned to seize natural deposits from the mudflats, but the police ground the salt back into the sand; the Mahatma did manage, however, to hold a mock auction, selling off a tiny fragment of salt for Rs1600.

The effects of the salt *satyagraha* were widespread; salt was made illegally and government salt works raided, while in Gujarat government servants resigned and refused to pay land revenues. The government responded with repression; picketing was made illegal, and peaceful protests were frequently met with police brutality. Gandhi was arrested on May 5, under an 1827 regulation that required neither a trial nor a sentence. Even behind bars, he exerted considerable influence, advising colleagues and holding meetings. Soon after his release, in January 1931, he met the British Viceroy, Lord Irwin, in Delhi, to sign the Gandhi-Irwin Pact, agreeing to a cessation of civil disobedience, the release of civil disobedience prisoners, restoration of lands to those who had refused to pay increased rates, and reinstatement of village officers. This led directly to the Round Table Conference in London, where Gandhi was to join in discussions on India's future.

The collection also includes some of the best examples anywhere of the *patola saris* woven in Patan (see p.571), as well as the extravagant *zari* work that gilds *saris* in heavy gold stitching, and can bring their weight to almost nine kilos. The Jain section features statues housed in a replica *haveli* temple, along with centuries-old manuscripts and *mandalas* painted on palm leaves; note the traditional symbols such as the snake-and-ladder motif representing rebirth and *karma*. Among exhibits from elsewhere in India are Kashmiri shawls, Kullu embroidery, glittering silk brocades from Varanasi, *Phulkari* folk art from the Punjab and masks and temple cars from Tamil Nadu. Tribal crafts such as Kutchi silk-and-cotton *mashru* weaving are displayed in spectacular wooden *havelis* from Patan and Siddhpur in northern Gujarat. Clearly labelled models and diagrams explain the weaving, dyeing and embroidery processes.

Sardar Patel Memorial Museum

Two hundred metres north up Shahibagh Rd, the **Sardar Patel Memorial Museum** (daily 9am–5.30pm; free) houses an exhibition of photos, clippings and mementos from the life and career Gandhi and Nehru's great ally, although the labelling is mostly in Hindi and the tribute is rather marred by an annexe of blatant propaganda for the controversial Narmanda dam project (see *Contexts*).

Gandhi Smarak

At the northern end of Ashram Road, set by the sublime gardens of Gandhi's **Sabarmati Ashram**, the **Gandhi Smarak** (daily 8.30am–7pm; free) displays the Mahatma's letters and possessions, along with a powerful collection of photographs of his years of fighting for freedom. It was here that Gandhi lived in humble apartments from 1917 until 1930 and held meetings with weavers and Harijans as he helped them find security and re-establish the manual textile industry in Ahmedabad. In keeping with the man's uncluttered lifestyle, the collection of his personal property is modest but poignant – wooden shoes, white seamless clothes and a pair of round spectacles. A **Sound and Light show** telling his life story runs in Gujarati (daily 7pm), Hindi (Mon, Tues, Thurs & Sat 8.30pm) and English (Sun, Wed & Fri 8pm), costs Rs5 and lasts 65 minutes. Tickets are sold at the door, or you can reserve on ☎748 3073. The ashram itself is no longer operating, but many people come here simply to sit and meditate.

Other museums

Ahmedabad's museums are strong in arts and crafts. Among them, the **Shreyas Folk Art Museum** (Tues–Sat 3–6pm, Sun 10am–noon & 3–6pm; free), way out to the west near the city limits (bus #41 from Lal Darwaja), displays the traditional work of Gujarat's many tribes. The **Tribal Museum** (Mon–Fri noon–5.30pm, Sat noon–5pm; free) in the northeastern corner of Gujarat Vidyapith, on Ashram Rd 100m south of Income Tax Circle, is equally informative, detailing the various peoples of the state and their customs, such as the painting of "magical" pictures by Bhils (see p.202) to ward off disaster. **N C Mehta Gallery** in the Indology Institute near Gujarat University (Tues–Sun 11am–noon & 3–5pm; free; bus #55 from Lal Darwaja), has a superb collection of miniatures from all over India. There's even a **Kite Museum** (Tues–Sun 10am–noon & 4–6pm) in Sanskar Kendra on Bhagtacharya Rd, west of the river.

Parks and gardens

Ahmedabad's quieter spots and open spaces provide welcome relief from the chaos of the busy streets. Just south of Bhadra the **Victoria Gardens** are suitably formal, with spacious lawns and tree-lined promenades around a pompous statue of Queen Victoria. Southwest of the old city, more picturesque gardens surround the artificial 34-sided **Kankaria Lake**. Dating from 1451, the lake has a fascinating ornate sluice gate on its eastern edge, a collection of Dutch and Armenian tombs on the west bank, and an island in the centre. The typically Indian **zoo** is not far north. It's best to visit in the cool of the evening; bus #32 runs frequently between Kankaria and Lal Darwaja.

Vishalla village

If you're not going to get the chance to make it to any genuine Gujarati villages, don't turn your nose up at **Vishalla village** (daily 11am–11pm), out on Sarkhej Rd, 4km south of town (bus #31). Designed this century by Surendra Patel, Vishalla is an admirably authentic collection of traditionally decorated mud huts where potters, weavers and *paan*-makers demonstrate their skills. The **Vechaar Utensils Museum** (daily 11am–10.30pm; Rs3) houses a vast collection of Gujarati metalware, including jewellery, knives and forks and odd-looking machinery for milking camels.

The village atmosphere can also be taken in during a leisurely evening trip, when dinner is served (7.30–11pm) to the accompaniment of local dance, music or puppet shows; the menu includes Gujarati dishes, super-sweet deserts and mugs of buttermilk. Lunch is served from 11am until 2pm, with snacks and juices available all day.

Accommodation

Ahmedabad's **hotels** range from grubby adequacy to polished luxury. Most are conveniently located in the west end of the old city, within walking distance of the bazaars, the local bus station, banks, the GPO and many of the sights. Cheaper places to stay cluster around the railway station, while north of Nehru Bridge on the east bank, in the rather classy Khanpur area, the hotels are smarter, if not luxurious.

In the west end of the old city

Alka Guest House, Shreenath Chamber, Salapose Rd (☎550 0830). One of the least expensive options with adequate facilities, clean rooms and a dormitory for men. ①–②.

Ashiana, Murtuza Manzil, Salapose Rd, Khas Bazaar (☎535 1114 or 5). Simple, tidy rooms with little ventilation. ②.

Balwas, 6751 Relief Rd (☎550 7135). Modern, well-kept place. Most rooms have a/c; all have clean private bathrooms with constant hot water. ④.

Bombay, 3rd floor, KB Commercial Centre (☎550 6296). Cramped, and not as clean as it might at first seem; but at least there's constant hot water. Some a/c rooms. ②–④.

Cadillac, Dr Tankaria Rd (☎550 7558 or 9). Small, colourful and very low-priced rooms, some with private bath. Dorm for men. ①–②.

Embassy, behind *Bank of Maharashtra*, Lal Darwaja (☎535 8463 or 73 or 91). Excellent, comfortable hotel in a modern building with all amenities. Good value. ③–⑥.

Esquire, Dr Tankaria Rd (☎550 6840). Opposite Sidi Sayyid's mosque. Rooms here are nothing special, though they are clean. Often full. ③.

Goodnight, Dr Tankaria Rd (☎550 6997 or 8). Spick and span modern hotel opposite Sidi Sayyid's mosque. Rooms with TV and private bathroom. ④.

Gujarat, Third Floor, Sneha Complex, Dr Tankaria Rd (☎356627). North of the clock tower. Attractive, modern and spotless, with swinging cane chairs on a leafy roof terrace. ④–⑤.

Gulmarg, 4th floor, Dr Tankaria Rd (☎550 7202 or 3). Opposite Dinbai Tower. Basic, reasonably clean rooms, some with balcony, some with a/c. ③–⑤.

Natraj, Dada Mavlankar Rd (☎550 6048). In a quiet area near Victoria Gardens. Clean rooms with private bathrooms (bucket of hot water), some with large balconies. ②.

Relax, Dr Tankaria Rd (☎550 7301). Modern, clean place in a noisy side street opposite *Advance Cinema*, with room service and constant hot water in private bathrooms. ③–④.

Sahil, Dr Tankaria Rd (☎550 7351 or 2; fax 350004). Friendly place next to *Relax Hotel*. Ordinary and a/c rooms, with carpets and private bathrooms. ④–⑤.

Around the railway station

A-One Guest House, Fanibunda Bldg, Station Rd (☎214 9823). Directly opposite the station, this offers very basic rooms and a dormitory for men, and is rarely cleaned. ①–②.

Manila, Lalbhai Chambers, Kapasia Bazaar (☎385876 or 7). Clean place with standard marble decor and some a/c rooms. ④–⑥.

Moti Mahal Guest House, Kapasia Bazaar (☎339091 or 2; fax 214 4132). Very well-kept, clean hotel offering rooms with bathroom and TV, some a/c. ④–⑤.

Shakunt, HK Bhavan, Reid Rd (☎214 5614 or 5). Smart reception area but the rooms are on the grubby side and have poor ventilation. ④–⑤.

Surya, Extra Commercial Complex, Sarangpur Kotri Rang, Panchkuva Sindhi Mkt (☎214 4151). Clean and homely carpeted rooms. ④–⑤.

Khanpur district

Alif International, Lady Vidyagauri Rd, opposite *Holiday Inn* and the *AA* (☎550 1270). Immaculate rooms, some a/c, but 9am checkout. ④–⑤.

Ambassador, Lady Vidyagauri Rd (☎550 2490; fax 550 2327). Large and modern with little character. 24hr checkout. ⑤–⑥.

Cama, Lady Vidyagauri Rd (☎550 5281 or 2; fax 550 5285). Luxurious rooms overlook River Sabarmati and a garden terrace with pool. All mod cons, restaurant, bar and coffee shop. Inconvenient 9am checkout. ⑧.

Stay Inn, Lady Vidyagauri Rd, by Khanpur Gate (☎550 0727; fax 469101). Smart and comfortable with partial a/c. 24hr checkout. ⑤–⑥.

Eating

Ahmedabad's **restaurants** are clustered around Salapose Rd and Relief Rd, while good stalls in Khas Bazaar serve kebabs and fresh, gloopy *dal*. Restaurants in Navrangpura, near the university 2km west of the river, offer Indian and Western dishes.

Advance, Dr Tankaria Rd. Good-value fixed veg meals, south Indian snacks and great sweet *lassi*. Open 8am–11pm, meals 11am–4pm & 6.30–10.30pm.

Anand Dining Hall, Salapose Rd, off Relief Rd. Small, very inexpensive veg place for Gujurati *thalis*. Open 10.30am–2.30pm & 6.30–9.30pm, except Sun evening. A branch across the street serves South Indian snacks 8am–10pm.

Balwas, Relief Rd, by the hotel of the same name. Comfortable, a/c restaurant serving reasonably priced non-veg and veg Indian food, and desserts including jelly and ice cream. Open 9am–11pm, meals noon–4pm & 7–11pm.

Bellur, Station Rd. Low-priced south Indian veg food in simple surroundings with a/c upstairs. Open 7am–11pm, meals served 10.30am–3.30pm & 6.30–11pm.

Chetna Dining Hall, Relief Rd. Popular veg place for excellent, cheap south Indian dishes noon–10pm, and sumptuous Gujarati *thalis*. 10.30am–3pm & 6.30–10pm.

Food Inn, under *Hotel Goodnight*, Dr Tankaria Rd. Smart, a/c restaurant with a wide variety of Indian and Chinese food, including non-veg. Open 9am–11pm, meals 11am–4pm & 6.30–11pm.

Gandhi Cold Drinks House, Khas Bazaar. Interesting, refreshing milk and ice cream concoctions, including Indonesian-style "Royal Faluda", unique to Ahmedabad, and saffron-flavoured *kesar* milk-shake. Remember to ask for no ice. Open 10.30am–11pm.

Gopi Dining Hall, Pritamrai Rd (☎657 6388). Great no-smoking veg place on the west side of Ellis Bridge. Gujarati and Punjabi *thalis* at unbeatable prices. Very popular, so reserve or queue. Open 10am–3pm & 6.30–10.30pm.

Kalapi, Dr Tankaria Rd. A/c no-smoking restaurant opposite *Advance Cinema*. The best veg food in Bhadra at easily affordable prices. Open 9am–11pm, meals 11am–4pm & 6–11pm.

Karnavati, Dr Tankaria Rd. The fixed Indian meals are great value, marred only by the vile scented air-conditioning. Also Chinese and continental dishes. Open 8am–11pm.

Mahendi Rang Lagyo Fruit Juice House, Relief Rd. Large stall with a wide selection of juices and shakes made to order. Open 6am–midnight.

Moti Mahal, Kapasia Bazaar, under the hotel of the same name. A stone's throw from the railway station, this non-veg restaurant and sweet centre is renowned for its service and quality. The salted *lassis* with cumin are great, but remind them to hold the ice. Open 5am–1am.

Nishat, Khas Bazaar. Very inexpensive, unelaborate place serving meat dishes. Open 5am–11pm.

Hotel Paramount, Bhadra. Despite its drab appearance, this a/c non-veg restaurant dishes up a wide selection of excellent Indian and Chinese dishes and desserts. Great for breakfast. Open 10am–11pm, meals 11.30am–4pm & 6–11pm.

Sanman, MG Rd, opposite the Jami Masjid. Gujarati and Punjabi veg dishes, filling inexpensive *thalis* and south Indian snacks. Open 9am–11pm, meals from 11am.

Toran Tourist Restaurant, opposite Gandhi Ashram, Ashram Rd. Veg place serving Punjabi food and Gujarati *thalis*. Reasonable but not worth going out of your way for. Open 7am–10pm.

Listings

Airlines Domestic: *East-West*, Agarwal Complex near the municipal market, Navrangpura (☎642 3311 or 2); *Indian Airlines*, on the road from Sidi Sayyid's Mosque to Nehru Bridge (☎353333); *Jet*,

Ashram Rd opposite Gujarat Vidyapith (☎656 2519); *Moduluft* c/o *Zeal Tours* in Radha Kishan Ave opposite Golden Triangle Stadium (☎466228); *NEPC*, 3rd floor of the City Centre, Navrangpura (☎642 6295); *Sahara, Hotel Sadat Palace*, Shahibagh (☎786 8469). International: *Air India*, off Ashram Rd near the High Court (☎642 5644 or 33); *Air France*, Paduban House near Ellis Bridge town hall; *British Airways*, at Fiveroads Junction, Panchvati (☎465621); *KLM*, in the Shefali Centre, Paldi (☎657 7677); *Delta* and *Swissair*, c/o *Samveg*, in the Surayarath Building behind the White House, Panchvati (☎640 2798); *Alitalia, Cathay Pacific* and *Kenya Airways*, c/o *Ajanta Travels*, off Ashram Rd 300m south of Income Tax Circle (☎405077).

Bookstores For maps, guides and books try *Sastu Kitab Ghar* on Relief Rd 100m east of Salapose Rd, or *People's Book House* 100m further. *The New Order Book Co*, on the west side of Ellis Bridge, sells books on Indian philosophy, architecture and crafts. *Mapin* at 31 Somnath Rd, just off Ashram Rd in Usmanpura publish glossy books on Indian art and culture, and stalls under Fernandes Bridge on MG Rd have a lot of tatty paperbacks among which you might find the odd gem.

Cinemas *Advance Cinema* on Salapose Rd opposite the *Hotel Sahil* and *Krishna Cinema* on Relief Rd by the *Chetna* restaurant are very popular.

Emergency services Police ☎100; Ambulance ☎102.

Hospitals *VS General*, Ellis Bridge (☎657 7621); *Akhhandanand Ayurvedic*, Akhandanand Rd (☎550 7796).

Motorbikes Buy an *Enfield* or have one repaired at *Shaik & Co Agency*, round the back of Swastik Supermarket, on Ashram Rd near the tourist office (☎449522).

▌ MOVING ON FROM AHMEDABAD

There are two daily express **trains** to **Bhavnagar** (5hr 30min), and two overnight trains to **Junagadh** (9–10hr) and **Veraval** (11–12hr), the better of which is the *Girnar Express* #9846. Of the six trains serving **Rajkot**, one continues to **Porbandar** (the overnight *Saurashtra Express* #9215); while of the three expresses to **Jamnagar**, the most convenient is the early morning *Saurashtra Mail* #9005, which also serves **Dwarka** and **Okha** (10hr 40min). There is a single direct overnight train to **Bhuj** (16hr 20min), but you can cut your journey time almost in half by taking the late night *Kutch Express* #9031 to Gandhidham and picking up a connection there. For **Vadodara**, there are no less than 24 trains daily, fifteen continuing to **Surat** (4hr 30min), eight to **Vapi** (for Daman; 6hr), and eight to **Bombay Central** (9hr) – to arrive early in the morning, catch one of the evening departures, the #9008, #9102 or #9006. Alternatively, the *Shatabdi Express* #2010 will speed you to Bombay in less than seven hours daily except Friday, calling at Vadodara (1hr 40min) and Surat (3hr 15min). Of the three metre-gauge services to **Delhi Sarai Rohilla**, the overnight *Ashram Express* #2906 is by far the fastest (17hr 45min) and most convenient, the other two taking a detour via **Jaipur** (17hr 15min). **Udaipur** has an overnight express (9hr), and a daytime passenger train (10hr 30min) which continues to **Chittaurgarh** (17hr); to Jodhpur, the best of the three trains is the overnight *Surya Nagari Express* #2908 (9hr 5min).

For journeys within Gujarat, it can be less hassle to opt for a **bus**, which at least travels at sociable hours. The **ST Bus Stand** serves a variety of local destinations including Gandhinagar (every 15min; 1hr), Dholka (for Lothal, half-hourly; 1hr 30min), and Nal Sarovar (1 morning departure; 2hr), Mehsana (every 10min; 2hr), and Dhranghadra (half-hourly; 3hr). In Rajasthan, there are buses to Mount Abu, Udaipur and Jaipur (overnight). There are also overnight services to Bombay, Indore and Bhopal, but none to Delhi. More comfortable and expensive **private buses** to various destinations in Gujarat and interstate are run by *Punjab Travels*, 3 Embassy Mkt, off Ashram Rd just north of the tourist office (☎656 9200 or 55) and *Shrinath Travel Agency* (☎44345) in the building next door, who organize various services to Rajasthan, including a night bus to Jaisalmer. Other private bus operators can be found near the ST stand and the railway station.

Flights to Bombay (1hr) are operated by *Indian Airlines* and *Jet* (both 2 daily), *East-West* (6 weekly) and *NEPC*.(3 weekly). To Delhi (1hr 25min) there's a choice of *Indian Airlines* (2 daily), *Jet* (1 daily), *Sahara* (5 weekly), and *Moduluft* (3 weekly). Other destinations served are Bhuj (*Indian Airlines*, 2 weekly; 45min), Bangalore (*Indian Airlines* and *NEPC*, 3 weekly), Madras (same flights), Jaipur (*Sahara* 5 weekly) and Calcutta (*Sahara* 4 weekly).

Photographic equipment *Gujarat Mercantile Co*, 100m south of the GPO on Salapose Rd (☎550 5421); *Scanner Fotoshop* on the first floor Padshah Pol, opposite *Pragati Co-op Bank*, Relief Rd, 100m east of the *Chetna* restaurant (☎535 7358).
Thomas Cook 208 Sakar III, off Ashram Rd near the High Court (☎405312).

Around Ahmedabad

The most obvious day trip from Ahmedabad is north to **Adalaj**, with its impressive step-well, and perhaps on a little further to the new capital of **Gandhinagar**, and its amazing Swaminarayan complex. South of town lie the lake, pavilions and mausoleums of **Sarkhej**. Further south, beyond the **Nal Sarovar** bird sanctuary is **Lothal**, and the excavation of an ancient Harappan site dating back four thousand years; the mosques in **Dholka** en route date back to the fourteenth century.

Adalaj Vav

One of Gujarat's most spectacular step-wells, or *vavs*, **Adalaj Vav**, stands in lovingly tended gardens about 1km from a bus stop on the route between Ahmedabad (19km) and Gandhinagar. Once a Hindu sanctuary, the well is now totally out of use; modern water taps nearby enable local women to wash clothes and cooking utensils.

The monument is best seen around noon, when sunlight penetrates to the bottom of the five-storey octagonal wellshaft. Steps lead down to the cool depths through a series of platforms raised on pillars. Alive with exquisite sculptures, the walls, pillars, cornices and niches portray erotica, dancing maidens, musicians, animals and images of Shiva in his terrible aspect, Bhairava. Stone elephants, horses and mythical animals parade around the sides of the shaft, where green parrots swoop down from outside to rest out of the glaring sun. Before descending you'll see several Sanskrit inscriptions etched into the walls just above eye level, one of which records the building of the well by Ruda, wife of a local chief, in 1498.

Gandhinagar

The second state capital after Chandigarh to be built from scratch since Independence, the uninspiring city of **GANDHINAGAR** is laid out in thirty residential sectors, in an ordered style influenced by the work of **Le Corbusier**, who designed Chandigarh, and had a hand in conceiving the layout of New Delhi. Its near-symmetrical numbered streets are wide and strangely quiet, lined with a total of 16 *lakh* trees – that's 26 per head of the city's population. There's little to warrant spending much time here, but the headquarters of the Swaminarayan sect, **Akshardam**, is worth a look. This vivacious Hindu revival movement, established in 1907 by Brahmaswarup Shastriji Maharaja, promotes Vedic ideals pronounced by Lord Swaminarayan (1781–1830). Born in Uttar Pradesh, the saint settled in Gujarat where he built six temples, wrote religious discourses and proclaimed that his presence would continue through a succession of saints, the most recent of whom is a Gujarati named Pramukh Swami Maharaja.

The Akshardam may advocate simplicity and poverty, but the colossal **Swaminarayan complex** on J Rd, Sector 20 (daily, but most attractions closed Mon, 7.30am–9.30pm), a centre for representing the precepts and practices of the sect, is hugely extravagant. Built of pink sandstone, all six thousand tonnes of it brought from Rajasthan, with domed roofs raised on almost one hundred profusely carved pillars, it's furnished inside with Karnataka rosewood, and the statues of Swaminarayan and two other prominent gurus shimmer with a gold leaf coating. The Hall of Holy Relics, containing possessions of Swaminarayan, also has a state-of-the-art display of images projected onto fourteen screens. There are three exhibition halls too (daily except Mon 10am–6.30pm; Rs15). In Nityanand Hall, fair-complexioned figures represent themes from the great Hindu epics, while the works of Indian mystical poets such as Tulsidas and Kabir are shown and models of *sadhus* tolerantly "discuss" world religions with a view to attaining universal harmony. There's a Centre for Applied Research in Social Harmony in the landscaped gardens.

Regular **buses** run between Gandhinagar and Ahmedabad (1hr), but there's only one train a day in each direction (1hr) and the station is rather inconveniently placed, out in Sector 14. Although the town sees few tourists, it does have a **tourist office** on Gha Rd in Sector 16, 200m north of Rd #4. Should you want to **stay**, the *Hotel Purnima* next to the tourist office (☎02712/22286; ①) is grubby and unwelcoming with a 9am checkout; the *Capital Guest House* in the same building (entrance round the back, ☎02712/2086; ③–⑤) is preferable. There's a **youth hostel** 300m behind them (☎02712/22364; ①) with clean dorms and a discount for cardholders, and the a/c *Hotel Haveli* (☎02712/24051 or 2; fax 24057; ⑥–⑦) in Sector 11, 300m behind the bus stand. Note that to telephone Gandhinagar from Ahmedabad you should use the code ☎82.

Sarkhej

Just under 10km southwest of Ahmedabad (bus #31 from Lal Darwaja) in the suburb of **Sarkhej** is a complex of beautifully fashioned monuments arranged around an artificial lake. The square tomb of the revered saint Sheikh Ahmed Khattu, the spiritual mentor of Ahmed Shah, who died in 1445, is the largest mausoleum in Gujarat, with scores of pillars inside supporting the domed roof, tracery work and inlaid marble on the upper walls and rows of arched wooden doors and brass screens on the outer wall. The mausoleum was constructed by Ahmed Shah's successor, Muhammad Shah, in 1446, and the later Sultan Muhammad Beghada (died 1511) so deeply admired Sheikh Ahmed that he built palaces, a harem and a vast lake at the site, and chose to have his own tomb here. Sarkhej became a retreat of Gujarati Sultans, who added gardens, pavilions and tombs to the elaborate complex. While some of the buildings are falling into ruin, it remains a charming place, usually teeming with brightly dressed Gujarati holidaymakers, and has a serene beauty comparable to that of Udaipur in Rajasthan.

Nal Sarovar reserve

A visit to **Nal Sarovar**, set in 121 square kilometres of wet grasslands some 50km southwest of Ahmedabad is best between November and February, when it attracts colonies of flamingoes, cranes, storks, pelicans, ducks and geese. Nal Sarovar is seen as a valuable asset by conservationists campaigning for the reduction of road building and industrial pollution, both fast drying out Gujarat's remaining expanses of wetland.

Dholka

A 35-kilometre journey southwest of Ahmedabad by bus or train brings you to **DHOLKA**, and its three majestic ruined mosques. The modestly proportioned **Masjid of Hilal Khan Qazi** (1333), featuring detailed tracery work, and the **Tanka Masjid** (1361), decorated with elaborate Hindu carvings, are both unaffected by Islamic design. More dilapidated, the **Mosque of Alif Khan** (1453) is distinctively Persian, dominated by solid square towers on either side of the facade. Dholka village is famous for its pomegranate and guava orchards, and also has a stunning wooden *haveli* temple.

Lothal

Remains of the **Harappan** (Indus Valley) civilization that spread across what are now western India and eastern Pakistan have been discovered in over fifty places in Gujarat. The largest excavated site is at **Lothal** (daily dawn–dusk), close to the mouth of the River Sabarmati, roughly 100km south of Ahmedabad, and an easy

THE INDUS VALLEY CIVILIZATION

Before the Mauryan empire took hold in the fourth century BC, the greatest empire in India was the **Indus Valley Civilization**. Well-planned, sophisticated settlements dating back to 2500 BC were first discovered in 1924 on the banks of the River Indus in present-day Sind, Pakistan, at **Mohenjo Daro** (which means "mound of the dead" in Sindi). Further excavations in 1946 on the banks of the River Ravi in Punjab revealed the city of **Harappa**, dating from the same era, which became a prototype of the entire Indus Valley Civilization for archeologists. In its prime, this great society spread from the present borders of Iran and Afghanistan to Kashmir, Delhi and southern Gujarat, covering an area larger than the Egyptian and Syrian dominions put together. It lasted until 1900 BC when a series of heavy floods swept away the towns and villages in the delta regions of major rivers in Sind, Saurashtra and south Gujarat.

A prosperous and literate society, importing raw materials from regions as far west as Egypt, and trading ornaments, jewellery and cotton cultivated in the fertile delta plains, it also had a remarkable, centrally controlled political system. Each town was almost identical, with separate areas for the ruling elite and the "workers", and all buildings built with bricks measured according to a system distinctly similar to that laid out in the Vedic *Shastras*, the earliest Hindu treatises. A uniform system of weights and measures, corresponding almost exactly to modern ounces, was used, and the complex, efficient drainage systems remained unmatched by any other pre-Roman civilization.

Towns established on river deltas were perfectly placed for trade. **Lothal**, close to the Gulf of Cambay in south Gujarat, was a major port, and also the source of shells which the Harappans made into jewellery. Some four thousand years later, Cambay is still the largest producer of shell jewellery in India, and south Gujarati artisans make their wonderful beadwork using barely altered materials and techniques.

Although much about this complex society remains unknown – including their impenetrable script – similarities do exist between the Indus Valley Civilization and present-day India. While their most important deity appears to have been a horned god, there was also a strong custom of worshipping a mother goddess, in the same way as the Hindus. The *peepal* tree was revered as it is by Buddhists today, and there is evidence, too, of phallic worship, still strong among Shaivites. In Lothal, altars bearing the remains of animal sacrifice have been discovered, and in every settlement large baths suggest a belief in the purifying quality of water. For more about the Indus Valley Civilization and its significance in Indian history, see *Contexts*.

journey by bus (change at Dholka) or train (3hr). Foundations, platforms, crumbling walls and paved floors are all that remain of the prosperous sea-trading community that dwelt here between 2400 and 1900 BC, when a flood all but destroyed the settlement.

A walk around the **central mound** reveals the old roads that ran past ministers' houses and through the acropolis, where you can see remains of twelve baths and a sewer. The lower town, evident today from a scattering of fragmented bricks and foundations, comprised a bazaar, workshops for coppersmiths, beadmakers and potters, and residential quarters. On the eastern edge of the site, shattered walls enclosing a rectangle indicate the existence of a dock – the only one discovered of its kind, suggesting that Lothal was probably a port serving a number of Harappan towns.

Evidence has been found here of an even older culture, perhaps dating from the fourth millennium BC, known because of its red pottery, as the **Red Ware Culture**. You can see remains from this period and from the Indus Valley civilization in the illuminating site **museum** (daily except Fri 10am–5pm). Among the jewellery collection, a necklace made from gold beads, each a mere 25mm in diameter, provides evidence of sophisticated skills and great wealth. Seals, delicately carved with animal motifs, were used by the Harappans to mark packages; one from Bahrain, imprinted with a dragon and a gazelle, is testimony to the extent of their trading links. A range of accurate weights and compasses testifies to the Harappans' knowledge of geometry and astronomy. From the Red Ware Culture, the museum displays bowls, jars, ceramic and terracotta pots and toys – including touchingly familiar spinning tops and marbles.

Northern Gujarat

North of Gandhinagar, the district of Mehsana was the Solankis' seat of government between the eleventh and thirteenth centuries. Some remains of their old capital – including the extraordinary **Rani-ki-Vav** step-well – still stand at **Anhilawada Patan**, just outside the modern city of **Patan**, which is home to Gujarat's last remaining *patola* weavers. From the city of **Mehsana**, at the province's centre, it's easy to get to the ancient and well-preserved sun temple at **Modhera**, or visit spectacular *havelis* in the small town of **Siddhpur**. Jain temples in the hills at **Taranga** and **Idar** can be reached from Mehsana, or directly from Ahmedabad.

Mehsana

The crowded residential city of **MEHSANA**, less than 100km north of Ahmedabad, doesn't merit a visit for its tourist sights – the one building of any interest is the old **Rajmahal** palace, now used as government offices. As the only place in the area to offer reasonable **accommodation**, it does, however, make an obvious base for visiting any of the towns in north Gujarat. The best bet is *Hotel Apsara* (☎02762/51027; ①–④) in Janta Supermarket on Rajmahal Rd, almost opposite the bus station, which has clean and simple ordinary and a/c rooms, some with balconies and all with private bath, and a food hall selling excellent and very low-priced *thalis*. Opposite the railway station, 300m down the road, you'll find a foursome of cheap and basic places, best of which is the *Avon Guest House* (☎02762/51394; ①). *Janta Supermarket*, in fact a concrete shopping precinct, contains a **post office** (Mon–Sat 10am–6pm), **telegraph office** (Mon–Sat 7am–10pm, Sun 8am–4pm), and three **banks**, including the *State Bank of India* (Mon–Fri 11am–3pm, Sat 11am–1pm). **Trains** link Mehsana to Ahmedabad (2hr), Delhi (23hr) via Abu Road (5hr) and Ajmer (14hr), and Jodhpur (11hr). There are also very slow steam trains to Patan (2hr) and an overnight fast service to Bhuj (14hr). **Buses** tend to be rather faster, serving Ahmedabad, Vadodara, Surat, Bhuj, Modhera, Abu Road, Ranakpur, Ajmer and Jodhpur.

Modhera

If you visit only one town in northern Gujarat, it should be **MODHERA**, where the eleventh-century **sun temple** (daily 8am–6pm) is the best example of Solanki temple architecture in the state. Almost a thousand years old, the temple has survived Muslim iconoclasm and nineteenth-century earthquakes; apart from a missing *shikhara* and slightly worn carvings, it remains largely intact.

The Solanki kings numbered Jains among their courtly advisers, and were probably influenced in their temple design by Jain traditions; deities and their vehicles, animals, full-breasted maidens and complex friezes adorn the sandy brown walls and pillars. Within the *mandapa*, or pillared entrance hall, twelve *adityas* set into niches in the wall portray the transformations of the sun in each month of the year – representations found only in sun temples. According to Indian convention, Modhera's sun temple is positioned so that at the equinoxes the rising sun strikes the images in the sanctuary, which at other times languish in a dim half-light. In front of the temple, a large tank with staggered steps and small shrines set into its four sides lies dry for most of the year. During the monsoon, however, it gives freshness to the temple, and the gardens around bloom with colour.

Modhera is linked by road to Mehsana (40min) and Ahmedabad (2–3hr). There are no **hotels**, but the state-run *Toran Cafeteria* in the temple grounds sells *thalis*, snacks and ice cream.

Patan and Anhilawada Patan

Modern, bustling **PATAN**, roughly 40km northwest of Mehsana, was founded in 1796. It has few monuments to speak of, but the streets of its older quarters are interesting enough, overlooked by the carved balconies and lintels of Muslim *havelis* and the marble domes and canopies of Jain temples. In an area called **Sadvi Wada** you can watch the complex weaving of silk *patola saris*, once the preferred garment of queens and aristocrats, and now made by just one family. Each *sari* takes from four to six months to produce, and is sold for up to Rs70,000 (more than US$2000). Silk threads are dyed in a set pattern before being woven on a complex loom, and the utmost care is taken to ensure completely even tension throughout the cloth. Patan is linked to Mehsana by six daily steam **trains** (2hr).

The big-city bustle of Patan is a far cry from the old Gujarati capital at **Anhilawada Patan**, 2km northwest. The original city served several Rajput dynasties, including the Solankis, between the eighth and the twelfth centuries, before being annexed by the Moghuls. It fell into decline when Ahmed Shah moved the capital to Ahmedabad in 1411. Little remains now except traces of fortifications scattered in the surrounding fields, and the stunning step-well, **Rani-ki-Vav**, built for the Solanki queen Udaimati in 1050 and extensively restored during the 1980s. The recent restorations, unlike those at the sun temple in Somnath (see p.595), are not obtrusively modern, and recreate as perfectly as possible the original carving.

Rani-ki-Vav is undoubtedly Gujarat's greatest step-well, with a deep octagonal shaft, wide flights of steps, and exquisite figures and foliate designs etched into dark grey stone walls and pillars. The well shaft, now home to a colony of particularly large bees, boasts most of its original decoration, and not one tiny area of stone has been missed by the *silavat* masons whose penchant for sculpting voluptuous and shapely maidens has left Rani-ki-Vav with almost as many round bosoms and tilted hips as Hindu friezes. Several sun motifs adorn the well shaft, dating from the era of pre-Hindu sun worship, but these are far outnumbered by sculptures of Vishnu and his various *avatars*, or incarnations. Look out for elephant-headed Ganesh figures.

Not far from the well is **Sashtraling Talou**, the "Thousand-*lingam* Tank" built at the turn of the twelfth century, but razed during Moghul raids. Only a few pillars remain of the Shiva temples that surrounded the tank. Sparse ruins of Rani Udaimati's house crumble nearby, on a hill that affords excellent views over the surrounding plains. The mosques and tombs that you see are within easy walking distance, and make for interesting exploration; many were constructed using pillars from Hindu temples.

Siddhpur

Roughly 40km north of Mehsana, the small town of **SIDDHPUR** is known for its **Rudramala temple**, built with delicate stone work and golden domes in the twelfth century and destroyed by Ala-ud-din Shah in 1297. The temple itself (from the bus stand up the train track to the railway station, then straight ahead past the clock tower and roughly straight on for 1km) is not that impressive – sorry ruins fenced off from the town and guarded by uniformed caretakers – but Siddhpur's architecture is more interesting. Neat *pols* feature wooden *havelis* and grand pillared mansions, built in imitation of the European structures in Bombay and Surat by Muslim merchants in the nineteenth century. Heading from the railway station to the temple, you'll pass a large number of these, particularly in the streets off on your right. For **accommodation**, the small *Ambaji Guest House* opposite the station on the corner, with only the word "welcome" on it in English (☎02732/20239; ①) offers cramped and dirty rooms. The bus stand is very near the station (the other side of the track, 100m north), with regular services to Mehsana, Ahmedabad and Abu Road. Trains also serve these places, but are slower and less frequent.

The Jain temples at Taranga and Idar

Although they're off the tourist trail, the hilltop temples at **Taranga** and **Idar** are easy to get to: 60km or so from Mehsana, both can be reached by bus, and Taranga is on the railway line (though the daily train chugs up from Mehsana at a snail's pace, taking almost three hours). Idar is also connected to Ahmedabad, over 100km south, by road.

Built during the Solanki period, the **Taranga** temples are particularly striking, and better preserved than more famous sites such as Mount Abu, Girnar and Shatrunjaya. Pilgrims and white-clad monks and nuns gather here year round to take blessings and pray at its shrines. The main temple, built of durable sandstone, is dedicated to Ajitanath, the second of twenty-four *tirthankaras* who represent the great teachers of Jainism. His image, complete with the jewelled eyes that adorn all Jain statues, gazes out from the main sanctuary, sturdy and still, while the rest of the temple is alive with a frenzied tangle of voluptuous maidens and musicians in smooth carved stone round the walls, pillars and ceilings, interspersed with rollicking animals and floral patterns.

The temples at **Idar** are less interesting, though they too are etched with numerous carvings. A plaque states that the larger Svetambara temple was built in 242 BC – it's more likely to date from the eleventh century, though the site itself may well have been a pilgrimage centre for centuries before. Most of what you see today is the result of recent renovation. Beside it, the Digambara temple is less ornate and more peaceful, decked with pictures of naked saints and ascetics who were shunned by the Svetambaras when the two sects formed. Used by Hindu and Jain meditators, the caves cut into the hills nearby are said to be sources of great spiritual power.

The town below the hill has a distinctly medieval feel, with few modern buildings and an abundance of delicately carved *havelis*. Now a quiet market town, it was once the home of the Maharaja of Idar and the capital of a large province; remnants of its rich past include an eerie ruined palace, twelfth-century Shiva temples overlooking a dry lake, a small dirty step-well and grand arched city gates. The adequate *Hotel Dreamland* on Highway Rd (☎02778/50597; ①), has basic, slightly grubby **rooms**.

Kutch

Bounded on the north and east by marshy flats and on the south and west by the Gulf of Kutch and the Arabian Sea, the province of **KUTCH** (also spelt Kuchchh or Kachchha) is a place apart. All but isolated from neighbouring Saurasthra and Sind, Kutch's largely arid landscape is shot through with the colour from heavily embroidered local dress. It's a land of legends recorded in stone statues, and folk customs reflected in popular craft and jewellery designs. Few tourists make it out to this beautiful region, much of which is off-limits to visitors without official permits, but those who do are invariably enchanted. With a little effort, you can head out from the central city of **Bhuj** to villages, ancient fortresses, medieval ports and isolated monasteries.

The treeless marshes to the north and east, known as the Great and Little **Ranns of Kutch**, can flood completely during a heavy monsoon, effectively transforming Kutch into an island. Home to the rare wild ass, the Ranns are also the only region in India where flamingoes breed successfully, during July and August, out of reach of any but the most determined bird watchers who can cross the marshes by camel. The southern district, known as **Banni**, was once among India's most fertile areas, and though drier today, still supports crops of cotton, castor-oil plants, sunflowers, wheat and

KUTCHI HANDICRAFTS

Kutch has long been known for its distinctive traditional crafts, from embroidery to jewellery-making and carving. The northern villages of Dhordo, Khavda and Hodko are home to the few remaining communities of **leather embroiderers** who soak hide in a solution of water, latex and lime in an underground earthen pot before stitching it with flower, peacock and fish motifs. The finished bags, fans, horse belts, wallets, cushion covers and mirror frames are sold in villages all through Kutch. Dhordo is also known for its **wood-carving**, while Khavda is one of the last villages to continue the printing method known as **ajrakh**. Cloth is dyed with natural pigments in a lengthy process similar to batik, but instead of wax, a mixture of lime and gum is used to resist the dye in certain parts of the cloth when new colours are added. Women in Khavda **paint terracotta** pots with dusky whites, reds and blacks, using cotton rags, and brushes made from bamboo leaves.

Rogan painting is now practised only in Biber in northern Kutch. A complex process turns hand-pounded castor oil into coloured dyes which are used to decorate cushion covers, bedspreads and curtains with simple geometric patterns. Craftsmen also make melodic **bells** coated in intricate designs of copper and brass, once used for communication among shepherds.

Kutchi **silver engraving** is a dwindling art form, practised mainly in Bhuj. Molten silver is poured into a mold, and, when dry, engraved by gentle taps with fine, sharp tools and small hammers. The final products, such as trays, pots, cups, pens and picture frames, are smoothed down and polished in an acid solution. Silver jewellery is common, featuring in most traditional Kutchi costumes. The anklets, earrings, noserings, bangles and necklaces are similar to those seen in Rajasthan, since much of it is made by the Ahir and Rabari communities who live in both areas. In Kutch, the silver is mixed with zinc to make it more malleable, and converted into wires and sheets. The main centres for silver are Anjar, Bhuj, Mandiri and Mundra.

The most common form of **cloth** printing is **bandhani**, or tie-dye, practised in most villages, but concentrated in Mandvi and Anjar. Kutchi clothes are distinctive for their fine embroidery and bold designs; one design unique to the area is *mushroo*-weaving (*ilacha*), a skill practised today by less than twenty artisans. The yarn used is silk, carefully dyed before it is woven in a basic striped pattern, with a complex design woven over the top in such fine detail that it seems to be embroidered. *Ilacha* cloth, made into *cholis* (blouses) and dresses, is hard to buy now; the best place to see it is Mandvi, or in the Calico Museum in Ahmedabad (see p.561).

groundnuts. Northern Kutch, on the other hand, is semi-desert, with dry shifting sands and no perennial rivers; villagers rely on income drawn from traditional crafts.

When **visiting Kutchi villages**, it goes without saying that you should be sensitive to local customs, removing your shoes before entering houses, and only taking photos with permission. Only the larger settlements are covered below; if you want to really get off the track, ask at the Bhuj tourist office.

Some history

Remains from the third millennium BC in eastern Kutch suggest that migrating Indus Valley communities crossed the Ranns from Mohenjo Daro in modern Pakistan to Lothal in eastern Gujarat. Traditional history recounts that Kutch belonged to the Yadavas, when it was known for rich grasses that flourished on ash manure that fell from heaven at the request of a wandering sage. Despite being so cut off, Kutch felt the effect of the Buddhist Mauryan empire, and later came under the control of Greek Bactrians, the Western Satraps and the powerful Guptas. The Arab invasion of Sind in 720 AD pushed refugees into Kutch's western regions, and tribes from Rajputana and Gujarat crossed its eastern borders. Later in the eighth century the region fell under the sway of the Gujarati capital Anhilawada (modern-day Patan), and by the tenth century the Samma Rajputs, later known as the Jadejas, had infiltrated Kutch from the west, and established themselves as rulers. Their line continued until Kutch was absorbed into the Indian Union in 1948.

When the Muslim Sultans ruled Gujarat, they made repeated unsuccessful attempts to cross into Kutch. It remained separate, with its own customs, laws and a thriving maritime tradition, while trade with Malabar, Mocha, Muscat and the African coast brought in spices, drugs, silks, rhino hides and elephant tusks. Connections with Africa also encouraged the slave trade, already common among the Portuguese in south Saurashtra. African deck hands and slaves arrived with merchants and sailors, and after the abolition of slavery in 1834 a small African community settled in north Bhuj. Their crafts, dances and music have been integrated into the region's tradtional arts.

Bhuj

Set in the heart of Kutch, the narrow streets and old bazaars of the walled town of **BHUJ** retain a medieval flavour unlike any other Gujarati city. Bhuj was established as the capital of Kutch in the mid-sixteenth century by Rao Khengarji, a Jadeja Rajput. The one interruption before 1948 in his family's continuous rule of the city was a brief period of British domination early in the nineteenth century. When the governance of the state was handed back to the rightful ruler, Maharao Desal, in 1834, the import of slaves from Africa was banned and Africans were given homes in the north of the city. With the establishment of the city of Gandhidham and the port of Kandla east of the capital, the economic centre of gravity shifted away from Bhuj, leaving it to carry on its traditions little affected by the modernizations of the twentieth century.

Arrival and information

Bhuj **airport** is 5km north of town, about Rs25–30 by auto-rickshaw, depending on your bargaining skills. Trains arrive at the **railway station** a little over 1km north of town, from where a rickshaw to a hotel costs roughly Rs15. The **bus station** is on ST Station Rd on the southern edge of the old city. The **tourist office** (daily except Thurs 9am–noon & 3–6pm; ☎20004) in Aina Mahal in the old city has a wealth of information on Bhuj and Kutchi villages, and details of **permits** required to travel to them (see p.581). On Sunday mornings, very cheap second-hand **books and magazines**, some in English, are traded in the Shroff Bazaar.

There's a branch of the **State Bank of India** in Prag Mahal (Mon–Fri 11am–3pm, Sat and the 18th and last working day of the month 11am–1pm), and one in New Station Rd (same hours; will change dollars and sterling cash or travellers' cheques only, and *Visa* cheques only if issued by *Barclays*). The **GPO** (Mon–Sat 10am–6pm) is south of Waniawad Gate.

> The telephone **area code** for Bhuj is ☎02832.

The Town

Bhuj is overlooked from the east by the old and crumbling fort on Bhujia Hill, while the vast **Hamirsar Tank**, with a small park on an island in its centre, stands on the western edge of town. The original city walls, built in 1715, were largely demolished in 1948 though parts remain, especially in the north. Near Bhid Gate a **pigeon tower**, built as an act of devotion and kindness to god's creatures, is maintained by a levy on the goods traded around it. Such towers are common in the villages of the region.

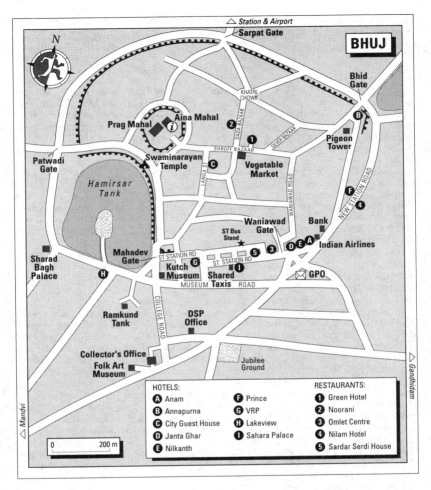

In the maze of winding streets that make up Bhuj's **old city**, the pace of life is in tune with the plod of camels that amble through the streets, past old vegetable markets and countless cloth stalls, mingling with the region's notoriously resilient cows and the Kutchi people dressed in heavily embroidered traditional clothes. Only some of the buildings of the beautifully preserved **palace complex**, guarded by sturdy walls and high heavy gates, are open to the public. Its most dazzling section, **Aina Mahal**, is now **Maharao Madansinji Museum** (daily except Sat 9am–noon & 3–6pm; Rs3). Built in the eighteenth century during the reign of Maharao Lakho, fondly known as Lakhpatji, Aina Mahal is a superb feat of architecture, its stunning interior designed by the Saurashtran, Ram Singh, who incorporated techniques picked up from as far afield as Europe. As a result, Lakhpatji's palace was decorated with a style unknown elsewhere in western India, a riot of finely blown glass lanterns, exquisite tile-work and detailed enamel designs. The first hall of the museum is given over to historical artefacts, including letters between Viceroy Mountbatten and the Maharao of Kutch in the final years of the Raj. You can also see sequined royal robes, classic Kutchi embroidery, and a painted scroll over 20m long depicting Maharao Pragmalji with an entourage of courtiers, cavalry and elephants, celebrating victory over the Moghuls in the 1850s.

Built of marble and decked with an exquisite mirrored design, the **Hall of Mirrors** is the most elaborate of the palace apartments. Next door is **Fuvara Mahal**, Lakhpatji's music room, lit by Venetian glass lanterns. The huge pool was once alive with the spray of fountains (*fuvara*), and dancers and bards performed before the king; note the musical instruments around the platform from where he watched all the fun. The coins on show beneath Kutchi paintings in the adjoining chamber are the *kori*, *dhingla* and *dokda* that were Kutch's currency from 1617 to 1948.

Lakhpatji's private room, **Hira Mahal**, contains his gilded bed, chiming clocks, glass ornaments and mechanical toys made by Ram Singh, along with remarkable Kutchi carpets. In the picture gallery, subjects include a very relaxed Lakhpatji smoking a *hookah*, attended by tiny African slaves; in another he is adorned with real pearls luxuriantly studded onto the surface of the portrait. The fabulous wooden door inlaid with ivory has been in the palace since 1708, despite more than one request by the British who wanted to add it to collections of Indian crafts in their own museums.

On the upper floor of the museum, Maharao Pragmalji's hand-drawn horoscope shows – not surprisingly – influential planetary positions, and there's a selection of illustrated manuscripts, as well as the (reconstructed) marriage room of Maharao Khengarji (1884). The throne for the betrothed couple is sheltered by a canopy of leaves and jewels, and flanked with towers of clay water pots.

The later **Prag Mahal** (daily except Sat 9am–noon & 3–6pm; Rs4, camera Rs15, video Rs50), built nearby in the 1860s, is unmistakably Victorian, combining Moghul, British, Kutchi and Italian architectural styles. A bemused-looking stuffed hippo head (coming apart at the seams) stares at you as you enter, and the main hall, used for *durbars* (state meetings) until 1948, holds a sad display of the spoils of royal hunts, unceremoniously laid out on the floor: scores of deer and blue bulls, 7 cheetahs, 7 tigers, 2 bears and 21 sets of deer horns, all killed in a single year. The main reason for entering the Prag Mahal is to enjoy views of the town from the top of the clock tower.

Nearby, on the road that runs along the east side of Hamirsar Tank, the gaily painted and lively **Swaminarayan Temple** belongs to the oldest of the three Hindu revivalist sects inspired by the spiritual guru Swaminarayan. Its decorative bold pinks, yellows, greens and soft blues are particularly vivid here in the sandy surroundings of Bhuj. Devotees gather and chat in the courtyard, and to one side gaudily dressed Hindu deities peer out from shrines shielded by silver grilles unlocked only during *pujas*. The temple is home to *sadhus* who follow the precepts of Vedic study, vegetarianism, chastity and moderation laid down by Swaminarayan, the "God Supreme", and grow vegetables in the private gardens behind the temple.

The plain building on the southeastern edge of Hamirsar Tank houses the **Kutch museum** (9am–noon, closed Wed and 2nd & 4th Sat of each month; Rs0.50, photos Rs2 each), not a patch on the Aina Mahal, but giving a more general overview of Kutchi culture. Archeological finds from Harappan times and ancient brass figures include Buddhas sitting with their hands poised in the *mudra* representing "no fear". A silver padlock in the shape of India is among the collection of gold and silver ornaments on the ground floor, most made in the nineteenth century and heavily influenced by European designs. A display of turbans on the upper floor explains the particular types worn by each tribe, albeit a little confusedly, and an impressive collection of musical instruments includes a *surando* (stringed instrument), a *transa* (drum) and a curious snake-like horn called a *nagfan*. The inevitable collection of

FESTIVALS IN AND AROUND BHUJ

Bhuj's **Tourist Festival**, held over five days in January or February, hosts a wide selection of traditional music – from religious and maritime songs to African drumming – as well as tribal and religious dance from Kutch and other parts of Gujarat. Stalls sell shoes, clothes and embroidered cloth.

Further afield in **Nakhatrana**, 50km west of Bhuj, a festival on the first Monday of Bhadrapada (Aug/Sept) commemorates the **Jakhs**, a mysterious horse-riding clan of 71 men and one lone woman who came to Kutch in the eleventh century. Their origins are unclear, though tales of their fair skin and medical skills could link them with the Zoroastrians from northern Iran who settled in Gujarat in the tenth century, and later formed communities in Bombay where they are known as Parsis. In Kutch they are worshipped as demi-gods and remembered as miracle workers able to cure barren women. During the festival bards and singers retell stories of their feats, and offerings are laid before equestrian images in hilltop temples.

stuffed animals includes, of course, the wild ass. You may see craftsmen stone-sculpting in the forecourt.

The road that skirts the southern edge of Hamirsar Tank leads to **Sharad Bagh Palace** (daily except Fri 9am–noon & 3–6pm; Rs1, camera Rs10, video Rs50), built in 1867 and the retreat of the last Maharao. The small porticoed buildings are delicately proportioned and include the plush drawing room, decked with hunting trophies, photographs and old clocks, and the dining room which contains Maharao Madansinjhi's coffin, which was shipped over from England after his death in 1991. The palace's most appealing feature, however, is its well-tended gardens, complete with pretty flower beds, giant bamboo trees, lofty palms and tennis courts.

Just south of the museum and west of College Rd, a path leads to the 250-year-old **Ramkund** tank, which is made of hard grey stone and shaded by trees. Decorated with skilfully crafted images of Kali, Vishnu, Nag and Ganesh, the tank also has small niches in the walls where oil lamps would glitter in the dusk as devotees prayed at the evening *puja*. Nearby is a set of sixteenth-century *sati* stones. Down at the other end of College Rd, off the Mandvi road just past the Collector's Office, the Bharatiya Sanskriti Darshan **Folk Art and Crafts Museum** (daily 9am–1pm; Rs2) has some lovely textiles, paintings and embroidery, but sadly no labels.

Accommodation

Bhuj's **hotels and lodges** cater almost exclusively for budget travellers, though a couple offer a/c and carpets for extra cash. If you're looking for something in the mid-range, and have no luck with those listed below, you could try a couple of hotels under construction at the time of writing, and due to open soon. They are the *Lake View* on the south side of Hamirsar Tank, and the *Sahara Palace* on ST Station Rd opposite the bus station. The grottier places around the bus station, such as *Nityanand Lodge* and *Jay Bharat Lodge* are not recommended.

Anam, New Station Rd (☎23397). Fresh, comfortable rooms with private bath, though most are invaded by traffic noise. "Deluxe" rooms have hot shower and a/c. The popular veg restaurant on the ground floor (10am–3pm & 7–10pm) serves high standard, affordable Gujarati *thalis*. ④–⑤.

Annapurna, Bhid Gate (☎20831). Small, friendly place, with clean, homely rooms (bucket of hot water). The restaurant serves tasty Kutchi veg *thalis* (10am–3.30pm & 7–11.30pm). Great value. ①.

City Guest House, Langa St (☎21067). Travellers' favourite. Clean, simple rooms around a small courtyard, some with private bath, and a cheap dorm. Hidden away in the old city, it can be hard to find (from the Aina Mahal and Prag Mahal, pass through the main gate and the stone gate beyond, go straight ahead and it's in the second street on the right). ①–②.

Janta Ghar, New Station Rd, near Waniawad Gate (☎24451 or 2; fax 20428). Dim, cell-like rooms on the ground floor, but some reasonable options with bath and hot shower, fan and window. ①.

Nilkanth Guest House, New Station Rd, a few doors east of the *Janta Ghar*, next door to *Hirani Sports* (☎22538). Clean rooms with attached bath, and a dorm for men. The one sign in English is way up on the side of the buiding and only visible from afar. ①.

Prince, New Station Rd (☎20370). Bhuj's one upmarket hotel. A/c, TV and private bath. Pay in foreign currency to avoid the "luxury tax". The restaurant (7.30–10am, 11am–2.30pm & 7.30–10.30pm) serves inviting Indian, Chinese and Western food as well as a superior *thali*. ①–⑤.

VRP Guest House, ST Station Rd (☎21388). Basic rooms in a three-storey complex opposite the taxi stand. The *Green Rock* restaurant (11am–3pm & 6–10.30pm) serves Punjabi dishes and South Indian snacks, but no hot drinks. ①.

Eating

Many of the best **places to eat** in Bhuj are in the hotels (see above); elsewhere, food is basic but adequate. Don't miss the all-you-can-eat **thalis**, which may have up to ten separate veg curries; the *Annapurna*'s (see above) are particularly good. A number of places near the bus station on ST Station Rd do **juices**, ice-creams and shakes; try the *Sardar Sereli House*, 20m west of the *Omlet Centre*, which has no English sign, but an open front and cane-crushing machine.

Green Hotel, Shroff Bazaar. Close to the old vegetable market, serving good, inexpensive Punjabi and south Indian food, milkshakes and ice cream. Open 9.30am–10.30pm.

Noorani, Dada Bazaar. One of the few non-veg restaurants in the old city. Good, inexpensive food, and lovely creamy curd. Open 8am–10pm.

Omlet Centre, ST Station Rd. Tiny, dim stall serving great eggy breakfasts with a choice between *deshi* (free range) and "farm" (battery) eggs. Open 8am–11.30pm.

Nilam Hotel, New Station Rd, opposite the *Hotel Prince*. Clean, pleasant and reasonably priced, with a wider choice of food than most, including passable vegetable chow mein. Open 8am–11pm.

MOVING ON FROM BHUJ

GSTC **buses** from the ST station serve Ahmedabad, Rajkot and Palanpur, along with Jamnagar (8 daily; 7hr), Porbandar (3 daily; 10hr), Mehsana (6 daily; 8hr) and Jaisalmer (1 daily; 14hr). *Helly Travels*, by the *Modern Talkies* cinema just west of the bus stand (☎22444), sells tickets for **private deluxe buses** to Rajkot (6 daily; 5hr) and Jodhpur (1 overnight; 10hr); *Patel Travels*, ST Station Rd opposite *VRP Guest House* (☎21499), for private bus services to Jamnagar (3 daily; 7hr), Ahmedabad (1 daily; 7hr), Dwarka (1 daily; 8hr 30min), and Bombay (1 daily; 15hr); and *Shree Sahjanand Travels*, in the same building as *VRP Guest House* (☎22236), for night sleeper buses to Ahmedabad (9hr).

Five daily **trains** run to Gandhidham for connections around Gujarat and to Bombay. There are direct daily trains to **Delhi** (8.15pm; 36hr) and Ahmedabad (1.45pm; 16hr 15min), but the fastest way to these destinations is to take the 8.15pm Delhi train as far as Gandhidham and change there for the *Intercity Express* #9104 to Ahmedabad (continuing to Vadodara), and again for Delhi. On Monday nights, you can also connect with the 4.05am Tuesday *Trivandrum Express* #6335 to Pune and all the way to Bangalore, Ernakulam and Thiruvananthapuram. By taking the 5.55pm train from Bhuj, you can change at Gandhidham for the 8.45pm *Kutch Express* #9032 to Bombay Central (arriving 11.45am); this train also calls at Ahmedabad (at 2.40am) as well as Vadodara (5am) and Surat (7.10am). The best route to **Rajasthan** is to travel to Palanpur and change (take the 8.15pm service); trains from there serve Abu Road, Ajmer and Jaipur, as well as Delhi Sarai Rohilla. If you don't want to trek up to the station to book, *Hemal Travels* near the bus stand on ST Station Rd north side, 100m west of the *Omlet Centre* (☎50311), make reservations for a Rs15 surcharge. Bhuj has its own quotas on trains out of Gandhidham, and you should usually be able to get tickets the day before.

Tickets for **flights** to Bombay can be booked through *Indian Airlines*, New Station Rd (Mon–Sat 10am–1.15pm & 2–5pm; ☎50204). There are no passenger **boat** services across the Gulf of Kutch. Note that to travel **north of Bhuj** you will need a **permit** – see below for details.

Villages around Bhuj

Bhuj is a useful base for visiting the **outlying villages**, whether by bus or the taxis that gather outside the **ST bus stand**. If you go by bus, you will have to do some walking to reach many of the most interesting Kutchi settlements, which lie a few kilometres from the nearest roads.

Due to the proximity of **northern Kutch** to the sensitive Pakistani border, you need a **permit** (see p.581) to visit villages north of Bhuj. Many trips in this area are best made by taxi as accommodation cannot be guaranteed, and bus services are infrequent. There are regular **shared taxis** for Mandvi, Mundra and Gandhidham, but for most other Kutchi destinations you will have to charter one.

Mandvi

The compact town of **MANDVI**, on the west bank of a wide tidal estuary 60km south of Bhuj, faces the Arabian Sea to the south and supports a dwindling *dhow*-building industry. In the late eighteenth century it was the docking point for a fleet of four hundred vessels exporting goods from a hinterland that encompassed Gujarat and the lands to the north as far as Jaisalmer. Merchants, seamen and later the British, were all keen to settle in this flourishing port; few remained, but they left behind grand mansions, imaginatively painted and carved in a style clearly influenced by European tastes.

Mandvi's **markets** are stocked with *bandhani* and silver, and one street crashes and clanks with the noise from the iron forgers' blackened stalls. It's a leisurely place, with several *chai* stalls set among old houses and cluttered shops that stretch west of the estuary, blocked in the south by the shifting sands of a long beach that's seldom used for swimming, but supports the tall windmills that power an electricity plant supplying the town. Beside the estuary you can see mighty Noah's Ark-style ships being hand-built from long wooden planks, with nails up to 1m long forged by local blacksmiths. Fifty men spend two years building each ship, many of which still make the long journey to ports in the west, often carrying Muslims to Mecca for the *haj* pilgrimage. Flamingos and other wader birds frequent the mud flats when the tide is out.

Mandvi's neglected and little-visited **Vijay Vilas Palace** (daily 8am–1pm & 2–6pm; Rs5, camera Rs25, video Rs100), 8km west of town (turn left after 4km), is a sandy-white domed building set in almost 700 acres of land, built as a summer retreat by Kutch's Maharao in the 1940s. Inside, Belgian, British and Italian furniture fills the high-ceilinged carpeted rooms, and hunting trophies deck the walls. A grand stairway leads to the ladies' quarters on the first floor; small apartments and cool marble courtyards open to the sky. A pavilion projecting from the roof catches fresh sea breezes and commands excellent views.

PRACTICALITIES

Hourly **buses** run between Bhuj and Mandvi (1hr 30min); **taxis** crammed with as many people as possible make the journey when full, for Rs20 a head. Of the town's three **guest houses**, the clean, modern *Sahara*, adjoining the city wall some 300m west of the bus stand (☎02834/20272; ①–③) is the best, and has a dorm; the *Shital*, near the bridge (☎02834/21160; ①) is cheap and cheerful. You can also stay in one of two guest houses at *Vijay Vilas Palace* (☎02834/20043; ④/⑥), which although characterful are not that good value by Indian standards; meals (Rs50) are served in the aristocratic dining room. Otherwise the best bet for **food** is *Zorba the Buddha Restaurant* on KT Shah Rd, west of the bus stand behind an old town gate (11am–2pm & 6–10pm), whose renowned *thalis* have over ten dishes, plus fresh chutneys, pickles and sweets.

Mundra

The small fishing port of **MUNDRA**, east of Mandvi, is best reached by bus (12 daily; 1hr) or shared taxi (Rs20) direct from Bhuj, 30km away, though it is also served by

KUTCHI TRIBES

Kutch has the most significant and conspicuous population of tribal communities in Gujarat, most of whom migrated from east and west from the seventh century onwards. Each tribe can be identified from its costume, and gains its income from pastoral farming or crafts such as weaving, painting, wood-carving and dyeing. Traditionally, each has concentrated on different crafts; the distinctions today are far less clear-cut.

The **Rabari** is the largest group in the Kutchi pastoral community, with three main tribes hailing from Marwad in Rajasthan. They rear cattle, buffalo, goats, sheep and camels, sell *ghee*, and weave, and are also known for fine **embroidery**. The men, most of whom sport a white turban, wear white cotton trousers tight at the ankle and in baggy pleats above the knee, a white jacket (*kehdiyun*) with multiple folds tucked around chest level and overlong sleeves, and a blanket thrown over one shoulder. Rabari women dress in black pleated jackets or open-backed blouses, full black skirts and tie-dyed head cloths, usually black and red, and always deck themselves with heavy silver jewellery and ivory bangles around the upper arms. Typical houses, made of mud or brick, are decorated inside with *gargomati* – a raised pattern of whitewashed mud and dung, inlaid with mirrors. Child marriages, customary among the Rabari, are performed over a four- or five-day period in the summer; immediately upon the birth of a daughter, a mother starts embroidering cloth to form the most valuable basis of her dowry. In **Bhujodi**, near Bhuj, the Rabari weave camel wool on pit looms into blankets and shawls.

Claiming descent from Krishna, the **Bharvad** tribes infiltrated Gujarat from Vrindavan, close to Mathura in Uttar Pradesh. Their dress is similar to that of the Rabaris, though the men are distinguishable from the peacock, parrot and flower motifs sewn into their *khediyun*, and the women by their bright backless shirts, *kapadun*, rarely covered by veils. Both men and women wear a thick *bori* cloth around the waist. Mass marriages take place among the Bharvad every few years; a custom originating as a form of protection in the Muslim period when single girls were frequently victims of abduction (the kidnapping of married girls was heavily punished). In the first week of each September the Bharvads gather at the Trinetresvar temple in **Tarnetar**, 65km from Rajkot, celebrating with dances and singing, sheltered under the shade of embroidered umbrellas made especially for the occasion.

The wandering **Ahir** cattle-breeders came to Gujarat from Sind, and settled as farmers in Kutch, and at Morvi in Saurashtra where they mixed with other tribes. Baggy trousers and *khediyun* are worn by the men, together with a white loosely wound headcloth, and the women dress like the Rabaris, with additional heavy silver nose rings. The children's bright *topis*, or skull-caps, overlaid with neat fragments of mirrors, are like those common in Pakistan. During Diwali, Ahirs lead their cattle through the streets to be fed by other local communities, which bestows merit on the giver and is good for *karma*.

The **Charans**, the long-established bards of Gujarat, encompass in their clans the Maldharis who raise prize cattle in southern Kutch and the Gir Forest, and the leatherworkers known as Meghavals. They claim descent from a celestial union between Charan and a maiden created by Parvati, and many gain almost divine status after death. The women are often worshipped by other tribes, since their connection with Parvati links them closely to the mother goddess, Ashpura, who is popular in Kutch, and the men's curses were once considered so powerful that they drove their opponents to kill themselves in the hope that the curse would be deflected upon the Charans: such "heroes" are remembered by stone monuments around Kutch depicting a man piercing his neck with a dagger.

Said to have migrated from Pakistan, the Kutchi **Jats** can be identified by their black dress. Young Jat girls have dainty plaits curving round the sides of their faces, and wear heavy nose rings. Traditionally semi-nomadic camel- and cattle-rearers, with houses made of reed (*pakha*) that are easily folded and carried from place to place, they have recently begun to settle more permanently.

buses from Mandvi (9 daily; 2hr). The road to Mundra runs through a dry red-brown rocky landscape, past broad fields of wheat and sunflowers, before approaching the thick walls that circle the town. Local crafts include batik prints, heavy silver jewellery and unusual woollen *namadas*; floor coverings, wall-hangings and camel saddles dyed in earthy maroons, blues, yellows and black. Several small Rabari and Jat villages lie a bus ride and a short walk from Mundra, and to the east, the Jain temples at **Bhadreswar** are a focus for pilgrims from all over Gujarat.

Southeast to Kandla

The 50-kilometre journey southeast from Bhuj to **KANDLA**, Kutch's main port, takes you past dry scrubland dotted with road signs proclaiming "Growing tree is symbol of living nation". In the small village of **Bhujodi**, less than 10km out of Bhuj, Rabari men weave thick shawls and blankets on pit looms dug into the floors of squat mud houses decorated with *gargomati*. You can buy their products from a small shop run by the Bhujodi Handweaving Co-op Society.

The first main town beyond Bhuj, **ANJAR** was the capital of Kutch until 1548. It's an important centre of bright and intricate Ahir embroidery, *bandhani*, batik, and nut-cracker making, and holds busy markets once or twice a week. Further east is **GANDHID-HAM**, the city planned for Sind refugees who came to Kutch after Partition. An industrial centre, supporting the modern port of Kandla at the mouth of the Gulf of Kutch, Gandhidham holds little attraction for tourists, though it's convenient for road and rail connections to Rajasthan and Gujarat. Buses run hourly between Bhuj and Gandhidham (1hr), and there are five trains a day, two of which continue to Kandla.

North of Bhuj

One bus a day from Bhuj makes the journey to the craft centres of **KHAVDA**, **HODKO** and **DHORDO**, where clusters of grass-roofed mud huts are decorated with traditional clay and whitewash patterns. You'll need to stay the night. Another popular craft centre, and an easy daytrip, is the village of **LUDIA**, though the painted mud huts and friendly people are more of a draw than the local embroidery, which is better at **Bhirendiara** and **Sumeraser** on the way. Bear in mind that Ludia is a fifteen-minute desert walk from the bus stop – you can't see the village from the road, but the path is clear – and Sumeraser also requires some walking to get to.

West of Khavda, the village of **THAN** is home to a small community of Hindu *sadhus* known as *Khanpata* ("split-ear") because of the heavy ornaments they wear in their ears. The order was founded by the twelfth-century saint, Dharamnath, who travelled to Kutch from Saurashtra and practised severe austerities for years on a nearby hill. A temple marking the spot is visited by *sadhus* year round, and may have been converted from an earlier sun temple by the Kathi tribe. The one daily bus currently leaves Bhuj at 5.15pm (3hr); you can **stay** overnight at Than's *dharamshala* for a donation.

PERMITS

Before heading into northern Kutch, it's obligatory to acquire a free **permit**, which should cover every place you intend to visit. Simply take your passport and a photocopy of the first three pages and your visa to the DSP (District Superintendant of Police) office just off the traffic circle at the southern end of College Rd (Mon–Sat 10.30am–6.10pm). They will tell you if permits are being issued for the places you want to visit (this varies slightly from time to time depending on the border situation) and issue an application form. Take that to the Collector's Office, just off College Rd nearby (Mon–Sat 10.30am–6pm; except for the 2nd & 4th Sat of the month) where your permit will be issued. The whole process takes about ninety minutes.

Near Than, the village of **BIBER** has a temple to Rama decorated with friezes depicting scenes from the *Ramayana*, executed using a long-forgotten technique known as *kamagar*. At neighbouring **NIRONA** you can see cloth painted in the ancient *rogan* style (though only one family there still does it). There are nine daily buses between Bhuj and Nironam (1hr 30min).

It's also possible to stay overnight in a *dharamshala* at the Gandhi Ashram in **Lilpur** northeast of Bhuj, or beyond that at **Rahpur**, enabling you to visit the archeological excavations at **DHOLAVIRA**, an island in the Rann where traces of the ancient Harappan civilization (see p.569) have been discovered. The bus from Bhuj to Dholavira (7hr) leaves in the morning.

Saurashtra

SAURASHTRA, also known as the **Kathiawar Peninsula**, forms the bulk of Gujarat state, a large knob of land spreading south from the hills and marshes of the north out to the Arabian Sea, cut into by the Gulf of Cambay to the east and the Gulf of Kutch to the west. This is Gujarat at its most diverse, with Hindu, Jain, Buddhist and Muslim architecture, modern urban centres and traditional bazaars, populated by cattle-rearing tribes and industrialists. Saurashtra boasts India's finest Jain temple city at **Shatrunjaya** near **Palitana**, Krishna temples at **Dwarka** and **Somnath** and Ashoka's Buddhist capital, **Junagadh**. Lions thrive in **Gir Forest**, while in the flat yellow grassland northeast of Bhavnagar India's largest herd of black buck live in a protected sanctuary at **Velavadar**. Gandhi's birthplace is still honoured in **Porbandar**; he is also remembered by a museum in **Rajkot** where he spent some years. The best place to head for to enjoy sun, sea and beaches is the island of **Diu**, just off the south coast.

Rajkot

Founded in the sixteenth century, **RAJKOT** was ruled by the Jadeja Rajputs until merging with the Union of Saurashtra after Independence, since when it has become a successful industrial centre. Best known for its associations with **Mahatma Gandhi**, who lived and worked here for some time, this quiet city has little to attract tourists except a museum and Gandhi's family home. Its central position, however, makes it a good base for trips to nearby Morvi, Wankaner and Whadwan.

Arrival, orientation and information
Three main roads radiate from the busy road junction at Sanganwa Chowk in the centre of Rajkot: **Dhebar Rd** heads south, past the ST bus station 100m away; **Lakhajiraj Rd** goes east, through the old city; and **Jawahar Rd** runs north, past Alfred High School (whose former pupils include M K Gandhi) and Jubilee Gardens towards **Rajkot Junction station** 2km northeast (get off here rather than at City Station if arriving by train), and the airport 4km northwest.

Rajkot's **tourist office** (Mon–Sat 10.30am–6pm; ☎31616) is off Jawahar Rd, north of Sanganwa Chowk behind the *State Bank of Saurashtra*. You'll find the **GPO** (Mon–Sat 8am–7.30pm, Sun 10am–4pm) on Sadar Rd, off Jawahar Rd opposite Jubilee Gardens.

The telephone **area code** for Rajkot is ☎0281.

The Town

In the most appealing area of Rajkot, the **old city**, typical Gujarati wooden-fronted houses, with intricately carved shutters veiling stained-glass windows, stand among more modern, faceless constructions. The Gandhis moved here from Porbandar in 1881; tucked away in the narrow streets on Ghitaka Rd, off Lakhajiraj Rd about 300m east of Sanganwa Chowk – the turning is marked by a blue signpost, but it's not easily spotted – the family house **Kaba Gandhi no Delo** (Mon–Sat 9am–noon & 3–6pm) has a small display of artefacts and photographs from the Mahatma's life.

Rajkot's chief tourist attraction, however, is the **Watson Museum** (daily except Wed and 2nd & 4th Sat of each month, 9am–12.30pm & 2.30–6pm; Rs0.50), in a robust nineteenth-century building in Jubilee Bagh. The museum, named after Colonel Watson, British Political Agent from 1886 to 1893, displays relics from 2000 BC to the nineteenth century, including findings from Indus Valley sites, medieval statues, manuscripts, miniatures and Rajput bronzes. On the ground floor a vast collection of portraits of Gujarat's rulers surrounds a staunch Queen Victoria, fashioned in 1899 by Alfred Gilbert who modelled Eros in London's Piccadilly Circus. Next door, the **Lang Library** (daily 9–10.50am & 5–6.50pm) is a grand but seldom used cobwebbed reading room, flanked with dusty English-language books though, unsurprisingly, most local people are more interested in the daily Gujarati newspapers.

Accommodation

Rajkot's inexpensive **hotels** leave much to be desired, but a few are adequate. It's worth spending a little more to find welcome relief from the noise and dirt of the city.

Babha Guest House, Panchnath Rd, off Jawahar Rd just south of Alfred High School (☎32187). The cleanest budget options, with small rooms. ①–③.

Galaxy, Jawahar Rd, 100m north of Sanganwa Chowk (☎55981; fax 55987). Spacious rooms – some a/c – on the third floor of a shopping complex. High standard of hygiene and service, but access is by elevator only – staff claim the stairs can be unlocked "immediately" in case of fire. ⑤.

Himalaya Guest House, Lakhajiraj Rd, just off Sanganwa Chowk (☎31736). Large place with reasonably clean rooms, all with private bathrooms and bucket of hot water. Often full. ①.

Jay Kishan, off Lakhajiraj Rd near Sanganwa Chowk (☎28703). Clean, tiny rooms.①.

Jyoti, Kanak Rd (☎25271). Behind the bus stand, with fairly pleasant rooms and a dorm. ①–②.

Kavrey, Kanak Rd (☎34942; fax 23421). Upmarket place set off a noisy road. Good comfortable rooms, some a/c, and suites. ⑤–⑦.

Milan, Shri Sadgnav Complex, 30/37 Karanpara (☎35049). Large hotel behind the bus stand with relatively clean and airy rooms and hot water round the clock. ③.

Samrat International, 37 Karanpara (☎22269; fax 32774). A little south of the *Milan*. Clean and well-managed, but not as good value as the *Galaxy*. ④–⑦.

Eating

Most **restaurants** in Rajkot serve unfailingly good Gujarati *thalis* with a wide range of sweet and sour tastes and often in unending supplies. Western food is only found in a few places in the more upmarket hotels. Most restaurants don't open until 10.30am, so early risers will have to survive on a cup of sweet tea until then. Cheap *dhabas* can, as you would expect, be found behind the bus station and opposite the railway station.

Havmor, Jawahar Rd, opposite Alfred High School. Comfortable a/c restaurant for good Punjabi food, Chinese and Western options, and their own selection of ice creams. Probably the best non-veg place in town. Open 10am–11pm.

Laxmi Lodge, Sanganwa Chowk. Popular dining hall serving cheap Gujarati *thalis*. Open 10.30am–3pm & 6.30–9.30pm.

Rainbow, Sanganwa Chowk. Small place for south Indian veg snacks, pizzas, and ice cream (no hot drinks) below the *Himalaya Guest House*. Open 10am–11pm (meals 11am–3.30pm & 7–11pm).

Samarkand, *Samrat International*. Good selection of international cuisine in comfortable a/c setting. Open 11.30am–3pm & 7–11pm.

Of Rajkot's two **train** services to Bombay, by far the better is the *Saurashtra Mail* #9006, leaving early evening and arriving at a civilized hour the next day. There's also a nighttime express and a daytime passenger train to Porbandar (4hr 30min), an express (the *Saurashtra Mail* in the other direction) and three fast passenger trains to Dwarka (5hr) and Okha (6hr), an overnight fast passenger train to Bhavnagar (8hr 30min), and four trains a day to Junagadh (3hr 15min), two continuing to Veraval (5hr 15min–6hr). The station to use is Rajkot Junction.

Frequent **buses** from the State Bus Terminal connect Rajkot with other Gujarati towns; private buses offer faster services for long-distance journeys, and also serve places like Pune, Bombay and Udaipur, but are invariably as full as the state buses. Book at *Shree Sadguru Travels* or other agents behind the bus station, where you can also pick up shared taxis to Junagadh.

The only destination accessible directly by **air** is Bombay, served daily by *UP Airways* (c/o *Nishit Travels* in the same building as the *Galaxy Hotel*, 2nd floor; ☎694300), six times weekly by *Gujarat Airways* (c/o *Devendra Travels*, Sterling Apartments, Jawahar Rd, opposite Alfred High School; ☎55862), and four times weekly by *NEPC* (also in Sterling Apartments; ☎57966) and *Indian Airlines* (Dhevar Rd, just north of Sanganwa Chowk; ☎0281/34122).

Vrindavan, *Kavrey*. Excellent veg restaurant decorated in traditional Gujarati village style. Gujarati and Punjabi dishes plus macaroni and pizza. Good service. Open 8–10am, 11am–3pm & 7–11pm.

Around Rajkot

The princes of Rajkot district left a rich legacy of elaborate residences whose architectural styles range from the delicate detail of the seventeenth century to bold 1930s Art Deco. The palaces at **Wankaner** and **Morvi** are easily seen in a day, while the older palace at **Halvad** a little further out can be combined with a trip to the wild ass sanctuary in the Little Rann of Kutch, accessible from **Dhrangadhra**.

Morvi

The delightful little town of **MORVI** (also spelt Morbi) two hours north from Rajkot on the banks of the River Machhu, once commanded a strategic defensive position, guarding against intrusions into the Kathiawar Peninsula from the Rann of Kutch in the north. Instability among neighbouring petty states left Morvi insecure until the mid-nineteenth century when the political climate changed and the town prospered. The eclectic **Mani Mandir**, built in 1880, married conflicting Venetian Gothic, Rajput and Saracenic styles, to produce a surprisingly fine and extremely unusual result. A suspension bridge, built in 1882, spans the river to the entrance of the palace. Closer to the main road, the later Art Deco **New Palace** (1931–44) is more imaginatively decorated than its plain two-storey granite exterior suggests. One of its fourteen bedrooms, embellished with erotic murals, lies underground, and there is a bathroom completely covered in sea shells. There are no fixed **visiting hours** for either building; Mani Mandir is now used as offices and only the courtyards are open to visitors. If you catch the caretaker of the New Palace on a good day you may be lucky enough to be permitted to see all the fascinating interior.

Wankaner

The flamboyant Ranjit Vilas Palace at **WANKANER**, 39km northeast of Rajkot, is still home to the family who once ruled the old state of the same name. Built between 1899 and 1914, the symmetrical building can be seen from far across the flat Saurashtran plains. Up close, its fancy arched facade shows a frenzy of Moghul, Italianate and Victorian Gothic styles, with large windows and domed towers, and scores of hunting trophies looming from the walls. You can **stay** here, in buildings separate from the palace, one of which is an Art Deco structure with a swimming pool and a preserved step-well (☎02828/20000; ⑦). Meals, taken in the palace, are included.

Dhrangadhra

The unassuming town of **DHRANGADHRA**, over 100km northeast of Rajkot, has little to detain visitors, but is the starting point for a visit to the **wild ass sanctuary** in the flat saline wilderness of the Little Rann of Kutch. The wild ass is distinguished from a common ass by the dark brown stripe down its back; you'll almost certainly see herds of them, dainty and small but very fast when they sprint over the dusty mud-flats.

Permission to visit the sanctuary should be sought from the Sanctuary Superintendent in Dhrangadhra; **jeeps** can be rented for Rs300 for a maximum period of five hours. It's possible to **stay** in the *Government Rest House* (①), which can be booked in advance from Ahmedabad by calling ☎0272/445068 or 448499.

Halvad

The seventeenth-century lakeside **palace** at **HALVAD**, 20km west of Dhrangadhra, features some superb wooden carvings and, nearby, a number of intriguing **tombstone monuments** (*pallias*) commemorating acts of bravery and heroism. Certain images recur; the symbol of a raised hand or arm indicates the death of a woman who has committed *sati* or self-immolation, while a mounted spear-bearing bard records the death of a courtly poet, offered by his lord as surety for a loan, and driven to suicide in the case of default. Halvad's *Rest House* (①) has simple **rooms**.

Jamnagar

Close to the northwest coast of Saurashtra, the busy, noisy city of **JAMNAGAR** preserves at its heart some fabulous architectural surprises. Founded in the sixteenth century, the walled city was built to the east of Ranmal Lake, centring on the circular Lakhota Fort. **KS Ranjitsinjhi**, the famously elegant cricketer who played for England alongside W G Grace, ruled Jamnagar for several years at the turn of the century, improving commercial contacts and replacing run-down buildings with attractive constructions that remain as testimony to a prosperous and efficient rule. The city is renowned for excellent *bandhani* (tie-dye), sold in its markets.

Arrival, orientation and information

The centre of town from a tourist's point of view is **Bedi Gate** near the shopping centre and office complex of **New Super Market**. As its name suggests, this junction was one of the gates of the old city, which lies to its south; most of the walls have long since been demolished. Northwest of Bedi Gate, Pandit Nehru Marg leads past **Teen Bati** and on towards the **railway station**, 6km out. The **bus station** (known as ST stand) is 2km or so west of Bedi Gate, past the **town hall** which is just south of Teen Bati, and the **airport** 8km west of that. Auto-rickshaw is the best way into town, though you could walk from the bus station, and some buses may drop you at **Three Gates**, a still-standing triple gateway to the east of Bedi Gate. The *State Bank of India* in New Super Market (Mon–Fri 11am–3pm, Sat 11am–1pm) will **change cash** or travellers' cheques.

The telephone **area code** for Jamnagar is ☎0288.

The City

The most remarkable of Ranjitsinjhi's constructions is **Willingdon Crescent**, the swooping arches of its curved facade overlooking the wide streets of Chelmsford Market. In the heart of town, just off Rangit Rd southwest of Bedi Gate, stands the late nineteenth-century **Ratan Bai Mosque**. This grand domed prayer hall, its sandalwood doors inlaid with mother-of-pearl, is the unlikely neighbour to a magnificent pair of **Jain temples**, one dedicated to Adinath (the first *tirthankara*) and one built to honour Shantinath (the sixteenth). The quality and quantity of the **murals** on the walls, ceilings and pillars of the temples is extraordinary. Hazy yellows, greens, pinks, oranges and blues depict a riot of flowers, people, gods and domestic objects, while tableaux tell the life stories of Jain saints. The most spectacular of the two, **Shantinath Mandir**, is a maze of brightly coloured columns, each section of roof between them highlighted with individual designs; the marble floor beneath is emblazoned with distinctive Jain patterns in yellow, black, white and red. Above the main sanctuary, an enormous dome rises in a series of concentric circles glinting with gold. The outer side of the large dome over **Adinath Mandir** is inlaid with gold and coloured mosaic, and both temples have cupolas enriched with a design of mirrors above the entrance porch.

The temples form the hub of **Chandni Bazaar**, an almost circular market area enhanced by doorways edged with mosaic panels. Small lanes flanked with the meticulously carved wooden doors and balconies of ancient homes lead off it.

Stretching west, far out of town, Ranmal Lake acts as a wide moat and defence for **Lakhota Fort** (daily except Wed and the 2nd & 4th Sat of the month, 10.30am–1pm & 3–6.30pm; Rs0.50), connected to solid land in both directions by a causeway. Thick circular walls studded with gun-holes protect the inner building. On entering you'll pass a guardroom containing muskets, swords and powder flasks; the **museum** on the upper floor holds a mediocre display of paintings, sculpture, folk art and coins. South of the lake stands the stolid **Bhujia Fort** (daily 8am–1pm & 5–7pm if you can find the caretaker – ask at the neighbouring filling station). To its northwest, on the edge of the old city, the **Bala Hanuman temple** has been the scene of round-the-clock non-stop chanting ("Shree Ram, Jay Ram, Jay Jay Ram") since 1964.

Accommodation

Acceptable **accommodation** is limited in Jamnagar. If you're on a budget you'll have to grit your teeth and face the bedbugs, or pay a little more than normal. Only those worth considering are listed below. Most of the cheap places are in and around New Super Market. The more expensive hotels are good, though there are few to choose from.

Anand, First Floor, New Super Market (☎78983). Rooms with bath are not bad, but standards of hygiene are basic. ①.

Aram, Nand Niwas, Pandit Nehru Marg (☎551701 or 2; fax 554957). Palatial old house with a garden restaurant 2km towards the railway station from Bedi Gate. The large a/c rooms, nostalgic for the days of the Raj and filled with European antiques, have a faded charm. ⑥–⑧.

Ashiana, 3rd Floor, New Super Market (☎76525). Carpeted deluxe rooms and grubbier ordinary ones; all have TV and bath with hot water. The best in New Super Market, but often full. ③–⑤.

Janki, Third Floor, Anjaria Chamber, KV Rd, near Bedi Gate (☎60822; fax 551165). Clean and spacious, the best mid-range bet. Hot water and TV in all rooms, and a/c for a little extra. ③–⑥.

President, Teen Bati (☎70516; fax 78634). Very clean, well-managed hotel with parking, bar, restaurant and currency exchange. Credit cards accepted. ⑤–⑧.

Punit, Pandit Nehru Marg, just northwest of Teen Bati (☎70559 or 60; fax 70966). Friendly, clean and popular, with a small roof terrace. More expensive a/c rooms. ④–⑥.

Shital, Narayan Cottage, opposite New Super Market (☎78885). Cheap and basic, with a dorm. ①.

Eating

A fairly wide choice of good inexpensive **restaurants**, in the main clustered around Teen Bati, serve veg dishes. Most places close at 10pm.

Amiras, *Hotel Ashiana*, New Super Market. Very tasty, great-value Punjabi and Gujarati dishes, south Indian snacks, and breakfast in humble surroundings. Open 8–10am for breakfast, 11am–2.30pm for lunch, 4–7.30pm for snacks, 7.30–10pm for dinner.

Kalpana, Teen Bati. Ageing decor but great, cheap veg food: south Indian, Punjabi, ice-cream, fruit juice and milkshakes. No hot drinks. Daily except Mon, 8.30am–10pm.

Rangoli, between *Kalpana* and New Super Market. South Indian and Punjabi dishes at higher than average prices. Daily except Wed, 9am–3pm & 5–11pm.

Seven Seas, *Hotel President*. A/c and dimly lit with comfortable seats. Indian, Chinese and Western dishes at moderate prices. Good if you fancy a meat feast. Open for snacks 6am–11pm, breakfast 6–11am, lunch 11am–3pm, dinner 7–11pm.

Shree Ram Dairy, Teen Bati, next to *Kalpana*. Ice-cream and jelly, milk-shakes and other childhood favourites: flavours include mango and *chiku*. Daily except Tues 10am–11pm.

MOVING ON FROM JAMNAGAR

Buses from the ST stand serve Porbandar, Dwarka, Junagadh, Rajkot and Ahmedabad, with a single very early morning departure to Una for Diu. The *Hotel Punit* keeps a list of current bus schedules. Travel agents opposite the bus stand sell tickets for private buses, and touts may approach you at the entrance. Main **train services** are the afternoon *Saurashtra Express* #9215 to Porbandar (3hr), the early afternoon *Saurashtra Mail* #9005, to Dwarka (3hr) and Okha (3hr 45min), and the same two trains in the other direction for Ahmedabad (7hr 15min), Vadodara (10hr), Surat (14hr) and Bombay Central (17hr 30min): the late evening *Saurashtra Express* #9216 is best for Ahmedabad, the afternoon *Saurashtra Mail* #9006 for Bombay. There is also a weekly direct train to Puri.

Indian Airlines (just west of the town hall; ☎552911) have four **flights** a week to Bombay, on the remaining three days you can get there with *NEPC*, whose office is directly north of there, in Centre Point just off Pandit Nehru Marg (☎550845).

The marine national park

The northwest coast of Saurashtra, bordering the heavily tidal Gulf of Kutch, is fringed with more than forty small islands, whose ever depleting mangrove population gives rise to some of the richest marine life off mainland India. In 1980, 295 square kilometres of the gulf was declared a marine sanctuary, and in 1982, over half of this was officially recognized as a **marine national park**.

The coast off Jamnagar has always been exploited for pearl fishing, and still supports a small population of pearl oysters. Permission to take a boat from Jamnagar to **Pirotan Island** – where the coral is particularly rich – can be sought from the Chief Conservator of Forests and Wildlife, Koti Annexe, Vadodara (see p.606); it may, however, not be granted. Besides abundant coral, the Gulf of Kutch shelters sea-turtles, snakes, dolphins, sharks and octopuses and attracts thousands of birds such as flamingoes, pelicans, harriers, cormorants, ibises and oyster-catchers.

Despite pressure from conservationists, the mangroves are still cut for firewood, and industries along the west coast of Saurashtra continue to pollute the sea with effluents. As the mangroves disappear, so does the aquatic life they support; mud from the coastline, no longer anchored by tree roots, is pushed from the shore to smother the coral reefs, thus denying fish their natural habitat.

Dwarka

In the very west of the peninsula, fertile wheat, groundnut and cotton fields, lightly ruffled by a cool sea breeze, emerge in vivid contrast to the arid expanses further inland. According to popular Hindu legend, Krishna fled Mathura (see p.241) to this coastal region, declaring **DWARKA** his capital. A labyrinth of narrow winding streets cluttered with temples, the town resonates today with the bustle of eager saffron-clad pilgrims and the clatter of celebratory drums. Dwarka really comes to life during the major Hindu festivals; the most fervent are Maha-Shivratri, dedicated to Shiva (Feb/March) and Janmashtami, Krishna's birthday (Aug/Sept).

The elaborately carved tower of **Dwarkadish temple** (daily 6am–12.30pm & 5–9pm) looms proudly 50m above the town. Inside, the sixteenth-century sanctuary, voluptuously sculpted and spilling out swirls of incense and murmured prayers, is surrounded by smaller shrines nestling in chiselled corners beneath sturdy pillars. Non-Hindus can enter only on signing a form declaring, at the very least, respect for religion. Get small change for donations from the change-*wallahs* at the east entrance.

When Krishna came to Dwarka he eloped with Princess Rukmini. One kilometre east of town, the small **Rukmini temple** – which local priests may tell you is 1500 years old, but in fact dates from the twelfth century – is, if anything, more architecturally impressive than the Dwarkadish temple, with carvings of elephants, flowers, dancers and Shiva in several of his aspects covering every wall.

Practicalities

Trains from Jamnagar (4 daily; 2hr 30min–4hr 40min) arrive at the station north of town from where tongas ferry visitors to hotels and the temple. The **bus stand** on the road to Okha has regular services to and from Jamnagar (8 daily; 3hr), Porbandar (6 daily; 3hr) and Veraval (hourly; 5–6hr).

Accommodation in Dwarka is, for the most part, cheap and unelaborate. The well-kept *Toran Guest House* (☎02892/313), out of town near the coast, offers dorms (①) and doubles (③), all with mosquito nets. The shabby *Radhika* (☎02892/754; ③), opposite the bus stand, has a/c and non-a/c rooms, but the restaurant is disappointing. Very near Dwarkadish temple, *Uttam Guest House* (☎02892/4234; ②) is homely enough, while towards the railway station *Hotel Meera* (☎02892/331; ①) is clean and comfortable, and serves undoubtedly the best **thalis** in town.

Bet Dwarka

A day trip to the tiny island of **Bet Dwarka**, also closely associated with the Krishna legend, is a must for any pilgrim to Dwarka, as its (architecturally uninspiring) temple is said to stand on the spot where Krishna died. Small, precariously full wooden dinghies transport pilgrims from the port of **OKHA**, on the westernmost point of the peninsula, to the island, where devotees scatter rupees and flowers towards Krishna's shrine and wait eagerly for the appearance of the priest who hands out *prasad*. Not surprisingly, fishing is a big source of income, but due to pollution, salt production and the destruction of mangroves, the quantity of fish is dangerously declining.

State **buses** run from Dwarka to Okha (1hr) every thirty minutes; private buses leave from the vegetable market; and there are frequent jeeps. There are no passenger boat services from Okha across the Gulf of Kutch.

Porbandar

Once an international port and state capital, **PORBANDAR**, smack in the middle of the 200km of coastline between Veraval and Dwarka, is inextricably associated with the family of **Mahatma Gandhi**, who was born here. In fact, he was just one in an important political line – his uncle, father and grandfather all served as prime minister to the Maharaja of the Jethwa Rajput state. In addition, and in common with much of the southwest coast of Saurashtra, Porbandar is linked with the legends of **Krishna** – in ancient times the settlement was called Sudampuri, after one of Krishna's comrades.

Today, shrouded in a dim haze of excretions from the cement and chemical factories on its outskirts, Porbandar has little to attract regular tourists, save, of course, Gandhi's house. However, it is from this town and the surrounding area that most of Gujarat's **diaspora** originate, and "NRIs" (that's Non-resident Indians) from Britain, Canada and East Africa are often here on visits to family and friends. It can be quite disconcerting when the person sitting next to you in a restaurant or on the bus, who you took to be a local, turns out to be from Leicester or Vancouver.

Arrival, orientation and information

Porbandar is bunched between the coast and a freshwater creek that curves around the north to meet the sea at the harbour – usually busy with shipbuilders and fishermen – in the west. A path follows the coast from east to west but the **beaches** in between, used as public toilets, are rather unpleasant. Porbandar's main street, not surprisingly, is called **Mahatma Gandhi (MG) Road**. It runs from a fountain at its eastern end, northeast of which is the **railway station**, to a **triple gateway** at its western end, near Gandhiji's house. In the middle, at the **main square**, it is bisected by Aria Sumaj Rd, which runs northwards across Jubilee Bridge, and southwards to the **GPO** (Mon–Sat 8am–6pm). Just east of that is the **ST bus station** (connected to MG Rd by ST Rd), and to its south the main beach. Another of India's founding fathers, Sardar Patel, is commemorated by SVP Rd, running parallel with MG Rd a block north. **Banks** along MG Rd change foreign currency and travellers' cheques.

> The telephone **area code** for Porbandar is ☎0286.

The Town

Mohandas Karamchand Gandhi was born in Porbandar in October 1869 and lived here until he was twelve. **Gandhi's birthplace** (free, but the guide will expect a donation) stands in the corner of a large courtyard in the west of town, in a narrow street entered through a large triple gateway and lined with carved wooden houses. There's barely anything to see inside the small three-storey structure; it is little changed since the family left in 1881, save for some fresh green paint on the wooden stairs and doorways. The whole place is empty, though some of the walls in the reading and prayer rooms on the upper floors bear faded traces of paintings.

The modern temple next to the house, **Kirti Mandir** (*kirti* means age), was donated to the city in 1950 by the industrialist Nanjibhai Kalidas, to commemorate Gandhi's 79 years; note the 79 lamps adorning its 79-foot-high spire. Upstairs, a **museum** has a display of photographs, hand-made Gujarati crafts and a bizarre collection of bottled seeds and oils – perhaps something to do with Gandhi's belief in self-sufficiency – while downstairs there's a small **bookstore**. A couple of kilometres north of town (over Jubilee Bridge, then straight on, bearing left after 20m, and turning left after another 50m) is the desperately old-fashioned **Planetarium** (shows in Gujarati 9.30, 10.30 & 11.30am, 3.30, 4.30, 5.30 & 6.30pm, but only if there are 20 or more people; Rs1; men and women must queue and enter separately), topped by a statue of Nehru. Directly opposite, set in a verdant garden, the airy pillared hall **Bharat Mandir** – another Kalidas benefaction – was built in memory of popular Hindi heroes. The divine, godly bodies of mythical figures are bright and distinct on the walls, and in the centre of the floor there's a large relief map of India.

Accommodation

Porbandar's **hotels** are a little bit pricier in general than their equivalents elsewhere (the *Rajkamal* excepted), though this may change since new ones are opening up all the time. Those on the coast are the best, with sea views; places in town are more cramped, and invaded by traffic noise. Checkout time is usually 10am.

Flamingo, MG Rd, 100m east of the main square (☎23123). Comfortable, clean hotel, British-owned, with ordinary inexpensive rooms and luxurious a/c suites. ②–⑤.

Kuber, off ST Rd (☎41289; fax 23888). Porbandar's poshest. ⑤–⑦.

Moon, ST Rd (☎41172). New hotel with immaculate, small rooms with bath. ③–⑥.

New Oceanic Hotel, Villa No 8, Chowpatty, by the beach (☎ & fax 20217). Cosy rooms, some a/c, in a modern sea-facing house. The terrace has a good restaurant, usually for residents only. ⑤.

Rajkamal Guest House, MG Rd, by the *Flamingo* (☎20374). The cheapest in town, often full. ①.

Rupalee, Rupalee Corner, junction of Aria Sumaj Rd and SVP Rd (☎22873). Clean, basic lodge opposite *Harish Talkies* (sign in Gujarati only). The restaurant serves filling *thalis*. ①.

Sheetal, Aria Sumaj Rd, opposite the GPO (☎23596; fax 41821). Curious, plush lodge. All rooms have bathrooms, and those with a/c offer a real treat – padded wardrobes and bath tubs. ③–⑥.

Toran Tourist Bungalow, Chowpatty, by the beach (☎21476). Large, clean rooms with sea-facing balconies. Two six-bed dorms, and bathrooms with constant hot water. A simple indoor restaurant facing the sea serves tasty but unimaginative dishes, if you order in advance. ③–⑤.

Eating

Although Porbandar is known for its **seafood**, you'll have a job finding it. Outside the hotel restaurants, there's a fairly uninspiring choice of **places to eat**; many seem to serve only one or two of the dishes listed on the menus. Breakfast can be a hard one – you may have to settle for buying a packet of biscuits to have with tea in one of the places in the little street off MG Rd just west of the *National* and the *Aadarsh*.

Aadarsh, MG Rd, next to the *National*. Popular, inexpensive veg restaurant for south Indian snacks. Open 10am–9.30pm.

National, MG Rd, 100m west of the main square. Muslim-run and pretty well the only place in town for meat. Open 10.15am–2.45pm & 6.30–10.30pm.

Royal, ST Rd. Tiny fish restaurant with no sign in English (coming from MG Rd, it's one block south on the right – look for the poster of Gulf fish on the wall inside). The pomfret is excellent if rather fiery, but prices are higher than you'd expect from the look of the place. Open 11am–11pm.

Swagat, MG Rd, 150m east of the main square. The best restaurant in town, softly lit and serving excellent, mid-priced Punjabi and south Indian veg dishes. Open 9am–3pm & 5.30–10pm.

MOVING ON FROM PORBANDAR

One express **train**, the *Saurashtra Express* #9216, leaves every evening for Bombay via Ahmedabad (10hr), Vadodara (13hr 50min) and Surat (16hr 40min). That and a morning passenger train both serve Jamnagar and Rajkot. To most destinations, however, the **bus** proves more convenient. Porbandar's **airport**, 4km northeast of town on the Junagadh road, serves Bombay (1hr 15min) only. Contact *Gujarat Airways*, c/o *Thanky's Tours*, MG Rd, 150m west of the main square (☎21128) or *NEPC*, Aria Sumaj Rd, just north of SVP Rd, ☎41889 or 90).

Around Porbandar

Inland from Porbandar, a scattering of ancient temples are easily visited in a day. **BILESHWAR**, an hour north, is a small village built round an early seventh-century Shiva temple. Though the temple's exterior is of little interest, coated in modern plaster, the inner sanctuary has a large monument dating from the Maitraka period (sixth to seventh centuries). Twenty kilometres further, in a serene wooded valley, **GHUMLI** boasts one of Gujarat's largest step-wells, **Vikai Vav**. Dating from the early twelfth century, it is superb, with richly carved pillars and pavilions topped by peaked pyramidal roofs; at the more dilapidated (thirteenth-century) **Naulakha temple** you can still see elaborate decorations beneath the collapsed roof. It's best to visit both sites early in the morning, as bus services back to Porbandar are poor (6 daily; 2hr–2hr 30min).

Junagadh

The friendly small town of **JUNAGADH** (also spelt Junagarh), less than 100km
inland from Diu, is an intriguing place, with a skyline broken by domes and
minarets and narrow streets whose shopfronts brim with spices piled in high powdery pyramids. It's fun to amble through the town's lively bazaars, and with a mixture of Buddhist monuments, Hindu temples, mosques, bold gothic archways and
mansions – not to mention the magnificent Jain temples on **Mt Girnar** – Junagadh
is an exciting city to explore for anyone with an interest in architecture and a taste
for history.

From the fourth century BC to the death of Ashoka (*c.* 232 BC), Junagadh was the
capital of Gujarat under the Buddhist Mauryas. The short reigns of the Kshatrapas and
the Guptas came to an end when the town passed into the hands of the Hindu
Chudasanas, who in turn soon lost out to Muslim invaders. Muslim sovereignty lasted
until Independence when, although the leaders planned to unite Junagadh with
Pakistan, local pressure ensured that it became part of the Indian Union.

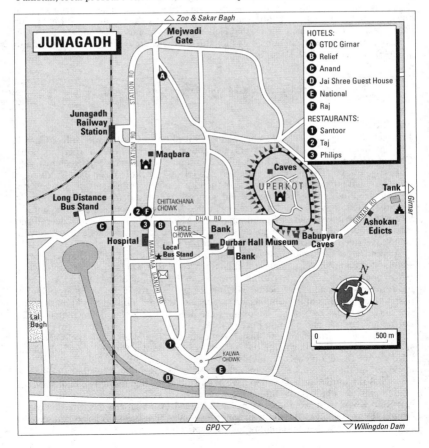

Because of the sanctity of Mt Girnar, the **Shivratri festival** (Feb/March) assumes particular importance in Junagadh, when thousands of saffron-clad *sadhus* come to camp around the town and in the surrounding hills. Fireworks, processions, chanting, *chillum*-smoking and demonstrations of body-torturing ascetic practices continue for nine days and nights. Tourists arriving in Junagadh at this time are in for a memorable experience, but rooms are at a premium; book well in advance.

Arrival and information

Arriving by bus or train, you're within easy walking distance of pretty well all the hotels (from the bus station, turn right, left at the main road and straight on across the railway tracks into the town centre; from the station, take a right down Station Rd, and left at the end by the filling station). Local transport is provided by **auto-rickshaws**, though **bicycles** are great for getting around; with a bit of leg-work you can even cycle to the foot of Mt Girnar. Run-of-the-mill bikes can be had from a shop just west of Chittakhana Chowk, or *Relief Hotel*.

The only useful **information** on the town's sites and the religious significance of Girnar is from the *National* or *Relief* hotels. The **GPO** (poste restante) is 2km south of town; a smaller branch next to the local bus depot sells stamps and aerograms. The *State Bank of India* opposite the Durbar Hall Museum changes dollar and sterling cash. To exchange travellers' cheques, head for the nearby *State Bank of Saurashtra* (both Mon–Fri 11am–3pm, Sat 11am–1pm).

The telephone **area code** for Junagadh is ☎0285.

The City

Junagadh is fairly compact, focusing around **Chittakhana Chowk** and **Kalwa Chowk** 1km further south. **Durbar Hall** with its modest museum is east of there in **Janta Chowk**, while nearby **Circle Chowk** fills a fine semi-circular terrace between towering Gothic gateways. The imposing fortified citadel of **Uperkot** (daily 6am–7pm) on a thickly walled mound in the northeast of the city, is a peaceful place with a rich history, colonized today by eagles, egrets and squirrels. Legend dates the fort's origins to the time of the Yadavas (Krishna's clan) who fled Mathura to settle in Dwarka, but historians believe it was built by Chandragupta the Mauryan in 319 BC. Rediscovered and repaired in 976 AD by Muslim conquerors, it regained importance as a defence, withstanding sixteen sieges in the next eight hundred years.

A grand set of three high gateways cut into solid rock during the Muslim occupation stands at the entrance, spanning a cobbled walkway that winds upwards past a *kund* (small pool) and some modern Hindu temples, to the summit of the raised fort, where the **Jami Masjid** stands abandoned to nature. Supporting the high roof, many of its 140 pillars were taken from the Chudasana palace and feature common Hindu motifs. The two fierce cannons opposite the mosque were used at Diu fort in defence against the Portuguese in 1530 and brought here in 1538.

Heading north from the Jami Masjid, you come to a complex of small cells arranged around courtyards cut down into the rock. These "**Buddhist Caves**" were built in the third or fourth century AD – much worn traces of figurines and foliage can still be made out on the columns in the lower level. Nearby, more than 170 steps descend to the well **Adi Chadi Vav**, believed to have been built at the bequest of two maidservants of the royal household in the fifteenth century. The more impressive eleventh-century **Navghan Kuva**, in the southeast of the citadel, consists of a superb staircase that winds around the well shaft to the dimly lit water level over 52m below. A large tank nearby collects water from the surrounding hills to supply the town.

Below the southern wall of the fort, the **Babupyara Caves**, hewn from the rock between 200 BC and 200 AD, were used by Buddhists until the time of Ashoka, and then by Jains. A little to the north of Uperkot, the slightly later, plainer **Khapra Kodia caves** remain in good condition, intersected with staircases, colonnades and passages.

East of the main entrance to Uperkot, in Janta Chowk, the **Durbar Hall Museum** (daily except Wed and the 2nd & 4th Sat of each month, 9am–12.15pm & 3–6pm; Rs0.50) takes up part of the former palace of the nawabs. Silver chairs in the great hall stand in regal splendour around a large carpet, valuable silver clocks encase scruffy stuffed birds, and huge coloured chandeliers hang from the ceiling. Surrounding rooms contain silver *howdahs* (elephant seats), weaponry, portraits, and a collection of textiles including 400-year-old cloth embroidered with gold thread, displayed alongside royal parasols overlaid with intricate needlework.

Junagadh's chief Muslim monuments are the boldly decorated **muqbara** – quite unlike any other in Gujarat – on Mahatma Gandhi Rd opposite the High Courts. Built for Muslim rulers in the nineteenth century, the mausolea, squat and square, are crowned with a multitude of bulbous domes, and smaller domes fronting balconies that overhang high curved arches cut into the tombs' sides. The most opulent is the 1892 sepulchre of Mahabat Khan I, but more outstanding, for its complex design, is that of Vizir Sahib Baka-ud-din Bhar, completed four years later and flanked on each corner by tall minarets hugged with spiral staircases. Next to the *muqbara* is a mosque whose multi-coloured pillars and gaily painted walls are oddly reminiscent of a *cassata*.

A group of smaller memorials to earlier nawabs stand in a peaceful graveyard, shielded by shops on Chittakhana Chowk and overgrown with coarse yellow grass. Delicate in both size and design, they boast fine carving on the eaves and stone lattice work cut from the walls. You'll have to scramble around the back of the shops to find the entrance: the rooftop of the *Relief Hotel* opposite gives good aerial views.

Ashokan edicts

East of town on the road to Girnar a rock engraved with the Buddhist **edicts of Ashoka**, Junagadh's most famous monarch (daily except Wed 8.30–11am & 2–6pm), remains where it was placed in the third century BC, its impact somewhat marred by a modern shelter and concrete platform. Written in the Prakrit dialect, the worn verses etched into the granite encourage the practice of *dharma* and equality, beseech different religious sects to live in harmony, and repent the evils of war. Situated on the route taken by pilgrims to the sacred hill of Girnar, the influence of Ashoka's edicts was strong; even as late as the seventh century AD there were about 3000 monks in Junagadh, and over 50 convents. Sanskrit inscriptions on the same rock were added during the reigns of King Rudraman (150 AD) and Skandagupta (455 AD).

Mt Girnar

Rising to a height of over 1100m, **Mt Girnar**, a steep-sided extinct volcano 4km east of Junagadh, is a major pilgrimage centre for both Jains and Hindus, and has been considered sacred since before the third century BC. Buses leave from Junagadh's local depot hourly, dropping passengers at the mountain base, from where five thousand irregular steps lead to the summit. It's best to start the ascent, which takes at least two hours, well before 7am, when the scorching sun rises from behind the peak. The path climbs through eucalyptus forests before zig-zagging across the sheer rock face, and there's a ready supply of *chai* and biscuits at stalls along the way.

On a plateau below the summit, roughly ninety minutes' climb from the base of the steps, the picturesque huddle of Jain temples has been slightly renovated since its erection between 1128 and 1500. **Neminath**, the 22nd *tirthankara*, said to have died on Mount Girnar after 700 years of meditation and asceticism, is depicted as a black figure sitting in the lotus position holding a conch in the marble **Neminath temple**, the first on the left as you enter the "temple city". The temple comprises a vast complex of court-yards, cloisters and lesser shrines, and has exquisite carving on its pillars and within the domed roofs, decorated outside with unusual coloured mosaic. Opposite, the **Mallinath temple** was built by the brothers Vastupal and Tejapala who also funded temples in Mount Abu and Shatrunjaya. Chequered black-and-white marble floors run through the three sanctuaries off the entrance porch. Carved musicians and dancers adorn the ceiling of the main shrine, and two smaller shrines feature images of *tirthankaras* raised on marble platforms.

It's well worth making the effort to climb the final two thousand steps to the summit of Mt Girnar. The views on the way are breathtaking. At the top, a temple dedicated to the Hindu goddess **Amba Mata** attracts both Hindu and Jain pilgrims, particularly new-lyweds who come here to be blessed by the mother goddess, and pray for a happy mar-riage. Steps lead down from this temple and then up again along a narrow ridge towards **Gorakhnath Peak**, where a small shrine covers what are supposedly the foot-prints of the pilgrim Gorakhnath, and further to a third peak where the imprints of Neminath's feet are sheltered by a small canopy. At the most distant point of the ridge, a shrine dedicated to the fierce Hindu goddess **Kalika**, the eternal aspect of Durga, is a haunt for near-naked **Aghora ascetics** who express their absolute renunciation of the world by ritually enacting their own funerals, living among corpses on burial grounds, and smearing themselves with ash from funeral pyres.

Sakar Bagh

The pleasant flower-filled Sakar Bagh, 3.5km north of Junagadh, encloses the **zoo** and the small **Junagadh Museum** (daily except Wed 9am–12.15pm & 3–6.15pm), which houses assorted pre- and proto-historic implements, medieval statues, manuscripts, ornaments and stuffed animals. The zoo, renowned for the successful breeding of endangered Asiatic lions, is home to wolves, tigers, birds and bears, all a little cramped in treeless cages, and a dim aquarium boasting nothing more impressive than goldfish.

Accommodation

Junagadh offers average, simple **accommodation**: a decent choice for budget trav-ellers, but few with any claims to comfort or mod-cons.

Anand, Bus Station Rd (☎22657). Clean and fresh with some a/c rooms, and they guarantee to change the sheets daily. ②–⑤.

GTDC Girnar, Mejwadi Gate (☎21201). Government-run hotel in the quiet outskirts of town: clean but impersonal with a reasonable restaurant that serves dinner from 6pm. ④–⑤.

Jay Shree, Jayshree Rd, off Kalwa Chowk (☎21032). Basic but friendly. ①–③.

National, Kalwa Chowk (☎27891). Carpeted, clean and comfy, and very good value. Delicious food – veg, fish and meat – in downstairs restaurant. ②–⑤.

Raj, Dhal Rd, Chittakhana Chowk (☎26236). Good-value, friendly Muslim-run hotel with large rooms and attached bathrooms, plus a dorm. ①.

Relief, Dhal Rd, Chittakhana Chowk (☎20280). Homely, if slightly grubby, rooms, some with attached bathroom and a/c. Average restaurant serves breakfast as early as 5am. The manager prides himself on supplying reliable tourist information. ②–⑤.

Eating

Hotel food halls are supplemented by streetside stalls, and one or two **restaurants**.

Philips, MG Rd, Chittakhana Chowk. Excellent value all-you-can-eat Gujarati *thalis* and thick *lassis* (the sign in English is vertical by the door). Open 11am–11pm.

Santoor, south of Chittakhana Chowk on MG Rd. Excellent, good-value south Indian and Punjabi dishes. Open 9.45am–3pm & 5–11pm.

Taj, Dhal Rd, Chittakana Chowk. Good place for fish, with great if underspiced *sabji*, and books on Gandhi to read while you wait. Open 9am–noon for breakfast, noon–2.30pm & 7–10.30pm for meals.

MOVING ON FROM JUNAGADH

Trains to Rajkot, Ahmedabad and the south coast call at Junagadh. The *Down* #352 leaves for Sasan Gir and Delvada (for Diu; 5hr 50min) early each morning. It's slow, but more civilized than the bus. Of the services to Rajkot, choose the fast passenger trains over the *Saurashtra Mail*); for Ahmedaba the overnight *Girnar Express* #9845 is the most convenient.

Buses from the central bus stand just west of Chittakhana Chowk serve destinations around the state; note that the bus to Diu takes only 5hr 30min (as opposed to 6hr 55min in the other direction). Bus #4 for **Girnar** (7 daily; 20min) leaves from the local bus stand 200m south of Chittakhana Chowk, or you can go by auto-rickshaw for around Rs20. Firms around Kalwa Chowk sell tickets for **private buses**, notably to Bombay (18hr).

Veraval and Somnath

On the Saurashtran coast, midway between Porbandar and Diu, the most lingering impression of the port of **VERAVAL** is its fishy stench. There's little to do here, unless you can endure the smells to watch the *dhow*-building in the docks, but Veraval is the jumping-off point for trips to **Somnath**, 5km east, whose temple is one of the twelve *jyotrilingas* of Shiva (see *Contexts*). Its shrines to Vishnu and connection with Krishna – who possibly lived here with the Yadavas during the time of the *Mahabharata* – make it equally important for Vaishnavites.

Somnath

SOMNATH consists of only a few streets and a bus station – even its famed sea-facing **temple** is little to look at, despite its many layered history. Legend has it that the site, formerly known as **Prabhas Patan**, was dedicated to Soma, the juice of a plant used in rituals and greatly praised for its enlightening and strengthening powers (and hallucinogenic influence) in the *Rig Veda*. The temple of Somnath itself is believed to have appeared first in gold, at the behest of the moon-god, next in silver, created by the sun-god, a third time in wood at the command of Krishna, and finally in stone, built by Bhimdeva, the strongest of the five Pandava brothers (from the *Mahabharata*).

The earliest definite record, however, dates the temple to the tenth century, when, rich from devotees' donations, it spilled over with precious stones and gold and rang to the sounds of musicians and dancing girls. Not surprisingly, such wealth came to the attention of the brutal iconoclast Mahmud of Ghazni, who captured and plundered so many of western India's cities (997–1030); the temple was battered and pillaged, and its riches taken to Afghanistan. The next seven centuries saw a cycle of rebuilding and sacking, though the temple lay in ruins for over two hundred years after a final sacking by Aurangzeb before the most recent reconstruction in 1950, funded by the wealthy Sardar Vallabhai Patel. Very little of the original structure remains, and although planned in the style of the Solanki period, the temple is built from unattractive modern stone. It's just possible, however, to imagine its former glory, from the height of the pillars supporting the towering *mandapa* and the fervour of the stream of devotees who pray in its airy halls. The main *pujas* are held at 7am, noon and 7pm.

In the small yard a little to the north, Somnath's fascinating **museum** (daily except Wed and 2nd & 4th Sat of month, 9am–noon & 3–6pm; Rs0.50) contains most of the architectural treasures saved from the temple – statues, lintels, sections of roof pillars, friezes and *toranas* from the tenth to twelfth centuries. It's all a bit cramped, but plans to move the collection to a new building opposite the bus stand will no doubt improve matters, and perhaps encourage the curators to invest in more explanatory labels.

Tongas and rickshaws gather outside the bus station, ready to take pilgrims to **temple sites east of Somnath**. Most important of these is **Triveni Tirth**, at the confluence of the Hiran, Saraswati and Kapil rivers as they flow into the sea: a peaceful place with a couple of new unspectacular temples. Before reaching the confluence, the road passes the ancient **Surya Mandir**, probably built during the Solanki period, and now cramped by a newer temple and concrete houses built almost against its walls. Close to the sea, **Triveni Ghat** marks the place where Krishna's body was supposedly cremated after he was killed by a hunter who mistook him for a deer.

Practicalities

Veraval is well-connected by road to Junagadh, Porbandar, Diu and Dwarka; the bus stand is west of town. **Trains**, from Junagadh (2hr 30min), Rajkot (4hr) and Ahmedabad (13hr), pull in north of town. For long journeys by train from Veraval it's best to change at Rajkot. To get to Somnath take the **bus** (every 15min) – it stops a few hundred metres east of the Shiva temple. **Auto-rickshaws** are also available.

Veraval has a wider choice of **accommodation** than Somnath, though the smell and dirt are enough to dissuade you from staying. The *Tourist Bungalow* on College Rd (✆02876/20488; ①–③), on the outskirts near the shore and the lighthouse, offers a dorm, spacious rooms and a modest restaurant. *Hotel Kasturi* (✆02876/22187; ②), tucked away in a narrow street south of the bus stand, is smarter. The best thing about the rapidly declining *Hotel Satkar*, which overlooks the noisy street directly opposite the bus stand (✆02876/20120; ②), is its restaurant. In **Somnath**, *Sri Somnath Guest House* (✆02876/20212; ①), on Triveni Rd opposite the bus station, has inexpensive, very simple rooms; those at the modern *Mayuram* (✆02876/20286; ③), almost immediately next door, are less spartan and cleaner. Twenty kilometres north along the coast, the old **summer palace** of the Junagadh nawabs at **CHORWAD** is now the GSTC *Palace Beach Resort* (✆0287688/556 or 7; ④–⑥), with separate cottages in well-tended gardens. There's nothing else to see or do here, which is a great part of its charm.

Food in Veraval and Somnath is unremarkable but easy to come by, usually in simple form in hotels or unelaborate roadside stalls.

Gir National Park

The **Asiatic lion**, which thanks to hunting, forest-cutting and poaching has been extinct in the rest of India since the 1880s, now survives in the wild in just 1150 square kilometres of the gently undulating Gir Forest. **Gir National Park** (Mid-Oct or Nov to mid-June daily 7–11am & 3–5.30pm), entered from **Sasan Gir**, 60km southeast of Junagadh and 45km northeast of Veraval, holds almost 300 Asiatic lions in its 260 square kilometres. They share the land with Maldhari cattle breeders, whose main source of income is buffalo milk. Many families have been relocated outside the sanctuary, but those who remain are paid compensation by the government for the inevitable loss of buffalo to marauding lions. Gir also shelters 200 **panthers**, more visible here than in any other Indian park.

Permits covering entry for up to three days can be obtained at the **park information centre** in the *Sinh Sadan Guest House* in Sasan Gir (Rs15 for three days – Rs5 per day thereafter, camera Rs7.50 per day, video Rs15 per day). You must enter the park in a jeep, which can take up to six people (Rs6 per km, plus Rs7.50 for a guide for three hours, Rs4 per additional hour, and a tip). Guides, although downright unenthusiastic at times, should know likely spots for sightings, and may be flexible enough to follow any route you wish to take (maps are available at the information centre). Two good tracks are "Deva Danga" and "Riley's", or out to the lake near Kamelshwar, just west of the park boundary, where there's a good chance of glimpsing a marsh crocodile.

Though sightings are far from certain, the lions are used to human noise, and seem not to be disturbed by jeeps, so if you are lucky enough to see one, you should be able to watch it for a while. Summer is the best time to catch them, as they gather at water-

THE ASIATIC LION

The rare **Asiatic lion** (*panthera leo persica*) is paler and shaggier than the more common African breed, with longer tail tassles, more prominent elbow tufts and a larger belly fold. Probably introduced to India from Persia, the lions were widespread in the Indo-Gangetic plains at the time of the Buddha, and in 300 BC Kautilya, the minister of Chandragupta Maurya, offered them protection by declaring certain areas *abharaya aranyas*, "forests free from fear". Later, in his rock-inscribed edicts, **Ashoka** admonished those who hunted the majestic animals – the emblem of Ashoka, printed on all Indian currency notes, shows four Asiatic lions standing back to back.

Such a symbol of potency was favourite game for India's nineteenth-century rulers, and by 1913, not long after it had been declared a protected species by the Nawab of Junagadh, the Asiatic lion population was reduced to twenty. Since then, Gir Forest has been recognized as a sanctuary (1969), and a national park (1975), and their number has swelled to over 250. While this is good news for the lions, they are starting to stray from the sanctuary, and recent attacks on humans and their livestock have caused justifiable concern. If plans to create a new sanctuary near Porbandar come to fruition, the lions should be assured security in their natural habitat.

holes to drink. For a failsafe guarantee, head for **Dewaliya** (daily dawn–dusk; Rs70), a small fenced-off area of the park known as the "interpretation centre". Regular jeeps and buses leave Sasan Gir for Dewaliya, and in the centre visitors are driven in a minibus past docile lions. It's certainly not *wild*, but you'll see them very close up.

Practicalities

Sasan Gir village is connected by **train** to Junagadh and Veraval, and by **bus** to Junagadh, Veraval and Una. The railway station, which also serves as a bus stand, is set back from the one main road that bisects the tiny town. There are just two **hotels**. The Forest Department's delightful *Sinh Sadan Guest House* (☎02877/5540; ②–⑤) on the main road, has large attractive rooms with mosquito nets, in an old house amid well-kept gardens. Book ahead by phone, or at a tourist office. Reasonably priced meals are available for residents, and the **park information centre** is in the grounds. Off the main road, past a small crocodile farm, the deluxe *Hotel Taj* (☎ & fax 02877/5528; ⑨) is the only other option. You can **eat** at the stall at the station end of the main road.

Diu

Set a little off the southern tip of Gujarat, the island of **DIU**, less than 12km long and just 3km wide, was until thirty years ago under Portuguese control. Today, along with Daman, governed as a Union Territory from Delhi, it stands apart, and has a relaxed atmosphere quite different from anywhere in central Saurashtra. Though its smallish beaches are nowhere near as idyllic as in Goa, most visitors stay longer than intended, idling in cafes, cycling around the island, or strolling along the cliffs. The leisurely pace is also due in part to the lack of alcohol restrictions: the island's many bars can ply you with a vast array of beers and various hard liquors.

Diu island is easy to explore by bike. Diu Town in the northeast is the focus, where a maze of alleys lined with distinctive Portuguese buildings form the hub of the **old town**, while the **fort** covers the eastern tip of the island and looks out to the Gulf of Cambay and the Arabian Sea. Along the northern coast the island's main road runs past salt pans that give way to mud-flats sheltering flocks of water birds, including flamingoes that stop to feed in early spring. The route skirting the south coast passes rocky cliffs and beaches, the largest of which is **Nagoa Beach**, before reaching the tiny fishing village of **Vanakbara** in the very west of the island.

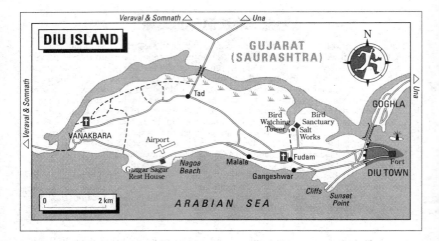

A brief history

The earliest records of Diu date from 1298, when it was controlled by the Chudasana dynasty. Soon after, like most of Gujarat, it fell into the hands of invading Muslims, and by 1349 was ruled by Muhammad bin Tughluq who successfully boosted the ship-building industry. Diu prospered as a Gujarati harbour, and in 1510 came under the government of the Ottoman Malik Ayaz, who repelled besieging Portuguese forces in 1520 and 1521. Well aware of Diu's strategic position for trade with Arabia and the Persian Gulf, and having already gained a toehold in Daman on the eastern edge of the Gulf of Cambay, the Portuguese did not relent. Under the leadership of Nuno da Cunha, they tried again, but failed, to take the island in 1531. In 1535 Sultan Bahadur of Gujarat agreed to sign a peace accord with Nuno da Cunha, but when the two leaders met, Bahadur was murdered and the Portuguese took control of Diu, immediately building the fort and a strong wall around the town.

While local traders and merchants thrived under the new rule, many resented paying taxes to boost Portuguese coffers already full with profits from customs duties levied on all vessels using the port. In defiance, local seamen made a series of unsuccessful raids on Portuguese ships. Moghul and Arab attacks were courageously resisted, too, but the Portuguese were finally forced out in 1961 by the Indian government, who after a swift bombing campaign declared Diu part of India.

Arrival and information

The usual point of entry to Diu island is by road, via **Goghla**, the small fishing village on the mainland that forms the northern edge of Diu territory. The three hotels here are nothing special, and most people head straight on to the island. Foreigners show passports and visas at a checkpoint before crossing the new bridge that meets the island at the northwestern edge of Diu Town. **Buses** usually pull in to the stand by the bridge, from where you'll have to walk to the town centre (one or two early morning arrivals, however, may drop you in the main square). **Una** and **Delvada** are connected to Diu by half-hourly buses; from Delvada, there are also tempos and auto-rickshaws.

The **tourist office** (Mon–Fri 9.30am–1.30pm & 2–6pm; ☎2653), 300m west of the main square on the north coast road, has maps and information. The **GPO** is on the west side of the main square, upstairs (Mon–Sat 8am–noon & 2–5pm). The most common way to get around is by **bike**, which you can rent at shops near the main square,

The telephone **area code** for Diu Town is ☎028758.

or close to the gate on the town's western edge. *Reshma Travels* opposite *Nilesh Hotel* rent cars and motorcycles. Auto-rickshaws are available, but if you're staying at Nagoa and want to get back from town at night expect high charges.

Diu Town

Cosy little **Diu Town** is protected by the fort in the east and a wall in the west. **Nagar Seth's Haveli**, one of the grandest of the town's distinctive Portuguese mansions, is on Makata Rd, hidden in the web of narrow streets that wind through the residential Old Portuguese District. Fisherfolk make daily trips from the north coast in wooden boats; women lay the silvery catch out on rugs to sell in the market near the mosque.

Although the Christian population is dwindling, along with the old language, a few **churches** built by the former European inhabitants are still used. Portuguese mass is celebrated beneath the high ceilings and painted arches of **St Paul's**, while the church of **St Thomas** to its north is now a museum (daily 8am–9am; free), and that of **St Francis of Assisi** to the south partly occupied by the local hospital.

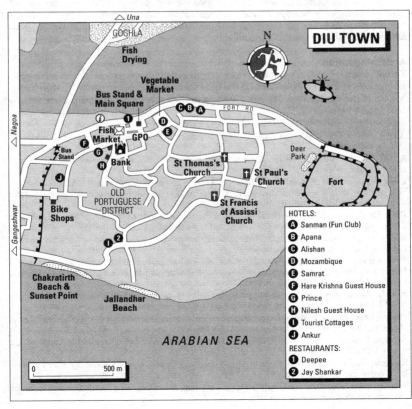

Diu's serene **fort** (daily 7am–6pm; free) stands robust, resisting the battering of the sea on three sides and sheltering birds, jackals and the town jail. Its wide moat and coastal position enabled the fort to withhold attack by land and sea, but there are obvious scars from the Indian government's airstrikes in 1961 – notice the hole above the altar of the church in the southwest corner. Now abandoned almost completely to nature, and littered with centuries-old cannon balls, it commands excellent views out to sea and over the island.

Around the island

Cliffs and rocky pools make up much of the southern coast of the island, giving way to the occasional sandy stretch. South of Diu Town is the small **Jallandhar Beach**; the larger **Chakratirth Beach** overlooked by a high mound, is a little to the west. By far the longest and most attractive beach, however, is at **Nagoa**, 7km west of town, where a single hotel offers simple facilities. Naturally, sunbathing is tempting on these sun-kissed sands, but many women visitors have reported hassle. **Buses** from Diu to Nagoa beach leave infrequently from the old bus stand at the end of the bridge (Diu–Nagoa 5 daily, Nagoa–Diu 7 daily). If you spend the day at Nagoa, or are staying at Nagoa and want to come into town, keep an eye on the time – missing the last bus (around 5pm) leaves you with little choice but to walk.

Not far out of town, a turning off the Nagoa Road leads to **FUDAM**, an attractive village of Portuguese houses washed in pale yellow and sky-grey, dominated by the smooth white bell towers of its church. One small outdoor **bar**, shaded by twisted palm fronds, stands in the centre of the village.

Accommodation

The atmosphere of Diu's **hotels**, concentrated in Diu Town, around the central open-air markets and along Fort Road on the northeast coast, is in keeping with the leisurely pace of the island. Most are low-priced, with their own restaurant, and a bar serving cold Indian beer.

Alishan, Fort Rd (☎2340). Clean rooms, some with bath. Balconies and views cost more. ③–⑤.

Ankur, between the western gate and the Main Bazaar (☎2388). Shabby and run-down, but with big airy rooms. ④–⑤.

Apana, Fort Rd (☎2112). Spacious rooms; the priciest have sea-facing balconies. Negotiable rates at slack times. ③–⑥.

Gangar Sagar Rest House, Nagoa Beach (☎2249). The only beachfront hotel (and restaurant). Very mellow, with a sea-facing courtyard. With prior permission, non-residents can enjoy great views and eat decidedly average food at the restaurant. ③.

Hare Krishna Guest House (☎2213), west of the centre, past the fish market. Small, cosy place with cheap, basic rooms, some with balcony, and a restaurant. ①.

Jay Shankar, Jallandhar Beach (☎2424). Basically a restaurant with rooms in a tiny family house. Peaceful, homely, simple and cheap. ①.

Mozambique, Market Square (☎2223). Good choice, but often full. Clean and airy rooms in a Portuguese building with balconies overlooking the vegetable market and beyond to the sea. Constant hot water. Pleasant bar on verandah and an unreliable restaurant. ①.

Nilesh, set back from the fish market (☎2319). Diu's poorest budget hotel, but handy if the others are full. Doubles with bath in the newer wing are not bad, but the restaurant is awful. ②–④.

Prince, Main Bazaar (☎2265). Large clean rooms with balconies (but not much of a view). Lacks character, though, and its restaurant serves only omelettes and bread. ③–④.

Samrat, Collectorate Rd (☎2354). Diu island's one "upmarket" hotel. Comfortable, carpeted a/c rooms with balconies, attached bathroom and constant hot water. ④–⑦.

Sanman (*Fun Club*), Fort Rd. Popular place facing the sea with a good verandah restaurant serving a varied menu. Large rooms with locally made rugs and high ceilings. ①.

Tourist Cottages, Jallandhar Beach (☎2654). Charming a/c cottages for two or four people on the coast overlooking the Arabian Sea. ⑤.

Eating

Sadly, the only vestiges of Portuguese influence on the dining scene in Diu is the free availability of alcohol. In general the **hotel restaurants** are disappointing, often dire. The selection below covers the exceptions. Most places close in the afternoon and after 9pm; stalls in the main square, however, mix excellent creamy *lassis* all day.

Aavkar, just off the main square. Spotless, good-value *thali* house. Open 9.30am–10pm.

Alishan, Fort Rd. Decent veg, meat and fish, with Chinese options. Breakfast 8–11.30am, lunch noon–3.30pm, dinner 7–11pm.

Apana, Fort Rd. Slightly posher and pricier than the *Alishan* next door. Lobster is usually available if ordered in advance. Open 7am–11pm.

Deepee, under the GPO. Good value, tasty Punjabi veg curries. Open 10am–2pm & 5–9pm.

Jay Shankar, Jallandhar Beach. Unpretentious, inexpensive little restaurant serving delicious fresh fish and seafood and good veg dishes. Open 8am–3pm & 4–10pm.

Samrat, Collectorate Rd. One of the best hotel restaurants, serving the earliest breakfast. Breakfast 7–11am, lunch 11am–3pm, dinner 6.30–11pm.

MOVING ON FROM DIU

There are few **direct state-run buses** from Diu, so it may be easier to take one to Una on the mainland and pick up a connection there. Buses to Delvada and Una (half-hourly; 40min) leave from the main bus stand, as do most of Diu's direct services: two in the morning to Rajkot (7hr 30min) via Veraval (2hr 30min) and Junagadh (5hr 30min), one in the morning to Ahmedabad (10hr 30min) via Bhavnagar (6hr 30min), and one at lunchtime to Porbandar (7hr). Two early morning services to Rajkot leave from the local bus stand in the main square, as do buses for Nagoa and Vanakbara, the last of which is at about 6pm. **Private buses** to destinations such as Ahmedabad, Bhavnagar, Rajkot, Porbandar and Bombay can be booked at *Reshma Travels* opposite *Nilesh Hotel*, *Radhika Travels* by the *State Bank of Saurashtra* (who also handle buses from Una to Surat and Vadodara), and *Panchmurti Travels* at the bus stand. The large central bus stand at **Una** is well connected to Gujarati destinations, and there's one bus in the early afternoon to Bombay (22hr) via Surat (13hr). The tourist office in Diu may be able to supply exact times.

Two **trains** a day leave from Delvada: one in the early afternoon to Sasan Gir (3hr) and Junagadh (6hr 55min), which is slower than the bus, but a more pleasant journey through the fields and forests of south Saurashtra, and one early in the morning for Veraval, which is so slow (4hr 15min) that only a serious rail enthusiast would consider it.

Gujarat Airways flies to Bombay (1hr) twice weekly from Diu **airport**, 5km west of Diu Town near the south coast. The main agent in town is *Reshma Travels* opposite *Nilesh Hotel* (π2383). There are no passenger **boat** services from Diu.

Bhavnagar

The coastal port of **BHAVNAGAR**, founded in 1723 by the Gohil Rajput Bhavsinghji, whose ancestors came to Gujarat from Marwar (Rajasthan) in the twelfth century, is an important trading centre whose principal export is cotton. With few sights of its own, Bhavnagar does, however, boast a fascinating bazaar in the old city, and is the obvious place to stay before heading southwest to the wonderful Jain temples of Palitana (see p.604). Incidentally, it is one of the few places (Ahmedabad is another) where you'll see hand-carts being pulled by man and wife, or women alone.

Arrival and information

Arriving by train, the way into town is straight ahead along Station Rd. From the ST bus station, turn right up ST Station Rd for the town centre. The *State Bank of Saurashtra* and the *Bank of India* have **money-changing** facilities (open usual Gujarati hours

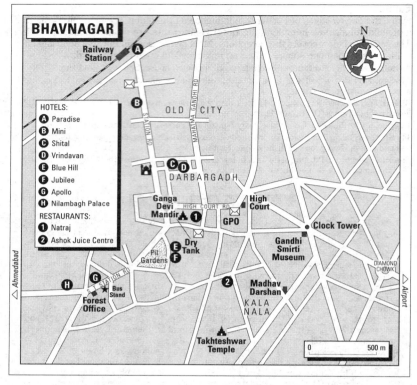

Mon–Fri 11am–3pm, Sat 11am–1pm); they're on Amba Chowk between the hotels *Shital* and *Vrindavan*. The **GPO** (Mon–Fri 10am–6pm, Sat 10am–1pm) is next to the High Court on High Court Rd, with branches just off Station Rd a block south of the station, and opposite the southeastern corner of the dried-up Ganga Jalia Tank. You can rent **bikes** from a shop less than 100m south of the *Mini Hotel* on Station Rd.

The telephone **area code** for Bhavnagar is ☎0278.

The City

The focus of interest in Bhavnagar is the **old city**, alive with character and charm, its vibrant markets overlooked by delicate wooden balconies and the plush pillared fronts of former merchants' houses. Sections of the old city are reserved for specific trades; there's a silver bazaar, a street lined with rope and tool stalls, a cloth bazaar where tailors perch like birds in tiny cubby holes above the shops, and a gold bazaar full of watchmakers and menders. Local handicrafts to look out for include *bhandani* and the elaborate beadwork characteristic of the region.

There are only a couple of formal attractions. The marble temple, **Ganga Devi Mandir**, by the dry tank in the centre of town, has a large dome and intricate lattice work on its walls, while the otherwise unspectacular **Takhteshwar temple**, raised on a hill in the south of town, at least affords a good view over the city to the Gulf of Cambay in the east. Southwest of the town centre on Diamond Chowk, the **Gandhi Smriti Museum** (daily except Sun and the 2nd & 4th Sat of each month, 9am–12.30pm & 2.30–6pm; free) exhibits Buddhist, Jain and Hindu statues, medieval bronzes, Harappan terracottas and a fossil display flanked by the four-metre jaw bones of a sperm whale. Labels are mostly in Gujarati. Upstairs is a display devoted to Gandhi's life, and a *Khadi Gramodyog* shop.

Accommodation

Bhavnagar has a reasonable choice of **places to stay**. There are a few budget hotels near the railway station, which also has retiring rooms; the more upmarket options are in Darbargadh, towards the bus stand, and around the bus stand itself.

Apollo, ST Station Rd, opposite the bus stand (☎425251; fax 428729). Carpeted, clean rooms with TV, some a/c. ⑤.

Blue Hill, opposite Pil Gardens (☎426951 or 2; fax 427313). Modern, well-maintained five-storey hotel with all mod cons, views over the gardens from front rooms, and a roof terrace. ⑥–⑦.

Jubilee, opposite Pil Gardens (☎ & fax 421740 or 1). Similar to the *Blue Hill*, but less smart. ⑥–⑦.

Mini, Station Rd (☎24415). Clean, well-kept rooms, some without windows. ②.

Nilambagh Palace, ST Station Rd (☎424241; fax 428072). The classiest hotel in Bhavnagar; an old palace set in vast gardens west of the bus stand. Large luxurious rooms. ⑦–⑧.

Paradise, by the station (☎423291). Cheap but not too clean. Doubles have attached bath. ①.

Shital, Darbargadh (☎428773). Small, basic hotel with 9am checkout and a men's dorm. ①.

Vrindavan, Darbargadh (☎427391). Immaculate but unelaborate rooms set in part of a massive old palace in the centre of town. The best value for budget travellers, with 24hr checkout. ②.

Eating

Most of Bhavnagar's **restaurants** adjoin the main hotels, and offer local, national and international cuisine; the most upmarket is the *Nilambagh Palace Hotel*. An excellent unnamed place behind the Police Chowk on Gandhi Rd stays open all day for low- priced local *thalis*.

Ashok Juice Centre, Kala Nala. Good ice-cream, shakes and juices. Open 10am–midnight.

Blue Hill, opposite Pil Gardens. Two high standard restaurants – the *Nilgiri* (Indian, Chinese and Western; snacks 7.30am–7pm, lunch 11.30am–3pm, dinner 7–11pm); and *Gokul* (Gujarati *thalis*; noon–3pm & 7–10pm), which is slightly cheaper.

MOVING ON FROM BHAVNAGAR

The usual way to get anywhere from Bhavnagar is by **bus**. From the ST satation services run to Ahmedabad, Bombay, Bhuj, Rajkot, Junagadh and Veraval, plus Vadodara (9 daily; 6hr) and Surat (4 daily; 8hr). There's only one direct service to Diu (6hr 30min), but seven to Una (6hr), where you can pick up buses to Diu every half-hour. To Palitana, there are hourly buses (1hr 15min), with three a day to Velavadar (1hr), and seven to Alang (1hr 30min). **Private buses**, operated by firms such as *Eddie Amin* opposite the ST station (☎421307 or 235), and *Punjab Travels* opposite the *Galaxy Cinema* in Kala Nala Rd (☎424582) serve destinations in Gujarat and interstate. Some pricier sleeper buses (with berths) are available.

Two daily express **trains** run from Bhavnagar to Ahmedabad (5hr 30min), where you'll have to change for anywhere beyond. There are also three fast passenger trains to Palitana, and one overnight to Rajkot. **Flights** to Bombay (50min–1hr 5min) are operated four days of the week by *Indian Airlines* (northwest of Ganga Jalia Tank; ☎426503 or 141), the other three days by *NEPC* (Madhav Darshan, Kala Nala, ☎411191). The airport is 5km southeast of town, best reached by auto-rickshaw.

Woodlands, in the *Jubilee Hotel*, opposite Pil Gardens. Decent veg place for Indian, Chinese and Western food on a pleasant terrace. Meals 11am–3pm & 7–11pm, sandwiches round the clock.

Manali, *Apollo Hotel*, ST Station Rd. Clean and fresh restaurant serving excellent meat, prawn and veg dishes. Open 11am–2.30pm & 7–10.30pm.

Mini Dining Hall, *Hotel Mini*, Station Rd. Supper-time Gujurati *thalis* at low prices. Open to non-residents 8.30–10.30pm.

Natraj, near Ganga Devi Mandir. Popular mid-range place, on the north side of Ganga Jalia Tank. Tasty veg south Indian and Punjabi food, and a great ice cream choice. Open 11am–3pm & 7–10pm.

Velavadar Black Buck Sanctuary

Outside the tiny village of **VELAVADAR**, 65km north of Bhavnagar, the **Black Buck Sanctuary** (best Nov–May) shelters the highest concentration of this Indian antelope anywhere in India. Although the area was officially declared a sanctuary in 1969, the buck were always protected by the Bishnoi tribe (see p.175). You can see the elegant black-and-white males strutting, chasing and jousting with their magnificent curved horns to define and defend their territories, each accompanied by a group of light-coloured females. It is also possible to walk in the park, and watch for wolves, now rare in India, who visit the water holes between dawn and dusk.

Buses leave Bhavnagar for Velavadar (1hr) twice daily in the afternoon, returning in the morning, so a visit to the sanctuary entails at least one night's **stay** at the small, perfectly located *Kaliyar Bhavan Forest Lodge* (②). **Permission** (Rs15 for 3 days, camera or video Rs5 per day) must be sought from Bhavnagar's Forest Office, in the cream and brown concrete government offices known as Multi-Storey Building, Annexe F/10, just west of the bus stand (daily except Sun and the 2nd & 4th Sat of each month, 10.30am–6.30pm; ☎0278/426425). Remember to ask about the availability of food – it's usually available but should be ordered in advance. **Guides** are not a necessity, but can be hired at a (ridiculously low) rate of Rs7.50 for three hours.

Palitana

For many visitors, the highlight of a trip to Saurashtra is a climb up the holy hill of **Shatrunjaya** (accessible 7am–7pm), India's principal Jain pilgrimage site, just outside **PALITANA**, 50km southwest of Bhavnagar. Almost nine hundred temples – many made of marble – crown this hill, said in legend to be a chunk of the mighty Himalayas where the Jains' first *tirthankara*, Adinath, and his chief disciple gained enlightenment. While records show that the hill was a *tirtha* as far back as the fifth century, the existing temples date only from the sixteenth century, anything earlier having been lost in the iconoclastic Muslim raids of the 1500s and 1600s.

Climbing the wide steps up Shatrunjaya takes roughly two hours, though as with all hilltop pilgrimage centres, *dholis* (seats on poles held by four bearers) are available for those unable, or unwilling, to walk. The view as you approach is magnificent, with spires and towers swooping upwards, hemmed in by mighty protective walls. You should allow at least two more hours to see even half the temples.

The individual *tuks* – temple enclosures – are named after the merchants who funded them. Together they create a formidable city, fortified by the thick walls and laid over the two summits of Shatrunjaya. Each *tuk* comprises courtyards within courtyards, chequered in black-and-white marble, and several temples, their walls exquisitely and profusely carved with saints, birds, animals, buxom maidens, musicians and dancers. Many temples are two, or even three storeys high, with perfectly proportioned pavilions crowning balconies, looming conical *shikharas* (spires), and within, ceilings rising to the highest point, swarming with carved figures that flow in concentric circles outwards from a central lotus blossom.

The largest temple, dedicated to **Adinath**, in the Khartaravasi *tuk* on the northern ridge, constantly hums with murmured prayers and blessings, and is usually full of masked nuns and monks, dressed in white and carrying white fly-whisks. The southern ridge, and the spectacular **Adishvara** temple in its western corner, is reached by taking the right-hand fork at the top of the path. On a clear day, the view from the summit takes in the Gulf of Cambay to the south, Bhavnagar to the north and the mountain range which includes Mt Girnar in the west.

The **museum** close to the bottom of the hill displays a collection of Jain artefacts, labelled in Gujarati but well worth seeing, and an ancient clock that invites much attention every hour when a model man emerges from a hole to hit a bell.

A path along the ridge and into the valley of Adipur, 13km away, is open for one day only, on the festival **Falgun Suth Tera** in celebration of Adinath, during the light half of the lunar month Falgun (Feb/March). Up to 50,000 pilgrims come to Shatrunjaya for this unique display of devotion, and are welcomed at the end of their *yatra* in a tented compound at Adipur with food and drink donated by Jain merchants.

Practicalities
Buses arrive from, and leave for, Bhavnagar (hourly; 1hr–1hr 30min), Junagadh (2 daily; 6hr) and Una (for Diu; 1 daily; 5hr). Three daily passenger **trains** connect Palitana with Bhavnagar (2hr). There is no **accommodation** on Shatrunjaya, so you'll have to stay in Palitana, either at one of many Jain *dharamshalas* in the old part of town that oblige guests to observe strict vegetarianism, or in a hotel nearer the bus stand. The comfortable GTDC *Hotel Sumeru* (☎02848/2327; ①–⑤) on Station Rd, between the bus stand and the railway station, has ordinary and a/c rooms, and dorms. Its restaurant serves lunchtime *thalis*, evening buffets and simple breakfasts. Accommodation at the *Hotel Shavrak* (☎02848/2428; ①–③), opposite the bus stand, is adequate, though less spacious; it also has inexpensive men-only dorms. In the narrow alley next to it, the basic, very cheap *Jagurti Restaurant* (10am–2pm & 6–9pm) serves excellent Gujarati meals and snacks, and is always busy.

Alang

Some 60km south of Bhavnagar, the coastal village of **ALANG** has become a massive breaker's yard for ships. Its "natural gift", a tide that brings large vessels in and leaves them beached on the shore with ease, has made it a major centre for the decommissioning of ships from around the world, especially Russia. While you are unlikely to be allowed into the yards, you can wander around the village and see secondhand parts being sold off to be reused in countries like Greece, Italy and Taiwan. Scrap iron is also sold by weight to Indian customers, and sundry ships' fittings and nautical knick-knacks are available. With a bit of hunting, you could pick up some unusual souvenirs, though it has to be said that most of the stuff (boilers, hatch covers, steel cable) are hardly essential buys. There's nowhere to stay in Alang, but it is easily reached from Bhavnagar by bus (7 daily; 1hr 30min–2hr), and connected by frequent tempos to nearby Talisa, on the main road from Bhavnagar to southern Saurashtra.

Southeastern Gujarat

The seldom visited **southeastern** corner of Gujarat, sandwiched between Maharashtra and the Arabian Sea, harbours few attractions to entice you off the road or railway line to or from Bombay. There's little to recommend **Vadodara** (Baroda), former capital of the Gaekwad rajas, but its proximity to the old Muslim town of **Champaner**, and the ruined forts and exotic Jain and Hindu temples that encrust **Pavagadh Hill**. Further south, the dairy pastures around **Anand** gradually give way to a swampy, malaria-infested coastal strip of banana plantations and shimmering salt pans that are cut by silty, sinuous rivers and peppered with mango trees and brick villages. The area's largest city is **Surat**, a sprawling modern industrial centre whose handful of colonial monuments are engulfed by some of the most chronically congested streets in South Asia. The historic port of **Bharuch**, overlooking the River Narmada, 66km north of Surat, is neither picturesque nor evocative; the only place of real interest in the far south of the state is the former Portuguese territory of **Daman**. Although nowhere near as appealing as its colonial cousins Goa and Diu, the twelve-kilometre-long enclave, whose main *raison d'être* is as a watering hole for alcohol-starved Gujarati men, does boast some impressive colonial architecture, and a couple of so-so beaches.

The west coast's main **transport** arteries, the NH8 and *Western Railway*, wind in tandem between Bombay and Ahmedabad. Even if you are only making short hops, stick to the trains: the highway, a graveyard of overturned buses and *Tata* trucks, is one of the most nail-bitingly terrifying roads in India.

Vadodara (Baroda)

The area between Ahmedabad and **VADODARA** (still commonly known as **Baroda**) is lush and fertile, but Vadodara itself is a heavily congested, noisy industrial city. Though the old city does retain some interest, with its beautiful ancient *havelis* and various bazaars, Vadodara has few tourist attractions. However, it does make the most convenient place to stay for trips to the ruined cities of **Champaner** and **Dabhoi**.

Prior to Independence, Vadodara was ruled by the Gaekwad Rajputs. Unlike their Rajasthani counterparts, they were little affected by the Indian government's withdrawal of privy purses, and continue to live in lavish **palaces**.

Arrival and information

The **railway station** and **bus stand** are very close together in the west of town, within easy walking distance of almost all the hotels. The airport is 6km northeast, or about Rs20 away by auto-rickshaw. There's a very helpful **tourist information desk** in the station (Mon–Sat 11am–5pm), which sells a leaflet with a map and a list of the city's main sights. They also arrange **city tours** (Tues, Wed & Fri 2pm–6pm) if there are ten or more takers; call ☎329656. Sterling and dollars **cash or travellers' cheques** can be changed at the *Bank of Baroda* international services branch in Sayaji Gunj behind Kadak Bazaar (Mon–Fri 11am–3pm). Otherwise, try the *Bank of South India* opposite, or the *State Bank of India* on R C Dutt Rd between the *Green* and *Welcomgroup* hotels, which will change dollar and sterling cash, and may do so on a Saturday (11am–1pm). The **GPO** is off Raopura Road in the centre of town. For secondhand **books**, try the stall on the corner of Tilak Rd by the *Jagdish Lodge* in Sayaji Gunj.

> The telephone **area code** for Vadodara is ☎0265.

The City

Vadodara's chief attractions are in **Sayaji Bagh**, the large green park whose main entrance is on Tilak Rd. It takes one or two hours to get round the large Indo-Saracenic **Baroda Museum and Picture Gallery** (daily 10am–5pm; Rs1), reached from University Rd, which holds art and textiles from all over the world, Gujarati archeological remains, Moghul miniatures and, as if to prove it's a *pukka* museum, an Egyptian mummy and a whale skeleton. Among the best exhibits are carved doors and lintels

△ Ahmedabad   △ Ahmedabad   △ Airport

TILAK RD

Indian
Airlines

Baroda Museum
■ Health Museum
SAYAJI
BAGH

Railway
Station   ST Bus Stand

RC DUTT RD

See
inset   SAYAJI
GUNJ   ❸

MS University   ■ Planetarium

TILAK ROAD

▲ Kirti Mandir

N

❶
RAOPURA RD   NAYA BAZAAR   Nazarbaug
Tambekarwada   Sarsagar   Laheri   Palace
Haveli ▪   ▫   Tank   Pura Gate ■   Pani
❺   Gate

DANDIA BAZAAR   M G   ROAD

❷ Yogikrupa   Nyaya   Mandvi
TILAK ROAD   Mandir   Gate

City
Buses ★

❹ ❻ ❼ ❽
❷ ❻ ❽   Laxmi   Gendi
❺ Bank   ❷   Niwas   Gate
Palace

Maharaja Fateh
■ Singh Museum

HOTELS:		RESTAURANTS:
Ⓐ Aditi	Ⓕ Green Hotel	❶ Hotel Gokul
Ⓑ Ambassador	Ⓖ Jagdish Hindu Lodge	❷ Kalyan Hotel
Ⓒ Baroda Municipal	Ⓗ Rama Inn	❸ Havmor
Corporation	Ⓘ Surya	❹ Radika
Ⓓ Chandan Mahal	Ⓙ Welcomgroup Vadodara	❺ Canara Coffee House
Ⓔ Delux		

0   500 m

VADODARA

▽ Surat   ▽ Surat

taken from Gujarat's *havelis*, and some fine fifth-century Jain bronzes excavated near-by. Works in the Picture Gallery are mostly British and European from the seventeenth to nineteenth centuries, including Poussin's *Christ and Mary Magdalene*, a Rubens portrait, and a painting by Johann Zoffany of David Garrick as Macbeth. As well as the museum, Sayaji Bagh contains a **Planetarium** (35min shows daily except Thurs in English at 4.30pm; Rs2), a pitiful **zoo**, a small **Health Museum** (11am–6pm; free), and a toy train running on what must be the narrowest gauge in India (10 inches).

From Sayaji Bagh, Tilak Rd continues east across the river past **Kirti Mandir**, the mausoleum of Vadodara's rulers, towards the old city, the centre of which is MG Rd, bounded at its western end by **Laheri Pura Gate** and **Nyaya Mandir** (literally "New Temple"), a fine Indo-Saracenic building which is now a law court. There's another gate (Pani Gate) at the eastern end of MG Rd, near the late nineteenth-century **Nazarbaug Palace,** and halfway between the two, the four-way **Mandvi Gate**, originally Moghul but much altered since. To the west of MG Rd is an artificial lake, the **Sursagar Tank** (check out *Pratap Talkies*, an over-the-top Art Deco pile at the northeastern corner), surrounded by glorious painted *havelis*. Other buildings worth a *look* include **Laxmi Vilas Palace** in the south of town, the most extravagant of Vadodara's palaces, now a heritage hotel. Glimpse it from the road, or from the dull **Maharaja Fateh Singh Museum** (daily except Mon, 10.30am–5.30; Rs10) in the palace grounds.

Accommodation

Vadodara's **hotels** are designed with business visitors in mind; there are several mid-range and upmarket places, and just a handful of inexpensive lodges which could all do with improved maintenance. Most of the hotels are grouped in the **Sayaji Gunj** area just south of the railway station.

Aditi, Sayaji Gunj (☎331188; fax 332259). A tall building just off Tilak Rd. Carpeted rooms with fridge, room service and TV, and clean bathrooms. ⑤–⑥.

Ambassador, Sayaji Gunj (☎327417; fax 310129). Clean and spacious rooms with TV and bath. A good mid-range option. Arranges air and railway reservations. ④–⑥.

Baroda Municipal Corporation, Pravasi Gruh (☎329656). Spartan and institutional, but clean and cheap. Guests must provide their own lock. ①.

Chandan Mahal, Sayaji Gunj (☎331822). Small, reasonably clean rooms in a pleasant old house with a central courtyard. Most rooms a little dusty, some have a/c. ①–④.

Delux, Kadak Bazaar (☎329604). Small, clean hotel in the heart of a lively bazaar just south of the railway station. ①.

Green Hotel, RC Dutt Rd (also called Racecourse Rd) (☎323111 or 2). The best low-budget option; rooms in a 100-year-old house with period furniture. Lacks a modern touch, but real character. ②.

Jagdish Hindu Lodge, Sayaji Gunj (☎330495). Clean and friendly. The rooms are not small, but only divided by wooden partitions. ①.

Rama Inn, Sayaji Gunj (☎330131or 2; fax 337735). Smart sizeable rooms in plush modern hotel with restaurants, health club, swimming pool and wine shop. Credit cards accepted. ⑤–⑦.

Surya, Sayaji Gunj (☎336500; fax 336504). Smart, but less upmarket than the *Rama*; no pool. ⑥–⑧.

Welcomgroup Vadodara, RC Dutt Rd (☎330033; fax 330050). Baroda's only five-star hotel, with predictably swanky and well-maintained rooms. ⑧.

Eating

With a large student population and a constant influx of business people, Vadodara has a choice of **restaurants** in all price ranges. Several upmarket hotels lay on buffet spreads; for fast food and snack stops, head for the bus and railway stations.

Canara Coffee House, *Pukka* coffee – a rarity in north India – and south Indian snacks at very low prices; a good place for breakfast. Open 7am–10pm.

Hotel Gokul, Koti Char Rasta. Small snack bar serving excellent south Indian, Punjabi and Gujarati *thalis* and ice-cream at very low prices. Open 10am–10pm.

MOVING ON FROM VADODARA

Vadodara **railway station** is often rather crowded and queues for tickets can be long (the reservation office is upstairs); you can bypass the hassle for a Rs20 fee if you buy your ticket from *Yogikrupa Travel Service* opposite (daily 8am–8pm; ☎327677). **New Delhi** is reached by five daily trains (16hr) via Kota (7hr 30min) and Sawai Madhopur (9hr), with one train a day to Jaipur (11hr 40min). Seven stop at Vapi (for Daman, 4hr). In addition, the faster and more expensive *Rajdhani Express* #2951/2952 serves Kota (6hr 45min), New Delhi (12hr 20min, overnight) and Bombay Central (5hr) daily except Monday, while the *Shatabdi Express* #2009/2010 serves Ahmedabad (2hr), Surat (1hr 30min) and Bombay Central (5hr) daily except Friday.

The **bus stand** on Tilak Rd, a little north, has regular, state-run services to other Gujarati towns, including Ahmedabad, Bharuch, Surat, Champaner (hourly; 1hr 30min), Bhavnagar (9 daily; 6hr) and Rajkot (12 daily; 8hr). Bombay (14hr) is served by eight buses, all in the evening, and none starting at Vadodara, so they may be full when they arrive. There are also services to Pune, Indore and Bhopal (1 daily; 16hr). Stalls selling tickets for **private buses** (to Bombay, Rajasthan and Madhya Pradesh) line Tilak Rd.

Indian Airlines **fly** daily to Bombay (1hr) and four days of the week to Delhi (1hr 30min). The office is in Fatehgunj, just north of Sayaji Bagh (☎329668). There are also three weekly flights to Ahmedabad (25min) with *Gujarat Airways*.

Havmor, Tilak Rd. Tasty Indian, Chinese and Western food with a/c and good service. Open noon–10.45pm (only snacks 3–7pm). Moderate to pricey.

Kalyan Hotel, Sayaji Gunj. Veg canteen extremely popular with students, a coffee shop specializing in Mexican snacks, and a restaurant; all reasonably priced. Open 7.30am–11pm.

Radika, Tilak Rd, Sayaji Gunj. Glass-fronted and very popular inexpensive *thali* house, with a red plastic sign in Gujarati (next door to *LM Kothari & Sons*). Open 8am–10pm.

Railway Refreshment Room, upstairs in the station. Not a great culinary experience but, like Indian Railways in general, solid, reliable and dirt cheap. Breakfast 8.30–10.30am, lunch noon–2.30pm, tea 4–5pm, dinner 7–9.30pm.

Hotel Surya, Sayaji Gunj. Two good, moderately priced veg restaurants: the *Vega*, offering filling buffets with dishes from all over the world (noon–3pm & 7–10.30pm); and the cheaper *Myra*, with delicious Gujarati *thalis* (11am–2.30pm & 7–10pm).

Around Vadodara

The Solanki kings, and later Muslim rulers, who between them held sway over Baroda for several centuries, left behind some fine architecture. A small town full of cloth and tailors' shops, **Dabhoi**, 24km southeast of Vadodara (1hr by bus), has four magnificent gateways. These, the only remnants of the thirteenth-century Solanki fortifications, are finely sculpted with gods, nymphs, animals and plants. The Kalika Mata temple next to the northern Mori Gate, though worn by time, features some excellent friezes.

Pavagadh and Champaner

The hill of **Pavagadh**, 45km northeast of Vadodara, rises 820m above the plains, overlooking the almost forgotten **Muslim city** of **CHAMPANER**. Take a jeep from Champaner, or walk up the path that ascends through battered gates and past the old walls of the Solanki fortress, to a mid-point where you can get snacks, souvenirs and a welcome cup of sweet *chai*. From here you can proceed by chairlift (7min) – or on foot up a well-trodden path – to the summit, where a number of Jain temples lie below a Hindu temple dedicated to Mataji, with a shrine to the Muslim saint Sadan Shah on its roof. The view stretches for miles over the patchwork plains of south Gujarat, and you can spot concrete barricades under construction along the Narmada canal.

In 1297 the Chauhan Rajputs made Pavagadh their stronghold, and fended off three attacks by the Muslims before eventually losing to Muhammad Begada in 1484: all the women and children committed *johar*, and the men who survived the battle were slain when they refused to embrace Islam. After his conquest, Muhammad Begada set to work on building Champaner, which took 23 years. The town was the political capital of Gujarat until the death of Bahadur Shah in 1536, when the courts moved to Ahmedabad and Champaner fell into decline.

Champaner today has a strange, time-warped atmosphere. The massive city walls with inscribed gateways still stand, encompassing several houses, exquisite mosques, Muslim funerary monuments, and newer Jain *dharamshalas* to accommodate and feed pilgrims visiting Pavagadh. Champaner's largest mosque, the exuberant **Jami Masjid**, is east of the walls. Towering *minars* stand either side of the main entrance, and the prayer halls are dissected by almost two hundred pillars supporting a splendid carved roof raised in a series of domes. The central dome, three times the height of the others, shelters an octagonal shaft trimmed with richly carved balconies. The *zenana*, or women's prayer section, is in the northwest corner behind perforated stone walls.

Buses from Vadodara leave hourly (via Halol; 1hr 30min) for Champaner, where there's a modest *chai* stall. There's also a direct service from Ahmedabad, every three hours. The *Hotel Champaner* (☎026765/45641; ①–④) halfway up Pavagadh, has adequate **rooms** with magnificent views over the vast plains of south Gujarat, and a dorm. The **restaurant** serves veg *thalis*.

Bharuch

The rarely visited provincial backwater of **BHARUCH** (formerly Broach), halfway between Vadodara and Surat, stands on the marshy north bank of the Narmada, 48km short of the Arabian Sea. A thriving port and mercantile capital since the first millennium AD, its heyday was during the seventeenth century, when its ships sailed for Southeast Asia, to fetch spices to trade at its now-ruined British and Dutch factories. Today, the coastal trade hurtles past on the NH8, and only if you have a penchant for jaded colonial trading posts will you find the tumbledown European houses and forlorn old quarter worth an hour or so out of a long train journey.

Clustered onto the two-kilometre-long narrow ridge that separates the bustling modern end of Bharuch from the sleepy right bank of the Narmada, the **old quarter** lies a ten-minute ride west of the railway station and bus stand: ask the rickshaw *wallah* to head for the **Jama Masjid**, a fourteenth-century mosque hemmed in by wooden balconies and flaking colour-washed walls. Its colonnaded courtyard, pierced by three doorways and crowned with a row of thirteen shallow domes, is a giant jigsaw puzzle of intricately carved masonry plundered from a Jain temple that formerly stood on the spot. Once you've checked out the richly decorated ceilings in the sanctuary hall, head downhill until you reach the town **walls**, erected by Shivaji to replace those destroyed by Aurangzeb in 1660. A walkway runs along the top of the ramparts, giving good views over marshy mud-flats, grazed by sleek grey water buffalo, to the river.

The walls veer north when they arrive at the edge of a dried-up creek, near a pale-blue Victorian clocktower, and the large colonial-style palace of an ex-nawab who frittered away his inheritance on opium. Drop down from here, and follow the river bank west through a putrid-smelling *basti*, to come out eventually at the old **quay**, now a fishing dock. Apart from their triangular sails (a legacy of Bharuch's trading links with the Arabian Gulf), the ramshackle flat-bottomed inshore fishing *dhows* here, built in the roadside carpenters' yards at the top of the hill, are identical to those that still fish the saltwater lagoons of central Portugal, hence their distinctive design.

Practicalities

Luggage can be left at the railway station parcel office, right of the main exit, while you explore town. Most of the **places to stay** are near the railway station. The best budget option is the *Hotel Classic* (☎02642/32264; ④), tucked behind the tall buildings on the south side of Station Rd, which offers en-suite doubles with carpets, *Star TV*, and balconies, or clean, windowless wood-partition cells. The *Hotel Palmland* (☎02642/31692; ④–⑤), around the corner from the bus stand, is nothing to write home about, but has clean and well-furnished rooms, some a/c, while the nearby *Hotel Plaza* (☎02642/30922; ⑥) offers central a/c and a posh restaurant.

The *Hotel Palmland*'s institutional *thali* joint is a reassuringly hygienic **place to eat**. Otherwise, take your pick from the lookalike veg cafes along Station Rd, a little west of the *Plaza*. Drinks and ice-creams are sold at stalls outside the railway station.

Surat

Packed around a tight bend in the River Tapti, 19km before it dumps its silty waters into the Gulf of Cambay, sprawling **SURAT** was the west coast's principal port before the meteoric rise of Bombay. These days, it is one of India's fastest growing industrial centres, but of no real interest to visitors, other than business travellers or die-hard colonial history buffs. Apart from a couple of melancholic European cemeteries, Surat's most memorable feature is its **traffic**, which, even by Indian standards, is appalling.

Founded by Parsi refugees in the twelfth century, Surat emerged as a minor trading post during the 1500s, when it was plundered and razed numerous times by the

Portuguese. In 1592, after a protracted siege, the town fell to Akbar, under whose patronage it became one of India's most prosperous mercantile capitals, as well as a key embarkation point for Muslims heading to Mecca. The **British** first appeared on the scene in 1612, after being granted permission by the Moghuls to trade in the area. Three years later, they routed the Portuguese in a navy battle off "Bloody Point", mouth of the nearby Swally estuary, opening a trading **"factory"** soon after. The Dutch and French followed, but saw their *godowns*, or warehouses, sacked by Shivaji's Marathas in 1664. The British, however, came through unscathed. By the end of the eighteenth century, their hold over the town and its shipyard was finally secure. Surat might eventually have become west India's number one city had it not been devastated by fire and floods in 1837. Many of the Jain and Parsi merchants fled south to Bombay, precipitating a decline from which Surat has only recently recovered.

Over the past decade, the city's booming textile, chemical and diamond-cutting businesses (a legacy of the Dutch trade-links) have generated a 60 percent growth in population. The resultant overcrowding and pressures on an already over-taxed infrastructure, however, are all too evident. In the winter of 1992–93, the packed commercial and Muslim districts around the main bazaar finally burst at the seams, erupting into some of the worst communal riots the state has ever seen.

Arrival and information

Surat, on the main line from Ahmedabad to Bombay, has very good **train** connections, and is served by regular **buses** from Gujarat and interstate. Both stations are on the eastern edge of the city centre, with the massive Ring Road stretching out leftwards from the major junction to your left as you come out of the railway station, to your right as you come out of the bus station. Private buses tend to leave you about 50m from the railway station, so ignore rickshaw *wallahs* who offer to take you there as you stagger sleepily off the overnight bus. The easiest way to **get around** town is to use auto-rickshaws. Although making reservations can be a major hassle, trains are still more convenient than buses when it comes to **moving on**. Agents around the ST station offer tickets on **private buses**, to destinations as far afield as Kerala, but also within Gujarat and to Rajasthan and Maharashtra.

GTDC's **tourist office** (daily except Sun and the 2nd & 4th Sat of each month, 10.30am–6pm; ☎26586), is hidden away at 1/847 Athugar St in Nanpura. The Rs20 auto-rickshaw ride from the railway station takes you 4km up the Ring Road to the junction called Athwa Gate (just before the elevated section), then right and up the first real street on the left, where it's 100m up on your left. They have city maps and can arrange visits to **diamond-cutting workshops**. The *State Bank of India* (Mon–Fri 11am–3pm, Sat 11am–1pm) is in the same street.

> The telephone **area code** for Surat is ☎0261.

The City

Surat's few sights are very spread out, but can be seen in an hour if you take an auto-rickshaw between them. A good spot to start is **Chowk**, the busy riverside intersection at the foot of Nehru Bridge. Facing the old British High Court building on one side, and the incongruous steeple of an Anglican church on the other, the **castle** is the city's oldest monument, erected in 1540 on the banks of the Tapti by the Sultan of Gujarat in an attempt to curtail the trading activities of the Portuguese. Although equipped with top-notch Turkish cannons (now removed), and protected on its landward side by a huge ditch (now filled in), the fort fell both to the Moghuls and the British. These days the bastion houses government offices, and is far from the imposing edifice it must have been when General Sir George Oxinden, erstwhile President of Surat and Bombay saw off the Marathas from its battlements. You can wander in and scale the ramparts, from where there are views upriver and over the old walled town to the east.

The only other of Surat's historic sites worth hunting out lies fifteen minutes northeast across town beside Kataragama Road, beyond the fortified gateway of the same name. Buzzing past in a rickshaw, you could easily mistake the domed mausolea of the weed-choked **English cemetery** for an oriental tomb garden. Now in a sorry state, the graveyard is locked and enclosed behind a low wall, which you can hop over behind the *peepal* tree on the pavement. Its most impressive sepulchre, a mildewing collection of pillars and arches crowned with crossed cupolas, is that of General Oxinden and his brother Christopher. The smaller of the two large tombs, on the left, is believed to be the final resting place of Gerald Aungier, of Bombay fame. Elsewhere in the cemetery, some four hundred more modest graves belong to young colonial officers and their families who succumbed to fever in what was, in the seventeenth century, a lonely, malaria-infested trading post.

Accommodation

Although you are unlikely to choose to stay in Surat, there are plenty of **hotels** near the station (many of them in Sufi Baug, the street running straight ahead opposite the entrance). Finding a room is only a problem towards the end of weekday afternoons, by which time most places are booked by visiting business travellers. Avoid a protracted hunt in the heat by phoning ahead: there are STD booths opposite the station.

Embassy, near the *Alfa* (☎443170 or 1; fax 443173). Stylish new three-star, carpeted throughout, with a/c, bathtubs, and "ozonated water around the clock". The best in its bracket. ⑦–⑧.

Holiday Inn, Bharti Park, Athwa Lines (☎666565; fax 667294). Surat's only five-star, 7km out in a peaceful residential suburb (Rs30–35 by auto-rickshaw from the station). Luxurious rooms and all the trimmings, including a pool. ⑦.

Omkar and **Vaibhav**, Eighth Floor, Omkar Chambers, Sufi Baug (☎419329 or 30). Two hotels with identical prices and a shared reception (with handy train timetable), attached or shared shower-toilets, room-service tea on tap, lots of coming and going, great if not exactly picturesque views, and optional *Star TV*. A good budget deal. ②–③.

Sarvajanik, Station Rd, more-or-less opposite the station (☎426434). Spotless en-suite singles, doubles, and hot water 4–10pm. Recommended. ④.

Eating

Most of Surat's **restaurants** are in the better hotels, while many of the cheaper lodges offer basic room-service menus.

Embassy Hotel, off Sufi Baug, opposite the railway station. Set breakfasts, *thalis* and Indian, Chinese and Western dishes in a clean, pleasant atmosphere. Open 7am–midnight.

Mossam, *Hotel Yuvraj*, off Sufi Baug, opposite the railway station. Stylish, moderately priced Gujarati cooking and south Indian snacks in sophisticated surroundings. Open 11.30am–11.30pm.

Sheer-e-Punjabi, below Omkar Chambers. Swanky *tandoori* house with marble floors, tablecloths and a varied non-veg menu. Open 9am–1am. Moderate to pricey; take-away available.

ST Refreshment Room, ST bus station. Handy for veg snacks and *thalis*; clean, very cheap and open round the clock.

Daman

Ask any Gujarati what they know about **DAMAN** and they'll probably say "liquor". As a Union Territory, independent of the dry state that surrounds it, Daman has liberal licensing laws and low duty on booze, making it something of a target at weekends for busloads of Gujarati men who drink themselves senseless, sway up and down the main street, and then crash out in cheap hotel rooms for the night, generally being pretty obnoxious. The rest of the time, however, Daman is a very pleasant, laid-back little town

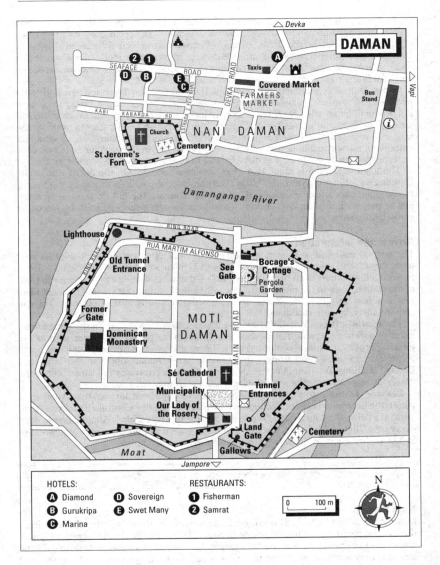

DAMAN

△ Devka

SEAFACE ROAD
ROAD

2 **1**
D **B** **E** **C**

Taxis

A

Covered Market

FARMERS
MARKET

Bus
Stand

ⓘ

DEVKA ROAD

KABI KABARDA RD

ESTRADA 2 DE FEVEREIRO

NANI DAMAN

△ Vapi

✝ Church

Cemetery

St Jerome's
Fort

Damanganga River

RING ROAD

Lighthouse

RUA MARTIM ALFONSO

Old Tunnel
Entrance

Sea
Gate

Bocage's
Cottage

Pergola
Garden

Cross

Former
Gate

MOTI
DAMAN

Dominican
Monastery

MAIN ROAD

RING ROAD

Sé Cathedral ✝

Municipality

Tunnel
Entrances

Our Lady of
the Rosery

Land
Gate

Cemetery

Moat

Gallows

Jampore ▽

HOTELS:
ⒶDiamond   Ⓓ Sovereign
ⒷGurukripa   Ⓔ Swet Many
ⒸMarina

RESTAURANTS:
❶ Fisherman
❷ Samrat

0   100 m

N

with excellent seafood, a small duty-free market, some immaculate Portuguese churches, houses and forts, and a couple of (admittedly uninspiring) beaches.

Straddling the mouth of the **Damanganga River**, which rises in the Sayadhri range
on the Deccan plateau, Daman made an obvious target for the Portuguese, who took it
in 1531 from the Sultan of Gujarat's Ethiopian governor, Siddu Bapita. The governor of
Goa, Dom Constantino de Bragança, cajoled the Sultan of Gujarat into ceding the terri-

tory 28 years later, after which it became the hub of the Portuguese trans-Arabian Sea trade with East Africa. The town's economic decline was precipitated by the British occupation of Sind in the 1830s, which effectively strangled its **opium** business. Colonial rule, however, survived until 1961 when, after a rather ineffective six-year barracade, Nehru lost patience with Portuguese refusal to negotiate a peaceful handover, and sent in the troops.

Today, Daman is administered from New Delhi as a Union Territory, along with the nearby ex-Portuguese colonies of Diu, and Dadra and Nagar Haveli. Apart from alcohol production and sales, its chief sources of income are coconuts, salt production, and smuggling. In recent years, the local tourist office has also been trying to promote the area as a mini-Goa. Don't be taken in: the unbroken stretch of palm-fringed sand that runs along its twelve-kilometre coastline may look idyllic in the brochures, but on closer inspection turns out to be a grubby fishing beach, used as a toilet by the locals.

The town of Daman is made up of two separate districts. On the north side of the Damanganga River is **Nani**, or "Little" **Daman**, where you'll find most of the hotels, restaurants, bars and markets; **Moti**, or "Great" **Daman**, the old Portuguese quarter, lies to the south, its baroque churches and Latinate mansions encircled by imposing stone battlements.

Arrival and information

The nearest **railhead** to Daman is 12km east at **Vapi** (check when you book that your train stops here). Shared *Ambassador* taxis to Daman will drop you on Seaface Rd, a five-minute walk east from most of the hotels – if none is waiting in the square in front of the station, walk to the main road, take a right and continue 500m until the next main junction. Just beyond is the ST **bus station**, with half-hourly buses to Daman. You can also get there by auto-rickshaw.

The **tourist office** (Mon–Fri 9.30am–1.30pm & 2–6pm; ☎35204), in the pink administrative building just south of the bus stand, hands out glossy brochures with lots of gushing prose, and **maps** of the territory. There are two **post offices**: one just north of the Damanganga Road bridge, the other in Moti Daman, opposite the Municipal Council building. You cannot currently change **foreign currency** in Daman, nor in the village of Somnath, despite what the local bank staff may tell you.

Leaving Daman, there are no direct buses to anywhere further than Vapi, from where the best transport connections are by train to Bombay Central (10 daily; 3–4hr), Surat (15 daily; 1hr 45min–3hr), Vadodara (9 daily expresses; 5hr), Ahmedabad (5 daily expresses; 7hr) and even, on the overnight *Saurashtra Janata Express* #9017, direct to Rajkot (12hr). *Gujarat Airways* fly to Bombay (3 weekly; 35min).

> The telephone **area code** for Daman is ☎02636.

Nani Daman

Most of the action in **Nani Daman** centres on **Seaface Road**, which runs west from the market past rows of hotels, seedy bars and IMFL (Indian Made Foreign Liquor) stores to the **beach**. Too polluted for a comfortable swim or sunbathe, Daman's dismal strand is only worth visiting around sunset, when the local fisherwomen hang strips of filleted pomfret on wooden racks to dry. At the opposite (east) end of Seaface Rd, the Portuguese **covered market** has a reputation as a purveyor of exotic contraband, although you won't find many packets of the fabled foreign cigarettes or bottles of whisky among the imported chocolate, Hindi film cassettes and cheap cotton clothes. More picturesque is the open-air **farmers' market** just behind it where, on weekday mornings, local women squat beside piles of fresh flowers, whole spices, fruit and veg.

Daman's noisiest trading, however, takes place at the **riverfront**. Head down here in the morning and you'll see scores of fishing boats moored at the quay, their bows hung with garlands of marigolds for good luck. While the night's catch is being landed, coolies haul heavy blocks of ice up the gangplanks to be hacked into pieces over baskets full of glistening fish that the fisherwomen, gathered on the beach below, then sell to the assembled housewives and restaurateurs. A good place from which to watch it all are the ramparts of **St Jerome's Fort**, directly behind the quay. Erected in the early seventeenth century to counter the threat of Moghul invasion, the citadel encircles a small *maidan*, a Catholic church, and a well-kept walled Portuguese graveyard.

Moti Daman

The town's most impressive monuments are across the river in the leafy colonial compound of **Moti Daman**, 2km south of Seaface Rd. Once inside the huge, heavily fortified walls that surround the quarter, you're worlds' away from the sandy cluttered streets of the new town: elegant double-storeyed mansions with sweeping staircases, wooden shutters, verandahs and colour-washed facades stand on sun-dappled courtyards. Now used as government offices, these residences were originally the homes of Portuguese nobles or *fidalgos* – the only people allowed to live inside the fort.

Moti Daman's highlights are its **churches**, which rank among the oldest and best-preserved Christian monuments in Asia. Grandest of all is the the **Sé Cathedral** (Church of Bom Jesus) on the main square. Built in 1603, its gigantic gabled baroque facade opens on to a lofty vaulted hall, at the end of which stands a gilded altar watched over by six statues of saints and a benign Madonna. On the opposite side of the square, the **Church of Our Lady of the Rosary** is crammed with ornate woodwork, notably some fine tableaux of the life of Jesus by the altar, while strings of fragrant jasmine and rose petals festoon its ceilings.

The **Main Road** linking Moti Daman's two **gates**, which were installed in the 1580s following a Moghul invasion, passes the **Pargola Garden**, a memorial to two Portuguese police officers who died in a mythical "uprising" in Dadra and Nagar Haveli. These former Portuguese enclaves, 80 percent of whose population are "tribals", were ceded by the Marathas in 1781 as an indemnity for two Portuguese ships they had sunk. Though both India and Portugal agreed on an official version – in which the locals rose up against the Portuguese and liberated the territory in 1954 – the reality was that Indian police officers in plain clothes acting on secret orders from the Maharashtra state government entered the territory, shot the policemen, and frightened the rest away with firecrackers. It is now a Union Territory, governed by the same authority as Daman and Diu.

A small cottage next to the northern ("sea") gate was once the home of the eighteenth-century Portuguese poet Bocage, while atop the bastion facing the southern ("land") gate is the cell where prisoners condemned to death in Portuguese times spent their final days. The wooden **gallows** on which they were hanged still stands beside it. Nearby are entrances to a couple of **tunnels**, the larger one, its destination unknown and possibly dangerously low in oxygen if you go in too far, is blocked by debris, while the smaller leads from the top to the bottom of the bastion. If you enter, take a light and beware of snakes, which hide in crevices in the walls, and may spring out if disturbed. At the western edge of the fort, a ruined **Dominican monastery** still has stellar carvings above what used to be the main altar. By the old **lighthouse** to its north, there are good views across the river.

Beaches

If you crave a beach, but are turned off by Nani Daman's drab sands, there are a couple of more appealing spots outside town. **Devka** (or Dwarka beach), backed by coconut plantations and a string of large resort hotels, can be reached in fifteen minutes by rickshaw, or by bus from the stop on the main road near the market. At the far southern end of the territory, also fifteen minutes' rickshaw ride from Nani Daman, **Jampore** is cleaner and less frequented, but no good for swimming as the tide recedes too far.

Accommodation

Most of Daman's **hotels** are in and around the grid of streets between the market and the beach. Aim for a first floor, west-facing room if you can, as these catch the best of the welcome sea breezes that blow in during the evenings.

Diamond, near the taxi stand (☎34235). Neat rooms in solid, respectable hotel. Some a/c. ④.

Gurukripa, Seaface Rd (☎35046; fax 34433). The poshest place to stay in town: spacious en-suite rooms, all with *Star TV*, and a roof garden, bar, and quality restaurant. Good value. ⑤.

Marina, Estrada 2 Fevereiro (☎34420). Simple rooms with period furniture in stylish, tatty colonial house. A bargain if you don't mind peeling plaster, dodgy plumbing and old beds. ③.

Sovereign, Seaface Rd (☎35023; fax 34433). Large, well-maintained hotel near the beach. Economy rooms have attached shower-toilets, fans and balconies, and are Daman's best budget deal. ③–⑤.

Swet Many, Seaface Rd (☎35069). Newly decorated and very spruce, with large, clean, and comfortable en-suite rooms: the ones on the top floor are best. ②.

Eating and drinking

The disproportionately large number of **places to eat** is due to the town's liquor laws, which oblige all bars to serve food with alcohol. Most of the "bar-restaurants" along Seaface Rd are restaurants in name only, and best avoided. **Seafood**, on offer all year (except during the monsoons), is especially good from late September to early November, when the fish market is glutted with fresh crabs, prawns and lobsters. Also seasonal is *papri*, a street snack consisting of beans baked in a pot with potatoes, sold with a special *masala* between January and April.

Though Daman is more than just a drinking centre, the abundance of cheap cold **beer** does add to the attraction of the place. **Tari** (palm wine), traditionally sold in earthenware pots, is best bought where you see the pots tied to trees to collect it; the Marwad area on the way to Devka is known for it, but that sold by the beach in town is likely to be watered down.

Fisherman, Seaface Rd. A bar with a large terrace out back, serving up reasonably priced tandoori pomfret and lobster, as well as Goan and Damanese specialities. Open 11am–3pm & 6–11pm.

Gurukripa, Seaface Rd. The place for a slap-up meal: veg and non-veg *tandoori*, seafood, pomfret stuffed with prawns, fish curries, plus Chinese dishes and Goan *fenni* nips. Open 7am–11pm.

Samrat, Seaface Rd. Spotless roadside restaurant that specializes in inexpensive, eat-till-you-burst Gujarati *thalis* that come with *namkeens*, a couple of different *dals*, and mouthwateringly mild veg dishes. Strictly "pure-veg" (read "no alcohol"), and excellent value. Open 11am–4pm & 7–11pm.

Sovereign, Seaface Rd. South Indian snacks, side dishes, and beers served indoors or *al fresco* on a breezy balcony. Breakfast and snacks 6.30–10.30am & 4–7pm, lunch 11am–3pm, dinner 6–10pm.

CHAPTER NINE

BOMBAY

Y oung, brash and oozing with the cocksure self-confidence of a maverick money-maker, **BOMBAY**, or **Mumbai** as it's now officially known, revels in its reputation as India's most dynamic and westernized city. Behind the hype, however, intractable problems threaten the Maharashtran capital; foremost among them, a chronic shortage of **space**. Crammed onto a narrow spit of land that curls from the swamp-ridden coast into the Arabian Sea, Bombay has, in less than five hundred years since its "discovery" by the Portuguese, metamorphosed from an aboriginal fishing settlement into a sprawling megalopolis of thirteen million people. Whether you are being swept along broad boulevards by endless streams of commuters, or jostled by coolies and hand-cart pullers in the teeming bazaars, Bombay always feels like it is about to burst at the seams.

The roots of the population problem lie, paradoxically, in the city's enduring ability to create **wealth**. Bombay alone generates 35 percent of India's GNP, its port handles half the country's foreign trade, and its **movie industry** is the biggest in the world. Symbols of prosperity are everywhere: from the phalanx of office blocks clustered on Nariman Point, Maharashtra's Manhattan, to the yuppie couples nipping around town in their shiny new *Maruti* hatchbacks. The flip side to the success story, of course, is the city's much chronicled **poverty**. Each day, hundreds of economic refugees pour into Bombay from the Maharashtran hinterland. Some find jobs and secure accommo-dation; many more (around a third of the total population) end up living on the already overcrowded streets, or amid the appalling squalor of Asia's largest slums, reduced to rag-picking and begging from cars at traffic lights.

However, while it would definitely be misleading to downplay its difficulties, Bombay is far from the ordeal some travellers make it out to be. Once you've overcome the major hurdle of finding somewhere to stay, you may even begin to enjoy its frenzied pace and crowded, cosmopolitan feel.

BOMBAY: CONTENTS

For a map of BOMBAY, see colour insert no.4 in the centre of this book

THE DONS AND THE BOMBS

For many years, despite intense competition for jobs and living space among its diverse ethnic and social groups, Bombay boasted of being one of India's most stable cities. While Delhi and Calcutta reeled under communal riots and terrorist attacks in the early 1980s, the great Maharashtran melting-pot remained outwardly calm. However, as early as 1982, Bombay's infra-structure was starting to buckle under the tensions of over-population. A bitter and protracted **textile strike**, or *bandh*, had impoverished tens of thousands of industrial workers. Unemployment and crime were spiralling, and the influx of immigrants into the city showed no signs of abating. Among the few beneficiaries of mounting discontent was the extreme right-wing Maharashtran party, the **Shiv Sena**. Founded in 1966 by Bal "the Saheb" Thackery, a self-confessed admirer of Hitler, the Sena's uncompromising stand on immigration and employment (jobs for "Sons of the Soil" first), found favour with the disenchanted mass of lower-middle-class Hindus in the poorer suburbs. The party's venom, at first focussed on the city's sizeable south Indian community, soon shifted to its 15-percent Muslim minority. Communal antagonism flared briefly in 1984, when ninety people died in riots, and again in 1985 when the Shiv Sena routed the Congress party in municipal elections, thereby sweeping into the mainstream.

The rise of the right coincided with an intensification of **organized crime**. Previously, the city's gangsters had confined their activities to small-scale racketeering in poor neighbourhoods. After the post-1970s real estate boom, however, many petty "landsharks" became powerful godfather figures, or **"dons"**, with multi-*crore* drug- and gold-smuggling businesses. Moreover, the corrupt politicians who had employed the gangs' muscle-power to rig elections, were now highly placed political puppets with debts to pay – a phenomenon dubbed as **"criminalization"**. The dividing line between the underworld and politics grew increasingly blurred as the decade progressed: in 1992, no less than forty candidates in the municipal elections had criminal records. Meanwhile, Shiv Sena had consolidated its support by striking up an alliance with the up-and-coming, and equally extreme-right Hindu party, the BJP.

Even to those who had been charting the communal situation, the events that followed the destruction by Hindu extremists of the **Babri Masjid** mosque in Ayodhya (see p.309) came as a shock. Between December 1992 and late January 1993 came two waves of **rioting**, affecting not only the Muslim ghettos and poor industrial suburbs, but, for the first time, much of downtown too. Around 150,000 citizens fled for the countryside, while 100,000 more moved into refugee camps. According to (conservative) official statistics, 784 people died, and around 5000 were injured – 70 percent of them Muslim. Although a great deal of blame for the madness must accrue to right-wing Hindu political groups such as Shiv Sena, some commentators believe other factions stood to gain from the situation, notably slum landlords whose tenants are protected under rent freezes imposed by the Bombay Rent Act. The thousands of slum dwellers who fled Bombay and their burning homes following the riots conveniently cleared the way, it is suggested, for property development.

Just as Bombay was regaining its composure, disaster struck again. Around mid-afternoon on March 12, 1993, ten massive **bomb blasts** ripped through the heart of the city, killing 317 people and gutting the Stock Exchange, the *Air India* building, the passport office and three swanky hotels near the airports. No one claimed responsibility, but the involvement of "foreign hands" (ie Pakistan) was suspected. Investigators claimed the bombs had been smuggled into India and planted by Muslim mobsters. The name of India's most wanted criminal, the *don* Dawood Ibrahim (presently exiled in Dubai), was bandied about in the press, although as yet neither he nor anyone else has been charged.

The city recovered from the explosions with astonishing speed. Most banks and offices reopened the next day, and slowly the paranoia, or "fear psychosis", subsided. It would, however, take more than the hoardings erected beside the motorways ("Bombay Bounces Back!", "It's My Bombay", "Bombay, I Love You") to fully restore the pride and ebullience with which India's most confident city had formerly gone about its business.

Conventional **sights** are thin on the ground. After a visit to the most famous colonial monument, the **Gateway of India**, and a look at the antiquities in the **Prince of Wales Museum**, the most rewarding way to spend time is simply to wander the city's atmospheric streets. **Downtown**, beneath the rows of exuberant **Victorian-Gothic** buildings, the pavements are full of noisy vendors and office-*wallahs* hurrying through clouds of wood-smoke from the *gram*-sellers' braziers. In the eye of the storm, encircled by the roaring traffic of beaten-up red double-decker buses, lie other vestiges of the Raj, the **maidans**. Depending on the time of day, these central parks are peppered with cricketers in white flannels, or the bare bums of squatting pavement-dwellers relieving themselves on the parched brown grass. North of the city centre, the broad thoroughfares splinter into a maze of chaotic streets. The **central bazaar** districts afford glimpses of the sprawling Muslim neighbourhoods, as well as exotic **shopping** possibilities, while Bombay is at its most exuberant along **Chowpatty Beach**, which laps against exclusive **Malabar Hill**. When you've had enough of the mayhem, the beautiful rock-cut Shiva temple on **Elephanta Island** – a short trip by launch across the harbour from the promenade, **Apollo Bunder** – offers a welcome half-day escape.

If you're heading for Goa or south India, you'll probably have to pass through Bombay at some stage. Its international airport, **Sahar**, is the busiest in the country; the **airline offices** downtown are handy for confirming onward flights, and all the region's principal air, road and rail networks originate here. Whether or not you choose to stay for more time than it takes to jump on a train or plane to somewhere else depends on how well you handle the burning sun, humid atmosphere and perma-fog of petrol fumes; and how seriously you want to get to grips with India of the late 1990s.

History

Bombay originally consisted of seven **islands**, inhabited by small Koli fishing communities. At different times, various dynasties held this insignificant outlying district; the city of Puri on **Elephanta** is thought to have been the major settlement in the region, until King Bimba, or Bhima, built the town of Mahim on one island, at the end of the thirteenth century. Hindus controlled the area until it was captured in the fourteenth century by the Muslim Gujarat Sultanate. In 1534 Sultan Bahadur of Ahmedabad ceded Bombay to the **Portuguese**, who felt the land to be of little importance, and concentrated development in the areas around Mahim and Bassein. They handed over the largest island to the English in 1661, as part of the dowry when the Portuguese Infanta Catherine of Braganza married Charles II; four years later Charles received the remaining islands and the port. This was the first part of India that could properly be termed a colony; elsewhere on the subcontinent the English had merely been granted the right to set up "factories", or trading posts. Because of its natural safe harbour and strategic position for trade, the **East India Company**, based at Surat, wanted to buy the land; in 1668 a deal was struck, and Charles leased Bombay to them for a pittance.

The English set about an ambitious programme of fortifying their outpost, living in the area known today as Fort. However, life was not easy. There was a fast turnover of governors, and malaria and cholera culled many of the first settlers. A chaplain of the East India Company, Revd Ovington, wrote at the end of the seventeenth century: "One of the pleasantest spots in India seemed no more than a parish graveyard, a charnel house . . . Which common fatality has created a Proverb among the English there, that two monsoons are the age of a man". **Gerald Aungier**, the fourth governor (1672–77), set out to plan "the city which by God's assistance is intended to be built", and by the start of the eighteenth century the town was the capital of the East India Company. The "father of Bombay" is credited with encouraging the mix that still contributes to the city's success, welcoming Hindu traders from Gujarat, Goans (escaping Jesuit persecution), Muslim weavers, and most visibly, the business-minded Zoroastrian **Parsis**.

Much of the British settlement in the old Fort area was destroyed by a devastating fire in 1803, and the European population remained comparatively low well into the 1800s. The arrival of the **Great Indian Peninsular Railway** in the 1850s improved communications, encouraging yet more immigration from elsewhere in India. In 1862 the first of many land-reclamation projects (still on-going) fused the seven islands; just a year later the rail link between Bombay and the cotton-growing areas of the Deccan plateau opened. **Sir Bartle Frere**, governor from 1862 to 1867, oversaw the construction of the city's distinctive colonial-Gothic buildings; the most extravagant of all, Victoria Terminus railway station, known simply as **VT**, is a fitting testimony to this extraordinary age of expansion. After the American Civil War, India replaced America as supplier of **cotton** to England, exporting the bulk of it via Bombay, and with the opening of the Suez Canal in 1869, and the construction of enormous docks, Bombay's access to European markets improved further.

Not all Bombay's grandest architecture is owed to the Raj; wealthy Jains and Parsis have also left their mark throughout the downtown area. As the most prosperous city in the nation, Bombay was at the forefront of the Independence struggle; Mahatma Gandhi used a house here, now a museum, to co-ordinate the struggle through three decades. Fittingly, the first British colony took pleasure in waving the final goodbye to the Raj, when the last contingent of British troops passed through the Gateway of India in February 1948. Despite its recent communal tensions, and growing crime-related violence, Bombay approaches the twenty-first century as the financial and commercial centre of India, with a cost of living almost equal to that in the US, and, in Malabar Hill in particular, some of the most expensive property in the world.

Arrival

Unless you arrive in Bombay by train at VT, be prepared for a long slog into the centre. The international and domestic airports are north of the city, way off the map (see colour insert), and 90min or more by road from the main hotel areas, while from Bombay Central railway or bus station, you face a laborious trip across town. **Finding a place to stay** can be even more of a hassle; phone around before you set off into the traffic.

By air

For many visitors, **Sahar**, Bombay's busy **international airport**, provides their first experience of India. The complex is divided into two "modules": one for *Air India* flights and the other for foreign airlines. Once through customs and the lengthy immigration formalities, you'll find a 24-hour *State Bank of India* exchange facility, government and state (MTDC) tourist information counters, car rental kiosks, cafes and a pre-paid taxi stand in the chaotic arrivals concourse. If you're on one of the few flights to land in the afternoon or early evening – by which time most hotels tend to be full – it's worth paying on the spot for a room at the **accommodation booking desk** in the arrivals hall. All of the domestic airlines also have offices outside the main entrance, and there's a handy 24-hour **left luggage** "cloakroom" in the car park nearby (Rs5–15 per day, depending on the size of your bag; maximum duration 90 days).

The "ex-servicemen's" *EAT* **bus** from Sahar (12 daily; 2.30am–10.30pm) is a cheap and convenient way to travel the 26km into the city, although departures tend to be frustratingly infrequent during the small hours. Heading down the west side of the peninsula, it passes Haji Ali's tomb, Chowpatty beach, and the *Air India* building at Nariman Point (the main drop) en route to the Gateway of India in Colaba. Tickets, bought on the bus, cost around Rs45. Many of the more upmarket hotels, particularly those near the airport, send out **courtesy coaches** to pick up their guests.

Taxis are more comfortable and not too extravagant. To avoid haggling over the fare, pay in advance at the taxi desk in the arrivals hall. The price on the receipt, which you hand to the driver on arrival at your destination, is slightly more than the normal meter rate, (around Rs200 to Colaba, or Rs100 to Juhu) but at least you can be sure you'll be

VICTORIA TERMINUS

Inspired by St Pancras station in London, F W Stevens designed **Victoria Terminus**, the most barmy of Bombay buildings, as a paean to "progress". **VT**, as it is known, is huge, built in 1887 as the largest British edifice in India; its extraordinary amalgam of domes, spires, Corinthian columns and minarets was succinctly defined by the journalist James Cameron as "Victorian-Gothic-Saracenic-Italianate-Oriental-St Pancras-Baroque".

Few of the two million or so passengers who fill almost a thousand trains every day notice VT's mass of decorative detail. A "British" lion and Indian tiger stand guard at the entrance, and the exterior is festooned with sculptures executed at the Bombay Art School by the Indian students of John Lockwood Kipling, Rudyard's father. Among them are grotesque mythical beasts, monkeys and plants and medallions of important personages. To minimize the sun's impact stained glass was employed, some designed with locomotives and elephant images. Above it all, "Progress" stands atop the massive central dome.

An endless frenzy of activity goes on inside, scuttling with passengers, hundreds of porters in red with impossibly oversize headloads, TTEs (Travelling Ticket Examiners) in black jackets and white trousers clasping clipboards detailing reservations, *chai-wallahs* with trays of tea, trundling magazine stands, crowds of bored soldiers smoking *bidis*, and the inexorable progress across the station of sweepers bent double. Amid it all, whole families spread out on the floor, eating, sleeping or just waiting and waiting.

taken by the most direct route. Taxi *wallahs* invariably try to persuade you to stay at a different hotel from the one you ask for. Don't agree; their commission will be added on to the price of your room.

Internal flights land at Bombay's more user-friendly **domestic airport, Santa Cruz**, which is divided into separate, modern terminals: the cream-coloured one (Module 1A) for *Indian Airlines*, and the blue-and-white (Module 1B) for private carriers. If you're transferring directly from here to an international flight at Sahar, 3km northeast, either take the *EAT* bus (Rs20), or the free "fly-bus" that shuttles every fifteen minutes between the two. The Indian government and MTDC both have 24-hour information counters in the arrivals hall, and there's a foreign exchange counter tucked away near the first-floor exit. Once again, the hourly *EAT* bus, which calls at Santa Cruz after leaving Sahar, is the cheapest way to get to the centre.

Don't be tempted to use the **auto-rickshaws** that buzz around outside the airports; they're not allowed downtown and will leave you at the mercy of unscrupulous taxi drivers on the edge of Mahim Creek, the southernmost limit of their permitted area.

By train

Trains to Bombay from most central, southern and eastern regions arrive at **Victoria Terminus** (aka "VT"), the main railway station at the end of the *Central Railway* line. From here it's a ten- or fifteen-minute ride to Colaba; either pick up a taxi at the busy rank outside the south exit, opposite the new reservation hall, or make your way to the main road and catch one of the innumerable buses.

Bombay Central, the terminus for *Western Railway* trains from northern India, is further out from the centre; take a taxi from the main forecourt, or cross the hectic road junction next to the station and catch a *BEST* bus from the top of Dr DN Marg (Lamington Rd); #66 and #71 run to VT, #70 to Colaba Causeway. Equally cheap, take a

ONWARD TRANSPORT

For **onward transport** from Bombay, including routes to **Goa**, see p.655 onwards.

suburban train from Bombay Central's local platform, across the footbridge. Four stops on is **Churchgate** station, the end of the line, a short taxi ride from Colaba (Rs15).

Some trains from south India arrive at more obscure stations. If you find yourself at **Dadar**, way up in the industrial suburbs, and can't afford a taxi, cross the Tilak Marg road bridge onto the *Western Railway* and catch a suburban train into town, or take *BEST* bus #70 to Colaba. **Kurla** station, where a few Bangalore trains pull in, is even further out, just south of Santa Cruz airport. The only alternative to a cab from here is to catch bus #91 to Bombay Central Station and change there to #70 for Colaba or a suburban train for Churchgate. Trying anything so complicated during a rush hour, however – especially if you're carrying heavy luggage – is more trouble than it's worth.

By bus

Nearly all inter-state **buses** arrive at **Bombay Central** bus stand, a stone's throw from the railway station of the same name. Again, you have a choice between municipal black and yellow taxis, the *BEST* buses (#66, #70 & #71), which run straight into town from the stop on Dr DN Marg (Lamington Rd), two minutes' walk west from the bus station, or a suburban train from Bombay Central's local platform over the footbridge.

Most Maharashtran state buses terminate at the **ASIAD** bus stand, a glorified parking lot beside the main street in **Dadar**. Taxis are on hand for the thirty- to sixty-minute trip down to Colaba, or you can make your way over Tilak Marg road bridge to Dadar railway station and pick up a local train to Churchgate.

Buses from Goa drop off at various points between central and downtown Bombay. Most of the private companies currently work from the roadside in front of the *Metro Cinema*, at the north end of MG Rd, while *Kadamba* (the Goan state transport corporation) buses stop nearby on the opposite (east) side of Azad Maidan, where they have a small ticket kiosk. Both places are an inexpensive taxi ride from the main hotel district.

Information and communications

The best source of **information** in Bombay is the excellent **India Government Tourist Office** (Mon–Fri 8.30am–6pm, Sat 8.30am–2pm; ☎203 3144) at 123 M Karve Rd, opposite Churchgate station's east exit. The staff here are exceptionally helpful and hand out a wide range of leaflets, maps and brochures both on Bombay and the rest of the country. There are also 24-hour tourist **information counters** at Sahar (☎832 5331) and Santa Cruz (☎614 9200) airports.

Maharashtra State Tourism Development Corporation's (**MTDC**) main office, on Madam Cama Rd (☎202 6731), opposite the LIC Building in Nariman Point, sells tickets for city sightseeing tours, and long-distance "luxury" buses (see p.658), and can reserve rooms in MTDC hotels. They too have information counters at Sahar and Santa Cruz, as well as at VT railway station and on CS Marg, near the Gateway of India.

Local publications

If you need detailed information about **what's on** in Bombay, ask at the government tourist office for a fortnightly listings pamphlet, or check out the "Entertainments" page in the *Indian Express*, whose city edition, and that of the *Times of India*, is available from street vendors around Colaba and the downtown area.

PHONE CODE AND NUMBER CHANGES

The telephone **area code** for Bombay is ☎022. Numbers in the city change constantly, so if you can't get through after several attempts, try **directory enquiries** on ☎197.

USEFUL BOMBAY BUS ROUTES

#1/3/6(Ltd)/11(Ltd)/16(Ltd)/ 19(Ltd)/103/124 Colaba bus station to Mahatma Phule (Crawford) Market, via VT (Nagar Chowk).

#43 Colaba bus station to GPO.

#70 Colaba to Dadar Station (W), via Bombay Central.

#103/106/107 Colaba to Kamala Nehru Park, via Chowpatty Beach.

#124 Colaba to Vatsalabai Desai Chowk, via Bombay Central.

#132 Colaba to Breach Candy, via Vatsalabai Desai Chowk.

#81 Churchgate to Santa Cruz, via Vatsalabai Desai Chowk (for Haji Ali's tomb and Mahalakshmi temple).

#66/71 Bombay Central to VT.

#91 Bombay Central to Kurla station.

For a detailed **map** of Bombay, look for *Karmarkar Enterprise*'s "*Most Exhaustive A–Z*" street plan (Rs60). It's fiendishly hard to find in bookstores (*Crossword* on Bhulabai Desai Rd usually have one or two in stock), but the pavement guidebook- and magazine-*wallahs* along VN Rd, between Churchgate and Flora Fountain, may have copies.

Banks

The logical place to change money when you arrive in Bombay is at the *State Bank of India*'s 24-hour counter in Sahar airport. Rates here are standard but you'll have to pay for an encashment certificate – essential if you intend to buy tourist quota railway tickets or an *Indrail* pass at the special counters in Churchgate or VT stations.

All the major **banks** downtown change foreign currency (Mon–Fri 10.30am–2.30pm, Sat 10.30am–12.30pm); some also handle **credit cards**. The *Andhra Bank* (☎204 4535), 18 Homi Modi St, near Flora Fountain, takes *Visa*, and the *Bank of America* (☎287 4959), in the Express Towers building, Nariman Point, deals with *Mastercard*. The fast and efficient *American Express* office (daily 9.30am–7.30pm; ☎204 8278), on Shivaji Marg, around the corner from the *Regal* cinema in Colaba, offers all the regular services (including poste restante) to travellers' cheque and card holders and is open to anyone wishing to change cash; they also have an office at 364 Dr DN Marg, near Flora Fountain. *Thomas Cook*'s big Dr DN Marg branch (Mon–Fri 9.30am–6.30pm, Sat 9.30am–4.30pm; ☎204 8556), between the *Khadi* shop and Flora Fountain, can also arrange money transfers from overseas, and is a good place to change money and cash travellers' cheques.

Mail and telecommunications

The **GPO** (Mon–Sat 9am–8pm, Sun 9am–4pm) is around the corner from VT Station, off Nagar Chowk. Its **poste restante** counter (Mon–Sat 9am–6pm, Sun 9am–3pm) is among the most reliable in India, although they trash the letters after four weeks. The much less efficient parcel office (10am–4.30pm) is behind the main building on the first floor. Packing-*wallahs* hang around on the pavement outside.

STD booths abound in Bombay. For rock-bottom **phone** and **fax** rates however, head for Videsh Sanchar Bhavan (open 24 hours), the swanky new government telecom building on MG Marg, where you can make **reversed charge calls** to destinations such as the UK, US and Australia. Receiving incoming calls costs a nominal Rs5.

City transport

Only a masochist would travel on Bombay's hopelessly overtaxed public **transport** for fun. For much of the day, traffic on the main roads crawls along at little more than walking speed, or grinds to a halt in endless jams at road junctions. On the plus side, it might take forever to ride across town on a dusty red double-decker **bus**, but it will never set you back more than a few rupees. Local **trains** get there faster, but are a real endurance test even outside rush hours. **Rickshaws** do not run downtown.

Buses

BEST (*Bombay Electric Supply and Transport*) operates a **bus** network of labyrinthine complexity, extending to the furthest-flung corners of the city. Unfortunately, neither the route booklets, maps nor *"Point to Point"* guides (which you can consult at the tourist office or at newsstands) make things any clearer. Finding out which bus you need is difficult enough. Recognizing it in the street can be even more problematic, as the numbers are written in Maharathi (although in English on the sides). Aim, wherever possible, for the "Limited" services, which stop less frequently, and avoid rush hours at all costs. Tickets should be bought from the conductor on the bus.

Trains

Bombay would be paralysed without its local **trains**, which carry millions of commuters each day between downtown and the sprawling suburbs in the north. One line begins at VT, running up the east side of the city as far as Thane. The other leaves Churchgate, hugging the curve of Back Bay as far as Chowpatty Beach, where it veers north towards Bombay Central, Dadar, Santa Cruz and Vasai, beyond the city limits. Services depart every few minutes from 5am until midnight, stopping at dozens of small stations. Carriages remain packed solid virtually the whole time, with passengers dangling precariously out of open doors to escape the crush, so start to make your way to the exit at least three stops before your destination. The apocalyptic peak hours are worst of all. Women are marginally better off in the "ladies carriages"; look for the crowd of *saris* and *salwar kamises* grouped at the end of the platform.

Taxis

With rickshaws banished to the suburbs, Bombay's ubiquitous black-and-yellow **taxis** are the quickest and most convenient way to nip around the city centre. In theory, all should have meters and a current rate card (to convert the amount shown on the meter to the correct fare); in practice, particularly at night or early in the morning, many drivers refuse to use them. If this happens, either flag down another or haggle out a fare. As a rule of thumb, expect to be charged Rs5 per kilometre after the minimum fare of around Rs10, together with a small sum for heavy luggage (officially Rs1 per article).

Boats

Ferry-boats regularly chug out of Bombay harbour, connecting the city with the far shore and some of the larger islands in between. The most popular with visitors is the **Elephanta Island** launch (see p.638) which departs hourly (9am–12.15am; Rs40) from the Gateway of India. Boats to **Rewas**, the jetty across the bay which is the transport hub for Chaul, Murud-Janjira and the rarely used coastal route south, leave from Ferry Wharf, 4.5km north of Colaba up P D'Mello (Frere) Rd.

Tours

Of MTDC's sightseeing **tours** around Bombay, the "City" tour (Tues–Sun 9am–1pm & 2–6pm; Rs60) is the most popular, managing to cram Colaba, Marine Drive, Jehangir Art Gallery, the Hanging Gardens, Kamla Nehru Park and Mani Bhavan into half a day; the "Suburban" tour (Tues–Sun 9.15am–6.15pm; Rs90) takes in Kanheri caves, Krishnagiri Upavan National Park, a lion safari and Juhu in a full day. Every Monday, "City-Suburban" tour combines the highlights of both, but wastes a lot of time in

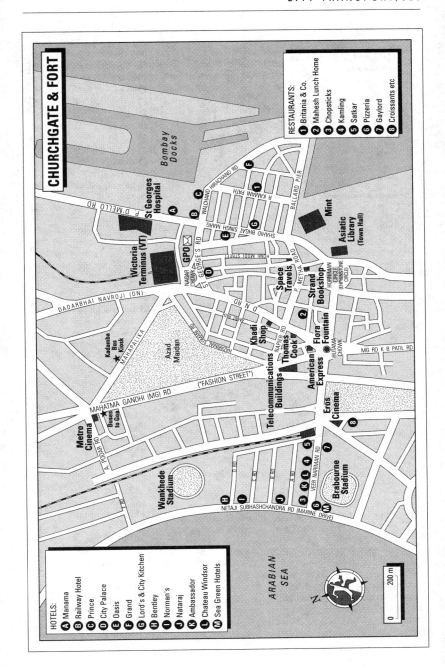

CHURCHGATE & FORT

RESTAURANTS:
❶ Britania & Co.
❷ Mahesh Lunch Home
❸ Chopsticks
❹ Kamling
❺ Satkar
❻ Pizzeria
❼ Gaylord
❽ Croissants etc

HOTELS:
Ⓐ Manama
Ⓑ Railway Hotel
Ⓒ Prince
Ⓓ City Palace
Ⓔ Oasis
Ⓕ Grand
Ⓖ Lord's & City Kitchen
Ⓗ Bentley
Ⓘ Norman's
Ⓙ Nataraj
Ⓚ Ambassador
Ⓛ Chateau Windsor
Ⓜ Sea Green Hotels

Bombay Docks

St Georges Hospital

Victoria Terminus (VT)

GPO

P. D'MELLO RD

WALCHAND HIRACHAND RD

R KAMANI PATH

BALLARD PIER

SHAHID BHGAT SINGH MARG

Mint

Asiatic Library (Town Hall)

NAGAR CHOWK

ST GEORGE'S RD

OMI MODI STREET

HORNIMAN CIRCLE (ELPHINSTONE CIRCLE)

Space Travels

Strand Bookshop

P. METHA RD

DADARBHAI NAVROJI (DN)

Kadamba Bus Kiosk

MAHAPALIKA

Azad Maidan

D N RD

Khadi Shop

Thomas Cook

Flora Fountain

HUTAMA CHOWK

MG RD   K B PATIL RD

("FASHION STREET")

American Express

Eros Cinema

Telecommunications Buildings

MAHATMA GANDHI (MG) RD

Metro Cinema

Buses to Goa

A PODAR RD

VEER NARIMAN RD

NAPIER RD

Wankhede Stadium

Brabourne Stadium

NETAJI SUBHASHCHANDRA RD (MARINE DRIVE)

ARABIAN SEA

0   200 m

N

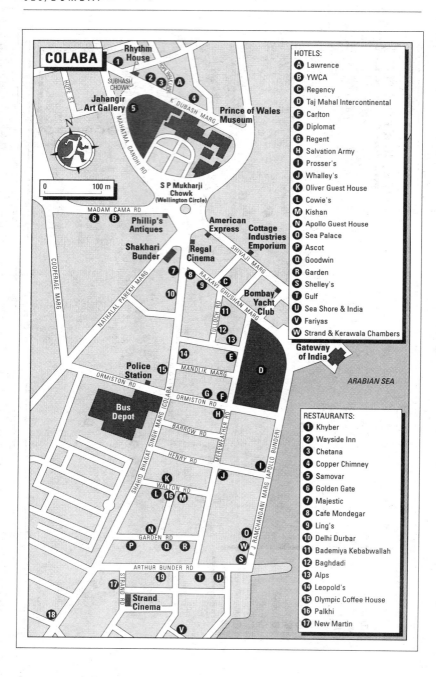

COLABA

Rhythm House

SUBHASH CHOWK

Jahangir Art Gallery

Prince of Wales Museum

S P Mukharji Chowk (Wellington Circle)

MADAM CAMA RD

Phillip's Antiques

Shakhari Bunder

Regal Cinema

American Express

Cottage Industries Emporium

Bombay Yacht Club

Police Station

Bus Depot

MANDLIK MARG

ORMISTON RD

Gateway of India

ARABIAN SEA

BARROW RD

HENRY RD

WALTON RD

GARDEN RD

ARTHUR BUNDER RD

Strand Cinema

HOPE ST

BOX WALLANE

K DUBASH MARG

MAHATMA GANDHI RD

COOPERAGE MARG

NATHALAL PAREKH MARG

RAJKAVI GHUSHAN MARG

SHIVAJI MARG

TULLOCH RD

COLABA

SHAHID BHAGAT SINGH MARG (COLABA)

MEREWEATHER RD

P J RAMCHANDANI MARG (APOLLO BUNDER)

STRAND RD

0   100 m

HOTELS:
- A Lawrence
- B YWCA
- C Regency
- D Taj Mahal Intercontinental
- E Carlton
- F Diplomat
- G Regent
- H Salvation Army
- I Prosser's
- J Whalley's
- K Oliver Guest House
- L Cowie's
- M Kishan
- N Apollo Guest House
- O Sea Palace
- P Ascot
- Q Goodwin
- R Garden
- S Shelley's
- T Gulf
- U Sea Shore & India
- V Fariyas
- W Strand & Kerawala Chambers

RESTAURANTS:
1. Khyber
2. Wayside Inn
3. Chetana
4. Copper Chimney
5. Samovar
6. Golden Gate
7. Majestic
8. Cafe Mondegar
9. Ling's
10. Delhi Durbar
11. Bademiya Kebabwallah
12. Baghdadi
13. Alps
14. Leopold's
15. Olympic Coffee House
16. Palkhi
17. New Martin

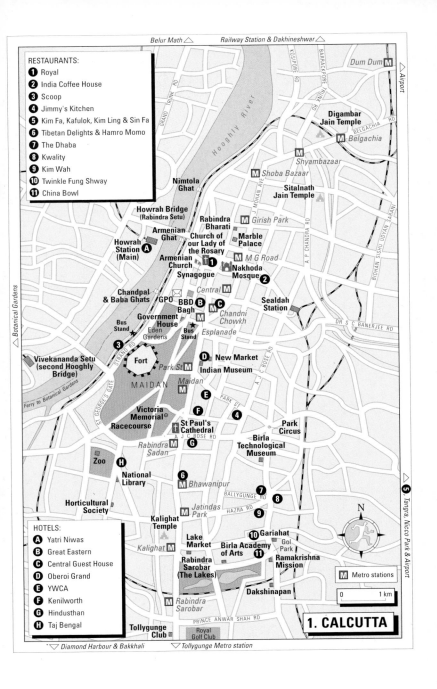

RESTAURANTS:
1. Royal
2. India Coffee House
3. Scoop
4. Jimmy's Kitchen
5. Kim Fa, Kafulok, Kim Ling & Sin Fa
6. Tibetan Delights & Hamro Momo
7. The Dhaba
8. Kwality
9. Kim Wah
10. Twinkle Fung Shway
11. China Bowl

HOTELS:
A. Yatri Niwas
B. Great Eastern
C. Central Guest House
D. Oberoi Grand
E. YWCA
F. Kenilworth
G. Hindusthan
H. Taj Bengal

M Metro stations

0   1 km

1. CALCUTTA

Belur Math △   Railway Station & Dakhineshwar △

Dum Dum M

△ Airport

KOSIPORE RD

BARRACKPORE TRUNK RD

Digambar
Jain Temple

M Belgachia

BELGACHIA RD

Hooghly River

GRAND TRUNK RD

Shyambazaar M

BIDHAN SISHU UDYAN SARANI

M Shoba Bazaar

Nimtola
Ghat

J MOHAN AVE

Sitalnath
Jain Temple

A P CHANDRA RD

Howrah Bridge
(Rabindra Setu)

Rabindra
Bharati

M Girish Park

Armenian
Ghat

Church of
our Lady of
the Rosary

Marble
Palace

Howrah
Station
(Main) A

Armenian
Church

1

M M G Road

Synagogue

Nakhoda
Mosque

2

Chandpal
& Baba Ghats

Central M

GPO

BBD B
Bagh M C

Sealdah
Station

DR S C BANERJEE RD

Government
House

M

Chandni
Chowkh

Bus
Stand

Eden
Gardens

Bus
Stand ★

Esplanade

Botanical Gardens

Vivekananda Setu
(second Hooghly
Bridge)

3

Fort

Park St M

D New Market

Indian Museum

A J C BOSE RD

STRAND RD

Ferry to Botanical Gardens

ST GEORGE'S GATE

MAIDAN

Maidan
M

PARK ST

Victoria
Memorial⊙
Racecourse

F
E

4

Park
Circus

St Paul's
Cathedral

Birla
Technological
Museum

Rabindra
Sadan M

A J C BOSE RD

G

Zoo

H

National
Library

6

M Bhawanipur

BALLYGUNGE RD

7

8

Horticultural
Society

Jatindas
Park M

HAZRA RD

9

Kalighat
Temple

Lake
Market

10 Gariahat

Gol
Park

Kalighat M

Birla Academy
of Arts

11

Ramakrishna
Mission

Rabindra
Sarobar
(The Lakes)

Dakshinapan

N

S Tangra, Nicco Park & Airport

M Rabindra
Sarobar

PRINCE ANWAR SHAH RD

Tollygunge
Club

Royal
Golf Club

·▽ Diamond Harbour & Bakkhali   ▽ Tollygunge Metro station

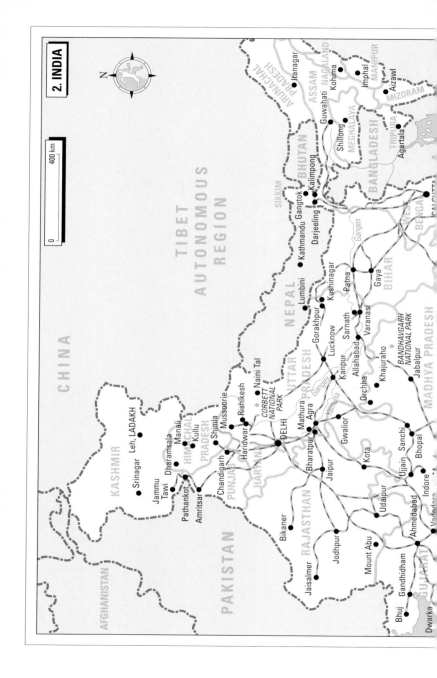

2. INDIA

0 _____ 400 km

CHINA

AFGHANISTAN

PAKISTAN

KASHMIR

Srinagar • Leh, LADAKH

Jammu •
Tawi
Pathankot • • Dharamsala • Manali
Amritsar • • Kullu HIMACHAL
• Chandigarh PRADESH
PUNJAB • Shimla
HARYANA • Mussoorie • Naini Tal
• Haridwar • Rishikesh
CORBETT
NATIONAL
PARK
DELHI • • Mathura
• Bharatpur • Agra

TIBET
AUTONOMOUS
REGION

Bikaner •
RAJASTHAN
Jaisalmer • • Jodhpur
• Jaipur
Mount Abu •
• Udaipur

Kota •

Gwalior •

Ganges
Yamuna

UTTAR
PRADESH
• Lucknow
Kanpur •
• Orchha
• Allahabad

NEPAL
• Lumbini
Kathmandu •
• Kushinagar
Gorakhpur •
• Sarnath
• Varanasi
Khajuraho •
BANDHAVGARH
NATIONAL PARK
• Jabalpur
MADHYA PRADESH

SIKKIM
Gangtok •
• Kalimpong
• Darjeeling
Ganges
Patna •
• Gaya
BIHAR

BHUTAN

ARUNACHAL
PRADESH
• Itanagar
ASSAM
• Guwahati
• Shillong
MEGHALAYA
BANGLADESH
TRIPURA
• Agartala

NAGALAND
• Kohima
• Imphal MANIPUR
MIZORAM
• Aizawl

CALCUTTA
WEST
BENGAL

Ujjain • • Sanchi
• Bhopal
Indore •
Vadodara •
Ahmedabad •
Gandhidham •
Bhuj •
GUJARAT
Dwarka

N

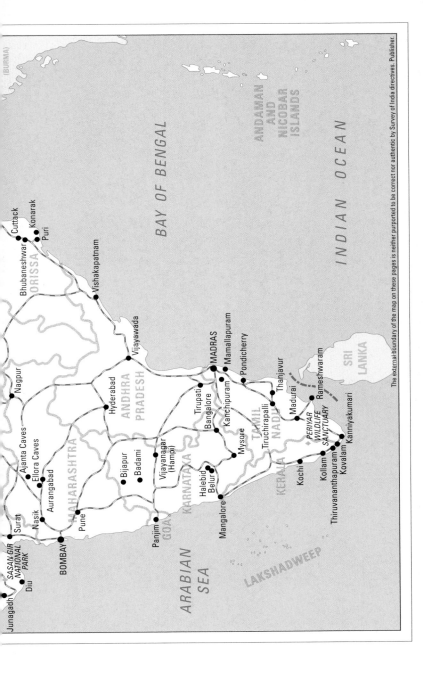

(BURMA)

BAY OF BENGAL

Cuttack
Konarak
Puri
Bhubaneshwar
ORISSA

Vishakapatnam

ANDAMAN
AND
NICOBAR
ISLANDS

INDIAN OCEAN

Nagpur

Vijayawada

Hyderabad
ANDHRA
PRADESH

MADRAS
Mamallapuram
Pondicherry

SRI
LANKA

Ajanta Caves
Ellora Caves
Aurangabad
MAHARASHTRA

Tirupati
Bangalore
Kanchipuram
TAMIL
NADU
Tiruchirapalli
Thanjavur
Rameshwaram
Madurai

Surat
Nasik
Bijapur
Badami
Vijayanagar
(Hampi)
KARNATAKA

Mysore
PERIYAR
WILDLIFE
SANCTUARY
Kanniyakumari

SASAN GIR
NATIONAL
PARK
Diu
BOMBAY
Pune
Panjim
GOA

Halebid
Belur

Mangalore
KERALA
Kochi
Kollam
Kovalam
Thiruvananthapuram

Junagadh

ARABIAN
SEA

LAKSHADWEEP

The external boundary of the map on these pages is neither purported to be correct nor authentic by Survey of India directives. Publisher.

3. DELHI

N

Yamuna River

Vijay Ghat
Shanti Vana
Raj Ghat
Firoz Shah Kotla
& Ashoka Pillar

Red Fort

GPO
Old Delhi

MAHATMA GANDHI RD

Interstate
Bus Station

GRAND TRUNK RD

MAHATMA GANDHI RD

SHAMNATH MARG

Ⓐ

Kashmiri
Gate

Old Delhi
Railway Station

Fatehpuri
Mosque

CHANDNI CHOWK

Gurudwara

Jami
Masjid

Ajmeri
Gate

Ⓑ

Delhi
Gate

Bengali
Market

★5

Pragati
Maidan

Foreigners'
Registration Office

VIRAS MARG

MATHURA RD

Ⓞ2

Zoo

Ⓟ

Ⓖ Humayun's

GRAND TRUNK RD

RANI JHANSI RD

RANI JHANSI RD

FAIZ RD

OUTUB RD

DESHBANDHU GUPTA RD

New Delhi
Railway Station

PAHARGANJ

Main
Bazaar

Connaught
Place

Jantar
Mantar

JANPATH

Napalese
Embassy

ASHOKA RD

India
Gate

Ⓜ

Ⓝ

Ⓞ3
Ⓞ4

Golf
Club

SANSAD MARG

Ⓓ Ⓔ Ⓕ

Ⓖ

Poste
Restante

GPO

RAJ PATH

Ⓞ1

Ⓛ

Lodi

MANDIR MARG

TALKATORA RD

Parliament

Rashtrapati
Bhavan

Secretariat

WILLINGDON CRES

Ⓞ6

Ⓞ5

KAUTILYA MARG

Ⓚ

SADHU VASWANI MARG

Buddha
Jayanti
Park

Mahavir
Jayanti
Park

Ⓙ

Ⓘ

Ⓗ

GURU GOBIND SINGH MARG

CAMP CINEMA RD

UPPER RIDGE RD

JODAPUR RD

ROHTAK RD

SHIVAJI MARG

NARAINA RD

2 km

0

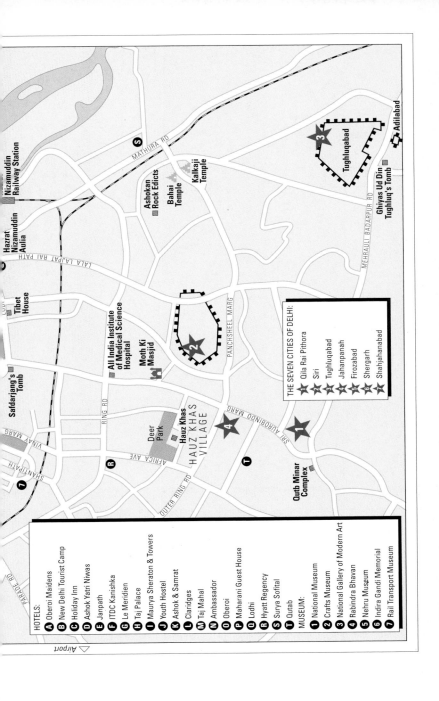

Airport ▽

PARADE RD

HOTELS:
Ⓐ Oberoi Maidens
Ⓑ New Delhi Tourist Camp
Ⓒ Holiday Inn
Ⓓ Ashok Yatri Niwas
Ⓔ Janpath
Ⓕ ITDC Kanishka
Ⓖ Le Meridien
Ⓗ Taj Palace
Ⓘ Maurya Sheraton & Towers
Ⓙ Youth Hostel
Ⓚ Ashok & Samrat
Ⓛ Claridges
Ⓜ Taj Mahal
Ⓝ Ambassador
Ⓞ Oberoi
Ⓟ Maharani Guest House
Ⓠ Lodhi
Ⓡ Hyatt Regency
Ⓢ Surya Sofital
Ⓣ Qutab

MUSEUM:
❶ National Museum
❷ Crafts Museum
❸ National Gallery of Modern Art
❹ Rabindra Bhavan
❺ Nehru Museum
❻ Indira Gandi Memorial
❼ Rail Transport Museum

VINAY MARG
SHANTIPATH

Safdarjang's Tomb

Tibet House

Hazrat Nizamuddin Aulia

Nizamuddin Railway Station
Ⓢ

MATHURA RD

LALA LAJPAT RAI PATH

LODI

All India Institute of Medical Science Hospital

Moth Ki Masjid

RING RD

AFRICA AVE

Deer Park

Hauz Khas

HAUZ KHAS VILLAGE

OUTER RING RD

PANCHSHEEL MARG

SRI AUROBINDO MARG

Qutab Minar Complex

Ⓣ

MEHRAULI BADARPUR RD

Ashokan Rock Edicts

Bahai Temple

Kalkaji Temple

Tughluqabad
★3

Ghiyas Ud Din Tughluq's Tomb

◇ Adilabad

THE SEVEN CITIES OF DELHI:
★ Qila Rai Pithora
★★ Siri
★★★ Tughluqabad
★★★★ Jahanpanah
★★★★★ Firozabad
★★★★★★ Shergarh
★★★★★★★ Shahjahanabad

★2

★4

★1

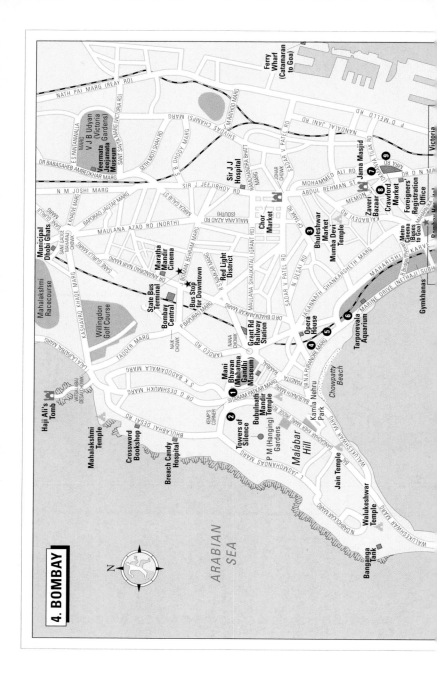

4. BOMBAY

N

ARABIAN SEA

Ferry Wharf (Catamaran to Goa)

NATH PAI MARG (REAY RD)

V J B Udyan (Victoria Gardens)
Jeermata Jeejamata Museum

ES PANTANWALLA MARG

SETH MOTI SHAH RD

S B DHODI MARG

SANT SAVTA MARG (VICTORIA RD)

SHIVDAS CHAMPSI MARG

M MATHOJI MARG

M MATHOJI MARG

NANDALAL JANI RD

P D'MELLO RD

DR BABASAHEB AMBEDKHAR MARG

Sir J J Hospital

RAMCHANDRA BHATT

JOHAR CHOWK

SADAR V PATEL RD

NANA TILAK RD

MAHA RD

Jama Masjid ⑦

N M JOSHI MARG

SIR J. JEEJIBHOY RD

MALAGAON (SOUTH)

MAULANA AZAD RD (SOUTH)

MOHAMMED ALI RD

ABDUL REHMAN ST

MEMON

DR D N MARG

Zaveri ⑧ Bazaar

Crawford Market

Foreigners' Registration Office

Municipal Dhobi Ghats

SANE GURUJI MARG

K KHADE MARG

BAPURAO JAGTAP MARG

MAULANA AZAD RD (NORTH)

Maratha Mandir Cinema

BOMAN BEHRAM MARG

R S NIMKAR MARG

Red Light District

Chor Market

MAULANA SHAUKATALI (GRANT RD)

GRANT RD

DR R BHADKAMKAR MARG

Bhuleshwar Market

Mumba Devi Temple ③

KALBADEVI RD

JAGANNATH SHANKARSHETH MARG

Metro Cinema (Buses to Goa)

MAHARSHI KARVE RD (QUEEN'S)

Victoria

Mahalakshmi Racecourse

KASHAVRAO KHADE MARG

Willingdon Golf Course

TARDEO MARG

State Bus Terminal

Bombay Central

P BAPURAO MARG

NAIK CHOWK

NANA CHOWK

TARDEO RD

Bus Stop for Downtown

Grant Rd Railway Station

SADAR V P DESAI RD

Opera House ④

⑤

DR N A PURANDARE MARG

MARINE DRIVE (NETHAJI SUBH)

MAHARISHI

Tarporevala Aquarium ⑥

Gymkhanas

Bombay Hos

Haji Ali's Tomb

VATSALABAI DESAI CHOWK

Mahalakshmi Temple

BHULABHAI DESAI RD

DR G DESHMUKH MARG

S K BARODAWALA MARG

KEMPS CORNER

Crossword Bookshop

Breach Candy Hospital

SITARAM PATKAR MARG

Mani Bhavan Mahatma Gandhi Museum ①

Towers of Silence ②

Bubulnath Mandir

P M (Hanging) Temple Gardens

Malabar Hill

BABULNATH MARG

KAMALA NEHRU MARG

Kamla Nehru Park

Chowpatty Beach

WALUKESHWAR MARG

JACHMOHANDAS MARG

Jain Temple

Walukeshwar Temple

N DABHOLKAR MARG

Banganga Tank

WALUKESHWAR MARG

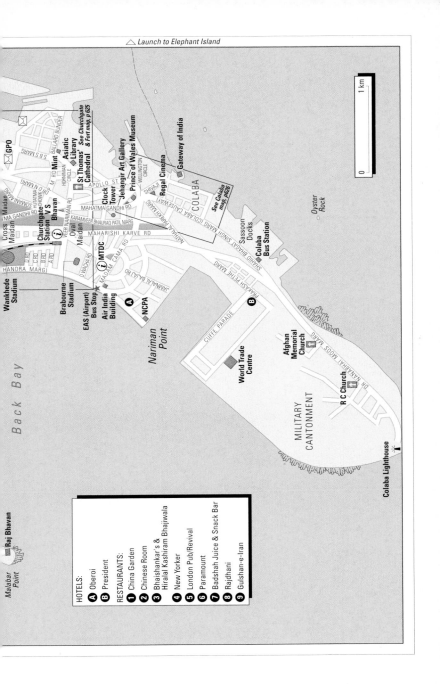

△ Launch to Elephant Island

1 km
0

Malabar
Point

Raj Bhavan

Back Bay

Wankhede
Stadium

Brabourne
Stadium

Cross Maidan

Churchgate
Station V S

Oval
Maidan

Nariman
Point

World Trade
Centre

CUFFE PARADE

EAS (Airport)
Bus Stop

Air India
Building

NCPA Ⓐ

MTDC

Ⓑ

MILITARY
CANTONMENT

R C Church

Afghan
Memorial
Church

Colaba Lighthouse

GPO

S B S MARG

Mint

Horniman
Circle

Asiatic
Library

St Thomas'
Cathedral

See Churchgate
& Fort map, p.625

Jehangir Art Gallery

Prince of Wales Museum

Gateway of India

WELLINGTON
CIRCLE

Regal Cinema

COLABA

See Colaba
map, p.626

Clock
Tower

APOLLO ST

MAHATMA GANDHI RD

MAHARISHI KARVE RD

Sassoon
Docks

Colaba
Bus Station

Oyster
Rock

HOTELS:
Ⓐ Oberoi
Ⓑ President

RESTAURANTS:
❶ China Garden
❷ Chinese Room
❸ Bhaishankar's &
   Hiralal Kashiram Bhajiwala
❹ New Yorker
❺ London Pub/Revival
❻ Paramount
❼ Badshah Juice & Snack Bar
❽ Rajdhani
❾ Gulshan-e-Iran

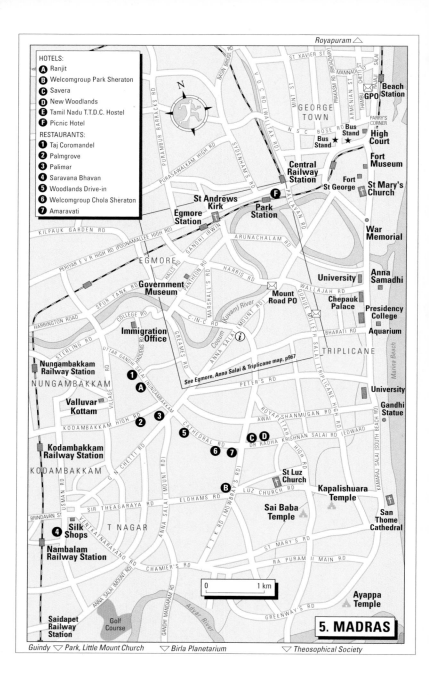

HOTELS:
- **A** Ranjit
- **B** Welcomgroup Park Sheraton
- **C** Savera
- **D** New Woodlands
- **E** Tamil Nadu T.T.D.C. Hostel
- **F** Picnic Hotel

RESTAURANTS:
- **1** Taj Coromandel
- **2** Palmgrove
- **3** Palimar
- **4** Saravana Bhavan
- **5** Woodlands Drive-in
- **6** Welcomgroup Chola Sheraton
- **7** Amaravati

Royapuram △

ST XAVIER ST
BASIN BRIDGE RD
ST X
MANNADI
PRAKASM RD (BROADWAY)
PURASAWALKAM HIGH RD
PUMBUR BARRACKS RD
N S C BOSE RD
V O C RD
1ST LINE
2ND LINE
ARMENIAN ST
THAMBU CHETTI ST
MINT
RAJAJI SALAI
GPO
Beach Station

GEORGE TOWN

PARRY'S CORNER

Bus Stand
Bus Stand ★
★ High Court

Central Railway Station
Fort St George
Fort Museum
St Mary's Church

KILPAUK GARDEN RD

St Andrews Kirk
Egmore Station
Park Station
F
PALLAVAN RD

GANDHI IRWIN RD
ARUNACHALAM RD

War Memorial

PERIYAR E V R HIGH RD (POONAMALLEE HIGH RD)
EGMORE
HALLS RD
PANTHEON RD
HARRIS RD
WALLAJAH RD

University
Anna Samadhi

SPUR TANK RD
Government Museum
MARSHALL'S RD
Mount Road PO
Chepauk Palace

HARRINGTON ROAD
COLLEGE RD
C-IN-C RD
Kuvam River
Coum
MOUNT RD
ANNA SALAI
Presidency College
Aquarium

STERLING RD
Immigration Office
GREAMES RD
ⓘ
BHARATI RD
TRIPLICANE

Nungambakkam Railway Station
UTTAR GANDHI SALAI NUNGAMBAKKAM
HADDOWS RD
See Egmore, Anna Salai & Triplicane map, p967
PETER'S RD
University

NUNGAMBAKKAM
1
A
Gandhi Statue

Valluvar Kottam
VILLAGE RD
ROYAPETTAH HIGH RD
ROYAPETTAH RD
AWAI SHANMUGAN RD
EDWARD

KODAMBAKKAM HIGH RD
2 **3**
CATHEDRAL RD
5
DR RADHA KRISHNAN SALAI RD
C **D**
6 **7**

Kodambakkam Railway Station
G N CHETTI RD
ANNA SALAI (MOUNT RD)
HIGH RD

KODAMBAKKAM
USMAN RD
St Luz Church
Kapalishuara Temple

B
ELDHAMS RD
LUZ CHURCH RD
SIR THEAGARAYA RD
BRINDAVAN ST
T K RD (MOWBRAY'S RD)
Sai Baba Temple
San Thome Cathedral

Silk Shops **4**
T NAGAR
VENKATNARAYANA RD
ST MARY'S RD

Nambalam Railway Station
CHAMIER'S RD
RA PURAM II MAIN RD

ANNA SALAI (MOUNT RD)
GANDHI MANDAPAM RD
0   1 km

Adyar River
Saidapet Railway Station
Golf Course
Ayappa Temple
GREENWAY'S RD

KAMARAJ SALAI (SOUTH BEACH RD)
Marina Beach

5. MADRAS

Guindy ▽ Park, Little Mount Church   ▽ Birla Planetarium   ▽ Theosophical Society stationary traffic. **Tickets** should be booked in advance from the MTDC counter next to the Gateway of India (the main departure point).

MTDC also run four-day "outstation tours" to the caves at **Ellora**, **Ajanta** and **Aurangabad**, and to **Nasik** and **Mahabaleshwar**. Either book all-in tickets, which include the cost of accommodation (Rs1000), or else pay the one-way fare of Rs140.

Car rental

Cars with drivers can be rented per day (around Rs600 for a non-a/c *Ambassador*, upwards of Rs1000 for more luxurious a/c cars), or per kilometre, from ITDC's counter at the government tourist office, or through good travel agents (see p.656). *Ramniranjan Kedia Rent-a-Car* (☎835 0559) are recommended if you want to book a vehicle on arrival at Sahar international airport.

Self-drive is also now available in Bombay, though the service seems to be intended more for middle-class Indians out to impress their friends ("They'll never know it's rented!"), than tourists. You will be a lot safer if you leave the driving to someone more at home with the city's racetrack rules of the road. If you're willing to risk it, try the *Transport Corporation of India* (in collaboration with *Hertz*), 16th Floor, Nariman Building, Nariman Point (☎202 3734 or 3343).

The City

Between the airports to the north and the southern tip of Bombay lies a thirty-kilometre-long, seething mass of streets, suburbs and relentless traffic. Even during the relatively cool winter months, exploring it can be hard work, requiring plenty of pit stops at cold drink stalls along the way. The best place to start is down at the far south end of the peninsula in **Colaba**, home to most of the hotels, restaurants and best-known sights, including the **Gateway of India**. Fifteen minutes' walk north takes you past the **Prince of Wales Museum** to the **Fort** area, home of all the banks and big stores, plus the cream of Bombay's ostentatious Raj-era buildings. The extravagant **Victoria Terminus** overlooks its northern limits, close to the impressive onion-dome of the **GPO**. The hub of the suburban train network, **Churchgate station**, stands 4km west, across the big *maidans* that scythe through the centre of town. Churchgate, and the **tourist office**, is a stone's throw from the sweeping curve of **Back Bay**. With **Nariman Point**'s skyscrapers at one end, lively **Chowpatty Beach** and the affluent apartment blocks of **Malabar Hill** at the other, the Bay is Bombay at its snazziest. But the area immediately north and east is ramshackle and densely populated. The **central bazaars** extend from **Crawford Market**, beyond VT station, right up to **J Boman (JB) Behram Marg**, opposite the other mainline train station, **Bombay Central**.

For a map of Bombay, see colour insert no.4 in the centre of this book.

Colaba

At the end of the seventeenth century, **Colaba** was little more than the last in a straggling line of rocky islands extending to the lighthouse that stood on Bombay's southernmost point. Today, the original outlines of the promontory (whose name derives from the **Koli** who first lived here) have been submerged under a mass of dilapidated colonial tenements, hotels, bars, restaurants and handicraft shops. If you never venture beyond the district, you'll get a very distorted picture of Bombay. In spite of being the main tourist enclave and a trendy hang-out for the city's rich young things, Colaba has retained the distinctly sleazy feel of the bustling port it used to be, with dodgy money-changers, dealers and pimps hissing at passers-by from doorways.

The Gateway of India

Bombay's most famous landmark, the **Gateway of India**, was built in 1924 by George Wittet, responsible for many of the city's grandest constructions. Commemorating the visit of King George V and Queen Mary in 1911, India's own honey-coloured Arc de Triomphe was originally envisaged as a ceremonial disembarkation point for passengers alighting from the *P&O* steamers. Ironically, today it is more often remembered as the place the British chose to stage their final departure from the country – on February 28, 1948, the last detachment of troops remaining on Indian soil set sail from here. Nowadays, the only boats bobbing about at the bottom of its stone staircase are the launches that ferry tourists across the harbour to Elephanta Island (see p.638).

The recently spruced-up square surrounding the Gateway is a popular place for a stroll during the evenings. At one end, an equestrian statue of **Shivaji**, the Maratha military adventurer who dogged the last years of the Moghul emperor Aurangzeb, looks sternly on. Shivaji has been appropriated as a nationalist symbol (the prototypical "Son of the Soil") by the extreme right-wing Shiv Sena, which explains the garland of marigolds often draped around the statue's neck.

Behind the Gateway

Directly behind the Gateway, the older hotel in the **Taj Mahal Intercontinental Hotel** complex stands as a monument to native hubris in the face of colonial oppression. Its patron, the Parsi industrialist J N Tata, is said to have built the old *Taj* as an act of revenge after he was refused entry to what was then the best hotel in town, the "whites only" *Watson's*. The ban proved their undoing. *Watson's* disappeared long ago, but the *Taj*, with its grand grey and white stone facade and red-domed roof, still presides imperiously over the seafront, the preserve of visiting diplomats, sheikhs and Bombay's jet-set. Lesser mortals are allowed in to sample the opulent tea-shops and restaurants.

From the *Taj*, you can head down the promenade, PJ Ramchandani Marg, better known as **Apollo Bunder** (nothing to do with the Greek sun god, the name is a colonial corruption of the Koli words for a local fish, *palav*, and quay, *bunda*), taking in the sea breezes and views over the busy harbour. Alternatively, Shivaji Marg heads northwest towards **Wellington Circle** (SPM Chowk), the hectic roundabout in front of the *Regal* cinema. The latter route takes you past the old **Bombay Yacht Club**, another idiosyncratic vestige of the Raj. Very little seems to have changed here since its smoky common rooms were a bolt hole for the city's *burrasahibs*. Dusty sporting trophies and models of clippers and *dhows* stand in glass cases lining its corridors, polished from time to time by bearers in cotton tunics. If you want to look around, seek permission from the club secretary; accommodation is available only to members and their guests.

Southwards along Colaba Causeway

To walk from Wellington Circle to the south of the peninsula, you have first to run the gauntlet of street-vendors and hustlers who crowd the claustrophobic pavements of **Colaba Causeway** (this stretch of Shahid Bhagat Singh Marg). It's hard to believe that such a chaotic city thoroughfare, with its hole-in-the-wall cafes, clothes stores and incense stalls, once lay beneath the sea. By the time you reach the tall wooden-galleried houses of **Arthur Bunder Rd**, however, even the Muslim perfumeries can barely smother the smell of fish wafting up the main street. The wholesale seafood market at **Sassoon Docks**, a kilometre or so south of central Colaba, provides an unexpected splash of rustic colour amid the drab urban surroundings. Koli fisherwomen, their cotton *saris* hitched *dhoti*-style, squat beside baskets of glistening pomfret, prawns and tuna, while coolies haul plastic crates of crushed ice over rickety gangplanks to the boats moored at the quay. The stench, as overpowering as the noise, comes mostly from the bundles of dried fish that are sold in bulk. **"Bombay duck"**, the salty local snack, has found its way to many a far shore, but you'll be hard pushed to find any in

Colaba's own restaurants. **Photography** is strictly forbidden, as the market is close to a sensitive military area.

From the docks, hop on any bus heading south down Colaba Causeway (#3, #11, #47, #103, #123, or #125) to the **Afghan Memorial Church of St John the Baptist**, built (1847–54) as a memorial to the British victims of the First Afghan War. Hemmed in by the cantonment area, the pale yellow church, with its tall steeple and tower, would look more at home beside the playing fields of Eton, in England, than the sultry waters of the Arabian Sea. If the door is unlocked, take a peep at the fine stained-glass marble plaques and windows inside.

Downtown Bombay

Aldous Huxley famously described Bombay as "one of the most appalling cities of either hemisphere", with its "lavatory bricks and Gothic spires". The critic Robert Byron, although a wholehearted fan of New Delhi, was equally unenthusiastic, feeling moved to refer to **downtown Bombay** in 1931 as "that architectural Sodom", claiming that "the nineteenth century devised nothing lower than the municipal buildings of British India. Their ugliness is positive, daemonic." Today, however, the massive erections of Empire and Indian free enterprise appear not so much ugly, as intriguing.

Prince of Wales Museum and Jehangir Art Gallery

Set back from Mahatma Gandhi (MG) Rd in an attractive garden is the unmissable **Prince of Wales Museum of Western India** (Tues–Sun 10.15am–6pm; Rs3; camera Rs15). This distinctive Raj-era building, crowned by a massive white Moghul-style dome, houses a superb collection of paintings and sculpture that you'll need several hours, or a couple of visits, to get the most out of. Its foundation stone was laid in 1905 by the future King George V, then Prince of Wales; the architect, George Wittet, went on to design the Gateway of India. The museum is undoubtedly the finest example of his work; the epitome of the hybrid **Indo-Saracenic** style, it is said to be an "educated" interpretation of fifteenth- and sixteenth-century Gujarati architecture, mixing Islamic touches with typically English municipal brickwork.

The **central hall**, overlooked by a carved wooden balcony, provides a snapshot of the collection with a few choice Moghul paintings, jade work, weapons and miniature clay and terracotta figures from the Mauryan (third century BC) and Kushana (first to second century AD) periods. From Bengal (first century AD) are horrible-looking *yakshis* (godlings or sprites) devouring lizards. Sculpture galleries on either side of the hall open onto the front garden; the one to the right houses the museum's **natural history** section, which contains a large and well-kept – if somewhat unfashionable – collection of stuffed birds, fish and animals.

The main **sculpture room** on the **ground floor** displays some excellent fourth- and fifth-century heads and figures from the Buddhist state of Gandhara, a former colony of Alexander the Great (hence the Greek-style statues). Important Hindu sculptures include a seventh-century Chalukyan bas-relief from Aihole depicting Brahma seated on a lotus, and a sensuously carved torso of Mahisasuramaraini, the goddess Durga with tripod raised ready to skewer the demon buffalo. On the way up to the **first floor** a display on the astonishingly urban **Indus Valley civilization** (3500–1500 BC) has models of typical settlements, mysterious seal moulds in an as-yet-undeciphered script, and jewellery. The main attraction, though, has to be the superb collection of **Indian painting**, including illustrated manuscripts and erotic Gita Govinda paintings in the pre-Moghul Sultanate style. **Moghul schools** are well represented, too, with fine portraits and folios from the reign of Akbar (1556–1605), and sublime drawings of animals and birds from the Jehangir (1605–28) school. The well-known portrait of the emperor Shah Jehan (1628–58) and his forefathers is also on display.

DABAWALLAHS

Bombay's size and inconvenient shape create all kind of hassles for its working population – not least having to stew for over four hours each day in slow municipal transport. One thing the daily tidal wave of commuters do not have to worry about, however, is finding an inexpensive and wholesome home-cooked lunch. In a city with a *wallah* for everything, it will find them. The members of the **Bombay Tiffin Box Suppliers Association**, known colloquially, and with no little affection, as "**dabawallahs**", see to that.

Every day, around four thousand *dabawallahs* deliver freshly cooked food from 125,000 suburban kitchens to offices in the downtown area. Each lunch is prepared early in the morning by a devoted wife or mother while her husband or son is enduring the crush on the train. She arranges the rice, *dhal*, *subzi*, curd and *parathas* into cylindrical aluminium trays, stacks them on top of one another and clips them together with a neat little handle. This **tiffin box**, not unlike a slim paint tin, is the lynchpin of the whole operation. When the runner calls to collect it in the morning, he uses a special colour code on the lid to tell him where the lunch has to go. At the end of his round, he carries all the boxes to the nearest railway station and hands them over to other *dabawallahs* for the trip into town. Between leaving the wife and reaching its final destination, the tiffin box will pass through at least half a dozen different pairs of hands, carried on heads, shoulder-poles, bicycle handlebars and in the brightly decorated handcarts that plough with such insouciance through the midday traffic. Tins are rarely, if ever, lost, and always find their way home again (before the husband returns from work) to be washed up for the next day's lunch.

To catch *dabawallahs* in action, head for **VT** or **Churchgate** stations around late morning time, when the tiffin boxes arrive in the city centre. The event is accompanied by a chorus of "lafka! lafka!" – "hurry! hurry!" – as the *dabawallahs*, recognizable in their white Nehru caps and baggy khaki shorts, rush to make their lunch-hour deadlines. Most collect about one rupee for each tin they handle, netting around Rs1000 per month in total. *Daba* lunches still work out a good deal cheaper than meals taken in the city restaurants, saving precious *paise* for the middle-income workers who use the system, and providing a livelihood for the legions of poorer immigrants from the Pune area who operate it.

Jade, porcelain and ivory can be seen on the **second floor**, along with a collection of **European art** that includes a minor Titian and a Constable. Among the weapon collection are the swords of emperors Shah Jehan and Aurangzeb, a shield of Akbar ornamented with the zodiac, and various daggers, maces and guns. The poorly lit **Indian textiles room** showcases brocaded *saris*, turbans, and antique Kulu and Kashmiri shawls, intricately patterned with flowers, birds, animals and abstract designs.

Technically in the same compound as the Prince of Wales Museum, though approached from further up MG Rd, the **Jehangir Art Gallery** (Mon–Fri 10am–5pm) is Bombay's best-known venue for contemporary art, with five small galleries specializing in twentieth-century arts and crafts from around the world. You never know what you're going to find – most exhibitions last only a week and exhibits are often for sale.

Around Oval Maidan

Karmaveer Bhaurao Patil Marg's southern edge holds a statue of Dr B R Ambedkar (1891–1956), who though born into an outcast Hindu community, converted to Buddhism. A great number of "untouchables" followed suit; many are now part of a militant movement calling themselves *dalits*, "the oppressed", eschewing Gandhi's reconstructed name of *Harijans*, "god's people". Some of Bombay's most important Victorian buildings line the eastern side of the vast green **Oval Maidan**, behind the statue, where impromptu cricket matches are held almost every day (foreign enthusiasts are welcome to take part, but should beware the *maidan*'s demon bowlers and less-than-even pitches). Partially obscured by police huts, the dull yellow **Old Secretariat** now serves as the City Civil and Sessions Court. Indian civil servant G W Forrest described it in 1903 as "a massive pile whose main features have been brought from Venice, but all the beauty has vanished in transhipment." Inside, you can only imagine the originally highly polished interior, which no longer shines, but buzzes with activity. Lawyers in black gowns, striped trousers and white tabs bustle up and down the staircases, whose corners are emblazoned with expectorated *paan* juice, and offices with perforated swing-doors give glimpses of text-book images of Indian bureaucracy – peons at desks piled high with dusty be-ribboned document bundles.

Across A S D'Mello Rd from the Old Secretariat, two major buildings belonging to **Bombay University** (established 1857) were designed in England by Sir Gilbert Scott, who had already given the world the Gothic extravaganza of London's St Pancras railway station. Access through the main gates is monitored by caretakers who only allow you in if you say you're using the library. Funded by the Parsi philanthropist Cowasjee "Readymoney" Jehangir, the **Convocation Hall** greatly resembles a church. Above its entrance, a huge circular stained-glass window features a wheel with spokes of Greek pilasters that separate signs of the zodiac, while the 79.2-metre-high **Rajabhai clock tower,** over the Library (daily 10am–10pm), is said to be modelled on Giotto's campanile in Florence. Until 1931 it chimed tunes such as *Rule Britannia* and *Home Sweet Home*. It's worth applying for a visitors' ticket (Rs5 a day, Rs10 for 3 days) just to see the interior. The magnificent vaulted wooden ceiling of the reading room, high Gothic windows and stained glass still evoke a reverential approach to learning.

Hutama Chowk (Flora Fountain)

A busy five-point intersection in the heart of the Fort area, **Flora Fountain** has been renamed **Hutama Chowk** ("Martyr's Square") to commemorate the freedom fighters who died to establish the state of Maharashtra in the Indian Union. The *chowk* centres on a statue of the Roman goddess **Flora**, erected in 1869 to commemorate Sir Bartle Frere. It's hard to see quite why they bothered– the Raj architecture expert, Philip Davies, was not being unkind when he said "The fountain was designed by a committee, and it shows."

Facing the Flora Fountain, a **statue of Dadabhai Naoroji** (1812–1917) shows the first Indian member of the British parliament (1892–95). You may want to tarry here a while to consult Machindra Govind Pawar, who for years has sat next to the statue daily (except Sunday) between 8am and 8pm. Signs explain his business, offering cures for "rheumatism, hair falling, piles, fistula and sex weakness". Sri Pawar, who hails from Pune, says he is a practitioner of *ayurveda* and operates on a basis that sounds like commercial suicide: he accepts no payment until his patients are cured.

Horniman (Elphinstone) Circle and the Town Hall

Elphinstone Circle, renamed **Horniman Circle** after a pro-Independence newspaper editor, was conceived in 1860 as a centrepiece of a newly planned Bombay by the then Municipal Commissioner, Charles Forjett, on the site of Bombay "Green". Forjett, a Eurasian, had something of a peculiar reputation; he was fond of disguising himself in "native" dress and prowling about certain districts of the city to listen out for seditious talk. In 1857, at the time of the First War of Independence (as it is now known by Indians; the British call it the Indian Mutiny), Forjett fired two suspected revolutionaries from a cannon on the Esplanade (roughly the site of the modern *maidans*).

It is often said that the design of Elphinstone Circle was based on Tunbridge Wells or Leamington Spa in England, with elegant Neoclassical buildings centring on a garden with a fountain. East of the square, the impressive Doric **Town Hall** on SBS Marg houses the vast collection of the **Asiatic Library** (see p.654).

St Thomas' Cathedral

The small, simple **St Thomas' Cathedral** (daily 6.30am–6pm), on Tamarind St, is reckoned to be the oldest English building in Bombay, blending Classical and Gothic styles.

Governor Aungier self-righteously envisaged it with "the main design of inviting the natives to repair thereunto, and observe the gravity and purity of our own devotions". After his death, the project was abandoned; the walls stood five metres high for forty-odd years until enthusiasm was rekindled by Richard Cobbe, a chaplain to the East India Company in the second decade of the eighteenth century. He believed the church's unfinished walls represented "a mark of derision for the natives for whose conversion they were partly raised [and] a reproach and a scandal to the English in Bombay". It was finally opened on Christmas Day 1718, complete with the essential "cannon-ball-proof roof". In those days the seating was divided into useful sections for those who should know their place, including one for "Inferior Women".

St Thomas' whitewashed and polished brass-and-wood interior looks much the same as when the staff of the East India Company worshipped here in the eighteenth century. Lining the walls are memorial tablets to English parishioners, many of whom died young, either from disease or in battle.

Marine Drive and Chowpatty Beach

Netaji Subhash Chandra Marg, better known as **Marine Drive**, is Bombay's seaside prom, an eight-lane highway with a wide pavement built in the 1920s on reclaimed land. Sweeping in an arc from the skyscrapers at Nariman Point in the south, Marine Drive ends at the foot of Malabar Hill and the old Chowpatty Beach. The whole stretch is a favourite place for a stroll; the promenade next to the sea has uninterrupted views virtually the whole way along, while the apartment blocks on the land side – most of which are ugly unpainted concrete and called something-or-other Mahal – are some of the most desirable and expensive addresses in the city.

It's a great place for people-watching. Early in the morning yuppies in shorts speed-walk or jog before breakfast while street kids, mother-and-babies and limbless beggars take up position at the traffic lights at major junctions to petition drivers and passengers for a rupee. Those one rung further up the social ladder have something to sell: twisted fun balloons or a newspaper. Some kids perfunctorily wipe a rag over the bodywork and do their best to wrest a few coins from momentarily captive people, 90 percent of whom stare resolutely ahead.

Evening sees servants walking their bosses' pekinese or poodles and children playing under the supervision of their *ayahs* (nannies). Sometime after 6pm the place magically transforms; the British called it the "Queen's Necklace". The massive red sun disappears into the sea, street lights snap on, 5-star hotels glow and neon lights blink. Innumerable couples materialize to take romantic strolls down to the beach, stopping on the way to buy from a peanut vendor or to pay off a *hijra*, eunuch (see p.195), threatening to lift up his *sari* and reveal all.

Just beyond the huge flyover, B Bridge, are a series of cricket pitches known as **gymkhanas**, where there's a good chance of catching a match any day of the week. A number are exclusive to particular religious communities. The first doubles as a swanky outdoor wedding venue for Parsi marriages; others include the Catholic, Islamic and Hindu pitches, the last of which has a classic colonial-style pavilion.

At the northern end of the gymkhanas, the **Tarporevala Aquarium** (Tues–Sat 10am–7pm, Sun & hols 10am–8pm) is less notable for its sea snakes, vibrant green and yellow trigger fish, glinting tin foil fish, and turtles, than its two aquatic miracles: the "Quran fish", inscribed with a line from the Koran, and the "Christ Crab" which has a holy cross on his back. No photography is allowed.

Chowpatty Beach

Chowpatty Beach is a Bombay institution, which really comes to life at night and on Saturday. People do not come here to swim (the sea is foul) but to wander, sit on the beach, let the kids ride a pony or a rusty Ferris wheel, have a massage, get ears cleaned or hair cut, listen to musicians, buy drugs, have a go on a rifle range, consult an astrologer, watch dreadlocked ascetics perform public austerities, get conned, and most importantly picnic on *bhel puri* and cups of *kulfi*. There are plenty of good ice-cream bars and restaurants across Marine Drive, opposite the beach (see p.648), where you'll also find *Wagh's Fine Art Studio,* whose curious collection of plaster figures in the window includes a much larger than life Gandhi plus Alsatian dog.

Amazingly enough, Chowpatty Beach is still home to a small Koli fishing village that carries on as if the vast city of Bombay didn't exist. Once a year in September the **Ganesh Chathurthi** festival (see p.652) draws gigantic crowds to participate in the immersion of idols, both huge and small, of the elephant-headed god Ganesh.

Mani Bhavan Mahatma Gandhi Museum

Mani Bhavan, 19 Laburnum Rd (daily 9.30am–6pm), was Gandhi's Bombay base between 1917 and 1934. Set in a leafy upper-middle-class road, the house is now a permanent memorial to the Mahatma with an extensive research library. Within the lovingly maintained polished wood interior, the walls are covered with photos of historic events and artefacts from the man's extraordinary life – the most disarming of which is a friendly letter to Hitler suggesting world peace. Gandhi's predictably simple sitting-cum-bedroom is preserved behind glass. Laburnum Road is a few streets along from the *Bharatiya Vidya Bhavan* music venue on KM Munshi Marg (see p.652) – if coming by taxi ask for the nearby Gamdevi Police Station.

Malabar Hill

Malabar Hill, the long, steep-sided promontory enfolding Chowpatty Beach at the north end of Back Bay, is Bombay's ritziest neighbourhood. Since the eighteenth century, its lush forests, fresh sea breezes and panoramic views have made the hill an attractive location for the grand mansions and bungalows of the city's merchants and governors. These days however, high-rise, high-rent apartment blocks have squeezed out all but a handful of the old colonial buildings to make way for Bombay's "new money" set – the in-crowd of politicians, millionaires, film stars and gangsters who flit across the glossy pages and gossip columns of India's popular magazines. Somehow, though, a few jaded remnants of the city's past have managed to weather the changes.

THE TOWERS OF SILENCE

High on the top of Malabar Hill, screened from prying eyes by an imposing wall and a dense curtain of vegetation, stand the seven Parsi **Towers of Silence**, or *Dokhmas*. If you know only one thing about the Parsis, it is probably that they dispose of their dead by leaving the corpses on top of tall cylindrical enclosures for their bones to be picked clean by vultures. This ancient mortuary ritual, thought to predate the 2500-year-old faith, was advocated by the prophet Zoroaster as a means of avoiding pollution of the four sacred elements (air, water, earth, and the holiest of all, fire). Recently, Parsis have been debating whether to switch to electric cremation as a sound, and more sanitary, alternative – supposedly because scraps of human flesh discarded by the over-fed vultures have been appearing on balconies, roof-tops and gardens near the Towers. Whatever they decide, no one will thank you for trying to peep at the *Dokhmas* themselves, which are off-limits to all living people other than the pall-bearers who put the corpses in place. Not to be put off, *Time-Life* once published a colour photograph of a funeral taken from the buildings overlooking the site. Enraged Parsis retorted by asking how the photographer would feel if he saw pictures of *his* mother's body being pecked to bits by birds?

Before heading up the hill from the busy roundabout at the far end of Chowpatty Beach, make a short diversion through the narrow backlanes to **Balbunath Mandir**, one of Bombay's most important Hindu temples. You'll have no trouble finding the entrance: just look for the melee of stray cattle and flower-sellers that forms here around *puja* times. The building itself, a clumsy modern agglomeration of towers, turquoise arches and staircases, makes a much less interesting spectacle than the stream of *pujaris* (priests) and pilgrims on the greasy stone steps leading to it.

The municipal parks and the Jain temple

From the Balbunath temple, the most pleasant and direct route up to Malabar Hill's main thoroughfare, **Ridge Road**, now re-named **Bal Gangadhar** (or BG) **Kher Marg**, is via the tangle of crumbling concrete paths through the woods below it. The trail emerges near a pair of dull but popular public parks. The larger, known as the "**Hanging Gardens**" (recently renamed "Pherozeshah Mehta Gardens") is full of loving couples smooching ostentatiously around its gravel paths and manicured flowerbeds. By contrast, the smaller **Kamala Nehru Children's Park** (across the road) is unlikely to appeal to anyone over the age of seven. The views of Back Bay are, in any case, better admired from the congenial terrace bars of the *Naaz Cafe* nearby.

A kilometre or so straight down the ridge from the parks stands Malabar Hill's **Jain temple**. Bombay's Jains originally came from Gujarat in the late seventeenth century to escape persecution by the Hindu Marathas. Since then, their legendarily sharp business sense has helped make these ultra-strict vegetarians one of the city's most prosperous minorities. According to an ancient dictum, Jains should, every day after bathing, walk barefoot to their local temple in a length of stitchless cloth to pray, a gesture of humility and renunciation that contrasts with the lavish decoration of the temples themselves. This temple, though on the small side, is no exception. Mirrors and colourful paintings cover the walls surrounding the approach to the central chamber, where the polished marble image of **Adinath**, the first of the twenty-four Jain teacher-prophets, or *tirthankaras*, is enshrined. In front of the image, devotees make rice patterns as offerings. The temple also runs a stall selling freshly baked pure-veg biscuits, sweets and cakes. It's to the left of the main entrance, near the racks where shoes and leather articles have to be deposited.

Walukeshwar Mandir and Banganga Tank

Beyond the Jain temple, Malabar Hill tapers off to a narrow spit that shelves steeply down to Back Bay on one side, and the rocky sea shore on the other. **Walukeshwar Mandir**, among the few of Bombay's ancient Hindu sites not buried under layers of conurbation, can be reached via a lane left off the main road. According to the *Ramayana*, Rama paused here during his journey south to rescue Sita from the clutches of the evil Ravana, and fashioned a *lingam* out of sand to worship Shiva. Over time, the Walukeshwar, or "Sand-Lord" shrine, became one of the western Indian coast's most important religious centres, venerated even by the marauding Malabar pirates who menaced the islands. Today's temple, erected in 1715 after the original had been destroyed by the Portuguese, is unremarkable and best bypassed in favour of the more impressive **Banganga tank**, below it. Hemmed in by a towering wall of apartment blocks, the spring that feeds the tank is believed to have been created by an arrow fired from Rama's own fabled bow. Today, it's a minor pilgrimage site, busy only on "white" (full-) or "black" (no-) moon days of the month. At other times, Banganga's stone *ghats*, numerous subsidiary shrines, and scum-covered greenish waters see little more than a trickle of bathers, drawn mostly from the slum encampments which have sprung up on the broken land lining the shore. A path picks its way past these shacks, and the washing lines of the *dhobis* who live in them, to the **cremation ghats** nearby.

North of Malabar Hill

Two of Bombay's most popular religious sites, one Hindu, the other Muslim, can be reached by following Bhulabhai Desai Rd **north from Malabar Hill** as far as Prabhu Chowk, through the exclusive suburb of **Breach Candy** (bus #132 from Colaba). Alternatively, make for Bombay Central and head due northwest to **Vatsalabai Desai Chowk** (also bus #132 from Colaba).

Mahalakshmi Mandir is joined to Bhulabhai Desai Rd by an alley lined with stalls selling *puja* offerings and devotional pictures. Bombay's favourite *devi*, **Lakshmi**, goddess of beauty and prosperity – the city's most sought-after attributes – is here propitiated with coconuts, sweets, lengths of shimmering silk and giant lotus blooms. At weekends, queues for *darshan* extend right the way across the courtyard and down the main steps beyond. Gifts pile so high that the temple *pujaris* run a money-spinning sideline reselling them. Their little shop, to the left of the entrance, is a good place to buy cut-price *saris* and brocades infused with lucky Lakshmi-energy. While you're here, find out what your future holds by joining the huddle of devotees pressing rupees onto the rear wall of the shrine room. If your coin sticks, you'll be rich.

A temple has stood on this rocky outcrop for well over a thousand years. Not until the eighteenth century however, when the hitherto swampy western edge of the city was drained, was the present building erected. Legend has it that the goddess herself told a contractor working on the project that unless her icon – which she said would soon reappear from the sea where it had been cast by Muslim invaders – was reinstated in a temple on the site, the breach-wall would not hold back the waves. Sure enough, the next day a Lakshmi deity was indeed fished out of the silt by workmen, to be installed on this small headland, where it has remained to the present day.

Another site shrouded in myth is the mausoleum of the Muslim saint, **Haji Ali**, occupying a small islet in the bay just north of the Mahalakshmi temple. Islamic lore says that the Afghan mystic lived and meditated on this spot, or, more picturesquely, that Haji Ali's coffin was washed ashore on these rocks after it had, on strict instructions from the saint, been cast into the sea off the coast of what is now Pakistan. The tomb is connected to the mainland by a narrow concrete **causeway**, only passable at low tide. When not immersed in water, its entire length is lined with beggars who change one-rupee pieces into ten-*paise* coins for pilgrims. The prime sites, closer to the snack bars that flank the main entrance, near the small mosque, and the gateway to the tomb itself, are allocated in a strict pecking order. If you want to make a donation, spare a thought for the unfortunates in the middle. After all the commotion, the **tomb** itself comes as something of a disappointment. Its white Moghul domes and minarets look a lot less exotic close up than when viewed from the shore, silhouetted against the sun as it drops into the Arabian Sea.

THE MUNICIPAL DHOBI GHATS

On the face of it, the idea of going out of your way to ogle Bombay's dirty washing sounds like a very perverse pastime. If you're passing however, the **municipal dhobi ghats**, near Mahalakshmi suburban railway station, are well worth hopping off the train to see. This huge open-air laundry is the centre of one of those miraculous Indian institutions which, like the *dabawallah*'s operation (see p.630), is usually regarded by Westerners with disbelief. Each morning, washing from all over Bombay is brought here to be thrown into soapy piles and thumped by the resident *dhobiwallahs* in the countless concrete tanks, barrels and shanty shacks inside the compound. The next day, after being aired, pressed, folded in newspaper and bound with cotton thread, the bundles are returned to whence they came. The bird's-eye view over the V-shaped rows of *dhobi ghats* from Mahalakshmi road bridge is one of Bombay's most bizarre photo opportunities.

A couple of kilometres further up the coast, the densely packed districts of central Bombay are broken by a huge, empty expanse of dusty brown grass. The optimistically named **Mahalakshmi racecourse**, founded in 1879, is the home of the *Bombay Turf Club* and a bastion of the city's Anglophile elite. Regular meetings take place here on weekends between November and March. If you fancy a hack yourself, the *Amateur Riding Club* also rents out horses during the week (except Wednesdays).

The central bazaars

Lining the anarchic jumble of streets north of Lokmanya Tilak (formerly Carnac) Rd, Bombay's teeming **central bazaars** are India at its most intense. You could wander around here for months without seeing the same shop front twice. In practice, most visitors find a couple of hours mingling with the crowds in the heat and din quite enough. Nevertheless, the market districts form a fascinating counterpoint to the wide and Westernized streets of downtown, even if you're not buying.

In keeping with traditional divisions of guild, caste and religion, most streets specialize in one or two types of merchandise – a pain if you want to see a smattering of all the goods on offer in a relatively short time. If you lose your bearings, the best way out is to ask someone to wave you in the direction of **Abdul Rehman St**, the busy road through the heart of the district, from where you can hail a cab.

Crawford Market

Crawford (aka Mahatma Phule) **Market**, ten minutes' walk north of VT station, is an old British-style covered market dealing in just about every kind of fresh food and domestic animal imaginable. When Bombayites crave a *bhaji* or a budgie, this is the first place they'll head for. Thanks to its pompous Norman-Gothic tower and prominent position at the corner of Lokmanya Tilak Rd and Dr DN Marg, the Crawford Market is also a useful landmark and a good place to begin a foray into the bazaars.

Before venturing inside, check out the **friezes** wrapped around its exterior – a Victorian vision of sturdy-limbed peasants toiling in the fields designed by Rudyard Kipling's father, Lockwood, as principal of the Bombay School of Art in 1865. Apart from the bare electric bulbs and fans dangling from the iron ribs of its high ceiling, the market itself must look much the same now as it did in Kipling's day. The **main hall** is still divided into different sections: pyramids of polished fruit and vegetables down one aisle; sacks of nuts or oil-tins full of herbs and spices down another. Sitting cross-legged on a raised platform in front of each stall, is its eagle-eyed owner, wearing starched *khadi* pyjamas and a Nehru cap, with a fresh red *tilak* smeared on his forehead.

Around the back of the market, in the atmospheric **wholesale wing**, the pace of life is more hectic. Here, noisy crowds of *coolies* mill about with large reed-baskets held high in the air (if they are looking for work) or on their heads (if they've found some). Underfoot, a messy compost of rotting vegetables, litter and straw accumulates as the day wears on, while clouds of dust kicked up by all the commotion catch beams of sunlight streaming through the tarpaulins and corrugated-iron roof.

At the epicentre of all this mayhem stands another of Lockwood Kipling's creations. Barely recognizable under a pile of empty boxes and hessian sacks, the **market fountain** was originally intended as a symbol of India's four great rivers. Its spouts, however, have long since run dry, much to the chagrin of the birds flitting around.

One place animal lovers should definitely steer clear of is Crawford Market's **pet** and **poultry** section, on the east side of the building. You never quite know what creatures will turn up here, cringing in rank-smelling, undersized cages. The **tobacco** market, by contrast, is altogether more fragrant. Look out for the Muslim *hookah* merchants selling picturesque smoking paraphernalia.

When you've had enough of Crawford Market, head past the shiny brass and hardware sections, and the stalls selling implausible wigs and false moustaches, to the west exits on Carnac (Lokmanya Tilak) Rd. Across the street, the famous *Badshah Juice and Snack Bar*'s **faloodas** (see p.648) and milk shakes make a great pick-me-up.

North of Crawford Market

The streets immediately **north of Crawford Market** and west of **Mohamed Ali Rd**, the main drag through Bombay's Muslim ghettoes, form one vast bazaar area. Ranged along both sides of narrow **Mangaldas Lane** the cloth bazaar, are small shops draped with lengths of bright silk and cotton. Low doorways on the left open on to a colourful **covered market** area, packed with tiny stalls where you'll be badgered to sit and take tea while the merchants tempt you with dozens of different *saris* and scarves.

At the far end of Mangaldas Lane from Carnac Rd, the pale green-washed domes, arches and minarets of the **Jama Masjid**, or "Friday Mosque" (1800), mark the start of the Muslim neighbourhoods. Hang around at this heaving crossroads for more than a few seconds and you'll be jostled and hissed by coolies and hand-cart pullers barging their way through dense crowds of shoppers. **Memon Street**, cutting north from the mosque, is the site of the **Zaveri Bazaar**, the jewellery market. Its rows of bright, air-conditioned shops, their windows glittering with gold and silver necklaces, rings and anklets, attract well-heeled family groups preparing for their daughters' weddings.

By the time the gleaming golden spire that crowns the **Mumba-Devi temple**'s cream and turquoise tower appears at the end of the street, you're deep in a maze of twisting lanes hemmed in by tall, wooden-balconied buildings. The temple is one of the most important centres of Devi-worship in India. Reached via a tiny courtyard where *pujaris* regale devotees with religious songs, its shrine houses a particularly revered, and unusual, deity. The mouthless "Maha-amba-aiee" (Mumba for short) is believed to have started her life as an obscure aboriginal earth goddess. Her present resting place was built early in the nineteenth century, when she was relocated from her former home to make way for VT Station. Mumba Devi's other claim to fame is that her name is the original root of the word "Bombay", as well as the newer, and more politically correct, Maharashtran version, "**Mumbai**", which the government has recently declared to be the city's official name.

The streets radiating off **Baiduni Chowk**, a short way northeast, are the place to shop for attractive hand-beaten **copper-** and **brass-ware**. Alternatively, jump in a taxi on the main road nearby for the two-kilometre trip north to the other concentration of markets around **Johar Chowk**. The most famous of these, **Chor** (literally "thieves") **Bazaar** (where vendors peevishly insist the name is a corruption of the Urdu *shor*, meaning "noisy"), is the city's largest **antiques**-cum-flea-market. Friday, the Muslim sabbath, is the best day to be here. From 9am onwards, the neighbourhood is cluttered with hawkers and hand-carts piled high with bric-a-brac and assorted junk being eagerly rummaged by men in skullcaps. At other times, the antique shops down on **Mutton Rd** are the main attraction. Once, you could hope to unearth real gems in these dark, fusty stores, but your chances of finding a genuine bargain nowadays are minimal. Most of the stuff is pricey Victoriana – old gramophones, chamber pots, chipped china – salvaged from the homes of Parsi families on the decline. The place is also awash with **fakes**, mainly small bronze votive statues, which make good souvenirs if you can knock the price down.

Press on north through Chor Bazaar and you'll eventually come out on to **Grant Rd** (Maulana Shaukatali Rd). Further north and west, in the warren of lanes below JB Behram Marg, lies the city's infamous **red-light district**. **Kamathipura's** rows of luridly lit, barred shop fronts, from where an estimated 25,000 prostitutes ply their trade, are one of Bombay's more degrading and unpleasant spectacles. Many of these so-called "**cage girls**" are young teenagers from poor tribal areas, and across the border in Nepal, who have been sold by desperate parents into **bonded slavery** until they can earn the money to pay off family debts. The area is definitely no place to wander around alone or on foot.

Bhuleshwar Market, Panjrapole Goshala and Flower Lane

Bhuleshwar Market, little visited by tourists, draws thousands of Bombayites for vegetables in the early morning or clothes bargains later in the day. The area is easiest approached from Charni Rd railway station (two stops from Churchgate). Make for CP Tank Circle (a crossroads on CP Tank Rd also served by buses #68, #103 and #107 from Flora Fountain), a short walk from the junction locally known as Kumbhar Tukda. By the afternoon this area is jam-packed; the following places are close together, but keep asking for directions. As you weave your way through you may notice the *Maganlal Dresswalla* shop, which supplies costumes for Hindi movies.

Walking along Bhuleshwar from *Hiralal Kashiram Bhajiawala* (see p.648) the first junction you come to is Panjrapole Corner. Panjrapole Rd, to the left, is full of steel kitchen utensil shops. At no. 200, *Mathalal Moortiwala & Sons* sells religious idols, to individuals and to temples. The best figures are made of white Rajasthani marble from Makrana, and painted in bright colours. Back at the corner, *Maganlal Kedarlal & Co.* sells soapstone and cheaper small figures plus white and black marble.

Compared with other Indian cities, the streets of Bombay are relatively cow-free. One contributory factor is the **Panjrapole Goshala**, or **cow shelter**, and animal sanctuary (daily 7am–6.30pm). It's a little tricky to find, tucked away on the other side of Panjrapole Rd, down a small lane, but any local will direct you if you ask for **Madhavbaug temple**, with which it is associated. A regular stream of devotees find their way to this little-known and, to the outsider, decidedly fun spot where you can gain religious merit by feeding the animals. At a counter inside the shelter, on the right-hand side of the courtyard filled with animal sheds, you exchange your ticket (Rs5 or Rs10) for a big plate of feed. You're then free to wander round and feed any of the 400 raspy-tongued residents, improving your *karma* as you go. The district also boasts a few good eating houses where you gain no merit at all by feeding yourself.

Back in Bhuleshwar, continue to the next junction, where another small turning to the left is **Phool Galli**, or **"Flower Lane"**, a short, narrow street devoted to supplying elaborate flower arrangements to temples and wedding functions. The skilled artists use jasmine, spider lilies, roses, hibiscus, ladies lace, a rare flower known as "snake champa" and blue, purple, orange and yellow marigolds, along with banana, *tulsi* and *gol pada* ("round foot") leaves. When admiring the blooms remember that to smell or touch them will render them useless for a temple and will lead to them being discarded. It is for the god to smell them first.

Elephanta

An hour's boat ride from Colaba, the tranquil, forested island of **ELEPHANTA** is one of the most atmospheric places in Bombay. Populated only by a small fishing community, it makes a wonderful contrast to the seething claustrophobia of the city, even when crowded with day-trippers at weekends. Originally known as **Gharapuri**, the "city of Ghara priests", the island was renamed in the sixteenth century by the Portuguese in honour of the carved elephant they found at the port (see p.640). Its chief attraction is its unique **cave temple**, whose massive **Trimurti** (three-faced) **Shiva sculpture** is as fine an example of Hindu architecture as you'll find anywhere.

"Deluxe" boats set off from the Gateway of India (hourly 9.00am–2.30pm; Rs50 including guide); book through MTDC on Madam Cama Rd or at their kiosk near the Gateway of India. Only three leave with a cave guide on board (8.45am, 11am & 2pm); if you take any of the others you can claim your guide from the ticket office on arrival. Luxury boats do not run during monsoon (June–Sept). **Ordinary ferries**, also from the Gateway of India, cost Rs35, do not include guides, and are usually packed. The journey takes about an hour.

Cool drinks and souvenir stalls line the way up the hill, and at the top, the MTDC *Chalukya* restaurant offers food and beer, and a terrace affording good views out to sea.

The Cave

Elephanta's impressive excavated **cave** (eighth century), covering an area of approximately 5000 square metres, is reached by climbing more than one hundred steps to the top of the hill. Inside, the massive columns, carved from solid rock, give the deceptive impression of being structural. To the right, as you enter, note the panel of **Nataraj**, Shiva as the cosmic dancer. Though spoiled by the Portuguese who, it is said, used it for target practice, the panel remains magnificent; Shiva's face is rapt, and in one of his left hands he removes the veil of ignorance. Opposite is a badly damaged panel of Lakulisha, Shiva with a club (*lakula*).

Each of the four entrances to the simple square main **shrine** – unusually, it has one on each side – is flanked by a pair of huge fanged *dvarpala* guardians (only those to the back have survived undamaged), while inside a large *lingam* is surrounded by coins and smouldering joss left by devotees. Facing the northern wall of the shrine another panel shows Shiva impaling the demon **Andhaka**, who wandered around as though blind, symbolizing his spiritual blindness. Shiva killed him as he attempted to steal a divine tree from heaven. The panel behind the shrine on the back wall portrays the marriage of **Shiva and Parvati**. Moving east, the next panel shows **Ganghadaran**, Shiva receiving the descending river Ganga, his lover, to live in his hair, while Parvati, his wife, looks on. A powerful six-metre-high bust of **Trimurti**, the three-faced Shiva, who embodies the powers of creator, preserver and destroyer, stands nearby, and to the west a sculpture shows Shiva as **Ardhanarishvara**, half male and half female. Near the second entrance on the east, another panel shows Shiva and Parvati on Mt **Kailasha** with Ravana about to lift the mountain. His curved spine shows the strain.

Uptown and the outskirts

Greater Bombay has crept inexorably northwards to engulf villages and swampland in a pall of chimneys, motorways and slums. These grim industrial areas hold few attractions, but possibilities for full- or half-day excursions include the quirky **Victoria and Albert museum and botanical gardens** in Byculla, and the **beach** at **Juhu**. All lie within reach of a suburban train station, although you will, in most cases, have to take a rickshaw or taxi for the last few kilometres. Beyond them to the north lie the Buddhist caves chiselled out of the hillside at **Kanheri**, and the crumbling Portuguese fort at **Bassein**.

Byculla and the Veermata Jeejamata (Victoria and Albert) museum

As the bedrock of Bombay's once-gigantic weaving industry, **Byculla**, immediately north of the central bazaar, epitomizes the grim legacy of nineteenth-century industrialization: idle chimney stacks, overcrowded chawls and pavements strewn with ragged, sleeping bodies. The cotton-mills and sweat-shops are still here, churning out cheap clothes for the massive domestic market, but few can claim the turnovers they enjoyed a hundred years ago. Today, eclipsed by their old Gujarati rivals in Surat and Ahmedabad, all but the larger nationalized mills teeter on the brink of bankruptcy.

Visitors are welcome to look around the few of Byculla's cotton-mills still in business, but a more common reason to come up here is to see the **Victoria and Albert museum** (renamed Veermata Jeejamata museum) on Dr Babasaheb Ambedkar Marg (daily except Wed 10am–5pm; free). Inspired by its namesake in London, this grand Victorian-Gothic building was built in 1871 to house artefacts relating to Bombay's history and development. Engravings, photographs and old maps are displayed in a small gallery on the first floor, along with sundry objets d'art. Downstairs in the main hall, the exhibits are more eclectic. Among the Victorian china and modest assortment of south Indian bronzes, are cases filled with papier-mâché parakeets, pick-axe heads and plastic models of vegetables. More instructive is the scale model of a Parsi Tower of Silence (see p.633), with a gruesome description of the mortuary rituals performed on the real ones on Malabar Hill.

The museum's oldest and most famous exhibit, however, is the **stone elephant** in the small garden to the rear of the building. Now somewhat forlorn and neglected in the shadows, this was the very beast that inspired the Portuguese to name the island in Bombay harbour "Elephanta" (see p.638). The crumbling figure was brought here for safe-keeping in 1863 from its original, and more fittingly prominent site alongside the landing stage that leads up to the cave temple.

A wrought-iron gateway beyond the elephant opens onto one of Bombay's most popular venues for an old-fashioned family day out. The peaceful and green **botanical gardens** (daily except Wed 8am–6pm) hold a huge collection of South Asian flora, plus Bombay's only **zoo**, where, after a trip around the predictably small and smelly cages, kids can enjoy an elephant or camel ride.

Both museum and botanical gardens can be reached either by *BEST* **bus** (#3 or #11(Ltd) from Colaba; #19 from Flora Fountain and Crawford Market) or by suburban **train** to Byculla station, on the opposite (western) side of the motorway.

Juhu Beach

With its palm trees, glamorous seaside apartment blocks and designer clothes stores, **Juhu**, 30km north of downtown, is Bombay's answer to Sunset Boulevard. Unless you're staying in one of the many 5-star hotels lining its five-kilometre strip of white sand, however, this affluent suburb holds little appeal. The beach itself is certainly no great shakes – thanks to an oily slick of raw sewage that seeps into the Arabian Sea from the slum bastis surrounding Mahim Creek to the south, sunbathing and swimming are out of the question. A more salubrious way to enjoy Juhu is to walk along the strand after office hours, when young families turn out in droves to enjoy the sunsets and sea breezes, attracting a bevy of *bhel puri-wallahs*, side shows, mangy camels and carts, and lads hawking cheap Taiwanese toys.

Further north up Juhu Rd, the headquarters of the International Society for Krishna Consciousness (ISKCON) deals with matters more spiritual. Its richly appointed **Krishna temple** (daily 4am–1pm & 4–9pm) draws local Hindus in their Sunday-best shirtings and *saris*, and well-heeled Westerners wearing kaftans, *kurtas* and *dhotis*. Rich visitors get to stay in what must surely rank as the world's most glamorous *dharamshala* – a modern, multi-storeyed hotel complex with its own veg restaurant, conference hall and theatre.

Kanheri Caves

The chief reason to make the day's excursion to the suburb of Borivli, 42km out at the northern limits of Bombay's sprawl, is to visit the Buddhist **caves** of **Kanheri** (daily 9am–5.30pm), ranged over the hills in virtually unspoilt forest. It's an interminable journey by road, so catch one of the many **trains** (50min) on the suburban line from Churchgate (marked "BO" on the departure boards; "limited stop" trains are 15min faster). When you arrive, take the Borivli East exit, and pick up an **auto-rickshaw** as far as the bottom of the hill near the caves, 3km along a wooded road from the entrance. Bring water and food, as the stalls here only sell cool drinks.

Kanheri may not be as spectacular as other cave sites, but some of its sculpture is superb – though to enjoy the peace and quiet that attracted its original occupants you should avoid the weekend and the crowds of day trippers. Most of the caves, which date from the second to the ninth centuries AD, were used simply for accommodation (*viharas*) during the four months of the monsoon, when an itinerant life was impractical – the season when the forest is at its most beautiful. They are connected by steep winding paths and steps; engage one of the friendly local guides at the entrance to find your way about, but don't expect any sort of lecture as their English is limited.

In **Cave 1**, an incomplete *chaitya* hall (a hall with a *stupa* at one end, an aisle and row of columns at either side), you can see where the rock was left cut, but unfinished. Two *stupas* from the Hinayana period stand in **Cave 2**; one was vandalized by a certain N Christian, whose carefully incised Times-Roman graffiti bears the date 1810. A panel shows seated Buddhas, portrayed as a teacher. Behind, and to the side, is the *bodhisattva* of compassion, Padmapani, while to the right the *viharas* feature rock-cut beds.

Huge Buddhas, with serenely joyful expressions and unfeasibly large shoulders, stand on either side of the porch to the spectacular **Cave 3**. Between them, you'll see the panels of "donor couples", thought to have been foreigners that patronized the community. Inside, leading to a *stupa* at the back, octagonal columns in two rows, some decorated with animal motifs, line the magnificent Hinayana *chaitya* hall.

The sixth-century **Cave 11** is a large assembly hall, where two long "tables" of rock were used for the study of manuscripts. Seated at the back, in the centre, is a figure of the Buddha as teacher, an image repeated in the entrance, to the left, with a wonderful flight of accompanying celestials. Just before the entrance to a small cell in **Cave 34**, flanked by two standing Buddhas, an unfinished ceiling painting shows the Buddha touching the earth. There must be at least a hundred more Buddha images on panels in **Cave 67**, a large hall. On the left side, and outside in the entrance, these figures are supported by *nagas* (snakes representing *kundalini*, yogic power).

Bassein

Trundling over the rickety iron bridge that joins the northern fringes of Bombay to the Maharashtran mainland, you could easily fail to notice the ruined fort at **Bassein** (or Vasai), 61km north of the city centre. Yet these mouldy stone walls, obscured by a carpet of palms and lush tropical foliage at the mouth of the milky-blue River Ulhas, once encompassed India's most powerful and prosperous colonial settlement. It was ceded to the Portuguese by Sultan Bahadur of Gujarat in 1534, in return for help in the Gujarati struggle against the Moghuls, and quickly became the hub of the region's maritime trade, "The Court of the North" from which the Portuguese territories at Goa, Daman and Diu were administered. In 1739, however, the **Marathas** laid siege to the city for three months, eventually wiping out the garrison, and a final death blow was dealt in 1780 by the cannons of the **British**. Bassein's crumbling remnants were left to be carried off for raw building material or reclaimed by the coastal jungle, and only a handful of weed-infested buildings still stand today.

If you don't mind spending hours in a crowded suburban **train** (around 1hr 15min from Churchgate, and no fun at all in rush hours), Bassein makes an atmospheric day trip from the city. Only a few express trains stop at the nearest mainline station, Vasai Rd, from where the onward trip (11km) involves jumping in and out of **shared autorickshaws**. These stop halfway at a busy market crossroads, where you catch another ride for the last stretch from a stand 100m up a road left from the crossroads. Ask for the "*kila*", the Marathi word for "fort". Stock up on food and drink at Vasai Rd; there's nowhere very sanitary to eat in Bassein.

The **fort** is entered through a large gateway in its slanting stone battlements. Once inside, the road runs past a modern monument to the Maratha leader, Shivaji, before heading towards the woods and the old Portuguese town. The ruins are a melancholy sight: *peepal* and tall palm trees poke through the chancels of churches and convents, while water buffalo plod listlessly past piles of rubble, and monkeys leap and crash through the canopy overhead.

By contrast, the small **fishing village**, under the archway from the rickshaw stand, is thriving. The spiritual legacy of the Portuguese has endured here longer than their architectural one, as shown by the painted Madonna shrines tucked into wall-niches and crucifixes gleaming on the singlets of the fishermen lounging in the local bar. On the **beach**, a short way down the narrow sandy footpath through the main cluster of huts, large wooden frames are hung with pungent-smelling strips of dried pomfret, while nearby, fishing boats bob around in the silt-laden estuary water.

Accommodation

Even though Bombay offers all kinds of **accommodation**, finding a room at the right price when you arrive can be a real problem. Budget travellers, in particular, can expect a hard time; standards at the bottom of the range are grim and room rates exorbitant. A windowless cell, with wood-partition walls and no running water can cost Rs300 and above, while a comfortable room in the centre of town, with an attached toilet and shower, and a window, may set you back the best part of Rs1000. The best of the relatively inexpensive places tend to fill up by noon, which can often mean a long trudge in the heat with only an overpriced flea-pit at the end of it, so you should really phone ahead as soon as (or preferably well before) you arrive. Prices in upmarket places are further inflated by the state-imposed "**luxury tax**" (between 4 and 30 percent depending on how expensive the room is), and "**service-charges**" levied by the hotel itself; such charges are included in the price symbols shown below.

Colaba, down in the far, southern end of the city, has dozens of possibilities in each price range and is where the majority of foreign visitors head first. A short way across the city centre, **Marine Drive**'s accommodation is generally a little more expensive, but more salubrious, with Back Bay and the promenade right on the doorstep. If you're arriving by train and plan to make a quick getaway, a room closer to **VT** station is worth considering. Alternatively, **Juhu**, way to the north near the airports, boasts a string of flashy 4- and 5-stars, with a handful of less expensive places behind the beach. For those who just want to crawl off the plane and straight into bed, there are plenty of options in the suburbs around **Sahar** and **Santa Cruz airports**, a short taxi ride from the main terminal buildings.

Finally, if you would like to **stay with an Indian family**, ask at the government tourist office in Churchgate, or at their information counters in Sahar and Santa Cruz (see p.622) about the popular "paying guest" scheme. Bed and breakfast-style accommodation in family homes, vetted by the tourist office, is available throughout the city at rates ranging from Rs200–1000.

ACCOMMODATION PRICE CODES

All **accommodation prices** in this book have been coded using the symbols below. In principle the prices given are for the least expensive double rooms in each establishment; however, some hotels, usually in category ①, offer rates per bed rather than per room. Local taxes are not included unless specifically stated. For more details, see p.35.

① up to Rs100	④ Rs225–350	⑦ Rs750–1200
② Rs100–150	⑤ Rs350–500	⑧ Rs1200–2200
③ Rs150–225	⑥ Rs500–750	⑨ Rs2200 and upwards

Colaba

A short ride from the city's main commercial districts, railway stations and tourist office, **Colaba** makes a handy base. It also offers more in the way of food and entertainment than neighbouring districts, especially along its busy main thoroughfare, "Colaba Causeway" (Shahid Bhagat Singh – SBS – Marg). The streets immediately south and west of the Gateway of India are chock-full of accommodation, ranging from grungy guest houses to India's most famous 5-star hotel, the *Taj Mahal Intercontinental*. Avoid at all costs the nameless lodges lurking on the top storeys of wooden-fronted houses along **Arthur Bunder Rd** – the haunts of not-so-oil-rich Gulf Arabs and touts who depend on commission from these rock-bottom hostels to finance their heroin habits. If, like many, you find all this sleaze a turn-off, Colaba's quieter, leafier backstreets harbour plenty of respectable, mid-range hotels.

For a map of Colaba, see p.626.

INEXPENSIVE

Carlton, 12 Mereweather Rd (☎202 0259). Popular budget hotel in advanced state of decrepitude. Pricier rooms have attached baths. Common verandah. ④–⑤.

India, 4th Floor, 1/39 Kamal Mansion, Arthur Bunder Rd (☎283 3769). Ceilingless, partitioned rooms with common baths (only those on the sea-facing side have windows). OK for a night and cheaper than *Sea Shore* upstairs. ④.

Kishan, Ground Floor, Shirin Manzil, Walton Rd (☎283 3886). Scruffy, but fairly clean and cool, and good for the price. Cheapest a/c option in the area. ④.

Lawrence, 3rd Floor, 33 Rope Walk Lane, off K Dubash Marg, opposite *Jehangir Art Gallery* (☎284 3618). Far and away Bombay's best-value cheap hotel. Six immaculate double rooms (1 single) with fans, common shower-toilet and breakfast included. Best to book in advance. ③.

Oliver Guest House, 6 Walton Rd (☎284 0291). Grubby and semi-derelict lodge, with slummy toilets and mattresses. Mentioned because it's the cheapest in Colaba – a dubious distinction. ②.

Prosser's, 2–4 Henry Rd (☎283 4937). Noisy, with mostly wood-partitioned rooms. ④.

Salvation Army, Red Shield House, 30 Mereweather Rd, directly behind *Taj* (☎284 1824). Rock-bottom bunk beds in cramped, stuffy dorms (lockers available), good-value doubles (some a/c), and a sociable travellers' scene. Cheap canteen food. Priority given to women. ①–⑤.

Sea Shore, 4th Floor, 1/49 Kamal Mansion, Arthur Bunder Rd (☎287 4237). Currently among the best budget deals in Colaba. The sea-facing rooms with windows are much better than airless cells on the other side. Try the cheaper *India* downstairs if it's full. Common baths only. ④–⑤.

YWCA, 18 Madam Cama Rd (☎202 0445). Relaxing, secure and quiet hostel with spotless dorms, doubles or family rooms. Rate includes membership, breakfast and filling buffet dinner. One month's advance booking (by money order) advisable. ③–⑥.

MODERATE

Apollo Guest House, Dhun Mahal, Garden Rd (☎284 0121). Grotty and overpriced, boxed into dingy ground floor flat. Avoid its namesake on Colaba Causeway – no connection – at all costs.

Cowie's, 15 Walton Rd (☎284 0232). Promising facade, but rooms are windowless, and non-a/c. ⑤.

Gulf, 4/36 Kamal Mansion, Arthur Bunder Rd (☎283 3742). Seedy surroundings, but respectable and recently redecorated, with clean, modern rooms. ⑤–⑥.

Kerawala Chambers, 3rd and 4th Floors, 25 PJ Ramchandani Marg (☎282 1089). Decent hotel tucked away above *Strand*, boasting the cheapest sea-facing rooms in Colaba. Good value. ⑤–⑥.

Regency, 18 Lansdowne House, Mahakari Bhusan Marg, behind *Regal* cinema (☎202 029; fax 287 3375). Well-appointed rooms, some rather cramped, and cheaper attic garrets with character. ⑥–⑦.

Strand, 30 PJ Ramchandani Marg (☎824 1624). Simple, spacious and reasonably comfortable rooms, although the sea-facing ones are way overpriced. Common or attached bathrooms. ⑦–⑧.

Whalley's, Jaiji Mansion, 41 Mereweather Rd (☎283 4206). Well-established, popular hotel in rambling colonial building, with 26 rooms (some very small), common or attached shower-toilets, pleasant verandah and some a/c. Reasonable value. ⑥–⑦.

EXPENSIVE

Ascot, 38 Garden Rd (☎287 2105; fax 204 6447). One of Bombay's oldest hotels. Comfortable, spacious rooms, with cable TV, room service etc. ⑧.

Diplomat, 24–26 PK Boman Behram Marg (☎283 0000). Hemmed in by the *Taj* across the road and in need of a face-lift, but the rooms are pleasant. ⑦–⑨.

Fariyas, 35 Arthur Rd (☎283 4892). Next on the scale down from the *Taj*. Relaxing roof garden, luxurious decor, pool, health club, central a/c and all the trimmings. ⑨.

Garden, 42 Garden Rd (☎824 1476). Rather bland option, with no single occupancy rates for its comfortable a/c rooms, but a reasonable restaurant and bar. ⑧.

Goodwin, Jasmine Building, Garden Rd (☎287 1592). Top class 3-star with restaurant, bar and 24hr room service. ⑧.

Regent, 8 Best Rd (☎287 1854; fax 202 0363). Luxurious, international-standard hotel on smaller scale, with all mod cons but smallish rooms. ⑦–⑧.

Sea Palace, 26 PJ Ramchandani Marg (☎285 4404; fax 284 1828). A touch shabby from the outside, but rooms are well-furnished and have bath tubs. Sea views at a premium. ⑦.

Shelley's, 30 PJ Ramchandani Marg (☎284 0229). Charmingly old-fashioned hotel in colonial mould. Period furniture, *pukka* dining hall and (more expensive) sea views. Recommended. ⑦–⑧.

Taj Mahal Intercontinental, PJ Ramchandani Marg (☎202 3366; fax 287 2711). The stately home among India's top hotels, and the haunt of Bombay's *beau monde*. Opulent suites in old wing or modern skyscraper; shopping arcades, outdoor pool, swish bars and restaurants. ⑧–⑨.

Marine Drive and Nariman Point

At the western edge of the downtown area, Netaji Subhash Chandra Marg, or **Marine Drive**, sweeps from the skyscrapers of Nariman Point in the south to Chowpatty Beach in the north. Along the way, 4- and 5-star hotels take advantage of the panoramic views over Back Bay and the easy access to the city's commercial heart, while a couple of inexpensive guest houses are worth trying if Colaba's cheap lodges don't appeal. Compared with Colaba, Marine Drive, and the arterial **VN Road** that connects it with Churchgate, are more open and relaxed. Families and office cronies plod along the promenade in the evening, approached more often by *gram-* and balloon-*wallahs* than junkies and money-changers. The hotels below are marked on the map on p.625

Ambassador, VN Rd (☎204 1131; fax 204 0004). Luxurious 4-star with excellent views from upper front-side rooms and revolving rooftop restaurant. No pool. ⑨.

Bentley's, 3rd Floor, Krishna Mahal, Marine Drive (☎203 1244). Run-down hotel on corner of D Rd. No lift, no a/c, no attached bathrooms and no frills (except windows). Breakfast included. ⑤.

Chateau Windsor, 5th Floor, 86 VN Rd (☎204 3376; fax 202 6459). Spotless single, double or group rooms (some on the small side), shared or attached bathrooms, optional a/c and self-catering for vegetarians. Very popular, so reservations recommended. ⑧–⑨.

Nataraj, 135 Marine Drive (☎204 4161; fax 204 3864). Swish 4-star overlooking Back Bay. ⑨.

Norman's, 127 Marine Drive (☎203 4234). Small, moderately priced ground-floor guest house, with neat, clean rooms, some attached shower-toilets and a/c. ⑥.

Oberoi/Oberoi Towers, Nariman Point (☎202 4343). The *Taj*'s main competitor – India's most expensive hotel – is glitteringly opulent, with a pool and Polynesian restaurant. ⑨.

President, 90 Cuffe Parade (☎215 0808). Formula 5-star boasting a pool, shopping mall, beauty parlour and good Italian restaurant. ⑨.

Sea Green, 145 Marine Drive (☎/fax 282 2294). Comfortable, efficient and clean hotel pitched at businessmen. Cable TV in all rooms. 24hr check out (8am for advance reservations). ⑧.

Sea Green South, 145-A Marine Drive (☎/fax 282 1613). Clone of *Sea Green* next door, only marginally cheaper. ⑧.

Around Victoria Terminus

Arriving in Bombay after a long train journey at **VT**, you may not feel like embarking on a room-hunt around Colaba. Unfortunately, the area around the station and the nearby GPO, though fairly central, has little to recommend it. The majority of places worth trying are mid-range hotels grouped around the crossroads of P D'Mello (Frere) Rd, St George's Rd and Shahid Bhagat Singh (SBS) Marg, immediately southeast of the post office (five minutes on foot from the station). VT itself also has **retiring rooms**, although these are booked up by noon. The hotels below are marked on the map on p.625.

City Palace, 121 City Terrace (☎261 5515; fax 267 6897). Large and popular hotel bang opposite the station. "Ordinary " rooms are tiny and windowless, but have a/c and are perfectly clean. ⑤–⑥.

Grand, 17 Sprott Rd, Ballard Estate (☎269 8211; fax 262 6581). Solid and very comfortable with faintly 1930s feel left by the British. Central a/c, restaurant and foreign exchange. ⑧.

Lord's, 301 Adi Mazban Path (Mangalore St) (☎261 0077). Above *City Kitchen* restaurant. Drab, but reasonably clean and cheap for the area. Mostly common bathrooms. ④–⑤.

Manama, opposite George Hospital, 221/5 P D'Mello Rd (☎261 3412). Reasonably clean, popular budget option with run-of-the-mill rooms. Book ahead. ⑤.

Oasis, 272 SBS Marg (☎269 7886). Small, well-maintained hotel close to VT. Few frills except 24hr running water. Some a/c. Good value. ④–⑤.

Prince, 34 Walchand Hirachand Rd, near Red Gate (☎261 2809). The best all-round economy deal in this area: modest, neat and respectable. Avoid the airless partition rooms upstairs. ⑤.

Railway, 249 P D'Mello Rd (☎261 6705; fax 265 8049). Spacious, clean and friendly, and the pick of the mid-range bunch around VT, though correspondingly pricey. ⑥–⑦.

Welcome, 257 SBS Marg (☎261 2196). Marble reception and OK furniture. ⑥–⑧.

Juhu Beach

Since the early 1970s, a crop of exclusive **resort-hotels** has been creeping steadily down the road that runs behind **Juhu Beach**, twenty minutes' drive from Santa Cruz airport. Most offer the predictable hermetically sealed five-star package, with bars, restaurants and a pool to lounge beside. It's hard to believe that anyone would come to India express-ly for this sort of thing, but if money's no object and you want to keep well away from all the hustle, bustle and poverty, you'll be spoiled for choice.

Vile Parle (pronounced *Veelay Parlay*) is the nearest suburban railway station to Juhu. All the hotels below lay on courtesy coaches from the airports, unless stated otherwise.

Centaur Juhu Beach, Juhu Tara Rd (☎611 3090; fax 6343). Gigantic 5-star with palatial foyer, sea views, pool, jogging track and "Tex-Mex" restaurant (among others). The full works. ⑨.

Citizen, 960 Juhu Beach (☎611 7273; fax 7170). Behind the Mahatma Gandhi statue. Backs on to the beach, with pleasant restaurant and views but no pool. ⑧.

Guestline, 462 AB Nair Rd (☎625 2222; fax 620 2821). Very plush, efficient and pricey. Roof top restau-rant and pool among the mod cons. ⑨.

Holiday Inn, Balraj Sahani Marg (☎620 4444; fax 4452). This recently re-vamped 5-star boasts two pools, terrace garden, shops, bars and formula furnishings. ⑨.

Sands, 39/2 Juhu Beach (☎620 4511; fax 5268). Plush 4-star; no pool. ⑨.

Sea Princess, Juhu Beach (☎612 2661; fax 611 3973). Five star with pool, smack on the beach. ⑧.

Seaside, 39/2 Juhu Beach (☎620 0293). Pleasant 3-star next to *Sun-n-Sand*. No pool. ⑥–⑦.

Sun-n-Sand, 39 Juhu Beach (☎620 1811; fax 2170). Longest established of the big 5-stars, with all amenities, including a pool. ⑨.

Around the airports

Hotels near Sahar and Santa Cruz **airports** cater predominantly for transit passengers and flight crews, at premium rates. If you're picking up your own tab, and arrive in Bombay at an inconvenient hour when most of the hotels in the city proper are closed or full, you may want to arrange less expensive accommodation in the nearby suburbs of **Santa Cruz**, **Vile Parle** or **Andheri**. Bookings can be made through the accommo-dation desk in the arrivals concourse at Sahar, or by phone. Nearly all the "moderate to expensive" hotels below have courtesy buses to and from the terminal building.

INEXPENSIVE

Airlines International, Plot #111, Fourth Rd, Prabhat Colony, Santa Cruz East (☎614 3069). Unremarkable economy hotel near domestic airport. Separate baths, single rates available. ⑤.

Airport Palace, Vakola Bridge, Bull's Royce Colony Rd (☎614 0057). Small, airless rooms, but all with fresh bed linen and lockable doors. ④.

Rang Mahal, Station Rd, Santa Cruz West (☎649 0303). Tucked away down lane behind (west of) Santa Cruz railway station. Cramped and stuffy, but fairly clean. No single rooms. ⑤.

MODERATE TO EXPENSIVE

Ashwin, near Marol Fire Station, Andheri Kurla Rd, Andheri East (☎836 7235). Medium-sized, international-standard hotel right outside Sahar. ⑧.

Centaur, Western Express Highway, Santa Cruz (☎611 6660; fax 611 3535). Circular building directly outside the domestic airport, with 5 stars, three restaurants, two bars and one pool. ⑨.

Host Inn, opposite Marol Fire Station, Andheri Kurla Rd, Andheri East (☎836 0105). In same mould as Ashwin, with identical prices. ⑦–⑨.
Kamat's Plaza, 70-C Nehru Rd, Vile Parle (☎612 3390; fax 612 5974). Plush 4-star with pool. ⑧–⑨.
Kumaria Presidency, Andheri Kurla Rd (☎834 2025; fax 837 3850). Facing the international airport. One of a string of 3-stars bookable through the accommodation desk in the airport arrivals hall. ⑧–⑨.
Leela Kempinski, Sahar (☎836 3636; fax 836 0606). Ultra-luxurious and best for sports. ⑨.
Samrat, Seventh Rd, Khar, Santa Cruz East, near Khar railway station (☎648 5441; fax 604 5503). Another comfortable transit hotel in quiet suburban backstreet. No courtesy bus. ⑤–⑥.
Satellite, 213/214 Dixit Rd, Vile Parle East (☎611 7452). Similar to the *Samrat*, but closer to domestic airport and with courtesy bus. All a/c. ⑥.

Eating and drinking

In keeping with its cosmopolitan credentials, Bombay (and Colaba above all) is crammed with interesting **places to eat and drink**, whether you fancy splashing out on a buffet lunch-with-a-view from a flashy 5-star revolving restaurant, or simply tucking into piping-hot *roti kebab* by gaslight in the street.

Restaurants, bars and cafes are listed below by district. The most expensive restaurants, particularly in the top hotels, will levy "service charges" that can add 30 percent to the price of your meal. Phone numbers have been given where we recommend you reserve a table for dinner.

STREET FOOD

Bombay is renowned for distinctive street foods – and especially **bhel puri**, a quintessentially Bombay *masala* mixture of puffed-rice, deep-fried vermicelli, potato, crunchy puri pieces, chilli paste, tamarind water, chopped onions and coriander. More hygienic, but no less ubiquitous, is **pao bhaji**, a round slab of flat-bread stuffed with meat or vegetables simmered in a vat of hot oil, and **kanji vada**, savoury doughnuts soaked in fermented mustard and chilli sauce. Even if all that doesn't appeal, a pit stop at one of the city's hundreds of **juice bars** probably will. There's no better way to beat the sticky heat than with a glass of cool milk shaken with fresh pineapple, mango, banana, *chikoo*, or custard apple. Just make sure they hold the ice – made, of course, with untreated water.

Colaba

Colaba (see map on p.626) has even more places to eat than it does hotels. In the space of just one kilometre, you can sample an amazing array of **regional cuisines**: pure-veg "Hindu hotels" serving delicious Gujarati and south Indian food stand cheek-by-jowl with Muslim cafes whose menus will delight die-hard carnivores. Nearby, within a stone's throw of the *Taj* and its expensive gourmet restaurants, are Bombay's oldest and best-loved Chinese joints. Other than during the monsoons (when choppy seas keep the fishing fleet in the polluted waters of the harbour), these offer fresh, safe **seafood** dishes of tiger prawns, crab or delicate white pomfret. Still in Colaba, traditional Iranian restaurants serve minced lamb and mutton specialities, while revamped cafe-bars dish up draught beer and reasonable Western food for tourists and local yuppies. Non-vegetarians will enjoy the succulent meats, smothered in the split lentil stew known as *dhansak*, in the Parsi restaurants, while Goan and Mangalorean "lunchhomes" crop up everywhere too – good for a pork *vindaloo* or a fiery fish curry.

The majority of Colaba's best cafes, bars and restaurants – among them the popular traveller's haunts, *Leopold's* and the *Cafe Mondegar* – are up at the north end of the Causeway. Those below are divided into price categories based on the cost of a main dish: inexpensive (below Rs50), moderate (Rs50–100), and expensive (above Rs100).

INEXPENSIVE

Bademiya, behind the *Taj* on Tulloch Rd. Legendary Colaba *kebab-wallah*; delicious flame-grilled chicken, mutton and fish steaks, in hot tandoori *rotis*, from benches on the sidewalk.

Kailash Parbat, 1 Pasta Lane, near *Strand* cinema. The outside doesn't look much, but the pure veg nibbles, hot snacks and sweets are worth the walk. Try their famous *makai-ka* (corn) *rotis*.

Majestic, near *Regal* cinema, Colaba Causeway. Large, traditional south Indian joint patronized by off-duty taxi *wallahs*, junior office staff and backpackers. Among the best value in this price range.

New Martin, near *Strand* cinema, Strand Rd. Unpromising formica booths, but famed for delicious Goan dishes such as prawn *pulao*, sausages, pork *vindaloo* and spicy fish curry. Does take-aways.

Olympic Coffee House, 1 Colaba Causeway. Old-fashioned, fin-de-siècle Iranian cafe with marble table tops, wooden wall panels and a mezzanine floor for "ladies". Decor more alluring than the menu of greasy meat dishes, but nonetheless, a good place for a coffee break.

MODERATE

Alps, Nawroji Fardunji Rd. Trendy, ersatz American restaurant serving lamb-burgers, fries, sizzling steaks and copious "mixed-grills".

Baghdadi, Tulloch Rd. Male-dominated place famous for its meat: mostly mutton and chicken steeped in spicy garlic sauce. Chauffeurs pick up take-aways for their bosses in the *Taj* from here.

Delhi Durbar, Colaba Causeway (☎202 0235). Popular branch of reputed Grant Rd restaurant specializing in classic Mughlai food with some vegetarian and Chinese alternatives. *Biriyanis* still cooked in traditional way – slowly over charcoal fire. Very reasonable prices.

Cafe Mondegar, 5a Colaba Causeway, next to the *Regal* cinema. Small, Western-style cafe-bar serving snacks (including tasty pizza) and light meals. Draught beer, by the pitcher or glass, loud CD juke box and murals by a famous Goan cartoonist are the main attractions, though the small tables can make life difficult for women on their own.

Leopold's, Colaba Causeway. Colaba's most famous cafe-bar is determinedly Western, with a clientele and prices to match. 400 items on the menu from scambled eggs to "drunken chicken", washed down with cold beer.

EXPENSIVE

Golden Gate, Madam Cama Rd, next to *YWCA* (☎202 6306). Classy a/c restaurant, best known for its buffet salad lunches. Also north Indian dishes, plus seafood and Chinese.

Ling's Pavillion, 19/21 Lansdowne Rd, behind *Regal* cinema (☎285 0023). Swanky Chinese restaurant; soft lighting, marble floors and gourmet Cantonese cuisine.

Menage à Trois, *Taj Hotel* (☎202 3366). Fussy French (*nouvelle*) cuisine – hors d'oeuvres and desserts only. Very expensive.

Palkhi, Walton Rd (☎284 0079). Over-the-top, quasi-medieval decor and traditional Mughlai cooking for the health-conscious (lighter on oil and spices). Lots of veg options too. Very reasonable.

Tanjore, *Taj Hotel* (☎202 3366). Opulent interior, rich Mughlai cuisine and classical Indian music and dance in the evening. Expense account prices.

Downtown

In the following list *Britania & Co.*, *City Kitchen* and *Mahesh Lunch Home* feature on the Churchgate and Fort map (see p.625); the others appear on the on the Colaba map (p.626).

Britania & Co., opposite the GPO, Sprott Rd, Ballard Estate. Definitive Iranian/Parsi food and decor. Try their special *"berry pulao"* or Bombay duck dishes. A real find, and cheap too.

Chetana, 34 K Dubash Marg (☎284 4968). Painstakingly prepared Rajasthani/Gujarati food, including set *thalis* and numerous à la carte dishes – absolutely the last word in fine veg cuisine. Expensive, but not extravagant. Reserve for dinner.

City Kitchen, 301 SBS Marg. Highly rated hole-in-the-wall Goan restaurant. Serves all the usual dishes – mostly fish and meat simmered in coconut milk and fiery spices. Inexpensive.

Copper Chimney, 18 K Dubash Marg (☎204 1661). Renowned tandoori house, recently renovated with wonderful ceramic murals; stylish renditions of standard north Indian dishes. Superb but expensive. Reservations essential.

Khyber, opposite *Jehangir Art Gallery*, Kala Ghoda (☎204 3227). Ultra-fashionable, with opulent Arabian Nights interior and uncompromisingly rich Mughlai/Punjabi cuisine. The chicken *makhanwallah* is legendary. Reservations essential.

Mahesh Lunch Home, 8-B Cawasji Patel St, Fort. Inexpensive Keralan restaurant serving authentic veg "meals" and delicious non-veg options – chicken fried in ginger or fish *masala* on groaning platefuls of rice.

Samovar, *Jehangir Art Gallery*, MG Rd. Very pleasant, peaceful semi-open-air cafe, with varying menu: *roti kebabs*, prawn curry, fresh salads and *dhansak* – and beer. Tues–Sat 10.30am–7.30pm.

Wayside Inn, opposite *Jehangir Art Gallery*, K Dubash Marg. Upmarket Parsi cafe, with red-chequered table cloths and solid English cooking. Nice place for a coffee after visiting the museum.

Churchgate and Nariman Point

Chopsticks, 90a VN Rd (☎204 9284). Wide choice of pricey meat, seafood and veg in fiery Szechuan and milder Cantonese style. Try the excellent *dim sum* or "ant climbing up the tree".

Croissants Etc, Industrial Insurance Building, opposite Churchgate station. Filled croissants, pricey pastries and other Western food, including delicious cakes. A/c.

Gaylord, VN Rd (☎282 1259). Surreal, Parisian-style terrace cafe in the heart of Bombay. Tandoori, sizzlers and some Western food. Wholewheat bread, baguettes and sticky buns in the patisserie.

Kamling, VN Rd (☎204 2618). Favourite for the title of oldest, best and most authentic Chinese in town. Southeast Asian flight crews and well-heeled locals tuck into delicious Cantonese dishes – try the mouthwatering "chimney soup" or the (expensive) seafood specialities.

The Outrigger, *Oberoi Hotel*, Nariman Point (☎202 3577). Polynesian specialities (Chinese with more fruit thrown in), tribal masks and a full-size canoe. Expensive.

Purohit's, VN Rd (☎204 6241). Justly popular traditional restaurant and coffee house serving good range of inexpensive *thalis*, main dishes and snacks. Recommended.

Rangoli, Nehru Centre, Nariman Point (☎233211). Excellent-value buffet lunches its forte, but the à la carte menu (including fish and strict Jain veg dishes) is gourmet standard and reasonably priced.

Satkar, opposite Churchgate station's western exit. Busy pure-veg terrace restaurant: great for south Indian "fast food" (*dosas*, *idlys*, *vadas* etc) and crowd-watching.

The Pizzeria, 143 Marine Drive. Delicious freshly baked pizzas served on terrace overlooking Back Bay, or to take away. Plenty of choice, and moderate prices.

The Top, *Ambassador Hotel*, VN Rd (☎291131). Revolving restaurant in glam 4-star hotel with panoramic views. Excellent lunch buffets are just the thing for a splurge. Reserve for dinner.

Trattoria, *Hotel President*, 90 Cuffe Parade (☎495 0808). Surprisingly authentic Italian cuisine. Pizza and pasta with fresh herbs, real Parmesan, and a big buffet lunch on Sundays (noon–3pm).

Crawford Market and the central bazaars

Badshah Juice and Snack Bar, opposite Crawford Market, Lokmanya Tilak Rd. Bombay's most famous *falooda* joint also serves delicious *kulfi*, ice-creams and dozens of freshly squeezed fruit juices. The ideal place to round off a trip to the market.

Bhaishankar's, near Bhuleshwar Market, CP Tank Circle. One of Bombay's oldest and most respected sweet shops. Try their Bengali *barfi*, cashew *kalingar* or *masala* milk (made with pistachio, almonds, saffron and nutmeg).

Gulshan-e-Iran, Palton Rd (☎265183). Popular Muslim breakfast venue on main road that does inexpensive *biryanis*, *kebabs*, chutneys and fresh bread. Open all day.

Hiralal Kashiram Bhajiwala, Kumbhar Tukda, Bhuleshwar Market. Cheap restaurant serving great *farsan* savouries, including *ponk vadas* (millet and garlic balls), *batata vadas* (made with sweet potatoes) and *kand bhajis* (deep-fried purple-yam), all with a tasty, fiery chutney.

Rajdhani, Mangaldas Rd (in the silk bazaar opposite Crawford market). Outstanding, eat-till-you-burst Gujarati *thalis* dished up by barefoot waiters to discerning aficionados. A little more expensive than usual, but well worth it.

Chowpatty Beach and Kemp's Corner

Chowpatty Beach is a popular venue for a picnic, crowded with vendors selling *kulfi* in clay cups and *bhel puri*, *kanji vada* and *pao bhaji*. **Kemp's Corner**, crouched under the hectic G Deshmukh flyover, fifteen minutes' walk north, boasts a clutch of very good places to eat – handy for visitors to Malabar Hill.

China Garden, Om Chambers, 123 August Kranti Marg (☎363 0841). Malabar Hill's glitterati don their finest for this place, which has expensive, authentic Chinese, Korean, Thai and Japanese food.

Chinese Rooms, Kwality House, Kemp's Corner (☎367 9771). A much less expensive alternative to *China Garden*, specializing in quality Sezchuan, Hunan and Cantonese cooking, with great seafood.

New Yorker, Fulchand Niwas, 25 Chowpatty Seaface. Western food – baked potatoes, pizzas, burgers, and some Tex-Mex options – dished up in a bustling a/c cafe. Moderate.

Paramount, Marine Drive, near the aquarium. Small Iranian cafe, which while it has a certain charm, with marble-top tables, wood-panelled and mirrored walls, applies strict rules: signs request that you "Do not spit", "Do not comb your hair", "Do not stretch legs on other pieces of furniture" and, most advisedly, "Do not sit unnecessarily a long time".

Revival, above *London Pub*, Chowpatty Seaface, near the footbridge. Fairly pricey 1930s retro-decor restaurant serving imaginative and tasty Western and Indian dishes.

Shopping

Bombay is a great place to shop, whether for last-minute souvenirs, or essentials for the long journeys ahead. Locally produced **textiles** and export-surplus clothing are among the best buys, as are **handicrafts** from far-flung corners of the country. With the exception of the swish arcades in the 5-star hotels, **prices** compare surprisingly well with other Indian cities. In the larger shops, rates are fixed and **credit cards** are often accepted; elsewhere, particularly dealing with street-vendors, it pays to **haggle**. Uptown, the **central bazaars** – see p.636 – are better for spectating than serious shopping, although the **antiques** and Friday flea-market in the **Chor**, or "thieves" **bazaar**, can sometimes yield the odd bargain. The **Zaveri** (goldsmiths') **bazaar** opposite Crawford Market is the place to head for new gold and silver jewellery.

Opening hours in the city centre are Monday to Saturday, 10am to 7pm. The Muslim bazaars, quiet on Friday, the Sabbath, are otherwise open until around 9pm.

Antiques

The Chor Bazaar area, and Mutton Street in particular, is the centre of Bombay's antique trade – even if it is no longer highly regarded by serious collectors. For a full account, see p.637. Another good, if much more expensive, place to sift through bric-a-brac is *Phillip's* famous antique shop, on the corner of Madam Cama Rd, opposite the *Regal* cinema in Colaba. This fascinating, old-fashioned store has changed little since it opened in 1860. Innumerable glass lamps and chandeliers hang from the ceiling, while antique display cases are stuffed with miniature brass, bronze and wood Hindu sculpture, silver jewellery, old prints and aquatints. Most of the stuff on sale dates from the twilight of the Raj – a result of the Indian government's ban on the export by foreigners of items more than a century old.

In the *Jehangir Art Gallery* basement, a branch of the antiques chain *Natesan's Antiqarts* offers a tempting selection of antique (and reproduction) sculpture, furniture, paintings and bronzes.

Clothes and textiles

Bombay produces the bulk of India's clothes, mostly the lightweight, light-coloured "shirtings and suitings" favoured by droves of uniformly attired office-*wallahs*. For cheaper Western clothing, you can't beat the long row of stalls on the pavement of MG Rd, opposite the Bombay Gymkhana. "**Fashion Street**" specializes in reject and export-surplus goods ditched by big manufacturers, selling off T-shirts, jeans, leggings, summer dresses, and trendy sweatshirts. Better quality cotton clothes (often stylish designer-label rip-offs) are available in shops along Colaba Causeway, such as *Cotton World*, down Mandlik Marg.

If you're looking for more traditional Indian clothes, head for the *Khadi Village Industries Emporium* at 286 Dr DN Marg, near the *Thomas Cook* office. As *Whiteaway & Laidlaw*, this rambling Victorian department store used to kit all the newly arrived *burra-sahibs* out with pith helmets, khaki shorts and quinine tablets. These days, its old wooden counters, shirt and sock drawers stock dozens of different hand-spun cottons and silks, sold by the metre or made up as vests, *kurtas* or block-printed *salwar kamises*. Other items include the ubiquitous white Nehru caps, *dhotis*, Madras-check *lunghis* and fine brocaded silk *saris*. Actually buying the stuff requires a number of separate manoeuvres: you select an item, get a chit, go to the cash desk, have the additions checked, pay for the goods, get a receipt, and go to the collection point, where your goods will be beautifully wrapped in paper bags just bursting to fall apart.

Another good place to pick up quality Indian clothes is the cloth bazaar on Mangaldas Lane, opposite Crawford Market, where touts lead you through a maze of stalls to backstreet shops crammed with inexpensive silk scarves, embroidered Kashmiri shawls and Gujarati tie-dye wall-hangings.

Handicrafts

Regionally produced **handicrafts** are marketed in assorted state-run emporia at the *World Trade Centre*, down on Cuffe Parade, and along Sir PM Rd, Fort. The quality is consistently high – as are the prices, if you miss out on the periodic holiday discounts. The same goes for the *Central Cottage Industries Emporium*, 34 Shivaji Marg, near the Gateway of India in Colaba, whose size and central location make it the single best all-round place to hunt for souvenirs. Downstairs you'll find inlaid furniture, wood- and metal work, miniature paintings and jewellery, while upstairs specializes in toys, clothing and textiles – Gujarati appliqué bedspreads, hand-painted pillowcases and Rajasthani mirror-work, plus silk ties and Noel Coward dressing-gowns. **Mereweather Rd**, directly behind the *Taj*, is awash with Kashmiri handicraft stores stocking over-priced papier-mâché pots and bowls, silver jewellery, woollen shawls and rugs. Avoid them if you find it hard to shrug off aggressive sales pitches.

Perfume is essentially a Muslim preserve. Down at the south end of Colaba Causeway, around Arthur Bunder Rd, shops with mirrored walls and shelves are stacked with cut-glass carafes full of syrupy, fragrant essential oils. **Incense** is hawked in sticks, cones and slabs of sticky *dhoop* on the sidewalk nearby (check that the boxes haven't already been opened and their contents sold off piecemeal). For bulk buying, the hand-rolled, cottage-made bundles of incense sold in the *Khadi Emporium* on Dr DN Marg (see above) are a better deal; it also has a handicraft department where, in addition to furniture, paintings and ornaments, you can pick up glass bangles, block-printed and calico bedspreads, and wooden votive statues produced in Maharashtran craft villages.

Books

Bombay's excellent English-language **bookshops** are well stocked with everything to do with India, and a good selection of general classics, pulp fiction and travel writing. Indian editions of popular titles cost a fraction of what they do abroad and include lots of interesting works by lesser-known local authors. If you don't mind picking through dozens of trigonometry textbooks, back issues of *National Geographic* and salacious 1960s paperbacks, the street-stalls between Flora Fountain and Churchgate station can also be good places to hunt for secondhand books.

Chetana, 34 Dubash Rd (Rampart Row). Exclusively religion and philosophy.

Crossword, Mahalakshmi Chambers, 22 Bhulabhai Desai Rd, Breach Candy (☎492 2548). Bombay's largest and most reputed retailer, a bus ride (#132) from the downtown area.

BOLLYWOOD THE CAPITAL OF THE HINDU FILM

For anyone brought up on TV, it's hard to imagine the power that films continue to wield in India. Every village has a cinema within walking distance, and with a potential audience in the hundreds of millions, film companies seem to have virtually cast-iron guarantees of vast profits. The Indian film industry is the largest in the world, producing around 750 full-length features each year. Regional cinema, catering for different language groups (in particular the Tamil cinema of Madras), though popular locally, has little national impact. Only Hindi film – which accounts for one-fifth of films made in India – has crossed regional boundaries to great effect, most particularly in the north. The home of the Hindi blockbuster, the "all-India film", is Bombay, famously known as **"Bollywood"**.

To overcome differences of language and religion, the Bollywood movie follows rigid conventions and genres; as in myth, its characters have predetermined actions and destinies. Knowing a plot need not detract from the drama, and indeed, it is not uncommon for Indian audiences to watch films numerous times. Unlike the Hollywood formula, which tends to classify each film under one genre, the Hindi film follows what is known as a **masala** format, including during its luxurious three hours a little bit of everything: especially romance, violence and comedy. Frequently the stories feature dispossessed male heroes fighting evil against all odds with a love interest thrown in. The sexual element is repressed, with numerous wet *saris* and dance routines featuring the tensest pelvic thrusts in the world. Other typical themes include male bonding and betrayal, family melodrama, separation and reunion and religious piety. Dream sequences are almost obligatory, too, along with a festival or celebration scene – typically Holi, when people shower each other with colour – a comic character passing through, and a depraved, alcoholic and mostly Western "cabaret", filled with strutting villains and lewd dancing. One way in which Bollywood has moved closer to Hollywood in recent years, however, has been the development, alarming to traditionalists, of films in which the "hero" is no longer necessarily a moral exemplar; violence can be fun, and good does not always triumph.

Film song is the most popular form of music in India; an average of six songs play an essential part in the narrative of each film. A song can transcend its filmic context, remaining popular years after the film it was composed for has been forgotten. However, the apposite marriage of film and song, through "picturization", means the story lives on in the mind of the listener. Equally, a good song released before the film acts as a trailer to help fill the theatres. The songs are created through the artistic collaboration of a film director, lyricist, music composer, arranger, studio instrumentalists, the "playback" singers (the most famous, Lata Mangeshkar, is in the *Guinness Book of Records* for the number of songs she has recorded), and finally the actor who mimes the song on screen.

The exploits of Bombay's **film stars** – on and off screen – and their lavish lifestyles in the city's clubs and millionaires' ghetto of Malabar Hill, are the subject of endless titillating gossip. Fanzines such as *Stardust, Star and Style, Film World* and *Cine Blitz* are snaffled up by millions, while the industry looks to the more sober *Screen*. Following the careers of the stars requires dedication; each may work on up to ten movies at once.

At one time specially arranged tours made it easy to get into a film studio to see a movie being made, but those days are gone. If you're very keen, try contacting *Mehboob Studios*, Hill Rd, Bandra West (☎642 8045); *Natraj Studios*, Western Express Highway, Andheri East (☎834 2371); or *Film City*, Goregaon East, Bombay 65 (☎840 1533).

Visitors to Bombay should have ample opportunity to sample the delights of a movie. To make an educated choice, buy *Bombay* magazine, which contains extensive listings and reviews. Otherwise, look for the biggest, brightest hoarding, and join the queue. Seats in a comfortable air-conditioned cinema cost around Rs20, or less if you sit in the stalls. Of the two hundred or so **cinemas**, only eight regularly screen **English-language** films. The most central and convenient are the *Regal* in Colaba, the *Eros*, opposite Churchgate station, and the *Sterling*, the *New Excelsior*, and the *New Empire*, which are all a short walk west of Victoria Terminus.

Nalanda, Ground Floor, *Taj*. An exhaustive range of coffee-table tomes and paperback literature.

Pustak Bharati, Bharatiya Vidhya Bhavan, KM Munshi Marg. Excellent small bookshop specializing in Hindu philosophy and literature, plus details of Bhavan's cultural programmes.

Shankar Book-Stand, outside the *Cafe Mondegar*, Colaba Causeway. Piles of easy-reads, guidebooks, classic fiction, and most of the old favourites on India.

Strand, next door to the *Canara Bank*, off PM Rd, Fort. The best bookshop in the city centre, with the full gamut of *Penguins* and Indian literature.

Music

The most famous of Bombay's many good **music shops** are near the *Moti* cinema along SV Patel Rd, in the central bazaar district. *Haribhai Vishwanath, Ram Singh* and *RS Mayeka* are all government-approved retailers of traditional Indian instruments, including *sitars, sarods, tablas* and flutes.

For **cassettes and CDs** try Subhash Chowk, next to the *Jehangir Art Gallery*. *Rhythm House* here is a veritable Aladdin's cave of classical, devotional and popular music from all over India, with a reasonable selection of Western rock, pop and jazz.

Nightlife and entertainment

Bombay never sleeps. No matter what time of night you venture out, there are bound to be others going about some business or other. However, like other parts of India, **nightlife** as Westerners know it is not that developed. A few **bars** and **discos** cater to young Westerners and Bombayites alike, but these are usually in the swanky hotels.

Of course, Bombay is also a cultural centre attracting the finest **Indian classical music** and **dance** artists from all over the country. Venues such as *Bharatiya Vidya Bhavan*, K M Munshi Marg – the headquarters of the international cultural (Hindu) organization – *Cowasjee Jehangir* (CJ) *Hall, Birla Matushri, Tejpal Auditorium, Shanmukhananda Hall* and the *National Centre for the Performing Arts* (NCPA) audi-

---

THE FESTIVALS OF BOMBAY

Bombay has its own versions of all the major Hindu and Muslim festivals, plus a host of smaller neighbourhood celebrations imported by its immigrant communities. Exact dates vary from year to year; check in advance at the government tourist office.

Elephanta Music and Dance Festival (Feb). MTDC-organized cultural event including floodlit performances by classical artists with the Shiva cave temple as backdrop.

Gokhulashtami (July/Aug). Riotous commemoration of Krishna's birthday; terracotta pots filled with curd, milk-sweets and cash are strung from tenement balconies and grabbed by human pyramids of young boys.

Nowroz (July/Aug). The Parsi New Year is celebrated with special ceremonies in the Fire Temples and feasting at home.

Ganesh Chathurthi (Aug/Sept). Huge effigies of Ganesh, the elephant-headed god of prosperity and wisdom, are immersed in the sea at Chowpatty Beach in a ritual originally promoted by freedom-fighters to circumvent British anti-assembly legislation. Recently it has seemed in danger of being hijacked by Hindu extremists such as the Shiv Sena, tinging it more with chauvinism than celebration.

Nariel Purnima (Sept). Koli fishermen launch brightly decorated boats to mark the end of the monsoon.

Ramadan (varies according to the Muslim calendar). Annual one-month bout of Muslim fasting and feasting; all-night food stalls in the bazaars, processions of Shi'ite flagellants commemorating the martyrdom of the Prophet's grandson at the battle of the Karbala.

Dussehra (Oct). Rama's victory over the evil king of Lanka, Ravana, is marked in Bombay by re-enactments of scenes from the *Ramayana* on Chowpatty Beach.

torium frequently present concerts and recitals. NCPA also offers modern Gujarati, Hindi, Marathi and English-language **plays** as well as Western **chamber music**, while a smattering of platinum-selling Western rock artists appear at Bombay stadia.

Bars and cabarets

Bombay has an unusually easy-going attitude to **alcohol**; popping into a bar for a beer is very much accepted (for men at least) even at lunchtime. Chowpatty Beach and Colaba Causeway, where *Leopold's* and the *Cafe Mondegar*, form the focus of the travellers' social scene, and are the main alternatives to the five-star hotels.

However, there is also a seamier side to the city's nightlife, concentrated around (illegal) late-night cabarets in the Grant Rd area. These dens of iniquity, where women dance before men-only crowds in clothes that might in the West be considered Victorian in their propriety but would be unheard-of anywhere else in India, are not places the casual visitor should dream of venturing into.

The Inside Story, *Cafe Mondegar*, Colaba Causeway, next to *Regal* cinema. The *Mondegar's* exclusive inner sanctum is a pricey ersatz English pub. With a mostly male clientele and bouncers.

Leopold Pub, 1st Floor, *Leopold's*, Colaba Causeway. Swanky, self-consciously Western-style bar-nightclub, with bouncers, serving expensive beers to Bombay's smart set. No single men admitted.

London Pub, 39D Chowpatty Seaface. Designer frosted-glass bar with prog-rock murals, quality sound system and uncomfortable bar stools.

The Tavern, *Fariyas Hotel*, Colaba. Another "English-style" pub, complete with wooden beams, loud music, and the local equivalent of lager louts.

Tiger Tim's, near the Stockmarket, Fort. Trendy bar with *MTV* sounds and clientele to match.

Discos

India has a long history of folk, classical and *filmi* dance, but people in general remain uncomfortable with free-style public frugging. The popularity of the bump'n'grind physicality of Apache Indian and the perennial "MJ", Michael Jackson, may free up the scene, but don't expect wild-abandon rave culture. Many clubs operate a "couples-only" entrance policy, and even those that don't may prohibit "stag" dancing (a male on his own). Most discos are seriously expensive and the clientele reflects this; those in the five-star hotels are usually open only to members and their guests.

The 1900s, *Taj Mahal*. Pounding disco, free to guests but otherwise for members only – a year's membership is a snip at Rs25,000.

The Cellar, *The Oberoi*. Hotel disco open to non-members as long as they're in a couple.

Go Bananas, *Kamat's Plaza* near Santa Cruz airport. Plays hit records and, on certain nights, allows singles onto its small dance floor.

Razzberry Rhinoceros, *Juhu Hotel*, Juhu Beach. A good size dance floor. Entrance is for couples only and they serve fairly pricey Chinese, Western and Indian food.

Sheetal Again, Juhu. Small pub with an enthusiastic crowd, tiny dance floor, loud sound system and DJs playing international dance hits. The barmen dress in denim dungarees and confederate caps. Although singles are allowed in, the comfortable seating is reserved for the paired-up. Woe betide any man who tries to dance on his own; the DJ will call for him to leave.

Listings

Ambulance ☎102, 534 1552 or 768 1010.

Hindi lessons *Kalina University*, in north Bombay, and a number of private academies run short courses. Ask at the tourist office in Churchgate (☎203 3144) for more details.

Hospitals The best hospital in the centre is the private *Bombay Hospital* (☎266 3343), New Marine Lines, just north of the government tourist office on M Karve Rd. *Breach Candy Hospital* on Bhulabhai Desai Rd, near the swimming pool, is also recommended by foreign embassies.

Left luggage If your hotel won't let you store bags with them, try the cloakrooms at Sahar and Santa Cruz airports (see p.620), or the one in VT station. Anything left here, even rucksacks, must be securely fastened with a padlock, or they'll refuse it. Luggage can be left for a maximum of 12 weeks, and don't, whatever you do, lose the receipt.

Libraries *Asiatic Society*, SBS Marg, Horniman Circle, Ballard Estate (Mon–Sat 10am–5.30pm); *British Council* (for British newspapers), "A" Wing, Mittal Towers, Nariman Point; *Alliance Francaise*, Theosophy Hall, 40 New Marine Lines; *Max Mueller Bhavan*, Prince of Wales Annexe, off MG Rd. *The KR Cama Oriental Institute*, 136 Bombay Samachar Marg (Mon–Fri 10am–5pm, Sat 10am–1pm, specializing in Zoroastrian and Iranian studies has a public collection of 22,000 volumes in European and Asian languages. *Bombay Natural History Society*, Hornbill House (Mon–Fri 10am–5pm, Sat 10am–1pm, closed 1st & 3rd Sat of the month), has an international reputation for the study of wildlife in India. Visitors may become temporary members which allows them access to the library, natural history collection, occasional talks and the opportunity to join organized walks and field trips.

Pharmacies *Real Chemist*, 1/51 Kaka Arcade and *Royal Chemists*, M Karve Rd, both close to *Bombay Hospital*, are open 24hr. *Kemps* in the *Taj* hotel also opens late.

Photographic studios and equipment *The Javeri Colour Lab*, opposite the *Regal* cinema in Colaba, stocks colour-print and slide film, as do most of the big hotels. A small boutique behind the florists in the *Shakhari Bunder* covered market does instant *Polaroid* passport photographs.

Police The main police station in Colaba (☎202 1122) is on the west side of Colaba Causeway, near the crossroads with Ormiston Rd. For emergencies call ☎100.

State tourist offices in Bombay include: *Gujarat*, Dhanraj Mahal, PJ Ramchandani Marg (Mon–Sat 10am–5pm; ☎202 4945); *Himachal Pradesh*, World Trade Centre, Cuffe Parade (Mon–Sat 10am–5pm; ☎218 1123); *Jammu and Kashmir*, World Trade Centre (Mon–Fri 10am–3pm; ☎218 9040); *Madhya Pradesh*, World Trade Centre (Mon–Sat 10am–5pm; ☎218 7603); *Rajasthan*, 230 Dr DN Marg (☎204 4162); *Tamil Nadu*, c/o *Peerless Hotels and Travels Ltd*, Ground Floor, Churchgate Chambers, New Marine Lines (Mon–Sat 9am–6pm; ☎266 6400); and *Uttar Pradesh*, World Trade Centre (Mon–Sat 10.30am–5.30pm, closed 2nd Sat of each month; ☎218 5458).

Swimming pools The snooty expat sports club at Breach Candy, north of Malabar Hill, is a popular place to beat the heat. A day's membership costs around Rs50.

Visa extensions Contact *Foreigners' Registration Office*, Office of the Police Commissioner, opposite Crawford Market (Mon–Fri 10am–1pm; ☎262 0446). Standard three-month extensions cost around Rs650, and take twenty-four hours to process.

CONSULATES AND HIGH COMMISSIONS

Although the many consulates and High Commissions in Bombay can be useful for replacing lost travel documents or obtaining visas, most of India's neighbouring states, including Bangladesh, Bhutan, Burma, Nepal and Pakistan, only have embassies in New Delhi and/or Calcutta (office hours 9am–5pm; see relevant city account).

Australia, 16th Floor, Maker Tower "E", Cuffe Parade (☎218 1071).

Canada, 41/42 Maker Chambers VI, Nariman Point (☎287 6028).

Denmark, L & T House, Narottam Moraji Marg, Ballard Estate (☎261 8181).

Germany, 10th Floor, Hoechst House, Nariman Point (☎283 2422).

Netherlands, 16 Queen's Rd (☎201 6750).

Norway, Navroji Mansion, 31 Nathelal Parekh Marg (☎284 2042).

Philippines, 116 Free Press House, Nariman Point (☎202 0375).

Singapore, 9th Floor, 941 Sakhar Bhavan, 230 Nariman Point (☎204 3209).

Sri Lanka, Sri Lanka House, 34 Homi Modi St, Fort (☎204 5861).

Sweden, 85 Sayani Rd, Subash Gupta Bhavan, Prabhadevi (☎436 0493).

Switzerland, 7th Floor, Manekh Mahal, 90 VN Rd (☎204 3003).

Thailand, 2nd Floor, Krishna Bagh, 43 Bhulabhai Desai Rd (☎363 1404).

United Kingdom, 2nd Floor, Maker Chamber IV, Nariman Point (☎283 0517).

USA, Lincoln House, 78 Bhulabhai Desai Rd (☎363 3611).

Onwards from Bombay

Most visitors feel like getting out of Bombay as soon as they can. Fortunately, Bombay is equipped with "super-fast" services to arrange or confirm **onward travel**. All the major international and domestic airlines have offices in the city, the railway networks operate special tourist counters in the main reservation halls, and dozens of travel agents and road transport companies are eager to help you on your way by bus.

Travel within India

Bombay is the nexus of several major internal flight routes, train networks and highways, and is the main transport hub for traffic heading towards south India. The most-travelled trails lead north up the Gujarati coast to **Rajasthan** and **Delhi**; northwest into the **Deccan** via Aurangabad and the caves at Ellora and Ajanta; and south, through Pune and the hills of Western Ghats towards **Goa** and the Malabar Coast. Public transport is cheap and frequent, but book in advance and be prepared for delays.

TRANSPORT SERVICES FROM BOMBAY

	Trains		Buses		Flights	
	Frequency	Time	Frequency	Time	Frequency	Time
Agra	2 daily	23hr 30min–27hr				
Ahmedabad	7 daily	9–12hr			6 daily	1hr
Aurangabad	2 daily	10hr	2 daily*	10hr	2 daily	45–65min
Bangalore	2 daily	24hr	3 daily*	24hr	4–5 daily	1hr 30min
Bhopal	4–5 daily	12–17hr			1 daily	2hr 10min
Bijapur			3 daily*	12hr		
Calcutta	4 daily	33–42hr			6–7 daily	2–3hr
Calicut	1–2 daily	34–39hr			4 daily	1hr 45min
Coimbatore	1–2 daily	30–35hr			3 daily	1hr 50min–3hr
Delhi	6–8 daily	17–33hr			12–16 daily	1hr 55min
Goa	2 daily	23–24hr	2 daily*	16–18hr	5 daily	1hr
Hyderabad	2 daily	14hr 20min–18hr	8 daily*	18hr	5 daily	1hr 15min
Indore	1 daily	14hr	2 daily*	16hr	6 weekly	55min
Jaipur	1 daily	22hr 30min			2–4 daily	1hr 30min–4hr
Jodhpur	1 daily	21hr 10min			1–2 daily	1hr 25min–2hr
Kochi	1–2 daily	35–60hr			4–5 daily	1hr 45min
Kolhapur	2 daily	11hr 30min	4 daily	10hr		
Madras	3 daily	24–31hr			4–7 daily	1hr 45min
Madurai					1–2 daily	2–3hr
Mahabaleshwar			2 daily	7hr		
Mangalore	1–2 daily	40–46hr	2 daily*	24hr	3 daily	1hr 15min
Nagpur	5 daily	14–17hr			1 daily	1hr 15min
Nasik	16 daily	4hr	6 daily**	4hr		
Pune	18 daily	3hr 30min–5hr	hourly**	4hr 30min	3–4 daily	30–75min
Thiruv'puram	1 daily	44hr 20min			2 daily	2–3hr
Udaipur	1 daily	24hr 30min			1 daily	1hr 15min
Ujjain	1 daily	14hr	1 daily*	17hr		
Varanasi	4 daily	27hr 30min–30hr			6 weekly	2hr 10min

* Buses from Bombay Central; ** Buses from ASIAD Dadar.   All flights from Santa Cruz.

Only **direct** trains are listed. For more details on transport to **Goa** see p.657.
Only state bus services are listed here; for details of private services, see p.658.

RECOMMENDED TRAINS FROM BOMBAY

The trains below are recommended as the **fastest** and/or **most convenient** services from Bombay. Most destinations are also accessible on other, slower trains – see p.617.

	Name	No.	From	Frequency	Departs	Total Time
Agra	Punjab Mail	1037	VT	daily	7.10pm	23hr 30min
Aurangabad	Devagiri Express	1003	VT	daily	9.20pm	10hr
Bangalore	Udyan Expess	6529	VT	daily	7.55am	23hr 45min
Bhopal	Pushpak Express	1033	VT	daily	8.10am	12hr 10min
Calcutta	Gitanjali Express	2859	VT	daily	6.05am	33hr 10min
	Bombay–Howrah Mail	8001	VT	daily	8.15pm	36hr 35min
Delhi	Rajdhani Express*	2951	BC	Tues–Sun	4.55pm	17hr
	Bombay–New Delhi a/c Express*	2953	BC	Mon, Wed, Sat	5.40pm	17hr 10min
	Frontier Mail	2903	BC	daily	9.10pm	21hr 50min
	Paschim Express	2925	BC	daily	11.35am	23hr
	Punjab Mail	1037	VT	daily	7.10pm	25hr
Gorakhpur	Kushi Nagar Express	1015	VT	daily	10.30pm	34hr 45min
Hyderabad	Hussain Express	7001	VT	daily	9.55pm	15hr 35min
Jaipur	Gujarat Express**	9011	BC	daily	5.45am	22hr 30min
Jodhpur	Saurashtra Mail**	9005	BC	daily	8.10am	21hr 10min
Kochi/Ernakulam	Kanniya Kumari Express	1081	VT	daily	3.35pm	39hr
Madras	Dadar–Madras Chennai Express	6063	Dadar	Tues, Fri, Sun	8pm	24hr 10min
Pune	Indrayani Express	1021	VT	daily	8.45am	3hr 45min
Thiruv'puram	Kanniya Kumari Express	1081	VT	daily	3.35pm	44hr 20min
Udaipur	Saurashtra Express**	9215	BC	daily	7.45am	24hr 30min
Varanasi	Bombay–Varanasi Ratnagiri Express	1065	VT	Mon, Wed, Thur	5am	27hr 05min

VT = Victoria Terminus. BC = Bombay Central.
* = a/c only. ** = Change to connecting train at Ahmedabad.

By plane

Indian Airlines and other domestic carriers fly out of Santa Cruz to destinations all over India. Computerization has made booking less of a lottery than it used to be, but availability on popular routes (Bombay–Goa–Bombay) should never be taken for granted. Check with the airlines as soon as you arrive; **tickets** can be bought directly from their offices (see p.659), or through any reputable travel agent, although you will have to pay the mandatory Rs300 **airport tax** when you get to Santa Cruz.

RECOMMENDED TRAVEL AGENTS IN BOMBAY

The following travel agents are recommended for booking domestic and international flights, and long-distance private buses where specified; most also sell tickets for *Damania*'s popular catamaran service to Goa (see opposite).

Agarwal Bros Travels, 24-D Krishna Building, Shop 3, SS Gaikwad Rd, Dhobi Talao Market, near *Metro* cinema (☎200 0600).

M/S Mgnum International Tours & Travels, Frainy Villa, Henry Rd, Colaba (☎284 1037).

Peerless Hotels & Travels Ltd, Ground Floor, Churchgate Chambers, 5 New Marine Lines (☎262 4811).

Sita Travels Pvt Ltd, 8 Atlanta Building, Nariman Point (☎284 0666).

Space Travels, 4th Floor, Nanabhoy Mansion, Pherozshah Mehta Marg, Fort (☎266 4749).

Windsor Travels, 5th Floor, 86 VN Rd (☎204 3376).

GETTING TO GOA

Many travellers only come to Bombay to pick up transport to Goa, 550km south. Since the suspension of the steamer service in 1987 (the Indian army commandeered the old boat to carry troops to Sri Lanka), there have been three main ways to make the journey.

By plane
At present, six domestic airline companies operate daily services to Goa (see p.659). If you can afford it, this is the most painless way to go, but competition for seats is fierce (particularly around Christmas–New Year) and you may well have to wait several days. The journey takes an hour and costs around Rs1700.

By train
Train services to **Goa** have been severely disrupted since autumn 1994 by the change-over from broad- to metre-gauge track. At present, services from Bombay VT only run as far as **Miraj**, 472km south of Bombay, from where buses ferry passengers the remaining four hours or so to Panjim. The upgraded line, which traverses the Western Ghats, should be up and running by the beginning of 1997, but in the meantime, you're better off catching an overnight bus, or shelling out for a plane or catamaran ticket. A brand new, faster coastal route – the *Konkan Railway* – is scheduled (optimistically) for completion by the end of 1997. When it's finally open, this line will make the train journey to Goa by far the best-value option.

With services in a state of flux, it would be pointless to list exact timings for trains to Goa. However, the government tourist office in Churchgate, and the *Central Railways'* booking office in VT station will have details of the revised timetables as soon as they are published.

By bus
The Bombay–Goa **bus** journey ranks among the very worst in India. Don't believe travel agents who assure you it takes thirteen hours. Clapped-out coaches, and appalling road surfaces along the sinuous coastal route, make eighteen hours a more realistic estimate.

Bus tickets start at around Rs240 for a push-back seat on a beaten-up *Kadamba* (Goan government) or *MSRTC* coach. Tickets for these services are in great demand in season, so book in advance at Bombay Central or *Kadamba*'s kiosks on the north side of Azad Maidan, near St Xavier's College (just up from VT station). More and more **private** overnight buses also run to Goa, costing from around Rs270 for a noisy front-engined *Tata* bus, to Rs550 for a place on a top-of-the-range imported a/c coach with pneumatic suspension, video and on-board toilet. **Tickets** should be booked at least a day in advance through a reputable travel agent (see opposite), though it's sometimes worth turning up at the car park opposite the *Metro* cinema, Azad Maidan, where most buses leave from, on the off chance of a last-minute cancellation. Make sure, in any case, that you are given both your seat and the bus registration numbers, and that you confirm the exact time and place of departure with the travel agent, as these frequently vary between companies.

By catamaran
Ever since the old steamer service ended, the powerful Goan bus lobby has managed to block any comeback by the Bombay–Goa passenger ferry. However, it's still possible to reach Goa by sea on the recently inaugurated **catamaran** service, operated by *Damania*. This is a fairly quick and comfortable way to do the trip, but feels more like air travel than an ocean cruise. Sailing just ten miles off shore, the Scandinavian-built catamaran, its reclining seats sealed inside air-conditioned cabins, takes seven hours to reach Panjim, leaving Bombay's **Baucha Chakka Ferry Wharf** dock every morning at 7am. Seats in economy class (lower deck) cost around US $45; a ticket in business class (upper deck with headphones and a choice of meals) will set you back US $60. Tourists are encouraged to pay in foreign currency, but note that the separate tariff works out more expensive than the rupee rate.

Tickets for the catamaran, which **does not operate during the monsoon** (roughly June–Sept), include the cost of two excellent meals, snacks and drinks, and are sold through most reputable travel agents in Bombay (see opposite). Alternatively, book through *Damania*'s Ferry Wharf office (☎373 5562 or 374 3737 for timetable information). Be sure to arrive at the dock, 3km north of VT along P D'Mello Rd, at least forty-five minutes before departure; buses run there from Colaba and Fort, but the trip is a lot less hassle by taxi.

In theory, it is also possible to book domestic air tickets abroad when you buy your original long-haul flight. However, as individual airlines tend to have separate agreements with domestic Indian carriers, you may not be offered the same choice (or rates) as you will through agents in Bombay. Note, too, that *Indian Airlines* is the only company offering 25-percent discounts (on all flights) to customers under the age of thirty.

By train

Two main networks converge on Bombay: the *Western Railway* runs to north and western India; the *Central Railway* connects Bombay to central, eastern and southern regions.

Nearly all services to Gujarat, Rajasthan, Delhi and the far north leave from **Bombay Central** station, in the mid-town area. Second-class tickets can be booked here through the normal channels, but the quickest place for foreign nationals to make **reservations** is at the efficient tourist counter (No.28) on the first floor of the *Western Railway*'s main booking hall, next door to the India government tourist office in Churchgate (Mon–Fri 9.30am–4.30pm, Sat 9.30am–2.30pm). This counter also has access to special "**tourist quotas**", which are released the day before departure if the train leaves during the day, or the morning of the departure if the train leaves after 5pm. The one catch is that you have to pay for tourist quota tickets in foreign currency (travellers' cheques will do), unless you can produce a recent encashment certificate. Change is always given in rupees. The same applies if you want to buy or book tourist quota tickets with *Indrail* passes. If the quota is "closed" or already used up, and you can't access the "**VIP quota**" (always worth a try), you will have to join the regular queue.

Bombay's other "Tourist Ticketing Facility" is in the snazzy new air-conditioned *Central Railway* booking office to the rear of VT (Mon–Sat 9.00am–1pm & 1.30–4pm; counter No.22, or No.21 on Sun), the departure point for most trains heading east and south. *Indrail* passes can also be bought here, and there's an MTDC tourist information kiosk in the main concourse if you need help filling in your reservation slips.

Just to complicate matters, some *Central Railway* trains to south India, including the fast *Dadar–Madras Chennai Express* #6063 to Madras, do not depart from VT at all, but from **Dadar** station, way north of Bombay Central. Seats and berths for these trains are reserved at VT. Finally, if you're booking tickets to Calcutta, make sure your train doesn't leave from **Kurla** station, which is even more inconvenient, up near the airports. Getting to either of these stations on public transport can be a major struggle.

By bus

The main departure point for long-distance **buses** leaving Bombay is the frenetic **State Transport Terminal** on JB Behram Marg, opposite Bombay Central railway station. State bus companies with counters here (daily 8am–8pm), include Maharashtra, Karnataka, Madhya Pradesh, Goa and Gujarat. Few of their services compare favourably with train travel on the same routes. Reliable timetable information can be difficult to obtain, reservations are not available on standard buses, and most long-haul journeys are gruelling overnighters. Among the exceptions are the **deluxe buses** run by MSRTC to Pune, Nasik and Kolhapur; the small extra cost buys you more leg-room, fewer stops and the option of advance booking. The only problem is, most leave from the **ASIAD** bus stand in Dadar, half an hour or so by road north of Bombay Central.

Other possibilities for road travel include the "super-fast" **luxury coaches** touted around Colaba. Most are run by private companies, guaranteeing breakneck speeds and noisy Hindi film videos. MTDC and ITDC also operate similarly priced, video-less services to the same destinations, which you can book direct from their main offices downtown or through the more conveniently situated India Government tourist office, 123 M Karve Rd, Churchgate. Two night buses leave Nariman Point every evening for the twelve-hour trip to **Aurangabad**, and there are morning departures to **Nasik** and **Mahabaleshwar**, which take six and seven hours respectively.

AIRLINE OFFICES IN BOMBAY

International Airlines

Aeroflot, Ground Floor, 241/242 Nirmal Building, Nariman Point (☎287 1942).

Air France, 1st Floor, Maker Chambers VI, Nariman Point (☎202 5021).

Air India, Air India Building, Nariman Point (☎202 4142).

Air Lanka, Ground Floor, Mittal Tower, C Wing, Nariman Point (☎282 3288).

Air Mauritius, Ground Floor, Air India Building, Nariman Point (☎202 8474).

Alitalia, Industrial Insurance Building, VN Rd, Churchgate (☎204 5023).

British Airways, 202-B, Vulcan Insurance Building, VN Rd, Churchgate (☎282 0888).

Canadian Airlines International, Podar House, 10 Marine Drive (☎204 2174).

Cathay Pacific, Ground Floor, Taj hotel, Colaba (☎202 9112).

Continental Airlines (USA), Ground Floor, 6 Maker Arcade, Cuffe Parade (☎218 1440).

Delta, Taj Hotel, Colaba (☎202 9020).

Emirates, 228 Mittal Chambers, Nariman Point (☎287 1645).

Gulf Air, Maker Chamber VI, Nariman Point (☎202 4065).

Japan Airlines, 2 Raheja Centre, Nariman Point (☎287 4036).

KLM, Khaitan Bhavan, 198 J Tata Rd, Churchgate (☎282 1185).

Lufthansa, 4th Floor, Express Towers, Nariman Point (☎202 3430).

Pakistan International Airlines, 7 Stadium House, VN Rd, Churchgate (☎202 1373).

Qantas Airways, 42 Sakhar Bhavan, Nariman Point (☎202 0343).

Royal Nepal Airlines, Sherbanoo, 111 Maharishi Karve Rd (☎283 6198).

Saudia, Ground Floor, Express Towers, Nariman Point (☎287 0656).

Scandinavian Airlines, Ground Floor, Podar House, 10 Marine Drive, Churchgate (☎202 7083).

South African Airways, Podar House, 10 Marine Drive (☎282 3450).

Swissair, Maker Chamber VI, 220 Nariman Point (☎287 2210).

Syrian Arab Airlines, 7 Stadium House, VN Rd, Churchgate (☎282 6043).

Thai Airways, Ground Floor, Podar House, 10 Marine Drive (☎282 3085).

Domestic Airlines

Indian Airlines, Air India Building, Nariman Point (Mon–Sat 8.30am–7.30pm, Sun 10am–1pm & 1.45–5.30pm; ☎202 3131); counter at the airport (☎611 7983).

Damania, Terminal B, Santa Cruz (☎610 2545).

East-West, 18 New Kantwadi Rd, Bandra West (☎643 6678), or Santa Cruz airport (☎610 3357).

Jet, Amarchand Mansion, Madam Cama Rd (☎285 5788).

Modiluft, Akash Ganga Building, 89 Bhulabhai Desai Rd (☎363 1921), or at Santa Cruz airport (610 3807).

NEPC, 2 Raheja Centre, Nariman Point (☎287 4936), or New Terminal Building, Santa Cruz airport (☎611 3517).

Leaving India

In spite of its prominence on trans-Asian flight routes (as detailed in the box on p.7), Bombay is no longer the bargain basement for **international air tickets** it used to be. Discounted fares are very hard to come by – a legacy of Rajiv Gandhi's economic reforms of the 1980s. If you do need to book a ticket, stick to one of the tried and tested agents listed on p.656.

All the major airlines operating out of Bombay have offices downtown where you can buy scheduled tickets or confirm your flight. The majority are grouped around Veer Nariman Rd, opposite the *Ambassador Hotel*, or else on Nariman Point, a short taxi ride west of Colaba.

CHAPTER TEN

MAHARASHTRA

Vast and rugged, the modern state of **MAHARASHTRA**, the third largest in India, was created in 1960, from the Marathi-speaking regions of what was previously Bombay State. As soon as you leave its seething port capital, **Bombay**, developed by Europeans, and now the epitome of modern, cosmopolitan, polyglot India – which as a law unto itself has its own chapter in this book – you enter a different world with a different history.

Undoubtedly, Maharashtra's greatest treasures are its extraordinary **cave temples** and **monasteries**. The finest of all are to be found near **Aurangabad**, renamed after the Moghul emperor Aurangzeb and still home to a sizeable Muslim population (as well as the "poor man's Taj Mahal", the Bibi-Ka-Maqbara). The busy commercial city is the obvious base for visits to the caves at **Ajanta**, with their fabulous and still-vibrant murals, and the monolithic temples of **Ellora**, where the Hindu **Kailash temple** may look like a structural building but was carved in its entirety from the rock. From the second century BC, this region was an important centre of Buddhism; artificial caves were excavated to shelter monks, and the finest artists sculpted magnificent cathedral-like halls for congregational worship.

Away from the cities, the most characteristic feature of the landscape is a plenitude of **forts** – as the western borderland between north and south India, Maharashtra's trade routes were always important, but could also bring trouble. **Inland**, parallel to the sea, and never further than 100km from it, the mighty Western Ghats rise abruptly. The areas of level ground that crowned them, endowed with fresh water, were easily converted into forts where small forces could withstand protracted sieges by large armies. Less aggressive modern visitors can scale such windswept fortified heights at Sinhagad, Pratapgarh, and **Daulatabad** – which briefly, bizarrely and disastrously replaced Delhi as capital in the fourteenth century.

During the last century, the mountains found another use. When the summer proved too much for the British in Bombay, they sought refuge in nearby **hill stations**, the most popular of which, **Mahabaleshwar**, now caters for droves of Indian holidaymakers. **Matheran**, 170km southeast of Bombay, and 800m higher, has a special attraction: quite apart from its cool, wet climate, it offers superb views and wooded paths. It is also closed to all motorized road traffic. Instead, visitors board a rickety miniature train that twists up the hill via 281 curves. Beyond the Ghats, the modern city of **Pune**, site of the

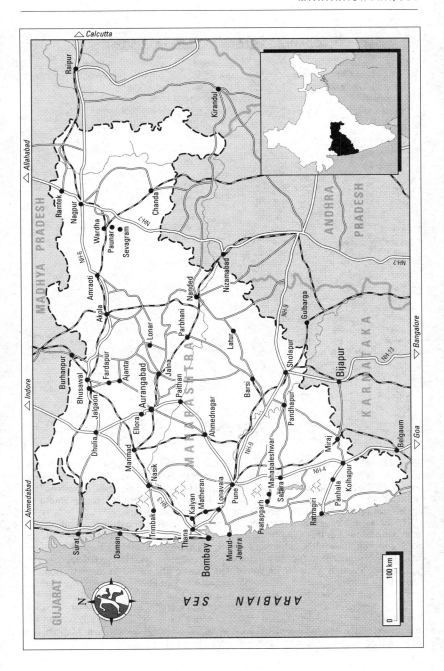

MAHARASHTRA TRAVEL DETAILS

	Trains		Buses		Flights	
	Frequency	Time	Frequency	Time	Frequency	Time
To and from AURANGABAD						
Ahmedabad			1 nightly	14hr		
Ajanta			hourly	3hr		
Bijapur			1 daily	12hr		
Bombay	2 daily	10hr	6 nightly	10–12hr	1–3 daily	40min
Delhi					1 daily	3hr 30min
Ellora			every 30min	45min		
Indore			2 daily	12hr		
Jaipur					daily	2hr 20min
Jalgaon			hourly	4hrs		
Nagpur			4 daily	12hr		
Nasik	1 daily	5hr	8 daily	5hr	1 daily	1hr
Pune			7 daily	5hr		
Udaipur			2 daily	7hr	daily	1hr 5min
To and from Jalgaon						
Agra	3–4 daily	14hr 20min–19hr				
Ajanta			hourly	1hr 40min		
Aurangabad			8 daily	4hr		
Bangalore	Sun only	24hr 25min				
Bhopal	3–4 daily	6hr–9hr 45min				
Bombay	11 daily	8–9hr	1 daily	10hr 30min		
Calcutta	4 daily	29hr–34hr 35min				
Delhi	3 daily	18–25hr				
Gwalior	3–4 daily	13hr				
Jhansi	3–4 daily	9hr 45min–12hr				
Madras	4 weekly	24hr				
Nagpur	5–6 daily	8hr–9hr 45min	1 daily	10hr		
Pune	1 daily	9hr 20min	5 daily	9hr		
Varanasi	4 daily	18hr–22hr 25min				
Wardha	5–7 daily	8hr–9hr 45min				

For transport connections **from Bombay**, see p.655 onwards.

internationally famous ashram founded by the new-age guru, Bagwan Rajneesh, presides over a semi-arid tableland of flat-topped hills and dusty wheat fields. Maharashtra extends 900km further east across the Deccan plateau to the geographical centre of the subcontinent, an area largely populated by tribal groups, where Mahatma Gandhi set up his headquarters at **Sevagram** during the Independence struggle.

To the west, Maharashtra occupies 500km of the Konkan **coast** on the Arabian Sea, from Gujarat to Goa; travelling has always been circuitous, as the coast winds back and forth with countless inlets, ridges and valleys, again peppered with forts. In the absence of its former seaborne traffic, this region of picturesque ports and deserted beaches cannot provide enough work for its young people, who are forced to move to Bombay, though the imminent advent of the controversial **Konkan Railway**, connecting Bombay with Goa and southern Karnataka, may well open it up to new opportunities. Close to Bombay, sleepy, old-fashioned **Murud-Janjira** has splendid beaches and an extraordinary island fort. More determined travellers with time to zigzag their way around will find more, all the way to Goa; places such as Jaigarh, Ratnagiri, Vijaydurg, Malwan, and Sindhudurg, each with its own history and a battle-scarred fort to prove it.

	Trains		Buses		Flights	
	Frequency	Time	Frequency	Time	Frequency	Time
To and from Nagpur						
Bhopal	13 daily	6hr 30min–9hr	1 daily	7hr		
Bhubaneshwar					3 weekly	1hr 15min
Bombay	4–5 daily	14hr–17hr 25min			1 daily	1hr 15min
Calcutta	4 daily	19–25hr			3 weekly	2hr 40min
Delhi	9 daily	16hr 25min–22hr				
Hyderabad	2–3 daily	11hr–12hr 35min			3 weekly	1hr 15min
Indore	1 daily	12hr	4 daily	11hr		
Jabalpur	6 weekly	10hr	9 daily	7hr		
Madras	3 daily	17hr 15min–24hr				
Pune	1 daily	18hr 20min	5 daily	16hr		
Ramtek	hourly	1hr 30min				
Varanasi	6 weekly	19hr 30min–22hr				
Wardha			hourly	2hr 30min		
To and from Nasik						
Agra	2–3 daily	17hr 30min–23hr				
Bhopal	3 daily	10–13hr				
Bombay	10–12 daily	4–6hr	6 daily	4hr		
Calcutta	3 daily	32–36hr				
Delhi	2 daily	21–29hr				
Jabalpur	7 daily	14hr 30min				
Nagpur	3 daily	11hr 30min–13hr				
Trimbak			hourly	45min		
To and from Pune						
Ahmedabad	1 weekly	12hr 35min				
Bangalore	1 daily	18hr 10min			3 weekly	45min
Bijapur			1 daily	8hr		
Bombay	18 daily	3hr 30min–5hr	hourly	4hr 30min	1–3 daily	35–45min
Delhi	1 daily	27hr 25min			6 weekly	2hr
Goa	2 daily	18hr	4 daily	15hr		
Hyderabad	1 daily	13hr 15min			3 weekly	1hr 30min
Kolhapur	3 daily	9hr	4 daily	12hr		
Madras	1 daily	22hr			3 weekly	3hr
Mahabaleshwar			3 daily	3hr		

Note that most individual routes appear only once in this chart; check against where you want to get to as well as where you're coming from.

For all the efforts of the Moghuls, Islam has made little impact on Maharashtra; eighty percent of the population is Hindu. **Nasik**, 187km northeast of Bombay, balances modern industry alongside ancient associations with the *Ramayana*; one of the four sites of the Kumbh Mela, when up to four million devotees bathe in the holy River Godavari, even during less auspicious times it is a magnet for pilgrims. A short distance west, one of India's most sacred Shiva shrines lies close to the source of the Godavari, reached by a short trek from **Trimbak**. Finally, in the far the south, the little-visited town of **Kolhapur**, almost at the Karnataka border, has retained plenty of old-fashioned character and makes a good place to break the long journey to Goa.

History
Although some paleolithic remains have been discovered, Maharashtra enters recorded history in the second century BC, with the construction of its first Buddhist caves. These lay, and still lie, in peaceful places of great natural beauty, but could never have been created without the wealth generated by the nearby caravan trade routes between north and south India.

The region's first Hindu rulers, based in Badami, appeared during the sixth century, but the eighth-century Rashtrakutas achieved a greater authority. Buddhism was almost entirely supplanted throughout the entire country by the twelfth century, in what has been characterized as a peaceful popular revolution attributable largely to the popular songs and teachings of poet-saints. The tradition they established continued to flourish throughout the thirteenth and fourteenth centuries, even when forced underground by Islam, reaching its zenith in the simple faith of the Ramdas, the "Servant of Rama" (1608–81).

Ramdas, ascetic and political activist, provided the philosophical underpinning behind the campaigns of Maharashtra's greatest warrior, **Shivaji** (1627–80). The fiercely independent Maratha chieftain united local forces to place insurmountable obstacles in the way of any prospective invader; so effective were their guerrilla tactics that he could even take on the mighty Moghuls. Shivaji progressively fought his way northwards, at a time when the Moghuls, who had got as far as capturing Daulatabad in 1633, were embroiled in protacted family feuds. A year after he succeeded in sacking the great port of Surat (Gujarat), in 1664, he was defeated in battle and imprisoned by Aurangzeb in Agra. He is said to have escaped by hiding in a package which the prison guards imagined was an innocent gift intended for local Brahmins; once outside, Shivaji simply walked away disguised as a religious mendicant. By the time he died, in 1680, he had managed to unite the Marathas into a stable and secure state, funded by the plunder gleaned through guerrilla raids as far afield as Andhra Pradesh.

Back at the Moghul court the following year, Aurangzeb's son Akbar rebelled briefly against his father, then fled to Maharashtra, where he sought protection from Shivaji's son Shambhuji, before going into exile in Iran. That was the trigger for Aurangzeb to move his operations south; Bijapur (1686) and Golconda (1687) fell, and Shambhuji was captured and summarily executed in 1689. Aurangzeb must have thought that the way was now clear, but the Marathas proved impossible to subdue; he was to spend 25 years in the region, unable to leave, fighting a long series of inconclusive battles until his death at the age of 89. The Marathas had meanwhile become a confederacy whose dominion extended as far east as Orissa. By the end of the eighteenth century, however, their power had weakened and the British were able to take full control.

Maharashtra claims a crucial role in the development of a nationalist consciousness. An organization known as the Indian National Union, originally convened in Pune, held a conference in Bombay in 1885 which it named the **Indian National Congress**. This loose aggregate of key figures from local politics around the country was to change the face of Indian politics. At first, its aim was limited to establishing a national platform to raise the status of Indians, and it remained loyal to the British; in the long term, of course, it was instrumental in the achievement of Independence 62 years later: many of Congress's factional leaders over the years were from Maharashtra.

With Independence, the Bombay Presidency, to which most of Maharashtra belonged, became known as Bombay State; Maharashtra as such was created in 1960. Its manufacturing industries, centered on Bombay and to a lesser extent cities such as Nagpur, Nasik, Aurangabad, Sholapur and Kolhapur, now account for a quarter of the nation's output. Textiles have long been important, but this is now also the premier region for electronics. However, the majority of Maharashtra's 79 million people are engaged in **agriculture**; main crops include sugar cane, cotton, peanuts, sunflowers, tobacco, pulses, fruit and vegetables. The western edge of the Deccan plateau has uncertain rainfall, and cultivation is concentrated close to rivers, while the southwestern monsoon sometimes halts in the mountains, leaving the rocky land to the east unwatered. Here, farmers rely on hardy staples such as millet and maize.

NORTHERN MAHARASHTRA

Beyond the seemingly endless concrete housing projects, petrochemical works and mosquito-infested swamplands of Greater Bombay, a wall of bare bluish-brown hills dominates the horizon. The **Western Ghats** form a series of huge steps that march from the narrow, humid coastal strip to the edge of the **Deccan** plateau – a vast, dry tableland punctuated with ridges of flat-topped hills and scruffy villages and market towns. **Northern Maharashtra's** main transport arteries, the NH3 and *Central Railway* line, wind in tandem through this stark landscape, following an ancient trade route that once linked the western ports with the prosperous cities further north. Over the centuries, a number of pilgrimage sites sprang up to take advantage of the lucrative through-traffic, and these form the principal points of interest in the region today.

The holy city of **Nasik** is a handy place to break journeys to or from Bombay, four hours away by road. Amid impressive scenery, the town of **Trimbak**, 10km west at the start of a steep half-day hike to the source of the sacred River Godavari, makes a more relaxing overnight stop. Most foreign visitors, however, head straight for the regional capital, **Aurangabad**, the jumping-off point for the rock-cut **caves** at **Ellora** and **Ajanta**. Among **Muslim monuments** to seek out here are Aurangabad's answer to the Taj Mahal, the **Bibi-Ka-Maqbara**, the dramatic hill-top fort at **Daulatabad**, and the tiny tomb town of **Rauza**, 5km from Ellora, where emperor Aurangzeb is buried.

From Aurangabad, a well-beaten track cuts through the middle of Madhya Pradesh, via **Jalgaon**, towards Varanasi and Nepal. Alternatively, you could head across central India to **Wardha** and **Nagpur**, in the far northeastern corner of the state, where a couple of **Gandhi ashrams**, and the picturesque whitewashed Hindu temple complex at **Ramtek** make pleasant pauses on long cross-country hauls.

Aurangabad

It's easy to see why many travellers regard **AURANGABAD** as little more than a convenient, though largely uninteresting, place in which to kill time on the way to Ellora and Ajanta. First impressions seem to confirm its dull reputation: wide streets, fast traffic, ugly building sites, and gaping patches of urban wasteland merge into a featureless ferro-concrete sprawl. Yet, given a little effort, northern Maharashtra's largest city can yield compensations for its architectural shortcomings. Scattered around its ragged fringes, the dilapidated remains of fortifications, gateways, domes and minarets – including those of the most ambitious Moghul tomb garden in western India, the **Bibi-Ka-Maqbara** – bear witness to an illustrious imperial past; the small but fascinating crop of **rock-cut Buddhist caves**, huddled along the flanks of the flat-topped, sandy yellow hills to the north, are remnants of even more ancient occupation.

The city, originally called **Khadke**, or "Big Rock", was founded in the early sixteenth century by **Malik Amber**, an ex-Abyssinian slave and prime minister of the independent Muslim kingdom of the Nizam Shahis, based at Ahmadnagar, 112km southwest. It was a perfect spot for a provincial capital: on the banks of the **Kham River**, in a broad valley separating the then-forested Sahyadri range to the north from the Satharas to the south, and at a crossroads of the region's key trade routes. Many of the **mosques** and palaces erected by Malik Amber still endure, albeit in ruins.

In 1629, Shah Jahan's redoubtable army swept south across the Deccan to usher in **Moghul** rule. As **Fatehnagar**, Aurangabad became the centre of operations for their protracted military campaign. It really rose to prominence, however, towards the end of the seventeenth century, when **Aurangzeb** decamped here from Delhi to supervise the subjugation of his troublesome enemies in the region. At his behest, the impressive

AURANGABAD

△ Bibi-Ka-Maqbara & Aurangabad Caves   △ Ajanta, Jalgaon & Taj Hotel

N

Ajanta Ambassador & Rama International Hotels & Airport ▷

Ellora, Rauza & Daulatabad ◁

Kham River

Makai Gate

Shivaji Maidan

KILA ARAK

Delhi Gate

Jama Masjid

Town Hall

Purwar Museum

Dargah & Pan Chakki

Police Station

Juna Bazaar Chowk

GPO

B A Z A A R

Shah Ganj Masjid

Himroo Factory

Bicycle Rental

Bicycle Rental

Gulmandi Square

Zaffar Gate

Weekly Market Ground

Bus Stand

Paithan Gate

Ⓐ

Ⓑ
❷

Indian Airlines Office

State Bank

Ⓒ
Ⓓ

Ⓕ
Ⓖ

DR. AMBEDKAR RD

DR. RAJENDRA PRASAD MARG

Kranti Chowk

JALNA ROAD

JALNA RD

❶

Ⓔ

❸

Osman Pura

Ⓗ

Ⓘ
❺
ⓘ
❻
Ⓙ
Ⓚ
Ⓝ Ⓜ
Ⓛ
Ⓞ

STATION RD EAST

STATION RD WEST

Railway Station

Manmad & Bombay ◁

Hyderabad ▷

0   500 m

RESTAURANTS:
❶ Agran Mistan
❷ Foodwala's Bhoj
❸ Mingling
❹ Rajdhika
❺ Chanakya
❻ Foodwala's Tandoori

HOTELS:
Ⓐ Green Palace
Ⓑ Devpriya
Ⓒ Printravel
Ⓓ Raviraj
Ⓔ Amarpreet
Ⓕ Youth Hostel
Ⓖ Panchavati
Ⓗ Rajdhani
Ⓘ Ashiyana
Ⓙ Tourist Home
Ⓚ Natraj
Ⓛ Vedant
Ⓜ MTDC Holiday Resort
Ⓝ Great Punjab
Ⓞ New Punjab

▽ Paithan

city walls and gates were raised in 1682 to withstand the persistent Maratha attacks that bedevilled his later years. Following his death in 1707, the city – renamed in his honour – changed hands once again. The new rulers, the **Nizam of Hyderabad**, somehow staved off the Marathas for the greater part of 250 years, until the city finally merged with Maharashtra in 1956.

Today Aurangabad is one of India's fastest growing commercial and industrial centres, manufacturing anything from pharmaceuticals to auto-rickshaws for a voracious Bombay market. It's a decidely upbeat kind of place, and a peaceful one which, despite the potentially uneasy combination of a local council dominated by the far-right Shiv Sena party, and a sizeable Muslim minority, has avoided the recent communal violence elsewhere in the region.

Arrival and information

Daily flights from Delhi, Bombay, Nagpur, Udaipur and Jaipur arrive at Aurangabad's **airport**, Chikal Thana, 8km east of the city. Metered **taxis** are on hand for the trip into town, and courtesy **minibuses** whisk away guests booked into the nearby five-star hotels. The mainline **railway station** stands on the southwest edge of the city centre, within easy reach of most hotels, and a 1.5km ride south down Station Rd from the **bus stand** – the hectic arrival point for all buses.

MTDC have helpful **tourist information** counters at the airport – open at flight times only – and in its *Holiday Resort* hotel (daily 7am–9.30pm; ☎331513). There's also an excellent government **tourist office** on Station Rd (Mon–Fri 8.30am–6pm, Sat 8.30am–12.30pm; ☎29817), which can arrange approved guides; their maps, however, aren't up to much. Nearly all hand out glossy maps and leaflets on local attractions, and can book you on to their respective **guided tours** of the city and Ellora and Ajanta caves (see below).

The most central places to **change money** are the *State Bank of India* (Mon–Fri 10am–2pm, Sat 10am–noon) on Kranti Chowk, and the *State Bank of Hyderabad*, off Shah Ganj square in the old city. The *Ashok* also has a foreign exchange facility, open to non-residents between 5pm and 10pm, and a counter at the aiport opens to coincide with the main flight times. The **GPO** (Mon–Sat 8am–8pm), and efficient poste restante counter, are at Juna Bazaar Chowk, on the north side of the old city. A sealing wax and sewing service is available outside, and stationery is on sale in the shop opposite.

A reliable and efficient *IATA*-approved **travel agent**, recommended for booking or reconfirming flights, is *MIP* in the *Hotel Amarpreet*, Jalna Rd.

> The telephone **area code** for Aurangabad is ☎0240.

City transport

Most of Aurangabad's sights lie too far apart to take in on foot. The city is, however, buzzing with **auto-rickshaws**, which, on the whole, will happily flag their meters – longer sightseeing trips work out much cheaper if you settle on a fare in advance (taking waiting time into account). **Taxis** hang around outside the 5-star hotels, and **cars** (with or without drivers) can be rented through the tourist offices, or travel agents such as *Classic Travel*, in the lobby of MTDC's *Holiday Resort* hotel, and *TSG Tours and Travels*, 168/A Shastri Nagar, Garkheda Rd (☎24262); *Budget* and *Hertz* also have counters in *Rama* and *Ambassador* hotels, and at the airport. Expect to pay around Rs750 per day, or slightly more if the driver is included.

Much the cheapest and most satisfying way to get around the city, however, is by **bicycle**. While the busy main streets and market can be hair-raising at times, a ride out to the sights in the north of town makes an enjoyable alternative to public transport – although women are rarely, if ever, seen cycling in Aurangabad. Two stalls just up the road from the bus stand have the best bikes, hourly rental, and require no deposit.

Tours

Various companies run daily guided **tours** of the area, all operating to the same itineraries and departure times; only the prices vary. The popular MTDC **"Ellora and City"** tour (depart 9.30am, return 6pm; Rs90) takes in the Bibi-Ka-Maqbara, Panchakki, Daulatabad fort, Aurangzeb's tomb at Rauza, and the Ellora caves (but not the Aurangabad ones), and is ridiculously rushed. The **Ajanta** tour (depart 8am, return 5.30pm; Rs125) goes to the caves only, and is a long round-trip to make in a day. If you want to spend more time at the site, either stay in Fardapur, or travel on to Jalgaon (see p.690 for both).

The departure point for the ITDC tour is the *Ashok Hotel* (book in advance from the tourist office on Station Rd, or *Ashok Tours and Travel* in the hotel lobby); MTDC leave from outside the *Holiday Resort*, and the (cheaper) *State Transport Corporation* tours start at the railway station (book at the ticket office at the city bus stand).

The City

Captains of industry and five-star hotels may have surplanted Moghul emperors and palaces, but Aurangabad has retained much of its Islamic feel. Head for the Muslim quarter around the **Chowk** area of the city and you'll see women veiled in long black *burkhas*, as well as **mosques** that continue to draw large crowds on Fridays. The old walled city, laid out on a grid by Malik Amber in the sixteenth century, still forms the core of Aurangabad's large **bazaar** area. It's best approached via **Gulmandi Square** to the south, along any of several streets lined with colourful shops and stalls. The bazaar lacks the character and intensity of those in larger Indian cities, but has a pleasant, workaday feel, and you'll not be approached by too many zealous salesmen.

Keep walking north, and you'll come out at a chaotic east–west thoroughfare. Close by, in a tiny backroom behind a shop on the north side of the main street, 100m east of the busy Chowk crossroads, stands the **Purwar Museum**. Housed in a beautiful old *haveli*, this impressive private collection of antiquities boasts a seventeenth-century Koran handpainted by Aurangzeb, superb bronzes, and a host of other wonderful objects accumulated by a retired doctor. Look for the sign above a doorway, and ask at the handicraft shop next door to be let in.

The unremarkable **Shah Ganj Masjid** (*c.* 1720) mosque that presides over the near-by main square is surrounded on three sides by small shops and a congested round-about-cum-racetrack. Anyone keen to see other remnants of Aurangabad's Moghul splendour should make for the city's largest and most impressive mosque, the **Jama Masjid**, 1km north. The present building is considerably older than its recent coat of pale-purple colourwash suggests; it's really an amalgam of parts begun by Malik Amber in 1612 and added to by Aurangzeb nearly a century later.

The ruins of Aurangzeb's former imperial headquarters, the **Kila Arak**, lie 200m east along the main road from the Jama Masjid, scattered around a boulder-strewn wasteland. Once this complex of palaces, battlements, gateways, tanks and gardens stretched all the way from Delhi Gate in the northeast of the city, to Mecca Gate on the west side of the river, and housed three princes and a retinue of thousands. Sadly, precious little of it is left, and only die-hard rubble fans are likely to enjoy a visit.

Finally, every Thursday, an excellent **weekly market** is held just west of the bus stand. Villagers from outlying areas pour in all morning on bullock carts, the women to set up eye-catching vegetable and spice stalls, the men to stand around in their best *dhotis* and Nehru caps while goats and glistening buffalo are put through their paces in the auction. The market gets into its stride around noon, winding up at about 5pm.

The Dargah and Pan Chakki

On the left bank of the River Kham, near Begampura Bridge, the **Dargah of Baba Shah Muzaffar** is a religious compound built by Aurangzeb as a memorial to his spiritual mentor, a *chisti* mystic. The principal point of interest is not so much the mosque, the modest tomb or ornamental gardens nearby, pleasant though these are, as the unusual adjoining **watermill** known as the **Pan Chakki**. Water pumped underground from a reservoir in the hills 6km away collects in a tank, now teeming with enormous *khol* fish, to drive a small grindstone once used to mill flour for the members of the *madrasa*, or theological college, next door. Directly beneath the fish tank, sealed

---

HIMROO

Marco Polo wrote of some fabric he was given in the Deccan region that it was "as fine as a spider's web, and Kings and Queens of any country will take pride in wearing it". The material in question could well have been woven in Aurangabad. Since well before the arrival of the Muslims in the thirteenth century, the region's weavers have skilfully combined local silk with gold thread to produce some of the most opulent and sought-after brocades in India. However, following the decline in the city's fortunes after the departure of the Moghuls few could afford this extravagant mixture, or **kamkhab**. Cotton was therefore blended with silk to create a cheaper alternative – **Himroo**, literally "similar".

At one time Aurangabad held hundreds of Himroo handlooms. Today, only one family, the Quraishis, continue to produce the fabric in the traditional way. You can see them and their employees in action on special double-sided looms in a tiny **factory** buried deep in the narrow back streets of the Mondhard district, near Zaffar Gate. This is also one of the few places in India where you can watch traditional **paithani saris** being made. Using designs set down more than two-thousand years ago, the Quraishis take six months or more to weave these famously elaborate brocaded lengths of cloth, some of which cost tens of thousands of rupees.

The Himroo factory is not easy to find, but most rickshaw *wallahs* know the way. If you feel like buying some fabric as a souvenir (not an obligation), the weavers keep a counter stocked with shawls and *saris*, as well as inexpensive batiks featuring scenes and motifs cribbed from the murals at Ajanta.

---

behind a wall at ground level by the river, is a large assembly hall supported by four rows of enormous pillars. The whole complex was an impressive engineering feat for its time, although visitors from wetter climes may regard Pan Chakki's charms with rather less enthusiasm than the water-crazy locals.

The Bibi-Ka-Maqbara

Were it not so flagrantly a (cheap) imitation of the Taj, Aurangabad's much maligned Moghul tomb-garden would probably attract a great many more admirers. In spite of being one of India's most impressive Islamic monuments, however, the **Bibi-Ka-Maqbara** (daily 8am to sunset; Rs1) is widely regarded as the definitive "also ran".

The mausoleum, completed in 1678, was dedicated to the memory of **Begum Rabi'a Daurani**, Aurangzeb's wife, by her son **Prince Azam Shah**. Originally intended by its designers to rival the Taj Mahal, lack of resources dogged the 25-year project, and the end result fell far short of expectations. The entrance to the complex is through an enormous brass-inlaid **door**, decorated with an elaborate geometric pattern said to be of Persian origin. An inscription around its edge names the maker, the year of its installation and the chief architect, **Ata Ullah**. Looking at the mausoleum from beyond the ornamental gardens and redundant fountains in front of it, you can see why commentators have been so ungenerous. The truncated minarets and ungainly entrance arch make the Bibi-Ka-Maqbara seem squat and ill-proportioned compared with the elegant height and symmetry of the Taj. The impression is not enhanced by the abrupt discontinuation of marble after the first 2m – a cost-saving measure.

Of the two entrances to the main tomb, one provides access to the inner balcony while the second leads down through another beautiful door to the **vault** itself (since a suicidal student jumped from a minaret, visitors may no longer climb them). Be sure to remove your shoes at the steps. Inside, an exquisite octagonal **lattice-screen** of white marble surrounds the raised plinth supporting Rabi'a Daurani's grave – like her husband's in nearby Rauza, "open" as a sign of humility. The unmarked grave beside it is said to be that of the empress's nurse. Through a slanted window on the back wall, the rays of the rising sun illuminate the tomb for three minutes each morning.

The caves

Carved out of a steep-sided spur of the Sahyadri range, directly overlooking the Bibi-Ka-Maqbara, Aurangabad's own **caves** bear no comparison to their cousins in nearby Ellora and Ajanta, but their fine **sculpture** makes a worthwhile introduction to rock-cut architecture. In addition, the infrequently visited site is peaceful and pleasant in itself, with commanding views over the city and surrounding countryside.

The caves themselves, all Buddhist, consist of two groups, eastern and western, numbered 1 to 9 by the ASI. The majority were excavated between the fourth and eighth centuries, under the patronage of two successive dynasties: the **Vakatkas**, who ruled the western Deccan from Nasik, and the **Chalukyas**, a powerful Mysore family who emerged during the sixth century. All except the much earlier cave 4, which is a *chaitya* hall, are of the *vihara* type, belonging to the Mahayana school of Buddhism.

Unless you cycle, the only practical way of **getting to the caves** is by auto-rickshaw or taxi; you'll be expected to shell out for waiting time, or the return fare. You could also, drop down on foot to the Bibi-Ka-Maqbara to pick up a scooter back into town.

The western group

The **western**, and oldest, group of caves is reached via a long flight of steps leading left off the main road. The first of interest, **Cave 2**, is a sixth-century *vihara*, with a columned verandah and a doorway flanked by two *bodhisattvas*. Inside, a small shrine containing a seated Buddha is surrounded by an unusual passage. **Cave 3** is a remarkably elaborate seventh-century *vihara*. Its most vivid friezes, depicting scenes from the lives of the Buddha, adorn the stone "beams" above the pillars in the main chamber.

Cave 4, the oldest at Aurangabad, may date from the first century AD, and is the only representative of the earlier and more austere Hinayana phase of architecture. Unlike its neighbours, the cave is a rectangular apsidal-ended *chaitya* hall, with a monolithic *stupa* as its focal point. The characteristic timber-style ceiling is thought to have been an imitation of earlier free-standing wooden structures.

The eastern group

If you only have time to visit one group, it should be the **eastern**, 1km further along the hillside. **Cave 6** contains some finely carved *bodhisattvas*, together with traces of painting on the ceiling of its porch, but the sculpture in **cave 7** is the real highlight. Its verandah has columned shrines to either side, with a lotus-holding Padmapani and Shakyamuni flanked by six goddesses; a chubby Panchika (guardian of the earth's treasures) and Hariti (goddess of prosperity) stand to the right. The panel on the left of the doorway shows the *bodhisattva* Avalokitesvara (lord of compassion) encircled by the eight mortal fears: fire, the sword, chains (imprisonment), shipwreck, lions, snakes, rampant elephants and the Demon of Death. Nearby, a couple of heavy-breasted *tara* figures bear witness to the increasing preoccupation with female creative energy – *shakti* – cults during the latter part of the Buddhist epoch. Finally, to the left of the preaching Buddha in the sanctuary is Aurangabad's most celebrated panel: a frieze showing a dancer in a classical pose accompanied by six female musicians.

The small unnumbered cave next to cave 6 has intrigued archeologists since its rediscovery in 1961. Unusually, the central deity here is the Hindu god **Ganesh**, while on the mural to its right an image of the Buddha provides graphic evidence of the overlap of Buddhism and Brahmanism in the eighth century.

Accommodation

Aurangabad's proximity to some of India's most important monuments, together with its new "boom-city" status, ensures a profusion of **hotels**. On the whole, standards tend

ACCOMMODATION PRICE CODES

All **accommodation prices** in this book have been coded using the symbols below. In principle the prices given are for the least expensive double rooms in each establishment; however, some hotels, usually in category ①, offer rates per bed rather than per room. Local taxes are not included unless specifically stated. For more details, see p.35.

① up to Rs100	④ Rs225–350	⑦ Rs750–1200
② Rs100–150	⑤ Rs350–500	⑧ Rs1200–2200
③ Rs150–225	⑥ Rs500–750	⑨ Rs2200 and upwards

to be high and prices very reasonable, particularly in the **budget** places, most of which are strung along the road between the bus stand and the railway station, and range from extremely basic Indian lodges to more pleasant travellers' hostels. All have 24-hour checkout unless otherwise stated. All the hotels in our "moderate to expensive" category have noon checkout times, some a/c rooms, and charge luxury tax.

Inexpensive

Devpriya, near Sidharth Gardens, Bus Stand Rd (☎339032). Neat, clean and efficiently run family hotel. Very good value, and there's a reputable massage service and steam bath. Recommended. ②.

Green Palace, opposite the bus stand (☎335501). Spartan but clean. Handy if you've just crawled off a bus and can't face a room hunt, and there's crop of good fall-backs nearby. ②.

Natraj, Station Rd (☎24260). Very traditional lodge run by two elderly Gujarati brothers. Spacious, clean, good-value rooms with shared bathrooms. No left luggage, and strictly no alcohol. ①.

New Punjab, opposite the railway station (☎21391). A large, functional, though clean, lodge with goodsized rooms, some with attached baths. Mostly men. ①.

Panchavati, Padampura, off Station Rd (☎28755). In a similar vein to the *New Punjab*, though with a popular restaurant. A convenient option if the nearby *Youth Hostel* is full. ①–②.

Tourist Home, Station Rd (☎337212). Congenial travellers' hostel with neat rooms, attached shower-toilets, and a sociable terrace where evening *thalis* are served. Excellent value. ②.

Youth Hostel, Padampura, off Station Rd (☎29801). Neat and clean segregated dorms (only Rs30) with mosquito nets, and reasonable private rooms, often booked in advance. Full board available. The cheapest option in town. Checkout 9am (closed 11am–4pm). ①.

Moderate to expensive

Amarpreet, Jalna Rd (☎332521; fax 332523). Central, well-appointed Punjabi-run hotel on airport road. Two restaurants, coffee shop, bar and foreign exchange. Some non-a/c rooms. ⑤–⑥.

Ambassador Ajanta, Chikalthana (☎82211; fax 84367). Luxurious 5-star near the airport, with over-the-top ersatz traditional interior. Excellent sports facilities. ⑧.

Ashiyana, Bansilal Nagar (☎29322). Immaculate if unexciting hotel just off Station Rd, near the tourist office. Peaceful and good value. ③–⑤.

Great Punjab, Station Rd (☎336482). Business-oriented hotel very near the railway station. All 42 rooms have bathrooms, balconies and TVs. Bland but very good value. ④–⑤.

MTDC Holiday Resort, Station Rd (☎334259). Spacious, comfortable rooms, if a touch shabby. Mosquito nets over beds. Good restaurant and garden. ④–⑤.

Printravel, Station Rd (☎29707). Faintly 1950s-style building near city centre. Common balcony with easy chairs and a good restaurant. Huge rooms (some a/c). ③–④.

Rajdhani, Railway Station Rd (☎27562). Comfortable (but rather pricey), with room service, satellite TV and carpets. Some a/c. ⑤.

Raviraj, Dr Rajendra Prasad Rd (☎27501). Classy, central chain hotel, with all amenities. ⑤.

Taj Residency, near Hersul Jail (☎333501). The newest and most impressive of the 5-stars. Well out of town, but palatial, peaceful and better value than its competitors near the airport. ⑧.

Vedant, Station Rd (☎333844; fax 331923). American-style 4-star with huge lobby, 24hr coffee shop, beauty parlour, gym and pool. Very central. ⑦.

Eating and drinking

Food in Aurangabad tends to be an incongruous mixture of strictly vegetarian **Gujarati** and meat-oriented north Indian Muslim dishes. Typically, "non-veg" is synonymous with dim lights, drawn curtains and a male clientele, while the veg restaurants attract families, and are particularly popular on Sunday evenings, when booking is recommended. Aurangabad has a conservative attitude to **alcohol**; on the whole, drinking is a male preserve, carried out in specially segregated bars (or **permit rooms**), with the exception of the larger and more tourist-oriented hotels and restaurants.

Agran Mistan, Aurangpura. Clean, no-nonsense restaurant on the southern edge of the old town, serving authentic, moderately-priced Gujarati food, mainly to visiting business people.

Chanakya, Dwarkapuri Rd. A big hit with the city's nouveau riche. Pretentious, but the food is excellent. Veg and non-veg (including fish) and alcohol served al fresco (bring mosquito repellent).

Foodwala's Bhoj, near Baba Petrol Pump. An old favourite, pure-veg restaurant at shiny new premises. Renowned for its meticulously prepared, good-value lunchtime Gujarati *thalis*.

Foodwala's Tandoori, Shyam Chambers, Station Rd. Upmarket a/c bar-restaurant with numerous à la carte chicken and mutton dishes. Pricey but worth it.

Kailas, *Hotel Amarpreet*, Jalna Rd. Authentic Punjabi cuisine and plenty of spicy Szechuan options, including *dim sum* starters.

Kailash, MTDC *Holiday Resort*. Standard veg and non-veg menu, with some Indian-style Chinese. Generous portions at reasonable prices.

Mingling, *Rajdoot Hotel*, Jalna Rd. Best Chinese in town, though a bit ostentatious and over-priced.

Radhika, *Hotel Nandanvan*. Justly popular, serving a large selection of inexpensive veg dishes (mainly south Indian) in garden. *Rathi* next door is equally good non-veg version, with cold beer, but dingy surroundings. Both are excellent value.

MOVING ON FROM AURANGABAD

Daily **flights** from Aurangabad to **Bombay** (40min) are operated by *NEPC* (7.45am), *Indian Airlines* (9.45am), and *East-West* (5.50pm). *Indian Airlines* also fly daily to **Delhi** (7.45am), calling at **Udaipur**, and **Jaipur**. Their office is on Jalna Rd (☎24864).

Both the state transport corporation (*MSRTC*) and MTDC run good-value "luxury" **night-buses** to **Bombay**. If you feel like a little more comfort, the *Royal Coach Company* also has an a/c bus; tickets, booked through *Classic Travels*, in the lobby of MTDC's *Holiday Resort*, cost a little more than the other buses. Getting to **Pune** is easy, on *MSRTC*'s "express" buses (7 daily; 5hr). **Nasik** buses are less frequent (5 daily; 3hr). Both *MSRTC* and *Royal* run buses to **Indore**, one at 5.30am, the other at 9pm. Anyone heading to **Udaipur** will need to take this, the first of two arduous twelve-hour journeys. The *MSRTC* bus to **Ahmedabad** is another gruelling overnighter.

Trains to and from Aurangabad are very limited, as the city is not on the main line. The two most useful services to **Bombay** are the heavily booked *Devagiri Express* #1004 (10hr) and the *Tapovan Express* #7618 (10hr), which leave at 9.00pm and 3.10pm respectively. You can also get to Hyderabad on the direct *Devagiri Express* (14hr) at 7.20am. Otherwise, the nearest mainline station, at **Jalgaon**, 108km north, is served by trains to Delhi, Agra, Bhopal, Calcutta and Madras.

Daulatabad (Deogiri)

Northwest of Aurangabad, the main Ellora road runs through fertile Deccani farmland punctuated by the occasional red-brick village or Muslim tomb crumbling in shady evergreen glades. Looming on the horizon of this serene and prosperous countryside is the stark profile of one of India's most imposing fortresses. Invading armies must have stopped dead when confronted with **DAULATABAD**, 13km northwest of

Aurangabad. The awesome hill-top citadel crowns a massive conical volcanic outcrop whose sides have been shaped into a sheer sixty-metre wall of granite. The fort's forbidding appearance is further accentuated by the slender victory **minaret** rising out of the ruins of the city that once sprawled from its base, like a pink finger in the face of the approaching enemy. If only for the panoramic **views** from its summit, Daulatabad makes an excellent pause en route to or from the caves at Ellora, 17km northwest.

Aside from the inevitable Buddhist and Jain hermits, occupation of the site – then known as **Deogiri**, "Hill of the Gods" – dates from its ninth-century role as bastion and capital of a confederacy of Hindu tribes. The **Yadavas** were responsible for scraping away the jagged lower slopes of the mount to form its vertical-cliff base, as well as the fifteen-metre deep moat that still encircles the upper portion of the citadel. Their prosperity eventually aroused the interest of the acquisitive Delhi Sultans, who stormed the fortress in 1294 and carried off a raja's ransom in gold, silver and precious stones.

Muslim occupation of Deogiri, however, began in earnest with the arrival in 1327 of Ghiyas-ud-din **Tughluq**. Convinced that the fort was the perfect base for campaigns further south, the Sultan decreed that his entire court should decamp here from Tughluqabad, the "third city" of Delhi (see p.76). The epic 1100-kilometre march cost thousands of lives, the Sultan's underfed and exhausted subjects dropping like flies by the wayside. Life in the new capital – which Tughluq prematurely renamed Daulatabad, or "Abode of Good Fortune" – was not much of an improvement. Within seventeen years, drought, famine and the growing threat of a full-scale Moghul invasion on his northern borders forced the beleaguered ruler to concede defeat and return to Tughluqabad. His audacious governor, Zafar Khan, seized the moment, and in 1327 mounted a rebellion to establish the **Bahmani** dynasty. Thereafter, the fortress fell to a succession of different regimes, including Shah Jahan's **Moghuls** in 1633, before it was finally taken by the **Marathas** midway through the eighteenth century.

The fortress

Daulatabad's labyrinthine **fortress** incorporates so many ingenious ways to snuff out unwanted intruders that it's almost inconceivable anyone ever managed to penetrate the formidable outer defences, let alone fight their way up the 183 metres of ramparts, moats and dark passages to the citadel at the top. The tone is set by the vicious, elephant-proof spikes that stick menacingly out of the main gates. Once inside, three **cannons** (two Persian and one Dutch – look for the engraving of a European sailing ship) lie discarded in the first of several claustrophobic courtyards – reminders of the aerial bombardment which by this stage would have been raining down upon the attackers. The proud **Chandminar**, or "Victory Tower", further along, was more of a psychological than a military deterrent. Soaring above the heart of the old town, of which only the scantest traces now remain, the majestic pink minaret was erected by Ala-ud-din Bahmani to celebrate his conquest of the fort in 1435. The Persian blue and turquoise tiles that once plastered it in complex geometric patterns have disappeared.

The **Jama Masjid**, directly opposite the Chandminar, is Daulatabad's oldest Islamic monument. Built by the Delhi Sultans in 1318, to chastise Deogiri's Hindu occupants for their refusal to pay annual tribute, the well-preserved mosque comprises 106 pillars plundered from the Hindu and Jain temples which previously stood on the site. Recently, the *masjid* was converted into a Bharatmata temple – much to the chagrin of local Muslims. Nearby, the large stone-lined "Elephant" **tank** was once a central component in the fort's extensive water-supply system. Two giant terracotta pipes channelled water from the hills into the Deogiri's legendary fruit and vegetable gardens.

Once beyond the open ground surrounding the tower, the main walkway heads through a series of interlocking bastions, fortified walls, moats and drawbridges before emerging from under the third gateway to the **Chini Mahal**, or "Chinese Palace", where the last Galconda ruler Abdul Hasan Tana Shah was imprisoned in 1687 by the Moghul emperor Aurangzeb. Following thirteen years of torture at the hands of his sadistic captors, Tana Shah is said to have begged, of all things, for a pot of curd which, once eaten, caused his head to explode. His corpse was then dragged behind an elephant to Rauza where it was finally entombed. The impressive ram-headed **Kila Shikan** ("Fort Breaker") cannon, inscribed with its name in Persian, rests on a stone platform nearby. From here onwards, a sequence of macabre traps lay in wait for the unwary intruder. First, a moat infested with man-eating crocodiles had to be crossed in order to reach the foot of the citadel, or **Bala Kot**. Next, the attackers had to crawl through a maze of pitch-black passageways cut from the fort's solid-rock foundations. At one point, these fork and rejoin again to dupe enemy soldiers into fighting each other in the darkness. If they survived that ruse, the suffocating toxic fumes emanating from the red-hot iron cover that sealed the only exit to the underground tunnel would probably finish them off. Their bodies would then be dumped down the slanting chutes in the side walls, to be devoured by the voracious crocodiles waiting in the moat below.

At the end of the tunnel, a broad flight of rock-cut steps climbs to an attractive twelve-pillared pavilion. The **Baradi** is thought to have been the residence of a Yadavi queen, though it was later used by emperor Shah Jahan during his visits to Daulatabad. The **views** from the flat roof of the building are superb. Note the tombs clinging to the foot of the barren brown hills to the east, and the street plan of the old town below, just discernible through the rubble-strewn wasteground beside the Jama Masjid. An even more impressive panorama is to be had from the **look-out post** perched on the summit of the hill, where you'll find another old cannon (the "Storm Creator") and an ancient rock-cut cave, home during the Moghul period to a renowned Hindu ascetic.

Practicalities

Although Daulatabad features on the MTDC guided **tour** of Ellora from Aurangabad (see p.667), you'll have more time to enjoy it if you travel there on one of the hourly shuttle **buses** between Aurangabad and the caves. The stop is directly opposite the main entrance to the fort, beside the string of *chai* and souvenir stalls and the good, small MTDC-run **restaurant**. Daulatabad holds no **accommodation** for visitors.

Khauldabad (Rauza)

As the silhouette of Daulatabad fort recedes into the haze on the horizon, the Ellora–Aurangabad road climbs a sun-bleached ridge called **Peepal Ghat**. Nestled on this saddle of high ground, 22km from Aurangabad and a five-kilometre ride from the caves, **KHAULDABAD**, also known as **Rauza**, is an old walled town famous for a bumper crop of tumbledown onion-domed **tombs**. Among the Muslim notables deemed worthy of a patch of earth in this most hallowed of burial grounds ("Khauldabad" means "Heavenly Abode"), were the emperor Aurangzeb, a couple of Nizams, and a fair few of the town's *chisti* founding fathers – the seven hundred mystic missionaries dispatched by the saint Nizam-ud-din Aulia to soften up local Hindus ahead of the Sultanate's invasion in the fourteenth century. Rauza's monuments are nowhere near as impressive as those in Delhi or Agra, but a couple harbour important **relics** and are still venerated for their miraculous properties. While they see a steady trickle of visitors, and even large crowds on festival days, the lesser mausoleums on the outskirts of the sleepy Muslim town lie deserted and all but forgotten, their old stone pavilions, bulbous domes and walled enclosures choked with weeds and grazed by herds of scruffy goats.

The Dargah of Sayeed Zain-ud-din

Khauldabad is encircled by tall granite battlements and seven fortified **gateways** raised by Aurangzeb before his death in 1707. The last of the great Moghuls is buried inside the town's most famous **dargah**, or shrine-tomb, midway between the North and South gates. Steps lead up from the main thoroughfare through a domed porch into a peaceful courtyard surrounded by whitewashed cloisters and minarets. **Aurangzeb's tomb** lies under the arch to the left. In keeping with the teachings of Islam, the grave itself is a humble affair, open to the elements instead of sealed in stone. The devout emperor insisted that it be paid for not out of the royal coffers, but with the money he had raised in the last years of his life by selling his own hand-quilted white skull-caps. The pierced-marble **screen** and walls that now surround the spot were erected much later by the British Viceroy, Lord Curzon, and the Nizam of Hyderabad.

Aurangzeb chose this as his final resting place primarily because of the presence, next door, of Sayeed **Zain-ud-din**'s tomb. The mausoleum of the Muslim saint, or *pir*, occupies a quadrangle separating Aurangzeb's grave from those of his wife and second son, Azam Shah. Its doors are beautifully inlaid with slabs of silver, brass and bronze, while the steps leading to it are encrusted with highly polished semi-precious stones donated by the wandering Muslim ascetics, or *fakirs*, who formerly came here on pilgrimages. Locked away behind a small door is Rauza's most jealously guarded relic. The **Robe of the Prophet** is revealed to the public once a year, on the twelfth day of the Islamic month of Rabi-ul-Awwal (usually around November), when the tomb becomes the focus of a festival attracting crowds of worshippers from all over India.

The other buildings in this *dargah* are a small **mosque** (on the west side of the main courtyard) and the **Nakkar Khanna**, or Music Hall, which, on high days and holy days, hosts performances of *qawwali*.

The Dargah of Sayeed Burhan-ud-din

Directly opposite Zain-ud-din's tomb is the **Dargah of Sayeed Burhan-ud-din**, a *chisti* missionary buried here in 1334. The shrine is said to contain hairs from the Prophet's beard which magically increase in number when they are counted each year. At the end of the fourteenth century, when a cash crisis had left the saint's disciples unable to provide for either themselves or the upkeep of the beloved *dargah*, a pair of "**silver trees**" miraculously sprouted in its central courtyard. These days, the only precious metal to be found in the tomb are the panels set into the doors of the shrine, although for a small donation the attendant will point out the two innocuous-looking lumps in the pavement nearby where the fabled trees once stood, and which are still said to secrete the odd drop of silver.

Around the town

Most of the other tombs on the outskirts of Rauza are difficult to locate without the help of a rickshaw *wallah*. Half a kilometre west of the two main *dargahs*, you'll find the *maqbara* of **Bani Begum**, the mistress of one of Aurangzeb's sons. This large walled garden tomb encloses some well-preserved Moghul-domed pavilions, pillars and arches set amid balding lawns and flower beds. The *dargah* of the Abyssinian ex-slave and founder of Aurangabad, **Malik Ambar**, is tucked away to the northwest, close to the whitewashed tomb of **Abdul Hasan Tana Shah**, the unfortunate ruler of Galconda who died after thirteen years of incarceration inside Daulatabad fort.

On the road down to the Ellora caves, you pass one of Rauza's few empty tombs. Commissioned by a foreign ambassador who fell ill here in the eighteenth century, this modest mausoleum was never occupied. Shortly after it was completed, the diplomat recovered from his supposedly terminal illness and limped home to Persia, where he eventually died, leaving his tomb to lie forever idle on this peaceful, west-facing ridge.

Practicalities

MSRTC **buses** pull in every half-hour or so at Rauza's small bus stand, a short walk west of the walls, en route between Aurangabad and the Ellora caves just down the hill. The only **place to stay** nearby is the *Government Rest House* (③), a wonderful *dak* bungalow converted by the British from the tomb of Nizam Shah Bhairi. Rooms are reserved for government servants or guests, and normally booked up well in advance, but there's no harm in trying to persuade the *chowkidar* to squeeze you in if he has a vacancy. If the prospect of **eating** in one of the insanitary sweet shops and *chai* stalls in Rauza's main bazaar doesn't appeal, you'll have to wait until you get to Ellora.

Ellora

Palaces will decay, bridges will fall, and the noblest structures must give way to the corroding tooth of time; whilst the caverned temples of Ellora shall rear their indestructible and hoary heads in stern loneliness, the glory of past ages, and the admiration of ages yet to come.

Captain Seely, *The Wonders of Ellora*

Maharashtra's most visited ancient monument, the **ELLORA caves**, 29km northwest of Aurangabad, may not enjoy as grand a setting as their older cousins at Ajanta (see p.683), but the amazing wealth of **sculpture** they contain more than compensates, and this is an unmissable port of call if you're heading to or from Bombay, 400km southwest. In all, thirty-four Buddhist, Hindu and Jain caves – some excavated simultaneously, in competition – line the foot of the two-kilometre-long Chamadiri escarpment as it tumbles down to meet the open plains. The site's principal attraction, the gargantuan **Kailash temple**, rears from a huge, sheer-sided cavity cut from the hillside. The world's largest monolith, this vast lump of solid basalt is fashioned into a spectacular agglomeration of interconnecting colonnaded halls, galleries, and sacred shrines.

The original reason why this apparently remote spot became the focus of so much religious and artistic activity was the busy **caravan route** that cut through here on its way between the prosperous cities to the north and the ports of the west coast. Profits from the lucrative overland trade fuelled a five-hundred-year spate of excavation, beginning midway through the sixth century AD at around the same time that Ajanta, 100km northeast, was abandoned. This was the twilight of the Buddhist era in central India; by the end of the seventh century, **Hinduism** had begun to reassert itself. The Brahmanical resurgence gathered momentum over the next three hundred years under the patronage of the Chalukya and Rashtrakuta kings – the two powerful dynasties responsible for the bulk of the work carried out at Ellora, including the eighth-century Kailash temple. A third and final flourish of activity on the site took place towards the end of the first millennium AD, after the local rulers had switched allegiance from Shaivism to the Digambara sect of the **Jain** faith. A small cluster of more subdued caves to the north of the main group stand as reminders of this age.

Unlike the isolated site of Ajanta, Ellora did not escape the iconoclasm that accompanied the arrival of the **Muslims** in the thirteenth century. The worst excesses were committed during the reign of **Aurangzeb** who, in a fit of piety, ordered the systematic destruction of the site's "heathen idols". Although Ellora still bears the scars from this time, most of its best pieces of sculpture have remained miraculously intact. The fact that they were cut from hard rock, beyond the reach of the monsoon downpours, has preserved the caves in remarkable condition.

The caves

All the **caves** are numbered, following a roughly chronological plan. Numbers 1 to 12, at the south end of the site, are the oldest, from the Vajrayana Buddhist era (500–750 AD). The Hindu caves, 17 to 29, overlap with the later Buddhist ones and date from between 600 and 870 AD. Further north, the Jain caves – 30 to 34 – were excavated from 800 AD until the late eleventh century. Because of the sloping hillside, most of the cave entrances are set back from the level ground behind open courtyards and large colonnaded verandahs or porches. **Admission** to all but the Kailash temple is free.

To see the oldest caves first, turn right from the car park where the buses pull in and follow the main pathway down to cave 1. From here, work your way gradually northwards again, avoiding the temptation to look around cave 16, the Kailash temple, which is best saved until late afternoon when the bus parties have all left, and the long shadows cast by the setting sun bring its extraordinary stonework to life.

The Buddhist group

The **Buddhist caves** line the sides of a gentle recess in the Chamadiri escarpment. All except number 10 are *viharas*, or monastery-halls, which the monks would originally have used for study, solitary meditation and communal worship, as well as the mundane business of eating and sleeping. As you progress through them, notice how the chambers grow steadily more impressive in scale and tone. Scholars attribute this to the rise of Hinduism and the need to compete for patronage with the more overtly awe-inspiring Shaivite cave-temples being excavated so close at hand.

CAVES 1 TO 5

Cave 1 is a plain, bare *vihara* containing eight small cells and very little sculpture, which may have been a granary for the larger halls. In the much more impressive **cave 2**, a large central chamber is supported by twelve massive, square-based pillars while the side walls are lined with seated Buddhas.

The doorway into the shrine room is flanked by two giant *dvarpalas*, or guardian figures: an unusually muscular **Padmapani**, the lotus-holding *bodhisattva* of compassion, on the left, and an opulent bejewelled **Maitreya**, the "Buddha-to-come", on the right. Both are accompanied by their consorts. Inside the sanctum itself, a stately Buddha is seated on a lion throne, looking stronger and more determined than his serene forerunners in Ajanta. **Caves 3** and **4**, slightly older and similar in design to cave 2, are in rather poor condition.

ROCK-CUT CAVES OF THE NORTHWESTERN DECCAN

The **rock-cut caves** scattered across the volcanic hills of the northwestern Deccan rank among the most extraordinary religious monuments in Asia, if not the world. Ranging from tiny monastic cells to colossal, elaborately carved temples, they are remarkable for having been hewn by hand from solid rock. Their third-century BC origins seem to have been as temporary shelters for Buddhist monks when heavy monsoon rains made their normal itinerant lifestyle impossible. Modelled on earlier wooden structures, most were sponsored by **merchants**, for whom the casteless new faith offered an attractive alternative to the old, discriminatory social order. Gradually, encouraged by the example of the Mauryan emperor Ashoka, the local ruling dynasties also began to embrace Buddhism. Under their patronage, during the second century BC, the first large-scale monastery-caves were created at **Karle**, **Bhaja** and **Ajanta**.

Around this time, the austere **Hinayana**, or "Lesser Vehicle", school of Buddhism predominated in India. In keeping with the original teachings of the Buddha, closed communities of monks had little or no interaction with the outside world. Caves cut in this era were mostly simple "worship halls", or **chaityas** – long, rectangular apsed chambers with barrel-vaulted roofs, and two narrow colonnaded aisles curving gently around the back of a monolithic **stupa** (see p.363). Symbols of the Buddha's Enlightenment, these hemispherical burial mounds provided the principal focus for worship and meditation, circumambulated by the monks during their communal rituals.

The **methods** employed to excavate the caves altered little over the centuries. First, the basic dimensions of the ornamental facade were sketched onto the cliff face. Next, gangs of stonemasons hacked out a rough hole (later to become the *chaitya's* graceful horseshoe-shaped window), through which they chiselled deep into the rock. As they worked their way down to floor level, using heavy iron picks, the labourers left chunks of raw rock for skilled sculptors to transform into pillars, devotional friezes and *stupas*.

By the fourth century AD, the Hinayana school was losing ground to the more exuberant **Mahayana**, or "Greater Vehicle", school. Its emphasis on an ever-enlarging pantheon of deities and **bodhisattvas** (merciful saints who postponed their accession to *nirvana* to help mankind towards Enlightenment) was accompanied by a transformation in architectural styles. *Chaityas* were superseded by lavish monastery-halls, or **viharas**, in which the monks both lived and worshipped, and the once-prohibited image of the Buddha became far more prominent. Occupying the circumambulatory recess at the end of the hall, where the *stupa* formerly stood, the colossal **icon** acquired the thirty-two characteristic attributes, or **lakshanas** (including the long dangling ear-lobes, cranial protuberance, short curls, robe and halo) by which the Buddha was distinguished from lesser divinities. The highwater mark of Mahayanan art came towards the end of the Buddhist age. Drawing on the rich catalogue of themes and images contained in ancient scriptures such as the **Jatakas** (legends relating to the Buddha's previous incarnations), Ajanta's exquisite and awe-inspiring wall **painting** may, in part, have been designed to rekindle enthusiasm for the faith, which was, by this point, already starting to wane in the region.

Attempts to compete with the resurgence of **Hinduism**, from the sixth century onwards, eventually led to the evolution of another, more esoteric religious movement. The **Vajrayana**, or "Thunderbolt" sect stressed the female creative principle, **shakti**, with arcane rituals combining spells and magic formulas. Ultimately, however, such modifications were to prove powerless against the growing allure of Brahmanism.

The ensuing shift in royal and popular patronage is best exemplified by **Ellora**, where during the eighth century, many of the old *viharas* were converted into temples, their shrines housing polished *shivalinga* instead of *stupas* and Buddhas. Hindu cave architecture, with its predilection for dramatic mythological **sculpture**, culminated in the tenth century with the magnificent **Kailash temple**, a giant replica of the free-standing structures that had already begun to replace rock-cut caves. It was Hinduism that bore the brunt of the iconoclastic medieval descent of Islam on the Deccan, Buddhism having long since fled to the comparative safety of the Himalayas, where it flourishes to this day.

Known as the **"Maharwada"** cave because it was used by local Mahar tribes-people as a shelter during the monsoon, **cave 5** is the grandest single-storeyed *vihara* in Ellora. Its enormous 36-metre-long rectangular assembly hall is thought to have been used by the monks as a refectory (note the two rows of **benches** carved out of the stone floor). At the far end, the entrance to the central shrine is guarded by two fine *bodhisattva* figures of Padmapani and Vajrapani – the "Thunderbolt Holder". The Buddha inside is seated, this time on a stool; his right hand touches the ground in the *mudra* denoting the "Miracle of a Thousand Buddhas", performed by the Master to confound a gang of heretics. Notice the delicate rendition of his long, flowing robe.

CAVE 6

The next four caves were excavated at roughly the same time in the seventh century, and are mere variations of their predecessors. On the walls of the antechamber at the far end of the central hall in **cave 6**, are two of Ellora's most famous and finely executed figures. **Tara**, the female consort of the *bodhisattva* Avalokitesvara, stands to the left, with an intense, kindly expression. On the opposite side, the Buddhist goddess of learning, Mahamayuri, is depicted with her emblem the peacock, while a diligent student sets a good example at his desk below. The parallels with Mahayuri's Hindu counterpart, Saraswati, are obvious (the latter's mythological vehicle is also a peacock), and show the extent to which seventh-century Indian Buddhism incorporated elements from its rival faith in an attempt to rekindle its waning popularity.

CAVES 10, 11 AND 12

Excavated in the early eighth century, **cave 10** is one of the last and most magnificent of the Deccan's rock-cut *chaitya* halls. Steps lead from the left of its large verandah to an upper balcony, where a trefoil doorway flanked by flying threesomes, heavenly nymphs, and a frieze of playful dwarves leads to an interior balcony. From here, you have a good view down into the long apsed hall, with its octagonal pillars and vaulted roof. The stone "rafters" carved out of the ceiling, imitations of the beams that would have appeared in earlier free-standing wooden structures, are the source of this cave's popular name, the **Sutar Jhopadi**, or "Carpenter's Workshop". At the far end, a seated Buddha is enthroned in front of a votive **stupa** – the hall's devotional centre-piece.

In spite of the rediscovery in 1876 of its hitherto hidden basement, **cave 11** continues to be known as the **Dho Tal**, or "two floors" cave. Its top storey is a long columned assembly hall housing a Buddha shrine and, on its rear wall, images of Durga and Ganesh, the elephant-headed son of Shiva – evidence that the cave was converted into a Hindu temple after being abandoned by the Buddhists.

Cave 12 next door – the **Tin Tal**, or "three floors" – is another triple-storeyed *vihara* approached via a large open courtyard. Again, the main highlights are on the uppermost level, once used for teaching and meditation. The shrine room at the end of the hall, whose walls are lined with five large *bodhisattvas*, is flanked on both sides by seven Buddhas – one for each of the Master's previous incarnations. Those on the left are shown in deep meditation, while those to the right are once more depicted in the *mudra* that signifies the "Miracle of a Thousand Buddhas".

The Hindu group

Ellora's seventeen **Hindu caves** are grouped around the middle of the escarpment, to either side of the majestic Kailash temple. Excavated at the start of the Brahmanical revival in the Deccan, during a time of relative stability, the cave-temples throb with a vitality absent from their restrained Buddhist predecessors. Gone are the rows of heavy-eyed, benign-faced Buddhas and *bodhisattvas*. In their place, huge **bas-reliefs** line the walls, writhing with dynamic scenes from the Hindu scriptures. Most are connected with **Shiva**, the god of destruction and regeneration (and the presiding deity in all of the Hindu caves on the site), although you'll also come across numerous images of Vishnu, the Preserver, and his various incarnations.

The same tableaux crop up time and again, a repetition that gave Ellora's craftsmen ample opportunity to refine their technique over the years leading up to their greatest achievement, the **Kailash temple** (cave 16). Covered separately on p.681, the temple is the highlight of any visit to Ellora, but you'll appreciate its beautiful sculpture all the more if you check out the earlier Hindu caves first. Numbers 14 and 15, immediately south, are the best of the bunch if you're pushed for time.

CAVE 14

Dating from the start of the seventh century AD, and among the last of the early excavations, **cave 14** was a Buddhist *vihara* converted into a temple by the Hindus. Its layout is similar to that of cave 8, with the shrine room set back from the wall and surrounded by a circumambulatory passage. The entrance to the sanctum is guarded by two impressive river goddesses, Ganga and Yamuna, while in an alcove behind and to the right, seven heavy-breasted fertility goddesses, the **Sapta Matrikas**, dandle chubby babies on their laps. The female aspect of Shiva's elephant-headed son, Ganesh, sits to their right beside two cadaverous apparitions, Kala and Kali, the goddesses of death. Superb **friezes** adorn the cave's long side walls. Starting at the front, those on the left (as you face the shrine) show Durga slaying the demon buffalo Mahisa; Lakshmi, the goddess of wealth, enthroned on a lotus as her elephant attendants shower her with water; Vishnu, in the form of the boar, Vahara, rescuing the earth goddess Prithvi from the primordial flood; and finally Vishnu, shown with his two wives. On the opposite wall, the panels are devoted exclusively to Shiva. The second from the front shows him playing dice with his wife Parvati; then doing the dance of death as Nataraja; and in the fourth frieze, blithely ignoring the demon Ravana's futile attempts to shake him and his consort off their heavenly abode, Mount Kailash.

CAVE 15

Like its neighbour, the two-storeyed **cave 15**, reached via a long flight of steps, began life as a Buddhist *vihara* but was hijacked by the Hindus and became a Shiva shrine. Skip the largely uninteresting ground floor, and make for the upper level to find some of Ellora's most magnificent sculpture. The cave's name, **Das Avatara**, is derived from the sequence of panels along the right wall, which show five of **Vishnu**'s ten incarnations (*avatars*). The one nearest the entrance shows Vishnu in his fourth manifestation as the Man-Lion, **Narashima**, which he adopted to slay a demon that could not be killed "by man nor beast, by day or night, inside or outside a palace" (Vishnu got him by lying in wait at dawn inside the entrance hall to his palace). Notice the demon's serene expession as he prepares to die, confident in the knowledge that he will attain salvation having been killed by a god. In the second frieze from the front, the Preserver appears as the "**Primordial Dreamer**", reclining on the coils of Anantha, the cosmic serpent of Infinity. His navel is about to sprout a lotus flower from which Brahma will emerge to begin the creation of the world.

A carved panel in a recess to the right of the antechamber shows Shiva emerging from a *lingam*. His rivals, Brahma and Vishnu, stand before the apparition in humility and supplication – symbolizing the supremacy of Shaivism in the region at the time the conversion work was carried out. Finally, halfway down the left wall of the chamber, as you're facing the shrine, the cave's most elegant piece of sculpture shows Shiva, as Nataraja, poised in a classical dance pose.

CAVES 17 TO 29

Only three of the Hindu caves strung along the hillside north of the Kailash temple are worth making the effort to visit. **Cave 21** – the **Ramesvara** – was excavated late in the sixth century. Thought to be the oldest Hindu cave at Ellora, it harbours some well-executed sculpture, including a fine pair of river goddesses on either side of the verandah, two wonderful door guardians and some sensuous loving couples, or *mithunas*, dotted around the walls of the balcony. Look out, too, for the superb panels featuring Shiva and Parvati. **Cave 25**, further along, contains a striking image of the sun-god **Surya** speeding in his chariot towards the dawn.

From here, the path picks its way past two more excavations, then drops steeply across the face of a sheer cliff to the bottom of a small river gorge. Once under the seasonal **waterfall**, the trail climbs the other side of the gully, to emerge beside **cave 29**, the **Dhumar Lena**. Dating from the late sixth century, the cave boasts an unusual cross-shaped floor plan similar to the Elephanta cave in Bombay harbour (see p.639). Pairs of rampant lions guard its three staircases, while inside, the walls are covered with huge **friezes**. Left of the entrance, Shiva skewers the Andhaka demon; in the adjacent wall panel he foils the many-armed Ravana's attempts to shake him and Parvati off the top of Mount Kailash (look for the cheeky dwarf baring his bum to taunt the evil demon). On the south side, a dice-playing scene shows Shiva teasing Parvati by holding her arm back as she prepares to throw.

The Kailash temple (cave 16)

Cave 16, the colossal **Kailash temple** (daily 6am–6pm; Rs2), is Ellora's masterpiece. Here, the term "cave" is not only a gross understatement, but a complete misnomer. For although the temple was, like the other excavations, hewn from solid rock, it bears a striking resemblance to the free-standing structures – at Pattadakal and Kanchipuram (see p.989) in south India – on which it was modelled. The monolith is believed to have been the brainchild of the Rashtrakuta ruler **Krishna I** (756–73). One hundred years and four generations of kings, architects and craftsmen elapsed, however, before the project was completed. Climb up the track leading along the lip of the compound's north-facing cliff, to the ledge overlooking the squat main tower, and you'll see why.

The sheer scale is staggering. Work began by digging three deep trenches into the top of the hill using pickaxes and lengths of wood which, soaked with water and stuffed into narrow cracks, expanded to crumble the basalt. Once a huge chunk of raw rock had been exposed in this way, the royal sculptors set to work. In all, a quarter of a million tonnes of chippings and debris are estimated to have been cut from the hillside, with no room for improvisation or error. The temple was conceived as a giant replica of Shiva and Parvati's Himalayan abode, the pyramidal **Mount Kailash** – a Tibetan peak, said to be the "divine axis" between heaven and earth. Today, all but a few fragments of the thick coat of white-lime plaster that gave the temple the appearance of a snowy mountain have flaked off, to expose elaborately carved surfaces of grey-brown stone beneath. Around the rear of the tower, these have been bleached and blurred by centuries of erosion, as if the giant sculpture is slowly melting in the fierce Deccani heat.

THE TEMPLE

The main **entrance** to the temple is through a tall stone screen, intended to mark the transition from the profane to the sacred realms. After passing between two guardian river goddesses, Ganga and Yamuna, you enter a narrow passage that opens on to the main forecourt, opposite a panel showing **Lakshmi**, the goddess of wealth, being lustrated by a pair of elephants – the scene known to Hindus as "Gajalakshmi". Custom requires pilgrims to circumambulate clockwise around Mount Kailash, so descend the steps to your left and head across the front of the courtyard towards the near corner.

From the top of the concrete steps in the corner, all three principal sections of the complex are visible. First, the shrine above the entrance housing Shiva's vehicle **Nandi**, the bull; next, the intricate recessed walls of the main assembly hall, or **mandapa**, which still bears traces of the coloured plaster that originally coated the whole edifice; and finally, the sanctuary itself, surmounted by the stumpy, 29-metre pyramidal tower, or **shikhara** (best viewed from above). These three components rest on an appropriately huge raised platform, borne by dozens of lotus-gathering elephants. As well as symbolizing Shiva's sacred mountain, the temple also represented a giant **chariot**. The transepts protruding from the side of the main hall are its wheels, the Nandi shrine its yoke, and the two life-sized trunkless elephants in the front of the courtyard (disfigured by marauding Muslims) are the beasts of burden.

Most of the main highlights of the temple itself are confined to its side walls, which are plastered with vibrant **sculpture**. Lining the staircase that leads up to the north side of the *mandapa*, a long, lively narrative panel depicts scenes from the *Mahabharata*. Below this, you may recognize episodes from the life of **Krishna**, including one, in the bottom right corner, in which the young god suckled the poisoned breast of a wet nurse sent to kill him by his evil uncle. Krishna survived, but the poison dyed his skin its characteristic blue. Continuing around the temple in a clockwise direction, the majority of the panels around the lower sections of the temple are devoted to **Shiva**. On the south side of the *mandapa*, in an alcove carved out of the most prominent projection, you'll find the relief widely held to be the finest piece of sculpture in the compound. It shows Shiva and Parvati being disturbed by the multi-headed demon **Ravana**, who has been incarcerated inside the sacred mountain and is now shaking the walls of his prison with his many arms. Shiva is about to assert his supremacy by calming the earthquake with a prod of his toe. Parvati, meanwhile, looks nonchalantly on, reclining on her elbow as one of her handmaidens flees in panic.

At this point, make a short detour up the steps at the bottom (southwest) corner of the courtyard, to the "**Hall of Sacrifices**", with its striking frieze of the seven mother goddesses, the **Sapta Matrikas**, and their ghoulish companions Kala and Kali (shown astride a heap of corpses), or head straight up the stairs of the main assembly hall, past the animated battle scenes in the dramatic **Ramayana frieze**, to the shrine room. The sixteen-columned assembly hall is shrouded in a gloomy half-light designed to focus worshippers on the presence of the deity within. Using a portable arc light, the *chowkidar* will illuminate fragments of painting on the ceiling, where Shiva, as **Nataraja**, performs the dance of death, as well as numerous erotic *mithuna* couples. The sanctum itself is no longer a living **shrine**, although it still houses a large stone *lingam* mounted on a *yoni* pedestal, symbolizing the dual aspects of Shiva's procreative energy.

The Jain group

Ellora's small cluster of four **Jain caves** is north of the main group, at the end of a curving asphalt road. They can be reached either from cave 29, by dropping down to the T-junction and bearing right, or directly from the Kailash temple. Either way, the two-kilometre round-trip is quite a hike in the heat, and you may feel like taking a rickshaw.

Excavated in the late ninth and tenth centuries, after the Hindu phase had petered out, the Jain caves are Ellora's swansong. After the exuberance of the Kailash temple, their modest scale and subdued interiors lack vitality and inspiration, although some of the decorative carving is very fine. Only one of the group is of any real note. **Cave 32**, the **Indra Sabha** ("Indra's assembly hall"), is a miniature version of the Kailash temple. The lower of its two levels is plain and incomplete, but the upper storey is crammed with elaborate stonework, notably the ornate **pillars** and the two *tirthankaras* guarding the entrance to the central shrine. The naked figure of **Gomatesvara**, on the right, is fulfilling a vow of silence in the forest. He is so deeply immersed in meditation that creepers have grown up his legs and animals, snakes and scorpions crawl around his feet. On the opposite doorway, **Parashvanath**'s protective coat of cobra heads is another mark of a spiritual superman. Note the massive lotus carved on the ceiling, and the traces of the original blue **painting** around it. The shrine houses a Buddha-like icon **Mahavira**, the twenty-fourth *tirthankara* and founder of the Jain faith.

The Grishneshwar Mandir

Rising above the small village west of the caves, the cream-coloured *shikhara* of the eighteenth-century **Grishneshwar Mandir** pinpoints the location of one of India's oldest and most sacred deities. The *lingam* enshrined inside the temple's cavernous inner sanctum is one of the twelve "self-born" **Jyotirlinga** ("*linga* of light"), thought to date back to the second century BC. Non-Hindus are allowed to join the queue for *darshan*, but men have to remove their shirts before entering the shrine itself.

Ellora practicalities

Most visitors use Aurangabad as a base for day trips to the caves, **getting to Ellora** either via the half-hourly *MSRTC* buses or one of MTDC's popular guided **tours** (daily, depart 9.30am, return 5.30pm; Rs65). These tours are very rushed, however; if you want to take in the caves at a more leisurely pace and climb Daulatabad Hill, either spend the night at Ellora or leave Aurangabad early in the morning.

Ellora offers a couple of decent **places to stay**. The new *Hotel Kailas* (☎02437/41043; fax 41067; ⑤–⑦) is a small campus of self-contained chalets insensitively positioned opposite the caves, but with good facilities, including a restaurant and an a/c bar. They also have a limited number of **dorm beds** in an adjacent wing, the *Nataraj* (②). The only other budget accommodation is *Vijay's Rock Art Gallery and Restaurant* (①–②), a little down the road from the *Kailas*. The rooms and washing facilities here are very basic, but the congenial guest house, run by a local painter for "visiting artists, writers and thinkers", is a nice place to stay if you've come to study the caves in any detail. You can also buy wonderful reproduction paintings of the Ajanta murals.

Tasty, moderately-priced **food** is available at MTDC *Food-Wallah*'s restaurant opposite the main bus stand. In addition to the usual veg and non-veg Indian dishes, they serve Chinese, good-value lunchtime *thalis* and cold beer – indoors under the fan or al fresco on the shady terrace. You can also order meals and filled rolls in the *Kailas'* slightly pricier *Heritage* restaurant, but their turnover is sluggish, especially during the week. Roadside stalls sell *bhajis*, *pakoras* and other greasy snacks.

Ajanta

Hewn from the near-vertical sides of a horseshoe-shaped ravine, deep in the semi-arid hills of the Deccan, the rock-cut caves at **AJANTA** occupy a site worthy of the spectacular ancient art they contain. Less than two centuries ago, this remote spot was known only to the local Bhil tribespeople – the shadowy entrances to its abandoned stone chambers lay buried deep under a thick blanket of creepers and jungle. The chance arrival in 1819, of a small detachment of scarlet-coated East India Company troops, however, brought the caves' obscurity to an abrupt end. The **rediscovery** reads like an *Indiana Jones* screenplay. Led to the top of the precipitous bluff that overlooks the gorge by a young "half-wild" aboriginal scout, the tiger-hunters spied, far below, what has now been identified as the facade of cave 10 protruding through the dense foliage.

The gung-ho British soldiers had made one of the most sensational archeological finds of all time. Further exploration revealed a total of twenty-eight colonnaded caves chiselled out of the chocolate-brown and grey basalt cliffs lining the River Waghora. More remarkable still were the exquisite and immaculately preserved **paintings**

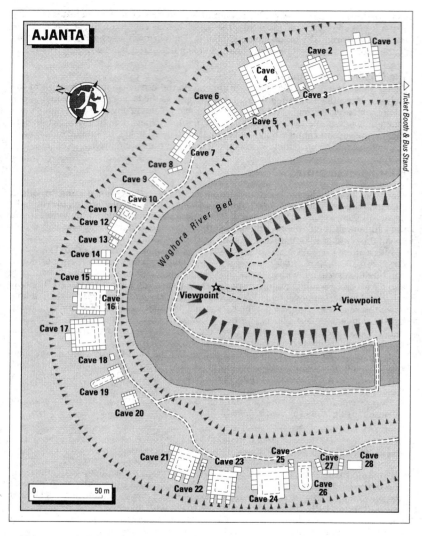

writing over their interior surfaces. For in addition to the phalanxes of stone Buddhas and other **sculpture** enshrined within them, Ajanta's excavations are adorned with a swirling profusion of multicoloured murals, depicting everything from battlefields to boudoirs, sailing ships to city streets and teeming animal-filled forests to snow-capped mountains. Even if you aren't wholly au fait with the narratives they portray, it's easy to see why these paintings rank among India's most beautiful treasures.

In spite of its comparative remoteness, Ajanta receives an extraordinary number of visitors. If you want to enjoy the site in anything close to its original serenity, avoid coming on a weekend or public holiday – it takes a fertile imagination indeed to picture Buddhist monks filing softly around the rough stone steps, when riotous schoolkids and holidaymakers are clambering over them. The best **seasons to visit** are either during the monsoon, when the river is swollen and the verdent gorge reverberates with the sound of the crashing waterfalls, or during the cooler winter months between October and March. At other times, the relentless Deccan sun beating down on the bare south-facing rock can make a trip around Ajanta a real endurance test. Whenever you come, bring a hat, some shades, a strong **flashlight** and plenty of drinking water.

Some history

Located close enough to the major trans-Deccan trade routes to ensure a steady supply of alms, yet far enough from civilization to preserve the peace and tranquillity necessary for meditation and prayer, Ajanta was an ideal location for the region's itinerant Buddhist monks to found their first permanent monasteries. Donative inscriptions indicate that its earliest cave excavations took place in the second century BC.

In its heyday, Ajanta sheltered over two hundred monks, as well as a sizeable community of painters, sculptors and labourers employed in excavating and decorating the cells and sanctuaries. Some time in the seventh century, however, the site was abandoned – whether because of the growing popularity of nearby Ellora, or the threat posed by the resurgence of Hinduism, no one knows. By the eighth century, the complex lay deserted and forgotten, overlooked even by the Muslim iconoclasts who wrought such damage to the area's other sacred sites during the medieval era.

Had the fateful tiger-hunting expedition not appeared over the horizon in 1819, Ajanta might have languished under a shroud of vegetation to this day. Instead, its wonders have been pored over by more prying eyes than just about any other Indian monument outside the "golden triangle" of Delhi, Agra and Jaipur. Early attempts to document the amazing discovery, however, met with such little success that Ajanta has been associated with a sinister **curse**. In 1866, after spending 27 years faithfully copying the paintings from his field-camp nearby, the artist **Robert Gill** lost his entire collection when London's Crystal Palace burned to the ground. The same fate befell another batch of facsimiles in the 1870s, which went up in smoke with London's Victoria and Albert Museum, while the efforts of a Japanese team were dramatically foiled when their rice-paper impressions of Ajanta's sculpture were crushed in an earthquake. Even **restoration** work has been dogged with misfortune. In 1920, the Nizam of Hyderabad (who then ruled the region) employed a pair of Italian experts to patch up some of the more badly damaged paintings. Unfortunately, the varnish they used to seal the flakier fragments of plaster to the cave walls darkened and cracked over time, causing further irreparable deterioration.

Nowadays, the job of restoration has fallen to the *ASI*. Among measures to minimize the impact of the hundreds of visitors who daily trudge through are a total ban on **flash photography**, and strict limits on the numbers allowed into a single cave at any given time – another good reason to avoid weekends. Recently, there has also been talk of a two-million-rupee investment to develop tourism. MTDC boldly boast of the snazzy new visitors' centre, three-star hotels and craft village that they hope to build nearby. So far though, the only commercialism to have hit Ajanta is the mushrooming collection of postcard and souvenir stalls around the bus stand below the main entrance. Just above these stands a handy **left luggage** hut (ask for the "cloakroom") where, for the princely sum of Rs3, you can stash your bags while you look around.

For more information on **rock-cut caves of the northwestern Deccan**, see p.678.

The caves

On arrival at the Ajanta **caves**, head straight through the pack of postcard- and gem-*wallahs* in the small bazaar-cum-bus stand, to the admissions kiosk on the other side of

CAVE PAINTING TECHNIQUES

The basic **painting techniques** used by the artists of Ajanta to transform the dull rock walls into lustrous kaleidoscopes of colour changed surprisingly little over the eight centuries the site was in use, from 200 BC to 650 AD. First, the rough-stone surfaces were primed with a six- to seven-centimetre coating of paste made from clay, cow-dung, and animal hair, strengthened with vegetable fibre. Next, a finer layer of smooth white lime was applied. Before this was dry, the artists quickly sketched the outlines of their pictures using red cinnabar, which they then filled in with a coating of *terre verte*. The **pigments**, all derived from natural water-soluble substances (kaolin chalk for white, lamp soot for black, glauconite for green, ochre for yellow and imported lapis lazuli for blue), were thickened with glue and added only after the undercoat was completely dry. Thus the Ajanta paintings are not, strictly speaking, frescoes (always executed on damp surfaces), but **tempera**. Finally, after they had been left to dry, the murals were painstakingly polished with a smooth stone to bring out their natural sheen.

The artists' only sources of **light** were oil-lamps and sunshine reflected into the caves by metal mirrors and pools of water (the external courtyards were flooded expressly for the purpose). Ironically, many of them were not even Buddhists, but Hindus employed by the royal courts of the day. Nevertheless, their extraordinary mastery of line, perspective and shading, which endows Ajanta's paintings with their characteristic other-worldly light, resulted in one of the great technical landmarks in Indian-Buddhist art history.

the rise (daily 9am–5.30pm; Rs0.50), to buy your entry and all-important Rs5 **light-tickets**. An obvious path leads from there to the grand **Mahayana** *viharas*; if you'd prefer to see the caves in chronological order, however, start with the smaller **Hinayana** group of *chaitya* halls at the bottom of the river bend (nos. 12, 10, 9 & 26), then work your way back up, via cave 17. If you need help getting up the steps, sedan chairporters, or *dhooli-wallahs*, stand in front of the stalls below. Official **guides** can be arranged through the ticket office; most have an interesting enough spiel, but you may well feel like taking in the sights again afterwards, at a more leisurely pace.

Cave 1

Cave 1 contains some of the finest and stylistically most evolved paintings on the site. By the time work on it began, late in the fifth century, *viharas* served not only to shelter and feed the monks, but also as places of worship in their own right – hence the addition to the rows of cells lining the front- and side-walls of a central **shrine room**. In common with most Mahayana *viharas*, the extraordinary **murals** lining the walls and ceilings depict episodes from the birth-story and former lives of the Buddha, the *Jatakas*. One of the most elaborate is the **Mahanjanaka**, which extends most of the way along the left-hand wall. This tells of a shipwrecked king who meets a solitary ascetic and decides to renounce all worldly attachments. On his return to his palace, his queen, with the help of a bevy of alluring dancing girls, unsuccessfully attempts to dissuade him. The last scene shows her husband leaving on a white horse, with a crowd of wailing courtesans in his wake.

Beyond the Mahanjanaka, left of the doorway into the main shrine, stands another masterpiece. **Padmapani**, the lotus-holding form of Avalokitesvara, is surrounded by an entourage of smaller attendants, divine musicians, lovers, monkeys and peacocks – his heavy almond eyes and languid hip-shot *tribhanga* (or "three-bend") pose exuding a distant and sublime calm. Opposite, flanking the right side of the doorway, is his counterpart, **Vajrapani**, the thunderbolt holder. Between them, these two *bodhisattvas* represent the dual aspects of Mahayana Buddhism, compassion and knowledge.

The real focal point of cave 1, however, is the gigantic sculpted Buddha seated in the shrine room – the finest such figure in Ajanta. Using portable electric spotlights, guides love to demonstrate how the expression on the Buddha's exquisitely carved face changes according to where the light is held: sombre to the left, blissful to the right, and serene when the light source is shone from below. On the pedestal below the statue, look for the wheel, symbolizing *dharma*, Buddha's teachings, and the deer which stands for the sermon he preached at Sarnath (see p.338).

On the way out, you may be able to spot this cave's other famous *trompe l'oeil*, crowning one of the pillars (on the third pillar from the rear as you face the shrine): the figures of four, apparently separate stags which, on closer inspection, all share the same head.

Cave 2

Cave 2 is another, similarly impressive, Mahayana *vihara*, dating from the sixth century. Here the ceiling, which seems to sag like a tent roof, is decorated with complex floral patterns, including lotus and medallion motifs. The design clearly takes its cue from ancient Greek art – a legacy of Alexander the Great's foray into the subcontinent half a millennium earlier. Sculpted friezes in the small subsidiary shrine to the right of the main chapel centre on a well-endowed fertility goddess, **Hariti**, the infamous child-eating ogress. When the Buddha threatened to give her a taste of her own medicine by kidnapping *her* child, Hariti flew into a frenzy (upper right), but was subdued by the Buddha's teachings of compassion (upper left). Below, a schoolroom scene shows a teacher waving a cane at a class of unruly pupils.

The side walls teem with lively **paintings** of the *Jatakas* and other mythological episodes. A frieze on the left verandah shows the birth of the Buddha, emerging from under his mother's arm, and his conception when a white elephant appeared to her in a dream (bottom left). Nearby, is one of several scenes portraying the "miracle of a thousand Buddhas", in which the Buddha, to confound a party of heretics, is said to have multiplied himself a thousand times.

Caves 3 to 9

Caves 3, 4 and 7 hold little of interest, but take a quick look into **cave 6**, a double-storeyed *vihara* with a finely carved door-jamb above its shrine room, a handful of octagonal pillars, and some peeling paintings above the entrances to its cells. Cave 8 is always closed; it contains the generator for the lights.

Cave 9, which dates from the first century BC, is the first *chaitya* you come to along the walkway. Resting in the half-light shed by a characteristic *peepal*-leaf-shaped window in the sculpted facade, the hemispherical **stupa**, with its inverted pyramidal reliquary, forms the devotional centrepiece of the fourteen-metre-long hall. The fragments of painting that remain, including the procession scene on the left wall, are mostly superimpositions over the top of earlier snake-deities (*nagarajas*).

Cave 10

Though partially collapsed, and marred by the unsightly wire meshing erected by the ASI to keep out bats, the facade of **cave 10**, a second-century BC *chaitya* hall – the oldest and most impressive of its kind in the ravine – is still a grand sight. The cave's main highlights, however, are far smaller and more subdued. With the help of sunlight reflected from a mirror held by an attendant, you may be able to pick out the fading traces of painting along the left wall (now encased in glass). The scene in which a raja and his retinue approach a group of dancers and musicians surrounding a garlanded *bodhi* tree – a symbol of the Buddha (the Hinayanas preferred not to depict him figuratively) – is believed to be the earliest surviving Buddhist mural in India. Elsewhere on the wall is graffiti scrawled by the British soldiers who rediscovered the caves in 1819.

The apsidal-ended hall itself, divided by three rows of painted octagonal pillars, is dominated by a huge monolithic **stupa** at its far end. If there's no-one else around, try out the *chaitya*'s amazing acoustics.

Cave 16

The next cave of interest, **cave 16**, is another spectacular fifth-century *vihara*, with the famous painting known as the "**Dying Princess**" near the front of its left wall. The "princess" was actually a queen named **Sundari**, and she isn't dying, but fainting after hearing the news that her husband, King Nanda (Buddha's cousin), is about to renounce his throne to take up monastic orders. The opposite walls show events from Buddha's early life as **Siddhartha**.

Cave 17

Cave 17, dating from between the mid-fifth and early sixth centuries, boasts the best preserved and most varied paintings in Ajanta. As with caves 1 and 2, only a limited number of visitors are allowed in at any one time. While you wait, have a look at the frescoes on the **verandah**. Above the door, eight seated Buddhas, including Maitreya, the Buddha to come, look down; to the left, an amorous princely couple share a last glass of wine before giving their worldly wealth away to the poor. The wall that forms the far left side of the verandah features fragments of an elaborate "Wheel of Life".

Inside the cave, the murals are, once more, dominated by the illustrations of the *Jatakas*, particularly those in which the Buddha takes the form of an animal to illustrate certain virtues. Running in a continuous frieze down the left aisle, the **Vishvantara Jataka** tells the story of a prince who was banished from the court by his father for giving away a magic rain-making elephant. Among the more poignant scenes in this long narrative is one where Vishvantara bids farewell to his queen in their four-poster bed before heading off to a hermitage in the forest. Nearby, on the wall to the left of the main shrine, is one of Ajanta's more gruesome highlights. In the **Sudasa Jataka**, a *bodhisattva* adopts the guise of a lioness to talk a prince out of eating his subjects. The artists have spared no detail, with gory illustrations of the cooking pots and chunks of human flesh being chopped up to put in them. Cannibalism is also the theme of the great **Simhala** frieze on the right-hand side of the cave. This relates the story of a merchant-adventurer and his band of mariners who, after being shipwrecked and washed ashore on a desert island, find themselves surrounded by voluptuous maidens. In a cruel twist (which would no doubt have Freud chuckling into his beard), these beautiful women turn, by night, into a horde of blood-crazed, man-eating ogresses. Luckily for the castaways, a *bodhisattva* appears in the form of a horse to lead them into a victorious battle against the evil she-demons.

The pillar separating the *Simhala Jataka* from a smaller frieze, which shows how the Buddha tore out his eyes to give to a blind *brahmin*, holds an exquisite and much-celebrated portrait of a sultry, dark-skinned princess admiring herself in a mirror while her handmaidens and a female dwarf look on. The *chowkidars* will demonstrate how, when illuminated from the side, her iridescent eyes and jewellery glow like pearls against the brooding dark background.

Cave 19

Excavated during the mid-fifth century, when the age of Mahayana Buddhism was in full swing, **cave 19** is indisputably Ajanta's most magnificent *chaitya* hall, its **facade** teeming with elaborate sculpture. On the columns flanking the walls, benign *bodhisattvas* in translucent robes are interspersed with meditating Buddhas, while on either side of the gracefully arched and pointed window, two pot-bellied, double-chinned demigods look smugly down. The penchant of the Mahayanas for theatrical luxuriance has been interpreted as a response to the concurrent rise of Brahmanism. This Hindu influence is even more manifest in the friezes that line the interior of the **porch**. On the left wall, crowned with a halo of cobra heads, the snake-king Nagaraja and his queen sit in a relaxed pose – reminiscent of the many Shiva and Parvati panels at Ellora, and of the indigenous snake-cult that formerly held sway here in the Waghora gorge.

Inside the hall, the faded frescoes are of less note than the sculpture around the tops of the pillars. The standing Buddha at the far end, another Mahayana innovation, is even more remarkable. Note the development from the stumpier *stupas* enshrined within the early *chaityas* (caves 9 & 10) to this more elongated version. Its umbrellas, supported by angels and a vase of divine nectar, reach right up to the vaulted roof.

Caves 21 to 26

Caves 21 to 26 date from the seventh century, a couple of hundred years after the others, and form a separate group at the far end of the cliff. Apart from the unfinished **cave 24**, whose roughly hacked trenches and pillars give an idea of how the original excavation was carried out here, the only one worth a close look is **cave 26**. Envisaged on a similarly grand scale to the other large *chaitya*, cave 19, this impressive hall was never completed. Nevertheless, the sculpture which the artisans had chiselled out here before they inexplicably downed tools is among the most vivid and dramatic at Ajanta. In the gloomy apse at the far end, the Buddha sits in front of a large cylindrical *stupa* ringed with *bodhisattvas*. In the "**Temptation of Mara**" frieze to his right (your left as you enter the cave), he appears again, this time impassively ensconced under a *peepal* tree as seven tantalizing sisters try to seduce him. Their father, the satanic Mara, watches from astride an elephant in the top left corner. The ruse to lead the Buddha astray fails, of course, eventually forcing the evil adversary and his daughters to retreat (bottom right). In contrast, the colossal image of **Parinirvarna**, Siddhartha reclining on his deathbed, along the opposite wall is a veritable pool of tranquillity. Check out the weeping and wailing mourners below, and the flying angels and musicians above, preparing to greet the sage as he drifts into *nirvana*. The soft sunlight diffusing gently from the doorway over Buddha's fine sensuously carved features completes the appropriately transcendent effect.

The viewpoint

The stiff thirty-minute climb to the "**viewpoint**" from where the British hunting party first spotted the Ajanta caves is well worth the effort – the panorama over the Waghora ravine and its surrounding walls of bare, flat-topped mountains is stunning. The easiest way to pick up the path is to head through the souvenir stalls outside the entrance to the caves and ford the river; alternatively, drop down the steps below caves 16/17 and follow the walkway until you reach a concrete footbridge. Turn left on the far side of the river, and then right when you see steps branching uphill. A right turn at the end of the bridge will take you further into the ravine, where there's an impressive waterfall: don't attempt this during **monsoon**, though, as water levels can be dangerously high.

Ajanta practicalities

The only way of **getting to Ajanta**, unless you have your own transport, is by **bus**. An hourly service makes the 100-minute climb into the hills from the nearest railhead at **Jalgaon**, 58km north. If you're coming from **Aurangabad** to the southwest, the 166-kilometre road trip takes three-and-a-half hours, with a pit stop at the market town of **Shillod** en route. The last buses leave Ajanta for Jalgaon at 6pm, and for Aurangabad at 5.45pm. Provided you catch an early enough bus up here, it's possible to see the caves, grab a bite to eat, and then head off again in either direction. Alternatively, you could do the round trip from Aurangabad on one of MTDC's rushed **tours** (daily depart 8am, return 5.30pm; Rs120). Tickets can be booked from any MTDC office.

There is no **accommodation** in Ajanta proper; most visitors stay in Aurangabad, or Jalgaon, to catch a train early the following day. If you want to stay within striking distance of the caves, choice is limited to MTDC's *Holiday Resort* (☎02438/3230; ④), in the one-horse village of **Fardapur**, a few kilometres down the Jalgaon road, where the rooms are reasonably clean, with fans and tatty mosquito nets; they also have a rock-bottom dorm (Rs50) if you don't mind sleeping on the floor. A small cafeteria, the *Vihara Restaurant*, serves unadventurous Indian and Chinese meals given a couple of hours advance warning. At the caves, the most popular place to **eat** is *Food-Wallah*'s very ordinary restaurant, next to the bus stand, but you can fill up on much cheaper freshly cooked *thalis* at the staff canteen next to the ticket office.

Jalgaon

Straddling an important junction in the *Central* and *Western Railway* networks, as well as the main trans-Deccan trunk road, NH6, **JALGAON** is a busy market town for the region's cotton and banana growers, and a key jumping-off point for travellers heading to or from the Ajanta caves, 58km south. Even though the town holds nothing of interest, you may find yourself obliged to hole up here to be well placed for a morning departure. If so, an early night with a good book should appeal considerably more than the dismal cafes and seedy permit-rooms (bars) outside the railway station.

Practicalities

Jalgaon is well-served by mainline **trains** between Delhi and Bombay, 420km southwest, and convenient for most cities to the north on the *Central Railway*. Express services also pass through en route to join the *Southeastern Railway* at **Nagpur**.

Buses to Indore (257km north) and Pune (336km) leave from the busy *MSRTC* bus stand, a ten-minute rickshaw ride across town from the train station. *Uncle Travels*, opposite the *Amram Guest House* on Station Rd, also operate luxury overnight video buses to Indore (depart 9.30pm; 8hr), Pune (depart 9.30pm; 9hr) and Bombay (depart 9pm; 10hr 30min). If you're heading to **Ajanta**, the fastest bus is the hourly service to **Aurangabad**, 166km south. Before buying your ticket, make sure that the bus does stop at the caves, or you might find yourself marooned at **Fardapur** (see above), fifteen minutes north of Ajanta.

You shouldn't have any difficulty finding **accommodation**. If you're not too squeamish about dirty toilets and a dawn chorus of throat-clearing, you could try the **retiring rooms** above platform 1 at the railway station (①–②). As well as the usual four- to six-bed dorms, some more expensive, but good-value rooms are tacked on the side. The rest of Jalgaon's places to stay are within easy walking distance. Among the cheap lodges around the station square and main street, *Amram Guest House* (☎0257/226549; ②)) is the most comfortable, with reasonably clean singles and doubles, fresh sheets, fans and some attached shower-toilets. Left off the main road down a little side street, the a/c *Hotel Chandan* (☎0257/226192; ②–⑤) offers plain, clean rooms. The best midrange option, however, has to be the very spruce *Hotel Plaza* on the left side of Station Rd (☎0257/224854; ②–③). Its economy rooms are particularly good, with immaculate tiled bathrooms, fans and 24-hour checkout; pricier rooms come with cable TV, and they'll provide tea in bed if you're leaving early in the morning. If these are all full, or if you're looking for more comfort, carry on to the roundabout at the end of Station Rd, where the *Tourist Resort* (☎0257/225192; ③–⑤) has rooms ranging from simple economy singles to a/c suites.

There's no better place to **eat** than the *Hotel Anjali*, immediately outside the station on the right. This small, spotless Gujarati restaurant opens at 7am for breakfast and does a good range of pure-veg south Indian snacks and main meals, including copious *thalis*, at other times of the day. Beer and other alcoholic drinks are available in the low-lit, curtained booths of the (men-only) permit-rooms nearby.

Nasik

Lying at the head of the main pass through the dark eroded hills of the Western Ghats, **NASIK** makes an interesting stopover on the lengthy journey to or from Bombay, 187km southwest. From the grim barrage of industrial estates, hoardings, *dhabas* and general conurbation creeping along its ring road, you'd be forgiven for thinking the city holds no interest for anyone other than truckers or travelling salesmen. However, this is one of the four sites of the world's largest religious gatherings, the triennial **Kumbh Mela** (see p.313). Every twelve years – next due in 2003 – millions of pilgrims descend on the temple and *ghat*-lined banks of the **River Godavari**, to take a purifying dip at one of the most auspicious moments in the Hindu calendar.

Even outside festival times, the riverside sees plenty of action. According to the *Ramayana*, Nasik was where Rama – Vishnu in human form – his brother Lakshmana, and wife Sita lived during their exile from Ayodhya, and the arch-demon Ravana carried off Sita from here in an aerial chariot to his kingdom, Lanka, in the far south. The scene of such episodes forms the core of the busy pilgrimage circuit – a vibrant enclave packed with religious specialists, beggars, *sadhus* and street vendors touting *puja* paraphernalia. However, Nasik has a surprising dearth of historical buildings – even the famous temples beside the Godavari only date from the **Maratha era** of the eighteenth century. Its only real monuments are the rock-cut caves at nearby **Pandav Lena**. Excavated at the high-water mark of Buddhist achievement on the Deccan, these two-thousand-year-old cells hark back to the days when, as capital of the powerful **Satavahana** dynasty, Nasik dominated the all-important trade routes linking the Ganges Plains with the ports to the west.

Today, the city continues to prosper, though the high profile of recently relocated Bombay businesses has done little to dampen its religious fervour. If anything, the extra cash has come as a boon for the local *pujaris*. Newly inaugurated temples, dripping with fairy lights and equipped with powerful hi-fi systems, stand cheek by jowl with glitzy *sari* emporia, shopping arcades and ice-cream parlours.

GOING DOOLALLY

In the days of the Raj, soldiers who cracked up under the stresses and strains of life in British India were invariably packed off to a military psychiatric hospital in the small Maharashtran cantonment town of **Deolali**, near Nasik, to recover. Its name became synonymous with nervous breakdown; hence the English idiom "to go doolally", meaning to become insane or eccentric.

Arrival and information

Buses from Bombay pull in at the **Mahamarga Bus Stand**, a ten-minute rickshaw ride from the city centre. Aurangabad buses terminate at the chaotic central **City Bus Stand** (aka the "CBS"), an easy walk from several cheap hotels and restaurants. Arrival by train is more problematic, as the **railway station**, Nasik Rd, lies 8km southeast. Buses meet incoming trains, but they tend to be sporadic or packed. Luckily, there's no shortage of shared taxis and auto-rickshaws. If you plan to leave Nasik by train, particularly on a weekend when the city booking counter, off MG Rd (Mon–Fri 10am–5pm) is closed, reserve your outward ticket on arrival.

Predictably for a city that sees so few foreign visitors, the MTDC **tourist office**, near the golf course on Old Agra Rd (☎0752/70059), is welcoming, but not worth the trouble to find. Their daily "Darshan Tour" of the city and its environs will only appeal to those with a passion for ferro-concrete temple architecture. To **change money**, the *State Bank of India* (Mon–Fri 10am–2pm, Sat 10am–noon) is just up from the City Bus Stand on Swami Vivekanand Rd. The **GPO** is around the corner on Trimbak Rd.

The City

After the hectic main streets of Nasik's commercial centre, the more colourful **riverbank** area comes as something of a surprise. Turn down any of the narrow back lanes behind MG Rd and you'll emerge eventually from the maze of dilapidated wooden houses and balconies of the old quarter at the open ground lining the Godavari (pronounced God*a*vri). The small stretch on the opposite bank, between the Holkar and Santar Gardi Mahara bridges, is the focal point. In 1991, during the Kumbh Mela, an estimated three-and-a-half million devotees converged here to bathe; usually, however, the site plays host to more secular pursuits, as *dhobiwallahs* gather on the *ghats* each morning to thump away at soapy bundles, and shoppers haggle over the produce piled neatly under rows of raffia sunshades at the **riverside market**.

South of the market, below Ram Situ footbridge, lies the eighteenth-century **Naro Sankar Mandir**. Built by the Marathas, this distinctive dark-stoned Shiva temple has some lively sculpture on the roof of its *mandapa*, and a bustling *devi* shrine. Originally, it was known as the Rameshvara Mandir; the name was changed when a local warrior, Sardar Naroshakar, installed an enormous church bell which he'd plundered from the Portuguese after their defeat at the battle of Vasai (Bassein) in 1739. The now clapperless bell is housed in a pavilion set in the wall of the western enclosure.

Ram Kund

A hundred metres further along the river bank, past the market and a lurid sky-blue and orange eight-metre-tall Hanuman, the **Ram Kund** is the reason most people come to Nasik. Surrounded by concrete viewing towers (built to alleviate the crush at the big *melas*), it looks more like an overcrowded municipal swimming pool than one of India's most ancient sacred places. Yet for the thousands of devout Hindus who avail themselves of its purifying properties each day, these murky waters are the holiest of holies.

Among the Ram Kund's more arcane attributes is its capacity to dissolve bones – a trick that has earned it the epithet of **"Astivilaya Tirth"** or "Bone Immersion Tank". Some of the more celebrated remains said to have ended up here are those of King Dasharatha of Ayodhya (Rama's father), Jawaharlal Nehru, his daughter Indira Gandhi, her son Rajiv, and a host of saints, musicians and movie stars.

Kala Ram Mandir

Follow the street opposite Ram Kund up the hill, past assorted *ashrams* and *dharamshalas*, to arrive at the city's second most important sacred site, the area around the **Kala Ram Mandir**, or "Black Rama Temple". Among well-known episodes from the *Ramayana* to occur here was the event that lead to Sita's abduction, when Lakshmana sliced off the nose of Ravana's sister after she had tried to seduce Rama in the form of a voluptuous princess. Sita's cave, or **Gumpha**, a tiny grotto known in the *Ramayana* as *Parnakuti* ("Smallest Hut"), is just off the square. On removal of shoes and payment of a small donation, you can squeeze into it to see where Sita spent all those lonesome hours while the boys were off doing battle with the forces of darkness and destruction.

The **Kala Ram temple** itself, at the bottom of the square, houses unusual jet-black deities of Rama, Sita and Lakshmana; these are very popular with visiting pilgrims, as access is free from all caste restrictions. The best time to visit is around sunset, after evening *puja*, when a crowd, mostly of women, gathers in the courtyard to listen to a traditional storyteller recounting tales from the *Ramayana* and other epics.

Pandav Lena

Halfway up one of the precipitous conical hills that overlook the Bombay–Agra road, 8km southwest of Nasik, is a small group of 24 rock-cut caves, some dating from the first century BC. The **Pandav Lena** site is famous for its well-preserved inscriptions in the ancient Pali language, and fine ancient stone sculpture.

Access to Pandav Lena is via a steep and uneven path. The caves themselves are numbered from right to left in chronological order; start with number **18**, left of the entrance. This small *chaitya* hall has a striking facade, with two leaf-shaped arches encasing auspicious Buddhist symbols. The two monastery caves, *viharas*, to either side, reached by flights of stone steps complete with their original railings, contain carved Buddhas – later additions made during the sixth century. Two further noteworthy caves are over on the other side of the group. **Caves 3 and 10**, both *viharas* dating from the second century AD, have superb stone carvings, as well as the famed **Pali inscriptions** above their doorways. These set out in elaborate detail the caves' benefactors (among them dynastic rulers, wealthy landowners, a writer and even a local Hindu worthy), as well as the complex financial provisions made for the monks who lived here.

The most straightforward way of **getting to Pandav Lena** without your own vehicle is by auto-rickshaw, though infrequent and crowded municipal buses also pass them. You can catch the buses in town from the second stop on the right, heading north away from the City Bus Stand on the main road (called the "Old Highway").

Accommodation

Most of Nasik's hotels are pitched at middle-class Bombay business travellers. The few noteworthy exceptions are the lodge-style budget places around the City Bus Stand *chowk*. These, however, tend to fill up early, soon after their noon checkout times.

Basera, Sivaji Rd (☎0253/575616). Very close to the City Bus Stand. Airy, comfortable rooms, some a/c, all with hot water and windows. Extra mattresses only Rs40. ④–⑤.

Padma, Sharampur Rd (☎0253/576837). Directly opposite the City Bus Stand. Safe, clean and convenient. All rooms have attached bathrooms and hot water. ④.

Panchavati, 430 Vakil Wadi (☎0253/575771). Nasik's largest hotel, right in the middle of town. Two restaurants, "Mexican-style" bar, foreign exchange and room service; some a/c rooms. ⑥.

Panchavati Yatri, 430 Vakil Wadi (☎0253/571273). The *Panchavati*'s good-value cheaper wing, with money exchange, 24hr coffee shop, bar and an excellent veg restaurant. Some a/c rooms. ⑤.

Raj Mahal Lodge, Sharampur Rd (☎0253/572880). Across the road from the bus stand. Very basic, though neat and clean. All rooms have hot water and TVs. The best-value budget hotel. ②.

Eating

By and large, Nasik's best-value **meals** are to be had in its traditional "keep it coming" *thali* restaurants. While they may not always be the cheapest option, for less than the price of a beer you can enjoy carefully prepared and freshly cooked food, often including such regional specialities as *bajra* (wholewheat *rotis*) and *bakri* (hot oatmeal biscuits), together with a plethora of tasty vegetable, pulse and lentil dishes. The city's religious associations tend to mean that meat and alcohol are rarer than elsewhere, but plenty of the larger hotels have bars and restaurants with permits.

Dhaba, *Panchavati*, Vakil Wadi. Classy Rajasthani-style *thalis*. Popular with families.

Khyber, *Panchavati*, Vakil Wadi. Standard north Indian, with some veg alternatives and a bar.

Pangat, *Panchavati Yatri*, Vakil Wadi. Mild but mouthwatering veg *thalis* at reasonable prices in pseudo-traditional Maharashtran ambience (mud walls and murals). Very good value.

Samrat, Swami Vivekanand Rd. Well-known *thali* joint, five minutes from the bus stand, doing a brisk trade in moderatel-priced, quality Gujarati food.

Suruchi, under *Basera*, Sivaji Rd. Clean, no-nonsense, south Indian fast-food cafe. Very cheap, spicy snacks and drinks. Crowds of office workers at lunch. Family/ladies room upstairs.

Trimbak

Crouched in the shadow of the Western Ghats, 10km west of Nasik, **TRIMBAK** – literally "Three-Eyed" in Marathi, another name for Lord Shiva – is yet another place of great significance for Hindus. This was the exact spot where one of the four infamous drops of immortality-giving *amrit*-nectar fell to earth from the *kumbh* vessel during the struggle between Vishnu's vehicle Garuda and the Demons – the mythological origin of the Kumbh Mela (see p.313). Trimbak is also near the source of one of India's longest and most sacred rivers, the **Godavari**; the spring can be reached via an ancient pilgrim-trail that cuts through a cleft in an awesome, guano-splashed cliff face. En route you pass colourful wayside shrines and a ruined **fort** (see below).

Hourly buses from Nasik pull in to Trimbak's little bus stand at the top end of the village. Make your way from there down the main street, past ramshackle shops selling vermilion powder and strings of wooden beads, to the entrance of the **Trimbakeshwar Mandir**. Numbering among India's most sacred centres for Shiva worship (it houses one of the twelve "self-born" *jyotirlinga* – see *Contexts*), the temple is unfortunately closed to non-Hindus. Its impressive eighteenth-century *shikhara* (tower), however, can also be glimpsed from the back streets nearby. Close to the temple, the **Kushawarth Tirth** is a small, stone-lined tank said to contain Ganges water. Its name is thought to derive from the *kush* grass used in *puja* ceremonies that once grew in profusion around it. Although the present *ghats* and temple date from 1750, myths relating to the Kushawarth Tirth occur in the *Puranas*, so it may have been used for 2500 years.

The Brahmagiri hike

The round-trip to **Brahmagiri**, the source of the Godavari, takes between two and three hours. It's a strenuous walk, particularly in the heat, so make sure you take adequate water. From the trailhead at the bottom of the village, the way is paved and stepped as far as the first level outcrop, where there are some welcome *chai* stalls and a small hamlet. Beyond that, either turn left after the last group of huts and follow the dirt trail through the woods to the foot of the **rock-cut steps** (20min), or continue straight on, to the three **shrines** clinging to the base of the cliff above. The first is dedicated to the goddess Ganga, the second – a cave containing 108 *linga* – to Shankar (Shiva), and the third to the sage Gautama Rishi, whose hermitage this once was.

The steps climb 550m above Trimbak to the remains of **Anjeri Fort** – a site that was, over the years, roughed up by the armies of both Shah Jahan and Aurangzeb before it fell into the hands of Shaha-ji Raj (father of the legendary rebel-leader Sivaji). The **source** itself is another twenty minutes further on, across **Brahmagiri Hill**, in the otherwise unremarkable Gaumukhu ("Mouth of the Cow") temple. From its rather unimpressive origins this paltry trickle somehow gathers sufficient momentum to flow for nearly 1000km east across the entire Deccan plateau to the Bay of Bengal.

Practicalities

Getting to Trimbak from Nasik is easy. Hourly **buses** leave from the depot opposite the main City Bus Stand (45min). To return you can catch a bus (until around 8pm), or one of the shared **taxis** that wait outside Trimbak bus stand; there's no difference in price as long as the car is full.

Although Trimbak makes an easy day trip from Nasik, it's a peaceful and atmospheric place to spend a night, with plenty of basic **accommodation**. The MTDC *Tourist Bungalow* (①/④) at the bottom of the village is the nicest option, with scruffy doubles with attached bathrooms, cheap dorm beds, and even tents pitched in the garden. In the unlikely event of it being full, head for *Alpobatchet Bhavan Rest House* (②) opposite the start of the Brahmagiri path, where the rooms are also pretty grubby.

For **food**, the only alternative to the grimy sweet-stalls around the bus stand is the small restaurant in the *Tourist Bungalow*. Given a little advance warning, they'll prepare basic veg and rice dishes for non-guests.

Nagpur

Geographically at the virtual centre of India, **NAGPUR** is the focus of government attempts to develop the remote northeastern corner of Maharashtra. It has no real sights to speak of, though its proximity to the Gandhian ashrams at **Sevagram** and **Paunar**, near **Wardha**, 77km southwest, and the hill-top temple complex at **Ramtek**, a 90-minute bus ride northeast, make it a good stop on a long cross-country journey.

Arrival and information

Nagpur's busy central mainline **railway station**, Nagpur Junction, is a short auto-rickshaw ride from the main hotel and market districts. MSRTC **buses** pull in at the state bus stand, 1500m southeast. Buses to and from Madhya Pradesh use the smaller *MPSRTC* bus stand, five minutes' walk south down the main road outside the station.

At the helpful MPTDC **tourist office**, on the fourth floor of the Lokmat Building, Wardha Rd (Mon–Fri 10am–5pm), you can book accommodation for Pachmarhi or Kanha National Park. The **GPO** is on Palm Rd, in the Civil Lines, 4km west of the centre. Large **banks** near the railway station include the *State Bank of India* (Mon–Fri 10.30am–2.30pm, Sat 10.30am–12.30pm) on Kingsway.

The Town

This site on the banks of the River Nag was first occupied in the tenth century by aboriginal Gonds, but Nagpur itself was founded by a family of militaristic local Hindu rulers, the Bhonslas, midway through the eighteenth century. In 1853, the Bhonslas fell foul of Lord Dalhousie's "Principle of Lapse" (a grossly iniquitous law which gave the British the right to take over any native state whose ruler died without a male heir), and Nagpur became the capital of the Central Provinces. Today, it's a thriving industrial and commercial centre, with a surprisingly affluent, easy-going and uncongested feel for a city of more than a million people. Ice-cream parlours line up alongside ritzy hotels and shopping malls, while "new-women" students in *salwar kamises* whizz around town on scooters – a far cry from the *khadi dhotis*, bullock carts, and mud and thatched villages of the surrounding countryside.

Nagpur's most prominent landmark, the **Sitabuldi Fort**, stands in the heart of the city, on a saddle between two low hills above the railway station. Strengthened by the British in the wake of the 1857 Mutiny, its ramparts and monuments have been annexed by the Indian territorial army and are closed to the public. Further reminders of colonial days survive in the **Civil Lines** area, immediately north and west of Sitabuldi Hill. The grand civic buildings and bungalows from which the British Commissioner administered the vast Central Provinces region (except in mid-summer, when he and his legions of *burrasahibs* decamped to Pachmarhi – see p.370) today house the university and government offices.

If you have an evening to fill in Nagpur, take an auto-rickshaw out to the **Ambazari Bagh**, the large artificial lake and gardens 5km southwest of the railway station, for a row and a *chai* at its waterside cafes.

Accommodation

Most of Nagpur's **places to stay** are either across the big railway bridge east of the railway station, along **Central Avenue**, or southwest of the fort around **Sitabuldi**, in the central bazaar. The railway station also has cheap **retiring rooms**.

Blue Diamond, 113 Central Ave, Dosar Chowk (☎0712/727461). Cheap and near the station. Good facilities; cable TV, a/c, attached bathrooms and "peep-out" balconies. 24hr checkout. ②–④.

Centre Point, 24 Central Bazaar Rd (☎0712/520910). The most established of Nagpur's top hotels, with all the trimmings, including a pool. ⑦.

Hardeo, Dr Munje Margi Marg, Sitabuldi (☎0712/529115). Fairly new, 3-star hotel in city centre. A/c rooms, quality restaurant, bar and 24hr coffee shop. Recommended. ⑥.

Jagson's Regency, Wardha Rd (☎0712/228111). Brand new luxury hotel next to the airport, boasting a rooftop restaurant, shopping arcade, gym and pool. 24hr checkout. ⑦–⑧.

Pal Palace, 25 Central Ave (☎0712/724724). Clean, comfortable and spacious rooms, some a/c, in slick and central 3-star. Foreign exchange facility. ④–⑦.

Skylark, 119 Central Ave (☎0712/724654). Close to railway station and best value in its class, with cable TV in all rooms and a good restaurant. Some credit cards accepted. ③–⑥.

Eating

While Nagpur's swish hotels, such as the *Hardeo* and *Jagson's Regency*, boast the majority of its top gourmet restaurants, a number of smaller, less pretentious **places to eat** around Central Ave and Sitabuldi offer excellent food at a fraction of the cost.

Continental, Central Ave. Low light, lurid decor, and a good selection of inexpensive spicy Indian food and chilled beer. Some veg options too.

Naivedhyam, off Rani Jhansi Chowk, Sitabuldi. Respectable first-floor family restaurant serving delicious veg food to a background of Hindi-Hawaiian music and fish tanks.

Parnakuti, Ambazari Rd, on the outskirts near the lake. Attractive restaurant noted for rustic decor and authentic, mouthwatering mid-priced Maharashtran cooking. Hard to find but well worth it.

Ramtek

The picturesque cluster of whitewashed hill-top temples and shrines at **RAMTEK**, 40km northeast of Nagpur on the main Jabalpur road (NH7), is one of those mysterious, alluring apparitions, espied from afar on long journeys through central India, which few travellers take the trouble to visit. According to the *Ramayana*, this craggy, scrub-strewn outcrop, marooned in a sea of yellowing wheat fields, was yet another spot where Rama, Sita and Lakshmana paused on their way back from Lanka. It is also allegedly the place where the greatest-ever Sanskrit poet and playwright, **Kalidasa**, penned the fifth-century *Meghdoota*, "the Cloud Messenger". Although few traces of these ancient times have survived (most of Ramtek's temples date from the eighteenth century), the site's old paved pilgrim trails, sacred lake, tumbledown shrines and fine views across the endless plains more than live up to its distant promise.

Ramtek's bus stand is 2km from the central market square, **Gandhi Chowk**, which is most easily reached in a shared auto-rickshaw. Once in the bazaar, head past the sweet stalls to the lane leading out of its top right-hand corner. At the T-junction, bear right and follow the track through the houses until it reaches open grazing land, on the far side of which a flight of stone steps climbs steeply up the rocky, south-facing side of Ramtek hill. The pathway eventually brings you out at a raised courtyard in front of the main entrance to the **temple complex**. Built in 1740 by Raghoji I, the Bhonsla ruler of Nagpur, it stands on the site of an earlier structure erected between the fourth and fifth centuries, of which only three small sandstone shrines remain.

The best **views** are to be had from the small onion-domed belvederes and whitewashed pavilions that surmount the flat roofs and battlements encircling the inner courtyard. To the southwest, you look out over the cluttered jumble of Ramtek town to the shining blue irrigation tanks on its outskirts, while the panorama in the other direction takes in a vast expanse of dead-flat and dusty wheat fields peppered with the occasional coppice of trees. At *puja* times, this is a good vantage point from which to watch the temple *pujaris* doing their rounds of the various shrines, ringing bells and waving smoky oil lamps before the deities.

Ambala Lake

Another of Ramtek's sacred sites is **Ambala Lake**, a holy bathing tank 1500m on foot from the hilltop. To pick up the flagstone pathway that leads down to it, head along the concourse opposite the temple's main entrance-porch to the edge of the plateau. From here, either turn left towards the small **Trivikarma Krishna temple**, clinging to the north slope of the hill, or continue down the main pilgrims' trail to the **lake**, which lies at the bottom of the gully, enfolded by a spur of parched brown hills. Its main attractions, at least for the shaven-headed pilgrims who make their way here in rented mini-vans for a *dhoti*-soaking dip in its holy waters, are the temples and *ghats* clinging to its muddy banks. More energetic visitors may wish to combine a look with a *parikama*, or circular **tour** of the tank, taking in the semi-derelict cenotaphs and weed-choked shrines that litter its more tranquil north and western shores.

Practicalities

Direct **buses** leave **Nagpur** (*MSRTC* stand) every hour for the hour-long trip to Ramtek. Long-distance *MPSRTC* buses also pass by en route to and from **Jabalpur**, although these will dump you on the main road, 3km from town. If you don't feel like hiking up to the temple, **auto-rickshaws** will whisk you up from the town bus stand, or from Gandhi Chowk (via Ambala Lake) for around Rs50.

The only **place to stay** in Ramtek, apart from the pilgrims' *dharamshalas* and ashrams around Ambala Lake, is the new MTDC *Holiday Resort* (☎07265/55213; ①–③) on the hill beside the main temple complex, offering cheap dorm beds and a couple of simple but clean self-contained rooms. **Food** can also be prepared here, though if you want anything more adventurous than *dal*, *subzi*-of-the-day and rice, you should phone ahead or, better still, book in advance through any MTDC tourist office. Finally, the PWD *Rest House* (②) in Ambala, opposite the big, red-and-white-painted fortified archway on the south bank of the lake, is also worth a try if you're stuck.

Sevagram

SEVAGRAM, Gandhi's model "Village of Service", is set deep in the serene Maharashtran countryside, 9km from the railroad town of **Wardha**. The Mahatma moved here from his former ashram at Sabarmati in Gujarat during the monsoon of 1936, on the invitation of his friend Seth Jamnalal Bajaj. Right at the centre of the sub-continent, within easy reach of the *Central Railway*, it made an ideal headquarters for the *Satyagraha* movement, combining seclusion with easy access to other parts of the country Gandhi needed in order to carry out his political activities.

These days, the small settlement is a cross between a museum and living centre for the promulgation of Gandhian philosophies. Interested visitors are welcome to spend a couple of days here, helping in the fields, attending discussions and prayer meetings, and learning the dying art of hand-spinning. The older ashramites, or **sadhaks**, are veritable fonts of wisdom when it comes to the words of their guru, Gandhiji.

The ashram

Named after the Mahatma's wife, the **Kasturba Gandhi Hospital**, on the corner of the main road, was set up by the ashram to provide cut-price health care for local farming communities. From the hospital, a short walk down the lane to the right takes you past fields and farmland to the **visitors' centre** (daily 10am–6pm), with its photos and documents relating to Gandhi's life.

The real focal point of the ashram is the main **compound** on the left side of the lane. These modest rustic huts, with their two-tiered terracotta roofs, smooth mud walls and shady courtyards, are little altered since Gandhi and his disciples lived out the last years of the Independence struggle. Men and women in simple handmade cotton clothes sit crosslegged on the wide verandahs, spinning thread and singing devotional songs, to the mild amusement of visitors from the city who look on with a peculiar mixture of respect for the Mahatma's memory and disdain for those who keep it alive. The first hut along the path has been converted into a small shop selling *khadi* goods and books about Gandhi. Nearby, the **Adi Niwas** was the Mahatma's first home in Sevagram. The interior of the **Bapu Kuti** opposite, Gandhi's main residence, has been kept exactly as it was in the 1930s, complete with its original bed, massage table and the few "luxuries" which Gandhi permitted himself: a foot-cleaner, the famous pair of tiny round specs, a spittoon and his beloved three brass monkeys.

Elsewhere, the compound holds the Mahatma's **secretariat**, or correspondence room, which enshrines a phone installed by the British as a pre-Independence "hotline"; the **Ba-Kuti**, where Kasturba lived; the **Parchure Kuti**, home of the Sanskrit scholar Shri Parchure Shashtri (the Mahatma's devotion to this close friend, a leprosy sufferer, did much to de-stigmatize the disease in India); and the **Akiri Niwas**, or "Final Home", where Gandhi stayed before leaving Sevagram for the last time.

Practicalities

Half-hourly, jam-packed local **buses** run from **Wardha** – on the *Central Railway* and accessible from Bombay (759km) – to the crossroads outside the Kasturba Gandhi Hospital. There are frequent "express" buses from Nagpur's *MSRTC* bus stand, 77km northeast, to Wardha (2hr 30min).

Accommodation is limited to the ashram's own *Yatri Niwas* (①) – a basic but spotless hostel. Simple and filling veg meals are shared with the *sadhaks* on a verandah in the main compound and, like the rooms, cost a nominal sum. Donations, which finance the ashram's adult education programme, are gratefully accepted. Occasionally, the rooms fill up with people attending conferences, so seek out the person in charge of bookings as soon as you arrive. The only other place to stay nearby, MTDC's **hotel** in Wardha (☎3172; ①–③), has 28 dorm beds and a dozen more costly self-contained rooms. Checkout time is 8am; reserve in advance through any MTDC office.

Paunar

Crowning a low hillock overlooking a rocky river bank at **PAUNAR**, 10km north of Wardha on the Nagpur road, Vinoba Bhave's ashram has an altogether more dynamic feel to it than its more famous cousin at Sevagram. Bhave, a close friend and disciple of Gandhi, best remembered for his successful Bhoondan or "**land gift**" campaign to persuade wealthy landowners to hand over farmland to the poor, founded the ashram in 1938 to develop the concept of **swarajya**, or "self-sufficiency". Consequently, organic gardening, milk-production, spinning and weaving have an even higher profile here than the regular meditation, prayer and yoga sessions. Another difference between this institution and the one up the road is that the *sadhaks* here are almost all female.

The ashram's living quarters, painted the pale blue worn by most of its inhabitants, are ranged like cloisters around an attractive square courtyard. At the far end, Vinoba's old **room** is now a shrine, its bare interior enlivened by fresh marigolds and incense. Stone steps lead down from the upper level to a small terrace looking out over the **ghats** where two small memorials mark the spots where a handful of Gandhi's, and later Vinoba's, ashes were scattered onto the river: Gandhi's is the circular plinth at the end of the long, narrow jetty, Bhave's the brass urn on the small *stupa*-shaped dome to the right. Every year on February 12, the *ghats*, which are immersed by floods for four months during the monsoon, are inundated with half-a-million people who come here to mark the anniversary of Gandhi's death.

Practicalities

Paunar can be reached by **bus** from either Nagpur (67km) or Wardha by jumping off at the old stone bridge across the river below it. Alternatively, you can **walk** the 3km from Sevagram. The path, a cart-track that runs over the hill opposite the hospital crossroads, comes out in the roadside village 1km west of the Paunar ashram.

As with Sevagram, it is possible to **stay** at Paunar in one of the visitors' rooms or dorms. Again, these are frequently booked up during conferences or seminars, so check when you arrive. Women are given preference if space is short. **Meals**, made from organic, home-grown produce, are available on request.

SOUTHERN MAHARASHTRA

Most tourists heading south from Bombay skip southern Maharashtra, but if you have a little time you can break up the journey profitably and ease the burden of covering vast distances in one go. **Pune** retains its Maratha character, in the old quarter at least, and also boasts a unique museum; some may also be attracted by its much-derided Osho Commune. Hill stations such as **Matheran** provide coolness, wooded walks and fine views, while **Murud-Janjira** has little-visited beaches, a picturesque old-fashioned town and a sea fort. From **Lonavala**, you can get to see the earliest Buddhist rock-cut art in the western Deccan, sometimes even in peaceful solitude, and **Kolhapur**, the last major city before Karnataka to the south, or Goa to the southwest, is a characterful place with a strange blend of Maratha and so-called Indo-Saracenic architecture.

Matheran

The little hill station of **MATHERAN**, 170km east of Bombay, is set on a narrow north–south ridge, 800m up in the Sahyadri Range. From viewpoints with such names as Porcupine, Monkey and Echo, at the edge of virtually perpendicular cliffs that plunge into steep ravines, you can see way across the hazy plains – on a good day, so they say, as far as Bombay. The town itself, shrouded in thick mist for much of the year, has for the moment one unique attribute; cars, buses, motorbikes and auto-rickshaws are prohibited. That, added to the journey up, on a **miniature train** that chugs its way through spectacular scenery to the crest of the hill, gives the town an agreeably quaint, time-warped feel. Brightly painted hand-pulled rickshaws trundle along dirt lanes, while monkeys crash across the rusting corrugated-iron roof tops of bungalows.

Matheran (literally "mother forest") has been a popular retreat from the heat of Bombay since the nineteenth century, when it was an exclusive bolt hole for British families. These days, however, few foreign visitors venture up here, and those that do only hang around a couple of days, killing time before a flight, or to sample one of India's most charming colonial-style hotels, **Lord's**. The season lasts from mid-September to mid-June (at other times it's raining or misty), and is at its most hectic between November and January (Diwali), April and May, or virtually any weekend. There's really nothing to do but relax, wander the woods on foot or horseback, and enjoy the fresh air and views.

As the crow flies, Matheran is only 6.5km from Neral on the plain below, but the train climbs up on 20km of track with no less than 281 curves, said to be among the sharpest on any railway in the world. From 1907, the demanding haul was handled by four complex steam engines. Sadly, they puffed their last in 1980 and were replaced by cast-off diesels from Darjeeling, Shimla and Ooty. The two-hour ride is a treat, especially if you can get a window seat; but be prepared for a squash and hard benches.

In 1974, the All India Rail Strike cut Matheran off. To combat the situation, the track was made passable for jeeps and finally in 1984 was tarred, up to Dasturi Naka, 2km from the town. A strong lobby wants to extend it to the centre, which if successful will undoubtedly destroy Matheran's character.

Arrival and information

To reach Matheran by train, you must first get to **Neral Junction**; the daily *Deccan Express* #1007 (depart VT 6.40am) and the *Koyana Express* #7307 (depart VT 8.45am) from **Bombay** pause here, but most express trains don't stop until **Karjat** (2–3hr), twenty minutes or so beyond Neral. However, backtracking by passenger train from there can involve a long wait, so catch one of the few direct services if you can. From **Pune** (2–3hr), the 6.50am *Sahyadri Express* #7304 stops at Neral. If you miss this, travel to Karjat and pick up a slower passenger service from there.

Narrow-gauge trains up from **Neral** to **Matheran** depart at 8.40am, 11am and 5pm (also 4.15pm, April & May; 2hr). These are timed to link up with incoming expresses, so don't worry about missing a connection if the train you're on is delayed – the toy train service should wait. Matheran **station** is in the centre of town on MG Rd, which runs roughly north–south.

All **motor vehicles**, including shared taxis and minibuses from Neral (Rs35 per head if the car is full, or Rs175 if you rent it for yourself), have to park at the taxi stand next to the MTDC *Holiday Camp* at Dasturi Naka, 2km north of the town centre. From here you can walk with a porter (Rs40), rent an aged horse and its keeper (Rs60), or take a labour-intensive cycle rickshaw (Rs120). If you're happy to carry your own bags, follow the rail tracks, which cut straight to the middle of Matheran, rather than the more convoluted dirt road. There is a little halt on the miniature railway near the Dasturi Nakataxi stand, but unless you've already booked a seat, you won't be allowed on. However you arrive, you must pay a **toll** to enter the town (Rs10). A small **tourist information** booth (daily 10am–6pm) opposite the railway station has maps and can help you get your bearings. You can **change money** at the bigger hotels only.

> The telephone **area code** for Matheran is ☎02148.

Accommodation and eating

Matheran has plenty of **hotels**, though few could be termed cheap. Most are close to the railway station on MG Rd and the road behind it, Kasturba Bhavan. Reduced rates may apply for midweek or long stays, and during the rainy off-season (when many places are closed altogether). Virtually all the hotels provide **full** or **half board** at reasonable rates, but if you want to eat out, or are on a tight budget, try one of the numerous *thali* joints around MG Rd.

Alexander, near Alexander Point, 2km south of the railway station (☎30251 or Bombay 492 6610). Pleasant wooded location with rooms, slightly dilapidated cottages (some a/c) and good Gujarati restaurant. ⑦.

Gujarat Bhavan, Maulana Azad Rd (☎30278 or Bombay 203 0876). Clean and comfortable pure-veg resort hotel, with a range of rooms and cottages (some a/c with TV). Full board only. ⑤.

Hope Hall, MG Rd, opp. *Lord's Central* (☎30253). The best of the budget bunch: large, clean en-suite rooms around a secluded yard at the quiet end of town. Great deals off-season, too. ②.

Lord's Central, MG Rd (☎30228 or Bombay 201 8008). Matheran's most characterful hotel, near the railway station. Genteel (non-c/c) Raj-era cottages with terraces, and superb views across the valley from a relaxing garden. Excellent veg and non-veg menu including Parsi and British food. ⑦.

MTDC Tourist Camp, Dasturi Naka (☎30277 or Bombay 202 6713). Cottages in a large old colonial house, and a cheap dorm, plus a simple open-air restaurant. Forty minutes walk from the centre of town, but a good option. ①–⑤.

Prasanna, MG Rd, opposite the railway station (☎3258). Fairly basic full-board budget lodge; close to the station. A touch pricey. ③–⑤.

Royal, Kasturba Rd (☎30247). Spruce and modern, with a large terrace and Matheran's only espresso machine. ④–⑦.

Rugby, Vithalrao Kotwal Marg (☎30291; fax 302532 or Bombay 202 1090). Two minutes' walk up the road opposite the railway station. Old hotel, now expanded, offering a range of rooms around a garden, with a good bakery attached. ⑧.

Murud-Janjira

The unspoilt, unhurried little coastal town of **MURUD**, 165km south of Bombay, was once part of the little-known state belonging to the Siddis of Janjira, descendants of Abyssinian sailor-adventurers. Modern development seems to have passed this quiet backwater by, and many of its characterful houses are largely built of wood, some brightly painted, fronted by pillared verandahs with built-in benches and gates. Nearing Murud, the undulating coast road from Bombay passes through attractive countryside with the sea slipping in and out of view, its shore lined with casuarinas, coconut and betel palms; inland is agricultural land used to cultivate rice and string-beans, and beyond lie forested hills, prowled, according to locals, by leopards.

The imposing **fort** of Janjira (2km south), which until the 1970s was inhabited by descendants of the Siddis, was built on an island in the Rajpuri creek in 1515. Even the Marathas, fort fanatics as they were, failed to penetrate its 15-metre-high walls. Shivaji attacked in 1659, followed by his son Shambhuji, who tried digging a tunnel and even attempted to fill the channel out to the island. The trip out by local *hodka* boat (around Rs50), from the jetty at the southern end of town, makes an excellent excursion.

You can get fine views of the bay and surrounding countryside by climbing more than 200 steps up to the small hilltop **Dattatreya Temple**, dedicated to the triple-headed deity comprising Vishnu, Shiva and Brahma. It's a simple structure, with an Islamic-style tower; inside, decorative tiles cover the floor of the wood-and-brick *mandapa* with flower and peacock designs, while European-looking angelic figures and landscapes adorn the ceiling. Left of the cell holding a Dattatreya image is a portrait of the nineteenth-century Maharashtran saint, **Gajanan Maharaj**, smoking *ganja*.

The dilapidated eighteenth-century **Nawab's Palace** – which bears more than a passing resemblance to the Addams Family residence – overlooks Janjira, 2km north of Murud. It was opened in 1991 as a museum, but soon closed due to vandalism, and today its present owner, the erstwhile Nawab Shah Siddi Mahmood Khan, lives elsewhere. If you find the caretaker, however, and ask him nicely enough, he may permit you to look around the hauntingly abandoned interior. Inside, the durbar hall, illuminated by a stained-glass ceiling of nine domes, is littered with furniture of marble and finely carved wood, interspersed with stuffed tigers, leopards and lions. Living quarters contain nineteenth-century Western furniture, badly in need of repair, and dusty, evocative photos, including a signed one of England's Queen Mary, and another showing the household in the days when the palace employed 350 servants.

Practicalities

Most **buses** from Bombay Central take five hours; there are two faster *Asiad* services (5.45am & 11am; 3hr 30min), which must be booked in advance. All stop on Murud's main street, Durbar Rd, parallel to the coast, where you'll find the post office, covered market, a few basic restaurants and the town's two **hotels**. Officially you're supposed to give fifteen days' notice to stay at the *Government Rest House* (①), but there's no harm in asking if one of their comfortable rooms is available (two have balconies overlooking the sea). Food is only cooked for groups, but you may be allowed to use the kitchen. The concrete bungalows of the MTDC *Murud Beach Resort* (☎278; ②) are gratifyingly quiet, inches from the virtually deserted beach, with a simple canteen-style restaurant.

Many visitors prefer to base themselves at **Kashid**, 15km north, where there's a fine beach, water sports and an upmarket hotel, the *Kashid Beach Resort* (☎8262; ⑥), which offers 17 very comfortable split-level rooms with balconies looking down on the sea, a good restaurant and swimming pool. The three-kilometre stretch of unspoilt beach, where you can rent a variety of water sports equipment, is a stone's throw away. Rooms can be booked in advance in Bombay at *Beacon Marketing & Reservation Services*, Munshaw House, 22 Rustom Sidhwa Marg (☎262 5406). All buses from Bombay to Murud go via Kashid, but you may have to ask the driver to stop.

Lonavala

Just thirty years ago, the town of **LONAVALA**, 100km southeast of Bombay and 62km northwest of Pune, was a quiet retreat in the Sahyadri Hills. Since then, the place has mush-roomed to cope with hordes of holidaymakers and second home owners from the state capital, and is now only of interest as a base for the magnificent **Buddhist caves** of **Karle**, **Bhaja** and **Bedsa**, some of which date from the Satavahana period (second century BC).

Arrival

Frequent buses arrive at Lonavala's central **bus stand**, just off the Bombay–Pune Rd (NH4), but the train is infinitely preferable. Lonavala is on the main railway line between Bombay (3hr) and Pune (1hr 30min), and all express trains stop here. The **railway station** is on the south side of town, close to the centre. With a car, or by tak-ing an early train, it's just about possible to take in the caves as day trip from Bombay, but it's better to allow yourself a full day to get around.

Accommodation

Lonavala has a wide range of **accommodation**, from very cheap to 5-star; many of its hotels lower their rates out of season (Oct–March) or for longer stays. Budget and mid-range places are concentrated in the centre, by the bus and railway stations.

Adarsh, behind the bus stand on Shivaji Rd (☎02114/72353). Spotless a/c and non-a/c rooms, some overlooking central courtyard. Dependable mid-range option, but can be noisy. ③–⑥.

Chandralok, Shivaji Rd (☎02114/72294). Clean, comfortable rooms with shower-toilets, 24hr hot water, friendly management and excellent Gujarati restaurant. The best deal in this category. ④–⑥.

DT Shahani Health Home, DJ Shahani Rd (☎02114/72784). Lonavala's best budget option: large, immaculate rooms in a modern block tucked down a suburban backstreet. Full board. ③.

Duke's Retreat, Pune–Bombay Rd, Khandala (☎02114/73826). Superb position overlooking ravine, with prizewinning garden and pool (open to non-residents, Rs100). Comfortable rooms and cottages; weekend packages include breakfast and dinner. Open-air cafe, a/c restaurant and bar. ⑧.

MTDC Karle Resort, Bombay–Pune Rd (☎02114/82230). On the Lonavala–Karle bus route, 2km from Malavli railway station. Range of comfortable accommodation (some a/c) in cottages, suites and economy doubles. Good restaurant and bar. ④–⑦.

Oriental, 158 Bombay–Pune Rd, opposite Power Station (☎02114/72552). Ten minutes' walk from the bus stand, with a certain eccentric charm. Don't be misled by the sign proclaiming "Luxury rooms available"; it's an old house with verandahs, ancient furniture and basic rooms (the cheapest is a single bed by the stairs). Food can be arranged. ②–⑤.

Pitale Lodge, Bombay–Pune Rd (☎021147/2657). Seven rooms in an old bungalow, with bar and restaurant. Characterful, friendly, basic and inexpensive. ②.

Eating

Most of the hotels in Lonavala lay on full board, and there is no shortage of small restaurants and snack bars on the main street catering for the brisk through trade. You'll also come across dozens of shops selling the local sweet speciality, **chikki** – a more-ish, but dentally challenging, amalgam of dried fruit and nuts set in rock-solid honey toffee. *Super Chikki* on the main street allow you to sample the many varieties before you buy, and they giftwrap the sticky blocks in attractively old-fashioned boxes. Their main competitors, *National Chikki*, further down, are also recommended, and are the best place to stock up on delicious deep-fried nibbles, the other local speciality.

Chandralok, *Hotel Chandralok*, Shivaji Rd. Wonderful and cheap "unlimited" Gujarati *thalis* served in a large canteen, with several kinds of bread and buttermilk dishes.

Guru Krippa, Bombay–Pune Rd. Sparkling new pure-veg joint on the main street: piping hot south Indian snacks, cheese toasties, and inexpensive Chinese and Punjabi main meals. Also a good selection of ice-creams, *kulfi* and full-on *faloodas*. Recommended.

Shabri, *Hotel Rama Krishna*, Bombay–Pune Rd. The well-heeled Bombay-*wallahs*' favourite. Spacious and clean, serving the full range of north and south Indian dishes and chilled beer.

The Buddhist caves of Karle, Bhaja and Bedsa

The three cave sites of **Karle**, **Bhaja** and **Bedsa** comprise some of the finest rock-cut architecture in the northwest of the Deccan region. Though not in the same league as Ajanta and Ellora, they harbour some beautifully preserved ancient sculpture, dating from the era when this region lay on several long-distance trade routes, and are definitely worth a look if you are passing.

The three sites lie some way from each other, all to the east of Lonavala. Covering Karle and Bhaja under your own steam by bus and or train is manageable in a day, if you're prepared for a good walk, but if you want to get out to Bedsa too, and can afford it, the easiest option is to rent an **auto-rickshaw** (around Rs300) or **car** (Rs400 for 4hr) for the day (usually found at Lonavala railway station). Finally, if you want to see the caves at their best, **avoid the weekends**, when they are inundated with bus loads of rowdy day trippers.

For a full run-down on the history and features of rock-cut cave architecture in the Deccan, see p.678.

Karle

KARLE (also spelled Karla and Karli) is 3km north of the town of Karle Caves Junction, 11km from Lonavala on NH4. Five buses (daily 6am, 9am, 12.30pm, 3pm & 6.30pm) call at the MTDC *Karle Resort*; the last bus back to Lonavala leaves Karle at 7pm.

The rock-cut Buddhist *chaitya* hall at Karle, reached by steps that climb 110 metres, is the largest and best preserved in India, dating from the first century AD. As you approach across a large courtyard, itself hewn from the rock, the enormous fourteen-metre-high facade of the hall towers above, topped by a horseshoe-shaped window and with three entrances below, one for the priest and the others for devotees. To the left of the entrance stands a *simhastambha*, a tall monolithic column capped with four lions.

In the porch of the cave, dividing the three doorways, are panels of figures in six couples, presumed to have been the wealthy patrons of the hall. Two rows of octagonal columns with pot-shaped bases divide the interior into three, forming a wide central aisle and, on the outside, a hall that allowed devotees to circumambulate the monolithic *stupa* at the back. Above each pillar's fluted capital kneels a finely carved elephant mounted by two riders, one with arms draped over the other's shoulders. Amazingly, perishable remnants survive from the time when the hall was in use; teak ribs on the vaulted ceiling show that the stone was carved to resemble a wooden structural model. Surmounting the *stupa* are the remains of a carved wooden umbrella.

Full views of the main entrance are obscured by the much later accretion, to the right, of a Hindu shrine to **Ekviri**, a goddess-oracle revered by Koli fishing communities. Fences are often erected outside it, to regulate the flow of worshippers who seek *darshan* or to consult the goddess. When questions are addressed to Ekviri, areca nuts are placed on silver discs above the head of the image. Depending on which nut falls to the ground, right or left, the answer is "yes" or "no". Tuesdays and Fridays are the busiest times, but Karle is at its most frenetic during the annual Chaitra (March/April) festival, when the blood of sacrificed chickens is smeared on the steps up the hill.

Bhaja

Although the eighteen caves at **BHAJA** may not be as elaborate as those at Karle, they're more atmospheric, giving visitors a much clearer sense of their original tranquillity (particularly during the rainy season, when monks traditionally ceased their wanderings). They lie 3km south of Karle Caves Junction, reached by following a path up from the village square near the railway station at Malavli, just 1km away. Regular passenger trains call here, and are the cheapest and most convenient way to get back to Lonavala if you're not travelling by rented rickshaw or car.

The caves at Bhaja are among the oldest in India, dating from the late second to early first centuries BC, during the earliest, Hinayana, phase of Buddhism. Most consist of simple halls (*viharas*) with adjoining cells that contain plain shelf-like beds; many are fronted by rough verandahs. Bhaja's apsidal *chaitya* hall (**#12**), which contains a *stupa*, but no figures, has 27 plain bevelled pillars, which lean inwards, mimicking the style of wooden buildings. Sockets in the stone of the exterior *chaitya* arch reveal that it once contained a wooden gate or facade. Further south, the last cave (**#19**), a *vihara*, is decorated with superb carvings. Mysteriously, scholars identify the figures as the Hindu gods, **Surya** and **Indra**, who figure prominently in the *Rig Veda* (*c.* 1000 BC). In Vedic mythology Surya, the sun god, is conventionally described flying through the sky as he banishes darkness; here, left of the entrance, he rides a chariot pulled by four horses and accompanied by two women who carry a parasol and fly-whisk. The chariot crushes the bodies of naked demonesses, who appear to float in the air. The panel to the right is thought to show Indra, who in the *Vedas* represents power, particularly lightning, thunder and rain, and thanks to the quantity of sacred *soma* drink that he quaffs, frequently becomes huge. In this striking sculpture, two figures are shown riding an elephant (Indra's vehicle), all gigantic in relation to the landscape. The elephant grasps what appears to be a little tree in his trunk.

Bedsa

It's quite possible you will not meet anyone else visiting the caves at **BEDSA**, which is one of its great attractions. Once you reach the village, which is 12km beyond Bhaja along NH4 or a three-kilometre bus ride from Kamshet, the nearest railway station, you'll have to ask the way to the unsigned path. If you're lucky, village kids hanging around will scramble up the steep hillside with you, for a fee.

Bedsa's **chaitya hall**, excavated later than that at Karle, is far less sophisticated. The entrance is extremely narrow, leading from a porch which appears to be supported, though of course it is not, by four octagonal pillars over 7m high, with pot-shaped bases and bell capitals; bulls, horses and elephants rest on inverted, stepped slabs on top. Inside, 26 plain octagonal columns lead to an unadorned monolithic *stupa*.

Pune (Poona)

At an altitude of 598m, **PUNE**, Maharashtra's second city, lies close to the Western Ghat mountains (known here as the Sahyadri Hills), on the edge of the Deccan plains as they stretch away to the east. The British chose Pune in 1820 as an alternative headquarters for the Bombay Presidency, to escape the summer heat and the monsoon deluge of the capital. Their military cantonment in the northwest of town is still used by the Indian army, and a number of British buildings, such as the Council Hall and Deccan College, survive.

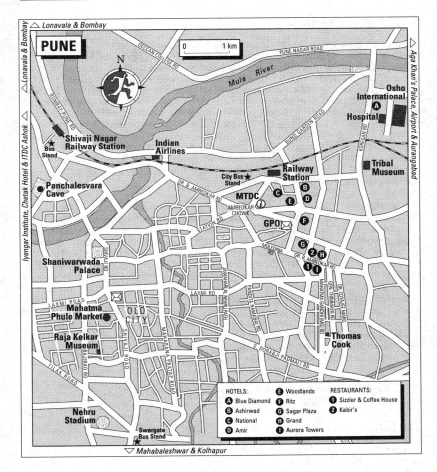

PUNE

Settlement on the site is thought to date back two thousand years, when Kasba, a fortified town, lay between the River Mula to the northwest and the Nagzari Nala creek to the east. Occupying a strategic position on trade routes between the Deccan and the Arabian Sea, the town prospered during the early Hindu period. Under the sixteenth-century Marathas, Pune became the capital and military headquarters of a sovereign state, until its rulers were deposed by the Brahmin Peshwa family, who dominated Pune during the eighteenth century before the arrival of the British.

Since colonial days, Pune has continued to develop as a major industrial city and a centre for higher education. But to most outsiders, it is notorious as the home of the **Osho Commune International**, founded in 1970 by the charismatic Bhagwan Rajneesh, or Osho (1931–90), whose syncretic and, to many Indians, scandalous philosophy of life lured thousands of neo-hippies from Europe and America.

Arrival and information

Pune's Lohagaon **airport**, 10km northeast of the centre, is served by flights from Bombay, Delhi, Madras, and Bangalore. Taxis, auto-rickshaws and a regular ("Ex-Servicemen") bus service are on hand for the fifteen-minute trip to the city centre. Pune is an important point on the southern express train routes from Bombay (3hr 30min–4hr 30min); the main **railway station** is in the centre of town, south of the river. Auto-rickshaws and tourist taxis wait outside the station – locals often use the shared long-distance taxis to get to Bombay. Of the three main **bus stands**, the one next to the railway station serves the city itself (though all the signs and timetables are in Marathi) and some destinations south, including Goa and Bombay. **Swargate**, about 3km south, close to Nehru Stadium, has services to Karnataka, while **Shivaji Nagar**, 3km west of the centre, has services from towns in the north, including Aurangabad and Lonavala. To establish exactly which station you need for which destination, ask at the enquiries hatch at the city bus stand.

Information

You can book MTDC long-distance buses and guided city tours, and seek advice about other bus services, at the **MTDC Tourist Information Counter** (Mon–Fri 10am–6pm & Sat 10am–1pm), opposite the railway station's First Class booking office. Like most government-run efforts, their three-hour **tour** of Pune (daily 8am & 3pm; Rs50) is far too rushed to be worthwhile. The other MTDC office, in the Central Office Building, Sassoon Hospital Rd, is of little use. The best places to **change money** are *Thomas Cook,* halfway along Gen Thimmaya Rd, which runs between MG Road and East St (Mon–Sat 10am–5.00pm; ☎648188; fax 643027), or the nearby *American Express* office around the corner from *Thomas Cook* on MG Rd (Mon–Sat 10am–6.30pm; ☎631848/9); both change travellers' cheques, and can also make airline and hotel reservations.

The best **bookshop** in Pune is *The Modern Bookshop* on Gen Thimmaya Rd (Mon–Sat 9.30am–1pm & 4–8.30pm; ☎633597), which stocks an impressive array of fiction, and has a good selection of maps and guidebooks of India.

> The telephone **area code** for Pune is ☎0212.

The City

Pune centre is bordered on the north by the **River Mula** and to the west by the **River Mutha** – the two join in the northwest to form the Mutha-Mula, at Sangam Bridge (previously Wellesley Bridge). The principal shopping area, and the greatest concentration of restaurants and hotels, is in the streets south of the railway station, particularly Connaught Road and further south, **MG Road**. The old Peshwa part of town, by far the most interesting to explore, is towards the west, between the fortified **Shaniwarwada Palace** and fascinating **Raja Dinkar Kelkar Museum**; old wooden *wadas*, palatial city homes, survive on these narrow, busy streets, and the Victorian, circular **Phule Market** is always a hive of activity.

Raja Dinkar Kelkar Museum

Dinkar Gangadhar Kelkar (1896–1990), aside from being a celebrated Marathi poet, published under the name Adnyatwass, spent much of his life travelling and collecting arts and crafts from all over the country. In 1975, he donated his collection to the Maharashtran government, as a permanent museum, dedicated to the memory of his son, Raja, who had recently died at the age of twelve.

Housed a huge old-town mansion, the **Raja Dinkar Kelkar Museum** (daily 8.30am–12.30pm & 3–6pm; Rs50 for foreigners, Rs10 for Indians), on 1378 Shukrawar Peth (reached on buses #72 or #74 from the railway station to City Market), is a wonderful pot-pourri, not only of objets d'art but also of humble everyday objects. Kitchen utensils include a camelskin oil container and a wooden noodle-maker which, like other Indian cooking tools such as coconut scrapers, requires its operator to sit astride it. Paraphernalia associated with *paan*, the Indian passion, includes containers in every conceivable design, made from silk, wood, brass and silver; some mimic animals or fish, or are egg-shaped and in delicate filigree, others are solid heavy-duty boxes built to withstand constant use. Lime applicators, nut-holders, and mortars are equally elaborate; nut-crackers often take the form of a loving couple. Also on show are musical instruments, superb Marathi textiles and costumes, toys, domestic shrines and furniture, beauty accessories and a model of Shaniwarwada Palace. Lavishly illustrated booklets (Rs75) are sold at the entrance.

Shaniwarwada Palace

In the centre of the oldest part of town, only the imposing high walls of the **Shaniwarwada Palace** (daily 8am–noon & 2–6pm; entrance free) survive, following fires in 1791, 1812 and 1828. The palace, founded by the Peshwa ruler Bajrao I in 1730 and the chief residence of the Peshwas until the British arrived in 1817, has little to excite interest today. Entrance is through the Delhi gate on the north, one of five set into the perimeter wall, whose huge teak doors come complete with nasty elephant-proof spikes. Just inside, faded murals show Ganapati, Vishnu and scenes from the *Ramayana*. Court musicians (drums and double-reed wind *shehnais*) played from the balconies above, a practice that is revived three times a year: January 26 (Republic Day), May 1 (Maharashtra Workers' Day) and August 15 (Independence Day). The interior of the palace is now grassed over, the seven-storey building entirely absent. Only one of the available guides, usually available in the afternoons, speaks English. Bus #3 runs the 2km southwest from the railway station to the palace.

Panchalesvara Cave

The **Panchalesvara** (aka Pataleshvar) **Cave**, on the west of town, just across the Mula River, lies in a rather surprising urban setting at the northern end of busy Jungli Maharaj Rd (bus #4 or #98). Hewn from rock in the same manner as the more elaborate examples elsewhere in Maharashtra, the cave dates from the Rashtrakuta period (eighth–ninth centuries). Steps lead from the pavement to a path which ends in a square courtyard and a circular roofed Nandi enclosure. Beyond it, the roughly excavated cave, with broad, square, plain pillars, is unfinished, bearing numerous chisel marks, and yet appears to have been in continuous use for a thousand years. Locals can be seen at prayer at most times of the day, or dozing in the shade during *tiffin* breaks. The central shrine contains a *shivalingam*, while to either side subsidiary cells hold figures of Lakshmi, Ganesh, Rama, his wife Sita and brother Lakshmana.

Aga Khan Palace and Gandhi Memorial

In 1942, Mahatma Gandhi, his wife Kasturba and other key figures of the freedom movement were interned at the **Aga Khan Palace** (daily 9am–12.30pm & 1.30–6pm), which is set in quiet leafy gardens, across the River Mula, 5km northeast of the centre (bus #1, #158 & #156). The Aga Khan donated the palace to the state in 1969, and it is now a small Gandhi museum, typical of many all over India, with captioned photos and simple rooms unchanged since they were occupied by the freedom fighters. A memorial behind the house commemorates Kasturba, who died during their imprisonment. A small *Khadi* shop sells handloom cloth and products made by village co-operatives.

BHAGWAN RAJNEESH

It is twenty-five years or so since the first disciple was initiated into the **Bhagwan Rajneesh** cult, latterly renamed Osho Commune International, a gradually evolving philosophy involving Buddhism, Sufism, Sexual Liberationism, Zen, Yoga, Hypnosis, Tibetan Pulsing, Disco, Video and unabashed materialism. The first Rajneesh ashram (the name for a hermitage more usually associated with Hindus who have foregone worldly attachments for a life of meditation) was founded in Pune in 1974. It rapidly attracted droves of Westerners and some Indians, who adopted new Sanskrit names and a uniform of orange or maroon cottons and bead necklace, attached to which was always a photo of the enlightened guru who, in classic style, sported long white hair and a beard. This costume immediately identified the wearer as a Rajneesh *sannyasin* (another term borrowed from Hinduism, particularly Shaivism, usually used to describe a renunciating mendicant who has attained a state of holiness).

Few early adherents denied that part of the attraction lay in Rajneesh's fun approach to fulfilment. His unapologetic dismissal of Christianity (dubbed "Crosstianity") as a miserably oppressive obsession with guilt, sin and the death of Jesus struck a chord with many, as did the espousal of liberation through sex. Within a few years, satellite ashrams were popping up throughout western Europe, most notably in Germany. Rajneesh assured his devotees that material comfort was not to be shunned and making money, at least for the ashram, was no bad thing. By 1980, outsiders and devotees alike could liberate themselves in plush Rajneesh discos with wacky names like *Zorba the Buddha* in big cities all over Europe.

Meanwhile, conscious of such potential threats to peace as pollution, nuclear war or accidents, AIDS and negative vibes, the Rajneesh organization was galvanized into action, pouring money and human energy into the Utopian project, **Rajneeshpuram**, on 64,000 acres of agricultural land in Oregon, USA – much to the dismay of their American neighbours. It was at this point that the tabloids and TV documentary teams really got interested in Rajneesh, who by now was said to be a multi-millionaire. His predilection for Rolls-Royces was big news; the fact that he couldn't drive and yet owned ninety of them was perfect grist to the mill. Baffled viewers watched as hordes of tambourine-banging, ecstatic devotees lined Main Street Rajneeshpuram, in order to catch a glimpse of the guru, bestowing beatific smiles as he swished by in decidedly non-ascetic transport.

Infiltrators leaked stories of the strange goings-on at Rajneeshpuram and before long his inner circle of high-powered female devotees/executives became the subject of police interest. Charges relating to tax evasion, drugs, fraud, arson and even a conspiracy to poison the population of the neighbouring town in order to sway the vote in local elections were all reported. Apparently unaware of such heinous crimes, Rajneesh nevertheless pleaded guilty to breaches of US immigration laws and was deported in 1985. Following protracted, futile attempts to gain permission to settle in up to 21 different countries, Rajneesh came home to India and finally back to Pune where, against all odds his commune has flourished, even since his death in 1990, at the age of 59.

Osho Commune International

Pune is the headquarters of the Bhagwan Rajneesh's avowedly non-religious **Osho Commune International**, 17 Koregaon Park (☎660963), 2km east of the railway station. Calling itself a "tasteful and classy resort" and claiming to attract more visitors than the Taj Mahal, the commune seems impervious to the sniping of cynical critics, quoting with pride the *Wall Street Journal*'s description of it as a "spiritual Disneyland for disaffected First World yuppies".

With a daily income of perhaps £40,000 during the peak season (Dec–March) and the dedicated toil of 700 volunteers, the commune has transformed its twenty acres into an exclusive playground with cafes, swimming pool, sauna, clinics and a shop selling Osho's 650 books, videos and cassettes. They have erected space-age, air-conditioned buildings, landscaped gardens, bored tube wells for water and planted trees to improve the air and organic vegetables to escape insecticide poisoning. Courses at the Multiversity (US$1000 per month) are offered in countless New Age and traditional techniques. Osho's own brand of jargon is extensive; tennis, for example, has been reborn as Zennis, which helps you to "get out of your body's way, bring the outer and the inner together" in "a unique synthesis of tennis and meditation". However, this eco-friendly environment-bubble also proudly follows a strict door policy: visitors who wish to spend longer in the commune than the daily hour-long guided tours (10.30am & 12.30pm; Rs10) must produce an HIV-negative certificate no less than thirty days old. If you don't have one and are still determined to look around, you'll have to take a blood test at the ashram clinic.

Tribal Museum

The Tribal Research and Training Institute, which runs the **Tribal Museum** (daily 10am–5pm), 2km east of the railway station at 28 Queen's Garden, is dedicated to the protection and documentation of the surviving culture of Maharashtra's numerous tribal groups, such as the Wagdheo, Bahiram, Danteshwari and Marai, who number more than five million. The museum's faded photos, costumes and artefacts serve as an excellent introduction to this little-known world, but the highlights are the wonderful collections of dance masks and Worli wedding paintings.

Parvati Hill

A ninety-step climb to the top of **Parvati Hill**, 4km south of the railway station (bus #4 and #99) and near Swargate bus stand, brings you to the small **Peshwa Museum** (daily 8am–noon & 3–6pm) dedicated to Pune's rulers, and an eighteenth-century **Ganapati temple**, built by the Peshwa ruler Balaji Baji Rao. There are good views over the city from here, the spot where Rao is said to have watched the British defeat his army at the battle of Kirkee.

Accommodation

Pune is well stocked with **hotels**, though in keeping with most big cities, prices are quite high for what you get. Most of the budget accommodation can be found in the area south of the railway station around Connaught Rd. The station itself also has better-than-average **retiring rooms**.

PUNE'S GANESH FESTIVAL

Pune's major festival, **Ganapati Chaturthi**, is dedicated to the elephant-headed Hindu deity Ganesh, the remover of obstacles and the most auspicious god for embarking on new endeavours. Once a domestic ritual, Ganesh Chaturthi was turned into a public rallying point for Hindus by the freedom fighter Bal Gangadhar Tilak in the late nineteenth century; both Pune and Bombay celebrate it in extravagant style each year.

On the first day, images of Ganesh, some huge and dripping with fairy lights, are erected in homes and public places, decorated with flowers and food, and worshipped. Over the next ten days or so events include arts and crafts displays, a village fair, sports competitions and a food festival, as well as Indian classical music and dance performances, usually featuring the most illustrious names in the country. On the last day the Ganesh images are taken in procession and immersed in water, the streets teeming with singing and dancing devotees.

Needless to say, Pune is very crowded during the festival, which takes place during late-August/early-September. MTDC organize the event, and can help arrange accommodation and all-in packages.

Inexpensive

Chetak, 1100/2 Model Colony (☎352681; fax 354078). Good value accommodation in the suburbs. Deservedly popular with students from nearby Iyengar Institute. Book in advance. ③.

Grand, opposite *Aurora Towers*, 8 Moldina Rd (☎668728). Single wood-partition "cabins" with common bathrooms, or simple but spacious en-suite doubles in an old colonial town house. Relaxing verandah, beer garden, cats and friendly management. ①–③.

National, 14 Sassoon Rd (☎68054). Rooms (some with wooden verandahs and attached bathrooms) in a dilapidated old building, or in basic modern "cottages", two minutes' walk from the railway station. Popular with budget travellers and Ba'hai devotees. ④.

MOVING ON FROM PUNE

Pune's **airport** (☎667538) sees regular *Indian Airlines* flights to **Delhi** (Mon, Wed, Fri & Sat depart 6.50pm; 2hr), and **Madras** (Mon, Wed & Fri depart 2pm; 3hr) via **Bangalore** (45min); tickets can be bought and confirmed at their office on Connaught Rd (☎664189; reservations ☎659939). There are also direct flights to **Bombay** (35–45min) on *East-West*, Amir Hotel Bldg, Sadhu Vaswani Rd (daily 6pm; ☎665862), and *Damania Airways*, 17 MG Rd; (Mon–Sat 8.30am; ☎640814), while *NEPC* fly the Pune–Bangalore–Madras route three times weekly (Tues, Thurs & Sat depart 4.30pm). Recommended agents for these private carriers include *Star Line Travels*, Darshan Apartments, Sadhu Vaswani Chowk, next to the *Woodland Hotel* (☎622130; fax 622095), and *Apple Travels*, in the *Amir* hotel on Connaught Rd (☎628189; fax 625421). The cheapest and most convenient way of **getting to the airport** is to take the *Indian Airlines* airport bus (Rs20), which leaves from in front of the *Amir* hotel.

As Pune is one of the last stops for around twenty long-distance trains on their way to Bombay, **rail services** are excellent. Many depart early in the morning, however, and some terminate at Dadar, so always check. The most convenient, if crowded, options for **Bombay VT** are *Deccan Queen Express* #2124 (7.15am), *Pragati Express* #1026 (7.30am) and *Sahyadhri Express* #7304 (6.50am). Direct express trains from Pune also run to Hyderabad (*Bombay–Hyderabad Express* #7031; daily depart 4.55pm), New Delhi (*Jhelum Express* #1077; daily depart 5.35pm), Madras (*Bombay–Madras Express* #6511; daily depart 6.20pm), Bangalore (*Gandhidam–Trivandrum* & *Rajkot–Cochin Express* #6335/7; depart Mon & Tues 10.50pm) and Thiruvananthapuram (#6335/7; details as per Bangalore). Though the daily service to Margao and Vasco da Gama, the 3pm *Goa Express* #2702/2704, has been disrupted for the past couple of years by conversion work, it should be running normally by mid-1997; ask at the station for details. Reservations should be made at the new Reservation Centre next to the station (Mon–Sat 8am–2pm & 2.15–8pm, Sun 8am–2pm).

Before travelling on the uncomfortable and crowded **state buses**, seek advice from the MTDC Tourist Information Counter at the railway station; the bus stands display no information in English. Services from the busy city stand next to the station head south, to Mahabaleshwar (3hr), Kolhapur (12hr), and Goa (depart 6.30pm & 8pm; 15hr; book in advance from the *Kadamba* hatch). *Asiad* buses to Bombay (4hr) also leave here every 15 minutes between 5.30am and 11.30pm, but must be booked a day or so in advance. If you're heading up to Lonavala or Aurangabad, you'll have to travel across the river to the Shivaji Nagar terminus.

Private luxury buses to Goa, Bangalore, Mangalore and Hyderabad can be booked through *Bright Star Tours & Travels*, 13 Connaught Rd, opposite Parmar Chambers (☎669647); to Ahmedabad, Vadodara, Indore, Surat and Goa from *Karan Travels*, 7 Konark Park, Dhole Patil Rd (☎663850); and for Aurangabad, Goa, Ahmedabad and Vadodara from *Prasanna Tours & Travels*, 396 Shaniwar Peth (☎431892). Finally, there's also a very handy direct bus service to **Bombay's** Sahar and Santa Cruz airports, leaving Pune at 4pm and arriving five hours later; tickets are sold through the *Thomas Cook* office on Gen Thimmaya Rd.

Ritz, Connaught Rd (☎62995). Friendly and characterful, though decrepit, and perennially popular with budget travellers. Excellent value evening *thalis*, too. ②.

Moderate to expensive

Amir, 15 Connaught Rd (☎621840). Good range of comfortable rooms and facilities including coffee shop, bar, health club, shops and three restaurants. Checkout 5pm. ⑥–⑦.

Ashirwad, 16 Connaught Rd (☎628885; fax 626121). Newish hotel near the station. Some a/c rooms with balconies and TV. Good veg restaurant, room service, exchange and travel desk. ⑤–⑦.

Aurora Towers, 9 Moledina Rd (☎631818; fax 631826). Upper-range place 2km from railway station, with 24hr room service and coffee shop, two good restaurants, shops and pool. ⑧.

Blue Diamond, 11 Koregaon Rd (☎663775). 5-star hotel, 2km northeast of railway station near the Osho ashram. Posh Indian and Chinese restaurants serving buffet lunches, 24hr coffee shop, swimming pool, and shops. ⑧.

ITDC Executive Ashok, 5 University Rd, Shivajinagar (☎357381). Business hotel with comfortable modern a/c rooms and pricey multi-cuisine restaurant, plus bar and coffee shop. ⑦–⑧.

Sagar Plaza, 1 Bund Garden Rd (☎622622; fax 622633). Medium-sized, flashy 4-star, 1km from railway station, with ritzy restaurant, 24hr coffee shop, bar, bookshop and swimming pool. ⑧.

Woodland, Sadhu Vaswani Circle (☎626161; fax 623131). Good-value rooms, mostly a/c, ten minutes' walk from the railway station. Veg restaurant, travel desk and foreign exchange. ⑥.

Eating

In addition to the hotel restaurants, there are numerous reasonably priced cafes and fast-food outlets around **Connaught** and **Moledina** roads, always busy in the evening. A sociable place to round off the day is the street running east from the GPO, where, from dusk until around 10pm, a string of pavement cafes serve up spicy snacks, cold drinks and fresh juices to young punters.

Coffee House, 2 Moledina Rd. A relaxing, upmarket south Indian snack joint that serves the best coffee, *dosas* and breakfasts in Pune. It's also a/c, and a good spot to beat the heat.

Kabir's, 6 Moledina Rd. Good selection of north Indian dishes for around Rs40–80, including lots of tasty *tandoori* options. Try to get a table outside. Serves beer.

Ritz, Connaught Rd. Traditional Maharashtran all-you-can-eat *thalis* served up in an old-style dining hall. Tasty, filling and cheap: the budget travellers' choice.

Sizzler, 7 Moledina Rd. Great fast food: chicken and mutton "sizzlers" and burgers, and plenty of Punjabi-style veg dishes. Popular with Pune's bright young things, and a little pricey.

Venky's, 2 Wellesley Rd. Another busy fast-food joint. This one does a good range of pizzas, as well as the usual burgers, fried chicken and milkshakes.

Sinhagad

The windswept, ruined fort of **SINHAGAD** (originally known as Kandana), 26km southwest of Pune at the top of an almost perpendicular cliff in the Bhuleshwar mountains, can easily be visited in a day trip from Pune by catching a bus (40min) from Swargate stand. This involves a stiff two-hour climb from the foot of the hill, but with your own transport you can drive a great deal closer. In 1647 Shivaji, the greatest chief of the Marathas, on hearing that his general Tanaji had died capturing the fort, lamented "I have won the fort, but lost the lion". To commemorate Tanaji's achievement, it was renamed Sinhagad, "lion fort". Tanaji had attacked on a moonless night, on the western side; the sheer size of the cliff was seen as such a deterrent that the fort was left undefended by the forces of Udai Bhan who were celebrating a wedding. However, according to legend, Tanaji had in his service the old campaigner Yashwanti, an iguana, which with a rope ladder tied to its tail was thrown onto the cliff face and, after three attempts, stuck securely. So strong was its grip that, before the night was out, three hundred of Tanaji's men had climbed into the fort.

Surprisingly, a few families live in simple houses within its twelve-metre-high walls. Some can serve you a cup of tea; other villagers from the plain are poor enough to climb up every day in the hope of selling pots of yoghurt to day trippers.

Mahabaleshwar

MAHABALESHWAR, 250km southeast of Bombay and the most visited hill resort in Maharashtra, is most easily reached from Pune (120km northeast). The highest point in the Western Ghats (1372m), it is subject to extraordinarily extreme **weather** conditions. The start of June brings heavy mists and a dramatic drop in temperature, followed by a deluge of Biblical proportions: up to seven metres of rain can fall in the hundred days up to the end of September. As a result, tourists only come here between November and May; during April and May, at the height of summer, the place is packed. The main attraction is the network of marked **hiking trails** through the woods, leading to waterfalls and assorted vantage points, with views over the peaks and down to the plains. You can also take boats out on the central **Yenna Lake**, and shop for strawberries, raspberries, locally made jams and honey in the market.

For most foreign visitors, Mahabaleshwar's appeal is primarily its convenient situation, mid-way between Bombay and Goa. However, to complete the short but rewarding walk to **Wilson's Point**, the highest spot on the ridge, you'll have to get here well before dusk. To pick up the (motorable) trail, head south through the bazaar (away from the bus stand) and straight over the crossroads at the end past the *Hotel Mayfair*; ten minutes further up the hill, you reach a red-and-white sign pointing left off the road. Wilson's Point lies another stiff ten minutes' up, crowned by a gigantic radio transmitter that is visible for miles. The sunset panoramas from here can be breathtaking.

Arrival and information

The central **State** ("ST") **bus stand**, at the north end of the bazaar, serves **Pune** (3 daily; 3hr), the most convenient railhead, as well as **Kolhapur** (3 daily; 7hr) and **Satara** (3 daily; 1hr), which is 17km from Satara Rd railway station, connected to Bombay via Pune and Miraj (for Goa). To get here from **Bombay**, much the best option is to catch the *MSRTC* luxury bus which departs from the Bombay Central Bus Stand each morning at 7am (7hr); buses back leave at 9am, 9.50am, 2.45pm and 9pm, and should be booked in advance from the reservations hatch at the far end of the concourse.

The telephone **area code** for Mahabaleshwar is ☎02168.

Accommodation and eating

As in many hill stations, despite an abundance of hotels, prices in Mahabaleshwar are well above average. The cheapest **places to stay** are on the road parallel with the main bazaar, **Murray Peth**, where, with a little haggling, you can pick up rooms for under Rs200. Accommodation is scarce during the monsoon (mid-June to mid-Sept), when most hotels close, and during peak season (Nov–May), when tariffs double.

The only commendable **places to eat**, other than the larger hotels, are the *Shreyas* (veg) and its (non-veg) neighbour, *Sher-e-Punjab*, both at the bus stand end of the main bazaar. Service in these is brisk, and the food fresh.

Ashoka, 289 Murray Peth (☎60622). One of a string of dependable, clean and essentially characterless places on this street. Restaurant, STD phone, but no views. ④.

Dreamland (☎60228). Large, established resort hotel below the bus stand. Rooms range from simple chalets ("cottages") to new a/c poolside apartments with stupendous views. The congenial garden cafe serves decent espresso. ⑤–⑥.

Fountain, opposite Koyna Valley (☎60227; bookable in Bombay through *Fountain's Fast Food Restaurant* 367 7182). Close to the centre. Posh doubles (some a/c with TV) and pure veg restaurant serving Indian, Western and Chinese dishes. ⑥–⑦.

Frederick's, near the bus stand (☎60240). Old hotel, with plain but comfortable double rooms. ⑤.

Grand, Woodlawn Rd (☎60322). Tucked away in a leafy and secluded spot, five minutes by taxi from the centre. Simpler than its name would suggest, but decent rooms with verandahs and very pleasant garden. ④.

MTDC Holiday Camp, 2km from the centre (☎060318 or Bombay 202 6713). Wide range of good-value no-frills accommodation, including cottages to sleep four, doubles, a dorm and a hall where you can crash on the floor. Simple restaurant and beer bar. ①–⑥.

Sai Niwas, 338 Koli Alley (☎60549). Newish, neat and clean rooms at the bottom of town, some with balconies. Among the best budget deals; the nearby *Suraj Plaza* is a good fall-back. ②.

Vyankatesh Lodge, Main Rd (☎60245). Run-of-the-mill budget lodge, near the bus stand. ②.

Pratapgarh

An hour's bus ride away from Mahabaleshwar, or a 24-kilometre hike, the seventeenth-century **fort** of **PRATAPGARH** stretches the full length of a high ridge. Reached by five hundred steps, it is famously associated with the Maratha chieftain, **Shivaji**, who lured the Moghul general Afzal Khan here from Bijapur to discuss a possible truce. Neither, it would seem, intended to keep to the condition that they should come unarmed. Khan attempted to knife Shivaji, who responded by killing him with the gruesome *wagnakh*, a set of metal claws worn on the hand. Modern visitors can see Afzal Khan's tomb, a memorial to Shivaji, and views of the surrounding hills.

Kolhapur

KOLHAPUR, on the banks of the River Panchaganga 225km south of Pune, is thought to have been since ancient times an important centre of the tantric cult associated with Shakti worship. The town probably grew up around the sacred site of the present-day **Mahalakshmi temple**, still important in the life of the city, although there are said to be up to 250 other temples in the area. With a population of over 500,000, Kolhapur has become a major industrial centre, but the city has retained enough Maharashtran character to make it worthy of a stopover.

Between the tenth and thirteenth centuries the city was ruled by the Yadavas; later it came under the Moghuls, and in 1675 it was conquered by the Maratha chief Shivaji. His descendants, the Chhatrapatis, ruled until Independence, having shifted their provincial capital here from Panhala (18km northwest) in 1708. In the late nineteenth century, Kolhapur played an important role in the development of the so-called **Indo-Saracenic** style of architecture. The architect Major Charles Mant, under the auspices of the Maharajah, blended Western styles with Islamic, Jain and Hindu ones, resulting in buildings that profoundly affected the evolution of colonial architecture. Mant's work, which can be seen all over the city, includes the **High School** and **Town Hall**; the **General Library**; the **Albert Edward Hospital**; and the **New Palace**, now a museum. Despite this prolific output, Mant lived in constant (unfounded) terror that his buildings would collapse; he commited suicide at the age of 42 in 1881.

Arrival and information

Two direct express **trains** leave Bombay VT for Kolhapur via Pune (9hr) each evening: the *Mahalaxmi Express* #1011 (11hr 30min) and the *Sahyadri Express* #7303 (11hr 40min). Heading in the other direction, the *Mahalaxmi Express*, bound for Pune and Bombay, pulls in at 8.20pm. The **railway station** is 500m from the **bus stand** on Station Rd, near the centre of town. A five-minute walk from here (turn right) brings you to the **MTDC Tourist Office**, in the Kedar Complex, also on Station Rd (Mon–Sat 8.30am–6.30pm), where you can sign up for a whistle-stop guided **tour** of Kolhapur and Panhala (Mon–Sat 10am–5.30pm; Rs50).

Mahalakshmi temple

The **Mahalakshmi temple**, whose cream-painted sanctuary towers soar above the town, is thought to have been founded in the seventh century by the Chalukyan king Karnadeva; following damage inflicted by the Moghuls. However, what you see today probably dates from the early eighteenth century. It is built from bluish-black basalt on the plan of a cross, with the image of the goddess Mahalakshmi beneath the eastern and largest of five domed towers. The *mandapa* hallways leading to the main shrine hold figures of Garuda, Vishnu's bird vehicle, and Ganapati, which devotees circumambulate prior to approaching the goddess, flanked by the goddesses Mahakali and Saraswati. Four-armed Mahalakshmi, in black stone, holds a mace and shield, fruit and a cup. Her head is crowned with a cobra whose hood stands over a *shivalingam*. A second storey above contains another *shivalingam*, Nandi and a *yantra*, or sacred diagram, intimately associated with the tantric rituals of the goddess cult. On Fridays the *devi* is brought out from the sanctum, seated in a palanquin, to process around the temple precincts.

Rajwada and the wrestling ground

Presiding over the square just up the road from the Mahalakshmi temple, the **Rajwada**, or Old Palace, is still occupied by members of the Chhatrapati family. Visitors can see the entrance hall (daily 10am–6pm) by passing under a pillared porch which extends out into the town square. This was once used for wedding ceremonies for the poor, financed by the Maharajah. Inside, overlooked by the private apartments, a large courtyard contains a shrine to the family deity, Bhavana. On display are sundry stuffed creatures and a statue of the late Maharajah, Shri Shahu Chhatrapati – still so revered by some locals that they bow when they pass it.

Kolhapur is famous as a centre for traditional wrestling, or *kusti*. On leaving the palace gates, turn right and head through the low doorway in front of you, from where a path picks its way past a couple of derelict buildings to the sunken *motibaug*, or **wrestling ground**. Come here between 5.30am and 5.30pm, and you can watch the wrestlers training, caked in red dirt. The main season is between June and September, the coolest time of year, but you may find them working out at other times. Hindus and Muslims train together, and it's fine to take photographs. Any men who want to pit their strength against the cream of Kolhapur's wrestling fraternity are welcome to join in: just bring some shorts, and be prepared for a pasting.

New Palace

The Maharajah's **New Palace** (Tues–Sun 9.30am–1pm & 2.30–6pm; Rs5), 2km north of the centre, was built in 1884, following a fire at the Rajwada. Designed by Major Mant, its style fuses Jain and Hindu influences from Gujarat and Rajasthan, and local touches from the Rajwada, while remaining indomitably Victorian, with a prominent clock tower. The present Maharajah lives on the first floor, while the ground floor holds an absorbing collection of costumes, weapons, games, jewellery, embroidery and paraphernalia such as silver elephant saddles. Other memorabilia includes a letter from 1900 from the British Viceroy and Governor General of India, who writes "to his highness Sir Shahu Chattrapati Maharaj GCSF of Kolhapur government. I hereby confer upon you the title of Maharajah as an hereditary distinction."

The taxidermist in the employ of Shahaji – the present Maharajah's grandfather – must have been kept very busy indeed. In a single room you'll find ten stuffed tigers, six tiger heads, wild dog, sloth bear, staring wild buffalo, lion, *dik dik* (tiny deer), black panther, wild boar, black buck, a number of other deer varieties, and a Himalyan black bear. Photos include one of the Maharajah with his hundredth dead tiger, elephant hunts and a series detailing how to train a cheetah.

Panhala fort

Regular buses (30min) run between Kolhapur and **Panhala fort**, 18km northwest. Although it has legendary connections with the god Parashurama (Rama with the axe), the fort was probably founded by King Raja Bhoja in the late twelfth century. It covers a vast area, with massive perimeter walls over 7km in length and a steep slope beneath. Nevertheless, Panhala could not reasonably be described as impregnable. Over the years it has fallen to the Devagiri Yadavas, various Maratha chieftains, and, in 1489, the Adil Shahi dynasty of Bijapur, who erected the ramparts that still stand. Shivaji took Panhala in 1659, only just managing to escape with his life a year later when it was retaken by the Bijapur army. According to tradition, he was saved because one of his lieutenants posed as the leader and was killed, allowing Shivaji to make a quick exit, and regain it later. After this, the fort fell to the Moghul Aurangzeb (1700), became Maratha state capital under Tarabai until 1782, and went to the British in 1827.

The Teen Darwaza "three door" gate meant successive doors could only be approached at an awkward angle, trapping troops in the inner courtyard and making it impossible to charge. A well in the corner was used to send word to allies; lemons with incised messages were dropped into the water, and would float to a lake outside.

A number of modern buildings have been erected within the fort, some of them palatial homes belonging, it is said, to wealthy personages such as "sugar barons" and the famous Hindi film song artist, Lata Mangeshkar. There are also a couple of **hotels**.

Accommodation and eating

Most of Kolhapur's **hotels** are central, around **Station Rd**, while there are two good options further out in the **Panhala fort**. Outside the hotels, the best **food** is to be had at *Diners*, Vishal Chambers, Sambhaji Bridge, Venus Corner, a comfortable, modern a/c restaurant, with a varied menu including good Maharashtran *thalis*. For cheaper south Indian-style snacks, meals and breakfast, try *Subraya* next door to *Samrat Hotel* at the top of Station Square, which does tasty *dosas*, *wada pao* and filling *pani puris*.

Hilltop Hotel, Panhala fort (☎0231/435048). Comfortable, spotless and overdecorated rooms, and a pleasant and simple outdoor garden restaurant. ④–⑤.

Maharaja, 514 Station Rd (☎0231/650829). Basic lodge, directly opposite the bus stand, with veg restaurant and dozens of simple clean rooms. The best cheap deal in town. ②.

MTDC Panhala, in a corner of the Panhala fort (☎0231/435048). Old-fashioned and slightly drab, but good value and comfortable, with a little courtyard. No restaurant, but room service. ②–④.

Opal, 2104 E Poona–Bangalore Rd (☎0231/653622). Small hotel, 1.5km from railway station, with non-a/c rooms with TV. The good restaurant specializes in Kolhapuri non-veg dishes. ④.

Shalini Palace, Rankala, A Ward (☎0231/650401). Dilapidated but characterful old palace, in peaceful gardens next to lake, 5km from the centre. Designed by Mant, with central a/c. ⑦.

Tourist, 204 E New Shahupuri, Station Rd (☎0231/650421). Spacious rooms (some a/c), with veg and non-veg Indian, Chinese and Western restaurants, and a bar. ④–⑤.

Woodlands, 204E, Tarabai Park (☎0231/650941; fax 633378). In a peaceful suburb, a five-minute rickshaw ride from the railway station. Range of a/c and non-a/c rooms with TV, 24hr coffee shop, tri-cuisine restaurant, garden and bar. Good value and popular, so book in advance. ⑨.

CHAPTER ELEVEN

GOA

amous for its soft white sand beaches, mesmeric sunsets, and for the laissez-faire
attitude of its inhabitants, the state of **GOA** has been renowned as one of India's
most irresistible destinations ever since the Portuguese navigator Vasco da Gama
sailed down the Malabar coast in 1498, in search of "Christians and spices". He
found neither, but the fort he founded at Cochin resulted, twelve years later, in the erstwhile Muslim port and its hinterland becoming a **Portuguese colony**, which it
remained until 1961. These days, the region's easygoing ambience, good food, and salubrious winter climate have made it one of the most popular spots in South Asia to
unwind and enjoy the simple, undemanding pleasures of life on the beach.

The very word "Goa" may be synonymous in some circles with hedonistic hippy holidays, but in reality, each of the countless beaches of this 100-kilometre-long state
seems to attract its own different kind of tourists, from Bombayites on weekend breaks,
to fortnighting European holidaymakers, as well as long-stay shoestring travellers.
Moreover, the fabled palm-fringed coastline, lapped by the warm waters of the Arabian
Sea, is only part of the picture. Separated from the rest of India by the jungle-covered
hills of the Western Ghats, Goa's heartland and most densely populated area is the alluvial strip **inland** from the beaches – a lush patchwork of paddy fields, coconut plantations, whitewashed churches, and gently meandering rivers.

Goa's 450 years under Portuguese domination produced a unique, syncretic blend of
East and West that is at once exotic and strangely familiar: Christmas and Carnival are
celebrated as enthusiastically by the 30-percent Christian minority as Diwali and Durga
puja are by the mainly Konkani-speaking Hindus. The state's separate identity is discernible in other ways too, most visibly in its Latin-influenced architecture, but also in
a fish- and meat-rich cuisine that would be anathema to most Indians. Another marked
difference is the prevalence of **alcohol**. Beer is cheap, and six thousand or more bars
around the state are licensed to serve it, along with the more traditional tipples of *feni*,
the local hootch, and *toddy*, a derivative of palm sap.

Thanks to a fecund tropical climate, and the well-watered soil of its seaward side,
Goan (as against "Goanese", which has undesirable colonial connotations) farmers
grow a wide array of **crops**, ranging from rice, the main staple, to cashew, areca (the
source of betel nuts), and fruit for export. On the coast itself, coconut cultivation and
fishing (both in-shore, with small boats, canoes and hand-nets, and off shore, with

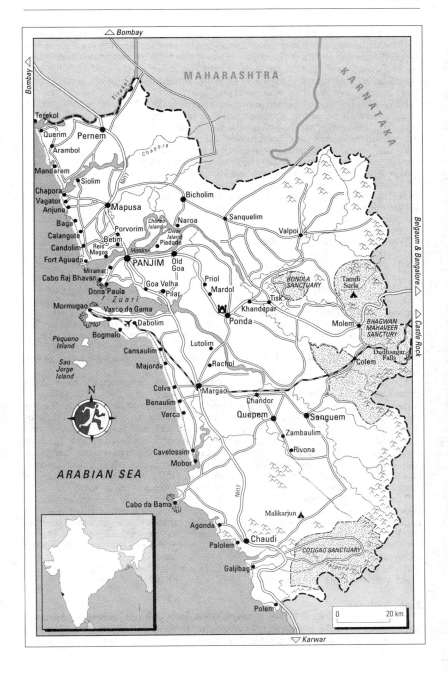

modern trawlers) are still the main sources of income. The recent discovery of **iron** in the hills to the east has also generated considerable revenue, and the economy is further fuelled by the stream of remittance cheques sent home by expatriate Goans working in Bombay and the Gulf states. The consequent higher standard of living has, inevitably, in turn stimulated a massive influx of **immigrants** from elsewhere in India, who comprise around a third of the total population.

Goa's other big money-spinner, of course, is **tourism**. Lured here in the 1960s by the locals' apparently permissive stance on drink, drugs and nudity – not to mention abundant cheap food and accommodation – the first foreigners to take advantage of the new state's pristine beaches were the "**hippies**". As the region's fame spread, however, the marginal minority was gradually squeezed out, leaving the more accessible stretches of coastline near Panjim free for development as **mainstream resorts**. Today, budget travellers taking time out from trips around the subcontinent, and package tourists over for a dose of winter sun, flock here in roughly equal numbers. The "alternative" contingent, meanwhile, has fled up the coast, ditching Pink Floyd along the way in favour of hard-edged, chest-thumping techno music. The legendary **full-moon parties** have also survived, despite numerous police crackdowns, and continue to attract thousands of revellers, especially around the Christmas–New Year period.

Which beach you opt for when you arrive largely depends on what sort of holiday you have in mind. Heavily developed resorts such as **Calangute** and **Baga**, in the north, and **Colva** (and to a lesser extent **Benaulim**), in the south, offer more "walk-in" accommodation, shopping and tourist facilites than elsewhere. Even if you don't fancy crowded bars and purpose-built hotels, it can be worth heading for these centres at first, as finding places to stay in less commercialized corners is often difficult. **Anjuna**, **Vagator**, and **Chapora**, where accommodation is generally more basic and harder to come by, are the beaches to aim for if you've come to Goa to party. To get a taste of what most of the state must have been like twenty or thirty years ago, however, you'll have to travel further afield – to **Arambol**, a sleepy fishing-village-cum-hippy-hang-out in the far north; or to **Agonda** and **Palolem**, near the Karnatakan border, where, as yet, tourism has made very little impact.

Foremost among worthwhile attractions **away from the coast** are the ruins of the Portuguese capital at **Old Goa**, 10km from Panjim – a sprawl of Catholic cathedrals, convents and churches that draws crowds of Christian pilgrims from all over India. Another popular day excursion is to Anjuna's Wednesday **flea market**, a sociable place to shop for souvenirs and the latest rave gear. Further inland, the thickly wooded countryside around **Ponda** harbours numerous temples, where you can check out Goa's peculiar brand of Hindu architecture. The *taluka* (district) of Salcete, and its main market town, **Margao**, is also littered with Portuguese mansions, churches and seminaries, whose gabled baroque facades nose tantalizingly above the tropical treeline. Finally, wildlife enthusiasts may be tempted into the interior to visit the nature reserve at **Cotigao** in the far south.

The best **time to come** to Goa is during the dry, relatively cool winter months between late September and early March. At other times, either the sun is too hot for comfort, or the monsoon rains make life miserable for everyone except the fisherfolk and hoteliers, who get to sit around all day snoozing and playing backgammon. During peak season, from mid-December to the end of January, the weather is perfect, with the temperature gauge rarely nudging above a manageable 32°C. Finding a room or a house to rent at that time, however – particularly over the Christmas and New Year fortnight when the tariffs double, or triple – can be a real hassle.

Some history

The sheer inaccessibility of Goa by land has always kept it out of the mainstream of Indian history; on the other hand, its control of the seas, and above all the lucrative spice trade, made it a much-coveted prize for rival colonial powers. Until a century

GOA TRAVEL DETAILS

	Trains		Buses		Flights	
	Frequency	Time	Frequency	Time	Frequency	Time
To and from VASCO DA GAMA						
Agra	1 daily	39hr				
Bangalore	1 daily	20hr	1 daily	16hr	6 weekly	1hr
Belgaum			5 daily	6hr		
Bhopal	1 daily	31hr 20min				
Bogmalo			hourly	20min		
Bombay	2 daily	24hr			4–5 daily	1hr
Delhi	1 daily	42hr 15min			2 daily	2hr 30min
Gwalior	1 daily	37hr 20min				
Hubli	1 daily	6hr 50min				
Hyderabad	1 daily				4 weekly	2hr 55min
Kochi					daily	1hr 10min
Kolhapur	2 daily	10hr 45min–11hr				
Madras					3 weekly	2hr 30min
Mangalore			2 daily	11hr		
Margao			every 15min	1hr		
Panjim			every 15min	45min		
Pune	3 daily	16hr–19hr 25min				
Thiruvan'puram					1 daily	2hr 15min
To and from MARGAO						
Belgaum			3 daily	5hr 30min		
Bombay	2 daily	23hr	2 daily	16hr		
Canacona / Chaudi			20 daily	1hr 40min		
Cavelossim			8 daily	30min		
Colva			12 daily	20–30min		
Gokarna			1 daily	4hr 30min		
Hubli	1 daily	5hr 50min	2 daily	6hr		
Karwar			20 daily	2hr		
Mangalore			2 daily	7hr		
Mapusa			10 daily	3hr		
Panjim			every 30min	1hr 30min		
Pune	3 daily	15hr–18hr 25min	1 daily	12hr		

Note that the same **trains** operate from Margao as from Vasco, usually leaving approximately one hour later.

By Bus

To and from PANJIM			**To and from PANJIM** (continued)		
Anjuna	4 daily	1hr	Pune	8 daily	12hr
Arambol	12 daily	2hr 25min	Terekol	2 daily	2hr 30min
Baga	every 30min	50min	Vagator	every 15min	55min
Bangalore	6 daily	14hr	Velha Goa	every 30min	30min
Belgaum	11 daily	5hr			
Bombay	24 daily	15–18hr	**To and from MAPUSA**		
Calangute	every 30min	45min	Anjuna	hourly	30min
Chapora	4 daily	1hr	Arambol	12 daily	1hr 45min
Hubli	8 daily	6hr	Baga	hourly	30min
Kolhapur	2 daily	9hr	Bombay	24 daily	14–17hr
Mangalore	5 daily	10–11hr	Calangute	hourly	45min
Mapusa	every 30min	35min	Chapora	every 15min	30–40min
Miraj	2 daily	9hr	Querim	4 daily	1hr
Mysore	1 daily	14–16hr	Vagator	every 15min	25min–35min

Train timings may well have changed since this book went to press due to conversion work on the line between Vasco, Margao and Karnataka.
Note that no individual route appears more than once in this chart; for any specific journey, check against where you want to get to as well as where you're coming from. For more detail on **onwards travel** from Goa, see p.730.

GETTING AROUND GOA

Before Independence, the many rivers that drain across Goa made **getting around** a problem. Nowadays, however, thanks to a network of road bridges (and the recent two-wheeler revolution), life is a lot easier.

As elsewhere in India, **cars** and **taxis** can be rented by the hour, or by the kilometre for excursions. Details of rates and rental companies are listed on p.725.

By ferry

If auto-rickshaws are the quintessentially Indian mode of transport, flat-bottomed **ferries** are their Goan equivalent. Crammed with cars, buses, commuters on scooters, fisher-women and clumps of bewildered tourists, these rusting blue-painted hulks provide an essential service, crossing the coastal backwaters where bridges have not yet been built. They're also incredibly cheap, and run from the crack of dawn until late in the evening.

The most frequented river crossings in Goa are Panjim to Betim, across the Mandovi (every 15min); Old Goa to Divar Island (every 15min); Siolim to Chopdem, across the Chapora River for Arambol and Pernem (every 15min); Querim to Terekol, over the Terekol River (every 30min); and Cavelossim, in the far south of Salcete *taluka*, to Assolna (every 20–30min)

By train

Goa's only rail route, a slow metre-gauge track currently being upgraded, runs east from Mormugao harbour, near Vasco da Gama, to join up with the main Bombay–Bangalore network. Along the way it winds through Margoa and the Ghats to the Karnatakan border, passing Dudhsagar Falls (see p.735). Services in Goa have been severely disrupted over the past few years by **line conversion work**, which looks set to continue through 1997–8. Check the temporary timetables at *Indian Railways* counter in Panjim's *Kadamba* bus stand, or at Vasco da Gama station, before making any travel plans. **Bookings** can be made at either of these places, and at Margao station; reservations on *Indrail* passes can only be made at Vasco.

By bus

The Goan transport corporation, **Kadamba**, runs long-distance services throughout the state from their main stands at Panjim, Mapusa and Margao. Private buses, serving everywhere else including the coastal resorts, are cheap, frequent, and more relaxed

before the arrival of the Portuguese adventurer **Vasco da Gama**, who landed near Kozhikode in Kerala in 1498, Goa had belonged for over a thousand years to the kingdom of Kadamba. In the interim it had been successfully conquered by the Karnatakan Vijayanagars, the Muslim Bahmanis, and Yusuf Adil Shah of Bijapur, but the capture of the fort at Panjim by **Afonso de Albuquerque** in 1510 signalled the start of a Portuguese occupation that was to last for 450 years.

As Goa expanded, its splendid capital (now Old Goa) came to hold a larger population than either Paris or London. Though Ismail Adil Shah laid siege for ten months in 1570, and the Marathas under Shivaji and later chiefs came nail-bitingly close to seizing the region, the greatest threat was from other European maritime nations. While the Dutch made several unsuccessful attacks, the British at first preferred the avenue of diplomacy. Their **East India Company** signed the **Convention of Goa** in 1642, granting them the right to trade with the colony, and use its harbours.

Meanwhile, conversions to **Christianity**, started by the Franciscans, gathered pace when St Francis Xavier founded the **Jesuit** mission in 1542. With the advent of the Inquisition soon afterwards, laws were introduced censoring literature and banning any faith other than Catholicism – even the long-established Syrian Christian community than many in India, although you should still brace yourself for a crush on market days and when travelling to major towns and tourist centres. Details on how to get around by bus are listed in the relevant accounts, and on p.719.

By motorcycle taxi
Goa's unique pillion-passenger **motorcycle taxis**, known locally as "**pilots**", are ideal for nipping between beaches or into town from the resorts. Bona fide operators ride black bikes (usually *Enfields*) with yellow mudguards and white number plates. Fares, which should be settled in advance, are comparable with auto-rickshaw rates: roughly Rs5 per km.

By rented motorcycle
Renting a motorcycle in Goa gives a lot of freedom but can be perilous. Every season, an average of one person a day dies on the roads; many are tourists on two-wheelers. Make sure, therefore, that the lights and brakes are in good shape, and be especially vigilant at night: many Goan roads are appallingly pot-holed and unlit, and stray cows and bullock carts can appear from nowhere.

Officially, you need an **international driver's licence** to rent, and ride, anything more powerful than a 25cc moped. Owners and rental companies rarely enforce this, but some local **police** use the rule to extract exorbitant *baksheesh* from tourists. If you don't have a licence with you, the only way around the problem is to avoid big towns such as Panjim, Margao and Mapusa (or Anjuna on market day), and only to carry small sums of money when driving. If you are arrested for not having the right papers, it's no big deal, though police officers may try to convince you otherwise; keep cool, and be prepared to negotiate. Some unlicensed operators attempt to rent out machines to unwary visitors; always make sure you get some evidence of rental and insurance.

Rates vary according to the season, the vehicle, and how long you rent it for; most owners also insist on a hefty deposit and/or passport as security. The range is pretty standard, with the cheapest choice, a 50cc **moped**, costing Rs50–100 per day. These are fine for buzzing to the beach and back, but to travel further try the stalwart **Enfield Bullet 350cc**, popular mainly for its pose value (upwards of Rs250 per day); the smaller but more reliable **Honda Kinetic 100cc**, which has automatic gears and is a good first-time choice (Rs100–120 per day); or the best all-rounder, the **Yamaha RD 100cc**: light, fast enough, reliable, economical, and with manual gears (Rs150–200 per day). The notoriously unreliable Indian-makes, **Rajdoot** and **Bajaj**, are best avoided.

were branded heretics. Hindu temples were destroyed, and converted Hindus adopted Portuguese names, such as da Silva, Correa and de Sousa, which remain common in the region. The transnational influence of the Jesuits eventually alarmed the Portuguese government; the Jesuits were expelled in 1749, which made it possible for Indian Goans to take up the priesthood. However, standards of education suffered, and Goa entered a period of decline. The Portuguese were not prepared to help, but neither would they allow native Goans equal rights. An abortive attempt to establish a Goan Republic was quelled with the execution of fifteen Goan conspirators.

A spin-off of the British conflict with Tipu Sultan of Mysore (an ally of the French) at the end of the eighteenth century, was the **British occupation** of Goa, a little-known period of the region's history, which lasted sixteen years from 1797. The occupation was solely military; the Goan authorities never gave up their administration. Despite a certain liberalization, such as the restoration of Hindus' right to worship, the nineteenth century saw widespread civil unrest. During British occupation many Goans moved to Bombay, and elsewhere in British India, to find work.

The success of the post-Independence Goan struggle for freedom from Portugal owed as much to the efforts of the Indian government, who cut off diplomatic ties with

POLICE, TROUBLE AND NUDISM

While the vast majority of visitors to Goa never encounter any **trouble**, tourism-related crime is definitely more prevalent than in other parts of the country. **Theft** is the most common problem – usually of articles left unattended on the beach. Don't assume your valuables are safe in a padlocked house or hotel room, either. Break-ins, particularly on party nights, are on the increase. The most secure solution is to rent a deposit box in a bank, which costs around Rs50, or to opt for one of the few guest houses with lockers.

The other eventuality to avoid, at all costs, is getting on the wrong side of the law. **Drugs** are the most common cause of serious trouble. Many travellers imagine that, because of Goa's free-and-easy reputation, drug-use is legal: it isn't. Possession of even a small amount of cannabis is a criminal offence, punishable by large fines or prison sentences of up to ten years. Arrests, however, rarely result in court appearances. The Goan police like to ensure that offenders are given the opportunity of leaving the country first, having relieved them of nearly all their spare cash and valuables.

Though violent crime is rare, women should think twice before wandering down deserted beaches on their own. **Sexual harassment** usually takes the form of a bit of unsubtle ogling, but there have also been several incidents of rape in recent years.

Finally, remember that **nudism** is prohibited. Visitors in the past all too often rode roughshod over local sensibilities, forgetting or wilfully ignoring the fact that Goa is part of India, and still predominantly Hindu. In case tourists miss the "NO NUDISM" signs posted at the entrances to most beaches, police regularly patrol the busier resorts to ensure that decorum is maintained. If you are tempted to drop your togs, check that there are no families within eyeshot. No-one is likely to object openly, but when you consider that wet Y-fronts and *saris* are about as risqué as beachwear gets for most Indians, you'll see why men in G-strings and topless women cause such a stir.

Portugal, as to the work of freedom fighters such as **Menezes Braganza** and **Dr Cunha**. After a "liberation march" in 1955 resulted in a number of deaths, the state was blockaded. Trade with Bombay ceased, and the railway was cut off, so Goa set out to forge international links, particularly with Pakistan and Sri Lanka. That led to the building of Dabolim airport, and a determination to improve local agricultural output. In 1961, Prime Minister Jawaharlal Nehru finally ran out of patience with his opposite number in Lisbon, the right-wing dictator Salazar, and sent in the armed forces. Mounted in defiance of a United Nations resolution, "**Operation Vijay**" met with only token resistance, and the Indian army overran Goa in two days. Thereafter, Goa (along with Portugal's other two enclaves, Daman and Diu) became part of India as a self-governing **Union Territory**, with minimum interference from Delhi

Since Independence, Goa has continued to prosper, bolstered by receipts from iron-ore exports and a booming tourist industry, but it is struggling to hold its own against a tidal wave of **immigration** from other Indian states. Its inhabitants voted overwhelmingly to resist merger with neighbouring Maharashtra in the 1980s, and successfully lobbied for Konkani to be granted offical-language status in 1987, when Goa was finally declared a fully-fledged state of the Indian Union.

Panjim and central Goa

Take any mid-sized Portuguese town, add a sprinkling of banana trees, auto-rickshaws and a dash of *garam masala*, drench annually with torrential tropical rain, and leave to simmer in fierce humid sunshine for at least one hundred and fifty years, and you'll end up with something similar to **PANJIM** (or Panaji – "land that does not flood"). The Goan capital has a completely different feel from any other Indian city. Stacked around the sides of a lush terraced hillside at the mouth of the River Mandovi, its skyline of red-tiled roofs, whitewashed churches, and mildewing concrete apartment blocks has more in common with Lisbon than Lucknow. This lingering European influence is most evident in the small squares and cobbled lanes of the town's old Latin quarter, **Fontainhas**. Here, Portuguese is still very much the lingua franca, the shopfronts sport names like *José Pinto* and *de Souza*, and the women wear knee-length dresses that would turn heads anywhere else in the country.

For centuries, Panjim was little more than a minor landing stage and customs house, protected by a hill-top fort, and surrounded by stagnant swampland. It became capital in 1843, after the port at Old Goa had silted up, and its rulers and impoverished inhabitants had fled the plague. Although the last Portuguese viceroy managed to drain many of the nearby marshes, and erect imposing public buildings on the new site, the town never emulated the grandeur of its predecessor upriver – a result, in part, of the Portuguese nobles' predilection for erecting their mansions in the countryside rather than the city. Panjim expanded rapidly in the 1960s and 1970s, without reaching the unmanageable proportions of other Indian state capitals. After Bombay, or even Bangalore, its uncongested streets seem easy-going, and pleasantly parochial. Sights are thin on the ground, but the palm-lined squares and atmospheric Latin quarter, with its picturesque Neoclassical houses and Catholic churches, make a pleasant backdrop for aimless wandering.

Some travellers see no more of Panjim than its noisy bus terminal – which is a pity. Although you can completely bypass the town when you arrive in Goa, either by jumping off the train or coach at Margao (for the south), or Mapusa (for the northern resorts), or by heading straight off on a local bus, it's definitely worth spending time here – if only a couple of hours en route to the ruined former capital at Old Goa.

The area **around Panjim** attracts far fewer visitors than the coastal resorts, yet its paddy fields and wooded valleys harbour several attactions worth a day or two's break from the beach. **Old Goa** is just a bus ride away, as are the unique temples around **Ponda**, an hour or so southeast, to where Hindus smuggled their deities during the Inquisition. Further inland still, the forested lower slopes of the Western Ghats, cut through by the main Panjim–Bangalore highway, shelter the impressive **Dudhsagar falls**, which you can only reach by rail.

Arrival and information

European charter planes and domestic flights from Bombay, Bangalore, Cochin, Delhi, Madras and Thiruvananthapuram arrive at Goa's **Dabolim airport**, 29km south of Panjim on the outskirts of Vasco da Gama. Pre-paid taxis into town (45min; Rs300), booked at the arrivals hall counter, can be shared by up to five people. *Kadamba* buses (Rs20) meet domestic flights, dropping passengers at the main bus stand and outside the *Indian Airlines* office on Dr D Bandodkar Rd, in the northwest of town.

Long-distance and local **buses** pull into Panjim at the town's busy **Kadamba bus terminal**, 1km east of the centre in the district of Pato. Ten minutes' walk from here across Ourem Creek to Fontainhas, brings you to several budget hotels. If you plan to stay in the more modern west end of town, flag down a motorcycle taxi or jump into an auto-rickshaw at the rank outside the station concourse.

Information

GTDC's handy **information** counter, inside the concourse at the main *Kadamba* bus stand (Mon–Fri 8am–6pm, Sat & Sun 9am–1pm & 2–5pm; ☎45620), keeps train and bus timetables, and can help you find accommodation. The equally efficient ITDC **tourist**

The telephone **area code** for Panjim is ☎0832.

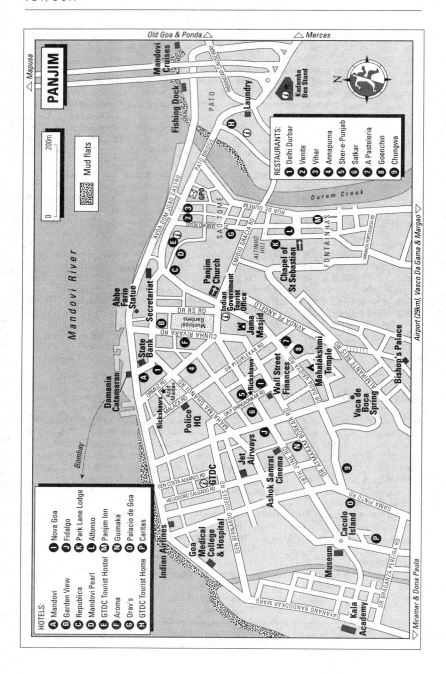

PANJIM

Mapusa △

Old Goa & Ponda △   △ Merces

Mandovi Cruises

Laundry

Kadamba Bus Stand

N

RESTAURANTS:
1 Delhi Durbar
2 Venite
3 Vihar
4 Annapurna
5 Sher-e-Punjab
6 Satkar
7 A Pasteleria
8 Goenchin
9 Chungwa

Fishing Dock

PATO

PATO BRIDGE

RIBANDAR CAUSEWAY

Mandovi River

200m

Mud flats

0

Ourem Creek

GPO

RUA DE OUREM

SAO TOMÉ

JANCHHO ROAD

AVDA DOM JOAO CASTRO

FONTAINHAS

Abbe Faria Statue

Secretariat

Panjim Church

EMIDIO GRACIA RD

ALTINHO HILL

Chapel of St Sebastian

Indian Government Tourist Office

DR RS RD

Municipal Gardens

CUNHA RIVARA RD

Jama Masjid

AVENIDA PE ANGELO

State Bank

ORMUZ RD

DR P SHIRGAONKAR RD

DR PISURLEKAR RD

MAHATMA GANDHI RD

Rickshaws

Damania Catamaran

Bombay

Rickshaws

Azad Maidan

MALACA RD

Police HQ

Wall Street Finances

Rickshaws

Mahalakshmi Temple

DR DADA VAIDYA RD

ALMIRANTE REIS RD

Vaca de Boca Spring

Bishop's Palace

Jet Airways

Ashok Samrat Cinema

18th JUNE RD

DR AMARAM BORKAR RD

GEN COSTA ALVARES RD

GTDC

HELIODORO SALGADO RD

GEN BERNARDO GUEDES RD

DAYANAND BANDODKAR MARG

Indian Airlines

Goa Medical College & Hospital

Caculo Island

Museum

Kala Academy

GAMA PINTO RD

DR BRAGANZA PEREIRA RD

Airport (29km), Vasco Da Gama & Margao ▽

Miramar & Dona Paula ▽

HOTELS:
A Mandovi
B Garden View
C Republica
D Mandovi Pearl
E GTDC Tourist Hostel
F Aroma
G Orav's
H GTDC Tourist Home

I Nova Goa
J Fidalgo
K Park Lane Lodge
L Alfonso
M Panjim Inn
N Guimaka
O Palacio de Goa
P Caritas

office is across town on Church Square (Mon–Fri 9.30am–5.45pm, Sat 9.30am–1pm; ☎43412). Alternatively, try GTDC's information desk inside the reception of their *Tourist Home* hotel in Pato (☎45715), on the east side of Ourem Creek near the bus stand. All three sell good state **maps** – invaluable if you plan to do any motorcycling.

Panjim's reliable **poste restante** counter (Mon–Sat 9.30am–1pm & 2–5.30pm) is next door to the **GPO**, 200m west of Pato Bridge.

Getting around

The most convenient way of **getting around** Panjim is by **auto-rickshaw** (around Rs20); flag one down at the roadside or head for one of the ranks around the city.

The only city **buses** likely to be of use to visitors run to Dona Paula from the main bus stand via several stops along the esplanade (including the Secretariat), and Miramar beachfront. If you feel up to taking on Panjim's anarchic traffic, **bicycles** can be rented (Mon–Sat only; Rs2 per hour) from the stall up the lane opposite the GPO, or from the *Daud M Agar* bike shop, in front of the National Theatre.

Cars with drivers are available for local sightseeing through GTDC, Trionora Apartments (☎43396), the ITDC office on Church Square, and from *Hertz*, opposite Dom Bosco School, Market Area (☎44304), from Rs400–600 (4hr) and Rs600–1000 (8hr). **Self-drive** costs around Rs700 (24hr) from *Budget Rent-a-Car*, c/o *Sai Service*, Mapusa Rd, Porvorim, on the north side of Mandovi bridge (☎217755); and *Hertz*.

The Town

Until recently, most visitors' first glimpse of **Panjim** was from the decks of the old Bombay steamer as it chugged into dock at the now-defunct ferry ramp. These days, however, despite the 1994 inauguration of *Damania*'s long-awaited catamaran service from Bombay, the town is most usually approached by road – from the north via the huge ferro-concrete bridge that spans the Mandovi estuary, or from the south on the recently revamped NH7, which links the capital with the airport and railhead at Vasco da Gama. Either way, you'll have to pass through the suburb of **Pato**, home of the main *Kadamba* bus terminal, before crossing Ourem Creek to arrive in Panjim proper. West of **Fontainhas**, the picturesque Portuguese quarter, the commercial centre's grid of long straight streets fans out west from Panjim's principal landmark, **Church Square**. Further north, the main thoroughfare, **Avenida Dom Joao Castro**, sweeps past the GPO and **Secretariat** building, before bending west along the waterfront towards the nearby beach resort of **Miramar**, and nearby **Dona Paula**.

Church Square

The leafy rectangular park opposite the ITDC tourist office, known as **Church Square** or the **Municipal Garden**, forms the heart of Panjim. Presiding over its east side is the town's most distinctive and photogenic landmark, the toothpaste-white Baroque facade of the **Church of Our Lady of the Immaculate Conception**. Flanked by rows of slender palm trees, at the head of a criss-crossing laterite walkway, the church was built in 1541 for the benefit of sailors arriving here from Lisbon. The weary mariners would stagger up from the quay to give thanks for their safe passage before proceeding to the capital at Old Goa – the original home of the enormous bell that hangs from its central gable.

The Secretariat

The road that runs north from the church brings you out at the riverside near Panjim's oldest surviving building. With its sloping tiled roofs, carved-stone coats of arms and wooden verandahs, the stalwart **Secretariat** looks typically colonial. Yet it was originally the summer palace of Goa's sixteenth-century Muslim ruler, the 'Adil Shah. Later, the Portuguese converted it into a temporary rest house for the territory's governors (who used to overnight here en route to and from Europe) and then a residence for the viceroy. Today, it accommodates the Goan State Legislature, which explains the presence of so many shiny chauffeur-driven *Ambassador* cars outside, and the armed guards at the door.

A hundred metres east, a peculiar statue of a man holding his hands over the body of an entranced reclining woman shows **Abbé Farin** (1755–1819), a Goan priest who emigrated to France to become one of the world's first professional hypnotists.

Fontainhas and Sao Tomé

Panjim's oldest and most interesting district, **Fontainhas**, lies immediately west of Pato, overlooking the banks of the oily green Ourem Creek. From the footbridge between the bus stand and town centre, a dozen or so blocks of Neoclassical houses rise in a tangle of terracotta rooftops up the sides of **Altinho Hill**. At siesta time, *Vespas* stand idle on deserted street corners, while women in Western clothes exchange pleasantries with their neighbours from open windows and leafy verandahs. Many buildings have retained their traditional coat of ochre, pale yellow, green or blue – a legacy of the Portuguese insistence that every Goan building (except churches, which had to be white) should be colour-washed after the monsoons.

At the southern end of the neighbourhood, the pristine whitewashed **Chapel of St Sebastian** is one of many Goan churches to remain faithful to the old colonial decree. It stands at the end of a small square where Fontainhas' Portuguese-speaking locals hold a lively annual street *festa* to celebrate their patron saint's day in mid-November. The eerily lifelike crucifix inside the chapel, brought here in 1812, formerly hung in the Palace of the Inquisition in Old Goa. Unusually, Christ's eyes are open – allegedly to inspire fear in those being interrogated by the Inquisitors.

Sao Tomé ward is the other old quarter, lying north of Fontainhas on the far side of Emilio Gracia Rd. This is the area to head for if you fancy a bar crawl: the narrow streets are dotted with dozens of hole-in-the-wall taverns, serving cheap, stiff measures of rocket-fuel *feni* under strip lights and the watchful gaze of colourful Madonnas. You'll feel less conspicuous in the neighbourhood's best known hostelery, the *Hotel Venite* (see below).

THE FESTIVALS OF GOA

Some of Goa's **festivals** are on fixed dates each year; ask at a tourist office for dates of the others. The biggest celebrations take place at Panjim and Margao.

Festa dos Reis (Jan 6). Epiphany celebrations include a procession of young boys decked out as the Three Kings to the Franciscan chapel of Reis Magos, near Panjim on the north bank of the Mandovi, 3km east of Fort Aguada. Other processions are held at Candelim and Chandor.

Carnival (Feb/March). Three days of *feni*-induced mayhem, centering on Panjim, to mark the run-up to Lent.

Shigmo (Feb/March). The Goan version of Holi is celebrated with big parades and crowds; drum and dance groups compete and huge floats, that threaten to bring down telegraph wires, trundle through the streets.

All Saints (March). On the fifth Monday in Lent, twenty-six effigies of saints, martyrs, popes, kings, queens and cardinals are paraded around the village of Velha Goa, near Panjim. A fair also takes place.

Igitun Chalne (May). Dhoti-clad devotees of the goddess Lairya enter trances and walk over hot coals at the village of Sirigao, Bichloim.

Pop, Beat and Jazz Music Festival (May). Local bands strut their stuff at the Kala Academy in Panjim.

Sanjuan (June 24). The festival of St John is celebrated all over Goa, but is especially important in the coastal villages of Arambol and Terekol. Youngsters torch straw dummies (representing St John's baptism, and thus the death of sin), while revellers in striped pants dive into wells after drinking bottles of *feni*.

Janmashtami (Aug). Ritual bathing in the River Mandovi, off Diwadi Island, to celebrate the birth of Krishna.

Dussehra (Sept/Oct). Nine days of festivities in which more effigies are burned on bonfires, and children perform episodes from the life of Rama.

Diwali (Oct/Nov). The five-day Hindu "festival of lights" features processions all over the region, often accompanied by fireworks, and the exchange of sweets by neighbours, regardless of their faith.

Christmas (Dec 24/25). Celebrated everywhere in Goa. Late-night mass is usually followed by music, dancing and fireworks, while tourist ravers party in Anjuna.

The museum

Moves are afoot to shift Panjim's small and mildly diverting **museum** to a purpose-built complex across town. For the time being, however, it occupies the dingy first floor of an office block at the far west end of the centre, near the **Caculo Island** intersection. The collection consists mostly of pre-colonial artefacts, including village deities, *puja* utensils, a handful of *sati* and hero stones, fragments of temple sculpture and some fine **Jain bronzes** rescued by Customs and Excise officers from smugglers. Also of interest are the Christian icons and pieces of antique furniture displayed in the small gallery devoted to **Western art**, and a series of **photographs** taken by a Portuguese colonial official around the turn of the century.

Accommodation

The town centre has plenty of **accommodation**, and finding a place to stay is only a problem during the festival of St Francis in early December, and during peak season (mid-Dec to mid-Jan), when tariffs double. At other times, hotels try to fill rooms by offering substantial discounts. The best inexpensive options are in Fontainhas, down by Ourem Creek, and in the back streets behind the esplanade. Standards are generally good, and even the cheapest rooms should have a window, a fan, running water and clean sheets. The rest of the hotels are mostly bland places in the more modern, west end of town.

Note that **checkout times** in Panjim vary wildly. Find out what yours is as soon as you arrive, or your hard-earned lie-in could end up costing you an extra day's rent.

Inexpensive

Alfonso, St Sebastian Chapel Square, Fontainhas (no phone). Modest family house in a picturesque backstreet, with large rooms (all with bath), and some self-catering. ③–④.

GTDC Tourist Home, around the corner from the bus stand, Pato; (☎45715). Run-of-the-mill dorm beds and inexpensive doubles – fine for a night if you can't face a room hunt. ①–③.

Guimaka, near *Ashok Samrat* cinema (☎22369). No-nonsense, neat and clean guest house in the centre of the shopping district. Attached or non-attached rooms, and a relaxing courtyard. ③.

Mandovi Pearl, PO Box #329, behind GTDC *Tourist Hostel* (☎46852). Idiosyncratic lodge, close to the riverfront, run by a garrulous landlord for salesmen and budget travellers. The rooms are roughish but good value. ②.

Orav's, 31 Janeiro Rd (☎46128). Bland modern building in the old quarter, with good-sized, comfortable rooms and small balconies. ④.

Park Lane Lodge, near Chapel of St Sebastian (☎220238). Spotless and characterful but cramped guest house in old colonial style family home. Pot plants, stuffed parrots, safe-deposit facilities and a relaxed, friendly atmosphere. Good off-season discounts, too. Recommended. ④.

Republica, near GTDC *Tourist Hostel* (☎224630). Good-value budget travellers' lodge with clean rooms, attached shower-toilets and river views from a large wooden verandah. ②.

Moderate to expensive

Aroma, Cunha Rivara Rd (☎43519; fax 224330). Very central and long-established hotel with a popular *tandoori* restaurant. Some rooms look onto Church Square. ⑤.

Caritas Holiday Home, south of the Caculo Island intersection, St Inez (☎220496). Shiny new place west of the town centre (near the museum), with spotless rooms but little character. ⑤.

Fidalgo, 18 June Rd (☎22629; fax 2250612). Large, well-established place with all mod cons, including central a/c, money exchange, *Star TV*, a health club, shopping arcade and travel agent. ⑧.

Garden View, opposite Municipal Gardens (☎47844; fax 44168). Large, modern, very clean and well-managed hotel. The more expensive rooms (some a/c) overlook the square. Good value. ⑥.

GTDC Tourist Hostel, Avda Dom Joao Castro (☎227103). Very popular hotel overlooking a busy thoroughfare and the river. Large, pleasant rooms, but no longer the bargain they used to be. Shops, a hair salon and tourist information in the lobby. ④–⑤.

Mandovi, Dr D Bandodkar Rd (☎226270; fax 225451). Grand waterside hotel with river views from front rooms, central a/c, shops, in-house travel agent and a pool. The best in this category. ⑦–⑨.

Nova Goa, Dr Atmaram Borkar Rd (☎46231; fax 224958). Panjim's newest and least expensive top hotel, in the heart of the shopping area. The usual comforts, plus bathtubs and a pool. ⑦–⑧.

Palacio de Goa, Gama Pinto Rd (☎44289). Kitsch, five-storey Neoclassical facade and pleasant but plain rooms with balconies, and a pure-veg restaurant. ⑤.

Panjim Inn, E-212, 31 Janeiro Rd, Fontainhas (☎226523; fax 228136). Grand old Portuguese town house, managed as an upmarket but homely hotel, with period furniture, individual balconies and a common verandah. Easily the best place in its class. ⑤–⑥.

Eating and drinking

Panjim is packed with good **places to eat**. Most are connected to a hotel (the *Hotel Venite* restaurant is the most popular with foreigners), but there are also plenty of smaller family-run establishments in the backstreets of Sao Tomé, where a plate of fish curry and rice and a cold *Kingfisher* will set you back less than Rs50; vegetarians will do better at the numerous south Indian-style cafeterias. Two of these, the *Satkar* and the *Vihar*, open at around 7am for blow-out **breakfasts** – great if you have just staggered into town after a night on the bus. Beer, *feni* and other spirits are available in all but the purest "pure veg" places, especially in the hole-in-the-wall taverns around Sao Tomé.

A Pasteleria, Dr Dada Vaidya Rd. Panjim's best bakery does dozens of Western-style cakes, biscuits and sticky buns, including brownies and fruit loaves. Takeaway only. Moderate.

Annapurna, Ormuz Rd. Traditional inexpensive south Indian *thalis* and snacks dished up by cotton-clad waiters in a large, clean, cool dining hall.

Chunghwa, *Hotel Samrat*, Dr Dada Vaidya Rd. Authentic, upscale Cantonese a/c restaurant with attentive service and a wide selection of moderately priced seafood, meat and veg dishes.

Delhi Durbar, behind the *Hotel Mandovi*. Recently opened branch of the famous Bombay restaurant, and the best place in Panjim to sample traditional Mughlai cuisine: mainly meat steeped in rich, spicy sauces. Patronized by an expense account crowd, but very reasonable.

Goenchin, off Dr Dada Vaidhya Rd. Glacial a/c and dim lighting, but unquestionably the best and most authentic Chinese food to be found in Goa. Expensive.

Satkar, 18 June Rd. Spotlessly clean and inexpensive south Indian cafe whose filling *dosas* come with chunks of fresh coconut.

Sher-e-Punjab, 18 June Rd, near the *Satkar*. North Indian food served up in crowded city-centre restaurant. Their speciality – butter chicken – is delicious, and there's a reasonable veg menu.

Venite, 31 Janeiro Rd. Deservedly popular hotel restaurant, serving great fresh seafood, including affordable lobster and crab, along with Western dishes, desserts, *feni* and cold beers. Wooden floors, balcony seats, candles and an eclectic cassette collection add to the ambience. Good breakfasts, too. Closed Sun.

Vihar, 31 Janeiro Rd, around the corner from *Venite*. Very well frequented Indian fast-food cafeteria with formica booths and barefoot waiters. Great *puri bhajis*, *dosas*, *wadas* and other snacks.

Listings

Airline offices in Panjim include: *Air India, Hotel Fidalgo*, 18 June Rd (☎224081); *British Airways*, 2 Excelsior Chambers, MG Rd (☎ & fax 224336); *Damania* (also for *Gulf Air, Air France* and *Air Canada*), Bernard Guedes Rd (☎220056); *East-West, Hotel Fidalgo*, 18 June Rd (☎224108; fax 220208); *Indian Airlines*, Dempo Building, Dr D Bandodkar Rd (☎223831); *Jet*, Rizvi Chambers, office #102, Caetano Albuquerque Rd (☎221476); *KLM* (also *PIA*), 18 June Rd, near *Titan* showroom (☎226678); *Modiluft*, Praca Commercio, Dr Atmaram Borkar Rd (☎225924).

American Express *Menezes Air Travel*, Rua de Ourem, near Pato Bridge (☎ & fax 225081).

Banks Foreign exchange facilities include the *State Bank of India*, opposite the *Hotel Mandovi*, Avda Dom João Castro; the *Bank of Baroda* (where you can draw money on *Visa* cards), Azad Maidan; the *Andhra Bank*, opposite the *Ashok Samrat* cinema (also good for *Visa*); and the *Corporation Bank* on Church Square, around the corner from the GTDC tourist office. Finally, *Thomas Cook* is near the *Indian Airlines* office, at 8 Alcon Chambers, Devanad Bandodkar Rd (☎221312; fax 221313). In addition to the usual exchange facilities, it also specializes in fast international money transfers.

Books The bookshops in the *Hotel Fidalgo* and the *Hotel Mandovi* stock a range of English-language fiction in paperback, and special interest titles and coffee-table tomes on Goa.

Consulate The British High Commission of Bombay has a Consular Assistant who can be useful in emergencies. Agnelo Godinho's office/home is 189 Avda Dom Joao Castro, around the corner from the GPO (☎46824).

Hospital Panjim's largest hospital, the Goa Medical College, is in the west of town at the far end of Avda Dom Joao Castro. For an ambulance, call ☎46300.

Music and dance Regular recitals of classical Indian music and dance are held at Panjim's school for the performing arts, the Kala Academy in Campal, at the far west end of town on Devanand Bandodkar Rd. For details of forthcoming events, consult the boards in front of the auditorium or the listings page of local newspapers.

MOVING ON FROM GOA

A full summary of road and air routes from Goa to the rest of India appears on p.719. When this book went to press, **rail services** were still badly disrupted by work being carried out on the line between Vasco da Gama and Miraj in Maharashtra, where Goa's metre-gauge track joins the main broad-gauge Bombay–Bangalore line. Until the work is completed (in 1997), services along most of this stretch will remain suspended. However, it is still possible to travel by bus as far as **Londa**, 119km east of Panjim, and pick up indirect trains to Bombay or Hubli from there, although most travellers find this more hassle than it's worth.

If you're heading north to **Bombay**, the quickest and easiest way is to fly. Four or five **planes** per day leave Dabolim airport, on the outskirts of Vasco da Gama (see p.754), for Santa Cruz (1hr). *Modiluft* currently offer the best value for money, with marginally cheaper fares than the similarly priced, but less reliable, *Indian Airlines*; *Jet*, *East-West* and *Damania* charge the most. *Damania*'s swish new **catamaran** is the next best option, leaving from the ferry quay opposite the *Hotel Mandovi* in Panjim at 9am, arriving in Bombay seven-and-a-half hours later (so make sure you have a room reserved in advance). Tickets (US $40 or around Rs1000) and should be booked as far in advance as possible. The food is good and they lay on a couple of films. The cheapest, though the most uncomfortable and nightmarish way to get to Bombay is by night **bus** (14–18hr), covering 500km of rough road at often terrifying speeds. For more on the different ways to travel between Goa and Bombay, see p.657.

The journey south down the Konkan coast towards **Mangalore** in Karnataka is a lot less gruelling, with better road surfaces and plenty of worthwhile places to pull over for a day or two. One direct **bus** per day leaves Panjim for **Gokarna** (see p.719); alternatively, catch one of the more frequent *Kadamba* services to **Mangalore** (10–11hr) and jump off at Ankola, from where private mini-vans cover the last leg to the coast. When the new Bombay–Mangalore Konkan Railway is finally up and running (scheduled optimistically for 1998), this trip will be a lot easier by rail.

Getting to **Hampi** from Goa will also be more straightforward with the completion of work on the line running east from Vasco; in the meantime, the only way to travel across the Ghats into Karnataka (unless you can afford a taxi) is by bus. One direct express service each day leaves Panjim for **Hospet** (depart 10.30am; 10–11hr). However, seats on this bus can be in short supply during peak season, and many travellers end up on the following day's service to **Hubli** (depart 6.30am), from where you can pick up hourly buses on to Hospet. Note that the buses *KSRTC* use for this route are even more decrepit than normal, and breakdowns are par for the course.

At present, the only way to get to **Delhi** direct is to fly (with *ModiLuft* or *Indian Airlines*). When the track conversion to Miraj is finished, there will also be a daily express train from Vasco and Margao; check with *Indian Railways* (see below) for more details.

Reservations, tickets and information:

Catamaran tickets can be booked direct at *Damania*'s office on Avda Dom Joao Castro (☎228711). Otherwise, *MGM International*, Mamai Camotim Building (near Secretariat), or *Tradewings Ltd*, Mascarenhas Buildings (near *Jolly Shoes*), Dr Akmaram Borkar Rd (☎22243), all specialize in **catamaran** and **air** tickets.

The **South Central Railway**'s Out Agency reservation counter (daily 10am–1pm & 2.30–5pm) is on Platform 5 of Panjim bus stand. The quota here is very limited, but it's worth trying, as the main booking office is at Vasco station – the only place to make reservations on *Indrail* passes, and on the elusive tourist quota. Book *Kadamba* **bus tickets** in advance at their offices in Panjim and Mapusa bus stands (daily 9–11am & 2–5pm); private companies sell theirs through the many travel agents immediately outside the bus stand in Panjim, and at the bottom of the square in Mapusa. **Information** on all departures and fares is available from Goa Tourism's counter inside Panjim's bus stand (Mon–Fri 9.30am–6pm, Sat 9.15am–1pm; ☎225620).

Reliable Panjim **travel agents** include: *AERO Mundial, Hotel Mandovi*, Dr D Bandodkar Rd (☎43773); *Menezes Air Travel*, Rua de Ourem (☎ & fax 225081); *TPH Travel*, Padmavati Towers, 18 June Rd (☎235365); and *Rauraje Deshprabhu*, Cunha Rivara Rd (☎221840).

Pharmacies *Hindu Pharma* (☎43176), near the tourist office on Church Square, stocks Ayurvedic, homeopathic and allopathic medicines. Alternatively, try *F Menezes*, oposite *Benetton*, on Avda Dom João Castro.

Police The Police Headquarters is on Malaca Rd, central Panjim. In emergencies, call ☎100.

Visa extensions The Foreigners' Registration Office is at Police Headquarters (Mon–Fri 9.30am–1pm; ☎46545).

Miramar and Dona Paula

West of Panjim, the coast road passes through the swish suburb of Campal, with its grand colonial residences (and their modern concrete counterparts), before swinging south towards the beach at **MIRAMAR**. Were this anywhere but Goa, you might be tempted to spend an afternoon here, enjoying the two-kilometre sweep of dark sand and the views across Aguada Bay. As it is, the beach's dodgy undercurrents, noisy bus parties, and over-zealous peanut-*wallahs*, make it far less attractive than most other resorts within easy reach of the capital. The same is true of nearby **DONA PAULA**, 9km west of Panjim. Nestled on the south side of the rocky, hammer-shaped headland that divides the Zuari and Mandovi estuaries, this former fishing village is nowadays a characterless and commercialized resort, and not somewhere you'd choose to spend much time – unless you're staying in one of the many 5-star campus hotels.

Practicalities

If you opt to **stay** in Miramar, the best option is GTDC's *Yatri Niwas* (☎227754; ④), a campus of double-storey chalets set in a sandy garden behind the beach. The rooms are spacious, breezy and clean, and very good value if you don't mind being a bus ride away from Panjim. A short way back up the main road towards town, tucked down a suburban backstreet, the *Youth Hostel* (☎225432; ①) offers much cheaper accommodation, although its large dorms get horrendously cramped and stuffy when block-booked by students. The only hotels in Dona Paula are overpriced resort complexes permanently booked out to European charter companies.

Buses to Miramar and Dona Paula leave every fifteen minutes from Panjim's *Kadamba* stand. You can also pick them up from the steamer jetty, and at various points along the waterfront. Travelling in the other direction, they leave from in front of Dona Paula's *Institute of Oceanograpahy*, and stop at Miramar's main roundabout, in front of the *Yatri Niwas*.

Old Goa (Velha Goa)

At one time a byword for splendour, with a population of several hundred thousand, Goa's erstwhile capital, **OLD GOA (Velha Goa)**, was virtually abandoned following malaria and cholera epidemics that plagued the city from the seventeenth century onwards. Today you need considerable imagination to picture the once-great capital as it used to be. The maze of twisting streets, piazzas and ochre-washed villas has gone, and all that remains are a score of extraordinarily grandiose churches and convents. Granted World Heritage Status by *UNESCO*, Old Goa today attracts bus loads of foreign tourists from the coast, and Christian pilgrims from around India, in roughly equal numbers. While the former come to admire the gigantic facades and gilt altars of the beautifully preserved churches, the main attraction for the latter is the tomb of **St Francis Xavier**, the renowned sixteenth-century missionary, whose remains are enshrined in the **Basilica of Bom Jesus**.

If you are staying on the coast and contemplating a day trip inland, this is the most obvious and accessible option. Just thirty minutes by road from the state capital, Old

Goa is served by buses every fifteen minutes from Panjim's *Kadamba* bus stand; alternatively, hop into an auto-rickshaw, or rent a taxi. GTDC also slot the site's highlights into several of their guided coach **tours**; further details and tickets are available at any GTDC hotel or tourist office.

Arch of the Viceroys and the Church of St Cajetan

Upon arriving at the river landing stage to the north, seventeenth-century visitors passed through the **Arch of the Viceroys** (1597), constructed to commemorate Vasco da Gama's arrival in India and built from the same porous red laterite as virtually all Old Goa's buildings. Above it a bible-toting figure rests his foot on the cringing figure of a "native", while its granite facade, facing the river, holds a statue of da Gama himself. It is hard to imagine today that these overgrown fields, and simple streets with a few cool drinks stands, were once the focus of a lively market, with silk and gem merchants, horse dealers and carpet weavers. The one surviving monument, known as **Adil Shah's Gate**, predates the Portuguese, and possibly even the Muslim, period. Hindu in style, it consists simply of a lintel supported by two columns in black basalt, to which are attached the remains of perforated screens. You can find it by turning left at the crossroads immediatley above the Arch of the Viceroys.

A short way up the lane from the Gate, the distinctive domed **Church of St Cajetan** (1651) was modelled on St Peter's in Rome by monks from the Theatine order, who believed in Divine Providence; they never sought charity, but simply expected it. While it does boast a Corinthian exterior, you can also spot certain non-European elements in the decoration, such as the cashew-nut designs in the carving of the pulpit. Hidden beneath the church is a crypt where the embalmed bodies of Portuguese governors were once kept in lead coffins before they were shipped back to Lisbon. Forgotten for over thirty years, the last batch (of three) was only removed in 1992 on the eve of the state visit to Goa of Portuguese President Mario Soares.

The Sé (St Catherines' Cathedral)

The Portuguese Viceroy Redondo (1561–64) commissioned the **Sé**, or **St Catherines' Cathedral**, southwest of St Cajetan's, to be "a grandiose church worthy of the wealth, power and fame of the Portuguese who dominated the seas from the Atlantic to the Pacific". Today it stands larger than any church in Portugal, although it was beset by problems, not least a lack of funds and Portugal's temporary loss of independence to Spain. It took eighty years to build and was not consecrated until 1640.

On the Tuscan-style exterior, the one surviving tower houses the **Golden Bell**, cast in Cuncolim (south Goa) in the seventeenth century. During the Inquisition, its tolling announced the start of the gruseome *auto da fés* that were held in the square outside. Reconstruction of parts of the roof, which once had overhanging eaves, has damaged some paintings inside. The scale and detail of the Corinthian-style interior is overwhelming; huge pillars divide the central nave from the side aisles, and no less than fifteen altars are arranged around the walls, dedicated among others to Our Ladies of Hope, Anguish and Three Needs. An altar to St Anne treasures the relics of the **Blessed Martyrs of Cuncolim**, whose failed mission to convert the Moghul emperor Akbar culminated in their murder by Muslims, while a chapel behind a highly detailed screen holds the **Miraculous Cross**, which stood in a Goan village until a vision of Christ appeared on it. Said to heal the sick, it is kept in a box; a small opening on the side allows devotees to touch it. The staggeringly ornate gilded main **altar** comprises nine carved frames and a splendid crucifix. Panels depict episodes from the life of St Catherine of Alexandria (died 307 AD), including an interchange of ideas with the pagan Roman emperor Maxim, who wished to marry her, and her subsequent flogging and martyrdom.

The Church of St Francis of Assisi and Archeological Museum

Southwest of the Cathedral is the ruined **Palace of the Inquisition**, in operation up until 1774, while to the west stands the **Convent of St Francis of Assisi**, built by Franciscan monks in 1517 and restored in the mid-eighteenth century. Today, the core of its **Archeological Museum** (daily except Fri 10am–5pm) is a gallery of portraits of Portuguese viceroys, painted by local artists under Italian supervision. Other exhibits include coins, domestic Christian wooden sculpture, and downstairs in the cloister, pre-Portuguese Hindu sculpture. Next door, the **Church of St Francis** (1521), features fine decorative frescoes and paintings on wood showing the life of St Francis of Assisi.

Basilica of Bom Jesus

Close to the convent of St Francis, the 1605 church of **Bom Jesus**, "Good" or "Menino Jesus" (Mon–Sat 9am–6.30pm, Sun 10am–6.30pm), is known principally for the **tomb of St Francis Xavier**. In 1946, it became the first church in India to be elevated to the status of Minor Basilica. On the west, the three-storey Renaissance facade encompasses Corinthian, Doric, Ionic and Composite styles.

ST FRANCIS XAVIER

Francis Xavier, the "Apostle of the Indies", was born in 1506 in the old kingdom of Navarre, now part of Spain. After taking a masters' degree in philosophy and theology at the University of Paris, where he studied for the priesthood until 1535, he was ordained two years later in Venice. He was then recruited by (Saint) **Ignatius Loyola** (1491–1556) along with five other priests into the new "Society of Jesus", which later became known as the **Jesuits**.

When the Portuguese king, Dom Joao III (1521–57), received reports of corruption and dissolute behaviour among the Portuguese in Goa, he asked Ignatius Loyola to despatch a priest who could influence the moral climate for the better. In 1541 Xavier was sent to work in the diocese of Goa, constituted seven years before, and comprising all regions east of the Cape of Good Hope. Arriving after a year-long journey, he embarked on a busy programme throughout southern India. Despite frequent obstruction from Portuguese officials, he founded numerous churches, and is credited with converting 30,000 people and performing such miracles as raising the dead and curing the sick with a touch of his beads. Subsequently he took his mission further afield to Sri Lanka, Malacca (Malaysia), China and Japan where he was less successful.

When Xavier left Goa for the last time, it was with the ambition of evangelizing in China; however, he contracted dysentery aboard ship and died on the island of San Chuan (Sancian), off the Chinese coast, where he was buried. On hearing of his death, a group of Christians from Malacca exhumed his body – which, although the grave had been filled with lime, they found to be in a perfect state of preservation. Reburied in Malacca, it was later removed and taken to Old Goa, where it has remained ever since, enshrined in the Basilica of Bom Jesus.

However, Saint Francis' incorruptible corpse has never rested entirely in peace. Chunks of it have been removed over the years by relic hunters and curious clerics: in 1614, the right arm was dispatched to the Pope in Rome (where it allegedly wrote its name on paper), a hand was sent to Japan, and parts of the intestines to southeast Asia. One Portuguese woman, Dona Isabel de Caron, even bit off the little toe of the cadaver in 1534; apparently, so much blood spurted into her mouth, it left a trail to her house and she was discovered.

Every ten years, the saint's body is carried in a three-hour ceremony from the Basilica of Bom Jesus to the Sé Cathedral, where visitors file past, touch and photograph it. During the 1995 "**Exposition**", which is rumoured to be the last one, an estimated two million pilgrims flocked for *darshan* or ritual viewing of the corpse, these days a shrivelled and somewhat unsavoury spectacle.

The interior is entered beneath the choir, supported by columns. On the northern wall, in the centre of the nave, is a cenotaph in gilded bronze to **Dom Jeronimo Mascaranhas**, the Captain of Cochin and benefactor of the church. The main altar, extravagantly decorated in gold, depicts the infant Jesus under the protection of St Ignatius Loyola; to each side are subsidiary altars to Our Lady of Hope and St Michael. In the southern transept, lavishly decorated with twisted gilded columns and floriate carvings, stands the **Chapel and Tomb of St Francis Xavier**. Constructed of marble and jasper in 1696, it was the gift of the Medici, Cosimo III, the Grand Duke of Tuscany; the middle tier contains panels detailing the saint's life. An ornate domed reliquary in silver contains his remains; on his feast day, December 3, the saint's finger is displayed to devotees.

Holy Hill

A number of other important religious buildings, some in ruins, stand opposite Bom Jesus on **Holy Hill**. The **convent of St Monica**, constructed in 1627, destroyed by fire in 1636 and rebuilt the following year, was the only Goan convent at the time and the largest in Asia. It housed around a hundred nuns, the Daughters of St Monica, and also offered accommodation to women whose husbands were called away to other parts of the empire. The **church** adjoins the convent on the south. As they had to remain away from the public gaze, the nuns attended mass in the choir loft and looked down upon the congregation.

Inside, a **Miraculous Cross** rises above the figure of St Monica at the altar. In 1636, it was reported that the figure of Christ had opened his eyes, motioned as if to speak and blood had flowed from the wounds made by his crown of thorns. The last Daughter of St Monica died in 1885, and since 1964 the convent has been occupied by the Mater Dei Institute for nuns.

Nearby, the **Convent of St John of God**, built in 1685 by the Order of Hospitallers of St John of God to tend to the sick, was rebuilt in 1953. At the top of the hill, the **Chapel of Our Lady of the Rosary**, built in 1526 in the Manueline style (after the Portuguese king Manuel I, 1495–1521), features Ionic plasterwork with a double-storey portico, cylindrical turrets and a tower that commands fine views across the river.

Ponda and around

Characterless, chaotic **PONDA**, 28km southeast of Panjim and 17km northeast of Margao, is Ponda *taluka*'s administrative headquarters and main market town, but not somewhere you're likely to want to stay. Straddling the busy Panjim–Bangalore highway (NH4), the town's ugly ferro-concrete centre is permanently choked with traffic, and guaranteed to make you wonder why you ever left the coast. Of the few visitors who stop here, most do so en route to the nearby **Hindu temples** or **wildlife reserves** farther east, or to take a look at Goa's best-preserved sixteenth-century Muslim monument, the **Safa Masjid**, 2km west on the Panjim road. Built in 1560 by the Bijapuri ruler Ibrahim 'Adil Shah, this small mosque, with its whitewashed walls and pointed terracotta tile roof, is renowned less for its run-of-the-mill architecture than for being one of only two Islamic shrines in Goa to survive the excesses of the Portuguese Inquisition.

Practicalities

Ponda is served by regular **buses** from Panjim (via Old Goa), and Margao, and lies on the main route east to Karnataka. The *Kadamba* bus stand is on the main square, next to the auto-rickshaw rank.

There are plenty of **places to stay** if you get stuck here. Best of the budget lodges is the *Padmavi* (no phone; ①) at the top of the square. For more comfort, try the *President* (☎08343/312287; ③–⑤), a short rickshaw ride up the Belgaum road, which has large, clean en-suite rooms (some with a/c). More upmarket is the 3-star *Atash*

(☎08343/312239; fax 313239; ⑤), 4km northwest on the NH4 at **Farmagudi**, whose comfortable a/c rooms have satellite TV, and there's also a restaurant and parking facilities. However, the best mid-range deal within striking distance of Ponda has to be GTDC's *Tourist Cottages* (☎08343/312932; ②–④), also at Farmagudi (look for the signpost on the roundabout below the Shivaji memorial), stacked up the side of a steep hill overlooking the highway, with spacious and clean en-suite chalets, and a small terrace restaurant serving a standard menu of spicy mixed cuisine.

Temples around Ponda

Scattered among the lush valleys and forests **around Ponda** are a dozen or so **Hindu temples** founded during the seventeenth and eighteenth centuries, when this hilly region was a Christian-free haven for Hindus fleeing persecution by the Portuguese. Although the temples themselves are fairly modern by Indian standards, their deities are ancient and held in high esteem by both local people and thousands of pilgrims from Maharashtra and Karnataka.

The temples are concentrated in two main clusters: the first to the north of Ponda, on the busy NH4, and the second deep in the countryside, around 5km west of the town. Most people only manage the **Shri Manguesh** and **Shri Mahalsa**, between the villages of **Mardol** and **Priol**. Among the most interesting temples in the state, they lie just a stone's throw from the main highway and are passed by regular **buses** between Panjim and Margao via Ponda. The others are farther off the beaten track, although they are not hard to find on motorbikes: locals will wave you in the right direction if you get lost. Alternatively, book one of GTDC's **guided tours**, the least rushed of which is the "Pilgrims' Special" (depart Panjim 9.30am, return 1pm; Rs50).

Mardol and Priol

Although the **Sri Manguesh** temple originally stood in a secret location in Cortalim, and was moved to its present site between **MARDOL** and **PRIOL** during the sixteenth century, what visitors see today dates from the 1700s. A gateway at the roadside leads to a paved path and courtyard that gives on to a water tank, overlooked by the white temple building, raised on a plinth. Also in the courtyard is a seven-storey *deepmal*, a tower for oil lamps. Inside, the floor is paved with marble, and bands of decorative tiles emblazon the white walls. Flanked by large *dvarpala* guardians, embossed silver doorways with floriate designs lead to the sanctum, which houses a *shivalingam*.

Two kilometres south, the **Mahalsa Marayani** temple was also transferred from its original site, in this case Salcete *taluka* further south, in the seventeenth century. Here, the *deepmal* is exceptionally tall, with twenty-one tiers rising from a figure of Kurma, the tortoise incarnation of Vishnu. Original features include a marble-floored wooden *mandapa* (assembly hall) with carved pillars, ceiling panels of parakeets and, in the eaves, sculptures of the incarnations of Vishnu.

Dudhsagar waterfalls

Measuring a mighty 600m from head to foot, the famous **waterfalls** at **DUDHSAGAR**, on the Goa–Karnataka border, are some of the highest in India, and a spectacular enough sight to entice a steady stream of visitors from the coast into the rugged Western Ghats. After pouring across the Deccan plateau, the headwaters of the Mandovi River form a foaming torrent that fans into three streams, then cascades down a near-vertical cliff face into a deep green pool. The Konkani name for the falls, which literally translated means "sea of milk", derives from clouds of foam kicked up at the bottom when the water levels are at their highest. Overlooking a steep, crescent-shaped head of a valley carpeted with pristine tropical forest, Dudhsagar is also set amid breathtaking **scenery** that is only accessible on foot or by train (the line actually passes over the falls on an old stone viaduct).

Practicalities

The best time to visit Dudhsagar is immediately after the monsoons (Oct–Dec), although the falls flow well into April. **Getting there** from the coast involves making a train journey from Vasco (2hr 45min) or Margao (2hr 15min): aim to catch the *Vasco Express* #7830, which leaves Vasco da Gama station at 7.15am. You can also pick this service up at **Colem** (not to be confused with Calem, the previous stop), in the Bhagwan Mahaveer Sanctuary near Molem at around 9.30am; check the departure times in advance with *Indian Railways* as timetables are currently being revised. GTDC also operate good-value guided **tours** to the falls; details and tickets are available at any of their offices or hotels.

North Goa

Beyond the mouth of the Mandovi estuary, the Goan coast sweeps **north** in a near-continuous string of beaches, broken only by the odd salt-water creek, rocky headland, and three tidal rivers – two of which, the Chapora and Arondem, have to be crossed by ferry. The most developed resorts, **Calangute** and **Baga**, occupy the middle and northern part of the seven-kilometre strip of pearl-white sand that stretches from the Aguada peninsula in the south to a sheer laterite promontory in the north. Formerly, the infamous colonies of Goa hippies gathered in these two villages during their annual winter migration; now both heave during high season with British charter tourists, bus loads of trippers from out-of-state and itinerant vendors hawking fruit and trinkets on the beach. The "scene", meanwhile, has shifted northwards, to the beaches around **Anjuna**, **Vagator**, and **Chapora**, where most Christmas–New Year parties take place.

Most of the tourist traffic **arriving in north Goa** from Bombay is syphoned off towards the coast through **Mapusa**, the area's main market town. For short hops between towns and resorts, **motorcycle taxis** are the quickest and most convenient way to get around, but **buses** also run to all the villages along the coast, via the **ferry crossings** at Siolim, 7km north of Anjuna, and Querim (for Terekol).

> All telephone area **phone codes** in North Goa are ☎0832.

Mapusa

The ramshackle market town of **MAPUSA** (pronounced *Map*sa) is the district headquarters of Bardez *taluka*. If you arrive by road from Bombay and plan to stay in one of the north Goan resorts, you can jump off the bus here and pick up a local service straight to the coast, rather than continue on to Panjim, 13km south.

A dusty collection of dilapidated modern buildings scattered around the west-facing slope of a low hill, Mapusa is of little more than passing interest in itself, although on Fridays it hosts a lively **market** (hence the town's name, which derives from the Konkani words for "measure", *map*, and "fill up", *sa*). Calangute and Anjuna may be better stocked with souvenirs, but this bazaar is more authentic. Visitors who have flown straight to Goa, and have yet to experience the rest of India, wander in on Friday mornings to enjoy the pungent aromas of fish, incense, spices and exotic fruit stacked in colourful heaps on the sidewalks. Local specialities include strings of spicy Goan sausages (*chouriço*), bottles of *todi* and large green plantains. You'll also encounter sundry freak shows, from run-of-the-mill snake charmers and kids dressed up as *sadhus*, to wide-eyed flagellants, blood oozing out of slashes on their backs.

Getting around

Other than to shop, you may want to visit Mapusa to arrange **onward transport**. All buses between Goa and Maharashtra pass through, so you don't need to travel to Panjim to book a ticket to Bombay, Pune, Bangalore or Mangalore. Reservations for private buses can be made at the numerous agents' stalls at the bottom of the square, next to where the buses pull in; the **Kadamba terminal** – the departure point for both long-distance state buses, and local services to Calangute, Baga, Anjuna, Vagator, Chapora, and Arambol – is five minutes' walk down the main road, on the southwest edge of town. You can also get to the coast from Mapusa on one of the **motorcycle taxis** that wait at the bottom of the square. Rides to Calangute and Anjuna take twenty minutes, and cost Rs30–40. **Taxis** charge considerably more, but you can split the fare with up to five people.

As soon as you step off the bus, you'll be pestered by touts trying to get you to rent a **motorbike**. They'll tell you that rates here are lower than on the coast – they're not. Another reason to wait a while is that Mapusa is effectively a "no-go zone" for rented motorbikes, especially on Friday, when the police set up road-blocks on the outskirts of town to collar tourists without international licences (see p.721).

Accommodation and eating

Nearly all long-distance buses pull in to Mapusa in the morning, leaving plenty of time to find **accommodation** in the coastal resorts nearby. If you have to spend the night here, though, there are plenty of places within easy walking distance of the *Kadamba* bus stand. The best deal is GTDC's *Tourist Resort* (☎262794; ③–⑤), on the roundabout below the square, which has spacious and clean rooms, a Goa **tourist information** counter, and a small *Damania Airways* office. *Hotel Trishul* (☎262700; ②–④), a large, no-frills lodge tucked away in the back streets above the main square, is a good fall-back. To find it, head along the lane up the hill past the Maruti (Hanuman) temple, and take the second turning on the right towards the Mapusa Clinic. For a little more comfort, try *Hotel Satyaheera* (☎262849; ③–⑤), at the top of the square opposite the temple, which offers some a/c rooms with bathrooms and hot water.

Mapusa's most relaxing **restaurant** is the *Ruchira*, on the top floor of the *Hotel Satyaheera*, which serves a standard Indian menu with Goan and Chinese alternatives, and cold beer. The *Hotel Vrindavan*, on the east side of the main square, dishes up Mapusa's best inexpensive Indian-style snacks, along with an impressive range of ice-creams and shakes. Cheaper but less salubrious Goan *thali* joints can be found in the streets east of the main square. Excellent fresh fruit and juice bars are dotted around the market.

Candolim, Aguada Fort and Sinquerim

Four or five years ago, **CANDOLIM**, at the far southern end of Calangute beach, was a surprisingly sedate resort, appealing to an odd mixture of middle-class Bombayites, and burgundy-clad *sanyasins* taking a break from the Rajneesh ashram at Pune. Times, however, have changed. Now, large-scale package holiday complexes jostle for space behind the dunes, and the increasingly crowded beach has sprouted ranks of over-priced sun beds. Worse still is the constant swoosh of speed boats, jet skis and huge inflatable banana-rafts through the surf: tourist Goa at its most gruesome.

Immediately south of Candolim, a long peninsula extends into the sea, bringing the seven-kilometre white sandy beach to an abrupt end. **AGUADA FORT**, which crowns the rocky flattened top of the headland, is the best-preserved Portuguese bastion in Goa. Built in 1612 to protect the northern shores of the Mandovi estuary from Dutch and Maharatha raiders, it is home to several natural springs, the first source of drinking water available to ships arriving in Goa after the long sea voyage from Lisbon. On the north side of the fort, a rampart of red-brown laterite juts into the bay to form a jetty between two small sandy coves. This picturesque spot, known as **SINQUERIM Beach**, was among the first places in Goa to be singled out for upmarket tourism. *Taj Group*'s *Fort Aguada* resorts, among the most expensive hotels in India, lords over the beach from the lower slopes of the steep-sided peninsula.

The ruins of the **fort** can be reached by road; head through the *Taj* village, and turn right when you see the sign. Nowadays, much of the site serves as a prison, and is therefore closed to visitors. It's worth a visit, though, if only for the superb views from the top of the hill where a four-storey Portuguese **lighthouse**, erected in 1864 and the oldest of its kind in Asia, looks down over the vast expanse of sea, sand and palm trees of Calangute beach on one side, and across the mouth of the Mandovi to Cabo Raj Bhavan, and the tip of the Mormugao peninsula, on the other.

Arrival and accommodation

Buses to and from Panjim stop every twenty minutes or so at the stand opposite the *Casa Sea Shell*, in the middle of Candolim. A few also continue south to the the *Fort Aguada Beach Resort* terminus, from where services depart every thirty minutes to the capital via Nerul village. **Taxis** wait outside the major resort hotels and can be flagged down on the main road.

Candolim is charter-holiday land, so **accommodation** tends to be expensive, and hard to find, for most of the season. The best place to look is at the end of the lane that leads to the sea opposite the *Canara Bank*, at the north side of the village.

Costa Nicola, Vaddi (☎0276343; fax 277343). Beautifully maintained Portuguese-style villa set in a relaxing garden. All rooms with verandahs; a recommended small-scale resort. ⑦.

Fort Aguada Beach Resort, including *Aguada Hermitage* and *Taj Holiday Village*, Sinquerim beach (☎77501; fax 277733). 5-star opulence in hermetically sealed, immaculately manicured vacation campus. Pools, but no private beach. Accused of infringing environmental laws. ⑨.

Manuel's, Murrod Vaddo (no phone). Small, friendly, inexpensive, and in a quiet location. ③–④.

Sea Shell Inn, Fort Aguada Rd, opposite the *Canara Bank* (☎276131). Comfortable hotel on the roadside with a so-so terrace restaurant. ⑤.

Ti Bhat, Murrod Vaddo (no phone). Simple attached rooms in one of Candolim's few remaining small, family-run guest houses. ③.

Xavier Beach Resort, Fort Aguada Rd, opposite the *State Bank of India* (no phone). Peaceful, with luxurious rooms, large verandahs and views from sea-facing windows. ⑥.

Eating and drinking

Candolim's numerous beach **cafes** are a cut above your average seafood shacks, with pot plants, state-of-the-art sound systems and prices to match. Basically, the farther from the *Taj* complex you venture, the more realistic the prices become. The main road is also dotted with restaurants serving the usual selection of fresh-fish dishes, with a handful of continental options thrown in.

Bom Successo, Fort Aguada Rd. Eclectic menu, occasional live jazz and classical Indian dance every Thursday.

Melza, near the *Fort Aguada Beach Resort*, Fort Aguada Rd. Tasty Chinese food and great seafood.

Nezvila, Dando. The best of the bunch down by the *Taj*, specializing in extravagant seafood dishes.

Sea Shell, Fort Aguada Rd. A congenial terrace restaurant that cooks seafood and sizzling meat meals to order – also good for vegetarians and anyone fed up with spicy Indian food.

GOAN FOOD AND DRINK

Goa has few of the dietary restrictions or taboos that apply in other regions of India, both Hindu and Muslim. Here the idea of vegetarianism is probably more equated with poverty than purity, and drinking alcohol is not the shameful activity it is elsewhere. The Goan palate relishes meat, especially pork, and all kinds of fresh seafood.

Not unnaturally, after 450 years of colonization, Goan cooking has absorbed a strong Portuguese influence. Palm vinegar (unknown elsewhere in India), copious amounts of coconut, garlic, tangy tamarind and fierce local chillies all play their part. Goa is the home of the famous vindaloo, originally an extra-hot and sour pork curry, but now made with a variety of meat and fish. If you like to pig-out on pork, try chouriço red sausages, sarpotel, a hot curry made from pickled pig's liver and heart, or suckling pig or balchaon, pork in a rich brown sauce. Delicious alternatives include vinegar chicken, spicy chicken or mutton xacutti, made with a sauce of lemon juice, peanuts, coconut, chillies and spices. The choice of seafood, often cooked in fragrant masalas, is excellent – clams, mussels, crab, lobster, giant prawns – while fish, depending on the type, is either cooked in wet curries, grilled, or baked in tandoor clay ovens. Try *apa de camarão*, a spicy prawn pie with a rice and semolina crust. *Sannam*, like the south Indian *iddli*, is a steamed cake of fermented rice flour, but here fermented with palm toddy. Sweet tooths will adore *bebinca*, a rich, delicious solid egg custard with coconut.

As for drinks, locally produced wine, spirits and beer are cheaper than anywhere in the country. Red wine tends to be sweet, not unlike port; white, both still and sparkling, is considered an unpretentious tipple. Whisky, brandy, rum, gin and vodka come in a variety of brand names for less than Rs10 a shot, but at half the price, local speciality *feni*, made from distilled cashew or from the sap of coconut palms, offers strong competition. Cashew *feni* is usually drunk after the first distillation, but you can also find it double-distilled, flavoured with ginger, cumin or sasparilla to produce a smooth liqueur.

Calangute

A mere 45-minute bus ride up the coast from the capital, **CALANGUTE** is Goa's busiest and most commercialized resort, and the flagship of the state government's recent bid for a bigger slice of India's package-tourist pie. In the 1970s and early 1980s, this once-peaceful fishing village epitomized Goa's popular reputation as a haven for hedonistic hippies. Indian visitors flocked by the bus load from Bombay and Bangalore to giggle at the tribes of dreadlocked Westerners lying naked on the vast white sandy beach, stoned out of their brains on local *feni* and cheap *charas*. The odd party of prurient day-trippers still arrives from time to time, but invariably leaves disappointed; Calangute has cleaned up its act. Apart from the handful of stalwart budget travellers' bars and guest houses on the edges of the town, the "scene" has been almost entirely squeezed out by more mainstream holiday culture. Hoteliers today joke about the old days, when they used to rent out makeshift shacks on the beach to backpackers. Now many of them manage tailor-made tourist settlements, complete with air-conditioned rooms, swimming pools and lush lawns, for groups of suitcase-carrying fortnighters.

Though heavily developed by Goan standards, Calangute is still a long way from the high-rise hell that many Asian resorts have become in recent years. Away from the narrow congested main road that runs from the bustling central market square to nearby Baga, most hotels are small, double-storeyed buildings, hidden among the dunes behind a noise-proof curtain of coconut trees. However, as the rash of construction sites around the outskirts blossom into larger resort complexes, what little charm Calangute retains looks set to disappear. Without adequate provision for sewage treatment or increased water consumption, it's only a matter of time before the town starts to stew in its own juices, putting off the very tourists the developers are trying to attract.

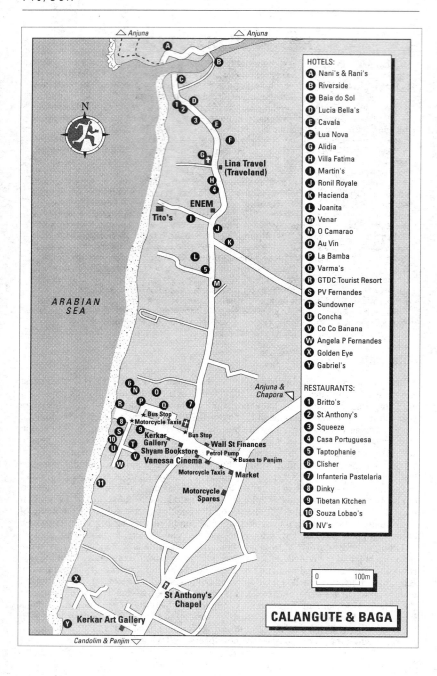

△ Anjuna   △ Anjuna

N

ARABIAN
SEA

HOTELS:
Ⓐ Nani's & Rani's
Ⓑ Riverside
Ⓒ Baia do Sol
Ⓓ Lucia Bella's
Ⓔ Cavala
Ⓕ Lua Nova
Ⓖ Alidia
Ⓗ Villa Fatima
Ⓘ Martin's
Ⓙ Ronil Royale
Ⓚ Hacienda
Ⓛ Joanita
Ⓜ Venar
Ⓝ O Camarao
Ⓞ Au Vin
Ⓟ La Bamba
Ⓠ Varma's
Ⓡ GTDC Tourist Resort
Ⓢ PV Fernandes
Ⓣ Sundowner
Ⓤ Concha
Ⓥ Co Co Banana
Ⓦ Angela P Fernandes
Ⓧ Golden Eye
Ⓨ Gabriel's

RESTAURANTS:
❶ Britto's
❷ St Anthony's
❸ Squeeze
❹ Casa Portuguesa
❺ Taptophanie
❻ Clisher
❼ Infanteria Pastelaria
❽ Dinky
❾ Tibetan Kitchen
❿ Souza Lobao's
⓫ NV's

Lina Travel
(Traveland)

ENEM

Tito's

Anjuna &
Chapora

Bus Stop
Motorcycle Taxis
Kerkar
Gallery
Shyam Bookstore
Vanessa Cinema
Bus Stop
Wall St Finances
Petrol Pump
Buses to Panjim
Motorcycle Taxis   Market
Motorcycle
Spares

0   100m

St Anthony's
Chapel

Kerkar Art Gallery

Candolim & Panjim ▽

CALANGUTE & BAGA

Arrival and information

Buses from Mapusa and Panjim pull in at the small bus stand-cum-market square in the centre of Calangute. Some continue to Baga, stopping at the crossroads behind the beach en route. Get off here if you can (as the main road veers sharply to the right); it's closer to most of the hotels. **Motorcycle taxis** hang around the little sandy square behind GTDC's *Tourist Resort*, next to the steps that drop down to the beachfront. Ask around here if you want to rent a **motorcycle**. Rates are standard; the nearest **filling station** ("petrol pump") is five minutes' walk from the beach, back towards the market on the right-hand side of the main road. **Bicycles** are also widely available for Rs20 to Rs25 per day.

There's a *State Bank of India* on the main street, but the best place to **change money** and travellers' cheques is *Wall Street Finances* (Mon–Sat 8.30am–7pm, Sun 10am–2pm), opposite the petrol pump and in the shopping complex on the beach front. If they are closed, try the fast and friendly *ENEM Finances* in Baga; they are open late (daily 8am–9pm), but offer poorer rates. For flight reconfirmation, and air, train and bus ticketing, try *MGM Travels* (☎0832/276703), on the roundabout opposite *Shyam Books*; *Royal Tours and Travels* (☎0832276109), opposite the GTDC *Tourist Resort*; or *Sea Breeze Travels* around the corner from *Royal Tours and Travels* on the main road.

The town and beach

The road from the **town** to the beach is lined with Kashmiri-run handicraft boutiques and Tibetan stalls selling Himalayan curios and jewellery. The quality of the goods – mainly Rajasthani, Gujarati and Karnatakan textiles – is generally high, as are the prices. Haggle hard and don't be afraid to walk away from a heavy sales pitch – the same stuff crops up every Wednesday at Anjuna's flea market. The **beach** itself is nothing special, with steeply shelving sand, but is more than large enough to accommodate the huge numbers of high-season visitors. Most of the action centres on the beachfront below GTDC's unsightly *Tourist Resort*, where crowds of Indian women in *saris* and straw hats stand around watching their sons and husbands frolic in the surf. Nearby, stray cows nose through the rubbish left by the previous bus party, while an endless stream of ice-cream and fruit sellers, *lunghi-wallahs*, ear cleaners and masseurs, work their way through the ranks of Western sun-worshippers.

To escape the melee, head fifteen minutes or so south of the main beachfront area, towards the rows of old wooden boats moored below the dunes. In this virtually hawker-free zone, you'll only come across teams of villagers hauling in hand-nets at high tide or fishermen fixing their tack under bamboo sun shades. Wherever you go, though, remember that Calangute's **"no nudism"** rule is for real and enforced by special police patrols; this includes topless bathing. In addition, several incidents of **sexual harassment** and attempted rape have occurred here in recent years.

Courses in Asthanya (Vinyasa) **yoga** are given by a British teacher at *The Practise Place*, down the lane behind the *Flying Dutchman* art gallery. Most participants book in the UK, arranging accommodation when they arrive, although walk-in punters are welcome if there are places.

Accommodation

Calangute is chock-full of **places to stay**. Demand only outstrips supply in the Christmas–New Year high season; at other times, haggle a little over the tariff, especially if the place looks empty. Most of the **inexpensive accommodation** consists of small rooms in family homes, or in concrete annexes tacked onto the backs of houses. Though bare and basic, these usually have running water and fans. For a little extra, you can get a verandah or a balcony, and an attached bathroom; nowhere is far from the shore, but sea views are more of a rarity. The **top hotels** are nearly all gleaming white, exclusive villa complexes with pools, and direct beach access. High-season rates in such places are staggeringly steep, as they cater almost solely for package tourists.

Angela P Fernandes, Umta Vaddo, south of beachfront. Calangute's most popular budget travellers' hang-out. Basic but fairly clean, with reliable water, fans and psychedelic murals. Cheaper rooms around the back. ①–②.

Au Vin, 5/193 Umta Vaddo, behind the bus park. Six neat, clean rooms (some attached) in a hospitable family guest house. Good home cooking, too. ②.

CoCo Banana, 5/139A Umta Vaddo, down the lane past *Meena Lobo's* restaurant (☎0832/276478). Very comfortable chalets, all with bath and balcony, grouped around a garden. Good value. ⑤.

Concha, Umta Vaddo (☎0832/276506). Stylish old-colonial villa, with banana plants in the garden, mosquito nets, verandahs and well-furnished rooms. Worth the extra. ⑦.

Gabriel's, just south of *Golden Eye*, Guara Vaddo (no phone). A congenial family-run guest house mid-way between Calangute and Candolim, and close to the beach. Recommended. ⑤–⑥.

Golden Eye, A-1/189 Gaura Vaddo (☎ & fax 0832/276187). Spacious rooms, balconies, sea views and a terrace restaurant, all on the beach. ⑥.

GTDC Tourist Resort, overlooking the steps to the beach (☎0832/276024). The last resort: a grim concrete block with marginally less hideous cottages adjacent. The rates aren't bad, though. ④–⑤.

La Bamba, next to GTDC *Tourist Resort* (☎0832/276108). Small, cosy and well-maintained guest house close to the beach. Some sea-facing rooms. ④.

O Camarão, 5/201 Umta Vaddo, just north of GTDC *Tourist Resort* (☎0832/276229). Spruce, blue-and white-painted bungalow with immaculate rooms, verandahs and a restaurant. Good value. ③.

P V Fernandes, near *Angela P Fernandes* (no phone). Old-fashioned Portuguese bungalow threatened by advancing dunes. Bare rooms with old beds and common shower-toilets. Overpriced. ③.

Sundowner Holiday Home, 5/128 Umta Vaddo, behind *Tibetan Kitchen* (no phone). Large, good-value rooms, some with fans and attached baths. ③.

Varma's Beach Resort, two minutes' east of GTDC *Tourist Resort* (☎0832/272222). Attractive a/c rooms, with balconies overlooking a leafy garden. Secluded but close to the centre of the village. ⑦.

Eating and drinking

Calangute's **bars** and **restaurants** are mainly grouped around the entrance to the beach and along the Baga road. As with most Goan resorts, the accent is firmly on **seafood**, though many places tack on a few token veggie dishes. Western breakfasts (pancakes, porridge, muesli, eggs, etc) also feature prominently.

Mr Cater's, GTDC *Tourist Resort*. Bustling terrace restaurant overlooking the beach and serving moderately priced *tandoori* seafood, meat sizzlers, *xacuti*, *cafreal* and a range of Indian veg dishes.

Clisher, north of GTDC *Tourist Resort*, behind the beach. Best of the beachside bar-restaurants, with the usual fresh seafood, good breakfasts, cold beer and sea views.

Dinky, beside the steps to the beach. Standard seafood and beer bar, with a pleasant verandah for crowd watching. Popular with budget travellers.

Gabriel's, near *Golden Eye*, Gaura Vaddo. Great Goan seafood and blow-out buffets for lunch.

Infantaria Pastelaria, near St John's Chapel, Baga Rd. Small roadside terrace packed out at breakfast time for piping-hot croissants or freshly baked apple pie.

NV's, south Calangute. A ten-minute trek down the beach, but well worth it for no-nonsense platefuls of grilled fish, calamari and crab, all fresh from the family boat.

Souza Lobo, on the beachfront. One of Goa's oldest restaurants and deservedly famous for its superb seafood; try their fish sizzlers or mouthwatering tiger prawns.

Tibetan Kitchen, off the beach road. Filling Tibetan food, including tasty cheese-fried *momo* and home-made cakes, Western and Chinese options, and breakfasts. New Age music and chess.

Nightlife and entertainment

Due to a concerted crackdown by the Goan police on beach parties and loud music, Calangute's **nightlife** is surprisingly tame. All but a handful of the **bars** wind up by 10pm, leaving punters to prolong the short evenings back at their hotels. One notable exception is *Tito's*, at the Baga end of the beach, which stays open until 11pm off season and into the small hours in late December and January. Calangute's trendiest (and priciest) night spot, this boasts a large sandy terrace overlooking the beach, a small dance floor and a powerful techno sound system. The only other places that consistently open late are a couple of dull hippy hangouts in the woods south of the beach road: *Pete's Bar*, a perennial favourite next door to *Angela P Fernandes*, is generally the liveliest, offering cheap drinks, backgammon sets and relentless reggae.

Farther afield, *Bob's Inn*, between Calangute and Candolim, is another popular bar, famed less for its tasty Western food than the group of ageing "heads" that holds court around a table in the back. Also worth a try while you're down that way are the shack bars around the *Golden Eye*, several of which host lively late-night drinking sessions.

The *Kerkar Art Gallery*, in Gaurwaddo, at the south end of town (☎276017), puts on evenings of **classical music and dance** (Tues & Sat 6.30–8pm), held in the back garden on a sumptuously decorated stage, complete with incense and evocative candlelight. The recitals, by students and teachers from Panjim's Kala Academy, are kept comfortably short, and are preceded by a short introductory talk. Tickets, available in advance or at the door, cost Rs150.

Baga

BAGA, 10km west of Mapusa, is basically an extension of Calangute; not even the locals agree where one ends and the other begins. Lying in the lee of a rocky, wooded headland, the only difference between this far northern end of the beach and its more congested centre is that the scenery here is marginally more varied and picturesque. A small river flows into the sea at the top of the village, below a broad spur of soft white sand, from where a dirt track strikes across an expanse of paddy fields towards Anjuna. The old red-tiled fishers' houses behind the dunes have long been swamped by bars, restaurants, handicraft shops and guest houses, but you don't feel quite so hemmed in as at Calangute. The river also marks the northernmost limits of mass tourism in Goa. Across the hideous concrete bridge that links Baga with the far bank, you enter a tranquil hinterland of coconut plantations peppered with tiny Hindu farming hamlets.

Most of the action in Baga revolves around the sandy square and bus park at the top of the village, where the main metalled road from Calangute peters out and the buses roll in from Mapusa and Panjim, 18km southeast. The restaurants nearby do a brisk trade during the day and stay open late in the evening, when they fill up with punters from the nearby resort hotels. Farther south, a row of lookalike bamboo beach bars compete for custom with uniformly raucous techno music systems.

Accommodation

Accommodation is harder to arrange on spec in Baga than Calangute, as most of the hotels have been carved up by the charter companies; even rooms in smaller guest houses tend to be booked up well before the season gets under way. If you're keen to stay, you may have to hole up farther down the beach for a night while you hunt around for a vacancy. The rough-and-ready places dotted around the fishing village usually have space; look for signs on the main square. Cheap houses and rooms for rent are also available on the quieter north side of the river, although these are like gold dust in December and January.

Alidia, Baga Rd (no phone). Attractive modern chalet rooms with good sized verandahs looking on to the dunes. Quiet and friendly. Recommended. ④.

Baia do Sol, on the square (☎276084). Baga's best (2-star) hotel is modern, immaculate and surrounded by a well-kept garden. No single occupancy in high season. Some a/c. ⑦.

Cavala, on the main road (☎276090). Modern building in tastefully traditional mould; simple rooms, bathrooms en suite and separate balconies. ⑥.

Hacienda, Baga Rd (☎277348). Nothing special but has big, airy rooms, balconies and a garden. ⑤.

BOATS TO THE ANJUNA FLEA MARKET

Every Wednesday, **boats** leave Baga beach for the flea market at Anjuna (see opposite), from around 9am until just before sunset. How much you pay for the twenty-minute trip depends on how many passengers the fishermen manage to cram on board, but it usually works out the same as a motorcycle taxi. If you go, pack your cameras and any valuables in a plastic bag. Accidents occasionally happen when the fishermen load their vessels to the gunwales and then try to save time and fuel by cutting through a narrow channel between two rocks – straightforward enough on calm days, but a hair-raising stunt when the sea is choppy.

Joanita, Baga Rd (no phone). Clean, airy rooms with attached baths and some double beds, all ranged around quiet garden. ③.

Lua Nova, north of the main road, near the *Cavala Hotel* (☎276288). Peaceful and cosy; sun beds on the lawn and individual balconies, though a bit boxed in by its multi-storey neighbour. ⑤.

Lucia Bella's, 7/173A Baga Rd (no phone). Cramped and not really pleasant enough for a lengthy stay, but fine as a stopover until you find your feet. ②.

Martin's, 1928 Cobra Vaddo (no phone). Eight simple rooms, some with balconies, in a small two-storey family house. Good value. ②.

Nani's and Rani's, north of the river (no phone). A handful of red-tiled, whitewashed cottages in a secluded back garden, popular with long-staying guests. Fans, common toilets, well water and an outdoor shower. Recommended. ②.

Riverside, on the square (☎6062). New, tasteful hotel with large comfy rooms, a good restaurant and river views. Moving into the package bracket, but the best value at this price. ⑤.

Ronil Royale, Baga Rd (☎276096). Ersatz Portuguese apartments overlooking two small pools, with a swish restaurant. A ten-minute walk from the beach. ⑦.

Venar, 1963 Cobra Vaddo (no phone). Large, immaculately neat rooms (some attached) in an old Portuguese-style house. Discount for singles. One of the best budget deals in town. ③.

Villa Fatima, Baga Rd (☎27605). Twenty-seven attached rooms around a sociable garden terrace. Popular with overlanders. Good value. ⑤.

Eating and drinking

Food options in Baga are confined to the open-air restaurants clustered around the square at the top end of the village and the no-frills **cafes** behind the beach. For a splurge, splash out on a candlelit dinner in the *Casa Portuguesa*, around the corner from Calangute's most popular nightclub, *Tito's* (see p.742).

For some reason *Vicky's* bar draws a bigger crowd than the others, but they all charge the same for a beer and swing well into the night during the season.

Britto's, on the square. Currently the most popular restaurant in the village, with a predictable menu of reasonably priced seafood and Western dishes, and some Goan specialities.

Casa Portuguesa, Baga Rd. Traditional Portuguese and Goan food served by candlelight inside this romantic colonial villa or *al fresco* on a leafy lawn. The gregarious owner serenades diners with Amelia Rodrigues *fados* most evenings. Pricey, but worth it for the atmosphere.

Nani's and Rani's, north of the river. Friendly family-run restaurant serving unremarkable but inexpensive food on a sociable verandah overlooking the river. Popular with budget travellers.

Squeeze, Baga Rd. Painstakingly prepared, healthy Western food with an Italian bias. Specialities include home-made pasta, hummus rolls and chocolate cake. Cocktails with a kick. Inexpensive.

St Anthony's, off the square. The place to watch the sunset accompanied by an icy beer and Indian classical music on a better-than-average sound system. The main meals are a touch pricey, though.

Taptophanie, Baga Rd. Laid-back terrace cafe and clothes store that's strong on Western food: brown bread, apple pie, muesli, cakes, light meals and espresso.

Valerio's, next door to *Hotel Baia do Sol*. Sophisticated bar-restaurant with good sea and river views from a pleasant first-floor terrace. Live music on Wednesdays after the flea market.

Anjuna

With its fluorescent-painted palm trees and infamous full-moon parties, **ANJUNA**, 8km west of Mapusa, is Goa at its most "alternative". Designer leather and lycra may have superseded cotton kaftans, but most people's reasons for coming are the same as they were in the 1970s: drugs, dancing and lying on the beach slurping tropical fruit. Depending on your point of view, you'll find the headlong hedonism a total turn-off or heaven-on-sea. Either way, the scene looks here to stay, despite government attempts to stamp it out, so you might as well get a taste of it while you're in the area, if only from the wings, with a day trip to the famous **flea market**.

One of the main sources of Anjuna's enduring popularity as a hippy hang-out is its superb **beach**. Fringed by groves of swaying coconut palms, the classical curve of soft white sand conforms more closely to the archetypal vision of paradise than any other beach on the north coast. Bathing is generally safer than at most of the nearby resorts, too, especially at the more peaceful southern end, where a rocky headland keeps the sea calm and the undertow to a minimum. North of the market ground, the beach broadens, running in an uninterrupted kilometre-long stretch of steeply shelving sand to a low red cliff. The village bus park lies on top of this high ground, near a crop of small cafes, bars and Kashmiri handicraft stalls. Every lunchtime, tour parties from Panjim pull in here for a beer, before heading home again, leaving the ragged army of sun-weary Westerners to enjoy the sunset. The season in Anjuna starts in early November, when most of the long-staying regulars show up, and peters out in late March, when they drift off again. During the Christmas

THE ANJUNA FLEA MARKET

Anjuna's Wednesday **flea market** is the hub of Goa's alternative scene, and *the* place to indulge in a spot of souvenir shopping. A few years ago, the weekly event was the exclusive preserve of backpackers and the area's semi-permanent population, who gathered here to smoke *chillums*, and to buy and sell clothes and jewellery they probably would not have the nerve to wear anywhere else: something like a small pop festival without the stage. These days, however, everything is more organized and mainstream. Pitches are rented out by the metre, drugs are banned and the approach roads to the village are choked solid all day with a/c buses and *Ambassador* cars ferrying in tourists from resorts farther down the coast.

The range of goods on sale has broadened, too, thanks to the high profile of migrant hawkers and stall-holders from other parts of India. Each region or culture tends to stick to its own corner. At one end, Westerners congregate around racks of New Age rave gear, Balinese batiks and designer beachwear. Nearby, hawk-eyed Kashmiris sit cross-legged beside trays of silver jewellery and papier-mâché boxes, while Tibetans, wearing jeans and T-shirts, preside over orderly rows of prayer wheels, turquoise bracelets and sundry Himalayan curios. Most distinctive of all are the Lamani women from Karnataka, decked from head to toe in traditional tribal garb, and selling elaborately woven multi-coloured cloth, which they fashion into everything from jackets to money belts, and which makes even the Westerners' party gear look positively funereal. Elsewhere, you'll come across dazzling Rajasthani mirrorwork and block-printed bedspreads, Keralan woodcarvings and a scattering of Gujarati appliqué.

What you end up paying for this exotic merchandise largely depends on your ability to **haggle**. Lately, prices have inflated as tourists not used to dealing in rupees will part with almost anything. Be persistent, though, and cautious, and you can usually pick things up for a reasonable rate.

Even if you're not spending, the flea market is a great place to sit and watch the world go by. Mingling with the sun-tanned masses are bands of strolling musicians, itinerant beggars, performing monkeys and snake charmers, as well as the inevitable hippy jugglers, clad in regulation waistcoats and billowing pyjama trousers.

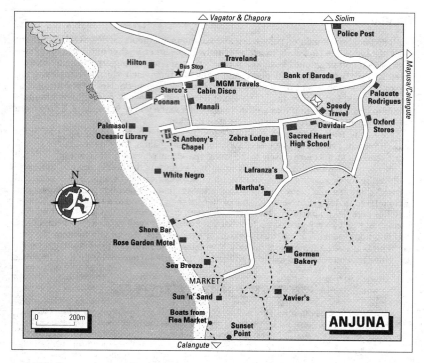

Vagator & Chapora △   *Siolim* △   *Mapusa/Calangute* △

Police Post

Hilton   Bus Stop   Traveland

Bank of Baroda

Starco's   MGM Travels
Cabin Disco   Palacete
Poonam   Rodrigues

Manali   Speedy Travel

Davidair   Oxford
Palmasol   Stores
Oceanic Library

St Anthony's   Zebra Lodge   Sacred Heart
Chapel   High School

White Negro   Lafranza's

Martha's

N

Shore Bar

Rose Garden Motel   German Bakery

Sea Breeze

MARKET

Sun 'n' Sand   Xavier's

Boats from
Flea Market   Sunset
Point   **ANJUNA**

0   200m

Calangute ▽

and New Year rush, the village is inundated with a mixed crowd of round-the-world back-packers, refugees from the British club scene and revellers from all over India, lured by the promise of the big beach parties. The rest of the time, though, Anjuna has a surprisingly simple, unhurried atmosphere – due, in no small part, to the shortage of places to stay. Most visitors who come here on market day or for the raves travel in from other resorts.

Whenever you come, keep a close eye on your valuables. **Theft**, particularly from the beach, is a big problem. Party nights are the worst; if you stay out late, keep your money and papers on you, or lock them somewhere secure (see below). Thieves have even been known to break into local houses by lifting tiles off the roof.

Arrival and information

Buses from Mapusa and Panjim drop passengers at various points along the tarmac road across the top of the village, which turns right towards Chapora at the main *Starco's* crossroads. If you're looking for a room, get off here as it's close to most of the guest houses. The crossroads has a couple of small **stores**, a **motorcycle taxi** rank, and functions as a *de facto* village square and **bus stand**.

BOATS

Fishing boats shuttle between Anjuna and Baga beach every Wednesday from just below the market ground. You can also catch a boat back to Arambol from here in the evening; see p.753.

WATER SHORTAGES

Because of the extra inhabitants it attracts over the winter, Anjuna has become particularly prone to **water shortages**. These tend not to affect many visitors, as the drought only begins to bite towards the end of March when the majority have already left. For the villagers, however, the problem causes genuine hardship. Use well water very sparingly and avoid water toilets if possible – traditional "dry" ones are far more ecologically sound.

The *Manali Guest House* and *Oxford Stores* **change money** for a hefty commission. Better rates are offered by the *Corporation Bank* in Vagator (see p.749). Note that the *Bank of Baroda* on the Mapusa road doesn't do foreign exchange, nor is it a good place to leave valuables, as thieves have previously climbed through an open window and stolen a number of "safe custody" envelopes. The **post office** is on the Mapusa road, 1km inland, with an efficient poste restante counter.

Accommodation

Most of Anjuna's very limited **accommodation** consists of small unfurnished houses, although finding one is a problem at the best of times – in peak season it's virtually impossible. By then, all but a handful have been let to long-staying regulars who book by post several months in advance. If you arrive hoping to sort something out on spec, you'll probably have to make do with a room in a guest house at first, although most owners are reluctant to rent out rooms for only one or two days at a time. Basically, unless you mean to stay for at least a couple of months, you're better off looking for a room in Calangute, Baga or nearby Vagator or Chapora.

Cabin Disco, next door to *Starco's* (☎273254). Unappealing cells with common bathrooms. OK for a night or two. ③.

Grandpa's Inn, east side of village on the main Mapusa road (☎273271; fax 274370). A bastion of Anjuna-style chic, pitched at well-heeled party lovers, with ten tasteful rooms, terrace restaurant, wet-bar, billiards room, karate and yoga lessons, and poolside jam sessions. ⑦–⑧.

Hilton, on the main road near the bus park (no phone). Characterless outbuilding, 500m behind the beach. Some attached shower-toilets. ④.

Manali, south of *Starco's* (no phone). Anjuna's best budget guest house has simple rooms around a yard, fans, safe deposit, money-changing, a sociable terrace-restaurant and shared bathrooms. Book in advance. ②.

Martha's, 907 Montero Vaddo (no phone). Five well-kept rooms run by a warm family. Basic amenities include kitchen space and running water. ②–⑤.

Palacete Rodrigues, near *Oxford Stores* (☎274304). Old-style Portuguese residence converted into an upmarket guest house. ⑥.

Palmasol Guest House, Praia de St Anthony, behind the middle of the beach (☎273258). Large, comfortable rooms very near the beach, with running water, verandahs and a relaxing garden. ⑤.

Poonam, east of the bus park (no phone). Double-storey purpose-built guest house with a garden and a cafe. Rooms are clean, but rudimentary and overpriced; larger suites are better value. ④.

Starco's, on the crossroads (no phone). Dark, cramped rooms around a yard. Good restaurant. ③.

White Negro, 719 Praia de St Anthony, south of the village (no phone). Pleasant chalets catching sea breezes, with attached bath and water. Has a lively restaurant and friendly management. ②–③.

Zebra Lodge and Camping, near Sacred Heart High School (no phone). Five neat, cheap rooms with common toilets, separate verandahs and a garden. Camping costs Rs10 per night. ①.

Eating and drinking

Both the beachfront and village at Anjuna are awash with good **places to eat and drink**. Most are simple semi-open-air, thatched palm-leaf affairs, specializing in fish and Western food. All serve cold beer, invariably with thumping techno music in the background. On the beach, you'll also be approached every ten minutes by women selling fresh **fruit**, including watermelons, pineapples and locally grown coconuts.

German Bakery, east of the market ground (look for the sign on the main road). Pricey but mouthwatering main meals and wholefood snacks, with real cream cheese, peanut butter, hummus, honey slices, sophisticated sounds and relaxing wicker chairs.

Lafranza's, south end of village on the road to market ground. The budget travellers' choice: big portions of tasty fresh fish and fries, with plenty of veg options.

Martha's Breakfast Home, near *Lafranza's*, off the road to the market. Secluded breakfast garden serving fresh Indian coffee, crêpes and American waffles, in addition to regular menu.

Rose Garden Motel, on the beach south of the *Shore Bar*. Not to be confused with the *Rose Garden Restaurant* in the village. The exhaustive menu here features superb, reasonably priced seafood sizzlers and tasty Indian veg dishes.

Sea Breeze, market ground. Does a roaring trade in cold beer and snacks on Wednesdays. At other times the vast *tandoori* fish is tasty and good value, especially for groups; order in advance.

Shore Bar, in the middle of the beach. Draws a dope-smoking crowd for sunset after the flea market and most Saturdays, with the best sound system in Anjuna. Meals served as well as drinks.

Starco's, on the crossroads. Sophisticated bar-restaurant, serving tasty *tandoori* seafood and Western dishes, inside or on the roadside terrace.

Sun 'n' Sand, market ground. Renowned for its whopping fresh-fruit salads served with crumbled coconut and curd. Great for inexpensive, healthy breakfasts.

Xavier's, east of market ground. Difficult to find, but worth it for its classy seafood and Chinese menu. Deservedly among Anjuna's most popular restaurants; the place for a splurge.

Nightlife

Anjuna has become a popular rave venue in recent years, attracting partygoers from all over the world. Most of the big events take place around the Christmas–New Year full-moon period, although smaller **parties** happen whenever their organizers manage to muster the increasingly large pay-offs demanded by local police (you'll know if they haven't got the cash together when the lanes become clogged by ravers roaring around on *Enfields* in search of some action). At other times, **nightlife** centres on the *Shore Bar*, in the middle of the beach, which has a pounding sound system. The biggest crowds show up after the Wednesday market to watch the sunset from the steps in front of the bar, accompanied by the latest ambient trance mixes from London. The music gains pace as the evening wears on, winding up around 11pm, when there's an exodus over to the *Guru Bar*, farther up the beach, or to the *Primrose Cafe* in Vagator, both of which stay open until after midnight.

Listings

Library The *Oceanic Circulating Library* (Mon–Sat 9am–2pm & 5–7pm; ☎273286), near the *White Negro Bar*, stocks a good selection of quality fiction and non-fiction. A labour of love run by a retired local woman, this place is a worthy recipient of any novels you might want to ditch before leaving.

Motorcycle repairs Anjuna's two motorcycle repair workshops are both up the road from the *Oxford Stores* department store. The smaller one, farther back from the roadside, is more helpful. Fuel and some spares, such as inner tubes and spark plugs, can be bought from the store on *Starco's* crossroads.

Pharmacy *St Michael's Pharmacy*, Soronto Vaddo, near *Starco's* crossroads, is open 24hr.

Photography *Oxford Stores* stock and process colour print film.

Travel agents *MGM* (☎274317) and *Traveland* (☎2773207) are both east of *Starco's* on the main Mapusa road; *Speedy* (☎273266) lies between the post office and *Rose Garden Restaurant*. All are reliable and efficient.

Vagator

Barely a couple of kilometres of cliff tops and parched grassland separate Anjuna from the southern fringes of its nearest neighbour, **VAGATOR**. A desultory collection of ramshackle farmhouses and picturesque old Portuguese bungalows scattered around a network of leafy lanes, the village is entered at the east via a branch off the Mapusa road, which passes a few small guest houses and restaurants before running down to the sea. Dominated by the red ramparts of Chapora fort, Vagator's broad white sandy beach – **Big Vagator beach** – is undeniably beautiful, spoiled only by the daily deluge of whisky-swilling, snap-happy tour parties that spill across it at lunchtimes.

Far better, then, to head to the next cove south. Backed by a steep wall of crumbling palm-fringed laterite, **Ozran**, or "Little", **Vagator beach** is more secluded and much less accessible than either of its neighbours. To get there, walk ten minutes from Big Vagator, or drive to the end of the lane off the main Chapora–Anjuna road, from where a footpath drops sharply down to a wide stretch of level white sand (look for the mopeds and bikes parked at the top of the cliff). At this southern end of the beach, a row of makeshift **cafes** provides shade and sustenance for a young, hip crowd. In spite of the Goan nudism laws, topless bathing is the norm; not that the locals, nor the odd groups of inebriated men that file past around mid-afternoon, seem in the least bit perturbed.

Like Anjuna, Vagator is a relaxed, comparatively undeveloped resort that appeals, in the main, to budget travellers with time on their hands. Accommodation is limited, however, and visitors frequently find themselves travelling to and from Baga every day until a vacancy turns up in one of the guest houses.

Arrival and information

Buses from Panjim and Mapusa, 9km east, pull in every fifteen minutes or so at the crossroads on the far northeastern edge of Vagator, near where the main road peels away towards Chapora. From here, it's a one-kilometre walk over the hill and down the other side to the beach, where you'll find most of the village's accommodation, restaurants and cafes. The *Corporation Bank* (Mon–Wed & Fri 10am–2pm, Sat 10am–noon) is 200m south of the main crossroads, on the Anjuna road. The only other official place in Vagator to **change money** – cash and travellers' cheques – is the *Primrose Cafe*, on the south side of the village, which charges at bank rates and hands out free encashment certificates. If you want to rent a **motorcycle**, try *Prakash Auto Service* (☎26 3214), near the *Sea Green Chinese Restaurant*.

Accommodation

Accommodation in Vagator revolves around a few family-run budget guest houses, a pricey resort hotel and dozens of small private properties rented out for long periods. The usual charge for a house is between Rs2000 and Rs4500 per month; ask around the cafes and back lanes south of the main road. **Water** is very short here, and should be used frugally at all times (see p.747).

Abu John's, between the crossroads and the beach (no phone). Comfortable self-contained chalets in quiet garden; all with bathrooms and running water. No off-season discounts. ④.

Anita Lodge, north of the road near the beach (☎274348). Five basic concrete rooms with Western toilets and small balconies, in a modern roadside bungalow. See the manager of *Anita Wine Shop* opposite for bookings, money-changing and STD telephone. ②.

Dolrina, north of the road near the beach (☎274347). Vagator's largest and most popular budget guest house, run by a friendly Goan couple; attached or shared bathrooms, a sociable common verandah and safe deposits. Breakfasts available. ④.

Jolly Jolly Jester, between the crossroads and Big Vagator beach (no phone). Pleasant doubles with bathrooms, plus a small restaurant, all in attractive woodland. Single occupancy possible. ③.

Mrs Bandobkhar's, next to the *Anita Wine Shop* (no phone). Good-value flats or five rooms in a brand-new building with running water. ①–②.

Oasis Guest House, west of the crossroads, near *Jerry's* (no phone). Concrete house surrounded by trees, with largish rooms, attached bath and running water. Nothing special. ④.

Sterling Resort, behind Big Vagator beach (☎373277). Upmarket resort hotel pitched at wealthy Bombayites. Cottages grouped around a large pool, two restaurants and lawns, in a palm grove. ⑦.

Eating, drinking and nightlife

Vagator's many cafes and restaurants are scattered along the main road and the back lanes that lead to Ozran beach. There are also several seafood joints behind Big Vagator beach, one or two of which serve Indian dishes in addition to the usual fish-rich Goan specialities. **Nightlife** focuses on the *Primrose Cafe*, out towards Anjuna, which boasts a beefier-than-average sound system, and a late bar.

Abu John's, between the crossroads and the beach. Recently opened terrace restaurant specializing in moderately priced seafood and meat barbecues.

Jolly Jolly Jester, between the village crossroads and Big Vagator beach. Not to be confused with *Julie Jolly's*, near the *Primrose*. This one's smaller and friendlier, offering a better selection of inexpensive seasonal seafood, salads and tasty Western-style veg dishes.

Lobo's, behind the beach. Best of the beach places. Mostly Goan-style seafood, with some unadventurous but cheap Western and veg alternatives.

Mango Tree, near the crossroads and bus stop. Moderately priced sizzlers, seafood and delicious stir-fries prepared in front of you by a resident Chinese chef.

Primrose Cafe and Restaurant, southern edge of the village. Goa's posiest cafe-bar livens up around 8pm and serves tasty German wholefood snacks, light meals, cakes, and drinks.

Ram Das Swami, above Ozran beach. Terrible service, but the portions are generous, the food tasty and inexpensive, and the sea views superb.

Chapora

Crouched in the shadow of a Portuguese fort on the opposite, northern side of the headland from Vagator, **CHAPORA**, 10km from Mapusa, is a lot busier than most north-coast villages. Dependent on fishing and boat-building, it has, to a great extent, retained a life of its own independent of tourism. The workaday indifference to the annual invasion of Westerners is most evident on the main street, lined with as many regular stores as travellers' cafes and restaurants. It's unlikely that Chapora will ever develop into a major resort, either. Tucked away under a dense canopy of trees on the muddy southern shore of a river estuary, it lacks both the space and the white sand that have pulled crowds to Calangute and Colva.

If you have your own transport, however, Chapora is a good base from which to explore the region: Vagator is on the doorstep, Anjuna is a short ride to the south, and the ferry crossing at Siolim – gateway to the remote north of the state – is barely fifteen minutes away by road. The village is also well connected by bus to Mapusa, and there are plenty of sociable bars and cafes to hang out in. The only drawback is that accommodation tends, again, to be thin on the ground. Apart from the guest houses along the main road, most of the places to stay are long-stay houses in the woods.

The only real sight to speak of is the **fort**, most easily reached from the Vagator side of the hill. At low tide, you can also walk around the bottom of the headland, via the anchorage, and the secluded coves beyond it, to Big Vagator, then head up the hill from there. The red-laterite bastion, crowning the rocky bluff, was built by the Portuguese in 1617 on the site of an earlier Muslim structure (whence the village's name – from *Shahpura*, "town of the Shah"). Deserted in the nineteenth century, it lies in ruins today, although the **views** up and down the coast from the weed-infested ramparts are still superb.

Practicalities

Direct **buses** arrive at Chapora three times daily from Panjim, and every fifteen minutes from Mapusa, with departures until 7pm. **Motorcycle taxis** hang around the old banyan tree at the far end of the main street, near where the buses pull in. Air, train, bus and catamaran **tickets** may be booked or reconfirmed at *Soniya Tours and Travels*, next to the bus stand.

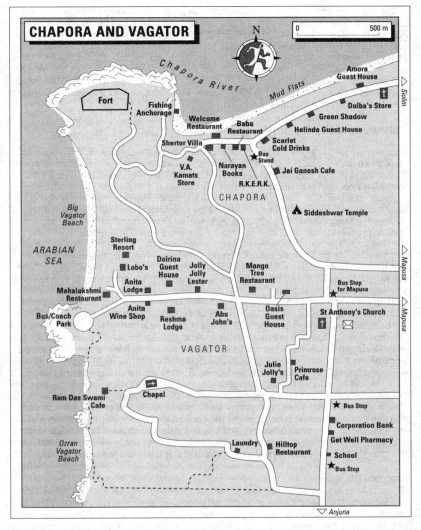

CHAPORA AND VAGATOR

N

0   500 m

Chapora River

Mud Flats

▷ Siolim

Fort

Amora
Guest House

Fishing
Anchorage

Welcome
Restaurant

Baba
Restaurant

Shertor Villa

Dulba's Store

Green Shadow

Helinda Guest House

Scarlet
Cold Drinks

Bus
Stand

V.A.
Kamats
Store

Narayan
Books

R.K.E.R.K.

Jai Ganesh Cafe

CHAPORA

Siddeshwar Temple

Big
Vagator
Beach

ARABIAN
SEA

Sterling
Resort

Lobo's

Dolrina
Guest
House

Jolly
Jolly
Lester

Mango
Tree
Restaurant

Bus Stop
for Mapusa

▷ Mapusa

▷ Mapusa

Mahalakshmi
Restaurant

Anita
Lodge

Anita
Wine Shop

Reshma
Lodge

Abu
John's

Oasis
Guest
House

St Anthony's Church

Bus/Coach
Park

VAGATOR

Julie
Jolly's

Primrose
Cafe

Ram Das Swami
Cafe

Chapel

Bus Stop

Corporation Bank

Get Well Pharmacy

School

Bus Stop

Ozran
Vagator
Beach

Laundry

Hilltop
Restaurant

▽ Anjuna

If you want to check in to a cheap guest house while you sort out more permanent **accommodation**, try the popular *Shertor Villa* (①–②), off the west side of the main street. Nearly all its rooms, ranged around a sheltered back yard, come with fans and running water. If this place is full, try the *Helinda* (①–③), at the opposite end of the village, which has rock-bottom options and more comfortable rooms with attached shower-toilets, and a good restaurant. As a last resort, the dilapidated *Amora* (①), between the *Helinda* and the chapel down the lane, has grotty rooms in an extension to the local fishing-tackle shop.

Finding somewhere to **eat** in Chapora is easy: just take your pick from the crop of inexpensive little cafes and restaurants on the main street. The popular *Welcome*, halfway down, offers a reasonable selection of cheap and filling seafood, Western and veg dishes, plus relentless reggae and techno music, and backgammon sets. The *Preyanka*, nearby, is in much the same mould, but has a few more Indian and Chinese options. Alternatively, try the more secluded *Green Shadow*, next door to the *Helinda*, which specializes in *tandoori* fish and chicken. If you're suffering from chilli-burn afterwards, *Scarlet Cold Drinks* and the *Sai Ganesh Cafe*, both a short way east of the main street, knock up deliciously cool fresh-fruit milkshakes.

Pernem and the far north

Sandwiched between the Chapora and Arondem rivers, the predominantly Hindu *taluka* of **Pernem** – in the *Novas Conquistas* area – is Goa's northernmost district and one of its least explored regions. Apart from the fishing village of **Arambol**, which attracts a trickle of backpackers seeking a rustic alternative to the resorts south of the River Chapora, the beautiful Pernem coastline of long sandy beaches, lagoons and coconut plantations has few settlements equipped to cope with visitors. However, the picturesque, if bumpy, journey north from Arambol to **Terekol fort**, on the Maharashtran border, provides ample incentive to spend a day away from the beach.

Heading to Pernem from Anjuna, Vagator, or Chapora, you have to travel a few kilometres inland to pick up the main Calangute road, as it runs north over a low ridge of laterite hills, to the river crossing at **Siolim**. Boatmen sometimes paddle tourists over the estuary from Chapora, too, although their dug-outs are unstable when laden with passengers and they can't carry motorbikes. The two **car ferries** that chug back and forth across the river from the ramp at Siolim charge a couple of rupees for the ten-minute trip, which is one of the high points of the journey north.

Once across the river, bear right until you reach a fork in the road, where a sign to "Harmal/Terekol" marks the quick route to Arambol. Alternatively, head left from the ferry dock and follow the scenic back road along the north bank of the Chapora, past a crumbling old Catholic church, as far as a deserted beach called **Morgim** (or Morji). A seemingly endless expanse of soft white sand stretches north from here, rounding a rocky headland where the local fishing fleet is beached, after which it widens and empties completely. If you really want to get away from everything, **Mandarem**, 3km further north, with its palm-fringed dunes and acres of space, is perfect. Apart from the odd fisherman or tourist buzzing along the hard sand at low tide, the only signs of life are a couple of makeshift **cafes** serving tea, soft drinks, fish *dal* and rice. The easiest way to get to Mandarem is to follow the road that cuts north along the coast from Morgim towards Davanvado; park your bike when you see a cafe on the left.

Arambol (Harmal)

Of the fishing settlements dotted along the north coast, only **ARAMBOL** (also known as **Harmal**), 32km northwest of Mapusa, is remotely geared to tourism – albeit in a very low-key, low-impact fashion. If you're happy with basic amenities, the village offers two very fine **beaches** and a healthy dose of peace and quiet. Parties are occasionally held here, drawing revellers across the river from Anjuna and Vagator, but these are rare intrusions into an otherwise tranquil, out-of-the-way enclave. However, this looks set to change if the local landowner and his cronies push through proposals to site a sprawling five-star resort here. The complex, which the planners hope to build atop the headland at the north end of the village, will, in addition to the usual water-guzzling swimming pools and lawns, comprise an eighteen-hole golf course, intended to pull in rich Japanese punters. Advocates claim it will bring greater prosperity to Arambol; the locals seem unanimously unconvinced.

Modern Arambol is scattered around an area of high ground west of the main coast road, where most of the buses pull in. From here, a bumpy lane runs downhill, past a large school and the village church, to the more traditional end of the village, clustered under a canopy of widely spaced palm trees. The main **beach** lies 200m farther along the lane. Strewn with dozens of old wooden fishing boats and a line of tourist cafe-bars, the gently curving bay is good for bathing, but much less picturesque than its neighbour around the corner.

The smaller and less frequented of Arambol's two beaches can only be reached on foot by following the stony track over the headland to the north. Beyond an idyllic, rocky-bottomed cove, the trail emerges to a broad strip of soft white sand hemmed in on both sides by steep cliffs. Behind it, a small freshwater lake extends along the bottom of the valley into a thick jungle. Hang around the banks of this murky green pond for long enough, and you'll probably see a fluorescent-yellow human figure or two appear from the bushes at its far end. Fed by boiling hot springs, the lake is lined with sulphurous mud, which, when smeared over the body, dries to form a surreal, butter-coloured shell. The resident hippies swear it's good for you and spend much of the day tiptoeing naked around the shallows like refugees from some obscure tribal initiation ceremony – much to the amusement of Arambol's Indian visitors. Nearby, in the woods immediately behind the lake, other members of the lunatic fringe have taken to living in the branches of an old tree; the scene resembles a cross between *Lord of the Flies* and *Apocalypse Now*.

PRACTICALITIES

Buses to and from Panjim (via Mapusa) pull into Arambol every half hour until noon, and every ninety minutes thereafter, at the small bus stand on the main road. A faster private **minibus** service from Panjim arrives daily opposite the *chai* stalls at the beach end of the village. **Boats** leave here every Wednesday morning for the ninety-minute trip to the Anjuna flea market. Tickets should be booked in advance from the *Welcome Restaurant* by the beach (Tues–Sun 8–9am & 8–9pm; Rs120), which also rents out **motorcycles**. The **post office**, next to the church, has a poste restante box; to **change money**, however, you'll have to head for Vagator, as Arambol's *State Bank of India* has no foreign-exchange facility.

Apart from a couple of purpose-built chalets on the edge of the village, most of Arambol's **accommodation** consists of simple houses in the woods behind the beach. Some of the more expensive places have fully equipped kitchens and showers, but the vast majority are standard-issue bare huts, with "pig" toilets and a well in the back garden. Long-stay visitors either bring their own bedding and cooking stuff, or kit themselves out at Mapusa market. The best place to stay if you only have a couple of days, however, is the *Ganesh Bar* (②–③), in the cove between the two main beaches. Scattered over the hillside directly above the cafe, it consists of a handful of small, new chalets with clean outhouses and superb sea views from their verandahs. The bar is also the best place in Arambol to enjoy the sunset over a chilled beer.

Finding **food** is, as ever, less problematic than finding a bed. The *Welcome Restaurant*, next to the main entrance to the beach, is a popular and sociable cafe serving a good range of locally caught seafood, with *todi* to order. The palm-leaf bar-restaurants on the beach itself are slightly pricier, but still good value. For inexpensive, filling food, though, you can't beat the no-nonsense *chai* stalls at the bottom of the village. *Sheila's* and *Siddi's* cheap and tasty *thalis* both come with *puris*, and they have a good travellers' breakfast menu of pancakes, eggs and curd. *Dominico's*, also at the bottom of the village (near where the road makes a ninety-degree bend), is renowned for its generous tropical fruit salads and milkshakes.

Terekol

North of Arambol, the sinuous coast road climbs to the top of a rocky, undulating plateau, then winds down through a swathe of thick woodland to join the River

Arondem, which it then follows for 4km through a landscape of vivid paddy fields, coconut plantations and temple towers protruding from scruffy red-brick villages. The tiny enclave of **TEREKOL**, the northernmost tip of Goa, is reached via a clapped-out car ferry (every 30min; 5min) from the hamlet of Querim, 42km from Panjim.

After the long and scenic drive, the old **fort** that dominates the estuary from the north is a bit of an anti-climax. Hyped as one of the state's most atmospheric historic monuments, it turns out to be little more than a down-at-heel country house recently converted into a low-key luxury hotel. If your visit coincides with the arrival of a guided tour, you may get a chance to look around the gloomy interior of the **Chapel of St Anthony**, in the fort's claustrophobic cobbled square; at other times it's kept locked.

PRACTICALITIES
The few visitors that venture up to Terekol tend to do so by motorbike, heading back at the end of the day to the relative comfort of Calangute or Baga. If you run out of fuel, the nearest service station is at Arambol. One of GTDC's daily **tours** from Panjim (see p.725) comes up here, as does one daily *Kadamba* **bus** from the capital; alternatively, the 7am bus from Siolim, on the Chapora, pulls in at the Querim ferry an hour later.

Accommodation is limited to the posh *Hotel Tirakhol Fort Heritage* (☎0834/220705; fax 283326; ⑥–⑧), whose rooms are pleasant and comfortable, but way overpriced at Rs500 for the no-frills (windowless) options, to around Rs1750 (plus taxes) for a luxury suite with sea views. The **restaurant** downstairs, kept busy in the daytime by bus parties, offers seafood, Indian and Chinese dishes, as well as beer.

South Goa

At present, tourism is a good deal less developed in **south Goa** than in the north. However, beyond the unattractive port city of **Vasco da Gama**, and its nearby airport, the southern reaches of the state harbour some of the region's finest **beaches**, with attractive Portuguese-style villages nestled in a hilly interior.

Many visitors base themselves initially at **Colva**, 6km west of Goa's second city, **Margao**. The most developed resort in the area, Colva stands slap in the middle of a spectacular 25-kilometre stretch of pure white sand, backed by a broad band of coconut plantations. Although increasingly carved up by the British charter industry, accommodation here is plentiful, with hotels and guest houses to suit most pockets. Longer staying budget travellers, however, tend to steer clear of Colva in favour of neighbouring **Benaulim**, 2km further south, which has thus far resisted encroachments by the package tour trade.

To escape the tourist scene altogether, rent a motorcycle, or jump on a long-distance bus bound for Goa's **far south**. Less than a couple of hours by road from Margao, **Canacona** district sees few visitors, yet its rocky coast shelters a string of beautiful beaches, set against a backdrop of forest-cloaked hills. **Palolem**, 2km west of the district's main settlement, **Chaudi**, is the only one really geared up for visitors.

Vasco da Gama

VASCO DA GAMA (commonly referred to as "Vasco"), 29km by road southwest of Panjim, sits on the narrow western tip of the Mormugao peninsula, overlooking the mouth of the Zuari River. Acquired by the Portuguese in 1543, this strategically important site was formerly among the busiest ports on India's west coast, and it remains a key shipping centre, with container vessels and iron-ore barges clogging the choppy river mouth.

Dominated by the unsightly oil storage tanks of *Hindustan Petroleum*'s oil refinery, Vasco is unremittingly drab and industrial. Many visitors, however, find themselves having to pass through at some point, either to book a ticket and catch a train from the station (Goa's principal railhead), or en route to nearby **Dabolim airport**. Apart from a browse around the small **bazaar**, crammed into the narrow streets northwest of the main square, there's absolutely nothing to see or do in the town. If you've time to kill, jump into a taxi or auto-rickshaw, or rent a bicycle from the stall on the square, and head off to **Bogmalo beach**, 8km southeast.

Dabolim Airport

Dabolim, Goa's airport, lies on top of a rocky plateau, 4km southeast of Vasco da Gama. This run-down naval aerodrome is a far cry from the sophistication of Western airports: check-in, passport control and disembarkation formalities for international arrivals take over an hour, and long delays are common.

Facilities in the terminal buildings include *State Bank of India's* **foreign-exchange desks** (open for flights), sub-post offices, and counters for domestic airlines. There's also a handy pre-paid **taxi counter** next to the exit in the arrivals hall. Fixed fares to virtually everywhere in the state are displayed behind the desk; pay here and give the slip to the driver when you arrive.

Kadamba **buses** (Rs30) meet domestic *Indian Airlines* flights, dropping passengers at the main bus stand in Panjim, and outside the *Indian Airlines* office on Dr D Bandodkar Rd, in the northwest of town. However, the least expensive way to get from the airport is to walk to the nearby main road (left out of the terminal building), and pick up a **local bus** to Vasco or Panjim – though this is more hassle than it's worth if you're weighed down with luggage.

Finally, if you're **leaving Goa** via Dabolim, don't forget the all-important Rs300 **airport tax**, which must be paid at the *State Bank* counter before you check in.

Arrival and information

Vasco is laid out in a grid, bordered by Mormugao Bay to the north, and by the railway line on its southern side. Apart from the cluster of oil storage tanks, the town's most prominent landmark is the **railway station** at the south end of the main Dr Rajendra Prasad Avenue. **Tickets** may be booked at the hatches inside the station, the only place in Goa where you can make reservations using *Indrail* passes.

Arriving in Vasco by **bus** from Panjim or Margao, you'll be dropped in the inconveniently situated interstate *Kadamba* terminus, 3km east of the town centre. Local **minibuses** ferry passengers from here to the more central market bus stand, at the top of the square. **Auto-rickshaws**, and *Ambassador* and motorcycle **taxis**, hang around on the corner of Swatantra Path and Dr Rajendra Prasad Ave, near the station and the small **cycle rental** stall.

If you need to **change money**, the *State Bank of India* (Mon–Fri 10am–2pm, Sat 10am–noon) is at the north end of F L Gomes Rd. For **tourist information**, head for GTDC's helpful counter in the lobby of the *Tourist Hostel* (daily 9.30–5pm).

Accommodation

Thanks to its business city status, Vasco boasts a better-than-average batch of **hotels**. Most are plush mid-range places, although there are several no-frills lodges near the railway station. The prices listed below apply to peak season; at other times, discounts can usually be negotiated.

Annapurna, Dattatreya Deshpande Rd (☎0834/513375). The best of the budget bunch. Neat, clean and close to the railway station, with a good restaurant. Book in advance. ③.

Citadel, Pe Jose Vaz Rd (☎0834/512097; fax 513036). The best value among Vasco's modern mid-range hotels: comfortable en-suite rooms, satellite TV, some a/c and good off-season discounts. ⑤.

GTDC Tourist Hostel, off Swatantra Path (☎0834/513119). Large rooms (some a/c) with fans and shower-toilets, plus an information counter, laundry and travel agent. Very good value. ③–④.

La Paz, Swatantra Path (☎0834/513302; fax 513503). The town's top hotel has central a/c rooms, plush bars and restaurants, a gym and courtesy buses to the beach and airport. Good value. ⑦.

Maharaja, opposite *Hindustan Petroleum* (☎0834/513075, fax 512559). Swanky marble reception and spacious, spotless rooms (some a/c), but dismal views over the refinery. ④–⑥.

Nagina, Dattatreya Deshpande Rd (☎0834/513674). Bland but central, secure and comfortable enough. Its cheapest rooms are a good deal. Some a/c. ③–⑤.

Urvashi, F L Gomes Rd (☎0834/510273). A comfortable budget hotel, east of the square, that would be more pleasant without the fishy fumes wafting from the nearby docks. Some a/c. ②–④.

Eating and drinking

The best **places to eat** are the restaurants attached to Vasco's classier hotels.

Annapurna, *Hotel Annapurna*, Dattatreya Deshpande Rd. Inexpensive pure-veg south Indian and Punjabi-style *thalis*, and traditional milk sweets, served in a plain but clean canteen.

Goodyland, Swatantra Path. Spanking new and self-consciously Western fast-food joint, with glacial a/c. Good for moderately priced pizzas, veg patties, Bengali sweets and milkshakes.

Gulzar, *Hotel Nagina*, Dattatreya Deshpande Rd. Goan and non-veg specialities, including reasonably priced chicken *cafreal*, mutton *xacuti*, and fresh fish. Delicious veg *makhanwalla*, too.

Nanking, off Swatantra Path, five minutes' walk east of railway station. Minimal decor but mountainous portions of cheap and tasty Chinese food.

Regency, *Hotel La Paz*, Swatantra Path. Expensive top-notch a/c restaurant with a mixed international menu, pot plants, and piped muzak.

Tradition, GTDC *Tourist Hostel*, off Swatantra Path. Inexpensive snacks and meals, mostly meaty Punjabi dishes with a few Chinese alternatives, served in a drab dining hall – or on a balcony if the barrage of Hindi videos gets too much.

Bogmalo

Immediately south of the airport, the Mormugao peninsula's sun-parched central plateau tumbles to a flat-bottomed valley lined with coconut trees and red-brick huts. The sandy **beach** at the end of the cove would be even more picturesque if not for the monstrous multi-storey edifice perched above it. Until *Oberoi* dumped a huge five-star hotel here, **BOGMALO** was just another small fishing village, hemmed in by a pair of palm-fringed headlands at the northern end of Colva Bay. The village is still here, complete with a tiny whitewashed chapel and gangs of hogs nosing through the rubbish, but its environs have been transformed. Pricey cafe-bars blaring Western music have crept up the beach, while the clearing below the hotel is prowled by assiduous Kashmiri handicraft vendors.

Even so, compared with Calangute or Colva, Bogmalo is still a small-scale resort. If you're staying at the *Oberoi*, and haven't come to Goa to get away from it all or party all night, then you'll find it congenial enough. The beach is clean and not too crowded, the water reasonably safe for swimming, and there are plenty of places to eat, drink and shop. If, on the other hand, you're looking for somewhere not yet on the package tourist map, you're better off farther south, at the far end of Colva beach or beyond.

Practicalities

Bogmalo can be reached by **bus** or **taxi** from Vasco da Gama, 8km northwest. It's also near enough to the airport for a last-minute dip before catching a plane. If you're thinking of staying, **accommodation** is very limited and best booked ahead. The *Oberoi Bogmalo Beach* (☎0834/52191; fax 52150; ⑨), overlooking the beach, offers formula five-star luxury, with a pool, central a/c and a sun terrace. The friendly *O Mar Beach Resort* (☎0834/510121; ③), on the opposite side of the village, behind the beach, is altogether more humble, with plain en-suite rooms, and a small covered verandah with a restaurant. Two minutes' walk from here stands *Joet's* (☎0834/514997; ⑤), a more modern and upmarket place complete with its own terrace restaurant; the small rooms, most of which are booked up by charter companies in high season, catch the sea breezes and have pleasant views.

What Bogmalo lacks in places to stay it makes up for in **bars** and **restaurants**. Most of the places dotted along the beach depend on a steady trickle of refugees from the *Oberoi*, and have whacked up their prices accordingly. The *Full Moon Kneipe*, outside the main hotel entrance, takes the lion's share of the overspill, though the menu, mainly seafood and chicken, is predictably expensive, and the portions are not overly generous. The *Sea Cuisine* opposite offers identical dishes and prices, but tends to be less crowded at lunchtimes. Farther up the beach, all the cafe-bars are in much the same mould; only the music changes.

Margao (Madgaon) and around

MARGAO, the capital of prosperous Salcete *taluka*, is regarded as Goa's second city, even though it's marginally smaller than Vasco da Gama, 30km northwest. Surrounded by fertile farmland, the town has always been an important agricultural market, and was once a major religious centre, with dozens of wealthy temples and *dharamsalas* – however, most of these were destroyed when the Portuguese absorbed the area into their *Novas Conquistas* ("New Conquests") during the seventeenth century. Today, Catholic churches still outnumber Hindu shrines, but Margao has retained a distinctly cosmopolitan feel, largely due to a huge influx of migrant labour from neighbouring Karnataka and Maharashtra. The resultant overcrowding has become a real problem in the town centre, whose 1950s municipal buildings and modern concrete blocks stew under a haze of traffic pollution.

The main reason to brave this melee, other than to get on or off a bus somewhere else, is to shop in Margao's excellent **bazaar**, a rich source of authentic souvenirs and a good place to browse. Stretching from the south edge of the main square to within a stone's throw of the railway station, the bazaar centres on a labyrinthine covered market, where you'll find everything from betel leaves and sacks of lime paste to baby clothes, incense, spices and cheap Taiwanese toys.

While you're here, take a short rickshaw ride north to the stately **Church of the Holy Spirit**, in the heart of a dishevelled but picturesque colonial enclave. Presiding over the dusty Largo de Igreja square, the church, built by the Portuguese in 1675, is one of the finest examples of late-Baroque architecture in Goa, boasting a pristine white facade and an interior dripping with gilt, crystal and stucco.

The picturesque farming villages strewn across the verdant countryside **around Margao** host a scattering of evocative colonial monuments and a handful of Hindu temples that can be visited on day trips from the coast.

Arrival and information

For travellers arriving in Goa at the **railway station**, 1km southeast of the town centre, Margao makes a much more congenial place to disembark than Vasco, one hour further down the line. **Auto-rickshaws** ferry passengers to the **city** (or "market") **bus stand**, on the chaotic Praça Jorge Barreto, from where local buses leave for a variety of destinations in south Goa (note that the stop for Colva and Benaulim is in front of the *Kamat Hotel*, on the east side of the square). Buses from north Goa and out of state pull into the **Kadamba bus stand**, 2km north, on the outskirts. You can pick up connections to Panjim, Mapusa, Chaudi (Canacona), Karwar and Gokarna (in Karnataka) here, or else head into town on one of the mini-van taxis or auto-rickshaws that line up near the exit on the main road.

Train tickets may be booked at the *Indian Railways* reservation and enquiry counter at Margao railway station (daily 8.30am–12.30pm & 2–5pm; ☎0834/22252). Note that reservations on *Indrail* passes can only be made at Vasco da Gama station.

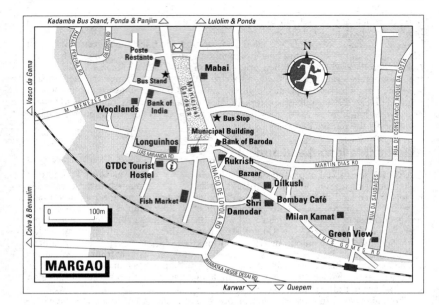

GTDC's **information office** (Mon–Fri 9.30am–5.30pm; ☎0834/222513), which sells tourist maps and keeps useful lists of train and bus times, is inside the lobby of the *Tourist Hostel*, on the southwest corner of the square.

Money-changing facilities are available at the *State Bank of India* (Mon–Fri 10am–2pm, Sat 10am–noon), off the west side of the square, and the *Bank of Baroda*, behind Grace Church on the lane that leads east from the market, where you can also draw money on *Visa* cards. The **GPO** is at the top of the municipal gardens, although its **poste restante** is in a different building, 200m west on the Rua Diogo da Costa.

Accommodation

With Colva and Benaulim a mere twenty-minute bus ride away, it's hard to think of a reason why anyone should choose to **stay** in Margao, but if you have an early-morning train to catch, or arrive here too late to get anywhere else, there are plenty of hotels within walking distance of the railway station and Praça Jorge Barreto.

Green View, Station Rd (☎0834/220151). Among the few cheerless cheapos outside the railway station licensed to take tourists. Attached rooms and a popular veg *thali* joint. ②.

GTDC Tourist Hostel, behind the Municipal Building (☎0834/220470). Standard good-value government block, with en-suite rooms (some a/c) and a restaurant. A safe budget option. ③–④.

Mabai, 108 Praca Jorge Barreto (☎0834/221658). The *Woodlands*' only real competitor is frayed around the edges, but clean and central. Some a/c. ④.

Milan Kamat, Station Rd (☎0834/221715). Standard budget lodge that's a good fall-back if the *Green View* is full. ②.

Rukrish, opposite the Municipal Building (☎0834/221709). Best of the rock-bottom lodges in the town centre, with passably clean rooms – some overlooking the main road and market. ①–②.

Woodlands, Miguel Loyola Furtado Rd (☎0834/221121). Margao's most popular mid-range hotel, around the corner from the *Tourist Hostel*. Its bargain "non-deluxe" rooms are often booked up. Reservations recommended. Some a/c. ③–④.

Eating and drinking

After a browse around the bazaar, most visitors make a beeline for *Longuinhos*, the long-established hang-out of Margao's English-speaking middle classes, and arguably the best place in town to eat. If you are on a budget, try one of the south Indian-style pure-veg cafes along Francisco Luis Gomes Rd. A couple of these, notably the *Bombay Cafe*, open early for breakfast.

Bombay Cafe, Francisco Luis Gomes Rd. Popular with office workers and shoppers for its cheap veg snacks, served on tin trays by young lads in grubby cotton uniforms. A mostly male clientele.

Dilkush, Francisco Luis Gomes Rd. Another good stand-up south Indian-style snack joint, offering plenty of cheap and filling veg dishes.

Longuinhos, opposite the *Tourist Hostel*, Rua Luis Miranda. Relaxing, old-fashioned bar-restaurant serving a reasonable selection of moderately priced meat, fish, and veggie main meals, freshly baked savoury snacks (including more-ish veg patties), cakes and drinks.

Shri Damodar, opposite Gandhi Market, Francisco Luis Gomes Rd. One of several inexpensive cafe and ice-cream parlours ranged around the temple square. This one is the cleanest, and has an air-cooled "family" (read "women's") room upstairs.

Lutolim

Peppered around the leafy lanes of **LUTOLIM**, 10km northeast of Margao, are several of Goa's most beautiful **colonial mansions**, dating from the heyday of the Portuguese empire when this was the country seat of the territory's top brass. Lying just off the main road, the village is served by eight daily **buses** from Margao, which drop passengers on the square in front of a lopsided-looking church. The cream of Lutolim's houses lie within walking distance of here, nestled in the woods, or along the road leading south. However, you shouldn't turn up at any of them unannounced; **visits have to be arranged in advance** through the Margao tourist office (☎0834/222513).

Pick of the crop in Lutolim is **Miranda house**, a stone's throw from the square. Fronted by a plain classical facade, the mansion was built in the 1700s, though renovated later following raids by a clan of rebel Rajput bandits. Today, it is occupied by a famous Goan cartoonist and his family, direct descendents of the wealthy areca planters who originally owned the surrounding estate. **Roque Caetan Miranda house**, two minutes' walk south of the square, and **Salvador Costa house**, tucked away on the western edge of the village, are other mansions worth hunting out; the latter is occupied by an elderly lady who only welcomes visitors by appointment.

Chandor

Thirteen kilometres east of Margao across the fertile rice fields of Salcete lies sleepy **CHANDOR** village, a scattering of tumbledown villas and farm houses ranged along shady tree-lined lanes. The only reason to venture out here these days is to visit the splendid **Perreira-Braganza/Menezes-Braganza house** (daily except holidays; donation), regarded as the grandest of Goa's colonial mansions. Dominating the dusty village square, the house, built in the 1500s by the wealthy Braganza family for their two sons, has a huge double-storeyed facade, with twenty-eight windows flanking its entrance. Braganza de Perreira, the great-grandfather of the present owner, was the last knight of the king of Portugal; more recently, Menezes Braganza (1879–1938) was a famous journalist and freedom fighter, one of the few Goan aristocrats to actively oppose Portuguese rule. Forced to flee Chandor in 1950, the family returned in 1962 to find their house, amazingly, untouched. The airy tiled interiors of both wings contain a veritable feast of **antiques**. Furniture enthusiasts, and lovers of rare Chinese porcelain, in particular, will find plenty to drool over, while anyone interested in religious relics should request a glimpse of St Francis Xavier's diamond-encrusted toenail, recently retrieved from a local bank vault and enshrined in the east wing's tiny chapel.

Visitors generally travel to Chandor by taxi, but you can also get there by bus from Margao (8 daily; 45min), or by train via Chandragoa station, 1km northwest. While many people turn up without an appointment, it is still a good idea to call ahead through the tourist office. Alternatively, contact the family business, *Agua de Fonte*, opposite the *Blue Fountain Cinema* in Margao (☎0834/223754).

Colva

A hot-season retreat for Margao's moneyed middle classes since long before Independence, **COLVA** is the oldest and largest – but least appealing – of south Goa's resorts. Its leafy outlying *vaddos*, or wards, are pleasant enough, dotted with colonial-style villas and ramshackle fishing huts, but the beachfront is dismal: a lacklustre collection of concrete hotels, souvenir stalls and fly-blown snack bars strewn around a bleak central roundabout. Each afternoon, bus loads of visitors from out of state mill around here after a paddle on the crowded foreshore, pestered by postcard-*wallahs* and the little urchins whose families camp on the outskirts. The ambience is not improved by heaps of rubbish dumped in a rank-smelling ditch that runs behind the beach, nor by the stench of drying fish wafting from the nearby village. If, however, you steer clear of this central market area, and stick to the cleaner, greener outskirts, Colva can be a pleasant and convenient place to stay for a while. Swimming is relatively safe, while the sand, at least away from the beachfront, is spotless and scattered with beautiful shells.

Arrival and information

Buses leave Margao (from outside the *Kamat Hotel* on Praça Jorge Barreto) every thirty minutes for Colva, dropping passengers at the main beachfront, and at various

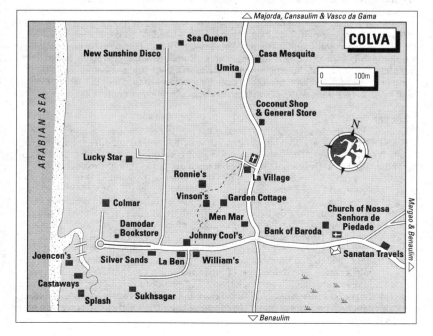

points along the main road. The thirty- to forty-minute trip costs virtually nothing, but can be a real endurance test towards the end of the day when the conductors pack on punters like sardines. Far better to jump in an **auto-rickshaw** for Rs40, or squeeze into a shared **taxi**. Heading in the opposite direction, from Colva to Margao, these pick up passengers at the entrance to the beach, along the main road leading to the village, and from the crossroads 200m west of the church. Regular mini-van and *Ambassador* taxis line up on the north side of the beachfront, next to the public toilets, and outside several of the upmarket resort hotels, including the *Silver Sands* and *Penthouse.*

To rent a **motorcycle**, ask around the taxi rank, or in front of *Vincy's Hotel*, where 100cc Yamahas are on offer at the usual rates. Their owners will advise you to avoid Margao if you haven't got a valid international drivers' licence, as the approach road passes the police post. **Fuel** is sold by the *Bisleri* bottle from a little house behind the Menino Jesus College, just east of *William's Resort* – the only fuel stop in Colva.

Sanatan Air Travel Agency (Mon–Sat 9.30am–7pm; ☎ & fax 0834/225876), 200m east of Colva church, exchanges **travellers' cheques** and **cash** at a little under bank rates; you can also draw cash on *Visa* and *Mastercard* here. The travel agent attached to *William's* in the middle of the village is another good place to change money. *Sanatan* also books and reconfirms domestic and international flights, and arranges deluxe bus, catamaran and train tickets to other parts of India.

The sub-**post office**, opposite the church in the village, has a small but reliable **poste restante** box. *Damodar Book Store*, on the beachfront, stocks a good selection of reasonably priced secondhand paperbacks in English. They also do part-exchange, and have the best range of postcards in Colva.

Tours out of Colva

GTDC operate a couple of **sightseeing tours out of Colva**, more popular with domestic tourists than foreigners, but better value than those run by the charter companies. Their "Traditional Tour" is the most tempting of the bunch, taking in a handful of monuments that include Old Goa and a few Hindu temples around Ponda. Tickets may be booked in advance through GTDC's *Tourist Cottages* complex on Colva beachfront.

A few private buses also leave Colva at 9am on Wednesday mornings for the **Anjuna flea market**. The trips cost Rs100 or so, but this works out cheaper than a taxi, and saves a lot of hassle: getting to Anjuna by public bus involves three changes and lots of waiting – hardly worth it if you're only going for the day. Tickets for the flea-market buses are sold at outlets along the main beach road, and at *La Village* guest house, which also organizes weekly **excursions to Palolem** (Rs100 including lunch).

Accommodation

Colva's plentiful **accommodation** ranges from bare cockroach-infested cells to swish campuses of chalets and swimming pools, with a fair selection of good-value guest houses in between. Most of the mid- and top-of-the-range places are strung out along the main beach road or just behind it. Budget rooms lie amid the more peaceful palm groves and paddy fields north of here: the quarter known as "Ward 4", which is accessible via the path that winds north from *Johnny Cool's* restaurant, or from the other side via a lane leading west off the main Colva–Vasco road.

Casa Mesquita, 194 Vasco Rd, Ward 3 (no phone). Large rooms, with rickety four-poster beds, no fans or attached shower-toilets, in fading old colonial-style house. Relaxing mosaic-floored verandahs, Western water toilet, and some cheap dorm beds available on request. Good value. ①.

Colmar, on the beachfront (☎0834/220485). Colva's oldest purpose-built hotel overlooks the beach, comprising comfortable chalets, and some cheaper non-attached rooms, grouped around a central lawn. No advance bookings, but good off-season discounts. Some a/c. ③.

Garden Cottages, Ward 4 (no phone). Immaculately maintained, attractive budget guest house in Colva's most tranquil quarter. Spacious twin-bedded en-suite rooms with fans, and a garden. Very popular and excellent value, so book ahead. ①.

La Ben, on the beach road (☎0834/222009). Neat, clean, and good value at this price, though better known for its rooftop restaurant. ⑤.

La Village, 333 Vasco Rd, Ward 4 (no phone). Relaxed and friendly roadside guest house geared to budget backpackers, with clean rooms (some attached), good wooden beds, mosquito nets, safe-deposit facility and terrace-cafe. ①.

Ronnie's, Ward 4 (no phone). Standard cell-block rooms, all with attached shower-toilets, and idyllic views west over the paddy fields from verandahs. ①.

Silver Sands, on the beach road (☎0834/221645). Average rooms (some a/c) ranged around a pool, with restaurant and health club. Facilities include car rental, money-changing and courtesy bus to airport. Popular with package companies, but shabbier than the others at this price. ⑥.

Sukhsagar, opposite the *Penthouse* (☎0834/220224). Nothing special from the outside, but its en-suite rooms are clean, light and airy, and the best deal in this price range. ④.

Vinson's, Ward 4 (no phone). Newest of this Ward's good-value cheapos; quiet and secluded. ①.

William's, on the beach road (☎0834/221077; fax 222852). Flashy package tour complex, 400m from the beach, with good facilities, some a/c, and a pool. Accepts walk-in customers. ⑥–⑦.

Eating and drinking

When the season is in full swing, Colva's beachfront sprouts a row of large seafood **restaurants** on stilts, some of them very ritzy indeed, with tablecloths, candles and smooth music. The prices in these places are top-whack, but the portions are correspondingly vast, and standards generally high. Budget travellers are equally well-catered for, with a sprinkling of **shack-cafes** at the less frequented ends of the beach, and along the Vasco Rd.

Joencon's, second restaurant south from beachfront. The classiest of Colva's beach restaurants. Agonizingly slow service and pricey, but the food is superb: try their flamboyant fish sizzlers, mouthwatering *tandoori* sharkfish or Chinese and Indian vegetarian specialities.

Johnny Cool's, opposite *William's Resort*, on the beach road. Inexpensive roadside cafe-bar with views across the fields behind. Serves different beers and spirits, and the best pizza in Goa.

La Ben's, on the beach road. Pleasant rooftop restaurant with a predictable moderately priced menu and sea views. A good sunset spot.

Men Mar, Vasco Rd. Their *lassis*, prepared with fresh fruit and home-made curd, are delicious. Open for breakfast.

Pasta Hut, on the beachfront. Western food, mostly pasta and some veg dishes, served on cramped terrace next to the unsightly rubbish-filled rivulet. A hit with 18–30 package tourists.

Sandcastle, north of the beachfront. Hippy beach hang-out bar-restaurant famed for its inexpensive pizza, pasta and apple pies.

Silver Sands, on the beach road. Swish indoor à la carte restaurant with an impressive selection of pricey Goan, Indian and continental dishes. Good place for a splurge.

Umita, Vasco Rd. Down-to-earth Goan and Indian veg cooking served up by a friendly Hindu family. Try their blow-out "special" *thalis* or whopping fresh-fruit-and-curd breakfasts. Opens early.

Nightlife

Although never an established rave venue, Colva's **nightlife** is livelier than anywhere else in south Goa, thanks to its ever-growing contingent of young package tourists. The two hippest nightclubs are down in the dunes south of the beachfront area: *Castaways* boasts a big *MTV* screen and music to match, and a late bar and disco that liven up around 10pm. A sandy plod just south of here, *Splash*'s dance floor is small but has a thumping Indian-ragga and techno sound system, and a sociable terrace littered with wicker easy chairs. In north Colva is the *New Sunshine*'s garden disco, which draws its custom from the *Sea Queen* package tour complex opposite. If you'd prefer to get plastered somewhere cheaper and less pretentious, try *Johnny Cool's*, midway between the beach and Colva crossroads. *Men Mar*, on the Vasco Rd, also serves beers, snacks and *lassis* until around 10.30pm, as does nearby *La Village*'s small terrace cafe.

Benaulim

According to Hindu mythology, Goa was created when the sage Shri Parasurama, Vishnu's sixth incarnation, fired an arrow into the sea from the top of the Western Ghats and ordered the waters to recede. The spot where the shaft fell to earth, known in Sanskrit as *Banali* ("place where the arrow landed") and later corrupted by the Portuguese to **BENAULIM**, lies in the centre of Colva Beach, 7km west of Margao. Only a decade ago, this fishing and rice farming village, scattered around the coconut groves and paddy fields between the main Colva–Mobor road and the dunes, had barely made it onto the backpackers' map. Now, the shady lane leading through it is studded with small guest houses and souvenir stalls. However, the tourist scene is still relatively low-key, most of Benaulim's visitors being budget travellers, young families and fugitives from more commercialized Colva.

Either side of the village's sand-blown beachfront, the gently shelving sands shimmer away almost to the horizon, littered with photogenic wooden fishing boats that provide welcome shade if the walk from the palm trees to the sea gets too much. Hawkers, itinerant masseurs and fruit-*wallahs* appear from time to time, but you can easily escape them by heading south towards neighbouring **Varca**, where tourism has thus far made little impact. Moreover, the sea is safe for swimming, being generally jellyfish-free, while the village itself boasts a few serviceable bars and restaurants, several telephone booths and a couple of stores. This all looks set to change if the monstrous concrete hotel complex currently being thrown up on the outskirts is the shape of things to come; for the time being, though, Benaulim is a wonderfully peaceful and friendly place to unwind.

Arrival and information

Buses from Margao, Colva, Varca, Cavelossim and Mobor roll through Benaulim every half hour, dropping passengers at the Maria Hall crossroads. Ranged around this busy junction are two well-stocked **general stores**, a couple of **cafe-bars**, a **bank**, **pharmacy**, **laundry** and the taxi- and auto-rickshaw rank, from where you can pick up **transport** 2km west to the beach.

Signs offering **bicycles** and **motorbikes** for rent are dotted along the lane leading to the sea: rates are standard, descending in proportion to the length of time you keep

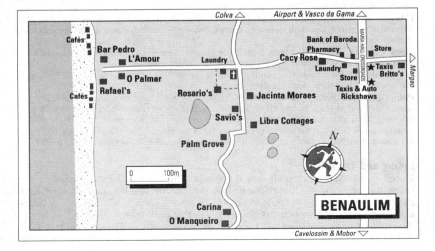

MUGGINGS IN BENAULIM

As this book went to press, reports reached the *Rough Guides* office that **muggings** had become a problem in Benaulim. During early 1996, dozens of tourists were robbed and assaulted on the road from the village to the beach. This is not a totally new phenomenon, but the attacks have clearly become more frequent and more violent over the past couple of seasons; one tourist had chilli pepper thrown in his eyes, and another's arm was broken during a scuffle. If you walk the road between the beachfront and Benaulim village after dark, do so in a group.

---

the vehicle. The nearest place to **change money** is the *Sanatan Travel Agency* in Colva (see p.761), or one of the banks in Margao (see p.758). Benaulim's *Bank of Baroda* (Mon–Fri 9am–1pm, Sat 9am–noon) only handles *Visa* card encashments; the *L'Amour Beach Resort* also has a foreign-exchange counter for guests. Finally, international and domestic **flights** can be booked or reconfirmed at *Sarken Tour Operators*, and *L'Amour*, which also does deluxe bus, train and catamaran ticketing for cities elsewhere in India.

Accommodation

Benaulim's **accommodation** consists largely of small budget guest houses, scattered around the lanes 1km or so back from the beach. Most are featureless annexes of spartan stone-tiled rooms with fans, and usually attached shower-toilets; the only significant difference between them is their location. As few places have telephones, the only way to find a vacancy is to hunt around on foot, although if you wait at the Maria Hall crossroads or the beachfront with a rucksack, someone is bound to ask if you need a room. During peak season, the village's few mid-range hotels tend to be fully booked, so reserve in advance if you want to stay in one of these.

Cacy Rose, 100m south of Maria Hall crossroads (no phone). A handful of basic rooms, mostly attached, above a sociable terrace bar-restaurant. ②.

Carina, Tamdi-Mati, Vas Vaddo (no phone). This good-value upmarket hotel lies in a tranquil location with a pool, bar-restaurant, foreign exchange and room service. Some a/c. ⑤–⑦.

Jacinta Morães, 1608/A Vas Vaddo (no phone). Half-a-dozen large-ish clean rooms with fans, attached shower-toilets and sound plumbing. Some Western toilets. ②.

L'Amour, on the beachfront (☎0834/223720). Benaulim's longest established hotel is a comfortable 30-room/cottage complex, with terrace restaurant, travel agent, money-changing and some a/c. No single occupancy. ④–⑤.

Libra Cottages, Vas Vaddo, Tambdi Mati (no phone). New double-storeyed complex of large rooms, all with attached bathrooms and twin beds. Excellent value. ②.

O Palmar, opposite *L'Amour* (no phone). A row of slightly shabby sea-facing chalets, virtually on the beach, and with their own verandahs. ④.

Palm Grove, Tamdi-Mati, Vas Vaddo (☎0834/222533). Secluded hotel surrounded by beautiful gardens, with a budget block around the back, some a/c, pleasant terrace restaurant and friendly management. A bike ride from the beachfront, but the most appealing place in its class. ③–⑥.

Rosario's, Vas Vaddo, off the second (west) crossroads (no phone). The village's most popular budget guest house, with common or attached bathrooms and small balconies (no views). ①–②.

Eating and drinking

Places to **eat** are scattered all over the village. The *Palm Grove*'s congenial garden restaurant, or any of the lookalike cafe-bars that dot the lane leading to it, offer alternatives if you're staying in south Benaulim, or fancy a change of scenery. The beach also sports a row of temporary seafood joints during peak season.

Cacy Rose, 100m south of Maria Hall. Large portions of inexpensive food (pancakes and porridge), with a fair choice of Goan, Indian and veg dishes, as well as breakfasts, served on roadside terrace.

Pedro's, on the beachfront. Long waits, but the food – mostly fish steaks served with home-made sauces – is cheap, freshly cooked and tasty.

Rafael's, on the beachfront. Rough-and-ready beach cafe serving all the usual stuff, plus fried rice, salads and deliciously stodgy oven-hot coconut pudding.

Solitary Gardens, *Palm Grove*, Tamdi-Mati, Vas Vaddo. Mostly Goan seafood, with some Indian and continental options, dished up al fresco in cosy garden cafe-restaurant. Worth the trip out here.

Tona, *L'Amour* hotel, on the beachfront. Their Chinese dishes are definitely worth a splurge, but the rest of the menu is overpriced, and the service poor.

Varca

If you're staying in Benaulim, you're bound at some point to visit **VARCA**: the row of beached wooden fishing boats 2km south of Benaulim belong to its community of Christian fisher-folk, whose palm-thatched long houses line the foot of the grassy dunes. Of the tourists that pedal past, few stay longer than a few hours crashed in the shade of an outrigger. However, it is possible to find **rooms to rent** in family houses by asking around the village. Facilities are ultra-basic, with well water and pig toilets, but if you're looking for somewhere authentically Goan, yet not too far off-track, Varca is worth considering. A bicycle and cooking equipment are essential for long spells.

The only blots on the otherwise unspoiled landscape around Varca are the *Resorte de Goa* (☎0834/245066; ⑨), a new three-star resort, whose rooms and bright chalets cluster around a pool and sun terrace, with two bars, restaurants and sea views; along with the large and swish *Ramada Renaissance* (☎0834/245200; ⑧–⑨), which boasts waterfalls in reception, a nine-hole golf course, Polynesian restaurant, poolside disco and casino.

Cavelossim and around

Sleepy **CAVELOSSIM**, straddling the coast road 11km south of Colva, is the last major settlement in southwest Salcete: its only claim to fame. A short way beyond the village's picturesque church **square**, a narrow lane veers left (east) across an open expanse of paddy fields to the Cavelossim–Assolna **ferry crossing** (last departures: 8.30pm from Cavelossim, 8.45pm from Assolna), near the mouth of the Sal River. If you're heading south to Canacona, turn left off the ferry – *not* right as indicated on local maps – and carry on as far as Assolna bazaar, clustered around a junction on the main road. A right turn at this crossroads puts you on track for Canacona.

The far south: Canacona

Ceded to the Portuguese by the Rajah of Sund in the Treaty of 1791, Goa's **far south** – **Canacona district** – was among the last parts of the territory to be absorbed into the the *Novas Conquistas*, and has retained a distinctly Hindu feel. The area also boasts some of the state's most outstanding scenery. Set against a backdrop of the jungle-covered Sahyadri Hills (an extension of the Western Ghat range), a string of pearl-white coves and sweeping beaches scoop its indented coastline, enfolded by laterite headlands and colossal piles of black boulders.

So far, tourism has made little impression on this beautiful landscape. With the exception of **Palolem**, whose near-perfect beach attracts a steady flow of day trippers and longer-staying travellers during high season, the coastal settlements remain rooted in a traditional fishing and *todi*-tapping economy. However, the red gash of the **Konkan Railway** currently being gouged through the district threatens to bring its days as a tranquil rural backwater to an end. When the controversial project is completed, Canacona will be reachable by direct "super-fast" express trains from Bombay, Panjim and Mangalore: the developers' bulldozers and concrete mixers are sure to follow.

The region's main transport artery is the NH17, which crawls across the Sahyadri and Karmali Ghats towards Karnataka via the district headquarters, **Chaudi**. Bus services between here and Margao are frequent; off the highway, however, bullock carts and bicycles far out number motor vehicles. The only way to do the area justice, therefore, is by motorcycle, although you'll have to rent one farther north and drive it down here as few are available *in situ*.

Chaudi

CHAUDI (aka Chauri, or Canacona), 33km south of Margao, is Canacona district's charmless headquarters. Packed around a busy junction on the main Panjim–Mangalore highway, it is primarily a transport hub, of interest to visitors only because of its proximity of Palolem, 2km west. Buses to and from Panjim, Margao, and Karwar in Karnataka *taluka* trundle in and out of a scruffy square on the main street, from where taxis and auto-rickshaws ferry passengers to the villages scattered across the surrounding fields. The area's only **pharmacy** stands just off the crossroads, handy if you're staying in Palolem.

Palolem

PALOLEM, 2km west of Chaudi, pops up more often in glossy holiday brochures than any other beach in Goa; not because the village is a major package tour destination, but because its crescent-shaped bay, lined with a swaying curtain of coconut palms, is irresistibly photogenic. Hemmed in by a pair of wooded headlands, a perfect curve of white sand arcs north from a pile of huge boulders to the spur of **Sahyadri Ghat**, which here tapers into the sea.

Until recently, foreign tourists were few and far between in Palolem. Over the past three or four years, however, increasing numbers of budget travellers have begun to pour in, and the village is now far from the undiscovered idyll it used to be, with a string of cafes, Karnatakan hawkers and a tent camp crowding the beach front. Souvenir stalls have also sprung up, catering mainly for the mini-van and boat parties of charter tourists on day-trips from resorts further north. In spite of these encroachments, Palolem remains a resolutely traditional village, where the easy pace of life is dictated more by the three daily rounds of *todi*-tapping than the exigences of tourism.

ARRIVAL AND INFORMATION

Buses run between Margao and Karwar (in Karnataka) via Chaudi (every 30min; 2hr), where you can pick up an **auto-rickshaw** (Rs30) or **taxi** (Rs50) to Palolem. Alternatively, get off at the Char Rostay ("Four-Way") crossroads, 1.5km before Chaudi, and walk the remaining kilometre or so to the village. A couple of buses each day also go all the way to Palolem from Margao; these stop at the end of the lane leading from the main street to the beachfront. The last bus from Palolem to Chaudi/Margao leaves at 4.30pm; check with the locals for the times, which change seasonally.

Cycles may be rented from a stall halfway along the main street for the princely sum of Rs2 per hour (with discounts for longer periods). The village has only a couple of **public telephones**: avoid the one in the *Beach Resort*, which charges more than double the going rate for international calls, and head for the cheaper ISD/STD booth next to the bus stop. At present, there is nowhere in Palolem or Chaudi to change money; the nearest bank with a foreign-exchange facility is in Margao (see p.758).

ACCOMMODATION

The most popular place to **stay** in the village is the *Palolem Beach Resort* (✆0834/643054; ②–③), slap on the beachfront, which offers eleven simple but clean rooms with attached shower-toilets and small verandahs, set in a shady walled compound. Between November and March, it also erects a handful of twin-bedded canvas tents (②), each with its own electric light, fan and locker. For a little more comfort, try *Tonrick's* (no phone; ④), two minutes' up the lane on the right, which boasts the village's only other mid-range rooms. If you're after something cheaper, ask at the *Fifth August Bar and Lodge* (☎0834/643173; ②), a short way north, whose eight pleasant sea-facing attached rooms have small verandahs facing the beach. Also worth enquiring about if these are full is a row of eight dingier cells around the back of the cafe (①). Palolem's only other accommodation is tucked away at the opposite end of the village in **private family houses**. *Dylan's Bar* on the beach is a good place to start looking, as they usually know which families have vacancies. Don't, however, expect anything too sophisticated: while the rooms tend to be spotless, and cheap, water is in short supply and the toilets are staffed by gangs of hungry hogs.

EATING AND DRINKING

Finding somewhere to **eat** is not a problem in Palolem, even though the locals have to buy in most of their fish from Margao (they only catch mackerel with their hand nets). Once again, the *Beach Resort* cleans up most of the custom, in spite of its indifferent and overpriced food and grating background music. Better, then, to choose one of the many cheap cafes dotted along the beach. They all serve the same standard and range of seafood dishes, washed down with cold beer.

For something a little more elegant, try the excellent *Classic* restaurant, tucked away two minutes' walk into the *todi* groves where the village's straight main street veers left toward Chaudi. An off-shoot of Anjuna's renowned *German Bakery*, this place serves tasty north Indian food, with a great selection of Western-style cakes, wholefoods, healthy breakfasts and desserts (including tiramisu to die for). Prices are well above average, but the food is worth it. The best all-round budget cafe-bar in the village has to be *Sun 'n' Moon*, half-way along the main street, which does all the usual snacks and fish dishes, with plenty of veg options, pancakes and puddings. Locally made *feni*, far better (and cheaper) than the bottled stuff sold in town, is available at most bars in Palolem (the village has a lucrative side-line in smuggling the stuff to Karnataka).

Agonda

AGONDA, 10km north of Chaudi, can only be reached along the sinuous coast road connecting Cabo de Rama with NH14 at Chaudi. No signposts mark the turning and few of the tourists that whizz past en route to Palolem pull off here, but the beach, fringed along its entire length by *todi* trees, is superb. Its remote location is not the only reason this three-kilometre spead of white sand has been bypassed by the bulldozers. Villagers here are opposed to any kind of tourist development. In 1982, when a group of absentee landlords sold off a chunk of the beach to a Delhi-based hotel chain, the locals refused to vacate the plot, insisting the proposed five-star and golf-course would ruin their traditional livelihoods. Faced with threats of violent resistance, and protracted legal battles, the developers eventually backed down, and the unfinished concrete hulk they left behind is today the only unsightly structure for miles.

At present, there's only one **place to stay** in Agonda. Situated at the far (south) end of the beach, the friendly *Dunhill Bar & Restaurant* has a handful of very basic rooms (①), with breezy verandahs and pig toilets around the back. It's a clean and peaceful place, and the friendly family who run it serve spicy Goan-style fried mackerel, rice and curry to order in their small terrace restaurant.

Cotigao Wildlife Sanctuary

The **Cotigao Wildlife Sanctuary**, 10km southeast of Chaudi, was established in 1969 to protect a remote and vulnerable area of forest lining the Goa–Karnataka border. Encompassing 86 square kilometres of mixed deciduous woodland, the reserve is certain to inspire tree lovers, but less likely to yield many wildlife sightings: its tigers and leopards were hunted out long ago, while the gazelles, sloth bears, porcupines, panthers and hyenas that allegedly lurk in the woods rarely appear. You do, however, stand a good chance of spotting at least two species of monkey, a couple of wild boar and the odd gaur (the primeval-looking Indian bison). Best visited between October and March, Cotigao is a peaceful and scenic park that makes a pleasant day trip from Palolem, 12km northwest. Any of the buses running south on NH14 to Karwar via Chaudi will drop you within 2km of the gates. However, to explore the inner reaches of the sanctuary, you really need your own transport. The wardens at the reserve's small **Interpretative Centre** will show you how to get to a 25-metre-high treetop watchtower, overlooking a **waterhole** that attracts a handful of animals around dawn and dusk. Written permission for an overnight **stay**, either in the watchtower or the Forest Department's small *Rest House* (①), must be obtained from the Deputy Conservator of Forests, 3rd Floor, Junta House, Panjim (☎0832/45926), as far in advance of your visit as possible. If you get stuck, however, the wardens can arrange a tent, blankets and basic food.

CHAPTER TWELVE

CALCUTTA AND WEST BENGAL

U nique among Indian states in stretching all the way from the Himalayas to the sea, **WEST BENGAL** is nonetheless explored in depth by few travellers. That may have something to do with the exaggerated reputation of its capital, **CALCUTTA**, which is actually a sophisticated and friendly city that belies its popular image as poverty-stricken and chaotic. Certainly the rest of Bengal holds an extraordinary assortment of landscapes and cultures, ranging from the dramatic hill station of **Darjeeling**, within sight of some of the highest mountains in the world, to the vast mangrove swamps of the **Sunderbans**, prowled by man-eating Royal Bengal tigers who share the seas with sharks and crocodiles. The narrow central band of the state is cut across by the huge River Ganges as it pours from Bihar into Bangladesh; its waters would virtually ignore West Bengal were it not for the **Farrakha Barrage**, which feeds south-flowing channels such as the River Hooghly, the lifeline of Calcutta.

At the height of British rule, in the nineteenth and early twentieth centuries, Bengal flourished both culturally and materially, nurturing a vibrant creative blend of West and East. The **Bengali Renaissance** produced thinkers, writers and artists such as Raja Ram Mohan Roy, Bankim Chandra Chatterjee, and above all **Rabindranath Tagore**, whose collective influence still permeates Bengali society a century later.

Not all of Bengal, however, is Bengali; the recent Nepalese-led separatist movement for the creation of a semi-autonomous "Gurkhaland" in the Darjeeling area has highlighted sharp differences in culture. Although the Hindu Nepalese largely displaced the

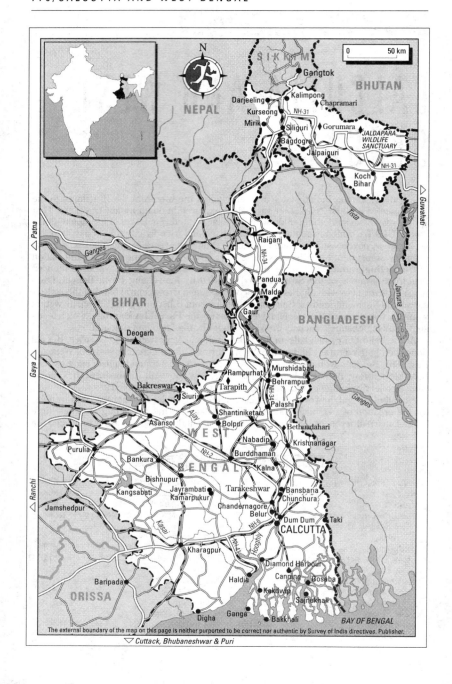

The external boundary of the map on this page is neither purported to be correct nor authentic by Survey of India directives. Publisher.

▽ Cuttack, Bhubaneshwar & Puri

WEST BENGAL TRAVEL DETAILS

	Trains		Buses		Flights	
	Frequency	Time	Frequency	Time	Frequency	Time
To and from CALCUTTA						
Agra	1 daily	30hr				
Agartala					1–2 daily	50min
Ahmedabad	1 daily	44hr				
Bagdogra (Siliguri)					1–2 daily	1hr
Bhubaneshwar	12 daily	7hr 30min–9hr	4 daily	8–10hr	1–2 daily	1hr
Bombay	3 daily	33–42hr			5–6 daily	2hr 30min
Delhi	7 daily	18hr–34hr 15min			7–9 daily	2–4hr
Dhaka					3–4 daily	1hr 10min
Guwahati					3–4 daily	1hr 10min–2hr 40min
Gwalior	4 weekly	26hr 30min				
Haridwar	1 daily	30hr				
Jabalpur	1 daily	21hr 15min				
Jaipur					4 weekly	3hr
Jalgaon	4 daily	28hr–34hr				
Kathmandu					7 weekly	1hr 35min–2hr 15min
Khajuraho					1 daily	5hr
Lucknow	5–6 daily	21hr 45min–28hr			8 weekly	3hr 30min–4hr
Madras	5–6 daily	27hr 30min–30hr			3–4 daily	3hr–5hr 30min
Nagpur	4 daily	19–25hr			3 weekly	2hr 40min
Patna	12 daily	7hr 30min–9hr			3 weekly	2hr
Port Blair					3 weekly	2hr
Puri	2 nightly	11hr 30min	2 daily	12hr		
Ranchi	1 daily	10hr			3 weekly	1hr
Shantiniketan (Bolpur)	7 daily	2hr 30min–4hr				
Shillong					1 daily	1hr 45min
Siliguri (NJP)	5 daily	12hr	8 daily	12hr		
Thiruv'puram	1 weekly	49hr				
Ujjain	2 weekly	33hr 40min				
Varanasi	5–8 daily	8hr 30min–20hr				
To and from BAGDOGRA (Siliguri)						
Bombay					2 daily	4hr 15min–7hr 30min
Delhi					1–3 daily	2hr–4hr
Guwahati					7 weekly	1hr
Madras					1 daily	3hr 50min

For more details on routes to and from **Siliguri** and **Darjeeling**, see pages 814 and 821 respectively.

indigenous tribal groups of the north during the nineteenth century, a new influx of Tibetans has revitalized the traditions of *lama*-ism. In the southwest, on the other hand, tribal groups such as the Santals and the Mundas still maintain a presence, and itinerant Baul **musicians** epitomize the region's traditions of song and dance. The Bauls are most often heard around Tagore's university at **Shantiniketan**, where his own musical form, *Rabindra Sangeet*, is a popular amalgam of influences including folk and classical. Other historical specialities of Bengal include the erection of ornate and delicate **terracotta temples**, as seen at Bishnupur, and the manufacture of **silk**, concentrated around Murshidabad, the last independent capital of Bengal.

Bengal's own brand of Hinduism emphasizes the mother goddess, who appears in such guises as the fearful Kali and Durga, the benign Saraswati, goddess of learning, and Lakshmi the goddess of wealth. The most mysterious of all is Tara, an echo of medieval links with Buddhism; her temple at **Tarapith** is perhaps the greatest centre of tantricism in the entire country. In recent years, however, the prayer flags have given way to red flags, and the new religion of politics.

A brief history of West Bengal

Although Bengal was part of the Mauryan empire during the third century BC, it first came to prominence in its own right under the Guptas, in the fourth century AD. So dependent was it on trade with the Mediterranean that the fall of Rome caused a sharp decline, only reversed with the rise of the Pala dynasty in the eighth century.

After a short-lived period of rule by the highly cultured Senas, based at **Gaur**, Bengal was brought under Muslim rule at the end of the twelfth century by the first Sultan of Delhi, Qutb-ud-din-Aibak. Sher Shah Suri, who usurped power from the Moghuls in the mid-sixteenth century, achieved much in Bengal; it was thanks to him that the Grand Trunk Road took its most developed form, running all the way to the Northwest Province on the borders of his native Afghanistan. Akbar took back the territory in 1574, just in time to face the advent of the Europeans.

The Portuguese, who were the first to set up a trading community beside the Hooghly, were soon joined by the British, Dutch and French and many others. Rivalry between them – all received some degree of sanction from the Moghul court – eventually resulted in the ascendancy of the **British**, with the only serious indigenous resistance coming from the tutelary kingdom of **Murshidabad**, led by the young Siraj-ud-Daula. His attack on the fledgeling British community of Calcutta in 1756 culminated in the infamous **Black Hole** incident, when British prisoners, possibly in error, were incarcerated in a tiny space that caused many to suffocate to death. Vengeance, in the form of a British army from Madras under **Robert Clive**, arrived a year later. The defeat of Siraj-ud-Daula at the Battle of Plassey heralded the start of British domination of the entire subcontinent. Bengal became the mainstay of the British East India Company, and its lucrative trading empire, until the company handed over control to the Crown in 1854.

Until 1905, Bengal encompassed Orissa and Bihar; then it was split down the middle by Lord Curzon, leaving East Bengal and Assam on one side and Orissa, Bihar and West Bengal on the other. That aroused bitter resentment, and the rift it created between Hindus and Muslims was a direct cause of the second Partition, in 1947, when East Bengal became East Pakistan. During the war with Pakistan in the early 1970s that resulted in the creation of an independent **Bangladesh**, up to ten million refugees fled into West Bengal; most have now returned. Shorn of its provinces, and with its capital Calcutta replaced by Delhi in 1911, the story of West Bengal in the twentieth century has largely been a chronicle of decline.

Economically, the **rice** grown in the paddy fields of the lowlands remains West Bengal's most important cash crop, though **tea** is a close second. The introduction of tea was largely the work of the British, who cleared the forests of the Himalayan foothills; they brought tea plants from China, but local Darjeeling tea soon developed a reputation of its own. The other great nineteenth-century industry, **jute**, has not fared so well. Most was grown in East Bengal – now Bangladesh – while the mills themselves were located along the River Hooghly around Calcutta. As a result, after 1947, the mills found it hard to obtain supplies; however, new jute-growing regions have since been developed.

Politics permeates almost every aspect of life in West Bengal today, which has largely returned to stability after several troubled decades. The state was all but brought to its knees in the 1960s and 1970s, when the **Naxalites** (Communist Party of

India – Marxist-Leninists) launched an abortive but bloody attempt at revolution. After a bitter three-way struggle between the Communist Party of India (Marxists), the Congress and the Naxalites, the CPI(M) finally emerged victorious. Since 1977, under the enigmatic leadership of Jyoti Basu, they have somehow succeeded in balancing rhetoric and old-fashioned socialism with a prudent practicality – and their strong rural base has enabled them to weather the collapse of world communism. Capitalism is allowed to survive, but made to support the political infrastructure.

CALCUTTA

One of the four great urban centres of India, Calcutta is to its proud citizens the equal of any city in the country in charm, variety and interest. Like Bombay and Madras, it is not an ancient city; its roots lie in the European expansion of the seventeenth century. The showpiece capital of the British Raj, this was the greatest colonial city of the Orient. Descendants of the fortune-seekers who flocked from across the globe to participate in Calcutta's eighteenth- and nineteenth-century trading boom remain conspicuous in its cosmopolitan blend of communities.

However, mass migrations of dispossessed refugees, occasioned by twentieth-century upheavals within the subcontinent, have tested the city's infrastructure to the limit. The resultant suffering – and the work of Mother Teresa in drawing attention to its most pathetic victims – has given Calcutta a reputation for **poverty** that its residents consider ill-founded. They argue that the city's problems are no longer as acute as those of Bombay or other cities across the world, and that the slum scenes familiar from the book and film *City of Joy* are distortions of the truth. In fact, though Calcutta's mighty Victorian buildings lie peeling and decaying, and its avenues have long been choked by its inability to expand any further, the image of a city struggling for survival belies a recent upsurge in its fortunes. Calcutta exudes a warmth that leaves few visitors unmoved, and with the return of political calm and the pragmatism of the Bengali government is buoyant with fresh optimism. The opening of India's first underground system in 1984 was seen as the first portent of a new beginning.

The Bengalis of Calcutta like to see themselves as the **intelligentsia** of India; a long-standing maxim states that "what Bengal does today, India will do tomorrow." This is a city where artistic endeavour is held in higher esteem than political and economic success, home to a multitude of **galleries** and huge Indian classical **music** festivals, with a thriving Bengali-language **theatre** scene and a tradition of **cinema** brought world renown by Satyajit Ray (see *Contexts*). Adding to the chaos and colour, Calcutta has a wonderful tradition of political posters and graffiti. Witty and flamboyant slogans compete with a forest of advertising hoardings to festoon every available surface.

Though Marxists may rule from the chief bastion of imperialism, the **Writers Building**, and the site of the notorious **Black Hole of Calcutta**, now obscured by the main post office, visitors still experience Calcutta first and foremost as a colonial city. Grand edifices in a profusion of styles include the imposing **Victoria Memorial** and the gothic **St Paul's Cathedral**, while the eclectic **Indian Museum**, one of the largest museums in Asia, ranges from natural history to art and archeology. Among numerous venerable Raj institutions to have survived are the race course, the polo ground, the reverence for cricket, and several exclusive gentlemen's clubs.

In terms of **climate**, Calcutta is at its best during its short winter, when the daily maximum temperature hovers around 27°C, and the markets are filled with vegetables and flowers. Before the monsoons, the heat hangs unbearably heavy; the arrival of the rains in late June brings relief, but usually also heavy floods that turn the streets into a quagmire. After a brief period of post-monsoon heat, October and November are quite pleasant; this is the time of the city's biggest festival, **Durga Puja**.

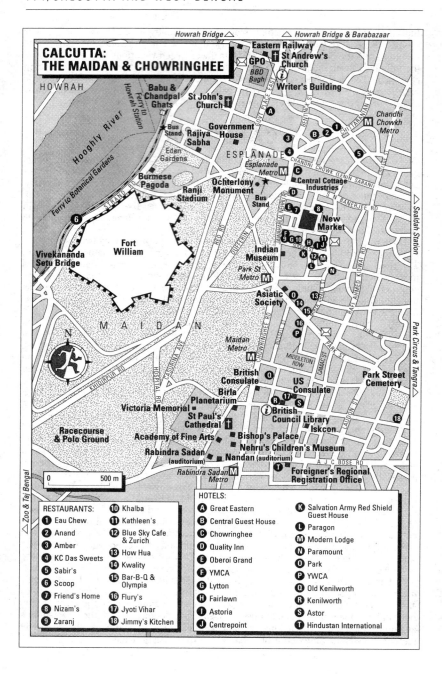

CALCUTTA:
THE MAIDAN & CHOWRINGHEE

HOWRAH

Hooghly River

Howrah Bridge △   △ Howrah Bridge & Barabazaar

Eastern Railway
GPO   St Andrew's
BBD   Church
Bagh
Writer's Building

Babu & Chandpal Ghats
St John's Church
Government House
Rajiya Sabha
Eden Gardens

Chandhi Chowkh Metro

ESPLANADE
Esplanade Metro
Central Cottage Industries

Burmese Pagoda
Ranji Stadium
Ochterlony Monument
Bus Stand

New Market

Indian Museum
Park St Metro

Fort William

Vivekananda Setu Bridge

Asiatic Society

M A I D A N

Maidan Metro

MIDDLETON ROW

British Consulate
US Consulate

Birla Planetarium
Victoria Memorial
St Paul's Cathedral
Academy of Fine Arts
Rabindra Sadan (auditorium)
Nandan (auditorium)
Rabindra Sadan Metro

Racecourse & Polo Ground

British Council Library
Iskcon
Bishop's Palace
Nehru's Children's Museum

Foreigner's Regional Registration Office

Park Street Cemetery

Sealdah Station

Park Circus & Tangra

Zoo & Taj Bengal

0   500 m

HOTELS:

RESTAURANTS:	
① Eau Chew	⑩ Khalba
② Anand	⑪ Kathleen's
③ Amber	⑫ Blue Sky Cafe & Zurich
④ KC Das Sweets	⑬ How Hua
⑤ Sabir's	⑭ Kwality
⑥ Scoop	⑮ Bar-B-Q & Olympia
⑦ Friend's Home	⑯ Flury's
⑧ Nizam's	⑰ Jyoti Vihar
⑨ Zaranj	⑱ Jimmy's Kitchen

Ⓐ Great Eastern	Ⓚ Salvation Army Red Shield Guest House
Ⓑ Central Guest House	Ⓛ Paragon
Ⓒ Chowringhee	Ⓜ Modern Lodge
Ⓓ Quality Inn	Ⓝ Paramount
Ⓔ Oberoi Grand	Ⓞ Park
Ⓕ YMCA	Ⓟ YWCA
Ⓖ Lytton	Ⓠ Old Kenilworth
Ⓗ Fairlawn	Ⓡ Kenilworth
Ⓘ Astoria	Ⓢ Astor
Ⓙ Centrepoint	Ⓣ Hindustan International

A history of Calcutta

By the time the remarkable **Job Charnock** established the headquarters of the **East India Company** at **Sutanuti** on the east bank of the Hooghly, in 1690, the riverside was already dotted with trading communities from European countries. Besides the British, previously based at Hooghly on the west bank, there were the French at Chandernagore, the Dutch and Armenians at Chinsurah, the Danes at Serampore, the Portuguese at Bandel, and even Greeks at Rishra and Prussians at Bhadeshwar.

Supported by Armenian funds, the East India Company bought land around Sutanuti, and in 1699 completed their first fort in the area – **Fort William**. A few years later the East India Company amalgamated Sutanuti and two other villages to form the town of **Calcutta**. The name may well derive from *Kalikutir*, the house or temple of Kali – a reference to the temple of **Kalighat**. Job Charnock, its first Governor, married an Indian wife who had been rescued from committing *sati* on her first husband's funeral pyre. With trading success came ambitious plans for development; in 1715 a delegation to the Moghul court in Delhi negotiated trading rights, along with several villages and towns on both banks of the Hooghly, to create a territory that was around fifteen kilometres long. The company built a moat around the perimeter to ward off possible Maratha attacks; known as the **Maratha Ditch**, it is marked by today's Circular Road. Later, the company entangled itself in the web of local power politics, with consequences both

THE BENGALI RENAISSANCE

Although a rich tradition of poetry existed in India long before the arrival of the Europeans – even scientific manuscripts were written in rhyming couplets – **prose** was all but unknown. Thus the foundation by the British of **Fort William College** in 1800 – primarily intended to assist administrators to learn Indian languages by commissioning prose in Bengali, Urdu and Hindi – had the unexpected side effect of helping to create a vital new genre in indigenous literature. Bankim Chandra **Chatterjee** (1838–99), a senior civil servant who wrote novels of everyday life, became known as the father of Bengali literature, while Michael Madhusudan **Dutt** (1829–73) introduced European poetic conventions into Bengali poetry. Simultaneously, Westernization began to sweep Bengali middle-class society, as they grew disenchanted with their culture and religion.

A leading figure in the new intelligentsia was Raja Ram Mohan **Roy** (1774–1833), born an orthodox Hindu, who travelled in Tibet before joining the East India Company, and eventually died in England as the ambassador of the Moghuls. Roy founded the **Brahmo Samaj**, a socio-religious movement that believed in a single god and set out to purge Hinduism of its idol worship and rituals, advocating the abolition of *sati* and child-marriage. Keshab Chandra **Sen**'s Navabidhan (New Dispensation), a synthesis of all the world's major religions, created a split in 1866 over its downplaying of the role of Hinduism. A renowned orator, Keshab Sen travelled to Britain to lecture, but actions such as marrying off two of his very young daughters – one to the Maharajah of Cooch Behar and the other to the Maharajah of Mayurbhanj – lost him much support.

The intellectual and cultural freedom of the Brahmo Samaj earned it an important influence over the Bengali upper classes that endures to this day. No single figure epitomized the **Bengali Renaissance** more than **Rabindranath Tagore**, a giant of Bengali art, culture and letters, who received the Nobel Prize for Literature in 1913. As well as writing several hymns, he set out the principles of the movement in *The Religion of Man*.

During and following the period of the Renaissance, several other religious leaders emerged in Calcutta. **Ramkrishna** (1836–86) was a great Kali devotee whose message was carried as far as North America by **Vivekananda**. **Paramhansa Yogananda** who wrote the renowned *Autobiography of a Yogi*, and **Sri Aurobindo** (1872–1950), who was a student in London before becoming a freedom fighter and later a philosopher. Preaching a return to a reformed esoteric Hinduism, he went on to establish his own ashram in Pondicherry.

unforeseen – as with the Black Hole (see p.784) – and most assiduously desired – as when the Battle of Plassey in 1758 made the British masters of Bengal. Recognized by Parliament in London in 1773, the company's trading monopoly led it to shift the capital of Bengal here from Murshidabad, and Calcutta became a clearing house for a vast range of commerce, including the lucrative exportation of opium to China.

At first, the East India Company brought young bachelors out from Britain to work as servants. Referred to as "writers", they lived in spartan conditions in communal mud huts, until the **Writers' Building** was eventually erected for their convenience. As they took to indigenous ways, and cohabited with local women, they were responsible for the emergence of the new **Eurasian** community. In time, Parliament rescinded the company's monopoly; when the doors of trade were thrown open, merchants and adventurers flocked in from far and wide, including Parsis, Baghdadi Jews, Afghans and Indians from other parts of the country. By 1857, such splendid buildings as the Court House, Government House, and St Paul's Cathedral, had earned Calcutta the soubriquet "City of Palaces". In truth, the humid and uncomfortable climate, putrefying salt marshes and the hovels that grew haphazardly around the city created unhygienic conditions that were a constant source of misery and disease.

The city's affluent elite – Bengali merchants included – came to be known as the "**bhadra log**", the good people. Although the term was lampooned by Kipling in *The Jungle Book*, in his depiction of the *Bandar Log*, the Monkey People, they were responsible for the great flowering of cultural and artistic expression known as the **Bengali Renaissance** (see box on p775). The decline of Calcutta as an international port came with the opening of the Suez Canal in 1869, the emergence of Bombay, and the end of the opium trade. In 1911, the days of glory came to a definitive end; the imperial capital of India was transferred to Delhi.

Arrival

Calcutta's **airport**, 20km north of the city centre, is served by international flights – although only a small proportion of visitors actually enter India here – as well as services from throughout the country. Officially "Netaji Subhash Bose International Airport", it is still universally known by its old name of **Dum Dum** – a name that became infamous during the Boer War, when the notorious (and now banned) exploding bullet was manufactured in a nearby factory. The dreary international terminal has money-changing facilities and a **pre-paid taxi** booth but little else. In complete contrast, the spanking new and modern **domestic terminal** has a much better range of amenities including an accommodation booking counter, tourist information, a railway reservation desk and a pre-paid taxi booth. Booked here, a **taxi** to the central Sudder Street area costs around Rs90; you'll pay a lot more if you attempt to make your own arrangements. Alternatively, an airport **bus** (Rs20) travels down Chowringhee to the *Indian Airlines* office and passes the western end of Sudder St. An a/c bus follows a similar route but has an erratic service and costs around Rs150. **Minibuses** run to BBD Bagh, but these can get crowded and prove to be an unwelcome introduction to the city. Another possibility is to take a taxi to the end of the **Metro** at Dum Dum, 3km away, and then take the underground line (Rs4) to Park St close to the top of Sudder St.

Of Calcutta's two main **railway stations**, neither of which is on the Metro system, **Howrah Station** – the point of arrival for major trains from the south and west, such as the *Rajdhani Express* from Delhi – stands on the far bank of the Hooghly a couple of kilometres west of the centre. To reach the central downtown area, traffic has to negotiate Howrah Bridge – a definitive introduction to the chaos of the city, especially during rush hours, which start late in the mornings. Long queues form at Howrah's **taxi rank** when main trains pull in – it works on a metered system, whereas touts and taxis who break the rank ask astronomical prices. **Minibuses** and **buses** (#5 and #6) also

The telephone **area code** for Calcutta is ☎033.

operate from Howrah, but tend to be far too crowded for comfort; the **trams** across town are a bit more bearable, if very slow. Probably the best alternative is to take a **ferry** ride to Babu Ghat, or the adjacent Chandpal Ghat, close to BBD Bagh, and pick up a taxi, bus or minibus from there.

Sealdah Station, used by trains from the north, is on the eastern edge of the centre, and much more convenient as you don't have to get across the river. Long-distance **buses** from the south terminate at **Babu Ghat Bus Stand**, not far from Fort William on the east bank, while some luxury buses, such as the *Rocket* from Darjeeling, arrive at **Esplanade Bus Stand**, under 1km north of Sudder St.

For **maps** of Calcutta, see map no.1 in the colour inserts and p.774

Information and communications

The recently revamped **Government of West Bengal Tourist Bureau**, 3/2 BBD Bagh East (☎248 8271), arranges tours of Calcutta and package trips around West Bengal, and in theory books accommodation in tourist bungalows all over the state, although communications are too poor for that service to be reliable. They also assist with permits and book tours and accommodation at the Sunderbans and Jaldapara wildlife parks, and maintain **tourist information counters** at the airport and at Howrah Station.

The helpful **Government of India Tourist Office**, 4 Shakespeare Sarani (☎242 5813), is probably easier to deal with, maintaining a useful if rather outdated database on sites and amenities throughout the region. Although their main task is to supply information, they provide passes for Marble Palace and assist in booking tours. An ITDC office, at 46c Chowringhee Rd, also provides information, and arranges tours.

English-language **newspapers** such as the *Statesman*, *Telegraph*, *Amrita Bazaar Patrika* and the *Hindusthan Standard* remain the primary source for information on **what's on**; WB Tourism also produce an occasional leaflet, available at all the tourist offices, called *Calcutta This Fortnight*.

Banks and currency exchange

Calcutta Airport has a 24-hour branch of the *State Bank of India*, as well as the *RN Dutta* bureau de change in the international departure lounge. Major **banks**, concentrated either in the vicinity of BBD Bagh or scattered around Jawaharlal Nehru Rd (Chowringhee Rd), include *Algemeene Bank Nederlands*, 18A Brabourne Rd; *American Express*, 21 Old Court House St; *Banque National de Paris*, 4a BBD Bagh East; *Bank of America*, 8 India Exchange Place; *Bank of Tokyo*, 2 Brabourne Rd; *Citibank*, 43 Jawaharlal Nehru Rd; *Grindlays*, 41 Jawaharlal Nehru Rd & 19 Netaji Subhas Rd; *Hong Kong & Shangai*, 8 Netaji Subhas Rd (24-hour service); *Standard Chartered*, 4 Netaji Subhas Rd; *State Bank of India*, 1 Strand Rd & 43 Jawaharlal Nehru Rd.

Among licensed brokers, whose exchange facilities are useful outside normal banking hours, are *RN Dutta*, Stephen House, 4–5 BBD Bagh East, 5&7 Kidderpore Dock and at the airport; *Maneek Lal Sen*, New Market; and *RR Sen*, 18 Jawaharlal Nehru Rd. *Thomas Cook* have their office in the Chitrakoot Building, 230 AJC Bose Rd (☎247 4560), and *American Express* (☎248 4464) is near the WB Tourist Bureau.

Mail services

Calcutta's imposing **GPO**, on the west side of BBD Bagh, houses the **poste restante** and has a philatelic department. The **Central Telegraph Exchange** is nearby at 8 Red

NEW AND OLD ROAD NAMES

Although many of Calcutta's old colonial **street names** have officially been changed over the last three decades, the original names continue to be widely used by Calcuttans.

Old Name	New Name
Bowbazar Street	Bepin Bihari Ganguly Street
Camac Street	Abanindranath Tagore Street
Chitpore Road	Rabindra Sarani
Chowringhee	Jawaharlal Nehru Road
Dalhousie Square	BBD Bagh
Dharamtala Street	Lenin Sarani
Free School Street	Mirza Ghalib Street
Harrington Street	Ho Chi Minh Sarani
Kyd Street	Dr Mohammed Ishaque Road
Landsdowne Road	Sarat Bose Road
Lower Circular Road	AJC Bose Road
Moria Street	Rev Martin Luther King Street
Red Road	Indira Gandhi Road
Ripon Street	Muzaffar Ahmed Street
Theatre Road	Shakespeare Sarani
Upper Lower	Acharya Prafulla
Circular Road	Chandra Road
Wellesley Street	Rafi Ahmed Kidwai Street
Wellington Square	Raja Subodh Mallick Square

Cross Place, close to Telephone Bhavan, the headquarters for Calcutta Telephones. If you're staying in the Sudder Street area, the **New Market Post Office**, Mirza Ghalib St, is much more convenient; sending parcels is easiest from the large and friendly post office on **Park Street**, where enterprising individuals make up the packaging and will handle the entire process for you for a negotiable fee.

Telephone and fax

Overseas phone calls can easily be made from the STD/ISD booths found all over the city. Most booths are digitalized and have convenient LED monitors showing the exact duration of each call, and the number dialled; many also have **fax** machines. Trying to put through **internal calls** can be frustrating in the extreme, though conditions are not as farcical as they were, when it was said to be easier to pass messages via relatives on the other side of the world. As digital technology is introduced, the city's telephone numbers are being progressively altered – which explains why some numbers have six digits and some seven. Published three times a year and available in bookshops, the *Infobase Neighbourhood Guide* or "ING" is a useful listings directory which gives the latest numbers.

City transport

Virtually all the different modes of transport that clog the streets of Calcutta – trams, buses, human rickshaws, auto-rickshaws, metered taxis, and minibuses – add to the problem of congestion rather than providing a solution. Only the city's pride and joy, India's first and only **Metro**, is an efficient way to get around (though even this consists of just one line). While using public transport beware of pickpockets, especially on crowded buses.

Increasingly, the **river** is being used for transport, with the *ghats* near Eden Gardens at the hub of a **ferry** system. The most pleasant way to beat the traffic is to take one of the very regular ferries from Chandpal Ghat to Howrah Station, while other sailings head downriver from Armenian Ghat, Chandpal or Babu Ghats to the Botanical

Gardens. Of more use to commuters than tourists, a **circular railway** loops south from Sealdah before moving up-river along the Strand and Princep Ghat, past Howrah Bridge and eventually to Dum Dum.

The Metro

Despite a couple of small fires in recent years, Calcutta's Russian-designed **Metro**, inaugurated in 1984, is every bit as good as its inhabitants proudly claim, a spotless contrast to the streets above, with trains operating punctually every few minutes, and videos on the platforms to keep passengers amused. Services start at 8am (3pm on Sun) and run until 8.30pm, with ticket prices from Rs2 to Rs4 for the entire distance from the centre to Dum Dum.

The entire single north–south line runs from Dum Dum, near the airport, to Tollygunge, taking in several convenient sights and following the main arteries including Chowringhee (Jawaharlal Nehru Rd), with convenient stations such as Park St, Kalighat, Esplanade and Rabindra Sadan.

Buses and minibuses

Calcutta supports a vast and complicated **bus** network, in operation each day between roughly 5am and 11pm, and subject to overcrowding and attendant pickpocketing problems. Red double-deckers and elongated trailer buses belonging to the *Calcutta Transport Corporation* – **CTC** – run the same routes, for much the same minimal fares, as a horde of private companies. Among potentially useful routes are **#8**, from Howrah via Esplanade and Gariahat Rd to Gol Park; **#S17**, from Chetla near Kalighat via Esplanade; and **#5** and **#6**, which both travel via Howrah and the Esplanade–Chowringhee area, and stop at the Indian Museum at the head of Sudder St.

In addition, private brown-and-yellow **minibuses** travel at inordinate speeds on ad-hoc routes; their destinations are usually painted boldly in Bengali and English on their sides, and conductors shout them out at bus stops or major junctions. Originally intended as fast seating-only commuter services, they now take on standing passengers; an incredibly uncomfortable way to travel, as unless you're absolutely tiny, you

---

CITY TOURS

City tours, run by West Bengal Tourism and the ITDC (see p.777) can involve more time contemplating heavy traffic than the sites themselves. Advance booking is necessary. They operate daily (except for holidays; and Mondays), costing around Rs75 for a full day; half-day tours have been suspended for the time being.

WB Tourism's tours start from their office in BBD Bagh East. Both last from 7.30am to 5pm, with a break for lunch. One takes in the Commercial area, Belur Math, Dakshineshwar, and the Sitalnath Jain temple, then returns via the Esplanade to the Indian Museum, Victoria Memorial, the Academy of Fine Arts, the Nehru Children's Museum and finally the zoo. On the other you'll see St Paul's Cathedral, the Botanical Gardens, the Sitalnath Jain temple, Nicco (theme) Park, the Birla Mandir and the riverside including Eden Gardens. ITDC's tours, booked through their office at 46c Chowringhee Rd or at the Government of India Tourist Office, 4 Shakespeare Sarani, follow similar itineraries and are better organized; tours depart from the tourist office at 8am.

Interesting walking tours of central Calcutta, taking in some of the traditional Bengali sectors, are organized by the Tourist Guide Association through the tourist offices and the Foundation for Conservation and Research of Urban Traditional Architecture (CRUTA), 67b Beadon St (☎554 6127). *Warren Travels*, 31 Chowringhee Rd (☎298274) arrange thematic tours on specific dates; options include the Art Treasures of Calcutta and a cultural river cruise taking in the Belur Math for around Rs250.

have to crouch. An empty minibus at Howrah may look like an attractive option, but will almost certainly soon be packed.

Taxis

Taxis in Calcutta are extremely good value. Most have working meters and drivers who refuse to use them should be avoided. However, what you pay is not the price actually shown on the meter, but a figure produced with the help of a fare conversion table, which drivers are required to carry; these are updated to keep up with the spiralling costs of diesel and petrol. Predictably, drivers make the conversions in their own favour. A modest excess charge, however, can seem reasonable as taxi-driving is a hazardous occupation due to the astronomical levels of pollution and chaos in the city. Note there is a small additional charge for placing your luggage in the "dicky" (the boot or trunk), which is invariably dusty and filled with oily rags.

Trams

Calcutta's cumbersome **trams**, barely changed since they started operating in 1873, are on their way out; their inability to deviate from fixed rails to cope with the city's crazy traffic makes them more of a nuisance than anything else. However, for all their grime and general dilapidation, they do have an odd quirky charm, and provide an interesting way of seeing the city; women travellers may well be glad of the rush-hour women-only coaches. Routes include **#25**, Sealdah to Ballygunge; **#35**, Sealdah via Esplanade to Behala; **#32** and **#21**, Howrah via Esplanade and Rashbehari to Ballygunge; and **#24**, Kalighat via Esplanade to Sealdah.

Rickshaws, auto-rickshaws and cycle rickshaws

Calcutta shares with Hong Kong the dubious honour of being the only cities in the world to have **human-drawn rickshaws**, which are only available in the central areas of the city, especially around New Market. These come into their own during the monsoons, when the streets get flooded to hip height and the rickshaw-men can extract healthy amounts of money for their pains. If you take one, take care not to lean back as your weight will unbalance the driver. Most of the rickshaw-pullers are Bihari pavement-dwellers, who live a short and difficult life; you'd have to be a strange sort of person to resent the fact that they invariably charge tourists extra. Some of them supplement their meagre income by soliciting for prostitutes or peddling drugs.

Auto-rickshaws, rare in the centre of town, are used as shared taxis on certain routes and link with Metro stations in suburbs such as Rashbehari and Gariahat. **Cycle rickshaws**, banned from much of the city, are only available in outlying suburbs.

Car rental

Car rental companies include *Car Rent Services*, 233–4A AJC Bose Rd (☎441285); *Durgapur Automobiles*, 113 Park St (☎294044); *New Lakshmi Travels*, 296 Rashbehari Ave (☎440 5317); *Rent-a-Car Service*, 1–5 Dover Lane (☎467186), *Sona International*, 17 Surya Sen St (☎241 6186) and *Wheels on Road*, 150 Lenin Sarani (☎273081). The Government of India Tourist Office and most large hotels also arrange cars. Typical charges are around Rs44 per hour plus Rs4.50 per km with a minimum charge of Rs250.

The City

Calcutta's crumbling weatherbeaten buildings and anarchic streets can create an intimidating first impression. Given a little time and patience, however, the huge metropolis starts to resolve itself into a fascinating conglomerate of styles and influences, with an uncontrollable profusion of buildings jockeying for attention.

The **River Hooghly**, which was until recently only spanned by the remarkable can-tilever Howrah Bridge, is not all that prominent in the life of the city. Instead its heart is the green expanse of the **Maidan**, which attracts Calcuttans from all walks of life for recreation, sports, exhibitions and political rallies. At its southern end stands the imposing white marble **Victoria Memorial**, and close by rise the tall gothic spires **of St Paul's Cathedral**. Next to the busy **New Market** area alongside looms the all-embracing **Indian Museum**. Further north, the district centered on BBD Bagh is filled with reminders of the heyday of the East India Company, dominated by the bulk of the **Writers' Building** with **St Andrew's Kirk** nearby; a bit further out, the **Armenian Church** stands on the edge of the frenetic, labyrinthine markets of **Barabazaar**, while the major temple of **Kalighat** is away to the south, in one of the city's more congested areas.

The Maidan, New Market and the Park Street area

The **Maidan** – literally "field" – which stretches from Esplanade in the north to the racecourse in the south, and is bordered by Jawaharlal Nehru Rd (**Chowringhee**) to the east and the Strand and the river to the west, is one of the largest city parks in the world. This vast area of open space stands in utter contrast to the chaotic streets of the city that surrounds it, big enough to swallow up several clubs, including the *Calcutta Ladies Golf Club*, and the immaculate greens of the *Calcutta Bowling Club*. It was created when the now-inconspicuous **Fort William** was laid out near the river in 1758, and Robert Clive cleared tracts of forest to give its guns a clear line of fire. Originally it was a haven for the elite, with a strictly enforced dress code. Now, early each morning, ordinary citizens come to exercise, shepherds graze their flocks, and riders on horseback canter along the old bridleways. In the late afternoons, it plays host to scores of impromptu cricket and football matches, as well as games of *kabaadi* (see p.51).

Esplanade
The 46-metre-tall vaguely Greek-style column of **Shahid Minar** (Martyrs' Memorial) towers over busy tram and bus terminals and market stalls at the northeast corner of the Maidan, known as Esplanade. As the **Ochterlony Monument**, it was built in 1828 to commemorate the memory of David Ochterlony, who led the East India Company troops to victory in the Nepalese Wars of 1814–16. Further northeast, in the small **Curzon Park** among the trees and fenced-off patches of greenery beyond the tram terminus, a colony of rats has burrowed a warren of holes. Local office workers spend their lunch hours feeding the fat and complacent rodents.

New Market and Chowringhee
Beneath its Gothic red-brick clock tower, the single-storey **New Market**, in the centre of cosmopolitan Calcutta, can have changed little since it opened in 1874. Its real name is Sir Stuart Hogg Market; supposedly, the ghost of Sir Stuart haunts the market, roaming the corridors at night crying out for peace. It would be easier to imagine that he was bemoaning the antics of its coolies, who drag willing and unwilling customers into the various shops in search of commission, and also double as black-market touts. At the north end of the market, a characterless multi-storey building has been erected to replace sections gutted by a fire in 1985. Many of the shops were housed in a temporary market on the Maidan, opposite the Indian Museum, before being rehoused here; that area is now something of an ugly shanty town.

The market itself stocks a vast array of household goods, luggage, ready-made garments, jewellery, curio shops, bookshops, textiles, and kitchenware, as well as meat, vegetables and fruit. Among shops that stand out from the rest, *Chamba Lama* sells Tibetan curios and antique items such as cosmetic and silver jewellery, and new bronzes. The *Symphony* music store has a good selection of classical and popular Indian music, while *Sujata's* is known for its silk, and *Nahoum & Sons* is a Jewish bakery (see p.793). Further up the corridor, condiment stalls offer cheese from Kalimpong, miniature rounds of salty Bandel cheese, and *amshat*, blocks made up of sheets of dried mango. *Dey Bros* is one of many bookshops in the southeastern part.

The formerly elegant colonnaded front of Chowringhee east of Esplanade, now in a sorry state of decay, is perpetually crowded with hawkers and shoppers. The only one of its grand institutions to survive relatively unscathed is the Victorian **Grand Hotel**, which after endless renovations and changes of management remains a haven of colonialism, with its palm court inspired by the famous *Raffles* of Singapore.

Indian Museum

27 J Nehru Rd (☎299853). Daily except Mon March–Nov 10am–5pm; Dec–Feb 10am–4.30pm. Rs2; Fri free.

At the corner of Chowringhee and Sudder St, a few metres south of the *Grand*, the stately **Indian Museum** is the oldest museum in India, founded in 1814. Built around a central courtyard, the present high-ceilinged building was opened to the public in 1878, and is probably the largest museum in Asia, ranging across a huge spectrum of exhibits from sculpture to natural history.

Visitors come to the museum in their thousands, many of them villagers who bring offerings to the *jadu ghar* or "house of magic". Its real showpiece is a collection of **stone and metal sculptures** obtained from sites all over India, which centres on a superb Mauryan polished sandstone **lion capital**, dating from the third century BC. One gallery houses the impressive remains of the second-century BC Buddhist *stupa* from Bharhut in Madhya Pradesh, partly re-assembled to display posts, capping stones, railings and gateways all made from red sandstone. Carvings depict human and animal figures, as well as scenes from the *Jataka* tales of the Buddha's many incarnations. There is also a huge collection of schist sculptures, dating from the first to the third century from the Gandhara region; themes include scenes from Buddha's life and other Buddhist divinities. You'll also see stone sculpture from **Khajuraho** and Pala bronzes, plus copper artefacts, stone-age tools and terracotta figures from other sites.

Along with an excellent exhibit of Tibetan *thangkas*, the museum holds Kalighat *pats* (see p.790) and paintings by the **Company School**, a group of mid-nineteenth-century Indian artists who emulated Western themes and techniques for European patrons. Finally, there's a spectacular array of fossils and stuffed animals, most of which look in dire need of a decent burial.

Park Street

Just around the corner from the museum, the **Asiatic Society** at 1 Park St, established in 1784 by orientalists including Sir William Jones, houses a huge collection of around 150,000 books and 60,000 ancient manuscripts, some of which date back to the seventh century. The society has a reading room open to the public (Mon–Fri 10am–8pm, Sat & Sun 10am–5pm; free) and a gallery of art and antiquities with paintings by Rubens and Reynolds, a large collection of coins and one of Ashoka's stone edicts.

Around 2km along Park Street from the Maidan, the disused but recently restored **Park Street Cemetery** is one of the city's most haunting memorials to its imperial past. Inaugurated in 1767, it is the oldest in Calcutta, holding a wonderful concentration of pyramids, obelisks, pavilions, urns and headstones, under which many well-known British personalities lie buried. The epitaphs make fascinating reading.

Fort William

A road leads west through the Maidan from the top of Park Street to the gates of **Fort William**. As the military headquarters of eastern command, this allows entry only to those who have sought permission in advance, although the public are allowed into certain sections on special occasions. Built on the site of the old village of Govindapur, and commissioned by the British after their defeat in 1756, the fort was completed in 1781 and named after King William III. A rough octagon, about 500m in diameter, whose massive but low bunker-like battlements are punctuated by six main gates, the fort was designed to hold all the city's Europeans in the event of attack. To one side it commanded a view of the Maidan, cleared to give a field of fire; to the other it dominated the river and its crucial shipping lanes. Water from the river was diverted to fill its surrounding moat. Eighteenth- and nineteenth-century structures inside include the Church of St Peter's (now a library), barracks and stables, an arsenal, strong rooms and a prison. Today, the army still controls the Maidan and any special construction or activity must be approved by them.

Victoria Memorial and the Calcutta Gallery

Daily except Mon, March–Oct 10am–3.30pm; Nov–Feb 10am–4.30pm. Rs2. Cameras must be deposited at the entrance. Sound and Light show held in English at 8.15pm; Rs5.

The dramatic white marble **Victoria Memorial** at the southern end of the Maidan, with its formal gardens and water courses, continues to be Calcutta's pride and joy. Other colonial monuments and statues throughout the city have been renamed or demolished, but the popularity of Queen Victoria seems to endure for ever; thirty years of attempts to change the name of the "VM" have come to nothing.

This extraordinary hybrid building, with Italianate statues over its entrances, Moghul domes in its corners, and tall elegant open colonnades along its sides, was conceived by Lord Curzon to commemorate the empire at its peak. Designed by Sir William Emerson, it was completed in 1921. Flanked by two ornamental tanks, a sombre statue of Queen Victoria gazes out towards the Maidan from a pedestal lined with bronze panels and friezes. Faced with Makrana marble from Jodhpur, the building itself is capped by a dome bearing a revolving five-metre-tall bronze figure of *Victory.*

The main entrance, at the Maidan end, leads into a tall chamber beneath the dome. The 25 galleries inside burst with mementoes of British imperialism – statues and busts of Queen Mary, King George V and Queen Victoria; paintings of Robert Clive and the Queen (again); a huge canvas of the future Edward VII entering Jaipur in 1876; French guns captured at the Battle of Plassey in 1758; and the black marble throne of a nawab defeated by Robert Clive. One air-conditioned chamber, converted and renamed the **Calcutta Gallery**, is dedicated to the Indians of the city and the Independence struggle. The evening **Sound and Light** show concentrates on the same theme.

Admission to the Victoria Memorial's popular gardens is free during the day. After they close at dusk, the Maidan in front of the gates is transformed. A seething mass of people come to enjoy the breeze, roadside snacks, and pony and *tikka* (open carriage) rides, and to watch the garish musical fountains.

St Paul's Cathedral and around

The gothic **St Paul's Cathedral**, a little way along from the Victoria Memorial, was erected by Major W N Forbes in 1847. Measuring 75m by 24m, its iron-trussed roof was then the longest span in existence. For improved ventilation, the lancet windows inside extend to plinth level, and tall fans hang from the ceiling. The most outstanding of the many well-preserved memorials and plaques to long-perished imperialists is the stained glass of the west window, designed by Sir Edward Burne-Jones in 1880 to honour Lord Mayo, assassinated in the Andaman Islands. The original steeple was destroyed in the 1897 earthquake; after a second earthquake in 1934 it was remodelled on the Bell Harry Tower at Canterbury Cathedral.

Immediately north of the cathedral, the **Birla Planetarium**, one of the largest in the world and certainly the largest in Asia, holds several shows every day, some in English (daily except Mon, 12.30–6.30pm; Rs10).

South of the cathedral, the **Academy of Fine Arts** on Cathedral Rd is a showcase for Bengali contemporary arts (daily except Mon 3–6pm; Rs1). As well as temporary exhibitions, it holds permanent displays of the work of artists such as Jamini Roy and Rabindranath Tagore. A cafe and pleasant grounds add to the appealing ambience. Rabindra Sadan, the large auditorium close by, regularly features programmes of Indian classical music and next door, **Nadan**, designed by the renowned film-maker Satyajit Ray, is a large and lively film centre with archives, library and auditoria.

Around the corner on Chowringhee, the small **Nehru Children's Museum**, 94/1 J Nehru Rd (daily except Mon noon–8pm; Rs2, under-12s Rs1), places a strong emphasis on the Hindu classics, illustrating the *Ramayana* and the *Mahabharata* with toys, puppets and picture shows.

Central Calcutta

The commercial and administrative hub of both Calcutta and West Bengal is **BBD Bagh**, which die-hard Calcuttans still insist on referring to as **Dalhousie Square**. The new official name, in a fine piece of official rhetoric, commemorates three revolutionaries hanged for trying to kill Lieutenant-Governor General Lord Dalhousie. In the centre of the square is the large Lal Dighi tank, or artificial pond.

Built in 1868 on the site of the original Fort William – destroyed by Siraj-ud-Daula in 1756 – the **GPO** on the west of the square hides the supposed site of the **Black Hole of Calcutta**. Quite what the truth of that much-mythologized incident may have been remains a matter for debate, but the British public was told that on a hot June night in 1756, 146 English prisoners were forced by Siraj-ud-Daula's guards into a tiny chamber with only the smallest of windows for ventilation, and that most suffocated to death by the next morning. A memorial to the victims that formerly stood in front of Writers' Building was removed in 1940 to the grounds of St John's Church south of the GPO. When Robert Clive regained control of Calcutta, he had learned his lesson. Fort William was not rebuilt in this virtually undefendable location in a built-up area, but in its current location on the Maidan, with clear visibility in all directions.

Now the seat of the West Bengal Government, **Writers' Building** to the north of the square was built in 1780 to replace the original structure used to house the clerks or "writers" of the East India Company. No official tours take in the building, but wandering in to any department reveals a world of endless corridors and vast chambers, where desks are piled high with dusty old files and clerks seem to exude apathy.

West of Writers' Building, beyond the headquarters of Eastern Railways on Netaji Subhash Rd, you come to the heart of Calcutta's **commercial district**, clustered around the Royal Stock Exchange at the corner of Lyon's Range. The warren of buildings, erected along the same lines as the contemporary business districts of Shanghai, houses all sorts of old colonial trading companies; Scottish names in particular still seem to be very much in evidence. One of its most extraordinary sights is **Exchange Lane**, where stockbrokers sit in brightly painted wooden cubicles armed with telephones and carry on business with punters on the street.

A further symbol of Calcutta's Scottish traditions is the grey spire of **St Andrew's Kirk**, which rises in the middle of the road at the northeast end of BBD Bagh. This Scottish church was built in 1818, in the face of intense opposition from Church of England representatives. To the east, the oldest street in the city, formerly known as Mission Row but now called RN Mukherjee Rd, holds the **Old Mission Church**, founded in 1770 by the Swedish missionary Johann Kiernander. South of the GPO, **St John's Church** was erected in 1787. Inside, along with memorials to British residents and to the first Bishop of Calcutta, Bishop Middleton, hangs an impressive painting by Johann Zoffany of The Last Supper, in which prominent Calcuttans are depicted as apostles. In the grounds, Calcutta's first graveyard holds the tomb of Job Charnock.

Dominating this area south of BBD Bagh, **Government House** (only open to the public with prior permission) overlooks the north end of the Maidan and the ceremonial Red Road, which was once used as an airstrip and is the only thoroughfare in the city without potholes. Until 1911, this was the residence of the British Governors-General and the Viceroys of India; now the official home of the Governor of Bengal, it is known as **Raj Bhavan**, which amounts to the same thing. When built at the very end of the eighteenth century, it was intended to be a palace, modelled on Kedleston Hall in Derbyshire, England. Sealed off by tall iron fencing from the rest of the city, Government House is approached through four ornamental gateways guarded by lions and sphinxes. Along with a throne room once used by George V, and a spectacular chandeliered ballroom, the interior holds Calcutta's first elevator introduced by Lord Curzon and still in working condition. Trophies littered around the formal grounds include a large bronze cannon mounted on a winged dragon, captured at Nanking during the Opium Wars, and brass cannons from the Afghan campaigns.

Nearby, opposite the **Assembly House** (Rajya Sabha) of West Bengal's Legislative Council, are the All India Radio building, and the sports complex of **Eden Gardens**, site of the huge world-famous cricket ground which periodically suffers riots and fires started by over-zealous fans, especially when their team is seen to be losing. Watching a test match here is an unforgettable experience as the 100,000 seat stadium resounds to the roar of the crowd and the sound of crackers thrown indiscriminately; if you want to avoid the missiles, sit in the covered sections. West of the sports complex, at the northwest corner of the Maidan, an ornamental park offers an artificial lake, a Burmese Pagoda, and pleasant walks along palm-strewn paths.

North Calcutta

The sprawling and amorphous area of **north Calcutta** was long part of the "native" town rather than the European sectors, and was where the city's prosperous nineteenth-century Bengali families created their little palaces. Today its markets continue to thrive unchanged, and the occasional church stands as a reminder of days gone by.

North of BBD Bagh, the area known as **Barabazaar** has played host to a succession of trading communities; the Portuguese were here even before Job Charnock landed at the fishing village that stood close by, and it later became home to Marwari and Gujarati merchants. The small and hectic lanes south of MG Rd are lined with shops and stalls that sell everything from glass bangles to textiles.

At the northwest corner of Barabazaar, near Howrah Bridge, is Calcutta's oldest church, the **Armenian Church of Our Lady of Nazareth**. Founded in 1724 by Cavond, an Armenian from Persia, it was built on the site of an Armenian cemetery in which the oldest tombstone dates to 1630. The Armenian community, drawn from both Armenia and Persia, was already highly influential at the courts of Bengal by the time the British arrived, and played an important role in the early history of the East India Company. Later they went on to help start the lucrative jute industry. Just around the corner on MG Rd at Murghihatta, the "Chicken Market", stands the Portuguese **Roman Catholic Cathedral**, built in 1797.

East of Barabazaar on Rabindra Sarani (formerly Chitpore Road), the huge red **Nakhoda Masjid**, whose two lofty minarets rise to 46 metres, is the great Jami Masjid (Friday mosque) of the city. Completed in 1942, it was modelled on Akbar's Tomb at Sikandra near Agra; its four floors can hold ten thousand worshippers. The traditional Muslim market that flourishes all around the mosque sells religious items along with clothes, dried fruit and sweets such as *firni*, made of rice. Down the road is Calcutta's most renowned Muslim restaurant, the *Royal*. North along Rabindra Sarani, musical instrument makers specialize in *sitars*, harmoniums and *tanburas*.

Until relatively recently, the chaotic jumble of streets to the south along Rabindra Sarani housed a thriving **Chinatown**, opium dens and all. Chinese families continue to live around Chhatawala Gully, where a small early-morning street market offers home-made pork sausages, noodles and jasmine tea. But the stalls serving *wonton* and *dim sum*, are rapidly disappearing and the legendary *Nanking* restaurant, once one of the most elegant in the city, has finally closed its doors. Today, the best Chinese restaurants can be found in the east of the city, in the new Chinatown in Tangra.

North of MG Rd, on the tiny Muktaram Babu St off Chittaranjan Ave, the controversial **Marble Palace** preserves its lavish, sensuous and sometimes tasteless treasures in less than satisfactory conditions (Tues–Wed & Fri–Sun; free). Visitors are supposed to obtain passes from the main tourist offices at BBD Bagh or Shakespeare Sarani, but a little *baksheesh* to the caretaker has not been unheard of; photography is forbidden. Built in 1835 by Raja Rajendro Mullick Bahadur, a wealthy *zamindar* educated by an English tutor, the colonnaded mansion epitomizes the incredible profusion of influences of the period, and is still maintained by the Raja's descendants, who live here. The palace earns its name from its ornate marble-paved chambers, which hold statues, European antiques, Venetian glass, chandeliers, mirrors and Ming vases. There are paintings by Rubens, Titian, Sir Joshua Reynolds and Gainsborough; supposedly there's even a statue by Michelangelo. At the centre of the building, part of an Italian courtyard is taken up by an aviary, while the grounds hold a small zoo.

North of Marble Palace is the city's main red-light area, **Sonagachi**. This is not a district into which travellers are advised to venture; those who do invariably come to harm, at the very least through finding themselves arrested by the police.

On Dwarkanath Tagore Lane, a short walk northeast of the Marble Palace, the small campus of Rabindranath Tagore's liberal arts university, **Rabindra Bharati**, preserves the house where he was born and died. Now the **Rabindra Bharati Museum**, currently undergoing restoration, it holds a large collection of his paintings (Mon–Fri 10am–5pm, Sat 10am–1.30pm; free). Next door, Bichitra Bhavan is used, as it was by Tagore himself, to stage theatrical performances. In September, it is the scene of a festival commemorating the Nobel Laureate.

Further east, **College Street** stretches along the edge of Calcutta University. Established in 1857 as the pride of Bengali learning, it still has one of the largest student bodies in the world. Senate House, one of its earliest buildings, was gutted during the turbulent days of the early Seventies. College St deals exclusively in books and supplies for students; its pavement stalls and shops are an excellent hunting ground for secondhand books, if not genuine antiques. Adjoining Albert St the famous **India Coffee House**, although now a bit jaded, continues to attract students and the intelligentsia. The small **Ashutosh Museum of Indian History**, at the Centenary Building on College St, has a good collection of Bengali art, handi-

POLLUTION AND FLOODS

With no controls on the emissions of its armada of diesel-engined vehicles, Calcutta is cursed with lethal atmospheric **pollution** – as any visitor to the city soon learns. For its residents, lung problems are part of everyday life. Rush hours are especially noxious, with grey fumes frequently obscuring the sunset. During the long months when the city holds its breath and waits for the monsoons to hit, the still and heavy air can be unbearable; and when the rains finally roll in at the end of June, Calcutta becomes a swamp. Being obliged to wade thigh-deep through filthy water, along roads riddled with potholes and open man holes, contributes to further health problems. Calcutta's **water table** is contaminated to a depth of over 20 feet, and gastric disease is endemic. Anyone who can afford it equips their home with its own purification systems or tube well. On top of all that, the Calcutta Corporation is hopelessly unequal to the task of keeping the city clean; streets are strewn with litter, and rubbish tips pile shoulder high.

crafts and fabrics as well as rare Buddhist manuscripts and statues (Mon–Fri 10.30am–4.30pm, Sat 10.30am–3pm; free).

North Calcutta has two large **Jain temples**. One, in **Belgachia** next to the bridge and the Metro station, is a simple red sandstone structure set in manicured lawns, dedicated to the Digambara sect. The other, at **Manicktolla**, known as the **Parasnath** Jain temple, consists of a group of temples set in an ornate garden which holds ponds full of carp. It honours **Sitalnath**, the lord of water and the tenth in the line of twenty-four *tirthankaras* (crossing-makers) that culimnated with Mahavira, born in Vaishali in 599 BC. Neoclassical marble and alabaster statues grace the grounds, while the main temple, another architectural hybrid, is crowned by an ornate cupola. Inside the chamber the image of Sitalnath is surrounded by gaudy marble-work studded with silver. An odd mixture of Venetian and post-Moghul, its assorted multi-hued chandeliers are offset by the surrounding glass and mirrors. Along with an information centre, the temple area has several Jain shrines and boarding houses.

Howrah and the River Hooghly

Although **Howrah** is technically a separate town, as the home of much of Calcutta's industry, as well as Howrah Station, it forms an integral part of the city. Until recently the antiquated **Howrah Bridge** was the only road link across the River Hooghly; since the opening of the tall and elegant **Vivekananda Setu**, the second Hooghly bridge, a few years ago, the west bank of the river is changing rapidly. Vivekananda Setu provides easy access to Shibpur and the beautiful **Botanical Gardens**, and onwards southwest to the open highways towards Orissa.

Howrah Station, across the river from central Calcutta, is a truly remarkable railway station, used by millions of passengers each day. Built in 1906, it's a striking red-brick building, topped by eight square towers. During the war in Bangladesh, in the early seventies, it found itself sheltering thousands of refugees in horrific conditions.

Until silting rendered it impractical for large ships, the **River Hooghly**, a distributary of the Ganges, was responsible for making Calcutta a bustling port. Unlike those at Varanasi, the *ghats* that line its east (Calcutta) bank have no great esoteric significance; they simply serve as real landings and places for ritual ablutions. Around 1.5km north of Howrah Bridge, **Nimtolla Ghat**, one of the city's main cremation grounds, is sealed off from the public gaze. The large steps alongside, and a Shiva temple, attract strange *sadhus* as they head through the city on their way to January's Ganga Sagar Mela (see p.797). A little further north, behind **Kumartuli Ghat**, a warren of lanes is home to a community of artisans who specialize in making the clay, straw and pith images of deities used for the major festivals. In the days leading up to the great *pujas*, especially that of Durga, **Kumartuli** is a fascinating hive of activity. As you walk north, you come next to **Baghbazaar Ghat**, where overloaded barges of straw arrive for the craftsmen of Kumartuli. Baghbazaar, the Garden Market, stands on the original site of Sutanuti, its grand but decaying turn-of-the-century mansions epitomizing the long-vanished lifestyle of the Bengali gentry, the *bhadra log*.

South of Howrah Bridge, but right in its shadow, the large **Armenian Ghat** is at its most animated soon after dawn, when traditional gymnasts and wrestlers, devotees of Hanuman the monkey god, do their morning practice, and a flower market is in full swing. Nearby, vehicles from trams to handcarts battle inch by inch to gain access to the Howrah Bridge. As the cobbled and much-potholed Strand heads south, it passes several warehouses on the way beyond Fairly Place to another cluster of *ghats*. **Babu Ghat** here, identified by its crumbling colonnade, is used for early-morning bathing, attended by *pujaris* (priests) and heavy-handed masseurs. Nearby, Babu Ghat's Bus Stand is one of Calcutta's main cross-country terminuses, while ferries from **Chandpal Ghat**, a couple of hundred metres north, provide an easy alternative to Howrah Bridge.

HOWRAH BRIDGE

One of Calcutta's most famous landmarks, **Howrah Bridge** – now also known by the new name of Rabindra Setu – is 97m high and 705m long, spanning the river in a single giant leap to make it the world's largest cantilever bridge. It was erected during World War II in 1943 to give Allied troops access to the Burmese front, replacing an earlier pontoon bridge that opened to let river traffic through. Looking like a giant version of something a child might make using a construction set, it's the world's busiest bridge, used by millions of commuters daily. Its eight lanes are perpetually clogged with vehicles, and it's so worn out that a man pushing his broken-down car is said to have fallen through a hole and disappeared. Don't let that put you off; joining the streams of perspiring pedestrians who walk across the bridge each day is a memorable experience.

Vivekananda Setu, the second Hooghly bridge, built 3km south to relieve the strain, was 22 years in the making. It's a vast toll bridge, high enough to let ships pass below, and with spaghetti-junction-style approaches.

Further south, past Eden Gardens, the Strand opens out into the promenades near Fort William, where the people of the city come to enjoy the cool evening river breezes. An ice-cream parlour overlooks the river and snack vendors are everywhere. A short boat trip to the new bridge and back costs around Rs30.

Botanical Gardens

The **Botanical Gardens** at Shibpur lie 10km south of Howrah Station on the west bank of the Hooghly. Although they were created in 1786 to develop strains of Indian tea, Calcuttans have only started to appreciate these 109 hectares once again since the opening of the second bridge. Populated by countless bird species, such as waders, cranes, and storks, the huge gardens are best seen in winter and spring and early in the mornings, when they're free from the grime of the metropolis. Their single most famous feature is the **world's largest banyan tree**, reaching up 24.5 metres high and embracing an astonishing circumference of 420 metres. Now over 240 years old, a survivor of cyclones in 1864 and 1867 that eventually caused it to lose its main trunk, its 1825 aerial roots drop from the overhead branches to create the effect of a small forest. Elsewhere, palm trees abound around the lakes, ponds and ornamental footbridges, and especially the brooding, atmospheric Palm House. The Orchid House, the Herbarium and the Fern Houses are also worth seeing, and there's an attractive riverside promenade.

As a rule, the gardens are empty during the week and busy at weekends. Much the nicest way to get here is by ferry from Armenian Ghat, Babu Ghat or Chandpal Ghat, though it's also accessible as a tedious road trip from Esplanade, by minibus or the ordinary ash-coloured C6 bus. Cafes within the gardens open at unpredictable hours.

South Calcutta

South of the Maidan and Park Street, Calcutta spreads towards suburbs such as **Alipore** and **Ballygunge**, both within easy distance of the centre. The thoroughfare that starts life as Jawaharlal Nehru Rd (Chowringhee) proceeds south from Esplanade past **Kalighat** to **Tollygunge**, following the Metro line which terminates near the luxurious *Tollygunge Club*, the mansion of an indigo merchant now surrounded by immaculate golfing fairways and bridle paths. Northeast of Tollygunge, beyond a white-tiled mosque built in 1835 by descendants of Tipu Sultan, the vast open area of the **Dhakuria Lakes** leads to **Ballygunge**, the home of Calcutta's Bengali middle classes.

Alipore

Around three kilometres south of Park Street, the crumbling nineteenth-century splendour of **Alipore** is slowly being engulfed by a forest of multi-storey buildings. Not far from the race course, opposite the luxury *Taj Bengal* hotel, the extremely popular **Calcutta Zoo** (daily 6am–5pm; Rs2) houses such weird and wonderful animals as a tigon, a cross between a lion and a tiger; a litigon, a cross between a tigon and a lion; a litatitigon . . . and so forth. Now threatened with closure, the zoo also has white tigers from Rewa, a reptile house, an aquarium (Rs1), a children's zoo, and four restaurants. The only real drawback is that many of the cages are cleaner than their litter-strewn surroundings.

Elegant triple-arched gates just south of the zoo lead to **Belvedere**, the former residence of the Lieutenant-Governor of Bengal, now the **National Library** (Mon–Fri 10am–6pm; separate periodical and newspaper reading room on Esplanade Mon–Fri 9am–2pm, Sat & Sun 10am–6pm; free). Presented to Warren Hastings by Mir Jafar, the building's original simplicity was enhanced by double columns and the sweeping staircase that leads to the Durbar Hall. When the capital shifted to Delhi, this library was left behind; today it houses a huge and extensive collection of books, periodicals and reference material, as well as rare documents in an air-conditioned chamber.

Half a kilometre south, Alipore's small **Horticultural Gardens**, popular with early morning walkers, cherish a wide assortment of plants and flowers (Sun–Tues 6–10am & 2–5pm; Rs1). The flower show here at the start of February is well worth a visit.

Kalighat

Calcutta's most important temple, **Kalighat**, 5km south of Park St along Ashutosh Mukherjee Rd, an extension of Jawaharlal Nehru Rd, stands at the heart of a congested and animated area. This plain but typically Bengali temple, built of brick and mortar in 1809 but capturing the sweeping curves of a thatched roof, is dedicated to Kali, the black goddess and form of Shakti. According to legend, Shiva went into a frenzy after the death of his wife Sati, dancing with her dead body and making the whole world tremble. The gods had attempted to stop him in various ways before Vishnu took his

---

MOTHER TERESA

Mother Teresa, Calcutta's most famous citizen, was born Agnes Gonxha Bojaxhiu to Albanian parents in 1910, and grew up in Skopje in the former Yugoslavia. After joining the Sisters of Loreto, an Irish order, she was sent as a teacher to Darjeeling, where she took her vows in May 1931 and became Teresa. In her work at St Mary's School in Calcutta, she became aware of the incredible poverty around her; in 1948, with permission from Rome, she put aside her nun's habit to clothe herself in the simple blue-bordered white *sari* that became the uniform of the **Missionaries of Charity**.

The best known of their many homes and clinics is Nirmal Hriday, a hospice for destitutes. In the face of local resistance, Mother Teresa chose its site at Kalighat – Calcutta's most important centre of Hinduism – in the knowledge that many of the poor specifically come here to die, next to a holy *tirtha* or crossing-place. Mother Teresa's simple piety and single-minded devotion to the poor have won her international acclaim, including the Nobel Peace Prize in 1979. In recent years she has also attracted a fair share of controversy with her fierce anti-abortion stance giving rise to accusations of fundamentalist Catholicism. She has also been accused by her detractors of disregarding modern advances in medicine in favour of saving the souls of the dying and destitute. Censure, however, seems iniquitous in the light of her immense contribuiton to humanity.

In principle Mother Teresa relies on charity and voluntary work. If you're interested, contact the Missionaries of Charity at Mother House, 54A Lower Circular Rd. However, they do occasionally have to turn casual volunteers away; it's not always possible to make constructive use of all the would-be helpers who arrive unannounced.

KALIGHAT PAINTINGS

Early in the nineteenth century, Kalighat was in its heyday, drawing pilgrims, merchants and artisans from all over the country. Among them were the **scroll painters** from elsewhere in Bengal, who developed the distinctive style now known as **Kalighat Pats** (paintings). Adapting Western techniques, they used paper and water-based paints instead of tempera, and gradually moved away from religious themes to depict contemporary subjects. By 1850, Kalighat *pats* had taken on a dynamic new direction, satirizing the middle classes in much the same way as today's political cartoons. As a result, their work serves as a witty record of the period, filled with images of everyday life. Kalighat *pats* can now be found in galleries and museums around the world, and in the Birla Academy here in Calcutta (see below).

solar discus and chopped the disintegrating corpse into 51 bits. The spot where each piece fell became a *pitha*, or pilgrimage site, for worshippers of the female principle of divinity – Shakti. The shrine here marks where her little toe fell.

The temple is open all hours, and always a frenzied hive of activity. Unless you manage to leave your shoes yourself at the entrance, greedy priests grab hold of them and whisk you downstairs to confront the dramatic monolithic image of the terrible goddess in the basement, with her huge eyes and bloody tongue.

The courtyard beyond the main congregational hall is used for sacrificing goats, especially during festivals such as Durga Puja and Kali Puja; supposedly, humans were formerly sacrificed here to appease the fertility goddess. To the north of the compound, a *lingam* is worshipped by women praying for children, while shops all around cater for pilgrims. Musical instrument makers around Kalighat Bridge specialize in *tablahs* and other percussion instruments, while the area in general is infamous for its prostitution, pickpockets and beggars. Nirmal Hriday, Mother Teresa's home for the destitute and dying, is nearby.

Ballygunge and the Lakes

At the junction of Gurusaday Rd and Gariahat Rd, 4km southeast of Park St, the **Birla Industrial and Technological Museum** (daily except Mon 10am-4.30pm; Rs5) is dedicated to Indian technology. Its large pleasant galleries set out to attract children in particular, with working models such as miniature mining scenes. A new science centre, inspired by Disney's Epcot centre in Florida, is about to open off the Eastern Bypass close to Tangra.

Turning left from Gurusaday Rd on to Gariahat Rd, past Calcutta Cricket Club, brings you to the huge unfinished **Lakshmi Narayan Temple**, also known as the Birla temple after its benefactors. Covered with bamboo scaffolding, the temple is designed on the model of the Lingaraj Temple at Bhubaneshwar in Orissa. Work has continued for over twenty years; it is said that according to a prophesy, the Birla family will meet with disaster if the air-conditioned monstrosity is ever finished.

Three kilometres south are the Bengali market of **Gariahat** and the **Gariahat Mor** intersection, whose pavement stalls are packed with evenings shoppers browsing through piles of *kurta pyjama*, traditional Bengali cotton *saris*, and contemporary clothing. The road to **Gol Park**, a busy roundabout 400m further south, is lined with vendors, including secondhand book and comic stalls. From here, a road branches southeast to Dhakuria, and the tree-lined Southern Avenue leads along the side of the **Dhakuria Lakes**, now also known as **Rabindra Sarobar**. These man-made lakes, with their tree-lined walkways, are the base of Calcutta's flourishing rowing clubs. There's a rather dirty open-air public swimming area.

A multi-storeyed building on Southern Avenue houses the **Birla Academy of Art and Culture**, also funded by the industrial Birla family (daily except Mon 3.30pm–8pm;

free). Its small auditorium puts on concerts and theatre, while galleries hold exhibitions of contemporary art, plus an eclectic collection of Indian art through the ages covering folk art, bronzes, stone sculptures, terracotta, miniatures, textiles and Kalighat paintings. Among artists of the Bengali Renaissance represented here are the trio of Tagores – Rabindranath, Abanindranath and Gaganendranath. In addition, there are Indian classical dance classes and art classes. The **Lake Kali Bari** alongside has grown in three decades from a small roadside Kali shrine to a major temple.

Accommodation

As soon as you arrive in Calcutta, taxi and rickshaw drivers are likely to assume that you'll be heading for the central **Sudder Street** area, next to New Market, which abounds in small and mid-sized hotels to suit short-stay overseas travellers. In fact, many visitors spend most of their time in this one enclave. However, the city's very top hotels are slightly further afield; the beautifully maintained *Oberoi Grand*, Calcutta's answer to the *Raffles* of Singapore, is around the corner on Chowringhee, and the luxurious *Taj Bengal* is in Alipore to the south.

ACCOMMODATION PRICE CODES

All **accommodation prices** in this book have been coded using the symbols below. In principle the prices given are for the least expensive double rooms in each establishment; however, some hotels, usually in category ①, offer rates per bed rather than per room. Local taxes are not included unless specifically stated. For more details, see p.35.

① up to Rs100	④ Rs225–350	⑦ Rs750–1200
② Rs100–150	⑤ Rs350–500	⑧ Rs1200–2200
③ Rs150–225	⑥ Rs500–750	⑨ Rs2200 and upwards

The many **guest houses** now on offer all over Calcutta – usually comfortable private houses or flats, with the use of a "cook-cum-bearer" – provide mid-budget travellers with an alternative to Sudder St. Be sure to clarify the food arrangements and all costs at the start of your stay. *The Guest* agency, a division of *Travel & Cargo Service*, 23 Shakespeare Sarani (☎247 9662), represents guest houses throughout the city.

Finally, well-heeled travellers might like to consider a stay at one of Calcutta's most exclusive **clubs**, the *Tollygunge Club*, at the southern end of the Metro line at 120 Deshapran Sasmal Rd (☎463141; fax 741923; ⑧). Accommodation involves temporary membership and includes the use of an eighteen-hole golf course, plus riding, swimming, tennis and squash facilities, as well as open-air and indoor restaurants and a good bar. You will need to contact the Secretary well in advance to reserve a room as the club is extremely popular with visiting businessmen.

Sudder Street area

Centrepoint Guest House, 20 Free School St (☎244 3928). Friendly and popular with a range of rooms (some a/c) and a travel service. ③–④.

Fairlawn, 13A Sudder St (☎245 1510). Famous hotel exuding a decadent Raj atmosphere, which is best sampled over a cup of tea or a beer on the lawn. Indian guests are not allowed. Room rates include unimaginative meals. ⑨.

Hilson, 4 Sudder St (☎249 0864). One of several similar run-of-the-mill places on the street. ③–④.

Lytton, 14 Sudder St (☎249 1872). The most modern and comfortable hotel on the street with central a/c, TV etc but otherwise lacking in character. Facilities include a bar and restaurants. ⑧.

Modern Lodge, 1 Stuart Lane (☎244 4960). Cramped but reasonably priced accommodation, popular with budget travellers since the 1960s. The roof terrace gets lively in the evenings. ①–③.

Palace, 13 Chowringhee Lane (☎244 6214). Old dilapidated building in need of a spring-clean and only good as a fall-back if everywhere else is booked up. ③.

Paragon, 2 Stuart Lane (☎ 244 2445). Friendly and justifiably popular with budget travellers, with a a dorm, pleasant courtyard cafe and lockers; rooms downstairs are dark. ②–③.

Paramount, 33/4 Free School St (☎294295). Close to Sudder St, reasonable and clean rooms all with attached baths and hot water by the bucket. A restaurant serves Indian and Chinese food. ④.

Plaza, 10 Sudder St. Friendly, clean and popular with visiting businessmen. ⑤.

Salvation Army Red Shield Guest House, 2 Sudder St, near the museum (☎245 2895). Good budget option, which is often booked up and has changed little over the years. Dorms and a few doubles; passing through its large gate is a welcome relief from the noise and pollution outside. ①.

Shilton, 5A Sudder St (☎245 1512). Large old building set behind a gateway. The rooms are pleasant but expensive. Breakfast is available, and food can be arranged but no restaurant as such. ④.

Times Guest House, Sudder St, near *Blue Sky Cafe* (☎245 1796). Small, friendly Sikh-run place with a dorm and a few double rooms. ①–③.

Tourist Inn, 4/1 Sudder St. Unattractive entrance leads up to a pleasant little lodge. ①–③.

YMCA, 25 J Nehru Rd (☎292192). Large, depressing establishment near the Indian Museum – popular for long-term stays, with table tennis and a well kept snooker table. ③–⑤.

YMCA, opposite *Lotus Cinema*, 42 SN Banerjee Rd (☎244 3814). Cheap rooms and a dorm. ②.

Elsewhere in the city

Astor, 15 Shakespeare Sarani (☎242 9950). Large Victorian house converted into a hotel, with three good restaurants and bars; the one in the garden serves excellent *tandoori* cuisine. ⑦.

Central Guest House, 18 Prafulla Sarkar St (☎274876). Within walking distance of BBD Bagh and Esplanade. Fairly priced but ordinary rooms; the entrance around the back is hard to find. ④.

Chowringhee, 1 J Nehru Rd (☎248 7905). Overlooking the most animated corner in Calcutta on the junction with Esplanade and Dharamtala, a large lodge with restaurant, well past its prime. ③.

Eastern Railway Yatri Niwas, Howrah Station (☎660 1742). Large place with small dorms and a/c suites, for travellers with long-distance or upper-class rail tickets only. 1-night maximum. ①–⑤.

Great Eastern, 1/3 Old Court House St (☎248 2311). Famous old hotel near BBD Bagh – as used by Mark Twain – where the marble floors and wood-panelled corridors have seen better days. Its recent aquisition by the Peerless Group may bring the hotel back to life. There are a handful of cheaper, non-a/c rooms including singles for under Rs300. ⑥–⑧.

Hindusthan International, 235/1 AJC Bose Rd (☎247 2394). Comfortable business hotel with indifferent service. An arcade with shops and travel services, plus an *Indian Airlines* office, restaurants and a swimming pool open to the public for a fee. Vastly overpriced in dollars. ⑨.

ITDC Airport Ashok, Calcutta Airport (☎552 9111). Handy for the airport but not the town; large featureless government-run luxury hotel with a health club and swimming pool. ⑨.

Kenilworth, 1 & 2 Little Russel St (☎242 8394). Comfortable and plush place not quite in the luxury bracket, consisting of an overpriced old block and a better-value new one, plus a bar, a restaurant and a pleasant garden. ⑨.

Oberoi Grand, 15 J Nehru Rd (☎249 2323). Completely revamped central hotel, part of the fabric of the city, whose white Victorian facade harks right back to the Raj. Very luxurious. ⑨.

Old Kenilworth, 7 Little Russell St (☎242 5325). Rambling and run-down old-world hotel – the original *Kenilworth*. Run by the eccentric Mrs Purdy. Full of character but musty and overpriced. ⑦.

Park, 17 Park St (☎249 7336). Modern hotel in a good location at the head of a cosmopolitan street, with all amenities including swimming pool, late checkout and good food at hand. Comfortable but overpriced and, despite a recent revamp, still characterless. ⑨.

Quality Inn, 12 J Nehru Rd (☎243 0301). Once the *Ritz*, now reopened after a strike closed it for years. Its shiny granite and marble interior has a very upmarket Bengali feel and the restaurant specializes in local cuisine. ⑧.

Taj Bengal, 24B Belvedere Rd, Alipore (☎248 3939). Opulent, showpiece hotel, attempting to amalgamate Bengali culture with the usual *Taj* grandeur but without the character of the *Grand*. Excellent Chinese and Indian restaurants and all mod cons including a pool and a disco. ⑨.

Youth Hostel, 10 Ananda Dutta Lane, Howrah (☎692869). Dingy dorms. ①.

YWCA, Middleton Row (☎290260). For women who plan to stay in town a while, there is no better place. Just off Park St, it is built around a pleasant courtyard with an immaculate tennis court. Minimum stay is one week and meals are included. ③.

Eating and drinking

Although Calcuttans love to **dine out**, traditional Bengali cooking is generally restricted to the home. Authentic Chinese cuisine, available in areas such as **Tangra** on the road to the airport, is the most popular option, though rich Muslim cooking can be sampled at places like the *Royal*, and Tibetan cafes fill the area around the Rabindra Sadan Metro. Most places in Tangra close at about 9.30pm, after which the area is deserted. The most cosmopolitan strip of the city for **bars** and restaurants is the western end of **Park Street**, where incongruous names such as *Blue Fox* and *Moulin Rouge* date back to the street's role in the 1960s and 1970s as host to a small but thriving pop and jazz scene. Restaurants and cafes around Sudder Street cater for Western travellers staying in the local hotels.

New Market and Sudder Street

Abdul Khalique, Marquis St. Cheap Muslim cafe near the corner of Stuart Lane, serving good *kati* and egg rolls.

Blue Sky Cafe, Sudder St. Around a corner, halfway down the strip. A haunt of budget travellers who stumble in for breakfasts of curd and fruit, porridge, burgers and milkshakes.

How Hua, 10 Mirza Ghalib St. Good Chinese food with an interesting regional menu. Closed Tues.

Kathleen's, 12 Mirza Ghalib St. Around the corner from Sudder St – good for *tandoori* food, ice-cream, teas and cold beer. They also have a popular bakery and patisserie. Closed Thurs.

Khalsa, Madge Lane. Simple but long-popular *dhaba* serving basic cheap food.

Nahoum & Sons, F20 New Market. Fruitcake, *chola* (Jewish braided bread), cheese straws, chicken patties, bagels and cream cheese – evidence of the dwindling Jewish presence.

Nizam's, 22–25 Hogg Market. Legendary if somewhat faded place behind New Market to the north, which specializes in the *kati roll*. These spicy *sheesh kebabs*, rolled into a *paratha* of white flour, are now sold throughout the city. Take away or eat in cubicles around the central halls.

Oasis, 2 Madge Lane. Small a/c multi-cuisine restaurant between Sudder St and New Market. A good breakfast menu includes sausage and mash. There's another branch at 33 Park Street. Closed Thurs.

Ruchika's, Chowringhee Centre, opposite *New Empire Cinema*. Snacks and ice-cream, as well as south Indian food.

Zaranj, 26 J Nehru Rd at Sudder St (☎299744). Part of the same excellent chain as the *Amber*, some feel it is even better. Upmarket and plush, specializing in North West Frontier food.

Zurich, 3 Sudder St. Around the corner from the *Blue Sky Cafe* and similarly pitched at travellers; more comfortable and restaurant-like, but, as yet, without the atmosphere.

Around Park Street

Bar-B-Q, 43 Park St. Good Chinese food in nice surroundings, and a bar downstairs. Closed Thurs.

Blue Fox, 55 Park St. Restaurant-cum-bar serving a range of cuisine.

Flury's, 18 Park St. Calcutta landmark, on the corner with Middleton Row. Good for tea, cakes and Swiss pastries – try the rum balls. They also make their own chocolates. Closed Mon.

Guptas, 18B Park St, on the corner with Mirza Ghalib St. Highly recommended Indian food.

Kwality, 17 Park St. Comfortable, plush and airy, one of Park St's best restaurants, with a range of food as well as ice-cream. Also serves alcohol. Closed Thurs.

Olympia, 21 Park St. A legend as a bar, it also serves good steak in the family restaurant upstairs.

Tandoor, 43 Park St. As the name suggests, it specializes in *tandoori* food, but it isn't in the same league as *Amber*. Closed Wed.

Trinca's, 17B Park St. Multi-cuisine restaurant, strong on Western food, with a bar. Once a popular night spot, it's now a bit faded, but still puts on occasional live music at a premium.

South Calcutta

China Bowl, Southern Ave, Gol Park. Dimly lit a/c Chinese restaurant which would otherwise be quite ordinary but for its location near the lakes.

The Dhaba, Ballygunge Phari. Sikh-run cafe, where the core menu of good Punjabi cooking in the mid-range restaurant upstairs has been extended to cover middle-class tastes. Recommended.

Hamro Momo, Suburban Hospital Rd (lane off Chowringhee, opposite Rabindra Sadan Metro). One of a handful of good Tibetan food cafes on this street.

Kim Wah, Garcha Rd, Ballygunge. Small but good Chinese restaurant close to Ballygunge Phari.

Kwality, Ballygunge Phari. Part of the famous chain with an indifferent ambience but good all-round menu and strong on ice-creams.

Lazeez, Shambhu Nath Pandit St, Bhowanipur. Comfortable if pricey, and good for both Indian and Western cooking.

Momo Plaza, 2A Suburban Hospital Rd (☎247 8250). Another good Tibetan cafe, specializing in *shyabhaley* – large flat *momos*.

Prema Villas, Lake Market, off Rashbehari Ave. Genuine south Indian local cafe near the Lakes, serving excellent milky coffee.

Radhu's, Lake Market. Snack bar serving fried fish and Bengali *alu dam* (steamed spicy potatoes).

Tibetan Delights, Suburban Hospital Rd. Down a lane just off the road, similar to *Momo Plaza* but with better ambience. Chicken *momos* are popular.

Twinkle Fung Shway, 1/1 Dover Lane, close to Gariahat Mor. Small, popular and new with an upbeat ambience; Calcutta's only Thai restaurant, with food spiced for Bengali tastes.

Tangra

Kafulok, South Tangra Rd. Versatile and reliably good restaurant with a good all-round menu.

Kim Fa, 9 South Tangra Rd. One of Tangra's best and most established Chinese restaurants – Thai soup, garlic prawns and chili king prawns which can be quite potent.

Kim Ling, South Tangra Rd. Good family-run restaurant – try the honey chicken, or the chicken with black mushrooms and baby corn.

Sin Fa, South Tangra Rd. Another recommended family-run Chinese restaurant.

Elsewhere in the city

Amber, 11 Waterloo St (☎283477). Legendary restaurant serving absolutely superb Mughlai and *tandoori* cooking. Plush and dimly lit, it covers three floors, and has a bar downstairs.

Anand, 19 Chittaranjan Ave. South Indian snacks as well as veggie burgers and milkshakes.

Chung Wah, Chittaranjan Ave. Chinese food in authentic but faded splendour.

Eau Chew, P-32 Mission Row Extension, Ganesh Chandra Ave (☎278260). A Chinese family-run restaurant above a petrol station. Excellent food but the best dishes like the *Chimney Soup* are off the menu and best ordered in advance.

India Coffee House, College St. Atmospheric historic cafe in the heart of the university area where students and intellectuals continue to meet and debate in faded surroundings.

Jimmy's Kitchen, AJC Bose Rd and Shakespeare Sarani crossing. Justifiably popular Chinese restaurant with specialities like mandarin fish.

Jyoti Vihar, 3A Ho Chi Minh Sarani. Inexpensive and deservedly popular a/c south Indian cafe near the US Consulate, which gets packed at lunch time.

Royal, near Nakhoda Masjid, Rabindra Sarani. Legendary restaurant serving excellent Muslim cuisine. Renowned for its *chanp* – a derivative of chop but cooked with spices and delicious with *rumali roti*, the super thin "kerchief" bread. The *biryanis* are highly recommended.

Sabir's, Chandni Chowk. Traditional, tasty but very rich Muslim restaurant behind the market. Try their *razala* – an aromatic meat curry.

Scoop, 71 Strand Rd, Man-o-War Jetty. Pleasant riverside location which gets crowded in the evenings. Renowned for its extravagant ice-creams, it also serves pizzas.

Suruchi, 89 Elliot Rd. Run by a charity – the All Bengal Women's Union – and one of the few places you can sample authentic Bengali cooking. Unpretentious atmosphere, and very reasonable prices. Look out for *macher jhol* (fish stew). Highly recommended. Closed Sat and Sun evenings.

Vineet, 1 Shakespeare Sarani. In the basement of the AC Market shopping complex – mid-priced vegetarian food plus snacks and ice-cream. Occasional live Hindi popular music.

Hotel restaurants

Astor, 15 Shakespeare Sarani (☎242 9950). This small hotel has a bar and several restaurants including the multi-cuisine *Serai* and the *Banyan Tree* serving Bengali food, but the best is *Kebab-e-Que* in the garden, which serves excellent *tandoori* food.

Fairlawn, 13A Sudder St (☎431510). Soak in the fossilized Raj atmosphere with tea on the lawn.

Lytton, 14 Sudder St (☎291872). Along with a bar, the hotel has two good restaurants including the *Dynasty* serving Chinese food and *Gaylords* serving Indian and Western.

Park, 17 Park St (☎297336). The *Zen* is an "oriental" restaurant serving dishes from China, Burma, Thailand and Indonesia.

Quality Inn, 12 J Nehru Rd (☎243 0222). Among its eating and drinking places is *Ahdee*, one of the few restaurants in town to serve genuine Bengali cuisine.

Taj Bengal, 24B Belvedere Rd, Alipore (☎283939). Smart and beautifully presented, the *Chinoiserie* offers some of Calcutta's best Chinese food; *Sonargaon* (Bengali for Golden Town) serves local delicacies and north Indian food; the *Coffee Shop* is open all hours and also serves meals; and the poolside barbecue prepares kebabs and griddle-based dishes.

Sweet shops

Milk-based sweets such as the small and dry *sandesh* are the Bengali speciality. Though confections such as the white *rosogulla*, the brown (deep-fried) *pantua* and the distinctive black *kalojam*, all in syrup, are found elsewhere in north India, they are nowhere as good as in Calcutta. Try also *lal doi* – a delicious red steamed yoghurt made with jaggery – or plain white *mishti doi* made with sugar. Sweet shops often serve savoury snacks in the afternoons such as *nimki* (literally salty), deep-fried light pastry strips, *shingara*, a delicate Bengali *samosa*, and *dal puri*, *paratha*-like bread made with lentils.

Bhim Chandra Nath, Surya Sen St, off College St. Best of several good sweet shops in the area.

Ganguram, 46C J Nehru Rd. Legendary sweet shop near Victoria Memorial with branches all over the city; unfortunately it has suffered a series of strikes over the last couple of years.

Girish Chandra Dey, 167N Rashbehari Ave. One of several good shops in the Gariahat area.

Jadav Chandra Das, 127A Rashbehari Ave. Another popular outlet in Gariahat.

KC Das, 11 Esplanade East and 1/433 Gariahat Rd. One of the city's most famous sweet shops.

Sen Mahasay, 171H Rashbehari Ave. Next to Gariahat Market, renowned for its *sandesh*.

Bars

Most of Calcutta's **bars** exude a tense all-male atmosphere; only the *Olympia* is a bit more welcoming. The obvious places to escape all that are the big hotels.

Amber, 11 Waterloo St. On the ground floor of a superb restaurant, with strong a/c and low lights.

Ashoka, 3B J Nehru Rd. Adjacent to Esplanade, and good for a cold beer.

Bar-B-Q, 43 Park St. Below the restaurant; one of the better bars on the strip.

Chowringhee Bar, *Oberoi Grand*, J Nehru Rd. Plush and well presented but pricey.

Esplanade, *Taj Bengal*, Alipore. Luxurious surroundings and an escape from the noise and grime of the city, but expensive.

New Cathay, Esplanade. Like the adjacent *Ashoka*, popular with office workers after hours.

Olympia, 21 Park St. Renowned address, with a legendary (albeit dead) clientele. Basic marble-floored downstairs bar, more comfortable "family room" upstairs. Also renowned for its steaks.

Sunset Bar, *Lytton Hotel*, Sudder St. Friendly and relaxed bar, popular with travellers.

Tippu Sultan Bar, Tollygunge Club. Grand colonial atmosphere, in the shade of large trees and surrounded by a golf course. For temporary membership contact the Secretary (see p.791).

Culture and entertainment

Calcutta's lively arts scene is well known for its **music** and Bengali **theatre**. A handful of galleries hold exhibitions of fine art, and the cultural centres of the various consulates (listed on p.800) also play an important role in the life of the city. Of the many non-religious festivals each year, the **Ganga Utsav**, held over a few weeks around the end of January at Diamond Harbour, involves music, dance and theatrical events.

Music

Calcuttan **music** audiences have a reputation as the most discerning in the country. The main concert season is winter and spring, with the huge week-long **Dover Lane Music Festival**, held under a marquee in south Calcutta around the end of January and early February, attracting many of India's best musicians. Other festivals to look out for include the **Sadarang Music Conference**, usually held in halls such as *Kala Bhavan* or *Rabindra Sadan* which also host regular performances of north Indian and Karnatik (south Indian) classical music and dance. The **Salt Lake Music Conference** is similar, while the **Ramakrishna Mission** hold a conference in January and both the **Kala Sangam** and the **Raja Sangit Academy** organize concerts at various venues.

Sangeet Research Academy, near Tollygunge Metro Station, is one of India's leading north Indian classical music research institutes. It offers long-term courses in various music forms and holds free Wednesday-evening concerts. **All India Radio Calcutta** is a good source for Indian classical music, folk music and Rabindra Sangit, the songs of Rabindranath Tagore. There is also a small but thriving Western classical music scene, with concerts at the **Calcutta Music School**, in Sunny Park, and the **Calcutta Jazz Festival** held sometimes in spring has been known to attract big names.

Cinemas

Cinemas that show English-language films three or four times each day can be found along Jawaharlal Nehru Rd near Esplanade and New Market. All are air-conditioned; some, like the *Lighthouse* on Humayan Place, are fine examples of art deco. Names to look for include *Elite*, SN Banerjee Rd; *Globe*, Lindsay St; *Metro*, J Nehru Rd; and *Minerva*, Chowringhee Place. *Nandan*, behind Rabindra Sadan on AJC Bose Rd, is the city's leading "art-house" cinema with library, archives and three auditoria.

Galleries

Bengal has a proud and lively tradition of contemporary art, with its few galleries showing a high standard of work.

Academy of Fine Arts, Cathedral Rd. Showplace for local artists and venue for international exhibitions of contemporary art. Permanent exhibitions include works by Rabindranath Tagore and Jamini Roy as well as sculpture.

Birla Academy of Art & Culture, Southern Ave. Exhibitions of visiting artists.

CIMA (Centre of International Modern Art), 2nd Floor, Sunny Towers, 43 Ashutosh Chowdhury Ave. Prestigious Ballygunge gallery, showing work by contemporary artists.

Gallery Katayun, Jassal House, Auckland Square. Close to Lower Circular Rd and the Rawdon St crossing with frequent exhibitions of contemporary artists.

Oxford Bookshop Gallery, 17 Park St. Recently renovated bookshop with a gallery holding special exhibitions on the mezzanine floor.

THE FESTIVALS OF CALCUTTA

Most of Calcutta's Hindu **festivals** are devoted to forms of the mother goddess, **Shakti**. As one of the last centres of north Indian Buddhism, Bengal reflects a unique blend of traditions; **tantric** Hinduism, closely related to Vajrayana Buddhism, continues to be evident in the devotion to mysterious deities such as **Tara** (see p.772 and p.810). Calcutta's own deity, the black goddess **Kali**, is an emanation of **Durga**, the consort of Shiva. Kali is depicted with four arms, standing on the prostrate Shiva after killing the demon Raktviya. This gory image conveys a simple truth. Her left top hand holds a bloody sickle, and the bottom a severed head; together they signify complete self-sacrifice to the truth; her right top hand, raised with its palm open, signifies fearlessness, which leads to deliverance shown by the bottom hand. Kali stands on Shiva, the female upon the male.

The two-week **Durga Puja** (Sept/Oct) is the most lavish festival of all. A symbol of victory, **Durga**, wife of Shiva, is shown with ten arms slaying the demon Mahisasura, who assumed the shape of a buffalo and threatened the gods. Durga either sits on a lion, or is accompanied by one. Other *pujas* honour **Lakshmi**, the goddess of wealth, whose festival falls in autumn, and **Saraswati**, the goddess of the arts and learning, who is shown as a beautiful fair woman sitting on a lotus playing a *sitar*-like instrument known as the *veena*.

During the festivals, images of straw, papier-mâché, or *sola pith*, originally moulded as voluptuous women with large rounded breasts and physical detail, then clothed and decorated, are carried in noisy procession to makeshift altars called *pandals*. Supported by donations from businesses and local residents, *pandals* often block off small streets and blare popular music through distorting loudspeakers. Competition between *pandals* can lead to street fights, when the image is taken for immersion to the river after *puja*.

Joydeb Mela (early Jan) Commemorating Joydeb, the author of the Gita Govinda revered by Bauls, and held in the village of Kenduli near Shantiniketan; the place to hear Baul minstrels in their element.

Ganga Sagar Mela (mid-Jan) During the winter solstice of Makar Sankranti, hundreds of thousands of Hindu pilgrims travel through Calcutta for a 3-day festival at Sagar Dwip, 150km south at the mouth of the Hooghly where the Ganges meets the sea. Many of the *sadhus* drawn to the *mela* stay at the Shiva temple at Nimtolla Ghat, north of Howrah Bridge.

Saraswati Puja (Jan/Feb) Important *pandal* festival to the goddess of learning, celebrated throughout the city.

Chinese New Year (Jan/Feb) Celebrated with a week-long festival of dragon dances, firecrackers and fine food, concentrated around the suburb of Tangra.

Shivratri (late Feb) The nationwide Shiva festival is celebrated all over the city.

Bakrid (Feb/March) Large parts of the Maidan are converted into a gigantic prayer ground when thousands of Muslims pray at the end of Ramadan. Id ul-Fitr is celebrated with feasting in Muslim restaurants.

Dol Purnima or **Holi** (Feb/March) The spring festival, when anyone foolhardy enough to go out is liable to be splashed and powdered in bright colours, is especially popular with Calcutta's Biharis.

Muharram (May/June) Shi'ite Muslims mark the anniversary of the martyrdom of Hussein by severe penance including processions where they flagellate themselves.

Rath Yatra (June/July) The chariot festival, heralding the monsoon, honours Jagganath, the Lord of the World. In Calcutta, festivities are organized by ISKCON.

Vishvakarma Puja (Sept) Dedicated to the God of Creation; craftsmen and artists decorate their tools with images of the deity.

Durga Puja (Sept/Oct) At the onset of winter, Durga Puja is very much the Bengali equivalent of Christmas. It climaxes on Mahadashami, the tenth day, when images are taken to the river for immersion. Elsewhere, the festival is known as Dussehra.

Lakshmi Puja (Oct/Nov) Held five days after Mahadashami on the full moon, to honour the goddess of wealth.

Kali Puja (Oct/Nov) Two weeks after Lakshmi Puja, Kali Puja is held on a moonless night when goats are sacrificed. Kali Puja coincides with Diwali, the festival of light.

Christmas (Dec 25) Park Street and the New Market are adorned with fairy lights and the odd Christmas tree. Plum pudding is sold at confectioners, and midnight mass is well attended.

Posh Mela (late Dec) Held in Shantiniketan just after Christmas, the *mela* attracts Bauls, the wandering minstrels who perform to large audiences (too large for some tastes).

Sports and swimming

Calcuttans are keenly interested in sport. **Football** matches, especially those between the two leading clubs, Mohan Bagan and East Bengal, and **cricket** test matches draw huge crowds. There are two major stadium complexes, the **Ranji Stadium** at Eden Gardens and the new **Salt Lake Stadium** on the edge of the city.

The **Maidan**, home to the *Calcutta Bowling Club* and the *Ladies Golf Club*, is a favourite venue for impromptu cricket and football matches, and the scene in winter and spring of regular race meetings. These are run by the *Calcutta Turf Club*, and bets can also be placed at their premises on Russell St. Also in winter, army teams play **polo** at the grounds at the centre of the race course. The curious sport of **kabaadi**, a fierce form of tag played by two teams on a pitch the size of a badminton court, can also be seen around the Maidan.

The easiest **swimming pool** for visitors to use is at the *Hindusthan Hotel*, 235-1 AJC Bose Rd (☎247 2394), which charges non-residents around Rs100 per day; the *Park Hotel* on Park St has a new pool which may open to non-residents.

Across the road from the superbly equipped **Tollygunge Club**, where with the right connections you might get to use the pool and tennis courts, the elite *Royal Calcutta Golf Club* is the world's second oldest **golf** club, after St Andrews in Scotland.

Shopping

Unlike Delhi, Calcutta is not geared towards tourism – a fact which is reflected, with one or two exceptions, by its **shops**. However, it does hold many characterful **markets**, including the wide-ranging New Market (see p.781), and local institutions such as Gariahat in the south (see p.790) and Barabazaar to the north (see p.785).

Among typical Bengali handicrafts to look out for are metal *dokra* items from the Shantiniketan region northwest of the city, in which objects such as animals and birds are roughly cast by a lost-wax process to give them a rough, wiry look. Long-necked, pointy-eared terracotta horses from Bankura, in all sizes, have become something of a cliché. *Kantha* fabrics display delicate line stitching in decorative patterns, while Bengali **leatherwork** features simple patterns dyed in subtle colours.

Emporia

Good selections of most handicrafts, including lace, can be found in various **state emporia**, many of which are located in the large **Dakshinapan** shopping complex south of Dhakuria Bridge near Gol Park. Offering fixed (if slightly high) prices, these are the simplest places to start shopping.

Aavishkar, 20K Park St. Popular shop on the corner with Middleton Row, stocking stationery and cards, music, pottery by local artists, and garden-fresh Darjeeling and Assam teas.

Assam, 8 Russell St. As part of Assam House, the emporium sells handicraft and textiles from Assam including fabrics in *pat* and *moga*, two techniques of silk manufacturing.

Bengal Home Industries, officially 57 J Nehru Rd but just around the corner on AJC Bose Rd. Very strong on furnishings and fabrics, plus Bengali handicrafts including terracotta.

Central Cottage Industries, 7 J Nehru Rd, Esplanade. Part of the national chain, selling handicrafts from all over India. Along with fabrics, leather, papier-mâché from Kashmir and furnishings, there is a small but interesting collection of silver jewellery, with some tribal bracelets.

Gujari, Dakshinapan complex, near Gol Park. An outstanding selection of Gujarati textiles, including handloom and mirrored cushion covers.

Kashmir Art, 12 J Nehru Rd. The usual Kashmiri handicrafts, including carpets and rugs.

Nagaland, 13 Shakespeare Sarani. A fine assortment of Naga shawls, with red bands and white and blue stripes on black backgrounds. As with Scots tartan, certain patterns denote particular tribes.

Orissa Handicrafts, Dakshinapan complex, near Gol Park. Very strong on silk and *ikat*.

Books

College Street with its street vendors and small bookshops has long been the prime hunting ground for book collectors. The month-long Calcutta Book Fair, held on the Maidan near Park Street in January and February, is now among the biggest of its kind in the country, and provides a good opportunity to pick up books at a discount.

Bookmark, 56D Mirza Ghalib St. A selection of books upstairs. One of several around Sudder St.

Cambridge Book & Stationery, 20D Park St. Small bookshop with a similar selection to the *Oxford Book & Stationery* down the road but dated in comparison.

Classical Books, Middleton Row. Small, friendly and well worth a browse.

Dey Bros, B47 New Market. One of several bookshops in this part of the market.

Family Book Shop, 1A Park St. On the Chowringhee end, small but crammed full of books.

W Newman & Company, 3 Old Court House St. Bookshop and stationers in the *Great Eastern* arcade near BBD Bagh, which has been around for a long time – and it shows.

Oxford Book & Stationery, 17 Park St. Completely and tastefully revamped with a/c, an art gallery and a music section; a limited collection of fiction, coffee-table books, maps, guides, magazines, stationery and postcards.

Objets d'art and antiques

Although Calcutta has surprisingly few antique shops, auction houses around Park Street deal with furniture and other objects. Along with the curios common to Tibetan shops, *Chamba Lama* in New Market occasionally has some interesting pieces.

Saroj, 3A Camac St, near Middleton Row. Serious collectors' shop, with an interesting mixture of antique furniture and objets d'art, old prints, good reproductions and jewellery.

Terra-Cottal, 158/2A Prince Anwar Shah Rd. Gallery and boutique near the lakes in south Calcutta specializing in everything terracotta, from jewellery to sculpted panels and tiles. Expensive.

Fabrics and clothing

Calcutta's dress sense, in general, is conservative, and the choice of ready-made garments is not very exciting. However, a wide range of fabrics is available, and all outlets should be able to point you towards a very good (and very cheap) tailor; there are several good ones around Mirza Ghalib St (Free School St) and Sudder St. A handful of upmarket boutiques such as *Burlingtons* and *Benetton*, both on Free School St, cater for the city's wealthy.

Cheong Seong, Chittaranjan Ave. One of the few Chinese shoe shops that still makes shoes to order. The place to come if you yearn for a pair of imitation cowboy boots.

Good Companions, 13C Russell St. Upmarket fabric and clothes shop just off Park St.

Handloom House, 2 Lindsay St. Near New Market, a government-run shop with a wide range of textiles including cotton and raw silks at reasonable fixed prices.

Indian Silk House, AC Market, 1 Shakespeare Sarani. Lots of printed silks.

Karma Kutir, 32 Ballygunge Place. A good place to pick up traditional decorative *kantha* work.

Khadi Gramodyog, 28 Chittaranjan Ave. Huge warehouse-like shop selling handloom fabric; supposedly in the tradition of Mahatma Gandhi, but poorly kept and a real disappointment.

Kolhapuri Centre, Gariahat Rd, Ballygunge Phari. Dedicated to selling Kolhapuri sandals and shoes – painful at first, but very comfortable if you persist; there's another branch on College St.

Nari Seva Sangh, Jodhpur Park. A women's cooperative that specializes in *kantha* embroidery.

Smartwear, Gariahat Rd, Gariahat Mor, Ballygunge. One of several good tailors in the city with a long tradition of formal men's tailoring including *sherwanis*, the long coat, made to order.

Musical instruments

Calcutta is renowned for its *sitar* and *sarod* makers – expect to pay from Rs5000 upwards for a decent instrument. Shops around Sudder St are strongest on Western instruments but their traditional instruments are invariably of inferior quality and may be beyond tuning; Rabindra Sarani (Chitpore Rd) has several shops but quality is suspect. Calcutta must produce more *tabla* players than any other city; *tabla*-makers can be found at **Kalighat**, next to Kalighat Bridge and at **Keshab Sen St** off College St.

Hemen Roy & Sons, Rashbehari Ave, Triangular Park. Once master instrument makers to Ali Akbar Khan, the *sarod* maestro, but have lost their crown to competition in recent years. Now make *sitars* and *tanburas* as well.

Hiren Roy & Son, Rashbehari Ave, Gariahat. The most famous *sitar* maker in the country whose clients include Imrat Khan, Vilayat Khan and Ravi Shankar; off-the-shelf instruments available.

Manoj Kumar Sardar & Bros, 8A Lalbazaar St, opposite Lalbazaar Police Station. Ashok Sardar makes very good *sitars* and *sarods* to order with a small selection of off-the-shelf instruments.

Naskar & Sons, 14 Ganga Prasad Mukherji Rd, Bhowanipur. Behind the busy market of Jhagu Bazaar off S P Mukherjee Rd, Naskar makes good *sitars* but is especially renowned for his *tanburas*, the drone instrument used to accompany singing.

Listings

Ambulance Ambulance services are provided by *Dhanwantary Clinic*, 1 National Library Ave (☎479 2290) and *Emergency Doctors' Service*, A 165 Lake Gardens (☎473 0604).

Consulates *Bangladesh*, 9 Circus Ave (☎247 5208); *Indonesia*, 128 Rash Behari Ave (☎762297); *Nepal*, 19 National Library Ave, Alipore (☎479 1003); *Netherlands*, Flat 5, 4 Russell St (☎290852); *Philippines*, 14 Government Place East (☎248 1507); *Singapore*, DBS Centre, Circular Court, 8 AJC Bose Rd (☎247 4990); *Sri Lanka*, Nicco House, 2 Hare St (☎28 5102); *Thailand*, 18B Mandeville Gardens (☎440 7836); *UK*, 1 Ho Chi Minh Sarani (☎242 5171); *USA*, 5/1 Ho Chi Minh Sarani (☎242 3611).

Cultural centres Cultural representatives of overseas countries in Calcutta, typically with reading rooms and facilities for performances and film shows, include *Alliance Francaise*, 24 Park Mansions, Park St (☎298793); the *British Council*, 5 Shakespeare Sarani (☎242 5370); the Russian *Gorky Sadan*, Gorky Terrace, near Minto Park; and the German *Max Mueller Bhavan*, 8 Pramathesh Barua Sarani (☎475 9398). Similar facilities can be found at the *Ramakrishna Mission Institute of Culture* in Gol Park, and *USIS*, American Centre, 38A J Nehru Rd (☎245 1221).

Foreigners' Registration *Foreigners' Registration Office*, 237 AJC Bose Rd (☎247 3301). Apply here for visa extensions, as well as permits if you plan to go to the Andaman Islands by boat.

Hospitals Cheap, **government-run hospitals** (notoriously mismanaged) include *Calcutta Hospital & Medical Research Institute*, 7–2 Diamond Harbour Rd (☎479 1921); *Calcutta National Medical College & Hospital*, 24 Gorachand Rd (☎244 0122); *Medical College Hospital*, 88 College St (☎241 1891); *N R S Medical College & Hospital*, 138 AJC Bose Rd (☎244 3213); *R G Kar Medical College & Hospital*, 1 Belgachia Rd (☎555 7656); *SSKM Hospital*, 244 Lower Circular Rd (☎248 9692). **Private medical care**, if expensive by comparison, is infinitely superior to government hospitals. *Belle Vue Clinic*, 9 Dr UN Brahmachari St (☎244 2321); *Tibetan Medical & Astro Institute*, 9 East Rd, Jadavpur; *Metropolitan Laboratory and Nursing Home*, 18 Shakespeare Sarani (☎432487); *Park Nursing Home*, 4 Victoria Terrace (☎244 3586); *Woodlands Nursing Home*, 8/6 Alipore Rd (☎479 1951).

Opticians *RC Ghose & Grandsons*, Gariahat Rd; *Himalaya Opticals*, 25 Camac St (☎402743); *Lawrence & Mayo*, 20E Park St (☎298310) and 11 Government Place East (☎248 1818; same-day delivery service); *Stephens Opticians*, 23 J Nehru Rd (☎291895).

Pharmacies *Blue Print*, 1 Old Court House St; *Dey's Medical Stores*, 20A Nelly Sengupta Sarani & 55 Gariahat Rd; *King & Co* (Homeopath), 29 Shyama Prasad Mukerjee Rd; *Singh & Roy*, 4–1 Sambhunath Pandit St (open daily, 24hr Wed–Sun); *Sterling & Co* (Homeopath), 91-C Elliot Rd; *Welmed*, 4–1 Sambhunath Pandit St (open daily, 24hr Mon & Tues).

Photography *Bombay Photo Stores*, 33–34 Park Mansions, Park St; *Camera Craft*, Park Centre, 1st floor, 24 Park St, for camera repairs; *Narains's Photo Cine Centre*, 20H Park St; *North East Colour Photo*, 14 Sudder St near New Market, offers 1-hour processing.

State Tourist Offices The most useful of the many tourist offices representing other states in Calcutta are those that cover the northeastern states, and issue whatever permits may be necessary (details of permit requirements can be found on p.868), and that of the Andaman and Nicobar islands. *Andaman & Nicobar*, 3A Auckland Place (☎244 6935); *Arunachal Pradesh*, 4B Chowringhee

For details on getting to the **Andaman Islands** from Calcutta, by air or sea, see p.952.

INTERNATIONAL AIRLINE OFFICES IN CALCUTTA

Aeroflot, 58 J Nehru Rd (☎242 3765).*

Air Canada, 230A AJC Bose Rd (☎247 7783).

Air France, 41 J Nehru Rd (☎242 6161).

Air India, 50 J Nehru Rd (☎242 2356).*

Air Lanka, 230A AJC Bose Rd (☎247 7783).

Alitalia, c/o *Jet Air*, 230A AJC Bose Rd (☎247 7394).

American Airlines, 2/7 Sarat Bose Rd, Vasundhara Building (☎475 1261).

Austrian Airlines, c/o *Jet Air*, 230A AJC Bose Rd (☎247 7783).

Bangladesh Biman, 30C J Nehru Rd (☎293709).*

British Airways, 41 J Nehru Rd (☎293453).*

Canadian Airlines, *IGAT*, Vasundhara, 2/7 Sarat Bose Rd (☎747622).

Canadian Pacific, *IGAT*, Vasundhara, 2/7 Sarat Bose Rd (☎475 0226).

Cathay Pacific, 1 Middleton St (☎403211).

Continental Airlines, *Stic Travels*, East Anglia House, 3C Camac St (☎292092).

Delta, 13D Russell St (☎290862).

Druk Air, 1A Ballygunge Circular Rd, 51 Tivoli Court (☎247 1301).*

Ethiopia Airlines, *Stic Travels*, East Anglia House, 3C Camac St (☎292092).

Gulf Air, 230A AJC Bose Rd (☎247 7783).

Japan Airlines, 35A J Nehru Rd (☎298370).

KLM Royal Dutch Airlines, 1 Middleton St, Jeevan Deep (☎247 4593).*

Kuwait Airlines, 230A AJC Bose Rd (☎247 7783).

Lufthansa Airlines, 30A/B J Nehru Rd (☎299365).

Malaysian Airlines, *Stic Travels*, East Anglia House, 3C Camac St (☎292092).

North West Airlines, 1 Middleton St, Jeevan Deep (☎247 4593).

Qantas, *Hotel Hindusthan International*, 235/1 AJC Bose Rd (☎247 0718).

Royal Brunei, *Stic Travels*, East Anglia House, 3C Camac St (☎294464).*

Royal Jordanian Airlines, Vasudhara Building, 2/7 Sarat Bose Rd (☎475 1272).*

Royal Nepal Airlines, 41 J Nehru Rd (☎298534).*

SAS, 2/7 Sarat Bose Rd (☎475 0226).

Singapore Airlines, 18D Park St (☎299297).*

Swissair, 46C J Nehru Rd (☎242 4643).

TWA, 230A AJC Bose Rd (☎247 5576).

Tarom Romanian, Landmark Building, 2/7 Sarat Bose Rd (☎40 3171 & 475 0226).*

Thai Airways International, 18G Park St (☎299846).*

United Airlines, 2/7 Sarat Bose Rd (☎747622).

* International airlines with direct flights in and out of Calcutta.

DOMESTIC AIRLINE OFFICES IN CALCUTTA

Indian Airlines, 39 Chittaranjan Ave, 012 (☎260730 or 263135).Also at *Hotel Hindusthan International*, 235/1 AJC Bose Rd, 020 (☎247 6606) and at *Great Eastern Hotel*, 1 Old Court House St (☎248 0073).

Archana Airways & **Deb Air**, 2 Palace Court, 1 Kyd St (☎292471).

Damania Airways & **NEPC**, 2/5 Sarat Bose Rd (☎475 6356).

East-West Airlines, 2A Sarat Bose Rd (☎745179).

Jet Airways, Chitrakoot Building, 230A AJC Bose Rd (☎408079).

Modiluft, 2 Russell St (☎298437).

Sahara Indian Airlines, 2/A Shakespeare Sarani (☎242 9075).

Vayudoot, 28D Shakespeare Sarani (☎247 7062, or 405316).

Place (☎248 6500); *Assam*, 8 Russell St (☎224 8067); *Bihar*, 26B Camac St (☎247 0821); *Manipur*, 25 Ashutosh Shastri Rd (☎350 4412); *Meghalaya*, 9 Russell St (☎249 0797); *Mizoram*, 24 Old Ballygunge Rd (☎247 7034); *Nagaland*, 11 Shakespeare Sarani (☎242 7255); *Orissa*, 55 Lenin Sarani (☎244 3653); *Sikkim*, 5 Russell St (☎249 9935); *Tripura*, 1 Pretoria St (☎245 5701).

For details of **flights** between Calcutta and **southeast Asia**, see p.7.

MOVING ON FROM CALCUTTA

By air

There is no central information system for flights from **Calcutta Airport** (see p.776); call the individual airlines listed on p.801 to confirm departure and arrival. Besides good domestic flight connections, Calcutta is served by several short and long-haul international flights. Major domestic routes from Calcutta are summarized in the "West Bengal Travel Details" on p.771.

By rail

Information on **train** connections is available around the clock: ☎131/220 3535 to 220 3544. Making **reservations** to leave Calcutta by train is easy, with computerized booking offices throughout the city. Unless you really need to get on the tourist quota, have an *Indrail* Pass or want to pre-book tickets from other stations, you may well prefer not to use the **Tourist Counter**, at the *Eastern Railways* office, off the northwest corner of BBD Bagh at 6 Fairlie Place (Mon–Sat 9am–1pm & 1.30–4pm, Sun & hols 9am–2pm; ☎242 2789 or 220 4025), which although helpful can get busy. Reservations up to 60 days in advance can be made for most trains out of the city and also for trains from other destinations; the latter should be confirmed as soon as possible after you get to the relevant city.

Other booking offices (same hours) include the *South Eastern Railway Booking & Information Centre*, Esplanade Mansions, opposite Raj Bhavan (☎248 9530); *Booking Office for Eastern and South Eastern Railways*, Alexandra Court, 61 J Nehru Rd, Rabindra Sadan; *Howrah Station*, 1st Floor; *Computerized Booking Office*, 3 Koilaghat St (☎248 0257); *New Koilaghat*, 14 Strand Rd (☎220 3496); *Sealdah Station*, 1st Floor (☎350 3496).

Among major trains departing from hectic **Howrah Station** are the a/c *Rajdhani Express* #2301 which covers the 1145km to **Delhi** in under 18hr, stopping at **Mughal Serai** (change for **Varanasi**), **Allahabad** and **Kanpur** en route; on Thursdays and Sundays as #2305 it travels via **Patna** as does the *Howrah–New Delhi Purva Express* #2303 (Mon, Tues, Fri & Sat). Confusingly, the similarly named *Howrah–New Delhi Delhi Purva Express* #2381 (Wed, Thur & Sun) stops at **Gaya** and **Varanasi** on the way to Delhi; the *Kalka Mail* #2311 follows a similar route to Old Delhi before proceeding on to **Kalka** in Himachal Pradesh; and the *Doon Express* #3009 travels via Gaya, Varanasi and **Lucknow**

Travel agents *American Express Travel Related Services*, 21 Court House St (☎248 1171); inbound tours and international flights. *AR-ES Travel*, 8 Sudder St (☎249 1724). *Seagull Travels*, opposite *Blue Sky Cafe*, 2/1 Sudder St (☎244 9908); domestic and international flights. *Sita*, 3B Camac St (☎249 7023). *Star Travels*, 10 Sudder St (☎245 1655); domestic and international flights. *Thomas Cook*, Chitrakoot Building, 230 AJC Bose Rd (☎247 5354); international flights and inbound tours. *Travel and Cargo Service*, 23 Shakespeare Sarani (☎247 5739); general travel services and also runs a number of guest houses. *Travel Media*, 40H Free School St (☎244 8353); multi-purpose shop selling international and domestic airline tickets as well as railway bookings. *Warren Travels*, 31 J Nehru Rd (☎296611); well-established service including international and domestic airlines, hotel bookings, group tours, and travel documents wherever possible.

Around Calcutta

The River Hooghly served for centuries as a lifeline for foreign traders; north of Calcutta, its banks are dotted with the remains of tiny European settlements. All these sites, together with the Hindu temples of **Dakshineshwar**, **Belur Math** and **Kalna**, and even the great Vaishnavite centre of **Nabadip** further north, can be taken in as day trips on local trains from Calcutta's Sealdah and Howrah stations. Some of the towns also offer limited accommodation in simple hotels.

to **Dehra Dun** and the **UP Hills** but is nearly always late. Other trains through Patna include the *Amritsar Mail* #3005. For **Bombay**, 1968km southwest, the best trains are the *Gitanjali Express* #2860 which takes over 33hr and the slightly slower early-morning *Howrah–Bombay Mail* #8002. Going south, the *Puri Express* #8007 leaves in the evening and heads via **Bhubaneshwar** to arrive at **Puri** early in the morning; the *Howrah–Bhubaneshwar Dhauli Express* #2821 departs early in the morning and gets to Bhubaneshwar around 1.30pm; the *Coromandal Express* #2841 departs early afternoon and takes around 28hr to cover the 1663km to **Madras** via Bhubaneshwar. By far the best train for **Bolpur**, the station for **Shantiniketan**, is the *Shantiniketan Express* #3015 that leaves Howrah at 9.55am.

Trains from **Sealdah** towards **Darjeeling** include the early-morning *Kanchenjunga Express* #2557, which pulls into **New Jalpaiguri** (NJP) just too late in the evening to get by road to **Darjeeling** or **Gangtok**; it continues to **Guwahati**. The *Kamrup Express* #5659 leaves Howrah at 5.35pm arriving at **NJP** at 7am before proceeding to Guwahati. The *Howrah Guwahati Express* #3045 leaves at 10pm stopping at **NJP** at 9.25am, arriving at Guwahati at 4pm. The slower *Darjeeling Mail* #3143 leaves Sealdah at 7.15pm and arrives at NJP at 8.30am, to connect with the "Toy Train" to Darjeeling. It has a/c coaches, but its chair-car is uncomfortable.

By road

The most famous of the main roads out of the city are the **Grand Trunk Road** (see p.531), which runs via Varanasi and Delhi all the way to Peshawar in Pakistan, and the **Bombay Trunk Road**.

Normally, you have to reckon on an average speed on Bengal's notoriously poor highways of around 30kph, but the *Rocket Bus* to **Siliguri** – handy for **Darjeeling** and **Sikkim** – covers the 560km journey overnight, if not in any great comfort (departs 8pm; Rs115). *Rocket Bus* is one of several companies based at the **Esplanade bus stand**.

Frequent buses for **Bhubaneshwar** and **Puri** in Orissa leave the **Babu Ghat Bus Stand**, where *Orissa Roadways* and *West Bengal State Transport* have booths. Buses from Babu Ghat also head to **Namkhana**, en route to **Bakkhali**, and there's an early-morning local service for **Basanti** and the **Sunderbans**. Buses leave both Babu Ghat and Esplanade for the beach at **Digha**.

Serampore

In 1799, the Englishman William Carey set up a press in Danish **SERAMPORE**, 25km north of Calcutta, and began to produce Bengali and Sanskrit bibles. He also pioneered Indian-language dictionaries, and established the Serampore College in 1819, which later became Asia's first modern university. Built on a high bank overlooking the river, the large Neoclassical building houses a small museum dedicated to Carey's life and work. Books in the accompanying library date back to the eighteenth century.

Dakshineshwar and Belur Math

At the outermost edge of Calcutta, 20km north of Esplanade on the east bank of the river, the popular temple of **DAKSHINESHWAR** (pronounced *Daukhineshwar*) stands in the shadow of Bally Bridge. Built in 1855 by Rani Rashmoni, a wealthy widow, it was a product of the Bengali Renaissance, consecrated at a time when growing numbers of middle-class Hindus were rejecting their faith. As the Rani was not a *brahmin*, she found it hard to employ a priest, but one of those she eventually contracted became renowned as the saint Ramakrishna. Set on a plinth in a vast courtyard, and ringed by a band of blood-red paint, the whitewashed main Kali temple is an ornate variation on the typical Bengali hut design, with a curved roof and second storey capped by nine *chhatris*, each with a beehive cupola, in the *nava-rattan* ("nine-jewelled") style. Ramakrishna's former room, beside the main gate, now preserves his personal effects.

Along the riverfront, perched above the *ghats*, twelve identical small temples contain *shivalinga*, while another temple houses images of Radha and Krishna. In the small park outside the complex, visitors feed tribes of rhesus monkeys.

Also in Dakshineshwar, not far from the main temple, **Yogoday Satsanga Math** is the headquarters of the Self-Realisation Fellowship, founded in California in 1925 by the author of *Autobiography of a Yogi*, Paramahansa Yogananda.

Across Bally Bridge from Dakshineshwar, 3km south along the west bank of the Hooghly, the massive riverfront temple at **BELUR MATH** was erected by a disciple of Ramakrishna, Swami Vivekananda, in 1938. A symbol of the resurgence in Bengali Hinduism, it incorporates elements from several world religions; the gate is inspired by early Buddhist sculpture, the windows by Islamic architecture, and the ground plan is based on the Christian cross.

Local trains run from Sealdah to Dakshineshwar, and from Howrah to Belur Math.

Chandernagore

Around 35km north of Howrah, the former French outpost of **CHANDERNAGORE** still bears traces of its colonial masters, who left in 1949 and officially seceded the town to India in 1952. Crumbling buildings along its grand riverside promenade, formerly the Quai Dupleix and now **the Strand**, include what was once the Hotel de Paris, while the Eglise du Sacré Coeur, set back from the river, houses an image of Joan of Arc. Nearby, the eighteenth-century mansion of the French administrator serves as the **Institut de Chandernagore**, with a library, a French-language school, and an interesting museum of documents, antiques, art and sculpture (Mon–Wed & Fri 4–6.30pm, Sun 11am–5pm; free).

Hooghly and Bandel

The next significant community as you continue north from Chandernagore is the former Armenian township of **Chinsurah**. A kilometre beyond that, **HOOGHLY** was a major East India Company trading post. Packed with Islamic monuments, it was devastated in turn by the Moghuls and the Marathas before being retaken by Robert Clive.

Eight kilometres out of Chandernagore, the grounds of the **Church of Our Lady of the Bandel**, one of eastern India's oldest churches and still a major centre of Catholic pilgrimage, sweep down to the river. Consecrated by Portuguese Augustinian friars in 1599, it was destroyed by the Moghuls in 1640. A cross marks the spot where an image known as Our Lady of Happy Voyages, which had been lost in the river during the siege, miraculously re-appeared some years later. The church was rebuilt around 1660; it has now been faced with polished granite, so lacks any great aesthetic value. Along with a cloistered courtyard, it holds a grotto and a large hall devoted to St Augustine.

The old cemetery next to the church, where the mast of a boat stands as a flagstaff, is a popular picnic spot, offering boat rides on the river. Trains from both Howrah and Sealdah call at a station 2km away, where cycle rickshaws are available.

Kalna

The small town of **KALNA**, just over 82km north of Howrah, is centered around a varied group of eighteenth- and nineteenth- century **terracotta temples**, built and still maintained by the family of the Maharajah of Burdwan. Its most unusual feature is a complex of 108 Shiva shrines, arranged in a *mandala* of two concentric circles, constructed by Maharajah Tek Chand in 1809; 108 is the holy number found on a *jap mala* or rosary. Opposite the shrines, gates lead into the main compound, where buildings in all states of repair include some that are still in use. Among them are the small Pratapesvara (1849), the *jor-bangla* (twin-roofed) Siddheshwari (1740), Ananta Vasudeva, which has superb detail on its facade (1754), the large Krishnachandra, which has a porch on three sides (1755), and the massive Lalji (1739).

Also at Kalna, **Gauridas Mandir** is related to Sri Chaitanya (see below) and his disciple Pandit Gauridas. Still maintained by a descendant of Gauridas, it houses an ancient manuscript and a paddle said to belong to the saint. ISKCON (see below) want to buy the site, but the local community seem determined to hang on to their heritage. The adjacent village of **Tantipara** is renowned for its silk and every household is involved with the production of *saris*, which are then sold across the river from Kalna, in the Sunday market of Shantipur.

Kalna's not very busy railway station is around 3km from the temples; you can also get here by bus from Bandel.

Nabadip and Mayapur

Pilgrims come in their thousands to the pleasant little town of **NABADIP** (also known as Nawadip), on the west bank of the Hooghly, 20km north of Kalna. However, although this was the eleventh-century capital of Bengal under the Sen dynasty, and later became famous as the home of **Sri Chaitanya** (1486–1533), one of the main inspirations behind the medieval Hindu revival, few of the many temples clustered around its Mayapur Ghat are of any great antiquity. The most important of these are **Gauranga Mahapur** and **Sonar Gauranga**, but the courtyards of virtually all are alive with devotees singing *kirtan* (devotional song). Enthusiastic worshippers perform the full 50-kilometre *padakrama*, a foot pilgrimage around sites connected with Chaitanya that spread across the nine nearby islands. The conspicuous *stupa*-like white temple on one of these, **MAYAPUR**, is a symbol of the contemporary face of Vaishnavism; it belongs to ISKCON, the "Hare Krishna" sect familiar the world over. Next door, lies the old temple and hermitage of **Gauriya Math** in tranquil surroundings. A relaxing way to take in both Nabadip and Mayapur is by boat trip from either one of the *ghats*.

Trains from Howrah run to Nabadip itself, while trains from Sealdah serve Nabadip Ghat on the river's east bank; **ferry** boats run to Mayapur and Nabadip from the adjacent Swarupganja Ghat. Mayapur is also serviced by direct *CSTC* **buses**, departing from Esplanade in Calcutta.

The plain **rooms** of *Nabadip Lodge* (②–④) at Poramatolla near the main ghat in Nabadip, command good views across the water, and there are simple cafes nearby. ISKCON's comfortable *Guest House* (①) in Mayapur is bookable through their temple in Calcutta, at 3C Albert Rd (off Shakespeare Sarani and Camac St); they also organize day trips. For a bit more comfort, the pleasant *Janhabi Tirtha Hotel* (☎03472/45258; ①–⑤) nearby, has a range of bungalow rooms (some a/c) looking on to the river, and provides meals.

COASTAL BENGAL

The coast of West Bengal consists of two very distinct sections, to either side of the **River Hooghly**. To the east are the **Sunderbans**, one of the largest estuarine deltas in the world covering an area of 2500 square kilometres, where a group of mangrove-covered islands large and small shelter the **Sunderbans Tiger Reserve**. This area is not all tigers and forest, however; it also includes the seaside resort of **Bakkhali**. West of the Hooghly, the unbroken beaches of the Bay of Bengal curve south towards Orissa, taking in **Digha** along the way.

Sajnekhali and the Sunderbans Tiger Reserve

The cluster of islands known as the **Sunderbans**, or "beautiful forest", lie in the Gangetic Delta, stretching east from the mouth of the Hooghly to Bangladesh. Incredibly, they are home to the legendary **Royal Bengal tiger**, a ferocious man-eater which has adapted remarkably well to this watery environment, and swims from island to island – covering distances of as much as 40km in one day. Other wildlife includes wild boar, spotted deer, Olive Ridley sea turtles, sharks, dolphins and large estuarine crocodiles. Among the people who find themselves sharing this delicate ecosystem with the mighty cats are honey collectors, woodcutters and fisherfolk. All, regardless of their official religion, worship Banbibi, the goddess of the forest; their occupations are so hazardous that wives take off all their married ornaments when their husbands go out to the forest, becoming widows until they return. As the tigers like to creep up from behind, the honey collectors and woodcutters wear masks at the back of their heads. Meanwhile, the women and children drag nets along the estuary shores to catch prawns – no less hazardous, considering they have to deal with crocodiles and sharks as well as tigers.

The main camp of the **Sunderbans Tiger Reserve**, at SAJNEKHALI, is sealed off from the jungle by wire fencing (though tigers still stray into the compound); permits (see below) are meticulously checked as you pass through. Guests stay in the *Sajnekhali Tourist Lodge* (④), a large ramshackle forest lodge built on stilts; the price includes meals. The Project Tiger complex has a mini zoo, a small museum and a watchtower. Food is left out for the wild animals in the late afternoons, which invariably attracts deer and monkeys but rarely tigers. However, the cats have been known to jump the fence and it's advised not to venture out after dark. Other Sunderbans watchtowers stand at Sudhannyakhali, Haldi and Netidhopani, near the ruins of a 400-year-old temple approached via caged pathways meant to protect you from the real threat of tiger attack.

All transport within the reserve is by **boat**; country boats can be rented with the help of the staff at the lodge for around Rs70 an hour or Rs400 for a whole day. You have to take along a Project Tiger guide. The loud diesel motors of the boats tend to scare wildlife away, but when they cut their engines the silence is awesome.

Getting to and from the Sunderbans

The **best time to visit** is in winter and spring. Getting to the Sunderbans **from Calcutta** is a laborious process. First you need to pick up a special **permit** from the Forestry Department, currently on the 6th floor at Writers' Building. Thankfully, these are soon to be issued at the tourist office in BBD Bagh East (see p.777) where you might well want to reserve **accommodation** in Sajnekhali at the same time, or just sign up for one of their two-day **tours** by bus and launch. These cost Rs600 if you sleep on the launch, Rs700 if you stay at Sajnekhali, or Rs1500 for a cabin on a luxurious yacht for one night and two days. The main disadvantage of a group tour is that the general noise of other people can all but preclude seeing any animals.

Whether you travel by **train** (from Sealdah; the route is outlined in reverse, below) or by **bus**, the journey from Calcutta to the Sunderbans by public transport is equally convoluted. To go by road, start by catching a bus from Babu Ghat to **Basanti** (4 daily; 3hr; Rs18); aim for the 7am one. From Basanti, you cross by ferry to **Gosaba** (Rs4), an hour-long trip through the delta rendered far more pleasant if you sit well away from the belching diesel engines. **Sajnekhali**, which comprises a Government Guest House (closed to the public) and a Forest Department complex but little else, is a six-kilometre cycle rickshaw ride from Gosaba, along a road that passes through some lovely flower-bedecked villages. Finally, to reach the Project Tiger compound itself, and the *Tourist Lodge*, you have to cross the estuary again, on a country boat from the further back and less likely looking of the two *ghats*, or jetties. There isn't usually a lot of traffic around here, so you may well have to wait or appeal to local boatmen.

When you go **back to Calcutta**, allow plenty of time to make all the connections; the last bus leaves Basanti around 4pm. Alternatively, shared auto-scooters from Basanti can take you to **Docghat** (30min; Rs6), to pick up a boat across the river to **Canning**, and then a local train to Sealdah via Ballygunge station. If you're unlucky enough to find that the tide is out when you get to Canning, you're faced with a laborious 500-metre wade through calf-deep squelchy mud. The faster you try to get out, the dirtier you get; the locals of course are well used to it, neatly roll up their trousers, and get through without a splash. A short walk through the town brings you to the station, where there are taps to wash the mud off. Your reward is the train ride itself, infinitely faster and more comfortable than the bus.

Along the Hooghly to the sea

As the Hooghly bends south on its way to the sea, it becomes larger and larger; when it reaches the Bay of Bengal at **Diamond Harbour**, 50km south of Calcutta, it is very wide indeed. The harbour was used by the East India Company, and a ruined fort is said to date back to Portuguese pirates. The trip down here from the city, by bus or train, is a popular day's excursion for Calcuttans, though it's also possible to stay the night at the *Sagarika Tourist Lodge* (☎03174/246; ③–⑤), which has some a/c rooms. Book through the tourist office on BBD Bagh.

Sagardwip, at the mouth of the Hooghly and accessible by ferry or bus from Diamond Harbour, is revered by Hindus as the point where the Ganges meets the sea. The actual confluence is venerated at the **Kapil Muni Temple**, on an island that bears the brunt of the savage Bay of Bengal cyclones and is gradually being submerged. On Makar Sankranti (mid-Jan), during the **Sagar Mela**, hundreds of thousands of pilgrims from all over India descend on the island, cramming into the water to bathe. A number of *dharamshalas* and ashrams offer cheap lodging, and a *Youth Hostel* can be booked through *Youth Services*, 32/1 BBD Bagh South, Calcutta 700 001 (☎248 0626).

The beach resorts

DIGHA, 175km southwest of Calcutta and almost halfway to Puri in Orissa, was originally conceived as a health sanatorium. Now it's a popular, if somewhat polluted seaside resort, with a disappointing beach of hard silt. The continental shelf is very shallow here, so the tide goes out a long long way. You can get to Digha from Calcutta by bus from the Esplanade Terminus, by train to Kharagpur and then a bus, or one of the daily bus tours organized by the WB Tourist Bureau which offers a one-way fare of Rs40. They can also reserve accommodation here, or you can just pick one of the many small hotels when you arrive.

If anything, the casuarina-lined beach at **BAKKHALI**, 80km south of Diamond Harbour on the east side of the Hooghly, is even harder than the one at Digha. However, it's much less developed and far more attractive, and at high tide gets some impressive surf. The journey here is an adventure in itself; from Calcutta, head first to **Namkhana**, either on an early bus from either Esplanade or Babu Ghat, or by train to Diamond Harbour and then a bus. From Namkhana take a country ferry, which can be alarmingly crowded, and then a bus on to Bakkhali via Fraserganj. The *Tourist Lodge*, behind the tree-lined dunes at Bakkhali (①–③), has recently been privatized, but can still be booked through Calcutta's tourist office, on BBD Bagh.

CENTRAL BENGAL

CENTRAL BENGAL may now seem quiet, rural and a long way from anywhere, but it was the site of the region's great early capitals. **Gaur**, on the outskirts of **Malda**, was the mightiest of all, until its glory passed, it began to sink back into the fields, and its building materials were plundered for use elsewhere. In **Bishnupur**, in its turn the capital of the Mallas, a cluster of exquisite terracotta temples now provides evidence of a forgotten art, while **Murshidabad**, north of Calcutta, was the capital of Bengal's last independent dynasty, supplanted by the British. Finally, the university of **Shantiniketan**, founded this century by Tagore, epitomizes the values of the Bengali Renaissance.

Bishnupur

The tranquil and attractive backwater of **BISHNUPUR**, around 150km northwest of Calcutta, is a famous centre of Bengali learning, renowned above all for its exquisite **terracotta temples**. It was for centuries the capital of the Malla rajas, under whose patronage one of India's greatest (and still-flourishing) schools of **music** developed. Largely beyond the sphere of Muslim influence in Bengal, Bishnupur's long tradition of temple building had its roots in the basic form of the domestic hut, which in East Bengal consisted of a bamboo frame supporting jute or reed woven walls, and a thatched roof curved along the eaves and ridge. Translated into temple architecture, built of brick as stone was rarely available, and faced with finely carved terracotta decoration (often depicting scenes from the *Ramayana*), the temples combine a striking simplicity of form with a vibrant texture. The harmonious colouring of the terracotta blends with the surrounding earth.

Several temples stand within the enclosure of the later Muslim fort. **Raas Mancha**, built around 1600 by Bir Hambir in a unique pyramidal style, is used to display the images of Krishna and Radha during the annual Raas festival. The tenth-century **Mrinmoyee temple** encloses the auspicious *nababriksha*, nine trees growing as one. An early example of the *pancharatna* design, **Shyam Rai** was built in 1643, with five (*panch*) brick spires and extensive decoration, even in the interior. The **Madan Mohan**, with its domed central tower, is one of the largest, dating from the late seventeenth century. Its facade panels depict scenes from the life of Krishna. The remains of the **Pathar Darwaza**, the laterite gate to the old Malla fort, can be seen, along with the remains of the strategically placed *bundhs* or reservoirs that doubled as moats.

Buses run to Bishnupur from **Tarakeshwar**, which is linked to Howrah Station, Calcutta, on the local *EMU* railway network. There's one direct train each day, while others travel to the main junction of **Kharagpur** on the Howrah–Jamshedpur–Puri line. **Accommodation** options in Bishnupur are restricted. Satyepirtola, the central market area, holds the basic *Tarama* and *Rangini* lodges (both ①), while the small, pleasant *Tourist Lodge* (②–④) is well situated, near a large tank close to the temples.

Shantiniketan

Far from the clamour and grime of Calcutta, **SHANTINIKETAN** is another peaceful haven, 136km northwest of the city. Founded by Rabindranath Tagore in 1921 on the site of his father's ashram, both the settlement, and its liberal arts university **Vishwa Bharati**, were designed to promote the best of Bengali culture. Towards the end of the Bengali Renaissance, Tagore's vision and immense talent inspired a whole way of life and art; the university and school still operate under this momentum, although few classes are now held in the open air in accordance with his original plan.

Centred around the **Uttarayan** complex of buildings, designed by Tagore, the university remains in perfect harmony with its surroundings, despite its recent growth as Calcuttans have settled or built holiday homes. Within the complex, the **Vichitra museum** (daily except Wed 10.30am–1pm & 2–4.30pm, Tues 1.30–4pm; Rs2) captures the spirit of Tagore's life and work with a collection of his paintings, manuscripts and personal effects. Well-known graduates include Indira Gandhi, and departments such as **Kala Bhavan** (art) and **Sangeet Bhavan** (music) are still attracting students from all over the world. **Chini Bhavan** – the China Department – is the largest of its kind in India; its superb collection of manuscripts was for years locked away due to tensions between India and China. **Kala Bhavan Gallery** houses twentieth-century Bengali

RABINIDRANATH TAGORE

The Bengali poet and literary giant, **Rabindranath Tagore** (1861–1941), has inspired generations of artists, poets and musicians. He developed an early interest in theatre, and set his poems to music – now, as *Rabindra Sangeet*, one of the most popular musical traditions in Bengal. Introduced to England and the West by the painter William Rothenstein and W B Yeats, Tagore had his collection of poems *Gitanjali* first published in translation in 1912, and the following year was awarded the Nobel Prize for Literature. Though he preferred to write in Bengali, and encouraged authors in other Indian languages, he was also a master of English prose. Not until he was in his seventies did his talent as an artist and painter emerge, developed from scribblings on the borders of his manuscripts. Among his many illustrious students were the painter Nandalal Bose, whose family is still associated with Shantiniketan, and the film-maker Satyajit Ray, who based several of his films on the works of Tagore.

sculpture and painting including works by eminent artists such as Abanendranath and Gaganendranath Tagore and Nandalal Bose (daily except Wed 1–5pm; free).

The centre of **Surul**, a village 4km from Shantiniketan (a 20-min cycle rickshaw ride), holds several small but delightful **terracotta temples**. These are scattered near the Rajbari, or "the house of the *zamindar*" – a sort of manor house, which with its large courtyard feels very much like a relic of nineteenth-century Bengal.

The large fair of **Posh Mela** (also known as Posh Utsav), is held between 22 and 25 December to commemorate the initiation of Rabindranath Tagore's father, Maharshi Debendranath Tagore, into the Brahmo Samaj (see p.775). Posh Mela features sports, dances and music, all with a strong Shantal and folk influence, but is most renowned for the Bauls who come to perform. In recent years culture-vultures from Calcutta have descended upon the *mela* with their tape recorders and cameras; it is still well worth the visit, however.

Arrival and information

Bolpur, 3km south of Shantiniketan, is the nearest **railway** station, on the main line between Calcutta and Darjeeling and also served by local trains between Burddhaman (or Burdwan) and Rampurhat. The best train to get to Bolpur **from Calcutta** is the *Shantiniketan Express* #3015, which leaves Howrah at 9.55am and terminates at Bolpur at 12.30pm. It can get quite crowded, but the atmosphere is great. Sometimes a fancy first-class lounge-coach, decorated with terracotta, is attached, but even then it's more fun to travel second-class, as Baul singers occasionally get on and busk.

If you're heading on from Shantiniketan **to Darjeeling**, your best option is the *Darjeeling Mail*, which *should* leave at 10.28pm and arrives in New Jalpaiguri at 8.30am the next morning in time to catch the 9am Toy Train into the hills (see p.813). Alternatively, the *Kanchenjunga* departs at 9.35am and arrives at NJP at 6.10pm, which means a night's stay in the Siliguri area before moving on to Darjeeling. Reservation quotas from Bolpur are tiny, so book early; there's another reservations counter near the post office in Shantiniketan.

Information is available at the Tourist Lodge, Bolpur, although the Public Relations Office at Vishwa Bharati is of more use, especially regarding the university.

Local **buses** from Bolpur use either the Bolpur bus stand, next to the station, or the Shantiniketan bus stand at Jamboni, 2km west towards Surul. Cycle rickshaws are the chief means of transport in the area; the ride from Bolpur to Shantiniketan costs around Rs12 but you are usually asked for more.

Accommodation and eating

The Shantiniketan area holds a reasonable amount of accommodation, with the university's *International Guest Houses* ideal if you're planning a medium- or long-term stay.

Bolpur Lodge, Bolpur (☎03463/52662). Although it may look like a hostel, the large lodge set off the main road has a pleasant leafy courtyard, a dorm, a/c rooms and a restaurant. ①–④.

Bolpur Railway Station Retiring Rooms. Very good value, if removed from the Shantiniketan ambience. The station restaurant is reasonable, and the a/c room is less than Rs100 per night! ①.

Chhuti, 241 Charu Palli, Jamboni (☎03463/52692). A bit ostentatious but comfortable and well laid out, with ethnic-look thatched cottages, some a/c, and a good restaurant. The most luxurious around Shantiniketan. ⑤–⑦.

International Guest House, Shantiniketan. The university runs two of these large guest houses – *Old* and *New* – although the old one looks newer. Large simple rooms and a cheap restaurant. ①.

Mayurakshi, Prantik (☎03463/52958). A concrete intrusion in a disappearing rustic landscape near Prantik station. Comfortable, if poorly-run, and accepts credit cards. ⑤–⑥.

Paushali, near Kala Bhavan. Limited accommodation; best known as a restaurant with Bengali home-cooking. ②.

Surabhi Lodge, Shantiniketan Rd (☎03463/52636). One of a handful of similar small lodges along this stretch of the main road from Bolpur. Plain rooms and poor location. ③.

Tourist Lodge, Bolpur Tourist Lodge Rd, (☎03463/52699). Large and rather institutional, but otherwise not too bad. A/c rooms, cottages, dorm, and a decent restaurant. ④–⑤.

Around Shantiniketan

The gentle rolling countryside that surrounds Shantiniketan is home to the **Shantal** people. Though now obliged to co-exist with Bengalis, they have managed to maintain their separate animist traditions. In the evenings, the country resounds with the sound of distant Shantal drums, used to accompany song and dance. The many **Bauls** – the legendary itinerant folk singers of Bengal, pronounced *ba'ul* – concentrated in this area can often be heard singing on the streets, on trains or busking from door to door.

Kankalitala

Across the railway track, roughly 9km south of Shantiniketan via Bolpur, the small Kali temple of **KANKALITALA** is unusual in having an oil painting of Kali as its central image. With its magnificent banyan tree, it makes a relaxing and attractive day trip. Behind the temple there's a *smashana* – cremation ground – used by tantrics (see below).

Tarapith

One of the most important centres of tantric Hinduism, **TARAPITH**, lies 8km from Rampurhat Railway Station, served by auto-rickshaws (Rs40 if you want one for yourself), cycle rickshaws and buses. There is a Tarapith station, but it is not connected by surfaced road to Tarapith itself. The temple and cremation ground, in a grove beside the river, are popular with tantric *sadhus*, and it is not uncommon to witness rituals involving skulls and cremation ashes. The temple itself is a simple building in the *bankura* style dedicated to *shakti* as Tara (the image has a silver face and large eyes); shrines litter the area, and the grove is populated by vociferous monkeys. Tarapith has various simple lodges and rest houses, with a very clean *dharamshala* near the temple.

Kendubilwa

The rural site of **KENDUBILWA**, also known as Kenduli, on the bank of a wide shallow river 42km from Shantiniketan, is the birthplace of Jaidev, the author of *Gita Govinda*, and the spiritual home of the Bauls. Its small terracotta temple, complete with sheltering banyan tree, is engulfed each year during the January *mela*, when hundreds of pilgrims, *yogis* and *sadhus* gather to hear the Bauls perform throughout the night. At that time, special buses leave from Bolpur (2hr) and Calcutta.

Bakreswar

A quiet but important temple town on the edge of the Chotanagpur Plateau, 58km north-west of Shantiniketan, **BAKRESWAR** is considered, along with Kalighat in Calcutta (see p.789), to be one of the 51 Sati *pithas*. The temple of **Mahishamardini** commemorates the spot where a part of Shakti's forehead fell, cut by Vishnu as the distraught and destructive Shiva carried her dead body. Shiva himself is venerated by the **Bakranath** temple. Nearby **hot springs** such as Agnikund, or "fire spring", have a high sulphur content, reach temperatures of 67°C, and are considered to have great therapeutic value. **Buses** for Bakreswar depart from the Jamboni bus stand to the west of Shantiniketan; change at Suri.

Murshidabad

Set in the brilliant green landscape of rural Bengal, historic **MURSHIDABAD** lies close to the commercial town of **Behrampur**. Several eighteenth-century monuments along the banks of the Hooghly stand as reminders of its days as the last independent capital of Bengal. Established early in the eighteenth century by the **Nawab Murshid Quli Khan**, Murshidabad was soon eclipsed when the forces of Siraj-ud-Daula were defeated by Robert Clive at the Battle of Plassey in 1757, as a result of which the British came to dominate Bengal, from the new city of Calcutta. Clive described Murshidabad as equal to London, with several palaces and seven hundred mosques; now it's not even a city, though it is still renowned today for such traditional crafts as silk weaving, hand-block printing, ivory carving and bell-metal ware.

Murshidabad's intriguing mixture of cultures is reflected in its architectural styles, which range from the Italianate **Hazarduari**, the Nawab's palace, designed by General Duncan Macleod of the Bengal Engineers, to the **Katra Mosque**, built by Murshid Quli Khan in the style of the mosque at Mecca. The palace, with its mirrored banqueting hall, circular durbar room, armoury, and library of fine manuscripts is now an impressive museum. Its gardens and riverside promenade are a popular recreational area, with shops nearby catering for tourists.

A large oxbow lake, the **Moti Jheel** or **Pearl Lake**, guards the desolate ruins of the palace where Siraj-ud-Daulah reigned before his defeat, subsequently occupied for a while by Clive. To the south, across the river, **Khushbagh**, the **Garden of Delight**, holds the tombs of many of the Nawabs, including Alivardi Khan and Siraj-ud-Daulah. Bengal's unique style of temple building, with its exquisite terracotta surface decoration, is also represented, in the **Rani Bhawani Temple** at Baranagar.

All travel to Murshidabad has to be via **Behrampur**, which is a five-hour **bus** ride from Calcutta's Esplanade. Behrampur is also served by **trains** from Calcutta (Sealdah Station), including the *Bhagirathi Express* and the *Lalgola Passenger*. Behrampur's *Tourist Lodge* (②–④) has some a/c **rooms** and a small dorm; the privately-run *Behrampore Lodge*, 30/31 RN Tagore Rd (☎03482/21830; ②–⑤), is welcoming, and serves meals. There's another cheaper branch at 5 RN Tagore Rd (☎03482/20952; ①–③). *Mayur*, 92/8 Pilkhana Rd, Ranibagan (☎03482/20893; ③–⑤), offers more comfort and the similar *Samrat* (③–⑤), on the main highway around 5km south of the centre.

Malda, Gaur and Pandua

The unattractive commercial town of **MALDA**, 340km north of Calcutta, is renowned for its local mango harvest. A natural port, at the confluence of two rivers, it was a prosperous trading post for silk and cotton; in the seventeenth and eighteenth centuries it housed Dutch, French and English factories. Little of interest has survived from that period, but Malda makes a good base to explore the historic sites of **Gaur** and **Pandua**, both earlier capitals of Bengal.

Malda is on the main line between Calcutta and Darjeeling, served by trains such as the *Gaur Express*, *Kanchenjunga Express* and the *Darjeeling Mail*. **Accommodation** includes the old-fashioned rooms leading off the central garden-courtyard of the *Malda Tourist Lodge*, Rathbari, English Bazaar (☎03512/6123; ①–⑤), which doubles as the local tourist office. *Meghdoot Lodge*, nearby (③–④), has a range of pleasant rooms (some a/c); the *Samrat* (③–④), opposite the *Tourist Lodge*, is similarly priced.

Gaur

Spread across a landscape of lush paddy fields, 16km south of Malda on the border with Bangladesh, **GAUR** was the seventh-century capital of King Sasanka, and then successively belonged to the Buddhist Pals and the Senas. The latter, the last Hindu kings of Bengal, were violently displaced by the Muslims at the start of the thirteenth century. The city was eventually sacked in 1537 by Sher Shah Suri, and its remaining inhabitants were wiped out by plague in 1575.

Deserted and overgrown, Gaur today is hard to relate to the city of one million inhabitants described by the Portuguese historian, Faria-y-Souza. He said it was so crowded during religious festivals that people were crushed to death; now it is only visited by Hindu pilgrims, performing rites at Sadulapur *ghat*. Nothing remains of the pre-Muslim period apart from large tanks, such as the **Sagar Dighi**, built in 1126 and almost 1500 metres long, and the embankments of the old city, which extend for several kilometres through the verdant rural landscape. **Dakhil Darwaza**, an impressive gateway built in 1425 of small red bricks, leads through the embankments surrounding the **Fort**, in the southeast corner of which a colossal 20-metre-high wall encloses the ruins of the old palace. Nearby are the **Qadam Rasul Mosque**, built in 1531 to contain the Prophet's footprint in stone, and the seventeenth-century tomb of Fateh Khan, one of Aurangzeb's generals, in Bengali hut style. Other remains of interest include the elegant **Tantipara Mosque**, with its finely detailed terracotta decoration, the Lattan or **Painted Mosque** where traces remain visible of the enamelled bricks that gave it its name, and the massive **Bara Sona Masjid**, "Great Golden Mosque", northeast of the Fort.

Pandua

In the opposite direction, 18km north of Malda, the remains of Fakhr-ud-Din's capital at **PANDUA** are also struggling to survive. The splendid **Adina Masjid**, built by Sikander Shah around 1370, and in its day the largest mosque in the subcontinent, now lies in ruins. These betray the origin of much of the building materials – carved basalt masonry from earlier Hindu temples was used to support 88 brick-built arches and 378 identical small domes, the orthodox design following that of the great eighth-century mosque of Damascus.

Most of the monuments of interest lie on or around the ten-kilometre length of the old brick paved road that runs through the town. These include the **Eklakhi mausoleum** – one of the first square brick tombs in Bengal, it is the tomb of the convert son of a Hindu Raja, with a carved Ganesh on the doorway. **Qutb Shahi Masjid**, called the Golden Mosque after the original yellow glazing on its minarets, was built to honour saint Nur Qutb-ul-Alam. His ruined shrine is nearby, with that of saint **Hazrat Shah Jalal Tabrizi**, known collectively as **Choti** and **Bari Dargah**.

NORTH BENGAL

NORTH BENGAL, where the Himalayas soar from the flat alluvial plains towards Nepal, Sikkim and Bhutan, holds some magnificent mountain panoramas, and also some of India's best **hill stations**. Most visitors pass as quickly as possible through **Siliguri** en route to **Darjeeling**, **Kalimpong** and Sikkim itself.

Further northeast, nearer Assam, the sub-Himalayan Duar Hills have much in common with the Brahmaputra Valley – not only climate, but also wildlife such as the one-horned rhino, sheltered in the **Jaldapara Wildlife Sanctuary**.

Siliguri and New Jalpaiguri

Rapidly emerging as a major commercial hub, the bustling and dusty town of **SILIGURI** has a thriving tea-auction centre and serves as the gateway to Darjeeling, Kalimpong, Sikkim and Bhutan. Together with its main railway station, **NEW JALPAIGURI** – commonly referred to as NJP – and the airport at Bagdogra, it forms an unavoidable link between the rail and air connections to Calcutta and Delhi, and the roads up into the mountains. The border with Nepal at **Kakarbitta** nearby is open to tourists.

Arrival and information
Bagdogra airport, 12km west of Siliguri and served by flights from Delhi, Calcutta and Guwahati, is connected not only with Siliguri itself, but also directly to Darjeeling – much the best alternative. **Taxis to Siliguri** charge around Rs100.

Most **buses** arriving at Siliguri terminate in or around the **Tenzing Norgay Bus Terminal** or the **Sikkim National Transport bus stand** on Hill Cart Rd, the road which runs all the way to Darjeeling. Recently renamed Tenzing Norgay Road, Hill Cart Road is Siliguri's central artery.

Siliguri does have its own railway station, used by the Toy Train, but the **New Jalpaiguri** (NJP) station, 4km east, is the largest railway junction in the region with trains to and from Calcutta, Delhi and Assam (Indian nationals only). Rickshaws into Siliguri from NJP cost around Rs12, auto-rickshaws more like Rs35; taxis are more expensive and take longer, as they can't take short cuts on the narrow lanes.

The Government of West Bengal's **Tourist Office** opposite *Hotel Vinayak*, on Hill Cart Rd (☎0353/431974) provides information and organizes weekend excursions to Jaldapara Wildlife Sanctuary (Mon–Fri 10.30am–4pm & Sat 10.30am–noon). Opposite the bus stand, the **Sikkim Tourist Information Centre**, SNT Colony (Mon–Sat, closed second Sat; ☎0353/24602 or 432646), in the same compound as the *Sikkim Nationalised Transport* stand, provides information and permits for

---

THE TOY TRAIN

Completed in 1889, the small-gauge **Toy Train** was designed as an extension of the *North Bengal State Railway*, climbing from **New Jalpaiguri**, via **Siliguri**, for a tortuous 90km up to **Darjeeling**. Pulled by ancient little steam engines, the train follows the Hill Cart Rd, which was designed so that even bullock carts could travel up its gradual incline from the plains, crossing it at regular intervals and even sharing it with traffic. Weather permitting, first-class coaches with large viewing windows provide magnificent views.

As the nine-hour journey progresses the scenery gradually unfolds; at the high pass at Jorebungalow near Ghoom, 7km short of Darjeeling, the magnificent High Himalayan panorama is suddenly revealed. Just beyond Ghoom, the train does a complete circle at the **Batasia Loop** – the most dramatic of five such loops along the way.

No longer an essential mode of transport, the Toy Train has fallen on hard times. The service has become unreliable, and despite talk of axing it completely, recent plans for privatizing the line have given this unique institution a glimmer of hope.

At present, two trains leave NJP each day, at 7.15am and 9am; they return, considerably quicker, in the late afternoon. If you don't have the patience required for the full trip, it's possible to soak in the ambience on a short round trip between Darjeeling and Ghoom.

Gangtok and West Sikkim but not for treks, which are only issued at Gangtok. Other information counters are located at Bagdogra airport and the stations at NJP and Siliguri. For **changing money**, the erratic *State Bank of India*, Mangaldeep Building, Hill Cart Rd (☎0353/431360) only accept *Amex* travellers' cheques in US dollars. There are **post offices** on Bidhan Rd, close to the *Central Railway Booking Office*, near Kanchenjunga Stadium, and Pradhan Nagar, near the Tenzing Norgay Bus Terminal.

Accommodation and eating

You might not actually choose to stay a night in Siliguri, but you may well have to anyway. The best of its **restaurants** are in its hotels.

Apsara, 18 Patel Rd, opposite Tenzing Norgay Bus Terminal, Pradhan Nagar (☎0353/24252). Overspill for the nearby *TSA Guest House*, with ample rooms. ③.

MOVING ON FROM SILIGURI

Flights from **Bagdogra Airport** have vastly improved with the coming of private airlines. *Indian Airlines* fly to **Calcutta**, **Delhi** and **Guwahati**; *Damania* fly to **Bombay**, **Madras** and Calcutta; *Sahara* fly to Guwahati and Delhi and *Jet Air* fly to Delhi, Bombay and **Bangalore**. *Indian Airlines* is in the *Hotel Mainak* Complex, Hill Cart Rd (☎0353/431509); *Jet* in the Hotel Vinayak Building, Hill Cart Rd (☎0353/435876); *Damania* on Hill Cart Rd (☎0354/436263) and at the airport (☎0354/450925); and *Sahara* in the *Hotel Sabera* Complex, Sevoke Rd (☎0353/434929).

All major **trains**, most terminating or starting at **Guwahati**, use NJP station, not Siliguri. Reservations can be made at the **Central Railway Booking Office**, Bidhan Rd, near Kanchenjunga Stadium (daily 8am–4pm). The main trains to **Calcutta** include the *Kanchenjunga Express* #2557/2558, *Darjeeling Mail* #3143/3144, and the *Kamrup Express* #5659/5660; trains to **Delhi** include the efficient *Rajdhani Express* #2423/2424 which departs on Wednesdays although there are plans to extend the service. The *Rajdhani*, like the *Superfast* or *North East Express* #2521/2522 and the *Brahmaputra Mail* #2455/2456, passes through **Patna** with connections for **Gaya** and **Bodh Gaya**, while the *Mahananda Link Express* #4083/4084 stops at **Mughal Sarai**, convenient for **Varanasi**.

To get to **Darjeeling**, either catch the Toy Train (see p.813), or take a bus from Siliguri's Tenzing Norgay Bus Terminal, or a shared taxi for around Rs100 from the stand on Hill Cart Rd (3–4hr, usually with a break in Kurseong). Shared jeeps also make the trip and, although crowded, cost less than the taxis. A luxury bus (Rs70) leaves WBTD *Mainak Tourist Lodge* at 8am for Darjeeling. Regular buses and shared jeeps also run to **Kalimpong**.

Overnight buses to **Calcutta** (12hr), such as the *Rocket Bus*, are much cheaper than the train, and have the advantage of depositing you in Esplanade, near the Sudder Street area. Whatever you're promised, be it "luxury bus" or "two by two", be prepared for a severe rattling.

If you're heading for **Kathmandu** in Nepal, you can share a taxi (Rs20), arrange an auto-rickshaw (Rs120) or catch a bus to the border at **Kakarbitta** (where it's possible to pick up a Nepalese visa for US$20) and make your own arrangements there. You could also book a ticket all the way through at various agencies at Siliguri including *Tourist Service Agency*, c/o *Overnight Express*, Pradhan Nagar (☎26547). The advantage of a pause in Kakarbitta is that it gives you a greater choice of onward buses; overnight buses (Rs240) leave around 4pm each day, arriving in Kathmandu around 9am the next morning.

Sikkim Nationalised Transport, Pradhan Nagar, Hill Cart Rd (☎0353/20528) and Booking Office (daily 10am–4pm; ☎0353/21496), run a good service to **Gangtok** and various other points in Sikkim (7am–2.30pm; Rs38–80). For Sikkim permits, see p.852. Shared jeeps are also available from here. Several agencies advertise the *Blue Hills* company (☎0353/26898), which runs by far the best bus service to **Guwahati**.

Chancellor, Sevoke Mor, corner of Sevoke and Hill Cart roads (☎0353/432360). Tibetan-run and friendly. Rooms have baths; the block at the back is quieter. Tibetan, Chinese and Indian food. ②–③.

Embassy, George Mehbert Rd (☎0353/435098). Surprisingly pleasant business hotel behind bustling Bidhan Market. ④–⑤.

Holidon, NJP Station Rd. Friendly and cheap hotel convenient for the main railway station. ①–③.

Mayor, Sevoke Rd (☎0353/342596). On a main road with spacious rooms but gruff management, all with attached baths. Popular bar and restaurant serving Indian and Chinese food. ③.

Ranjit, Hill Cart Rd (☎0353/431680). Part of a complex of hotels, restaurants and bars including the *Saluja* (☎433684; ②–⑥), a clean Sikh-run hotel off the main drag with a good vegetarian restaurant and a range of prices – the cheaper rooms tend not to have windows. ①–⑤.

Sikkim, George Manbert Rd, behind Bidhan Market (☎0353/430422). Simple budget hotel in a busy part of town with a cafe serving *momos* and the usual Chinese and Indian food. ①–②.

Tourist Service Agency Guest House, Pradhan Nagar (☎0353/430872). A bungalow on a quiet street being expanded with a new floor. Good value and friendly, but often full. ③.

WBTD Mainak Tourist Lodge, Pradhan Nagar (☎0353/430986). Set in large grounds with friendly, welcoming staff and comfortable rooms. Car rental, restaurant and bar. ⑤–⑦.

Jaldapara Wildlife Sanctuary

Apart from Darjeeling and the hills, most of North Bengal is far off the beaten track; few travellers venture off the Darjeeling–Sikkim–Nepal road. Probably the best reason to do so is to visit the small **JALDAPARA WILDLIFE SANCTUARY**, roughly 124km east of Siliguri. The sanctuary was established in 1943 to help protect wildlife against the encroachment of tea cultivation. Consisting of tracts of tall elephant grass on the banks of the River Torsa, and set against the backdrop of forested foothills, it now shelters around fifty highly endangered greater **one-horned rhinoceroses**, as well as tiger, leopard, wild elephant, *sambar*, and hog deer.

Jaldapara is open from November to the end of April, with March being the best month to view animals, as they graze on new shoots. Much the best way to explore it is on elephant back. The easiest way to get here is on a package **tour** organized by the WB *Tourist Office* in Siliguri (☎0353/431974), bookable in Siliguri or Calcutta, which leaves Siliguri at noon on Saturday and returns early evening on Sunday (around Rs640). However, it is possible to travel by train or bus from Siliguri to the town of **Madarihat**, 7km from the sanctuary, from where taxis run to **Hollong** in the heart of the forest for around Rs100. **Accommodation** and **food** are available at the *Madarihat Tourist Lodge* (which can also be booked through the WB *Tourist Bureau* in Calcutta; ☎248 5917; ③–⑤), or at the *Hollong Forest Lodge* (③), also booked through the WB *Tourist Office* in Siliguri; the lodge tends to get full due to its proximity to Phuntsholing on the border with Bhutan.

Darjeeling

Part Victorian holiday resort, part major tea-growing centre, **DARJEELING** (from *Dorje Ling*, "the place of the thunderbolt") straddles a ridge 2200m up in the Himalayas and almost 600km north of Calcutta. Fifty years after the British departed, the town remains as popular as ever with holiday-makers from the plains, and promenades such as the Mall and the Chowrasta still burst with life. Although the infrastructure created under the Raj is now struggling to cope, and Darjeeling is plagued by acute shortages of water and electricity, it's a fascinating and cosmopolitan place. Above all (literally), the greatest appeal for visitors has to be its stupendous mountain vistas – the equal of any hill station in India, with Kanchendzonga (also spelt Kanchenjunga), the third highest mountain in the world, dominating the northern horizon. The best seasons to come – and to attempt the magnificent trek to Sandakphu, to see Everest – are after the monsoons and before winter (late Sept to late Nov), and spring (mid-Feb to May).

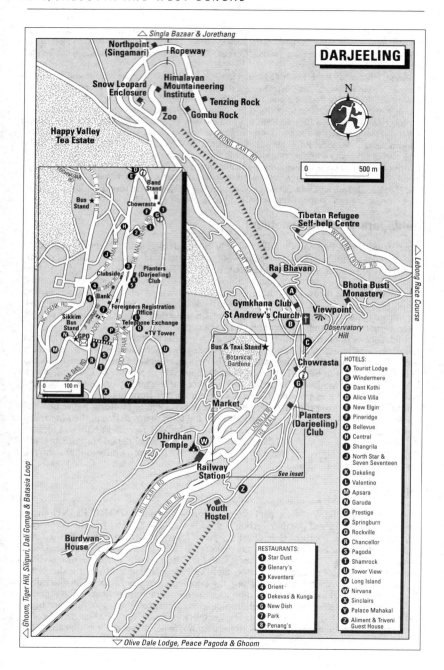

DARJEELING

Singla Bazaar & Jorethang

Northpoint (Singamari) — Ropeway

Himalayan Mountaineering Institute

Snow Leopard Enclosure

Tenzing Rock

Zoo — Gombu Rock

Happy Valley Tea Estate

N

0   500 m

Lebong Race Course

KOCHNAGAR RD
HILL CART RD

Bus Stand
Band Stand
Chowrasta

THE MALL (NEHRU RD)

HD MAMA RD

Bus Stand

Tibetan Refugee Self-help Centre

WESTERN LEBONG RD

Planters (Darjeeling) Club

Clubside
Bank
Foreigners Registration Office
Telephone Exchange
TV Tower

Raj Bhavan

Sikkim Bus Stand
GPO

COOCH BEHAR RD

Gymkhana Club
St Andrew's Church

Bhotia Busti Monastery

Viewpoint

Observatory Hill

Bus & Taxi Stand
Botanical Gardens

Chowrasta

SM DAS RD

100 m

Market

Planters (Darjeeling) Club

Dhirdhan Temple

Railway Station

See inset

HILL CART RD

D B GIRI RD

Youth Hostel

Burdwan House

HOTELS:
- **A** Tourist Lodge
- **B** Windermere
- **C** Dant Kothi
- **D** Alice Villa
- **E** New Elgin
- **F** Pineridge
- **G** Bellevue
- **H** Central
- **I** Shangrila
- **J** North Star & Seven Seventeen
- **K** Dekeling
- **L** Valentino
- **M** Apsara
- **N** Garuda
- **O** Prestige
- **P** Springburn
- **Q** Rockville
- **R** Chancellor
- **S** Pagoda
- **T** Shamrock
- **U** Tower View
- **V** Long Island
- **W** Nirvana
- **X** Sinclairs
- **Y** Palace Mahakal
- **Z** Aliment & Triveni Guest House

RESTAURANTS:
- **1** Star Dust
- **2** Glenary's
- **3** Keventers
- **4** Orient
- **5** Dekevas & Kunga
- **6** New Dish
- **7** Park
- **8** Penang's

Ghoom, Tiger Hill, Siliguri, Dali Gompa & Batasia Loop

Olive Dale Lodge, Peace Pagoda & Ghoom

Until the nineteenth century, Darjeeling belonged to **Sikkim**. However, in 1817, after a disastrous war with Nepal, Sikkim was forced to concede the right to use the site as a health sanatorium to the **British**, who had helped to broker a peace settlement. Darjeeling soon became the most popular of all hill resorts, especially after the Hill Cart Road was built in 1839 to link it with Siliguri. **Tea** arrived a few years later, and with it an influx of Nepalese labourers, and the virtual disappearance of the forests that previously carpeted the hillsides. The town's growing economic significance led Britain to force a treaty on the Sikkimese in 1861, thereby annexing Darjeeling and Kalimpong. (Part of the aim was to develop trade via the two towns with Tibet; when the Tibetans demurred, Colonel Younghusband was despatched into the mountains, where his troops pulverized the ill-equipped and archaic Tibetan army at Gyantse in 1904.) In the early 1900s, Darjeeling had a reputation of being one of the most glamorous and far-flung outposts of the British empire, attracting socialites and adventurers in equal numbers.

Meanwhile, the advent of the **Nepalese** had changed the face of the hills, so that its main language is now Nepali. After Independence the region joined West Bengal, administered from Calcutta, but calls for autonomy grew, taking shape in the **Gurkhaland** movement of the 1980s. Led by the Gurkha National Liberation Front (GNLF) under the leadership of Subhash Ghising, a long and frequently very violent campaign ended a few years ago in what some see as a compromise, and others as a sell-out. The GNLF now controls the Darjeeling Hill Council, still under the aegis of the West Bengal government, but running vital services such as tourism and transport. Cracks are beginning to reappear in the unhappy arrangement with various calls for total autonomy from West Bengal, a merger with Nepal, or even independence.

Arrival, information and transport

Virtually all travellers arriving in Darjeeling from the plains come via Siliguri (and Bagdogra, its airport; see p.813), whether by the Toy Train, shared taxi or bus. Taxis and buses draw in at the **bus stand** in the bottom half of the town. Those taxis which aren't continuing anyway up to the **Clubside** taxi stand at the top of town – a lot nearer most of the hotels – can usually be persuaded to do so for around Rs40.

The town itself is best explored on foot – in fact much of it, such as the Mall and the Chowrasta, is closed to all vehicles, but shared taxis, buses and jeeps are available for journeys away from the centre. In particular, if you want to get to Tiger Hill for the sunrise (see p.824), jeeps wait at Clubside for the 4am run. This is also the place to arrange **car rental**.

Staff at Darjeeling's **Tourist Bureau**, 1 The Mall (**☎**0354/54050), on the **Chowrasta** above the *Indian Airlines* office, can fix up transport for local sightseeing, and sell tickets for *DGHC* buses to Siliguri and Bagdogra. **DGHC Tourism**, Silver Fir, The Mall (**☎**0354/54214), below *Hotel Windermere*, is more administrative, but also assists with arranging tours. Indira Gongba of *Trek-Mate*, who runs a little stall at Ajit Mansions, opposite the Tourist Bureau, is an invaluable source of sound advice and information. The main **post office** and **banks** such as the *State Bank of India* and *ANZ Grindlays*, are all located close to each other on Laden La Rd.

If you're planning to head on to **Sikkim**, you'll have to get yourself a **permit** in Darjeeling if you haven't got one already. Pick up a form from the District Magistrates Office (Mon–Fri 9am–5pm), below the Gymkhana Club; take it to be okayed by the **Foreigners' Registration Office** on Laden La Rd; then return to the DM's office for the final stamp. That may all sound complicated, but it only takes around an hour. You have to specify where you intend to go; you can choose to go direct to western Sikkim. At present, trekking permits to Dzongri are only issued at Gangtok, but check with agencies such as *Trek Mate* to see if there have been any changes.

The Town

The heart of Victorian Darjeeling, the **Chowrasta** – the word means "crossroads", and it's a large flat promenade where locals and tourists alike take the air – stands above the hectic bazaar on Hill Cart Rd. A small group of interesting shops line one side, with a bandstand at the northern end and a line of stables to the south, offering pony rides to tourists who often outweigh the emaciated beasts. One of the four roads that meet at the Chowrasta is **The Mall**, recently renamed **Nehru Road**. This extension of the promenade descends gradually to Clubside, below the prestigious **Planters' Club**. Established in 1868, and otherwise known as the Darjeeling Club, this venerable institution was once the centre of Darjeeling high society. Not much seems to have changed since the days when tea planters from all over the territory rode here to attend social occasions, but visitors who take temporary membership are welcome to stay, and facilities such as the snooker room are available for a day-use fee. A short walk down Laden La Rd from Clubside stands **Haden Hall**, an unremarkable building which houses an art and crafts centre with workshops and an outlet specializing in carpets and woollen garments.

Taking the right fork from the northern end of the Chowrasta, near the bandstand, brings you to a viewpoint where you can survey the Kanchendzonga massif and almost the entire state of Sikkim. From near the *Windermere Hotel* steps, ascend the pine-covered hillside to **Observatory Hill**, another viewpoint and the site of the monastery which gave Darjeeling its name. Accompanied by streams of Buddhist prayer flags, the shrine at the summit, dedicated to the wrathful Buddhist deity Mahakala, who Hindus equate with Shiva, has been influenced by Hinduism, creating a garish hybrid of styles. A steep road leads down from the Chowrasta to **Bhotia Busti**, the focus of Darjeeling's community of Bhotias, a people of Tibetan origin. Amid a warren of lanes stands the **Bhotia Busti Monastery**, with its beautifully painted facade. This small *gompa* was founded at the end of the nineteenth century, but is now almost empty.

Another Raj-era institution, now in sad decline, stands near Observatory Hill. The **Gymkhana Club** (☎0354/54341; Rs30 per day) hit rock bottom during the Gurkhaland movement when a para-military outfit set up camp in its skating hall. It's now once again possible for visitors to drop in and play billiards, snooker, badminton, table tennis, tennis, squash and even roller skate; there is also a small library, a bar and bridge tables. Below the club, a dreary **Natural History Museum** holds a huge but somewhat faded assortment of stuffed animals and birds (daily except Thurs 10am–4pm; Rs1). Further away from the Chowrasta, and a steep drop down from Government House, the extensive **Tibetan Self-Help Centre** stands above the road to the disused Lebong race course. Founded in 1959, it houses around 700 refugees, most of whom make carpets or Tibetan handicrafts. Tourists are welcome to wander through and watch the activity in the workshops; among items on sale are clothes, hats and leather items, and Tibetan boots made of embroidered cloth and leather soles. Whether ready-made or made to order, the carpets themselves are far from cheap.

A kilometre further on, north towards the high mountains and just above the gothic **St Joseph's College** (or Northpoint), the **Passenger Ropeway** is a cable car that in theory provides access to the tea gardens and Singla Bazaar in the Rangit Valley far below. When working, it offers a return trip to the Takvar tea estate for Rs30, but the tea factory is not open to the public. On the way to the ropeway, Darjeeling's **Zoo** (daily except Thurs, 9am–4.30pm; Rs3) is worth a visit, not so much for its tigers, bears and wolves as for the enclosure of **snow leopards**, tucked away in the woods and reached by a separate entrance. Snow leopards are fluffier than ordinary leopards, with large bushy tails, and more approachable, even playful. Officially an endangered species, they rarely breed in captivity; a breeding programme here is having mixed success.

Nearby Birch Hill is the home of the **Himalayan Mountaineering Institute**, reached via the zoo and covered by the same ticket. This is possibly India's most important training centre for climbers, holding countless courses (for Indians only) all year round. Its first

DARJEELING TEA

Although the original appeal of Darjeeling for the British was as a hill resort with easy access from the heat of the plains, inspired by their success in Assam, they soon realized its potential for growing tea. As the British East India Company first cleared the forests to introduce Chinese tea, they discovered that some of the plants they were discarding were indigenous strains. Today, Darjeeling continues to flourish, producing China Jat, China Hybrid and Hybrid Assam. A combination of factors, including altitude and sporadic rainfall, have resulted in a relatively small yield – only 3 percent of India's total – but Darjeeling is a delicate black tea that is considered one of the finest in the world. It is also one of the most expensive; the world record is held by a grade from Castleton, an estate near Kurseong, which sold at auction a few years ago for an astronomical Rs13500 a kilo.

Grades such as Flowery Orange Pekoe (FOP) or Broken Orange Pekoe (BOP) are determined by quality and length of leaf during a production process that includes withering, crushing, fermenting and drying. The word Pekoe comes from the Chinese *pakho* and alludes to the soft down of a child's cheek, thought to resemble the fine down on one side of new tea leaves which appear as *flushes*. The plucking season (March–Dec) in Darjeeling produces two *flushes*, the best of which is the second. Then comes a monsoon tea of inferior quality, and finally, a vintage *autumnal*. If you're interested in learning at first hand just how tea is dried and processed, call in at the **Happy Valley Tea Estate** beyond the Botanical Gardens (Tues–Sat 8am–noon & 1–4.30pm, Sun 8am–noon; free).

As for **buying tea**, vendors with good reputations include *RN Agarwal*, who have a stall on the Mall, and *Nathmull's* on Laden La Rd, a large shop where they are only too happy to sit and explain the virtues, vices and vicissitudes of various teas. Such vendors usually trade in unblended tea, bought directly from tea gardens. Being independent, they are able to pick and choose according to quality and do not necessarily stock tea from the same garden every year. The typical cost of a kilo of good middle-grade tea is around Rs500. *Nathmull's* are happy to ship tea home for you.

Director was **Sherpa Tenzing Norgay**, the conqueror of Everest, who lived and died in Darjeeling; his nephew Nawang Gombu is now the Director. All the instructors are Sherpas or Bhotia mountain men, but the Principal is a representative of the armed forces, for whom the HMI plays a vital role. In the heart of the beautiful leafy complex are two fascinating exhibition halls (daily 9am–1pm & 2–4pm; additional Rs3). The **HMI Museum** is dedicated to the history of mountaineering, with equipment old and new, a relief map of the Himalaya, and a collection of costumes of different hill people, while the **Everest Museum** tells the story of the conquest of the highest mountain in the world. Photographs from early expeditions culminate with Tenzing and Hillary's successful climb in 1953. A huge telescope pointing at Kanchendzonga, known as "Hitler's telescope" because it was given by Hitler to a Nepalese general, provides remarkable views on a clear day.

Back in town, a road winds down from the bus stand in the bazaar to enter the **Botanical Gardens**, where pines, willows and maples cover the hillside and pleasant walks zigzag down to the dilapidated central greenhouses, filled with ferns and orchids. One final prominent sight you're bound to notice is the multi-roofed **Dhirdham Temple** below the railway station; built as a replica of the great Shiva temple of Pashupatinath, on the outskirts of Kathmandu, it is otherwise entirely lacking in significance.

Accommodation

Darjeeling has no shortage of **hotels**; in fact new ones spring up all the time, placing further strains upon the infrastructure. The main thing to establish before you check in anywhere is the **water** situation; many of the cheaper places only provide water in buckets, and charge extra if you like it hot. Off-season (late June–Sept & late Nov–April) **discounts** can be as much as 50 percent.

Alice Villa, 41 HD Lama Rd (π0354/54181). At crossroads near Chowrasta, a quaint Victorian facade hides a modern block with spacious but characterless rooms. ⑥.

Aliment, 40 Dr Zakir Hussein Rd. Poky rooms, but cheap and popular travellers' hangout with a welcoming cafe and friendly management. ①.

Bellevue, The Mall (π0354/54075). Above the Tourist Bureau, and dominating the Chowrasta, this place, run by a welcoming Tibetan family, has very pleasant rooms, a bar and a restaurant. ⑤–⑥.

Central, Robertson Rd (π0354/54480). An old and prestigious establishment which despite its new wing, is a faded reminder of better days. ⑦.

Chancellor, 5 Dr SM Das Rd (π0354/2956). Comfortable hotel with good facilities including a restaurant and pastry shop. Although poorly located, the rooftop terrace makes up for it. ⑦.

Dant Koti, CR Das Rd (π0354/54120). Literally the "tooth house" and until recently a dentist's surgery. Two excellent rooms upstairs with balconies and great views. ⑤–⑥.

Dekeling, 51 Gandhi Rd, above *Dekevas* restaurant (π0354/54159). Well situated, friendly and welcoming with comfortable rooms and running hot water; recommended. ③–⑥.

Long Island, 11/A/2 Dr Zakir Hussein Rd (π0354/2043). Near Tower View and good for an overspill with basic, characterless rooms but a pleasant cafe upstairs. ②.

New Elgin, Robertson Rd (π0354/54114). Comfortable and well-maintained old-world atmosphere, if a bit formal. Rates include all meals. ⑨.

Nirvana, 8 Dr SK Paul Rd, near railway station (π0354/2909). The best of a poor lot around the station but cheap and good for late arrivals. ①.

North Star, 25 HD Lama Rd (π0354/54499). Possibly the best of the new breed of overpriced, fully featured hotels along this stretch. An unflattering location. ⑦.

Olive Dale, Gandhi Rd, above Dali Gompa (π0354/2784). A bit far from the centre but quiet with the added advantage of cooking facilities. There is also a separate cottage with a kitchen. ⑥.

Pagoda, 1 Upper Beechwood Rd. Close to Laden La Rd but surprisingly quiet, with reasonably priced rooms and a fire in the lounge. ③.

Palace Mahakal, Cooch Behar Rd (π0354/2026). Extraordinary and garish art and decor but the comfortable rooms with balconies provide great views. ⑥–⑦.

Pineridge, The Mall (π0354/54074). Well situated next to the Chowrasta and part of a large mansion with spacious old-fashioned rooms but little atmosphere. ⑥.

Planters' Club, also known as the *Darjeeling Club* (π0354/54348). Guests have to take out temporary membership (Rs50 for the first three days, reduced thereafter). Facilities include a billiard room, bar, restaurant and library. See also p.818. ⑥–⑦.

Prestige, above GPO, Laden La Rd (π0354/3199). Running hot water, good discounts and reasonable rooms makes this a popular place for travellers, on the steep steps up to Gandhi Rd. ③–④.

Rockville, 4 Rockville Rd (π0354/2513). Newish place with running hot water, electric and coal fires and the best rooms upstairs. ④–⑤.

Shamrock, Upper Beechwood Rd (π0354/3387). Atmospheric and friendly Bhutanese-run establishment with a dorm and a cosy kitchen. Popular with budget travellers for some years. ①–③.

Shangrila, The Mall (π0354/54149). Spacious old-world wood-lined rooms with fireplaces above a popular family restaurant that serves good Indian, Chinese and Tibetan dishes. ⑥.

Tower View, 8/1 Dr Zakir Hussein Rd, Rockville. Near the TV tower with good views and friendly. A variety of rooms, a dorm and a cosy restaurant. If full you'll be directed to the *Green Valley* (①) annexe next door. ①–③.

Triveni Guest House, 85/1 Dr Zakir Hussein Rd (π0354/3114). Roomier than the *Aliment* opposite, but not as popular, with a clean and more formal restaurant. Good views from the sun deck. ①.

Valentino, 6 Rockville Rd (π0354/2228). Modern Chinese-run place situated in a warren of hotels above the telephone exchange. Clean and well run. ⑥–⑦.

Windermere, Observatory Hill (π0354/54041). The most celebrated of Darjeeling's hotels, which has accommodated a pantheon of rich and famous guests. Old-world atmosphere but with recent complaints of poor managment and unsatisfactory catering. ⑨.

Youth Hostel, Zakir Hussein Rd. On top of the ridge with wonderful views but now very run down. The friendly management assist with equipment and in planning treks to Sandakphu and the trekkers' log book is essential reading. Dorms and a couple of double rooms. ①.

Eating

Darjeeling has plenty of choice for **eating out**; the more touristy of its restaurants are around the top of town. Many of the hotels, such as the *Windermere, Central* and *New Elgin*, have good multi-cuisine restaurants, and the *Windermere* also has a cosy bar; the cafe in the *Aliment* is a favourite, while the restaurant in the Chinese-owned *Valentino* is pricey but good.

Dekevas, 51. A relaxed ambience popular with travellers and locals alike, with the usual mixed menu and a very good value breakfast.

MOVING ON FROM DARJEELING

The nearest **airport** to Darjeeling is **Bagdogra**, 100km south (see p.813), with *Indian Airlines, Damania, Jet Air* and *Sahara Airlines* flying to **Calcutta**, **Delhi** and **Guwahati**. A *DGHC* bus leaves the *Tourist Lodge* and Clubside around 8am each day to connect with flights; book at the Tourist Bureau. *Indian Airlines* have an office on the Mall, at Chowrasta (☎0354/54230). *Clubside Tours & Travels*, JP Sharma Rd, below the GPO (☎0354/54646) books flights for the other airlines.

To get to **Siliguri**, take an express bus (hourly; Rs42) from the bus stand at the bazaar, or a shared taxi (Rs80) from the bazaar or Clubside. Shared jeeps leave from the bus stand to Siliguri (every 10min; Rs41), and *KMTS* jeeps depart for **Kalimpong** (Rs50) every hour.

Two buses each day run to **Gangtok**; an ordinary one from the *Sikkim Nationalised Transport Office*, below the GPO on Laden La Rd, while *Diamond Tours & Travels*, Supermarket, have an express leaving from the Bus Stand at 7am (Rs65). Shared jeeps leave from the bus stand to **Jorethang** in **West Sikkim** requiring a change for Legship, Ghezing and **Pelling**.

The **Toy Train** (see p.813) departs for **Siliguri** and **New Jalpaiguri** (8.30am & 10am), and an afternoon train travels to Kurseong. Check the current timetable as the service is erratic and may soon be privatized. **Railway reservations** (daily 10am–noon & 2–4pm) for mainline trains out of NJP can be made at Darjeeling's station a couple of days before departure.

Although it's possible to buy bus tickets for **Kathmandu**, you still have to change buses at Siliguri; it can be easier to make your own arrangements there and there is more choice across the Nepal border at Kakarbitta (see p.814).

TREK AND TOUR OPERATORS

Greenland Tours & Travels, 21 Beechwood, Laden La Rd (☎0354/3011). Low-key, friendly travel, tour and trek operator, with a book exchange next to the *Prestige*.

Himalayan Adventures, 15 The Mall (☎0354/54090). Upmarket tour and trekking operation, run by Sheila Pradhan of *Das Studios* in conjunction with *The Trekking Company*, 11 Lonsdale St, Braddon ACT 2601, Australia (☎0354/257 6494).

Himalayan Nature & Adventure Foundation, 3 Belomber Rd, opposite Dhirdham temple (☎0354/2237). Run by Nima Tashi, Field Director of the HMI, a good organizer used to working with large expeditions. Singalila, Dzongri and Teesta valley treks.

Himalayan Travels, 18/1 Gandhi Rd (☎0354/54544). A major trek operator in West Sikkim as well as Sandakphu.

Kanchenjunga Treks & Tours, DB Giri Rd. Run by Tenzing's son with the main base in the US.

Moktan Mountain Treks & Tours, c/o *Youth Hostel*, Dr Zakir Hussein Rd. Friendly family-run concern, arranging treks to the Sandakphu and Sikkim.

Shikhar Trekking, PO Maneybhanjan, Via Sukhia Pokhari, Darjeeling District, DGHC. Conveniently based for the Sandakphu trek.

Trek-Mate, Pine Ridge, Ajit Mansions, opposite Tourist Bureau, The Mall. Indira Gongba arranges tailor-made tours as well as treks to Sandakphu and western Sikkim. She can provide guides and porters and rents sleeping bags, down jackets and day packs.

Glenary's, The Mall. For years Darjeeling's most reputable eating place, now completely revamped with a restaurant-cum-bar serving the best *tandoori* food in town, and a great coffee shop and patisserie.

Keventers, Clubside. Snack bar serving hearty ham-and-bacon breakfasts. The terrace above the crossroads is excellent for people-watching, even if the service is poor.

SINGALILA TREKS

The single ridge of the **Singalila Range** rises near Darjeeling and extends all the way to the summit of Kanchendzonga. The relatively easy trails along its initial sections, to **Sandakphu** (3636m) and **Phalut** (3600m) don't stray onto glacial terrain, and provide magnificent views of the higher ranges. Lightweight expeditions are made possible by the existence of trekking huts (where the quilts are inadequate when it gets cold) and simple food stalls along the way. Several organizations in Darjeeling can arrange itineraries and guides, which are not absolutely essential for experienced trekkers, and rent equipment (see p.821). If you do plan to venture out alone, be sure to call in at the *Youth Hostel* in Darjeeling, where an incredibly useful log book records comments and descriptions from those who have done various treks and combinations of treks in the area.

Views from the Sandakphu–Phalut trail include four of the five highest mountains in the world – Everest, Kanchendzonga, Makalu and Lhotse. If you want to keep the panorama in sight rather than behind you, trek northwards from Sandakphu towards Phalut. The best time to trek is after the monsoons (Oct & Nov), and during spring (Feb–May). It does get hot at the end of April and into May, but this is an especially beautiful season, with the rhododendrons in bloom.

Maneybhanjan, a small town and roadhead 27km from Darjeeling, is the most usual starting point for the route. Foreigners are expected to register with the police at Sukhiapokhari and Maneybhanjan, though they don't check. Taking a taxi the early-morning bus to Maneybhanjan (7am; 1hr 30min) from Darjeeling enables you to start the trek the same day, or you can **stay** in the basic *Pradhans* (①), the *Goperna Lodge* (②), or the simple but comfortable rooms above *Wangdi Tibetan Restaurant* (①). As far as Sandakphu, the steep trail is accompanied by a rough jeep track; if you're desperate, you can take a jeep all the way from Darjeeling to Sandakphu for Rs1500.

Assuming you start from Maneybhanjan, **DAY 1** begins with a sharp climb to **Meghma**, then eases to the hut at **Tonglu** (3070m). Most trekkers continue from Meghma to the small town of **Jaubari** in Nepal, with its handful of small cheap lodges such as the *Everest Lodge* (①), *Indira Lodge* (①), *Teacher's Inn* (①) and places to eat. Officials, well used to trekkers passing through, look the other way. On **DAY 2**, the Jaubari trail rejoins the main one at **Gairibas**, continues to **Kalipokhari** and **Bikhaybhanjan**, then rises steeply to **Sandakphu** (3636m), which has a trekkers' hut with blankets, a small friendly lodge near the memorial stone, and a couple of PWD bungalows.

The panorama opens out as you leave Sandakphu on **DAY 3**, and the trek follows the ridge to **Sabarkum**. There's no shelter or food there, but you can find both by dropping down to the right for half an hour to **Molley**, where there is an inhospitable DGHC trekkers' hut. On **DAY 4**, retrace your steps to Sabarkum and continue along the ridge to **Phalut** (3600m) where there's a trekkers' lodge. The panorama from here is particularly impressive. Either retrace your steps to Sandakphu on **DAY 5**, or follow the trail from Phalut via **Gorkhey**, which has a trekkers' hut, to **Rammam** (2560m), home of the *Sherpa Lodge* (①).

The final day, **DAY 6**, leads to **Rimbik** (2286m); check with locals before setting off as the route is confusing. Accommodation options in Rimbik include the friendly *Shiva Pradhan* (①), which has hot water but an unflattering location, and the warm and cosy *Sherpa Lodge* (①), who will help arrange bus tickets to Darjeeling; another option is the *New Sherpa Tenzing* (①) with common baths and hot water by the bucket. Rimbik is a roadhead served by buses and taxis for Darjeeling, or you can walk for another (long) day's walk to Bijanbari, which also has transport to Darjeeling.

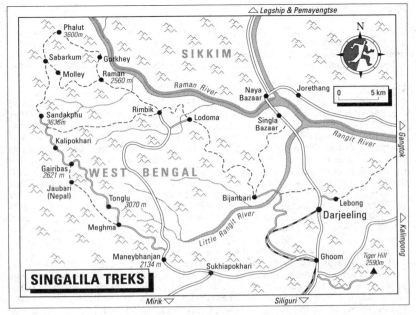

New Dish, JP Sharma Rd. Excellent Chinese food, prepared by Suyan, the former chef to the Bhutan royal family. A favourite with the local Chinese community, it was rebuilt after a fire in 1992.

Park, opposite *State Bank of India*, Laden La Rd. Plush new restaurant, strong on Chinese food.

Penang's, opposite GPO, Laden La Rd. At the bottom of the steps leading to *Prestige*, a popular local haunt serving cheap Chinese and Tibetan food, including *momo* and *thukpa*.

Star Dust, Chowrasta. Open-air restaurant serving coffee and snacks; the great terrace makes up for the dull food.

Triveni, 85/1 Dr Zakir Hussein Rd. A good and cleaner alternative to *Aliment*, opposite, but without the relaxed atmosphere.

Listings

Bookshops *Oxford Books & Stationery*, Chowrasta.

Car Rental *Darjeeling Transport Corporation*, Laden La Rd (☎0354/2074) is one of the more established operators; others are centred around Clubside.

Cultural Centres *Manjushree Centre of Tibetan Culture*, 8 Burdwan Rd. Seminars and talks on various topics covering culture, religion and medicine as well as Tibetan language courses.

Foreigners' Regional Registration Office, Laden La Rd, opposite *State Bank of India*.

Hospitals *Planters' Hospital*, Planter's Club, The Mall (☎0354/54327).

Pharmacies *Frank Ross & Co*, The Mall; *Puri & Co*, The Mall.

Photography *Das Studios*, The Mall; *Darjeeling Photo Stores*, The Mall.

Shopping Apart from tea, Darjeeling is a good place to buy curios, semi-precious stones and Tibetan costumes and jewellery. The best shops in which to browse include *Lhasa Curio*, on Gandhi Rd near the *Hotel Tara*, and the confusing but rewarding *Habib Mullick's* on the Chowrasta.

Tibetan Medicine The *Tibetan Medical & Astro Institute*, Hotel Seven Seventeen, 26 HD Lama Rd, is part of the Dalai Lama's medical organization, *Men-Tsee-Khang*, and has a clinic and a well-stocked dispensary.

Around Darjeeling

One really unmissable part of the Darjeeling experience is the early-morning mass exodus to **Tiger Hill**, to watch the sunrise. That readily combines with a visit to the old monastery of **Ghoom**, and the huge monastery at **Sonada** on Hill Cart Rd towards Siliguri. The picturesque lake at **Mirik** near the Nepal border attracts weekend crowds.

Tiger Hill

Jeeps and taxis packed with tourists leave Darjeeling around 4am each morning, careering 12km through Ghoom and the woodlands to catch the sunrise at **TIGER HILL**. Tickets are required to enter either of the two floors of the **viewing tower** at the top of the hill; the top floor costs Rs7, the lower one Rs2, and both rates include tea and biscuits. This incredible viewpoint (2585m) provides an unparalleled 360° Himalayan panorama, with the steamy plains bordering Bangladesh to the south, the Singalila range with Everest beyond to the west, Kanchendzonga and Sikkim to the north, and the Bhutanese and Assam Himalayas trailing into the distance to the northeast. From left to right, the peaks around Everest include Lhotse (which actually looks larger than Everest), Everest itself, and Makalu, then after a long gap the rocky summit of Kang on the Sikkim–Nepal divide, Jannu in Nepal, Rathong, Kabru South, Kabru North, Talung, Kanchendzonga Main, Central, South, Pandim, Simvo, Narsing and the fluted pyramid of Siniolchu. As the sun rises from the plains, it lights each in turn; not yet obscured by the haze of the day, they are bathed in pastel hues.

It's also possible to walk up during the day and camp for the night near the top. The *Tourist Bungalow*, on the plain below the summit, offers cheap **accommodation** including a dorm bed, and dinner for Rs80. Night treks to Tiger Hill used to be popular, but are no longer recommended unless in significant groups; if the bandits don't get you the dogs will. *Juniper Tours & Travels*, Police Stand, Laden La Rd (Clubside), is one of several operators arranging **jeeps** to Tiger Hill. Shared jeeps cost around Rs40 per head and depart from Clubside at 3.30am in summer and 4am in winter.

Ghoom and other monasteries

Although one of the many monasteries along Hill Cart Rd announces itself on a billboard as the "Ghoom Monastery", it isn't; it is in fact the new monastery of **Samten Choling**, beautifully sited looking over the mountains but historically unimportant.

Yiga Choling, the real **GHOOM MONASTERY**, is hidden above the road behind the brash new Sterling Resort – built on land sold by the monks to raise funds – and is reached via a side road that rises 200m beyond Ghoom railway station towards Darjeeling, passes through a small market, then winds up to end at the monastery. Built by Sharap Gyatso in 1850, a renowned astrologer, the monastery comprises a single chambered temple, with a few residential buildings and an outhouse. Inside the prayer hall stands a huge image of Maitreya, the Buddha of the future. Adorned with *katas* (ceremonial scarves), he is unusually depicted seated on a chair; his eyes are blue, as according to one belief he will appear from the west. A beautiful painting of the demonic Mahakala is always covered with red cloth; he is considered too fierce to be looked at directly. The murals on the wall are being carefully repainted by local Darjeeling *thangka* artists. At the doorway is a donation box with a suggested charge per photograph.

Unfortunately the Sterling Resort's huge, noisy generator, housed in a building next to the monastery gates, has all but destroyed the ambience of the place.

Buses, shared taxis and trucks connect Ghoom with Darjeeling, but the nicest ways to travel have to be walking the 8km along the top road, or catching the Toy Train.

In the small hamlet of **Rongbul**, south of Ghoom and below the Hill Cart Rd, next to the small Nyingmapa **Gonjan Monastery**, the *School of Tibetan Thangka Painting* is run by the artist Lama Tsondu Sangpo, whose work, sometimes for sale, displays a distinctive fluid style. Further down Hill Cart Rd, the huge **Sonada Monastery**, founded in the 1960s, was the seat of Kalu Rinpoche who developed a large American and French following. It has recently been extensively renovated to house Kalu Rinpoche's young *tulku* or re-incarnation. Rooms are available for retreat.

Mirik

MIRIK, 45km southwest of Darjeeling near the border with Nepal, before the initial rise of the Singalila Range, is being promoted as a new resort, but for the moment it remains quiet and low-key except on weekends. On the edge of the orange orchards above the picturesque central lake, the large **Mirik Gompa**, belonging to the Gelug-pa Sect, is lively with young acolytes. Surrounded by huge tea estates, Mirik is a pleasant place to come and enjoy a walk through the surrounding pine forests, with occasional glimpses of the distant snows.

Most of the **accommodation** is restricted to the newer **Krishnagar** settlement at the southern end of the lake. At the bottom of the road leading to the *gompa*, *Inny's Lodge* (②–③) is the most pleasant budget option. Small and friendly, *Jagjeet* (⑤–⑦) is comfortable and has a good restaurant; *Sadhbhawana* (③–④), behind a line of lake-side cafes, is newer. One of the older lodges, the reasonable and clean *Chinari* (②), stands right beside the lake; the *Tourist Lodge* is combined with the *Youth Hostel* (①–⑤) and has a dorm, double rooms and a cottage suite with good views of the lake. Above the lake, the overpriced DGHC *Mirik Motel* (⑥–⑦) offers self-catering cottages on a bald hill with great views. Krishnagar also has several **restaurants** and cafes. Buses and shared taxis run to and from Darjeeling.

Kalimpong

Though it may seem quite grubby at first, the hill station of **KALIMPONG** – a sort of small sister to Darjeeling – has a lot to offer anyone who cares to explore, including an extraordinary profusion of spectacular flowers and orchids. Unlike Darjeeling, this was never a tea town or resort; it was a trading town on the vital route to Tibet, and may indeed be so again one day. Tensions between India and China over the last few decades have meant that local roads were also strategic military lifelines, and the whole region was closed to foreign tourists, but Kalimpong itself, and the hills around it, are now once more opening up. For the present it lies somewhat dormant, having suffered during the political upheavals of the Gurkhaland movement, and prone to severe water shortages as a result of the total neglect of its infrastructure – although the army is still here, remaining aloof in the cantonment area. Several walks explore the hills to the south of Kalimpong, which are still home to Lepchas, the tribal community that once covered most of Sikkim and the Darjeeling region.

Kalimpong spreads along a curving ridge to either side of its main **market area**, known as **Tenth Mile** which, with the exception of the *Arts and Craft Cooperative Centre* (Mon–Sat 9.30am–3.30pm & Sun 9am–noon) selling tapestry and copperware made by local women, lacks the curio and tourist shops so common in Darjeeling and Gangtok. However, Tenth Mile comes to life on Wednesdays and Sundays when villagers flock in from the surrounding areas for the principal weekly markets. A few Tibetan stalls sell food as well as bags and jewellery.

Rinkingpong Hill, which looms above the town to the southwest, was once a surveying point; hence the local name *Durpin Dara*, which means "binocular ridge". It is now firmly in the hands of the army, who allow tourists through in taxis but occasionally stop those on foot. At its highest point, entirely surrounded by the army, is the **Zong Dog Palri Fobrang Monastery**, consecrated by the Dalai Lama in 1976. As well as a large image of Guru Rinpoche, also known as Padma Sambhava, the patron saint and founder of the Nyingmapa order – it holds some impressive frescoes, and an

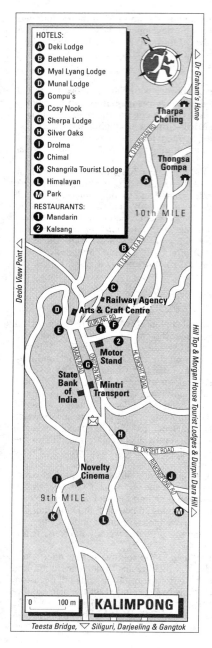

HOTELS:
- **A** Deki Lodge
- **B** Bethlehem
- **C** Myal Lyang Lodge
- **D** Munal Lodge
- **E** Gompu's
- **F** Cosy Nook
- **G** Sherpa Lodge
- **H** Silver Oaks
- **I** Drolma
- **J** Chimal
- **K** Shangrila Tourist Lodge
- **L** Himalayan
- **M** Park

RESTAURANTS:
- **1** Mandarin
- **2** Kalsang

Dr Graham's Home

Tharpa Choling

Thongsa Gompa

KHAPRADHAN RD

10th MILE

RISHI ROAD

Deolo View Point

Railway Agency

Arts & Craft Centre

GURUNG RD

Motor Stand

MANI ROAD

ONGDEN RD

H.D.DIKSHIT ROAD

State Bank of India

Mintri Transport

Hill Top & Morgan House Tourist Lodges & Durpin Dara Hill

BL DIKSHIT ROAD

RINKINGPONG RD

Novelty Cinema

9th MILE

0   100 m

KALIMPONG

Teesta Bridge, ▽ Siliguri, Darjeeling & Gangtok

excellent collection of *thangkas* (not always on display). Upstairs there's an image of the thousand-armed Chenrazee, or Avalokitesvara, and an ornate wooden model of heaven.

At the other end of town, half an hour's walk up Deolo Hill brings you to the **Tharpa Choling Gompa**, a Gelug-pa or "Yellow Hat" monastery, founded in 1892 and recently completely rebuilt. Below and closer to town is the **Thongsa Gompa**, a small Bhutanese monastery founded in 1692 and also recently rebuilt. The strong impact of Christian missionaries in the area is evident in **Dr Graham's Home**, further up the hill. Founded in 1900 by the Scotsman, the Rev Dr John Anderson Graham, as a home for six orphans, this famous school today has around 900 students, and has inspired several similar schools for the destitute and the handicapped. It also runs its own dairy. Kalimpong used to be known for its **cheese**, manufactured by a Swiss dairy; despite efforts to revive the dairy after disruption during the Gurkhaland movement, it has ceased to exist and what little production there is, is being carried out by redundant workers. Above Dr Graham's Home, **Deolo View Point** offers superb views of the town, the Teesta Valley below, and even, on a clear day, the snows and the passes of Nathula and Jelepla into Tibet. Nearby **Deolo Lake** is the town's inadequate reservoir.

Kalimpong is renowned for its **horticulture** and especially its orchid culture with around fifty nurseries such as *Sri Ganesh Mani Pradhan* specializing in new hybrids as well as cacti, amaryllis and other species of plants. Although the best time to see orchids in bloom is between mid-April and mid-May, Kalimpong's flower festival is usually held in October.

Arrival and information

Kalimpong, only accessible by **road**, is served by regular buses, taxis and jeeps from Darjeeling (3hr 30min) and Siliguri (2hr 30min). Coming from Gangtok, you may have to change buses at Teesta Bazaar, on the River Teesta. As soon as you cross the river (no photos as you go over the bridge), at a sweltering 300m, you're confronted by a sign welcoming you to Kalimpong, although the town itself is 15km further on, and over 1000m higher up.

Most transport pulls in at the **Motor Stand** in the central market area. This is the place to pick up buses to Darjeeling (run by the *Kalimpong Motor Syndicate* and the *Darjeeling Gurkha Hill Council*), Gangtok (*Sikkim Nationalised Transport*; ☎03552/55319), and Siliguri (*North Bengal State Transport* among others). The last buses leave in the early afternoon; shared jeeps cost more – around Rs50 – and are a bit more faster.

Kalimpong has no tourist office. However, a number of organizations arrange **walking** and **cycling** tours and other activities in the area, prime among them the efficient if expensive *Gurudongma Holidays*, Hilltop Rd, near *Hotel Silver Oaks* (☎03552/55304). The head office of the Darjeeling Gurkha Hill Council, Silver Fir Building, The Mall, Darjeeling, can advise on the latest political situation.

The **post office** is close to the centre of town, above the bazaar area near the police station, and there's a *State Bank of India* (☎03552/55310) further up on Main Rd.

Accommodation and eating

Kalimpong's acute **water** problems are likely to influence your choice of **accommodation** – few of the lower-range options have running water. Both the market area and the Motor Stand are centres for budget hotels. The Victorian **youth hostel** is sadly in a terrible state. The best **restaurants** are in the hotels – especially the *Kalimpong Park and Gompus* – but alternatives to look out for include the *Myal Lyang*, a very good Chinese restaurant on Rishi Rd, and the *Mandarin*, at the Motor Stand, and the basic but friendly *Kalsang*, tucked around the corner from the Motor Stand.

Bethlehem, Rishi Rd, 10th Mile (☎03552/55185). Same management as *Sherpa Lodge*. New and comfortable with running hot water and, so far, clean bathrooms. ③–④.

Cosy Nook, Motor Stand (☎03552/55541). Family hotel, run by Anil Pradhan. There's a dorm but the new rooms have running water and a bit more elbow room. ①–③.

Deki Lodge, Tripai Rd, 10th Mile (☎03552/55095). Ten minutes' walk from the Motor Stand, and marked *T Temba Cottage*. Clean, friendly and recommended budget hotel with cheapest rooms in the wooden block at the back. There's running water and a cosy kitchen. ①–③.

Drolma, Evening Side, 9th Mile, near *Novelty Cinema* (☎03552/55909). Welcoming family hotel with a special place in Tibetan history – run by Jigme Shakabpa the grandson of Tsepon Shakabpa, the last Finance Minister of free Tibet. Pleasant garden and great views. ③–⑥.

Gompu's, Dambar Chowk (☎03552/55818). Landmark hotel in the heart of the market area, with atmospheric wooden rooms which have seen better days. The bar and restaurant (great *momos*) are straight out of a film set. Proprietor Sonam Gompu is helpful and friendly. ③.

Himalayan (☎03552/55248). Historic hotel, set amid exquisite gardens in the former residence of David Macdonald, an interpreter with the Younghusband Mission to Lhasa in 1904 who helped the 13th Dalai Lama to escape Tibet in 1910. The Macdonald family still run the hotel, which boasts oak ceilings, teak pillars and fireplaces in rooms filled with memorabilia. Price includes meals. ⑦.

Kalimpong Park (☎03552/55304). A hotel with a bit of a split personality; the main building is old and quaint, but most guest rooms are in the spacious but characterless modern block behind. A helpful travel counter and a very good restaurant; credit cards accepted. ⑥–⑦.

Munal Lodge, Malli Rd (☎03552/55404). New characterless block with airy and clean rooms, below *Gompu's*. ③.

Sherpa Lodge, Dr Ongden Rd (☎03552/55572). Basic but friendly hotel, above the playground near the Motor Stand; the rooms at the back are cheaper. ②–④.

Silver Oaks (☎03552/55296 or 55368). Comfortable and plush, Kalimpong's premier (4-star) hotel has a rather drab grey brick and glass exterior and generally lacks character. 20 rooms with telephones, and all amenities including currency exchange. Price includes full board. ⑨.

WBTDC Hill Top Tourist Lodge, Hill Top (☎03552/55384). Large and reasonably pleasant Victorian lodge. In the middle price range, but with a dorm and food included in price. ③–⑤.

WBTDC Shangrila Tourist Lodge, near *Novelty Cinema* (☎03552/55230). Budget lodge, offering characterless double rooms as well as a dorm. ③–⑤.

WBTDC Morgan House Tourist Lodge, Durpin Hill (☎03552/55384). Grand grey lodge, set in fabulous gardens and built for a British jute merchant. The equally beautiful annexe, the *Tashiding Tourist Lodge*, belonged to Jigme Dorji, a premier of Bhutan who was mysteriously murdered. ⑨.

Around Kalimpong

Although the **Lepchas,** the original inhabitants of the area, have lost their traditional way of life in most other parts of Darjeeling and Sikkim, their lifestyle has remained relatively untouched in the unspoilt forest covered hills and deep river valleys to the south of Kalimpong. Lying on an old trade route to Bhutan, the small hamlet of **LAVA**, 35km from Kalimpong and accessible by shared jeep, makes an ideal base for exploring the nature trails abundant with orchids, birds and other wildlife. Lava is also convenient for approaching the **Rachela Pass** (3152m) on the Sikkim–Bhutan border which provides excellent views of the Chola range including Chomalhari (7314m), the sacred mountain of Bhutan on its border with Tibet. Basic accommodation in Lava includes the *Forest Rest House* (①), booked through the Forest Department in Kalimpong. Pleasant trails lead west from Lava towards **Budhabare**, a weekly market town in the Git River valley which has a sprinkling of Lepcha, Gurkha and Bhutia villages. The track continues through forest to **Kafer** and **Lolegaon**, where there is another *Forest Rest House* (①); the trail north from here crosses the Relli River near the village of the same name and returns directly to Kalimpong.

CHAPTER THIRTEEN

BIHAR

One of India's poorest states, **BIHAR** occupies the flat eastern Gangetic basin, south of Nepal between Uttar Pradesh and West Bengal. The land of the Buddha – born in Lumbini in Nepal, he spent much of his life wandering through the kingdoms of the Ganges – Bihar's very name comes from "*vihara*", monastery. In his quest for truth during the sixth century BC, Prince Gautama visited **Vaishali** and **Rajgir**, before moving on to **Bodh Gaya** and gaining enlightenment under the Bodhi Tree. Only during the nineteenth century was it demonstrated that the major events of the Buddha's life took place in identifiable sites here in north India, but the region now draws Buddhist pilgrims from all over the world. As well as being the first centre of Buddhism in north India, Bihar was its last bastion; the university of **Nalanda** stands as a poignant reminder of the extent of the faith. In addition, the state capital **Patna** (ancient Pataliputra) is sacred to Sikhs as the birthplace of Guru Gobind Singh, the tenth guru; **Gaya** is holy to Hindus; and the founder of Jainism, Mahavira, a contemporary of the Buddha who also lived and taught around Bihar, gained enlightenment at **Pawapuri** close to Nalanda.

Historically, Bihar's greatest moments came early. During the sixth century BC, this was the heartland of the **Magadhas**, whose King Bimbisara was converted by the Buddha at his capital of Rajagriha (now Rajgir). Shortly after the Magadhas shifted their capital to Patna, they were overthrown around 321 BC by the dynamic **Chandragupta Maurya**, said to have met Alexander the Great. The next major dynasty to rule Bihar were the **Guptas**, around the fourth century AD, whose advent marked the return of Hinduism. Extraordinarily, even after the Muslim Sultanate swept the region at the end of the twelfth century, and the Moghuls came to rule all northern India from Delhi three hundred years later, the Buddhist centre of Bodh Gaya continued to thrive. Bihar was incorporated into Bengal in 1764, soon fell under British jurisdiction, and eventually became a province and finally a state of modern India.

Due to intense poverty, inter-caste violence and general lawlessness, Bihar today has a reputation as one of the worst-run states in the country. The best that can be said for it is that its government (a coalition under the Janata Party, led by Lalu Prasad Yadav) is at least committed to secularism, even though it is virtually controlled by the Thakurs, a clan of caste-based landlords who maintain a Mafia-like grip on the state. During the traumatic aftermath of events in Ayodhya in late 1992, Bihar was one of the few north Indian states to escape violence. However, it is characterized by an almost complete absence of law and order – kidnappings, banditry, murder and rape are commonplace. Although the ordinary visitor or Buddhist pilgrim is usually unaffected, no one chooses to travel the roads of Bihar at night.

Bihar has tracts of highly arable land, producing rice along the border with Nepal and fruit in the region of Muzaffarpur. There are also vast mineral deposits in the southeast, including coal around **Dhanbad** and iron in the vicinity of **Jamshedpur**. Despite this, the state has been unable to exploit its natural resources and today is firmly entrenched in the "cow-belt" – a backward region plagued by out-dated caste values. After the torrential monsoons hit the Himalaya, much of central Bihar is annually submerged by floods; rivers like the Kosi burst their banks, and the Ganges is in

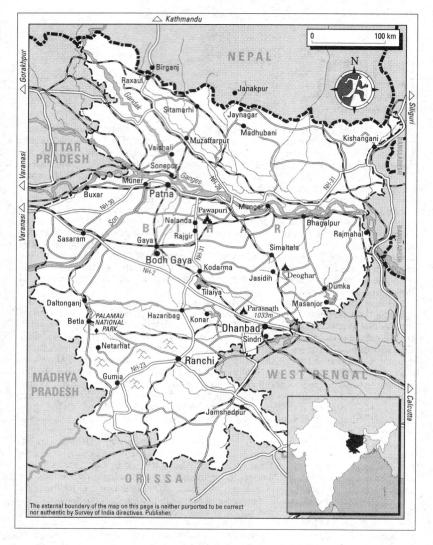

spate. At other times, parts of the Gangetic basin are racked by drought. Much of the central belt of the state around Gaya is dry, arid and desperately poor, while far to the south red hills rise up to the Chotanagpur plateau, home to the tribes of Jharkand. Here, around industrial **Ranchi** and **Jamshedpur**, large tracts of forest still cover much of the land and the remote southwestern region holds the wildlife sanctuary of **Palamau National Park**.

BIHAR TRAVEL DETAILS

	Trains		Buses		Flights	
	Frequency	Time	Frequency	Time	Frequency	Time
To and from PATNA						
Agra	1 daily	14hr 30min				
Allahabad	4 daily	13hr				
Bombay	3 daily	33hr–36hr				
Calcutta	12 daily	7hr 30min–10hr	6 weekly	1hr		
Darjeeling (NJP)	5 daily	8hr 30min–26hr 20min				
Delhi	13 daily	12hr 15min–15hr	daily	3hr		
Gaya	12 daily	2hr 30min–4hr	hourly	3hr		
Guwahati	5 daily	20hr 45min–26hr				
Jammu	1 daily	29hr 15min				
Lucknow	3 daily	9hr–14hr	3 weekly	1hr		
Madras	1 weekly	53hr				
Puri	1 daily	19hr 30min				
Ranchi	3 daily	10hr 50min–15hr	4 daily	12hr–14hr	6 weekly	45min
Raxaul			9 daily	5hr		
Vaishali			2 daily	3hr		
Varanasi	3 daily	4hr 30min–6hr	4 daily	6hr 30min		
To and from GAYA						
Allahabad	3 daily	2hr 20min–6hr 35min				
Bodh Gaya	hourly	30min				
Bombay	1 daily	24hr 15min				
Calcutta	16 daily	5hr 30min–8hr				
Dehra Dun	1 daily	25hr 50min				
Delhi	9 daily	11hr 15min–16hr 20min				
Haridwar	1 daily	23hr 20min				
Jammu	1 daily	36hr 40min				
Kalka	1 daily	27hr 10min				
Lucknow	3 daily	10hr–12hr 40min				
Mughal Sarai	13 daily	4hr–5hr	6 daily	5hr		
Parasnath	11 daily	2hr 30min–4hr				
Puri	4 weekly	16hr 35min–19hr 20min				
Sasaram	10 daily	1hr 10min–3hr	8 daily	3hr		
Varanasi	4 daily	4hr 20min–5hr	6 daily	5hr 30min		
To and from RANCHI						
Allahabad	1 daily	18hr				
Calcutta (Howrah)	1 daily	8hr 15min	3 weekly	2hr 25min		
Daltonganj	1 daily	7hr 20min	4 daily	8hr		
Delhi	1 daily	29hr 30min	6 weekly	1hr 25min		
Dhanbad	3 daily	4hr–6hr 30min	6 daily	5hr		
Gaya	3 daily	8hr 20min	8 daily	8hr		
Jasidih	2 daily	9hr				
Netarhat	2 daily	5hr				

Note that no individual route appears more than once in this chart; check against where you want to get to as well as where you're coming from.

Patna

The capital of Bihar, **PATNA**, dates back to the sixth century BC, which makes it one
of the very oldest cities in India. Today, it's a nice enough place, but one which holds
only the barest of indications of its former glory, as the centre of the Magadhan and
Mauryan empires. The sprawling metropolis hugs the south bank of the Ganges,
stretching for around 15km in a shape that has changed little since Ajatasatru (491–459
BC) shifted the Magadhan capital here from Rajgir.

The first Mauryan emperor, **Chandragupta**, established himself in what was then
Pataliputra, in 321 BC, and pushed the limits of his empire as far as the Indus; his grandson **Ashoka** (274–237 BC), among the greatest of all Indian rulers, held sway over even
greater domains. To facilitate Indo-Hellenic trade, the Mauryans built a Royal Highway
from Pataliputra to Taxila in Pakistan, which later became the Grand Trunk Road, and
similar highways reached towards the Bay of Bengal and along the east coast. The city
experienced two later revivals. The first Gupta emperor, also named **Chandra Gupta**,
made Patna his capital early in the fourth century AD, and a thousand years later it was
rebuilt by the brilliant Afghan ruler Sher Shah Suri (1540–45), who constructed the Sher
Shahi Mosque in the east of the city. Nearby, the beautiful *gurudwara* of **Har Mandir** was
built to honour the birthplace of the tenth and most militant Sikh Guru – Guru Gobind
Singh. In his honour, the old quarter of the city is often referred to as Patna Sahib.

Arrival, transport and information

Patna has three railway stations, but all main-line services arrive at **Patna Junction**, in
the west of the city in the Bankipur area. Frazer Road (now Mazharul-Raq Path) is the
main drag, immediately north of the station. Patna's **airport** is 5km west of here (a
Rs20 cycle rickshaw ride into town, or Rs70 by taxi); a few hundred metres west of the
station, the main private **Harding Park bus stand** offers connections to Gaya,
Varanasi, and the Nepal border at Raxaul. North of Frazer Rd, on the northern (river)
side of the large oval Gandhi Maidan, the **Gandhi Maidan bus stand** is a *Bihar
Roadways* terminal serving destinations throughout the state.

Cycle rickshaws and auto-rickshaws are the most common means of transport;
shared *Vikram* auto-rickshaws cross the city east to west for around Rs8 with a change
at Gandhi Maidan for Patna Sahib.

The inadequate **Bihar Tourist Office**, Frazer Rd (☎225295), provides information
and organizes weekend tours, taking in Patna, Nalanda, Rajgir and Pawapur. The inconveniently located ITDC **Tourist Office**, in a office block close to the railway bridge at
Sudama Palace, Kankarbagh Rd (Mon–Fri 9am–6pm, Sat 9am–1pm; ☎345776), runs a
guide service and is more helpful. A number of agents (see p.835) also organize tours
and arrange **car rental**. The *State Bank of India*, on West Gandhi Maidan (☎226134),
handles **foreign exchange**, and the **GPO** is on Buddha Marg.

> The telephone **area code** for Patna is ☎0612.

The Town

In the most interesting area of Patna – the older part of town, 10km east of the centre
– tiny congested lanes, crammed with vehicles of all kinds, lead to **Har Mandir Sahib**,
the second holiest of the four great Sikh shrines known as *takhts* (thrones), and dedicated to Guru Gobind Singh, born in Patna in 1660. Visitors are obliged to remove their
shoes and cover their heads before entering the central onion-domed marble temple,
set in an expansive courtyard off the main road. Stairs lead up to a small museum containing relics from the Guru's life; one room focusses on the theme of martyrdom.

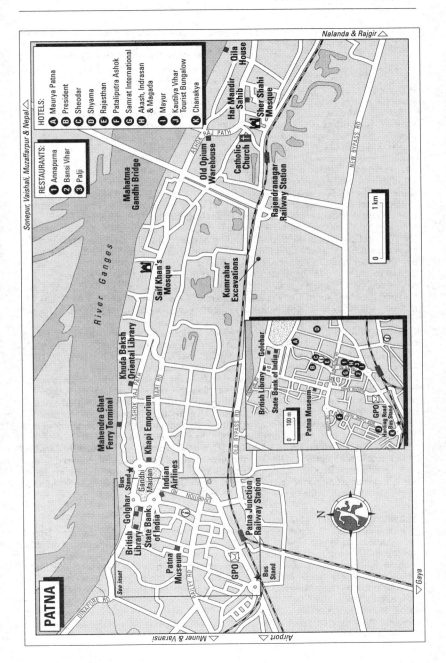

PATNA

HOTELS:
A Maurya Patna
B President
C Sheodar
D Shyama
E Rajasthan
F Pataliputra Ashok
G Samrat International
H Akash, Indrasan & Magada
I Mayur
J Kautilya Vihar Tourist Bungalow
K Chanakya

RESTAURANTS:
1 Annapurna
2 Bansi Vihar
3 Palji

Nalanda & Rajgir
Sonepur, Vaishali, Muzaffarpur & Nepal
Qila House
Har Mandir Sahib
Sher Shahi Mosque
NEW BYPASS RD
ASHOK RAJ PATH
Old Opium Warehouse
Catholic Church
Rajendranagar Railway Station
Mahatma Gandhi Bridge
River Ganges
Saif Khan's Mosque
Kumrahar Excavations
Khuda Baksh Oriental Library
BARI RD
ASHOK RAJ PATH
OLD BYPASS RD
Mahendra Ghat Ferry Terminal
Khapi Emporium
Gandhi Maidan
Indian Airlines
Bus Stand
Golghar
British Library
State Bank of India
Patna Museum
BAILEY RD
DINAPORE RD
GPO
Patna Junction Railway Station
Bus Stand
EXHIBITION
See inset
British Library
Golehar
State Bank of India
Patna Museum
Harding Road
Bus Stand
GPO
100 m
1 km
N
Airport
Muner & Varansi
Gaya

A little way north, the private **Qila House** (or Jalan Museum), on Jalan Ave, holds a fine collection of art including Chinese paintings and Moghul filigree work in jade and silver (call ahead for permission from the Jalan family; ☎225070). Among the antiques are porcelain that once belonged to Marie Antoinette, and Napoleon's four-poster bed. Further east, close to the river, the **Old Opium Warehouse** at **Gulzaribagh**, now a printing press, allows visitors to view the East India Company halls. Beyond it lies a small mosque known as **Saif Khan's Mosque** or the "mosque of stone".

A few fragments of a Mauryan hall, and a single highly polished sandstone pillar, stand at **Kumrahar** in south Patna, between Patna Junction and Rajendranagar stations, as the most significant surviving relics of the golden days of Pataliputra (daily except Mon 9am–5pm; Rs1). Though not the most dramatic of sites, the surrounding gardens are attractive, and a small museum displays assorted finds. The massive hall once covered 77 square metres and was built on three storeys; most of it was made of wood, which may explain why it did not endure. The Chinese traveller Fa Hien, who came here in the fifth century AD, reported that it had already stood for 700 years.

Patna's most remarkable monument – and oddly mundane – dates from the British era. This huge grain storage house known as **Golghar**, the "round house" – now a symbol of the city – was built in 1786 by John Garstin at the behest of the then administrator, Warren Hastings, in the hope of avoiding a repetition of the terrible famine in 1770. Mercifully it never needed to be used. Overlooking the river and the *maidan*, it looks like the upper half of a gigantic off-white Easter egg, decorated with two sets of stairs that spiral their way to the summit, 29m above the road. These were designed so that *coolies* could carry grain up one flight, deliver their load through a hole at the top, and descend the other stairs. Constructed with stone slabs, the base of the structure is 125 metres wide, with 3.6-metre-thick walls. Sightseers now clamber up for views of the mighty river and the town itself.

Within walking distance, close to the new Indira Gandhi Planetarium, the **Patna Museum**, though faded and run-down, has an excellent collection of sculpture (daily except Mon 10am–4.30pm; Rs0.50). Among its most famous pieces is a polished sandstone female attendant or *yakshi*, holding a fly-whisk, found at Didarganj and dating from the third century BC. Some Jain images from the Kushana period, and a group of Buddhist *bodhisattvas* from the Gandhara region (northwest Pakistan), belong to the second and third centuries AD. Natural history exhibits feature several stuffed animals, including a few freaks, and a gigantic fossilized tree thought to be 200 million years old. The museum also houses Chinese art, and the second floor is devoted to some superb Tibetan *thangkas* (scroll paintings), albeit in dire need of restoration.

Founded in 1900, the **Khuda Bhaksh Oriental Library**, east of Gandhi Maidan, has a remarkable selection of books from all over the Islamic world, all gathered by one man. Besides rare Persian and Arabic manuscripts, it houses Moghul and Rajput miniatures, and manuscripts rescued from the Moorish University at Cordoba in Spain. One of its more unusual exhibits is a tiny Koran measuring just 25mm wide.

Accommodation and eating

Patna has an ample choice of **accommodation**. Cheaper hotels can be found on "Hotel Lane", around the station end of Frazer Rd, while the top end can offer pricier options. Apart from those in the upmarket hotels, Frazer Rd holds several good **restaurants**, such as the *Annapurna*, which serves north and south Indian food, and the *Bansi Vihar*, a good-value south Indian veg place. Many of the a/c restaurants along this stretch double as bars. Most are male-dominated except for the reasonably priced *Palji* at Krishna Chowk.

Akash, Hotel Lane, off Frazer Rd (☎239599). Better than most in the lane, but not any roomier. ②.

Indrasan, Hotel Lane, off Frazer Rd (☎226872). One of the roomier budget hotels along the lane; close to all amenities. ②.

Maurya Patna, Frazer Rd, South Gandhi Maidan (☎222060). The only real luxury hotel in town with numerous facilities and a nice location. Pleasant bar and restaurant. ⑨.

Mayur, Frazer Rd (☎224149). Currently being refurbished under new management. A reasonable restaurant, a large dimly lit bar and affordable if ordinary rooms with running hot water. ③–④.

Pataliputra Ashok, Beer Chand Patel Path (☎226270). Friendly staff make up for this large, comfortable chain hotel, now looking frayed at the edges. Pleasant restaurant and pool. ⑧.

President, behind LIC office, off Frazer Rd (☎220600). Off the busy thoroughfare, a popular business hotel close to the *Rajasthan* with reasonable rooms, including some a/c. ④–⑥.

Rajasthan, Frazer Rd (☎225102). A friendly and well managed, old Indian-style hotel, with some air-cooled rooms and a recommended vegetarian restaurant. ④–⑤.

Samrat International, Frazer Rd (☎220560). The fanciest hotel in this part of town. Close to amenities, with comfortable rooms (some a/c), and a few restaurants including one on the roof. ⑦–⑧.

Sheodar, Frazer Rd (☎227210). Small but clean and one of the best of the cheaper hotels around the top end of Frazer Rd, with reasonable doubles and a choice of a/c rooms. ③–④.

Shyama, Exhibition Rd (☎655539). One of the better budget hotels on this busy road with cheap rooms and attached baths. ②.

MOVING ON FROM PATNA

Patna Junction is the most important **railway** station in the region, connected to **Gaya, Delhi, Varanasi, Darjeeling** (NJP), **Calcutta, Bombay** and **Madras**. The best train to Calcutta (Howrah) is the fast *Rajdhani Express* #2306; other principal trains to Calcutta are the *Poorva Express* #2304 and the *Amritsar Mail* #3006. The *Patna Delhi Shramjeevi Express* #2401 also stops at Varanasi and most major trains stop at **Mughal Sarai**, not far from Varanasi. Among others, the *Rajdhani Express* #2305 and the *Poorva Express* #2303 travel to Delhi. The *Guwahati Dadar Express* #5646 travels to Bombay and in the other direction, on its way to **Guwahati**, stops at **New Jalpaiguri**, handy for Darjeeling and **Sikkim**; more convenient trains to the northeast include the *NE Express* #5622. The *Patna Puri Express* #8450 travels to **Puri** on the Orissa coast; of the three *Patna Hatia Expresses* following the same route, the #8623 is more convenient for **Ranchi**, travelling at night, while the #8624, departing in the mornings, is best for the short journey to Gaya and **Bodh Gaya**.

Patna Airport is linked by *Indian Airlines*, at City Office, South Gandhi Maidan (☎222554), to **Calcutta, Ranchi, Delhi** and **Lucknow**; *NEPC* flies to Varanasi and Calcutta (3 weekly), and *Sahara Indian Airlines* flies daily to Delhi. Flights to **Kathmandu** have been suspended for the time being. Although it is just as easy to make your own arrangements, travel companies offer bus tickets to Kathmandu, with a voucher for the bus across the border. **Buses** for the Nepal border at **Raxaul** (5hr; see p.837) depart from the Harding Road bus stand, as do buses to **Gaya, Vaishali**, and via **Muner** to **Varanasi**. Buses to Vaishali also leave from the Gandhi Maidan bus stand. You'll have to change at **Bihar Sharif** as there are no direct buses to **Rajgir, Nalanda** and **Pawapuri**.

Reliable **travel agents** include *Ashok Travel & Tours*, in the *Hotel Pataliputra Ashok*; *Inter Travel Shop*, Frazer Rd (☎221337); and *Travel Corporation of India*, Maurya Patna Complex (☎221699).

Around Patna

Patna makes a popular base for exploring Nalanda and Rajgir, as well as Vaishali to the north, but there are also places of interest closer at hand. The fabulous *dargah* – Sufi mausoleum – at **Muner**, on the road to Varanasi, is the prime attraction, but if you're in the area between early November and early December, don't miss the **Sonepur Mela**, an enormous month-long **cattle fair** held across the huge Gandhi Bridge, 25km north of Patna at the confluence of the Gandak and Ganges. Cattle, elephants, camels, para-keets and other animals are brought for sale, pilgrims combine business with a dip in the Ganges, *sadhus* congregate, and festivities include song and dance performances as well as a large funfair with stalls and a circus. Bihar Tourism (☎225411) organizes tours and maintains a tourist village at Sonepur during the Mela, with a bungalow and sever-al huts providing a range of accommodation (①–④).

Muner

The imposing but somewhat neglected red sandstone **mausoleum** of the Sufi saint Yahia Muneri overlooks a lake 27km west of Patna on the busy Varanasi road, 1km west of **MUNER** – an easy bus ride from the city. The shrine itself, built in 1605 by Ibrahim Khan, the governor of Gujarat under Jahangir, stands atop a hillock; the beautifully maintained gardens below are the responsibility of Sufi caretakers, whose timeless lifestyle provides an intriguing glimpse of days gone by. Every year, around February, a three-day *Urs* or festival in the saint's honour attracts pilgrims from far and wide, including *qawwals*, the renowned Sufi minstrels of the Chistia orders of Delhi and Ajmer. If you do come to Muner, it's worth knowing that the town is famous for its **sweets**, and especially *ladoos*, made of lentils.

North Bihar

The one area of Bihar capable of growing reliable crops is the fertile agricultural belt along the Himalayan foothills north of the Ganges. Other than passing through en route to Nepal via the large town of **Muzaffarpur**, most visitors only pause to explore the remains of the abandoned Buddhist city of **Vaishali**, although the region also holds a handful of shrines and temple towns associated with the *Ramayana*.

Vaishali

Set amid the paddy fields, 55km north of Patna, the quiet hamlet of **VAISHALI** is sig-nificant to both Buddhists and Jains. Archeological excavations are still in progress, and only a fraction of this ancient city, buried deep in the silted floodplains on the banks of the River Gandak and dating from the sixth century BC, has yet to been unearthed. This was where the Buddha preached his last sermon, before he died in Kushinagara

---

MADHUBANI PAINTINGS

Jitwarpur, a village on the outskirts of the small town of Madhuban, in the district of Mithila in north Bihar, is the home of a vibrant tradition of Indian folk art. **Madhubani paintings** started out as decorations for the outside of village huts, executed by the women using natural dyes. Illustrations of mythological themes, incorporating images of local deities as well as Hindu gods and goddesses, the paintings were eventually trans-ferred onto handmade paper, often using bright synthetic primary colours, mixed in unique ways, to fill the strong black line drawings. You do see plain black and white pic-tures, but more familiar now are paintings dominated by reds, pinks and blues and off-set by yellow, on a white background.

Fabrics printed with Madhubani designs have become very chic; usually in one colour only, these days they tend to be professionally made elsewhere, and are sold in the expensive boutiques of India's major cities.

Buses connect Patna to Madhubani (5hr 30min) where there is some basic accom-modation. Rickshaws can take you to Jitwarpur.

around 483 BC, and a silver urn containing ashes found in a *stupa* close to the Coronation Tank is said to contain his remains.

Named after King Visala, who is mentioned in the *Ramayana*, some historians believe Vaishali to have been the first city state in the world to practise a democratic, republican form of government. After leaving Nepal and renouncing the world and his family, Prince Gautama studied here, then rejected his master's teachings to continue on the path which eventually led to his becoming the Buddha. He returned on three occasions; on his last visit, he announced his final liberation – *Mahaparinirvana* – and departure from the world. One hundred years later, in 383 BC, the Second Buddhist Council was held in Vaishali, and two *stupas* were erected. For a further thousand years, under Pataliputra (Patna) as capital, Vaishali continued to prosper.

At the centre of the main site, surrounded by trees, the rectangular **Coronation Tank** (or Abhishekh Pushkarni) bears little evidence of its past; considered holy, its waters were used to anoint the leaders of the city. On one side of the tank, near the visitors' centre, a small but well-presented **archeological museum** is dedicated to the local excavations. Along with terracotta, seals, pottery, coins and sculpture from elsewhere, it provides a fascinating picture of the ancient Buddhist world (daily except Fri 10am–5pm; free). A short path next to the tank leads off to the remains of the *stupa*, now covered by a roof, where the supposed ashes of the Buddha were found.

Two kilometres north at **Kolhua**, reached via the left fork of the main road, stands the remarkably well-preserved **Ashokan Pillar**, erected by the Mauryan emperor (273–232 BC) to commemorate the site of the Buddha's last sermon. Out of the thirty such pillars throughout his immense kingdom, this is one of only two still on its original site. Known locally as Bhimsen-ki-lathi (Bhimsen's staff), the 18.3-metre-high pillar, made of polished red sandstone, is crowned by a lion sitting on an inverted lotus, which faces north towards Kushinagara. Alongside, near the remains of a large *stupa*, the elaborate remains of the brick-built **Monkey Tank** are gradually being excavated. According to legend, it was built by monkeys as an offering to the Buddha, after he was given honey by a monkey who was later re-incarnated as his disciple.

Jains of the Svetambara sect, who believe that the last *tirthankara*, Mahavira, was born in Vaishali in 599 BC, have erected a shrine in the fields 1km east of Kolhua.

Practicalities

Vaishali is near enough to Patna that most visitors come on day trips. Companies such as the *Travel Corporation of India* can arrange transport, or you can make your own way by bus as far as Sonepur or Hajipur, and change onto one of the overcrowded local shared taxis. Direct buses leave from Gandhi Maidan but are few and far between.

The village has limited facilities if you want to stay a night or two. The small *Tourist Lodge* (②) on the main road has simple but reasonable rooms, and there's a pleasant and superbly located *Rest House* (①) at the Coronation Tank. At the other end of the strip the welcoming *Youth Hostel* (①) has a dorm and simple canteen.

The road to Nepal

Travellers heading from Patna towards **Nepal** have to cross the border at **Raxaul**. To get there, take one of the few, crowded direct buses (hourly from 6am; 5hr 30min) from Harding bus stand, or a government bus from Gandhi Maidan in Patna. After 2pm expect a change or even a stay at **Muzaffarpur**, where there is limited **accommodation** near the bus stand and in the town centre near the railway station. Muzaffarpur has unreliable train connections to Raxaul.

Raxaul itself is an unattractive, grubby town with limited amenities, infested with mosquitoes and flies, so you're better off staying at Birganj across the Nepal border. If you have **to stay**, the clean *Railway Retiring Rooms* are the best bet (①), but guests have to have a rail ticket and pay a small incentive. The *Ajanta* on Ashram Rd (②) is the best that Raxaul has to offer, with attached baths and meals prepared to order; the more basic *Asia*, also on Ashram Rd, is cheaper (①). **Cafes** along the main road include one at the cinema, serving a local delicacy of kebab and *muri* (puffed rice).

The border itself, between Raxaul and the Nepalese town of **Birganj**, 5km away (a Rs20 rickshaw ride), is open 24 hours for foreigners but in practice the Nepal side is often left unmanned and closes from 7pm to 5am. If you don't already have a visa, you are expected to pay in cash (US$25). Early-morning buses and one at night run from Birganj to Kathmandu (12hr) and Pokhara (10hr). Minibuses (8hr) cost slightly more – book early to ensure a seat.

Jasidih and Deogarh

JASIDIH, a small industrial town 220km southeast of Patna on the main line to Calcutta, has started to attract travellers due to the international popularity of the ascetic Swami Satyananda and his **Rikhya Yoga Ashram**, 12km from the centre. Note, however, that the ashram is open to the public only a few select days every year; visitors are expected to donate clothes and medicine. **Yoga** courses are run by his disciple Niranjan within the walls of the old fort at **Monghyr**, 60km to the north near the town of Jamalpur, 180km east of Patna.

Baidyanath Dham, the Shiva temple at **DEOGARH**, 6km to the east on the Ganges, has been an important pilgrimage centre for centuries; legend has it that this is where the evil Ravana rested on his way to Lanka after abducting Sita. Deogarh's tranquillity is shattered during the annual *mela*, held during the monsoon month of Shravan (July/Aug) when around 100,000 pilgrims visit the temple every day. Jasidih and Deogarh provide convenient bases for exploring the pleasant surrounding tribal country, home to the Santals, where the forested hills teem with waterfalls, hot springs and wildlife.

Practicalities

Almost midway between Patna and Calcutta (Howrah), Jasidih is easily accessible by train, and several buses link Monghyr, Jamalpur and Jasidih.

Jasidih's small selection of **hotels** includes the reasonable *Yatrik* (☎06432/70280; ③), the vast *Arog Bhavan*, with a very cheap dorm and a/c rooms (①–⑤), and the amazing *Mitra Garden* (☎06432/70280; ④), with air-cooled rooms, a restaurant, and indoor and outdoor pools – the proprietor will have you picked up from the station and also organizes trips to nearby Santal villages. Options near the ashram include the *Sita* (③) and *Dreamland* (☎06432/22250; ④). In Deogarh the small *Yatrik* (☎06432/22299; ④) and *Baidyanath* (☎06432/23112; ③) have very reasonably priced a/c rooms. Besides *Neelkamal* which serves excellent veg meals, the best **eating** to be had is in the hotels; *Mitra Garden*'s restaurant is the best around.

Central Bihar

South of the Ganges, and north of the hills of the Chotanagpur plateau, **CENTRAL BIHAR** contains some of north India's most important Buddhist sites. The greatest shrine of all, a focus for Buddhists from around the world, is the Bodhi Tree at **Bodh Gaya** where the Buddha gained enlightenment. His contemporary Mahavira, the Jain patriarch, achieved *his* final liberation at **Pawapuri**, where a beautiful shrine marks his passing, not far from the ancient Buddhist university of **Nalanda**. The auspicious and holy city of **Gaya** attracts Hindus from all over India who come to make offerings for their deceased ancestors.

Rajgir

Twelve kilometres south of Nalanda, the small market town of **RAJGIR** nestles in the rocky hills that witnessed the meditations and teachings of both the Buddha and Mahavira. The capital of the Magadha kingdom before Pataliputra, this was where King Bimbisara converted to Buddhism. Today the picturesque and quiet environs, visited by international pilgrims, are also enjoyed as a health resort because of its **hot springs**. The pools are always open, but can get unpleasantly crowded.

Several sites bear witness to the Buddha's many visits. A Japanese shrine at **Venuvana Vihara** marks the spot where a monastery was built for the Buddha to live in, while it was at **Griddhakuta** (Vulture's Peak) that the Buddha set in motion his second Wheel of Law. Each year, during the three-month rainy season, he preached to his disciples here. The massive modern *stupa* that now dominates the hill can be reached by a chair lift (Rs8 return), a fifteen-minute round trip offering wonderful views. Look out for the 26 Jain shrines on top of these hills, reachable by a challenging trek attempted almost solely by Jain devotees. On an adjacent hill, in the **Saptaparni cave**, the first Buddhist council met to record the teachings of the Buddha after his death.

Rajgir is connected by **bus** to Gaya, Bodh Gaya and Patna, which usually involves a change at Bihar Sharif. You can also get here on **tours** from Patna. **Kund Market**, near the main hot springs (Brahma Kund), is home to *Siddharta Hotel* (①–③), which has budget **rooms**, some with attached baths. The main bazaar 500m north has several cheap options, including the *Rajgir* (☎06119/5266; ③), with a pleasant garden, attached baths but ordinary rooms. *Centaur Hokke* (☎06119/5245; ⑨), an impressive Japanese luxury hotel combines simplicity and comfort, serving Japanese and Indian cuisine in its a/c restaurants. Cheap **cafes**, such as the *Green Hotel*, are around Kund Market.

Nalanda

The richly adorned towers and the fairy-like turrets, like the pointed hill-tops, are congregated together. The observations seem to be lost in the vapours of the morning, and the upper rooms tower above the sky . . . All outside courts, in which are the priests' chambers, are of four stages. The stages have dragon projections and coloured eaves, the pearl-red pillars carved and ornamented, the richly adorned balustrades, and the roofs covered with tiles that reflect the light in a thousand shades. These things add to the beauty of the place.
Hiuen Tsang, who spent twelve years at Nalanda as student and teacher.

Founded in the fifth century AD by the Guptas, the great monastic **Buddhist university** of **NALANDA** flourished, with thousands of international students and teachers, until it was sacked by the Afghan invader Bhaktiar Khilji in the twelfth century. Excavations have revealed nine levels of occupation on the site, dating back to the time of the Buddha and the Jain founder Mahavira, in the sixth century BC. Most of it is now in ruins, but the orderliness and scale of what remains is staggering evidence of the strength of Buddhist civilization in its prime. Nalanda is now part of the modern Buddhist pilgrimage circuit, but even the casual tourist will appreciate taking the time to walk through the extensive site, or climb its massive *stupa* for commanding views.

Courses taught at Nalanda included the study of scriptures of the Mahayana and Hinayana Schools of Buddhism, Brahmanical and Vedic texts, philosophy, logic, theology, grammar, astronomy, mathematics and medicine. Education was provided free, supported by the revenue from surrounding villages, and by benefactors such as the eighth-century King of Sumatra, who requested permission to endow a monastery.

The site has the remains of *stupas*, temples and eleven monasteries, most aligned north to south and built of red brick, with their thick walls impressively intact. Most of the monasteries consist of small cells leading off a verandah, surrounding an open central courtyard, with a guarded entrance to the west, and a shrine room to the east. Evidence has been found that the **great stupa**, more than 31m high, is built above seven previous structures. Smaller *stupas* surround it, with plaster *bodhisattvas* and seated Buddhas set into the walls. Informative booklets available at the ticket booth render the solicitous guides unnecessary.

Nalanda Museum houses antiquities found here and at Rajgir, including Buddhist and Hindu bronzes and a number of undamaged statues of the Buddha (daily except Fri 10am–5pm; free with Rs0.50 ticket to the site). Other sculptures produced here during the eighth- to tenth-century Pala period are displayed at the Indian Museum, Calcutta, the National Museum, New Delhi and the Patna Museum. **Nava Nalanda Mahavihara**, the Pali postgraduate research institute, houses many rare Buddhist manuscripts, and is devoted to study and research in Pali literature and Buddhism.

Shared **jeeps** ply regularly between Bihar Sharif and Rajgir, stopping at the turning to Nalanda from where an assortment of transport, including shared tongas, is available for the remaining 2km to the gates of the site.

Pawapuri

PAWAPURI, 38km from Rajgir and 26km from Nalanda, is where Mahavira, founder of the Jain religion, gained enlightenment, and also where he died and was cremated on the bank of a large lake overflowing with lotus flowers. Today, however, its stunning beauty is unfortunately offset by clouds of mosquitoes. **Jalmandir**, the white marble temple in the centre of the lake is a centre of Jain pilgrimage, along with **Samosharan**, another temple nearby. Pawapuri lies 1km off the main road; buses from Nalanda and Rajgir serve the nearby town of Bihar Sharif.

Barabar and Nagarjuna caves

The mysterious caves of **Barabar** and **Nagarjuna**, which provided the inspiration for E M Foster's *A Passage to India*, are set in wild and inhospitable bandit country, 35km north of Gaya. Few travellers pass this way, and those who do make sure they leave on the same day; travel in the evenings is not recommended. The safest option if you do want to come is to arrange a tour through operators such as *Shiva Travels* in Bodh Gaya (see p.841); solo visitors may even want to take the precaution of hiring a policeman from the police station at Bela (around Rs30 for the day), or hiring a police jeep that is free (in theory) except for the petrol.

The caves lie at the end of a 15-kilometre detour along a narrow and dreadfully potholed road that leads to the right off the main Gaya–Patna road just beyond **Bela**, 18km north of Gaya. They date back to the third century BC, when the emperor Ashoka, who, despite his embrace of Buddhism, allowed non-Buddhists to practise their faith, helped establish this as a centre for alternative religion.

The **BARABAR CAVES** consist of temples and sanctuaries hacked out of huge granite outcrops. Inspired by ordinary huts, they are designed to look as if they're made of wood; the facade of the **Lomas Rishi** cave is sculpted to resemble lattice screens. Their interior surfaces are remarkably smooth, and some are thought to have served as retreats for Jain monks. The three smaller caves at **NAGARJUNA**, 1km northeast, bear inscriptions that date them to around fifty years later.

Gaya

The fly-blown and densely packed town of **GAYA**, 100km south of Patna, serves as an essential transit point for visitors to **Bodh Gaya** 13km away. Far from appealing in itself, it is however of great significance to Hindus, who traditionally come here to honour their parents a year after death by offering *pind* – a gift of funeral cakes. Legend has it that a good demon called Gaya, appalled by the sorrow caused by death, complained to Vishnu, and as a protest died for the world. Impressed by his resolve, Vishnu blessed Gaya with the power to absolve sinners. Like Varanasi, and many other riverside towns, Gaya is said to be a *tirtha* – a crossing across the celestial divide.

On the banks of the River Phalgu, the massive **Vishnupad temple** is believed to have been built over Vishnu's footstep (*pad*); its main image is a footprint imprinted in a rock and surrounded by a silver basin. What you see today – if you're not a Hindu, you'll only be able to get a glimpse from an adjacent building within the complex – was entirely rebuilt in 1787 by Rani Ahalyabai of Indore. Final rites for the dead are held beneath the **Akshayabat**, the immortal banyan tree that stands in the courtyard, under which the Buddha is said to have meditated.

After the monsoons, when the river is in spate, pilgrims bathe in the river and present their offerings. During the dry season, they have to content themselves with holes dug into the river bed to the water level.

Practicalities

Gaya is a major junction on the main railway line between **Calcutta**, **Varanasi** and **New Delhi**; it is also connected to Puri on the Orissa coast and Jodhpur in Rajasthan. The new airport halfway on the road to Bodh Gaya is yet to see regular commercial flights. *Bihar Roadways* run buses from the **Gandhi Maidan bus stand** to points such as **Patna** and **Ranchi**, while buses for **Rajgir** leave from the **Gaurakshini bus stand** on the outskirts of town. A few buses for Bodh Gaya depart from the station with more choice, including crowded mini-buses, from the **Zila School bus stand**, 1km south of the station; shared auto-rickshaws for Bodh Gaya are also available here as well as at the **Kacheri** stand. Taxis, tongas and auto-rickshaws at the railway station don't follow a shared system. Cycle and auto-rickshaws are available for transport around town.

If you're heading onto Bodh Gaya, there's no point **staying** at Gaya unless you arrive after dark; the route between the two is becoming increasingly dangerous and is best avoided at night. There are fairly clean *Railway Retiring Rooms* at the station (①–②), with a dorm and good-value a/c rooms, while the *Ajatsatru*, opposite on Station Rd (☎0631/21514; ②–⑤), has a wide range of rooms with attached baths, and a restaurant with an extensive menu. Gaya's most prestigious hotel, the *Siddharta International*, in its own compound on Station Rd (☎0631/21254; ⑦), has a/c rooms and a plush multi-cuisine restaurant, and handles foreign exchange. Budget options on Station Rd include the friendly *Siddharta* (①), the bigger *Ajit Rest House* (☎0631/420198; ②) and the quieter *Pal Rest House* (☎0631/433139; ①), set back from the road. A rickshaw ride (Rs5) away from the bustle of the station, the newish *Surya*, Swarajpuri Rd (☎0631/24004; ③), is a good alternative to the *Ajatsatru*.

Bodh Gaya

BODH GAYA, sacred to Buddhists as the place where the Buddha gained enlightenment after years of penance, lies 13km south of Gaya beside the River Phalgu. A small market town has grown along the approach to its majestic **Mahabodhi temple**, and a shopping precinct caters for the constant flow of pilgrims, while the **Bodhi Tree** alongside is an offshoot of the original *peepal* tree under which the Buddha sat.

Although the site dates back to the period immediately following the Buddha's passing, the temple complex probably began to take its present shape in the seventh century AD, around the time the Chinese pilgrim Hiuen Tsang visited it. Even after the sack of Nalanda and the virtual demise of Buddhism in north India, it continued to

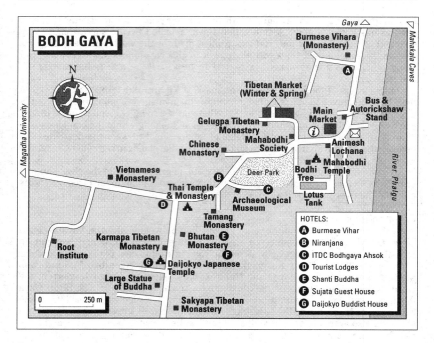

BODH GAYA

N

Gaya △

▽ Mahakala Caves

Burmese Vihara
(Monastery)

Ⓐ

Tibetan Market
(Winter & Spring)

Bus &
Autorickshaw
Stand

Main
Market

Gelugpa Tibetan
Monastery

ℹ

Animesh
Lochana

Chinese
Monastery

Mahabodhi
Society

Mahabodhi
Temple

Vietnamese
Monastery

Ⓑ

Deer Park

Bodhi
Tree

△ Magadha University

Thai Temple
& Monastery

Ⓒ

Lotus
Tank

River Phalgu

Ⓓ

Archaeological
Museum

Tamang
Monastery

HOTELS:

Karmapa Tibetan
Monastery

Bhutan Ⓔ
Monastery

Ⓐ Burmese Vihar

Root
Institute

Ⓕ

Ⓑ Niranjana

Ⓖ

Daijokyo Japanese
Temple

Ⓒ ITDC Bodhgaya Ahsok

Ⓓ Tourist Lodges

Large Statue
of Buddha

Ⓔ Shanti Buddha

Ⓕ Sujata Guest House

0   250 m

Sakyapa Tibetan
Monastery

Ⓖ Daijokyo Buddist House

flourish during the Muslim period. After the sixteenth century, it began to decline, falling into the hands of *brahmin* Hindu priests, who professed to be baffled by its origins when the first British archeologists turned up here early in the nineteenth century. Once excavations had shown the site's true provenance, it was rejuvenated by overseas Buddhists, and is now the most important pilgrimage site of international Buddhism, with all Buddhist nations represented in its many scattered monasteries, temples and shrines.

From November to February, Bodh Gaya is the home of an animated community of exiled **Tibetans**, including the Dalai Lama himself (although recent reports suggest that he has become jaded with the place), as well as a stream of shaven-headed international Tibetophiles. Hinayana and Mahayana meditation courses attract others, while large monasteries from places like Darjeeling bring their international followers to attend ceremonies and lectures under the Bodhi Tree, where Buddhists from around the world rub shoulders. In summer, from mid-March to mid-October, long after the Dalai Lama's official and unofficial entourage has left for the hills, the region becomes oppressively hot, and Bodh Gaya returns once again to its quiet ways.

Unfortunately all is not right at this holiest of holy shrines. The Mahabodhi temple is also sacred to Hindus, who see the Buddha as an incarnation of Vishnu, and, strangely, the committee that looks after it is controlled by a Hindu majority, despite strong protests from the Buddhist world. The resultant unhappiness is all too apparent, and is exacerbated by contrasting forms of worship – while the Buddhists continue a solitary inward approach, Hindus tend towards spectacle and noisy ceremony. A group of militant Buddhists have threatened to march on the temple while others are campaigning to remove all commercial activity and to restore Bodh Gaya to a monastic settlement.

Arrival and information

Several government-run *Nagar Seva* **buses** journey each day to Bodh Gaya from the railway station in **Gaya** (last service 6pm; Rs3), as do private buses from the **Zila School bus stand**, 1km south of the station. Auto-rickshaws cost around Rs80, while horse drawn *tongas* (1hr 30min) charge Rs50. At night only travel by **taxi** (Rs250); after 7pm very little traffic moves along the route which is considered dangerous.

All buses – including the few direct services from Patna and Rajgir – stop on the main road north of the Mahabodhi temple. Most sites are within walking distance, but **bicycles** can be rented from the *Root Institute* (Rs15 per day plus deposit; see "Accommodation"), and cars through ITDC, at the *Ashok Hotel*. *Buddha Travels*, near the Tibetan temple, *Shiva Travel and Consultancy* and *Shashi Travels & Tours*, both in the small commercial precinct opposite the Mahabodhi temple, also arrange car rental and tours, including trips to the Mahakala Cave and the Barabar Caves. The same precinct houses the local **Tourist Office** (daily except Sun 10am–5pm), which provides information on the area and assistance with tours. **Money** can be changed at the *State Bank of India* in the shopping precinct or at the *Bank of India* near the *Tourist Lodge*.

The Mahabodhi Temple and the Bodhi Tree

The elegant single spire of the **Mahabodhi temple**, rising to the lofty height of 55 metres above the trees of its leafy compound at the centre of Bodh Gaya, is visible from all over the surrounding countryside. Within the temple complex, which is liberally sprinkled with small *stupas* and shrines, the main brick temple stands in a hollow encircled by a stone railing dating from the second century BC. Only three quarters of the railing remains in place, other sections are in the site museum (see below) and museums in Calcutta and London.

Unlike most popular temples in India, the Mahabodhi temple exudes an atmosphere of peace and tranquillity, where diverse forms of religious activity co-exist in seeming harmony. Extensively renovated during the nineteenth century, it is supposed to be a replica of the seventh-century structure that in turn stood on the site of Ashoka's original third-century shrine. Its busy detail includes niches and short towers on all four corners. Inside the temple a single chamber holds a large gilded image of the Buddha, while upstairs are a balcony and a small plain meditation chamber.

At the rear of the temple to the west, the large **Bodhi Tree** grows out of an expansive base, in pleasant grounds that attract scholars and meditators. For all its holiness, this is in fact only a distant offshoot of the original tree beneath which the Buddha gained *nirvana*, which legend relates was destroyed by Ashoka before his conversion to the faith. His daughter Sanghamitta took a sapling to Sri Lanka, and planted it at Anuradhapura, where its offshoots were nurtured, and a sapling was brought back and replanted here. Pilgrims tie coloured thread to its far-reaching branches, decorated by prayer flags, and Tibetans accompany their rituals with long lines of butter lamps. A sandstone slab with carved sides next to the tree is believed to be the **Vajrasana** or "thunder-seat" upon which the Buddha sat facing east (towards the temple).

The small white **Animeshlochana temple** to the right of the compound entrance – a miniature version of the main one – marks the spot where the Buddha stood and gazed upon the Bodhi Tree in gratitude. It now obscures the view of the tree, but not the long raised platform known as the **Chankramana** along the northern wall where the Buddha paced in meditation. Remains of a row of columns suggest that it may once have been covered. Numerous ornate *stupas* from the Pala period (seventh–twelfth centuries AD) are littered around the grounds. Next to the temple compound to the south is the rectangular Lotus Pool where the Buddha may have bathed.

Entry to the temple compound (daily 6am–noon & 2–6.30pm) is from the east; shoes are tolerated within the grounds but not inside the temple, and can be left here. In theory you are liable to pay a camera fee of Rs10, but in practice no one bothers to impose the rule. The west gate, leading straight to the Bodhi Tree, is sometimes open.

MEDITATION COURSES IN BODH GAYA

A visit to the Bodhi Tree is enough to inspire most visitors to meditate. Especially during the high season, in winter, short- and long-term **meditation courses** are available in either of two distinct traditions of Buddhism – Mahayana (the Great Vehicle), epitomized by the various forms of Tibetan Buddhism, and Hinayana (the Lesser Vehicle), as practised in Sri Lanka, Thailand and other parts of southeast Asia. During the winter, check noticeboards in places such as the *Om Cafe*, and the pages of the occasional *Bodhi News* or ask at the *Root Institute* or the Burmese Vihar.

Along with seminars, the **Root Institute for Wisdom Culture**, in a rural setting 1.5km west of the main temple, organizes short and week-long residential courses, mostly focussing on the Mahayana tradition. The institute does not belong to any religious order, and has a low-key approach, working with the local community on education and health projects. Mud huts are available for retreats, and guests who appreciate a quiet environment are also welcome. The ambitious Maitreya Project being organized by the Institute plans to construct a 170ft-high statue of the Buddha near the university. Another centre of activity is the **Burmese Vihar** where, besides meditation courses, there are opportunities to be involved with voluntary social work such as a school for poor children run by Westerners.

Two ten-day courses in the Vipasana tradition of Hinayana, run by Christopher Titmus, a Western Buddhist, are held every January at the **Thai temple**; the price (US\$50) includes food and lodging – ask at the Burmese Vihar or Thomas Jost at the Thai temple; information can also be obtained in advance from Gaia House, Woodland Rd, Denbury, Devon TQ12 6DY, UK (☎01803/813188). The **International Meditation Centre**, opposite, runs ten-day beginners' courses in the Goenka school of Vipasana, and thirty-day courses for the more experienced. Donations are accepted, as there are no fixed fees. Their new and underdeveloped site, 5km away near the university, the **Dhamma Bodhi International Meditation Centre** (☎0631/400437), also organizes ten-day courses and offers a motley collection of basic bungalows and tents. Several other courses take place throughout the winter.

Temples and monasteries

Numerous monasteries and temples are located around Bodh Gaya, some simple and others, like the Thai temple, elaborate reproductions. The **Tibetan temple**, a monastery belonging to the Gelug-pa (Yellow Hat) sect, is located within the Tibetan quarter northwest of the main shrine. Built over the last four decades in the style of a traditional *gompa*, the complex includes a central prayer hall, a large prayer wheel and residential buildings. Each winter, this area of Bodh Gaya is transformed by its annual influx of Tibetans, who erect a small market and open restaurants and cafes. The bigger of the two other Tibetan monasteries further west belongs to the **Karmapa** sect; its spacious main prayer hall is decorated with beautiful modern murals, Buddha images and a large *Dharma Chakra* or Wheel of Law.

Next to the Karmapa monastery, the **Daijokyo Japanese Monastery** captures in concrete some elements of a traditional Japanese temple. Opposite that, the **Indosan Nipponji temple** has an elegant and simple hut-like roof and a beautiful image of Buddha inside its main hall. Further north, at the junction with the main road, the unmistakable **Thai temple** is built as a typical *wat* with a terracotta roof of overlapping eaves. In a decorative garden at the end of a short road, the 25-metre-tall Japanese-style **Giant Buddha Statue** was consecrated by the Dalai Lama in 1989. The Sri-Lankan-based **Mahabodhi Society**, responsible for reviving Bodh Gaya in the nineteenth century, maintains a small complex northwest of the Mahabodhi temple.

Bodh Gaya's **archeological museum**, a short way west of the Deer Park near the *Ashok Hotel*, holds a collection of locally discovered sculpture, and ninth-century Pala bronzes of Hindu and Buddhist deities (daily except Fri 10am–5pm; free).

Accommodation and eating

Recent building activity has resulted in several new, mediocre and overpriced **hotels** and a large Tibetan guest house near the temple. Most pilgrims stay in their respective temples, monasteries or pilgrim guest houses, where guests are expected to abide by the rules and respect the environment. There are several **cafes** in the Mahabodhi temple Market Complex, north of the temple, and Tibetan cafes, such as the traveller-friendly *Om Cafe* and the *Dragon Cafe*, which serves Bhutanese food in the temporary tented market around the Tibetan temple. Similar tent-cafes such as the *Gautam* and the *Pole Pole*, near the *Burmese Vihar*, provide a popular alternative in winter.

Burmese Vihar, Gaya Rd. Set in a pleasant garden. A long-time favourite with Westerners, which is run on a donations system; very spartan, but there is a new wing under construction. ①.

Daijokyo Buddhist House, near Giant Buddha Statue (☎0631/400747). Beautifully maintained for visiting Japanese pilgrims and tour groups; others are allowed to stay on discretion – book by telephone first. An excellent kitchen specializes in Japanese cuisine. ⑥.

ITDC Bodhgaya Ashok, near the Museum (☎0631/400725). Comfortable bungalow-type accommodation with a pleasant lawn, an upmarket restaurant and several facilities including a travel desk; now showing its age and a bit expensive for what it is. ⑧.

Mahabodhi Society Pilgrim Rest House (*Sri Lanka Guest House*). Popular with pilgrims and often full. A dorm and a handful of rooms, plus a reasonable vegetarian canteen. ①.

Root Institute, past Thai temple (☎0631/400714). Meditation centre which offers reasonably priced huts for retreats and accommodation including a dorm in the main building and two comfortable if simple new blocks. A pleasant rustic environment with a community spirit, but arm yourself with mosquito repellent. Meals are provided and bicycles are available for rent. ①–④.

Sujata Guest House, near the Thai temple (☎0631/400481). The smartest of the new hotels, where the lobby is far more impressive than the mediocre but exorbitantly priced rooms. ⑦.

Around Bodh Gaya: Mahakala Caves

The **MAHAKALA** (or Dungeshwari) **CAVES**, in remote, almost desert-like surroundings on the far side of the Phalgu 18km northeast of Bodh Gaya, are the site where the Buddha did the severe penance that resulted in the familiar image of him as a skeletal, emaciated figure. After years of extreme self-denial at Mahakala, he realized its futility and walked down to Bodh Gaya, where he received rice as a gift. A short time later, after a final battle with temptation, he achieved *nirvana* under the Bodhi Tree.

During the dry season, a turnoff to the right from the Gaya road, 9km out of Bodh Gaya, leads across the large dry river bed and winds its way through three villages including Khiriyama. This walk should only be attempted in winter; at other times it gets far too hot. Wild dogs along the way, and desperately poor and deprived villagers, provide additional obstacles, making it advisable not to travel alone.

If you do make it to the base of the impressive cliff, a short climb leads to a Tibetan monastery and the small caves themselves. A Buddhist shrine inside the main cave is run by Tibetans, although a Hindu priest has recently set himself up in competition. Very few visit this place, and the occasional car or bus that does arrive gets mobbed by urchins and beggars. Offers by international Buddhist communities to help build roads and some sort of infrastructure have been rejected by the Bihar government.

Sasaram

Dreary, unattractive **SASARAM**, 17km west of the main railway junction of Dehri-on-Sone and the three-kilometre-long Sone River Bridge, is noteworthy as the site of the impressive **mausoleum of Sher Shah Suri**. It is one of two majestic Muslim monuments built by the same master architect, Aliwal Khan, which bear the distinctive heavy lines of the early Lodi monuments of Delhi. Of Afghan extraction, Sher Shah briefly interrupted the Moghul domination of India in 1540 by his displacement of Humayun (see p.77). In his brief reign he created the efficient system of government and administration that was adapted so successfully by Humayun's son Akbar.

The well-maintained five-storey sandstone mausoleum, capped by a massive dome, stands in the middle of a 430-square-metre artificial lake, beside the Grand Trunk Road around 1km west of the railway station. Originally approached by boat, it was later connected to the north shore of the lake by the still-existing causeway, entered through the gatehouse. Close inspection of this plain building reveals that it was once adorned by red, white, blue and yellow geometrical designs, and the dome, once white, topped with a golden lotus. A curious re-alignment means that the mausoleum is now at an angle of 8º to its base, to orient it with the points of the compass. At its centre, a large octagonal chamber contains the tomb itself, while pavilions mark each corner of the plinth, and steps lead down to the water.

Around 500m east, visible from the upper storeys of Sher Shah's mausoleum, is the tomb of his father, **Hasan Sur Khan**. Built in 1535 within a walled enclosure, and lacking a plinth let alone a lake, it has been engulfed by the rustic town of Sasaram and is in a somewhat dilapidated condition. Despite its status as a protected monument, some of the flagstones are being removed. Local people do not always take kindly to visitors.

Practicalities

Sasaram is halfway between **Varanasi** and **Gaya** (both 3hr) on the main railway line. Few expresses stop here apart from the *Doon Express* #3009, and the *Howrah–Bombay Mail* #3003 (which stops at Mughal Serai rather than Varanasi itself), but several passenger trains do – check the timetables carefully, for what they're worth – so it's probably best to think of it as a day trip, not an overnight stop. Cycle rickshaws provide the main means of local transport.

The *Retiring Rooms* at the railway station have a double room for just Rs20 per head, there are plenty of simple hotels and restaurants on the main road nearby, and the basic *Tourist Lodge* (②) has some extremely good-value air-cooled rooms.

South Bihar: Chotanagpur

On the eastern extremities of the Vindhya Hills, at the northern fringes of the Deccan, lie the forested hills and escarpments of the rugged **Chotanagpur plateau**. Its largest town is **Ranchi**, although **Jamshedpur** in the southeast corner is one of eastern India's most important industrial towns, the headquarters of the steel conglomerate *TISCO*. The forests that surround Jamshedpur, at the edge of the plateau, are home to aboriginal tribes such as the Santals, Oraon and Munda, who amount to around 60 percent of the region's population. Christian missionaries have had a strong impact here, and some Munda villages display shrines to the Virgin, but much of the area is **unsafe** for travellers due to general lawlessness and fringe left-wing guerrilla groups.

This area was formerly renowned for its **wildlife**. Sadly, the beautiful forests of the **Palamau** or **Betla National Park** on the southwest edge of Chotanagpur, have been damaged by years of drought. Its tigers are now severely endangered species, and the situation is worse at the **Hazaribagh Wildlife Sanctuary**, north of Ranchi near the town of **Hazaribagh**, whose name means "a thousand tigers".

Ranchi

Industrial **RANCHI**, at the heart of the Chotanagpur plateau over 300km south of Gaya, is hardly a major-league tourist destination, but it does make a good base from which to explore some attractive rolling countryside, thick with lakes and waterfalls. This was once the summer capital of Bihar, but its tea-gardens have long since been abandoned in favour of heavy industry. The climate remains pleasant, however, which may explain the presence of ashrams such as the extensive and central **Yogoda Math Ashram**.

The **Ranchi Museum** on Morabadi Rd has an interesting ethnographic collection of tribal artefacts, costumes, implements and earthenware objects (daily except Fri 10.30am–5pm; free). A smaller replica of the temple at Puri, the **Jaganath temple**, 6km southwest, is the scene of an annual Rath (chariot) festival.

Arrival and information

Several major **trains** – connecting with, among other places, Calcutta, Delhi, Patna, Dattoganj, Dhanbad, Jasidih, and Jamshedpur – either call at Ranchi station, near the southern end of the Main Road, or terminate at Hatia, 7km away.

From the **Main bus stand** near the railway station, regular *Nagar Seva* buses travel to *Gaya* (7hr), Hazaribagh, Netarhat, Jamshedpur, and to **Daltonganj**, headquarters of the Palamau (Betla) National Park, 160km west. Ranchi's **airport**, a 5-kilometre taxi ride east of the centre (Rs100), is connected by *Indian Airlines* flights to Calcutta, Patna and Delhi, though they occasionally "overfly" Ranchi leaving passengers stranded. *Indian Airlines* offices are at 4 Welfare Centre Enclave, and Jawan Bhavan, both on Main Rd (☎206160 and 308692).

Ranchi's **tourist office**, at Tourist Complex, *Hotel Birsa*, Main Rd (Mon–Sat 8am–8pm; ☎314826), is friendly but offers little more than dusty brochures. They also have an information booth at the railway station. *Holiday Travellers*, Patel Chowkh (☎300573) offers organized **tours** to the waterfalls around Ranchi, Betla and Netarhat.

The telephone **area code** for Ranchi is ☎0651.

Accommodation and eating

Most of Ranchi's **hotels** are along, or just off, the long Main Road. If you'd rather not eat in your hotel, *Friends Restaurant*, Station Rd, is a cheap and basic cafe serving south Indian snacks; *Suttor*, on Club Rd, is a good multi-cuisine restaurant; the recommended *Kaveri*, Church Complex, Main Rd, is a very reasonably priced veg restaurant despite its upmarket ambience, while *Krishna*, downstairs, is a bit cheaper.

Amrit, Station Rd (☎311068). Reasonable rooms, but a bit expensive for what it is. ③–⑤.

Birsa Vihar, Tourist Complex, Main Rd (☎305352). Poorly-run tourist lodge but with adequate rooms, a dorm and a quiet location set back from the main road and close to amenities. ①–③.

Embassy, Station Rd (☎314764). One of the better budget hotels along this stretch; reasonably clean with attached baths. ②.

Highland Inn, Old Hazaribagh Rd (☎309537). Old-world, simple bungalow, with atmospheric if faded rooms; within walking distance of the railway station and bus stand. ②–④.

Kwality Inn, Station Rd (☎305469). Justifiably popular with central a/c and smart, comfortable rooms, and one of the best restaurants in town – the *Nook*. ⑤–⑦.

Ranchi Ashok, Doranda (☎500441). Ranchi's most prestigious, with central a/c, and all facilities including a bar and an expensive restaurant; part of a poorly-run government chain. ⑧.

South Eastern Railway, Station Rd (☎208048). Capturing an old-world atmosphere, with pleasant gardens, and bungalows with sizeable rooms and pillared verandahs. ⑤–⑥.

Yuvraj, Main Rd, Doranda (☎300403). Popular hotel with a good restaurant. ④–⑥.

Around Ranchi

Macluskieganj, 40km northwest of Ranchi, was originally designed as a haven for Anglo-Indians. These days it's in a peculiar state of limbo, with most of its original community having long since left. Some of its garden cottages are dilapidated, others house retired urbanites and army officers. A few visitors make their way here to savour its vaguely Victorian ambience, and to enjoy pleasant walks along wooded paths, through flower gardens and orchards separated by large tracts of tall *sal* trees.

The most picturesque of the many waterfalls near Ranchi, all at their most dramatic towards the end of the monsoons, are the **Hundru Falls**, 45km northeast off the Purulia road. They're not on a bus route, but *Bihar Tourism* occasionally run tours out here. A small single-track road bears left from the highway, heading past the beautiful lake of Getalsud set against a backdrop of red, wooded hills. Negotiating the edge of the plateau, the road passes through densely forested tribal country then disintegrates as it approaches the small complex above the falls. A couple of tea shops and a haunted-looking *Forest Bungalow* (①) look down on the 100-metre-high falls, created by the River Subarnarekha as it drops from the plateau along great rocky steps. A staircase descends to the bottom of the falls, where several pools are good for swimming.

Palamau (Betla) National Park

In a remote and lawless corner of the state, 170km west of Ranchi, the beautiful forests of the **PALAMAU NATIONAL PARK** (also known as Betla), cover around 1000 square kilometres of hilly terrain rising south towards Madhya Pradesh. Part of the **Project Tiger** scheme (see *Contexts*), Palamau has been hard hit by drought, and even optimistic estimates of its tiger population stand at a mere sixty. Tiger sightings, more common in the hot season, are proudly announced on a noticeboard at the park offices.

Like many national parks, Palamau consists of a buffer zone, open to visitors, surrounding a core area which is not; the tigers are known to roam around 20km a day, but tend to concentrate in the core area. The fact that several villages are located within the park boundaries has not helped the protection of animals, despite a scheme of compensation for owners of cattle killed by tigers. Other animals found in the park include wild elephants, best seen after the monsoons, *nilgai* (antelope), leopard, *gaur* (bison), Indian wolf, wild boar and wild dogs.

Passing through the main gates at **Betla** brings you into a slightly surreal area, where a picturesque and well-maintained road leads through avenues of great trees. Deer that have grown used to human presence wander peacefully nearby, perhaps to escape predators in the deep jungles. The road soon descends into thick forest along ravines rich in bamboo; its total 25-kilometre circuit seems to be over all too quickly.

The best way to see the park is from the back of an **elephant**, and the earlier in the morning you go the more animals you're likely to spot. Elephant rides set out from Betla each morning at 5.30am and 7am (1hr; Rs50). Cars and jeeps (both Rs50), minibuses, buses and trucks are allowed in, accompanied by a guide (Rs15 per hour); they penetrate further, but animals usually shy away from the noise and smell of their engines. Night tours also go into the park, using spotlights to dazzle the animals; an efficient way to spot different creatures, if one that many visitors find objectionable.

Practicalities

The official headquarters of the park, **Daltonganj**, 25km from Betla, is served by direct buses and a branch railway line from Ranchi. Five buses each morning and three each afternoon (first at 7.30am; last at 4.30pm) run from Daltonganj to Betla, which is 6km off the main Ranchi–Daltonganj road. If you're coming from Ranchi, you could try to change buses at the turnoff and get to Betla without going through Daltonganj. There have been several armed robberies in the area over the last few months and even a few hold-ups on the highway.

Next to the **Betla** gates, the main park entrance, a small complex holds administration offices, rest houses and an **information centre**, where entry tickets, elephant rides and accommodation in any of the Forest Department's rest houses can be arranged. All arrangements, including car or jeep rental and accommodation, can also be made at Daltonganj through the Director, Project Tiger, Jail Compound.

Forest Department Rest Houses in Betla itself include the main one (②), which prioritizes visiting civil servants but is comfortable and offers attached baths, and the very cheap and basic *Janata* and *Shyama* lodges (①).

There are also a couple of new **hotels**. The privately run *Naihar* (☎504; ①–④), 300m from the park gates, has a nice garden, a dorm, a/c rooms, and a reasonable restaurant serving Chinese and Indian food, while the grand-looking *Van Vihar* (③–④), recently opened by Bihar Tourism, offers spacious rooms (some a/c), and also has a restaurant. Simple **cafes** can be found opposite the gates at Betla.

Netarhat

The popular but undeveloped hill station of **NETARHAT** – the only one in Bihar, and known as "the Queen of Chotanagpur" – occupies the crest of a high ridge 120km south of the Palamau park, and served by direct buses from both Betla and Ranchi, 156km east (5hr; Rs50). Set at a pleasant altitude of 1138m, Netarhat is comfortable throughout the year, despite the occasional touch of frost in winter. Rambling walks through the hills around town offer superb views, especially at sunrise and sunset; Magnolia Point, 10km away, looks out to the Palamau plateau to the north, while the cascading Burhaghagh Falls are right on the edge of town. Unfortunately the forests around Netarhat are being threatened with Army plans for a firing range as well as a hydroelectric project that will submerge large tracts of land and displace the local tribal population. The best place **to stay** in Netarhat is the *Prabhat Vihar*, the tourist bungalow (③–④), which has its own restaurant.

Parasnath

Towering 1000m above the plains, beside the Calcutta–Gaya railway line 30km west of Dhanbad, the crag of **PARASNATH** is rendered holy to Jains by its associations with the life of Mahavira. It is covered with dense forests, where Jain belief has it that even the tigers are vegetarian. Twenty-four shrines – one per *tirthankara* – are sprinkled along its lofty crest, including the main **Parasnath temple** on the westernmost and highest summit. Pilgrims, on foot or carried on palanquins, follow a trail that winds its way up from the village of **Madhuban** (not to be confused with Madhubani, in North Bihar). Most come back down on the same day, as the facilities on top are limited. The final rise to the main temple is along a marble staircase, which echoes to the sound of bare feet. Sited on a rocky pinnacle, the pristine white temple, where tiny marble feet represent the footprints of the saint, repays the effort with superb views.

Just below the temple, a *Forest Bungalow* provides basic accommodation and views of beautiful sunsets (①), while Madhuban itself has a **Tourist Reception Centre** and several Jain *dharamshalas*. Cycle rickshaws and buses connect the village with **Parasnath Railway Station**, served by local trains to the major junctions of Dhanbad and Gaya. The town of Parasnath lies on NH2, a major east–west bus route. **Car** rental is available at Dhanbad.

CHAPTER FOURTEEN

SIKKIM

The tiny but beautiful land of **SIKKIM** lies just south of Tibet, sandwiched between Nepal to the west and Bhutan to the east. Though measuring just 65km by 115km – the size of Switzerland – it ranges from sweltering deep valleys a mere three hundred metres above sea level to lofty snow peaks such as Kanchendzonga (or Kanchenjunga; 8586m), the third highest mountain in the world. Few roads penetrate this rugged Himalayan wilderness; most of those that do are in the eastern part of the state, around its capital **Gangtok**.

For centuries, until war with China in the early 1960s led the Indian government to see it as a crucial corridor between Tibet and Bangladesh, Sikkim was an isolated, independent Buddhist kingdom. As a result of its annexation by India in 1975, it has experienced dramatic changes. Now a fully-fledged Indian state, it is predominantly Hindu, with a population made up of 75 percent **Nepalese Gurungs**, and less than 20 percent **Lepchas**, its former rulers. Smaller proportions survive of **Bhotias**, of Tibetan stock, and **Limbus**, also possibly of Tibetan origin, who gave the state its name – *sukh-im*, "happy homeland". Nepali is now the lingua franca and the Nepalese are socially and politically the most dominant people in the state. The ruling minority in neighbouring Bhutan, having observed this transition with alarm, has adopted an aggressive stance towards the Nepalese, and there has been ugly violence on both sides.

Sikkim holds a special status within the Indian union, exempt from income tax and attracting government subsidy. Only Sikkimese can hold major shares in property and businesses. The resultant prosperity is evident as soon as you cross the border from West Bengal – the roads in particular are very good, though this of course is largely the work of the Indian Army, for its own ends. Few maps may show them, but several of the old trade routes in northern Sikkim are now rough but motorable roads.

Culturally, historically and spiritually, Sikkim's strongest links are with **Tibet**. For those visitors who now make their way here, the main reasons to come – apart from the lure of the mountains themselves – are its **Buddhist monasteries**. There are over 250 monasteries, mostly belonging to the ancient Nyingmapa sect. Some, such as **Pemayengtse** in the west, are all but deserted except for special occasions, but others like **Tashiding** and **Rumtek** are thriving centres of Mahayana Buddhism.

Sikkim is where the monsoons that rush in off the Bay of Bengal hit the Himalaya; its gigantic mountain walls and steep wooded hillsides, drained by torrential rivers such as the **Teesta** and the **Rangit**, are a botanist's dream. The lower slopes abound in **orchids**; sprays of cardamom carpet the forest floor, and the land is rich with apple orchards, orange groves and terraced paddy fields (to the Tibetans, this was **Denzong**, "the land of rice"). At higher altitudes, monsoon mists cling to huge tracts of lichen-covered forests, where every conceivable species of rhododendron and giant magnolia trees punctuate the deep cover. Higher still, approaching the Tibetan plateau, dwarf rhododendron provide vital fuel for yak herders. All over Sikkim, forests and wilderness areas are inhabited by snow leopards, *tahr* (wild ass on the

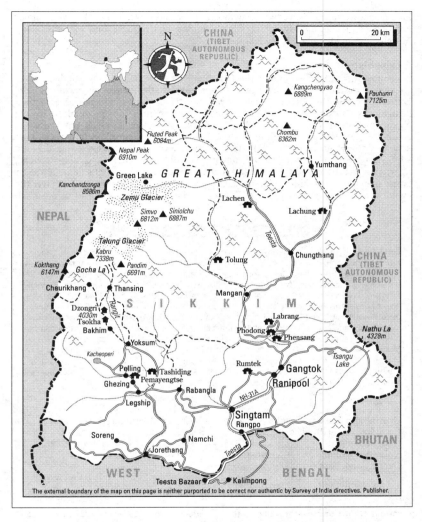

The external boundary of the map on this page is neither purported to be correct nor authentic by Survey of India directives. Publisher.

Tibet plateau), *bharal* or blue sheep, and the symbol of Sikkim – the endangered **red panda**.

The **best time to visit** Sikkim is between mid-March and June but especially, April and May, when the rhododendrons and orchids bloom – although temperatures can be high, especially in the valleys. Any earlier than that, and the lingering winter snow makes trekking too difficult. During the monsoons, from the end of June until early September, rivers and roads become impassable, though plants nurtured by the incessant rain erupt again into bloom towards the end of August. October, when orchids bloom once again, and November tend to have the clearest weather of all. As December approaches, it gets bitterly cold at high altitudes, and remains that way until early March, despite long periods of clear weather.

A brief history

No one knows quite when or how the **Lepchas** – or the Rong, as they call themselves – came to Sikkim, but their roots can be traced back to the animist Nagas of the Indo-Burmese border. **Buddhism,** which arrived from Tibet in the thirteenth century, took its distinctive Sikkimese form four centuries later, when three Tibetan monks of the old Nyingmapa order, disenchanted with the rise of the reformist Gelug-pas, migrated south and gathered at Yoksum in western Sikkim. Having consulted the oracle, they sent to Gangtok for a certain Phuntsog Namgyal, whom they crowned as the first **Chogyal** or "Righteous King" of Denzong in 1642. Both the secular and religious head, he was soon recognized by Tibet, and set about sweeping reforms. His domain was far larger than today's Sikkim, taking in Kalimpong and parts of western Bhutan. Over the centuries, territory was lost to the Bhutanese, the Nepalese and the British. Sikkim

PERMITS AND RESTRICTIONS

Until recently, it was virtually impossible for foreigners to enter Sikkim; now, though much of the north and east remains closed or restricted, getting hold of a **permit** to visit Gangtok and the west is a mere formality. These are initially issued for either ten or fifteen days; you must specify in advance exactly which areas and places you intend to visit. Extensions and permits for specific areas such as west Sikkim are available in Gangtok – see p.855 – but as you might otherwise not go there, it's worth arranging whatever permissions you need before you arrive. Certain **restricted areas**, like Tsangu Lake, Yumthang and Dzongri, only allow foreigners in groups of a minimum of four, accompanied by representatives of approved travel agents. In addition, travellers are not allowed to stray off the cited routes. Three-day **extensions** on the Sikkim permit are available in Gangtok and involve first going to the Foreign Section, State Home Department, Tashiling Secretariat, and then the Foreigners' Regional Registration Office, Special Branch, Yangthang Building, Kazi Rd, to have it stamped.

Permitted Areas

Central and Eastern Sikkim: Gangtok (including Rumtek), Phodong, Tsangu Lake (restricted).
North Sikkim: Mangan, Chungthang, Lachung and Yumthang (all restricted).

Western Sikkim: Jorethang, Naya Bazaar, Pemayengtse and Pelling, Tashiding and Yoksum, Dzongri and Gocha La (restricted).

Offices issuing Permits

Indian High Commissions all over the world, when applying for a visa.
Airport immigration at the four main entry points – Delhi, Bombay, Calcutta, Madras.
Foreigners' Regional Registration Offices in Delhi, Bombay, Calcutta and Madras.
Resident Commissioner, Sikkim House, 14 Pancsheel Marg, New Delhi.

Sikkim Tourist Centre, SNT Bus Stand, Siliguri.
Deputy Commissioner, below the Gymkhana Club, Darjeeling.
Deputy Secretary, Home Dept, Writers' Building, BBD Bagh, Calcutta.
Assistant Resident Commissioner, Sikkim Govt, 4C Poonam, 5 Russell St, Calcutta.

TREKKING INTO SIKKIM

Trekking in Sikkim is confined to the western part of the state, and severely restricted. The fact that trekking permits do not extend your total stay in Sikkim places a great constraint on time, while high charges, payable in US dollars, ensure that only the rich or the very curious get to see certain areas. In addition, most Sikkimese trekking operators and guides are not as yet of a very high calibre, and there have been a number of complaints.

Trekking permits are only available from the Sikkim Tourism offices in Gangtok and Delhi. Trekking or tour operators in Gangtok, listed on p.859, can make the necessary arrangements; if they do, check the papers before you set off, as the slightest error can lead to problems later on. Trekking parties have to consist of at least four people – numbers are usually made up by operators who charge an official daily rate of US$40 per head, but you can usually find an operator who will do it for less.

The only high-altitude trek currently on offer is the **Dzongri–Gocha La** route, detailed on p.862. Although mountains such as Thingchen Khang (5818m) and Jopuno (5805m) were designated as "trekking peaks" over two years ago, bureaucratic wrangles mean that permission is still not forthcoming – check the latest situation with the Indian Mountaineering Federation in Delhi. At the moment Dzongri bears the brunt of the entire trekking industry in the state and the pressure is beginning to tell severely on the environment.

Recently, the Mountain Institute, based in Nepal, have launched the **Biodiversity Conservation Network** in order to develop tourism, while protecting natural resources and the environment. Their aims include support of local communities and the development of a sustainable and healthy infrastructure. For more information contact their project officer Renzino Lepcha, 31A NH, opposite Krishi Bhavan, Tadong, Gangtok, or The Mountain Institute, Dogwood and Main streets, Franklin, WV 26807, USA.

---

originally ceded Darjeeling to the East India Company as a spa in 1817, but were forced to give up all claims to it in 1861. The British set out to diminish the strong Tibetan influence by importing workers from Nepal to work in the tea plantations of Sikkim, Darjeeling and Kalimpong; they soon outnumbered the indigenous population.

After Indian Independence, the reforming and intensely spiritual eleventh Chogyal, Tashi Namgyal, strove hard until his death in 1962 to prevent the dissolution of his kingdom. Officially Sikkim was a protectorate of India, and the role of India became increasingly crucial with the Chinese military build-up along the northern borders that culminated in an actual invasion early in the 1960s. His son Palden Thondup, the last Chogyal, married an American, Hope Cook, whose reforms as Gyalmo (queen), did not prove popular. The embattled Chogyal eventually succumbed to the demands of the Nepalese majority, and Sikkim was annexed by India in 1975; he remained as a figurehead until his death in 1981, by which time Hope Cook had abandoned him and returned to the United States with their children. Some of the Chogyal's family continue to live in seclusion in Gangtok.

Gangtok

The capital of Sikkim, the overgrown hill town of **GANGTOK**, occupies a rising ridge in the southeast of the state, on what used to be a busy trade route into Tibet. Due to rapid development and new wealth, it now retains only a few traditional Sikkimese elements; instead it sports an ugly assortment of concrete multi-storeyed buildings and is growing, virtually unchecked, all the time. However, a short amble soon leads you away from the hectic central market area, while longer walks out into the surrounding countryside provide glimpses of the full grandeur of the Himalaya. On a good day, you can see Kanchendzonga and the fluted pyramid of Siniolchu.

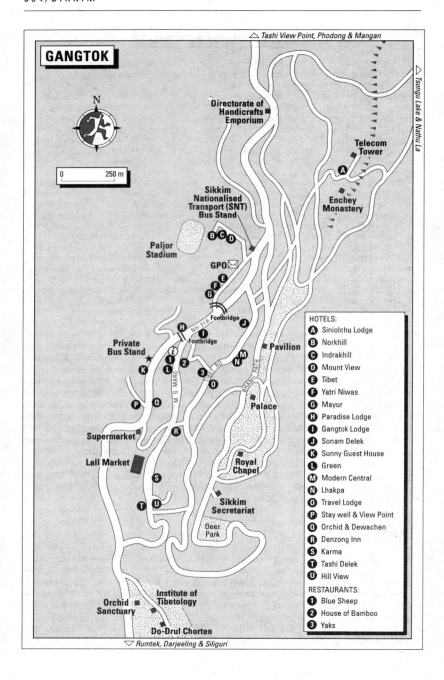

△ *Tashi View Point, Phodong & Mangan*

GANGTOK

N

0   250 m

△ *Tsongu Lake & Nathu La*

Directorate of
Handicrafts
Emporium

Telecom
Tower

Enchey
Monastery

Sikkim
Nationalised
Transport (SNT)
Bus Stand

Paljor
Stadium

GPO

Footbridge

NH-31A

Footbridge

Private
Bus Stand

M G MARG

TIBET RD

BHANU PATH

Pavilion

Palace

Supermarket

Lall Market

Royal
Chapel

Sikkim
Secretariat

Deer
Park

Institute of
Tibetology

Orchid
Sanctuary

Do-Drul Chorten

▽ *Rumtek, Darjeeling & Siliguri*

HOTELS:
A Siniolchu Lodge
B Norkhill
C Indrakhill
D Mount View
E Tibet
F Yatri Niwas
G Mayur
H Paradise Lodge
I Gangtok Lodge
J Sonam Delek
K Sunny Guest House
L Green
M Modern Central
N Lhakpa
O Travel Lodge
P Stay well & View Point
Q Orchid & Dewachen
R Denzong Inn
S Karma
T Tashi Delek
U Hill View

RESTAURANTS:
1 Blue Sheep
2 House of Bamboo
3 Yaks

Although modern Gangtok epitomizes the recent changes in Sikkimese culture and politics, its Buddhist past is the root of its appeal for visitors, and remains evident at the impressive **Institute of Tibetology**, the charming **Enchey Monastery** and the marvellous **Rumtek Monastery** not far away. However, the **Palace** used by the Chogyals between 1894 and 1975 is now out of bounds, occupied by the new regime and not acknowledged as part of Sikkimese heritage. Sikkim's pride and joy, the **orchid**, is nurtured at several sites in and around Gangtok, and celebrated every spring in a flower show held near **White Hall**, the Governor's residence on the ridge above town.

Arrival and information

Gangtok is not served directly by rail or by air; most travellers arrive by bus or shared taxi from **Siliguri** in West Bengal (4hr 30min; see p.814), where **Bagdogra** airport has flights to Calcutta, Guwahati and Delhi, and **New Jalpaiguri**, a major railhead.

All buses run by **Sikkim Nationalised Transport** (*SNT*), the state carrier, use the **SNT bus stand** on Paljor Stadium Rd, but arriving passengers may prefer to be dropped off earlier at the main crossing on MG Rd, which is more convenient for the tourist office. Non-*SNT* buses stop at the **Private bus stand**, below the National Highway a couple of hundred metres before the crossing; there are some reasonable hotels nearby. Shared taxis and jeeps for Kalimpong and Darjeeling also stop here or along MG Rd; jeeps and taxis for other destinations in Sikkim terminate at a stand at **Childrens' Park**, just above MG Rd. For details of buses to and from Siliguri, and around Sikkim – all subject to disruption during the monsoons – see p.814.

Sikkim Tourism's **Tourist Information Centre**, MG Rd (mid-March to mid-June and mid-Sept to Nov 8.30am–7.30pm, off season 10am–4pm; ☎22064), provides poor-quality maps, arranges transport in high season and organizes occasional city tours including Rumtek and Inchey. This is also the place to pick up **West Sikkim permits** (available 10am–4pm in season, 10–11am off-season) to cover Jorethang, Pemayengtse, Pelling, Kacheoperi and Yoksum. For details of **trekking permits**, see p.852.

There's a *State Bank of India*, near the tourist office; the *State Bank of Sikkim* at the crossing with Paljor Stadium Rd will also change cash. The main **post office** is further down Paljor Stadium Rd.

The telephone **area code** for Gangtok is ☎03592.

The Town

Though central Gangtok – which means "the hilltop" – is concentrated immediately below the Palace, its unchecked urban sprawl begins almost as soon as the road rises from the valley floor at Ranipool, 10km southwest. Most of the town itself looks west; one explanation for the lack of development east of the ridge is that tradition dictates that houses face northwest, towards Kanchendzonga, Sikkim's guardian.

The town's liveliest markets are the **New Market** on MG Rd, with workshops such as the *Sakya Metal Works* specializing in bronzes and silver jewellery, and the local produce bazaar of **Lall Market**, where stalls sell dried fish, yak's cheese (*churpi*), and yeast for making the local beer (*tomba*). At the huge complex run by the **Directorate of Handicrafts and Handloom**, on the National Highway north of the centre, visitors can watch rural Sikkimese create carpets, handloom fabrics, *thangka* paintings and wooden objects, and buy their work in a showroom. Curio shops on MG Rd and near the *Tibet* hotel on Paljor Stadium Rd sell turquoise and coral jewellery, and religious objects such as silver ritual bowls and beads.

Right at the top of town, just below a colossal and ugly telecom tower, 3km up from MG Rd and reached by several roads, of which the most picturesque follow the west side of the ridge, **Enchey Monastery** is a small two-storey Nyingmapa *gompa*. Surrounded by tall pines, and housing over a hundred monks, it's a real gem of a place. Built by the Chogyal in the middle of the nineteenth century, on traditional Tibetan lines, its beautifully painted porch holds murals of protective deities and the wheel of law, while the conch shells that grace the doors are auspicious Buddhist symbols. Enchey holds an annual *chaam,* or masked *lama* dance, each December or January according to the lunar calendar.

Although in theory guards deny entry to the **Royal Palace** to anyone without permission, visitors not carrying cameras are occasionally granted access to **Tsuklakhang,** the yellow-roofed royal chapel at its far end, to see its impressive murals, Buddhist images and vast collection of manuscripts. Here too there's a *lama* dance, known as *kagyat,* at the end of December, during which the main gates are open to the public; some years the *kagyat* takes place in Pemayengtse instead.

Beyond the chapel, below the small **Deer Park** (Mon–Sat 8–11am & Sun 8am–5pm). but above the National Highway, set in wooded grounds 3km from the centre, is the museum-cum-library of the **Institute of Tibetology**. Here you can see an impressive collection of books and rare manuscripts, as well as religious and art objects such as exquisite *thangkas* (scrolls), embroidered in silk, commissioned for the ordination of the present Dalai Lama (daily 10am–4pm; Rs2). It's hard to believe that the adjacent **Orchid Sanctuary** boasts 200 species as it is so poorly maintained. The blooms are best seen in April and May (daily 8am–4pm).

A couple of hundred metres beyond the Institute on the brow of the hill, an imposing whitewashed *chorten* (see p.502), known as the **Do-Drul Chorten,** dominates a large lively monastery, home to young acolytes. The *chorten* is capped by a gilded tower, whose rising steps signify the thirteen steps to *nirvana*; the sun and moon symbol at the top stands for the union of opposites and the elements of ether and air. The 108 prayer-wheels that surround it – each with the universal prayer *Om mani padme hum,* "Hail to the Jewel in the Lotus" – are rotated clockwise by devotees as they circumambulate the *stupa.* Nearby, a prayer hall houses a large image of Padmasambhava, also known as **Guru Rinpoche,** the patron saint of Nyingmapa Buddhism, who arrived in Tibet in 747 AD and founded *lama*-ism, which incorporated existing local beliefs. He is supposed to have travelled through Sikkim hiding precious manuscripts in caves, for discovery at a future date. Curiously, part of the head of the image projects into the ceiling protected by a raised section of roof; belief has it that the image is slowly growing.

Accommodation and eating

Gangtok's hotels are expensive in **high season** – each hotel defines its own seasons, but broadly speaking April to June and September to November – but at other times offer discounted rates. Most of the hotels listed here as being on NH31-A are clustered close to each other near the private bus stand, five minutes' walk from the crossing near the tourist office. A greater choice of budget options exists along Paljor Stadium Rd past the GPO and above the Mall on Tibet Rd.

The best places to **eat** are the hotel restaurants, although there is an increasing number of new restaurants cropping up. The relaxed and fairly priced *Blue Sheep*, MG Rd, next to the *Tourist Information Office,* has a bar and good Indian and Chinese food. Opposite, the *House of Bamboo* is popular with locals, especially in the evenings. For snacks and "fast food", try *Porkey's*, at the Super Market. *Yaks Restaurant*, on Tibet Rd, is a small cafe serving Sikkimese and Tibetan food, and *tomba*. **Sikkimese food** is a melange of Nepalese, Tibetan and Indian influences; rice is a staple, and *dal* is readily available, while *gyakho* is a traditional soup served on special occasions.

Most restaurants serve alcohol. "Foreign" liquor such as brandy and beer is cheap enough, but look out for **tomba**, a traditional drink consisting largely of fermented millet, with a few grains of rice for flavour, served in a wooden or bamboo mug, and sipped through a bamboo straw. The mug is occasionally topped up with hot water; once it's been allowed to sit for a few minutes, you're left with a pleasant milky beer. *Tomba* is usually found in less salubrious places including the *Hotel Sikkim*, on Paljor Stadium Rd, and *Cholay Hotel*, on Tibet Rd, although most hotels will arrange for one on request. Note that the Sikkimese have alcohol-free days during full moon.

Denzong Inn, Lall Bazaar Rd, New Market (☎22692). Flashy establishment in the heart of the bazaar, with comfortable rooms and *Gufa*, a fast food restaurant with piped music. ⑤.

Gangtok Lodge, near Tourist Office, MG Rd (no phone). Overlooking the crossroads, friendly but basic, with a restaurant and travel and tour operators. ②.

Green, MG Rd (☎23354). A wide range of rooms, most without views. Its legendary, busy restaurant serves good inexpensive food. ③–⑥.

Hill View, MG Rd, New Market (☎23545). Opposite *Tashi Delek*. Quietly situated in a charming little garden compound above the road. Airy rooms and friendly staff. ⑤.

Indrakhill Lodge, Paljor Stadium Rd (☎22108). Just below the road, small and cheap but reasonable with hot water by the bucket. ①–②.

Karma, MG Rd, New Market (no phone). Budget accommodation with single rooms, doubles and dorms; the rooms at the top are the best. Good off-season discounts but no food. ②–③.

Lhakpa, Tibet Rd (☎23002). Cheap, atmospheric hotel-restaurant above the main bazaar. A bar as much as a restaurant, it serves Sikkimese food with prior notice. ②–④.

Modern Central Lodge, Tibet Rd (☎23417). Friendly and welcoming family hotel, popular with travellers. Running hot water, a restaurant downstairs and even snooker. ②–④.

Norkhill, Paljor Stadium Rd (☎23187). Luxurious former guest house of the Chogyal. All facilities including a good restaurant, but pricey, and an unfortunate location right next to the stadium. ⑨.

Orchid, NH31-A (☎23151). An old favourite with budget travellers. Nice enough rooms, especially those that face outwards. The restaurant is good for cheap Chinese and Tibetan food. ①–④.

Siniolchu Lodge, above Gangtok, near the prison and Enchey *gompa* (no phone). Extremely good value, except that it is a Rs35 taxi ride up from the bazaar, and a brisk twenty-minute walk back again. Recommended if you want to get away from it all. ②–③.

Sonam Delek, Tibet Rd (☎22566). High above the bazaar, with a range of comfortable and clean rooms. The best provide fine views of the snows. ③–⑤.

Stay Well, Arithang Rd, off the National Highway (☎22963). Comfortable, but overpriced. The food – Indian, Chinese, Sikkimese and *momos* – is better than the accommodation. ⑤.

Sunny Guest House, near Private Bus Stand, NH31-A (☎22179). No single rooms but pleasant with great triples on the rooftop. *Hungry Jack* next door does good *tandoori* food. ③–④.

Tashi Delek, MG Rd, New Market, Gangtok 737 101 (☎22038). An easily missed entrance off the market area hides one of Gangtok's most prestigious addresses – a plush, extensive but unremarkable complex. Full board only; the multi-cuisine *Blue Poppy* restaurant and adjoining rooftop cafe serve Sikkimese and Tibetan dishes, and club sandwiches. ⑨.

Tibet, Paljor Stadium Rd (☎22523 or 23468). Linked to the Dalai Lama's trust – popular with visiting Western Buddhists. Friendly, comfortable and recommended, but the rooms are ordinary and small; the best face out to the hills. The *Snow Lion* restaurant is the best in town, and serves Chinese, Indian and Japanese food, but excels in Tibetan dishes. ⑤–⑦.

Travel Lodge, Tibet Rd (☎23858). New and pleasant family hotel. All rooms have balconies, baths and running water; the best rooms are on the top floor and provide good views. ④–⑤.

View Point Lodge, Arithang Rd, off the National Highway (☎22549). Just below the *Orchid*. Clean mid-range establishment with good views. Rooms on the higher floors are more expensive. ④–⑤.

Yatri Niwas, Paljor Stadium Rd. Between the *Mayur* and *Tibet*, and an attractive and cheaper alternative; clean, comfortable and brand new. ④–⑥.

Around Gangtok

The most obvious destinations for day trips from Gangtok are the great Buddhist monasteries of **Rumtek** to the southwest, and **Phodong** to the north. On the road to Phodong, **Tashi View Point**, 8km out of Gangtok, provides views of the eastern aspects of Kanchendzonga, whose tent-like appearance here is radically different from the way it looks from Darjeeling, and the snowy pyramid of Siniolchu (6888m), which the pioneering mountaineer Eric Shipton ranked among the most beautiful in the world.

Several operators, including Sikkim Tourism, *Hangu* and *Bayyul*, run excursions to **Tsangu Lake**, 35km northeast of Gangtok on the military road to Nathu La. Not long opened to foreign tourists, this has long been popular with Indian visitors as an accessible and easy opportunity to sample the high mountain environment and experience snow. The *SNT* bus to Tsangu is by far the cheapest way to get there.

Rumtek

Visible from Gangtok, a 24-kilometre road trip southwest of the capital, the large *gompa* (monastery) of **RUMTEK** is the headquarters of the Karmapa branch of the reformist Kargyudpa sect. Familiarly known as the "**Black Hats**", Karmapa was founded during the twelfth century by Karmapa Ranchun Dorje, as a reversion to the old magical ways of the Nyingmapa, the original school of Tibetan Buddhism. According to legend, hordes of celestial maidens descended upon the first Karmapa Rinpoche, and a crown was woven using a single hair from each one. That crown is invisible to the ordinary person, but the Empress of China later presented a black hat which all could see. Unless the Rinpoche holds onto the hat whenever he wears it, its magical powers will cause it to fly away.

Rumtek monastery was founded in 1740, but had to be rebuilt during the 1960s after an earthquake. Construction of the lavish four-level complex was made possible by international funding attracted by the sixteenth Karmapa Rinpoche, who established around 200 Karmapa centres all over the world. His death in 1981 led to a struggle between the two abbots, Samar Rimpoche and Situ Rimpoche, over the replacement *tulku* or incarnate *lama*; in 1993, the Dalai Lama came to Sikkim, performed the Kalachakra (Wheel of Time) ceremony at Gangtok, and resolved the conflict in favour of Situ Rimpoche. Unfortunately, the feuding has flared up again, fuelled by financial interests vying for control of the wealthy, but bitterly divided, monastery.

Rumtek's ornate facade is covered with intricate brightly-painted wooden lattice work. Large red columns support the high roof of the **prayer hall**, where the walls are decorated with murals and *thangkas*. Visitors can attend daily rituals, when lines of monks sit chanting. A chamber off the hall, used for tantric rituals, is painted with gold against a black background and depicts wrathful protective deities (no photography).

Behind the main temple is the most ornate of all the buildings, built in 1984 along Tibetan lines. Monks spend a minimum of nine years studying at the *Karma Shri Nalanda Institute of Buddhist Studies*, followed by an optional three-year period of isolated meditation. The main hall on the third floor is decorated with magnificent murals, and holds images including the Buddha Shakyamuni – the historic Buddha – and the sixteenth Karmapa Rinpoche. His remains are contained in a gilded *chorten* or *stupa*, studded with semi-precious stones, opposite the institute.

During Lohsar, the Tibetan New Year (Feb), the main courtyard stages *chaam* dance spectacles, in which Black Hat ceremonial dancers in colourful costumes spin and move to the magical and ponderous sounds of horns, drums and clashing cymbals.

Below the new monastery and Rumtek village, a path leads to the simple original Rumtek *gompa*, in an attractive wooded clearing and surrounded by empty outbuildings in traditional Sikkimese alpine style, with latticed wooden windows.

The one-day city tours run by the tourist office in Gangtok (see p.855) include an hour in Rumtek, which is not nearly long enough. There's also one *SNT* bus from Gangtok each day, which leaves at 4pm and returns the next morning. **Rooms** of a pretty low standard are available opposite the main gates of the *gompa* (①), and a couple of *chai* shops next door serve basic meals. The more salubrious *Sangay Hotel* (①), a couple of hundred metres down the Gangtok road, has an adjacent tea shop, while further down the *Kunga Delek Tourist Lodge* (①) has cheap cottages.

Phodong

PHODONG, 38km north of Gangtok on the Mangan road, is another living monastery, but a far less ostentatious one. Lying on a spur of the hill 1km above the main road, and commanding superb views, it consists of a simple square main temple, plus several out-houses and residential quarters. Also built in 1740, this was Sikkim's pre-eminent Kargyudpa monastery until the growth of Rumtek in the 1960s. It too hosts colourful

MOVING ON FROM GANGTOK

The busiest route in and out of Sikkim is the road between Gangtok and **Siliguri** in West Bengal, site of the nearest airport and railway station (see p.810). Flights from Bagdogra can be booked at the *Indian Airlines* office on Tibet Rd in Gangtok (☎23099); trains from New Jalpaiguri at the *SNT Out Agency* on Paljor Stadium Rd (☎22016). *Josse & Josse*, MG Rd (☎24682), are agents for *Jet Air*, *Damania* and *Sahara*, all of which fly out of Bagdogra (see p.814).

As outlined on p.855, *SNT* state **buses** use a different stand to the assorted private operators. *SNT* run several ordinary buses each day to Siliguri (6am–2pm); the super deluxe *Sikkim Queen* leaves at 7am, and there's also one *SNT* bus straight to Bagdogra airport (7am). Bookings may be made in advance from their office on Paljor Stadium Rd (daily 9am–noon & 1–2pm). Private companies such as *Apsara*, *Sikkim Beauty*, *Tashi Delek* and *Sikkim Glory* travel the same route (7am–3pm) leaving from the Private Bus Stand. Also from here, slightly quicker, cramped shared taxis – mainly jeeps – leave regularly for Siliguri (Rs60); jeeps cost around Rs1200.

Both **Kalimpong** (8.30am) and **Darjeeling** (7am) are served by one *SNT* bus per day; there are three private buses to Kalimpong and one to Darjeeling. You can also get to Darjeeling or Kalimpong by taking any Siliguri bus and changing at **Teesta Bazaar**. Shared jeeps also run to Kalimpong, the last service leaving in the afternoon.

Apart from tour buses, only one *SNT* bus leaves for **Rumtek** each day; shared jeeps for Rumtek are available from Lall market. *SNT* buses for western Sikkim include those to **Ghezing** via **Rabangla** (2 daily), and direct services to **Jorethang** (2 daily), where you can pick up connections to Darjeeling, Ghezing and **Pemayengtse** via **Legship**. Buses to **Phodong** take around two hours (3 daily). Shared jeeps for destinations in Sikkim leave from **Children's Park** taxi stand above MG Rd and the Tourist Office.

Trekking and Tour Operators

Bayyul Tours and Travels, 27 Super Market (☎737101). Treks to Dzongri, Chaurikhang, Bikbari and Goechala. They are usually helpful and often have reductions.

Hangu Travels, MG Rd (☎23517). Treks and tours of Sikkim, Darjeeling, Nepal and Bhutan, plus domestic airline tickets, entry permits into Sikkim, visas for Bhutan, and foreign exchange.

Mahayana Tours & Treks, 23 Super Market (☎23885). Along with the usual tours and treks, they organize monastery treks and visits to the four holy caves of Sikkim.

Namgyal Sherpa, Tibet Rd (☎23701). High-altitude trek and expedition operator; Nepal specialist.

Orchid Tours & Treks, 15 Supermarket (☎22197). A reliable operator charging

US$35 a day for treks to Dzongri and trips to Yumthang.

Potala Tours & Treks, Paljor Stadium Rd (☎22041). One of several identity-kit agents along this stretch, specializing in Yumthang and Dzongri.

Sikkim Tours & Travels, top floor, Supermarket & Church Rd (☎22188). Luku is friendly and adaptable and one of the central figures in the new Biodiversity Conservation Network.

Tashila Tours and Travels, NH31-A (☎22979). Experienced operator offering trekking, river rafting from Singtam to Rangpo (US$40 or Rs1000), yak safaris, angling, and monastery tours.

Yoksum Tours and Treks, below High Court, National Highway (☎23473). Treks to Dzongri and Goechala from US$45 per day.

lama dances, like the *chaam* of Rumtek, each December. A rough road leads for 4km up to another renovated old monastery – the unusual octagonal **Labrang**.

Despite the presence of several new hotels, the *Yak & Yeti* (②), 2km beyond the Phodong monastery turnoff, in the hamlet on the main road, is still a good bet with a basic restaurant and reasonable budget rooms; *Evergreen* (②) is another option. The bus to Gangtok stops at the hamlet around 4pm; shared jeeps also ply the route.

Western Sikkim

All trekking in Sikkim is currently confined to the area west of the River Teesta. On the far west, along the border with Nepal, the watershed of the Singalila range rises along a single ridge, with giants such as Rathong and Kabru culminating in Kanchendzonga itself. This beautiful land, characterized by great tracts of virgin forests and deep river valleys, holds ancient monasteries such as **Pemayengtse** and **Tashiding**; the old capital, **Yoksum**, lies at the start of the trail towards Dzongri and Kanchendzonga.

Permit restrictions (see p.852) mean that trekkers can only follow well-beaten trails within a limited period of time; as western Sikkim is nearer Darjeeling than Gangtok, it makes sense to arrange permits before you enter the state. Although only one high-altitude trail is currently available, several low-altitude treks, free from trekking restrictions, provide pleasant and undemanding walking through relatively unspoiled terrain.

Jorethang and Legship

The most important town in western Sikkim, **JORETHANG**, lies in the very south of the state, just across the River Rangit from Singla Bazaar in West Bengal and a mere 30km north of Darjeeling, barely visible across the tea plantations. Set on an extensive shelf, which makes it feel oddly flat despite the huge hills that rise in every direction, it's a surprisingly pleasant and well-ordered place, with a good market and even a couple of decent budget hotels.

Although Jorethang is well connected by bus with the rest of Sikkim, and there is a direct bus to Siliguri, no buses cross the border due south into West Bengal. Shared jeeps (Rs50), however, do venture along the perilous road to Darjeeling which winds its way up through the tea estates. The territory around Singla Bazaar south of the river from Naya Bazaar, Jorethang's twin town, is not particularly safe and vehicles are occasionally forced to pay an unofficial "tax"; few jeeps leave Jorethang after 1pm.

LEGSHIP, in the deep Rangit Valley 26km north of Jorethang, is the first town you come to if you approach western Sikkim from Gangtok, just under 100km east. It's an important regional road junction, but not an interesting destination. A police checkpost near its main crossroads checks all permits, and the nearby *Hotel Trishna* (①), the only local restaurant, has a few basic rooms. Buses and shared taxis connect Legship with Gangtok, Ghezing and Yoksum via Tashiding, and also with Jorethang.

Ghezing

Although of no great appeal in itself, the unattractive market town of **GHEZING**, 110km west of Gangtok, is the transport hub of western Sikkim, with a major *SNT* bus terminal. It's a good place to stock up on provisions, and has a handful of basic **hotels** around the main square, including the *Kanchenjhunga* (①), which has a restaurant, the *Mayalu* (①), the *West End* (①), and the *No Name* (①), with a bar, and a restaurant serving Chinese and Indian food. The most pleasant address is the *PWD Bungalow* above town, which has to be booked through the department at Gangtok.

An *SNT* **bus** to Ghezing (5hr) leaves Gangtok at 7am, and arrives at noon, in time to catch the 2.30pm bus (one of several daily services) to **Pelling**, 9km north (see below), or walk to **Pemayengtse**. Going back to Gangtok, the bus leaves around 8.30am. With the road via Pelling to Yoksum currently under repair, daily buses to **Yoksum** (7.30am & 1pm) travel via **Tashiding**, and there's a direct service to **Siliguri** (7am). Shared taxis occasionally run to Yoksum and Pelling, and slightly more regularly to Legship, Jorethang, Gangtok and Siliguri.

Pemayengtse and Pelling

Perched at the end of a ridge parallel to (and visible from) that of Darjeeling, the haunting monastery of **PEMAYENGTSE**, 118km from Gangtok, is poised high above the River Rangit as it snakes towards its confluence with the Teesta on the West Bengal border. The main road from Ghezing takes nine kilometres to wind up there, but a steep four-kilometre short cut through the woods leads past a line of *chortens* and the otherwise uninteresting ruins of Sikkim's second capital, **Rabdentse**.

"Perfect Sublime Lotus", founded in the seventeeth century by Lhatsun Chempo, one of the three *lamas* of Yoksum, and extended in 1705 by his re-incarnation, is the most important *gompa* of the Red Hat sect. A place of impressive solitude, it now has few resident monks; though used daily for morning and evening worship, it is generally quiet. Surrounded by exquisite outhouses, with intricate woodwork on the beams, lattice windows and doors, the main *gompa* itself is plain in comparison. Built on three floors, it centres around a large hall which contains images of Guru Rinpoche and Lhatsun Chempo, and an exquisite display of *thangkas* and murals. Upstairs, one of several ritual chambers holds a magnificent model of paradise, protected in a large glass case. Carved in wood and painted by Dungzin Rinpoche, a former abbot of Pemayengtse, it depicts Zandogpalr, the celestial abode of Guru Rinpoche, rising above the carnage of hell. Detail includes demons, animals, birds, Buddhas and *bodhisattvas*, *chortens* and flying dragons. An annual *chaam* – masked dance – is held here during the Tibetan New Year (Feb), and attracts visitors from all over Sikkim. A meditation centre in one of the outhouses runs occasional courses administered through the orphanage school on the way to Pelling.

Both Pemayengtse and the small, quiet town of **PELLING**, 1.5km beyond, look north towards the glaciers and peaks of Kanchendzonga. High above the forest-covered hills, in an amphitheatre of cloud, snow and rock, the route to the Rathong Glacier over Dzongri La is displayed in near entirety, from its start at Yoksum.

A trail rises westwards for around 4km from Pelling, exiting left from a playing field through some sites associated with Guru Rinpoche to reach the small monastery of **Sange Choling**. One of Sikkim's oldest *gompas*, built in 1697, this is another of Lhatsun Chempo's creations, and is highly venerated among the Nyingmapa. Gutted by fire, it has been rebuilt and houses some of the original clay statues.

Practicalities

The large and impersonal *Mount Pandim* **hotel**, just below the monastery in Pemayengtse, offers the smartest and most comfortable accommodation in western Sikkim (☎03593/50765; ⑤–⑥), with magnificent views and a restaurant. Divided into upper and lower settlements, Pelling has recently been declared a market town and is set to drastically change, with several new hotels already under construction.

The loose collection of buildings at the crossroads includes a handful of small hotels and lodges such as the traveller-friendly *Garuda* (☎03593/50614; ①), which has small but clean rooms, shared bathrooms, and the best rooftop cafe in Sikkim; a new wing is under construction. *Kabur Lodge and Restaurant*, 300m away, is more comfortable but less atmospheric, and has a good restaurant next door. Immediately above the crossroads, the comfortable *Sikkim Tourist Centre* (☎03593/50855; ⑤), not really a tourist lodge, has running hot water and attached baths, but is expensive for what it is. The pleasant and undiscovered *View Point* (☎03593/50638; ①–②), near the helipad, has a dorm, simple rooms and a more comfortable block with running hot water. Choices in lower Pelling include the Bengali-run *Pemachen* (☎03593/50641; ③–④), which has a restaurant, the ordinary *Pelling* (☎03593/50707; ③), and the simple *Samtenhling* (③), with plain but clean rooms and shared baths. Pelling is a good place to sample *tomba* (see p.855), available everywhere.

Shared jeeps regularly ply between Pelling and Ghezing; some buses from Pelling to Ghezing continue to Jorethang, on the main route to Darjeeling. Shared jeeps also depart from near Garuda to **Gangtok** (6am). The daily direct bus service to **Yoksum** leaves from Ghezing (see p.861); other services include one to Kacheoperi Lake.

Kacheoperi Lake

Surrounded by dense forests and hidden in a mountain bowl (2000m) 33km to the north of Pelling, **KACHEOPERI LAKE**, known as the "Wishing Lake", is sacred to the Lepchas. Legend has it that if a leaf drops onto the lake's surface a guardian bird swoops down and picks it up, thereby maintaining the purity of the water. Kacheoperi can be taken in on a low level trek from Pelling, or by public transport, which will usu-

---

THE DZONGRI TRAIL

The one **high-altitude trek** currently allowed in Sikkim, from **Yoksum** to **Dzongri**, in the very shadow of Kanchendzonga, passes through huge tracts of forest and provides incredible mountain vistas. Trekkers must have special **permits** (see p.852), travel in groups organized by authorized agencies (see p.859), complete with largely superfluous guides and a liaison officer, and pay a daily rate of around US$35. You need to sort out food arrangements before you set off, and bring adequate clothing – including protective headgear to cope with the heat of the river valleys – boots, and sleeping bags. For general advice on trekking equipment and health issues, see *Basics*.

Although Dzongri is the junction of several trails, the prescribed route onwards leads to **Gocha La** via Zemanthang and Samiti Lake. Though yak herders also use the trail, it can at times seem too narrow for man or beast, but it penetrates surprisingly high into the mountains considering its brevity. Well marked, and dotted with basic accommodation, the trail is at its best in May, when the rhododendrons bloom.

DAY 1 consists of getting to **Yoksum**, either by bus or, more enjoyably, walking 18km from **Pelling** (see p.861). The route from Pelling starts by dropping down to a footbridge across a mountain river. Then you ascend diagonally to the right to join the motor road, and follow it past a tea shop and a small hamlet to pick up another trail which leads down again to a precarious bamboo bridge over the turbulent Rathong Chu. Beyond the white sandy beach and boulders, a steep trail climbs to a motor road and a tiny hamlet, then rises to catch the same road again. Turn left and follow this all the way past the school at Yoksum to the police station, near the end of the motor road.

DAY 2 takes 7hr to climb 18km from **Yoksum** to **Tsokha**. You begin by crossing the cultivated mountainside almost horizontally; then the trail reaches deep forest cover, to undulate past waterfalls and across minor bridges before arriving at the Parekh Chu above its confluence with the Rathong. The next 3 or 4km involve a knee-grinding ascent past the rambling *Forest Rest House* at **Bakhim**. You have now entered the lichen zone and cloud forests. **Tsokha** (3048m), 1.5km further on, and around 300m higher, is set-tled by Tibetan yak herders. It has a *Trekkers Hut* and several rustic houses, where guests are offered Tibetan tea – a salty brew made with rancid butter – sitting in the kitchen beneath rafters blackened by smoke and hung with slowly curing chunks of yak meat.

ally drop you off at the Kacheoperi turnoff from where it's an 11-kilometre hike up a rough but motorable road to the lake.

Facilities at Kacheoperi are dire – there's a basic *Trekkers Hut* (①), and a large, comfortable *Rest House* (①) at the entrance to the lake, which is not always open; the tea shops next door serve basic meals but don't encourage travellers to stay overnight.

Yoksum

The sleepy, spread-out hamlet of **YOKSUM**, which occupies a large shelf at the entrance to the Rathong Chu gorge, 40km north of Pemayengtse at the end of the motor road, holds a special place in Sikkimese history. This was the spot where the three *lamas*, including Lhatsun Chempo, arrived across high and difficult passes to establish Tibetan Buddhism in Sikkim, in the form of the **Red Hat** or Nyingmapa sect. However, although Yoksum was once the capital of the state, and the first Chogyal was crowned here, little evidence of its past remains. Abandoned by modern Sikkim, its main role these days is as the start of the **Dzongri Trail**.

Lhatsun Chempo is supposed to have buried offerings in Yoksum's large white **Norbugang Chorten** after the enthronement of the first Chogyal, Phuntsog Namgyal. Nearby, past the *Trekkers Hut*, a path branches left through a traditional part of the

It makes good sense to spend **DAY 3** acclimatizing yourself to the altitude at Tsokha, perhaps with a short trek of around 5km towards Dzongri, to a watchtower which (weather permitting) has superb views of Kanchendzonga.

The hike from **Tsokha** to **Dzongri** on **DAY 4** takes 5hr to cover 16km. The trail rises through beautiful pine and rhododendron forests before a final steep and gruelling ascent brings you out suddenly at the tracts of dwarf rhododendron of **Phedang Meadows**, before dipping down to the hut at desolate, snow-covered **Dzongri** (4030m).

Once again, it's worth staying around Dzongri on **DAY 5** for further acclimatization. That gives you the opportunity to climb Dzongri Hill above the hut, for early-morning and early-evening views of Kanchendzonga's rocky triple-buttressed South Summit. Also look out for the black tooth of Kabur, a forbidding-looking holy mountain that towers above Dzongri La. Several trails meet at the meadows at Dzongri – one descends to cross the Rathong Chu and rises again to the demanding pass of Kang La into Nepal; another crosses Dzongri La (4800m), descends around 450m and rises again to the HMI base camp at Chaurikhang and the Rathong Glacier.

On **DAY 6**, the trek from **Dzongri** to **Thangsing** (4hr; 14km) descends against an incredible backdrop of peaks to a rhododendron forest, crosses a bridge and continues through woods to the *Trekkers Hut* at **Thangsing** (3800m), at the end of a glacial valley.

DAY 7's route crosses varied terrain from **Thangsing** to **Samiti Lake** (4hr; 10km). First the trail follows a stream and alpine meadows past a yak-herders' hut, then it traverses glacial moraine before again crossing meadows and a rocky landscape before arriving at the emerald-green **Samiti Lake** (4060m). The camping ground here is next to a giant boulder, which provides some shelter from cold winds or storms; if you are still going strong, you could continue to **Zemanthang** where there's a *Trekkers Hut*.

DAY 8, very much the climax of the trek, is also by far its most difficult section – not because of any technicalities, but simply due to its high altitude. In a round trip of 14km, you climb from **Samiti Lake** up to **Gocha La** (4hr) and back down again (2hr 30min). Leaving Samiti Lake, the trail follows glacial moraine, drops to a dry lake at Zemanthang, then makes a final grinding rise alongside cairns decorated with the occasional prayer flag to the defile at **Gocha La** (4940m). Kanchendzonga South is clearly visible above the pass, while to the left glaciers tumble off Kabru Dome.

Most of **DAY 9**'s long hike, from **Samiti Lake** back to **Tsokha** (8hr; 24km) is downhill, taking a short cut to avoid Dzongri. Crossing the bridge and following the path to a junction signed to the left puts you back above **Tsokha**, to rejoin the trail to Yoksum.

village to a small grove where the simple stone throne of the first Chogyal stands in front of a *chorten* built with stones and earth from different parts of Sikkim.

High above the town, prayer flags announce the site of the **Dubdi Monastery**, built in 1701. From the end of the road at the hospital, a path threads past water-wheels and a small river and rises through the forest to arrive at the dramatically situated *gompa*, looking out over Yoksum and Pemayengtse. Unless you've made prior arrangements, there's unlikely to be anyone around to let you have a look inside.

Visitors with West Sikkim permits are welcome in Yoksum, but unless you have a Dzongri Trek permit you're not supposed to venture any further. The police are quite vigilant, so there's not much chance of a surreptitious high-mountain trek, but so long as you're not carrying a backpack they may allow a day trip along the main trail to the Parekh Chu and its confluence with the Rathong Chu – a 28-kilometre round trip. You won't see the high Himalaya, but you do pass through some beautiful forest scenery (visibly being eroded to feed the increasing demands of the trekking industry). Yaks – or rather *dzo*, a more manageable cross between yak and domestic cattle – travel this route, with supplies for trekking parties and isolated communities.

Practicalities

The *Demazong* (②) at the bus stand in Yoksum is the cleanest and most comfortable **hotel** in town, with reasonable rooms and a restaurant serving basic meals. Behind it, in the middle of a field, the chalet-like *Trekkers Hut* has plain wooden rooms (①), out-house toilets and allows camping. The best of the few basic **cafes** is the friendly *Dzongrila* (①), opposite the *Demazong*, which also provides accommodation. There are two good *Forest Rest Houses* (①), bookable in Gangtok; #1 is approached through gates near the police station, #2 is about 1km beyond the *Trekkers Hut* on the Dzongri trail. **Buses** to Tashiding, Legship and Ghezing leave from in front of the *Dzongrila* (7am); shared jeeps also connect Yoksum to Legship and one goes as far as Siliguri.

Tashiding

The beautiful *gompa* of **TASHIDING** occupies the point of a conical hill 19km south of Yoksum, high above the confluence of the Rangit and the Rathong. "The Devoted Central Glory" was built in 1717, after a rainbow was seen to connect the site to Kanchendzonga. A wide path, lined with tall fluttering prayer flags, leads to the monastery complex, where traditional buildings, *chortens* and an impressive *mani* wall (inscribed with the mantra *Om mani padme hum*) are located around the unassuming main temple, which was recently rebuilt using some of the features and wooden beams of the original. Around February, on the fifteenth day of the first month of the Tibetan lunar calendar, devotees from all over Sikkim gather in Tashiding for the **Nyingmapa Bhumchu festival**. They are blessed with the holy water from an ancient bowl said by legend never to dry up; oracles consult the water's level to determine the future. The 200 resident monks and acolytes are friendly, and invite visitors to share Tibetan tea.

Around 2km below the *gompa*, Tashiding's tiny bazaar is situated near a saddle that separates the mountainside from the monastery hill. Basic **accommodation** in the bazaar includes the *Gupta Tea Shop* (①) and the friendly *Blue Bird* (①), which serves simple wholesome food; there's a small *Tourist Lodge* (①) higher up on the Yoksum road. Three **buses** travel daily to Yoksum and in the other direction to Legship (18km); shared jeeps are an alternative. On foot, short-cuts through the forests lead to Pemayengtse, a hard and confusing climb up on the far side of the Rathong (ask for directions), or to Legship, over the Rangit.

North Sikkim

Most of spectacular **NORTH SIKKIM** is closed to visitors. Until 1993 no one was allowed to venture past Phodong, but now, groups armed with special permits, arranged through travel and tour operators in Gangtok, are allowed as far as **Yumthang**, at the edge of the Tibetan plateau.

The road north of Gangtok follows the deep Teesta gorge past Phodong (see p.859), across what is said to be the highest bridge in the world (no photographs), before reaching the quiet little town of **Mangan**, after 60km. The administration centre for north Sikkim, it has a couple of basic hotels and cafes on the main road. A small and unremarkable *gompa* above the road around 5km north provides incredible views, especially early in the morning, of the huge east face of Kanchendzonga. Although a magnificent valley branches northwest from Mangan towards Kanchendzonga, this area is reserved as the Lepcha heartland and is closed to all non-Lepchas.

A further 40km north lies **Chungthang**, a dark and grubby town, set in a deep valley at the confluence of the Lachen and Lachung rivers, with a large military presence. There is a large PWD bungalow here as well as a couple of basic hotels including the *Neelam* (②) on the main road, with a decent but simple restaurant.

Beyond Chumthang, the valleys fork; these are border areas and the military who maintain the rough roads are very sensitive – photography, even of harmless monasteries, is not tolerated. The road to the right climbs rapidly to the small settlement of **Lachung**, the "big pass", a mere 15km west of Tibet. Across the river, **Lachung Monastery** is a two-storey Tibetan-style *gompa* belonging to the Nyingmapa sect. As the area opens up to tourism, one or two lodges are under construction; for now try the *Apple Valley Inn* (②) and the *Alpine Resort* (③).

Twenty-four kilometres further north, the valley becomes even more spectacular. Craggy snow-bound peaks rise as high as 6000m to either side, and there are large tracts of rhododendron and pine forests around **Yumthang**, which has hot sulphur springs but no accommodation. *Yaksey Lodge* (④), half-way between Lachung and Yumthang, provides a base from which to discover the valley.

CHAPTER FIFTEEN

THE NORTHEASTERN HILL STATES

C ertainly the most mysterious, and arguably the most beautiful region of India, the **NORTHEASTERN HILL STATES** have long been all but sealed off from the outside world – a lot of people here still talk about India as a foreign country. Only now, with government restrictions gradually being eased, are the states opening up to travellers. Although the entire region was the single state of **ASSAM** until the 1960s, separatist pressures since then have progressively split it up into seven states. Assam itself now consists of the low-lying valley of the **Brahmaputra**, while the others occupy the hills on all sides. The capital of Assam, **Guwahati**, is the gateway to the entire region; all the other states are heavily dependent on the transport routes of the Assam Valley.

The surrounding hill states are quite stunningly different from Assam. In **ARUNACHAL PRADESH** to the north, with its vast array of different peoples, the Himalaya rise to 6500m, while **MEGHALAYA**, on the Shillong Plateau to the south, is predominantly Christian, in common with **NAGALAND** and **MIZORAM** to the east. As in **MANIPUR**, which sits uneasily between those two, the people look East Asian and speak languages quite unrelated to Assamese, let alone Hindi (Mizo, for example, is tonal, like Thai or Chinese). In some of these places, English is spoken as a second language in preference to Hindi. Only **TRIPURA**, nestling against Bangladesh west of Mizoram, and cut off from its traditional connection with the plains by the 1947 Partition, still feels more like the rest of India than the rest of the northeastern hill states. Bengali is the main language here, and not much English is spoken.

The main appeals of visiting the northeast are its extraordinary diversity of peoples and its spectacular **landscapes**. One of the wettest monsoon belts in the world, most of the region was, until recently, rich in teak forests and wild elephants. Although elephant stockades are now rare, the lower-lying forests are being rapidly depleted, and many ecosystems are under severe strain, it still holds large tracts of bamboo, mixed deciduous and evergreen forests, and an astounding array of flora and fauna. Of its many **wildlife sanctuaries**, the most famous is **Kaziranga** in Assam, home of the Indian one-horned rhino; others, such as **Namdapha** in the farthest corner of Arunachal, remain miles off any normal tourist circuit. The recommended **time to visit** any part of the northeastern hill states is in winter and spring, when the sanctuaries are open. It rains heavily from May to the end of September, and you have to be prepared for rain at any time of year.

There are two major reasons why the Indian government has been wary of encouraging tourism to the northeastern hill states. Quite apart from the **insurgences** that have plagued the region since Independence (see p. 871), Indian military thinking sees the area as extremely vulnerable, connected to the rest of the country only by a 20km wide "chicken's neck" of land between Bhutan and Bangladesh. This vulnerability was made cruelly apparent by the **Chinese**, whose 1962 invasion reached the outskirts of Tezpur in the Brahmaputra Valley.

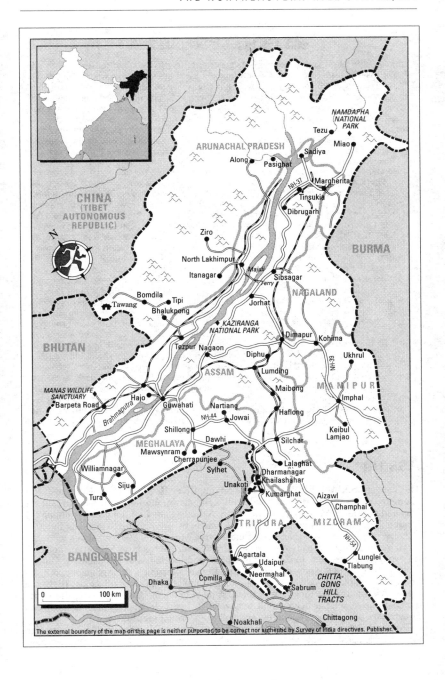

The external boundary of the map on this page is neither purported to be correct nor authentic by Survey of India directives. Publisher.

ACCESS AND PERMITS

Although the long-standing **restrictions** governing entry to the northeast for foreign and Indian visitors have recently eased substantially, there are still places where you cannot go, and others which you may only visit in a group. The trend at present is towards further liberalization, but this may depend on political developments. In the hope that more areas will soon be accessible to travellers, we have in this chapter covered some destinations which at present are not yet open to foreigners, and can only advise would-be visitors to check the current situation when they arrive in India. Interestingly, much of the pressure to lift restrictions comes from the states themselves; it's central government that appears keen to keep the lid on what it regards as highly sensitive border areas.

The situation in 1996 is as follows: **Assam**, **Meghalaya** and **Tripura** are completely open and you may visit them at will, enter by any route, and travel within them more or less wherever you like. Indian citizens may also visit **Manipur**, for which foreigners require a **Restricted Area Permit**. Tourists are only granted these if in a group of four or more, and may possibly have to prove that they have been travelling together; even then, the permit only applies to certain areas, probably only Imphal and Lake Loktak. Foreign tourists are likewise only admitted to **Mizoram** with permits and in groups of at least four, though they can travel anywhere within the state. Indian visitors to Mizoram require an **Inner Line Permit**. With insurgency in the state apparently sorted out, however, Mizoram may open up completely in the near future, all being well. **Arunachal Pradesh** is also only open to foreigners in groups of four or more on a stated itinerary. Permits cover four areas (Bhalukpong and Tipi in the west, Itanagar and Ziro, and Along and Pasighat in the centre, and Miao and Namdapha National Park in the east); however, even if you don't accept the state government's rather pricey package tours (US$150 per person per day), you still have to pay US$50 per person per day just to be in the state. Indian citizens require an Inner Line Permit, but can in principle obtain permission to travel anywhere not considered to be "of defence importance". Word is that restrictions on visiting Arunachal Pradesh could be eased, but this may not affect the money requirement, and will certainly not apply to sensitive areas close to the Chinese border. **Nagaland** is the most sensitive state of all, with insurgency still rife and public opinion not entirely on the side of the government. For now Nagaland is closed to foreigners, and even Indian citizens are unlikely to get an Inner Line Permit if their only reason for wishing to do so is tourism. The **railway** line from Lumding to Dibrugarh passes through Nagaland, with a stop at Dimapur; you can use the line without a permit so long as you do not attempt to disembark at Dimapur.

Assam

The state of **ASSAM** is dominated by the mighty **River Brahmaputra**, whose lush 700-kilometre valley is sandwiched between the Himalayan foothills to the north and the hills and plateau of Meghalaya to the south. Although much of the valley is under cultivation, large tracts of woodland make this one of the most forested states in India.

Assam produces more than half of India's **tea**. Most of its 800 tea estates were laid down by the British, who created a basic infrastructure of roads, as well as one golf club for every fifteen estates, to relieve the tedium and loneliness of the planters. Though most of the estates are now owned by large Indian companies, their managers are still known as "tea planters". The state also holds some of India's few **oil** fields; **Digboi** in Upper Assam (the northeast) was the first oil refinery in Asia. However, the earthquake-prone region has been unable to develop its hydroelectric potential. Bamboo and forestry are other major resources, and still use working **elephants**.

Political violence has wracked Assam over the last two decades. In 1979, a campaign against Bangladeshis registering to vote in a by-election led to strikes and protests against

Permits

To obtain **Inner Line Permits**, Indian citizens should apply with two passport photographs to representatives of the state governments concerned. Applications should only take a day to process (a lot longer in the case of Nagaland) and are valid for a week in the first instance, but can be extended for up to six months in the relevant state capital. Again, Nagaland is the exception, where you will probably end up with a maximum of four specified days, even if you can get a permit. Foreigners in the requisite groups of four plus can also now apply for a **Restricted Area Permit** to the state government representatives of Manipur, Mizoran or Arunachal Pradesh at least two weeks in advance (preferably more), and will usually be allowed two weeks in each state. Foreigners with a good reason wanting to travel alone or in groups of less than four should apply to the Ministry of Home Affairs, Foreigners' Division, Lok Nayak Bhavan, near Khan Market in New Delhi, at least four weeks in advance, and expect to make several visits before any permit is granted. You may be able to enlist the aid of state government representatives, and it's a good idea to consult them first anyway. We have heard of tourists getting round the group requirement (usually by having the right connections), but such cases are definitely the exception rather than the rule.

State Government Representatives

Arunachal Pradesh Arunachal Bhawan, Kautilya Marg, Chanakyapuri, Delhi (☎011/301 3915); Roxi Cinema Hall, Chowringee Rd, Calcutta (☎033/248 6500); Arunachal Bhawan, Bhaskar Nagar, off RG Baruah Rd, near Commerce College, Guwahati (☎0361/562859).

Manipur Manipur Bhawan, Sardar Patel Marg, Chanakyapuri, Delhi (☎011/301 3311); Manipur Bhawan, 25 Ashutosh Shastri Rd, Calcutta (☎033/365012 or 3); Manipur Bhawan, Rajgarh Rd, Chandmari, Guwahati (☎0361/540707).

Mizoram Mizoram Bhawan, Circular Rd behind the Sri Lankan Embassy, Chanakyapuri, Delhi (☎011/301 5951); Mizoram House, 24 Old Ballygunge Rd, Calcutta (☎033/757034); Mizoram House, GS Rd, just north of the junction with RG Baruah Rd, Bhangagarh, Guwahati (☎0361/564626); Mizoram Circuit House, Sunai Rd, Silchar Rangir Kharia, Silchar (☎03842/20142).

Nagaland 29 Aurangzeb Rd, Delhi (☎011/379 3019); Nagaland House, 13 Shakespeare Sarani, Calcutta (☎033/225247); Nagaland House, Nongrim Hill, Shillong (☎0364/230083).

Bengali immigrants, largely organized by the All Assam Students Union (AASU). The unrest culminated in a boycott of the 1983 state assembly elections and a series of pogroms that left more than 3000 dead. Two years later, a coalition (the AGP) based on the AASU won control of the state, but infighting and incompetence dogged the regime, while a more extreme group, the United Liberation Front of Asom (ULFA) began an armed struggle for independence. Kidnappings and murders generated an atmosphere of terror that threatened to close the tea industry, but in 1991 the Indian Army's Campaign Rhino struck at the heart of the organization and forced them to the negotiating table. Some ULFA cadres however, loath to lose the income their activities generated, refused to give up, and the problem remained unresolved. At the same time, Assamese nationalism sparked opposition from Bodos, Cachars and other ethnic minorities, giving rise to further insurgences.

The capital of Assam, **Guwahati**, which once controlled a far greater area, is a busy town that continues to provide the key to the entire northeast region, with its vital air, rail and road connections. It is also the site of one of India's most important Kali temples, the *shaktipath* of **Kamakhya**, and the temple of **Navagraha**, once a great centre of astrology and astronomy. Within easy access of Guwahati, the bountiful grasslands of the wildlife sanctuary at **Kaziranga** are renowned for their one-horned **rhinoceroses** – the state symbol.

AHOMS AND BODOS

Migration of people has played a major role in the history of the northeastern hill states. Originally called the Shan, the **Ahom**, Buddhists from Thailand, invaded in 1228 and settled in the northeast corner of the valley of the Brahmaputra. Establishing their capital at Sibsagar, they named the region *Assam*, "undulating land". By the end of the sixteenth century the fiery and tenacious Ahoms had displaced the Kacharis and Koche of northeastern Bengal and western Assam, and they later repelled several Muslim invasions from Bengal.

Intermingling with the mostly Bengali Aryans of the lowlands, they became accomplished cultivators; as they adopted Hindu socio-religious traditions, a new Assamese identity emerged. In the eighteenth century, the formal conversion of the Ahom chief to Hinduism prompted a rebellion, which was quelled with the help of the Burmese. The Burmese then absorbed the entire kingdom, which marked the end of Ahom rule, and it was united with India when they eventually ceded it to the British in 1826.

The term **Bodo**, derived from *Bhotia* (ie people from Bhot – another name for Tibet), serves to describe several trans-Himalayan tribes, including the Monpas, Daflas and Mishmis of Arunachal Pradesh, groups in the Cachar Hills of Tripura, and the Garos of Meghalaya. The Bodos have recently come to be regarded as a single ethnic group, and a campaign for Bodo autonomy has grown over the last decade, with the Bodo Army, formerly the Bodo Security Force (BdSF) now one of the state's most troublesome insurgent groups.

Guwahati

The most striking feature of **GUWAHATI** (also spelt Gauhati), the capital of Assam and gateway to the northeastern hill states, is the **Brahmaputra**, whose muddy swollen channel is so vast that the far shore is often invisible. Guwahati lies at the point where the wooded hills at the edge of the Shillong Plateau touch the southern banks of the river, with the flat alluvial plains of the Assam valley stretching away to the north. Busy and interesting markets occupy the town centre, while avenues radiate away to suburbs that nestle in the foothills. Of its many mysterious temples, **Kamakhya** and **Navagraha** overlook the river, while **Umananda** sits marooned on an island crag.

Guwahati's main business, **tea**, is booming, with the new *Assam Tea Auction Centre* (8km down GS Rd in Dispur) holding auctions of the *CTC* (*Crush, Tear and Curl*) variety that previously took place as far away as Calcutta and London (Tues & Wed 9.30am–1pm & 2.30–6pm). In addition, Noonmati, on the northern outskirts, is the region's largest oil refinery. Despite Guwahati's recent prosperity and rapid growth, however, the town retains an appealing old-world atmosphere.

Arrival, information and public transport

The **railway station** is in the centre of town, with the state **bus stand**, and most private bus companies, in Paltan Bazaar just behind it. From the **airport**, 18km east of the centre, taxis into town cost around Rs150; buses, including those run by *Indian Airlines*, are more like Rs20.

The Assamese government's **tourist office** shares premises with the *Tourist Lodge* on Station Rd (daily except Sun and the 2nd & 4th Sat of the month, 10am–5pm; ☎544475), and organizes local and longer tours; those to Kaziranga are particularly good value. Branch offices in the station and the airport keep the same hours. The **ITDC Tourist Office**, BK Kakati Rd, Ulubari (Mon–Fri 9am–5pm, Sat 10am–1pm; ☎547407), can provide information on the entire northeastern region.

For **foreign exchange**, *ANZ Grindlays* on GNB Rd opposite the State Museum will change US and Australian dollars, or pounds sterling, cash and travellers' cheques,

TROUBLE IN THE NORTHEASTERN HILL STATES

Since Independence, the northeastern states have been dogged by conflicts and insurgences that have made them the most unstable region in India. Most of the troubles stem from **claims for autonomy, statehood** and **independence**. If the northeast as a whole has long been neglected by the centre, so the hill tribes have also faced callous disregard by the state of Assam, and both these factors have given rise to separatist movements, from Nagas struggling for complete independence to Mizos wanting independence but settling for statehood, Bodos still fighting for their own state, and smaller groups simply demanding more local autonomy. All too often, it is the contempt with which these claims have been met that has turned them into violent uprisings.

A second ingredient in the troubles has been **ethnic rivalry**. The current spate of murderous violence between Nagas and Kukis in Manipur is just the latest of a series of inter-ethnic hatreds that have bubbled to the surface, especially in Manipur and parts of Assam. Often the rivalry is between hill people and plainspeople, or tribals and Assamese, competing for land in a mainly agricultural economy at its heart. The biggest ethnic conflict, however, stems from the influx of Bengalis, putting pressure on a region where land is already scarce. To a Westerner, it's easy see the **anti-Bengali agitation** that has affected even the region's most peaceful states as akin to the kind of racism we know from home, but on closer examination there is more to it than that. Bengalis and other outsiders have been coming into the region since colonial times, often to do the jobs that Assamese people have refused. This has led to political problems, with Pakistan claiming Assam at Independence due to its huge Muslim Bengali population; only some wily politicking by Assam Congress leader Gopinath Bardoloi (who had to enlist Gandhi's help and agree to the hiving-off of Sylhet) kept it for India. Since then, the influx of Bengalis has been seen as a political threat, yet Bangladesh's massive overpopulation and land shortages have meant constant large-scale illegal immigration. In Tripura, Bengalis are now the majority, and within Bangladesh, Bengali Muslims have displaced the mainly Buddhist Chakmas of the Chittagong Hill Tracts, whose ever increasing numbers as **refugees**, along with Bhutanese Nepalis, has also led to anti-immigrant agitation, especially in Arunachal Pradesh.

Separatism and ethnic or anti-outsider feelings frequently combine, with separatist groups occasionally indulging in "ethnic cleansing", and antipathy between hill-dwellers and plains people a major factor in campaigns for autonomy. The United Liberation Front of Asom (ULFA), one of the region's largest and most troublesome insurgent groups, started out demanding the expulsion of Bengalis, but gradually became a group fighting for Assamese independence. ULFA's history illustrates very well many of the **features of local insurgency**. It has formed links with other militants in the region, most importantly the National Socialist Council of Nagaland (NSCN), the region's oldest insurgent group, and together they have supplied and shared experience, training and sources of arms. Groups in neighbouring Burma have also been involved, and from the governments of Pakistan, China and Bangladesh they have obtained arms, funds, training sanctuary, or just a blind eye, in the hope of weakening India or its hold on the northeast. Nor have the authorities in India been as unconnected to the insurgents as you might suppose, with ULFA and the NSCN in particular having strong connections at state level, and friends in all local political parties. Agreements between insurgents and state governments usually fail to work however, because as the leadership makes a deal, extremists within the group break away and the insurgency continues – this happened in Nagaland in 1975, and to ULFA in 1992. Part of the reason is that activists develop a taste for fundraising (robbery and extortion), and the politics becomes little more than an excuse. Only in Mizoram did the extremist factions eventually fizzle out.

The best historical account of the region's problems can be found in Sanjoy Hazarika's book, *Strangers of the Mist*, available in paperback throughout India, with current developments covered well in the fortnightly *North-East Sun*.

while the *State Bank of India*, on MG Rd 50m west of ARB Rd, will change US or sterling cash, travellers' cheques, and may change other hard currencies (both Mon–Fri 10am–2pm, Sat 10am–noon; note that banks may not have the day's rates early on, and are unlikely to have them on Saturday, which means that they will not change money then). The **GPO** on ARB Rd (Mon–Sat 10am–6pm) is around the corner from the *State Bank of India*, with the **telegraph office** (24hr) just around the corner from that.

Guwahati has an efficient and extensive system of minibuses, known as **canters**, whose conductors call out their destinations at each stop. Cycle rickshaws tend to stay close to the centre, while auto-rickshaws cover a wider area. The main terminal for river **ferries** is at **Sukreswar Ghat**.

> The telephone **area code** for Guwahati is ☎0361.

The Town

Although strictly speaking Guwahati is split in two by the Brahmaputra – only crossed by the **Saraighat Bridge** and the ferries – "Guwahati" is taken to refer to the main town south of the river, while **North Guwahati** is virtually a separate town. The main roads out of town are the **Assam Trunk Road** (AT Rd) to Upper Assam, and the **Guwahati-Shillong Road** (GS Rd) to Meghalaya.

Paltan Bazaar, Pan Bazaar and **Fancy Bazaar**, Guwahati's main shopping areas, are bunched in the centre on either side of the railway, with the older residential areas north of the tracks. Most of the bazaars deal simply in provisions; **silk** and other Assamese crafts are sold at several good shops on GNB Rd east of *Grindlays* bank.

Archeological and ethnographic displays in Assam's **State Museum**, near the centre of town, include stone and copper plate inscriptions dating from the fifth century, a twelfth-century sculpture of Surya, terracotta and costumes (Tues–Sat 10am–4.15pm, 5pm in summer, Sun 9am–1pm; closed the 2nd & 4th Sat of the month, ticket counter closed 1–1.30pm; Rs2).

The Shiva temple of **Umananda**, reached by motor launches and public ferries from **Umananda Ghat** (whose position may shift slightly according to the level of the river), stands on an island bluff in the middle of the Brahmaputra. Its location, at the top of a flight of steep steps up from the jetty, is more dramatic than the temple itself. A couple of shops sell offerings at the temple gates, and the trees house beautiful golden langur, well used to being fed by passing pilgrims and happy to pose for a close-up.

On the commanding Nilachal Hill, overlooking the river 8km west of the centre, the important Kali temple of **Kamakhya**, with its beehive-shaped *shikhara*, is a fine example of the distinctive Assamese style of architecture. Said to occupy the site of a Khasi sacrificial ground, and to mark the place where Shakti's *yoni* (vulva) fell when her body disintegrated into 108 pieces, it has a somewhat eerie atmosphere, despite having been rebuilt in 1665 after a priest who converted to Islam burned down the original structure. Small shops selling offerings crowd its main entrance, which throngs in the morning with priests clad in Tantric red and saffron awaiting their clients. Myriads of pilgrims come up the hill by bus or car, while the poor and devout trudge up on foot. Animal sacrifice is a standard part of ritual; kid goats are bathed in the ceremonial tank and then led to slaughter behind the temple hall. Non-Hindus are allowed to enter the inner sanctum, which involves walking barefoot on a floor sprinkled lightly with sacrificial blood. A short walk up the hill brings you to a smaller and emptier temple, with great views of the Brahmaputra and Guwahati.

Another hill in east Guwahati holds the atmospheric **Navagraha** temple – the "temple of the nine planets", an ancient seat of astrology and astronomy – surrounded by large trees that shelter tribes of monkeys. Housed in a single red dome, again in the beehive style, the central *lingam* is encircled by a further nine representing the plan-

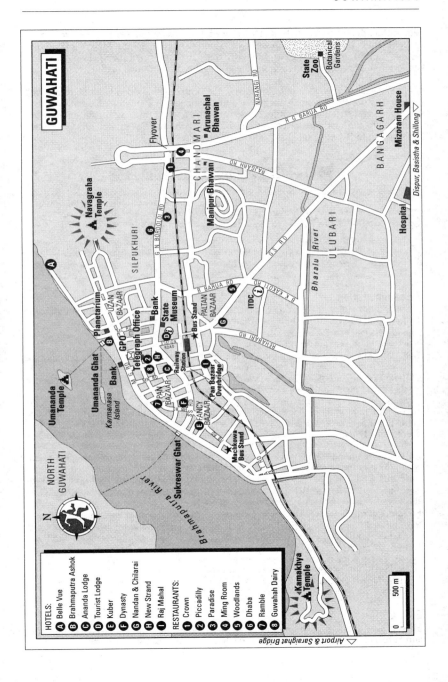

GUWAHATI

N
NORTH
GUWAHATI

Umananda
Temple

Navagraha
Temple

SILPUKHURI

CHANDMARI

State
Zoo

Botanical
Gardens

Flyover

Arunachal
Bhawan

Manipur Bhawan

NARANGI RD

R G BARUA RD

RAJGARH RD

BANGAGARH

Mizoram House

Dispur, Basistha & Shillong ▷

Hospital

ULUBARI

Bharalu River

G S RD

G N BORDOLOI RD

Planetarium

UZAN
BAZAAR

Bank

State
Museum

Bus Stand

B BARUA RD

PALTAN
BAZAAR

B K KAKOTI RD

ITDC

GPO

Telegraph
Office

Umananda Ghat

Bank

Karmanasa
Island

STATION
ROAD

Railway
Station

PAN
BAZAAR

Pan Bazaar
Overbridge

FANCY
BAZAAR

M L NEHRU RD

S S RD

Machkowa
Bus Stand

Sukreswar Ghat

Brahmaputra River

REHABARI RD

HOTELS:
Ⓐ Belle Vue
Ⓑ Brahmaputra Ashok
Ⓒ Ananda Lodge
Ⓓ Tourist Lodge
Ⓔ Kuber
Ⓕ Dynasty
Ⓖ Nandan & Chilarai
Ⓗ New Strand
Ⓘ Raj Mahal

RESTAURANTS:
❶ Crown
❷ Piccadilly
❸ Paradise
❹ Ming Room
❺ Woodlands
❻ Dhaba
❼ Ramble
❽ Guwahah Dairy

Kamakhya
Temple

◁ Airport & Saraighat Bridge

0   500 m

ets. Although limited by the lack of telescopes, Indian astronomers managed to discern seven planets (*graha*) – Sun (Surya, Ravi), Moon (Chandra, Soma), Mercury (Buddha), Venus (Sukra), Mars (Mangala), Jupiter (Brhaspati) and Saturn (Sani). Two more were added, Rahu and Ketu, the dragon's head and the dragon's tail, or the ascending and descending nodes of the moon.

At the base of a wooded hill, 5km east of the centre stands Guwahati's leafy and well-managed **Zoo**. Prize animals include clouded leopards – a small leopard with a large bushy tail and strikingly beautiful markings – and a white tiger. At the far end, the zoo blends into the ornamental **Botanical Gardens** (both daily except Fri, Oct–March 8am–4pm, April–Sept 7am–4.30pm; Rs3, camera Rs5, video Rs250).

ACCOMMODATION PRICE CODES

All **accommodation prices** in this book have been coded using the symbols below. In principle the prices given are for the least expensive double rooms in each establishment; however, some hotels, usually in category ①, offer rates per bed rather than per room. Local taxes are not included unless specifically stated. For more details, see p.35.

① up to Rs100	④ Rs225–350	⑦ Rs750–1200
② Rs100–150	⑤ Rs350–500	⑧ Rs1200–2200
③ Rs150–225	⑥ Rs500–750	⑨ Rs2200 and upwards

Accommodation

Guwahati has a strong selection of **places to stay**. In addition to the budget options in Paltan Bazaar, several new hotels compete for the business market.

Ananda Lodge, MN Rd, Pan Bazaar (☎544832). A very good-value budget lodge, with a clean courtyard atmosphere but dingy rooms. Food is available. ①.

Belle Vue, MG Rd, opposite Raj Bhavan (☎ & fax 540847 or 8). On a wooded hill overlooking the river, away from the noise of the bazaars. Although showing its age, it still has some charm. ⑤–⑧.

Chilarai Regency, off GS Rd, Paltan Bazaar (☎541350; fax 547917). In a side street by the *Nandan*, another luxury hotel with 44 rooms, restaurant and bar. ⑤–⑥.

Dynasty, SS Rd, Fancy Bazaar (☎542868 or 9; fax 522112). Right in the heart of the market area; classier than many of the smart new hotels, with understated decor and two good restaurants. ⑦.

ITDC Brahmaputra Ashok, MG Rd (☎541064 or 5; fax 540870). The best hotel in Guwahati, near the river and 1km from the railway station, with a restaurant serving Indian, Chinese and European food. Bar and car rental facilities. ⑧.

Kuber International, Hem Barua Rd (☎520807 or 8; fax 541465). Guwahati landmark, right in the centre of Fancy Bazaar. Comfortable if slightly shabby. ⑤–⑥.

Nandan, GS Rd, Paltan Bazaar (☎521476 or 7; fax 542634). Large 3-star near the bus stand. ⑥–⑦.

New Strand, GNB Rd, Pan Bazaar (☎32245). Close to the railway station – clean and pleasant for a simple budget hotel and very competitively priced. ②–③.

Railway Retiring Rooms. Two double rooms and a small dorm. Book at the enquiry counter. ①.

Raj Mahal, AT Rd, Paltan Bazaar (☎522476; fax 521559). Garish 3-star with all mod cons. ⑦–⑧.

Space Lodge, MN Rd, Pan Bazaar (☎548898). Basic but decent, though the rooms are small. ①.

Tourist Lodge, Station Rd (☎547475). In the same complex as the tourist office, not far from the railway station. A few a/c rooms. Handy and quite clean, but unremarkable, though connoisseurs of the supernatural may want to try out room 303, which is said to be haunted. ③.

Urvashi, Airport (☎84219/26). Comfortable hotel, well out of town but very convenient for catching flights – complimentary transfers. ⑤–⑥.

Eating

Most of Guwahati's middle and more expensive hotels have multi-cuisine **restaurants** and bars, concentrating on Mughlai and Chinese food. Only the *Paradise* specializes in

Assamese cuisine – pleasantly mild, and reminiscent of Bengali food in its emphasis on fish. For breakfast, various places around the bus stand open early for tea and omelettes, or you can treat yourself to a buffet breakfast at *Chopstix* in the *Dynasty*. Many *chai* shops offer the choice of black tea, even sometimes with lemon, which you may well prefer since milk is invariably powdered.

Crown Hotel, GNB Rd, Chandmari. Just a simple *dhaba*, but does good tea, curd, omelettes and low-priced curries. Open 9am–10pm.

The Dhaba, GNB Rd, Silpukhuri. Good, moderately priced north Indian meat dishes and *tarka dal* served in traditional Assamese decor of cane and bamboo. Open noon–10.30pm.

Dynasty Hotel, SS Rd. Two good restaurants: *Tandoor*, for north Indian and *tandoori* (noon–3pm & 7–11pm); and the slightly cheaper *Chopstix*, a multi-cuisine restaurant serving good Chinese food, burgers, vindaloo and even fish fingers (open 24hr for snacks, 7–10.30am for breakfast, 10.30am–12.30pm & 3–7.30pm for meals).

Guwahati Dairy, MN Rd, Pan Bazaar. Good samosas, sweets and curd. Open 7.30am–8pm.

Madras Cabin, AT Rd, Paltan Bazaar. Tasty cheap south Indian food, very handy for breakfast before catching that early morning bus or train. Open 4.30am–10pm.

Ming Room, Chandmari, next to the flyover, just south of the train track. A bit of a way from the centre but the best Chinese food in town, at higher prices than elsewhere. Open noon–10pm.

Orbit, *Kuber International Hotel*, HB Rd, Fancy Bazaar (☎520807 or 8). Revolving restaurant with a view. Open 7am–10pm, serving breakfast, snacks and full meals.

Paradise, GNB Rd, Silpukhuri. Excellent Assamese restaurant, especially good for lunch, with *thalis*, non-veg curries and Chinese food. Open 10am–3.30pm & 6–9.30pm.

Piccadilly, MN Rd, Pan Bazaar. The food (Indian or Chinese) is good, but service is slow. Open 8.30am–8.30pm.

Ramble, HB Rd, Pan Bazaar. Dependable local and Chinese dishes, including meat curries and fish. Open 10am–9.30pm.

Woodlands, GS Rd, Ulubari. Great north and south Indian veg restaurant, serving *thalis*, *masala dosas* and real coffee. Open 8am–9pm, *thalis* 11am–3pm & 7–9pm.

Listings

Airlines *British Airways*, c/o *Pelican Travels*, *Brahmaputra Ahok Hotel* (☎545149); *Indian Airlines*, GS Rd, near the junction with RG Baruah Rd, Dispur (☎564420 or 1); *Jet*, GNB Rd, Silpukhuri (☎520255); *Modiluft*, c/o *Patson Tours*, just behind *Indian Airlines*, (☎565082); *NEPC* (☎566437) and *Air India* (c/o *Aryna Travels*, ☎561881), next to each other on GS Rd, Bhangagarh, 3km from the centre; *Sahara India*, GS Rd, northwest of BK Kakoti Rd (☎547808).

Books There are a number of bookshops in Pan Bazaar, notably *Western Book Depot*, Josovanta Rd just off HB Rd, with a good selection of fiction, and titles on the northeast, the *Advanced Study Centre* on MN Rd opposite *Ananda Lodge*, and the *Modern Book Depot* on HB Rd near MN Rd.

Hospital *Guwahati Medical College Hospital*, Bhangagarh, south of the junction of GS Rd and Rajgarh Rd (☎561477).

Pharmacy *Life Pharmacy* on GS Rd (just south of B Baruah Rd) is open 24 hours a day.

Photography *New Frontier Colour Lab*, SS Rd, Lakhtokia, 50m west of Pan Bazaar Over Bridge (☎34686); *S Ghoshal*, HB Rd, Pan Bazaar near *Ramble* restaurant.

Travel agents *Jungle Travels*, GNB Rd, Silpukhuri (☎524121) are agents for *American Express* and can make bookings on domestic and international airlines. Air tickets out of Guwahati can also be booked through *Rhino Travels*, MN Rd, Pan Bazaar (☎540666) and *Link* just north of GNB Rd by the flyover in Chandmari (☎524234). *Blue Hill* bus company behind the *Hotel Nandan* in Paltan Bazaar (☎547911) operate tours and can make railway bookings.

Around Guwahati

Guwahati is well placed for excursions to Kaziranga and Manas, as well as day and weekend breaks to the cooler climes of Shillong in Meghalaya. Closer to hand are the temples of **Basistha** and, across the Brahmaputra, **Hajo**, while more distant **Tezpur** makes a convenient base for the small wildlife sanctuary of **Orang**.

MOVING ON FROM GUWAHATI

State-run **buses** from the *ASTC* stand in AT Rd (☎510984) serve Shillong (hourly until 5.30pm; 3hr), Tezpur (hourly until 4pm plus one evening departure; 4hr), Kaziranga (14 daily; 4hr), Jorhat (9 daily; 6hr 30min), Sibsagar (7 daily; 8hr), Silchar (3 daily; 12hr), Itanagar (2 daily; 9hr), Dimapur (1 daily; 9hr) and Siliguri (3 daily; 12hr). **Private companies** run the same routes; their offices are in Paltan Bazaar, including *Blue Hill*, behind the *Hotel Nandan* (☎547911), *Network*, GS Rd opposite the *Nandan* (☎522007), *Assam Valley*, GS Rd (☎31523), and *Green Valley*, on GNB Rd in Silpukhuri (☎544636). As well as the aforementioned destinations, they also serve places like Agartala (25hr), Aizawl (21hr), Kohima (11hr) and Imphal (23hr via Silchar – you can't travel on services via Nagaland without a permit). Buses for Hajo (6 daily; 1hr 15min) run from Machkowa bus stand off MG Rd southwest of the centre, with additional services from Adabari bus stand, 4km out of town on AT Rd near Guwahati University (reached by city bus or autorickshaw from MG Rd).

Of the three daily **trains** to New Delhi, the best is the *North–East Express* #5621 (36hr), but is often extremely late. The *Rajdhani Express* #2423 is faster (3 weekly; 28hr), but pricier. To Calcutta, the best of two daily services is the *Kanchenjunga Express* #5658 to Sealdah (in theory 21hr 35min). There are also trains to Bhubaneshwar (3 weekly; 31hr 10min) and Madras (3 weekly; 53hr), Bombay Dadar (2 weekly; 53hr 35min), and Bangalore (1 weekly; 61hr), Kochi (1 weekly; 67hr 15min) and Thiruvananthapuram (1 weekly; 72hr) – all are likely to be outrageously late. In the interior, there are services to Lumding (3 daily; 4–6hr), two of which continue to Dimapur (7hr). On the metregauge line, the *Arunachal Express* #5813 serves Rangapara (5hr), North Lakhimpur (11hr 10min) and Silapathar (14hr 15min), from where you can travel on to, respectively, Tezpur, Bhalakpung and Along.

You can **fly** to Calcutta (1hr 10min) with *Indian Airlines* (at least daily), *Jet* (daily), *Modiluft* (5 weekly) and *NEPC* (4 weekly); to Delhi (2hr 25–4hr 40min) with *Jet* (daily) and *Indian Airlines* (2 weekly), and *Sahara India* (3 weekly; the only non-stop service). You can also get to Imphal on *NEPC* (daily; 50min) and *Indian Airlines* (2 weekly), while Agartala is served by *Indian Airlines*, (2 weekly; 40min) and Dimapur by *NEPC* (4 weekly; 50min) whose flights continue to Jorhat (1hr 50min). The thrice-weekly *Pawan Hans* **helicopter** service to Itanagar can be booked through *Rhino Travels* (see *Listings*, p.875) or the Arunachal Tourist Dept. (see p.900).

Basistha

Beside a picturesque waterfall, 11km southeast of Guwahati, two small red-domed temples at **BASISTHA**, in Assamese beehive style, commemorate Vasistha Muni, the author of the *Ramayana*. Nestling within an impressive copse of trees, with rock carvings in the stream to add to the air of antiquity, Basistha is popular with pilgrims and picnickers alike. City buses for Basistha can be picked up outside the library on GNB Rd by the junction of Station Rd, or anywhere along GNB Rd from there to the flyover, and then on RG Baruah Rd.

Hajo

The small town of **HAJO**, 32km northeast of Guwahati, has a special place in Assamese culture, having been sacred even before the Ahom arrived as Buddhists, let alone after their conversion to Hinduism. Now holy to Buddhists, Hindus and Muslims, it attracts pilgrims from all the faiths, in apparent harmony. A long palm tree-lined stone staircase climbs a hill to the small Hindu temple of **Haigriba Madhab** where, some say, the Buddha gained *nirvana*. Praying at the mosque of **Pao Mecca** nearby grants Muslims a quarter (*pao*) of the spiritual benefit of Mecca. Hajo is easily accessible from Guwahati's Machkowa bus stand (6 daily; 1hr 15min) and is also served from Adabari bus stand. The nearby village of **Sualkuchi** is known for its production of golden *muga* silk, which involves virtually every household.

Madan Kamdev

Some 40km northwest of Guwahati, **MADAN KAMDEV** is the site of a Tantric temple to Shakti (Durga) dating back to the Pallava dynasty (eleventh and twelfth centuries). The temple, which is mentioned in the Tantric scriptures known as the *Yogini Tantra* was evidently destroyed, though the cause is unknown. Much of the site remains unexcavated, but a **museum** preserves many finds including figures in, naturally, various erotic postures. Madan Kamdev can be reached by bus from Guwahati's Adabari bus stand to Baihata Chariali, from where it's a six-kilometre walk or auto-rickshaw ride.

Tezpur

Amid tea gardens and military cantonments on the north bank of the Brahmaputra, 181km east of Guwahati, the pleasant little town of **TEZPUR**, built around several lakes, stands on the site of **Sonitpur** (City of Blood). According to legend, this was the scene of a terrible battle involving no less than Lord Krishna, who journeyed here from Gujarat to rescue his grandson, imprisoned by the local ruler, King Asura, for an illicit affair with and secret marriage to the latter's daughter. Despite opposition from Shiva, whose disciple Asura was, Krishna won the day and the lovers were reunited. In more recent fighting, in 1962, Tezpur was almost captured by the Chinese.

Nehru Maidan, the triangular green behind the *Tourist Lodge*, features a pretty little church and the small **District Museum** (Tues–Sun 10am–4.30pm; free), with old manuscripts and sculptures ancient and modern (notably a very Assamese-looking Gandhi), labelled in Assamese and English. Opposite the *Tourist Lodge*, in the middle of a lake, **Cole Park** was established by a British Deputy Commissioner in the 1800s to house remnants of Asura's palace excavated during construction of the Court. The main market, **Chowk Bazaar**, is on MC Rd 1km or so north of the *Tourist Lodge*, with the ancient **Mahabhairab temple** still further north. A kilometre east along the river, **Agnigarh** is a hill commanding a view over town and river, where Asura is said to have imprisoned his daughter, Usha, while all that remains of **Da-Parbatia temple**, 6km west of town, is its finely carved doorway.

Tezpur is an ideal base for visiting the wildlife sanctuary of **Orang**, 65km away (see p.878), and the nature reserve of **Bhalukpung**, 60km north on the border of Arunachal Pradesh, where an *Eco-Camp* (④), offering trekking, rafting and "angling to conserve" (you tag the fish for identification), can be booked through Assam (Bhorelli) Anglers Association in Tezpur (☎03712/20004; fax 21583) or Guwahati (☎ & fax 0361/545847).

TEZPUR PRACTICALITIES

Tezpur's **state bus stand** is on KK Rd, 500m north of the central *Tourist Lodge*. The **tourist office**, in the *Tourist Lodge*, is on KP Agarwalla Rd in the centre of town (Mon–Sat 10am–4.30pm; ☎03712/21016). There's a **GPO** on Nehru Maidan, on SC Rd; the *State Bank of India* near the *ASTC* bus stand does not change foreign currency.

Hotels, aside from the *Tourist Lodge* (☎03712/21016; ③), include the posher *Luit* in Ranu Singh Rd, a large white building 100m north of the state bus stand, with hot water and some a/c rooms (☎03712/21220; ⑤–⑥), and the cheap but reasonable *Meghdoot* on KK Rd, 500m north of the *ASTC* bus stand and near Chowk Bazaar (☎03712/20714; ①). For **food**, *Raj Chinese Hotel* on Nehru Maidan, has excellent Chinese food.

The **state bus stand** has *ASTC* buses to Guwahati (13 daily; 4hr 30min), Jorhat (5 daily; 4hr) via Kaziranga (1hr 30min), and Sibsagar (2 daily; 5hr 30min), as well as *APSTS* departures to Itanagar (Sat–Thurs 3 daily; Fri 1 daily; 5hr), Bomdila (Sat–Thurs 3 daily; Fri 2 daily; 6hr) via Balakpung (1hr 30min), and Tawang (3 weekly; 14hr). State buses dry up around 3pm. **Private bus** companies such as *Blue Hill* and *Green Valley* have offices just opposite, though their buses tend to leave from a stand west of the *Tourist Lodge* by the river, where there are frequent departures to Guwahati and Jorhat (via Kaziranga), with one or two to Siliguri, Sibsagar and Tinsukia.

The **railway station**, a little way beyond the private bus stand, sees four daily departures to North Rangapara, none of them very convenient for onward connections. Trains out of Guwahati can be booked at the Movement Control Office on the left just before you reach the station (8.30–10.30am), or at the *Blue Hill* on Nehru Maidan. Only *Indian Airlines* serve the **airport**, north of town, on and from Calcutta (2 weekly; 1hr 15min), and to, but not from, Imphal (30min). *Indian Airlines'* office is two doors from the *Tourist Lodge*; they provide buses to the airport to meet their flights.

The Wildlife Sanctuaries

Most of Assam's magnificent **Wildlife Sanctuaries** are in the Brahmaputra Valley, where the large tracts of grasslands on the flood plains are home to the Indian one-horned rhino and other beasts. On such terrain, as opposed to the thick jungle cover of most other Indian parks, sightings of animals are all but assured.

Kaziranga, the greatest park of all, is renowned for its elephant grass and rhino, but also incorporates some forest; the rarely visited, smaller, but no less beautiful **Orang** nearby occupies a similar habitat north of the Brahmaputra, near Tezpur. **Manas**, also known for its rhinos, extends over varied territory, taking in hills and river valleys on the border with Bhutan. The **Nambor Reserve Forest** in upper Assam, not far from Jorhat, consists of hill country away from the flood plains and grasslands.

Kaziranga

Covering an area of 430 square kilometres on the southern bank of the Brahmaputra, **KAZIRANGA NATIONAL PARK**, 217km east of Guwahati, occupies the vast valley floor against a backdrop of the forest-covered Karbi Anglong Hills. Rivulets and *bhils* (shallow lakes), and the semi-evergreen forested "Highlands", just out of reach of the Brahmaputra's annual floods, blend into marshes and flood plains covered with tall elephant grass. Animal sightings are guaranteed, with rhinos, deer and herds of wild buffalo grazing close to the park entrance not far from the administrative centre of **Kohora**. Rich birdlife includes egrets, herons, storks, fish-eating eagles and a grey pelican colony settled among the red cotton trees. However, few tracks penetrate this sea of grass, and the wild elephants seldom venture into it anyway, preferring to remain in the forested Highlands, while tigers are incredibly elusive. In addition, with the grasslands bordering onto cultivated fields and domestic cattle encroaching into the sanctuary and introducing epidemics, the wild animals are under increasing threat – poaching is rife, with rhino horns fetching astronomical prices as aphrodisiacs.

Kaziranga's large concentration of one-horned **rhino** – at over a thousand, the most in the subcontinent – are best seen from the back of an elephant, early on a winter's morning. Each of the **elephant rides** (5.30am & 7am) lasts around one hour, costing Rs55 per person plus Rs100 for a six-person jeep to get you to the starting point and back; book at 7.30pm the evening before at the park offices at Kohora. Although the elephants do not penetrate far into the sanctuary, merely travelling in a three or four kilometre circle, it is incredible how much wildlife can be seen in this small area – the dawn ride is the best if you can get up that early. The mild-mannered rhinos seem oblivious to camera-clicking tourists – unlike the unpredictable wild buffalo, equipped with lethal horns and potentially ferocious. Although **jeeps** (arranged through the Deputy Director of Tourism at Kohora, or *Wild Grass*; see below) penetrate deeper into the forest, they cannot approach wild animals anything like as closely.

Kaziranga is open from mid-November to early April only. During the monsoons (Jun–Sept), the Brahmaputra bursts its banks, flooding the low-lying grasslands and causing animals to migrate from one area to another within the park. Deer and even leopard often cross the main road, heading for the hills until the waters recede.

KAZIRANGA PRACTICALITIES
The main gate for Kaziranga at **Kohora** on NH37 (the AT Road) consists of a handful of cafes and a small local market. *ASTC* and private buses stop here on their way to and from Guwahati, Tezpur and Upper Assam; some private buses retain a seat quota for Kaziranga passengers. The most convenient way to come, however, is on the daily tourist bus from the *Guwahati Tourist Lodge* (see p.874), who also arrange complete tours, including a night's accommodation and an elephant ride.

The **Directorate of Tourism** (☎037765/423) is buried a few hundred metres off the road to the north, in the *Bonani Lodge*. All visitors have to sign in here, before making for the **park headquarters** alongside, where you can book elephant and jeep rides, and rooms in the nearby lodges. *Aranya* (☎037765/429; ⑤) is the largest and most comfortable, with a/c and non-a/c rooms with baths, private balconies, room service, and the best restaurant; *Bonani* is smaller, with five a/c rooms and a restaurant (④). *Bonoshree* (③) has eight doubles and a four-bedded room, all with bath, while the budget option, *Kunjaban*, has a dorm but provides no linen (①).

A kilometre and a half off the road, 4km east of Kohora, *Wild Grass* (④–⑥) is a highly recommended **luxury resort** at the foot of the Karbi Hills on the River Diring. Endorsed by the World Wildlife Fund and Project Tiger, it can book jeep safaris and elephant rides in the park and **fishing trips** at the *Eco-Camp* at Bhalukpung (see p.877). In summer, when the park is closed, they offer a swimming pool, tours to view wildlife from the park's boundary, rafting and elephant rides. *Wild Grass* also have a thatched lodge 6.5km inside the park, and can pick you up from Guwahati airport and even arrange your entire itinerary in Assam. Reserve through *Wild Grass*, PO Kaziranga, Dist Golaghat 785109 (☎037765/81437), or Barua Bhavan, 1st Floor, 107 MC Rd, Uzanbazar, Guwahati (☎0361/546827; fax 541186).

Most people staying in the park take the inexpensive **meals** provided at fixed times in *Bonani Lodge* (order in advance), although better food at more flexible times can be had at *Aranya Lodge*. You can also get tasty, very cheap Assamese dishes at *Rhinorica*, run by the *Blue Hill* bus company at the bus stop at Kohora (8am–midnight).

Manas
Bordering Bhutan, on the banks of the River Manas 176km west of Guwahati, **MANAS**, Assam's only **Project Tiger** sanctuary (Dec–April), is an absolutely spellbinding place, now reopened after being closed to visitors for several years thanks to the activities of the Bodo autonomous movement. As it emerges from the jungle-covered Himalayan foothills, the snow-fed river has a reputation as one of the best fishing grounds for the legendary *mahseer*, a pike-like game fish renowned as a fighter. Manas also has rhino, wild elephant, the rare hispid hare and the pigmy hog.

The Forest Department's two very basic **bungalows** at **Mathanguri** can be reserved through the Field Director, Tiger Project, Barpeta Rd (☎03666/153; ①). **Eating** arrangements are inadequate and food should be brought in. The big problem is **transport**: the nearest bus stop and railway station are 40km away at **Barpeta Road**, with regular services to Guwahati, and an information office and *Tourist Lodge* run by Assam Tourism (☎03712/2149; ③), but there is no regular public transport to the park, and taxis charge around Rs1000 each way. The more intrepid have been known to hitch, but by far the best way to get to Manas is on the conducted tour organized by the *Blue Hill* bus company from Guwahati (☎0361/520604 or 547911).

Upper Assam

Stretching northeast from Guwahati along the valley, Assam penetrates the complex Brahmaputra watersheds at the eastern extremity of the Himalaya, in the area known as **Upper Assam**. Road and rail networks provide access to the mountainous interiors of Arunachal Pradesh and Nagaland, and vital communications to the most industrialized region of the northeastern states.

Jorhat

JORHAT, 310km east of Guwahati, has research establishments dedicated to the tea industry, and an annual tea festival. The town is not of great interest, but you will probably have to stop here if coming to or from Majuli. **Buses** stop on the main drag, AT Rd, part of the NH37 highway; the *ASTC* terminal is half a block north of the private companies' offices/bus stops. Assam Tourism's **tourist office** is at the *Tourist Lodge* on MG Rd, 300m south of AT Rd (Mon–Sat, closed the 2nd & 4th Sat of the month, 10am–4pm; ☎0376/321579). The **GPO** is on Post Office Rd, off AT Rd between the *ASTC* stand and MG Rd. US dollars and sterling cash and travellers' cheques can be exchanged at the *State Bank of India* on AT Rd just west of Post Office Rd (Mon–Fri 10am–2pm, Sat 10am–noon: you may have trouble changing money on Sat).

The *Tourist Lodge* has large, comfortable, carpeted **rooms** (③), but if you want hot running water, you'll have to head for the *Paradise*, down a lane off AT Rd by the *ASTC* station (☎0376/321521; ④–⑤). Hotels down the same lane include the *Dilip* (☎0376/321610; ②) and the *Neera* (☎0376/322618; ②–④). The budget *Broadway* on the corner of Gar Ali and Thana Rd, about 200m east of the *Tourist Lodge* (☎0376/320192;①), is clean, and keeps a list of *ASTC* bus departures. All these hotels provide mosquito nets.

You can **eat** in all the above hotels (those in the lane by the bus station also have bars). Alternatives include the *Oasis* on MG Rd, south of the *Tourist Lodge* near the junction with KB Rd (10am–9pm), and *Treats*, 200m east up KB Rd (Mon–Sat 8.30am–8.30pm, Sun 2.30–8.30pm), both of which offer the usual local food as well as eccentric but not unpalatable versions of Chinese dishes. The *Mayur*, opposite *Treats* (7am–8pm), specializes in chicken and is also open for breakfast (serving only coffee, no tea), while the *Cherry Garden* bakery on KB Rd by the corner of MG Rd (9am–8.30pm) has excellent cakes and savoury snacks, including pizza.

ASTC **buses** run to Guwahati (16 daily; 6–7hr), Tezpur (5 daily; 4hr), Sibsagar (10 daily; 1hr 3min), Tinsukia (6 daily; 4hr 30min), and Dimapur (1 daily; 3hr 30min). Kaziranga (2hr 30min) is served by buses to Guwahati and Tezpur. For Itanagar, change at Bagdugra (daily; 8hr). The best of the **private companies** are *Blue Hill*, *Green Valley*, *Assam Valley* and *Network*, who run services to Guwahati, Sibsagar, Tinsukia and Dimapur. On MG Rd, which meets AT Rd 200m east of the *ASTC* station, a local stand offers frequent services to Sibsagar and the nearest main line railway station at Mariani, and also two daily connections for the ferry from to Majuli. From Mariani, two daily passenger **trains** and two expresses run to Tinsukia (4hr 20min–6hr 30min), the expresses continuing to Margherita, while the other way, three trains reach Dimapur (4hr 45min–5hr 45min), with two to Lumding (7hr– 8hr 15min). Jorhat is connected to Guwahati (50min) by four weekly **flights** on *NEPC* (c/o *Pelican Tours* on MG Rd near KB Rd; ☎0376/321128), and to Calcutta (2hr 15min) and to (but not from) Dimapur (35min) by two weekly flights on *Indian Airlines* (off AT Rd some 400m west of the *ASTC* station; ☎0376/320970). The airport, 5km out of town, can be reached by rickshaw, auto-rickshaw or *Indian Airlines*' bus.

Majuli

Ferries run twice a day from **Nimatighat**, 12km north of Jorhat, to **MAJULI**, the largest river island in the world, which holds several important Vaishnavite *sattras*. Upper Majuli is inhabited by the Mising and Deori tribes.

ASSAMESE VAISHNAVISM

Vishnu worship was established in Assam by the seventh century, and by the middle of the fifteenth century was already eclipsing Shaivism and Tantric Shakti-worship. Its distinctive Assamese form was developed by **Srimanta Sankardeva** (1449–1569), a poet, playwright, musician, composer, and theologian, who opposed ritual and image-worship, and rejected all other Hindu gods in favour of simple devotion to Vishnu, whom he saw as all-encompassing and formless (though he recognized Vishnu's avatars, particularly Krishna). Sankardeva's ideas were developed by his disciples, primarily Madhavdeva, and in the eighteenth century, followers of a mainly low-caste offshoot, the **Moamarias**, led a rebellion against the Ahoms and carved out a state covering the island of Majuli and a large chunk of Upper Assam.

The main institution of Assamese Vaishnavism is the **sattra**, the first founded by Sankardeva at his birthplace, Bardowa, 15km northwest of Nargaon. The *sattra* is not only a temple, but also a monastery, school and centre of the arts, including poetry, folk music, literature, sculpture and dance, often in combination (as in *dhulia*, a theatrical dance with masks recreating episodes from the *Ramayana* or the *Mahabharata*). *Sattras* consist of a prayer hall (*namghar*) open on all sides and supported by pillars (usually eight pairs), surrounded by living quarters for devotees and *ghats* for bathing. The *namghar* has three parts: a roofed gate (*karapat*), the main body of the hall (*kirtanghar*), and a closed shrine (*bhanjghar*), which may be a separate building, in which case it is called the *manikot*. Although "idol worship" is eschewed, Vaishnavites are not as strict about this as, say, Muslims: images of Vishnu's avatars often decorate the *sattra*, though they are never prayed to.

From the ferry station (whose position shifts with the level and course of the river), buses run to the village of **Kamalabari** (some 5km away), and 5km beyond to the island's "capital" at **Garamur**. Garamur and Kamalabari (connected by 6 daily buses) each have a couple of **sattras**, but you'll have to travel a few kilometres out of Kamalabari to see the more interesting ones: **Auniati**, 4km west, keeps royal artefacts from the Ahom kingdom, while **Bengenati**, 4km east, built in the early seventeenth century, has a very friendly caretaker who is happy to show visitors around. **Samoguri** 6km beyond Bengenati, is a centre for making clay and bamboo masks – sculptures in their own right – used for traditional festivals and performances. There are also *sattras* at **Bongaori**, 8km beyond Samoguri, and **Dakhinpat** 5km south of that.

PRACTICALITIES

Although distances are short, **transport** is inconvenient. For the able-bodied, the most relaxing way to take in the *sattras* is on foot over a couple of days. Alternatively, you could hire a taxi in Garamur or Kamalabari, for around Rs500; an auto-rickshaw from Kamalabari costs about half that.

Most visitors **stay** at the *Circuit House* in Garamur (①); obtain permission from the SDO (Civil), whose office is conveniently next-door. All foreign visitors should also register with the police at Garamur. In Kamalabari there is a small and very basic hotel (①), and it is possible to stay at the guest house in the *sattra* for a donation. Arrangements for **food** are best made where you are staying.

From Majuli, public ferries for Nimatighat leave at 9am and 3pm; private services leave slightly earlier. Connecting buses leave Garamur about two hours earlier, calling at Kamalabari. The whole journey back to Jorhat takes four or five hours. It is also possible to travel north from Majuli, with two daily ferries from Luhitghat, 3km north of Garamur, to Khabalughat on the north bank, from where there are buses to North Lakhimpur, and thence buses to Itanagar or Tezpur, and even a train to Guwahati.

Sibsagar

The former capital of the Ahoms, one of the oldest towns in Assam, **SIBSAGAR** – "The Ocean of Shiva" – lies 60km east of Jorhat and 369km from Guwahati. Now at the centre of an important tea- and oil-producing district, its cluster of monuments from six centuries of Ahom rule still holds cultural and historic resonance for modern Assam. A huge artificial tank, constructed by Queen Madambika in 1734, lies at the heart of the complex. Rising from its southern shore, the massive, plain 32-metre-high **Shivadol** is the tallest Shiva temple in India, flanked by smaller temples dedicated to Durga and Vishnu. On the western shore of the lake next to a park, a **Tai Ahom Museum** (Mon–Thurs & Sat, 10.30am–3.30pm; free) contains a few ill-labelled artefacts.

Temples and palaces in varying degrees of abandonment dot the local area, including the **Rang Ghar**, a two-storey oval pavilion 6km out, built by King Pramatta Singha in the eighteenth century to stage elephant fights and other sporting events. In 1979 it was scene of a secret 1979 meeting that led to the foundation of ULFA. Nearby, isolated against a flat and bare countryside, are the ruined eighteenth-century palaces of the **Kareng Ghar** and the **Talatal Ghar**, with another at **Gargaon**, 13km east of Sibsagar. *Maidams* (tombs) of the early Ahom kings can be found at their original thirteenth-century capital of **Charaideo**, 28km east of Sibsagar, and there are further tank and temple complexes like Sibsagar's at **Rangpur**, **Rudrasagar** and **Gaurisagar**, all within a 12km radius of Sibsagar.

The best place to **stay** is the *Tourist Bungalow* by the southwestern corner of Sibsagar Tank (☎03842/22394; ③), which also serves as the **tourist office**. Alternatives include the *Hotel Kareng* in Temple Rd, 100m in front of Shivadol temple (☎03842/22713; ②), and the *Annapurna Lodge*, with its reception at the private bus stand, and the rooms themselves two blocks behind (☎03842/22218; ②–③). All provide mosquito nets. For **food**, the *Annapurna* by the private bus stand has cheap set meals (5am–7pm), while the *Kushboo* in Temple Rd, 20m in front of Shivadol temple, does a passable *masala dosa*, and chow mein in the evenings (7.30am–7.30pm).

The **Post Office** is south of the lake, opposite the Durga temple, with a 24hr telecom office. There are no foreign exchange facilities. From the *ASTC* **bus stand**, 300m east at the junction of Hospital Rd and AT Rd, you'll find services to Jorhat (10 daily; 1hr 30min), Kaziranga (9 daily; 3hr), Guwahati (7 daily; 8hr), Tezpur (2 daily; 6hr) and Tinsukia (4 daily; 3hr 30min). The **private bus stand** is across AT Rd. Simaluguri, the nearest railhead, 20km east, is served by very frequent buses from the junction 200m north, all passing through Gargaon. Charaideo is served by three daily buses from the Saheli stand by the same junction. For Gaurisagar, tempos can be picked up at the central market. Other local destinations are best reached by auto-rickshaw.

South Assam

South Assam, ridged by the Cachar Hills, is the crossing point for the surrounding states of Meghalaya, Tripura, Mizoram, Manipur and Nagaland. While the main town, **Silchar**, contains little of interest, places further afield, notably the low-key hill station of **Haflong**, are far more appealing.

Silchar

The nondescript town of **SILCHAR** is south Assam's main transport nexus. There's little to do here but wait for a bus or train out, but you may find yourself having to **stay** the night. The *Tourist Lodge*, 300m down Park Rd from its junction with Central Rd (☎03842/32376; ③) has a small information office; other options include the reasonably clean *Swagat* in Central Rd (☎03842/30667; ①–③), the good-value *Nataraj* off Club Rd opposite *Network Travel* (☎03842/30084; ②–④), and the *Monoranjan* not far away in Steamer Ghat Rd by Sadarghat Bridge (☎03842/20583; ③–④). The *Geetanjali* in Club

---

SILCHAR TRANSPORT CONNECTIONS

The **state bus stand** is near the *Devdoot* cinema, where Central Rd and Club Rd meet Circuit House Rd. Served also by *Meghalaya Transport Corporation* and *Tripura Road Transport Services*, the stand sees buses for Guwahati (3 daily; 12hr), Dharmanagar (5 daily; 4hr), and Agartala (2 daily; 12hr), Shillong (2 daily; 9hr) and Haflong (2 daily; 5hr). Most **private bus companies** have offices in Circuit House Rd (except *Network*, at the other end of Club Rd), with usually one or two daily departures for the same destinations, as well as Aizawl (9hr), Imphal (11hr) and places around Assam such as Tezpur (16hr), North Lakhimpur (26hr), Sibsagar (17hr) and Tinsukia (20hr). *Manipur State Bus Corporation* also run a very early morning bus to Imphal from Rangpur, over Sadarghat Bridge on the other side of the river, and *Mizoram State Transport Corporation* have two daily departures for Aizawl from outside Mizoram House in Sunai Rd.

The **railway station** is 3km out of town in Tarapur, with trains to Dharmanagar (1 daily; 5hr 35min), Haflong (2 daily; 6hr) and Lumding (2 daily; 10hr 45min), where you can pick up connections to Guwahati. Silchar's **airport**, 13km away, can be reached by shared taxi from outside the *Indian Airlines* office in Club Rd (Rs35). *Indian Airlines* (☎03842/20072) have flights to Calcutta (6 weekly; 1hr 5min) and Imphal (3 weekly; 35min), while *Modiluft* (c/o *Commercial Travels*, next door, ☎03842/32355) fly to Calcutta (2 weekly), and to, but not from, Guwahati (2 weekly; 35min). *NEPC* are also represented by *Choudhury (Lokenath) Travels* opposite (☎03842/22607).

Rd has similar rooms to the *Natraj* and the *Monoranjan* at higher prices, but its **restaurant** is the best place to eat in town (7am–10pm).

Haflong and around

The scenic hill-resort of **HAFLONG**, 84km north of Silchar, is the seat of the North Cachar Hills Autonomous District Council, where members of several ethnic groups including Dimasas, Hmars, Nagas and Mizos, belonging to different religious denominations – Christian, Hindu and Buddhist – live together in apparent harmony. Give or take, that is, the odd ruction in support of statehood or at least further autonomy, and the odd consignment of arms or militants en route to Manipur or Nagaland.

Haflong is spread along **Main Road**, which winds up from Silchar. The **market**, off Main Rd in the centre of town, is at its most bustling and colourful on Saturday, when it expands into an enclosure further down Main Rd, and stands spilling over with fresh betel nut, banana flowers and *dju* (rice beer) crowd for space. For the best views, head out towards the *ASTC* bus stand.

Within easy reach of Haflong, **Jatinga** lies 9km south on the road to Silchar. Legend says that birds commit suicide in this beautiful spot – the more brutal truth is that on certain foggy, moonless nights in autumn, local migrant birds can become disorientated while flying up the valley over the saddle of the hill and are attracted with lights by local people, who clobber them to death with bamboo poles and eat them. There is a **birdwatching centre** in Jatinga, where you may be able to stay if you can get permission from the District Forestry Office in Haflong. Buses to Silchar pass through, but it is more convenient to come by auto-rickshaw (around Rs50) – don't forget, however, to arrange your journey back.

HAFLONG PRACTICALITIES

Private **buses** pull in on Main Rd 100m above the market by *Hamringdi* cinema, with departures early morning and midday for Silchar (5hr), plus one overnight deparure to Guwahati (9hr). The *ASTC* bus stand, 1km further out, sees morning and noon departures to Silchar, and one daily to Nagaon (7hr). There should be a bus from *Hamringdi* cinema to connect with these. If coming by **train**, Lower Haflong is the station you want, 3km from town, with departures to Lumding – a slow but very scenic ride (3 daily; 5hr–6hr 15min), Silchar (2 daily; 6hr 30min), and Dharmanagar (1 daily; 9hr 30min) and Kumarghat (1 daily; 12hr).

The best **hotel** in town, though hardly deluxe, is the *Elite*, just above the *Hamringdi* cinema (☎03842/2708; ②), though you may be able to stay in the *Circuit House*, off Main Rd two junctions below the market (①), with permission from the District Commissioner. Other basic options include the *Joyeswary* just below *Hamringdi* cinema (☎03842/2484; ①–②), the *Eastern*, about 200m further down, below the post office (☎03842/2476; ①) and the very similar *Rahamaniya* almost opposite (☎03842/2230; ①). All have basic **restaurants**, but the best place in town to eat is the *Elite* (7am–9pm), which does non-veg curries and fish. There are no exchange facilities in Haflong.

Meghalaya

Created in 1972 from a section of Assam, **MEGHALAYA**, one of the smallest states in India, occupies the plateau and rolling hills between Assam and Bangladesh. Its people, predominantly Christian and belonging to three distinct ethnic groups (see p.886), are strikingly different from those of Assam, as is its landscape. Much of Meghalaya, "the land of the rain-clouds", is covered with lush forests, rich in orchids. These "blue hills", catch the main force of the monsoon-laden winds off the Bay of Bengal, and are among the wettest places on earth; stupendous waterfalls can be seen near the capital, **Shillong**, but the most dramatic of all plummet from the plateau to the south, around **Cherrapunjee**. The hills of Meghalaya rise to just under 2000m, which makes for a pleasant year-round climate, a welcome refuge from the steamy valleys of Assam. Teaching in Meghalayan schools is usually in English, widely spoken as a result.

Shillong

With its rolling hills and tall elegant pines, **SHILLONG** has often been called "the Scotland of the east"; the impression is first brought to mind by **Barapani**, the loch-like reservoir on its fringes. At an altitude of around 1500m, Shillong was a favourite holiday resort for the British, who built it on the site of a thousand-year-old Khasi settlement and made it the capital of Assam in 1874. Much of the original Victorian town is still evident; the large gardens around **Ward Lake** at its centre conjure up images of colonial masters longing for a home far away. However, political uncertainty throughout the northeast, and violent unrest in Meghalaya, have left Shillong all but abandoned, with its Golf Club and Polo Ground gradually falling into decay.

Away from the centre, post-colonial Shillong hasn't worn well. An acute water shortage and a general lack of planning have resulted in haphazard growth, and the surrounding hills have been subjected to severe deforestation. Migration has created intense communal pressures over the years, with the Khasi population reacting with hostility to the influx of Bengalis and other outside groups.

Arrival and information

Buses from outside the state pull in at the **Police Bazaar** area at the heart of town – if coming from Guwahati sit on the right-hand side of the bus for a view over Barapani Lake. Though neither offers much local information, the state **Tourist Information Centre** on Jail Rd opposite the *MTC* bus stand (Mon–Sat 7.30am–5pm, Sun 7.30–11am;

The telephone **area code** for Shillong is ☎0364.

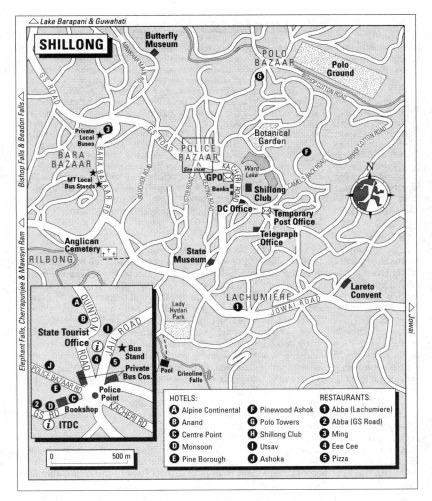

☎226220) is the place to make reservations on guided tours of Shillong, or out to Cherrapunjee (minimum 15 people), while the **Government of India Tourist Office** nearby on GS Rd (Mon–Fri 9.30am–5.30pm; ☎225632) provides a hotel booking service. The *Modern Book Depot* opposite the ITDC tourist office on GS Rd has city maps and a good selection of **books** on the northeastern region.

The **GPO** on Kacheri Rd, opposite the Shillong Club, has been at a temporary location down the road by the Deputy Commissioner's Office during rebuilding; the **telegraph office** is near the temporary GPO. You can **change** US and sterling cash and *Amex* or *Thomas Cook* travellers' cheques at the *State Bank of India* opposite the Shillong Club, Kacheri Rd, or the *Indian Overseas Bank* nearby (Mon–Fri 10am–2pm).

KHASIS, GAROS AND JAINTIAS

The most prominent of the three main hill peoples of Meghalaya, the **Khasis**, who dominate the centre of the state, belong to the Mon-Khmer group. Their origins go back to southern China, and they are related to the Mundas of north central India, who also erect stone monuments to their dead ancestors. Curiously, the Khasi word for "stone" is *men*, as in the ancient European words *dolmen* and *menhir*. The **Garos**, many of whom migrated to the Garo Hills of western Meghalaya from East Pakistan (now Bangladesh) in 1964, are said to have Tibetan origins; certainly, their language belongs to the Tibeto-Burman linguistic group. Until the coming of the British, they were animists who practised human sacrifice; thanks to the missionaries, Christianity is now the dominant religion among the Garos just as it is with all the other groups. The **Jaintias**, based in the Jaintia Hills in the east of the state around Jawai, have a similar ancestry to the Khasis. Meghalayans have matrilineal, exogamous clans, said to be descended from the mythical "mother of the root". Though private land can be acquired by both sexes, the property of a woman is inherited by her daughter, while that of a man is inherited by his mother's family. Children take their mothers' names.

The Town

Life in Shillong revolves around the decorative, serpentine **Ward Lake**, set in poorly maintained gardens. In the exclusive European Ward next to it, the large bungalows set in generous pine-shadowed gardens include Government House, the official residence of the governor. The atmosphere here is seemingly unaffected by the chaos around **Police Bazaar**, where emporia of the various northeastern states sell cane furniture, handicrafts, shawls and textiles. Here you'll see Khasi women wearing the toga-like *jainsem*, often in checked patterns including gingham and tartan, and Khasi men smoking rough chiselled pipes, which resemble home-made briars. **Bara Bazaar** further west, is even more hectic, attracting locals and tribals from the hills to its warren of stalls and shops. Primarily, it is a produce and provisions market, but you may come across interesting jewellery and handicrafts. Bara Bazaar is the scene of Meghalaya's oldest and most important market, **Iewdah**, held every eight days, when it will be at its most active, although there are stalls and shops open every day.

Meghalaya's **State Museum**, Lachumiere, near Ward Lake, has exhibits depicting tribal customs, and a weaker collection of ancient sculptures from elsewhere in India (Mon–Sat, summer 10am–4.30pm, winter 10am–4pm, closed the 2nd & 4th Sat of the month; free). More unusual is the tiny **Butterfly Museum**, based in the home of Mr Wankhar, in the Riatsamthiah area, which holds an extensive collection of rare butterflies and moths (Mon–Fri 10am–4pm, Sat 10.30am–1pm; Rs5; ☎0364/223411). Since 1939, Mr Wankhar has run a breeding farm in the Khasi Hills to the south, shipping eggs and cocoons all over the world.

Although Shillong's **Botanical Gardens**, below the lake, across a viaduct, are not really worth a visit, **Lady Hydari Park**, about 1km away (daily 8.15am–4pm; Rs2, camera Rs10, video Rs1000), is an attractive ornamental park, modelled on a Japanese garden. A small forestry museum, a mini zoo and a deer enclosure are tucked away among the pines. The garden at the **Crinoline Falls** nearby holds bonsai and orchids and there is also a swimming pool (summer daily 9am–5pm; Rs5). The actual flow of water at the falls, however, is unreliable; dependable alternatives include **Beadon Falls** and **Bishop Falls**, off the Guwahati road at **Mawprem**, 3km north, and **Elephant Falls**, set amid fern-covered rocks 12km south, which have been turned into a picnic site, with walkways leading down to the lowest pool. Both are accessible by taxi. Lovers of old churchyards will want to seek out the **Anglican cemetery** in Rilbong, with gravestones dating back to the last century, including several soldiers killed in the Lushai campaign in Mizoram.

THE ARCHERY STAKES

Shillong's unique **Archery Stakes** started out as a genuine competition, which became such a focus of illegal gambling that the Stakes were eventually legalized by the state, in order to levy taxes on winnings. On most days of the year, two of the many clubs in the *Khasi Archers' Association* repeatedly shoot a set amount of arrows in four-minute bursts at a cylindrical bamboo target in a corner of the Polo Ground. The object of the game is to predict the last two digits of the number of arrows that stick – a matter of luck not judgement. The results of each competition are relayed throughout Shillong. If you expect a colourful pageant, you may be disappointed; the whole affair is geared specifically towards gambling, and the actual shooting of arrows is over relatively quickly. The archers squat in a semicircle; as the day progresses, most of them tend to become a little inebriated from imbibing *kakiad*, the local rice wine, in the bookmakers' and refreshment stalls.

Accommodation

Shillong has a healthy range of **accommodation,** with traditional old hotels clustered near and around Ward Lake, newer ones springing up in the congested Police Bazaar area, and a number of basic options along Quinton Road, behind Police Bazaar. The owner of the *Eee Cee* restaurant plans to open a **campground** on Lake Barapani, 1km off the Guwahati–Shillong Road at the at the northern end of the lake – enquire at the *Eee Cee* for further details.

Alpine Continental, Quinton Rd (☎220991; fax 220996). Comfortable 3-star with room service, restaurant and bar, and hot running water. ⑤–⑦.

Anand, Quinton Rd (☎223466). Simple, clean vegetarian hotel with basic restaurant and shared bathrooms (hot water 7.30–9.30pm daily). ①.

Ashoka, Police Bazaar (☎223690). Basic but cheap with shared bathrooms. ①.

Centre Point, Police Bazaar (☎225210; fax 224647). Plush hotel in the heart of town; all mod cons and a good range of facilities, including a nice restaurant. ⑥–⑦.

Monsoon, GS Rd, opposite the ITDC office (☎227106). Simple hotel with attached bathrooms and solar-heated water. ③.

Pine Borough, in the middle of Police Bazaar (☎227523). Adequate rooms with attached baths, restaurant and bar, and a good tour and travel service. ④.

Pinewood Ashok, Rita Rd, European Ward (☎223116; fax 224176). Grand old hotel, straight out of the Raj, built in 1917 for British tea planters. Dotted around the landscaped grounds are cottages with Burma teak panels, carpeted wooden floors and fireplaces. The hotel arranges golfing facilities at nearby *Shillong Golf Club*, and has a billiards and snooker room. ⑥–⑦.

Polo Towers, Polo Rd (☎222341 or 2; fax 220090). Modern hotel with comfortable rooms. ⑥–⑦.

Shillong Club, Kacheri Rd (☎226938; fax 221840). One of India's famous old clubs, offering temporary membership along with accommodation in its residential quarters. ⑤.

Utsav, Jail Rd, opposite *MTC* interstate bus stand (☎226715). Homely place with cosy rooms. ③–④.

Eating

Eating places in **Police Bazaar** include a popular south Indian cafe at Centre Point; **Bara Bazaar** too has a few simple restaurants and cafes. Otherwise, the obvious place to eat is in your hotel. The more adventurous might want to seek out the tiny unnamed shack on Mawkhar Main Rd (Mon–Sat 8am–7pm) known among local cognoscenti for its excellent home-style Khasi cooking.

Abba, Main Rd, Malki Point, Lachumiere. The best Chinese restaurant in Shillong, with another, more central, branch on GS Rd. Both open Mon–Sat 11am–7pm.

Eee Cee, Jail Rd. Good Chinese and non-veg Indian food, and great sweets. Open 8am–7.30pm.

La Galarie, *Hotel Centre Point*, Police Bazaar. One of Shillong's plushest restaurants serving fine Indian and Chinese food. Good chicken in oyster sauce and wun tun soup. Open 11.30am–9.30pm (till 10pm Sat & Sun).

Ming Restaurant, Bara Bazaar. No-nonsense Chinese and Tibetan grub. Open 9.30am–7.30pm.
Pizza, Jail Rd, opposite *Eee Cee*. Indian snacks, passable pizzas and burgers – in principle to take away, but there is space to sit and eat. Open noon–8pm.

MOVING ON FROM SHILLONG

Buses from the *MTC* depot in Jail Rd run hourly or half-hourly, depending on demand, to Guwahati (last bus 5pm; 3hr), with buses to Silchar (2 daily; 9hr) and Tura (2 daily; 12hr). There are also departures to Aizawl (2 weekly; 18hr) and Agartala (5 weekly; 22hr). Private firms such as *Blue Hill*, *Network* and *Assam Valley* are up the road by the police point in Police Bazaar, offering regular services to these destinations as well as Dimapur (13hr), Kohima (17hr) and Imphal (24hr). *Nagaland State Transport* run a daily bus to Dimapur from Nagaland House on Nongrim Hill southeast of town. *MTC* also run buses from a stand in Bara Bazaar, serving Cherrapunjee (2 daily; 2hr), Mawsynram (2 daily; 3hr) and Jowai (2 daily; 1hr 30min); private buses to the same destinations leave 100m north of here.

There are no passenger **flights** out of Meghalaya's Umroi airport, but bookings on most airlines can be made through *Sheba Travels*, Police Bazaar Point (☎23015). The border crossing to **Bangladesh** at Dawki, southeast of Cherrapunjee, is served by private buses from Bara Bazaar. The nearest places to get a visa are Calcutta and Agartala.

Cherrapunjee and around

The important market town of **CHERRAPUNJEE**, 56km south of Shillong, was considered until recently to be the wettest place in the world. The greatest amount of rainfall ever recorded in a single day fell here in 1876 – an unbelievable 104cm in 24 hours. Cherrapunjee has now lost its crown to nearby Mawsynram, but impressive waterfalls south of the town still plunge down the high escarpments on the edge of the plateau. Deep wooded ravines amid the lush rain-fed vegetation conceal a network of large caves. Once the administrative centre of the Khasis, the bustling market of **Cherra Bazaar** (market day is on the eight-day cycle, four days after Iewdah) is famous for its honey and tribal jewellery.

A popular day trip, Cherrapunjee is easily accessible from Shillong by bus (2 *MTC* buses daily from Bara Bazaar, plus several private buses; 2hr) or shared taxi (from Jail Rd, generally mornings only, especially market day); *Meghalaya Tourism* and a number of hotels organize tours. The only **place to stay** is the *Circuit House* (①) – apply to the Deputy Commissioner's office in Kacheri Rd, Shillong, near the Shillong Club.

Mawsynram and Jakrem

MAWSYNRAM, the town which has usurped Cherrapunjee's title of "world's wettest place", is just 12km away as the crow flies, but there is no direct transport between the two – you will have to come back at least as far as Upper Shillong. Buses from Shillong leave from Bara Bazaar (2 *MTC* plus several private buses daily; 3hr); ask to be dropped off at the turnoff to the town, which is 2km off the road. Mawsynram's main attraction is **Mawjinbuin Cave**, where a stalagmite in the form of a *shivalingam* receives regular drips of water from a rock shaped like a breast. The only place to **stay** in Mawsynram is the *Inspection Bungalow* (①) – seek permission from the Deputy Commissioner's Office in Shillong. **JAKREM**, 21km off the main road 44km out of Shillong, has hot sulphur springs, but is not as yet served by public transport.

Elsewhere in Meghalaya

Siju in the Garo Hills in the west of Meghalaya is home to the state's most spectacular limestone caves, accessible by public transport only from Tura, which is itself best reached from Guwahati (there are two daily *MTC* buses to Tura from Jail Rd in Shillong, but they travel via Guwahati in any case). The **Jaintia Hills** in the east of the state are more easily accessible, with buses from Shillong's Bara Bazaar (2 *MTC* plus several private buses daily; 1hr 30min) to **Jowai**, the main town of the region, whose market is held on the same day as Cherrapunjee's. Some 24km north of here, and best reached by taxi, **Nartiang** is the former capital of the Jaintia kings, full of huge and ancient monoliths, the tallest of them 8m high. It also boasts a fifteenth-century Durga temple, and remains of the Jaintia Kings' palace.

Tripura

Tucked away in a corner of the northeast, surrounded by Bangladesh on three sides, the wooded hills and lowlands of **TRIPURA** have long served as a meeting place for a huge assortment of peoples and races. Over the last few centuries, however, its closest ties have been with Bengal. If the northeast has a very different feel from the rest of India, then Tripura in turn has a very different feel from the rest of the northeastern states. The majority of its people are Bengali, largely as a result of events in the last fifty years, though the Partition of India and the subsequent creation of Bangladesh have left it somewhat cut off from the heartland of Bengali culture. Nonetheless, away from the tribal areas, Tripura seems more akin to the Indian plains than to Assam and other neighbouring states.

The **history** of the kingdom of Tripura, and its Manikya rulers, who claimed descent from far-off Rajput *kshatryas*, is presented in a curious Bengali poem of uncertain age, the *Rajmala*. Udai Manikya (1585–96), who founded the city of **Udaipur** on the site of the old capital of Rangamati, adorned it with beautiful tanks, buildings and temples. The **Tripura Sundari temple** here is one of India's most important *shaktipiths*, or centres of female power. After staving off the Muslim rulers of Bengal, the Manikyas finally submitted to the Moghuls, but continued to rule over their states until they were eventually swallowed into British India. Maharaja Birchandra Manikya, who came to the throne in 1870 and was heavily influenced both culturally and spiritually by Bengal – and by his close relationship with Rabindranath Tagore, the Bengali poet, author and painter – established Bengali as the language of the court. Since Independence, migrations of Hindus from Bangladesh have put Bengalis in a majority of about four to one over "tribals" in Tripura. The largest tribe are the Tripuris, living mostly in the west, with sizeable numbers of Jamatias in the south and Reangs in the north.

TROUBLE IN TRIPURA

Although Tripura is now routinely open to tourism, **insurgency** continues in many areas. For this reason buses from Silchar to Agartala currently travel in convoy with a military escort from Kumarghat as far as Teliamura. You are not likely to meet any trouble in most places of tourist interest, but you should always keep your ear to the ground and take advice from local people, especially if you plan to visit the more obscure parts of the state.

The insurgent groups, primarily the **NLFT** (National Liberation Front of Tripura), the **ATTF** (All Tripura Tiger Force) and the **TRA** (Tripura Resurrection Army), are fighting for tribal autonomy or even independence and expulsion of Bengalis, but some claim they are not all they seem; allegedly, political parties encourage guerrilla activities in the run-up to elections, promising rewards in return for "surrender" if they take power. Certainly, state elections are often followed by mass surrenders of militants, who then get jobs and money.

Tripura's forests were once famed for their **elephants**, praised by the Moghul chronicler Abu Fazal in his *Ain-e-Akbari*. Sadly, due to the widespread and uncontrolled practice of slash and burn agriculture, and general pressure on the land, wildlife has come under severe threat. A handful of sanctuaries such as **Gumti**, **Rowa**, **Trishna**, and **Sepahijala** strive, largely in vain, to protect the few forests that remain.

Along the roadside you will see a large number of quite graphic clay sculptures of **Kali**, Bengal's favourite goddess; these are made by households for their monthly *puja*. The other thing you will see often is the hammer and sickle; Tripura is a **Communist** state, regained by the CPI(M) in 1993 after its loss to Congress five years earlier. One thing you will *not* see is bars: **alcohol** is allowed, but must be consumed in private (which includes clubs, but not hotels). **English** is not widely spoken, although it is used for many roadsigns ("Better Mr Late than the late Mr" and the like).

Agartala

AGARTALA, the capital of Tripura, is a laid back administrative centre very reminiscent of towns in Bangladesh, just 2km away. Its main monument of interest is the gleaming white **Ujjayanta Palace**, completed in 1901. Set amid formal gardens and artificial lakes, this huge building, whose main block now houses the State Legislative Assembly, covers an area of around 800 acres. One of the many temples located within its grounds, the **Jaganath** temple, an orange tower rising from an octagonal plinth, is open to the public. Other temples of interest include **Umamaheswar** temple directly opposite Jaganath across the Palace gardens, and the Buddhist **Venuban Vihar** (7–11am & 4–7pm), 1km north on Airport Rd. The rather unusual **Gedu Mian Mosque** near the Motor Stand is encrusted with a mosaic of crockery pieces.

Most of Agartala's amenities, bazaars, bus stands and civil administration are concentrated in the centre, immediately south of the palace. Although the **markets** are hectic, almost all sell provisions and supplies rather than interesting artefacts. At Post Office Chowmuhani (*chowmuhani*, used in many addresses, means "crossing" or "four roads"), the **State Museum** displays interesting ethnographical and archeological exhibits (Mon–Sat 10am–5pm; free). One gallery is devoted to the excavations at Unakoti in the forests of northern Tripura (see p.893).

Arrival, information and transport

Arriving by bus, you will probably be dropped off either at the office of one of the private companies, mostly on Laxmi Narayan Bari Road (LN Bari Rd for short), or at the state bus depot at Krishna Nagar on Durga Bari Rd, a continuation of LN Bari Rd, 1km or so to the west. From the airport, there are buses and taxis to the Motor Stand 100m south of LN Bari Rd.

The local **tourist office** (Mon–Sat 10am–5pm, Sun 3–5pm; ☎225930) is in a wing of the palace – in theory it's the only part of the palace open to the public, but they may be able to get you a visitor's pass for the main part if you're interested. They also organize tours and arrange transport for sightseeing. The main **bank** is the *State Bank of India* on HGB Rd, Melarmath, Bartala, and the **post office** (Mon–Sat 7am–6pm) is at Post Office Chowmuhani nearby, with the **telegraph office** (daily 7am–8.30pm) in LN Bari Rd, just west of the main gate to the Palace. The **Bangladeshi Visa Office** off Airport Rd, 1km out of town (down a lane on the right around 200m after Venuban Vihar Buddhist temple; Mon–Fri 8.30am–1pm & 2.30–4.30pm; ☎224807) can issue visas the same day, but first you'll have to deposit the fee, which varies according to your

The telephone **area code** for Agartala is ☎0381.

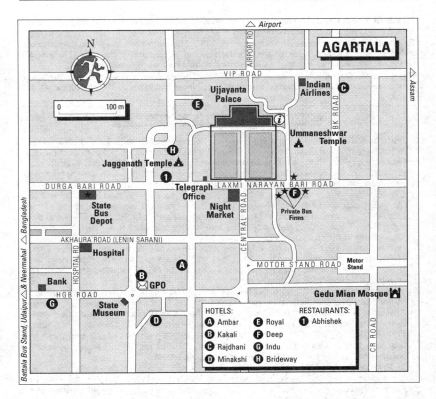

nationality, in their account at the *State Bank of India*; you will also need two passport photos.

Cycle rickshaws and auto-rickshaws are plentiful. For longer journeys, jeeps can be chartered at the Motor Stand.

Accommodation and eating

Agartala has a small but good selection of **hotels** – nothing fancy, but something for everyone. All places listed provide mosquito nets. Choice of **eating places** is more limited: your hotel is the obvious place. Otherwise, apart from cheap *dhabas*, you could try the *Abhishek* in Durgabari Rd (10am–9pm), which offers indoor or outdoor tables, with separate veg and non-veg dining rooms.

Ambar, SD Barman Sarani (☎223587). Near all amenities, with reasonably priced a/c rooms, and a restaurant serving basic, filling non-veg meals (7am–9pm). ③–④.

Brideway, JB Rd, near the west side of the palace (☎227523). Clean rooms, some a/c, with large bathrooms attached. ②–⑤.

Deep Guest House, LN Bari Rd (☎227482). A small place, clean, comfortable and friendly, with carpets and attached bathrooms, though the single rooms lack windows. ③.

Indu Guest House, 69 HGB Rd (no phone). Simple but clean with no frills. ①.

Kakali, PO Chowmuhani, Mantri Bari Rd (☎223234). Close to the museum, and the post office; prettily decorated on the outside with a moth and flowers. ③.

Minakshi, Khosh Bagan, Hawkers' Corner Rd (☎223430). In a quiet spot, but handy for the bazaar area. A good range, from budget cubby holes to a/c rooms. ①–④.

Rajdhani, BK Rd, near *Indian Airlines* office (☎223387). Mid-range hotel, away from the market but within walking distance of the palace. Comfortable but without much character. The *Panchali* restaurant, which serves Indian and Chinese food, should be booked in advance. ③–⑤.

Royal Guest House, Palace Compound (☎225652). Tucked down a side street near the palace. Roomy and comfortable, with a good restaurant for Chinese and Indian food (8am–10pm). ④–⑤.

MOVING ON FROM AGARTALA

State buses leave from Kadam Tuli depot, on the corner of Hospital Rd and LN Bari Rd in Kishangarh, with departures to Shillong (5 weekly; 22hr), four of which continue to Guwahati (25hr). There are also departures for Silchar (2 daily; 12hr) and Kailashahar (2 daily; 7hr). For most of these destinations, however, it makes more sense to take the more comfortable and more frequent **private buses** operated by firms such as *Network*, *Capital*, *Green Valley* and *Assam Valley*, mostly to be found on LN Bari Rd, 100m east of the palace entrance. Buses heading northeast from Agartala have to travel in one of the twice-daily army-escorted convoys from Teliamura to Kumarghat, so they all leave at the same times (around 6am and 4pm). That also applies to private buses for Kailashahar which leave in the morning from the Motor Stand. Kumarghat (7hr) is also the nearest railhead to Agartala (see North Tripura; p.893). Buses to Udaipur (every 15min; 2hr), Melaghar (for Neermahal; every 30min; 2hr) and Kamala Sagar (5 daily; 1hr) run from Battala bus stand at the western end of HGB Rd, as do shared jeeps – faster but more cramped – for the same destinations.

Agartala's **airport**, 12km north of the centre, can be reached by bus or taxi from the Motor Stand, by bus from the beginning of Airport Rd, or by auto-rickshaw. *Indian Airlines* (VIP Rd, just west of BK Rd; ☎224570) have daily flights – two on some days – to Calcutta (50min), and two a week to Guwahati (40min) while *Modiluft* (c/o *Travel Plus*, 28 Akhaura Rd; ☎222125) have flights five times a week to Calcutta and three to Guwahat, and *Sahara India* (c/o *Sagar Travels*, LN Bari Rd, 100m east of the palace entrance, ☎222013) are about to introduce a Calcutta service.

To **cross the border into Bangladesh**, walk or take a rickshaw to the checkpoint a couple of kilometres down Akhaura Rd. Rickshaws on the Bangladeshi side can take you to Akahura Junction station, 4km away, from where there are trains to Comilla, Sylhet and Dhaka. There are seven official border crossings in Tripura, but this is the most convenient.

Around Agartala

Five kilometres east of the modern town, **Old Agartala**, or Puran Haveli, the previous capital of Tripura, holds the unusual **Chaturdas Devata** or "fourteen deities" temple. This otherwise unassuming temple's tribal roots are revealed in July every year, when the festival of Karchi Puja draws people from all over the region. It is best reached by auto-rickshaw, although buses and jeeps from the Motor Stand can take you to Khayerpur, from where it's a short walk.

On the border with Bangladesh, 27km south of Agartala, the large lake of **Kamala Sagar** is overlooked by a small but important Kali Temple. Its twelfth-century sandstone image of Mahisa-Mardini, a form of Durga, has a *shivalingam* in front of it. A single bus shuttles from Battala bus stand in Agartala to the lake (5 daily; 1hr).

Some 30km south of Agartala, **Sipahijala** is a small reserve with a lake, zoo and botanical gardens. Permission to **stay** at the *Forest Bungalow* (①) should be sought in person at the Forestry Office in Agartala (2km up Airport Rd, then off on the left, ☎0381/222224). Regular buses run to Udaipur, Melaghar (for Neermahal) and Agartala, taking about an hour to each.

Udaipur

The former capital of the Manikyas, **UDAIPUR** retains an atmosphere of antiquity not found in the metropolis of Agartala 52km north. Now an important market town, with even a **tourist office** (☎0381/22432), it nestles among paddy fields and low forested hills. On the southwest bank of the artificial lake **Jaganath Dighi**, the dome and vaulted roof of the ruined **Jaganath** temple reflect its strong Muslim influence, while the seventeenth-century **Moghul Masjid** shows that Udaipur was the very furthest outpost of the Moghul empire.

Otherwise known as **Matabari** or "mother's [Kali's] house", **Tripura Sundari**, the most important temple in the area, stands 5km outside Udaipur, on a small hillock in front of a holy lake which is teeming with carp. Built in typical Bengali-hut style with a square sanctum and large meeting hall in front, this is one of the 51 *pithasthan* sacred to the Tantras, and celebrates the spot where a leg of the disintegrating Shakti is supposed to have fallen. It is appropriately painted blood red.

Although most people visit Udaipur on a day trip from Agartala, you can **stay** at the *Pantha Niwas Tourist Lodge* (no phone; ➀); book through the tourist office here or in Agartala. Regular **buses** run to Agartala's Battala bus stand (every 15min; 2hr) and Melaghar (for Neermahal; every 30min; 30min). There are also frequent shared jeeps.

Neermahal

One of India's most picturesque spots, the fairy-tale water palace of **NEERMAHAL**, 55km south of Agartala, was built early in the twentieth century onto **Rudrasagar Lake**. Inspired by Moghul architecture, its bridges, moats, towers and pavilions stretch over the lake in prolific confusion. The lake is 1km from the town of **Melaghar**, which is connected by half-hourly buses and frequent shared jeeps to Agartala's Battala bus stand (2hr) and to Udaipur (30min).

Neermahal makes an easy day-trip from Agartala, either on its own or combined with Udaipur, but should you want to stay, the *Sagarmahal Tourist Lodge* (no phone; ➀) at the lakeside can be booked through the tourist office in Agartala. The rooms are pleasant if a bit shabby – some of them have great views of the palace across the lake – and there's a dorm. Food is available for guests. Directly opposite the *Tourist Lodge*, a small **restaurant** run by the local fishermen's co-op serves basic, good food (9.30am–4.30pm). Here you can rent boats to cross the lake to the palace (motorboats Rs125 per hour for up to 12 people; punts Rs50 per ninety minutes for up to eight people), a very pleasant journey among lily-pads, dragonflies, ducks and cormorants. The palace itself (daily 9am–4pm; Rs2) is rather derelict on the inside, but the tourist department have recently taken it over, done up the outside, restored the gardens and installed floodlighting, with complete renovation scheduled for the near future.

North Tripura

In the northeastern corner of Tripura, 20km from Dharmanagar and 180km from Agartala, **UNAKOTI** is one of the most intriguing archeological sites in the northeast. The site consists of several gigantic rock-cut images scattered across a hillside, so vast that they remain relatively unscarred after a thousand years or more of neglect. Most of the images are as yet unexplained; this is considered to be an eighth-century Shaivite site, and certainly Shiva, Durga and Vishnu, as well as a particularly enormous Ganesh, can be discerned, but there is also strong evidence of Buddhist occupation.

The nearest accommodation is at **Kailashahar**, the District Headquarters for North Tripura, 10km away. Neither the *Forest Rest House* (➀) and *Dak Bungalow* (➀) is really designed for tourists, and you'll need to seek permission from the local Forestry Office (☎03824/22224) for the former, and the local Deputy Commissioner's Office for the latter. Kailashahar is connected by bus to Agartala (2 daily; 7hr) and to the nearest railhead at **Dharmanagar** (7 daily; 1hr 30min). From there, a tortuously slow night train runs to Lumding (17hr) via Karimganj (4hr 40min) and Haflong (11hr), with one in the afternoon for Silchar (6hr 15min). Taking an afternoon bus from Agartala (7hr), you can also pick up the Lumding train where it starts at **Kumarghat**.

Mizoram

As you head south from the Assam Valley into the hills of **MIZORAM**, "the Land of the Highlanders", the change is instantaneous – from green paddy fields and tea estates to forests and bamboo-covered hills. Despite the difficult terrain, Mizoram is a gentle pastoral land, and the **Mizos** a friendly and welcoming people. Whitewashed Christian churches dot the landscape, making the region feel more like Central America than a state squeezed between Burma (Myanmar) and the Chittagong Hill Tracts of Bangladesh.

Even as late as the end of the last century, the Mizos, who had migrated to the area in the eighteenth century from the Chin Hills in Burma, were regularly raiding tea plantations in the Assam Valley; only in 1924 did the British administration finally manage to bring about some semblance of control. They opened the doors of what were then the **Lushai Hills** to missionaries, who were so successful that now just a handful of animists remain, along with pockets of Buddhists in the west. Mizoram became a state in 1986, after a violent twenty-year struggle to secede from India altogether (see below).

Mizoram is now one of the most peaceful states in the country, with an optimism epitomized by **Aizawl**, its busy and cosmopolitan capital. Here in the heart of the state, traditional Mizo communities occupy the crests of a series of ridges, each village still dominated by its chief's house and *zawlbuk*, or bachelors' dormitory. An egalitarian people, without sex and class distinction, the Mizos remain justifiably proud of their age-old custom of *Tlawmgaihna*, a code of ethics which governs hospitality. Among surviving traditions are the **Cheraw**, "bamboo dance", performed for mothers who die in childbirth to welcome them to *Pialral*, the realm of the dead, and the weaving of local costumes such as the *puan*, characterized by white, black and red stripes.

THE INSURGENCY THAT ENDED

Mizoram's two main species of bamboo flower every fifty years (one 18 years after the other), attracting hordes of rats and boosting their fertility rate fourfold. The rats devour crops in the fields, leaving famine in their wake. The first time this happened after Independence, in 1959, unpreparedness and apparent callousness on the part of Delhi and Assam led **Laldenga**, a clerk on the District Council, to found the **Mizo Famine Front** (MFF). Set up at first simply to fight the famine, it gradually transformed into the **Mizo National Front** (MNF), a guerrilla group fighting for secession. The government's heavy-handed response in 1967, rounding up Mizos from their homes into guarded villages under curfew, not only boosted support for the MNF, but also wiped out the traditional Mizo way of life at a stroke. Bangladeshi independence was a bitter blow to the MNF, who relied on Pakistani support, and moderates on both sides eventually brought them to the negotiating table, where statehood was granted in 1986 in return for an end to the insurgency. Laldenga became chief minister of the new state, but his administration proved rather a damp squib, and he lost to Congress in the following elections. The MNF have been in peaceful opposition ever since. A few diehards tried to continue the armed struggle, but without their leader, and with no popular support, they did not last for long. For the last few years, Mizoram has been at peace.

> The telephone **area code** for the entire state of Mizoram is ☎0389.

The Mizo villages now look down on hillsides that are all but denuded of trees by the effects of *jhum* (slash and burn agriculture), and planted instead with large tracts of bamboo. Most of the untouched forests lie further south and east. Apart from Aizawl itself, the most likely destination to benefit if tourism opens up further is the **Blue Mountain National Park** near **Phawngpui**, close to the southern border with Burma and rich in orchids and butterflies.

Aizawl

One of India's remotest state capitals, the picturesque and pleasant town of **AIZAWL** perches precariously on the steep slopes of a sharp ridge, straddling the watershed between the Tlawng and the Tuirial river valleys and given a comfortable year-round climate by its altitude of 1100m. Although it may lack a snowy Himalayan backdrop, it has something of the feel of a Himalayan hill station, though without the tourists and largely without the infrastructure to cope with visitors. There's little to see, but the markets are interesting, and you can easily walk out to the very rural surroundings.

The road from the north makes a dramatic entrance through a deep cleft in the rocky ridge, emerging from the shadows, to provide a first glimpse of Aizawl. A huge white cross stands guard at the entrance of the pass.

Arrival, information and transport

Virtually all visitors to Aizawl arrive by **bus** from **Silchar**, 180km north in Assam. Most Aizawl to Silchar services run overnight, except for *Mizoram State Transport*'s two basic (and heavily over-subscribed) morning buses. Allow plenty of time to book tickets at *MST*'s chaotic office, near the GPO and below Zodin Square, where you can also arrange **rail** tickets for use on the network in Assam; the nearest major junction is at Lumding, a further 180km north of Silchar. Companies operating deluxe buses to and from Silchar, as well as Shillong and Guwahati, include *Capital Travels* and *Barak Travels*, both based at the other end of town in **Zarkawt**.

Of the minibuses that run between central Aizawl and the suburbs, the most useful head from the top of town near the GPO and Zodin Square to Chandmari in the north – a tiring two-kilometre walk.

The friendly and hospitable staff of the Mizoram government's **Directorate of Tourism**, Chandmari (Mon–Fri 9am–5pm; ☎21227), provide advice, information and transport, and can book tourist lodges throughout Mizoram – including the one here in Aizawl. The landmark **post office** is on Treasury Square, near the main branch of the *State Bank of India*, which handles foreign exchange.

The Town

Thanks to its precipitous setting, much of Aizawl does not see the sun for significant parts of the day, and the new multi-storey concrete edifices clinging to the hillsides add to the overall greyness. The only relief from its monotonous sprawl is the Assam Rifles sports ground at the top of town. **Chaltlang Hill**, high above Chandmari in the north, with an approach road rising on stilts, provides an excellent overall viewpoint.

Busy central markets include **Bara Bazaar**, which ranges from recordings of Mizo music to Chinese cobblers which still make shoes to measure. Further up the hill, Solomon's Cave in **Zodin Square** is an indoor market selling fabrics, garments and music; traditional stuff is notably absent. The *District Industries Centre* in Upper Bazaar stocks local handicrafts such as shawls and bags. The **Mizoram State Museum**, in an unsuitable building on MacDonald Hill (Tues–Fri 10am–4pm, Mon noon–4pm; free), has a small but interesting collection of Mizo costumes and implements. Staff are only too happy to guide you around.

Accommodation and eating

Several **hotels** in Aizawl are geared towards low- and mid-budget travellers, and its simple cafes, especially around Bara Bazaar, serve **Mizo food**. Lentils, fish, rice and bamboo shoots are popular; the mild dishes can be a welcome change from most north Indian cooking.

Ahimsa, Zarkawt (☎21133). One of Aizawl's better hotels. Very central, with a popular restaurant serving a good multi-cuisine range. ④.

Chawlhna, Zarkawt (☎22292). Budget hotel. Dingy, but with a busy canteen-like restaurant. ①.

Embassy, Chandmari (☎22570). Competitively priced and conveniently situated at the northern end of town, near the tourist office. Boasts one of Aizawl's best multi-cuisine restaurants. ③.

State Guest House, Bawngkawn (☎20131 or 2). Formerly Aizawl's most prestigious hotel, with all mod cons and a restaurant with a good reputation for Indian and Chinese cooking. ④.

Raji International, Treasury Square (☎22532). Good value and convenient location. ②–③.

Ritz, Bara Bazaar (☎23131). Friendly, comfortable, and popular with business travellers. Shared baths, and mid-range suites. Well-furnished, recommended, multi-cuisine restaurant. ②.

Tourist Lodge, Chaltlang (☎21083). Beautifully situated, perched on a sharp hill with a terrace providing dramatic views. Large comfortable rooms and a restaurant serving Mizo food with prior notice. The long steep walk from the centre can be an effort, but you can always get a taxi. ③.

Around Aizawl: Luangmual

The **Durtlang Hills** constitute a natural barrier immediately south of Aizawl, their high ridges punctuated by Mizo villages and Christian missions, and provide pleasant rambling country. In **LUANGMUAL**, dramatically poised on a high spur 7km west of Aizawl, the *Luangmual Handicrafts Centre* is a low-key institution that sets out to revive Mizoram's ailing indigenous crafts. Workers weave traditional water-resistant *khumbeu* hats – very reminiscent of straw baseball hats – out of *h'manthial* leaves.

Luangmual has a basic *Youth Hostel* (☎32263; ①) and a large, modern, and often deserted *Tourist Lodge* (②), bookable through the tourist office in Aizawl.

Manipur

The state of **MANIPUR**, stretching along the border with Burma (Myanmar), centres on a vast lowland area watered by the lake system south of its capital **Imphal**. This almost forgotten region is home to the **Meitheis**, who have created in isolation their own fascinating version of Hinduism. Though the area around Imphal is now all but devoid of trees, the outlying hills are still forested, and shelter such exotic birds and animals as the spotted linshang, Blyths tragopan, the curiously named Mrs Hume's barbacked pheasant, slow loris, Burmese pea-fowl and the beautifully marked clouded leopard, as well as numerous unclassified varieties of orchids. Probably its most unusual natural habitat is the floating mass of vegetation on **Loktak Lake**, south of Imphal, inhabited by the unique *sangai* deer.

Manipur's **history** can be traced back to the foundation of Imphal in the first century AD. Despite periodic invasions from Burma, it has also had long periods of independent and stable government. Manipur was first incorporated into India at the end of the Indo-Burmese war in 1826, but only came under British rule in 1891 as a result of the Battle of Kangla. During World War II, most of Manipur was occupied by the Japanese, who used it as a base from which to strike towards the Assam Valley. Having been part of Assam, and later a Union Territory, Manipur became a fully fledged Indian state within the union in 1972. Since then it has been subjected to waves of violent unrest, initially as a result of self-rule campaigns and more recently through a brutal war between Kukis and Nagas; inter-communal hostilities came to a head in 1993, when several villages were destroyed and many innocent people brutally slaughtered. Since then, **disturbances** have been on the increase, with curfews in force in Imphal and elsewhere; at the time of writing, tourists were being advised to stay away, and were not allowed to spend the night anywhere outside the capital. You are advised to check the current situation before visiting the state.

Imphal

Overlooked by a circle of distant hills, the capital of Manipur, **IMPHAL**, lies in an almost completely flat basin at an altitude of around 785m. Though devoid of dramatic monuments, it is at least given a sense of openness by its large avenues; but even the rivers and canals that run through the town are unable to give it any visual appeal. Instead, the real interest in Imphal is supplied by its people, whose handsome Meithei faces are adorned with the long and distinctive *tikki* (forehead mark) of Vishnu. Although the valley is predominantly Hindu, Imphal feels more like southeast Asia than India, and visitors tend to be confronted by a **language** barrier: most people understand neither English nor Hindi.

Arrival and information

Imphal's **airport**, 6km south of town, is connected by *Indian Airlines* to Calcutta (5 weekly; 1hr 5min), Silchar (3 weekly; 35min), and Delhi (2 weekly; 3hr 10min). *NEPC* fly daily to Guwahati (1hr 5min). The *Indian Airlines* office is on MG Rd (☎220999). However, **schedules** for flights are occasionally disrupted, so do check either in Calcutta, or once you're in Imphal.

State **buses** arrive at the stand next to the Polo Ground and private buses at their individual offices. Bus connections with **Guwahati** are good, but the 579-kilometre journey takes around twenty hours. *Manipur Golden Travels*, on MG Rd (☎221332), provides by far the best service. National Highway 39 – "The Burma Road" – links Imphal with the closest railhead at **Dimapur**, 215km away, via Kohima in Nagaland;

THE FESTIVALS AND PERFORMING ARTS OF MANIPUR

Manipuri dance, like the associated colourful traditions of Burma (Myanmar), Indonesia and Thailand, is replete with Hindu themes and influences. Considered one of India's main classical dance forms, it centres around the story of Krishna cavorting with the *gopis* (milkmaids), a theme repeated throughout northern India. Here the *gopis* are dressed in elaborate crinoline-like skirts, while the accompanying music includes energetic group drumming, with large barrel drums suspended across the shoulders. The *Jawaharlal Nehru Manipur Dance Academy*, North AOC, Imphal, Manipur's premier dance institution, arranges occasional recitals and hosts an annual dance festival.

The **martial arts** of Manipur are currently going through something of a revival with performances by men and women being choreographed for the stage. **Thang-Ta** is a dynamic form utilizing *thang*, the sword and *ta*, the spear. Fast, furious and seemingly extremely dangerous, performances take place each May during **Lai Haraoba**, a ritual dance festival held at Moirang (see p.899).

Finally, the annual **Heikru Hitongba Boat Race** is held every September as part of a celebration to commemorate the founding of the two major Vaishnavite temples of Imphal, Bijoy Govinda and Govindjee. Two teams of rowers, standing in long dugout canoes race on the Thangapat moat near the Bijoy Govinda temple.

The telephone **area code** for Imphal is ☎0385.

you need a permit for Nagaland to travel this way. The 200-kilometre bus ride to **Silchar** with *Kangleipak Tours & Travels*, MG Rd (☎222911), may look tempting, but anti-smuggling checkpoints along the way make it a nightmare of up to fourteen hours.

With prior notice, Manipur's **Directorate of Tourism**, based at *Hotel Imphal* (Mon–Sat 9.30am–5pm; ☎224603), organizes tours every Sunday of Imphal and the surrounding area, including Sendra Island on Loktak Lake. The **ITDC tourist office**, on Jail Rd, provides information only (Mon–Sat 9.30am–5.30pm; ☎221131). There's a *State Bank of India* on MG Rd, and a **post office** on Secretariat Rd.

Auto- and cycle rickshaws are the main means of **transport** within Imphal, and taxis and rental cars can be booked through hotels. Rather intimidatingly, and of no great help in bridging the language barrier, the cycle rickshaw men of Imphal wear waterproof straw caps, and wrap their faces in cloth to keep out dust and fumes.

The Town

Imphal's small and congested centre is sandwiched between the stately avenue of Kanglapat on the east and the somewhat stagnant River Nambu on the west. The town's **Polo Ground** dominates the area; according to popular legend, the Manipuri game of *Sagol Kangjei* is the original form of the modern game of polo. In one corner, the Shaheed Minar commemorates the Meithei revolt in 1891 against British occupation, while just southeast, the **Manipur State Museum** focusses on tribal costumes, jewellery and weapons along with geological, archeological and natural history displays (Mon–Fri 9.30am–4.30pm; Rs0.50).

At the heart of Imphal, the fascinating market of **Khwairamband** – also known as *Nupi Keithel* and *Ima Bazaar* or "Mothers' Market" – is run solely by Meithei women, making it one of India's largest women's markets. One of its two sections is devoted to textiles, selling shawls and fabrics including the *moirangphee*, the traditional Meithei dress. This distinctive striped skirt comes in two pieces; for a small fee, women with sewing machines will stitch them together with amazing speed. Across the road, the other half of the market sells local fish and vegetables, along with basic provisions, while smaller markets nearby include one dedicated to cane and wicker. If you prefer not to bargain, fixed-price shops include *Sangai Handloom and Handicrafts*, at GM Hall, near the clock tower, and the *Handloom House* in Paona Bazaar.

Next to the ruins of the **Old Palace**, 2km east, is **Shri Govindjee**, Manipur's preeminent Vaishnavite temple. Otherwise a disappointing mix of twentieth-century buildings, Shri Govindjee is crowned by two gold domes and has an impressive large prayer hall preceding the courtyard and main temple. Covering around 200 acres with more than a hundred species of orchids, the **Khonghampat Orchidarium**, the orchid centre of the Forest Department, lies 12km from Imphal on NH39 and is best visited in April and May when the orchids are in bloom.

Accommodation and eating

Imphal has a few simple **hotels** in the market area, and a handful of mid-range ones scattered all over town. Similarly the choice of **restaurants** is small – the best bets apart from the hotels are the *Airlines Hotel*, opposite *Indian Airlines* on MG Rd, and the *Meitei Hotel*, on Kangla Pat. There are no **bars** – this is a dry state.

Excellency, Airport Rd (☎223231). The best that Imphal has to offer with all mod cons including a popular multi-cuisine restaurant. ⑤–⑥.

ITDC Imphal, North AOC Point, Imphal Dimapur Rd (☎220459). Rather resplendent government-run hotel-cum-tourist lodge with nice large rooms, and a canteen-like restaurant. ③–④.

Pintu, North AOC, NH39 (☎222743). Away from the noise and dust of the centre, a large, clean and friendly hotel with a multi-cuisine restaurant open to non-residents. ③–④.

Thampa, North AOC, NH39 (☎221486). Cheap and simple hotel, with no restaurant but conveniently placed near small *dhabas* and the bus stands.①.

Around Imphal – Loktak Lake

South of Imphal, the huge and complex body of water known as **LOKTAK LAKE**, fed by numerous rivers and dotted with islands, is home to a unique community of fishermen who live on large rafts made of reeds. Rare and endangered dancing *sangai*, brow-antlered deer, live on the floating vegetation that covers much of the lake, sharing their habitat with other species including the hog deer. Much of the lake is taken up by the **Keibul Lamjao National Park**, 53km from Imphal, which attracts a host of waterfowl and migratory birds between November and March. A 40-room hill-top *Tourist Bungalow* on **Sendra Island**, 48km from Imphal, providing a good vantage point from which to view the wildlife, is due to open when the political situation allows. The state tourist department has in the past organized transport from Imphal.

On the more populated western shore of Loktak, 45km south of Imphal, the small town of **MOIRANG** is the traditional centre of Meithei culture, with a temple devoted to the pre-Hindu deity **Thangjing**. The Indian National Army, which fought for Independence alongside the Japanese, against the British Indian Army, during World War II, first unfurled its flag on Indian soil here at Moirang; a memorial and museum commemorates the event. Guided tours of Loktak sometimes take in Moirang, and regular buses from the private bus stand at Keishampat, near the centre of Imphal, also run here, taking around an hour.

Arunachal Pradesh

ARUNACHAL PRADESH, "the land of the dawn-lit-mountains", is one of the last unspoilt wildernesses in India, dropping eastwards from the high Himalaya near Bhutan towards Burma, with the mountains of Tibet away to the north. Scarcely any roads penetrate this vast state, formerly known as the Northeast Frontier Agency (NEFA), whose new capital, **Itanagar**, is just across the border from Assam. Entering Arunachal, the road to **Tawang** runs through rugged hills, engulfed by virgin forests, with silver ribbons of rivers far below; a complete contrast to the denuded paddy bowls of Assam, though most of the Himalayan foothills must once have looked like this.

Only very recently have foreign tourists been permitted to visit Arunachal (see p.869 for permits). This long-standing isolation is partly due to cultural considerations, and partly to political factors, as the border with the Chinese is still under dispute. The big attraction is the state's dazzling array of flora and fauna, in a habitat that combines glacial terrain, alpine meadows and sub-tropical rainforests. **Namdapha National Park**, in the northeast, is home to the rare Hoolock gibbon; other animals include the legendary snow leopard, tigers, musk deer, bears, panda and elephant, while Arunachal also abounds in bamboo and cherishes over 500 species of orchids.

Itanagar

The town of **ITANAGAR**, just under 400km northeast of Guwahati, has been developed as the capital of the state largely because of its convenient location, and holds little to interest visitors. It is built on a saddle overlooked by two hills, one occupied by the Governor's house and the other by a new Buddhist temple; new lightweight earth-quake-proof houses mingle with older traditional structures, a market and offices. Facilities are shared with its twin town, **Naharlagun**, 10km away in the Assam Valley.

THE TRIBES OF ARUNACHAL

The successive river valleys of Arunachal, separated by forbidding north–south ridges, enable distinct micro-cultures to flourish in what can be very small areas. The **Monpas**, who have a strong affinity with the Bhutanese, occupy the valleys north of Bomdila; their largest town, Dirang, with its *dzong* (fort), is just before the pass at Sela. Although they practise Buddhism, focussed around the great monastery of Tawang, they retain many of their original animist-shamanist beliefs. They are easily recognized by their dress – a *chuba* or short cloak, made of coarse wool dyed red with madder.

The **Sherdukpens** live south of the Bomdila Range, in the valleys of the Tengapani, and have close affinities with their Monpa neighbours. They wear distinctive *gurdams*, or yak's hair skullcaps, from which jut tassel-like projections that serve as guttering – this part of Arunachal sees very heavy rainfall. Traditionally Sherdukpen men wear a sword in a scabbard tucked into their waist or on a strap. Although they have a reverence for *lama*-ism, their religious beliefs are a curious blend of Buddhism and shamanism, with *jijis*, or priests, practising witchcraft to counteract malevolent spirits.

Further southeast are the **Akas**, literally "painted", who paint their faces with resin and charcoal. East of Kameng, the menfolk of the sturdy hill people known as the **Daflas** wear a distinctive wicker helmet surmounted by the red-dyed beak of a hornbill. Protruding in front of their foreheads is a bun of plaited hair called *podum*, skewered horizontally with a large brass pin. The Daflas trace their descent from Abo Teni, a mythical primeval man, as do the neighbouring **Apa Tanis**, who thanks to the work of European anthropologists are the best known of all the tribal groups. Occupying a 26-square-kilometre stretch of hanging valley in the central region of Subansiri, the Apa Tanis are experts at terraced rice cultivation. They too wear a hat and *podum* on their foreheads but do not sport the distinguishing yellow ribbon of the Daflas; both men and women tattoo their faces.

Consecrated by the Dalai Lama, the **Buddhist temple** reflects the extensive Tibetan influence in this frontier land, and provides good views of Itanagar and the surrounding countryside. An extensive ethnographic collection devoted to local tribes in the **Jawaharlal Nehru State Museum** includes wood carvings, musical instruments, textiles, handicrafts and archeological finds (Tues–Sat 9.30am–5pm; Rs1), while a workshop in the *Handicrafts Centre* specializes in traditional cane manufacture. The adjacent salesroom sells tribal handicrafts. The emerald **Gyaker Sinyi** (Ganga Lake), 6km away, is surrounded by primeval vegetation, providing a small taste of the magnificent forests of the state.

Practicalities

The nearest **airport** to Itanagar, at **Lilabari** in Assam, 67km away, and served by connecting buses, is served by *NEPC* flights to and from Guwahati (2hr 20min) and to, but not from, Dibrugarh (45min). There is also a thrice weekly *Pawan Hans* helicopter service between Itanagar and Guwahati. Fast passenger **trains** from Guwahati run as far as Harmuti, 33km away in Assam. Overnight *Blue Hill* buses connect Itanagar with Guwahati (9hr), and *Arunachal State Transport* run an extensive if basic service throughout the state, as well as to Assam and Meghalaya.

Information is available from the **Tourist Department** at Naharlagun (☎03781/44115), who also arrange transport. Unmetered taxis and shared taxis are available and cycle rickshaws are common in Naharlagun. Accommodation can be found in both Itanagar and Naharlagun. The *Donyi-Polo Ashok* (☎0360/22627; fax 22611; ⑦) is Itanagar's prime address, with a restaurant. Simple options in Ganga Market include the *Ganga* (☎0360/22294; ①) and the *Himalaya* (☎0360/22210; ①). In Naharlagun the *Hornbill* (☎0360/44419; ①–③) has a range of rooms.

West Arunachal

Hemmed in by Bhutan and Tibet, the isolated hills and valleys of western Arunachal climb to some of the remotest glaciers and peaks in the Himalayas. Besides named peaks such as Gori Chen (6858m) and Nyegi Kangsang (7047m), around twenty mountains of above 6000m remain completely unknown. Tezpur (see p.877) is the nearest major railhead and airport.

The great River **Jia Bharali**, renowned for its fish, drains the watersheds of the north, then meanders through deep forested valleys to emerge at **Tipi**, where an orchid house nurtures 500 species. **Accommodation** is available here at the *Forest Inspection Bungalow* (①; apply for permission to the Divisional Forest Officer in Bhalakpung, 3km away on the Assamese border).

Points beyond Tipi are currently closed to foreign tourists, and the one highway that winds up through the forests to Bomdila sees little traffic beyond the occasional military convoy. During the Sino-Indian War of 1962, it was the scene of heavy fighting, when the Chinese took the Indians by surprise and reached the outskirts of Tezpur. The Indian army gradually fought their way back, and the road is littered with memorials to fallen comrades. Somehow, thankfully, the forests here have survived the large military concentrations further up.

Bomdila, a peaceful unspoiled town set among apple orchards on a spur of the Thagla Ridge, marks the dividing line between the rainforests to the south and the subalpine valleys to the north. It has a couple of Buddhist monasteries, a small local museum, a tourist officer, and a couple of places to stay.

Around 180km beyond Bomdila and cut off from the rest of Arunachal by a high ridge breached by the inhospitable and dramatic Sela Pass, the great monastery of **Tawang** dominates the land of the Monpas. Perched at the end of a high ridge at over 3000m above deep valleys, the largest Buddhist monastery in India looks out onto a semicircle of snow-capped peaks that seem close enough to touch. The birthplace of the sixth Dalai Lama, Tawang was established in the seventeenth century and has a renowned collection of manuscripts and *thangkas*.

Central and East Arunachal

The picturesque hill station of **Ziro**, 150km northeast of Itanagar on the Apa Tani plateau, can be reached by bus from Itanagar or North Lakhimpur. Accommodation is available at the *Circuit House* (①) and the *Inspection Bungalow* (①). Further east, **Along** and **Pasighat**, the district headquarters respectively of West and East Siang, are best reached from North Lakhimpur, or from Dibrugarh via ferry to Oiramghat. Pasighat has a few basic hotels; in Along you can stay at the *Circuit House* (①; apply to the Deputy Commissioner; ☎037832/221). The **Dr D Ering Memorial Wildlife Sanctuary** near Pasighat is home to buffalo, tiger, hispid hare and a variety of birdlife.

In eastern Arunachal, the remote valleys of **Dibang** and **Lohit**, inhabited by tribes such as the Mishmis, descend from snow-covered passes to sub-tropical forests, where the rivers draining the east Himalaya flow into the Brahmaputra. The sacred Hindu sites of **Parasuramkund** and **Brahmakund**, on the banks of the River Lohit, are associated in myth with the birth of the River Brahmaputra.

Further south, the huge **Namdapha National Park** (Oct–April) ranges from altitudes of 200m to 4500m along the border with Burma. Its inhabitants include tigers, leopards, clouded leopards and snow leopards, as well as red pandas. The park headquarters are at **Miao**, where a *Tourist Lodge* (①) provides rental cars. Accommodation is also available at the *Forest Inspection Bungalow* (①).

Buses to and from Miao pass through **Margherita**, 64km west and **Tinsukia**, 40km further on, both connected by bus to Sibsagar and Guwahati; Tinsukia has two daily trains to Dimapur (9–10hr) and Lumding (11hr 40min–13hr 25min). **Dibrugarh**, 47km beyond Tinsukia, has flights to Guwahati and Delhi.

Nagaland

On the border with Burma (Myanmar), south of Arunachal Pradesh and east of Assam, **NAGALAND** is physically and conceptually at the very extremity of the subcontinent. Many of its hills and valleys, home to the fiercely independent Nagas, were uncharted until recently, and the eastern regions, remain far beyond the reach of the skeletal road system, despite the fact that the forested mountains rarely exceed 3000m in height. Today this remains the most politically sensitive of the Northeastern hill states, and is all but closed to foreigners.

The British administrators of Nagaland who arrived at a truce with the Nagas towards the end of the nineteenth century, agreed not to penetrate beyond certain boundaries, so their maps left numerous blank areas. Based in the Angami village of Kohima, the Deputy Commissioner occasionally toured the territories to collect taxes and administer justice and came to hold a certain authority among the various tribes. Some developed a loyalty to the British, others saw them as intruders. In 1879 the **Khonoma Angami** rebellion against Kohima was relieved through assistance by loyal Kohima Angamis who helped to smuggle a message through to British lines in the Assam Valley. When the Indian flag replaced the Union flag in 1947, it was promptly removed by Nagas, who had come to accept the British presence but did not want to join India. For many years, the Nagaland National Council (NNC) under **Angami Zapu Phizo**, and with Chinese support, fought a bitter war for independence. In 1974, a section of it broke away and, as the United Democratic Front, won election to the state government, then signed the **Shillong Accord** and laid down their arms. But the rump of the NNC fought on, splitting in 1980 when Phizo's lieutenant, Thengaling Muivah, broke away to form the National Socialist Council of Nagaland (NSCN), still fighting to this day. Armed patrols through the streets of Kohima are common, and the volatility of the border with Burma means that the state is still highly unstable.

Kohima

Although the capital of Nagaland, **KOHIMA**, 74km east of Dimapur in the Assam Valley, was built by the British in the nineteenth century, it was never a hill station, and lacks Victorian promenades, villas and public gardens. It was founded here – alongside the large Angami village known as **Kohima Village**, or in the adopted Hindusthani as **Bara Basti** (the large village) – strictly for the purposes of administration, and continues in much the same vein under a new regime. A more intimate glimpse of traditional Naga life is offered by the walk up to Bara Basti, or the short trip to **Khonoma**, 20km beyond Kohima, the Nagas' once impregnable stronghold, sacked by the British in 1879 and again by the Indian army in 1956.

Arrival, information and public transport

Kohima lies on the Dimapur–Imphal road, three or four hours by road from the railhead and airport of **Dimapur**, in the Assam valley to the west (see p.904), and six hours from Imphal in Manipur to the south. *Nagaland State Transport* **buses** from Dimapur terminate in the market area in the centre of town; *Blue Hill* "luxury" services from Guwahati (11hr) stop at their office, 2km uphill beyond the *Japfu Ashok*. Taxis and minibuses are the main forms of public transport, though the central area is small enough to explore on foot. The **Directorate of Tourism** (Mon–Fri 10am–4pm; ☎22214), is on the National Highway south, beyond the *Japfu* and below the Cathedral.

THE NAGAS

From villages perched high on the mountain ridges to either side of the valleys of Nagaland, **Naga** tribespeople survey their separate domains. Headhunters until not so long ago, the Nagas have long been feared and respected throughout the northeast, although in truth they are a warm and welcoming people. They seem originally to have lived in northeast Tibet, then moved through southwest China into Burma, Malaya and Indonesia, as well as eastern Assam. In Nagaland, they can be divided into sixteen main groups, including the **Angamis** around Kohima, the **Konyaks, Ao, Lothas, Semas** and **Wanchus**. Despite their fierce reputation, all are essentially farmers who cultivate terraced fields and tend cattle.

Traditionally, Nagas differentiated between the soul, a celestial body, and the spirit, a supernatural being, believing that the human soul resided in the nape of the neck and could only be set free by beheading, while the spiritual being, in the head, brought good fortune. Heads of enemies and fallen comrades were collected to add to those of the community's own ancestors. Some tribes decorated their faces with tattoos of swirling horns to mark success in headhunting. Trophies were hoarded in each village in the men's meeting house, or **morung**, which also served as the boys' dormitory. This large open hall was decorated with fantastic carvings of animals, elephant heads and tusks. Constructed of wood and bamboo, *morungs* were frequently destroyed by fire, along with the precious collection of heads; however, the benevolent spirits were retained by the re-creation of the lost collection in carved wood. In addition, the Naga still construct **megalithic monuments**, which line the approaches to villages, and come to personify those who erect them after death. Menhirs stand in pairs or in long double rows, to honour fame and generosity or enhance the fertility of a field. The Angamis were never ruled by chiefs; the closest equivalent is the *Tevo*, a descendant of the founder of the village and mediator between the community and the supernatural world. Each village is sub-divided into *khel*, which in the past often had independent inter-tribal policies, and who settled their own disputes by bloody fights. Relations between the sexes traditionally were conducted with great openness and equality. Few first marriages led to a permanent union, and in spite of the Christian influence divorce remains common.

Although each tribe has its own dialect, a pidgin drawn from various Naga languages, Assamese and even Nepalese, has developed into the common **Nagamese** tongue. As the Nagas have been integrated into the modern world, their traditions are under threat. In an effort to realign society along so-called civilized lines, boys are encouraged to live at home with their parents, and *morungs* are discouraged and left to fall into ruin.

The Town

Spread loosely over a saddle joining two large hills, Kohima forms a pass that played a strategic role during World War II. The highway from Imphal to Dimapur – the route along which the Japanese hoped to reach the plains of India – crosses the saddle at the foot of the **Second World War Cemetery**, which dominates the town. These immaculate gardens stand as a memorial to the Allies who died on this very spot during the three-month **Battle of Kohima**, which ended in April 1944.

Alongside the cemetery, central Kohima consists of busy markets and shopping precincts. Shawls, bags, decorative spears and other handicrafts are available at the *Nagaland Sales Emporium* near the bus stand. Weaving is a tradition passed on from generation to generation; each Naga tribe has its own distinctive design on its shawls such as the red, black and white *Tsungkotepsu* of the Ao Nagas.

The large Naga settlement of **Bara Basti**, or **Kohima Village**, is set on a high hill overlooking Kohima. Few of its buildings are now in traditional Naga style, with pitched

The telephone **area code** for Kohima is ☎0370.

roof and crossed "house-horns" on the gable, but with its tightly knit lanes and labyrinth of small houses the village maintains a definite Naga feel. Carved heads to signify family status, a huge grain basket in front of the house, and a trough used to make rice beer are among distinctive features.

The highlight of the fascinating **State Museum** (Mon–Fri 10am–4pm), 1.5km north of Kohima and a nice walk or easy minibus trip, is a small but stunning collection of Naga jewellery, dominated by yellow, red and dark blue beads. A wooden war canoe that is too large for the rivers of Nagaland reflects the belief that the Nagas may have originated from Sumatra.

Accommodation and eating

Kohima has few **accommodation** choices, though standards aren't bad. **Naga food** is refreshingly simple and under-spiced, with boiled vegetables, chicken and ginger stew, pork, and in season, frogs. Chinese and Tibetan food is also widely available at basic cafes on Main Bazaar. The *Embassy Hotel*, near the Art College, Main Bazaar, is a little more upmarket, while nicest of all is the *Naga Japanese Hotel*, near Secretariat. They serve Chinese dishes, and with notice, Naga food. Service is friendly, and it's a good place to meet young Kohimans.

Japfu Ashok, PR Hill (☎22721). Nagaland's showpiece hotel; spacious rooms and restaurants. ⑦.

Pine, Midland, Phool Bazaar (☎22234). Popular hotel with clean rooms and attached baths. ④.

Valley View, Bus Station (☎22728). Moderately clean, central, budget to mid-range hotel. ②–③.

Dimapur

DIMAPUR, the "City of the River People", 74km west of Kohima, is Nagaland's largest and most industrialized town – and the only one not in the hills. In fact, its vital communications may explain why it was included within the state, for it has absolutely no resemblance and affinity with the rest of Nagaland. The main entry point into the state, it's a fly-blown place that has pushed back the forest, polluted the river and encroached on the numerous large water tanks.

Dimapur was established by the **Kachari**, a Tibeto-Burmese people who erected huge carved fertility symbols. This was at a time when Hinduism had not conquered the Assam Valley, and these symbols are not directly connected to the Shaivite *lingam*. After the power of the Kachari kings had been shattered by attack from the **Ahoms** during the sixteenth century, they migrated southwest and set up their own kingdoms, which lasted until the British occupation in 1830.

Practicalities

The only railhead in Nagaland, Dimapur is served by **trains** to Simaluguri (for Sibsagar), Tinsukia and Dibrugarh in Upper Assam, and two for Lumding, of which the *Kamrup Express* #5906 connects for Guwahati. Services to Guwahati and even Delhi will almost certainly be reintroduced when track conversion to broad gauge is completed. Dimapur's **airport** is served by *Indian Airlines*, with flights to Calcutta, and *NEPC*, with flights to Guwahati and to, but not from, Jorhat. **Buses** run to Guwahati and towns throughout the northeastern hill states; *Blue Hill* and several *Nagaland State Transport* services go to and from Kohima.

Accommodation in Dimapur includes a *Tourist Lodge* (☎03862/20147; ②), and a basic *Youth Hostel* (①).

CHAPTER SIXTEEN

ORISSA

Despite being one of India's poorest regions, **ORISSA** is among its most distinctive and vibrant. Protected by the thickly forested mountains of the Eastern Ghats to the west and open to the Bay of Bengal on the east, the strip of fertile alluvial plains lining the coast forms a long, low-lying delta, across which the mighty Mahanandi and Brahmani rivers meander towards the sea. Thanks to its location, Orissa's densely populated "rice-bowl" heartland has historically been ravaged less often by malevolent invaders than by floods and famine. Nor has the recent advent of dams and weather satellites entirely insulated rural communities from the notorious tropical climate. A heavier than average monsoon or, even worse, a cyclone sweeping in from the sea can still rupture river banks and irrigation channels to spoil the crops. Most of the time however, the Orissan countryside looks deceptively prosperous and picturesque. The extreme brevity of the dry season (it can rain here any time between March and December) means that whenever you visit the state, its countless thatched villages, with their water tanks, palmgroves and whitewashed temple towers, are likely to be surrounded by a patchwork of vivid green and mud-brown paddy fields.

The coastal plains also claim the highest concentration of historical and religious monuments – Orissa's principal tourist attractions. **Puri**, site of the famous **Jagannath temple** and venue for one of the world's most spectacular devotional processions, the Rath Yatra, combines the heady intensity of a Hindu pilgrimage centre with the more hedonistic pleasures of the beach. Just a short hop off the main Calcutta–Madras road and railway, the town has in recent years become something of a backpackers' hang-out, with a good crop of budget accommodation and an easy social scene. **Konarak**, a short hop up the coast, has the ruins of Orissa's most ambitious medieval temple. Hidden for years under a gigantic sand dune, its surfaces writhe with exquisitely preserved sculpture, including some eyebrow-raising

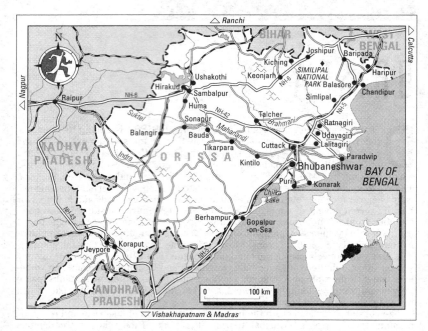

erotica. The ancient rock-cut caves and ornate sandstone temples of **Bhubaneshwar**, the state capital – all too often skipped by visitors – hark back to the era when it ruled a kingdom stretching from the Ganges delta to the mouth of the River Godavari.

Away from the central "golden triangle" of sights, tourism has yet to make much of an impact. In these outlying districts, **wildlife reserves** are the main incentive to brave the rigours of minimal infrastructure and over-taxed public transport. The **Simlipal National Park**, deep in the *sal* forests of the far northeast, boasts some spectacular scenery, wild tigers and elephants, and hundreds of other species of animals, birds and reptiles that have all but disappeared from more populated areas. In winter, the small islands dotted around **Chilka Lake**, a huge salt-water lagoon south of Bhubaneshwar, become a bird watcher's paradise, while in the **Bhita Kanika Sanctuary** at the end of Orissa's river delta, a remote stretch of beach is the nesting site for a school of giant marine turtles that migrate here every year from the South American coast.

From the number of temples, pilgrims and wayside shrines in Orissa, you'd be forgiven for thinking Hinduism was its sole religion. In fact, nearly 25 percent of the population are **adivasi**, or "tribal" (literally "first") people, thought to be descended from the area's pre-Aryan aboriginal inhabitants. In the more inaccessible corners of the state, such as the tract of near-impenetrable hill country running the length of the interior, many of these groups have retained unique cultural traditions and languages. Thus far, the scourge of "ethnic" tourism – so destructive elsewhere in Asia – has been less of a threat to the Adivasis' way of life than encroachments by dam builders, missionaries and "advancement programmes" of the state government.

Orissa enjoys a fairly congenial **climate** for most of the year, with average temperatures ranging from 17°C between November and March, to a bearable-if-humid

32° in summer. The monsoon blows in around mid-June, just in time for Rath Yatra. The cool winter months are the **best time to visit**, particularly around Makar Sankranti, in January, when Orissan villages celebrate the end of the harvest with colourful festivals.

Getting around presents few practical problems if you stick to the more populated areas. National Highway 5 and the Southeast Railway, which cut in tandem down the coastal plain via Bhubaneshwar, are the main arteries of the region. A metre-gauge branch line also runs as far as Puri, connecting it by frequent, direct express **trains** to Delhi, Calcutta and Madras. Elsewhere, **buses** are the way to go. Regular government and private services cover all the main routes and most of the more remote stretches.

ORISSA TRAVEL DETAILS

	Trains		Buses		Flights	
	Frequency	Time	Frequency	Time	Frequency	Time
To and from BHUBANESHWAR						
Agra	1 daily	39hr				
Balasore	8–11 daily	4hr	every 30min	6hr		
Bangalore	Mon & Thurs	22hr				
Baripada			hourly	7hr–7hr 30min		
Berhampur	5–8 daily	2hr 20min–3hr	hourly	4–5hr		
Bombay	1 daily	38hr				
Calcutta	6–9 daily	7hr 30min–12hr	4 nightly	8–10hr	8 weekly	55min
Cuttack	8–11 daily	40min	every 15min	45min–1hr		
Delhi	2–3 daily	30–43hr			5 weekly	2hr 10min
Hyderabad	2 daily	20–23hr 30min			3 weekly	3hr 10min
Kochi	4 weekly	36hr				
Konarak			1 daily	1hr 30min		
Madras	2–4 daily	22–24hr			2 weekly	2hr 40min
Pipli			every 15min	20–30min		
Puri	10 daily	2–3hr	every 15min	1hr 30min–2hr		
Thiruvananthapuram	Tues	40hr				
Varanasi	3 weekly	20hr 30min				
To and from PURI						
Agra	1 daily	40hr				
Balasore	6–7 daily	5hr 30min				
Calcutta	3 daily	10–14hr	2 daily	12hr		
Chilka Lake			6 daily	2hr–3hr 30min		
Delhi	3 daily	32–40hr				
Konarak			every 30min	1hr		
Varanasi	3 weekly	22hr				
To and from Balasore						
Baripada			hourly	1hr 15min		
Calcutta	6–9 daily	4–8hr	5 daily	5–6hr		
Chandipur			5 daily	30min		
To and from Berhampur						
Gopalpur-on-Sea			every 15min	30min		
Koraput			1 daily	13hr		
Rayagada			1 daily	3hr		
Taptapani			hourly	1hr 15min		

Note that no individual route appears more than once in this chart; check against where you want to get to as well as where you're coming from.

History

Other than scattered fragmentary remains of prehistoric settlement, Orissa's earliest archeological finds date from the fifth century BC and the appearance at **Sisupalgarh**, near modern Bhubaneshwar, of a fortified city. Little is known about the **Kalinga** dynasty, whose capital this was, except that its power was founded on domination of the lucrative land and maritime trade routes leading south. The existence of such rich pickings so close to his frontiers was too strong an enticement for the ambitious Mauryan emperor **Ashoka**. In the third century BC, he descended on ancient Kalinga with his imperial army, and routed the kingdom in a battle so bloody that the carnage was supposed to have inspired his legendary conversion to **Buddhism**. Rock edicts erected around the empire extol the virtues of the new faith, *dharma*, as well as the principles that Ashoka hoped to instil in his vanquished subjects. With the demise of the Mauryans, Kalinga enjoyed something of a resurgence. Under the imperialistic **Chedi** dynasty, followers of the Jain faith, vast sums were spent expanding the capital and on carving elaborate monastery caves into the nearby hills of **Khandagiri** and **Udaigiri**. In the course of the second century BC, however, the kingdom gradually splintered into warring factions and entered a kind of dark age. The influence of Buddhism waned, Jainism all but vanished, and **Brahmanism**, disseminated by the teachings of the Shaivite zealot Lakulisa, started to resurface as the dominant religion.

By the seventh century, Orissa's rise to prominence was well under way. Over the next five hundred years, a succession of powerful and prosperous Hindu dynasties ruled the region, creating some of the finest artistic and architectural achievements in the history of South Asia. When the **Eastern Gangas** took control early in the twelfth century, this "golden age" reached its zenith. Fuelled by the gains from a thriving trade network (extending as far east as Indonesia), the Ganga kings erected magnificent **temples** at Bhubaneshwar, Puri and Konarak, in which the Shiva worship and arcane tantric practices espoused by earlier Orissan rulers were replaced by new forms of devotion to Vishnu. The shrine of the most popular royal deity of all, Lord Jagannath at Puri, was by now one of the four most hallowed religious centres in India.

With the exception of a brief incursion by Firuz Sultan in the fourteenth century, Hinduism in Orissa came through the Muslim occupation of Bihar and Bengal comparatively unscathed. Such good fortune, however, was not to last. In the fifteenth century, the **Afghans of Bengal** swept south to annexe the region, with Man Singh's **Moghul** army hot on their heels in 1592. That even a few medieval Hindu monuments escaped the excesses of iconoclasm that ensued is miraculous; thankfully some did, though ever since non-Hindus have never been allowed to enter the most holy temples in Puri and Bhubaneshwar (Indira Gandhi was refused entry to the Jagannath temple because of her marriage to a Parsi). In 1751 the **Maharathas** from western India ousted the Moghuls as the dominant regional power. The East India Company, meanwhile, was also making inroads along the coast, and 28 years after Clive's victory at Plassey in 1765, Orissa finally came under **British rule**.

Since **Independence**, the state has sustained rapid **development** without the accompanying political instability that has dogged some of its neighbours. Discoveries of coal, bauxite, iron ore and other minerals have stimulated considerable industrial growth and infrastructural improvements. German-backed steel works and townships have been created at Rourkela in the north and new high-grade roads built to transport goods to and from the main port at Paradwip. Nevertheless, Orissa has remained, first and foremost, a poor rural state, heavily dependent on agriculture to provide for the basic needs of its 32 million inhabitants.

Bhubaneshwar

At first impression, **BHUBANESHWAR** may strike you as surprisingly dull for a city with a population approaching half a million and a history of settlement stretching back over two thousand years. Featureless Fifties architecture and rows of rapidly decaying concrete shopping arcades stand where you might expect exotic bazaars, while long tree-lined avenues diffuse the usual intensity of a busy state capital. Beyond the confines of the modern planned city, however, things improve considerably. Hidden among the backstreets and wastegrounds of the messier southern suburbs are the remnants of some of India's finest medieval **temples**, evidence of a much earlier and infinitely more inspired building boom than the one that followed Independence. These are indisputably the main attractions, made all the more atmospheric by the animated religious life that continues to revolve around them, particularly at festival times.

The Bhubaneshwar area first appears in history during the fourth century BC, as the capital of ancient **Kalinga**. It was soon to be the target of Ashoka's ferocious onslaught, which was responsible for the introduction of Buddhism, and the erection of one of the subcontinent's best preserved rock edicts – still in place near the site of the campaign's

decisive battle at **Dhauli**, 5km south of the present city. Under the **Chedis**, who succeeded the Mauryans a century or so later, ancient Kalinga gained control over the region's thriving mercantile trade, and became the northeast seaboard's most formidable power. The elaborate sculpture adorning a complex of Jain caves cut from the hillsides of **Khandagiri** and **Udaigiri**, which overlook the capital, provides a taste of the military might and opulent royal lifestyles enjoyed by its rulers.

Not until the fifth century AD, long after the Chedis had disappeared, did Bhubaneshwar re-emerge as a regional force. As home to the revolutionary Pasupata sect, the city, known by this time as **Ekamrakshetra**, became a key centre for the promulgation of Shaivism – worship of Shiva and his female counterpart Shakti. When the **Sailodbhavas** made it their capital in the seventh century, wealth and power were coupled with the mounting religious fervour and Bhubaneshwar embarked in earnest upon its "golden age". Nothing is so expressive of the prosperity and self-confidence of this era as its religious architecture. Between the seventh and twelfth centuries some 7000 sandstone temples are said to have been erected around the **Bindu Sagar**, or "Ocean Drop Tank". Intended both as offerings to the gods and as symbols of authority, the temples evolved from the relatively modest proportions favoured by the Bhauma-Karas and Somavamsis, to the Gangas' gigantic creation, the **Lingaraj** – home of Tribhubaneshwara, or "Lord of Three Worlds" from which the city eventually took its name. Their passion for architecture did not however prevent Bhubaneshwar's medieval rulers from retaining an army strong enough to hold off the eastward advance of Islam until the end of the fifteenth century. When the Moghuls did eventually take the city, they made up for lost time by razing all but a few of the temples. Thereafter, Bhubaneshwar was consigned to relative obscurity. Only after Independence, when Cuttack had reached bursting point, was it officially declared the new state capital.

Arrival and information

There's no regular bus service into the centre of Bhubaneshwar from its domestic **airport** on the southwest outskirts, but unmetered taxis and auto-rickshaws wait to meet

> The telephone **area code** for Bhubaneshwar is ☎0674.

incoming flights. Long-distance **buses** terminate at the inconveniently situated Baramunda Bus Stand, 5km out on the northwestern edge of town, though not before making a whistlestop tour of the centre. Ask to be dropped at **Station Square** (look for a statue of a horse in the middle of a large roundabout), which is near most hotels. If you miss the stop, frequent local buses head back to the city bus stand (aka old bus stand), on Raj Path. The **railway station** is right in the centre of town close to many of the mid-range hotels. For **cheaper rooms**, leave the station via platform 4 and catch a rickshaw from there down to Kalpana Square, 1km south.

Moving on from Bhubaneshwar you can pick up buses to Puri, Pipli and Cuttack from Jayadev Nagar opposite the *Kalinga Ashok Hotel* and near the railway station. See p.918 for the numbers to call for **train** and **bus enquiries**, and for a list of **travel agents** that can fix up reservations and tours.

Information

Both the **OTDC** office on Jayadev Nagar (aka Lewis Rd and Puri Rd), near the *Panthaniwas Hotel* (Mon–Sat 10am–5pm; ☎431299), and the counter at the railway station hand out useful free maps of Orissa and can arrange taxis for local sightseeing. The helpful **India Government tourist office** around the corner from the *Panthaniwas* on BJB Nagar (Mon–Fri 10am–5pm; ☎432203) has a large selection of leaflets and city plans for other parts of the country.

The **post office** is on the corner of Mahatma Gandhi Marg and Sachivalaya Marg. For poste restante ask at "enquiries" on the middle counter. A *pan-wallah* by the main entrance packs and seals parcels. To **change money**, if you're not staying in a hotel with a foreign exchange counter, try the *State Bank of India* (Mon–Fri 10am–2pm, Sat 10am–noon; no *Amex* travellers' cheques) on Raj Path, opposite New Market, or the *Indian Overseas Bank* on the corner of Station Square and Janpath. The latter will change travellers' cheques if you show receipt of purchase.

City transport

Modern Bhubaneshwar is too spread out to explore on foot; you'll need to take an **auto-** or **cycle rickshaw**. Sights outside the city, such as Dhauli or the Udaigiri and Khandagiri caves, can reached by local **buses** from the city bus stand near Capital Market, by auto-rickshaw or on one of OTDC's **luxury bus tours**. Private *Ambassador* **taxis** can also be arranged through most travel agents (see p.918), the OTDC office on Jayadev Nagar, or at large hotels such as the *New Kenilworth* or the *Kalinga Ashok*. Expect to pay anywhere between Rs400 and 800 for a full day.

Tours

Tickets for OTDC's rather rushed **city tours** (Tues–Sun 9.30am–5.30pm; Rs75, a/c Rs100) are available from the office on Jayadev Nagar; their trips to **Puri** and **Konarak** (Mon–Sat 9am–6.30pm; Rs85, a/c Rs130), also involve too much time on the bus and not enough looking around the sights. More upmarket **package tours** of Bhubaneshwar, Puri and Konarak, with four-star accommodation, transport in an a/c car and guides, can be arranged through *Swosti Travels*, 103 Janpath (☎408526) – ask too about their specialist "wildlife", "tribal" and "architectural" tours.

Visits to *Mahila Vikash Samabaya Niga*, a government-run women's development co-operative set up to promote cottage industries, may be arranged by telephoning ☎401852.

The temples

Of the five hundred or so **temples** that remain in Bhubaneshwar, only a handful are of interest to any but the most ardent templo-phile. They are all in the south of the city, and quite spread out, but thanks to the city's ubiquitous rickshaw *wallahs*, who will find you long before you need them, it's possible to see most of the highlights in a morning.

Most visitors see the temples in more or less chronological order. Apart from giving a sense of the development of Orissan architecture over the years, this also delays the onset of temple fatigue by leaving the most impressive monuments until last. The majority are active places of worship, so dress appropriately, remove your shoes (and any leather items) at the entrance and seek permission before taking photographs, particularly inside the buildings. The resident *brahmin* will expect a donation if he's shown you around, of course, but don't necessarily believe the astronomical amounts recorded in the ledgers you'll be shown.

The central group

The compact **central group**, just off Jayadev Nagar beyond the museum and *Panthaniwas Hotel*, includes some of Bhubaneshwar's most celebrated temples. In order to see the oldest first, follow the footpath from the main road past the more recent Muktesvara Mandir and its adjacent water tank, as far as a small square lined with cold drink stalls and souvenir shops.

PARASUMARESVARA MANDIR

The best preserved and most beautiful of Bhubaneshwar's early temples, the lavishly decorated **Parasumaresvara Mandir**, stands in the shade of a large *banyan* tree just beyond the square. Art historians rave about this temple, which with its plain, rectangular assembly hall (*jagamohana*), simple stepped roof and squat beehive-shaped tower (*deul*), typifies the predominant style of late seventh-century Orissa. In addition to the sheer quality of its exterior sculpture, Parasumaresvara is significant in marking the then-recent transition from Buddhism to Hinduism. The *brahmin* may point out panels depicting **Lakulisha**, the proselytizing Shaivite whose sect was largely responsible for the Hinduization of Orissa in the fifth century. On the east side of the tower he appears with four disciples at his feet, while on the west, above the relief showing Shiva as Nataraj, Lord of the Dance, he adopts the full-blown lotus position, looking every bit the meditating Buddha. Around the corners of the *deul* are even more blatant assertions of Hindu supremacy. Look for the **rampant lions** with their heads thrown back, crouched or standing above elephants, symbols of the beleaguered Buddhist faith.

Elsewhere the sculpture concentrates mainly on the Hindu pantheon and scenes from mythological narratives. Highlights include the marriage of Shiva and Parvati on the east side of the sanctuary tower, and the intricate friezes that line the north wall of the assembly hall. Among these stands a row of seven Mother Goddesses (*Sapta Matrikas*), with the emaciated Chamunda (Shiva's consort Durga in her terrifying aspect) to the right; an unusual depiction of Ganesh, Shiva's other (elephant-headed) son, here shown with a human face and a trunk growing from his chin; and further to the left, a dreadlocked *rishi*, or saint, counting on his rosary while strapped into an uncomfortable looking yogic pose. In the far corner of the courtyard, an intriguing *lingam*, the **Sahasralingam**, is decorated with a thousand miniature versions of itself.

MUKTESVARA MANDIR

Back towards the main road, the **Muktesvara Mandir**, set in its own low-walled courtyard, is often described as the "gem" of Orissan architecture. During the two hundred years after the Parasumaresvara was constructed, a new, more elaborate style evolved in Bhubaneshwar. The *jagamohana* here has the complex pyramidal roof normally

ORISSAN TEMPLES

Orissan temples constitute one of the most distinctive regional styles of religious architecture in South Asia. To make sense of the buildings, you need to be able to identify their common features. Many of these conventions have endured for thousands of years, and are recorded in the **Shilpa Shastras** – Sanskrit canonical texts that set out, in meticulous detail, ancient building specifications and their symbolic significance. Exactitude was a hallmark of ancient architecture; as one of the *Shastras* says: " . . . if the measurements are perfect, there will be perfection in the Universe."

Unlike Christian churches or Muslim mosques, Hindu temples are not simply places of worship, but are *objects* of worship in themselves – recreations of the "Divine Cosmic Creator-Being" or the particular deity enshrined within them. For a Hindu, to move through a temple is akin to entering the very body of the God to be glimpsed in the shrine-room during the moment of *darshan*, or ritual viewing of the deity – the culmination of an act of worship. In Orissa, this concept also finds expression in the technical terms used in the *Shastras* to designate the different parts of the structure: the foot (*pabhaga*), shin (*jangha*), torso (*gandi*), neck (*kantha*), head (*mastaka*) and so forth.

Most temples are made up of two main sections. The first and most impressive of these is the **deul**, or sanctuary tower. A soaring, curvilinear spire with a square base and rounded top, the *deul* symbolizes the Divine Mountain from which the sacred Ganges flows into the world. Its intricately ribbed sides, which in later buildings were divided into rectangular projections known as *raths*, usually house images of the accessory deities, while its top supports a lotus-shaped, spherical *amla* (a motif derived from an auspicious fruit used in Ayurvedic medicine as a purifying agent). Above that, the vessel of immortality, the *kalasha*, is crowned by the presiding deity's sacred weapon, a wheel (Vishnu's *chakra*) or trident (Shiva's *trichul*). The actual deity occupies a chamber inside the *deul*. Known in Oriya as the **garbha griyha**, or inner sanctum, the shrine is shrouded in a womb-like darkness intended to focus the mind of the worshipper on the image of God.

The **jagamohana**, or "World Delighter", which adjoins the sanctuary tower, is a lighter porch where the congregation gathers for readings of religious texts and other important ceremonies. Its pyramidal roof, made up of layers of receding steps, contrasts sharply with the gently curving lines of the tower. Larger temples, such as the Lingaraj in Bhubaneshwar and the Jagannath in Puri, also have additional structures that were tacked on to the main porch when music and dance were more commonly performed as part of temple rituals. Like the *jagamohana*, the roofs of the **nata mandir**, the dancing hall, and **bhoga-mandapa**, the hall of offerings, are pyramidal. The whole structure, along with any smaller subsidiary shrines (often earlier temples erected on the same site), is usually enclosed in a walled courtyard.

Over the centuries, as construction techniques and skills improved, Orissan temples became progressively grander and more elaborate. It's fascinating to chart this transformation as you move from the earlier buildings in Bhubaneshwar to the acme of the region's architectural achievement, the stunning Sun temple at Konarak. Towers grow taller, roofs gain extra layers, and the **sculpture**, for which the temples are now famous all over the world, attains a level of complexity and refinement unrivalled before or since.

associated with Orissan temples, while the *deul*, though similar in shape to its predecessor, places more emphasis on vertical than horizontal lines. Once again, the sandstone **sculpture** is the most striking feature. Directly in front of the main entrance, the ornamental **gateway** (*torana*), topped by two reclining female figures, is the Muktesvara's masterpiece. The grinning lions and dwarves around the windows on the side of the porch, known as the *bho* motif, come a close second. Witty touches include the lice-picking monkeys around the latticed windows, and the little panel hidden amid the ornamentation along the side walls, whose geometric pattern, when partially covered, reveals two separate dancing nymphs.

Between the Muktesvara and the road, the murky green waters of the small **Marichi Kund** tank are believed to cure infertility – which doesn't altogether explain its popularity with noisy adolescent boys. Still, the *ghats* surrounding the tank are a pleasant place to sit and enjoy the temple. Around the frame of the door leading to it Lakulisha crops up again, this time encircled by students and ascetics reading books.

Finally, on the edge of Muktesvara's terrace stands an example of the mature phase of Orissan temple building. The unfinished **Siddhesvara** was erected at more or less the same time as the Lingaraj, in the eleventh century, but is nowhere near as impressive. The lesser deities around the tower, Ganesh and Karttikeya (Shiva's sons), are about its only remarkable points.

The eastern group

To reach the first of the more scattered **eastern group** of temples, ten to fifteen minutes' walk from Muktesvara, head back up Jayadev Nagar as far as the crossroads, turn right down Tankapani Rd, and keep going until you reach the park on the right.

RAJRANI MANDIR

Even though it was never completed, the majestic eleventh-century **Rajrani Mandir** is among the very finest of Bhubaneshwar's later temples. From the far end of the well-watered gardens in which it stands, the profile of the *deul*, with its successive tiers of projections rising to form an elegant eighteen-metre tower, is the building's most unusual feature. Closer to, you can make out the profusion of sculpted figures for which Rajrani is equally famous. The best are about 3m off the ground surrounding the sides of the tower. The **Dikpalas**, or Guardians of the Eight Directions, are the deities who "protect" the main shrine. Identifiable by their respective vehicles and attributes, they form a marked contrast to the languid and alluring poses of the exquisite female figures (*nayikas*) that stand between them. Among the more distinctive of the Dikpalas are (moving clockwise) Yama (south), the Judge of the Dead, with his club and noose; Nritti (southwest), the God of Misery holding a severed head; Varuna (west), the serene God of Light, shown standing on his vehicle, a sea monster; Kubera (north), God of Prosperity, complete with pot-belly and jar full of gem stones; Ishana (northeast), a form of Shiva whose erect phallus has seen an untimely end; and next to him Indra (east), the Storm God with his corn-on-the-cob-like thunderbolt.

Compared to the sanctuary tower, the Rajrani's porch looks plain and unfinished. Of considerably more interest to some may be the palm-leaf manuscripts being hawked in the temple gardens. Spurred on no doubt by Khajuraho's money-spinning example, enterprising local artists have tried to make up for Bhubaneshwar's comparative lack of erotic sculpture by applying this most ancient of Orissan skills to illustrating the *Kama Sutra*. The results sometimes verge on the surreal.

BRAHMESVARA MANDIR

From Rajrani, a fair walk leads up Tankapani Rd to the turn off for the **Brahmesvara Mandir**, 500m on the right. Along the way you cross a canal, originally dug by King Kharavela in the first century BC, and an open stretch of ground to the left of the road with an odd-shaped temple in the middle. The **Bhaskaresvara** is unfinished, but has an interesting three-metre *lingam*, or phallus, enshrined in its double-storeyed interior which archeologists claim was formerly a Mauryan column.

Unlike most of its neighbours, the eleventh-century Brahmesvara temple itself, at the end of the dirt lane opposite the entrance to the Bhaskaresvara, still houses a living deity, as indicated by the saffron pennant flying from the top of the sanctuary. The gateway in the high enclosure wall brings you out opposite a small cloth-covered image of Lakshmi. Here too you can see guardian figures (*dikpalas*) on the corners, and a fierce Chamunda on the western facade (shown astride a corpse and holding a trident and severed head), as well as curvaceous maidens admiring themselves in mirrors or, in the panels around the tower, responding with some abandon to the advances of their male consorts. An inscription, now lost, records that one Queen Kovalavati once made a donation of "many beautiful women" to this temple – proof perhaps that **devadasis**, the dancers-cum-prostitutes who were to become a prominent feature of Orissan temple life in later years, made an early appearance here. Unfortunately, the temple *brahmins* are reluctant to allow non-Hindus into the strongly atmospheric shrine room for *darshan*, or a view of the *shivalingam*. There's a majestic Nandi, Shiva's bull, with testicles polished by years of worshippers giving them a propitious rub on the way in; and an inner sanctum, richly carved and lit by butter lamps, which is filled with incense smoke and the heady scent of oil-soaked flowers left as *puja* offerings.

The Bindu Sagar group

By far the largest group of temples is clustered around the **Bindu Sagar**, or "Ocean Drop Tank", 2km south of the city centre. This small artificial lake, mentioned in the *Puranas*, is itself a place of great religious importance. Said to contain nectar, wine and water drawn from all of the world's most sacred rivers, the tank is the main bathing place both for pilgrims visiting the city and for the Lingaraj deity, who is taken to the pavilion in the middle once every year during Bhubaneshwar's annual **Car Festival** (Ashokastami) for his ritual purificatory dip. The hours around sunrise and sunset are the most evocative time for a stroll here, when the residents of the nearby *dharamshalas* file through the smoky lanes and huddles of stray cattle to pray at the *ghats*.

LINGARAJ MANDIR

Immediately south of the Bindu Sagar stands the most stylistically evolved temple in all Orissa. Built early in the eleventh century by the Ganga kings, one hundred years before the Jagannath temple at Puri, the mighty **Lingaraj Mandir** has remained very much a "living" shrine. The small square in front of the main gateway still throngs with pilgrims clutching bananas and coconuts, bought at the colourful stalls nearby, to be offered as *prashad* to Tibhuvaneshwar, the "Lord of Three Worlds". Unfortunately, the square is about as close to the inside as most foreign visitors are allowed. Although the temple is open to all castes, non-Hindus (in practice non-Asians) have to be content with a peep from the top of the **viewing platform** overlooking the north wall, around the corner from the main entrance. From this vantage point you can still see all four of the principal sections of the building. The two nearest the entrance, the *bhoga-mandapa* (the Hall of Offering) and the *nata mandir* (the Hall of Dance, associated with the rise of the *devadasi* system – see p.936) are both later additions to the complex. If you have binoculars you may just be able to pick out some of the beautiful **sculpture**, depicting the music and dance rituals that would once have taken place inside.

Even more than the huge *jagamohana*, loaded with fancy stonework and the characteristic pyramidal roof, the immense 45-metre *deul* is the literal and aesthetic high point of the Lingaraj. Notice the rampant lion projecting from the curved sides of the tower, and the downtrodden elephant beneath him – again, the triumph of Hinduism over Buddhism. On the top, the typical Orissan motif of the flattened, ribbed sphere (*amla*) supported by gryphons, is crowned with Shiva's trident. As in the Brahmesvara temple, the long saffron pennant announces the living presence of the deity below.

The **shrine** inside is very unusual. The powerful 2.5-metre-thick Svayambhu (literally "self-born") *lingam* that it contains, one of the twelve *jyotrilinga* in India, is known as "Hari-Hara" because it is considered to be half Shiva, half Vishnu – an extraordinary amalgam that is thought to have resulted from the ascendancy of Vaishnavism over Shaivism in the twelfth and thirteenth centuries. Unlike other *linga*, which are bathed every day in a concoction prepared from hemlock, Svayambhu is offered a libation of rice, milk and *bhang* by the *brahmins*. Another peculiar feature of the shrine room is that it lacks a ceiling. Instead, the roof reaches right to the top of the tower.

VITAL DEUL MANDIR

Anyone not totally templed-out by this stage should head left from the Lingaraj viewing platform and up the main street to the fascinating **Vital Deul**, one of the group's oldest buildings and a real feast of tantric art. The temple was built around 800 AD in a markedly different style from most of its contemporaries in Bhubaneshwar, drawing heavily on earlier Buddhist influences (the south Indian style tower, called *kakhara* after an Orissan pumpkin, resembles the distinctive *chaitya* arches found in rock-cut caves). The Vital Deul also boasts some very accomplished stonework. Among the panels of Hindu deities encrusting its outer walls, you may occasionally come across examples of some of India's earliest **erotic sculpture**, thought to catalogue positions exploited in the tantric rituals that took place inside.

Once your eyes adjust to the darkness of the **interior**, you swiftly realize that this was no ordinary temple. Even if you missed the tell-tale post outside the entrance (a four-faced *lingam* used for tethering the sacrificial offerings) the grotesque images adorning the walls of the *jagamohana* graphically convey the macabre nature of the esoteric rites once performed here. Durga, in her most terrifying aspect as **Chamunda**, peers out of the half-light from behind the grille at the far end of the hall – her withered body, garlanded with skulls and flanked by an owl and a jackal, stands upon a rotting corpse. In front of her, to the right of the door, an even more nightmarish figure of a man picks himself up from the floor, having filled his skull-cup with blood from the decapitated body nearby. The whole gruesome frieze is littered with severed heads and jackals gnawing at corpses; you'll need a torch to see it all properly.

Orissa State Museum

Bhubaneshwar's **museum** (Tues–Sun 10am–1.30pm & 2.30–5pm; Rs1), a port of call on the OTDC tour, is housed in a large modern building at the top of Jayadev Nagar. Its collection of "tribal" artefacts, illuminated manuscripts and various archeological finds are worth an hour or so en route to the temples.

On display in the downstairs galleries are pieces of religious sculpture, coins and donative inscriptions on stone and copper plates salvaged from the city's temples. The upstairs rooms feature ethnographic material from indigenous Orissan societies. As well as heavy jewellery, musical instruments, weapons, tools and moth-eaten traditional costumes, there are reproductions of **chitra muriya**, the folk murals seen on walls and floors in village houses around Puri. The museum's real highlight, however, has to be its collection of antique **painting** and illuminated **palm-leaf manuscripts** (see p.922), kept in the small room at the end of the corridor on the first floor. Only the National Museum in New Delhi holds finer examples of this traditional Orissan art form.

The Tribal Research Institute or "Museum of Man"

Hidden away on the northwestern edge of town, close to Baramunda bus stand, the *Tribal Research Institute*'s anthropological **Museum of Man** (Mon–Sat 10am–5pm) is given over solely to "tribal" art and culture. Material collected from across the state is exhibited in the garden, in traditional-style huts built and decorated by *adivasi* specialists. While most of the buildings are evidently idealized versions of the real thing, some of the **murals** decorating their walls are more authentic.

Accommodation

As state capital, Bhubaneshwar has a disproportionate number of hotels for its size, ranging from luxurious five-stars to the filthiest of lodges. While the better-class hotels are spread out all over the city, the inexpensive places tend to be grouped around the

ACCOMMODATION PRICE CODES

All **accommodation prices** in this book have been coded using the symbols below. In
principle the prices given are for the least expensive double rooms in each establishment;
however, some hotels, usually in category ①, offer rates per bed rather than per room.
Local taxes are not included unless specifically stated. For more details, see p.35.

① up to Rs100	④ Rs225–350	⑦ Rs750–1200
② Rs100–150	⑤ Rs350–500	⑧ Rs1200–2200
③ Rs150–225	⑥ Rs500–750	⑨ Rs2200 and upwards

railway station, or a five-minute rickshaw ride away near the busy **Kalpana Square**
junction at the bottom of Cuttack Rd. Many of these can be pretty dreadful, but paying
just a fraction more will get you clean sheets, a fan that works and a private bathroom.
By far the best deals are the budget-price rooms offered by some mid-range hotels. The
railway station also has **retiring rooms** if you're really stuck. Reservations must be
made in advance at the counter in the main hall.

Inexpensive

Aristo Lodge, Kalpana Square (☎417963). Very basic, but friendly, and some rooms even have
fuzzy black-and-white TV. ①.

Bhagwat Niwas, 9 Buddha Nagar (☎417708). Right behind the *Pushpak*. Cheap and cheerful, managed by an Aurobindo devotee. Basic but clean and good value. ②.

Lingaraj, Old Station Bazaar (☎416342). Clean and good-value, near the platform 4 station exit. ②.

Pushpak, Kalpana Square (☎415545). Popular budget hotel with fairly clean, large rooms, attached
bathrooms, balconies and a small restaurant downstairs. Good value. ①.

Yatri Niwas, Cuttack Rd (☎416438). Institutional hostel run by the local authority, with cheap beds
in large dorms or smaller rooms. ①.

Moderate

Anarkali, 110 Kharvel Nagar (☎404031). Two minutes from the station. Upmarket place with all
mod-cons including *Star TV*, bar and a/c restaurant. Some good-value budget rooms too. ③–⑤.

Bhubaneshwar, Cuttack Rd (☎416977). Very clean and comfortable with attached bath, 24-hour
hot water, balconies, a generator and pleasant little restaurant. Some a/c. Excellent value. ②–⑤.

Jajati, Kharvela Nagar (☎400352). Modern chain hotel at the top of Station Square. A little
frayed around the edges, but very reasonably priced. Budget and more comfortable a/c
rooms. ③–⑤.

Meghdoot, 5-B Sahid Nagar (☎405802). Rooms from basic non-a/c "coir-rug" variety to luxurious
suites with wall-to-wall carpets, bath tubs and colour TV. Also quality restaurant, coffee shop and foreign exchange. The best value in its class, but way up the top of town. ④–⑦.

OTDC Panthaniwas, Jayadev Nagar (☎432515). Government hotel close to museum and temples.
Nothing fancy, but comfortable with three restaurants and TV in reception. Some a/c. ④–⑤.

Richi, 12a New Station Square (☎406619). Opposite the railway station. Large, functional, well-run
place with hot water in all rooms and a back-up generator. ③–⑤.

Expensive

Keshari, 113 Station Rd (☎408801). The full works from in-house movies to a craft shop in the lobby.
A bar, plus a restaurant serving local specialities. Some cheaper non-a/c rooms. ⑤–⑧.

New Kenilworth, 86/A-1 Gautam Nagar (☎411723). Plush 5-star in the centre of town with an
excellent restaurant, bar, pool and tempting pastry shop. ⑧.

Oberoi Bhubaneshwar, Nayapalli (☎56116; fax 0675/56269). Indisputably the city's top hotel. A
modern building, exquisitely furnished using antique textiles, stone and metalwork. Two restaurants with international menus, 24-hr coffee shop and a pool. Way out to the north of town. ⑧.

Prachi, 6 Janpath (☎402689). Established upmarket hotel with a/c, pool, beauty parlour, exchange and travel agent. Also two good restaurants, one serving (almost) authentic Chinese food. ⑦.

Swosti, 103 Janpath (☎404178; fax 0675/407524). Award-winning, central, American-style 4-star. Luxurious rooms, all with *Star TV*, two top-class restaurants and bar. Highly recommended. ⑧–⑨.

Eating

Eating out in Bhubaneshwar is usually a simple matter of choosing between the predictable five-star food dished up in the a/c comfort of places such as the *New Kenilworth*, or cheap and chilli-ful south Indian dishes served in rather less salubrious surroundings. The one or two restaurants that make an effort to include traditional **Orissan cuisine** on their menus are worth seeking out; seafood dishes combining prawns or delicate white "pomfret" fish with rice, fresh vegetables, yoghurt and spices are common in the coastal villages, but you rarely see them in the city. One traditional delicacy you're sure to come across however is the **coconut milk** sold by street vendors – just make sure the straws are as fresh as the fruit.

Athiti Bhavan, Lingaraj Rd. A short way down the lane opposite the temple. Wide range of veg, non-veg, tandoori and Chinese dishes, plus superb Bengali *thalis* and cold beers. Very reasonable.

Fahien and **Mohini**, OTDC *Panthaniwas*, see p. 917. Identical menus of standard Indian, Chinese and western food. The *Fahien* is the most comfortable of the two.

Hare Krishna, Janpath. Waiters in dinner jackets not *dhotis*, but the food is strictly *ISKON*-style vegetarian and delicious. A/c and quite expensive.

Padma, Kalpana Square, under *Pushpak Hotel*. The best of the cheap south Indian restaurants. Does a roaring trade in unfeasibly large *dosas* and opens early for breakfast.

Sangam, *New Kenilworth Hotel*, see p. 917. High-quality food with unusual dishes in classy surroundings. Not as expensive as you might think.

Swosti, 103 Janpath. Absolutely the best restaurant for a slap-up meal. Authentic Orissan dishes, such as mouth-watering *dahi machho* (river fish in yoghurt sauce), served with advance warning.

Vineeth, off Station Square. Dingy interior, but the pure veg snacks and meals are tasty, fresh and cheap. Popular with families.

Listings

Airlines *Indian Airlines* main booking office is on Raj Path, near New Market (Mon–Fri 10am–5.30pm; booking ends 4.15pm; ☎401084). NEPC office ☎413612.

Ambulance (Red Cross) ☎400688.

Ayurvedic hospital Between the *Panthaniwas* and the Ramesvara temple (☎51347).

Bookstores The *Modern Bookshop* at the top of Station Square has a rack of pulp fiction. The *Bookshop*, across the square in Ashoka Market, stocks a much more eclectic range with titles from Harold Robbins to Indian literature in translation. Also lots on politics, religion and history.

Bus enquiries Baramunda bus stand ☎400540.

Dance Visits or lessons can be arranged through the *Odissi Dance Academy*, Plot no. 459/4962, near Airport Chowk (☎406797). For more on Odissi dance see p.936.

Hospital The Capital Hospital (and homeopathic clinic) is near the airport. Casualty is on ☎400688.

Music The only venue staging regular performances of Indian classical music and *ghazaals* is the *New Kenilworth Hotel* (☎411723). The *Meghdoot* (☎405802) also advertises recitals.

Photography Film and colour processing available from *Neel Kamal*, 29 West Market Building (☎401491) or from *Photomakers*, 28 West Tower, New Market (☎400700).

Police station Near the *State Bank of India* (☎401232).

Railway enquiries Best to go in person or ask at a travel agency; otherwise call ☎402233.

Travel agents The *Keshari*, *New Kenilworth*, *Meghdoot*, *Oberoi* and *Prachi* hotels all have in-house travel agents. *Swosti Travels* at 103 Janpath (☎408526) has a good reputation. *Prime Tours and Travels* in the Pushpak Complex on Kalpana Square do car rental, tickets and sort out train reservations.

Around Bhubaneshwar

A number of places around Bhubaneshwar are worth combining with a day trip to the city. Fifteen minutes by rickshaw out of the centre, the second-century BC caves at **Khandagiri** and **Udaigiri** offer a glimpse of the region's past prior to the rise of Hinduism. **Dhauli**, just off the main road to Puri, boasts an even older monument: a rock edict dating from the Mauryan era, commemorating the battle of *c.* 260BC that gave the emperor Ashoka control of the eastern seaports, and thus enabled his missionaries to export the state religion across Asia.

Udaigiri and Khandagiri caves

Six kilometres west of Bhubaneshwar, beyond the leafy avenues of its exclusive neighbourhoods and the point where the green belt is broken by the busy Calcutta–Madras highway, a pair of low bony hills rises from the coastal plain. More than 2000 years ago, caves chiselled out of their malleable yellow sandstone were home to a community of **Jain monks**. Nowadays, they lie virtually deserted, left for troupes of black-faced langur monkeys and occasional parties of tourists to clamber over. Though by no means in the same league as the caves of the Deccan, **Udaigiri** and **Khandagiri** (daily 8am–6pm) rank, nevertheless, among Orissa's foremost historical monuments.

Inscriptions show that the **Chedi** dynasty, which ruled ancient Kalinga from the first century BC, was responsible for the bulk of the work. Apart from providing the monks with cells for meditation and prayer, the excavations enabled the rulers to show off their wealth and worldly achievements. Hallways, verandahs and facades outside several caves are encrusted with **sculpture** depicting court scenes, lavish processions, hunting expeditions, battles, dances and a host of domestic details from the daily life of Kalinga's cool set. The later additions, by contrast (from medieval times, when Jainism no longer enjoyed royal patronage in the region), are more austere, showing the twenty-four heroic Jain prophet-teachers, or *tirthankaras* ("crossing-makers").

Every year, Udaigiri and Khandagiri also play host to a **sadhu convention**. For a week or so in late January, the caves and surrounding woodland are claimed by dozens of itinerant holy men, resplendent in their saffron robes and coiled dreadlocks, who gather on the hillside to intone verses from the *Gita* into crackly PA systems. Predictably, the event has grown into something of a funfair. Crowds of exuberant day-trippers pour in on buses to enjoy the religious spectacle and the many market traders, travelling theatre groups and circus acts who set up along the roadside.

From Bhubaneshwar, the caves are approached via a road that follows the route of an ancient **pilgrimage path** (leading, archeologists believe, to a now-defunct *stupa*). As you face the hills with the highway behind you, Khandagiri ("Broken Hill") is on your left and Udaigiri ("Sunrise Hill") on your right. Best to begin with the latter, which has the finest of the early stonework.

Udaigiri

The **Udaigiri** caves occupy a fairly compact area around the south slope of the hill. To reach the largest and most impressive in the group, walk up the main pathway and take the track off to the right. **Cave 1**, the **Rani Gumpha** or "Queen's Cave", is tucked away around the corner. Its best sculpture is to be found over the pillars, arches and to the rear of the courtyard on the lower level, and across the back wall of the upper storey, where a long frieze shows rampaging elephants, panicking monkeys, sword fights and the abduction of a woman. Nobody, as yet, has managed to string all these scenes into a coherent narrative, though some are thought to illustrate episodes from the life of Kalinga's King Kharavela. As you return along the same path, the first caves of interest are numbers 3 and 4 – a double-storeyed cave containing sculptures of a lion holding its prey, elephants with snakes wrapped around them and pillars topped by pairs of peculiar winged animals. **Cave 9**, up the hill and around to the right, also has two storeys. Inside the lower, between the second and third doors, a badly damaged relief shows figures worshipping a long-vanished Jain symbol. The one wearing what looks like a crown (second from the left) is thought to be the Chedi king, Vakradeva, whose donative inscription can still be made out near the roof.

To reach **cave 10**, return to the main steps and climb towards the top of the hill. Its popular name, Ganesh Gumpha, is not derived from the elephants in front of the cave, but from the appearance on the rear wall of the cell on the right of the elephant-headed Ganesh. From here, follow the path up to the ledge at the very top of Udaigiri hill for good views and the ruins of an old **chaitya hall**. This was probably the main place of worship for the Jain monks who lived below and may even once have housed the legendary **Kalinga Jina**, a kind of votive cult object-cum-Holy Grail that Kharavela recovered after it had been removed by the King of Magadha (south Bihar).

Below the ruins are **cave 12**, shaped like the head of a tiger, and **cave 14**, the Hathi Gumpha known for the long **inscription** in ancient Magadhi carved onto its overhang. This relates in glowing terms the life history of King Kharavela, whose exploits, both on and off the battlefield, brought in the fortune needed to finance the cave excavation. Guides take great delight in pointing out the hole in the rear wall that they insist was "the Queen's shitting place" – scatological conjecture perhaps, but the channels next to it do seem to lead from ruined reservoirs on the hill above.

Khandagiri

The caves on the opposite hill, **Khandagiri**, can be reached either by the long flight of steps leading from the road, just up from the main entrance to the Udaigiri caves, or by cutting directly across from Hathi Gumpha via the steps that drop down from cave 17. The latter route brings you out at **caves 1** and **2**, known as the "Parrot Caves" for the carvings of birds on their doorway-arches. Cave 2, excavated in the first century BC, is the larger and more interesting. On the back wall of one of its cells, a few faint lines in red *brahmini* script are thought to have been scrawled 2000 years ago by a monk practising his handwriting. The reliefs in **cave 3**, the Ananta Gumpha or "Snake Cave" – serpents decorate the doorways – contain the best of the sculpture on Khandagiri hill, albeit badly vandalized in places. **Caves 7** and **8**, left of the main steps, were former sleeping quarters, remodelled in the eleventh century as sanctuaries. Both house reliefs of *tirthankaras* on their walls as well as Hindu deities which had, by the time conversion work was done, become part of the Jain pantheon. **Cave 9**, the last of any real note, was also reconverted in medieval times. It too contains *tirthankaras*, though only the three standing images of Rishabanatha (in black chlorite stone) are any good.

The best place to wind up a visit to Khandagiri is the modern **Jain temple** at the top of the hill. Aside from some old *tirthankaras* in the shrine room, the building itself, erected during the nineteenth century on the site of a much earlier structure, is rather less inspiring than the **view** across the plains from its terrace. The Jain monks who lived here would have been able to look out over the ancient city at Sisupalgarh, 9km southeast, on which they depended for alms. Today, the ruins are upstaged by the white peace pagoda at Dhauli and by the Lingaraj temple – Bhubaneshwar's most prominent feature, despite competition from an unsightly water-tower nearby.

Nandankanan Botanical Gardens and Zoo

March–Sept Tues–Sun 7.30am–5.30pm; Oct–Feb Tues–Sun 8am–5pm; Rs2 Indians, Rs10 foreigners.

Set amid the open grassland and natural forest on the banks of Kanjia Lake, 20km north of Bhubaneshwar, is **Nandankanan** ("Garden of Pleasure"), India's largest **zoo**. While the enclosures are certainly luxurious and well-maintained by Indian standards, wildlife enthusiasts will find the sight of animals in captivity no less depressing here than anywhere else. Kids, however, should enjoy the place enormously. Novelty attractions include a rare albino crocodile and the world's only **white tigers** to have bred successfully in captivity. Apparently, one mated with a wild tigress who scaled the perimeter fence in 1967 and then stayed on to give birth to her cubs. If you get fed up with the zoo, try a trip across the lake by pedalo or rowing boat to the peaceful **botanical gardens**. Failing that, there's always the toy train ride, to the left of the main entrance, or a popular **lion safari** by minibus around an enormous fifty-acre reserve.

The simplest way to **get to** Nandankanan, apart from the OTDC **tour**, is to catch one of the hourly state transport **buses** from the bus stand in town. Otherwise, it's a pleasant 90-minute trip by **bicycle**, though finding a bike to rent in Bhubaneshwar isn't easy.

Sisupalgarh and Dhauli

Emerging from the ramshackle fringes of southern Bhubaneshwar, the Puri road crosses an old canal, then heads into open farmland towards the confluence of the Bhargubi and Daya rivers. The kilometre-long bank of earth to the left of the road at **SISUPALGARH** is a section of the ramparts that surrounded ancient **Kalinganagara**. Founded by the Kalingas in the fourth century BC, the city is thought to have been the region's capital until it was mysteriously deserted by the Chedis 700 years later. These days, all that's left are overgrown fortifications, a couple of gateways and the occasional patch of decaying brickwork – hardly worth getting off a bus to see.

Across the Daya, the stark profile of the Shanti Stupa at **DHAULI**, standing on top of a lone sandstone outcrop, is the flat riverine countryside's most dominant feature. The *stupa* overlooks the spot where the Mauryan emperor **Ashoka** defeated the Kalingas in the decisive battle of 265 BC. Apart from bringing the prosperous Orissan kingdom to its knees, the victory also led the emperor, allegedly overcome by remorse at having slain 150,000 people, to renounce the path of violent conquest in favour of the spiritual one preached by Gautama Buddha. Thereafter, he set about promoting the maxims of his new-found faith in **rock edicts** installed at key sites around the empire (see "History" section in *Contexts*). One such inscription, in ancient **Brahmi**, the ancestor of all non-Islamic Indian scripts, still stands on the roadside at the foot of Dhauli hill. A translation erected by the ASI nearby gives some idea of its contents: a typically colourful mixture of rambling philosophical asides, discourses on animal rights and tips on how to treat your slaves. The Dhauli edict also includes the famous "All men are my children . . ." line, but diplomatically omits the account that crops up elsewhere describing how many poor Kalingas Ashoka had to put to the sword before he finally "saw the light".

Carved out of the rock directly above the inscription is a very lifelike, frontal view of an **elephant**. Among the oldest of its kind on the subcontinent, the sculpture is thought to represent *dharma*, Ashoka's name for Buddhism, and was probably placed here to announce the location of the edict to passers-by. Nowadays, the gleaming white **Shanti Stupa** on top of Dhauli Hill does a much better job. Built by an order of Japanese Buddhists in 1972, the "peace pagoda" stands as a memorial both to the battle that prompted Ashoka's legendary change of heart and to the zealous dissemination of *dharma* across Asia that ensued. Panels around the sides illustrate episodes from the life of the emperor (below) and the Buddha (above), while the umbrella-like projections on the top symbolize the five cardinal Buddhist virtues of faith, hope, compassion, forgiveness and non-violence. Alongside the *stupa*, somewhat eclipsed by its futuristic neighbour, there's also a recently renovated Shiva temple – the **Dhabaleshwara Mandir**. From the terrace on top of Dhauligiri, the **views** over the surrounding geometrically patterned rice fields are serene. Arrive here early enough and you might just

ORISSAN ART AND ARTISTS

Few regions of India retain as rich a diversity of **traditional art forms** as Orissa. While a browse through the bazaars and emporia in Puri and Bhubaneshwar provides a good idea of local styles and techniques, a trip out to the **villages** where the work is actually produced is a much more memorable way to shop. On the whole, different villages specialize in different crafts – a division that harks back to the origins of the caste system in Orissa. Patronage from the nobility and wealthy temples during medieval times allowed local artisans, or *shilpins*, to refine their skills over generations. As the market for arts and crafts expanded, notably with the rise of **Puri** as a pilgrimage centre, **guilds** were formed to control the handing down of specialist knowledge and separate communities established to carry out the work. Today, the demand for **souvenirs**, particularly easily transportable ones, has given many old art forms a new lease of life.

Stone sculpture With modern temples increasingly being built out of reinforced concrete, life for Orissa's **stone sculptors** is getting tougher. Nevertheless, the work of a few small communities remains on a par with that of their illustrious forebears at Konarak and Bhubaneshwar. At **Lalitgiri**, the Buddhist monument northeast of Cuttack, families of sculptors claim to own tools used by their ancestors to build the eighth- and ninth-century monasteries nearby; the Santal villages near **Lulung**, in the Simlipal National Park, have lately had to diversify from stone phalluses to pressure cookers to stay in business; while in Pathuria Sahi ("Stonecarvers' Lane") and the famous *Sudarshan Workshop* in **Puri**, mastercraftsmen and apprentices still fashion Hindu deities and other votive objects according to specifications laid down in ancient manuals.

Painting *Patta chitra*, classical Orissan **painting**, is closely connected with the Jagannath cult. Traditionally, artists were employed to decorate the inside of the temples in Puri and to paint the deities and chariots used in the Rath Yatra. Later, the same vibrant colour schemes and motifs were transferred to lacquered cloth or palm-leaves and sold as sacred souvenirs to visiting pilgrims. In the village of **Raghurajpur** near Puri, where the majority of the remaining artists, or *chitrakaras*, now live, business is still booming. Specialities include devotional images of Lord Jagannath, scenes from the *Gita Govinda* and sets of **ganjiffa** – small round cards used to play a trick-taking game based on the struggle between Rama and the demon Ravana, as told in the *Ramayana*.

Palm-leaf manuscripts Palm leaves, or *chitra pothi*, have been used as writing material in Orissa for centuries, and the basic techniques have changed little. Using a sharp stylus called a *lohankantaka*, the artist first scratches the text or design on to the surface of palm leaves, then applies a paste of turmeric, dried leaves, oil and charcoal. When the residue is rubbed off, the etching stands out more clearly. Some scholars claim that the rounded Oriya script may have developed to cope with the problems of writing on palm leaves, the

catch the last of the morning mist hanging over the tiny hamlets and gently meandering water courses that line the bend in the River Daya nearby.

If you don't have your own vehicle and are not on a tour, **getting to Dhauli** involves a bit of a walk. Ask to be dropped off the bus at **Dhauli Chowk**, the junction on the main Puri–Bhubaneshwar road, and make your way along the avenue of cashew trees to the rock edict. The road to the *stupa* begins its short climb up the hill here, ending at a small car park surrounded by postcard and *chai* stalls – 2km in all.

Pipli

Fifteen minutes or so beyond Dhauli on the Puri road, splashes of bright colour in the shop fronts ranged alongside the main street announce your arrival in **PIPLI**, Orissa's **appliqué** capital (see above). Much of what the artisans produce here nowadays on their hand-powered sewing machines is shoddy kitsch compared with the painstaking work traditionally undertaken for the Jagannath temple. Express enough interest, though, and you'll be shown some of the better-quality pieces for which Pipli is justly straight lines of other Indian languages being more likely to pierce their surface. Today, *patta chitra* artists in **Raghurajpur** bind strips of palm leaves together to make canvases, and in the **Raghunandan Library** in Puri, students diligently copy old manuscripts to sell to tourists. The best places to see genuine **antique books** however are the national museum in New Delhi or the state musuem in Bhubaneshwar.

Textiles Distinctive **textiles** woven on hand looms are produced throughout Orissa. Silk *saris* from **Berhampur** and **Sambalpur** are the most famous, combining bands of rich colours and brocade with traditional geometric and figurative designs, though **ikat**, which originally came to Orissa via the ancient trade links with southeast Asia, is also typical. It is created using a "tie-dye", or *bandha*, technique in which bundles of thread are wrapped and dyed in different colours, and the pattern emerges automatically when they are woven together. The same principle is employed by weavers from the village of **Nuapatna**, 70km from Bhubaneshwar, who produce silk *ikats* covered in verses from the scriptures for use in the Jagannath temple.

Appliqué The village of **Pipli** (see below), between Bhubaneshwar and Puri, has the monopoly on **appliqué**, another craft rooted in the Jagannath cult. Geometric motifs and stylized birds, animals and flowers are cut out of brightly coloured cloth and sewn on to black backgrounds. Pipli artists are responsible for the chariot covers used in the Rath Yatra as well as for the small canopies, or *chhatris*, suspended above the presiding deity in Orissan temples. These days, the more entrepreneurial among them are turning their hands to garish secular goods, with wall-hangings, bedspreads, lampshades, handbags, beach-brollies and heart-shaped shields(*tarasa*) among the current favourites.

Metalwork *Tarakashi*, silver filigree, is Orissa's best known **metalwork** technique (*tara* = woven; *kashi* = wire). Using lengths of wire made by drawing strips of silver alloy through small holes, the smiths create distinctive ornaments, jewellery and utensils for use in rituals and celebrations. The **designs** are thought to have come to India from Persia with the Moghuls, though the existence of an identical art form in Indonesia, with whom the ancient Orissan kingdoms used to trade, suggests that the technique itself may be even older. *Tarakashi* is now only produced in any quantity in Cuttack (see p.937); thanks to a preference among Hindus for gold jewellery rather than silver, the gradual take-over of the trade by rip-off middle men, and a reluctance on the part of the artisans to change their designs with the times, it's becoming a dying art form.

Dhokra The "lost-wax" *dhokra* metal-casting technique practised by *adivasi* communities in Mayurbhunj and Keonjhar districts has done very well out of the recent revival of interest in "ethnic" art. You can spot *dhokra* objects – usually figurines depicting animals or tribal deities – by the distinctive woven-wire patterns that used to decorate them. The effect is achieved by adding threads to the original wax image, before it is covered with a clay mould which is filled with molten metal.

famed. Bedspreads, wall-hangings and small awnings, or *chhatris*, normally hung above household and temple shrines, are about the most authentic goods on offer – though who's to say Lord Jagannath doesn't use napkins.

Puri

A true-hearted pilgrim does not fear to measure kingdoms with his feeble footsteps.
Old Hindu saying

Whenever you approach the Orissan coast through its hinterland of lush green palm-groves and paddy fields, it's hard not to feel a sense of expectation. Never is this more true than upon arrival at **PURI** – the state's premier temple town and tourist resort. As the site of the famous **Jagannath temple** – which soars out of the narrow packed streets and colonial suburbs like some kind of misplaced space rocket – as well as the

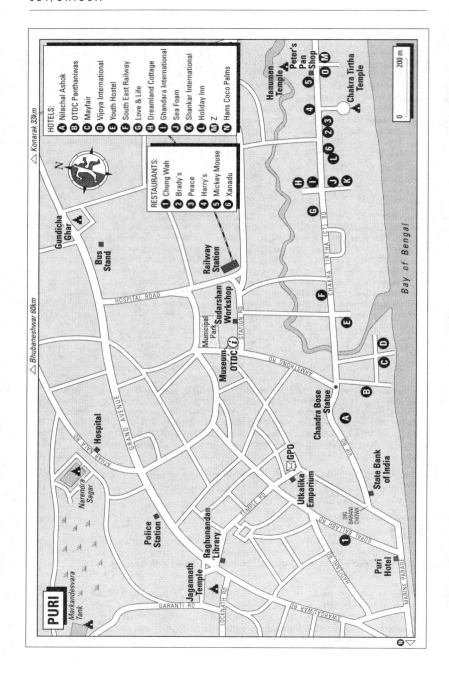

PURI

HOTELS:
- **A** Nilachal Ashok
- **B** OTDC Panthaniwas
- **C** Mayfair
- **D** Vijoya International
- **E** Youth Hostel
- **F** South East Railway
- **G** Love & Life
- **H** Dreamland Cottage
- **I** Ghandara International
- **J** Sea Foam
- **K** Shankar International
- **L** Holiday Inn
- **M** Z
- **N** Hans Coco Palms

RESTAURANTS:
- **1** Chung Wah
- **2** Brady's
- **3** Peace
- **4** Harry's
- **5** Mickey Mouse
- **6** Xanadu

Konarak 33km
Bhubaneshwar 60km

Markandesvara Tank
Jagannath Temple
GARANTI RD
LOCKNATH RD
Raghunandan Library
Police Station
Narendra Sagar
Hospital
ATHAR NALA RD
GRAND AVENUE
Gundicha Ghar
Bus Stand
HOSPITAL ROAD
Municipal Park
Sudarshan Workshop
Museum
OTDC
Railway Station
STATION RD
AMSTRONG RD
CHAKRA TIRTHA (CT) RD
Chandra Bose Statue
GPO
Utkalika Emporium
TEMPLE RD
State Bank of India
GOPAL BALLABH RD
DIG BARANI CHOWK
HADISAHI RD
SWARGADWAR RD
MARINE PARADE
Puri Hotel
Hanuman Temple
Peter's Pan Shop
Chakra Tirtha Temple
Bay of Bengal

0   200 m

location of one of India's most spectacular religious festivals, the annual **Rath Yatra**, Puri has been attracting visitors in their thousands since long before the hippy trail found its way here in the early 1970s.

Three distinct contingents come to Puri: middle-class Bengalis lured by the combined pleasures of the promenade and a *puja* in the nearby temple; young Western and Japanese visitors keen to discover Puri's small **travellers' scene**, and the thousands of pilgrims who flock in to see Lord Jagannath. Over the years the three have staked out their respective ends of town and stuck to them. It all makes for a rather bizarre, but not unpleasant atmosphere, where you can be transported from the maelstrom of religious devotion, to the sea, and back again to the relative calm of your hotel verandah at the turn of a bicycle wheel.

History

The early history of Puri before its rise to prominence as a Hindu religious centre is rather obscure. It's known that the surrounding forests were once the territory of the Sabaras, a pre-Aryan group, and that the sacred Buddhist site of **Dantapura** ("Town of the Tooth"), where one of the Buddha's teeth was enshrined, may also have been here, but few traces of these ancient times have survived.

Until the seventh and eighth centuries Puri was little more than a provincial outpost along the coastal trade route linking eastern India with the south. Then, thanks to its association with the Hindu reformer **Shankaracharya**, the town began to feature on the religious map. Shankara made Puri one of his four *mathas*, or centres for the practice of a radically new, and more ascetic form of Hinduism. Holy men from across the whole subcontinent came here to debate the new philosophies – a tradition carried on in the town's temple courtyards to this day. With the arrival of the **Gangas** at the beginning of the twelfth century, this religious and political importance was further consolidated. In 1135 Anantavarman Chodaganga founded the great temple in Puri, and dedicated it to **Purushottama**, one of the thousand names of Vishnu – an ambitious attempt to integrate the many feudal kingdoms recently conquered by the Gangas. Under the Gajapati dynasty in the fifteenth century Purushottama's name changed to Jagannath, "Lord of the Universe". Henceforth **Vaishnavism** and the devotional worship of Krishna, an incarnation of Vishnu, was to hold sway as the predominant religious influence in the temple. Puri is nowadays one of the four most auspicious pilgrimage centres, or *dhams*, in India. It's impossible to estimate the exact number of people who travel here each year, but in high season as many as 5000 pour daily through the bus and railway stations, while during the annual Rath Yatra or "Car Festival", the population temporarily swells to nearly a million.

By comparison, western-style leisure **tourism**, centred firmly on the town's long sandy beach, is a new phenomenon. The British were the first to spot Puri's potential as a resort. When they left, the Bengalis took over their bungalows, only to find themselves sharing the beach with an annual migration of young, *chillum*-smoking Westerners attracted to the town by its freely available hashish. Today, few vestiges of this era remain. Thanks to a concerted campaign by the municipality to clean up Puri's image, the "scene" has dwindled to little more than a handful of rather dismal cafes, and is a far cry from the swinging hippy paradise some still arrive here hoping to find.

Arrival and information

The none-too-welcome sight of rickshaw *wallahs* sprinting alongside incoming **buses** to grab a fare is most visitors' first experience of Puri. This little ritual takes place at the Athar Nala–Grand Avenue crossroads, close to the Jagannath temple in the heart of town, where buses drop their passengers before heading off to the main bus stand, fur-

> The telephone **area code** for Puri is ☎06752.

ther east. Arriving by **train** is marginally more sedate. Puri's end-of-the-line station lies on the eastern edge of Hospital Rd, a short ride from the beach and the hotels.

Puri is reasonably compact and flat, so **cycle rickshaws** are the best way to **get around**, at least when you first arrive – once you've got your bearings, you can rent a **bicycle** from any one of the numerous stalls in the travellers' enclave. **Auto-rickshaws** are thin on the ground, though one or two are always hanging around the railway station. Keep an eye out too for **Enfield motorbikes**, rented out by a couple of travel agents for full or half days and useful for trips up the coast to Konarak. In-house **travel agents** at the larger hotels can help with all transport arrangements, though the most reliable all-round place for ticket booking, flights, car/motorcycle/bike rental and so on is *Heritage Tours*, currently based at the *Mayfair Beach Resort* (☎23656).

Information

Unless you collect outdated leaflets on Orissa, the OTDC **tourist office** (Mon–Sat 10am–5pm; ☎22664) on Station Rd and the 24-hour counter at the railway station are a waste of time. Travel arrangements are best made or checked directly with the station itself or else through a travel agent.

Puri's main **post office** is on Temple Rd (Mon–Fri 10am–5pm, Sat 10am–noon); for poste restante (Mon–Fri 9am–noon & 4–6pm, Sat 9am–noon), use the side door on the left side of the building. If you need to **change money**, the *State Bank of India* (Mon–Fri 10am–2pm, Sat 10am–noon, Sun 11.30am–1.30pm) is on Dig Barani Chowk, just up the road from the *Nilachal Ashok Hotel*; the *Allahabad Bank* on Temple Rd, 200m towards the temple from the head post office, is speedy and efficient.

The Jagannath temple

The mighty **Jagannath temple** in Puri is for Hindus one of the four holy *dhams*, or "Abodes of the Divine". Every year millions of pilgrims, or *yatris*, make their way here to spend three auspicious days and nights near Lord Jagannath, the presiding deity. Non-Hindu visitors, obliged despite the temple's long-standing "caste no bar" rule to

---

PANDAS

Few non-Hindu visitors to Puri are aware of the world of the **yatri panda**, or pilgrimage priests. The *panda*'s job is basically to "look after" the pilgrims during their stay: to fix them up with board and lodging, to make sure they take in all the sites in the correct order, and, as *brahmins*, to offer prayers for them at the temple. In return, the pilgrims are expected to leave a generous goodbye tip, or **bidagi**, when they leave. Apart from bringing "good luck" in the next life, the *bidagi* system is also, needless to say, highly lucrative for the *pandas*.

No surprise then that each one, and the *dharamshalas* to which they are connected, has his own exclusive rights to the rich pickings. Every town and village in the country is carved up according to long-established links recorded in special **ledgers**. The first thing the *pandas* have to ascertain from the new arrivals therefore, is their place of birth, family name and caste. Once these are established, the pilgrims are ushered from the station back to the appropriate *dharamshala* and shown the records of visits made by previous generations from their village or family. Woe betide anyone who tries to poach clients. When they're not relieving hapless *yatris* of their rupees or indulging in that time-honoured Puri tradition of drinking *bhangas* (a sugar and milk-based preparation containing ground cannabis leaves), *pandas* spend their days **wrestling** in Puri's old-style gyms.

THE JAGANNATH DEITIES AND RATH YATRA

Stand on any street corner in Orissa and you'd be hard pushed not to spot at least one image of the black-faced **Jagannath deity**, with his brother **Balabhadra** and sister **Subhadra**. This faintly grotesque family trio, with glaring eyes, stumpy legless bodies, and undersized arms protruding menacingly from heavily garlanded heads, seems to crop up everywhere – from buses and cycle rickshaws, to *beedee* wrappers and bags of nuts.

The origins of this peculiar national symbol are shrouded in **legend**. One version relates that the image of Lord Jagannath looks the way it does because it was never actually finished. King Indramena, a ruler of ancient Orissa, once found the god Vishnu in the form of a tree stump washed up on Puri beach. After performing all the necessary prostrations, he carried the lump of wood to the temple and, following instructions from Brahma, called the court carpenter Visvakarma to carve out the image. Visvakarma agreed to perform the task on condition that no-one so much as set eyes on the deity until it was completed. The king, however, unable to contain his excitement, peeped through a crack in the door of the carpenter's workshop during the night to see how the job was progressing. Visvakarma spotted him, downed tools just as he had promised and cast a spell on the deity so that no-one else could finish it.

These days, new versions have to be produced about every twelve years (they rot in the humidity) by specially trained temple priests in a sacred ceremony known as **Nava Kalebara**, literally "new embodiment". The culmination of highly secret, nocturnal ritual takes place when the "divine essence" of the old Lord Jagannath is removed from his hollowed-out chest and placed inside that of the new incumbent.

The Jagannath deities are also the chief focus of Puri's annual "Car Festival", the **Rath Yatra**. For a couple of weeks in midsummer, the town is saturated with visitors who come to witness the procession of the colossal Jagannath chariots, or *raths*, down Puri's Grand Avenue. Rath Yatra is just one episode in a long cycle of rituals that begins in the full moon phase of the Oriya month of Djesto (June/July). In the first of these, the **Chandan Yatra**, special replicas of the three temple deities are taken to the **Narendra Sagar** where for twenty-one consecutive days they are smeared with *chandan* (sandalwood paste) and rowed around in a ceremonial, swan-shaped boat. At the end of this period, in a ceremony known as **Snana Yatra**, the three go for a dip in the tank, after which they head off for fifteen days of secluded preparation for Rath Yatra.

The Car Festival proper takes place during the full moon of the following month, Asadho (July/Aug). Lord Jagannath and his brother and sister are placed in their chariots and dragged by 4200 honoured devotees through the assembled multitudes to their summer home, the **Gundicha Ghar** ("Garden House"), 1.5km away. If you can find a secure vantage point and escape the crush, it's an amazing sight. The immense chariots are draped with brightly coloured cloth and accompanied down Grand Avenue by elephants, the local Raja (who sweeps the chariots as a gesture of humility and equality with all castes), and a cacophony of music and percussion. Each has a different name and a different coloured cover, and is built anew every year to rigid specifications laid down in the temple's ancient manuals. Balabhadra's *rath*, the green one, leads; Subhadra is next, in black; and lastly, in the thirteen-metre-tall chariot with eighteen wheels and a vivid red and yellow drape, sits Lord Jagannath himself. It takes eight hours or more to haul the *raths* to their resting place. After a nine-day holiday, the sequence is performed in reverse, and the three deities return to the temple to resume their normal lives.

Conventional wisdom has it that the procession commemorates Krishna's journey from Gokhul to Matheran; historians cite the similarity between the *raths* and temple towers to claim it's a hangover from the time when temples were made of wood. Whatever the reason for the Car Festival, its devotees take it very seriously indeed. Early travellers spoke of fanatics throwing themselves under the gigantic wheels as a short cut to eternal bliss (whence the English word "**Juggernaut**", meaning an "irresistible, destructive force"). Contemporary enthusiasts are marginally more restrained, but like most mass gatherings in India the whole event teeters at times on the brink of complete mayhem.

observe proceedings from a nearby rooftop, will find the spectacle of the gigantic tower and surrounding compound thronging with devotees absolutely extraordinary.

The present structure, modelled on the older Lingaraj temple in Bhubaneshwar, was erected by the Ganga ruler Anantavarman Chodaganga, at the start of the twelfth century. The best place to see it from is the flat roof of the **Raghunandan Library** (Mon–Sat 10am–noon & 4–8pm) directly opposite the main gate. One of the librarians, wielding a long stick to fend off the monkeys, will show you up the stairs via their collection of dusty tomes and **palm-leaf manuscripts**, to the vantage point overlooking the East Gate – you should make a donation for this service, but again, some of the amounts registered in the ledger beggar belief. From here you have a fine view of the immense **deul**, at 65m by far the loftiest building in the entire region. To the Dutch sailors passing the Orissan coast three centuries or more ago the tower was known as "the Black Pagoda". More recently, archeologists chipping away at its distinctively plastered surface have begun to expose elaborate **carving** simular to that on the Lingaraj. The work being carried out at present is intended to restore this sculpture to its original state. Crowning the very top, a long scarlet pennant and the eight-spoked wheel(*chakra*) of Vishnu announce the presence of Lord Jagannath within.

In imitation of a ridge of mountain peaks, the pyramidal roofs of the temples' adjoining halls, or *mandapas*, rise in steps towards the tower. The one nearest the sanctuary, the *jagamohana* (assembly hall), is part of the original building, but the other two, the smaller *nata mandir* (dance hall) and the *bhoga-mandapa* (hall of offerings) nearest the entrance, were added in the fifteenth and sixteenth centuries. These halls still see a lot of action during the day as worshippers file through for *darshan*, while late every night they become the venue for devotional music and dance performances. Women and transvestite dancers (*maharis* and *gotipuras*) perform episodes for the amusement of the Lord Jagannath and his "brother" and "sister" from Jayadev's *Gita Govinda*, the much-loved story of the life of Krishna.

Outside the main building, in the walled compound surrounding the temple, stand dozens of subsidiary shrines that the pilgrims are supposed to honour during their visit. Nearby, on the left of the enclosure, are the **kitchens**. The food prepared here, known as *mahaprashad*, is blessed by Lord Jagannath himself before being eaten. It's said to be so pure that even a morsel of it taken from the mouth of a dog and fed to a *brahmin* by a *harijan* (an "untouchable") will cleanse the body of sin. Among the 10,000 or so daily recipients of the *mahaprashad* are the 6000 employees of the temple itself. These **servants** are divided into ninety-six hereditary and hierarchical orders known as *chhatisha niyoga*, and include the priests who minister to the needs of the deities (teeth cleaning, dressing, feeding, getting them ready for afternoon siesta, and so forth), as well as the teams of craftspeople who produce all the materials required for the daily round of rituals.

A good place to sample the atmosphere of the temple is in front of its main (East) gate. The elaborate doorway is usually jammed with groups of *yatris*, some newly alighted from special buses, others making their way barefoot through the crowds from nearby *dharamshalas*. In front of the gateway, its base splashed with vermilion and flowers, is a **column** that once stood before the Surya temple in Konarak. It was brought here in the eighteenth century by the Maharathas and is topped by a figure of Aruna, the charioteer of the sun god.

Around the temple

The crowded streets **around the Jagannath temple** are buzzing with activity – commercial as much as religious. **Grand Avenue**, Puri's broad main street, is lined with a frenetic **bazaar**, many of its stalls specializing in *rudrat* and sandalwood beads, Ayurvedic cures and the ubiquitous images of Lord Jagannath. Look out too for the wonderful "religious maps" of Puri. Hindu mythology traditionally represents the pilgrimage site in the form of a conch shell made up of seven concentric layers, with the deities' platform as the innermost core and the outer third under the sea. Not much help for finding your way around, but superb souvenirs.

Leading south from the main square, the dingy **Swargadwar** ("Cremation") **Rd** plunges you into a world of acrid smells, tea stalls and heaps of oily sweets swarming with flies. For most of the day the entire length of the lane is lined with beggars sitting in front of rice and ten-paise coins tossed by passing pilgrims. You're also likely to see bare-chested *brahmins* from the temple performing their ablutions, sacred threads tucked safely over their ears to preserve purity (the ear is the purest part of the body in Hinduism, being associated with the source of the Ganges). Keep going down Swargadwar Rd for long enough and you eventually surface to the glaring sunshine and sea breezes of the main promenade. The cremation ground itself, situated well beyond the south corner of the beach, is among India's most auspicious mortuary sites. Inquisitive tourists, especially those wielding cameras, are definitely not welcome.

A more enjoyable foray from the main square is the trip up to the **sacred tanks** in the north of town (best attempted by bicycle). Follow the north wall of the Jagannath temple up to the little road junction in the far corner, then turn right and stick to the same narrow twisting backstreet for about five minutes until you arrive at the **Markandesvara tank**. This large, steep-sided bathing place is said to have been the spot where Vishnu once resided in the form of a *neem* tree, while his temple, the precursor of the current one in Puri, was buried deep under a sand dune. There's no sign of the tree, but the temples on the south side are worth a look, particularly the smaller of the group, which contains images of the Jagannath trio.

If you retrace your route from here back down the lane as far as the first road junction, then bear left and continue another mile or so, you'll emerge at the **Narendra Sagar** – Puri's most holy tank. In the middle stands a small temple, joined to the *ghats* by a narrow footbridge. During the annual **Chandan Yatra**, or "Swimming Festival", a replica deity of Lord Jagannath, Mandan Mohan, is brought here every day for his dip. The temple itself is plastered with vivid **murals** that you can photograph on payment of the set fee listed nearby. The list also advertises the range of services offered by the temple *pujaris*, including the unlikely sounding "Throw of Bone" and "Throw of Hair" – references to the tank's role as another of Puri's famous mortuary ritual sites.

Museum and Sudarshan workshop

Puri's small **museum** (Tues–Sun 10am–5pm), tucked away above the tourist office on Station Rd, houses tacky reproductions of the Jagannath deities' ceremonial garb, along with models of the *raths* used in the Car Festival. You won't find much information, but the handful of displays are clearly labelled and supplemented by photos.

Further down the road towards the station, close to the Shinto shrine, the **Sudarshan workshop** is one of the few traditional stone carvers' yards left in Puri. For once, the sculptors and their apprentices seem more interested in pursuing their art than selling it to tourists, but gladly point potential customers in the direction of the factory **shop** next door. Most of the pieces here are large religious icons beautifully carved out of khondalite – the multi-coloured stone used in the Sun temple at Konarak.

The beach

If a peaceful swim and a lie in the sun are your top priorities, you may be disappointed with **Puri beach**. It's not just the constant stream of hawkers that's the problem. Thanks to a combination of an open **sewer** trickling into the sea slap in the middle of the beach, and a stiff on-shore breeze to spread the contents around the shallows, bathing, at least along certain stretches, can be something of a health risk. Keep to the area south of the *Mayfair Hotel*, well away from the outlet.

Pollution aside, Puri's strand makes an excellent place for a stroll. The bottom end is traditionally the preserve of Calcutta's salary men and their families. While the higher-ranking among them enjoy the use of company bungalows in the suburbs, the majority squeeze into rooms on the beach-front hotels overlooking the promenade – with its knick-knack stalls and cafes, faintly reminiscent of a shabby British seaside resort.

Local fishermen patrol the beach as **lifeguards**; recognizable more by their triangular straw hats and *dhotis* than their strapping physiques, they wade with their punters into the surf and literally hold their hands to keep them on their feet. This may seem a little excessive to anyone used to choppier water, but the undertow claims victims every year, so weak swimmers should be careful. When not saving lives, the fishermen are busy at the other end of the beach, engaged in the more traditional industries of mending nets and boats. The **fishing village** is one of the biggest in Orissa, with dozens of tiny triangular sails tacking to and fro off the coast during the day. Once landed, the catch is transferred to baskets for women to carry to the **fish market** in the village, and the heavy collapsible boats are split in two and dragged up the beach. The best time to pay a visit is around dawn, when the sight of the little fleet putting out towards the sun rising over the sea can make Puri seem truly exotic after all.

Around Puri

Back inland among the coconut palms, rice paddies, muddy lakes and rivers, are many traditional *brahmin* villages, most of them Vaishnavite. Two such places, about 12km from Puri just off the main Bhubaneshwar road are **BIRAPRATAPUR** and **GANGA-NARAYANPUR**, where you can see thatched houses of baked clay and wood, many painted with gay designs, and small temples fronted by stone frames used for suspending the deity during festivals. You may even chance upon the house of an astrologer and have your fortune told. For those not quite up to puffing around the area by bike, *Heritage Tours* (☎23656) in Puri arrange guided tours of a couple of villages for around Rs700 per car, including food.

Accommodation

Virtually all Puri's **hotels** stand on or near the beach – a five-minute ride from the railway station through the bumpy back streets. A strict distinction is observed between hotels pitched at domestic tourists – lined up behind the promenade, Marine Drive, on the west end of the beach – and those oriented towards budget-conscious Westerners, sandwiched further east between the high-rise, upmarket resort hotels and the fishing *bastee*. This latter district around Chakratirtha (CT) Rd, known as **Pentakunta**, has become a real tourist enclave, and for many foreign visitors counts as Puri's main attraction. Literally dozens of places are tucked away down lookalike sandy lanes, most offering basic concrete-walled rooms, some dorm beds, lockers, fans and hot water. If you find the smaller lodges too cramped, the slightly decaying colonial buildings on the main street tend to be more comfortable. Many have wide verandahs, balconies and courtyards full of potted plants, where you can relax during the hot afternoons.

The less expensive hotels are quiet during the summer months, but the **pricier accommodation** tends to be booked solid well in advance over Rath Yatra, which coincides with the Bengali holiday season – make your reservations as early as possible.

Dreamland Cottage, off CT Rd (☎24122). Not exactly roses around the door, but homely and relaxed with a leafy, secluded garden. ①.

Ghandara International, CT Rd (☎24117). Considerately managed for the budget traveller, with rock-bottom, clean rooms around a courtyard, roof space, lock-up, generator, free washing machine and drinking water in the fridge. Some dorm beds. Excellent value. ①–⑦.

Hans Coco Palms, Marine Drive (☎22638). Modern complex in a superb setting 2km south of the centre; all rooms overlook the sea. Central a/c, bar and restaurant. ⑦–⑧.

Holiday Inn, CT Rd (☎23782). Clinical but comfortable western-style hotel with simple, pleasant rooms, some overlooking the beach. ⑤–⑥.

Love and Life, CT Rd (☎24433). Very popular with the many young Japanese visitors to Puri. Easy-going atmosphere, relaxing garden and a good restaurant. ①–④.

Mayfair Beach Resort, CT Rd (☎24041). New, fashionable hotel. Luxury chalets, backing on to a pool and the beach. 5-star facilities, including an excellent restaurant. Recommended. ⑧.

Nilachal Ashok, Raj Bhavan, VIP Rd (☎23651). Typically austere modern building set in its own grounds. Formulaic furnishings, now a touch jaded. All the usual comforts, and all rooms a/c. ⑦.

OTDC Panthaniwas, off CT Rd (☎22562). Impersonal hotel, where some of the plain but spacious rooms catch sea breezes, some are a/c. Bar, restaurant and coffee shop. Good value. ④–⑤.

Sea Foam, CT Rd (☎23226). Another old favourite, offering very basic creature comforts including hot water and safe deposit. A new extension promises more of the same with less grime. ①–②.

Shankar International, off CT Rd (☎22696). Slightly old-fashioned, though well-run, with rooms at assorted prices on three floors, sea views and a lawn with wicker chairs. ②–⑤.

South East Railway Hotel, CT Rd (☎22063). Nothing has changed here since it was the premier bolt hole for Calcutta's *burra-* and *mem-sahibs*. Turbaned bearers with big belts pad barefoot around the verandahs; a must for Raj-ophiles. ⑥–⑦.

Sri Balajee Lodge, CT Rd (☎23388). Some way beyond most of the other hotels, this small lodge with simple rooms around a courtyard offers discounts for longer stays. ②–③.

Toshali Sands, Konarak Rd (☎22888). Self-styled "ethnic village" 9km north of town. Cottages grouped around a garden and pool, with good restaurant, gym and sauna. Ideal for families. ⑧.

Vijoya International, off CT Rd (☎22702). Faceless giant, with all the usual facilities including central a/c, exchange, restaurant and "unending comforts". Also direct access to the beach. ④–⑦.

Youth Hostel, off CT Rd. Stuffy, segregated dorms and a 10pm curfew. Not a place to hang around during the evenings, but cheap and convenient if everywhere else is full. ①.

Z, CT Rd (☎22554). An institution, the "Z" (pronounced *jed*) made its name for providing cheap, clean and comfortable rooms in congenial surroundings. Prices are higher now, but the rooms are still pleasant and there's a common room with satellite TV. Some dorm beds. ③–④.

Eating

Inexpensive eating options around Pentakunta are limited to the handful of cafes along CT Rd, most of which are of the "write your own order" ilk and seem to be staffed by twelve-year-olds. The food they dish up rarely amounts to anything more exciting than copious bland platefuls with a western bias – though the Chinese and Indian dishes are sometimes passable. In season, fresh **seafood** features prominently, as do puddings steeped in that great Indian-English tedium reliever, known here as "caustered".

Better food is to be found in the restaurants at the nearby resort hotels. Most serve a reasonable range of veg and non-veg Indian dishes, including fish, with a few Chinese alternatives thrown in for form. After the rough-and-ready style of the CT Rd coffee houses, the middle-class Bengali atmosphere in these places can seem rather stilted.

Brady's, CT Rd. A good meeting place, with standard budget travellers' menu.

Chung Wah, Armstrong Rd, off Marine Drive. Hard to find, but worth the effort. Popular, family-run restaurant serving authentic, inexpensive Chinese food.

Harry's, CT Rd. The most popular place for a budget breakfast. Good fish, too, and a cheap fax service. Opens early.

Holiday Inn, CT Rd. Characterless surroundings, but the mostly Indian food is carefully prepared, delicious and not too pricey.

Holiday Resort, CT Rd. Classy a/c hotel restaurant. The upmarket western decor is less appealing than the food, which includes superb Bengali *thalis* (lunch only), and is not too expensive.

Love and Life, CT Rd. In addition to the staple travellers' favourites, this recently renovated road-side joint serves more costly Japanese dishes with an accent on fresh fish.

Mayfair, CT Rd. Sophisticated and expensive. A top-class resident Chinese chef and an unusually adventurous menu make this the best place for an extravagant evening away from *dal* and rice.

Mickey Mouse, CT Rd. The loudest music and the most original lampshades. Very laid-back service too, though chess sets are considerately provided.

Peace, CT Rd. Unremarkable if inexpensive food, served to an exclusively international clientele.

South East Railway Hotel, CT Rd. Idiosyncratic colonial charm, with checked table cloths, silver butter dishes and waiters in *pukka* turbans and belts. The poor-value set menus are less memorable. Non-residents should give a couple of hours' warning.

Xanadu, CT Rd. Easily the best of the cheapies with a pleasant garden and huge menu.

Listings

Medical emergencies Puri's main "HQ" hospital (☎22062) is well outside the town centre. Hotels such as the *Panthaniwas*, or *Heritage Tours* at the *Mayfair*, can help find a doctor in an emergency.

Shopping and markets *Utkalika* and the other hand-loom emporiums, just up from the head post office on Temple Rd, stock a good range of local crafts at fixed prices. *Surdarshan* on Station Rd (close to the OTDC tourist office) is the best place to buy traditional stone sculpture. *Holiday Inn* and *Brady's* cafe have some jewellery, textiles and filigree, but are not the cheapest places in town. For reproductions of the Jagannath deity, look in the bazaar around the temple. There's a lively market on the beach off Marine Drive, south of *Puri Hotel*, every evening until around 10pm.

Tours OTDC run tour buses from in front of the *Panthaniwas* to nearby attractions including Bhubaneshwar and environs (Rs75), and Chilka Lake (Mon, Wed & Fri; Rs80).

MOVING ON FROM PURI

Puri is joined to the main Calcutta–Madras routes by a branch line of the busy South East Railway network and a good metalled road through Bhubaneshwar, so it's well-connected with most other major Indian cities. Travel agents at major hotels, especially the *Mayfair Beach Resort*, can book tickets.

By train

A couple of direct express trains take 32–36hr to link Puri with **Delhi**, some calling at **Varanasi** and **Agra** en route. Avoid the evening *Kalinga–Utkal Express*; it's much slower and frequently late. The quickest and most convenient train to **Calcutta** is the *Jagannath Express* #8410, which leaves Puri at 9.10pm for the 11hr overnight trip.

If you're heading for **south India**, either pass through Bhubaneshwar or change at Khurda Road, 44km from Puri, to pick up daily trains to **Madras** (22hr). Two of these (*Howrah/Guwahati–Bangalore Express* #2611/2674) carry on to Bangalore on Wed and Thurs, while on Fri, Sat, Sun and Mon there's a direct service to Kochi. On Tues you can even go all the way to Thiruvananthapuram on the *Guwahati–Trivandrum Express* #2602.

Getting to **Bombay** also involves changing at Bhubanashwar and a total journey time of more than 40hr. For **Central Indian** destinations such as Jabalpur or Nagpur, take the *Kalinga–Utkal Express* #8477 as far as Bilaspur and change there.

Computerized **reservations** can be made at the main station (Mon–Sat 8am–3pm, Sun 8am–1pm) or, for second-class tickets only, at the city booking office on Grand Avenue (opposite the police station).

By bus

Minibuses are definitely the easiest way to travel between Puri and **Bhubaneshwar**. Services are fast (1hr) and frequent until 5pm, but make sure that it's "non-stop" before you get on. The same applies to **Konarak** buses, which also leave more or less hourly from the main city bus stand in the east of town, near the Gundicha Ghar. Jeeps ply the same route much more frequently for the same price, departing from the bus stand when full.

If you plan to head south by road along the Orissan coast, OTDC run a direct, non-stop "luxury" bus to the *Panthaniwas* at Balugaon on **Chilka Lake**. It leaves from the Puri *Panthaniwas* on Mon, Wed and Fri mornings, and costs Rs85.

Konarak

Time runs like a horse with seven reins,
Thousand-eyed, unageing, possessing much seed.
Him the poets mount; His wheels are all beings.
                    The *Artharva Veda*

If you visit only one temple in Orissa, it should be **KONARAK**. Standing imperiously in its compound of lawns and casuarina trees, 35km north of Puri on the coast road, this majestic pile of oxidizing sandstone is considered to be the apogee of Orissan architecture and one of the finest religious buildings anywhere in the world.

The temple is all the more remarkable for having languished under a huge mound of sand since it fell into neglect three hundred or so years ago. Not until early this century, when the dune and heaps of collapsed masonry were cleared away from the sides, did the full extent of its ambitious design become apparent. A team of seven galloping horses and twenty-four exquisitely carved wheels found lining the flanks of a raised platform showed that the temple had been conceived in the form of a colossal chariot for the sun god **Surya**, its presiding deity. Equally as sensational was the re-discovery among the ruins of some extraordinary **erotic sculpture**. Konarak, like Khajuraho (see p.387), is plastered with loving couples locked in ingenious amatory postures drawn from the *Kama Sutra* – a feature that may well explain the comment made by one of Akbar's emissaries, Abdul Fazl, in the sixteenth century: "Even those who are difficult to please," he enthused, "stand astonished at its sight."

Apart from the temple, a small **museum** and a fishing **beach**, Konarak **village** has little going for it. In recent years, cafes and hotels have mushroomed around its dusty bus stand to service the stream of bus parties that buzz in and out during the day, spilling out crowds of day trippers to clamber over the ruins in their best silk *saris* and shirtings. Sundays and public holidays in particular are best avoided if you're hoping for some peace and quiet. In any case, aim to be around at sunset after most of the tour groups have left, when the rich evening light works wonders on the natural colours in the khondalite sandstone.

History

As with all important temples, Konarak has its own popular **origin myth**. Samba, one of Krishna's sons, was caught spying on his stepmothers while they were bathing in the river. Enraged by his son's prurience, Krishna is said to have cursed him with leprosy and expelled him from the palace. Twelve years of penances later, Surya (who is also the divine healer of skin complaints) took pity on the boy and cured him of the disease, in return for which Samba built a temple dedicated to the sun god nearby.

History, as ever, has a different version of events. Inscription plates attribute the founding of the temple to the thirteenth-century Ganga monarch **Narashimadeva**, possibly to commemorate his military successes against the Muslim invaders. The mighty sun temple, with its 70-metre tower, was a landmark for European mariners sailing off the shallow Orissan coast (who knew it as the "**Black Pagoda**"; see p.928) as well as an obvious target for raids on the region. In the fifteenth century Konarak was sacked by the Yavana army. Though unable to raze the temple or destroy its deity, which had been smuggled away by the priests to Puri, the marauding Muslims nevertheless managed to damage it sufficiently to allow the elements get a foothold. As the sea receded, sand slowly engulfed the building and salty breezes set to work on the spongy khondalite, eroding the exposed surfaces and weakening the superstructure. By the end of the nineteenth century, the tower had disintegrated completely, and the porch lay buried up to its waist, prompting one art historian of the day to describe it as "an enormous mass of stones studded with a few peepal trees here and there".

Restoration only really began in earnest at the start of this century. After putting an end to the activities of the local Raja, who had been plundering the ruins for masonry and sculpture to use on his own temple, government archeologists set about unearthing the immaculately preserved hidden sections of the building and salvaging what they could from the rest of the rubble. The porch was shored up with rocks and sand, large chunks of the walls were rebuilt, and chemicals applied to the stonework to prevent further deterioration. Finally, trees were planted to shelter the compound from the corrosive winds, and a museum opened to house what sculpture was not shipped off to Delhi, Calcutta and London. Today, Konarak is one of India's most visited ancient monuments, and the flagship of OTDC's bid to promote the area as an alternative to the "golden triangle" of Delhi, Agra and Jaipur.

The temple

The main entrance to the **temple** complex on its eastern, sea-facing side brings you out directly in front of the **bhoga-mandapa**, or "hall of offerings". Ornate carvings of amorous couples, musicians and dancers decorating the sides of its platform and stocky pillars suggest that the now roofless pavilion, which was a later addition to the temple, must originally have been used for ritual dance performances.

To get a sense of the overall scale and design, stroll along the low wall that bounds the south side of the enclosure before you tackle the ruins proper. As a giant model of Surya's war chariot, the temple was intended both as an offering to the Vedic sun god and as a symbol for the passage of time itself – believed to lie in his control. The seven **horses** straining to haul the sun eastwards in the direction of the dawn (only one is still intact) represent the days of the week, while the **wheels** ranged along the base stand for the twelve months. Originally, a **stone pillar** crowned with an image of Aruna, Surya's charioteer, also stood in front of the main door, though this has since been moved to the eastern gateway of the Jagannath temple in Puri.

With the once-lofty **sanctuary tower** now reduced to little more than a clutter of sandstone slabs tumbling from the western wing, the **porch**, or *jagomohana*, has become Konarak's real centrepiece. Its impressive pyramidal roof, rising to a height of 38m, is divided into three tiers by rows of uncannily lifelike statues – mostly musicians and dancers serenading the sun god on his passage through the heavens. Among the figures on the bottom platform are a four-headed, six-armed Shiva, garlanded with severed heads and performing the dance of death. Though now blocked up, the huge cubic **interior** of the porch was a marvel of medieval architecture. The original builders ran into problems installing its heavy ornamental ceiling, and had to forge ten-metre iron beams as support – a considerable engineering feat for the time.

Amazingly elaborate **sculpture** embellishes every conceivable nook and cranny of the outside of the porch – and most other parts of the temple – in a bewildering profusion of deities, animals, floral patterns, mythical beasts and aquatic monsters. This is what attracts the majority of visitors to Konarak – above all, the infamous **erotica**. Look at any carved surface for long enough and you're sure to come across a voluptuous maiden striking an alluring pose or a richly bejewelled couple sharing a tender moment. Some of Konarak's most beautiful erotic pieces are to be found in the niches halfway up the walls of the porch, where a keen eye may be able to spot the telltale pointed beards of *sadhus*, clearly making the most of a lapse in their vows of chastity. Bawdier scenes also appear in miniature along the sides of the platform and around the two remaining intricate door-frames on the main building – just look for the groups of tittering teenagers. Though sculpture of this kind is not uncommon in India, only rarely does it run to such rampant excesses. Many theories have been advanced over the years to explain the phenomenon. In Konarak's case, it seems likely that the erotic art was meant as a kind of metaphor for the ecstatic bliss experienced by the soul when it fuses with the divine cosmos – a notion central to **tantra** and the related worship of the female principle, **shakti**, which were prevalent throughout medieval Orissa.

Moving clockwise around the temple from the south side of the main staircase, the intricately worked faces of the **platform** are what first grab most people's attention. Check out the detail on the **wheels**, and the extraordinary **friezes** that run in narrow bands above and below them. These depict military processions (inspired by King Narashimadeva's tussles with the Muslims) and hunting scenes, and feature literally thousands of rampaging **elephants**. If you want to keep any children busy for a while, tell them to find the **giraffe** which crops up somewhere on the top frieze (south side) – proof that trade with Africa took place during the thirteenth century.

Once past the porch you arrive at a double staircase that leads up to a shrine containing a **statue of Surya** himself. Carved out of top-quality green chlorite stone, this serene image – one of three around the base of the ruined sanctuary tower – is a real masterpiece. Notice his characteristic tall riding boots and the little figure of Aruna, the charioteer, holding the reins of the seven horses at his feet. The other two statues in the series are also worth a look, if only to compare their facial expressions which, following the progress of the sun around the temple, change from wakefulness in the morning (south) to heavy-eyed weariness at the end of the day (north). Before working your way around the far side of the porch, you can also climb down into the remains of the **sanctum sanctorum** where the deity was once enshrined. At the foot of the western wall there's an altar-like platform covered with carving: the kneeling figure in its central panel is thought to be King Narashimadeva, the donor of the temple.

Elsewhere in the compound

The first and largest of the two small **shrines** in the southwest corner, the **Mayadevi temple** (formerly dedicated to Surya's wife, the shadow goddess), is the most interesting of the other sites in the compound. Positioned at the north and south ends of the compound, now occupying their own separate pedestals, are the impressive **colossi** that once guarded the temple entrances: harnessed elephants to the north and rearing war-horses led by soldiers to the south. The lions that used to flank the eastern gateway have been moved to a spot near the "hall of offerings".

Some way outside the compound near the *Yatri Niwas* restaurant, the sculpture at the **archeological museum** (daily 9am–5pm) is neither particularly inspiring nor informatively displayed, most of the juicy pieces having been taken off to Delhi. Of more interest is the small shed in the northeast corner of the enclosure. The stone architrave inside it, bearing images of **nine planet deities**, the Navagrahas, originally sat above one of the temple's ornamental doorways and is now kept as a living shrine.

Practicalities

The easiest way to get to Konarak from Puri, 33km down the coast, is by **bus** or **jeep**. There are regular services in both directions and the journey only takes an hour or so, which makes it possible to do the round trip in a day. Buses from Bhubaneshwar are much less frequent and take between two and four hours to cover the 65km (with a change at Pipli), depending on whether you catch the one direct express "tourist" bus, which leaves from the town stand at 10am. Alternatively, you could join one of OTDC's whistle stop **tours**, though as these combine Konarak with a string of other attractions they don't leave you nearly enough time to do the temple justice. The tour from Puri (Tues–Sat depart 6.30am, return 6.30pm; Rs75) takes in Bhubaneshwar and environs, while the one from Bhubaneshwar (Tues–Sat depart 9am, return 6.30pm; Rs85, a/c Rs130) includes Pipli and Puri. Both leave from in front of the *Panthaniwas*.

Accommodation, eating and entertainment

With Puri only an hour down the road, few people end up staying in Konarak. If, however, you want to enjoy the temple at a more leisurely pace or just fancy spending the night somewhere a little more peaceful, there's plenty of **accommodation** in the village. Not far from the main entrance to the monuments, the OTDC *Panthaniwas* (☎06758/8823; ②–③) is nothing special but has clean and reasonably priced rooms, and is responsible for four a/c rooms at the tiny *Travellers' Lodge* (☎06758/8831; ④), tucked behind the *Yatri Niwas* (☎06758/8820; ②), up past the main bus stand a short way before the museum. The rooms at the latter are neat and pleasant, and unlike the other two, cost less if you're travelling alone. In the unlikely event of these three being full, there are also a couple of shabbier places around the village. Another decent place, a short way down the beach road, is the *Labanya Lodge* (☎06758/8824; ①), with clean, good-value rooms and friendly management.

ODISSI DANCE

Even visitors who don't normally enjoy classical dance cannot fail to be seduced by the elegance and poise of Orissa's own regional style, **Odissi**. Friezes in the Rani Gumpha at Udaigiri (see p.919) attest to the popularity of dance in the Orissan courts as far back as the second century BC. By the time the region's Hindu "golden age" was in full swing, it had become an integral part of religious ritual, with purpose-built dance halls, or *nata mandapas*, being added to existing temples and corps of dancing girls employed to perform in them. **Devadasis**, literally "wives (or slaves)" of the god, were handed over by their parents at an early age and symbolically "married" to the deity. They were trained to read, sing and dance and, as one disapproving early nineteenth-century chronicler put it, to "make public traffic of their charms" with male visitors to the temple. Gradually, ritual intercourse (a legacy of the tantric influence on medieval Hinduism) degenerated into pure prostitution, and dance, formerly an act of worship, grew to become little more than a form of commercial entertainment. By the colonial era, Odissi was all but lost, its secrets frozen in ancient sculpture or absorbed into the popular traditions of musical plays that toured provincial towns and villages.

This would probably have heralded the end of Odissi altogether, had it not been for the rediscovery in the 1950s of the **Abhinaya Chandrika**, a fifteenth-century manual on classical Orissan dance. Like Bharatanatyam, India's most popular dance style, Odissi has its own highly complex language of poses and steps. Based on the *tribhanga* "hip-shot" stance, movements of the body, hands and eyes convey specific emotions and enact episodes from well-known religious texts – most commonly the **Gita Govinda** (the Krishna story). Using the *Abhinaya* and temple sculpture, dancers and choreographers were able to reconstruct this grammar into a coherent form and within a decade Odissi was a thriving performance art once again. Today, dance lessons with a reputed guru have become *de rigueur* for the young daughters of Orissa's middle classes – an ironic reversal of its earlier associations.

Few types of dance match Odissi for sheer style. The dancers deck themselves out in extravagant costumes of pleated silk brocades, silver jewellery, bells, jasmin flowers and distinctive *dhotis*, while in front of the stage, musicians and singers recite hypnotic *talas* – cycles of devotional poetry set to music. Unfortunately, catching a **live performance** is largely a matter of being in the right place at the right time. The only regular recitals take place in the Jagannath temple. If, however, you're not a Hindu, the annual **festival of dance** at Konarak, in the last week of November, is your best chance of seeing Orissa's top performers. While the atmosphere might not be as authentic as in the temple, the dancing is superb and the flood-lit backdrop spectacular. Failing that, the state television station broadcasts Odissi quite regularly, especially on public holidays. If you're keen to learn, a number of dance academies in Bhubaneshwar run intensive **courses** for beginners (see p.918).

For **food** you have a choice between the row of snack and tea stalls opposite the temple or a more substantial meal in one of the hotel restaurants. The *Panthaniwas'* very popular and inexpensive *Gitanjali* cafe serves the usual range of veg and rice dishes. Further afield, the *Yatri Niwas* is also open to non-residents and less likely to be packed out at lunchtime with tour parties.

Power cuts permitting, the sun temple is **floodlit** most evenings (May–Sept 7–10pm, Oct–April 5.30–9.30pm). In early December it also hosts one of India's premier **dance festivals**, drawing an impressive cast of both classical and folk/"tribal" dance groups from all over the country. For the exact dates, line-up and advance bookings, contact OTDC in Bhubaneshwar (☎0674/431299) or Delhi (☎01/344580).

Around Konarak

Unless you like beaches, few attractions **around Konarak** are likely to tempt you. Konarak's own picturesque **beach,** 3km from the temple along the Puri road, is a good place to watch the local fishing fleet at work, but far from an ideal place to swim or sunbathe. For more privacy, catch a local bus heading south and jump off after a couple of kilometres when you see a track leading from the main road through the woods and dunes to the sea. Chances are you'll have long stretches of white sand to yourself. To get back again, flag down a bus or jeep from the roadside.

A stone's throw away from Konarak beach lies the sacred pond where Samba was cured of leprosy – the miracle that allegedly inspired the founding of the sun temple. For a couple of days every year during the full or "white" moon phase of Magha (Jan/Feb), **CHANDRABHAGA** is also the site of a big religious festival, the **Magha Saptami Mela**. Thousands of pilgrims converge on the pool during the small hours to take a holy dip in its curative waters, then shuffle off to the beach where, in accordance with an age-old custom mentioned in the *Puranas*, they watch the sun rise over the sea. The event is followed by a *puja* at the Navagrahas.

Cuttack

After the comparative serenity of the surrounding countryside, **CUTTACK** comes as something of a shock. Orissa's former capital and most densely populated city is packed onto a narrow island amid a tangle of tributaries and sandbanks in the River Mahanandi. Without the benefit of suburbs to break you in gently, its noisy, traffic-filled streets can seem all the more claustrophobic. Nevertheless, if you're in no hurry and like crowded, old-fashioned bazaars, Cuttack has its enjoyable aspects.

The site has possessed great strategic importance since the warlike Keshari ("Lion") dynasty founded a *kataka*, or "military camp", here in 989 AD. As the major river crossing for the busy north–south land trade route, as well as a nexus for the canals that connect the Orissan interior with the sea, the island proved an ideal platform from which to dominate the region's economy. It was the Kesharis, in the eleventh century, who were responsible for building the impressive granite **embankment** still visible along the south of the island. Apart from making the site less vulnerable to attack, the walls also strengthened it against the ravages of Cuttack's other perennial threat – the annual monsoon floods. In the fourteenth century, the **Barbati Fort** was added on the north bank. Two hundred years later, Orissa's last independent Hindu ruler, Mukunda Harichandan, built a much grander, nine-storey palace on the same site. The Raja never had much of a chance to enjoy it however, as only eight years after his succession the Moghuls and, soon after, the Afghans of Bengal annexed the city.

Under the Maharathas, who took over in the eighteenth century, Cuttack expanded still further. Lucrative trade with the British on the coast financed the construction of new temples and, thanks to a particularly liberal administration, of **mosques** for the city's sizeable Muslim minority. When the British finally merged the region's twenty-six princedoms, Cuttack was a logical choice as state capital. Its prominence however was shortlived; constant floods and chronic overcrowding ensured that the capital had, eventually, to be moved to the drier and far less constricted site at Bhubaneshwar.

Apart from some big cricket matches played in the Barbati stadium, Cuttack only tends to hit the news nowadays in conjunction with the infamous "hooch scandal" of 1992, when 170 people died after drinking (poisonous) illegal liquor. The tragedy made national headlines and cost a number of prominent government ministers their jobs.

The City

Congestion, as you'll quickly discover, is Cuttack's big problem. The main arterial route between Calcutta and Madras scythes straight across one end of the island, and the combination of narrow streets and brisk business make the town centre chaotic. Your first priority should be to work your way east, away from the mayhem outside the bus stand, towards the more atmospheric **old quarter**.

Dozens of small jewellers' shops line the bustling main streets of **Nayasarak** and **Balu bazaars**, close to the incongruous British High Court building. They're loaded with glittering *tarakashi* **filigree** work (see p.923), unique to Cuttack and practised here for many centuries. Only a few elderly artisans survive; you're unlikely to see them in action, unless you ask one of the shopkeepers to take you to meet their suppliers. A stone's throw away from the silver bazaar, the **Kadam-i-Rasul** is one of the few interesting buildings in Cuttack. A complex of domed mosques and shrines, it houses among other things a round stone carved with the footprints of the Prophet. The spirit of religious tolerance symbolized by the Kadam-i-Rasul – its construction was sponsored by the Hindu Maharathas – has fallen foul of the recent wave of communalism, and non-Muslims are no longer allowed to enter.

Towards the northwest corner of the city, the twisting, crowded streets of the bazaar peter out into the leafier and more spacious district around the Barbati stadium. The ruins of Barbati **fort**, Cuttack's only real monument, lie on the opposite side of the nearby *maidan*. Apart from the moats, a lone-standing gateway and an unimpressive mosque, most of this once grand complex, likened by one eighteenth-century traveller to Windsor Castle, has been reduced to rubble. The citadel in the middle looks slightly more promising, but is currently under excavation and not accessible to visitors.

After Barbati, the road follows the river bank out as far as **Chahata Ghat**, on the westernmost point of the island. Ferries cross the Mahanandi from here to the picturesque local pilgrimage spot of **Dhabaleshwar**, where there's a small Shiva temple and an OTDC *Panathasala*. The accommodation, which is cheap and very rudimentary, should be arranged through the tourist office in advance so that they can warn the poor unfortunate who's posted there to expect you.

Practicalities

Cuttack's **railway station** lies east of the city centre, in the middle of the island. **Buses** in both directions turn west off NH5, which runs parallel with the railway line, towards the city bus stand, 2km further up Link Rd. Halfway between the two, the Arunodhya Market building is the site of the ineffectual state government **tourist office** (daily 10am–5pm; ☎0671/23525), which also has a counter at the railway station (☎0671/25107).

The majority of the cheap **hotels** are near the silver bazaar in Choudury Bazaar. Best bet is the *Veena* (☎0671/24326; ①); the cheaper *Adarsh* (☎0671/25498; ①) on Chandi Chowk is tolerable. More expensive, but a much better deal, the OTDC *Panthaniwas* (☎0671/23867; ④–⑤) on Buxa Bazaar has a range of simple, clean rooms, all with hot water, and a reasonable restaurant. The two most **expensive** hotels in town are the

Akbari Continental on Haripur Rd (☎0671/25242; ④–⑤) which has central a/c, restaurant, bar and foreign exchange, and the similar *Ashoka* on Ice Factory Rd, near College Square and the railway station (☎0671/25708; ③–⑤). These two and the *Panthaniwas* are also by far the best **places to eat** in Cuttack.

Ratnagiri, Udayagiri and Lalitgiri

Hidden away in the well-watered backcountry south of the River Brahmani, 65km northeast of Cuttack, lie the remains of three ancient Buddhist universities, **Ratnagiri**, **Udayagiri** and **Lalitgiri**. Although interesting in themselves and very scenically situated, they're as yet virtually inaccessible by public transport. The easiest way to get there from Cuttack is on a full-day *Ambassador* trip (around Rs600–650 – the OTDC *Panthaniwas* has the best rates). **Getting there independently** involves catching a bus north up NH5 from Bhubaneshwar or Cuttack as far as the **Chandikohl crossroads** and then picking up an auto-rickshaw for the (costly) 60-kilometre round trip. Alternatively, you can wait for a bus heading from Chandikohl to Paradwip, on the coast, and get down at Patharajpur – the turnoff for two of the three sites. It's a long hike from there however, and unless you're able to hitch a ride you'll find it impossible to see the ruins and return to Bhubaneshwar in a day. Luckily, there's a small **OTDC hostel** (*Panthasala*; ①), a short way east of the Ratnagiri turnoff on the main road; the warden will arrange food if given warning.

Ratnagiri
RATNAGIRI, the most impressive of the sites, lies 20km from the main road, on the top of a hill overlooking the River Keluo. When the Chinese chronicler Hiuen T'sang visited the university in 639 AD, it had already been a major Buddhist centre for at least two hundred years. In those days the sea reached much further inland, and would have been visible from this point – which may in part account for the choice of location. **Missionaries** were trained in such places before being sent abroad to spread the Buddha's message in China and southeast Asia.

The focal point of the site is the enormous **stupa** at the top of the hill. A stone casket containing gold and silver artefacts, believed to be relics of the Buddha, was found inside it during excavations in the 1970s. Nearby, just below the *stupa*, lie two **monasteries**. The larger and better preserved of the pair, dating from the seventh century, has a paved courtyard surrounded by cells and a beautifully carved doorway made from local blue-green chlorite stone. Inside the shrine there's a large seated Buddha.

Dotted around the complex is a rich array of carvings of *bodhisattvas* and female deities, piles of fallen masonry and several Buddha heads. Between the monasteries and the *stupa* a more recent small Hindu temple presents the unusual spectacle of a tree growing from the cracks in its *deul*.

Udayagiri
Ten kilometres back towards the main road, a signpost leads to the most recently discovered of the three sites, **UDAYAGIRI**, which is still undergoing excavation. Its main structure is a large *stupa*, better preserved than its counterpart at Ratnagiri, standing on a square pedestal with a carving of the Buddha in different postures on each face. Further along the path, nestling in the basin of a green ridge, are two more monasteries, only one of which has been excavated. It features a large seated Buddha in its central shrine and an intricately carved entrance to match that at Ratnagiri, along with an inscribed step-well. More rock-cut sculptures adorn the crest of the hill behind the monastery but it's a long awkward climb through thick brush to reach them.

Lalitgiri

The turning for **LALITGIRI**, the most accessible of the three Buddhist sites, is about 10km further along the main road towards Paradwip; the Archaeological Survey of India is still excavating, so officially you're not allowed to take photographs. Most of the ruins on the two adjacent hills are thought to date from the ninth century, though an inscription in the ancient *brahmini* script has recently come to light that suggests that it may have been occupied seven hundred years earlier. It is also thought that Lalitgiri is the Puspagiri described in glowing terms by Hiuen T'sang for its *stupa* that "emitted brilliant light because of its sacredness". Though the best of the sculpture has been placed in a small **museum** (officially Tues–Sun 10am–5pm, but the paucity of visitors means that it's often closed), or incorporated into the modern Hindu temple up on Parabhadi hill, some pretty impressive chunks are still lying around the place – most notably the huge head of a Buddha that has become emblematic in OTDC's attempts to promote the site. The large renovated *stupa* at the top of the hill above the museum affords a splendid view across the lush green paddy fields of the plain below to the hills of the sister sites. A small community of **stone carvers** who live at the foot of the hill claim to be descended from the craftsmen who worked on the original Buddhist buildings (see p.922).

North from Cuttack

As you head **north from Cuttack** and the Mahanandi, the profile of the Eastern Ghats recedes temporarily into the haze on the horizon leaving a flat expanse of paddy fields, palm trees and mud-walled villages. The main railway line, and NH5 that twists alongside it, follow the path of the famous **pilgrim trail**, the *Jagannath Sadak*, that once led from Calcutta to Puri. Until the end of the nineteenth century this now hectic route was no more than a mud track. Then, following the 1865 famine that wiped out nearly a quarter of Orissa's population, the British were pressured into completing a road and rail link with more prosperous parts of the country. With the addition of iron bridges in the 1960s, the highway became the stream of trucks, ramshackle old buses, *dhabas* and *chai*-stalls it is today.

Balasore

The first town of any note along the way, **BALASORE** (literally "Town of the Young Lord" – Krishna) was one of the earliest British outposts in India. In 1636 it was given by the emperor Shah Jahan to a British surgeon, Mr Gabriel Broughton, after he had

---

SUBAI ROPE

Drive along any of Mayurbhunj's country roads while the sun is shining and you're sure at some point to see villagers laying out strips of what look like jungle creepers on the asphalt. It's all part of the region's principal cottage industry, the production of **subai rope**. With the depletion of forest resources, many local people have had to turn to less traditional sources of subsistence; for villagers in areas where the soil is too poor to grow rice, *baliba* grass has proved a literal lifeline. This hardy, indigenous plant stands up well to the Orissan sun, and helps prevent soil erosion during the monsoon. After harvesting, the *baliba* is twisted to make *subai* rope and sun-dried on the nearest road. Then it's rubbed against tree trunks or telegraph poles to make it smooth, bound into one-kilogram bundles, and finally taken to Baripada market on the back of a bicycle to be sold to buyers from the city.

successfully cured the Moghul princess of burns (her clothes had caught fire during a sea voyage). If the port hadn't silted up in the eighteenth century, Balasore might well have become Calcutta. As it is, the sea is now 13km away, and the town is little more than a collection of market stalls grouped around a crossroads and a railway station.

Practicalities
The chances are that if you end up in Balasore it'll only be a pit stop en route to somewhere else. The main line **railway station** is a short way off the main street. From here it's a ten-minute cycle-rickshaw ride over the railway bridge to the **bus stand** where you can catch regular buses to Baripada, Bhubaneshwar, Cuttack and Chandipur. **Accommodation** is not hard to come by. Unless you're catching an early morning train, avoid the dives around the station. The hotels on Sahadevkhunta Rd, just up from the bus stand on the other side of the tracks, are a much better deal. The well-run *Hotel Swarnachuda* (☎06782/73440; ①–⑤) has a range of rooms, some a/c, with a small restaurant and bar. Further down, the *Suraj* (☎06782/72657; ①–②) only has cheaper rooms, none a/c, and a small restaurant. If you've got your own vehicle and are looking for something a little more comfortable, you couldn't do better than the *Hotel Torrento* (☎06782/73481; ⑤–⑦), 3km further out of town near NH5. It has large rooms, most with central a/c, a spacious garden and a superb restaurant serving à la carte tandoori, Mughlai, veg and Chinese dishes. There's nowhere in Balasore to **change money**, although the manager of the *Torrento* may be able to help you out if you're desperate.

Chandipur

From the main market square in Balasore, a narrow, surfaced road winds its way out through the remnants of the old town to the open fields and picturesque villages beyond. After running along 16km of flood-proof embankment it eventually arrives at the nearest seaside settlement, **CHANDIPUR**. The village has two claims to fame, neither likely to inspire much enthusiasm among foreign visitors. The first is that at low tide the sea here retreats 5km from Chandipur's white sandy **beach**. This has proved something of a godsend for the locals who, with their dugouts and hand nets, are able to fish the parts the big fleets down the coast fear to reach. The second is the presence just outside the village of a test-firing range for the Indian army's infamous Agni rockets. Periodically, the army turfs out the disgruntled villagers so that they can take potshots at targets positioned on Chandipur's famous sand-flats – the cause of a protracted controversy in the Orissan government and media.

Apart from the occasional rocket launches, and limitless possibilities for paddling in miles of silty sea water, there's not a great deal to do in Chandipur. It's a relaxing enough place though, and one that rarely attracts more than a handful of visitors.

Practicalities
Getting to Chandipur is straightforward: hop on one of the five daily buses from Balasore, which you can pick up at the crossroads near the railway station. Auto-rickshaws also do the trip, though expect to have to pay the return fare.

Apart from during public holidays, when Chandipur is swamped with trippers from Calcutta, finding somewhere to **stay** is also relatively easy. The *Yarica Yatri Niwas* (☎06782/72234; ①–⑤) has modern rooms around a courtyard and some cheaper dorms. They also serve food, though there isn't a proper restaurant. On the road that turns down to the beach, you'll find good rooms at the *Hotel Chandipur* (☎06782/72313; ②); the *Shubham* (☎06782/72025; ④–⑤) opposite boasts an attractive garden. In a colonial building overlooking the beach, the OTDC *Panthaniwas* (☎06782/72251; ①–⑤) has two cheap dorms and a good restaurant serving fresh fish (if given a couple of hours' notice). **Tours** of the area's attractions, including some off-the-beaten-track tem-

ples that are hard to visit without your own transport, are supposed to depart from here (7.30am & 1.30pm; Rs50); unfortunately, they tend to be reluctant to leave unless the minibus is full, which it rarely (if ever) is outside holiday times. *Maharaja Tours*, a private company based in the village, also run sightseeing trips from Chandipur.

Baripada and Mayurbhunj

A little way north of Balasore, the highway crosses the River Burhabalanga and splits in two, the right fork towards the Bengal border and the left towards the hills of the Orissan interior. Further inland, the intensively cultivated alluvial plains of the coastal strip gradually give way to patches of deciduous forest and red-laterite soil, punctuated by termite mounds and neatly thatched villages. **BARIPADA**, headquarters of **Mayurbhunj** district (pronounced *marvunj*) and gateway to the nearby **Simlipal National Park**, appears after about ninety minutes.

As the main **market** town for some widely scattered farming communities, Baripada is unexpectedly busy. There are no real sights to speak of, but if you're not in a hurry it's a good place to get an idea of small-town Orissan life. The district is also the traditional home of the **Santal** tribe. Comprising around 70 percent of the local *adivasi* (tribal) population, the Santals are predominantly settled agriculturalists who practise a blend of ancestor worship and Hinduism. They're known for having developed a written form of their tribal language, Olchikki, and for their festivals and dances.

The **town** itself is a typically Indian mixture of tumbledown shops and houses, quietly decaying bungalows and grand, but time-worn civic buildings erected by the local Maharaja during the days of the Raj. Mayurbhunj was among the last of the princely states to join independent India. For centuries it remained under the **Bhanja** kings, a reputedly "progressive" ruling family favoured by the British, whose present incumbent still lives in an incongruous neo-classical mansion overlooking the river in the north of town. The older **palace**, now a college on the main street, was an even more ostentatious affair. Among its more extravagant features is a swimming pool that the local council have converted into a library.

Apart from the whitewashed **Jagannath temple**, a miniature of Puri's, the one "sight" in town is Baripada's small **museum** (Tues–Sun 10am–5pm). Awkwardly situated in the backstreets to the east of town, it houses a dusty collection of sculpture, coins, pottery and inscriptions that once belonged to the Maharaja.

FESTIVALS IN MAYURBHUNJ

In addition to celebrating all the usual Hindu festivals, which have in many cases been distinctively adapted by the *adivasi* population, the Mayurbhunj district also has its own totally unique festivals, rarely experienced by outsiders. The dates vary from year to year in accordance with the astrological calendar, so enquire in advance at a tourist office or consult an Oriya calendar at a newspaper stall.

Karam Puja (mid-Jan). A harvest festival celebrated by the Mahanta (Kshatriya) caste and *munda* tribals. Large gatherings, plus a procession to the river where women plant seeds in the sand, with music and dance.

Chaitra Parbar (mid-April). This Hindu end-of-spring bash is marked by tribal *Chhou* dancing, a form of dance developed from pre-battle warm-up routines.

Rath Yatra (June/July). Baripada's very own Car Festival is lively and memorable,

albeit upstaged by Puri's. Subhadra's chariot is pulled exclusively by women.

Damorda Yatra (Sept/Oct). Tribal ancestor worship ritual, which involves the immersion of a deceased relative's ashes in the local tank.

Tusu Parbar (Nov/Dec). Unmarried girls carry an effigy of a local (anti-Moghul) resistance heroine to the tank and submerge it, while crowds of men tear apart a chicken thrown from the town *neem* tree.

Practicalities

Arriving in Baripada, **buses** pass the temple at the bottom of the broad main street and then head up the hill to the bus stand and market. From here it's a five-minute walk to the most central **hotels**: the simple *Bishram* (☎06792/53535; ①), and the *Hotel Ambika* (☎06792/52557; ②–④), a shabby but adequate place with variously priced rooms, all with attached baths and frames for the much-needed mosquito nets. Downstairs is Baripada's best **restaurant**. The surroundings look none too salubrious but they serve a good selection of Indian veg and non-veg and above average Chinese dishes.

A rather less convenient option is the *Durga* (☎06792/52338; ①–②), in an old British-style building 3km out of town past the temple. The OTDC **tourist office** (Mon–Fri 10am–5pm), five minutes' walk from the bus stand in the other direction, is not worth the trouble to find. If you want to arrange transport to Simlipal or rent a bicycle, the manager at the *Ambika* is much more helpful. His travel information, however, is not always entirely up-to-date, so it's best to double check.

Simlipal National Park

West of Baripada, the landscape changes suddenly from open fields to the thickly wooded slopes and ridges of the Eastern Ghats. At more than 1000m, **Khairbhuru**, the peak visible from the outskirts of town, is the highest in the region and one of the last true wildernesses in eastern India. The mixed deciduous forests, perennial streams and glades of savannah grasslands draped around its flanks have allowed for an uncommonly rich diversity of flora and fauna.

In 1957 the whole area around the mountain was declared a wildlife sanctuary – primarily in an attempt to revive its dwindling population of **tigers** (see *Contexts*). Prior to this it had been the exclusive preserve of the Maharaja of Mayurbhunj, who used the woods as a private hunting ground and source of timber (the narrow-gauge railway running from Baripada to the main line on the coast was built to carry the lumber out). Fifteen years later **SIMLIPAL** was officially designated a national park, and the following year became the site of one of India's first Project Tiger reserves.

Simlipal deserves be one of eastern India's major attractions. The fact it isn't has less to do with the amount of wildlife within its borders – abundant by any standards – than with its comparative **inaccessibility**. Unlike its counterparts in neighbouring states, transport to and around the park is a real problem, accommodation is rudimentary and advance permits (essential for overnight stays) difficult to arrange. If you overcome all these obstacles, the rewards are more than compensate. Apart from the elusive tigers – park rangers, perhaps a touch optimistically, claim they number almost one hundred – the reserve boasts leopards, langurs, barking and spotted deer, gaur, sloth bears, mongoose, flying squirrels, porcupines, turtles, monitor lizards, pythons and the very rare (and ominous-sounding) **mugger crocodile**. Herds of wild **elephant** are also common (too common for the unfortunate villagers, who have to spend the night in tree houses in order to scare rampaging pachyderms away from their crops) and there are reportedly 231 species of **birds** flying around. All this to a backdrop of some beautiful granite hills and as tranquil and pristine an old-growth forest as you're likely to find anywhere. If nothing else, it's a perfect antidote to the frenzy of the coastal cities.

Park practicalities

The first major obstacle to be negotiated before you arrive in Simlipal (open only Nov 1–June 15) is to obtain a **permit**. Officially, anyone intending to spend a night in the park (essential if you want to see any animals) must reserve accommodation, at least one month in advance, by writing to the Field Director of Project Tiger, Baripada 757002, Mayurbhunj District, Orissa (☎06792/52593). Include the exact dates of your visit and the names of the lodges you'd like to stay in. Before you set off, it's also important to confirm the reservation with the office in Baripada, 300m past the big radio transmitter at the top of town (when it's closed, call ☎06792/52773).

Much the easiest way to visit Simlipal is on an organized **tour**. *Swosti Travel* in Bhubaneshwar (☎0674/408526), and *Heritage Tours* in Puri (☎06752/23656) are reputable. They will arrange permits, transport, accommodation and guides at very short notice and charge reasonable rates. Without your own vehicle, the only alternative way to **get around** the park is to rent a **jeep**. This can be arranged through the manager at the *Ambika* in Baripada, or through the less reliable taxi *wallahs* hanging around the bus stand. In any case, expect to pay up to Rs1000 per day. If you're on a budget, you may be able to cushion the blow by getting a group together, though the chances of meeting people on arrival at Baripada are at best slim and this should be organized well in advance. Another way to cut costs is to use **JOSHIPUR** as an alternative base for visiting the park: closer to most of the points of interest than Baripada, it also features a couple of extremely basic lodges, and you can cut costs by renting a jeep from there.

The park itself covers a total area of 2750 square kilometres, but the majority of the tigers are supposed to hang out in the 845-acre "core zone", which for the most part is out of bounds. There are two main **entrances**: one at Joshipur in the west (convenient if you're driving from Calcutta, and close to most of the lodges), and one at Pithabata near Baripada on the eastern side. You have to pay an entry fee (Rs50 per vehicle plus Rs5 for Indians and Rs50 for foreigners per person) and as much again for camera permits if you intend to take photographs or film inside the park. From here, unsurfaced but motorable roads link up the lodges with the numerous waterfalls, panoramas, grazing areas and water holes in the buffer zone.

Where to go in Simlipal is largely dictated by the location of the **lodges**. There are six dotted around the park, but the best from the point of view of spotting wildlife is **Chahala** (83km from Baripada) – one of the Maharaja's former hunting lodges, just inside the core zone near a salt-lick where animals congregate in the evenings. As with all accommodation, facilities there are very basic. You have to take in your own food (which the *chowkida* will cook for you). The other lodges are Barheipani (73km), near a waterfall with impressive views; Newana (60km), believe it or not a "frost-prone area"; Gudugudia (25km from Joshipur) said to be particularly good for bird-watching; and Joranda (64km from Baripada) which has a bit of everything. The only lodge not requiring advance permission is the *Aranya Niwas* at **Lulung**, on the Baripada side. You're unlikely to see much wildlife here, but the rooms are pleasant and inexpensive; there's a cheap dorm and a restaurant, and the compound, surrounded by an elephant-proof ditch, is right in the heart of the forest. They even have **solar panels** to provide electricity.

Southern Orissa

Few places along the south coast are likely to inspire more than a cursory glance out of a bus or train window. Between the long stretches of dishevelled roadside settlements and rural stations, however, a couple of minor resorts may tempt you to break a long journey. Three hours south of the capital, at the foot of a barren, sea-facing spur of the Eastern Ghats – which here creep almost up to the coast – is India's largest salt-water lake. **Chilka**'s main attractions are the migratory birds that nest here in winter, and leisurely boat trips to its islands. Seventy or so kilometres further on, **Gopalpur-on-Sea** is sufficiently remote to have remained a decidedly low-key beach town. Out of season, the only crowds are families from the local fishing community. **Berhampur**, 16km inland, is southern Orissa's biggest market town, and the main transport hub for the sinuous route west through the hills to the tribal districts of **Koraput** and **Jeypore**.

Chilka Lake

Were it not for its glass-like surface, **CHILKA LAKE**, Asia's largest lagoon, could easily be mistaken for the sea. From its mud-fringed foreshore you can barely make out the narrow strip of marshy islands and sand-flats that separate the 1100-square-kilometre expanse of brackish water from the Bay of Bengal. Come here between December and February, though, and you'll see dozens of **migratory bird species** from as far afield as Persia and Siberia, including avocets, ruffs, pelicans, ospreys, flamingoes and rare cranes. *Chital* and black buck can also sometimes be spotted on the shore. Elsewhere around the lake, several **islands** (some inhabited by small subsistence fishing communities) are popular destinations for daily **boat trips**. By and large, the fishing villages and fabled island "kingdom" of **Parikud** on the eastern side of the lake, home to one of India's whackier maharajas, are passed up in favour of the *devi* shrine on **Kalijai** island. Legend has it that a local girl once drowned here on the way to her wedding across the lake. Since no suitable male member of the family could be found to accompany the girl on the journey, her father stepped in at the last minute – a serious breach of Hindu custom. En route, a retributory storm blew in from the sea and overturned the boat. When they had all but given up the search for survivors, some fishermen claimed to have heard the girl's voice calling from under the water that she had become a goddess and that a shrine should be inaugurated in her name. Over the years the miracle has become associated with **Kali** (Shiva's consort Durga in her terrifying aspect) and the place it occurred something of a sacred site. Each year at *makar sankrati*, after the harvest, pilgrims flock to the tiny island from all over Orissa and West Bengal to leave votive offerings in the cave where the deity was enshrined.

Practicalities

The best **place to stay** on the lake is the excellent value *Yatri Niwas* (①) at **Satapada** on the coastal side, just 45km from Puri and linked by several daily buses. Rooms can be booked from Puri's tourist office. Neither of the other two hotels on the lake are at all attractive, although the OTDC *Panthaniwas* (☎06756/20488; ④–⑤) at **Balugaon** is passable. Rooms are shabby and over-priced, but come with bath and mosquito nets (you won't get a wink of sleep without one). A verandah downstairs overlooks an unkempt garden where they serve fresh, if ordinary, **food**. **Getting there** involves taking the bus to **Barkul**, 7km away, and then finding a rickshaw to do the last leg. From Puri, a direct OTDC **tour bus** (daily; Rs85–Rs120) leaves from the *Panthaniwas*.

Though considerably cheaper and more accessible, the other *Panthaniwas* (☎06814/346; ②), near the railway station at **Rumbha** 34km further south, is even more lacklustre and best avoided. The only plus is that it's better placed for walks around the more scenic southern corner of the lake.

A couple of OTDC motor launches, and rowing boats manned by local villagers, operate **boat trips** from the jetty below the Balugaon *Panthaniwas*. The round trip to **Kalijai island**, the most popular option with domestic tourists, takes around two hours, while the bird sanctuary of **Nalabana island** takes four. The manager at the *Panthaniwas* can arrange seats; rates are charged per hour. Rowing boats also depart from Rumbha, though the fishermen who run them seem to be more intent on attending to their nets than ferrying passengers to the islands.

Gopalpur-on-Sea

Two thousand or more years ago, when the Kalingas were piling up wealth from the pearl and silk trade with southeast Asia, **GOPALPUR-ON-SEA**, formerly the ancient port of Paloura, must have been a swinging place. Today, the only time you're likely to encounter much action here is during the monsoon, when the village is temporarily inundated with promenading Bengali holiday-makers. For the rest of the year, its desultory collection of crumbling bungalows and seafront hotels stands idle, left to the odd backpacker blown off-course by the promise of an undiscovered beach paradise, and the armies of industrious fishermen hauling in hand-nets on Gopalpur's endless empty shoreline. Paradise it certainly isn't, but if you're looking for a spot along the coast to unwind and enjoy the warm sea breezes, this could be just the place.

The village has plenty of accommodation, much of it heavily discounted in the off-season, and there's a reasonable choice of places to eat. Despite appearances to the contrary however, Gopalpur's long white sandy **beach** is far from an ideal place to swim and sunbathe. For the local fishing community (*katias*), the rare spectacle of a white (read "rich and apparently insane") person strolling half-naked through their workplace is a major distraction; a swim in the sea, let alone a discreet doze in the sun, is a veritable crowd-puller. Still, if you don't mind being the centre of attention and are content to watch the locals fish, dressed in their traditional pointed straw bonnets and bright *saris,* the beach is an enjoyable place to while away a few hours.

Getting there is easiest via Berhampur, from where frequent minibuses and jeeps depart the central bus stand for the 16-kilometre trip. You'll be dumped at the top of Gopalpur's "main street", ten minutes' walk from the seafront and most of the hotels.

Accommodation and eating

Gopalpur's many **rooms** tend to cost considerably more than elsewhere, and you may well feel inclined to haggle. Only during holiday times, however, are they liable to be booked up in advance. The rates below all refer to the off-season period.

As for **eating**, considering the amount of fish pulled out of the sea, there's a surprising dearth of **seafood** in Gopalpur. Some restaurateurs can however be cajoled into cooking the odd "pomfret", given sufficient warning. Apart from the hotel restaurants, try *Naz Snack Bar*, overlooking the beach, for hot drinks, fresh *samosas, pakoras* and

---

SEA TURTLES

Every year around February and March, a strip of beach at the end of Orissa's central river delta witnesses what must surely be one of the world's most extraordinary natural spectacles. Having swum right across the Pacific and Indian oceans, 200,000 female **Olive Ridley marine turtles** crawl onto the sand; each looks for a safe spot, then sets about digging a hole with its hind flippers in which to lay its annual batch of eggs. Twenty minutes later, after a quick breather, they're off again into the surf, to begin the journey back to their mating grounds on the other side of the world.

No one knows quite why they travel such distances, but for the local villagers the arrival of the giant turtles has traditionally been something of a boon. Turtle soup for breakfast, lunch and tea . . . and extra cash from market sales. Over the years the annual slaughter began to turn into something of a green gold rush and turtle numbers plummeted drastically. At the personal behest of Indira Gandhi, a special wildlife reserve was set up to protect them. Today, the *Bhita Kanika Sanctuary* on **Gahirmatha beach**, 130km from Bhubaneshwar, is a safe haven for the creatures. Weeks before the big three-or-four-day invasion, coastguards monitor the progress of the schools as they approach the Orissan shoreline and armed rangers ensure that poachers are kept at bay. For wildlife enthusiasts it's a field day. Thanks to the fact that during their labour the preoccupied turtles are, not surprisingly, oblivious to the presence of humans, you can watch the whole sequence at close range.

Visits to Gahirmatha are allowed, though you should ask at the OTDC tourist office in Bhubaneshwar to find out exactly when the turtles are expected. **Transport, food** and **accommodation** can be a problem unless you are prepared to rough it or to pay through the nose for a rental car, as the sanctuary is well off the beaten track.

other nibbles on rickety old furniture, or *Rohini*, halfway up the main street, a cafe-bar that boasts adventurous-sounding Chinese dishes.

Holiday Inn, near the lighthouse. Couldn't be less like its North American namesake – a handful of very basic rooms around a yard with bucket baths and no running water. The friendly family allow guests to use their kitchen. ①.

Mermaid, on the north side of the beach (☎0680/82050). Plain, upmarket place pitched at wealthy Calcuttans. Tariffs include full board; non-residents can eat at the restaurant (carefully prepared Bengali *thalis* plus veg and non-veg options) with advance notice. ⑤–⑥.

Oberoi Palm Beach (☎0680/82021). Cosy, characterful self-contained 5-star. Chalets around central lawn, jogging track, lots of palm trees and easy access to beach. The snazzy restaurant serves plush, expensive buffet spreads; the bar is more reasonably priced. ⑨.

Rosalin, on the seafront (☎0680/82071). Chaotic, family-run establishment with cells around a small garden-cum-courtyard and a very informal restaurant in reception for standard omelette, tea and toast breakfasts or *dal*, veg and rice dinners. Cheap and cheerful. ①–②.

Sea Side Breeze, north side of the beach (☎0680/82075). Simple but pleasant enough, with spacious, neat rooms, some opening on to the sea. ④.

Berhampur

Having squeezed around the narrow strip of flat land at the southern fringes of the lake, the railway line skirts the bottom of an eroded hillside, then heads out across a fertile river basin towards **BERHAMPUR**, the last major town before Andhra Pradesh. A bustling provincial market, with noisy streets crammed full of trucks and little shops serenading passers-by with film music, the only real reason you might conceivably want to stop here is to catch a bus or train somewhere else. Sights are non-existent, except perhaps the **weavers' quarter** around the temple where Berhampur's famous silk *saris* are still produced using traditional hand looms.

Moving on is most people's first priority. From Berhampur it's possible to catch **buses** up the coast to Bhubaneshwar; north to Sambalpur and the Hirakud Dam; west past Taptapani towards Rayagada and Koraput; and east to Gopalpur-on-Sea. Private buses leave from the new bus stand, some way across town, while the state transport company works out of the more central bus stand in the square. The main line **railway station** is ten minutes' rickshaw ride to the south.

If you need to spend the night, there are several decent **places to stay**. Much the best value is the *Government Rest House* (☎0680/200466; ①) opposite the cricket stadium and five minutes' walk from the central bus stand; most rooms are pretty grungy but it's very cheap and central. The more upmarket *Hotel Moti* (☎0680/203641; ②–⑤), just around the corner, is a pleasant alternative with some a/c rooms and a restaurant. If all else fails the **railway retiring rooms** at the station will do for a night. For **food**, the *Rest House* has a decent restaurant, and the *Hotel Poonam* on bus stand square is a safe bet, though it doesn't open for breakfast.

Taptapani

One possible foray from Berhampur, if you're tempted by the lure of the nearby hills, is the trip up to **TAPTAPANI**, a spa village nestled in the Ghats 51km to the west. The road leads out through Berhampur's hectic commercial district to a broad, flat-bottomed river valley strewn with huge black granite boulders and poor-looking villages. Along the way, patches of rice paddy and red-brown soil are enlivened by glimpses of local women hard at work in their blue and green cotton *saris*. An hour or so out, the increasingly bumpy road gradually narrows and loses most of its traffic. The hills and *sal* forest begin to close in and the bus, stuffed full with villagers heading upcountry, starts to crawl around the hairpins towards the pass. Among the passengers you're likely to see a number of **Tibetans** from the Chandragiri refugee camp, 45km off the main road beyond Taptapani. Following the Chinese invasion in 1957 the refugees were given land by the Orissan government on which to settle and have lived there ever since, weaving carpets and breeding ferocious guard dogs for a living.

After the journey up the valley, Taptapani itself comes as a marked disappointment. Little more than a line of dingy snack-stalls and mildewed bungalows deep within dense forest, it's the kind of place to which government servants pray not to be posted. Even the legendary **hot springs**, believed to cure infertility, look jaded. The boiling sulphurous water bubbles listlessly out of a cleft in the mountainside and is piped into a small tank set just below the road. Women seeking to avail themselves of its curative effects are supposed to grope under the surface for seeds that fall off the tree overhanging the pond – an act of endurance that can take days to accomplish.

If you choose to **stay** in Taptapani, you can enjoy the water in the privacy of your own hotel; it's pumped into capacious bathtubs in some rooms at the atmospheric OTDC *Panthaniwas* (☎06814/2531; ③–⑤), a short way down the hill from the springs and commanding fine views over the trees and valley to the hills in the distance. Although the *Panthaniwas* is rarely full, there's absolutely nowhere else to stay for miles around, so it's safest to reserve a room through an OTDC office in advance.

Beyond Taptapani

Beyond Taptapani, you're soon worlds away from the congested roads and towns of Orissa's coastal plains. Traffic dries up, villages become even poorer and less frequent and rice cultivation is squeezed out by thick forest. The appearance of pots attached to sago palms and windowless mud huts with low thatched roofs indicate that you've arrived in Orissa's *adivasi* homeland. The pass above Taptapani is the start of the **Saora**'s traditional land. Further west around the Koraput and Jeypore area live the **Dongria Kondh**, the **Koya** and the **Bondas**.

Officially, you're not allowed into the district without first obtaining a **permit** from the state government. Paranoia about **naxalites** hiding out in the forests along the Andhran border, coupled with a marked reluctance to allow foreigners into tribal zones, make these notoriously difficult to obtain. Theoretically it's still possible to move freely around the various towns and villages in Orissa's wild west, though in practice it's hard to know which, if any, are worth the hassle of minimal infrastructure, rudimentary accommodation and infrequent transport. If you're really keen to visit *adivasi* villages, the best, though far from the cheapest, way is to arrange a trip through a specialist **travel agent** in Bhubaneshwar or Puri. They'll take care of the permits, sort out food and rooms and, if they're any good, have local contacts to make sure you behave appropriately in the villages and markets. *Heritage Tours* (☎06752/23656) in Puri arrange 6–10 day trips for roughly Rs1000 per person per day and make every effort not to intrude where outsiders are not welcome. Whichever way you look at it though, turning up in an isolated and culturally sensitive place with an *Ambassador* car and a camera has got to be a pretty unsound way of "meeting" the locals.

CHAPTER SEVENTEEN

THE ANDAMAN AND NICOBAR ISLANDS

The **ANDAMAN AND NICOBAR ISLANDS** lie in the Bay of Bengal, over 1000km off the east coast of India and accessible from either Calcutta or Madras. The islands are thickly covered by deep green jungle – inhabited by unique bird species – and fringed with clean sandy beaches, but the real attraction for tourists lies offshore, in crystal-clear seas that harbour some of the world's richest and least spoilt marine reserves. Filled with dazzling fish and kaleidoscopic corals, and roamed by schools of dolphins and sharks, the waters are perfect for **snorkelling** and **scuba diving**.

The two groups comprise over 300 islands, summits of a submarine mountain range that stretches for 755km from north to south, populated in parts by indigenous tribes whose numbers have been slashed dramatically by the effects of nineteenth-century European settlement and rampant deforestation. Today felling is restricted, and 86 percent of the islands' forest is protected – nevertheless, *padauk* and teak are still used for building materials and made into furniture and tourist knick-knacks. Foreign tourists are only permitted to visit parts of the **Andaman** group, over 200 islands separated by the deep Ten Degree Channel from the nineteen islands further south that constitute the **Nicobars**, access to which is at present restricted to Indians.

The main island of the Andamans, and the point of arrival for boats and planes, is **South Andaman**, where the Indian and Burmese community in the small but busy capital, **Port Blair**, accounts for almost half the total population. **Permits** obtainable on the mainland or on arrival are initially granted for a stay of fifteen days, which allows just enough time to explore a few islands, or take a scuba-diving course; this can be extended to a maximum of one month. The most beautiful beaches and coral reefs are found on outlying islands. A healthy get-up-and-go spirit is essential if you plan to explore these, as connections and transport are erratic and severely limited, especially on the smaller islands, means you may need your own camping supplies.

The **climate** remains tropical throughout the year, with temperatures between 24° and 35°C. By far the best time to visit is between November and May. From mid-May to October, heavy rains flush the islands, often bringing violent cyclones that leave west-coast beaches strewn with fallen trees, and in November and December less severe rains arrive with the northeast monsoon. Dense tree cover, marshy swamps, humidity and high rainfall combine to provide perfect breeding ground for mosquitoes, and **malaria** is very common. Despite being so far east, the islands run on Indian time, so the sun rises at 4am and darkness falls soon after 5pm.

A little history

The earliest mention of the Andaman and Nicobar Islands is found in **Ptolemy**'s geographical treatises (second century AD). Other records from the Chinese Buddhist monk I'Tsing (seventh century) and Arabian travellers who passed by in the ninth cen-

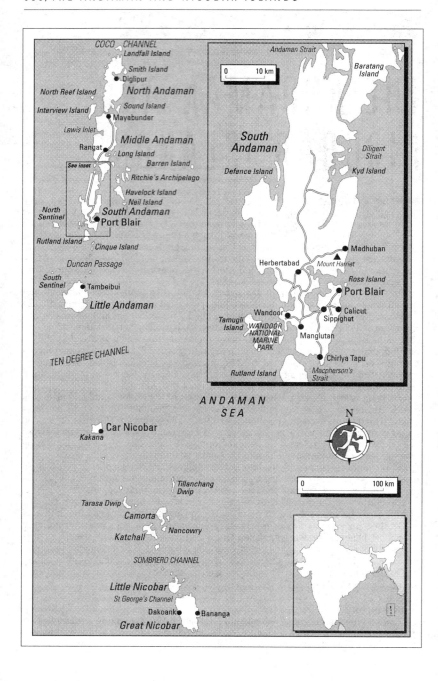

tury, depict the inhabitants as fierce and cannibalistic. **Marco Polo** arrived in the islands in the thirteenth century and could offer no more favourable description of the natives: "The people are without a king and are idolaters no better than wild beasts. All the men of the island of Angamanian have heads like dogs . . . they are a most cruel generation, and eat everybody they catch . . ." It is unlikely, however, that the Andamanese were cannibals, as the most vivid reports of their ferocity were propagated by Malay pirates who held sway over the surrounding seas, and needed to keep looters well away from trade ships that passed between India, China and the Far East.

NATIVE PEOPLE OF THE ANDAMAN AND NICOBAR ISLANDS

Quite where the indigenous population of the Andaman and Nicobar Islands came from is uncertain. Negrito communities may have migrated here from the east and north when the islands were connected to Burma, or the sea was sufficiently shallow to allow transport by canoe. Their survival has been threatened by traders and colonizers, who introduced disease and destroyed their territories by widespread felling. Of perhaps 5000 aborigines in 1858, only 5 percent remain, from six of the twelve native tribal groups.

On the Nicobar Islands, the Mongoloid **Nicobarese**, who claim descent from a Burmese prince and were identified as *lojenke* (naked people) by I'Tsing, have integrated to some extent with recent settlers, and while they continue to live in small communities of grass huts raised on stilts, have adopted modern agricultural methods, raising pigs rather than hunting. The **Shompen** of Great Nicobar have not assimilated, however, and less than 200 remain, living on the coast, where they barter in honey, cane and nuts with the Nicobarese, and in isolated pockets further inland.

The Andaman communities, divided into *eramtaga* (jungle-dwellers), and *ar-yuato* (coast dwellers), subsist on fish, turtles, turtle eggs, pigs, fruits, honey and roots. They acknowledge an anthropomorphic deity, Phalgun, who is feared for his wrath in the form of storms, but do not worship him. Dreams are considered significant, and ancestors said to be able to influence events and cause earthquakes when angry. Daily ritual dances, central to communal life, are held on land enclosed by huts. Most tribes affix great importance to trees in their territory, and each male marks a tree as his own.

Less than twenty **Great Andamanese** remain, settled today on Strait Island, north of South Andaman. In the 1860s, the Rev H Corbyn set up a "home" for them to learn English on Ross Island, insisting that they wear clothes and abandon body-painting. From the settlers the Andamanese contracted diseases such as syphilis, measles, mumps and influenza, and within three years almost the entire population had died.

The **Jarawas**, who shifted from their original homes when land was cleared to build Port Blair, now live on the western coasts of Middle and South Andaman, hemmed in by the Andaman Trunk Road which since the 1970s has cut them off from hunting grounds and fresh water supplies. Some contact with settlers has been made through gift-exchange at each full moon when the Jarawas sing and dance, and in apparent friendliness fart in the face of the visitors. Nevertheless, they remain unwilling to mix, and are determined to retain their land, firing arrows at settlers whose cattle and fields encroach upon vital resources.

Once used by the Chinese and Japanese to dive for valuable shells in exchange for alcohol and opium, the **Onges** are today the largest tribe on the Andaman Islands, living on Little Andaman and Rutland Island. Unlike other tribes, the Onges do not practice tattooing, but they paint their bodies with white clay and ochre, and the women smear themselves with yellow dye from orchids. They live in communal shelters (*bera*) and construct temporary thatched huts (*korale*) where they live for forty or fifty days at a time before moving on. In areas on Little Andaman, wooden huts have been built for the Onges by Indians, in an attempt to compensate for loss of land.

The most elusive tribe of all, the **Sentinelese**, live on North Sentinel Island west of South Andaman. Some contact was made with them in 1991, after a team put together by the local administration had left gifts on the beaches every month for two years.

During the eighteenth and nineteenth centuries **European missionaries** and trading companies turned their attention to the islands with a view to colonization. A string of unsuccessful attempts to convert the Nicobarese to Christianity was made by the French, Dutch and Danish, all of whom were forced to abandon their plans in the face of hideous diseases and a severe lack of food and water. Though the missionaries seldom met with any hostility, several fleets of trading ships that tried to dock on the islands were captured, and their crews murdered, by Nicobar people.

In 1777 the British Lieutenant Blair chose the South Andaman harbour now known as **Port Blair** as the site for a penal colony, based on the deportation of criminals that had proved successful in Sumatra, Singapore and Penang. Both this scheme, and an attempt to settle the Nicobar Islands in 1867, were thwarted by adverse conditions. However, the third go at colonization was more successful, and in 1858 **Port Blair** finally did become a penal settlement, where political activists who had fuelled the Mutiny in 1857 were made to clear land and build their own prison. Out of 773 prisoners, 292 died, escaped or were hanged in the first two months. Many lost their lives in attacks from Andamanese tribes who objected to forest clearance, but the settlement continued to fill with people from mainland India, and by 1864 the number of convicts had grown to three thousand. In 1896 work began on a jail made up of hundreds of tiny solitary cells, which was used to confine political prisoners until 1945. The prison still stands, one of Port Blair's few "tourist attractions".

In 1919, the British government in India decided to close down the penal settlement, but it was subsequently used to incarcerate a new generation of freedom fighters from India, Malabar and Burma. During World War II the islands were occupied by the **Japanese**, who tortured and murdered hundreds suspected of collaborating with the British, and bombed homes of the Jarawa tribes. British forces moved back in 1945, and at last abolished the penal settlement. After Partition, refugees, mostly Hindus from Bangladesh and Bengal, were given land in Port Blair and on the Nicobar Islands, where yet more woodland was cleared and new industries established. This replanted population, which has mixed with ex-convicts who chose to stay, now greatly outnumbers the indigenous people; contact between the two societies is limited, and not always friendly.

Getting to the Andaman Islands

Port Blair, on South Andaman, is served by *Indian Airlines* **flights** from **Calcutta** (Wed, Fri & Sun; 2hr) and **Madras** (Tues, Thurs & Sat; 2hr 5min). *East–West* now also has a service from Madras (Mon, Wed & Fri; 2hr 5min). Both outward and return journeys should be booked well in advance at the respective airline offices anywhere on the mainland. The *Indian Airlines* flights, in particular, are usually full up months ahead.

It's also possible to get to Port Blair by **ship**; sailings leave Calcutta, Vishakapatnam and Madras every one or two weeks. Although far cheaper than flying, the crossings are long (3–4 days), uncomfortable and often delayed by bad conditions and bureaucracy. **Tickets** cost from Rs690 for a simple, crowded bunk to Rs2500 for a deluxe a/c cabin. Meals of *dal*, rice and vegetables are served for around Rs100 per day, but vary little, so take some supplementary snacks and fruit. It's best to arrange journeys in advance through the Shipping Corporation of India (**SCI**) at their offices at First Floor, 13 Strand Rd, Calcutta (☎2482354), AV Bhanoji Row Garude, Pattbhiramaya & Co, Vishakapatnam port (☎565597) or Jawahar Building, near Customs House, Rajaji Rd, Madras (☎5220841). Most boats on the Madras sector are under the auspices of the directorate of shipping opposite Customs House, Rajaji Rd, Madras (☎5220841). You'll need three passport photos, and should confirm your place on the boat 48 hours before leaving. There's also an **information centre** for the islands at F 104 *Curzon Road Hostel*, Kasturba Gandhi Marg, New Delhi (☎387015).

Tourists arriving by plane can pick up the **permit** necessary to visit the islands on arrival at Port Blair airport; ship passengers should obtain one at a shipping office or Foreigners' Registration office before leaving India. The superintendent of police in Port Blair's Aberdeen Bazaar can **extend** your initial fifteen-day visa up to a maximum of thirty days.

South Andaman Island

South Andaman is today the most heavily populated of the Andaman Islands – particularly around the capital, **Port Blair** – thanks in part to the drastic thinning of the tree cover to make way for settlement. Foreign tourists can only visit its southern reaches – including the beaches at **Corbyn's Cove** and **Chirya Tapu**, and the fine reefs on the western shores at **Wandoor**, 35km southwest of Port Blair – and stretches of the northern region near **Mount Harriet** and **Madhuban** on the east coast, where elephants are trained for felling.

With your own transport it's easy to find your way along the narrow bumpy roads that connect small villages, weaving through forests and coconut fields, and skirting the swamps and rocky outcrops that form the coastline.

Port Blair

PORT BLAIR, a characterless cluster of tin-roofed houses, shops, restaurants and offices, meeting the sea in the north, east and west and fields and forests in the south, merits only a short stay. There's little to see here – just the **Cellular Jail** and a few small **museums** – but as the point of arrival for the islands, and the only place with a bank, tourist offices and hotels, it can't be avoided.

Arrival and information

Taxis wait at **Phoenix Bay Jetty**, where the **boats** come in, to cover the two-kilometre drive south to the town centre. The Marine Department at the jetty (☎20742) has the latest information on boats and ferries to other islands. The **airport** is 5km south of Port Blair; unless you're staying at the *Andaman Beach Resort*, which lays on a free airport shuttle bus, you'll have to rely on taxis (Rs30–40) to get to a hotel, although some hotels tout for custom by offering free transport too.

A counter at the airport has leaflets listing accommodation and sights around South Andaman Island, while the **ITDC tourist office** is in Super Shoppe complex, Junglighat, near the airport (Mon–Fri 10am–5pm; ☎21006). The more informative and efficient **Andaman and Nicobar tourist office**, next to the Secretariat and opposite *Indian Airlines*, on the southern edges of the town (Mon–Sat 10am–5pm; ☎20694), has details on tours (see below) and ferry crossings to other islands. For information on island wildlife and forest tracks in areas such as Mount Harriet and Chirya Tapu, head for the **chief wildlife warden**'s office in Haddo, west of Phoenix Bay Jetty (☎21459). Government-run hotels can also help with maps and information.

Road names are not used much in Port Blair, with most establishments addressing themselves simply by their local area. The name of the busiest and most central area is **Aberdeen Bazaar**, where you'll find the superintendent of police (for permit extensions), the SCI office for onward bookings by sea (☎21347), and the *State Bank of India* (Mon–Fri 1–4.30pm). Some hotels will change travellers' cheques. Flights can be reserved at *Indian Airlines*, Middle Point (Mon–Fri 10am–1pm & 2–4pm; ☎20946), and through *Shompen Travels* at *Shompen Hotel* (☎20360), for *East–West* flights.

The telephone **area code** for Port Blair is ☎03192.

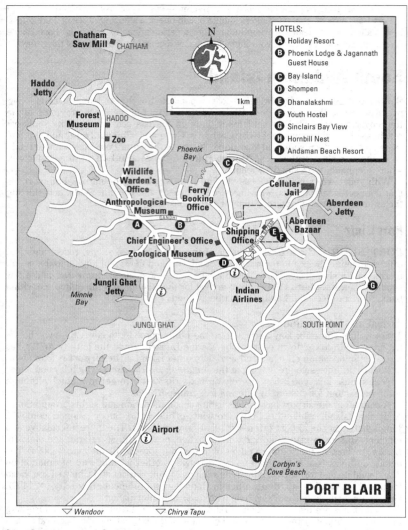

Local transport and tours

Walking is tiring and time-consuming in hilly Port Blair, even taking into account the minimal amount of sightseeing the place offers – and transport to get from place to place is essential. Yellow-top **taxis** gather at the west end of Gandhi Rd, opposite the bus stand. They all have meters, but negotiating the price before leaving is usual practice. Expect to pay Rs50 for a trip from the centre of town to Corbyn's Cove. No rickshaws, auto- or otherwise, operate on the island.

Local **buses** run infrequently from the bus stand in central Port Blair to Wandoor and Chirya Tapu, and can be used for day trips, though it's best to rely on your own transport to get around South Andaman. **Bicycles** can be rented from Aberdeen Bazaar, but the hilly roads to the coasts are most easily covered on a **Vespa** or **motorcycle**, both available for rent at *TSG Travels* (Mon–Sat 9am–5pm; ☎20894) on Babu Lane in the centre of town or from *Singh Travels* (☎21757), near the clock tower in Aberdeen Bazaar, at Rs120–200 per day. The petrol pump is on the crossroads west of the bus stand and there's another on the road towards the airport.

By far the best way to see Port Blair is on a **tour**. Good-value half-day bus tours to the jail, museums and sawmill are organized by the Andaman and Nicobar tourist office (daily; Rs450), *Shompen Travels* in *Shompen Hotel* (on demand; Rs100) and *Andaman Beach Resort* (daily; Rs100). **Harbour cruises** (daily 3–5pm; book at the Marine Dept, ☎20725) depart from Phoenix Bay Jetty, drift around the floating docks, and make a fleeting visit to **Viper Island** (see p.960).

The Town

Port Blair's only firm reminder of its gloomy past, the sturdy brick **Cellular Jail** (Mon–Sat 9am–noon & 2–7pm), overlooks the sea from a small rise in the northeast of town. Built between 1896 and 1905, its tiny solitary cells were quite different and far worse than the dormitories in other prison blocks erected earlier. Only three of the seven wings that originally radiated from the central tower now remain; visitors can peer into the 13m-by-7m cells, and imagine the grim conditions under which the prisoners existed. Cells were dirty and ill-ventilated, drinking water was limited to two glasses per day, and the convicts were expected to wash in the rain as they worked clearing forests and building prison quarters. Food, brought from the mainland, was stored in vats where the rice and pulses became infested with worms; more than half the prison population died long before their twenty years' detention was up. Protests against conditions led to hunger strikes in 1932, 1933 and 1937, resulting in yet more deaths, and frequent executions took place in full view of the cells, at the gallows that still stand in squat wooden shelters in the courtyards. The **sound and light show** (in English Wed, Sat & Sun 7.15pm; in Hindi daily 6pm; not in the rainy season) outlines the history of the prison, and a small **museum** by the entrance gate (same hours as prison) exhibits lists of convicts, photographs and grim torture devices.

South of the jail, you can see tanks brimming with exotic fish and coral from the islands' reefs at the **marine museum** (daily 8.30am–12.30pm & 1.30–5pm), which includes a salt-water crocodile farm that breeds and releases crocodiles into the coastal mangrove swamps. In the Haddo area in the west of town, the **anthropological museum** (Mon–Sat 9am–noon & 1–4pm) illustrates the lives of Andaman and Nicobar tribes with photographs and miniature models.

Further north, on the knobby peninsula that marks the northernmost edge of Port Blair, **Chatham sawmill** (daily 7am–2.30pm) is one of the oldest and largest timber processing plants on Indian territory. The seasoning of beautiful and rare woods taken from various islands is sad testimony to continuing felling; photography is prohibited. Lumbering methods are clearly explained in the adjoining **forest museum** (Mon–Sat 9am–noon & 2–4pm), which also displays local types of wood used in the timber industry such as *padauk*, rosewood and marble wood. The **zoo** nearby (Mon–Sat 7am–noon & 2–5pm; Rs1) is small, but gives an impression of the rich variety of animals and reptiles on the islands, many of which, like the agile luminous-green Andaman gekko, are seen nowhere else in the world.

Accommodation

Port Blair's **hotels** offer something to suit every pocket. Budget accommodation is concentrated in the centre of town – spend a little more and you can stay in secluded lodges with gardens and views over the sea. Note that the tourist authority has started charging foreigners double the normal tariff for government hotels such as the *Hornbill Nest*. As darkness falls at around 5pm it's a good idea to find a hotel that has verandahs and a bar where you can while away the evening.

Andaman Beach Resort, Corbyn's Cove (☎21463). Perfect setting amid gardens of palms, jasmine and bougainvillea, opposite a white sandy beach. Balconied a/c rooms, intimate cottages, bar, and a medium-priced restaurant where the evening buffet doesn't always match up to what is served in simpler places elsewhere. Table tennis and TV hall upstairs. Ideal for families. ⑧.

Bay Island, Marine Hill, Port Blair (☎20881). Port Blair's best hotel by far; elegant, airy and finished with polished dark wood. All rooms have carpets, en suite bathrooms and balconies overlooking Phoenix Bay and the seas; the less expensive ones are a little cramped. The restaurant is superb for a splurge, with good Indian specialities and seafood, and a well-stocked bar. Lush gardens and open-air sea-water swimming pool. ⑨.

Dhanalakshmi, Aberdeen Bazaar, Port Blair (☎21953). Friendly hotel with dim but spacious rooms, and an excellent restaurant, preparing Indian dishes and seafood to order. ③–⑤.

Holiday Resort, Premnagar, 15-minute walk from the centre (☎30516). Clean and spacious rooms in this friendly new hotel. *Star TV* lounge. ④.

Hornbill Nest, 1km from Corbyn's Cove (☎20018). Clean, roomy cottages on a hill by the coast. Good food available if you order well in advance. ⑤.

Jagannath Guest House, Moulana Azad Rd (☎21140). One of the best value basic lodges. ①.

Shompen, Middle Point (☎20360). Unjustified prices for stuffy, tatty rooms, but you can negotiate rates. Travel counter and good seafood in rooftop restaurant. ⑤–⑥.

Sinclairs Bay View, on the coast road to Corbyn's Cove (☎21159). Clifftop hotel with spotless carpeted rooms, balconies and en suite bathrooms. Dramatic views, bar and restaurant. ⑤–⑥.

Youth Hostel, eastern edge of town (☎20459). Small lodge with basic facilities at very low rates. ①.

Eating

It can be well worth forfeiting the convenience of the hotel restaurants reviewed above, and trying something a little different. Between them, Port Blair's restaurants offer dishes from north and south India, Burmese specialities, and a wide variety of seafood. Don't miss the local **spiced fish** – the heads are considered to be the most delicious part. Roadside stalls sell plates of grilled fish for less than Rs20.

Annapurna Cafeteria, Aberdeen Bazaar, towards the post office. Great *dosas* and other snacks.

Avanti, opposite bus stand. Popular place for fixed meals, *dosas*, and northern dishes such as *chola bathura* (spicy chickpeas served with huge crispy *puris*). Good food, but dim surroundings.

China Room, near Phoenix Bay Jetty. By booking well in advance at this small family-run restaurant you can guarantee some superb Burmese-style seafood dishes at very reasonable prices.

Daawath, Premnagar, beneath the *Holiday Resort*. Good north and south Indian food in smart dark room. Friendly but slow service.

Hotel Ashoka, Gandhi Rd. Small hole-in-the-wall joint not far from the bus stand. Tiffins, coffee, *lassis* and an assortment of breads all day long; also, inexpensive, hearty south Indian meals.

Around the island

South Andaman's best spot for swimming and sunbathing is 10km southeast of Port Blair at **Corbyn's Cove**, a small stretch of smooth white sand fringed with palms. Bear in mind, though, that lying on the beach scantily clothed will bring you considerable attention from crowds of local workers. The long white beach at **Wandoor** is littered with the dry, twisted trunks of trees torn up and flung down by annual cyclones, and fringed not with palms, but with dense forest teeming with birdlife. You should only snorkel here at high tide. Boats leave Wandoor jetty, sailing through wide creeks that lap against mangrove swamps and out to nearby islands that constitute a **national park**, boasting exquisite coral and fish colonies.

At the southern tip of South Andaman, an hour's drive from Port Blair, is the tiny hook of **Chirya Tapu**, or Bird Island, where swamps give way to shell-strewn beaches, sharp rocks and vast coral reefs. The path from Chirya Tapu's small fishing village to its beach leads through thick humid jungle overhung with twisting creepers, echoing with bird calls and the shrill hum of insects, and passes massive termite mounds and streams trickling through deep red soil – don't return to the village too late, as walking through this looming jungle in semi-darkness can be pretty eerie.

Ferries from Phoenix Bay Jetty also make the short trip (30min) to Bamboo Flat, from where you can catch a bus to **Madhuban**, a felling area where elephants work alongside men. If you want to take your own vehicle to Madhuban, there's a car ferry from Chafham jetty to Bamboo Flat, which saves a long drive over poor roads on the route from Port Blair. Not far from Madhuban, **Mount Harriet** (400m) is one of the highest points on South Andaman. Permission to climb the nature trails that weave through dense forest to its summit must be obtained from the chief wildlife warden in Haddo. Although in theory Madhuban and Mount Harriet can only be visited as day trips from Port Blair, the warden might also give you permission to stay in the **forest rest house** at Mount Harriet, which technically is reserved for VIPs and visiting wildlife officers; the same goes for another rest house at Chirya Tapu.

Middle and North Andaman Islands

The other two large islands, Middle and North Andaman, which, together with South Andaman, form the backbone of the group and account for the vast majority of the total land mass, are linked to Port Blair both by ship and the Andaman trunk road with shorter ferry crossings. Although foreigners can only officially stay at **Rangat**, **Mayabunder** and **Diglipur**, in practice it seems possible to roam further afield and it is certainly permissible to travel through the islands by bus though there is the possibility of having your vehicle ambushed by bow-wielding Jarawas during the section that runs through their territory. As a precaution against this occasional occurrence, armed guards board the bus for the relevant part of the journey.

Neither of the islands offers anything outstanding in the way of natural or cultural beauty and are certainly not geared up to tourism – mineral water is not available, for example – so many may consider the time and effort involved in getting to them unrewarding. However, they do exude a certain back-of-beyond frontier feeling. The only decent accommodation available is in the APWD rest houses, for which permission can be obtained from the office of the Chief Engineer in Port Blair (☎21050), although it does not guarantee a place and is not an absolute requirement.

Middle Andaman Island

The main settlement in the southern part of the island is **Rangat**, an unattractive conglomeration of concrete, wood and corrugated iron that sprawls across one end of a fertile valley of rice paddies, 8km from the harbour at Rangat Bay. To **get there**, you can either take a ferry (several weekly; 7–9hr) from Port Blair, some via Havelock Island, or an express bus (4 daily; 6hr). The APWD rest house (☎74237; ①), pleasantly situated up a winding hill from the bazaar with views across the valley, is also the best place to eat, providing good filling fish *thalis*. There are a couple of grim lodges in the bazaar, of which the *Hare Krishna* (①) is preferable to the *Chandra Mohan* (☎74219; ①).

The nearest sandy beach to Rangat is Betapur, 19km along the road to Mayabunder. Another possible trip is to Bakultala, 8km in the other direction and accessible by a regular bus service. Here, a young man named Paritosh Biswas has opened an office of the *Humanist Association of India*, offering to guide visitors to remote villages on day-long treks by foot and canoe through jungle and mangrove swamps (around Rs150).

Nearly three hours further north by road, perched on a long promontary right at the top of the island and surrounded by mangrove swamps, is **Mayabunder**. The village is more spread out and more appealing than Rangat, but again there is little to hold your interest for long. The APWD rest house (☎73214; ①) near the jetty is comfortable, has a pleasant garden overlooking the sea and also serves good set meals. The only other accommodation is at the dilapidated and grotty *Lakshminarayan Lodge* (①). Otherwise, there's the usual string of small shops, food and *chai* stalls and government offices as well as a sub-post office. Confusingly, Mayabunder is counted as part of the North Andaman administration, although it is geographically attached to Middle Andaman.

Moving on

Until the last stretch of the Andaman trunk road is completed and a bridge across the narrow strait to North Andaman island constructed just west of Mayabunder, the shortest crossing is the ferry ride to Kalighat (2 daily; 2hr 30min) and then onto Diglipur by bus. Some ferries take the long route round to Diglipur's Arial Bay (4hr 30min).

North Andaman

Diglipur, the northernmost point of the whole Andaman chain accessible to foreigners, is another disappointing ramshackle bazaar, 9km inland from its harbour at Arial Bay. If you want to stay, the APWD rest house (☎72203; ①) is quite acceptable; the smaller APWD rest house on a hillock down at Arial Bay is more pleasant. You can swim at a small beach beside the mangrove swamps near a saw mill just the other side of the jetty from the tiny bazaar, but there is a better sandy beach 11km further on at Kalipur, which is connected by bus. Still further in the same direction is thickly forested **Saddle Peak**. Permission to make the three- to four-hour climb must be obtained from the Range Officer at Arial Bay. You can also get a permit there to visit nearby Austin Island, but you have to negotiate a price to get there with a local dingy owner. From Arial Bay the boat that has made its way up with long layovers at Rangat and Mayabunder usually returns direct (13–14hr) to Port Blair, often overnight.

Other islands

The rest of the islands open to foreign visitors fall into two categories: those that you can stay on and those that can only be visited by day.

It's possible to stay at **Havelock, Neil** and **Long islands**, though accommodation is very limited. You can camp though and equipment can be rented from the government run *Andaman Teal House* in Port Blair. They are all accessible by ferry from Phoenix Bay Jetty. You can charter a boat from here or from *Shompen Travels* at *Shompen Hotel* (☎20360), which saves time, but is expensive at about Rs10,000 per day per boat.

Day trips (only) can be made from Port Blair to **Ross** and **Viper islands**, north of the harbour and to **Cinque island**, three hours to the south. Travel agents also organize daily trips to **Red Skin** and **Jolly Buoy**, which are part of Wandoor national park.

Havelock Island

Havelock Island, the largest of a scattering of islets northeast of Port Blair, can be reached by ferry (several weekly, departs 6.30am; book at the Marine Department; ☎20725), on a four-hour route that passes colonies of playful dolphins.

SCUBA DIVING IN THE ANDAMAN ISLANDS

The seas around the Andaman and Nicobar Islands are some of the world's finest, relatively unexplored, unspoiled and dazzlingly colourful. Many species of fish and coral are unique to the area and fascinating life systems exist in ash beds and cooled lava around the eastern volcanic island of Barren.

For a quick taste of marine life, you could start by **snorkelling**; most hotels can supply masks and snorkels, though some equipment is in dire need of replacement. However, the only way to get really close, and venture out into deeper waters, is to **scuba dive**. The experience of weaving in and out of coral beds, coming eye to eye with fish or swimming with dolphins and barracudas is unforgettable, and at prices that are among the lowest in the world, it's an opportunity not to be missed.

The recently established **Andaman and Nicobar Scuba Diving Society** is run by Mr Chowdhary, a highly experienced and very competent instructor who can be contacted through the *Bay Island Hotel* on Marine Hill, Port Blair (☎20881; fax 21389). If you're a qualified diver with a valid certificate, you can rent equipment and make two dives with an instructor for Rs1500 per day. **Courses** for learners that result in PADI (Professional Association of Diving Instructors) certificates take four or five days (Rs6500), but it's possible to do the one day Discover Scuba course (Rs1500) that doesn't lead to a certificate but gives a taster; training in advanced open water diving and rescue are also on offer (2–3 days; Rs4500). Gaining the certificate of Dive Master requires a three-week course (Rs15,500).

It's not uncommon to come across schools of sharks, which rarely turn hostile, but one thing to watch out for and avoid is the **black-and-white sea snake**. Though the snakes seldom attack – and, since their fangs are at the back of their mouths, would find it difficult to get a grip on any human – their bite is more deadly than that of the cobra.

It's essential to respect your environment when diving and snorkelling. Increased tourism inevitably puts pressure on the delicate marine eco-system, and poorly funded wildlife organizations can do little to prevent damage from insensitive visitors. Divers and snorkellers should never touch or pick coral; most of the reefs remain undamaged, but the dead coral in the shallow waters on the shores at Wandoor is an early sign of what happens if coral is walked on or picked.

The island, popular for its long white beaches, is slightly hilly and very fertile – much of the forest has been cleared so that fruit and vegetables can be grown for sale on South Andaman. **Accommodation** is available in clean double rooms at the new *Dolphin Yatri Nivas* (☎21328; ④–⑤) about 3km from the jetty – an *ANTO* bus meets the ferry (book at the Andaman and Nicobar tourist office in Port Blair), where you can also get reasonable but unexciting food. The only other hotel is the poor *VS Lodge* (④), not far from the jetty, where there are also a few shops and basic meal joints. The wide beach close to the hotel is good for sunbathing, and the sea is very shallow, but the best waters for swimming lie off the beach at **Radhnagar**, 10km from the jetty at the end of a narrow and poorly surfaced road; watch for pesky sandflies, especially in the evenings. There's no guarantee of transport to Radhnagar – the best thing to do is to bring a moped (plus fuel) or bicycle with you from Port Blair.

Neil Island

Many of the ferries from Port Blair to Havelock either call first at or continue south to the smaller and more densely populated **Neil Island**, settled by Bengalis in the years following Partition. The largest of Neil's wide and deserted beaches is at Sitapur, on the east coast. There's an APWD rest house (①) for which an introductory letter can be obtained from the Chief Engineer's Office in Port Blair (☎20206), or else you can camp.

Long Island

Up near the southeastern coast of Middle Andaman, this sparsely populated and attractive island boasts fine beaches and good coral reefs, but is less well connected with only one boat a week on average. It also has an APWD rest house, which is run by the same Chief Engineer's department as the one on Neil Island.

Cinque Island

South of Chirya Tapu, uninhabited **Cinque Island** emerges from some of the finest coral reefs open to tourists, and is shrouded in jungle. Until the proposed tourist rest house is built, visitors to Cinque must provide their own shelter in tents, and stock up with plenty of food – ferries between Phoenix Bay and the island run only once a week (3hr), though it is sometimes possible to get a ride on a fishing boat from Chirya Tapu.

Viper and Ross islands

Viper and Ross islands, northeast and west of Port Blair, are closely associated with the British. Harbour cruises from Port Blair (daily 3–5pm; Rs20) include a short stop on **Viper Island**, where convicts were made to stay for a month to deter them from breaking prison discipline. Gallows, whipping posts and crumbling walls remain as relics of a punishment area.

A short boat tour from Phoenix Bay Jetty (daily except Wed, 8.30am, 10.30am, & 12.30pm; Rs13) allows an hour on **Ross Island**, where the Rev H Corbyn established his home for the Andamanese and the British set up their administrative headquarters. It's interesting to see how quickly nature has regained its hold – the semi-ruined buildings are today withdrawing into the tangled branches and vines of trees and creepers, that will eventually hide some of the last monuments to British occupation of the islands.

Red Skin and Jolly Buoy islands

Part of the Wandoor national park, **Red Skin** and **Jolly Buoy islands** boast a stunning array of coral and fish. Travel agents organize daily trips to these uninhabited islands (departures from Wandoor jetty, daily except Mon, 10am; 90min; Rs75 for Jolly Buoy, Rs50 for Red Skin). Food and drink are usually provided on the organized tours, which also provide transport from Port Blair to Wandoor. If you don't arrange a trip through an agent or your hotel, it's possible to buy a ticket at the jetty and board the 10am launch, though you'll have to bring your own food and snorkelling equipment. Although the trips give less than three hours to explore fabulous reefs, they are still worthwhile. Transfers onto glass- or fibre-bottomed boats constitute part of the trips, allowing those fearful of entering the water to get a glimpse of life around the coral.

CHAPTER EIGHTEEN

TAMIL NADU

TAMIL NADU, the cradle of south Indian temple architecture, is a living museum of styles that originated in the seventh century and matured in the huge temple complexes studded with towering gateways – *gopuras* – that soar above the markets of almost every town. Physically, the state brims with green paddies and palm fields on its eastern edge, where flat alluvial plains roll to the **Coromandel coast** to meet the Bay of Bengal, while in the west and north high rocky hills, in parts shrouded in forest, border Kerala, Karnataka and Andhra Pradesh. Apart from the **Kaveri**, the state has few perennial rivers: complex irrigation systems and tanks, often connected to temples, help maintain a water supply.

Despite its seafront fort, grand mansions and excellence as a centre for the performing arts, the state capital **Madras** is probably its least appealing destination; a scruffy, dusty, noisy city with faint echoes of the Raj. Much the best place to start a **temple tour** is nearby **Mamallapuram**, a seaside village that, quite apart from some exquisite **Pallava** rock-cut architecture (fifth–ninth centuries), boasts a long stretch of beach. Inland, the pilgrimage city of **Kanchipuram** is filled with reminders of an illustrious past under successive dynastic rulers, while further down the coast is one of India's rare French colonial possessions, **Pondicherry**, where Auroville has found a new role in the "New Age". The road south from Pondicherry puts you back on the temple trail, leading to the tenth-century **Chola kingdom** and the extraordinary architecture of **Chidambaram**, **Gangaikondacholapuram**, **Kumbakonam** and **Darasuram**. For the best Chola bronzes, however, and a glimpse of the magnificent paintings that flourished under Maratha rajas in the eighteenth century, travellers should head for **Thanjavur**. Chola capital for four centuries, the city boasts almost a hundred temples and was the birthplace of **Bharatanatyam** dance, famous throughout Tamil Nadu.

In the very centre of Tamil Nadu, **Tiruchirapalli**, a commercial town just northwest of Thanjavur, held some interest for the Cholas, but reached its heyday under later dynasties, when the temple complex in neighbouring **Srirangam** became one of south India's largest. Among its patrons were the Nayaks of **Madurai**, whose erstwhile capi-

tal further south, bustling with pilgrims, priests, peddlers, tailors and tourists, is an unforgettable destination. Here south India's most profusely carved temple dapples with light that seeps through countless pillared halls, and reflects from shimmering oil lamps onto gods, saints and maidens peeping from every wall, column and gateway.

Rameshwaram, on the long spit of land reaching towards Sri Lanka, and **Kannyakumari**, at India's southern tip (the auspicious meeting point of the Bay of Bengal, the Indian Ocean and the Arabian Sea) are both important pilgrimage centres, with the added attraction of welcome cool breezes and vistas over the sea.

While Tamil Nadu's temples are undeniably its major attraction, it would take months to see them all, and there is plenty else to distract even the most ardent architecture buff. In the west of the state, where the hill stations of **Kodaikanal** and **Ooty** are the premier attractions, verdant hills offer mountain views and a network of trails winds through forests and tea and coffee plantations. **Mudumalai Wildlife Sanctuary**, a vast spread of deciduous forest dominated by teak, offers a good chance of spotting elephants and *dholes*, wild pack-hunting dogs, and you might even see tigers and leopards. **Anamalai sanctuary**, closer to Kodaikanal in the Palani hills, is better known for its lion-tailed macaques (black-maned monkeys). The wetlands of the coast provide perfect resting places for migratory birds, whose numbers soar during the winter monsoon at **Vedanthangal**, near Madras, and **Point Calimere**.

Temperatures in Tamil Nadu, which usually hover around 30°C, peak in May and June, when they often soar above 40°, and the overpowering heat makes all but sitting in a shaded cafe exhausting. The state is barely affected by the southwest monsoon that pounds much of India from June to September: it receives most of its **rain** between October and January. Cooler, rainy days bring their own problems; widescale flooding can disrupt road and rail links, and imbue everything with an all-pervasive dampness.

Accommodation prospects are good; all but the smallest towns and villages have something for every budget. Most hotels have their own dining halls which, together with local restaurants, sometimes serve sumptuous *thalis*, tinged with tamarind and presented on banana leaves. **Indigenous dishes** are almost exclusively vegetarian; for north Indian or Western alternatives, head for the larger hotels or more upmarket city restaurants.

Some history

Since the fourth century BC, Tamil Nadu has been shaped by its majority **Dravidian** population, of uncertain origins but physically quite different from north Indians. Their language developed separately, as did their social organization; the difference between high-caste *brahmins* and low-caste workers has always been more pronounced here than in the north. The influence of the powerful *janapadas*, established in the north by the fourth and third centuries BC, extended as far south as the Deccan, but they made few incursions into **Dravidadesa** (Tamil country). Incorporating what are now Kerala and Tamil Nadu, it was ruled by three dynasties: the **Cheras**, who held sway over much of the Malabar coast (Kerala), the **Pandyas** in the far south, and the **Cholas**, whose realm stretched along the eastern Coromandel coast. Indo-Roman trade in spices, precious stones and metals flourished at the start of the Christian era, when **St Thomas** arrived in the south, but dwindled when trade links began with southeast Asia.

The prosperity of the early kingdoms having faded by the fourth century AD, the way was clear for the **Pallavas**, who emerged in the sixth century as leaders of a kingdom centred around **Kanchipuram**. By the seventh century the successors of the first Pallava king, Simhavishnu, were engaged in battles with the southern Pandyas and the forces of the Chalukyas, based further west in Karnataka. However, the centuries of Pallava dominion are not marked simply by battles and territorial expansion; this was also an era of social development. **Brahmins** became the dominant community, responsible for lands and riches donated to temples. The emergence of *bhakti*, devotional worship, placed temples firmly at the centre of religious life (see p.1003), and the inspirational *sangam* literature of saint-poets fostered a tradition of dance and music that has become Tamil Nadu's cultural hallmark.

The **Vijayanagars**, who gained a firm footing in Hampi (Karnataka) in the fourteenth century, resisted Muslim incursions from the north and spread to cover most of south India by the sixteenth century, heralding a new phase of architectural development by building new temples, expanding older ones and introducing colossal *gopuras*, or towers. In **Madurai** Vijayanagar governors, **Nayaks**, set up an independent kingdom whose impact spread as far as **Tiruchirapalli**. For a short period (1740–48) the

TAMIL NADU TRAVEL DETAILS

	Trains		Buses		Flights	
	Frequency	Time	Frequency	Time	Frequency	Time
To and from MADRAS						
Bangalore	7 daily	5hr 30min–7hr	32 daily	9–11hr	2–5 daily	45min
Bhubaneshwar	7 daily	20hr–23hr 30min			2 weekly	1hr 40min
Bombay	2 daily	36hr 30min			6–11 daily	1hr 50min
Calcutta	4–6 daily	28hr–32hr 30min			2–3 daily	2–3hr
Chengalpattu	10 daily*	1hr 10min	60 daily	1hr 30min–2hr		
Chidambaram	5 daily*	5hr 30min	20 daily	5–7hr		
Coimbatore	10 daily	8–9hr	9 daily	11–13hr	2–3 daily	1hr 15min
Delhi	3 daily	33hr 45min–48hr			3–4 daily	2hr 30min–2hr 40min
Dindigul	6 daily*	6hr 30min–12hr	10 daily	10–11hr		
Hyderabad	2 daily	14–15hr	1 daily	18–20hr	2–3 daily	1hr
Kanchipuram			46 daily	1hr 30min–2hr		
Kanniyakumari	1 daily	19hr 30min	9 daily	16–18hr		
Kochi	3 daily	13–14hr			1–2 daily	1hr 35min–2hr
Kodaikanal Road	3 daily*	10–13hr	1 daily	14–15hr		
Kumbakonam	3 daily*	7hr 20min	17 daily	7–8hr		
Madurai	6 daily*	7hr 40min–14hr	37 daily	10hr	1–2 daily	50min–1hr 15min
Mamallapuram			80 daily	2–3hr		
Mysore			2 daily	15hr 30min		
Pondicherry			70 daily	4–5hr		
Port Blair					6 weekly	2hr 5min
Pune	3 daily	20–26hr			3 weekly	2hr 55min
Rameshwaram	2–3 daily*	14hr 30min–24hr	1 daily	14hr		
Salem	10 daily	4–5hr	20 daily	5–7hr		
Thanjavur	3 daily*	8–9hr	18 daily	8hr 30min		
Thiruv'puram	1–2 daily	18hr 10min	3 daily	16–18hr	1 daily	1hr 10min–2hr 35min
Tindivanam			40 daily	3–4hr		
Tiruch'palli	11 daily*	5hr 30min–11hr	46 daily	8–9hr	9 weekly	45min
Tirupati	2 daily	3hr	43 daily	4–5hr		
Tiruvannamalai			23 daily	4–6hr		
Udhagamandalam			2 daily	16hr		
Vedanthangal			3 daily	2–3hr		
Vellore			30 daily	3–4hr		
Vijayawada	13 daily	7–11hr	1 daily	13–16hr		

* Trains from Egmore; all others from Central

To and from Chengalpattu						
Kanchipuram	2 daily	1hr	20 daily	1hr		
Kodaikanal Road	3 daily	9–12hr	1 daily	14hr		
Kumbakonam	3 daily	6hr–6hr 30min	3 daily	6–7hr		
Mamallapuram			30 daily	1hr		
Rameshwaram	2 daily	13–15hr				
Thanjavur	3 daily	7–8hr				
Vedanthangal			4 daily	1hr		

To and from Chidambaram						
Chengalpattu	5 daily	4hr 30min	20 daily	4hr 30min–5hr		
Kodaikanal Road	1 daily	7hr 10min				
Kumbakonam	4 daily	1hr 40min	58 daily	2hr 30min		
Rameshwaram	1 daily	11hr				
Thanjavur	4 daily	2hr 30min–3hr	21 daily	4hr		
Tiruch'palli	4 daily	4hr	9 daily	5hr		
Tirupati	2 daily	5–6hr				
Tiruvannamalai	2 daily	4hr 50min	5 daily	3hr 30min		
Vellore			5 daily	4hr 30min		

	Trains		**Buses**		**Flights**	
	Frequency	Time	Frequency	Time	Frequency	Time
To and from Coimbatore						
Bangalore	1 daily	9hr 30min	2 daily	8–9hr	6 weekly	50min
Bombay	1–2 daily	9hr 50min–11hr			1–3 daily	1hr 40min–2hr 10min
Calcutta	2 weekly	39hr 30min			3 weekly	3hr
Delhi	1–2 daily	35–43hr				
Hyderabad	1 daily	20hr 50min				
Kanniyakumari	2 daily	12hr 35min–14hr	3 daily	14hr		
Kochi	8 daily	6hr–6hr 30min				
Kodaikanal Road			2 daily	6hr		
Rameshwaram	1 daily	12hr 20min	2 daily	14hr		
Salem	4 daily	3hr	40 daily	3–4hr		
Thiruv'puram	4 daily	9hr 50min–11hr	2 daily	12hr		
Tiruch'palli	1 daily	5hr	11 daily	6hr		
To and from Kanchipuram						
Tiruvannamalai			8 daily	3hr		
Vellore			20 daily	2hr 30min		
To and from Kanniyakumari						
Bombay	1 daily	48hr				
Delhi	Fri only	58hr				
Kochi	2–3 daily	7hr 30min–9hr				
Salem	1 daily	15hr				
Thiruv'puram	2–3 daily	2hr–2hr 30min	20 daily	2hr		
To and from Madurai						
Bangalore	1 daily	12hr 50min	17 daily	8–9hr		
Chengalpattu	6 daily	10hr–12hr 40min	37 daily	9hr		
Chidambaram	2 daily	8hr–9hr 30min	5 daily	7–8hr		
Coimbatore	3 daily	5hr 50min–7hr	55 daily	10hr		
Kochi			4 daily	10hr		
Kodaikanal Road	6 daily	40min–1hr	11 daily	4hr		
Pondicherry			2 daily	9–10hr		
Rameshwaram	3 daily	6hr 15min–7hr	26 daily	4hr		
Thanjavur	2 daily	4hr 35min–6hr	36 daily	5–6hr		
Thiruv'puram			18 daily	7hr	1 daily	35min
Tiruch'palli	8 daily	2hr 20min–4hr	60 daily	2hr 30min–3hr		
Tirupati	1 daily	18hr 20min	6 daily	15hr		
Tiruvannamalai	1 daily	12hr 20min				
Vellore	1 daily	14hr 30min				
To and from Pondicherry						
Bangalore			4 daily	8hr		
Kanchipuram			8 daily	3hr		
Mamallapuram			9 daily	3hr		
Thanjavur			4 daily	5hr		
Tiruch'palli			4 daily	6hr		
To and from Tiruchirapalli						
Chengalpattu	9 daily	6hr 30min–9hr 20min	46 daily	7–8hr		
Kanchipuram			2 daily	6–7hr		
Kodaikanal Road	5 daily	2hr 40min	1 daily	5hr		
Thanjavur	4 daily	1hr 40min	60–70 daily	1hr–1hr 30min		
Tiruvannamalai			2 daily	4–5hr		

Note that no individual route appears more than once in this chart; for any specific journey, check against where you want to get to as well as where you're coming from. Bear in mind, also, that there is only room here for a general summary; see the "Moving On" sections in specific cities for more details.

Marathas, a strong force further north, took power in Madurai, Thanjavur and Tiruchirapalli, but they made little impact on the south's development.

Much more significant was the arrival of **Europeans**. First came the Portuguese, who landed in Kerala and monopolized Indian trade for about a century before they were joined by the British, Dutch and French. Though mostly on cordial terms with the Indians, the Western powers soon found themselves engaged in territorial disputes. The most marked were between the French, based in **Pondicherry**, and the British, whose stronghold since 1640 had been Fort St George in **Madras**. After battles at sea and on land, the French were confined to Pondicherry, while British ambitions reached their apex in the eighteenth century, when the East India Company occupied Bengal (1757) and made firm its bases in Bombay and Madras.

As well as rebellions against colonial rule, Tamil Nadu also saw anti-*brahmin* protests, in particular those led by the Justice Party in the 1920s and 1930s. Independence in 1947 signalled the need to reorganize state boundaries, and by 1956 areas had been demarcated on a linguistic basis. Andhra Pradesh and Kerala were formed, along with Mysore state (later Karnataka) and **Madras Presidency**, a slightly smaller area than that governed from Madras by the British, where Tamil was the predominant language. In 1965 Madras Presidency became Tamil Nadu, the latter part of its name coming from the Chola agrarian administrative units known as *nadus*.

Since Independence, Tamil Nadu's industrial sector has mushroomed. Initially the state was led by Congress, but in 1967 the **DMK** (Dravida Munnetra Kazhagam), championing the lower castes and reasserting Tamil identity, won a landslide victory. Anti-Hindi and anti-centre, the DMK flourished until the film star "**MGR**" (MG Ramachandran) broke away to form the **All India Anna Dravida Munnetra Kazhagam** (AIADMK), and won an easy victory in the 1977 elections. Virtually deified by his fans-turned-supporters, MGR remained successful, promoting welfare schemes but rejecting industrial development, until his death in 1988, when the Tamil government fell back into the hands of the DMK. Soon after, the AIADMK were reinstated, led by **Sri Jayalalitha Jayaram**, an ex-film star and dancer once on close terms with MGR. In 1996, the AIADMK, in alliance with Congress, was routed conclusively by the DMK, and Jayalalitha, increasingly plagued by corruption scandals, lost her seat.

Madras

In the northeastern corner of Tamil Nadu on the Bay of Bengal, **MADRAS** is India's fourth largest city, with a population nudging six million. Hot, congested and noisy, it is the major transportation hub of the south – the international airport makes a marginally less stressful entry point to the subcontinent than Bombay or Delhi – and most travellers stay just long enough to book a ticket somewhere else. The attractions of the city itself are sparse, though it does boast fine specimens of Raj architecture, pilgrimage sites connected with the apostle "Doubting Thomas", superb Chola bronzes at its chief museum, and plentiful music and dance performances.

The **capital** of Tamil Nadu, Madras is, like Bombay and Calcutta, a comparatively modern creation. It was founded by the **British East India Company** in 1639, on a narrow five-kilometre strip of land between the Cooum and Adyar rivers, a few kilometres north of the ancient Tamil port of **Mylapore** and the Portuguese settlement of San Thome, established in 1522. The site had no natural harbour; it was selected by Francis Day, the East India Company agent, in part because he enjoyed good relations with the Nayak governor Dharmala Ayyappa, who could intercede with the Vijayanagar Raja of Chandragiri, to whom the territory belonged. In addition, the land was protected by water on the east, south and west; cotton could be bought here 20 percent cheaper than elsewhere; and, apparently, Day had acquired a mistress in San Thome. A fortified trad-

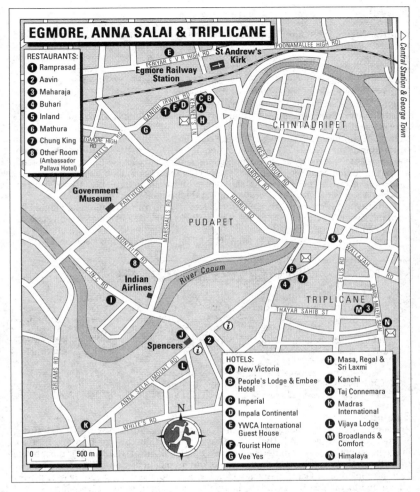

EGMORE, ANNA SALAI & TRIPLICANE

RESTAURANTS:
1 Ramprasad
2 Aavin
3 Maharaja
4 Buhari
5 Inland
6 Mathura
7 Chung King
8 Other Room
(Ambassador
Pallava Hotel)

Central Station & George Town

POONAMALLEE HIGH RD
PERIYAR E V R HIGH RD
St Andrew's Kirk
Egmore Railway Station
SANDHI IRWIN RD
KENNETS LN
EGMORE HIGH RD
HALLS RD
CHINTADRIPET
WEST COOUM RD
GARDEN RD
HARRIS RD

Government Museum
PANTHEON RD
MARSHALLS RD
MONTIETH RD
C IN C RD
PUDAPET
WALLAJAH RD
ELLIS RD
QAIDE MILETH SALAI

Indian Airlines
River Cooum
TRIPLICANE
THAYAR SAHIB ST

GREAMS RD
ANNA SALAI MOUNT RD
WHITE'S RD

N

0   500 m

HOTELS:
A New Victoria
B People's Lodge & Embee Hotel
C Imperial
D Impala Continental
E YWCA International Guest House
F Tourist Home
G Vee Yes

H Masa, Regal & Sri Laxmi
I Kanchi
J Taj Connemara
K Madras International
L Vijaya Lodge
M Broadlands & Comfort
N Himalaya

ing post, completed on St George's Day (April 23) 1640, was named **Fort St George**. By 1700, the British had acquired neighbouring territory including Triplicane and Egmore, while over the course of the next century, as capital of the **Madras Presidency**, which covered most of south India, the city mushroomed to include many surrounding villages. The British were repeatedly challenged by the French who, in 1746, destroyed much of the city. **Robert Clive** ("Clive of India"), then a clerk, was taken prisoner, an experience said to have inspired him to become a campaigner. Clive was among the first to re-enter Madras when it was retaken three years later, and continued to use it as his base. Following this, fortifications were strengthened and the British survived a year-long French siege (1759), completing the work in 1783. By this time, however, Calcutta was in the ascendancy and Madras lost its national importance.

Arrival

Madras Meenambakkam airport is comprehensively served by international and domestic flights; the two terminals are a minute's walk from each other, 16km south-west of the city centre on NH45. Out in the main hall of the international terminal, you'll find a 24-hour post office, several STD telephones, and a couple of snack bars. It's by no means certain that anyone will be staffing the **Government of Tamil Nadu Tourist Information Centre** booth at the arrivals exit, but if you're lucky you may be able to fix up accommodation from here.

To **get away from the airport**, there are pre-paid minibus and taxi counters at the international arrivals exit. **Taxis** cost around Rs200–225 for the thirty-minute ride to the main hotels or railway stations; rickshaws considerably less. A taxi to **Mamallapuram** (see p.981) is in the region of Rs700. An express **bus** (Rs60) runs to the large hotels, Egmore and Central Stations and Thiruvalluvar (Express) bus stand, according to demand. For Anna Salai, walk to the main road and take any bus marked Broadway from the near side. Ask to be let off at the central LIC (*Life Insurance Company*) stop, close to hotels, restaurants and tourist information.

Trains run every 15 or 20 minutes (4.30am–11pm) from **Trisulam** station, 500m from the airport on the far side of the road, to Park, Egmore and North Beach stations, taking roughly 45 minutes.

For a **map** of Madras, see colour insert no.5 in the centre of this book or p.967.

ROAD NAMES IN MADRAS

The names of several roads in Madras have changed over the last few years; confusingly, both old and new names remain in use. We have used the new names throughout the chapter. Thus Mount Rd, the main shopping road through the centre of town, is now **Anna Salai**; to the east, Triplicane High Rd has become **Quaide Milleth Salai**; Poonamallee High Rd, running east–west across the north of the city is **Periyar EVR High Rd**; North Beach Rd, along the eastern edge of George Town is known as **Rajaji Salai**; South Beach Rd, the southern stretch of the coastal road, is **Kamaraj Salai**; running west, Edward Elliot's Rd has been renamed **Dr Radha Krishnan Salai**; Mowbray's Rd is also known as **TTK Rd**, and Nungabamkkam High Rd is now **Uttamar Gandhi Salai**.

By train

Arriving in Madras by train, you come in at one of two **long-distance railway stations**, 1.5km apart on Periyar EVR High Rd, towards the north of the city. **Egmore Station**, in the heart of the busy commercial Egmore district, is the arrival point for most trains from Tamil Nadu and Kerala; on the whole, others pull in at **Central Station**, further east, on the edge of George Town, which has a 24-hour left luggage office, and STD phone booths outside the exit. Information kiosks at both stations are poorly staffed and badly equipped, but both have plentiful taxis and auto-rickshaws – Central has a pre-paid auto-rickshaw booth in the forecourt.

By bus

Buses from elsewhere in Tamil Nadu arrive at two bus stands, **Thiruvalluvar** (also known as Express), and **Broadway**, opposite each other in George Town, near the High Court complex off NSC Bose Rd. Though both stations are unbearably crowded and confusing, Broadway, which also sees services from Karnataka and Andhra Pradesh, is marginally worse: little more than a dirty, chaotic, pot-holed yard, and a nightmare to negotiate with luggage. It can also be a real problem to pick up a rickshaw. For details of buses to **Mamallapuram** from Broadway, see p.980.

Information and communications

At the highly efficient and very helpful **Government of India Tourist Office** (GITO) at 154 Anna Salai (Mon–Fri 9.15am–5.45pm, Sat 9.15am–1pm; ☎852 4785 or 852 4295), you can pick up leaflets, arrange accommodation and organize tours by rented car. They also supply approved **guides** by the day (Rs300–650) or half-day (Rs200–400).

Not far north, the **Tamil Nadu Tourism Development Corporation** (TTDC), 143 Anna Salai (Mon–Fri 10am–5pm; ☎830752), has plenty of information on Madras, and organizes its own tours of the city. Advance bookings for ITDC hotels can be made, and tours of the city arranged, at the ITDC office at 29 Victor Crescent, C-in-C Rd (Mon–Sat 6am–8pm, Sun 6am–2pm; ☎827 8884). Tourist offices for **other states**, including Himachal Pradesh, Kerala, Rajasthan and Uttar Pradesh, are at 28 C-in-C Rd; *Hallo! Madras* (see below) has full details of these and other state offices.

Banks and exchange

Tourists have few difficulties **changing money** in Madras: there are plenty of banks, and the major **hotels** offer exchange facilities to residents. The following places provide efficient service: *American Express*, G-17, Spencer Plaza, 769 Anna Salai (daily 9.30am–7.30pm); *Central Bank of India*, Anna Salai and *Thomas Cook*, Rajaji Salai (Mon–Fri 10am–5pm).

Post and telephone

The **head post office**, with poste restante, is just beyond Parry's Corner on Rajaji Salai (daily 8am–8pm; ☎512011). Madras' other main post office, **Mount Road Post Office** (same hours) at the northern end of Anna Salai, also has a poste restante, but only holds letters addressed to Mount Road PO. The post office on Quaide Milleth Salai (Mon–Sat 7am–3pm) is convenient if you're staying at *Broadlands* or *Himalaya Hotel*.

Telegram and **telephone** services are most efficient at the head post office. Trying to make a local or international call from Mount Road Post Office requires tiresome form-filling, queuing and deposits – if you're in the area head for a phone booth advertising STD/PCO/ISD on a yellow sign, where you'll rarely have to wait in line.

> The telephone **area code** for Madras is ☎44.

Publications

The long-established *Hallo! Madras* (monthly; Rs5, free in some tourist offices) is an accurate directory to all the city's services, with full moon dates (useful for estimating temple festivals), a guide to Tamil for tourists, exhaustive flight and train details, and an outline of Madras bus timetables. *Variety Travel and Shopping Guide* (monthly; Rs15) is packed with travel details and comprehensive listings. Neither guide has a "What's On" section: for forthcoming music and dance performances, contact the venues or ask at the tourist office.

City transport

The offices, sights, railway stations and bus stands of Madras are spread over such a wide area that it's impossible to get around without using some form of **public transport**. Much the best way is by **bus**, a network relieved by an efficient **train** system that operates like an above-ground metro.

Incidentally, the city's drastic water shortage explains the **water carriers** trundling along its congested streets. Watch out for unofficial ones as you cross the road; tractors pulling tankers so heavy that they either topple over or fail to stop when brakes are applied, causing fatal accidents.

Buses

To ride the bus in most Indian cities you need to be incredibly resilient, a master of the art of hanging onto open doorways with two fingers. Buses in Madras, on the other hand, are regular, reliable, inexpensive, well-labelled, and only cramped during rush-hours. On Anna Salai, they have special stops – on smaller streets, flag them down, or wait with the obvious crowd. Buses in Egmore gather opposite the railway station.

Trains

If you want to travel south from central Madras to Guindy (Deer Park), St Thomas Mount, or the airport, the easiest way to go is by **train**. Services run every 15 minutes (on average) between 4.30am and 11pm, prices are minimal, and you can guarantee a seat at any time except rush hour (9am & 5pm). First-class carriages substitute padded seats for wooden slatted benches, and are a little cleaner. Buy a ticket before boarding.

City trains follow the route: North Beach (opposite the head post office), Fort, Park (for Central), Egmore, Nungambakkam, Kodambakkam, Mambalam (for T Nagar and silk shops), Saidapet (for Little Mount Church), Guindy, St Thomas Mount, and Trisulam (for the airport).

Taxis and rickshaws

Madras' yellow-top *Ambassador* **taxis** gather outside Egmore and Central railway stations, and at the airport. All have meters, but they often prefer to set a fixed price before

---

USEFUL BUS ROUTES IN MADRAS

From Broadway Bus Station
#18A, #52B, D, E, F, #54T, #60A Broadway Bus St – Guindy – St Thomas Mt
#88 Broadway – Egmore RS
#18RR, #RR18 Broadway – Guindy – Airport
#19R Broadway – VGP Golden Beach
#52J Broadway – Little Mount – Guindy – Airport

From Egmore Railway Station
#22A, #27, #27B, #27H, #29A Egmore RS –Triplicane – Anna Square
#M4 Egmore RS – Periyar EVR High Rd – Central RS
#1JJ Egmore RS – Rajaji Salai – Parry's – Anna Salai – Triplicane
#23J & #29R Egmore RS – Anna Salai – Adyar

Northbound
#7J, #31, #32 & #32A Triplicane – Anna Square – Chepauk – Secretariat – Parry's
#18C St Thomas Mt – Guindy
#23A & B Adyar Bus Station – Egmore RS

From George Town
#9, #9B, #17D, E, K & T Parry's – Central RS – Egmore RS
#9A Parry's – Egmore RS – Nungambakkam (Income Tax Office and Foreigners' Registration Office)
#18E, T & G Parry's – Central RS – Guindy
#21E, #51R Parry's – Secretariat – Adyar – Guindy RS – St Thomas Mount
#J1 Parry's – Anna Salai – Guindy – National Airport
#6JJ Beach Station – Parry's – Triplicane – San Thome
#1, #45J Parry's – Secretariat – Triplicane
#R18, #36R Beach Station – Anna Salai – Guindy
#19RR High Court – Anna Salai PO – Mylapore – Adyar – VGP Golden Beach
#21J High Court – Secretariat – Chepauk – Adyar – Guindy – National Airport

From Anna Salai
#40 Anna Square – Triplicane – Egmore RS
#45B Anna Square – Triplicane – Anna Salai – Guindy RS – Butt Rd (St Thomas Mount)

TOURS IN MADRAS AND TAMIL NADU

One good way to get around the sights of Madras is on an ITDC or TTDC **bus tour**: bookings are taken in the relevant offices. Albeit inevitably rushed, they're good value, and the guides can be very helpful.

ITDC tours from their office at 26 C-in-C Rd (daily 1.30–6pm; Rs60) visit Fort St George and the fort museum, St Mary's Church, the Government Museum and art gallery, Valluvar Kottam, memorials to Gandhi, Rajaji and Kamaraj, the children's park, Snake Park and Kapalishvara temple.

The **TTDC half-day tour** (daily: 7.30am–1.30pm or 1.30–6.30pm; Rs65) starts at 143 Anna Salai, and picks up passengers at the Express bus stand near the High Court in George Town. It takes in Fort St George, the Government Museum, the Snake Park, Kapalishvara temple and Elliot's Beach, and stops at Marina Beach.

Among longer TTDC tours are good-value **daytrips** to Mamallapuram, Kanchipuram, Crocodile Bank, Muttukadu boat house and VGP Golden Beach (daily 6.20am–7pm; Rs150, Rs220 for a/c bus). Meals are included. The **8-day Tamil Nadu tour** whistles through twelve towns that deserve more time: among them Chidambaram, Thanjavur, Rameshwaram, Kodaikanal, Pondicherry, Kannyakumari, Thiruvananthapuram, Madurai, and Trichy (dep Sat 7am; Rs2250–3500).

leaving, and invariably charge a return fare, whatever the destination. At around Rs120 for Central to Triplicane, they're practically pricing themselves out of business.

Flocks of auto- and cycle rickshaws wait patiently outside tourist hotels, and not so patiently outside railway stations. **Auto-rickshaw** drivers in Madras are notorious for their demand for high fares from locals and tourists alike. All rickshaws have meters; a few drivers use them if asked, but in many cases you'll save a lot of frustrating bargaining by offering a small sub above the meter-reading. If you need to get to the airport or station early in the morning, you can book a rickshaw, and negotiate the price, the night before (the driver may well sleep in his rickshaw outside your hotel). Typical fares from Anna Salai or Triplicane to Egmore or Central are Rs20–25.

Only take **cycle rickshaws** on the smaller roads; riding amid Madras traffic on a fragile tricycle seat can be extremely hair-raising.

Car and bike rental

Car rental, with driver, is available from agencies, and many of the upmarket hotels. It's a great, relatively stress-free way to get about if you can afford it – *Hertz* (☎459962) charge around Rs1200 per day and self-drive is even more expensive.

Anyone interested in renting a **moped** or **motorcycle** for short rides around the city, or tours of Tamil Nadu, should head for the *U-Rent Services* offices at 36 2nd Main Rd, Gandhi Nagar, Adyar (Mon–Sat 8am–8pm; ☎414222), or *Picnic Hotel*, 1132 Periyar EVR High Rd (Mon–Sat 6am–10pm; ☎588828). You'll need an international driving licence. Prices range from Rs100 to Rs300 per day.

The City

Madras divides into three main areas. The northern district, separated from the rest by the River Cooum, is the site of the first British outpost in India, **Fort St George**, and the commercial centre, **George Town**, that grew up during British occupation. At the southern end of Rajaji Salai, **Parry's Corner**, George Town's principal landmark – look for the tall grey building labelled *Parry's* – is a major bus stop.

Central Madras, sandwiched between the Cooum and Adyar rivers, and crossed diagonally by the city's main thoroughfare, **Anna Salai**, is dominated by modern commercial and residential areas, and gives way in the east to a long straight **coastline**

men mend nets and set small boats out to sea, and tourists hitch up *saris* and trousers for a quick paddle. South of here, near the coast, **Mylapore**, inhabited in the 1500s by the Portuguese, boasts **Kapalishvara temple** and **San Thome Church**, both tourist attractions and places of pilgrimage. Further out, south of the Adyar, the Portuguese church on **St Thomas Mount** overlooks **Guindy National Park**, the only city national park in India.

For a **map** of Madras, see colour insert no.5 in the centre of this book or p.967.

Fort St George

Quite unlike any other fort in India, **Fort St George** stands amid state offices facing the sea in the east of the city, just south of George Town on Kamaraj Salai. It looks more like a complex of well-maintained colonial mansions than a fort; indeed many of its buildings are used today as offices, roamed during the week by businessmen passing between the Secretariat and State Legislature.

The fort was the first structure of Madras city, and the first territorial possession of the British in India. Construction began in 1640, but most of the original buildings had to be replaced later that century, after being damaged during French sieges. The most imposing structure is the eighteenth-century colonnaded **Fort House**, coated in deep slate grey and white paint. Next door, in the more modestly proportioned **Exchange Building** – site of Madras' first bank – is the fort **museum** (daily except Fri 10am–5pm). The collection within faithfully records the central events of the British occupation of Madras with portraits, regimental flags, weapons, coins minted by the East India Company, medals, stamps and letters written by figures such as Robert Clive. The squat cast-iron cage on the ground floor was brought to Madras from China, where for more than a year in the nineteenth century it had been used as a particularly sadistic form of imprisonment for a British captain. The upper floor, once the Public Exchange Hall where merchants met to gossip and trade, is now an **art gallery**, where portraits of prim officials and their wives sit side-by-side with fine sketches of the British embarking at Madras in aristocratic finery, attended by Indians in loin cloths.

South of the museum, past the State Legislature, is the oldest surviving Anglican church in Asia, **St Mary's Church** (daily 9am–5pm), built in 1678, and partly renovated after the battle of 1759. The church, built with thick walls and a strong vaulted roof to withstand the city's many sieges, served as a store and shelter in times of war. It's distinctly English in style, crammed with plaques and statues in memory of British soldiers, politicians and their wives. The grandest plaque, made of pure silver, was presented by Elihu Yale, former Governor of Fort St George (1687–96), and founder of Yale University in the USA. A collection of photographs of visiting dignitaries, including Queen Elizabeth II, is on display in the entrance porch, while the ageing mural of the Last Supper above the altar in the eastern wing, probably painted by a student of Raphael, was looted from the French headquarters in Pondicherry. The cemetery outside contains the graves of yet more soldiers, and smaller headstones commemorating young children struck down by disease. Nearby, **Robert Clive's house** is in a rather sorry state, used by the Archaeological Survey of India as offices.

George Town

North of Fort St George, the former British trading centre of **George Town** remains a focus for banks, offices and shipping companies. This confusing – if well-ordered – grid of streets harbours a fascinating medley of architecture: eighteenth- and nineteenth-century churches, Hindu and Jain temples, and a scattering of mosques, interspersed with grand mansions. However, despite its potential charm, this is Madras' most chaotic and crowded area, a dirty and uninviting warren clogged by particularly persistent hawkers and thick traffic. Probably the best way to appreciate the area is from its edges. In the east, on Rajaji Salai, the **head post office** occupies a robust earth-red Indo-Saracenic building, constructed in 1884. George Town's southern extent is marked by the bulbous white domes and sandstone towers of the **High Court**, and the even more opulent towers of the **Law College**, both showing strong Islamic influence.

It can be fun to take a quick root around George Town's **bazaars**, lines of rickety stalls selling clothes, bags, umbrellas, watches, shoes and perfume, concentrated along Rajaji Salai and NSC Bose Rd. Further south, the pavements are crowded by stalls selling balloons, fruit, flowers and lottery tickets.

Government Museum

Pantheon Rd, south of Egmore Railway Station. Daily except Fri 9am–5pm. Rs3, camera Rs10.

It's well worth setting aside at least half a day to explore the Madras **Government Museum** for its remarkable archeological finds from south India and the Deccan, stone sculptures from major temples, and unsurpassed collection of Chola bronzes.

A deep red circular structure, fronted by Italian-style pillars and built in 1851, the **main building** stands opposite the entrance and ticket office. Inside, the first gallery is devoted to archeology and geology, with tools, pots, jewellery and weapons from the Stone and Iron ages, and maps of principal excavations. Later exhibits include a substantial assortment of dismantled panels, railings and statues from Amaravati (see p.1198), carved with episodes from the Buddha's life and scenes from the *Jataka* stories from early Hinayana Buddhist texts. To the left of this gallery, high arcaded halls full of stuffed animals and the like lead to the **ethnology gallery**, where models, clothes and weapons, along with photographs of expressionless faces in orderly lines, illustrate local tribal societies, some long since wiped out. A fascinating display of wind and string instruments, drums and percussion includes the large predecessor of today's *sitar* and several very old *tabla*. Nearby, a group of wooden doors, lintels and window frames from Chettinad, a region near Madurai, are exquisitely carved with floral and geometric designs much like those found in Gujarati *havelis*.

The museum's real treasure, however, is the modern, well-lit gallery, left of the main building, which contains the world's most complete and impressive selection of **Chola bronzes** (see p.1013). Large statues of Shiva, Vishnu and Parvati stand in the centre, flanked by glass cases containing smaller figurines, including several sculptures of Shiva as **Nataraja**, the Lord of the Dance, encircled by a ring of fire, and standing with his arms and legs poised and head provocatively cocked. One of the finest models is **Ardhanarishvara**, the androgynous form of Shiva (united with Shakti in transcendence of duality) familiar from Chola temples. The left side of the body is female and the right male, and the intimacy of detail is astounding. A rounded breast, a delicate hand and tender bejewelled foot are counterpoints to the harsher sinewy limbs and torso, and the male side of the head is crowned with a mass of matted hair and serpents.

A **children's museum** demonstrates the principles of electricity and irrigation with marginally diverting, semi-functional models, while the magnificent Indo-Saracenic **art gallery** houses old British portraits of figures such as Clive and Hastings, Rajput and Moghul miniatures, and a small display of ivory carvings.

St Andrew's Kirk

Just northeast of Egmore station, off Periyar EVR High Rd, **St Andrew's Kirk**, consecrated in 1821, is a fine example of Georgian architecture. Modelled on London's St Martin-in-the-Fields, it is one of just three churches in India with a circular seating plan, beneath a huge dome painted blue with gold stars and supported by a sweep of Corinthian columns. A staircase leads onto the flat roof, surrounding the dome, from where you can climb further up into the steeple past the massive bell and patiently ticking clock mechanism to a tiny balcony affording excellent views of the city.

Valluvar Kottam

In the south of the Nungambakkam district, at the corner of Village Rd and Kodambakkam High Rd, the **Valluvar Kottam** is an intriguing construction, built in classical style in 1976 as a memorial to the first-century Tamil poet Thiruvalluvar. Most impressive is the 34m high stone chariot, carved from just three blocks of granite in a likeness of the great temple car of Thiruvarur, east of Thanjavur; adjoining this veritable juggernaut is a vast public auditorium, one of the largest in Asia, with a capacity of 4000. A stroll along the auditorium roof past shallow rectangular ponds brings you to a large statue of the poet saint, within a shrine carved into the upper reaches of the chariot. Among the many reliefs around the monument, look out for the cat in human pose, reminiscent of the figure at Arjuna's Penance in Mamallapuram.

Marina

One of the longest city beaches in the world, the **Marina** (Kamaraj Salai, aka South Beach Rd) stretches 5km from the harbour at the southeastern corner of George Town, to San Thome Cathedral. The impulse to transform Madras' "rather dismal beach" into a Marina, styled "from old Sicilian recollections" which would function as a "lung" for the city, was conceived by Mountstuart Elphinstone Grant-Duff (Governor 1881–86) who had otherwise won himself the reputation for being "feeble, sickly" and a "failure". Over the years, numerous buildings, some of which undoubtedly would not have figured in memories of Sicily, have sprung up.

The **beach** itself is a sociable stretch, peopled by idle paddlers, picnickers and pony-riders; on Sunday afternoons crowds gather for a market. Swimming and sunbathing are neither recommended nor approved – if you're desperate, however, you could try one of the shabby swimming pools. There's also a rather neglected aquarium, and two parks at the northern end, the **Anna Park** and **MG Ramachandran Samadhi**. The **landward** side reveals a wealth of colonial architecture; at the north, one of the oldest of the city's University buildings is the **Senate House** (1879), an uncharacteristically Byzantine-influenced design by Robert Fellowes Chisholm (1840–1915). He was one of the British leaders in developing the Indo-Saracenic hybrid style, incorporating Hindu, Jain and Muslim elements along with solid Victorian British brickwork.

Continuing south, past the Indo-Saracenic **Presidency College** (1865–71), a number of stolid Victorian University buildings include the **Lady Willingdon Teacher Training College**. Next door, the college's hostel, a huge lump of a building with a semicircular frontage painted white and yellow, was until 1870 Madras' Ice House, storing huge blocks of ice imported from New England.

Mylapore

Long before Madras came into existence, **Mylapore**, south of the Marina, was an important settlement; the Greek geographer Ptolemy mentioned it in the second century AD as a thriving port. During the Pallava period (fifth–ninth centuries) it was second only to Mamallapuram (see p.981).

An important stop – with Little Mount and St Thomas Mount – on the St Thomas pilgrimage trail, **San Thome Cathedral** (daily 6am–8pm) marks the eastern boundary of Mylapore, lying close to the sea at the southern end of the Marina. Although the present neo-Gothic structure dates from 1896, San Thome stands on the site of two earlier churches (the first possibly erected by Nestorian Christians from Persia during the tenth century) built over the tomb of St Thomas; his relics are kept inside. Behind the church, a small **museum** houses stone medallions, stones inscribed in Tamil, Sanskrit (twelfth-century Chola) and early Portuguese, and a map of India dated 1519.

The **Kapalishvara**, less than 1km west, is the most famous temple in Madras, its principal shrine to Shiva. Seventh-century Tamil poet-saints sang its praises, but the present structure probably dates from the sixteenth century. Until then, the temple is thought to have occupied a site on the shore; sea erosion or demolition at the hands of the Portuguese led it to be rebuilt inland. Dominating the eastern and main entrance, the huge (40m) *gopura*, covered in stucco figures, is comparatively recent (1906). Surrounding an assortment of busy shrines, where priests offer blessings for devotees and non-Hindus alike, the courtyard features an old tree where a small shrine to Shiva's consort, Parvati, shows her in the form of a peahen worshipping a *lingam*. This commemorates the legend that she was momentarily distracted from concentrating on her Lord by the enchanting dance of a peacock. Shiva, miffed at this dereliction of wifely duty, cursed her, whereupon she turned into a peahen (*mayil*). To expiate the sin, Parvati took off to a place called Kapalinagar, and embarked upon rigorous austerities. To commemorate her success, the town was named Mayilapore or **Mylapore**.

The oldest artefacts in the Kapalishvara temple are the movable bronze images of deities and the 63 Shaivite Nayanmar poet-saints, two of whom came from Mylapore. Unusually, the main shrine faces west, towards a space that appears vast in this cramped suburban district, and is dominated by an eighteenth-century water lily tank.

Important **festivals** held here include Tai Pusham (Jan/Feb), when the bronze images of Shiva and Parvati are pulled around the temple tank in a decorated boat to the accompaniment of music. Brahmotsava (March/April) celebrates the marriage of Shiva and Parvati; on the eighth day, in the afternoon, all 63 bronze images of the Nayanmar saints are clothed and garlanded and taken out in palanquins along the streets to meet the bejewelled images of Shiva and Parvati. Vasantha (May/June), the summer festival, is marked by concerts.

In the busy **market streets** that surround the temple, amid stalls selling pots and pans, flowers, religious paraphernalia and vegetables, glittering shops spill over with gold wedding-jewellery. Exquisite *saris* are unfolded for scrutiny in silk emporia; the finest quality comes from Kanchi, delicately embroidered with gold and silver thread that can add as much as Rs30,000 to the cost of a wedding.

A little further west, before you come to TTK Rd, the **Luz Church**, on Luz Church Rd, is thought to be the earliest in Madras, built by the Portuguese in the sixteenth century. Its founding is associated with a miracle; Portuguese sailors in difficulties at sea were once guided to land and safety by a light which, when they tried to find its source, disappeared. The church, dedicated to Our Lady of Light, was erected where the light left them.

Little Mount

St Thomas is said to have sought refuge from persecution in the **Little Mount caves**, 8km south of the city centre, now 200m off the road between the Maraimalai Adigal Bridge and the Residence of the Governor of Tamil Nadu. Entrance to the cave is beside steps leading to a statue of Our Lady of Good Health (see p.1017). Inside, next to a small natural window in the rock, are impressions of what are believed to be St Thomas' handprints, made when he made his escape through this tiny opening.

Behind the new circular church of Our Lady of Good Health, together with brightly painted replicas of the Pietà and Holy Sepulchre, is a natural **spring**. Tradition has it that this was created when Thomas struck the rock, so the crowds that came to hear him preach could quench their thirst; samples of its holy water are on sale.

St Thomas Mount

Tradition has it that St Thomas was speared to death (or struck by a hunter's stray arrow), while praying before a stone cross on **St Thomas Mount**, 11km south of the city centre, close to the airport. **Our Lady of Expectation church** (1523) is reached by 134 granite steps marked at intervals with the fourteen stations of the cross. At the top of the steps, a huge old banyan tree provides shade for devotees who come to fast, pray and sing. Inside the church, St Thomas' cross is said to have bled in 1558; above the altar which marks the spot of the Apostle's death, a painting of the Madonna and Child is credited to St Luke. A memento stall stands nearby and cool drinks are available in the adjacent Holy Apostle's Convent.

The Theosophical Society Headquarters

The **Theosophical Society** was established in New York in 1875 by Colonel Olcott and the eccentric Madame Petrovna Blavatsky, who claimed occult powers and telepathic links with "Mahatmas" in Tibet. Claiming to believe in the equality and truth of all religions, the society in fact propagated a modern Hinduism, praising all things Indian and shunning Christian missionaries – so its two founders were greeted enthusiastically when they transferred their operations to Madras in 1882, establishing their headquarters near Elliot's Beach in the south. Even after Madame Blavatsky's psychic powers were proved to be bogus, the society continued to attract Hindus and Western visitors, and its buildings still stand today, sheltering several shrines and an excellent library of books on religion and philosophy (Tues–Sun 8–11am & 1.30–5pm; ☎413528). Quite simply one of the most serene places on earth, this is a superb spot to sit and restore spirits away from the noise and heat of the city streets; a vast **banyan tree** in the gardens, a tangle of wide branches and hanging roots that form subsidiary trunks, is said to be the second largest in the world.

Guindy National Park

South of Elliot Beach Road, not far from Guindy railway station, the peaceful **Guindy National Park** is home to a healthy community of **black buck, chital** (spotted deer), mongooses and monkeys. However, it's rather neglected, and many visitors leave disappointed, without spotting any animals. One section is fenced off as a **Snake Park** (daily 9am–5.30pm; Rs2, camera Rs5, video Rs100), but its reptilian residents are neither unusual nor plentiful. Dotted along the north side of the park are three large memorials to Kamaraj, Gandhi and Rajaji.

Accommodation

Finding a **place to stay** in Madras can be a problem, as hotels are often full. Demand has pushed prices up, so only a couple of places offer anything for less than Rs100. Standards in the less expensive places are not high – in contrast Madras' top-notch hotels are truly palatial, immaculately clean and very well run.

The main concentration of mid-range and inexpensive hotels is in **Egmore**, around the railway station. Head for the ones listed below first; if they're full, a bit of hunting around should turn up a reasonable fall-back. Other popular areas include **Anna Salai**, which tends to be more expensive, and Triplicane, further east. The bulk of the top hotels are in the south of the city; several offer buses to and from the airport.

Due to frequent shortages, visitors should use **water** as sparingly as possible.

ACCOMMODATION PRICE CODES

All **accommodation prices** in this book have been coded using the symbols below. In principle the prices given are for the least expensive double rooms in each establishment; however, some hotels, usually in category ①, offer rates per bed rather than per room. Local taxes are not included unless specifically stated. For more details, see p.35.

① up to Rs100	④ Rs225–350	⑦ Rs750–1200
② Rs100–150	⑤ Rs350–500	⑧ Rs1200–2200
③ Rs150–225	⑥ Rs500–750	⑨ Rs2200 and upwards

Egmore

Embee, 12a Whannels Rd (☎830444). Functional, with budget singles. Doubles are less good. ③.

Impala Continental, 12 Gandhi Irwin Rd (☎825 0484). Large hotel with impersonal but clean rooms, all with bath and some with hot water. Good value and often full. Reasonable restaurant. ⑤.

Imperial, 6 Gandhi Irwin Rd (☎825 0376). Set back from the road. Assorted rooms, comfortable a/c suites. Restaurant, nightclub and travel services. ⑤–⑥.

Masa, 15/1 Kennet's Lane (☎825 2966). Smart, modern place with TV; some 4-bed rooms. ④–⑤.

New Victoria, 3 Kennet's Lane (☎825 3638). Newish hotel; all rooms a/c with hot shower and some with balconies. ⑦–⑧.

People's Lodge, 18 Whannels Rd (☎835 9380). Basic, grubby and cheap, and often full. ①.

Regal, 15 Kennet's Lane (☎825 1967). One of the better budget options. ②–③.

Sri Laxmi Lodge, 16 Kennet's Lane (☎825 4576). Standard non-a/c rooms opening onto dim corridors; clean and functional. ②.

Tourist Home, 21 Gandhi Irwin Rd (☎825 0079). Popular hotel directly opposite the railway station: fresher and better ventilated than many. Rooms (some a/c) with showers, telephones, clean sheets and towels. Good value and often full. ④–⑤.

Vee Yes, 35 Gandhi Irwin Rd (☎825 2547). Average small hotel, badly ventilated but clean enough. Carpeted, a/c rooms with hot showers. ③–⑤.

YWCA International Guest House, 1086 Periyar EVR High Rd (☎532 4234). Attractive hotel in quiet gardens. Spotless rooms and a good restaurant. ⑤–⑥.

Anna Salai and Triplicane

Broadlands, 16 Vallabha Agraham St, Triplicane (☎845573 or 848131). Whitewashed old house, around a courtyard; the kind of budget travellers' enclave you either love or loathe. Large roof terrace and clean rooms, a few with shower and balcony. Left-luggage, bike rental and snacks, drinks and beer to order. The in-house masseur is not recommended. Indians not allowed. ④.

Comfort, 22 Vallabha Agraharam, Triplicane (☎845117). Good value, roomy new hotel. Rooms with *Star TV*, and travel service available. ③–④.

Himalaya, 54 Quaide Milleth Salai (☎847522). Clean, spacious rooms and efficient service. TV, table and chair, hot shower and balcony in all rooms; some a/c. ④–⑤.

Kanchi, 28 C-in-C Rd (☎827 1100). Good-value mid-priced hotel with non- and a/c rooms, two restaurants (one rooftop) and bar. ④–⑤.

Madras International, 693 Anna Salai (☎852 4111). Reasonable hotel with range of rooms, shops, veg and non-veg restaurant and bar. ⑦–⑧.

Taj Connemara, Binny Rd (☎852 0123; fax 852 3361). A Madras institution; near Anna Salai but a world away from its traffic. The best rooms are the big, characterful old ones, with dressing room and verandah overlooking the pool. Good service, restaurants and all facilities. ⑨.

Vijaya Lodge, 3 Patullos Rd, off Anna Salai (☎852 5437). Basic, simple and reasonably clean. ②.

Outside the centre

New Woodlands Hotel, 72–75 Dr Radha Krishnan Salai (☎827 3111). Clean, spacious rooms with hot showers. ⑥.

Ranjit, 9 Nungambakkam High Rd (☎827 0521). Spotless rooms (some a/c) with *Star TV*. Veg and non-veg restaurants. ⑥.

Savera, 69 Dr Radha Krishnan Salai (☎827 4700). Modern hotel boasting all mod-cons and a swimming pool, bar and restaurant. Smart rooms, including huge deluxe suites. ⑧.

Tamil Nadu TTDC Hostel, 3 Periyar EVR High Rd (☎589132). Basic dorms or doubles, about the only reasonable option in walking distance of Central Station. ④.

Trident, 1/24 GST Rd (☎234 4747; fax 234 6699). Comfortable 5-star hotel in lovely gardens with swimming pool. Near the airport (3km), but long (albeit complimentary) drive into town (12km). Good restaurants, one of which serves Thai cuisine. ⑨.

Welcomgroup Park Sheraton, 132 TTK Rd (☎499 4101; fax 499 7101). Last word in American-style, executive luxury, with bow-tied valets and in-room fax machines. Three excellent restaurants (see below), 24hr coffee shop and other 5-star facilities. ⑨.

Eating

Madras is jam-packed with **restaurants**, from the predictable range of standard "meals" joints, to places where you can sample the very best in south Indian cuisine. For budget experimentation you can't beat *Saravana Bhavan* in the T Nagar market area; with a fistful of cash, head for the luxurious *Park Sheraton* and *Connemara*.

Aavin, Anna Salai. Blissfully cooling milk and ice-cream parlour, a few steps north of the Government Tourist Office. Takeaway only.

Amaravati, Cathedral Rd. Excellent, inexpensive Andhra food, with particularly good *biryanis*.

Buhari, 83 Anna Salai. A/c and non-a/c dining rooms and open-air terrace with a homely atmosphere, veg and non-veg south and north Indian food, plus freshly baked cakes.

Chung King, Anna Salai, down an alley next to *Buhari*. Genuine cuisine prepared by Chinese chef.

Taj Connemara, see above. Irresistible buffet lunches at the *Verandah* coffee shop, costing around Rs240. Excellent veg and non-veg Indian and Western dishes, wicked desserts – breakfast is just as good. In the evening, the outdoor *Rain Tree* specializes in spicy dishes from Chettinad; live Carnatic classical music and Bharatanatyam performances add to the atmosphere.

Imperial, 6 Gandhi Irwin Rd, Egmore. Imaginative menu, featuring superb steaks, served at indoor and outdoor tables in an enjoyable family atmosphere.

Inland, Anna Salai. Cosy, with small rooftop terrace and a/c room serving reasonably priced variety of Indian snacks and meals.

Maharaja, 307 Quaide Milleth Salai. Simple restaurant, popular with budget travellers. Excellent value set meals and a good range of other veg dishes. Open till midnight.

Mathura, Tarapore Towers, 827 Anna Salai. High-quality veg meals in large, well-decorated, a/c hall. Roof terrace not always open.

Other Room, *Ambassador Pallava Hotel*, 53 Monteith Rd. North Indian cuisine with live bands and dance floor in the evening; lunchtime buffet for around Rs 200.

Palimar, 48 Ground Floor, Parsn Manere, 602 Anna Salai. Good value snack-oriented dishes (mostly south Indian, some *tandoori*) in smart a/c rooms, plus daily specials noon–3pm.

Palmgrove, 5 Kodambakkam High Rd. Two veg restaurants: *Oorvasi*, with *tandoori* dishes and "meals"; the cheaper *Menaka* has south Indian snacks and good lunch *thalis*.

Picnic, 1132 Periyar EVR High Rd, 300m from Central Station. Relaxing haven for travellers in transit with time to kill: cool, friendly, clean, and serves excellent tiffin.

Ramprasad, 22 Gandhi Irwin Rd, Egmore. Small, simple dining hall attached to hotel. Standard south Indian dishes, fresh chutneys, and strong hot coffees. Great for breakfast.

Saravana Bhavan, Thanigai Murugan Rathinavel Hall, 77 Usman Rd, T Nagar. Off the tourist trail, near Ranganathan St Market (Mambalam railway station), but an excellent and very crowded place to eat authentic, inexpensive south Indian veg food. For tasty curries, and all the trimmings, try the deluxe "Tamil Nadu meal". The a/c first floor is more expensive than the hectic "leaf meals" canteen on the top floor, while the ground floor serves south Indian snacks, ice-creams and sweets.

Taj Coromandel, 17 Nungambakkam High Rd. Two main restaurants: *Mysore* for a variety of Indian food and *Golden Dragon* for fine Chinese. The *Pavilion Coffee Shop* is good for blow-out buffet breakfasts.

Welcomgroup Chola Sheraton, 10 Cathedral Rd (☎499 4101). Upmarket hotel with two good restaurants; the *Peshawari* serves lavish (and expensive) northwestern frontier food, while the excellent rooftop *Sagari* specializes in Chinese dishes.

Welcomgroup Park Sheraton, see above. More – extremely good – upmarket hotel restaurants. The *Residency* serves Indian, Western and Chinese, the *Khyber* is a meaty poolside barbecue, but best of all is the south Indian *Dakshin*. Excellent choice of unusual veg dishes, seafood and fish in marinaded spices, plus spicy chicken from Andhra, Karnataka mutton *biryani*, and *meen moilee*. Piping-hot *idiappam* and *appam* made on the spot. Live Carnatic music.

Woodlands Drive-In, 30 Cathedral Rd. Pure veg tiffin joint, in garden setting, popular with young people on scooters and families in cars. Transport, however, is not compulsory. Best for breakfast.

THE MADRAS FESTIVAL AND THE SABHAS

The **sabhas** of Madras – the city's arts societies and venues, of which the most illustrious is the *Madras Music Academy* – stage regular public performances of Carnatic classical music and Bharatanatyam dance, where ambitious artists have to undergo the scrutiny of an often fanatical audience and a less-than-generous bevy of newspaper critics, whose reviews can make or break a career.

Musicians are expected to interpret correctly the subtleties of any given composition, *raga* or *tala*. The sets of notes that make up a *raga* occupy a place midway between melody and scale; they must be played imaginatively in improvisation, but in strict sequences and with correct emphasis. The worst crime, the sign of an amateur, is to slip accidentally into a different *raga* that might share the same scale. *Tala*, the rhythmic cycle and bedrock of the music, will often be demonstrated by someone on stage, and consists of a series of claps and waves; unlike in north India, this element is overt in the south and the audience delights in clapping along to keep the often-complex time signatures. The pleasure is heightened during percussion improvisations on the barrel-shaped *mridangam* drum or *ghatam* clay pot that accompany many performances.

During the second half of December and early January, the two- to three-week **Madras Festival** stages up to 500 events in an orgy of classical music and dance recitals, during which many of India's greatest artistes – from both north and south – can be seen at work.

Female vocalists to look out for include MS Subbulakshmi, Mani Krishnaswamy, Charumathi Ramachandran, Sudha Raghunathan and Bombay Jayashree; duos such as the Bombay and Hyderabad Sisters are also popular. Top-ranking **male singers**, KV Narayanaswamy, Thanjavur M Thiagarajan, B Rajam Iyer and younger artists like Thrissur Ramachandran and TN Seshagopalan should not be missed. Among the best of the **instrumentalists** are Balachandar, Kalyana Krishna Bhavatar, E Gayatri and Rama Varma on the gentle melodic *vina*, a stringed instrument unique to the south; Ramani on flute; violinists such as TN Krishnan, D Ananda Raman; and N Ravikiran on *gottuvadyam*, a rare member of the *vina* family, laid flat on the floor and played much like a slide guitar.

The predominant **dance** style is Bharatanatyam, as performed by stars such as Alarmail Valli, and the Dhananjayans. Dance dramas are also staged by the *Kalakshetra Academy*, a school of dance and music set in a beautiful 100-acre compound near the sea in Tiruvanmiyur, on the southern outskirts of the city.

Outside the festival, to find out about **performances of music and dance**, ask at tourist offices, consult local papers, or contact the following *sabhas* and dance halls:

Indian Fine Arts Society, 15 Stringers St, Madras 18 (☎580015).
Kalaivanar Arangam, Govt Estate, Wallajah Rd (☎565669).
Kamaraj Memorial Hall, Anna Salai (☎451355).
Music Academy, 115E TTK Rd, Madras 14 (☎827 5619).
Mylapore Fine Arts Club, 160 Oliver Rd, Madras 4 (☎499 2660).
Naranda Gana Sabha, 254 TTK Rd, Madras 18 (☎499 3201).
Rani Seethai Hall, 603 Anna Salai (☎827 4863).
Sri Krishna Gana Sabha, 8 Griffith Rd, T Nagar, Madras 17 (☎828 0806).
Sri Thyaga Brahma Gana Sabha, Vani Bhavan, 50 GN Chetty Rd, Madras 17 (☎828 2166).
Tamil Issai Sangam, Raja Annamalai, Esplanade (☎561425).

Listings

Bookstores *Higginbothams* on Anna Salai is Madras' largest bookshop, with a vast assortment of books at reasonable prices. The hole-in-the-wall *Giggles Bookshop* in the *Connemara Hotel* has an excellent collection of novels and coffee-table books; *Giggles & Scribbles*, Wellingdon Estate, 24 C-in-C Rd (Mon–Sat 9.30am–7.30pm) is a larger branch, set back 50m from the road, selling rare

MOVING ON FROM MADRAS

Transport connections between Madras and the rest of India are summarized on p.964; flights between Madras and **southeast Asia** are listed on p.7; and details on how to get to the **Andaman islands** by sea or air are given on p.952.

By air

Cities served by **daily flights** from Madras include **Bangalore** (4 daily, 5 on Mon, Tues, Thurs & Sat, 2 Sun; 45min), **Bombay** (6–11 daily; 1hr 50min), **Calcutta** (2 daily, 3 on Mon, Wed, Fri & Sun; 2hr 10min–3hr), **Coimbatore** (2 daily, 3 on Mon, Wed & Fri; 1hr 15min), **Delhi** (3 daily, 4 on Wed & Sun; 2hr 40min), **Hyderabad** (3 daily, 2 on Sun; 1hr), **Madurai** (daily, 2 on Tues, Thurs & Sat; 50min–1hr 15min), and **Thiruvananthapuram** (1hr 10min–2hr 35min). You can also fly to **Pune** (Mon, Wed & Fri; 2hr 55min), **Port Blair** (Mon–Sat; 2hr 5min) and **Tiruchirapalli** (Mon–Sat, 2 on Mon, Thurs & Fri; 45min).

Airline offices, mostly open Mon–Fri 10am–5am, Sat 10am–1pm, include: *Air India*, 19 Marshalls Rd (☎827 4477, airport ☎234 7400); *Air France*, 769 Anna Salai (☎825 0326); *Air Lanka*, 758 Mount Chamber, Anna Salai (☎852 5301); *British Airways*, Khaleeli Centre, Monteith Rd (☎827 4272); *Gulf Air*, 52 Montieth Rd (☎826 7872); *Indian Airlines*, 19 Marshalls Rd (Mon–Sat 10am–1pm & 1.45–5.30pm; ☎825 1677); *Lufthansa*, 171 Anna Salai (☎826 9095); *Qantas*, Eldorado Building, 112 Nungambakkam High Rd (☎827 8680); *Swissair*, 191 Anna Salai (☎825 4783); *Thai International*, Swan Travels, Avarti Buildings, 189 Anna Salai (☎826 9140). For *American, Air Canada, Biman, Philippine, Royal Jordanian* and *TWA*, contact *Jetair*, Apex Plaza, 3 MG Rd (☎826 2409).

By train

Trains to Trichy, Thanjavur, Pudukottai, Rameswaram, Kodaikanal Road, Madurai and Kollam leave from **Egmore Station**. All other departures are from **Central**. Left of the main building, on the first floor of the Moore Market Complex, the efficient **tourist reservation counter** (Mon–Sat 8am–8pm, Sun 8am–2pm) sells tickets for trains from either station. The booking office at Egmore, up the stairs left of the main entrance (same hours), also handles bookings for both stations, but has no tourist counter.

Most destinations are served by more than one daily train. For the long haul to **Delhi** the best service is the *Tamil Nadu Express* #2621 (daily 9pm; 33hr 45min). To save time on a journey to **Madurai**, opt for the fastest of six daily trains, the *Vaigai Express* #2635 (12.25pm; 7hr 40min) – all the other services run overnight, arriving early in the morning. The *Madras–Trivandrum Mail* #6319 runs daily to **Thiruvananthapuram** (6.55pm; 17hr), supplemented by an additional service on Sundays. The closest railhead to **Ooty** is Mettupalayam, served by the nightly *Nilgiri Express* #6005 (9.05pm; 10hr 15min). For **Kodaikanal**, take a train to Kodaikanal Road (3 daily) or Dindigul (5 daily).

By bus

Getting away from **Thiruvalluvar** or **Broadway** bus stands can be confusing: few of the buses, run by several different operators, are marked in English. Both serve other towns in Tamil Nadu, but only Thiruvalluvar serves Karnataka and Andhra Pradesh. Thiruvallavur operates a reasonably efficient booking system; Broadway is far more chaotic. Here you'll have to rely on asking others, or accept the help offered by gangs of children (who expect tips) to find the bus you want. Buses to **Mamallapuram** leave from Broadway. The fastest services are #188, #188 A/B/D/K (less than 2hr); #19A, #19C, #119 and #119A take a little longer; #108B (via the airport and Chengalpattu) takes at least 3hr.

In theory, you can pick up most buses at Parry's Corner, Anna Salai and Adyar, but the struggle to hail the right one, get through the crowds, and find a seat is best avoided.

Travel agents

Most travel agents book bus, train and air tickets for a small fee. Reliable operators include *American Express*, G-17 Spencer Plaza, 768/769 Anna Salai (☎852 3592); *Asian Travels*, 39 Anna Salai (☎827 6451); *Popular Travels, Hotel Imperial*, 6 Gandhi Irwin Rd, Egmore (☎825 8601); *Sita World Travels*, Fagun Mansion, 26 C-in-C Rd (☎827 8861); *Thomas Cook*, Chebroos Centre, Monteith Rd, Egmore (☎827 3092).

reprints of historical books on India and Indian music cassettes, and with an efficient mail-order system. *Karnatic Music Book Centre*, 14 Sripuram First St, Royapettah, Madras 14 is an excellent bookshop for Carnatic classical music and Indian dance fanatics, with mail-order service.

Cinemas Cinemas such as *Abhirami* and *Lakshmi* along Anna Salai show English-language films.

Consulates *Germany*, 22 C-in-C Rd (☎827 1747; 9am–noon); *Norway*, 44 Rajaji Salai (☎517950; 10am–5pm *Sri Lanka*, 9-D Nawab Habibullah Rd (☎827 2270); *Sweden*, 6 Cathedral Rd (☎827 5792; 9.30am–1pm); *UK*, 24 Anderson Rd, Nungambakkam (☎827 3136); *USA*, 220 Anna Salai (☎827 3040; Mon–Fri 8am–5.15pm).

Cultural institutions *Alliance Française*, 3/4-A College Rd, Nungabakkam (☎827 2650); *British Council*, 737 Anna Salai (☎826 9402; Mon–Fri 10am–5pm); *Max Mueller Bhavan*, 13 Khadar Nawaz Khan Rd (☎826 1314).

Hospitals *Apollo Hospital* (private), 21/22 Greams Rd (☎827 7447); *KJ Hospital*, 496 Periyar EVR High Rd (☎664513).

Left luggage Counters at Egmore and Central railway stations store bags for Rs2–4 per day; they usually require proof of train-booking. Some hotels also guard luggage at a daily rate.

Music stores *Musee Musical*, 67 Anna Salai (☎849380), stocks *sitars*, percussion, flutes and poor quality guitars. *Audiocon*, 10 Plaza Centre, 3 Anna Salai, has a wide selection of cassettes.

Opticians Eye tests, glasses and contact lenses are available at *Lawrence and Mayo*, 68 Anna Salai.

Pharmacy *Lalitha's Medical and General Store*, 11 Gandhi Irwin Rd; *Spencer & Co*, Spencer Plaza, Anna Salai (Mon–Sat 8am–7pm; ☎826 3611).

Photographic equipment *Photo Emporium*, 46 Anna Salai, for film and developing. For camera repair try one of the string of shops on Meeran Sahib St, off Anna Salai near the *Casino Theatre*.

Tax clearance To get a tax clearance certificate (see *Basics*) take exchange documents and passport to 121 Uttamar Gandhi Rd, and allow for 3–4hr of tedious form-filling.

Visa extension and permits Foreigners' Registration Office, Shastri Bhavan Annexe, Haddows Rd (☎827 5424; Mon–Fri 9.30am–6pm).

Yoga *Prof T Krishnamacharya's Yoga Mandiram*, 103 St Mary's Rd (☎499 7602); *International Shivananda Yoga Centre*, Vedanta Centre, 78 C P Ramaswamy Iyer Rd, Kottapuram (☎418431).

The northeast

Most visitors get out of Madras as fast as they can, heading for the extraordinary rock sculptures and shore temple of **Mamallapuram**, a seaside village just a couple of hours south along the coast. Further inland, in **Kanchipuram**, the Pallava capital, early structures are set beside later, larger temples that totally dominate the town, for centuries a place of pilgrimage. **Pondicherry**, the former **French** capital of India and today a Union Territory, expounds a spirituality of a different kind at its Sri Aurobindo Ashram and "new age" village, **Auroville**.

Mamallapuram (Mahabalipuram)

MAMALLAPURAM (aka Mahabalipuram) is set in a boulder-strewn landscape, 58km south of Madras on the Bay of Bengal. Although a perfectly feasible day trip from Madras, it has become in the last couple of decades a magnet for long-stay travellers. Many are drawn solely by the miles of unspoilt **beach**, but Mamallapuram was once a major port of the Pallavas, who ruled south India between the fifth and ninth centuries, and it boasts some of India's most sublime **rock-cut art**, for which it has been declared a World Heritage Site by UNESCO.

Little is known about life in the ancient port, and it is only possible to speculate about the purpose of much of the boulder sculpture littering the area. It does appear, however, that the community has always been a centre for sculpture, and that some of the temples were not made for worship at all, but rather as a showcase for the talents of local artists. Due in no small part to the maritime activities of the Pallavas, their style

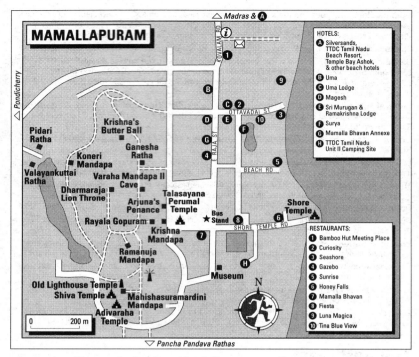

MAMALLAPURAM

△ Madras & Ⓐ

HOTELS:
Ⓐ Silversands,
TTDC Tamil Nadu
Beach Resort,
Temple Bay Ashok,
& other beach hotels
Ⓑ Uma
Ⓒ Uma Lodge
Ⓓ Magesh
Ⓔ Sri Murugan &
Ramakrishna Lodge
Ⓕ Surya
Ⓖ Mamalla Bhavan Annexe
Ⓗ TTDC Tamil Nadu
Unit II Camping Site

RESTAURANTS:
❶ Bamboo Hut Meeting Place
❷ Curiosity
❸ Seashore
❹ Gazebo
❺ Sunrise
❻ Honey Falls
❼ Mamalla Bhavan
❽ Fiesta
❾ Luna Magica
❿ Tina Blue View

△ Pondicherry

Pidari Ratha
Krishna's Butter Ball
Ganesha Ratha
Koneri Mandapa
Valayankuttai Ratha
Varaha Mandapa II Cave
Dharmaraja Lion Throne
Arjuna's Penance
Talasayana Perumal Temple
Rayala Gopuram
Krishna Mandapa
Ramanuja Mandapa
Shore Temple
Bus Stand
Old Lighthouse Temple
Shiva Temple
Mahishasuramardini Mandapa
Museum
Adivaraha Temple

OTTAVADAI ST
E RAJA ST
KOVALAM RD
BEACH RD
SHORE TEMPLE RD

0   200 m

▽ Pancha Pandava Rathas

of art and architecture had wide-ranging influence, spreading from south India as far north as Ellora (see p.676), as well as to southeast Asia.

Mamallapuram art divides into four categories: open-air **bas-reliefs**, structured **temples**, man-made **caves** and **rathas** ("chariots", carved in situ from single boulders, to resemble temples or the chariots used in temple processions). The famous bas-reliefs, **Arjuna's Penance** and the **Krishna mandapa**, adorn massive rocks near the centre of the village, while the beautiful **Shore temple** towers over the waves behind a protective breakwater. Sixteen man-made caves, in different stages of completion, are scattered through the area, but the most complete of the nine *rathas* are in a group, named after the five Pandava brothers of the *Mahabharata*.

Arrival and getting around

Numerous daily **buses** ply to and from Madras, along three different routes: via Kovalam, aka Covelong (#19c, #119a & any #188 express), Thirupperur (#19a & #119) and Chengalpattu/Madras airport (49km north; #108b). About half a dozen run to Kanchipuram (2hr), and nine express buses run south to Pondicherry (2hr 30min; #188a/b/d/k). The bus stand is in the centre of the village. The nearest **railway station**, at Chengalpattu (Chingleput), 29km northeast on the bus route to Kanchipuram, is on the main north–south line, but not really a convenient access point. A **taxi** from Madras costs around Rs700.

Mamallapuram itself is little more than a few dusty roads. By far the best way to get to the important sites, if you're up to it, is by **bicycle**, which you can rent from shops on E Raja St, on Kovalam Rd opposite the entrance to the *Temple Bay Ashok Beach Resort*, or through many of the hotels. **Scooters** and **Enfield** motorbikes are also available (Rs150–300 a day), from *Indhu Motor Works*, opposite the Township Office, or *Metro Tours*, 137 E Raja St (☎42456), whose friendly owner is also a mine of local information. Government-approved guides must be arranged from Madras, at either of the tourist offices on Anna Salai. **Taxis** and **auto-rickshaws** gather by the bus stand.

> The telephone **area code** for Mamallapuram is ☎04113.

Information
The **Government of Tamil Nadu Tourist Office** (supposedly Mon–Sat 10am–5.45pm; ☎42232) is one of the first buildings you see in the village, next to a smelly fish market, as you come in from Madras. You can **change money** at the bigger hotels or the *Canara* and *Indian Overseas* banks on E Raja St.

The Krishna mandapa and Arjuna's Penance
At the heart of the village, the enormous bas-relief known as the **Krishna mandapa** shows Krishna raising Mt Govardhana aloft in one hand. The sculptor's original intention must have been for the rock above Krishna to represent the mountain, but the seventeenth-century Vijayanagar addition of a columned *mandapa*, or entrance hall, prevents a clear view of the carving. Krishna is also depicted seated, milking a cow, and standing, playing the flute. Other figures are *gopas* and *gopis*, the cowboys and girls of his pastoral youth. Lions sit to the left, one with a human face, and above them a bull.

Another bas-relief, **Arjuna's Penance** – also referred to as the "Descent of the Ganges" – is a few metres north, opposite the modern Talasayana Perumal temple. The surface of this rock erupts with detailed carving, most notably the endearing and naturalistic renditions of animals. A family of elephants dominates the right side, with tiny offspring asleep beneath a great tusker. Further still to the right, separate from the great rock, is a free-standing sculpture of an adult monkey grooming its young.

On the left-hand side, Arjuna, one of the Pandava brothers and a consummate archer, is shown standing on one leg. He is looking at the midday sun through a prism formed by his hands, meditating on Shiva, who is nearby represented by a statue, fashioned by Arjuna himself. The *Shiva Purana* tells that Arjuna made the journey to a forest on the banks of the Ganges to do penance, in the hope that Shiva would part with his favourite weapon, the *pashupatashastra*, a magic staff or arrow. Shiva eventually materialized in the guise of Kirata, a wild forest-dweller, and picked a fight with Arjuna over a boar they both claimed to have shot. Arjuna only realized he was dealing with the deity after his attempts to drub the wild man proved futile; narrowly escaping death at the playful hand of Shiva, he was finally rewarded with the weapon. Not far away, mimicking Arjuna's devout pose, an emaciated (presumably ascetic) cat stands on hind legs, surrounded by mice.

To the right of Arjuna, a natural cleft represents the **Ganges**, complete with *nagas*, water spirits in the form of cobras. Near the bottom, a fault in the rock that broke a *naga* received a quick-fix of cement in the 1920s. Evidence of a cistern and channels remain at the top, which at one time must have carried water to flow down the cleft, simulating the great river. It's not known if there was some ritual purpose to all this, or whether it was simply an elaborate spectacle to impress visitors. You may see sudden movements among the carved animals; lazing goats often join the permanent features.

A little way north of Arjuna's Penance, precipitously balanced on the top of a ridge, is a massive, natural, almost spherical boulder called **Krishna's Butterball**. Picnickers and goats often rest in its perilous-looking shade.

THE TEMPLES OF TAMIL NADU

No Indian state is more dominated by its **temples** than Tamil Nadu, where temple architecture catalogues the tastes of successive dynasties, and testifies to the centrality of religion in everyday life. Most temples are built in honour of Shiva and Vishnu and their consorts; all are characterized not only by their design and sculptures, but by constant activity – devotion, dancing, singing, *pujas*, festivals and feasts. Each is tended by *brahmin* priests, recognizable by their *dhotis* (loincloths), a sacred thread draped over the right shoulder, and marks on the forehead. One to three horizontal (usually white) lines distinguish Shaivites; vertical lines (yellow or red), often converging into a near-V shape, are common among Vaishnavites.

Dravida, the temple architecture of Tamil Nadu, first took form in the **Pallava** port of **Mamallapuram**. A step up from the cave retreats of Hindu and Jain ascetics, the earliest Pallava monuments were **mandapas**, shrines cut into rock faces and fronted by columns. The magnificent **bas-relief** at Mamallapuram, Arjuna's Penance, shows the fluid carving of the Pallavas at its most exquisite. This sculptural skill was transferred to freestanding temples, **rathas**, carved out of single rocks and incorporating the essential elements of Hindu temples: the dim inner sanctuary, the *garbhagriha*, capped with a modest tapering spire featuring repetitive architectural motifs. In turn, the Shore temple was built with three shrines, topped by a *vimana* similar to the towering roofs of the *rathas*; statues of Nandi, Shiva's bull, later to receive pride of place, surmount its low walls. In the finest structural Pallava temple, the Kailasanatha temple at **Kanchipuram**, the sanctuary, again crowned with a pyramidal *vimana*, stands within a courtyard enclosed by high walls. The projecting and recessing bays of the walls, carved with images of Shiva, his consort and ghoulish mythical lions, *yalis*, were the prototype for later styles.

Pallava themes were developed in Karnataka by the Chalukyas and Rashtrakutas, but it was the Shaivite **Cholas** who spearheaded Tamil Nadu's next architectural phase, in the tenth century. In **Thanjavur**, Rajaraja I created the Brihadeshvara temple principally as a status symbol. Its proportions far exceed any attempted by the Pallavas; set within a vast walled courtyard, the sanctuary, fronted by a small pillared hall (*mandapa*), stands beneath a sculpted *vimana* that soars over 60 metres high. Most sculptures once again feature Shiva, but the *gopuras*, or towers, each side of the eastern gateway to the courtyard, were a new innovation, as were the lions carved into the base of the sanctuary walls, and the pavilion erected over Nandi in front of the sanctuary. The second great Chola temple was built in **Gangaikondacholapuram** by Rajendra I. Instead of a mighty *vimana*, he brought new elements, adding subsidiary shrines and placing an extended *mandapa* in front of the central sanctuary, its pillars writhing with dancers and deities.

By the time of the thirteenth-century **Vijayanagar** kings, the temple was central to city life, the focus for civic meetings, education, dance and theatre. The Vijayanagars extended earlier structures, adding enclosing walls around a series of *prakaras*, or courtyards, and erecting free-standing *mandapas* for use as meeting halls, elephant stables, stages for music and dance, and ceremonial marriage halls (*kalyan mandapas*). Raised on superbly decorated columns, these *mandapas* became known as **thousand-pillared halls**. **Tanks** were added, doubling as water stores and washing areas, and used for festivals when deities were set afloat in boats surrounded by glimmering oil lamps.

Under the Vijayanagars, the *gopuras* were enlarged and set at the cardinal points over the high gateways to each *prakara*, to become the dominant feature. Rectangular in plan, and embellished with images of animals and local saints or rulers as well as deities, *gopuras* are periodically repainted in pinks, blues, whites and yellows, a sharp and joyous contrast with the earthy browns and greys of halls and sanctuaries beyond. **Madurai** is *the* place to check out Vijayanagar architecture, and experience the timeless temple rituals. Dimly lit halls and sun-drenched courtyards hum with murmured prayers, and regularly come alive for festivals in which Shiva and his "fish-eyed" consort are hauled through town on mighty wooden chariots tugged by hordes of devotees. Outside Tiruchirapalli, the temple at **Srirangam** was extended by the Vijayanagar Nayaks to become south India's largest. Unlike that in Madurai, it incorporates earlier Chola foundations, but the ornamentation, with pillars formed into rearing horses, is superb.

Ganesha ratha and Varaha cave

Just north of Arjuna's Penance a path leads west to a single monolith, the **Ganesha ratha**. Its image of Ganesh dates from this century; some say it was installed at the instigation of England's King George V. An interesting sculpture at one end, of a protecting demon with a tri-corn headdress, is reminiscent of the Indus Valley Civilization's 4000-year-old horned figure known as the "proto-Shiva" (see *Contexts*).

Behind Arjuna's Penance, southwest of the Ganesha *ratha*, is the **Varaha-mandapa II** cave, whose entrance hall has two pillars with horned lion-bases and a cell flanked by two *dvarpalas*, or guardians. One of four **panels** shows the boar-incarnation of Vishnu, who stands with one foot resting on the *naga* snake-king as he lifts a diminutive Prithvi, the earth, from the primordial ocean; another is of Gajalakshmi, the goddess Lakshmi seated on a lotus being bathed by a pair of elephants. Trivikrama, the dwarf *brahmin* who becomes huge and bestrides the world in three steps to defeat the demon king Bali, is shown in another panel, and the fourth depicts a four-armed Durga.

The Shore temple

East of the village, a distinctive silhouette above the crashing ocean, Mamallapuram's **Shore temple** dates from the early eighth century and is considered to be the earliest stone-built temple in south India. The design of its two finely carved towers was profoundly influential; today, due to the combined forces of wind, salt and sand, much of the detailed carving has eroded, giving the whole a soft, rounded appearance.

The taller of the towers is raised above a cell that faces out to sea – don't be surprised to see mischievous monkeys crouching inside. Approached from the west through two low-walled enclosures lined with small Nandi (bull) figures, the temple comprises two *lingam* shrines (one facing east, the other west), and a third shrine between them housing an image of the reclining Vishnu. Recent excavations, revealing a tank containing a structured stone column thought to have been a lantern, and a large Varaha (boar-incarnation of Vishnu) aligned with the Vishnu shrine, suggest that the area was sacred long before the Pallavas chose it as a temple site.

The Lighthouses and the Mahishasuramardini Cave

At the highest point in an area of steep paths, unfinished temples, ruins, scampering monkeys and massive rocks, south of Arjuna's Penance, the **New Lighthouse** affords fine views east to the Shore temple, and west across paddy fields and flat lands littered with rocks. Next to it, the **Olakanesvara** ("flame-eyed" Shiva), or **Old Lighthouse temple**, used as a lighthouse until the beginning of the twentieth century, dates from the Rajasimha period (674–800 AD) and contains no image.

Nestling between the two lighthouses is the **Mahishasuramardini Cave**, whose central image portrays Shiva and Parvati with the child Murugan seated on Parvati's lap. Shiva's right foot rests on the back of the bull Nandi, and Parvati sits casually, leaning on her left hand. On the left wall, beyond an empty cell, a panel depicts Vishnu reclining on the serpent, his attitude of repose contrasted with the weapon-brandishing demons, Madhu and Kaithaba. Other figures seek Vishnu's permission to chase them.

Opposite, in one of the most celebrated sculptures in Indian art, a carved panel shows the eight-armed goddess **Durga** as Mahishasuramardini, the "crusher" of the buffalo demon **Mahishasura**. The story goes that Mahishasura became so powerful that he took possession of heaven, causing great misery to its inhabitants. To deal with such a dangerous foe, Vishnu and Shiva hit upon the idea of combining all the gods' powers into a single entity. This done, fiery jets appeared, from which emerged the terrifying "mother of the universe", Durga. In the ensuing battle, Durga caught Mahishasura with a noose, and he changed into a lion; she beheaded the lion, and he transformed into a human wielding a sword; she fired off a flight of arrows, only to see him turn into a huge trumpeting elephant; and she cut off his trunk, whereupon the buffalo returned. Now furious, Durga partook of her favourite beverage – blood, "the supreme wine". Climbing on top of the buffalo, she kicked him about the neck and stabbed him with her trident. The impact of her foot forced him halfway out of his own mouth, only to be beheaded by his own sword, at which point he fell. The panel shows Durga riding a lion, in the midst of the struggle. Accompanied by dwarf *ganas*, she wields a bow and other weapons; Mahishasura equipped with a club, can be seen to the right, in flight with fellow demons.

The tiny **Archaeological Survey of India Museum** (daily 9am–1pm & 2–5pm) on W Raja St, near the Lighthouse, has a collection of Pallava sculpture found in and around Mamallapuram, and sells quality postcards at low prices.

Pancha Pandava rathas

In a sandy compound 1.5km south of the village centre stands the stunning group of monoliths known for no historical reason as the **Pancha Pandava** *rathas*, the five chariots of the Pandavas. Dating from the period of Narasimhavarman I (*c*.630–70 AD), and consisting of five separate free-standing sculptures that imitate structured temples plus some beautifully carved life-size animals, they were either carved from a single gigantic sloping boulder, or from as many as three distinct rocks.

The "architecture" of the *rathas* reflects the variety of styles employed in temple building of the time, and stands almost as a model for much subsequent development in the **Dravida**, or southern, style. The Arjuna, Bhima and Dharmaraja *rathas* show strong affinities with the Dravidian temples at Pattadakal in Karnataka and caves 32 and 16 at Ellora in Maharashtra (see p.681–2). Carving was always executed from top to bottom, enabling the artists to work on the upper parts with no fear of damaging anything below. Any unfinished elements there may be are always in the lower areas.

Intriguingly, it is thought that the *rathas* were never used for worship. A Hindu temple is only complete when the essential pot-shaped finial, the *kalasha*, is put in place – which would have presented a physical impossibility for the artisans, as the *kalasha* would have had to have been sculpted first. *Kalashas* can be seen next to two of the *rathas* (Dharmaraja and Arjuna), but as part of the base, as if they were perhaps to be put in place at a later date.

The southernmost and tallest of the *rathas*, named after the eldest of the Pandavas, is the pyramidal **Dharmaraja**. Set on a square base, the upper part comprises a series of diminishing storeys, each with a row of pavilions. Four corner blocks, each with two panels and standing figures, are broken up by two pillars and pilasters supported by squatting lions. Figures on panels include Ardhanarishvara (Shiva and female consort in one figure), Brahma, the king Narasimhavarman I, and Harihara (Shiva and Vishnu combined). The central tier includes sculptures of Shiva Gangadhara holding a rosary with the adoring river goddess Ganga by his side and one of the earliest representations in Tamil Nadu of the dancing Shiva, Nataraja, who became all-important in the region. Alongside, the **Bhima** *ratha*, the largest of the group, is the least complete, with tooling marks all over its surface. Devoid of carved figures, the upper storeys, like in the Dharmaraja, feature false windows and repeated pavilion-shaped ornamentation. Its oblong base is very rare for a shrine.

The Arjuna and Draupadi *rathas* share a base. Behind the **Arjuna,** the most complete of the entire group and very similar to the Dharmaraja, stands a superb unfinished sculpture of Shiva's bull Nandi. **Draupadi** is unique in terms of rock-cut architecture, with a roof that appears to be based on a straw thatched hut (a design later copied at Chidambaram; see p.1001). There's an image of Durga inside, but the figure of her lion vehicle outside is aligned side-on and not facing the image, a convincing reason to suppose this was not a real temple. To the west, close to a life-size carving of an elephant, the *ratha* named after the twin brothers **Nakula** and **Sahadeva** is, unusually, apsidal ended. The elephant may be a visual pun on this, as the Sanskrit technical name for a curved ended building is *gajaprstika*, "elephant's backside".

The road out to the *rathas* resounds with incessant chiselling from sculptors' workshops. Much of their work is excellent, and well worth a browse – the sculptors produce statues for temples all over the world and are used to shipping large-scale pieces. Some of the artists are horrifyingly young; children often do the donkey work on large pieces, which are then completed by master craftsmen.

Government College of Sculpture

A visit to the **Government College of Sculpture**, 2km from Mamallapuram on the Kovalam (Covelong) Rd, gives a fascinating insight into the processes of training. You can watch anything from preliminary drawing, with its strict rules regarding proportion and iconography, through to the execution of sculpture, both in wood and stone, in the classical Hindu tradition. Contact the college office (☎42261) to make an appointment.

Tiger Cave

Set amid groves close to the sea, 5km north from Mamallapuram on the Kovalam (Covelong) Rd, the extraordinary **Tiger Cave** contains a shrine to Durga, approached by a flight of steps that passes two subsidiary cells. Following the line of an irregularly shaped rock, the cave is remarkable for the elaborate exterior, which features multiple lion heads surrounding the entrance to the main cell.

Tirukalikundram

The village of **TIRUKALIKUNDRAM**, 16km east on the road to Kanchipuram, is locally famous for its hill-top Shiva temple where two Neophran vultures swoop down from Varanasi daily at noon to be fed by the priests. Be prepared, however, after climbing more than 400 red-hot stone steps at the appointed time, for the fact that the vultures may decide not to call after all. Added to that, any interest you may have had in looking at the temple could well evaporate in the effort required to disabuse various individuals, including the priests, of the impression that you need their multifarious services and paid company. Visits to the village are made more worthwhile if you take the time to explore the vast **Vijayanagar temple** at its heart.

Crocodile Bank

The **Crocodile Bank** (daily 8am–5.30pm) at Vadanemmeli, 15km north of town on the road to Madras, was set up in 1976 by the American zoologist Romulus Whittaker, to protect and breed indigenous crocodiles. The bank has been so successful (fifteen crocs to five thousand in the first fifteen years) that its remit now extends to saving endangered species, such as turtles and lizards, from around the world.

Low-walled enclosures in its garden compound house hundreds of inscrutable crocodiles, soaking in ponds or sunning themselves on the banks. Breeds include the fish-eating, knobbly-nosed gharial, and the world's largest species, the saltwater *crocodylus porosus*, which can grow to 8m in length. You can watch feeding time at about 4.30pm each Wednesday. The temptation to take photos is tempered by the sight of those hungry saurians clambering over each other to chomp the chopped flesh, within inches of the top of the wall. Not surprisingly, excited kids ignore the sage advice not to lean over the walls.

Another important field of work is conducted with the collaboration of local Irula people, whose traditional expertise is with snakes. Cobras are brought to the bank for **venom collection**, to be used in the treatment of snakebites. Elsewhere, snakes are repeatedly "milked" until they die, but here at the bank only a limited amount is taken from each snake, enabling them to return to the wild. Coastal route buses #19C and #119A stop at the entrance.

Accommodation

With more than twenty years' experience of tourism, Mamallapuram is not short on **accommodation**, with new places appearing yearly. The bulk of cheap to **mid-range** lodges are within the village, some distance from the **beach**, which is the preserve of the more expensive places. Large hotels of varying standards sit side by side along a six-kilometre stretch of coast. Without a bike, getting to these can prove a bit of a hassle; it's easy enough to take a rickshaw out there from the village, but not in the other direction. However, the walk back into Mamallapuram, either along the beach or the Kovalam Rd (to which they are all connected by long driveways) is pleasant – if you're not carrying luggage.

Long-term stays can be arranged in the south village behind the sculptors' workshops on the way to the Pancha Pandava *rathas*. Both R Kuppuswamy and the *Canary* are basic, but wholesome, and charge around Rs200 a week.

IN THE VILLAGE

Magesh, E Raja St (☎42201). Basic, clean rooms in the centre of the village. No restaurant. ①–③.

Hotel Mamalla Bhavan, opposite the bus stand. Basic, very Indian rooms above a restaurant. ①.

Mamalla Bhavan Annexe, E Raja St (☎42260). Very good value place, right in the centre of the village; spotless a/c rooms – functional, not luxurious – overlooking a courtyard. Non-a/c rooms with mosquito nets. Room service, *Star TV*. ③–④.

Ramakrishna Lodge, 8 Ottavadai St (☎42331 or 42431). In the village, near a lake. Clean, well-maintained rooms, all with bathroom but no a/c, set round a pretty courtyard. Sea views from the terrace on top floor. No restaurant, but room service. ②.

Sri Murugan Guest House, Ottavadai St (☎42552). New, great value place, next door to the *Ramakrishna*. Small and peaceful, with good service: one of the nicest options in the village. ②.

Surya, off Ottavadai St (☎42239). Lakeside hotel set in a tranquil leafy compound dotted with sculptures (including a replica Buddhist gateway). Simple, well-maintained rooms (some a/c); mosquito nets are available and, considering the proximity of the lake, essential. ④.

Uma, 138 E Raja St (☎42422). Basic but fair-sized rooms in newish building. Non-veg restaurant. ②.

Uma Lodge, 15 Ottavadai St (☎42322). Close to the main road, acceptable for the price. ①–②.

ON THE BEACH

Golden Sun, 3km from town, 59 Kovalam Rd (☎42245; fax 836247). In an attractive garden compound; sea-facing rooms are the best value. Health club and good pool. ⑥.

Ideal Beach Resort, 4km from town, Kovalam Rd (☎42240). Very appealing cottages a little way before the Tiger Cave. Fine pool, inexpensive restaurant and friendly management. ⑤–⑥.

Mamalla Beach Resort, 2.5km from town, Kovalam Rd (☎42375). One of the less luxurious complexes along the beach road, with reasonable rates. ④.

Silversands, Kovalam Rd (☎42228). Huge luxury complex of cottages between the road and beach. Several craft shops. Splendid restaurant on the sand. Non-a/c and a/c; the priciest rooms have swings, balconies and private bathrooms. The new *Silver Inn* budget complex is cheaper. ④–⑥.

Taj Fisherman's Cove, Covelong Beach, 30min drive north from Mamallapuram (☎04128/2304). Four-star hotel, with bar and restaurants. Rooms in main building overlook a beachside garden, while circular cottages stand at the ocean's edge. ⑨.

Temple Bay Ashok (ITDC) Beach Resort (☎42251; fax 42257). Despite its great location – on the beach near the village, with views of the Shore temple – this place is somewhat overpriced, geared towards conference bookings. Basic cottages on the beach all have sea-facing balconies, and there are huge rooms in the main building. Swimming pool and restaurant. ⑧.

TTDC Hotel Tamil Nadu Beach Resort, Kovalam Rd (☎42235). Huge split-level cottages (some non-a/c) with sea-facing sit-outs. Good value. Lovely swimming pool, and restaurants. ⑤.

TTDC Hotel Tamil Nadu Unit II Camping Site, Kovalam Rd (☎42287). Dorm, new a/c rooms, and standard non-a/c – those facing the sea are more expensive. Pay extra for TV (not *Star*). ③–⑤.

Eating

The village is full of cheap, shack-style restaurants, specializing in **seafood**. Prices are higher at the **beach hotels**, but the atmosphere, and often the food, is usually worth it.

Bamboo Hut Meeting Place, Kovalam Rd, just before the tourist office. Friendly, inexpensive little place, with just two fans, serving seafood, chicken, snacks, and omelettes.

Curiosity, Ottavadai St. Popular with Westerners for its breakfasts and selection of fresh fish.

Fiesta, Shore Temple Rd. Variety of dishes served in a mellow "tropical" courtyard.

Gazebo, 101 E Raja St. Very friendly restaurant in a pleasant airy room. Fresh seafood, such as tiger prawns and lobster, cooked on a charcoal grill or barbecue. Open 6am–midnight.

Honey Falls, Shore Temple Rd. Tiny little place specializing in grilled fish and lobster.

Ideal Beach Resort, 4km from town, Kovalam Rd. Sri Lankan, Chinese, Indian and Western food in a great location.

Luna Magica, beyond Ottadavai St. Tasty food – the usual mix of Indian, Western and seafood – served with sangria.

Mamalla Bhavan, opposite the bus stand. Superb, inexpensive Indian "meals" and good *tandoori*.

Mamalla Bhavan Annexe, E Raja St. Plush cafe in a relaxed courtyard setting, serving the best veg food in the village, and wonderful ice-cream sundaes.

Pumpernickel Bakery, 15 Ottavadai St. German-run place, above the *Uma Lodge*, serving good bread and cakes, Chinese food and strong beer. Often closed in the summer.

Seashore Restaurant, at the end of Ottavadai St. Great seafood, but dubious Western dishes. Airy, though, and with a good view.

Silversands, Kovalam Rd. Over-commercialized hotel restaurant on the sand serving good Indian, Western and Chinese dishes, and superb south Indian seafood.

Sunrise, Beach Rd. Specialists in *masala*-fried fish, shark steak, tiger prawns and fresh lobster at great prices.

Tina Blue View, 152 Ottavadai St. Breakfasts, seafood, Chinese and steaks. Nice rooftop location, with a gaudy mural, and views of the sea in the distance, but slow service and ordinary food

Kanchipuram

Once protected by robust walls, the modest-sized fly-blown city of **KANCHIPURAM** was for thousands of years a major arena for artistic and architectural achievement; the temple *gopuras* that soar above its narrow streets can be seen from far across the vast plains. Today, as the holiest Hindu city in south India – the only such site to be sacred to both Shaivites and Vaishnavites – it is a busy pilgrimage centre, humming with activity around its extraordinary temple precincts.

Established by the **Pallava** kings in the fourth century AD, Kanchipuram served as their capital for five hundred years, and continued to flourish throughout the Chola, Pandya and Vijayanagar eras. Under the Pallavas, it was an important scholastic forum, and a meeting point for Jain, Buddhist and Hindu cultures; today Hindu **temples** alone dominate the town, spanning the years from the peak of Pallava construction to the seventeenth century, when the ornamentation of the *gopuras* and pillared halls was at its most elaborate (for more on Tamil Nadu's temples, see p.984). All can be easily reached by foot, bike or rickshaw, and all close between noon and 4pm. You'll be offered a panoply of services – from sanctuary priests, shoe bearers, guides, women giving out food for fish in the temple tanks, and well-trained temple elephants that bless you with their trunks – so be prepared with a pocketful of change. Always animated, they really come alive during major festivals such as the **Car Festival** (May) and **Navaratri** (Oct/Nov).

Arrival and information

Flanked on the south by the River Vagavathi, Kanchipuram lies 70km southwest of Madras, and about as far from the coast. **Buses** from Madras (2hr), Mamallapuram

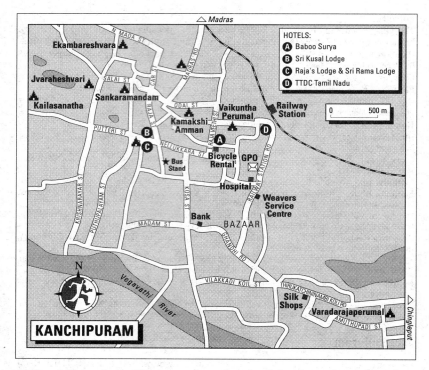

HOTELS:
A Baboo Surya
B Sri Kusal Lodge
C Raja's Lodge & Sri Rama Lodge
D TTDC Tamil Nadu

0   500 m

KANCHIPURAM

(2hr), and Chengalpattu (1hr) stop at the potholed and chaotic stand in the centre on Raja St. The **railway station** in the northeast is used by two daily services from Chengalpattu and two from Anakkonam (8.20am & 5.45pm).

There's no official **tourist office** in Kanchipuram, but you can glean a little information from the detailed map at the TTDC *Tamil Nadu Hotel*. The easiest way to **get around** is by **bicycle** – available for minimal daily rates at stalls west and northeast of the bus stand. Kanchipuram's vegetable markets, hotels, restaurants and bazaars are concentrated in the centre of town, near the bus stand.

Ekambareshvara temple

Kanchipuram's largest temple and most important Shiva shrine, the **Ekambareshvara temple** – also known as Ekambaranatha – is easily identified by its colossal white-washed *gopuras*, which rise almost 60m north of town. The main temple contains some Pallava work, but was mostly constructed between the sixteenth and seventeenth centuries, and stands within a vast walled enclosure beside some smaller shrines and a large fish-filled water tank.

Entrance, through a high arched passageway beneath an elaborate *gopura* in the south wall, leads to an open courtyard and a majestic "thousand-pillared hall", *kalyan mandapa*, whose slightly decaying grey stone columns are modelled as nubile maidens, animals and deities. This hall faces the tank in the north and the sanctuary (inaccessible to non-Hindus) in the west that protects the emblem of Shiva (here in his form as **Kameshvara**, Lord of Desire), an "earth" *lingam* that is one of five *linga* in Tamil Nadu that represent the elements. Legend connects it with the goddess **Kamakshi** (Shiva's consort, "having eyes of desire"), who angered Shiva by playfully covering his eyes and plunging the world into darkness. Shiva reprimanded her by sending her to fashion a *lingam* from the earth in his honour; once it was completed, Kamakshi found she could not move it. Local myths tell of a great flood that swept over Kanchipuram and destroyed the temples, but did not move the *lingam*, to which Kamakshi clung so fiercely that marks of her breasts and bangles were imprinted upon it.

Behind the sanctum, accessible from the covered hallway around it, an eerie bare hall lies beneath another profusely carved *gopura*, and in the courtyard a venerable mango tree represents the tree under which Shiva and Kamakshi were married. This union is celebrated during a festival each April, when many couples are married in the *kalyan mandapa*.

The somewhat neglected twelfth-century **Jvaraheshvari temple**, in leafy gardens to the south, is the only Chola (tenth–twelfth centuries) structure in Kanchipuram not to have been modified and overshadowed by later buildings. Unlike the Pallava constructions, it is built of hard grey stone; its sculpted pyramidal roof is an early form of the *gopuras* used extensively by the Pandyas.

Kailasanatha temple

The **Kailasanatha temple**, the oldest structure in Kanchipuram and the finest example of Pallava architecture in south India, is situated among several low-roofed houses just over 1km west of the town centre. Built by the Pallava king Rajasimha early in the eighth century, its intimate size and simple carving distinguish it from the town's later temples. Usually quieter than its neighbours, it becomes the focus of vigorous celebrations during the **Mahashivratri festival** each March. Like the contemporaneous Shore temple at Mamallapuram, it is built of soft sandstone, but its sheltered position has spared it from wind and sand erosion, and it remains remarkably intact.

Topped with a modest pyramidal spire, the small temple stands within a rectangular courtyard, enclosed by a wall inlaid with tiny meditation chambers and sculpted with images of Shiva, Parvati and their sons, as well as rearing mythical lions (*yalis*). On the south side of the spire Shiva is depicted as a begging ascetic (Bhikshatana); on the north he's in the pose of the dance of destruction (Samhara-Tandava). Walls in the dim interior bear traces of frescoes, and the ceilings are etched with religious verses written in Pali. The sanctum (inaccessible to non-Hindus) shelters a sturdy sixteen-sided black *lingam*, guarded by elephant-headed Ganesh and Shiva's other son, Skanda, the god of war, with whom the king Rajasimha was closely associated. Double walls were built round the sanctuary to support the weighty tower above; the passage between them is used as a circumambulatory path as part of the ritual worship of Shiva.

Vaikuntha Perumal temple

Built shortly after the Kailasanatha temple at the end of the eighth century, the smaller **Vaikuntha Perumal temple**, a few hundred metres west of the railway station, is dedicated to Vishnu. Its lofty carved *vimana* (towered sanctuary) crowns three shrines containing images of Vishnu, stacked one on top of the other. Unusual scenes carved in the walls enclosing the temple yard depict events central to Pallava history, among them coronations, court gatherings and battles with the Chalukyas who ruled the regions to the northwest. The temple's pillared entrance hall was added by Vijayanagar rulers five centuries later, and is very different in style, with far more ornate sculpting.

Kamakshi Amman temple

Built during Pallava supremacy and modified in the fourteenth and seventeenth centuries, the **Kamakshi Amman temple**, northwest of the bus stand, combines several styles, with an ancient central shrine, gates from the Vijayanagar period, and high *gop-*

uras set above the gateways much later. The *gopuras* and the *vimanas* are a dazzling sight, painted a riot of gold, pink and blue. To the right of the central shrine, inaccessible to non-Hindus, a raised *mandapa* is now an art gallery, housing many pictures of the recent **Acharyas** (see below).

This is one of India's three holiest shrines to Shakti, Shiva's cosmic energy depicted in female form, usually as his consort. The goddess Kamakshi, a local form of Parvati, shown with a sugar cane bow and arrows of flowers, is honoured as having lured Shiva to Kanchipuram, where they were married, and thus having forged the connection between the local community and the god. In February or March, deities are wheeled to the temple in huge wooden "cars", decked with robed statues and swaying plantain leaves. For the rest of the year the bulky but delicately carved temple cars, balanced on colossal wheels, are kept on Gandhi Road.

Varadarajaperumal temple

The Vaishnavite **Varadarajaperumal temple** stands within a huge walled complex in the far southeast of town, guarded by high gates topped with *gopuras*. The inner sanctuary boasts superb carving and well-preserved paintings, but non-Hindus only have access to the outer courtyards, and the elaborate sixteenth-century pillared hall close to the western entrance gate. The outer columns of this *mandapa* are sculpted as lions, and warriors on rearing horses, to celebrate the military vigour of the Vijayanagars, who believed their prowess was inspired by the power of Shakti.

Sankaramandam

Kanchipuram is the seat of a line of holy men bearing the title **Acharya**, whose line dates back, according to different versions, as far as 1300–482 BC to the saint Adi Sankaracharya. The 68th Acharya, the highly revered Sri Chandrasekharendra Sarasvati Swami, died in January 1994 at the age of 100. His mortal remains are kept in a *math*, **Sankaramandam**, where there is a *samadhi* shrine in his honour and a small meditation hall – there's little to see here, but it's a profoundly atmospheric place.

SHOPPING IN KANCHIPURAM

Kanchipuram has long been renowned for the superb quality of its hand-produced **silk**; *saris* are still made using methods little changed since Pallava times, when the industry supplied kings and queens with splendid fabrics. The high prices charged by its large specialist shops, south of the centre along Thirukatchininambi Koli Rd, are determined by weight. The most expensive, and spectacular, are fringed with borders of pure gold or silver thread. The silk is dyed with natural pigments and woven with complex but subtle patterns, which usually feature peacock, parrot or fruit motifs. You can see the weaving process at the *Weavers' Service Centre* (Mon–Fri 9.15am–5.45pm), 20 Station Rd.

Accommodation and eating

There's not a great choice of **accommodation** in Kanchipuram, but its hotels are sufficient for a short stay, and all except *Hotel Tamil Nadu* are right in the centre. The less expensive lodges offer minimal comfort, while the pricier places, if not exactly elaborate, are clean and comfortable and serve generally good south Indian dishes in their own **restaurants**. If you don't want to eat in your hotel, you can guarantee a hearty meal at any of the **thali dhabas** lining Kamaraj Rd just west of the bus stand.

Baboo Surya, 85E Raja Veethi St (☎04112/22555). Large, modern hotel with immaculate a/c and non-a/c rooms and a very good restaurant. *Star TV*, car rental and exchange facilities. ⑨.

Raja's Lodge, 20 Nellukkara St (☎04112/22603). Very cheap and very basic, with small rooms. ①.

Sri Kusal Lodge, 68C Nellukkara St (☎04112/22356). New lodge, the best of the bunch. ②–③.
Sri Rama Lodge, 21 Nellukkara St (☎04112/22435). Good, fairly clean budget lodge with attached bathrooms and some a/c rooms. ①–④.
TTDC Tamil Nadu, Railway Station Rd (☎04112/22553). State-run hotel near the railway station. Comfortable, spacious rooms, some a/c, and a small restaurant serving uninspired food. ③.

Vellore

The uninspiring city of **VELLORE**, close to the River Palar just under 150km west of Madras, is dominated by towering granite fort walls that enclose government offices and a stunning sixteenth-century **temple**. There are no other buildings of interest to tourists in this confusion of dusty, crowded markets and streets, and for most Indians, Vellore is significant only as the home of an excellent hospital for tropical diseases.

The approach to the **fort** (daily 8am–8pm) is from the east, over a modern bridge that straddles the wide moat, once filled with crocodiles. Headquarters in the fourteenth century of the Vijayanagar governor Chinna Bomma Reddi, and enclosed by two thick walls, the fort held off attacks until it fell to the Muslim Adi Shahis of Bijapur in the seventeenth century. Later the Marathas ousted their Muslim enemies, only to be overthrown in turn by Daud Khan of Delhi early in the eighteenth century. British officers took control in 1768, and remained overlords until Independence.

Close to the northern wall, the magnificent *kalyan mandapa* (pillared hall) in the outer courtyard of the **Jalakanteshvara temple** boasts a vitality and richness of carving matched only at Srirangam (see p.1021). The outer pillars depict rearing steeds, mythical dragons and warriors, while the central columns support sculptures of *yalis*, mythical lions prominent in much earlier Pallava temples. The temple shrine is dedicated to Shiva, represented by a *lingam*, and guarded by Nandi, the god's bull.

A **cemetery** to the right of the fort entrance holds the graves of the British soldiers who died during a swiftly defeated mutiny in 1806, when *sepoys* rose in protest against demands for them to shave their beards and adopt a common dress code.

Practicalities

Regular **buses**, from the bus stand just east of the fort, connect Vellore to Madras (every 30min; 3–4hr), Kanchipuram (every 30min; 2hr 30min) and Bangalore (10 daily; 5–6hr). **Trains** from Tirupati and Tiruvannamalai arrive at Vellore Station in the south; Katpadi Station, thirty minutes' north of the city, is on the Madras–Bangalore line.

Vellore is best visited as a day trip from Kanchipuram, but if you're looking for inexpensive **lodgings**, head for the eastern area of town, where the clean and basic *VDM Lodge* (☎0416/24008; ①), with some a/c rooms, and *Srinivasa Lodge* (☎0416/26389; ①), are both on Beri Bakkali St near the hospital. On Babu Rao St, further south, the well-kept, simple hotels *Balaram* (☎0416/22476; ①) and *Mayura* (☎0416/25488; ①) offer similar standards. Most upmarket is the partly a/c *Hotel River View* (☎0416/22349; ③), a modern, comfortable place on Katpadi Rd north of the city.

Hotel River View has three **restaurants**, but you can get good south Indian meals and tiffin in restaurants nearer the fort on Ida Scudder Rd. The reasonably priced *Susil* has a roof terrace and a broad menu of Indian dishes, while nearby the *Geetha* and *Best* specialize in south Indian food. *Chinatown*, a small, friendly place with excellent Chinese dishes, is on Gandhi Rd, which runs south of Ida Scudder Rd.

Vedanthangal

One of India's most spectacular mixed heronries lies roughly 1km east of the village of **VEDANTHANGAL**, a cluster of squat brown houses set in a patchwork of vivid green paddy fields 30km from the east coast and 86km southwest of Madras. It's a tiny, relaxed place, bisected by one road and boasting just two *chai* stalls.

The **sanctuary** (daily, dawn–dusk; Rs 1) a low-lying area less than half a kilometre square, is at its fullest between December and February, when it is totally flooded. The rains of the northeast monsoon, sweeping through in October or November, bring indigenous water birds ready to nest and settle until the dry season (usually April), when they leave for wetter areas. Abundant trees on mounds above water level provide perfect nesting spots, alive by January with chirping fledglings, some of which fall prey to kites, eagles, scavenger vultures or migratory harriers that swoop when the parents are away from the nest. Visitors can watch the goings-on from a path at the water's edge, or from a watchtower; binoculars make a big difference, as does timing – try to come at sunset, when the birds return from feeding. Common Indian species to look out for are openbill storks, spoonbill pelicans, black cormorants, and **herons** of several types: the eastern grey heron, the smaller, duller night heron that nests in low branches, and the spritely pond heron whose wings flash white in flight against an unremarkable brown plumage. You may also see ibises, robust grey pelicans, migrant cuckoos and sandpipers, egrets, which paddle in the rice fields, and tiny, darting bee-eaters. Some migrant birds pass through and rest on their way between more permanent sites; swallows, terns and redshanks are common, while peregrine falcons, wigeons and doves are less regularly spotted.

Practicalities

Getting to Vedanthangal can present a few problems. The nearest town is Maduranthakam, 8km east, on NH45 between Chengalpattu and Tindivanam. Head here to wait for the hourly buses to the sanctuary, or catch one of the four daily services from Chengalpattu. Taxis make the journey from Maduranthakam for Rs175–250, but cannot be booked from Vedanthangal.

Vedanthangal's only accommodation is the three-roomed **forest lodge** (①) near the bus stand, school and *chai* stall. Rooms, spacious and comfortable with attached bath, can be booked through the Wildlife Warden, 50 4th Main Gandhi Nagar, Adyar, Madras (☎413947) – if you turn up on spec, it may well be full, especially in December and January. They'll prepare excellent home-cooked food if given enough notice.

Tiruvannamalai

Set in arid plains beneath a high conical hill at the northern end of the Shevaroy range, just over 100km south of Kanchipuram, **TIRUVANNAMALAI** is a small, quiet town dominated by the grand **Arunchaleshvara temple**. This is one of the most important Shaivite towns in south India, focused on its **agnilingam**, or fire-*lingam*, one of the five in Tamil Nadu associated with the elements. Smaller temples in town are dedicated to Ganesh and Shiva's consort, Parvati, often depicted in her wrathful form as **Durga**. The town is also associated with the nineteenth-century spiritual master **Ramakrishna** – teacher of Vivekananda and forefather of modern Hinduism worldwide – who spent much of his early life here.

Tiruvannamalai's calendar is punctuated with festivals, when Shiva and his accompanying deities (Parvati, plus Ganesh and Subrahmanya, their sons) are wheeled through town on huge wooden temple cars, or floated upon tanks dedicated to three of the guardians of the directions: Agni, Indra and Ishana. The largest celebrations are for **Karttigai**, the fire festival, in November/December. For ten days, the town's population doubles as devotees gather to witness the lighting of a fire on the summit of the hill (this, rather than the image in the temple, is technically the fire-*lingam* to which the town is devoted), and circumambulate its base in a procession led by images of Shiva. Devotees also walk around the hill during the curious two-day festival (end of Jan) that re-enacts *tiruvudal*, the holy love-quarrel, a popular theme in Tamil literature, normally involving Nataraja (Shiva as Lord of the Dance) and his consort. The quarrel is mimed in the temples, and acted with vigour by temple singers in the streets.

Arunchaleshvara temple

The **Arunchaleshvara temple**, built over a period of almost a thousand years, and incorporating several distinct styles, consists of four courtyards whose gateways are topped by tapering *gopuras*, the largest of which cover the east and north gates. On the way to the main gate in the east wall, you pass through a covered bazaar that resonates with the bangs and clashes of metal being knocked into shape. The shops here are full of shiny brass, iron and copper pots, trunks, bells, horns and cooking utensils piled in perilous, clanking metallic pyramids and weighed on immense scales.

The eastern gateway leads through the thick outer wall, carved with images of deities, local saints and teachers, and opens into a large courtyard. The large stepped Shivaganga tank to the left originally lay outside the temple precincts; on the right stands a vast "thousand-pillared" *mandapa*, where the temple elephant lives when not taking part in rituals. This outer courtyard usually presents a lively scene: fruit and nut sellers shaded by black umbrellas share space with *sadhus* and dozing devotees, while young boys swim in the tank and children gape at the elephant. In the basement of a raised hall to the right before entering the next courtyard is the Parthala *lingam*, where **Ramakrishna** is said to have sat in a state of Supreme Awareness while ants devoured his flesh.

The second enclosure, built a couple of centuries earlier, in the 1200s, is much smaller, with a large Nandi bull facing the sanctuary and a shrine to the Goddess (Shiva's consort) on its northern edge. In the temple kitchens, in its southeastern corner, food is prepared for the gods. A nineteenth-century roof shelters the central courtyard, surveyed by numerous deities etched into its outer walls, among them Shiva, Parvati, Venugopala (Krishna), Lakshmi, Ganesh and Subrahmanya. In the dim interior, arcaded cloisters supported by magnificently carved columns lead to the main shrine to Shiva, open to non-Hindus: a *lingam* raised on a platform bearing tenth-century inscriptions. This is the location of six daily *pujas*, or worships, when the *lingam* is bathed, clothed and strewn in flower garlands amid the heady smell of incense and camphor and the sound of bells and steady chanting.

In one of the outer courtyards on the north side, drenched devotees, most of them women, circumambulate an ancient hybrid *neem* and *bodhi* tree, draping it with offerings for the health of offspring and the success of married life.

Virupaksha and Skandasraman caves

Opposite the northwestern corner of the temple complex, a path leads up a holy hill (15min) to the **Virupaksha cave**, where Ramakrishna stayed between 1899 and 1916. He personally built the bench outside and the hill-shaped *lingam* and platform inside, where all are welcome to meditate in peace. When this cave became too small, constantly crowded with relatives and devotees, Ramakrishna shifted to another, hidden away in a clump of trees a few minutes further up the hill. He named this one, and the small house built onto it, **Skandasraman**, and lived there 1916–22. The inner cave here is also set aside for meditation, and the front patio affords splendid views across the temple, town and surrounding plains. Both caves are administered by the **Ramanasram ashram** on the other side of the hill, where it is possible to stay and study.

Practicalities

Most visitors arrive in Tiruvannamalai by **bus** at the stand roughly 2km north of the temple on the main road to Gingee, though drivers often drop passengers much closer to the temple. Tiruvannamalai's **railway station**, 500m north of the bus stand, is on the line between Tirupati and Madurai, with a daily service in each direction. A sprinkling of **rickshaws** gathers at the bus and railway stations.

Tiruvannamalai can be visited in a day, but if you're seduced by the peace and quiet, choose from three simple **lodges**. The most basic is *Aruna Lodge*, 82 Kosamadam St, 200m east of the north temple entrance (☎04175/323291; ①), which has good temple views from the roof. To the south, at 57A Car St, *Udipi Brindhavan Hotel* (☎04175/22693; ①) has spartan rooms with private bath, and an excellent *thali* hall, where meals are filling and cheap. Smartest of the lot is the new *Sri Kalaimagal Lodge*, almost opposite the north entrance to the temple at 14 Vadaothavadai St (☎04175/24215; ①).

Near Tiruvannamalai: Gingee

West of the outskirts of **GINGEE**, the eighteenth-century capital of a Maratha kingdom whose boundaries spread east to Pondicherry and west to Tiruvannamalai, **Gingee** fort (daily 9am–5pm; Rs0.50, free on Fri) covers the crests of three hills. Now deserted, with the plains grasses creeping into nooks and crevices of grey-brown crumbling walls and forgotten temples, its ramparts offer outstanding views, and the peaceful location makes a relaxing change from the bustle of temple cloisters. A narrow path to the fort passes a shrine to **Komalakanni Amman**, one of the seven guardian deities of Gingee, who is still worshipped today, and offered animal sacrifices on festival days. Other temples enclosed within the crenellated ramparts lie still and empty beside the remains of granaries, a palace and harem, a dilapidated mosque and an audience hall. Most of the fort was built in the 1500s by the Vijayanagars, and modified by later occupants: Marathas, Moghuls, the French and British.

Gingee is served by hourly buses from Tiruvannamalai, 37km west (in which case you come to the fort before the town; ask the driver to drop you off), and Pondicherry, 70km southeast; there's no accommodation, but a few hours is adequate for a leisurely perusal. Arrive early to avoid having to make the twenty-minute climb to the fort in the burning midday sun.

Pondicherry

PONDICHERRY, on the Bay of Bengal 160km south of Madras, lies amid flat scrubland, dotted with low thatched huts, tall palmyra palms, bamboo, casuarina and tamarind trees. Relatively few visitors make it down here from Madras, though that may change with the completion of the new coastal highway, partly financed by the World Bank. Once the capital of French India, it became in 1954 the headquarters of the **Union Territory of Pondicherry**, administering former French enclaves scattered over south India. The Gallic presence is still tangible: for anyone more familiar with the British colonial imprint, it can induce culture shock to to see the profusion of richly ornamented Catholic churches, French road names and good French restaurants, not to mention hearing French spoken in the streets.

Set on either side of a canal, Pondicherry splits neatly into two parts. To the west is a bustling Indian market town; to the east, towards the sea, the streets are emptier, cleaner and decidedly European. The seaside promenade, **Goubert Salai** (formerly Beach Rd), has the forlorn look of an out-of-season French resort, complete with its own white Hôtel de Ville. Tanned sun-worshippers share space with grave Europeans in white Indian costume, busy about their spiritual quest; **Sri Aurobindo Ghose** (1872–1950), a leading figure in the freedom struggle in Bengal, was given shelter here after it became unwise to live close to the British in Calcutta, and his **ashram** attracts thousands of devotees from all around the world, most particularly from Bengal.

Ten kilometres north, the Utopian experiment-in-living **Auroville** was inspired by Aurobindo's disciple, the charismatic Mirra Alfassa, a Parisian painter, musician and mystic better known as "The Mother". Today this slightly surreal place is populated by numbers of expats and visited by long-stay Europeans eager to find inner peace.

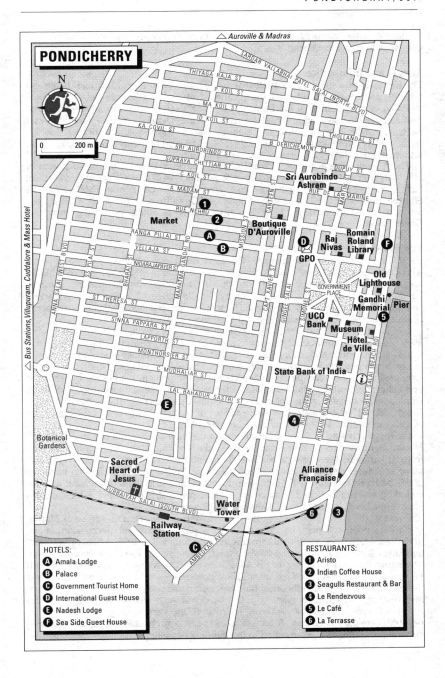

PONDICHERRY

N

0   200 m

Auroville & Madras

Bus Stations, Villupuram, Cuddalore & Mass Hotel

SARDAR VALLABHAI ZATEL SALAI (NORTH BLVD)

THIYAGA RAJA ST

P KOIL ST

MA KOIL ST

ID KOIL ST

KA COVIL ST

SRI AUROBINDO ST

SUPRAYA CHETTIAR ST

C KOIL ST

A MADAM ST

RUE NEHRU

RANGA PILLAI ST

VELLAJA ST

NIDARAJAPAYER ST

ST THERESA ST

SINNA PAPPARA ST

LAPPORTH ST

MONTHORSIER ST

C. MUDHALIAR ST

LAL BAHADUR SASTRI S

ANNA SALAI WEST BLVD

SS PILLAI ST

BHARATI ST

MAHATMA GANDHI RD

MISSION ST

CANTEEN ST

CAPT XAVIER ST

GINGEE SALAI

ST SIMONEL ST

RUE SUFFREN

ROMAIN ROLAND ST

B DERICHEMONT ST

THOLLANDAL ST

DUPUY ST

RUE DE LA MARINE

F MARTIN ST

GOUBERT SALAI (BEACH RD)

Market

Boutique
D'Auroville

Sri Aurobindo
Ashram

Raj
Nivas

GPO

Romain
Roland
Library

Old
Lighthouse

GOVERNMENT
PLACE

Gandhi
Memorial / Pier

UCO
Bank

Museum

Hôtel
de Ville

State Bank of India

i

Botanical
Gardens

Sacred
Heart of
Jesus

Alliance
Française

SUBBAIYAH SALAI (SOUTH BLVD)

Water
Tower

Railway
Station

AMBEDKAR AVE

HOTELS:
A Amala Lodge
B Palace
C Government Tourist Home
D International Guest House
E Nadesh Lodge
F Sea Side Guest House

RESTAURANTS:
1 Aristo
2 Indian Coffee House
3 Seagulls Restaurant & Bar
4 Le Rendezvous
5 Le Café
6 La Terrasse

More dissolute visitors find solace in the fact that Pondicherry levies no tax on alcohol. **Beer** is extremely cheap.

Arrival and information

The two main **bus** stands, **Thiruvalluvar** (state buses), and **New Moffussil** (state and private), are near each other in the southwest of town on Maraimalai Adigal Salai (NH45a), a continuation of Lal Bahadur Sastri St. Both serve substantially the same destinations; for a summary of routes, see the "Travel Details" on p.964. Pondicherry's **railway station** is in the south, five minutes' walk from the sea; on a branch line, it's connected by four daily trains to the main line at Villupuram (departures 8am, 10.50am, 4.45pm & 9pm; 2hr). The **airport** is closed indefinitely.

The friendly staff at the tiny **Pondicherry Tourism Development Corporation** office on Goubert Salai (daily 8am–1pm & 2–7pm; ☎0413/39497) can give you their leaflet, arrange **city tours** (half-day 8am & 2pm; Rs25) or **car rental** (Rs625). You can **change money** at the *State Bank of India* on Rue Suffren or the *UCO Bank* on the south side of Government Place. The **post office** is in the northwest corner of Government Place.

The Town

Pondicherry's beachside promenade, **Goubert Salai**, is a favourite place for a stroll, with cafes and bars to idle in and cooling breezes coming in off the sea. There's little to see, other than the world go by, but Hôtel de Ville, today housing the Municipal Offices building, is still impressive, and a four-metre Gandhi memorial, surrounded by ancient columns, dominates the northern end. Nearby, on the land side, a French memorial commemorates French Indians who lost their lives in World War I.

Just north of the Hôtel de Ville, a couple of streets back from the promenade, is the leafy old French-provincial-style square now named **Government Place**. A fountain stands at the centre, and among its paths and lawns are a number of sculptures carved in nearby Gingee. On its northern side, guarded by policemen in red *képis*, the impressive, gleaming white **Raj Nivas**, official home to the present Lieutenant Governor of Pondicherry Territory, was built late in the eighteenth century for Joseph Francis Dupleix, who became governor of French India. Unfortunately, the home of Ananda Ranga Pillai (1709–61) *dubash*, or close adviser of Dupleix – once one of the highlights of a visit to Pondicherry – is now closed to the public.

On the south side of Government Place on rue Romain Roland, the **Pondicherry Museum** (daily except Mon 10am–5pm) holds Neolithic and 2000-year-old remains from Arikamedu, a few Pallava (sixth–eighth centuries) and Buddhist (tenth-century) stone sculptures, bronzes, weapons and paintings. Perhaps most intriguing, however, is the bizarre assembly of French salon furniture and bric-a-brac from local houses, including a velvet S-shaped "conversation seat", piano, drinks cabinet, tables, carved cupboards, beds, lacquer boxes, long-case clock and plates.

Focus of the Aurobindo Society, the **Sri Aurobindo Ashram** on rue de la Marine (daily 8am–noon & 2–6pm; no children under 3; photography with permission) is one of the best-known and wealthiest ashrams in India, founded in 1926. A beautifully maintained small rockery, cactus and flower garden greets you as you enter the compound. The **samadhi**, or mausoleum, of Sri Aurobindo and The Mother is covered daily with flowers and usually surrounded by supplicating devotees with their hands and heads placed on the tomb. Inside the main building, an incongruous and very bourgeois-looking Western-style room complete with three-piece suite, is where The Mother and Sri Aurobindo chilled out. Make sure not to tread on the Persian carpet on the floor, as devotees prostrate here also. A bookshop in the next room sells tracts, and frequent cultural programmes are presented in the building opposite.

In the southwest of town, near the railway station, you can hardly miss the huge cream-and-brown **Sacred Heart of Jesus**, one of Pondicherry's finest Catholic churches, built by French missionaries in the 1700s. Nearby, the shady **Botanical Gardens** established in 1826, offer many quiet paths to wander (daily 8.45am–5.45pm). The French planted 900 species here, experimenting to see how they would do in Indian conditions; one, the *khaya senegalensis*, has grown to a height of 25m. You can also see an extraordinary fossilized tree, found about 25km away in Tiravakarai.

Auroville

The most New Age place anywhere in India must surely be **AUROVILLE**, the planned "City of Dawn", 10km north of Pondicherry, just outside the Union Territory in Tamil Nadu. Founded in 1968, Auroville was inspired by The Mother, the spiritual successor of Sri Aurobindo. Around 800 families live in communes with such names as Fertile, Certitude, Sincerity, Revelation and Transformation, in what it is hoped will eventually be an ideal city for a population of 50,000. Architecturally experimental buildings, combining modern Western and traditional Indian elements, are set in a rural landscape of narrow lanes, deep red earth and lush greenery. Income comes from agriculture, handicrafts, alternative technology, educational and development projects and *Aurolec*, a computer company. Although the avowed aim is to live in harmony, a life made meaningful through hard physical work backed up by spiritual discipline, the place has had its ups and downs, not least of which have been the disputes between the community and the Sri Aurobindo Society over ownership ever since The Mother's death in 1973. In addition, although Auroville is supposedly an international community, with lots of well-off Westerners buzzing around on mopeds and motorbikes, Pondicherriens tend to assert that most of the Indians involved today are delegated to the status of labourers.

Still under construction, the **Matri Mandir** is a gigantic, costly, almost-spherical, hitech meditation centre intended as the focal point of Auroville (daily, temple 4–5pm, grounds 8am–5pm). In 1970 it was stated that "The Matri Mandir wants to be a symbol of the Divine's answer to man's inspiration for perfection. Union with the Divine manifesting in a progressive unity". Earth from 126 countries was symbolically placed in an urn, and is kept in a concrete cone from which a speaker can address an audience of 3000 without amplification, in the amphitheatre adjacent to Matri Mandir. The **Boutique d'Auroville** (daily except Sun 9am–1pm & 2–5.30pm) nearby sells New Age souvenirs, books, Mother postcards, healing gems and joss sticks. Next to it is a smart, modern, vegetarian cafe and an exhibition on The Mother's philosophy.

Auroville does not actively encourage sightseeing, although the PTDC city tour (see p.998) calls at Matri Mandir. If you have a genuine interest, contact the *Boutique d'Auroville* in rue Nehru, Pondicherry. As Auroville is so spread out, covering fifty square kilometres, it's best to come with your own transport – at the very least a bike. Buses only run as far as the villages of Periyamudaliarchavadi and Chinnamudaliarchavadi on the coastal road, and an auto-rickshaw trip to Matri Mandir from town costs around Rs100.

Accommodation

Pondicherry's **basic lodges** are concentrated around the main market area, Ranga Pillai St and rue Nehru. Guest houses belonging to the **Sri Aurobindo Ashram** come with a lot of baggage apart from your own (regulations, curfews and overpowering "philosophy of life" notices). Although supposedly open to all, they are not keen on advertising, or on attracting misguided individuals indulging in "spiritual tourism". Travellers on a tight budget can try the Railway Retiring Rooms.

If you want to stay in **Auroville**, where rooms range from the most basic to reasonably comfortable, contact the *Boutique d'Auroville* in Pondicherry; they too do not encourage common or garden tourists.

Amala Lodge, 92 Ranga Pillai St (☎0413/38910). Decent basic option, in the heart of town. ①.

Government Tourist Home, Ambedkar Ave, near the railway station (☎0413/36376). Spartan, clean place not far from the sea. 42 rooms (8 a/c), but often full. Snacks-only restaurant. ①.

International Guest House, Gingee Salai, near the head post office (☎0413/36699). An Aurobindo establishment with a range of rooms, some a/c. ①–④.

Mass, Maraimalai Adigal Salai (☎0413/37221). Near the bus stands, in the southwest of town. All rooms a/c with *Star TV*. Veg and non-veg restaurants. ⑤.

Nadesh Lodge, 539 Mahatma Gandhi Rd (☎0413/39221). Basic, reasonable rooms ranged round a leafy, elongated courtyard. Small library. ①.

Palace, 29–31 Ranga Pillai St (☎0413/34477). Smart, well-kept place with large rooms. ②–④.

Palms Beach Cottage Centre, Chinnamudaliarchavadi bus stand, 9km from Pondicherry on the old coastal road to Mamallapuram, near Auroville. Two double and four single cottages, with shared bath, in a beautiful little garden. A real hippy hideaway. ①.

Pondicherry Ashok, Chinnakalapet, 12km from Pondicherry on the old coastal road to Mamallapuram, near Auroville (☎0413/852160). Twenty comfortable rooms in a quiet, breezy location on the seashore. *Star TV*, children's park, restaurant, barbecue and bar. ⑦.

Sea Side Guest House, 14 Goubert Salai (☎0413/26494). Aurobindo guest house in an old, converted house. Often full as there are only eight, sizeable, rooms (2 a/c). ②–④.

Eating

Pondicherry has several places where you can eat by the waves, in the open air, drinking beer – and best of all, a couple of very good **French restaurants**.

Ajantha, Goubert Salai. Hotel restaurant on the land side overlooking the sea and promenade. Tables outside are quite pleasant, but the north Indian menu is fairly uninspiring. Best go just for a drink, alcoholic or otherwise, in the cool breeze.

Anugraha, *Hotel Surguru*, 104 Sardar Vallabhai Patel Salai (North Blvd). Good pure veg, north Indian, Chinese and Western dishes. Snacks served after 4pm.

Aristo, rue Nehru. Delightful rooftop restaurant below plant-filled arbour, filled with twittering budgies in cages. Good north Indian, Western non-veg and some veg dishes.

Le Café, Goubert Salai. A balcony cafe which at high tide is only inches from the sea; selling drinks and snack food, dosas, omelettes and ice-cream. Popular with students. Open 6am–9pm.

Indian Coffee House, rue Nehru. Not their cleanest branch, but the coffee is as good as usual.

Le Rendezvous, 30 rue Saffren. Excellent restaurant run by hearty Indian cordon bleu chef. French, Indian and Chinese plus hamburgers and pizza. Roof terrace and pleasantly decorated interior. Alcohol not on menu, but served discreetly.

Seagulls Restaurant and Bar, rue Damas. Reasonably priced, open-air rooftop restaurant in breezy spot right next to the sea, new pier and cargo harbour. Huge menu, with veg dishes, meat, seafood, Indian, Chinese and even some Italian (pizza, risotto, spaghetti).

La Terrasse, 5 Subiah Salai. Close to *Seagulls*, this friendly place serves good seafood, Indian and Chinese in a small courtyard. No alcohol.

The Chola heartland

Continuing south of Pondicherry along the Coromandel coast, you enter the flat landscape of the Kaveri (aka Cauvery) Delta. This was the very heartland of the mighty **Chola** empire, which was at its peak in the tenth century AD (see p.963). Much as the Cholas originally intended, every visitor is immediately awed by their huge temples, not only at cities such as **Chidambaram**, **Kumbakonam** and **Thanjavur**, but also out in the countryside at places like **Gangaikondacholapuram**, where the temple is all that remains of a once-great city. Exploring the area for a few days will also bring you into contact with the more delicate side of Chola artistic expression, such as the magnificent **bronzes** of Thanjavur.

Chidambaram

CHIDAMBARAM, 58km south of Pondicherry, is so steeped in myth that its history is hard to unravel. As the site of the *tandava*, the cosmic dance of Shiva as **Nataraja**, king of the dance, it is one of the holiest sites in south India. A visit to the **Sabhanayaka temple** affords a fascinating glimpse into ancient Tamil religious practice and belief. The legendary king **Hiranyavarman** is said to have made a pilgrimage here from Kashmir, seeking to rid himself of leprosy by bathing in the temple's Shivaganga tank. In thanks for a successful cure, he enlarged the temple. He also brought 3000 *brahmins*, of the Dikshitar caste, whose descendants are to this day the ritual specialists of the temple, distinguishable by top-knots of hair at the front of their heads.

Few of the fifty *maths*, or monasteries, that once stood here remain, but the temple itself is still a hive of activity and hosts numerous **festivals**. The two most important are ten-day affairs, building up to spectacular finales: on the ninth day of each, temple chariots process through the four Car streets (**"Car Festival"**), while on the tenth, **Abhishekham**, the principal deities in the Raja Sabha (thousand-pillared hall) are anointed. For exact dates (one is in May/June, the other in Dec/Jan), contact any TTDC tourist office; plan well ahead, as they are very popular. Other local festivals include fire-walking and Kavadi folk dance (dancing with decorated wooden frames on the head) at the Thillaiamman Kali (April/May) and Keelatheru Mariamman (July/Aug) temples.

The town also has a hectic market, and a large student population, based at Annamalai University to the east, a centre of Tamil studies. Among the simple thatched huts in the local flat, sparsely populated countryside, which becomes very dry and dusty in summer, the only solid-looking structures are small roadside temples. Many honour Aiyannar, the village deity who protects borders, and are accompanied by *kudirais*, brightly painted terracotta or wooden figures of horses.

Arrival and information

The town revolves around the Sabhanayaka temple and the busy market area that surrounds it, along North, East, South and West Car streets. Though little more than a country halt, the **railway station**, 2km southeast of the centre, has good connections both north and south, and boasts retiring rooms and, on platform 1, a **post office** (Mon–Sat 9am–1pm & 1.30–5pm). Buses from Madras, Thanjavur, Pichavaram, Mamallapuram, Nagapattinam and Madurai pull in at the **bus stand**, also in the southeast, but nearer the centre, about 1km from the temple.

Staff at the TTDC **tourist office**, next to TTDC *Hotel Tamil Nadu* on Railway Feeder Rd, are charming and helpful, but only have a small pamphlet to give visitors. You can **change money** at the *State Bank of India*, Pava Mudali St; *Central Bank*, 62 Bazaar St, and *Indian Bank*, 64 S Car St. The **main post office** is on N Car St.

Sabhanayaka Nataraja temple

The **Sabhanayaka Nataraja temple** complex (daily 4am–noon & 4.30–10pm) covers about 55 acres, divided by four concentric walls. The oldest parts now standing were built under the Cholas, who adopted Nataraja as their chosen deity and crowned several kings here. The rectangular outermost wall, of little interest in itself, affords entry on all four sides, so if you have the time the best way to tackle the complex is to work slowly inwards from the third enclosure in clockwise circles. **Guides** are readily available but tend to shepherd visitors towards the central shrine too quickly. Frequent **ceremonies** take place at the innermost sanctum, the most popular being at 5pm. On Friday nights before the temple closes, during a particularly elaborate *puja*, Nataraja is carried on a palanquin accompanied by music and attendants carrying flaming torches and tridents. At other times, you'll hear ancient devotional hymns from the *Tevaram*.

THE THIRD ENCLOSURE

Four gigantic *gopura* towers rise out of the irregular third wall, each with a granite base and a brick-built superstructure of diminishing storeys covered in a profusion of carved figures. The western *gopura* is the most popular entrance, as well as being the most elaborately carved and probably the earliest (*c.*1150 AD). Turning north (left) from here, you come to the colonnaded **Shivaganga tank**, the site of seven natural springs. From the broken pillar at the tank's edge, all four *gopuras* are visible.

Facing the tank, on the left side, is the **Shivakamasundari temple**, devoted to Parvati, consort of Shiva. Step inside to see the Nayak (sixteenth-century) ceiling paintings arranged in cartoon-like frames in muted browns and greens, outlined in black. On the right as you enter, the story of the leper king Hiranyavarman (see above) is illustrated, and, at the back, frames form a map of the temple complex. Next door, in the northwest corner, a shrine to Subrahmanya, the son of Shiva, is adorned with paintings illustrating stories from the *Skanda Purana*. Beyond this, in front of the northern *gopura*, stands a small shrine to the Navagraha (nine planets).

In the northeast corner, the largest building in the complex, the **Raja Sabha** (fourteenth–fifteenth century) is also known as "the thousand-pillared hall"; tradition holds that there are only nine hundred and ninety-nine actual pillars, the thousandth being Shiva's leg. During festivals the deities Nataraja and Shivakamasundari are brought here and mounted on a dais for the anointing ceremony, *abhishekha*.

The importance of **dance** at Chidambaram is underlined by the reliefs of dancing figures inside the east *gopura* demonstrating 108 *karanas* (a similar set is to be found in the west *gopura*). A *karana* (or *adavu*, in Tamil) is a specific point in a phase of movement prescribed by the extraordinarily comprehensive Sanskrit treatise on the performing arts, the *Natya Shastra* (*c.*200 BC–200 AD) – the basis of all Indian classical dance, music and theatre. A caption from the *Natya Shastra* surmounts each *karana* niche. Four other niches are filled with images of patrons and *stahapatis* – the sculptors and designers responsible for the iconography and positioning of deities.

A pavilion at the south *gopura* houses an image of Nandi, Shiva's bull. Although not accessible from here, the central Nataraja shrine faces south; as with all Shiva temples, Nandi sits opposite the god. In the southwest corner, a shrine contains one of the largest images in India of the elephant-headed son of Shiva, Ganapati (Ganesh). If you stand inside the entrance *mandapa* with your back to Ganapati, you'll see at the base of the two pillars nearest the shrine, carvings of the two important devotees of Nataraja at Chidambaram (see below). To the right is the sage Patanjali, with a snake's body, and on the left Vyaghrapada, with a human body and tiger's feet.

THE SECOND ENCLOSURE

To get into the square second enclosure, head for its **western entrance** (just north of the west *gopura* in the third wall), which leads into a circumambulatory passageway. Once beyond this second wall it's easy to become disorientated, as the roofed inner enclosures see little light and are supported by a maze of colonnades. The atmosphere is immediately more charged, reaching its peak at the very centre.

On the north side, the **Mulasthana** houses the *svayambhulingam* worshipped by Patanjali and Vyaghrapada. The **Devasabha**, or "hall of the gods", on the east, shelters as many as a hundred bronze images used in processions, and is a meeting place for members of the 300 Dikshitar *brahmin* families who own and maintain the temple. Beyond it lies the other, eastern entrance to the second enclosure.

The **Nritta Sabha**, or dance hall, stands on the site where Shiva outdanced Kali (see p.1004), now the southwest corner of the second enclosure. Probably the oldest surviving structure of the two inner areas, its raised platform was fashioned in stone to resemble a wooden temple chariot, or *ratha*. Before they were inexplicably concreted over in the mid-1950s, the east and west sides of the base were each adorned with a wheel and a horse; all that can be seen now are fragments.

BHAKTI AND THE TAMIL POETS

From the eighth century onwards, the devotional form of Hinduism known as **bhakti**, which blossomed in Tamil Nadu, spread north into the rest of India to become, as it still is, the dominant strain of Hinduism throughout the country. It was essentially a popular movement, whose emphasis that each individual devotee could form a personalized, emotionally charged relationship with a chosen god (*ishtadevata*) revolutionized Hindu practice by offering a religious path and goal open to all castes.

The great champions of *bhakti* were the **poet-saints** of Tamil Nadu, often said to have "sung" the religions of Jainism and Buddhism out of south India. Although in practice a variety of deities were worshipped, the movement had two strands – the **Nayanmars**, devoted to Shiva, and the **Alvars**, centred on Vishnu. Collections of their poetry, the greatest literary legacy of south India, remain popular today, and the poets themselves are almost deified, featuring in carvings in many temples.

The four most prominent of the 63 Nayanmar poet-saints were **Campantar**, who converted the king of Madurai from Jainism and had a great cult centre at Chidambaram; **Cuntarar**, a *brahmin* who had two low-caste wives; **Appar**, himself a convert from Jainism; and **Manikkavachakar**, whose mystical poems are still sung in homes and temples throughout Tamil Nadu. The Vaishnavite movement centred on Srirangam (near Trichy), its poets including men and women of all social classes. The most celebrated Alvar was **Nammalvar**, a *shudra* who spent his life in fasting and meditation. **Antal**, the most popular female Alvar, who is said to have married Vishnu's statue at Srirangam, was thereafter regarded as an incarnation of Vishnu's consort, Shri.

All the poems tell of the ecstatic response to intense experiences of divine favour, an emotion frequently described in terms of conjugal love, and expressed in verses of great tenderness and beauty. They stress selfless love between man and god, claiming that such love alone can lead to everlasting union with the divine. Devotees travelled the south, singing, dancing and challenging opponents to public debates.

By the tenth century the **Srivaishnava** sect had been formed around Alvar teachers. The most famous of these, **Ramanuja** (traditionally dated 1017–1137), was for a time head teacher at Srirangam. His works include philosophical treatises, commentaries on the *Bhagavad Gita* and the *Brahmasutra*, devotional poems and a manual of daily practice, written in Sanskrit to reach a wider audience. His new philosophical school, **Visishtadvaita**, proposed God (Vishnu) as the source of all created things and the ruler of the universe. Rejecting Shankara's concept that all except God is illusion, or *maya*, Ramanuja upheld the reality of God, souls and the world, stressing the dependence of all on Vishnu, whom he called **Narayana**, and envisioning the final "union" of the soul with God as an eternal relationship between two distinct entities. God was seen as desiring to offer his grace to all who made themselves open to it. Ramanuja emphasized ritual as the first step to surrender (*prapatti*), and the increased participation of worshippers at all levels spread from Srirangam to Vaishnavite centres all over the south.

Out of Nayanmar poetry a parallel movement arose among Shaivites who, in the tenth century, developed the **Shaiva Siddhanta** system with the compilation of their poems in the **Tirumurai**. Focussing on ultimate union with Shiva, the Shaiva Siddhanta stresses that the human soul is sunk in evil, and can only obtain release through knowledge of God, initiated by Shiva's grace and the soul's love for him. Shiva is thought to appear as a guru, to entice the devotee.

The final major works of the Shaiva teachers were the **Umapati**, supposedly written by a Vaishnavite-turned-Shaivite at Chidambaram. In these, Shiva as Lord of the Dance, **Nataraja**, dances through the world in ceaseless activity to liberate souls. Though Shiva is transcendent, he is made imminent on earth through his power, or *shakti*, personified in iconography by his female consort. Temple festivals mark marriage, quarrels and other exploits of the couple. The Shaiva Siddhanta became firmly established at teaching centres in the south, based on *brahmin* institutions known as *maths*, but led by non-*brahmin* gurus, whose presence strengthened the position of *shudras*, not in a rejection of caste distinction, but in an assertion that the teachings were open to all.

THE DANCE COMPETITION BETWEEN SHIVA AND KALI

The thousand-headed cosmic serpent, **Adisesha**, upon whose coiled body Vishnu reclines in the primordial ocean, once expressed a wish to see Shiva's famed dance. Having arranged time off from his normal duties with Vishnu, Adisesha prayed to Shiva, who was so impressed by the serpent's entreaties that he promised to dance in the forest of Tillai (the site of Chidambaram). Adisesha was reborn as the human sage **Patanjali** (represented as half-man, half-snake) and made straight for Tillai. There he met another sage, **Vyaghrapada** – "Tiger Feet", who had been granted the claws of a tiger to help him climb trees and pluck the best flowers to offer Shiva – who shared his wish to see Shiva dance. Together, they worshipped a *svayambhulingam*, a *shivalingam* that had "self-manifested" in the forest, now housed in the Mulasthana shrine of Sabhanayaka temple. However, the guardian of the forest, who turned out to be the goddess **Kali**, refused to allow Shiva to dance when he arrived. In response, he challenged her to a **dance competition** for possession of the forest. Kali agreed but, perhaps due to modesty, could not match a pose of Shiva's which involved raising the right foot above the head. Defeated, Kali was forced to move off a little way north, where a temple now stands in her honour.

THE INNERMOST ENCLOSURE

Passing through the southern entrance (marked by a gold flagstaff) to the **innermost enclosure** brings you immediately into a hallway, which leads west to the nearby **Govindaraja shrine**, dedicated to Vishnu – a surprise in this most Shaivite of environments. Govindaraja is attended by non-Dikshitar *brahmins*, who, it is said, don't always get along with the Dikshitars. From outside the shrine, non-Hindus can see through to the most sacred part of the temple, the **Kanaka Sabha** and the **Chit Sabha**, adjoining raised structures, roofed with copper and gold plate and linked by a hallway. Two huge bells and extremely loud *nagaswarams* (double-reed wind instruments), *tavils* (drums) and *nattuvangams* (cymbals) call worshippers for ceremonies. The only entrance – closed to non-Hindus – is up five silver-plated steps into the Chit Sabha, guarded by the devotees Vyaghrapada and Patanjali and lit by an arc of flickering oil lamps.

The Chit Sabha houses bronze images of Nataraja and his consort Shivakamasundari. Behind and to the left of Nataraja, a curtain, sacred to Shiva and strung with rows of leaves from the bilva tree, demarcates the most potent area of all. Within it lies the **Akashalingam**, known as the Rahasya, or "secret", of Chidambaram: made of the most subtle of the elements, Ether (*akasha*) – from which Air, Fire, Water and Earth are born – the *lingam* is invisible.

A crystal *lingam*, said to have emanated from the light of the crescent moon on Shiva's brow, and a small ruby Nataraja are worshipped in the Kanaka Sabha. They are ritually bathed in the flames of the priests' camphor fire or oil lamps six times a day.

Accommodation and eating

To cope with the influx of tourists and pilgrims, Chidambaram abounds in budget **accommodation**, but there are no upper-bracket options. If you'd prefer not to **eat** in the hotel restaurants, there are basic "meals" places on and around the Car streets, the *Get In*, opposite the TTDC tourist office, is a favourite with the Chidambaram student set, and there's an *Indian Coffee House*, on Venugopal Pillai St.

Akshaya, 17/18 E Car St (☎20191). Modern hotel, backing onto the temple wall, with 30 rooms (3 a/c; non-a/c is better value). The *Aswini* restaurant serves veg Chinese and Indian dishes (cheaper at lunch), and you can eat non-veg dishes on the lawn next to the temple. ③–④.

The telephone **area code** for Chidambaram is ☎04144.

Railway Retiring Rooms, ask at the Station Master's Office, platform 1. The best deal in town – huge clean rooms, though the bathrooms are a little dilapidated. ①.

Saradharam, 19 Venugopal Pillai St, opposite the bus stand (☎22966). Large, clean and well-kept rooms (a/c ones have *Star TV*) in modern buildings, with a small garden. There's a bar, and the a/c restaurant serves chicken and mutton as well as veg food. ③.

Shameer Lodge, 6 Venugopal Pillai St (☎22983). Well-kept, basic lodge, with largish rooms. ①.

Star Lodge, 101 S Car St (☎22743). Near the temple, welcoming, and oddly stylish for such a cheap place. Good, inexpensive veg meals in the *Babu* restaurant. Hot water at 6am. ①.

TTDC Hotel Tamil Nadu, Railway Feeder Rd, between railway station and bus stand (☎20056). Friendly, but some rooms are woefully neglected: check bedding, and if the a/c works. Also hostel lodging, and decent, reasonably priced veg and non-veg south Indian snacks and meals. ①–⑤.

Gangaikondacholapuram

Devised as the centrepiece of a city built by the Chola king Rajendra I (1014–42) to celebrate his conquests, the magnificent **Brihadishwara temple** stands in the tiny village of **GANGAIKONDACHOLAPURAM**, in Trichy District, 35km northeast of Kumbakonam. The tongue-twisting name means "the town of the Chola who took the Ganges"; under Rajendra I, the Chola empire did indeed stretch as far as the great river of the north, an unprecedented achievement for a southern dynasty. Aside from the temple, nothing of the city remains, although the site of Rajendra's palace, 2km east at Tamalikaimedu, long a source of bricks for local villagers, is being excavated. Hourly **buses** run here from Kumbakonam, and it is also served by some between Trichy and Chidambaram. Facilities are minimal, little more than a few cool drinks stands, so be sure not to get stuck here between noon and 4pm when the temple is closed. Parts of the interior are extremely dark, and a torch is useful.

Brihadishwara temple

The **Brihadishwara temple** (daily 6am–noon & 4–8pm) is enclosed by a rectangular wall; visitors enter through a gateway to the north, separated from the main road by a car park. From here you arrive at a well-maintained, grassy courtyard, flanked by a closed *mandapa* hallway. Over the sanctuary, to the right, a massive pyramidal tower (*vimana*) rises 55m in nine diminishing storeys. Though smaller than the one at Thanjavur, the tower's graceful curve gives it an impressive refinement.

Turning left (east) inside the courtyard, you pass a small shrine to the goddess **Durga**, containing an image of Mahishasuramardini (see p.985). Just beyond, steps climb from a large seated lion, known as Simha-kinaru and made from plastered brickwork, to a well. King Rajendra is said to have had Ganges water placed in it to be used for the ritual anointing (*abhishekha*) of the *lingam* in the main temple.

Set into the east wall, the remains of a *gopura* entranceway lead directly to a large water tank. Directly in front, before the eastern entrance to the temple, stands a small altar for offerings (*bali-pitha*) and a huge Nandi bull. Two flights of steps on the north and south ascend to a porch, the *mukhamandapa*, where a large pair of *dvarpala*s flank the entrance to the long pillared *mahamandapa* hallway. Here you're likely to meet the ASI caretakers, who are worth taking as guides, especially if you'd like to climb up onto the roof for views of the vicinity and of the tower. Access is from within the temple, up steep steps. Immediately inside, on either side of the doorway, sculptures of Shiva in his various benevolent (*anugraha*) manifestations include him blessing Vishnu, Devi, Ravana and the saint Chandesha (see p.1009). In the northeast corner an unusual square stone block features carvings of the nine planets (*navagraha*). A number of **Chola bronzes** (see p.1013) stand on the platform; the figure of Karttikeya, the war god, carrying a club and a shield, is thought to have had particular significance.

The *mahamandapa* leads to the small pillared antechamber (*ardhamandapa*) which has an entrance and stairway at the north and south. Beyond it, the square sanctum sanctorum (*garbha griha*) houses a massive *shivalingam*. Back outside, turning right from the *mukhamandapa* to the southern side of the temple you pass the staircase to the *ardhamandapa*, protected by a pair of *dvarpala* door guardians. In the southwest corner of the courtyard are two **shrines**. The first is to Shiva as Kailasanatha; the other contains a large image of Ganesh, his trunk gleefully curling around a glut of sweets.

The base of the main temple sanctuary is decorated with lions and scrollwork. Above, running from the southern to the northern entrance of the *ardhamandapa*, a series of sculpted figures in pilastered niches portray different images of Shiva. The most famous is at the northern entrance, showing Shiva and Parvati garlanding the saint Chandesha, who here is sometimes identified as Rajendra I. For more on the temples of Tamil Nadu, see p.984.

Two minutes' walk east along the main road (turn right from the car park), the tiny **Archeological Museum** (daily except Fri 10am–1pm & 2–5.45pm) contains Chola odds and ends, discovered locally. The finds include terracotta lamps, coins, weapons, tiles, bronze, bangle pieces, palm-leaf manuscripts and an old Chinese pot.

Kumbakonam

The Cholas are said to have kept a high-security treasury in **KUMBAKONAM**, on the River Kaveri (Cauvery) 74km southwest of Chidambaram and 38km northeast of Thanjavur. Long a sacred site, it still boasts eighteen **temples** and numerous water **tanks**, but it's now also the chief commercial centre for the Thanjavur region. The main bazaar, **Big Street**, sells cotton, plantains, brassware and quality costume jewellery. Quite apart from its own attractions, the town is within easy reach of the magnificent examples of **Chola architecture** at Darasuram and Gangaikondacholapuram; if time is short, make those your priority.

Arrival and information

Kumbakonam's small **railway station**, in the southeast, 2km from the main bazaar, is well-served by trains both north and south, and has a left luggage office (24hr) and decent **retiring rooms** (①). The busy and dusty **Moffussil** (local) and **Aringannar** (long-distance) bus stands are opposite each other in the southeast of town, between the railway station and the Mahamakham tank. All the timetables are in Tamil, but there's a 24-hour enquiry office. Buses leave for **Gangaikondacholapuram** hourly, and **Thanjavur** every few minutes, many via Darasuram. Frequent services run to Madras, several daily to Bangalore and Pondicherry.

To **change money**, the *State Bank* and *Indian Bank* are opposite each other on TSR Big St. The **post office** is, startlingly, on Head Post Office Rd, near Mahamakham tank.

The Town

According to legend, Kumbakonam's seventeenth-century **Kumbareshwara temple** centres on a *lingam* fashioned by Shiva himself. Apparently, a pot (*kumba*) of **amrita**, the beverage of immortality, was washed by a great deluge from atop sacred Mt Meru in the Himalaya, and carried all the way here. Shiva, who happened to be passing in the guise of a wild forest-dwelling hunter, for some reason fired an arrow at the pot, causing it to break. From the broken pieces, he made this very *lingam*.

The temple's east entrance is approached via a covered market selling a huge assortment of cooking pots, a local speciality, as well as the usual glass bangles and trinkets. As you enter, you pass the temple elephant, with painted forehead and necklace of bells. Beyond the flagstaff, a *mandapa* hallway, whose columns feature painted *yali* (mythical beast) brackets, leads to the principal *gopura* entranceway. A figure of Shiva's bull-vehicle, Nandi, faces the main sanctuary. There's also a fine collection of silver *vahanas*,

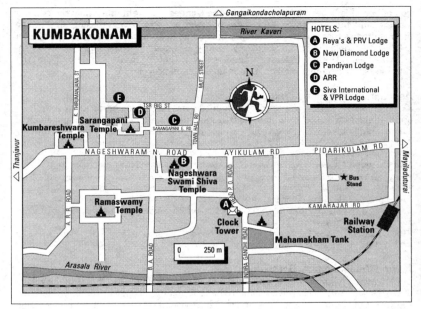

KUMBAKONAM

HOTELS:
A Raya's & PRV Lodge
B New Diamond Lodge
C Pandiyan Lodge
D ARR
E Siva International & VPR Lodge

vehicles of the deities, used in festivals, and *pancha loham* (compound of silver, gold, brass, iron and tin) figures of the 63 Nayanmar poet-saints (see p.1003).

The principal and largest of the Vishnu temples in Kumbakonam is the thirteenth-century **Sarangapani temple**. Entry, into a hundred-pillar hallway from the seventeenth century (Nayak period), is through a ten-storey pyramidal *gopura* gate, more than 40m high. Passing through a smaller *gopura* leads into a second courtyard, containing another columned *mandapa* and to the right, a shrine to Lakshmi. The **central shrine** dates from the late Chola period with many later accretions. Its entrance, within the innermost court, is guarded by huge *dvarpalas*, identical to Vishnu whom they protect. Between them are carved stone *jali* screens, each different, and in front of them stands the sacred, square *homam* fireplace. During the day, pinpoints of light from ceiling windows penetrate the darkness around the sanctum, designed to resemble a chariot with reliefs of horses, elephants and wheels. A painted cupboard contains a mirror for Vishnu to see himself when he leaves the sanctum sanctorum.

Possibly the oldest in Kumbakonam, the small **Nageshwara Swami Shiva temple**, one of the finest early Chola temples, noted for the quality of its sculpture, is thought to have been completed a few years into the reign of Parantaka I (907–*c*.940). Standing in a courtyard, the principal shrine to Shiva is connected to a columned *mandapa*. Both share a base carved with scenes from the epics and lotus petals. The main niches on the sanctum wall contain **sculptures**; on the north, Dakshinamurti ("south-facing" Shiva as teacher), on the west Ardhanarishvara (male Shiva and female Shakti in one figure) and Brahma on the south. Joining them are high-relief near-life-size sculptures of unidentified figures, perhaps worshippers, donors or royalty. Within the courtyard, a shrine to **Nataraja** features rearing horses and wheels, with tiny figures as spokes.

The most famous and revered of many sacred **water tanks** in Kumbakonam, the **Mahamakham** in the southeast of town, is said to have filled with ambrosia collected from the pot broken by Shiva. Every twelve years, when Jupiter passes the constellation of Leo, it is believed that water from the Ganges and eight other holy rivers flows into the tank, thus according it the status of *tirtha*, or sacred river crossing. At this auspicious time as many as two million pilgrims come here to take an absolving bathe; in 1992, sixty people died in an accident variously ascribed to a collapsing wall or to general mayhem. During a lesser annual festival (Feb/March) the deity from the Kumbareshwara temple is taken to Mahamakham in procession.

Accommodation and eating

Kumbakonam is not a major tourist location, and has limited **accommodation**, with no upper-range hotels; the good news is that most places are clean and well-maintained. There's nothing very exciting about **eating out**; your best bet is to dine in the hotels.

ARR, 21 TSR Big St (☎0435/21234). Reasonable rooms, some a/c, deluxe ones with *Star TV*. Veg restaurant serves south Indian snacks in the evening and "leaf-meals" at lunchtime. ③–⑤.

New Diamond Lodge, 93 Nageswaram N St (☎0435/20870). Inexpensive and clean. ①.

Pandiyan Lodge, 52 Sarangapani E St (☎0435/20397). Clean rooms; some are windowless. Cheap veg and "deluxe" meals (with mutton); the *Arul Restaurant* opposite is also good. ①.

PRV Lodge, 32 Head Post Office Rd (☎0435/21820). Basic lodge with veg restaurant. ②.

Raya's, 28–29 Head Post Office Rd (☎0435/22545). Smallish, but very clean a/c and non-a/c rooms. *Star TV*. Veg and non-veg restaurants. ④–⑤.

VPR Lodge, 101/3 TSR Big St (☎0435/21045). Shares a reception desk with *Siva International*, a modern tower hotel; but is far more basic, with non-a/c rooms only and no *Star TV*. ①.

Around Kumbakonam: Darasuram

The **Airavateshwara temple**, built by King Rajaraja II (*c*.1146–73), stands in the village of **DARASURAM**, an easy five-kilometre bus trip (on the Thanjavur route) or bike ride southwest of Kumbakonam. This superb if little-visited Chola monument ranks alongside those at Thanjavur and Gangaikondacholapuram; but while they are grandiose, emphasizing heroism and conquest, it is far smaller, exquisite in proportion and detail and said to have been decorated with *nitya-vinoda*, "perpetual entertainment", in mind. Shiva is here known as Airavateshwara, because he was worshipped at this temple by Airavata, the white elephant of the king of the gods, Indra.

Entrance is through a large *gopura* gateway, 1m below ground level, in the main wall, which is topped with small reclining bull figures. Inside, the main building is set in a spacious courtyard. Next to the inner sanctuary, fronted by an open porch, the steps of the closed *mandapa* feature elegant curled balustrades decorated with elephants and *makaras* (mythical crocodiles with floriate tails). At the corners, rearing horses and wheels make the whole into a chariot. Elsewhere, clever sculptural puns include the head of an elephant merging with that of a bull.

Fine Chola black basalt images in wall niches in the *mandapa* and the inner shrine include **Nagaraja**, the snake-king, with a hood of cobras, and **Dakshinamurti**, the "south-facing" Shiva as teacher, expounding under a banyan tree. One rare image shows Shiva as **Sharabha**, part man, beast and bird, destroying the man-lion incarnation of Vishnu, Narasimha – indicative of the animosity between the Shaivite and Vaishnavite cults. Sharabha, in his own separate small *mandapa*, is approached by a flight of steps. Fanged *dvarpala* door guardians in *raudra* (furious) mood flank the shrine entrance. Each possesses a club, their four hands in an attitude denoting threat (*tarjani*) with Shiva's trident, the *trishula*, wound into their hair.

Outside, a unique series of somewhat gruesome panels, hard to see without climbing on to the base, form a band along the top of the basement of the closed *mandapa* and the sanctum sanctorum. They illustrate scenes from Sekkilar's **Periya Purana**, one of the great works of Tamil literature. The poem tells the stories of the Tamil Shaivite saints, the Nayanmars, and was commissioned by King Kulottunga II, after the poet criticized him for a preoccupation with erotic, albeit religious, literature. Sekkilar is said to have composed it in the Raja Sabha at Chidambaram; when it was completed the king sat every day for a year to hear him recite it.

Each panel illustrates the lengths to which the saints were prepared to go to demonstrate devotion to Shiva. The boy **Chandesha**, for example, whose job it was to tend the village cows, discovered one day that they were involuntarily producing milk. He decided to bathe a *lingam* with the milk as part of his daily worship. Appalled by this apparent waste, the villagers complained to his father, who went to the field, cursed the boy, and kicked the *lingam* over. At this affront to Shiva, Chandesha cut off his father's leg with an axe; he is shown at the feet of Shiva and Parvati, who have garlanded him. Another panel shows a man who frequently gave food to Shiva devotees. When his wife was reluctant to welcome and wash the feet of a mendicant who had previously been their servant, he cut off her hands. Elsewhere, a Pallava queen has her nose cut off for inadvertently smelling a flower, rendering it useless as an offering to Shiva. The last panel shows the saint **Sundara** who, by singing a hymn to Shiva, rescued a child who had been swallowed by a crocodile.

On the lowest portions of the base, rows of *yali*s (mythical lions) and *gana*s, the dwarf attendants of Shiva, dance and play musical instruments. Surrounding the main shrine, a four-metre-wide channel, created by a very low wall, is decorated with lotus patterns and badly damaged Nandis. At one time, this was filled with water, so the temple appeared to float in a pool.

Thanjavur

Although its history and treasures give it a crucial significance to south Indian culture, the bustling country town of **THANJAVUR** (aka Tanjore), 55km east of Tiruchirapalli and 35km southwest of Kumbakonam in one of the main rice-growing regions of the Kaveri (Cauvery) Delta, is often overlooked by travellers.

Thanjavur is roughly split in two by the east–west **Grand Anicut Canal**. The **old town**, north of the canal and once entirely enclosed by a fortified wall, was between the ninth and the end of the thirteenth centuries chosen as the capital of their extensive empire by all the Chola kings save one. None of their secular buildings survives, but you can still see as many as ninety temples – notably the magnificent **Brihadishwara temple**, an eloquent statement of the power and patronage of Rajaraja I (985–1014). Under the Cholas, as well as the later Nayaks and Marathas, literature, painting, sculpture, Carnatic classical music and Bharatanatyam dance all thrived here; quite apart from its own intrinsic interest, the Nayak **royal palace compound** houses an important library and museums including a superb collection of Chola bronzes.

Of major local **festivals,** the most lavish celebrations at the Brihadishwara temple are associated with the birthday of King Rajaraja, in October. An eight-day celebration of **Carnatic classical music** is held each January at the Panchanateshwara temple at **Thiruvaiyaru**, 13km away, to honour the great Carnatic composer-saint, Thyagaraja.

Arrival and information
Buses from Madras, Pondicherry, Madurai and Tiruchirapalli pull in at the long-distance Thiruvalluvar stand, opposite the city bus stand, off Hospital Rd in the south of the old town. Other services from Tiruchirapalli, and those to local destinations such as Kumbakonam, stop at the new bus stand, 4km southwest of the centre.

The **railway station**, south of the centre, has a new computerized system (Mon–Sat 8am–2pm & 3–5pm, Sun 8am–2pm), for booking trains to Madras (3 daily; the *Cholan Express* #6154 leaves at 8.50am), Madurai (2 daily), Tiruchirapalli (4 daily), Rameshwaram (1 daily; 5am). There are also several fast passenger services daily to Thiruvarur, Nagapattinam and Nagore. The red-and-cream station itself has an antiquated air, with its decorated columns in the main hall, and sculptures of dancers and

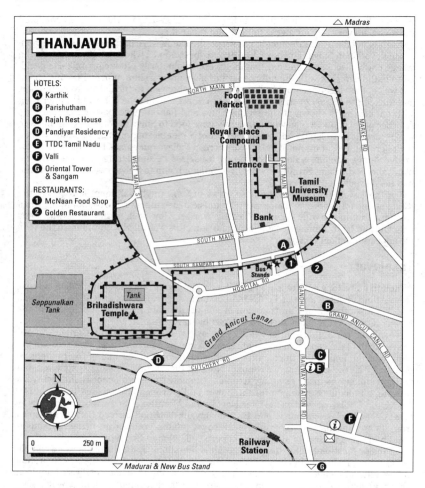

THANJAVUR

HOTELS:
Ⓐ Karthik
Ⓑ Parishutham
Ⓒ Rajah Rest House
Ⓓ Pandiyar Residency
Ⓔ TTDC Tamil Nadu
Ⓕ Valli
Ⓖ Oriental Tower & Sangam

RESTAURANTS:
❶ McNaan Food Shop
❷ Golden Restaurant

△ Madras

NORTH MAIN ST
Food Market
Royal Palace Compound
Entrance
Tamil University Museum
Bank
WEST MAIN ST
EAST MAIN ST
MARKET RD
SOUTH MAIN ST
SOUTH RAMPART ST
Bus Stands
HOSPITAL RD
Seppunalkan Tank
Tank
Brihadishwara Temple ▲
Grand Anicut Canal
GANDHIJI RD
GRAND ANICUT CANAL RD
CUTCHERY RD
RAILWAY STATION RD
N
0   250 m
Railway Station
▽ Madurai & New Bus Stand
▽ Ⓖ

musicians. Luggage can be left in the Parcel Office in a separate building. The nearest **airport** to Thanjavur is at Tiruchirapalli (64km).

The **post office** and most of the hotels and restaurants lie on or around **Gandhiji Rd** (aka Railway Station Rd), which crosses the canal and leads to the railway station in the south. The **TTDC Tourist Office**, opposite the post office (Mon–Fri 10am–5.45pm; ☎23017) is a good source of local information; there's a smaller branch in the compound of TTDC *Hotel Tamil Nadu I* on Gandhiji Rd (daily 8am–4pm).

You can **change money** at *Canara Bank* on South Main St, the *State Bank of India*, Hospital Rd, and *Hotel Parishutham* – useful out of banking hours. The Government

The telephone **area code** for Thanjavur is ☎04362.

Hospital is on Hospital Rd, and there are plenty of pharmacies on Gandhiji Rd. At no. 162, opposite Irattai Mastan Dharga mosque, *National Studio & Video* sells film.

Brihadishwara temple

Thanjavur's skyline is dominated by the huge tower of the **Brihadishwara temple**, which for all its size lacks the grandiose excesses of later periods. The site has no great significance; the temple was constructed as much to reflect the power of its patron, King Rajaraja I, as to facilitate the worship of Shiva. Profuse **inscriptions** on the base of the main shrine provide incredibly detailed information about the organization of the temple. They show it to have been rich, both in financial terms and in ritual activity. Among recorded gifts from Rajaraja, from booty acquired in conquest, are the equivalent of 600lb of silver, 500lb of gold, and 250lb of assorted jewels, plus income from agricultural land throughout the Chola empire, set aside for the purpose. No less than 400 female dancers, **devadasis** (literally "slaves to the gods", married off to the deity), were employed, and each provided with a house. Other staff – another 200 people – included dance teachers, musicians, tailors, potters, laundrymen, goldsmiths, carpenters, astrologers, accountants and attendants for all manner of rituals and processions.

Entrance to the complex is on the east, through two **gopura** gateways some way apart. Although the outer one is the larger, both are of the same pattern: massive rectangular bases topped by pyramidal towers with carved figures and vaulted roofs. At the core of each is a monolithic sandstone lintel, said to have been brought from Tiruchirapalli, over 50km away. The outer facade of the inner *gopura* features mighty fanged *dvarpala* door guardians, mirror images of each other, and thought to be the largest monolithic sculptures in any Indian temple. Panels illustrating scenes from the *Skanda Purana* decorate the base, including the marriage of Shiva and Parvati.

Once inside, the gigantic **courtyard** gives plenty of space to appreciate the temple buildings. A sixteenth-century pavilion, fronted by a tall lamp column and facing the main temple, holds the third largest Nandi (Shiva's bull-vehicle) in India.

The **main temple**, constructed of granite, consists of a long pillared *mandapa* hallway, followed by the *ardhamandapa*, or "half-hall" which in turn leads to the inner sanctum, the *garbha griha*. The plinth of the central shrine measures 46 square metres; above it, the pyramidal *vimana* tower (at just under 61m high, the largest and tallest in India) rises in thirteen diminishing storeys, the apex being exactly one third of the size of the base. Such a design is quite different from later temples, where the *vimanas* become smaller as the *gopura* entranceways increasingly dominate – a desire to protect the sanctum sanctorum from the polluting gaze of outsiders.

The long pillared *mandapa* from the Vijayanagar period (sixteenth century) has been roughly adjoined to the *ardhamandapa*; you can see the mouldings do not match. Inside, the walls are decorated with eighteenth-century Maratha portraits. The *vimana* is an example of a "structured monolith", a stage removed from the earlier rock-cut architecture of the Pallavas, whereby blocks of stone are assembled and then carved. The profusion of carvings, aside from the inscriptions, include *dvarpala* door guardians, Shiva, Vishnu, Durga, Ganapati (Ganesh), Bhu-devi (the female goddess Earth) and Lakshmi, arranged on three sides in two rows.

As the stone that surmounts the *vimana* is said to weigh eighty tons, there is considerable speculation as to how it got up there; the most popular theory is that it was hauled up a four-mile-long ramp. Others have suggested the use of a method comparable to the Sumer Ziggurat style of building, whereby logs were placed in gaps in the masonry and the stone raised by leverage. The simplest answer, of course, is that perhaps it's not a single stone at all.

You can enter the *vimana* tower at the north and south by large stairs leading to the **ardhamandapa**, where Chola bronzes include one of Rajaraja himself. The black *shivalingam*, over 3.5m high, in the inner sanctum is called Adavallan, "the one who can dance well" – a reference to Shiva as Nataraja, the King of the Dance, who resides at Chidambaram and was the *ishtadevata*, chosen deity, of the king. The *lingam* is not always on view, but during *puja* ceremonies (8 & 11am, noon & 7.30pm), to the accompaniment of clanging bells, a curtain is pulled revealing the god to the devotees.

Surrounding the *garbha griha*, an **ambulatory passage** contains three massive sculptures of Shiva on the south, west and north sides. Along the upper register, a sculpted series of 108 classical dance poses predates the famous sets at Chidambaram (see p.1001), though here Nataraja is depicted as the dancer. Paintings on the ceiling and walls, currently being restored, are the oldest to survive from the Chola period.

Outside, the walls of the courtyard are lined with **colonnaded passageways** – the one along the northern wall is said to be the longest in India. The one on the west, behind the temple, contains 108 *linga* from Varanasi and painted panels from the Maratha period. At the centre stands a small shrine to Varuna (the Vedic god, associated with water and the sea), next to an image of goddess Durga, usually kept clothed.

Other **shrines** inside the enclosure include one behind the main temple to a devotee-saint, Karuvurar, supposedly able to cure barrenness. To the northwest, a seventeenth-century temple to Subrahmanya (a son of Shiva) has a base finely decorated with sculptures of dancers and musicians. Close to the figure of Nandi is a thirteenth-century Devi shrine; in the northeast corner, a *mandapa* houses images of Nataraja, his consort and a devotee, and is also used for decorating icons prior to processions.

In the southwest corner of the courtyard, the small **Archeological Museum** (daily 9am–1pm & 4–8pm) houses an interesting collection of sculpture, including an extremely tubby, damaged Ganesh, before-and-after photos detailing restoration work to the temple in the 1940s and displays about the Cholas. You can also buy the excellent ASI booklet *Chola Temples*, which gives detailed accounts of Brihadishwara and the temples at Gangaikondacholapuram and Darasuram. A path leads from between the two *gopuras* the length of the main wall where, behind the temple, the manicured lawn lined with benches is a haven of quiet. The temple water tank lies just beyond, next to the northwest corner. For more on Tamil Nadu's temples, see p.984.

The Royal Palace compound

The **Royal Palace** compound, where members of the erstwhile royal family still reside, is on E Main St (a continuation of Gandhiji Rd), 2km northeast of Brihadishwara temple. Dotted around the compound are several reminders of Thanjavur's past under the

---

CHOLA BRONZES

Originally sacred temple objects, **Chola bronzes** are the only art form from Tamil Nadu to have penetrated the world art market. The most memorable bronze icons are the **Natarajas**, or dancing Shivas. The image, standing on one leg, encircled by flames, with wild locks caught in mid-motion, has become almost as recognizably Indian as the Taj Mahal, and few Indian millionaires would feel their sitting rooms complete without one.

The principal icons of a temple are usually stationary and made of stone. Frequently, however, ceremonies require an image of the god to be led in procession outside the inner sanctum, and even through the streets. According to the canonical texts known as *Agamas*, these moving images should be made of metal. Indian bronzes are made by the **cire-perdu**, "lost-wax", process. Three layers of clay mixed with burned grain husks, salt and ground cotton are applied to a figure crafted in wax, with a stem left protruding at each end. When that is heated, the wax melts and flows out, creating a hollow mould into which molten metal can be poured through the stems. After the metal has cooled, the clay shell is destroyed, and the stems filed off, leaving a unique completed figure.

Knowledge of bronze-casting in India goes back at least as far as the Indus Valley Civilization (2500–1500 BC), and the famous **"Dancing Girl"** from Mohenjo Daro. The earliest produced in the south were made by the Andhras, whose techniques were continued by the Pallavas, the immediate antecedents of the Cholas. The few surviving **Pallava** bronzes show a sophisticated handling of the form; figures are characterized by broad shoulders, thick-set features and an overall simplicity that suggests all the detail was completed at the wax stage. The finest bronzes of all are from the **Chola** period, in the late ninth to the early eleventh centuries. As the Cholas were predominantly Shaivite, Nataraja, Shiva and his consort Parvati (frequently in a family group with son Skanda) and the 63 Nayanmar poet-saints are the most popular subjects. Chola bronzes display more detail than their predecessors. Human figures are invariably slim-waisted and elegant, with the male form robust and muscular and the female graceful and delicate.

The design, iconography and proportions of each figure are governed by the strict rules laid down in the **shilpa shastras**, which draw no real distinction between art, science and religion. Measurement always begins with the proportions of the artist's own hand and the image's resultant face-length as the basic unit. Then follows a scheme which is allied to the equally scientific rules applied to classical music, and specifically *tala* or rhythm. Human figures total eight face-lengths, eight being the most basic of rhythmic measures. Figures of deities are *nava-tala*, nine face-lengths.

Those bronzes produced by the few artists practising today invariably follow the Chola model; the chief centre is now **Swamimalai**, 8km west of Kumbakonam. Original Chola bronzes are kept in many Tamil temples, but as temple interiors are often dark it's not always possible to see them properly. Important **public collections** include the Nayak Durbar Hall Art Museum at Thanjavur, the Government State Museum at Madras and the National Museum, New Delhi.

Nayaks and the Marathas, including an exhibition of oriental manuscripts and a superlative museum of Chola bronzes. The dusty and run-down **Tamil University Museum** contains coins and musical instruments, while near the entrance to the complex, the new **Royal Museum** (daily 9am–6pm; Rs1) houses a modest collection of costumes, portraits, musical instruments, weapons, manuscripts and courtly accessories.

The palace buildings have been in a sorry state for years; hopes were raised for their preservation when the responsibility for maintenance passed in 1993 to the Indian National Trust for Cultural Heritage (INTACH), but almost immediately some suffered extensive damage in storms. The Sarja Madi, "seven-storey" bell tower, built by Serfoji II in 1800, is closed to the public due to its unsafe condition.

Work on the palace began in the mid-sixteenth century under Sevappa Nayak, the founder of the Nayak kingdom of Thanjavur; additions were made by the Marathas from the end of the seventeenth century onwards. Remodelled by Shaji II in 1684, the **Durbar Hall**, or hall of audience, houses a throne canopy decorated with the mirrored glass distinctive to Thanjavur. Although damaged, the ceiling and walls are elaborately painted. Five domes are striped red, green and yellow, and on the walls, friezes of leaf and pineapple designs, and trumpeting angels in a night sky show European influence.

Niches in the walls hold sculptures of deities, and figures including the Shiva devotee Patanjali (see p.1004), with a snake winding around his leg, and an Englishman said to be in the unlikely position of learning classical dance from a young woman, to whom he is presenting a gift. Visible on the left wall, as you face the throne, are traces of a Nayak mural of deer in a forest. Next to this, two holes in the floor, once entrances to a secret passageway, are home to cobras and not recommended for exploration. Some of the later paintings portray the entertainers who as recently as the 1960s revelled in the now overgrown square outside – fighters, circus performers and wrestlers.

SARASWATI MAHAL LIBRARY MUSEUM

The **Saraswati Mahal Library**, one of the most important oriental manuscript collections in India, is closed to the public, but used by scholars from all over the world. Over 80 percent of its 44,000 manuscripts are in Sanskrit, many on palm-leafs, and some very rare or even unique. The Tamil works include treatises on medicine and commentaries on works from the Sangam period, the earliest literature of the south.

A small **museum** (daily except Wed 10am–1pm & 1.30–5.30pm) displays a bizarre array of books and pictures from the collection. Among the palm-leaf manuscripts is a calligrapher's tour-de-force, in the form of a visual mantra, where each letter in the inscription "Shiva" comprises the god's name repeated in microscopically small handwriting. Most of the Maratha manuscripts, produced from the end of the seventeenth century, are on paper; they include a superbly illustrated edition of the *Mahabharata*. Sadists will be delighted to see the library managed to hang on to their copy of the explicitly illustrated **Punishments in China**, published in 1804. Next to it, full rein is given to the imagination of French artist, **Charles Le Brun** (1619–90), in a series of pictures on the subject of physiognomy. Animals such as the horse, bullock, wolf, bear, rabbit and camel are drawn in painstaking care above a series of human faces which bear an uncanny, if unlikely, resemblance to them. You can buy postcards of this scientific study and exhibits from the other palace museums in the **shop** next door.

NAYAK DURBAR HALL ART MUSEUM AND RAJARAJA CHOLAN MUSEUM

A magnificent collection of **Chola bronzes** – all discovered locally – fills the **Nayak Durbar Hall Art Museum** (daily 9am–1pm & 3–6pm; Rs2), a high-ceilinged audience hall with massive pillars, dating from 1600. The elegance of the figures and delicacy of detail is exquisite. A tenth-century statue of Kannappa Nayannar, a hunter-devotee, shows minutiae right down to his embroidered clothing, fingernails and the fine lines on his fingers. The oldest bronze shows Vinadhra Dakshinamurti ("south-facing Shiva") who, with a deer on one left hand, would have originally been playing the *vina* – the musical instrument has long since gone. Along with several dynamic examples of Nataraja, Shiva as the King of the Dance, there's a fine Kalyanasundaramurti, where Shiva, with his arm draped around the shy Parvati, is about to be married.

The **Rajaraja Cholan Museum** (same hours) houses Chola stone sculpture and small objects excavated at Gangaikondacholapuram (see p1005) such as tiny marbles, games boards, bangles and terracotta pieces. Two illuminated maps show the remarkable extent of the Chola empire under the great kings Rajaraja I and his son, Rajendra I. Towering over these buildings is the Nayak-period **arsenal**, cunningly designed to resemble a temple *gopura*, with fine views of Thanjavur from the top.

TANJORE (THANJAVUR) PAINTING

The name **Tanjore painting** is given to a distinctive form of southern picture-making that came to prominence in the eighteenth century, encouraged by the Maratha Raja of Thanjavur, Serfoji. The term "painting", however, is misleading, and inadequate to describe work of the Tanjore school. It is distinctive because, aside from a painted image, details such as clothing, ornaments, and any (typically baroque) architectural elements are raised in low plaster relief from the surface, which is then decorated by the sumptuous addition of glass pieces, pearls, semi-precious or precious stones and elaborate gold leaf work. Other variations include pictures on mica, ivory and glass.

Figures are delineated with simple outlines; unmixed primary colours are used in a strict symbolic code, similar to that found in the make-up used in the classical dramas of Kerala, where each colour indicates qualities of character. Other schools of painting normally show Krishna with blue-black skin; in the Tanjore style, he is white.

Traditionally, most depicted Vaishnavite deities, with the most popular single image probably that of **Balakrishna**, the chubby baby Krishna (see p.244). In the tenth-century Sanskrit *Bhagavata Purana*, Balakrishna was portrayed as a rascal who delighted in stealing and consuming milk, butter balls and curd. Despite his naughtiness, all women who came into contact with him were seized with an overflowing of maternal affection, to the extent that their breasts spontaneously oozed milk. Thanks to such stories, Krishna as a child became the chosen deity par excellence of mothers and grandmothers. Tanjore paintings typically show him eating, accompanied by adoring women.

Although Tanjore painting went into decline after the nineteenth century, in recent years there has been a new demand for domestic, rather than temple, shrines. High-quality work is produced in Thanjavur, Kumbakonam and Tiruchirapalli.

Accommodation and eating

Most of Thanjavur's **hotels**, which as a rule charge higher rates than you'd pay elsewhere in the state, are concentrated in the area between the railway station and bus stands; a flurry of building activity in the run up to the 1995 World Tamil Conference has led to a proliferation of upper-range options, many of them south of the centre. There are plenty of straightforward **restaurants** around Gandhiji Rd; the rooftop *Golden Restaurant*, just around the corner on Hospital Rd has good veg specialties.

Karthik, 73 S Rampart St, near the bus stand (☎22116). Very overpriced, grotty a/c rooms, but the popular restaurant serves good, low-priced veg "meals", and south Indian snacks at night. ③–⑤.

Oriental Tower, 2889 Srinivasam Pillai Rd, 1–2km south of town (☎21467). Huge, all mod-cons hotel-cum-shopping complex with swimming pool. Excellent, inexpensive restaurant. ⑧.

Pandiyar Residency, 14 Cutchery Rd (☎20574). Across the canal from the Brihadishwara temple; all rooms (6 a/c) have *Star TV*, and deluxe ones have temple views. ④–⑤.

Parishutham, 55 Grand Anicut Canal Rd (☎21801). Comfortable, clean but expensive rooms with balcony, cable and *Star TV*. Craft shop, pool and foreign exchange. Rather pricey veg and non-veg restaurants where the varied menus include barely-warmed soups "from the boiling kettle". ⑧.

Railway Retiring Rooms, contact Matron on the first floor of the railway station. Six big, clean double rooms opening out onto a large communal verandah, overlooking station approach. ①.

Rajah Rest House, Gandhiji Rd (☎20515). Down a lane next to the *Hotel Tamil Nadu*. Basic, but peaceful and clean enough. ①.

Sangam, Trichy Rd, 2km south of centre (☎24805). New luxury complex with pool and all facilities. ⑦.

TTDC Tamil Nadu, Gandhiji Rd, 10min from the bus and railway stands (☎21024). Once the Raja's guest house; good value, good service. Large, comfortable carpeted rooms (a few more expensive with a/c and *Star TV*), set around a garden. Restaurant serving veg and non-veg "meals" and south Indian snacks, including tasty onion *utthapam* (thick pancakes), and a bar. ④–⑤.

Valli, 2948 MKM Rd (☎21584). In a cul-de-sac near the railway station, alongside the car mechanics of Thanjavur. All the not-so-clean rooms have cable TV, and there's a veg restaurant. ②–④.

Thiruvarur

Often overlooked by visitors travelling between Thanjavur and the coast, quiet, dusty **THIRUVARUR**, 55km east of Thanjavur, is famed as the birthplace of the musical saint Thyagaraja, to whom the town's huge temple is dedicated. According to Hindu myth, the first temple was built on this spot after Shiva and Parvati, at rest in a garden at the foot of Mt Kailash, were disturbed by a handful of bilva leaves scattered over them by a playful monkey. Shiva, delighted, blessed the beast, who was reincarnated as the kindly King Muchukunda of the Manu dynasty. The king built many temples but later got involved in a fight with the demon Vala, who was finally killed by the god Indra. Muchukunda was offering *pujas* in thanks for his salvation when Shiva appeared and instructed him to build a temple at Thiruvar. Today, the **Thyagarajaswamy temple**, on the north side of town, dating mainly from the fourteenth and fifteenth centuries, measures nearly 300m by more than 200m. Its three successive enclosed courtyards contain a number of shrines, including one to Thyagaraja with an unusual line of the nine *navagralias* peering in at the saint's image. The inner sanctum houses a bronze *lingam* crowned with a seven-headed cobra, its outer walls and ceilings brightly painted with vivid images of Shiva and accompanying deities.

In March the town hosts the **Arulmigu Thyagarajaswamy car festival**, when for ten days animated crowds pull, push and wish the great temple car (the largest in Tamil Nadu) and its smaller companions on their laborious path around the surrounding streets – well worth stopping for.

Practicalities

Frequent **buses** and **trains** arrive in Thiruvarur from Thanjavur and Nagapattinam; there are also a few train services from Mayiladuturai in the north. The railway station and bus stand are five minutes' walk apart in the south of town. To reach the temple, cross the bridge just north of the bus stand, and carry on straight for ten or so minutes. It's not difficult to find **somewhere to stay**, even during the car festival. Several adequate lodges (all ①) stand close to the bus stand on Thanjavur Rd: try *VPK Lodge* (☎04366/22309); *President* (☎04366/22748) or *Sekar* (☎04366/22525), which is next to the post office.

Nagapattinam and around

NAGAPATTINAM, 170km south of Pondicherry and 90km east of Thanjavur at the mouth of the Kaveri, was the key port of the Chola empire. Nowadays unprepossessing, it warrants little more than an overnight stop on the way to the pilgrimage sites of **Nagur** and **Velankanni**, where devotees of all faiths testify to the region's tradition of religious tolerance. In the flat **Kaveri Delta**, paddy fields stretch as far as the eye can see, broken up by tamarind, palmyra and coconut trees, and occasional fields of maize. Roads pick their way through a tangle of rivers, which most of the year are more sand than water. In December, however, destructive **cyclonic storms** render the area extremely dangerous, when the already poor roads become veritable rivers with potholes of depths best left unplumbed. The surrounding villages, clusters of thatched huts with long sloping roofs, are largely Muslim, but the nearer you get to Nagapattinam the more red flags and hammer-and-sickle symbols you see. Here too are tight-knit, impoverished fishing communities that frequently come under suspicion of harbouring Tamils who arrive under cover of night from Sri Lanka.

Nagur

In the village of **NAGUR**, 10km north of Nagapattinam, the 500-year-old **dargah** of the Muslim saint Hazrat Mian Sahib comprises five golden-domed mosques set in a warren of paths, open courtyards and hallways teeming with pilgrims. Elaborately embossed silver steps decorate the shrines, while the paths and walls are covered in white tiles with patterned friezes. At the back of the mosques, people bathe in the large **Pirkulam** tank in the hope of being granted good health. In a little shelter at the water's edge, barbers busily shave the heads of children and adults who dispense with their hair as a form of penance. Stalls throughout the complex sell the blue, black or gold hats, similar to Nehru caps, worn by many male visitors, colourful Mecca and Koranic verse pictures, and *bhartia*: little baskets of sugar, joss and *shambrani* incense for offerings.

Nagapattinam is connected by **train** to Thanjavur and Madras, and frequent **buses** from Nagur and Velankanni (both 20min), Madras, Thanjavur and Trichy call at the Thiruvalluvar bus stand. The only decent **accommodation** in the village is at *Hotel Tamil Nadu*, Thonitthurai Salai, near the railway station (☎04365/22389; ③–④). The rooms, some of them a/c, lack charm but staff are friendly and the basic restaurant is a little more attractive than the "meals" places elsewhere. The **post office** is ten minutes' walk away, in the centre of town.

Velankanni

At **VELANKANNI**, 11km south of Nagapattinam, a strong atmosphere of devotion pervades the white, spired Roman Catholic church of **Our Lady of Good Health**, the Lourdes of south India. Families hold lighted candles, up to 1m tall, in front of the altar, while officials wave their carrier bags of offerings in front of the image of the Virgin. Rows of display cases in the **museum** (daily 9am–6pm) contain silver and gold models of parts of the body – arms, legs, feet, livers, hearts – and of objects such as cars, cows, stethoscopes and houses. Each is accompanied by a testimonial and photograph of the person whom Our Lady has helped. Also on show is a case of various gold jewellery stated to have been stolen on November 20 1987, and recovered by police "with miraculous help of Our Lady" on November 20 1988, as well as hundreds of notes, in Tamil and English, thanking Her for enabling couples to have children (especially the male variety) and students to pass their exams. Next door to the museum a shop sells plastic finger rings, postcards and novelty picture key-rings that flash between images of Our Lord and Our Lady. Close by are several simple "meals" **restaurants**.

Kodikkarai (Point Calimere)

On a small knob of land jutting out into the sea, 65km south of Nagapattinam and 80km southeast of Thanjavur, **KODIKKARAI BIRD SANCTUARY** plays host to around 250 species in an area of swampland, known as "the great swamp", and dry evergreen forest. On the way to the sanctuary, you pass through fifty thousand acres of salt marshes around **Vedaranyam**, the nearest town, 11km north – vast salt fields, traditionally the mainstay of the local economy, line the road, the salt drying in thatched mounds. During the Independence struggle this was an important site for demonstrations in sympathy with Gandhi's famous salt protest (see p.562). Over the last few years, however, salt has been pushed into second place by prawn cultivation, which brings a good income, but has necessitated widespread forest clearance and has reduced the numbers of birds visiting Kodikkarai.

The **best time** to visit the sanctuary is between November and February, when migratory birds come, mostly from Iran, Russia and Poland, to spend the winter. The rarest species include black bittern, barheaded goose, ruddy shelduck, Indian blackcrested baza and eastern steppe eagle. During December and January the swamps host spotted billed pelicans and around 10,000 flamingoes – who live on tiny shrimp (the source of the lurid pink colouring of their plumage), and whose numbers have dropped from the 30,000 that wintered here in the days before prawn production took off. The deep forest is the home of one of the most colourful birds in the world, the Indian pitta (*pitta brachyura*), which, though little bigger than a sparrow, sports a black, orange and white head, orange and yellow stomach, brown, blue, black, light and dark green wings each with a white spot and a tail of red, blue and black.

Prodigiously well-informed local **guides**, equipped with powerful binoculars, can take you to key wildlife haunts. The Forest Department works with the Bombay Natural History Society to ring birds and trace their migrating patterns, and occasionally the BNHS organizes **field trips** around the area.

From the jetty, you might be lucky enough to spot a school of **dolphins**. To do so, however, you need to seek permission from the Navy Command – Kodikkarai is only 40km across the Palk Strait from Jaffna, and from the grounds of the *Rest House* (see below) the navy monitors all seaborne activity between Sri Lanka and the Indian coast.

Practicalities

Kodikkarai can only be reached (by regular bus) via Vedaranyam, connected by **bus** to Nagapattinam, Thanjavur, Trichy, Madras and Ramanathapuram (for Rameshwaram). Madras buses can be booked in advance in a house next door to *Shitharthan Medical Stores* on Vedaranyam's E Main St (over the road from the bus stand). The nearest **railway station** is 30km away at Tiruthuraipondi.

The only **accommodation** in the area, the Forest Department's exceptionally inexpensive *Poonarai Rest House* (reserve through *DFO*, 281/1846 W Main St, Thanjavur; ①), has ten plain, spacious rooms, each with chairs, desk, fan, bedding, bath and balcony. Apart from in January, when the rest house is invariably full, it's usually possible to turn up without a reservation. **Food** is limited to a couple of *chai* shops outside the gate, although staff will bring it in if asked. If you need to eat in **Vedaranyam** turn left out of the bus stand, and again at a T-junction, into the main bazaar, Melai St. The best place is the simple *Karaivani*, on the left-hand side, which serves veg "leaf" meals.

Tiruchirapalli and around

TIRUCHIRAPALLI – more commonly referred to as **Trichy** – stands in the plains between the Shevaroy and Palani hills, just under 100km north of Madurai. Dominated by the dramatic Rock Fort, it's a sprawling commercial centre with a modern feel; the town itself holds little attraction, but pilgrims flock to **temples** such as the spectacular **Ranganathaswamy temple** in **Srirangam**, 6km north. You'll need at least a day to make the most of a visit to this structure, taking time to meander through cloisters and open courtyards and to discover some of the finest masonry in the south.

The precise date of Trichy's foundation is uncertain, but though little early architecture remains it is clear that between 200 and 1000 AD control of the city passed between the Pallavas and Pandyas. The Chola kings who gained supremacy in the eleventh century embarked upon ambitious building projects, reaching a zenith with the Ranganathaswamy temple. In the twelfth century, the Cholas were subverted by the Vijayanagar kings of Hampi, who stood proudly against invading Muslims until they were eventually overcome in 1565 by the Sultans of the Deccan. Less than fifty years later the Nayaks of Madurai came to power, constructing the fort and firmly establishing Trichy as a trading city. After almost a century of struggle against the French and British, who both sought lands in southeast Tamil Nadu, the town came under British control until it was declared part of Tamil Nadu state in 1947.

Arrival and information

Trichy's **airport**, 8km south of the centre, serves Madras (Mon, Thurs & Fri; 2hr 20min) and Madurai (daily except Sun; 30min). The journey into town, by taxi (Rs60–80) or bus (#7, #28, #59, #63, #122 or #K1) takes less than half an hour; for

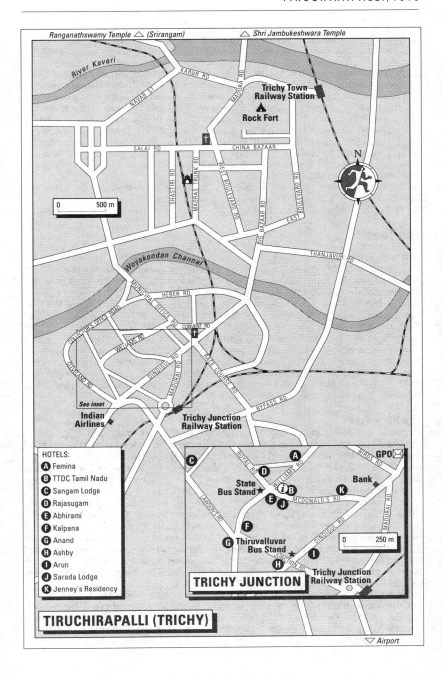

Ranganathswamy Temple △ (Srirangam)   △ Shri Jambukeshwara Temple

Trichy Town Railway Station

Rock Fort

River Kaveri

KARUR RD

NAVAB ST

MADURA RD

SALAI RD

CHINA BAZAAR

SHASTIRI RD

MADRAS TRUNK RD

WEST BOULEVARD RD

BIG BAZAAR RD

EAST BOULEVARD RD

N

0   500 m

Woyakondan Channel

THANJAVUR RD

MUNICIPAL OFFICE RD

HEBER RD

COLLECTORS OFFICE ROAD

WILLIAMS RD

CONVENT RD

RAMELAND RD

DINDIGUL RD

MADURAI RD

RACE COURSE RD

BYPASS RD

See inset

Indian Airlines

Trichy Junction Railway Station

HOTELS:
A Femina
B TTDC Tamil Nadu
C Sangam Lodge
D Rajasugam
E Abhirami
F Kalpana
G Anand
H Ashby
I Arun
J Sarada Lodge
K Jenney's Residency

GPO

BIRDS RD

ROYAL RD

WILLIAMS RD

State Bus Stand

Bank

MADURAI RD

McDONALD'S RD

LAWSON'S RD

Thiruvalluvar Bus Stand

JUNCTION RD

DINDIGUL RD

0   250 m

TRICHY JUNCTION

Trichy Junction Railway Station

TIRUCHIRAPALLI (TRICHY)

▽ Airport

---

enquiries and bookings go to *Indian Airlines* on Dindigul Rd (☎463116). There are also two weekly flights from **Colombo** on *Air Lanka* (based in the *Hotel Femina*; ☎460844).

Trichy's main railway station, **Trichy Junction** – which has given its name to the southern district of town – provides frequent rail links with Madras, Madurai and the east coast. From here you're within easy reach of most hotels, restaurants and banks, as well as the **bus stands**. State transport and Thiruvalluvar buses run frequently to major towns such as Madurai – during the day, Thiruvalluvar buses depart from the central bus stand, and only go from their own stand after 6pm. The efficient local service (#1) is the most convenient way of getting to the Rock Fort and Srirangam. **Rickshaws** are also widely available.

The **tourist office** (Mon–Fri 10.30am–5.45pm; ☎460136), stocked with maps and information, is opposite the State bus stand in Trichy Junction just outside *Hotel Tamil Nadu*. **Banks** for foreign exchange include the *State Bank of India* on Dindigul Rd.

The Town

Although Trichy conducts most of its business in **Trichy Junction**, the southern district, the main sights are at least 4km north. The **bazaars** immediately north heave with locally made cigars, textiles and fake diamonds made into inexpensive jewellery and used for dance costumes. As you follow the northbound Big Bazaar Rd (a continuation of Dindigul Rd), you're confronted by a looming solid stone hill, **Rock Fort**, an unexpected vision in the otherwise flat town, topped by a seventeenth-century Vinayaka (Ganesh) temple.

North of the fort, the wide River Kaveri marks the boundary between Trichy's crowded streets and its more serene temples; the **Ranganathaswamy temple** is so large it holds much of the village of Srirangam within its courtyards. Also north of the Kaveri is the elaborate **Shri Jambukeshwara temple**, while several British **churches** in Trichy town make for an interesting contrast. The **Shantivanam ashram**, a bus ride away, is open to visitors year round.

The Rock Fort

Dramatic and downright incongruous, Trichy's **Rock Fort** (daily 6am–8pm; Rs0.50 camera Rs10), looms over the bazaars and a rectangular water tank in the north of town. The massive sand-coloured rock towers to a height of more than 80m, its irregular sides smoothed by wind and rain. The Pallavas were the first to cut into it, building temples in cool recesses, but it was the Nayaks who grasped the site's potential as a fort, adding only a few walls and bastions as fortifications.

Once you've craned your neck up to look at the Rock Fort from the outside, a walk through China Bazaar leads past shops and stalls overflowing with jewellery, clothes, imitation designer perfumes, films, transistors and clocks, to the fort's entrance, just beyond a pair of whitewashed Jain temples. At the entrance, where a weary elephant gives blessings in exchange for a few coins, the atmosphere becomes cool and clammy, and the passageway leads to a shrine at the base of the rock. A broad flight of painted steps ascends from here, passing Pallava and Pandya rock-cut temples, notable for their simple design, and closed to non-Hindus.

Near the top, you emerge into daylight to join a sloping path up to the simple rectangular **Ganesh temple** on the very summit. The temple is closed to non-Hindus, but anyone can enjoy the **views**, which take in the Ranganathaswamy and Jambukeshwara temples to the north, their *gopuras* rising from a sea of palms; to the south, red-brown tiled roofs and yellow-washed houses stretch as far as the eye can see.

Shri Jambukeshwara temple

By the side of the Madras-bound road north out of Trichy, the **Shri Jambukeshwara temple**, dedicated to Shiva, is smaller and later than the Ranganathaswamy temple. Much of it is closed to non-Hindus, but the sculptures that adorn the walls in its outer courts, of an extravagance typical of the seventeenth-century Nayak architects, are worth the short detour.

Srirangam: Ranganathaswamy temple

The **Ranganathaswamy temple** at **Srirangam**, 6km north of Trichy, is among the most revered shrines to Vishnu in south India, and also one of the largest and liveliest, engulfing within its outer walls homes, shops and markets. Enclosed by seven rectangular walled courtyards and covering more than sixty hectares, it stands on an island defined by a tributary of the River Kaveri. This location symbolizes the transcendence of Vishnu, housed in the sanctuary reclining on the coils of the snake Adisesha, who in legend formed an island for the god, resting on the primordial Ocean of Chaos. Frequent **buses** from Trichy pull in and leave from outside the southern gate.

The temple is approached from the south. A gateway topped with an immense and heavily carved *gopura*, plastered and painted in bright pinks, blues and yellows, and completed as recently as 1987, leads to the outermost courtyard, the latest of seven built between the fifth and seventeenth centuries. Most of the present structure dates from the late fourteenth century, when the temple was renovated and enlarged after a disastrous sacking by the Delhi armies in 1313. The outer three courtyards, or *prakaras*, form the hub of the temple community, housing ascetics, priests, and musicians, and the streets are lined with food stalls and shops selling souvenirs, ritual offerings and plump fresh flower garlands to be presented to Vishnu in the inner sanctuary.

At the fourth wall, the entrance to the temple proper, visitors remove footwear before passing through a high gateway, topped by a magnificent *gopura* and lined with small shrines to teachers, hymn-singers and sages. In earlier days, this fourth *prakara* would have formed the outermost limit of the temple, and was the closest members of the lowest castes could get to the sanctuary. It contains some of the finest and oldest buildings of the complex, including a temple to the goddess **Ranganayaki** in the northwest corner where devotees worship before approaching Vishnu's shrine. On the east side of the *prakara*, the heavily carved "thousand pillared" *kalyan mandapa*, or hall, was constructed in the late Chola period. During the month of Margali (Dec/Jan) Tamil hymns are recited from its southern steps as part of the Vaikuntha Ekadasi festival.

The pillars of the outstanding **Sheshagiriraya Mandapa**, south of the *kalyan mandapa*, are decorated with rearing steeds and hunters armed with spears. These are splendid examples of **Vijayanagar** style, which depicts chivalry defending their temple against Muslim invaders, and represents the triumph of good over evil. On the southern side of the *prakara*, the Venugopala shrine, dedicated to Krishna, probably dates from the Nayak period (late sixteenth century). Its pillars are carved with beautiful maidens leaning on trees, playing musical instruments and gazing into mirrors. Inside the porch, paintings show Krishna playfully courting his *gopis* (cowgirls). The western side of the courtyard is taken up by a large pond, which blossoms with lotus flowers in spring, when Vishnu is laid upon its waters in a barge at the height of a three-day festival. To the right of the gateway into the fourth courtyard, a small **museum** (daily 10am–noon & 3–5pm) contains a modest collection of stone and bronze sculptures, and some delicate ivory plaques. For a small fee you can climb to the roof of the fourth wall and take in the view over the temple rooftops and *gopuras*, which increase in size from the centre outwards. The central tower, crowning the holy sanctuary, is coated in gold and carved with images of Vishnu's *avatars*, or incarnations, on each of its four sides.

Inside the gate to the third courtyard – the final section of the temple open to non-Hindus – is another pillared hall, the **Garuda Mandapa**, carved throughout in typical

Nayak style. Maidens, courtly donors and Nayak rulers feature on the pillars that surround the central shrine to Garuda, the man-eagle vehicle of Vishnu. Other buildings in the third courtyard include the vast kitchens, which emanate delicious smells as *dosas* and *vadas* are prepared for the deity, while devotees ritually bathe in the tanks of the moon and the sun in the northeast and southeast corners.

Chola structures and more recent shrines added by Vijayanagar and Nayak donors fill the second courtyard, while the dimly lit innermost courtyard, the most sacred part of the temple, shelters the image of Vishnu in his aspect of Ranganatha, reclining on the serpent Adisesha. The shrine is usually entered from the south, but for one day each year, during the **Vaikuntha Ekadasi festival**, the north portal is opened; those who pass through this "doorway to heaven" can anticipate great merit. Most of the temple's daily festivals take place in the courtyard, beginning each morning with *vina*-playing and hymn-singing as Vishnu is awakened in the presence of a cow and an elephant, and ending just after 9pm with similar ceremonies.

For more on Ranganathaswamy and Tamil Nadu's other great temples, see p.984.

Around Tiruchirapalli: Shantivanam ashram

The fascinating **Shantivanam** (Sanskrit for "Peace Forest") **ashram** (☎04323/3060) is in the small village of **THANNEEPALLI**, about forty minutes by bus on the route to Kullithalai, northwest of Trichy. The programme here is based on a fusion of Christianity and Hinduism, the work of an extraordinary Benedictine monk, Bede Griffiths, who died in 1993 at an advanced age. In the ashram's chapel, lines from the *Bhagavad Gita* and Om symbols share space with crosses and Biblical verses. Visitors can participate in as much or as little of the programme as they wish, staying in dorms or private rooms, and sharing meals, in exchange for a donation and chores. The ashram is usually full during Christian celebrations.

Accommodation and eating

Trichy has no shortage of **hotels** to accommodate the thousands of pilgrims that visit the town. Close to the bus stand you'll find an assortment of basic inexpensive lodges and some characterless but comfortable more upmarket hotels. If you want to stay in **Srirangam** the only option is the simple, minimally clean *Dandayuthapani Lodge* (①).

For **eating**, your best bet is the hotels, most of which serve good, reasonably priced south Indian food at a higher standard than the town's basic "meals" houses. Most places also have at least some Chinese dishes on the menu.

Abhirami, 10 McDonald's Rd (☎460001). Tower block opposite the State bus stand. Clean, anonymous rooms, and one of the best restaurants in town. ③–⑤.

Anand, 1 Racquet Court Lane (☎460545). Very clean, sizeable rooms (some with a/c) with attached bath and towels provided. The good restaurant serves standard south Indian dishes. ③–⑤.

Arun, 24 Dindigul Rd (☎461421). Large hotel near the Thiruvalluvar bus stand. Impersonal, but clean enough. Restaurant and travel counter. ③–④.

Ashby, 17A Junction Rd (☎460652). Pleasant place facing Thiruvalluvar bus stand. Dim, big rooms (some a/c) with verandahs around a leafy courtyard. Small bar and restaurant, serving north and south Indian dishes and a few Chinese options; very slow service, and Western clientele. ③–⑤.

Femina, 14C Williams Rd (☎461551). Well-maintained place east of the State bus stand. Rooms and suites, some with balconies looking to the Rock Fort. Plush restaurants, 24hr coffee bar. ⑤–⑥.

Jenney's Residency, 3/14 McDonald's Rd (☎461302). Smart, homely carpeted a/c and non-a/c rooms; some family suites. "Wild West" bar, and two good restaurants – including an upmarket Chinese place – cocktail bar and swimming pool, open to non-residents for Rs50. ⑥–⑦.

Kalpana, 9A Rockins Rd (☎460011). Simple and comfortable lodge with spartan rooms. ②.

Rajasugam, 13-B/1 Royal Rd (☎460636). Clean rooms, and a popular open-air veg restaurant. ③.

Sangam, Collector's Office Rd (☎464700). The most upmarket place in town, with all facilities. ⑦.

Sarada Lodge, McDonald's Rd (☎460216). Comfortable, quiet place, set off the road. ②.

TTDC Tamil Nadu, McDonald's Rd (☎460383). Good, well-kept rooms with large clean bathrooms overlooking a quiet gardened compound. ③.

Madurai

One of the oldest cities in south India, the seat of power for the ancient Pandya dynasty, **MADURAI**, on the banks of the River Vaigai, is an archetypal Hindu city, a swirl of life revolving around its mighty **Meenakshi-Sundareshwarar temple**. Any day of the week no less than 15,000 people pass through its gates; increasing to 25,000 on Friday, sacred to the fish-eyed Meenakshi (see p.1026). The temple's ritual life spills out into the streets in an almost ceaseless round of festivals and processions.

Madurai is the subject of an extraordinary number of myths. Its origins stem from a *sthala* (a holy site where legendary events have taken place) where Indra, the king of the gods, bathed in a holy tank and worshipped Shiva. Hearing of this, the Pandyan king Kulashekhara built a temple on the site and installed a *shivalingam*, around which the city grew. The name Madurai is popularly derived from the Tamil word *madhuram*, meaning "sweetness"; according to legend, Shiva shook his matted locks over the city, coating it with a fine sprinkling of *amrita*, the nectar of immortality.

Madurai's urban and suburban sprawl creates traffic jams to rival India's very worst. Chaos on the narrow, potholed streets is exacerbated by demonstrations and processions, wandering cows – demanding right of way with a peremptory nudge of the haunch – and put-upon pedestrians forced onto the road by ever-increasing numbers of street traders. Open-air kitchens extend from *chai*-shops, where competing *paratha-wallahs* literally drum up custom for their fresh breads with a tattoo of spoon-on-skillet signals. Given the traffic problems, it's just as well that Madurai, with a profusion of markets and intriguing corners, is an absorbing city to walk around. When some respite from the clamour of the city is required, the River Vaigai is close by.

A little history

Although invariably interwoven with myth, the traceable history and fame of Madurai stretches back well over 2000 years. Numerous natural **caves** in local hills and boulders, often modified by the addition of simple rock-cut beds, were used both in prehistoric times and by ascetics, such as the Ajivikas and Jains, who practised withdrawal and penance. In the third century BC, the Greek ambassador **Megasthenes** told of the city's splendour, and of its queen, Pandai, "a daughter of Herakles".

Madurai appears to have been the capital of the Pandyan empire without interruption for at least a thousand years. It became a major commercial city, trading with Greece, Rome and China; *yavanas* (a generic term for foreigners), frequent visitors to Pandyan seaports, were employed as palace guards and policemen. Long a seat of Tamil culture, under the Pandyas Madurai is credited with being the site of three literary **sangams**, "academies", said to have lasted 10,000 years and supported some 8000 poets. Despite this fanciful reckoning, the most recent of these academies does have an historical basis; the "Sangam period" is generally taken to mean the first three to four centuries of the Christian era.

The Pandyas' capital fell in the tenth century, when the **Chola** King Parantaka took the city; they briefly regained power in the thirteenth century, but early in the 1300s the notorious **Malik Kafur**, the Delhi Sultanate's "favourite slave", made an unprovoked attack during a plunder-and-desecration tour of the south, and destroyed much of the city. Forewarned of the raid, the Pandya king, Sundara, fled with his immediate family and treasure, leaving his uncle and rival, Vikrama Pandya, to repel Kafur. Nevertheless, the latter returned to Delhi with booty said to consist of "six hundred and twelve elephants, ninety-six thousand *mans* of gold, several boxes of jewels and pearls and twenty thousand horses".

Shortly after this raid Madurai became an independent Sultanate; in 1364, it joined the Hindu **Vijayanagar** empire, ruled from Vijayanagar/Hampi (see p.1163) and administered by governors, the **Nayaks**. In 1565, the Nayaks asserted their own independence. Under their supervision and patronage, Madurai enjoyed a renaissance, being rebuilt on the pattern of a lotus centring on the Meenakshi temple. Part of the palace of the most illustrious of the Nayaks, **Thirumalai** (1623–55), survives today.

The city remained under Nayak control until the mid-eighteenth century when the **British** gradually took over. A hundred years later the British de-fortified Madurai, filling its moat to create the four Veli Streets that today mark the boundary of the old city.

Arrival and information

Madurai's small airport, 16km south of the city, is served by flights to and from Madras, Bombay and Thiruvananthapuram. Theoretically you should be able to get information at the **Government of Tamil Nadu Tourist Information Centre** booth by the exit, but it's not always open to meet flights. Very simple snack meals ("bread-omelette") are served at the **restaurant** (daily 9am–5pm). There's also a bookshop and a branch of *Indian Bank*, but they can't change money. **Taxis** into the city charge a fixed rate of around Rs125. Airport buses leave hourly either from near the exit or to the left, near the staff canteen.

Arriving in Madurai by **bus**, you come in at one of four stands, all served by long-distance and city buses. The largest, and nearest to the centre, is the **TTC stand** (Madras, Kerala, Karnataka and Andhra Pradesh) on W Veli St in the west of the old city, close to the railway station and most accommodation. **Arapalayam stand** (some services within the state, and Kerala) is in the northwest, close to the south bank of the river, about 2km from the railway station. **Palankanathan stand** (also written as Pazhanganatham; south Tamil Nadu and south Kerala) is in the southwest, 5km from the centre, and **Anna stand** (points north, such as the Chola cities) is 5km out in the northeast, north of the Vaigai.

The **railway station** is just west of the centre off W Veli St. You can leave your luggage at the office (24hr) next to the **reservations office** in the main hall where you'll also find a *Higginbothams* bookstall, STD telephone and a branch of the **Tourism Department Information Centre** (daily 6.30am–8.30pm; ☎33888), where you can make onward reservations (see p.1032). There's a veg **canteen** on Platform 1, and, unusually, a **pre-paid auto-rickshaw booth** outside the main entrance, open to coincide with train arrivals. There are no pre-paid taxis.

> The telephone **area code** for Madurai is ☎0452.

Information

In addition to the offices at the railway station and airport (see above), the **Tourist Dept Main Office**, W Veli St (Mon–Fri 10am–5.45pm, sometimes Sat 10am–1pm; ☎34757), provides useful information about Madurai and surrounding areas. They have details of **car rental** and will also arrange, with a little notice, **city tours** with one of the Government-approved **guides**, who can usually be found at the southern entrance to the temple. Find out their names first at the tourist office as they're a much better bet than the other guys hanging around; the latter, however well-meaning, may be ill-informed and more than likely will want to get you into a shop double-quick. Official guided tours, for one to four visitors, cost around Rs200 for a half-day, and Rs300 for up to eight hours. The fee for a temple tour is negotiable.

Madurai's **post office** is at the corner of Scott Rd and N Veli St. For postal services, enter on the Scott Rd side (Mon–Sat 8am–7.30pm, Sun & hols 9am–4.30pm; speedpost 10am–7pm); for fax and **telephone**, go in by the N Veli St side (Mon–Fri 8am–8pm). You can **change money** at the *State Bank of India*, 6 W Veli St, and the *Central Bank of India*, 15 Meenakshi Koil St. *Mastercard* and *Visa* are accepted at the *Andhra Bank* on W Chitrai St, but no currency or travellers' cheques. For **visa extensions**, call at the Foreigners' Regional Registration Office, Commissioner of Police, S Chithirai St.

Bike rental at low rates is available at *SV*, W Tower St, near the west entrance to the temple, or the stall on W Veli St, opposite the *Hotel Tamil Nadu*.

The City

The **old city** of Madurai, south of the River Vaigai and centred on the Meenakshi temple, is where you'll find the main markets, tourist office, post office, railway station, three of four main bus stands, and all the budget and mid-range accommodation. Principal streets are laid out concentrically around the temple and prefixed North, South, East or West, which helps somewhat with orientation. **North of the river** are a number of expensive hotels, the Gandhi Museum and the Anna bus stand.

Shri Meenakshi-Sundareshwarar temple

Enclosed by a roughly rectangular six-metre-high wall, in the manner of a fortified palace, the **Meenakshi-Sundareshwarar temple** (daily 5am–12.30pm & 4–9.30pm) is one of the largest temple complexes in India. Much of it was constructed during the Nayak period between the sixteenth and eighteenth centuries, but certain parts are very much older. The principal shrines (closed to non-Hindus) are those to Sundareshwar (Shiva) and his consort Meenakshi; unusually, the goddess takes precedence.

For the first-time visitor, confronted with a confusing maze of shrines, sculptures and colonnades, and unaware of the logic employed in their arrangement, it's very easy to get disorientated. However, if you're not in a hurry, this should not deter you. Quite apart from the estimated thirty-three million sculptures to arrest your attention, the life of the temple is absolutely absorbing, and many visitors find themselves drawn back at several different times of the day. Be it the endless round of *puja* ceremonies, loud *nagaswaram* and *tavil* music, weddings, *brahmin* boys under religious instruction in the *Vedas*, the prostrations of countless devotees, the busy glittering market stalls inside the east entrance, or, best of all, a festival procession, something is always going on to make this quite simply one of the most compelling places in Tamil Nadu.

Approximately fifty priests work in the temple, and live in houses close to the north entrance. They are easily identified – each wears a white *dhoti* (*veshti* in Tamil) tied between the legs; on top of this, around the waist, is a second, coloured cloth, usually of silk. Folded into the cloth, a small bag contains holy white ash. The bare-chested priests invariably carry a small towel over the shoulder. Most wear earrings and necklaces including *rudraksha* beads, sacred to Shiva. As Shaivite priests, they place three horizontal stripes of white ash on the forehead, arms, shoulders and chest and a red powder dot, sacred to the goddess, above the bridge of the nose. The majority wear

---

MEENAKSHI, THE FISH-EYED GODDESS

The goddess **Meenakshi** of Madurai emerged from the flames of a sacrificial fire as a three-year-old child, in answer to the Pandyan king Malayadvaja's prayer for a son. The king, not only surprised to see a female, was also horrified that she had three breasts. In every other respect, she was beautiful, as her name, Meenakshi ("fish-eyed"), suggests – fish-shaped eyes are classic images of desirability in Indian love poetry. Dispelling his concern, a mysterious voice told the king that Meenakshi would lose the third breast on meeting her future husband.

In the absence of a son, the adult Meenakshi succeeded her father as Pandyan monarch. With the aim of world domination, she then embarked on a series of successful battles, culminating in the defeat of Shiva's armies at the god's Himalayan abode, Mt Kailasah. Shiva then appeared at the battlefield; on seeing him, Meenakshi immediately lost her third breast. Fulfilling the prophecy, Shiva and Meenakshi travelled to Madurai, where they were married. The two then assumed a dual role, firstly as king and queen of the Pandya kingdom, with Shiva assuming the title Sundara Pandya, and secondly as the presiding deities of the Madurai temple, into which they subsequently disappeared.

their long hair tied into a knot, with the forehead shaved. Inside the temple they also carry brass trays holding offerings of camphor and ash.

Madurai takes the **gopura** so prominent in other southern temples to its ultimate extreme. The entire complex has no less than twelve such towers; set into the outer walls, the four largest rise to a height of around 46m, and are visible for miles outside the city. Each is covered with a profusion of gaily painted stucco gods and demons, with the occasional live monkey scampering and chattering among the divine images. It is sometimes possible, for a small fee, to climb the southern and tallest tower, to enjoy superb views over the town.

The most popular **entrance** is on the east side, where the *gopura* gateway has reopened after a period of closure following the inauspicious suicide of a temple employee who leapt from the top. You can also enter nearby through a towerless gate which is directly in line with the Meenakshi shrine deep inside. In the **Ashta Shakti Mandapa** ("Eight Goddesses Hallway"), a sparkling market sells *puja* offerings and souvenirs, from fat garlands of flowers to rough-hewn sky-blue plaster deities. Sculpted pillars illustrate different aspects of the goddess Shakti, and Shiva's sixty-four miracles at Madurai. Behind this hall, to the south, are stables for elephants and camels.

If you continue straight on from here, cross E Ati St, and go through the seven-storey **Chitrai gopura**, you enter a passageway leading to the eastern end of the **Pottamarai Kulam** (Tank of Golden Lotuses), where Indra bathed before worshipping the *shivalingam*. From the east side of the tank you can see the glistening gold of the Meenakshi and Sundareshwarar *vimana* towers. Steps lead down to the water from the surrounding colonnades, and in the centre stands a brass lamp column. People bathe here, prior to entering the inner shrines, or just sit, gossip and rest on the steps.

The ceiling paintings in the corridors are modern, but Nayak murals around the tank illustrate scenes from the *Gurur Vilayadal Puranam* which describes Shiva's Madurai miracles. Of the two figures located halfway towards the Meenakshi shrine on the north side, one is the eighth-century king Kulashekhara Pandyan, said to have founded the temple; opposite him is a wealthy merchant patron.

On the west side of the tank is the entrance to the **Meenakshi shrine** (closed to non-Hindus), popularly known as **Amman Koyil**, literally the "mother temple". The immovable green stone image of the goddess is contained within two further enclosures that form two ambulatories. Facing Meenakshi, just past the first entrance and in front of the sanctum sanctorum, stands Shiva's bull-vehicle, Nandi. At around 9pm, the movable images of the god and goddess are carried to the **bed chamber**. Here the final *puja* ceremony of the day, the **lalipuja**, is performed, when for thirty minutes or so the priests sing lullabies (*lali*), before closing the temple for the night.

The corridor outside Meenakshi's shrine is known as the **Kilikkutu Mandapa** or Parrot Cage Hallway. Parrots used to be kept just south of the shrine as offerings to Meenakshi; a practice discontinued in the mid-1980s, as the birds suffered due to "lack of maintenance". Sundareshwarar and Meenakshi are brought every Friday (6–7pm) to the sixteenth-century **Oonjal Mandapa** further along, where they are placed on a swing (*oonjal*) and serenaded by members of a special caste, the Oduvars. The black and gold, almost fairground-like decoration of the *mandapa* dates from 1985.

Across the corridor, the small **Rani Mangammal Mandapa**, next to the tank, has a detailed eighteenth-century ceiling painting of the marriage of Meenakshi and Sundareshwar, surrounded by lions and elephants against a blue background. Sculptures in the hallway portray characters such as the warring monkey kings from the *Ramayana*, the brothers Sugriva (Sukreeva) and Bali (Vahli), and the indomitable Pandava prince, Bhima, from the *Mahabharata*, who was so strong that he uprooted a tree to use as a club.

Walking back north, past the Meenakshi shrine, through a towered entrance, leads you to the area of the Sundareshwarar shrine. Just inside, the huge monolithic figure

TEMPLE FESTIVALS AT MADURAI

Date	Name	No. of days	Date	Name	No. of days
Jan/Feb	Teppa	12	July/Aug	Ati Mulaikkottu	10
Feb/March	Machi Mantala	10	Aug/Sept	Avani Mula	12
March/April	Kotaivasanta	9	Sept/Oct	Navaratri	9
April/May	Chittirai	12	Oct/Nov	Kolatta	6
May/June	Vasanta	10	Nov/Dec	Tirukkarttikai	10
June/July	Unchal	10	Dec/Jan	Ennai Kappu	9

The date of each of the Madurai temple's **annual festivals** varies each year; check with a tourist office when you plan your visit. The principal and most exciting component of most of them is the **procession** (*purappatu*, or "setting forth"), held on the morning and evening of every day. Each procession is accompanied by officiating *brahmins*, temple employees bearing royal insignia, umbrellas, silver staffs and, at night, flaming torches. The entourage is invariably preceded by the penetrating orchestra of **tavil** (barrel drum), hand cymbals, and the distinctive **nagaswaram** (double-reed oboe-like wind instrument), for which the Madurai area is particularly famous.

Processions circumambulate clockwise inside the temple, and many leave its precincts, starting from the east entrance, passing along the Chittirai, Avani Mula or Masi streets and, on special occasions such as the **floating festival** (days 10 and 11 of the Teppa ceremonies), leave the centre of the city altogether. Locals and visiting pilgrims crowd the streets for *darshan*, a view of the deities. The evening processions, weaving through the starlit night, are undoubtedly the most atmospheric.

Icons from the temple, special movable images, are taken out, lavishly clothed in silk and ornaments of rubies, sapphires, pearls, silver and gold. When the festival celebrates both Meenakshi and Sundareshwar, the contingent is usually led by Vinayaka (Ganesh, son of Shiva), as the "remover of obstacles", followed in succession by Subrahmanya (another son of Shiva), Sundareshwara (a multiple image of the marriage of Shiva), Meenakshi and Chandeshwara (another form of Shiva). On some occasions, the deities are enshrined by simple canopies, but on others they ride on silver or gold vehicles (*vahanas*) such as horses, elephants or, most auspiciously, huge silver bulls.

At the **Avani Mula** festival, the coronation of Shiva is celebrated and his Madurain miracles are enacted in a series of plays (*lilas*). During the greatest festival of all, **Chittirai**, more plays are staged, telling the story of Meenakshi. The eighth day sees the goddess crowned as queen of the Pandyas, and, on the tenth, her marriage to Shiva draws as many as 50,000 people to the temple. Out in the streets the next morning, mayhem ensues when the most elaborate transport is brought into use for procession. The god and goddess travel in fifteen-metre-high chariots, with giant wooden wheels, hauled through the streets by hundreds of devotees, all tugging on long ropes. Rising from a wooden platform, the massive pyramidal bamboo superstructures are decorated in colourful appliqué and fronted by a row of rearing wooden horses.

The god and goddess are taken to the banks of the River Vaigai, to meet Meenakshi's brother who, in southern mythology, is Lord Kallalagar (Vishnu). The icon of Vishnu is brought from the forested hilltop temple at Alagarkovil, 20km northeast of Madurai. Vishnu travelled to Madurai to give his sister away at the wedding, only to find on reaching the river that the ceremony had already occurred. Because of this, to appease the deity, the festivities always take place on the northern bank of the river.

of Ganesh, **Mukkuruni Vinayaka**, is said to have been found during the excavation of the Mariamman Teppakulam tank (see p.1029). Chubby Ganesh is well-known for his love of sweets, and during his annual **Vinayaka Chathurti festival** (Sept), a special *prasad* (gift offering of food) is concocted from ingredients including 300 kilos of rice, 10 kilos of sugar and 110 coconuts.

Around a corner, a small image of the monkey god **Hanuman**, covered with *ghee* and red powder, stands on a pillar. Devotees take a little with their finger for a *tillak*, to mark the forehead. A figure of Nandi and two gold-plated copper flagstaffs face the entrance to the **Sundareshwarar shrine** (closed to non-Hindus). From here, outsiders can just about see the *shivalingam* beyond a blue and red neon Tamil Om sign.

Causing a certain amount of fun, north of the flagstaffs are figures of Shiva and Kali in the throes of their dance competition (see p.1004). A stall nearby sells tiny **butter balls** from a bowl of water, which visitors throw at the god and goddess "to cool them down". If you leave through the gateway here, on the east, you'll find in the northeast corner the fifteenth-century **Ayirakkal Mandapa**, or thousand-pillared hall, now transformed into the temple **Art Museum**. In some ways it is a great shame, as screens have been erected and dusty educational displays replace a clear view of this gigantic hall. However, there's a fine, if rather dishevelled, collection of wood, copper, bronze and stone sculpture, an old nine-metre-high teak temple door and general miscellanea.

For more on the temples of Tamil Nadu, see p.984.

Vandiyur Mariamman Teppakulam tank and the floating festival

At one time, the huge **Vandiyur Mariamman Teppakulam** tank in the southeast of town (bus #4 or #4A; 15min) was full with a constant supply of water, flowing via underground channels from the Vaigai. Nowadays, thanks to a number of accidents, it is only filled during the spectacular Teppa **floating festival** (Jan/Feb), when pilgrims take boats out to the goddess shrine in the centre. Before their marriage ceremony, Shiva and Meenakshi are brought in procession to the tank, where they are floated on a raft, decorated with lights, which devotees pull by rope, three times encircling the shrine.

During the rest of the year the tank and the central shrine remain empty. Accessible by steps, the tank is most often used as an impromptu cricket green, and the shade of the nearby trees makes a popular gathering place. Tradition states that the huge image of Ganesh, Mukkuruni Vinayaka, in the Meenakshi temple, was uncovered here when the area was originally excavated to provide bricks for the Thirumalai Nayak Palace.

Thirumalai Nayak Palace

Roughly a quarter survives of the seventeenth-century **Thirumalai Nayak Palace** (daily 9am–1pm & 2–5pm; Rs1), 1.5km southeast of the Meenakshi temple. Much of it was dismantled by Thirumalai's grandson, Chockkanatha Nayak, and used for a new palace at Tiruchirapalli. What remains was renovated in 1858 by the Governor of Madras, Lord Napier, and again in 1971 for the Tamil World Conference. The palace originally consisted of two residential sections, plus a theatre, private temple, harem, royal bandstand, armoury, and gardens.

The surviving building, the **Swargavilasa** ("Heavenly Pavilion"), is a rectangular courtyard, flanked by 18-metre-tall colonnades. As well as occasional live performances of music and dance, the Tourism Department arranges a nightly **Sound and Light Show** (in English 6.45–7.30pm; Rs2–5), which relates the story of the Tamil epic, *Shilipaddikaram*, and the history of the Nayaks. Some find the spectacle edifying, and others soporific – especially when the quality of the tape is poor. In an adjoining hall, the palace **museum** (same hours) includes Pandyan, Jain and Buddhist sculpture, terracottas and an eighteenth-century print showing the palace in a dilapidated state.

All that remains of the **Rangavilasa**, the palace where Thirumalai's brother Muthialu lived, are just ten pillars, wedged in a tiny back street. Take Old Kudiralayam St, right of the palace as you face it, pass the Archaeological Department Office and turn right into Mahal Vadam Pokki St. The third turning on the left (opposite the *New India Textile Shop*) is the unmarked Ten Pillars South Lane. One pillar contains a **shivalingam** which is worshipped by passers-by.

Tamukkam Palace: the Gandhi and Government museums

Across the Vaigai, 5km northeast of the centre near the Central Telegraph Office, stands **Tamukkam** (bus #3; 20min), the seventeenth-century multi-pillared and arched palace of Queen Rani Mangammal. Built to accommodate such regal entertainments as elephant fights, Tamukkam was taken over by the British, used as a courthouse and collector's office, and in 1955 became home to the Gandhi and Government museums.

Madurai's **Gandhi Museum** (daily 10am–1pm & 2–5.30pm), far better laid out than most of the species, charts the history of India since the landing of the first Europeans, viewed in terms of the freedom struggle. Generally the perspective is national, but where appropriate, reference is made to the role played by Tamils. Wholeheartedly critical of the British, it states its case clearly and simply, quoting the Englishman, John Sullivan: "We have denied to the people of the country all that could raise them in society, all that could elevate them as men; we have insulted their caste; we have abrogated their laws of inheritance; we have seized the possessions of their native princes and confiscated the estates of their nobles; we have unsettled the country by our exactions, and collected the revenue by means of torture." One chilling artefact, kept in a room painted black, is the bloodstained *dhoti* the Mahatma was wearing when he was assassinated. Next door to the museum, the **Gandhi Memorial Museum Library** (daily except Wed 10am–1pm & 2–5.30pm) houses a reference collection, open to all, of 15,000 books, periodicals, letters and microfilms of material by and about Gandhi.

Opposite, the small **Government Museum** (daily except Fri 9am–5pm; closed 2nd Sat each month) displays stone and bronze sculptures, musical instruments, paintings (including examples of Tanjore and Kangra styles) and folk art such as painted terracotta animals, festival costumes and hobby horses. There's also a fine collection of

---

SHOPPING AND MARKETS IN MADURAI

Old Madurai is crowded with **textile and tailors' shops**, particularly in W Veli, Avani Moola and Chitrai streets and Town Hall Rd. Take up the offers you're bound to receive to go into the shops near the temple, where locally produced textiles are generally good value, and tailors pride themselves on turning out faithful copies of favourite clothes in a matter of hours. Many shops in the immediate vicinity also offer an incentive by allowing visitors to climb up to their roofs for views over the Meenakshi complex. S Avani Moola St is packed with **jewellery**, particularly gold, shops, while at 10 N Avani Moola St, you can plan for the future at the *Life & Lucky Number Numerology Centre*.

Madurai is also a great place to pick up south Indian **crafts**. Among the best outlets are *All India Handicrafts Emporium*, 39–41 Town Hall Rd; *Co-optex*, W Tower St, and *Pandiyan Co-op Supermarket*, Palace Rd, for handwoven textiles; and *Surabhi*, W Veli St, for Keralan handicrafts. For souvenirs such as sandalwood, temple-models, carved boxes and oil lamps head for *Poompuhar*, 12 W Veli St (☎25517), or *Tamilnad Gandhi Smarak Nidhi Khadi Gramodyog Bhavan*, W Veli St, opposite the railway station, which sells crafts, oil lamps, Meenakshi sculptures and *khadi* cloth and shirts.

The old purpose-built, wooden-pillared fruit and vegetable market, between N Chitrai and Avani Moola streets, provides a slice of Madurai life that can't have changed for centuries; beyond it, on the first floor of the concrete building at the back, the **flower market** (24hr) is a riot of colour and fragrance. Weighing scales spill with tiny white petals and plump pink garlands hang in rows. Varieties such as orange, yellow or white marigolds (*samandi*), pink jasmine (*arelli*), tiny purple spherical *vanameli* and holy *tulsi* plants come from hill areas such as Kodaikanal and Kumili. These are bought in bulk and distributed for use in temples, or to wear in the hair; some are made into elaborate wedding garlands (*kalyanam mala*). The very friendly traders will show you each and every flower, and if you've got a camera will more than likely expect to be recorded for posterity. It's a nice idea to offer to send them a copy of any photograph you take.

shadow puppets, said to have originated in the Thanjavur area and probably exported to southeast Asia during the Chola period. A small house in which **Gandhi** once lived stands in a garden within the compound. Beside it, a number of unfinished latrines may have been intended as an exhibit, or a public amenity. It's rather hard to tell.

Kochadai Aiyannar temple

The village of **Kochadai**, a northwestern suburb of Madurai, has a beautifully maintained temple dedicated to **Aiyannar**, the Tamil village deity and guardian of the borders. Travelling in Tamil Nadu, you often see such shrines from the road, but it may not always be possible, or appropriate, to investigate them. Here, however, they are accustomed to visitors. Flanked by two huge garish *dvarpalas* (doorkeepers), the entrance opens directly onto two gigantic horses with riders and furious-looking armed attendants. The shrine on the left houses the god Rama and his brother Lakshmana and, facing the entrance, is the shrine to Aiyannar. To the right, the *alamaram* tree, also a shrine, apparently houses a **cobra**, fed with eggs and milk. According to the priests he only comes out during full moon.

During a big **festival** in the Tamil month of Panguni (March/April), Aiyannar is taken around the village to the accompaniment of music and fireworks. Kochadai is served by frequent buses (#68 or #54) en route to Solavandan.

Accommodation

Madurai has a wide range of **accommodation**, from rock-bottom lodges to good, clean mid-range places that cater for the flocks of pilgrims and tourists. There's a cluster of hotels on **W Perumal Maistry St**: if those listed below are full, you could also try the *Grand Central* (no 47; ②), *Keerthi* (no 40; ③) and *TM Lodge* (no 50; ③). Upmarket options lie a few kilometres out of the town centre, north of the Vaigai.

Aarathy, 9 Perumalkoil, W Mada St (☎31571). Great location, overlooking a temple near the TTC bus stand. All rooms with TV, some with a/c and balcony, and a superb open-air restaurant that is especially popular when the temple elephant is led through each morning. Only hampered by occasionally surly staff. ③.

Duke, 6 N Veli St close to the junction with W Veli St (☎26314). Modern hotel, a 10min walk from railway. Every surface is clean, but you may need to ask for acceptable bedsheets. Hot water, *Star TV* and room service, but no restaurant. Non-a/c options are the best value. ③–⑤.

International, 46 W Perumal Maistry St (☎31552). Standard and deluxe doubles with *Star TV* and balconies overlooking the street. No restaurant. ③.

Madurai Ashok, Alagarkoil Rd (☎42531). Plush hotel with 24hr room service, bar, currency exchange, craft shops and a swimming pool that costs Rs70 per day for non-residents. ⑨.

New College House, 2 Town Hall Rd (☎24311). Huge maze of a place; good budget option. ②.

Pandiyan, Race Course, north of the river (☎42471). Comfortable hotel with a good restaurant, bar, exchange facilities, travel agency, bookstores and several craft shops. Nice garden, too. ⑧.

Prem Nivas, 102 W Perumal Maistry St (☎37531). Fairly small, clean rooms, all with *Star TV*. Some a/c options and an a/c veg restaurant. ③–④.

Railway Retiring Rooms, first floor, stairway on platform 1 (turn right from the main entrance hall). Huge, clean rooms (some a/c) in this busy station. Often full. ①–②.

Sree Devi, 20 W Avani Moola St (☎36743). Good-value rooms (some a/c). No TV, or restaurant, but room service will send out for food. Great view over temple from the roof. ②.

Supreme, 110 W Perumal Maistry St (☎540330). Large hotel; all rooms with *Star TV*, and deluxe options with balcony and temple view. A duplex gives views of Yanna Malai hill range and railway line. Rooftop and vegetarian restaurants. ④.

Taj Garden Retreat, Pasumalai Hills (☎601020). Madurai's most exclusive hotel; a refurbished colonial house in the hills over the city, 6km out. Fifteen a/c rooms, restaurant, pool and bar. ⑧–⑨.

Thilaga, 111 W Perumal Maistry St (☎30762). Small, clean rooms with fan, in new building. ③–④.

TTDC Hotel Tamil Nadu I, W Veli St (☎37470). Busy but comfortable, with some a/c rooms and a restaurant. ③.

TTDC Tamil Nadu II (Star), Alagarkoil Rd (☎42462). The posher of Madurai's two government hotels, north of the river, 5km from the centre. Good-sized rooms (some a/c) and restaurant. ④.

Eating

As with accommodation, the range of places to eat in Madurai is gratifyingly wide, and standards are high, whether you're eating at one of the many utilitarian-looking "meals" places around the temple, or in a swanky hotel.

MOVING ON FROM MADURAI

By air
Indian Airlines, 7a W Veli St (☎26795) flies to **Madras** (Wed, Fri & Sun; 50min), **Bombay** (Tues, Fri, Sat & Sun; 1hr 50min) and Kozhikode (Tues, Thur & Sat; 45min). Daily flights to **Bombay** via **Thiruvananthapuram** are run by *East–West*, 119 W Perumal Maistry St (☎37595). *NEPC*, Ramnivas, 279 Goods Shed St (☎24520) have daily flights direct to Madras. In every case check in advance, as all flights are subject to change.

By train
To make onward train reservations, the **Tourism Department Information Centre** (see p.1025) in the entrance hall of the station is particularly helpful; with a member of staff, foreign visitors can shamelessly jump the long queue.

Madurai is well-connected to destinations in the south, but there are no direct trains to Bombay or Delhi. The fastest of the four daily services to **Madras**, the *Vaigai Express* #2636 (6.45am), calls at Trichy (2hr 20min), Villupuram (5hr) and Madras Egmore (7hr 40min). Slower Madras trains take 15hr, going via Thanjavur (5hr 10min), Kumbakonam (6hr), Chidambaram (8hr), Villupuram (11hr) and Chengalpattu (13hr 10min).

The three daily trains to **Rameshwaram** (4.45am, 2pm & 11.30pm; 5hr 30min–6hr 30min) call at Ramanathapuram (3hr–4hr15min). For **Ooty** and the **Nilgiris**, you have to take one of the two daily services to Coimbatore, and change there. The best is the sleeper *Coimbatore Express* #6116 (9.45pm; 7hr). One train daily, at an ungodly hour, runs to **Kanniyakumari** – the *Madras–Kanniyakumari Express* #6019 (4.10am; 6hr). From Kanniyakumari it's a 2hr hop to **Thiruvananthapuram**; otherwise, the daily *Madurai–Quilon Express* #6161 stops at Kollam (7.10pm; 10hr 40min), where you can change for Kottayam, Kochi and Thiruvananthapuram. There is one daily service each to **Bangalore** (*Madurai–Bangalore Express* #6531; 7.30pm; 12hr 30min) and express to **Tirupati** in Andhra Pradesh (*Madurai–Tirupati Express* #6800; 10.30am; 18hr 30min).

By bus
At the last count, four different stations operated long-distance **buses** from Madurai (see p.1025); check on the current situation with the tourist office, to avoid unscrupulous hustlers who may take you under their wing and charge inflated prices.

From the **TTC** stand, numerous *TTC* buses leave day and night to **Madras** (11hr). Destinations in **Karnataka** include Bangalore, of which there are 19 *TTC* (first 6am, last 10.15pm) and two *KSRTC* (7.45am & 10.30pm) buses. There are two per day to Mysore (4pm & 9.30pm) and one to Mangalore (4pm).

For **Kerala** there are three *JJTC* and two *PRC* buses a day to Kozhikode (12hr) via Palakaad (Palghat), and the same number to Ernakulam (10hr), for Kochi, via Kottayam. Five *TTC* buses daily run to Tirupati (14hr) in Andhra Pradesh.

Buses to **Coimbatore** (10hr) leave from the **Arapalayam** stand every 15min during the day and every 30min during the night. There are 11 a day to Kodaikanal (4hr). You can also get buses to Kumily (for Periyar Wildlife Sanctuary) every 30min, and one a day to Palakaad (9hr). The **Anna** stand offers regular buses to destinations north such as Thanjavur, Tiruchirapalli and Kumbakonam. Long-distance buses from **Palankanathan** stand include hourly services to both Kanniyakumari and Thiruvananthapuram.

Amutham, Town Hall Rd. Western, Chinese and Indian non-veg snacks and "meals".
Chettinad, Chitraikara St. A local favourite for country-style cooking.
Jaya Vilas Mess, E Avani Moola St. Popular with visitors from surrounding villages, in for a day's shopping. Non-veg meals at ridiculously low prices; a little extra for chicken and mutton gravy.
Madurai Ashok, see above. Smart hotel restaurant serving Indian, Chinese and Western food. Open 6am–11pm.
Mahal, Town Hall Rd. Acceptable a/c veg and non-veg restaurant; popular with backpackers.
Pandiyan, see above. Hotel restaurant with a reasonably priced lunchtime buffet and a varied evening menu; mostly Chinese and north Indian, with a few south Indian options.
Park Plaza, 114 W Perumal Maistry St. Rooftop non-veg restaurant with temple views.
Prem Nivas, see above. A/c veg restaurant, serving the usual Indian and Chinese dishes.
Supreme, see above. Mid-priced rooftop hotel restaurant with views of the temple, serving Indian, Western and Chinese veg dishes; pleasant in the evening. The downstairs *Surya* is also strictly veg.

Rameshwaram and around

The sacred island of **RAMESHWARAM**, 163km southeast of Madurai and less than 20km from Sri Lanka across the Gulf of Mannar, is a major Hindu pilgrimage site. Hindus tend to be followers of either Vishnu or Shiva, but Rameshwaram brings them together, being where the god Rama, an incarnation of Vishnu, worshipped Shiva in the *Ramayana*. The **Ramalingeshwara temple** complex, with its magnificent pillared walkways, is the most famous on the island, but there are several other small temples of interest, such as the **Gandhamadana Parvatam**, sheltering Rama's footprints, and the **Nambunayagi Amman Kali temple**, frequented for its curative properties. **Danushkodi**, "Rama's bow", at the eastern end of the peninsula, is where Rama is said to have bathed, and the boulders that pepper the sea between here and Sri Lanka, known as "Adam's Bridge", are the stepping stones used by Hanuman in his search for Rama's wife, Sita, after her abduction by Ravana, the demon king of Lanka.

Rameshwaram is always crowded with day trippers, and ragged mendicants who camp outside the Ramalingeshwara and the **Ujainimahamariamman**, the small goddess shore temple. An important part of their pilgrimage is to bathe in the main temple's sacred tanks and in the sea; the narrow strip of beach is shared by groups of bathers, relaxing cows and *mantra*-reciting *swamis* sitting next to sand *linga*. As well as fishing – prawns and lobsters for packaging and export to Japan – shells are a big source of income in the coastal villages.

Arrival and information

NH49, the main road from Madurai, connects Rameshwaram with Mandapam on the mainland via the impressive two-kilometre-long Indira Gandhi Bridge. Armed guards at checkposts at either end keep a watchful eye on travellers. **Buses** from Madurai (via Ramnad), Trichy, Thanjavur, Kanniyakumari and Madras pull in at the bus stand, 2km west of the centre. The **railway station**, 1km southwest of the centre, is the end of the line for trains from Madras, Coimbatore, Madurai and Ramnad, and boasts decent **retiring rooms**, a veg restaurant and a left luggage office (5.30am–10pm). There are two daily express trains to Madras and one to Coimbatore via Madurai. Buses run every half hour to Madurai and eight times daily to Kunniyakumari. Travel agents around the temple run faster and more comfortable **minibuses** around south India.

Red and white city buses run every ten minutes from the stand to the main temple; otherwise, **local transport** consists of unmetered cycle and auto-rickshaws that gath-

The telephone **area code** for Rameshwaram is ☎04573.

er outside the bus stand. Jeeps are available for rent near the railway station, and bicycles can be rented from shops in the four Car streets around the temple. There is no **ferry service** to and from Sri Lanka, due to the troubles there.

The tiny TTDC **tourist office**, 14 E Car St (Mon–Fri 10am–5pm; ☎21371), gives out information about guides, accommodation and boat trips. TTDC also have a counter at the railway station (to coincide with arriving trains; ☎21373), and a small booth at the bus stand (daily except holidays 10am–5.45pm). The **post office** is on Pamban Rd, the road to the bus stand.

Ramalingeshwara temple

If a man goes with an impure mind into a temple he adds to the sins that he had already and goes home a worse man than when he left it . . . If sin is committed in any ordinary place it can easily be removed; but sin in a Tirtha [place of pilgrimage] *cannot be removed . . . He who sees Shiva in the poor, in the weak and the diseased, really worships Shiva; and if he sees Shiva only in the image his worship is only preliminary. He who has served and helped one poor man seeing Shiva in him, without thinking of his caste or creed or race, Shiva is more pleased with him than with the man who sees Him only in temples . . . Unselfishness is the test of religion. And if a man is selfish, even though he has visited all the temples, seen all the places of pilgrimage and painted himself like a leopard, he is still further off from Shiva.*

From a speech by Swami Vivekananda at Ramalingeshwara,
inscribed in stone at the temple.

The core of the **Ramalingeshwara** (or Ramanathaswamy) **temple** was built by the Cholas in the twelfth century to house two much-venerated **shivalinga** associated with the *Ramayana*. After rescuing his wife Sita from the clutches of Ravana, Rama was advised to atone for the killing of the demon king – a *brahmin* – by worshipping Shiva. Rama's monkey lieutenant, Hanuman, was despatched to the Himalayas to fetch a *shivalingam*, but when he failed to return by the appointed day, Sita fashioned a *lingam* from sand (the *Ramanathalingam*) so the ceremony could proceed. When Hanuman eventually showed up with his *lingam*, in order to assuage the monkey's guilt Rama decreed that in future, of the two, Hanuman's should be worshipped first. The *linga* are now housed in the inner section of the Ramalingeshwara, not usually open to non-Hindus. Much of what can be visited dates from the 1600s, when the temple received generous endowments from the Sethupathi rajas of Ramnad (see p.1035).

High walls enclose the temple, forming a rectangle with huge pyramidal *gopura* entrances on each side. The gateways lead to a spacious closed ambulatory, flanked to either side by continuous platforms with massive pillars set on their edges. These **corridors** are the most famous attribute of the temple, their extreme length – 205m, with 1212 pillars on the north and south sides – giving a remarkable impression of receding perspective. Delicate scrollwork and brackets of pendant lotuses supported by *yalis*, mythical lion-like beasts, adorn the pillars.

Before entering the inner sections, pilgrims are expected to bathe in water from each of the twenty-two **tirthas** (tanks) in the temple; hence the groups of dripping wet pilgrims, most of them fully clothed, making their way from one tank to the next to be doused in a bucket of water by a temple attendant. Each tank is said to have special benefits: the Rama Vimosana Tirtha provides relief from debt, the Sukreeva Tirtha gives "complete wisdom" and the attainment of *Surya Loka*, the realm of the Sun, and the Draupadi Tirtha ensures long life for women and "the love of their spouses".

Monday is Rama's auspicious day, when the Padilingam *puja* takes place. **Festivals** of particular importance at the temple include **Mahashivaratri** (10 days during Feb/March), **Brahmotsavam** (10 days during March/April), and **Thirukalyanam** (July/Aug), celebrating the marriage of Shiva to Parvati.

Minor temples

The **Gandhamadana Parvatam** (daily 6–11am & 3.30–6.30pm), on a hill 2km north of Rameshwaram town centre, is a venerable shrine housing Rama's footprints. On some days, ceremonies are conducted here after the 5.30am *puja* at the Ramaling-esh-wara temple, encouraging pilgrims to climb the hill to continue their devotions. From the roof, fine views extend over the surrounding country; on clear nights you can see the lights of Jaffna.

Three kilometres east of town towards the old fishing village of Dhanushkodi, the small **Nambunayagi Amman Kali temple**, set in a quiet sandy grove 200m off the main road, attracts people in search of cures for illnesses. Inside a banyan tree next to it is a shrine dedicated to the spirit Retatalai, "the two-headed". A pair of wooden san-dals with spikes, said to belong to the spirit, is left in the shrine and locals say they can hear them clip-clopping at night when Retatalai chooses to wander. Pieces of cloth are tied to the branches of the tree to mark thanks for such boons as pregnancy after bar-renness and the healing of family feuds. The bus terminates at Dhanushkodi, from where you can walk along the ever-narrowing spit of sand until the sea finally closes in and the island peters out, tantalizingly short of Sri Lanka.

Accommodation

Apart from the TTDC hotels, **accommodation** in Rameshwaram is restricted to basic lodges, mostly in the Car streets around the temple. The temple authorities have a range of rooms for pilgrims; ask at the Devasthanam Office, E Car St (☎21292).

Chola Lodge, N Car St (☎21307). Basic place in the quietest of the Car streets. ①.

Maharaja's, 7 Middle St (☎21271). Good clean rooms next to the temple's west gate, two with a/c and TV. Temple views from balconies. No restaurant, but management will bring food in. ②.

Railway Retiring Rooms. Six large double and three triple rooms, generally cleaner (and quieter) than town lodges for the same price, plus a dorm. ①.

Santhiya Lodge, 1 W Car St (☎21329). Shabby, but very cheap. ①.

TTDC Hotel Tamil Nadu (Mandapam), 13km away, close to the mainland side of the Indira Gandhi bridge (☎41512). 12 double cottages on the beach, in a bay harbouring fishing boats. Primarily used by tour groups, so quite likely to be full. ②.

TTDC Hotel Tamil Nadu, near the beach (☎21277). The best place in Rameshwaram, in a pleas-ant location and with bar and restaurant. Comfortable, sea-facing rooms, some a/c; also cheaper dorm and hostel beds. Often full – book in advance from another TTDC hotel or office. ①–④.

TTDC Hotel Tamil Nadu II, near the railway station on Railway Feeder Rd (☎20171). New hotel, far cheaper than the above, and in a far less attractive location. ①.

Eating

Eating in Rameshwaram is more about survival than delighting the taste buds. Most places serve up fairly unexciting "meals".

Arya Bhavan and **Kumbakonam**, W Car St. Both run by the same family; standard veg "meals".

Ashok Bhavan, W Car St. Regional varieties of *thalis*.

Hotel Guru, E Car St. Delicious veg "meals" and snacks.

TTDC Hotel Tamil Nadu, near the beach. Gigantic, noisy, high-ceilinged glasshouse near the sea, serving good south Indian snacks and "meals" – many items on the menu are unavailable, however.

Around Rameshwaram: Ramnad (Ramanathapuram)

RAMNAD offers a possible break on the bus or train between Madurai (120km north-west) and Rameshwaram (36km east). It's worth stopping here to see the neglected but atmospheric **Ramalinga Vilas**, palace of the Sethupati rajas, who by tradition were guardians of the mythical Sethu bridge built by Rama to cross to Lanka.

The entrance to the palace (daily except Fri 9am–1pm & 2–5pm; Rs2), 2km from the bus stand, takes you into the big and dusty **Durbar Hall**, whose central aisle is hung with oil portraits of the rajas of the last few hundred years. Ceilings and walls throughout the building are decorated with early eighteenth-century murals depicting subjects such as business meetings with the English and battles with the Maratha king Sarabhoji, as well as scenes from the epics. One battle scene shows soldiers fighting with boomerangs, and there's a real Indian boomerang on display. Also on show are palm-leaf manuscripts, a Ravi Varma painting with appliquéd brocade, and sculptures of Vishnu from the eighth and thirteenth centuries. From the **throne room**, a secret passageway once gave an escape route to a local temple. The Raja's throne, supported on carved elephant legs, is decorated with a coat of arms, given by the British, featuring a lion and unicorn. As further proof of the royal family's compliance with the foreign power, the Raja, at the end of the eighteenth century, allowed them to use the bedchambers upstairs – decorated with erotic murals – as a meeting hall. This cosy relationship did not find unanimous approval among his subjects. Influential local landowners showed their contempt for the British by responding to tax demands with bags of stones and, in 1798 and 1801, rebellions took place, sometimes dubbed the "South Indian War of Independence". In 1803, at the request of the British, the Ramnad Raja was obliged to accept the lesser rank of Zamindar (feudatory chieftain).

On the roof is a stone bed on which the Raja would lounge in the evenings to enjoy panoramic views of the town and surrounding country. The buildings immediately below were royal guest houses, in one of which a descendant of the rajas now lives.

Kanniyakumari

KANNIYAKUMARI, at the southernmost extremity of India, is almost as compelling for Hindus as Rameshwaram. It is significant, not only for its association with a virgin goddess, Kanya Devi, but also as the meeting point of the Bay of Bengal, Indian Ocean and Arabian Sea. Watching the sun rise and set is the big attraction, especially on full moon day in April, when it's possible to see both the setting sun and rising moon on the same horizon. Although Kanniyakumari is in the state of Tamil Nadu, most foreign visitors arrive on day trips from Thiruvananthapuram, the capital of Kerala, 86km northwest. While the place is of enduring appeal to pilgrims, others may find it bereft of atmosphere, with nature's power to engender wonder in the human spirit obliterated by ugly buildings and hawkers selling shells and trinkets.

Arrival and local transport

Trains from Thiruvananthapuram, New Delhi, Bombay, Bangalore and even Jammu – at 86hr, the longest rail journey in India – stop at the **railway station** in the north of town, 2km from the seafront. The new Thiruvalluvar **bus stand**, near the lighthouse west of town, is served by buses from Thiruvananthapuram, Kovalam, Madurai, Rameshwaram (change at Madurai during the rainy season in Nov and Dec) and Madras. Taxis and auto-rickshaws provide **local transport**.

The Town

The seashore **Kumari Amman temple** (daily 4.30–11.30am & 5.30–8.30pm) is dedicated to the virgin goddess **Kanya Devi**, who may originally have been the local guardian deity of the shoreline, but was later absorbed into the figure of Devi, or Parvati, consort of Shiva. One version of Kanya Devi's story relates how she did penance to win the hand of Shiva. The god was all in favour and set out from Suchindram for the wedding, due to take place at midnight. The celestial *devas*, however, wanted Kanya Devi to remain a virgin, so that she could retain her full quota of *shakti* or divine power, and hatched a plot. Narada the sage assumed the form of a cock and crowed; on hearing this, Shiva, thinking that it was dawn and that he had missed the auspicious time for the ceremony, went home. The image of Kanya Devi inside the temple wears a diamond nose stud of such brilliance that it's said to be visible from the sea. Male visitors must be shirtless and wear a *dhoti* before entering the temple; non-Hindus are not allowed in the inner sanctum. It is especially auspicious for pilgrims to wash at the bathing *ghat* here.

The **Gandhi mandapam** (daily 6.30am–12.30pm & 3–7.30pm), 300m northwest of the Kumari Amman temple, is a curious modern imitation of an Orissan temple, so designed that the sun strikes the auspicious spot where the ashes of Mahatma Gandhi were laid, prior to their immersion in the sea, at noon on his birthday, October 2.

Possibly the original sacred focus of Kanniyakumari are two rocks, about 60m apart, half-submerged in the sea 500m off the coast, which came to be known as the Pitru and Matru *tirthas*. In 1892 they attracted the attention of the Hindu reformer Vivekananda, who swam out to the rocks to meditate. Incorporating elements of architecture from around the country, the 1970 **Vivekananda Memorial** (daily except Tues 7–11am & 2–5pm), reached by the Poompuhar ferry service from the jetty on the east side of town (every 30min; same hours), houses a statue of the saint. The footprints of Kanya Devi can also be seen here, at the spot where she performed her penance.

Accommodation and eating

As Kanniyakumari is a "must see" for Indian tourists and pilgrims, **hotels** can fill up early. However, recent developments have raised standards, and relieved the pressure on space. Aside from the usual "meals" places and hotel dining rooms, there are a few popular non-veg **restaurants** in the centre of town near the main shopping area, such as *Chicken Corner*.

Ganga Lodge, Main Rd (☎04653/71399). Decent basic rooms, popular with pilgrims. ①.

Kerala House, Seafront (☎04653/71229). Institututional-looking place whose cavernous doubles (2 a/c have dressing rooms and bathrooms, and some sea views. Food can be ordered in advance. ⑤.

Lakshmi Tourist Home, E Car St (☎04653/71333). Smart rooms, many facing the sea. Excellent non-veg restaurant. ②–④.

Manickam Tourist Home, N Car St (☎04653/71387). Good non-a/c, a/c and deluxe rooms with *Star TV*. Faces the sunrise and the Vivekananda rock. ③–⑤.

Samudra, Sannathi St (☎04653/71162). Smart new hotel near the temple entrance, with well-furnished deluxe rooms facing the sunrise. Star TV and veg restaurant. ④–⑥.

Tri-Sea Lodge, Bus Stand Rd (☎04653/71283). One of the best budget options, with some sea-facing rooms. ①–②.

TTDC Hotel Tamil Nadu, Seafront (☎04653/71257). Cottages (some a/c) and clean rooms (a/c first floor), most with sea view. Cheaper "mini" doubles at the back and a youth hostel dorm. Good square meals served in functional surroundings. ①–⑤.

Suchindram

Construction of the **Stanunathaswami temple** at SUCHINDRAM (12km northwest of Kanniyakumari) extended over a period of at least six hundred years. Parts date back as far as the ninth or tenth century, others from the fifteenth century, and a huge seven-storey pyramidal *gopura* was erected during the sixteenth. Although its main sanctuary houses a *shivalingam*, the temple is jointly dedicated to Brahma, Vishnu and Shiva. Its proudest boasts are "musical" pillars, which emit a chime when struck, and an extra-ordinarily tall (3m) figure of Hanuman. A special *puja* takes place at sunset (around 6pm) every Friday, with music and a procession. Male visitors must remove their shirts before entering.

The Ghats

The Eastern and Western Ghats, which separate Tamil Nadu from Karnataka and
Kerala, may not exactly rival the Himalayas, but like their counterparts further north
were much appreciated in the days of the Raj as escapes from the blast of the summer
sun. Much the best known of the **hill stations** – in fact better known, and more visited, than it deserves – is **Udhagamandalam** (formerly Ootacamund, still often "Ooty"),
in the **Nilgiris** (from *nila-giri*, "blue mountains"). The ride up to Ooty, on the **miniature railway** via Coonoor, is fun, and the views incredible, but in general, unless you
can afford to stay in the best hotels, the town itself comes as a rude shock.

The other main hill resorts are **Kodaikanal**, further south not far from Madurai, and
Yercaud, a low-key alternative within easy reach of Madras.

Salem and Yercaud

Situated in the low western ranges of the Shevaroy Hills, 100km northwest of Trichy,
the busy industrial town of **SALEM** spreads over gently undulating hills at the base
of the road that snakes 33km up to the peaceful hill station of **Yercaud**. Most of
Salem's temples, and its fort, are badly ruined, and overshadowed by modern concrete buildings; all it really has to offer is a small **museum** (daily except Fri
9am–12.30pm & 1–5pm) on Omalur Rd, with an uninspiring display of long-dead animals and a small collection of Chola bronzes. Every Tuesday, hundreds of traders
converge in the **bazaar** near Salem Market Station to sell locally made textiles in
makeshift stalls.

Few tourists make the detour to **YERCAUD**, but in contrast to the congestion and
clamour of Salem, this quiet, undisturbed town is a perfect spot to unwind and a convenient stop-off between Madras and Madurai or Coimbatore. Lower than Tamil Nadu's
other hill stations, at just 1515m, Yercaud more than makes up for its lack of views by
a picturesque setting among coffee plantations and thickly forested slopes, and supports a wide variety of flowers in its nurseries, parks and orchid house. Like any true
hill station, it also has a small artificial **lake**, fed by waters that flow from the higher
hills, forming a 300-metre waterfall just 3km away.

Practicalities

Salem is connected to Coimbatore, Cuddalore, Vellore and Madras by **train**; daily
buses include two or three from Trichy, Pondicherry and Coimbatore, and one from
Madras. A frequent bus service from Salem to Yercaud takes just under an hour.

What little **accommodation** there is in **Yercaud** is of a high standard. *Shevaroys* on
Hospital Rd (☎04281/22288; ⑤–⑦), near the lake, is the best hotel, with several cottages, well-maintained rooms, private bathrooms, a good restaurant and bar. The smaller, reasonably comfortable TTDC *Hotel Tamil Nadu* (☎04281/22273; ③–④) on Ghat Rd
is typical of the chain, with some a/c rooms and an inexpensive restaurant. Cheapest of
all is the simple TTDC *Youth Hostel* (①), not far from *Hotel Tamil Nadu*.

Hotels in **Salem** are more expensive, and less ideally located. The best of its dim,
grotty and inexpensive lodges is *Coimbatore Lodge* (☎0427/63649; ①) on Venkatroa St,
where rooms, with common bathrooms, are small and spartan. The *National*
(☎0427/54100; ④–⑥) on Bangalore Rd is smart but unimaginative, with a restaurant
and bar, and cottages in the grounds. Salem's grandest hotel is the modern *Salem
Castle* (☎0427/448702; ⑥–⑦) at A/4 Bharathi St, Swarnapuri; it has mirrored marble
halls, spotless rooms with TV and big bathrooms, and a swimming pool, bar and
restaurant.

Coimbatore

Visitors tend only to use the busy textile city of **COIMBATORE** as a stopover on the way to Ooty, 90km northwest. There's little to do here, but you could weave your way along the cacophonous shopping area near the bus stand, crowded with what seem like hundreds of tailors' shops, traders plying fragrant garlands of flowers piled on rough blankets on the ground, and canny shoeshine boys clamouring for your trade.

The telephone **area code** for Coimbatore is ☎0422.

Arrival and moving on

Coimbatore's two main **bus stands**, Central and Thiruvalluvar, are close together towards the north of the city centre; the busy town bus stand is sandwiched in between. From Central stand, on Dr Nanjappa Rd, buses leave for Ooty every thirty minutes. Buses to Bangalore and Mysore can be booked in advance at the **reservation office** (9am–noon & 1–8pm). There's also a frequent service to Ooty from the Thiruvalluvar stand on Cross Cut Rd, as well as regular buses to Madurai, Madras and Tiruchirapalli (Trichy). A third stand, Ukkadam, serves **local towns** such as Pollachi and Palghat; it's 4km from the others, in the southwest of the city next to the lake.

The **railway station**, 2km south of the bus stands, is well connected to major southern destinations. To meet up with the *Nilgiri Blue Mountain Railway* to Ooty (see p.1043), join the *Nilgiri Express* #6005 from Madras, which leaves Coimbatore at 6.30am, and change onto the narrow-gauge railway at Mettupalayam (7.45am). If you're catching this early train, try to stay near the railway station, or arrange transport the night before, as auto-rickshaws are few and far between at this hour of the morning.

Several overnight services leave for **Madras**, including the *Nilgiri Express* #6006 (8.35pm) and the *Cochin–Guwahati Express* #6313 (10.10pm). The daily *Rameshwaram Express* goes to Rameshwaram via Madurai; other daily trains are the *Nagercoil–Bangalore Express* #6525 for Bangalore (8.55pm; 9hr30min); *Trichy–Cochin Express* #6365 for Kochi (12.55am; 5hr 30min); and the *Mangala Link Express* #2617 for Delhi Hazrat Nizamuddin (8.10pm; 43hr).

From Coimbatore **airport**, 11km northeast and served by buses to and from the town bus stand, *Indian Airlines* fly four times a week to Bombay (via Madurai), Kozhikode and Madras. They have an office (☎213569) on Trichy Rd, 1km or so from the railway station. *Jet Air* (☎212037) run daily flights to Bombay, while *East–West* (☎210286) go daily except Saturday. Finally, *NEPC* (☎216741) goes daily to Madras, and daily except Sunday to Bangalore.

Accommodation and eating

Most of Coimbatore's **accommodation** is around the bus stands. The cheapest places line Nehru St and Sastri Rd. As for **eating**, your best bets are the bigger hotels, many of which serve splendid south Indian food to a predominantly business clientele.

Blue Star, 369 Nehru St (☎230635). Highly designed rooms, some without windows (non-a/c half the price of a/c). Veg and non-veg restaurant. ③–④.

City Tower, just off Dr Nanjappa Rd, 2-min walk south of the Central bus stand (☎230681). Modern interiors, heavy on leatherette and vinyls, but clean and decent (some a/c) with balconies. Superb veg and non-veg restaurants; the rooftop *Cloud 9* is especially recommended. ⑥–⑦.

Gateway, 517B Oppanakara St (☎391133). Good value; handy for the Ukkadam bus stand. ③–⑤.

Jothi, 8/80 Geetha Hall Rd (☎212077). Basic lodge in road opposite the railway station. ①.

Sri Aarvee, 311A Gandhipuram (☎433677). Clean business-style hotel, opposite the town bus stand. A/c and cheaper non-a/c rooms (all with *Star TV*). Good Andhra restaurant. ⑤.

Sri Ganapathy, 1 Sastri Rd (☎234814). Adequate lodge behind the Central bus stand. ②.

Srinivasa, 365 Nehru St (☎230116). Near the bus stands and just about OK for the price. ①.

TTDC Tamil Nadu, Dr Nanjappa Rd (☎236311). Opposite Central bus stand. Convenient clean and reliable; many rooms with *Star TV*. Light and airy veg and non-veg restaurant. ③–⑤.

Vaidurya, 72 Geetha Hall Rd (☎214582). Modern hotel with *Star TV*, near the railway station. ④.

Coonoor

COONOOR, a busy Indian town on the *Nilgiri Blue Mountain Railway* (see p.1043) lies at the head of the Hulikal ravine, 27km north of Mettupalayam and 19km south of Ooty, at an altitude of 1858m, on the southeastern side of the Dodabetta mountains. Often considered to be second best to its more famous neighbour, Coonoor has avoided Ooty's over commercialization, and can make a pleasant place for a short stop.

The steep hills and valleys surrounding Coonoor are carpeted with tea bushes, interspersed with eucalyptus and silver oak. **Tea-pickers** work the slopes, carrying wicker baskets of fresh leaves and bamboo rods that they use like rulers to ensure that each plant is evenly plucked. Once the leaves reach the factory, they're processed within a day, producing seven grades of tea. Orange Pekoe is the best and most expensive; the seventh and lowest grade, a dry dust of stalks and leaf swept up at the end of the process will be sold on to make instant tea. To visit a tea or coffee plantation, contact *UPASI* (United Planters' Association of Southern India), "Glenview", Coonoor.

Coonoor loosely divides into two sections, with the bus stand (regular services to Mettupalayam, Coimbatore and elsewhere in the Nilgiris), railway station and market huddled together in **Lower Coonoor**. In Upper Coonoor, **Sim's Park** is a fine botanical garden on the slopes of a ravine, with hundreds of rose varieties. Nearby **viewpoints** include Lamb's Rock (5km), overlooking Mettupalayam far away on the plains, and Dolphin's Nose (9km) which has spectacular views onto St Catherine's Falls on one side and Coonoor and Kotagiri streams, tributaries of the Bhavani, on the other.

Accommodation and eating

When it comes to finding somewhere to **stay** or **eat**, there's not a lot of choice in Coonoor, and it's not a good idea to leave it too late in the day to be looking for a room. By and large the hotels are dotted around Upper Coonoor within around 4km of the station; you'll need an auto-rickshaw to find most of them.

Blue Hills, Mount Rd (☎04264/20103). Standard, clean doubles with soulless formica furnishing. "Blue Hills" bus stop outside; 1km from central bus stand. Good non-veg restaurant. ④.

Monarch Ritz, Ritz Rd (☎04264/20484). Russian-designed building in Upper Coonoor, near Sim's Park. Needs refurbishment, but the pleasant garden has a reasonable restaurant and bar. ⑥.

Sri Lakshmi Tourist Home, Kamrajpuram, Rockby (☎04264/21022). Basic lodge with plain restaurant. ②–③.

Taj Garden Retreat, Hampton Manor (☎04264/20021). Excellent, expensive old hotel with cottage accommodation and real character. The restaurant, overlooking the pretty garden, is the best place to eat in town – try the spectacular lunchtime buffet. ⑨.

Venkateswara Lodge, Cash Bazaar (☎04264/22309). Very basic option near the bus stand. ②.

YWCA Guest House, Wyoming, near the hospital (☎04264/20326). Beautiful, characterful old building in peaceful garden. Five clean doubles and seven cheaper singles with hospital-style beds. Dining hall serves wholesome food. Very small and often full, so try phoning ahead. ④.

Udhagamandalam (Ootacamund)

Originally a Toda village, **UDHAGAMANDALAM**, established by the British in the nineteenth century as a retreat from the heat of the plains below, is still known as "Ooty", the "Queen of Hill Stations". Until the mid-1970s "Snooty Ooty" was home to

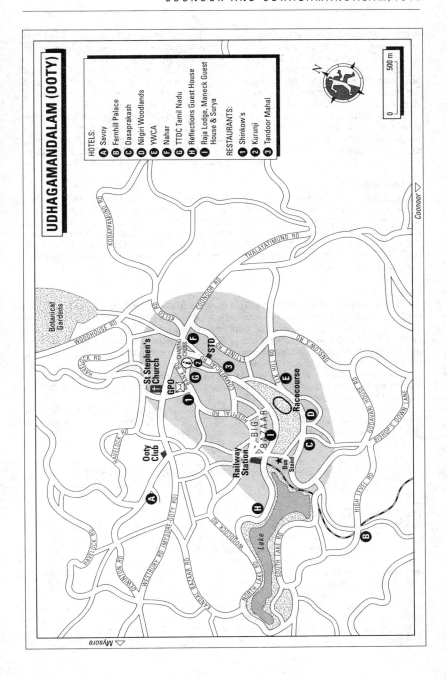

UDHAGAMANDALAM (OOTY)

HOTELS:
- Ⓐ Savoy
- Ⓑ Fernhill Palace
- Ⓒ Dasaprakash
- Ⓓ Nilgiri Woodlands
- Ⓔ YWCA
- Ⓕ Nahar
- Ⓖ TTDC Tamil Nadu
- Ⓗ Reflections Guest House
- Ⓘ Raja Lodge, Maneck Guest House & Surya

RESTAURANTS:
- ❶ Shinkow's
- ❷ Kurunji
- ❸ Tandoor Mahal

0   500 m

English bungalows, schools, shops and churches and to the last colonial inhabitants who chose to "stay on", living out their last days on tiny pensions that only here would allow them to keep a lifestyle to which they had become accustomed.

Since Independence, travellers have continued to be attracted by Ooty's cool climate and peaceful green hills, forest and grassland. However, if you come in the hope of finding quaint vestiges of the Raj, you're likely to be disappointed; what with indiscriminate development and a deluge of holidaymakers, they're few and far between.

The **best time to come** is between January and March, avoiding the high-season crowds (April–June & Sept–Oct). In May, the summer festival brings huge numbers of people and a barrage of amplified noise; worlds away from the peaceful retreat envisaged by the *sahibs*. From June to September, and during November, it'll be raining and misty, which appeals to some. From November to February it can get really cold.

Arrival and local transport

Most visitors arrive in Ooty either by bus from Mysore in Karnataka (the more scenic, if steeper, route goes via Masinagudi), or on the **miniature mountain railway** from Coonoor and Mettupalayam. The bus and railway stations are fairly close together, at the western end of the big bazaar and racecourse. **Local transport** consists of autorickshaws and taxis, which meet incoming trains and gather outside the bus stand and on Commercial Rd around Charing Cross. You can **rent bikes** but the steep hills make cycling very hard work.

Information

The **TTDC tourist office** (daily; ☎43977) in Super Market Building, Charing Cross, is eager to help, but information is not always reliable. You can book tours here, among them "Ooty, Pykara and Mudumalai" (daily 9am–7.30pm; Rs150), which calls at Pykara dam, falls and boathouse and Mudumalai Wildlife Sanctuary, making a very long day, and "Ooty and Coonoor" (daily 9am–6pm; Rs75), which goes to Sim's Park, the botanical gardens, the lake, Dodabetta Peak, Lamb's Rock and Dolphin's Nose.

Ooty's **post office**, northwest of Charing Cross at Town West Circle, off Spencers Rd and near St Stephen's Church, has a poste restante counter (enquiries and stamps Mon–Fri 9am–5pm; parcels Mon–Fri 9am–3pm & Sat 9am–2pm).

To arrange elephant rides, transport and accommodation at Mudumalai Wildlife Sanctuary, see the **Wildlife Officer**, in the Mahalingam & Co Building on Coonoor Rd (☎44098). It's almost inevitable that you'll need to book well in advance to get in.

The telephone **area code** for Udhagamandalam (Ooty) is ☎0423.

The Town

Ooty sprawls over a large area of winding roads and steep climbs. The obvious focal point is **Charing Cross**, a busy junction on dusty **Commercial Road**, the main, relatively flat, shopping street that runs south to the big bazaar and vegetable market. Goods on sale range from jewellery to fat plastic bags of cardamom tea, and presentation packs of eucalyptus oil. A little way northeast of Charing Cross, the **Botanical Gardens** (daily 8am–6.30pm; Rs5, camera Rs5, video Rs25), laid out in 1847 by gardeners from London's Kew Gardens, consist of twenty hectares of immaculate lawns, lily ponds and beds, with more than a thousand varieties of shrubs, flowers and trees. There's a refreshment stand, and shops outside sell candy floss, peanuts and snacks.

Northwest of Charing Cross, the small gothic-style **St Stephen's Church** was one of Ooty's first colonial structures, built in the 1820s on the site of a Toda temple; timber

THE NILGIRI BLUE MOUNTAIN RAILWAY

The famous **narrow-gauge Mountain Railway** climbs up from Mettupalayam on the plains, via Hillgrove (17km) and Coonoor (27km) to Udhagamandalam, a journey of 46km through forest, tea plantations, sixteen tunnels and more than 250 bridges. It's a slow journey of three-and-a-half to four hours – sometimes the train moves little faster than walking pace – but the views are absolutely magnificent.

In theory, trains up from Mettupalayam set off at 7.45am, but this depends on what time the *Nilgiri Express* (an overnight service leaving Madras at 9.15pm) arrives. If you're in Coimbatore, you can pick up the *Nilgiri Express* there, ostensibly at 6.30am. Some visitors prefer to come by shared taxi or bus from Mettupalayam, and take the train from Ooty to Coonoor as an excursion later on. During the peak season (April–June) there are three trains a day down from Ooty; the 6pm terminates at Coonoor, but the earlier two at 9.35am and 3pm go through to Mettupalayam where you can pick up regular trains to Coimbatore and beyond. The popular *Nilgiri Express* #6006 to Madras departs at 7.25pm.

for its bowed teak roof was taken from Tipu Sultan's Palace at Srirangapatnam and hauled up here by elephant. The area around the church gives some idea of what the hill station must have looked like in the days of the Raj; on the way up to it you'll pass **Spencer's** store on Church Hill, opened in 1909, which still serves from old wooden counters. Over the road from the church, tucked away, the charming little branch of **Higginbotham's** is still the best place to buy books. Nearby, in the same compound as the post office, gowned lawyers buzz around the red-brick **Civil Court**, a quasi-gothic structure with leaded diamond-shaped windows, corrugated iron roofs and a clock tower capped with a weather vane. Over the next hill (west), the most snooty of Ooty institutions, the **Club**, dates from 1830. Originally the house of Sir William Rumbold, it

TREKKING IN THE NILGIRIS

The best way to appreciate the Nilgiri Hills is to get well away from the towns by **trekking**; assorted routes, dotted with basic accommodation, wind through the local Reserved Forest. None is particularly difficult, but many lead through remote areas where help in an emergency is difficult to come by, and access is restricted to protect the environment.

If you arrive on spec, it can take up to a week to get the necessary permission from the relevant District Forest Officer (there are North and South divisions) at the **Nilgiri Wildlife and Environment Association**, based at the District Forest Department, North Division, Mt Steward Hill, Ooty (Mon–Fri 9am–5pm; ☎43968; postal address: Udhagamandalam, Nilgiris 643001). They can also advise about routes and guides.

Treks in the **west** of the region (best Dec–May) take you through largely uninhabited country with spectacular views, springs, rivers and rivulets, grassland, natural forest (*shola*) where wild flowers include rhododendron and orchids, and man-made forest of eucalyptus, wattle and pine. On the far west, at the edge of the escarpment that forms the western border of Mukurti Sanctuary, 1000-metre drops plummet to the heavy evergreen rainforest of Kerala. **Animals** include Nilgiri *tahr* and *sambar* (deer), wild dog, elephant, and even panther and tiger. The bird population is small: grey jungle fowl, hawks and harriers. At higher altitudes, bright daytime sunshine with temperatures of around 20°C is followed by a dramatic cooling to freezing point at night; warm clothing is essential.

The lower areas in the **north** and **east** are completely different; a dry, rough, rocky terrain with patches of dense thorny scrub, populated by diverse wildlife, including *sambar*, sloth bear and some *gaur* (Indian bison). Trekking is possible all year round, but the intense heat between March and May is not conducive to long walks.

became a club in 1843 and expanded thereafter. Entry is strictly restricted to members and their guests or members of affiliated clubs. Further along Mysore Rd, the modest **Government Museum** (daily except Fri & 2nd Sat of month 9am–1pm & 2–5pm) houses a few paltry tribal objects, sculptures and crafts.

West of the railway station and racecourse (races mid-April to mid-June), the **Lake**, constructed in the early 1800s, is one of Ooty's main tourist attractions, despite being heavily polluted. Honeymoon couples in particular go boating (8am–6pm; rowing, paddle and motor Rs20–100) and horse riding (short rides Rs10–40, or Rs80 per hour).

Fernhill Palace, close to the southeast end of the Lake and once the summer residence of the Maharaja of Mysore, is now run as a hotel (see below). It's an extraordinary pile, built in the fullest expression of Ooty's characteristic Swiss-chalet style, with carved wooden bargeboards and ornamental cast iron balustrades. Among the compound of firs, cedars and monkey puzzle trees, a bizarre church-like building was erected as an indoor badminton court.

Local walks along the leafy lanes around Ooty are not what they once were, due to the volume of traffic, but it is still possible, at least out of the main seasons, to get some peace and magnificent views on parts of Wenlock Downs (8km on the Gudalur Rd), Dodabetta Peak (10km east, off the road to Kotagiri), Avalanche (24km) which is part of the *shola* forest with wild flowers and Pykara Dam (19km).

Accommodation

Ooty is a lot more expensive than many places in India; during April and May the prices below can double. It also gets very crowded, so you may have to hunt around to find what you want. The best by far are the grand old Raj-era places; otherwise, the choice is largely down to average hotels at above-average prices. In winter (Nov–Feb), when it can get pretty cold, most hotels provide heating at extra cost.

Dasaprakash, south of racecourse (☎42434). Old-style Indian hotel, clean and reasonably quiet. No TV in standard rooms; Rs50 extra for heating. Two veg restaurants. Travel agent. ④–⑤.

Fernhill Palace (☎43910). Characterful old place, set in 40 acres of garden and woodland. Built by the British in the mid-1800s, it was sold to the Maharajah of Mysore soon afterwards, and only fell into the hands of the *Taj* group in 1991. It has yet to be refurbished, and its unique suites, antique furniture, carved teak details, ballroom and "Hunt Bar" give it a gloriously faded charm. ⑧–⑨.

Maneck Guest House, Main Bazaar (☎43138). Friendly, clean Jain hotel. ①–④.

Nahar, Charing Cross (☎42173). Decent rooms (best in the modern building at the back) with *Star TV*. Tariff halves in winter; Rs75 extra for heater. Two veg restaurants (see below). ⑤.

Nilgiri Woodlands, Racecourse Rd, 1km from bus stand and railway station (☎42551). Arrange to be collected from the station. Raj-era building, with wood-panelled lobby and bare, clean rooms (phone and TV; Rs75 for heater). Dorm available for groups of 10 minimum. Restaurant. ④–⑥.

Raja Lodge, Lower Bazaar (☎43512). Very basic, but one of the cheapest in town, and just two minutes from the bus stand. ①.

Reflections Guest House, North Lake Rd (☎43834). Pleasant cottage-style hotel by the lake five minutes from the railway station. ②.

Savoy, 77 Sylkes Rd (☎44142). Long-established *pukka* hotel, now run by the *Taj* group, with manicured lawns and bushes (quiet classical music seeps from the leaves). Immaculate and chintzy old-world cottages with working fireplaces, wood and brass fittings. Restaurant, bar, travel agent. ⑨.

Surya Holiday Inn, 11 Upper Bazaar (☎42567). Smallish, clean rooms (heater Rs25) in fairly recent and central hotel. ③.

TTDC Hotel Tamil Nadu, Wenlock Rd (☎44010). Reached by steps by the tourist office. Good value, with large, clean rooms. Restaurant, bar and billiards room. ③–⑤.

TTDC Youth Hostel, Charing Cross (☎43665). Cheaper unit with doubles and dorms. ①/③.

YWCA, Ettines Rd (☎42218). Very popular place tucked behind the east end of the racecourse, with a range of accommodation including double rooms with bathroom and dorms. Restaurant. ①–④.

THE TODAS AND THE THREAT TO THE NILGIRIS

Until the arrival of the British, the **Todas** of the Nilgiri Hills maintained their own language and customs in villages (*munds*) of wagon-shaped huts of bamboo, thatch and reeds. Today the Toda tribal community still exists, albeit in depleted numbers. Some wear traditional costume; plain white waist-cloths under thick white woven cloaks striped with red and black. Once, all adult women had their upper body tattooed, their hair oiled and curled into long ringlets at the front; feminine beauty is judged by the narrowness of the feet and facial hair is admired. Men keep their hair and beards long.

Toda culture centres around the **buffalo**, held sacred; the only product they use is its milk, consuming it in vast quantities. Toda temples are dairies, off-limits to everyone save the officiating priests. The community is divided into fourteen patriarchal clans, though its polyandrous social system is fast breaking down. "Marriages" were arranged at birth with partners from another clan; at the age of fifteen the female moved in with the husband's family and automatically became the wife of his younger brothers too. She could also seek further partners from other families, with the permission of her principal partner, who would generally assume the paternal role for any resultant offspring.

The Todas lived in interdependence with three other tribal groups, based on a barter system under which their main responsibility was to supply the others with dairy products; the **Kotas** were ironsmiths and potters, and provided music for rituals, while jungle-dwelling **Kurumbas**, known for their aptitude in magic, also gathered honey and wood. The **Badagas**, who arrived in the fourteenth century, kept the others in grain and beans.

At present there are about 1500 Todas, of whom a quarter are Christian. Due to high infant mortality and the introduction of life-threatening diseases by the British, by the 1940s their population had dwindled to little more than 600. This alarming situation was dramatically reversed, largely through the efforts of an exceptional Toda woman, **Evam Piljain-Wiedemann**, who trained as a nurse in England, and succeeded in winning the confidence of other Todas to take advantage of a mobile medical clinic. She continues to work to secure rights for the Todas, and to protect the natural environment.

Blame for the threat to the Nilgiris cannot simply be laid at the door of colonial exploitation, though the story does begin with the arrival of the British in 1821. Despite their penchant for hunting (panther, tiger and deer) and fishing, the British were aware, within the vision of the time, of protecting the natural landscape. The worst came after Independence. From 1952, a series of "five-year plans" towards "development" were implemented. Widespread planting of exotic trees, principally eucalyptus, wattle and pine, provided a generous income for the government, but had far-reaching effects on local ecology. A new synthetic fibre industry, established in the foothills, requires huge amounts of pulp to make fibre. Despite local fears and protests, including a *satyagraha*-style public fast, more and more acreage is cleared in order to feed factories.

Traditional *shola* forest, once destroyed, takes thousands of years to replace, while the newly planted eucalyptus draws water from miles around. For the first time in its history, this once swampy region suffers from **water shortages**. The Todas can no longer get enough thatching grass to build houses and temples, and their traditional homes are being replaced by concrete. Nothing grows under eucalyptus and pine, and the sacred buffalo have nowhere to graze. Many Todas have been forced to sell their stock, and barely enough are left to perform the ceremonies at the heart of Toda life.

Eating

Many of the mid-range hotels serve up good south Indian food, but Ooty has yet to offer a gourmet restaurant. The *Savoy* and *Fernhill Palace*, however, are well worth checking out for the colonial ambience.

Fernhill Palace, see above. Pricey, high-quality food served in palatial surroundings.

Kurinji Snack Bar, Commercial Rd. Fast food outlet, open to the street; popular with Ooty youth.

Nahar, see above. Hotel with two good veg restaurants, and a snack bar serving milk shakes, *dosa, aloo chaat* and the like, with some tables set outside.

Nilgiri Woodlands, see above. The speciality is beefsteak, but the inexpensive *thalis* are good too. Checked tablecloths and cane chairs give it the look of a village hall. No alcohol.

Sabari, near Mariamman temple and vegetable market. Basic budget veg snacks and "meals".

Savoy, see above. Not the cheapest, but the best of the old colonial places. The food is good with a mixed menu of Indian, Chinese and Western; and the verandah overlooking the garden is a pleasant place for an alcoholic drink or a tray of tea.

Shinkows, 42 Commissioners Rd (☎42811). Good value, authentic Chinese food.

Tandoor Mahal, Commercial Rd. Central, very good value non-veg restaurant; serves beer too.

MOVING ON FROM OOTY

Ooty **railway station** has a reservation counter (10am–noon & 3.30–4.30pm) and a booking office (6.30am–7pm). For details of services on the narrow-gauge railway, see p.1043.

You can also book **buses** in advance, at reservation offices for both state buses (daily 9am–12.30pm & 1.30–5.30pm) and the local company, *Cheran Transport* (daily 9am–1pm & 1.30–5.30pm). Towns served include Bangalore and Mysore (buses to both pass through Mudumalai), Kodaikanal, Thanjavur, Thiruvananthapuram and Kanniyakumari, as well as Kotagiri, Coonoor and Coimbatore nearer to hand. **Private buses** to Mysore, Bangalore and Kodaikanal can be booked at hotels, or agents in Charing Cross; even when advertised as "super-deluxe", many turn out to be cramped minibuses.

Mudumalai Wildlife Sanctuary

Set 1140m up in the Nilgiri Hills, **MUDUMALAI WILDLIFE SANCTUARY** is one of the most accessible in the south, covering 322 square kilometres of deciduous forest, split by the main road from Ooty (64km) to Mysore (97km). The approach from Ooty is spectacular, twisting and turning down 36 hairpin bends, through wooded hills and past waterfalls (in season). Monkeys dart and play in the trees, and you may glimpse a tethered elephant from the camp at **Kargudi,** where wild elephants are tamed for work in the timber industry.

Mudumalai has one of the largest populations of elephants in India, along with wild dogs, *gaur* (Indian bison), common and Nilgiri langur and bonnet macaque (monkeys), jackal, hyena and sloth bear – even a few tigers and panthers. On a brief foray, such as the organized tour from Ooty (see p.1042), you're not likely to see much wildlife, and to make the most of a visit, you'll need to stay overnight, and trek out into the park. Even then, pressure on numbers means that time in the sanctuary is severely rationed.

Arrival and information

You can only get to Mudumalai by road. The fastest and most spectacular route is not negotiable by large vehicles, but private minibuses and a regular Cheran Transport bus service run to Masinagudi (1hr) from Ooty. Standard buses to Mysore and Bangalore from Ooty take 2hr 30min to reach Theppakkadu, which is connected to Masinagudi, 7km away, by bus and jeep.

At **Theppakkadu,** the main access point to the sanctuary, you can book van tours (1hr; Rs25) and elephant rides (1hr; Rs125) into the forest from the **Wildlife Sanctuary Reception and Administration Centre** (daily 6.30–9am & 4–6pm; ☎0423/56235). The **Elephant Camp show** (daily 6pm; Rs20) is fine if you're into seeing put-upon pachyderms playing soccer to a Boney M accompaniment.

Accommodation and eating

Accommodation standards in Mudumalai are high, often in gorgeous, peaceful settings. The best places are up to 5km off the main road from Masinagudi. Book in advance, and arrange for your hosts to pick you up from the bus stop – taxis or jeeps are rare in the village. Most places expect guests for full board, as Masinagudi only has a few simple restaurants, and will arrange tours of the park for residents.

There is also basic **dorm accommodation** in the park. To make sure of securing a place you should book well in advance, at the Wildlife Office in Ooty (see p.1043), but you can always ask Forest Department officials at Theppakkadu on the off chance.

Bamboo Banks Guest House, 2km from the main road, Masinagudi (☎0423/56222). Two rooms, and four cottages, in a very attractive setting. Excellent food served outdoors. ⑥.

Blue Valley Resort, 1km off the main road, Masinagudi (☎0423/56244). Comfortable rooms, two restaurants. Will collect from the village, and can arrange trekking and jeep tours (Rs5 per km). ⑥.

Jungle Hut, 5km from the road, Bokkapuram, Masinagudi (☎0423/56240). Twelve comfortable cottages, and a swimming pool. Excellent food, including barbecues. Will arrange trekking, elephant rides and pick up from Theppakkadu. ⑥.

Monarch Safari Park, Bokkapuram, Masinagudi (☎0423/56250). Fourteen rooms in *machans* (cottages on stilts) with *Star TV*; full and half board. Open restaurant, also on stilts. Safari rides, riding, cycling, trekking, golf, indoor games and meditation centre. ⑤–⑦.

Mountania Lodge, Masinagudi (☎0423/56237). Cabins in Masinagudi's only roadside lodge. ④.

TTDC Hotel Tamil Nadu, Theppakkadu (☎0423/56249). Functional, clean four-bed rooms and dorms. Meals by arrangement, seven-night maximum stay. Book at the TTDC office in Ooty, but you may be lucky on spec if they're not full. ①.

Kodaikanal

High on the southern ridges of the Palani hills, just over 100km northwest of Madurai, **KODAIKANAL**, also known as **Kodai**, is one of the south's more popular hill stations, but even so, like the others, it seldom detains tourists for more than a day or two. Kodai's greatest plus is its hilltop position, which affords views south over the plains and north to the smooth blue-green reaches of the Palani range. Raj-era houses and gardens flooded with the hues of flowers from all over the world add atmosphere, while short walks out of the centre lead to rocky outcrops, waterfalls and dense forest.

Kodaikanal's history, with an absence of wars, battles for leadership and princely dominion, is uneventful, and the only monuments to its past are the neat British bungalows that overlook the lake and Law's Ghat Road on the eastern edge of town. The British first moved here in 1845, to be joined later by members of the American Mission who set up schools for European children. One remains as Kodai International School; despite the name, it has an almost exclusively Indian student population. The school lays a strong emphasis on music, particularly guitar playing, and occasionally holds workshops, and concerts on the green just east of the lake.

After a while in the plains of south India a retreat to Kodai's cool heights is more than welcome. However, in the height of summer (June–Aug), when temperatures compete with those in the lowlands, it's not worth the trip – nor is it a good idea to come during the monsoon (Oct–Dec), when the town is shrouded in mists and drenched by heavy downpours. In late February and early March the nights are chilly; the busiest tourist season is from April to June, when prices soar.

Arrival, information and getting around

The **buses** from Madurai and Dindigul that climb the spectacular road up the steep hillside to Kodai from the plains pull in at the bus stand in the centre of town. Unless you're coming from as far as Madras or Tiruchirapalli, the bus is much more convenient than

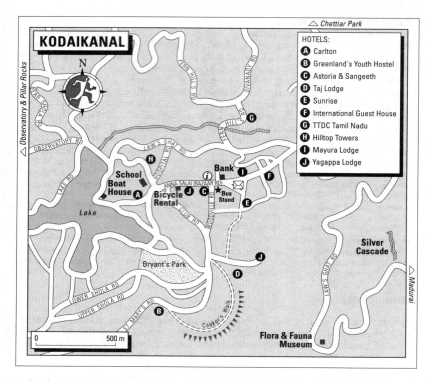

train: the nearest **railhead**, Kodaikanal Road – also connected to Dindigul (30min) and Madurai (50min) – is three hours away by bus. Rail tickets for onward journeys from Kodaikanal Road can be booked at an office above the *Hilltop Inn* restaurant next to *Hilltop Towers Hotel* on Club Rd (Mon–Sat 9am–1pm & 1.30–5pm, Sun 1.30–5pm), or at *King Tours and Travels* on Woodville Rd, which will also reserve buses and planes within south India. The **tourist office** (daily 10am–5.30pm), on the main road, Anna Salai (Bazaar Rd), offers little except unclear sketch maps of the area.

Hotel Tamil Nadu runs **tours** (2 daily; 4hr) taking in all the town's sights and most of the viewpoints. Alternatively, **taxis** line Anna Salai in the centre of town, offering sightseeing tours at high but fixed rates. However, most tourists prefer to amble around at their own pace. Compact and hilly as it is, Kodaikanal is best explored on foot, or you could rent a **bicycle** from a stall on Anna Salai for Rs15–20 per day; it may be fun to freewheel *down* hills, but most journeys will involve a hefty push.

If you need to **change money**, head for the *State Bank of India* on Anna Salai.

The Town

Kodai's focal point is its **lake**, sprawling like a giant amoeba over a full 24 hectares just west of the town centre. This is a popular place for strolls, or bike rides along the five-kilometre path that fringes the water's edge (a booth rents out bikes at low rates), and pedal- or rowboats can be rented on the eastern shore (Rs10–30 for 30min). Lakeside horse riding is also an option, prices varying from Rs20 for a guided ride to Rs100 per hour on your own. Shops, restaurants and hotels are concentrated in a rather congested area of brick, wood and corrugated iron buildings east and downhill from the lake. To the south is **Byrant's Park**, with tiered flower beds and a backdrop of pine, eucalyptus, rhododendron and wattle, which stretches southwards to Shola Rd, less than 1km from the point where the hill drops abruptly to the plains. A path, known as **Coaker's walk**, skirts the hill, winding from *Taj Lodge* to *Greenland's Youth Hostel* (10min), offering remarkable views that on a clear day stretch as far as Madurai.

One of Kodai's most popular natural attractions is **Pillar Rocks**, a series of granite cliffs rising more than 100m above the hillside, 7km south of town. To get there, follow the westbound Observatory Rd from the northernmost point of the lake (a moderate uphill slope) for roughly 4km, until you come to a crossroads. The southbound road passes the gentle **Fairy Falls** on the way to Pillar Rocks. Observatory Rd continues west to the **Astrophysical Observatory**, perched at Kodai's highest point (2347m). Visitors cannot go in, but a small **museum** (daily 10am–noon & 2–5pm; Fri only outside peak season) displays assorted instruments. Closer to the north shore of the lake, **Bear Shola Falls** are at their strongest early in the year, just after the monsoon.

East of the town centre, about 3km south down Law's Ghat Rd (towards the plains), the **Flora and Fauna Museum** (daily except Sun 10am–noon & 3–5pm; Rs1) has a far from inviting collection of stuffed animals. However, the orchid house is spectacular, and well worth a look on the way to **Silver Cascade** waterfalls a further 2km along.

Chettiar Park, on the very northwest edge of town, around 3km from the lake at the end of a winding uphill road, flourishes with trees and flowers all year round, and every twelve years is flushed with a haze of pale-blue **Kurinji blossoms** (next flowering 2006). These unusual flowers are associated with the god Murugan, the Tamil form of Karttikeya (Shiva's second son), and god of Kurinji, one of five ancient divisions of the Tamil country. A temple in his honour stands just outside the park.

Accommodation

Kodaikanal's inexpensive **lodges** are grouped at the lower end of Anna Salai. Many are dim and poky, however, so hunt around. Always ask whether blankets and hot water are provided. **Mid-range hotels** are usually good value, especially if you get a room with a view, but hike their prices drastically during high season (April–June).

Astoria, Anna Salai (☎40525). Well-kept hotel opposite the bus stand, with homely rooms and a good, mid-priced restaurant. ⑤.

Carlton, off Lake Rd (☎40056). The most luxurious hotel in Kodaikanal. Spacious, tastefully renovated and well-maintained colonial house overlooking the lake, with a bar and comfortable lounge. Cottages within the grounds are available at higher prices; all rates include meals. ⑨.

Greenland's Youth Hostel, St Mary's Rd (☎41099). Attractive old stone house offering unrivalled views, simple rooms and a cosy bunk-bed dorm. One of the best budget options. ①–③.

Hilltop Towers, Club Rd (☎40413). Modern rooms and good service, very near the lake. ⑤.

International Guest House, Anna Salai (☎45420). One of the better low-priced lodges, with clean small rooms, some with attached bath, and hot water available by the bucket. ①–②.

Mayura Lodge, Anna Salai. Friendly lodge with spartan washing facilities and simple rooms. ①.

Sangeeth, opposite the bus stand (☎40456). Reasonably sized, comfortable rooms with bath. Central, but with no views over the plains. Pay extra for a TV. ③.

Sunrise, Post Office Rd (☎41358). Cheap lodge with poky run-down rooms (those at the front have great views), and attached baths with water heaters. ②.

Taj Lodge, off Club Rd (☎40940). Comfortable hotel in pleasant gardens with excellent views. All rooms have attached bathrooms, but you'll have to get hot water by the bucket. ②–③.

TTDC Tamil Nadu, Fern Hill's Rd (☎41336). Large, well-run hotel northwest of town. Many rooms have *Star TV*, and there's a deluxe cottage and cheap dorm. Quite good views, too. ①–⑥.

Yagappa Lodge, off Club Rd (☎41235). Nice, quiet rooms in wooden building with fine views. ③.

The telephone **area code** for Kodaikanal is ☎04542.

Eating

If you choose not to eat in any of the **hotel restaurants,** head for the food stalls along **Hospital Rd** just west of the bus stand. Menus include Indian, Chinese, Western and Tibetan dishes, and some cater specifically for vegetarians. Look out, too, for the bakeries, with their wonderful fresh, warm bread and cakes each morning.

Carlton, *Carlton Hotel,* Lake Rd. Expensive, tasty food. A buffet spread is laid out each evening and there's a well-stocked bar.

Chefmaster, Hospital Rd. The best place for Keralan dishes, including unbeatable *thalis.* Reasonable Chinese food and Western-style meals, including great chicken sizzler.

Manna Bakery, Bear Shola Rd. Friendly place for fresh doughnuts, bread, rolls, cakes and pizza.

Hotel Punjab, Hospital Rd. Great Indian cuisine and reasonably priced *tandoori* specialities.

Silver Inn, Hospital Rd. Exclusively Western menu; reasonable rates. Often full.

Tibetan Brothers Restaurant, Hospital Rd. Tibetan dishes ranging from thick bread to *momos* and noodles, and some Indian and Chinese options.

Wangs Kitchen, Hospital Rd. Smart new Chinese restaurant.

Palani

Few foreigners venture further into the Palani hills than Kodaikanal, but the spectacular bus ride over them and down to **PALANI** on the other side, fringed by tea gardens roughly 60km north, is a worthwhile detour or alternative route north.

Palani's modern hilltop **Shri Dandayudhapani temple** attracts pilgrims all year round, but the town comes alive most in April, when it hosts a festival in honour of **Murugan,** Shiva's son (also known as Skanda). Hundreds of devotees, mostly male and clad in black *dhotis,* trudge up the winding flight of more than 600 steps to worship the image, said to be formed from an aggregate of poisonous minerals, that, if mixed with coconut milk, fruits and flowers, produces medicinal herbs. A smaller festival takes place in Feb/March. The streets around the hill are crammed with stalls selling the usual religious paraphernalia, plastic toys and bric-a-brac, buzzing with activity as worshippers meander between the main temple and some smaller ones. Those unable to climb the steps can ascend in a carriage pulled slowly up the steep incline by winch (Rs1) but it can take a lot of queuing to get on.

Apart from the numerous simple *dharamshalas* aimed at the flocks of pilgrims, Palani has two proper **hotels**: a small new unit of *TTDC Tamil Nadu,* W Giri St, opposite the winch station (☎04545/41156; ③–④) and the smart new *Subam Hotel,* 7 N Giri St near the main temple entrance (☎04545/42672; ②–④). **Buses to Palani** from Kodaikanal (every 1hr 30min; 3hr) are often full, so it's wise to reserve. The town is also well-connected by train and bus to Coimbatore, via Pollachi (for the Indira Gandhi wildlife sanctuary), and Madurai.

Indira Gandhi (Anamalai) Wildlife Sanctuary

Anamalai Wildlife Sanctuary, officially renamed the **Indira Gandhi Wildlife Sanctuary,** is a 958 square kilometre tract of forest on the southern reaches of the Cardamom Hills, south of the busy junction town of **Pollachi.** Vegetation ranges from dry deciduous to tropical evergreen, and the sanctuary is home to lion-tailed **macaques** (black-maned monkeys), wild elephants, crocodiles, *sambar,* spotted and barking deer, as well as fifteen elusive **tigers** at the last count.

Rooms in simple **forest lodges** (①) at **Topslip,** within the sanctuary, can be arranged at the Wildlife Warden offices, 178 Meenkarai Rd, Pollachi (☎04259/25356); in Topslip you can hook up with vans or elephant rides into the forest. Two buses a day (10.30am & 5.30pm) run to Topslip from Pollachi, which, on the main rail and road link between Madurai and Coimbatore, has good connections in both directions.

CHAPTER NINETEEN

KERALA

solated at the southwestern tip of India, sandwiched between the Arabian Sea and the forested Western Ghat mountains, the state of **KERALA**, around 550km long and 120km wide at its broadest point, is blessed with unique geographical and cultural features. Its overpowering tropical greenness, with 41 rivers and countless waterways, fed by two annual monsoons, intoxicates every newcomer. Equally, Kerala's arcane rituals and spectacular festivals stimulate even the most jaded imagination, continuing centuries of tradition that has never strayed far from the realms of magic.

Travellers weary of daunting metropolises find no such problems here. Kerala's cities are small-scale, relaxed and generally a good deal less expensive than elsewhere. For visitors, the most popular is undoubtedly the great port of **Kochi** (Cochin), where Kerala's extensive history of peaceable foreign contact is evocatively evident in the atmospheric old quarters of Mattancherry and Fort Cochin, hubs of a still-thriving tea and spice trade. The capital, **Thiruvananthapuram** (Trivandrum), almost as far south as you can go and a gateway to the nearby palm-fringed beaches of **Kovalam** provides visitors with varied opportunities to sample Kerala's rich cultural and artistic life.

However, more so than anywhere in India, the greatest joy of exploring Kerala is the actual travelling – above all, by **boat**, in the spell-binding Kuttanad region, near historic **Kollam** (Quilon) and **Alappuzha** (Alleppey). Vessels from cruisers to wooden longboats ply the **backwaters** in day-long voyages, well worth taking for the chance of a close-up view of village life in India's most densely populated state. Furthermore, it's always easy to escape the heat of the lowlands by taking off to the **hills**. Roads through a landscape dotted with churches and temples pass spice, tea, coffee and rubber plantations, and natural forest, en route to wildlife reserves such as **Peppara** or **Periyar**, roamed by herds of mud-caked elephants.

Kerala is short on the historic monuments prevalent elsewhere in India, mainly because wood is the building material of choice. Moreover, what ancient temples there are remain in use, more often than not closed to non-Hindus. Nonetheless, distinctive

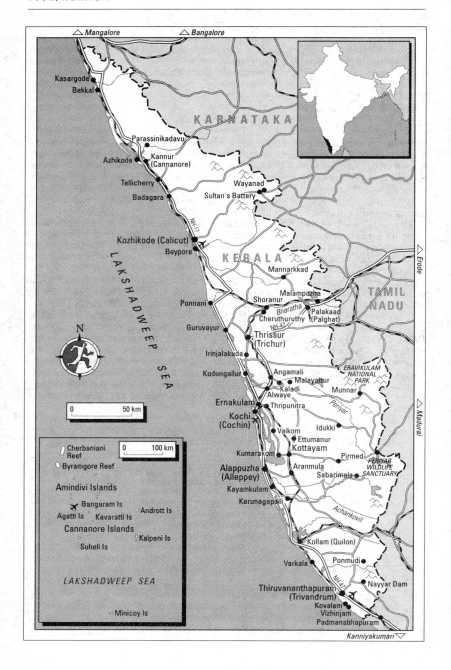

KERALA TRAVEL DETAILS

	Trains		Buses		Flights	
	Frequency	Time	Frequency	Time	Frequency	Time
To and from THIRUVANANTHAPURAM						
Alappuzha	3 daily	2hr 50min–3hr 30min	15 daily	3hr 15min		
Bangalore	1–2 daily	18hr 30min			4 weekly	1hr 5min
Bombay	1–2 daily	40hr–45hr 30min			2–3 daily	1hr 55min
Calcutta	1 weekly	49hr				
Colombo					7 weekly	50min
Delhi	2–3 daily	44hr 30min–56hr 40min			1 daily	4hr 30min
Kanniyakumari	3 daily	2hr 25min	12 daily	2hr		
Kochi	8 daily	4hr–4hr 40min	20 daily	5–6hr	1 daily	40min
Kollam	hourly	1hr 10min–1hr 45min	15 daily	1hr 30min		
Kottayam	6–7 daily	3hr–3hr 25min	5 daily	4hr		
Kozhikode	3 daily	9hr 30min–10hr 30min				
Madras	1–2 daily	17hr 45min–18hr 20min	4 daily	17hr	1 daily	1hr 30min
Madurai			10 daily	7hr		
Malé (Maldives)					1 daily	40min
Periyar			3 daily	8hr		
Ponmudi			4 daily	2hr 30min		
Thrissur	5–6 daily	5hr 30min–6hr 45min				
Varkala	8 daily	55min	hourly	1hr 30min		
To and from KOCHI/ERNAKULAM						
Alappuzha	2 daily	1hr 20min	15 daily	1hr 30min		
Bangalore	1 daily	13hr			2 daily	50min
Bombay	1–2 daily	40–58hr			2 daily	1hr 45min
Coimbatore	5 daily	4hr 45min				
Delhi	2 daily	40hr 30min–49hr			6 weekly	4hr
Goa					1 daily	1hr 10min
Kanniyakumari	4 daily	7hr	6 daily	9hr		
Kollam	5 daily	3–4hr	15 daily	3hr		
Kottayam	5 daily	1hr 5min	15 daily	1hr 30min–2hr		
Kozhikode	5 daily	4–5hr			1 daily	30min
Lakshadweep					3 weekly	1hr 30min
Madras	3 daily	13–14hr			1–2 daily	1hr 35min
Palakaad	5 daily	3hr 20min				
Periyar			10 daily	6hr		
Thrissur	5 daily	1hr 30min–2hr	7 daily	2hr		
To and from Periyar						
Kottayam			every 30min	3–4hr		
Kozhikode			every 30min	6hr		
Madurai			10 daily	5hr		
To and from Thrissur						
Guruvayur			10 daily	40min		
Madras	3 daily	11hr 30min	1 daily	14hr		
Mysore			2 daily	10hr		
Palakaad			6 daily	2hr		

For details of **ferry** services on the **backwaters** – primarily between Alappuzha and Kollam – see p.1079.

Note that most individual routes appear only once in this chart; check against where you want to get to as well as where you're coming from.

buildings throughout the state eschew grandiosity in favour of elegant understatement. Following an unwritten law, few buildings, whether houses or temples, are higher than the surrounding trees; from high ground in urban areas this can create the miraculous illusion that you're surrounded by forest. Typical features of both domestic and temple architecture include long, sloping tiled and gabled roofs that minimize the excesses of both rain and sunshine, and pillared verandahs; the definitive example is **Padmanabhapuram Palace**, just south of the border in neighbouring Tamil Nadu and easily reached from Thiruvananthapuram.

Phenomenal amounts of money are lavished upon many, varied, and often all-night **entertainments** associated with Kerala's temples. Fireworks rent the air, while processions of gold-bedecked elephants are accompanied by some of the loudest (and deftest) drum orchestras in the world. The famous **Puram** festival in Thrissur is the most astonishing, but smaller events take place throughout the state – often outdoors, with all welcome to attend.

Theatre and **dance** styles abound in Kerala; not only the region's own female classical dance form, **Mohiniattam** ("dance of the enchantress"), but also the martial-art-influenced **Kathakali** dance drama, which has for four centuries brought gods and demons from the *Mahabharata* and *Ramayana* to Keralan villages. Its 2000-year-old predecessor, the Sanskrit drama **Kutiyattam**, is still performed by a handful of artists, while localized rituals known as **Teyyam**, in which dancers wearing nine-metre-tall masks become "possessed" by temple deities, continue to be a potent ingredient of village life in the north. Few visitors ever witness these extraordinary all-night performances first hand, but between December and March, you could profitably spend weeks hopping between village festivals in northern Kerala, experiencing a way of life that has altered little in centuries.

History

The god Parashurama, "Rama with the battle axe", the sixth incarnation of Vishnu, is credited with creating Kerala. Born a brahmin, he set out to re-establish the supremacy of the priestly class, whose position had been usurped by arrogant *kshatryas*, the martial aristocracy. Brahmins were forbidden to engage in warfare, but he embarked upon a campaign of carnage, which only ended when Varuna, the all-seeing god of the sea, gave him the chance to create a new land from the ocean, for brahmins to live in peace. Its limits were defined by the distance Parashurama could throw his axe; the waves duly receded up to the point where it fell. Fossil evidence suggests that the sea once extended to the Western Ghats, so the legend reflects a geological truth.

Ancient Kerala is mentioned as the land of the Cheras in a third-century BC Ashokan edict, and also in the *Ramayana* (the monkey king Sugriva sent emissaries here in search of Sita), and the *Mahabharata* (a Chera king sent soldiers to the Kurukshetra war), while the Tamil *Silappadikaram* ("The Jewelled Anklet") was composed here and provides a valuable picture of life around the time of Christ. Early foreign accounts, such as in Pliny and Ptolemy, testify to thriving trade between the ancient port of Muziris (now known as Kodungallur) and the Roman Empire.

Little is known about the early history of the Cheras; their dominion covered a large area, but their capital Vanji has not been identified. Other contemporary rulers included the Nannanas in the north and the Ay chieftains in the south, who battled with the Pandyas from Tamil Nadu, in the eighth century. At the start of the ninth century, the Chera king Kulashekhara Alvar – a poet-saint of the Vaishnavite *bhakti* movement known as the *alvars* – established his own dynasty. His son and successor, Rajashekharavarman, is thought to have been a saint of the parallel Shaivite movement, the *nayannars*. The great Keralan philosopher Shankaracharya, whose *advaita* ("non-dualist") philosophy influenced the whole of Hindu India, lived at this time.

Eventually, the prosperity acquired by the Cheras through trade with China and the Arab world proved too much of an attraction for the neighbouring **Chola** empire, who embarked upon a hundred years of sporadic warfare with the Cheras at the end of the tenth century. Around 1100, the Cheras lost their capital at Mahodayapuram in the north, and shifted south to establish a new capital at Kollam (Quilon).

When the **Portuguese** ambassador/general Vasco da Gama and his fleet first arrived in India in 1498, people were as much astounded by their recklessness in sailing close to Calicut during monsoon, as by their physical and sartorial strangeness. Crowds filled the streets of Calicut to see them, and a Moroccan found a way to communicate. Eager to meet the king, whom they believed to be a Christian, the Portuguese were escorted over 29km in torrential rain to his palace. However, da Gama soon found that the gifts he had brought from the King of Portugal had not made a good impression. The Zamorin (Raja) wanted silver and gold, not a few silk clothes and a sack of sugar.

Vasco da Gama, after such diplomatic initiatives as the kidnapping, mutilation and murder of assorted locals, nevertheless came to an agreement of sorts with the Zamorin, then pressed on to demand exclusive rights to the spice trade. He was determined to squeeze out the Keralan Muslim (Mappila) traders who for centuries had been a respected section of the community, acting as middlemen between local producers and traders in the Middle East. Exploiting an already existing enmity between the royal families of Cochin and Calicut, da Gama turned to Cochin, which became the site of India's first Portuguese fortress in 1503. The city's strategic position enabled the Portuguese to break the Middle Eastern monopoly of trade with western India; unlike previous visitors, they introduced new agricultural products such as cashew and tobacco, and for the first time turned coconut into a cash crop, having recognized the value of its by-products, coir rope and matting.

The rivalry between Cochin and Calicut allowed other colonial powers to move in; both the Dutch, who forcibly expelled the Portuguese from their forts, and the British, in the shape of the East India Company, established themselves early in the seventeenth century. During the 1700s, first Raja Martanda Varma, and then Tipu Sultan of Mysore, carved out independent territories, but the defeat of Tipu Sultan by the British in 1792 left the British in control right up until Independence.

Kerala today can claim some of the most startling **radical** credentials in India. In 1957 it was the first state in the world democratically to elect a communist government and despite having one of the lowest per capita incomes in the country it has the most equitable land distribution, due to uncompromising reforms during the 1960s and 1970s. In 1996, the Left Democratic Front, led by CPI (M) retook the state from the Congress-led United Democratic Front, who had been in power for five years. Poverty is not absent, but it appears far less acute than in other parts of India. Kerala is also justly proud of its reputation for health care and education, with a literacy rate that stands, officially at least, at 100 percent. However, industrial development is negligible, with potential investors from outside tending to fight shy of dealing with a politicized workforce. Many Keralans find themselves obliged to leave home to seek work, especially in the Gulf. The resultant influx of petro-dollars seems only to have the negative effect of increasing inflation.

Thiruvananthapuram

Kerala's capital, the coastal city of **THIRUVANANTHAPURAM** (still widely known as **Trivandrum**), is set on seven low hills, 87km from the southern tip of India. Despite its administrative importance – demonstrated by wide roads, multi-storey office blocks and gleaming white colonial buildings – it's a decidedly easygoing city, with an attractive mixture of narrow backstreets, traditional red-tiled gabled houses and acres of palm trees and parks breaking up the bustle of its modern concrete centre.

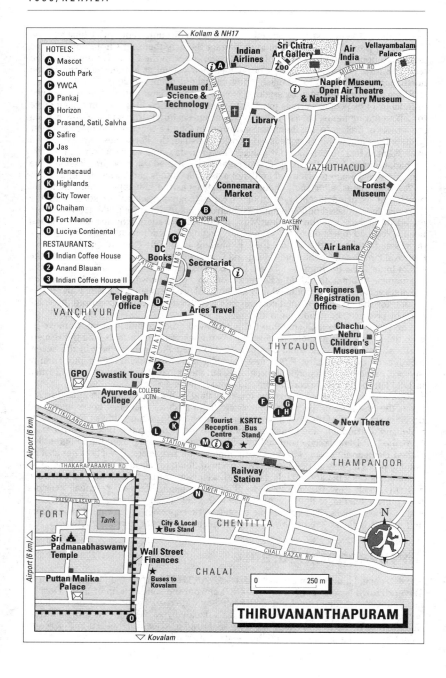

△ Kollam & NH17

HOTELS:
Ⓐ Mascot
Ⓑ South Park
Ⓒ YWCA
Ⓓ Pankaj
Ⓔ Horizon
Ⓕ Prasand, Satil, Salvha
Ⓖ Safire
Ⓗ Jas
Ⓘ Hazeen
Ⓙ Manacaud
Ⓚ Highlands
Ⓛ City Tower
Ⓜ Chaiham
Ⓝ Fort Manor
Ⓞ Luciya Continental
RESTAURANTS:
❶ Indian Coffee House
❷ Anand Blauan
❸ Indian Coffee House II

Indian Airlines
Sri Chitra Art Gallery
Zoo
Air India
Vellayambalam Palace
Napier Museum, Open Air Theatre & Natural History Museum
MUSEUM RD
Museum of Science & Technology
Library
Stadium
VAZHUTHACUD
Connemara Market
Forest Museum
SPENCER JCTN
BAKERY JCTN
DC Books
Secretariat
Air Lanka
Telegraph Office
Aries Travel
VANCHIYUR
PRESS RD
Foreigners Registration Office
Chachu Nehru Children's Museum
THYCAUD
GPO
Swastik Tours
Ayurveda College
COLLEGE JCTN
MANJALIKULAM RD
S.S. COIL RD
ARISTO ROAD
TALKAD HOSPITAL
VAZHUTHACUD ROAD
New Theatre
Tourist Reception Centre
KSRTC Bus Stand
STATION RD
CHETTIKULANGARA RD
Airport (6 km)
THAKARAPARAMBU RD
Railway Station
THAMPANOOR
PADMAVILASAM RD
FORT
Tank
PanHOUSE RD
Sri Padmanabhaswamy Temple
City & Local Bus Stand
CHENTITTA
Airport (6 km)
Wall Street Finances
CHALAI BAZAR RD
Puttan Malika Palace
CHALAI
Buses to Kovalam
0   250 m

THIRUVANANTHAPURAM

N

▽ Kovalam

THE CITY OF THE SNAKE ANANTHA

Thiruvananthapuram was the capital of the kingdom of Travancore from 1750 until 1956, when the state of Kerala was created. Its name (formally re-adopted to replace "Trivandrum"), derives from *thiru-anantha-puram* – "the holy city of Anantha", the coiled snake on which the god Vishnu reclines in the midst of the cosmic ocean.

Vishnu is given a special name for this non-activity – *Padma-nabha*, "lotus-navel" – and is invariably depicted lying on the sacred snake with a lotus growing umbilically from his navel. The god Brahma sits inside the lotus, which represents the beginning of a new world age. Padmanabha is the principal deity of the royal family of Travancore, and of Thiruvananthapuram's **Shri Padmanabhaswamy temple**.

Although it has few monuments as such, Thiruvananthapuram is an ideal first stop in the state, as a window on Keralan culture. The oldest, most interesting, part of town is the **Fort** area in the south, around the **Shri Padmanabhaswamy temple** and **Puttan Malika palace**, while important showcases for painting, crafts and sculpture, the **Shri Chitra Art Gallery** and **Napier Museum**, stand together in a park in the north. In addition, schools specializing in the martial art Kalarippayat, and the dance/theatre forms of Kathakali and Kutiyattam, offer visitors an insight into the Keralan obsession with physical training and skill.

Many travellers choose to pass straight through Thiruvananthapuram, lured by the promise **Kovalam**'s palm-fringed beaches. A mere twenty-minute bus ride south, this popular resort is close enough to use as a base to see the city, although the recent upsurge in package tourism means it's far from the low-key, inexpensive travellers' hang-out it used to be.

Arrival and information

The **airport** (connected to most major Indian cities, as well as Sri Lanka, the Maldives, and the Middle East) is 6km southwest of town; bus #14, auto-rickshaws and taxis run to the centre. The long-distance *KSRTC* **Thampanoor bus stand** (☎71029) and **railway station** (☎64585) face each other across Station Rd in the southeast of the city, a short walk east of Overbridge Junction, where Thiruvananthapuram is bisected by the long north–south **MG Road**.

Local buses (to Kovalam for example) are five minutes' walk from the stations, at the City bus stand, East Fort. **Rickshaws** also run to Kovalam for around Rs60–70.

The telephone **area code** for Thiruvananthapuram is ☎0471.

Information and communications

KTDC has helpful **tourist offices** at the airport (daily 8am–8pm; ☎451085); Thampanoor bus stand; and next door to the *Indian Coffee House* and *Chaithram Hotel* on Station Rd (daily 6am–10pm; ☎330031). As well as booking accommodation in their good-value hotel chain, they give information about trains, and sell tickets for their **guided tours**. Most of these, including the city tour (daily 8am–7pm; Rs70), are far too rushed, but if you're pushed for time try the **Cape Comorin** tour (daily 7.30am–9pm; Rs150), which takes in Padmanabhapuram Palace (except Mon), Kovalam, Suchindram temple, and Kanniyakumari.

The **GPO**, with poste restante (daily 8am–6pm), is in Vanchiyur district, a short distance west of MG Rd. The **Telegraph Office**, opposite the Secretariat on MG Rd, is open around the clock. **Money** can be changed at the *State Bank of India*, near the Secretariat on MG Rd (Mon–Fri 10am–2pm, Sat 10am–noon), or more efficiently at *Wall Street Finances* (Mon–Sat 10am–6pm), behind the *Lucia Continental Hotel* in East Fort, and at the *Central Reserve Bank* in the lobby of the KTDC *Chaithram Hotel*. *American Express* cash credit card and travellers' cheques through *The Great Indian Tour Company*, Mullassery Tavern, Vanross Junction (☎331422 or 331516; fax 330579), east off MG Rd. *Thomas Cook* has an office at *Tour India*, MG Rd (☎ & fax 331407).

The City

The historical and spiritual heart of Thiruvananthapuram is in the **Fort area**, at the southern end of **MG Road**, which encloses the Shri Padmanabhaswamy Vishnu temple. Following MG Rd north leads you through the main shopping district, busy all day, and especially choked when one of the frequent, but generally orderly, political demonstrations converges on the grand colonial **Secretariat** building halfway along. The whole centre can be explored easily on foot, though you might be glad of a rickshaw ride back from the museums and parks, close to the top end of the road.

Fort area

A solid but unremarkable fort gateway leads from near the Kovalam bus stand at East Fort to the **Shri Padmanabhaswamy temple**, which is still controlled by the Travancore royal family. Unusually for Kerala it is in the Dravidian style of Tamil Nadu, with a tall *gopura* gateway, but it's surrounded by high fortress-like walls, and is closed to non-Hindus; little can be seen from outside, apart from the seven-storey *gopura*.

Most of the temple buildings date from the eighteenth century, added by Raja Marthanda Varma to a much older shrine. According to legend, the temple was founded after Vishnu, disguised as a beautiful child, merged into a huge tree in the forest, which immediately crashed to the ground. There it transformed into an image of the reclining Vishnu, a full 13km long. Divakara, a sage who witnessed this, was frustrated by his limited human vision, and prayed to Vishnu to assume a form that he could see in its entirety. Vishnu complied, and the temple appeared. The area in front of the temple, where devotees bathe in a huge tank, is thronged with stalls selling religious souvenirs, shell necklaces, *puja* offerings, jasmine and marigolds, along with the ubiquitous plaster-cast models of Kathakali masks. As you approach, the red-brick *CVN Kalari Sangam*, a **martial arts** gymnasium, is on the left. From 6.30am to 8am you can watch students doing Kalarippayat fighting exercises. Foreigners may join courses in the gym, arranged through the head teacher, although prior experience of martial arts and/or dance is a definite advantage. You can also come here for a traditional **Ayurvedic massage**, and to consult the gym's expert Ayurvedic doctors.

A path along the north side of the tank leads past the north, west and southern entrances to the temple, all guarded by bare-chested doormen armed with sticks, apparently to keep dogs away. It's an atmospheric walk, particularly in the early morning and at dusk, when devotees make their way to and from prayer (a closed iron gate bars the northern side, but everybody climbs through the gap). These neat little streets, in the old days of Kerala's extraordinary caste system, would have been a "no go" area, possibly on pain of death, to some members of the community.

Behind the temple on West Fort, set back from the road across open ground, the *Margi* school of **Kathakali** dance drama and **Kutiyattam** theatre (see p.1110) is housed in Fort High School. With prior notice you can watch classes; this is the place to ask about authentic Kathakali performances.

Puttan Malika Palace

The **Puttan Malika palace** (daily 8.30–12.30pm & 2–5.30pm; no cameras; Rs20), immediately southeast of the temple, became the seat of the Travancore rajahs after they left Padmanabhapuram at the end of the nineteenth century. To generate funds for much-needed restoration, the royal family have opened the palace to the public for the first time in more than 200 years. Although much of it remains off-limits, you can wander around some of the most impressive wings, which have been converted into a **museum**. Cool chambers, lined with delicately carved wooden screens and highly polished plaster floors, house a crop of dusty Travancore heirlooms. Among the predictable array of portraits, royal regalia and weapons are some genuine treasures, such as a solid crystal throne given by the Dutch, and some fine murals. The real highlight, however, is the typically understated, elegant Keralan architecture. Beneath sloping red tiled roofs, hundreds of wood pillars carved into the forms of rampant horses prop up the eaves, with airy verandahs projecting onto the surounding lawns.

The royal family have always been keen patrons of the arts, and the tradition is maintained with an open-air **Carnatic music festival**, held in the grounds (Jan/Feb). Performers sit on the palace's raised porch, flanked by the main facade, with the spectators seated on the lawn. For details, ask at the KTDC tourist office.

MG Road: markets and shopping

An assortment of craft shops along **MG Road** north of Station Rd sell sandalwood, brass and Keralan bell-metal oil lamps (see p.1107). The Gandhian *Khadi Gramodyog*, between Pazhavangadi and Overbridge junctions, stocks handloom cloth (dig around for the best stuff), plus radios and cassette machines manufactured by the Women's Federation. *Natesan's Antique Arts*, further up, is part of a chain that specializes in paintings, temple wood carvings and so forth. Prices are high, but they usually have some beautiful pieces, among them some superb reproduction Thanjur paintings and traditional inlaid chests for Kathakali costumes.

Most of the **bookstores** in the area are somewhat disappointing, largely intended for exam entrants. However, the a/c *Continental Books* on MG Rd stocks a good choice of titles in English, mostly relating to India and with a fair selection of fiction. Smaller, but with an equally wide array of English-language fiction is *DC Books*, Statue Rd, on the first floor of a building above Statue Junction.

Almost at the top of MG Rd, on the right hand side, the excellent little **Connemara Market** is the place to pick up essentials like plastic buckets, dried fish, fruit, vegetables, coconut scrapers, crude wooden toys, coir, woven winnowing baskets and Christmas decorations. It also holds the workshops of several **tailors**.

Public Gardens, Zoo and museums

A minute's walk east from the north end of MG Rd, opposite the Information Centre, you come to the entrance to Thiruvananthapuram's **Public Gardens**. As well as serving as a welcome refuge from the noise of the city – its lawns usually filled with courting couples, students and picnicking families – the park holds the city's best museums. The **Zoo** is in a nice enough setting, just inside the gate on the left, but the depressing state of the inmates, and the propensity of some visitors to get their kicks by taunting them, makes it eminently missable (daily except Mon 9am–4.45pm; tickets sold at the Shri Chitra Art Gallery, Rs5).

The extraordinary **Government (Napier) Museum** of arts and crafts (Tues & Thurs–Sun 9am–5pm, Wed 1–5pm), completed in 1880, was an early experiment in what became known as the "Indo-Saracenic" style, with tiled double-storey gabled roofs, garish red-black-and-salmon-patterned brickwork, tall slender towers, and, above the main entrance, a series of pilasters forming Islamic arches. The spectacular interior boasts stained-glass windows, a wooden ceiling and loud turquoise, pink, red and yellow stripes. The architect, Robert Fellowes Chisolm (1840–1915), set out to incorporate Keralan elements into colonial architecture; the museum was named after his employer, Lord Napier, the Governor of the Madras Presidency. Highlights include fifteenth-century Keralan woodcarvings from Kulathupuzha and Thiruvattar, gold necklaces and belts, minutely detailed ivory work, a carved temple chariot (*rath*), wooden models of Guruvayur temple and an oval temple theatre (*kuttambalam*), plus twelfth-century Chola and fourteenth-century Vijayanagar bronzes.

The attractive **Shri Chitra Art Gallery** (same hours), with its curved verandah and tiled roof, houses some splendid paintings from the Rajput, Moghul and Tanjore schools, as well as China, Tibet and Japan. The oil paintings by Raja Ravi Varma (1848–1906) have been criticized for their sentimentality and Western influence, but his treatment of Hindu mythological themes is both dramatic and beautiful.

In the ethnographic collection at the **Natural History Museum** (same hours), there's a model of a Nayar *taravad* (manor house). Kerala is littered with traditional houses that follow this *nalekettu* ("four-sided") design, built around an open courtyard. Grander ones can have as many as four such courtyards – all hidden from prying eyes.

Away from the centre

The **Chachu Nehru Children's Museum** (Mon–Fri 10am–5pm), in Thycaud in the east of the city, serves as a rather dusty testament to the enthusiasm of some anonymous donor, presumably back in the 1960s. One room contains ritual masks, probably

---

FESTIVALS OF THIRUVANANTHAPURAM

The **Arat** festival, centered around the Shri Padmanabhaswamy temple, takes place bi-annually, in Meenam (March/April) and Thulam (Oct/Nov). Each time, ten days of festivities inside the temple (open to Hindus only) culminate in a procession through the streets of the city, taking the deity, Padmanabhaswamy, to the sea for ritual immersion. Five caparisoned elephants, armed guards, a *nagasvaram* (double-reed wind instrument) and *tavil* drum group are led by the Maharaja of Travancore, in his symbolic role as *kshatrya*, the servant of the god. Instead of the richly apparelled figure that might be anticipated, the Maharaja, no longer officially recognized, wears a simple white *dhoti*, with his chest bare save for the sacred thread. Rather than riding, he walks the whole way, bearing a sword. To the accompaniment of a 21-gun salute and music, the procession sets off from the east gate of the temple at around 5pm, moving at a brisk pace to reach Shankhumukham Beach at sunset, about an hour later. The route is lined with devotees, many of whom honour both the god and the Maharaja. After the seashore ceremonies, the cavalcade returns to the temple at about 9pm, to be greeted by another gun salute. An extremely loud firework display rounds off the day.

For ten days in March, Muslims celebrate **Chandanakkutam** at the Beemapalli mosque, 5km southwest of the city on the coastal road towards the airport. The Hindu-influenced festival commemorates the anniversary of the death of Beema Beevi, a woman revered for her piety. On the first, most important, day, pilgrims converge on the mosque carrying earthenware pots decorated with flowers and containing money offerings. Activities such as the sword-form of *daharamuttu* take place inside the mosque, while outside there is dance and music. In the early hours of the morning, a flag is brought out from Beema Beevi's tomb and taken on a procession, accompanied by a *panchavadyam* drum-and-horn orchestra and caparisoned elephants, practices normally associated with Hindu festivals. Once more, the rest of the night is taken up with fireworks.

from Bengal, Rajasthan and Orissa, but the rest of the place is taken up with stamps, health education displays, and over 2000 dolls featuring figures in Indian costume, American presidents, gonks, Disney characters and British Beefeaters.

Also on the eastern side of town, visitors can by arrangement watch classes at the *PS Balachandran Nair Kalari* **martial arts gymnasium**, Kalariyil, TC 15/854, Cotton Hill (daily 6–8am & 6–7.30pm; ☎65140). Built in 1992 along traditional lines, in stone, the *kalari* fighting pit is overlooked from a height of 4m by a viewing gallery. Students, some as young as eight, train both in unarmed combat and in the use of weapons. Traditionally, the art of battle with long razorblade-like *urumi* is only taught to the teacher's successor. The school arranges short courses in Kalarippayat, and can also provide guides for forest trekking.

Accommodation

Thiruvananthapuram's mid-range and expensive **hotels** are, in general, cheaper than in most state capitals, but are not concentrated in any one district. Budget hotels are grouped mainly in the streets around **Central Station Road**. Good areas to start looking are **Manjalikulam Road**, five minutes' walk west from the railway station, or the lanes off **Aristo Junction**; note that the best of the budget places tend to be full by late afternoon. If you prefer to base yourself at the beach, head for Kovalam (see p.1064).

ACCOMMODATION PRICE CODES

All **accommodation prices** in this book have been coded using the symbols below. In principle the prices given are for the least expensive double rooms in each establishment; however, some hotels, usually in category ①, offer rates per bed rather than per room. Local taxes are not included unless specifically stated. For more details, see p.35.

① up to Rs100	④ Rs225–350	⑦ Rs750–1200
② Rs100–150	⑤ Rs350–500	⑧ Rs1200–2200
③ Rs150–225	⑥ Rs500–750	⑨ Rs2200 and upwards

Inexpensive

Hazeen, off Aristo Rd (no phone). Among the best budget lodges within easy reach of the station; the usual green-walled rooms, but the bed linen is fresh and the tiled bathrooms immaculate. ②.

Manacaud, Manjalikulam Rd (☎330360). Nothing special, but the best maintained of several cheap hotels on this lane. Attached bathrooms, though small windows and no balconies. ②.

Prasand Tourist Home, Aristo Rd, opposite *Horizon Hotel* (☎67180). One of a crop of rock-bottom guest houses around a courtyard near the station. Reputable and family run. *Satil* and *Salvha*, next door, are similar. ②.

YWCA, Spencer Junction (☎77308). Spotless en-suite doubles in modern block. Friendly, efficient and central, and by far the city's best economy deal; book ahead by phone. Men welcome, and single rates available. ③.

Moderate to expensive

Fort Manor, Power House Junction (☎462222; fax 460560). Slap in the centre, this huge semi-circular building is the city's top hotel, offering large rooms (many with good views), roof-top garden terrace and a mini-gym. ⑧–⑨.

Jas, Aristo Junction (☎64881; fax 64443). Good-value 2-star in a quiet hilltop location near the stations. Plain but pleasant rooms, all with TVs, Western toilets and easy chairs. ⑤–⑦.

Highlands, Manjalikulam Rd (☎68200). Dependable mid-range option; clean, well run and a short walk from the stations. In a multi-storey block, it's also the easiest place in the area to find. ④–⑤.

Horizon, Aristo Rd, 10min by taxi north of the railway station (☎66888; fax 67642). Plush Western-style place with good-value non-a/c rooms and a/c suites, restaurant and bar. 24hr check out. ④–⑦.

KTDC Chaithram, Station Rd (☎330977). Large, modern hotel opposite the railway station, with spacious rooms (some a/c), a/c veg restaurant, bank, travel agent, car rental, beauty parlour, book-shop and bar. Good value at this price. ④–⑤.

Luciya Continental, East Fort (☎463443; fax 463347). An upscale complex near the temple, with 104 rooms plus "fantasy suites". Mod cons include a restaurant, coffee shop and travel agent. ⑥–⑦.

Pankaj, opposite Secretariat, MG Rd (☎76667). Stylish, well maintained, modern hotel. Some rooms have beautiful views over trees, as does the fifth-floor restaurant. Some a/c. ⑥–⑦.

South Park, MG Rd (☎65666; fax 68861). Comfortable, business-oriented 4-star with a/c rooms, a restaurant and 24-hr coffee shop. Central reservation through any *Welcomgroup* hotel. ⑧.

Eating

Thiruvananthapuram is crying out for a **restaurant** specializing in delicious Keralan home-cooking. In the meantime, the upscale hotels have the best **places to eat**, with generalized Indian and Western cuisine at moderate prices. Some, such as the *Fort Manor* and *Pankaj*, have roof-top restaurants with views over the city.

Anand Bhawan, opposite Secretariat, MG Rd. Cheap, simple restaurant near the *Pankaj*, offering regional veg "meals".

Indian Coffee House, Spencer Junction, MG Rd. Small, colonial-style building, set back from the road and a sociable place to meet local students. Serves good-value snack meals and coffee.

Indian Coffee House (II), Central Station Rd. Unbeatable for breakfast or a quick snack. Turbaned waiters serve *dosas*, *wadas*, omelettes and hot drinks in a bizarre spiral building designed by eccentric British architect. Obligatory pit-stop.

KTDC Chaithram, Central Station Rd. Two restaurants: one pure veg and the other *Mughlai*-style. The former, a tastefully decorated air-cooled place, is the best, offering good-value Keralan special-ities and a standard range of rice-based north Indian dishes. Recommended.

Sandha, *Pankaj Hotel*, opposite Secretariat, MG Rd. Fifth-floor restaurant with a mixed menu and good-value lunch buffet; and a ground-floor restaurant open for breakfast.

Listings

Car rental *Best Travels*, Pandit's Building, Palayam (☎61616); *Inter-Car*, Ayswarya Buildings, Press Rd (☎67964); *Nataraj Travels*, Thampanoor (☎63064); *Travel India*, Convent Rd (☎78208).

Dance and drama For Kathakali and Kutiyattam check with the *Margi School* (see p.1058), or the tourist office on Station Rd (see p.1057), which organizes free dance performances at the open-air *Nishagandhi Auditorium* (Sept–March Sat 6.45pm).

Hospitals General Hospital, Vanchiyur; Ramakrishna Mission Hospital, Sastamangalam.

Travel agents *Aries Travels* (specialists for tours to the Maldives), Ayswarya Building, Press Rd (☎330964); *Jaihind Travels*, nr PMG Circle, opposite the Science Musem (☎447821); *Swastik Tours and Travel*, Puthenchantai, MG Rd (☎331713; fax 331270); *The Great Indian Tour Company*, Mullassery Towers, Vanross Jctn (☎331516); *Airtravel Enterprises* (good for air tick-ets), LMS Jctn (☎67182); and *Channakya Group Travels*, St Joseph Press Building, Cotton Hill (☎65498).

Visa extension The City Police Commissioner's office (Mon–Sat 10am–5pm; ☎60555), on Residency Rd, near the Women's College, Thycaud. The process takes three days to one week.

Yoga The *Shivananda Yoga Ashram* at 27/1929 Airport Rd, Palkulangara, West Fort (☎450942) holds daily classes at various levels, which you can arrange on spec. Better still, head for Neyyar Dam, 28km east of town, where their world-famous ashram offers excellent two-week introductory courses amid idyllic mountain surroundings (see p.1069 for more).

MOVING ON FROM THIRUVANANTHAPURAM

Thiruvananthapuram is the main transport hub for traffic along the coast and cross-country. Towns within a couple of hours of the capital – such as Varkala and Kollam – are most quickly and conveniently reached by **bus**, although for longer hauls you're better off travelling by **train** as both the private and state (*KSRTC*) buses tend to hurtle along the recently upgraded coastal highway at terrifying speeds; they're also more crowded.

For a **full rundown** of travel services to and from Thiruvananthapuram, see Kerala Travel Details on p.1053.

By air
Thiruvananthapuram's **airport**, 6km south of the centre, sees daily flights to **Bombay** (1hr 55min) on *Indian Airlines* and *East–West*. *Air India*'s six weekly flights to Bombay only accept passengers connecting with international flights. *Indian Airlines* also fly to **Bangalore, Madras** and **Delhi** via **Kochi**. International flights go to **Colombo** in Sri Lanka on *Indian Airlines* and *Air Lanka*, and **Malé** in the **Maldives** on *Indian Airlines*.

Indian Airlines have offices at *Air Centre*, Mascot Jctn (π436870), and the airport (π451537). *Air India* are at Museum Rd, Velayambalam Circle (π434837), and the airport (π451426), while *Air Lanka* are based at Geethanjali Building, Geethanjali Hospital Rd, Vazhuthacaud (π63209). *Gulf Air*, who operate regular flights to various Gulf sates, are across town in Vellayambalam (π67988); and *Maldives Airways* are c/o *S&J Sales Corporation*, Glass House Building, Panavila Jctn (π66105).

By bus
From the long-distance *KSRTC* Thampanoor **bus stand** (π63886), frequent services run north through Kerala to Kollam and Ernakulam/Kochi via Alappuzha (3hr 15min). Three buses a day go up to Kumily for the Periyar Wildlife Reserve, and one an hour to Kanniyakumari. Most buses running south are operated by the Tamil Nadu state road transport corporation, *Thiruvallar*; these include regular services to Madurai and Madras. **Tickets** for all the services listed above may be booked in advance at the reservations hatch on the main bus stand concourse; note that *Thiruvallar* have their own counter.

By train
Kerala's capital is well connected **by train** with other towns and cities in the country, although getting seats at short notice on long-haul journeys can be a problem. **Reservations** should be made as far in advance as possible from the computerized booking office at the station (Mon–Sat 8am–2pm & 2.15–8pm, Sun 8am–2pm). Sleepers are sold throughout Kerala on a first-come, first-served basis, not on local stations' quotas.

The following trains are recommended as the **fastest** and/or **most convenient** from Thiruvananthapuram.

Destination	Name	Number	Frequency	Departs	Total time
Bangalore	*Kanniyakumari–Bangalore Express*	#6525	daily	7.20am	18hr 25min
Bombay	*Trivandrum–Bombay Express*	#6332	Sat	4.30am	40hr
	Kanniyakumari Express	#1082	daily	7.30am	45hr 35min
Calcutta	*Trivandrum–Guwahati Express*	#6321	Thurs	12.45pm	49hr
Delhi	*Rajdhani Express*	#2431*	Fri	8pm	44hr 30min
	Kerala Express	#2625	daily	9.45am	53hr 30min
Ernakulam/Kochi	*Kerala Express*	#2625	daily	9.45am	4hr 30min
Kanniyakumari	*Kanniyakumari Express*	#1081	daily	12.20pm	2hr 15min
Kollam	*Kanniyakumari Express*	#1082**	daily	7.30am	1hr 30min
Kozhikode	*Trivandrum–Cannanore Express*	#6347	nightly	8.35pm	9hr 50min
Madras	*Trivandrum–Madras Mail*	#6320	daily	1.10pm	17hr 45min
Mangalore	*Malabar Express*	#6029	daily	5.40pm	16hr

* a/c only
** connects with the Kollam–Alappuzha backwater cruise

Around Thiruvananthapuram

Although for virtually its entire 550-kilometre length the **Keralan coast** is lined with sandy beaches, rocky promontories and coconut palms, **Kovalam** is the only place where swimming in the sea is not considered eccentric by locals, and which offers accommodation to suit all budgets. When it gets too hot at sea level, **Ponmudi**, a bus ride away in the Cardamom hills through forest, spice and tea plantations, makes a refreshing break. Another easy excursion from Thiruvananthapuram is its predecessor as capital of Travancore, **Padmanabhapuram**, site of a magnificent palace.

Kovalam

The coastal village of **KOVALAM** may lie just 10km south from Thiruvananthapuram, but as Kerala's most developed **beach resort** it's becoming ever more distanced from the rest of the state. Each year greater numbers of Western visitors – budget travellers and jet-setters alike – arrive in search of sun, sea and palm-fringed beaches. For many travellers it has become, with Goa and Mamallapuram, the third essential stop on a tri-angular tour of tropical south Indian "paradises" – or indeed just another leg of the trail along the coasts of South Asia.

Europeans have been visiting Kovalam since the 1930s, but not until hippies started to colonize the place some thirty years later were any hotels built. As the resort's popularity began to grow, more and more paddy fields were filled and the first luxury holiday complexes sprang up. These soon caught the eye of European charter companies scouting for "undiscovered" beach hideaways to supplement their Goa brochures, and by the mid 1990s plane-loads of fortnighting package tourists were flown here direct from the UK. This latest influx has had a dramatic impact on Kovalam. Prices have rocketed, rubbish lies in unsightly piles at the roadsides, and in high season the beach – recently enlarged to make way for even more cafés, souvenir stalls and fish restaurants – is packed nose-to-tail. Add to this a backdrop of rapidly deteriotating concrete hotels, and you can see why Kovalam's detractors call it "the Costa del Kerala".

Arrival, information and getting around

Heading along the recently upgraded approach road from the capital (now lined by more stone-breakers and publicity hoardings than trees), the frequent #9 **bus** from Thiruvananthapuram (East Fort; 20min) loops through Kovalam, and stops at the gates to the *Ashok* complex, at the northern end of the middle bay. Anyone carrying heavy bags who wants to stay by the sea (and not at the *Ashok*), should alight earlier, either at the road to the lighthouse, or the road leading down to the *Sea Rock* hotel. It's also possible to take an auto-rickshaw or taxi all the way from Thiruvananthapuram.

The only **bank** is the *Central Bank of India* (Mon–Fri 10.30am–2pm, Sat 10.30am–noon) at the *Ashok*. You can also change money at *Wilson's Hotel* any time (at bank rates), and at the *Moonlight Tourist Home*. Opposite the bus stand, *Western Travels* (daily 8am–8pm; ☎481334) is a reliable agent for flight confirmations and ticketing, and can arrange **car rental**. Surfboards can be rented through *Santana* restaurant on Lighthouse Beach. **Cycles** are also available through the Tourist Information Centre in the grounds of the *Ashok Hotel* (Rs5 per hour; Rs50 for 24hr).

The telephone **area code** for Kovalam is ☎0471.

Kovalam's beaches

Kovalam consists of four successive small crescent beaches; the southernmost, known for obvious reasons as **Lighthouse Beach**, is where most visitors spend their time. Roughly five minutes' trudge through the sand from end to end (none of it is paved), it's bordered with cheek-to-cheek low-rise guest houses and restaurants. The red-and-white **lighthouse** (daily 2–4pm; max stay 15min), on the promontory at the southern end of the beach, gives superb views across to Vizhinjam mosque (see below).

Hawah, the middle beach, overlooked from a rocky headland by the 5-star *Ashok* resort, functions each morning as a base for local fishermen, who drag a massive net through the shallows to scoop up thrashing multi-hued minnows, coiling endless piles of coir rope as they work. North of the *Ashok*, though in full view of its distinctive sloping terraces, the final, northermost beach, **Samudra**, is the least affected of all by the changing times, dotted with a few rudimentary wooden fishing vessels.

WARNING: SWIMMING SAFETY

Due to unpredictable rip currents and an often strong undertow, **swimming** from Kovalam's beaches is not always safe. The recent introduction of lifeguards has reduced the annual death toll, but at least a couple of tourists still drown here each year, and many more get into difficulties, so follow the warnings of the safety flags at all times and keep a close eye on children. If you do find yourself swept out into the bay, hold one arm in the air and try to swim parallel with the beach towards the rocks.

Pozhikkara beach and Pachalloor village

Heading north along Samudra for around 3km you'll eventually arrive at a point where the sea merges with the backwaters to form a salt-water lagoon. Although only thirty minutes' walk from the *Ashok*, the sliver of white sand dividing the two, known as **Pozhikkara beach**, is a world away from the headlong holiday culture of Kovalam. Here, the sands are used primarily for landing fish and fixing nets, while the thick palm canopy shelters a mixed community of Hindu fishermen and Christian coir makers. The tranquil village of **PACHALLOOR**, behind the lagoon, is a good alternative base to Thiruvananthapuram or Kovalam. A single guest house, the wonderful *Lagoona Beach Resort* (☎443738 or 480049; ⑤), provides four basic en-suite rooms that open on to the water. Lazing in a hammock in the garden, you can watch villagers paddling past in their long dug-outs, and sand-*wallahs* diving to fill buckets with silt. The guest house also organizes its own (recommended) **backwater trips**. Accompanied by a knowledgable guide, you're punted around the neighbouring villages, with stops to see coir being made and to identify an amazing wealth of tropical fruit trees, spices and birds. The **food** served at *Lagoona* is also exceptional, with authentic Keralan village dishes that you're unlikely to encounter elsewhere, and, power-cuts permitting, chilled beer. To get to *Lagoona* direct from Thiruvananthapuram, take an auto-rickshaw 6km along the highway towards Kovalam (Rs40–50), bearing right along the "by-pass" where the road forks (just after the Thiruvallam Bridge). After another 1km or so, a sign on the right of the road points through the trees to the guest house; if you've booked ahead by phone (strongly recommended) one of the staff should be there to meet you.

Vizhinjam (Vilinjam)

The unassuming village of **VIZHINJAM** (pronounced *Virinyam*), on the opposite (south) side of the headland from Lighthouse Beach, was once the capital of the Ay kings, the earliest dynasty in south Kerala. During the ninth century the Pandyans inter-

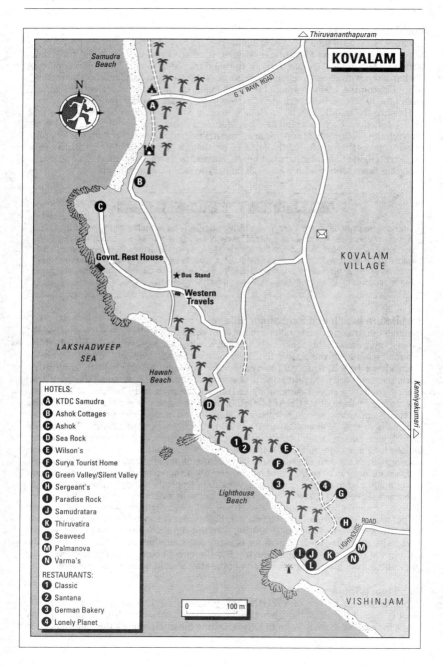

mittently took control, and it was the scene of major Chola–Chera battles in the eleventh century. A number of small simple shrines survive from those times, and can be made the focus of a pleasant afternoon's stroll along quiet paths. They're best approached from the village centre, beyond a fishing community, rather than via the coast road. However, if you do walk along the coast road from Kovalam to the north side of Vizhinjam, you can't fail to be struck by the contrast; from the conspicuous consumption of a tourist resort you find yourself in a poor fishing village, where a huge modern pink **mosque** on the promontory overlooks a bay of tightly packed thatched huts.

For centuries, the Muslim fishermen here were kept at arm's length by the Hindu orthodox, perpetually forced into debt by the combination of low prices for their produce with the exorbitant interest charged by moneylenders on loans for boats and nets (as much as 10 percent per day). Cooperatives have recently started to arrange interest-free loans and sell fish on behalf of individuals, but the mutual antipathy between the two communities persists, flaring up in the early 1990s in a series of violent riots during which numerous local people died. Today, Hindus and Muslims are divided by a 300-metre stretch of no-man's-land, patrolled by police, which only tourists can cross without risking a severe beating. Needless to say, you're not likely to be popular if you use Vizhinjam as a photo opportunity.

On the far side of the fishing bay, in the village centre, 50m down a road opposite the police station, a small unfinished eighth-century rock shrine features a carved figure of Shiva with a weapon. The **Tali Shiva** temple, reached by a narrow path from behind the Govt primary school, may mark the original centre of Vizhinjam. The simple shrine is accompanied by a group of *naga* snake statues, a reminder of Kerala's continuing cult of snake worship that survives from pre-Brahmanical times.

The grove known as **Kovil Kadu** ("temple forest") lies near the sea, ten minutes' walk from the main road in the village along Hidyatnagara Rd. Here a small enclosure contains a square Shiva shrine and a rectangular one dedicated to the goddess **Bhagavati**. Thought to date from the ninth century, these are probably the earliest structural temples in Kerala, although the Bhagavati shrine has been renovated.

Kovalam accommodation

Kovalam is crammed with **accommodation**, ranging from sandy-floored cells to 5-star hilltop chalets. Only rock-bottom rooms are hard to find, as all but a handful of the many budget travellers' guest houses that formerly crowded the beach front have been recently upgraded. Touts hang around the bus stand, but if you follow one remember that their "commission" tends to be tacked on to the tariff.

Prices are extortionate compared with the rest of Kerala, soaring in peak season (Dec to mid-Jan), when you'll be lucky to find a basic room for less than Rs250. At other times, haggling should bring the rate down, especially if you stay over a week.

INEXPENSIVE

Sergeant's, Lighthouse Beach (no phone). Dilapidated guest house run by garrulous retired army sergeant. Rooms are basic, but the atmosphere is sociable, and the rates rock-bottom. ①–②.

Silent Valley/Green Valley, Lighthouse Beach (☎480636). Set amid the paddy fields, this pair of jointly owned hotels offers the best budget accommodation in Kovalam, with pleasant en-suite rooms ranged around leafy and secluded courtyards. Restaurant on site. ④.

Surya Tourist Home, Lighthouse Beach (no phone). One of a clutch of no-frills places tucked behind the main beach, with small-ish rooms and low tariffs. Plenty of fall-backs nearby. ②.

Thiruvathira, Lighthouse Beach (☎480787). Attached rooms with verandahs and sea views, though slightly boxed in. Martial arts and massage courses available. Good value. ③.

Wilson's, behind the *Neelkantha Hotel* (☎480051). At the top of this range, but worth the extra for spacious en-suite rooms, balconies, garden, friendly staff and proximity to the beach. The massage parlour is also recommended (for men or women), and they do foreign exchange. ③–④.

MODERATE TO EXPENSIVE

Ashok, Kovalam Beach (☎480101; fax 480242). Four complexes of chalets and "cottages" in Charles Correa's award-winning hilltop block. Bars, restaurants, pools, yoga centre and tennis courts make this Kovalam's swankiest option. Tariffs from Rs4000–5000 per night (taxes extra). ⑨.

KTDC Samudra, Kovalam Beach (☎480089; fax 480242). Posh government-run 2-star set away from other hotels, with good access to beach. Open-air restaurant, bar and ayurvedic massage. ⑨.

Palmanova, Lighthouse Rd (☎480494; fax 480495). Well-appointed rooms in a modern concrete building, surrounded by palms and with fine views from individual terraces. Restaurant on site. ⑧.

Paradise Rock, Lighthouse Rd (☎480658) Variously priced, large en-suite rooms overlooking the main beach. Clean and welcoming, though no single occupancy. ④–⑥.

Samudratara, Lighthouse Rd (☎480653). Three-storey concrete block set back from beach, with comfortable rooms and individual balconies. Peaceful, and popular with older visitors. ⑤–⑦.

Sea Rock, Hawah Beach (☎480422). One of Kovalam's oldest established hotels. Slap on the seafront, with views of Hawah Beach from the more expensive front rooms (those at the back cost half). Good off-season discounts. ⑤–⑦.

Sea Weed, Lighthouse Rd (☎480391; fax 480806). Neat, clean and breezy hotel with rooftop restaurant and leafy central courtyard. Again, rooms with views cost extra. ⑤–⑦.

Varma's, Lighthouse Rd (☎480478). Most attractive of the upper-mid-range places. Superb views and tastefully furnished rooms with carved wood and tiled interiors, plus sea-facing terraces. ⑧.

Kovalam eating and nightlife

Lighthouse Beach is lined by cafés and restaurants. Most specialize in **seafood**: you pick from the fresh fish, lobster, tiger prawns, crab and mussels on display, which is then weighed, grilled over a charcoal fire, and served with salad and chips. Meals are pricey by Indian sandards – typically between Rs120–150 per head for fish, and double that for lobster or prawns – and the service is often painfully slow, but the ambience of the beachfront terraces is convivial enough. Beer, spirits and local *feni* (distilled palm wine) are also served, to a background of soft reggae or Pink Floyd (the rave scene has yet to hit Kovalam). For **breakfast** you can chose from any number of typical trans-Asia-budget-traveller cafés with the usual brown bread menus.

  Nightlife in Kovalam is pretty laid back, revolving around the beach, where Westerners lounge about drinking and playing backgammon until the wee hours. A couple of restaurants also offer **video nights**, screening pirate copies of the latest American hits. You may be offered *charas*, but bear in mind cannabis is illegal in Kerala, as everywhere else in India, and that the local police regularly arrest foreigners for possession.

Classic, Lighthouse Beach. Unpretentious beachside café, popular with budget travellers for its wide menu of inexpensive snacks and meals, techno system and negotiable prices. Try their full-on Rs50 breakfasts of fruit juice, muesli, toast and eggs.

German Bakery, Lighthouse Beach. Breezy rooftop terrace at the south end of the beach, serving tasty (mostly healthy) Western food and lots of tempting cakes (try the waffles with chocolate sauce). Breakfasts include a "full English" and "French" (croissants with expresso and a cigarette).

Lonely Planet, behind Lighthouse Beach, near the *White House Hotel*. Congenial, generally inexpensive, veg restaurant tucked away in the paddy fields. The place to come if you're pining for Indian food, and one of the few places you can get *iddlies* for breakfast.

Santana, Lighthouse Beach. The best of the seafood joints on the beach, with a great BBQ and *tandoori* fish and chicken, and Kovalam's best sound system. Stays open later than most.

Ponmudi and Peppara Wildlife Sanctuary

In the tea-growing region of the **Cardamom** (or Ponmudi) **Hills**, about 60km northeast of Thiruvananthapuram at an altitude of 1066m, the hill station of **PONMUDI** – not a town, or even a village, but merely some accommodation of a pretty minimal standard – commands breathtaking views out across the range as far as the sea.

The main reason anyone comes up here is that it serves as the only practical base for visits to the 53 square kilometres of forest set aside as **Peppara Wildlife Sanctuary**, which protects elephants, *sambar*, lion-tailed macaques, leopard, and assorted birds. Although Peppara is theoretically open all year, the main season is from January until May; check before you go with the District Forest Officer, Thiruvananthapuram Forest Division, Thiruvananthapuram (☎60637).

The beautiful drive up, via the small towns of Nedumangad and Vithura, runs along very narrow roads past areca nut, clove, rubber and cashew plantations, with first the Kavakulam and then the Kallar river close at hand. The bridge at **Kallar Junction** marks the start of the real climb. Twenty-two hairpin bends (numbered at the roadside) lead slowly up, firstly in the foothills, past great lumps of black rock and thick clumps of bamboo (*iramula*), then through the Kallar teak forest. You finally emerge into tea plantations; the temperature is noticeably cooler and, once out of the forest, the views across the hills and the plains below become truly spectacular.

Practicalities

Four daily **buses** run from Thiruvananthapuram to Ponmudi, via Vithura; the first is at 5.30am and the last at 3.30pm. They return between 12.30pm and 6.30pm. In 1992, the River Kallar broke its banks in freak December rains, killing a number of people, and the havoc caused may still be evident. Check that the road is safe before attempting the journey in your own vehicle.

The KTDC *Ponmudi Guest House* (☎0471/89230; closed June & July; ①–②) has 24 **rooms**, a dorm, and seven cottages. Meals have to be ordered in advance, so it's worth bringing some provisions. The main building, which originally belonged to the Raja of Travancore, has lost any charm it may once have possessed, and the huge plate-glass windows of its canteen-like restaurant rattle disconcertingly in the wind, but views from the terrace make up for all that. Weekends get lively, thanks to the beer parlour.

SWANANDA YOGA VEDANTA DHANWANTARI

Located amid the serene hills and tropical forests around **Neyyar Dam**, 28km east of Thiruvananthapuram, the **Swananda Yoga Vedanta Dhanwantari** is one of India's leading **yoga** ashrams. It was founded by Swami Shivananda – dubbed the "Flying Guru" because he used to pilot light aircraft over war-stricken areas of the world scattering flowers and leaflets calling for peace – as a centre for meditation, yoga and traditional Keralan martial arts and medicine.

Aside from training teachers in advanced *raja* and *hatha* yoga, the ashram offers excellent **introductory courses** for beginners. These comprise four hours of intensive tuition per day (starting at 5.30am), with background lectures that provide helpful theory. During the course, you have to stay at the ashram and comply with a regime that some Western students find disconcertingly strict (smoking, alcohol, drugs, sex and even "rock music" are prohibited, the diet is pure veg, and you have to get up at the crack of dawn). However, if you are keen to acquire the basic techniques and knowledge of yoga, this is a good place to start. For more details, contact the ashram itself (☎0472/54493), or their branch in Thiruvananthapuram (27/1929 Airport Rd, West Fort; ☎0471/450942).

Padmanabhapuram

Although now officially in Tamil Nadu, **PADMANABHAPURAM**, 63km southeast of Thiruvananthapuram, was the capital of Travancore between 1550 and 1750, and therefore has a far more intimate connection with the history of Kerala. For anyone with even a minor interest in Keralan architecture, this small palace is an irresistible attraction. However, **avoid weekends**, when the complex gets overrun with bus parties.

Set in neat gravelled grounds in a quiet location away from the main road, the predominantly wooden **Padmanabhapuram Palace** (daily except Mon 9am–4.30pm; cameras Rs5) epitomizes Keralan architecture. It is reached by crossing the main road from the bus station (see below), turning left, and then following a road on the right for a pleasant 10- or 15-minute walk through the paddy fields. The substantial walls of the palace compound delimit a small village.

Against a backdrop of steep-sided hills, the exterior of the palace – parts of which date back to the town's earliest days – displays a perfect combination of clean lines and gentle angles, with the sloping tiled roofs of its various interconnecting buildings broken by triangular projecting gables enclosing delicately carved screens. The whole ensemble is excellently maintained by the Archaeological Survey of India; all visitors have to be shown around by the informative **guides**.

In the **entrance hall** (a verandah), a brass oil lamp hangs from an ornate teak, rosewood and mahogany ceiling carved with ninety different lotus flowers. Beautifully ornamented, the revolving lamp inexplicably keeps the position in which it is left, seeming to defy gravity. The Raja rested from the summer heat on the cool polished granite bed in the corner. On the wall is a collection of *onamvillu*, ceremonial bows painted with reclining Vishnus (or more properly Padmanabha), which local chieftains would present to him during the Onam festival.

Directly above the entrance, on the first floor, is the **mantrasala** or council chamber, gently illuminated through panes of coloured mica. Herbs soaking in water were put into the boxed bench seats along the front wall, as natural air-conditioning. The highly polished black floor was made from a now-lost technique using burnt coconut, sticky sugar-cane extract, egg whites, lime and sand.

The oldest part of the complex is the **Ekandamandapam** – "the lonely place". Built in 1550, it was used for rituals for the goddess Durga which typically employed *kalam ezhuttu*, elaborate floor paintings (see p.1095). A loose ring attached to a column is a tour de force of the carpenter: both ring and column are carved from a single piece of jackwood. Nearby is a *nalekettu*, the four-sided courtyard found in many Keralan houses, open to the sky and surrounded by a pillared walkway. A trapdoor once served as the entrance to a secret passageway leading to another palace, since destroyed.

The Pandya-style stone-columned **dance hall** stands directly in front of a shrine to the goddess of learning, Saraswati. The women of the royal household had to watch performances through screens on the side, and the staff, through holes in the wall from the gallery above. Typical of old country houses, steep wooden ladder-like steps, ending in trapdoors, connect the floors. Belgian mirrors and Tanjore miniatures of Krishna adorn the chamber forming part of the **women's quarters**, where a swing hangs on plaited iron ropes. A four-poster bed, made from sixteen kinds of medicinal wood, dominates the **Raja's bedroom**. Its elaborate carvings depict a mass of vegetation, human

---

TRAVANCORE AND THE SERVANTS OF VISHNU

In front of a depiction of the god in the meditation, or prayer room, at Padmanabhapuram Palace lies a sword. In 1750, **Raja Marthanda Varma** symbolically presented this weapon to Padmanabha, the god Vishnu, who reclines on the sacred serpent Anantha in the midst of the cosmic ocean, and thereby dedicated the kingdom of Travancore to Vishnu. From that day, the Raja took the title of Padmanabhadasa ("servant of Padmanabha"), and ruled as a servant of the god.

Thus Travancore belonged to Vishnu, and the Raja was merely its custodian – a spiritual, and presumably legal, loophole which is said to have proved invaluable in restricting the power of the British in Travancore to the installation of a British Resident.

figures, birds and as the central motif, the snake symbol of medicine, associated with the Greek physician Asclepius.

The **murals** for which the palace is famous – alive with detail, colour, graceful form and religious fervour – adorn the walls of the **meditation room**, used by the Raja and the heirs apparent, directly above the bedroom. Unfortunately, this is now closed – allegedly because the stairs are shaky, but in fact to preserve the murals, which have been severely damaged by generations of hands trailing along the walls.

Further points of interest in the palace include a **dining hall** intended for the free feeding of up to 2000 brahmins, and a 38-kilo stone which, it is said, every new recruit to the Raja's army had to raise above his head 101 times.

Practicalities

Frequent **buses** run to Padmanabhapuram from Thiruvananthapuram's Thampanoor station; hop on any service heading south towards Nagercoil or Kanniyakumari and get down at **Thakkaly** (sometimes written Thuckalai). If you're determined to see Padmanabhapuram, Kanniyakumari and Suchindram in one day, leave the city early to arrive when the palace opens at 9am. Seats are harder to come by on the way back, but with luck not all the passengers will be going right the way to Thiruvananthapuram. Note that two express buses leave Thakkaly for the capital during the afternoon, at 2.30pm and 3.30pm.

The area around the bus station, being on the NH47, is noisy and dirty. It's better to get **refreshment** from the *chaiya*-cum-food and "cool drinks" shops inside the outer walls of the palace. Just outside the inner gate you can usually find tender **coconuts**.

Varkala

Long known to Keralans as a place of pilgrimage, **VARKALA**, 54km northwest of Thiruvananthapuram and 20km southeast of Kollam, is drawing more and more foreign visitors, who see the beautiful beach and cliffs 1500m beyond the village as a quiet, unspoiled alternative to Kovalam. Centred on a handful of budget guest houses and palm-thatch cafés, the tourist scene has so far been relatively low-key. However, things look set to change following the completion of *Taj Group*'s luxury resort, which will bring package tourists here for the first time in the winter of 1996–7. The local council has big plans for the place, too, so enjoy it while you can; this tranquil spot could well go the same way as Kovalam – a sorry prospect indeed.

Arrival and information

Varkala's railway station, 2km east of the village, is served by express and mail **trains** from Thiruvananthapuram, Kollam (hourly; 45min), and most other Keralan towns on the main line. An auto-rickshaw to the beach costs around Rs20–30. Regular **buses** also run from Thiruvananthapuram's Thampanoor stand, and from Kollam (40min). Some go all the way to the beach, but most stop in the village centre, a five-minute auto-rickshaw ride away.

For general **tourist information** head for the privately run *Tourist Helping Centre* (aka *Mama House*) on the lane leading to the beach, who can arrange motorbike rental and advise you about train times. Their main raison d'etre, however, is to recruit punters for their **elephant trips** through the forest 30km away. The full day costs a little over Rs600, including all food and travel, and is well worthwhile. There are no official places to **change money** in Varkala, although your hotel or guest house owner will probably be able to exchange hard currency.

The telephone **area code** for Varkala is ☎0472.

The village

Known in Malayalam as Papa Nashini ("sin destroyer"), Varkala's beautiful white-sand **beach** has long been associated with ancestor worship. Devotees come here after praying at the **Janardhana Swamy** temple (said to be over 2000 years old) to bring the ashes of departed relatives for "final rest". A small government hospital at its north end, opened by Indira Gandhi in 1983, was set up to benefit from three **natural springs**, and take advantage of the sea air, said to boost the health of asthma sufferers.

Backed by a sheer red laterite cliffs and drenched by rolling waves off the Arabian Sea, Papa Nashini is imposingly scenic and still a relatively peaceful place to soak up the sun, with few hawkers and only the odd group of ogling men. Its religious significance means attitudes to (female) public nudity are markedly less liberal than other coastal "resorts" in India. Bikinis don't necessarily cause offence, but you'll attract a lot less attention if you wear a full-length cotton sarong while bathing.

Few of Varkala's Hindu pilgrims wander up to the **cliff-top area**, reached by several steep footpaths, or by the metalled road from the village that was built to service a helipad in advance of Mrs Gandhi's visit. However, those that do invariably seem less enthralled by the splendid sea views, than by the sight of *sari*- and *kurta*-clad Westerners meditating and pulling yoga poses under the palm trees. This faintly cheesy New Age scene centres on the small *Scientific School of Yoga*, which offers two-week courses in yoga, as well as regular Ayurvedic massage. Their small shop, *Prakruthi Sores*, stocks honey, essential oils, herbs and hand-made soaps, as well as books on yoga, meditation and massage.

Sivagiri Hill, at the eastern edge of the village, harbours a more traditional **ashram** that attracts pilgrim devotees of Shri Narayana Guru, a saint who died here in 1922. Born into the low *ezhava* caste, he fought orthodoxy with a philosophy of social reform ("one caste, one religion, one God for man"), which included the consecration of temples with an open-door policy to all castes, and had a profound effect on the "upliftment" of the untouchables.

Accommodation

Varkala has a fair choice of **places to stay**; most are basic rooms with shared (or outside) shower-toilets. If you're on a tight budget, head first for the cliff-top area (rickshaws can make it up there), where there are several family-run guest houses in the coconut trees behind the row of cafés. On the way, it's worth stopping to see if the wonderful *Government Guest House* has vacancies. Otherwise, choose from a scattering of places amid the paddy fields, and along the metalled road leading to the village. Accommodation is tight in **peak season** (late Nov–Jan), when you should call ahead.

Akshay Beach Resort, Beach Rd, Papanasam (☎402668). Clean guest house with en-suite rooms (one a/c), massage and helpful management. Dull location, but handy for the beach. ②–⑤.

Government Guest House, five minutes' walk north of the temple, near the *Taj* hotel (☎402227). Former Maharajah's hoilday palace, converted into a characterful guest house, with eight enormous rooms and meals available on request. Superb value. ①.

Green House, behind Yoga School, cliff-top area (no phone). Secluded and only 2min from the cliff edge, in an unhurried hamlet, and with plenty of similarly priced fall-backs nearby (try *White House* or *Red House*). It's actually blue and purple, not green. ①.

Hilltop Palace, north end of cliff (☎411737). Newish concrete building in a great spot, with pleasant, breezy rooms, attached shower-toilets and relaxing terrace restaurant. Good value. ③.

Marine Palace, behind the beach (☎403204). En-suite rooms in a modern, pale green building near the sea. Pricier front rooms have sea views and balconies; the thatched annexe is cheaper. ③.

Mama House (*Tourist Helping Centre*), Beach Rd (no phone). Rock-bottom rooms in crudely converted farm compound. Shared toilets and well water only; the cheapest in Varkala. ①.

Motal Beach Palace, off beach road (☎402453). Marooned in the paddy fields behind the beach, with cosy en-suite rooms around a fish pond. Easy to find – it's bright blue with palm-thatch roofs – but no road access. ③.

Eating

Seafood lovers will do well in Varkala's increasingly sophisticated cliff-top café-restaurants, some of which have upper storeys raised on stilts for better sea views. Prices are quite high, but the superb location more than compensates.

Motal Beach Palace, off beach Rd. The food is nothing to rave about, but the small pavilion on stilts in the middle of their fish pond is a novel place for beer. Inexpensive.

Sea Fish, cliff-top area. The largest of the cliff-top cafés, serving moderately priced *tandoori* meat and fish on a sandy terrace with relaxing wicker chairs and optimum views.

Shri Padman, next to temple, Varkala village. The large rear terrace of this unpromising, grubby-looking "meals" joint is the main travellers' hang-out in Varkala. The (Indian veg) food is cheap and delicious (try the coconut-rich *navrattan*, deep-fried cheese, garlic *chapatis*, or filling *biriyanis*), and the location atmospheric, especially at breakfast time, when villagers come to the tank to bathe.

Kollam (Quilon)

One of the oldest ports of the Malabar coast, **KOLLAM** (pronounced *Koillam*, and previously known as Quilon), 74km northwest of Thiruvananthapuram and 85km south of Alappuzha, was once at the centre of the international spice trade. The sixteenth-century Portuguese writer Duarte Barbossa described it as a "very great city with a right good haven", which was visited by "Moors, Heathen and Christians in great numbers", and stated that "a great store" of pepper was to be found there. In fact, the port flourished from the very earliest times, trading amicably with the Phoenicians, Arabs, Persians, Greeks, Romans and Chinese.

Nowadays, Kollam is chiefly of interest as one of the entry or exit points to the backwaters of Kerala (see p.1078), and most travellers simply stay overnight en route to or from Alappuzha. The **town** itself, sandwiched between the sea and the Ashtamudi ("eight inlets") lake, is less exciting than its history might suggest. It's a typically sprawling Keralan market community, with a few characterful old tiled wooden houses and winding backstreets, kept busy with the commercial interests of coir, cashew nuts (a good local buy), pottery, aluminium and fishery industries. The missable ruins of **Tangasseri** fort (3km from the centre) are the last vestiges of colonial occupation.

Arrival and information

The **boat jetty** (for boat details, see p.1079) and **bus stand** are close together on the edge of Ashtamudi Lake; note that the ATDC ferry leaves from a pier 100m west of its rival – see map). Bookable express **buses** are available south to Thiruvananthapuram (1hr 30min) and north to Kochi (3hr 30min) via Alappuzha (1hr 15min).

The **railway station** is on the east of town, a three-kilometre auto-rickshaw ride from the jetty. Numerous daily trains each way run to Ernakulam (3hr) and Thiruvananthapuram (1hr 10min–1hr 45min) and beyond. On platform 4, the tiny **Tourist Information Counter** (Mon–Sat 9am–12.30pm & 1.30–5pm; ☎72558) offers an excellent service. They will book hotels for travellers even outside the state; you have to pay one night in advance, but the only extra charge is for the phone calls.

Accommodation and eating

The most congenial **places to stay** are outside the town, across Ashtamudi Lake from the main jetty (easy to get to by auto-rickshaw, but more difficult to return from). Apart from the hotel restaurants, other places to **eat** include the *Indian Coffee House* on Main Rd, and *Guru Prasad*, a little way along, which serves great south Indian veg "meals".

The telephone **area code** for Kollam is ☎0474.

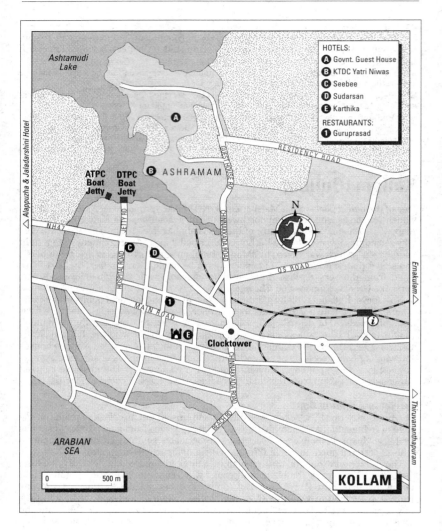

HOTELS:
- **Ⓐ** Govnt. Guest House
- **Ⓑ** KTDC Yatri Niwas
- **Ⓒ** Seebee
- **Ⓓ** Sudarsan
- **Ⓔ** Karthika

RESTAURANTS:
- **❶** Guruprasad

KOLLAM

Govt Guest House, 3km out, by Ashtamudi Lake (☎70356). Characterful Euro-Keralan building, once the British Residency, with curved tiled roof and verandahs, in a vast compound. Ye olde British furniture in cavernous spaces, but just 5 rooms (unbelievable value at Rs50). Boats are available for rent on the lake, simple meals are served by arrangement, and you can reserve your backwater tickets here. Book in advance; some travellers come to Kollam purely to stay here. ①.

Jaladarshini, Thevally, 2km west of town (☎203414). A/c and non-a/c rooms in a small, modern lakeside complex. Peaceful, with a good restaurant. ③–⑤.

KTDC Yatri Nivas, across from the jetty (☎78638). Modern, clean rooms (2 a/c) in a great location overlooking the lake; the best fall-back if the *Govt Guest House* is full. Good restaurant with south Indian snacks and, as always with KTDC, a beer parlour. ②.

Railway Retiring Rooms, first floor of railway station. Spacious, clean, and very cheap. ①.

Sea Bee, Jetty Rd (☎75371). Big, recently renovated hotel, near the bus station and jetty. Some a/c rooms, restaurant, bar, and foreign exchange. ④–⑤.

Sudarsan, Parameswar Nagar (☎75322). Central and popular, with varying rooms, some with a/c and TV. Busy, dark a/c restaurant with a white plaster *Last Supper* at one end and a TV at the other. Large Indian and Chinese menu, though not all is necessarily available, and a bar. ③–⑦.

Around Kollam: Kayamkulam and Karunagapalli

KAYAMKULAM, served by (non-express) buses between Kollam and Alappuzha, was once the centre of its own small kingdom, which after a battle in 1746 came under the control of Travancore's king Marthanda Varma. In the eighteenth century the area was famous for its spices, particularly pepper and cinnamon. The Abbé Reynal claimed that the Dutch exported some two million pounds of pepper each year, one-fifth of it from Kayamkulam. At this time, the kingdom was known also for the skill of its army, fifteen thousand Nayars (Kerala's martial caste).

Set in a tranquil garden, the dilapidated eighteenth-century **Krishnapuram Palace** (Tues–Sat 10am–4.30pm) is imbued with Keralan grace, constructed largely of wood, with gabled roofs and rooms opening out onto internal courtyards. It's now a museum, but unlike the palace at Padmanabhapuram (see p.1070), with which it shares some similarities, the whole place is in great need of restoration. So few visitors ever find their way here that the motivation for upkeep must be minimal.

The collection inside is dusty, poorly labelled and neglected. A display case contains *puja* ceremony utensils and oil lamps, some of which are arranged in an arc known as a *prabhu*, placed behind a temple deity to provide a halo of light. Fine miniature *panchaloha* ("five-metal" bronze alloy, with gold as one ingredient) figures include the water god Varuna, several Vishnus, and a minuscule worshipping devotee. Small stone columns carved with serpent deities were recovered from local houses.

The prize exhibit is a huge **mural** of the classical Keralan school, in muted ochre-reds and blue-greens, measuring over fourteen square metres, which depicts **Gajendra Moksha** – the salvation of Gajendra, king of the elephants. In the tenth-century Sanskrit *Bhagavata Purana*, the story is told of a Pandyan king, Indrayumna, a devotee of Vishnu cursed by the sage Agastya to be born again as an elephant. One day, while sporting with his wives at the edge of a lake, his leg was seized by a crocodile whose grip was so tight that Gajendra was held captive for years. Finally, in desperation the elephant called upon his chosen deity Vishnu, who immediately appeared, riding his celestial bird/man vehicle, Garuda, and destroyed the crocodile.

The centre of the painting is dominated by a dynamic portrayal of Garuda about to land, with huge spread wings and a facial expression denoting *raudra* (fury); stark contrast to the compassionate features of the multi-armed Vishnu. Smaller figures of Gajendra, in mid-trumpet, and his assailant are shown to the right. As with all paintings in the Kerala style, every inch is packed with detail. Bearded sages, animals, mythical beasts and forest plants surround the main figures. The outer edges are decorated with floriate borders which, at the bottom, form a separate triptych-like panel showing Balakrishna, the child Krishna, attended by adoring females.

At a quiet spot just outside the small town of **KARUNAGAPALLI**, 23km north of Kollam on the NH47 towards Alappuzha, it's possible to watch the construction of traditional **kettu vallam** ("tied boats"). These long cargo boats, a familiar sight on the backwaters, are built entirely without the use of nails. Each jackwood plank is

---

KETTU VALLAM CRUISES

Groups of up to ten can charter a *vallam* moored at **Karunagapalli** for a day's **cruise** on the backwaters (see p.1078). The boat has comfortable cane chairs and a raised central platform where passengers can laze on cushions, and a toilet on board. Cool drinks can be made available. Sections of the curved roof of wood and plaited palms open out to provide shade and allow uninterrupted views. Whether powered by local gondoliers or by sail, the trip is as quiet and restful (at least for the passenger) as you could possibly want. Though not cheap (around Rs3000 for the day), the luxury is well worth it. For longer trips a second *vallam* has been converted into a houseboat with two bedrooms and a kitchen. A cook will also be provided. To book, call *Tourindia*, MG Rd, Thiruvananthapuram (☎0471/79407 or 79437).

KTDC also rent out houseboats for cruises on Vembanad Lake, moored at their *Kumarakaram Tourist Village*, near the Kumarakom Bird Sanctuary (see p.1081), Alappuzha (☎0481/92258). Rates start at around Rs2000 per boat per day, which includes the services of crew and cook. These *kettu vallam* can also be rented for shorter cruises (Rs600 per hour).

---

sewn to the next with coir rope, and then the whole is coated with a caustic black resin made from boiled cashew kernels. With careful maintenance they last for generations.

Karunagapalli is best visited as a day trip from Kollam; regular **buses** pass through on the way to Alappuzha. One daytime **train**, #6525, leaves Kollam at 11.55am, arriving at Karunagapalli at 12.30, but you have to get a bus back. On reaching the bus stand or railway station, ask an auto-rickshaw to take you to the boatyard of the *vallam asharis*, the boat carpenters. The boatbuilders are friendly and willing to let visitors watch them work. In the shade of palm trees at the edge of the water, some weave palm leaves, others twist coir strands into rope, and craftsmen repair the boats. Soaking in the shallows nearby are palm leaves, to use for thatch, and coconut husks for coir rope. If you want to buy a *vallam* you'll need more than *lakh* (100,000) rupees.

Alappuzha

Under its former appellation of Alleppey, **ALAPPUZHA**, roughly midway between Kollam (85km south) and Kochi (64km north), is another romantic and historic name from Kerala's past. It was one of the best-known ports along the coast of Malabar, and tourist literature is fond of referring to it as "Venice of the East", but while it may be full of interconnecting **canals**, there the resemblance ends. Alappuzha is a bustling, messy town of ramshackle wood and corrugated iron-roof houses, chiefly significant in the coir industry, which accounts for much of the traffic on its oily green-brown waterways. Emanating from the slicks of raw sewage, diesel spills and aquatic weed that coagulate on their surfaces, the stomach-churning stench these give off each time a ferry chugs through is something many travellers wince about for weeks afterwards.

Despite its insalubrious canals and frequent power cuts, Alappuzha is prominent on the tourist trail as one of the major centres for **backwater boat trips**, served by ferries to and from Kollam and Kottayam in particular. Most visitors stay just one night, catching a boat or bus out early the next morning. No special sights demand attention, but the bazaar along the main street, **Mullakal Road**, is worth a browse, with a better-than-average crop of lurid Keralan *lunghis*.

Alappuzha really comes alive on the second Saturday of August, in the depths of the rainy season, when it serves as the venue for one of Kerala's major spectacles – the Nehru Trophy **snakeboat race**. This event, first held in 1952, is based on the tra-

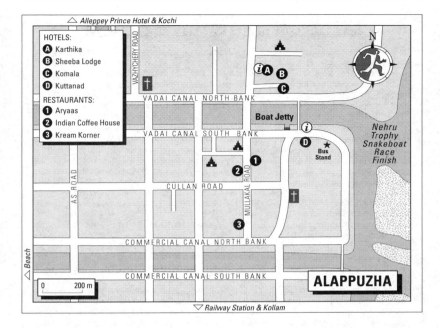

ditional Keralan enthusiasm for racing magnificently decorated long boats, with raised rears designed to resemble the hood of a cobra. More than enthusiastically powered by up to 150 singing and shouting oarsmen, scores of boats take part, and Alappuzha is packed with thousands of spectators. Similar races can be seen at Aranmula (p.1081), and at Champakualm, 16km by ferry from Alappuzha. The ATDC information office (see below) will be able to tell you the dates of these events, which change every year.

Arrival and information

The shambolic *KSRTC* **bus stand**, on the east of town, is served by half-hourly buses to Kollam (3hr) and Thiruvananthapuram (3hr 15min), and to Ernakulam (2hr); less frequent buses run to Kottayam, Thrissur and Palakaad. The **boat jetty** is just one minute's walk west from the bus stand. As the backwaters prevent **trains** from continuing south beyond Alappuzha, only a few major daily services depart from the **railway station**, 3km southwest of the jetty. Among these are the *Steel City Express* #8690 to Ernakulam Junction, at 6am, and the *Alleppey–Madras Express* #6042, to Ernakulam Junction and Thrissur, at 3.10pm. You can also catch direct daily trains to Thiruvananthapuram, Bombay and Delhi.

The ATDC **tourist information office** (daily 7.30am–8.30pm; ☎3462) at the *Karthika Tourist Home* across the canal from the jetty sells tickets for their ferries and charter boats (maximum 20 people Rs750 per day) – good for group excursions into less visited backwaters. For details of **ferries** to and from Alappuzha, see p.1079.

The telephone **area code** for Alappuzha is ☎0477.

KUTTANAD: THE BACKWATERS OF KERALA

One of the most memorable experiences available to travellers in India – even those on the lowest of budgets – is the opportunity to take a boat journey on the **backwaters of Kerala**. The area known as **Kuttanad** stretches for 75km from Kollam in the south to Kochi in the north, sandwiched between the sea and the hills. This bewildering labyrinth of shimmering waterways, composed of lakes, canals, rivers and rivulets, is lined with dense tropical greenery, and preserves rural Keralan lifestyles that are completely hidden from the road.

Views change from narrow canals and dense vegetation to open vistas and dazzling green paddy fields. Homes, farms, churches, mosques and temples can be glimpsed among the trees, and every so often you might catch the blue flash of a kingfisher, or the green of a parakeet. If you're lucky enough to be in a boat without a motor, at times the peace will be broken only by the squawking of crows and the occasional film song from a distant radio. Day-to-day life is lived on and beside the water. Some families live on tiny pockets of land, with just enough room for a simple house, yard and boat. They bathe and wash their clothes – sometimes their buffaloes too, muddy from ploughing the fields – at the water's edge, while you often pass villagers standing up to their necks in water, far from the banks and busy with impenetrable sub-aquatic chores. Traditional Keralan longboats, *kettu vallam*, glide past, powered both by gondolier-like boatmen with poles and by sail. Often they look on the point of sinking, laden with heavyweight cargo with water lapping perilously over the edge. Fishermen work from rowing boats or operate massive Chinese nets on the shore.

Coconut trees at improbable angles form shady canopies, and occasionally you pass under simple curved bridges. Here and there basic drawbridges can be raised on ropes, but major bridges are few and far between; most people rely on boatmen to ferry them across the water to connect with roads and bus services, a constant criss-crossing of the waters from dawn until dusk (a way of life beautifully represented in the visually stunning film *Piravi*, by Keralan director Shaji). Poles sticking out of the water indicate dangerous shallows.

The **African moss** that often carpets the surface of the narrower waterways, incidentally, may look attractive, but is a menace to small craft traffic and starves underwater life of light. It is also a symptom of the many serious **ecologial problems** currently affecting the region, whose population density ranges from between two and four times that of other coastal areas in southwest India. This has put growing pressure on land, and hence a greater reliance on fertilizers, which eventually work their way into the water causing the build up of moss. Illegal land reclamation, however, poses the single greatest threat to this fragile eco-system. In a little over a century, the total area of water in Kuttanad has been reduced by two-thirds, while mangrove swamps and fish stocks have been decimated by pollution and the spread of towns and villages around the edges of the backwater region.

Accommodation

Alappuzha's choice of **lodgings** is uninspiring – the cheapest places seem to regard the fact that tourists tend to stay only a single night as a disincentive to raise standards. If money's not to tight, spoil yourself in the *Alleppey Prince*, which has a pool.

Alleppey Prince, AS Rd, 2km north of the jetty (☎3752; fax 3758). The poshest option, all rooms a/c. Private backwater trips, and classical music or Kathakali staged by the pool. Book ahead. ⑥.

Karthika Tourist Home, Kathiyani Rd, across the canal, opposite the jetty (☎5524). Good value non-a/c rooms, some with bath and wicker chairs. Room 31 has large bay windows. ①–②.

Komala, Zilla Court Ward, north of the jetty canal, 5min by rickshaw from the bus stand (☎3631). Large hotel, easily the best in its class, and with the town's nicest restaurant. Some a/c. ②–⑤.

Routes and practicalities

There are numerous backwater routes to choose from, on vessels ranging from local ferries, through chauffeur-driven speedboats offered by upmarket hotels such as the *Malabar* in Kochi, to customized *kettu vallam* (see p.1076). Much the most popular excursion is the full-day journey between **Kollam** and **Alappuzha**; you can cover part or all of the route in a day, returning to your original point of departure by bus during the evening, or, more comfortably, staying the night at either end. All sorts of private hustlers offer their services, but the basic choice lies between boats run by the Alleppey Tourism Development Co-op (ATDC) and the District Tourism Promotion Council (DTPC), which run one boat daily on alternate days from Monday through Saturday (there is **no service on Sundays**); from December to May they lay on two boats per day. The double-decker boats depart at 10.30am, and tickets, which can be bought in advance at the jetties, or from ATDC/DTPC counters in Alappuzha and Kollam, cost Rs150. Both companies make around five stops during the 8hr 30min journey, including one for lunch, and another at the renowned **Mata Amritanandamayi Mission** at Amritapuri. Foreigners are welcome to stay at the ashram, which is the home of the renowned female guru, Shri Amritanandamayi Devi, known as the "hugging Mama" because she gives each of her visitors and devotees a big, power-imparting hug during the daily *darshan* sessions.

Although it is by far the most popular backwater trip, many tourists find the Alappuzha–Kollam route overlong and at times uncomfortable, with crowded decks and intense sun. There's also something faintly embarassing about being cooped up with a crowd of fellow tourists madly photographing any signs of life on the water or canal banks, while gangs of kids scamper alonside the boat screaming "one pen ! . . . one pen ! . . .". You can sidestep the tourist scene completely by catching **local ferries**. These are a lot slower, and the crush can be worse, but you're far less conspicuous than on the ATDC/DTPC boats and gain a more intimate experience of life on the water. The trip from Alappuzha to Kottayam is particularly recommended; take the 2.30pm departure for the best light, and arrive early so you can get a place on the bow, which affords uninterrupted views. The scenery on this route is more varied than between Alappuzha and Kollam, begining with open lagoons and winding up on narrow canals through densely populated coconut groves and islands; the ticket costs one tenth of the price.

Whichever boat you opt for, take a sun hat and plenty of water, and **check the departure times** in advance, as these can vary from year to year.

From Alappuzha, ATDC (based at *Karthika Tourist Home*; ☎0477/3462) depart on Mon, Wed and Fri at 10.30am; from Dec–May, they lay on wo boats per day. There are also 11 daily departures by local ferry to **Kottayam** (Rs5; 2hr 30min; first at 5am, last 9pm), one every other day to **Kochi** (noon; 6hr), and one daily to Kumarakom (3pm; 2hr 30min). Noisy speedboats can be chartered from ATDC for Rs300 per hour, or Rs700 per day.

From Kollam, the ATDC boat departs at 10.30am on Tues, Thurs and Sat only. Shorter trips are available to Kapapuzha and Guhanandapuram (2hr), if you don't have time for a full-day excursion.

From Kottayam, there are 11 daily ferries to Alappuzha (Rs5; 2hr 30min; first at 7.30am, last 8.30pm).

Kuttanad Tourist Home, by the *KSRTC* bus station (☎61354). Very basic rooms (some a/c). Not particularly clean, but close to the jetty. The restaurant serves excellent fish. ②.

Eating

Virtually every foreign visitor to Alappuzha ends up **eating** in the *Komala Hotel*'s *Arun* restaurant, although there are plenty of other servicable, and cheaper, places. For a splurge, slip on some clean clothes and catch a rickshaw out to the *Alleppey Prince*, whose a/c *Vembanad* restaurant offers the town's classiest menu, and beer by the pool.

Arun, *Komala Hotel*, Zilla Court Ward. Tasty Chinese noodles and Indian veg (including delicious *dal makhini*, *malai kofta* and *subzis*), but avoid the continental food. If it's busy, settle in for a wait.

Aryaas, Mullakal Rd. The town's best Udupi restaurant, serving south Indian breakfasts and excellent *rawa masala dosas* after 6pm. Recommended if you're on a tight budget.

Kream Korner, Mullakal Rd. Recently re-vamped non-veg-restaurant-cum-ice-cream parlour. Mostly chicken and mutton, with a selection of snacks, milkshakes and ice creams.

Thoppi, *Karthika Hotel*. Very modest but clean and friendly place with an ambitious, inexpensive Indian and Chinese menu. They open early for standard "omelette-bread-butter-jam" breakfasts.

Kottayam

The busy commercial centre of **KOTTAYAM** is strategically located between the backwaters to the west and the spice, tea and rubber plantations, forests, and the mountains of the Western Ghats to the east, 76km southeast of Kochi and 37km northwest of Alappuzha. Most visitors come here on the way somewhere else – foreigners take short backwater trips to Alappuzha or set off to **Periyar Wildlife Sanctuary**, while Ayappa devotees pass through en route to the forest temple at Sabarimala (see p.1084).

Kottayam's long history of **Syrian Christian** settlement is reflected by the presence of two thirteenth-century churches on a hill 5km northwest of the centre, which you can get to by rickshaw. Two eighth-century Nestorian stone crosses with Pahlavi and Syriac inscriptions, on either side of the elaborately decorated altar of the **Valliapalli** ("big") church, are probably the earliest solid evidence of Christianity in India, while the visitors book contains entries from as far back as the 1890s, including one by the Ethiopian King, Haile Selassie, and a British Viceroy. The interior of the nearby **Cheriapalli** ("small") church is covered with lively, naive paintings, thought to have been executed by a Portuguese artist. If the doors are locked, ask for the key at the church office (9am–1pm & 2–5pm).

Arrival and information

Kottayam's *KSRTC* **bus stand**, 500m south of the centre on TB Rd (not to be confused with the private stand for local buses on KK Rd), is an important stop on routes to and from major towns in south India. Four of the frequent buses to Kumily/Periyar (3–4hr) each day go on to Madurai, in Tamil Nadu (7hr), and there are regular services to Thiruvananthapuram, Kollam and Ernakulam. The **railway station** (2km east of the centre) sees a constant flow of traffic between Thiruvananthapuram and points north. **Ferries** from Alappuzha and elsewhere dock at the weed-clogged jetty, 3km south of town. For details of backwater trips from Kottayam, see p.1079.

You are defied to get any useful information from the booth that serves as the **Tourist Information Office**, Central Junction, but you may want to use their STD phone. Tourism enquiries get a more sympathetic ear at the *KTDC Aiswarya*; see below.

The telephone **area code** for Kottayam is ☎0481.

Accommodation and eating

Kottayam has a good choice of mid-range **hotels**. If you're not pressed for time, stay on the outskirts away from the noise. Two new luxury hotels in the backwaters near Kumarakom make appealing alternatives. There are basic "meals" **restaurants** in the centre, such as the *Black Stone*, close to the bus station on TB Rd, and there's a fairly dingy *Indian Coffee House* on TB Rd, but for an evening out, the lovely lakeside *Vembanad Lake Resort*, where you eat on a *kettu vallam* rice boat, definitely wins.

Ambassador, KK Rd (☎563293). Well run economy hotel with some a/c rooms. Frayed around the edges, but basically clean and fine for a night. ③–④.

Anjali, KK Rd, 2km from railway station, close to the square, downtown (☎563661). Comfortable upscale *Casino* group hotel with international and Chinese restaurants and bar. All a/c. ⑦.

Green Park, Kurian Uthup Rd, Nagampadam, near station and private bus stand (☎563331 or 563243). Modern business hotel. Good value, with decent rooms, a bar and two restaurants. ②–③.

Homestead Hotel, opposite *Manorama*, KK Rd, 1km from the station (☎560467; fax 560740). Comfortable budget hotel; clean, central and good value. ③–⑤.

KTDC Aiswarya, Thirunakkara, near bus stand and jetty (☎61256). Simply furnished modern tower block; lacks character, but the staff are friendly and the rooms (a/c and non-a/c) spacious. Superb views from the upper storeys. Restaurant, beer parlour, 24hr room service. ③–④.

Vembanad Lake Resort, Kodimatha, 2km from town and bus station (☎564866). Western-style motel, with large, simply furnished modern chalets (4 a/c) in pleasant gardens beside an inlet of Lake Vembanad. The restaurant has good Indian, Western and Chinese dishes, including seafood. Eat outside in a lakeside garden or on a moored *kettu vallam* long boat – gorgeous at night. ④–⑤.

Around Kottayam

Some of Kerala's most attractive scenery lies within easy access of Kottayam. Probably the ideal destination for a day trip – it also has some wonderful accommodation – is the **Kumarakom** bird sanctuary, in the backwaters to the west. **Aranmula** to the south is one of the last villages still making *kannady* metal mirrors, and has a Krishna temple that organizes a ritual "non-competitive" boat race. The Mahadeva temple at **Ettumanur**, a short way north of Kottayam, is known to devotees as the home of a dangerous and wrathful Shiva, and to art lovers as a sublime example of temple architecture, adorned with wood carvings and murals.

Kumarakom

KUMARAKOM, 16km west of Kottayam, is technically an island on Vembanad Lake. Although right in the thick of a tangle of lush tropical waterways, it can be reached by bus from Kottayam (every 10min), via an horrendously pot-holed road. The peak time to visit the **Bird Sanctuary** (daily 10am–6pm) is between November and March, when it serves as a winter home for many migratory birds, most of them from Siberia. Species include the darter or snake bird, little cormorant, night heron, golden-backed woodpecker, crow pheasant, white-breasted water hen and tree pie. Enthusiasts should seek permission to enter the sanctuary at dawn, the best time for bird viewing.

Next to the sanctuary, set in lovely waterside gardens, a refurbished colonial bungalow that once belonged to a family of Christian missionaries and rubber planters forms the nucleus of a new luxury **hotel**. *The Taj Garden Retreat* (☎048192/668377; ⑧) has a couple of dozen "cottages" and a *kettu vallam* long boat grouped around a landscaped garden. However, it's not nearly as impressive as *Casino Group*'s *Coconut Lagoon Hotel* (☎048192/668221; fax 668001; ⑧), 1km northwest and reached by launch (you can telephone for the boat from a kiosk at the canal side). Superbly crafted from fragments of ruined Keralan palaces, with beautiful wood carvings and brass work, the building alone merits a visit. It was designed in traditional Keralan style, and its air of low-key elegance is set off perfectly by the location on the edge of Vembanad Lake. Even if you can't afford to stay here, consider eating Keralan specialities at the **restaurant**.

The only other place to eat is KTDC's decidedly uninspiring café at the *Tourist Complex* near where the bus from Kottayam pulls in. You can rent *kettu vallams* through them for Rs1500 per day, or more if you fancy a cruise across the lake.

Aranmula

The village of **ARANMULA** is another appealing day trip – so long as you start early – from Kottayam, 30km south of the town and 10km beyond Chengannur. Its ancient temple is dedicated to Parthasarathy, which was the name under which Krishna acted as

CHRISTIANITY IN KERALA

The history of Kerala's **Christians** – who today represent 21 percent of the population – is said to date back to the first century AD, some three centuries before Christianity received official recognition in Europe. These days, the five main branches among a bewildering assortment of churches are the **Nestorians** (confined mainly to Thrissur and Ernakulam), **Roman Catholics** (found throughout Kerala), **Syrian Orthodox Church** (previously known as the Jacobite Syrians), **Marthoma Syrians** (a splinter group of the Syrian Orthodox), and the Anglican **Church of South India**.

A legend, widely believed in Kerala but the object of academic scepticism, states that **St Thomas** the Apostle – "Doubting Thomas" – landed on the Malabar coast in AD 52, where he converted several Brahmins and others, and founded seven churches. Muziris, his first port of call, has been identified as Kodungallur (see p.1107); the traditional accounts of Jews who arrived there in AD 68 state that they encountered a Christian community. Their number was augmented in the fourth century by an influx of Syrians belonging to seven tribes from Baghdad, Nineveh and Jerusalem, under the leadership of the merchant Knayi Thoma (Thomas of Cana).

Christians gradually came to the forefront as traders, and eventually gained special privileges from the local rulers. The early communities followed a liturgy in the **Syriac language** (a dialect of Aramaic). Latin was introduced by missionaries who visited Kollam in the Middle Ages; once the Portuguese turned up, in 1498, a large community of **Latin Christians** developed, particularly on the coast, and came under the jurisdiction of the Pope. In the middle of the seventeenth century, with the ascendancy of the Dutch, part of the Church broke away from Rome, and local bishops were appointed through the offices of the Jacobite Patriarch in Antioch.

During the nineteenth century, the Anglican Church amalgamated with certain "free" Churches, to form the Church of South India. At the same time, elements in the Syrian Church advocated the replacement of Syriac with the local language of Malayalam. The resultant schism led to the creation of the new Marthoma Syrian Church.

Christmas is an important festival in Kerala; during the weeks leading up to Dec 25, innumerable star-shaped lamps are put up outside shops and houses, illuminating the night and identifying followers of the faith.

Arjuna's charioteer during the bloody Kurekshetra war recorded in the *Mahabharata*, and the guise in which he expounded the *Bhagavad Gita*. Each year towards the end of the Onam festival (Aug/Sept), when a **Snakeboat Regatta** is celebrated as part of the temple rituals, crowds line the banks of the River Pampa to cheer on the thrusting longboats (similar to those seen at Alappuzha; see p.1076).

Aranmula is also known for manufacturing extraordinary *kannady* **metal mirrors**, produced, using the "lost wax" technique, with an alloy of copper, silver, brass, lead and bronze. Once a prerequisite of royal households, these ornamental mirrors are now exceedingly rare; only two master craftsmen, Subramanian and Arjun Asary, and their families, still make them. The most modest models cost in the region of Rs300, while custom-made mirrors can cost as much as Rs 50,000.

The **Vijana Kala Vedi Cultural Centre** offers ways of "experiencing traditional India through the study of art and village life". Introductory courses are offered in Kathakali, Mohiniattam and Bharatanatyam dance, woodcarving, mural painting, cooking, Kalarippayat, ayurvedic medicine, and several Indian languages. Courses cost upwards of $200 per week; book by writing to the Director, *Vijana Kala Vedi Cultural Centre*, Tarayil Mukku Junction, Aranmula, Kerala 689533.

Ettumanur

The magnificent Mahadeva temple at **ETTUMANUR**, 12km north of Kottayam on the road to Ernakulam, features a circular shrine, fine woodcarving and one of the earliest (sixteenth-century) and most celebrated of Keralan **murals**. The deity is Shiva in one of his most terrible aspects, described as *vaddikasula vada*, "one who takes his dues with interest" and is "difficult to please". His predominant mood is *raudra* (fury). Although the shrine is open to Hindus only, foreigners are allowed to see the painting, which may be photographed only after obtaining a camera ticket from the hatch to the left of the main, *gopura* entranceway. The four-metre mural depicts Nataraja – Shiva – executing a cosmic *tandava* dance, trampling evil under-foot in the form of a demon. Swathed in cobras, he stands on one leg in a wheel of gold, with his matted locks fanning out amid a mass of flowers and snakes. Outside the wheel, a crowd of celestials are in attitudes of devotion. Musical accompaniment is courtesy of Krishna on flute, three-headed Brahma on cymbals, and, playing the copper *mizhavu*, the holiest and most ancient of Keralan drums, Shiva's special rhythm expert Nandikesvara.

Ettumanur's ten-day **annual festival** (Feb/March) reflects the wealth of the temple, with elaborate celebrations including music. On the most important days, the eighth and tenth, priests bring out figures of elephants, fashioned from 210 pounds of gold, presented in the eighteenth century by Marthanda Varma, the Raja of Travancore.

Periyar Wildlife Sanctuary

One of the largest and most visited wildlife reserves in India, the **Periyar Wildlife Sanctuary** occupies 777 square kilometres of the Cardamom Hills region of the Western Ghats. The majority of its many visitors come in the hope of seeing **tigers** and **leopards** – and are disappointed, as the few that remain very wisely keep their distance, and there's only a slight chance of a glimpse even at the height of the dry season (April/May). However, there are plenty of other animals: elephant, *sambar*, wild pig, Malabar flying squirrel, *gaur*, stripe-necked mongoose and over 260 species of birds including Nilgiri wood pigeon, blue-winged parakeet, white-bellied tree pie, laughing thrushes and flycatchers. Located close to the Kerala–Tamil Nadu border, the park makes a convenient place to break the long journey across the Ghats between Madurai and the coast. It's also a good base for day trips into the Cardamom Hills, with a couple of tea factories, spice plantations, the trailhead for the Sabarimala pilgrimage (see p.1084), and view points and forest waterfalls within striking distance.

Periyar lies at cool altitudes (750–1500m), just over 100km east of Kottayam, and centres on a vast artificial **lake**, created by the British in 1895 to supply water to the drier parts of neighbouring Tamil Nadu, around Madurai. The royal family of Travancore, anxious to preserve favourite hunting grounds from the encroachment of tea plantations, declared it to be a Forest Reserve, and built the Edapalayam Lake Palace to accommodate their guests in 1899. It expanded as a wildlife reserve in 1933, and once again when it became part of **Project Tiger** in 1979 (see *Contexts*).

Seventy percent of the protected area, which is divided into core, buffer and tourist zones, is covered with evergreen and semi-evergreen forest. The **tourist zone** – logically enough, the part accessible to casual visitors – surrounds the lake, and consists mostly of semi-evergreen and deciduous woodland interspersed with grassland, both on hilltops and in the valleys. Although excursions on the lake are the standard way to experience the park, you can get much more out of a visit by **walking** with a local guide in a small group, or, especially, staying in basic accommodation away from the crowd. However, avoid the period immediately after the monsoons, when **leeches** make hiking virtually impossible. The **best time to visit** is from December until April, when the dry weather draws animals from the forest to drink at the lakeside.

Getting to Periyar

Travellers heading for the sanctuary have first to make their way to the small tea and spice market village of **Kumily**, 4km short of the park entrance at **Thekkady**, on the northwest of the reserve. Kumily is served by **buses** from Kottayam (every 30 min; 4hr), Ernakulam (10 daily; 6hr), and Madurai in Tamil Nadu (frequent service; 5hr 30min); most of these terminate at the scruffy bus stand east of Kumily bazaar, from where a minibus shuttles visitors to the park, although some continue through to the *KTDC Aranya Nivas*, inside the sanctuary.

The pothole-filled road that winds through the undulating hills up to Kumily from Ernakulam and Kottayam makes for a very long slow drive, but it gives wonderful

---

THE AYAPPA CULT

During December and January, Kerala is jam-packed with crowds of men in black or blue *dhotis*, milling about railway stations and filling trains on their way to the Shri Ayappa forest temple (also known as Hariharaputra or Shasta) at **Sabarimala**, in the Western Ghat mountains, around 200km from both Thiruvananthapuram and Kochi. The **Ayappa devotees** can seem disconcertingly ebullient, chanting "*Swamiyee Sharanam Ayappan*" (give us protection, god Ayappa) in a call and response style reminiscent of Western sports fans.

Although he is primarily a Keralan deity, Ayappa's appeal has spread phenomenally in the last thirty years across south India, to the extent that this is said to be the **second largest pilgrimage in the world**, with as many as a million devotees each year. A curious story relates to the birth of Ayappa. One day, when the two male gods, Shiva and Vishnu, were together in a pine forest, Shiva asked to see Vishnu's famed female form Mohini, the divine enchantress. Vishnu refused, having a fair idea of what this could lead to. However, Shiva was undeterred, and used all his powers of persuasion to induce Vishnu to transform. As a result of the inevitable passionate embrace, Vishnu became pregnant, and the baby Ayappa emerged from his thigh.

Pilgrims, however, are required to remain celibate; they must abstain from intoxicants, keeping to a strict vegetarian diet for a period of 41 days prior to setting out on the four-day walk through the forest from the village of **Erumeli** (61km, as the crow flies, northwest) to the shrine at Sabarimala. Rather less devoted devotees take the bus to the village of Pampa, and join the five-kilometre queue. When they arrive at the modern temple complex – a surreal spread of concrete sheds and walkways in the middle of the jungle – pilgrims who have performed the necessary penances may ascend the famous eighteen **gold steps** to the inner shrine. There they worship the deity, throwing donations down a chute that opens onto a subterranean conveyer belt, where the money is counted and bagged for the bank. In recent years, the mass appeal of the Ayappa cult has brought in big bucks for the temple, which now numbers among India's richest, despite being open for only a few months each year. Funds also pour in from the shrine's innumerable spin-off businesses, such as the sale of coconut oil and milk (left by every pilgrim) to a soap manufacturer.

Although males of any age and even of any religion can take part in the pilgrimage, females between the ages of nine and fifty are barred. This rule, still vigorously enforced by the draconian temple oligarchy, was contested in 1995 by a bizarre court case. Following complaints to local government that facilities and hygiene at Sabarimala were sub-standard, the Local Collector, a 42-year-old woman, insisted she be allowed to inspect the site. The temple authorities duly refused, citing the centuries-old ban on women of menstrual age, but the High Court, who earlier upheld the gender bar, were obliged to over-rule the priests' decision. The Collector's triumphant arrival at Sabarimala soon after made headline news, but she was still not allowed to enter the shrine proper.

For advice on how to visit Sabarimala, via a back route begining at Kumily near the Periyar Sanctury, see p.1087.

views across the Ghats. The route is dotted with grand churches among the trees, and numerous jazzy roadside shrines to St Francis or the Virgin Mary – a charming Keralan blend of ancient and modern. Once you've climbed through the rubber-tree forests into Idukki District, the mountains get truly spectacular, and the wide-floored valleys are carpeted with lush tea plantations.

KTDC runs hectic and uncomfortable **weekend tours** to Periyar from Kochi, calling at Kadamattom and Idukki Dam en route (see p.1092; Sat 7.30am–Sun 8pm), and an even more rushed tour from Thiruvananthapuram. Unless you love being cooped up for days in video buses, give them a miss.

Boat trips and walking in the park

Tickets for the **boat trips** (7am & 4pm; 2hr; Rs50 for open upper deck; Rs25 enclosed lower deck) on the lake are sold through the Forest Department at their hatch just above the main Visitors Centre. Although it is unusual to see that many animals from the boats – engine noise, and the presence of a hundred other people, make sure of that – you might spot a family group of elephants, wild boar and sambar deer by the water's edge. The upper deck is best for game viewing, although the seats are invariably block-booked by the upscale hotels. Turn up half-an-hour early, however, and you may be allocated any no-show places, either at the ticket hatch, or by slipping the boatman some *baksheesh*. To maximize your chances, take the earliest boat at 7am (wear something warm). At this hour, the mist rises over the lake and hills as you chug past dead trees, now bird perches, that were never cleared when the valley was flooded. You could also consider renting your own boat (Rs300 for 6 passengers, again at the jetty). Note that after heavy rain, chances of good sightings are very slim as the animals only come to the lake when water sources inside the forest have dried up.

Group trekking is possible (9am–noon; Rs20 per head), but it's more enjoyable by far to hire a **private guide** to take you walking in the forest (under Rs100 for 3hr for two or three people; longer trips are negotiable). They'll approach you in Kumily or near the park gates at Thekkady. Guides point out anything of interest, reassuring you that the fresh elephant dung on the path is nothing to worry about.

Accommodation and eating inside the sanctuary

The star attraction of Periyar has to be the prospect of staying in the Forest Department **watchtowers**, reached by boat from Thekkady and the best way to get a hands-on experience of the jungle. For the *Lake Palace*, *Periyar House* and the *Aranya Niwas* you should book in advance at the KTDC offices in Thiruvananthapuram or Ernakulam – essential if you plan to come on a weekend, a public holiday, or during **peak season** (Dec–March), when rooms are often in short supply.

Forest Department Rest House, Edappalayam. Very basic accommodation in the woods on the far side of the lake (you have to catch the 4pm boat and then hike, so a guide is recommended). Bring your own food and bedding. Reserve in advance at the Forest Department's Visitors Centre in Thekkday, above the boat jetty; you'll be lucky to get in on a weekend or in December. ②.

Forest Department Watchtowers, Edappalayam and Manakkavala. Even more primitive than the *Rest House*, but the best way of sighting game: the towers overlook waterholes in the buffer zone. Book through the Visitors Centre, and take along food, candles, matches, a torch and plenty of warm blankets and clothes. Again, you have to catch the 4pm boat and trek from the jetty, so a guide is useful. Don't consider this if it's been raining, when leeches plague the trail. ①.

KTDC Aranya Niwas, just above the boat jetty, Thekkady (☎04869/22023; fax 22282). Plusher than *Periyar House*, with a top-notch multi-cuisine restaurant and a pretty garden. Upper deck tickets on the boat trips are included in the tariff. ⑦–⑧.

KTDC Lake Palace, across the lake. The sanctuary's flagship luxury hotel, a converted Maharajah's game lodge surrounded by forest, with wonderful views. This has to be one of the few places in India where you stand a chance of spotting tiger and wild elephant while sipping gin and tonic on your own verandah. Rates start at Rs6000. ⑨.

KTDC Periyar House, mid-way between the park gates and the boat jetty, Thekkady (☎04869/22026; fax 22282). This comfortable mid-range hotel recently had a face-lift and is no longer the excellent value it used to be, although it's close to the lake, with a restaurant, bar, and balcony overlooking the monkey-filled woods leading down to the waterside. Ask for a lake-facing room. ⑤.

Accommodation outside the sanctuary: Kumily

With beds inside the sanctuary in such short supply, most visitors end up staying in or near **Kumily**, 2km north of the park gates. Clustered along the main trans-ghat highway, the village centre is a long, gritty bazaar full of raucous traffic and lined with hardware and spice shops. In the middle of the melee stands the area's main **cardamom auction**, where you can watch tribal women sifting and sorting the fragrant green pods in heart-shaped baskets; it's easy to find – just follow your nose.

Kumily has **accommodation** to suit all pockets. Thankfully, most of it lies well outside the bazaar area, dotted along the Thekkady Road leading to the park. Nearly every establishment has its own café-restaurant, ranging from the *Spice Village*'s smart a la carte terrace, to the more traveller-oriented *Coffee Inn*. If you're on a really tight budget, however, the best place to eat in Kumily is the *Hotel Saravana*, one of several no-frills "meals" joints on the main bazaar. Their *thalis*, served on plantain leaves, are tasty, cheap and always freshly cooked, and they serve up deliciously crisp *dosas*.

Ambadi, next to turn-off for Mangaladevi temple, Thekkady Rd (☎04869/22193; fax 22192). Pleasant hotel, with coir mats and tasteful wood carving, whose non-a/c "cottages" are very good value. The restaurant serves good chicken, but avoid the meat if there have been power cuts. ⑤–⑦.

Claus Garden Home, five minutes' walk south of the main bus stand (no phone). Difficult to find, but worth the effort. Simple, pleasant rooms in cosy house, owned by a non-resident German, with sociable verandahs and *mandala* murals, surrounded by pepper plantations. Great breakfasts of *poothay* (steamed coconut cakes) with hot buffalo milk, banana, and cardamom tea. ②.

Coffee Inn, Thekkady Rd (no phone). Good budget accommodation: a handful of simple rooms (one en-suite) around a covered terrace and garden. Their "Wild Huts" annexe has six rooms (and two rafia tree houses) with shared shower and toilet, and a spacious enclosed garden with a pond. The (pricy) café serves delicious home-made Western food including fresh bread. ②.

Lake Queen, opposite the Thekkady turn-off, Kumily Bazaar (☎04869/22084). Dilapidated multi-storey hotel, with good views from the top floors, but a far cry from the forest. ③–④.

Spice Village, Thekkady Rd (☎04869/22315; fax 22317). Trendy new (and terrifically eco-conscious) campus of thatched huts, ranged around a pool, with staff in quasi-tribal garb. The best upmarket option after the *Lake Palace*. ⑧.

Woodlands, Thakkady Rd (☎04869/22071). The cheapest place to stay in Kumily, and very rudimentary, although clean enough for a short stay, and with friendly management. ①.

Around Periyar and Kumily: the Cardamom Hills

Nestled amid soaring, mist-covered mountains and dense jungles, Periyar and Kumily are convenient springboards from which to explore Kerala's beautiful **Cardamom Hills**. Guides will approach you at Thekkady with offers of trips by jeep-taxi; if you can get a group together, these work out good value. Among the more popular destinations is the **Mangaladevi temple**, 14km east of Kumily. When this book went to press, the rough road to this tumbledown ancient ruin deep in the forest, was closed due to flood damage, but when open the round trip takes about five hours. With a guide, you can also reach remote waterfalls and mountain view points, offering panoramic vistas of the Tamil Nadu plains. Rates vary according to the season, but expect to pay between Rs400 and 500 for the taxi, and an additional Rs150 for the guide.

Of places that can be visited under your own steam, the fascinating **High Range Tea Factory** (☎04868/77038 or 77043) lies at Puttady (pronounced "Poo-*tee*-dee"), 19km north on the Munnar road. Regular buses leave from Kumily bus stand; get down at

Puttady crossroads, and pick up a rickshaw from there to the factory. Driven by whirring canvas belts, old-fashioned English-made machines chop, sift, and ferment the leaves, which are then dried by wood-fired furnaces and packed into sacks for delivery to the tea auction rooms in Kochi. The affable owner, Mr PM James, or one of his clerks, will show you around; you don't have to arrange the visit, but it's a good idea to phone ahead to check they are open.

The other possible day trip from Kumily, though one that should not be undertaken lightly (or, because of Hindu lore, by pre-menopausal women), is to the Sri Ayappan forest shrine at **Sabarimala** (see p.1084). This remote and sacred site can be reached in a long day, but you should leave with a pack of provisions, as much water as you can carry, and plenty of warm clothes in case you get stranded. Jeep taxis wait outside Kumily bus stand to transport pilgrims to the lesser frequented of Sabarimala's two main access points, at a windswept mountain top 13km above the temple (2hr; Rs40 per person if the jeep is carrying ten passengers). Peeling off the main Kumily–Kottayam road at **Vandiperiyar**, the route takes you through tea estates to the start an of appallingly rutted forest track. After a long and spectacular climb, this emerges at a grass-covered plateau where the jeeps stop. You proceed on foot, following a well-worn path through superb old-growth jungle – complete with hanging creepers and monkeys crashing through the high canopy – to the temple complex at the foot of the valley. Allow at least two hours for the descent, and an hour or two more for the climb back up to the road head, for which you'll need plenty of drinking water. Given the very real risks involved with missing the last jeep back to Kumily (the mountain top is prime elephant and tiger country), it's advisable to get a group together and rent a 4WD for the day (Rs800, plus waiting time).

Munnar and around

MUNNAR, 130km east of Kochi and four-and-a-half hours by bus north of Periyar, is the centre of Kerala's principal tea growing region. Although billed in tourist bumpf as a "hill station", it is less a Raj-style resort than a scruffy, workaday settlement of corrugated-iron-roofed cottages and factories, surrounded by mile upon mile of rolling green **tea plantations**. All the same, it's easy to see why the pioneering Scottish planters that first developed this hidden valley in the 1900s felt so at home here. At an altitude of around 1600m, the town enjoys a refreshing climate, with crisp winter mornings and relentlessly heavy rain during the monsoons. Hemmed in by soaring mountains – including peninsular India's highest peak, **Anamudi** (2695m) – it also boasts a spectacular setting; when the river mist clears, the surrounding summits form a wild backdrop to the carefully manicured plantations carpeting the valley floor and sides.

Munnar's greenery and cool air have attracted increasing numbers of well-heeled honeymooners from Bombay and Bangalore. Foreign visitors, however, remain few and far between. Those that do make it up here tend to come for the spellbinding bus ride from Periyar, which takes you across the high ridges and lush tropical forests of the Cardamom Hills, or for the equally spectacular climb across the Ghats from Madurai. Once in the town, there's little to do other than enjoy the views and fresh air, although several interesting sights, and a superb **hike**, lie within reach of day trips.

Arrival and information

Munnar can be reached by **bus** from Kochi (5 daily; 4hr 30min), Kottayam (5 daily; 5hr), Kumily (1 daily; 4hr 30min) and Madurai (1 daily; 5hr). State-run and private services pull into the stand in the bazaar at north end of town, near the river confluence and *Tata* headquarters; for the hotels south of the centre you should ask to be dropped near the friendly but ineffectual KSTDC **tourist office**. If you need **information** on transport, accommodation and day trips, including to Eravikulam, seek out the extra-ordinarily helpful **Joseph Iype**, who runs a small information office of his own on the main bazaar. Immortalized in Dervla Murphy's *On a Shoestring to Coorg*, this self-appointed tourist officer has become something of a legend. In addition to handing out useful **maps** and newspaper articles, he'll arrange rickshaws and taxis for excursions, and bombard you with background on the area.

The Town and around

Raj-ophiles will enjoy the prospect of verandahed British bungalows clinging to the valley's sides, and the famous **High Range Club** on the southeast edge of town, with its manicured lawns and golf course. Beyond the club sprawl some of the valley's 37 thousand-acre plantations, most of which are owned by the Parsi industrial giant, *Tata*. Their regional headquarters in the centre of town is the place to arrange visits to **tea factories** in the area.

Encompassing 100 square kilometres of moist evergreen forest and grassy hilltops in the Western Ghats, **ERAVIKULAM NATIONAL PARK** (Rs50; Rs100 per person in a vehicle), 17km northeast of Munnar, is the last stronghold of one of the world's rarest mountain goats, the **Nilgiri tahr**. Its innate friendliness made the tahr pathetically easy prey during the hunting frenzy of the colonial era (during a break in his campaign against Tipu Sultan in the late 1790s, the future Duke of Wellington reported that his soldiers were able to shoot the unsuspecting goats as they wandered through his camp), and by Independence it was virtually extinct. Today, however, numbers are healthy, and the animals have regained their tameness, largely thanks to the efforts of the American biologist, Cifford Rice, who studied them here in the early 1980s. Unable to get close enough to properly observe the creatures, Rice followed the advice of locals and attracted them using salt. Soon, whole herds were congregating around his camp. The tahrs' salt addiction also explains why so many hang around the park gates at **Vaguvarai**, where visitors – despite advice from rangers – slip them salty snacks.

The park gates mark the start of an excellent **hike** up the most accesible of the Anamudi massif's three peaks, for which you'll need sturdy footwear, plenty of water, a fair amount of stamina and a head for heights. Follow the road as it winds through the sanctuary, cutting across the switchbacks until you reach the pass forming the Kerala-Tamil Nadu border (rickshaw-*wallahs* and jeep-taxis will drive you this far, although you'll have to fork out the higher entrance cost if you enter the park in a vehicle). Leave the road here and head up the ridge to your right; the path, which becomes very steep, peters out well before you reach the summit, and many hikers find the gradient too hair-raising to continue. But the panoramic views from the top are well worth the effort, and you may be rewarded with a glimpse of tahr grazing the high slopes.

Another popular excursion is the 32-kilometre uphill climb by bus through the subcontinent's highest tea estates to **TOP STATION**, a tiny hamlet on the Kerala–Tamil Nadu border with superb views across the plains. It's renowned for the very rare **Neelakurunji plant** (*Strobilatanthes*), which grows in profusion on the mountainsides but only flowers once every twleve years, when crowds descend to admire the cascades of violet blossom spilling down the slopes. Top Station can be reached by **bus** from Munnar (8 daily; 1hr), and taxi-jeeps will do the round trip for Rs400.

Accommodation and eating

Thanks to its status as an up-and-coming hill resort, Munnar has plenty of **accommodation**, although budget options are limited. Visitors generally **eat** in their hotels; the *Royal Retreat*'s plush à la carte restaurant is particularly recommended, with an eclectic menu and attentive service, while *Woodlands*, in the old bazaar opposite the government High School is a characterful old-style coffee shop serving south Indian snacks.

For tasty, filling and cheap meals, however, you can't beat the *Poopada*, whose small, no-frills restaurant is open to non-residents.

East End, Temple Rd, across the river from the bus stand (☎04865/40351; fax 30227). Immaculate upmarket hotel with "cottages" in a big garden, and a multi-cuisine restaurant. ⑥–⑧.

Government Guest House, Mattupatty Rd, near the main bazaar, on the far side of the river (☎04865/30385). Run-down, characterful old British bungalow with tatty, very cheap rooms. Meals by arrangement. ①.

Hillview, Kannan Devan Hills (☎04865/30567; fax 30241). Large, well-run Western-style hotel at the south end of town. All rooms are en-suite; some have good views. ⑥–⑧.

Poopada, Kannan Devan Hills, on the Manukulam Road (☎04865/30223). Good-sized, en-suite rooms, and about the best cheap eating in town, along with fine valley views and secluded location. Booking recommended on weekends. ④.

Royal Retreat, Kannan Devan Hills (☎04865/30240). Spacious rooms, some with brick fire places and cane furniture, in a new motel-style complex at the south end of town. The best upscale option, though its north side has been boxed in by the *Hillview* next door. ⑥.

Shree Narayana ("SN") Tourist Home, Kannan Devan Hills, on the main road near the tourist office (☎04865/30230). Far and away Munnar's best economy lodge, although there are much cheaper (and grottier) places further north in the bazaar. Shared or en-suite bathrooms. ③–④.

Kochi (Cochin) and Ernakulam

The venerable city of **KOCHI** (long known as Cochin), Kerala's prime tourist destination, spreads across islands and promontories in a stunning location between the Arabian Sea and backwaters. Its main sections – modern **Ernakulam**, in the east, and the old districts of **Mattancherry** and **Fort Cochin** on a peninsula in the west – are linked by a complex system of ferries, and distinctly less romantic bridges. Although most visitors end up staying in Ernakulam, Fort Cochin and Mattancherry are the focus of interest, where the city's extraordinary history of foreign influence and settlement is reflected in an assortment of architectural styles. During a wander through their narrow lanes, you'll stumble upon spice markets, Chinese fishing nets, a synagogue, a Portuguese palace, India's first European church, Dutch homes, and a village green that could have been transported from England's Home Counties. The city is also one of the few places in Kerala where, at any time of year, you can be assured of seeing **Kathakali dance**, either in one of several special tourist theatres, or at a more authentic performance by a temple-based company.

Kochi sprang into being in 1341, when a flood created a natural safe port that swiftly replaced Muziris (Kodungallur, 50km north) as the chief harbour on the Malabar coast. The royal family transferred here from Muziris in 1405, after which the city grew rapidly, attracting Christian, Arab and Jewish settlers from the Middle East. Its name probably derives from *kocchazhi*, meaning the new, or small, harbour.

The history of European involvement in Kochi from the early 1500s onwards is dominated by the aggression of, successively, the Portuguese, Dutch and British, competing to control the port and its lucrative spice trade. From 1800, the state of Cochin was part of the British Madras Presidency; from 1812 until Independence in 1947, its administration was made the responsibility of a series of *diwans*, or financial ministers. In the 1920s, the British expanded the port to make it suitable for modern ocean-going ships; extensive dredging created Willingdon Island, between Ernakulam and Fort Cochin.

Arrival and local transport

Kochi's busy **airport** – served by several flights daily from **Bombay**, one each from **Kozhikode** and **Madras**, most days from **Delhi**, and twice weekly from **Goa** and the **Lakshadweep islands** – is at the southern end of Willingdon Island, connected to

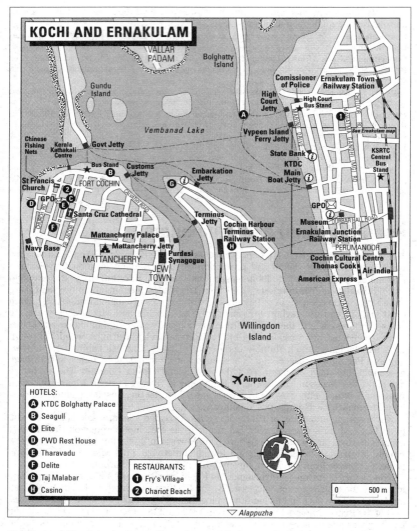

KOCHI AND ERNAKULAM

VALLAR PADAM

Bolghatty Island

Gundu Island

Vembanad Lake

Chinese Fishing Nets

Kerala Kathakali Centre

Govt Jetty

Bus Stand **Ⓑ** Customs Jetty

St Francis Church

GPO **Ⓒ**

FORT COCHIN

Ⓓ

Ⓔ

Santa Cruz Cathedral

Ⓕ

Navy Base

Mattancherry Palace

Mattancherry Jetty

MATTANCHERRY

Purdesi Synagogue

JEW TOWN

Embarkation Jetty

Ⓖ

Terminus Jetty

Cochin Harbour Terminus Railway Station

Ⓗ

Comissioner of Police

Ernakulam Town Railway Station

High Court Jetty

High Court Bus Stand

Ⓐ

Vypeen Island Ferry Jetty

State Bank

KTDC Main Boat Jetty

Ⓘ

KSRTC Central Bus Stand

GPO

Museum

DURBAR HALL ROAD

Ernakulam Junction Railway Station

PERUMANOOR

Cochin Cultural Centre

Thomas Cook

Air India

American Express

BROADWAY

See Ernakulam map

Willingdon Island

✈ Airport

N

HOTELS:
Ⓐ KTDC Bolghatty Palace
Ⓑ Seagull
Ⓒ Elite
Ⓓ PWD Rest House
Ⓔ Tharavadu
Ⓕ Delite
Ⓖ Taj Malabar
Ⓗ Casino

RESTAURANTS:
❶ Fry's Village
❷ Chariot Beach

0   500 m

▽ *Alappuzha*

Ernakulam (5km) by buses, taxis and auto-rickshaws. There are three **railway stations – Ernakulam Junction**, closest to the centre, is the most important; Ernakulam Town lies 4km to the north. No trains run to Fort Cochin or Mattancherry. The Cochin Harbour Terminus, on Willingdon Island, is useful only for people using the airport or staying in one of the luxury hotels on the island.

The *KSRTC* **Central bus station** (☎372033), beside the rail line a short way east of MG Rd and north of Ernakulam Junction, is the principal and most convenient station for long-distance buses. There are two bus stands for the much slower private buses, which are not officially permitted to use the state highways, stop more frequently and tend to be more crowded; **Kaloor stand** (rural destinations to the south and east) is across the bridge from Ernakulam Town railway station on the Alwaye Rd, and the High Court stand (buses to Kumily, for Periyar Wildlife Reserve, and north to Thrissur, Guruvayur and Kodungallur) is opposite the High Court ferry jetty.

Although **auto-rickshaws** are plentiful and reliable in Ernakulam, and to a slightly lesser extent across the water in Mattancherry and Fort Cochin, everyone uses Kochi's **ferry system**. **Bicycles** for exploring Mattancherry and the rest of old Kochi can be rented from a small shop on Bazar Rd between *Hotel Seagull* and Fort Cochin.

The telephone **area code** for Kochi and Ernakulam is ☎0484.

Tours and backwater trips

KTDCs half-day **Kochi Boat Cruise** (daily 9am–12.30pm & 2–5.30pm; Rs50) is a good way to orientate yourself, though as it doesn't stop long in Mattancherry or Fort Cochin, you should give it a miss if time is short. Departing from the High Court Jetty on Shanmugham Rd, Ernakulam, it calls at the Synagogue, Mattancherry Dutch Palace, St Francis Church, the Chinese fishing nets, and Bolghatty Island. Book at the KTDC Reception Centre on Shanmugham Rd (☎353234).

KOCHI BY FERRY

Half the fun of visiting Kochi is getting about on the cheap **local ferries**. When it's not downright impossible, catching a bus, rickshaw or taxi the long way round to most parts of the city takes much longer and is far less interesting.

The map opposite shows Ernakulam's four jetties. Theoretically, the routes below should work in reverse. However, play safe, and don't rely on getting the last boat. Timings are available from the ticket hatches by the jetties, and from the helpful Tourist Desk at the Main Boat Jetty in Ernakulam.

Ernakulam to Mattancherry
From Ernakulam (Main Jetty), via **Fort Cochin** (Customs Jetty), for Chinese fishing nets, St Francis Church, Dutch Cemetery; Willingdon Island (Terminus Jetty); and **Mattancherry Jetty** for Jewish Synagogue and Dutch Palace. Journey time 20min.
First boat 7am, last 9.30pm.

Ernakulam to Vypeen
From Ernakulam (Main Jetty). This frequent service has two routes: one via Willingdon Island (Embarkation Jetty; 25min), and a fast one to Vypeen (Govt Jetty; 15min). First boat 7am, every 30min until 9.30pm.

Fort Cochin to Vypeen
Privately operated service, intended mainly for locals. Journey time 10min. First boat 6.30am, every 30min until 9pm.

Willingdon Island to Fort Cochin
From the Tourist Office Jetty (Willingdon Island) to Customs Jetty (Fort Cochin). Journey time 10min.
First boat 6.30am, every 30min until 6.15pm.

Ernakulam (High Court Jetty) to Bolghatty Island
Journey time 10min. First boat 6.30am, last 9pm; there are also speed boat taxis (Rs15).

Ernakulam to Varapuzha
Local ferry service that provides a chance to see the **backwaters** (see p.1078) if you can't travel further south than Kochi. First boat 7.40am, last 6.45pm; 2hr each way. There's little to see at Varapuzha, apart from paddy fields and coconuts, so it makes sense to take the 2.30pm boat and stay on it, returning to Ernakulam just after dusk at 6.30pm.

KTDC and a couple of private companies also operate popular **backwater trips** (see p.1078) out of Kochi. Taking in a handful of coir-making villages north of the city, these are a leisurely and enjoyable way to experience rural Kerala, from small hand-punted canoes. KTDC's cost Rs300, including the car or bus trip to the departure point, 30km north, and a knowledgable guide. Better value is a similar trip run by the Tourist Desk at the Main Boat Jetty (daily depart 9am, return 1.30pm or depart 2pm, return 6.30pm; Rs250). Reserve at least a day in advance for either tour.

Information and communications

The helpful Government of India **Tourist Office** (Mon–Fri 9am–5.30pm, Sat 9am–noon; ☎668352), between the *Malabar Hotel* and Tourist Office Jetty on Willingdon Island, offers information on Kerala and beyond, and can provide guides. KTDC's **Reception Centre**, on Shanmugham Rd, Ernakulam (☎353234), will book hotels in their chain (including the popular *Bolghatty Palace Hotel*) and runs sightseeing and backwater tours (see above). Further KTDC counters can be found at the airport and at the Old Collectorate, Park Ave, Ernakulam. The tiny independent **Tourist Desk** (daily 9am–5pm), at the entrance to the Main Boat Jetty in Ernakulam, is very helpful and friendly, and the best place to check ferry and bus timings. This is also the only place for free city maps, and is a mine of information on ritual theatre and temple festival dates around the state.

The city's **tourist police** are on hand at to answer queries and assist if you get into difficulties. Staffed by helpful English-speaking graduates, they have counters next to the KTDC office on Shanmugham Rd (☎353234), at Fort Cochin, Mattancherry Palace, the railway station, and airport (☎666076).

Banks and post offices

Banks along MG Rd in Ernakulam include *ANZ Grindlays* (☎361301), *State Bank of India* (☎366376), which also has a branch opposite the main KTDC tourist office on Shanmugham Rd, and *State Bank of Travancore* (☎352309); the latter is virtually the only place in the state where you can trade in torn bank notes. However, to exchange travellers' cheques, the best place is *Thomas Cook* (Mon–Sat 9.30am–6pm; ☎373829) near the *Air India* Building at Palal Towers, MG Rd.

The **Head Post Office** is on Hospital Rd, not far from the Main Jetty (Mon–Fri 8.30am–8pm, Sat 9.30am–2.30pm & 4–8pm, Sun 10am–4pm); the city's **poste restante** is at the **GPO**, behind St Francis Church in Fort Cochin.

Mattancherry

With high-rise development restricted to Ernakulam, across the water, the old-fashioned character of **Mattancherry** and **Fort Cochin** remains intact. Within an area small enough to cover on foot, bicycle or auto-rickshaw, glimpses of Kochi's variegated history greet you at virtually every turn. As you approach by ferry (get off at Mattancherry Jetty), the shoreline is crowded with tiled buildings painted in pastel colours – a view that can't have changed for centuries.

Despite the large number of tourists visiting daily, trade is still the most important activity here. Many of the streets are busy with barrows loaded with sacks of produce trundling between *godowns* (warehouses) and little shops where dealers do business in tea, jute, rubber, chillies, turmeric, cashew, ginger, cardamom and pepper.

Jew Town

The road heading left from Mattancherry Jetty leads into the district known as **Jew Town**, where *NX Jacob's* tailor shop and the offices of *JE Cohen*, advocate and tax con-

THE JEWS OF KOCHI

According to tradition, the first Jews to arrive on the Malabar Coast were fleeing from the occupation of Jerusalem by Nebuchadrezzar, in 587 BC. Trading in spices, they remained respected members of Keralan society until the Portuguese embarked upon a characteristic "Christian" policy of persecution of non-believers, early in the sixteenth century.

At that time, when Jews were being burned at the stake in Goa, and forced to leave their settlements elsewhere on the coast, the Raja of Cochin gave them a parcel of land adjoining the royal palace in Mattancherry. A new Jewish community was created in the area now known as Jew Town, and a synagogue was built.

There were formerly three distinct groups of Jews in Kochi; **Black** (Myuchasim), **Brown** (Meshuchrarim) and **White** (Pardesi, "foreign") Jews. The Black Jews were employed as labourers in the spice business, and their community of some thousands resulted from the earliest Jewish settlers marrying and converting Indians; the Brown Jews are thought to have been slave converts. Both groups were considered inferior by the White Jews. In the early 1950s, however, most of Kochi's Jews disappeared, when they were given free passage to Israel. The remaining White Jews are on the verge of extinction. At the time of writing only seven families survive, a total of 22 people with just enough males over the age of thirteen to perform the rituals in the synagogue – and no rabbi.

sultant, serve as reminders of a once-thriving community. Nowadays many of the shops sell antiques, Hindu and Christian woodcarvings, oil lamps, wooden jewellery boxes and other bric-a-brac.

Turning right at the India Pepper & Spice Trade Building, usually resounding with the racket of dealers shouting the latest spice prices, and then right again, brings you into Synagogue Lane. The **Pardesi (White Jew) Synagogue** (daily except Sat 10am–noon & 3–5pm) was founded in 1568, and rebuilt in 1664. Its interior is an attractive, if incongruous, hotchpotch; note the floor, paved with hand-painted eighteenth-century blue and white tiles from Canton, each unique, depicting a love affair between a mandarin's daughter and a commoner. The nineteenth-century glass oil-burning chandeliers suspended from the ceiling were imported from Belgium. Above the entrance, a gallery supported by slender gilt columns was reserved for female members of the congregation. Opposite the entrance, an elaborately carved Ark houses four scrolls of the *Torah* (the first five books of the Old Testament) encased in silver and gold, on which are placed gold crowns presented by the maharajas of Travancore and Cochin, testifying to good relations with the Jewish community. The synagogue's oldest artefact is a fourth-century copperplate inscription from the Raja of Cochin.

An attendant is usually available to show visitors around, and answer questions; his introductory talk features as part of the KTDC guided tour (see p.1091).

Mattancherry Palace

Mattancherry Palace (daily except Fri 10am–5pm) stands on the left side of the road a short walk from the Mattancherry Jetty in the opposite direction to Jew Town. The gateway on the road is, in fact, its back entrance; although the most sensible side to approach from the ferry, it inexplicably remains locked with a loose chain. Visitors slim enough can, and do, enter through the gap, saving the walk around the block. In the walled grounds stands a circular, tiled Krishna temple (closed to non-Hindus).

Although known locally as the **Dutch Palace**, the two-storey palace was built by the Portuguese as a gift to the Cochin Raja, Vira Keralavarma (1537–61), and the Dutch were responsible for subsequent additions. While its appearance is not particularly striking, squat with whitewashed walls and tiled roof, the interior is captivating.

KERALAN MURALS

The quality and unique style of the **murals** at Mattancherry Palace in old Kochi (see below), along with those in as many as sixty other locations in Kerala, are probably the best kept secrets in Indian art. Most are on the walls of functioning temples, not marketable, transportable, or indeed even *seen* by many non-Hindus. Few date from before the sixteenth century, depriving them of the aura of extreme antiquity; their origins may go back to the seventh century, probably influenced by the Pallava style of Tamil Nadu, but only traces in one tenth-century cave temple survive from the earliest period. The traveller Castaneda, who accompanied Vasco da Gama on the first Portuguese landing in India, described how he strayed into a temple, supposing it to be a church, and saw "monstrous looking images with two inch fangs" painted on the walls, causing one of the party to fall to his knees exclaiming, "if this be the devil, I worship God".

Technically classified as **Fresco-Secco**, Kerala murals employ vegetable and mineral colours, predominantly ochre reds and yellows, white and blue-green, and are coated with a protective sheen of pine resin and oil. Their ingenious design, strongly influenced by the canonical text, *Shilparatna*, incorporates intense detail with clarity and dynamism in the portrayal of human (and celestial) figures; subtle facial expressions are captured with the simplest of lines, while narrative elements are always bold and arresting. In common with all great Indian art, they share a complex iconography and symbolism.

Non-Hindus can see fine examples in Kochi, Padmanabhapuram (see p.1069), Ettumanur (see p.1082) and Kayamkulam (see p.1075). Visitors interested in how they are made should head for the *Mural Painting Institute* at Guruvayur (see p.1108). A paperback book, *Murals of Kerala*, by MG Shashi Bhooshan (Kerala Govt Dept of Public Relations) serves as an excellent introduction to the field.

The **murals** that adorn some of its rooms are among the finest examples of Kerala's much underrated school of painting; friezes illustrating stories from the *Ramayana*, on the first floor, date from the sixteenth century. Packed with detail and gloriously rich colour, the style is never strictly naturalistic; the treatment of facial features is pared down to the simplest of lines for the mouth, and characteristically aquiline noses. Downstairs, the women's bedchamber holds several less complex paintings, possibly dating from the 1700s. One shows Shiva dallying with Vishnu in his female form, the enchantress Mohini; a second portrays Krishna holding aloft Mount Govardhana; another features a reclining Krishna surrounded by *gopis*, or cowgirls. His languid pose belies the activity of his six hands and two feet, intimately caressing adoring admirers.

While the paintings are undoubtedly the highlight of the palace, the collection also includes interesting Dutch maps of old Cochin, coronation robes belonging to past maharajas, royal palanquins, weapons and furniture. Without permission from the Archaeological Survey of India, photography is strictly prohibited.

Fort Cochin

Moving northwest from Mattancherry Palace along Bazar Rd, you pass wholesale emporia where owners, sitting behind scales surrounded by sacks of spices, may well be prepared to talk about their wares. After about half an hour's leisurely walk, cross the canal to find yourself in **Fort Cochin**. The architecture of the quiet streets in this enclave is very definitely European, with fine houses built by wealthy British traders, and Dutch cottages with split farmhouse doors. At the water's edge there's a bus stand, boat jetty and food and drinks stalls. This area, and nearby Princess St (which has a few budget hotels) attract backpackers and the consequent local hustlers.

Chinese fishing nets

The huge, elegant **Chinese fishing nets** that line the northern shore of Fort Cochin – adding grace to an already characterful waterside view, and probably the single most familiar photographic image of Kerala – are said to have been introduced to the region by traders from the court of Kublai Khan. Known in Malayalam as *cheena vala*, they can also be seen throughout the backwaters further south. The nets, which are suspended from arced poles and operated by levers and weights, require at least four men to control. You can buy fresh fish from the tiny market here and have it grilled on the spot at one of the ramshackle stalls.

St Francis Church

Walking on from the Chinese fishing nets brings you to a typically English village green. In one corner stands the church of **St Francis**, the first European church in India. Originally built in wood and named Santo Antonio, it was probably associated with Franciscan friars from Portugal. Exactly when it was founded is not known, but the stone structure is likely to date from the early sixteenth century. The facade, with multi-curved sides, became the model for most Christian churches in India. Vasco da Gama was buried here in 1524, but his body was later removed to Portugal.

Under the Dutch, the church was renovated and became Protestant in 1663, then Anglican with the advent of the British in 1795 and since 1949 has been attached to the Church of South India. Inside, various tombstone inscriptions have been placed in the walls, the earliest of which is from 1562. One hangover from British days is the continued use of *punkahs*, large swinging cloth fans on frames suspended above the congregation; these are operated by people sitting outside pulling on cords.

The interior of the twentieth-century **Santa Cruz Cathedral**, south of St Francis church, will delight fans of the colourful – verging on the downright gaudy – Indo-Romano-Rococo school of decoration.

KALAM EZHUTTU

The tradition of **kalam ezhuttu** (pronounced "kalam-*erroo*-too") – detailed and beautiful ritual drawings in coloured powder, of deities and geometric patterns (*mandalas*) – is very much alive all over Kerala. The designs usually cover an area of around thirty square metres, often outdoors and under a *pandal*, a temporary shelter made from bamboo and paddy fronds. Each colour, made from rice flour, turmeric, ground leaves and burnt paddy husk, is painstakingly applied using the thumb and forefinger as a funnel. Three communities produce *kalams*; two come from the temple servant (*amblavasi*) castes, whose rituals are associated with the god Ayappa (see p.1084) or the goddess Bhagavati; the third, the *pullavans*, specialize in serpent worship. Iconographic designs emerge gradually from the initial grid lines and turn into startling figures, many of terrible aspect, with wide eyes and fangs. Noses and breasts are raised, giving the whole a three-dimensional effect. As part of the ritual, the significant moment when the powder is added for the iris or pupil, "opening" the eyes, may well be marked by the accompaniment of *chenda* drums and *elatalam* hand-cymbals.

Witnessing the often day-long ritual is an unforgettable experience. The effort expended by the artist is made all the more remarkable by the inevitable destruction of the picture shortly after its completion; this truly ephemeral art cannot be divorced from its ritual context. In some cases, the image is destroyed by a fierce-looking **vellichapad** ("light-bringer"), a village oracle who can be recognized by shoulder-length hair, red *dhoti*, heavy brass anklets and the hooked sword he brandishes either while jumping up and down on the spot (a common sight), or marching purposefully about to control the spectators. At the end of the ritual, the powder, invested with divine power, is thrown over the onlookers. *Kalam ezhuttu* rituals are not widely advertised, but check at tourist offices.

Ernakulam

ERNAKULAM presents the modern face of Kerala, with more of a city feel than Thiruvananthapuram, but small enough not to be daunting. Other than the fairly dull **Parishath Thamburan Museum** (daily except Mon 9.30am–noon & 3–5.30pm) in Darbar Hall Rd, there's little in the way of sights; along the busy, long, straight **Mahatma Gandhi (MG) Road**, which more or less divides Ernakulam in half 500m back from the sea, shopping, eating and movie-going are the main activities. Here you can fax and phone to your heart's content, and choose from an assortment of great

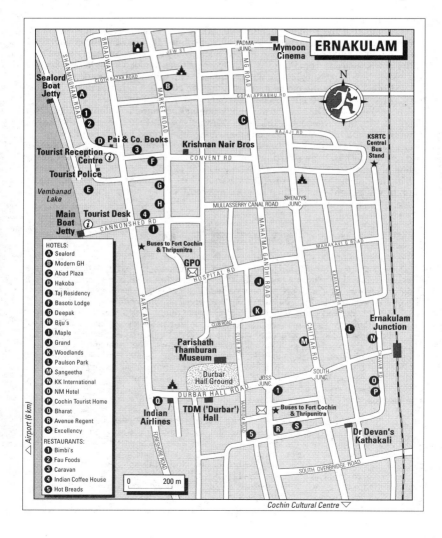

HOTELS:
- **A** Sealord
- **B** Modern GH
- **C** Abad Plaza
- **D** Hakoba
- **E** Taj Residency
- **F** Basoto Lodge
- **G** Deepak
- **H** Biju's
- **I** Maple
- **J** Grand
- **K** Woodlands
- **L** Paulson Park
- **M** Sangeetha
- **N** KK International
- **O** NM Hotel
- **P** Cochin Tourist Home
- **Q** Bharat
- **R** Avenue Regent
- **S** Excellency

RESTAURANTS:
- **1** Bimbi's
- **2** Fau Foods
- **3** Caravan
- **4** Indian Coffee House
- **5** Hot Breads

Cochin Cultural Centre ▽

KATHAKALI IN KOCHI

Kochi is the only city in the state where you are guaranteed the chance to see live **Kathakali**, the uniquely Keralan form of ritualized theatre (see p.1110). Whether in its authentic setting, in temple festivals held during the winter, or at the shorter tourist-oriented shows that take place year round, these mesmerizing dance dramas are an unmissable feature of Kochi's cultural life.

Three venues in the city hold daily recitals. Beginning at 6.30pm, the hour-long shows are preceeded by an introductory talk. You can also watch the dancers being made-up if you arrive an hour or so early. Tickets cost Rs50 and can be bought on the door. Most visitors only attend one show, but you'll gain a much better sense of what Kathakali is all about if you take in at least a couple, followed, ideally, with an all-night recital at a temple festival, or at least one of the recitals given by the *Ernakulam Kathakali Club* (for either contact the Tourist Desk at the Main Boat Jetty, Ernakulam). Keen photographers should arrive well before the start to ensure a front-row seat.

Cochin Cultural Centre, Souhardham, Manikath Rd (☎367866). The least commendable option: the dancing at this a/c theatre ("sound-proof, insect-proof, and dust-proof") is accomplished, but performances are short, with only two characters, and you can't see the musicians. Worst of all, large tour groups monopolize the front seats, and the PA speakers at the back are excruciatingly loud.

Kerala Kathakali Centre, Cochin Aquatic Club, River Rd (near the bus stand), Fort Cochin waterfront. Performed by a company of young graduates of the renowned Kalamandalam Academy (see p.1110), and hugely enjoyable. What the actors lack in expertise they make up for with enthusiasm, and the small, dilapidated performance space, whose doors open on to the water, adds to the atmosphere. You also get to see three characters, and the music is particularly good. Come early to see them getting into their costumes.

Dr Devan's Kathakali, *Devan Gurukulam*, Kalathiparambil Lane, near Ernakulam railway station (☎369471 or 371759). The oldest-established tourist show in the city, introduced by the inimitable Dr Devan, who steals the stage with his lengthy discourse on Indian philosophy and mythology. Entertaining, but maybe too much chat and not enough Kathakali.

places to eat Keralan food. This area is particularly good for cloth, with an infinite selection of colours. If there's a jazzy style in *lunghis* this year, you'll get it on MG Rd.

An eight-day annual **festival** at the Shiva temple in Ernakulam (Jan/Feb) features elephant processions and *panchavadyam* (drum and trumpet groups) out in the street. As part of the festival, there are usually night-time performances of Kathakali, and the temple is decorated with an amazing array of electric lights: banks of coloured tubes and sequenced bulbs imitating shooting stars.

Thripunitra

The small suburban town of **THRIPUNITRA**, 12km southeast of Ernakulam, is worth a visit for its dilapidated colonial-style **Hill Palace** (daily except Mon 9am–12.30pm & 2–4pm), now an eclectic museum a short auto-rickshaw ride from the busy bus stand. The royal family of Cochin ("Honour is our family treasure") at one time maintained around forty palaces. This one was confiscated by the state government after Independence, and has slipped into dusty decline over the past decade.

One of the museum's finest exhibits is an early seventeenth-century wooden *mandapa* removed from a temple in Pathanamthitta, featuring excellent carvings of the coronation of the monkey king Sugriva and other themes from the *Ramayana*. Of interest too are silver filigree jewel boxes, gold and silver ornaments, and ritual objects associated with grand ceremonies. The **epigraphy** gallery contains an eighth-century

THE ISLANDS OF LAKSHADWEEP

Visitors to Kochi who really want to get away from it all, and have time and a lot of money to spare, could do no better than to head for **LAKSHADWEEP**, the "one hundred thousand islands", which lie between 200 and 400km offshore, in the deep blue of the Arabian Sea. The smallest Union Territory in India consists of lagoons, reefs, sand banks and 27 tiny coconut-palm-covered coral islands. Only ten are inhabited, with a total population of just over 50,000, the majority of whom are Malayalam-speaking Sunni Muslims, said to be descended from seventh-century Keralan Hindus who converted to Islam. The main sources of income are fishing, coconuts and related products. Fruit, vegetables and pulses are cultivated in small quantities but staples such as rice and many other commodities have always had to be imported. The Portuguese, who discovered the value of coir rope, a by-product of the coconut, controlled Lakshadweep during the sixteenth century; when they imposed an import tax on rice, locals retaliated by poisoning some of the 40-strong Portuguese garrison. Terrible reprisals followed. As Muslims, the islanders enjoyed friendly relations with Tipu Sultan of Mysore. That naturally aroused the ire of the British, who moved in at the end of the eighteenth century and remained until Independence, when Lakshadweep became a Union Territory.

At present, only one island can be visited by non-residents of India. The teardrop-shaped uninhabited islet of **Bangaram** welcomes a limited number of tourists, and expects them to pay handsomely for the privilege. Bangaram is the archetypal tropical paradise, edged with pristine white sands and sitting in a calm lagoon where average water temperature stays around 26°C. Beyond the lagoon lies coral reef and the technicolour world of the deep, home to sea turtles, dolphins, eagle rays, lionfish, parrotfish, octopus and predators like barracudas and sharks. Islanders come to Bangaram and its uninhabited neighbours to fish and to harvest coconuts.

It's theoretically possible to visit Bangaram all year round; the hottest time is April and May, when the temperature can reach 33°C; the monsoon (May–Sept) attracts approximately half the rainfall seen in Kerala, in the form of passing showers, not a deluge, although seas are rough. The island remains staggeringly peaceful, and compared to other resorts, at least attempts to minimize its ecological impact. The *Bangaram Island Resort* (⑨) accommodates thirty couples in simple thatched cottage rooms, each with a verandah; cane tables and chairs sit outside the restaurant on the beach, and a few hammocks are strung up between the palms. There's no air-conditioning, TV, radio, telephone, newspapers or shops, let alone discos. The tariff, if expensive for India, compares favourably with other exotic holiday destinations; during the peak season (mid-Dec to mid-Jan) it rises to around US$120 per person full board in a twin-bedded room; in low season (April–Sept except Aug) it may be as much as 25 percent less. Facilities include scuba diving (from US$45 per dive; lessons with qualified instructor); glass-bottomed boat trips to neighbouring uninhabited islands (2hr; $30); and deep-sea fishing (Oct to mid-May; US$50–75). Kayaks, catamarans and a sail boat are available free.

At present, the only way to reach Bangaram is on the staggeringly expensive NEPC 20-seater plane from **Kochi** (2 weekly; 1hr 30min) to the island of Agatti, 8km southwest. The connecting boat journey from Agatti takes two hours, picking its way through the shallows to avoid the corals; during the monsoon, helicopters are used. All arrangements, including accommodation and the necessary entry permit, are handled by the *Casino Hotel*, Willingdon Island, Kochi (☎668221; fax 668001). Some foreign tour operators, however, offer all-in packages combining Lakshadweep with another destination, usually Goa.

Jewish *Torah*, and Keralan stone and copperplate inscriptions. Sculpture, ornaments and weapons in the **bronze** gallery include a *kingini katti* knife, whose decorative bells belie the fact that it was used for beheading, and a body-shaped cage in which condemned prisoners would be hanged for birds to peck them to death. Providing the place isn't crowded with noisy school groups here to see the nearby deer park, the **garden** behind the palace is a peaceful spot to picnic beneath the cashew trees.

Performances of theatre, classical music and dance, including consecutive all-night Kathakali performances, are held over a period of several days during the annual **festival** (Oct/Nov) at the **Shri Purnatrayisa** temple, on the way to the palace. Inside the temple compound, both in the morning and at night, massed drum orchestras perform *chenda melam* in procession with fifteen caparisoned elephants. At night, the outside walls of the sanctuary are covered with thousands of tiny oil lamps. Although the temple is normally closed to non-Hindus, admittance to appropriately dressed visitors is usually allowed at this time.

Accommodation

Despite its romantic atmosphere, **Fort Cochin** holds a regrettably small selection of accommodation, limited to a handful of low-budget guest houses and one mid-range hotel. Most visitors end up staying in **Ernakulam**, which, although it lacks the old-world ambience, is far more convenient. **Bolghatty Island**, site of the city's most congenial and best value mid-price hotel, is a comfortable, but isolated, alternative.

Ernakulam
Ernakulam has plenty of accommodation, although its guest houses and hotels tend to fill up by late-afternoon, so book in advance.

INEXPENSIVE
Basoto Lodge, Press Club Rd (☎352140). Clean, dependable backpackers' lodge that has hiked its prices, although it is still cheap. Two rooms have small balconies and attached shower-toilets. Advance booking recommended. ①.

Biju's Tourist Home, corner of Canon Shed and Market roads (☎369881). Pick of the budget bunch, with 28 basic but clean and spacious rooms, close to the main boat jetty. TVs may be rented, and they have an inexpensive same-day laundry service. ③.

Cochin Tourist Home, opposite railway station (☎364575). Cleanest of the cheap hotels lined up outside Ernakulam Junction, but often full. Single occupancy available, and there's a resident astro-palmist. If it's full, try *KK International* (☎366010; ③), or *NM Hotel* (③), both nearby. ②.

Hakoba, Shanmugham Rd (☎353933). Between Main and High Court boat jetties, near KTDC tourist office. Dowdy, but adequate for a night, with good "meals" joint on the ground floor. Their front rooms overlooking the street and harbour are the best deals. ②.

Maple Guest House, XL/271 Canon Shed Rd (☎355156). After *Biju's*, the best deal in the district. The rooms are spartan, but clean, cheap and central. ②.

Modern Guest House, XL/60667, Market Rd (☎352130). Simple rooms above (noisy) Keralan veg restaurant, all en-suite and with fans. Popular budget option; book ahead. ②.

MODERATE TO EXPENSIVE
Abad Plaza, MG Rd (☎361636). Comfortable business-style high-rise, with restaurant and bar, in the centre of Ernakulam. ⑥.

Avenue Regent, MG Rd (☎372660; fax 370129). Very comfortable, centrally a/c 4-star, close to the railway station and main shopping area. Restaurant, 24-hr coffee shop, and most mod cons. ⑧.

Bharat, Durbar Hall Rd (☎353501; fax 370502). Large, well-run hotel near the harbour and city centre. Clean and comfortable rooms, 24-hr coffee shop and three restaurants. ⑤–⑦.

Excellency, Nettipadam Rd, Jos Junction (☎337001; fax 374009). Close to MG Rd. Smart, modern mid-range place with mostly a/c rooms. Credit cards accepted. ⑤–⑥.

Grand, MG Rd (☎353211). Two-part hotel near Woodlands Junction in central Ernakulam; the cheaper rooms are on the bottom floors, which have a faintly 1950s feel. Restaurant on site. ⑤–⑦.

Paulson Park, Carrier Station Rd (☎354002). Close to Ernakulam Junction. Good value, with large, well-appointed rooms and a ground-floor restaurant featuring surreal fake rock garden. ②–④.

Sangeetha, 36/1675 Chittoor Rd, near stations (☎368736). Comfortable rooms, if small for the price; the non-a/c ones can be stuffy. Left luggage and foreign exchange. ⑥–⑦.

Sealord, Shanmugham Rd (☎352682; fax 370135). Modern, comfortable high-rise near High Court jetty. Standard rooms are excellent value; the best are on the top floor. Rooftop restuarant, bar and foreign exchange. ⑤–⑦.

Taj Residency, Marine Drive (☎371471; fax 371481). Erankulam's top hotel enjoys a prime location overlooking the harbour. All the luxuries, minus a pool. ⑧.

Woodlands, Woodlands Junction, MG Rd (☎351372). In the centre, a stylish Indian-style middle-class hotel with fine veg restaurant. A/c and non-a/c rooms have sofas and easy chairs, and spot-less marble bathrooms. Recommended. ③–④.

Fort Cochin

Delite, opposite the Parade Ground (☎228658). Recently opened, and already established as the best all-round budget option in Fort Cochin. Six spacious, airy rooms around a leafy courtyard, run by a friendly family. Breakfasts available. ②.

PWD Rest House, Dutch Cemetery Rd. Near the water. Three gigantic rooms with colonial fur-niture. Intended for government employees, but others can stay when it's not busy. Dilapidated. ①.

Seagull, Calvathy Rd (☎228128). Between Mattancherry and Fort Cochin at the water's edge. Assorted rooms, a couple with a/c, but none make the most of the location (stand on a chair to see out of the window). Bar and restaurant. ③–⑤.

Tharavadu Tourist Home, Quiros St (the road behind the post office), Fort Cochin (☎226897). Eight simple, clean rooms (2 without bath) in old house. Friendly staff can provide breakfast and cool drinks, and there's cheap laundry service. The best choice after *Delite*. ②–③.

Willingdon and Bolghatty islands

Casino, Willingdon Island, 2km from airport, close to Cochin Harbour Terminus railway station (☎666821; fax 668001). Fairly modern and comfortable, with good service, swimming pool, travel agent, foreign exchange, and a choice of restaurants. ⑧.

KTDC Bolghatty Palace, Bolghatty Island (☎355003 or 354879). Renovated palace in beautiful location, a short hop by ferry from the High Court Jetty, Ernakulam. Huge rooms in main building, built by the Dutch in 1744 and later home of the British Resident, and "honeymoon" cottages in the grounds. Check by phone, or at the KTDC office on Shanmugham Rd, to make sure they have vacancies, and arrive armed with mosquito repellent. Highly recommended. ⑤–⑧.

Malabar, Willingdon Island, by Tourist Office Jetty (20min ferry from Ernakulam), near Cochin Harbour Terminus railway station (☎668010; fax 668297). One of India's best hotels, owned by the *Taj* group. Superb waterside location with waterside gardens and views of old Mattancherry. Two restaurants, swimming pool and excellent service. ⑧.

Eating

Unusually for Keralan cities, Kochi offers a wide choice for **eating out**, from the deli-cious fresh-cooked fish by the Chinese fishing nets at Fort Cochin, to the sophistication of the *Malabar Hotel*. Between the two extremes, various popular, modest places in Ernakulam serve real Keralan food. The *Elite* bakery on Princess St in Fort Cochin, long a budget travellers' haunt, has recently been the cause of many an upset stomach and should be avoided.

Ernakulam

Fry's Village Restaurant, adjacent to *Mymoor Cinema*, Chittoor Rd. Moderately priced, ultra-spicy Keralan and "ethnic" specialities you rarely find served in such style, including Calicut Muslim del-icacy *patthri*, wafer-thin rice pancakes, *idliappam* dumplings, and *puthoo*, steamed rice cakes.

Bimbi's, Shanmughan Rd and Jos Junction. Brisk new Indian-style fast food joints. Hugely popular for inexpensive Udupi, north Indian and Chinese snacks and meals, and the tangiest *wada-sambars* in town. They also do a great selection of shakes and ice-creams.

The Brasserie, *Taj Residency*, Marine Drive. Luxury coffee shop serving snacks and a particular-ly good range of Western cakes (Dundee, plum, palmettes and fudge). Expensive.

Caravan, Broadway, near the KTDC tourist office. A/c ice-cream parlour that's a good place to chill out over a banana split or milkshake. Closes at midnight so you can nip in for a late dessert.

Fau Foods, Shanmughan Rd. Busy, clean and popular roadside restaurant serving veg and non-veg meals, including blow-out *thalis* and good-value "dish of the day". For dessert, try their Bombay-style *faloodas*, vermicelli steeped in syrup.

Hot Breads, Warriom Rd. Freshly baked cakes, pastries and breads, including delicious chocolate croissants, to take away.

Indian Coffee House, corner of MG Rd and Durbar Hall Rd. The usual excellent coffee (ask for "pot coffee" if you don't want it with sugar) and simple snacks such as *dosa* and scrambled egg. There's another branch at the corner of Canon Shed Rd and Park Ave.

Lotus Cascades, *Woodlands Hotel*, Woodlands Junction, MG Rd. Classy veg Indian food, with plenty of *tandoori* options, at bargain prices. Great service, too. Recommended.

Sealord, Shanmugham Rd. Pricey rooftop restaurant serves good Chinese, Indian and sizzlers – but the portions are not too generous, and the view is not what it was since the shopping centre opposite was built. Great for a beer, though.

Utsav, *Taj Residency*, Marine Drive. Top Indian restaurant with great views over the harbour, and an a la carte menu at expense-account prices. Their lunch-time buffets are better value.

Fort Cochin

Chariot Beach, Princess St. Huge seafood and Chinese menu, at reasonable prices, and you can eat al fresco on their small terrace.

Seagull, Calvetty Rd. Average restaurant, in good location overlooking the water. Their seafood in Chinese sauces is particularly tasty, but be preapred for a long wait. Serves beer and spirits.

Willingdon Island

Casino (☎340221). Good lunchtime buffet and evening meals in dark indoor restaurant, and excellent outdoor poolside seafood restaurant, often accompanied by south Indian classical music.

Malabar (☎340010). Two restaurants: the *Jade Pavilion* for Chinese and *Rice Boats* serving Western, north Indian and Keralan in a beautiful waterside location. The food is excellent and prices reflect this; the lunchtime buffet is less expensive.

Listings

Airlines *Indian Airlines*, Durbar Hall Rd (daily 9.45am–1pm & 1.45–4.45pm; ☎353901); *NEPC* in the Chandrika Building, also on MG Rd (☎366888); *Air India*, 35/1301 MG Rd, Ravipuram (☎360380); *British Airways*, c/o *Nijhwan Travels*, MG Rd (☎364867); *Delta*, 35/2433 MG Rd, Ravipuram (☎360843); *Egypt Air*, c/o *ABC International*, Old Thevara Rd (☎353457); *Kuwait Airways*, c/o *National Travels*, MG Rd (☎360123); *Moduluft*, at the airport (☎0484/668558); *PIA*, c/o *ABC International*, Old Thevara Rd (☎353457); *Saudia*, c/o *Arafat Travels*, MG Rd (☎352689); *Singapore Airlines* & *Swissair*, 35/2433 MG Rd, Ravipuram (☎367911 or 360380); *TWA*, c/o *Jet Air*, Warriam Rd (☎369142). *Spencer & Co*, Arya Vaidya Sala Buildings, 35/718 MG Rd (☎373997) are the local agents for *Air Maldives, Cathay Pacific, KLM* and *Northwest Airlines*.

Audio cassettes *Sargam*, XL/6816 GSS Complex, Convent Rd, opposite Public Library (☎374216), stocks the best range of music tapes in the state, mostly Indian (Hindi films, and lots of Keralan devotional music), with a couple of shelves of Western rock and pop.

Bookstores *Bhavi Books*, Convent Rd (☎354003); *Higginbothams*, TD Rd (☎368834); *Pai & Co*, MG Rd (☎355835), Broadway (☎361020), and New Rd (☎225607).

Cinemas *Sridhar Theatre*, Shanmughan Rd, near the *Hotel Sealord*, screens English-language movies daily; check the listings pages of the *Indian Express* or *Hindu* (Kerala edition) to find out what's on. For the latest Malayalam and Hindi releases, head for the comfortable a/c *Mymoon Cinema* at the north end of Chitoor Rd, or the *Saritha Savitha Sangeetha*, at the top of Market Rd.

Handicrafts *CI Company*, Broadway (☎352405); plus *Kairali* (☎354507), *Khadi Bhavan* (☎355279); *Khataisons Curio Palace* (☎367472), *Surabhi Kerala State Handicrafts* (☎353063), all on MG Rd.

Hospitals General, Hospital Rd (☎361251); Lissie, Lissie Jnct (☎352006); Lourdes, Pachalam (☎351507).

MOVING ON FROM KOCHI/ERNAKULAM

For a **full rundown** of travel services to and from Kochi/Ernakulam, see "Kerala Travel Details" on p.1053.

By Air
Kochi airport, 5km south of the city centre on Willingdon Island, is served by daily *Indian Airlines* and *Modiluft* flights to **Bombay**. You can also fly direct with either *Indian Airlines*, *Modiluft*, or *NEPC* to **Bangalore**, **Madras**, and **Delhi**. The daily *IA* Delhi fight calls in at Goa (1hr 10min), although this stop may be discontinued. The only other scheduled domestic departures from Kochi are to the Lakshadweep Islands, on *NEPC*'s expensive **Agatti** flight (2 weekly; 1hr 20min).
    For details of the airlines, see under *Listings*, above; for general ticketing and flight confirmation, the *IATA*-approved travel agents *PL Worldways*, at 35/1389 MG Rd are recommended.

By Bus
Buses leave Ernakulam's *KSRTC* Central bus stand for virtually every town in Kerala, and some beyond; most, but not all, are bookable in advance. Travelling south, dozens of buses per day run to **Thiruvananthapuram**; most go via **Alappuzha** and **Kollam**, but a few go via **Kottayam**. It is also possible to travel all the way to Kanniyakumari (9hr). However, for destinations further afield in Karnataka and Tamil Nadu, you're much better off on the train.

By Train
Kochi lies on Kerala's main broad-gauge line, and sees frequent trains down the coast to Thiruvananthapuram, via Kottayam, Kollam and Varkala. Heading north, there are plenty of services to Thrissur, and thence northeast across Tamil Nadu to Madras, but only a couple run north to Mangalore, where a poorly served branch line veers inland to Hassan and Mysore in Karnataka.
    Although most long-distance express and mail trains depart from **Ernakulam Junction**, a short way southeast of the city centre, a couple of key services leave from **Ernakulam Town**, 2km north. To confuse matters further, some also start at Cochin Harbour station, on Willingdon Island, so be sure to check the departure point when you book your ticket. The main reservation office, good for trains leaving all three stations, is at Ernakulam Junction (☎353100 for general enquiries); take a good book with you as there is no special fast-track counter for tourists.
    The following trains are recommended as the fastest and/or most convenient services from Kochi. If you're heading to **Alappuzha** for the backwater trip to Kollam, take the bus, as the only train that can get you there in time invariably arrives late. Note, too, that until the completion of the Konkan Railway (scheduled for late 1997) there will be no through trains to Goa; you have to catch one of the two daily serices to Mangalore, and pick up a bus from there.

Destination	Name	Number	Station	Departs	Total time
Bangalore	*Kanniyakumari–Bangalore Express*	#6525†	ET	3.27pm	13hr
Bombay	*Kanniyakumari Express*	#1081†	EJ	12.55pm	40hr
Delhi	*Rajdhani Express*	#2431*	EJ	12.05am	40hr 30min
	Kerala Express	#2625†	EJ	5.05am	48hr 45min
Madras	*Trivandrum–Madras Mail*	#6320†	ET	5.50pm	12hr 25min
Mangalore	*Malabar Express*	#6029†	ET	10.55pm	10hr 30min
	Parsuram Express	#6349†	ET	11am	10hr
Thiruvananthapuram	*Ernakulam–Trivandrum Express*	#6341†	EJ	6.45am	4hr 10min
Varkala	*Kanniyakumari Express*	#1081†	EJ	6.55am	4hr 10min

EJ = Ernakulam Junction
ET = Ernakulam Town
* = a/c only, Fri only
† = daily

Musical instruments *Manual Industries*, Bannerji Rd, Kacheripady Jnct (☎352513) is the best for Indian classical instruments. For traditional Keralan drums, ask at Thripunitra bazaar (see p.1097).
Photographic supplies *Krishnan Nair Bros*, Convent Rd (☎352098) stock the best range of camera film, including black-and-white, *Kodachrome* and *Fujichrome*, and professional colour transparency; *Royal Studio*, Shanmugham Rd (☎351614) are also worth a try.
Visa extensions Apply in person to City Police Commissioner, Marine Drive (☎31700); take two passport photos. Extensions normally take between five and ten working days to process.

Thrissur

The welcoming town of **THRISSUR** (Trichur), roughly midway between Kochin (74km south) and Palakaad (79km northeast) on the NH47, is an obvious base for exploring the cultural riches of central Kerala. Near the Palghat (Palakaad) Gap – an opening in the natural border made by the Western Ghat mountains – it presided over the main trade route into the region from Tamil Nadu and Karnataka, and was for years the capital of Cochin State, controlled at various times by both the Zamorin of Kozhikode and Tipu Sultan of Mysore. The town centres on Kerala's largest temple complex, **Vadakkunatha**, surrounded by a *maidan* (green) that sees all kinds of public gatherings, not least Kerala's most extravagant, noisy and sumptuous festival, **Puram**.

Arrival and information
The principal point of orientation in Thrissur is the Round, a road subdivided into North, South, East and West, which encircles the Vadakkunatha temple and *maidan* at the centre. Once you've established which side of the Round you're on, you can save yourself long walks along the busy pavement by striking out across the green.

Thrissur's **railway station** is 1km southwest of Round South, near the *KSRTC* **long-distance bus stand. Priya Darshini** (also known as "North", "Shoranur" and "Wadakkancheri") bus station, close to Round North, serves Palakaad and Shoranur. The **Shakthan Thampuran** stand, on TB Rd, 2km from Round South, serves local destinations south such as Irinjalakuda, Kodungallur and Guruvayur.

The KTDC **tourist office**, where you can pick up maps of Thrissur, but little else, is on Palace Rd, opposite the Town Hall (five minutes' walk off Round East); KTDC also have a small information counter at their hotel *Yatri Niwas*, Stadium Rd (☎27383). The main branch of the *State Bank of Travancore* (Mon–Fri 10am–2pm, Sat 10am–noon) on the first floor next to the Paramekkavu temple, Round East, accepts *American Express* travellers' cheques, but not *Thomas Cook* or *Mastercard*. Opposite the same temple, the *State Bank of India* (same hours) refuses all travellers' cheques but will change dollars and sterling. Finally, the GPO is on the southern edge of town, neat the *Casino Hotel* off TB Road.

The telephone **area code** for Thrissur is ☎0487.

Vadakkunatha temple
Vadakkunatha temple (closed to non-Hindus), is a walled complex of fifteen shrines, dating from the twelfth century and earlier, the principal of which is dedicated to Shiva. Inside the walls, the grassy compound is surprisingly quiet and spacious, with a striking apsidal shrine dedicated to Ayappa (see p.1084). Sadly, many of the temple's treasures, such as wood carving and murals, are not as well-maintained as they might be.

Once an essential ingredient of the temple's cultural life, but now under-used and neglected, the long, sloping-roofed **Kuttambalam theatre** with carved panels and

PURAM

Thrissur is best known to outsiders as the venue for Kerala's biggest festival, **Puram**, which takes place on one day in April/May. Introduced by the Kochi (Cochin) Raja, Shaktan Tampuran (1789–1803), Puram is today the most extreme example of the kind of celebration seen on a smaller scale all over Kerala, whose main ingredients invariably include **caparisoned elephants**, **drum music** and **fireworks**.

On this day, at the hottest time of year, the centre of Thrissur fills to capacity with a sea of people gravitating towards Round South, where a long wide path leads to the southern entrance of the **Vadakkunatha temple** complex. Two processions, representing the Tiruvambadi and Paramekkavu temples in Thrissur, compete to create the more impressive sights and sounds. They eventually meet, like armies on a battlefield, facing each other at either end of the path. Both sides present fifteen tuskers sumptuously decorated with gold ornaments, each ridden by three brahmins clutching objects symbolizing royalty: silver-handled whisks of yak hair, circular peacock feather fans and orange, green, red, purple, turquoise, black, gold or patterned silk umbrellas fringed with silver pendants. At the centre of each group, the principal elephant carries an image of the temple's deity. Swaying gently, the elephants stand still much of the time, ears flapping, seemingly oblivious to the mayhem engendered by the crowds, bomb-like firework bangs and the huge orchestra that plays in front of them.

Known as **chenda melam**, this quintessentially Keralan music, featuring as many as a hundred loud, hard-skinned, cylindrical *chenda* drums, crashing cymbals and wind instruments, mesmerizes the crowd while its structure marks the progress of the procession. Each kind of *chenda melam* is named after the rhythmic cycle (*tala* or, in Malayalam, *talam*) in which it is set. Drummers stand in ranks, the most numerous at the back often playing single beats. At the front, a line of master drummers, the stars of Keralan music, try to outdo each other with their speed, stamina, improvisational skills and showmanship. Facing the drummers, musicians play long double-reed, oboe-like *kuzhals* (similar to the north Indian *shehnai*) and C-shaped *kompu* bell-metal trumpets. The fundamental structure is provided by the *elatalam* – medium-sized, heavy, brass hand cymbals that resolutely and precisely keep the tempo, essential to the cumulative effect of the music. Over an extended period, the *melam* passes through four phases of tempo, each a double of the last, from a majestic dead slow through to a frenetic pace.

The arrival of the fastest tempo is borne on a wave of aural and visual stimulation. Those astride the elephants stand at this point, to manipulate their feather fans and hair whisks in co-ordinated sequence while behind, unfurled umbrellas are twirled in flashes of dazzling colour and glinting silver in the sun. Meanwhile, the cymbals crash furiously, often raised above the head, requiring extraordinary stamina (and causing nasty weals on the hands). The master drummers play their loudest and fastest, frequently intensified by surges of energy emanating from single players, one after another. A chorus of trumpets, in ragged unison, make an ancient noise.

All this is greeted by firework explosions and roars from the crowd. Many people punch the air, some fairly randomly much like heavy metal fans in the West, while others are clearly *talam branthans*, rhythm "madmen", who follow every nuance of the structure. When the fastest speed is played out, the slowest tempo returns and the procession edges forward, the *mahouts* leading the elephants by the tusk. Stopping again, the whole cycle is repeated. At night, the Vadukannatha temple entrances are a blaze of coloured lights and a spectacular firework display takes place in the early hours of the morning.

If you venture to Thrissur for Puram, be prepared for packed buses and trains. Needless to say, accommodation should be booked well in advance. An umbrella or hat is recommended. Women travellers should be aware that the densest parts of the crowd are almost entirely male; Keralan women usually look on from a distance.

Similar but much smaller events take place, generally from September onwards, with most during the summer (April & May). Enquire at a tourist office or your hotel, or ask someone to check a local edition of the newspaper, *Mathrabhumi*, for local performances of *chenda melam*, and other drum orchestras such as *panchavadyam* and *tyambaka*.

lathe-turned wooden pillars, is the venue for the ancient Sanskrit performance forms Chakyar Kuttu and Kutiyattam (closed to non-Hindus).

The Town
The **State Art Museum** and **Zoo** (both daily except Mon 10am–5pm) stand together on Museum Rd, ten minutes' walk from Round East, in the northeast of town (turn right at the end of Palace Rd and walk 200m down the right-hand side). Although small, the museum has excellent local bronzes, jewellery, fine wood carvings of fanged temple guardians and a profusion of bell-metal oil lamps. The zoo, however, houses a miserable set of tenants, and although it can be grimly fascinating to observe the variety of snakes that slither locally (king cobra, krait, viper), you may also be expected to watch an attendant prod cobras with a stick so they spit at the glass that separates you from them.

One of the most important churches for Thrissur's large Christian population is the Syrian Catholic **Lourdes Cathedral**, just over 1km east of the Medical College Hospital on Round East, along St Thomas College Rd. Three daily masses serve a regular congregation of nine hundred. Like many of Kerala's Indo-Gothic churches, the exterior of dome and spires is more impressive than the interior, with its unadorned metal rafters and corrugated iron ceiling. Steps lead down from the altar to the crypt, a rather dilapidated copy of the grotto in Lourdes.

Shopping
Thrissur is a great place to pick up distinctive Keralan **crafts**. The main shopping area is on the Round; on Round West, the *Kerala State Handicraft Emporium* specializes in wood, while a few doors along, a small branch of *Khadi Gramodyog* sells a limited range of handloom cloth. A far better selection of handloom can be found in *Co-optex* at the top of Palace Rd (a one-minute walk from Round East). At *Chemmanur's*, Round South, near the *Elite Hotel*, you'll find the usual carved wooden elephant type souvenirs, and, on the ground floor, a high-kitsch Aladdin's Cave of nodding dogs, Jesus clocks, Mecca table ornaments and parabolic nail-and-string art. *Sportsland*, further west on Round South, aside from sports equipment, also sells crudely painted wooden toys, such as buses and cars.

Kuruppam Road, which leads south towards the railway station from the western end of Round South, is one of the best places in Kerala to buy **bell-metal** products, particularly oil lamps made in the village of Nadavaramba, near Irinjalakuda (see p.1107). *Nadavaramba Krishna & Sons* and *Bell-metal Craft* both specialize in brass, bronze and bell-metal. Lamps cost Rs70–25,000, and "superfine" bell-metal is sold by weight, at over Rs250 per kilo. Continuing south on Kuruppam Rd to the next junction with Railway Station Rd, you'll find a number of small shops selling cheap Christian, Muslim and Hindu pictures etched on metal, and places that supply festival accessories, including umbrellas similar to those used for Puram (see opposite).

Accommodation
Thrissur has a fair number of mid-price hotels, but there's a dearth of decent budget places. The one bargain in this bracket is the palatial *Government Rest House*, which offers star-hotel comfort at economy lodge rates.

Binni Tourist Home, Round North, near the Priya Darshini bus stand (☎335703). Shabby lodge, a fall-back if the *Rest House* and *Yatri Niwas* are full, but not recommended for women. ①.

Casino, TB Rd, near the railway station (☎2469; fax 3390379). Thrissur's poshest hotel, with a multi-cuisine restaurant, bar and foreign exchange for residents (they'll accept travellers' cheques as partial payment if you eat here). ⑤.

Elite International, Chembottil Lane, off Round South (☎21033). Pronounced *Ee-light*. Thrissur's first "modern" hotel, with 82 rooms. Friendly staff, good restaurant and very central; some balconied rooms overlook the green (booked months ahead for Puram, when they cost ten times more than normal). ④–⑥.

KTDC Yatri Niwas, off Museum Rd (☎27383). Clean and reasonable place with a beer parlour and "omelette-bread-jam"-style restaurant. The best budget option after the *Rest House*. ②.

Luciya Palace, Marar Rd (☎24731). Recently revamped Neoclassical/traditional Keralan fantasy; a very good mid-range choice. Some a/c rooms, but the standard non-a/c rooms, with coir mats and cane furniture, are the best deals. Single occupancy possible. ④–⑤.

Ramanilayam Government Rest House, Palace Rd (☎20300). Very good value, huge, clean, comfortable suites with balconies. It's officially for VIPs, and they're not obliged to give you a room, but smart dress will help. It's hugely popular, and often full; if you're alone, the rate doubles after three nights. Breakfast served; other meals by advance order only. ②.

Siddartha Regency, Veliyannur Rd, Kokkalai (☎24774). Modernish, comfortable Indian hotel in the southwest corner of town, near the railway, *KSRTC* and Shakthan Thampuran bus stations. Restaurant, garden and some a/c. ④.

Eating and drinking

Thrissur's big **hotels** offer Indian, Western and Chinese food, and Keralan lunches, while several quality, inexpensive "meals" places are clustered near **the Round**. Late at night, on the corner of Rounds South and East, opposite the Medical College Hospital, you'll find a string of *chai* and omelette stalls, frequented by auto-rickshaw *wallahs*, hospital visitors, itinerant mendicants, Ayappa devotees and student revellers.

Bharata Lodge, Chembottil Lane, next door to *Elite Hotel*. Inexpensive, good-quality south Indian breakfasts, snacks and "meals" at lunchtime.

Indian Coffee House, Round South. The better of two in town. Very busy, serving snacks and the usual excellent coffee. The branch on Station Rd is very run-down.

Kerala Bhavan, Railway Station Rd. Recommended for breakfast and low-priced regional "meals". A 10-min walk south of Round South (most rickshaw-*wallahs* know where it is).

Luciya Palace, Marar Rd (☎24731). Indian and Chinese dishes. The main appeal is that they serve food at night in a pleasant garden illuminated by fairy lights.

Ming Palace, Pathan Building, Round South. Inexpensive "Chindian", serving chop suey, noodles and lots of chicken and veg dishes, under dim light and with cheesy muzak.

Pathan's, Round South. Deservedly popular veg restuarant, with a cosy a/c family (female) annexe and a large canteen-like dining hall. Generous portions and plenty of choice, *koftas*, *kormas* and lots of *tandoori* options, as well as Keralan *thalis* and wonderful Kashmiri *nan*.

Around Thrissur

The chief appeal of exploring the area around Thrissur is for the chances it provides to get to grips with Kerala's cultural heritage. Countless festivals, at their peak before the monsoon hits in May, enable visitors to catch some of the best drummers in the world, **Kathakali** dance drama and **Kutiyattam**, the world's oldest surviving theatre form.

Irinjalakuda

The village of **IRINJALAKUDA**, 20km south of Thrissur, has a unique temple, five minutes' walk west from the bus stand, dedicated to **Bharata**, the brother of Rama. Visitors are usually permitted to see inside (men must wear a *dhoti*), but as elsewhere, the inner parts of the temple are closed to non-Hindus. It boasts a superbly elegant tiled *kuttambalam* **theatre** within its outer courtyard, built to afford an unimpeded view for the maximum number of spectators (drawn from the highest castes only), and known for excellent acoustics. A profusion of painted woodcarvings of mythological animals and stories from the epics decorate the interior. On the low stage, which is enclosed by painted wooden columns and friezes of female dancers, stand two large copper *mizhavu* drums, for use in the Sanskrit drama Kutiyattam (see p.1111), permanently installed in wooden frames into which a drummer climbs to play. Traditionally, *mizhavus* were considered sacred objects;

NADAVARAMBA BELL-METAL OIL LAMPS

Keralan nights are made more enchanting by the use of **oil lamps**; the most common type, seen all over, is a slim floor-standing metal column surmounted by a spike that rises from a circular receptacle for coconut oil, and using cloth or banana plant fibre wicks. Every classical theatre performance keeps a large lamp burning centre-stage, all night. The special atmosphere of temples is also enhanced by innumerable lamps, some hanging from chains; others, *deepa stambham*, are multi-tiered and stand metres-high.

The village of **Nadavaramba**, near Irinjalakuda, is an important centre for the manufacture of oil lamps and large cooking vessels, known as *uruli* and *varppu*. Alloys made from brass, copper and tin are frequently used, but the best are from bell-metal, said to be 80 percent copper, and give a sonorous chime when struck. Shops in Thrissur that specialize in Nadavaramba ware arrange visits to see the craftsmen at work.

Nandikeshvara, Shiva's rhythm expert and accompanist, was said to reside in them. The drama for which they provided music was a holy ritual, and in the old days the instrument was never allowed to leave the temple and only played by members of a special caste, the Nambyars. Since then, outsiders have learned the art of *mizhavu* playing; some are based near the temple, but the orthodox authorities do not allow them to play inside.

Natana Kairali is an important cultural centre dedicated to the performance, protection and documentation of Kerala's lesser-known, but fascinating and vibrant theatre arts, including Kutiyattam, Nangiar Koothu (female mono-acting), shadow and puppet theatres. Left of the Bharata temple as you leave, it is based in the home of one of Kerala's most illustrious acting families, Ammanur Chakyar Madhom; cite that name when you ask for directions. *Natana Kairali*'s director, Shri G Venu, is a mine of information about Keralan arts, and can advise on forthcoming performances.

Irinjalakuda is best reached by **bus** from the Shakthan Thampuran stand at Thrissur rather than by train, as the railway station is an inconvenient 8km east of town.

Kodungallur

Virtually an island, surrounded by backwaters and the sea, the small country town of **KODUNGALLUR** (Cranganore), 35km south of Thrissur, is rich in Keralan history. The dearth of information regarding the modern town contrasts with tales of its illustrious past, and travellers may find that Kodungallur's "sights", with one exception, require some imagination. The town is best visited in a day trip by **bus** from Thrissur's Shakthan Thampuran stand (1hr 30min), or en route between Thrissur and Kochi.

Standing on a large piece of open ground at the centre of Kodungallur, the ancient and typically Keralan **Kurumba Bhagavati temple** is the site of an extraordinary annual event that some residents would prefer didn't happen at all. The **Bharani** festival, held during the Malayalam month of Meenom (March/April), attracts droves of devotees, both male and female, mainly from "low caste" communities previously excluded from the temple. Their devotions consist in part of drinking copious amounts of alcohol and taking to the streets to sing Bharani *pattu*, sexually explicit songs about, and addressed to, goddess Bhagavati, which are considered obscene and highly offensive by many other Keralans. On Kavuthindal, the first day, the pilgrims run en masse around the perimeters of the temple three times at breakneck speed, beating its walls with sticks. Until the mid-1950s, chickens were sacrificed in front of the temple; today, a simple red cloth symbolizes the bloody ritual. An important section of the devotees are the crimson-clad village oracles, wielding scythe-like swords with which they sometimes beat themselves on the head in ecstatic fervour, often drawing blood. Despite widespread disapproval, the festival draws plenty of spectators.

Kodungallur has been identified as the site of the ancient cities of **Vanji**, one-time capital of the Chera kingdom, and **Muziris**, described in the first century AD by the Roman traveller, Pliny, as *Primum Emporium Indiae*, the most important port in India. Other accounts describe the harbour as crowded with great ships, warehouses, palaces, temples and *Yavanas* (a generic term for foreigners) who brought gold, and left with spices, sandalwood, teak, gems and silks. The Romans are said to have built a temple in Kodungallur; nothing remains, but their presence has been shown through finds of coins, the majority of which date from the reigns of Augustus to Nero (27 BC–68 AD). Its life as a great port was curtailed in 1341 by floods that silted up the harbour, leading to the development of Kochi (Cochin).

Kodungallur is also reputed to be the site where the Apostle Thomas ("**Doubting Thomas**") landed in 52 AD, bringing Christianity to the subcontinent. Jews fleeing the fall of Jerusalem arrived in 69 AD, and, although the advent of Islam in India is usually associated with invading land armies arriving from the northwest in the twelfth century, Kerala claims an earlier date. The region had long enjoyed peaceable relations with the Arab world, thanks to its sea trade. **Cheraman Perumal**, the legendary Keralan king who converted to Islam, abdicated, and emigrated to Mecca, is said to have founded the Cheraman Juma Masjid in Kodungallur in the seventh century, making it the earliest mosque in India. The supposed site of his palace, Cheraman Parambu, is today nothing more than a few broken columns on open ground.

Cheraman Juma Masjid, 1500m from Kodungallur centre, is thought to be the earliest mosque in India, founded in the seventh century. The present building, which dates from the sixteenth century, was until recently predominantly made of wood, of a style usually associated with Keralan Hindu temples. Unfortunately, due to weather damage, it has recently had to be partly rebuilt, and the facade, at least, is now rather mundane, with concrete minarets. The wooden interior remains intact, however, with a large Keralan oil lamp in the centre. Introduced five centuries ago for group study of the Koran, the lamp has taken on great significance to other communities, and Muslims, Christians and Hindus alike bring oil for the lamp on the auspicious occasion of major family events. In an ante-room, a small mausoleum is said to be the burial place of Habib Bin Malik, an envoy sent from Mecca by the convert king Cheraman Perumal. Women are not allowed into the mosque at any time ("they pray at home"), but interested male visitors should contact the assistant *mukhari* (*imam*, or priest), KM Saidumohamed, who lives directly opposite and will show you around.

The **Mar Thoma Pontifical Shrine**, fronted by a crescent of neoclassical colonnades at Azhikode (pronounced "Arikode") Jetty (2km) marks the place where the Apostle Thomas is said to have arrived in India, soon after the death of Christ. It's a nice enough spot, on the edge of backwaters, but not worth a detour unless you're desperate to see the shard of the saint's wrist bone enshrined within the church.

Guruvayur

Kerala's most important Krishna shrine, the high-walled temple of **GURUVAYUR**, 29km northwest of Thrissur, attracts a constant flow of pilgrims, second only in volume to Ayappa's at Sabarimala (see p.1084). Its deity, **Guruvayurappan**, has inspired numerous paeans from Keralan poets, most notably Narayana Bhattatiri who wrote the *Narayaniyam* during the sixteenth century, when the temple, whose origins are legendary, seems to have first risen to prominence.

One of the richest temples in Kerala, **Guruvayar temple** (3am–1pm & 4–10pm) is from very early morning to late at night awash with pilgrims in their best white clothes, often trimmed with gold. Some visitors find the intense activity of the market around the temple perimeter too commercial, full of glitter and trinkets such as two-rupee plastic Guruvayurappan signet rings, but nevertheless there is a palpable air of excitement, particularly when events inside spill out into the streets. Closed to non-Hindus, the temple has turned away many famous people in its time, including, ironically, the most vocal of Guruvayurappan's devotees, the Keralan film song artist Jesudas. Though born into a Christian family (his name literally means "servant of Jesus"), Jesudas has earned millions of fans by his sincere rendition of Hindu devotional songs. Many temples, including this one, play his records, but he is not allowed past the door unless he formally converts and produces a certificate to prove it. One of his songs describes how he has, in any event, already had *darshan* of Guruvayurappan "in his mind".

Of the temple's twenty-four **annual festivals**, the most important are Ekadashi and Ulsavam. During the eighteen days of Ekadashi, in the month of Vrischikam (Nov/Dec), marked by processions of caparisoned elephants outside the temple, the exterior of the building may be decorated with the tiny flames of innumerable oil lamps. On certain days (check dates with a KTDC office) programmes staged in front of the temple attract the cream of south Indian classical music artists.

During Ulsavam, in the month of Kumbham (Feb/March), tantric rituals are conducted inside, an **elephant race** is run outside on the first day and elephant processions take place during the ensuing six days. On the ninth day, the Palivetta, or "hunt" occurs; the deity, mounted on an elephant, circumambulates the temple accompanied by men dressed as animals, who represent human weaknesses such as greed and anger, and are vanquished by the god. The next night sees the image of the god taken out for ritual immersion in the temple tank; devotees greet the procession with oil lamps and throw rice. It is considered highly auspicious to bathe in the tank at the same time as the god.

The Punnathur Kotta Elephant Sanctuary

When they are not involved in races and other arcane temple rituals, Guruvayur's tuskers hang out at the **Punnathur Kotta Elephant Sanctuary** (daily 9am–6pm; free; camera Rs25), 4km north of town. Forty animals, aged from three to ninety-three, live here, munching for most of the day on specially imported piles of fodder. Most were

---

THE FOUNDING OF GURUVAYUR TEMPLE

The founding of the **Guruvayur temple** is associated with the end of Krishna's life. After witnessing the massacre of family and compatriots, Krishna returned to his capital, Dvarka, in Gujarat, to end his earthly existence. However, knowing that Dvarka would disappear into the sea on his death, he was concerned that the form of Vishnu there, which he himself worshipped, should be spared its fate.

Krishna invited Brihaspati, also known as Guru, the preceptor of the gods, and a pupil, Vayu, the god of wind, to help him select a new home for Vishnu. By the time they arrived at Dvarka, the sea (Varuna) had already claimed the city, but the wind managed to rescue Vishnu. Krishna, Guru and Vayu travelled south, where they met Parashurama, who had just created Kerala by throwing his axe into the sea (see p.1054). On reaching a beautiful lake of lotuses, Rudratirtha, they were greeted by Shiva and Parvati who consecrated the image of Vishnu; Guru and Vayu then installed it, the temple was named after them, and so the deity received the title **Guruvayurappan** ("Lord of Guruvayur").

either gifted by wealthy patrons or else rescued from slavery and starvation in other parts of India. Though hobbled for much of day, they appear content enough, cared for by their two personal *mahoots*, who wash and scrub them each evening in the sanctuary pond – a great photo opportunity. One exception is the giant bull elephant that

KERALAN RITUAL AND RITUALIZED THEATRE

Among the most magical experiences a visitor to Kerala can have is to witness one of the innumerable ancient rituals, ritualized theatre or dance styles that play such an important, and unique role in the cultural life of the region. The dance drama **Kathakali** is the best known; other less publicized forms, which clearly influenced its development, include the classical Sanskrit **Kutiyattam** and the village hero-worship ritual **Teyyam**.

Many Keralan forms share broad characteristics. A prime aim of each performer is to transform the mundane to the world of gods and demons; his preparation is highly ritualized, involving other-worldly costume and mask-like make-up. In Kathakali and Kutiyattam, this is rigorously codified and part of a classical tradition, whereas the much wilder appearance of Teyyam differs from village to village. One-off **performances** of various types take place throughout the state, building up to fever pitch during April and May before pausing for the monsoon (June, July & Aug). Finding out about such events requires a little perseverance, but it's well worth the effort; enquire at tourist offices, or buy a Malayalam daily paper such as *Mathrabhumi* and ask someone to check the listings. **Temple festivals**, where most of the action takes place, are invariably announced. Tourist Kathakali is staged in Kochi (see p.1097) but to find authentic performances, contact **performing arts schools** such as Thiruvananthapuram's *Margi* (see p.1058) and Cheruthuruthy's *Kerala Kalamandalam*. Kutiyattam artists work at both, as well as at *Natana Kairali* at Irinjalakuda (see p.1107).

Kathakali

Here is the tradition of the trance dancers, here is the absolute demand of the subjugation of body to spirit, here is the realization of the cosmic transformation of human into divine.

Mrinalini Sarabhai, classical dancer

Kathakali dance drama, Kerala's most popular theatre form, is recognized as one of the four major classical Indian styles. The image of a Kathakali actor in a magnificent costume with extraordinary make-up and a huge gold crown has become Kerala's trademark, seen on anything from matchboxes to TV adverts for detergents. Traditional performances, of which there are still many, usually take place on open ground outside a temple, beginning at 10pm and lasting until dawn, illuminated by the flickers of a large brass oil lamp centre stage. Virtually nothing about Kathakali is naturalistic, because it depicts the world of gods and demons. Both male and female roles are played by men.

Standing at the back of the stage, two musicians play driving rhythms, one on a bronze gong, the other on heavy bell-metal cymbals; they also sing the dialogue. Actors appear and disappear from behind a handheld curtain and never utter a sound, save the odd strange cry. Learning the elaborate hand gestures, facial expressions and choreographed movements, as articulate and precise as any sign language, requires rigorous training which can begin at the age of eight and last ten years. At least two more drummers stand left of the stage; one plays the upright **chenda** with slender curved sticks, the other plays the *maddalam*, a horizontal barrel-shaped hand drum. When a female character is "speaking", the *chenda* is replaced by the hourglass-shaped *ettaka*, a "talking drum" on which melodies can be played. The drummers keep their eyes on the actors, whose every gesture is reinforced by their sound, from the gentlest embrace to the gory disembowelling of an enemy.

Although it bears the unmistakable influences of Kutiyattam and indigenous folk rituals, Kathakali, literally "story-play", is thought to have crystallized into a distinct theatre rocks manically back and forth in the corner of the compound, making menacing noises at passersby; he killed two people a few years back, and it's a credit to the animal-loving temple authorities that they haven't put him down. Just don't get too close to any of the elephants unless their handlers say it's safe to do so.

form during the seventeenth century. The plays are based on three major sources: the Hindu epics *Mahabharata*, *Ramayana* and the *Bhagavata Purana*. While the stories are ostensibly of god-heroes such as Rama and Krishna, the most popular characters are those that give the most scope to the actors – the villainous, fanged, red-and-black-faced, *katti* ("knife") anti-heroes. These types, such as the kings Ravana and Duryodhana, are dominated by lust, greed, envy and violence. David Bolland's handy paperback *Guide to Kathakali*, widely available in Kerala, gives invaluable scene-by-scene summaries of the most popular plays and explains in simple language a lot more besides.

When attending a performance, arrive early to get your bearings before it gets dark, even though the first play will not begin much before 10pm. (Quiet) members of the audience are welcome to visit the dressing room before and during the performance. The colour and design of the mask-like make-up, which specialist artists take several hours to apply, reveal the character's personality. The word *pacha* means both "green" and "pure"; a green-faced *pacha* character is thus a noble human or god. Red signifies *rajas*, passion and aggression, black denotes *tamas*, darkness and negativity, while white is *sattvik*, light and intellect. Once the make-up is completed, elaborate wide skirts are tied to the waist, and ornaments of silver and gold are added. Silver talons are fitted to the left hand. The transformation is complete with a final prayer and the donning of waist-length wig and crown. Visitors new to Kathakali will almost undoubtedly get bored during such long programmes, parts of which are very slow indeed. If you're at a village performance, you may not always find accommodation, so you can't leave during the night. Be prepared to sit on the ground for hours, and bring some warm clothes. Half the fun is staying up all night to witness, just as the dawn light appears, the gruesome disembowelling of a villain or a demon *asura*.

Kutiyattam

Three families of the Chakyar caste and a few outsiders perform the Sanskrit drama **Kutiyattam**, the oldest continually performed theatre form in the world. Until recently it was only performed inside temples and then only in front of the uppermost castes. Visually it is very similar to its offspring, Kathakali, but its atmosphere is infinitely more archaic. The actors, eloquent in sign language and symbolic movement, speak in the bizarre, compelling, intonation of the local *brahmins'* Vedic chant, unchanged since 1500 BC.

A single act of a Kutiyattam play can require ten full nights; the entire play forty. A great actor, in full command of the subtleties of gestural expression, can take half an hour to do such a simple thing as murder a demon, berate the audience, or simply describe a leaf fall to the ground. Unlike Kathakali, Kutiyattam includes comic characters and plays. The ubiquitous **Vidushaka**, narrator and clown, is something of a court jester, and traditionally has held the right openly to criticize the highest in the land without fear of retribution.

Teyyam

In northern Kerala, a wide range of ritual "performances", loosely known as **Teyyam,** are extremely localized, even to particular families. They might include *bhuta* (spirit or hero worship), trance dances, the enactment of legendary events, and oracular pronouncements. Performers are usually from low castes, but during the ritual, a brahmin will honour the deities they represent, so the status of each individual is reversed.

Although Teyyam can now be seen in government-organized cultural festivals, the powerful effect is best experienced in the courtyard of a house or temple, in a village setting. Some figures, with painted faces and bodies, are genuinely terrifying; costumes include metres-high headgear, sometimes doubling as a mask, and clothes of leaves and bark.

Practicalities

Buses from Thrissur (40min) arrive at the main **bus stand** at the top end of E Nada St, five minutes east of the temple. **Accommodation** is concentrated along this street; it's often packed to the gills with pilgrims, but the two KTDC hotels are usually good bets. *Mangalya* (③–④) has a/c and non-a/c rooms, but can be noisy as it is so near the temple entrance; *Nandanam* (②–④) is a better option, set back from the road near the bus stand. Rooms are spacious, if a little dowdy, and there's a restaurant and laundry on site. As you'd expect, the town is crammed with pure veg "meals" **restaurants**, and an *Indian Coffee House* on the southern side of E Nada St serves south Indian snacks.

Cheruthuruthy

The village of **CHERUTHURUTHY** is an easy day trip 32km north of Thrissur through gently undulating green country. It consists of a few lanes and one main street, that runs south from the bank of Kerala's longest river, the **Bharatapuzha** (pronounced *Bharatapura*). Considered holy by Hindus, the great river has declined in recent years, leaving a vast expanse of sand. Although of little consolation to locals, who have to deal with the problems of a depleted water supply, it has produced landscape of incomparable beauty.

Cheruthuruthy is famous as the home of **Kerala Kalamandalam**, the State's flagship training school for Kathakali and other indigenous Keralan performing arts, which was founded in 1927 by the revered Keralan poet Vallathol (1878–1957). At first patronized by the Raja of Cochin, the school has been funded by both state and national governments and has been instrumental in the large-scale revival of interest in Kathakali, and other unique Keralan artforms. Despite conservative opposition, it followed an open-door recruitment policy, based on artistic merit, which produced "scheduled caste", Muslim and Christian graduates along with the usual Hindu castes, something that was previously unimaginable. During the 1960s Kalamandalam's dynamic leadership forged international links with cultural organizations. Foreign students were accepted and every attempt was made to modernize, extending into the way in which the traditional arts were presented. Kalamandalam artists perform in the great theatres of the world, many sharing their extraordinary skills with outsiders; luminaries of modern theatre, such as Grotowski and Peter Brook, are indebted to them. Nonetheless, many of these trained artists are still excluded from entering, let alone performing in, temples, the most popular venue for Hindu artforms.

Non-Hindus can see Kathakali, Kutiyattam and Mohiniattam performed in the school's superb theatre, which replicates the wooden, sloping-roofed traditional theatres, known as *kuttambalams*, found in Keralan temples. If you've got more than a passing interest in how this extraordinary technique is taught, don't miss the chance to sit in on the rigorous training sessions, which have to be seen to be believed (Mon–Fri 4.30–6.30am, noon–1pm & 3.30–5.30pm; closed March 31, June 15, public hols, April & May). A handful of foreigners each year also come to the Kalamandalam academy to attend full-time **courses** in Kathakali and other traditional dance and theatre forms, usually for the minimum period of three months, and occassionally for a year or more. Fees are Rs750 per term, and previous experience of a related discipline is normally required. Applications may be made from abroad (write to the Secretary, Kerala Kalamandalam, Vallathol Nagar, Cheruthuruthy, Thrissur Dist, Kerala 675 531), but it's a good idea to visit before committing yourself. The students' lot here is not an easy one – to say the least. For information contact the school office (☎04926/2418).

Practicalities

Cheruthuruthy's only **accommodation** is the very basic *Government Rest House* (☎04929/2498; ②) near the riverbank, where eight simple doubles share a verandah.

Food may be available by arrangement, and there are simple "meals" shops in the village; of these, the *Mahatma* is much the best. **Buses** heading to Shoranur from Thrissur's Wadakkancheri stand stop outside Kalamandalam, just before Cheruthuruthy. The nearest **railway** station is Shoranur Junction, 1km south. It's on the main line and served by express trains to and from Mangalore, Madras and all major stations south of here on the coastal route through Kerala.

Palakaad

PALAKAAD (Palghat), surrounded by paddy fields, lies on NH47 between Thrissur (79km) and Coimbatore, Tamil Nadu (54km) and on the railway line from Karnataka and Tamil Nadu. Historically, thanks to the natural twenty-kilometre-wide Palakaad Gap in the Western Ghats, this area has been one of the chief entry points into Kerala. The environs are beautiful, but the town itself doesn't warrant a stop, unless to break a journey. The well-preserved **fort**, built in 1766 by Haider Ali of Mysore, is the nearest thing to a "sight"; it gets plenty of visitors at weekends, despite having little to offer. However, many travellers in search of **Kathakali** and **Teyyam** performances find themselves directed here. Particularly during April and May, hundreds of one-off events take place in the area. The local Government Carnatic Music College has an excellent reputation, and a small open-air amphitheatre next to the fort often hosts first-class music and dance performances. Ask at the tourist office (see below) for details.

Practicalities

Palakaad is well-connected to the rest of Kerala; the **railway station** (☎0491/535231) is 6km northeast of town and the *KSRTC* **bus stand** is slap in the centre. Most **accommodation** is in Indian-style lodges. *Hotel Kairali* (☎0491/534611; ②), near the *KSRTC* bus stand, is the best budget option. Far more upmarket, the modern concrete *Hotel Indraprastha*, English Church Rd (☎0491/534641; ⑥–⑦), boasts large a/c rooms, a gloomy but blissfully cool a/c restaurant serving a mixed menu of Indian, Western and Chinese cuisine, and a bar. *Fort Palace*, W Palace Rd (☎0491/534626; ③–④), is also reasonable, with some a/c rooms and a restaurant for good Indian food.

Both these last two hotels **change money**; as, in theory, does the *State Bank of India*, next door to the *Indraprastha*.

Kozhikode (Calicut)

The busy coastal city of **KOZHIKODE** (Calicut), 225km north of Kochi, occupies an extremely important place in Keralan legend and history. It is also significant in the story of European interference in the subcontinent, as Vasco da Gama first set foot in India at Kozhikode in 1498. However, as a tourist destination, it's a dud, with precious few remnants of its historic past. The few foreigners that pause here invariably do so only to break the long journey between Mysore and Kochi.

Kozhikode's roots are shrouded in myth. According to Keralan tradition, the powerful king Cheraman Perumal is said to have converted from Hinduism to Islam and left for Mecca "to save his soul", never to return. Before he set sail he divided Kerala between his relatives, all of whom were to submit to his nephew, who was given the kingdom of Kozhikode and the title Zamorin, equivalent to emperor. The city prospered and, perhaps because of the story of the convert king, became the preferred port of Muslim traders from the Middle East in search of spices, particularly pepper. During the Raj, it was an important centre for the export of printed Indian cotton, whence the term "calico", an English corruption of the name Calicut – itself an anglicized version of the city's original Malayalam name, now reinstated.

Arrival and information

The railway station is close to the centre, while the most important of the three bus stands is the KSRTC stand, Mavoor Rd, from where buses run to destinations as far afield as Bangalore, Mysore, Ooty, Madurai, Coimbatore and Mangalore. From the New Mafussil private stand, 500m away, on the other side of Mavoor Rd, you can get local buses and services to northern Kerala. The Palayam stand is for infrequent long-haul buses and destinations further south, such as Palakaad, Thrissur, and Guruvayur. Kozhikode's airport (connections only to Thiruvananthapuram, Bombay and the Gulf countries) lies at Karippur, 23km south of the city.

The **KTDC Information Centre** (☎76101) in their *Malabar Mansion Hotel*, at the corner of SM St, can supply limited information and "sketch maps" of the centre.

> The telephone **area code** for Kozhikode is ☎0495.

The City

Few traces remain of the model city laid out in the fourteenth century, which followed a Hindu grid formula based on a sacred diagram containing the image of the cosmic man, Purusha. The axis and energy centre of the diagram was dictated by the position of the ancient **Tali Shiva temple** (closed to non-Hindus), which survives to this day. Everything, and everybody, had a place. The district around the port in the northwest was reserved for foreigners. Here, a Chinese community lived in and around Chinese St (now Silk St) and, later, the Portuguese, Dutch and British occupied the area. Keralan Muslims (Mappilas) lived in the southwest. The northeast of the city was a commercial quarter, and in the southeast stood the Tali temple. Here too was a palace and fort; all the military *kalaris*, martial art gymnasia, that stood around the perimeter have now gone.

Considering its history, there is very little to see in Kozhikode, though it is quite good for **shopping**. Around SM St, many good fabric and ready-made clothes shops sell the locally produced plain white cotton cloth. This district is also a good place to try the local *halva* sweets, especially popular with the large Mappila community. Some shops also specialize in piping-hot banana chips, straight from the frying pan.

Locals enjoy a promenade on or near the **beach** (3km from the centre) in the late afternoon and early evening. Although not suitable for swimming, it's a restful place, where you can munch on roasted peanuts sold in the many stalls while scanning the seas for jumping dolphins. After dark it's difficult to find an auto-rickshaw to take you back into town, but on the land side of the road regular buses run into the centre.

The **Pazhassirajah and Krishnamenon Museums and Art Gallery** (Tues & Thurs–Sun 10am–12.30pm & 2.30–5pm, Wed 2.30–5pm) stand together 5km from the centre on East Hill. The Pazhassirajah collection includes copies of murals, coins, bronzes and models of the umbrella-shaped, stone megalithic remains peculiar to Kerala, while the museum houses a collection of memorabilia associated with the left-wing Keralan politician VK Krishnamenon, and a gallery of works by Indian artists.

Accommodation and eating

Kozhikode's reasonably priced city centre **hotels** can fill up by evening, especially during conventions. The beach area is a quiet alternative. Your best bet for a proper **meal** is to eat at your hotel, though you can get snacks in town at the dependable *Indian Coffee House* on Kallai Rd. The open-air *Park Restaurant*, by Mananchira tank, makes an appealing oasis in the evenings in the city centre.

Alakapuri Guest House, MM Ali Rd, near the railway station, 1km from *KSRTC* bus stand (☎73361). Built around a courtyard, some rooms have huge bathtubs, polished wood and easy chairs; the cheaper, non-a/c, options are rather spartan. The first-floor café serves great south Indian food all day; in the evening go to the restaurant on the ground floor. Singles available. ③–⑤.

Kalpaka Tourist Home, Town Hall Rd (☎60220). Five storeys ranged around a weirdly shaped courtyard-cum-sari store make for a space-station like interior. The views from the east side are best. Some a/c, and 24-hr check-out. ③–⑤.

KTDC Malabar Mansion, SM St (☎65391). Modern high-rise hotel, near the railway station at the top of the main street. Huge a/c suites, reasonable non-a/c rooms, beer parlour and restaurant. Good value, but usually block-booked weeks in advance. ②.

Paramount Tower, Town Hall Rd, near railway station (☎62731). Large (53 room) hotel with some non-a/c rooms. Restaurant on site, and car rental. ④–⑤.

Sasthapuri, Jail Rd, Palayam (☎60381). Small, functional, well-maintained rooms; the best budget option near the station. It's tucked away down a side street off the main road (MM Ali/Jail Rd) that runs east into town from the railway station. ②.

Sea Queen, Beach Rd, 2km from centre (☎58504). Quiet, comfortable, middle-class hotel over the road from the beach, whose prime location is marred only by the nasty smells from across the road. A/c and non-a/c rooms, plus popular ground-floor restaurant and bar. ④–⑤.

North of Kozhikode

The beautiful coast of Kerala, **north of Kozhikode**, is a seemingly endless stretch of coconut palms, wooded hills and virtually deserted beaches. However, the towns hold little of interest for visitors, most of whom bypass the area completely. The main reason to stop here today is to look for **Teyyam**, the extraordinary masked trance dances that take place in villages throughout the region during winter.

Kannur (Cannanore)

KANNUR (Cannanore), 92km north of Kozhikode, was for many centuries the capital of the Kolathiri rajahs, who prospered from the thriving martime spice trade through its port. In the early 1500s, after Vasco da Gama passed through, the Portuguese took it and erected an imposing bastion, **St Angelo's fort**, overlooking the harbour, but this is today occupied by the Indian army and closed to visitors. If you come to Kannur at all, it will probably be on the trail of **Teyyam**, spectacular spirit-possession rituals that are an important feature of village life in the area from late December until March (see p.1111). Locating them is not always easy, but if you ask at the local tourist office, they should be able to point you in the right direction, and it's well worth heading out to the daily ritual at **Parassinikadavu** (see below).

Practicalities

Straddling the main coastal transport artery between Mangalore and Kochi/Thiruvananthapuram, Kannur is well connected by **bus** and **train** to most major towns and cities in Kerala. Modest, good value **accommodation** is available at KTDC's *Yatri Niwas* (☎0497/500717; ②–④), just across the tracks from the railway station, or a five-minute rickshaw ride from the bus stand, which has large, clean en-suite rooms and a simple restaurant and beer parlour. More upscale is the business-oriented *Kamala International* (☎0497/66911; ⑤–⑦), in the town centre on SM Rd, where most rooms are a/c, with colour TVs and room service. They also have a small 24-hour coffee shop and a rooftop garden restaurant. If you have your own vehicle, another option is KTDC's small *Motel Araam* (②), fifteen minutes' drive north of Kannur on the main highway, where a couple of simple rooms overlook a roadside garden terrace; book through *Yatri Niwas*.

Parassinikadavu

The only place you can be guaranteed a glimpse of Teyyam is the village of **PARASSINIKADAVU**, 20km north of Kannur beside the River Valapatanam, where the head priest, or *madayan*, of the **Parassini Madammpura** temple performs daily before assembled devotees. Elaborately dressed and accompanied by a traditional drum group, he becomes possessed by the temple's presiding deity – Lord Muthappan, Shiva in the form of a *kiratha*, or hunter – and enacts a series of complex offerings. The two-hour ceremony culminates when the priest/deity dances forward to bless individual members of the congregation. Even by Keralan standards, this is an extraordinary spectacle, and well worth taking time out of a journey along the coast for.

Regular local buses leave Kannur **for Parassinikadavu** from around 7am, dropping passengers at the top of the village, ten minutes on foot from the temple. However, if you want to get there in time for the dawn Teyyam, you'll have to splash out on one of the *Ambassador* taxis that line up outside Kannur bus stand. The cabbies sleep in their cars, so you can arrange the trip on the spot by waking one up. Alternatively, head out to Parassinikadavu for the early afternoon ritual, which starts around 2pm, allowing you plenty of time to get there and back by bus, with half-an-hour or so to browse the temple bazaar (whose stalls do a great line in kitsch Lord Muthappan souvenirs). Note that the second performance of the day does not always take place; if you should miss the ritual and are still determined to see it at dawn the following day, but can't afford a taxi from Kannur, look for accommodation in one of the village's small *dharamshalas* grouped around the temple at the riverside. Plenty of small *dhabas* serve *dosas* and other spicy vegetarian snacks in the temple bazaar.

Kasargode and Bekkal

The old-fashioned little town of **KASARGODE**, 153km north of Kozhikode, near the Karnataka border, is principally a fishing community – though some say smuggling is not unknown. It currently gets few foreign visitors, but the number is sure to increase, as it is the nearest town of any size to the beaches and fort at **BEKKAL** (16km south), now earmarked for development. At present, this is as unexploited an area as you could hope to find, with nary a beachside shack cafe, let alone a 5-star hotel. However, don't come expecting an undiscovered Kovalam. The local fishermen are completely un-used to the sight of semi-naked Westerners, while large stretches of sand serve as communal toilets. The undertow can also be dangerously strong in some places.

A popular weekend day-trip destination, Bekkal's **fort** stands on a promontory between two long, classically beautiful palm-fringed **beaches**. Although this is one of the largest forts in Kerala and has been under the control of various powers including Vijayanagar, Tipu Sultan and the British, it's nothing to get excited about. The bastion's commanding position, with views across the bays to north and south, is impressive enough, but only four watchtowers and the outer walls survive.

Practicalities

The nearest major town to Kasargode is Mangalore, 50km north in Karnataka, a ninety minute bus ride away. Long-distance **buses** usually call at both its bus stands, a new one on the outskirts and another in town. Among regular buses along the coast road, those to Kanhangad stop at Bekkal. Kasargode **railway station** is 3km from town.

Accommodation at Bekkal is limited to the *Travellers Bungalow* (☎04995/502; ①), which has two basic rooms in a superb location at the furthest point of the promontory inside the fort. It's a great place to spend a night, except at weekends, when bus-loads of ghetto-blaster-toting day-trippers hang out on the verandah. Unless you don't mind sleeping rough, don't come at the end of the day without booking (through the Kasargode District Collector, Civil Station, Kasargode; ☎04995/20666), as there is nowhere else in the village to stay, and local people do not rent out rooms. Near the bus stand in Kasargode, the *Enjay Tourist Home* (☎04995/1164; ②–③) has some a/c rooms, a south Indian restaurant and car rental, and *Aliya Lodge* (☎04995/22897; ①–②), also offering a/c rooms, has a restaurant.

CHAPTER TWENTY

KARNATAKA

C reated in 1956 from the princely state of Mysore, **KARNATAKA** – the name is a derivation of the name of the local language, Kannada, spoken by virtually all of its 46 million inhabitants – marks a transition zone between northern India and the Dravidian deep south. Along its border with Maharashtra and Andhra Pradesh, a string of medieval walled towns, studded with domed mausoleums and minarets, recall the era when this part of the Deccan was a Muslim stronghold, while the coastal and hill districts that dovetail with Kerala are quintessential Hindu south India, profuse with tropical vegetation and soaring temple *gopuras*. Between the two are scattered some of the peninsula's most extraordinary historic sites, notably the ruined Vijayanagar city at Hampi, whose lost temples and derelict palaces stand amid an arid, boulder-strewn landscape of surreal beauty.

Karnataka is one of the wettest regions in India, its **climate** dominated by the seasonal monsoon, which sweeps in from the southwest in June, dumping an average of 4m of rain on the coast before it peters out in late September. Running in an unbroken line along the state's palm-fringed coast, the **Western Ghats**, draped in dense deciduous forests, impede the path of the rain clouds east. As a result, the landscape of the interior – comprising the southern apex of the triangular Deccan trap, known here as the **Mysore Plateau** – is considerably drier, with dark volcanic soils in the north, and poor quartzite-granite country to the south. Two of India's most sacred rivers, the Tungabhadra and Krishna, flow across this sun-baked terrain, draining east to the Bay of Bengal.

Broadly speaking, Karnataka's principal attractions are concentrated at opposite ends of the state, with a handful of lesser-visited places dotted along the coast between Goa and Kerala. Road and rail routes dictate that most itineraries take in the brash state capital, **Bangalore**, a go-ahead, modern city that epitomizes the aspirations of the country's new middle classes, with glittering malls, fast-food outlets and a nightlife unrivalled outside Bombay. The state's other major city, **Mysore**, appeals more for its old-

fashioned ambience, nineteenth-century palaces and vibrant produce and incense markets. It also lies within easy reach of several important historical monuments. At the nearby fortified island of **Srirangapatnam** – site of the bloody battle of 1799 that finally put Mysore State into British hands, by defeating the Muslim military genius **Tipu Sultan** – parts of the fort, a mausoleum and Tipu's summer palace survive.

A clutch of other unmissable sights lie further northeast, dotted around the dull railroad town of **Hassan**. Around nine centuries ago, the Hoysala kings sited their grand dynastic capitals here, at the now middle-of-nowhere villages of **Belur** and **Halebid**, where several superbly crafted temples survive intact. More impressive still, and one of India's most extraordinary sacred sites, is the eighteen-metre Jain colossus at **Saravanabelgola**, which stares serenely over idyllic Deccani countryside.

West of Mysore, the Ghats rise in a wall of thick jungle cut by deep ravines and isolated valleys. You can either traverse the range by rail, via Hassan, or explore some of its scenic backwaters by road. Among these, the rarely visited coffee- and spice-growing region of **Kodagu (Coorg)** has to be the most entrancing, with its unique culture and lush vistas of misty wooded hills and valleys. Most Coorgi agricultural produce is shipped out of **Mangalore**, the nearest large town, of little interest except as a transport hub whose importance can only increase when the long-awaited, and highly controversial, Konkan Railway finally starts to operate all the way from Bombay to Kerala. Situated mid-way between Goa and Kerala, it's also a convenient – if uninspiring – place to pause on the journey along Karnataka's beautiful **Karavali coast**. Interrupted by countless mangrove-lined estuaries, the state's 320-kilometre-long red laterite coast has always been difficult to navigate by land, and traffic along the recently re-vamped highway remains relatively light. Although there are plenty of superb beaches, facilities are, with rare exceptions, non-existent, and locals often react with astonishment at the sight of a foreigner. Again, that may well change when the Konkan Railway gets going – with as-yet-unguessable consequences for the fishing hamlets, long-forgotten fortresses and pristine hill and cliff scenery along the way. For now, few Western tourists visit the famous Krishna temple at **Udupi**, an important Vaishnavite pilgrimage centre, and fewer still venture into the mountains to see India's highest waterfall at **Jog Falls**, set amid some of the region's most spectacular scenery. However, atmospheric **Gokarn**, further north up the coast, is an increasingly popular beach hideaway for budget travellers. Harbouring one of India's most famous *shivalinga*, this seventeenth-century Hindu pilgrimage town enjoys a stunning location, with a high headland dividing it from a string of exquisite beaches.

Winding inland from the mountainous Goan border, NH4A and the rail line comprise sparsely populated **northern Karnataka**'s main transport artery, linking a succession of grim industrial centres. This region's undisputed highlight is the ghost city of Vijayanagar, better known as **Hampi**, scattered around boulder hills on the south banks of the Tungabhadra River. The ruins of this once splendid capital occupy a magical site, while the village squatting the ancient bazaar is a great spot to hole up for a spell. The jumping-off place for Hampi is **Hospet**, from where buses leave for the bumpy journey north across the rolling Deccani plains to **Badami**, **Aihole** and **Pattadakal**. Now lost in countryside, these tiny villages were once capitals of the **Chalukya** dynasty (sixth–eighth centuries). The whole area is littered with ancient rock-cut caves and finely carved stone temples.

Further north still, in one of Karnataka's most remote and poorest districts, craggy hilltop citadels and crumbling wayside tombs herald the formerly troubled buffer zone between the Muslim-dominated northern Deccan and the Dravidian-Hindu south. The bustling walled market town of **Bijapur**, capital of the Bahmanis, the Muslim dynasty that oversaw the eventual downfall of Vijayanagar, harbours south India's finest collection of Islamic architecture, including the world's second largest free-standing dome, the Golgumbaz. The first Bahmani capital, **Gulbarga**, site of a famous Muslim shrine

KARNATAKA TRAVEL DETAILS

When this book went to press, the changeover from metre- to broad-gauge track was disrupting some **train services** in Karnataka. If you're planning to travel to Goa, Hubli or Hassan by rail, check the current situation with *Indian Railways* first.

	Buses		Trains		Flights	
	Frequency	Time	Frequency	Time	Frequency	Time
To and from BANGALORE						
Ahmedabad			6 weekly	37hr	6 weekly	2hr 5min
Bombay	3 daily	24hr	4 daily	22hr 30min–24hr	9–10 daily	1hr 20min
Calcutta			1 weekly	26hr 15min	1–2 daily	2hr 20min
Coimbatore	2 daily	9hr	3 daily	18–20hr	8 weekly	40min
Delhi			2 daily	33hr 15min–41hr 45min	6–7 daily	2hr 20min
Goa	5 daily	14hr			3 weekly	1hr
Gulburga	2 daily	15hr	2 daily	12hr		
Hassan	every 30min	4hr				
Hospet	3 daily	8hr	1 daily	10hr		
Hubli	6 daily	9hr	2 daily	7hr 30min–9hr 20min		
Hyderabad	10 daily	16hr	1 daily	16hr 15min	2 daily	50min
Jog Falls	1 nightly	8hr				
Karwar	3 daily	12hr				
Kodaikanal	1 nightly	12hr				
Kochi (Ernakulam)	6 daily	12hr	2 daily	13hr 10min–16hr 20min	1 daily	50min
Kozhikode (Calicut)	6 daily	10hr			2 weekly	45min
Madikeri	16 daily	6hr				
Madras	9 daily	9hr	4–5 daily	5–7hr	3–5 daily	40min–1hr
Madurai	2 daily	8hr				
Mangalore	10 daily	8hr	3 weekly	18–24hr	3 weekly	40min
Mysore	every 15min	3hr	3–4 daily	2hr 30min–3hr		
Pondicherry	2 daily	9hr				
Pune			2 weekly	20hr	6 weekly	1hr 25min
Thiruvananthapuram			1 daily	18hr	4 weekly	50min
Udhagamandalam	7 daily	8hr				
To and from HOSPET						
Badami	4 daily	5hr				
Bidar	1 nightly	10hr				
Gokarn	1 daily	10hr				
Hampi	every 30min	20min				
Hyderabad	2 daily	12hr				
Mangalore	2 daily	10hr				
Mysore	3 daily	7–8hr				
Panjim	1 daily	10hr				
Vasco da Gama	1 daily	10hr				

Note that no individual route appears more than once in this chart; check against where you want to get to as well as where you're coming from.

and theological college, has retained little of its former splendour, but the more isolated **Bidar**, where the Bahmanis moved in the sixteenth century, definitely deserves a detour en route to or from Hyderabad, four hours east by bus. Perched on a rocky escarpment, its crumbling red ramparts harbour Persian-style mosaic-fronted mosques, mausoleums and a sprawling fort complex evocative of Samarkhand and the great silk route.

	Buses		Trains		Flights	
	Frequency	Time	Frequency	Time	Frequency	Time
To and from MYSORE						
Channarayapatna	hourly	2hr				
Jog Falls*	hourly	7hr				
Kannur	5 daily	7hr				
Kochi	5 daily	12hr				
Kozhikode	hourly	8hr				
Madikeri	hourly	2hr 30min				
Udhagamandalam	12 daily	5hr				
Somnathpur	every 30min	20min				
Srirangapatnam	every 30 min	20min				
To and from Bijapur						
Aurangabad	2 daily	14hr				
Badami	5 daily	4hr	5 daily	4hr 20min		
Bidar	2 daily	7hr 30min				
Bombay	3 daily	12hr				
Gadag			5 daily	6hr		
Gulbarga	4 daily	3hr 30min				
Hospet	4 daily	5hr				
Hubli	hourly	6hr				
Hyderabad	1 daily	1hr 30min				
Pune	1 daily	8hr				
Sholapur	9 daily	3hr	5 daily	3hr 30min		
To and from Hassan						
Channarayapatna	hourly	1hr				
Halebid	15 daily	1hr				
Hospet	1 daily	10hr				
Mangalore	hourly	4hr	1 daily	8hr		
Mysore	15 daily	7–8hr	3 daily	4hr		
To and from Mangalore						
Bombay					2 daily	1hr 15min
Bijapur	1 daily	16hr				
Chaudi	6 daily	8hr				
Kochi (Ernakulam)			3 daily	21hr 50min		
Gokarn	1 daily	7hr				
Hassan			2 daily	6hr 30min		
Karwar	9 daily	8hr				
Kollam			3 daily	25hr 30min		
Kozhikode			3 daily	5hr		
Madikeri	hourly	4hr				
Mysore	hourly	7hr	2 daily	11hr		
Panjim	6 daily	10hr 30min				
Thiruvananthapuram			3 daily	16hr		
Udupi	hourly	1hr				

*via Shimoga

A little history

Like much of southern India, Karnataka has been ruled by successive Buddhist, Hindu and Muslim dynasties. The influence of Jainism has also been marked; India's very first emperor, **Chandragupta Maurya**, is believed to have converted to Jainism in the fourth century BC, renounced his throne, and fasted to death at Sravanabelgola, now one of the most visited Jain pilgrimage centres in the country.

During the first millennium AD, this whole region was dominated by power struggles between the various kingdoms, such as Vakatakas and the Guptas, who controlled the western Deccan and at times extended their authority as far as the Coromandel coast, now in Tamil Nadu. From the sixth to the eighth centuries, only interrupted by thirteen years of Pallava rule, the **Chalukya** kingdom included Maharashtra, the Konkan coast on the west, and the whole of Karnataka. The **Cholas** were powerful in the east of the region from about 870 until the thirteenth century, when the Deccan kingdoms were overwhelmed by General Malik Kafur, a convert to Islam.

By the medieval era, Muslim incursions from the north had forced the hitherto warring and fractured Hindu states of the south into close alliance, with the mighty **Vijayanagars** emerging as overlords. Founded by the brothers Harihara and Bukka, their lavish capital, Vijayanagar, ruled an empire stretching from the Bay of Bengal to the Arabian Sea and south to Cape Comorin. The Muslims' superior military strength, however, triumphed in 1565 at the Battle of Talikota, when the **Bahmanis** laid siege to Vijayanagar, reducing it to rubble and plundering its opulent palaces and temples.

Thereafter, a succession of Muslim sultans held sway over the north, while in the south of the state, the independent **Wadiyar Rajas** of Mysore, whose territory was comparatively small, successfully fought off the Marathas. In 1761, however, the brilliant Muslim campaigner Haider Ali, with French support, seized the throne. Haider Ali, and his son Tipu Sultan, turned Mysore into a major force in the south, before Tipu was killed by the British at the **battle of Srirangapatnam** in 1799.

Following Tipu's defeat, the British restored the Wadiyar family to the throne. They kept it until riots in 1830 led the British to appoint a Commission to rule in their place. Fifty years later, the throne was once more returned to the Wadiyars, who remained governors until Karnataka was created by the merging of the states of Mysore and the Madras Presidencies in 1956.

Bangalore and around

Once across the Western Ghats the cloying air of Kerala and the Konkan coast gradually gives way to the crisp skies and dry heat of the dusty **Mysore Plateau**. The setting for E M Forster's acclaimed Raj novel, *A Passage to India*, this southern tip of the Deccan – a vast, open expanse of gently undulating plains dotted with wheat fields and dramatic granite boulders – formed the heartland of the region's once powerful princely state. Today it remains the political hub of the region, largely due to the economic importance of **BANGALORE**, Karnataka's capital, which, with a population racing towards eight million is said to be the fastest growing city in Asia. A major scientific research centre at the cutting edge of India's technological revolution, its trendy high-speed self-image ensures that it is quite unlike anywhere else in south India.

In the 1800s, Bangalore's gentle climate, broad streets, and green public parks made it the "Garden City". Until well after Independence, senior citizens, film stars and VIPs flocked to buy or build dream homes amid this urban idyll, which offered such unique amenities as theatres, cinemas, and a lack of restrictions on alcohol. However, during the last decade or so, Bangalore has undergone a massive transformation. The wide avenues, now dominated by tower blocks, are choked with traffic, and water and electricity shortages have become the norm. Even the climate has been affected.

Many foreigners turn up in Bangalore without really knowing why they've come. What little there is to see is no match for the attractions elsewhere in the state, and the city's very real advantages for Indians are two-a-penny in the west. That said, Bangalore is a transport hub, especially well served by plane and bus, and there is some novelty in a Westernized Indian city that not only offers good shopping, eating and hotels, but also is the only place on the subcontinent to boast anything resembling a pub culture.

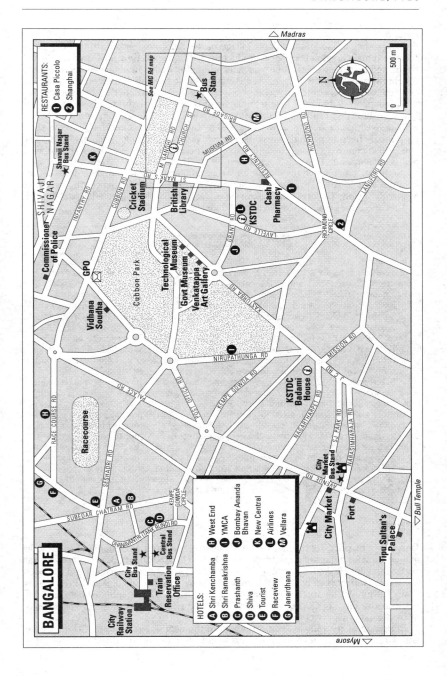

△ Madras

500 m

N

RESTAURANTS:
1 Casa Piccolo
2 Shanghai

Shivaji Nagar
Bus Stand

Bus Stand

SHIVAJI NAGAR

Commissioner
of Police

INFANTRY RD

CUBBON RD

Cricket
Stadium

M

K

CHURCH ST

M GANDHI RD

See MG Rd map

MUSEUM RD

ST MARK'S RD

BRIGADE RD

RICHMOND RD

LANGFORD RD

British
Library

H

RESIDENCY RD

Cash
Pharmacy

1

i L KSTDC

GRANT RD

LAVELLE RD

RICHMOND
CIRCLE

2

J

GPO

Cubbon Park

Technological
Museum

Govt Museum

Venkatappa
Art Gallery

KASTURBA RD

Vidhana
Soudha

i

NIRUPATHUNGA RD

PALACE RD

POST OFFICE RD

KEMPE GOWDA RD

MISSION RD

KSTDC
Badami
House

i

SJ PARK RD

RACE COURSE RD

H

Racecourse

SESHADRI RD

NAGARTHPET RD

NARASIMHARAJA RD

BANGALORE

G
F

E
A
B

SUBEDAR CHATRAM RD

KEMPE
GOWDA
CIRCLE

C
D

DHANAVANTHRI (TANK BUND) RD

City
Bus Stand

Central
Bus Stand

Train
Reservation
Office

City Market
Bus Stand

AVENUE RD

City Market

A

Fort

Tipu Sultan's
Palace

City Railway
Station

HOTELS:
A Shri Kenchamba
B Shri Ramakrishna
C Prashanth
D Shiva
E Tourist
F Raceview
G Janardhana

H West End
I YMCA
J Bombay Ananda
   Bhavan
K New Central
L Airlines
M Vellara

△ Mysore

▽ Bull Temple

History

Bangalore began life as the minor "village of the half-baked *gram*"; to this day *gram* (beans) remain an important local product. In 1537, Magadi **Kempe Gowda**, a devout Hindu and feudatory chief of the Vijayanagar empire, built a mud fort and erected four watchtowers outside the village, predicting that it would, one day, extend that far; the city now, of course, stretches way beyond. During the first half of the seventeenth century, Bangalore fell to the Muslim Sultanate of Bijapur; changing hands several times, it returned to Hindu rule under the Mysore Wadiyar Rajas of Srirangapatnam. In 1758, Chikka Krishnaraja Wadiyar II was deposed by the military genius Haider Ali, who set up arsenals here to produce muskets, rockets and other weapons for his formidable anti-British campaigns. Both he and his son, **Tipu Sultan**, greatly extended and fortified Bangalore, but Tipu was overthrown by the British in 1799. The British set up a cantonment, which made the city an important military station, and passed the administration over to the Maharaja of Mysore in 1881. After Independence, the erstwhile Maharaja became Governor of Mysore state. Bangalore was designated capital in 1956, and retained that status when Karnataka state was created in 1973.

THE SILICON RUSH

It comes as a surprise to many visitors to learn that India is the second-largest exporter of computer software after the US. Generating sales of around $720 million per year, the centre of this hi-tech boom is the Electronic City Industrial Park on the outskirts of Bangalore, dubbed "**Silicon Valley**" by the Indian press.

Bangalore's meteoric industrial rise began in the early 1980s. Fleeing the crippling costs of Bombay and Delhi, a clutch of hi-tech Indian companies re-located here, lured by the comparatively cool climate, and an untapped pool of highly skilled, English-speaking labour (a consequence of the Indian government's decision to concentrate its telecommunications and defence research here in the 1960s). Within a decade, Bangalore had become a major player in the software market, and a magnet for multinationals such as *Motorola* and *Texas Instruments* (who have their own satellite link with head office in Dallas).

For a while, Bangalore revelled in a spending frenzy that saw its centre sprout gleaming skyscrapers, swish stores and shopping malls. Soon, however, the price of prosperity became apparent. At the height of the boom, millions of immigrants poured in, eager for a slice of the action; it is estimated that in less than five years the population more than doubled to 7.5 million. However, too little municipal money was invested in infrastructure, and today, Bangalore is buckling under the weight of numbers. Designed to hold 700 people, its airport, for example, sees around 6000 passengers daily, while levels of traffic **pollution** approach those of Delhi and **power cuts** are routine. All this is having a disastrous effect on business and industry: the multinationals are now moving out as quickly as they moved in, forcing the city's big-spending ex-pats and computer whizz kids to leave with them. Old Bangaloreans, meanwhile, wonder what became of their beloved "Garden City".

Arrival

Bangalore airport, 13km north of the city centre, serves cities throughout south India and beyond; for details of departures, see p.1131. The **KSTDC desk** in the arrivals hall (daily 7am–2pm & 2.30–8.30pm; ☎526 8012) stocks leaflets on Karnataka and can book hotel rooms. Branches of the *State Bank of Mysore* (daily 8am–7pm) and *Vijaya Bank* (daily 8.30am–12.30pm) **change money**, and there's an STD telephone booth. You can get **into the city** on *KSRTC* buses (Rs15), by taxi (Rs170; book at the pre-paid desk), or by the auto-rickshaws that gather outside.

Bangalore City railway station is east of the centre, near Kempe Gowda Circle, and across the road from the main bus stands (for the north of the city, get off at

Bangalore Cantonment station). As you come into the entrance hall from the platforms, the far left-hand corner holds a **pre-paid taxi counter** (daily 8.30am–2pm & 2.30–5pm) and an **ITDC booth** (daily 7am–5.30pm; ☎220 4277), where you can rent cars and book tours. The **KSTDC tourist information office** (daily 6.30am–8pm; ☎287 0068), to the right, also book tours and accommodation.

Innumerable **long-distance buses** (listed on p.1120) arrive at the big, busy **Central** (*KSRTC*) **stand**, opposite the railway station. A bridge divides it from **City stand**, used by local services. **City Market**, 2km southeast, has two stands: one for domestic buses and one for the surrounding area, while **Shivaji Nagar stand**, in the northeast, is only for local services, including the outskirts.

> The telephone **area code** for Bangalore is ☎080.

Information

For information on Bangalore, Karnataka and neighbouring states, go to the excellent **Government of India Tourist Office** (Mon–Fri 10am–6pm, Sat 9.30am–1pm; ☎558 5417), in the KFC Building, 48 Church St (parallel to MG Rd between Brigade and St Mark's roads). They run city **tours**, as well as two-day packages to Mysore and Ooty.

Apart from the desks at the City railway station and airport (see above), **KSTDC** has two city offices: one at Badami House, NR Square (☎227 5883), where you can book the tours outlined below, and another on the second floor of 10/4 Mitra Chambers, Kasturba Rd, Queen's Circle (☎221 2901).Their useful *Downtown Bangalore* map (Rs30) features the latest bars and restaurants, while for up-to-the-minute information about what's on, restaurants and shops, check the trendy and ubiquitous free listings paper *Bangalore This Fortnight*.

The **Post Office** (Mon–Sat 10am–7pm, Sun 10.30am–1.30pm), on the corner of Raj Bhavan Rd and Cubbon St, at the northern tip of Cubbon Park, is about ten minutes' walk from MG Rd. The best place to **change money** is *Thomas Cook*, 55 MG Rd, on the corner of Brigade Rd; the slower *State Bank of India*, is further down at 87 MG Rd (Mon–Fri 10.30am–2.30pm & Sat 10.30am–12.30pm). Alternatively, try the fast and efficient *Wall Street Finanaces*, 3 House of Lords, 13/14 St Mark's Rd (Mon–Sat 9.30am–6pm; ☎227 1812). For *Visa* and *Mastercard* encashments – but not travellers' cheques – go to *Bank of Baroda*, 70 MG Rd (same hours). **Cars** can be rented from ITDC at the railway station, and through agents such as *Brindavan Travels*, 62/3 Mission Rd (☎223 3692), or *Europcar*, Sheriff House, 85 Richmond Rd (☎221 9502).

Tours

KSTDC operate a string of conducted **tours** from Bangalore. Though rushed, these can be handy if you're short of time. The twice-daily **City Tour** (9am–2pm or 2–7pm; Rs60), calls at the museum, Vidhana Soudha, Ulsoor Lake, Lalbagh Gardens, Bull temple and Tipu Sultan's palace, and winds up with a long stop at the Government handicrafts emporium. **Outstation tours** include the long daytrip to Srirangapatnam and Mysore (daily 7.15am–11pm; Rs160), and the weekend tour to Hampi (Fri 9pm–Sun 10pm; Rs420). Their day trip to Belur, Halebid and Sravanabelgola is not recommended unless you're happy to spend more than eight hours on the bus.

The City

The centre of modern Bangalore lies about 5km east of Kempe Gowda Circle and the bus and railway stations. On **MG Road** you'll find most of the mid-range accommodation, restaurants, shops, tourist information and banks. Leafy **Cubbon Park**, and its less than exciting museums, lie on its eastern edge, while the oldest, most "Indian" part of the city extends south, a warren of winding streets at their most dynamic in the hub-bub of the **City** and **Gandhi markets**. Bangalore's tourist attractions are spread out; monuments such as **Tipu's Summer Palace** and the **Bull temple** are some way south of the centre. Most, if not all, can be seen on a half-day tour; if you explore on foot, be warned that Bangalore has some of the worst pavements in south India.

Cubbon Park and museums

A welcome green space in the heart of the city, shaded by massive clumps of bamboo, **Cubbon Park** is entered from the western end of MG Rd, presided over by a statue of Queen Victoria. On Kasturba Rd, which runs along its southern edge, the poorly labelled and maintained **Government Museum** (daily except Wed 10am–5pm) features Vijayanagar, Hoysala and Chalukya sculpture, musical instruments, Thanjavur paintings and Deccani and Rajasthani miniatures. Next door, the missable **Venkatappa Art Gallery** (same ticket) exhibits twentieth-century landscapes and abstract wood sculpture, and occasional contemporary art shows. Further along, the **Technological and Industrial Museum** (daily except Mon 10am–5pm; Rs2) is geared towards kids.

Vidhana Soudha

Built in 1956, Bangalore's vast State Secretariat, Vidhana Soudha, northwest of Cubbon Park, is the largest civic structure of its kind in the country. K Hanumanthaiah, Chief Minister at the time, wanted a "people's palace" that, following the transfer of power from the royal Wadayar dynasty to a legislature, would "reflect the power and dignity of the people". In theory its design is entirely Indian, combining local models from Bangalore, Mysore and Somnathpur with features from Rajasthan and the rest of India, but its overall effect is not unlike the bombastic colonial architecture built in the so-called Indo-Saracenic style.

Lalbagh Botanical Gardens

Inspired by the splendid gardens of the Moghuls and the French botanical gardens at Pondicherry in Tamil Nadu, Haider Ali set to work in 1760 laying out the **Lalbagh Botanical Gardens** (8am–8pm), south of the centre. Originally covering forty acres, just beyond his fort – where one of Kempe Gowda's original watchtowers can still be seen – the gardens were expanded under Ali's son Tipu, who introduced numerous

---

SHOPPING IN BANGALORE

Bangalore has many fine shops, particularly if you're after **silk**. A wide range is sold at *Karnataka Silk Industries Corporation* and *Vijayalakshmi Silk Kendra*, both on Gupte Market, Kempe Gowda Rd. **Handicrafts** such as soapstone sculpture, brass, carved sandalwood and rosewood are also good value; emporia include *Central Cottage Industries Emporium*, 144 MG Rd, *Cottage Industries Exposition Ltd*, 3 Cunningham Rd, and *Gulshan Crafts*, 12 Safina Plaza, Infantry Rd. For **silver**, try looking on and around Commercial St (north of MG Rd) and at KR Market, on Residency Rd. At 64 MG Rd, *Natesan's Antiqarts* sells antiques and beautifully made reproduction sculpture, furniture and paintings, at international art house prices.

Bangalore is also a great place to pick up hard-to-find **books**. The first floor of *Gangarams*, 72 MG Rd, offers a wide selection on India (coffee-table art books and academic) plus the latest paperback fiction, and a great selection of Indian greetings cards. *Higginbotham's*, 68 MG Rd, is also good. *Premier*, 46/1 Church St, around the corner from the ITDC office, crams a huge number of books in a tiny space. The shop belonging to renowned publishers *Motilal Banarsidas*, 16 St Mark's Rd, close to the junction with MG Rd, offers a superb selection of heavyweight Indology and philosophy titles. The best **music** shops in the city centre, selling Indian and Western tapes, are *HMV*, on Brigade Rd or St Mark's Rd, and *Rhythms*, at 14 St Mark's Rd, beneath the *Nahar Heritage* hotel.

exotic species of plants. The British brought in gardeners from Kew in 1856 and – naturally – built a military bandstand and a glasshouse, based on London's Crystal Palace, which hosts wonderful flower shows. Now spreading over 240 acres, the gardens are pleasant to visit during the day, but tend to attract unsavoury characters after 6pm.

Tipu's Summer Palace
A two-storey structure built in 1791, mostly of wood, **Tipu's Summer Palace** (9am–5pm), southwest of the City Market, is similar to the Daria Daulat Palace at Srirangapatnam, but in a far worse state, with most of its painted decoration destroyed. Next door, the **Venkataramanaswamy temple**, dating from the early eighteenth century, was built by the Wadiyar Rajas. The *gopura* entranceway was erected in 1978.

Bull temple
About 6km south of the City bus stand (bus #34 & #37), in the Basavanagudi area, Kempe Gowda's sixteenth-century **Bull temple** (open to non-Hindus; daily 7.30am–1.30pm & 2.30–8.30pm) houses a massive monolithic Nandi bull, its grey granite made black by the application of charcoal and oil. The temple is approached by a path lined with mendicants and snake charmers; inside, for a tip, the priest will offer you a string of fragrant jasmine flowers.

Accommodation

Arrive in Bangalore towards the end of the day, and you'll be lucky to find a room at all, let alone one at the right price, so book at least a couple of days ahead or at least phone around as soon as you arrive. **Budget accommodation** is concentrated around the railway station (which itself has good-value but often full *Retiring Rooms*; ①–④) and Central bus stand. Standards in this area can be very low; better options are dotted around Subedar Chatram Rd, five minutes' walk east; Dhanavanthri Rd, a little way south, and the Racecourse, a short rickshaw trip east. **Mid-range hotels** are more scattered; of the many near MG Rd, the *Victoria* is definitely the most characterful.

ITDC's **paying guest scheme** offers rooms in family homes for around Rs200–450, though most are well outside the city centre. Enquire at their office on Church St.

ACCOMMODATION PRICE CODES

All **accommodation prices** in this book have been coded using the symbols below. In principle the prices given are for the least expensive double rooms in each establishment; however, some hotels, usually in category ①, offer rates per bed rather than per room. Local taxes are not included unless specifically stated. For more details, see p.35.

① up to Rs100	④ Rs225–350	⑦ Rs750–1200
② Rs100–150	⑤ Rs350–500	⑧ Rs1200–2200
③ Rs150–225	⑥ Rs500–750	⑨ Rs2200 and upward

Around the railway station and Central bus stand
Prashanth, 21 E Tank Rd (☎287 4041). Among the better lodges opposite the Central bus stand. All rooms with windows and shower-toilets. The *Mayura* nearby is the best fall-back. ④–⑤.

Shiva, 14 Dhanavantri (formerly "Tank Bund") Rd (☎228 1778). Recently revamped, renamed, and now the poshest option within easy striking distance of the station. Balconies cost extra. ⑤–⑥.

Shri Kenchamba, 197 Ananthashrama Lane (☎225 4131). Clean rooms in newish concrete complex, ranged around a courtyard (the top floor has great views). The best budget deal in the area. Ask for the *Kapali* cinema. ④.

Shri Ramakrishna, Subedar Chatram Rd (☎226 3041). Modern mega-lodge with 250 simple (ensuite) rooms in a colossal concrete block. ④.

Around the Racecourse and Cubbon Park

Janardhana, Kumara Krupa Rd (☎225 4444). Neat, clean and spacious rooms with balconies and baths. Well away from the chaos and good value at this price (despite hefty service charges). ⑤.

Raceview, 25 Race Course Rd (☎220 3401). Run-of-the-mill mid-range hotel whose upper front-side rooms overlook the racecourse. Safe deposit, foreign exchange and some a/c. ⑤–⑥.

Tourist, Ananda Rao Circle (☎226 2381). Bangalore's best all-round budget lodge, with 120 small rooms, long verandahs, and friendly family management. No reservations. ③.

West End, Race Course Rd (☎225 5055; fax 220 0010). Faintly Gothic-looking hotel, parts of which date from 1887. The most characterful rooms are in the old wing, with deep verandahs overlooking acres of gardens. Check out the colonial-era red letter box, too. ⑨.

Windsor Manor Sheraton, 25 Sankey Rd (☎226 9898; fax 226 4941). Ersatz palace run by *Welcomgroup* as a luxurious 5-star, mainly for businesspeople. Facilities include voice mail, modems, gym, jacuzzi and pool. ⑨.

YMCA, Nirupathanga Rd, Cubbon Park, mid-way between the bus stand and MG Rd (☎221 1848). Large, clean rooms and cheaper dorm beds for men. Rock-bottom rates, but often full. ②–④.

Around MG Road

Airlines, 4 Madras Bank Rd (☎227 3783). Respectable budget hotel in its own grounds, with lively terrace restaurant. Among the best options at this end of town, so it's usually full. Some a/c. ②–⑥.

Ajantha, 22-A MG Rd (☎558 4328). Good value, with larger than average en-suite rooms. Close to the shops, and often booked up days in advance. ④.

Berry's, 46 Church St (☎558 7221). Not a particularly good deal (the rooms are a bit musty), but the views are great, and there are nearly always vacancies. ④.

Bombay Ananda Bhavan, 68 Vittal Mallya (☎221 4581). Immaculate Raj-era mansion, in a lovely garden, with stylish rooms (bath tubs, shutters and stucco ceilings). Recommended. ⑦.

Brindavan, 40 MG Rd (☎558 4000). Old-style economy hotel with some a/c rooms and an excellent south Indian "meals" restaurant. A little dowdy, but still excellent value for money. ③–⑤.

Gautam, 17 Museum Rd (☎558 8461). Shabby concrete block south of MG Rd. The largest of the "economy" hotels in this area, so more likely than most to have vacancies. Overpriced. ⑤–⑥.

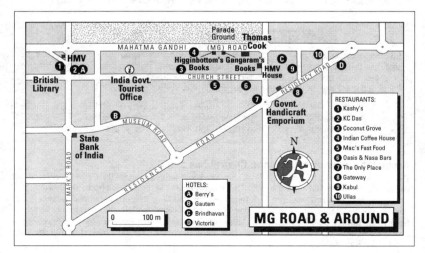

Oberoi, 37–9 MG Rd (☎558 5858; fax 558 5960). Ultra-luxurious 5-star, with a clutch of swish restaurants, beautiful landscaped garden and a pool. Expense account prices. ⑨.

Taj Residency, 41/3 MG Rd (☎558 4444; fax 558 4748). Not in quite the same league as the *Oberoi*, but a fully fledged 5-star, with all the trimmings. ⑨.

Vellara, 283 Brigade Rd, opposite Brigade Towers (☎556 9116). Good-value rooms from no-frills "standard", to light and airy "deluxe" on the top floor (with sweeping city views). Avoid *Sunflower* next door. ④–⑤.

Victoria, 47–8 Residency Rd (☎558 4077; fax 558 4945). Set in its own leafy compound and arguably the best mid-range hotel in Bangalore, with heaps of old-world style. Rooms open on to a pretty garden; "deluxe" buys you a verandah. Book well ahead. ⑥.

Eating

With unmissable sights thin on the ground, but tempting cafés and restaurants on every corner, you could easily spend most of your time in Bangalore **eating**. Nowhere else in south India will you find such gastronomic variety. Around **MG Rd**, ritzy ice-cream parlours and gourmet French restaurants stand cheek by jowl with Bombay *chaat* cafés and snack bars where, in true Bangalorean style, humble *thalis* masquerade as "executive mini–lunches".

Casa Piccolo, Devata Plaza, 131 Residency Rd. A dozen different tasty pizzas, *wienerschnitzel*, steaks, fried chicken and ice cream. Tables outside and flower baskets give the place a European ambience. Patronized by the well-heeled, sunglass-wearing studenty set and travellers.

Coconut Grove, Church St (☎558 8596). Mouthwatering and moderately priced gourmet coastal cuisine: vegetarian, fish and meat preparations simmered in coconut oil and spices, and served in traditional copper *thalis* on a leafy terrace. Recommended.

Gateway, 66 Residency Rd (☎558 4545). The *Peacock* serves a fairly undistinguished selection of Mughlai and other north Indian dishes, while the *Karavalli* specializes in west coast dishes from Goa to Kerala, including seafood and veg. Very attractive room in traditional southern style with wooden ceiling – plus tables outside under an old tamarind tree. Reservations essential. Expensive.

Indian Coffee House, MG Rd. The usual cheap south Indian snacks, egg dishes and good filter coffee, served by dapper waiters in turbans and cummerbunds. Best for breakfast.

Kabul, 43/4 Gopal Krishna Complex, Residency Rd. One of two northwest frontier restaurants in Bangalore, serving Afghan *biriyanis*, *kebabs* and Muslim-style mutton in rich almond and cream sauces. Moderately priced.

Kashy's, St Mark's Rd, next to British Library. Spacious old-style café with cane blinds, pewter tea pots and cotton-clad waiters. Bangalore's most congenial meeting place. Serves snacks and alcohol.

KC Das, 38 Church St (corner of St Mark's Rd). Traditional steam-cooked Bengali sweets, many soaked in syrup and rose water. Try their definitive *rasgullas*. Eat in or take away.

Mac's Fast Food, Church St. Cramped, not at all bad burger joint that also does stroganoffs, passable pizzas and fish and chips.

Mavalli Tiffin Rooms, Lalbagh Rd. Indian fast-food restaurant, serving superb value set menus (4–8.30pm), and good snacks (including the best *masala dosas* in Bangalore) during the day. Also pure fruit juices and *lassis* sweetened with real honey.

The Only Place, Mota Royal Arcade, Brigade Rd. Bangalore's most rated Western food, including a near-legendary lasagne and great apple pie, at reasonable prices.

Shanghai, G3–4 Shiva Shankar Plaza, 19 Lalbagh Rd, Richmond Circle. Among the city's top Chinese restaurants. Excellent beancurd veg soup and Hunan peppered fish, deep-fried with ginger, garlic and spring onions in a black pepper sauce.

Shiva Refreshments, *Brindhavan Hotel*, MG Rd. Deservedly popular traditional south Indian "meals" restaurant, packed out for unlimited *thalis* served on plantain leaves.

Ullas, First Floor, Public Utility Building, MG Rd. Bustling, inexpensive south Indian snack bar packed with office workers for its *chaat*, *dosas* and Punjabi meals. They also do a good selection of shakes, *kulfi* and ice-creams, served indoors, or on a terrace overlooking the street.

Nightlife

The big boom may be over, but Bangalore's bright young things still have money to spend, and **nightlife** in the city is thriving. A night on the town generally kicks off with a bar crawl along **Brigade Rd** and **Church St**, where scores of swish "**pubs**" compete with tacky theme decor, *MTV*, lasers and thumping sound systems. Drinking alcohol does not have the seedy connotations here it does elsewhere in India; you'll even see young Indian women enjoying a beer with their mates. There is, however, a ban on alcohol sales between 2.30 and 5.30pm, imposed in 1993 by ex-Chief Minister Veerappa Moily because of the number of school kids skipping school to booze; this only seemed to start them off earlier, or had them staying later.

Bangalore is also a major centre for **cinema**, with a booming industry and dozens of theatres showing the latest releases from India and abroad. Check the listings page of the *Deccan Herald* to find out what's on. Western movies are often dubbed into Hindi, although their titles may be written in English; check the small print in the newspaper. Cinema fans should head for **Kempe Gowda Circle**, which is crammed with extraordinarily colourful posters, hoardings and larger-than-life-size cardboard cut-outs of the latest stars, strewn with spangly garlands. To arrange a visit to a local movie studio phone *Chamundeshwari Studio* (☎226 8642) or *Shree Kanteera Studio* (☎337 1008).

Pubs

Black Cadillac, 50 Residency Rd. Theme pub with car fetish decor, and some tables outside.

Guzzlers Inn, 48 Rest House Rd, off Brigade Rd. Popular and established pub offering *MTV*, *Star Sport* and draught beer.

High Spirits, Brigade Rd, below *Kwality Restaurant*. Loads of mirrors and glass, quasi-tribal terracota designs and TV sets, but ludicrously loud sounds. Mostly men.

Nasa, 1/4 Church St. Karaoke and space-age decor, with the usual combination of big-screen *MTV* and in-your-face music.

Oasis, Church St. Low light and unobtrusive sound system: the chill-out option.

Listings

Airlines *Air Canada*, 131–132 Residency Rd (☎221 5416); *Air France*, Sunrise Chambers, Ulsoor Rd (☎558 9397); *Air India*, Unity Building, JC Rd (☎222 4303); *British Airways*, St Mark's Rd (☎227 4304); *Damania Airlines,* 102/3 Manipal Centre, Dickenson Rd (☎558 8866); *East-West*, 1/A MG Rd (☎558 8282); *Gulf Air*, Unity Buildings, JC Rd(☎223 7741); *Indian Airlines*, Cauvery Bhavan, Kempegowda Rd (☎221 1914); *Jet*, Sunrise Chambers, 22 Ulsoor Rd (☎558 6977); *KLM, Taj West End*, Race Course Rd (☎225 9281); *Lufthansa*, Dickenson Rd (☎558 8791); *Malaysian Airlines*, Richmond Circle (☎221 3030); *Modiluft*, 45 Vinayak Complex, Residency Rd (☎558 2202); *NEPC*, 138A Brigade Gardens, Church St (☎559 4860); *Pakistan International Airlines*, Brigade Rd (☎558 3074); *Qantas*, Westminster Cunningham Rd (☎226 4719); *Sahara Indian Airlines*, 1 Church St (☎558 6976); *Singapore Airlines*, Richmond Rd (☎221 2822); *Swiss Air*, 51 Richmond Rd (☎221 1983); *Thai Airlines*, Richmond Rd (☎221 9810).

Emergencies Police ☎100; ambulance ☎102.

Libraries The *British Council* (English-language) library, 29 St Mark's Rd (Tues–Sat 10.30am–6.30pm), has newspapers and magazines that visitors are welcome to peruse in a/c comfort, as do the *Alliance Française*, (French), 16 GMT Rd, and *Max Mueller Bhavan* (German), 3 Lavelle Rd.

Pharmacies Open all night: *Al-Siddique Pharma Centre*, opposite Jamia Masjid near City Market; *Janata Bazaar*, in the Victoria Hospital, near City Market; *Sindhi Charitable Hospital*, 3rd Main S R Nagar. During the day, head for *Santoshi Pharma*, 46 Mission Rd.

Photographic equipment *Adlabs*, Mission Rd, Subbaiah Circle, stocks transparency film. *GG Welling*, 113 MG Rd and *GK Vale*, 89 MG Rd sell transparency and Polaroid film.

Swimming pools Five-star hotel pools open to non-residents include: the *Taj Residency* (Rs165 includes sauna, jacuzzi and health club); *Holiday Inn* (Rs110); and *Taj West End* (Rs165).

Travel agents For flight booking and reconfirmation, try *Merry Go Round Tours*, 41 Museum Rd, opposite *Berry's Hotel* (☎/fax 558 6946); *Marco Polo Tours*, Janardhan Towers, 2 Residency Rd (☎227 4484; fax 223 6671; or *Sita Travels*, 1 St Mark's Rd (☎558 8892).

Visa extensions Commissioner of Police, Infantry Rd (☎75272).

MOVING ON FROM BANGALORE

Bangalore is south India's principal transport hub. Fast and efficient computerized booking facilities make **moving on** relatively hassle-free, although availablity of seats should never be taken for granted; book as far in advance as possible. For a **full rundown** of travel services to and from Bangalore, see "Karnataka Travel Details" on p.1120.

Bangalore's **airport** is the busiest in south India, with international and domesic departures. The most frequent flights are to **Bombay**, operated by *Indian Airlines, East-West, Damania, Jet, Modiluft, Sahara Indian,* and *NEPC.* There are also six or seven daily flights to **Delhi**. For precise departure times, bookings or confirmations, contact the airlines (see "Listings", above). Most of the wide range of long-haul **buses** from the **Central stand** (listed on p.1120) can be booked in advance at the computerized counters near bay #13 (6.30am–8.30pm). Aside from *KSRTC*, state bus corporations represented include Andhra Pradesh, Kerala, Maharashtra and Tamil Nadu. Timings and ticket availability for the forthcoming week are posted on a large board left of the main entrance. For general enquiries, call ☎287 3377.

When this book went to press, some **rail** routes in Karnataka were disrupted while *Southern Railways* converted to broad gauge. Check the situation when you arrive. Bangalore City station's **reservations** office (Mon–Sat 8am–2pm & 2.15–8pm, Sun 8am–2pm; phone enquiries: 7am–2pm & 2.15–9pm; ☎132) is in a separate building, east of the main station. Counter #14 is for foreigners. If you have an Indrail Pass, go to the Chief Reservations Supervisor's Office on the first floor (turn left at the top of the stairs), where "reservations are guaranteed". If your reservation is "waitlisted", or you are required to confirm the booking, you may have to go on the day of departure to the Commercial Officer's office, in the Divisional Office – yet another building, this time to the west, accessible from the main road. There are two 24-hour **telephone information** lines; one handles timetable enquiries(☎131), the other reels off a recorded list of arrivals and departures (☎133).

Recommended trains from Bangalore

The following **trains** are recommended as the fastest and/or most convenient from Bangalore.

Destination	Name	Number	Departs	Total time
Bombay	*Udyan Express*	#6530	daily 8.30pm	24hr
Calcutta (Howrah)	*Howrah Express*	#6312	Fri 11.30pm	26hr 15min
Cochin (Ernakulam)	*Kanyakumari Express*	#6526	daily 9pm	16hr 25min
Delhi	*Karnataka Express*	#2627	daily 6.25pm	41hr 45min
	*Rajdhani Express**	#2627	daily 6.45am	33hr 15min
Hospet (for Hampi)	*Hampi Express*	#6592	daily 9.55pm	10hr
Hyderabad	*Hyderabad Express*	#7086	daily 5.05pm	16hr 20min
Madras	*Lalbagh Express*	#2608	daily 6.41am	5hr
	*Shatabdi Express**	#2008	daily except Tues 4.30pm	4hr 45min
Mysore	*Kaveri Express*	#6222	daily 8.25am	2hr 30min
	Tippu Express	#6206	daily 2.25pm	2hr 25min
	Chamundi Express	#6216	daily 6.30pm	3hr
	*Shatabdi Express**	#2007	daily 10.55am	2hr
Thiruvananthapuram	*Kannyakumari Express*	#6526	daily 9pm	15hr 10min

*= a/c only

Around Bangalore

Many visitors to Bangalore are on the way to or from Mysore. The **Janapada Loka Folk Arts Museum**, between the two, gives a fascinating insight into Karnataka culture, while anyone wishing to see or study classical dance in a rural environment should check out **Nrityagram Dance Village**.

Janapada Loka Folk Arts Museum

The **Janapada Loka Folk Arts Museum** (daily 9am–6pm), 53km southwest of Bangalore on the Mysore road, includes an amazing array of Karnatakan agricultural, hunting and fishing implements, weapons, ingenious household gadgets, masks, dolls and shadow puppets, carved wooden *bhuta* (spirit-worship) sculptures and larger-than-life temple procession figures, manuscripts, musical instruments and *Yakshagana* theatre costumes. In addition, 1600 hours of **audio and video recordings** of musicians, dancers and rituals from the state are available for viewing on request.

To get to the museum, take one of the many slow Mysore buses (not the non-stop ones) from Bangalore. After the town of Ramanagar, alight at the 53rd km stone by the side of the road. A small **restaurant** serves simple food, and dorm **accommodation** (①) is available. For more details contact the *Karnataka Janapada Trust*, 7 Subramanyaswami Temple Rd, 5th Cross, 4th Block, Kumara Park West, Bangalore.

Nrityagram Dance Village

NRITYAGRAM is a purpose-built model village, 30km west of Bangalore, designed by the award-winning architect Gerard de Cunha and founded by the dancer Protima Gauri, who specializes in Orissa's Odissi dance (see p.936). It hosts regular performances and lectures on Indian mythology and art, and also offers courses in different forms of Indian dance. **Guided tours** of the complex cost Rs250. **Accommodation** for longer stays (②) promises "oxygen, home-grown vegetables and fruits, no TV, telephones, newspapers or noise". Contact their Bangalore office (☎558 5440 or 226188).

Mysore

A centre of sandalwood-carving and incense production, 159km southwest of Bangalore, **MYSORE**, the erstwhile capital of the Wadiyar Rajas, is one of south India's most popular attractions. Considering the clichés that have been heaped upon the place, however, first impressions can be disappointing; like anywhere else, you are not so much greeted by the scent of jasmine blossom or gentle wafts of sandalwood when you stumble off the bus or train, as by the usual cacophony of careering autorickshaws and noisy buses, bullock carts, and tongas. Nevertheless, Mysore is certainly lovely: an old-fashioned, undaunting town dominated by the spectacular **Maharaja's Palace**, just one of several beautiful residences dotted around the wide, attractive streets. The magnificent Hoysala temple of **Somnathpur** lies little more than an hour's drive away.

In the tenth century Mysore was known as "Mahishur" – "the town where the demon buffalo was slain" (by the goddess Durga). Presiding over a district of many villages, the city was ruled from about 1400 until Independence by the Hindu **Wadiyars**, its fortunes inextricably linked with those of Srirangapatnam (15km northeast; see p.1139), which became headquarters from 1610. Their rule was only broken from 1761, when the Muslim Haider Ali and son Tipu Sultan took over. Two years later, the new rulers demolished the labyrinthine old city to replace it with the elegant grid of sweeping, leafy streets and public gardens that survive today. However, following Tipu Sultan's defeat 1799 by the British Colonel, Arthur Wellesley (later the Duke of

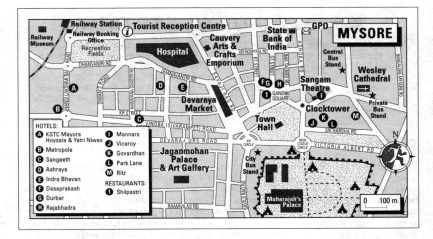

Wellington), Waidya power was restored. As the capital of Mysore state, the city there-after dominated a major part of southern India. In 1956, when Bangalore became capital of newly formed Karnataka, its Maharaja was appointed Governor.

Arrival and information

Mysore's nearest airport is at Bangalore. The **railway station**, 1500m northwest of the centre, is served by three or four daily trains to the state capital, with connections to and from Madras. Mysore has three bus stands: major long-distance *KSRTC* services pull in to **Central**, near the heart of the city, where there's a handy KSTDC information counter (good for bus times and tour tickets); the **Private** stand, just a dusty patch of road, lies a little way south, opposite the *Ritz Hotel*, and is used by buses to and from Somnathpur. Local buses, including services for Chamundi Hill and Srirangaptnam, stop at the **City** stand, next to the northwestern corner of the Maharaja's Palace.

Ten minutes' walk southeast of the railway station, on a corner of Irwin Rd in the Old Exhibition Building, the helpful **Tourist Reception Centre** (daily 10am–5.30pm) will book accommodation by phone and make an effort to answer queries, though there's not much you can take away with you. The **KSTDC office** (daily 7.30am–8.30pm), in the same building, is of little use except to book one of their tours. The whistlestop **city tour** (7.30am–8.30pm; Rs85) makes for a long day, covering Jaganmohan Palace Art Gallery, Maharaja's Palace, St Philomena's Cathedral, the Zoo, Chamundi Hill, Somnathpur, Srirangapatnam and Brindavan Gardens. It only leaves with a minimum of 10 passengers, so you may not know for sure whether it will run when you buy your ticket. The **long-distance tour** and the **Ooty** tours are not recommended; you spend far too much time on the bus. There's another, more helpful KSTDC office at *Hotel Mayura Hoysala*, Jhansi Laxmi Bai Rd.

The main **post office** (poste restante) is on the corner of Ashoka and Irwin roads, and there's a *State Bank of Mysore* on the corner of Sayaji Rao and Sardar Patel Rd.

The telephone **area code** for Mysore is ☎0821.

WILDLIFE SANCTUARIES AROUND MYSORE

Mysore lies within striking distance of three wildlife sanctuaries, all of which require forward planning if you want to get the most out of them. Accommodation at **Bandipur** (see p.1140) and **Nagarhole** (see p.1141) must be booked as far in advance as possible through the Chief Warden, *Aranya Bhavan*, Ashokpuram; ☎0821/520901 (6km south of the centre, on bus #61 from the city stand). To arrange accommodation at **Mudumalai**, across the border in Tamil Nadu, you'll have to phone ahead (see p.1047). Note that the Forest Department's *Rest Houses* can only be booked in Ooty.

The City

In addition to its official tourist attractions, Mysore is a great city simply to stroll around. The characterful, if dilapidated, pre-Independence buildings lining market areas such as **Ashok Road** and **Sayaji Rao Road** lend an air of faded grandeur to the busy centre, teeming with vibrant street life. Souvenir stores spill over with the famous **sandalwood**; the best place to get a sense of what's on offer is the *Government Cauvery Arts and Crafts Emporium* on Sayaji Rao Rd (closed Thurs), which stocks a wide range of local crafts that can be shipped overseas. Finally, the famous **Devaraja Market** on Sayaji Rao Rd is one of south India's most atmospheric produce markets: a giant complex of covered stalls groaning with green bananas, luscious mangoes, blocks of sticky *jaggery*, and conical heaps of lurid *kunkum* powder.

Maharaja's Palace

Mysore centre is dominated by the walled **Maharaja's Palace** (daily 10.30am–5.30pm), a fairytale spectacle topped with a shining brass-plated dome surmounting a single tower; especially magnificent on Sunday nights and during festivals, when it is illuminated by no less than 5000 lightbulbs. Designed in the hybrid "Indo-Saracenic" style by Henry Irwin, the British consultant architect of Madras state, it was completed in 1912 for the twenty-fourth Wadiyar Raja, on the site of the old wooden palace that had been destroyed by fire in 1897. Twelve temples surround the palace, some of them of much earlier origin. Although there are six gates in the perimeter wall, entrance is on the south side only. Shoes and cameras must be left at the cloakroom inside.

An extraordinary amalgam of styles from India and around the world crowds the lavish **interior**. Entry is through the Gombe Thotti or **Dolls' Pavilion**, once a showcase for the figures featured in the city's lively Dussehra celebrations and now a gallery of European and Indian sculpture and ceremonial objects. Halfway along, the brass **Elephant Gate** forms the main entrance to the centre of the palace, through which the Maharaja would drive to his car park. Decorated with floriate designs, it bears the Mysore royal symbol of a double-headed eagle, now the state emblem. To the north, past the gate, are dolls dating from the turn of the century, a wooden *mandapa* glinting with mirrorwork, and at the end, a ceremonial wooden elephant *howdah* (frame to carry passengers). Elaborately decorated with 84kg of 24-carat gold, it appears to be inlaid with red and green gems – in fact the twinkling lights are battery-powered signals to let the *mahout* know when the Maharaja wished to stop or go.

Walls leading into the octagonal **Kalyana Mandapa**, the royal wedding hall, are lined with a meticulously detailed frieze of oil paintings illustrating the great Mysore Dussehra festival of 1930, executed over fifteen years by four Indian artists. The hall itself is magnificent, a cavernous space featuring cast-iron pillars from Glasgow, Bohemian chandeliers, and multi-coloured Belgian stained glass arranged in peacock designs in the domed ceiling. A mosaic of English floor-tiles repeats the peacock motif. Beyond here lie small rooms cluttered with grandiose furniture, including a pair of silver chairs and others of Belgian cut-crystal made for the Maharaja and Lord Mountbatten, the last Viceroy of India. One of the rooms has a fine ceiling of Burma teak carved by local craftsmen.

Climbing a staircase with Italian marble balustrades, past an unnervingly realistic life-size plaster of Paris figure of Krishnaraja Wadiyar IV, lounging comfortably with his bejewelled feet on a stool, you come into the **Public Durbar Hall**, an orientalist fantasy often compared to a setting from *A Thousand and One Nights*. A vision of brightly painted and gilded colonnades, open on one side, the massive hall affords views out across the parade ground and gardens to Chamundi Hill. The Maharaja gave audience from here, seated on a throne made from 280kg of solid Karnatakan gold. These days, the hall is only used during the Dussehra festival, when it hosts classical concerts. Paintings by the celebrated artists Shilpi Siddalingaswamy and Raja Rama Varma, from the Travancore (Kerala) royal family, adorn the walls. The whole is crowned by white marble, inlaid with delicate floral scrolls of jasper, amber and lapis lazuli in the Moghul style. Somewhat out of synch with the opulence, a series of ceiling panels of Vishnu, painted on fire-proof asbestos, date from the 1930s. The smaller **Private Durbar Hall** features especially beautiful stained glass and gold-leaf painting. Before leaving you pass two embossed silver doors – all that remains of the old palace.

Nearby, behind the main palace building but within the same compound, a small **museum** run by the royal family shows paintings from the Thanjavur and (see p.1015) Mysore schools, some inlaid with precious stones and gold leaf.

Jaganmohan Palace: Jayachamarajendra Art Gallery

Built in 1861, the **Jaganmohan Palace** (daily 8am–5pm; no cameras) was used as a royal residence until turned into a picture gallery and museum in 1915 by the Maharaja Krishnaraja Wadiyar IV. Most of the "contemporary" art on show seems to date from the 1930s, when a revival of Indian painting was spearheaded by EB Havell and the Tagore brothers Abandrinath and Ganganendranath in Bengal.

On the ground floor, a series of faded black-and-white photos of ceremonial occasions shares space with elaborate imported clocks. Twentieth-century paintings dominate the first floor; Raja Rama Varma's mediocre oils show epic themes such as the demon king Ravana absconding with Rama's wife Sita. Games on the upper floor include circular *ganjeeb* playing cards illustrated with portraits of royalty or deities, and board games delicately inlaid with ivory. There's also a cluster of musical instruments, among them a brass *jaltarang* set and glass xylophone, and harmonicas and clarinet played by Krishnaraja Wadiyar IV himself. Another gallery, centring on a large wooden Ganesh seated on a tortoise, is lined with paintings, including Krishnaraja Wadiyar sporting with the "inmates" of his *zenana* (women's quarter of the palace) during Holi.

MYSORE DUSSEHRA FESTIVAL

Following the tradition set by the Vijayanagar kings, the ten-day festival of **Dussehra** (Sept/Oct), to commemorate the goddess Durga's slaying of the demon buffalo, Mahishasura (see p.985), is celebrated in grand style at Mysore. Scores of cultural events include concerts of south Indian classical (Carnatic) music and dance performances in the great Durbar Hall of the **Maharaja's Palace**. On Vijayadasmi, the tenth and last day of the festival, a magnificent procession of mounted guardsmen on horseback and caparisoned elephants – one carrying the palace deity, Chaamundeshwari, on a gold *howdah* – marches 5km from the palace to Banni Mantap. There's also a floating festival in the temple tank at the foot of **Chamundi Hill**, and a procession of chariots around the temple at the top. A torchlight parade takes place in the evening, followed by a massive firework display and much jubilation on the streets.

Chamundi Hill

Chamundi Hill, 3km southeast of the city, is topped with a temple to the chosen deity of the Mysore Rajas; the goddess Chamundi, or Durga, who slew the demon buffalo Mahishasura (see p.985). It's a pleasant, easy bus trip (#101 from the City stand) to the top; the walk down, past a huge Nandi, Shiva's bull, takes about thirty minutes. Pilgrims, of course, make the trip in reverse order. Take drinking water to sustain you, especially in the middle of the day – the walk isn't very demanding, but by the end of it, after more than 1000 steps, your legs are likely to be a bit wobbly.

Seats to the left of the bus give the best views of the plain surrounding Mysore. Don't be surprised if, at the top of the hill, dominated by the temple's forty-metre *gopura*, you're struck by a feeling of déja vu – one of the highly educational displays at the **Godly Museum** states that "5000 years ago at this time you had visited this place in the same way you are visiting now. Because world drama repeats itself identically every 5000 years". Another exhibit goes to the heart of our "problematic world: filthy films, lack of true education, blind faith, irreligiousness, bad habits and selfishness". Suitably edified, you can proceed along a path from the bus stand, past trinket and tea stalls, to the temple square. Immediately to the right, at the end of this path, are four bollards painted with a red stripe; return here for the path down the hill.

Non-Hindus can visit the twelfth-century **temple** (daily 8am–noon & 5–8pm; leave shoes opposite the entrance), staffed by friendly priests who will plaster your forehead in vermillion paste. The Chamundi figure inside is solid gold; outside, in the courtyard, stands a fearsome, if gaily coloured, statue of the demon Mahishasura. On leaving, if you continue by the path instead of retracing your steps, you can return to the square via two other temples and various buildings storing ceremonial paraphernalia and animal figures used during Dussehra. You'll also come across loads of scampering monkeys, and the odd dreadlocked *sadhu* who will willingly pose for your holiday snaps, for a consideration. The magnificent five-metre **Nandi**, carved from a single piece of black-granite in 1659, is an object of worship himself, adorned with bells and garlands and tended by his own priest. Minor shrines, dedicated to Chamundi and the monkey god Hanuman among others, line the side of the path; at the bottom, a little shrine to Ganesh lies near a *chai*-shop. From here it's usually possible to pick up an auto-rickshaw or bus back into the city, but at weekends the latter are often full. If you walk on towards the city, passing a temple on the left, with a big water tank (the site of the floating festival during Dussehra), you come after ten minutes to the main road between the Lalitha Mahal Palace and the city; there's a bus stop, and often auto-rickshaws, at the junction.

Accommodation

Mysore has plenty of **hotels** to suit all budgets. Finding a room is only a problem during Dussehra, by which time the popular places have been booked up weeks in advance. Cheap lodges are concentrated on and around **Dhanavantri Rd**, a little way south of the tourist office on Irwin Rd, and close to **Gandhi Square** further east. Mid-range to expensive hotels are more spread out, but a good place to start is **Jhansi Laxmi Bai Rd**, which runs south from the railway station. If you're looking for a palace, then head straight for ITDC's opulent *Ashok Lalitha Mahal*.

Inexpensive

Govardhan, opposite *Opera* "talkies", Sri Harsha Rd (☎34118). Basic budget rooms close to Ghandi Square. Frayed around the edges, but clean enough. ③.
Indra Bhavan, Dhanavantri Rd (☎23933). Dilapidated and characterful old lodge, with en-suite singles and doubles. Their "ordinary" rooms are a little grubby, but the good-value "deluxe" have squeaky-clean tiled floors and open on to a wide common verandah. ②.

KSTDC Yatri Niwas, 2 Jhansi Llaxmi Bai Rd (☎25349). The government-run *Mayura Hoysala*'s economy wing: simple rooms around a central garden, with beer garden and terrace restaurant next door, and a cheap dorm. ①–②.

Mannars, Chandragupta Rd (☎35060). Newish budget hotel, near the bus stand and Ghandi Square. No frills, except the TV and sofas in reception. Deservedly popular with backpackers. ②.

Park Lane, 2720 Curzon Rd (☎30400). Six pleasant rooms over a popular beer-garden/restaurant. One of the best deals at this price, but with some drawbacks: clouds of mozzies, noise from the bar until 11.30pm and dodgy plumbing. Avoid room 8 (it's next to the generator). ③.

Rajabhadra, Gandhi Square (☎23023). Best value of several look-a-like lodges on the square. The front rooms are great if you don't mind being in the thick of things. Some singles. ②.

Ritz, Bangalore–Nilgiri Rd (☎22668). Wonderful colonial-era hotel, a stone's throw from the private bus stand. At the top of this category, but worth the extra. Only four rooms, so book ahead. ③.

Sangeeth, 1966 Narayana Shastry Rd, near the Udipi Krishna temple (☎24693). Mysore's best all-round budget deal: bland and a bit boxed in, but central, friendly and very good value. ①–②.

Moderate to expensive

Aashraya, Rajmal Talkies Rd, Dhanavantri Rd Cross (☎27088 or 26570). Run-of-the-mill hotel on the edge of the market area. Attached rooms are small, but comfortable and reasonable value. ④.

Dasaprakash, Gandhi Square (☎24444 or 22821). Modern multi-storey hotel; clean and efficient, though lacking character. Some a/c rooms, and a veg restaurant. ③–④.

Green, Chittaranjan Palace, 2270 Vinoba Rd, Jayalakshmipuram (☎512536; fax 516139). Former royal palace refurbished as an elegant, eco-conscious 2-star, in large gardens on the western outkirts. Spacious rooms, lounges, verandahs, a croquet lawn and well-stocked library; they even keep mosquito-eating fish in the pond. All profits to charities and environmental projects. ⑥–⑦.

ITDC Ashok Lalitha Mahal Palace, T Narasipur Rd (☎571265; fax 571770). On a slope overlooking the city, and visible for miles around, this white, Neoclassical palace was built in 1931 to accommodate the Maharaja's foreign guests. Now it's a Raj-style fantasy; popular with tour groups and film crews. Tariffs are astronomical by Indian standards, ranging from $160 to $600 per night for the "Viceroy Suite". The tea lounge, restaurant and pool are open to non-residents. ⑨.

KSTDC Mayura Hoysala, 2 Jhansi Laxmi Bai Rd (☎25349). Reasonably priced, well-maintained rooms in restored colonial-era building. Terrace restaurant and beer garden. Good value ④.

Metropole, 5 Jhansi Laxmi Bai Rd (☎520681; fax 520854). Charming old-fashioned hotel in Maharaja's former guest house: large (some huge) rooms, wicker chairs, long verandahs and a relaxing garden add to the 1940s feel. Highly recommended. ⑥–⑦.

Viceroy, Sri Harsha Rd (☎24001; fax 25410). Snazzy new business-oriented hotel, with most mod cons and views over the park to the palace from front rooms. Mostly a/c. ⑥–⑦.

Eating

Mysore has scores of **places to eat**, from numerous south Indian "meals" joints dotted around the market to the opulent *Lalita Mahal*, where you can work up an appetite for a gourmet meal with a few lengths of the pool. Avoid the *Durbar*, opposite the *Shilpastri*, which, notwithstanding its popular rooftop, dishes up poor food.

Akshaya, *Hotel Dasaprakash*. Very good south Indian veg "meals" joint, serving various *thalis* (try the "special"), ice-creams and cold drinks. Low on atmosphere, but the food is delicious and cheap.

Gopika, *Govardhan Lodge*. Inexpensive "meals" restaurant on the ground floor of a busy hotel; opens early for Indian breakfasts of *idlys*, *wada*, *pakora* and big glasses of hot-milk coffee.

KSTDC Bamboo Grove, *Mayura Hoysala*. Simple terrace-garden restaurant, with split-cane blinds and the usual multi-cuisine menu. Serves alcohol.

Lalitha Mahal. Sample the charms of this palatial 5-star with an expensive hot drink in the turn-of-the-century tea lounge, or an à la carte lunch in the grand dining hall, accompanied by live sitar music. The old-style bar also boasts a full-size billiards table.

Metropole, 5 Jhansi Laxmi Bai Rd. Recommended more for the characterful colonial-style ambience than the food. Some tables outside in the garden, where there's often an evening barbecue (bring mosquito repellent). Moderate to expensive.

Park Lane, 2720 Curzon Park Rd. Congenial courtyard restaurant-cum-beer garden, with tasty, moderately priced veg and non-veg food (meat sizzlers are a speciality), pot plants and loud *filmi* music. Popular with foreign travellers.

Ritz, Bangalore–Nilgiri Rd. Central and secluded, and a nice escape from the city streets for a drink, or veg and non-veg meals. The best tables are in courtyard at the back. Opens at 8.30am for "omlette-bread-butter-jam" breakfasts.

Shilpastri, Gandhi Square. Quality north Indian-style food, with particularly tasty *tandoori* (great chicken *tikka*). Plenty of good veg options, too, including lots of *dals* and curd rice. Serves alcohol. Another popular roof-top meeting place, the *Durbar*, opposite, dishes up poor food.

MOVING ON FROM MYSORE

If you're contemplating a long haul, the best way to travel is by **train**, usually with a change at **Bangalore**. Four express services leave Mysore each day for the Karnatakan capital, taking between 1hr and 2hr 50min to cover the 139km. The fastest of these, the a/c *Shatabdi Express* (#2008, daily except Tues) continues on to Madras (6hr 55min); the others terminate in Bangalore, where you can pick up long-distance connections to a wide range of Indian cities (see p.1120). Reservations can be made at Mysore's computerized booking hall inside the station (Mon–Sat 8am–2pm & 2.15–8pm, Sun 8am–2pm). There's no tourist counter; take a good book.

Reservations are not required for Bangalore (except on the *Shatabdi Express*), so you shouldn't ever have to do the trip by **bus**, which takes longer and is a lot more terrifying. However, several destinations within a day's ride of Mysore can only be reached by road. Long-distance services operate out of the Central bus stand, where you can book computerized tickets up to three days in advance. English timetables are posted on the wall inside the entrance hall, and there's a helpful enquiries counter in the corner of the compound. Regular buses leave here for **Hassan**, jumping-off place for the Hoysala temples at Belur and Halebid, and for Channarayapatna/**Saravanabelgola** (hourly; 2hr). Heading south to **Ooty** (5hr), there's a choice of a dozen or so buses, all of which stop at **Bandipur National Park**. Mysore is also connected by direct services to **Hospet**, the nearest town to Hampi, and several cities in **Kerala**, including Kannur, Kozhikode and Kochi. Until work on the train line to **Goa** is completed, the only way to travel direct to Panjim is on the 4pm overnight bus. Most travellers, however, break this long trip into stages, heading first to **Mangalore** (12–15 daily; 7hr), and working their way north from there, usually via **Gokarn** – which you can also reach by direct bus (1 daily; 14hr) – or **Jog Falls**. Another possible place to head for after Mysore is **Madikeri**, capital of Kodagu (Coorg), served by hourly buses. For details of services to **Somnathpur** and **Srirangapatnam**, see the relevant accounts below.

Mysore doesn't have an airport (the nearest one is at Banglaore), but you can confirm and book *Indian Airlines* flights at their office in the KSTDC *Mayura Hoysala* (Mon–Sat 10am–1.30pm & 2.15–5pm; ☎516943).

For a **full rundown** of travel services to and from Mysore, see "Karnataka Travel Details" on p.1120.

Around Mysore

Mysore is a jumping-off point for some of Karnataka's most popular destinations. At **Srirangapatnam**, the fort, palace and mausoleum date from the era of Tipu Sultan, the "Tiger of Mysore", a perennial thorn in the side of the British. The superb **Hoysala temples** (see p.1144) of **Somnathpur**, and further out, **Belur** and **Halebid**, are architectural masterpieces. Also near Hassan, the Jain site of **Sravanabelgola** attracts busloads of pilgrims and tourists to see the monolithic naked statue of Gomateshvara.

The Western Ghat mountains are easily accessible from Mysore: just three hours away by road, the capital of the coffee-growing Kodagu (Coorg) region, **Madikeri**, makes a congenial stop on the journey to or from the coast. If you're heading south towards Ooty, **Bandipur National Park**'s forests and hill scenery offer another possible escape from the city, although your chances of spotting any rare animals are slim. The same is true of **Nagarhole National Park**, three hours southwest of Mysore in the Coorg region, which recently suffered severe fire damage.

Srirangapatnam

The island of **SRIRANGAPATNAM**, in the River Kaveri, 14km north of Mysore, measures 5km by 1km. Long a site of Hindu pilgrimage, it is named for its tenth-century Sriranganathaswamy Vishnu temple, which in 1133 served as a refuge for the philosopher Ramanuja, a staunch Vaishnavite, from the Shaivite Cholas in Tamil Nadu. The Vijayanagars built a fort here in 1454, and in 1616 it became the capital of the Mysore Wadiyar Rajas. However, Srirangapatnam is more famously associated with **Haider Ali**, who deposed the Wadiyars in 1761, and even more so with his son **Tipu Sultan**. During his seventeen-year reign – which ended with his death in 1799, when the future Duke of Wellington took the fort at the bloody battle of "Seringapatnam" – Tipu posed a greater threat than any other Indian ruler to British plans to dominate India.

Tipu Sultan and his father were responsible for transforming the small state of Mysore into a major Muslim power. Born in 1750, of a Hindu mother, Tipu inherited Haider Ali's considerable military skills; unlike his illiterate father, he was also an educated, cultured man who introduced radical agricultural reforms. His burning life-long desire to rid India of the hated British invaders naturally brought him an ally in the French. He obsessively embraced his popular name of the "**Tiger of Mysore**", surrounding himself with symbols and images of tigers; much of his memorabilia is decorated with the animal or its stripes, and, like the Romans, he is said to have kept tigers for the punishment of criminals. Tipu's Srirangapatnam was largely destroyed by the British, but parts of the fort area in the northwest survive, including gates, ramparts, the grim dungeons (where chained British prisoners were allegedly forced to stand neck-deep in water), and the domed and minareted Jami Masjid mosque.

The former summer palace, the **Daria Daulat Bagh** (daily 10am–5pm), literally "wealth of the sea", 1km east of the fort, was used to entertain Tipu's guests. At first sight, this low, wooden colonnaded building set in an attractive formal garden fails to impress, as most of it is obscured by sunscreens. However, the superbly preserved interior, with its ornamental arches, tiger-striped columns and floral decoration on every inch of the teak walls and ceiling, is remarkable. A much-repainted mural on the west wall relishes every detail of Haider Ali's victory over the British at Pollilore in 1780. Upstairs, a small collection of Tipu memorabilia, European paintings, Persian manuscripts on hand-made paper and a model of Srirangapatnam are on show.

An avenue of cypresses leads from an intricately carved gateway to the **Gumbaz mausoleum**, 3km further east. Built by Tipu Sultan in 1784 to commemorate Haider Ali, and later also to serve as his own resting place, the lower half of the grey granite edifice is crowned by a dome of white-washed brick and plaster, spectacular against the blue sky. Ivory-inlaid rosewood doors lead to the tombs of Haider Ali and Tipu, each covered by a pall (tiger stripes for Tipu), and an Urdu tablet records Tipu's martyrdom.

Practicalities

Frequent **buses** from Mysore City bus stand and all the Mysore–Bangalore **trains** pull in near the temple and fort. Srirangapatnam is a small island, but places of interest are quite spread out; tongas, auto-rickshaws and bicycles are available on the main road

---

THE RANGANATHITTU BIRD SANCTUARY

Some 2km southwest of Srirangapatnam, the **Ranganathittu Bird Sanctuary** (daily 9am–6pm; Rs100) is a must for ornithologists, especially during October/November, when the lake, fed by the River Kaveri, attracts huge flocks of migrating birds. At other times it's a tranquil spot to escape the city, where you can enjoy boat rides through the backwaters to look for crocodiles, otters and dozens of species of resident waders, wildfowl and forest birds. The easiest way to **get there** is by rickshaw from Srirangapatnam.

---

near the bus stand. The KSTDC **hotel**-cum-restaurant, *Mayura River View* (☎52114; ④), occupies a pleasant spot beside the Kaveri, 3km from the bus stand.

Bandipur National Park

Situated among the broken foothills of the Western Ghat mountains, **Bandipur National Park**, 80km south of Mysore, covers 880 square kilometres of dry decid-uous forest, south of the River Kabini. The reserve was created in the 1930s from the local Maharajah's hunting lands, and expanded in 1941 to adjoin the Nagarhole National Park to the north, and Madumalai and Wynad Sanctuaries to the south in Tamil Nadu. These now collectively comprise the huge **Nilgiri Biosphere Reserve**, one of India's most extensive tracts of protected forest. However, as a tourist destin-ation, Bandipur, in spite of its good accommodation and well-maintained metalled jeep tracks, is a disappointment. Glimpses of anything more exciting than a langur or spot-ted deer are rare outside the core area, which is off-limits to casual visitors, while the noisy diesel bus laid on by the Forest Department to transport tourists around the accessible areas of park scares off what little fauna remains. If you're hoping to spot a tiger, forget it.

On the plus side, Bandipur is one of the few reserves in India where you stand a good chance of sighting wild **elephants**, particularly in the wet season (June–Sept), when water and forage are plentiful and the animals evenly scattered. Later in the mon-soon, huge herds congregate on the banks of the Kabini River, in the far north of the park, where you can see the remnants of an old stockade used by one particularly zeal-ous nineteenth-century British hunter as an elephant trap. Bandipur also boasts some fine scenery: at **Gopalswamy Betta**, near the park HQ, a high ridge looks north over the Mysore Plateau and its adjoining hills, while to the south, the "**Rolling Rocks**" afford sweeping views of the craggy, 260-metre-deep "**Mysore Ditch**".

Practicalities

Beds in the park are very limited, and it is essential to **book accommodation in advance** through the Forest Department's offices in Bangalore (Aranya Bhavan, 18th Cross, Malleswaram; ☎080/334 1993), or Mysore (Project Tiger, Aranya Bhavan, Ashokpuram; ☎0821/520901). The **best time to visit** is during the rainy season (June –Sept); unlike neighbouring parks, Bandipur's roads do not get washed out by the annu-al deluge, and elephants are numerous at this time. By November/December, however, most of the larger animals have migrated across the state border into Madumalai, where water is more plentiful in the dry season. Whenever you come, **avoid weekends**, when the park is inundated with bus loads of noisy day trippers.

Getting to Bandipur by bus is easy; all the regular *KSRTC* services to Ooty from Mysore's Central bus stand (12 daily; 2hr 30min) pass through the reserve (the last one back to Mysore leaves at 5pm), stopping outside the Forest Department's reception centre (daily 9am–4.30pm), where you can confirm **accommodation** bookings. The rooms on offer are basic, but good value, ranging from the "VIP" *Gajendra Cottages*

(③), which have en-suite bathrooms and verandahs, to beds in large, institutional dorms (Rs25). The *chowkidars* will knock up simple meals by arrangement.

Unless you have your own vehicle, the only **transport around the park** is the hopeless Forest Department bus, which makes two tours daily (7.30am & 4.30pm; 1hr; Rs160, camera Rs10). You may see a deer or two, but nothing more, on the half-hour **elephant ride** (Rs10) around the reception compound.

Nagarhole National Park

Bandipur's northern neighbour, **Nagarhole** ("Snake River") **National Park**, extends 640 square kilometres north from the Kabini River, dammed in 1974 to form a picturesque artificial lake. During the dry season (Feb–June), this perennial water source attracts large numbers of animals, making it a potentially prime spot for sighting wildlife. The forest here is of the moist-deciduous type – thick jungle with a thirty-metre-high canopy – and more impressive than Bandipur's drier scrub.

However, disaster struck Nagarhole in 1992, when friction between local pastoralist "tribals" and the park wardens over grazing rights and poaching erupted into a spate of arson attacks. Thousands of acres of forest were burned to the ground. The trees have grown back in places, but it will be decades before animal numbers completely recover. Meanwhile, Nagarhole is only worth visiting at the height of the dry season, when its muddy river banks and grassy swamps, or *hadlus*, offer better chances of sighting *gaur* (Indian bison), elephant, *dhole* (wild dog), deer, boar, and even the odd tiger or leopard, than any of the neighbouring sanctuaries.

Practicalities

Nagarhole is open year-round, but avoid the monsoons, when floods wash out most of its dirt tracks, and leeches make hiking impossible. To get there from Mysore, catch one of the two daily **buses** from the Central stand to **Hunsur** (3hr), 10km from the park's north gate, where you can pick up transport to the Forest Department's two *Rest Houses* (①). These have to be booked well in advance through the Forest Department offices in Mysore or Bangalore (see Bandipur, above). Turn up on spec, and you'll be told accommodation is "not available". It is also essential to arrive at the park gates well before dusk, as the road through the reserve to the lodges closes at 6pm, and is prone to "elephant blocks". The only other accommodation in Nagarhole is the luxury *Kabini River Lodge* (book through *Karnataka Jungle Lodges* in Bangalore; ☎080/559 7022; ⑨), approached via the village of **Karapura**, 3km from the park's south entance. Set in its own leafy compound on the lakeside, this former Maharajah's hunting lodge offers expensive all-in deals that include transport around the park with expert guides. It's impossible to reach by public transport, so you'll need to rent a car to get there.

Somnathpur

Built in 1268 AD, the exquisite **Keshava Vishnu temple**, in the sleepy hamlet of **SOMNATHPUR**, was the last important temple to be constructed by the Hoysalas; it is also the most complete and, in many respects, the finest example of this singular style (see p.1144). Somnathpur itself, just ninety minutes from Mysore by road, is little more than a few neat tracks and some attractive simple houses with pillared verandahs.

Like other Hoysala temples, the Keshava is built on a star-shaped plan, but, as a triple shrine, represents a mature development from the earlier constructions. ASI staff can show you around and also grant permission to clamber on the enclosure walls, to get a marvellous bird's-eye view of the modestly proportioned structure. It's best to do this as early as possible, as the stone gets very hot to walk on in bare feet.

The temple is a *trikutachala*, "three-peaked hills" type, with a tower on each shrine – a configuration also seen in certain Chalukya temples, and three temples on Hemakuta hill at Vijayanagar (Hampi; see p.1163). Each shrine, sharing a common hallway, is dedicated to a different form of Vishnu. In order of "seniority" they are Keshava in the central shrine, Venugopala to the proper right and Jagannath to the left. The Keshava shrine features a very unusual *chandrasila*, "moonstone" step at its entrance, and, diverging from the usual semi-circular Hoysala style, has two pointed projections.

The Keshava's high plinth (*jagati*) provides an upper ambulatory, which on its outer edge reproduces the almost crenellated shape of the structure and allows visitors to approach the upper registers of the profusely decorated walls. Among the many superb images here are an unusually high proportion of Shaivite figures for a Vishnu temple. As at Halebid, a lively frieze details countless episodes from the *Ramayana*, *Bhagavata Purana* and *Mahabharata*. Intended to accompany circumambulation, the panels are "read" (there is no text) in a clockwise direction. Unusually, the temple is autographed; all its sculpture was the work of one man, named Malitamba.

Outside the temple stands a *dvajastambha* column, which may originally have been surmounted by a figure of Vishnu's bird vehicle Garuda. The wide ground-level ambulatory that circles the whole building is edged with numerous, now empty, shrines.

Practicalities

Very few Mysore **buses**, if any, go direct to Somnathpur. Buses from the Private stand run to T Narasipur (1hr), served by regular buses to Somnathpur (20min). Everyone will know where you want to go, and someone will show you which scrum to join. Alternatively, join one of KSTDC's guided tours (see p.1133).

Aside from the odd coconut or watermelon seller, the only **food** and **drink** on offer in Somnathpur is at the KSTDC outpost, *Hotel Mayura Keshava* (no phone; ①), which serves basic snacks until 5pm and meals by arrangement later in the day. Their four clean and basic rooms, with bathroom, cannot be booked in advance; you'll have to go back to the cheap "meals" hotels at T Narasipur if you're desperate.

Hassan

The unprepossessing town of **HASSAN**, 118km northwest of Mysore, is visited in disproportionately large numbers because of its proximity to the Hoysala temples at **Belur** and **Halebid**, both northwest of the town, and the Jain pilgrimage site of **Sravanabelgola**, southeast. Some travellers end up staying a couple of nights, killing time in neon-lit *thali* joints and dowdy hotel rooms, but with a little forward planning you shouldn't have to linger here for longer than it takes to get on a bus somewhere else. Set deep in the serene Karnatakan countryside, Belur, Halebid and Saravanabelgola are much more congenial places to stay.

Arrival and information

Hassan's **bus stand** is in the centre of town, at the northern end of Bus Stand Rd which runs south past the post office to **Narsimharaja Circle**. Here you'll find the *State Bank of Mysore*, where you can change money but not *Thomas Cook* travellers' cheques, and most of the town's accommodation. Winding its way east–west via this junction is the Bangalore–Mangalore Road (BM Rd); along here to the east are the **tourist office** (1km), which won't tell you anything that you can't find out from your hotel, and the

The telephone **area code** for Hassan is ☎08172.

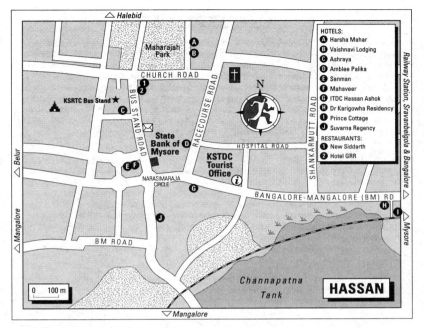

railway station (2km), served by slow passenger trains to Mysore and Mangalore. Note that the line from here across the Ghats to the coast is usually closed by flooding between June and early September.

Accommodation

Considering the number of tourists who pass through, Hassan is oddly lacking in good accommodation. Most of the budget options are of a pitiful standard: the few exceptions are within walking distance of the bus stand, around **Narsimharaja Circle**. Wherever you stay, call ahead, as most hotels tend to be full by early evening.

Ashraya, near the bus stand (☎68024). Run-of-the-mill rooms, some literally overlooking the bus stand. Clean enough, but noisy. ①.

DR Karigowda Residency, BM Rd, 1km from railway station (☎64506). Immaculate new mid-range place: friendly, comfortable and amazing value. Single occupancy possible; no a/c. ④.

ITDC Hassan Ashok, BM Rd, near Narsimharaja Circle (☎68731; fax 67154). On the left as you approach from the railway station. Overpriced hotel for tour groups and VIPs. Uninspiring but comfortable veg and non-veg restaurant, craft shops and bar. ⑧.

Mahaveer, BM Rd, near Narsimharaja Circle (☎68885). Cleanish rooms (some with TVs and mosquito nets) and good but dilapidated veg restaurant, the *Abhiruchi*. ①–②.

Prince Cottage, BM Rd, behind *Bhanu Theatre* (☎573201). Small, neat guest house tucked away off the main road. Good value and handy for the railway station. ②.

Sanman, Municipal Office Rd (☎68024). Decent rooms with squeaky-clean white-tiled floors, frames for mozzie nets, attached bath, and small balconies looking on to main bazaar. ②.

Suvarna Regency, PB 97, BM Rd (☎64006; fax 66774). The swankiest hotel in town, with lots of lights, shiny marble lobby, comfortable rooms and a rooftop BBQ. Recently opened, good value and a much better choice than the *Ashok*. Some a/c. ⑤–⑥.

HOYSALA TEMPLES

The **Hoysala** dynasty ruled southwestern Karnataka between the eleventh and thirteenth centuries. From the twelfth century, after the accession of King Vishnu Vardhana, they built a series of distinctive temples centred primarily at three sites: **Belur** and **Halebid**, close to modern Hassan, and **Somnathpur**, near Mysore.

At first sight, and from a distance, Hoysala temples appear to be modest structures, compact and even squat. On closer inspection, however, their profusion of fabulously detailed and sensuous sculpture, covering every inch of the exterior, is astonishing. Detractors are prone to class Hoysala art as decadent and overly fussy, but anyone with an eye for craftsmanship is likely to marvel at these jewels of Karnataka art.

The intricacy of the carvings was made possible by the material used in construction: a soft steatite soapstone that on oxidization hardens to a glassy, highly polished surface. The level of detail, similar to that seen in sandalwood and ivory work, became increasingly freer and fluid as the style developed, and reached its highest point at Somnathpur. Beautiful bracket figures, often delicate portrayals of voluptuous female subjects, were placed under the eaves, fixed by pegs top and bottom. A later addition (except possibly in the Somnathpur temple), these serve no structural function.

Another technique more usually associated with wood is the unusual treatment of the massive stone **pillars**: lathe-turned, they resemble those of the wooden temples of Kerala. They were probably turned on a horizontal plane, pinned at each end, and rotated with the use of a rope. It may be no coincidence that, to this day, wood turning is still a local speciality. Only the central shaft of each pillar seems to have been turned; in the base and capitals, a less precise, presumably handworked imitation of turning is evident.

The architectural style of the Hoysala temples is commonly referred to as **vesara**, or "hybrid" (literally "mule"), rather than belonging to either the northern, *nagari*, or southern Dravidian styles. However, they show great affinity with *nagari* temples of western India, and represent another fruit of contact, like music, painting and literature, facilitated by the trade routes between the north and the south. All Hoysala temples share a star-shaped plan, built on high plinths (*jagati*) that follow the shape of the sanctuaries and *mandapas* to provide a raised surrounding platform. Such northern features may have been introduced by the designer and artists of the earliest temple at Belur, who were imported by Vishnu Vardhana from further north in Andhra Pradesh. Also characteristic of the Hoysala style is the use of *ashlar* masonry, without mortar. Some pieces of stones are joined by pegs of iron or bronze, or mortice and tenon joints. Ceilings inside the *mandapas* are made up of corbelled domes, looking similar to those of the Jain temples of Rajasthan and Gujarat; in the Hoysala style they are only visible from inside.

Vaishnavi Lodging, Harsha Mahal Rd (☎67413). Hassan's best budget lodge, with big clean rooms and veg restaurant. Reservations essential. Turn left out of the bus stand, right onto Church Rd and it's on the corner of the first left turn. *Harsha Mahal* next door (☎68533; ③) is an OK fall-back. ②.

Eating

Most of the **hotels** listed above have commendable restaurants, or you can take your pick from the string of cheap snack bars and *thali* joints outside the bus stand.

Harsha Mahal, below *Harsha Mahal* lodge, Harsha Mahal Rd. No-nonsense veg canteen that serves freshly cooked *idly* and *dosa* breakfasts from 7.30am.

Hotel GRR, opposite the bus stand. Traditional, tasty and filling "mini-meals" served on plantain leaves, with a wide choice of non-veg dishes and some ice creams.

New Mangola, next to *Amblee Palika Hotel*, Race Course Rd. A posher-than-average first-floor "meals" restaurant: low light and Carnatic background music set the tone. No smoking.

New Siddarth, around the corner (north) from *Hotel GRR* and bus stand, on first floor. The most popular inexpensive restaurant in Hassan, offering a great selection of North Indian dishes, including delicious butter *paneer masala*, veg *khurma* and spicy *malai kofta*, along with noodles, *raithas* and milk shakes. Ask for a window seat.

GETTING FROM HASSAN TO BELUR AND SRAVANABELGOLA

Unless you're on a tour from Mysore or Bangalore, the only way to see Sravanabelgola, Belur and Halebid in one day is **by car**, which some visitors share; most of the hotels can fix this up (at least Rs800). Travelling **by bus**, you'll need at least two days. Belur and Halebid can be comfortably covered in one day; it's best to take the first (8am) of fifteen daily buses to Halebid (1hr) and move on to Belur (30min), from where services back to Hassan during the evening are more frequent (6.30am–6.15pm; 1hr 10min). **Sravanabelgola**, however, is in the opposite direction, and not served by direct buses; you have to head to **Channarayapatna** (from 6.30am; 1hr) on the main Bangalore highway and pick up one of the regular buses (30min) from there. If you want to get to Sravanabelgola in time to visit the site and move on the same day (to Mysore or Bangalore), aim to catch one of the private luxury buses to Bangalore that leave from the road just below the *Vaishnavi Lodge* before dawn (5.30–6am); they all stop briefly in Channarayapatna. Bear in mind, too, that there are places to stay in both Belur and Halebid; arrive in Hassan early enough, and you can travel on to the temple towns before nightfall, although you should definitely phone ahead to check rooms are available.

Halebid

Now little more than a scruffy hamlet of brick houses and *chai* stalls, **HALEBID**, 32km northwest of Hassan, was once the capital of the powerful Hoysala dynasty, who held sway over south Karnataka from the eleventh until the early fourteenth centuries. Once known as **Dora Samudra**, the city's name was changed to *Hale-bidu*, or "Old City", in 1311 when Delhi Sultanate forces under the command of Ala-ud-Din-Khalji swept through and reduced it to rubble. Despite the sacking, several large Hoysala temples (see opposite) survive, two of which, the Hoysaleshvara and Kedareshvara, are superb, covered in exquisite carvings. A small **archeological museum** (daily except Fri 10am–5pm) next to the Hoysaleshvara temple houses a collection of Hoysala art and other finds from the area.

The Hoysaleshvara temple

The **Hoysaleshvara** temple was started in 1141, and after some forty years of work remained incomplete; this possibly accounts for the absence here of the type of towers that feature at Somnathpur, for example. It is no longer known which deities were originally worshipped, though the double shrine is thought to have been devoted at one time to Shiva and his consort. In any event, both shrines contain *shivalinga* and are adjoined by two linked, partly enclosed *mandapa* hallways in which stand Nandi bulls.

Like other Hoysala temples, the whole is raised on a high plinth (*jagati*) which follows the star-shaped plan and provides an upper ambulatory; the *mandapas* are approached by flights of steps flanked by small free-standing, towered shrines. Inside, the lower portions of the black polished stone pillars were lathe-turned, though the upper levels appear to have been hand-carved to reproduce the effect of turning.

Hoysaleshvara also features many Vaishnavite images. The **sculptures**, which have a fluid quality lacking in the earlier work at Belur, include Brahma aboard his goose vehicle Hamsa, Krishna holding up Mount Govardhana, another where he plays the flute, and Vishnu (Trivikrama) bestriding the world in three steps. One of the most remarkable images is of the demon king **Ravana** shaking Shiva's mountain abode, Mount Kailasa, populated by numerous animals and figures with Shiva and Parvati seated atop. Secular themes, among them dancers and musicians, occupy the same register as the gods, and you'll come across the odd erotic tableau featuring voluptuous, heavily bejewelled maidens. A narrative frieze, on the sixth register from the bottom, follows the length of the Nandi *mandapas* and illustrates scenes from the *Bhagavata* and Vishnu *Puranas*, *Mahabharata* and *Ramayana*.

The Kedareshvara temple

About 600m south of the Hoysaleshvara, a group of Jain *bastis* (temples) stand virtually unadorned; the only sculptural decoration consists of ceiling friezes inside the *mandapas* and elephants at the entrance steps, where there's an impressive donatory plaque. The *chowkidar* will demonstrate various tricks made possible by the carved pillars' highly polished surfaces; some are so finely turned they sound metallic when struck.

To the east, there's a smaller Shiva temple, **Kedareshvara** (1217–21), also built on a stellate plan. Unfortunately, due to instability, it's not possible to get inside. Many fine images decorate the exterior, including an unusual stone Krishna dancing on the serpent demon Kaliya – more commonly seen in bronze and painting.

Practicalities

Frequent **buses** run between Halebid (the last at 8.45pm) and Hassan, and to Belur. The private mini-buses that work from the crossroads outside the Hoysaleshvara temple take a lot longer and only leave when crammed to bursting.

The monuments lie within easy walking distance of each other, but if you fancy exploring the surrounding countryside, rent a **bicycle** from the stalls by the bus stand (Rs2 per hour); the road running south past the temples leads through some beautiful scenery, with possible side-hikes to hilltop shrines. **Accommodation** in the village is limited to KSTDC's "cottages" (☎018177/3224; ②) opposite the main temple. Set in a small garden by the road, these consist of two comfortable doubles with verandahs, plus a seven-bed dorm (Rs45), both of which should be booked in advance. Plans are afoot to construct a larger complex further south; ask at any KSTDC tourist office.

After 6pm, when the *chai* stalls at the crossroads are closed, the only place to **eat** is KSTDC's grotty canteen, which only seems to serve omelettes and toast.

Belur

BELUR, 37km northwest of Hassan, on the banks of the Yagachi, was the Hoysala capital prior to Halebid, during the eleventh and twelfth centuries. Still active (open to non-Hindus), the **Chennakeshava temple**, a fine and early example of the singular Hoysala style, was built by King Vishnuvardhana in 1117 to celebrate his conversion from Jainism, victory over Chola forces at Talakad and his independence from the Chalukyas. Today, its grey-stone *gopura*, or gateway tower, soars above a small, bustling market town – a popular pilgrimage site from October to December, when busloads of Ayappan devotees stream through en route to Sabarimala (see p.1084).

Built on a star-shaped plan, Chennakeshava stands in a huge walled courtyard, surrounded by smaller shrines and columned *mandapa* hallways. Lacking any form of superstructure, terminating at the first floor, it appears to have a flat roof. If it ever had a tower, it would have disappeared by the Vijayanagar (sixteenth-century) period – above the cornice, a plain parapet, presumably added at the same time as the east entrance *gopura*, shows typically Vijayanagar Islamic influences. Both the sanctuary and *mandapa* are raised on the usual plinth (*jagati*). Double flights of steps, flanked by minor towered shrines, afford entry to the *mandapa* on three sides; this hallway was originally open, but in the 1200s, pierced stone screens, carved with geometric designs and scenes from the *Puranas*, were inserted between the lathe-turned pillars.

The quantity of **sculptural decoration**, if less mature than in later Hoysala temples, is staggering. Carvings on the plinth and lower walls, in successive and continuous bands, start at the bottom with elephants, each different, and then garlands and arches with lion heads; stylized vegetation with dancing figures, birds and animals; pearl garlands; projecting niches containing male and female figures and seated *yakshas*, or spirits; miniature pillars alternating with female figures dressing or dancing; miniature temple towers interspersed with dancers, and above them lion heads. Above the screens, a series of 42 bracket figures, added later, shows celestial nymphs hunting, playing music, dancing and beautifying themselves.

Columns inside, each unique, feature extraordinarily detailed carving, with more than a hundred deities on the central **Narasimha pillar**. The inner sanctum contains a black image of Chennakeshava, a form of Krishna who holds a conch (*shankha*, in the upper right hand), discus (*chakra*, upper left), lotus (*padma*, lower right) and mace (*gada*, lower left). He is flanked by consorts Shri Devi and Bhudevi. Within the same enclosure, the **Kappe Channigaraya temple** has some finely carved niche images and a depiction of Narasimha (Vishnu as man-lion) killing the demon Hiranyakashipu. Further west, fine sculptures in the smaller **Viranarayana** shrine include a scene from the *Mahabharata* of Bhima killing the demon Bhaga.

Practicalities

Buses from Hassan and Halebid pull into the small bus stand in the middle of town, ten-minutes' walk along the main street from the temple. If you're in a rush, rent a cycle from one of the stalls along the way. The KSTDC *Mayuri Velapuri* (☎08177/22209; ①–③), near the temple, is a good **place to stay**, with immaculately clean and airy rooms in its new block, or dingy ones in the older wing. The large dorm is rarely occupied, other than between March and May, when the hotel tends to be block-booked by pilgrims. The *Swagath Tourist Home* (no phone; ①), further up the road towards the temple, is basic and boxed in, but fine as a fall-back. For **food**, steer clear of the KSTDC *Velapuri*'s filthy canteen in favour of one of the veg *dhabas* by the temple.

Sravanabelgola

The sacred Jain site of **SRAVANABELGOLA**, 49km southwest of Hassan and 93km north of Mysore, consists of two hills and a large tank. On one of the hills, Indragiri (also known as Vindhyagiri), stands an extraordinary eighteen-metre-high monolithic statue of a naked male figure, **Gomateshvara**. Said to be the largest free-standing sculpture in India, this tenth-century colossus, visible for miles around, as well as the nearby *bastis* (Jain temples) make Sravanabelgola a key pilgrimage centre, though surprisingly few Western travellers find their way out here. Spend a night or two in the village, however, and you can climb Indragiri Hill before dawn to enjoy the serene spectacle of the sun rising over the sugar cane fields and outcrops of lumpy granite that litter the surrounding plains – an unforgettable sight.

Sravanabelgola is linked in tradition with the Mauryan emperor Chandragupta, who is said to have starved himself to death on the second hill in around 300 BC, in accordance with a Jain practice. The hill was renamed Chandragiri, marking the arrival of Jainism in southern India. At the same time, a controversy regarding the doctrines of Mahavira, the last of the 24 Jain **tirthankaras** (literally "crossing makers", who assist the aspirant to cross the "ocean of rebirth"), split Jainism into two separate branches. *Svetambara*, "white-clad" Jains, are more common in north India, while *digambara*, "sky-clad", are usually associated with the south. Truly ascetic *digambara* devotees go naked, though few do so away from sacred sites.

All the *tirthankaras* are represented as naked figures, differentiated only by their individual attributes: animals, inanimate objects (such as a conch shell), or symbols (such as the *svastika*). Each of the 24 is also attached to a particular *yaksha* (male) or *yakshi* (female) spirit; such spirits are also evident in Mahayana Buddhism, suggesting a strand of belief with extremely ancient origins. *Tirthankaras* are represented either sitting cross-legged in meditation – resembling images of the Buddha, save for their nakedness – or *kayotsarga*, "body upright", where the figure stands impassive; here Gomateshvara stands in the latter, more usual posture.

The monuments at Sravanabelgola probably date from no earlier than the tenth century, when a General Chamundaraya is said to have visited Chandragiri in search of a Mauryan statue of Gomateshvara. Failing to find it, he decided to have one made. From the top of Chandragiri he fired an arrow across to Indragiri Hill; where the arrow landed he had a new Gomateshvara sculpted from a single rock.

Indragiri Hill

Gomateshvara is approached from the tank between the two hills by around 700 steps, cut into the granite of **Indragiri Hill**, which pass numerous rock inscriptions on the way up to a walled enclosure. Shoes must be deposited at the stall to the left of the steps, and you can leave bags at the site office nearby. Anyone unable to climb the steps can be carried up by chair. Entered through a small wagon-vaulted *gopura*, the **temple** is of the type known as *betta*, which instead of the usual *garbhagriha* sanctuary consists of an open courtyard enclosing the massive sculpture. Figures and shrines of all the *yaksha* and *yakshi* spirits stand inside the crenellated wall, but the towering figure of Gomateshvara dominates. With elongated arms and exaggeratedly wide shoulders, his proportions are decidedly non-naturalistic. The sensuously smooth surface of the white granite "trap" rock is finely carved: particularly the hands, hair and serene face. As in legend, ant-hills and snakes sit at his feet and creepers appear to grow on his limbs.

GOMATESHVARA AND MAHAMASTAKABHISHEKA

Gomateshvara, or Bahubali, who was the son of the legendary King Rishabdev of Ayodhya (better known as Adinath, the first *tirthankara*), had a row with his elder brother, Bharat, over their inheritance. After a fierce fight, he lifted his brother above his head, and was about to throw him to the ground when he was gripped by remorse. Gently setting Bharat down, Gomateshvara resolved to reject the world of greed, jealousy and violence by meditating until he achieved *moksha*, release from attachment and rebirth. This he succeeded in doing, even before his father.

As a *kevalin*, Gomateshvara had achieved *kevalajnana*, "sole knowledge" acquired through solitude, austerity and meditation. While engaged in this non-activity, he stood "body upright" in a forest. So motionless was he that ants built their nest at his feet, snakes coiled happily around his ankles, and creepers began to grow up his legs.

Every twelve years, at an auspicious astrological conjunction of certain planets, the Gomateshvara statue is ritually anointed in the **Mahamastakabhisheka** ceremony (the last was in December 1993). The process lasts for several days, culminating on the final morning when 1008 *kalashas* (pots) of "liberation water", each with a coconut and mango leaves tied together by coloured thread, are arranged before the statue in a sacred diagram (*mandala*), on ground strewn with fresh paddy. A few priests climb scaffolding, erected around Gomateshvara, to bathe him in milk and *ghee*. After this first bath, prayers are offered. Then, to the accompaniment of temple musicians and the chanting of sacred texts, a thousand priests climb the scaffold to bathe the image in auspicious unguents including the water of holy rivers, sandal paste, cane juice, saffron and milk, along with flowers and jewels. The ten-hour 1993 ceremony reached a climax when a helicopter dropped 20kg of gold leaf and 200 litres of milk on the colossus, along with showers of marigolds, gem stones and multi-hued powders. The residue formed a cascade of rainbow colours down the statue's head and body, admired by *lakhs* of devotees, Jain *sadhus* and *sadhvis* (female *sadhus*), and the massed cameras of the world. A satellite township, Yatrinagar, provides accommodation for 35,000 during the festival, and eighteen surrounding villages shelter pilgrims in temporary *dharamshalas*.

Bhandari Basti and monastery (math)

The road east from the foot of the steps at Chandragiri leads to two interesting Jain buildings in town. To the right, the **Bhandari Basti** (1159), housing a shrine with images of the 24 *tirthankaras*, was built by Hullamaya, treasurer of the Hoysala Raja Narasimha. A high wall encloses the temple, forming a plain ambulatory which contains a well. Two *mandapa* hallways, where naked *digambara* Jains may sometimes be seen discoursing with devotees clad in white, lead to the shrine at the back. Pillars in the outer *mandapa* feature carvings of female musicians, while mythical beasts adorn the entrance to the inner, *navaranga*, hallway.

At the end of the street, the *math* (monastery) was the residence of Sravanabelgola's senior *acharya*, or guru. Thirty male and female monks, who also "go wandering in every direction", are attached to the *math*; normally a member of staff will be happy to show visitors around. Among the rare palm-leaf manuscripts in the library, some more than a millennia old, are works on mathematics and geography, and the *Mahapurana*, hagiographies of the *tirthankaras*. Next door, a covered walled courtyard contains a number of shrines; the entrance is elaborately decorated with embossed brass designs of *yali* mythical beasts, elephants, a two-headed eagle and an image of Parshvanath, the twenty-third *tirthankara*, here shown as Padmavati. Inside, the courtyard is edged by a high platform on three sides, on which a chair is placed for the *acharya*. A collection of tenth-century bronze *tirthankara* images is housed here, and vibrant murals detail the various lives of Parshvanath. The hills where the *tirthankaras* stood to gain *moksha* are represented in a model, somewhat resembling a jelly mould, with tacked-on footprints.

Chandragiri Hill

Leaving your shoes with the keeper at the bottom, take the rock-cut steps to the top of the smaller **Chandragiri Hill**. Miraculously, the sound of radios and rickshaws down below soon disappears. Fine views stretch south to Indragiri and, from the north on the far side, across to a river, paddy and sugarcane fields, palms and the village of **Jinanathapura**, where there's another ornate Hoysala temple, the Shantishvara *basti*.

Rather than a single large shrine, as at Indragiri, Chandragiri holds a group of *bastis* in late Chalukya Dravida style, within a walled enclosure. Caretakers, who don't speak fluent English, will take you around and open up the closed shrines. Save for pilasters and elaborate parapets, all the temples have plain exteriors. Named after its patron, the tenth-century **Chamundaraya** is the largest of the group, dedicated to Parshvanath. Inside the **Chandragupta** (twelfth century), superb carved panels in a small shrine tell the story of Chandragupta and his teacher Bhadrabahu. Traces of painted geometric designs survive and the pillars feature detailed carving. Elsewhere in the enclosure stands a 24-metre-high *manastambha*, "pillar of fame", decorated with images of spirits, *yakshis* and a *yaksha*. No fewer than 576 inscriptions dating from the sixth to the nineteenth centuries are dotted around the site, on pillars and the rock itself.

Practicalities

Sravanabelgola, along with Belur and Halebid, features on **tours** from Bangalore and Mysore (see p.1125 & p.1133). However, if you want to look around at a civilized pace, it's best to come independently. There are plenty of **dharamsalas**, managaged by the temple authorities, offering simple, scrupulously clean rooms, many with their own bathrooms and sit-outs, ranged around gardens and courtyards, and costing less than Rs100 per night. The 24-hr accommodation desk, where you will be allocated a room, is located inside the *SP Guest House*, next to the bus stand (look for the clock tower). *Hotel Raghu*, opposite the main tank, is the best of the many small local **restaurants**.

Crisscrossed by winding back roads, the idyllic (and mostly flat) countryside around Sravanabelgola is perfect cycling terrain. **Bicycles** are available for rent (Rs2 per hour) at *Saleem Cycle Mart*, on Masjid Rd, opposite the northeast corner of the tank.

Kodagu (Coorg)

The hill region of **Kodagu**, formerly known as **Coorg**, lies 100km west of Mysore in the Western Ghats, its eastern fringes merging with the Mysore Plateau. Comprising rugged mountain terrain interspersed with cardamom jungle, coffee plantations and swathes of lush rice paddy, it's one of south India's most beautiful areas. Little has changed since Dervla Murphy spent a few months here with her daughter in the 1970s (the subject of her classic travelogue, *On A Shoestring To Coorg*) and was entranced by the landscape and people, whose customs, language and appearance set them apart from their neighbours.

Today tourism is still virtually non-existent, and the few travellers that pass through rarely venture beyond **Madikeri** (Mercara), Kodagu's homely capital. However, if you

---

THE KODAVAS

Theories abound as to the origins of **the Kodavas**, or **Coorgis**, who today comprise less than one sixth of the hill region's population. Fair-skinned and with their own language and customs, they are thought to have migrated to southern India from Kurdistan, Kashmir and Rajasthan, though no one knows exactly why or when. One popular belief holds that this staunchly martial people are descended from Roman mercenaries who fled here following the collapse of the Pandyan dynasty in the eighth century; some even claim connections with Alexander the Great's invading army. Whatever their origins, the Kodavas have managed to retain a distinct identity apart from the freed plantation slaves, Moplah Muslim traders and other immigrants who have settled here. More akin to Tamil than Kannada, their language is Dravidian, yet their religious practices, based on ancestor veneration and worship of nature spirits, differ markedly from those of mainstream Hinduism.

Spiritual and social life for traditional Kodavas revolves around the **Ain Mane**, or ancestral homestead. Built on raised platforms to overlook the family land, these large, detached houses, with their beautiful carved wood doors and beaten-earth floors, generally have four wings and courtyards to accommodate various branches of the extended family, as well as shrine rooms, or **Karona Kalas**, dedicated to the clan's most important forebears. Key religious rituals and rites of passage are always conducted in the *Ain Mane*, rather than the local temple. However, you could easily travel through Kodagu without ever seeing one, as they are invariably away from roads, shrouded in thick forest.

You're more likely to come across traditional Kodava **costume**, which is donned for all auspicious occasions, such as marriages, funerals, harvest celebrations and clan get-togethers. The men wear dapper knee-length coats called *kupyas*, bound at the waist with a scarlet and gold cummerbund, and daggers (*peechekathis*) with ivory handles. Most distinctive of all, though, is the unique flat-bottomed turban; sadly, the art of tying these is dying, and most men wear ready-made versions (which you can buy in Madikeri bazaar). Kodava women's garb of long, richly coloured silk *saris*, pleated at the back and with a *pallav* draped over their shoulders, is even more stunning, enlivened by heaps of heavy gold and silver jewellery, and precious stones. Women also wear headscarves, in the fields as well as for important events, tying the corners behind the head, Kashmiri style.

Like all traditional Indian cultures, this one is on the decline, not least because young Kodavas, predominantly from well-off land-owning families, tend to be highly educated and move away from home to find work, weakening the kinship ties that have for centuries played such a central role in the life of the region.

plan to cross the Ghats between Mysore and the coast, the route through Kodagu is definitely worth considering. Facilities are relatively undeveloped, and "sights" few, but the countryside is idyllic and the climate refreshingly cool, even in summer.

Some history

Oblique references to Kodagu crop up in ancient Tamil and Sanskrit scriptures, but the first concrete evidence of the kingdom dates from the eighth century, when it prospered from the salt trade passing between the coast and the cities on the Deccan Plateau. Under the Hindu **Haleri Rajahs**, the state repulsed invasions by its more powerful neighbours, including Haider Ali and his son Tipu Sultan, the infamous Tiger of Mysore. A combination of hilly terrain, absence of roads (a deliberate policy on the part of defence-conscious Kodagu kings) and the tenacity of its highly trained army, ensured Kodagu was the only Indian kingdom never to be conquered.

Peace and prosperity prevailed through the 1700s, when the state was ruled by a line of eccentric rajahs, among them the paranoid Dodda Vira (1780–1809), who reputedly murdered most of his relatives, friends, ministers and palace guards. The monarchy was more accountable during the reign of his successor, Chickavirarajah Rajendra, known as **Vira Rajah**, but eventually lapsed into decadence and corruption. Emulating his father's brutal example, Vira Rajah imprisoned or assassinated his rivals and indulged his passion for women and spending. The king's ministers eventually appealed to the British Resident in Mysore for help to depose the despot. Plagued by threats from Vira Rajah, the colonial administration was eager for an excuse to intervene; they got it in 1834, when the unruly rajah killed his cousin's infant son. Accusing him of maladministration, the British massed troops on the border and forced a short siege, at the end of which Vira Rajah (and what remained of his family) fled into exile.

Thereafter, Kodagu became a princely state with nominal independence, which it retained until the creation of Karnataka in 1956. During the Raj, **coffee** was introduced and, despite plummeting prices on the international market, this continues to be the lynchpin of the local economy, along with pepper and cardamom.

Madikeri (Mercara)

Nestling beside a curved stretch of craggy hills, **MADIKERI (Mercara)**, capital of Kodagu, is 117m up in the Western Ghats, roughly midway between Mysore and the coastal city of Mangalore. Few foreigners travel up here, but it's a pleasant enough town, with red-tiled buildings and undulating roads that converge on a bustling bazaar.

The **Omkareshwara Shiva** temple, built in 1820, features an unusual combination of red-tiled roofs, Keralan Hindu architecture, Gothic elements and Islamic-influenced domes. The fort and palace, worked over by Tipu Sultan in 1781 and rebuilt in the nineteenth century, now serve as offices and a prison. Also worth checking out are the huge square **tombs of the Rajahs** which, with their Islamic-style gilded domes and minarets, dominate the town's skyline. **St Mark's Church** holds a small **museum** of British memorabilia, Jain, Hindu and village deity figures and weapons (daily except Mon 9am–5pm). At the western edge of town, **Rajas' Seat**, next to *Hotel Valley View*, is a belvedere, said to be the Kodagu kings' favoured place to watch the sunset.

Practicalities

You can only reach Madikeri by road, but it's a scenic three-hour **bus** ride from Mysore, 120km southeast (unless you mistakenly get on one of the few buses that goes via Siddapura, which take more than an hour longer). Regular services also connect Madikeri with **Mangalore**, 135km northwest across the Ghats. The *KSTRC* state **bus stand** is at the bottom of town, below the main bazaar; private buses from villages around the region pull into a parking lot at the end of the main street. The small local

tourist office lies five minutes' walk along the Mysore road, at the *PWD Travellers' Bungalow* (daily 10am–5.45pm).

Accommodation in Madikeri can be hard to come by, particularly in the budget range. The best upmarket option is the *Coorg International* on Convent Rd (☎08272/293390; fax 28073; ⑦–⑧), ten minutes by rickshaw from the centre. It's a large, modern hotel with comfortable Western-style rooms, a multi-cuisine restaurant, exchange facilities, and shops. Better value is the more characterful KSTDC *Hotel Mayura Valley View* (☎08272/26387; ④), well away from the main road, near Raja's Seat, and with excellent views. Rooms are huge and the restaurant serves beer. Hail a rickshaw to get there, as it's a stiff twenty-minute uphill walk from the bus stand. If it's full, try the more modern *Rajdarshan* (☎08272/26142; ⑥), just down the hill on the left. Budget accommodation is concentrated around the bazaar and bus stand. Nowhere stands out, but the *Vinayaka Lodge* (☎08272/26230; ②), left outside the *KSRTC* stand, is adequate for a night, and they offer single rates. As well as the **restaurants** in the better class hotels, there are a couple of "meals" joints on the main road: choose the one that's most crowded and you can't go wrong.

Bhagamandala and Talakaveri

A good bus excursion from Madikeri takes you to the quiet village of **Bhagamandala** (35km west), and from there to the sacred site of **Talakaveri** (9km), said to be the source of the holy Kaveri (Cauvery) River. The hill scenery is superb, and you can opt to walk part of the way on blissfully quiet country roads.

Wearing something warm, take the 6.30am bus from Madikeri's private stand to **BHAGAMANDALA**. You should arrive around 8am, with just enough time to grab a good breakfast of *parathas* and local honey at the *Laxmi Vilas* tea shop, next to where the bus to Talakaveri leaves at 8.30am. At Bhagamandala, the holy spot where the Kaveri merges with two streams, Kanike and Sujyothi, the **Bhagandeshwara temple** is a fine example of Keralan-style architecture, with tiled roofs and courtyards.

At **TALAKAVERI** the bus stops on the slopes of Brahmagiri Hill by the entrance to the sacred tank and **temple**. In October, thousands of pilgrims come here to witness a spring, thought to be the goddess Kaveri, known as Lopamudra, the local patron deity, suddenly spurting into a small well; to bathe in the tank at this time is considered especially sin-absolving. Whenever you come you're likely to find wild-haired *sadhus* and bathing pilgrims, the surrounding walls swathed in drying *dhotis* and *saris*. Two small shrines stand at the head of the tank, one containing an image of Ganesh and the other a metal *lingam* with *naga* snake canopy. Steep granite steps to the right lead up to the peak of **Brahmagiri Hill**, which affords superb 360° views over Kodagu.

Mangalore

Many visitors only come to **MANGALORE** on their way somewhere else. As well as being fairly close to Madikeri and the Kodagu (Coorg) hill region, it's also a stopping-off point between Goa and Kerala, and is the nearest coastal town to the Hoysala and Jain monuments near Hassan, 172km east.

Mangalore was one of the most famous ports of south India. It was already famous overseas in the sixth century, as a major source of pepper, and the fourteenth-century Muslim writer Ibn Batuta noted its trade in pepper and ginger and the presence of merchants from Persia and the Yemen. In the mid-1400s, the Persian ambassador Abdu'r-Razzaq saw Mangalore as the "frontier town" of the Vijayanagar empire (see p.1165) – which was why the Portuguese captured it in 1529. In Haider Ali's time, during the eighteenth century, the city became a shipbuilding centre. Nowadays, the modern port, 10km north of the city proper, is principally known for the processing and export of cof-

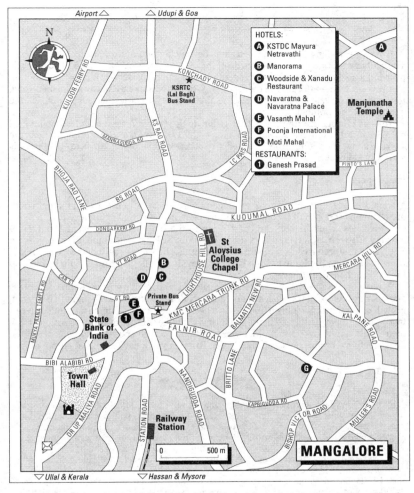

fee and cocoa (much of which comes from Kodagu), and cashew nuts from Kerala, Karnataka as well as granite. It is also a centre for the production of *bidi* cigarettes.

Arrival and information

Mangalore's busy *KSRTC* **bus stand** (known locally as the "Lal Bagh" bus stand) is 2km north of the town centre at the bottom of Kadri Hill. From here, frequent services run south to Madikeri and Kerala and north to Udupi; daily longer hauls include Goa, Mysore, Bangalore and Hassan. **Bajpe airport**, 22km north of the city (bus #47A), is served by *Indian Airlines* to Bombay and Bangalore. The airline office is at the *Moti Mahal Hotel*, Falnir Rd (☎44669).

> The telephone **area code** for Mangalore is ☎0824.

If you're travelling to Kerala, the train is far quicker and more relaxing than the bus. The **railway station**, on the south side of the city centre, sees daily services to cities all over India, including Delhi, Agra, Hyderabad, Bangalore, Madras, Thiruvananthapuram and Hassan (except during the monsoons). When the Konkan Railway is finished (optimistically set for late 1997), you'll also be able to take "super-fast express" trains all the way to Goa and Bombay.

You can **change money** at *TT Travels*, inside the *Poonja International* shopping mall on KS Rao Rd (Mon–Sat 9.30am–5.30pm; ☎426817); the *State Bank of India*, near the Town Hall on Hamilton Circle (Mon–Fri 10.30am–2.30pm & Sat 10.30am–12.30pm), is somewhat slower.

The City

Mangalore's strong Christian influence can be traced back to the arrival further south of St Thomas (see p.1082). Some 1400 years later, in 1526, the Portuguese founded one of the earliest churches on the coast close to the old port; the present **Most Holy Rosary Church**, however, with a dome based on St Peter's in Rome, dates only from 1910. Fine restored fresco, tempera and oil murals, the work of an Italian artist, Antonio Moscheni, adorn the Romanesque-style **St Aloysius College Chapel**, built in 1885, on Lighthouse Hill, near the centre.

At the foot of Kadri Hill, 3km north, Mangalore's tenth-century **Manjunatha temple** is an important centre of the Shaivite and Tantric **Natha-Pantha cult**. Thought to be an outgrowth of Vajrayana Buddhism, the cult is a divergent species of Hinduism, similar to certain cults in Nepal. Enshrined in the sanctuary, a number of superb **bronzes** include a 1.5-metre-high seated Lokeshvara (Matsyendranatha), made in 958 AD and considered the finest southern bronze outside Tamil Nadu. To see it you'll have to visit at *darshan* times

KAMBLA

If you're anywhere between Mangalore and Bhatkal from October to April and come across a crowd gathering around a water-logged paddy field, pull over and spend a day at the races – Karnatakan style. Few Westerners ever experience it, but the unique and spectacular rural sport of **Kambla**, or **bull racing**, played in the southernmost district of coastal Karnataka (known as Dakshina Kannada), is well worth seeking out.

Two contestants, usually local rice farmers, take part in each race, riding on a wooden plough-board tethered to a pair of prize bullocks. The object is to reach the opposite end of the field first, but points are also awarded for style, and riders gain extra marks – and roars of approval from the crowd – if the muddy spray kicked up from the plough board splashes the special white banners, or *thoranam*, strung across the course at a height of 6 to 8m.

Generally, race days are organized by wealthy landowners on fields specially set aside for the purpose. Villagers flock in from all over the region, as much for the fair, or *shendi*, as the races themselves: men huddle in groups to watch cock fights (*korikatta*), women haggle with bangle sellers, and the kids roam around sucking sticky *kathambdi goolay*, the local bon-bons. It is considered highly prestigious to be able to throw such a party, especially if your bulls win any events or, better still, come away as champions. Known as *yeru* in Kannada, racing bulls are thoroughbreds who rarely, if ever, are put to work. Pampered by their doting owners, they are massaged, oiled and blessed by priests before big events, during which large sums of money are often won and lost.

(6.30–9am & 6.30–9pm). Manjunatha's square and towered sanctuary, containing an unusual *lingam*, is surrounded by two tiled and gabled colonnades with louvred windows, showing strong affinity with the temple complexes further south in Kerala. Nine water tanks adjoin the temple. Opposite the east entrance, steps lead via a laterite path to a curious group of minor shrines. Beyond this complex stands the **Shri Yogishwar Math**, a hermitage of Tantric *sadhus* set round two courtyards, one of which contains shrines to Kala Bhairava (a form of Dakshinamurti, the southern aspect of Shiva and deity of death), Durga and god of fire, Agni. Nearby, cut into the side of the hill, a tiny unadorned cave is credited with being one of the "night halts" for the Pandava brothers from the *Mahabharata*.

If you're looking to escape the city for a few hours, head out to the village of **ULLAL**, 10km south, whose long sandy **beach**, backed by whispy fir trees, stretches for miles in both directions. It's a deservedly popular place for a stroll, particularly in the evening when families and courting couples come out to watch the sunset, but a strong undertow makes swimming difficult, and at times unsafe. You're better off checking in to the excellent *Summer Sands Beach Resort* (see below), immediately behind the beach, and using their pool. Local **buses** (#44A) run to Ullal from the junction at the south end of KS Rao Rd. As you cross the river en route, look out for the brick chimney stacks clustered on the banks at the mouth of the estuary. Using quality clay shipped downriver from the hills, these factories manufacture the famous terracotta red **Mangalorean roof tiles**, which you see all over southern India.

Accommodation and eating

Mangalore's **accommodation** standards seem to be forever improving; it even has a modern 5-star. The main area for hotels, **KS Rao Rd**, runs south from the bus stand, but the best budget option, the KSTDC *Mayura Netravathi*, lies on the north side of town, 1km from the main bus stand. With a little more to spend, you can also stay out of town by the beach in **Ullal**.

The best **places to eat** are in the bigger hotels. If you're on a tighter budget, try one of the inexpensive café-restaurants opposite the bus stand, or the excellent canteen inside the bus stand itself, which serves great *dosas* and other south Indian snacks. Also recommended for delicious, freshly cooked and inexpensive "meals" is the *Ganesh Prasad*, down the lane alongside of the *Poonja International*. For something a little more sophisticated, head for the a/c *Xanadu*, connected to the *Woodside Hotel*, also on KS Rao Rd, which offers classy non-veg cuisine. It's too dingy for lunch, but fine for dinner, when its kitsch fish tanks and resident duck colony are illuminated.

KSTDC Mayura Netravathi, 1km north of the bus stand, Lighthouse Hill Rd (☎411192). Established government hotel, the best of the budget bunch, with large, good-value in-suite rooms (most with twin beds and mozzie nets), although some are a little on the grubby side. None of the rickshaw-*wallahs* know where it is, so ask for the "Circuit House", next door. ②.

Manorama, KS Rao Rd (☎440306 or 7). A 65-room concrete block with spartan, large and very clean rooms (some a/c). Good value; the best fall-back if the *Mayura Netravathi* is full. ③–⑤.

Moti Mahal, Falnir Rd (☎441411). Large hotel (some a/c) with 24-hr room service and coffee shop, bar, pool, shops, exchange and travel desk. *Mangala* non-veg and *Madhuvan* veg restaurants serve Indian, Chinese and Western food. ⑤–⑥.

Navaratna, KS Rao Rd (☎440520). Clean, dependable, good-value hotel, slap in the centre. Some deluxe rooms with TV, 24-hr room service and laundry. *Navaratna Palace* (☎441104) nearby is more upmarket, with two good a/c restaurants: *Heera Panna* and *Palimar* (pure veg). Both ④–⑤.

Summer Sands Beach Resort, Chota Mangalore, Ullal, 10km south of the city (☎467690 or 1). Spacious rooms and cottages (some a/c) near the beach, originally built as a campus for ex-pats, with pool, and bar-restaurant serving local specialities, Indian and Chinese food. Foreign exchange for guests. Highly recommended. Take bus #44A from town. ⑤–⑥.

Vasanth Mahal, KS Rao Rd (☎22311). Large but run-down budget lodge, with bathrooms and few frills. The best that can be said about it is that it's handy for the railway station. ②.

Welcomgroup Manjarun, Old Port Rd, 2km from railway station (☎420420). Modern business hotel; some rooms with sea view and all a/c. Travel desk, exchange, pool, bar and 24-hr coffee shop. The pricey restaurant, *Galley*, serves Indian and Western food; *Embers* is a poolside BBQ. ⑥–⑦.

Woodside, KS Rao Rd (☎440296). Old-fashioned hotel offering a range of rooms (their economy doubles are the best deal), but "no accommodation for servants". Some a/c. ④–⑤.

MOVING ON FROM MANGALORE

Mangalore is a major crossroads for tourist traffic heading along the Konkan coast between Goa and Kerala, and between Mysore and the coast. For a **full rundown** of travel services to and from Mangalore, see "Karnataka Travel Details" on p.1120.

If you're moving on to **Goa**, you'll have to take the bus, at least until the completion of the Konkan Railway. Six services leave the *KSRTC* Lal Bagh stand daily, taking around 10hr 30min to reach Panjim. You can jump off at Chaudi (for Palolem) en route, and some buses also go via Margao (for Colva beach), but it's best to check, as most travel direct to the Goan capital. Tickets should be booked in advance (preferably the day before) at *KSRTC*'s well-organized computer booking hall (daily 7am–8pm), or from the *Kadamba* office on the main concourse. The Goa buses are also good for **Gokarn**; hop off at **Kumta** on the main highway, and catch an onward service from there. The only direct bus to Gokarn leaves Mangalore at 1.30pm.

Heading south down the coast towards **Kerala**, most travellers opt for the train. Three services leave Mangalore station every day for Thiruvananthapuram, via Kozhikode, Ernakulam/Cochin, Kottayam and Kollam. Leaving at the red-eyed time of 4.15am, the *Parsuram Express* (#6350) is the fastest of the lot.

For **Mysore**, **Bangalore**, **Hassan** and **Madikeri**, take the bus; trains do run inland, but they are far less regular, and generally slower.

North of Mangalore: coastal Karnataka

Until the completion of the Konkan Railway, transport along the **Karnatakan (Karavali) coast** is confined to the busy NH14, southern India's smoothest highway. The ten-hour bus journey between Goa and Mangalore ranks among the most scenic anywhere in the country. Crossing countless palm- and mangrove-fringed estuaries, the recently upgraded road, dubbed by the local tourist board as "The Sapphire Route", scales several spurs of the Western Ghats, which here creep to within a stone's throw of the sea, with spellbinding views over long, empty beaches and deep blue bays. Highlights are the pilgrim town of **Udupi**, site of a famous Krishna temple, and **Gokarn**, a bustling village that provides access to exquisite unexploited beaches. A couple of bumpy back roads wind inland through the mountains to **Jog Falls**, India's biggest waterfall, most often approached from the east. Infrequent buses crawl from the coast through rugged jungle scenery to this spectacular spot, but you'll enjoy the trip more by motor bike; it is possible to rent one in Goa and ride down the coast from there, stopping off at secluded beaches, falls and viewpoints en route.

Udupi

UDUPI (also spelt Udipi), on the west coast, 58km north of Mangalore, is one of south India's holiest Vaishnavite centres. The Hindu saint **Madhva** (1238–1317) was born here, and the **Krishna temple** and *mutts* (monasteries) he founded are visited by *lakhs* of pilgrims each year. The largest numbers congregate during the late winter, when the town hosts a series of spectacular **car festivals** and gigantic, bulbous-domed chariots are hauled through the streets around the temple. Even if your visit doesn't coincide with a festival, Udupi is a good place to break the journey along the Karavali coast. Thronging with *pujaris* and pilgrims, its small sacred enclave is wonderfully atmospheric, and you can take a boat from the nearby fishing village of **Malpé beach** to St **Mary's Island**, the deserted outcrop of hexagonal basalt where Vasco da Gama erected a crucifix prior to his first landfall in India.

Incidentally, Udupi also lays proud claim to being the birthplace of the nationally popular **masala dosa**; these crispy stuffed pancakes, made from fermented rice flour, were first prepared and made famous by the Udupi *brahmin* hotels.

The Krishna temple and mutts

Udupi's **Krishna temple** lies five minutes' walk east of the main street, surrounded by the eight **mutts** founded by Madhva in the thirteenth century. Legend has it that the idol enshrined within was discovered by the saint himself, after he prevented a shipwreck. The grateful captain of the vessel concerned offered Madhva his precious cargo as a reward, but the holy man asked instead for a block of ballast, which he broke open to expose a perfectly formed image of Krishna. Believed to contain the essence (*sannidhya*) of the god, this deity draws a steady stream of pilgrims, and is the focus of all but constant ritual activity. It is cared for by *archaryas*, or pontiffs, from one or other of the *mutts*. The only people allowed to touch the idol, they perform *pujas* (5.30am–8.45pm) that are open to non-Hindus. As the *acharya* approaches the shrine, the crowd divides to let him through, while *brahmin* boys fan the deity with cloths, accompanied by a cacophony of clanging bells and clouds of incense smoke.

A stone tank adjacent to the temple, known as the **Madhva Sarovara**, is the focus of a huge festival every two years (usually Jan 17/18), when a new head priest is appointed. Preparations for the **Paryaya Mahotsava** begin thirteen months in advance, and culminate with the grand entry of the new *archarya* into the town, at the head of a huge procession. Outside in the street, a window in the wall affords a view of the deity; according to legend, this is the spot where a Harijan, or "untouchable" devotee, denied entry due to his caste, was worshipping Krishna from outside when the deity turned to face him. A statue of the devotee stands opposite. Nearby, there's a magnificent gold-painted temple chariot (*rath*), wood-carved in the distinctive Karnatakan style, its onion-shaped tower decked with thousands of scraps of paper, cloth and tinsel.

At the **Regional Resources Centre for the Performing Arts**, in the MGM College, staff can tell you about local festivals and events that are well off the tourist trail; the collection includes film, video and audio archives. The pamphlet *Udupi: an Introduction*, on sale in the stalls around the sacred enclave, is another rich source of background detail on the temple and its complex rituals.

Malpé, Thottam and St Mary's Island

Udupi's weekend picnic spot, **Malpé beach**, 5km north of the centre, is disappointing, marred by a forgotten concrete block that was planned to be a government-run hotel. After wandering around the smelly fish market at the harbour you could take a local boat (Rs500) out to **St Mary's Island**, an extraordinary rockface of hexagonal basalt. Vasco da Gama is said to have placed a cross here in the 1400s, prior to his historic landing at Kozhikode in Kerala. From a distance, the sandy beach at **Thottam**, 1km north of Malpé and visible from the island, is tempting; in reality it's an open sewer.

Practicalities

Udupi's two **bus stands** are a short walk from the main street in the centre of town: the "City" stand handles private services to nearby villages, including Malpé, while the *KSRTC* stand is for long-distance government buses to and from Mangalore, Bangalore, Gokarn and Goa, and other towns along the coastal highway.

Udupi has a good choice of **places to stay**. The *Hotel Sharada International* (☎08252/22912; ③–④), 1km out of town on the highway, has a range of rooms from singles to carpeted a/c, veg and non-veg restaurants and a bar. *Kediyoor*, near the bus stand (☎08252/22381; ③–④) is much the same, but with three restaurants – the a/c *Janata* serves the town's best *thalis* – while the *Shri Ramakrishna Hotel* (☎08252/23189; ④–⑤) also has a good, but slow, non-veg restaurant and bar. All are pretty swish by Udupi standards, and take credit cards. If you're looking for somewhere cheaper, try the *Vyavahar Lodge*, on Kankads Rd (☎08252/22568; ①), between the bus stand and temple. This excellent, if bland, hotel has simple, clean rooms, some of them en-suite and looking over the temple precinct. The small restaurant serves good "meals".

Jog Falls

Hidden in a remote, thickly forested corner of the Western Ghats, **JOG FALLS**, 240km northeast of Mangalore, are the highest **waterfalls** in India. These days, they are rarely as spectacular as they were before the construction of a large dam upriver, which impedes the flow the River Sharavati over the sheer red-brown sandstone cliffs. However, the surrounding scenery is spectacular at any time, with dense scrub and jungle carpeting sparsely populated, mountainous terrain. The views of the falls from the scruffy collection of *chai* stalls on the opposite side of the gorge is also impressive, unless, that is, you come here during the monsoons, when mist and rain clouds envelop the cascades. Another reason not to come here during the wet season is that the extra water, and abundance of leeches at this time, make the excellent **hike** to the floor valley dangerous. So if you can, head up here between November and January, and bring stout footwear. The trail starts just below the bus park and winds steeply down to the water. Confident hikers also venture further downriver, clambering over boulders to other pools and hidden viewpoints, but you should keep a close eye on the water level and take along a local **guide** to point out the safest path.

Practicalities

Getting to Jog Falls by public transport is not easy. A single daily bus leaves Karwar (8hr) around mid-morning, arriving after dark and returning early the next day. From Mysore, Bangalore or Hassan, head for Sagar (30km southeast) via Shimoga, and pick up a local service from there. With a car or motorbike, you can approach the falls from the coast along one of several scenic routes through the Ghats. The easiest and best maintained of these heads inland from Bhatkal, but for a truly unforgettable experience, risk the tortuous, bumpy back route from **Kumta**, which takes you through some breathtaking landscape. There are very few villages, and no fuel stops, along the way, so stock up beforehand, and make sure your vehicle is in good shape.

Accommodation is limited, to say the least. The *PWD Inspection Bungalow* (①), on the north side of the gorge, has great views from its spacious, comfortable rooms, but is invariably full and has to be booked in advance from Shimoga. The small *Youth Hostel*, ten minutes' walk down the Shimoga road, is filthy and unfriendly. Most travellers make do with a raffia mat on the floor of one of the houses behind the *chai* stalls ranged around the square. One local family offer a room with bathroom and freshly cooked meals for Rs50 per person – the owner meets incoming buses. The only **food** available in Jog Falls are the uninspiring (eggy) snacks served up at the *chai* stalls.

Gokarn

Set behind a broad white-sand beach, with the forest-covered foothills of the Western Ghats forming a blue-green backdrop, **GOKARN**, (also spelled Gokarna), seven hours by bus north of Mangalore, is among India's most scenically situated sacred sites. Yet this compact little coastal town – a Shaivite centre for more than two millennia – remained largely "undiscovered" by Western tourists until a little under a decade ago, when it began to attract dreadlocked and didjgeridoo-toting travellers fleeing the commercialization of Goa. Now, it's firmly on the tourist map, although the Hindu pilgrims pouring through still far outnumber the foreigners that flock here in winter.

Even if you're not tempted to while away weeks on isolated beaches, Gokarn is well worth a short detour from the coastal highway. Like Udupi, it is an old-established pilgrimage place, with a markedly traditional feel: shaven-headed *brahmins* sit cross-legged on their verandahs murmuring Sanskrit verses, while Hindu pilgrims file through a bazaar crammed with religious paraphernelia to the sea for a holy dip.

Arrival and information

Both *KSRTC* and private services terminate half way down the main bazaar, within easy walking distance of Gokarn's limited accommodation. The town is well connected by direct daily **bus** to Goa (5hr), and several towns in Karnataka, including Bangalore (13hr), Hospet/Hampi (10hr) and Mysore (14hr), via Mangalore (7hr) and Udupi (6hr). You can also pick up **tempos** to the town from Kumta and Ankola on the main highway. For current bus timings, ask at the *KSRTC* counter on Car St.

The nearest place to **change money** is the *State Bank of India* in the busy market town of **Karwar**, ninety minutes north on the main highway; catch the 8.15am Panjim bus to get there. If you find yourself with a long wait for a Gokarn bus to get back again, hop on any service heading south towards Mangalore and get off at Ankola, where you can pick up a *tempo* for the last leg to the coast.

The Town

Gokarn **town**, a hotch-potch of wood-fronted houses and red terracotta roofs, is clustered around a long L-shaped bazaar, its broad main road – known as **Car Street** – running west to the town beach, a sacred site in its own right. Hindu mythology indentifies it as the place where Rudra (another name for Shiva) was re-born through the ear of Mother Earth from the underworld after a period of penance. Gokarn is also the home of one of India's most powerful *shivalinga* – the **pranalingam**, which came to rest here after being carried off by Ravana, the evil king of Lanka, from Shiva's home on Mount Kailash in the Himalaya. Sent by the gods to reclaim the sacred object, Ganesh, with the help of Vishnu, tricked Ravana into letting him look after the *lingam* while he prayed, knowing that if it touched the ground it would take root and never be moved. When Ravana returned from his meditation, he tried to pick the *lingam* up, but couldn't, because the gods had filled it with "the weight of three worlds".

The *pranalingam* resides in Gokarn to this day, enshrined in the medieval **Shri Mahabaleshwar temple**, at the far west end of the bazaar. It is regarded as so auspicious that a mere glimpse of it will absolve a hundred sins, even murder of a *brahmin*. Local Hindu lore also asserts that you can maximize the *lingam*'s purifying power by shaving your head, fasting, and taking a holy dip in the sea before *darshan*, or ritual viewing of the deity. For this reason, pilgrims traditionally begin their tour of Gokarn with a walk to the beach. They are aided and instructed by their personal *pujari* – one of the bare-chested priests you see around town, wearing sacred caste threads, and with single tufts of hair sprouting from their shaven heads – whose job it is to guide the pilgrims. Next, they visit the **Shri Mahaganpati temple**, a stone's throw east of Shri Mahabaleshwar, to propitiate the elephant-headed god Ganesh; non-Hindus are welcome to visit both shrines. En route, check out the splendid **rath**, or chariot, that stands at the end of the bazaar next to the Mahaganpati temple. During important festivals, notably Shiva's "birthday", **Shivratri** (Feb), deities are installed inside this colossal carved-wood cart and hauled by hand along the main street, accompanied by drum bands and watched by huge crowds.

The beaches

Notwithstanding Gokarn's numerous temples, shrines and tanks, most Western tourists come here for the beautiful **beaches** situated south, beyond the lumpy laterite headland that overlooks the town. The hike to them takes in some superb coastal scenery, but be sure to carry plenty of water and wear a hat.

To pick up the trail, head along the narrow alley opposite the south entrance to the Mahaganpati temple, and follow the path uphill through the woods. After twenty minutes, you drop down from a sun-baked rocky plateau to **Kootlee beach** – a wonderful kilometre-long sweep of pure white sand sheltered by a pair of steep-sided promontories. Drinks and simple food can be ordered from the palm-leaf *chai* stalls and seasonal cafés that spring up here during the winter, and some of the villagers offer very basic accommodation in huts. However, well-water is in short supply, toilets are non-existent, and you have to bring your own bedding.

It takes around forty minutes to hike from Kootlee to the next beach, scaling the headland to the south and following the steep gravel path as it zig-zags down the other side to the sea. The views along the way are stunning, especially when you first glimpse exquisite **Om beach**, so-named because its distinctive twin cresent-shaped bays resemble the auspicious Om symbol. For the past decade or so, this has been the all but exclusive preserve of a hard-core hippy fringe, many of whom spend months here wallowing in a *charas*-induced torpor. However, the arrival of a dirt road from Gokarn, and the recent acquisition of the land by developers, may well squeeze the scene out. If the concrete mixers ever do descend, it's unlikely they'll ever reach Gokarn's two most remote beaches, which lie another forty- to sixty-minute walk over the hill. Tantalizingly inaccessible and virtually devoid of fresh water, **Half-Moon** and **Paradise** beaches, reached via difficult dirt paths across a sheer hillside, are only for intrepid sun lovers happy to pack in their own supplies. If you're looking for near-total isolation, this is your best bet.

Accommodation

Gokarn has a small, but not bad, choice of **guest houses**. After staying in the village for a couple of days, however, many visitors strike out for the **beaches**, where apart from the handful of picturesque brick-and-mortar huts on the north side of Kootlee beach (invariably booked out to long-staying tourists from late-Sept through March), accommodation consists of primitive palm-leaf shacks with beaten-earth floors, scattered in the trees. If you're lucky, you might find one with a lockable wooden door and a well nearby, but don't bank on it. Many people end up sleeping rough on the sand, but the nights can be chilly, and robberies are common, so come prepared. Leave your luggage and valuables behind in Gokarn (most guest houses will store your stuff for a fee), and if you plan to spend any time on the beaches, consider investing in a cheap mattress from the bazaar – you can always sell it on when you leave.

As a last resort, you can nearly always find a bed in one of the pilgrims' hostels, or **dharamshalas**, dotted around town. With dorms, bare, cell-size rooms and basic washing facilities, these are intended mainly for Hindus, but Western tourists are welcome if there are vacancies: try the *Prasad Nilaya*, just down the lane from *Om Hotel*.

KSTDC Tourist Home, high on a hill above Gokarn (look for the sign on the left as you arrive). Large rooms, each with tiled bathroom, sit-out and garden overlooking the coast and out to sea. The staff are helpful, and serve meals to order. Good option if you have your own transport. ②.

Nimmu House (no phone), a minute's walk from the temples. Gokarn's best budget guest house, with six clean rooms (shared showers). Roof space for Rs15, and a reliable left luggage facility. ①.

Om Hotel, five minutes down the lane leading north off Car St (☎08386/46440). Conventional economy hotel pitched at middle-class Indian pilgrims, with plain, good-sized en-suite rooms and a dingy bar that serves cold beer – a rarity in Gokarn. The next best option after the *Nimmu*. ③.

Shastri's (☎08386/46220). The best of the uniformly drab and run-down guest houses lining the main street, with attached and non-attached rooms, and rock-bottom single occupancy rates. ①.

Vaibhav Nivas, off the main road, five minutes across town from the bus stop (☎08386/46289). Friendly, popular place, with very cramped rooms, mostly without bathrooms, but clean enough. You can eat here, too, and leave luggage if you're heading off to Om beach. ①.

Eating

Gokarn town offers a good choice of **places to eat**, with a crop of busy "meals" joints along Car St and the main road. Most popular, with locals and tourists, is the brightly lit *Pai Restaurant*, which dishes up fresh and tasty veg *thalis*, *masala dosas*, crisp *wadas*, teas and coffees until late. The other commendable "meals" canteen, around the corner on Car St, is also called the *Pai Hotel*; it's much smaller, but their snacks are excellent, and the milk coffee delicious. *Shree Shakti Cold Drinks*, also on Car St, serves mouthwatering fresh cheese, hygienically made to an American recipe and served with rolls, garlic and tomato; the friendly owner also makes his own peanut butter, and serves filling toasties and *lassis*. Round this off with an ice-cream, either here, or at any number of places along the road. Every café does its own version of *gad-bads*, several layers of different ice-creams mixed with chopped nuts and chewy dried fruit. A popular tourist pastime in Gokarn is discussing the relative merits of each.

Hospet

Charmless **HOSPET**, ten hours by bus east of Goa, is of little interest except as a transport hub: in particular, it is the jumping-off place for the extraordinary ruined city of Vijayanagar (Hampi), 13km northeast. If you arrive late, or want somewhere fairly comfortable to sleep, it makes sense to stay here and catch a bus or taxi out to the ruins the following morning. Otherwise, hole up in Hampi, where the setting more than compensates for the basic facilities.

Arrival and information

Hospet's **railway station**, 1500m north of the centre, is served by the overnight *Hampi Express* #6592 from Bangalore and services from Hyderabad, via Guntakal Junction. When this book went to press, the line running west to Gadag (for Badami and Bijapur), Hubli and Vasco da Gama in Goa was being upgraded and trains were suspended; things should be back to normal after late 1997. Auto-rickshaws are thin on the ground, and the only way to get into town is by cycle rickshaw (Rs20).

The **long-distance bus stand** is nearer the centre, 250m down MG (Station) Rd, which runs south from the railway station. The most frequent services are from Bangalore and Hubli, and there are daily arrivals from Mysore, Badami, Bijapur, Hassan, Gokarn, Mangalore and Goa. For a rundown see "Karnataka Travel Details" on p.1120. **Bookings** for long-distance routes can be made at the ticket office on the bus stand concourse (daily 8am–noon & 3–6pm), where there's also **left luggage**.

You can **change currency** at the *State Bank of India* (Mon–Fri 10.30am–2.30pm & Sat 10.30am–12.30pm). The *State Bank of Mysore* (same hours) on MG Rd changes travellers' cheques; or try the reception desk at the *Hotel Malligi*.

Getting to Hampi

KSTDC's daily guided **tour** only stops at three of the sites in Hampi and spends an inordinate amount of time at the far less interesting Tungabhadra Dam. Even so, it can be worth it if you're short of time. It leaves from their office at Rotary Circle (Taluk Office Circle), east of the bus station (9.30am–5.30pm; Rs70 including lunch).

Frequent **buses to Hampi** run from the bus stand between 6.30am and 7.30pm; the journey takes thirty minutes. If you arrive late, either stay in Hospet, or take a taxi or

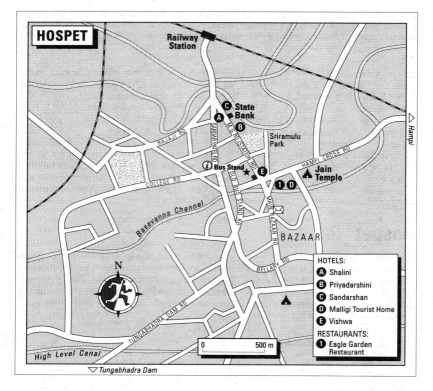

one of the rickshaws that gather outside the railway station. It is also possible to catch a bus to **Kamalpura**, at the south side of the site, and explore the ruins from there, catching a bus back to Hospet from Hampi Bazaar at the end of the day. **Bicycles** are available for rent at several stalls along the main street, but the trip to, around, and back from the site is a long one in the heat; you'd have to be made of sturdy stuff to do it on foot. Finally, some hotels in Hospet can organize for you to hook up with **trained guides** in Hampi; ask at the *Malligi* or *Priyardarshini*.

Accommodation and eating

Accommodation in Hospet, concentrated around MG Rd, ranges from budget to mid-price. By far the most popular place to stay is the *Malligi Tourist Home*, but the *Priyadarshini* is equally good value, and nearer the bus and railway stations.

There's little to do in Hospet, so you'll probably pass a fair amount of time **eating and drinking**. Many of the hotels have good dining rooms, but in the evening, the upscale though affordable *Eagle Garden*, behind the *Malligi*, is the most congenial place to hang out, serving *tandoori* and chilled beer from 7pm to 11pm (bring lots of mosquito repellent). *Shanbhog*, an excellent little Udupi restaurant next to the bus station, is a perfect pit stop before heading to Hampi, and opens early for breakfast.

Malligi Tourist Home, 6/143 Jambunatha Rd, 2min walk east of MG Rd (look for the signs) and the bus stand (☎08394/58101; fax 57038). Friendly, Western-style hotel with 116 clean, comfortable rooms (some a/c). They sell the otherwise hard-to-find journal *Homage to Hampi*, and offer foreign exchange. The al fresco *Madhu Paradise* restaurant/bar serves great veg food. ③–⑤.

Priyadarshini, MG Rd, over the road from the bus stand, towards the railway station (☎08394/58838). Rooms from rock-bottom singles to doubles with TV and a/c (some balconies). Large, and bland, but spotless and very good value. Two good restaurants: the veg *Chalukya* and, in the garden, non-veg *Manasa*, which has a bar. ②–⑤.

Sandarshan, MG Rd, between the railway station and bus stand (☎08394/58574). Budget rooms, some with bath. ②–③.

Shalini, MG Rd, across the canal on the right-hand side as you approach from the railway station (☎08394/58910). Very basic, small lodge; some rooms with bath. ①.

Vishwa, MG Rd, right opposite the bus stand (☎08394/57171). No-frills lodge, with mostly en-suite rooms. The *Shanthi* canteen serves breakfast, south Indian snacks, and unlimited veg "meals". ②.

Hampi (Vijayanagar)

> *The city of Bidjanagar [Vijayanagar] is such that the pupil of the eye has never seen a place like it, and the ear of intelligence has never been informed that there existed anything to equal it in the world. . . . The bazaars are extremely long and broad. . . . Roses are sold everywhere. These people could not live without roses, and they look upon them as quite as necessary as food. . . . Each class of men belonging to each profession has shops contiguous the one to the other; the jewellers sell publicly in the bazaars pearls, rubies, emeralds and diamonds. In this agreeable locality, as well as in the king's palace, one sees numerous running streams and canals formed of chiselled stone, polished and smooth. . . . This empire contains so great a population that it would be impossible to give an idea of it without entering into extensive details.*
>
> Abdu'r-Razzaq, the Persian ambassador, who visited Vijayanagar in 1443.

The ruined city of **Vijayanagar**, "the City of Victory" (also known as **HAMPI**, the name of a local village), spills from the south bank of the Tungabhadra River, littered among a surreal landscape of golden-brown granite boulders and leafy banana fields. According to Hindu mythology, the settlement began its days as Kishkinda, the monkey kingdom of the *Ramayana*, ruled by the monkey kings Vali and Sugriva and their ambassador, Hanuman; the weird rocks – some balanced in perilous arches, others heaped in colossal, hill-sized piles – are said to have been flung down by their armies in a show of strength.

Between the fourteenth and sixteenth centuries, this was the most powerful Hindu capital in the Deccan. Travellers such as the Portuguese chronicler Domingo Paez, who stayed for two years after 1520, were astonished by its size and wealth, telling tales of markets full of silk and precious gems, beautiful, be-jewelled courtesans, ornate palaces and joyous festivities. However, in the second half of the sixteenth century, the dazzling city was devastated by a six-month Muslim siege. Only stone, brick and stucco structures survived the ensuing sack – monolithic deities, crumbling houses and abandoned temples dominated by towering *gopuras* – as well as the sophisticated irrigation system that channelled water to huge tanks and temples.

Thanks to the Muslim onslaught, most of Hampi's monuments are in disappointingly poor shape, seemingly a lot older than their four or five hundred years. Yet the serene riverine setting and air of magic that lingers over the site, sacred for centuries before a city was founded here, make it one of India's most extraordinary locations. Even so, mainstream tourism has thus far made little impact: along with streams of Hindu pilgrims, and tatty-haired *sadhus* who hole up in the more isolated rock crevices and shrines, most visitors are budget travellers straight from Goa. Many find it difficult to leave, and spend weeks chilling out in cafés, wandering to whitewashed hilltop temples and gazing at the spectacular sunsets.

The **best time to come** to Hampi, weather-wise, is from October to March, when daytime temperatures are low enough to allow long forays on foot through the ruins. From Christmas through early January, however, the site is swamped by an exodus of travellers from Goa that has been increasing dramatically over the past few years; there have even been Anjuna-style full-moon parties, complete with techno sound systems and bus-loads of Israeli ravers. The influx also attracts its share of dodgy characters, and crime has become a problem in the village at this time; so if you want to enjoy Hampi at its best, come outside peak season.

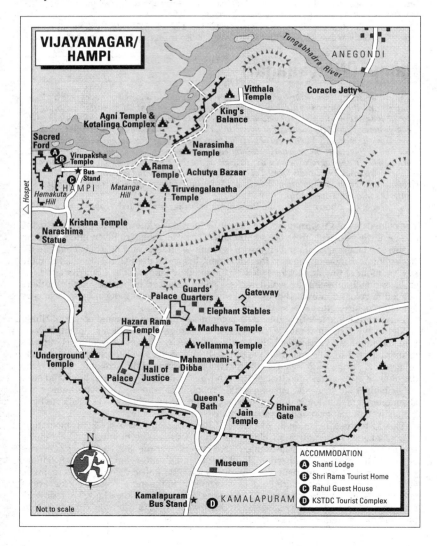

VIJAYANAGAR/ HAMPI

ANEGONDI

Tungabhadra River

Vitthala Temple

King's Balance

Coracle Jetty

Agni Temple & Kotalinga Complex

Sacred Ford

Narasimha Temple

Virupaksha Temple

Bus Stand

Rama Temple

Achutya Bazaar

HAMPI

Matanga Hill

Tiruvengalanatha Temple

Hemakuta Hill

Krishna Temple

Narashima Statue

Guards' Quarters

Gateway

Palace

Elephant Stables

Hazara Rama Temple

Madhava Temple

Yellamma Temple

'Underground' Temple

Palace

Hall of Justice

Mahanavami-Dibba

Queen's Bath

Jain Temple

Bhima's Gate

N

Museum

Kamalapuram Bus Stand

KAMALAPURAM

ACCOMMODATION
A Shanti Lodge
B Shri Rama Tourist Home
C Rahul Guest House
D KSTDC Tourist Complex

Not to scale

POLICE, THIEVES AND MOSQUITOES

Hampi is generally a safe site to wander around, but a spate of armed attacks on tourists over the past three or four years means that you ought to think twice before venturing on your own to a number of known trouble spots. Foremost among these is **Matanga Hill**, to the right of Hampi Bazaar as you face away from the Virupaksha temple, dubbed by local guides as "sunrise point" because it looks east. Muggers have been jumping Westerners on their way to the temple before dawn here, escaping with their cameras and money into the rocks. If this has happened recently, the police will prevent you from walking the path up to the temple, but even at other times it's advisable to go in a group, and to leave valuables behind.

The other hassle to watch out for in Hampi is the **police** themselves, who are not averse to squeezing the odd backhander from tourists. You'll see *chillums* smoked in the cafés, but possession of hashish (*charas*) is a serious offence in Karnataka, liable to result in a huge bribe, or worse. There have also been reports of local cops arresting, and extracting *baksheesh* from, Western men who walk around shirtless. Another reason to stay fully dressed in Hampi, particularly in the evenings, is that it is a prime **malaria** zone. Sleep under a mosquito net if you have one, and smother yourself in insect repellent well before sunset.

A little history

This was an area of minor political importance under the Chalukyas; the rise of the **Vijayanagar empire** seems to have been a direct response, in the first half of the fourteenth century, to the expansionist aims of Muslims from the north, most notably Malik Kafur and Muhammad-bin-Tughluq. Two Hindu brothers from Andhra Pradesh, Harihara and Bukka, who had been employed as treasury officers in Kampila, 19km east of Hampi, were captured by the Tughluqs and taken to Delhi, where they supposedly converted to Islam. Assuming them to be suitably tamed, the Delhi Sultan despatched them to quell civil disorder in Kampila, which they duly did, only to abandon both Islam and allegiance to Delhi shortly afterwards, preferring to establish their own independent Hindu kingdom. Within a few years they controlled vast tracts of land from coast to coast. In 1343 their new capital, Vijayanagar, was founded on the southern banks of the River Tungabhadra, a location long considered sacred by Hindus. The city's most glorious period was under the reign of **Krishna Deva Raya** (1509–29), when it enjoyed a near monopoly on the lucrative trade in Arabian horses and Indian spices passing through the coastal ports.

Thanks to its natural features and massive fortifications, Vijayanagar was virtually impregnable. In 1565, however, following his interference in the affairs of local Muslim Sultanates, the regent Rama Raya was drawn into a battle with a confederacy of Muslim forces, 100km away to the north, which left the city undefended. At first, fortune appeared to be on the side of the Hindu forces, but there were as many as 10,000 Muslims in their number, and loyalties may well have been divided. When two Vijayanagar Muslim generals suddenly deserted, the army fell into disarray. Defeat came swiftly; although members of his family fled with untold hoards of gold and jewels, Rama Raya was captured and suffered a grisly death at the hands of the Sultan of Ahmadnagar. Vijayanagar then fell victim to a series of destructive raids, and its days of splendour were brought to an abrupt end.

The site

Although spread over 26 square kilometres, the ruins of Vijayanagar are mostly concentrated in two distinct groups: the first lies in and around **Hampi Bazaar** and the nearby riverside area, encompassing the city's most sacred enclave of temples and *ghats*; the second centres on the **"royal enclosure"** – 3km south of the river, just northwest of **Kamalpuram** village – which holds the remains of palaces, pavillions, elephant stables, guard houses and temples. Between the two stretches a long boulder-choked hill and swathe of banana plantations, fed by ancient irrigation canals.

Frequent buses run from Hospet to Hampi Bazaar and Kamalpuram, and you can start your tour from either; most visitors prefer to set out on foot or bicycle from the former. After a look around the soaring **Virupaksha temple**, work your way east along the main street and river bank to the beautiful **Vitthala temple**, and then back via the **Achyutaraya** complex at the foot of Matanga Hill. From here, a dirt path leads south to the royal enclosure, but it's easier to return to the bazaar and pick up the tarred road, calling in at **Hemakuta Hill**, a group of pre-Vijayanagar temples, en route.

On KSTDC's whistlestop **guided tour** (see p.1161), it's possible to see most of the highlights in a day. If you can, however, set aside at least two or three days to explore the site and its environs, crossing the river by **coracle** to **Anegondi** village, with a couple of side hikes to hilltop view points: the west side of Hemakuta Hill, overlooking Hampi Bazaar, is best for sunsets, while **Matanga Hill**, though plagued by thieves in recent years, offers what has to be one of the world's most exotic sunrise vistas.

Arrival and information
Buses from Hospet terminate halfway along the main street in Hampi Bazaar, a little east of the Virupaksha temple. On the opposite side of the street, the **tourist information counter** might be able to put you in touch with a guide, but not much else; if you're coming from Hospet, you'd do best to organize a guide from there (see p.1162). Rented **bikes**, available in the bazaar for Rs5 per hour, are only really of use if you're planning to explore Anegondi across the river; most paths around Vijayanagar are too rough to cycle. The only place in Hampi with a licence to **change money** (including travellers' cheques) is the *Swambhu Restaurant* opposite *Shanti Lodge*. However, their rates are poor, and most visitors use the *Mallingi Hotel*'s facility in Hospet.

FESTIVALS AT VIJAYANAGAR

Vijayanagar's main **festivals** include, at the **Virupaksha temple**, a Car Festival with street processions each February, and in December the marriage ceremony of the deities, which is accompanied by drummers and dances. An annual music festival, Purandaradas Aradhana (Jan/Feb), takes place in the **Vitthala temple**, to celebrate the birth anniversary of the poet-composer Purandaradasa. Concerts of Carnatic (south Indian) classical music take place over three days in the temple's *mandapa*.

Hampi Bazaar, the Virupaksha temple and riverside path
Lining Hampi's long, straight main street, **Hampi Bazaar**, which runs east from the eastern entrance of the Virupaksha temple, you can still make out the remains of Vijayanagar's ruined, columned bazaar, partly inhabited by today's lively market. Landless labourers live in many of the crumbling 500-year-old buildings.

Dedicated to a local form of Shiva known as Virupaksha or Pampapati, the functioning **Virupaksha temple** (daily 8am–12.30pm & 3–6.30pm) dominates the village, drawing a steady flow of pilgrims from all over southern India. The complex consists of two courts, each entered through a towered *gopura*. The larger gateway, on the east, is approximately 56m high, each storey with pilastered walls and sculptures flanking an open window. It is topped by a single wagon-vault and *kalasha*, pot-shaped finial. In the southwest corner a water channel runs along a large columned *mandapa*.

A colonnade surrounds the inner court, usually filled with pilgrims dozing and singing religious songs; in the middle the principal temple is approached through a *mandapa* hallway whose carved columns feature rearing animals. Rare Vijayanagar-era paintings on the *mandapa* ceiling include aspects of Shiva, a procession with the sage Vidyaranya, the ten incarnations of Vishnu, and scenes from the *Mahabharata*; the style of the figures is reminiscent of local shadow puppets. Faced by a brass image of Nandi, a *shivalingam* is housed in the small sanctuary, its entrance decorated with painted *makaras*, semi-aquatic mythical animals whose bodies end with foliage instead of a tail. Blue water spouts from their mouths, while above them flicker yellow flames. Just outside the main temple's wall, immediately to the north, is a small earlier temple, thought to have been the "ancestor" of the Virupaksha.

The sacred **ford** in the river is reached from the Virupaksha's north *gopura*; you can also get there by following the lane around the temple past *Shanti Lodge*. A *mandapa* overlooks the steps that originally led to the river, now some distance away. **Coracles** ply from this part of the bank, just as they did five centuries ago, ferrying villagers to the fields and tourists to the popular *Uma-Shankar Café* on the other side. The path through the village also winds to an impressive ruined bridge, and on to the hilltop Hanuman shrine – a recommended round walk described on p.1168.

To reach the Vitthala temple, walk east from the Virupaksha, the length of Hampi Bazaar. At the end, a path on the left, staffed at regular intervals by conch-blowing *sadhus* and an assortment of other ragged mendicants, follows the river past a café and numerous shrines, including a Rama temple – home to hordes of fearless monkeys. Beyond at least four Vishnu shrines, the paved and colonnaded **Achutya Bazaar** leads due south to the **Tiruvengalanatha temple**, whose beautiful stone carvings – among them some of Hampi's famed erotica – are being restored by the *ASI*. Back on the main path again, make a short detour across the rocks leading to the river to see the little-visited waterside **Agni temple** – next to it, the Kotalinga complex consists of 108 (an auspicious number) tiny *linga*, carved on a flat rock. As you approach the Vitthala temple, to the south is an archway known as the **King's Balance**, where the rajas were weighed against gold, silver and jewels to be distributed to the city's priests.

Vitthala temple

Although the area of the **Vitthala temple** does not show the same evidence of early cult worship as Virupaksha, the ruined bridge to the west probably dates from before Vijayanagar times. The bathing *ghat* may be from the Chalukya or Ganga period, but as the temple has fallen into disuse it seems that the river crossing (*tirtha*) here has not had the same sacred significance as the Virupaksha site. Now designated a World Heritage Monument by UNESCO, the Vitthala temple was built for Vishnu, who according to legend was too embarrassed by its ostentation to live there. The tower of the principal Vishnu shrine is made of brick – unusual for south India – capped with a hemispherical roof; in front is an enclosed *mandapa* with carved columns, the ceiling of which has partly collapsed. Two doorways lead to a dark passageway surrounding the sanctuary.

The open *mandapa* features slender monolithic granite **pillars**. As in so many Indian temples, guides gleefully make them "sing" different notes in a scale by tapping them. Outer columns sport characteristic Vijayanagar rearing horses, while friezes of lions, elephants and horses on the moulded basement display sculptural trickery – you can transform one beast into another simply by masking one portion of the image.

In front of the temple, to the east, a stone representation of a wooden processional **rath**, or chariot, houses an image of Garuda, Vishnu's bird vehicle. Now cemented, at one time the chariot's wheels revolved. The three *gopura* entrances, made of granite at the base with brick and stucco multi-storey towers, are now badly damaged.

Anegondi and beyond

With more time, and a sense of adventure, you can head across the Tungabhadra to **ANEGONDI**, a fortress town predating Vijayanagar and the city's fourteenth-century headquarters. The most pleasant way to go is to take a **putti**, a circular rush-basket cor-acle, from the ford 1500m east of the Vitthala temple; they also carry bicycles.

Forgotten temples and fortifications litter Anegondi village and its quiet surround-ings. The ruined **Huchchappa-matha temple**, near the river gateway, is worth a look for its black stone lathe-turned pillars and fine panels of dancers. **Aramani**, a ruined palace in the centre, stands opposite the home of the descendants of the royal family; also in the centre, the **Ranganatha temple** is still active.

A huge wooden temple chariot stands in the village square. To complete a five-kilo-metre loop back to Hampi from here (best attempted by bicycle), head left (west) along the road, winding through sugar cane fields towards the sacred **Pampla Sarovar**, sign-posted down a dirt lane to the left. The small temple above this square bathing tank, tended by a *swami* who will proudly show you photos of his pilgrimage to Mt Kailash, holds a cave containing a footprint of Vishnu.

Another worthwhile detour from the road is the hike up to the tiny whitewashed **Hanuman temple**, perched on a rocky hilltop north of the river, from where you gain superb views over Hampi. The steep climb up to it takes around half an hour. Keep fol-lowing the road west for another 3km and you'll eventually arrive at an impressive old **stone bridge** dating from Vijayanagar times. The track from the opposite bank cross-es a large island in the Tungabhadra, emerging after twenty minutes at the sacred ford and coracle jetty below the Virupaksha temple. This rewarding round walk can, of course, be completed in reverse, beginning at the sacred ford. With a bike, it takes around three hours, including the side trips outlined above; allow most of the day if you attempt it on foot, and take plenty of water.

Hemakuta Hill and around

Directly above Hampi Bazaar, **Hemakuta Hill** is dotted with pre-Vijayanagar temples that probably date from between the ninth and eleventh centuries (late Chalukya or Ganga). Three are of the *trikutachala*, "three-peaked hills" type, with three shrines fac-ing into a common centre. Aside from the architecture, the main reason to clamber up here is to admire the **views** of the ruins and surrounding countryside. Looking across miles of boulder-covered terrain and banana plantations, the sheer western edge of the hill is Hampi's number one sunset spot, attracting a crowd of blissed-out tourists most evenings, along with a couple of entrepreneurial *chai-wallahs*.

A couple of interesting monuments lie on the road leading south towards the main, southern group of ruins. The first of these, a walled **Krishna temple complex** to the west of the road, dates from 1513. Although dilapidated in parts, it features some fine carving and shrines. On the opposite side of the road, a fifty-metre-wide processional path leading east through what's now a ploughed field, with stray remnants of colon-nades straggling on each side, is all that remains of an old market place.

Hampi's most-photographed monument stands just south of the Krishna temple in its own enclosure. Depicting Vishnu in his incarnation (*avatar*) as the Man-Lion, the monolithic **Narashima** statue, with its bulging eyes and crossed legs strapped into meditation pose, is one of Vijayanagar's greatest treasures.

The southern and royal monuments

The most impressive remains of Viyayanagar, the city's **royal monuments**, lie some 3km south of Hampi Bazaar, spead over a large expanse of open ground. Before tack-ling the ruins proper, it's a good idea to get your bearings with a visit to the small **Archeological Museum** (daily except Fri 10am–5pm) at Kamalapuram, which can be reached by bus from Hospet or Hampi. Turn right out of the Kamalapuram bus stand, take the first turning on the right, and the museum is on the left – two minutes' walk. Among the sculpture, weapons, palm-leaf manuscripts and painting from Vijayanagar and Anegondi, the highlight is a superb scale-model of the city, giving an excellent bird's-eye view of the entire site.

To walk into the city from the museum, go back to the main road and take the nearby turning marked "Hampi 4km". After 200m or so you reach the partly ruined massive **inner city wall**, made from granite slabs, which runs 32km around the city, in places as high as 10m. The outer wall was almost twice as long. At one time, there were said to have been seven city walls; coupled with areas of impenetrable forest and the river to the north, they made the city virtually impregnable.

Just beyond the wall, the **citadel area** was once enclosed by another wall and gates of which only traces remain. To the east, the small *ganigitti* ("oil-woman's") fourteenth-century **Jain temple** features a simple stepped pyramidal tower of undecorated horizontal slabs. Beyond it is **Bhima's Gate**, once one of the principal entrances to the city, named after the Titan-like Pandava prince and hero of the *Mahabharata*. Like many of the gates, it is "bent", a form of defence that meant anyone trying to get in had to make two 90° turns. Bas-reliefs depict such episodes as Bhima avenging the attempted rape of his wife, Draupadi, by killing the general Kichaka. Draupadi vowed she would not dress her hair until Kichaka was dead; one panel shows her tying up her locks, the vow fulfilled.

Back on the path, to the west, the plain facade of the fifteen-metre-square **Queen's Bath** belies its glorious interior, open to the sky and surrounded by corridors with 24 different domes. Eight projecting balconies overlook where once was water; traces of Islamic-influenced stucco decoration survive. Women from the royal household would bathe here and umbrellas were placed in shafts in the tank floor to protect them from the sun. The water supply channel can be seen outside.

Continuing northwest brings you to **Mahanavami-Dibba** or "House of Victory", built to commemorate a successful campaign in Orissa. A twelve-metre pyramidal structure with a square base, it is said to have been where the king gave and received honours and gifts. From here he watched the magnificent parades, music and dance performances, martial art displays, elephant fights and animal sacrifices that made celebration of the ten-day Dussehra festival famed throughout the land (the tradition of spectacular Dussehra festivals is continued at Mysore; see p.1135). Carved reliefs of dancers, elephant fights, animals and figures decorate the sides of the platform. Two huge monolithic doors on the ground nearby may have once been part of a building atop the platform, of which no signs remain. To the west, another platform – the largest at Vijayanagar – is thought to be the basement of the **King's Audience Hall**. Stone bases of a hundred pillars remain, in an arrangement that has caused speculation as to how the building could have been used; there are no passageways or open areas.

The two-storey **Lotus Mahal**, a little further north and part of the **zenana enclosure**, or women's quarters, was designed for the pleasure of Krishna Deva Raya's queen: a place where she could relax, particularly in summer. Displaying a strong Indo-Islamic influence, the pavilion is open on the ground floor, whereas the upper level (no longer accessible by stairs) contains windows and balcony seats. A moat surrounding the building is thought to have provided water-cooled air via tubes.

Beyond the Lotus Mahal, the **Elephant Stables**, a series of high-ceilinged, domed chambers, entered through arches, are the most substantial surviving secular buildings at Vijayanagar – a reflection of the high status accorded to elephants, both ceremonial and in battle. An upper level, with a pillared hall, capped with a tower at the centre, may have been used by the musicians who accompanied the royal elephant processions. Tender coconuts are usually for sale under the shade of a nearby tree. East of here, recent archeological excavations have revealed what are thought to have been the foundations of a series of Vijayanagar administration offices, which until 1990 had remained buried under earth deposited by the wind.

Walking west of the Lotus Mahal, you pass two temples before reaching the road to Hemakuta Hill. The rectangular enclosure wall of the small **Hazara Rama** ("One thousand Ramas") temple, thought to have been the private palace temple, features a series of medallion figures and bands of detailed friezes showing scenes from the *Ramayana*. The inner of two *mandapas* contains four finely carved, polished, black columns. Many of the ruins here are said to have been part of the Hazara Rama Bazaar, which ran northeast from the temple. Much of the so-called **Underground Temple**, or Prasanna Virupaksha, lies below ground level and spends part of the year filled with rainwater. Turning north (right) onto the road that runs west of the Underground Temple will take you back to Hampi Bazaar, via Hemakuta Hill.

Accommodation

If you're happy to make do with basic amenities, Hampi is a far more enjoyable place to stay than Hospet, with a couple of congenial **guest houses** and plenty of cafés to hang out in after a long day in the heat. Staying in the village also means you can be up and out early enough to catch the sunrise over the ruins – a mesmerizing spectacle.

Deservedly the most popular place to stay is *Shanti Lodge* (☎08394/51368; ①), just north of the Virupaksha temple (follow the lane around the side of the temple enclosure; the lodge is 30m further on the right). Run by atheist yoga-teacher Mr Shivanand and his two sons, it comprises a dozen or so twin-bedded cells ranged on two storeys around a leafy inner courtyard, it's basic (showers and toilets are shared), but spotless, and all rooms have fans and windows. Roof space is also available if the lodge is fully booked. After *Shanti*, the next best is the spartan *Rahul Guest House* (no phone; ①), on the opposite side of the bazaar, with rudimentary washing and toilet facilites. The *Shri Rama Tourist Home*, next to the Virupaksha temple, offers rock-bottom accommodation mainly for Hindu pilgrims. The only remotely upscale place to stay within reach of the ruins is KSTDC's *Hotel Mayura Bhavaneshwari* (☎08394/5374) at Kamalapuram. It's pleasant enough, with clean en-suite rooms and a restaurant, but the village lacks the charm of Hampi Bazaar.

Eating

During the season, Hampi spawns a rash of travellers' cafés and temporary tiffin joints, as well as a number of laid-back shack bars tucked away in more secluded corners. Among the many **restaurants** in the bazaar, *Welcome* and *Krishna* are firm favourites with Western tourists, serving a predictable selection of pancakes, porridge, omelettes and veggie food. *Swambhu*, opposite *Shanti Lodge*, is another typical travellers' joint, renowned for its fresh pasta and soft cheese (steer clear of the latter if there have been lots of power cuts). A relative newcomer to Hampi's café scene is *Suresh* behind the *Shri Rama Tourist Home*, whose delicious *shak-sheeka* is served on banana leaves; it's also a good place for breakfast.

Manmasa, at the top of the bazaar past the Hospet turning, serves up a better than average selection of Indian food, prepared by an experienced Rajasthani chef (his *korma* is superb). You can also get filling *thalis* and a range of freshly cooked snacks in the *Rahul Guest House*. However, the prize for Hampi's best all-round café has to go to the *Mango Tree*, hidden away in the banana plantations beyond the coracle jetty. The food is fairly run-of-the-mill, but the relaxing riverside location is hard to beat.

You can get authentic Western-style bread and **cakes** through *Shanti Lodge*; place your order by early evening, and the cakes are delivered the following day.

Monuments of the Chalukyas

Now quiet villages, **BADAMI**, **AIHOLE** and **PATTADAKAL**, in northwest Karnataka, were once the capital cities of the **Chalukyas**, who ruled much of the Deccan between the fourth and eighth centuries. The astonishing profusion of **temples** in the area beggars belief, and it is hard to imagine the kind of society that can have made use of them all. Most visitors use Badami, which can offer a few basic lodges, as a base; Aihole boasts a single rest house, and no rooms are available at Pattadakal.

Badami and Aihole's cave temples, stylistically related to those at Ellora (see p.676), are some of the most important of their type. Among the many structural temples are some of the earliest in India, and uniquely, it is possible to see both northern (*nagari*) and southern (Dravida) architectural styles side by side. Clearly much experimentation went on, as several other temples (commonly referred to, in art historical terms, as "undifferentiated") fit into neither system. None is now thought to date from before the late sixth century, but at one time scholars got very excited when they believed the famous Lad Khan temple at Aihole, for example, to be even older.

Although some evidence of **Buddhist** activity around Badami and Aihole exists, the earliest cave and structural temples are assigned to the period of the Chalukya rise to power in the mid-sixth century, and are mostly **Hindu**, with a few Jain examples. The first important Chalukyan king was Pulakeshin I (535–66), but it was Pulakeshin II (610–42) who captured the Pallava capital of Kanchipuram in Tamil Nadu and extended the empire to include Maharashtra to the north, the Konkan coast on the west and the whole of Karnataka. Although the Pallavas subsequently, and briefly, took most of his territory, including Badami, the capital at the end of his reign, Pulakeshin's son, Vikramaditya I (655–81) later recovered it, and the Chalukyas continued to reign until the mid-eighth century. Some suggest that the incursion of the Pallavas accounts for the southern elements seen in the structural temples.

Badami

Surrounded by a yawning expanse of flat farm land, **BADAMI**, capital of the Chalukyas from 543 AD to 757 AD, extends east into a gorge between two red sandstone hills, topped by two ancient fort complexes. The south is riddled with cave temples, and on the north stand early structural temples. Beyond the village, to the east, is an artificial lake, Agastya, said to date from the fifth century.

Arrival

Badami **bus stand** – in the centre of the village on Main (Station) Rd, very near two of the village's few places to stay – sees daily services to Gadag, Hospet, Hubli, Bijapur and Kolhapur, and frequent buses to Aihole and Pattadakal. The **railway station** is 5km north, along a road lined with *neem* trees; buses, tongas and auto-rickshaws are usually available for the journey into town. Services are mostly slow passenger trains to and from places further south such as Gadag, Hospet and Hubli, and to Bijapur, and to the main-line junction of Sholapur to the north (where you can pick up express trains to and from Bombay) – but check first because of conversion work on the tracks.

Southern Fort cave temples

Badami's earliest monuments, in the Southern Fort area, are a group of sixth-century **caves** cut into the hill's red sandstone, each connected by steps leading up the hillside. About 15m up the face of the rock, **Cave 1**, a Shiva temple, is probably the earliest. Entrance is through a triple opening into a long porch raised on a plinth decorated with images of Shiva's dwarf attendants, the Ganas. Outside, to the left of the porch, a *dvarpala* door guardian stands beneath a Nandi bull. On the right is a striking 1.5m-high image of a sixteen-armed dancing Shiva. He carries a stick-zither-type *vina*, which may or may not be a *yal*, a now-extinct musical instrument, on which the earliest Indian classical music theory is thought to have been developed. In the ante-chamber, a panel on the left shows Harihara (Shiva and Vishnu combined), accompanied by consorts Lakshmi and Parvati and the gods' vehicles Nandi and Garuda. On the right

Ardhanarishvara (Shiva combined with Parvati; half male, half female) is accompanied by Nandi and the skeleton Bringi. Ceiling panels include a coiled Naga snake deity, flying couples, and Shiva and Parvati. Inside, a columned hall, divided into aisles, leads to a small, square sanctuary at the back, containing a *lingam*.

A little higher, the similar **Cave 2**, a Vishnu shrine, is approached across a courtyard with two *dvarpala* door guardians at the end. The porch contains a panel to the left of Varaha, the boar incarnation of Vishnu, and, to the right, Trivikrama, Vishnu as a dwarf *brahmin* who inflates in size to cross the earth in three steps. On the ceiling nearby, Vishnu is shown riding his bird Garuda. A central square of the ceiling features a lotus encircled by sixteen fish; other decoration includes *svastika* designs and flying couples. Traces of painting show how colourful the caves originally were.

Steps and slopes lead on upwards, past a natural cave containing a smashed Buddha image, and steps on the right in a cleft in the rock lead up to the fort. **Cave 3** (578 AD) stands beneath a thirty-metre-high perpendicular bluff. The largest of the group, with a facade measuring 21m from north to south, it is also considered the finest, for the quality of its sculptural decoration. Eleven steps lead up to the plinth decorated with dwarf *ganas*. Treatment of the pillars is extremely elaborate, featuring male and female bracket figures, lotus motifs and medallions portraying amorous couples.

To the east of the others, a Jain temple, **Cave 4**, overlooks Agastya Lake and the town. It's a much simpler shrine, dating from the sixth century. Figures, both seated and standing, of the 24 *tirthankaras*, mostly without their identifying emblems, line the walls. Here, the rock is striped.

After seeing the caves you can climb up to the fort and walk east where, hidden in the rocks, a carved panel shows Vishnu reclining on the serpent Adisesha, attended by a profusion of gods and sages. Continuing, you can skirt the gorge and descend on the east to the Bhutanatha temples at the lakeside. Before you get to them, there's another rock carving of a reclining Vishnu and his ten incarnations.

North Fort

North of Agastya Lake a number of structural temples can be reached by steps. The small **Archeological Museum** (daily except Fri 10am–5pm) nearby contains sculpture from the region. Although now dilapidated, the **Upper Shivalaya temple** is one of the earliest Chalukyan buildings. Scenes from the life of Krishna decorate the base and various images of him can be seen between pilasters on the walls. Only the sanctuary and tower of the **Lower Shivalaya** survive. Perched on a rock, the **Malegitti Shivalaya** (late seventh century) is the finest southern-style early Chalukyan temple. Its shrine is adjoined by a pillared hallway with small pierced stone and a single decor image on each side: Vishnu on the north and Shiva on the south.

Mahakuta

Another crop of seventh-century Chalukyan temples lies 5km out of Badami at **Mahakuta**. Occasional buses run to the site, but the 2–3-hr **walk** there, via an ancient paved pilgrims trail, is well worthwhile. The path starts a short way beyond the museum (before you reach the first temple complex and tank). Peeling left up the hill, it winds past a series of crumbling shrines, gateways and old water courses, and peters out into the flat plateau. The turning down to Mahakuta is easy to miss: look for a stone marker post that reads "RP", which leads you to a steep, roughly paved stairway. At the bottom, the main temple complex, ranged around a spring-fed tank and shady courtyard dominated by a huge banyan tree, centres on the whitewashed **Mahakutesvara temple**, around whose base are wrapped some fine stone friezes. Those on the south-west corner, depicting Shiva and Parvati with Ravana, the demon-king of Lanka, are particularly accomplished. More carvings adorn the entrance and ceilings of the **Mallikarjuna temple** on the opposite side of the tank, while in the clearing outside the nearby **Sangameshwar temple** stands a gigantic stone-wheeled chariot used during the annual festival in May.

Accommodation and eating

Badami has a handful **places to stay and eat**. By far the most comfortable is the *Hotel Badami Court* (☎08357/65230; ⑤–⑥), 2km west of town towards the railway station. Ranged around a garden on two storeys, its 21 en-suite rooms are plain, but spacious; they serve meals and beer, and nearly always have vacancies. Far cheaper, the KSTDC *Hotel Mayura Chalukya* (☎08357/3246; ③), at the south side of town on Ramdurg Rd, has ten basic rooms with decrepit plumbing and peeling plaster, but the gardens are pleasant and the staff helpful, and there's a restaurant. The only other options are the grungy budget lodges opposite the bus stand; the *Satkar* (☎08357/3217; ①–②) is best, followed by the *Shri Laxmi Vilas* (☎08357/3277 or 3299; ①–②), which has a good restaurant. You may be able to talk the *chowkidar* of the spartan but clean *PWD Inspection Bungalow* (①) into letting you have one of his four double rooms for a night, but these should in theory be booked ahead through the Assistant Engineer, Badami.

Aihole

No fewer than 125 temples, dating from the Chalukyan and the later Rashtrakuta periods (sixth–twelfth centuries), are found in the tiny village of **AIHOLE** (Aivalli), near the banks of the River Malaprabha. Lying in clusters within the village, in surrounding fields and on rocky outcrops, many of the temples are remarkably well-preserved, despite being used as dwellings and cattle sheds. Reflecting both its geographical position and spirit of architectural experimentation, Aihole boasts northern (*nagari*) and southern (Dravida) temples, as well as variants that failed to survive subsequent stylistic developments.

Two of the temples are **rock-cut caves** dating from the sixth century. The Hindu **Ravanaphadigudi**, northeast of the centre, a Shiva shrine with a triple entrance, contains fine sculptures of Mahishasuramardini (see p.985), a ten-armed Nateshan (the precursor of Shiva Nataraja) dancing with Parvati, Ganesh and the Sapta Matrikas ("seven mothers"). A central lotus design surrounded by mythical beasts, figures and foliate decoration adorn the ceiling. Near the entrance is Gangadhara (Shiva with the River Ganga in his hair) accompanied by Parvati and the skeleton Bringi. A two-storey cave, plain save for decoration at the entrances and a panel image of Buddha in its upper verandah, can be found partway up the hill to the southeast, overlooking the village. At the top of that hill, the Jain **Meguti** temple, which may never have been completed, bears an inscription on an outer wall dating it to 634 AD. The porch, *mandapa* hallway and upper storey above the sanctuary, which contains a seated Jain image, are later additions. You can climb up to the first floor for fine views of Aihole and surrounding country.

The **Durga temple** (*c.* late seventh–early eighth centuries), one of the most unusual, elaborate and large in Aihole, stands close to others on open ground, near the centre of the village. It derives its name not from the goddess Durga but from the Kannada *durgadagudi*, meaning "temple near the fort". Its apsidal-ended sanctuary shows influence from earlier Buddhist *chaitya* halls; another example of this curved feature, rare in Hindu monuments, can be seen in one of the *rathas* at Mamallapuram in Tamil Nadu. Here the "northern"-style tower is probably a later addition, and is incongruously square-backed. The temple is raised on a plinth featuring bands of carved decoration. A series of pillars – many featuring amorous couples – forming an open ambulatory continue from the porch around the whole building. Other sculptural highlights include the decoration on the entrance to the *mandapa* hallway and niche images on the outer walls of the now-empty semi-circular sanctum. Remains of a small and early *gopura* gateway stand to the south. Nearby, a small **Archeological Museum** (daily except Fri 10am–5pm) displays early Chalukyan sculpture and sells the booklet *Glorious Aihole*, which includes a site map and accounts of the monuments.

Further south, beyond several other temples, the **Ladh Khan** (the name of a Muslim who made it his home) is perhaps the best known of all at Aihole. Now thought to have been constructed at some point between the end of the sixth century and the eighth, it was dated at one time to the mid-fifth century, and was seen as one of the country's temple prototypes. The basic plan is square, with a large adjoining rectangular pillared porch. Inside, twelve pillars support a raised clerestory and enclose a further four pillars; at the centre stands a Nandi bull. A small sanctuary containing a *shivalingam* is next to the back wall. Both *lingam* and Nandi may have been later additions, with the original inner sanctum located at the centre.

Practicalities

Regular **buses** run to Aihole from Badami (2hr) via Pattadakal (30min). The only place to **stay and eat** (apart from a few *chai*-shops) in Aihole is the small, clean and spartan KSTDC *Tourist Rest House* (✆Aminagad 641; ①) about five minutes' walk up the main road north out of the village, next to the ASI offices. They've got a "VIP" room, two doubles with bath plus two doubles and four singles without. Simple, tasty food is available by arrangement – and by candlelight during frequent power cuts. The *Kiran Bar* on the same road, but in the village, serves beer and spirits.

Pattadakal

The village of **PATTADAKAL**, next to the River Malaprabha, served as the site of Chalukyan coronations between the seventh and eighth centuries; in fact it may only have been used for such ceremonials. Like Badami and Aihole, Pattadakal boasts fine Chalukyan architecture, with particularly large mature examples; and as at Aihole, both northern and southern styles can be seen. The main group of monuments stand together in a well-maintained compound, close to the village.

Earliest among the temples, the **Sangameshvara**, also known as **Shri Vijayeshvara** (a reference to its builder, Vijayaditya Satyashraya; 696–733), shows typical southern features, such as the parapet lined with barrel-vaulted miniature roof forms and walls divided into niches flanked by pilasters. To the south, both the **Mallikarjuna** and the enormous **Virupaksha**, side by side, are in the southern style, built by two sisters who were successively the queens of Vikramaditya II (733–46). The temples were inspired by the Pallava Kailashanatha temple at Kanchipuram in Tamil Nadu, complete with enclosure wall with shrines and small *gopura* entranceway. Along with the Kanchi temple, the Virupaksha was probably one of the largest and most elaborate in India at the time. Interior pillars are carved with scenes from the *Ramayana* and *Mahabharata*, while in the Mallikarjuna the stories are from the life of Krishna. Both temples have open Nandi *mandapa* hallways and sanctuaries housing black polished stone *linga*.

The largest northern-style temple, the **Papanatha**, further south, was probably built after the Virupaksha in the eighth century. It features two long pillared *mandapa* hallways adjoining a small sanctuary with a narrow internal ambulatory. Outside walls feature reliefs (some of which, unusually, bear the sculptors' autographs) from the *Ramayana*, including, on the south wall, Hanuman's monkey army.

About 1km south of the village, a fine **Rashtrakuta** (ninth–tenth century) **Jain temple** is fronted by a porch and two *mandapa* hallways with twin carved elephants at the entrance. Inexplicably, the sanctuary contains a *lingam*. In the first *mandapa*, on the right, a stone staircase leads up to the roof, where there's a second, empty sanctuary. The porch is lined with bench seats interspersed with eight pillars; the doorway is elaborately decorated with mythical beasts.

Pattadakal is connected by regular **buses** to Badami (90min) and Aihole (30min). Aside from a few tea shops, "cool drinks" and coconut stalls, there are no **facilities**.

Bijapur

Boasting some of the Deccan's finest Muslim monuments, **BIJAPUR** is often billed as "The Agra of the South". The comparison is partly justified: for more than three hundred years, this was the capital of a succession of powerful rulers, whose domed mausoleums, mosques, colossal civic buildings and fortifications recall a lost golden age of unrivalled prosperity and artisitic refinement. Yet there the similarities between the two cities end. A provincial market town of just 210,000 inhabitants, modern Bijapur is a world away from the urban frenzy of Agra. With the exception of the mighty **Golgumbaz**, which attracts bus-loads of day trippers, its historic sites see only a slow trickle of tourists, while the ramshackle town centre is surprisingly laid-back, dotted with peaceful green spaces and colonnaded mosque courtyards. At the same time, this is a conservative Muslim town, with a definite north Indian ambience, and women travellers in particular may find it less than relaxing at times.

Some history
Bijapur began life in the tenth century as **Vijayapura**, the Chalukyas' "City of Victory". Taken by the Vijayanagars, it passed into Muslim hands for the first time in the thirteenth century with the arrival of the Sultans of Delhi. The Bahmanis administered the area for a time, but it was only after the local rulers, the **Adil Shahis**, won independence from Bidar by expelling the Bahmani garrison and declaring this their capital that Bijapur's rise to prominence began.

Burying their differences for a brief period in the late sixteenth century, the five Muslim dynasties that issued from the breakdown of Bahmani rule – based at Galconda, Ahmednagar, Bidar and Gulbarga – formed a military alliance to defeat the Vijayanagars. The spoils of this campaign, which saw the total destruction of Vijayanagar (Hampi), funded a two-hundred-year building boom in Bijapur during which the city acquired its most impressive monuments. However, old enmities between rival Muslim sultanates on the Deccan soon resurfaced, and the Adil Shahi's royal coffers were gradually squandered on fruitless and protracted wars. By the time the British arrived on the scene in the eighteenth century, the Adil Shahis were a spent force, locked into a decline from which they and their capital never recovered.

Arrival, information and transport

State and interstate **buses** from as far afield as Bombay and Aurangabad (a full list of services appears on p.1120), pull into the *KSRTC* bus stand on the southwest edge of the town centre; ask at the enquiries desk for exact timings, as the timetables are all in Kannada. Most visitors head off to their hotel in a horse-drawn *tonga*, and there are plenty of (unmetered) auto-rickshaws. Just a stone's throw away from the Golgumbaz, outside the old city walls, the **railway station**, 3km northeast of the bus stand, is a more inspiring point of arrival. However, services have been severely disrupted over the past few years by track conversion work, and only five passenger trains per day pass through in either direction: south to Badami and Gadag, where you change for onward express services to Bangalore; and north to Sholapur, for Bombay and most points

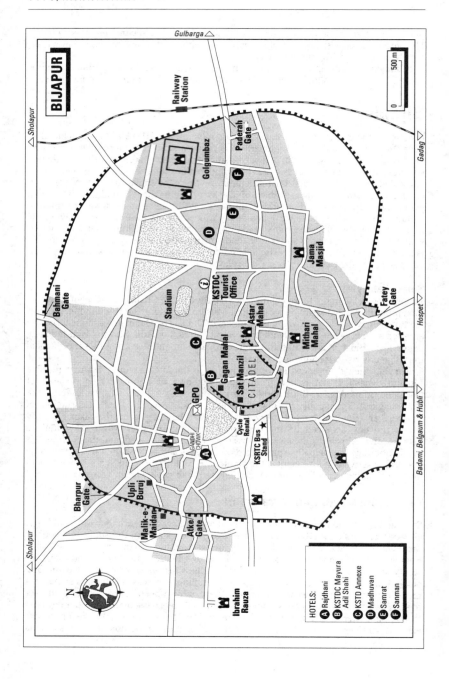

BIJAPUR

Gulbarga △

△ Sholapur

Railway Station

Paderah Gate

Golgumbaz

F

E

D

KSTDC Tourist Office

Stadium

ⓘ

Astar Mahal

Jama Masjid

Fatey Gate

Gagan Mahal

C

B

Sat Manzil

CITADEL

Mithari Mahal

Hospet ▷

GPO

Bahmani Gate

Cycle Rental

KSRTC Bus Stand ★

Badami, Belgaum & Hubli ▷

GANDHI CHOWK

A

Bharpur Gate

Upli Buruj

Malik-e-Maidan

Atke Gate

Gadag ▷

△ Sholapur

N

Ibrahim Rauza

500 m
0

HOTELS:
Ⓐ Rajdhani
Ⓑ KSTDC Mayura Adil Shahi
Ⓒ KSTD Annexe
Ⓓ Madhuvan
Ⓔ Samrat
Ⓕ Sanman

north. The only reliable source of information on train departures is the station itself, although most hotels keep a timetable in reception.

The KSTDC **tourist office**, half-way along Station Rd, has little to offer visitors. If you need to **change money** (or travellers' cheques), head for the *Canara Bank*, a short walk north up the road from the vegetable market.

Bijpaur is flat, compact, relatively uncongested, and generally easy to negotiate by **bicycle**; rickety *Heros* are available for rent from several stalls outside the bus stand for around Rs20 per day, or staff at the KSTDC *Mayura Adil Shahi* can sort you out a bike. Auto-rickshaws are a more expensive and far less satisfying way of getting around the monuments, and charge through the nose for waiting time.

> The telephone **area code** for Bijapur is ☎08352.

The town and monuments

Unlike most medieval Muslim strongholds, Bijapur lacked natural rock defences and had to be strengthened by the Adil Shahis with huge **fortified walls**. Extending some 10km around the town, these ramparts, studded with cannon emplacements (*burjes*) and watchtowers, are breached in five points by *darwazas*, or strong gateways, and several smaller postern gates (*didis*). In the middle of the town, a further hoop of crenellated battlements encircled Bijapur's **citadel**, site of the sultans' apartments and durbar hall, of which only fragments remain. The Adil Shahis' **tombs** are scattered around the outskirts, while most of the important **mosques** lie southeast of the citadel.

It's possible to see Bijapur's highlights in a day, although most people stay for three or four nights, taking in the monuments at a more leisurely pace. Our account covers the sights from east to west, beginning with the Golgumbaz – which you should aim to visit at around 6am, before the bus parties descend – and ending with the exquisite Ibrahim Rauza, an atmospheric spot to enjoy the sun set.

The Golgumbaz

The vast **Golgumbaz** mausoleum (daily 6am–6pm; Rs0.50), Bijapur's most famous building, soars above the town's east walls, visible for miles in every direction. Built towards the end of the Adil Shahis' reign, it is a fitting monument to a dynasty on its last legs – pompous, decadent and ill-proportioned, but conceived on an irresistibly awesome scale.

The cubic tomb, enclosing a 170-square-metre hall, is crowned with a single hemispherical **dome**, the largest in the world after St Peter's in Rome (which is only 5m wider). Spiral staircases wind up the four, seven-storey octagonal towers that buttress the building to the famous **Whispering Gallery**, a three-metre passage encircling the interior base of the dome. Get here just after opening time and you can experiment with the extraordinary acoustics; by 7am, though, the cacophony generated by bus-loads of whooping and clapping tourists means you can't hear yourself think, let alone make out whispering 38m away. A good antidote to the din are the superb **views** from the mausoleum's ramparts, which overlook the town and its monuments to the dark-soiled Deccan countryside beyond, scattered with minor tombs and ruins.

Set on a plinth in the centre of the hall below are the gravestones of the ruler who built the Golgumbaz, **Muhammed Adil Shahi**, along with those of his wife, daughter, grandson and favourite courtesan, Rambha.

The Jama Masjid

A little under 1km southwest of the Golgumbaz, the **Jama Masjid** (Friday Mosque) presides over the quarter that formed the centre of the city during Bijapur's ninetheenth-century nadir under the Nizam of Hyderabad. It was commissioned by Ali Adil Shahi, the ruler credited with constructing the city walls and complex water supply system, as a monument to his victory over the Vijayanagars at the battle of Talikota in 1565, and is widely regarded as one of the finest mosques in India.

Approached via a square *hauz*, or ablutions tank, the main **prayer hall** is surmounted by an elegantly proportioned central dome, with thirty-three smaller shallow domes ranged around it. Simplicity and restraint are the essence of the colonnaded hall below, divided by gently curving arches and rows of thick plaster-covered pillars. Aside from the odd geometric design and trace of yellow, blue and green tile work, the only ornamentation is found in the *mihrab*, or west- (Mecca-) facing prayer niche, which is smothered in gold leaf and elaborate calligraphy. The marble floor of the hall features a grid of 2500 rectangles, known as *musallahs* (after the *musallah* prayer mats brought to mosques by worshippers). These were added by the Moghul emporer Aurangzeb, allegedly as recompense for making off with the velvet carpets, long golden chain and other valuables that originally filled the prayer hall.

The Mithari and Astar Mahals

Continuing west from the Jama Masjid, the first monument of note is a small, ornately carved gatehouse on the south side of the road. Although of modest size, the delicate three-storey structure, known as the **Mithari Mahal**, is one of Bijapur's most beautiful buildings, with ornate projecting windows and minarets crowning its corners. Once again, Ali Adil Shahi erected it, along with the mosque behind, using gifts presented to him during a state visit to Vijayanagar. The Hindu rajas' generosity, however, did not pay off. Only a couple of years later, the Adil Shahi and his four Muslim allies sacked their city, plundering its wealth and murdering most of its inhabitants.

The lane running north from opposite the Mithari Mahal brings you to the dilapidated **Asar Mahal**, a large open-fronted hall propped up by four green-painted pillars and fronted by a large stagnant step-well. Built in 1646 by Muhammed Adil Shahi as a Hall of Justice, it was later chosen to house hairs from the Prophet's beard, thereby earning the title *Asar-i-Sharif*, or "place of illustrious relics". In theory, women are not permitted inside to view the upper storey, where fifteen niches are decorated with mediocre, Persian-style pot-and-foliage murals, but for a little *baksheesh*, one of the girls who hang around the site will unlock the doors for you.

The citadel

Bijapur's **citadel** stands in the middle of town, hemmed in on all but its north side by battlements. Most of the buildings inside have collapsed, or have been converted into government offices, but enough remain to give a sense of how imposing this royal enclave must once have been.

The best-preserved monuments lie along, or near, the citadel's main north–south artery, Anand Mahal Rd, reached by skirting the southeast wall from the Asar Mahal, or from the north side via the road running past KSTDC's *Mayura Adil Shahi Hotel*. The latter route brings you first to the **Gagan Mahal**. Originally Ali Adil Shahi's "Heavenly Palace", this now ruined hulk later served as a durbar hall for the sultans, who would sit in state on the platform at the open-fronted north side, watched by crowds gathered in the grounds opposite. West off Anand Mahal Rd, the five-storeyed **Sat Manzil** was the pleasure palace of the courtesan Rambha, entombed with Muhammed Adil Shahi and his family in the Golgumbaz. In front stands an ornately carved water pavilion, the **Jal Mandir**, now left high and dry in an empty tank.

Malik-i-Maidan and Upli Buruj

Guarding the principal western entrance to the city is one of several bastions (*burje*) that punctuate Bijapur's battlements. This one, the Burj-i-Sherza ("Lion Gate") sports a colossal cannon, known as the **Malik-i-Maidan**, literally "Lord of the Plains". It was brought here as war booty in the sixteenth century, and needed four hundred bullocks, ten elephants and an entire batallion to haul it up the steps to the emplacement. Inscriptions record that the cannon, whose muzzle features a relief of a monster swallowing an elephant, was cast in Ahmednagar in 1551.

A couple more discarded cannons lie atop the watchtower visible a short walk northwest. Steps wind around the outside of the oval-shaped **Upli Burj**, or "Upper Bastion", to a gun emplacement that affords unimpeded views over the city and plains.

The Ibrahim Rauza

Set in its own walled compound less than 1km west of the ramparts, the **Ibrahim Rauza** represents the high watermark of Bijapuri architecture. Whereas the Golgumbaz impresses primarily by its scale, the appeal of this tomb complex lies in its grace and simplicity. Beyond the reach of most bus parties, it's also a haven of peace, with cool colonnaded verandahs and flocks of viridescent parakeets careening between the mildewed domes, minarets and gleaming golden finials.

Opinions differ over whether the tomb was commissioned by Ibrahim Adil Shah (1580–1626), or his favourite wife, Taj Sultana, but the former was the first to be interred here, in a gloomy chamber whose only light enters via a series of exquisite pierced stone (*jali*) windows. Made up of elaborate Koranic inscriptions, these are the finest examples of their kind in India. More amazing stonework decorates the exterior of the mausoleum, and the equally beautiful **mosque** opposite, the cornice of whose facade features a stone chain carved from a single block. The two buildings, bristling with minarets and domed cupolas, face each other from opposite sides of a rectangular raised plinth, divided by a small reservoir and fountains. Viewed from on top of the walls that encloses the complex, you can see why its architect, Malik Sandal, added a self-congratulatory inscription in his native Persian over the tomb's south doorway, describing his masterpiece as " . . . A beauty of which Paradise stood amazed".

Accommodation and eating

Accommodation standards are pretty low in Bijapur, although finding a room is rarely a problem. Most budget tourists head for the KSTDC *Mayura Adil Shahi*, which, despite its shabbiness, has a certain charm; it's also cheap and central. The old-fashioned *Annexe*, around the corner, is more comfortable, but the only modern mid-range place is the *Madhuvan*. **Eating** is largely confined to the hotels, with the *Mayura Adil Shahi*'s dingy beer-bar-restaurant cleaning up most of the foreign tourist trade.

KSTDC Mayura Adil Shahi, Anand Mahal Rd (☎20943). Stone-floored rooms ranged around a leafy courtyard-garden, all with very grubby attached bathrooms, fans, holed mozzie nets, clean sheets and towels. Hot and cold drinks from the restaurant are served on the verandahs by helpful staff. The service at the restaurant itself is incredibly slow, and the food – a standard mix of veg- and non-veg Indian, with some Chinese and Continental dishes – is very ordinary, but they do serve chilled beer; just be sure not to peek into the kitchen before you order. ②.

KSTDC Mayura Adil Shahi Annexe, Station Rd (☎20401). Almost as dowdy as the main wing, but with larger, cleaner rooms and individual sit-outs. No restaurant. ③.

Madhuvan, Station Rd (☎25572). The cleanest, newest and best-appointed place in town, with a variety of rooms, from "economy" doubles to more comfortable a/c "deluxe" options. The restaurant serves good-value thalis at lunchtime. ②–⑤.

Rajdhani, opposite *Laxmi Talkies*, near Old Head Post Office, Station Rd (☎24994). Most bearable of the rock-bottom lodges in the centre, with clean rooms. Sandwiched between two cinemas. ①.

Samrat, Station Rd (☎21260). Newly opened lodge at the east end of town. Institutional, and not all that neat, but a fall-back if the *Mayura Adil Shahi* is full. Don't risk the restaurant, though. ①.

Sanman, opposite the Golgumbaz, Station Rd (☎21866). Best value among the budget places, and well placed for the railway station. Good-sized rooms with mozzie nets and clean attached shower-toilets. The Udupi canteen is a stop for the bus parties, so the their south Indian snacks are all fresh-ly cooked; try the popular *puri korma* or delicious *sadar masala dosas*. ①.

Gulbarga

GULBARGA, 165km northeast of Bijapur, was the founding capital of the Bahmani dynasty and the region's principal city before the court moved to Bidar in 1424. Later captured by the Adil Shahis and Moghuls, it has remained a staunchly Muslim town, and bulbous onion domes and mosque minarets still soar prominently above its ram-shackle concrete-box skyline. The town is also famous as the birthplace of the *chisti*, or saint, Hazrat Bandah Nawaz Gesu Daraz (1320–1422), whose tomb, situated next to one of India's foremost Islamic theological colleges, is a major shrine.

In spite of Gulbarga's religious and historical significance, its **monuments** pale in comparison with those at Bijapur, and even Bidar. Unless you're particularly interested in medieval Muslim architecture, few are worth breaking a journey to see. The one exception is the tomb complex on the northeast edge of town, known as **the Dargah**. Approached via a broad bazaar, this marble-lined enclosure, plastered in mildew-streaked limewash, centres on the tomb of Hazrat Gesu Daraz, affectionately known to his devotees as "**Bandah Nawaz**", or "the long-haired one who brings comfort to oth-ers". The saint was spiritual mentor to the Bahmani rulers, and it was they who erect-ed his beautiful double-storeyed mausoleum, now visited by hundreds of thousands of Muslim pilgrims each year. Women are not allowed inside, and must peek at the tomb – surrounded by a mother-of-pearl-inlaid wooden screen and draped with green silk – through the pierced-stone windows. Men, however, can enter to leave offerings and admire the elaborate mirror-mosaic ceiling. The same gender bar applies to the neigh-bouring tomb, whose interior has retained its exquisite Persian paintings. The *Dargah*'s other important building, open to both sexes, is the **Madrasa**, or theological college, founded by Bandah Nawaz and enlarged during the two centuries after his death. The syllabus here is dominated by the Koran, but the saint's own works on Sufi mysticism and ethics are also still studied.

After mingling with the crowds at the *Dargah*, escape across town to Gulbarga's deserted **fort**. Encircled by 16-metre thick crenellated walls, fifteen watchtowers and an evil-smelling stagnant moat, the great citadel now lies in ruins. Its only surviving building is the beautiful fourteenth-century **Jama Masjid**, whose elegant domes and arched gateways preside over a scrubby wasteland. Thought to have been modelled by a Moorish architect on the great Spanish mosque of Cordoba, it is unique in India for having an entirely domed prayer hall.

Arrival and information

Daily *KSRTC* **buses** from Bijapur, Bidar and Hospet pull in to the state bus stand on the southwest edge of town. Private mini-buses work from the roadside opposite, their conductors shouting for passengers across the main concourse. Don't be tempted to take one of these to Bidar; they only run as far as the fly-blown highway junction of Humnabad, 40km short, where you'll be stranded for hours. Gulbarga's main-line **rail-way station**, with services to and from Bombay, Pune, Hyderabad, Bangalore and Madras, lies 1km east of the bus stand. **Station Road**, the town's main artery, runs due north of here past three hotels and a large artificial lake to the busy **Chowk** crossroads, at the heart of the bazaar.

Gulbarga's main sights are well spread out, so you'll need to **get around** by auto-rickshaw; fix fares in advance. For medical help, head for the town **hospital**, east of the centre next door to the *Hotel Santoosh*, which has a well-stocked pharmacy. There is nowhere in Gulbarga to **change money**.

Accommodation and eating

Gulbarga is well provided with good-value **accommodation**, and even travellers on tight budgets should be able to afford a clean room with a fan and small balcony. The one place to avoid is the grim KSTDC *Mayura Bahmani*, more of a drinking den than a hotel, and plagued by mosquitoes; the *Adithya* opposite is a far better deal.

All the hotels listed below have **restaurants**, mostly pure-veg places with a no alcohol rule (to discourage boozers from across the border in dry Andhra Pradesh).

Adithya, Station Rd, opposite Public Gardens (☎08472/202039). Unbeatable value economy doubles, or posher a/c options, in a new building. Their impeccably clean pure-veg Udupi restaurant, *Pooja*, on the ground floor does great *thalis* and snacks. ③–⑤.

Pariwar, Station Rd, near the railway station (☎08472/21522; fax 22060). The town's top hotel, and excellent value. Book ahead if you want an economy room, which fill up by noon. The *Kamakshi Restaurant* (6am–10pm) serves quality south Indian food, but no beer. Some a/c. ③–⑥.

Raj Rajeshwari, Vasant Nagar, Mill Rd (☎08472/25881). Just 5min from the bus stand, and good value. Well-maintained modern building with large en-suite rooms with balconies, plus a reasonable veg restaurant (strictly no alcohol). ③.

Santosh, Bilgundi Gardens, University Rd (☎08472/22661; fax 231991). Upscale, efficient chain hotel peacefully located on the eastern outskirts, with big, comfortable rooms (some a/c), sit-outs, veg- and non-veg restaurants and a bar. Recommended only if you have your own vehicle. ④–⑤.

Bidar

In 1424, following the break-up of the Bahmani dynasty into five rival factions, Ahmad Shah I shifted his court from Gulbarga to a less constricted site at **BIDAR**, spurred, it is said, by grief at the death of his beloved spiritual mentor, Bandah Nawas Gesu Daraz. Revamping the town with a new fort, splendid palaces, mosques and ornamental gardens, the Bahmanis ruled from here until 1487, when the Barid Shahis took control. They were succeeded by the Adil Shahis from Bijapur, and later the Moghuls under Aurangzeb, who annexed the region in 1656, before the Nizam of Hyderabad finally acquired the territory in the early eighteenth century.

Lost in the far northwest of Karnataka, Bidar, 284km northwest of Bijapur, is nowadays a provincial backwater, better known for its fighter-pilot training base than the monuments gently decaying in, and within sight of, its medieval walls. Yet the town, half of whose 140,000 population are still Muslim, has a gritty charm, with narrow red-dirt streets ending at arched gates and open vistas across the plains. Littered with tile-fronted tombs, rambling fortifications and old mosques, it merits a visit if you're travelling between Hyderabad (150km east) and Bijapur, although expect little in the way of Western comforts, and more than the usual amount of curious approaches from locals. Lone women travellers, especially, may find the attention more hassle than it's worth.

Bidar's sights are too spread out to be comfortably explored on foot. However, autorickshaws tend to be thin on the ground away from the main streets, and are reluctant to wait while you look around the monuments, so it's a good idea to rent a **bicycle** for the day from the stall on the roundabout (*chowk*) east of the *Maura Badri Shahi Hotel*, next door to the *Kamat* restaurant.

The old town

The heart of Bidar is its medieval **old town**, encircled by crenellated ramparts and eight imposing gateways (*darwazas*). This predominantly Muslim quarter holds many Bahmani-era mosques, *havelis* and *khanqahs* – "monasteries" set up by the local rulers

---

BIDRI

Bidar is renowned as the home of a unique damascene metalwork technique known as **Bidri**, developed by the Persian silversmiths that came to the area with the Bahmani court in the fifteenth century. These highly skilled artisans engraved and inlaid their traditional Iranian designs on to a metal alloy composed of lead, copper, zinc and tin, which they blackened and polished. The resulting effect – swirling silver floral motifs framed by geometric patterns and set against black backgrounds – has since become the hallmark of Muslim metalwork in India.

Bidri objets d'art are displayed in museums and galleries all over the country. But if you want to see *pukka bidri-wallahs* at work, take a walk down Bidar's **Siddiq Talim Road**, which cuts across the south side of the old town, where skull-capped artisans tap and burnish vases, goblets, plates, spice boxes, betel-nut tins, and ornamental *hookah* pipes, as well as less traditional objects – coasters, ashtrays and bangles – that crop up (at vastly inflated prices) in silver emporiums as far away as Delhi and Calcutta.

---

for Muslim cleric-mystics and their disciples – but its real highlight are the impressive ruins of **Mahmud Gawan's Madrasa**, or theological college, whose single minaret soars high above the city centre. Gawan, a scholar and Persian exile, was the *wazir*, or prime minister, of the Bahmani state under Muhammed Bahmani III (1463–1482). A talented linguist, mathematician and inspired military strategist, he oversaw the dynasty's expansion into Karnataka and Goa, bequeathing this college as a thank-you gift to his adoptive kingdom in 1472. The distinctively Persian-style building, originally surmounted by large bulbous domes, once housed a world-famous library. However, this burnt down after being struck by lightning in 1696, while several of the walls and domes were blown away when gunpowder stored here by Aurangzeb's occupying army caught fire and exploded. Today, the *madrasa* is little more than a shell, although its elegant arched facade has retained large patches of the vibrant Persian glazed-tile-work that once covered most of the exterior surfaces. This includes a beautiful band of Koranic calligraphy, and striking multi-coloured zigzags wrapped around the base of the one remaining *minar*, or minaret.

The fort

Presiding over the dark-soiled plains from atop a sheer-faced red laterite escarpment, Bidar's **fort**, at the far north end of the street running past the *madrasa*, was founded by the Hindu Chalukyas and strengthened by the Bahmanis in the early fifteenth century. Despite repeated sieges, it remains largely intact, encircled by 10km of ramparts that drop away in the north and west to 300-metre cliffs. The main southern entrance is protected by equally imposing man-made defences: gigantic fortified gates and a triple moat formerly crossed by a series of drawbridges. Once inside, the first building of note (on the left after the third and final gateway) is the exquisite **Rangin Mahal**. Mahmud Shah built this modest "Coloured Palace" after an unsuccessful uprising of Abyssinian slaves in 1487 forced him to relocate to a safer site inside the citadel. The palace's relatively modest proportions reflect the Bahmanis' declining fortunes, but its interior comprises some of the finest surviving Islamic art in the Deccan, with superb wood carving above the door arches and Persian-style mother-of-pearl inlay on polished black granite surfaces. If the doors to the palace are locked, ask for the keys at the near-by *ASI* **museum** (daily 8am–1pm & 2–5pm; free), which houses a missable collection of Hindu temple sculpture, weapons and Stone-Age artefacts.

Opposite the museum, an expanse of gravel is all that remains of the royal gardens. This is overlooked by the austere **Solah Khamb** mosque (1327), Bidar's oldest Muslim monument, whose most outstanding feature is the intricate pierced-stone *jali* calligraphy around its central dome. From here, continue west through the ruins of the former royal enclosure – a rambling complex of half-collapsed palaces, baths, *zenanas* (womens' quarters) and assembly halls – to the fort's west walls. You can complete the round of the **ramparts** in ninety minutes, taking time out to enjoy the views over the red cliffs and across the plains.

Ashtur: the Bahmani tombs

As you look from the fort's east walls, a cluster of eight bulbous white domes float alluringly above the trees in the distance. Dating from the fifteenth century, the mausoleums at **Ashtur**, 3km east of Bidar (leave the old town via Dulhan Darwaza gate), are the final resting places of the Bahmani sultans and their families, including the son of the ruler who first decamped from Gulbarga, Alauddin Shah I. His remains by far the most impressive tomb, with patches of coloured glazed tiles on its arched facade, and a large dome whose interior surfaces writhe with sumptuous Persian paintings. Reflecting sunlight on to the ceiling with a small pocket mirror, the *chowkidar* picks out the highlights, among them a diamond, barely visible among the bat droppings.

The tomb of Allaudin's father, the ninth and most illustrious Bahmani sultan, Ahmad Shah I, stands beside that of his son, decorated with Persian inscriptions. Beyond this are two more minor mausoleums, followed by the partially collapsed tomb of Humayun the Cruel (1458–61), cracked open by a bolt of lightning. Continuing along the line, you can chart the gradual decline of the Bahmanis as the mausoleums diminish in size, ending with a sad handful erected in the early sixteenth century, when the sultans were no more than puppet rulers of the Barid Shahis.

Crowning a low hillock half-way between Ashtur and Bidar, on the north side of the road, the **Chaukhandi of Hazrat Khalil Ullah** is a beautiful octagonal-shaped tomb built by Allaudin Shah for his chief spiritual advisor. Most of the tiles have dropped off the facade, but the surviving stonework and calligraphy above the arched doorway, along with the views from the tomb's plinth, deserve a quick detour from the road.

The Badri Shahi tombs

The **tombs of the Badri Shahi** rulers, who succeeded the Bahmanis at the start of the sixteenth century, stand on the western edge of town, a little under 1km beyond the bus stand on the Udgir road. Although not as impressive as those of their predecessors, the mausoleums, mounted on raised plinths, occupy an attractive site. Randomly spaced rather than set in a chronological row, they are surrounded by lawns maintained by the *ASI*. The most interesting is the tomb of **Ali Barid** (1542–79), whose Mecca-facing wall was left open to the elements. A short distance southwest lies a mass grave platform for his 67 concubines, who were sent as tribute gifts by vassals of the Deccani overlord from all across the kingdom.

Practicalities

Bidar lies on a branch line of the main Bombay–Secunderabad–Madras rail route, and can only be reached by slow passenger **train**. The few visitors that come here invariably arrive **by bus**, at the *KSRTC* bus stand on the far western edge of town, which has direct services from Hyderabad (3hr 30min), Gulbarga (3hr 30min), and Bijapur (8hr).

Auto-rickshaws are on hand for the short hop east along the main road to the town's two only decent **hotels**. The best is the *Bidar International* (no phone; ②–③), a newish concrete building 1km from the bus stand, with large rooms with attached shower-toilets and fans. However, patronized largely by refugees from nearby Andhra Pradesh's liquor prohibition, it does get rowdy at night. The rat-infested KSTDC *Mayura Barid Shahi* (☎08482/6571; ①), 500m down the road, is best avoided.

Finding somewhere good to **eat** is much less of a problem, thanks to the excellent open-air garden restaurant next to the *Mayura Barid Shahi*. The food here – mostly North Indian with a handful of Chinese options – is fresh and tasty (try the delicious veg *malai kofta*, or spicy chicken *tikka*), and the service attentive; they also do chilled beer and ice-cream. Also recommended, and much cheaper, is the popular *Udupi Krishna* restaurant, five minutes east of the *Mayuri Badri Shahi*, overlooking the *chowk*, which serves up unlimited pure-veg *thalis* for lunch; they have a "family room" for women, too, and open early (around 7.30am) for piping hot south Indian breakfasts.

CHAPTER TWENTY ONE

ANDHRA PRADESH

Although Andhra Pradesh occupies a great swathe of eastern India, stretching for over 1200km along the coast from Orissa to Tamil Nadu and reaching far inland from the fertile deltas of the Godavari and Krishna rivers to the semi-arid Deccan Plateau, it's not a place that receives many tourists. Most foreign travellers pass through en route to its more attractive neighbours, and it's not hard to see why; exploring Andhra Pradesh takes a lot of time and effort that you may well end up feeling would have been better spent elsewhere. Its infrastructure is rudimentary – in particular, if you don't have your own vehicle you're at the mercy of an extremely poor public transport system that does little more than connect the major towns.

The state capital, **Hyderabad**, is a run-down but undoubtedly atmospheric city dating from the late sixteenth century. Its endless bazaars, eclectic Salar Jung museum

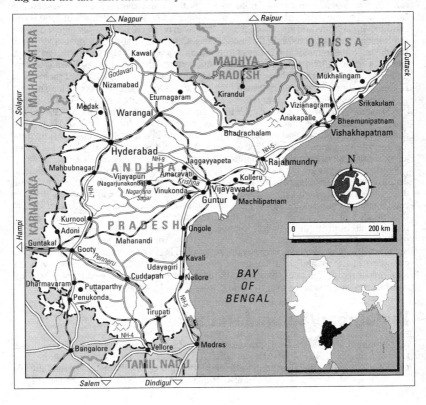

and, nearby, the mighty **Golconda Fort** make it an absorbing place to spend a day or two. By contrast, its modern twin, commercial **Secunderabad**, excels only in characterlessness. **Warangal**, 150km northeast of Hyderabad, has both Muslim and Hindu remains from the twelfth and thirteenth centuries, while the region's Buddhist legacy – particularly its superb sculpture – is preserved in museums at sites such as **Nagarjunakonda** (south of Hyderabad) and **Amaravati**, the ancient Satavahana capital. In the east, the big cities of **Vishakapatnam** and **Vijayawada** have little to recommend them, though the latter makes a convenient access point for Amaravati. However, the temple town of **Tirupati** in the far southeast – best reached from Madras in Tamil Nadu – is one of India's great Hindu phenomena, a fascinating and impossibly crowded pilgrimage site, said to be more popular even than Mecca. In the southwest of the state, the small town of **Puttaparthy** attracts a more international pilgrim crowd, drawn here by the prospect of *darshan* from spiritual leader Sai Baba.

Although modern industries have grown up around the capital and shipbuilding, iron and steel are important on the coast, most people in Andhra Pradesh remain poor. Away from the Godavari and Krishna deltas, where the soil is rich enough to grow rice and sugar cane, the land is in places impossible to cultivate.

Some history

Earliest accounts of the region, dating back to the time of **Ashoka** (third century BC), refer to a people known as the Andhras. The **Satavahana dynasty** (*c*. second century BC–second century AD), also known as the Andras, came to control much of central and southern India from their second capital at Amaravati on the Krishna. They enjoyed extensive international trade with both eastern Asia and Europe, and were great patrons of Buddhism. Subsequently, the Pallavas from Tamil Nadu, the Chalukyas from Karnataka, and the Cholas all held sway. By the thirteenth century, the Kakatiyas of Warangal were under constant threat from Muslim incursions, while later on, after the fall of their city at Hampi, the Hindu Vijayanagars transferred operations to Chandragiri near Tirupati.

The next significant development was in the mid-sixteenth century, with the rise of the Muslim **Qutb Shahi dynasty**. In 1687, the son of the Moghul emperor Aurangzeb seized Golconda. Five years after Aurangzeb died in 1707, the Viceroy of Hyderabad declared independence and established the Asaf Jahi dynasty of Nizams. In return for allying with the British against Tipu Sultan of Mysore, the Nizam was allowed to retain a certain degree of autonomy even after the British had come to dominate all India.

During the struggle for Independence, harmony between Hindus and Muslims in Andhra Pradesh disintegrated. **Partition** brought matters to a climax, as the Nizam desired to join other Muslims in the soon-to-be created state of **Pakistan**. In 1949 the capital erupted in riots, the army was brought in and Hyderabad state was admitted to the Indian Union. Andhra Pradesh state was created in 1956 from Telegu-speaking regions (although Urdu is widely spoken in Hyderabad) that had previously formed part of the Madras Presidency on the east coast and the princely state of Hyderabad to the west. Today almost 90 percent of the population is Hindu, with Muslims largely concentrated in the capital. In 1995, under pressure from militant wives upset with the wasteful drinking habits of their men, the state government imposed a **total ban on alcohol**, making Andhra Pradesh India's second major dry state after Gujarat.

Hyderabad/Secunderabad

A melting-pot of Muslim and Hindu cultures, the capital of Andhra Pradesh comprises the twin cities of **HYDERABAD** and **SECUNDERABAD**. The latter, of little interest to visitors, is the modern administrative city founded by the British, whereas the old city, with its seething **bazaars**, **Muslim monuments** and **Salar Jung Museum** has

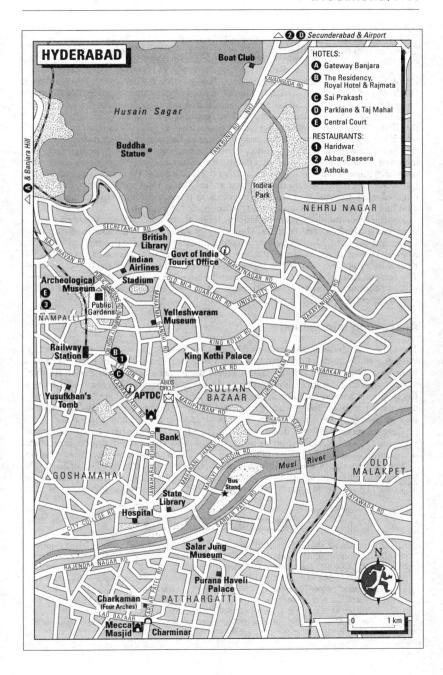

HYDERABAD

△ ❷ ⓓ *Secunderabad & Airport*

Boat Club

Husain Sagar

Buddha Statue

KAVADIGUDA RD

TANKBUND RD

HOTELS:
ⓐ Gateway Banjara
ⓑ The Residency, Royal Hotel & Rajmata
ⓒ Sai Prakash
ⓓ Parklane & Taj Mahal
ⓔ Central Court

RESTAURANTS:
❶ Haridwar
❷ Akbar, Baseera
❸ Ashoka

Indira Park

NEHRU NAGAR

△ ⓐ & Banjara Hill

& Banjara Hill

RAJ BHAVAN RD

SECRETARIAT RD

British Library

Indian Airlines

Govt of India Tourist Office ⓘ

HIMAYATNAGAR RD

Archeological Museum △

ⓔ
❸

Stadium

OLD MLA QUARTERS RD

UNIVERSITY RD

NARAYANGUDA RD

NAMPALLI

Public Gardens

PUBLIC GARDENS RD

MAHATMA GANDHI RD

Yelleshwaram Museum

KING KOTHI RD

VIR SAVARKAR RD

Railway Station

ⓑ ❶

STATION RD

MUKARRAM JAHI RD

ⓒ

ⓘ **APTDC**

ABIDS CIRCLE ✉

King Kothi Palace

TILAK RD

TIRREAZKHAN RD

SULTAN BAZAAR

MAHIPATRAM RD

BHAGYA REDDY RD

Yusufkhan's Tomb

Bank

JAWAHARLAL NEHRU RD

MAHRANI JHANSI RD

MAULVI ALAUDDIN RD

Musi River

OLD MALAKPET

GOSHAMAHAL

△

State Library

Hospital

CITY COLLEGE RD

Bus Stand ★

SARDAR PATEL RD

VIJAYAWADA RD

Salar Jung Museum

RAJENDRA NAGAR RD

Purana Haveli Palace

PATTHARGATTI

SARDAR PATEL RD

N

Charkaman (Four Arches)

LAD BAZAAR

Mecca Masjid

Charminar

0   1 km

> As Hyderabad/Secunderabad is very much the transportation hub for Andhra Pradesh, this chapter has no **"Travel Details"**; see p.1193 for "Moving On from Hyderabad".

heaps of charm. Despite this, Hyderabad has been in decline since Independence. While 45 percent of the population inhabit the old city, a mere 25 percent of the city's budget is spent on it, exacerbating a tension that is never far from the surface.

Hyderabad was founded in 1591 by **Muhammad Quli Shah** (1562–1612), beside the River Musi, 8km east of Golconda, the fortress capital of the Golconda empire which by now was suffering from overcrowding and a serious lack of water. Unusually, this new city was laid out on a grid system, with huge arches and stone buildings that included Hyderabad's most famous monument, **Charminar**. At first it was a city without walls; these were only added in 1740, as defence against the Marathas. Legend has it that a secret tunnel linked the spectacular **Golconda Fort** with the city, dotted with dome-shaped structures at suitable intervals to provide the unfortunate messengers who had to use it with the opportunity to come up for fresh air.

For the three hundred years of Muslim reign, there was harmony between the predominantly Hindu population and the minority Muslims. Hyderabad was the most important focus of Muslim power in south India at this time; the princes' fabulous wealth derived primarily from the fine gems, particularly diamonds, mined in the Kistna Valley at Golconda. In the 1600s, Golconda was the diamond centre of the world. The famous **Koh-i-Noor** diamond was found here – the only time it was ever captured was by Moghul emperor Aurangzeb, when his son seized the Golconda Fort in 1687. It ended up, cut, in the British royal crown.

Arrival and information

The old city of **Hyderabad** straddles the River Musi. Most places of interest lie south of the river, while much of the accommodation is to the north. Further north, separated from Hyderabad by the Husain Sagar Lake, is the modern twin city of **Secunderabad**, where some long-distance trains terminate. Hyderabad **airport**, 8km north of the city at Begumpet, is served by auto-rickshaws, taxis, and buses #9m/10 via Nampally, and a number of routes including #10, #45, #47 and #49 from Secunderabad. **Hyderabad railway station** (also known as Nampally) is close to all amenities and offers a fairly comprehensive service to major destinations. You can reserve trains here for Secunderabad services, too (see p.1193). The well-organized, brand new **long-distance bus stand** occupies an island in the middle of the Musi River, 3km southeast of the railway station.

The best source of **tourist information** in Hyderabad is the **APTDC office** in the Gagan Vihar building, MJ Rd (☎557531), five minutes' walk from the railway station; the other APTDC office, at Yatri Nivas, Sardar Patel Rd, Secunderabad (☎843931), is of lit-

---

CONDUCTED TOURS

APTDC operate a number of conducted tours. All times quoted below are when the tours set off from the Secunderabad office; pick-up time in Hyderabad is 45min later. The **city tour** (daily 7.45am–6.30pm; Rs75) includes Husain Sagar, the Birla temple and planetarium, Qutb Shahi tombs (not Fri), Salar Jung Museum (not Fri), Charminar and Golconda. The **Nagarjuna Sagar tour** (daily 6.30am–9.30pm; Rs150) travels 360km in total, and is rather rushed, but is a convenient way to get to this fascinating area (see p.1194). There's a tour to **Tirupati** (Fri 3.30pm–Sun 7am; Rs525 including hotel), though it's better to get there from Madras. APTDC also organize trips to Golconda Fort's **sound and light** show (Rs40 including entrance fee), leaving from Yatri Niwas at 5pm.

tle use unless you want to book one of their tours. The **Government of India tourist office**, Sandozi Buildings, Himayatnagar Rd, Hyderabad, offers a few brochures.

To **change money**, head for Abids Circle, where there's a branch of the *State Bank of India* and the *Andhra Bank*, which appears to be on Nehru Rd although its official address is Sultan Bazaar, and where they'll change travellers' cheques up to US$200 and accept *Mastercard* and *Visa* encashments. For **car rental**, with or without driver, head for *Alpha Motors*, 17 Abids Shopping Centre, opposite *Hotel Emerald*, Chirag Ali Lane (☎201306). *Hertz* is based at *Hotel Viceroy*, near Tank bund (☎618383 or 618777).

The City

Hyderabad is divided into three: **Hyderabad** the old city; **Secunderabad**, the new (originally called Husain Shah Pura); and **Golconda**, the old fort. The two cities are basically one big sprawl, separated by a lake, **Husain Sagar**, which was created in the 1500s and named after Husain Shah Wali, who had helped Ibrahim Quli Qutb Shah recover from a serious illness. A huge stone Buddha stands in the centre of the lake.

The most interesting area, south of the River Musi, holds the **bazaars**, **Charminar** and the **Salar Jung Museum**. It must be a long time since the Musi amounted to very much. Even after the rains the river is about a tenth the width of the bridge; most of the area under the bridge is grassed over, some planted with palms and paddy. North of the river, the main shopping areas are centred around Abids Circle and the Sultan Bazaar (ready-made clothes, fruit, veg and silk), ten minutes' walk east of the railway station. Abids Circle is connected to MG Rd, which runs north to Secunderabad and metamorphoses into Nehru Rd in the south.

Salar Jung Museum

The unmissable **Salar Jung Museum** (daily except Fri 9.30am–5.15pm; Rs5), on the south bank of the Musi, houses part of the huge collection of Salar Jung, one of the Nizam's prime ministers, and his ancestors. A well-travelled man of wealth, with an eye for objets d'art, he bought whatever took his fancy from both the east and west, from the sublime to, in some cases, the ridiculous. His extraordinary hoard includes Indian jade, miniatures, furniture, lacquer work, Moghul opaque glassware, fabrics, bronzes, Buddhist and Hindu sculpture, manuscripts, and weapons. There are also good examples of *bidri*, decorated metalwork cast from an alloy of zinc, copper and tin, that originated in Bidar in northern Karnataka. Avoid weekends, when it gets very crowded.

Charminar, Lad Bazaar and the Mecca Masjid

A maze of bazaars teeming with people, the old city has at its heart the **Charminar**, a triumphal arch built at the centre of Muhammad Quli Shah's city in 1591 to commemorate an epidemic. It features four graceful minarets, each 56m high, housing spiral staircases to the upper storeys. Although a secular building, it has a mosque (now closed) on the roof; the oldest in Hyderabad, it is said to have been built to teach the royal children the Koran. The yellowish colour of the whole building is thanks to a special stucco made of marble powder, gram and egg yolk.

Charminar marks the start of the fascinating **Lad Bazaar**, as old as the town itself, which leads to Mahboob Chowk, a market square featuring a mosque and Victorian clocktower. Lad Bazaar specializes in everything you could possibly need for a Hyderabadi marriage; it's full of bangle shops, old stores where you can buy rosewater, herbs and spices, exotic materials and more mundane *lunghis*. You'll also find silver filigree jewellery, antiques and *bidri* ware, as well as boxes, plates, *hookah*-paraphernalia and the like, delicately inlaid with silver and brass. Hyderabad is the centre of the pearl trade; **pearls**, so beloved of the Nizams that they not only wore them but apparently liked nothing more than having them ground into powder to eat, can be bought in the markets near the Charminar. Southeast of Lad Bazaar, the complex of **Royal Palaces** includes Chaumahalla, four palaces set around a central courtyard.

Southwest, behind the Charminar, is **Mecca Masjid**, the sixth largest mosque in India, constructed in 1598 by the sixth king, Abdullah Qutb Shah, from locally hewn blocks of black granite. Small red bricks from Mecca are slotted over the central arch. The mosque can hold 3000 followers with up to 10,000 in the courtyard; on the left of the courtyard are the tombs of the Nizams. Outside the mosque is a stall where they will change your torn, cut rupee bills at good rates.

The **Charkaman**, or Four Arches, north of Charminar, were built in 1594 and once led to the parade ground of royal palaces (now long gone). The surrounding narrow streets spill over with interesting small shops; through the western arch, **Doulat-Khan-e-Ali** (which originally led to the palace), stores sell lustrous brocade and old *saris*. The arch itself is said to have been once hung with rich gold tapestries.

North of the river

Just north of the railway station, set in Hyderabad's tranquil public gardens, the **archeological museum** (Mon–Sat 10.30am–5pm) displays a modest but well-labelled collection of bronzes, prehistoric tools, copper inscription plates, weapons, household utensils and even an Egyptian mummy. There's a gallery of modern art in the new extension, too. The **Birla Venkateshwara temple** (daily 7am–noon & 3–9pm), on Kalabahad ("black mountain") Hill, north of the Public Gardens, is open to all, irrespective of caste, creed or nationality. Constructed in Rajasthani white marble in 1976 by the Birla Trust, it was set up by the wealthy industrialist Birla family. Although the temple itself is not of great interest, it affords fine views. Nearby, and built by the same organization, is the **planetarium**, whose shows are in English (Mon–Thurs 11.30am, 4pm & 6pm; every 2nd and last Fri from 3pm; Sun 11.35am, 3.45pm & 6pm; Rs10).

Golconda Fort and the Tombs of the Qutb Shahi Kings

Golconda, 122m above the plain and 11km west of old Hyderabad, was the capital of the seven Qutb Shahi kings from 1518 until the end of the sixteenth century, when the court moved to Hyderabad. Its outer wall reached 18m, and the citadel boasted 87 semi-circular bastions and eight mighty gates, four of which are still in use, complete with gruesome elephant-proof spikes.

To get **to the fort**, buses #119 and #80R run from Nampally. Both the #66G direct bus from Charminar and #80D from Secunderabad stop outside the main entrance. **For the tombs**, take #123 and #142S from Charminar. From Secunderabad the #5, #5S, #5R all go to Mehdipattanam, where you should hop onto #123. Or, of course, you could take a rickshaw and spare yourself the bother (agree a waiting fee in advance). Set aside a day to explore the fort, which covers an area of around forty square kilometres; it's well worth hiring one of the many guides who gather at the entrance, or at least buying one of the handy little pamphlets, including map, sold by vendors.

Entering the **fort** by the Balahisar Gate, you come into the Grand Portico, where guards clap their hands to show off the fort's acoustics; the claps can be clearly heard at the Durbar Hall at its highest point. To the right is the **mortuary bath**, where the bodies of deceased nobles were ritually bathed prior to burial. If you follow the arrowed anti-clockwise route, you then pass along a straight walled path before coming to the two-storey residence of ministers Akkana and Madanna, and starting the proper ascent to Durbar Hall. Halfway along the steps, which pass assorted water channels and wells, you come to a small dark cell named after the court cashier **Ramdas**, who while incarcerated here produced the clumsy carvings and paintings that litter the gloomy room. Nearing the top, you come across the small, pretty mosque of Ibrahim Qutub Shah; beyond here, set beneath two huge granite stones, is an even tinier temple to Durga in her manifestation as Mahakali.

The steps are crowned by the three-storey **Durbar Hall** of the Qutb Shahs, on platforms outside which the monarchs would sit and survey their domains. Their accompaniment was the lilting strains of court musicians, as opposed to the cacophony of incessant clapping from far below. As you head back down to the palaces and harems, you pass the tanks that supplied the fort's water system.

The ruins of the **queen's palace**, once elaborately decorated with multiple domes, stand in a courtyard centred on an original copper fountain that used to be filled with rosewater. You can still see traces of the "necklace" design on one of the arches, at the top of which a lotus bud sits below an opening flower with a cavity at its centre that once contained a diamond. Petals and creeper leaves are dotted with tiny holes that formerly gleamed with rubies and diamonds; parrots, long gone, had rubies for their eyes. Today visitors can only speculate how splendid it must all have looked, especially at night, when flaming torches illuminated the glittering decorations. At the entrance to the **palace** itself, four chambers provided protection from intruders. Passing through two rooms, the second of which is overgrown, you come to the **Shahi Mahal**, the royal bedroom. Originally it had a domed roof and niches on the walls that once sheltered candles or oil lamps. It is said that the servants used silver ladders to get up there to light them. Golconda's **sound and light** show (English; March–Oct Sun & Wed 7pm; Nov–Feb 6.30pm; Rs15) is suitably theatrical.

There are 82 **tombs** (daily except Fri 9am–4.30pm) about 1km north of the outer wall. Set in peaceful gardens, they commemorate commanders, relatives of the kings, dancers, singers and royal doctors, as well as all but two of the Qutb Shahi kings. Faded today, they were once brightly coloured in turquoise and green; they all have an onion dome on a block, with a decorative arcade. You can reach them by road or, more pleasantly, by picking your way across the quiet grassy verges and fields below the fort's battlements.

Accommodation

The area in front of **Hyderabad railway station** (Nampally) has the cheapest accommodation, but you're unlikely to find anything basic for less than Rs150. The real

bargains are more in the mid- to upper-range hotels, which offer better facilities for lower rates than in other big cities. About 2km north of Secunderabad railway station, decent places line **Sarojini Devi Rd**, near the Gymkhana Ground.

Central Court, Lakdi-ka-Pul (continuation of Raj Bhavan Rd) (☎233262; fax 232737). Smallish, new hotel, 2km from railway, with standard as good as many twice the price. Comfortable rooms with *Star TV* and 24hr room service. Travel desk, coffee shop and restaurant. ⑥.

Gateway Banjara, Rd No 1, Banjara Hill (☎222222; fax 222218). *Taj* group hotel with usual facilities, overlooking lake, 4km from the centre of Hyderabad on the top of Banjara Hill. Good restaurant and coffee shop. ⑧–⑨.

Parklane, 115 Park Lane, Secunderabad (☎84066). Large rooms ("ordinary" and deluxe), with views onto other buildings, very clean bathrooms, *Star TV*, restaurant and friendly staff. ⑤–⑥.

Rajmata, Nampally High Rd, opposite railway station (☎201000). Set back from the road near the various *Royal* lodges. Next door to the *Lakshmi* restaurant. Largish, clean non-a/c rooms. ④.

The Residency, Nampally High Rd (☎204060). Swish, modern hotel; the most upmarket option near the station. The restaurant serves good veg food, beautifully presented in plush surrounds. ⑦.

Royal Hotel, opposite railway station (☎201020). Decent, basic lodge; non-a/c with *Star TV*. ③.

Sai Prakash, Station Rd (☎511726). Near railway, 2km from bus stand. Modern hotel, complete with capsule lift. Comfortable, carpeted rooms (all with *Star TV*) set around atrium. High standards (non-a/c in particular), and very popular. Good restaurants and bar. ⑤.

Taj Mahal, 88 Sarojini Devi Rd, Secunderabad (☎812105). Old-fashioned hotel with character, built in 1949, that bears no detectable relation to the Taj Mahal. Rooms are clean, comfortable and spacious, although a bit dark. Veg restaurant with snacks and hot Andhra meals. No bar. ④.

Eating

In addition to the hotel restaurants, plenty of "meals" places around town specialize in **Hyderabadi cuisine**, such as authentic *biryanis*, or the famously chilli-hot Andhra cuisine, often non-veg.

Akbar, 1-7-190 MG Rd, Secunderabad. Hyderabadi cuisine at moderate prices.

Ashoka, 6-1-70 Lakdi-ka-Pul. Hotel with a/c *Saptagiri* cafeteria serving good-value south Indian snacks and some north Indian dishes.

Baseraa, 9-1-167/168 Sarojini Devi Rd, Secunderabad. The simply furnished *Daawat* serves veg, south Indian snacks, breakfasts and north Indian food in the evenings. The posher *Mehfill* is heavy on Mughlai meat dishes with a few Chinese and Western thrown in. It also has a bar.

Central Court, Lakdi-ka-Pul. Good Hyderabadi non-veg plus some veg options and barbecue kebabs on small patio; also Mughlai, Western and Chinese food. Lunch buffet, evenings à la carte.

Gateway Banjara, Rd No 1, Banjara Hill. *Dakhni* serves excellent, pricey, authentic south Indian cuisine, and Hyderabadi specialities.

Haridwar, next to *Residency Hotel*. Excellent, tasty stand-up *dosas*, *vadai* and other snacks.

Sai Prakash, Station Rd. The *Woodlands* serves good-value veg south Indian snacks and north Indian dishes. *Rich'n'Famous* is much posher and pricier, with comfy chairs and imaginative daily specials including crab, prawns and specialities from Hyderabad and further afield.

Listings

Bookstores *Higginbothams*, 1 Lal Bahadur Stadium, Hyderabad (☎237918); *Gangarams*, 62 DSD Rd, near *Garden Restaurant* in Secunderabad (☎820691).

Crafts *Utkalika* (Government of Orissa handicrafts), House no. 60-1-67, between *Ravindra Bharati* and *Hotel Ashoka*, sells silver filigree jewellery, handloom cloth, *ikhat* tie-dye, Jagannath papier-mâché figures and buffalo bone carvings. *Cheneta Bhavan* is a modern shopping complex a little south of the railway station, stuffed with handloom cloth shops from various states, including Tamil Nadu, Uttar Pradesh, Rajasthan, Madhya Pradesh and Andhra Pradesh. For Kanchi and other silks, head for *Sanchi Kamakshi Silks*, shop no. 4-4-6/1, "Beside Dilshad Talkies" (now demolished) and *Thunga Sambaiah*, "opposite Dilshad Talkies", Sultan Bazaar, Kothi.

Library The British Library, Secretariat Rd (Tues–Sat 10am–6pm; ☎230774) has a wide selection of books and recent British newspapers. You must be a member or a British citizen to get in.

Pharmacies *Apollo Pharmacy* (☎231380) and *Health Pharmacy* (☎210618) are both 24hr.

Photography and film *Jyoti Foto*, 5-4-730 Station Rd, sells colour print and trannies; *Moorty & Sons*, Gandhi Rd has accessories; *Royal Image*, next to the *Royal Hotel*, sells print film only.

Travel agents *Alam Tours and Travels*, 5-9-189/104 1st floor, Lenaine Estate, next to SBH Gunfoundry, Abids Rd (☎203761); *Sita World Travels*, Sita House, 3-5-874 Hyderguda; *Travel Corporation*, 102 Regency House, 680 Somajiguda, Greenlands Rd (☎212722), are all in Hyderabad.

MOVING ON FROM HYDERABAD

Domestic airlines serving Hyderabad include *Indian Airlines* (☎140; pre-recorded flight info: ☎142; office: ☎599333), *East-West* (☎813568), *Jet* (☎230979), *Modiluft* (☎243783) and *NEPC* (☎241660). There are up to three daily flights to Bangalore (1hr; *Indian Airlines, NEPC*), at least five to Bombay (1hr 15min; *Indian, East-West, Jet*), two daily to Delhi (2hr; *Indian Airlines)*, two or three to Madras (1hr; *Indian, East-West*) and daily except Monday to Calcutta, via Bhubaneshwar on three of those days (1hr 55min; *Indian Airlines*).

From the Central Bus Stand regular services run to Amaravati (2 daily; 7hr), Bangalore (10 daily; 13hr), Bombay (8 daily; 17hr), Madras (1 daily; 16hr) and Tirupati (10 daily; 9hr).

Daily services **from Hyderabad** railway station include *Hyderabad Express* #7085 to Bangalore (6.10pm; 17hr); the *Hyderabad–Bombay Express* #7032 to Bombay (8.20pm; 17hr); *Charminar Express* #6060 to Madras (6.40pm; 15hr); *Rayasaleena Express* #7429 to Tirupati (5pm; 16hr); and the *Godavari Express* #7008 to Vijayawada (5.15pm; 7hr). All northeast-bound services call at Warangal (3hr). **From Secunderabad,** the daily *Ajanta Express* #7551 runs to Aurangabad (6.30pm; 12hr 15min) and the *Howrah Express* #8046 (6.45am; 33hr) to Calcutta. For Delhi, choose from the *Andhra Pradesh Express* #2723 to New Delhi (6.30am; 26hr) or the *Hazrat Nizamuddin Express* #7029 (8pm; 26hr).

The **reservations office** (Mon–Sat 8am–2pm & 2.30–8pm, Sun 8am–2pm) is to the left as you enter the station. Counter #213 (next to enquiry counter) is supposedly for tourist reservations, but it's also used for group bookings and lost tickets. Foreign visitors can make bookings at the Chief Reservation Inspector's Office on platform 1 (daily 9am–5pm). All trains from Secunderabad can be booked from Hyderabad.

Warangal

WARANGAL – "one stone" – 150km northeast of Hyderabad, was the Hindu capital of the Kakatiyan empire in the twelfth and thirteenth centuries. Like other Deccan cities, it changed hands many times between the Hindus and the Muslims – something that is reflected in its architecture and the remains you see today.

Warangal's **fort** (4km south) is famous for its two circles of fortifications: the outer made of earth with a moat, and the inner of stone. Four roads into the centre meet at the ruined temple of **Svayambhu** (1162), dedicated to Shiva. At its southern, free-standing gateway, another Shiva temple, from the fourteenth century, is in much better shape; inside, the remains of an enormous *lingam* came originally from the Svayambhu shrine. Also inside the citadel is the **Shirab Khan**, or **Audience Hall**, an early eleventh-century building very similar to Mandu's Hindola Mahal (see p.419).

The largely basalt Chalukyan-style **"thousand-pillared" Shiva temple**, just off the main road, beside the slopes of Hanamkonda Hill (6km north), was constructed by King Rudra Deva in 1163. A low-roofed building, on several stepped stages, it features superb carvings and three shrines to Vishnu, Shiva and Surya the sun god. They lead off the *mandapa* whose numerous finely carved columns give the temple its name. In front, a polished Nandi bull was carved out of a single stone. A Bhadrakali temple stands at the top of the hill.

Practicalities

If you make an early start, it's just about possible to visit Warangal in a day trip from Hyderabad. Frequent buses and trains run to the site (roughly 3hr 30min). Warangal's **bus stand** and **railway station** are opposite each other, served by local buses and auto-rickshaws. The easiest way to cover the site is to **rent a bicycle** from one of the stalls on Station Rd. As you follow Station Rd from the station, for the fort turn left just beyond the post office, under the railway bridge and left again at the next main road. For Hanamkonda turn right at the next main junction after the post office, left at the next major crossroads, and right at the end on to the Hanamkonda main road. The temple and hill are on the left.

Accommodation is limited; the *Hotel Ashok* (☎78491; ③–⑤) on Main Rd, Hanamkonda, 6km from the railway and bus stand, has a/c rooms, a restaurant and bar, while basic lodges near the railway on Station Rd include the *Vijaya* (☎25851; ①), which is the closest and best value, and *Venkateshwara* (☎26455; ①). The slightly posher *Hotel Ratna* (☎60645; ③–④) is further down on M G Rd.

Nagarjunakonda

NAGARJUNAKONDA, or "Nagarjuna's Hill", 166km south of Hyderabad and 175km west of Vijayawada, is all that now remains of the vast area, rich in archeological sites, submerged when the huge Nagarjuna Sagar Dam was built across the River Krishna in 1960. Ancient settlements in the valley were first discovered in 1926; extensive excavations carried out between 1954 and 1960 uncovered more than one hundred sites dating from the early Stone Age to late medieval times. Nagarjunakonda was once the summit of a hill, where a fort towered 200m above the valley floor; now it's just a small oblong island near the middle of Nagarjuna Sagar Lake, accessible by boat from the mainland. Several Buddhist monuments have been reconstructed, in an operation reminiscent of that at Abu Simbel in Egypt, and a **museum** exhibits the more remarkable ruins of the valley. **VIJAYAPURI**, the village on the shore of the lake, overlooks the colossal dam itself, which stretches for almost 2km. Torrents of water flushed through its 26 flood gates produce electricity for the whole region and irrigate an area of almost 800 square kilometres. Many villages had to be relocated on higher ground when the valley was flooded.

Nagarjunakonda and the museum

Boats arrive on the northeastern edge of Nagarjunakonda island, unloading passengers at what remains of one of the gates of the fort, built in the fourteenth century and considerably renovated by the Vijayanagar kings in the mid-sixteenth century. Low, damaged stone walls skirting the island mark the edge of the fort, and you can see ground-level remains of the Hindu temples that served its inhabitants.

Well-kept gardens lie between the jetty and the museum, beyond which nine Buddhist monuments from various sites in the valley have been rebuilt. West of the jetty, there's a reconstructed bathing *ghat*, built entirely of limestone during the reigns of the Ikshvaku kings (third century AD). A series of levels and steps leads to the water's edge; boards etched into some of its slabs were probably used for dice games.

The **maha-chaitya**, or *stupa*, constructed at the command of King Chamtula's sister in the third century AD, is the earliest Buddhist structure in the area. It was raised over relics of the Buddha – said to include a tooth – and has been reassembled in the southwest of the island. Nearby, a towering **statue** of the Buddha stands draped in robes beside a ground plan of a monastery that enshrines a smaller *stupa*. Other **stupas** stand nearby; the brick walls of the *svastika chaitya* have been arranged in the shape of swastikas, common emblems in early Buddhist iconography.

In the **museum** (daily except Fri 9am–5pm), **Buddhist sculptures** include large stone friezes decorated with scenes from the Buddha's life: his birth; his mother's vision of an elephant and a lotus blossom; his renunciation, and his subversion of evil as he meditated and realized enlightenment under the *bodhi* tree. Twelve statues of standing Buddhas – one of which reaches 3m – show the Buddha in various postures of teaching or meditation. Many pillars are undamaged, profusely carved with Buddha images, bowing devotees, elephants and lotus medallions.

Earlier artefacts include 200,000-year-old stone tools and pots from the Neolithic age (third millennium BC), and metal axe heads and knives (first millennium BC). Among later finds are several inscribed pillars from Ikshvaku times, recording in Prakrit or Sanskrit the installation of Buddhist monasteries and statues. The final phase of art at Nagarjunakonda is represented by medieval sculptures: a thirteenth-century *tirthankara* (Jain saint), a seventeenth-century Ganesh and Nandi, and a set of eighteenth-century statues of Shiva and Shakti, his female consort. Also on display is a model showing the excavated sites in the valley.

Practicalities

Organized **APTDC tours** from Hyderabad to Nagarjunakonda (see p.1188) – taking in the sites and museum, the nearby Ethiopothala Waterfalls and an engraved third-century Buddhist monolith known as the Pylon – can be a bit rushed: if you want to spend more time in the area you can take a bus from Hyderabad (5hr) or Vijayawada (6hr; a direct service runs daily at 11am and frequent services leave from Guntur).

Accommodation at Vijayapuri is limited. The APTDC *Vijay Vihar Complex* (☎2125; ③) in south Vijayapuri, near the jetty, can be booked through any APTDC office; it offers clean, spacious rooms (some a/c) with balconies, and excellent south and north Indian food in the restaurant. APTDC *Project House* (☎2040; ①), is more basic and less convenient, 3km from the jetty. Budget options include *Golden Lodge* (☎2348; ①), opposite the hospital and 1km down the hill from *Vijay Vihar Complex*.

Tickets for **boats** to the island (9.30am & 1.30pm; 1hr) are on sale 25 minutes before departure (Rs18–25). Each boat leaves the island thirty minutes after it arrives, which permits a quick dash round the museum but not enough time to visit the monuments: if you want to spend longer, take the morning boat and return in the afternoon. A cafeteria on the island serves drinks and, occasionally, snacks.

Puttaparthy

Deep in the southwest of the state, amid the arid rocky hills bordering Karnataka, a thriving community has grown up around the once insignificant village of **PUTTA-PARTHY**, birthplace of spiritual leader Sai Baba, whose followers believe him to be the new incarnation of God. Centring on **Prasanthi Nilayam**, the ashram where Sai Baba resides from July to March, the town has schools, a university, hospital and sports centre which offer up-to-date and free services to all. There's even a small airport. The **ashram** itself is a huge complex with room for thousands, with canteens, shops, a museum and library, and a vast assembly hall where Sai Baba gives *darshan* twice daily (6.45–7am & 3.45–4pm). Queues start more than an hour before the appointed time, and a lottery decides who gets to sit near the front. The **museum** (daily 10am–noon) contains a detailed, fascinating display on the major faiths with illustrations and quotations from their sacred texts, punctuated by Sai Baba's comments.

SHRI SATYA SAI BABA

Born **Satyanarayana Raju** on 23 November 1926 in Puttaparthy, then an obscure village in the Madras Presidency, Satya is reported to have shown prodigous talents and unusual purity and compassion from an early age. His apparently supernatural abilities initially caused some concern to his family, who took him to Vedic doctors and eventually to be exorcised. Having been pronounced to be possessed by the divine rather than the diabolical, at the age of fourteen he calmly announced that he was the new incarnation of **Sai Baba**, a saint from Shirdi in Maharashtra who died eight years before Satya was born.

Gradually his fame spread, and a large following grew. In 1950 the **ashram** was inaugurated and a decade later Sai Baba was attracting international attention; today he has millions of devotees worldwide, a considerable number of whom turn out for his birthday celebrations in Puttaparthy, when he delivers a message to his devotees. Just 5ft tall, with a startling Hendrix-style Afro, his smiling, saffron-clad figure is seen on representations all over south India in particular. Though his **miraculous powers** reportedly include the ability to materialize *vibhuti*, sacred ash, with curative properties, Sai Baba claims this to be an unimportant activity, aimed at those firmly entrenched in materialism, and emphasizes instead his message of **universal love**. Whatever your feelings about the divinity of Sai Baba, the atmosphere around the ashram is undeniably peaceful, and the growth of such a vibrant community in this once-forgotten backwater is no small miracle in itself.

Practicalities

Puttaparthy is most accessible from Bangalore in Karnataka (see p.1122), from where five daily **buses** (4hr) run to the stand outside the ashram entrance. The town is also connected to Hyderabad (3 daily; 10hr) and Madras (1 nightly; 11hr). Regular buses make the 42-kilometre run to **Dharmavaram**, the nearest **railhead**, which has good services north and south. There are also two **flights** a week from Bombay and Madras.

Most visitors **stay** at the ashram in large bare sheds (4 for foreigners), or smaller rooms if available. Except in the case of families, accommodation is strictly segregated by sex. Costs are minimal, and though you can't book in advance, you can enquire about availability at the secretary's office (☎08555/87583). Outside the ashram, places are rather overpriced. *Sai Ram Lodge* (☎08555/87412; ②) is about the cheapest; at the other end of the scale, try *Sai Towers* (☎08555/87270; ⑦). Even non-residents can **eat** in the ashram canteen, and there are simple snack stalls along the main street.

Eastern Andhra Pradesh

Perhaps India's least visited area, **eastern Andhra Pradesh** is sandwiched between the Bay of Bengal in the east and the red soil and high peaks of the Eastern Ghats in the north. Its one architectural attraction is the ancient Buddhist site of **Amaravati**, near the city of **Vijayawada**, whose sprinkling of historic temples is far overshadowed by impersonal, modern buildings. Some 350km north, the major port of **Vishakapatnam** is little better – a crowded, dirty place that barely warrants a stop. For anyone with a strong desire to explore, however, pockets of natural beauty along the coast and in the hills of eastern Andhra Pradesh can offer rich reward. In this sleepy landscape, little affected by modernization, bullocks amble between swaying palms and the rice fields are viridescent against rusty sands. Unless you have the patience to endure the excruciatingly slow public transport system, your own vehicle is essential.

Vijayawada

Almost 450km north of Madras, a third of the way to Calcutta, **VIJAYAWADA** is a bustling commercial centre on the banks of the Krishna delta, hemmed in by bare granite outcrops 90km from the coast. This unattractive city is seldom visited by tourists, but does, however, make the obvious stop-off point for visits to the third-century Buddhist site at **Amaravati**, 60km west.

A handful of temples in Vijayawada merit a quick look. The most important, raised on the low Indrakila Hill in the east, is dedicated to the city's patron goddess **Kanaka Durga** (also known as Vijaya), goddess of riches, power and benevolence. Though it is believed to be thousands of years old, with the exception of a few pillared halls and intricate carvings what you see today is largely renovated (and freshly whitewashed). Across the river, roughly 3km out of town, there's an ancient, unmodified cave temple at **Undavalli**, a tiny rural village set off the main road, easily reached on any Guntur-bound bus, or the local #13 service. The temple is cut out of the granite hillside in typical Pallava style: simple, solid and bold. Each of its five levels contains a deep low-roofed hall, with small rock-cut shrines to Vishnu, Shiva and Parvati, and pillared verandahs guarded by sturdy grey statues of gods, saints and lions. Views from the porches take in a sublime patchwork of rivulets, paddy fields and banana plantations.

Practicalities

Vijayawada's **railway station**, on the main Madras–Calcutta line, is in the centre of town. Buses arriving from Vishakapatnam, Guntur, Amaravati and as far afield as Hyderabad and Madras pull into the **bus stand** further east. Specific ticket offices cater for each service, and a **tourist office** has details on local hotels and sights. Between the bus stand and railway station, Ryes Canal flows through the heart of town.

Vijayawada is a major business centre, with a good selection of mid-range **hotels**, all less than 2km from the railway station and bus stand. Most have reasonably priced restaurants serving Andhra *thalis* and Western food. Budget options include *Monica's* (①), just off Elluru Rd about 500m from the bus stand: very simple, and slightly grubby. The better-value *Santhi* (☎0866/65056; ②–④), close to *Apsara Theatre* on Elluru Rd, offers spotless rooms, private bathrooms with hot water, room service, and excellent food in its veg restaurant. Vijayawada's top hotel is the *Illapuram* on Besant Rd (☎0866/61282; ④–⑦), roughly 1km from the railway station. Its rooms (some a/c) are immaculate, spacious and well lit, with private bath; the carpeted suites are excellent value. Veg and non-veg restaurants on the ground floor serve a wide range of south Indian dishes, and the travel desk arranges tours and transport for guests.

Amaravati

AMARAVATI, a small village on the banks of the Krishna 30km west of Vijayawada, is the site of a Buddhist settlement, formerly known as Chintapalli, where a *stupa* larger than those at Sanchi (see p.360) was erected over relics of the Buddha in the third century BC, during the reign of Ashoka. The *stupa* no longer stands, but its great size is evident from the large mound that formed its base. It was originally surrounded by grey stone railings with a gateway at each of the cardinal points, one of which has been reconstructed in an open courtyard. Its decoration, meticulously carved and perfectly preserved, shows the themes represented on all such Buddhist monuments: the Buddha's birth, renunciation and life as an emaciated ascetic, enlightenment under the *bodhi* tree (see p.843), his first sermon in the Deer Park, and *parinirvana*, or death. Several foundation stones of monastic quarters remain on the site.

Exhibits at the small but fascinating **museum** (daily except Fri 10am–5pm) range in date from the third century BC to the twelfth century AD. They include statues of the Buddha, with lotus symbols on his feet, a head of tightly curled hair, and long ear lobes, all traditional indications of an enlightened teacher. Earlier stone carvings represent the Buddha through such symbols as the *chakra* (wheel of *Dharma*), a throne, a *stupa*, a flaming pillar or a *bodhi* tree, all being worshipped. The lotus motif, a central symbol in early Buddhism, is connected with a dream the Buddha's mother had shortly after conception, and has always been a Buddhist symbol of essential purity: it appears repeatedly on railings and pillars. Later sculptures include limestone statues of the goddess Tara and *bodhisattva* Padmapani, both installed at the site in medieval times when the community had adopted Mahayana teachings in place of the earlier Hinayana doctrines. What you see here are some of the finer pieces excavated from the site – other remains have been taken to the Madras Government Museum and the British Museum in London.

Practicalities

Just one **bus** daily runs direct from Vijayawada to Amaravati (4.30pm; 2hr), so it's best to take a bus to Guntur (every 30min; 30min), where you can pick up a connection on to Amaravati (1hr–1hr 30min). Buses return to Guntur every half hour, and during the monsoon **boats** gather at the jetty in Amaravati and follow the River Krishna all the way to Vijayawada. The excavated site and museum are roughly 1km from the bus stand. Tri-shaws – miniature carts attached to tricycles and brightly painted with chubby film stars – take tourists to the site and the river bank, where there are several drink stalls. Amaravati has no **hotels**, though APTDC have plans for a guest house.

Vishakapatnam

One of India's most rapidly growing industrial cities, and its fourth largest port, **VISHAKAPATNAM** (also known as Vizag), 350km north of Vijayawada, is an unpleasant city choked with the smells and dirt of a busy shipbuilding industry, an oil plant and a steel factory. Such is its sprawl that it has overtaken and polluted the neighbouring town of Waltair, once a health resort. Although there's little to warrant a stop at Vishakapatnam – even its wide stretch of beach is not that clean – remnants of older communities lie within a day's journey from the city.

At **Bheemunipatnam**, 30km north, you can see the remains of a Dutch fort and a peculiar cemetery where slate-grey pyramidal tombs are abandoned to nature. **Borra**, 70km inland on a minor road that winds through the Eastern Ghats and the Araku forests, boasts a set of eerie limestone caves whose darkness is pierced with age-old stalactites and stalagmites. You'll need a car to get to **Mukhalingam**, 100km north of Bheemunipatnam, where three Shaivite temples, built between the sixth and twelfth centuries, rest in low hills. Their elaborate carving and well-preserved towering *shikharas* display slight local variations to the otherwise standard Orissan style (see p.913). There's nowhere to stay in Mukhalingam.

Practicalities

Vishakapatnam's **railway station**, on the Madras–Calcutta coastal route, is in the old town, close to the port. The ride to Delhi takes a tedious two days. The **bus stand**, known as "complex", is in a newer area, 3km from the coast. There's an **airport**, 12km west of town, with daily connections to Hyderabad and Bombay, and several weekly to Calcutta and Bhubaneshwar. Irregular **ships** make the three-day crossing to Port Blair on the Andaman islands.

If you arrive late by bus, head for the well-maintained **retiring rooms** (①) in the bus stand. Otherwise, most **hotels** are in the old town, near the railway station. The best is *Hotel Karanths*, 33-1-55 Patel Marg (☎0891/60347; ②–④), whose spotless rooms have balconies, pressed sheets and attached bathrooms. The downstairs restaurant serves unbeatable *thalis* and *tiffin* at low prices. Next door, *Dakshayani* (☎0891/61798; ①) offers simple grotty rooms, some with private bathrooms. Closer to the port in Poorna Market, the *Ashoka* (☎0891/61049; ②–③) is cleaner and more spacious than the insalubrious surroundings suggest. Vishakapatnam's nicest upmarket hotel, the *Park* on Beach Rd (☎0891/54861; ⑧), has luxurious rooms, swimming pool, bar and restaurant, and access to the beach; watch for currents if you swim in the sea.

Tirupati

Set in a stunning position, surrounded by wooded hills capped by a ring of vertical red rocks, the **Shri Venkateshvara temple** at Tirumala, a hair-raising drive 700m up in the Venkata hills, 11km from **TIRUPATI** and 170km northwest of Madras, is said to be the richest and most popular place of pilgrimage in the world, drawing more devotees than either Rome or Mecca. If you are not a devotee of Shri Venkateshvar, and not particularly keen on waiting in line for hours at a time, choose the day of your visit with care; avoid weekends, public and school holidays, and particularly special festivals, as you are likely to meet at least 10,000 other visitors.

Arrival and information

The best way of **getting to Tirupati** is by train from Madras; the trip can be done in a day if you get the earliest of the three daily services (3hr 30min). From Hyderabad it takes sixteen hours. An information counter at the **railway station** is accessible from the entrance hall and platform 1, where there's a 24-hour left-luggage office and a self-service veg refreshment room. Stands sell English copies of TKT Viraraghava Charya's *History of Tirupati*, and there's a Vivekananda religious bookshop next door. Tirupati's *APSRTC* Central **bus station** – also with 24-hour left luggage – is about 1km from the railway station. Frequent express services run from Madras (4hr), but the train is far more comfortable. Local transport is provided by beautifully decorated **cycle rickshaws**, with silver backs, colourfully painted, some with coverings of appliquéd cloth.

Getting a bus **to Tirumala** and the Venkateshvara temple often requires a lot of waiting in line. If you can manage it, try for one of the earliest services, at about 4am. This avoids queues at the stand and the temple, though is no good on Friday when an elaborate *abhisekham* ceremony means that there's no special *darshan* until 10am. An alternative is to go on a **conducted tour** (see below). The easiest option is to take a **taxi**, but be warned that some of the guys outside the railway station are not licensed and your trip may be curtailed by the Tirumala police. APTDC at the railway station can provide tourist taxis.

The telephone **area code** for Tirupati is ☎08574.

There are several **tourist offices** in Tirupati: *AP Tourism Regional Office*, 139 TP Area (☎232208), *AP Government State Information Centre*, Govindaraja Car St (☎4818) and *TTD Information Centres*, at 1 New Chowltry (☎22777) and the railway station. Daily APTDC **tours** (10am–5pm; Rs50; ☎20602) leave from the bus station, calling at the railway station and including the Padmavati, Venkataswara and Kapilateertham temples, among others, and Chandragiri Fort (not Fri). Where necessary, customers are required to buy "Special Entrance" tickets.

Tirumala Hill, the Venkateshvara temple and Kapilateertham

Not for nothing is there a small shrine to Ganesh at the foot of **Tirumala Hill**. The journey up is hair-raising, to say the least, and any driver, or passenger for that matter, should say a quick prayer when embarking on it. Overtaking is strictly forbidden, but drivers do anyway; virtually every bend is labelled "blind" and every instruction to drive slowly is blithely ignored. The fearless sit on the left for the best views; the most devout, of course, climb the hill by foot. When you get to the top, you will see barbers busying themselves giving pilgrims tonsures as part of their devotions. This is one of the very few temples where non-Hindus are permitted to enter the inner sanctum, but for everyone *darshan*, a view of the god, is the briefest of brief experiences. Temple funds support a university, hospital, orphanages and schools at Tirupati as well as providing cheap, and in some cases free, accommodation for pilgrims.

The **Venkateshvara Vishnu temple**, started in the tenth century, has been recently renovated to provide facilities for the thousands of pilgrims who visit daily; a rabbit warren of passages and waiting rooms wind their way around the complex in which pilgrims interminably shuffle towards the inner sanctum. Unless your visit is intended to be particularly rigorous, on reaching the temple you should follow the signs for the special *darshan* that costs Rs30. This will reduce the time it takes to get inside by hours, if not days (no *darshan* 10am–noon).

Once inside, you'll see the somewhat incongruous sight of *brahmins* sitting at video monitors, observing the goings-on in the inner sanctum; the constant to-ing and fro-ing includes temple attendants bringing in supplies, truckloads of oil and other comestibles, and huge cooking pots being carried across the courtyard. You may also catch deities being hauled past on palanquins to the accompaniment of *nagesvaram* (a south Indian oboe-like double-reed wind instrument) and *tavil* drum, complete with an armed guard. At the entrance is a colonnade, lined with life-sized statues of royal patrons, in copper or stone. The *gopura* gateway leading to the inner courtyard is decorated with sheets of embossed silver; a gold *stambha* (flagstaff) stands outside the inner shrine next to a gold upturned lotus on a plinth. Outside, opposite the temple, is a small museum, the **Hall of Antiquities** (daily 8am–8pm). **Kapilateertham**, a temple at the bottom of the hill, has a gaily painted little Hindu pleasure garden at the entrance; after the rains, a powerful waterfall crashes into a large tank surrounded by colonnades, and everyone piles in for a bath, ensuing in typically good-natured pilgrim bedlam.

Tiruchanur Padmavati temple

Between Tirupati and Tirumala Hill, the **Tiruchanur Padmavati temple** is another popular pilgrimage halt. A gold *vimana* tower with lions at each corner surmounts the sanctuary, which contains a black stone image of goddess Lakshmi with one silver eye. At the front step, water sprays to wash the feet of the devotees. A Rs5 ticket allows you to jump the line to enter the sanctuary. If you'd like to donate a *sari* to the goddess, you may do so, on payment of Rs1200. Cameras are prohibited.

Chandragiri Fort

In the sixteenth century, **Chandragiri**, 11km southwest of Tirupati, became the third capital of the Vijayanagars, whose power had declined following the fall of the city of Vijayanagar (Hampi) in Karnataka. It was here that the British negotiated the acquisition of the land to establish Fort St George, the earliest settlement at what is now Madras. The original fort, thought to date from *c*.1000 AD, was taken over by Haider Ali in 1782, followed by the British in 1792. A small **museum** of sculpture, weapons and memorabilia (daily except Fri 10am–5pm) is housed in the main building, the Indo-Saracenic Raja Mahal. Another building, the **Rani Mahal**, stands close by, while behind that is a hill with two free-standing boulders that was used as a place of public execution during Vijayanagar times. A small temple from the Krishna Deva Raya period and a freshwater tank stand at the top of the hill behind the Raja Mahal.

Accommodation and eating

Unless you're a pilgrim seeking accommodation in the *dharamshalas* near the temple, all the decent places to stay are in Tirupati, near the railway and bus stand. The *Bhima* chain are probably the best-maintained hotels in town. **Eating** is recommended in the bigger hotels; there are, of course, cheap "meals" places in town and near the temple.

Bhimas Deluxe, 34-38 G Car St, near railway station (☎20121). Decent, comfortable rooms (some a/c). *Maya* veg restaurant serves south Indian snacks in the morning and north Indian, some Chinese dishes in the evenings. Very reasonable prices. ⑤.

Bhimas Paradise, Renigunta Rd (☎25747). Spotless, functional rooms (pristine leatherette but no carpet), some a/c, and tiny balconies. *Star TV*, pool, garden, 24hr coffee shop. The restaurant, *Bharani*, is clean and dark, serving veg south Indian snacks, *thalis* and north Indian dishes. ⑤–⑥.

Mayura, 209 TP Area (☎25251). Well-maintained hotel with some a/c rooms, *Star TV*, exchange and travel desk. *Surya* restaurant serves south Indian breakfast and north Indian evening meals. ④.

Mini Bhimas, Railway Station Rd (☎25930). No-frills bottom of the range lodge. ③.

Vishnu Priya, opposite Central Bus Stand (☎25070). Dilapidated rooms (some a/c with TV) with views over the bus stand. Veg food, and travel desk. US$ travellers' cheques accepted. ④–⑤.

PART THREE

THE
CONTEXTS

A BRIEF HISTORY OF INDIA

The earliest human activity in the Indian sub-continent can be traced back to the Early, Middle and Late Stone Ages (400,000–200,000 BC). Implements from all three periods have been found from Rajasthan and Gujarat in the west to Bihar in the east, from the northwest of what's now Pakistan to the tip of the peninsula; and rock paintings of hunting scenes can be seen in the Narmada Valley and elsewhere in central India.

These Paleolithic peoples were semi-nomadic **hunters and gatherers** for many millennia. Indeed, some isolated hill tribes continued to be hunters and gatherers or to practice the transitional "slash and burn" type of agriculture into the twentieth century. Five main peoples are known to have been present when the move to an agricultural lifestyle took place, in the middle of the ninth millennium BC: The **Negrito** race, believed to be the earliest; the **Proto-Australoid**; the **Mediterranean** peoples; the **Mongoloid** elements (confined to the north and northeast); and the western **Brachycephals** or **Alpine** peoples.

The first evidence of **agricultural settlement**, at Mehrgarh on the western plains of the Indus, is roughly contemporaneous with similar developments in Egypt, Mesopotamia and Persia. Village settlements in western Afghanistan, Baluchistan and the Sind gradually developed over the next five thousand years as their inhabitants began to use copper and bronze, domesticate animals, make pottery and trade with their western neighbours.

The distinct styles of pottery discovered at Nal and Zhob in the Brahui hills of Baluchistan, Kulli on the Makran coast and the lower Indus, and Amri in the Sind indicate the development of several independent cultures. **Terracotta figurines** of goddesses, bulls and phallic emblems echo the fertility cults and Mother Goddess worship found in early agricultural communities in the Mediterranean region and the Middle East; they also prefigure elements which were to re-emerge as aspects of the religious life of India.

THE FIRST GREAT INDIAN CIVILIZATION

From the start of the fourth millennium BC, the individuality of early village cultures began to be replaced by a more homogeneous style of pottery at a large number of sites throughout the **Indus Valley**; by the middle of the third millennium, a uniform culture had developed at settlements spread across nearly 500,000 square miles, including parts of the Punjab, Uttar Pradesh, Gujarat, Baluchistan, the Sind and the Makran coast. Two great cities on the Indus, **Harappa** in the north and **Mohenjo Daro** in the south, were supported by the agricultural surplus produced by such settlements. Recent archeological research has unearthed further sites, almost as large as the first two and designed on the same plan, at Kalibangan, on the border of India and Pakistan, at Kot Diji east of Mohenjo Daro, at Chanhu Daro further south on the Indus, and at Lothal in Gujarat.

The emergence of the first great Indian civilization, around 2500 BC, is almost as remarkable as its stability for nearly a thousand years. All the cities were built with baked bricks of the same size; the streets were laid out in a grid with an elaborate system of covered drains; and the houses, some with more than one storey, are large. Vast granaries and a citadel built on higher ground with a gigantic adjoining bath at Mohenjo Daro, together with the absence of royal palaces and the large numbers of religious figurines, suggest that it was a theocratic state of priests, merchants and farmers.

By now, farmers had domesticated various **animals**, including hump-backed (Brahmani) cattle, goats, water buffaloes and fowls. They cultivated wheat, barley, peas and sesamum, and were also probably the first to grow and make clothes from **cotton**. Excavations at Lothal have uncovered a **harbour**; merchants were certainly involved in extensive trading by both sea and land, for they imported metals, including gold, silver and copper, and semi-precious stones from the Indian peninsula, Persia, Afghanistan, central Asia and Mesopotamia. While the main export was probably cotton yarn or cloth, they may have exported surplus grain as well. Indus seals found at Ur confirm the continuity of trading links with Sumer between 2300 and 2000 BC.

The sheer quantity of **seals** discovered in the Indus cities suggests that each merchant or mercantile family had its own. They are usually square, and made of steatite (a kind of soapstone), engraved and then hardened by heating. All bear inscriptions, which remain undeciphered, although nearly 400 different characters have been identified. The emblems beneath the inscriptions – iconographic scenes and animals, such as the bull, buffalo, goat, tiger and elephant – are more enlightening. One of the most notable depicts a horned deity sitting cross-legged in an ithyphallic posture, surrounded by a tiger, an elephant, a rhinoceros, a water buffalo and two deer. He appears on two other seals, and it seems certain that he was a fertility god; indeed, he has been called a "**proto-Shiva**" because of the resemblance to Pashupati, the Lord of the Beasts, a major representation of the fully developed Hindu god, Shiva. Other seals provide evidence that certain trees, especially the *peepal*, were worshipped, and thus anticipate their sacred status in the Hindu and Buddhist religions.

No monumental sculpture survives, but large numbers of human figurines have been discovered, including a steatite bust of a man thought to be a priest, a striking bronze "dancing girl", brilliantly naturalistic models of animals, and countless terracotta statuettes of a Mother Goddess. This goddess is thought to have been worshipped in nearly every home of the common people, but the crude style of modelling suggests that she was not part of the cult of the priestly elite.

The sudden demise of the Indus civilization in the last quarter of the second millennium BC used to be explained by invasions of barbarian tribes from the northwest; but recent research has established that tectonic upheavals in about 1700 BC caused a series of floods, and these are now considered primarily to blame.

THE VEDIC AGE 1500–600 BC

The written history of India begins with the invasions of the charioteering **Indo-European** or **Aryan** tribes, which spelt the final collapse of the Indus civilization. This period takes its name from the earliest Indian literature, the **Vedas**, collections of hymns (*samhitas*) composed in Vedic Sanskrit. Though composed between 1500 and 1000 BC, the *Rig Veda* was not written down until as late as 900 or 800 BC. Although essentially a religious text, in use to this day, it sheds great light on the social and political life of the period.

The Aryans belonged to the barbarian tribes, who broke out of the vast steppeland that stretches from Poland to central Asia to maraud and eventually colonize Europe, the Middle East and the Indian subcontinent from the start of the second millennium BC. They probably entered the Punjab via the Iranian plateau in successive waves over several hundred years; the peaceful farmers of the Indus would have been powerless against their horsedrawn chariots. Aryan culture was diametrically opposed to the Indus civilization, and Vedic literature relates how their war god, Indra, destroyed hundreds of urban settlements.

Semi-nomadic hunters and pastoralists when they first settled the region known as the *Sapta-Sindu* or seven "Induses" (from Kabul to the desert of Rajasthan), as the Aryans spread eastwards into the plain between the upper Ganges and the Yamuna, known as the Doab, they adopted the techniques of settled farming from the peoples they had conquered. The tribes began to organize themselves into village communities, governed by tribal councils (*sabha* and *samiti*) and warrior chiefs (*raja*), who offered protection in return for tribute; the sacrifices of the chief priest or *purohita* secured their prosperity and martial success.

The hymns describe the inter-tribal conflicts characteristic of the period, but there was an underlying sense of solidarity against the indigenous peoples, known as Dasas. Originally a general term for "enemies", it came to denote "subjects" as they were colonized within the land of the Aryans (*aryavarta*). The Dasas are described as negroid phallus worshippers, who owned many cattle and lived in fortified towns or villages (*pur*). The Aryans began to emphasize the purity of blood as they settled among the darker aboriginals, and their original class divisions of nobility and ordinary tribesmen were hardened to exclude the Dasas. At the same time, the priests, the sole custodians and extrapolators of the increasingly complex oral traditions of the sacrificial religion, began to claim high privileges for their skill and training.

By 1000 BC, a fourfold division of society had been given religious sanction in a hymn, which describes how the four classes (*varna*, literally "colour") emanated from the mouth, arms, thighs and feet of the primeval man (*purusha*). The *varna* of priest, warrior, peasant and serf (*brahmin, kshatrya, vaishya* and *shudra*) have persisted as the fundamental structure of society to the present day. The first three encompassed the main divisions within the Aryan tribes, which later assumed the status of "twice-born" (*dvija*); the Dasas and other non-Aryan peoples became the *shudras*, who served the three higher classes.

During the later Vedic period, between 1000 and 600 BC, the centre of Aryan culture and power shifted from the Punjab and the northwest to the Doab, whence their influence continued to spread eastwards and southwards. The sacred texts of the *Sama, Yajur* and *Atharva Vedas*, the *Brahmanas* and the *Upanishads* all originate in this period. Like the *Rig Veda*, they tell us much about developments in religious life, but only offer glimpses of the Aryanization of the subcontinent.

One of the *Brahmanas* relates how Agni, the Aryan fire-god, travelled eastwards destroying the jungle until his advance was arrested by the River Gandak. The Aryans refused to cross the river because Agni had not purified the land beyond until the fire-god ordered a warrior called Videgha Mathava to transport him across the river. The story provides an insight into how colonization occurred, both in terms of the gradual progress eastward of Aryan culture, represented by the fire-god, and of the manner in which the jungle was cleared as the migrating tribes established new settlements.

The great epic poems, the *Mahabharata* and the *Ramayana*, and the *Puranas* claim to relate to this period. Though they are unreliable as historical sources, being overlaid with accre-

> The account of **Hinduism** on p.1228 includes more about the *Mahabharata*, the *Ramayana*, and the development of caste divisions.

tions from later centuries, it is possible to extract some of the facts entwined with the martial myths and legends.

The great battle of **Kurukshetra** – the central theme of the *Mahabharata* – is certainly historical, and took place near modern Delhi some time between the ninth and eighth centuries BC. It was the culmination of a dynastic dispute among the Kurus, who, with their neighbours the Panchalas, were the greatest of the Aryan tribes. Archeological evidence has been found of the two main settlements mentioned in the epic, Indraprastha (Delhi) and Hastinapura, further north on the Ganges; the latter was the capital of the Kurus, two of whose kings, Parikshit and Janamejaya, are described as mighty conquerors in the Vedic literature.

By the time of Kurukshetra, the Aryans had advanced into the mid-Gangetic valley to establish **Kosala**, with its capital at **Ayodhya** – according to the *Ramayana*, the realm of Rama, the god-hero. Vedic literature mentions neither Rama nor his father Dasharatha, but does refer to Rama's father-in-law, Janaka of Videha. Certainly the extension of Aryan influence to south India, reflected in the myth of Rama's invasion of Sri Lanka to rescue Sita, did not occur until much later. At this time, the megalithic cultures of Madras, Kerala and Mysore remained untouched by the Aryan invaders. The Aryanization of north India, however, continued throughout the period, and began to penetrate central India as well.

The migrating tribes pushed east beyond Kosala to found the kingdoms of **Kashi** (the region of Varanasi), **Videha** (east of the River Gandak and north of the Ganges), and **Anga** on the border of Bengal. The **Yadava** tribe settled around Mathura, on the Yamuna; a branch of the Yadavas is said later to have colonized Saurashtra in modern Gujarat. Further east, down the Yamuna, the **Vatsa** kingdom established its capital at Kaushambi. Other tribes pushed southwards down the River Chambal to found the kingdom of **Avanti**; some penetrated as far as the Narmada, and by the end of the period Aryan influence probably extended into the northwest Deccan.

This territorial expansion was assisted by significant developments in Aryan civilization. When they arrived in India Aryan knowledge of **metallurgy** was limited to gold, copper and bronze, but later Vedic literature mentions tin, lead, silver and iron. The use of iron, together with the taming of elephants, facilitated the rapid clearance of the forests and jungles for settlement. They now grew a large range of crops, including rice; specialized trades and crafts grew considerably, and merchants re-established trade with Mesopotamia, curtailed since the days of the Indus civilization.

Vedic culture and society was transformed by mutual acculturation between the Aryans and indigenous peoples. By the end of the Vedic period, the Aryan tribes had consolidated into little kingdoms, each with its capital city. Some were republics, but generally the power of the tribal assemblies was dwindling, to be replaced by a new kind of politics centred on a **king**, who ruled a geographical area. His relatives and courtiers formed a rudimentary administrative system – known as "Jewel Bearers" (*ratnins*), they included the chief priest, the chamberlain and palace officials.

Kingship was becoming more absolute, limited only by the influence of the priesthood; a relationship between temporal and sacred power that became crucial. The *Brahmana* literature, compiled by the priests, contains instructions for the performance of sacrifices symbolizing royal power, such as the royal consecration ceremonies (*rajasuya*) and the horse sacrifice (*ashvamedha*). Thus, the priests sustained belief in the association of kingship with divinity through their rituals and assisted new political institutions to emerge.

Not all religious specialists were committed to these political developments, and the evolution of Aryan civilization in the late Vedic period also involved a degree of introspection and pessimism. The disintegration of tribal identity created a profound sense of insecurity, which combined with doubts as to the efficacy of sacrificial rituals led to the emergence of non-conformists and ascetics. Their teachings were set down in the metaphysical literature of the *Upanishads* and the *Aranyakas*, which laid the foundations for the various philosophical systems developed in later periods.

THE AGE OF THE BUDDHA 600–321 BC

The age of the Buddha was marked by great intellectual endeavour and spiritual agitation. Though mystics and ascetics rejected the norms of Vedic society, major political and commercial developments continued; the emergence of kingdoms and administrative systems encouraged rulers to think in terms of empire.

By 600 BC, the association of tribes with the territories they had colonized had resulted in the consolidation of at least sixteen republics and monarchies, known as **mahajanapadas** (territories of the great clans). Some, like **Kuru** and **Panchala**, represented the oldest and earliest established kingdoms; others, like **Avanti**, **Vatsa** and **Magadha** had come into existence more recently. The hereditary principle and the concept of divinely ordained kings, tended to preserve the status quo in the monarchies, while the republics provided an atmosphere in which unorthodox views were able to develop. The founders of the "heterodox" sects of Buddhism and Jainism were both born in small republics of this kind (see pp.1235 & 1237).

The consolidation of the *mahajanapadas* was based on the growth of a stable agrarian economy and the increasing importance of **trade**, which led to the use of coins and a script (Brahmi, from which the current scripts of India, Sri Lanka, Tibet, Java and Burma derive) and encouraged the emergence of towns, such as Kashi (Varanasi), Ayodhya, Rajagriha (first capital of Magadha), Kaushambi in the Ganges Valley, and Ujjain on the Narmada. The resultant prosperity stimulated conflict, however, and by the fifth century BC the four great kingdoms of Kashi, Koshala, Vatsa and Magadha and the republic of the Vrijjis between them held sway over all the others.

Eventually, **Magadha** emerged supreme, under Bimbisara (543–491 BC), a resolute and energetic organizer, and Ajatashatru (491–461 BC), who conquered Kashi and Koshala, broke up the Vrijji confederacy, and built a strong administration. Both kings set out to control the trade of the Ganges Valley and its rich deposits of copper and iron.

Magadha expanded over the next hundred years, moving its capital to **Pataliputra** (Patna) and annihilating the other kingdoms in the

Ganges Valley or reducing them to the status of vassals. In the middle of the fourth century BC, the **Nanda** dynasty usurped the Magadhan throne; Mahapadma Nanda conquered Kalinga (Orissa and the northern coastal strip of Andhra Pradesh) and gained control of parts of the Deccan. The disputed succession after his death coincided with significant events in the northwest; out of this confusion the first and perhaps greatest of India's empires was born.

Darius I, the third Achaemenid emperor of Persia, had claimed Gandhara in the northwest as his twentieth satrapy, and advanced into the Punjab near the end of the sixth century BC; but a second invasion in the fourth century BC was more significant. **Alexander the Great** defeated Darius III, the last Achaemenid, crossed the Indus in 326 BC, and overran the Punjab. He was in India for just two years and although he left garrisons and appointed satraps to govern the conquered territories, his death in 323 BC made their position untenable. Chandragupta Maurya was quick to take advantage of the political vacuum.

THE MAURYAN EMPIRE 321–104 BC

The accession to the throne of **Chandragupta Maurya**, who overthrew the last of the Nanda dynasty of Magadhan about 321 BC, marked the beginnings of the first Indian empire. He is said to have met Alexander the Great and was probably inspired by his exploits; his 500,000-strong army drove out the Greek garrisons in the northwest, and annexed all the lands east of the Indus. When Seleucus Nicator, Alexander's general, attempted to regain control of Macedonian provinces in India, Chandragupta defeated him and forced the surrender of territories in what is now Afghanistan as a reward.

According to tradition, Chandragupta was assisted by an unscrupulous *brahmin* adviser called Kautilya or Chanakya, the reputed author of the *Arthashastra*, a famous treatise on political economy. The Mauryan empire developed a highly bureaucratic state administration, which controlled economic life and employed a very thorough secret service system. From about 297 BC onwards, Chandragupta's son Bindusara extended the empire as far south as Mysore.

Bindusara was succeeded in around 269 BC by his son, **Ashoka** – the noblest ruler of India, whom the Buddhists called a universal emperor (*chakravartin*). Ashoka's political pragmatism and imperial vision, complemented by his humanity, practical benevolence and tolerance, mark him out as a statesman and a reformer far ahead of his times. He ruthlessly consolidated his power for the first eight years of his reign, before invading and subduing the tribal kingdom of Kalinga (Orissa), his only campaign of violent conquest, in 260 BC. Two and a half years later,

THE EDICTS OF ASHOKA

Edict 1 denounces animal slaughter for sacrifices and festivities, and details the reduced consumption by the royal household from hundreds of beasts to only two peacocks and one deer per day.

Edict 2 records the import and cultivation of herbs, roots and fruits for the treatment of humans and animals, and the building of highways and wells.

Edict 3 instructs *Mahamatras* ("Officers of Righteousness") to carry out *dharma*.

Edict 4 embellishes Edict 3.

Edict 5 requests Ashoka's subjects to aid the families of prisoners and wean criminals away from evil.

Edict 6 says Ashoka is available for council at any time.

Edict 7 recommends self-control and purity of thought so that religious sects may live in harmony.

Edict 8 tells of Ashoka's pilgrimages and acts of charity.

Edict 9 encourages the practice of *dharma* in place of superstitious rites.

Edict 10 praises the modesty brought about by *dharma*, and denounces fame and glory.

Edict 11 propounds the beneficial results of *dharma*.

Edict 12 advises *Mahamatras* to expound the principles of all religions.

Edict 13 apologizes for the devastation at Kalinga.

Edict 14 summarizes the previous thirteen.

his conversion to **Buddhism** caused Ashoka to espouse non-violence (*ahimsa*), and consequently to abandon territorial aggression in favour of conquest by the **Law of Righteousness** (*dharma*). The fourteen **edicts** in which he laid down its principles were engraved in the Brahmi script on eighteen great rocks and thirty polished sandstone pillars throughout the empire.

Ashoka sought to neutralize the regional pluralism within the empire by his proclamation of the *dharma*, a code of conduct designed to counteract the social tensions created by the *varna* distinctions of class, sectarian conflicts and economic differences. It inculcated social responsibility, encouraged socio-religious harmony, sought to ensure human dignity and expressed a paternal concern for his subjects' well-being and happiness. His social reforms included the restriction of animal slaughter and the prohibition of animal sacrifices in Pataliputra, which encouraged vegetarianism; the cultivation of medicinal herbs and the establishment of healing centres. The system of communications was improved by planting roadside fruit trees and by the construction of wells and rest houses. He also replaced the annual royal hunt with a pilgrimage of righteousness (*dharma yatra*), which gave him the opportunity to visit the distant corners of the empire personally and exhibit himself as the living symbol of imperial unity.

His adoption of Buddhism and this new ethical system, however, did not interfere with his imperial pragmatism, and despite his avowed remorse after the Kalinga campaign he continued to govern the newly acquired territory, retained his army without reduction and warned the wilder tribesmen that he would use force to subjugate them if they continued to raid the civilized villages of the empire.

Ashoka's empire extended from Assam to Afghanistan and from Kashmir to Mysore; only the three Dravidian kingdoms of the Cholas, Cheras and Pandyas in the southernmost tip of the subcontinent remained independent. Diplomatic relations were maintained with Syria, Egypt, Macedonia and Cyrene, and all the states on the immediate borders. The Mauryan empire was built on military conquest and a centralized administration — its well-organized revenue department ensured a strong fiscal base — but Ashoka's imperial vision, his shrewd-

ness, and above all the force of his personality and the loyalty he inspired, held it all together.

After Ashoka's death in 232 BC, the empire began to fall apart. While princes contested the throne, the provincial governors established their independence. Inter-regional rivalries and further invasions from central Asia exacerbated matters, and in 184 BC the last of the Mauryans, Brihadratha, was assassinated by his *brahmin* general, Pushyamitra Shunga. The Mauryans had ruled India for nearly 140 years; Ashoka's importance was recognized more than two thousand years later, when Nehru adopted the lion capital of his Sarnath pillar as the emblem of the newly independent India.

THE AGE OF INVASIONS
104 BC–320 AD

Although economic prosperity and cultural enrichment endured for five hundred years after the death of Ashoka, India became politically fragmented. Successive invasions, and the emergence of regional monarchies in the south, reduced Magadha to one of many quasi-feudal kingdoms struggling for regional power.

The dynasty founded by Pushyamitra Shunga ruled Magadha until 72 BC, when the last Shunga monarch was deposed by his servant Vasudeva Kanva. Pushyamitra was an orthodox *brahmin*, but Buddhism continued to be generously patronized; elaborate stone *stupas* were erected at Sanchi and Bharhur during Shunga times. Magadha still included Bengal, Bhopal and Malwa within its boundaries, though the Punjab and the northwestern territories had been lost.

The Bactrian Greeks, who had asserted their independence from the Seleucids of Syria and recaptured Gandhara (the Peshawar region of Pakistan) in 190 BC, were the first invaders. When the Mauryan empire collapsed, the Indo-Greek rulers occupied the Punjab and extended their control as far as Mathura in Uttar Pradesh. One Indo-Greek king, Milinda or Menander, who ruled the Swat Valley and the Punjab from Sagala (Sialkot) between 155 and 130 BC, became famous for his conversion to Buddhism by the philosopher Nagasena. Another example of acculturation is found on the Garuda pillar at Besnagar (Bhilsa), by Heliodorus, the Greek envoy to the Shunga court, to commemorate the Bactrian conquests of northwestern India. Its inscription proclaimed Heliodorus to be a worshipper of Vasudeva, a god later identified with Krishna, the Lord of the *Bhagavad Gita*.

The next wave of invasions, in the second century BC, saw Parthians (Pahlavas) from Iran take control of Bactria. Soon large-scale movements of central Asian Yueh-Chi nomads had precipitated the migration of the Scythians (Shakas), who displaced the Parthians. During the first century AD, the Kushan branch of the Yueh-Chi in turn drove the Shakas out of northwestern India into Gujarat and Malwa around Ujjain, where they settled and became Indianized, while Kujula Kadphises established the **Kushan** dynasty in the northwest.

The third and greatest of the Kushan kings, **Kanishka**, who reigned for more than twenty years around 100 AD, extended his rule as far east as Varanasi and as far south as Sanchi. Kanishka's empire prospered through control of trade routes between India, China and the West, and his court attracted artists and musicians as well as merchants. Ashvaghosha, one of the first classical Sanskrit poets, wrote a Life of the Buddha (*Buddha Charita*) and is credited with converting the emperor to Buddhism.

While the tribal republics of northern and central India absorbed invaders from the northwest, the kingdoms of Ayodhya and Kaushambi continued to be important in the Gangetic valley; but the first great kingdom of southern India was flexing its muscles. Between the second century BC and the second century AD the **Andhra** or **Satavahana** dynasty, which originated in the region between the rivers Godavari and Krishna, spread its control across much of south and central India.

Having unsuccessfully challenged the Shakas in Malwa and Gujarat, they brought the northwest Deccan under their control and created a capital at Paithan on the Godavari, northeast of Pune in Maharashtra. The Satavahanas overthrew the Kanva dynasty of Magadha in 27 BC and pushed south to the Tungabhadra and Krishna rivers. Their second capital, at **Amaravati** on the Krishna, prospered on trade with Rome and southeast Asia, but by the middle of the third century the Satavahana kingdom had collapsed. The Pallavas took control of their territories in Andhra Pradesh, while the Vakatakas gained supremacy in the central and northwestern regions of the Deccan in the latter half of the third century, only to be subsumed within the Gupta empire by the end of the fourth century.

Further south, the three kingdoms of the **Cheras** on the Malabar coast in the west, the **Pandyas** in the central southern tip of the peninsula, and the **Cholas** on the east coast of Coromandel – together comprising much of present-day Tamil Nadu and Kerala – had been developing almost completely independently of north India. **Madurai**, the Pandyan capital, and still one of the major temple cities of the south, had become a centre of Tamil culture. Between 300 BC and 200 AD, colleges or academies (**sangam**) of poets produced a body of literature which describes an indigenous Tamil culture and society only gradually being influenced by the Aryan traditions of the north. The early kingdoms were matriarchal, and the Dravidian kinship system was endogamous, being based on cross-cousin marriage, in sharp contrast to the Indo-Aryan system of exogamy, which prescribed marriage to outsiders. Society was divided into groups based on the geographical domains of hills, plains, forest, coast and desert rather than class or *varna*, though *brahmins* did command high status. Although agriculture, pastoralism and fishing were the main occupations, trade in spices, gold and jewels with Rome and southeast Asia underpinned the region's prosperity.

The three kingdoms initially balanced individual struggles for political hegemony with alliances to withstand the aggression of their northern neighbours; but after the middle of the first century BC conflicts between themselves became more frequent. This enervating warfare rendered them vulnerable; early in the fourth century AD, the **Pallavas** overran the Chola capital of Kanchipuram, and by 325 AD they were in control of Tamil Nadu. The Pallavas remained a dominant power in the south until the ninth century AD, and thus became one of the longest ruling dynasties in Indian history.

Despite the disintegration of the Mauryan empire and the proliferation of fiercely rival kingdoms from 200 BC to 300 AD, this was also a period of unprecedented economic wealth and cultural development. The growing importance of the mercantile community encouraged the monetization of the economy and stimulated the growth of urban centres all over India. Merchants and artisans organized themselves into guilds (*shreni*), which along with the ruling dynasties, minted their own coins.

External **trade**, overland and maritime, opened up lines of communication with the outside world. The main highway from Pataliputra to Taxila gave India access to the old **Silk Road**, the most important trade route of the time, linking China to the Mediterranean via central Asia. Maritime trade traversed the coastal routes between the seaports in Gujarat and southern India and as far as south Arabia; and Indian merchants established trading communities in various parts of south Asia.

The invasion of foreign peoples, the growth of trade and urbanization together had a considerable impact on the structure of society. Foreign conquerors and traders, who had to be integrated within the *varna* system, the burgeoning importance of the *vaishya* class of merchants and artisans, and the influence of urban liberalism, all presented serious challenges to law and social order. The Law Books (*Dharmashastras*) were composed in this period in an attempt to accommodate these changes and redefine social, economic and legal rights and duties. Important developments in India's religions can also be linked to socio-economic changes. Radical schisms occurred in both Buddhism and Jainism, and may be attributed to the increasing participation and patronage of the *vaishyas*; while the Vedic religion, which had been the exclusive domain of the *brahmins* and *kshatryas*, underwent fundamental transformations to widen its social base.

THE CLASSICAL AGE 300–650 AD

The era of the imperial Guptas (320–550 AD) and the reign of Harsha Vardhana (606–647 AD) of Kanauj, during which north India was re-unified, comprises the **Classical Age** of Indian history.

Chandra Gupta I (no relation to the Mauryan Guptas) struck gold coins in 320 AD to celebrate his coronation and marriage to Princess Kumaradevi of the Licchavi tribe, which had re-established itself in the neighbouring territory of Vaishali, north of the Ganges. Chandra Gupta I thus established a powerful kingdom, centred on Magadha, Koshala and Ayodhya, in the Gangetic plain, which controlled the vital East–West trade route, and claimed the title of Great King of Kings (*maharajadhiraja*).

His son and heir, Samudra Gupta (*c*.335–376 AD), expanded the frontiers of the realm from Punjab to Assam; an inscription in Allahabad claimed that he "violently uprooted" nine kings of northern India, humbled eleven more in the south and compelled another five to pay tribute

as feudatories. The martial tribes of Rajasthan and the Shakas, who had ruled Malwa and Gujarat for over two hundred years, never did more than pay homage; but Samudra had built the foundations for the second largest empire in pre-medieval India, which reached its apogee under his successor.

Chandra Gupta II (376–415 AD) finally subjugated the Shakas in Gujarat to secure access to the trade of the western coast at the end of the fourth century AD, and re-unified the whole of northern India, with the exception of the northwest. He extended his influence by marrying Kuvera, a queen of the Nagas, and marrying his daughter Prabhavati to Rudrasena II of the Vakatakas, whose kingdom included parts of modern Madhya Pradesh, Maharashtra and northwestern Andhra Pradesh.

Fa Hsien, a Chinese Buddhist monk who visited India during the reign of Chandra Gupta II, noted the palaces and free hospitals of Pataliputra and the fact that all respectable Indians were vegetarian. He also mentions discrimination against the untouchables, who carried gongs to warn passers-by of their polluting presence; but generally, he describes the empire as prosperous, happy and peaceful. The Guptas performed Vedic sacrifices to legitimize their rule, and patronized popular forms of Hinduism, such as devotional religion (*bhakti*) and the worship of images of Vishnu, Shiva and the Goddess in temples, which were crystallizing during the period; but Buddhism continued to thrive and Fa Hsien mentions thousands of monks dwelling at Mathura as well as hundreds in Pataliputra itself.

Patronage of art and literature under the Guptas facilitated the development of a classical idiom that became the exemplar for subsequent creative endeavours. Secular **Sanskrit literature** reached its perfection in the works of Kalidasa, the greatest Indian poet and dramatist, who was a member of Chandra Gupta II's court. The cave paintings of **Ajanta** and **Ellora** inspired Buddhist artists throughout Asia, and Yashodhara's detailed analysis of painting in the fifth century prescribed the classical conventions for the new art form. In **sculpture**, the images of the Buddha produced in Sarnath and Mathura embodied the simple and serene quality of classicism; but there were also the voluptuous mother goddesses of Hinduism.

The formative stages of the northern style of **Hindu temple**, which became India's classic architectural form, also occurred in this era; a fine example survives at **Deogarh**, near Jhansi in central India. Early Hindu temples were comparatively small and simple; an inner sanctuary (*garbha griha*) housing the deity was connected to a larger hall (*mandapa*), where the devotees could congregate to worship. This prototype of the northern Hindu temple persisted from Gupta times to the present day, but these humble origins subsequently evolved into extravagantly ornate structures.

The era of the Guptas produced great thinkers as well: six systems of **philosophy** (*Nyaya, Vaisheshika, Sankhya, Yoga, Mimamsa* and *Vedanta*) evolved, which refuted Buddhism and Jainism. *Vedanta* has continued as the basis of all philosophical studies in India to this day. In the fifth century, the great **astronomer**, Aryabhata, argued that the earth rotated on its own axis while revolving around the sun, and his terse commentary on an anonymous mathematical text assumes an understanding of the decimal system of nine digits and a zero, with place notation for tens and hundreds. The Arabs acknowledged their debt to the "Indian art" of mathematics; and many Western European discoveries and inventions would have been impossible if they had remained encumbered by the Roman system of numerals.

Though the Gupta empire remained relatively peaceful during the long reign of Kumara Gupta, who succeeded Chandra Gupta II, by the time Skanda Gupta came to the throne in 454 AD, western India was again threatened by invasions from Central Asia. Skanda managed to repel White Hun raids, but after his death their disruption of central Asian trade seriously destabilized the empire. By the end of the fifth century, the Huns had wrested the Punjab from Gupta control, and further incursions early in the sixth century were the death blow to the empire, which had completely disintegrated by 550 AD. In the sixth century another wave of central Asian tribes, including the Gurjaras, displaced the older tribes in Rajasthan and became the founders of the **Rajput** dynasties.

After the demise of the Guptas, northern India again split into rival kingdoms; but the Pushpabhutis of Sthanvishvara (Thanesvar, north of Delhi) had established supremacy by the time **Harsha Vardhana** came to the throne

in 606 AD. He reigned for 41 years over an empire that ranged from Gujarat to Bengal, including the Punjab, Kashmir and Nepal, and moved his capital to **Kanauj** in the wake of his eastern conquests. Even the king of Assam acknowledged his influence, but his attempts to advance into the Deccan were emphatically repulsed by Pulakeshin II of the Chalukyas. Harsha possessed considerable gifts as well as untiring energy; in addition to his martial achievements and ceaseless touring, he wrote three dramas and found time to indulge a love of philosophy and literature. The life of Harsha (*Harshacharita*) by Bana, his court poet, is the first historically authentic Indian biography.

Harsha's empire was essentially feudal, with most of the defeated kings retaining their thrones as vassals, and when he died without heirs in 647 AD north India once again fragmented into independent kingdoms.

KINGDOMS OF CENTRAL AND SOUTH INDIA 500–1250 AD

After the collapse of Harsha's empire, significant events took place in the Deccan and Tamil Nadu. Aryan influences were assimilated into Dravidian culture throughout the era of the **Pallavas**, which began when they captured Kanchipuram early in the fourth century and lasted until they were overthrown by a revived Chola dynasty in the ninth century. The upper strata of society increasingly adopted Aryan ideas, but as the indigenous culture reacted to assert itself among the lower strata, a distinctive Tamil culture emerged from the synthesis.

The history of the period was dominated by conflicts between three major kingdoms. The **Pandyas** of Madurai had their own regional kingdom by the sixth century; the **Chalukyas** of Vatapi (Badami in Mysore) had expanded their kingdom into the Deccan when the Vakataka dynasty collapsed in the middle of the sixth century; and the **Pallavas** had supplanted the Satavahanas in the Andhra region and made Kanchipuram their capital.

Under Mahendravarman I, a contemporary of Harsha at the start of the seventh century, the Pallavas came into conflict with the Chalukyas over the region of Vengi in the Krishna-Godavari valley. They remained at war until the middle of the eighth century, intermittently harassed by the Pandyas further south. Both the Pallavas and the Chalukyas enlisted the support of other kingdoms at different times during the protracted struggle – the **Cheras** of Kerala, who made alliances with both sides, avoided direct involvement in the conflict – but their military strength was so evenly matched that neither was able to gain the ascendancy. Eventually the Chalukya dynasty was overthrown in 753 by a feudatory, Dantidurga, the founder of the Rashtrakuta kingdom. The Pallavas survived their arch enemies by about a hundred years, then succumbed to a combined attack of the Pandyas and the Cholas.

The **Rashtrakutas** exploited the instability in the north by attempts to capture the trade routes of the Ganges Valley, and Indra III gained possession of Kanauj for a brief period, but ultimately the campaigns drained the kingdom's resources.

Meanwhile, the **Cholas** were on the ascendant in Tamil Nadu; they conquered the region of Thanjavur in the ninth century, and Parantaka I, who came to power in 907 AD, captured Madurai from the Pandyas. The Rashtrakutas defeated the Cholas in the middle of the tenth century, but when they were replaced by the revived "Later" Chalukyas in 973 AD the Cholas were able to regain their lost territories, and expand further during the eleventh and twelfth centuries.

Rajaraja I campaigned against the allied powers of Kerala, Ceylon and the Pandyas to break their control of western trade and combat competition from the Arab traders, who were supported by Kerala. **Rajendra I**, who succeeded his father in 1014 AD, annexed the southern territories of the Chalukyas, renewing the campaigns against Kerala and Ceylon, and initiating a northern offensive, which reached the banks of the Ganges. Rajendra did not hold his northern conquests for long, but was successful in protecting Indian commercial interests in southeast Asia.

By the end of the eleventh century the Cholas were supreme in the south, but incessant campaigning had exhausted their resources. Ironically, their destruction of the Chalukyas laid the seeds of their own downfall. Former Chalukya feudatories, such as the **Yadavas** of Devagiri in the northern Deccan and the **Hoysalas**, around modern Mysore, set up their own kingdoms; the latter attacked the Cholas from the west while the Pandyas directed a new offensive from the south. By the thirteenth cen-

tury, the **Pandyas** had superseded the Cholas as south India's major power; the Yadavas and the Hoysalas controlled the Deccan until the advent of the Turkish Sultans of Delhi in the fourteenth century.

Despite constant political conflicts this period was very much the classical age of the south. The ascendancy of the Cholas was complemented by the crystallization of Tamil culture; the religious, artistic, and institutional patterns of this period dominated the culture of the south and influenced developments elsewhere in the peninsula. In the sphere of religion for instance, the great philosophers **Shankara** and Ramanuja, as well as the Tamil and Maharashtran saints, had a significant impact on Hinduism in north India.

REGIONAL KINGDOMS IN NORTH INDIA 650–1250 AD

In north India, Harsha's death was followed by a century of confusion, with assorted kingdoms competing to control the Gangetic valley. In time, the **Pratiharas**, descendants of the Rajasthani Gurjaras, and the **Palas** of Bihar and Bengal emerged as the main rivals.

The Pala king Dharmapala (770–810) was the first to gain the initiative, by taking Kanauj; however, the Pratiharas wrested it back soon after his death. They remained in the ascendant during the ninth century, but were weakened by repeated incursions from the Deccan by the **Rashtrakutas**, who briefly occupied Kanauj in 916. The Pratiharas regained their capital, but the tripartite struggle sapped their strength and they were unable to repel the Turkish invasion of Kanauj in 1018. At the start of the eleventh century the Palas again pushed west as far as Varanasi, but had to abandon the campaign to defend their homelands in Bengal against the Chola king Rajendra.

The struggle for possession of Kanauj depleted the resources of the three competing powers and resulted in their almost simultaneous decline. In northern India, just as in the south, the tendency of feudatories of large kingdoms to assert their independence brought several small states into being. Kingdoms such as Nepal, Kamarupa (Assam), Kashmir, Orissa, the eastern Chalukyas and the Gangas of the east coast developed their own cultural identities. Regional histories and dynastic genealogies were written, local customs and literature were patronized, and the kingdoms competed to outdo each other in building temples.

In **Orissa**, small kingdoms in the Mahanadi and Brahmani valleys had co-existed for nearly five hundred years when the Somavamshi dynasty united western and central Orissa in the eleventh century, and established its capital at **Bhubaneshwar**. The temples they constructed demonstrate a notable continuity from the earliest days in the eighth century, to the magnificent Lingaraja temple, dated around 1000 AD. The royal cult of Jagannath (Vishnu), with its "juggernaut" car festival and the gigantic temple at **Puri** were cultural manifestations of the political unification completed by the eastern Gangas of Kalinga in the twelfth century. The stunning chariot temple dedicated to the sun god Surya at **Konarak** in the thirteenth century represents the aesthetic climax of these regional developments.

The **Rajputs**, so influential in the culture and politics of medieval India, were descended from the sixth-century central Asian invaders. They attained respectability in keeping with the Puranic traditions by acquiring solar and lunar genealogies and adopting *kshatrya* status. By the tenth century, the most important clans, like the Pariharas (a branch of the Pratiharas) of south Rajasthan, the Chamanas or Chauhans of Shakambhari and Ajmer, and the Chaulukyas or Solankis of Kathiawar, had all established regional kingdoms. Rajput clans in western and central India included the **Chandellas** of Bundelkhand, who produced the magnificent group of temples at **Khajuraho**, the Guhilas of Chittaurgarh, the Tomaras in Haryana, and the Kalachuris of Tripuri near Jabalpur.

The Rajputs fought among each other incessantly, however, and failed to grasp the significance of a new factor, which entered the politics of north India at the start of the eleventh century. **Mahmud**, a Turkish chieftain who had established a powerful kingdom at Ghazni in Afghanistan, made seventeen plundering raids into the plains of India between 1000 and 1027. Mathura, Thanesvar, Kanauj and Somnath in Saurashtra were all looted to enhance the greatness of Ghazni and only the astuteness of the Chandellas of Bundelkhand, who agreed to pay tribute, saved the temples of Khajuraho from destruction.

The three most powerful Rajputs of northern India, Prithviraja Chamana, Jahacchandra

Gahadavala and Paramardideva Chandella, were in a state of three-way war when Muhammad of Ghur supplanted the line of Mahmud, seized the Ghaznavid possessions in the Punjab at the end of the twelfth century, and focussed his attention on the wealthy lands further east. **Prithviraja III**, the legendary hero of the Chauhans, patched together an alliance to defeat the Turkish warlord at **Tarain** (near Thanesvar) in 1191; but Muhammad returned the next year with a superior force, defeated the Rajputs, and had Prithviraja executed. Muhammad went home, leaving his generals to complete the conquest and establish what became known as the **Slave Dynasty**.

THE DELHI SULTANATE 1206–1526 AD

The **Delhi Sultanate** was to be the major political force in north India from the thirteenth to the sixteenth century, its power and territories fluctuating with the abilities of successive rulers. Although it never succeeded in welding together an all-India empire, the impact of Islam on Indian culture reverberated for centuries throughout the subcontinent.

Muhammad was assassinated in 1206 within a few years of his return to Ghur. His empire disintegrated, to leave his Turkish slave general, **Qutb-ud-din-Aiback**, as the autonomous ruler of the Indian territories and founder of the first "slave dynasty" of the Sultanate. Aiback died four years later – before the Qutb Minar, his victory tower, in Delhi could be completed – and his son-in-law **Iltutmish** (1211–36) inherited the task of securing the Sultanate's tenuous hold on northern India. When Genghis Khan annihilated the world from which the ancestors of Iltutmish had come, it gave him an added incentive to consolidate his power base in India. Iltutmish had extended the Sultanate's territories from the Sind to Bengal by the time he died in 1236, but the subsequent three decades were critical. His daughter, Sultana Raziyya, succeeded but was murdered in 1240, and not until Balaban, Raziyya's chief huntsman and member of her father's palace guard, took control in 1266 did the Sultanate attain any degree of stability.

Meanwhile, the **Mongols** had returned in 1241. Although internecine strife within the Mongol empire from 1260–61 offered a temporary reprieve, the accession of the Khalji dynasty in 1290 coincided with a renewed threat from the Chaghatai Mongols. Their raids extended beyond the Punjab and even laid siege to Delhi for two months in 1303. Nevertheless, **Ala-ud-din-Khalji** (1296–1315) energetically enforced Islamic rule over the autonomous Hindu states, which were a constant source of aggravation. Having conquered Gujarat and the Rajput fortresses of Ranthambor, Chittaurgarh, Sevana and Jalor in a series of expeditions between 1299 and 1311, he turned his attention to the Deccan and the south where he exacted tribute from the Yadavas of Devagiri, the Kakatiyas of Telengana, and the Pandyas. His aspirations to build a stable empire were dashed, however, when Gujarat, Chittaurgarh and Devagiri all re-asserted their independence before his death in 1315.

A fresh imperial impetus came from the **Tughluq** dynasty, which succeeded the Khaljis in 1320. Under **Muhammad bin Tughluq** (1325–51), the Sultanate reached its maximum extent, comparable in size to Ashoka's empire. Unfortunately, Muhammad weakened the empire by his attempts to finance his ambitions. He provoked a peasant uprising in the Doab by increasing the revenue demand to pay for an expedition to Khurasan in central Asia, and later tried to introduce a token currency to pay the troops, which had to be withdrawn. He then made a controversial and abortive attempt to relocate his capital in a more central position at Devagiri (renamed Daulatabad) in the Deccan. Revolts signalled the first phase in the collapse of the Delhi Sultanate: Malabar, Bengal and Telengana all seceded between 1334 and 1339. The Bahmani dynasty became the autonomous rulers of the Deccan in 1347, and the new Hindu kingdom of **Vijayanagar** took advantage of the decline of the Sultanate's authority to extend its influence. From its capital near Hampi, Vijayanagar dominated the region south of the Krishna and Tungabhadra rivers between the middle of the fourteenth century and 1565, when an alliance of Muslim kingdoms brought it down.

Firoz Shah Tughluq (1351–88), who re-established the capital at Delhi, stemmed the tide to some extent with the comparative mildness of his rule. He is credited with an impressive list of public works, including the building of mosques, colleges, reservoirs, hospitals, public baths, bridges and towns – especially **Jaunpur**, near Varanasi, which became a major

centre of Islamic culture. However, by reverting to a decentralized administrative system he fostered the rise of semi-independent warlords, who became increasingly antagonistic under the last of the Tughluqs.

Family squabbles over the throne after Firoz Shah's death in 1388 further weakened the Sultanate, and the degeneracy of his successors made it vulnerable to external predators. After **Timur**, the central Asian conqueror known to the West as Tamberlane, sacked Delhi in 1398, autonomous sultanates emerged in Jaunpur, Malwa and Gujarat; the Hindu kingdoms of Marwar and Mewar were established in Rajasthan; and small principalities even nearer the capital appeared at Kalpi, Mahoba and Gwalior. The Delhi Sultanate had been reduced to just one of several competing Muslim states in northern India.

After the death of the last Tughluq, Delhi was seized by Khizr Khan (1414–21), who had been an officer of the governor of Multan and Lahore appointed by Timur before he left India. In 37 years, Khizr's **Sayyid** dynasty lost Multan and were repeatedly harassed by the Sharqi sultans of Jaunpur. The Sultanate experienced a modest revival under the more energetic rule of the Afghan Lodis, especially **Sikander Lodi** (1489–1517), who annexed Jaunpur and Bihar; but his successor, Ibrahim, was unable to overcome the dissension among his Afghan feudatories. Eventually, one enlisted the support of Babur, the ruler of Kabul, who defeated Ibrahim at Panipat in 1526.

By the time of the Sultanate, India had considerable experience of assimilating foreigners; Greeks, Scythians, Parthians and Huns had all been absorbed over the centuries, politically, socially and culturally. However, the Sultanate brought its own theologians and social institutions. **Islam** presented a new pattern of life, far less easy for the xenophobic Hindu social system to accommodate. Nonetheless, a process of mutual acculturation did slowly evolve. Despite the Muslims' iconoclastic zeal, Hinduism found common ground with some aspects of Islam: elements of Sufi mysticism and Hindu devotionalism were combined in the teachings of many saints. **Kabir** (1440–1518), in particular, denied any contradiction between Muslim and Hindu conceptions of god, preached social egalitarianism and was claimed by adherents of both creeds as their own. The replacement of

Sanskrit by Persian as the official language of the administration encouraged regional languages; **Urdu** resulted from a fusion of Hindi and Persian using an Arabic script. A stylistically unified architecture began to develop, which flourished under the **Moghuls**; and new social ideas were introduced which became integral to Indian life.

THE MOGHUL EMPIRE 1526–1761

Babur, a descendant of both Timur and Genghis Khan, had gained control of Delhi and Agra by defeating Ibrahim; but his position was threatened by the Rajput confederacy, led by Rana Sanga of Mewar, south of Agra, and by the Afghan chiefs, who had united under the Sultan of Bengal. Babur reacted vigorously by declaring a religious war (*jihad*) against the Rana; he annihilated the Mewar forces at the battle of Kanwaha in 1527, and then turned his attention to the Afghan uprisings in the east. Although he crushed the allied armies of the Afghans and the Sultan of Bengal in 1529, his failing health forced him to retire to Lahore, where he died in 1530.

Babur possessed many talents: as well as a brilliant military campaigner, he was a skilful diplomat, a poet and a man of letters. He constructed a loosely knit empire, extending from Badakshan and Kabul to the borders of Bengal, in just four years. His personal magnetism commanded loyalty and inspired his warrior chiefs to fresh endeavours when they yearned to depart the hot and dusty plains of India for the cool mountains of their homeland. His very readable memoirs, moreover, reveal a man of sensibility, taste and humour, who loved music, poetry, sport and natural beauty.

Humayun, his son and successor, was by contrast a volatile character, who alternated between bursts of enthusiastic activity and indolence. He subdued Malwa and Gujarat, only to lose both while he "took his pleasure" in Agra. **Sher Khan Sur** of south Bihar soon assumed the leadership of the Afghan opposition and after two resounding defeats Humayun had to seek refuge in Persia. Sher Khan set up an administrative system in Delhi, set out to re-assess the land revenue, and continued his campaigns against the Rajputs; but Humayun took advantage of the chaos after Sher Khan's death in 1545 to stage a return. Humayun's armies, led by Bairam Khan and Prince Akbar,

crushed Sikander Sur at Sirhund in 1555; but he died the following year after a fall in the Purana Qila in Delhi leaving **Akbar**, his major contribution to the Moghul empire, to succeed where he had failed.

Akbar, aged only 13, was lucky to have Bairam Khan as regent to help him survive the crisis of the first four years. Bairam, a loyal general and an experienced politician, overcame the challenge of the Hindu general Hemu at the second battle of Panipat in 1556, recovered Gwalior and Jaunpur, and handed over a consolidated kingdom of north India to Akbar in 1560. The young emperor quickly established his own control of the government in dramatic fashion; he personally executed Adham Khan, who had murdered the prime minister, and had him thrown from the palace walls.

Akbar's first military campaigns were against the **Rajputs**; within a decade he secured the flank of the Moghul bases at Delhi and Agra by subduing all the Rajput domains except Mewar (Udaipur). Akbar possessed the personal magnetism of his grandfather and was a brilliant general, who above all had the gift of rapid movement. In 1573 he marched his army 600 miles in nine days to defeat astonished insurgents in Gujarat. He had secured Bengal, the richest province, by 1576, and by the end of his reign in 1605 he controlled a broad sweep of territory north of the River Godavari, which reached from the Bay of Bengal to Kandahar and Badakshan, with the exception of Gondwana and Assam.

Akbar was a very clever politician and administrator as well as a successful general. After subduing the Rajputs, he diplomatically bestowed imperial honours on their chiefs by making them military commanders and provincial governors. By giving them autonomy within their own states, he made the Rajputs partners in the empire and thereby secured the acquiescence of the whole Hindu community. His marriage to a Jaipur princess was an important symbolic statement of this partnership.

The imperial service, in which Akbar involved both Moghuls and Rajputs, was carefully crafted to ensure that the nobility were hereditary as an aristocratic class but not as individuals. His officers – *mansabdars*, holders of commands – were arranged in grades that indicated how many troops they were obliged to maintain for imperial service. A commander of five thousand was both an important state official and a noble; but the titles were not hereditary, being conferred by appointment and promotion, and the *mansabdars* salaries were paid in cash so that they lacked a territorial basis for insurrection.

The creation of an administrative framework, which sustained the empire through its efficient collection of revenue, was one of Akbar's most enduring achievements. He collected information about local revenue, productivity and price variations to arrive at a schedule, acceptable to the peasant farmers but also generating maximum profit for the state. Akbar recruited leaders of local communities and holders of land rights (*zamindars*) to collect the revenue in cash.

In addition to involving Hindu *zamindars* and nobles in economic and political life, Akbar adopted a conscious policy of religious toleration aimed at widening the base of his power. In particular, he abolished the despised poll-tax on non-Muslims (*jizya*), and tolls on Hindu pilgrimages. A mystical experience in about 1575 inspired him to instigate a series of discussions with orthodox Muslim leaders (*ulema*), Portuguese priests from Goa, Hindu *brahmins*, Jains and Zoroastrians at his famous house of worship (*ibadat khana*) in Fatehpur Sikri. The discussions culminated in a politico-religious crisis and a revolt, organized by the alienated *ulema*, which Akbar ruthlessly crushed in 1581. He subsequently evolved a theory of divine kingship incorporating the toleration of all religions, and thereby restored the concept of imperial sanctity with which the early Hindu emperors had surrounded themselves, while declaring his non-sectarian credentials.

Akbar was a liberal patron of the arts and his eclecticism encouraged a fruitful Muslim-Hindu dialogue. Music, which he loved, was especially enriched by this mutual acculturation. Akbar ranks alongside Ashoka as one of the great statesmen of the world, and his reign laid the foundations for a century of stable government under the succeeding Moghuls.

The reigns of **Jahangir** (1605–27) and **Shah Jahan** (1628–57) together represent the great age of the Moghuls, whose reputation for magnificence, pomp and luxury did not escape the notice of Europe and is recorded in the writings of Bernier and Dryden. It was a time of brisk economic activity notable for artistic and architectural splendour, as well as the excesses of imperial indulgence.

Despite his reputation for drunken cruelty, Jahangir was a connoisseur of art. It was under his patronage that the art of the **miniature**, imported from Persia, reached its perfection in Moghul painting before being further evolved and enriched by Hindu artists, especially in Rajasthan. Jahangir is best remembered for his great devotion to Nur Jahan, which he celebrated with a special issue of gold coins (*mohur*). Nur Jahan commissioned the building of the beautiful Itmad-ud-Daulah, a magnificent tomb for her parents in Agra, sometimes said to be the blueprint for the Taj Mahal.

In the political sphere, Jahangir settled the conflict with Mewar, extended the empire by subjugating the last of the Afghan domains in east Bengal and Orissa, and restrained the threat from the Deccan by defeating the combined forces of the Nizamshahi kingdom and the Adilshahis of Bijapur in 1620. However, the combination of failing health and political intrigues involving his beloved Nur Jahan prevented him from completing his Deccan campaign, and Persia's capture of Kandahar in 1622 dented his prestige.

When Shah Jahan came to power in 1628, he ruthlessly executed all the male descendants of his brothers and uncles. He displayed all the imperial qualities of administrative and military ability and, like his predecessors, was a great lover and patron of the arts, especially architecture. Delhi's **Red Fort** and **Jami Masjid**, Agra Fort, and the splendid **Taj Mahal**, the mausoleum he created for his wife Mumtaz, are the results of his personal inspiration and artistic direction. Thus he actively participated in the apogee of Indo-Persian culture, although his political achievements were less notable.

Shah Jahan attempted to deal with the ascendancy of the Marathas in the Deccan by conquering the Nizamshahi kingdom in 1636. He then concentrated on extending the empire on the Assam border and the containment of the Uzbek threat in the northwest. He regained Kandahar from the Persians, but it was lost again in 1649. Meanwhile, a crisis was brewing. The revenue schedule had not been reviewed, and the system now tended to enrich local intermediaries at the expense of the empire. Powerful *zamindars* began to resist paying the full revenue to the treasury. The empire's total dependence on the rural aristocrats to collect the land revenue indirectly fostered the agencies of its disintegration.

Shah Jahan governed India firmly for thirty years, but in his later years he became increasingly sensual. He ended his days a pathetic prisoner in the Agra Fort, gazing nostalgically across the Yamuna at the mausoleum of his beloved Mumtaz; a sad old man who had lost everything through self-indulgence.

Aurangzeb, the last of the great Moghuls, seized power in a dramatic civil war, eliminated his brothers, a son and a nephew, and imprisoned his father in the Agra Fort. Though lacking the charisma of Akbar or Babur, he evoked an awe of his own and he proved to be a firm and capable administrator, who retained his grip on the increasingly unsettled empire until his death at the age of 88. In contrast to the pomp of the other Moghuls, his lifestyle was pious and disciplined. In later life the ruthless statesman became an austere sage, who fasted and spent long hours in prayer.

In the first 23 years of his rule, Aurangzeb maintained a continuity with Shah Jahan's administration and ostensibly contained disruptive elements; but he failed to solve the problems which eventually erupted after his death and caused the dissolution of the empire. The **Maratha** chief, **Shivaji**, who humiliated the Moghul army early in Aurangzeb's reign, was a constant threat. Although he was defeated by the Rajput Jai Singh and forced to visit the Moghul court in 1666, Shivaji made a daring escape from Agra, rallied his resources, and was soon again the master of a compact and well-organized kingdom in western India, to which the Muslim kingdoms of Bijapur and Golconda were eager to ally themselves against the imperialism of Aurangzeb.

The militant separatism of the **Sikhs** was brutally suppressed when Guru Tegh Bahadur was executed in 1675 for refusing to embrace Islam; but his son, Guru Gobind, transformed the religious community into a military sect which became increasingly powerful in the Punjab. Aurangzeb's confrontation with the Rajputs over the Jodhpur succession in 1678 resulted in another war, and the alienation of most of the Rajput partners in empire.

Meanwhile, religious and economic discontent turned the passive support of the Hindu community, cultivated by Akbar, into indifference, disdain and even armed conflict. Aurangzeb aligned himself with the orthodox Sunni Muslims of the *ulema*, who rejected the

syncretism encouraged by Akbar's non-sectarian policies. Hindu places of worship were again the object of iconoclasm, the tax on non-Muslims (*jizya*) was re-introduced, religious fairs were banned, and discriminatory duties were imposed on Hindu merchants. The Jats and the Satnamis of the Agra-Delhi region rebelled over insufferable increases in land revenue demands, and elsewhere peasant farmers rallied behind Maratha, Sikh and Rajput landholders to oppose imperial exploitation.

Aurangzeb crushed the agrarian rebellions and turned his attention to expansion. He transferred his base to the Deccan in 1681 and spent the rest of his life overseeing the subjugation of the Bijapur and Golconda kingdoms and trying to contain the Maratha rebellion. In 1689, he succeeded in capturing and executing Shivaji's son, Shambhuji, and by 1698 the Moghuls had overrun almost the whole of the peninsula. The Marathas had been suppressed, but they re-emerged under the Peshwa leadership in the eighteenth century to harass the remnants of Moghul power and even to challenge the political ambitions of the British.

Aurangzeb did manage to extend the empire during his long reign of over 48 years; but the newly acquired lands in the south were difficult to administer, his nobles were divided by factionalism, and the disruptive consequences of his policies were to be critical in the eighteenth-century collapse of the empire.

Bahadur Shah, Aurangzeb's son, succeeded in 1707 and briefly restored the situation, but after his death in 1712 the disintegration of the empire and power struggles between would-be successors dominated events. By the 1720s the Nizam of Hyderabad and the Nawabs of Avadh and Bengal were effectively independent; the Marathas overwhelmed the rich province of Malwa in 1738; Hindu landholders everywhere were in revolt; and Nadir Shah of Persia dealt a serious blow to the empire's prestige when he invaded India, defeated the Moghul army and sacked Delhi in 1739.

The **Maratha** kingdom had by now been transformed into a confederacy under the leadership of a hereditary *brahmin* minister, called the Peshwa. By 1750 the Marathas had spread right across central India to Orissa, had attacked Bengal, and were insinuating themselves in the imperial politics of Delhi. When Delhi was again looted in 1757, this time by an independent Afghan force led by Ahmad Shah Abdali, distraught Moghul ministers called in the Marathas to rescue the situation. The Marathas drove the Afghans back to the Punjab; but Ahmad Shah advanced again in 1761 and overwhelmed them at the third battle of Panipat. Any designs he had on the imperial throne were dashed, however, when his soldiers mutinied for their arrears of pay.

New centres of Moghul culture developed, notably at Murshidabad, Lucknow, Hyderabad, and Faizabad, but the political strength of the empire had fragmented and north India was left in a power vacuum for the next forty years. It was against this background that the European trading companies, and the East India Company in particular, were able to establish their trading posts and develop their ambitions.

THE EAST INDIA COMPANY 1600–1857

The prosperity of foreign trade in India attracted European interest as early as 1498, when **Vasco da Gama** landed on the Malabar coast. During the ensuing hundred years Portuguese, Dutch, English, French and Danish companies all set up coastal trading centres exporting textiles, sugar, indigo and saltpetre.

The **East India Company**, established by eighty London merchants in 1599 and chartered by Queen Elizabeth I on December 31, 1600, arrived in Surat in 1608. The Company had established 27 trading posts by 1647, including **Fort George** on the Coromandel coast, out of which Madras developed. The enclave of Bombay, part of Catherine of Braganza's dowry in her marriage to Charles II, became crown property in 1665, was leased to the Company from 1668, and soon replaced Surat as its headquarters. The Moghul emperor permitted the Company to establish a new settlement at **Fort William**, which grew into Calcutta, and in 1701 the British received a grant of the revenues of the Twenty-Four Parganas near Calcutta from Aurangzeb, in recognition of the growing importance of their trade in the economy of Bengal.

It was in the **south**, however, that European trading initiatives first took on a political significance, after the onset of the War of the Austrian Succession in 1740. Armed conflict between the French and English trading companies along the Carnatic coast developed into a war over the succession of the Nizam of

Hyderabad. The British victory and the Peace of Paris in 1763 eclipsed French ambitions in India. Meanwhile, **Robert Clive**'s defeat of the rebellious young Nawab of Bengal at Plassey in 1757 had decisively augmented British power; by 1765 the enervated Moghul emperor legally recognized the Company as an Indian potentate by granting the revenue management (*diwani*) of Bengal, Bihar and Orissa to Lord Clive.

Ironically, the Company's mastery of the rich province soon brought it to the brink of bankruptcy, provoking parliamentary intervention in its affairs. The **Regulating Act** of 1773 appointed a Governor-General of the Company's three provinces in Calcutta, Bombay and Madras; and in 1784 the India Act established a President of the Board of Control in London to oversee the Governor-General in Calcutta.

Warren Hastings, the first Governor-General, made the Company's colony in Bengal politically viable, successfully defending it against the jealous governors of Bombay and Madras, and the internal dissensions of his Council in England. His major achievement was to protect Bombay and Madras against the assaults from a coalition of Marathas, the Nizam of Hyderabad and Haidar Ali, the Sultan of Mysore; but he also laid the foundations of British administration in India by replacing the Indian revenue-collecting deputies with a Board of Revenue in Calcutta and English collectors in the districts. **Lord Cornwallis** completed the reforms by fixing the land revenues in the Permanent Land Settlement of 1793; by dividing Company service into separate political and commercial branches; and by a further Europeanization of the administration.

The Governor-Generals were charged with non-aggression and administrative reform until the end of the eighteenth century, but the Napoleonic Wars allowed **Lord Wellesley** to follow his imperial instincts. His swift defeat of **Tipu Sultan** of Mysore, the company's best organized and most resolute enemy, a confrontation with the Marathas, and the subjugation of the Nizam of Hyderabad resulted in the annexation of considerable territories in Andhra Pradesh, Tamil Nadu, Mysore, the Upper Doab, Gujarat and Maharashtra; nearly all the other rulers in India recognized British suzerainty by 1805. There was a brief respite in the expansion until Napoleon's defeat in 1815; but the last vestiges of Maratha opposition were crushed by

1823, and the absorption of Sind, the Sikh king-dom of the Punjab, Kashmir, Assam, Chittagong and Lower Burma by 1852 established **British supremacy** in India.

The new British dominion, however, was in a state of social and economic collapse as a result of the almost incessant conflicts of the previous hundred years. High revenue assess-ments had depressed the condition of both peasants and *zamindars*; peasants deserted their lands, land revenue receipts were falling, and there were local revolts and grain riots in the 1830s. Gangs of robbers (dacoits) had reached epidemic proportions, and their activi-ties curtailed commerce between states and towns. The cult of the **Thugs**, who robbed and murdered in honour of the goddess Kali, spread terror all over central and northern India.

Inspired by Burke's ideas, Utilitarianism and the Radical humanism in Europe, **Lord William Bentinck**'s reforms as Governor-General did lit-tle to alleviate the situation. The campaign against the Thugs received general approval, but his suppression of the practice of widows joining their husbands on funeral pyres (*sati*) was seen as an attack on the values of tradi-tional Hindu society.

The Company's policy of government patron-age for Indian learning was replaced after 1835 by a resolution to promote "European literature and science". Schools and colleges imparting Western knowledge through the medium of the English language were established, and English replaced Persian as the official state language. The educated elite and intellectuals like Ram Mohan Roy had already adopted Western ideas, but such cultural imperialism aggravated the unrest and distrust of the majority.

James Andrew Broun Ramsey, Marquess of Dalhousie, Governor-General between 1848 and 1856, was a firm believer in the benefits of **Westernization**. He promoted Western educa-tion by initiating plans for the first three Indian universities with Sir Charles Wood, and embarked on a series of public works, including the development of the railway and telegraph systems. These were commendable achieve-ments, but their Westernizing influence increased social tension. His controversial poli-cy of annexing dependent but autonomous states, which brought **Oudh**, two Maratha king-doms and five other states under direct admin-istration, caused considerable resentment among the dispossessed and alarm among the Indian ruling classes.

Against this general background of unease, discontent had been growing in the army, which had been increasingly deployed overseas during the previous two decades – a practice resented on religious grounds by the many *brahmins* it contained. The cows' and pigs' grease on the cartridges of the new Enfield rifle, polluting to both Hindus and Muslims, convinced the sol-diers that there was a conspiracy against their religious beliefs and sparked the revolt. The **Indian Mutiny** – the "First War of Independence" – started with a rising at Meerut on May 10, 1857, and Delhi was seized the next day. The last Moghul emperor Bahadur Shah in Delhi, the dispossessed court at Lucknow, and the exiled members of the Maratha court at Kanpur all supported the cause and some land-lords participated in the rebellion.

The British authorities were caught by sur-prise. The Crimean War had reduced the num-ber of their regiments in India, and their forces were concentrated around Calcutta or the Punjab. However, the revolt failed to cut their lines of communication, and crucially the **Sikh** regiments in the Punjab remained loyal. Delhi was retaken by a column from the Punjab in late September, **Kanpur** (Cawnpore) was relieved in the same month, and the final recapture of **Lucknow** in March 1858 effectively broke the back of the Mutiny. The rebels fought on under the leadership of Tantia Topi, and the valiant Rani of Jhansi in central India, until they too were crushed in June 1858. The governing pow-ers of the East India Company were abolished and the British crown assumed the administra-tion of India through an appointed Viceroy in the same year.

THE RAJ AND INDIAN NATIONALISM 1857–1947

India played a key role in the politics of **British imperialism**, especially in the rivalry with France and Russia during this period. Its army became an instrument of British foreign policy, in the Afghan Wars attempting to create a buffer state to block Russia's advance in central Asia, and in the Anglo-Burmese Wars to check the French expansion in Indo-China. It was also used to protect British interests beyond the Indian subcontinent as far afield as Abyssinia and Hong Kong.

As a British colony, India assumed a new position in the world economy. Its trade benefited from the British development of the railways, and Indian businessmen began to invest in a range of industries, including the manufacture of textiles, iron and steel; but India subsidized the British economy as a source of cheap raw materials and as a market for manufactured goods. Its own economy and agriculture remained underdeveloped, and the growth of the gross national product was outstripped by increases in population.

British civil servants dominated the higher echelons of the administration, imposing Western notions of progress on the indigenous social structure. Tenurial systems based on ownership rather than land use, irrigation schemes, the suppression of social customs offensive to humanist ideals, the railways and the introduction of a Western judiciary often involved policies contrary to existing Indian interests. At the same time, the propagation of the English language and the Western knowledge to which it gave access resulted in the emergence of a new **middle class** of civil servants, landlords and professionals, whose consciousness of an Indian national identity steadily increased.

Within thirty years of the Mutiny, the history of the British in India becomes essentially a chronicle of the struggle for **Independence**. By the start of the twentieth century the British conception of empire involved a contradiction between liberal rhetoric and the fact of territorial, economic and intellectual expansion. By World War I, the imperial incentive had been swept away by the realization that Indian independence was unavoidable; the only problem remaining was how to relinquish suzerainty.

Awareness of national identity first found expression in local associations and public demonstrations about specific issues; but when the liberalism of Gladstone was confronted by a growing Indian disaffection while Lord Ripon was Viceroy, the British showed their willingness to conciliate the Indian educated classes by giving their official blessing to the foundation of the first all-India political organization, the **Indian National Congress**, in 1885. It began modestly with only seventy affluent public men as delegates, who advocated limited reforms and a consolidation of union with Britain; but by 1900 Gopal Krishna **Gokhale**

and Bal Gangadhar **Tilak**, both Maratha *brahmins*, had emerged as leaders of the Moderates and the Extremists respectively. By 1905 Tilak had persuaded Congress to adopt self-government as a political aim.

Lord Curzon, a romantic imperialist, who believed that it was Britain's duty to protect India's past and educate it for the future, began his second term of office as Viceroy by sending the Younghusband expedition to Lhasa in 1904. When he decided on the equally controversial partition of Bengal in 1905, it precipitated the first major confrontations with the government. There were widespread protests: Tilak proposed a no-tax campaign and a boycott of British goods, and when the government crushed the protests Bengali terrorists employed even more radical tactics.

In 1906, concerns about the predominantly Hindu interests of Congress led to the foundation of the **All-India Muslim League** to represent the Muslims, who made up a quarter of India's population. A Liberal landslide in Great Britain produced the Morley-Minto Reforms in 1909, which paved the way for Indian participation in provincial executive councils and made allowance for separate Muslim representation. Tilak was imprisoned that year for incitement to violence. The reversal of the partition of Bengal was announced at the **Great Durbar** of 1911, held in honour of the new king George V and his queen, and the capital was moved to **Delhi**.

During World War I, the British conflict with the Sultan of Turkey – still considered to be the spiritual head (*khalifa*) of Indian Muslims – provoked further demonstrations. Tilak returned to found a **Home Rule League** in 1916, and made the Lucknow Pact with the Muslims in support of their *khalifa* movement. The British responded with the Royal Proclamation of 1917, which promised a gradual development of dominion-style self-government; and two years later the Montagu-Chelmsford Reforms attempted to implement the declaration. However, legislation authorizing internment without trial, also passed in 1919, seemed to contradict these promises; the Muslim population were alarmed by the collapse of Turkey and the masses were becoming more restless.

At this point, **Mohandas Karamchand Gandhi** – hailed as the Mahatma or "Great Soul" by Rabindranath Tagore upon returning from his campaign of passive resistance against the government in South Africa – took up the initiative. The Indian-style one-day strike (*hartal*) he proposed was organized in all the major cities; but feelings ran so high that there were riots, which were mercilessly crushed by the government. In particular, General Dyer dispersed the Jallianwalla Bagh meeting in **Amritsar** on April 13, 1919 by firing without warning on the unarmed crowd, killing 379 and wounding 1200. The racial bitterness invoked by the atrocity inspired Gandhi's **Non-Cooperation Movement**; but by 1922 further acts of violence induced him to call off the campaign just before he was imprisoned.

Mahatma Gandhi, born in Porbander in Gujarat, had been educated as a lawyer in England. Over the years he was influenced by Christian, Hindu, liberal and humanitarian ideas; but the doctrine of non-violence (*ahimsa*) and the pursuit of truth (*satya*) became the philosophical cornerstones of his endeavours to achieve a united independent India. His belief in the rights of man, and especially his championing of the Untouchables, whom he renamed the Children of God (*Harijan*), put him in opposition to *brahmin* orthodoxy; but he won the hearts of the people in 1921 when he discarded European clothes for the homespun cotton *dhoti* and shawl, to identify with the masses. His personal charisma and all-India appeal inspired the Independence movement throughout the period, whether he was in prison, organizing the rejection of imported cloth in his *swadeshi* campaign, leading acts of civil disobedience, or fasting to bring about the cessation of Hindu-Muslim community violence.

Gandhi was released from prison in 1924. Despite liberal concessions by the British, by 1928 Congress was demanding complete Independence (*purna swaraj*). The government offered talks, but the more radical elements in Congress, now led by the young **Jawaharlal Nehru**, were in a confrontational mood. Their declaration of Independence Day on January 26 1930 forced Gandhi's hand; he responded with a well-publicized 60-mile march from his ashram in Sabarmati to make **salt** illegally at Dandi in Gujarat (see p.562). This demonstration of non-violent civil disobedience (*satyagraha*) caught the people's imagination, leading to more processions, strikes, and the imprisonment of a hundred thousand of his followers by the end of the year. Abortive round-table talks, the Irwin-

Gandhi truce, Gandhi's trip to London for further talks, and more civil disobedience culminated in the **Government of India Act** in 1935, which still fell short of aspirations for complete Independence. Congress remained suspicious of British intentions, and despite Gandhi's overtures refused to accommodate Muslim demands for representation.

The idea of a **separate Muslim state** was first raised in 1930 by the poet Sir Muhammad Iqbal and Chaudhuri Rahmat Ali, and a group of fellow students at Cambridge coined the name **Pakistan**, literally meaning "Land of the Pure". **Muhammad Ali Jinnah**, a lawyer from Bombay who assumed the leadership of the Muslim League in 1935, initially promoted Muslim-Hindu co-operation, but he soon despaired of influencing Congress and by 1940 the League passed a resolution demanding an independent Pakistan.

Confrontations between the government, Congress and the Muslim League continued throughout World War II. Mahatma Gandhi introduced the "**Quit India**" slogan and proposed another campaign of civil disobedience; the government immediately responded by imprisoning the whole Working Party of Congress in Pune. Jinnah, meanwhile, preached his "two nations" theory to the educated, and inspired mass Muslim support with his rhetoric against "Hinduization". A spate of terrorist activities left a thousand dead and sixty thousand imprisoned; by the end of the war, the government accepted that complete Independence would have to be negotiated.

British attempts to find a solution that would preserve a united India and allay Muslim fears after the war disintegrated in the face of continued intransigence from both sides, and they gradually realized that Partition was inevitable. In 1946 Jinnah provoked riots in Calcutta with his call for Direct Action, and Hindus retaliated with atrocities against Muslims in Bihar and Uttar Pradesh. The British cabinet appointed **Lord Mountbatten** as Viceroy to supervise the handover of power in 1948. Mahatma Gandhi desperately sought to avert the escalating Hindu-Muslim violence and find a resolution to secure a united India, while Nehru was persuaded that a separate Pakistan would be preferable to the anarchy of communal killings.

Lord Mountbatten brought Independence forward: the subcontinent was **partitioned** on

August 15, 1947 and Pakistan came into existence, even though several princely states had still to decide which of the two new countries they would join. The new boundaries cut through both Bengal and the Punjab; Sikhs, Muslims and Hindus who had been neighbours became enemies overnight. Five million Hindus and Sikhs from Pakistan, and a similar number of Muslims from India, were involved in the ensuing two-way exodus, and the atrocities cost half a million lives. Mahatma Gandhi, who had devoted himself to ending the communal violence after Partition, was **assassinated** in January 1948 by Hindu extremists antagonized by his defence of the Muslims. India had lost its "Great Soul", but the profound shock of the Mahatma's last sacrifice at least contributed to the gradual cessation of the violence.

INDEPENDENT INDIA 1947–1996

Jawaharlal Nehru, India's first and longest running Prime Minister, proved to be a dynamic, gifted and extremely popular leader during his seventeen years of premiership. He built the foundations of a democratic, secular state, and guided the first stages of its agricultural and industrial development. Nehru's first task, however, was to consolidate the Union.

His able deputy Prime Minister, **Sardar Vallabhai Patel**, was made responsible for incorporating the 562 princely states within the federal Union. The Nizam of **Hyderabad**, who resisted even though the majority of the state's population were Hindus, had to be persuaded by an invasion of Indian troops. The Hindu Maharaja of **Kashmir** also prevaricated, as three quarters of his subjects were Muslims, and by October 1947 he had to appeal to India for help against a tribal invasion supported by Pakistan. Kashmir's accession to India resulted in the first outbreak of hostilities between the two countries; the United Nations intervened in 1949 to enforce a ceasefire line. The **French** enclaves at Pondicherry and Chandernagar were incorporated in the 1950s; but the **Portuguese** refused to accept the new situation and in 1961 Nehru had to annex **Goa**. The **Naga** people were brought within the federal Union as the Nagaland state in the same year.

The Constitution for India's "Sovereign Democratic Republic and Union of States" became law on January 26, 1950, the twentieth anniversary of "Independence Day". The franchise was made universal for all adults, and with 173 million eligible to vote in 1951 India became the **world's largest democracy**. Hindi was designated the "official language of the Union"; but south India, in particular, was adamant in its opposition to Hindi, and Nehru re-aligned the several state borders on linguistic principles. By 1961 the Union consisted of sixteen states and six centrally administered territories. The Punjabi-speaking Sikhs had to wait until 1966 for their state to be separated from Hindu-dominated Haryana.

Nehru sought to achieve the constitutional aims of justice, liberty, equality and fraternity with a vigorous programme of social and economic reforms. He redressed the iniquities of caste by abolishing "untouchability" in 1955 and radically improved the status of women. The national average literacy was increased to 23.7 per cent by 1961 and free elementary education became more readily available, although it still fell short of aspirations.

On the **economic** front, Nehru engineered the first three of India's **Five Year Plans** to improve production capability and eradicate poverty. Population growth and the failures of the monsoon in 1952 and 1953 eroded the mainly agricultural aims of the first plan (1951–56); but food grain production increased from 52 million to over 65 million tons by 1956, and to 80 million tons by the end of the second plan (1956–61), which also injected capital into industry. Under the third plan (1961–66), a nuclear energy programme was inaugurated, and foreign aid and technical assistance secured to speed up industrialization.

Foreign policy was Nehru's biggest disappointment. He adopted a policy of non-aligned peaceful co-existence, but **China** threatened his aim of promoting Asian unity. He attempted to dispel the tensions created by the Chinese invasion of Tibet in 1950 by concluding a trade treaty with China in 1954, which included a declaration of mutual respect for each other's territories; but this did not deter the Chinese from building a road across a remote area of Ladakh in 1957, and India sustained losses during a confrontation in 1959. In 1962, sporadic conflicts in the Northeast Frontier Agency (**Assam**) escalated into a war; the Chinese army proved to be far superior and advanced unhindered over India's northeast frontier. Their unilateral decision to withdraw, on November 21, 1962, added humiliation to defeat and spelt the end of India's policy of non-alignment. Nehru immediately made a defence treaty with the US, and set about creating a new elite Border Security Force.

The whole nation, loyal throughout the China crisis, mourned his death in 1964, which prevented him from witnessing the restoration of India's military prestige in the **Second Indo-Pakistan War** of 1965. Indian tanks had advanced to within three miles of a virtually defenceless Lahore when the UN ceasefire was agreed on September 23. Lal Bahadur **Shastri**, who had led the interim government, died shortly after in January 1966 leaving Nehru's daughter, **Indira Gandhi**, to establish her superiority as leader of the Congress left, over Morarji Desai's right wing of the party.

Mrs Gandhi swiftly secured American financial support for India's fourth Five Year Plan (1966–71); but her devaluation of the *rupee* in June 1966 aroused considerable opposition and elections the next year radically reduced her majority. Two years later, Congress split under the pressure of internal dissensions. Mrs Gandhi embraced the socialist principle by nationalizing the banks, and enlisted the support of the Communists, the Sikhs and the Dravidian Progressive Federation (DMK) to form a coalition government. By this time, India had made a spectacular agricultural breakthrough with its **Green Revolution**, as a result of the introduction of high-yield grains, and in 1969 industrial growth was over seven percent. Mrs Gandhi pressed on with her socialist reforms, abolishing the former maharajas' privy purses and privileges after she had consolidated her mandate in fresh elections in 1971.

Meanwhile, Yahya Khan's brutal repression of the struggle for independence in **East Pakistan** had caused a mass exodus of refugees; by April 1971 Bengali civilians were pouring across into India at the rate of sixty thousand a day. Mrs Gandhi astutely waited until she had the moral support of the international community, signed a Treaty of Peace, Friendship and Co-operation with the Soviet Union, and launched simultaneous attacks in West and East Pakistan on December 4. India had total air superiority, as well as the support of the East Pakistan population, and by December 15 the Pakistani general capitulated and signed the Instrument of Surrender of "all Pakistan armed forces in Bangla Desh".

If the liberation of Bangla Desh was the crowning glory of Mrs Gandhi's premiership, her abandonment of the democratic ideals so dear to her father was its lowest ebb. After widespread agrarian and industrial disturbances and protests against the rate of inflation and corruption within the Congress in 1974, the clamour of protest rose to a crescendo in June 1975, and when the opposition coalition under the joint leadership of JP Narayan and Morarji Desai threatened to oust India's "iron lady", she declared a **State of Emergency** on June 26, which suspended all civil rights, including habeas corpus, and silenced all opposition by internment and strict censorship of the press.

Her administrative and economic reforms had the desired effect of cutting inflation and curbing corruption, but the enforced sterilization of men with two or more children, and brutal slum-clearances in Delhi supervised by her son **Sanjay**, alienated millions of her supporters. When she finally released her opponents and called off the Emergency in January 1977, the bitterness she had engendered resulted in her ignominious defeat in the March elections. The ensuing **Janata** coalition under **Morarji Desai** fell apart within two years, and his premiership was terminated by a vote of no confidence in 1979. Mrs Gandhi, who had rebuilt her Congress-I Party with Sanjay's help, swept back into office in January 1980. Sanjay died in a plane crash a few months later; four years later, Mrs Gandhi made the second, fatal, mistake of her career.

A group of terrorists demanding a separate "nation" – Khalistan – for Sikhs, took control of the **Golden Temple** in Amritsar early in 1984, and organized a campaign of violence from its precincts. Hundreds of Hindus and moderate Sikhs fell victim to terrorist attacks, and the whole nation was calling for positive action to end the atrocities. Indira sent in her tanks in June 1984, but two days of raging combat desecrated the Sikhs' holiest shrine as well as generating the first martyrs of Khalistan. In October that year, her Sikh bodyguards avenged their brotherhood and faith by assassinating Mrs Gandhi at her house in Delhi.

Rajiv Gandhi came to power in December 1984 on a wave of sympathy boosted by his reputation as "Mr Clean", given added meaning by the **Bhopal** gas tragedy just two weeks before the elections. The honeymoon was short-lived;

the political accords he reached with the Punjab, Assam and Mizoram deteriorated into armed conflict; more than two years of "peace-keeping" by the Indian army failed to disarm Tamil guerrillas in Ceylon; and allegations of corruption tarnished his image. By the end of the 1980s the opposition had rallied under the leadership of **VP Singh**, a former Congress minister. The December 1989 elections did not give VP Singh's Janata Party a majority, but he managed to form a coalition government with the support of the "Hindu first" Bharatiya Janata Party (**BJP**), led by **LK Advani.**

Singh was immediately confronted by problems in the Punjab and Kashmir, as well as upper-caste Hindu protests against his planned implementation of proposals for a sixty percent reservation of civil service jobs for lower castes and former "untouchables"; but it was an even more emotive issue which brought down his government in less than a year. Advani had assumed the leadership of a popular Hindu revivalist movement, which was demanding that the Babri Masjid mosque in **Ayodhya**, built by Babur in the sixteenth century, should be replaced by a Hindu temple on the supposed site of the birthplace of Rama, god-hero of the epic *Ramayana*.

Singh, utterly committed to secularism, pleaded with Advani to desist; undeterred Advani set off towards Ayodhya in October 1990, seated on a golden chariot pushed by his followers and thousands of devout Hindus, with the avowed intention of destroying the mosque and building a temple for Rama. Singh ordered Advani's arrest; within two weeks the inevitable withdrawal of the BJP support from his coalition government resulted in a vote of no confidence on November 7, 1990. Rajiv Gandhi declined the offer to form an interim government, hopeful that he could improve his party's position in an election. His campaign went well and it was assumed that Congress would win; but then, on a tour of Tamil Nadu in May 1991, he was assassinated by Tamil Tigers seeking revenge for India's active opposition to their "freedom fight" in Ceylon.

PV Narasimha Rao skilfully steered Congress Party through the elections, and formed a government with the support of the Muslim League, the Communist "Left Front" and Tamil Nadu's most powerful party (AIADMK). At the same time, the BJP ominously increased its

seats in the Lok Sabha from 80 to 120, Advani became leader of the opposition, and the enormous popular support for the rebuilding of Rama's temple in Ayodhya encouraged the *Vishwa Hindu Parishad* to take up the crusade. VP Singh countered by leading a march of 500 secularists to Ayodhya; but the BJP had won control of the Uttar Pradesh state government, making them responsible for law and order, and this time it was Singh who found himself arrested and imprisoned.

In December 1992, when the situation came to a head again, the central government could not prevent extremists inciting the crowds of fanatical devotees to tear down the mosque in a blaze of publicity (see p.310). The demolition of the Babri Masjid was followed by terrible **riots** in many parts of the country, especially Bombay and Gujarat, where Muslim families and businesses were targeted. A few months later, in retaliation against the extreme Hindu violence, **bombs** were planted in Bombay (see p.618) by underground Muslim groups. As a result of the Babri Masjid episode, the BJP-led state governments of UP, Himachal Pradesh, Madhya Pradesh, Rajasthan and Delhi were suspended. Elections in these states in late 1993 showed that the popularity of the BJP, and its call for the creation of **Hindutva**, a Hindu homeland, was fading. They re-asserted control of Delhi, which has always been a stronghold of the Hindu right, barely hung on in Rajasthan, and lost the rest.

The electoral results provided a much needed boost for Narashima Rao, whose grip over the leadership of the Congress Party seemed to be slippng. Accused by the opposition and press of lacking decisive policies, and dogged by allegations that he had accepted a suitcase of money as a bribe from a prominent businessman (the so-called "Harsha scandal"), the prime minister was under increasing pressure to step down. However, he weathered an unsuccessful no confidence motion mounted by the BJP, and the surprise election victories in November temporarily silenced his rivals, among them minister Arjun Singh, who would later engineer a split in the Congress Party in an attempt to wrest power from Rao.

National morale during this post-Ayodhya period was shaky. After a year blighted by bomb blasts, riots and the rise of religious extremism, it seemed as if India's era as a secular state was doomed. To rub salt in the wounds, 15,000 people died in a massive **earthquake** around the northwest Maharashtran city of Latur, and soon after, Surat, in southern Gujarat, was at the centre of an outbreak of a disease ominously resembling bubonic **plague**. Thousands fled the city and the international community panicked, cancelling export orders and axing flights. The "plague" turned out to be a flash-in-the-pan, but the damage to India's self-image was done.

Against this backdrop of uncertainty, the rise of right-wing Hindu-fundamentalist parties gathered pace. Temporarily cowed by the Babri-Masjid debacle, the BJP took advantage of the power struggle in the Congress Party to rekindle regional support. Expediently sidelining the contentious *Hindutva* agenda, the new rallying cry was **Swadeshi** – a campain against the Congress-led programme of **economic liberalization** and, in particular, the activities of multi-nationals such as *Coca Cola*, *Pepsi* and *KFC* (one of whose branches was forced to close by the BJP-controlled Delhi municipality). Bal Thackeray's proto-fascist **Shiv Sena** party also made ground in Maharashtra, eventually winning the State Assembly elections there in March 1995.

In **Kashmir**, meanwhile, the armed struggle by Pakistani-backed militants for greater autonomy intensified into a full-blown guerrilla war, fuelled by a series of bloody clashes with the Indian army. The first of these was the **Sopone massacre**, when security forces, in retaliation for a grenade attack on an army barracks, shot dead fifty militants. Then, in November 1993, a re-run of Operation Bluestar and the Golden Temple fiasco seemed inevitable as heavily armed militants occupied one of the region's holiest shrines, the Hazratbal mosque. This siege, however, ended with a government climb-down (the militants were allowed safe passage out of the mosque), although twenty-two protestors were shot by the army in its wake.

After the Hazratbal siege, there ensued a period of relative calm; curfews were suspended and the Jammu & Kashmir Liberation Front (JKLF)'s leader, Javed Mir, was captured. With pressure being brought to bear on India by the US for a speedy resolution of the crisis, the peace seemed likely to result in long-awaited elections, until yet another stand-off between troops and militants stalled negotiations. In May 1995, a Muslim shrine near Srinagar, the **Char-e-Sharief**, was burned down while surrounded by the army, killing twenty Kashmiris and sparking off riots in the capital. For the first time tourists were targeted as a means of internationalizing the independence struggle. An attempt to abduct and incarcerate three Westerners in Delhi was foiled by police, but shortly afterwards a group of foreign Muslim extremists, Al-Faran, kidnapped five tourists; one, a Norwegian, was beheaded and, at the time of going to press (September 1996), the others were still missing. The actions of a minority of extremists aside, the Kashmir situation at last looks set to improve, with elections imminent – the first since the troubles began in the late 1980s.

The political landscape has altered at national level, too, since the **general election** of May 1996. Polling 194 of the Lok Sabha's 534 seats, the BJP emerged as the single largest party. They attempted to form a government, they could not, despite much behind-the-scenes wheeling and dealing, muster a majority and were ousted a couple of weeks later, out-manoeuvered by a hastily formed coalition, the **Unified Front,** led by **HD Deve Gowda**. Ironically, the UF had to rely on the support of the Congress Party (I) – the principal opponent of many of its thirteen constituent parties – to establish a working majority. It remains to be seen whether Gowda can forge a common programme from this hotch-potch of apparently incongruous poilitical groups; a period of instability seems inevitable as they jockey for postition. One potential advantage of the situation is that, for the first time, minority groups such as the Backward Classes, farmers and regional parties should enjoy unprecedented influence in the Indian parliament, although women remain hopelessly under-represented.

THE RELIGIONS OF INDIA

For the majority of Indians, **Hinduism** permeates every aspect of life, from commonplace daily chores to education and politics. The vast pantheon of Hindu deities is manifest everywhere – not only in temples, but in shops, rickshaws and even on *bidi* packets and matchboxes. Beside Hindus, **Muslims** are the most prominent religious group; they have formed an integral part of Indian society since the twelfth century, and mosques are almost as common as temples. Though **Jains** and **Buddhists** are now a tiny fraction of the population, their impact is still felt, and their magnificent temples are among the finest in India. Both these ancient faiths, like the more recently established **Sikh** community, formed in reaction to the caste laws and ritual observances of Hinduism. In addition, there are small communities of **Zoroastrians**, descended from Iranians, and **Christians**, here since the first century (see p.1082).

Hindu practices, such as caste distinction, have crept into most religions, and many of the **festivals** – see p.62 – that mark each year with music, dance and feasting, are shared by all communities. Each has its own **pilgrimage** sites, **heroes**, **legends** and even culinary specialities, mingling in a unique diversity that is the very pulse of society.

HINDUISM

Contemporary **Hinduism** – the "religion" of over eighty-five percent of Indians – is the product of several thousand years of evolution and assimilation. It has neither founder nor prophet, no single creed, and no single prescribed practice or doctrine; it takes in hundreds of gods, goddesses, beliefs and practices, and widely variant cults and philosophies. Some are recognized by only two or three villages, others are popular right across the subcontinent. Hindus (from the Persian word for Indians) call their beliefs and practices *dharma*, which envelops natural and moral law to define a way of living in harmony with a natural order, while achieving personal goals and meeting the requirements of society.

EARLY DEVELOPMENTS

The foundations of Hinduism were laid by the **Aryans**, semi-nomads who entered northwest India during the second millennium BC, and mixed with the indigenous Dravidian population (see p.1206). With them they brought a belief in gods associated with the elements, including **Agni**, the god of fire and sacrifice, **Surya**, the sun-god, and **Indra**, the chief god. Most of these deities faded in later times, but Indra is still regarded as the father of the gods, and Surya, eternally present in his magnificent chariot-temple in **Konarak** (Orissa), was widely worshipped until the medieval period.

Aryan beliefs were set out in the **Vedas**, scriptures "heard" (*shruti*) by "seers" (*rishis*). Transmitted orally for centuries, they were finally written, in Sanskrit, between 1000 BC and 500 AD. The earliest were the *Samhitas*, or hymns; later came the *Brahmanas*, sacrificial texts, and *Aranyakas*, or "forest treatises".

The earliest and most important *Samhita*, the **Rig Veda**, contains hymns to deities and *devas* (divine powers), and is supplemented by other books detailing rituals and prayers for ceremonial use. The **Brahmanas** stress correct ritual performance, drawing heavily on concepts of **purity and pollution** that persist today, and concentrating on sacrificial rites. Pedantic attention to ritual soon supplanted the importance of the *devas*, and they were further undermined by a search for a single cosmic power thought to be their source, eventually conceived of as **Brahma**, the absolute creator, personified from earlier mentions of Brahman, an impersonal principle of cosmic unity.

The *Aranyakas* focussed upon this all-powerful godhead, and reached their final stage in the *Upanishads*, which describe in beautiful and emotive verse the mystic experience of unity of the soul (*atman*) with Brahma, ideally attained through asceticism, renunciation of worldly values and meditation. In the *Upanishads* the concepts of **samsara**, a cyclic round of death and rebirth characterized by suffering and perpetuated by desire, and **moksha**, liberation from *samsara*, became firmly rooted. Fundamental aspects of the Hindu world view, both are accepted by all but a handful of Hindus today, along with the belief in **karma**, the belief that one's present position in society is determined by the effect of one's previous actions in this and past lives.

HINDU SOCIETY

The stratification of Hindu society is rooted in the **Dharma Shashtras** and **Dharma Shutras**, scriptures written from "memory" (*smriti*) at the same time as the *Vedas*. These defined four hierarchical classes, or **varnas**, each assigned specific religious and social duties known as **varnashradharma**, and established Aryans as the highest social class. In descending order the *varnas* are: **brahmins** (priests and teachers), **kshatryas** (rulers and warriors), **vaishyas** (merchants and cultivators) and **shudras** (menials). The first three classes, known as "twice-born", are distinguished by a sacred thread worn from the time of initiation, and granted full access to religious texts and rituals. Below all four categories, groups whose jobs involve contact with dirt or death (such as undertakers, leather workers and cleaners) were classified as **Untouchables**. Though discrimination against Untouchables is now a criminal offence, in part thanks to the campaigns of Gandhi – he renamed Untouchables *Harijans*, "Children of God" – the lowest stratum of society has by no means disappeared.

Within the four *varnas*, social status is further defined by **jati**, classifying each individual by family and precise occupation (for example, a *vaishya* may be a jewellery seller, cloth merchant, cowherd or farmer). A person's *jati* determines his **caste**, and lays restrictions on all aspects of life from food consumption, religious obligations and contact with other castes, to the choice of marriage partners. In general, Hindus marry members of the same *jati* – marrying someone of a different *varna* often results in ostracism from both family and caste, leaving the couple stranded in a society where caste affiliation takes primacy over all other aspects of individual identity. There are almost three thousand *jatis*; the divisions and restrictions they have enforced have become, time and time again, the substance of reform movements and the target of critics.

A Hindu has three aims in life: **dharma**, fulfilling one's duty to family and caste and acquiring religious merit (*punya*) through right living; **artha**, the lawful making of wealth; and **kāma**, desire and satisfaction. These goals are linked with the four traditional stages in life. The first is as a child and student, devoted to learning from parents and guru. Next comes the stage of householder, expected to provide for a family and raise sons. That accomplished, he or she may then take up a life of celibacy and retreat into the forest to meditate alone, and finally renounce all possessions to become a homeless ascetic, hoping to achieve the ultimate goal of *moksha*. The small number of Hindus, including some women, who follow this ideal life assume the final stage as **sannyasis**, saffron-clad **sadhus** who wander throughout India, begging for food, and retreat to isolated caves, forests and hills to meditate. They're a common feature in most Indian towns, and many stay for long periods in particular temples. Not all have raised families: some assume the life of a *sadhu* at an early age as *chellas*, pupils, of an older *sadhu*.

THE POPULAR DEITIES

Alongside the *Dharma Shashtras* and *Dharma Shutras*, the most important works of the *smriti* tradition, thought to have been completed by the fourth century AD at the latest, were the **Puranas**, long mythological stories focused on the Vedic gods and their heroic actions, and Hinduism's two great epics, the **Mahabharata** and **Ramayana**. Through these texts, the main gods and goddesses became firmly embedded in the religion. Alongside **Brahma**, the creator, **Vishnu** was acknowledged as the preserver, and **Shiva** ("auspicious, benign"), referred to in the *Rig Veda* as Rudra, was recognized for his destructive powers. The three are often depicted in a trinity, *tri-murti*, but in time Brahma's importance declined, and Shiva and Vishnu became the most popular deities.

Other gods and goddesses who came alive in the mythology of the *Puranas*, each depicted in human or semi-human form and accompanied by an animal "**vehicle**", are still venerated across India. River goddesses, ancestors, guardians of particular places, and protectors against disease and natural disaster are as central to village life as the major deities.

PHILOSOPHICAL TRENDS

The complications presented by Hinduism's view of deities, *samsara*, *atman* (the human soul), and *moksha* naturally encouraged philosophical debate, and led eventually to the formation of six schools of thought, known as the **Darshanas**. Each presented a different exposition of the true nature of *moksha* and how to attain it.

Foremost among these was the **Advaita Vedanta** school of **Shankara** (*c.*788–850 AD), who interpreted Hinduism as pure monotheism verging on monism (the belief that all is one: in this case, one with god). Drawing on Upanishadic writings, he claimed that they identified the essence of the human soul with that of God (*tat tvam asi*, "that thou art"), and that all else – the phenomenal world and all *devas* – is an illusion (*maya*) created by God. Shankara is revered as saint-philosopher at the twelve *jyotirlinga*: sacred Shaivite sites associated with the unbounded *lingam* of light, which as a manifestation of Shiva once persuaded both Brahma and Vishnu to acknowledge Shiva's supremacy.

Another important *Darshana* centred around the age-old practice of **yoga** (literally "the action of yoking [to] another"), elucidated by

Patanjali (second century BC) in his *Yoga Sutras*. Interpreting yoga as the yoking of mind and body, or the yoking of the mind with God, Patanjali detailed various practices, which used in combination may lead to an understanding of the fundamental **unity** of all things. The most common form of yoga known in the West is *hatha-yoga*, whereby the body and its vital energies is brought under control through physical positions and breathing methods, with results said to range from attaining a calm mind to being able to fly through the air, enter other bodies or become invisible. Other practices include *mantra-yoga*, the recitation of formulas and meditation on mystical diagrams (*mandalas*), *bhakti-yoga* (devotion), *jnana-yoga* (knowledge) and *raja*, or royal, *yoga* the highest form of yoga when the mind is absorbed in God.

THE MAHABHARATA

Eight times as long as the *Iliad* and *Odyssey* combined, the **Mahabharata** is the most popular of all Hindu texts. Written around 400 AD, it tells of a feuding *kshatrya* family in upper India (Bharata) during the fourth millennium BC. Like all good epics, the *Mahabharata* recounts a gripping tale, using its characters to illustrate moral values. In essence it attempts to elucidate the position of the warrior castes, the *kshatryas*, and demonstrate that religious fulfilment is as accessible for them as it is for *brahmins*.

The chief character is **Arjuna**, a superb archer, who with his four brothers – Yudhishtra, Bhima, Nakula and Sahadeva – represents the **Pandava** clan, upholders of righteousness and supreme fighters. Arjuna won his wife **Draupadi** in an archery contest, but wishing to avoid jealousy she agreed to be the shared wife of all five brothers. The Pandava clan are resented by their cousins, the evil **Kauravas**, led by Duryodhana, the eldest son of Dhrtarashtra, ruler of the Kuru kingdom.

When Dhrtarashtra handed his kingdom over to the Pandavas, the Kauravas were far from happy. Duryodhana challenged Yudhishtra (known for his brawn but not his brain) to a gambling contest. The dice game was rigged; Yudhishtra gambled away not only his possessions, but also his kingdom and his shared wife. The Kauravas offered to return the kingdom to the Pandavas if they could spend thirteen years in exile, together with their wife, without being recognized. Despite much schem-

ing, the Pandavas succeeded, but on return found that the Kauravas would not fulfil their side of the bargain.

Thus ensued the great battle of the *Mahabharata*, told in the sixth book, the **Bhagavad Gita** – immensely popular as an independent story. Vishnu descends to earth as **Krishna**, and steps into battle as Arjuna's charioteer. The *Bhagavad Gita* details the fantastic struggle of the fighting cousins, using magical weapons and brute force. Arjuna is in a dilemma, unable to justify the killing of his own kin in pursuit of a rightful kingdom for himself and his brothers. Krishna consoles him, reminding him that his principal duty, his *varnashradharma*, is as a warrior. What is more, Krishna points out, each man's soul, or *atman*, is eternal, and transmigrates from body to body, so Arjuna need not grieve the death of his cousins. Krishna convinces Arjuna that by fulfilling his *dharma* he not only upholds law and order by saving the kingdom from the grasp of unrighteous rulers, he also serves God in the spirit of devotion (*bhakti*), and thus guarantees himself eternal union with the divine in the blissful state of *moksha*.

The Pandavas finally win the battle, and Yudhishtra is crowned king. Eventually Arjuna's grandson, Pariksit, inherits the throne, and the Pandavas trek to Mount Meru, the mythical centre of the universe and the abode of the gods, where Arjuna finds Krishna's promised *moksha*.

PRACTICE

The primary concern of most Hindus is to reduce bad *karma* and acquire merit (*punya*), by honest and charitable living within the restrictions imposed by caste, and by worship, in the hope of attaining a higher status of rebirth. Strict rules address purity and pollution, the most obvious of them requiring high-caste Hindus to limit their contact with potentially polluting lower castes. All bodily excretions are polluting (hence the strange looks Westerners receive when they blow their nose and return the handkerchief to their pocket). Above all else, **water** is the agent of purification, used in ablutions before prayer, and revered in all rivers, especially Ganga (the Ganges).

In most Hindu homes, a chosen deity is worshipped daily in a shrine room, and scriptures are read. Outside the home, worship takes place in temples, and consists of **puja**, or devotion to God – sometimes a simple act of prayer, but more commonly a complex process when the god's image is circumambulated, offered flowers, rice, sugar and incense, and anointed with water, milk or sandalwood paste (which is usually done on behalf of the devotee by the temple priest, the *pujari*). The aim in *puja* is to take **darshan** – glimpse the god – and thus receive his or her blessing. Whether devotees simply worship the deity in prayer, or make requests – for a healthy crop, a son, good results in exams, a vigorous monsoon or a cure for illness – they leave the temple with *prasad*, an offering of food or flowers taken from the holy sanctuary by the *pujaris*.

Communal worship and get-togethers en route to pilgrimage sites are celebrated with *kirtan* or *bhajan*, singing of hymns, perhaps verses in praise of Krishna taken from the *Bhagavad Purana*, or repetitive cries of "Jay Shankar!" (Praise to Shiva). Temple ceremonies are conducted in Sanskrit by *pujaris* who tend the image in daily rituals that symbolically wake, bathe, feed and dress the god, and finish each day by preparing the god for sleep. The most elaborate is the evening ritual, **arthi**, when lamps are lit, blessed in the sanctuary, and passed around devotees amid the clanging of drums, gongs and cymbals. In many villages, shrines to *devatas*, village deities who function as protectors and may bring disaster if neglected, are more important than temples.

Each of the great stages in life – birth, initiation (when boys of the three twice-born *varnas* are invested with a sacred thread, and a *mantra* is whispered into their ear by their guru), marriage, death and cremation – is cause for fervent prayer, energetic celebration and feasting. The most significant event in a Hindu's life is **marriage**, which symbolizes ritual purity, and for women is so important that it takes the place of initiation. Feasting, dancing, and singing among the bride and groom's families, usually lasting for a week or more before and after the marriage, are the order of the day all over India. The actual marriage is consecrated when the couple walk seven times round a sacred fire, accompanied by sacred verses read by an officiating *brahmin*. Despite efforts to reduce the importance of a **dowry**, a valuable gift from the bride's family to the groom, dowries are still demanded, and among wealthier families may include televisions, videos, and cars in addition to the more common items of jewellery and money. Burning of wives whose dowry is below expectations is still known to occur.

Life transitions are by no means the only cause for celebration among Hindus, whose year is marked by **festivals** devoted to deities, re-enacting mythological stories and commemorating sacred sites. The grandest festivals are held at places made holy by association with gods, goddesses, miracles, and great teachers, or rivers and mountains; throughout the year these are important **pilgrimage** sites, visited by devotees eager to receive *darshan*, glimpse the world of the gods, and attain merit. The journey, or *yatra*, to a pilgrimage site is every bit as significant as reaching the sacred location, and bands of Hindus (particularly *sadhus*) often walk from site to site. Modern transport, however, has made things easier, and every state lays on pilgrimage tours, when buses full of chanting families roar from one temple to another, filling up with religious souvenirs as they go.

Perhaps India's single most sacred place is the ancient city of **Varanasi** (also known as Benares or Kashi), on the banks of the Ganges. The river has been sacred since the time of the earliest Aryan settlements, and is personified as the beneficent goddess Ganga. At Varanasi it holds the redeeming quality common to all rivers, but bathing in its waters, and more particularly, dying or being cremated there, is a pre-

HINDU GODS AND GODDESSES

VISHNU

The chief function of **Vishnu**, "pervader", is to keep the world in order, preserving, restoring and protecting. With four arms holding a conch, discus, lotus and mace, Vishnu is blue-skinned, and often shaded by a serpent, or resting on its coils, afloat on an ocean. He is usually seen alongside his half-man-half-eagle vehicle, Garuda.

Vaishnavites, often distinguishable by two vertical lines on their foreheads, recognize Vishnu as supreme lord, and hold that he has manifested himself on earth nine times. These incarnations, or *avatars*, have been as fish (Matsya), tortoise (Kurma), boar (Varaha), man-lion (Narsingh), dwarf (Vamana), axe-wielding *brahmin* (Parsuram), Rama, Krishna and Balaram (though some say that the Buddha is the ninth *avatar*). Vishnu's future descent to earth as Kalki, the saviour who will come to restore purity and destroy the wicked, is eagerly awaited.

The most important *avatars* are Krishna and Rama. **Krishna** is the hero of the *Bhagavad Gita*, in which he proposes three routes to salvation (*moksha*): selfless action (*karmayoga*), knowledge (*jnana*), and devotion to god (*bhakti*), and explains that *moksha* is attainable in this life, even without asceticism and renunciation. This appealed to all castes, as it denied the necessity of ritual and officiating *brahmin* priests, and evolved into the popular *bhakti* cult that legitimized love of God as a means to *moksha*, and found expression in emotional songs of the quest for union with God. Through *bhakti*, Krishna's role was extended, and he assumed different faces: most popularly he is the playful cowherd who seduces and dances with cowgirls (*gopis*), giving each the illusion that she is his only lover. He is also pictured as a small, chubby, mischievous baby, known for his butter-stealing exploits, who inspires tender motherly love in women. Like Vishnu, Krishna is blue, and often shown dancing and playing the flute.

Popular legend has it that Krishna was born in **Mathura**, today a major pilgrimage centre, and sported with his *gopis* in nearby **Vrindavan**. He also established a kingdom on the far western coast of Gujarat, at **Dwarka**.

Rama is the chief character in the *Ramayana*. Born a prince in Ayodhya, he was denied succession to the throne by one of his father's wives, and was exiled for fourteen years, together with his wife Sita. The *Ramayana* details his exploits during these years, and his defeat of the demon king of Lanka, Ravana. When Rama was reinstated as king in Ayodhya, he put Sita through "trial by fire" to prove that she had remained pure while in the clasps of Ravana. Sita passed the trial unharmed, and is held up as the paradigm of women – faithful, pure and honest.

SHIVA

Shaivism, the cult of **Shiva**, was also inspired by *bhakti*, requiring selfless love from devotees in a quest for divine communion, but Shiva has never been incarnate on earth. He is presented in many different aspects, such as **Nataraja**, Lord of the Dance, **Mahadev**, Great God, and **Maheshvar**, Divine Lord, source of all knowledge. Though he does have several terrible forms, his role extends beyond that of destroyer, and he is revered as the source of the whole universe.

Shiva is often depicted with four or five faces, holding a trident, draped with serpents, and bearing a third eye in his forehead. In temples, he is identified with the *lingam*, or phallic symbol, resting in the *yoni*, a representation of female sexuality. Whether as statue or *lingam*, Shiva is guarded by his bull-mount, Nandi, and often accompanied by a consort, who also assumes various forms, and is looked upon as the vital energy, *shakti*, that empowers him. Their erotic exploits were a favourite sculptural subject between the ninth and twelfth centuries, most unashamedly in carvings on the temples of **Khajuraho**, in Madhya Pradesh.

While Shiva is the object of popular devotion all over India, as the terrible **Bhairav** he is also the god of the Shaivite **ascetics**, who renounce family and caste ties and perform extreme meditative and yogic practices. Many, though not all, smoke *ganja*, Shiva's favourite herb; all see renunciation and realization of God as the key to *moksha*. Some ascetic practices enter the realm of **tantrism**, in which confrontation with all that's impure, such as alcohol, death, and sex, is used to merge the sacred and the profane, and bring about the profound realization that Shiva is omnipresent.

GANESH

Chubby and smiling, elephant-headed **Ganesh**, the first son of Shiva and Parvati, is invoked before every undertaking (except funerals). Seated on a throne or lotus, his image is often placed above temple gateways, in shops and houses; in his four arms he holds a conch, discus, bowl of sweets (or club) and a water lily, and he's always attended by his vehicle, a rat. Credited with writing the *Mahabharata* as it was dictated by the sage

Vyasa, Ganesh is regarded by many as the god of learning, the lord of success, prosperity and peace.

DURGA

Durga, the fiercest of the female deities, is an aspect of Shiva's more conservative consort, Parvati (also known as Uma), who is remarkable only for her beauty and fidelity. In whatever form, Shiva's consort is *shakti*, the fundamental energy that spurs him into action. Among Durga's many aspects, each a terrifying goddess eager to slay demons, are Chamunda, Kali and Muktakeshi, but in all her forms she is Mahadevi (Great Goddess). Statues show her with ten arms, holding the head of a demon, a spear, and other weapons; she tramples demons underfoot, or dances upon Shiva's body. A garland of skulls drapes her neck, and her tongue hangs from her mouth, dripping with blood – a particularly gruesome sight on pictures of Kali. Durga is much venerated in Bengal; in all her temples, animal sacrifices are a crucial element of worship, to satisfy her thirst for blood and deter her ruthless anger.

LAKSHMI

The comely goddess **Lakshmi**, usually shown sitting or standing on a lotus flower, and sometimes called Padma (lotus), is the embodiment of loveliness, grace and charm, and the goddess of prosperity and wealth. Vishnu's consort, she appears in different aspects alongside each of his *avatars*; the most important are Sita, wife of Rama, and Radha, Krishna's favourite *gopi*. In many temples she is shown as one with Vishnu, in the form of Lakshmi Narayan.

KARTTIKEYA

Though some legends claim that his mother was Ganga, or even Agni, **Karttikeya** is popularly believed to be the second son of Shiva and Parvati. Primarily a god of war, he was popular among the northern Guptas, who worshipped him as Skanda, and the southern Chalukyas, for whom he was Subrahmanya. Usually shown with six faces, and standing upright with bow and arrow, Karttikeya is commonly petitioned by those wishing for male offspring.

HANUMAN

India's great monkey god, **Hanuman**, features in the *Ramayana* as Rama's chief aide in the fight against the demon-king of Lanka. Depicted as a giant monkey clasping a mace, Hanuman is the deity of acrobats and wrestlers, but is also seen as Rama and Sita's greatest devotee, and an author of Sanskrit grammar. As his representatives, monkeys find sanctuary in temples all over India.

SARASWATI

The most beautiful Hindu goddess, **Saraswati**, the wife of Brahma, with her flawless milk-white complexion, sits or stands on a water lily or peacock, playing a lute, *sitar* or *vina*. Associated with the River Saraswati, mentioned in the *Rig Veda*, she is seen as a goddess of purification and fertility, but is also revered as the inventor of writing, the queen of eloquence and goddess of music.

SANI

Closely linked with the planet Saturn, **Sani** is feared for his destructive powers. His image, a black statue with protruding blood-red tongue, is often found on street corners; strings of green chillies and lemon are hung in shops and houses each Saturday (*Saniwar*) to ward off his evil influences.

KHAMDENU

Mention must also be made of the **sacred cow**, Khamdenu, who receives devotion through the respect shown to all cows, left to amble through streets and temples all over India. The origin of the cow's sanctity is uncertain; some myths record that Brahma created cows at the same time as *brahmins*, to provide *ghee* (clarified butter) for use in priestly ceremonies. To this day cow dung and urine are used to purify houses (in fact the urine keeps insects at bay), and the killing or harming of cows by any Hindu is a grave offence. The cow is often referred to as mother of the gods, and each part of its body is significant: its horns symbolize the gods, its face the sun and moon, its shoulders Agni (god of fire) and its legs the Himalaya.

condition to entering heaven (*svarga*) and achieving release from rebirth. *Ghats*, steps leading to the water's edge, are common in all river- or lakeside towns, the abode of priests who offer *puja* to a devotee's chosen deity.

The source of the Ganges, high in the mountains of western Uttar Pradesh at **Gangotri**, is held in great reverence, as are the five ancient temples nearby, known as **Panch Kedar**, deep in the Himalaya. Equally important are *sangams*, or *tirthas*, the points where two rivers meet. Every twelve years, when India's largest festival, the **Kumbh Mela**, is held at Allahabad, the *sangam* of the Ganges and the Yamuna, the *ghats* turn into a seething mass of bodies, overrun by near-naked ascetics who are the first of millions to bathe in the holy waters. Lesser *melas* are held at three-yearly intervals at the *tirthas* of Haridwar, Nasik, and Ujjain.

Not only river confluences are auspicious: at Kanniyakumari, the southern tip of India, the waters of the Indian Ocean, the Bay of Bengal and the Arabian sea are thought to merge. Pilgrimages here are often combined with visits to the great temples of **Tamil Nadu**, where Shaivite and Vaishnavite saints established cults, and India's largest temples were constructed. Madurai, Thanjavur, Chidambaram and Srirangam are major pilgrimage centres, representing the pinnacle of the architectural development that began at Mamallapuram. Their festivals often involve the tugging of deities on vast wooden chariots through the streets, a practice most vigorously played out at **Puri**, in Orissa, when Lord Jaganath is taken from the temple during *Rath Yatra* for a foray through the town.

As well as specific temples sacred to particular gods – Brahma in **Pushkar**, Kali at **Calcutta**, or Shiva at the twelve *jyotirlinga* – historical sites, such as the caves of **Ellora**, and the former Vijayanagar capital at **Hampi**, remain magnets for pilgrims. More than a common ideology, it is this sacred geography, entwined with popular mythology, that unites hundreds of millions of Hindus, who have also been brought together in nationalistic struggles, particularly in response to Christian missionaries and Muslim and British domination.

ISLAM

Indian society may be dominated by Hindus, but **Muslims** – some ten percent of the population – form a significant presence in almost every town, city and village. The belief in only one god, Allah, the condemnation of idol worship, and the observance of strict dietary laws and specific festivals set Muslims apart from their Hindu neighbours, with whom they have co-existed for centuries. Such differences have often led to communal fighting, most notably during Partition, and in 1993 riots all over north India followed the destruction by Hindus of the Babri Masjid mosque in Ayodhya.

Islam, "submission to God", was founded by **Muhammad** (570–632 AD), regarded as the last in a succession of prophets, who transmitted God's final and perfected revelation to mankind through the writings of the divinely

revealed "recitation", the **Koran** (Quran). The true beginning of Islam is dated at 622 AD, when Muhammad and his followers, exiled from Mecca, made the *hijra*, or migration, north to Yathrib, later known as Medina, "City of the Prophet". The *hijra* marks the start of the Islamic lunar calendar: the Gregorian year 1995 is for Muslims 1416 AH (*Anno Hijra*).

From Medina, Muhammad ordered raids on caravans heading for Mecca, and led his community in battles against the Meccans, inspired by *jihad*, or "striving" on behalf of God and Islam. This concept of holy war was the driving force behind the incredible expansion of Islam – by 713 Muslims had settled as far west as Spain, and on the banks of the Indus in the east. When **Mecca** was peacefully surrendered to Muhammad in 630, he cleared the sacred shrine, the Ka'ba, of idols, and proclaimed it the pilgrimage centre of Islam.

The Koran, the authoritative scripture of Islam, contains the basics of Islamic belief: that there is one god, Allah (though he is attributed with 99 names), and his prophet is Muhammad.

Muhammad was succeeded as leader of the *umma*, the Islamic community, by Abu Bakr, the prophet's representative, or Caliph, the first in a line of Caliphs who led the orthodox community until the eleventh century AD. However, a schism soon emerged when the third Caliph, Uthman, was assassinated by followers of Ali, Muhammad's son-in-law, in 656 AD. This new sect, calling themselves **Shi'as**, "partisans" of Ali, looked to Ali and his successors, infallible *Imams*, as leaders of the *umma* until 878 AD, and thereafter replaced their religious authority with a body of scholars, the *ulema*.

By the second century after the *hijra* (ninth century AD), orthodox, or **Sunni**, Islam had assumed the form in which it endures today. A collection of traditions about the prophet, **Hadith**, became the source for ascertaining the **Sunna**, customs, of Muhammad. From the Koran and the Sunna, seven major **items of belief** were laid down: the belief in God, in angels as his messengers, in prophets (including Jesus and Moses), in the Koran, in the doctrine of predestination by God, in the Day of Judgement, and in the bodily resurrection of all people on this day. Religious practice was also standardized under the Muslim law, **Sharia**, in the **Five Pillars of Islam**. The first "pillar" is the confession of faith, *shahada*, that "There is no god but God, and Muhammad is his messenger". The other four are prayer (*salat*) five times daily, almsgiving (*zakat*), fasting (*saum*), especially during the month of Ramadan, and, if possible, pilgrimage (*hajj*) to Mecca, the ultimate goal of every practising Muslim.

The first Muslims to settle in India were traders who arrived on the south coast in the seventh century, probably in search of timber for shipbuilding. Later, in 711, Muslims entered Sind, in the northwest, to take action against Hindu pirates, and dislodged the Hindu government. Their presence, however, was short-lived. Much more significant was the invasion of north India under **Mahmud of Ghazni**, who rampaged through the Punjab in search of temple treasures, and in the spirit of *jihad*, engaged in a war against infidels and idolaters. More Turkish raids followed in the twelfth century, resulting in the colonization of India and the provision of a homeland for refugees pushed out of Persia by the Mongols. The Turks set themselves up in Delhi as **Sultans**, the forerunners of the **Moghuls** (see p.1217).

Many Muslims who settled in India intermarried with Hindus, Buddhists and Jains, and the community spread. A further factor in its growth was missionary activity by **Sufis**, who emphasized abstinence and self-denial in service to God, and stressed the attainment of inner knowledge of God through meditation and mystical experience. In India, Sufi teachings spread among Shaivites and Vaishnavites, who shared their passion for personal closeness to God. Their use of music (particularly *qawwali* singing) and dance, shunned by orthodox Muslims, appealed to Hindus, for whom *kirtan* (singing) played an important role in religious practice. One *qawwali*, relating the life of the Sufi saint Waris Ali Shah, draws parallels between his early life and the childhood of Krishna – an outrage for orthodox Muslims, but attractive to Hindus, who still flock to his shrine in Deva Sharief near Lucknow. Similar shrines, or *dargars*, all over India bridge the gap between Islam and Hinduism.

Muslims are enjoined to pray five times daily, following a routine of utterances and positions. They may do this at home or in a **mosque** – always full at noon on Friday, for communal prayer. (Only the Druze, an esoteric sect based in Bombay, hold communal prayers on Thursdays.) Characterized by bulbous domes

and high minarets, from which a *muezzin* calls the faithful to prayer, mosques always contain a *mihrab*, or niche indicating the direction of prayer (to Mecca), a *mimbar* or pulpit, from which the Friday sermon is read, a source of water for ablutions, and a balcony for women. Firm reminders of Muslim dominance, mosques all over India display a bold linear grandeur quite different to the delicacy of Hindu temples. India's largest mosque is the Jami Masjid ("Friday Mosque") in **Delhi**, but magnificent structures, including tombs, schools and substantial remains of cities are scattered throughout north India and the Deccan, with especially outstanding examples in Hyderabad, Jaunpur, Agra and Fatehpur Sikri.

The position of **women** in Islam is a subject of great debate. It is customary for women to be veiled, though in larger cities many women do not cover their head, and in strictly orthodox communities most wear a *burqa*, usually black, that covers them from head to toe. Like other Indian women, Muslim women take second place to men in public, but in the home, where they are often shielded from men's eyes in an inner courtyard, they wield great influence. In theory education is equally available to boys and girls, but girls tend to forgo learning soon after sixteen, encouraged instead to assume the traditional role of wife and mother. Contrary to popular belief, polygamy is not widespread; while it does occur, and Muhammad himself had several wives, many Muslims prefer monogamy, and several sects actually stress it as the duty of Muslims. In marriage, women *receive* a dowry (Hindu women must provide one) as financial security.

BUDDHISM

For several centuries, **Buddhism** dominated India, with adherents in almost every part of the subcontinent. However, having reached its height in the fifth century, it was all but eclipsed by the time of the Muslim conquest. Today Buddhists are a tiny fraction of the population, but superb monuments are firm reminders of the prior importance of the faith, and essential elements in India's cultural legacy.

The founder of Buddhism, **Siddhartha Gautama**, known as the **Buddha**, "the awakened one", was born into a wealthy *kshatriya* family in Lumbini, north of the Gangetic plain in present-day Nepal, around 566 BC. Brought up in luxury as a prince and a Hindu, he married at an early age, and renounced family life when he was thirty. Unsatisfied with the explanations of worldly suffering proposed by Hindu gurus, and convinced that asceticism did not lead to spiritual realization, Siddhartha spent years in meditation, wandering through the ancient kingdom, or *janapada*, of Magadha. His enlightenment (*bodhi*) is said to have taken place under a *bodhi* tree in **Bodhgaya** (Bihar), after a night of contemplation during which he resisted the worldly temptations set before him by the demon, Mara. Soon afterwards he gave his first sermon in **Sarnath**, now a major pilgrimage centre. For the rest of his life he taught, expounding *Dharma*, the true nature of the world, human life and spiritual attainment. Before his death (*c*.486 BC) in Kushinagara (UP), he had established the *sangha*, a community of monks and nuns, who continued his teachings.

The Buddha's view of life incorporated the Hindu concepts of *samsara* and *karma*, but remodelled the ultimate goal of religion, calling it *nirvana*, "no wind". Indefinable in worldly terms, since it is by nature free from conditioning, *nirvana* represents a clarity of mind, pure understanding and unimaginable bliss. Its attainment signals an end to rebirth, but no communion of a "soul" with God; neither has independent existence. The most important concept outlined by the Buddha was that all things, subject to change and dependence, are characterized by **impermanence**, and there is **no self**, no permanent ego, so **attachment** to anything (possessions, emotions, spiritual attainment and *devas*) must be renounced before impermanence can be grasped, and *nirvana* realized.

Disregarding caste and priestly dominance in ritual, the Buddha formulated a teaching open to all. His followers took refuge in the three jewels: *Buddha*, *Dharma*, and *Sangha*. The teachings became known as **Theravada**, or "Doctrine of the Elders". By the first century BC the **Tripitaka**, or "three Baskets" (a Pali canon in three sections), had set out the basis for early Buddhist practice, proposing *dana*, selfless giving, and *sila*, precepts which aim at avoiding harm to oneself and others, as the most important guidelines for all Buddhists, and the essential code of practice for the lay community.

Carried out with good intentions, *sila* and *dana* maximize the acquisition of good *karma*, and minimize material attachment, thus making the individual open to the more religiously oriented teachings, the **Four Noble Truths**. The first of these states that all is suffering (*dukkha*), not because every action is necessarily unpleasurable, but because nothing in the phenomenal world is permanent or reliable. The second truth states that *dukkha* arises through attachment, the third refers to *nirvana*, the cessation of suffering, and the fourth details the path to *nirvana*. Known as the **Eightfold Path** – right understanding, thought, speech, action, livelihood, effort, mindfulness and concentration – it aims at reducing attachment and ego and increasing awareness, until all four truths are thoroughly comprehended, and *nirvana* is achieved. Even this should not be clinged to – those who experience it are advised by the Buddha to use their understanding to help others to achieve realization.

The Sanskrit word *bhavana*, referred to in the West as **meditation**, translates literally as "bringing into being". Traditionally meditation is divided into two categories: **Samatha**, or calm, which stills and controls the mind, and **Vipassana**, or insight, during which thought processes and the noble truths are investigated, leading ultimately to a knowledge of reality. Both methods are taught in Buddhist centres across India.

At first, Buddhist iconography represented the Buddha by symbols such as a footprint, *bodhi* tree, parasol or vase. These can be seen on *stupas* (domed monuments containing relics of the Buddha) built throughout India from the time of the Buddhist emperor Ashoka (see p.1209), and in ancient Buddhist caves, which served as meditation retreats and *viharas* (monasteries). The finest are at **Ellora** and **Ajanta**; like the remarkable *stupas* at **Sanchi**, they incorporate later designs which depict the Buddha in human form, standing and preaching or sitting in meditation, distinguished by characteristic marks, and indicating his teaching by hand gestures, or *mudras*.

This artistic development coincided with an increase in the devotional side of Buddhism, and a recognition of *bodhisattvas* – those bound for enlightenment who delayed self-absorption in *nirvana* to become teachers, spurred by selfless compassion and altruism.

The importance of the *bodhisattva* ideal grew as a new school, the **Mahayana**, or

"Great Vehicle", emerged. By the twelfth century it had become fully established and, somewhat disparagingly, renamed the old school **Hinayana**, or "Lesser Vehicle". Mahayanists proposed emptiness, *sunyata*, as the fundamental nature of all things, taking to extremes the belief that nothing has independent existence. The **wisdom** necessary to understand *sunyata*, and the **skilful means** required to put wisdom into action in daily life and teaching, and interpret emptiness in a positive sense, became the most important qualities of Mahayana Buddhism. Before long *bodhisattvas* were joined in both scripture and art by female consorts who embodied wisdom.

Hinayana Buddhism survives today in Sri Lanka, Burma, Thailand, Laos and Cambodia. Mahayana Buddhism spread from India to China, Japan, Korea and Vietnam, where it incorporated local gods and spirits into a family of *bodhisattvas*. In many places further evolution saw the adoption of magical methods, esoteric teachings, and the full use of sense experience to bring about spiritual transformation, resulting in a separate school known as **Mantrayana** or **Vajrayana** based on texts called *tantras*. Mantrayana encouraged meditation on *mandalas* (symbolic diagrams representing the cosmos and internal spiritual attainment), sexual imagery, and sometimes sexual practice, in which the female principle of wisdom could be united with skilful means.

Buddhism was introduced to **Tibet** in the seventh century, and integrated to a certain extent with the indigenous **Bön** cult, before emerging as a faith considered to incorporate all three vehicles – Hinayana, Mahayana and Vajrayana. Practised largely in Ladakh, along with parts of Himachal Pradesh, Sikkim and Bihar, Tibetan Buddhism worships historical Buddha, known as Shakyamuni, alongside other Buddhas and a host of *bodhisattvas* and protector deities. Elaborate rituals and ceremonies incorporating music and dance mark important dates in the Buddhist calendar. There is a heavy emphasis on teachers, *lamas* (similar to gurus), and reincarnated teachers, known as *tulkus*. The **Dalai Lama**, the head of Tibetan Buddhism, is the fourteenth in a succession of incarnate *bodhisattvas*, the representative of Avalokitesvara (the *bodhisattva* of compassion), and the leader of the exiled Tibetan community whose headquarters are in **Dharamsala** (HP).

For Buddhist monks and nuns, and some members of the lay community, meditation is an integral part of religious life. Most lay Buddhists concentrate on *dana* and *sila*, and on auspicious days, such as *Vesak* (marking the Buddha's birth, enlightenment and death), make **pilgrimages** to Bodh Gaya, Sarnath, Lumbini and Kushinagar. After laying offerings before Buddha statues, devotees gather in silent meditation, or join in chants taken from early Buddhist texts. *Uposathas*, full moon days, are marked by continual chanting through the night when temples are lit by glimmering butter lamps, often set afloat on lotus ponds, among the flowers that represent the essential beauty and purity to be found in each person in the thick of the confusing "mud" of daily life.

Among Tibetan communities, devotees hang prayer flags, turn prayer wheels, and set stones carved with *mantras* (religious verses) in rivers, thus sending the word of the Buddha with wind and water to all corners of the earth. Prayers and chanting are often accompanied by horns, drums and cymbals.

JAINISM

Though the **Jain** population in India is small – accounting for less than one percent of the population – it has been tremendously influential for at least 2500 years. A large proportion of Jains live in Gujarat, and all over India they are commonly occupied as merchants and traders. Similarities to Hindu worship, and a shared respect for nature and non-violence, have contributed to the decline of the Jain community through conversion to Hinduism, but there is no antagonism between the two sects.

Focused on the practice of **ahimsa** (non-violence), Jains follow a rigorous discipline to avoid harm to all **jivas**, or "souls", which exist in animals and humans, and in plants, water, fire, earth and air. They assert that every *jiva* is pure, omniscient, and capable of achieving liberation, or *moksha*, from existence in this universe. However, *jivas* are obscured by **karma**, a form of subtle matter that clings to the soul, is born of action, and binds the *jiva* to physical existence. For the most orthodox Jain, the only way to dissociate *karma* from the *jiva*, and thereby escape the wheel of death and rebirth, is to follow the path of asceticism and meditation, rejecting passion, wrong view, attachment, carelessness and impure action.

The Jain doctrine is based upon the teachings of **Mahavira**, or "Great Hero", the last in a succession of 24 *tirthankaras* ("crossing-makers") said to appear on earth every 300 million years. Mahavira (*c.*599–527 BC) was born as Vardhamana Jnatrputra into a *kshatrya* family near modern Patna, in northeast India. Like the Buddha, Mahavira rejected family life at the age of thirty, and spent years wandering as an ascetic, renouncing all possessions in an attempt to conquer attachment to worldly values. Firmly opposed to sacrificial rites and caste distinctions, after gaining complete understanding and detachment, he began teaching others, not about Vedic gods and divine heroes, but about the true nature of the world, and the means required for release, *moksha*, from an endless cycle of rebirth.

His teachings were written down in the first millennium BC, and Jainism prospered throughout India, under the patronage of kings such as Chandragupta Maurya (third century BC). Not long after, there was a schism, in part based on linguistic and geographical divisions, but mostly due to differences in monastic practice. On the one hand the **Digambaras** ("sky-clad") believed that nudity was an essential part of world renunciation, and that women are incapable of achieving liberation from worldly existence. The ("white-clad") **Svetambaras**, however, disregarded the extremes of nudity, incorporated nuns into monastic communities, and even acknowledged a female *tirthankara*. Today the two sects worship at different temples, but the number of naked Digambaras is minimal. Many Svetambara monks and nuns wear white masks to avoid breathing in insects, and carry a "fly-whisk", sometimes used to brush their path; none will use public transport, and they often spend days or weeks walking barefoot to a pilgrimage site.

Practising Jain householders vow to avoid injury, falsehood, theft (extended to fair trade), infidelity and worldly attachment. Jain **temples** are wonderfully ornate, with pillars, brackets and spires carved by *silavats* into voluptuous maidens, musicians, saints, and even Hindu deities; the *swastika* symbol commonly set into the marble floors is central to Jainism, representing the four states of rebirth as gods, humans, "hell beings", or animals and plants. Worship in temples consists of prayer and *puja* before images of the *tirthankaras*; the devotee circumambulates the image, chants sacred verses and makes offerings of flowers, sandalwood paste, rice, sweets and incense. It's common to fast four times a month on *parvan* (holy) days, the eighth and fourteenth days of the moon's waxing and waning periods. While reducing attachment to the body, this emulates the fast to death (while in meditation), or *sallekhana*, accepted by Jain mendicants as a final rejection of attachment, and a relatively harmless way to end worldly life.

To enter a monastic community, lay Jains must pass through eleven *pratimas*, starting with right views, the profession of vows, fasting and continence, and culminating in renunciation of family life. Once a monk or nun, a Jain aims to clarify understanding through meditational practices, hoping to extinguish passions and sever the ties of *karma* and attachment, entering fourteen spiritual stages, *gunasthanas*, to emerge as a fully enlightened, omniscient being. Whether pursuing a monastic or lay lifestyle, however, Jains recognize the rarity of enlightenment, and religious practice is, for the most part, aimed at achieving a state of rebirth more conducive to spiritual attainment.

Pilgrimage sites are known as **tirthas**, but this does not refer to the literal meaning of "river crossing", sacred to Hindus because of the purificatory nature of water. At one of the foremost Svetambara *tirthas*, **Shatrunjaya** in Gujarat, over nine hundred temples crown a single hill, said to have been visited by the first *tirthankara*, Rishabha, and believed to be the place where Rama, Sita and the Pandava brothers (incorporated into Jain tradition) gained deliverance. An important Digambara *tirtha* is **Shravan Belgola** in Karnataka, where a 57-

THE 24 TIRTHANKARAS

1 Adinath/Rishabha	13 Vimala
2 Ajitanath	14 Ananta/Anantajita
3 Sambhava	15 Dharma
4 Abinandana	16 Santi/Shantinath
5 Sumati/Suminath	17 Kunthu
6 Padmaprabha	18 Ara
7 Suparsva	19 Malli
8 Chandraprabha	20 Munisuvrata
9 Puspadanta	21 Nami
10 Sitala	22 Nemi/Neminath
11 Sreyansa	23 Parshva/Parshvanath
12 Vasupujya	24 Mahavira

feet-high image of Bahubali (recognized as the first human to attain liberation), at the summit of a hill, is anointed in the huge *abhisheka* festival every twelve years.

In an incredibly complicated process of philosophical analysis known as **Anekanatavada** (many-sidedness), Jainism approaches all questions of existence, permanence, and change from seven different viewpoints, maintaining that things can be looked at in an infinite number of valid ways. Thus it claims to remove the intellectual basis for violence, avoiding the potentially damaging result of holding a one-sided view. In this respect Jainism accepts other religious philosophies, and it has adopted, with a little reinterpretation, several Hindu festivals and practices.

SIKHISM

Sikhism, India's youngest "religion", remains dominant in the Punjab, while its adherents have spread throughout northern India, and several communities have grown up in Britain, America and Canada.

Guru Nanak (1469–1539) was the movement's founder. Born into an orthodox Hindu *kshatrya* family in Talwandi, a small village west of Lahore (in present-day Pakistan), he was among many sixteenth-century poet-philosophers, sometimes referred to as Sants, who formed emotional cults, drawing elements from both Hinduism and Islam. Nanak declared "God is neither Hindu nor Muslim and the path which I follow is God's"; he regarded God as *Sat*, or truth, who makes himself known through gurus. Though he condemned ancestor worship, astrology, caste distinction, sex discrimination, auspicious days, and the rituals of *brahmins*, Nanak did not attack Islam or Hinduism – he simply regarded the many deities as names for one supreme God, and encouraged his followers to shift religious emphasis from ritual to meditation.

In common with Hindus, Nanak believed in a cyclic process of death and rebirth (*samsara*), but he asserted that liberation (*moksha*) was attainable in this life by all women and men, regardless of caste, and religious practice can and should be integrated into everyday practical living. He contested that all people are characterized by *humai*, a sense of self-reliance that obscures an understanding of dependence on god, encourages attachment to temporal values

(*maya*), and consequently results in successive rebirths. For Sikhs, the only way to achieve release from human existence is to conquer *humai*, and become centred on God (*gurmukh*). The only people believed to have realized the ultimate truth embodied by God are the Sikh gurus.

Guru Nanak, who died in 1539, was succeeded by a disciple, Lehna, known as **Guru Angad** ("limb"), who continued to lead the community of Sikhs ("disciples"), the **Sikh Panth**, and wrote his own and Nanak's hymns in a new script, **Gurumukhi**, which is today the script of written Punjabi.

After Guru Angad's death in 1552, eight successive gurus acted as leaders for the Sikh Panth, each introducing new elements into the faith and asserting it as a separate and powerful religious movement. Guru Ram Das (1552–74) founded the sacred city of **Amritsar**; his successor, Guru Arjan, compiled the gurus' hymns in a book called the **Adi Granth**, and became Sikhism's first martyr when he was executed at the hands of Jahangir.

The last leader, **Guru Gobind Singh**, was largely responsible for moulding the community as it exists today. In 1699 he founded the **Khalsa Brotherhood**, requiring members to renounce tobacco, *halal* meat, and sexual relations with Muslims, and to adopt the **five Ks**: *kesh* (unshorn hair), *kangha* (comb), *kirpan* (sword), *kara* (steel wristlet) and *kachch* (short trousers). This code, assumed at initiation, together with the replacement of caste names with Singh ("lion") for men and Kaur ("princess") for women, and the wearing of turbans by men, created a distinct cultural identity. Guru Gobind Singh compiled a standardized version of the *Adi Granth*, which contains the hymns of the first nine gurus as well as poems written by Hindus and Muslims, and installed it as his successor, naming it **Guru Granth Sahib**. This became the Sikh's spiritual guide, while political authority rested with the Khalsa, or *sangat*.

Demands for a separate Sikh state – Khalistan – and fighting in the eighteenth century, and later after Independence, have burdened Sikhs with a reputation as military activists, but Sikhs regard their religion as one devoted to egalitarianism, democracy and social awareness. Though to die fighting for the cause of religious freedom is considered to lead to liberation, the use of force is officially sanctioned only when other methods have failed.

The main duties of a Sikh are *nam japna*, *kirt karni*, and *vand chakna*; keeping God's name in mind, earning honest means, and giving to charity. Serving the community (*seva*) is a display of obedience to God, and the ideal life is uncontaminated by the **five evil impulses**: lust, covetousness, attachment, anger and pride.

Sikh **worship** takes place in a **gurudwara** ("door to the guru") or in the home, providing a copy of the *Adi Granth* is present. There are no priests, and no fixed time for worship, but congregations often meet in the mornings and evenings, and always on the eleventh day (*ekadashi*) of each lunar month, and on the first day of the year (*sangrand*). During *Kirtan*, or hymn singing, a feature of every Sikh service, verses from the *Adi Granth* or *Janam Sakhis*, stories of Guru Nanak's life, are sung to rhythmic clapping. The communal meal, *langar*, following prayers and singing, reinforces the practice laid down by Guru Nanak that openly flaunted caste and religious differences.

Gurudwaras – often schools, clinics or hostels as well as houses of prayer – are generally modelled on the Moghul style of Shah Jahan, considered a congenial blend of Hindu and Muslim architecture; usually whitewashed, and surmounted by a dome, they are always distinguishable by the *nishan sahib*, a yellow flag introduced by Guru Hargobind (1606–44). As in Islam, God is never depicted in pictorial form. Instead, the representative symbol *II Oankar* is etched into a canopy that shades the *Adi Granth*, which always stands in the main prayer room. In some *gurudwaras* a picture of a guru is hung close to the *Adi Granth*, but it's often difficult to distinguish between the different teachers: artistically they are depicted as almost identical, a tradition that unites the ten gurus as vehicles for god's words, or *mahalas*, and not divine beings.

Important occasions for Sikhs, in addition to naming of children, weddings and funerals, are **Gurpurbs**, anniversaries of the birth and death of the ten gurus, when the *Adi Granth* is read continuously from beginning to end.

ZOROASTRIANISM

Of all India's religious communities, Western visitors are least likely to come across – or recognize – **Zoroastrians**, who have no distinctive dress, and few houses of worship. Most live in Bombay, where they are known as **Parsis** (Persians) and are active in business, education, and politics; the Tata family are leading industrialists who until recently had a virtual monopoly on Indian truck building, and control many major chemical factories. Zoroastrian numbers (roughly ninety thousand) are rapidly dwindling, due to a falling birth rate and absorption into wider communities.

The religion's founder, **Zarathustra** (Zoroaster), who lived in Iran in 6000 BC (according to Zoroastrians), or between 1700 and 1400 BC, was the first religious prophet to expound a dualistic philosophy, based on the opposing powers of good and evil. For him, the absolute, wholly good and wise god, **Ahura Mazda**, together with his holy spirit and six emanations present in earth, water, the sky, animals, plants and fire, is constantly at odds with an evil power, **Angra Mainyu**, who is aided by *daevas*, or evil spirits.

Mankind, whose task on earth is to further good, faces judgement after death, and depending on the proportion of good and bad words, thoughts and actions, will find a place in heaven, or suffer the torments of hell. Zarathustra looked forward to a day of judgement, when a saviour, **Saoshyant**, miraculously born of a seed of the prophet and a virgin maiden, will appear on earth, restoring Ahura Mazda's perfect realm and expelling all impure souls and spirits to hell.

The first Zoroastrians to enter India arrived on the Gujarati coast in the tenth century, soon after the Arabian conquest of Iran, and by the seventeenth century most had settled in Bombay. Zoroastrian practice is based on the responsibility of every man and woman to choose between good and evil, and to respect God's creations. Five daily prayers, usually hymns (*gathas*), uttered by Zarathustra and standardized in the main Zoroastrian text, the **Avesta**, are said in the home or in a temple, before a fire, which symbolizes the realm of truth, righteousness and order. For this reason, Zoroastrians are often, incorrectly, called "fireworshippers".

Members of other faiths may not enter Zoroastrian temples, but one custom that is evident to outsiders is the method of disposing of the dead. A body is laid on a high open rooftop (or isolated hill) known as *dakhma* (often referred to as a "tower of silence"), for the flesh to be eaten by vultures, and the bones cleansed by sun and wind. Recently, some Zoroastrians, by necessity, have adopted more common methods of cremation or burial; in order not to bring impurity to fire or earth, they only use electric crematoria, and shroud coffins in concrete before laying them in the ground.

No Ruz, or "New Day", which celebrates the creation of fire and the ultimate triumph of good over evil, is the most popular Zoroastrian festival; the oldest sacred fire in India, in **Udwada**, just north of Daman in south Gujarat, is an important pilgrimage site.

Harriet Podger

INDIAN CINEMA

Travellers to India cannot help but be struck by the overwhelming presence of the **cinema**. Stridently non-naturalistic film hoardings, in bright primary colours, loom large in the urban landscape, and every city rings with the sounds of the latest popular **film songs** (pop music *is* film music in India), relayed through millions of radios.

Any attempt to understand modern Indian culture must entail coming to grips with the popular cinema, if only on account of the sheer volume of its product. India's film industry is the largest in the world; so large, in fact, that it scarcely makes sense to speak of it as being a single industry. The most obvious factor contributing to its diversity has been the existence, ever since the advent of sound, of a number of **regional language** cinemas. Although the Tamil cinema of Madras is responsible for producing the greatest number of films, the best known and most influential of the regional cinemas is the **Bombay film**. The Hindi market is the largest linguistic market, and one on which the southern studios and stars keep a vigilant eye, through direct production, dubbing regional works into Hindi, and attempting to transform regional stars into national ones.

Indian popular cinema has long been misrepresented and misunderstood, both within India and in the rest of the world. Urban sophisticates obsessed with realist and classical canons of film-making forever charge it with a dependence on simple melodrama, a wilful failure to

consider individual pyschology, and an uncontrollable tendency to take recourse in song and dance sequences at every conceivable juncture. In India, such critiques have their roots in the late 1940s and 1950s, and the emergence of an Indian "art cinema", led by **Satyajit Ray**. Ray argued for a cinema that developed its own iconography and addressed the everyday "reality" of Indian life. Quite apart from the universal debate concerning notions of "high" and "low" art, these arguments display a narrow-mindedness as to what may or may not be the "correct" way to portray India, and Indianness.

THE EARLY DECADES

Cinema in India emerged as an art form in the late nineteenth century. As an import from the West, at a time when India was under the political control of the British, it is not surprising that it interacted with European conventions. At the time, Victorian **theatrical melodrama** was one of the most popular and influential forms of entertainment. The earliest Indian films blended melodramatic themes – family conflict, mistaken identity, heart-rending experiences, and a denouement centring on a triumphant disclosure of virtue – with indigenous traditions of narrative and performance. Moral questions, and the role of the family, still tend to be more significant than the secular public domain, and the notions of individual choice and self-determination around which so many Western narratives revolve.

Issues of morality and duty permeate what is often referred to as the first Indian feature film, *Raja Harishcandra*, directed by DG Phalke (1913), in which female roles were played by men, as was the custom of the time. Its story, drawn from an episode in the ancient *Mahabharata* epic, details the suffering undergone by the king of the title and his family in order to fulfil a vow of penance. It inaugurated a genre known as the **mythological**, which was to be a staple of popular cinema well into the 1950s.

Despite the occasional gesture, the British never really encouraged the Indian film industry. What little remains of Indian silent cinema up to 1931 barely fills six video-cassettes in the National Film Archives of India, but it is remarkable for the way traditional "theatrical" framing (static characters, faced front on by the camera) is animated by a considerable investment in location shooting, both in natural surroundings and in the city. This is evident not only in *Raja Harishcandra*, but also in historical-cum-stunt films such as *Diler Jigar/Gallant Hearts* (SS Agarwal; 1931) and *Gulaminu Patan/The Fall of Slavery* (SS Agarwal; 1931), and in the international co-productions directed by Himansu Rai and the German Franz Osten. Among these, *Light of Asia* (1925), about the Buddha, and *Shiraz* (1928), about the origins of the Taj Mahal, referred to as **"Romances from India"** by their producers, render "India" as a startling, exotic assemblage: scenes of ancient and medieval court life, attended by the ritual of courtly gesture, and by spectacular processions of elephants and camels, are juxtaposed with a glittering naturalism, impressionist in its capturing of sunlight on leaves as the wind courses through the trees. The orientalist, touristic conception of the Osten/Rai films is underlined in the way *Light of Asia* begins, with a series of views of Hindu, Muslim and Buddhist culture, as they are presented to a group of White tourists. An "oriental" disposition, of worldly renunciation, and unrequited romantic desire is outlined as the ultimate destiny of Gautama (the Buddha) and Shiraz (the artisan who, obsessed with the Empress Nur Jahan, designs the Taj Mahal in her memory). Another aspect of the portrait of "essential" Indian traits is that of the brave Rajput, the warrior caste of north India, who serves to present the past in a heroic, romantic mould.

THE TALKIES

In 1931, India's first talkie, *Alam Ara*, was released, dubbed into Hindi and Urdu. As the talkies emerged over the next decade, so too did a new series of issues. The most prominent of these, of course, was language, and **language markets**; alongside, there are considerations of regional identity, of the different places that separately and together make up India. Many films of the time were produced both in the regional language (Bengali, Marathi), and in Hindi, so that they could be oriented to the larger Hindi-speaking market. However, through the development of a genre known as the **devotional film**, very specific religious and cultural traditions could be addressed by using the **music** of the region. Films like the Bengali *Chandidas* (Debaki Bose; 1932), and the Marathi *Sant Tukaram* (Fatehlal and Damle; 1937) both about popular "saints" from regional devotional traditions that coun-

tered Brahmanical orthodoxy, were not released in Hindi versions.

Ironically, the genre that might have added to this sense of specific place and particular custom, the **"social film"**, conceived by the industry to represent contemporary social life, swiftly acquired a pan-Indian homogeneity. While addressing social differences of caste, class and the relations between the sexes, the social films of the 1930s adopted a modern reformist outlook in an essentially converging view of society, and their studio settings further distanced them from any sense of particular place. Nonetheless, many showed great innovation. The Marathi director, V Shantaram, for example, was alert to world trends in film-making, deploying expressionist effects intelligently in such works as *Amrit Manthan* (Prabhat Talkies; 1934). In what was probably the most important film of the period, *Devdas* (1935), the director Pramathesh Barua created a startlingly edited climax to a tale of love frustrated by social distinction and masculine ineffectuality. Released in Bengali, Hindi and Tamil, *Devdas* created an oddly ambivalent hero for this period (and again, through a Hindi re-make directed by Bimal Roy in 1955), predicated on indecision, frustration and a focus on failure and longing rather than on achievement.

By the 1940s the social film further delimited its focus by excluding particularly fraught issues, especially of caste division. A representative example, prefiguring the kind of entertainment extravaganza that has become the hallmark of the **Bombay film**, was *Kismet/Fate* (Gyan Mukerji; Bombay Talkies; 1943), which broke all box-office records and ran for more than two years. Family and class become the key issues in the representation of society, and the story's location is an indeterminate urban one. As a child the hero loses a respectable family identity, is precipitated into a life of glamorous crime, and eventually comes to recover his rightful position. Made at the height of **World War II**, in a climate that saw fortunes lost and made thanks to inflation, the film appears to speak to the excitement and anxiety of a new social moment. Social mobility, rather than the rigidity associated with caste, was to become a recurrent theme. However, the melodrama of *Kismet* is woven in with a pageant of nationalist mobilization; social divisions are reconciled by bringing everyone into the family through marriage. Although this became the model for popular cinema, especially after the decline of regional industries in Maharashtra and Bengal by the end of the 1940s, different strains are observable in the Tamil films of the same period.

In the 1930s, the **Tamil cinema** gained national recognition with the costume extravaganza, *Chandralekha*, directed by SS Vasan for Gemini studios, and called by its director a "pageant for our peasants" (a large section of the audience would have been illiterate). Its story, of the conflict for the inheritance of an empire, is laden with overblown set-pieces and crowds of extras. Even more significant than this investment in the spectacular was its "Tamil-ness"; the recognition of a national existence different to that portrayed in the Bombay output. In films inspired by the anti-high caste Tamil nationalist movement, the Dravida Kazhagam, the Tamil region becomes the Tamil nation, distinct from, and frequently oppressed by, the Hindi-speaking north. Such anti-Brahmanical, anti-north ideology is much in evidence in films like *Parasakthi/ The Goddess* (1949), although by then some of the radicalism of these positions was already being watered down. From that time onwards, film in Tamil Nadu, and neighbouring Andhra Pradesh, became a key vehicle of politics, facilitating the rise to power of the movie stars MG Ramachandran and NT Rama Rao to the chief ministerships of the two states.

THE 1950s

By the start of the 1950s, Bombay was ascendant in the Hindi film market, while Pune and Bengal were in decline, transformed into struggling regional language centres, and Madras was on the way to becoming a large-scale producer. Calcutta, now disestablished as focus of a thriving commercial film industry, became the vanguard of the art cinema, with the emergence of the **film society movement** at the end of the 1940s and Satyajit Ray's *Pather Panchali/ Song of the Road*, produced with West Bengal state government support in 1955.

Post-Independence, despite a relatively sympathetic government enquiry in 1951, the industry became the object of considerable moral scrutiny and criticism, and was subject to severe taxation. A covert consensus emerged between proponents of art cinema and the state, all focussing on the imperative to create a "better" cinema. The Film and Television Institute of India was established at Pune in 1959 to develop technical skills for an industry seen to be lacking in this field. However, active support for **parallel cinema**, as it came to be called, only really took off at the end of the 1960s, under the aegis of the government's *Film Finance Corporation*, set up in 1961 to support new film-makers.

Ironically, this pressure and vocal criticism occurred at a time when arguably some of the most interesting work in popular cinema was being produced. Radical cultural organizations, loosely associated with the Indian Communist Party, had organized themselves as the *All India Progressive Writers Association* and the *Indian People's Theatre Association* (*IPTA*). This latter had produced *Dharti ke Lal/ Sons of the Soil* (KA Abbas; 1943), and its impact on the industry can be seen in the work of radical writers such as Abbas, lyricists such as Sahir Ludhianvi, and directors such as Bimal Roy and Zia Sarhady. In addition, directors such as Raj Kapoor, Guru Dutt and Mehboob Khan, while not directly involved in *IPTA*, created films that reflected a passionate concern for questions of social justice.

Largely studio-based, the films of this era nevertheless incorporated vivid stylistic experimentation, influenced by **international currents** in film-making. For example, the expressionist *chiaroscuro* of Hollywood *film noir* was frequently employed to create layers of darkness and light, portraying the shadowy city as a place of economic insecurity and social indignity. Such effects are evident in *Awara/ The Vagabond* (Raj Kapoor; 1951; script by KA Abbas), *Awaaz/ The Call* (Zia Sarhady; 1956) and *Pyaasa/ Craving* (Guru Dutt; 1957). The First International Film Festival, held in Bombay in 1951, showed Italian works for the first time in India; the influence of Neorealism can be seen in films such as *Do Bigha Zamin/ Two Measures of Land* (Bimal Roy; 1953), a portrait of father and son eking out a living in Calcutta that strongly echoes the narrative of Vittorio de Sica's *Bicycle Thief* (1948). Mehboob Khan's *Andaz/ Style* (1949), an upper-class love triangle founded on a tragic misunderstanding, draws on codes of psychological representation – hallucinations and dreams – that feature strongly in 1940s Hollywood melodrama, especially in what has come to be known as the "women's film".

Mehboob's tendency to make a visual spectacle of his material, and his involvement with populist themes and issues make him a good example of popular cinema of the time. His movies are emblazoned with kitsch ornamentation, and the overall effect of the excesses, the signs of privilege (butlers, valets, cooks, gardeners) and modes of dress (riding clothes, dressing-gowns, sports jackets, ballroom gowns) is that of contamination by the "West".

ART CINEMA

India's emergent **art cinema**, led by the Bengali directors Ray, Mrinal Sen and Ritwik Ghatak reacted against such spectacle. **Satyajit Ray**'s world-famous debut, *Pather Panchali* (1955), is based on many of the themes that engaged contemporaneous popular filmmakers of the time, such as loss of social status, economic injustice, uprootment, but sets them within a naturalistic, frame which put a special value on the Bengali countryside, locating it as a place of nostalgia, to which the urban protagonist, Apu, looked with longing.

In Ray's later work on urban middle-class existence, *Mahanagar/Big City* (1963), *Charulata* (1964), *Seemabadha/Company Limited* (1971), *Pratidwandi/The Protagonist* (1970), and *Jana Aranya/The Middleman* (1975), his rational, humanist vision is at the same time at home in the city, and repulsed by it; overarching estrangement is relayed through images of futile job interviews, cynical corporate schemes, murky deals in respectable cafes.

When Ray tries to step out of the cityscape, however, into a broader sphere, he falls flat. The tribal woman character of *Aranyer din Ratri*, played by the glamorous Bombay film star, Simi Garewal, is grotesque; while the director's well-meaning attempt to capture the horror of the great Bengal famine of 1943 through the perspective of a *brahmin* priest, in *Ashani Sanket/Distant Thunder* (1973), is ineffectual. Films from the latter part of his career, such as *Ghare Baire/Home and the World* (1984), *Ganashatru/Enemy of the People* (1989), *Shakha Proshakha/Branches of a Tree* (1990), and *Agantuk/The Visitor* (1992), show these failings magnified. Wedded to the traditions of the nineteenth-century intelligentsia, he finds society wanting, vilifies it for its ignorance and corruption, and oversees the malignant terrain below with a lofty disdain. In these last works,

women characters, once his forte, dwindle to assume a conventional moral role, critical of men who wander from the straight and narrow; a great pity, for his *Charulata*, starring the wonderful Madhabi Mukherjee, must stand as one of the great woman's roles of the Indian cinema, subtly evoking the intellectual and erotic frustration that circumscribe the life of the female protagonist in late-nineteenth-century Calcutta. Indeed, Ray's women, such as the mother, Sarbojaya of *Pather Panchali*, the tomboy Aparna Sen of *Samapti/The End* (1961), Mukherjee in *Charulata* and *Mahanagar*, and Kaberi Bose in *Aranyer din Ratri*, are splendidly drawn portraits in the realist tradition.

In contrast to Ray, his contemporaries **Mrinal Sen** and Ritwik Ghatak set out to expose the dark underside of India's lower middle-class and unemployed. Sen, after a phase of uneven, didactic political cinema at the height of the Maoist-inspired Naxalite movement of the early 1970s – marked by the trilogy *Interview* (1971), *Calcutta 71* (1972) and *Padatik/The Guerrilla Fighter* (1973) – made two films, *Akaler Sandhane/In Search of Famine* (1980) and *Khandar/Ruins* (1983), about film-making itself, exploring its inherent distance and disengagement, and the problems entailed in trying to record "reality". In his later works he took on the role of the social raconteur, portraying the claustrophobia, constrained lives and hypocrisy of the lower middle class in a series of interesting films: *Ek din pratidin/And Quiet Rolls the Day* (1979), *Chaalchitra/Kaleidoscope* (1981) and *Kharij/The Court Is Closed* (1982). Bringing the themes together, the intense *Mahaprithivi/This Great Earth* (1992) tells the story of a mother (the remarkable Geeta Sen) who commits suicide after the fall of the Berlin wall; the death of the communist dream seems to have made a mockery of the death of her idealist son in a police shoot-out twenty years earlier.

Perhaps the most outstanding figure of this generation, fulfilling the potential of the radical cultural initiatives of the *IPTA*, was the great **Ritwik Ghatak**. Disruption, the problems of locating oneself in a new environment, and the indignities and oppression of common people are the recurrent themes of this poet of Partition, who lamented the division of Bengal in 1947. Disharmony and discontinuity could be said to be the hallmark of *Nagarik/Citizen* (1952) and *Meghe Dhaka Tara/Cloud-capped*

Star (1960), where studio sets of street corners mingle uneasily with live-action shots of Calcutta. There is something deliberately jarring about the rhythms of editing, the use of sound, and the compositions, as if the director refuses to allow us to settle into a comfortable, familiar frame of viewing. In *Aajantrik/Man and Machine* (1958) and *Subarnarekha* (1952; released 1965) he juxtaposes the displaced and transient urban figure with tribal peoples; placing the human figure at the edge of the frame, dwarfed by majestic nature.

THE 1970s AND THE 1980s

During the 1960s, popular cinema had shifted its social concerns towards more romantic genres, showcasing such new stars as Shammi Kapoor, Raj's younger brother – a kind of Indian Elvis – and later, Rajesh Khanna, a soft, romantic hero. The period is also notable for a more assertive Indian **nationalism**. Following the Indo-Pakistan wars of 1962 and 1965, the Indian officer, and especially the fighter pilot, came to be a glamorous rallying point for the national imagination in films such as *Sangam/Meeting of Hearts* (Raj Kapoor; 1964) and *Aradhana/Adoration* (Shakti Samanta; 1969).

However, the political and economic upheaval of the following decade saw a return to social questions across the board, in both the art and popular cinemas. The accepted turning point in the popular film was the angry, violent *Zanjeer/The Chain* (Prakash Mehra; 1973), which fed into the anxieties and frustrations generated by the quickening but lopsided pace of **industrialization** and **urbanization**. Establishing Amitabh Bachchan as the biggest star of the next decade and beyond, its policeman hero is ousted from service through a conspiracy, and takes the law into his own hands to render justice and to avenge his long-dead parents. The considerable **political turmoil** of the next few years, including the railway strike of 1974 and the Nav Nirman movement led by JP Narayan in Bihar and Gujarat, ultimately led to the declaration of Indira Gandhi's Emergency in 1975. It was as if the state and the people had split apart. As the cities grew, so did the audiences. The popular cinema generated an ambiguous figure to express this alienation; whether he represented the state or the people is another question.

At the level of images, there was a greater investment in the stresses of everyday life and, unlike the 1950s, in location shooting. In *Zanjeer*, the casual killing of a witness on Bombay's commuter trains conjures up the perils of life in the metropolis; this is echoed in images of the dockyard, taxi-rank, railtrack and construction site in *Deewar/The Wall* (Yash Chopra; 1975), also starring Amitabh Bachchan. Here his construction worker takes to a life of crime to maintain his family, and is ultimately killed by his police-officer brother in a rite of moral cleansing that glamorizes the persona of the rebellious outsider. From this period until the present day, popular movies are full of images of a fraught urban scenario, drawing out fantastic and often nightmarish scenes of melodramatic conflict.

The recurrent narrative of these films, of protagonists uprooted from small town and rural families to the perils of the city, is shared by the street children researched by professional sociologists in Mira Nair's *Salaam Bombay!* (1988). It can, however, be argued that Nair's realism, for all its international acclaim, is not an adequate way to represent the experience of the modern city. Here the Bombay film's very excesses, its grand gestures, and the priority it gives to emotion and excitement may more truly reflect the dominant rhythms of urban life in India. At the level of plot and character, however, the Bombay film simultaneously simplifies and collapses our sense of India, reducing the enormous variety of identity – social, regional, ethnic and religious – that makes up Indian society. Where these identities appear, they do so as caricatures and objects of fun. To counter this, the **art cinema of the 1980s** diversified from its Bengali moorings of the earlier period under the aegis of the *Film Finance Corporation*. Works by Shyam Benegal, Gautam Ghose, Saeed Mirza, BV Karanth, Girish Kasaravalli, Mrinal Sen, MS Sathyu, Ray, and Kundan Shah, among others, actively addressed questions of social injustice: problems of landlord exploitation, bonded labour, untouchability, urban power, corruption and criminal extortion, the oppression of women, and political manipulation. Ghatak in particular had addressed many of these issues earlier, but never had there been such an outpouring of the social conscience, nor such a flowing of new images – of regional landscapes, cultures, and social structures. Many of the films may seem didactic and uncomplex, undercutting the attention to form that had marked the earlier period – but not all.

Benegal's first two films indicate an unusual concern with the psychology of domination and subordination; *Ankur/The Seedling* (1974) is particularly striking not only for this and for the open, fluid way it captures the countryside. Among Kannada directors, working in south India, Kasaravalli in *Ghattashradha* (1981) effected an intimate vision of the oppression of widows through the view of a child. And special mention must be made of Kundan Shah's *Jaane Bhi Do Yaaron/Let Sleeping Dogs Lie* (1984), a wonderful exercise in farce and slapstick that is also a brilliant portrait of Bombay.

THE SOUTH

The most notable of the directors who speak specifically about their own cultures, and about the possibilities of change, are – as well as Kumar Shahani and Mani Kaul, who work in Hindi – Adoor Gopalakrishnan and Aravindan from **Kerala**. A key to their productivity was the overall development of film culture in Kerala, India's most literate state. In his films **Gopalakrishnan** transformed the lush countryside, busy towns and animated culture of Kerala into a strange, dissociated place, fraught with communicative gaps, menacing, inexplicable characters, and an overall sense of the impenetrable. Subjects range from the mounting tragedies that beset a young couple in the city (*Swayamvaram/One's Own Choice*; 1972), and the effete authoritarianism of a declining feudal landlord (*Elippathayam/The Rat-Trap*; 1984), to the mysterious spiritual decline of a popular communist activist (*Mukha Mukham/Face to Face*; 1987). Gopalakrishnan was a markedly controlled director, and his modernist framing of the world could be said either to constrain our vision of it, or to illuminate it from an unconventional angle. *Kodiyettam/Ascent* (1981), his second film about the life of a ne'er-do-well, shot in black-and-white with an eye for the space and texture of the Keralan countryside, breathes more easily in comparison.

The late **Aravindan**, sometime cartoonist and employee of the Kerala Rubber Board, had something of the mystic in him, but went through a range of styles, including a *cinéma-vérité* approach, as in *Thampu/The Circus Tent* (1978), in which circus performers speak direct to the camera. His episode from the *Ramayana*, *Kanchana Sita/Golden Sita*, places the action against the grain of the high Hindu tradition by situating it among tribes in the verdant landscape of the Kerala forests. At his best, his narrative style refuses a didactic approach, generating a whimsical sense of how destinies are shaped.

CONTEMPORARY CURRENTS

In the 1990s, **video**, national and satellite/cable television have resulted in the development of a prolonged crisis in India's movie industry, where commercial and art films are equally at risk of failing at the box office. The problems of the latter are mainly due to a persistent failure to find distribution outlets; now, more and more film-makers of both streams look to **television**; the state film finance unit (now named the *National Film Development Corporation*) has a major stake in the expansion of the national network.

There have been two responses to this crisis. The first, at the economic level, has been to try and curb film piracy, and to systematize the relationship of film to video. The second is an investment in **new technology**, and in new forms of story-telling. The Telugu and Tamil industries, and directors such as Ram Gopal Varma and Mani Ratnam, are at the forefront of such moves, showing a lively interest in new techniques in American cinema. Varma's *Shiva* (1990) and *Raat/Night* (1991) showcase the use of steadicam – in the latter, to the exclusion of any serious narrative. The technical virtuosity of Mani Ratnam's works, as well as their elegant story-telling and restrained performances have attracted a following among film buffs across the country, who identify with his style and, implicitly, with the image of a dynamic, modern identity. In 1993, Ratnam made an important breakthrough with *Roja*, a love story about a young Tamil peasant woman and her husband, a cryptographer who decodes messages for military intelligence. The couple are transported to Kashmir, presently subject to sustained separatist extremism. Embroiling the Tamil couple in a national issue that might have seemed remote to an earlier generation, the film identified a new pan-Indian field of interest. Dubbed into Hindi, it was a national success, giving rise to the dubbing of a number of southern films. Whether this is a positive development, or will collapse India's many voices into a modern anonymity, remains to be seen.

Ravi S Vasudevan

THE MUSIC OF INDIA

The origin of north Indian (Hindustani) classical music is shrouded in obscurity. There is a tendency in India to attribute the invention of any ancient art form to one of the many Hindu deities, and the resulting synthesis of myth and legend is often taken as literal truth. But in reality north Indian classical music as it exists today is the result of a long process of integrating many diverse cultural influences. Not only is there a rich and varied tradition of regional folk musics, but all through its history India has absorbed the culture and traditions of foreign invaders, the most influential being the Muslim Moghuls.

The introduction of Turko-Persian musical elements is what primarily distinguishes north Indian classical music from its predecessor, Carnatic, now restricted to southern India. The latter is a complex, rich and fascinating musical tradition in its own right, and even an untrained ear can usually distinguish between the two.

TEACHERS AND PUPILS

In the north, both Hindu and Muslim communities have provided outstanding artists. While music recognizes no religious differences – indeed it is something of a religion in its own right – distinguished musicians of Hindu origin customarily take the title of *pandit* (and become known as gurus), while their Muslim counterparts add the prefix *ustad* (meaning "master") to their names. An *ustad* may teach anything – not only his own particular art or instrument. It is not unusual for *sitar* maestros to teach *sarod* or vocal techniques to their pupils.

The **teaching** of north Indian classical music is a subject in itself. One thing that strikes a Westerner is the spiritual link between teacher and pupil. Quite often the two may be blood rela-

Features on **music**, **dance** and **performing arts**, scattered throughout this book, include:

tions anyway, but where they are not, a spiritual relationship is officially inaugurated in a ceremony in which the teacher ties a string to the wrist of the pupil to symbolize the bond between them.

Apart from actual musical form and content, north Indian music has various extra-musical traditions and rituals, usually taught through musical families and ***gharanas*** ("schools"). Traditionally, Indian music is taught on a one-to-one basis, often from father to son. Many academies and colleges of music now follow the modern style, but traditionalists still adhere to the *gharana* system, and great importance is still attached to membership of a musical family or an impressive lineage. A *gharana*, which may be for singing, for any or all kinds of instruments, or for dance, is more a school of thought than an institution. It suggests a particular belief, or a preference for a certain performance style. *Gharanas* differ not only in broad terms, but also in minute details: how to execute a particular combination of notes, or simply the correct way to hold an instrument. They are usually founded by musicians of outstanding ability, and new styles and forms are added by exceptionally talented musicians who may have trained with one particular *gharana* and then evolved a style of their own.

SCALES OF PURITY AND IMAGINATION

Singing is considered the highest form of classical music, after which instruments are graded according to their similarity to the human voice. The two main vocal traditions are *dhrupad*, the purest of all, devoid of all embellishment and entirely austere in its delivery, and *khayal*, which has a more romantic content and elaborate ornamentation and is the more popular today. Less abstract vocal forms include the so-called light classical *dadra*, *thumri* and *ghazal* as well as *qawwali*, religious music of the Sufi tradition. The degree of musical purity is assigned according to a scale which has music at one extreme and words at the other. As words become more audible and thus the meaning of lyrics more important, so the form is considered to be musically less pure.

Indian musicologists talk about two **kinds of sound** – one spiritual and inaudible to the human ear, the other physical and audible. The inaudible sound is said to be produced from the ether, and its function is to liberate the soul. But to feel it requires great devotion and concentration which the average person can never really attain. Audible sound, on the other hand, is actually "struck" and is said to have an immediate and pleasurable impact.

Indian music always has a **constant drone** in the background, serving as a reference point for performer and listener alike. In north Indian music this drone is usually played on the four-stringed *tambura*. The privilege of accompanying a teacher's performance on the *tambura* is often accorded to advanced students.

Indian music does not so much describe a mood (as some European music does) as help to create that mood, and then explore it to its depths. Where Western classical music starts at a particular point and then progresses from it, Indian classical music revolves around the point, probing it from every angle, yet maintaining a dignified restraint. It is this restraint that distinguishes Indian classical music from the carefree abandon of Indian pop and film music.

RAAGS AND RHYTHMS

The mainstay of all north Indian classical music is the **raag** (or *raga*), an immensely intricate system of scales and associated melodic patterns. Each of the 200 main *raags* is defined by its unique combination of scale-pattern, dominant notes, specific rules to be obeyed in ascending or descending and associated melodic phrases. While Indian classical music is renowned for improvisation, this only takes place within the strictly defined boundaries of a particular *raag*. If the improviser wanders away from the main musical form of the *raag* his or her performance ceases to be regarded as "classical" music. The mark of a good performer is the ability to improvise extensively without abandoning the set of defining rules.

Some *raags* are linked with particular seasons; there is a *raag* for rain, and one for spring; *raags* can be "masculine" or "feminine"; and musicologists may categorize them according to whether they are best suited to a male or female voice. Each *raag* is allotted a time of day, a time identified with the spiritual and emotional qualities of the *raag*. *Raags* are specifically allocated to early morning (either before or after sunrise), mid-morning, early afternoon, late afternoon, early evening (either before or after sunset), late evening, late night and post-midnight. This system causes a few problems in northern latitudes, for there is some argument as to whether a *raag* should be heard by clock-time or sun-time. Purists adhere to the archaic tradition of a "*raag* timeable" even if they're only listening to records.

The performance of a *raag*, whether sung or played on a *sitar*, *sarod* or *sarangi*, follows a set pattern. First comes the *alaap*, a slow, meditative "mood-setter" in free rhythm which explores the chosen *raag*, carefully introducing the notes of the scale one by one. The *alaap* can span several hours in the hands of a distinguished performer, but may only last a matter of minutes; older aficionados allege that most present-day listeners cannot sustain the attention required to appreciate a lengthy and closely argued *alaap*. As a result, performers have felt under pressure to abbreviate this section of the *raag*, to reach the faster middle and end sections as soon as possible. This became customary in the recording studio, although the advent of the CD, which does not force the music to fit into 25 minutes as the LP did, has initiated a move back to longer performances.

In the next two sections, the *jorh* and the *jhala*, the soloist introduces a rhythmic element, developing the *raag* and exploring its more complex variations. Only in the final section, the *gath*, does the percussion instrument – usually the *tabla* or *pakhavaj* – enter. The soloist introduces a short, fixed composition to which he or she returns between flights of improvisation. In this section rhythm is an important structural element. Both percussionist and soloist improvise, at times echoing each other and sometimes pursuing individual variations of rhythmic counterpoint, regularly punctuated by unison statements of a short melody known as "the composition". The *gath* itself is sub-divided into three sections: a slow tempo passage known as *vilambit*, increasing to a medium tempo, called *madhya*, and finally the fast tempo, *drut*.

Just as the *raag* organizes melody, so the rhythm is organized by highly sophisticated structures expressed through cycles known as *taals*, which can be clapped out by hand. A *taal* is made up of a number of beats (*matras*), each beat defined by a combination of rhythm pattern and timbre. It is the unique set of patterns (*bols*)

MUSICAL INSTRUMENTS

STRING INSTRUMENTS

The best-known instrument is the **sitar**, invented by Amir Khusrau in the thirteenth century and played with a plectrum. It has six or seven main strings, of which four are played and the other two or three are used to supply a drone or a rhythmic ostinato. In addition there can be between eleven and nineteen sympathetic strings. The two sets of strings are fitted on different bridges. Twenty brass frets fastened to the long hollow neck can be easily moved to conform to the scale of a particular *raag*, and their curvature allows the player to alter the pitch by pulling the string sideways across the fret to provide the gliding portamento so characteristic of Indian music.

The **surbahar** ("spring melody"), effectively a bass *sitar*, is played in the same way. Developed by Sahibdad Khan, the great-grandfather of Vilayat and Imrat Khan, it produces a deep, dignified sound. The neck is wider and longer than that of the *sitar* but its frets are fixed. Thanks to its size, and longer strings, the sound can be sustained for longer, and the range of the portamento is wider.

The **sarod** is a descendant of the Afghani *rebab*. Smaller than a *sitar*, it has two resonating chambers, the larger made of teak covered with goatskin, and the smaller, at the other end of the metal fingerboard, made of metal. Ten of its 25 metal strings are plucked with a fragment of coconut shell. Four of these carry the melody; the others accentuate the rhythm. The rest are sympathetic strings, underneath the main strings. The *sarod* was hugely improved by Ustad Allaudin Khan, whose pupils Ustad Ali Akbar Khan and Ustad Amjad Ali Khan are now its best-known exponents.

The **sarangi** is a fretless bowed instrument with a very broad fingerboard and a double belly. The entire body of the instrument – belly and fingerboard – is carved out of a single block of wood and the hollow covered with parchment. There are three or four main strings of gut and anything up to forty metal sympathetic strings. Some claim it is the most difficult musical instrument to play in the world. Certainly the technique is highly unusual. While the right hand wields the bow in the normal way, the strings are stopped not by the fingertips of the left hand, but by the nails. The *sarangi* is capable of a wide range of timbres and its sound is likened to that of the human voice, so it is usually used to accompany vocal recitals. Originally this was its only function, but in recent years it has become a solo instrument in its own right, thanks

available within a particular *taal* that define it. There are literally hundreds of *taals*, but most percussionists use the same few favourites over and over again, the most common being the sixteen-beat *teentaal*.

The most unfamiliar aspect of *taal* to the Western ear is that the end of one cycle comes not on its last beat, but on the first beat of the following one, so that there is a continual overlap. This first beat is known as *sum*, a point of culmination which completes a rhythmic structure, and performers often indicate it by nodding to each other when they arrive at it. Audiences do the same to express satisfaction and appreciation.

Among smaller, more discerning audiences, verbal applause such as "Wah!" (Bravo!), or even "Subhan-Allah" (Praise be to God!), is considered the standard form of appreciation. Only in Western-style concert halls, where such exclamations would be inaudible, has hand-clapping come to replace these traditional gestures of approval.

LIGHT CLASSICAL MUSIC

Many concerts of classical music end with the performance of a piece in one of the styles collectively referred to as "light classical". Although they obey the rules of classical music with respect to *raag* and *taal*, they do so less rigorously than is required for a performance of *dhrupad*, *khayal* or other pure classical styles. The *alaap* is short or non-existent, and the composition is frequently derived from a folk-melody. Indeed, it could be said that light classical music is essentially a synthesis of folk and classical practice. The two most important and widespread types are *thumri* and *ghazal*.

The origin of **thumri** is popularly ascribed to Nawab Wajid Ali Shah, who governed Lucknow (Avadh) from 1847 to 1856. Although little interested in matters of state, he was a great patron of the arts and during his reign music, dance, poetry, drama and architecture flourished. *Thumri* employs a specific set of *raags* and is particularly associated with *kathak* dance; the mainly to the efforts of Ustad Sultan Khan and Pandit Ram Narayan.

The *santoor*, a hammered zither of trapezoid shape and Persian origin, has only recently been accepted in classical music. It has over a hundred strings, pegged and stretched in pairs, parallel to each other. Each pair passes over two bridges, one on each side of the instrument. The strings are struck by two curving wooden sticks. Its most notable exponent is Pandit Shiv Kumar Sharma.

The *surmandal* resembles a zither, and is used by vocalists to accompany themselves in performance. Even though its primary function is to provide the drone, singers sometimes also play the basic melody line on this instrument.

WIND INSTRUMENTS

The *shehnai*, the traditional instrument for wedding music, is a double-reed, oboe-type instrument with up to nine finger holes, some of which are stopped with wax for fine tuning to the scale of a particular *raag*. It demands a mastery of circular breathing and enormous breath control. A drone accompaniment is provided by a second *shehnai*.

The word *bansuri* refers to a wide variety of bamboo (*banse*) flutes, most end-blown, but some, such as Krishna's famous *murli*, are side-blown. Despite offering a range of less than two octaves, it now appears as a solo concert instrument.

DRUMS

The *tabla* is a set of two small drums played with the palms and fingertips to produce an incredible variety of sounds and timbres, in a range of one octave. Its name is short for *tabla-bayan* – the *tabla* is on the right and the *bayan* ("left") on the left. Its invention is attributed to Amir Khusrau, creator of the *sitar*. Both drum heads are made of skin, with a paste of iron filings and flour in the centre, but while the body of the *tabla* is all wood, the *banya* is metal. The *tabla* is usually tuned to the tonic, dominant or sub-dominant notes of the *raag* by knocking the tuning-blocks, held by braces on the sides of the instrument, into place.

Pre-dating the *tabla*, the *pakhavaj* is nearly a metre long and was traditionally made of clay, although now wood is more popular. It has two parchment heads, each tuned to a different pitch, again by knocking the side blocks into place. A paste of boiled rice, iron filings and tamarind juice is applied to the smaller head and a wheat flour paste on the larger helps produce the lower notes.

The *pakhavaj* has a deep mellow sound and is used to accompany *dhrupad* singing and *kathak* dancing. A smaller version of the *pakhavaj*, the *mridangam*, is widely used in south Indian music.

---

graceful movements of the dancer are echoed in the lyricism of the musical style. Although classical instrumentalists in concert frequently perform a *thumri* to relax from the intensity of the pure classical style, most *thumri* is vocal, and sung in a language known as Braj Bhasha, a literary dialect of Hindi. The singer is always accompanied by the *tabla*, as well perhaps as the *tambura*, the *sarangi* or the *surmandal*, and sometimes the violin or harmonium.

The lyrics of *thumri* deal with romance. Love songs, written from a female perspective, they stress themes like dressing up for a tryst, the heartache of absence and betrayal, quarrels and reconciliation, and the joyful return from a meeting with a husband or lover. Such themes are often expressed metaphorically, with references in the lyrics to the (suggestive) flute-playing of the god Krishna, the symbol of young love. Despite the concentration on the woman's point of view, some of the greatest singers of *thumri* have been men, notably Ustad Bade Ghulam Ali Khan. As male singers are frequent-ly middle-aged and overweight, there is a certain initial incongruity about the spectacle of this depiction of the gentle and delicate emotions of a beautiful young woman. Yet a fine artist, fat and balding though he may be, can make a song like this one infinitely affecting: "My bracelets keep slipping off/My lover has cast a spell on me/He has struck me with his magic/What can a mere doctor do?" Her bracelets have slipped off because, while pining for her absent lover, she has starved herself to the point of emaciation.

Still more songlike than the *thumri* is the *ghazal*. In some ways the Urdu counterpart of *thumri*, the *ghazal* was introduced to India by Persian Muslims and is mainly a poetic rather than a musical form. Although some *ghazal* tunes are based on the *raag* system, others do not follow any specific mode. The *taals* are clearly derived from folk music; at times the *ghazal* shades into the area of sophisticated pop song. Indeed, at the more commercial end of the scale – the so-called film *ghazal* – sophistication gives way to mere charm. The *ghazal* has played an important part in the cultures of India, Pakistan and Afghanistan since the early eighteenth century, when it was one of the accomplishments required of a courtesan. Modern *ghazal* singers usually come from a more "respectable" background.

While *thumri* singers take on a female persona, emotions in the *ghazal* are almost always expressed from the male point of view. Some of the finest performers of *ghazals* are women – Begum Akhtar and Shobha Gurtu among them. Many favourite *ghazals* are drawn from the works of great Urdu poets.

A patriotic poem by Faiz Ahmed Faiz, *Mujhse Pehli Si Muhabbat Mere Mehboob Na Maang* (Do not ask me my love, to love you the way I used to love you), proved a milestone in the advance of art poetry into the realm of the film *ghazal*. Sung by the popular Pakistani singer Noor Jehan in her inimitable style, her interpretation is said to have so impressed the poet Faiz that he formally relinquished all claims to it in her favour.

TALES OF THE GOLDEN AGE

Ghazals can be heard every day on the radio or on films either in India or Pakistan or in Asian communities abroad. But pure classical music is, for those who don't get invited to a *mahfil*, most often heard in concert – a far cry from the golden age of Indian classical music, when its chief patrons were nawabs, maharajahs and *zamindar* landlords. At this time Indian classical music was essentially court music, and its forms and practices, perfected within this framework, were clearly aimed at a leisured elite able to appreciate the subtleties that the musicians were developing.

Many traditional tales tell of this period. For instance, the Prince of Mysore would take his court musicians to a neighbouring district, inhabited by deadly snakes. The performers would then play the *poongi*, a kind of wind instrument. As the sounds grew louder, the snakes would venture from their holes and slide towards the musicians. The snakes would encircle the players completely and sway in perfect rhythm, as if intoxicated by the sound. As soon as the music stopped, they would glide away quietly without biting anyone. Another story is that of Tan-Sen, the greatest singer that India ever produced and court musician to the emper-

or Akbar. Tan-Sen was said to have such extraordinary power over his music that one day, when he began singing a late-night *raag* at noon, the world was plunged into darkness.

If another story is to be believed, there was a singer even greater than Tan-Sen. One day, as Tan-Sen sang the fiery *Raag Deepak*, the whole palace went up in flames. A young water-carrying maiden who happened to be passing by saw the flames, and taking a deep breath began to sing the *Raag Megh* (associated with rain). She sang with such emotion and sincerity that the heavens poured forth torrents and the flames caused by the great Tan-Sen were extinguished. Even in modern times, skilful performers are often credited with averting famine by singing *Raag Megh*. But *Raag Deepak* is superstitiously avoided these days.

Nearly every Indian musician has such tales attached to his or her name. Another one relates to Ustad Imdaad Khan, court musician at Indore and exponent of the *surbahar*. One night, as he accompanied the Maharajah's entourage on a tiger hunt, there was concern about a mad elephant on the rampage. As night set in and everyone prepared to settle down and remain quiet for fear of the elephant, Imdaad upset the whole party by getting his *surbahar* out for his usual practice. When he had been playing a while, a most unusual sight was seen outside his tent – a huge elephant, swaying to the sound of the *surbahar* as though hypnotized. From then on, all through the hunt, Imdaad was ordered to play the *surbahar* each night in order to keep the elephant quiet.

SOUND OF THE SOUTH

Southern India's **Carnatic** classical music is essentially similar to Hindustani classical music in outlook and theoretical background but differs in many details, usually ascribed to the far greater Islamic influence in the north. To the Western ear, Carnatic music is emotionally direct and impassioned, without the sometimes sombre restraint that characterizes much of the north's music. For instance the ***alaapaana*** section, although it introduces and develops the notes of the *raag* in much the same way as the *alaap* of north Indian music, interrupts its stately progress with sparkling decorative flourishes. Often, too, the *alaapaana* is succeeded by a set of increasingly complex elaborations of a basic melody in a way that is more easily grasped than the abstract, sometimes severe improvisations of the Hindustani masters. Compositions, both of "themes" and the set variations upon them, play a much greater role in Carnatic musical practice than in Hindustani.

The *raags* of Carnatic music, like those of Hindustani music, are theoretically numbered in the thousands and musicians are expected to be familiar with them all. In practice, however, only a few hundred are ever played, and probably only fifty or sixty are in common use.

Song is at the root of south Indian music, and forms based on song are paramount, even when the performance is purely instrumental. The vast majority of the texts are religious, and the temple is frequently the venue for performance. The most important form is the *kriti*, a devotional song, hundreds of which were written by the most influential figure in the development of Carnatic music, the singer **Tyagaraja** (1767–1847). He was central to the music, not only for his compositions but also for the development of techniques of rhythmic and melodic variations. Southern India's biggest music festival, held annually near Thanjavur on the banks of the River Kaveri, is named after him.

Although the vocal tradition is central to this music, its singers are perhaps less well known in the West than instrumentalists. MS Subbulakshmi and Dr M Balamurali Krishna are among the famous names, but the most celebrated is probably Ramnad Krishnan, who has taught in America.

The instruments of Carnatic music include the **vina**, which resembles the *sitar* but has no sympathetic strings (Carnatic musicians appear not to like the somewhat hollow timbre that they give to the instrument), the *mridangam* double-headed drum, and the enormous *nadasvaram*, a type of oboe nearly four feet long which takes great experience and delicacy to play. The violin is widely used – listen to the playing of Dr L Subramaniam or his brother L Shankar, better known for his fusion experiments with guitarist John McLaughlin than for his classical recordings. The mandolin is growing in popularity and the saxophone has made a strikingly successful appearance in the hands of Kadri Gopalnath. Among *vina* players look out for S Balachander and KS Nayaranaswami.

Percussion is very important, perhaps more so than in Hindustani music, and percussion ensembles frequently tour abroad. In addition to

the *mrindangam* percussion instruments include the *ghatam*, a clay pot played with tremendous zest and sometimes tossed into the air in a burst of high spirits. "Vikku" Vinayakram is its best-known player.

NEW PATHS

In earlier times the job of musician was more or less hereditary: would-be musicians began their musical education at the age of four, and music (as a profession) was considered beneath the dignity of the well-to-do and the academic classes. However, in recent years traditional restrictions have been relaxed, and music is no longer the province of a few families. Many educated Indians are becoming involved in both performance and composition, and as public performance loses its stigma so too the requirement for musicians to begin their training at a very early age becomes less forceful. Women instrumentalists too are making their mark – a startling innovation in a male-dominated musical culture. Two women with particularly high reputations are violinist Sangeeta Rajan and *tabla* player Anuradha Pal, both of whom have recorded in India. Several *gharanas* have been set up abroad, notably the one in California run by *sarod* player **Ali Akbar Khan**, who is probably Indian music's most influential living figure, and there is a steady trickle of Westerners who are willing to subject themselves to the disciplines of study.

However, the importance of the old families is barely diminished. Among the younger generation of players are such names as *sarod* player Brij Narayan, son of Ram Narayan, Nikil Banerjee, who studied *sitar* with his father Jitendra Nath Banerjee, and Krishna Bhatt, who studied with Ravi Shankar and also comes from a family of musicians. Other important figures to listen out for are sitarist Rais Khan and vocalist Rashid Khan. These, like the other names mentioned, bear witness to the remaining vitality and richness of the classical music tradition in India and abroad.

FOLK MUSIC OF INDIA

There are very many kinds of **Indian folk**, but the main regional strands are the folk musics of Uttar Pradesh, Rajasthan, the Punjab (spread across both India and Pakistan), and Bengal (including Bangladesh). In the Northwest Frontier Province of Pakistan, folk music shows a definite affinity with that of Afghanistan. Kashmir produces its own distinctive folk sound, and the music of many of India's tribal peoples more closely resembles that of southeast Asia or even Borneo than anything else in the sub-continent. Apart from obvious linguistic differences, the folk songs of each region have their own distinct rhythmic structures and are performed on or accompanied by different musical instruments. Some classical instruments are used, but the following are mostly associated with less formal folk occasions.

In **Rajasthan**, music is always played for weddings and theatre performances, and often at local markets or gatherings. There is a whole caste of professional musicians who perform this function, and a wonderful assortment of earthy-sounding stringed instruments like the *kamayacha* and *ravanhata* that accompany their songs. The *ravanhata* is a simple, two-stringed fiddle that, skilfully played, can produce a tune of great beauty and depth. Hearing it played by a fine street musician behind the city walls of Jaisalmer, it seems the perfect aural background for this desert citadel.

The *satara* is the traditional instrument of the desert shepherds. A double flute, it has two pipes of different lengths, one to play the melody, the other to provide the drone, rather like bagpipes without the bag. The bag is the musician himself, who plays with circular breathing. Local cassettes of these instruments are available in small stores across Rajasthan.

As well as drums, India boasts a variety of tuned **percussion instruments**. The most popular in this category is the *jaltarang* – a water-xylophone – consisting of a series of porcelain bowls of different sizes, each containing a prescribed amount of water. The bowls are usually struck with a pair of small sticks, but sometimes these are abandoned as the player rubs the rims of the bowls with a wet finger. The small brass, dome-shaped cymbals called *manjira* or *taal* are the best known of the many kinds of bells and gongs.

FOLK AND FILM

There are songs for all kinds of work and play. Almost every activity is represented in song,

and there is an extensive repertoire of dance music. Inevitably, film music has drawn heavily from this folk tradition, but sadly has also become a relatively effortless substitute for most of it. In some instances, "pop" adaptations of traditional folk music have served to revitalize and add a fresh lease of life to the original form – *bhangra*, the folk music of Punjab, is a very good example of this. British "*bhangra*-rock" has created a fresh interest in the original *bhangra* of the Punjabi farmers.

Folk music is now beginning to awaken greater interest, particularly with non-Indian record companies, and largely as a result of the growing Western interest in different kinds of Indian music. Perhaps this overseas interest has come just in time, for although it is still practised in the old way in more traditional settings and for particular rituals – weddings, births, harvest time and so on – folk music on the whole, if it is to be defined as the "music of the people", has largely been eclipsed by the output of the Indian film industry.

Whereas in the past traditional wedding songs would have been sung by the neighbourhood women all through the festivities, it is now more usual to hear film songs blaring away at Indian weddings. Nonetheless, fears that traditional music is vanishing altogether seem unwarranted: in Pakistan the unique sound of the *sohni* bands – clarinet-led brass bands which play at weddings – fills the air with wild melody, and in Rajasthan members of the traditional musicians' castes still make their living by playing at ceremonies and for entertainment. The radio and cassette player are by no means all-conquering.

Jameela Siddiqi, David Muddyman and Kim Burton

This account has been condensed and slightly altered from articles that appear in the *Rough Guide to World Music* (1994), which includes even more extensive coverage of the music of the Indian subcontinent, together with recommended discographies.

GREEN ISSUES IN INDIA

As the **population** of India continues relentlessly to rise – one in every seven people on the planet lives in India – so too does the threat to its **resources**, despite the fact that the average Indian consumes much less than an inhabitant of a typical Western country.

A large proportion of Indians live in close contact with nature, meeting their needs directly from the land around them. They draw food from the land; fuel, fodder, building materials and fruit from trees; manure for the fields from animals and composted leaves; and the raw materials for crafts and rural industry from all sorts of different plants. Once land has been denuded or eroded, or a river polluted, people can find themselves unable to earn a living, and there may be little alternative employment. If India is successfully to feed over a billion people during the next century, protecting its natural assets and safeguarding their use by villagers is an essential and urgent task.

Dams and mining have destroyed vast expanses of land, while industrial pollution (of which the **Bhopal** tragedy, see p.354, was a potent example) threatens the quality of life in both rural and urban areas. Almost half the industrial output of India draws on raw materials such as cotton, paper, rubber, jute, tobacco, and sugar. As these industries expand, their demands on land increase and cash crops progressively replace food crops.

The most controversial environmental issues in India today are the uneven distribution of **water**, and the rapid pace of **deforestation**. Since the days of the Chipko movement in the early 1970s (see p.1257), mass protests against state policy have burgeoned. India's fledgeling green movement has achieved striking if limited successes, and attracted international attention.

DAM SCHEMES

The massive post-Independence **river valley projects** of the 1950s – such as the Bhakra-Nangal dam in Punjab, the Tungabhadra project in Andhra Pradesh, the Hirakud dam in Orissa, and the Rihand dam in Uttar Pradesh – affected tens of thousands of people, but encountered little resistance. However, during the 1980s, similar projects from Tehri in the north to Silent Valley in the south, and from Koel Karo in the east to the Narmada Valley in the west, became the subject of bitter criticism. Campaigners argue that government justifications for dam projects invariably over-estimate benefits and under-estimate costs, that siltation rates have usually been much higher than anticipated (and so the life of each reservoir has been shorter), that the construction of large dams seriously disrupts fish breeding and assists the spread of water-borne diseases, and that the high incidence of waterlogging and the wholesale submergence of forests and wildlife is simply unacceptable.

However, above all else, the **social implications** of dam building have evoked the most significant response. Over the last four decades, more than 20 million people have been displaced from their homes by development projects, and many of them put into unfamiliar surroundings without appropriate compensation or proper re-housing.

THE NARMADA DAM PROJECT

The 800-mile-long **River Narmada**, the only major Indian river to flow west, rises in the central state of Madhya Pradesh and follows a tortuous route through Maharashtra and Gujarat. Hindus, who believe that its waters spring from the body of Shiva, perform a ritual 1600-mile-long *pradaksina* (ceremonial circumnavigation) by walking all the way along one of its banks, and then back down the other.

The idea of harnessing the river to supply water to some of India's most drought-prone areas, and power to some of its poorest people, was first put forward by Jawaharlal Nehru. The ambitious scheme involves the construction along the entire Narmada Valley of thirty large and over one hundred smaller dams by the year 2025, as well as a huge irrigation project in Gujarat. In addition to providing water for human consumption and irrigation to several million acres of Madhya Pradesh, Maharashtra, Gujarat and Rajasthan, the scheme is intended to alleviate flooding and create up to one million jobs. At the heart of the controversy is the colossal 1500-metre-wide **Sardar Sardovar** dam. Work is nearing completion, and the gleaming white spectacle is viewable for miles around.

In theory, up to thirty million people will eventually benefit from the scheme. However, prospects for the rural population, largely indigenous Bhil tribespeople ("tribals") and low-caste Hindus, are far from rosy. As many as 200,000 people may be displaced, with over 100 villages disappearing beneath the waters.

"**Project Affected People**" (PAPs), as the official jargon has it, are to be resettled away from the valley. The *Gujarat Dam Association* has promised that each relocated family will be given a new home, electricity, water on tap, and initial financial support. However, as the dam wall inches upwards, the protest and unrest of tribal peoples has coalesced into a widespread movement. Many villagers have already been forced to leave the "submergence zone" around the village of Manibeli, and often sent to live in temporary tin huts in areas with little or no water, fuel or grazing.

Activists from all over India have participated in mass demonstrations, both in Delhi and in the villages, and been incarcerated for their pains, while hunger strikers have attempted to shame the Indian government into changing its policies.

Only part of the $3.5 billion funding for the dam has been raised. The World Bank, which at first endorsed the project, has pulled the plug on further funding, and decided to hold back $187 million it originally pledged. Ostensibly, this is because the Indian authorities could not guarantee to meet its deadlines, but it seems likely that civil unrest played a part. Cynics argue that by fulfilling the initial tranches of payment, the World Bank has financed the construction of the dam, while withholding the final tranche will mean that the costs of such items as resettlement payments and tree planting cannot be met. As a result of the withdrawal of the World Bank, other major sponsors may well remain jittery; Japan is thought unlikely to release $200 million earmarked for turbines and generating equipment, which was frozen in 1990.

Many local politicians have reconsidered their support for the dam as costs have escalated, and the prospect of its aims being achieved has receded thirty years into the future. The finances of the state of Gujarat have been drained by drought and civil disorder; it was only able to find forty percent of the funds budgeted for the dam in 1993.

In spring 1994, the then Indian prime minister Narashima Rao overruled an order from the Ministry of Environment, which had halted work on the dam on the grounds that the Gujarati government was not fulfilling its commitment to relocate villagers.

The *Narmada Bachao Andalon* movement (Save Narmada Movement, or *NBA*), has long been at the forefront of the campaign against the dam. As this book went to press, protesters were focussing on the actions of project engineers who have defied a court ruling by closing sluices on the dam, which were designed to allow construction to continue without a build-up of water upstream, several months ahead of schedule. Allegedly, this is for reasons of safety; the effect has been to flood villages from which people had not yet been resettled.

THE GREEN REVOLUTION

The much heralded **Green Revolution**, the radical transformation in agricultural practices which followed Independence, has had a profound effect on the environment and on rural lifestyles. Traditionally, Indian agriculture favoured labour-intensive, rotational farming methods; as many as five different crops were grown in a single field, a practice known as **intercropping** which had been refined over many generations. Such diversity ensures that if one crop type fails, not all food production is lost, and also increases nitrogen levels in the soil. Fertility was further retained and enhanced by the use of cow-dung and leaf compost.

After Independence, Western aid and government programmes encouraged India to intensify agricultural production. High-yield strains of crops were introduced, along with modern machinery and high-input techniques, such as the purchase of seeds and chemicals and the development of extensive irrigation schemes.

Although successful in the production of large quantities of wheat and rice, which enabled India to survive national drought in 1988, and even to donate food aid during the African Sahelian famines of the 1980s, the longer-term benefits of the Green Revolution are under scrutiny. For example, production of high-protein foodstuffs such as pulses and other cereals – staple food sources for many of India's poorest people – have actually declined.

High-yielding crop varieties can damage the environment, removing nutrients from the soil and producing fewer by-products such as fodder for cattle. The copious irrigation they require often leads to waterlogging and salinization of the soil; in marginal areas, intensive farming practices cause soil erosion. Artificial fertilizers tend to leave high levels of nitrate in the soil, which can pollute water supplies.

The gap between rich and poor farmers has widened in recent years. While better-off farmers have been able to afford new technology such as tractors, farm machinery, high-yielding seeds, and pesticides, this has not been possible for their smaller counterparts, many of whom have ended up in debt, obliged to sell their land to larger businesses. In addition, the high profits and bumper harvests for large-scale farmers have made them want to maximize their land-holdings, and consequently force out their tenants and sharecroppers.

This "shake-down" has had a tremendous impact – there has been a massive trend of **rural to urban migration** in states such as Uttar Pradesh, Haryana, Rajasthan and Madhya Pradesh, as former agricultural workers drift towards towns and cities to find work. Slum settlements adjacent to and within urban areas have mushroomed, placing an ever-greater strain on urban facilities and services.

DEFORESTATION

Prior to the escalation of the dam debate, the exploitation of **forest** resources, by the commercial timber industry, supported by state forestry policy, was the major concern of Indian environmentalists.

In the tribal areas of central India, hunter-gatherers, shifting cultivators, peasants, pastoral nomads and artisans alike depend on forests for fodder, water and fuel – effectively, for their very survival. Until 1864, and the establishment of the Indian Forest Department, there was little state intervention in the management of forested areas; opposition to commercial forestry has grown ever since.

During the 1960s, extensive plantations, often of one sole species of tree (monoculture) were created. Together with development projects such as dams and mines, they served to erode forest areas. Popular protests came to a head during the 1970s, in formerly well-forested states like Bihar, Orissa, Madhya Pradesh, Maharashtra and Andhra Pradesh, though villagers tended to minimize the element of out-right confrontation with authority, and simply continued with the illegal grazing of animals or gathering of fuel wood.

Coherent and widespread opposition was crystallized in 1973 by the emergence of the **Chipko** movement, when the peasants of Mandal, a village high in the Garhwal Himalayas, prevented logging operations in a nearby forest by threatening to "hug" the trees. Campaigners found a common national cause in the coordinated opposition to the government's Draft Forest Bill of 1982, which sought to strengthen the powers of the Forest Department. Dozens of grassroots environmental organizations lobbied hard against the proposed legislation, and the government was finally forced to withdraw it. Popular feeling has also led to notable changes in state forestry policy, such as the abandonment of programmes for the clear-felling of natural forests in order to replace them with plantations of industrially useful exotic species.

Although campaigners stress the importance of returning control of the forests to their inhabitants, it has to be pointed out that a major factor in forest loss is the use of timber to fuel domestic fires. By extension, sheer pressure of population means that the forests are being used up faster than they can hope to regenerate, despite programmes to introduce fast-growing species.

Today, true forest covers around thirteen percent of the total land area of India. Studies in Karnataka have shown a variety of reasons for the ongoing loss, thought to be mirrored countrywide. Among them are the extension of cultivation (30 percent), mining (19 percent), hydroelectric projects (18 percent), direct submersion (16 percent), and the resettlement of displaced persons (11 percent).

Many of India's **mines** are located in forested regions, and the extraction of minerals such as iron ore, bauxite, copper, zinc, gypsum and limestone is increasingly at the expense of the former forest cover. Even more directly, the Indian **paper** industry – India is one of the twenty largest producers of paper in the world – requires the cutting down of several million trees annually.

With forests dwindling by an estimated 15,000 square kilometres per year, competition for living space between the human population and forest **animals** is intensifying. Alarm bells are already sounding for some of the better-known forest creatures. Since the 1930s, the density of the human population per square kilometre has trebled, while the number of **tigers** has declined to eight percent at best of its previous total. The many forest national parks, may be well protected, but they have

THE INDIAN TIGER

Feared, adored, immortalized in myth and used to endorse everything from breakfast cereals to petrochemicals, few animals command such universal fascination as the **tiger**. Only in India, however – thanks to drastic conservation measures – can this rare and enigmatic big cat still be glimpsed in the wild, stalking through the teak forests and *terai* grass to which it is uniquely adapted. A solitary predator, at the apex of the food chain, it has no natural enemies save one.

As recently as the turn of the century, up to 40,000 tigers still roamed the subcontinent. However, **shirkar**, tiger hunting, had long been the "sport of kings"; an ancient dictum held it auspicious for a ruler to notch up a tally of 109 dead tigers, and nawabs, maharajas and Moghul emperors all indulged their prerogative to devastating effect. The trigger-happy British brought tiger hunting to its most gratuitous excesses. Photos of pith-helmeted, bare-kneed *burrasahibs* posing behind mountains of striped carcasses became a hackneyed image of the Raj. Even Prince Philip (now President of the Worldwide Fund for Nature) couldn't resist bagging one during a royal visit to India.

In the years following Independence, **demographic pressures** nudged the Indian tiger perilously close to extinction. As the human population increased in rural districts, more and more trees were cleared to open up land for farming – thereby depriving large carnivores of their main source of game and of the cover they needed to hunt. Forced to turn on farm cattle as an alternative, tigers were drawn into direct conflict with man; some animals, out of sheer desperation, even turned **man-eater** and attacked human settlements.

Poaching too has taken its toll. The black market has always paid high prices for live animals, and for pieces of them believed to hold magical or medicinal properties. Tiger meat is used to ward off snakes; its brain to cure acne; its spore for piles; its powdered bones to mix in traditional medicines; and kidney fat, applied liberally to the afflicted organ, as an antidote to male impotence.

By the time an all-India moratorium on tiger shooting was declared in 1972, numbers had plummeted to below two thousand. A radical response came the following year, with the inau-

guration of **Project Tiger**. At the personal behest of Indira Gandhi, nine areas of pristine forest were set aside for the last remaining tigers. Displaced farming communities were resettled and compensated, and armed rangers employed to discourage poachers. Today, there are nineteen Project Tiger sites, while a further 3000 tigers are thought to live in other areas of protected forest not incorporated into the scheme. However, despite its best intentions, Project Tiger has been almost helpless in the face of falling numbers. The population rise indicated by counts based on pug marks – thought to be like human finger prints, unique to each individual – that gave such encouragement in the early 1990s has been declared inaccurate.

The continued demand for tiger parts is keeping poachers in business, aided by an organized smuggling ring. Since 1988 the overall population should, through natural regeneration, have increased by well over a thousand; instead it has fallen. In August 1993, undercover wildlife investigators recovered a 400kg-haul of tiger bones, together with forty fresh carcasses, from a team of Tibetan smugglers in Delhi who had promised to supply 1000kg more on demand. Sadly, much of the illegal trade seems to be centred on the very reserves set up to protect the animals in the first place. Well-organized guerrilla groups operate out of remote national parks, including Corbett, Dudhwa and Kanha, where inadequate numbers of poorly armed and poorly paid wardens offer little more than token resistance. Increased use of poison among poachers is making it more and more difficult to track killings, while the death of dominant males or established matriarchs can severely damage regeneration prospects. Project Tiger officials are understandably reluctant to jeopardize lucrative tourist traffic by admitting that sightings are getting rarer, but the prognosis looks very gloomy indeed. Some experts even claim that at the present rate of destruction, India's most exotic animal could face extinction by 2000.

For now, your best chances of seeing a wild tiger in India are at Kanha and Bandhavgarh (MP, see p.406 & 408); Ranthambore (Rajasthan, see p.160); Corbett and Dudhwa (UP, see p.287); Manas and Kaziranga (Assam, see p.879), and Bandipur (Karnataka, see p.1140).

become island oases amid intensively farmed land, where nothing goes to waste. At the edges of the forests, farmers spend their nights huddled in flimsy wooden towers, guarding their crops against deer and wild pigs.

On occasion, larger forest animals such as elephants and tigers explicitly threaten the livelihood of farmers. In January 1994, for example, a herd of fifty elephants was driven from their forest in Bihar by forest fires. After blundering through fields, villages and small towns, they were finally driven back to their forest, but not before six people had been trampled to death. Although tigers who spend too much time in close proximity to humans have been known to develop man-eating habits, for many forest creatures avoidance of man and his activities is becoming increasingly difficult.

Indian farmers traditionally view such encroachment onto their land with mistrust. Anti-animal feelings run high; deer are poached, and tigers have been poisoned. Attempts to involve local people with the protection of their forests and its creatures have been encouraged in some areas through the growth of new organizations. In northern India, the Ranthambore Foundation, set up to protect the tigers of Ranthambore, has developed incentives for local people, such as the more efficient management of livestock, the planting of trees and the improvement of local livelihoods.

OVERFISHING

Distinct groups of **fishing** peoples have for millennia worked the rivers and lengthy coastline of India. Until very recently, the coastal fishing economy was controlled by artisanal fisherfolk, operating small, unmechanized craft, and supplying fish to inland markets. In the 1960s, larger businesses realized the potential of fish stocks in Indian waters, and mechanized trawler fleets moved in to exploit the resource. After an initial rapid increase in the quantity of fish landed, stagnation followed, and then the industry began to decline.

The state worst affected by these changes was **Kerala** in the south, where major changes in the ecology and economy of fisheries took place. Some of its fishermen were able to make the transition to a more capital and resource-intensive system, but the majority faced the direct competition from the trawler fleets. This conflict gave rise to a widespread movement, in which smaller fishermen pressed for restrictions on the operation of trawlers. Strikes, processions, and violent clashes with trawler owners ensued. The movement also called for a ban on trawling during the monsoon, the breeding season for several major species of fish. When a partial ban was finally imposed in the late 1980s, it did in fact result in an increased harvest following the monsoon months. At the same time, the creation of co-operative fishing villages by many communities has made local people more self-reliant — fish is now marketed co-operatively and money for new boats and equipment is borrowed from within the co-op rather than from outside money-lenders.

In the case of **inland fisheries**, the chief threat to fish stocks is from industrial pollution. However, in some instances, an almost feudalistic control is still exerted over fishing rights. The best known example of this in recent years has involved fishermen in the Bhagalpur district of Bihar, where two families claim the hereditary right to control fishing on a fifty-mile stretch of the Ganga (Ganges). Thanks to an anomaly in the provisions of the law abolishing landlord-ism (*zamindari*), enacted after 1947, these "waterlords" continue to levy taxes on some 40,000 fishermen, according to "**panidari**" (water) rights that date back to Moghul times. Since the early 1980s, the fishermen have been organized by young socialists into the "*Ganga Mukti Andolan*" (Free the Ganga) movement, but despite a protracted court case they have so far failed to escape their antiquated obligations.

BOOKS

The following list is a personal selection of the books that proved most useful or enjoyable during the preparation of this guide. Most of them are available in India itself, as are countless inexpensive editions of Indian and English classics.

HISTORY AND SOCIETY

Alberuni *Alberuni's India*. Lucid, fascinating account by the traveller, adventurer and chronicler in thirteenth-century India – possibly the first guide book on the sub-continent.

AL Basham *The Wonder that was India*. Learned survey of Indian history, society, music, art and literature from 400 BC to the coming of the Muslims. Volume II, by S A Rizvi, brings it up to the arrival of the British.

Judith M Brown *Gandhi and Civil Disobedience*. Pragmatic view of Gandhi's politics, which, refreshingly, doesn't resort to hagiography.

Larry Collins and Dominique Lapierre *Freedom at Midnight*. Readable, if shallow, account of Independence, highly sympathetic to the British, and particularly to Mountbatten, who was the authors' main source of information.

Trevor Fishlock *India File*. The latest edition of this now classic analysis of contemporary Indian society includes essays on the Golden Temple siege and the rise of Rajiv Gandhi. Recommended as an all-round introduction, or an enlightening read while travelling.

Dorf Hartsuiker *Sadhus: Holy Men of India*. The weird world of India's itinerant ascetics exposed in glossy colour photographs and erudite but accessible text.

Sanjoy Hazarika *Strangers of the Mist* (Penguin India). Comprehensive and incisive investigation into the problems and insurgences of India's troubled northeastern region.

Gita Mehta *Karma Cola*. Satirical look at the psychedelic 1970s freak scene in India, with some hilarious anecdotes, and many a wry observation on the whackier excesses of spiritual tourism. Mehta's charming and magically Indian *A River Sutra* is also well worth a read.

Ved Mehta *New India*. In-depth exploration of the Emergency, shot through with scathing criticism of Indira Gandhi. The sequel, *A Family Affair*, continues in the same spirit to peruse Indian politics after the Emergency.

Prafulla Mohanti *Changing Village, Changing Life*. Insightful, entertaining portrait of life in an east Indian village through the eyes of an anglicized expat. Essential if you plan to visit Orissa.

Geoffrey Moorhouse *Calcutta, the City Revealed*. Fascinating, if politically out of date, glimpse of the great city in the early 1970s.

VS Naipaul *India: A Wounded Civilisation*. Naipaul, a Trinidadian Indian, is one of the country's harshest critics, accusing it of narrowmindedness and barbaric selfishness amid debilitating poverty and misguided faith; inspired by the revelations of the Emergency. The novelist's *A Million Mutinies Now* is a penetrating, superbly crafted mosaic of individual lives from around the subcontinent. Hard going in places, but worth sticking with.

Jawaharlal Nehru *The Discovery of India* (Asia Publishing). Nehru's view of India, its history and its destiny.

Christine Noble *A Home in the Himalayas*. Life among the hill people of Himachal Pradesh.

Helena Norberg-Hodge *Ancient Futures: Learning From Ladakh*. The traditional culture and present development dilemmas of Ladakh.

John Pemble *The Raj, the Indian Mutiny and the Kingdom of Oudh 1801–1859*. Honest discourse on the events that led to the Mutiny, and an account of its aftermath.

Janet Rizvi *Ladakh: Crossroads of High Asia*. Excellent all-round introduction to Ladakh, past and present: particularly strong on history.

Percival Spear *Master of Bengal: Clive and His India.* Critical and historical analysis of the adventurer and opportunist who went on to help establish the British Raj.

Romila Thapar *History of India Volume I.* Concise paperback account of early Indian history, ending with the Delhi Sultanate. Percival Spear's *History of India Volume II* covers the period from the Moghul era to the death of Gandhi.

Gillian Tindall *City of Gold.* Definitive, if rather dry biography of Bombay, from colonial trading post to modern metropolis.

Mark Tully *No Full Stops in India.* Earnest, but highly readable dissection of contemporary India by the former BBC correspondent, incorporating anecdotes and first-hand accounts of political events over the past twenty years.

Mark Tully and Satish Jacob *Amritsar: Mrs Gandhi's Last Stand.* Aptly named examination of the storming of the Golden Temple and the prime minister's eventual assassination.

Col. Henry Yule and AC Burnell *Hobson–Jobson – a Glossary of Colonial Anglo-Indian Words and Phrases and of Kindred Terms, Etymological, Historical, Geographical, and Discursive* (Munshiram Manoharlal, India). The definitive Victorian reference manual and dictionary on life and customs in India; fascinating on any number of levels.

TRAVEL

Penelope Chetwode *Kullu: The End of the Habitable World.* A quintessentially English *memsahib* returns to her childhood haunts in Himachal Pradesh. Quirky and nostalgic, with detailed descriptions of PWD bungalows and the region's temples.

William Dalrymple *City of Djinns.* Modern Delhi vividly brought to life with a wealth of fascinating historical detail.

Alexander Frazer *Chasing the Monsoon.* Frazer's wet-season jaunt up the west coast and across the Ganges plains.

Norman Lewis *A Goddess in the Stones.* Veteran English travel writer's accomplished account of his trip to Calcutta and around the backwaters of Bihar and Orissa, with some vivid insights into tribal India.

Dervla Murphy *On a Shoestring to Coorg.* Evocative account of Murphy's stay with her young daughter in the little-visited tropical mountains of Coorg, Karnataka. Arguably the most famous modern Indian travelogue, and a manifesto for budget travel.

Eric Newby *Slowly down the Ganges.* England's most celebrated living travel writer's record of his mammoth journey from Haridwar to the mouth of the Hooghly in the 1960s. Though dated in places, his deft prose and wry humour evoke the timelesss allure of the countryside and cultures lining the subcontinent's holiest river.

Joe Roberts *Three-Quarters of a Footstep.* New, deftly written Englishman Abroad-style travelogue, mainly focussed on south and central India. Crammed full of anecdotes, literary asides, and rich contextual snippets.

Mark Shand *Travels on My Elephant.* Award-winning account of a 600-mile ride on an elephant from Konarak in Orissa to Bihar, accompanied by a drunkern mahout, among others; full of incident, humour and pathos. For the sequel, *Queen of the Elephants*, Shand teams up with an Assamese princess who's the country's leading elephant handler.

Heather Wood *Third-Class Ticket.* A party of elderly Bengalis leave their home village for the first time to tour the subcontinent by train. Absorbing and poignant, though the ersatz fictional style grates after a while.

Michael Wood *The Smile of Murugan.* Writer and broadcaster Wood tours pilgrimage sites in the south on video buses. A serious and affectionate portrait of the region and its people in the mid 1990s that manages to avoid sentimentality.

FICTION

Stephen Atter and Wimal Dissanayake *The Penguin Book of Indian Short Stories.* Ragbag of twentieth-century fiction translated from various languages.

EM Forster *A Passage to India.* Forster's most acclaimed novel, a withering critique of colonialism set in the 1920s. Memorable as much for its sympathetic portrayal of middle-class Indian life as for its insights into cultural misunderstandings.

Ruth Prawer Jhabvala *Out of India*. One of many short story collections that shows India in its full colours: amusing, shocking and thought-provoking. Other titles include *How I Became a Holy Mother*, *Like Birds, Like Fishes*; *Heat and Dust*; and *In Search of Love and Beauty*.

Rudyard Kipling *Kim*. Cringeingly colonialist at times, of course, but the atmosphere of India and Kipling's love of it shine through in this – often surprisingly enlightened – story of an orphaned white boy. Kipling's other key works on India are two books of short stories: *Soldiers Three* and *In Black and White*.

Dominique Lapierre *City of Joy*. Melodramatic story of a White man's journey into Calcutta's slums, loaded with anecdotes about Indian religious beliefs and customs.

Rohinton Mistry *Such a Long Journey*. Highly acclaimed account of a Bombay Parsi's struggle to maintain personal integrity in the face of betrayals and disappointments.

RK Narayan *Gods, Demons and Others*. Classic Indian folktales and popular myths told through the voice of a village story teller. Many of Narayan's beautifully crafted books, full of subtly drawn characters and good-natured humour, are set in the fictional south India territory of Malgudi.

Salman Rushdie *Midnight's Children*. This story of a man born at the very moment of Independence, whose life mirrors that of modern India itself, won Rushdie the Booker Prize and the emnity of Indira Gandhi, who had it banned in India. His latest novel, *The Moor's Last Sigh*, is the subject of a defamation case brought by Shiv Sena leader Bal Thackeray.

Vikram Seth *A Suitable Boy*. Vast, all-embracing tome set in UP shortly after Independence; wonderful characterizations and an impeccable sense of place and time make this an essential read for those long train journeys.

Kushwant Singh *Train to Pakistan* (Ravi Dayal, Delhi). Short, striking focus on life in a village on the edge of the Partition line in the summer of 1947; a chillingly realistic portrayal of the tragic massacres of the time. Singh's other works include *Delhi: A Novel*, a series of voices from the city's past interrupted by an old man's quest for sexual satisfaction in the present; *Sex, Scotch and Scholarship*, a collection of wry short stories, and several non-fiction

investigations into the history of Punjab, the Sikhs and the Khalistan question.

Rabindranath Tagore *The Home and the World*. Tragic, romantic novel by renowned Bengali poet, focussing on one woman's struggle to escape the confines of her marriage and find happiness with a radical leader.

Mark Tully *The Heart of India*. Arguably Tully's best short stories, revealing through amusing narrative the loyalties and deceptions of village life in UP.

BIOGRAPHY AND AUTOBIOGRAPHY

JR Ackerley *Hindoo Holiday*. During the 1920s, a gay and eccentric pal of EM Forster steps into the bizarre world of an even more gay and eccentric Maharajah seeking a tutor for his eighteen-month-old son. . .

Charles Allen *Plain Tales from the Raj*. First-hand accounts from erstwhile *sahibs* and *memsahibs* of everyday British India in the twentieth century.

James Cameron *An Indian Summer*. Affectionate, funny and honest view of the country; the veteran British journalist describes his visit to India in 1972, and his marriage to an Indian woman.

Louis Fischer *The Life of Mahatma Gandhi*. Meticulously written, authoritative biography.

MK Gandhi *Experiments with Truth*. Gandhi's fascinating records of his life, including the spiritual and moral quests, changing relationship with the British Government in India, and gradual emergence into the fore of politics.

Jawaharlal Nehru *Nehru – An Autobiography*. Examination of pre-Independence power struggles, written by India's first prime minister.

WOMEN

Elizabeth Bumiller *May You Be the Mother of a Hundred Sons*. Lucid exploration of the Indian woman's lot, drawn from dozens of first-hand encounters by an American journalist. Subjects tackled include dowries, arranged marriages, *sati*, magazines, and film stars.

Sashi Deshpande *The Binding Vine*. Disturbing story of one woman's struggle for independence, and her eventual acceptance of the position of servitude traditionally assumed by an Indian wife.

Atia Hossain *Sunlight on a Broken Column*. A novel set in the 1930s about a Muslim family and the lead-up to Independence.

Patricia Jeffrey *Frogs in a Well*. The meaning of *purdah* in Muslim society, treated from a female perspective.

Anees Jung *New Moon*. Revealing and poetic stories woven around interviews with Muslim women from all sectors of Indian society. Jung's *Unveiling India* is a compelling account of the life of a Muslim woman who has chosen to break free from orthodoxy.

Sarah Lloyd *An Indian Attachment*. Life in a Punjabi plains village through the eyes of a young Western woman, whose relationship with an opium-addicted Sikh forms the essence of this honest and enlightening book.

Sara Mitter *Dharma's Daughters*. Gripping account of Indian women's lives, influenced by mythical heroines and constrained by social expectations, and the attitudes of women's groups.

Karma Lekshe Tsomo (ed) *Daughters of the Buddha*. Opinions, concerns and stories gathered from Buddhist women around the world, compiled after the first International Conference of Buddhist Nuns in 1987.

In Other Words (Kali for Women, Delhi). Collection of stories by Indian women; not all feminist.

THE ARTS AND ARCHITECTURE

William Archer *Kalighat Paintings* (HMSO). A catalogue and introduction to the unique artform that blended indigenous and Western traditions and lampooned nineteenth-century society in Calcutta.

Roy Craven *Indian Art*. Concise general introduction to Indian art, from Harappan seals to Moghul miniatures, with lots of illustrations.

Basil Gray *The Arts of India*. Early to modern art forms catalogued in a historical context, and well illustrated.

Mohan Khokar *Traditions of Indian Classical Dance* (Clarion Books, India). Detailing the religious and social roots of Indian dance, this lavishly illustrated book, with sections on regional traditions, is an excellent introduction to the subject.

George Michell *The Hindu Temple*. A fine primer, introducing Hindu temples, their significance, and architectural development.

GHR Tillotson *The Rajput Palaces*. Excellent, illustrated catalogue of the history and architecture of northwest India's Rajput palaces. Also in the series is *Mughal India*.

Bonnie C Wade *Music in India: The Classical Traditions* (Manmohar, India). A scrupulous catalogue of Indian music, outlining the most commonly used instruments (with illustrations and musical scores).

Stuart Cary Welch *India: Art and Culture 1300–1900*. Originally produced for an exhibition at New York's Metropolitan museum, this exquisitely illustrated and accessibly written tome covers every aspect of India's rich and varied culture, with sections on the classical Hindu tradition of the south, the tribal art of rural India, the Muslim courts, the Rajputs and the Raj. Highly recommended.

RELIGION

Mary Boyce *Zoroastrians. Their Religious Beliefs and Practices*. A survey of Zoroastrian history, both secular and religious.

WO Cole and P Singh Sambhi *The Sikhs: Their Religious Beliefs and Practices*. Informative study of Sikhism.

Paul Dundas *The Jains*. Up-to-date, comprehensive study of Jainism.

Diana L Eck *Banaras – City of Light*. Thorough discourse on the religious significance of Varanasi, and a good introduction to Hindu cosmology in practice.

Richard Gombrich *Theravada Buddhism*. History of Theravadin beliefs and practices from their beginnings to the present day.

Roger Hudson *Travels through Sacred India*. Erudite and accessible introduction to modern India, with lively essays on temples, *sadhus*, gurus and sacred sites; a gazeteer of holy places, and listings for ashrams. Hudson derives much of his material from personal encounters, which brings the subjects to life. Includes sections on all India's main faiths, and an excellent bibliography.

Trevor Ling *The Buddha's Philosophy of Man.* Select Pali texts detailing the Buddha's social outlook and the early ordering of the community.

Ajit Mookerjee *Kali the Feminine Force.* Discussion of the art and beliefs of the *shakti* tradition.

Wendy O'Flaherty (transl.) *Hindu Myths.* Translations of popular Hindu myths, providing an insight into the foundations of Hinduism.

Chakravarti Rajagopalachari *Ramayana* and *Mahabharata* (Bharatiya Vidya Bhavan, India).

Comprehensive, accessible novelized versions of the great Hindu epics.

Andrew Rippin *Muslims; Their Religious Beliefs and Practices.* The essential guide to Islamic history and beliefs.

Paul Williams *Mahayana Buddhism.* Comprehensive study of Mahayana history and philosophy.

RC Zaehner *Hinduism.* Lively, accessible and often amusing catalogue of Hinduism and Indian society.

GLOSSARY

ACHARYA religious teacher.

ADIVASI official term for tribal person.

AGARBATI incense.

AHIMSA non-violence.

AKHANDPATH continuous reading of the Sikh holy book, the *Adi Granth*.

AMRITA nectar of immortality.

ANGREZI general term for Westerners.

ANNA coin, no longer minted (16 annas to one rupee).

APSARA heavenly nymph.

ARAK liquor distilled from rice or coconut.

ARATA evening temple *puja* of lights.

ASANA yogic seating posture; small mat used in prayer and meditation.

ASHRAM centre for spiritual learning and religious practice.

ASURA demon.

ATMAN soul.

AVATAR reincarnation of Vishnu on earth, in human or animal form.

AYAH nursemaid.

AYURVEDA ancient system of medicine employing herbs, minerals and massage.

BABA respectful term for a *sadhu*.

BAGH garden, park.

BAITHAK reception area in private house.

BAKSHEESH tip, donation.

BANDH general strike.

BANDHANI tie-and-dye.

BANIYA another term for a *vaishya*; a money lender.

BANYAN vast fig tree, used traditionally as a meeting place, or shade for teaching and meditating. Also, in south India, a cotton vest.

Note that a separate glossary of **Architectural Terms** appears on p.1270; that many **religious** terms are explained in detail in the section which begins on p.1228; and **musical** instruments and other terms on p.1248 onwards.

BASTEE slum area.

BAUL Bengali singer.

BAZAAR commercial centre of town; market.

BEGUM Muslim princess; Muslim women of high status.

BETEL leaf chewed in *paan*, with the nut of the areca tree: loosely applies to the nut, also.

BHAJAN song.

BHAKTI religious devotion expressed in a personalized or emotional relationship with the deity.

BHANG pounded marijuana, often mixed in *lassis*.

BHAWAN (also *bhavan*) palace or residence.

BHOTIA Himalayan people of Tibetan origin.

BHUMI earth, or earth goddess.

BIDI tobacco rolled in a leaf; the "poor man's puff".

BINDU seed, or the red dot (also *bindi*) worn by women on their foreheads as decoration.

BODHI TREE / BO TREE *peepal* tree, associated with the Buddha's enlightenment (*ficus religiosa*).

BODHI enlightenment.

BODHISATTVA Buddhist saint.

BRAHMIN a member of the highest caste group; priest.

BUNDH general strike.

BURKHA body-covering shawl worn by orthodox Muslim women.

BURRA-SAHIB colonial official, boss or a man of great importance.

CANTONMENT area of town occupied by military quarters.

CASTE social status acquired at birth.

CHAAT snack.

CHADDAR large head-cover or shawl.

CHAKRA discus; focus of power; energy point in the body; wheel, often representing the cycle of death and rebirth.

CHANDAN sandalwood paste.

CHANDRA moon.

CHANG Ladakhi liquor distilled from wheat or rice.

CHAPPAL sandals or flip-flops (thongs).

CHARAS hashish.

CHARPOI string bed with wooden frame.

CHAURI fly whisk, regal symbol.

CHELA pupil.

CHIKAN Lucknow embroidery.

CHILLUM cylindrical clay or wood pipe for smoking *charas* or *ganja*.

CHOLI short, tight-fitting blouse worn with a *sari*.

CHOR robber.

CHOULTRY quarters for pilgrims adjoined to south Indian temples.

CHOWGAN green in the centre of a town or village.

CHOWK crossroads or courtyard.

CHOWKIDAR watchman/caretaker.

COOLIE porter/labourer.

CRORE ten million.

DABBA packed lunch.

DACOIT bandit.

DALIT "oppressed", "out-caste". The term, introduced by Dr Ambedkar, is preferred by so called "untouchables" as a description of their social position.

DANDA staff, or stick.

DARSHAN vision of a deity or saint; receiving religious teachings.

DAWAN servant.

DEG cauldron for food offerings, often found in *dargahs*.

DEVA god.

DEVADASI temple dancer.

DEVI goddess.

DEVTA deity from Himachal Pradesh.

DHABA food hall selling local dishes.

DHAM important religious site, or a theological college.

DHARAMSHALA rest house for pilgrims.

DHARMA sense of religious and social duty (Hindu); the law of nature, teachings, truth (Buddhist).

DHOBI laundry.

DHOLAK double-ended drum.

DHOLI sedan chair carried by bearers to hilltop temples.

DHOOP thick pliable block of strong incense.

DHOTI white ankle-length cloth worn by males, tied around the waist, and sometimes hitched up through the legs.

DHURRIE woollen rug.

DIGAMBARA literally "sky-clad": a Jain sect, known for the habit of nudity among monks, though this is no longer commonplace.

DIKPALAS guardians of the four directions.

DIWAN (*dewan*) chief minister.

DOWRY payment or gift offered in marriage.

DRAVIDIAN of the south.

DUPATTA veil worn by Muslim women with *salwar kamise*.

DURBAR court building; government meeting.

EVE-TEASING sexual harassment of women, either physical or verbal.

FAKIR ascetic Muslim mendicant.

FENI Goan spirit, distilled from coconut or cashew fruits.

GADA mace.

GADI throne.

GANDA dirty.

GANDHARVAS Indra's heavenly musicians.

GANJ market.

GANJA marijuana buds.

GARI vehicle, or car.

GHAT mountain, landing platform, or steps leading to water.

GHAZAL melancholy Urdu songs.

GHEE clarified butter.

GOONDA ruffian.

GONCHA ankle-length woollen robe worn by Ladakhi women.

GOPI young cattle-tending maidens who feature as Krishna's playmates and lovers in popular mythology.

GURU teacher of religion, music, dance, astrology etc.

GURUDWARA Sikh place of worship.

HAJ Muslim pilgrimage to Mecca.

HAJJI Muslim engaged upon, or who has performed, the *haj*.

HARIJAN title – "Children of God" – given to "untouchables" by Gandhi.

HARTAL one-day strike.

HIJRA eunuch or transvestite.

HINAYANA literally "lesser vehicle": the name given to the original school of Buddhism by later sects.

HOOKAH water pipe for smoking strong tobacco or marijuana.

HOWDAH bulky elephant-saddle, sometimes made of pure silver, and often shaded by a canopy.

IDGAH area laid aside in the west of town for prayers during the Muslim festival Id-ul-Zuhara.

IMAM Muslim leader or teacher.

IMFL Indian-made foreign liquor.

ISHWARA God; Shiva.

JAGHIDAR landowner.

JATAKAS popular tales about the Buddha's life and teachings.

JATI caste, determined by family and occupation.

JAWAN soldier.

JHUTA soiled by lips: food or drink polluted by touch.

-JI suffix added to names as a term of respect.

JIHAD striving by Muslims, through battle, to spread their faith.

JINA another term for the Jain *tirthankaras*.

JOHAR old practice of self immolation by women in times of war.

JYOTIRLINGA twelve sites sacred by association with Shiva's unbounded *lingam* of light.

KAILASA or KAILASH Shiva's mountain abode.

KALAM school of painting.

KĀMA satisfaction **KAMISE** women's knee-length shirt, worn with *salwar* trousers.

KARMA weight of good and bad actions that determine status of rebirth.

KATCHA the opposite of *pukka*.

KAVAD small decorated box that unfolds to serve as a travelling temple.

KHADI home-spun cotton; Gandhi's symbol of Indian self-sufficiency.

KHAN honorific Muslim title.

KHOL black eye-liner, also known as *surma*.

KHUD valley side.

KIRTAN hymn-singing.

KOTWALI police station.

KSHATRYA the warrior and ruling caste.

KUMKUM red mark on a Hindu woman's forehead (widows are not supposed to wear it).

KUND tank, lake, reservoir.

KURTA long men's shirt worn over baggy *pajamas*.

LAKH one hundred thousand.

LAMA Tibetan Buddhist monk and teacher.

LATHI heavy stick used by police.

LINGAM phallic symbol in places of worship representing the god Shiva.

LOKA realm or world, eg *devaloka*, world of the gods.

LUNGHI male garment; long wrap-around cloth, like a *dhoti*, but usually coloured.

MADRASA Islamic school.

MAHADEVA literally "Great God", and a common epithet for Shiva.

MAHALLA neighbourhood.

MAHARAJA (Maharana, Maharao) king.

MAHARANI queen.

MAHATMA great soul.

MAHAYANA "Great Vehicle": a Buddhist school that has spread throughout southeast Asia.

MAHOUT elephant driver or keeper.

MAIDAN large open space or field.

MALA necklace, garland or rosary.

MANDALA religious diagram.

MANDI market.

MANDIR temple.

MANI STONE stone etched with Buddhist prayers by Tibetans and laid in piles or set in streams.

MANTRA sacred verse.

MARG road.

MASJID mosque.

MATAJI female *sadhu*.

MATH Hindu or Jain monastery.

MAUND old unit of weight (roughly 20kg).

MAYUR peacock.

MEHENDI henna.

MELA festival.

MEMSAHIB respectful address to European woman.

MITHUNA sexual union, or amorous couples in Hindu and Buddhist figurative art.

MOKSHA blissful state of freedom from rebirth aspired to by Hindus and Jains.

MOR peacock.

MUDRA hand gesture used in Vedic rituals, featuring in Hindu, Buddhist and Jain art and dance, and symbolizing teachings and life stages of the Buddha.

MUEZZIN man behind the voice calling Muslims to prayer from a mosque.

MULLAH Muslim teacher and scholar.

MUTT Hindu or Jain monastery.

NADI river.

NAGA mythical serpent; person from Nagaland.

NALA stream gorge in the mountains.

NATAK dance.

NATYA drama.

NAUTCH performance by dancing girls.

NAWAB Muslim landowner or prince.

NILGAI blue bull.

NIRVANA Buddhist equivalent of *moksha*.

NIZAM title of Hyderabad rulers.

NULLAH stream gorge in the mountains.

OM (aka *AUM*) symbol denoting the origin of all things, and ultimate divine essence, used in meditation by Hindus and Buddhists.

PAAN betel nut, lime, calcium and aniseed wrapped in a leaf and chewed as a digestive. Mildly addictive.

PADMA lotus; another name for the goddess Lakshmi.

PAISE there are a hundred paisa in a rupee.

PAJAMA men's baggy trousers.

PALI original language of early Buddhist texts.

PANCHAYAT village council.

PANDA pilgrims' priest.

PARIKRAMA ritual circumambulation around a temple, shrine or mountain.

PARSI Zoroastrian.

PIR Muslim holy man.

POL residential quarters, common in Gujarat.

PRANAYAMA breath control, used in meditation.

PRASAD food blessed in temple sanctuaries and shared among devotees.

PRAYAG auspicious confluence of two or more rivers.

PUJA worship.

PUJARI priest.

PUKKA correct and acceptable, in the very English sense of "proper".

PUNYA religious merit.

PURDAH seclusion of Muslim women inside the home, and the general term for wearing a veil.

PURNIMA full moon.

PUROHIT priest.

QAWWALI devotional singing popular among Sufis.

RAAG or **RAGA** series of notes forming the basis of a melody.

RAJ rule; monarchy; in particular the period of British Imperial rule 1857–1947.

RAJA king.

RAJPUT princely rulers who once dominated much of north and west India.

RAKSHASA demon (demoness: *rakshasi*).

RANGOLI geometrical pattern of rice powder laid before houses and temples.

RAWAL chief priest (Hindu).

RINPOCHE highly revered Tibetan Buddhist *lama*, considered to be a reincarnation of a previous teacher.

RISHI "seer"; philosophical sage or poet.

RUDRAKSHA beads used to make Shiva rosaries.

RUMAL handkerchief, particularly finely embroidered in Chamba state (HP).

SADAR "main"; eg. *sadar bazaar*.

SADHU Hindu holy man with no caste or family ties.

SAGAR lake.

SAHIB respectful title for gentlemen; general term of address for European men.

SALABHANJIKA wood nymph.

SALWAR KAMISE long shirt and baggy ankle-hugging trousers worn by Muslim women.

SAMADHI final enlightenment; a site of death or burial of a saint.

SAMSARA cyclic process of death and rebirth.

SANGAM sacred confluence of two or more rivers, or an academy.

SANGEET music

SANNYASIN homeless, possessionless ascetic (Hindu).

SARAI resting place for caravans and travellers who once followed the trade routes through Asia.

SARI usual dress for Indian women: a length of cloth wound around the waist and draped over one shoulder.

SATI one who sacrifices her life on her husband's funeral pyre in emulation of Shiva's wife. No longer a common practice, and officially illegal.

SATSANG teaching given by a religious figurehead.

SATYAGRAHA Gandhi's campaign of non-violent protest, literally "grasping truth".

SCHEDULED CASTES official name for "untouchables".

SEPOY an Indian soldier in European service.

SETH merchant or businessman.

SEVA voluntary service in a temple or community.

SHAIVITE Hindu recognizing Shiva as the supreme god.

SHANKHA conch, symbol of Vishnu.

SHASTRA treatise.

SHIKAR hunting.

SHISHYA pupil.

SHLOKA verse from a Sanskrit text.

SHRI respectful prefix; another name for Lakshmi.

SHULAB public toilet.

SHUDRA the lowest of the four *varnas*; servant.

SINGHA lion.

SOMA medicinal herb with hallucinogenic properties used in early Vedic and Zoroastrian rituals.

STHALA site sacred for its association with legendary events.

SURMA black eyeliner, also known as *khol*.

SURYA the sun, or sun god.

SUTRA (*sutta*) verse in Sanskrit and Pali texts (literally "thread").

SVETAMBARA "white-clad" sect of Jainism, that accepts nuns and shuns nudity.

SWAMI title for a holy man.

SWARAJ "self rule"; synonym for independence, coined by Gandhi.

TALA rhythmic cycle in classical music; in sculpture a *tala* signifies one face-length.

TALUKA district.

TANDAVA vigorous, male form of dance; the dance of Shiva Nataraja.

TANDOOR clay oven.

TAPAS literally "heat": physical and mental austerities.

TEMPO three-wheeled taxi.

THALI combination of vegetarian dishes, chutneys, pickles, rice and bread served, especially in south India, as a single meal; the metal plate on which a meal is served.

THANGKA Tibetan religious scroll painting.

THERAVADA "Doctrine of the Elders": the original name for early Buddhism, which persists today in Sri Lanka and Thailand.

THUG member of a north Indian cult of professional robbers and murderers.

TIFFIN light meal.

TIFFIN CARRIER stainless steel set of tins used for carrying meals.

TILAK red dot smeared on the forehead during worship, and often used cosmetically.

TIRTHA river crossing considered sacred by Hindus, or the transition from the mundane world to heaven; a place of pilgrimage for Jains.

TIRTHANKARA "ford-maker" or "crossing-maker": an enlightened Jain teacher who is deified – 24 appear every 300 million years.

TOLA the weight of a silver rupee: 180 grains, or approximately 11.6g.

TONGA two-wheeled horse-drawn cart.

TOPI cap.

TRIMURTI the Hindu trinity.

TRISHULA Shiva's trident.

TULKU reincarnated teacher of Tibetan Buddhism.

UNTOUCHABLES members of the lowest strata of society, considered polluting to all higher castes.

URS Muslim saints day festival.

VAHANA the "vehicle" of a deity: the bull Nandi is Shiva's *vahana*.

VAISHYA member of the merchant and trading caste group.

VARNA literally "colour"; one of four hierarchical social categories: *brahmins, kshatryas, vaishyas* and *shudras*.

VEDAS sacred texts of early Hinduism.

WALLAH suffix implying occupation, eg: *dhobi-wallah*, rickshaw *wallah*.

WAZIR chief minister to the king.

YAGNA Vedic sacrificial ritual.

YAKSHA pre-Vedic folklore figure connected with fertility and incorporated into later Hindu iconography.

YAKSHI female *yaksha*.

YALI mythical lion.

YANTRA cosmological pictogram, or model used in an observatory.

YATRA pilgrimage.

YATRI pilgrim.

YOGI *sadhu* or priestly figure possessing occult powers gained through the practice of yoga (female: *yogini*).

YONI symbol of the female sexual organ, set around the base of the *lingam* in temple shrines.

YUGA aeon: the present age is the last in a cycle of four *yugas, kali-yuga*, a "black-age" of degeneration and spiritual decline.

ZAMINDAR landowner.

ARCHITECTURAL TERMS

AMALAKA repeating decorative motif based on the fluted shape of a gourd, lining and crowning temple towers: a distinctive feature of northern architecture.

ANDA literally "egg": the spherical part of a *stupa*.

BAGH garden.

BAOLI step-well in Gujarat and western India.

BHAWAN building or house.

BHUMIKA storey.

BIRADIRI summer house; pavilion.

CELLA chamber, often housing the image of a deity.

CENOTAPH ornate tomb.

CHAITYA Buddhist temple.

CHARBAGH garden divided into quadrants (Moghul style).

CHAUMUKH image of four faces placed back to back.

CHHATRI tomb; domed temple pavilion.

CHORTEN monument, often containing prayers, texts or relics, erected as a sign of faith by Tibetan Buddhists.

CUPOLA small delicate dome.

DARGAH tomb of a Muslim saint.

DARWAZA gateway; door.

DEUL Orissan temple or sanctuary.

DIWAN-I-AM public audience hall.

DIWAN-I-KHAS hall of private audience.

DUKHANG main temple in a *gompa*.

DUKKA tank and fountain in courtyard of mosque.

DURBAR court building, hall of audience, or government meeting.

DVARPALA guardian image placed at sanctuary door.

FINIAL capping motif on temple pinnacle.

GARBHA GRIHA temple sanctuary, literally "womb-chamber".

GARH fort.

GODOWN warehouse.

GOMPA Tibetan, or Ladakhi, Buddhist monastery.

GONKHANG temple in a *gompa* devoted to protector (*gon*) deities.

GOPURA towered temple gateway, common in south India.

HAMMAM sunken hot bath, Persian style.

HAVELI elaborately decorated (normally wooden) mansion, especially in Rajasthan.

IMAMBARA tomb of a Shi'ite saint.

INDO-SARACENIC overblown Raj-era architecture that combines Muslim, Hindu, Jain and Western elements.

IWAN the main (often central) arch in a mosque.

JAGAMOHANA porch fronting the main sanctuary in an Orissan temple.

JALI lattice work in stone, or a pierced screen.

JANGHA the body of a temple.

KABUTAR KHANA pigeon coop.

KALASHA pot-like capping stone characteristic of south Indian temples.

KANGYU LANG book house in a *gompa* storing sacred Tibetan texts and manuscripts.

KOT fort.

KOTHI residence.

KOTLA citadel.

KOVIL term for a Tamil Nadu temple.

LIWAN cloisters in a mosque.

MAHAL palace; mansion.

MAKARA crocodile-like animal featuring on temple doorways, and symbolizing the River Ganges. Also the vehicle of Varuna, the Vedic god of the sea.

MANDAPA hall, often with many pillars, used for various purposes: eg *kalyana mandapa* for wedding ceremonies and *nata mandapa* for dance performances.

MEDHI terrace.

MIHRAB niche in the wall of a mosque indicating the direction of prayer (to Mecca). In India the *mihrab* is in the west wall.

MIMBAR pulpit in a mosque from which the Friday sermon is read.

MINARET high slender tower, characteristic of mosques.

PADA foot, or base, also a poetic metre.

PAGODA multi-storeyed Buddhist monument.

POLE fortified gate.

PRADAKSHINA PATHA processional path circling a monument or sanctuary.

PRAKARA enclosure or courtyard in a south Indian temple.

QABR Muslim grave.

QILA fort.

RATH processional temple chariot of south India.

REKHA DEUL Orissan towered sanctuary.

SHIKHARA temple tower or spire common in northern architecture.

STAMBHA pillar, or flagstaff.

STUPA large hemispherical mound, representing the Buddha's presence, and often protecting relics of the Buddha or a Buddhist saint.

TALA storey.

TORANA arch, or free-standing gateway of two pillars linked by an elaborate arch.

TUK fortified enclosure of Jain shrines or temples.

VAV step-well, common in Gujarat.

VEDIKA railing around a *stupa*.

VIHARA Buddhist or Jain monastery.

VIMANA tower over temple sanctuary.

ZENANA women's quarters; segregated area for women in a mosque.

USEFUL HINDI WORDS AND PHRASES

India has fifteen main languages, and around seven hundred minor languages and dialects. Most Indians are, at least, bi-lingual; **Hindi**, the language of Delhi, is widely spoken and understood everywhere except the far south. **English**, however, remains the language of officialdom.

There are two broad language groups— the older, **southern**, or Dravidian group includes Tamil, Malayalam (spoken in Kerala), and Kannada (Karnataka). The main languages of the **north**, such as Hindi, Bengali, Punjabi, and Gujarati, belong to the Indo-Aryan group and are related to Sanskrit. The odd one out is **Urdu** (literally **Greetings** "camp"), which developed in the first Muslim camps and settlements in the twelfth century, adding central Asian, Persian, Turkish and Arabic words to the structure of what is now Hindi.

Greetings

Greetings	*Namaste* (said with palms together at chest height as in prayer – not used for Muslims)	Goodbye (to a Muslim)	*Khudaa Haafiz* (may god bless you)
		How are you? (formal)	*Ap kaise hain*
Hello	*Namaskar* (not used for Muslims)	How are you? (familiar)	*Kya hal hai*
Greetings reply – ale	(to a Muslim) *Aslaam alequm* in *qum aslaam*	Brother (a common address to a stranger)	*bhaaii* or *bhaayaa*
We will meet again (goodbye)	*phir milenge*	Sister	*didi*
		Sir	*Hazuur* (Muslims only)
		Sir (Sahib)	*Saaheb*

Basic words

Yes	*han*	You (formal)	*ap*	Good	*achhaa*	Go	*jaao*
OK	*achhaa*	You (familiar)	*tum*	Bad	*kharaab*	Run	*bhaago*
No	*nahin*	How	*kaise*	Come	*aao*	(also "take a run" or "scram")	
Me	*main*	How much	*kitna*	Please come	*aaiiye*		

Basic phrases

My name is . . .	*Mera nam . . . hai*	I don't speak Hindi	*Main Hindi nahin bol sakta hun*
What is your name? (formal)	*Aapka naam kya hai*		
What is your name? (familiar)	*Tumhara naam kya hai*	Please speak slowly	*Aaiste se boliye*
		Please forgive me (I am sorry)	*Mujhe maaf kiijiiye*
I (male) come from . . .	*Main . . . se aa rahaa hun*	It is OK	*Thiik hai*
I (female) come from . . .	*Main . . . se aa rahii hun*	How much?	*Kitna paisa?*
		How much is this?	*Iskaa daam kyaa hai?*
Where do you come from?	*Kahan se aate hain*	What work do you do?	*Kya kaam karte hain?*
I don't know	*Maalum nahin*	Do you have any brothers or sisters?	*Bhaai behan hai?*
I don't understand	*Samaj nahin aayaa*		
I understand	*Samaj gayaa*		

Getting Around

Where is the . . . ?	*. . . kahaan hai?*	Which is the bus for Gwalior?	*Gwalior kaa bas kahaanhai?*
I want to go to . . .	*Main . . . jaanaa chaataa hun.*	What time does the train leave	*Gaarii kab chhutegii?*
Where is it?	*Kahaan hai?*	Stop	*ruko*
How far?	*Kitnaa duur?*	Wait	*thero*

Accommodation

I need a room	*Mujhe kamraa chaahiye*	I am staying for one night	*Main ek raat ke liiye tehr rahaa hun*
How much is the room?	*Kamraa kaa bhaaraa kyaa hai?*		

Medicinal

I have a headache	*Sir me dard hai*	Where is the pharmacy?	*Dawaiikhaanaa kahaa hai?*		
I have a pain in my stomach	*Meraa pet me dardhai*				
The pain is here	*Dard yahaan hai*	Medicine	*dawaii*	Nose	*naakh*
Where is the doctor's surgery?	*Daaktarkhaanaa kahaan hai?*	Pain	*dard*	Ear	*kaan*
		Stomach	*pet*	Back	*piit*
Where is the hospital?	*Haspitaal kahaan hai?*	Eye	*aankh*	Foot	*paao*

INDEX

The following abbreviations are used throughout this index

Amsterdam	1-85828-086-9	£7.99	US$13.95	CAN$16.99
Andalucia	1-85828-094-X	8.99	14.95	18.99
Australia	1-85828-141-5	12.99	19.95	25.99
Bali	1-85828-134-2	8.99	14.95	19.99
Barcelona	1-85828-106-7	8.99	13.95	17.99
Berlin	1-85828-129-6	8.99	14.95	19.99
Brazil	1-85828-102-4	9.99	15.95	19.99
Britain	1-85828-208-X	12.99	19.95	25.99
Brittany & Normandy	1-85828-126-1	8.99	14.95	19.99
Bulgaria	1-85828-183-0	9.99	16.95	22.99
California	1-85828-181-4	10.99	16.95	22.99
Canada	1-85828-130-X	10.99	14.95	19.99
Corsica	1-85828-089-3	8.99	14.95	18.99
Costa Rica	1-85828-136-9	9.99	15.95	21.99
Crete	1-85828-132-6	8.99	14.95	18.99
Cyprus	1-85828-182-2	9.99	16.95	22.99
Czech & Slovak Republics	1-85828-121-0	9.99	16.95	22.99
Egypt	1-85828-188-1	10.99	17.95	23.99
Europe	1-85828-159-8	14.99	19.95	25.99
England	1-85828-160-1	10.99	17.95	23.99
First Time Europe	1-85828-210-1	7.99	9.95	12.99
Florida	1-85828-184-4	10.99	16.95	22.99
France	1-85828-124-5	10.99	16.95	21.99
Germany	1-85828-128-8	11.99	17.95	23.99
Goa	1-85828-156-3	8.99	14.95	19.99
Greece	1-85828-131-8	9.99	16.95	20.99
Greek Islands	1-85828-163-6	8.99	14.95	19.99
Guatemala	1-85828-189-X	10.99	16.95	22.99
Hawaii: Big Island	1-85828-158-X	8.99	12.95	16.99
Hawaii	1-85828-206-3	10.99	16.95	22.99
Holland, Belgium & Luxembourg	1-85828-087-7	9.99	15.95	20.99
Hong Kong	1-85828-187-3	8.99	14.95	19.99
Hungary	1-85828-123-7	8.99	14.95	19.99
India	1-85828-200-4	14.99	23.95	31.99
Ireland	1-85828-179-2	10.99	17.95	23.99
Italy	1-85828-167-9	12.99	19.95	25.99
Kenya	1-85828-192-X	11.99	18.95	24.99
London	1-85828-231-4	9.99	15.95	21.99
Mallorca & Menorca	1-85828-165-2	8.99	14.95	19.99
Malaysia, Singapore & Brunei	1-85828-103-2	9.99	16.95	20.99
Mexico	1-85828-044-3	10.99	16.95	22.99
Morocco	1-85828-040-0	9.99	16.95	21.99
Moscow	1-85828-118-0	8.99	14.95	19.99
Nepal	1-85828-190-3	10.99	17.95	23.99
New York	1-85828-171-7	9.99	15.95	21.99

Pacific Northwest	1-85828-092-3	9.99	14.95	19.99
Paris	1-85828-125-3	7.99	13.95	16.99
Poland	1-85828-168-7	10.99	17.95	23.99
Portugal	1-85828-180-6	9.99	16.95	22.99
Prague	1-85828-122-9	8.99	14.95	19.99
Provence	1-85828-127-X	9.99	16.95	22.99
Pyrenees	1-85828-093-1	8.99	15.95	19.99
Rhodes & the Dodecanese	1-85828-120-2	8.99	14.95	19.99
Romania	1-85828-097-4	9.99	15.95	21.99
San Francisco	1-85828-185-7	8.99	14.95	19.99
Scandinavia	1-85828-039-7	10.99	16.99	21.99
Scotland	1-85828-166-0	9.99	16.95	22.99
Sicily	1-85828-178-4	9.99	16.95	22.99
Singapore	1-85828-135-0	8.99	14.95	19.99
Spain	1-85828-081-8	9.99	16.95	20.99
St Petersburg	1-85828-133-4	8.99	14.95	19.99
Thailand	1-85828-140-7	10.99	17.95	24.99
Tunisia	1-85828-139-3	10.99	17.95	24.99
Turkey	1-85828-088-5	9.99	16.95	20.99
Tuscany & Umbria	1-85828-091-5	8.99	15.95	19.99
USA	1-85828-161-X	14.99	19.95	25.99
Venice	1-85828-170-9	8.99	14.95	19.99
Vietnam	1-85828-191-1	9.99	15.95	21.99
Wales	1-85828-096-6	8.99	14.95	18.99
West Africa	1-85828-101-6	15.99	24.95	34.99
More Women Travel	1-85828-098-2	9.99	14.95	19.99
Zimbabwe & Botswana	1-85828-186-5	11.99	18.95	24.99

Phrasebooks

Czech	1-85828-148-2	3.50	5.00	7.00
French	1-85828-144-X	3.50	5.00	7.00
German	1-85828-146-6	3.50	5.00	7.00
Greek	1-85828-145-8	3.50	5.00	7.00
Italian	1-85828-143-1	3.50	5.00	7.00
Mexican	1-85828-176-8	3.50	5.00	7.00
Portuguese	1-85828-175-X	3.50	5.00	7.00
Polish	1-85828-174-1	3.50	5.00	7.00
Spanish	1-85828-147-4	3.50	5.00	7.00
Thai	1-85828-177-6	3.50	5.00	7.00
Turkish	1-85828-173-3	3.50	5.00	7.00
Vietnamese	1-85828-172-5	3.50	5.00	7.00

Reference

Classical Music	1-85828-113-X	12.99	19.95	25.99
Internet	1-85828-198-9	5.00	8.00	10.00
Jazz	1-85828-137-7	16.99	24.95	34.99
Rock	1-85828-201-2	17.99	26.95	35.00
World Music	1-85828-017-6	16.99	22.95	29.99

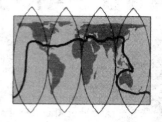